THE STEPHEN BECHTEL FUND 
IMPRINT IN ECOLOGY AND THE ENVIRONMENT

The Stephen Bechtel Fund has established this imprint to promote understanding and conservation of our natural environment.

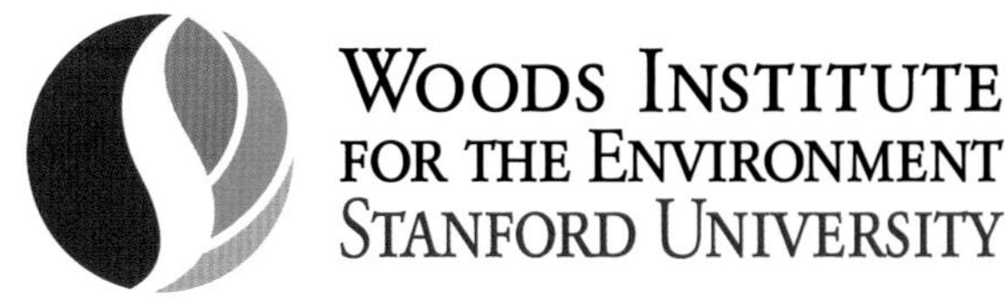

FROM THE PUBLISHER

We gratefully acknowledge the generous contribution to this book provided by the Stephen Bechtel Fund.

We gratefully acknowledge the generous contribution to this book provided by the International Community Foundation/JiJi Foundation Fund.

FROM THE AUTHORS

We are indebted to the following institutions—the S. D. Bechtel, Jr. Foundation, the California Academy of Sciences, the David and Lucile Packard Foundation, and the Stanford University Woods Institute for the Environment—for their generous contributions in support of the production of this volume and the outreach efforts to make it accessible to a diverse audience.

ECOSYSTEMS OF CALIFORNIA

Ecosystems of California

Edited by

HAROLD MOONEY and ERIKA ZAVALETA

Graphics edited by

MELISSA C. CHAPIN

UNIVERSITY OF CALIFORNIA PRESS

University of California Press, one of the most distinguished university presses in the United States, enriches lives around the world by advancing scholarship in the humanities, social sciences, and natural sciences. Its activities are supported by the UC Press Foundation and by philanthropic contributions from individuals and institutions. For more information, visit www.ucpress.edu.

University of California Press
Oakland, California

Library of Congress Cataloging-in-Publication Data

Ecosystems of California / edited by Harold Mooney and Erika Zavaleta ; graphics editor, Melissa Chapin.
pages cm
Includes bibliographical references and index.
ISBN 978-0-520-27880-6 (cloth : alk. paper)
ISBN 978-0-520-96217-0 (ebook)
1. Ecology—California. 2. Ecosystem management—California.
I. Mooney, Harold A., editor. II. Zavaleta, Erika, 1972–editor.
QH105.C2E36 2016
577.09794—dc2 2015016442

Manufactured in China

22 21 20 19 18 17 16
10 9 8 7 6 5 4 3 2 1

The paper used in this publication meets the minimum requirements of ANSI/NISO Z39.48-1992 (R 2002) (*Permanence of Paper*). ⊗

To our students, whose enthusiasm inspired and motivated us
to craft something more substantial than we could have on our own

To our families, whose love and support make our work possible

In memory of Rafe Sagarin, 1971–2015

CONTENTS

CONTRIBUTORS

JOHN T. ABATZOGLOU
University of Idaho
Moscow, Idaho

DAVID D. ACKERLY
University of California
Berkeley, California

PETER S. ALAGONA
University of California
Santa Barbara, California

EDITH B. ALLEN
University of California
Riverside, California

PETER ALPERT
University of Massachusetts
Amherst, Massachusetts

TANYA ATWATER
University of California
Santa Barbara, California

HELEN BAILEY
University of Maryland
Solomons, Maryland

DENNIS D. BALDOCCHI
University of California
Berkeley, California

MICHAEL G. BARBOUR
University of California
Davis, California

PATRICK L. BARNARD
U.S. Geological Survey
Santa Cruz, California

JAMES W. BARTOLOME
University of California
Berkeley, California

ERIN BELLER
San Francisco Estuary Institute
Richmond, California

JAYNE BELNAP
U.S. Geological Survey
Moab, Utah

ERIC P. BJORKSTEDT
NOAA Southwest Fisheries Science Center
Trinidad, California

CAROL A. BLANCHETTE
University of California
Santa Barbara, California

STEVEN J. BOGRAD
NOAA Southwest Fisheries Science Center
Monterey, California

ABRAHAM BORKER
University of California
Santa Cruz, California

RICHARD D. BRODEUR
NOAA Northwest Fisheries Science Center
Newport, Oregon

MATTHEW L. BROOKS
U.S. Geological Survey
Oakhurst, California

ANDRZEJ BYTNEROWICZ
USDA Forest Service
Riverside, California

JOHN C. CALLAWAY
University of San Francisco
San Francisco, California

MARK H. CARR
University of California
Santa Cruz, California

DANIEL R. CAYAN
Scripps Institution of Oceanography / USGS
La Jolla, California

REBECCA CHAPLIN-KRAMER
Stanford University
Stanford, California

NONA R. CHIARIELLO
Stanford University
Stanford, California

RICARDO CISNEROS
University of California
Merced, California

ELSA E. CLELAND
University of California
San Diego, California

JAMES E. CLOERN
U.S. Geological Survey
Menlo Park, California

BRANDON COLLINS
USDA Forest Service
Davis, California

PAUL W. COLLINS
Santa Barbara Museum of Natural History
Santa Barbara, California

SCOTT D. COOPER
University of California
Santa Barbara, California

TARA CORNELISSE
Canisius College
Buffalo, New York

DON CROLL
University of California
Santa Cruz, California

FRANK W. DAVIS
University of California
Santa Barbara, California

TODD DAWSON
University of California
Berkeley, California

MICHAEL L. DEAS
Watercourse Engineering, Inc.
Davis, California

LESLEY A. DEFALCO
U.S. Geological Survey
Henderson, Nevada

MARK W. DENNY
Stanford University
Pacific Grove, California

NOAH S. DIFFENBAUGH
Stanford University
Stanford, California

LOWELL DILLER
Green Diamond Resources
Korbel, California

CHRISTOPHER R. DOLANC
Mercyhurst University
Erie, Pennslyvania

WALTER G. DUFFY
U.S. Geological Survey
Arcata, California

JENIFER E. DUGAN
University of California
Santa Barbara, California

JOHN M. ENGLE
University of California
Santa Barbara, California

KATHERINE ENNIS
University of California
Santa Cruz, California

LA'SHAYE ERVIN
University of Utah
Salt Lake City, Utah

ANDREW B. ESCH
University of California
Santa Barbara, California

TODD C. ESQUE
U.S. Geological Survey
Henderson, Nevada

VALERIE T. EVINER
University of California
Davis, California

KATE FAULKNER
Channel Islands National Park
Ventura, California

MARK FENN
USDA Forest Service
Riverside, California

ROBERT S. FERANEC
New York State Museum
Albany, New York

CHRISTOPHER B. FIELD
Carnegie Institution for Science
Stanford, California

JOHN C. FIELD
NOAA Southwest Fisheries Science Center
Santa Cruz, California

JOSEPH FLESKES
U.S. Geological Survey
Dixon, California

JENNIFER L. FUNK
Chapman University
Orange, California

PHILIP GARONE
California State University Stanislaus
Turlock, California

ROBERT C. GRAHAM
University of California
Riverside, California

J. LETITIA GRENIER
San Francisco Estuary Institute
Richmond, California

BRENDA J. GREWELL
University of California
Davis, California

EDWARD D. GROSHOLZ
University of California
Davis, California

ROBIN GROSSINGER
San Francisco Estuary Institute
Richmond, California

KACEY HADICK
Far Western Anthropological Research Group
Davis, California

ELIZABETH A. HADLY
Stanford University
Stanford, California

NADIA HAMEY
Hamey Woods
Santa Cruz, California

SUSAN HARRISON
University of California
Davis, California

ELLIOTT L. HAZEN
NOAA Southwest Fisheries Science Center
Monterey, California

BRENT HELM
DBA Helm Biological Consulting
Sheridan, California

BRIAN HELMUTH
Northeastern University
Boston, Massachusetts

KATHRYN HIEB
California Department of Fish and Wildlife
Stockton, California

JAMES T. HOLLIBAUGH
University of Georgia
Athens, Georgia

PETER HOPKINSON
University of California
Berkeley, California

RICHARD E. HOWITT
University of California
Davis, California

DAVID M. HUBBARD
University of California
Santa Barbara, California

LYNN HUNTSINGER
University of California
Berkeley, California

SAM F. IACOBELLIS
Scripps Institution of Oceanography
La Jolla, California

G. DARREL JENERETTE
University of California
Riverside, California

TERRY L. JONES
California Polytechnic State University
San Luis Obispo, California

SHARON KAHARA
Humboldt State University
Arcata, California

TODD KEELER-WOLF
California Department of Fish and Wildlife
Sacramento, California

JON E. KEELEY
U.S. Geological Survey
Three Rivers, California

NOAH KNOWLES
U.S. Geological Survey
Menlo Park, California

SARAH J. KUPFERBERG
University of California
Berkeley, California

SUZANNE LANGRIDGE
University of California
Santa Cruz, California

ANDREW W. LEISING
NOAA Southwest Fisheries Science Center
Monterey, California

CHENG LI
Stanford University
Stanford, California

MILTON LOVE
University of California
Santa Barbara, California

JAMES A. MACMAHON
Utah State University
Logan, Utah

LISA MANDLE
Stanford University
Stanford, California

JESSICA MARTER-KENYON
University of California
Santa Barbara, California

SARA M. MAXWELL
Old Dominion University
Norfolk, Virginia

ALEX MCCALLA
University of California
Davis, California

KATHYRN MCEACHERN
U.S. Geological Survey
Ventura, California

JOHN MELACK
University of California
Santa Barbara, California

ADINA M. MERENLENDER
University of California
Berkeley, California

CONSTANCE I. MILLAR
USDA Forest Service
Albany, California

LUKE P. MILLER
Hopkins Marine Station
Pacific Grove, California

HAROLD MOONEY
Stanford University
Stanford, California

PETER MOYLE
University of California
Davis, California

KARINA J. NIELSEN
San Francisco State University
Tiburon, California

MALCOLM NORTH
USDA Forest Service
Davis, California

A. TOBY O'GEEN
University of California
Davis, California

ELISSA M. OLIMPI
University of California
Santa Cruz, California

FLAVIA C. DE OLIVEIRA
University of California
Santa Cruz, California

V. THOMAS PARKER
San Francisco State University
San Francisco, California

JAE R. PASARI
Pacific Collegiate School
Santa Cruz, California

DIANE E. PATAKI
University of Utah
Salt Lake City, Utah

TIM PAULSON
University of California
Santa Barbara, California

STEPHANIE PINCETL
University of California
Los Angeles, California

ROGER POWELL
North Carolina State University
Raleigh, North Carolina

MARY E. POWER
University of California
Berkeley, California

R. BRANDON PRATT
California State University
Bakersfield, California

PAULO QUADRI BARBA
University of California
Santa Cruz, California

ELIZABETH RAUER
Khaled bin Sultan Living Oceans Foundation
Landover, Maryland

ROSEMARY RECORDS
Colorado State University
Fort Collins, Colorado

DANIEL C. REED
University of California
Santa Barbara, California

DANIEL V. RICHARDS
Channel Islands National Park
Ventura, California

LAURA ROGERS-BENNETT
California Department Fish and Wildlife
Bodega Bay, California

PHILIP W. RUNDEL
University of California
Los Angeles, California

HUGH D. SAFFORD
USDA Forest Service
Vallejo, California

MARIA JOÃO FERREIRA DOS SANTOS
Utrecht University
Utrecht, The Netherlands

S. GEOFFREY SCHLADOW
University of California
Davis, California

BENKTESH SHARMA
University of California
Berkeley, California

M. REBECCA SHAW
Environmental Defense Fund
San Francisco, California

JOSEPH SILVEIRA
U.S. Fish and Wildlife Service
Willows, California

BARRY SINERVO
University of California
Santa Cruz, California

SARAH A. SKIKNE
University of California
Santa Cruz, California

JAYSON R. SMITH
California State Polytechnic University
Pomona, California

DENA SPATZ
University of California
Santa Cruz, California

SHERI SPIEGAL
University of California
Berkeley, California

BRONWEN STANFORD
University of California
Santa Cruz, California

RICK STARR
University of California
San Diego, California

NATHAN L. STEPHENSON
U.S. Geological Survey
Three Rivers, California

WILLIAM STEWART
University of California
Berkeley, California

KATHARINE N. SUDING
University of Colorado
Boulder, Colorado

MARTHA SUTULA
Southern California Coastal Water Research Project
Costa Mesa, California

ROBERT SWIERS
North Carolina State University
Raleigh, North Carolina

BERNIE TERSHY
University of California
Santa Cruz, California

TARA L. E. TRAMMELL
University of Delaware
Newark, Delaware

CLAUDIA M. TYLER
University of California
Santa Barbara, California

SAMUEL VELOZ
Point Blue Conservation Science
Petaluma, California

KERSTIN WASSON
Elkhorn Slough National Estuarine Research Reserve
Royal Oaks, California

TERRELL WATT
Terrell Watt Planning Consultants
San Francisco, California

ROBERT H. WEBB
University of Arizona
Tucson, Arizona

ALISON WHIPPLE
San Francisco Estuary Institute
Richmond, California

AMELIA A. WOLF
University of California
Santa Cruz, California

WALLACE B. WOOLFENDEN
USDA Forest Service, retired
Swall Meadows, California

ROB YORK
University of California
Berkeley, California

ERIKA ZAVALETA
University of California
Santa Cruz, California

PREFACE AND ACKNOWLEDGMENTS

Every place on earth is special but, as the saying goes, some places are more special than others. California stands out as truly unique in its physical, biological, and societal diversity. This book documents aspects of California's diversity and the ecological dynamism that both maintains and arises from it. The project rose out of the need to have access to up-to-date knowledge on the nature of California's ecological wealth. Students needed it, because until now there has not been an available resource covering the large array of California's ecosystems for the many classes on this subject taught throughout the state. The book also serves the state's many and diverse practitioners who deal with conservation and resource management as scientists, managers, and decision makers.

Meeting the goals for this book was challenging because the enormity of the topic constantly did battle with our desire to craft a single, ideally portable, volume. The forty-one chapters cover the state's main ecosystem types, but each possesses so many variants that regrettably we had to leave out some areas and topics of value because of space limitations. However, we are extremely pleased about the amazing amount of knowledge that has been brought together by an enormous team of experts. In this volume we have assembled information on both terrestrial and marine systems. Although these systems interact in many ways, they are usually dealt with separately in overviews of California. This reflects in part an academic cultural divide that we hope fades in the future.

In addition to documenting and focusing on California's ecosystems today, we have looked to the geological and historical past to illuminate how we got here and what has changed. We have also considered the future to examine what is in store for these systems in light of the rapid regional and global changes, both ongoing and projected. Thus we strove to view the past, the present, and the future of the state's natural capital. We have taken a broad view of California's ecosystems and have therefore included chapters on the state's managed and built ecosystems as well as the more natural entities. Most of the chapters, across the spectrum of natural to managed ecosystems, discuss the services each ecosystem provides to illustrate the ways that they provision human well-being as well as the trade-offs involved in changing these systems.

This book could not have come to be without the dedication and work of an immense group of people. Foremost is the hugely talented group of experts on California's ecosystems who crafted these chapters. We thank them for their attention to endless details and their patience with us through many rounds of review and revision. At the production stage we had the extraordinary assistance of Melissa Chapin, who went above and beyond as graphics editor. We would like to particularly thank Chuck Crumly, formerly with the University of California Press, for his enthusiastic support of this venture from its inception. Merrik Bush-Pirkle, Blake Edgar and Kate Hoffman, also of UC Press, championed and saw this project through to completion. Parker Welch and Aaron Cole with the Center for Integrated Spatial Research (CISR) at the University of California–Santa Cruz worked diligently to produce the set of distribution maps for the book. Amy Smith Bell expertly tackled the enormous copy editing job. Emily Saarman, Diane Delaney, Astoria Tershy and Arica Mooney provided additional production input.

For improving the entire manuscript with their careful eyes and incisive suggestions, we thank Peter Moyle, Mike Allen, and Jessica Blois. Terry Chapin carefully reviewed the hundreds of figures and figure captions. We are grateful to the members of the project advisory committee who contributed early in the process to developing the book concept and structure: Bruce Baldwin, Mark Carr, Frank W. Davis, R. A. Dahlgren, Valerie T. Eviner, Jon E. Keeley, John Melack, Adina M. Merenlender, Diane E. Pataki, Stephanie Pincetl, Mary Power, Philip W. Rundel, and Heather Tallis. We thank all of our external chapter reviewers—Larry Allen, John Battles, Richard D. Brodeur, Sarah Carvill, Oliver Chadwick, David Charlet, Jeff Corbin, Hall Cushman, Carla D'Antonio, Frank W. Davis, Sandy DeSimone, Tim Duane, Jonna Engel, Jack Engle, Ned (Chip) Euliss, Valerie T. Eviner, Lynn Fenstermaker, Robert S. Feranec, Jerry Franklin, Rebecca Franklin, Mike Foster, Melvin George, Dave Graber, Gary Griggs, Greg Gilbert, Kathy Hilimire, Richard Hobbs, David Igler, Paul Koch, Julie King, Lara Kueppers, Steve Lonhart, Georgina Mace, Blair McLaughlin, Adina M. Merenlender, Peter Moyle, Karina J. Nielsen, Jeanne Panek, Mitchell Pavao-Zuckerman, Bill Peterson, Stacy Philpott, Andrea Pickart, Daniel Press, Marcel Rejmanek, Torben Rick, Dylan Schwilk, Jim Sickman, Lisa Sloan, Loren Smith, Scott Smith, Scott Starratt,

Scott Stephens, John Stuart, Kerstin Wasson, and Will White, as well as those reviewers who asked not to be named.

Finally, we thank our families for their tremendous support and patience. And to those whom we have forgotten to mention here, we beg your forgiveness. This book has been an incredible eight-year odyssey for us. We could not have done it without the hundreds who have given their time, brilliance, and intimate knowledge of this great state. As the project comes to completion, we cannot help but reflect on the community it has helped to build among us. California is blessed to have so many scientists and scholars dedicated to its understanding and stewardship. We hope above all for that community and its collective knowledge to carry on and thrive in subsequent generations. If this book helps in service toward that goal, it will have been more than worth the effort.

Erika Zavaleta and Harold Mooney
July 2015

MARINE ECOSYSTEMS

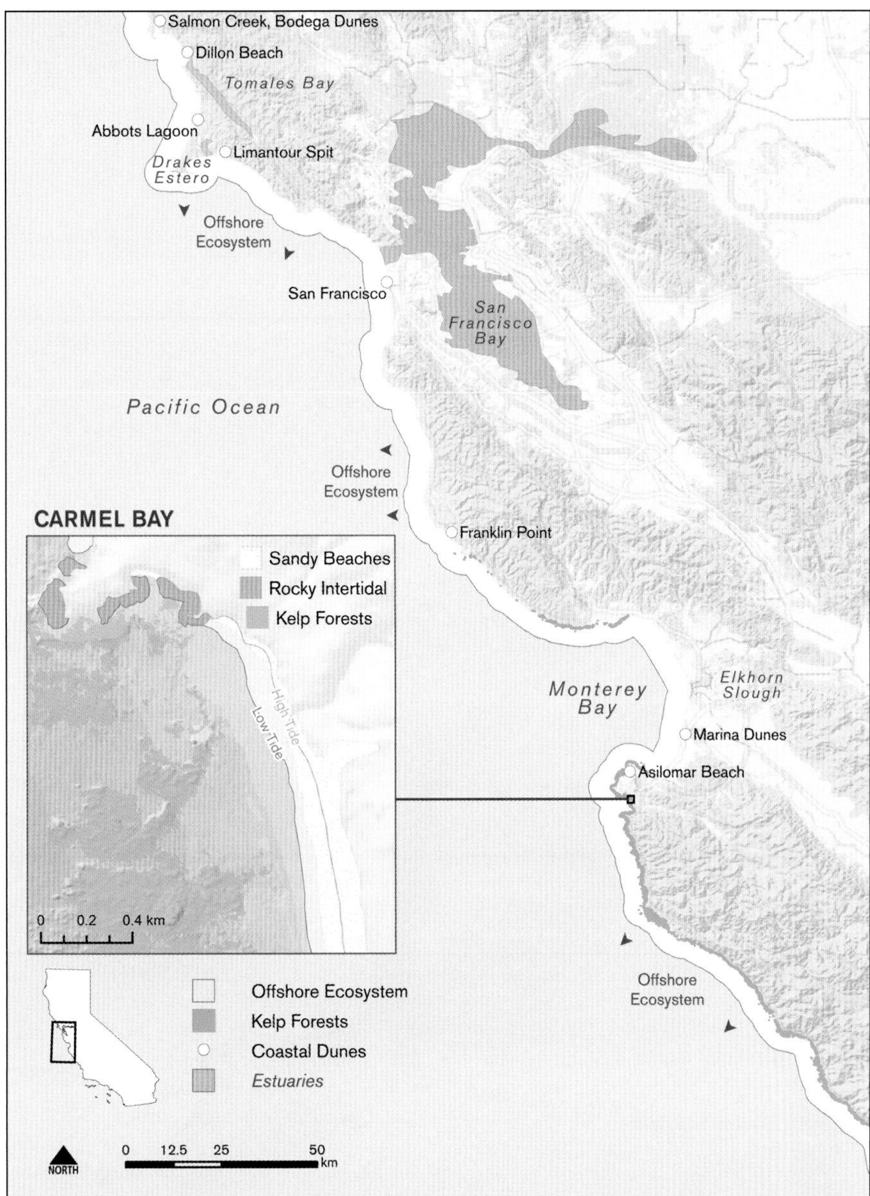

Marine ecosystems of California, depicted for just a subset of the state's coastline in order to visualize their narrow extents and fine interrelationships. At the regional scale, for the San Francisco Bay/Central Coast, distributions are shown for the offshore ecosystem (>3 km from the coastline), kelp forests and estuaries, and selected current and former coastal dune sites (labeled). Major interstate (white) and state (light orange/red) area roads are shown. At the scale of the individual site, within Carmel Bay, distributions are shown of kelp forest, rocky intertidal, and sandy beach ecosystems, in relation to daily mean lower low tides and daily mean higher high tides, with blue ocean shading indicating depth and bathymetry. Data from the U.S. Geological Survey, National Hydrography Dataset (NHD); California Department of Fish and Wildlife, Ocean Imaging; the Seafloor Mapping Lab of California State University–Monterey Bay; and ESRI. Map: Parker Welch (Center for Integrated Spatial Research [CISR], UC Santa Cruz), Emily Saarman.

TERRESTRIAL ECOSYSTEMS

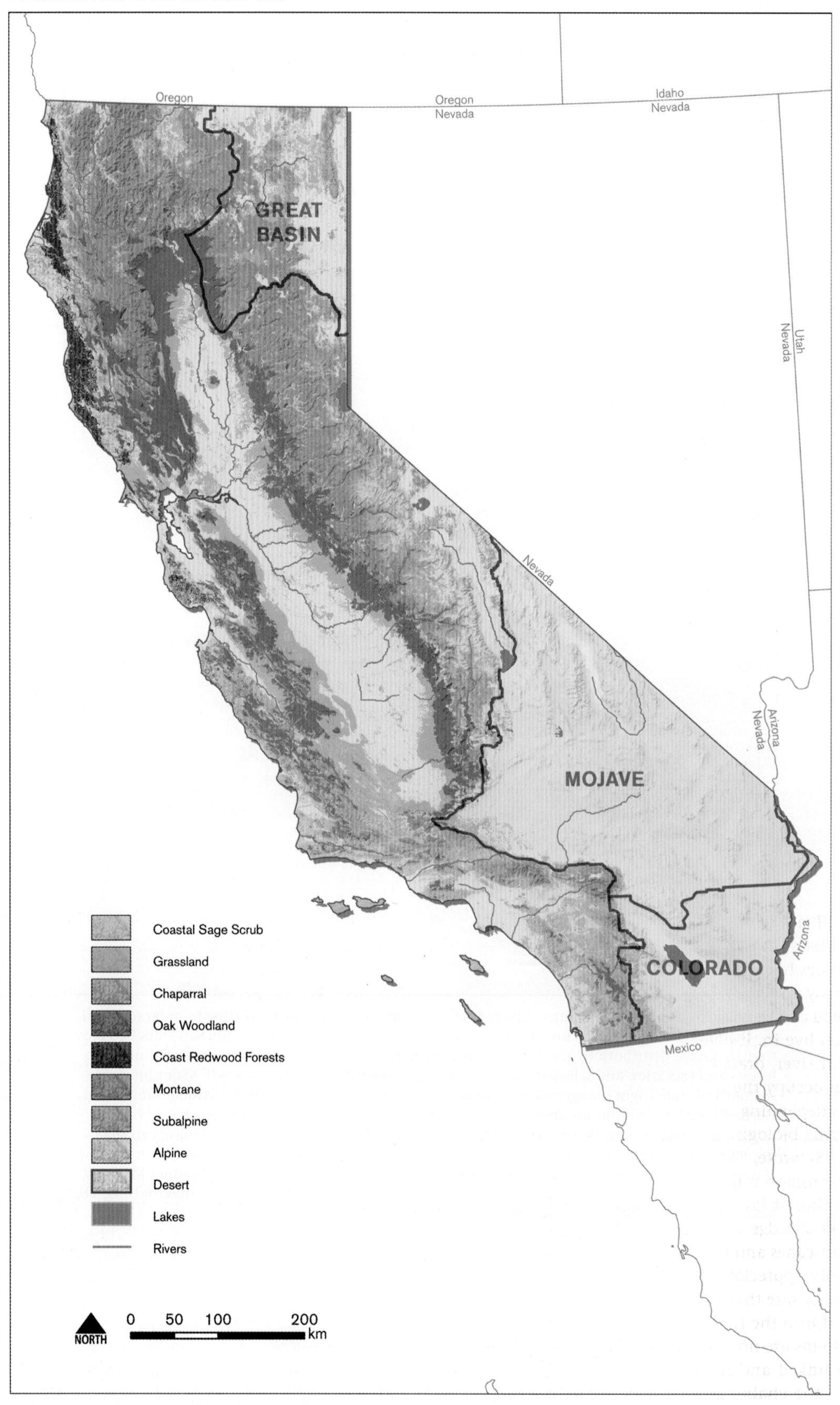

Terrestrial ecosystems of California. The state's three major desert regions are labeled: Great Basin, Mojave, and Colorado. Data from the U.S. Geological Survey, Gap Analysis Program (GAP); Cal Fire, Fire Resource and Assessment Program (FRAP); and the U.S. Geological Survey, National Hydrography Dataset (NHD). Map: Parker Welch (CISR, UC Santa Cruz).

ONE

Introduction

ERIKA ZAVALETA and HAROLD MOONEY

It is no small task to understand the characteristics of the various ecosystems that occupy California, since there are more different types here than anywhere else in the United States. This is the joy and marvel of living in a state where in a short distance, you can be in a completely different landscape from the one you live in. It could be the coast, a beautiful lake, a magnificent river, dramatic deserts, or the rich and diverse forests that occupy the state—or, for that matter, all of those landscapes depending on the direction you pick. As pioneering California biologist and university president David Starr Jordan (1898) wrote, "There is from end to end of California scarcely a common mile."

The task that we lay out in this book is to bring together the necessary knowledge to understand the nature of California's diverse landscapes and their biotic and social character so we can not only appreciate their uniqueness but also position ourselves to ensure that they are being utilized sustainably, at present and into the future. We take the position that these diverse systems are not totally isolated from one another but rather are linked and interacting to varying degrees. Thus we take on the challenge of assembling information on all of California's systems, managed and natural, terrestrial and aquatic. We look not only at the status and dynamics of these systems at present but also at how these systems came to be and how they are likely to look in the future. We understand that although California is somewhat of an ecological island, isolated by mountains and climate from much of the continent that it bounds, it is not unconnected from the rest of the nation and world. The lessons we gather from a comprehensive look at this singularly diverse and complex state can, we hope, inspire integrative and dynamic thinking about ecological systems elsewhere.

The Need for This Book

More great books about the natural world and our connections to it have been written about California than probably anywhere else. So far, however, these books have not included a comprehensive, process-oriented ecology of the entire state. California contains more distinct ecosystem types by far than any other U.S. state. California has also had a long, complex, and unique history as a dynamic social-ecological system. It is both the most biodiverse and the most demographically diverse state in the nation. It hurtles towards a complex, unique, and uncertain future. In this book we strive to focus on process in every sense—on the cross-scale processes that define the boundaries and character of each of California's ecosystems; the interacting social and ecological dynamics that have shaped the ecosystems we see today and continue to shape them going forward; the articulations between systems defined ecologically and systems defined by human enterprise, from fisheries to agriculture to cities; and the prospects for stewardship now and in the coming century. The result is a book with twice as many chapters as we first planned, and even so with gaps.

Why did we feel we needed this book? First, although many courses are taught about California's ecology in the state's institutions of higher learning, there has been no comprehensive text available to cover the diverse ecosystems of the state from terrestrial to aquatic to marine; their distribution, structure, and composition and functional attributes; and least of all the range of natural and managed systems. We both have been teaching university courses about California's ecology for a long time without an accompanying text. One of us (Hal) taught *Ecosystems of California* at Stanford for some forty years using materials culled from a great variety of sources. Especially in a state renowned globally for its university system, it ought to be easier for people to teach and learn about California's tremendous diversity of ecological systems. Beyond the classroom, a comprehensive overview of the state of knowledge about California's many ecosystems could serve as a valuable reference for researchers, decision makers, and stewards. Among other things, each of the chapters in this book addresses knowledge gaps that highlight opportunities and needs for new scholarship; history that provides context for what we see today; and past, current, and future threats and losses that highlight opportunities and needs for policy and management action. The volume is intended as a source book for teaching and for conservation, policy, planning, and decision-making in California.

Second, we wanted to capture the complexity and dynamism of a more comprehensive set of systems in California than other works have. The field of ecology has evolved over the past several decades to embrace perpetual dynamism, historical contingency, cross-scale interactions, and emergent features. This approach has replaced a more static view and a focus on structure, inviting more attention to function and processes. Much of this contemporary perspective on ecology has been explored but not synthesized in California, and it deserved to be brought together in one place. Finally, an up-to-date treatment of the history, ecology, management, and future of each of California's ecosystems could undergird targeted research, informed management and stewardship, and inspired decision-making and citizenship. It could make plain what we know—and what we need to know. It could also provide a view of the state's ecology as integrated with and dependent on, rather than artificially separated from, the state's economy, culture, and human communities. Because we care about the diversity and ecology of California, we want to explore and articulate how contingent its past has been and its future will be on our collective choices and decisions.

Photo on previous page: California brown pelicans (*Pelecanus occidentalis californicus*) and early winter swell, Scotts Creek, California. Listed as endangered in 1970 due to severe DDT exposure throughout the U.S., brown pelicans recovered gradually after DDT was banned in the early 1970s and were officially delisted in 1999. Their recovery reminds us that California's ecosystems today reflect a history of conservation successes as well as human impacts. Photo: Ed Dickie (eddickie.com).

The Early Development of Ecology in California: A Different Path Taken

What we know best and least about California's ecosystems is colored by the unique development of ecology as a science in this state. California is an island ecologically, and it was also an island in the way our knowledge of natural systems developed through time. This yielded both innovations originating in the state and gaps peculiar to California. Michael Smith (1987) noted, for example, that early Californian scientists were influenced by their "observation of California's physical environment [that] profoundly affected their thinking—both about science and about their new home. The peculiarities of their social environment influenced the ways in which they sought support for science and eventually prompted their efforts to arbitrate between the land and its occupants. These forces, compounded by geographic separation from other scientists, contributed to a professional role for earth and life scientists that differed in significant ways from that of their Eastern counterparts" as did the "rich intermingling of environmental influences [that] checkerboards California with dissimilar ecosystems . . . [that] compress into dramatic adjacency in California" in contrast to the gradual nature of ecosystem change (through space) in other parts of the country.

California did not achieve statehood until 1850, three-quarters of a century after the establishment of the United States. In 1853 a small group of citizens in San Francisco founded the California Academy of Sciences to provide a home for the state's growing natural history collections. The San Francisco Bay Area became the initial hot spot for the early buildup of local scientific capacity at the academy as well as at the emerging universities. In 1868 the University of California was founded, and early faculty including Joseph LeConte, E. L. Greene, Willis Lynn Jepson, and Joseph Grinnell combed the state to catalog its geological, plant, and animal diversity. They rapidly accumulated deep knowledge about both the state's biogeography and the ecological and behavioral traits of the specimens that they collected. The scientific basis for the optimal use of California's natural resources by society was fostered from the outset because the new University of California was designated from its beginnings as a land grant university. A College of Agriculture was established in 1875, and in 1913 a forestry division was added.

In much of the U.S. and beyond, scientists involved directly in studying natural systems often avoided those with a human presence. In California, environmental science and protection of natural systems coevolved more closely, reducing the lines dividing ecology from conservation. In the early twentieth century, leading ecologists in the state became alarmed at the extensive overexploitation of its natural wealth and took direct actions to ensure its protection. They became directly involved in conservation efforts and helped ignite a national conservation movement through their roles in founding the Sierra Club and the Sempervirens Club. Then as now, California had the opportunity for leadership in bridging scientific knowledge to sound conservation and resource management policies and actions.

Emergent Patterns

The chapters in this book were written by a diverse cadre of experts on California's ecosystems. Each team of authors, of

FIGURE 1.1 Wildfire sunrise in Lassen Volcanic National Park. Photo: Ed Dickie (eddickie.com).

course, brought its own set of perspectives to the chapter in question and chose to a large degree how best to structure the chapter to reflect its subject. This inevitably produced differences in the emphases of each chapter on particular ecological scales, taxonomic groups, trophic levels, and so on. Nevertheless, we strived for strong coverage in every chapter across ecological scales (from organismal adaptations to species interactions to feedbacks and interactions between community and ecosystem scales), time periods (from historical to future), and applications (from basic ecology to conservation, management, and policy implications). As a result, variation among chapters reflects genuine differences in knowledge, state, and stressors of each system, among other things. For example, it became clear in the process of developing the chapter on alpine ecosystems (29) that very little research has been done on the ecosystem ecology of California's alpine; this is reflected in the chapter's coverage of that topic.

By the same token, consistency among chapters reveals some genuine, emergent patterns that we did not necessarily expect at the outset. A strong pattern emerging across many ecosystems from chapters here deals with the historic moment we inhabit in California's conservation trajectory. Chapter after chapter describes the recovery of species and systems from a nadir of environmental quality that occurred roughly forty to fifty years ago. To a surprising extent, some trends have been successfully reversed, such as declining air quality in California's cities (see, e.g., Chapters 7 and 39) and declining species from island endemic plants to peregrine falcons to sea otters in the face of stressors from DDT to overharvesting and invasive species (see, e.g., Chapters 11 and 34). Older legacies, like the widespread damage caused by overgrazing and gold mining in the nineteenth century, have both continued to fade with time and been actively addressed by restoration and remediation efforts (see, e.g., Chapters 5, 19, and 33) and changes for the better in management of such forces as fire and grazing (see, e.g., Chapters 3, 23, and 37) (Figure 1.1). These successes are tempered by at least two other trends: the ongoing loss of habitat to continued urban and exurban development (see, e.g., Chapters 5, 22, 25, and 31) and the emergence of climate change as a growing, ubiquitous force influencing California's ecosystems (see, e.g., Chapters 14, 17, 26, 27, and 29, among many others).

California's ecosystems can be profound integrators of the complexity around interacting environmental changes at various temporal and spatial scales; for example, the acid neutralizing capacity of Emerald Lake in the Sierras declined steadily from about 1920 to 1970 before beginning to climb from the late twentieth century to the present, possibly reflecting first the effects of rising fossil fuel burning and acid deposition, then the effects of advancing snowmelt under increasing temperatures (Chapter 32). Examples from throughout the volume make clear the prevalence of interactions of this nature across ecosystems. Across the state, matter and energy move downstream, such as the movement of sediment, nutrients, and other compounds from forest to river to estuary to intertidal and kelp forest ecosystems (Chapters 17–19, 28, and 33); and upstream, such as in the fires that burn from the montane forest up into the subalpine forest (Chapters 3 and 28), the nutrients moved by anadromous fishes from the ocean to freshwaters and nearby terrestrial settings (Chapters 33 and 35), and the air masses that carry moisture, pollutants, and even propagules from the coast to the mountains (e.g., Chapters 2, 7, and 27). Source and sink relationships abound; entire heterotrophic ecosystems in California, subsidized by flows of energy and matter from other ecosystems, range from its estuaries (Chapter 19) to its cities (Chapter 39). Offshore, upwelling associated with the California current generates tremendous marine diversity and productivity that move among the porous boundaries of intertidal, rocky reef, estuarine, open ocean, and sandy beach ecosystems (Chapters 16–20) in forms ranging from carcasses to suspended particulate organic matter.

A third, emergent pattern from across systems concerns north-south distinctions in dynamics, threats, and in some cases perspectives on ecology that arise from differences in what studies have emphasized as well as in the underlying systems themselves. These contrasts and gradients across the latitudinal range of the state are most clear for ecosystem types that span a large part of the state. For example, the dynamics and dominance of invasive plant species vary markedly from south to north in coastal sage scrub (Chapter 22) and grasslands (Chapter 23). The historical and present roles of fire vary from south to north in chaparral ecosystems (Chapter 24); treeline elevation shifts (Chapters 28 and 29); and dominant species turnover in systems ranging from desert scrub (Chapter 30) to montane forests (Chapter 27) and kelp forests (Chapter 17). Finally, although statewide development patterns have altered coastal, low-elevation ecosystems more and interior, high-elevation ecosystems less (e.g., highly altered and fragmented coastal sage scrub, intermediate desert [low, interior], and relatively unfragmented subalpine and alpine), the condition of particular ecosystems tends to vary more, and in complex ways, along north-south lines than from west to east. For example, coast redwood forests (Chapter 26) experienced historically high rates of clearing throughout the coast but are now more affected by fire, climate change, and disease to the south than in the state's north. Grasslands (Chapter 23) are more fragmented, converted, and invaded in the south than in the north within the coastal and interior valley grassland types.

Structure of the Book

We designed this book to be used in a variety of ways to reflect a diversity of needs. We provide this brief overview as a road map to the book and a guide for selecting sections and chapters for reference, teaching, and study. Throughout the volume, chapters include recommended further readings and chapter-specific glossaries of technical terms not described in the text. We also chose to keep the references with each chapter to facilitate use of individual chapters for reference and teaching.

The first part of the book following this introduction examines overarching drivers of patterns and processes on the California landscape ("Drivers," Chapters 2–7). Although we initially conceived of them as more or less abiotic drivers, in reality they occupy a range from strongly abiotic (e.g., oceanography, climate) to largely influenced by biotic forces (e.g., fire, soils). All incorporate, again to varying degrees, the effects of human activities. In particular, the chapters on atmospheric chemistry (7) and population and land use (5) explicitly focus on human drivers, and the chapter on fire as an ecosystem process (3) deals extensively with human effects on fire regimes. The chapter on population and land use is a hybrid between a historical and a driver chapter; it is the abridged story of how human population and land use dynamics and in the postcolonial era have shaped the lay of the land today. We felt that if we placed it in the history part of the book ("History," Chapters 8–10), we would erroneously convey that land use and human habitation are less-than-critical drivers of ecosystem patterns and processes in California.

The next three chapters focus on history: the paleohistory of vegetation and animals, respectively, and an ecological history of indigenous Californians and their roles in shaping the California we see today. The chapter on paleovegetation (8) necessarily tackles the stage for vegetation history in the region and covers the geomorphological, climate, and ecosystem history of California. The chapter on vertebrate prehistory (9) focuses on mammals as the best-understood group in the paleorecord and traces their history in the region from sixty million years ago. The chapter on indigenous California (10) illustrates the degree to which scholarly debate and changing political contexts can influence, over time, conceptions of how people related to and shaped their environment in the past, and how that history has influenced today's ecosystems.

The next five chapters ("Biota," Chapters 11–15) describe overarching biotic patterns, threats, and concepts as a foundation for the rest of the book. The chapter on biodiversity (11) provides an overview of the state's biological diversity and its spatial distribution, threats, and success stories across five focal taxonomic groups (plants, birds, mammals, invertebrates, and herptiles [amphibians and reptiles]). Subsequent chapters give an overview of the state's major patterns of terrestrial vegetation (12) and of the special, widespread issues of biological invasions (13) and climate change impacts (14) in relation to the state's ecology. The final chapter in this section (15) describes emerging understanding and framing of the relationships among biological diversity, ecosystem functioning, ecosystem services, and natural capital, which recur in nearly every subsequent chapter.

The next part of the book describes the state's ecosystems ("Ecosystems," Chapters 16–33). This section proceeds roughly from the offshore Pacific Ocean towards land, then inland and upward in elevation, and finally down the eastern mountain slopes to the desert. Chapters 31–33 double back and tackle the major freshwater systems (wetlands, lakes, rivers) distributed across the state's terrestrial ecosystems. Each chapter in this part describes the process-based ecology of an ecosystem: its distribution and the factors that shape it; key constituent species, species interactions and processes such as disturbance regimes; ecosystem dynamics, including trophic interactions and the cycling of elements; and ecological history, including the influences of people. Each chapter also describes the services to society associated with that ecosystem; the threats and challenges it faces; and likely future trends, challenges, and opportunities for its management.

In this section we had to make some tough decisions about how to lump and split, and where to accept uneven coverage that reflected space constraints as well as knowledge gaps. For example, we decided not to split estuarine subtidal and salt marsh systems into separate chapters but to include both within a single chapter on estuaries (19), or to split deserts (30) into the various desert types that characterize eastern California but to combine them in one large chapter. Enough is known about each subsystem for a book, but this book had to fit between one set of covers. The chapters vary in length and balance among components, reflecting author choices as well as varying availability of knowledge about particular systems. For example, the chapter on alpine ecosystems (29) focuses especially on geomorphological processes and biotic communities, with less emphasis on ecosystem dynamics, simply because less is known about them specifically in California's alpine.

The next part of the book describes managed ecosystems ("Managed Systems," Chapters 34–39), defined variously by the societal endeavors that created them and proceeding roughly from less to more strongly human-altered managed systems. California's islands (Chapter 34) are a microcosm of many of California's coastal systems but are distinct both ecologically, as islands, and in terms of their management for diverse purposes ranging from military to conservation to recreation. California's marine fisheries (Chapter 35) are defined by the organisms they harvest, while forestry (Chapter 36) is an activity defined by the ecosystems that can support it, and range (Chapter 37) is what livestock do when they are let out to forage. The chapter on agriculture (38) emphasizes the history and economy of an activity that defines much of the state's landscape and water use and supplies much of the country. The chapter on urban ecosystems (39) enters relatively new terrain, applying ecological concepts to the city as an ecosystem and examining how it supports biodiversity and ecosystem services in unique ways.

The final two chapters in the book return to stewardship ("Policy and Stewardship," Chapters 40 and 41). The chapter on regulation for resource conservation (40) traces efforts to regulate land use and stewardship over California's history. The chapter on stewardship, conservation, and restoration in the context of environmental change (41) pulls together themes and cases from across the book to examine effective paths to sustain California's ecological legacy into the future.

We live in exciting times; California is in a state of accelerating change, but so is our knowledge about its ecological dynamics and their articulation with conservation and management efforts. In keeping with the spirit of pervasive dynamism that kindled this effort, we have already begun to think about the next edition of this volume; we would be grateful for your feedback. Finally, we hope this book will build understanding and guide stewardship of California's incredible diversity, with appreciation for the layers of historical and dynamic forces reflected in the landscapes of this great state.

Recommended Reading

A diversity of great books tackle California's ecology from many angles. They include the literary—from John Muir's *The Mountains of California* (1875) to John McPhee's "Los Angeles against the Mountains" (1989) and *Assembling California* (1993) to the anthology of Jack London's California works, *Golden State* (Haslam 1999). They include the taxonomic—from Jim Hickman's great *Jepson Manual* of the state's vascular plants (1993), now in its second edition (Baldwin et al. 2012), to *Inland Fishes of California* (Moyle 2002). They include a great many natural histories, including Allan Schoenherr's *A Natural History of California* (1995) as well as scores of guides to particular systems, regions, groups of organisms, weather, glaciers, ethnobotany, and geology. They include conservation surveys—the *Atlas of the Biodiversity of California* (Parisi 2003) summarizes tremendous information and knowledge in maps; while *Life on the Edge: A Guide to California's Endangered Natural Resources* centers on wildlife, threats, and their management (Thelander and Crabtree 1994).

We cannot fail to mention the works of historical ecology, like Laura Cunningham's *A State of Change* (2010) and the carefully researched *California Grizzly* (Storer and Tevis 1996); the comprehensive *Manual of California Vegetation* (Sawyer et al. 2009) and *Terrestrial Vegetation of California* (Barbour et al. 2007); and the many whole volumes exploring the ecology of individual ecosystems (like *California Grasslands*, Stromberg et al. 2007), processes (like *Fire in California's Ecosystems*, Sugihara et al. 2006), and threats (like biological invasions in *California's Fading Wildflowers*, Minnich 2008). Many books—from Ray Dasmann's rousing *Destruction of California* (1965) to the cautious optimism of volumes like *In Our Own Hands* (Jensen et al. 1993)—lay plain the conservation challenges that we face in California and impel us to act.

Finally, a number of valuable California ecosystem resources exist online. The California Naturalist Program (http://calnat.ucanr.edu/) provides naturalist certification and training to members of the public interested in stewardship. It is one of many excellent efforts to build citizen science and service in the state. Considerable data and educational resources reside on the websites of the California Academy of Sciences, Berkeley's Jepson Herbarium and Museum of Vertebrate Zoology, the California Invasive Plant Council, the California Native Plant Society, and many state agency sites.

We have surely forgotten to mention volumes and efforts that we cherish, but their sheer numbers make it hard to call them all up at once.

References

Baldwin, B. G., D. H. Goldman, D. J. Keil, R. Patterson, T. J. Rosatti, and D. H. Wilken, editors. 2012. The Jepson manual: Vascular plants of California. Second edition. University of California Press, Berkeley, California.

Barbour, M., T. Keeler-Wolf, and A. Schoenherr. 2007. Terrestrial vegetation of California. University of California Press, Berkeley, California.

Cunningham, L. 2010. A state of change: Forgotten landscapes of California. Heyday Books, Berkeley, California.

Dasmann, R. F. 1965. The destruction of California. Macmillan Company, New York.

Haslam, G., editor. 1999. Jack London's Golden State: Selected California writings. Heyday Books, Berkeley, California.

Jensen, D. B., M. S. Torn, and J. Harte. 1993. In our own hands: A strategy for conserving California's biological diversity. University of California Press, Berkeley, California.

Jordan, David S. 1898. California and the Californians. The Atlantic Monthly 82:793–801.

McPhee, J. 1993. Assembling California. Farrar, Strauss & Giroux, New York.

———. 1989. Los Angeles against the mountains. Pages 183–272 in J. McPhee. The control of nature. Farrar, Strauss & Giroux, New York.

Minnich, R. A. 2008. California's fading wildflowers: Lost legacy and biological invasions. University of California Press, Berkeley, California.

Moyle, P. B. 2002. Inland fishes of California. University of California Press, Berkeley, California.

Muir, J. 1875. The mountains of California. The Century Company, New York.

Parisi, M. 2003. Atlas of the biodiversity of California. California Department of Fish and Game, Sacramento.

Sawyer, J., T. Keeler-Wolf, and J. Evens. 2009. A manual of California vegetation. Second edition. California Native Plant Society, Sacramento.

Schoenherr, A. 1995. A natural history of California. University of California Press, Berkeley, California.

Smith, M. L. 1987. Pacific visions. California scientists and the

environment 1850–1915. Yale University Press, New Haven, Connecticut.
Storer, T. I., and L. P. Tevis. 1996. California grizzly. University of California Press, Berkeley, California.
Stromberg, M., J. Corbin, and C. D'Antonio. 2007. California grasslands: Ecology and management. University of California Press, Berkeley, California.
Sugihara, N. G., J. W. van Wagtendonk, K. E. Shaffer, J. Fites-Kaufman, and A. E. Thode. 2006. Fire in California's ecosystems. University of California Press, Berkeley, California.
Thelander, C. G., and M. Crabtree, editors. 1994. Life on the edge: A guide to California's endangered natural resources: Wildlife. Biosystems Books, Santa Cruz, California.

PART ONE

DRIVERS

TWO

Climate

SAM F. IACOBELLIS, DANIEL R. CAYAN, JOHN T. ABATZOGLOU,
and HAROLD MOONEY

The Nature of the California Climate

California is one of the most geographically and ecologically diverse regions in the world, with landscapes ranging from sandy beaches to coastal redwood rainforests to snow-covered alpine mountains to dry desert valleys. Despite the variety of landscapes, much of California experiences what is termed a "Mediterranean-type" climate, sharing very similar climate and vegetation with other low- to mid-latitude regions on the west sides of continents, including the (European) Mediterranean Basin (e.g., di Castri and Mooney 1973, Minnich 2006), parts of South Africa, south and southwestern Australia, and central Chile. All of these regions have cool winters with intermittent wetness and hot, dry summers. This type of climatic regime has characterized California for millions of years and started to develop between 7 and 4 Ma ago as the California Current became colder and blocked entry of the seasonal North American monsoons emanating from Mexico (Adams and Comrie 1997). By 2.6 Ma ago, California's vegetation elements resembled what we see today (see Chapter 8, "Ecosystems Past: Vegetation Prehistory").

In today's California the basic progression of temperature and precipitation throughout the year is the same in nearly all parts of the state—although the actual amount of precipitation and the temperatures obtained are very dissimilar and explain to a large degree the variability of ecosystems that exist (Figure 2.1). The shading in the bottom row of Figure 2.1 indicates significant variability in monthly precipitation throughout the state—monthly precipitation commonly ranges from less than 50% to over 150% of its long-term average, and the highest variations occur in the winter months when mean precipitation is greatest. In fact, the ups and downs of precipitation are a fundamental feature of California climate, not only within daily and monthly totals but also over annual and longer periods. California has the highest variability of year-to-year precipitation in the conterminous United States (Figure 2.2a). Within these fluctuations are multiyear periods of consecutive wet or dry years, notorious spells that impact ecosystems throughout the state. Reconstruction of the past four hundred years of northern California winter precipitation from tree ring analysis (Figure 2.2b) provides evidence that the high level of interannual variability observed in recent decades by weather instruments is not unusual, and that consecutive wet or dry years can last up to a decade or longer.

The decoupling of moisture and energy of the Mediterranean climate type poses "problems" for organisms. In winter,

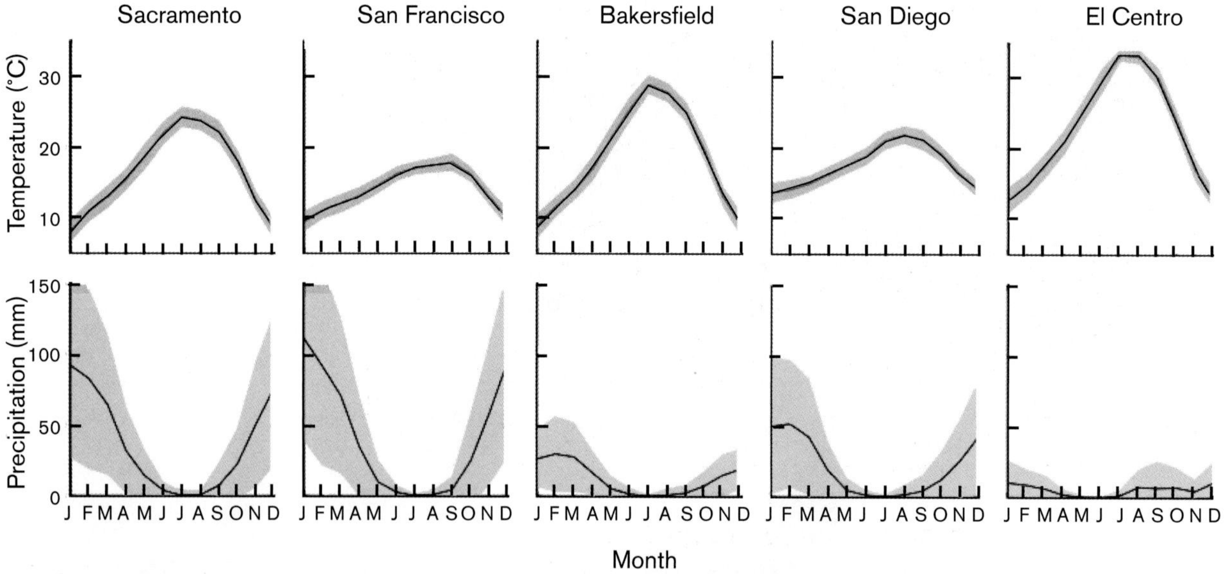

FIGURE 2.1 Climatological monthly mean temperature (top row) and precipitation (bottom row) at five sites in California. Values computed using available station records of at least sixty years from the National Weather Service (NWS) Cooperative Observer Program (COOP). The shading represents the standard deviation around the monthly means.

when moisture is available, temperatures are too low for high rates of metabolic activity. In contrast, during summer, when energy is ample and temperatures are favorable for growth, little or no water often is available (Figure 2.3). The activities of virtually all organisms in California can be related to the juxtaposition of available water and suitable temperatures. Warm summers and autumns are occasionally punctuated by hot, extremely dry air masses, sometimes with strong winds from the interior, that stress vegetation and other organisms. Dry, windy conditions promote wildfires, which in turn affect the evolution and patterning of the vegetation on the landscape.

For many ecosystems in California, biotic activity tends to be limited to the spring. This is the crossover point of adequate moisture and equable temperatures. During the dry summer months, vegetation becomes water-limited. The biota of vast areas of the state goes into dormancy to avoid the extended drought period. Those plants that can find a water supply, such as by a stream or lakeside, or those with roots that can penetrate deeply into the soil where water reserves are held, can remain active during the seasonal dry period. Although there are important variations in different regions and individual landscapes, discussed below in this chapter, this basic pattern of alternating dry and wet period is found in all areas of the state.

It is often remarked that California experiences a drought every year during the summer period, owning to the absence of storms, clear skies, and high amounts of solar radiation reaching the surface, which produces high evaporative demand. Actual evapotranspiration (AET) is the combined flux of water to the atmosphere from soil surfaces and plants by evaporation and transpiration. AET is driven by solar energy and wind but depends on the availability of water. Potential evapotranspiration (PET) is the atmospheric demand of water from the soil and free water surfaces, which represents the amount of evapotranspiration that would occur if water were not a limiting factor. There are marked seasonal and spatial structures of PET and AET in California, where PET peaks in summer due to strongest energy availability and AET peaks in spring and early summer when water and the evaporative demand are jointly high (see Figure 2.3). Arid and semiarid areas have PET in considerable excess of AET and are thereby water-limited. Wetter areas of the state and those at high elevations, where energy is lower, exhibit AET values that are closer to PET and are energy-limited. During persistent dry spells, the landscape shifts toward a greater proportion of water-limited area, while during wet spells it shifts toward more energy-limited area (Hidalgo et al. 2005). Recent investigation of tree mortality indicates that increased water limitation is a primary mechanism of tree mortality in California's lower-elevation forests (Das et al. 2013).

Photo on previous page: Visible satellite image of California and the adjacent Pacific Ocean, January 17, 2011. While sunny conditions prevailed over most of California on this winter day, dense tule fog extended throughout the Central Valley, and marine stratus hugged the coastline in the northern portion of the state. Embedded within the marine stratus are ship tracks created as aerosols from ship exhaust alter cloud radiative and reflective properties. The snow-capped Sierra Nevada Range and brown desert regions in the southeast part of the state further illustrate the diversity present in California's climate at a moment in time. Geostationary Earth Orbiting Satellite (GOES) image courtesy of the National Oceanic and Atmospheric Administration (NOAA).

General Climate Features

The North Pacific High pressure system, among all of the large-scale features of global atmospheric circulation, has the most immediate impact on California climate. A network of subtropical high pressure centers, including the North Pacific High, result from the uneven heating of the Earth's surface. A net radiative influx (more solar radiation reaching the Earth's surface than is vented from the surface by terrestrial infrared radiation) within latitudes equatorward of approximately 38° and a net loss of radiation poleward of approximately 38° results in low surface pressure near the equator and higher surface pressure near latitudes of 30°N and 30°S. Due to the position of the land masses, these high-pressure systems do

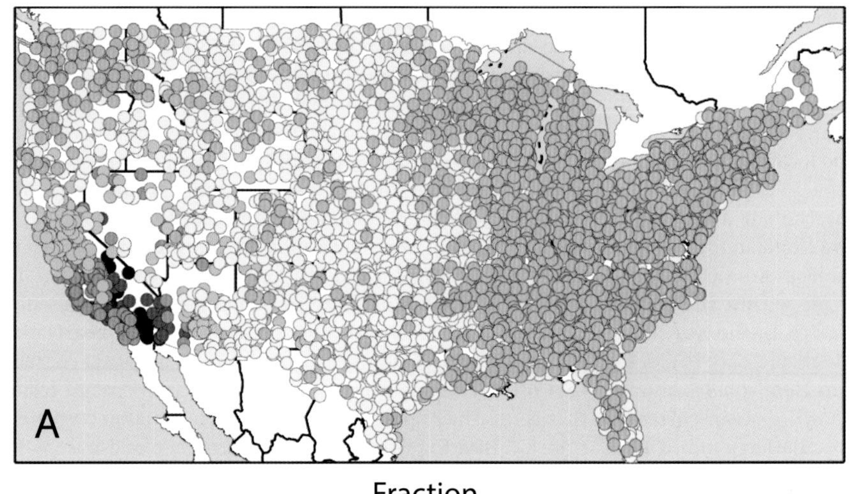

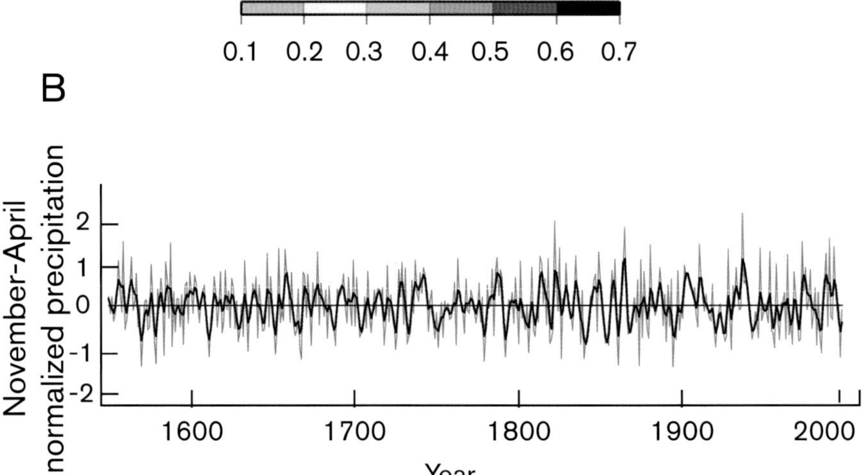

FIGURE 2.2 California precipitation variability.

A Coefficient of variation (standard deviation/mean) of water year (October–September) precipitation at long-term monitoring stations across the conterminous United States, from water year 1951–2008. Source: From Dettinger et al. 2011.

B Reconstructed winter precipitation (normalized by the standard deviation) for northern California Coast ranges based on analysis of blue oak (*Quercus douglasii*) tree rings. Annual estimates are plotted in blue and a five-year smoothed version is plotted in black. Source: From Stahle et al. 2013.

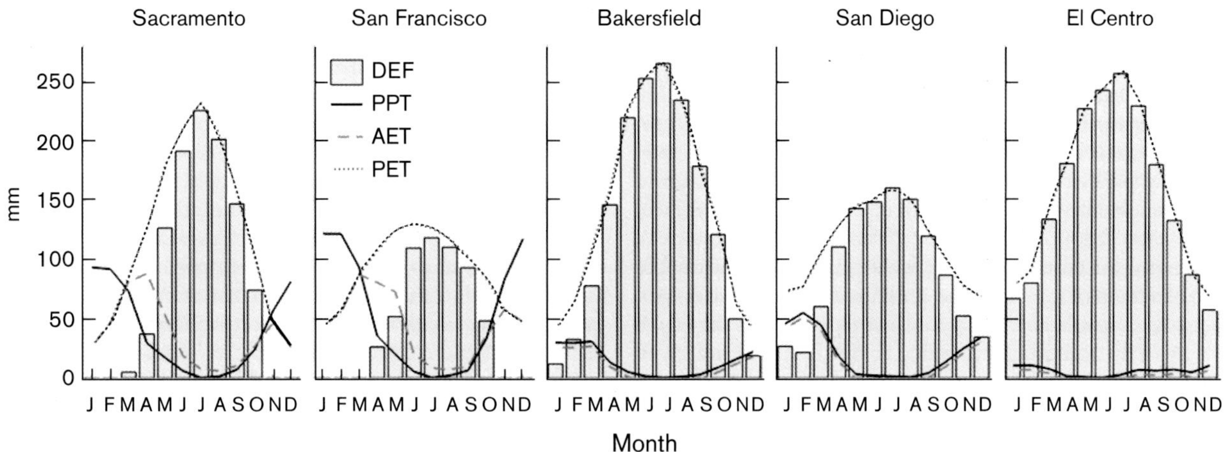

FIGURE 2.3 Climatological monthly water balance at five sites in California estimated using a modified Thornthwaite soil water balance model. Individual components include precipitation (PPT), potential evapotranspiration (PET), actual evapotranspiration (AET), and the deficit (DEF, defined as the difference between PET and AET). When AET is greater than PPT, the difference is obtained from soil moisture. Evapotranspiration values obtained using the Penman-Monteith method for a reference grass surface and a prescribed soil water holding capacity of 150 mm. Source: Necessary climatic data was obtained from the PRISM Climate Group, Oregon State University, <http://prism .oregonstate.edu>.

not form a continuous belt but rather form distinct high-pressure centers. The North Pacific High is a prominent example of these systems and is normally centered between the Hawaiian Islands and the west coast of North America. It is referred to as "semipermanent" because it is nearly always present in the region even though the strength and location of the high-pressure system varies over time.

Within the high-pressure system, the air from aloft descends, inhibiting vertically extensive cloud and storm formation. As the air descends, it also warms ADIABATICALLY, decreasing relative humidity, so the air within the high-pressure system is generally warm and dry. In the Northern Hemisphere the air flow around the high pressure is clockwise (counterclockwise in the Southern Hemisphere) and is responsible for the general clockwise-flowing ocean currents in much of the North Pacific. The circulation around the North Pacific High also exposes much of California to prevailing NORTHWESTERLY WINDS. However, local wind patterns can vary greatly due to the diverse topographic features in the state and the related thermal conditions.

Warm Season

The North Pacific High reaches its maximum intensity and furthest northward extent during the summer months (Figure 2.4a). Associated with the expansion of the high-pressure system, the North Pacific storm track becomes less active and recedes northward. Descending air within the high suppresses upward motion and inhibits rainfall. These two factors create dry conditions—precipitation occurs very rarely in summer months throughout most of California, except for occasional thunderstorms in the mountains and desert areas.

Because they lie on the eastward and northward flanks of the Pacific High, California coastal waters are driven by northwesterly winds that prevail throughout spring, summer, and early fall. The northwesterly winds "push" surface water away from the coast that is then replaced by the UPWELLING of colder water from below. Upwelling along with the southward flow of cool water by the California current (see Chapter 6, "Oceanography") maintains relatively cold water, between 50°F and 60°F (10–15°C), along most of the California coastline during summer. The relatively cool water along the California coast helps to promote a cool and moist marine layer in the lowest 300 to 1,000 meters of atmosphere.

A key feature that distinguishes California from other regions of the United States is a low-level TEMPERATURE INVERSION, which is a crucial feature in developing the marine layer and low-level clouds (Iacobellis and Cayan 2013) and also in trapping and accumulating particulates and pollution (Iacobellis et al. 2009; see Chapter 7, "Atmospheric Chemistry"). Normally, air temperature cools with height, but below the top of a temperature inversion air temperature increases with height. Controlled by the strength and position of the North Pacific High and other large-scale factors, temperature inversions are a persistent feature along the California coast and inland valleys. Along the coast the inversion is known as a "subsidence inversion," caused by descending air in the North Pacific High combined with the cool air above the ocean surface. Interior valleys also frequently experience inversions, especially at night in the winter season due to low solar insolation, radiative cooling of land surfaces, and drainage of cool air into low-lying areas. During strong inversions the afternoon temperature at San Diego near sea level along the coast can be 8°C cooler than that at Alpine, in the adjacent mountains at 530 meters (approximately 1,730 feet) elevation. The subsidence inversion is present, to varying degree, throughout much of the year, especially in spring and summer.

Because the density of air under the inversion is vertically stacked and very stable, the low-level temperature inversion forms a "cap" that inhibits vertical mixing of surface air. This can lead to elevated pollutant levels near the surface, particularly in coastal areas with mountainous topography to the east (e.g., Los Angeles and San Joaquin Valley air basins). The stability of the temperature inversion also leads to a lens of horizontally extensive MARINE STRATUS clouds, a nearly ubiquitous spring and summer feature of the California coastline that often extends from well offshore across coastal terrain that is less than approximately 600 meters (2,000 feet) elevation. Coastal fog occurs when the stratus cloud base is low enough to intersect the ground or the ocean surface. These clouds are most dense in evening through morning hours but still reflect considerable incoming solar radiation, which suppresses daytime temperatures along the coast. The marine layer and stratus regime is an important regulator that affects a wide variety of ecosystems through its moderation of solar radiation, temperature, and humidity.

Periodically during summer months, a pulse of warm moist air flows northeastward into the southern part of the state from the Gulf of California, mainland Mexico, and sometimes the eastern subtropical Pacific. These pulses are part of the Southwest MONSOON, which commonly operates in northern Mexico, Arizona, and New Mexico, leading to frequent summer thunderstorms. When conditions align, the warm, moist air stream can be augmented by the remnants of hurricanes dissipating off the Pacific coast of Mexico. The warm and moisture-laden air often permits thunderstorm development and large precipitation events in the desert regions of southeasterly California. In contrast to most of California, these southeasterly deserts receive a substantial fraction of their annual precipitation during the summer months (see panel for El Centro in Figure 2.1).

During spring and summer, winds in the coastal regions are usually from the northwest. The prevailing northwesterly direction may be broken along the Southern California Bight when winds take a southerly direction during periods when the CATALINA EDDY takes hold. This eddy forms in the lee of the mountainous coastline, which takes an abrupt change in the direction at Point Conception. The Catalina Eddy most commonly occurs during periods of moderate-to-strong northwesterly winds off the Central California coastline (Kanamitsu et al. 2013). Some of California's windiest locations occur in the vicinity of mountain passes, which direct air from cooler climates (usually coastal) to that of the warmer climates (often deserts or valleys). One such location separates the cool, coastal climate of the San Francisco Bay region from that of the Central Valley (Altamont Pass); another lies in the cool upper reaches of the Tehachapi Mountains located close to the hot Mohave Desert (Tehachapi Pass); and the third separates the southern California coastal plain from the Colorado Desert (San Gorgonio Pass). These winds tend to be strongest and most prevalent during summer, when the coast-to-interior temperature contrast is largest. As the interior region warms up and air near the surface rises, cooler marine air from the west rushes in through the mountain passes to replace it. These winds have a strong diurnal character and are the strongest in the afternoon when daytime heating and resulting thermal gradients are greatest.

A. Strong Pacific High

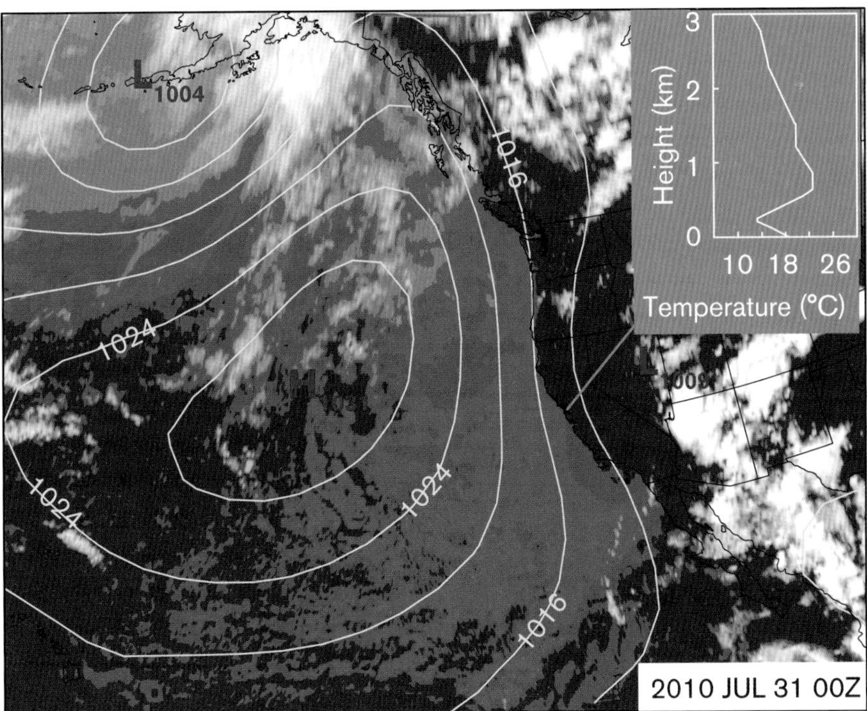

B. Weak Pacific High

FIGURE 2.4 Satellite infrared imagery overlaid with surface pressure isobars (yellow lines) on days when the North Pacific High was strong (A) and weak (B). The inset in the upper right corner of each plot shows the vertical temperature at Oakland, California, for each day. A strong temperature inversion is evident on the day with the strong North Pacific High, but nonexistent on the day with the weak North Pacific High.

Cool Season

During winter months the North Pacific High weakens and shifts to the southeast. At the same time, the North Pacific storm track also migrates southward and intensifies due to a strengthened north-south atmospheric temperature gradient. As a consequence, the storms that form along the JET STREAM are more intense and more likely to directly impact California because blocking by the North Pacific High is reduced (see Figure 2.4b). The winter storms that impact California generally are spawned to the west and north over the North Pacific and propagate over the state in a northwest to southeast direction. Sometimes they can also move in a more westerly or occasionally southwesterly direction. The direction of the storm center, and most important the direction of the winds within the storm, is critical due to the strength and orientation of the winds with respect to topographic features (Dettinger et al. 2004). Interaction of storm winds and mountain ranges can create very heavy precipitation—as air encounters the mountains, it is forced upward and cools. If the air cools to the condensation threshold, the water vapor in the air will condense, leading to enhanced precipitation. When the direction of the wind is perpendicular to the orientation of the mountain range, precipitation is maximized. As discussed later, California's mountain ranges present a variety of directional orientations and thus exhibit differing responses to a given wind direction.

Many areas of California, particularly high elevations and mountain passes, are prone to strong winds as winter storms move through the state. As a typical storm approaches from the northwest, winds near the surface are generally from the southwest and then swing around to westerly and finally northwesterly as the storm leaves the region. Certain locations are more susceptible to winds during different phases of storm passage due to topographic features such as the directional orientations of canyons and passes.

Atmospheric Rivers

Occasionally, relatively narrow streams of air with high concentrations of moisture originating from the tropics or subtropics intercept the coast of California (Figure 2.5). Interaction of these moisture belts with storms forming along the jet stream can result in extreme amounts of precipitation (Dettinger et al. 2011). These moisture-laden air streams have sometimes been called a "pineapple express" but are now referred to as an atmospheric river. Because they often reside over a given location for several hours, retaining their active dynamics and generating heavy precipitation, atmospheric rivers can be extremely productive and are now understood to be the source of many of the floods along the West Coast. A study by Ralph et al. (2006) found that all of the significant floods from October 1997 to February 2006 in the Russian River area were associated with atmospheric rivers crossing the California coastline. In many cases, atmospheric rivers transport warm moist air into California so that storm precipitation occurs as rain up to unusually high elevations before transitioning to snow. These high-elevation snow levels can add to the heavy precipitation in producing flood flows due to the larger fraction of the landscape generating rainfall runoff along with possible melting of low- and mid-elevation snowpack due to rain-on-snow.

There is evidence that unusually severe and lengthy atmospheric river episodes can appear in California, perhaps every couple of hundred years. A legendary historical event began on Christmas Eve in 1861, when high amounts of precipitation starting falling in the Sierra Nevada and lowland watersheds. Reports indicate that precipitation, in some form, persisted for forty-three days in central California and that virtually the whole state was affected by this wet spell. With the copious runoff, the Central Valley turned into a gigantic lake and the tidal inflow into San Francisco Bay was curtailed by freshwater discharge from the Sacramento and San Joaquin River runoff (Brewer 1930, Roden 1967). It is estimated that some eight hundred thousand cattle died and parts of Sacramento, the state capital, were submerged at times under 3 meters of flood water (Dettinger and Ingram 2013).

The warm-moisture "conveyer belt" that operates during atmospheric river storms can also cause considerable flood damage at higher elevations. During a vigorous atmospheric river during December 26, 1996, through January 3, 1997, large amounts of warm rainfall fell in the northern and central Sierra Nevada. Along an elevational gradient, this storm produced 9.4 centimeters (3.7 inches) of rain in Sacramento, 24.4 centimeters (9.6 inches) in Auburn, and 75.4 centimeters (29.7 inches) in Blue Canyon and melted snow above the 3,050-meter level (about 10,000 feet). Copious runoff overwhelmed dams, and widespread flooding occurred. In addition to the climate-related hazards associated with atmospheric rivers, they are important contributors to annual precipitation across much of California. Dettinger et al. (2011) found approximately 30% to 45% of the annual precipitation fell in association with atmospheric river events, and Dettinger (2013) identifies atmospheric rivers as important "drought busters."

Ocean Influence

The climate of California is strongly influenced by its proximity to the Pacific Ocean. Water has a much larger HEAT CAPACITY than air or soil, so an enormous reservoir of heat can be stored in the upper ocean. As a result, the ocean is much more difficult to cool or warm than are the nearby land masses. Thus the ocean and its marine air masses do not change temperature as much and the diurnal and annual variation of the ocean surface temperature and the air above it are much less than those of the air over land masses. In most cases, the ocean is cooler than the adjacent land in summer and warmer than land in winter. A similar relationship generally holds during the course of a day, with the ocean being cooler than land during the day and warmer than land during night. Consequently, the ocean creates an "air-conditioned" zone that pervades across the coastal lowlands to locations inland where marine air can easily penetrate.

Ocean temperature offshore of California is relatively cool (compared to similar latitudes) due to frequent upwelling and horizontal ADVECTION of cold water in the California current system (see Chapter 6,"Oceanography"). Sea surface temperatures (SSTs) along California's coast vary from about 10°C to 15°C (50°F to 59°F) north of Point Conception. South of Point Conception within the Southern California Bight, where the northwesterly winds are interrupted so that upwelling is diminished and the transport of the California current is reduced, SSTs are generally warmer, especially in summer, and have a larger seasonal variation of about 13°C to 22°C (55°F to 72°F).

Because the upper ocean holds a massive amount of heat,

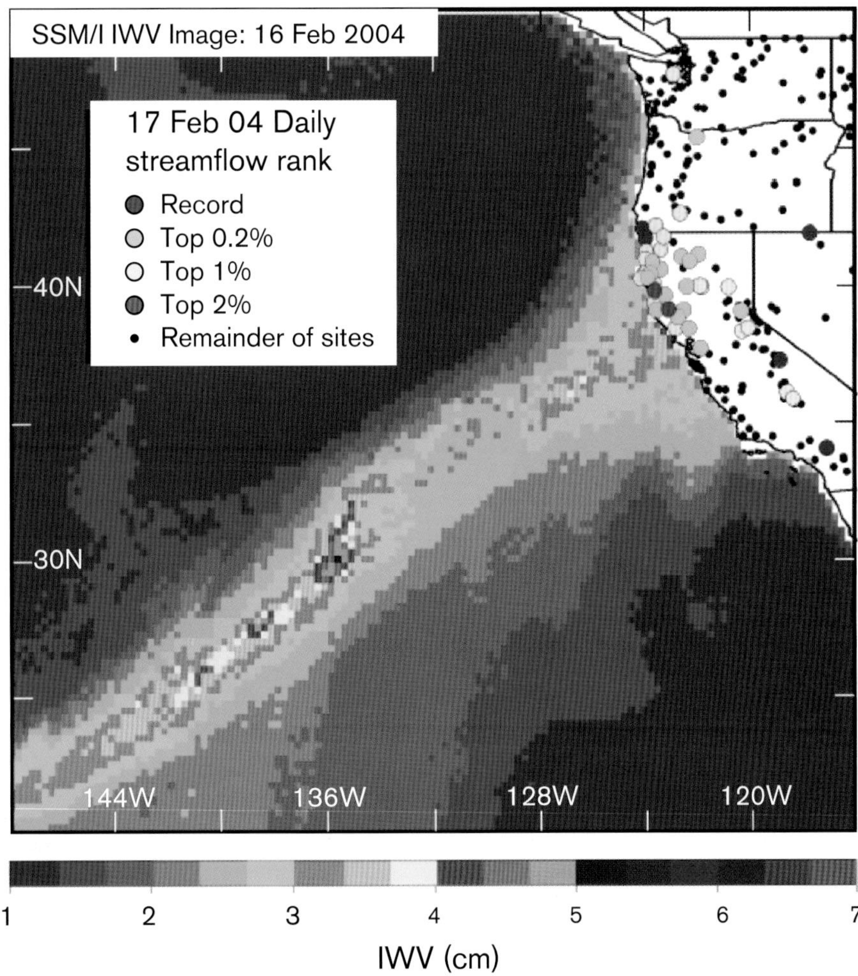

FIGURE 2.5 Composite satellite image of integrated water vapor (IWV) in centimeters (color scale at bottom of map) constructed from multiple polar-orbiting swaths during an atmospheric river event on February 16, 2004, between approximately 1400 and 1830 UTC (Coordinated Universal Time). The impact on river systems along the U.S. West Coast is shown using percentile rankings of daily streamflow on the following day, February 17, 2004, LST (Local Standard Time) (add eight hours for UTC) as indicated by the color-filled circles (e.g., red, yellow, and green circles indicate daily streamflow at the 98th, 99th, and 99.8th percentile levels, respectively; a daily streamflow greater than any previously recorded value is denoted by a blue circle). Gauges with less than thirty years of recorded data are not shown. Source: From Ralph et al. 2006.

the sea surface temperature is relatively resistant to change. Due to molecular and turbulent exchanges, the air in the boundary layer over the ocean tends to quickly equilibrate to the SST. Prevailing northwesterly winds transport this cool ocean air onto the California coastal regions and into accessible inland valleys. This marine layer influence moderates the range of temperatures that would otherwise exist in these regions, an effect that is particularly noticeable during summer months. In addition, since most of the storms that impact California track from over the ocean, the surface air within these systems is usually close to the ocean temperature. As a result, coastal and inland valleys of California are generally insulated from the cold winter conditions found at similar latitudes at other locations in the United States.

El Niño and La Niña

Next to the annual cycle, the most important pattern of climate variation in California is the El Niño / Southern Oscillation (ENSO). El Niño and its opposing phase partner, La Niña, are parts of a coupled ocean-atmosphere phenomenon rooted in the tropical Pacific and involving fluctuations in heat content, ocean surface temperature, and tradewinds. ENSO has a variety of global expressions but can be quite strongly felt in California's oceanic and atmospheric climate. Through transfers of heat, moisture, and momentum, tropical ENSO conditions are transmitted (teleconnected) to the mid-latitude ocean and atmosphere including the California region. Near the equator, surface winds (the TRADEWINDS) generally blow from east to west. Ocean surface currents, driven by the tradewinds, transport water in a westward direction, resulting in a sea level about a half of a meter higher in the western than in the eastern Pacific. Movement of the water away from the coast of South America drives the upwelling of colder deep water. During "normal" conditions, sea surface temperature (SST) decreases from west to east along the equatorial Pacific, with relatively cold water along the South American coast and very warm water (SST >30°C) in the Western Tropical Pacific sometimes

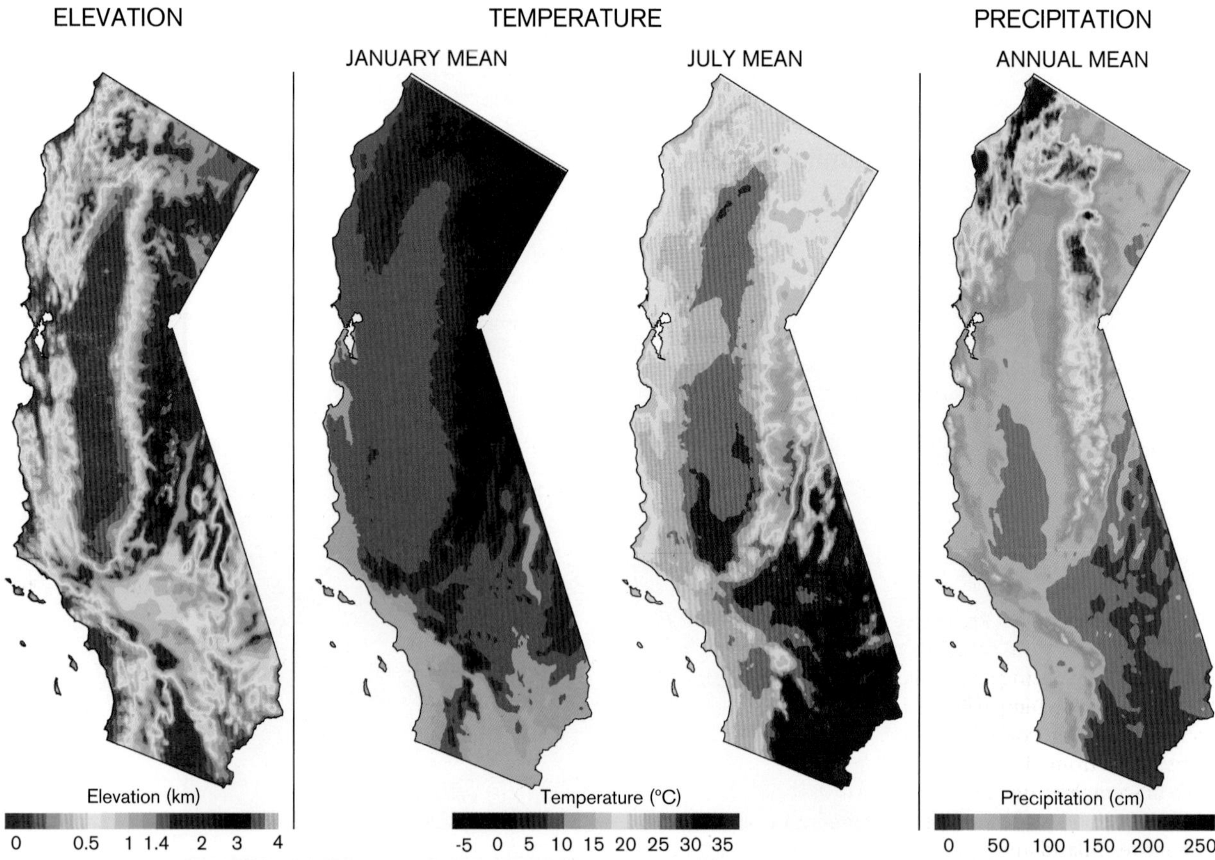

FIGURE 2.6 Maps showing (from left to right) elevation, January mean temperature, July mean temperature, and annual mean precipitation throughout California. Data obtained from the PRISM Climate Group, Oregon State University, http://prism.oregonstate.edu.

referred to as "the warm water pool." Associated with this warm water are low surface pressures, strong atmospheric convection, and resulting deep cumulus clouds and heavy precipitation.

Periodically, at irregular intervals of about two to seven years, the easterly tradewinds over the tropical Pacific slacken or occasionally even reverse direction (Rasmussen and Carpenter 1982, Philander 1990). In response, the SST increases in the Central and Eastern Tropical Pacific, upwelling diminishes along the equator and along the South American coast, CONVECTIVE activity shifts from the western toward the central and eastern equatorial Pacific, and dryness sets in over central America. This condition is called El Niño and can have a dramatic impact on weather and ecosystems both locally, in the Tropical Pacific, and with recognized global manifestations (Rasmussen and Wallace 1983, Philander 1990, Wolter and Timlin 2011) as well as strong regional impacts along the U.S. West Coast, particularly in California (Sette and Isaacs 1960, Monteverdi and Null 1997).

During El Niño, the increase in SST in the Central and Eastern Tropical Pacific often consumes a vast region that alters heat and moisture fluxes to the extent that it impacts global atmospheric circulation patterns. One primary impact is a shift and intensification of the subtropical branch of the jet stream across the Pacific that bring winter storms further south during winter toward California. As a result, California can be (but is not always) subjected to more frequent winter storminess and precipitation during an El Niño event (Redmond and Koch 1991, Gershunov and Barnett 1998, Cayan et al. 1999). During the exceptionally strong El Niño events of 1982–1983 and 1997–1998, California experienced enormous storm sequences and extraordinarily heavy precipitation, snowpack, and coastal storm impacts (Flick 1998, Bromirski et al. 2003, National Research Council 2012). In addition, these storms are generally warmer, contain more atmospheric moisture, and tend to track in a more westerly or southwesterly direction as they cross the California coast.

The La Niña phase of the ENSO phenomenon occurs when tradewinds in the tropical Pacific become stronger than normal. In contrast to El Niño, La Niña SSTs are cooler than normal in the Central and Eastern Tropical Pacific, convection is strong in the far western equatorial Pacific, and upwelling along the equator and along South America is strong. In many La Niña events, associated atmospheric circulation changes result in a northerly shift in the jet stream across the North Pacific, limiting the frequency of winter storms and precipitation in California. In contrast to the often-increased California precipitation during El Niño years, La Niña years have quite consistently yielded subpar winter precipitation (Redmond and Koch 1991). This La Niña–diminished precipitation association, like its El Niño-increased precipitation counterpart, is strongest in southern California and fades in northern California.

The Wide Range of Climates in California

Most of California is dominated by cool, intermittently wet winters and warm dry summers. Overlain on this general pattern is extraordinary spatial and temporal variability. Considerable spatial variability arises from the inherent structure within the atmosphere and because of the influence of California's varied setting and complex landscape. For example, Abatzoglou et al. (2009) used objective measures to identify eleven regional modes of temperature and precipitation variability within California. This variability is an inextricable part of California's climate and ecosystems.

Spatial Variability of Temperature

As expected, the broad-scale view of surface air temperature in California shows an increase from north to south. However, there is considerable complexity and spatial variation in temperature that cannot be explained simply by latitude (Figure 2.6).

Coastal Influence

Throughout the state, coastal regions generally tend to be warmer in winter and cooler in summer than interior regions due to the moderating effect caused by the large thermal inertia of the ocean. Temperatures over the land that are closely connected to the coast are influenced by marine air masses transported from directly over the ocean (Lebassi et al. 2009), with air temperatures very close to the SST (Figure 2.7). The oceanic influence on surface air temperatures decreases as one moves inland and is sharply limited by coastal hills and mountains. In some cases, such as along the Big Sur coast of central California, this transition can occur over distances less than 3 kilometers due to the confluence of maritime air and steep topography, resulting in dramatic gradients in temperature and humidity. The oceanic influence on air temperatures has important consequences for annual range of temperature. Coastal locations have a low range of temperatures, while further inland the difference between summer maximum and winter minimum temperatures increases sharply. This temperature range is an important determinant of the distribution and adaptability of species and ecosystems across the region.

Deserts

The desert regions of southeastern California are warmer than most other regions of the state throughout the year. This is partly due to their southerly location but is highly dictated by the year-round influence of the descending (and warming) air on the flank of the North Pacific High. Another factor that contributes to the region's relative warmth is the adiabatic compressional heating of eastward-flowing air masses that traverse the Peninsular and Transverse ranges. In addition, during daytime hours, due to the lack of moisture and vegetation, incoming solar radiation quickly warms the surface since little solar energy is used to evaporate water, resulting in higher maximum temperatures. Conversely, at night, radiational cooling of the surface is very efficient because of the lack of clouds and extreme lack of water vapor in the air, so the surface can get very cold. As a result, deserts exhibit very strong diurnal temperature changes—this impacts the distribution and adaptability of ecosystems in these regions.

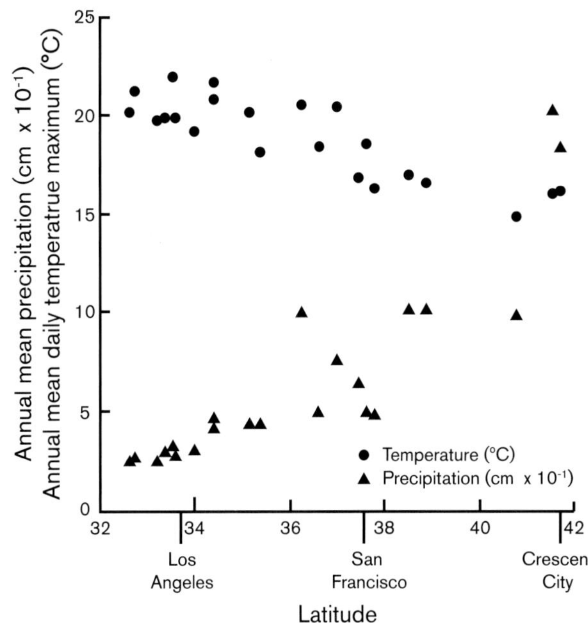

FIGURE 2.7 Plot showing the latitudinal dependence of annual precipitation (triangles) and annual mean daily temperature maximum (circles) at coastal California locations based on COOP (Cooperative Observer Program) station measurements.

Elevation and Slope

Throughout the year in most situations, relatively cool temperatures are found at the higher elevations, particularly along the Coast Ranges and the Sierra Nevada. As elevations rise from sea level, atmospheric pressure decreases. Since air temperature depends strongly on pressure, temperatures also generally decrease with height (an exception is the inversion layer discussed earlier in this chapter). On average in the free atmosphere air temperature decreases with height at a rate of 6.5°C per kilometer. The marked topographic features in California mean that associated air temperature changes due to elevation are large, as are the changes in species and ecosystems (e.g., Thorne et al. 2009). The patterning of the biota of California is also strongly influenced by the effect of topography on MICROCLIMATE. Aspect (slope direction) also affects radiation, local temperature, and hence site water balance. These in turn determine biological processes and the distribution of organisms. North-facing slopes in the Northern Hemisphere receive considerably less radiation, particularly in the winter, than do south-facing slopes.

Seasonal and Diurnal Temperature Variation

The range of temperatures is a critical factor for the viability of many species. Given its diverse landscapes, California has a broad range of temperature variation. Temperature variability, both diurnally and seasonally, along California's coast is moderated by the insulating effects of the Pacific Ocean. Further inland, temperature variation is much greater (Figure 2.8). The largest annual temperature variations are found in the southeastern deserts of California. There, daytime temperatures during summer can exceed 120°F (approximately 50°C). At night, the surface cools quickly through

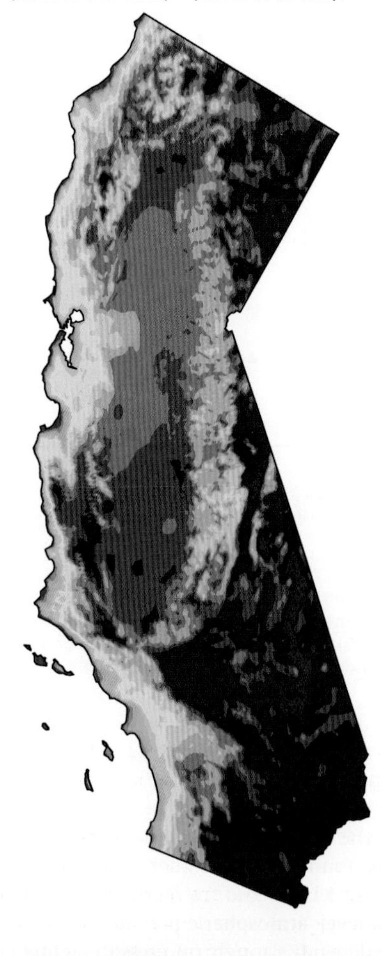

FIGURE 2.8 Annual temperature variation as measured by the difference between the mean July daily maximum and mean January daily minimum temperatures. Source: Data based on years 1981 through 2010 obtained from the PRISM Climate Group, Oregon State University, http://prism.oregonstate.edu.

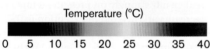

the emission of INFRARED RADIATION. This radiational cooling is enhanced by the low concentration of atmospheric water vapor and cloud-free skies generally found in the desert regions. During winter, when the nights are longer, minimum temperatures can fall as low as 30°F (-1°C). The spatial distribution of diurnal temperature variations is similar to the annual values shown in Figure 2.6; however, the magnitude of the differences are considerably lower.

Spatial Variability of Precipitation

California displays enormous variation in annual precipitation, ranging from <5 cm year^{1} in Death Valley to >300 cm year^{1} along its northern coastal regions (see, e.g., Minnich 2006). This remarkable spatial variability in precipitation results from the strong amplification or suppression of precipitation by mountain and lowland topography, along with the larger-scale changes in precipitation that occur over the north-to-south and west-to-east extents of California's boundaries.

Topography

When moisture-laden air within storm systems sweeps over mountains such as the Sierra Nevada, the air is forced upward in a process known as OROGRAPHIC UPLIFT. As the air rises, it cools due to decreasing atmospheric pressure. If the air cools sufficiently, it will reach its SATURATION POINT and water vapor will begin to condense, forming clouds and precipitation along the WINDWARD side of the mountain range. Orographic lifting amplifies precipitation along the windward side of mountain ranges. Conversely, an opposing "rain shadow" effect occurs on the LEEWARD side, where the air mass begins to sink and warm as the atmospheric pressure increases with declining altitude. This effectively ends further condensation, and the clouds often quickly evaporate. Also, the air on the lee side is drier because moisture in the air mass has been depleted by precipitation on the windward side. Increased precipitation on the windward sides and rain shadows on the leeward sides are most pronounced when the air is flowing across (perpendicular to) the orientation of the mountain range. Most regions on the leeward side of California's mountain ranges exhibit rain shadows—notable examples are found on the east side of the Coast Range and the east side of the Sierra Nevada (Figure 2.9). A "rain-out" of moisture also occurs as storm-driven Pacific air masses cross the mountain blocks in California, as evidenced by the much drier, sparsely vegetated west slope of the White Mountains compared to the west slopes of the Coast Range and Sierra Nevada.

Figure 2.9 shows seven locations along an east-west transect across central California, where the mountain ranges lie mostly parallel to the coast. As storm air masses move off the Pacific and across the state, larger amounts of precipitation are observed on the windward sides and smaller amounts on the leeward sides. The Sierra Nevada, with the highest elevations, exhibits the largest difference between windward and leeward precipitation and experiences greatest precipitation during storms with westerly to west-southwesterly wind flow (Pandey et al. 1999) and during warm storms with moist air masses (Cayan and Riddle 1993). While most of California's mountain ranges are generally oriented north-south, others, such as the Transverse Mountains of southern California, lie in a more east-west configuration. Some winter storms—for example, during some of California's strong El Niño winters, contain relatively warm air and large amounts of moisture and produce a circulation with southwesterly or southerly winds. These storm systems tend to produce large amounts of precipitation in just a few hours along the windward side of the Transverse Range. Such high-intensity precipitation events can lead to disastrous results, including landslides and debris flows, particularly if a recent wildfire has denuded the mountain slopes (USGS 2005).

Latitude

In addition to the variability created by the numerous mountain ranges, precipitation generally increases with latitude.

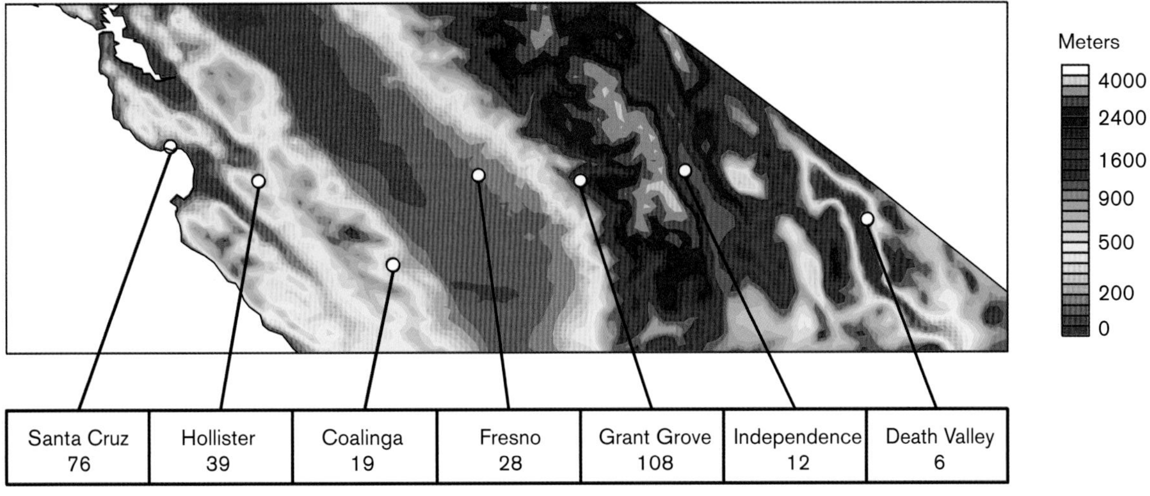

FIGURE 2.9 Annual mean precipitation values at selected sites along an approximate latitudinal transect across California. The color map denotes elevation. Precipitation data based on selected COOP (Cooperative Observer Program) station measurements with at least forty years of data.

This is easiest to see along the immediate coastline, where the impact of mountain ranges on precipitation is minimized (see Figure 2.7). Most, but not all, winter storms are disturbances that are embedded in the fast, upper-level atmospheric jet stream. Typically these storms initially make landfall along the north coast of California and then propagate south and east. As these storms move in a general southeastward direction across California, they often weaken to the point that there is less frequent storm activity in southern California than areas north of Point Conception.

In contrast to the more frequently occurring frontal storm system are "cut-off low" circulations that often form at lower latitudes and may deposit rain and snow in southern California but not to its north. Cut-off lows, as eddy-like circulations that are separate from the primary flow at upper levels, often propagate very slowly or remain stationary and can produce many hours of precipitation that is sometimes quite heavy. Overall, however, the southern portions of the state experience diminished storminess and less precipitation, which creates a south-to-north precipitation gradient—compare mean annual precipitation in San Diego (32° 44'N) of about 25 centimeters to that in Eureka (40° 48') of about 100 centimeters. In contrast, air temperatures along the immediate coastline display only a modest variation with latitude of about 7°C due to the moderating influence of the eastern North Pacific.

Interannual Variability of Precipitation

From an ecological as well as economic point of view, highly variable precipitation is one of the most important characteristics of California's climate. The relatively short seasonal window of precipitation (see Figure 2.1) compounds the influence of strong variability in the winter storm track across the northeastern Pacific. Variability in precipitation from synoptic to multiyear time scales in California occurs throughout the state (see Figure 2.2). In relative terms, the variability of California precipitation is the greatest in the United States (Dettinger et al. 2011). This arises from the off-and-on activity of storminess in California and its tendency to take a more northerly track across the North Pacific in some years and a southerly track in others (Dettinger et al. 1998). Examination of yearly records at locations throughout the state finds frequent, multiyear periods of either deficit or surplus precipitation amounts (see, e.g., Figure 2.2b). Extended periods of either deficit or surplus precipitation can place significant stress on both terrestrial and marine ecosystems.

During winter, much of the precipitation that falls over the Sierra Nevada and higher-elevation watersheds in other mountain ranges is in the form of snow. The snow at these high elevations typically remains frozen until temperatures warm later in spring (Lundquist and Loheide 2011) (Figure 2.10). This explains why the water content in the Sierra snowpack usually reaches a maximum during March or April, while precipitation amounts peak during January. During heavy precipitation years such as the great El Niño of 1982–1983, high snow depths can extend into May (Figure 2.10; California Department of Water Resources 1983).

The natural water storage provided by mountain snowpack has important implications for many ecosystems, since it prolongs the presence of water in the soil and allows for more gradual runoff than occurs in settings that are rainfall-dominated. Snow-fed watersheds produce less damaging flood conditions compared to rainfall basins or those whose snow melts immediately after falling. This is also a major concern of climate change adaptability studies. Projected increases in temperature are expected in California to result in both (1) less snow and more rain, leading to more immediate runoff; and (2) an earlier period of snowmelt (see Chapter 14, "Climate Change Impacts"). Through these effects warmer winters and springs, especially if they include heavy precipitation events, could lead to increased potential for damaging floods. Changes in the timing of the spring runoff due to snowmelt would have important consequences for soil moisture values at many locations in the state. Stewart et al. (2005) describe an advance of snowmelt–driven streamflow across much of the western U.S. since 1950, and Hoerling et al. (2013) found that streamflow maxima in many snowmelt-fed streams of the southwestern U.S. occurred earlier during 2001–2010, compared to the 1950–1999 base period. An earlier runoff

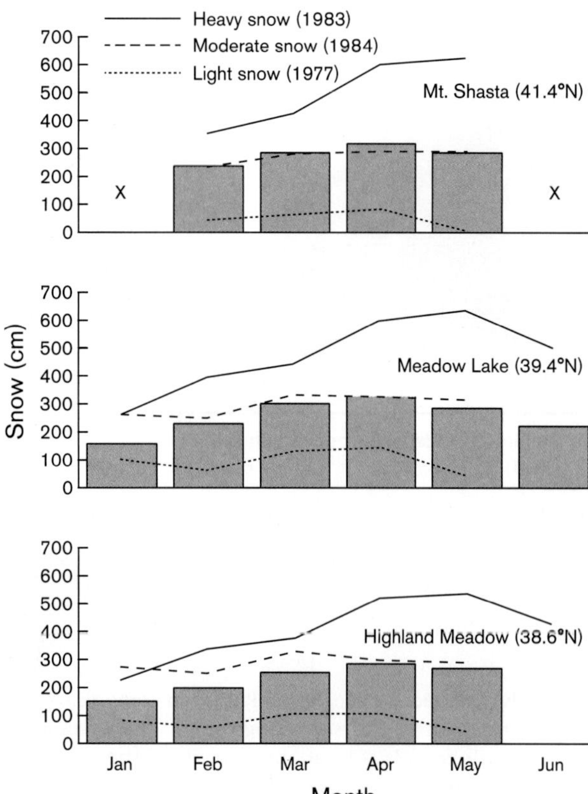

FIGURE 2.10 Monthly snow depth at three California locations. Bars indicate monthly averages over the 1950–1999 period. The lines represent selected years when the snow depth was low, moderate, or high. Source: California Department of Water Resources Snow Survey Records.

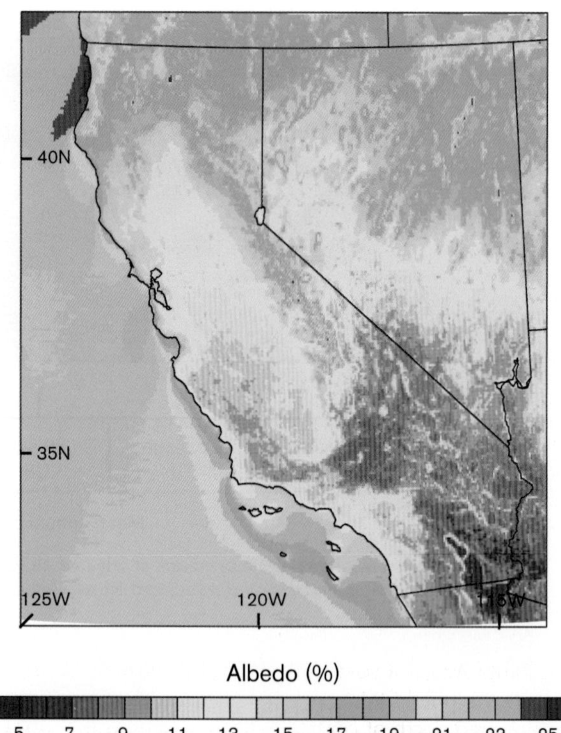

FIGURE 2.11 Annual mean cloud albedo (solar reflectance) measured by Geostationary Orbiting Environmental Satellites (GOES) imagery over the 1996–2012 period. Source: Satellite data obtained from the National Oceanic and Atmospheric Administration (NOAA) Comprehensive Large Array-data Stewardship System (CLASS) website at <http://www.nsof.class.noaa.gov> and the University of Wisconsin Space Science and Engineering Center.

would generally lead to reduced soil moisture later during in the summer months when soils are already critically dry due to the normal summer drought.

Spatial Variation of Incoming Surface Solar Radiation

The amount as well as spatial and temporal distribution of solar radiation supplies the energy needed by organisms to photosynthesize. Solar radiation also provides much of the energy needed to melt snow and to drive evaporative processes. At the top of the atmosphere, the amount of incoming solar radiation is a function of latitude and time of year and is easily calculated. However, how much of that solar radiation reaches the surface is not so trivial. Solar radiation at the surface is determined by slope and aspect of the land surface and is also strongly affected by cloud cover, with AEROSOL and water vapor concentrations playing a minor role.

A major producer of clouds in California is CYCLONIC storm systems, which are especially frequent and generally best developed in the northern part of the state, and more common in winter than in summer. Rain shadows of numerous mountain ranges inhibit cloud formation and thus add complexity to the distribution of clouds (and of sunshine) within the state (Figure 2.11). The far southeastern part of the state is rarely impacted by northerly cyclonic storms and lies more or less in a large rain shadow, under the influence of a regional descending air mass (described earlier in the chapter). This region has a large number of cloudless days that, in part, determines the high temperatures that prevail in this region. These cloudless zones are among the most arid regions of the state, which have a strong influence on the flora and fauna there and have led to the development of new solar energy generation facilities (see Chapter 30, "Deserts").

Marine stratus clouds play a major role along the coast of California and are a key factor in determining the amount of solar radiation reaching the surface. These clouds, produced by the effects of the North Pacific High and the cool SSTs off the California coast, are most frequent during summer months when available solar radiation is at its highest, which amplifies their impact. They create a marked seasonal increase in cloud ALBEDO (equivalent to decrease in surface solar radiation) along California's coastline (see Figure 2.11). The contrast is largest in the northern portions of the state and decreases southward. The reduction of solar radiation by marine stratus along the immediate coastline is an important contributor to the relatively cool temperatures in these regions.

Regional Features

Heat Waves

Summer heat waves impose a major stress on ecosystems in California, often occurring during periods when soil and plant moisture have already declined and temperature is already relatively hot. Heat waves usually occur just a few times in a given summer and typically persist for just a few days, but they have been observed to last for more than one week (Gershunov et al. 2009). Heat wave events whose strongest expression is during daytime hours have occurred irregularly during the past several decades, but without major upward or downward trends. A rising trend has been observed of nighttime heat waves, anomalously warm during the day but with exceptionally warm nighttime temperatures (Gershunov et al. 2009, Guirguis et al. 2014). The atmospheric circulation anomalies responsible for most great daytime- and nighttime-type California heat waves are remarkably similar, consisting of a prominent anticyclone aloft above Washington State. This feature reinforces a strong, surface pressure gradient between a high-pressure anomaly over the Great Plains and a low off the California coast. In contrast to daytime heat waves, which are generally characterized by low relative humidity, nighttime heat waves have been accompanied by heightened humidity. The lack of relief from hot daytime conditions when nighttime temperatures remain elevated can have harsh consequences for ecosystems, livestock, and people.

Santa Ana Winds

The Santa Ana is a FOEHN-like wind in southern California that results when high pressure develops over the interior to the east and north of coastal California. Often this configuration arises when a cool, dry air mass flows downslope from high-elevation basins in the western North American interior toward lower atmospheric pressures off the Pacific coast. As the air descends to lower elevations, it undergoes compression and warms. Since the air is sourced from higher altitudes, it is already dry, and as it warms its relative humidity is further reduced. Compression of this air mass through mountain passes often produces winds of 40 to 60 km hr^{1} and in extreme cases may yield wind speeds in excess of 100 km hr^{1}.

Hot, dry conditions in summer in California are conducive to wildfires and are especially common in California's mountain forest zones (Wildfire Today 2013). These summer wildfire conditions are distinct from Santa Ana events (Westerling et al. 2003), which are most common during fall and winter and are especially dangerous in spawning fires at lower elevations west of the mountain fronts in southern California (Hughes et al. 2011). Santa Anas are a regional phenomenon expressed most strongly within the coastal margin and nearby mountain passes of southern California. In many cases Santa Ana winds are set up by much larger-scale weather patterns that drive northeasterly winds along and across the gradient of high-amplitude atmospheric pressure cells that develop in the West Coast and Great Basin region during fall and winter (Abatzoglou et al. 2013). These hot, dry winds frequently occur toward the end of the dry season, when soils and watersheds are at their driest after the long summer drought, and thereby severely increase the environmental stress on many ecosystems. If fuel moistures remain low in early fall due to lack of widespread wetting rains, the potential for Santa Ana–driven wildfires heightens.

Santa Ana winds are often responsible for the rapid expansion of destructive wildfires, (Westerling et al. 2004) as occurred in southern California in October 2003 (Figure 2.12). The October 2003 fires, emblematic of other strong Santa Ana–driven fires in southern California (Keeley et al. 2013), burned vast areas of native grassland and chaparral—and also destroyed many homes and businesses when the paths of these fires ran into developed areas. Because of the extreme winds and drying in Santa Anas, resulting wildfires can rapidly cover enormous areas; the October 2003 fires burned more than 300,000 hectares, destroying ecosystems and causing more than three billion dollars in damage.

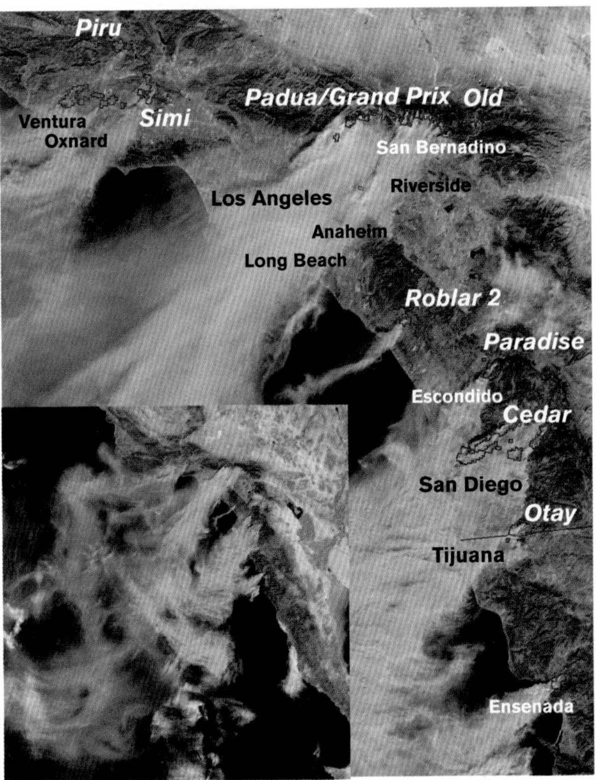

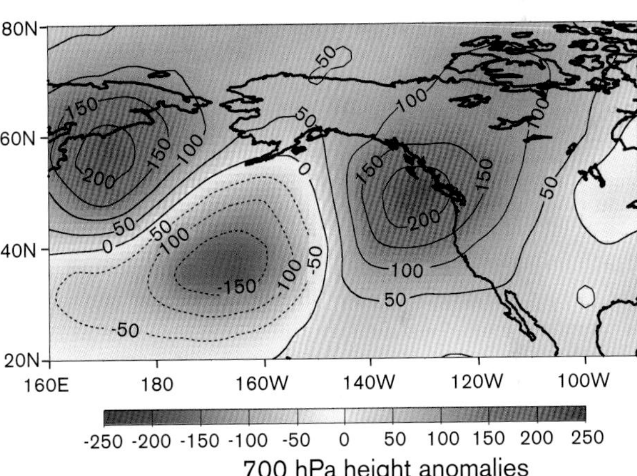

FIGURE 2.12 (Top) Smoke from southern California wildfires (named in italics) on October 26, 2003, as seen from NASA/MODIS (Moderate Resolution Imaging Spectroradiometer) satellite imagery. Active fire perimeters are outlined in red. (Bottom) The bottom panel shows the 700 hPa geopotential height anomalies on October 25, 2003 (ignition date). Source: From Westerling et al. 2004.

Sea Breeze

Because of the high heat capacity of water, land surfaces are usually much warmer than the ocean during summer daytime hours. This horizontal land-ocean temperature gradient creates a pressure minimum over the warm land, which sets up a circulation that draws in cool air from over the ocean. This wind system is called a sea breeze and is most common and most pronounced during the summer, when the land-ocean temperature contrast is at a maximum. The onshore flow of cool marine air helps to moderate the temperatures along the coastal margin, providing cooler and moister conditions on days when the sea breeze develops. Larger-scale synoptic weather patterns can reinforce the sea breeze or create an opposing PRESSURE GRADIENT negating the sea breeze. During periods when the sea breeze is suppressed, coastal areas can become much warmer than normal, increasing stress on ecosystems (and humans) accustomed to the normally cool coastal temperatures.

As the sun sets, the land cools more quickly than the ocean, and the temperature gradient can reverse—with low pressure forming over the water and a breeze blowing from land to the water. This is called a land breeze and primarily occurs during winter when the nights are longer, giving the land more time to cool. A particular example of a sea breeze with important impacts on a large region occurs during summer east of the San Francisco Bay. On most summer days, the inland Sacramento Valley quickly warms during morning hours. At the same time, the land-ocean thermal gradient increases rapidly and a sea breeze develops. Advection of this cool moist marine air advances inland through the San Joaquin Delta and often into the western Sacramento Valley and is known as the Delta Breeze. The Delta Breeze is most pervasive when subsiding air from the overhead North Pacific High is weakened, allowing a deeper marine layer. With a deep marine layer, the cool Delta Breeze can penetrate into Sacramento and beyond into the Sacramento Valley, bringing substantial relief from hot summer temperatures.

Tule Fog

During winter months, light winds are a typical feature in the San Joaquin and Sacramento Valleys. In winter, the ground is often wet enough to moisten the boundary layer. At night, cold air drains down the sides of the Sierra Nevada to the east and the Coast Ranges to the west, facilitating the formation of a strong nocturnal temperature inversion. With little wind mixing and sufficient humidity, shallow radiation fog easily forms overnight underneath this inversion. This radiation fog is also known as tule fog after the tule grass wetlands in the region.

During daylight hours the fog drastically reduces visibility and reflects large amounts on incoming solar radiation, preventing the surface from warming and aiding the persistence of the fog. Although it is relatively shallow (approximately 60 meters thick), the fog can endure through much of the day and often will not dissipate at all, setting the stage for even greater production the following night. The daily cycle of fog is interrupted by increasing winds of approaching winter storms that mix the air and break down the thermal inversion. It is not unusual each winter season to have prolonged periods of fog (two to three weeks) due to a lack of storm activity. Air temperatures in the coastal mountains and Sierra Nevada are typically above normal during such prolonged events due to high-pressure subsidence and ample sunshine on landscapes that lie above the inversion. Fog keeps the surface cool during the day by reflecting sunlight but also keeps the surface warmer at night by absorbing and reemitting infrared energy. The resulting consistent, cool temperatures are an asset to fruit tree production, a major agricultural business in these valleys.

Lightning

Lightning strikes play a key role in igniting wildfires in California (e.g., Abatzoglou and Brown 2009). The occurrence of lightning varies greatly according to geography and topography, season, and weather pattern (Figure 2.13). Lightning occurrence is highest in summer, peaking in August when surface warming is greatest, and tends to occur most frequently in afternoon hours with peak heating of the land surface and enhanced tendency for rising atmospheric motions. Lightning strikes are more frequent at higher elevations. Weather patterns that promote lightning in most California regions exhibit strengthened high-pressure cells stationed over the western U.S. (van Wagtendonk and Cayan 2008). These circulations deploy moist, monsoonlike air masses, and favor hot afternoon temperatures that promote rising motions, especially over mountain terrain. The occurrence of lightning strikes is highest in California's mountains and deserts and lowest in coastal and valley regions. In the mountains relatively frequent lightning occurrence falls on forest ecosystems with heavy fuel loads. This combination can result in active wildfires. Fortunately, lightning usually does not occur during strong winds, and lightning is suppressed during Santa Ana events when vertical motions are downward, so this ignition source is quelled during some of the most extreme fire weather conditions.

Summary

California's Mediterranean climate, comprised of cool, wet winters and hot, dry summers, together with numerous mountain ranges and valleys throughout the state produce a unique and diverse set of ecological landscapes. The seasonal pattern of precipitation and temperature is a stress on many ecosystems during summer, when temperatures are conducive to growth but necessary water is lacking. Precipitation in California is strongly linked to seasonal variations in the North Pacific High and the extratropical storm track. During summer months the North Pacific High is at peak intensity and greatest poleward extent, effectively blocking storm systems from California. The North Pacific High weakens and moves equatorward away from California during winter months, allowing storm systems forming over the North Pacific to track across the state. California's desert regions experience considerably less precipitation than other parts of the state and receive the bulk of their precipitation during the summer months due to thunderstorm activity.

Annual precipitation amounts throughout California vary significantly over a range of time scales, from synoptic periods to decades. This extremely high variation is an important factor for ecosystems and subjects them to large year-to-year and even extended, multiyear periods of below- or above-average moisture availability. Some of this strong variability stems from the occurrence of El Niño and La Niña events, which often result, respectively, in significantly higher and lower than normal annual precipitation totals throughout much of the state. Spatially, the variation across the Califor-

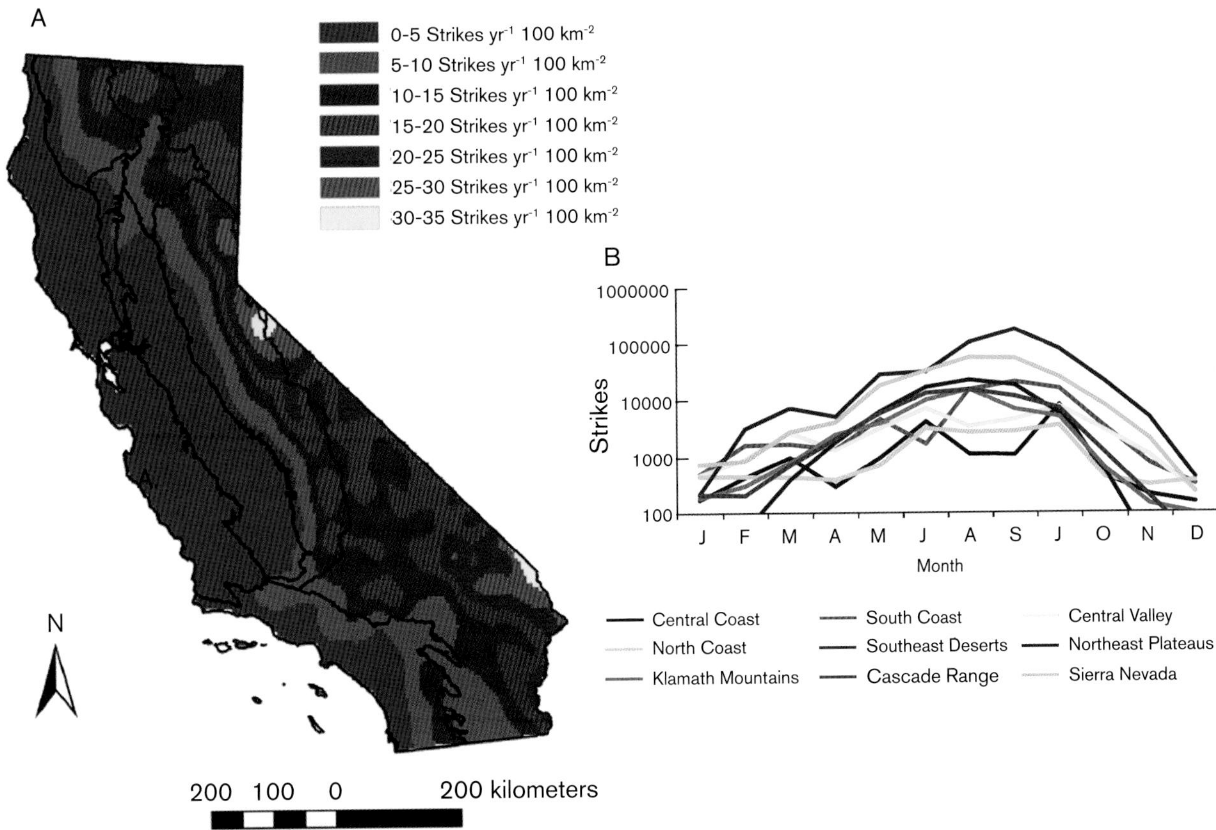

FIGURE 2.13 Lightning strikes. Source: From van Wagtendonk and Cayan 2008.

A Lightning strike density (strikes yr^{-1} 100 km^{-2}) in California, for the period 1985 through 2000.

B Number of lightning strikes by month and bioregion in California, for the period 1985 through 2000. The monthly pattern is consistent with more strikes occurring during the summer months than during the winter months.

nia landscape of temperature and precipitation is strongly associated with latitude and topography. There is a general trend of cooler temperatures and increasing precipitation with increasing latitude. However, topography plays a strong role also, as the height and orientation of the numerous mountain ranges have profound influence on precipitation distribution. In general, as winds within storm systems encounter mountainous terrain, precipitation is enhanced on windward slopes and reduced on the leeward sides.

A diverse array of regional climatic features throughout California have a profound impact on ecosystems. Cloud cover from wintertime cyclonic storms and summer marine stratus along California's coast strongly regulate the solar radiation reaching the surface. Santa Ana winds aggravate wildfire threat by producing unseasonably dry and warm conditions at many locations in southern California. During summer months sea breezes transport cool marine air along California's coastal regions. Prolonged periods of tule fog often occur each winter in the San Joaquin and Sacramento Valleys, reducing visibility and resulting in consistently cool daytime and nighttime temperatures. Thunderstorm activity, most commonly in California's mountain and desert regions, reaches a maximum frequency during summer months, with associated lightning strikes playing an important role in igniting wildfires in California.

Acknowledgments

The authors would like to acknowledge the California Nevada Applications Program (CNAP), one of the NOAA RISA centers, and the Southwest Climate Science Center (SWCSC), sponsored by the Department of Interior, for funding a portion of this work.

Recommended Reading

Cayan, D. R., K. T. Redmond, and L. G. Riddle. 1999. ENSO and hydrologic extremes in the Western United States. Journal of Climate 12:2881–2893.

Dettinger, M. D., F. M. Ralph, T. Das, P. J. Neiman, and D. R. Cayan. 2011. Atmospheric rivers, floods, and the water resources of California. Water 3:445–478.

Gershunov, A., D. R. Cayan, and S. F. Iacobellis. 2009. The Great 2006 heat wave over California and Nevada: Signal of an increasing trend. Journal of Climate 22:6181–6203.

Iacobellis, S. F., and D. R. Cayan. 2013. The variability of California summertime marine stratus: Impacts on surface air temperatures. Journal of Geophysical Research: Atmospheres 118:9105–9122.

Luers, A. L., D. Cayan, G. Franco, M. Hanemann, and B. Croes. 2006. Our changing climate—assessing the risks to California: A summary report from the California Climate Change Center, California Energy Commission Report CEC-500-2006-077. <www.energy.ca.gov/2006publications/CEC-500-2006-077/CEC-500-2006-077.PDF>. Accessed March 12, 2015.

Minnich, R. A. 2006. California climate and fire weather. Pages 13–37 in N. G. Sugihara, J. W. VanWagtendonk, K. E. Shaffer, J. Fites-Kaufman, and A. E. Thode, editors. Fire in California's ecosystems. University of California Press, Berkeley, California.

Pierce, D. W., editor. 2012. California climate extremes workshop report. Scripps Institution of Oceanography. <http://meteora.ucsd.edu/cap/pdffiles/CA_climate_extremes_report_SIO_Dec2011.pdf>. Accessed March 12, 2015.

Westerling, A. L., D. R. Cayan, T. J. Brown, B. L. Hall, and L. G. Riddle. 2004. Climate, Santa Ana winds, and autumn wildfires in southern California. EOS, Transactions, American Geophysical Union 85:289–296.

Glossary

ADIABATIC An adiabatic process is one that takes place without heat being exchanged between the system and its surroundings.

ADVECTION The horizontal transfer of any atmospheric property by the wind.

AEROSOL Solid particles suspended in atmosphere. These tiny particles are produced from both natural or anthropogenic sources such as fossil fuel burning.

ALBEDO The percentage of incident solar radiation on a surface that is reflected back into space.

CATALINA EDDY A localized circulation feature along the southern California coast. The Catalina Eddy develops when northwesterly flow along the central California coast moves south of Point Conception and develops cyclonic circulation centered near Santa Catalina Island.

CONVECTIVE Fluid motions that transport and mix properties of the fluid. Convection is often associated with upward vertical motion initiated by warm surface temperatures.

CYCLONIC Circulation that moves in a counterclockwise direction in the Northern Hemisphere (clockwise in the Southern Hemisphere) and is associated with low pressure systems and rising air.

FOEHN A wind that descends along the leeside of a mountain range. As the air descends, the pressure increases and the temperature rises due to adiabatic compression.

HEAT CAPACITY The amount of heat absorbed (or released) by an object divided by the temperature increase (or decrease).

INFRARED RADIATION Electromagnetic radiation with wavelengths between 0.7 and 1000 microns. In general, components of Earth's climate system are at temperatures that cause them to emit radiation in the infrared range.

JET STREAM A concentrated band of strong winds in the atmosphere. While there are several different jet streams in the atmosphere, the term usually refers to the polar jet stream, which is conducive for the formation of mid-latitude cyclonic storm systems.

LEEWARD Refers to the direction in which the wind is moving. Also known as "downwind."

MARINE STRATUS These are low sheet-like clouds that form over ocean surfaces. These clouds are generally horizontally expansive with limited vertical growth.

MICROCLIMATE The climate of a localized region that differs in some respect from the climate of the surrounding area.

MONSOON A wind circulation system that changes direction seasonally and is caused by the uneven heating rates of land and water regions.

NORTH PACIFIC HIGH A semipermanent area of high pressure centered around 30°N off the west coast of North America. The location and intensity vary seasonally.

NORTHWESTERLY WIND Wind that originates from the northwest and moves toward the southeast. This convention (direction ending with "-ly") is also applied to other wind directions.

OROGRAPHIC UPLIFT The uplift of air as it encounters such terrain features as mountains.

PRESSURE GRADIENT The change in pressure over a distance.

SATURATION POINT The maximum amount of water vapor that can exist in an air mass for a given temperature and pressure.

SYNOPTIC SYSTEMS Weather systems with horizontal-length scales from several hundred to several hundred to a few thousand kilometers and time scales of days to a week or more. Hurricanes and mid-latitude cyclones are examples of synoptic weather systems.

TEMPERATURE INVERSION A vertical region of the atmosphere where the temperature increases with height. A temperature inversion represents very stable conditions that can limit the vertical mixing of air beneath.

TRADEWINDS The prevailing surface winds found in the tropical regions between the equator and approximately 25°. These winds generally are northeasterly in the Northern Hemisphere and southeasterly in the Southern Hemisphere.

UPWELLING Ocean water that rises from depth to replace surface water. Upwelled water is generally cold and nutrient rich.

WINDWARD Refers to the direction from which the wind originates. Also known as "upwind."

References

Abatzoglou, J. T., and T. J. Brown. 2009. Influence of the Madden-Julian oscillation on summertime cloud-to-ground lightning activity over the continental United States. Monthly Weather Review 137:3596–3601.

Abatzoglou, J. T., K. T. Redmond, and L. M. Edwards. 2009. Classification of regional climate variability in the state of California. Journal of Applied Meteorology and Climatology 48:1527–1541.

Abatzoglou, J. T., R. Barbero, and N. J. Nauslar. 2013. Diagnosing Santa Ana winds in southern California with synoptic-scale analysis. Weather and Forecasting 28:704–710.

Adams, D. K., and A. C. Comrie. 1997. The North American monsoon. Bulletin of the American Meteorological Society 78:2197–2213.

Brewer, W. H. 1930. Up and down California in 1860–1864. Yale University Press, New Haven, Connecticut.

Bromirski, P. D., R. E. Flick, and D. R. Cayan. 2003. Storminess variability along the California coast, 1858–2000. Journal of Climate 16:982–993.

California Department of Water Resources. 1983. Water conditions in California, Report 4. May 1, 1983. <http://cdec.water.ca.gov/cgi-progs/products_b120hist_sno/Bull120-83_May.pdf>. June 7, 2015.

Cayan, D. R., and L. Riddle. 1993. Atmospheric circulation and precipitation in the Sierra Nevada. Pages 771–720 in R. Herrmann, editor. Managing water resources during global change: An international conference: AWRA 28th annual conference and symposium. American Water Resources Association, Middleburg, Virginia.

Cayan, D. R., K. T. Redmond, and L. G. Riddle. 1999. ENSO and hydrologic extremes in the western United States. Journal of Climate 12:2881–2893.

Das, A. J., N. L. Stephenson, A. Flint, T. Das, and P. J. van Mantgem. 2013. Climatic correlates of tree mortality in water- and energy-limited forests. PLOS ONE 8(7), e69917. <doi:10.1371/journal.pone.0069917>.

Dettinger, M. D. 2013. Atmospheric rivers as drought busters on the US west coast. Journal of Hydrometeorology 14:1721–1732.

Dettinger, M. D., and B. L. Ingram. 2013. The coming megafloods. Scientific American 308:64–71.

Dettinger, M. D., D. R. Cayan, H. F. Diaz, and D. M. Meko. 1998. North-south precipitation patterns in western North America on interannual-to-decadal timescales. Journal of Climate 11:3095–3111.

Dettinger, M. D., F. M. Ralph, T. Das, P. J. Neiman, and D. R. Cayan. 2011. Atmospheric rivers, floods, and the water resources of California. Water 3:445–478.

Dettinger, M., K. Redmond, and D. Cayan. 2004. Winter orographic precipitation ratios in the Sierra Nevada—Large-scale atmospheric circulations and hydrologic consequences. Journal of Hydrometeorology 5:1102–1116.

di Castri, F., and H. A. Mooney. 1973. Mediterranean type ecosystems: Origin and structure. Springer Verlag, Berlin, Germany.

Flick, R. E. 1998. Comparison of tides, storm surges, and mean sea level during the El Niño winters of 1982–83 and 1997–98. Shore and Beach 66:7–17.

Gershunov, A., and T. P. Barnett. 1998. ENSO influence on intraseasonal extreme rainfall and temperature frequencies in the contiguous United States: Observations and model results. Journal of Climate 11:1575–1586.

Gershunov, A., D. R. Cayan, and S. F. Iacobellis. 2009. The great 2006 heat wave over California and Nevada: Signal of an increasing trend. Journal of Climate 22:6181–6203.

Guirguis, K., A. Gershunov, A. Tardy, and R. Basu. 2014. The impact of recent heat waves on human health in California. Journal of Applied Meteorology and Climatology 53:3–19.

Hidalgo, H. G., D. R. Cayan, and M. D. Dettinger. 2005. Sources of variability of evapotranspiration in California. Journal of Hydrometeorology 6:3–19.

Hoerling, M. P., M. Dettinger, K. Wolter, J. Lukas, J. Eischeid, R. Nemani, B. Liebmann, and K. E. Kunkel. 2013. Present weather and climate: Evolving conditions. Pages 74–100 in G. Garfin, A. Jardine, R. Merideth, M. Black, and S. LeRoy, editors. Assessment of Climate Change in the Southwest United States: A Report Prepared for the National Climate Assessment. Island Press, Washington D.C.

Hughes, M., A. Hall, and J. Kim. 2011. Human-induced changes in wind, temperature, and relative humidity during Santa Ana events. Climatic Change 109:S119–S132.

Iacobellis, S. F., and D. R. Cayan. 2013. The variability of California summertime marine stratus: Impacts on surface air temperatures. Journal of Geophysical Research: Atmospheres 118:9105–9122.

Iacobellis, S. F., J. R. Norris, M. Kanamitsu, M. Tyree, and D. R. Cayan. 2009. Climate variability and California low-level temperature inversions. California Climate Change Center Publication CEC-500-2009-020-F. <http://www.energy.ca.gov/2009publications/CEC-500-2009-020/CEC-500-2009-020-F.PDF>. June 7, 2015.

Kanamitsu, M., E. Yulaeva, and H. Li. 2013. Catalina Eddy as revealed by the historical downscaling of reanalysis. Asia-Pacific Journal of Atmospheric Sciences 49:467–481.

Keeley, J., A. Syphard, and C. J. Fotheringham. 2013. The 2003 and 2007 wildfires in southern California. Pages 42–52 in S. Boulter et al., editors. Natural Disasters and Adaptations to Climate Change. Cambridge University Press, New York.

Lebassi, B., J. Gonzalez, D. Fabris, E. Maurer, N. Miller, C. Milesi, P. Switzer, and R. Bornstein. 2009. Observed 1970–2005 cooling of summer daytime temperature in coastal California. Journal of Climate 22:3558–3573.

Lundquist, J. D, and S. P. Loheide. 2011. How evaporative water losses vary between wet and dry water years as a function of elevation in the Sierra Nevada, California, and critical factors for modeling. Water Resources Research 47. <doi:10.1029/2010WR010050>.

Minnich, R. A. 2006. California climate and fire weather. Pages 13–37 in N. G. Sugihara, J. W. Van Wagtendonk, K. E. Shaffer, J. Fites-Kaufman, and A. E. Thode, editors. Fire in California's ecosystems. University of California Press, Berkeley, California.

Monteverdi, J., and J. Null. 1997. El Niño and California rainfall. NOAA Western Region Technical Attachment, No. 97-37. November 21, 1997.

National Research Council. 2012. Sea-level rise for the coasts of California, Oregon, and Washington: Past, present, and future. National Academies Press, Washington, D.C.

Pandey, G. R., D. R. Cayan, and K. P. Georgakakos. 1999. Precipitation structure in the Sierra Nevada of California during winter. Journal of Geophysical Research 104:12019–12030.

Philander, S. G. 1990. El Nino, La Nina, and the southern oscillation. Academic Press, Waltham, Massachusetts.

Ralph, F. M., P. J. Neiman, G. A. Wick, S. I. Gutman, M. D. Dettinger, D. R. Cayan, and A. B. White. 2006. Flooding on California's Russian River: Role of atmospheric rivers. Geophysical Research Letters 33. <doi:10.1029/2006GL026689>.

Rasmussen, E. M., and J. M. Wallace. 1983. Meteorological aspects of the El Nino/southern oscillation. Science 222:1195–1202.

Rasmussen, E. M., and T. H. Carpenter. 1982. Variations in tropical sea surface temperature and surface wind fields associated with the southern oscillation/El Nino. Monthly Weather Review 110:354–384.

Redmond, K. T., and R. W. Koch. 1991. Surface climate and streamflow variability in the western United States and their relationship to large-scale circulation indices. Water Resources Research 27:2381–2399.

Roden, G. I. 1967. On river discharge into northeastern Pacific Ocean and Bering Sea. Journal of Geophysical Research 72:5613–5629.

Sette, O. E., and J. D. Isaacs, editors. 1960. Symposium on "The changing Pacific ocean in 1957 and 1958." CalCOFI Reports 7:13–217.

Stahle, D. W., R. D. Griffin, D. M. Meko, M. D. Therrell, J. R. Edmondson, M. K. Cleaveland, L. N. Stahle, D. J. Burnette, J. T. Abatzoglou, K. T. Redmond, M. D. Dettinger, and D. R. Cayan. 2013. The ancient blue oak woodlands of California: Longevity and hydroclimate history. Earth Interactions 17. <doi:10.1175/2013EI000518.1>.

Stewart, I. T., D. R. Cayan, and M. D. Dettinger. 2005. Changes toward earlier streamflow timing across Western North America. Journal of Climate 18:1136–1155.

Thorne, J. H., J. H. Viers, J. Price, and D. M. Stoms. 2009. Spatial patterns of endemic plants in California. Natural Areas Journal 29:344–366.

U.S. Geological Survey (USGS). 2005. Southern California—wildfires and debris flows. U.S. Geological Survey Fact Sheet 2005–3106.

van Wagtendonk, J. W., and D. R. Cayan. 2008. Temporal and spatial distribution of lightning strikes in California in relation to large-scale weather patterns. Fire Ecology 4:34–56.

Westerling, A.L., D. R. Cayan, T. J. Brown, B. L. Hall, and L. G. Riddle. 2004. Climate, Santa Ana winds and autumn wildfires in southern California. EOS, Transactions, American Geophysical Union 85:289–296.

Westerling, A. L., T. J. Brown, A. Gershunov, D. R. Cayan, and M. D. Dettinger. 2003. Climate and wildfire in the western United States. Bulletin of the American Meteorological Society 84:595–604.

Wildfire Today. 2013. Wildfire today, California: Rim fire at Yosemite NP. <http://wildfiretoday.com/2013/08/21/california-rim-fire-west-of-yosemite-np>. Accessed November 13, 2014.

Wolter, K., and M. S. Timlin. 2011. El Niño/southern oscillation behaviour since 1871 as diagnosed in an extended multivariate ENSO index (MEI.ext). International Journal of Climatology 31:1074–1087.

THREE

Fire as an Ecosystem Process

JON E. KEELEY and HUGH D. SAFFORD

Introduction

Any land surface with sufficient precipitation to produce moderate levels of plant biomass and a seasonal climate that dries the vegetation is likely to be fire-prone. California's MEDITERRANEAN-TYPE CLIMATE makes the landscape particularly predisposed to fires: rains occur during winter and because of the ocean influence, temperatures are relatively mild, leading to abundant plant growth that can produce densely vegetated landscapes of potential fuels. The warm, annual summer drought makes this vegetation highly flammable. In combination, these factors contribute to frequent wildfires that can burn extensive parts of the landscape. Droughts in California are an annual event that result in a more predictable fire regime than in most other parts of the U.S., where severe fire weather might occur only every few years, decades, or centuries due to long-period oscillations in synoptic weather conditions (Minnich 2006, Keeley et al. 2012).

Fire is an important ecosystem process in many California ecosystems (Sugihara et al. 2006). Prior to EURO-AMERICAN settlement, more than 40% of the state supported high fire frequencies (FIRE RETURN INTERVALS less than thirty-five years on average), and another 15%–20% supported moderate fire frequencies (fire return intervals of thirty-five to one hundred years) (Table 3.1). Ecosystems that burned infrequently include subalpine forests, moist forests in northwesternmost California, and desert vegetation.

Fire influences ecosystem composition, structure, and function in many ways, and ecosystems themselves strongly influence fire. As a disturbance, fire is unique in that its intensity and frequency depend on the growth rate of the medium (vegetation) it destroys. Because of this, there is a broadly inverse relationship between fire frequency and intensity, with the strength of that relationship varying by ecosystem type (Huston 2003). Worldwide, fire is a keystone process in Mediterranean-type climate ecosystems, determining structural and distributional patterns of both flora and fauna and influencing biodiversity on both ecological and evolutionary time scales (Keeley et al. 2012). In many ecosystems fire is a principal consumer of plant biomass, and it removes, recycles, and renews various nutrients in plants and soils (Sugihara et al. 2006). In many ways it is an important component of the trophic pyramid in ecosystems in that it competes with other herbivores (Bond and Keeley 2005).

Although fire is a natural process integral to the long-term sustainability of many California ecosystems, it is mislead-

TABLE 3.1

Major fire regime groupings for California and their percentage of California area and mean pre-Euro-American settlement fire return intervals (FRI)

Fire regime (frequency and severity)	Vegetation-type groups	Percentage of California area[A]	Presettlement FRI[B] (years)
High frequency/low to moderate severity	Yellow pine, mixed conifer	14.7	13.5[C]
	Oak woodland	9.3	12
	Interior grassland	12.5	<10
	Redwood	2.2	23
	Mixed evergreen	3.2	29
SUBTOTAL		**41.9**	
Moderate frequency/low to moderate severity	Red fir	1.8	40
Moderate frequency/moderate to high severity	Great Basin sagebrush, sagebrush steppe	3.8	35
Moderate frequency/high severity	Chaparral, coastal sage scrub, serotinous conifers	10.8	60[C]
SUBTOTAL		**16.4**	
Low frequency/ moderate to high severity	Subalpine forests	2	133
	Pinyon-juniper and juniper steppe	3.2	133[C]
	Northwestern moist forests	1.9	236[C]
Very low frequency/high severity	Desert shrub ecosystems	24.4	610
SUBTOTAL		**31.5**	

NOTE: Subtotals add to 90%. Some vegetation types from Barbour et al. 2007 have been excluded due to lack of fire frequency data, and California also includes water bodies and areas free of vegetation (barren rock, sand, etc.).

A. Data from Barbour et al. 2007.

B. Data from Van de Water and Safford 2011.

C. Fire return intervals from weighted average of component vegetation types (not all listed).

ing to think of species as being fire-adapted per se. Rather, they are adapted to a particular temporal and spatial pattern of burning. This is captured in the concept of a *fire regime*, which includes (1) types of fuels consumed, such as herbaceous, dead surface litter, live and dead canopy branches; (2) intensity (or severity, a related term) of the fire; (3) pattern of spread and size of patches burning at different intensities; (4) fire frequency; and (5) season of burning (Keeley et al. 2009). Fires are often referred to as disturbances, which are natural ecosystem processes often crucial to maintaining ecosystem character and dynamics. Perturbations to this disturbance regime that lie outside the historical (or natural) range include anthropogenically increased fire frequency as well as the suppression and exclusion of fire. Humans invariably modify natural fire regimes wherever they interact with flammable vegetation, and such changes can create significant challenges to conservation, management, and the sustainability of ecosystems (Cochrane et al. 1999, Noss et al. 2006).

Photo on previous page: Aerial retardant drop on a chaparral wildfire in coastal southern California, taken July 5, 2008, in the foothills of the Los Padres National Forest. Photo: Dan Lindsay.

Types of Fuels Consumed

Organic materials consumed by fire are referred to as fuels. Fuels in ecosystems are heterogeneously distributed, vertically as well as horizontally. The types of fuels consumed leads to different descriptors for the types of fires. Surface fires consume fuels on the ground, which can be either herbaceous biomass that is annually replenished or dead leaf and stem material that accumulates over time. CROWN FIRES burn in the canopies of shrubs and trees. *Passive crown fires* spread in surface fuels and then are carried into the canopy by ladder fuels such as dead branches and saplings, whereas *active crown fires* spread in both surface fuels and canopy fuels. *Independent crown fires* are not linked to surface fires and generally require rather dense spacing of canopies and sufficient wind or steep terrain to carry fire from canopy to canopy. These are typical of chaparral and other shrubland fire regimes. All of these fire types are characterized by flaming combustion, whereas *ground fires* spread slowly by smoldering combustion through duff (or peat) and can be sustained at relatively high fuel moisture conditions (Miyanishi 2001). Ground fires and surface fires can smolder for weeks or longer, thus "storing" lightning-ignitions that often occur when weather conditions

FIGURE 3.1 (A) Mixed conifer forests in the Sierra Nevada that commonly burn in low-intensity surface fires, in contrast to (B) lower-elevation southern California chaparral shrublands that burn in high-intensity crown fires. Photos: Jon Keeley.

are not suitable for active burning but later irrupt into surface or crown fires as the weather changes.

Surface fires and crown fires (Figures 3.1) represent very different ecosystem processes, and they are often associated with the evolution of very different plant traits. For example, in pines (*Pinus*), thick bark and self-pruning of lower branches are common traits in species that have historically been subject to surface fire regimes; but thin bark, retention of dead branches, and serotinous cones are traits associated with crown fire regimes (Keeley 2012). Another example is in the oaks (*Quercus*), in which savanna species have evolved thick bark to defend against surface fires, while scrub oaks in shrublands have thin bark due to the unlikelihood of surviving high-intensity crown fires (Zedler 1995). Some ecosystems (e.g., ponderosa pine (*Pinus ponderosa*) forests; see Figure 3.1A) characteristically experience mostly low-intensity surface fires, whereas others (e.g., chaparral shrublands) typically burn in high-intensity crown fires (Figure 3.1B). Most ecosystems fall somewhere on a gradient between these two fire types, and many fire regimes—including those in ponderosa pine forests—include some level of both surface and crown fire. The proportion of burning by surface versus crown fires in an ecosystem is a function of, among other things, the species involved, the time since last fire, site productivity (which dictates rate of fuel accumulation), antecedent drought, and severity of fire weather.

Fire Intensity or Severity

Fire intensity is a term that is often used interchangeably with fire severity. Although the terms are related, they refer to different fire parameters (Figure 3.2). Intensity is the measure of energy released during a fire. Because it needs to be measured directly from the fire, intensity measurements are rarely available from a wildfire. A commonly used surrogate for fire intensity is fire severity, which is a measure of biomass loss and can be assessed after the fire (Keeley 2009). Although intensity and severity are strongly correlated, the relationship is imperfect because different plant species have different tolerances to fire, and other factors like water relations and plant stress play a role in how the intensity of fire is translated into biomass loss and mortality (e.g., Van Mantgem et al. 2013). Fire severity can be measured in a number

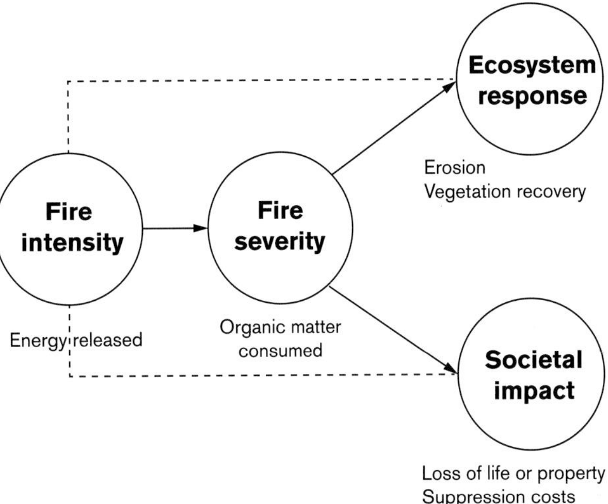

FIGURE 3.2 Schematic depiction of the relationship of fire intensity, fire severity, postfire ecosystem response, and societal impacts.

of ways. Fire severity to vegetation (often called "vegetation burn severity") measures the loss of vegetation biomass due to a fire event. Today, vegetation burn severity can be measured using paired remotely sensed images from before and after fire and is called the DIFFERENCED NORMALIZED BURN RATIO OR DNBR (Figure 3.3; Miller and Thode 2007). Another commonly used severity measure is soil burn severity, which measures loss of soil organic matter and direct effects on soil structure. Soil burn severity maps are sometimes confused with vegetation severity maps, but they are not equivalent (Safford et al. 2008). Fire intensity and severity are primarily of interest because the magnitude of these parameters has important implications for ecosystem responses to fire and their impacts on adjacent natural and urban resources. Relevant responses include soil erosion, resprouting and other vegetation regeneration, restoration of community structure, and faunal recolonization. Some authors have used the terms "fire severity" and "burn severity" to include ecosystem responses, but there is value in keeping separate the direct effects of the fire on charring and biomass loss as well as the ecosystem responses that constitute postfire recovery processes (see Figure 3.2).

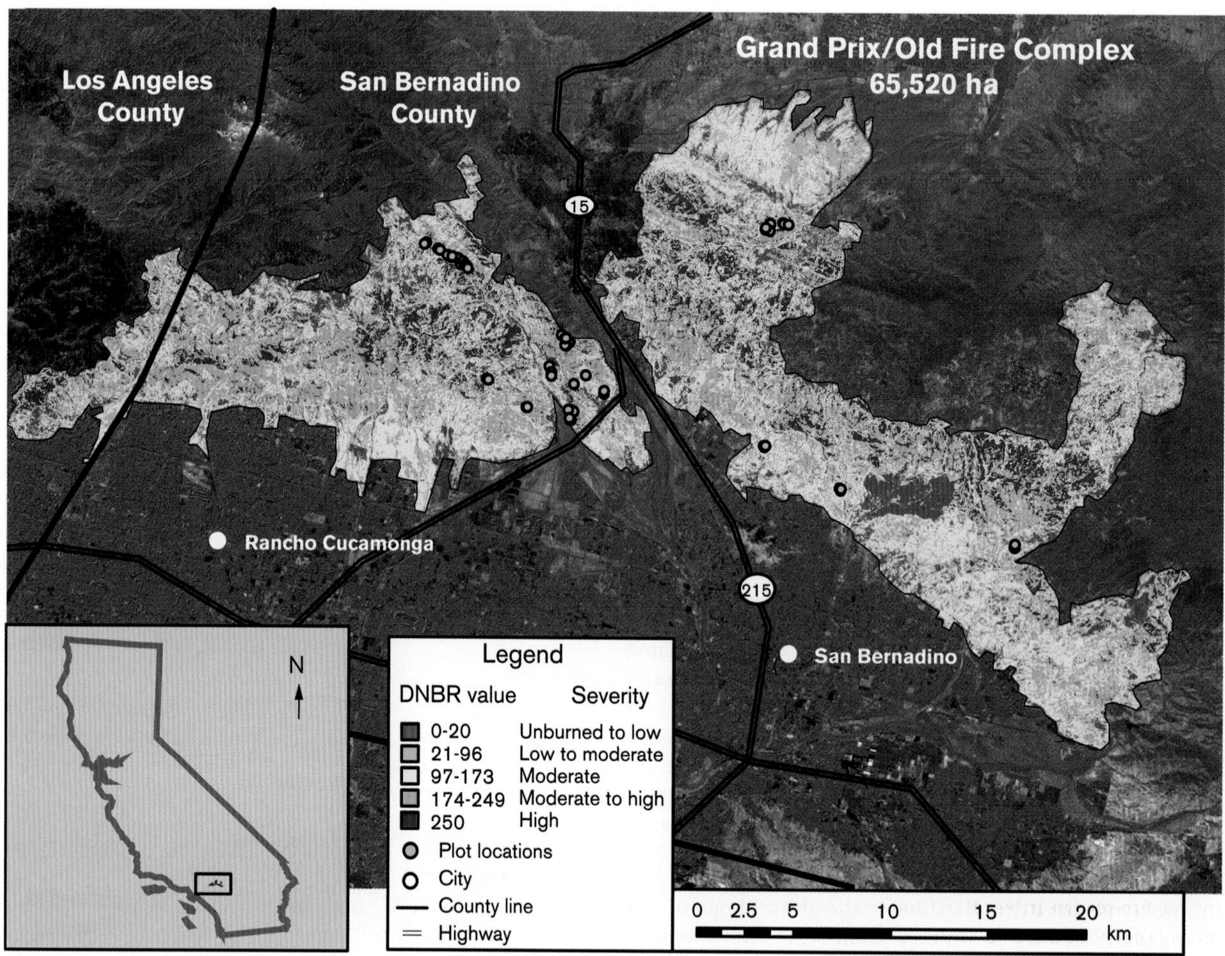

FIGURE 3.3 Fire severity for a single, large fire estimated from the normalized difference vegetation index (NDVI). This was done using the differenced Normalized Burn Ratio (dNBR, equal to reflectance in the months prior to the fire minus reflectance immediately after fire). Source: From Keeley et al. 2008, which provides further description of plots and study.

Patterns of Fire Spread

Different ecosystems are characterized by different spatial patterns of burning. Ecosystems typified by infrequent, high-severity fire (e.g., chaparral, wet/high-elevation forest) tend to support a COARSE-GRAINED, hard-edged patchiness, where the boundaries between successional stages are easy to recognize and where significant ecological changes occur across those boundaries (e.g., changes in light, nutrient, and water availability; in plant and animal dispersal and levels of competition). Vegetation stands in such ecosystems are often even-aged due to synchronous regeneration after fire. On the other hand, ecosystems typified by frequent, low- and moderate-severity fire (e.g., ponderosa pine, mixed conifer) tend to support a FINE-GRAINED PATCHINESS, where edges between successional stages are more graded, even-aged stands of vegetation area are rare, and spatial variation in ecological conditions is less pronounced. In such systems ecological patchiness can be more pronounced in the understory than in the tree canopy. Mosaic patterns of burning, where patches of unburned, low-severity, moderate-severity, and high-severity fire are juxtaposed or interspersed (e.g., see the dNBR illustration in Figure 3.3), can increase landscape diversity of both plants and animals (Smith et al. 2000). Landscape patterns of burning also potentially affect the success of non-native plant and animal invasions (Zouhar et al. 2008).

Fire Frequency

Fire frequency has been greatly modified by humans in many California ecosystems. For example, in many ecosystems humans have greatly increased fire frequency by providing ignitions, outpacing the natural frequency on most California landscapes. This occurs particularly in densely populated, lowland, coastal landscapes but also throughout the state (Table 3.2). This pattern has persisted for most of the past century up to the present (although the ratio of human ignitions to lightning ignitions has been dropping in conifer forests of northern and eastern California; Miller et al. 2012). An opposite effect of humans on fire frequency has limited fire spread through aggressive fire suppression action. While this has no effect on numbers of ignitions, it has caused significant reductions in frequency of burning over large expanses of forested landscape (Safford and Van de Water 2014).

Fire frequency is expressed various ways. For a given area, such as an individual National Forest or a watershed, the time required to burn an area equivalent to the entire forest is termed the *fire rotation period*. A more site-specific term is the *fire return interval*, which describes the time between fires for a given site. Different landscapes in California historically had very different fire frequencies before Euro-American settlement. For example, montane coniferous forests had relatively frequent fires occurring at ten- to thirty-year intervals

TABLE 3.2
Fire incidence by region for the three decades and percentage due to human ignitions

	Number of fires per million hectares			Percentage due to human ignitions		
Region	1920	1960	2000	1920	1960	2000
Cal Fire						
North coastal	822	3,475	4,044	95	91	93
North interior	991	4,325	5,195	95	90	93
Sierra Nevada	609	2,608	5,209	97	90	97
Central coast	643	2,456	3,277	100	98	99
Southern California	4,403	5,026	6,138	99	96	98
USFS						
North coastal	2,477	2,636	2,125	73	62	63
North interior	2,920	3,888	2,365	72	61	63
Sierra Nevada	1,434	3,983	2,115	73	60	67
Central coast	622	849	621	96	80	87
Southern California	2,057	4,548	4,353	86	78	86

SOURCE: Data from Keeley and Syphard 2015.

(Swetnam and Baisan 2003) and mostly as low-intensity surface fires. Lower-elevation foothills are thought to have had longer fire return intervals of many decades to a century or more (Keeley and Davis 2007), due largely to landscape patterns of lightning ignitions, which are abundant at the upper elevational limit of chaparral but sparse at lower elevations. Today humans override this natural frequency gradient, as they did on a more localized extent prior to Euro-American contact.

Season of Burning

Historically, fires ignited from lightning were restricted to summer and early autumn, when occasional monsoon conditions brought unstable air into California from the east; as a consequence, lightning ignitions are a rare occurrence in coastal California and an order of magnitude more frequent in the interior mountains (Minnich 2006). In average years large fire events were concentrated in late summer and autumn; but in anomalous years when spring rains ceased early, large fire events began earlier (Dennison et al. 2008). Today humans have not only greatly increased the number of ignitions (see Table 3.2) but also have significantly changed their seasonal distribution. In contrast to lightning-ignited fires, human-caused fires are more broadly distributed throughout the year. Lighting-ignited fires often occur under weather conditions not conducive to rapid fire spread, but if unchecked they can burn for months at a time. If weather conditions remain moderate, such long-lived fires might burn only small areas before they are extinguished by precipitation. However, periods of high winds and/or extremely dry conditions can cause such fires to irrupt and spread more widely. Human-ignited fires have a greater potential to start during severe fire-weather conditions and are more likely to give rise to large, catastrophic fire events.

As a general rule, most area is burned in summer and fall, depending on the region. Montane coniferous forests experience a well-documented latitudinal gradient in the timing of peak fire season, with northern California forests experiencing most fire in the late summer, central California forests in the mid- to late summer, and coastal California and Baja California in early to mid-summer (Stephens and Collins 2004, Skinner et al. 2008). Lower-elevation, nonforested landscapes in southern California experience the most severe fire weather conditions in the autumn when foehn winds, known as SANTA ANA WINDS or Diablo winds, produce a high-velocity, offshore flow of air coupled with extremely low humidity. These wind events follow a four- to six-month drought, thus the vegetation is at its lowest level of fuel moisture, and these conditions result in some of the state's worst fire events. During these wind events lighting storms are nonexistent, so most such fires today are ignited by humans. However, it has been suggested that late-summer, lightning-ignited fires that persisted until autumn would have resulted in Santa Ana wind–driven fires and likely constituted the bulk of the area burned historically (Keeley and Zedler 2009). Today, humans provide a more reliable and widespread source of ignitions, and evidence indicates that Santa Ana wind–driven fires are more frequent today than in the past.

Climatic warming over the past few decades has expanded the fire season in many regions of the western U.S., including California. For conifer forests across the West, Westerling et al. (2006) found that the average period between the first report of a wildfire and the date of overall control expanded by over two months from 1970 to 2003. Perhaps the most notable expansion of the fire season has been in southern California, where it is now common for firefighters to be battling fires every month of the year.

Fire Regime Types

Fire regime parameters do not vary independently; as a result, consistent combinations are captured in different fire regime types. Two that are widely distributed in California are *crown fire regimes* and *surface fire regimes*. The former is characteristic of chaparral fires, which kill most aboveground biomass and consume all foliage. These fires occur at moderate to long intervals of fifteen to more than one hundred years (Sawyer et al. 2009) and are of high intensity with flame lengths often exceeding 30 meters. Because these shrublands occur in contiguous expanses, fires in them tend to be large and coarse-grained, encompassing associated vegetation such as grasslands, woodlands, and sage scrub. Fire season for this type is a function of annual precipitation patterns and can occur any month of the year but is usually in summer and autumn.

Ponderosa pine forests (prior to fire suppression) are an example of surface fire regimes, in which low-intensity fires consume understory surface fuels but, due to a gap in fuels between the surface and the tree canopy, most larger trees survive. Historically such forests burned frequently and at mostly low intensity, every five to thirty years on average (Van de Water and Safford 2011) and largely during summer and early autumn. Landscape patterns of burning were typically fine-grained, small, patchy burns—but occasionally due to decadal-scale droughts, fires spread across larger landscapes. Today such forests burn much less frequently. Limited fire, together with other human management practices, have led to greatly altered forest and fuel structure and consequently to a different fire regime characterized by fewer but larger, more intense and more severe fires (Mallek et al. 2013).

California has a diversity of plant communities, each with its own fire regime characteristics. Most of these fall along a gradient between the crown fire and surface fire regimes (see Sugihara et al. 2006b for a detailed description of the fire regimes of major vegetation types in the state). People often refer to "mixed-severity" fire regimes that occupy the middle ground of this gradient, but in truth all fire includes areas of high, moderate, and low severity (Thode et al. 2011). It is important to note that the fire regime is an abstract concept that describes a modal pattern for a given ecosystem, but internal variability exists in all of the associated parameters, both spatially and temporally. For example, many of California's conifer forests are well-described as having a surface fire regime historically dominated by frequent, low-intensity understory fires. However, on a landscape basis this regime was often juxtaposed with patches of high-intensity, passive crown fires where the entire tree canopy was consumed. Thus, on a landscape basis, the fire regime is best characterized as a mosaic of fire intensities and fire behavior. The fire regime likewise can vary over time, with the size of patches varying from one fire to the next. Fully capturing these variations in different fire regime types is elusive, and authors have taken very different approaches to handling this problem (c.f., Sugihara et al. 2006a; Bradstock 2010).

Fire in a Historical Context

Many of the plant species that comprise contemporary ecological communities in California have had a long evolutionary association with fire extending back to the early geological period known as the TERTIARY, more than fifty million years ago (Keeley et al. 2012). Although earlier paleoecological studies tended to discount the evolutionary importance of fire (e.g., Axelrod 1980, 1989), there is now abundant evidence that fire has been an important ecosystem process throughout land plant evolution (Pausas and Keeley 2009). The Tertiary is divided into five epochs marked by very different climatic patterns of temperature and precipitation, and in concert with these changes the importance of fire most likely waxed and waned over time. The Eocene epoch that began fifty-four million years ago has often been characterized as equable—warm and wet with very little seasonality and little, if any, fire (Raven and Axelrod 1972). However, evidence suggests in California that the Eocene exhibited seasonality at various temporal scales and that some parts of the landscape were fire-prone (Frederickson 1991). Certainly by the mid-Miocene epoch fifteen million years ago, parts of California were subject to periodic wildfires (Keeley et al. 2012) and have been continuously since then.

Evolutionary responses of biota, especially plants, to fire have been variable across the California landscape. Chaparral is known as a hotspot of adaptation to relatively predictable but infrequent high-severity fires that reset the successional clock and create a plethora of postfire regeneration niches. Many (mostly herbaceous) species in chaparral spend the vast majority of their life cycles as seeds in the soil and only emerge to flower, fruit, and reproduce after severe fire has removed the dense, overlying cover of shrubs. The reproduction of many woody species in chaparral is also tied to fire, with physical or chemical cues from heat, smoke, and/or ash necessary for germination. In yellow pine and mixed conifer forests, on the other hand, little exists in the way of a specialized postfire flora, which speaks to the relative rarity of highly intense and severe fire on evolutionary timescales (Grubb 1977; Keeley et al. 2003; Keeley et al. 2012, chapter 10). Nonetheless there is substantial reason to believe that fire has played an important role in the life history evolution of many pine species (Keeley 2012).

In many of California's plant communities, the ecological process of fire has been as important a factor in determining the community assemblage of species as physical environmental factors like climate and soils. Ponderosa pine occurs under a wide range of climatic conditions, from North Dakota with severe winters and summer rains to the California climate of mild winters and summer droughts. However, across all climate regimes ponderosa pine occurs on sites with a long history of frequent, low-intensity surface fires, and it is reasonable to surmise that frequent fires have been as important in determining its range as climate and soils (Keeley et al. 2012, chapter 5). This is supported by the results of a century of fire suppression, where populations of ponderosa pine and associated tree species are succumbing to strong competition from more shade-tolerant trees like white fir (*Abies concolor*) and incense cedar (*Calocedrus decurrens*).

Human Impacts

While certain plant communities such as chaparral and ponderosa pine forest have been present somewhere on the landscape for millions of years, the particular current landscape distribution of communities is far younger. Summer lightning storms have long been and still are an important ignition source for fires, but with the arrival of humans in the late

Pleistocene about thirteen thousand years ago anthropogenic impacts on fire regimes became a major factor.

Human impacts have varied both temporally and spatially. The earliest populations were sparse and their impacts on fire regimes likely more limited. But as food economies changed, in particular with the development of an acorn-based food system in the mid-HOLOCENE (Erlandson 1994), substantial increases in human population growth occurred along with increasing potential for ecological impacts. Some surmise that Native Americans did not use fire as a regular management tool in California (e.g., Chapter 10, "Indigenous California"). Although we lack firsthand information on how early people managed their landscapes, there are many reasons why they would have used fire, and historical documents and ethnographic accounts support the idea that fire was an important management tool (Lewis 1973, Blackburn and Anderson 1993, Anderson 2005, Keeley 2002, Lightfoot et al. 2013). At the time of contact with Europeans, Native Americans occupied lowland landscapes in California that would have supported expanses of dense, impassable vegetation in the absence of human interventions, and fire was the only tool available to these people that could modify vegetation at the appropriate scale (Pyne 1995).

Prior to the Euro-American invasion of California, Native American impacts on fire regimes were likely variable across the landscape. For a given subregion, important factors would have been the density of people and the frequency of natural lightning ignitions (Pinter et al. 2011). Where natural sources of fire ignitions from lightning were common, humans would have contributed little to changing the fire regime. Where natural lightning was less abundant, humans had much greater potential for affecting fire regimes. It is likely that in California, Native Americans had little impact on fire regimes in mountainous regions due to the lack of year-round settlements and high frequency of lightning-ignited fires at higher elevations. The foothills and plains had higher population densities and a low frequency of lightning; thus the high rates of fire found in the paleorecord for many of these landscape must have been influenced by human agency (Keeley 2002). Even within a region, Native American impacts likely varied through space. Cooper (1922) contended that throughout the Coast Ranges, Native Americans dominated the valley bottoms and played a substantial role in type converting shrublands and woodlands to grasslands or other herbaceous associations. As one moved from the valleys to the foothills, Cooper argued, vegetation changed to a mosaic of grassland and shrublands due to less-intense human burning. Just one set of hills further into the mountains, dense shrublands might have occurred as a result of very little Native American impact.

With repeated waves of human settlement in California, first by Europeans then by Mexicans followed by Euro-Americans, fire frequency increased in many low-lying areas of the state, due largely to the need for increased rangeland for livestock production. By the late 1800s grazing lands had been exploited, and it was a well-accepted practice to burn shrublands to enhance their rangeland value. Such repeated burning often type converted these to open range (Burcham 1957, Brown and Show 1944). *Rangeland improvement* was institutionalized through state-approved programs of prescription burning with the sole intention of limiting woody plant growth and encouraging herbaceous vegetation. However, as population growth expanded across more of California, such burning programs were eliminated due to the dangers associated with wildland fires infringing on the urban environment (Keeley and Fotheringham 2003). In montane conifer landscapes the story was somewhat different. Euro-American contributions to the fire regime generally included reduced frequencies of fire overall but with an increase in periodic large, severe fires set by humans (Sudworth 1900, Barbour et al. 1993, Cermak 2005). As Native American populations declined and were extirpated and protection of timber resources became a major management goal, fire suppression policies were adopted and fire frequencies dropped even further.

Landscape Patterns of Burning

California has a rich fire history database that provides a view of how fires have changed on the landscape over the past century. Although sporadic reports of fires date to the late nineteenth century, the longest continuous record comes from U.S. Forest Service (USFS) lands throughout the state from about 1910 to the present (Figure 3.4a–e). In California's interior mountain ranges, USFS lands are mostly conifer forest–dominated landscapes at mid- to high elevation, but in coastal central and southern California USFS lands are dominated by a mosaic of shrublands, grasslands, and oak woodlands with small (higher-elevation) stands of conifers. Lands outside USFS jurisdiction, and not under the responsibility of other federal agencies such as the National Park Service (NPS) and the Bureau of Land Management (BLM), are mostly state responsibility areas protected by the state fire agency Cal Fire (Figure 3.4f–j). These are predominantly nonforested landscapes in the southern half of the state with increasing levels of woodland and forest further north.

The fire history of the state shows that fire activity on both USFS and Cal Fire lands peaked in the 1920s and declined markedly over the next half century in most parts of the state. In the National Forests, area burned began to increase again in the 1970s throughout the state (see Figure 3.4a–e). However, on the Cal Fire lands this increase is only evident in southern California (see Figure 3.4f–j). There are also remarkable spatial differences. In the northern half of the state during the first half of the twentieth century, much more burning occurred on the lower-elevation Cal Fire lands; this has not been the case since then. In the central coastal region, burning has been much higher on USFS lands in most decades than on Cal Fire lands (see Figure 3.4d and 3.4i). Throughout the period of record, southern California has dominated the state in area burned on both USFS and Cal Fire lands (see Figure 3.4e and 3.4j).

Factors influencing historical and modern patterns of fire activity are diverse and likely have changed over time. The early peak in fire activity in the 1920s has also been observed on other USFS lands in the western U.S. (Miller et al. 2009, Littell et al. 2009). More limited fire suppression capacity early in the twentieth century might have played a role (Agee 1993, Barbour et al. 1993, Barbour et al. 2007, Sugihara et al. 2006), but other factors should be considered as well. In the 1920s automobile usage expanded by an order of magnitude with a consequent increase in road building into remote landscapes, changing the timing and frequency of ignitions (Keeley and Fotheringham 2003). Climate is also a potential factor, as the 1920s were a dry decade in many parts of California. It has been demonstrated for Sierra Nevada forests that warmer and drier spring conditions are associated with

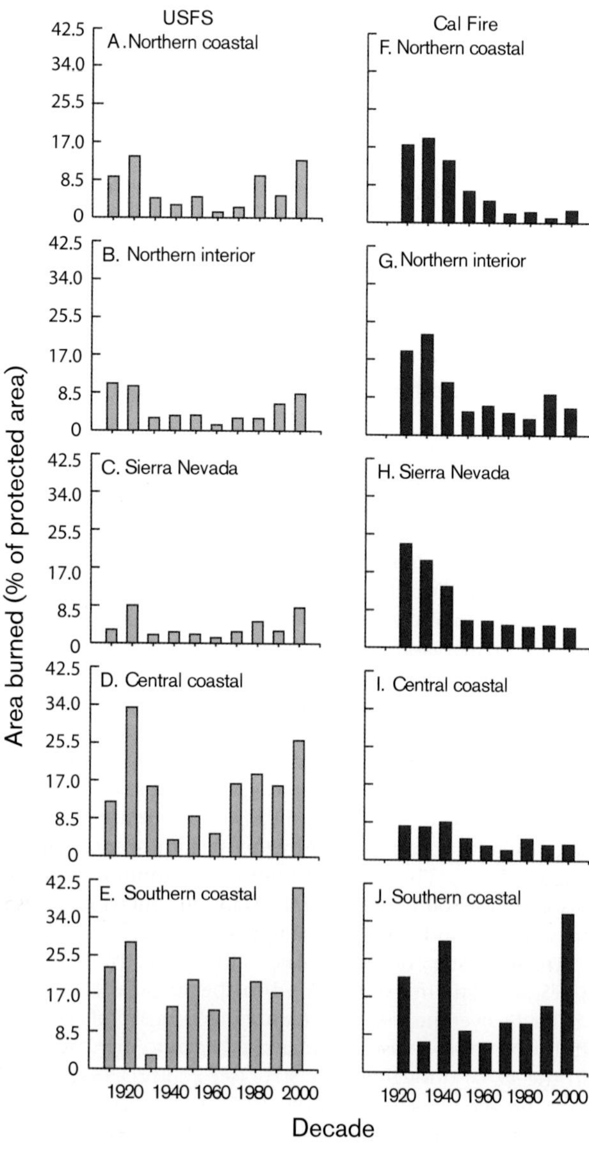

FIGURE 3.4 Fire history illustrating decadal area burned (as a percentage of protected area) for (A–E) mostly montane U.S. Forest Service landscapes and (F–J) mostly lower elevation Cal Fire lands dominated largely by grasslands, shrublands, and woodlands. Source: From Keeley and Syphard 2015.

significantly higher area burned since record-keeping began in 1910 (Keeley and Syphard 2015).

More recent burning patterns across the western U.S. likewise appear to track annual climate anomalies, with warm dry springs an important factor leading to high-fire years (Westerling et al. 2006). Changes in fire management practices on USFS lands could also be a factor. In the early 1970s, in response to numerous issues including recognition of the important ecological role of fire in western forests, the so-called 10am Policy was replaced with a policy of "constrain and contain." The former policy mandated aggressive suppression of all fires with the goal of having the fire extinguished by the morning following fire discovery, whereas the new policy stressed fire "management" instead of suppression and allowed the use of wildfire for ecological purposes in certain predetermined locations (mostly remote wilderness areas). Fire suppression strategies employed over the subsequent decades have evolved greatly, and direct attack on large, complex fires has been replaced to a great extent with indirect attack methods that use fire modeling, weather forecasting, topography, and the geographic distribution of fuels and human infrastructure (among other things) to determine when and where different fire suppression tactics will be employed. As a result, fires that escape initial attack burn longer as conditions are evaluated and fire containment lines are built in propitious locations ahead of the growing blaze. Changes in fire suppression tactics thus almost certainly contribute to the increase in area burned on USFS lands over the past several decades (see Figure 3.4a–e).

Topography and weather play major roles in driving fire behavior, and patterns of burning on California landscapes reflect the effects of both. Santa Ana winds arise in the southern California interior between early fall and spring and blow towards the coast. Topographic gaps in the southern California mountains funnel these winds and result in well-known corridors of east-west trending megafires that occur when ignitions (usually human) coincide with Santa Ana wind events. In northern California large fires are more often driven by the prevailing westerlies, in interaction with canyon alignment and topographic complexity. The landscape of the northernmost Sierra Nevada and southern Cascades is relatively subdued due to less geologic uplift and the submergence of mountainous terrain under volcanic rocks. Fires in this landscape tend to spread from southwest to northeast, in alignment with the wind as well as with the general trends of the river canyons. In the absence of wind, fires in these landscapes can be surprisingly round in shape, with fire spread driven by plume growth and collapse. On the other hand, the Klamath Mountains are steep and topographically complex, and river canyons and mountain ridges spread in many directions. Fire shape and size in that landscape is less predictable and more driven by daily and weekly changes in weather conditions, which depend greatly on the interaction between maritime and continental air masses and the formation of air temperature inversions. Inversions can greatly suppress fire below the inversion layer due to low winds and humid, cooler air but allow for very active burning above the inversion, where air temperatures are higher, humidities lower, and winds more active (Robock 1988, Skinner et al. 2006).

Fire Departure Index

One of the most significant changes wrought by humans on California ecosystems has been the widespread alteration of fire regimes. Two major types of change have occurred: decreased fire frequencies in vegetation types naturally typified by high frequencies of low-severity fires, and increased fire frequencies in vegetation types naturally characterized by infrequent but severe fire.

FIRE RETURN INTERVAL DEPARTURE (FRID) is a useful way to depict spatial and temporal patterns of fire frequency alterations across California (Figure 3.5). FRID analysis quantifies the difference between current and presettlement fire frequencies and can be based on average fire frequencies over the past century or simply the time since last fire (van Wagtendonk et al. 2002, Safford and Van de Water 2014). In both cases the modern metrics are scaled against average fire frequencies from the centuries preceding Euro-American settlement (about 1500 to 1850).

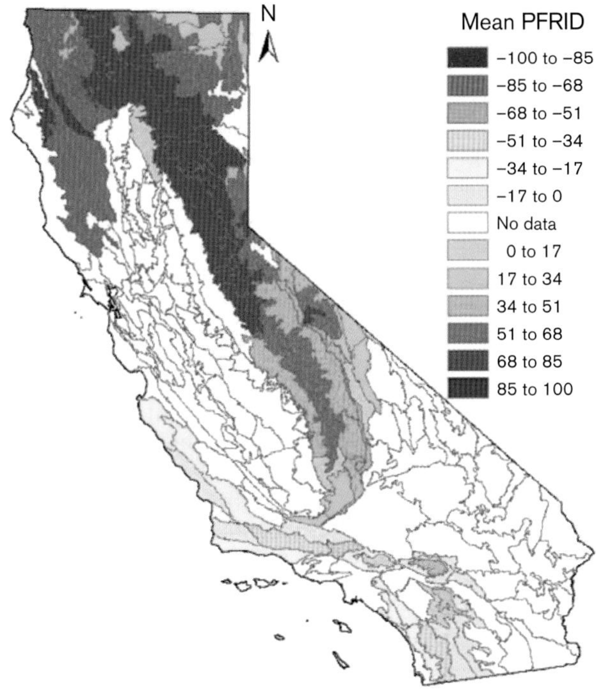

FIGURE 3.5 Deviation of twentieth-century burning frequency from the historical regime, illustrated by mean percentage fire return interval departure index (mean PFRID), one measure of FRID. Negative values (warm colors) indicate areas where fire frequencies since 1910 are higher than under presettlement conditions; positive values (cool colors) are areas where fire frequencies over the past century are lower than under presettlement conditions (based on Safford and Van de Water 2014). Values are generalized to the Forest Service's ecological subsection map (Miles and Goudey 1997) from Forest Service and National Park Service lands in each subsection; subsections with negligible USFS or NPS lands are left blank (Safford and Van de Water 2014). By convention, areas within approximately 33% of zero change (-33 to +33) are considered minimally or not departed; and areas with greater than 67% departure (either positive or negative) are considered substantially departed (Safford and Van de Water 2014).

Much of northwestern California and the Sierra Nevada (mostly conifer forest) has missed multiple fire cycles due to fire suppression, while southern California (mostly shrublands) is characterized by large areas burning at higher frequencies than under presettlement conditions. Overall, low- and middle-elevation vegetation types show the greatest departures from presettlement fire frequencies: oak woodlands, yellow pine, and mixed conifer forests have missed the most fire cycles, while coastal fir, coastal sage scrub, and chaparral (mostly in southern California) are generally experiencing shorter fire return intervals than under presettlement conditions (Safford and Van de Water 2014). These broad patterns underline the very different fire management situations in southern and northern California. In the former, all-out fire suppression is a management necessity on much of the landscape, from the standpoints of both human security and ecological sustainability. In the latter (and also in the high-elevation conifer forests in southern California, as blue islands in Figure 3.5), fire suppression itself is a major perturbation and has resulted in ecosystem modifications that have profoundly changed ecological composition, structure, and function across large landscapes (Agee 1993, Barbour et al. 1993, Barbour et al. 2007, Sugihara et al. 2006)

Postfire Recovery of Plant Communities

Postfire recovery of vegetation determines future conditions for ecosystems, including their biodiversity, ecosystem services, and future fire activity. Recovery trajectories vary greatly among ecosystem types and as function of fire severity; individual plant strategies (of populations, species) drive the overall patterns of vegetation recovery observed over time. Plant populations exhibit four modes of recovery following fire:

1. ENDOGENOUS REGENERATION from resprouts or fire-triggered seedling recruitment,
2. delayed seedling recruitment from postfire resprout seed production,
3. delayed seedling recruitment from in situ surviving parent plants, or
4. colonization from unburned METAPOPULATIONS.

Endogenous Regeneration

Endogenous regeneration refers to recovery in the first postfire growing season from vegetative resprouts and/or dormant seed banks. It is common in most crown fire regimes where all or most aboveground stems are killed by fire. Resprouting from vegetative structures that survive fire can occur from basal resprouts from stem bases, RHIZOMES, bulbs, CORMS, or roots; or on aboveground stems known as epicormic resprouts. Resprouting is almost a universal recovery mechanism in woody plants following top-kill from fire (although it is relatively less common in tropical wet forests), but since it also has adaptive value following damage from other disturbances (drought, wind, freezing, browsing, etc.), it is difficult to assign primacy to any single one of these disturbance factors.

OBLIGATE RESPROUTERS are species present in the first year after fire as vegetative resprouts with no seedling recruitment. A seemingly specialized resprouting mode is evident in a diverse array of woody species that resprout from swollen, lignified structures at the base of the stems, known as basal burls or LIGNOTUBERS. This adaptation to surviving intense fire is found in chaparral shrub species across many genera. In contrast to postfire seeders, obligate resprouters have propagules designed for more widespread dispersal, and their seedling recruitment tends to be restricted to the understory of the vegetation canopy on sites free of fire for extended periods of time (Williams et al. 1991, Keeley 1992) or in gaps of adjacent woodlands (Keeley 1990). In both woodlands and shrublands, recruitment by these seeds appears to be tied to years of high precipitation. Epicormic resprouting occurs from dormant buds under the bark of scorched trunks of some trees. Species with this feature include some oaks as well as the conifer big-cone Douglas-fir (*Pseudotsuga macrocarpa*). Their epicormic resprouts can produce seeds that recruit seedlings during the early postfire years.

Many species regenerate after fire from dormant seeds in the soil that recruit in a single, postfire pulse of seed germination. Some of these species regenerate from a combination of resprouting and seedling recruitment; these are termed FACULTATIVE SEEDERS. OBLIGATE SEEDERS are woody species that lack resprouting capacity and depend entirely on postfire seedling recruitment. These species are highly sensitive to short fire intervals, as they require a sufficient period without fire to develop a seed bank to keep from being extirpated from a site after a short-interval fire (Jacobson et al. 2004, Keeley and Brennan 2012).

Postfire seeders typically produce and disperse seeds between fire events and accumulate dormant, soil-stored seed banks. Their seeds have innate barriers to germination and are triggered to germinate by fire-related cues. They include many shrubs and a huge number of ephemeral species, the latter of which spend most of their lifetime as dormant seed banks (Keeley and Fotheringham 2000). Fire-stimulated germination of soil seed banks may be triggered by heat or chemicals from the combustion of biomass. These are often considered rather specialized germination mechanisms; however, there is evidence that the combustion chemical-cued germination mechanism could be rather ancient, found in basal TAXA within several different lineages (Pausas and Keeley 2009). A few conifers in crown fire ecosystems from the genera *Pinus* (pines) and *Hesperocyparis* (cypresses) have serotinous cones, ones that delay opening of cones or fruits until fire triggers the synchronous opening and dispersal of seeds into postfire seedbeds. In these species seeds are not dormant but are unable to germinate until released from the cones.

Delayed Seedling Recruitment from Postfire Resprouts

Many woody and herbaceous taxa in crown fire regimes recover by resprouts that grow rapidly and flower in the first postfire growing season, producing copious seeds that then recruit in the following year. These include many sage scrub subshrubs and herbaceous perennials such as geophytes and bunchgrasses. These taxa typically have very limited seed dormancy, thus first-year seed crops often will germinate en masse in the second growing season. In terms of their immediate response to fire, these taxa are usually referred to as obligate resprouters, but since seedling recruitment often is most prolific in postfire environments they might be considered fire-dependent reproducers. As noted earlier, in woodlands epicormic resprouting allows parent trees to survive fire. In these cases seed production and seedling recruitment in early postfire years could be particularly important for regeneration, although they also occur throughout the fire interval.

Delayed Seedling Recruitment from in Situ Surviving Parent Plants

Surface fire regimes have selected for a very different suite of adaptive traits in the dominant overstory species. Trees in this fire regime self-prune lower dead branches, creating a midstory gap between surface fuels and canopy fuels that prevents surface fire spread into crowns. Trees in this context also have thick bark that further enhances survival of surface fires. Regeneration depends on the survival of parent trees in proximity to fire-created gaps (Keeley and Zedler 1998, Keeley 2012). The classic examples of such species in California include ponderosa pine and Jeffrey pine (*Pinus jeffreyi*), whose needles and cones are also very flammable, promoting high-fire frequencies and permitting their dominance on sites where they are not competitive in the absence of disturbance. When cones or fruits are present at the time of fire, recruitment can occur in the first growing season after fire; however, recruitment is often delayed until subsequent fruiting cycles (Keeley and van Mantgem 2008). Many trees in surface fire regimes have MASTING cycles of reproduction. If a fire coincides with a mast year, there will be abundant seedling recruitment in the first postfire year. Following fires that do not coincide with mast years, recruitment can be delayed and substantially reduced. The longer the interval between fire and a mast year, the greater the competitive inhibition of tree seedlings by understory vegetation. Thus a certain level of serendipity shapes successional trajectories in these systems depending on the relative timing of fires and seed production events.

Colonization from Unburned Metapopulations

Some fire-sensitive species decimated by fire, or species that are transitory on sites, are generally absent from recently burned areas and ultimately enter those communities through colonization. The role of colonization is quite variable between different vegetation types. For example, in California chaparral all dominant shrubs recover endogenously and colonization during early succession typically accounts for a minor part of community (Keeley et al. 2005). In contrast, in semiarid parts of western North America the dominants in woodlands, pinyon (*Pinus* spp.), juniper (*Juniperus* spp.), and sagebrush (*Artemisia tridentata*) all recover slowly from crown fires by recolonization, often from unburned patches that result from uneven patterns of burning.

When a forest fire is severe enough to kill many trees and fire patch sizes are large, most tree species in California and elsewhere will rely for regeneration on seedling dispersal from surviving adults outside of the burned area. The mix of species in the seedling crop will depend on relative densities of different species in surviving stands, seedling production of those adult trees, dispersability of the seeds (e.g., size, shape, presence of seed wings, relationships with animal dispersers), and conditions at the site of seed arrival. If severely burned patches are not too large, seed crops are sufficient and moisture is available after fire, most forests will quickly fill a gap with seedlings. However, if patches are large (e.g., >100–150 meter radius), conifer and hardwood recruitment can be delayed by many years and shrubs can dominate much of the site, further delaying forest succession. Assuming they do not reburn, very large areas of stand-replacing fire can remain free of forest for many decades.

Fire Effects on Animal Communities

Animals exhibit a diversity of strategies for dealing with fire. Some invertebrates can persist as dormant diaspores in the soil, similar to the bulbs of many herbaceous perennial geophytes. Smaller mammals "shelter-in-place" and survive by seeking refugia such as rock outcrops, moist ravines, and burrows within the burn perimeter. Others, including birds and larger mammals, flee the fire and must subsequently recolonize from the unburned landscape. As a consequence, animals can exhibit different sensitivities to fire regime attributes than do plants within the same ecosystem types. For example, recovery of chaparral vegetation generally is not greatly affected by fire size. However, for chaparral animals that must flee the fire and recolonize afterward, fire size and size of high-severity patches can be immensely important. In contrast to chaparral plants, for some animals the metapopulation dynamics of source populations in the surrounding landscape, including their sizes and dispersion as well as their connectivity to each other and the burned site, are critically important to recovery rate after large fire events. The degree of habitat fragmentation outside the burn perimeter can also strongly affect animal recolonization (Sauvajot et al. 1998). For example, habitat of the federally endangered California gnatcatcher (*Polioptila californica*) in mature sage scrub has been severely impacted by urban growth, diminishing source populations, and thus its potential for recolonizing burned areas (Beyers and Wirtz 1995).

Fire behavior can also affect animal recovery. Fast-moving fires can harm animals that must flee the fire but might have little direct effect on species that shelter-in-place in burrows, mesic riparian sites, or other refugia such as rock outcrops. For these species slow-moving fires often generate greater volumes of smoke and longer lasting heat, which can greatly reduce survival (Shaffer and Laudenslayer 2006). Seasonality is another fire regime attribute that can play a greater role in animal than plant response. For example, nesting birds and other animals with new offspring are particularly vulnerable to spring burning in many vegetation types (Smith et al. 2000, Shaffer and Laudenslayer 2006). Seasonality also affects fire behavior; spring fires are likely to burn vegetation with greater moisture and potentially greater smoke production. Changes in fire seasonality can threaten some animal species. For example, the sage grouse (*Centrocercus urophasianus*), once a very common bird in the western U.S. and Canada, is now a candidate for listing under the Endangered Species Act. This bird depends on Great Basin shrublands dominated by sagebrush (*Artemisia*), which historically experienced summer and fall burns. With the invasion of the annual cheatgrass (*Bromus tectorum*), which produces contiguous, fine fuels, the fire season begins earlier and fires lack historical patchiness (see Chapter 30, "Deserts"). The new fire regime disadvantages both the sagebrush and the grouse that depends on it (Baker 2006).

Some components of the fauna are well-insulated from fire effects. For example, some flightless insects like the wingless walking-stick (*Timema cristinae*) enter diapause and survive fires as a tough egg stage buried in the soil (Sandoval 2000); many other arthropods likely survive fire in a similar manner. In this respect, these invertebrates are like plants such as geophytes that persist through the dry season (and consequently the fire season) as dormant bulbs buried in the soil. Each year they might emerge during the wet season, regardless of whether or not a fire occurred.

Once fire has passed, animal recovery is influenced by the magnitude of changes in vegetation structure (Smith et al. 2000). Ground-dwelling HERBIVORES and GRANIVORES are often food-limited for many months following fire and can be forced to temporarily migrate outside the burn perimeter for forage. As a consequence, animal recovery can often parallel plant recovery (e.g., Rochester et al. 2010). In some animals such as deer the enhanced nutritional value of plant regrowth leads to significant population increases (Hiehle 1961). In crown fire ecosystems the loss of vegetation cover can have profound impacts on visibility of foragers to predators and can enhance mammalian carnivore populations (Schuette et al. 2014) as well as hawks and owls (Lyon et al. 2000). Indeed, postfire habitats are the preferred habitat for a diversity of organisms. Noteworthy are bark beetles like *Dendroctonus* and *Ips* species (Furniss and Carolin 1977) and fire beetles (*Melanophila* species), which are drawn to forest fires even while they are still burning and seek out sites for ovipositing on burned logs (Hart 1998). Other forest species attracted to high-severity crown fires include several woodpecker species adapted to forage on recently charred trees (Smucker et al. 2005).

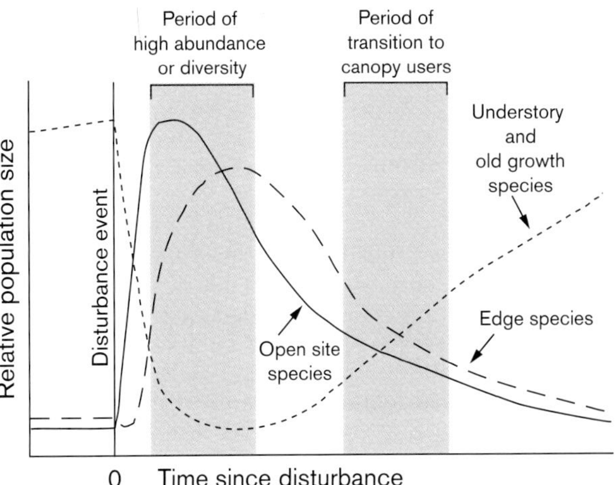

FIGURE 3.6 Hypothetical patterns of change in animal populations relative to postfire changes in forest structure. Source: Huff and Smith 2000.

Certain species groups benefit from the habitats and food sources (e.g., bark beetles) that result when most of the dominant vegetation is killed. Examples include many rodents, woodpeckers, and other birds that forage on the ground or in brush (Raphael et al. 1987, Smith et al. 2000). However, in forests with mixtures of surface and crown fire, increasing proportions of the latter can greatly slow recolonization by many animal species (Smith et al. 2000). Some of the most contentious resource management issues in California revolve around the increasing severity of fire in low- and middle-elevation conifer forests caused by the combined effects of fire suppression and climate warming (Miller et al. 2009, Van Mantgem et al. 2013). Management actions are increasingly necessary to ameliorate the effects of severe fire on populations of rare mesocarnivores that require older, long-unburned forest for part of their life cycle (e.g., spotted owl [*Strix occidentalis*], Pacific fisher [*Martes pennant*], and goshawk [*Accipiter gentilis*]).

Though few long-term studies have examined animal responses to fire in California's ecosystems, work in other regions shows that species-specific animal traits result in changing peak abundances with time since fire. For example, long-term studies of postfire animal responses in the Mediterranean-type shrublands in Australia found that fire influences reptile occurrence over century-long time scales (Nimmo et al. 2012). Preliminary postfire studies in California chaparral show that some species dominate early, while others depend more on later successional stages (Rochester et al. 2010). Huff and Smith (2000) have pointed to the diversity of vertebrates' responses to fire; some initially increase, some decrease, and others remain unchanged (Figure 3.6).

Fire can also have important, mostly indirect effects on organisms living in streams and lakes. Postfire increases in turbidity and nutrients change water quality, and channel scouring from debris flows and heavy sediment loads can greatly modify aquatic habitat. Major sediment and nutrient pulses after fire can kill aquatic organisms, but most aquatic effects of fires are ephemeral. Studies of stream impacts of fire find relatively little in the way of long-term damage to aquatic ecosystems, except where burned landscapes are already compromised by other stressors such as human land use (Gresswell 1999, Minshall 2003).

Fire Effects on Soils, Hydrology, and Carbon Storage

Depending on goals and on the variables and time period of interest, fire can have both positive and negative effects on soil, water, and carbon resources. Here we summarize some of the most salient fire effects, but for a more comprehensive treatment we direct the reader to excellent summaries in Debano et al. (1998) and Wohlgemuth et al. (2006).

Soils

Fire effects on soil depend on the amount and duration of heat output in conjunction with the physical and chemical properties of the soil itself. Temperatures of 100°C are lethal to most organisms, and these temperatures are readily exceeded by fires at the soil surface. However, temperature pulses are ephemeral, and soil depth strongly attenuates heating as well. At 5 centimeter depth, wildfire-caused temperatures rarely exceed the 100°C threshold, except where fuels are heavy or large logs induce long-term smoldering. Low-intensity fires burning in surface litter and/or herbaceous vegetation, as were historically common in yellow pine and mixed-conifer ecosystems, have little soil impact (except in the surface litter), whereas today's fires of typically higher intensity have deeper, more widespread effects on soils. High-intensity fires common in chaparral and in conifer forest areas with heavy fuels can drive surface temperatures above 500°C for periods of ten to twenty minutes and temperatures at 2.5 centimeter depth to 100°C to 200°C (Debano 1981). At these higher surface temperatures most nitrogen and organic phosphorus volatilize, and soil physical and chemical structures are greatly altered. However, recent studies have shown that the relationship between fuel load and soil temperatures during fire are much more complicated than previously assumed (Stoof et al. 2013).

Different soils and soil conditions vary in sensitivity to the heating effects of fire. Coarse textured soils with relatively low carbon content, such as are common in soils weathered from granitic rocks in many of California's major mountain ranges, generally show little fire-induced change in their bulk density and relatively little change in porosity. Finer-textured soils (e.g., those with higher clay content) with higher levels of carbon are much more sensitive to high temperatures, and their soil structure can be greatly altered, leading to reduced water infiltration and postfire erosion under sustained rainfall (Wohlgemuth et al. 2006). Soil water content is also an important variable, as moist soils are greatly protected from the downward transmission of heat from fire (Busse et al. 2005). Fire effects on soil water repellency, known as *soil hydrophobicity*, depend on complex interactions among fire heating, soil and plant chemistry, soil texture and moisture, and characteristics of the litter layer.

Fire's most significant impacts to soil chemistry revolve around soil organic matter and macronutrients. Fire consumes soil litter and carbon compounds in the upper soil, causing important changes in soil structure (loss of aggregation), reduced soil water-holding capacity, and reduced CATION EXCHANGE CAPACITY. Severely burned soils with high loss of organics can be largely transformed to ash, and windy conditions during and after fire can lead to local soil losses. The loss of carbon also produces major changes in the soil microflora, which in turn typically causes a release of soluble nitrogen compounds. Nitrogen and phosphorus are largely volatilized by fire, but the net loss of both minerals is often offset by an increase in their soluble, bio-available forms. A (usually short-term) flush of important nutrients is thus typically available to those plants that can use them quickly, such as resprouters and seedlings that germinate in the first year after fire. Much of the nutrient pulse is lost to water transport offsite during the rainy season (Wohlgemuth et al. 2006).

Water

Fire's effects on hydrology depend to a great extent on the soil effects described earlier and on vegetation responses. Since fire removes biomass, it can greatly increase the proportion of precipitation that directly hits the soil. Decreased canopy interception of rain and loss of litter and soil organic matter, which reduce soil infiltration, increase the erosional actions of rainsplash and the transport of water by overland flow. Lower plant cover leads to greater ground accumulation of snow (depending also on wind patterns) but also speeds melting during warm, sunny weather. Burning changes the balance between evaporation and transpiration, increasing the former while reducing the latter. Dry springs commonly begin to flow again after fire, and stream levels are usually enhanced, especially during storm events. Extensive scientific study of this effect has documented over one-thousand-fold increases in stream flow depending on factors including burn severity and precipitation patterns (Tiedemann et al. 1979).

One of the major impacts of fire is that it often initiates sediment transport processes including DRY RAVEL, erosion, and debris flows (Cannon et al. 2010, Moody and Martin 2001, Lamb et al. 2013). Models to predict these processes include many soil characteristics such as particle size; organic matter content; soil thickness; underlying rock type; slope incline and aspect; rainfall frequency, duration, and intensity; prefire vegetation and fire severity impacts. Contributing to sediment loss is hydrophobicity. In high-intensity chaparral fires, water-repellent chemicals on the surface can be destroyed and reformed as a hydrophobic layer at deeper levels, leading to major surface soil erosion when subsequent rainfall saturates the upper soil and is then detoured horizontally by the hydrophobic lens. The importance of this layer is greatly influenced by subsequent rainfall patterns and in some cases might not contribute significantly to soil loss (Hubbert and Oriol 2005).

Although hillslope erosion is greatly increased by fire, it can return to prefire levels within a few years. The timing of extreme precipitation events in relation to the fire is an important variable (Oliver et al. 2012). Since stream flows are so sensitive to fire, stream channel erosion and sediment transport are both greatly affected by fire as well. A typical pattern is one where hillslope erosion fills smaller channels with sediment, while later storms promote downcutting through these deposits, transporting the accumulated sediment to lower stream reaches. Sometimes channel scour can occur catastrophically, in the form of fast-moving and very destructive debris flows (Wohlgemuth et al. 2006). Finally, fire affects water quality. Suspended solid particles, mostly ash and soil, increase stream turbidity and often carry high levels of soil nutrients into the stream system. This erosional pulse is usually short-lived, however. Longer-term effects to streams leaving the fire area include elevated temperatures due to loss of vegetation shading and increases in dissolved concentrations of various nutrients such as nitrogen, phosphorus, and calcium (Tiedemann et al. 1979, Oliver et al. 2012).

Carbon

Since fire burns biomass, it always results in a short-term loss of carbon. The actual amount lost to burning is highly variable, and overall carbon balances for a given ecosystem are generally expected to equilibrate over time (due to vegetation regrowth) as long as the fire regime is not changing (Kashian et al. 2006). Carbon losses from the soil can strongly affect ecosystem processes. For example, lost organic compounds reduce the cation exchange capacity of the soil and the ability of water to infiltrate and be retained within the soil. Carbon loss also affects nutrient availability for plants, as less carbon substrate for microbes causes bacterial and fungal mortality and subsequent release of nitrogen into the soil (Wohlgemuth et al. 2006).

Carbon losses due to fire include both direct losses to combustion and longer-term losses to decomposition. Combustion of biomass averages 20% to 30% for tree boles and large branches in temperate forests affected by high-severity fires, while greater proportions of needles/leaves, cones, and fine branches are consumed (Tinker and Knight 2000, Schuur et al. 2003, Stephens, Boerner, Moghaddas et al. 2012). Carbon combustion also affects the organic layers in soil; these losses can exceed 60% of the prefire carbon. Over the longer term, vegetation killed by fire will decompose, and over decades the overall carbon emissions from decomposition can be five times greater or more than the carbon lost to combustion (Auclair and Carter 1993).

Attempts to reduce fire-related carbon loss via forest thinning and other fuel treatments are most likely to realize actual long-term carbon balance gains in ecosystems that have ecological and evolutionary associations with frequent, low-intensity fire, such as ponderosa pine or mixed-conifer forests. Such practices are more likely to negatively affect long-term carbon sequestration in ecosystems where fire is rare and/or combustion typically less complete, such as wet forests of the northwest coast and coastal mountains (Hurteau et al. 2008, Mitchell et al. 2009). Changes towards increased summer drought and fire frequency in these wet forests—as are generally projected by future climate and fire models—could increase the amount of biomass held in young successional forests, which would reduce carbon sequestration on the ground and increase emissions to the atmosphere.

Fire in Social Context

Fires pose an important hazard for people in California, in a state prone to many hazards such as earthquakes, floods, and landslides. Based on written records from the late nineteenth century, the largest fire in the state's history occurred in Orange County in 1889, burning more than 100,000 hectares. No one died, and no homes were lost, from that fire (Keeley and Zedler 2009). Today, such large wildfires still occur, but due to explosive population growth during the twentieth century (see Chapter 5, "Population and Land Use"), they now account for substantial losses of property and lives. Since the middle of the twentieth century, the state has averaged more than five hundred homes lost per year from fires, and in the past decade the rate has doubled (Keeley et al. 2013).

Most of California's population growth has occurred in the lower-elevation foothills, valleys, and coastal plains, where humans are responsible for igniting nearly all fires (see Table 3.2). Thus one of the important means of reducing fire losses has been through public campaigns aimed at fire prevention. Since the early twentieth century, county, state, and federal agencies have taken on the responsibility of fighting fires, and suppression tactics have grown increasingly sophisticated over this time. Thus prevention and suppression are the primary responses to fires that threaten human developments. In past several decades there has been increasing emphasis on trying to alter fire outcomes through vegetation management that seeks to change fuel patterns on the landscape. More recently, emphasis has been placed on greater personal responsibility of homeowners to increase the fire resistance of their homes through construction improvements and landscape maintenance. The last avenue for managing fire risk to urban developments has been through changes in local community planning decisions. Just as the history of flood hazards in the state has been partially solved through flood zoning regulations, the future may hold greater fire zoning restrictions as one part of the fire solution.

Fire Management

Because of the prevalence of fires in California and mounting losses of resources, property, and lives, fire management has unavoidably become a central focus of federal, state, and local agencies across California. Together, these agencies spend over three billion dollars annually in wildfire prevention and suppression, and the costs of fighting fire are rising rapidly (Safford 2007).

Prefire

Prefire management essentially involves manipulating fuels on the landscape with the goals of preventing ignitions from becoming significant fires, allowing for quicker suppression of fires that do occur and reducing the amount of resource damage caused by fires. Prefire fuel treatments can be very effective in slowing or stopping fire and protecting human infrastructure, depending on location, method, and ease and safety of firefighter access (Syphard et al. 2011, Martinson and Omi 2013). In frequent-fire forest ecosystems (e.g., yellow pine, mixed conifer), typical fuel treatment practices include mechanized thinning of medium and smaller trees (usually focused on shade-tolerant species), hand or mechanical reduction of surface fuels, and prescribed fire or fuel pile burning. Data from both northern and southern California show that treatments that incorporate all or most of these steps are effective at reducing fire severity and carbon loss to fire (North and Hurteau 2011, Carlson et al. 2012, Safford et al. 2012). Since fire regimes, forest structure and composition, and fuel loadings in these forest types have been greatly modified by human intervention, fuel reduction treatments—especially where they incorporate some form of fire reintroduction—are generally benign and even restorative in terms of their ecological and environmental effects (Stephens, McIver, Boerner et al. 2012). Various meta-analyses have found mostly positive or neutral effects of these types of treatments on a wide variety of taxonomic groups (Kalies et al. 2010, Verschuyl et al. 2011).

On the other hand, fuel treatments in shrubland landscapes that are burning much more frequently today than before Euro-American settlement—the general case in sage scrub and chaparral landscapes in southern California—contribute little to ecological restoration and in some cases may cause environmental damage. For example, invasive species generally increase with reduced native shrub cover (Merriam et al. 2006, Keeley and Brennan 2012), and areas with reduced shrub cover, whether by fire or treatment, are sources of hillslope erosion, stream sedimentation, and stream channel debris flows in the wet season (Wohlgemuth et al. 2006). In such highly flammable and often densely populated landscapes, fuel treatments are a management necessity to protect human lives and property, but strategic thinking is necessary to properly balance the positive features of treatment networks with their potential negative environmental impacts. Fuel treatments in places like southern California can also be conducted for ecological purposes—for example, to protect older stands of chaparral or coastal sage scrub or to shield regenerating populations of species threatened by overly frequent fire, such as cypresses (e.g., Tecate cypress, *Hesperocyparis forbesii*) or rare, fire-sensitive habitats. In these cases the treatments themselves would be viewed as environmental sacrifices made on a local scale to realize landscape-level ecological benefits.

Postfire

Human management of postfire landscapes can have major effects on ecosystem succession and can generate both positive and negative effects on the native biota. Federal management agencies have tended to focus on short-term issues arising from severe wildfires. Immediately after fire, BURNED AREA EMERGENCY RESPONSE (BAER) teams work to identify areas of high erosion hazard and non-native plant invasion (among other things). Treatments implemented based on BAER reports can notably reduce soil loss and decrease exotic invasion of postfire landscapes (Robichaud et al. 2009). In the longer term, tree planting efforts can stabilize populations of rare species, accelerate successional processes, and begin to resequester carbon lost to fire. However, it is critically important that trees appropriate for the site are chosen for such projects.

At the same time, postfire management can have negative effects on ecosystems. For example, timber harvest of dead trees from severely burned areas has become controversial because it often disturbs the soil and reduces the density of forest structures known to be important for a number of animal species (Peterson et al. 2009). In some cases such harvest may reduce the amount of fuel available for future combustion, but depending on the method used, fine fuels may actually increase. Many calls have been made for longer-term perspectives in postfire resource management, especially as fire activity and burned area increase in certain ecosystems (Robichaud et al. 2009, Cerdá and Robichaud 2009), but funds are usually lacking to effect such recommendations.

A primary concern after fire is soil loss and excessive water flow off recently burned slopes that can lead to floods and debris flows. Approaches to address this problem seek to stabilize slopes to reduce erosion and runoff. One approach includes seeding of fast-growing grasses to stabilize slopes prior to winter rains. Another tactic is to distribute hay or other organic matter on burned slopes to attenuate the impact of torrential rainfall. Another approach, rather than to reduce erosion, is to construct barriers that capture debris and prevent runoff from entering drainages that lead to urban environments or other values at risk. Postfire aerial seeding as a management practice has its roots in southern California as a flood control measure. It arose partly from incomplete understanding of the natural capacity for rapid recovery in chaparral ecosystems. For example, one document (Los Angeles River Watershed 1941) stated: "Severe burning so depletes the chaparral cover that artificial measures are necessary to hasten its re-establishment."

However, we know from countless studies over the past fifty years that this is not true; chaparral possesses an extraordinary capacity for regeneration from resprouting of rootstocks and dormant seed banks. In addition, many studies over this time have shown that seeding both exotic and native species is a precarious undertaking that fails more often than not. There are several reasons why seeding is not practical on southern California landscapes, but the primary one is that these seeds require gentle and continuous autumn rains to establish root systems capable of holding soil back from winter rains. The first rains of the year commonly occur as intense torrents in late autumn and winter that wash seeds off the surface of steep slopes before they have an opportunity to establish. Such is not the fate of native seeds that are buried and better protected from transport by these rains. Perhaps a more important reason for not depending on seeding is that other methods for reducing slope erosion, such as mulch or hay bales, have proven to be more effective and far more predictable than seeding.

Seeding also has the potential for negative impacts on the conservation of naturally functioning chaparral ecosystems. On those occasions where the rains do cooperate and exotic seeded species establish, they can outcompete native species and sometimes escape to become aggressive invaders. Black mustard (*Brassica nigra*), which was the favored exotic species used to seed after fires in southern California during the first half of the twentieth century, today is a widespread pest throughout the region. Physical barriers created by mulch and hay bales also can introduce exotic species; as a consequence, more and more such projects are requiring "weed-free" hay.

Global Changes

Climate Change

Current and projected future climatic trends appear likely to increase the potential for fire in most California wildlands. This reflects the interactions of various factors, including increasing temperatures, changing precipitation patterns, decreasing snowpack, higher probability of drought events, increasing forest fuels, greater fuel continuity (due to both fire suppression and faster growth under warmer climates), and increasing human ignitions (Miller and Urban 1999; Westerling et al. 2006; Lenihan et al. 2008; Flannigan et al. 2009; Miller et al. 2009; National Research Council 2011; Safford, North, and Meyer 2012). Projections based on dynamic vegetation models linked to down-scaled GENERAL CIRCULATION MODELS (GCMs) suggest that the geographic distributions of major ecosystem types in California could change substantially by the end of the twenty-first century, with much of the change mediated by changes in fire activity and severity (Hayhoe et al. 2004, Lenihan et al. 2008; see Chapter 14, "Climate Change Impacts").

Lenihan et al.'s (2008) projections for California's Sierra Nevada and southern coast vary notably among climate scenarios, but some notable commonalities emerge. Under all scenarios the Sierra Nevada section is projected to experience a reduction in conifer forest (evergreen conifer and subalpine) and shrubland and an increase in hardwood-dominated forest (mixed forest and woodland) and grassland. In the south coast section all scenarios predict a loss of shrubland and an increase in grassland. In both sections these projected changes are largely due to increased fire activity, with grassland replacing shrubland and forest due to the inability of woody life forms to regenerate under greatly increased fire frequencies, and hardwoods replacing conifers due to the resprouting ability of hardwoods after fire and increased fitness of hardwoods under warmer conditions (especially where precipitation does not decrease substantially and if anthropogenic nitrogenous inputs are maintained or increased) (Lenihan et al. 2008). Notably, these projections extend trends already apparent in both ecological sections. For example, hardwood density has already increased in the Sierra Nevada section over the past seventy-five years (Bolsinger 1988, Dolanc et al. 2014), and grassland is already replacing shrubland across large areas of lowland southern California (Keeley 2006).

Restoration

Ecological restoration typically requires identification of some reference state to provide a target for management and to allow measurement of restoration progress. Because anthropogenic alterations to ecosystems and the global environment have been so ubiquitous, contemporary, unaltered reference ecosystems are difficult to identify. Thus restorationists are often forced to rely on historical information to construct reference states (Safford, Hayward et al. 2012). Historical ecology has provided invaluable evidence of conditions before human degradation occurred, but directional changes in—among other things—population, air and water pollution, and climate have led many to suggest that past conditions might no longer represent reasonable management targets for restoration planning (Millar et al. 2007, Wiens et al. 2012).

Long-lived, woody structures in semiarid and arid environments can store centuries of fire occurrence information in the form of fire scars. This has allowed development of historically based management guidance for many western U.S. forest types, but rapid global change requires some reconsideration of management strategies that rely implicitly on an assumption of environmental stasis. Since most western U.S. forests will likely experience even more potential for fire than during the centuries before Euro-American settlement (the usual historical reference period, which coincided with the Little Ice Age), current focus on reintroducing fire and creating forest structures resistant or resilient to fire seems entirely justified. Our current efforts seem paltry when measured against the scale of changes taking place (North et al. 2012). The current focus on preserving "pristine" conditions (i.e., with high fidelity to historical environments) in many ecosystems will likely need to be amended to embrace both the inherent dynamism of ecological systems and the directional changes now well under way (Cole and Yung 2010; Safford, Hayward et al. 2012; Wiens et al. 2012).

Summary

Fire is a natural ecosystem process throughout much of California. Historically, humans have played a substantial role in perturbing natural fire regimes. These impacts have differed substantially between montane, coniferous forests and lower-elevation, nonforested environments. Although humans today are responsible for over half of all fires ignited in forested landscapes, lightning has historically been an abundant source of ignition. Many California forests have had a long history of frequent, low-, and moderate-intensity surface fires, and the primary human impact has been suppression of the natural fire regime. These surface fires have been amenable to fire attack, rendering the history of fire suppression largely equivalent to fire exclusion. One consequence has been an anomalous accumulation of surface fuels and ingrowth of young trees, both of which have contributed to the potential for a fire regime shift to high-intensity crown fires.

Shrublands and other nonforested landscapes in the state have historically burned in high-intensity crown fires; as a result, fire suppression activities have been unable to exclude fire as in conifer forests. These landscapes have historically low lightning frequency; since human occupation, people have been the dominant source of ignitions. With increasing population growth, fire suppression efforts have worked hard to keep up with increasing numbers of fires. However, twentieth-century fires have been more abundant in central and southern coastal California than historically was the case. This increase in fire frequency has had negative ecosystem impacts by type-converting native shrublands to non-native grasslands throughout many parts of the region. Future global changes are likely to have very different impacts on these two landscapes, with global warming playing a significant role in forests and demographic growth and urban development playing larger roles in coastal plains and foothills.

Acknowledgments

This research was supported by the U.S. Geological Survey, Fire Risk Scenario project. Any use of trade names is for descriptive purposes only and does not imply endorsement by the U.S. government.

Recommended Reading

Bond, W. J., and B. W. van Wilgen. 2005. Fire and plants. Chapman and Hall, New York, New York.

Ford, R., Jr. 1991. Santa Barbara wildfires: Fire on the hills. McNally & Loftin, Santa Barbara, California.

Keeley, J. E., W. J. Bond, R. A. Bradstock, J. G. Pausas, and W. Rundel. 2012. Fire in Mediterranean climate ecosystems: Ecology, evolution, and management. Cambridge University Press, Cambridge, UK.

Kennedy, R. G. 2006. Wildfire and Americans: How to save lives, property, and your tax dollars. Hill and Wang, New York, New York.

Sugihara, N. G., J. W. van Wagtendonk, K. E. Shaffer, J. Fites-Kaufman, and A. E. Thode. 2006. Fire in California's ecosystems. University of California Press, Los Angeles, California.

Wuerthner, G., editor. 2006. The wildfire fire reader: A century of failed forest policy. Foundation for Deep Ecology by arrangement with Island Press, Sausalito, California.

Glossary

BURNED AREA EMERGENCY RESPONSE (BAER) A federal program that evaluates and makes recommendations for postfire management.

CATION EXCHANGE CAPACITY Used as a measure of soil fertility it is the total level of nutrients a soil is capable of holding and available for exchange with the soil solution.

COARSE-GRAINED VERSUS FINE-GRAINED PATCHINESS Coarse-grained environments are composed of large patches of a particular type, and fine-grained are small patches.

CORMS Modified stems used for underground storage of carbohydrates, inorganic nutrients, and buds.

CROWN FIRES Fires that burn the canopy of woody vegetation and are typically high intensity.

DIFFERENCED NORMALIZED BURN RATIO (DNBR) A remote sensing index that provides a measure of biomass before and after fire and is a measure of fire severity, or as is sometimes used, burn severity.

DRY RAVEL Also known as dry creep, describes the dry gravitational movement of soil particles, often driven forward by wetting/drying or freeze-thaw cycles and common especially in southern California.

ENDOGENOUS REGENERATION Plants that reproduce by seeds or resprouts from within the burn perimeter and do not depend on colonization from outside the burned area.

EURO-AMERICANS Americans with ancestry in Europe.

FACULTATIVE SEEDERS Plants that regenerate following fire by resprouting and from germination of dormant seed banks after canopies are killed by crown fire.

FIRE RETURN INTERVAL Time between fires for a spatially explicit area.

FIRE RETURN INTERVAL DEPARTURE (FRID) The difference between current and presettlement fire frequencies.

GENERAL CIRCULATION MODELS (GCMS) A type of mathematical climate of the general circulation of planetary atmosphere used to forecast future climates.

GRANIVORES Animals that feed largely on seeds.

HERBIVORES Animals that feed largely on herbaceous material.

HOLOCENE Along with the Pleistocene, one of the two epics of the Quaternary geological period; it is the current epoch that began ten thousand years ago.

LIGNOTUBER Woody swelling that develops at the base of a stem, which has buds capable of initiating new shoots, typically after fire.

MASTING A boom-and-bust pattern of seed production, where a population has synchronous seed production in one year followed by years of little or no seed production.

MEDITERRANEAN-TYPE CLIMATE Moderate precipitation during winter when temperatures are mild alternating with hot summer droughts, typical of regions between 30–38° latitude and on the western side of five continents. These include southern Europe and northern Africa, California, central Chile, the Cape of South Africa, western Australia, and south Australia.

METAPOPULATION Populations connected by colonization, which are important sources of recovery when a population is extirpated.

OBLIGATE RESPROUTERS Plants that regenerate following fire only by resprouting after canopies are killed by crown fire.

OBLIGATE SEEDERS Plants are completely killed by crown fires and that regenerate from germination of formerly dormant seed banks.

RHIZOMES Underground stems that spread laterally.

SANTA ANA WINDS Known by meteorologists as foehn winds, they develop from a high-pressure system in the interior of western North America that drives high-velocity offshore winds towards a coastal low pressure cell.

SURFACE FIRES Fires that burn fuels near the ground, including herbaceous materials and dead leaves and other litter and are typically of low intensity.

TAXA A taxonomic unit such as species, genus, family, and so on.

TERTIARY The geological period lasting from 65 million to 1.8 million years, including the epochs Paleocene, Eocene, Oligocene, Miocene, and Pliocene.

References

Agee, J. K. 1993. Fire ecology of Pacific Northwest forests. Island Press, Washington, D.C.

Anderson, M. K. 2005. Tending the wild. University of California Press, Los Angeles, California.

Auclair, A. N., and T. B. Carter. 1993. Forest wildfires as a recent source of CO_2 at northern latitudes. Canadian Journal of Forest Research 23:1528-1536.

Axelrod, D. I. 1989. Age and origin of chaparral. Pages 7-19 in S. C. Keeley, editor. The California chaparral: Paradigms reexamined. Natural History Museum of Los Angeles County, Los Angeles, California.

———. 1980. History of the maritime closed-cone pines, Alta and Baja California. University of California Publications in Geological Sciences 120:1–143.

Baker, W. L. 2006. Fire and restoration of sagebrush ecosystems. Wildlife Society Bulletin 34:177–185.

Barbour, M. G., T. Keeler-Wolf, and A. A. Schoenherr, editors. 2007. Terrestrial vegetation of California. Third edition. University of California Press, Los Angeles, California.

Barbour, M. G., B. Pavlik, F. Drysdale, and S. Lindstrom. 1993. California's changing landscapes: Diversity and conservation of California vegetation. California Native Plant Society, Sacramento, California.

Beyers, J. L., and W. O. Wirtz. 1995. Vegetative characteristics of coastal sage scrub sites used by California gnatcatchers: Implications for management in a fire-prone ecosystem. Pages 81–89 in Proceedings: First conference on fire effects on rare and endangered species and habitats, Coeur d'Alene, Idaho. International Association of Wildland Fire, Missoula, Montana.

Blackburn, T. C., and K. Anderson. 1993. Before the wilderness: Environmental management by Native Californians. Ballena Press, Menlo Park, California.

Bolsinger, C. L. 1988. The hardwoods of California's timberlands, woodlands, and savannas. Resource Bulletin PNW-RB-148. USDA Forest Service, Pacific Northwest Research Station, Portland, Oregon.

Bond, W. J., and J. E. Keeley. 2005. Fire as a global "herbivore": The ecology and evolution of flammable ecosystems. Trends in Ecology and Evolution 20:387–394.

Bradstock, R. A. 2010. A biogeographic model of fire regimes in Australia: Current and future implications. Global Ecology and Biogeography 19:145–158.

Brown, W. S., and S. B. Show. 1944. California rural land use and management: A history of the use and occupancy of rural lands in California. USDA Forest Service, California Region, Berkeley, California.

Burcham, L. T. 1957. California range land: An historic-ecological study of the range resources of California. State of California, Department of Natural Resources, Division of Forestry, Sacramento, California.

Busse, M. D., K. R. Hubbert, G. O. Fiddler, C. J. Shestak, and R. F. Powers. 2005. Lethal soil temperatures during burning of masticated forest residues. International Journal of Wildland Fire 14:267–276.

Cannon, S. H., J. E. Gartner, M. G. Rupert, J. A. Michael, A. H. Rea, and C. Parrett. 2010. Predicting the probability and volume of postwildfire debris flows in the intermountain western United States. Geological Society of America Bulletin 122:127–144.

Carlson, C. H., S. Z. Dobrowksi, and H. D. Safford. 2012. Variation in tree mortality and regeneration affect forest carbon recovery following fuel treatments and wildfire in the Lake Tahoe Basin, California, USA. Carbon Balance and Management 7:7. <doi:10.1186/1750-0680-7-7>.

Cerdá, A., and P. R. Robichaud. 2009. Fire effects on soils and restoration strategies. Science Publishers, Enfield, New Hampshire.

Cermak, R.W. 2005. Fire in the forest: A history of fire control on the national forests in California, 1898-1956. R5-FR-003. USDA Forest Service, Pacific Southwest Region, Albany, California.

Cochrane, M. A., A. Alencar, M. D. Schulze, C. M. Souza, D. C. Nepstad, P. Lefebvre, and E. A. Davidson. 1999. Positive feedbacks in the fire dynamic of closed canopy tropical forests. Science 284:1832–1835.

Cole, D. N., and L. Yung, editors. 2010. Beyond naturalness: Rethinking park and wilderness. Stewardship in an era of rapid change. Island Press, Washington, D.C.

Cooper, W. S. 1922. The broad-sclerophyll vegetation of California: An ecological study of the chaparral and its related communities. Publication No. 319. Carnegie Institution of Washington, Stanford, California.

DeBano, L. F. 1981. Water repellent soils: A state-of-the-art. General Technical Report PSW-GTR-46. USDA Forest Service, Pacific Southwest Forest and Range Experiment Station, Berkeley, California.

DeBano, L. F., D. G. Neary, and P. E. Folliott. 1998. Fire's effects on ecosystems. John Wiley and Sons, New York, New York.

Dennison, P. E., M. A. Moritz, and R. S. Taylor. 2008. Evaluating predictive models of critical live fuel moisture in the Santa Monica Mountains, California. International Journal of Wildland Fire 17:18–27.

Dolanc, C. R., H. D. Safford, S. Z. Dobrowksi, and J. H. Thorne. 2014. Twentieth century shifts in abundance and composition of vegetation types of the Sierra Nevada, CA, US. Applied Vegetation Science 17:442–455.

Erlandson, J. M. 1994. Early hunter-gatherers of the California coast. Plenum Press, New York, New York.

Flannigan, M. D., M. A. Krawchuk, W. J. de Groot, B. M. Wotton, and L. M. Gowman. 2009. Implications of changing climate for global wildland fire. International Journal of Wildland Fire 18:483–507.

Frederiksen, N. O. 1991. Pulses of middle Eocene to earliest Oligocene climatic deterioration in southern California and the Gulf Coast. Palaios 6:564–571.

Furniss, R. L., and V. M. Carolin. 1977. Western forest insects. Volume 1339. USDA Forest Service, Washington, D.C.

Gresswell, R. E. 1999. Fire and aquatic ecosystems in forested biomes of North America. Transactions of the American Fisheries Society 128:193–221.

Grubb, P. J. 1977. The maintenance of species richness in plant communities: The importance of the regeneration niche. Biological Reviews 52:107–145.

Hart, S. 1998. Beetle mania: An attraction to fire. BioScience 48:3–5.

Hayhoe K, C. Cayan, C. Field, P. Frumhoff, E. Maurer, N. Miller, S. Moser, S. Schneider, K. Cahill, E. Cleland, L. Dale, R. Drapek, R. Hanemann, L. Kalkstein, J. Lenihan, C. Lunch, R. Neilson, S. Sheridan, and J. Verville. 2004. Emission pathways, climate change, and impacts on California. Proceedings of the National Academy of Sciences 101:12422–12427.

Hiehle, J. L. 1961. Measurement of browse growth and utilization. California Fish and Game 50:148–151.

Hubbert, K. R., and V. Oriol. 2005. Temporal fluctuations in soil water repellency following wildfire in chaparral steeplands, southern California. International Journal of Wildland Fire 14:439–447.

Huff, M. H., and J. K. Smith. 2000. Fire effects on animal communities. Pages 35–42 in J. K. Smith, L. J. Lyon, M. H. Huff, R. G. Hooper, E. S. Telfer, and D. S. Schreiner, editors. Wildland fire in ecosystems: Effects of fire on fauna. General Technical Report RMRS-GTR-42. Volume 1. USDA Forest Service, Rocky Mountain Research Station, Ogden, Utah.

Hurteau, M. D., G. W. Koch, and B. A. Hungate. 2008. Carbon protection and fire risk reduction: Toward a full accounting of forest carbon offsets. Frontiers in Ecology and the Environment 6:493–498.

Huston, M. A. 2003. Understanding the effects of fire and other mortality-causing disturbances on species diversity. Pages 37–70 in I. Abbott and N. Burrows, editors. Fire in ecosystems of south-west Western Australia: Impacts and management. Symposium proceedings, volume 1, Perth, Australia, April 16–18, 2002. Backhuys Publishers, Leiden, The Netherlands.

Jacobson, A. L., S. D. Davis, and S. L. Babritius. 2004. Fire frequency impacts non-sprouting chaparral shrubs in the Santa Monica Mountains of southern California. No pagination in M. Arianoutsou and V. P. Panastasis, editors. Ecology, conservation, and management of Mediterranean climate ecosystems. Millpress, Rotterdam, The Netherlands.

Kalies, E. L., C. L. Chambers, and W. W. Covington. 2010. Wildlife responses to thinning and burning treatments in southwestern conifer forests: A meta-analysis. Forest Ecology and Management 259:333–342.

Kashian, D. M., W. H. Romme, D. B. Tinker, M. G. Turner, and M. G. Ryan. 2006. Carbon storage on landscapes with stand-replacing fires. BioScience 56:598–606.

Keeley, J. E. 1990. Demographic structure of California black-walnut (*Juglans californica*) woodlands in southern California. Madroño 37:237–248.

———. 1992. Recruitment of seedlings and vegetative sprouts in unburned chaparral. Ecology 73:1194–1208.

———. 2002. Native American impacts on fire regimes in California coastal ranges. Journal of Biogeography 29:303–320.

———. 2006. South coast bioregion. Pages 350–390 in N. G. Sugihara, J. W. van Wagtendonk, K. E. Shaffer, J. Fites-Kaufman, and A. E. Thode, editors. Fire in California's ecosystems. University of California Press, Los Angeles, California.

———. 2009. Fire intensity, fire severity, and burn severity: A brief review and suggested usage. International Journal of Wildland Fire 18:116–126.

———. 2012. Ecology and evolution of pine life histories. Annals of Forest Science 69:445–453.

Keeley, J. E., G. H. Aplet, N. L. Christensen, S. G. Conard, E. A. Johnson, P. N. Omi, D. L. Peterson, and T. W. Swetnam. 2009. Ecological foundations for fire management in North American forest and shrubland ecosystems. General Technical Report PNW-GTR-779. USDA Forest Service, Pacific Northwest Research Station, Corvallis, Oregon, USA.

Keeley, J. E., W. J. Bond, R. A. Bradstock, J. G. Pausas, and P. W. Rundel. 2012. Fire in Mediterranean ecosystems. Ecology, evolution, and management. Cambridge University Press, Cambridge, UK.

Keeley, J. E., and T. Brennan. 2012. Fire driven alien invasion in a fire-adapted ecosystem. Oecologia 169:1043–1052.

Keeley, J. E., T. Brennan, and A. H. Pfaff. 2008. Fire severity and ecosystem responses following crown fires in California shrublands. Ecological Applications 18:1530–1546.

Keeley, J. E., and F. W. Davis. 2007. Chaparral. Pages 339–366 in M. G. Barbour, T. Keeler-Wolf, and A. A. Schoenherr, editors. Terrestrial vegetation of California. Third edition. University of California Press, Los Angeles, California, USA.

Keeley, J. E., and C. J. Fotheringham. 2000. Role of fire in regeneration from seed. Pages 311–330. in M. Fenner, editor. Seeds: The ecology of regeneration in plant communities. Second Edition. CAB International, Oxon, UK.

Keeley, J. E., and C. J. Fotheringham. 2003. Impact of past, present, and future fire regimes on North American Mediterranean shrublands. Pages 218–262 in T. T. Veblen, W. L. Baker, G. Montenegro, and T. W. Swetnam, editors. Fire and climatic change in temperate ecosystems of the western Americas. Springer, New York, New York, USA.

Keeley, J. E., C. J. Fotheringham, and M. Baer-Keeley. 2005. Determinants of postfire recovery and succession in Mediterranean-climate shrublands of California. Ecological Applications 15:1515–1534.

Keeley, J. E., D. Lubin, and C. J. Fotheringham. 2003. Fire and grazing impacts on plant diversity and alien plant invasions in the southern Sierra Nevada. Ecological Applications 13:1355–1374.

Keeley, J. E., and A. D. Syphard. 2015. Different fire-climate relationships on forested and non-forested landscapes in the Sierra Nevada ecoregion. International Journal of Wildland Fire 24:27–36.

Keeley, J. E., A. D. Syphard, C. J. Fotheringham. 2013. The 2003 and 2007 wildfires in southern California. Pages 42–52 in S. Boulter, J. Palutikof, D. J. Karoly, and D. Guitart, editors. Natural disasters and adaptation to climate change. Cambridge University Press, Cambridge, UK.

Keeley, J. E., and P. J. van Mantgem. 2008. Community ecology of

seedlings. Pages 255–273 in M. A. Leak, V. T. Parker, and R. L. Simpson, editors. Seedling ecology and evolution. Cambridge University Press, Cambridge, UK.
Keeley, J. E., and P. H. Zedler. 1998. Evolution of life histories in *Pinus*. Pages 219–251 in D. Richardson, editor. Ecology and biogeography of pines. Cambridge University Press, Cambridge, UK.
Keeley, J. E., and P. H. Zedler. 2009. Large, high intensity fire events in southern California shrublands: Debunking the fine-grained age-patch model. Ecological Applications 19:69–94.
Lamb, M. P., M. Levina, R. A. DiBiase, and B. M. Fuller. 2013. Sediment storage by vegetation in steep bedrock landscapes: Theory, experiments, and implications for postfire sediment yield. Journal of Geophysical Research: Earth Surface 118:1147–1160.
Lenihan, J. H., D. Bachelet, R. P. Neilson, and R. Drapek. 2008. Response of vegetation distribution, ecosystem productivity, and fire to climate change scenarios for California. Climatic Change 87 (suppl. 1): S215–S230.
Lewis, H., 1973. Patterns of burning in California: Ecology and ethnohistory. Ballena Press, Menlo Park, California.
Lightfoot K. G., R. Q. Cuthrell, C. M. Boone, R. Byrne, A. S. Chavez, L. Collins, A. Cowart, R. R. Evett, P. V. A. Fine, D. Gifford-Gonzalez, M. G. Hylkema, V. Lopez, T. M. Misiewicz, and R. E. B. Reid. 2013. Anthropogenic burning on the central California coast in late Holocene and early historical times: Findings, implications, and future directions. California Archaeology 5:371–390.
Littell, J. S., D. McKenzie, D. L. Peterson, and A. L. Westerling, 2009. Climate and wildfire area burned in western U.S. ecoprovinces, 1916–2003. Ecological Applications 19:1003–1021.
Los Angeles River Watershed. 1941. Survey report for the Los Angeles River watershed. U.S. Government Printing Office. 67 pp.
Lyon, L. J., E. S. Telfer, and D. S. Schreiner. 2000. Direct effects of fire and animals responses. Pages 17–23 in J. K. Smith, L. J. Lyon, M. H. Huff, R. G. Hooper, E. S. Telfer, and D. S. Schreiner, editors. Wildland fire in ecosystems: Effects of fire on fauna. General Technical Report RMRS-GTR-42, volume 1. USDA Forest Service, Rocky Mountain Reserch Station, Ogden, Utah.
Mallek, C. R., H. D. Safford, J. H. Viers, and J. Miller. 2013. Modern departures in fire severity and area vary by forest type, Sierra Nevada and southern Cascades, California. Ecosphere 4(12): 1–28.
Martinson, E. J., and P. N. Omi. 2013. Fuel treatments and fire severity: A meta-analysis. Research Paper RMRS-RP-103. USDA Forest Service, Rocky Mountain Research Station, Fort Collins, Colorado.
Merriam, K. E., J. E. Keeley, and J. L. Beyers. 2006. Fuel breaks affect nonnative species abundance in California plant communities. Ecological Applications 16:515–527.
Miles, S. R., and C. B. Goudey. 1997. Ecological subregions of California: Section and subsection descriptions. Technical Paper R5-EM-TP-005. USDA Forest Service, San Francisco, California.
Millar, C. I., N. L. Stephenson, S. L. Stephens. 2007. Climate change and forests of the future: Managing in the face of uncertainty. Ecological Applications 17:2145–2151.
Miller, C., and D. L. Urban. 1999. Forest pattern, fire, and climatic change in the Sierra Nevada. Ecosystems 2:76–87.
Miller, J. D., H. D. Safford, M. Crimmins, and A. E. Thode. 2009. Quantitative evidence for increasing forest fire severity in the Sierra Nevada and southern Cascade Mountains, California and Nevada, USA. Ecosystems 12:16–32.
Miller, J. D., C. N. Skinner, H. D. Safford, E. E. Knapp, and C. M. Ramirez. 2012. Trends and causes of severity, size, and number of fires in northwestern California, USA. Ecological Applications 22:184–203.
Miller, J. D., and A. E. Thode. 2007. Quantifying burn severity in a heterogeneous landscape with a relative version of the delta Normalized Burn Ratio (dNBR). Remote Sensing of Environment 109:66–80.
Minnich, R. A. 2006. California climate and fire weather. Pages 13–37 in N. G. Sugihara, J. W. van Wagtendonk, K. E. Shaffer, J. Fites-Kaufman, and A. E. Thode, editors. Fire in California's ecosystems. University of California Press, Los Angeles, California.
Minshall, G. W. 2003. Responses of stream benthic macroinvertebrates to fire. Forest Ecology and Management 178:155–161.
Mitchell, S. R., M. E. Harmon, and K. E. O'Connell. 2009. Forest fuel reduction alters fire severity and long-term carbon storage in three Pacific Northwest ecosystems. Ecological Applications 19:643–655.
Miyanishi, K. 2001. Duff consumption. Pages 437–475 in E. A. Johnson and K. Miyanishi, editors. Forest fires: Behavior and ecological effects. Academic Press, San Diego, California.
Moody, J. A., and D. A. Martin. 2001. Initial hydrologic and geomorphic response following a wildfire in the Colorado Front Range. Earth Surface Processes on Land 26:1049–1070.
National Research Council. 2011. Climate stabilization targets: Emissions, concentrations, and impacts over decades to millennia. National Academies Press, Washington, D.C.
Nimmo, D. G., L. T. Kelly, L. M. Spence-Bailey, S. J. Watson, A. Haslem, J. G. White, M. F. Clarke, and A. F. Bennett. 2012. Predicting the century-long post-fire response of reptiles. Global Ecology and Biogeography 21:1062–1073.
North, M. P., B. M. Collins, and S. Stephens. 2012. Using fire to increase the scale, benefits, and future maintenance of fuels treatments. Journal of Forestry 110:392–401.
North, M. P., and M. D. Hurteau. 2011. High-severity wildfire effects on carbon stocks and emissions in fuels treated and untreated forest. Forest Ecology and Management 261:1115–1120.
Noss, R. F., J. F. Franklin, W. L. Baker, T. Schoennagel, and P. B. Moyle. 2006. Managing fire-prone forests in the western United States. Frontiers in Ecology and the Environment 4:481–487.
Oliver, A. A., J. E. Reuter, A. C. Heyvaert, and R. A. Dahlgren. 2012. Water quality response to the Angora fire, Lake Tahoe, California. Biogeochemistry 111:361–376.
Paleoindian migrations. Quaternary Science Reviews 30:269–272.
Pausas, J. G., and J. E. Keeley. 2009. A burning story: The role of fire in the history of life. BioScience 59:593–601.
Peterson, D. L., J. K. Agee, G. H. Aplet, D. P. Dykstra, R. T. Graham, J. F. Lehmkuhl, D. S. Pilloid, D. F. Potts, R. F. Powers, and J. D. Stuart. 2009. Effects of timber harvest following wildfire in western North America. General Technical Report PNW-GTR-776. USDA Forest Service, Pacific Northwest Research Station, Portland, Oregon.
Pinter, N., S. Fiedel, and J. E. Keeley. 2011. Fire and vegetation shifts at the vanguard of
Pyne, S. J. 1995. World fire. The culture of fire on earth. Henry Holt and Company, New York, New York.
Raphael, M. G., M. L. Morrison, and M. P. Yoder-Williams. 1987. Breeding bird populations during twenty-five years of postfire succession in the Sierra Nevada. Condor 89:614–626.
Raven, P. H., and D. I. Axelrod. 1972. Plate tectonics and Australasian paleobiogeography. Science 176:1379–1386.
Robichaud, P. R., S. A. Lewis, R. E. Brown, and L. E. Ashmun. 2009. Emergency post-fire rehabilitation treatment effects on burned area ecology and long-term restoration. Fire Ecology 5(1):115–128.
Robock, A. 1988. Enhancement of surface cooling due to forest fire smoke. Science 242:911–913.
Rochester, C. J., C. S. Brehme, D. R. Clark, D. C. Stokes, S. A. Hathaway, and R. N. Fisher. 2010. Reptile and amphibian responses to large-scale wildfires in southern California. Journal of Herpetology 44:333–351.
Safford, H. D. 2007. Man and fire in southern California: Doing the math. Fremontia 35(4):25–29.
Safford, H. D., G. Hayward, N. Heller, and J. A. Wiens. 2012. Climate change and historical ecology: Can the past still inform the future? Pages 46–62 in J. A. Wiens, G. Hayward, H. D. Safford, and C. M. Giffen, editors. Historical environmental variation in conservation and natural resource management. John Wiley and Sons, New York, New York.
Safford, H. D., J. Miller, D. Schmidt, B. Roath, and A. Parsons. 2008. BAER soil burn severity maps do not measure fire effects to vegetation: A comment on Odion and Hanson (2006). Ecosystems 11:1–11.
Safford, H. D., M. North, and M. D. Meyer. 2012. Climate change and the relevance of historical forest conditions. Pages 23–46 in M. P. North, editor. Managing Sierra Nevada forests. General Technical Report PSW-GTR-237. USDA Forest Service, Pacific Southwest Research Station, Albany, California.
Safford, H. D., J. T. Stevens, K. Merriam, M. D. Meyer, and A. M. Latimer. 2012. Fuel treatment effectiveness in California yellow pine and mixed conifer forests. Forest Ecology and Management 274:17–28.
Safford, H. D., and K. M. Van de Water. 2014. Using fire return interval departure (FRID) analysis to map spatial and temporal changes

in fire frequency on National Forest lands in California. Research Paper PSW-RP-266. USDA Forest Service, Pacific Southwest Research Station, Albany, California.

Sandoval, C. 2000. Persistence of a walking-stick population (Phasmatoptera: Timematodea) after a wildfire. Southwestern Naturalist 45:123–127.

Sauvajot, R. M., M. Buechner, D. A. Kamradt, and C. M. Schonewald. 1998. Patterns of human disturbance and response by small mammals and birds in chaparral near urban development. Urban Ecosystems 2:279–297.

Sawyer, J. O., T. Keeler-Wolf, and J. M. Evens. 2009. A manual of California vegetation. Second edition. California Native Plant Society, Sacramento, California.

Schuette, P., J. Diffendorfer, D. Deutschman, S. Tremor, and W. Spencer. 2014. Carnivore distributions across chaparral habitats exposed to wildfire and rural housing in southern California. International Journal of Wildland Fire 23 (4), 591–600.

Schuur, E. A., S. E. Trumbore, M. C. Mack, and J. W. Harden. 2003. Isotopic composition of carbon dioxide from a boreal forest fire: Inferring carbon loss from measurements and modeling. Global Biogeochemical Cycles 17(1):1–9.

Schwilk, D. W., J. E. Keeley, E. E. Knapp, J. McIver, J. D. Bailey, C. J. Fettig, C. E. Fiedler, R. J. Harrod, J. J. Moghaddas, K. W. Outcalt, C. N. Skinner, S. L. Stephens, T. A. Waldrop, D. A. Yassey, and A. Youngblood. 2009. The National Fire and Fire Surrogate Study: Effects of alternative fuel reduction methods on forest vegetation structure and fuels. Ecological Applications 19:285–304.

Shaffer, K. E., and W. F. Laudenslayer. 2006. Fire and animal interactions. Pages 118–144 in N. G. Sugihara, J. W. van Wagtendonk, K. E. Shaffer, J. Fites-Kaufman, and A. E. Thode, editors. Fire in California's ecosystems. University of California Press, Los Angeles, California.

Skinner, C. N., J. H. Burk, M. G. Barbour, E. Franco-Vizcaíno, and S. L. Stephens. 2008. Influences of climate on fire regimes in montane forests of north-western Mexico. Journal of Biogeography 35:1436–1451.

Skinner, C. N., A. H. Taylor, and J. K. Agee. 2006. Klamath Mountain Bioregion. Pages 170–194 in N. G. Sugihara, J. W. van Wagtendonk, K. E. Shaffer, J. Fites-Kaufman, and A. E. Thode, editors. Fire in California's ecosystems. University of California Press, Los Angeles, California.

Smith, J. K., L. J. Lyon, M. H. Huff, R. G. Hooper, E. S. Telfer, and D. S. Schreiner, editors. 2000. Wildland fire in ecosystems: Effects of fire on fauna. General Technical Report RMRS-GTR-42. USDA Forest Service, Rocky Mountain Research Station, Fort Collins, Colorado.

Smucker, K. M., R. L. Hutto, and B. M. Steele. 2005. Changes in bird abundance after wildfire: Importance of fire severity and time since fire. Ecological Applications 15:1535–1549.

Stephens, S. L., R. E. J. Boerner, J. J. Moghaddas, E. E. Y. Moghaddas, C. Edminster, C. E. Fiedler, B. R. Hartsough, J. E. Keeley, E. E. Knapp, J. D. McIver, C. N. Skinner, and A. Youngblood. 2012. Fuel treatment impacts on estimated wildfire carbon loss from forests in Montana, Oregon, California, and Arizona. Ecosphere 3(5): article 38. <http://dx.doi.org/10.1890/ES11-00289.1>.

Stephens, S. L., and B. M. Collins. 2004. Fire regimes of mixed conifer forests in the north-central Sierra Nevada at multiple spatial scales. Northwest Science 78:12–23.

Stephens, S. L., J. D. McIver, R. E. J. Boerner, C. J. Fettig, J. B. Fontaine, B. R. Hartshough, P. L. Kennedy, and D. W. Schwilk. 2012. The effects of forest fuel-reduction treatments in the United States. BioScience 62:549–560.

Stoof, C. R., D. Moore, P. M. Fernandes, J. J. Stoorvogel, R. E. S. Fernandes, A. J. D. Ferreira, and C. J. Ritsema. 2013. Hot fire, cool soil. Geophysical Research Letters 40:1–6. <doi:10.1002/grl.50299>.

Sudworth, G. B. 1900. Stanislaus and Lake Tahoe Forest Reserves, California, and adjacent territories. Pages 505–561 in Twenty-first annual report of the U.S. Geological Survey, Part 5, Forest Resources. Government Printing Office, Washington, D.C.

Sugihara, N. G., J. W. van Wagtendonk, and J. Fites-Kaufman. 2006a. Fire as an ecological process. Pages 58–74 in N. G. Sugihara, J. W. van Wagtendonk, K. E. Shaffer, J. Fites-Kaufman, and A. E. Thode, editors. Fire in California's ecosystems. University of California Press, Los Angeles, California.

Sugihara, N. G., J. W. van Wagtendonk, K. E. Shaffer, J. Fites-Kaufman, and A. E. Thode, editors. 2006b. Fire in California's ecosystems. University of California Press, Los Angeles, California.

Swetnam, T. W., and C. H. Baisan. 2003. Tree-ring reconstructions of fire and climate history in the Sierra Nevada and Southwestern United States. Pages 158–195 in T. T. Veblen, W. L. Baker, G. Montenegro, and T. W. Swetnam, editors. Fire and climatic change in temperate ecosystems of the western Americas. Springer, New York, New York.

Syphard, A. D., J. E. Keeley, and T. J. Brennan. 2011. Comparing the role of fuel breaks across southern California national forests. Forest Ecology and Management 261:2038–2048.

Thode, A. E., J. W. van Wagtendonk, J. D. Miller, and J. F. Quinn. 2011. Quantifying the fire regime distributions for severity in Yosemite National Park, California, USA. International Journal of Wildland Fire 20: 223–239.

Tiedemann, A. R., C. E. Conrad, J. H. Dieterich, J. W. Hornbeck, W. F. Megahan, L. A. Viereck, and D. D. Wade. 1979. Effects of fire on water, a state-of-knowledge review. General Technical Report WO-GTR-10. USDA Forest Service, Washington, D.C.

Tinker, D. B., and D. H. Knight. 2000. Coarse woody debris following fire and logging in Wyoming lodgepole pine forests. Ecosystems 3(5):472–483.

Van de Water, K. P., and H. D. Safford. 2011. A summary of fire frequency estimates for California vegetation before Euro-American settlement. Fire Ecology 7:26–58.

Van Mantgem, P. J., J. C. Nesmith, M. Keifer, E. E. Knapp, A. Flint, and L. Flint. 2013. Climatic stress increases forest fire severity across the western United States. Ecology Letters 16:1151–1156.

van Wagtendonk, J. W., K. A. van Wagtendonk, J. B. Meyer, and K. J. Paintner. 2002. The use of geographic information for fire management planning in Yosemite National Park. Applied Geography 19:19–39.

Verschuyl, J., S. Riffell, D. Miller, and T. B. Wigley. 2011. Biodiversity response to intensive biomass production from forest thinning in North American forests—A meta-analysis. Forest Ecology and Management 261:221–232.

Westerling, A. L., H. G. Hidalgo, D. R. Cayan, and T. W. Swetnam. 2006. Warming and earlier spring increases western U.S. forest wildfire activity. Science 313:940–943.

Wiens, J. A., G. D. Hayward, H. D. Safford, and C. M. Giffen, editors. 2012. Historical environmental variation in conservation and resource management. Wiley-Blackwell, Oxford, UK.

Williams, K. S., S. D. Davis, B. L. Gartner, and S. Karlsson. 1991. Factors limiting the establishment of a chaparral oak, *Quercus durata* Jeps., in grassland. Pages 70–73 in Proceedings of the symposium on oak woodlands and hardwood rangeland management, October 31–November 2, 1990, Davis, California. General Technical Report PSW-GTR-126. USDA Forest Service, Pacific Southwest Research Station, Berkeley, California.

Wohlgemuth, P. M., K. Hubbert, and M. J. Arbaugh. 2006. Fire and physical environment interactions: Soil, water, and air. Pages 75–93 in N. G. Sugihara, J. W. van Wagtendonk, K. E. Shaffer, J. Fites-Kaufman, and A. E. Thode, editors. Fire in California's ecosystems. University of California Press, Los Angeles, California.

Zedler, P. H. 1995. Are some plants born to burn? Trends in Ecology and Evolution 10:393–395.

Zouhar, K., J. Kapler, S. Sutherland, M. L. Brooks. 2008. Wildland fire in ecosystems: Fire and nonnative invasive plants. General Technical Report RMRS-GTR-42, volume 6. USDA Forest Service, Rocky Mountain Research Station, Ogden, Utah.

FOUR

Geomorphology and Soils

ROBERT C. GRAHAM and A. TOBY O'GEEN

Overview of Geologic Processes

California's highly diverse geologic setting is the result of the interplay of tectonics, sediment accumulation, emplacement and alteration of oceanic rocks, intrusion of magmas, extrusion of volcanic rocks, glaciation, and lateral displacement of rocks along faults. These conditions—coupled with dramatic differences in climate, biota, topography, and landscape age—give rise to a diversity of soils. Nevertheless, the state can be divided into distinct physiographic provinces (Figure 4.1) to discuss the relationships between geology and climate that have interacted to produce distinct soils and ecosystems. The majority of the chapter is organized by physiographic province, beginning with the Sierra Nevada, moving west to the Central Valley and Coast Ranges, then north to the Klamath and Cascade Mountains and the Modoc Plateau, then down and around through the desert Basin and Range, Transverse and Peninsular Ranges, and back up California's coast. Although we present an overview of the kinds of soils present in the state, our emphasis is on soil processes and interactions with ecosystems.

California's landscapes and LITHOLOGIES are inextricably related to the convergence of two tectonic plates: the Pacific plate pushes and scrapes northwest along the North American plate at a rate of about five centimeters per year. The San Andreas fault along California's western edge expresses the boundary between the two plates, but numerous other faults result from the tectonic forces. Lateral and vertical movements along the faults create valleys, uplift mountain ranges, and shape stream courses. Erosion of continually uplifted terrain has kept mountain landscapes rugged and unstable and has produced huge amounts of sediment that fill valleys (Harden 2004).

The types of rocks that form soils to support California's ecosystems owe their formation, or at least their exposure, to tectonic movement. As the Pacific plate has been subducted beneath the North American plate in the area of northern California, oceanic sediments have been accreted against the plate margin. In some places slabs of ULTRAMAFIC mantle rock are lodged into these sediments. Both the sediments and ultramafic rocks have been uplifted and exposed—in the northern Coast Ranges, the western Sierra Nevada, and the Klamath Mountains. These rocks have been metamorphosed by the high pressures and temperatures caused by deep burial. As the Pacific plate is further subducted, its rocks melt and magma rises up through the North American plate causing

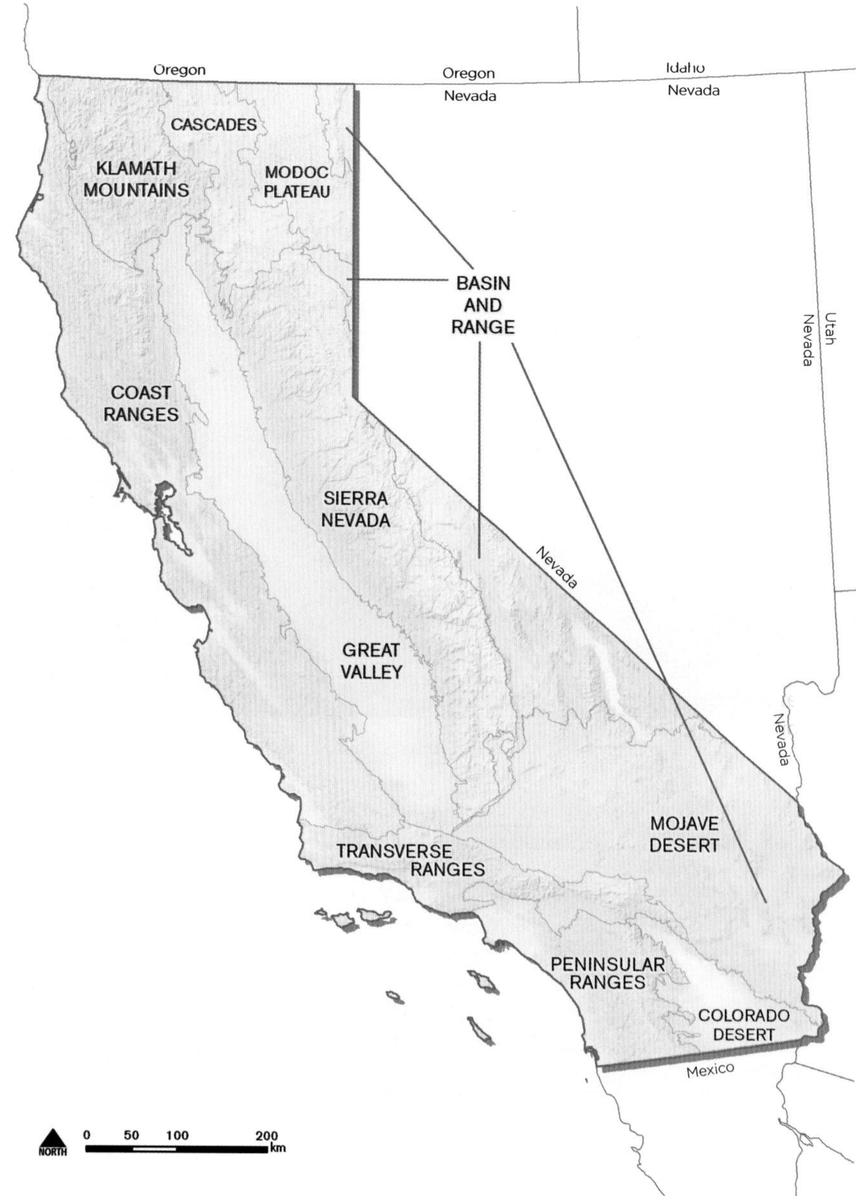

FIGURE 4.1 Physiographic regions of California. Map: Parker Welch (UC Santa Cruz).

volcanic extrusions, mostly in the eastern part of the state. GRANITES in the Sierra Nevada and elsewhere in the state are also the result of melted subducted Pacific plate rocks that intruded upward into the North American plate but cooled before reaching the surface, and that faulting later uplifted and erosion exposed (Harden 2004). Sediments have accumulated in the deep trough of the Great Valley as they have been shed off the surrounding mountains. More recently, the higher elevations of the Klamath Mountains, the Cascade Range, and especially the Sierra Nevada were shaped by glaciation that exposed fresh bedrock and deposited moraines and glacial outwash material at lower elevations.

Photo on previous page: Coastal landscape at Cambria showing two elevations of marine terraces: a lower one with grass and a higher one with trees on the skyline. The soil on the lower terrace (center of photo) has a thick, dark horizon. Photo: Tom Rice.

Sierra Nevada

Geology and Geomorphology

The Sierra Nevada occupies approximately 70,000 square kilometers, extending from its southern end east of Bakersfield to just south of Lassen Peak in the north. The mountain range is asymmetric, consisting of a gradually sloping western face created by a west-tilted fault block and a steep eastern escarpment, which represents the normal faulting that delineates the western edge of the Basin and Range province. Elevation at the crest is highest in the south due to greater uplift, with peaks over 4,000 meters, and decreases to between 1,800 and 2,450 meters at the northern end. The topographic and altitudinal trend of the southern Sierra is more complex compared to the rest of the west slope, with a westward-stepped topography that dips toward the south from the latitude of Mount Whitney (Clark et al. 2005).

The southern Sierra and much of the high country across the mountain range is an exposed granitic BATHOLITH. The Sierran Batholith, emplaced 210 million to 80 million years ago, consists of granitic rocks, interspersed with small PLUTONS of more MAFIC rocks. Metamorphic rocks are also found in the Sierra as roof pendants, which are remnants of the rock that once covered the batholith. The metamorphic cap has been removed by erosion at high elevations and throughout the southern Sierra but remains in parts of the central and northern Sierra and throughout the northern half of the foothill region where uplift has been less. Uplift and faulting was accompanied by volcanic activity. Volcanism was common in the northern Sierra between twenty million and five million years ago. Volcanic activity that originated east of what is now the Sierra crest extruded massive BASALTIC lava flows and ANDESITIC mudflows that followed ancient drainage systems all the way to the Sacramento Valley floor. The remnants of these deposits can be seen as table mountains throughout the region. This inverted topography was formed where ancient river valleys were filled with volcanic flows and the surrounding older terrain was removed by erosion.

Topographic trends are governed by lithology and the general asymmetry of the mountain range. The east slope landscapes are characterized by very steep mountains drained by steep V-shaped canyons at elevations below where glaciation has occurred. Slopes become moderate to gently sloping near the base of the east slope, where glacial till, outwash, and QUATERNARY ALLUVIAL FAN deposits exist. At high elevations (1,830 to 3,050 meters) within the exposed batholith, terrain consists of gently to moderately sloping plateaus, steep mountains, and U-shaped valleys sculpted by glaciers. At lower elevations (920 to 1,830 meters) of the west slope, granitic terrain gives rise to steep slopes drained by very steep-sided canyons, particularly in the southern Sierra. The metamorphic terrain of the west slope and foothill region consists of a moderately steep plateau dissected by major rivers. The granitic foothill landscapes are typically more hilly, with rounded summits, convex and concave hillslopes, and a network of small interconnected lowlands.

Soil Formation Influences

Along the west slope of the Sierra, the orographic effect of air masses cooling with increasing elevation creates a strong climatic gradient that produces systematic patterns in soil development. The mean annual precipitation (MAP) in the foothills ranges from 200 millimeters in the south to 1,020 millimeters in the central and northern foothills. As elevation increases, MAP increases to a maximum of 2,290 millimeters at the highest northern and central peaks. MAP decreases dramatically on the steep east side, ranging from 200 to 1,270 millimeters, depending on elevation. Precipitation generally increases in a northerly direction. Mean annual air temperatures decrease from 18°C in the foothill region to 4°C at the crest.

A bioclimatic gradient exists across the Sierra. Vegetation progresses from blue oak and live oak woodlands at low elevations through ponderosa pine, mixed conifer, and red fir forests at mid-elevations and alpine lodgepole pine systems at highest elevations, as described in Chapter 12, "Vegetation," and Chapter 27, "Montane Forests." Soil development trends correspond to this altitudinal gradient, which imposes a weathering environment that is limited by moisture at low elevations and by low temperature at high elevations. A zone of high-weathering intensity exists along the entire Sierra Nevada at mid-elevations (1,000 to 2,500 meters). This belt of intense soil development occurs in all parent materials and reflects the combined influence of mild temperatures and high precipitation, predominantly as rain (Dahlgren et al. 1997, Rasmussen et al. 2007).

At high elevation (above approximately 3,000 meters), landscape age is generally constrained to the end of the last glacial maximum. Here soil cover and weathered bedrock were scoured by advancing ice sheets, resetting the pedologic clock at approximately ten thousand years before present. It is likely that soils formed at lower elevations (e.g., below approximately 3,000 meters) are significantly older. Moreover, soils formed from glacial material such as outwash and till can have a wide range of ages as a result of multiple glaciations. Soils formed on older glacial deposits (older than eighty thousand years) contain reddish BT HORIZONS (Birkeland and Janda 1971). In some of these older soils, subsoil horizons are cemented by PEDOGENIC silica. Soils formed in till deposited fourteen thousand to twenty-one thousand years ago are less developed, with only weak B horizons. Soils younger than this are only slightly weathered and have colors that are close to those of the parent material (olive brown and yellowish brown) (Birkeland and Janda 1971).

Soils of Granitic Terrain

Elevation-controlled climate strongly influences chemical and physical properties of soils on granitic terrain in the Sierra Nevada (Dahlgren et al. 1997). For example, soil pH decreases approximately two units from around neutral (pH = 6.5–7.5) in the foothills to strongly acidic (pH = 4.7–5.5) at elevations greater than 2,000 meters, where BASE CATIONS are removed by greater leaching. Carbon:nitrogen ratios in the upper 18 centimeters of soil increase with elevation from a low of 12.4 in the oak woodlands of the foothill region to a maximum of 32.0 at elevations above 2,000 meters, where coniferous plant residues are more resistant to microbial decomposition due to lower N levels and higher lignin and polyphenol content.

Soil organic carbon (SOC) content summed for the A AND B HORIZONS, shows a bell-shaped relationship with elevation (Figure 4.2). Relatively warm soil temperatures throughout the year in the low foothills accelerate microbial decomposition of plant residues, resulting in low SOC (~5 kg m^{-2}). SOC is highest at mid-elevations (~14 kg m^{-2}) due to the tremendous biological productivity there. SOC decreases at upper elevations (~10.5 kg m^{-2}) because cold temperatures limit primary productivity. Soil depth, clay content, and pedogenic iron oxides follow a trend similar to that of SOC, with highest levels at mid-elevations. This is due to the intense weathering facilitated by high precipitation and mild temperatures in that elevation range (Dahlgren et al. 1997).

Soil morphologies reflect differences in soil forming processes. At high elevations (higher than 2,500 meters), cold temperatures limit pedogenesis to the extent that litter accumulation and darkening of the soil profile by soil organic carbon are the dominant processes. Soils are coarse textured (sands and loamy sands) and often have an abrupt transition to hard bedrock in areas where glaciation occurred. These soils are ENTISOLS. At elevations between 1,800 and 2,500 meters, Bw horizons have slight ILLUVIAL clay accumulation, more intense colors, and development of soil structure. At somewhat lower elevations, soils are deep and more highly

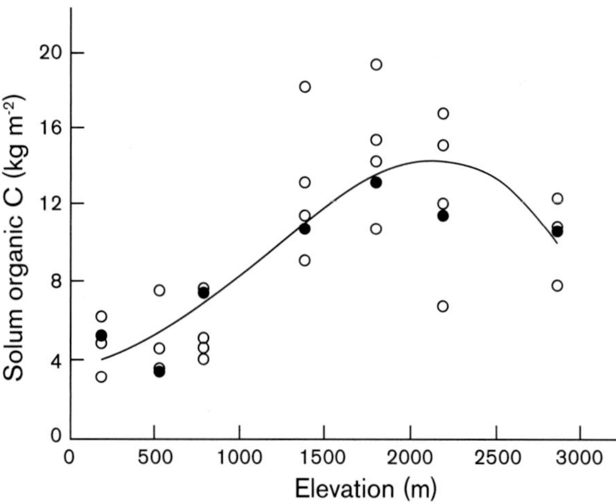

FIGURE 4.2 Organic carbon content in the solum (A + B horizons) of soils in granitic terrain along an elevation transect in the Sierra Nevada. Black dots represent data generated by Dahlgren et al. (1997), open circles are from soil survey characterization data, and the line is generated from the means at the different elevations. Source: Adapted from Dahlgren et al. 1997.

weathered and are underlain by thick zones of weathered bedrock. Soil textures are commonly sandy loams in surface horizons, abruptly transitioning to sandy clay loams in Bt horizons. High concentrations of pedogenic iron give rise to well-aggregated soils, which promote rapid infiltration and drainage.

A fundamental role of soil is to regulate water and nutrients to the ecosystem. Deeply weathered, crumbly granite bedrock is a characteristic of Sierran landscapes that contributes to the fertility and productivity of this ecosystem. This weathered bedrock is an important source of plant-available water (Graham, Rossi, and Hubbert 2010) and nutrients such as P, Ca, Mg, and K that would otherwise be unavailable. The stored water that weathered bedrock supplies during the dry season governs the productivity and survival of coniferous forests (Arkley 1981, Witty et al. 2003, Bales et al. 2011). Weathered bedrock is a more important source of water for plant transpiration during the summer than are overlying soils (Anderson et al. 1995; Hubbert, Beyers, and Graham 2001; Hubbert, Graham, and Anderson 2001; Rose et al. 2003).

Soils of Volcanic Terrain

Many soils in the region are formed from volcanic materials and have what are known as ANDIC PROPERTIES. Some of these properties, such as low bulk density, high plant-available water retention, and high soil organic carbon contents, promote forest productivity (Shoji et al. 1993, Rasmussen et al. 2007). But these soils also require careful consideration relative to some of their characteristics, including PH-DEPENDENT CHARGE, low CATION EXCHANGE CAPACITY, PHOSPHATE FIXATION, and high susceptibility to erosion (Dahlgren et al. 2004). Compared to soils derived from granite and many other parent materials, soils formed from volcanic materials tend to be more developed due to the abundance of highly weatherable components such as glass, pyroxenes, biotite, and amphiboles. Nevertheless, soils derived from andesite, a common volcanic rock in the Sierra, show weathering trends similar to those outlined for granite, with the same strong dependence on elevation. At mid-elevations soil textures are typically loams and sandy loams in surface horizons, gradually transitioning to clay loams and clays in the subsoil. Clay mineralogy of these soils is dominated by KAOLIN and amorphous iron and aluminum oxides. Many soils in volcanic terrain of the Sierra are ULTISOLS. ALFISOLS are common where precipitation is lower and leaching is less. At upper elevations ANDISOLS and INCEPTISOLS are prevalent (Rasmussen et al. 2007). Soils with andic properties are found in winter-snow–dominated landscapes between 1,700 and 2,150 meters. Mineral transformations are minimal at higher elevations.

Soils of the Foothills

The oak-grassland foothill region (Figure 4.3) has a north-south trending sequence of parent material lithology. The northern foothill region consists mainly of metavolcanic and volcanic rocks (greenstone, basalt, and andesite). The central foothill region consists of a complex mixture of rock types including metasedimentary, metavolcanic, sedimentary, volcanic, and intrusive igneous. The southern foothill region is largely granitic with some volcanic rocks interspersed. Soils developed from marble, serpentinite, andesite, and metavolcanic rocks are most developed. These soils typically have subsurface clay contents that exceed 30% and strong red colors throughout much of the profile. Soils derived from greenstone (metavolcanic) often have a CLAYPAN (see Figure 4.3). These horizons create seasonal perched water tables that, in sloping terrain, result in subsurface lateral flow that supplies a significant component of streamflow in ephemeral streams (O'Geen et al. 2010, Swarowsky et al. 2012). Foothill soils derived from metasedimentary and granitic rocks tend to show less morphologic development. They are less red, indicating lower pedogenic iron content, and their clay contents tend to gradually increase with depth, typically to a maximum of 30%. With the exception of soils derived from granite, most foothill soils contain abundant rock fragments, with median values exceeding 20%, particularly in the subsoil.

Soil depth is perhaps the most important soil property governing the quantity of water and nutrients in semiarid landscapes. Soils derived from granite are most deeply weathered, often exceeding 160 centimeters in thickness. Soils derived from marble and metasedimentary rocks also tend to be very deep. Soils derived from metavolcanic rock tend to reach 1 meter in thickness. Soils derived from serpentinite and slate are commonly less than 1 meter deep and in many instances are shallow (less than 50 centimeters deep).

Soils of Montane Valleys

A little less than 10% of the Sierra Nevada consists of upper montane meadows (Ratliff 1985). These meadowlands perform many important ecosystem services such as flood water retention, maintenance of summer streamflows, forage production for grazing animals, carbon sinks, and hotspots of biodiversity (Norton et al. 2011). Soil properties of the meadows are influenced by water table dynamics. In meadows that are saturated with water during most of the growing season, the limited supply of oxygen slows microbial decomposition of plant residues resulting in a buildup of organic residues. The soils are HISTOSOLS. Drier meadows have mineral soils, typically MOLLISOLS. Meadow landscapes are vulnera-

FIGURE 4.3 The oak grasslands in the foothills of the Sierra Nevada (above) have soils with claypans (very clayey Bt horizons) when formed from metavolcanic rock. Here, the claypan is the bottom zone where the knife is propped up. Note the vertical cracks in the dry clay.

ble to encroachment by surrounding coniferous forest if they dry out. Meadow drying can occur due to long-term climatic changes or by channel incision that lowers the groundwater table of the entire system.

There are a variety of other types of valley landscape positions in the Sierra. Rapid uplift has resulted in steeply incised canyons with narrow valley floors in settings where glaciation has not occurred. These soils are highly variable in terms of chemical and physical composition because they are a product of the depositional environment. For example, landforms that experience high-energy flood events have coarse-textured soils with high rock fragment content and areas that experience low-energy flooding have fine-textured soils and may be rich in organic matter because imperfect drainage impedes its decomposition. Many soils in these landscapes are stratified with abrupt transitions between horizons that have very different textures. In the central and northern foothills many valley soils have formed in tailings and debris deposits produced by placer mining operations during the Gold Rush. These landscapes can have a wide range of soil properties but typically consist of stratified deposits of stony, cobbly, and gravelly material with enough fine sand or silt to support annual grasses. Soil thickness can be highly variable in these landscapes.

The Central Valley

Geology and Geomorphology

The Central Valley is one of the most productive regions in the world. The valley is approximately 58,000 square kilometers stretching around 650 kilometers in length. It is often considered as two regions separated by the San Joaquin Delta, the Sacramento Valley to the north and the San Joaquin Valley to the south. The Sacramento and San Joaquin river systems converge at the delta, which is at sea level. The valley gently slopes to an elevation of 120 meters at its southern end and approximately 245 meters at its northernmost reach.

The region consists of an elongate asymmetric syncline, once a large inland sea that began filling with sediment approximately 150 million years ago. The ancient sediment has been estimated to be as much as 13 to 15 kilometers thick and is capped by PLEISTOCENE alluvium (Alt and Hyndman

2000). Gently sloping, nearly level alluvial fans exist across the valley, derived from granitic, metamorphic, sedimentary, and volcanic rock sources. Fans created by the Mokelumne, Stanislaus, Tuolumne, Merced, San Joaquin, Kings, Kaweah, and Cosumnes Rivers have drainage basins that connect to glaciated portions of the Sierra Nevada, whereas the fans created by the Calaveras, Chowchilla, and Fresno Rivers, and minor fans produced by many smaller rivers, have drainage basins that are limited to nonglaciated regions (Weissmann et al. 2005). Gently sloping floodplains and terraces are found along streams and rivers. Both gently and steeply undulating Pleistocene terraces occupy the valley margins. These terraces are remnants of fans that document depositional and erosional response to Quaternary climate change and regional uplift (Weissmann et al. 2005). During the initial stages of Sierran uplift, the mountains were capped with metamorphic rock. As uplift continued, the mountain caps were removed by erosion, exposing the underlying granitic batholith. Thus a great deal of the early ALLUVIUM from metamorphic rock was buried by subsequent alluvium from granitic sources. However, uplift and erosion has exposed older portions of the alluvial fan by stripping more recent alluvial cover at valley margins (O'Geen, Pettygrove et al. 2008). This alluvial sequence grades entirely into granitic alluvium in the southern part of the valley.

The agriculturally rich landscapes of the Central Valley contain an incredibly diverse array of soils, perhaps more so than any other agricultural area of similar size in the United States. This soil variability reflects the influence of multiple parent materials spanning a range of ages, from modern-day stream deposits to ancient GEOMORPHIC SURFACES that are among the oldest in the country. Soils of the Central Valley have formed from thick alluvium that has accumulated over thousands to millions of years. Most of the sediment has come from the Sierra because of its large rivers and the vast volume of sediment supplied by glacial outwash. The absence of glaciation and the smaller watersheds of the Coast Range have limited its sediment deposition to the western margin of the Valley. Within the basin floor, meandering rivers have mixed Coast Range and Sierran alluvium. Terraces and alluvial fans exist as a sequence of buried alluvial deposits, where younger alluvium overlies older deposits. Older alluvium remains exposed at the valley margins, isolated from younger deposition by uplift of the Sierra and Coast Range. These old terraces have soils with very different properties compared to recent alluvium.

Soils of the Basin and East Side

On the east side of the Central Valley, soils have formed from alluvium of mixed sources that has accumulated over thousands of years from erosion of the Sierra Nevada. Systematic spatial patterns in soil exist because the parent materials have been deposited by water over time (Figure 4.4). A typical sequence from the basin floor (center of the valley) east to the foothill region includes four alluvial soil landscapes.

1. *Weakly developed soils in basin alluvium and recent floodplain deposits.* These formed between the present and about ten thousand years ago. Floodplains along major river systems contain sandy soils with little pedogenic alteration. A typical soil profile of this landscape position is layered, reflecting the energetics of the depositional environment, where high-energy flood events deposit coarse-grained materials and low-energy events deposit fine-grained material. Since deposition is often event-based, soil profiles commonly have large and abrupt changes in texture with depth. Much of the basin experienced moderate to low energy sediment deposition, resulting in fine-textured soils with poor drainage conditions and SMECTITE clays, many of them VERTISOLS, which are difficult to manage. Their change in volume in response to moisture status destroys roads, foundations, structures, and sidewalks. These soils also damage tree roots, making them more susceptible to disease. Vertisols are commonly flooded for rice production because they are slowly permeable when wet. Many basin soils are poorly drained due to a seasonally high water table that extends to the soil surface or within the root zone. The poor drainage slows organic matter decomposition, resulting in soils with high soil organic matter content (Mollisols).
2. *Weakly developed soils on basin margins and broad alluvial fans.* These were emplaced from approximately ten thousand to seventy thousand years ago. Large expanses of this landscape exist, derived from rivers (Mokelumne, Cosumnes, Stanislaus, Tuolumne, Kern, and Kings Rivers) that deposited glacial sediment as massive alluvial fans in the valley floor. Soils on these fans are typically coarse-textured and show little evidence of soil formation; the main process being accumulation of organic carbon in an A horizon. As a result, soils are typically Entisols and Mollisols.
3. *Highly developed soils on low terraces.* These deposited approximately 130,000 to 330,000 years ago. Large expanses of this soilscape rise above more recent alluvial fan deposits. Much of the landscape has microtopographic highs and lows (patterned ground) and the soils, formed in granitic alluvium, often contain DURIPANS and claypans that restrict water and root penetration. The dominant soil of this region is the San Joaquin series, California's state soil.
4. *Highly developed soils on dissected high terraces (deposited more than 600,000 years ago) on the eastern edge of the valley.* The landscape consists of alluvial fans that have been dissected by erosion into remnant "islands" (high terraces) with ancient soils. The soils have duripans and/or claypans and abundant resistant GRAVELS and COBBLES composed primarily of quartzite and chert. Clay content often exceeds 40% in the Bt horizons. The pH decreases with depth from moderately acidic in the A horizon to strongly acid in horizons below. The clay mineralogy is dominantly kaolinitic, indicating that these soils are highly weathered (O'Geen, Pettygrove et al. 2008). In places, erosion and terrace dissection have removed much of the upper parts of these very old soils.

In the past, soils with restrictive horizons, such as duripans and claypans, limited the agricultural possibilities to annual crops. As prices of fruit, nuts, and grapes increased, these soils were developed for production through the destruction of restrictive horizons by deep tillage and mixing. Currently, soils with restrictive horizons are rare in the San Joaquin Valley to the extent that they have become endangered (Amundson et al. 2003). Land leveling is another common land management practice that has altered the Central Valley

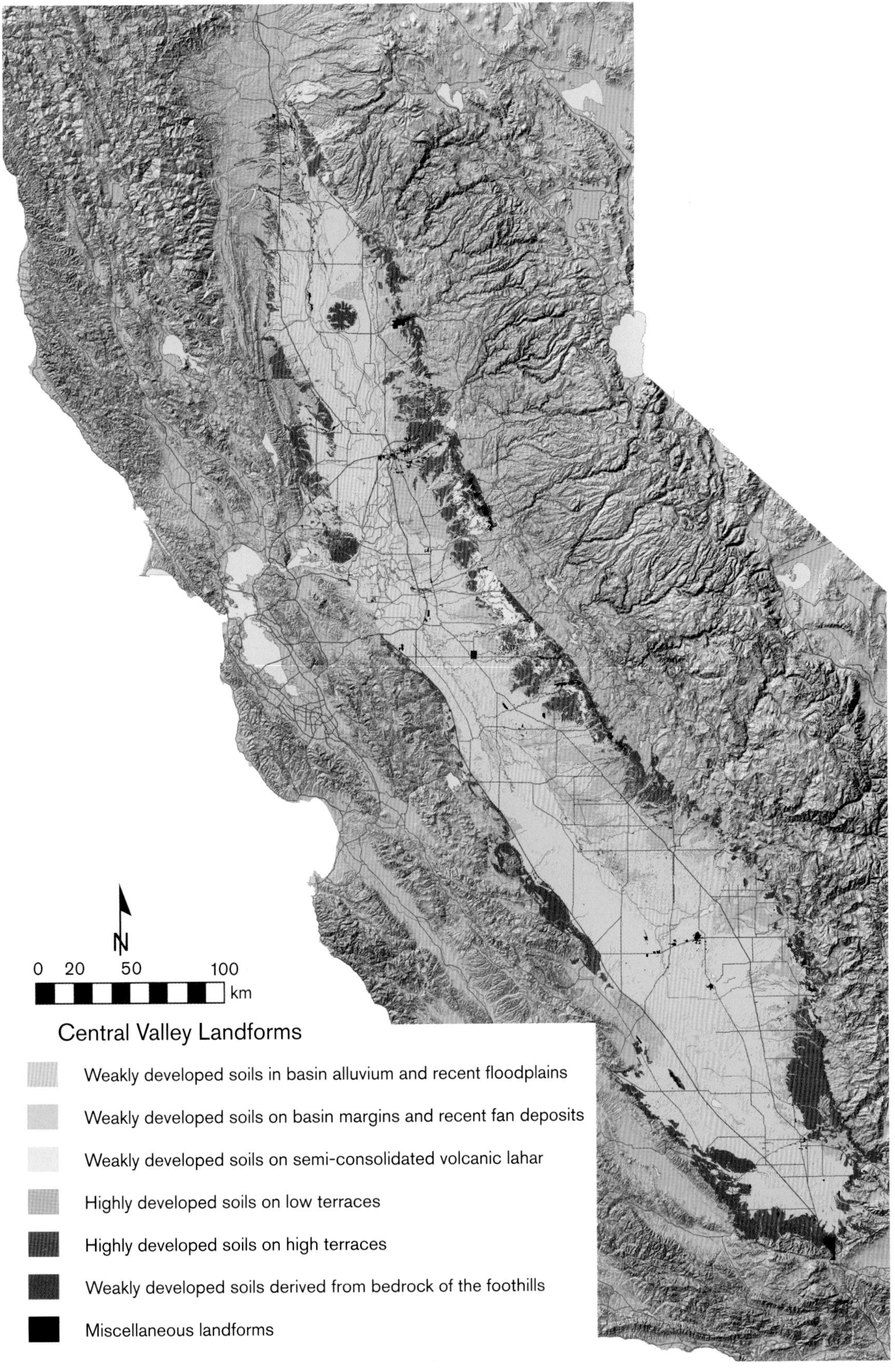

FIGURE 4.4 The spatial extents of soil landscapes of the Central Valley. Map developed by V. Bullard, M. Walkinshaw, T. Harter, and A. T. O'Geen using the U.S. Department of Agriculture–Natural Resources Conservation Service SSURGO (Soil Survey Geographic) Database.

landscapes for irrigation purposes. These agricultural practices, coupled with urban expansion, mean that soils in the Central Valley have been, and continue to be, subject to significant changes.

Soils of the West Side

The west side of the valley displays a sequence of soils that increases in age and soil development up fan (see Figure 4.4). Alluvium from the Coast Range tends to be finer-textured compared to east side alluvium, resulting in slower drainage. Geologic conditions give rise to an extensive area of salt-affected soils, particularly in the San Joaquin Valley. The Coast Ranges consist of oceanic sediments that are high in sodium and other soluble salts. The flushing of salts via deep percolation is impeded by a slowly permeable clay lens, creating a regionally high groundwater table. Coast Range parent materials also weather to relatively fine-textured soils, which drain slowly, so soil water is held close to the surface, where it is subject to evaporation and salts are left behind. SALINE, SODIC, and SALINE-SODIC SOILS are present under these conditions, especially at the interface of the eastern edge of alluvial fans and the basin margin. Saline soils have soluble salt concentrations with ELECTRICAL CONDUCTIVITY (EC) values that exceed 4 ds m^{-1}, a level that many standard crops cannot tolerate. Sodic soils have low EC but high exchangeable sodium percentage (ESP), >15% on cation exchange sites.

Sodicity disperses clays, thereby clogging pores and drastically decreasing permeability. The pH of sodic soils is also extremely high, often greater than 9. Saline-sodic soils have EC above 4 ds m^{-1} and ESP above 15%. These soils do not have restricted permeability, but do cause osmotic stress in plants. In the past, saline soils were reclaimed by leaching, while sodic and saline-sodic soils were treated with gypsum and then leached. This practice has been largely discontinued because there is no safe place to dispose of the leachate, which can be high in selenium. Many innovative practices are now employed to manage salt-affected soils on the west side. One example involves segregating land for high-value salt-intolerant crops and reusing drain waters on adjacent fields for salt-tolerant crops.

Soils of the Delta

The delta is a triangular-shaped inland marsh. The landscape is not a true delta in that it has expanded in an eastern direction rather than westward toward the ocean (Shlemon and Begg 1975). This is because converging Sacramento and San Joaquin Rivers encounter a topographic constriction caused by the Montezuma Hills and the Coast Ranges on the downstream side. Water is impounded in an eastern direction and constrained by alluvial fans at its eastern edge. The California Delta Region occupies almost 300,000 hectares, much of which consists of peat (Histosols). Peat deposits were formed during the HOLOCENE as melted continental glaciers created sea level rise, which flooded inland channels within the region. The growth of dense wetland vegetation, primarily tules, provided the organic residues that have aggraded through time because microbial decomposition is inhibited by the water-saturated conditions. Peat accumulations reach depths of 9 to 15 meters in the thickest part and thin to the east and along the delta margins. The delta does not consist solely of peat. The network of sloughs, rivers, and tributaries creates a series of natural levee deposits. These formed before human modifications to the delta landscape through the deposition of coarse-textured sediment during flood events along floodplains of stream/river channels. This process created microtopographic highs that grade down to near sea level with increasing distance from the channel. Most levee deposits have been leveled for agriculture or during anthropogenic levee construction, but the sand patches remain interstratified with poorly drained thick peat deposits.

Before the arrival of settlers of European descent, the delta was one of California's most dynamic landscapes, subject to change from daily tides, annual floods, droughts, shifts in climate, and sea level rise. A network of anthropogenic levees and drainage systems were completed by the late 1930s that "reclaimed" approximately 3,000 square kilometers for agricultural use (Ingebritsen et al. 2000). Drainage of peat soils has resulted in land subsidence due to microbial oxidation and compaction by dewatering. A significant portion of the delta has subsided as much as 15 meters, reducing its elevation in places to 3 meters below sea level. Over one billion cubic yards of soil are projected to be lost by 2050 from microbial oxidation alone. As a result, the delta has become a very unstable manufactured landscape where levees are prone to failure due to earthquakes and flooding. The subsidence-induced susceptibly to levee failures threatens not only local communities and agriculture, but the drinking water for more than twenty-five million people as well. A levee breach in the wrong location could cause a saltwater intrusion that would destroy water quality.

Vernal Pool Soils

California vernal pools are seasonal, freshwater wetlands commonly formed by perched water above a low-permeability layer, such as a duripan, claypan, or bedrock. Vernal pools are found in low areas of gently undulating topography. Vernal pool landscapes consist of integrated and unintegrated drainages composed of a series of basins and mounds. Seasonal pools in the basins are typically small (tens of square meters), with maximum water depth seldom greater than 50 centimeters. They rarely remain saturated for more than sixty to ninety consecutive days.

Vernal pools experience hydrologic extremes in California's Mediterranean climate, where they become inundated with standing water, experience episodes of saturated conditions during winter and spring, then become completely desiccated during summer and fall. In many instances seasonally submerged soils of the basins meet hydric soil criteria (and jurisdictional wetland definitions) but may represent just 3% to 5% of the vernal pool landscape area. While the surrounding microtopographic highs (mounds) do not meet current hydric soil criteria (O'Geen et al. 2007), subsurface hydraulic connectivity links water and nutrient transport in the soils across vernal pool landscapes (Rains et al. 2006). Disturbance of up-gradient vernal pool landscapes may have appreciable impacts on hydrological and biogeochemical processes in all down-gradient vernal pools. Thus it is important that these landscapes are not unnaturally divided into well-drained (mound) and poorly drained (basin) areas for land-use purposes. Due to complex spatial and temporal patterns associated with vernal pools, delineating, conserving, and managing these landscapes result in many challenges and conflicts.

Coast Ranges

Geology and Geomorphology

The Coast Range Province extends from the Transverse Ranges to the Oregon border for approximately 1,000 kilometers. From the Pacific Ocean, the Range extends roughly 130 kilometers to the Central Valley. The east-west extension of the Coast Range is considerably less in northern California, where it borders the Klamath Mountains. The Ranges were created by transform motion and compression along the Pacific and North American plate boundary approximately 3.5 million to 5 million years ago. Thus the Coast Ranges are quite young and the associated topography reflects this, with steeply sloping dissected uplands separated by ephemeral stream valleys (Harden 2004).

The Coast Ranges are derived from rocks of the Franciscan Assemblage, Great Valley sequence, and Salinian block. The Franciscan Assemblage and Great Valley sequence consist primarily of interbedded sandstone and shale. Chert, conglomerates, schists, and serpentinite occur to a lesser extent. Uplift, faulting, compression, and folding of the interbedded marine deposits has resulted in a highly complex sequence of contrasting lithologies throughout the Coast Ranges. The Salinian block occurs west of the San Andreas fault, primarily in the southern half of the Coast Ranges. It is mainly granite. Volcanic rocks consisting of RHYOLITE, basalt, PYROCLASTIC FLOWS, and andesite are exposed along the central coast and east of the San Andreas fault. The age of these rocks becomes progressively younger from the south where rocks are up to fifteen million years old, to the north in the Clear Lake volcanic fields where they are as young as ten thousand years (Harden 2004).

A common geomorphic feature, particularly in hillslopes formed from sandstone and shale, are spoon-shaped hollows, which are concave hillslopes mantled by thick COLLUVIUM. They are formed by landslides caused by rapid uplift and slope failure along contact zones of different rock types and along joints and fractures. Over time, these hollows fill with sediment. Periodically, during winter storm events, soils toward the base of these hollows become saturated with water, and high pore water pressures cause debris flows (Dietrich and Dorn 1984). The hummocky landscape throughout the Franciscan terrain reflects the dynamic nature of this landscape.

TABLE 4.1

Geographic distribution of the dominant soils inventoried by soil survey in the Coast Ranges

Soil order	Percentage of region	Geographic extent
Entisols	19	Steep slopes where erosion outpaces the rate of soil development, or along floodplains
Inceptisols	15	Convex ridge tops and backslopes throughout the region
Mollisols	35	Valley floors footslopes, toeslopes, and concave hillslopes
Alfisols	19	Throughout the Coast Ranges
Ultisols	0.8	Found on older stable landforms in areas of high precipitation
Vertisols	8	Lowlands and lower slope angles of hillslopes across the region
Aridisols	3	Southeastern side of the Coast Ranges and on some south-facing slopes throughout the southern half
Histosols	0.03	Found in wetlands
Other	0.4	Typically rock outcrop, water, and urban landscapes

SOURCE: USDA-NRCS Soil Survey Geographic Database

Soils

Despite the complex lithology and topography of the region, soil variability is relatively low from a taxonomic standpoint (Table 4.1). Mollisols are common throughout the west side of the Coast Range, where temperatures are mild relative to warmer inland soils. The milder temperatures may encourage soil organic matter accumulation by slowing microbial activity and the decomposition of plant residues. Mollisols are also common in soils derived from shale, because this rock weathers rapidly to smectite clays and soil organic matter accumulates preferentially on smectite (Gonzalez and Laird 2003).

Alfisols, with thinner A horizons and less soil organic matter than Mollisols, are common throughout the inland areas of the Coast Ranges, where precipitation is moderate and temperatures are high. Weakly developed soils (Entisols and Inceptisols) occupy steep slopes, convex landforms, and steep, south-facing slopes in semiarid regions of the Coast Ranges (Beaudette and O'Geen 2008). They are common on granitic parent materials. Desert soils (ARIDISOLS and Entisols with an ARIDIC SOIL MOISTURE REGIME) are found in the southeastern Coast Ranges, particularly on south-facing slopes. Highly weathered Ultisols are on old, stable landscape positions in the northern Coast Ranges, where precipitation is high. Soils derived from volcanic rocks, such as the Pinnacles Formation, are mostly Mollisols, and some Entisols on steep south-facing slopes. Vertisols are common in lowland positions, where fine-textured alluvium has been deposited and downslope drainage yields high silica and base cation concentrations favorable for smectite clay formation. The eastern zone of the southern and central Coast Ranges is dominated by the Moreno shale, which is old sea floor material containing selenium-rich pyrite (iron sulfide). As the shale weathers, the sulfides are oxidized to sulfuric acid, creating an extremely acidic soil environment (pH <4). Many arid soils in this zone are rich in selenium, which substitutes for sulfur in sulfide and sulfate minerals. Toxic levels of selenium are encountered in drainwater from these soils (Tanji et al. 1986, O'Geen et al. 2007).

A distinctive region of soils occurs in the mountainous New Idria area, northwest of Coalinga. Here, a 12,400 hectare body of serpentinite consists mainly of highly sheared, soft, friable ASBESTOS. The serpentinite provides a harsh geochemical environment for plants, so the vegetation is sparse and stunted, consisting of leather oak (*Quercus dumosa*), manzanita (*Arctostaphylos glauca, A. pungens*), chamise (*Adenostoma fasciculatum*), as well as scattered Coulter pine (*Pinus coulteri*), gray pine (*P. sabiniana*), and Jeffrey pine (*P. jeffreyi*). Many slopes are completely barren. Shallow Entisols occur on steep slopes and barrens, and Mollisols with ARGILLIC HORIZONS occur on the more stable, vegetated shoulder and summit positions. The area is laced with prospect pits and abandoned asbestos mines and was a popular off-road vehicle recreation destination until its closure in 2008 due to potential health risks from asbestos fibers. The risk of asbestos fiber release is greatest where the soil is disturbed. Among the undisturbed sites, fiber release potential is greatest for Entisols. In the Mollisols the fibers are degraded by weathering and are aggregated by organic matter in the A horizons and smectite clay in the argillic horizons. Erosion to below the argillic horizon exposes fresh fibers that can be redistributed by wind and water (Rice and Graham 1993).

In sandstone terrains, hillslope positions that shed water and sediment, such as convex positions and steep slopes, have shallow soils with low organic carbon content and more sand and gravel relative to clay. In contrast, landscape positions that accumulate water and sediment, such as concave positions, footslopes, and toeslopes, have deep soils with thick, carbon-rich A horizons (Gessler et al. 2000, Beaudette and O'Geen 2008). On the more gentle slopes, where erosion is minimal, well-developed soils with argillic horizons have formed. Burrowing by pocket gophers (*Thomomys bottae*) is a dominant soil process in the Coast Range. Gopher burrowing creates homogenized soils having thick, well-mixed A horizons (Yoo and Amundson 2005). Moreover, soil mixing by gopher activity brings subsoil material to the surface, where it is subsequently transported downslope (Black and Montgomery 1991). In soils derived from shale, thickening of the soil profile at downslope positions has been attributed to SHRINK-SWELL processes, slow gravitational soil movement, and mixing by animals (McKean et al. 1993).

Klamath Mountains

Geology and Geomorphology

The Klamath Mountains Province, in northwestern California and southwestern Oregon, contains several mountain ranges, including the Siskiyou, Marble, Trinity, and Salmon Mountains. There is a general concordance of summits of these mountain ranges, at the 1,500 to 2,100 meter level, reflecting a precursor plain that has been incised by rivers as the area has been uplifted over the course of several million years. The Klamath and Trinity Rivers and their tributaries now flow in deep canyons amid exceptionally steep and rugged terrain (Harden 2004). The highest peaks reach about 2,750 meters and the lowest canyon bottoms on the western side of the province are on the order of 100 meters above sea level.

The Klamath Mountains are composed of accreted oceanic terranes; that is, oceanic-derived rocks were emplaced as the Pacific plate collided with the North American plate. As a result, the rocks become successively older to the east, but the composition of these terranes is similar in that they include metasedimentary and metavolcanic rocks, intruded in places by plutons of granitic rocks. Of particular note are the belts of ultramafic rock that are sandwiched between the north-south-trending accreted terranes. They represent the basement rocks upon which the oceanic sediments and volcanic materials were deposited before being metamorphosed and accreted onto the North American plate (Harden 2004).

Surficial processes have shaped the landscapes of the Klamath Mountains during the Quaternary. Rotational slumps are common where the bedrock, such as serpentinite and schist, has low mechanical strength. Debris flows occur on extremely steep slopes at soil-bedrock interfaces when soils are saturated by extreme rainstorms. Stabilized landslide deposits form some of the more gentle slopes amid an overall extremely steep and rugged mountainous terrain. During the Pleistocene, glaciers scoured the highest north-facing slopes, mostly above 1,800 meters, producing cirques in the upper parts of valleys and depositing till as moraines down the canyons, sometimes as low as 1,220 meters in elevation. Alluvium has been deposited where tributaries enter the larger rivers, such as at Happy Camp and Seiad Valley along the Klamath River and in the intermontane Scott Valley.

Soils in the Klamath Mountains have formed in response to a wide variety of environmental influences. Lithologies include granitic, ultramafic, marble, schist, greenstone, chert, and phyllite. Soils form in the RESIDUUM of these rocks but also in colluvium, alluvium, and glacial till. Slopes range from nearly level on alluvial terraces, ground moraines, landslide benches, and broad ridgetops to extremely steep (as much as 100% slope) on mountain sideslopes. Overprinted on this geological complexity is a climatic gradient that is dry in the east (mean annual precipitation = 500 millimeters) to wet in the west (2,790 millimeters). Precipitation amounts, and the proportion of it as snow, increase with elevation. All of the soils (except for wet meadows) have a XERIC MOISTURE REGIME, but mean annual soil temperatures range from 15°C to 22° C at the lowest elevations to 0°C to 8°C at the highest, north-facing sites (Foster and Lang 1994).

Soils of Ultramafic Terrain

Ultramafic rocks are a geochemical extreme compared to the aluminosilicate-rich rocks that predominate in the Earth's crust (Table 4.2). Ultramafic rocks contain very little aluminum, almost no potassium, low levels of calcium, and very high amounts of magnesium. As a result, the nutritional requirements for calcium and potassium are not satisfied for most plants growing on ultramafic soils. Furthermore, high levels of heavy metals, specifically nickel and chromium, may be at phytotoxic levels. These geochemical conditions produce the "SERPENTINE syndrome," with sparse and stunted vegetation and endemic species (Alexander et al. 2007).

PERIDOTITE and serpentinite are the two types of ultramafic rock that occur in the Klamath Mountains. While the chemical composition of the two rocks is essentially the same, their mineralogy is different. Peridotite is composed of olivine and pyroxene, both of which are iron/magnesium silicates that are relatively easily weathered in the soil environment. As a result, soils derived from peridotite are generally rich in iron oxides, particularly hematite, which imparts a red color. Serpentinite is a hydrothermal alteration product of peridotite in which the magnesium and silica have formed the mineral serpentine and the iron has been segregated into the separate oxide phase of magnetite. Magnetite is very resistant to weathering, so less iron is released to form pedogenic iron oxides. Consequently, soils on serpentinite are mostly grayish rather than red like those on peridotite. The two different

TABLE 4.2
Elemental composition of two common rock types in the Klamath Mountains

Rock type	Si	Al	Fe	Mg	Ca	K
Serpentinite	18.9%	0.3%	6.9%	23.9%	0.9%	0.0%
Phyllite	19.6%	9.3%	6.9%	9.1%	2.9%	2.8%

SOURCE: Graham et al. 1990

rock types produce different topographies as well. Peridotite is a massive rock that is more structurally competent than serpentinite, which has extensive fracturing with slick fracture planes and is highly susceptible to landsliding. Because serpentinite slopes fail rather than persist at steep angles, peridotite terrain generally has steeper slopes (Alexander and DuShey 2011). Peridotite tends to produce soils with larger rock fragments (cobbles and STONES) than soils derived from serpentinite (mostly gravel). Much of the ultramafic terrain in the Klamath Mountains consists of serpentinized peridotite; that is, it is somewhat of a mix between the two rock types.

In an east-west climatic transect from about 500 millimeters mean annual precipitation near Yreka to 2,800 millimeters near Gasquet, soils on serpentinite mountain slopes show an increase in maximum clay content (20% to almost 60%), decrease in pH (7.5 to 6.5), decrease in BASE SATURATION (85% to 60%), increase in pedogenic iron oxides (1% to 10% Fe), and an increase in organic carbon storage (5 to 15 kg/m^2 to 1-m depth). Soils on the eastern, drier end tend to be Mollisols, while those on the wetter end tend to be Alfisols. Irrespective of mean annual precipitation, the soils have argillic horizons and low exchangeable calcium/magnesium ratios (≤0.1 in the B horizon, 0.3–0.7 in the A horizon). Lack of aluminum in the parent rock limits the kind of clay minerals that can form, so all of the soils have smectite as the dominant clay mineral.

Landslide topography is common in serpentinite terrain. Rotational slumps leave a scarp (>30% slopes) at the source and a bench (≤15% slopes) where the material is deposited. Groundwater flow exposed by the landslide produces springs, so stabilized landslide benches often have wet meadows with a dense growth of rushes, sedges, forbs, and grasses. Topographic convergence of water in the wet meadows gives the soils an AQUIC MOISTURE REGIME and predominantly reducing conditions that inhibit organic matter decomposition. Consequently, soils are organic-rich Mollisols and in some places they are Histosols. Soils on the surrounding well-drained landscape, including the landslide scarp and flanks, have a xeric moisture regime reflective of the climate (Lee et al. 2004). Weathering in the xeric soils produces smectite clay that accumulates as clayey argillic horizons. These soils are Mollisols. Erosion from the surrounding landscape, particularly after forest fires, delivers fine sediments to the wet meadows. These fines, together with smectite precipitated from soil solutions that drain from upslope, yield thick, clayey sediments in the wet meadows.

Soil development is minimal at high elevations, on young deposits, and on steep, eroded slopes. Soils on these sites are generally Inceptisols. Aluminosilicate-rich rock within ultramafic terrain gives rise to soils and vegetation that stand in contrast to those of the ultramafic areas. This is particularly true if the rock contains Ca-bearing minerals (Lee et al. 2001). Volcanic ash from the Cascade volcanoes to the east, present in small amounts in most A horizons of this region, is another exogenous source of potassium, calcium, and aluminum in these ultramafic soils (Lee et al. 2004).

Soils of Metamorphic Terrain

At low and mid-elevations, most soils derived from metasedimentary and metavolcanic rock have argillic horizons. Maximum clay contents range between 15% and 45% and aluminum-rich clay minerals dominate (e.g., kaolin; Graham et al. 1990), regardless of mean annual precipitation (MAP). In the wetter, western part of the Klamath Mountains, leaching has depleted base cations so the soils are Ultisols. In the drier, eastern part of the region, leaching is less and the soils are Alfisols, with Mollisols at the driest margins. Inceptisols are on the younger, less stable, or higher elevation sites. At MAPs of 500 to 1,800 millimeters, soil pH is mostly between 5.5 and 7, but at higher MAP soil pH drops as low as 4.5 due to accumulation of aluminum on cation exchange sites. Nevertheless, the ratio of exchangeable Ca:Mg is always above 0.3, mostly above 1, and as high as 12.

In general, forest vegetation on nonultramafic soils does not experience a harsh geochemical environment, but at high elevations, such as on the Siskiyou crest, the dense red fir forest is interrupted in places by barren areas. These areas are predominantly on quartz muscovite schist. Their origin is unclear but may be related to effects of wildfire and overgrazing (Atzet and Wheeler 1982). Severe herbivory by gophers keeps these barrens devoid of tree seedlings. Only sparse, low-growing herbaceous plants inhabit the barrens, leaving the soil open to rainsplash and sheetwash erosion. Nevertheless, the organic matter that is produced by the herbaceous plants is mixed deeply by the gophers, resulting in 70-centimeter-thick A horizons, while those in the red fir forests, where there are no gophers, are only half as thick (Laurent et al. 1994). In some cases extreme acidity results when ammonium released from the mica structure undergoes nitrification (Dahlgren 2005). Levels of exchangeable calcium in the upper 30 centimeters of soil are four times higher under red fir compared to the barren areas (Laurent et al. 1994). Landslide topography is prevalent in metasedimentary terrain, resulting in scarps with poorly developed soils and benches with deep, productive colluvial soils. As in serpentinitic terrain, landslide benches may contain springs and small wetlands.

Other Mountain Soils

Soils derived from granitic rock tend to be light yellow–brown and are coarser-textured than those from metamorphic or ultramafic rock. Granite contains a substantial amount of quartz, which is resistant to weathering and persists as sand grains in the soils. Soil textures are generally loamy sand to loam. Weathering of feldspars and biotite produces clays, which, under conditions of sufficient geomorphic stability, are translocated to the subsoil to form an argillic horizon. In the wetter western side of the province, soils are more leached of base cations and are Ultisols. In the drier eastern side, soils are Alfisols. At high elevations, or on less stable geomorphic positions, soil development is less and the soils are Inceptisols. Soil pH is typically in the range of 6 to 7 and increases upward in the soil profile. In the western higher rainfall areas, soil pH is about one unit lower. When the parent rock contains more mafic minerals, as in diorite or gabbro, the soils have more clay (sandy clay loam textures) and are redder.

At mid- and low elevations both metamorphic and granitic bedrocks are fractured to such an extent that they provide access to woody roots, and weathering has made them porous enough to hold appreciable plant available water. At higher elevations soils are more likely to be underlain by hard rock because cold temperatures have impeded weathering and glaciation has scoured to hard bedrock within the past ten thousand years. In some of the high-elevation basins, with seasonally perched or high water tables, Spodosols have formed because the coarse textures allow thorough leaching by the abundant snowmelt. Organic acids from conifers, shrubs, and litter layers are dissolved in the soil solution. They act as chelates to keep iron and aluminum soluble so they can be translocated to the subsoil to form the characteristic Spodosol morphology. Soils on marble and limestone are less acidic than soils on metamorphic and granitic parent materials, with pH values as high as 8.2 in the lowest horizons and decreasing upward to about 6.5 in A horizons. These soils are thin on exceptionally steep, rocky slopes and are thick in deep colluvium on lower slopes. They are mostly loamy Mollisols.

Valley Soils

Soils in the intramontane valleys are formed in alluvium, including some glacial outwash, such as on the west side of Scott Valley. Soils of floodplains and alluvial fans of the larger tributaries to the valleys are Entisols. They are very coarse-textured and have very low water-holding capacities. In the basins of large valleys, such as Scott Valley, soils have a finer texture (e.g., loam, sandy clay loam, silty clay loam), a seasonally high water table that results in reducing conditions and gray subsoil colors, and accumulation of humified organic matter resulting in black A horizons. These soils are Mollisols with an aquic moisture regime. Some of them may be alkaline, with pH values ranging from 8.2 to 9.

Soils in wide parts of river canyons, such as at Happy Camp and Seiad Valley, are formed in alluvium of floodplains and successively older, higher terraces. The floodplain soils are very coarse-textured Entisols with low water-holding capacities. On successively higher terraces, soils are progressively older, more weathered (Inceptisols-Alfisols-Ultisols), contain more clay, and have higher water-holding capacities. While some floodplain soils are in riparian areas, the older terrace soils are elevated and may be some distance from the current stream channel.

Cascade Range

Geology and Geomorphology

Cascade volcanoes have produced a spectrum of extrusive igneous rocks (basalt, andesite, rhyolite) that span a range of susceptibility to weathering. Volcanic activity in the Cascade Range is caused by subduction of the Gorda plate beneath the North American plate. Many of the volcanoes in the Cascade region have a classic cone shape created by multiple sequences of eruptions. Mount Shasta and Mount Lassen are the two largest volcanoes of the Californian Cascade region. Much of the land area in this region consists of volcanic plateaus and lava flows that extend for great distances. For example, the Tuscan Volcanic Plateau extends from near Lassen Peak to the Sacramento Valley. The Medicine Lake Highland region, east of Mount Shasta, consists of more than one hundred cinder cones, domes, and lava flows superimposed on a basalt shield volcano (Southard and Southard 1989).

Many of the steeply sloping mountains are prone to slope failure, particularly if their rocks have been hydrothermally altered such that primary minerals have been converted to clay, thereby destabilizing the bedrock. High-elevation peaks have been shaped by water erosion and powerful glacial activity. Intermediate elevations experienced thinner sheet-like glacial ice advances. Plateaus are nearly level in the Sacramento Valley and become steeper toward the source. Dissection by streams and rivers has produced deep canyons, but the intervening uplands tend to undulate gently (Alexander et al. 1993). Glacial outwash and recent alluvium occupy valley landscape positions. Much of the region has experienced recent volcanic activity, and as a result, rhyolitic ash blankets a significant part of the terrain. The complex terrain and sequence of volcanic and glacial events has produced soils on a variety of parent materials such as lava, volcanic ash, mudflows, alluvium, colluvium, and glacial till.

Soil Landscape Relationships

The degree of soil mineral weathering dictates the spatial distribution of soil orders across the region. Soil development in volcanic materials evolves over the trajectory from Entisols-Andisols-Inceptisols-Alfisols and/or Ultisols. Entisols are found in relatively recent deposits of volcanic ejecta where soil formation has been limited to the accumulation of soil organic matter (Figure 4.5). Over time, volcanic parent materials are altered to poorly crystalline minerals that impart unique chemical and physical behaviors and result in soils classified as Andisols. With increasing time and weathering, more crystalline minerals such as kaolin are formed. This intermediate stage of weathering gives rise to Inceptisols. As time progresses, clays are translocated into subsurface layers, creating argillic horizons in Alfisols and Ultisols (Takahashi et al. 1993).

Andisols occupy 15% of the California Cascade region and the distribution of these soils is controlled by elevation and proximity to volcanic activity. Andisols are common in areas where volcanic ejecta have been replenished regularly throughout the Holocene. They are also commonly found at higher elevations (approximately 1,700 to 2,050 meters) where weathering is limited by cool temperatures. They are generally not found at highest elevations where cold temperatures inhibit weathering that produces poorly crystalline minerals. Conditions that encourage the evolution of Andisols into Alfisols and Ultisols include a combination of mild to hot temperatures and high precipitation, which promotes the illuvial translocation of clays and leaching of base cations. These conditions tend to exist at intermediate elevations, around 500 to 1,500 meters, where precipitation falls predominantly as rain. Alfisols are the most extensive soil order in the California Cascades, covering 39% of the region. Ultisols form in this region only under optimal conditions, including stable landscapes with gentle slopes, warm temperatures, and high rainfall. Thus the distribution of these soils is limited, occupying about 2% of the region. Inceptisols and Entisols together cover 38% of the region and are found at the

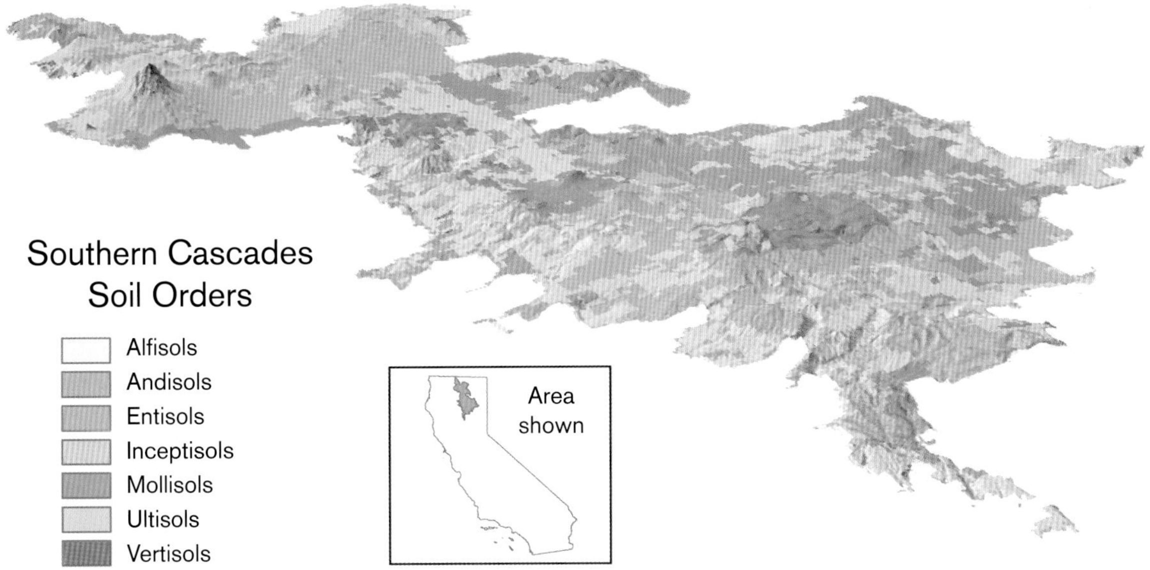

FIGURE 4.5 Geographic extent of soil orders in the California Cascade region. The high peak in the upper left is Mount Shasta. Map by California Soil Resource Lab http://casoilresource.lawr.ucdavis.edu/. Source: USDA-NRCS Soil Survey Geographic Database upscaled to 1 km grid.

highest elevations, on very steep slopes, or on recent lava and mud flows. The degree of weathering and distribution of soils is constrained by proximity to recent volcanic activity where intermittent deposition of volcanic ash supplies new material, rejuvenating the profile and resetting the pedogenic time clock. In addition, a slope threshold was recognized for this region where soil development was found to be greatest on slopes less than 30% (Alexander et al. 1993).

As is the case throughout the state, climate and the climate-moderating effects of topography have a strong influence on soil development. In an elevation gradient extending from 270 to 2,030 meters in the southwestern Cascades, soil base saturation and pH decrease with increasing elevation due to increased leaching of the soil profile and changes in vegetation (Alexander et al. 1993). Clay content and soil depth are greatest in the lower portion of the mixed conifer zone at elevations between 500 and 1,000 meters, reflecting the favorable weathering conditions associated with mild temperatures and high precipitation. Soil organic carbon content is constant below 1,700 meter elevation where temperatures are warmest, but increase at higher elevations. The relationship between elevation and soil organic matter is likely driven by differences in soil temperature. Cold temperatures slow microbial activity, resulting in a greater stock of soil organic residues. Warm temperatures stimulate microbial activity, promoting rapid decomposition of soil organic matter.

The degree of weathering as regulated by the age of volcanic deposits is illustrated by a CHRONOSEQUENCE of mudflows on the slopes of Mount Shasta. Soils formed on deposits ranging in age from twenty-seven to twelve hundred years (Dickson and Crocker 1953a, 1953b, 1954). Soil properties—including pH, base saturation, organic matter, and water-holding capacity—changed rapidly over this short pedological timeframe. For example, soil organic matter was found to reach steady state within five hundred years. Valley and basin soils are typically very deep. Many basin soils are poorly drained due to a high groundwater table. The mild temperatures and poor drainage give rise to soils with large carbon stocks. Many lowland soils are Mollisols.

The Cascade Range contains active and inactive hydrothermal areas, which have a large impact on soil properties. Soil temperature, acidity, and chemical/mineralogical properties vary dramatically over short distances in hydrothermal areas and impact vegetation establishment and succession. An active fumarole in Lassen Volcanic National Park produced a thermal gradient ranging from 100°C to 15°C, along which soil pH increased from strongly acid (pH <4) to slightly acid (pH = 6.5) (Diaz et al. 2010). Pedogenic alteration was greatest at high temperature sites despite the lack of vegetation. The combination of low pH, high temperature, high exchangeable Al^{3+}, and low nutrient status of soils in active thermal areas deterred vegetative establishment.

Volcanic Soil Properties

Andisols and other soils developed from volcanic ejecta are typically highly productive soils because of their high plant-available water-holding capacity (Dahlgren et al. 2004). In Mediterranean-type climates and semiarid environments, water-holding capacity is arguably the most important soil property governing the establishment and maintenance of many plant communities. Andisols formed from volcanic ash have the highest water-holding capacity because they have a large volume of pores of the ideal size to maximize retention of plant-available water.

Soils derived from volcanic materials contain abundant poorly crystalline minerals and crystalline iron and aluminum oxides in the more strongly weathered Alfisols and Ultisols. These soil constituents have sorption sites that retain phosphate, sulfate, and nitrate to varying degrees (Strahm and Harrison 2007). In particular, phosphate is bound strongly in forms unavailable for plant uptake. Sulfur can also become a limiting nutrient as a result of sulfate sorption in these soils (Kimsey et al. 2005). These soils have pH-dependent charge, so at slightly acid pH positively charged sites develop that retain exchangeable (plant-available) nitrate. Unlike many forest systems in California, forest productivity in the southern Cascades may be limited by nutrient availability rather than water.

Andisols have low bulk densities (<0.90 g cm^{-3}), reflecting high porosities, which are favorable for root penetration and seedling emergence. Despite their native low bulk density, Andisols are highly susceptible to compaction, which reduces their capacity to infiltrate and supply water (Geist et al. 1989, Cullen et al. 1991, McDaniel and Wilson 2007). While some studies have reported that Andisols are resistant to erosion because they are strongly aggregated and have high infiltration rates (Nanzyo et al. 1993, Dahlgren et al. 2004), others have found that the low bulk density and particle density of volcanic ash–derived soils make them highly susceptible to wind and water erosion (Kimble et al. 2000, Arnalds et al. 2001). Andisols are particularly vulnerable to erosion when vegetation and surface litter layers are removed (McDaniel and Wilson 2007).

Modoc Plateau

Geology and Geomorphology

The Modoc Plateau is related to two distinctly different provinces, it is structurally linked to the Basin and Range and lithologically related to the Cascade Ranges (Miles and Goudey 1997). The region's typical fault block topography has transformed what was once relatively flat volcanic landscape into a series of northwest-trending mountains and ridges interspersed with broad, down-faulted basins. Lava flows, shield volcanoes, and cinder cones are present throughout this terrain (Miles and Goudey 1997). Rhyolitic lava and ash were deposited throughout the region in the late Miocene. Valleys have accumulated fine-grained alluvium, LOESS, ash, and LACUSTRINE deposits.

The geomorphology of the region is mainly a gently to moderately sloping volcanic plateau, although steep hillslopes are present along mountains, shield domes, and stratovolcanoes. Elevation ranges from 912 to 3,010 meters. A series of closed basins and small depressions supported lakes in wetter periods of the Holocene and late Pleistocene that have since dried. The main geomorphic processes are faulting, fluvial erosion, freeze-thaw, and deposition of sediment by wind and water (Miles and Goudey 1997). As an area situated between the Cascade Ranges and the Basin and Range Provinces, the region reflects a transition from xeric to aridic soil moisture regimes. Temperatures fluctuate widely on a daily basis with a mean annual air temperature of approximately 1.5°C to 11°C. Precipitation ranges from 200 to 760 millimeters. This climatic transition zone is moderated by the water-holding capacity of soils, which is governed by texture but also by andic soil properties.

Upland Soils

A key differentiating characteristic of soils on the Modoc Plateau is the thickness of volcanic ash in the soil profile. Landscape positions proximal to recent volcanic activity have soil profiles thickened by volcanic ejecta. These soils are typically deep (100-150 centimeters) or very deep (>150 centimeters) and classified as Andisols. Soils distal to recent volcanic activity tend to be shallow (<50 centimeters) or moderately deep (50–100 centimeters) and are classified as Alfisols, Inceptisols, and Entisols. Entisols are typically found on ridgetops and convex hillslopes. Inceptisols are typically found on sideslopes. Alfisols exist where water is focused by the terrain at concave areas and lower slope positions.

A significant portion of the Modoc Plateau consists of lava plateaus strongly influenced by volcanic ejecta. The soils on these plateaus are deep and typically transition from sandy loams in surface horizons to clay loams in the subsoil where clay has been concentrated by illuvial transport. Despite having a strong volcanic influence, many soils of this landscape are not Andisols but are typically Alfisols and Mollisols. The relatively planar nature of these landforms facilitates weathering processes that transform poorly crystalline clays into stable crystalline forms such as kaolin, thus these soils do not display andic soil properties. Andisols exist in areas where ash deposition is more recent. Despite being shallow, upland soil landscapes distal from volcanoes tend to show very large increases in clay. Some soils have layers cemented by silica overlying bedrock. The highly weatherable basic igneous rocks, coupled with the semiarid climate, give rise to the formation of smectite clays, which display strong shrink-swell behavior during drying-wetting cycles. Soils in these landscapes are typically Vertisols and Mollisols. Most Mollisols form in landscapes that have grasses as a significant component of the plant community, which tends to occur in areas that receive between about 380 to 760 millimeters mean annual precipitation.

Valley Soils

Soils in lowlands have formed on stream terraces, floodplains, basin floors, alluvial fans, and even glacial outwash. The combination of poor drainage and cold temperatures facilitates soil organic matter accumulation, thus lowland soils in this region are typically Mollisols. Soils with duripans are common on fan deposits and stable stream terraces. Volcanic flows periodically dammed drainage systems, forming large lakes in pluvial times that collected sediment and volcanic ejecta from the surrounding landscape. The lakes are no longer present in the current drier climate, but the lacustrine sediments are enriched in silica and base cations that promote the formation of smectite and Vertisols.

Basin and Range Province

Geology and Geomorphology

The Basin and Range is an extensive physiographic province in the western United States and northern Mexico. It covers virtually all of Nevada and spreads into eastern California where it includes the Mojave and Colorado Deserts as well as the colder deserts to the north in Inyo, Mono, and eastern Modoc Counties. The topography of the region has been shaped by extensional thinning of the crustal zone, resulting in large north-south-trending normal faults. These faults bound valleys that have been down-dropped relative to the adjacent mountains.

The southern part of the region contains large areas of sedimentary rocks, including limestone and dolomite, which accumulated between 600 million and 250 million years ago. Magma generated by subduction of the Pacific plate intruded these rocks, forming granitic batholiths at depth or volcanic

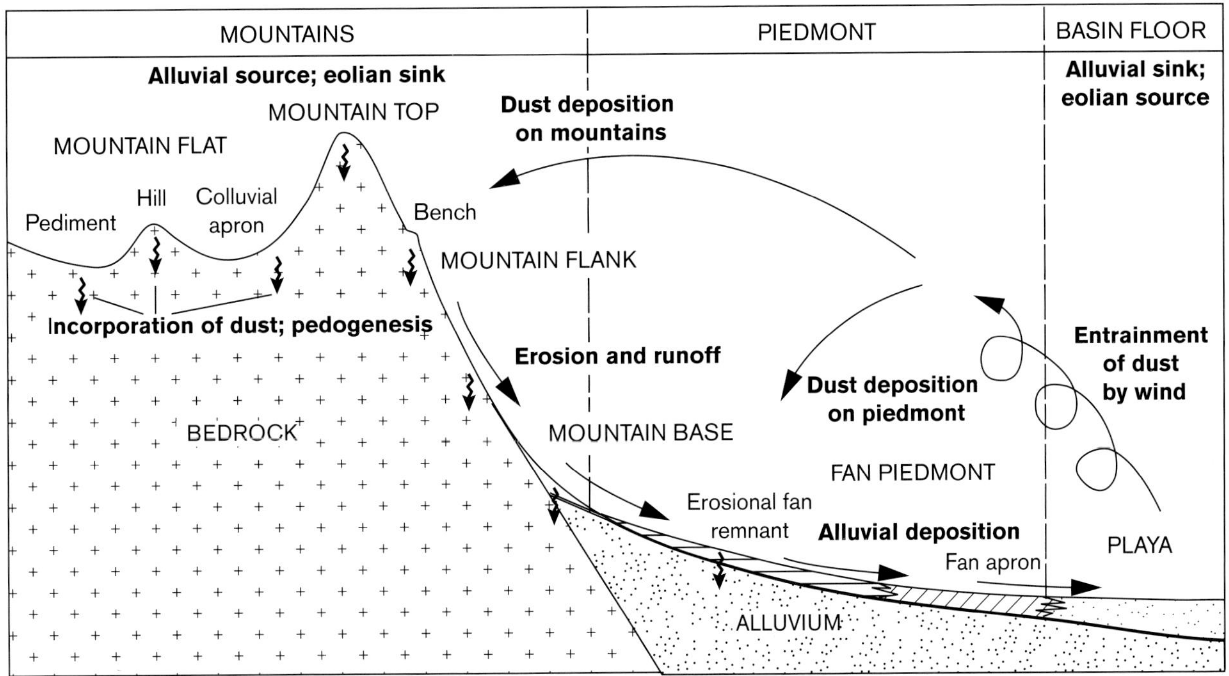

FIGURE 4.6 Conceptual geomorphic model of mountain-piedmont-basin floor interactions in the Mojave Desert. Source: Hirmas et al. 2011.

extrusions at the surface. Subsequently, right-lateral shearing associated with the San Andreas Fault Zone, Garlock Fault, and Eastern California Shear Zone modified the landscapes, displacing lithologies and creating mountains and intervening valleys. During the past nineteen million years, large volcanic eruptions occurred, producing lava flows, cinder cones, and extensive deposits of volcanic ash (Harden 2004).

Water runoff during extreme storm events has eroded the mountains, generating debris flows and alluvium that are deposited in alluvial fans as the floodwaters leave the narrow confines of the mountain channels (McDonald et al. 2003). The mountain ranges throughout the desert are aproned by coalescing alluvial fans known as bajadas (Peterson 1981). These landforms have been dissected by alluvial channels, producing terraces of different elevations. The highest terraces are the oldest, and the lowest, adjacent to the active washes, are the youngest. In places, the broad surface that slopes away from the mountains, though it resembles an alluvial fan, is actually a PEDIMENT. The valley center may be occupied by a large axial wash or, if it is a closed basin, a dry lakebed (i.e., PLAYA). The zone between the mountain front and the playa—incorporating both alluvial fan and pediment—is termed the PIEDMONT. Thus the general landform types can be summarized as mountains, piedmonts, and playas, although some valleys have no playa and the alluvial fans extend to the valley center.

During the Pleistocene, alternating wet and dry periods, coinciding with glacial and interglacial episodes, had major impacts on the Basin and Range landscapes. During glacial periods, precipitation increased across the region, including in the high mountains that border the region (e.g., the San Bernardino Mountains, Sierra Nevada, and Warner Mountains) that are the headwaters of rivers that flow into the desert. Increased water flow created numerous lakes in the basins, but these dried up during the interglacial periods to form playas (Harden 2004). During the dry, interglacial periods, the freshly exposed sediments in lakebeds and dry washes were mobilized by strong winds, producing sand dunes and extensive blankets of loess downwind. During pluvial times the lakebeds were filled with water and the dust sources, and their impacts on soils, were severely curtailed (Reheis 2006). The cycles of wet and dry periods persisted through the Quaternary and continue to this day. The deposition of dust across the landscape has had major impacts on soils and ecosystems in the desert. The soils of California's deserts cannot be thoroughly understood without recognition of the erosional-depositional linkages among the playa, piedmont, and mountain components of the landscapes (Figure 4.6; Hirmas et al. 2011). Soils in this region are Aridisols, except those that are young and have no subsoil development (Entisols) or are at higher elevations and have accumulated enough soil organic matter to be Mollisols.

Playa Soils

Because they are mostly barren of plants (Figure 4.7a), there has been little emphasis on discerning the variability in soil characteristics among playas. However, playas, playa margins, and the washes that empty onto them are major sources of dust, and eolian dust has an overarching effect on soil processes in the desert. A major distinction can be made between wet playas and dry playas (Reheis 2006, Reynolds et al. 2007).

Wet playas are those that have, at least seasonally, a water table shallow enough (roughly <5 meters) that the CAPILLARY FRINGE reaches the surface; that is, water from the water table wicks up and moistens the soil all the way to the surface. The groundwater is enriched in salts because it is water that has drained from the whole basin, dissolving minerals en route. When the water evaporates from the soil at the surface, the salts are left behind. As long as capillarity brings water to the surface, evaporation continues and so does precipitation of salts. As a result, a layer of salts accumulates on the soil surface. As the salts crystallize, they lift up soil mineral grains,

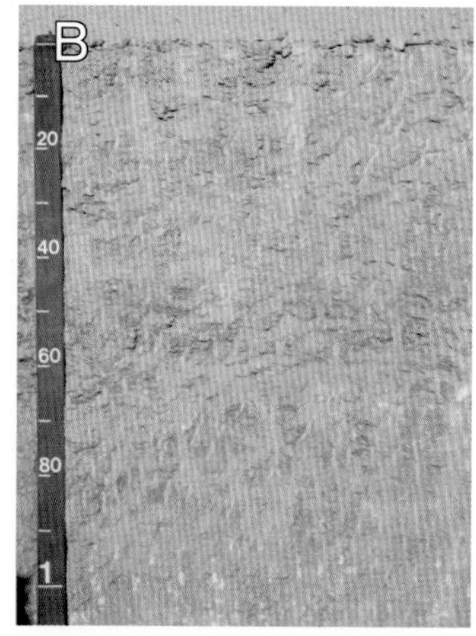

FIGURE 4.7 Geomorphic and soil features in the Mojave Desert. Photos kindly provided by Daniel Hirmas (A–C), Nathan Bailey (D, E), Judy Turk (F), and Robert C. Graham (G).

A Dry playa with mountains in the background.

B Soil (Entisol) profile in the playa.

C Soil profile in the mountains showing irregular depth to bedrock.

D Alluvial fan surface (as seen from a small hill) showing dark gray, barren desert pavement surface cut by washes where shrubs grow in a more favorable soil-water environment.

E Desert pavement with tightly interlocked clasts on a piedmont surface.

F Vesicular horizon underlying a desert pavement.

G Petrocalcic horizon outcropping along the edge of a very old alluvial fan terrace.

loosening them and making them more susceptible to wind erosion. Not only does the salt make the soil a harsh environment for plants, one in which only sparse halophytes can survive, but it also is a source of loose salts and entrained silicate mineral grains that are readily eroded by wind and transported to other parts of the landscape (Reynolds et al. 2007). Dust from wet playas can contain high levels of potentially hazardous elements, such as arsenic in the dust from Owens Dry Lake (Reheis et al. 2009).

Dry playas have a water table so deep (roughly >5 meters) that the capillary fringe does not reach the surface; that is, water does not wick up far enough to moisten the surface soil (see Figure 4.7b). Consequently, salts are not continually concentrated at the surface and the surface soil is not salty. A dry playa generally has a dense, crusted, cracked surface of silty clay (see Figure 4.7a). Minimal dust blows off the surface, except after the occasional flooding brings in fresh sediment or when the surface is disturbed by human activity. The dust that does blow off has a low salt content compared to that from a wet playa (Reynolds et al. 2007). Playa margins are dominated by relict shoreline features, such as wave-cut terraces, depositional beach ridges, and offshore bars and spits. Soil-forming processes in these locations are similar to those on other depositional features in the desert, involving dust accumulation, DESERT PAVEMENT and VESICULAR HORIZON formation, and the progressive accumulation of calcium carbonate, gypsum, and salts (McFadden et al. 1992). Sand dunes form at the downwind ends of playas. Less commonly, sand-size clay aggregates can similarly form dunes. Soil development is inhibited in dunes that are actively moving. Groundwater seep zones at playa margins, or where faults create hydrologic barriers, produce soil conditions similar to those described for wet playas.

Mountain Soils

Contrary to appearances, the mountains are not entirely covered by rock outcrops and shallow, minimally developed soils. In granitic mountains in the southern Mojave, fewer than half the soils are shallow (<50 centimeters thick) over soft or hard bedrock (Hirmas and Graham 2011). Furthermore, soils vary by geomorphic position. For example, argillic, CALCIC, and PETROCALCIC HORIZONS are most common on mountaintops and benches, reflecting the geomorphic stability of these positions compared to mountain flanks or bases (Hirmas and Graham 2011). Hard bedrock is most likely to underlie mountain flanks (see Figure 4.7c), where debris flows periodically remove soils and softer bedrock.

In mostly granitic mountains of the west-central Mojave Desert, soil properties, such as thickness and calcium carbonate accumulation, have high spatial variability (Crouvi et al. 2013). Generally, soil thickness increases downslope. Soils are often less than half a meter thick on upper slopes but increase to over a meter thick at the base of the slope. Calcium carbonate content also is highest at the base of slopes, such that the soil matrix is engulfed (calcic horizon) or cemented (petrocalcic horizon) by carbonates. Eolian dust is a major component of soils in desert mountains, often accounting for 5% to 20% of the soil volume. Since the dust originates from playas and active washes, the mineralogy of the soils may contrast sharply with that of the underlying rock (Crouvi et al. 2013). The dust is concentrated in near surface horizons but extends throughout the soil profile and even into fractures in the underlying bedrock (Hirmas and Graham 2011). Its spatial distribution is controlled by sources, wind directions relative to slope orientation, and dust-trapping capabilities (i.e., surface roughness) of the site (Hirmas et al. 2011). The fine texture of the dust increases the water-holding capacity of the otherwise coarse-textured mountain soils, but the dust also contains salts and carbonates that significantly change the soil chemistry (Hirmas and Graham 2011).

Soils in the White Mountains, east of the Sierra Nevada, contain eolian materials, which constitute more than half of their volume in some places. Much of this consists of volcanic ash from the Mono Craters area (Marchand 1970). At elevations up to about 3,000 meters, soils in INTERSPACES between shrubs have desert pavements underlain by vesicular horizons composed of this eolian material. At higher, moister elevations, the tundra-like vegetation cover is continuous (or virtually absent on the highest summits and extremely steep slopes) and the eolian material is mixed into the profile by frost heave and rodent burrowing. Permafrost is present only at the highest elevations (Graham, Blake et al. 2010), but relict features formed by intense freezing and thawing are found in subsoils at 3,800 meters. Despite the widespread eolian input, different lithologies (e.g., limestone, granitic, dolomite, basalt) support different plant assemblages, so the underlying rock does have an important influence on soil properties. Chemical conditions, such as low available phosphorus, potassium, and iron in soils on carbonate rocks, are a primary determinant of plant distribution (Marchand 1973), but other factors may be important as well. For example, granitic rocks weather deeply, producing intact bedrock that is porous and holds plant available water (Graham, Rossi, and Hubbert 2010). Jointing in granites provides ready access for plant roots to reach the stored water.

Piedmont Soils

Because alluvial fans are deposited, and subsequently incised, by water, the ages of alluvial terraces are correlated with paleoclimatic conditions (McDonald et al. 2003). Each terrace represents a discrete interval of time and a series of them records changes in soils as a function of time—that is, a chronosequence. Distinctive soil characteristics correspond to the different landform ages, but even on a single geomorphic surface, soils formed in interspaces (areas between shrubs) are different from those formed under shrubs, and the differences are exaggerated with age (Caldwell et al. 2012, Pietrasiak et al. 2014).

The young soils (on the order of hundreds of years old) are found in active washes and associated low terraces. Very little soil development has occurred and differences between interspace and shrub soils are minimal. Biological soil crusts (biocrusts; Chapter 30, "Deserts") are most abundant on the stony parts of these alluvial deposits, but also in the shrub zones (Pietrasiak et al. 2014). The soils are coarse-textured throughout and consequently have very high infiltration rates. Plant roots are not impeded by soil horizonation, although root penetration may be impeded at stratigraphic boundaries—for example, the contact between a fine sandy layer and a coarse gravelly layer. Materials that blow in with the dust—such as clay, calcium carbonate, gypsum, and soluble salts—have not accumulated to any significant extent.

Intermediate-aged soils (a few thousand years old) are found on somewhat higher terraces. Interspace soils have moderately developed desert pavements underlain by thin vesicular horizons that have formed in accumulated eolian dust. Clay content, although still minimal, has increased in the upper part compared to the young soils due to dust influx. The desert pavement and vesicular horizon have reduced the infiltration rate of the soil, so leaching has decreased and some carbonates, gypsum, and soluble salts have accumulated. Soils under shrubs have a finer texture than the young soils because eolian dust trapped by the shrubs has been mixed into the soils by rodent burrowing (Caldwell et al. 2012). But the mixing also homogenizes the soil, preventing the development of desert pavement and vesicular horizons. Infiltration rates under shrubs remain high and soluble salts are leached from the profile. Calcium carbonate may accumulate because CO_2 respiration in the biologically rich soil favors calcite precipitation. The shrubs also produce organic litter that either accumulates where it drops or blows elsewhere to be trapped and accumulated under other shrubs. The organic matter is mixed into the soils by rodents and enhances the soil fertility. Biological soil crusts occur equally in shrub zones and the stony areas (Pietrasiak et al. 2014).

Old soils (tens of thousands of years old) are on the high, long-stable geomorphic surfaces. Desert pavements are well developed in interspaces, cover large areas, and are essentially devoid of plants and biological soil crusts (see Figure 4.7d; Pietrasiak et al. 2014). The CLASTS comprising the pavement are tightly interlocked and are embedded in the soil (see Figure 4.7e). Most clasts (excepting easily weathered ones, such as limestone or dolomite) have strong desert varnish—black from manganese oxides on top and red from iron oxides underneath. The desert pavement rests on a vesicular horizon that is 5 to 15 centimeters thick, with columnar structure parting to platy structure (see Figure 4.7f). This grades into a NATRIC HORIZON. The vesicular horizon, with its lack of interconnected pores, effectively inhibits infiltration (Young et al. 2004), so the soils are very dry. The lack of leaching causes accumulation of abundant soluble salts, gypsum, and carbonates. The low infiltration rates also result in water runoff during rainstorms. Water flows across the interspaces to adjoining shrub zones (Graham et al. 2008) where desert pavements, vesicular horizons, and natric horizons have been destroyed, or prevented from forming, by burrowing animals (McAuliffe and McDonald 2006). The water flows into the bioturbated soil material and the rodent burrows themselves. Consequently, soils in shrub zones are deeply leached of soluble compounds and receive extra water beyond what the mean annual precipitation would indicate.

Very old soils (hundreds of thousands of years old) are on the highest, relict surfaces. They have strong desert pavements and vesicular horizons. Calcium carbonate and opaline silica have accumulated in the subsoil to the extent that they plug and cement it (Harden, Taylor, Hill et al. 1991; Harden, Taylor, Reheis et al. 1991), forming petrocalcic horizons or duripans (see Figure 4.7g). These cemented subsoil horizons prevent deep rooting as effectively as hard rock. The overlying soils have often been eroded to some degree by surface runoff, because infiltration has been severely restricted by vesicular horizons and subsoil accumulation of clay, carbonates, and opaline silica (Wells et al. 1985). The cemented soil horizons may be exposed at the surface, particularly as outcrops around the margins of the eroded fan remnant.

The rough surfaces of lava flows are particularly effective at trapping dust (Wells et al. 1985, McFadden et al. 1987). On flows no older than a few thousand years, soils form in pockets where dust has accumulated. On older flows (tens of thousands to hundreds of thousands of years old) huge amounts of dust have leveled out the irregular surfaces. As time passed, the clasts of the desert pavement were lifted up by the dust that was trapped and accumulated under them (McFadden et al. 1987, Anderson et al. 2002). The desert pavements are very tightly interlocked and are underlain by a strongly developed vesicular horizon and a natric horizon formed in the thick accumulation of dust. These soils have the same hydrologic behavior as described for those on alluvial fans (Wood et al. 2005).

Soils capped by desert pavement and vesicular horizons contain high levels of nitrate (150–800 mg/kg NO_3-N) within the upper 50 centimeters (Graham et al. 2008). The depth distribution of nitrate coincides with that of chloride, so both are almost certainly blown in as salts from playas, trapped by the desert pavement, and leached to a shallow depth in the soil. While playa soils have been found to have high levels of nitrate (Vasek and Lund 1980, Hirmas and Graham 2011), the origin of the nitrate in playas is unknown. Soils under shrubs, where infiltration rates are high, have very low levels of nitrate (and chloride) due to deep leaching. It is unknown whether the shrubs can access the nitrate in the immediately adjacent desert pavement soils. The high levels of nitrate are only fractions of a meter away, but the soil is also very salty and may be inhospitable to plant roots.

Transverse and Peninsular Ranges

Geology and Geomorphology

The Transverse Ranges consist of east-west trending mountain ranges with intervening valleys. The major mountain ranges include the San Bernardino, San Gabriel, Santa Monica, and Santa Ynez Mountains. The valleys include San Gabriel, San Fernando, Simi, Santa Clara, Ojai, Ventura, and Santa Ynez. These sequences of mountains and valleys have developed in relation to the San Andreas fault and numerous smaller, associated faults. The topography of this region is the direct result of compressional forces where the San Andreas fault bends to an east-west orientation. Because the Pacific plate's movement is dominantly northwestward, it pushes against the North American plate as it encounters this bend in the fault. This compression causes uplift that is very active to this day. The highest peaks are Mount San Gorgonio (3,505 meters) in the San Bernardino Mountains and Mount San Antonio (3,068 meters) in the San Gabriel Mountains. The Transverse Ranges are composed of sedimentary rocks, especially in the western part, and granitic and metamorphic rocks primarily in the east (Harden 2004).

The Peninsular Ranges run north-south and include the Santa Ana, San Jacinto, and Santa Rosa Mountains in southern California. They also extend south the entire length of the Baja California peninsula. The Peninsular Ranges are dominated by granitic rocks whose origin is related to that of the Sierra Nevada batholith. The highest point is San Jacinto Peak (3,302 meters), whose eastern escarpment drops abruptly to Palm Springs (elevation 150 meters). The Peninsular Ranges in southern California contain, and are shaped by, numerous faults. The Santa Ana Mountains are bounded on the east by the Elsinore fault, and the San Jacinto and Santa Rosa Mountains are bounded by the San Jacinto fault on the west and the San Andreas fault on the east. Erosion of granitic bedrock and deposition of sediments in basins has created broad plains between the major mountain ranges. These areas of low relief, such as the Perris Plain in western Riverside County and inland parts of San Diego County, have broad, gentle pediment slopes with residual soils over weathered granitic rock. They are broken by numerous bedrock hills. The Peninsular Ranges, with the exception of the San Jacinto Mountains, are relatively tectonically stable compared to the Transverse Ranges (Norris and Webb 1990).

The rapid and continuing uplift in the Transverse Ranges, on the order of 0.1 to 1.5 meters per thousand years (Blythe et al. 2002), and in the San Jacinto Mountains ensures that much of the terrain is unstable and subject to high rates of natural erosion, on the order of 1.5 meters per thousand years (Graham et al. 1988). The extremely steep, chaparral-covered slopes are subject to continuous erosion. During the summer, erosion known as dry ravel is triggered when the slightest disturbance, such as a lizard skittering across the slope, dislodges a small rock fragment, which in turn dislodges more debris as it falls downslope, producing a cascade of sand and rock fragments. Heavy winter or monsoonal rains initiate debris flows and landslides. Erosion is dramatically increased after slopes are denuded by fire. The few stable parts of the landscape include nearly level ridgetops and older remnants of alluvial fans and stream terraces that have been isolated from stream erosion.

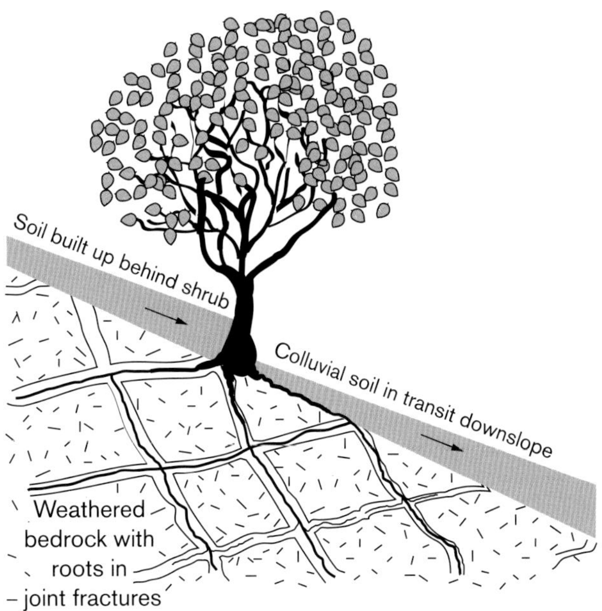

FIGURE 4.8 Idealized cross-section showing how chaparral shrubs are primarily rooted in the weathered bedrock in steep upland areas. Roots extend several meters deep along fractures in the porous bedrock and extract stored water. The thin soil is in transit downslope past the shrubs but temporarily accumulates on their upslope sides. During fires, the shrubs burn and accumulated soil is eroded downslope. Source: de Koffe et al. 2006. Illustration: Melissa Chapin.

Mountain Soils

The soils on steep mountain slopes are mostly shallow to bedrock and are Entisols. Many of these soils are only 10 or 20 centimeters thick and hold insufficient moisture to support the chaparral or forests that grow on them. Instead, the plants extend their roots deep (3–10 meters) into the highly fractured bedrock. The rock has been made so crumbly and porous by weathering that it can store appreciable plant-available water, and it is this rock-held water that supports the chaparral and forest ecosystems on mountain slopes. While roots are confined to fractures, the hyphae of the mycorrhizal fungi that symbiotically infect the roots are small enough to penetrate the capillary pores in the weathered bedrock matrix to extract the stored water and deliver it to the plant root (Egerton-Warburton et al. 2003, Bornyasz et al. 2005). On the steeper slopes the thin mantle of soil is in continual transit, moving downslope around and past the shrubs or trees, which are securely rooted in the bedrock (Graham et al. 1988, Jones and Graham 1993) (Figure 4.8). While the soils are ineffectual at storing water, they may still be important sources of nutrients. Organic debris from plants, together with wood ash from fires, accumulates in the thin soils, especially downslope. Nutrients are supplied by wood ash and released from organic matter by microbial decomposition and can be taken up by fine roots that occupy the relatively unstable soil.

On the more stable parts of the mountain landscapes, erosion is minimal, so soils are thicker and more developed. On toeslopes, in hollows, and on stable alluvial deposits, soils often have thick, dark A horizons from the decomposition and incorporation of plant organic matter (Mollisols). On landscape positions that have been stable for tens of thousands of years, such as broad ridgetops and high stream terraces, soils are often reddish with clay-enriched subsoils (Alfisols). Vernal pools with Vertisols are present on basalt flows of the Santa Rosa Plateau (Weitkamp et al. 1996). On those parts of the landscape where Santa Ana winds are channeled, dust from the Mojave Desert is trapped by chaparral shrubs and eventually is washed down and incorporated into the soil. This process significantly increases the silt and clay content of the soils and enhances their water-holding capacity (McFadden and Weldon 1987). Type of parent material can strongly influence the kinds of soils that form. Fine-grained sedimentary rocks, such as siltstones, mudstones, and shales, have fine-textured soils. These soils tend to be thicker, hold more water, support more biomass, and therefore accumulate more organic matter than soils formed on coarse-grained rocks, such as granite. They are often Mollisols or Vertisols.

Fire is common in ecosystems of the Transverse and Peninsular Ranges, and it influences soils in several important ways. Most critically, it removes vegetation and plant litter cover, leaving the soil open to erosion. In southern California, severe wildfires often occur during episodes of Santa Ana winds. These strong winds not only drive the fire, but they also scour and erode the soil left bare by the fire. When powerful gusts hit ridgetops and windward slopes, dust explodes from the soil, becomes airborne, and can be transported long distances, even out to sea, before being deposited. On steep chaparral-covered slopes, woody debris, shrub stems, and ground-level branches all serve to trap gravity-transported sediment. This accumulated colluvium is released when the woody materials are combusted by fire, resulting in a large pulse of sediment off the slopes and into first-order channels (Florsheim et al. 1991, de Koff et al. 2006). This initial postfire erosion can occur as dry ravel, but rainfall will trigger more erosion and intense runoff will flush accumulated colluvium from hillslope channels, producing highly destructive debris flows. Soils formed on debris flow deposits are mostly Entisols because they are generally eroded or buried by subsequent debris flows (Turk et al. 2008).

Fire frequently changes the physicochemical nature of the soil in a way that exacerbates erosion. Chaparral litter contains waxes that are vaporized as the plant material burns. During the fire some of these vapors condense in the cooler part of the soil, a few centimeters below the surface, coating the soil mineral grains with a thin film of wax. This zone with the wax coating is water repellent, so it inhibits infiltration of percolating rainwater. The thin layer of soil above the water-repellent zone becomes saturated with water during rain storms and flows off the steep slopes, creating debris flows that gain material and erosive power as they move downslope (DeBano et al. 1998). Fortunately, these water-repellent layers are relatively short-lived because soil fauna, especially ants and gophers, almost immediately begin to dig through them and break them up.

Nutrients contained within plant material are released upon burning. Some are lost from the site as they literally go up in smoke, but wood ash remaining on site is composed of oxides of nutrient cations such as Ca, K, and Mg (Ulery et al. 1993). On stable sites, wood ash provides readily available nutrients as plants reestablish after a fire. Initially wood ash is extremely alkaline (pH 10–12), but within a month or so the oxides react with atmospheric CO_2 to form carbonates, and the pH drops to about 8.2. Thus wood ash can modify acidic soils in the mountains to pH levels more favorable to nitrogen-fixing bacteria that may infect colonizing leguminous plants. In steep terrain, wood ash is often eroded by wind and water, so nutrients are lost from the site. On the other hand, larger particles of charcoal remain on the soil and with time are incorporated into it and comminuted (MacKenzie et al. 2008). Charcoal has been shown to increase soil fertility by increasing cation exchange capacity, water-holding capacity, beneficial microbial habitats, and nitrification (Briggs et al. 2012). Fire can alter soil minerals, but this happens only where the heat has become very intense, generally under a completely combusted log. The soils become brick red as a result of the thermal transformation of the common yellow-brown iron oxyhydroxide, goethite, to the red iron oxides, hematite and maghemite (Ulery and Graham 1993, Goforth et al. 2005). The structures of certain clay minerals are destroyed or disrupted as well (Ulery et al. 1996).

Lowland Soils

Soils in the lowland areas are either formed in valley sediments or have formed into weathered bedrock. In either case, these soils are thicker than those on mountain slopes. Alluvial fans extending from the mountain ranges cover large areas in this region, including the San Fernando Valley, San Gabriel Valley, Los Angeles Basin, and San Bernardino Basin. The alluvium of these fans is sorted by distance from the mountain fronts. As the streams debouch from the mountain canyons, the heaviest material is deposited first and the lighter material is transported the farthest. Consequently, the soils closest to the mountains are sandy with abundant gravel, cobbles, and boulders. Farther down fan, the soils become finer-textured, such as fine sandy loams, and contain no rock fragments. Soils near the active washes are Entisols, but those on long-stable geomorphic surfaces are Alfisols, reflecting weathering and clay translocation that has occurred over tens of thousands of years (McFadden and Weldon 1987). On the oldest highest terraces, soils are cemented by pedogenic silica (Kendrick and Graham 2004). Where strong winds scour active river washes, such as Lytle Creek near Cajon Pass, sand dunes have formed downwind. These dunes host distinctive species, such as the endangered Delhi Sands flower-loving fly (*Rhaphiomidas terminatus abdominalis*). Particularly fine-textured soils have formed in the lowest parts of basins such as Lake Elsinore, San Jacinto, and San Bernardino Valleys. Prior to flood control and artificial drainage infrastructures, these areas were wetlands formed by shallow lakes or fault-controlled hydrologic barriers. The soils are clayey, often with a large silt component, and are dark colored due to humified organic matter. Most of the soils are Mollisols, but the more clay- and smectite-rich soils are Vertisols.

Soils that have formed over bedrock on the granitic pediment slopes of the Peninsular Ranges vary with topographic position (Nettleton et al. 1968). Soils on the smooth hilltops and upper backslopes are yellow-brown Inceptisols with a relatively uniform sandy loam texture throughout. Morphologic development in these soils is inhibited by extensive burrowing by ground squirrels. On the more moist middle and lower parts of backslopes, soils are Alfisols with a reddish-brown, sandy clay loam argillic horizon. Soils on the footslopes are even more moist due to downslope flow of water. The subsoils have a clay texture and sodium released from feldspars during weathering is abundant on cation exchange sites. On still lower and even moister slopes, soils are dark Vertisols. Weathered granitic bedrock underlies the soils along the entire slope transect. The bedrock is friable and relatively easily excavated, but it retains the original rock structure. On upper slope positions, ground squirrels burrow into the weathered bedrock, disrupting it and thereby increasing the soil depth. Lower on the slope, clay has been leached into the bedrock, plugging pores and making it hard for animals to burrow into. Instead, rock fabric is disrupted by shrink-swell activity resulting from the increased clay content (Frazier and Graham 2000).

Coastal California

Geology and Geomorphology

The coastline of California is 1,800 kilometers long and its overriding influence on geomorphology, microclimate, and atmospheric chemistry extends inland for several kilometers (California Coastal Commission 1987). Coastal processes of erosion and deposition have shaped the landscape. The impact of these processes is preserved where the land has been raised relative to the active shoreline by a combination of tectonic uplift and eustatic drop in sea level. During times of shoreline stability, wave action cuts a broad, bench-like platform parallel to the shoreline. These platforms become covered by beach sands, which serve as soil parent material when the platforms are uplifted (or sea level lowers) and preserved as marine terraces (Harden 2004). Flights of marine terraces record snapshots of geomorphic time, from the youngest at the active beach environment to the highest terrace, which is often hundreds of thousands of years old (Merritts and Bull 1989). Marine terraces occur throughout the length of the California coast and are interspersed with rocky headlands of wave-resistant rock, dune fields, and wetlands.

The formation of coastal dunes requires a sand supply and effective onshore winds (Orme and Tchakerian 1986). Sediment deposited at the mouths of rivers is transported by longshore currents until a seaward projection of land facilitates its accumulation as a sandbar, from which it is moved by waves onto the beach (California Coastal Commission 1987). Beach sand is blown inland to accumulate as dunes. Typically the more inland dunes are stabilized by vegetation and may be thousands of years old, whereas the seaward dunes are young and not stabilized. Dunes make up about 23% of the California coastline. River channels that were cut deeply when sea level was lower during the Pleistocene have been flooded by sea level rise since glaciers have melted in the Holocene. The resulting estuaries, together with lagoons and other coastal waterways, create abundant wetlands along the California coast.

Marine Terrace Soils

Marine terraces form chronosequences—that is, the terraces become progressively older with increasing elevation. Soils of these chronosequences have been studied along the length of the coast to help interpret tectonic movement, sea level changes, and geochemical and pedogenic processes (Mendocino: Merritts et al. 1991; Santa Cruz: Schulz et al. 2010; San Luis Obispo: Moody and Graham 1995; Ventura: Harden et al. 1986; Channel Islands: Muhs et al. 2008). The Mendocino and Channel Islands chronosequences provide examples of soils and processes of the northern and drier southern coastal chronosequences.

The Mendocino chronosequence receives an average of about 1,000 millimeters of rainfall per year, which promotes weathering of primary minerals to produce clays (Merritts et al. 1991). The high rainfall also supports lush vegetation, in this case mostly bunchgrasses, which, together with cool temperatures, results in a rapid accumulation of organic matter in the soils, although the rate of soil organic carbon accumulation levels off after about thirty thousand years. The older soils are appreciably leached of base cations. On some high marine terraces in this area, the soils are so depleted of nutrients and so acidic (pH as low as 2.8) that forest vegetation (Bishop pine [*Pinus muricata*], Bolander pine [*Pinus contorta* ssp. *bolanderi*], Mendocino cypress [*Cupressus goveniana* ssp. *pygmaea*]) is severely stunted. This is the area of the "pygmy forest" at Jug Handle State Natural Reserve that was studied and described by Jenny (1980). The soils of the pygmy forest experience large fluctuations in the water table because infiltrating rainwater collects on the basal rock surface under the soil.

During the rainy season the water table rises so that it saturates the soil completely to the surface. The rising water table is coffee-colored from dispersed organic acids, and these acids chelate iron and carry it in solution. By late spring, evapotranspiration and lateral seepage lower the water table and the soil is thoroughly dried out. The extreme acidity and the wetting and drying have dissolved and removed weatherable minerals leaving a quartz-rich, sandy to sandy loam Spodosol with a thick, white E HORIZON overlying a B horizon enriched with iron oxides. In fact, the rising and falling of the water table promotes the formation of a concrete-like, iron-cemented hardpan at about the 50-centimeter depth. The extreme acidity, low levels of nutrients (Ca, K, Mg, N, P), root-limiting hardpan, and the wide fluctuations in water content make these soils an exceptionally difficult place for most plants to grow.

The islands off the coast of southern California have very distinct marine terraces that range in age from a few thousand to hundreds of thousands of years old (Muhs 1983, Muhs et al. 2008). The soils are notable because their upper horizons, up to 20 centimeters thick, are composed of eolian dust transported by Santa Ana winds from the Mojave Desert and river valleys of the coastal mountains in southern California (Muhs et al. 2008). On San Clemente Island the mean annual precipitation is low (165 millimeters) but is supplemented by considerable fog drip, so the subsoils are clayey, smectite-rich, and strongly developed, having weathered from marine sediments that were later capped by the contrasting eolian silt mantles. The soils also have high levels of exchangeable sodium, which has promoted the dispersion and translocation of clay, resulting in clayey natric horizons in the soils ≤ two hundred thousand years old. Older soils are Vertisols, with cracks at least 1-centimeter wide extending from the surface to well over 50 centimeters in depth. Shrink-swell activity has mixed eolian silt materials into the highly clayey, smectitic subsoils. Significant accumulations of soluble salts and gypsum in the Vertisols are due to the influx of sea spray (Muhs 1983).

Dune Field Soils

Soil development is initially impeded by dune activity, but as dunes gain distance from the coast (e.g., by tectonic uplift), they begin to stabilize. Establishment of vegetation is key to further dune stabilization and soil horizon formation, but this is difficult because the sandy (≥98% sand) dune materials have a very low plant-available water capacity (Crawford et al. 1983). Upon stabilization and colonization by vegetation, organic matter begins to accumulate to form an A horizon. A weak B horizon forms as iron oxides coat subsoil sand grains and thin (≤5 millimeters) lamellae of clay and iron oxides form in the lower B horizon (Moody and Graham 1995). These subsoil lamellae are deposited by wetting fronts and are common features in very sandy soils. With time the clay accumulated in lamellae increases the soil water-holding capacity (Torrent et al. 1980), making the soils more favorable for vegetation.

Coastal Wetland Soils

Coastal wetland soils are at the interface between land and sea, and are influenced by both. Fine-grained sediments from low-gradient streams are the parent material in which the soils form, and tidal movements affect the aeration and chemistry of the soils. Various hydrophytic plants, such as reeds and tules, contribute organic matter. Water tables are at or near the surface and the soils are saline Inceptisols or Entisols. If the upper A horizons are exposed during low tide, they may partially drain to create an oxidizing environment, but overall these soils are strongly reduced. Iron and manganese oxides precipitate in localized oxidizing environments, such as around roots or in larger pores of the surface horizons, creating yellow-red mottles and iron/manganese nodules. Under saturated conditions, oxygen is absent and the microbes must use alternative electron acceptors as they decompose the dead plant material. Iron and manganese oxides are reduced in the subsoils, producing gleyed (blue-green) colors. Redox potentials typically are so low that sulfate from the seawater is reduced, producing hydrogen sulfide, which smells like rotten eggs. This further reacts with dissolved ferrous iron to precipitate iron sulfides, including pyrite, which impart a black color. If the reduced soils are drained, the oxidation of pyrite produces sulfuric acid and the pH drops from the range of 7 to 8.5 in the natural soil to 3.5 to 4 in the drained soil. The yellow potassium-iron-sulfate mineral, jarosite, forms around pores in the drained, oxidized soils (Lynn 1964, Doner and Lynn 1989).

Soils of Redwood Forests

Redwood forests occur along much of the northern California coast, where rain and fog create a moist environment favorable for their growth. Although rainfall is minimal during the summer, soils are kept moist by fog drip from the forest canopy, which can account for over a third of the annual hydrologic input (Dawson 1998). The soils that support redwoods (*Sequoia sempervirens*) are on marine terraces, alluvial fans and terraces, and on mountain slopes and ridges. They are mostly loamy to clayey Ultisols and Inceptisols and tend to be several meters deep. Deep-seated and shallow landsliding is common in the mountainous terrain, and soils are formed in colluvium or colluvium overlying residuum. On gentle mountain slopes, the soils are deep Ultisols with red, clayey argillic horizons; on steeper midslope positions the soils are still Ultisols but are more brown and not as clay-rich; and on the steepest slopes the soils are loamy Inceptisols only about a meter deep over soft, fractured sedimentary or metasedimentary bedrock (Marron and Popenoe 1986). In these latter cases, the weathered bedrock extends the rooting depth to several meters and effectively serves as soil. In general, soils on north-facing slopes are more developed (more clay, redder) than on south-facing slopes, and soils on steep slopes adjacent to higher-order streams are maintained as weakly developed Inceptisols due to landsliding.

Soils also form in the canopies of the redwood trees themselves. These "arboreal soils" develop in organic debris that accumulates in tree crotches and on massive limbs more than 50 meters above the forest floor. They are up to a meter thick, have distinct soil horizons and soil structure, and support epiphyte communities. The soils are entirely organic and are classified as Histosols. Accumulation of the organic debris is favored by low decomposition rates due to extreme acidity (pH 3.1–4.0), seasonally low moisture contents, and recalcitrant litter components (Enloe et al. 2006, 2010).

Summary

By virtue of its tectonic setting, California is endowed with a plethora of rock types, and the terrain of these lithologies has been shaped by geomorphic processes driven by climate and tectonics. The resulting landscapes, with their distinct geochemical foundations and climatic influences, support a diverse array of ecosystems and coevolved soils. The characteristics of these soils reflect the environmental influences they experienced during their formation, be that a few hundred years on a landslide scarp or a million years of stability on an ancient river terrace. The soil properties that coevolved with landscapes and ecosystems took thousands of years to form but can be disrupted by humans in days. The future of soil conditions in the state is in the hands of humans.

The equilibrium between soils and their natural environments was largely undisturbed by humans until the massive influx of immigrants began in the mid-nineteenth century. Placer and hydraulic mining destroyed thousands of hectares of soils. Early agricultural operations had modest effects on soils, but as land modification increased in the form of land leveling and deep ripping, the long-evolved characteristics of the soils have been lost forever, traded for enhanced agricultural production. Virtually all agriculture in California relies on irrigation, and the altered water budget changes the soils themselves. Certain timber management practices, such as scalping to control brush and promote reestablishment of conifers after logging, physically disrupt the native soils. Forest and chaparral fires, made larger and more severe by a century of suppression, expose bare soil to erosion. Fire suppression activities themselves, such as firebreaks and access roads, cause soil erosion. Currently, the construction of solar and wind power facilities is physically disturbing huge expanses of native soils in the deserts. We are rapidly reaching a point where native, undisturbed soils are rare. The extent to which the loss of native soils is justified by resource production is open to interpretation, but once soils are altered from their native state, the ecosystems they support will no longer be truly natural.

Recommended Reading

Buol, S. W., R. J. Southard, R. C. Graham, and P. A. McDaniel. 2011. Soil genesis and classification. John Wiley & Sons, West Sussex, UK.

Harden, D. R. 2004. California Geology. Pearson Prentice Hall, Upper Saddle River, NJ.

O'Geen, A.T., and D.E. Beaudette. http:// casoilresource.l awr.ucdavis .ed u/soilweb- apps/. Accessed June 2015.

U.S. Department of Agriculture. Accessed June 2015. Soil survey information by region. <http://soils.usda.gov/survey/>.

Glossary

A HORIZON A soil layer that occurs at or near the surface and is enriched in humified organic matter but is dominantly composed of mineral particles.

ALFISOLS Soils that have an argillic horizon with a relatively high base saturation and do not have a thick, dark A horizon.

ALLUVIAL FAN A fan-shaped deposit of alluvium that has its apex at the point where a narrow canyon debouches into a valley.

ALLUVIUM Sediment deposited by flowing water.

ANDESITE A type of volcanic rock with a predominance of sodium/calcium feldspar and some mafic minerals.

ANDIC PROPERTIES Properties typical of soils developed in volcanic materials, including relatively low bulk density, adsorption of phosphate, and amorphous iron oxides and aluminosilica materials.

ANDISOLS Soils that form in volcanic materials and have andic properties.

AQUIC SOIL MOISTURE REGIME The condition where soils are completely saturated with water (to the surface) at least some time during the year.

ARGILLIC HORIZON A subsoil horizon that has accumulated significant clay, which has been translocated in suspension with percolating water and deposited in that location (illuvial clay).

ARIDIC SOIL MOISTURE REGIME The condition where soils are almost always dry.

ARIDISOLS Soils that have an aridic soil moisture regime and have some degree of subsoil development (i.e., they are not Entisols).

ASBESTOS Term for silicate minerals that occur as strong, thin fibers.

BASALT A dark-colored volcanic rock with a predominance of calcium feldspar and mafic minerals.

BASE CATIONS Calcium, magnesium, potassium, sodium.

BASE SATURATION The percentage of a soil's cation exchange capacity that is occupied by base cations.

BATHOLITH A huge body of intrusive igneous rock.

B HORIZON A subsoil layer that has been altered from the parent material by soil-forming processes.

BT HORIZON A type of B horizon in which clay has accumulated.

CALCIC HORIZON An uncemented subsoil horizon with accumulation of pedogenic calcium carbonate.

CAPILLARY FRINGE The zone above the water table that is wetted by water that is wicked up into the soil by capillary forces in very small diameter pores.

CATION EXCHANGE CAPACITY The capacity of a soil to adsorb cations due to its inherent negative electrical charge.

CHRONOSEQUENCE A sequence of soils (or vegetation communities or landforms) that represent a time series of development. In the case of soils, other environmental factors such as climate, vegetation, parent material, and topography are supposed to remain constant through time.

CLASTS Rock fragments.

CLAYPAN A dense, clayey subsoil horizon that has an abrupt transition from an overlying more sandy horizon.

COBBLES Rock fragments that are 75 to 250 millimeters in diameter.

COLLUVIUM Sediment that was deposited after being transported by gravity.

DESERT PAVEMENT A monolayer of rock fragments that form a tight mosaic on the surface of certain desert soils. It is generally underlain by a vesicular horizon that has rafted the layer of rocks upward during its formation.

DURIPAN An extremely hard subsoil horizon cemented by pedogenic amorphous silica (opal).

E HORIZON A light-colored, near-surface, sandy soil horizon from which organics and iron oxides have been removed by water leaching through it.

ELECTRICAL CONDUCTIVITY (EC) A measurement reflecting the salt content in soils. Soil samples are saturated with water in the lab, dissolving any salts that are present. The water is suctioned out and its ability to conduct electricity is measured. The ability of water to conduct electricity is directly proportional to its salt content.

ENTISOLS Soils that have little or no pedogenic development—that is, they are very young and not much changed from the original geologic material in which they are forming.

GEOMORPHIC SURFACE A land surface feature with definite spatial boundaries that was formed by processes acting during a specific time period. It may include several landforms and its formation may have involved erosion, deposition, or both. It is two-dimensional (a surface only) and has no thickness. Examples include a stream terrace, a moraine (both depositional), a hillslope that grades to a valley (erosional in the upper part, depositional in the lower part).

GRANITE An intrusive igneous rock composed of abundant quartz and potassium/sodium feldspar; often with some biotite and hornblende.

GRAVELS Rock fragments that are 2 to 75 millimeters in diameter.

HISTOSOLS Soils composed largely of organic matter (e.g., peat).

HOLOCENE The period of time extending from the end of the Pleistocene (11,700 years ago) to the present.

ILLUVIAL The process of colloidal material (usually clay) being transported from the upper soil horizons to the subsoil.

INCEPTISOLS Soils that have rather weak B horizon development but do not have a thick, dark A horizon, nor an aridic soil moisture regime.

INTERSPACE The largely unvegetated areas between shrubs in the desert.

KAOLIN A clay mineral in which aluminum and silicon are dominant components.

LACUSTRINE Of, or pertaining to, a lake.

LOESS A deposit composed of wind-blown, silt-rich sediment.

LITHOLOGY A description of a rock unit's visible physical characteristics, such as texture, grain size, and color.

MAFIC Minerals or rocks that are rich in magnesium and iron.

MOLLISOLS Soils that have a thick, dark A horizon and a high base saturation.

NATRIC HORIZON A subsoil horizon of illuvial clay concentration that has abundant sodium on its cation exchange sites.

PEDIMENT A relatively smooth surface eroded into weathered bedrock and covered with a veneer of sediment.

PEDOGENIC Related to, or formed by, processes active in the soil.

PERIDOTITE An intrusive igneous rock composed almost entirely of mafic minerals.

PETROCALCIC HORIZON An extremely hard subsoil horizon cemented by pedogenic calcium carbonate.

PH-DEPENDENT CHARGE Electrical charge in soils that varies with pH, becoming more negative at high pH, and thereby adsorbing more cations, and becoming positive at low pH, thereby adsorbing anions. In contrast, most soils have a permanent negative charge and adsorb cations.

PHOSPHATE FIXATION The condition whereby phosphorus is incorporated into soil minerals and made unavailable to plants.

PIEDMONT Includes the landforms that skirt the base of a mountain.

PLAYA A barren, dry lake bed.

PLEISTOCENE The time period spanning from 2,588,000 to 11,700 years ago; includes the most recent periods of glaciation.

PLUTON A body of intruded igneous rock.

PYROCLASTIC FLOW A fast-moving, fluidized mass of volcanic debris and hot gases.

QUATERNARY The period of time consisting of the Pleistocene and the Holocene.

RESIDUUM Material that has not moved laterally as it weathered from bedrock to soil.

RHYOLITE A volcanic rock composed of abundant quartz and potassium/sodium feldspar.

SALINE-SODIC SOIL A soil that has the properties of both saline and sodic soils.

SALINE SOIL A soil with a salt content high enough to impair the growth of most plants (electrical conductivity >4 dS/m).

SERPENTINE A clay mineral in which iron, magnesium, and silicon are dominant components (the rock composed of serpentine is called serpentinite).

SHRINK-SWELL SOILS Clayey soils that shrink when dry and swell when wet.

SMECTITE A silica- and magnesium-rich clay mineral that swells when wet and shrinks when dry.

SODIC SOIL A soil in which sodium fills more than 15% of the cation exchange capacity.

SPODOSOLS Soils that have an E horizon underlain by a brown horizon of illuvial accumulation of colloidal organic matter and iron oxides.

STONES Rock fragments that are 250 to 600 millimeters in diameter.

ULTISOLS Soils that have an argillic horizon with a low base saturation and do not have a thick, dark A horizon.

ULTRAMAFIC ROCK Rock that is composed almost entirely of mafic minerals (e.g., peridotite, serpentinite).

VERTISOLS Clayey, smectite-rich soils that exhibit strong shrink-swell activity.

VESICULAR HORIZON A surface soil horizon that forms in a thin layer of loess in arid regions. It is permeated by vesicles (bubbles) that form when air is trapped as the soil is wetted and are preserved as it dries. It forms in barren areas under desert pavement or in interspaces where the soil surface is sealed by crusting.

XERIC SOIL MOISTURE REGIME The condition in which the soil is moist in the winter and dry in the summer, reflective of a Mediterranean climate.

References

Alexander, E. B., and J. DuShey. 2011. Topographic and soil differences from peridotite to serpentinite. Geomorphology 135:271–276.

Alexander, E. B., J. I. Mallory, and W. L. Colwell, 1993. Soil-elevation relationships on a volcanic plateau in the southern Cascade Range, northern California, USA. Catena 20:113–128.

Alexander, E. B., R. G. Coleman, T. Keeler-Wolf, and S. P. Harrison. 2007. Serpentine geoecology of western North America: Geology, soils, and vegetation. Oxford University Press, New York.

Alt, D., and D. W. Hyndman. 2000. Roadside geology of northern and central California. Mountain Press Publishing Company, Missoula, Montana.

Amundson, R., Y. Guo, and P. Gong. 2003. Soil diversity and land use in the United States. Ecosystems 6:470–482.

Anderson, K., S. Wells, and R. Graham. 2002. Pedogenesis of vesicular horizons, Cima Volcanic Field, Mojave Desert, California. Soil Science Society of America Journal 66:878–887.

Anderson, M. A., R. C. Graham, G. J. Alyanakian, and D. Z. Martynn. 1995. Late summer water status of soils and weathered bedrock in a giant sequoia grove. Soil Science 160:415–422. <doi:10.1097/00010694-199512000-00007>.

Arkley, R. J. 1981. Soil moisture use by mixed conifer forests in a summer-dry climate. Soil Science Society of America Journal 45:423–427. <doi:10.2136/sssaj1981.03615995004500020037x>.

Arnalds, O., F. O., Gisladottir, and H. Sigurjonsson. 2001. Sandy deserts of Iceland. Journal of Arid Environments 47:359–371.

Atzet, T., and D. L. Wheeler. 1982. Historical and ecological perspectives on fire activity in the Klamath geological province of the Rogue River and Siskiyou National Forests. U.S. Forest Service Publication PNW R-6 Range-102. Pacific Northwest Forest and Range Experiment Station, Portland, Oregon.

Bales, R. C., J. W. Hopmans, A. T. O'Geen, M. Meadows, P. C. Hartsough, P. Kirchner et al. 2011. Soil moisture response to snowmelt and rainfall in a Sierra Nevada mixed-conifer forest. Vadose Zone Journal 10:786–799. <doi:10.2136/vzj2011.0001>.

Beaudette, D., and A. T. O'Geen. 2008. Quantifying the aspect effect: An application of solar radiation modeling for soil survey. Soil Science Society of America Journal. 73:1345–1352.

Birkeland, P. W., and R. J. Janda. 1971. Clay mineralogy of soils developed from Quaternary deposits of the eastern Sierra Nevada, California. Geological Society of America Bulletin 82:2495–2514.

Black, T. A., and D. R. Montgomery. 1991. Sediment transport by burrowing mammals, Marin County, California. Earth Surface Processes and Landforms 16:163–172.

Blythe, A. E., M. A. House, and J. A. Spotila. 2002. Low-temperature thermochronology of the San Gabriel and San Bernardino Mountains, southern California: Constraining structural evolution. Pages 231–250 in A. Barth, editor. Contributions to Crustal Evolution of the Southwestern United States. Geological Society of America Special Paper, Boulder, Colorado.

Bornyasz, M. A., R. C. Graham, and M. F. Allen. 2005. Ectomycorrhizae in a soil-weathered granitic bedrock regolith: Linking matrix resources to plants. Geoderma 126:141–160.

Briggs, C., J. M. Breiner, and R. C. Graham. 2012. Physical and chemical properties of *Pinus ponderosa* charcoal: Implications for soil modification. Soil Science 177:263–268.

Caldwell, T. G., M. H. Young, E. V. McDonald, and J. Zhu. 2012. Soil heterogeneity in Mojave Desert shrublands: Biotic and abiotic processes. Water Resources Research 48:W09551. <doi:10.1029/2012WR011963>.

California Coastal Commission. 1987. The California coastal resource guide. University of California Press, Berkeley, California.

Clark, M. K., G. Maheo, J. Saleeby, and K. A. Farley. 2005. The non-equilibrium landscape of the southern Sierra Nevada, California. GSA Today 15, no. 9:4–10. <doi:10:1130/1052 5173(2005)015<4:TNELOT>2.0.CO;2>.

Crawford, T. W., L. D. Whittig, E. L. Begg, and G. L. Huntington.1983. Eolian influence on development and weathering of some soils of Point Reyes Peninsula, California. Soil Science Society of America Journal 47:1179–1185.

Crouvi, O., J. D. Pelletier, and C. Rasmussen. 2013. Predicting the thickness and aeolian fraction of soils in upland watersheds of the Mojave Desert. Geoderma 195–196c:94–110.

Cullen, S. J., C. Montagne, and H. Ferguson. 1991. Timber harvest trafficking and soil compaction in western Montana. Soil Science Society of America Journal 55:1416–1421.

Dahlgren, R. A. 2005. Geologic nitrogen and as a source of soil acidity. Soil Science and Plant Nutrition 51:719–723.

Dahlgren, R. A. J. L. Boettinger, G. L. Huntington, and R. G. Amundson. 1997. Soil development along an elevational transect in the western Sierra Nevada, California. Geoderma 78:207–236.

Dahlgren, R. A., M. Saigusa, and F. C. Ugolini. 2004. The nature, properties, and management of volcanic soils. Pages 113–182 in D. L. Sparks, editor. Advances in Agronomy, volume 82. Elsevier Academic Press, Amsterdam, The Netherlands.

Dawson, T. E. 1998. Fog in the California redwood forest: Ecosystem inputs and use by plants. Oecologia 117:476–485.

DeBano, L. F., D. G. Neary, and P. F. Folliott. 1998. Fire's effects on ecosystems. John Wiley & Sons, New York, New York.

de Koff, J. P., R. C. Graham, K. R. Hubbert, and P. M. Wohlgemuth. 2006. Pre- and post-fire erosion of soil nutrients within a chaparral watershed. Soil Science 171:915–928.

Diaz, F., A. T. O'Geen, C. Rasmussen, and R. A. Dahlgren. 2010. Pedogenesis along a thermal gradient in a geothermal region of the southern Cascades, California. Geoderma 154:495–507.

Dickson, B. A., and R. L. Crocker. 1954. A chronosequence of soils and vegetation near Mt. Shasta, California. III. Some properties of the mineral profile. Journal of Soil Science 5:173–191.

———. 1953a. A chronosequence of soils and vegetation near Mt. Shasta, California. I. Definition of the ecosystem investigated and features of the plant succession. Journal of Soil Science 4:123–141.

———. 1953b. A chronosequence of soils and vegetation near Mt. Shasta, California. II. The development of the forest floors and the carbon and nitrogen profiles of the soils. Journal of Soil Science 4:142–156.

Dietrich, W. E., and R. Dorn. 1984. Significance of thick deposits of colluvium on hillslopes: A case study involving the use of pollen analysis in the coastal mountains of northern California. Journal of Geology 92:147–158.

Doner, H. E., and W. C. Lynn. 1989. Carbonate, halide, sulfate, and sulfide minerals. Pages 279–330 in J. B. Dixon and S. B. Weed, editors. Minerals in Soil Environments. Soil Science Society of America, Madison, Wisconsin.

Egerton-Warburton, L. M., R. C. Graham, and K. R. Hubbert. 2003. Spatial variability in mycorrhizal hyphae and nutrient and water availability in a soil-weathered bedrock profile. Plant and Soil 249:331–342.

Enloe, H. A., R. C. Graham, and S. C. Sillett. 2006. Arboreal Histosols in old-growth redwood forest canopies, northern California. Soil Science Society of America Journal 70:408–418.

Enloe, H. A., S. A. Quideau, R. C. Graham, S. C. Sillett, S-W. Oh, and R. E. Wasylishen. 2010. Soil organic matter processes in old-growth redwood forest canopies. Soil Science Society of America Journal 74:161–171.

Florsheim, J. L., E. A. Keller, and D. W. Best. 1991. Fluvial transport in response to moderate storm flows following chaparral wildfire, Ventura County, southern California. Geological Society of America Bulletin 103:504–511.

Foster, C. M., and G. K. Lang 1994. Soil survey of Klamath National Forest Area, parts of Siskiyou County, California and Jackson County, Oregon. U.S. Government Printing Office, Washington, D.C.

Frazier, C. S., and R. C. Graham. 2000. Pedogenic transformation of fractured granitic bedrock, southern California. Soil Science Society of America Journal 64:2057–2069.

Geist, J. M., J. W. Hazard, and K. W. Seidel. 1989. Assessing physical conditions of some Pacific Northwest volcanic ash soils after forest harvest. Soil Science Society of America Journal 53:946–950.

Gessler, P. E., O. A. Chadwick, F. Chamran, L. Althouse, and K. Holmes. 2000. Modeling soil-landscape and ecosystem properties using terrain attributes. Soil Science Society of America Journal 64:2046–2056.

Goforth, B. R., R. C. Graham, K. R. Hubbert, C. W. Zanner, and R. A. Minnich. 2005. Spatial distribution and properties of ash and thermally altered soils after high-severity forest fire, southern California. International Journal of Wildland Fire 14:343–354.

Gonzalez, J. M., and D. A. Laird. 2003. Carbon sequestration in clay mineral fractions from 14C-labeled plant residues. Soil Science Society of America Journal 67:1715–1720.

Graham, R. C., A. M. Rossi, and K. R. Hubbert. 2010. Rock to regolith conversion: Producing hospitable substrates for terrestrial ecosystems. GSA Today 20:4–9. <doi:10.1130/GSAT57A.1>.

Graham, R. C., B. E. Herbert, and J. O. Ervin. 1988. Mineralogy and incipient pedogenesis of Entisols in anorthosite terrane of the San Gabriel Mountains, California. Soil Science Society of America Journal 52:738–746.

Graham, R. C., D. R. Hirmas, Y. A. Wood, and C. Amrhein. 2008. Large near-surface nitrate pools in soils capped by desert pavement in the Mojave Desert, California. Geology 36:259–262.

Graham, R. C., E. W. Blake, A. M. Boner, J. H. Blanchard, and J. A. Frisbie. 2010. A Gelisol near White Mountain Peak, California. Soil Survey Horizons 51:56–58.

Graham, R. C., M. M. Diallo, and L. J. Lund. 1990. Soils and mineral weathering on phyllite colluvium and serpentinite in northwestern California. Soil Science Society of America Journal 54:1682–1690.

Harden, D. R. 2004. California geology. Pearson Prentice Hall, Upper Saddle River, New Jersey.

Harden, J. W., A. M. Sarna-Wojcicki, and G. R. Demroff. 1986. Soils developed on coastal and fluvial terraces near Ventura, California. U.S. Geological Survey Bulletin 1590-B. U.S. Government Printing Office, Washington, D.C.

Harden, J. W., E. M. Taylor, C. Hill, R. K. Mark, L. D. McFadden, M. C. Reheis, J. M. Sowers, and S. G. Wells. 1991. Rates of soil development from four soil chronosequences in the southern Great Basin. Quaternary Research 35:383–399.

Harden, J. W., E. M. Taylor, M. C. Reheis, and L. D. McFadden. 1991. Calcic, gypsic, and siliceous soil chronosequences in arid and semiarid environments. Pages 1–16 in W. D. Nettleton, editor. Occurrence, characteristics, and genesis of carbonate, gypsum, and silica accumulations in soils. Special Publication No. 26. Soil Science Society of America, Madison, Wisconsin.

Hirmas, D. R., and R. C. Graham. 2011. Pedogenesis and soil-geomorphic relationships in an arid mountain range, Mojave Desert, California. Soil Science Society of America Journal 75:192–206.

Hirmas, D. R., R. C. Graham, and K. J. Kendrick. 2011. Soil-geomorphic significance of land surface characteristics in an arid mountain range, Mojave Desert, USA. Catena 87:408–420.

Hubbert, K. R., J. L. Beyers, and R. C. Graham. 2001. Roles of weathered bedrock and soil in seasonal water relations of *Pinus jeffreyi* and *Arctostaphylos patula*. Canadian Journal of Forest Research 31:1947–1957.

Hubbert, K. R., R. C. Graham, and M. A. Anderson. 2001. Soil and weathered bedrock: Components of a Jeffrey pine plantation substrate. Soil Science Society of America Journal 65:1255–1262. <doi:10.2136/sssaj2001.6541255x>.

Ingebritsen, S. E., M. E. Ikehara, D. L. Galloway, and D. R. Jones. 2000. Delta subsidence in California: The sinking heart of the state. U.S. Geological Survey publication # FS-005-00.

Jenny, H. 1980. The soil resource: Origin and behavior. Springer-Verlag, New York, New York.

Jones, D. P., and R. C. Graham. 1993. Water-holding characteristics of weathered granitic rock in chaparral and forest ecosystems. Soil Science Society of America Journal 57:256–261.

Kendrick, K. J., and R. C. Graham. 2004. Pedogenic silica accumulation in chronosequence soils, southern California. Soil Science Society of America Journal 68:1295–1303.

Kimble, J. M., C. L. Ping, M. E. Sumner, and L. P. Wilding. 2000. Andisols. Pages E209–224 in M. E. Sumner, editor. Handbook of Soil Science. CRC Press, Boca Raton, Florida.

Kimsey, M., P. McDaniel, D. Strawn, and J. Moore. 2005. Fate of applied sulfate in volcanic ash influenced forest soils. Soil Science Society of America Journal 69:1507–1515.

Laurent, T. E., R. C. Graham, and K. R. Tice. 1994. Soils of the red fir forest-barrens mosaic, Siskiyou Mountains crest, California. Soil Science Society of America Journal 58:1747–1752.

Lee, B. D., R. C. Graham, T. E. Laurent, and C. Amrhein. 2004. Pedogenesis in a wetland meadow and surrounding serpentinitic landslide terrain, northern California, USA. Geoderma 118:303–320.

Lee, B. D., R. C. Graham, T. E. Laurent, C. Amrhein, and R.M. Creasy. 2001. Spatial distributions of soil chemical conditions in a serpentinitic wetland and surrounding landscape. Soil Science Society of America Journal 65:1183–1196.

Lynn, W. C. 1964. A study of chemical and biological processes operative in reclaimed and unreclaimed tidal marsh sediments. PhD dissertation. University of California, Davis, California.

MacKenzie, M. D., E.J.B. McIntire, S. A. Quideau, and R. C. Graham. 2008. Charcoal distribution affects carbon and nitrogen contents in forest soils of California. Soil Science Society of America Journal 72:1774–1785.

Marchand, D. E. 1973. Edaphic control of plant distribution in the White Mountains, eastern California. Ecology 54:223–250.

———. 1970. Soil contamination in the White Mountains, eastern California. Geological Society of America Bulletin 81:2497–2506.

Marron, D. C., and J. H. Popenoe. 1986. A soil catena on schist in northwestern California. Geoderma 37:307–324.

McAuliffe, J. R., and E. V. McDonald. 2006. Holocene environmental change and vegetation contraction in the Sonoran Desert. Quaternary Research 65:204–215.

McDaniel, P. A., and M. A. Wilson. 2007. Physical and chemical characteristics of ash-influenced soils of inland northwest forests. Pages 31–45 in D. Page-Dumroese, R. Miller, J. Mital, P. McDaniel, and D. Miller, editors. Volcanic-Ash-Derived Forest Soils of the Inland Northwest: Properties and Implications for Management and Restoration. November 9–10, 2005, Coeur d'Alene, Idaho. Proceedings RMRS-P-44. U.S. Department of Agriculture, Forest Service, Rocky Mountain Research Station, Fort Collins, Colorado.

McDonald, E. V., L. D. McFadden, and S. G. Wells. 2003. Regional response of alluvial fans to the Pleistocene-Holocene climatic transition, Mojave Desert, California. Pages 189–205 in Y. Enzel, S. G. Wells, and N. Lancaster, editors. Paleoenvironments and paleohydrology of the Mojave and southern Great Bassin Deserts. Geological Society of America Special Paper 368. Geological Society of America, Boulder, Colorado.

McFadden, L. D., and R. J. Weldon. 1987. Rates and processes of soil development in Cajon Pass, California. Geological Society of America Bulletin 98:280–293.

McFadden, L. D., S. G. Wells, and J. J. Jercinovich. 1987. Influences of eolian and pedogenic processes on the origin and evolution of desert pavements. Geology 15:504–508.

McFadden, L. D., S. G. Wells, W. J. Brown, and Y. Enzel. 1992. Soil genesis on beach ridges of pluvial Lake Mojave: Implications for Holocene lacustrine and eolian events in the Mojave Desert, southern California. Catena 19:77–97.

McKean, J. A., W. E. Dietrich, R. C. Finkel, J. R. Southon, and M. W. Caffee 1993. Quantification of soil production and downslope creep rates from cosmogenic 10Be accumulations on a hillslope profile. Geology 21:343–346.

Merritts, D. J., and W. B. Bull. 1989. Interpreting Quaternary uplift rates at the Mendocino triple junction, northern California, from uplifted marine terraces. Geology 17:1020–1024.

Merritts, D. J., O. A. Chadwick, and D. M. Hendricks. 1991. Rates and processes of soil evolution on uplifted marine terraces, northern California. Geoderma 51:241–275.

Miles, S. R., and C. B. Goudy. 1998. Ecological subregions of California: Section and subsection descriptions. U.S. Department of Agriculture, Forest Service, Pacific Southwest Region. Publication R5-EM-TP-005, 211 pages. San Francisco, CA.

Moody, L. E., and R. C. Graham. 1995. Geomorphic and pedogenic evolution in coastal sediments, central California. Geoderma 67:181–201.

———. 1994. Pedogenic processes in thick sand deposits on a marine terrace. Pages 41–55 in D. L. Cremeens, R. B. Brown, and J. H. Huddleston, editors. Whole Regolith Pedology. Soil Science Society of America Special Publication 34. Madison, WI.

Muhs, D. R. 1983. Quaternary sea-level events on northern San Clemente Island, California. Quaternary Research 20:322–341.

Muhs, D. R., J. R. Budahn, D. L. Johnson, M. Reheis, J. Beann, G. Skipp, E. Fisher, and J. A. Jones. 2008. Geochemical evidence for airborne dust additions to soils in Channel Islands National Park, California. Geological Society of America Bulletin 120:106–126.

Nanzyo, M., S. Shoji, and R. Dahlgren. 1993. Physical characteristics of volcanic ash soils. Pages 189–207 in S. Shoji, M. Nanzyo, R. Dahlgren, editors. Volcanic ash soils—Genesis, properties, and utilization. Elsevier, Amsterdam, The Netherlands.

Nettleton, W. D., K. W. Flach, and G. Borst. 1968. A toposequence of soils in tonalite grus in the southern California Peninsular Range. Soil Survey Investigations Report No. 21. U.S. Department of Agriculture Soil Conservation Service, Washington, D.C.

Norris, R. M., and R. W. Webb. 1990. Geology of California. John Wiley & Sons, New York, New York.

Norton, J. B., J. L. Jungst, U. Norton, H. R. Olsen, K. W. Tate, and W. R. Horwath. 2011. Soil carbon and nitrogen storage in upper montane riparian meadows. Ecosystems 14:1217–1231.

O'Geen, A. T., G. S. Pettygrove, R. J. Southard, H. Minoshima, and P. Verdegaal, 2008. Soil-landscape model helps predict potassium supply in vineyards. California Agriculture 62:195–201.

O'Geen, A. T., R. A. Dahlgren, and D. Sanchez-Mata. 2008. California soils and examples of ultramafic vegetation. Pages 71–106 in M. G. Barbour, T. Keller-Wolf, and A. A. Schoenherr, editors. Terrestrial Vegetation of California. Third edition. University of California Press, Ltd. London, UK.

O'Geen, A. T., R. A. Dahlgren, A. Swarowsky, K. W. Tate, D. J. Lewis, and M. J. Singer. 2010. Research connects soil hydrology and stream water chemistry in California oak woodlands. California Agriculture. 64:78–84.

O'Geen , A. T., W. A. Hobson, R. A. Dahlgren, and D. B. Kelley. 2007. Soil properties and horizon stratigraphy in vernal pool landscapes of northern California. Soil Science Society of America Journal. 72:727–740.

Orme, A. R., and V. P. Tchakerian. 1986. Quaternary dunes of the Pacific Coast of the Californias. Pages 149–175 in W. G. Nickling, editor. Aeolian Geomorphology. Allen and Unwin, Boston, Massachusetts.

Peterson, F. F. 1981. Landforms of the Basin and Range Province: Defined for soil survey. Technical Bulletin 28. Nevada Agricultural Experiment Station, University of Nevada, Reno, Nevada.

Pietrasiak, N., R. E. Drenovsky, L. S. Santiago, and R. C. Graham. 2014. Biogeomorphology of a Mojave Desert landscape: Configurations and feedbacks of abiotic and biotic land surfaces during landform evolution. Geomorphology 206:23–36.

Rains, M. C., G. E. Fogg, T. Harter, R. A. Dahlgren, and R. J. Williamson. 2006. The role of perched aquifers in hydrological connectivity and biogeochemical processes in vernal pool landscapes, Central Valley, California. Hydrologic Processes 20:1157–1175.

Rasmussen, C., N. Matsuyama, R. A. Dahlgren, R. J. Southard, and N. Brauer. 2007. Soil genesis and mineral transformation across an environmental gradient on andesitic lahar. Soil Science Society of America Journal 71:225–237.

Ratliff, R., 1985. Meadows in the Sierra Nevada of California: State of knowledge, GTR PSW-84. U.S. Forest Service, Berkeley, California.

Reheis, M. C. 2006. A sixteen-year record of eolian dust in southern Nevada and California, USA: Controls on dust generation and accumulation. Journal of Arid Environments 67:487–520.

Reheis, M. C., J. R. Budahn, P. J. Lamothe, and R. L. Reynolds. 2009. Compositions of modern dust and surface sediments in the Desert Southwest, United States. Journal of Geophysical Research-Earth Surface 114:F01028.<doi:10.1029/2008JF001009>.

Reynolds, R. L., J. C. Yount, M. Reheis, H. Goldstein, P. Chavez, R. Fulton, J. Whitney, C. Fuller, and R. M. Forester. 2007. Dust emission from wet and dry playas in the Mojave Desert, USA. Earth Surface Processes and Landforms 32:1811–1827.

Rice, T. J., and R. C. Graham. 1993. Environmental considerations for serpentinite-derived soils in the California Central Coast Ranges. Pages 210–218 in J. M. Kimble, editor. Proceedings of 8th International Soil Management Workshop, Sacramento, California, July 18, 1992. USDA-Soil Conservation Service, Washington, DC.

Rose, K. L., R. C. Graham, and D. R. Parker. 2003. Water source utilization by *Pinus jeffreyi* and *Arctostaphylos patula* on thin soils over bedrock. Oecologia 134:46–54. <doi:10.1007/s00442-002-1084-4>.

Schulz, M. S., D. Vivit, C. Schulz, J. Fitzpatrick, and A. White. 2010. Biologic origin of iron nodules in a marine terrace chronosequence, Santa Cruz, California. Soil Science Society of America Journal 74:550–564.

Shlemon, R. J., and E. L. Begg. 1975. Late Quaternary evolution of the Sacramento–San Joaquin Delta, California. Pages 259–266 in R. P. Cresswell, editor. Quaternary Studies. The Royal Society of New Zealand, Wellington, New Zealand.

Shoji, S., M. Nanzyo, and R. Dahlgren. 1993. Volcanic ash soils—genesis, properties, and utilization. Elsevier, Amsterdam, The Netherlands.

Southard, S. B., and R. J. Southard. 1989. Mineralogy and classification of andic soils in northeastern California. Soil Science Society of America Journal 53:1784–1791.

Strahm, B. D., and R. B. Harrison. 2007. Mineral and organic matter controls on the sorption of macronutrient anions in variable-charge soils. Soil Science Society of America Journal 71:1926–1933.

Swarowsky, A., R. A. Dahlgren, and A. T. O'Geen. 2012. Linking subsurface lateral flowpath activity with stream flow characteristics in a semiarid headwater catchment. Soil Science Society of America Journal 76:532–547.

Takahashi, T., R. Dahlgren, and P. Vansusteren. 1993. Clay mineralogy and chemistry of soils formed in volcanic materials in the xeric moisture regime of northern California. Geoderma 59:131–150.

Tanji, K., A. Lauchli, and J. Meyer. 1986. Selenium in the San Joaquin Valley. Environment 28:6–39.

Torrent, J., W. D. Nettleton, and G. Borst. 1980a. Clay illuviation and lamellae formation in a Psammentic Haploxeralf in southern California. Soil Science Society of America Journal 44:363–369.

Turk, J. K., B. R. Goforth, R. C. Graham, and K. J. Kendrick. 2008. Soil morphology of a debris flow chronosequence in a coniferous forest, southern California, USA. Geoderma 146:157–165.

Ulery, A. L., and R. C. Graham. 1993. Forest fire effects on soil color and texture. Soil Science Society of America Journal 57:135–140.

Ulery, A. L., R. C. Graham, and C. Amrhein. 1993. Wood-ash composition and soil pH following intense burning. Soil Science 156:358–364.

Ulery, A. L., R. C. Graham, and L. H. Bowen. 1996. Forest fire effects on soil phyllosilicates in California. Soil Science Society of America Journal 60:309–315.

USDA-NRCS (Natural Resources Conservation Service). 2007. Soil survey of the Tahoe Basin Area, California and Nevada. http://www.nrcs.usda.gov/wps/portal/nrcs/surveylist/soils/survey/state/?stateId=CA. Accessed June 28, 2015.

Vasek, F. C., and L. J. Lund. 1980. Soil characteristics associated with a primary plant succession on a Mojave Desert dry lake. Ecology 61:1013–1018.

Weissmann, G. S., G. L. Bennett, and A. L. Lansdale. 2005. Factors controlling sequence development of Quaternary fluvial fans, San

Joaquin Basin, California, USA. Pages 169–186 in A. M. Harvey, A. E. Mather, and M. Stokes, editors. Alluvial Fans: Geomorphology, Sedimentology, Dynamics. Geological Society, London, Special Publications, 251. The Geological Society of London, UK.

Weitkamp, W. A., R. C. Graham, M. A. Anderson, and C. Amrhein. 1996. Pedogenesis of a vernal pool Entisol-Alfisol-Vertisol catena in southern California. Soil Science Society of America Journal 60:316–323.

Wells, S. G., J. C. Dohrenwend, L. D. McFadden, B. D. Turrin, and K. Mahrer. 1985. Late Cenozoic landscape evolution on lava flow surfaces of the Cima volcanic field, Mojave Desert, California. Geological Society of America Bulletin 96:1518–1529.

Witty, J. H., R. C. Graham, K. R. Hubbert, J. A. Doolittle, and J. A. Wald. 2003. Contributions of water supply from the weathered bedrock zone to forest soil quality. Geoderma 114:389–400.

Wood, Y. A., R. C. Graham, and S. G. Wells. 2005. Surface control of desert pavement pedologic process and landscape function, Cima volcanic field, Mojave Desert, California. Catena 59:205–230.

Yoo, K., and R. Amundson. 2005. Erosion of upland hillslope soil organic carbon: Coupling field measurements with a sediment transport model. Biogeochemical Cycles 19. <doi:10.1029/2004GB002271>.

Young, M. H., E. V. McDonald, T. G. Caldwell, S. G. Benner, and D. G. Meadows. 2004. Hydraulic properties of a desert soil chronosequence in the Mojave Desert, USA. Vadose Zone Journal 3:956–963.

FIVE

Population and Land Use

PETER S. ALAGONA, TIM PAULSON, ANDREW B. ESCH,
and JESSICA MARTER-KENYON

Introduction

California is the third largest state in the nation by land area at around 424,000 square kilometers and has the largest population with just over thirty-eight million residents, almost a third more than the second largest state (Walker and Lodha 2013). California's population is the most diverse in the country and has the greatest percentage of foreign-born immigrants. California is also the most urban state, with a majority of its residents living in major cities along the Pacific coastline. Beyond these great coastal metropolises lie vast, thinly populated rural regions, as well as the largest area in designated parkland and wilderness of any state other than Alaska. Almost half of California is publicly owned, and more than 90 percent of this land is federal property. Unlike many other populous states with more evenly dispersed residents, California's population history is almost entirely a story of urban growth. As a result, a relatively small fraction of the state's inhabitants have played a direct role in shaping land use outside its cities. Over the past 250 years, however, Californians as a group have subjected the state's ecosystems to an extraordinary diversity of uses, sometimes reaping great profits but also transforming the environment in myriad ways.

This chapter explores the history and geography of California's human population and land use, and the relationships between them. It begins with a discussion of the complex relationships between population and land use, and their implications for environmental change. The second part of the chapter tells the story of California's population history, arranged chronologically by period from the beginning of the Mission era in 1769 to the present. As one might expect, this section focuses mainly on URBAN AREAS. The third part of the chapter explores California's land use history, organized into sections focusing on six distinctive regions: coastlines, deserts, hardwood rangelands, mountains, northwest forests, and agricultural valleys. These sections deal mainly with land use, leaving discussions of the environmental effects of human activities for other chapters in this volume. For the sake of clarity and organization, this chapter discusses population and land use in separate parts, but it is important to remember that the two interact in numerous, complex ways.

The Relationships between Population and Land Use

For centuries, scholars from diverse disciplines and intellectual traditions have sought to understand the relationships between human populations and their biophysical environments. Until the 1960s, most theories relied on mechanistic explanations that considered resource use, commodity production, and environmental impacts as functions of total human population. If population increased, then demands on natural systems would also increase, leading to resource depletion, environmental decline, and social dislocation. In recent decades, however, numerous researchers have challenged these simple overarching theories, revealing the diversity, complexity, and contingency of the relationships between human populations and their environments (Harrison and Pearce 2000). Today, most scholars view population as a dynamic, multidimensional set of patterns and processes that plays an important—but not determinative—role in shaping land use and environmental change (de Sherbinin et al. 2007).

Understanding human populations requires much more than counting the total number of people in a given area (Xie 2000). Demographers consider population as a collection of variables that includes age, ethnicity, gender, language, income, mobility, and others. The composition and relative importance of these variables change over time and space. For example, population age structures vary dramatically from fast-growing developing countries in sub-Saharan Africa that contain large percentages of young people, to slow-growing, highly developed countries in northern Europe that house older populations. California represents a middle ground between these two extreme examples; the state's population is continuing to expand, but the average age of its residents is increasing as its total growth rate declines (Myers 2013) (Table 5.1). California experienced massive growth during and immediately after the Gold Rush. The state has continued to grow, but its growth rate has declined since World War II, and the gap between California's growth rate and the national average has narrowed over time.

Two variables are particularly important to consider when studying the relationships between population and the environment. The first is the percentage of the population living in rural versus urban areas, which is related to labor markets and the political and economic importance of agriculture, ranching, mining, and other resource-dependent industries. Today, globally as well as in California and the United States, the vast majority of population growth is occurring in and around cities (U.S. Census Bureau 2012b). But this has not always been the case. During the 1930s and 1940s, for example, many Dust Bowl refugees from the Great Plains and immigrants from Mexico moved to California's rural Central Valley in search of farm employment (Gregory 1989). A second, related variable is the relative importance of "natural" population growth or decline, meaning births and deaths of residents, versus total growth or decline, which also includes immigration and emigration. In recent decades much of California's population growth has occurred in the form of migration from other states and countries. With birth rates and immigration both on the decline, California's population is beginning to stabilize (Pitkin and Myers 2012).

Photo on previous page: Aerial view of highway U.S. 101 in Sonoma County, California, looking south. Courtesy of FloridaStock/Shutterstock.

Environmental change is at least as complicated a topic as population. Natural changes have occurred throughout Earth's history in land, water, air, soils, plant and animal populations, marine environments, and of course climates. Such changes may occur at spatial scales from the local to the global, and at time scales from the momentary to the geological. Changes may be cyclical, meaning that they occur in a repetitive rotation, or secular, meaning that they represent long-term directional or qualitative shifts. Changes can result from both large-scale driving forces and specific proximate causes. Even in the absence of human action, environmental changes in Earth's history were rarely caused by a single factor. More often, they stemmed from numerous sources or from a combination of influences. Understanding environmental change becomes even more complex when we add humans to the equation.

Human societies have always shaped and been shaped by their environments. These reciprocal relationships can be transformative, but they are not necessarily destructive. It is more accurate therefore to think of the relationships between populations and environments as dynamic interactions than as one-directional impacts. The changes associated with these interactions have been under way for many thousands of years, but they have increased dramatically since the Industrial Revolution in the eighteenth and nineteenth centuries (Steffen et al. 2007). The European colonization of California, beginning at the outset of the Mission Era in 1769, coincides with this global transformation. This was also the period when scholars began to think in earnest about the connections between expanding human populations and the natural resources upon which those populations depend.

The figure of Thomas Malthus (1766–1834) looms large over all debates about population and the environment (Turchin and Nefedov 2009). A British political economist and demographer, Malthus (1798) argued against his optimistic Enlightenment contemporaries, predicting that human population growth would hinder social progress by straining resources. This growth could not continue indefinitely, however, because it was limited by the earth's ability to produce the resources necessary for human survival, including food. George Perkins Marsh (1864) adopted this theme in the mid-nineteenth century when he wrote about the degradation of soils, along the shores of the Mediterranean in southern Europe, due to destructive agricultural and timber-harvesting practices that led to deforestation and soil erosion. Scholars have often pointed to Marsh as the first American environmentalist, and so it is not surprising that subsequent generations adopted similar ideas about the central role of human population in land use and environmental change.

These ideas experienced a period of heightened popularity during the 1960s and 1970s, when elite think tanks such as the Club of Rome (Meadows et al. 1972) and prominent public intellectuals like the ecologist Paul Ehrlich (1968) advanced neo-Malthusian theories claiming that human populations were approaching the planet's CARRYING CAPACITY, and that overpopulation would cause an ecological catastrophe (Robertson 2012). Most scholars now regard MALTHUSIAN thinking as overly simplistic due to its failure to account for cultural change, technological innovation, political institutions, gender equity, economic trends, labor relations, long-distance trade, physical geography, and other factors. Even the idea of carrying capacity, which suggests that a given area can hold only a fixed number of people based on the limits of its resources, no longer plays a role in most studies of human populations.

TABLE 5.1
Populations and ten-year growth rates for California and the United States

Year	Population		Decade	Ten-year growth rate	
	California	U.S.		California	U.S.
1850	92,597	23,191,876	—	—	—
1860	379,994	31,443,321	1850–60	310.4%	35.6%
1870	560,247	39,818,449	1860–70	47.4%	26.6%
1880	864,694	50,189,209	1870–80	54.3%	26.0%
1890	1,213,398	62,947,714	1880–90	40.3%	25.4%
1900	1,485,053	76,212,168	1890–1900	22.3%	21.1%
1910	2,377,549	92,228,496	1900–10	60.1%	21.0%
1920	3,426,861	106,021,537	1910–20	44.1%	15.8%
1930	5,677,251	122,775,046	1920–30	65.7%	16.2%
1940	6,907,387	132,164,569	1930–40	21.7%	7.6%
1950	10,586,223	150,697,361	1940–50	53.3%	14.0%
1960	15,717,204	179,323,175	1950–60	48.5%	19.0%
1970	19,971,069	203,302,031	1960–70	27.0%	13.4%
1980	23,667,764	226,545,805	1970–80	18.6%	11.4%
1990	29,760,021	248,709,873	1980–90	25.7%	9.8%
2000	33,871,653	281,421,906	1990–2000	13.8%	13.2%
2010	37,253,956	308,745,538	2000–10	10.0%	9.7%

SOURCE: Based on U.S. Census Data from 1850 to 2010, Minnestoa Population Center (2011).

Current thinking about the complexity of population-environment relationships falls into three general categories (Jolly 1994).

The first of these approaches emerged during the early 1970s with the introduction of the now famous I=PAT equation, which postulates that environmental impact (I) is the product of population (P) multiplied by affluence (A) times technology (T) (Ehrlich and Holdren 1971). This simple formula incorporates two variables that previously had received little attention: affluence, which is related to consumption, and technology (Curran and de Sherbinin 2004, Goklany 2009). In the years since its introduction, scholars have developed this equation into several more detailed forms that account for a larger and more diverse set of variables (Dietz et al. 2007). The I=PAT framework thus maintains population as an important driving force, but acknowledges that population alone provides an insufficient basis for explaining environmental change.

A second alternative approach to MALTHUSIANISM, known as CORNUCOPIANISM and embraced by many neoclassical economists, holds that the Earth's resources have no meaningful limits because humans have an essentially infinite ability to overcome resource scarcity through the application of their knowledge and technology (Simon 1981 and 1986, Gleditsch and Urdal 2002). Because population growth increases this capacity, it is seen as beneficial for human development and at worst a neutral factor in environmental change (Boserup 1965). Cornucopianists do not deny that environmental degradation can occur, but they point to market failures, often caused by misguided government policies, as the causes of such damage.

A third approach includes the work of critical social scientists who regard population-environment relationships as complex, multivariate, and profoundly influenced by history and geography. For these scholars, issues such as the relationship of the state to civil society, social inequality, globalization, and legacies of past political regimes play crucial roles in shaping the ways that human populations use their lands and resources. Numerous studies have shown, for example, that in postcolonial developing countries corrupt governments have exploited forests, fisheries, soils, water, and other resources for the benefit of a privileged few, often forcing rural people to adopt unsustainable practices just to survive (Peluso 1994). In their efforts to build international support and consolidate power, cynical officials then blame their impoverished citizens for causing environmental degradation (Forsyth 2002). Population growth may exacerbate environmental problems, but in such contexts population-environment relationships are inextricable from issues of governance, power, and poverty. Much of the research on these relationships has focused on the connections between land use and land cover change (Lambin et al. 2001). "Land use" refers to human activities that require the allocation of geographic space, while "land cover change" refers to alterations in the ecological structure, functioning, and appearance of the land itself. In many cases, the two are indivisible—changes in land use affect land cover and vice versa—and each can be either a cause or a consequence of environmental change.

Over the past two decades, scholars have moved away from simple explanations for shifting patterns of land use and their environmental consequences (Lambin et al. 2001). No single variable, equation, ideology, or approach can fully account for the diversity, complexity, and contingency of population-environment relationships. What scholars do agree on is that land use acts as a major driver and component of environmental change worldwide, at multiple spatial and temporal scales, with consequences for air, water, climate, biodiversity, agriculture, and ecosystem services, as well as for the resilience of human communities and their social and economic systems.

Population

In 1949 the journalist and historian Carey McWilliams argued that California's tremendous growth, and the conditions under which it had occurred, made the state a "great exception" in American history (McWilliams 1971, p. 7). Historians and demographers have debated California's exceptionalism ever since. Today, most agree that although some of California's growth patterns track larger national trends, the state's population history is unusual in at least four ways. First, since achieving statehood, California has housed a population far more diverse—in terms of ethnicity, language, and country of origin—than the United States as a whole. Second, California's infamous booms and busts have often exceeded national economic cycles (State of California 2005), prompting greater swings in the rate of population growth than in other parts of the country. Third, despite these cycles, the state has experienced a population growth rate much higher than the national average (Table 5.2). And fourth, after more than a century of such growth, in 1962 California became the largest state and remains so today. By 2012 it had a population of 38,041,430, around 12 percent of the U.S. total, and some twelve million more than Texas, the second largest state (U.S. Census Bureau 2012a).

California also has an unusual population geography shaped by the interaction of natural and social factors (Walker and Lodha 2013). Mountain ranges, protected harbors, perennial water sources, and other natural features influenced the location of indigenous communities, siting of missions, development of farms, and growth of cities. Social forces that have shaped California's population geography include commodity production, labor markets, land ownership, infrastructure development, and migration patterns.

One result of these processes is that California's residents are more unevenly distributed, spatially, than those of most other populous states. People in California have always congregated near the coast, beginning long before European contact with some of the largest indigenous communities in temperate North America (Fagan 2004). Franciscan priests established their missions close to Native American settlements, and some of the state's major cities grew up around these mission sites. By the middle of the twentieth century, two-thirds of Californians lived on the coastal 1 percent of the state's land (Gregor 1963, Klein 2012). As of the 2010 census, nearly 70 percent of the state's residents, more than twenty-six million people, lived in coastal counties (California Department of Finance 2011), compared to 39 percent nationwide.

Within this coastal belt, populations are further clustered in the San Francisco–Oakland, San Jose, Los Angeles, and San Diego areas, which together really comprise two giant megalopolises, one in the north and one in the south. Indeed, since its establishment, California has been one of the most urbanized states. In 2010 it had the country's largest proportion of urban residents, at 94.95 percent. It ranked second in total urban land area with more than 21,000 square kilometers of cityscape, but just eleventh in population density with an average of 244.2 inhabitants per square mile, and only twenty-third in its proportion of urban land area at just 5.28 percent (U.S. Census Bureau 2010). What all of this means is that, in addition to being the most biologically diverse state, California has the largest, most diverse, and most urban human population. It also means that the history of California's human population, since the time of European colonization, has been largely a tale of urban growth (see also Chapter 39, "Urban Ecosystems"). The remainder of this section examines the patterns and processes in California's history that created its contemporary population geography through a series of periods spanning from the beginning of the Mission era in 1769 to the present.

Mission and Rancho Eras, 1769–1848

The most important population trend during the Spanish mission and Mexican rancho eras was the decline of California's Native American population. Anthropologists estimate that at least 350,000 diverse indigenous people lived in what is now California at the beginning of the Mission era (Chapter 10, "Indigenous California"). Between 1769 and 1834, however, the number of Native Americans living near the coast from San Diego to Sonoma declined by a catastrophic 75 percent. By 1855 there were only around fifty thousand indigenous people left in California, and their population declined further to as low as twenty-five thousand by 1860. This well-documented demographic calamity resulted from a combination of disease, migration, dispossession, assimilation, and violence (Cook 1976, Hackel 2005). Hispanic priests, soldiers, and settlers established their coastal missions, presidios, ranchos, and pueblos during this period, but their population remained low, probably numbering no more than fourteen thousand at any point. The only surviving contemporary estimate places this number even lower, at five thousand. Most of these immigrants were Europeans of mixed Spanish descent. The ones who remained became known as Californios, with small communities concentrated in the rancho settlements (Haas 1995, Heidenreich 2009).

Ecological changes stemming from European contact were probably well under way by the beginning of the Mission era. During the late eighteenth and early nineteenth centuries, however, this small population of colonizers sparked a social and biological transformation. They introduced and spread new plant and animal species and diseases (see Chapter 13, "Biological Invasions") and brought California into contact with distant powers and economies. According to the historian Alfred Crosby, these processes resulted in the "Europeanization" of North America. As native species, indigenous populations, traditional lifeways, and economic systems declined, New World landscapes increasingly resembled the colonizers' homeland (Crosby 2003, 2004). This process never resulted in a complete transformation, but it did have qualitative consequences in a state whose Mediterranean climates and ecosystems already had much in common with the famil-

TABLE 5.2
Population growth of California's ten largest cities, 1850–2010

1850		1900		1950		2010	
Largest cities	Population	Largest cities	Population	Largest cities	Population	Largest cities	Population
San Francisco	35,000	San Francisco	342,782	Los Angeles	1,970,358	Los Angeles	3,792,621
Sacramento	6,820	Los Angeles	102,479	San Francisco	775,357	San Diego	1,307,402
Placerville and vicinity	5,623	Oakland	66,960	Oakland	384,575	San Jose	945,942
Nevada City	2,683	Sacramento	29,282	San Diego	334,387	San Francisco	805,235
Middle Fork, American River	1,722	San Jose	21,500	Long Beach	250,767	Fresno	494,665
Los Angeles	1,610	San Diego	17,700	Sacramento	137,572	Sacramento	466,488
South Fork, American River	1,386	Stockton	17,506	Berkeley	113,805	Long Beach	462,257
Auburn and vicinity	1,302	Alameda	16,464	Pasadena	104,577	Oakland	390,724
Cosumnes	1,092	Berkeley	13,214	Richmond	99,545	Bakersfield	347,483
Monterey	1,092	Fresno	12,470	Glendale	95,702	Anaheim	336,265
TOTAL POPULATION OF LARGEST CITIES	**58,330**		**640,357**		**4,266,645**		**9,349,082**
Percentage Bay Area	60.0%		72.0%		64.6%		22.9%
Percentage Southern California	2.8%		18.8%		32.2%		63.1%
Percentage elsewhere	37.2%		9.3%		3.2%		14.0%

SOURCE: Minnesota Population Center (2011).

iar Iberian landscapes its colonizers had left behind in the Old World (Alagona et al. 2013).

Early Statehood Era, 1849–1889

Large-scale immigration to California began with the discovery of gold near Sutter's Mill in the western Sierra Nevada foothills in 1848. During the height of the Gold Rush, most immigrants went to mining towns (McEntire 1946). The influx of would-be miners and mining-related commerce also made San Francisco the Pacific Coast's first major urban center, with a population that grew from 1,000 in 1848 to at least 35,000 in 1850 (Figure 5.1). By 1880, San Francisco had 233,959 residents—compared to a population of 282,494 in Oregon, Washington, and Idaho combined—making it the ninth largest city in the country. As late as 1900, the Bay Area accounted for 20 percent of all U.S. residents living west of the continental divide (White 1998, p. 51).

Unlike the Eastern and Midwestern states, California never developed a large and dispersed rural farming population comprising a significant fraction of its total population. Beginning in 1849, population growth in the interior occurred mainly in the Sierra foothills and around the state capitol of Sacramento, which was really an outpost of San Francisco. As early as the 1860s, outmigration from the Sierra Nevada facilitated the growth of agriculture in the Central Valley. Yet most former miners chose to pursue commercial opportunities in the city rather than farming in the country. At the time, the United States was urbanizing and farm employment was declining as a fraction of the labor force. In California, opportunities for families to enter into agriculture were especially scarce. The state lacked much land that could be farmed without sizable investments in dredging or irrigation, it still contained large single-owner parcels derived from the Spanish land grant ranchos, and land speculators and agribusiness firms accumulated vast holdings, shutting many would-be family farmers out of the real estate market (Klein 2012, Igler 2001). Despite the increasing economic importance of agriculture in California, the state thus continued to urbanize.

Progressive Era, 1890–1920

The Progressive era was a period of rapid population growth in California, as in much of the rest of the United States. From 1900 to 1910 alone, California's population increased by 60 percent, or nine hundred thousand residents. Between 1890 and 1920, the state's population nearly tripled in size, reach-

FIGURE 5.1 San Francisco in 1851. Courtesy of the United States Library of Congress.

ing 3.4 million. As before, much of this growth occurred in the San Francisco Bay Area. By 1890, San Francisco's population numbered about three hundred thousand, with the nine Bay Area counties accounting for 45 percent of California's 1.2 million residents (California Department of Finance 2011).

Despite the Bay Area's growth, the geographical center of California's population began to shift southward. In the late nineteenth century, the expansion of citrus and orchard crops drove economic development in Southern California, contributing to the state's booming agricultural industry (Walker 2001). By 1910 Southern California also had become one of the country's most important petroleum-producing regions (Sabin 2004). Boosterism contributed to growth by promoting the area as a favorable climate for Easterners seeking to improve their health, get rich, or if already wealthy, then lead a life of leisure (Gendzel 2008, Culver 2010). Land speculation, the expansion of service industries such as entertainment and tourism, the development of transportation networks, and infrastructure investments that enabled the long-distance importation and storage of water also encouraged coastal Southern California's growth and development.

Interwar Era through World War II, 1920–1950

From 1920 to 1950, California's population growth rate was 3.6 times the national average. The state reached its greatest twentieth-century growth rate in the decade from 1920 to 1930, when its population increased by 65 percent, adding 2.25 million people (Minnesota Population Center 2011). Much of this growth involved migration to California from the Eastern and Midwestern states, as young people moved westward for employment opportunities. The growth of manufacturing, the continued productivity of the Southern California petroleum industry, poverty in Mexico, and the Dust Bowl agricultural crisis in the southern Great Plains all attracted new residents to the state (Gordon 1954, Otterstrom and Earle 2002).

Urban expansion continued throughout this period (Figure 5.2). By 1930, Los Angeles had become the country's fifth largest city—behind New York, Chicago, Detroit, and Philadelphia—with 1,233,561 residents. San Francisco had fallen to a distant second in California, with 637,212 inhabitants, though it remained a center of culture, commerce, industry, and finance. Meanwhile, former satellite towns, such as Long Beach and Oakland, became important cities in their own right, with New Deal–era infrastructure projects in the form of ports, highways, and bridges facilitating their development. The legacy of this growth is still visible today in the extensive neighborhoods of Craftsman-style homes dating from this era.

During the Great Depression, California's rural population grew faster than before. The 1940 census reported that, for the first and only time in the state's history, the percentage of Californians living in rural areas increased, despite a decrease in the percentage living on farms (Gregor 1963). This apparent contradiction resulted from the state's first major wave of suburban growth. Development on the urban fringes continued in subsequent decades, but later censuses erased much of it by remapping the state's metropolitan areas to include its burgeoning suburbs (U.S. Census Bureau 1995).

Postwar Era, 1950–1990

Two patterns, continued growth and SUBURBANIZATION, characterized the postwar era in California's population history (Figure 5.3). In 1950, California's population was 10.59 million; by 1990 it had nearly tripled to 29.76 million. During the same period, the state's largest city, Los Angeles, grew from 1.97 million to 3.46 million residents. The state's second largest city, San Diego, which had just 17,700 residents in 1900, grew from 333,865 in 1950 to 1.11 million in 1990 (California Department of Finance 2011). FERTILITY doubled in California during the postwar BABY BOOM, from 1946 to 1964, but immigration still accounted for significant population

FIGURE 5.2 Los Angeles sprawl. Photo: William Garnett, 1954, courtesy of the J. Paul Getty Museum.

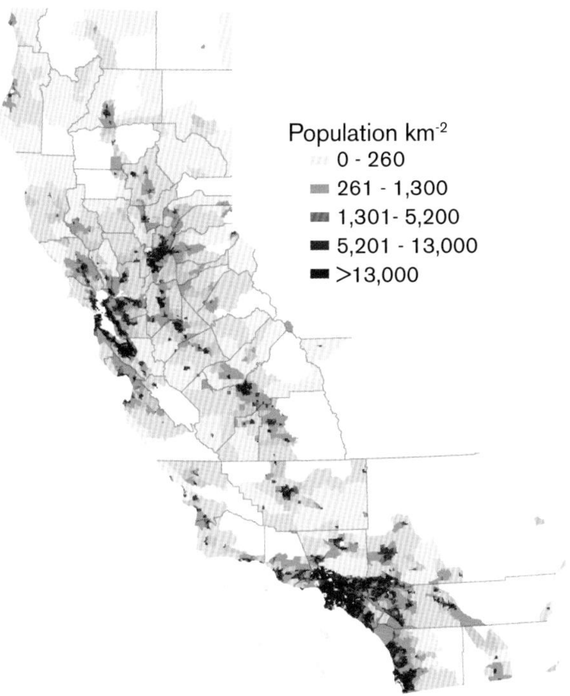

FIGURE 5.3 California population density by 2010 census tract. California is both the most populous and the most urban state. Courtesy of Mike Bostock.

growth. During the 1980s and 1990s, many Californians, particularly young families and retirees, relocated to other parts of the American West, such as Arizona and Colorado, seeking a lower cost of living. But California experienced a smaller "baby boom echo" around 1990, and newcomers continued to flock to the state to take advantage of its educational, lifestyle, and economic opportunities, including employment in the technology, entertainment, aerospace, and other industries (California Department of Finance 2013).

During the postwar era, growth rates in the older urban cores tended to decline, while suburbs and newer cities expanded. For example, in the Bay Area, San Francisco and Oakland grew only moderately, while once-outlying cities, including Fremont and Sunnyvale, grew to several times their wartime populations. By the 1950s, California had become famous for its car-oriented geography and commuter culture. Growth in these formerly outlying areas was not a simple or natural process—it relied on a complex combination of factors, including water policy, transportation planning, real estate speculation, tax structures, and inner-city decay—but its results were unmistakable (Wolch et al. 2004). As early as 1990, San Jose, a once sleepy suburb, had surpassed San Francisco in population; San Jose is now the state's third and the country's tenth largest municipality, with nearly one million residents.

This pattern of growth, in which formerly secondary cities rise to the status of important urban centers, has continued to the present. In Southern California, Anaheim grew to 22 times its 1950 population by 2010, making it the state's tenth largest city (California Department of Finance 2011). Meanwhile, Sacramento more than tripled its population, Fresno grew more than fivefold, and Bakersfield ballooned to nine times its former size. Between 2000 and 2010, the Orange County city of Irvine grew at an average annual rate of 4.8 percent; by 2012 it was the fastest growing city in California and the eighth fastest growing municipality in the country, with 230,000 residents. Beginning in the 1970s, smaller cities and rural communities also began to experience significant growth, placing pressure on unprepared local governments and meager public services. The population of Nevada County, in the Sierra Nevada northeast of Sacramento, boomed during the Gold Rush, but its population declined and then stabilized for a century. In 1960 it had about twenty thousand residents, roughly the same number as in 1860. By 1990 an influx of EXURBAN refugees and retirees had caused the population to more than quintuple (Duane 1999, Walker and Fortmann 2003).

This does not mean that the state's older city centers remained static. By 1990, after a generation of white flight and urban decay, redevelopment projects had begun in central business districts and industrial areas around the state. In other areas, CHAIN MIGRATION created bustling neighborhoods of recent immigrants in communities defined by language, culture, and country of origin.

One consequence of these processes is that California's older cities have increased their population densities (see Figure 5.3). For example, although Los Angeles is often cast as the archetype of suburban SPRAWL, as of 2013 the Los Angeles–Long Beach–Anaheim metropolitan area was the most densely populated urban region in the United States, with almost 7,000 people per square mile. The San Francisco–Oakland and San Jose metropolitan areas were the country's second and third most densely populated. New York–Newark was fifth, with 5,319 residents per square mile (U.S. Census Bureau 2012b, Lotchin 2008). Seen in this way, the low-rise urban form of California cities such as Los Angeles, which is probably best described as "dense sprawl," is less the result of misguided planning than it is a function of their sheer size, rapid growth, physical geography, and relative youth. In the coming years, this pattern of densification will likely continue, particularly in Los Angeles, where city planners and construction firms are preparing for a boom in high-rise development.

Current Era, 1990–present

Since 1990, California's population has continued to grow, reaching more than thirty-eight million by 2013. Indeed, the

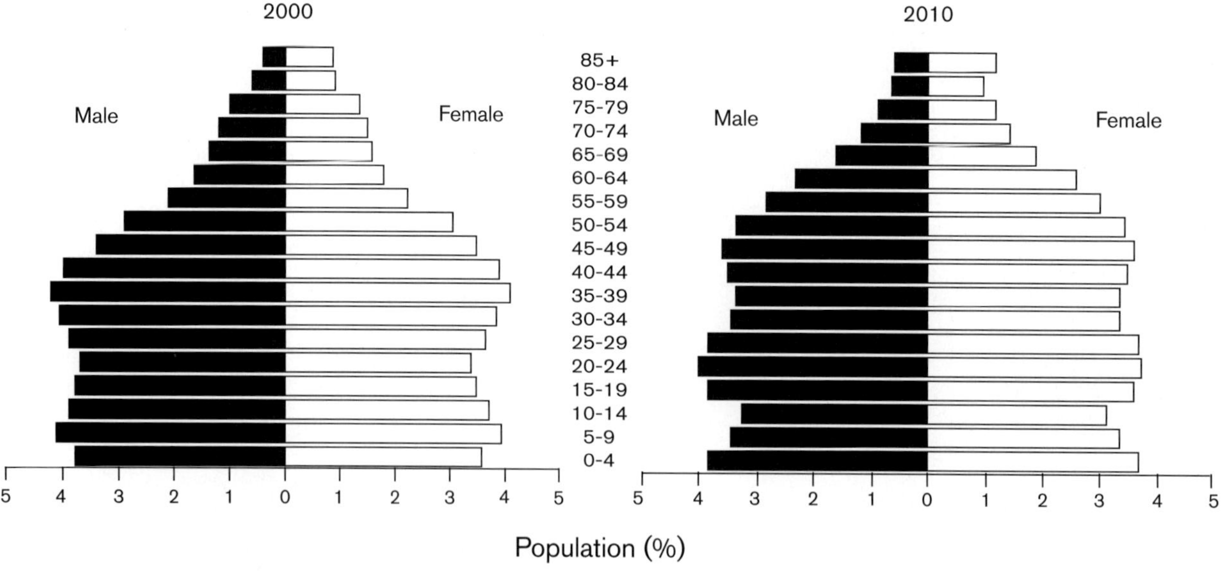

FIGURE 5.4 California population pyramids, 2000 and 2010. Two baby booms are visible in the state's age distribution, and overall California's population is growing older. Source: U.S. Census Bureau 2005.

total number of residents added during the 2000s exceeded the number added during the 1920s, when California experienced its highest growth rate (Minnesota Population Center 2011). Over the past two decades, however, the state's rate of growth has declined—relative to both its historical rate and the national average—and demographers agree that it will decline even further in the years to come (Pitkin and Myers 2012).

This drop in California's growth rate stems from reductions in both fertility and immigration. Birth rates have declined in every major racial and ethic group, so that by 2013 the average rate stood at just 1.94 children per woman, well below the REPLACEMENT LEVEL of around 2.1. In 1970 children under the age of eighteen comprised 33 percent of California's population, but by 2030 that number is projected to drop to 21 percent (Myers 2013) (Figure 5.4). Although they represent a smaller percentage of the state's population than in previous eras, their generation is distinguished by its extraordinary diversity, comprised of 51.2 percent Hispanic or Latino, 27.4 percent non-Hispanic whites, 10.7 percent Asian or Pacific Islanders, 5.6 percent African Americans, and 5.1 percent coming from other ethnic or racial groups.

Since the mid-twentieth century, California has served as the main gateway for immigrants coming to the United States. In 1970 only 4.6 percent of U.S. residents were foreign born; by 2009 the proportion had increased to 12.5 percent, or one-eighth of the population. By contrast, in 2011 about 27 percent of Californians were foreign born. Around 53 percent of the immigrants residing in California today came from Latin America. Between 2007 and 2011, however, the same sized majority, about 53 percent, hailed from Asia. Today, Mexico, the Philippines, and China are the leading sources of California's new immigrants (Johnson and Mejia 2013). Immigration to the state has declined since 1990, however, and projections suggest that the percentage of foreign-born residents will remain relatively stable over the next few decades.

Much remains uncertain about the future of California's population. What we do know is that over the next few decades, the state will grow considerably, probably reaching fifty million before the middle of the century even as its growth rate continues to decline. The state's population will remain overwhelmingly urban, although growth rates in the interior areas will probably outpace rates in the coastal CONURBATIONS (Public Policy Institute of California 2013). Its proportion of immigrants will remain steady, while its percentage of residents born in California will continue to rise. Finally, the proportion of children will decline as the population ages. These demographic processes, some of which are unprecedented in the state's history, will have social and economic consequences affecting land use and the environment in California in numerous complex ways.

Land Use

This section explores the land use histories of six California regions: coastlines, deserts, hardwood rangelands, mountains, northwest forests, and agricultural valleys. Each of these regions has experienced unique events and processes, but some of their stories overlap or follow similar trajectories and all are part of California's broader environmental history.

Coastlines

Californians have subjected their coastlines to an extraordinarily diverse array of uses. Although the state is known worldwide for its beautiful and diverse coast, this thin strip where land and water meet is perhaps the most intensively used and extensively altered of its major biophysical regions. Prior to European colonization, indigenous populations clustered near the coastline to access its diverse and productive resources. Thousands of archaeological sites attest to the state's pre-European population geography and provide a rich record of this long history of human occupation. Until recently, most researchers believed that despite their long-term presence, Native Americans did not significantly change their coastal or marine environments. Yet recent research, in areas such as the northern Channel Islands, suggests that fishing, marine mammal hunting, and shellfish collecting

FIGURE 5.5 Aerial photographs of Marina del Rey, Los Angeles County, in 1938 and 1968. Over three decades the area was converted from an agricultural landscape at the mouth of Ballona Creek into a densely populated suburban area with an extensive harbor complex. Courtesy of the Map & Imagery Laboratory at the University of California, Santa Barbara.

may have altered animal populations and predator-prey relationships, causing qualitative, if temporary, shifts in ecosystem dynamics (Rick et al. 2008).

Scholars have often described California's nineteenth-century economic history as a progression from animal to mineral to vegetable. Indeed, the state's first "gold rush" was really a fur rush. The California sea otter harvest began in earnest shortly after 1800, when ships from around the world arrived to exploit this most valuable (by weight) of North American commodities (Ogden 1975). By 1830 the hunt was all but finished, and by 1900 most naturalists believed that sea otters had gone extinct in the state's waters. It was not until the 1930s that the animals began appearing again in small numbers off the California coast. Commercial salmon fishing picked up after the decline of the otter harvest, getting its start in the San Francisco Bay Delta in the 1850s. After 1900 salmon fishing moved offshore, which resulted in the establishment of a chain of fishing communities along the California coast (Yoshiyama et al. 1998).

During the first two decades of the twentieth century, interests representing the tourism and resource extraction industries began their long history of conflict along the California coast. Guests at Monterey's luxurious Del Monte Hotel traveled there to enjoy the scenery and ocean breezes, but instead they often discovered putrid smells wafting in from the nearby canneries and ramshackle neighborhoods populated by the sardine industry's immigrant laborers and their families (Chiang 2008). The tourism and resource extraction industries also clashed in Santa Barbara, where local residents fought against oil drilling when that community emerged as an early site in Southern California's petroleum boom (Sabin 2004).

URBANIZATION began along the California coast in the mid-nineteenth century with the development of ports first at San Francisco and later at Oakland, which became the terminus of the Transcontinental Railroad in 1868 (White 1991). Manufacturing and shipping hubs thrived along the shore of San Francisco Bay during the growth years of the 1920s and again during World War II. In Southern California the Los Angeles city center emerged fifteen miles from the nearest coastline, partly due to the availability of fresh water in that area, but seaside development began at the nearby town of Santa Monica as early as the 1870s. In 1904 the author, CONSERVATIONIST, land developer, and all-around Renaissance man Abbot Kinney began the construction of Venice-by-the-Sea, now known as Venice Beach, which soon became one of Los Angeles County's most popular tourist attractions (Deverell and Hise 2010).

Between 1945 and 1965, major reclamation, infrastructure, and development projects took place along several stretches of the California coast. Deep-water ports expanded in cities such as Long Beach and San Diego, fueling economic development. The state's coastal strip had long served as a corridor for boulevards and railroads, but the Federal Aid Highway Act of 1956 greatly increased the size and quality of California's transportation system, converting bumpy state roads into modern interstate highways, including stretches of the 101 and 5 freeways paralleling the Southern California coast. Ambitious development projects also occurred at Mission Bay in San Diego County and Marina del Rey in Los Angeles County (Figure 5.5), both occupying the former sites of coastal wetlands.

In 1972, California voters, partly in response to the 1969 Santa Barbara oil spill and a plan for a massive new development on the Sonoma County coast, passed Proposition 20, creating a California Coastal Commission with temporary authority to review and regulate development (Pincetl 1999). The California Coastal Act of 1976 further defined the role and authority of the commission and made it a permanent state agency. Today, the Coastal Commission is charged with protecting the natural and cultural resources of the California coast by promoting pubic access and habitat conservation, sustaining agriculture, fisheries, scenery, and water quality, regulating industrial sites from oil refineries to power plants and ports, and reviewing proposals for infrastructure projects such as the construction of harbors, seawalls, and breakwaters. The commission is known for a cautious, conservation-oriented approach that has earned it high marks from environmental groups. Yet its work has often proven controversial, especially among landowners who protest restrictions on the development of valuable real estate (Los Angeles Times 2013).

Despite the commission's work, California has lost large portions of its most diverse and productive seaside habitats, including the coastal dune, strand, lagoon, and wetland systems that provide crucial habitat for numerous fish and wildlife species. Development has, however, spared some areas. Marine Corps Base Camp Pendleton in San Diego County and Vandenberg Air Force Base in Santa Barbara County contain large areas of relatively undisturbed habitat with little or no public access. A string of state and national parks and other nature reserves—including jewels such as Montana de Oro State Park in San Luis Obispo County, the Big Sur State Parks in Monterey County, the Redwood State and National Parks complex near the Oregon border, and the Bureau of Land Management's Kings Range National Conservation Area, also known as the Lost Coast—provide superb examples of undeveloped California coastlines.

Habitat conservation has also moved offshore. In 1999 the California Legislature passed the landmark Marine Life Protection Act, which required the state's Department of Fish and Game to redesign, and in many cases greatly expand, its system of marine PROTECTED AREAS. In the years since, the department, along with its many partners and citizen participants, has developed plans for increasing conservation through the creation of a network of state marine reserves, parks, conservation areas, and recreational management areas designed to protect threatened species, restore degraded systems, and increase the productivity of commercial and sport fisheries (California Department of Fish and Wildlife 2013).

Deserts

Relatively few people live in California's arid southeastern quarter, and to casual observers it can appear empty or even timeless. Yet it has a long and complex history, and human activities—from ranching and mining to military training, tourism, and conservation—have profoundly shaped the landscape that exists there today (Pavlik 2008). Indeed, perhaps more than any other region of the state, the legacies of this history remain visible, for those who are willing to look, in the sparse desert environment (Hunter et al. 2003).

The first broad category of land use that has shaped California's deserts is commodity production. During the second half of the nineteenth century, mining for gold, silver, borax, and other minerals spread throughout the region. These excavations caused significant local damage, but harm to the desert environment was usually limited to sites in and around the mines and settlements (Webb and Newman 1982). Mining in the California desert has waxed and waned over the years in response to commodity prices; activity declined during the 1990s, for example, but bounced back somewhat during the 2000s along with increases in the price of gold and other precious metals.

Ranching also expanded during the late nineteenth century. Desert rangelands probably never produced enough forage for a sustainable livestock industry, but optimistic cattlemen pressed forward nonetheless (Lovich and Bainbridge 1999). They overstocked the land during wet years and watched their herds starve during frequent dry periods (Hereford et al. 2004). Grazing peaked on California desert lands during the 1920s, and since the 1990s, it has continued to decline, reaching the lowest levels for 150 years in many areas. Much of the California desert region's nonlivestock farm production occurs in the Imperial Valley, an area discussed in the agricultural valleys section later in this chapter.

A second category of land use, infrastructure, makes commodity production and other land uses possible in California's deserts. Infrastructure development, often in the form of linear corridors, began with access roads for mines and ranches but then grew dramatically with the construction of railroads, canals, pipelines, and highways. The LA Aqueduct and All-American Canal, both built in the early twentieth century, supply water for coastal cities and Imperial Valley farms. The completion of Route 66 during the 1930s and a web of interstate highways during the 1950s provided access to the region's new national and state parks, which constructed their own scenic byways, trails, and campgrounds. Infrastructure development reached a new level on the military facilities that expanded and proliferated during World War II. The Department of Defense now operates nine major bases and several smaller installations throughout the California desert, making it one of the country's most important regions for military training. The economies of many desert towns, such as Barstow and Ridgecrest, rely on defense-related activities and personnel.

The largest urban areas in the California desert are the Lancaster-Palmdale area in Los Angeles County, the Apple Valley–Victorville area in San Bernardino County, and the Coachella Valley, including such cities as Palm Springs and Indio, in Riverside County. Although most of the Mojave Desert lies in California, the Mojave's largest conurbation, by far, is the Las Vegas metropolitan area in Clark County, Nevada, with around two million residents. Unlike the California desert's more remote outposts, its major cities serve primarily as exurban vacation, retirement, and bedroom communities with close economic ties to the coastal Southern California megalopolis.

Tourism and recreation in the California desert region commenced with the development of Palm Springs as a vacation resort in the early twentieth century. The era of desert parks began in the 1930s with the establishment of Death Valley and Joshua Tree National Monuments as well as Anza Borrego, the country's largest state park. Recreational use of the California desert increased dramatically during the early 1970s, particularly on the vast areas administered by the Bureau of Land Management (BLM). The BLM lacked the statutory authority to administer these lands until Congress passed the Federal Land Policy and Management Act in 1976, which provided the bureau with a multiple-use, sustained-yield mandate similar to that of the U.S. Forest Service. In 1980 the Department of the Interior approved the BLM's California Desert Conservation Area Plan, which still serves as the guiding document for land and resource management in this 10 million hectare region (Alagona and Smith 2012).

The California desert, particularly the Mojave portion, is now one of the most "protected" areas in the United States in terms of parks, WILDERNESS areas, and other nature reserves. Much of this is due to the California Desert Protection Act of 1994, which expanded Death Valley and Joshua Tree National Monuments and upgraded both to national park status, transferred the East Mojave Scenic Area from the BLM to the National Park Service and renamed it the Mojave National Preserve, and set aside seventy-one new wilderness areas encompassing 1.5 million hectares (Wheat 1999, Nystrom 2003). A series of other federal laws, purchases, partnerships, and land swaps in the years since have created hundreds of thousands of hectares of new reserves.

Yet "protection" is a relative term. Large areas of the California desert are now designated as parks and nature reserves, but debates about conservation, recreation, and land use continue. The region's infamous battles over off-road vehicles, which began in the 1970s, have led to increased restrictions but also the allocation of special sites set aside for this purpose (Darlington 1996). Residential and commercial development in places such as the Coachella Valley boomed from the 1980s through the early 2000s, leading to conflicts over zoning, water, and habitat conservation for the region's many rare, endemic, and endangered species. Since 2008, renewable energy development, in the form of utility-scale wind and solar facilities, has also emerged as a major source of strife among local residents, conservationists, public officials, entrepreneurs, and indigenous communities (Alagona and Smith 2012). Finally, climate change poses considerable threats to fragile ecosystems and imperiled species—including those that exist in parks and nature reserves (see also Chapter 30, "Deserts").

Hardwood Rangelands

The hardwood rangeland—California's bucolic countryside of rolling grasslands, oak savannas, and mixed oak-evergreen woodlands—is among the state's most familiar and beloved rural landscapes (see also Chapter 23, "Grasslands," and Chapter 25, "Oak Woodlands"). The history of this region is best understood as a series of phases in which owners and managers subjected the land to new use regimes, sometimes with profound social and ecological consequences. Cultural traditions, agricultural economics, and conservation philosophies have all influenced this history, but at its core this is a story about changing modes and conceptions of productivity.

By the beginning of the nineteenth century, Spanish military and religious colonists had established a chain of missions, presidios, pueblos, and ranchos in hardwood rangelands from San Diego to Sonoma. Their initial goals were to find riches, secure their country's northern frontier in the New World, and convert the native people, but they soon established a livestock empire in the hardwood rangelands. By the 1820s, California's twenty-one missions had claimed about 6.9 million hectares of land, on which they grazed around three hundred thousand sheep and four hundred thousand head of cattle (Alagona et al. 2013). During the period between Mexican independence in 1821 and the Treaty of Guadalupe Hidalgo, which ended the Mexican-American War in 1848, the Mexican government sought to grow the population of Alta California to secure its northern province against Russian, British, and American economic exploitation and territorial ambitions. By the time the war began in 1846, however, there were still only about 110,000 people living in the region, just a small fraction of whom were Mexican citizens of predominantly Spanish descent.

These naturalized Hispanic settlers, known as Californios, enjoyed their status as landed gentry for little more than a single human lifetime. In the decades after the Gold Rush, Anglo immigrants and interlopers used the American court system to usurp Californio lands and supplant the rancho culture and economy. Once in control, they replaced the rancho system with a capitalist livestock market based on their belief in unlimited rangeland resources. By the 1860s, industrial cattle corporations had acquired vast holdings in the Great Central Valley and neighboring foothills (Igler 2001). The floods and droughts of that decade took a major toll on the industry, however, and over the next four decades the cattlemen saw their access to prime seasonal pastures increasingly restricted by barbed wire protecting valley farms and federal rangers guarding mountain forest reserves. By 1900 most cattlemen had lost their ability to engage in transhumant livestock cultivation. They settled in the hardwood rangelands, where they sought to increase productivity by clearing brush to make way for grasslands and removing trees they thought blocked sunlight and reduced soil moisture. Yet intensive, year-round grazing in these seasonally arid landscapes proved risky. Overstocked cattle denuded the vegetation during dry years, and the once widely held belief in limitless rangeland resources gave way to a sense of inevitable decline (Burcham 1981).

Beginning around 1920, the first generation of professional range managers argued that rangeland resources were neither infinite nor doomed; ranchers could maintain the long-term productivity of their operations through a modest program of conservation and restoration. Arthur Sampson, the first professor of range management at the University of California, encouraged ranchers to observe sustainable stocking levels, adopt efficient grazing rotation schedules, protect water sources, and preserve moderate canopy cover for shelter and shade (Sampson 1923). By the 1930s, Sampson had helped organize the ranchers into cooperative units to promote conservation activities that would ensure the viability of their industry.

After World War II, improvement replaced restoration as the conservation goal. A new generation of scientists and managers sought to convert unruly rangelands into efficient machines that would produce beef and wool for a booming population. They received support from agribusiness corporations, industry associations, and state and federal governments in the form of subsidies and other programs. During this era of "big conservation," experts and officials recommended the increased use of fertilizers and heavy machinery, the widespread application of chemical pesticides, and the aggressive control of predators that threatened livestock. They also convinced many ranchers that productivity would increase if the ranchers removed large numbers of the oak trees on their properties. Between 1951 and 1973, range improvement programs resulted in the clearance of approximately 365,000 hectares, or 10 percent, of the state's oak woodlands (Alagona 2008).

Beginning in the 1970s, some scientists and environmentalists started to question these approaches to hardwood range management, as well as the philosophy of maximum livestock productivity on which they were based. This new group argued that rangelands served multiple functions beyond just livestock production, including contributing to watershed, wildlife, scenic, open space, and recreational values (Standiford and Howitt 1993). In particular, they questioned the assumption that removing oak trees would increase productivity, since the trees provided nutrients to the soil through leaf litter and shade during the long, dry summer. These opposing views fueled a series of conflicts over land use, conservation, and environmental regulation—including widespread efforts to protect the remaining oak woodlands. By the mid-1980s scientists and managers had responded with new research, education, and outreach programs dedicated to developing a more holistic, integrated approach to hardwood range management (see also Chapter 37, "Range Ecosystems").

The 1990s and 2000s was a period of tremendous social and ecological change in the hardwood rangelands (Huntsinger et al. 2010). The growth of the wine grape industry resulted in the conversion of large areas of rangelands to intensive agriculture. Suburban and exurban development continued to encroach on once-rural communities. This led to the clearing of thousands of hectares of woodlands, while large oaks became isolated as old trophy trees in newly developed neighborhoods. Population growth produced changes in the demographic composition of some hardwood rangeland areas, increases in property values and taxes, and shifts away from livestock production on large parcels toward subdivision and residential development. Beginning in the early 2000s, the spread of sudden oak death, a disease caused by the pathogen *Phytophthora ramorum*, caused considerable damage in California and Oregon (see Chapter 13, "Biological Invasions"). During the economic downturn of the late 2000s, the State of California slashed its budgets for education and conservation programs, including those that supported hardwood range research, education, and management. Land conversions also declined during this period. Yet this decrease may prove to be a temporary consequence of the Great Recession as construction returns to California's oak-dominated landscapes, which still rank among the most attractive in the state for residential development.

Mountains

California is one of the country's most topographically rugged and diverse states. Its major mountain chains—the Sierra Nevada, Coast Ranges, Transverse Ranges, and Cascades—form an enormous ring around the Great Central Valley, profoundly shaping the state's climate and ecology as well as its economy and population geography. Today, Californians tend to think of these mountains as sanctuaries of nature, conjuring up images of spectacular valleys, dramatic waterfalls, solitary volcanoes, peaceful meadows, rushing rivers, and jagged granite peaks all nestled within the welcoming boundaries of national parks and forests. Despite their unspoiled appearance, however, California's mountains have a long record of intensive human use, including some of the first sites of industrial resource extraction on the Pacific Coast of North America—a history that is increasingly hidden among the sweeping vistas and verdant vegetation.

Few explorers or settlers visited the state's mountains before the 1840s. Between 1848 and 1884, however, mining emerged as the dominant form of land use. By 1858 tens of thousands of prospectors had extracted $550 million of gold from the Sierra Nevada and other California mountain ranges. Yet this initial stage had a comparatively minor effect on the state's landscapes and ecosystems, since most prospectors worked alone or in small syndicates and used simple technologies like pans or short sluices. After 1858 gold was harder to find, but the industry compensated by becoming more fully capitalized, with small-scale, low-technology operations giving way to large firms capable of mobilizing greater resources and introducing new extraction methods. Chief among the new methods introduced by firms during the 1850s was hydraulic mining, which used pressurized water, delivered to mining sites through elaborate flume systems, to erode hillsides and liberate the underlying minerals from their surrounding rock and soil. From 1858 to 1874, firms extracted $400 million in gold from California's mountains. By 1883 hydraulic mining operations had impounded about 215 million cubic meters of water, about half the current capacity of Hetch Hetchy Reservoir in Yosemite National Park (Isenberg 2005).

The debris that flowed from these denuded slopes clogged mountain streams, decimating fisheries, polluting the water, and causing a series of winter floods and mud flows that reached all the way to Central Valley farms and cities, including the state capitol of Sacramento (Isenberg 2005, Garone 2011). Downstream farmers and property owners responded by taking the mining companies to court. This legal battle culminated in 1884, when Justice Lorenzo Sawyer, of the Ninth Circuit Court of the United States in San Francisco, handed down his famous *Woodruff v. North Bloomfield Mining and Gravel Company* decision. The Sawyer decision, as it is now known, effectively ended hydraulic mining in the state by prohibiting North Bloomfield and other firms from dumping mining debris into mountain rivers with the knowledge that doing so would cause downstream property damage. More broadly, the Sawyer decision signaled a transition from mining to agriculture as a driver of the state's economy and led to the further depopulation of California's mining boomtowns.

One of the most crucial resources for gold miners, in addition to labor and water, was mercury, also known as quicksilver, which the miners used to separate the gold from its ore. Between 1850 and 1981, miners extracted about 100 million kilograms of mercury from the state's Coast Ranges, around 12 million kilograms of which was used for California gold mining, mainly in the Sierra Nevada and Klamath-Trinity Mountains (Alpers and Hunerlach 2000). Much of this highly toxic heavy metal filtered into the water and soil downstream from the gold mining sites, where it remains in significant quantities today (Isenberg 2005, Beesley 2004). The State of California still maintains advisory warnings for fish in more than a dozen major water-bodies, including the San Francisco Bay Delta, containing potentially dangerous levels of methylmercury derived from historic mining activities (State of California 2003) (see Chapter 19, "Estuaries: Life on the Edge").

Before its decline in the 1880s, the mining industry catalyzed the growth of several other related industries in California's mountains, including logging (Sackman 2008) (see Chapter 36, "Forestry"). In the nineteenth century, wood was both the primary building material and a source of fuel. A large timber industry thus developed to exploit the Sierra Nevada's sugar pine and sequoia forests. Initially, Sierra Nevada logging was extremely profitable, and as many as 150 mills may have operated there during in the mid-nineteenth century. By the 1890s, however, more than 90 percent of the mills had closed due to the lack of an accessible supply, a decline in demand from local mines, competition from northwest forest timber operations, and other factors (Isenberg 2005, Brechin 2006, Beesley 2004). The exact extent of deforestation is impossible to determine, but in 1886 the California Board of Forestry estimated that one-third of the Sierra Nevada's timber already had been harvested, and U.S. Geological Survey reports from 1900 and 1902 suggest that up to 90 percent of the timber near the large mining sites was gone (Beesley 2004).

Californians began expressing concern about depleted forests and polluted waterways in the Sierra Nevada as early as the 1850s. In 1864 the federal government transferred 8,000 hectares of public land, including Yosemite Valley and the Mariposa Grove of Giant Sequoias, to California as a nature reserve for conservation and recreation (Beesley 2004). Poor funding and management conflicts led the federal govern-

FIGURE 5.6 Photographs of Howland Flat in Plumas County, taken in 1880 and 1993, show a California mountain region transformed by land use change (Gruell 2001). Between 1849 and 1890, logging and fires eliminated most of the area's forest cover. By 1993 cessation of logging and fire suppression resulted in the establishment of verdant—and highly flammable—new forests. Photos courtesy of George Gruell and Mountain Press.

ment to take back control of these sites in 1906 (Sawyer 2006). By the end of the nineteenth century, Yosemite and Sequoia/Kings Canyon National Parks had become major tourist destinations, with around ten thousand visitors annually, requiring considerable investment in services and infrastructure.

As early as the 1870s, some observers argued that public ownership alone would not prevent the degradation of park resources and that a program of active conservation would be necessary to maintain these sites in perpetuity (Beesley 2004). The establishment of the U.S. National Park Service in 1916 signaled Congress's willingness to support the institutionalization and professionalization of federal park conservation efforts. It was not until the 1930s, however, that the NPS began to develop a scientifically grounded research and management program, which initially was based on the campus of the University of California in Berkeley. Many of these programs were discontinued during World War II, and in the immediate postwar era of the 1950s and 1960s the NPS focused more on building infrastructure to accommodate tourists than protecting park resources. In the decades since, California's national parks, like parks nationwide, have continued to struggle to balance their dual mandates of use and preservation (Sellars 2009).

Beginning in the 1890s, large areas of California's mountains became federal forest reserves and then national forests after the establishment of the U.S. Forest Service in 1906. Like the national parks, the national forests have a complicated history. National forests operate under a multiple-use, sustained-yield mandate, which means that they host extractive uses as well as recreation and conservation. The balance among these uses varies from place to place and has changed over time. During the early twentieth century, federal foresters sought to restore degraded landscapes and adopted a deliberate, conservation-oriented approach to resource extraction. Timber harvest on national forests increased dramatically over time, however, from less than 1.2 million cubic meters nationwide in the late 1930s, to a high of nearly 33 million cubic meters in the late 1980s, before declining again to less than 5 million cubic meters in the early 2000s (Bosworth and Brown 2007).

One of the most important legacies of public land management in California's mountains involves the region's long history of fire suppression. During the nineteenth century, sheepherders set fires to clear vegetation and stimulate forage growth, often following age-old patterns of seasonal ignitions established by the region's indigenous peoples. But mining operations and railroads sparked dozens of unintended and uncontrolled fires that ravaged ancient groves, devastated watersheds, and left moonscapes in the place of forests. State and federal officials sought to curtail this damage by prosecuting arsonists, launching public education programs, and aggressively attacking fires once they began. These efforts succeeded in reducing fire damage, and today green forests have returned to many areas. These new forests differ, however, from past forests in their structure and composition, with younger, more flammable trees and understory bushes clumped more closely together. The result is that forests, in large parts of the Sierra Nevada and elsewhere, now appear extremely lush by historical standards (Figure 5.6), but they have become so stocked with woody fuel that they are more flammable—and more dangerous—than at any time in recorded history (Sugihara 2006, Gruell 2001).

Private recreational development also has shaped California's mountain landscapes. Resorts emerged around Lake Tahoe by the 1920s and in Southern California and the eastern Sierra Nevada in the 1940s (Loeffler 2006). Today, many of these communities are struggling to maintain their status as attractive vacation destinations, with development pressures and climate change threatening to diminish the scenic beauty and recreational opportunities that constitute their economic lifeblood. Public and private organizations around Lake Tahoe are working to maintain the water quality responsible for the lake's legendary clarity, while residents in the communities of Arrowhead, Big Bear, and June Lake have found themselves depending on increasingly sporadic snowfalls to entice both winter and summer visitors.

Current land use in California's mountains includes a complex mix of conservation, recreation, resource extraction, and residential and commercial development. All of these activities require extensive infrastructure networks, and in many areas these networks are among the most visible expressions of contemporary land use. From highways and power lines to aqueducts and ski lifts, California's mountain landscapes host a wide variety of infrastructure nodes, links, facilities, and corridors. Water is the most important natural resource that comes from California's mountain ranges, and water capture and delivery structures, including dams and reservoirs, remain divisive symbols of competing political agendas, contrasting cultural values, and ecological change. Yet they also remind us that California's mountains, despite being relatively remote and thinly populated, remain intimately connected to the state's economy and population.

Northwest Forest

The northwest forest, which begins in central California with a few patchy groves of low-elevation conifers in San Luis Obispo County and reaches its greatest development on the windward slopes of the Coast Ranges north of the San Francisco Bay Area, is defined by its trees. Although this region contains a great diversity of tree species, one stands out among the rest. Reaching more than 115 meters and living more than fifteen hundred years, coast redwoods, which dominate the most productive forests in this region, are the tallest trees on Earth and among the most beautiful. When mature, a single individual can contain 95–235 cubic meters of high-quality timber, making the redwood California's most valuable tree species. This dichotomy—trees as ecological monuments versus valuable commodities—has shaped the land use history of California's northwest forests for more than 150 years (see also Chapter 26, "Coast Redwood Forests").

Several industries have exploited California's northwest forests since the nineteenth century—including fishing, mining, farming, and ranching—but logging began early and has long dominated land use in the region. Spanish settlers harvested redwood lumber for missions starting in 1773, and Russian traders and settlers began felling redwoods after 1809. Timber harvests increased even before 1849, but the Gold Rush diverted most able-bodied men from lumbering in the northwest to mining in the Sierra Nevada, and early timber operations failed to attract the labor necessary to fell, transport, and mill the region's giant trees. In the 1850s, most lumbering in California occurred in the Sierra Nevada, but harvesting also took place on the hills and mountains in and around the San Francisco Bay Area. Redwood logging in more remote areas took off in the 1870s, as loggers depleted the sugar pines of the Sierra Nevada and railroads increased access to new stands and markets (Isenberg 2005, Palais 1974, Sawyer 2006).

During the mid-nineteenth century, the federal, state, and local governments helped open up the northwest forest for private timber harvests. In 1858, the United States government placed 202,000 hectares of prime Humboldt County timberland up for sale, and the Stone and Timber Act of 1878 extended the transfer of forests on the public domain to private industry for a fee of just \$6.18 ha^{-1} (\$2.50/acre), the equivalent of about \$148.26 ha^{-1} (\$60/acre) in 2012 dollars. Timber companies also took advantage of the Homestead Act of 1862, which Congress passed as a way to transfer public land to family farmers, by having their employees stake claims that the companies, which controlled the labor and machinery to clear the land, would then purchase outright or acquire the permission to log, at a bargain price.

Timber firms soon developed new technologies and factory-style labor processes to increase their efficiency and profits. In the 1850s, logging was seasonal and labor intensive. It relied on oxen and waterpower, and the immense size of the redwoods actually hindered the harvest. In the 1860s, mills began using steam-powered circular saws to cut down the mighty redwoods at an unprecedented pace. In 1868 sixteen mills in Mendocino County harvested 113,000 cubic meters of timber, while ten mills in Humboldt County cut 59,000 cubic meters. By 1874, Mendocino and Humboldt operations together were felling an average of 260,000 cubic meters annually (Isenberg 2005). In the 1880s, timber firms replaced animal and water power with the mechanical winched "donkey engine," which allowed them to skid trees to landing areas where the logs could be transferred for further shipment and processing (Rajala 2011).

These new techniques and technologies increased efficiency so rapidly that the industry produced redwood lumber faster than available markets could consume it. Profit margins narrowed, and during the depression of 1873 the price for 300 meters of redwood lumber plummeted from \$18 to \$11 in San Francisco markets (Isenberg 2005). A timber cartel formed to impose supply restrictions, but once the price began to rise in the 1880s individual mills increased production. Midwestern corporate capital poured into the industry, and these firms greatly increased the capacity of the redwood mills—in some cases even tripling output, and once again flooding the market.

Redwood harvesting in the nineteenth century was not only aggressive—it was also wasteful. Up to 20 percent of the redwoods felled shattered when they hit the ground, and most of these were abandoned on the forest floor (Palais 1974). According to one estimate, in 1850 California's redwood forest contained approximately 78 million cubic meters of timber. By 1890—without accounting for sawdust, scrap, mill fuel, or shattered logs—the northwest forest timber industry had brought at least 28 million cubic meters to market (Isenberg 2005). This represented an enormous amount of inexpensive building material as well as a tremendous disturbance to the region's terrestrial and aquatic ecosystems (Figure 5.7).

Industrial logging left an even greater mark on the northwest forest after World War II. Previously, loggers had selected only the best trees in a given area, but better road access and the use of tractors, among other factors, helped facilitate the transition to clearcutting (Sawyer 2006). Tractors also disrupted the soil, encouraging the growth of less valuable hardwoods, which necessitated the use of herbicides to control these so-called weed species. Postwar logging in California's four North Coast counties (Sonoma, Mendocino, Humboldt, and Del Norte) peaked by 1955 at about 7 million cubic meters. In the decades that followed, the depletion of mature timber stocks, as well as competition from abroad, new environmental regulations, and a variety of other economic, ecological, and political factors, led to a gradual decline in northwest forest timber harvests. By 2010 the four North Coast counties were producing less than 700,000 cubic meters of timber per year, about 10 percent of the mid-twentieth-century maximum. Of the 800,000 hectares of coast redwood that existed in 1850, more than 95 percent have been logged at least once (Standiford 2012).

The northwest forest differs from other forested areas of California, such as the Sierra Nevada and the Cascades, in that much of it is still in private ownership. State and federal agencies have shaped markets by selling land and providing access to it, but private owners are responsible for most forest management in the region. Beginning in 1900, with the creation of the Sempervirens Club, private citizens began to push for the preservation of the region's remaining old-growth forests by founding a network of redwood parks for conservation and recreation. In 1901 the state allocated \$250,000 to purchase its first such park, at Big Basin in

FIGURE 5.7 Logging in the northwest forest during the late nineteenth century. Courtesy of the Bancroft Library, University of California, Berkeley.

Santa Cruz County, and in 1908 Congressman William Kent donated a grove in Marin County to the federal government as Muir Woods National Monument (Schrepfer 2003). In 1918 these efforts expanded under the auspices of the Save-The-Redwoods League, which raised money to purchase and fund more parks and led the movement to establish the California State Parks System in 1927. Northwest forest conservation reached a milestone in 1968 with the establishment of Redwood National Park. The park expanded in 1978, and in 1994 it entered into a collaborative management agreement with several nearby state parks (Sawyer 2006, Miles 1967). The combined Redwood National and State Parks now cover 53,800 hectares and account for 45 percent of the remaining uncut redwood.

The 1990s saw yet another period of conflict involving efforts to harvest the few unprotected stands of what, by that time, many environmentalists were calling "ancient forests." These debates resulted in the purchase of new state parklands and allocation of endangered species habitat conservation areas. The timber wars of the 1990s subsided with the passage of the Northwest Forest Plan in 1994, but they never entirely concluded and conflicts occasionally rekindle. Today the northwest forest appears to be entering a new era in which sustainable forestry, tourism, and ecological restoration are becoming major engines of the regional economy.

Agricultural Valleys

Considered together, California's agricultural valleys—including the Sacramento, San Joaquin, Salinas, Imperial, and others—comprise the most intensely farmed nontropical region in the world. Three processes characterize the history of California agriculture: increases in productivity, intensification, and diversification (see also Chapter 38, "Agriculture"). Because California's agricultural regions always have had a small permanent workforce relative to the state's total population, and because the state's agribusiness firms have increasingly produced goods for global markets, these three processes are better understood as the responses of capitalist corporations to macroeconomic trends than from changes in local or regional markets (Walker 2004).

During the Spanish and Mexican periods, agriculture in Alta California included subsistence farming for the mission and pueblo settlements, as well as extensive livestock cultivation on the rancho land grants, as discussed in the hardwood rangelands section earlier in this chapter (Liebman 1983). Modern capitalist production began with the Gold Rush, as Anglo-American settlers introduced new varieties of cattle, sheep, and grains. These efforts were so successful that by 1870 the state's annual farm receipts had surpassed gold production in total revenue, and agriculture employed more workers than the mining industry (Walker 2004). This transition from subsistence to industrial agriculture began with a crop that is nearly absent from the state today: wheat. In the 1850s, agriculture concentrated around San Francisco Bay, but by the 1860s farmers began raising wheat in more remote areas of the Sacramento Valley. By 1890, California had more than 1.6 million hectares sown with wheat and barley, it ranked second in the country for total wheat production with more than 40 million bushels produced annually, and wheat accounted for almost 80 percent of the state's total agricultural revenue. The forty-year wheat boom ended between 1900 and 1910—probably due to a combination of soil depletion, a slump in wheat prices, and the growth of markets for other farm commodities—when production declined by 75 percent and many Sacramento Valley farmers shifted to rice production (Walker 2004).

Between 1890 and 1914, the number of farms in California increased, their average size declined, and the state saw a shift from extensive grain production to the intensive cultivation of fruits and nuts, particularly in the San Joaquin Valley and Southern California. By 1919, California farmers grew more than half of the country's oranges and plums, more than three-quarters of its grapes and figs, and almost all of its apricots, almonds, walnuts, olives, and lemons (Olmstead and Rhode 2003). This shift from grain to specialty crop production continued throughout the twentieth century with the further development of areas such as the Salinas, Imperial, and Napa Valleys. By 1929, California had become the nation's top agricultural state, with more than $1 billion in total farm revenue (U.S. Department of Agriculture 2013). California remains in this position, with more than $16.3 billion in net farm income ($43.5 billion in gross receipts), which is about 13.8 percent of the U.S. total and around $5.5

billion more than the second largest producing state, Iowa. California agriculture differs, however, from other top producing states in its diversity. Whereas most other large farming states produce no more than a dozen significant CASH CROPS, California farmers grow more than two hundred major and another two hundred minor cash crops.

The increasing productivity, intensification, and diversification of California agriculture has resulted from several factors (Olmstead and Rhode 2003). California's valleys contain rich alluvial soils deposited over millennia through runoff from the state's mountain streams, and their Mediterranean climates allow for year-round cultivation in many areas. Improvements in transportation infrastructure, from railroads and ports to the interstate highway system, provided better linkages for once remote California farms to far-flung consumers. Shifts in agricultural markets, such as the growing demand for high-value and value-added goods, from dairy products to olive oil to wine, also has benefited California growers. Farms in the state rank among the most mechanized in the world, with a long history of investments in the heavy machinery necessary for intensive production. California growers also owe their success to a large pool of mobile, foreign-born laborers, mostly of Mexican and Central American descent. Unfortunately, the state's agricultural labor force, which accounts for 27 percent of all U.S. farmworkers, has long suffered under poor working and living conditions. Despite the richness of California's farms, some of the state's agricultural areas—such as the southern San Joaquin Valley, where these problems are at their worst—rank among the poorest places in the United States (Daniel 1981, Cowan 2005).

Perhaps the most important factor in the development of California's modern agricultural economy is its vast water infrastructure, which enables farmers to grow crops year-round despite the state's seasonally arid climate and frequent droughts. The Central Valley Project began as a state plan, but the Franklin D. Roosevelt administration adopted it during the Great Depression when California failed to raise the requisite funds. The State Water Project, which began in the 1960s and remains under California control, is the largest public works project ever undertaken by a state. These two systems, along with several smaller systems such as those operated by the cities of San Francisco and Los Angeles, capture water that falls as rain and snow in the Sierra Nevada and other mountain ranges in a series of reservoirs, then redistribute it via an elaborate system of canals, aqueducts, pipelines, pumping stations, and other facilities. Farms throughout the state rely on this water, but those in especially dry areas, such as the southern San Joaquin Valley, have become utterly—and in some cases precariously—dependent on these oversubscribed systems.

As of 2011, California had 81,500 farms and ranches operating on 10.3 million hectares. The average value of this farmland was $17,000 ha^{-1}, with irrigated cropland selling at around $28,400 ha^{-1}. Fresno was the state's top agricultural county, with more than $6.8 billion in revenue, followed by Tulare, Kern, Monterey, and Merced Counties. California was home to nine of the top ten agricultural counties in the United States. California's top agricultural commodity was dairy, followed by almonds, grapes, cattle, nursery plants, and berries (California Department of Food and Agriculture 2012). Cannabis is also a major source of revenue, with some estimates placing it among the state's top two or three most lucrative agricultural commodities, but no accurate statistics exist for this partly elicit crop grown mainly in the northwest forest region.

Two trends run counter to the story of growth, intensification, and diversification in California valley agriculture. First, by 1959 the state emerged as a national leader in cotton production, trailing only Texas (Olmstead and Rhode 2003). Cotton farming in California is intensive, with levels of mechanization and yields per land area exceeding that of other cotton producing states; it is also extensive, forming a vast and breathtakingly uniform monoculture in the southern San Joaquin Valley where it is grown. Yet even this botanical juggernaut is gradually giving way. Cotton production peaked at around 650,000 hectares in the late 1970s and then shrunk to around 400,000 hectares by 2000. Cotton in California has continued to decline even further in recent years due to lower prices and strong competition from other more valuable crops. A second important countertrend involves the loss of farmland to urbanization. From around 1910 until the 1950s, Los Angeles was the largest producing agricultural county in the United States, with robust citrus, dairy, grape, and vegetable industries. By the 1970s, urban growth had pushed farms out of many areas, and Los Angeles did not even rank among the top ten agricultural counties in California. Similar processes have unfolded in Orange, Riverside, San Diego, and Santa Clara Counties. Today, some of the country's best farmland lies below pavement in California cities.

Conclusion

California is probably not the "great exception" that Carey McWilliams imagined, but over the past 250 years the state has experienced a fascinating and momentous environmental history. The legacies of this history remain visible in California's contemporary human population, which is distinctive among the American states in its size, diversity, cosmopolitanism, urban-ness, and affinity for the coast. California may not be *exceptional*, to use McWilliams's term, but in all of these ways it is clearly *remarkable*.

The relationships between the state's population and land use history are complex. During eighteenth and nineteenth centuries, populations that would be considered tiny by today's standards transformed vast areas of the state, from the interior valleys to the foothill woodlands to the great rivers and forests of the Sierra Nevada and Coast Ranges. California's 2014 population of more than 38 million people continues to place pressure on the state's ecosystems and infrastructure, with myriad environmental problems from air and water pollution to soil erosion, biodiversity loss, and the elimination of prime farmland. Yet the state still retains vast wildland areas, and some endangered species and degraded ecosystems have started to bounce back.

Continued population growth does not spell environmental doom for the Golden State. What will matter in the future, as in the past, are the decisions we make. Future Californians, who will be even more diverse and numerous than today, will face difficult choices about how to manage their lands and use their resources. It will be these collective decisions—not the number or color or background of the people who make them—that will shape the environments future Californians pass on to their children.

Summary

California is the largest state by population and third largest by land area. It was once home to a widely dispersed collection of indigenous peoples. Since the late nineteenth century, the state's population has diversified to include immigrants from around the world. Today, California has the largest urban population in the United States, both by percentage and total number of residents. The vast majority of this population resides in major metropolitan areas along the southern and central California coastlines and adjacent valleys. As a result, the state's population history is largely a story of urban growth, and its contemporary population geography is dominated by a handful of enormous urban regions that rank among the most sprawling and densely populated in the country.

With most of its human inhabitants living on a small fraction of its total land base, California still contains vast, remote regions with low population density. Government agencies now manage large portions of the state's forests, mountains, and deserts as parks, wilderness areas, or multiple use wildlands. Many of these areas appear relatively untrammeled today, but most have experienced long histories of land use and resource extraction, with profound and lingering ecosystem effects. Mining, ranching, forestry, and the harvesting of wild animal species rank among the most important of these historic activities, though all have declined in economic importance since the late nineteenth century. The most lucrative land uses in California today are commercial and residential development associated with continued urban growth, and agriculture, which remains one of the state's largest, most diverse, and most dynamic industries.

Recommended Reading

Beesley, D. 2004. Crow's range: An environmental history of the Sierra Nevada. University of Nevada Press, Reno, Nevada.

Garone, P. 2011. The fall and rise of the wetlands of California's great Central Valley. University of California Press, Berkeley, California.

Gruell, G. E. 2001. Fire in Sierra Nevada forests: A photographic interpretation of ecological change since 1849. Mountain Press Publishing Company, Missoula, Montana.

Isenberg, A. C. 2005. Mining California: An ecological history. Hill and Wang, New York, New York.

Hunter, L. M. 2000. The environmental impacts of population dynamics. Rand Corporation. Santa Monica, California.

Klein, H. S. 2012. A population history of the United States. Cambridge University Press, Cambridge, UK.

McWilliams, C. 1971. California: The great exception. Greenwood Publishing Group, Westport, Connecticut.

Merchant, C. 1998. Green versus gold: Sources in California's environmental history. Island Press, Washington, D.C.

Pincetl, S. 1999. Transforming California: A political history of land use and development. Johns Hopkins University Press, Baltimore, Maryland.

Sawyer, J. O. 2006. Northwest California: A natural history. University of California Press. Berkeley, California.

Walker, R. A. 2004. The conquest of bread: 150 years of agribusiness in California. New Press, New York, New York.

Walker, R. A., and S. K. Lodha. 2013. Atlas of California: Mapping the challenge of a new era. University of California Press, Berkeley, California.

White, R. 1991. It's your misfortune and none of my own: A new history of the American West. University of Oklahoma Press, Norman, Oklahoma.

Wolch, J. R., M. Pastor, and P. Dreier. 2004. Up against the sprawl: Public policy and the making of Southern California. University of Minnesota Press, Minneapolis, Minnesota.

Glossary

BABY BOOM In the United States, the baby boom is usually defined as the period from 1946 to 1964, when birth rates increased from a low of around 1.85 percent in the 1930s to more than 2 percent, reaching a high of about 2.65 percent in the late 1940s. Around seventy-nine million Americans were born during this eighteen-year postwar period.

CASH CROP Any agricultural product grown for sale on the market rather than for subsistence use.

CHAIN MIGRATION The process by which immigrants from a particular city or region follow each other to a new place. Chain migration has led to the formation of neighborhoods populated by people from distant regions as ethnic enclaves in many American cities.

CONSERVATIONISM A theory of natural resource management that emerged in the nineteenth century based on the idea that resources should be managed, according to utilitarian principles, for the benefit of the most people for the longest time. Conservationism soon diversified into numerous traditions and approaches, including preservationism, which holds that some areas should be spared from resource exploitation and left to natural processes.

CONURBATION A large area of industrial or developed space formed from previously separate towns and cities.

CORNUCOPIANISM The belief that the needs of a growing human population can be met through increased knowledge and technology.

EXURBAN AREAS Exurban areas are outlying commuter, or "bedroom," communities that lie beyond traditional suburbs. Such communities may be as far as one hundred miles from their closest urban cores and are generally thought to have emerged after World War II. Exurban areas multiplied in California beginning in the 1970s, when families and retirees began leaving urban areas to seek a higher quality of life and lower cost of living.

FERTILITY The average number of children per woman in a population.

MALTHUSIANISM A theory of population and environment, first introduced by the British economist and demographer Thomas Malthus in his *Essay on the Principle of Population* (1798), postulating that human population continues to grow until checked by resource scarcity or the conflicts that result from it. Malthusianism experienced a resurgence of popularity during the 1960s and 1970s, during a time of concern about Earth's capacity to accommodate continued human population growth.

PROTECTED AREA Any area of land or water specifically dedicated to nature conservation, including parks, sanctuaries, wilderness areas, marine protected areas, or other nature reserves.

REPLACEMENT LEVEL The average number of children per woman necessary to maintain a stable population size, not accounting for immigration or emigration.

SPRAWL The tendency of modern cities to expand outward into outlying areas. In North America and Europe, the term "sprawl" is often used to describe inefficient, low-density development. Yet sprawl may also be a stage of urban development to be followed by increasing densification.

SUBURBANIZATION Growth and development of outlying areas surrounding the traditional downtown core, often with lower population densities than the city center. Suburbs are connected to and contiguous with the city, unlike exurbs, but they often have distinctive neighborhoods and may be autonomous political entities.

URBAN AREA In the United States the Census Bureau defines "urban areas" as areas with core census blocks or block groups with a population density of at least one thousand people per square mile and surrounding blocks with at least five hundred people per square mile.

URBANIZATION The growth, development, and geographic expansion of cities. Urbanization may take many forms and involve several stages of development.

WILDERNESS Any area set aside for conservation or recreation, where mechanized or motorized forms of transportation are restricted or prohibited. These include areas of federal land designated as wilderness under the Wilderness Act of 1964 as well as some state, local, and private lands managed in this manner. California contains the second largest area of wilderness of any state after Alaska.

References

Alagona, P. S. 2008. Homes on the range: Cooperative conservation and environmental change on California's privately owned hardwood rangelands. Environmental History 13:287–311.

Alagona, P. S., and C. F. Smith. 2012. Mirage in the making. Boom: A Journal of California 2:25–44.

Alagona, P. S., A. Linares, P. Campos, and L. Huntsinger. 2013. History and recent trends. Pages 25–28 in P. Campos, L. Huntsinger, J. L. Oviedo, P. F. Starrs, M. Diaz, R. B. Standiford, and G. Montero, editors. Mediterranean Oak Woodland Working Landscapes. Springer, New York, New York.

Alpers, C.N. and M.P. Hunerlach. 2000. Mercury Contamination from Historic Gold Mining in California. United States Geologic Survey Fact Sheet FS-061-00.

Beesley, D. 2004. Crow's range: An environmental history of the Sierra Nevada. University of Nevada Press, Reno, Nevada.

Boserup, E. 1965. The conditions of agricultural growth. Earthscan, London, UK.

Bosworth, D. and H. Brown. 2007. After the Timber Wars: Community-Based Stewardship. Journal of Forestry 105: 271-273.

Brechin, G. 2006. Imperial San Francisco: Urban power, earthly ruin. University of California Press, Berkeley, California.

Burcham, L. T. 1981. California rangelands in historical perspective. Rangelands 3:95–104.

California Department of Finance. 2011. Historical census populations of counties and incorporated cities in California, 1850–2010. <http://www.dof.ca.gov/research/demographic/state_census_data_center/historical_census_1850-2010/view.php>. Accessed March 14, 2013.

California Department of Finance. 2013. History of the California economy. <http://www.dof.ca.gov/html/fs_data/historycaeconomy/>. Accessed August 1, 2013.

California Department of Fish and Wildlife. 2013. California Department of Fish and Wildlife (2013). Marine Protected Areas Update.

California Department of Food and Agriculture. 2012. California agricultural statistics review 2012–2013. California Department of Food and Agriculture, Sacramento, California.

Chiang, C. 2008. Shaping the shoreline: Fisheries and tourism on the Monterey Coast. University of Washington Press, Seattle, Washington.

Cook, S. F. 1976. The population of the California Indians, 1769–1970. University of California Press, Berkeley, California.

Cowan, T., editor. 2005. California's San Joaquin Valley: A region in transition. Congressional Research Service, Washington, D.C.

Crosby, A. W. 2004. Ecological imperialism: The biological expansion of Europe, 900–1900. Cambridge University Press, Cambridge, UK.

———. 2003. The Columbian exchange: Biological and cultural consequences of 1492. Greenwood Publishing Group, Westport, Connecticut.

Culver, L. 2010. The frontier of leisure: Southern California and the shaping of modern America. Oxford University Press, Oxford, UK.

Curran, S., and A. de Sherbinin. 2004. Completing the picture: The challenges of bringing "consumption" into the population-environment equation. Population and Environment 26:107–31.

Daniel, C. E. 1981. Bitter harvest: A history of California farmworkers, 1870–1941. Cornell University Press, Ithaca, New York.

Darlington, D. 1996. The Mojave: A portrait of the definitive American desert. Henry Holt and Company, New York, New York.

de Sherbinin, A., D. Carr, S. Cassels, and L. Jiang. 2007. Population and environment. Annual Review of Environment and Natural Resources 32:345–373.

Deverell, W., and G. Hise. 2010. A companion to Los Angeles. John Wiley and Sons, Malden, Massachusetts.

Dietz, T., E. A. Rosa, and R. York. 2007. Driving the human ecological footprint. Frontiers in Ecology and the Environment 5:13–18.

Duane, T. P. 1999. Shaping the Sierra: Nature, culture, and conflict in the changing West. University of California Press, Berkeley, California.

Ehrlich, P. R. 1968. The population bomb. Ballantine Books, New York, New York.

Ehrlich, P. R., and J. P. Holdren. 1971. Impact of population growth. Science 171:1212–1217.

Fagan, B. M. 2004. Before California: An archaeologist looks at our earliest inhabitants. Rowman Altamira, Walnut Creek, California.

Forsyth, T. 2002. Critical political ecology: The politics of environmental science. Routledge, London, UK.

Garone, P. 2011. The fall and rise of the wetlands of California's great Central Valley. University of California Press, Berkeley, California.

Gendzel, G. 2008. Not just a golden state: Three Anglo "rushes" in the making of Southern California, 1880–1920. Southern California Quarterly 90:349–378.

Gleditsch, N. P., and H. Urdal. 2002. Ecoviolence? Links between population growth, environmental scarcity and violent conflict in Thomas Homer-Dixon's work. Journal of International Affairs 56:283–302.

Goklany, I. M. 2009. Have increases in population, affluence, and technology worsened human and environmental well-being? Electronic Journal of Sustainable Development 1:1–28.

Gordon, M. S. 1954. Employment expansion and population growth, the California experience: 1900–1950. University of California Press, Berkeley, California.

Gregor, H. F. 1963. Spatial disharmonies in California population growth. Geographical Review 53:100–122.

Gregory, J. N. 1989. American exodus: The Dust Bowl migration and Okie culture in California. Oxford University Press, Oxford, UK.

Gruell, G. E. 2001. Fire in Sierra Nevada forests: A photographic interpretation of ecological change since 1849. Mountain Press Publishing Company, Missoula, Montana.

Haas, L. 1995. Conquests and historical identities in California, 1769–1936. University of California Press, Berkeley, California.

Hackel, S. W. 2005. Children of coyote, missionaries of Saint Francis: Indian-Spanish relations in colonial California, 1769–1850. University of North Carolina Press, Chapel Hill, North Carolina.

Harrison, P., and P. Pearce. 2000. AAAS atlas of population and environment. University of California Press, Berkeley, California.

Heidenreich, L. 2009. This land was Mexican once: Histories of resistance from northern California. University of Texas Press, Austin, Texas.

Hereford, R., R. H. Webb, and C. I. Longpre. 2004. Precipitation history of the Mojave Desert region, 1983–2001. Fact Sheet 117-03. United States Geological Survey, Flagstaff, Arizona.

Hunter, L. M. De J., G. Gonzalez, M. Stevenson, K. S. Karish, R. Toth, T. C. Edwards Jr., R. J. Lilieholm, and M. Cablk. 2003. Population and land use change in the California Mojave: Natural habitat implications of alternative futures. Population Research and Policy Review 22:373–397.

Huntsinger L., M. Johnson, M. Stafford, and J. Fried. 2010. California hardwood rangeland landowners, 1985–2004: Ecosystem services, production, and permanence. Rangeland Ecology and Management 63:325–334.

Igler, D. 2001. Industrial cowboys: Miller and lux and the transformation of the far west, 1850–1920. University of California Press, Berkeley, California.

Isenberg, A. C. 2005. Mining California: An ecological history. Hill and Wang, New York, New York.

Johnson, H., and M. C. Mejia. 2013. Immigrants in California. Public Policy Institute of California. Sacramento, CA.

Jolly, C. L. 1994. Four theories of population change and the environment. Population and Environment 16:61–90.

Klein, H. S. 2012. A population history of the United States. Cambridge University Press, Cambridge, UK.

Lambin, E.F., B. L. Turner, H. J. Geist, S. B. Agbola, A. Angelsen, J. W. Bruce, O. T. Coomes, R. Dirzo, G. Fischer, C. Folke, P. S. George, K. Homewood, J. Imbernon, R. Leemans, X. Lin, E. F.

Moran, M. Mortimore, P. S. Ramakrishnan, J. F. Richards, H. Skånes, W. Steffen, G. D. Stone, U. Svedin, T. A. Veldkamp, C. Vogel, and J. Xu. 2001. The causes of land-use and land-cover change: Moving beyond the myths. Global Environmental Change 11:261–269.

Liebman, E. 1983. California farmland: A history of large agricultural land holdings. Rowan and Allanheld, Totowa, New Jersey.

Loeffler, J. O. 2006. Northwest California: A natural history. University of California Press, Berkeley, California.

Los Angeles Times. 2013. In the news: California Coastal Commission. <http://articles.latimes.com/keyword/california-coastal-commission>. Accessed August 1, 2013.

Lotchin, R. W. 2008. Population concentration in Los Angeles, 1940–2000. Pacific Historical Review 77:87–101.

Lovich, J. E., and D. Bainbridge. 1999. Anthropogenic degradation of the Southern California desert ecosystem and prospects for natural recovery and restoration. Environmental Management 24:309–326.

Malthus, T. R. 1798. An essay on the principle of population as it affects the future improvement of society. Johnson, London, UK.

Marsh, G. P. 1864. Man and nature: Or, physical geography as modified by human action. Scribner, New York, New York.

McEntire, D. 1946. The population of California: A report of a research study made by authorization of the board of governors of the Commonwealth Club of California. Parker Printing Company, San Francisco, California.

McWilliams, C. 1971. California: The great exception. Greenwood Publishing Group, Westport, Connecticut.

Meadows, D. H., D. L. Meadows, J. Randers, and W. W. Behrens. 1972. The limits to growth: A report for the Club of Rome's project on the predicament of mankind. Universe Books, New York, New York.

Miles, J. G. 1967. The Redwood Park question. Forest History 11:6–11.

Minnesota Population Center. 2011. National Historical Geographic Information System. University of Minnesota, Minneapolis. <www.nhgis.org>. Accessed July 1, 2013.

Myers, D. 2013. California's diminishing resource: Children. USC Price School of Public Policy, Los Angeles, California.

Nystrom, E. C. 2003. From neglected space to protected place: An administrative history of Mojave National Preserve. Department of the Interior, National Park Service, Great Basin Cooperative Ecosystem Studies Unit, Washington, D.C.

Ogden, A. 1975. The California sea otter trade, 1748–1848. University of California Press, Berkeley, California.

Olmstead, A. L., and P. W. Rhode. 2003. The evolution of California agriculture, 1850–2000. Pages 1–28 in J. Siebert, editor. California agriculture: Dimensions and issues. University of California, Berkeley, California.

Otterstrom, S. M. and C. Earle. 2002. The settlement of the United States from 1790 to 1990: Divergent rates of growth and the end of the frontier. Journal of Interdisciplinary History 33:59–85.

Palais, H. 1974. Pioneer redwood logging in Humboldt County. Forest History 17:18–27.

Parsons, J. A. 1986. A geographer looks at the San Joaquin Valley. Geographical Review 76:371–389.

Pavlik, B. M. 2008. The California deserts: An ecological rediscovery. University of California Press, Berkeley, California.

Peluso, N. 1994. Rich forests, poor people: Resource control and resistance in Java. University of California Press, Berkeley, California.

Pincetl, S. 1999. Transforming California: A political history of land use and development. Johns Hopkins University Press, Baltimore, Maryland.

Pitkin, J., and D. Myers. 2012. Generational projections of the California population by nativity and year of immigrant arrival. USC Price School of Public Policy, Los Angeles, California.

Public Policy Institute of California. 2013. California population. Public Policy Institute of California, Sacramento, California.

Rajala, R. A. 2011. Clearcutting the Pacific rain forest: Production, science, and regulation. University of British Columbia Press, Vancouver, Canada.

Rick, T. C., J. M. Erlandson, T. J. Braje, J. A. Estes, M. H. Graham, and R. L. Vellanoweth. 2008. Historical ecology and human impacts on coastal ecosystems of the Santa Barbara Channel Region, California. Pages 77–102 in T. C. Rick and J. M. Erlandson, editors. Human impacts on ancient marine ecosystems: A global perspective. University of California Press, Berkeley, California.

Robertson, T. 2012. The Malthusian moment: Global population growth and the birth of American environmentalism. Rutgers University Press, New Brunswick, New Jersey.

Rome, A. W. 2001. The bulldozer in the countryside: Suburban sprawl and the rise of American environmentalism. Cambridge University Press, Cambridge, UK.

Sabin, P. 2004. Crude politics: The California oil market, 1900–1940. University of California Press, Berkeley, California.

Sackman, D. C. 2008. Nature and conquest: After the deluge of '49. Pages 175–191 in W. Deverell and D. Igler. A companion to California history. Blackwell, Malden, Massachusetts.

Sampson, A. W. 1923. Pasture and range management. Stanhope Press, Boston, Massachusetts.

Sawyer, J. O. 2006. Northwest California: A natural history. University of California Press, Berkeley, California.

Schrepfer, S. R. 2003. The fight to save the Redwoods: A history of the environmental reform, 1917–1978. University of Wisconsin Press, Madison, Wisconsin.

Sellars, R. W. 2009. Preserving nature in the National Parks: A history. Yale University Press, New Haven, Connecticut.

Simon, J. L. 1986. Theory of population and economic growth. Basil Blackwell, New York, New York.

———. 1981. The ultimate resource. Princeton University Press, Princeton, New Jersey.

Standiford, R. 2012. Forest research and outreach. Trends in harvest levels and stumpage prices in coastal California. <http://ucanr.edu/blogs/blogcore/postdetail.cfm?postnum=8623>. Accessed July 1, 2013.

Standiford, R. B., and R. E. Howitt. 1993. Multiple use management of California's hardwood rangelands. Journal of Range Management 46:176–182.

State of California. 2005. Revenue volatility in California. Legislative Analyst's Office, Sacramento, California.

———. 2003. Methylmercury in sport fish: Information for fish consumers. Office of Environmental Hazard Assessment, Sacramento, California.

Steffen, W., P. J. Crutzen, and J. R. McNeill. 2007. The Anthropocene: Are humans now overwhelming the great forces of nature? AMBIO 36:614–621.

Sugihara, N. G. 2006. Fire in California's ecosystems. University of California Press, Berkeley, California.

Turchin, P., and S. A. Nefedov. 2009. Secular cycles. Princeton University Press, Princeton, New Jersey.

U.S. Census Bureau 2012a. American fact finder. <http://factfinder2.census.gov/faces/nav/jsf/pages/index.xhtml>. Accessed July 1, 2013.

U.S. Census Bureau. 2012b. Growth in urban population outpaces rest of nation, Census Bureau Reports. Press release dated March 26. Washington, D.C.

U.S. Census Bureau. 2010. 2010 Census urban and rural classification and urban area criteria. <http://www.census.gov/geo/reference/ua/urban-rural-2010.html>. Accessed July 1, 2013.

U.S. Census Bureau, Population Division, Interim State Population Projections, 2005.

U.S. Census Bureau. 1995. Urban and rural definitions. <http://www.census.gov/population/censusdata/urdef.txt>. Accessed April 29, 2013.

U.S. Department of Agriculture. 2013. USDA Economic Research Service. Farm sector income and finances. <http://www.ers.usda.gov/topics/farm-economy/farm-sector-income-finances.aspx#.Ud7gHGBiY6I>. Accessed July 1, 2013.

Walker, P., and L. Fortmann. 2003. Whose landscape? A political ecology of the "exurban" Sierra. Cultural Geographies 10:469–491.

Walker, R. A. 2004. The conquest of bread: 150 years of agribusiness in California. New Press, New York, New York.

———. 2001. California's golden road to riches: Natural resources and regional capitalism, 1848–1940. Annals of the Association of American Geographers 91:167–199.

Walker, R. A., and S. K. Lodha. 2013. Atlas of California: Mapping the challenge of a new era. University of California Press, Berkeley, California.

Webb, R. H., and E. B. Newman. 1982. Recovery of soil and vegetation in ghost-towns in the Mojave Desert, southwestern United States. Environmental Conservation 9:245–248.

Wheat, F. 1999. California desert miracle. Sunbelt Publications, El Cajon, California.

White, R. 1998. The Gold Rush: Consequences and contingencies. California History 77:42–55.

———. 1991. It's your misfortune and none of my own: A new history of the American West. University of Oklahoma Press, Norman, Oklahoma.

Wolch, J., M. Pastor, and P. Dreier. 2004. Up against the sprawl: Public policy and the making of Southern California. University of Minnesota Press, Minneapolis, Minnesota.

Yoshiyama, R. M., F. W. Fisher, and P. B. Moyle. 1998. Historical abundance and decline of Chinook salmon in the Central Valley region of California. North American Journal of Fisheries Management 18:487–521.

SIX

Oceanography

STEVEN J. BOGRAD, ANDREW W. LEISING,
and ELLIOTT L. HAZEN

Introduction

The California Current System (CCS) is a dynamic and highly productive region dominated by a large southward surface flow that extends from near the U.S.–Canadian border, south to the southern tip of the Baja Peninsula, and offshore to several hundred kilometers. The physics of the system are controlled primarily by atmospheric forcing, which causes direct response of the ocean. In turn, the resulting physical features of the ocean drive ecosystem responses. Hence the CCS is thought of as a "bottom up"–driven ecosystem. Although highly variable, the major feature of the atmospheric forcing is a somewhat reliable spring and summertime condition wherein strong southward winds eventually lead to enhanced growth of plants and animals in the nearshore—a process known as coastal UPWELLING. The southward flowing California Current also generates considerable meanders, eddies, and jets, which may act to further enrich the ecosystem. As a result, the CCS is one of the most highly productive, and seasonally predictable, marine ecosystems on the earth. The dynamic nature of the physical structure of the CCS, both in space and time, not only leads to variability in the marine ecosystem but also affects coastal terrestrial ecosystems. Hence an understanding of the forces, variability, and likely future changes driving the CCS is key to understanding both marine and coastal ecosystems for the entire west coast of North America.

Atmospheric Forcing

Persistent, large-scale atmospheric patterns over the North Pacific drive the dynamics of the CCS. The dominant atmospheric pressure centers over the North Pacific are the ALEUTIAN LOW (AL) and NORTH PACIFIC HIGH (NPH). Climatologically, the AL is centered over the Gulf of Alaska and is strongest (lowest sea-level pressure) in winter, when its lower limb directs storms into northern California and the Pacific Northwest. The NPH is a broad, high-pressure system over the North Pacific Subtropical Gyre. It strengthens (highest sea-level pressure) in summer and, along with a deepening thermal low pressure center over the southwestern continental U.S., produces the cross-shore pressure gradient that drives coastal upwelling in the CCS.

Oceanic Response

Upwelling

Coastal upwelling is the dominant physical process in the CCS and is largely responsible for maintaining its highly productive and diverse ecosystem. The cross-shore pressure gradient between the strong summertime NPH and the deepening continental thermal low drives persistent alongshore (equatorward) winds offshore of the U.S. West Coast. These winds in turn drive an offshore flow in the surface EKMAN LAYER, leading to upwelling of cold, salty, nutrient-rich, low pH and oxygen-poor waters near the coast (Figure 6.1). In contrast, poleward alongshore winds drive an onshore Ekman flow and thus downwelling at the coast. Downwelling occurs commonly in winter, especially in the northern CCS. Typical upwelling velocities are 10 to 20 m d^{-1} (Huyer 1983, Checkley and Barth 2009). The cool upwelled waters are separated from the warmer offshore waters by a surface thermal front that is generally parallel to the coast. This "upwelling front" often provides a dynamic boundary between nearshore and offshore ecosystem components. When upwelling is sustained for a period of a few days or more, a GEOSTROPHIC BALANCE between the cross-shore pressure gradient (due to the horizontal density difference between the upwelled and offshore waters) and the Coriolis force establishes a strong equatorward surface-intensified current, the "upwelling jet" (Huyer 1983, Checkley and Barth 2009). This jet, with speeds up to ~1 m s^{-1}, is strongest where the cross-shore density difference is greatest—that is, at the upwelling front.

The characteristics of upwelled waters can be highly variable. Water that is upwelled can have different physical, chemical, and/or biological characteristics, depending on the depth at which they originate, the strength and persistence of the upwelling winds, and the stratification of the water column. When coastal waters are highly stratified, for example, the source of upwelled waters would be higher in the water column and would have different biogeochemical properties than waters originating near the bottom boundary layer (Smith 1981). Upwelled waters having different nutrient and oxygen contents can yield different biological responses, including a different phytoplankton community structure (Kudela et al. 2008). There is significant variability in both the timing and strength of coastal upwelling along the meridional extent of the CCS. The climatological upwelling season is nearly year-round at the southern end of the CCS. It gets progressively shorter, with a later spring transition to upwelling and earlier fall transition away from it, at more northerly latitudes (Bograd et al. 2009). Off northern California, where the magnitude of summertime upwelling is typically strongest, the upwelling season typically spans the period March–September, although there is significant interannual variability in these dates (see below). Orographic variation along the coastline can also lead to variability in upwelling. Such variation can lead to regions of strong wind-stress curl and amplified upwelling (Beardsley et al. 1987) as well as "upwelling shadows" with weaker upwelling in the lee of prominent topographic and bathymetric features (e.g., Cape Blanco, Cape Mendocino, Monterey Bay) (Graham 1993, Barth et al. 2000, Castelao and Barth 2005, Woodson et al. 2009). These regions

Photo on previous page: Long-exposure image of night waves on the rocky shore, Big Sur, California. Photo: Elliott L. Hazen.

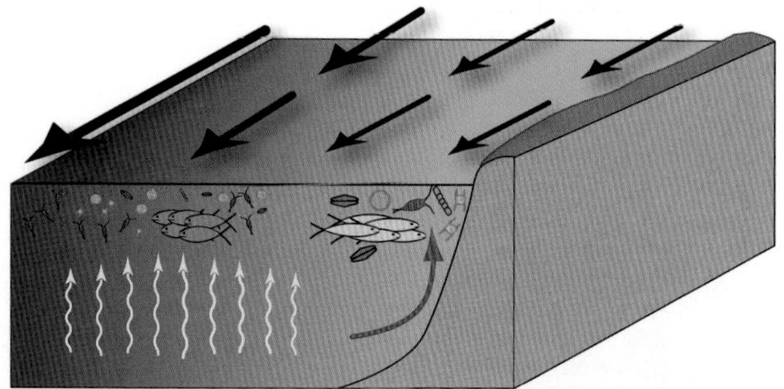

FIGURE 6.1 Conceptual diagram displaying the hypothesized relationship between wind-forced upwelling and the pelagic ecosystem. Alongshore, equatorward wind stress results in coastal upwelling (red arrow), supporting production of large phytoplankters and zooplankters. Between the coast and the wind-stress maximum, cyclonic wind-stress curl results in curl-driven upwelling (yellow arrows) and production of smaller plankters. Anchovy (gray fish symbols) prey on large plankters, whereas sardine (blue fish symbols) specialize on small plankters. Black arrows represent winds at the ocean surface, and their widths are representative of wind magnitude. Source: Rykaczewski and Checkley 2008.

can serve as important nearshore retention sites for planktonic organisms (Graham and Largier 1997).

In addition to coastal upwelling, there is another process that brings water to the surface from below, known as curl-driven upwelling. Cross-shore variation in the strength of the alongshore winds leads to spatially variable Ekman transports and to regions of convergence and divergence that are compensated for by vertical motions. This results in broad offshore areas of upwelling driven by positive wind-stress curl (see Figure 6.1; Pickett and Paduan 2003, Rykaczewski and Checkley 2008). Although the offshore, curl-driven upwelling is an order of magnitude weaker (~0.1–0.2 m d^{-1}), it occurs over a larger region and can thus represent a substantial fraction of the total upwelling in the CCS (Pickett and Paduan 2003). Rykaczewski and Checkley (2008) argued that these contrasting upwelling domains drive different pelagic ecosystems with, for example, rapid wind-driven upwelling near the coast supporting large phytoplankton and zooplankton favored by anchovy, and slow curl-driven upwelling offshore supporting smaller plankters (planktonic organisms) favored by sardines.

Circulation

Three currents comprise the CCS: the California Current, the California Undercurrent, and the Inshore Countercurrent (sometimes called the Davidson Current). The dominant feature is the equatorward-flowing California Current (CC), which is the eastern limb of the North Pacific Subtropical Gyre. The CC is a slow (~10–20 cm s^{-1}), meandering flow, which transports relatively cool, fresh waters of subarctic origin towards coastal California (Hickey 1979, Hickey 1998). The CC is a broad feature, typically extending several hundred kilometers offshore, with strongest flow in the surface layer. It is difficult to define an offshore boundary of the CC, although in a broad sense it can be considered to extend out to the southeastern extension of the Subarctic Frontal Zone, 800 to 900 km off the California coast (Sverdrup et al. 1942, Lynn and Simpson 1987). Based on seasonal variation of the physical characteristics of the CC, Lynn and Simpson

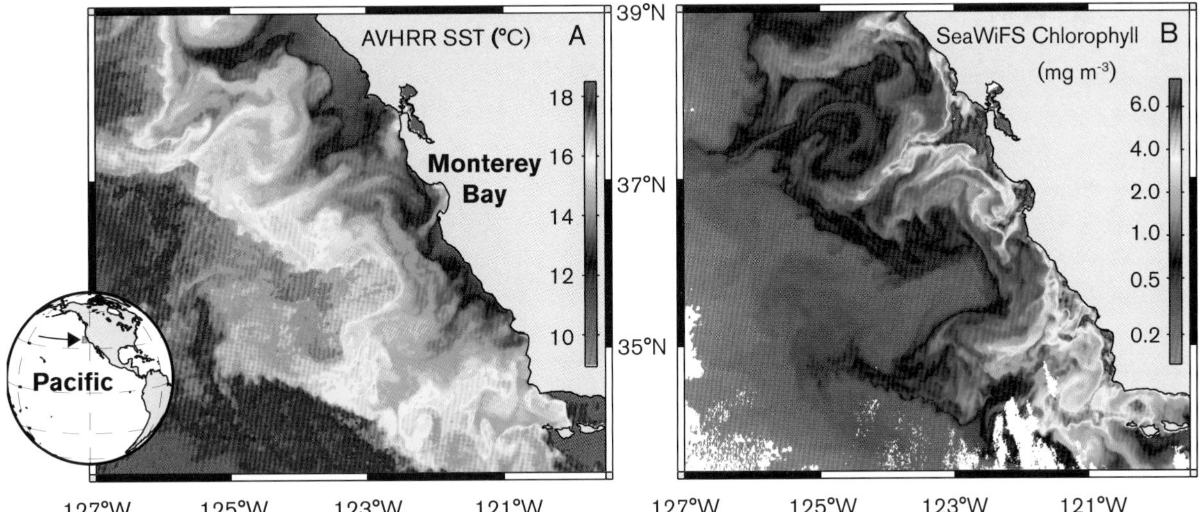

FIGURE 6.2 Satellite remote sensing imagery of the central California Current upwelling system. (A) Sea surface temperature (SST) from the Advanced Very High Resolution Radiometer (AVHRR) on August 14, 2000, and (B) surface chlorophyll from the Sea-viewing Wide Field-of-view Sensor (SeaWiFS) on August 16, 2000. Upwelled waters are characterized by cooler waters with higher chlorophyll content. Source: Ryan et al. 2005.

(1987) defined three cross-shore domains: an offshore oceanic regime, a coastal regime, and an intervening transition zone centered approximately 200 to 300 km offshore. This transition zone is a region of high mesoscale activity (eddies and meanders), characterized by highly variable dynamic height (Lynn and Simpson 1987). Interannual variations in the water properties and transport of the CC can have significant downstream impacts on biological structure (Chelton et al. 1982, Chelton 1984, Kiester et al. 2011).

The other dominant current in the CCS is the poleward-flowing California Undercurrent (CUC). This current is a narrow (~10–40 km) and relatively weak (~2–10 cm s^{-1}) flow centered at depth (~200–300 m) along the continental slope (Wooster and Jones 1970, Hickey 1979, Hickey 1998, Lynn and Simpson 1987). The CUC transports warm, salty, low-oxygen, low-nitrate waters originating in the eastern tropical Pacific into the CCS. The CUC has been observed to be continuous along the full latitudinal extent of the CCS (Pierce et al. 2000) and appears to be utilized by Pacific hake (whiting) undergoing northward migrations (Agostini et al. 2006). Finally, the Inshore Countercurrent (IC), or Davidson Current, is a weak (~5 cm s^{-1}) poleward surface flow observed seasonally north of Point Conception, generally confined to a narrow region near the coast (Lynn and Simpson 1987). The IC may result from the shoaling of the CUC in late fall through winter.

Mesoscale Structure

While the currents described in the previous section represent the dominant circulation features of the CCS, there is in fact considerable spatial variability in the CCS on the mesoscale (scales of tens to a couple of hundred kilometers). This rich mesoscale structure is evident in any satellite image of surface properties of the CCS (Figure 6.2). The equatorward-flowing CC is characterized by large-scale meanders, which often break off to form mesoscale eddies. The coastal upwelling jet is also highly unstable, and filaments of cold, upwelled waters are often observed extending several hundred kilometers offshore from prominent topographic features (Strub et al. 1991). The development of mesoscale variability in the CCS is highest in late summer to early fall. It results from an accumulation of energy supplied to the mean CCS flow through seasonal wind forcing, and the subsequent transfer of energy via instabilities to smaller scales (Strub and James 2000, Centurioni et al. 2008, Checkley and Barth 2009). Mesoscale features in the CCS are often associated with enhanced biological activity. This is due both to fine-scale circulation patterns that support high primary productivity and to the aggregation of planktonic organisms and their subsequent utilization by predators up the food pyramid (Logerwell and Smith 2001, Mantyla et al. 2008, Checkley and Barth 2009).

Temporal Variability

SEASONAL PHENOLOGY

The physical processes driving ecosystem variability in the CCS vary across a spectrum of temporal scales, from daily to decadal (Woodson et al. 2008, McGowan et al. 2003, Baumgartner et al. 1992). Many marine organisms have life histories adapted to this temporal periodicity. The largest and most consistent physical and biological changes take place on seasonal time scales, forced by the annual cycle of large-scale atmospheric patterns that drive coastal upwelling. As upwelling-favorable winds become established in the spring, coastal sea level drops, temperatures on the continental shelf decrease, and strong alongshore flow develops, that is, the coastal upwelling jet (Huyer et al. 1979, Huyer 1983, Strub and James 1988, Strub and James 2000, Lynn et al. 2003). This "spring transition" typically occurs in March through April and is followed by the peak upwelling season and a subsequent "fall transition" back to winter conditions around October through November (Strub and James 1988 and 2000). The spring transition is accompanied by a rapid increase in primary productivity, as can be seen in satellite images of surface ocean color (see Figure 6.2).

Because of this strong seasonal forcing, many marine organisms in the CCS have life histories adapted to seasonal events in the environment (Abraham and Sydeman 2004,

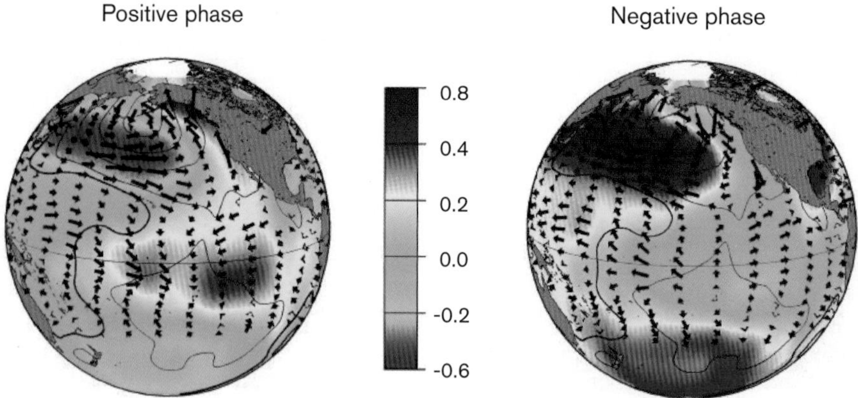

FIGURE 6.3 Typical wintertime sea surface temperature (colors), sea level pressure (contours), and surface wind stress (arrows) anomalies during the positive (warm; left) and negative (cool; right) phases of the Pacific Decadal Oscillation. Source: The Pacific Decadal Oscillation (PDO), <http://jisao.washington.edu/pdo/>.

Bograd et al. 2002, Bograd et al. 2009). Changes in the timing and amplitude of coastal upwelling can have profound impacts on the CCS ecosystem. This was particularly evident in 2005, when a significant delay in the spring transition (Kosro et al. 2006, Schwing et al. 2006, Barth et al. 2007) led to ecosystem changes at multiple trophic levels from primary production (Thomas and Brickley 2006) to zooplankton (Mackas et al. 2006) to fish, birds, and mammals (Brodeur et al. 2006, Sydeman et al. 2006, Weise et al. 2006). This ecosystem disruption can be generally attributed to mismatches between physical forcing and the productivity and life cycles of predator and prey (Cushing 1990, Beare and McKenzie 1999, Stenseth and Mysterud 2002, Durant et al. 2007). Since upwelling can have a cumulative effect on ecosystem productivity and structure, Bograd et al. (2009) used a cumulative upwelling index to describe long-term and latitudinal variability in the timing of coastal upwelling in the CCS. They identified extended periods of high or low seasonally integrated upwelling and a long-term trend towards a later and shorter upwelling season in the northern CCS.

INTERANNUAL/ENSO

The CCS is also driven by significant interannual variability, of which the El Niño–Southern Oscillation (ENSO) cycle is the most prominent source. One of the first studies of climate-driven ecosystem change occurred at the 1960 California Cooperative Oceanic Fisheries Investigations (CalCOFI) conference, when a number of prominent oceanographers described the unusual physical and ecological conditions observed off California following the strong 1957–1958 El Niño event (Sette and Isaacs 1960). Effects of El Niño events reach the CCS via both atmospheric and oceanic teleconnections. El Niño years are often characterized by a stronger than usual Aleutian Low, resulting in more southerly storm tracks and high precipitation in California (Horel and Wallace 1981, Emery and Hamilton 1985, Schwing et al. 2002).

The El Niño signal often reaches the southern CCS via poleward-propagating coastal Kelvin waves (Chelton and Davis 1982; Clarke and Van Gorder 1994; Chavez et al. 2002b; Lynn and Bograd 2002, Strub and James 2002). With a lag of several months from the El Niño onset in the equatorial Pacific, coastal temperatures in the CCS warm, and the pycnocline deepens. These anomalies are associated with low productivity (Chavez et al. 2002b; Lynn and Bograd 2002). Quick transitions from El Niño to La Niña conditions can take place in the tropics, with a similarly quick transition from warm, low productivity to cool, high productivity conditions in the CCS (Bograd and Lynn 2001; Lynn and Bograd 2002; Chavez et al. 2002a; Chavez et al. 2002b). Some of the largest physical and biological perturbations observed in the CCS have been associated with strong El Niño events (notably the 1957–1958, 1982–1983, and 1997–1998 events), although not all El Niño events trigger the same response in the CCS (Chavez et al. 2002a; Chavez et al. 2002b; Mendelssohn et al. 2003).

DECADAL/PDO-NPGO

The CCS is also impacted by atmospheric forcing and oceanic responses at much lower frequencies, on the time scale of decades. Several large-scale indices have been developed to characterize aspects of the physical (atmospheric and oceanic) state of the North Pacific region. Foremost among these is the Pacific Decadal Oscillation (PDO) (Mantua et al. 1997, Hare and Mantua 2000), defined as the leading principal component of sea surface temperature (SST) variability in the North Pacific (Figure 6.3). Time series of the PDO show extended (decadal) periods of positive values (warm SSTs along the North American coast and cooler SSTs in the ocean interior) or negative values, punctuated by rapid transitions from one state to the other. These transitions between climate states have been referred to as regime shifts and have been the topic of significant research effort over the past fifteen to twenty years (see Steele 2004 and references therein). Periods of positive PDO are characterized by a stronger Aleutian Low pressure system, weaker coastal upwelling, anomalously warm SSTs in the CCS, and generally lower levels of productivity.

Negative PDO regimes are characterized by opposite conditions. Many studies have presented evidence of the ecosystem impacts of these climate regimes, including low-frequency transitions between sardine- and anchovy-dominated forage bases in the CCS (Lluch-Belda et al. 1992, Schwartzlose et al. 1999, Chavez et al. 2003, Checkley et al. 2009). An apparent regime shift from cool (negative PDO) to warm (positive PDO) conditions occurred in 1976–1977, with substantial ecosystem changes in the CCS and throughout the North Pacific (Miller et al. 1994, Roemmich and McGowan 1995, Bograd and Lynn 2003, Brinton and Townsend 2003, McGowan et al. 2003). Some authors have argued that another regime shift, back to cool conditions in the CCS, occurred in 1999, following the high-amplitude 1997–1999 El Niño–La Niña cycle (Bograd et al. 2000, Bond et al. 2003, Peterson and Schwing 2003).

Another leading climate index is the North Pacific Gyre Oscillation (NPGO) (Di Lorenzo et al. 2008). The NPGO is defined as the second principal component of sea surface height variability in the North Pacific. Variations in the NPGO describe low-frequency changes in the strength of the North Pacific Current, the eastward-flowing current across the basin that marks the boundary between the subarctic gyre (the Alaskan Gyre) to the north and the subtropical gyre (the North Pacific Subtropical Gyre) to the south. Positive values of the NPGO correspond to a stronger North Pacific Current, what Cummins and Freeland (2007) refer to as a "breathing mode," indicative of stronger flow in the basin-scale gyres. The NPGO represents the leading mode of decadal variability in surface salinity and upper-ocean nutrients over the full extent of the CCS, with a positive NPGO corresponding to higher nutrient levels (Di Lorenzo et al. 2009). Thus, at decadal time scales, nutrient variability in the CCS is driven largely by changes in the basin-scale circulation.

Both the PDO and NPGO are the oceanic expressions of large-scale atmospheric patterns. These patterns can be described by indices of the relative strength of the dominant sea-level pressure patterns over the North Pacific—that is, the Aleutian Low and the North Pacific High. The leading mode of sea-level pressure variability over the North Pacific corresponds to out-of-phase variations in these pressure centers and to PDO cycles in oceanic conditions. The NPGO corresponds to the second mode of sea-level pressure variability, with in-phase changes in the pressure centers. Although driven by large-scale changes in atmospheric forcing, the mechanisms of decadal variability in CCS physics and biology, and in particular the nature and causes of regime shifts, remain a subject of ongoing research.

Future Changes in the California Current System

The CCS is a biologically rich and highly dynamic ecosystem, susceptible to both bottom-up and top-down (including human) impacts across a spectrum of temporal scales (King et al. 2011). It is therefore important to consider the impacts of climate change on the productivity, structure, and functioning of the CCS. We review a few of the potential changes to the CCS we might anticipate under climate change and their impacts on the ecosystem.

Changes in Upwelling

Upwelling is expected to change in response to broader climate change. Bakun (1990) presented a hypothesis that anthropogenic climate change (i.e., global warming) could result in the intensification of coastal upwelling in the eastern boundary current systems. The argument is that under expected climate change scenarios, the rate of heating over land would be enhanced relative to that over the ocean, resulting in a stronger cross-shore pressure gradient between the continental low and oceanic high pressure centers and a proportional increase in alongshore winds and resultant upwelling (Bakun 1990, Bakun et al. 2010). Although there have been several studies suggesting an increase in the amplitude of coastal upwelling in the CCS over the past few decades (Schwing and Mendelssohn 1997, García-Reyes and Largier 2010, Narayan et al. 2010, Black et al. 2011), as well as observations of increasing satellite-observed chlorophyll-*a* (Kahru et al. 2012), the time series are too short to definitively attribute these trends to anthropogenic climate change. A recently completed meta-analysis of the upwelling intensification hypothesis has found general support for it but with significant spatial (latitudinal) and temporal (intraseasonal) variability between and within the eastern boundary current systems (Sydeman et al. 2014).

Similarly, there is little consensus among climate models on this issue, with some supporting (Snyder et al. 2003, Auad et al. 2006) and others opposing (Mote and Mantua 2002) the upwelling intensification hypothesis. The ambiguity in these modeling studies is likely due to issues of scale, with some models resolving coastal upwelling better than others. Improved regional downscaling of climate models will be needed to better resolve changes in the upwelling process. It should be noted that climate change may also impact the timing of coastal upwelling and other processes, which may have even broader ecosystem impacts than changes in upwelling amplitude (Diffenbaugh et al. 2004, Diffenbaugh 2005, Rykaczewski et al. 2015).

A warming of the upper ocean could have additional effects on ocean structure and productivity. Warming could lead to an increase in water column stratification and thus a stronger THERMOCLINE (Palacios et al. 2004). This could counter the effects of upwelling intensification by reducing the ability of coastal upwelling to deliver nutrients to the euphotic zone. Enhanced stratification in the southern CCS has been implicated in an observed long-term decline in zooplankton biomass (Roemmich and McGowan 1995, McGowan et al. 2003), although a decline in the abundance of pelagic tunicates may also be responsible (Lavaniegos and Ohman 2003, Lavaniegos and Ohman 2007). However, some modeling studies (Auad et al. 2006) suggest that increases in upwelling-favorable winds would overcome enhanced thermal stratification, potentially resulting in enhanced productivity. Warming conditions also have the potential to increase jellyfish production (Brotz et al. 2012). Changes in the water mass characteristics of upwelled waters could also have unforeseen consequences on ecosystem productivity and structure. Rykaczewski and Dunne (2010) used an earth system model to explore changes in California Current productivity under expected climate change scenarios. They found enhanced nitrate supply and productivity during the twenty-first century even with increased stratification and a limited change in upwelling. They attributed this nutrient increase to enrichment of deep source waters resulting from decreased ventilation of the North Pacific. They also noted that future ecosystem states in the CCS may be distinctly unlike those seen in the historical record (Rykaczewski and Dunne 2010).

Shoaling Oxygen Minimum Zone and Ocean Acidification

Another potential consequence of climate change is a reduction in mid-ocean dissolved oxygen content. Climate models driven by increasing greenhouse gases predict a decline in dissolved oxygen as a result of enhanced stratification and reduced ventilation (Sarmiento et al. 1998, Keeling and Garcia 2002, Keeling et al. 2010). Large-scale ocean circulation would transport these modified waters to the CCS and other regions (Deutsch et al. 2005). The OXYGEN MINIMUM ZONE (OMZ), a region of permanently low oxygen found at mid-depths throughout the eastern Pacific, is typically found at depths of 700 to 1,000 m within the CCS. A reduction in mid-depth dissolved oxygen content would effectively lift the OMZ to depths from which upwelled waters are derived. Indeed, long time series from CalCOFI have revealed a long-term trend towards declining oxygen content in the southern CCS, with the hypoxic boundary (defined as the depth at which dissolved oxygen is 60 μMol/kg) shoaling by up to 80 m over the period 1984–2006 in the Southern California Bight (Bograd et al. 2008, McClatchie et al. 2010). Similar trends have been observed at the northern end of CCS (Whitney et al. 2007) as well as the western subarctic Pacific (Whitney et al. 2013). This shoaling of the OMZ could have complex and far-ranging ecosystem impacts (Diaz and Rosenberg 1995). Benthic organisms found in regions where the OMZ intersects the continental margin could be directly impacted by declining oxygen levels (Levin 2003), while pelagic species could find their viable habitat significantly compressed (Bograd et al. 2008, McClatchie et al. 2010, Stramma et al. 2010, Stramma et al. 2011, Koslow et al. 2011). Habitat shifts and broad changes in community structure could result from persistently lower oxygen levels in the CCS.

In the northern CCS, hydrographic observations have revealed a recent increase in the frequency and severity of hypoxic events, and even occasional water-column anoxia, on the inner continental shelf (Grantham et al. 2004, Chan et al. 2008). These events appear to be driven by enhanced coastal productivity and subsequent increases in respiration, combined with generally lower levels of dissolved oxygen at depth on the inner continental shelf (Grantham et al. 2004, Chan et al. 2008). The biological impacts of these events can be catastrophic, with widespread mortality of macroscopic benthic organisms observed on the Oregon continental shelf (Grantham et al. 2004). High-frequency, low-oxygen (but not anoxic) events have also been observed in Monterey Bay (Booth et al. 2012) and the inshore Southern California Bight (Nam et al. 2011, Send and Nam 2012, Frieder et al. 2012).
Another consequence of rising atmospheric CO_2 concentrations is OCEAN ACIDIFICATION, a reduction in oceanic pH. This will lead to large-scale changes in seawater carbonate chemistry, with major negative impacts on shell-building organisms including some plankton, molluscs, and corals (Doney et al. 2009). Indeed, the seasonal upwelling of low-pH ("corrosive") waters has been observed in the CCS decades earlier than predicted by models (Feely et al. 2008, Gruber et al. 2012, Leinweber et al. 2013). Taken together, these recent observations highlight the potential for severe, climate-driven ecological disruptions in the CCS.

Climate Change Projections

Offshore of the California Current, the less productive subtropical gyre is expanding and is projected to continue expanding (Polovina et al. 2008, Polovina et al. 2011). This expansion will result in altered habitat available offshore of the CC upwelling front and reduced productivity along important corridors such as the northward-moving transition zone (Polovina et al. 2011, Hazen et al. 2013). Long-term climate change effects on California Current ecosystems are more difficult to predict, as much depends on trends and variance in upwelling and in acidity of upwelled waters. Upwelling will continue to provide nutrient-rich and cooler waters in the context of a warming North Pacific. Increases in upwelling may make the CCS an increasingly important hotspot for top predators into the future (Cheung et al. 2009, Hazen et al. 2013, Woodworth-Jefcoats et al. 2013). Large fish abundance is projected to decrease in the North Pacific as a whole, while large fish in the CCS are predicted to increase (Woodworth-Jefcoats et al. 2013).

Consequences of increased upwelling and lower dissolved oxygen include additional habitat compression for HYPOXIA-sensitive species (Stramma et al. 2011) and reduced maximum body sizes for fish species in the CCS (Cheung et al. 2012). If increased upwelling also results in lowered surface pH, planktonic communities could shift (Field et al. 2006) because shell-bearing species (particularly a type of pelagic snail known as a pteropod, which can be a major food source for fish; Armstrong et al. 2005) will have increasing difficulty in building their shells. As illustrated by the periodic expansion of Humboldt squid in the CCS and by recruitment failures of Cassin's auklet and Chinook salmon in recent years (Sydeman et al. 2006, Field et al. 2007, Lindley et al. 2009, Stewart et al. 2012), changing environmental conditions will most certainly result in some species expanding their niches while others contract.

We can use anomalous upwelling years and El Niño events to hypothesize how climate change may influence CCS ecosystems and to identify species most likely to be affected (Sydeman et al. 2006, Sydeman et al. 2009, King et al. 2011). With warming waters in the future, CCS species such as albacore tuna and Chinook salmon are predicted to have restricted habitat, closer to shore. Meanwhile, migratory top predators like sharks, seabirds, and marine mammals can switch prey resources and follow their prey, potentially buffering their population responses (King et al. 2011). Changes in timing of upwelling could lead to mismatches between the timing of energy-intensive life history strategies and the periods of greatest food availability. This was documented in Cassin auklet reproductive failure due to delayed upwelling in 2005 (Sydeman et al. 2006, Sydeman and Bograd 2009). Ultimately, a suite of approaches including mechanistic ecosystem models and spatially explicit regression models coupled with climate change scenarios are needed to predict which species and physical features underlying hotspots are most likely to change over the next century. The dynamic nature of the CCS, particularly the pelagic ecosystem, highlights the need for adaptive management in the face of climate change (Doney et al. 2012, Hazen et al. 2013).

Summary

The California Current System, although generally highly productive, is also known for its high variability. Variability occurs across a wide spectrum of spatial and temporal scales, and in both the forcing and response of the system. In some cases a climate event can force large, temporary changes in overall productivity or community composition, as occurred during the large 1997–1998 El Niño event (Bograd and Lynn 2001) or the delayed upwelling in 2005 (Barth et al. 2007). In other cases, climate-driven regime shifts can alter the overall community structure of the system, changing it, for example, from a sardine-dominated to an anchovy-dominated forage base (Chavez et al. 2003). The CCS can therefore be characterized as both resilient (quick to recover from disturbances) and robust (able to maintain ecosystem function and relatively high productivity) to natural climate variability, sustaining many species of high commercial and conservation value. However, the scale of future responses to anthropogenic climate change may be beyond the historical scales of variability (Sydeman et al. 2013), making forecasts of the response of the CCS to climate change difficult.

Acknowledgments

The authors thank the external reviewers for useful comments on earlier drafts of the chapter. We thank Ryan Rykaczewski for permission to use Figure 6.1, and John Ryan for permission to use Figure 6.2. The authors also thank Hal Mooney and Erika Zavaleta for providing editorial support and leadership in developing this book.

Recommended Reading

Several manuscripts provide comprehensive reviews of the dominant physical processes and ecosystem responses in the CCS. Huyer (1983) provides a detailed account of coastal upwelling processes. Hickey (1979) and Lynn and Simpson (1987) provide thorough reviews of the seasonal dynamics of the CCS, the latter focusing on the southern end of the system. Hickey (1998) provides a broad review of CCS dynamics over a range of temporal scales. Checkley and Barth (2009) provide a more recent review of both the physical forcing and ecosystem response in the CCS, and King et al. (2011) review potential climate change impacts on the California Current ecosystem. McClatchie (2014) provides a history of the CalCOFI program. In addition, several textbooks provide a thorough review of the physical processes that are important in the CCS (e.g., Tchernia 1980). The current physical and biological status of the CCS is reviewed in the *State of the California Current* reports published annually in CalCOFI Reports (e.g., Bjorkstedt et al. 2012). Additional resources are listed below:

Checkley, D. M., Jr., and J. A. Barth. 2009. Patterns and processes in the California Current System. Progress in Oceanography 83:49–64.

Doney, S. C., M. Ruckelshaus, J. E. Duffy, J. P. Barry, F. Chan, C. A. English, H. M. Galindo, J. M. Grebmeier, A. B. Hollowed, N. Knowlton, J. Polovina, N. N. Rabalais, W. J. Sydeman, and L. D. Talley. 2012. Climate change impacts on marine ecosystems. Annual Reviews of Marine Science 4:11–37.

Doney, S. C., V. J. Fabry, R. A. Feely, and J. A. Kleypas. 2009. Ocean acidification: The other CO_2 problem. Annual Reviews of Marine Science 1:169–192.

Hickey, B. M. 1998. Coastal oceanography of western North America from the tip of Baja California to Vancouver Island. Pages 345–393 in A. R. Robinson and K. H. Brink, editors. The Sea, the Global Coastal Ocean, volume 11. John Wiley & Sons, New York, New York.

———. 1979. The California current system—hypotheses and facts. Progress in Oceanography 8:191–279.

King, J. R., V. N. Agostini, C. J. Harvey, G. A. McFarlane, M.G.G. Foreman, J. E. Overland, E. Di Lorenzo, N. A. Bond, and K. Y. Aydin. 2011. Climate forcing and the California Current ecosystem. ICES Journal of Marine Science 68(6):1199–1216.

Lynn, R. J., and J. J. Simpson. 1987. The California Current System: The seasonal variability of its physical characteristics. Journal of Geophysical Research 92:12947–12966.

Glossary

ALEUTIAN LOW A semipermanent region of low sea-level pressure (cyclonic circulation) located near the Aleutian Islands in winter. One of the main centers of action in the atmospheric circulation over the North Pacific.

EKMAN LAYER The thin horizontal layer of water riding on top of the ocean that is affected by wind.

GEOSTROPHIC BALANCE The balance of the horizontal pressure gradient and the acceleration provided by the spinning of Earth—that is, the Coriolis force. Determines the first-order circulation patterns in the open ocean.

HYPOXIA A phenomenon that occurs in aquatic environments when dissolved oxygen becomes reduced in concentration to levels detrimental to organisms.

KELVIN WAVES A wave in the ocean or atmosphere that balances Earth's Coriolis force against a topographic boundary such as a coastline or a waveguide such as the equator. Kelvin waves associated with El Niño events impact coastal California.

NORTH PACIFIC HIGH A semipermanent region of high sea-level pressure (anticyclonic circulation) located over the northeast Pacific. It is strongest in summer (when it drives coastal upwelling) and shifts southward during winter (when the Aleutian Low is more active).

OCEAN ACIDIFICATION Decrease in the pH of Earth's oceans, caused by the uptake of anthropogenic carbon dioxide from the atmosphere.

OXYGEN MINIMUM ZONE The zone in which oxygen saturation in the ocean is at its lowest, typically around 200 to 1,000 m in depth in eastern boundary current systems.

PHENOLOGY The study of periodic life cycle events and how these are influenced by seasonal and interannual variations in climate.

PYCNOCLINE The oceanic layer in which density changes more rapidly with depth than it does in the layers above or below.

REGIME SHIFT Large, abrupt, and persistent changes in the structure or function of a system—for example, a marine ecosystem.

THERMOCLINE The oceanic layer in which temperature changes more rapidly with depth than it does in the layers above or below.

UPWELLING An oceanic process that involves wind-driven motion of dense, cooler, and usually nutrient-rich water towards the ocean surface, replacing the warmer, usually nutrient-depleted surface water.

References

Abraham, C. L., and W. J. Sydeman. 2004. Ocean climate, euphausiids, and auklet nesting: Interannual trends and variation in phenology, diet, and growth of a planktivorous seabird, Ptychoramphus aleuticus. Marine Ecology Progress Series 274:235–250.

Agostini, V. N., R. C. Francis, A. B. Hollowed, S. D. Pierce, C. Wilson, and A. N. Hendrix. 2006. The relationship between Pacific hake (*Merluccius productus*) and poleward subsurface flow in the California Current System. Canadian Journal of Fisheries and Aquatic Sciences 63:2648–2659.

Armstrong J. L., J. L. Boldt, A. D. Cross, J. H. Moss, N. D. Davis, K. W. Myers, R. V. Walker et al. 2005. Distribution, size, and interannual, seasonal, and diel food habits of northern Gulf of Alaska juvenile pink salmon, *Oncorhynchus gorbuscha*. Deep Sea Research II 52:247–265.

Auad, G., A. Miller, and E. Di Lorenzo. 2006. Long-term forecast of oceanic conditions off California and their biological implications. Journal of Geophysical Research 111, C09008.

Bakun, A. 1990. Global climate change and intensification of coastal ocean upwelling. Science 247:198–201.

Bakun, A., D. B. Field, A. Redondo-Rodriguez, and S. J. Weeks. 2010. Greenhouse gas, upwelling-favorable winds, and the future of coastal ocean upwelling ecosystems. Global Change Biology 16:1213–1228.

Barth, J. A., B. A. Menge, J. Lubchenco, F. Chan, J. M. Bane, A. R. Kirincich, M. A. McManus, K. J. Nielsen, S. D. Pierce, and L. Washburn. 2007. Delayed upwelling alters nearshore coastal ecosystems in the northern California Current. Proceedings of the National Academy of Sciences USA 104(10):3719–3724.

Barth, J. A., S. D. Pierce, and R. L. Smith. 2000. A separating coastal upwelling jet at Cape Blanco, Oregon, and its connection to the California Current System. Deep Sea Research II 47:783–810.

Baumgartner, T. R., A. Soutar, and V. Ferreira-Bartrina. 1992. Reconstruction of the history of the Pacific sardine and northern anchovy populations over the past two millennia from sediments of the Santa Barbara Basin, California. California Cooperative Oceanic Fisheries Investigations Reports 33:24–40.

Beardsley, R. C., C. E. Dorman, C. A. Friehe, L. K. Rosenfeld, and C. D. Winant. 1987. Local atmospheric forcing during the coastal ocean dynamics experiment. I. A description of the marine boundary layer and atmospheric conditions over a northern California upwelling region. Journal of Geophysical Research 92:1467–1488.

Beare, D. J., and E. McKenzie. 1999. Connecting ecological and physical time series: The potential role of changing seasonality. Marine Ecology Progress Series 78:307–309.

Bjorkstedt, E., R. Goericke, S. McClatchie, E. Weber, W. Watson, N. Lo, B. Peterson, R. Brodeur, S. J. Bograd, T. Auth, J. Fisher, C. Morgan, J. Peterson, R. Durazo, G. Gaxiola-Castro, B. Lavaniegos, F. Chavez, C. A. Collins, B. Hannah, J. Field, K. Sakuma, P. Warzybok, R. Bradley, J. Jahncke, W. Sydeman, S. A. Thompson, J. Largier, S. Y. Kim, S. Melin, R. DeLong, and J. Abell. 2012. The state of the California Current, 2011–2012: Ecosystems respond to local forcing as La Niña wavers and wanes. California Cooperative Oceanic Fisheries Investigations Reports 53:41–76.

Black, B. A., I. D. Schroeder, W. J. Sydeman, S. J. Bograd, B. Wells, and F. B. Schwing. 2011. Winter and summer upwelling modes and their biological importance in the California Current Ecosystem. Global Change Biology 17:2536–2545.

Bograd, S., F. Schwing, R. Mendelssohn, and P. Green-Jessen. 2002. On the changing seasonality over the North Pacific. Geophysical Research Letters 29(9):47-1.

Bograd, S. J., and R. J. Lynn. 2003. Long-term variability in the southern California current system. Deep Sea Research II 50(14–16):2355–2370.

———. 2001. Physical-biological coupling in the California Current during the 1997–99 El Niño–La Niña cycle. Geophysical Research Letters 28:275–278.

Bograd, S. J., C. G. Castro, E. Di Lorenzo, D. M. Palacios, H. Bailey, W. Gilly, and F. P. Chavez. 2008. Oxygen declines and the shoaling of the hypoxic boundary in the California current. Geophysical Research Letters 35.

Bograd, S. J., I. Schroeder, N. Sarkar, X. Qiu, W. J. Sydeman, and F. B. Schwing. 2009. The phenology of coastal upwelling in the California Current. Geophysical Research Letters 36, L01602.

Bograd, S. J., P. DiGiacomo, R. Durazo, T. L. Hayward, K. D. Hyrenbach, R. J. Lynn, A. Mantyla, F. Schwing, T. Baumgartner, B. Lavaniegos, and C. S. Moore. 2000. The state of the California Current, 1999–2000: Forward to a new regime? CalCOFI Reports 41:26–52.

Bond, N. A., J. E. Overland, M. Spillane, and P. Stabeno. 2003. Recent shifts in the state of the North Pacific. Geophysical Research Letters 30.

Booth, J.A.T., E. McPhee-Shaw, P. Chua, E. Kingsley, M. Denny, R. Phillips, S. J. Bograd, L. D. Zeidberg, and W. F. Gilly. 2012. Natural intrusions of hypoxic, low pH water into nearshore marine environments on the California coast. Continental Shelf Research 45:108–115.

Brinton, E., and A. Townsend. 2003. Decadal variability in abundances of the dominant euphausiid species in southern sectors of the California Current. Deep Sea Research II 50(14–16):2449–2472.

Brodeur, R. D., S. Ralston, R. L. Emmett, M. Trudel, T. D. Auth, and A. J. Phillips. 2006. Anomalous pelagic nekton abundance, distribution, and apparent recruitment in the northern California Current in 2004 and 2005. Geophysical Research Letters 33, L22S08.

Brotz, L., W.W.L. Cheung, K. Kleisner, E. Pakhomov, and D. Pauly. 2012. Increasing jellyfish populations: Trends in Large Marine Ecosystems. Hydrobiologia 690:3–20.

Castelao, R. M., and J. A. Barth. 2005. Coastal ocean response in a region of alongshore bottom topography variations off Oregon during summer upwelling. Journal of Geophysical Research 110, C10S04.

Centurioni, L. R., J. C. Ohlmann, and P. P. Niiler. 2008. Permanent meanders in the California current system. Journal of Physical Oceanography 38:1690–1710.

Chan, F., J. A. Barth, J. Lubchenco, A. Kirincich, H. Weeks, W. T. Peterson, and B. A. Menge. 2008. Emergence of anoxia in the California Current large marine ecosystem. Science 319(5865):920.

Chavez, F. P., C. A. Collins, A. Huyer, and D. Mackas, editors. 2002a. El Niño along the west coast of North America. Progress in Oceanography 54:1–511.

Chavez, F. P., J. Ryan, S. E. Lluch-Cota, and M. Niquen. 2003. From anchovies to sardines and back: Multidecadal change in the Pacific Ocean. Science 299: 217–221.

Chavez, F. P., J. T. Pennington, C. G. Castro, J. P. Ryan, R. P. Michisaki, B. Schlining, P. Walz, K. R. Buck, A. McFadyen, and C. A. Collins. 2002b. Biological and chemical consequences of the 1997–1998 El Niño in central California waters. Progress in Oceanography 54:205–232.

Checkley, D. M., Jr., and J. A. Barth. 2009. Patterns and processes in the California Current System. Progress in Oceanography 83:49–64.

Checkley, D. M., Jr., J. Alheit, Y. Oozeki, and C. Roy. 2009. Climate change and small pelagic fish. Cambridge University Press, Cambridge, UK

Chelton, D. B. 1984. Seasonal variability of alongshore geostrophic velocity off central California. Journal of Geophysical Research 89:3473–3486.

Chelton, D. B., and R. E. Davis. 1982. Monthly mean sea-level variability along the west coast of North America. Journal of Physical Oceanography 12:757–784.

Chelton, D. B., P. A. Bernal, and J. A. McGowan. 1982. Large-scale interannual physical and biological interaction in the California Current. Journal of Marine Research 40:1095–1125.

Cheung, W.W.L., J. L. Sarmiento, J. Dunne, T. L. Frölicher, V.W.Y. Lam, M. L. Deng Palomares, R. Watson, and D. Pauly. 2012. Shrinking of fishes exacerbates impacts of global ocean changes on marine ecosystems. Nature Climate Change 3:254–258.

Cheung, W.W.L., V.W.Y. Lam, J. L. Sarmiento, K. Kearney, R. Watson, and D. Pauly. 2009. Projecting global marine biodiversity impacts under climate change scenarios. Fish and Fisheries 10:235–251.

Clarke, A. J., and S. Van Gorder. 1994. On ENSO coastal currents and sea levels. Journal of Physical Oceanography 24:661–680.

Cummins, P. F., and H. J. Freeland. 2007. Variability of the North Pacific current and its bifurcation. Progress in Oceanography 75:253–265.

Cushing, D. H. 1990. Plankton production and year-class strength in fish populations: An update of the match-mismatch hypothesis. Advances in Marine Biology 26:249–293.

Deutsch, C., S. Emerson, and L. Thompson. 2005. Fingerprints of climate change in North Pacific oxygen. Geophysical Research Letters 32, L16604.

Diaz, R. J., and R. Rosenberg. 1995. Marine benthic hypoxia: A review of its ecological effects and the behavioral responses of benthic macrofauna. Annual Review of Oceanography and Marine Biology 33:245–303.

Diffenbaugh, N. S. 2005. Response of large-scale eastern boundary current forcing in the twenty-first century. Geophysical Research Letters 32: L19718.

Diffenbaugh, N. S., M. A. Snyder, and L. C. Sloan. 2004. Could CO_2-induced land-cover feedbacks alter nearshore upwelling regimes? Proceedings of the National Academy of Sciences of the USA 101:27–32.

Di Lorenzo E., J. Fiechter, N. Schneider, A. Bracco, A. J. Miller, P.J.S. Franks, S. J. Bograd, A. M. Moore, A. C. Thomas, W. J. Crawford, A. Peña, and A. Hermann. 2009. Nutrient and salinity decadal variations in the central and eastern North Pacific. Geophysical Research Letters 36, L14601.

Di Lorenzo, E., N. Schneider, K. M. Cobb, P.J.S. Franks, K. Chhak, A. J. Miller, J. C. McWilliams, S. J. Bograd, H. Arango, E. Curchitser, T. M. Powell, and P. Riviere. 2008. North Pacific Gyre oscillation links ocean climate and ecosystem change. Geophysical Research Letters 35.

Doney, S. C., M. Ruckelshaus, J. E. Duffy, J. P. Barry, F. Chan, C. A. English, H. M. Galindo, J. M. Grebmeier, A. B. Hollowed, N. Knowlton, J. Polovina, N. N. Rabalais, W. J. Sydeman, and L. D. Talley. 2012. Climate change impacts on marine ecosystems. Annual Reviews of Marine Science 4:11–37.

Doney, S. C., V. J. Fabry, R. A. Feely, and J. A. Kleypas. 2009. Ocean acidification: The other CO2 problem. Annual Reviews of Marine Science 1:169–192.

Durant, J. M., D. O. Hjermann, G. Ottersen, and N. C. Stenseth. 2007. Climate and the match or mismatch between predator requirements and resource availability. Climate Research 33:271–283.

Emery, W., and D. Hamilton. 1985. Atmospheric forcing of interannual variability in the northeast Pacific Ocean: Connections with El Niño. Journal of Geophysical Research 90:857–868.

Feely, R. A., C. L. Sabine, J. M. Hernandez-Ayon, D. Ianson, and B. Hales. 2008. Evidence for upwelling of corrosive "acidified" water onto the continental shelf. Science 320:1490–1492.

Field, D. B., T. R. Baumgartner, C. D. Charles, V. Ferreira-Bartrina, and M. Ohman. 2006. Planktonic foraminifera of the California Current reflect twentieth-century warming. Science 311:63–66.

Field, J. C., K. Baltz, A. J. Phillips, and W. A. Walker. 2007. Range expansion and trophic interactions of the jumbo squid, *Dosidicus gigas*, in the California Current. California Cooperative Oceanic Fisheries Investigations Reports 48:131–146.

Frieder, C. A., S. H. Nam, T. R. Martz, and L. A. Levin. 2012. High temporal and spatial variability of dissolved oxygen and pH in a nearshore California kelp forest. Biogeosciences 9:3917–3930.

García-Reyes, M., and J. Largier. 2010. Observations of increased wind-driven coastal upwelling off central California. Journal of Geophysical Research 115, C04011.

Graham, W. M. 1993. Spatio-temporal scale assessment of an "upwelling shadow" in northern Monterey Bay, California. Estuaries 16:83–91.

Graham, W. M., and J. L. Largier. 1997. Upwelling shadows as nearshore retention sites: The example of northern Monterey Bay. Continental Shelf Research 17:509–532.

Grantham, B. A., F. Chan, K. J. Nielsen, D. S. Fox, J. A. Barth, A. Huyer, J. Lubchenco, and B. A. Menge. 2004. Upwelling-driven nearshore hypoxia signals ecosystem and oceanographic changes in the northeast Pacific. Nature 429:749–754.

Gruber, N., C. Hauri, Z. Lachkar, D. Loher, T. L. Frolicher, and G.-K. Plattner. 2012. Rapid progression of ocean acidification in the California Current. Science 337:220–223.

Hare, S. R., and N. J. Mantua. 2000. Empirical evidence for North Pacific regime shifts in 1977 and 1989. Progress in Oceanography 47:103–145.

Hazen, E. L., S. Jorgensen, R. R. Rykaczewski, S. J. Bograd, D. G. Foley, I. D. Jonsen, S. A. Shaffer, J. P. Dunne, D. P. Costa, L. B. Crowder, and B. A. Block. 2013. Predicted habitat shifts of Pacific top predators in a changing climate. Nature Climate Change 3:234–238.

Hickey, B. M. 1998. Coastal oceanography of western North America from the tip of Baja California to Vancouver Island. Pages 345–393 in A. R. Robinson and K. H. Brink, editors. The Sea, the Global Coastal Ocean, volume 11. John Wiley & Sons, New York, New York.

———. 1979. The California current system—hypotheses and facts. Progress in Oceanography 8:191–279.

Horel, J., and J. M. Wallace. 1981. Planetary-scale atmospheric phenomena associated with the Southern Oscillation. Monthly Weather Review 109:813–829.

Huyer, A. 1983. Coastal upwelling in the California Current System. Progress in Oceanography 12:259–284.

Huyer, A., E.J.C. Sobey, and R. L. Smith. 1979. The spring transition in currents over the Oregon continental shelf. Journal of Geophysical Research 84:6995–7011.

Kahru, M., R. M. Kudela, M. Manzano-Sarabia, and B. G. Mitchell. 2012. Trends in the surface chlorophyll of the California Current: Merging data from multiple ocean color satellites. Deep Sea Research II.

Keeling, R. F., A. K. Kortzinger, and N. Gruber. 2010. Ocean deoxygenation in a warming world. Annual Review of Marine Sciences 2:199–229.

Keeling, R. F., and H. E. Garcia. 2002. The change in oceanic O_2 inventory associated with recent global warming. Proceedings of the National Academy of Sciences USA 99:7848–7853.

Keister, J. E., E. DiLorenzo, C. A. Morgan, V. Combes, and W. T. Peterson. 2011. Copepod species composition is linked to ocean transport in the northern California Current. Global Change Biology 17: 2498–2511.

King, J. R., V. N. Agostini, C. J. Harvey, G. A. McFarlane, M.G.G. Foreman, J. E. Overland, E. Di Lorenzo, N. A. Bond, and K. Y. Aydin. 2011. Climate forcing and the California Current ecosystem. ICES Journal of Marine Science 68:1199–1216.

Koslow, J. A., R. Goericke, A. Lara-Lopez, and W. Watson. 2011. Impact of declining intermediate-water oxygen on deepwater fishes in the California Current. Marine Ecology Progress Series 436:207–218.

Kosro, P. M., W. T. Peterson, B. M. Hickey, R. K. Shearman, and S. D. Pierce. 2006. Physical versus biological spring transition: 2005. Geophysical Research Letters 33, L22S03.

Kudela, R. M., N. S. Banas, J. A. Barth, E. R. Frame, D. A. Jay, J. L. Largier, E. J. Lessard, T. D. Peterson, and A.J.V. Woude. 2008. New insights into the controls and mechanisms of plankton productivity in coastal upwelling waters of the northern California Current System. Oceanography 21:46–59.

Lavaniegos, B. E., and M. D. Ohman. 2007. Coherence of long-term variations of zooplankton in two sectors of the California Current System. Progress in Oceanography 75:42–69.

———. 2003. Long-term changes in pelagic tunicates of the California Current. Deep Sea Research II 50:2473–2498.

Leinweber, A., and N. Gruber. 2013. Variability and trends of ocean acidification in the southern California Current System: A time-series from Santa Monica Bay. Journal of Geophysical Research <doi:118:3622-3633>.

Levin, L. A. 2003. Oxygen minimum zone benthos: Adaptation and community response to hypoxia. Oceanography and Marine Biology 41:1–45.

Lindley, S. T., C. B. Grimes, M. S. Mohr, W. T. Peterson, J. E. Stein, J. J. Anderson, L. W. Botsford, D. L. Bottom, C. A. Busack, and T. K. Collier. 2009. What caused the Sacramento River fall Chinook stock collapse? Pre-publication report to the Pacific Fishery Management Council, U.S. Department of Commerce, NOAA-NMFS, Southwest Fisheries Science Center, Fisheries Ecology Division, Santa Cruz, CA.

Lluch-Belda, D., R. A. Schwartzlose, R. Serra, R. Parrish, T. Kawasaki, D. Hedgecock, R.J.M. Crawford. 1992. Sardine and anchovy regime fluctuations of abundance in four regions of the world oceans: A workshop report. Fisheries Oceanography 1:339–347.

Logerwell, E. A., and P. E. Smith. 2001. Mesoscale eddies and survival of late stage Pacific sardine (*Sardinops sagax*) larvae. Fisheries Oceanography 10:13–25.

Lynn, R. J., and J. J. Simpson. 1987. The California Current System: The seasonal variability of its physical characteristics. Journal of Geophysical Research 92:12947–12966.

Lynn, R. J., and S. J. Bograd. 2002. Dynamic evolution of the 1997–1999 El Niño–La Niña cycle in the southern California Current System. Progress in Oceanography 54:59–75.

Lynn, R. J., S. J. Bograd, T. K. Chereskin, and A. Huyer. 2003. Seasonal renewal of the California Current: The spring transition off California. Journal of Geophysical Research-Oceans 108.

Mackas, D. L., W. T. Peterson, M. D. Ohman, and B. E. Lavaniegos. 2006. Zooplankton anomalies in the California Current System before and during the warm ocean conditions of 2005. Geophysical Research Letters 33, L22S07.

Mantua, N. J., S. H. Hare, Y. Zhang, J. M. Wallace, and R. C. Francis. 1997. A Pacific interdecadal climate oscillation with impacts on salmon production. Bulletin of the American Meteorological Society 78:1069–1079.
Mantyla, A. W., S. J. Bograd, and E. L. Venrick. 2008. Patterns and controls of chlorophyll-*a* and primary productivity cycles in the Southern California Bight. Journal of Marine Systems 73:48–60.
McClatchie, S. 2014. Regional fisheries oceanography of the California Current System: The CalCOFI program. Springer Press, Dordrecht, Netherlands.
McClatchie, S., R. Goericke, R. Cosgrove, G. Auad, and R. Vetter. 2010. Oxygen in the Southern California Bight: Multidecadal trends and implications for demersal fisheries. Geophysical Research Letters 37(19).
McGowan, J. A., S. J. Bograd, R. J. Lynn, and A. J. Miller. 2003. The biological response to the 1977 regime shift in the California Current. Deep Sea Research II 50:2567–2582.
Mendelssohn, R., F. B. Schwing, and S. J. Bograd. 2003. The spatial structure of subsurface temperature variability in the California Current System, 1950–1993. Journal of Geophysical Research 108:3093.
Miller, A. J., D. C. Cayan, T. P. Barnett, N. E. Graham, and J. M. Oberhuber. 1994. Interdecadal variability of the Pacific Ocean: Model response to observed heat flux and wind stress anomalies. Climate Dynamics 9:287–302.
Mote, P. W., and N. J. Mantua. 2002. Coastal upwelling in a warmer future. Geophysical Research Letters 29:2138–2141.
Nam, S. H., H. J. Kim, and U. Send. 2011. Amplification of hypoxic and acidic events by La Niña conditions on the continental shelf off California. Geophysical Research Letters 38, L22602.
Narayan, N., A. Paul, S. Mulitza, and M. Schulz. 2010. Trends in coastal upwelling intensity during the late twentieth century. Ocean Sciences 6:815–823.
Palacios, D. M., S. J. Bograd, R. Mendelssohn, and F. B. Schwing. 2004. Long-term and seasonal trends in stratification in the California Current, 1950–1993. Journal of Geophysical Research-Oceans 109.
Peterson, W. T., and F. B. Schwing. 2003. A new climate regime in northeast Pacific ecosystems. Geophysical Research Letters 30.
Pickett, M. H., and J. D. Paduan. 2003. Ekman transport and pumping in the California Current based on the U.S. Navy's high-resolution atmospheric model (COAMPS). Journal of Geophysical Research 108.
Pierce, S. D., R. L. Smith, P. M. Kosro, J. A. Barth, and C. D. Wilson. 2000. Continuity of the poleward undercurrent along the eastern boundary of the mid-latitude North Pacific. Deep Sea Research II 47:811–829.
Polovina, J. J., E. A. Howell, and M. Abecassis. 2008. Ocean's least productive waters are expanding. Geophysical Research Letters 35:L03618.
Polovina, J. J., J. P. Dunne, P. A. Woodworth, and E. A. Howell. 2011. Projected expansion of the subtropical biome and contraction of the temperate and equatorial upwelling biomes in the North Pacific under global warming. ICES Journal of Marine Science 68:986-995.
Roemmich, D., and J. A. McGowan. 1995. Climatic warming and the decline of zooplankton in the California Current. Science 267:1324–1326.
Ryan, J. P., F. P. Chavez, and J. G. Bellingham. 2005. Physical-biological coupling in Monterey Bay, California: Topographic influences on phytoplankton ecology. Marine Ecology Progress Series 287:23–32.
Rykaczewski, R. R., and D. M. Checkley Jr. 2008. Influence of ocean winds on the pelagic ecosystem in upwelling regions. Proceedings of the National Academy of Sciences USA 105:1965–1970.
Rykaczewski, R. R., and J. P. Dunne. 2010. Enhanced nutrient supply to the California Current ecosystem with global warming and increased stratification in an earth system model. Geophysical Research Letters 37, L21606. <doi:10.1029/2010GL045019>.
Rykaczewski, R.R., J.P. Dunne, W.J. Sydeman, M. Garcia-Reyes, B.A. Black, and S.J. Bograd, 2015. Modeled changes in upwelling-favorable winds in the ocean's eastern boundary currents through the 21st century. Geophysical Research Letters, in press.
Sarmiento, J. L., T.M.C. Hughes, R. J. Stouffer, and S. Manabe. 1998. Simulated response of the ocean carbon cycle to the anthropogenic climate warming. Nature 393:245–248.
Schwartzlose, R. A., J. Alheit, A. Bakun, T. R. Baumgartner, R. Cloete, R.J.M. Crawford, W. J. Fletcher, Y. Green Ruiz, E. Hagen, T. Kawasaki, D. Lluch-Belda, S. E. Lluch-Cota, A. D. MacCall, Y. Matsuura, M. O. Nevarez-Martinez, R. H. Parrish, C. Roy, R. Serra, K. V. Shust, M. N. Ward, and J. Z. Zuzunaga. 1999. Worldwide large-scale fluctuations of sardine and anchovy populations. South African Journal of Marine Science 21:289–347.
Schwing, F. B., and R. Mendelssohn. 1997. Increased coastal upwelling in the California Current System. Journal of Geophysical Research 102:3421–3438.
Schwing, F. B., N. A. Bond, S. J. Bograd, T. Mitchell, M. A. Alexander, and N. Mantua. 2006. Delayed coastal upwelling along the U.S. West Coast in 2005: A historical perspective. Geophysical Research Letters 33.
Schwing, F.B., T. Murphree, L. deWitt, and P. M. Green. 2002. The evolution of oceanic and atmospheric anomalies in the northeast Pacific during the El Niño and La Niña events of 1995–2001. Progress in Oceanography 54:459–491.
Send, U., and S. H. Nam. 2012. Relaxation from upwelling: The effect on dissolved oxygen on the continental shelf. Journal of Geophysical Research—Oceans 117, C04024.
Sette, O. E., and J. D. Isaacs. 1960. Symposium of the changing Pacific Ocean in 1957 and 1958. California Cooperative Oceanic Fisheries Investigations Reports 7:13.
Smith, R. L. 1981. A comparison of the structure and variability of the flow field in three coastal upwelling regions: Oregon, Northwest Africa, and Peru. Pages 107–118 E. A. Richards, editor. Coastal Upwelling. American Geophysical Union, Washington, D.C.
Snyder, M. A., L. C. Sloan, N. S. Diffenbaugh, and J. L. Bell. 2003. Future climate change and upwelling in the California Current. Geophysical Research Letters 30:1823–1826.
Steele, J. H. 2004. Regime shifts in the ocean: Reconciling observations and theory. Progress in Oceanography 60:135–141.
Stenseth, N. C., and A. Mysterud. 2002. Climate, changing phenology, and other life history traits: Nonlinearity and match-mismatch to the environment. Proceedings of the National Academy of Sciences of the USA 99:13379–13381.
Stewart, J. S., E. L. Hazen, D. G. Foley, S. J. Bograd, and W. F. Gilly. 2012. Marine predator migration during range expansion: Humboldt squid (*Dosidicus gigas*) in the northern California Current System. Marine Ecology Progress Series 471:135–150.
Stramma, L., E. D. Prince, S. Schmidtko, J. Luo, J. P. Hoolihan, M. Visbeck, D.W.R. Wallace, P. Brandt, and A. Körtzinger. 2011. Expansion of oxygen minimum zones may reduce available habitat for tropical pelagic fishes. Nature Climate Change 2:33–37.
Stramma, L., S. Schmidtko, L. A. Levin, and G. C. Johnson. 2010. Ocean oxygen minima expansions and their biological impacts. Deep Sea Research I 57:1–9.
Strub, P. T., and C. James. 2002. Altimeter-derived surface circulation in the large-scale NE Pacific gyres: Part 2. 1997–1998 El Niño anomalies. Progress in Oceanography 53:185–214.
———. 2000. Altimeter-derived variability of surface velocities in the California Current System: Part 2. Seasonal circulation and eddy statistics. Deep Sea Research II 47:831–870.
———. 1988. Atmospheric conditions during the spring and fall transitions in the coastal ocean off western United States. Journal of Geophysical Research 93:15561–15584.
Strub, P. T., P. M. Kosro, A. Huyer, and CTZ Collaborators. 1991. The nature of the cold filaments in the California Current System. Journal of Geophysical Research 96:14743–14768.
Sverdrup, H. U., M. W. Johnson, and R. H. Fleming. 1942. The oceans: Their physics, chemistry, and general biology. Prentice-Hall, Upper Saddle River, New Jersey.
Sydeman, W. J., and S. J. Bograd. 2009. Marine ecosystems, climate, and phenology: Introduction. Marine Ecology Progress Series 393:185–188.
Sydeman, W. J., J. A. Santora, S. A. Thompson, B. M. Marinovic, and E. Di Lorenzo. 2013. Increasing variance in North Pacific climate relates to unprecedented ecosystem variability off California. Global Change Biology 19:1662–1675.
Sydeman, W. J., K. L. Mills, J. A. Santora, S. A. Thompson, D. F. Bertram, K. H. Morgan, M. A. Hipfner, B. K. Wells, and S. G. Wolf. 2009. Seabirds and climate in the California Current—a synthesis of change. CalCOFI Reports 50:82–104.

Sydeman, W. J., M. Garisol-Reyes, D. Schoeman, R. Rykaczewski, B. A. Black, and S. J. Bograd. 2014. Climate change and wind intensification in coastal upwelling systems. Science 345:77–80.

Sydeman, W. J., R. W. Bradley, P. Warzybok, C. L. Abraham, J. Jahncke, K. D. Hyrenbach, V. Kousky, J. M. Hipfner, and M. D. Ohman. 2006. Planktivorous auklet *Ptychoramphus aleuticus* responses to ocean climate, 2005: Unusual atmospheric blocking? Geophysical Research Letters 33.

Tchernia, P. 1980. Descriptive regional oceanography. Volume 253. Pergamon Press, Oxford, UK.

Thomas, A. C., and P. Brickley. 2006. Satellite measurements of chlorophyll distribution during spring 2005 in the California Current. Geophysical Research Letters 33, L22S05.

Weise, M. J., D. P. Costa, and R. M. Kudela. 2006. Movement and diving behavior of male California sea lion (*Zalophus californianus*) during anomalous oceanographic conditions of 2005 compared to those of 2004. Geophysical Research Letters 33, L22S10.

Whitney, F. A., H. Freeland, and M. Robert. 2007. Persistently declining oxygen levels in the interior waters of the eastern subarctic Pacific. Progress in Oceanography 75:179–199.

Whitney, F. A., S. J. Bograd, and T. Ono. 2013. Nutrient enrichment of the subarctic Pacific Ocean pycnocline. Geophysical Research Letters 40: 2200–2205.

Woodson, C. B., D. I. Eerkes-Medrano, A. Flores-Morales, M. Foley, S. Henkel, M. Hessing-Lewis, D. Jacinto, L. Needles, M. Nishizaki, J. O'Leary, C. E. Ostrander, M. Pespeni, K. Schwager, J. A. Tyburczy, K. A. Weersing, A. R. Kirincich, J. A. Barth, M. A. McManus, and L. Washburn. 2008. Diurnal upwelling driven by sea breezes in northern Monterey Bay: A local mechanism for larval delivery to the intertidal? Continental Shelf Research 27:2289–2302.

Woodson, C. B., L. Washburn, J. A. Barth, D. J. Hoover, A. R. Kirincich, M. A. McManus, J. P. Ryan, and J. A. Tyburczy. 2009. Northern Monterey Bay upwelling shadow front: Observations of a coastally and surface-trapped buoyant plume. Journal of Geophysical Research 114, C12013.

Woodworth-Jefcoats, P. A., J. J. Polovina, J. P. Dunne, and J. L. Blanchard. 2013. Ecosystem size structure response to twenty-first-century climate projection: Large fish abundance decreases in the central North Pacific and increases in the California Current. Global Change Biology 19:724–733.

Wooster, W. S., and J. H. Jones. 1970. California undercurrent off northern Baja California. Journal of Marine Research 28:235–250.

SEVEN

Atmospheric Chemistry

ANDRZEJ BYTNEROWICZ, MARK FENN, EDITH B. ALLEN, and RICARDO CISNEROS

Introduction

In this chapter we discuss air pollution effects on mixed conifer forests and other ecosystems in California with a major focus on the most ecologically influential pollutants, OZONE (O_3) and various nitrogen (N) compounds. From the perspective of human health effects, we focus on fine PARTICULATE MATTER ($PM_{2.5}$) and ozone. We discuss other pollutants briefly in the context of potential toxic effects or impacts on climatic changes. Air quality issues in California have a long history. In precolonial times, long before the modern-day smog problem emerged in the 1940s (Jacobs and Kelley 2008), air quality was almost certainly poor at times due to emissions from lightning-caused fires and those set by Native Americans (Minnich 2008). The Spanish explorer Juan Rodriguez Cabrillo, after sailing into what is now San Pedro Harbor in 1542, named it La Bahia de las Fumas (the bay of smokes) after the darkened skies caused by fires set by Native Americans (Jacobs and Kelly 2008). Approximately 1.8 million hectares burned annually in precontact California, equivalent to 88% of the land area burned in the entire U.S. during extreme wildfire years (Stephens et al. 2007). As a result, skies were likely smoky during much of the summer and fall in that era.

On modern-day air pollution in California, Char Miller (Pomona College, Claremont, California) shared the following personal retrospective: "The postcard on my desk is almost forty years old. Angelenos of a certain age will recognize it—a wide-angled, aerial shot of the downtown core of Los Angeles and its then, much-more modest skyline. Framed by the intersection of the Santa Monica and Harbor freeways, the whole scene is muffled in a brown smear of smog. Barely visible in the deep background, just poking above the thick toxic stew, is a snow-capped Mt. Baldy, the tallest of the San Gabriels. Reads the arch caption: 'Greetings from Los Angeles.' I first spotted the card in the fall of 1972 when I came to Southern California to attend Pitzer College, and immediately sent a steady stream of them to family and friends back east. They got its black humor, which I reinforced when I confessed (and perhaps bragged) that my dorm room was within five miles of Mt. Baldy yet I almost never saw its bold face. Now I see it every day, often with stunning clarity, as if the entire range was etched out of a blue true dream of sky" (Miller 2011).

Summer 1943 marked the beginning of smog in Los Angeles, or at least of public awareness of the approaching air pollution tidal wave. On July 26, 1943, the fourth and by far the most severe smog episode reported that month abruptly appeared in Los Angeles as a thick, suffocating, and noxious haze (City Hunting 1943). Something corrosive was in the air—women's nylon stockings repeatedly developed runs and holes (Jacobs and Kelley 2008), and tire manufacturers noticed that rubber disintegrated faster in Los Angeles than anywhere in the country (SCAQMD 1997). In 1944 plant pathologists at the University of California–Riverside first observed unusual symptoms on agricultural crops in the Los Angeles Basin, which they attributed to a new kind of air pollution: Los Angeles smog (Middleton et al. 1950). It wasn't until the early 1950s that a group led by Ariel Haagen-Smit, a Dutch biochemist at Cal Tech (California Institute of Technology in Pasadena), identified the atmospheric compounds and photochemical reactions responsible for this new kind of air pollution (Finlayson-Pitts and Pitts 2000, Haagen-Smit and Fox 1954).

Since the mid-1940s, air quality in California, especially in its southern part, has been among the worst in the nation. We now know that the infamous Los Angeles PHOTOCHEMICAL smog is a result of uncontrolled emissions of VOLATILE ORGANIC COMPOUNDS (VOCs), carbon monoxide (CO), and NITROGEN OXIDES (NO_x) from millions of motor vehicles and other pollution sources. These compounds undergo photochemical reactions under conditions of high temperatures, light intensity, and THERMAL INVERSIONS typical in summer in the Los Angeles Basin, bounded by several mountain ranges. Thousands of secondary chemical compounds are formed during such reactions, including highly toxic ozone, NITRIC ACID VAPOR (HNO_3), peroxyacetyl nitrate (PAN), and many other compounds toxic to vegetation and humans (Seinfeld and Pandis 1998, Finlayson-Pitts and Pitts 2000).

Unusual symptoms of decline in ponderosa pine (*Pinus ponderosa*) trees were first observed in 1953 in the western portions of the San Bernardino Mountains east of the Los Angeles Basin (Asher 1956). Since the cause of the symptoms was initially unknown, the observed phenomenon was described as "X-disease" by local foresters (Parmeter et al. 1962, Richards et al. 1968, Ohmart 1980, Little 1992). James Asher, a timber management assistant on the San Bernardino National Forest, described his observations of the tree decline in his historic report: "The foliage deterioration, affecting an increasing percentage of the ponderosa pine forest stands within the Arrowhead Ranger District, has been noted with growing concern. This effect, known as the 'X Disease' or 'Needle Dieback' is causing loss of vigor and thus a lessening of annual increments on an alarming number of trees. Though the causative agent is classed as 'unknown,' mortality is occurring." The report suggested possible causes of the malady, but in Asher's view the decline was due to "a heavy concentration of air pollutants borne onto the foliage of the ponderosa pine" (Asher 1956, Little 1992). Subsequent groundbreaking studies conducted by Paul Miller, a U.S. Forest Service scientist, with the use of controlled fumigation of seedlings and branches of mature trees, later showed that ozone was responsible for so-called X-disease, or chlorotic decline (Miller et al. 1963). Symptoms on native ponderosa and Jeffrey pines (*Pinus jeffreyii*) in the San Bernardino Mountains were eventually found to include CHLOROTIC MOTTLE, premature needle loss, reduction of terminal and diameter growth, deterioration of root systems, greater susceptibility to bark beetles, and eventual death of trees (Grulke et al. 2009, Miller 1992).

Since smog became an undeniable problem in the Los Angeles Basin in the 1940s, it has taken decades of struggle on the local, state, and national levels to build the political capital and legislative clout needed to pass emissions control regulations that have made possible major improvements in the air quality of California (Jacobs and Kelly 2008). Various science-based air pollution regulations have been introduced by the California Air Resources Board and local Air Quality Management Districts (http://www.arb.ca.gov/html/brochure/history.htm). As a result of these regulations and their enforcement, air pollution in the Los Angeles Basin has been improving since the 1970s. Air pollution regulation initiated in California strongly influenced the passage of the CLEAN AIR ACT and the development of national standards for controlling major toxic air pollutants (http://www.epa.gov/air/caa/) (Table 7.1).

Temporal and Spatial Patterns of Air Quality: An Overview

While naturally produced air pollution is important (e.g., volcanic emissions of sulfurous gases and AEROSOLS, ozone and nitric acid vapor produced by lightning, emissions of methane (CH_4) from bogs and marshes, dust released from deserts and other arid areas), presently air pollution caused by various anthropogenic activities have much larger effects on human and ecosystem health (Finlayson-Pitts and Pitts 2000, Chapin et al. 2011). Anthropogenic air pollution has been affecting terrestrial ecosystems in California for many decades. In the past, high concentrations of sulfur dioxide (SO_2) or hydrogen fluoride (HF) emitted from point sources such as power plants or metal smelters had only local negative effects on vegetation. Rapid urbanization, increase of automobile traffic, and expansion of various anthropogenic activities (industry, agriculture, residential emissions, and many small business enterprises) made poor air quality a major problem in the Los Angeles Basin and other areas, especially the Central Valley and the San Francisco Bay Area. Agricultural emissions significantly contribute to severe air pollution problems in the Central Valley and in portions of the eastern Los Angeles Basin with high density of dairy farms (Carle 2006). Changes in landscape use, such as the massive movement of dairy farms from the Los Angeles Basin into the Central Valley in the 2000s, have significantly changed the spatial distribution of agricultural emissions in the state (Farrell 2005).

In the seventy years since the first episodes of severe smog in the Los Angeles Basin occurred, air quality in California has generally improved (Pollack et al. 2013). This has resulted from active, science-based implementation of strict air pollution measures, such as the introduction of catalytic converters, reformulation of gasoline, reduced consumption of gasoline in cars and other vehicles, and elimination of most heavy-emitting stationary and mobile pollution sources. These trends are reflected more broadly in a continuing decrease in emissions of nitrogen oxides and reactive organic gases (ROG) in California (Figure 7.1).

However, emissions of fine particulate matter (<2.5 µm in diameter, $PM_{2.5}$) and coarse particulate matter (<10 µm in diameter, PM_{10}) have not decreased or even slightly increased.

Photo on previous page: Air masses contaminated by San Joaquin Valley photochemical smog affect air quality in Sequoia National Park, August 2014. Photo: A. Bytnerowicz.

TABLE 7.1
Air pollutants exhibiting significant effects on California terrestrial ecosystems

Pollutant	Typical concentration ranges in remote areas	Mode of action	Sensitive receptor	Ecological response	References
Ozone (O_3)	1 hour: 0–150 ppb; summer average: 20–80 ppb	Oxygen free radical damage to chloroplasts	Ponderosa and Jeffrey pines	Foliar damage, growth decrease, and increased sensitivity to drought and bark beetle attacks	Bytnerowicz and Grulke 1992, Bytnerowicz et al. 2008
Ammonia (NH_3)	0.2–18.5 $\mu g/m^3$ (summer average)	Direct toxicity to oligotrophic lichens; contribution to N deposition	Oligotrophic lichens; native forbs	Changes in lichen communities; increased invasion of grasses (for effects of N deposition, see Table 7.2)	Bytnerowicz and Fenn 1996, Bytnerowicz et al. 2007, Fenn et al. 2011
Nitrogen oxides (NOx)	NO: < 25 ppb NO_2: < 50 ppb	Contribution to N deposition and ozone formation	Various natural vegetation communities	As above	Bytnerowicz et al. 1998
Nitric acid vapor (HNO_3)	0.3–17.5 $\mu g/m^3$ (summer average)	Direct toxicity to plant cuticles; contribution to N deposition	Various natural vegetation communities	As above	Bytnerowicz and Fenn 1996, Bytnerowicz et al. 2007
Semivolatile organic compounds (SOCs)	Differ for various compounds	Movement in food chain; accumulation of toxic compounds in animal tissue	Sensitive wildlife species, including pollinators, fish, and mammals	Effects increase with higher position in a food chain	Landers et al. 2010

Many areas in California, especially in its southern part and in the Central Valley, suffer from poor air quality and frequent violations of air pollution standards for ozone and particulate matter. In January 2014 extremely high fine particulate matter levels, exceeding by about three times the national air quality standard of 35 mg m^{-3}, were recorded near Fresno and Bakersfield in the Central Valley. Such levels are caused by high pollution emissions, lack of rain that typically cleans the air, stagnant conditions, and prolonged thermal inversions that keep polluted air masses near the ground. Concentrations of fine particulates and other pollutants are largely driven by weather conditions (pers. comm., Dr. Barbara Finlayson-Pitts, University of California–Irvine). Chemical reactions that convert nitrogen oxides and other gases from cars, diesel trucks, trains, ships, and factory emissions into haze-forming fine particles are further accelerated by greater humidity when fog blankets the area (Barboza 2014). Five of ten of the most polluted U.S. urban areas (Bakersfield; Los Angeles–Long Beach–Riverside; Visalia-Porterville; Hanford-Corcoran; and Fresno-Madera) are in California (American Lung Association 2013). Emissions from these pollution source areas influence air quality in remote areas of California, with pronounced ecological effects. For example, the San Bernardino Mountains and the Sierra Nevada Mountains are strongly affected by air pollution from, respectively, the Los Angeles Basin and the Central Valley (Figure 7.2).

Elevated levels of ambient ozone and atmospheric NITROGEN DEPOSITION, though much lower than several decades

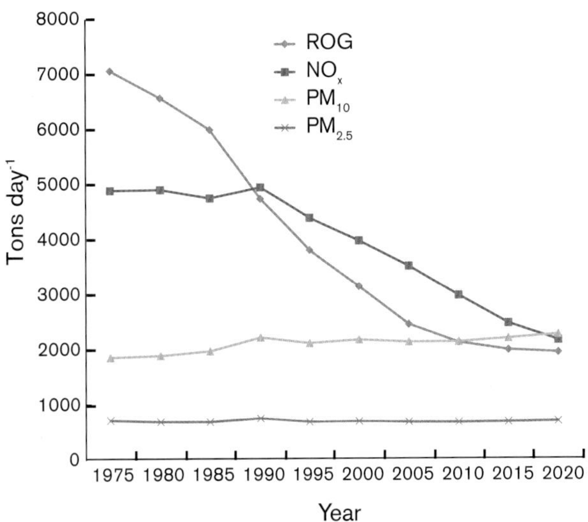

FIGURE 7.1 Changes in air pollution emissions in California: totals for reactive organic gases (ROG), nitrogen oxides (NOx), particulate matter <2.5 µm in diameter ($PM_{2.5}$) and particulate matter <10 µm in diameter (PM_{10}). Source: California Air Resources Board. http://www.arb.ca.gov/aqd/almanac/almanac.htm. Accessed June 10, 2015.

FIGURE 7.2 Photochemical smog.

A Over the Los Angeles Basin, view from the San Bernardino Mountains, June 2003. Photo: Andrzej Bytnerowicz.

B Over the San Joaquin Valley, view from Moro Rock, September 2014. Photo: Andrzej Bytnerowicz.

ago, still pose severe threats to vegetation in California. Long-range transport of polluted air masses from Mexico (Wang et al. 2009) or across the Pacific from Asia also contribute substantially to elevated ozone levels (Vingarzan 2004). Increased ozone concentrations could also result from climate change in California. Prolonged lack of precipitation and stagnant conditions resulted in serious smog problems in downtown Los Angeles and its coastal areas in January 2014 (Barboza 2014). Other potentially toxic pollutants, such as PESTICIDES from extensive agricultural operations or deposition of mercury (Hg) from combustion processes, can be transported long-distance and deposited to sensitive ecosystems in remote areas of California. The long-term biogeochemical effects of these pollutants on aquatic and terrestrial ecosystems are of concern.

Statewide Atmospheric Circulation Patterns and Their Implications for Air Pollution Transport

Pollutant transport is a complex phenomenon. Sometimes transport can be straightforward, as when wind blows from one area to another at ground level and carries polluted air masses with it. However, most often transport patterns are three-dimensional and can take place either at the surface or high above the ground (aloft). Winds can blow in different directions at various heights above the ground. To further complicate matters, winds can shift during the day, moving polluted air masses in multiple directions. Therefore accurate determinations of the impacts of pollution transported from a source area to a downwind area require complex analyses and modeling (Austin et al. 2001).

Air masses in California broadly tend to move from the coast inland. Typical summer wind patterns for California (Figure 7.3) involve northwesterly winds, which are a consequence of GEOSTROPHIC BALANCE between the subtropical ANTICYCLONE over the eastern Pacific Ocean and thermal low pressure over the California, Nevada, and Arizona deserts driving air masses onshore to the coastal ranges (Fujioka et al. 1999). In the San Francisco Bay area, at the gap of the coastal ranges, these onshore winds diverge into two streams: one flowing northward into the Sacramento Valley and the other southward into the San Joaquin Valley. The marine layer (or marine air mass trapped by thermal inversion) over the California coast usually dissipates in the Central Valley due to ADIABATIC HEATING and mixing with warm air aloft. Warm, boundary layer air masses overlaying the Central Valley are stratified by a weak thermal inversion at 1,000 to 1,300 meters. Daytime land heating generates local ANABATIC WINDS from the southwest and west along the western Sierra Nevada slopes, moving polluted air masses eastward into the Sierra crest. Finally, marine air funnels through low passes in the Sierra Nevada into the Mojave Desert and the Modoc Plateau (Minnich and Padgett 2003). In the upper half of the state, the fall and spring wind patterns are quite similar to those in summer, although generally much weaker. However, during winter the combination of strong horizontal mixing aloft in the presence of the jet stream, weak INSOLATION, and strong thermal inversions overlaying the Central Valley shifts wind patterns and reduces transport of polluted air masses into the Sierra Nevada (Hayes et al. 1992, Minnich and Padgett 2003).

In southern California during warm summers, cool winds flow inland from the Pacific Ocean (Figure 7.4). These winds mostly consist of the "onshore south" and "sea breeze" types, which constitute approximately 70% of all summer winds (Hayes et al. 1992). Pacific high pressure affects air pollution transport in the South Coast Air Basin primarily through a SUBSIDENCE INVERSION, which caps the mixing layer and promotes cloud-free conditions above the inversion. In the resulting absence of clouds, temperatures rise faster over land than over the ocean. This causes a sea breeze from the Pacific Ocean moving eastward and inland. Cloudless skies above the inversion also make more sun available for photochemical reactions inside the inversion layer, resulting in formation of high concentrations of ozone and other secondary air pollutants. Since the sea breeze is typically capped at relatively low elevation (~1,000 meters above sea level), the polluted air masses are trapped inside the Los Angeles Basin (Fujioka et al. 1999). With air moving eastward in the late afternoon hours, the western slopes of the San Bernardino and San Gabriel Mountains experience very high ozone concentrations (Bytnerowicz et al. 2008). The Transverse and Peninsular mountain ranges form barriers to the movement of sea breezes further inland. While spring wind patterns are quite similar to those in summer, fall and especially winter patterns are quite different. They involve

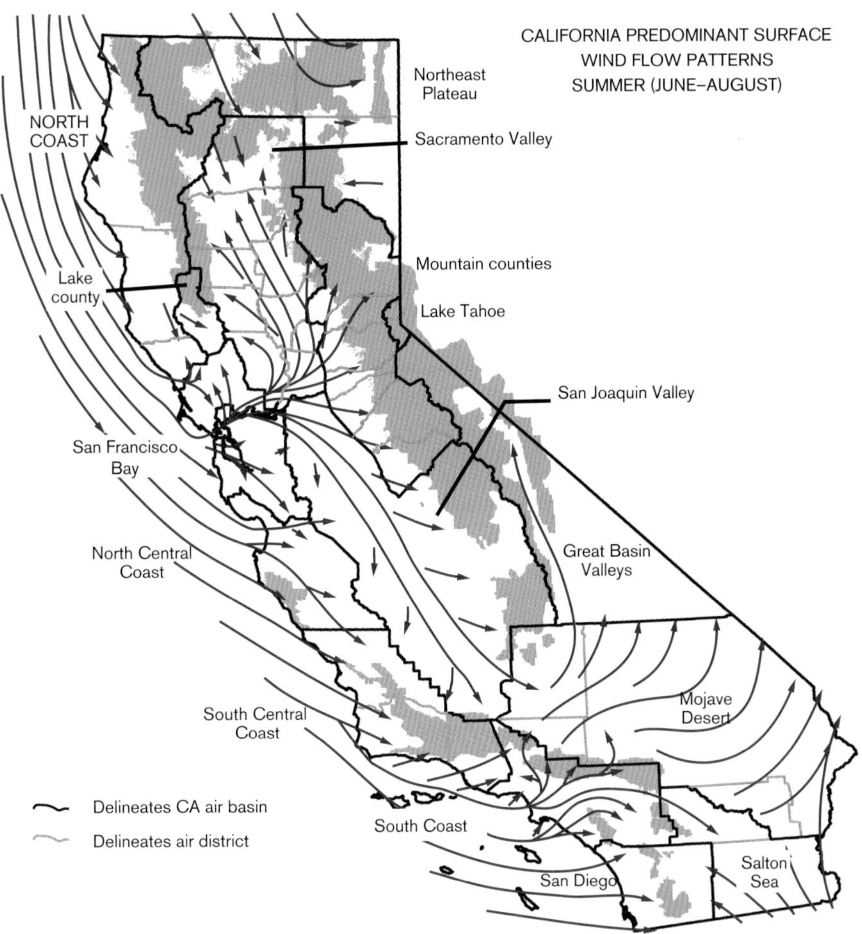

FIGURE 7.3 Typical summer (June–August) wind flow patterns in California. Green shaded areas are forests on federal lands. Source: Hayes et al. 1992.

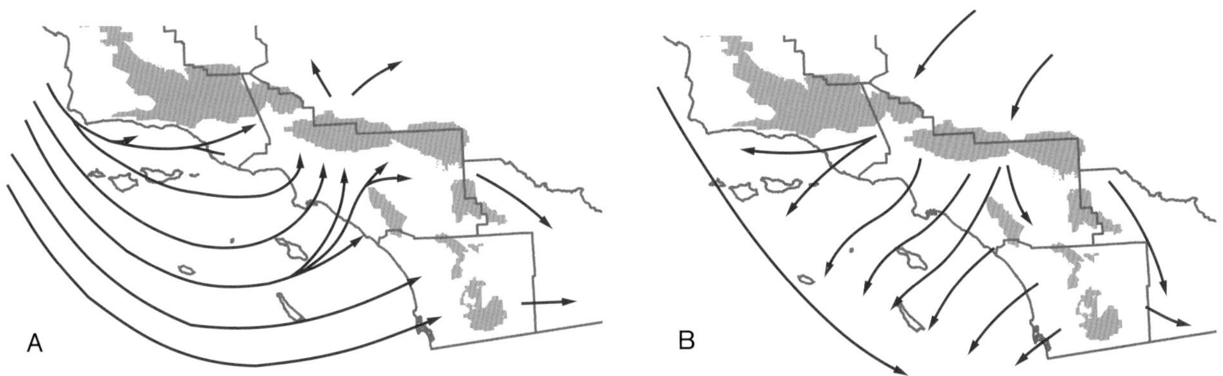

FIGURE 7.4 Examples of wind patterns in the South Coast Air Basin. Green shaded areas are forests on federal lands. Source: Hayes et. al. 1992.

A Summer, onshore south.

B Winter, full Santa Ana winds.

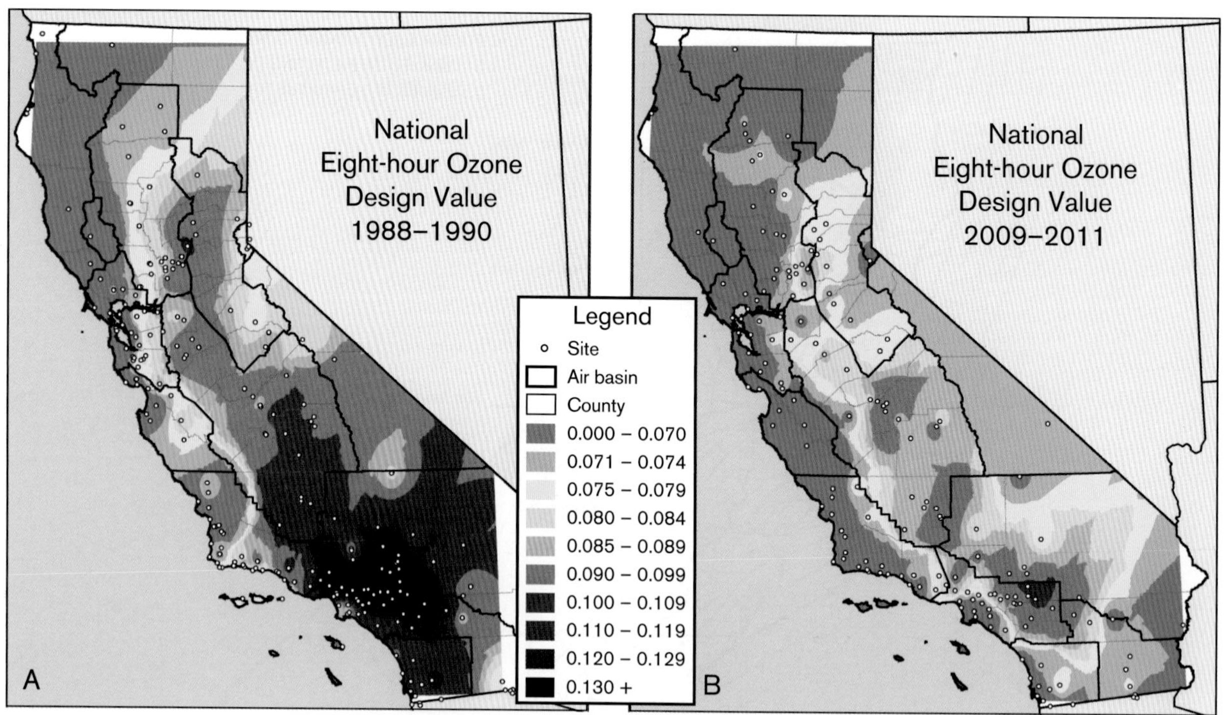

FIGURE 7.5 Three-year average of fourth-highest daily maximum eight-hour average ozone concentrations (ppm, parts per million) for (A) 1988–1990 and (B) 2009–2011. Values >0.075 ppm indicate exceedance of the federal primary air pollution standard. Source: California Air Resources Board.

much higher occurrence of the southerly, downslope/transitional, and strong SANTA ANA WINDS (Hayes et al. 1992), which sweep the air from the Los Angeles Basin into the Pacific Ocean (see Figure 7.4) (see also Chapter 2, "Climate").

Ozone Distribution in Space and Time

California still has the highest ozone air pollution and associated highest risks to human health in the U.S. (CASTNET 2013). However, recent progress in ozone air quality in California is impressive (Figure 7.5), and further improvement in O_3 air quality is expected. Part of this improvement mirrors broader geographic trends. Many Northern Hemisphere sites that showed increasing ozone concentrations fifteen to thirty years ago also show slightly decreasing or flattening patterns in the past ten to fifteen years (Oltmans et al. 2013). In California's urban areas maximum hourly ozone concentrations declined drastically between the 1970s and mid-1990s and have continued to shrink since, but at a more moderate rate (Pollack et al. 2013). The most improved ozone air quality took place in the South Coast Air Quality Management District (AQMD) followed by the San Diego AQMD. The Sacramento, San Francisco, and San Joaquin AQMDs had much smaller decreases in ozone concentrations (Figure 7.6). Similar to urban area trends, significant improvement of ozone air quality has also been observed in remote areas in California, including the San Bernardino Mountains (Bytnerowicz et al. 2008, Bytnerowicz, Fenn et al. 2013).

Projections based on recent data (approximately fifteen years of data) at the highly polluted San Bernardino Mountains site of Crestline indicate that by 2100, ozone levels could become similar to those before the photochemical smog episodes started occurring in the Los Angeles Basin in the 1940s (Bytnerowicz, Fenn, et al. 2013). These long-term projections have very large uncertainty because of many factors—especially demographic, economic, and technological—that will affect future air pollution emissions, levels, and spatial distribution. From an ecological perspective, information on ozone distribution in remote forested areas is essential. Because the reliability of pollution transport models in complex mountain terrain is limited (Austin et al. 2001), the USDA Forest Service has developed methods for ground-level air pollution monitoring in remote California areas using PASSIVE SAMPLERS. Samplers provide long-term average (weeks, months) concentrations of various air pollutants, and their results are spatially displayed as geostatistically generated maps (Arbaugh and Bytnerowicz 2003, Frączek et al. 2003, Panek et al. 2013). Because evaluations of the phytotoxic potential of ozone also requires information on its real-time concentrations, portable battery and solar-panel operated UV-absorption O_3 monitors are also used (Bognar and Birks 1996).

Results of 1999 air pollution monitoring conducted over the entire range of the Sierra Nevada Mountains show the highest summer ozone averages in its southern portion (Frączek et al. 2003). High levels of the pollutant are caused by LONG-RANGE TRANSPORT of polluted air masses containing ozone and its precursors (nitrogen oxides, volatile organic compounds, carbon monoxide) from the California Central Valley (on the southwestern Sierra slopes) and southern California (on the southeastern Sierra slopes). Further north, ozone concentrations are generally lower, although the mid-elevation western slopes, including Sequoia and Kings Canyon and Yosemite National Parks, may experience very high levels at times (Bytnerowicz et al. 2002, Burley and Ray 2007). Ozone can penetrate into the eastern portions of the Sierra Nevada along canyons and valleys crossing the range, as shown by high concentrations sustained along the southwest-northeast tran-

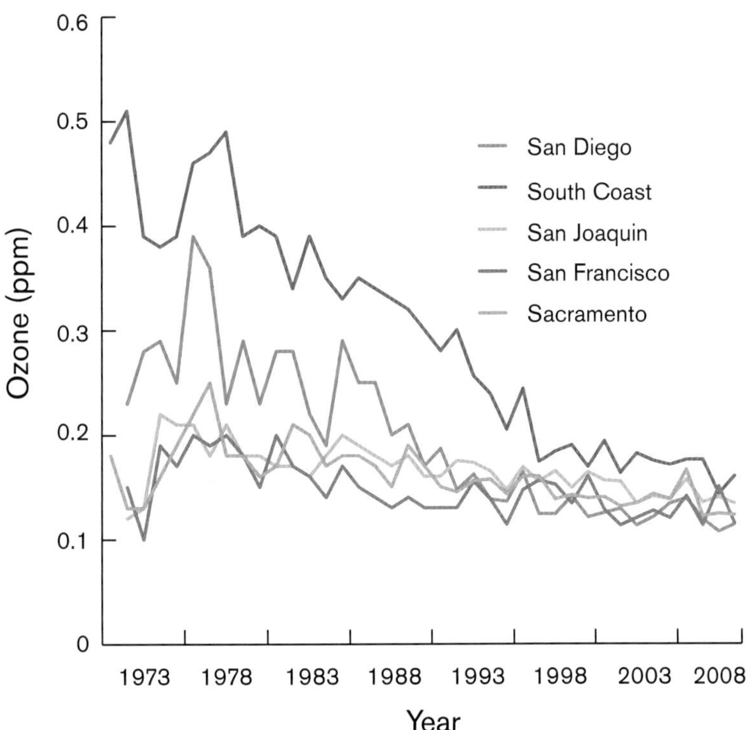

FIGURE 7.6 Changes in maximum one-hour ozone concentrations (ppm, parts per million) in selected Air Quality Management Districts in California. http://www.arb.ca.gov/aqd/almanac/almanac.htm. Accessed June 10, 2015.

sect of the San Joaquin River drainage (Cisneros et al. 2010). However, high mountain ranges can also create barriers to the movement of the polluted air masses (Frączek et al. 2003). For example, polluted air masses from the California Central Valley are blocked from entering the Lake Tahoe Basin by the high elevation massif of the Desolation Wilderness (Gertler et al. 2006). Ozone air pollution in the Lake Tahoe Basin is thus generally low and mainly results from local ozone generation. Because levels of other pollutants are also low, air quality in the Lake Tahoe Basin is generally good, with high visibility during most of the summer. Occasionally, at some of the most polluted sites on the eastern side of the Lake Tahoe Basin, elevated ozone occurs due to long-range transport of polluted upper layers of tropospheric air (Gertler et al. 2006).

Ozone concentrations decline as air masses move over forested slopes due to stomatal uptake of the pollutant, as was reported in the western portions of Sequoia and Kings Canyon National Park (Bytnerowicz et al. 2002). This is in contrast to only slightly decreasing ozone concentrations when air masses move over a sparsely forested landscape (Cisneros et al. 2010). Generally, the lowest ozone pollution in a remote eastern Sierra Nevada site (Devils Postpile National Monument) occurred when air masses originating from over the Pacific Ocean crossed the California Central Valley at high elevation (3–5 kilometers). The highest ozone pollution at Devils Postpile occurred when air masses swept at low altitudes over the highly polluted San Francisco Bay Area and the San Joaquin Valley (Bytnerowicz, Burley et al. 2013).

Ozone distribution in southern California generally shows strong west-to-east concentration gradients, as seen in the San Bernardino Mountains, with very high concentrations on their western side and low concentrations, close to CONTINENTAL BACKGROUND levels, in their eastern portion near Big Bear Lake (Bytnerowicz et al. 2008). A similar pattern occurs in the most O_3-polluted national park in the U.S., Joshua Tree National Park in the western Mojave Desert (Burley et al. 2014). Finally, southwest-to-northeast winds move polluted air masses from the Los Angeles Basin, causing elevated ozone concentrations in the Owens Valley and southeastern Sierra Nevada Mountains (Figure 7.7).

Biological Effects of Ozone

Ozone effects on vegetation depend on its concentrations, and more specifically on the dose of ozone taken up by plants as well as their physiological and biochemical defense mechanisms. Negative effects of ozone on plants include chlorophyll damage, reduced stomatal conductance, premature foliar senescence, and lower root mass, resulting in decreased photosynthesis (Grulke 2003). Various abiotic and biotic characteristics, especially water availability, ambient temperature, and the presence of pests and diseases, influence the extent of ozone phytotoxic effects (Bytnerowicz and Grulke 1992).

Severe ozone effects of this type on sensitive ponderosa and Jeffrey pines in the San Bernardino Mountains continued through about 1978. Subsequently and through 1988, tree condition improved as ozone concentrations decreased (Miller et al. 1989). Values for several PHYTOTOXIC INDICES calculated for the 1980–2010 period at Crestline, the most highly ozone-polluted site in the San Bernardino Mountains, indicate pronounced decreases during the 1980–1995 period and much slower decreases since 1995. Values at this site still place the western side of the San Bernardino Mountains as the forested area with the highest ozone exposure in the U.S. and with high potential for negative effects (Bytnerowicz et al. 2008, Vollenweider et al. 2013).

Ozone injury in forests of the Sierra Nevada Mountains was

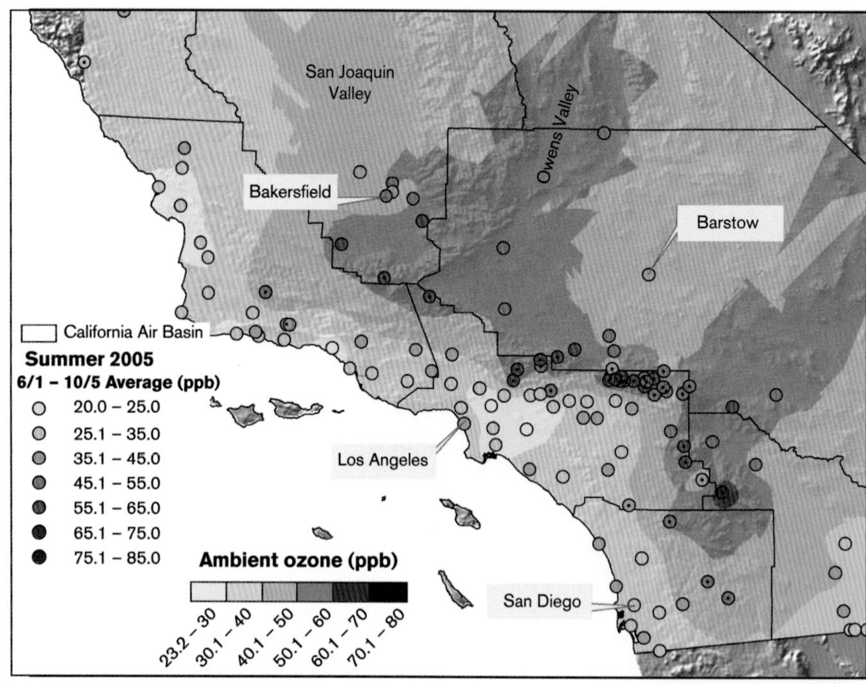

FIGURE 7.7 Influence of southern California smog on ozone air pollution in the Owens Valley and eastern Sierra Nevada, summer 2005 (1ppb = 10^{-3} ppm). Source: A. Bytnerowicz, unpublished.

first observed in the western portions of Sequoia National Forest and Sequoia National Park in the early 1970s (Miller and Millecan 1971, Williams et al. 1977). In the 1970s and 1980s ozone injury symptoms were discovered over most of the Sierra Nevada, with more than 20% of the evaluated ponderosa and Jeffrey pines affected. The lowest ozone injury was detected in the northern Sierra Nevada, while in the southwestern portion of the range the most severe symptoms occurred (with the worst injury at elevations lower than 1,800 meters). Injury declined along the west-to-east direction across the Sierra Nevada as distance from the highly polluted California Central Valley increased (Carroll et al. 2003). The most severe injury of pines was found in Sequoia and Kings Canyon and Yosemite National Parks (respectively 39% and 29% of trees with injury symptoms). Ozone injury evaluations repeated in 2000 on a subset of monitoring plots in the Sierra and Sequoia National Forests showed a gradual increase in the number of trees with chlorotic mottle—from 21% of all trees in 1977 to 40% in 2000. In the southern Sierra Nevada Mountains plots, tree mortality reached 7% during that period. Ozone was the primary cause of tree death (36.5%), with bark beetles and wood borers responsible for 27.9% of mortality, followed by forest fire (15.4%) and other less significant factors such as broken tops, mistletoe, logging damage or windthrow (Carroll et al. 2003). Ozone is a predisposing damaging factor in tree mortality in California, while other factors (such as drought and infestations by various species of bark beetles) are the ultimate cause of mortality (Fenn et al. 2003, Minnich and Padgett 2003).

Nitrogen Air Pollution and Atmospheric Deposition: Forms and Spatial Trends

Contrary to patterns of wet deposition of nitrogen for the U.S., the highest levels of nitrogen deposition in the country, particularly to forested areas, occur in certain areas of California and are caused mainly by dry nitrogen deposition (Fenn et al. 2012). As with other air pollutants, spatial distribution of nitrogen-containing pollutants and resulting nitrogen deposition depend on the location and size of emission sources as well as geographic and climatic characteristics. In California's Mediterranean climate more than 85% of precipitation occurs in winter. In the mountains most of the winter precipitation occurs as snow, except the coastal ranges that receive mostly rainfall (Aschmann 1973). Summer precipitation is scarce and occurs as short-lasting storms. Generally winter precipitation does not contain high concentrations of nitrogenous ions because it mostly brings very clean Pacific moisture and is typically quite evenly distributed throughout the state (Bytnerowicz and Fenn 1996). Because of low concentrations of locally generated gaseous pollutants in winter, SCAVENGING of those compounds does not result in high concentrations of nitrate (NO_3^-) or ammonium (NH_4^+) in precipitation, except within or downwind of major urban or agricultural emissions sources (Fenn and Bytnerowicz 1997). Most of the elevated levels of nitrogen deposition in southern and central California (Figure 7.8) therefore result from high dry summer deposition of various reactive nitrogen species.

An important exception is in regions where fog events occur. Fog water, when coinciding with nitrogen emissions sources, contains ionic concentrations typically one to two orders of magnitude greater than in precipitation (Collett et al. 1990, Fenn et al. 2000). As a result, in many montane regions of California, inputs from fog or cloud water are an important nitrogen deposition pathway (Fenn and Bytnerowicz 1997, Fenn and Poth 2004). As much as one-third of total annual deposition inputs may occur from fog water in forested sites of California with regular fog occurrence (Collett et al. 1989, Fenn et al. 2000, Fenn and Poth 2004).

The dominance of dry deposition is magnified in airsheds with frequent thermal inversions, such as the Los Angeles

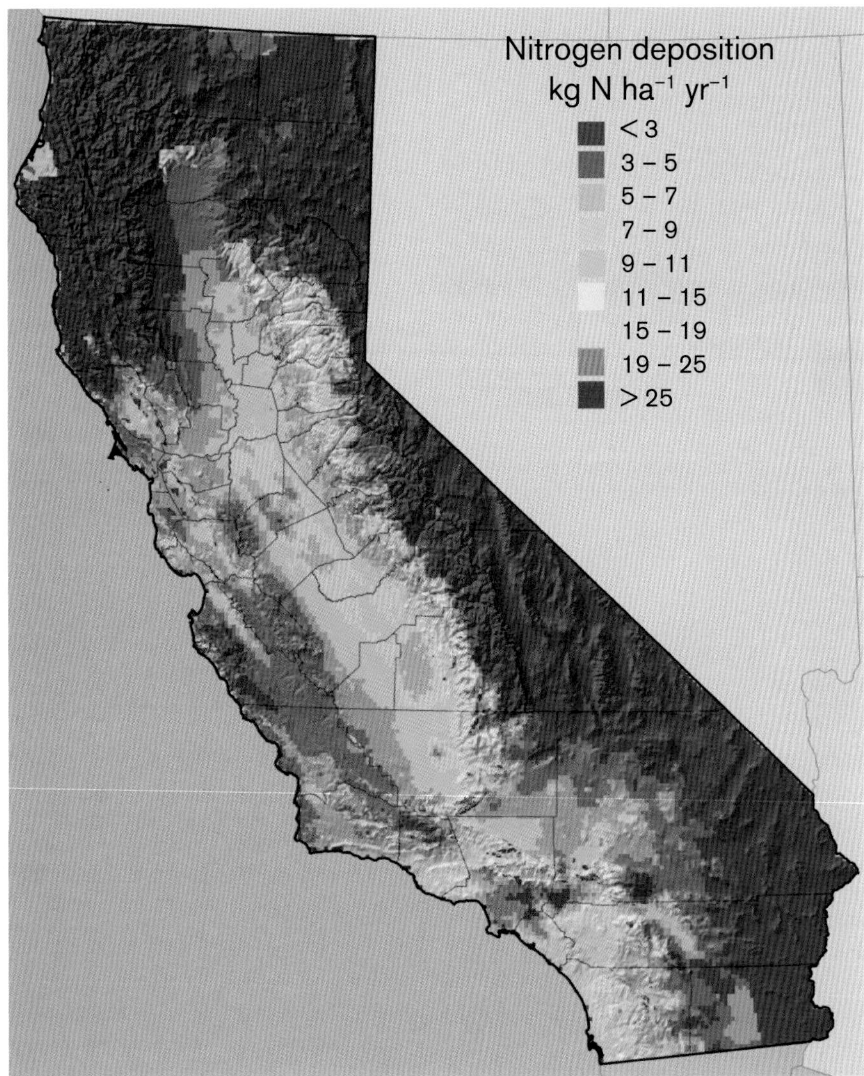

FIGURE 7.8 Map of nitrogen deposition in California. Source: Fenn et al. 2010.

and San Joaquin Valley air basins. In general, nitrogen dry deposition to California ecosystems is dominated by surface deposition of nitric acid vapor and AMMONIA (NH_3), particulate nitrate and ammonium, and stomatal uptake of gaseous nitrogenous pollutants such as nitrogen oxides, ammonia, and nitric acid vapor. The importance of ammonia and nitric acid vapor in California reflects high ambient concentrations of these compounds as well as their high deposition velocities, which result in very high fluxes (Bytnerowicz and Fenn 1996). In addition to inorganic nitrogen deposition involving the compounds discussed earlier, organic reactive nitrogen species can significantly contribute to total nitrogen deposition (Greaver et al. 2012).

The use of passive samplers has allowed us to understand the distribution of major contributors to inorganic nitrogen deposition in southern California (Figure 7.9). In summer 2005 a major monitoring effort showed highly elevated concentrations of ammonia, especially near Riverside and along Interstate 10 leading to Palm Springs and beyond, with concentrations decreasing from west to east. High ammonia concentrations in the Riverside area are most likely caused by agricultural emissions from the nearby, upwind dairy operations in Norco and Chino. However, emissions of ammonia from combustion engines equipped with three-way catalytic converters (Bishop et al. 2010, Kean et al. 2000) also contribute to high concentrations of the pollutant in California. High ammonia concentrations were not observed in the San Bernardino Mountains, probably due to few local emissions sources of this pollutant and to its effective deposition onto various landscape receptors. However, eastern portions of Joshua Tree National Park experienced elevated ammonia concentrations. Highest concentrations of nitrogen dioxide were recorded in the Riverside area, most likely due to its generation from nitric oxide emitted by local traffic and also to long-range transport of the pollutant from upwind Los Angeles. High concentrations of nitrogen dioxide were also observed near Palm Springs, indicating effects of traffic on Interstate 10. Concentrations of nitric acid vapor were also highest in the Riverside and Palm Springs areas. This can be explained by (1) photochemical production of the pollutant from its precursors in the Los Angeles area and along local transportation routes and (2) eastward movement of the polluted air masses with the onshore summer winds. These findings illustrate how passive monitoring networks for measuring concentrations of nitrogen pollutants can greatly increase our understanding of spatial and temporal dynamics of the

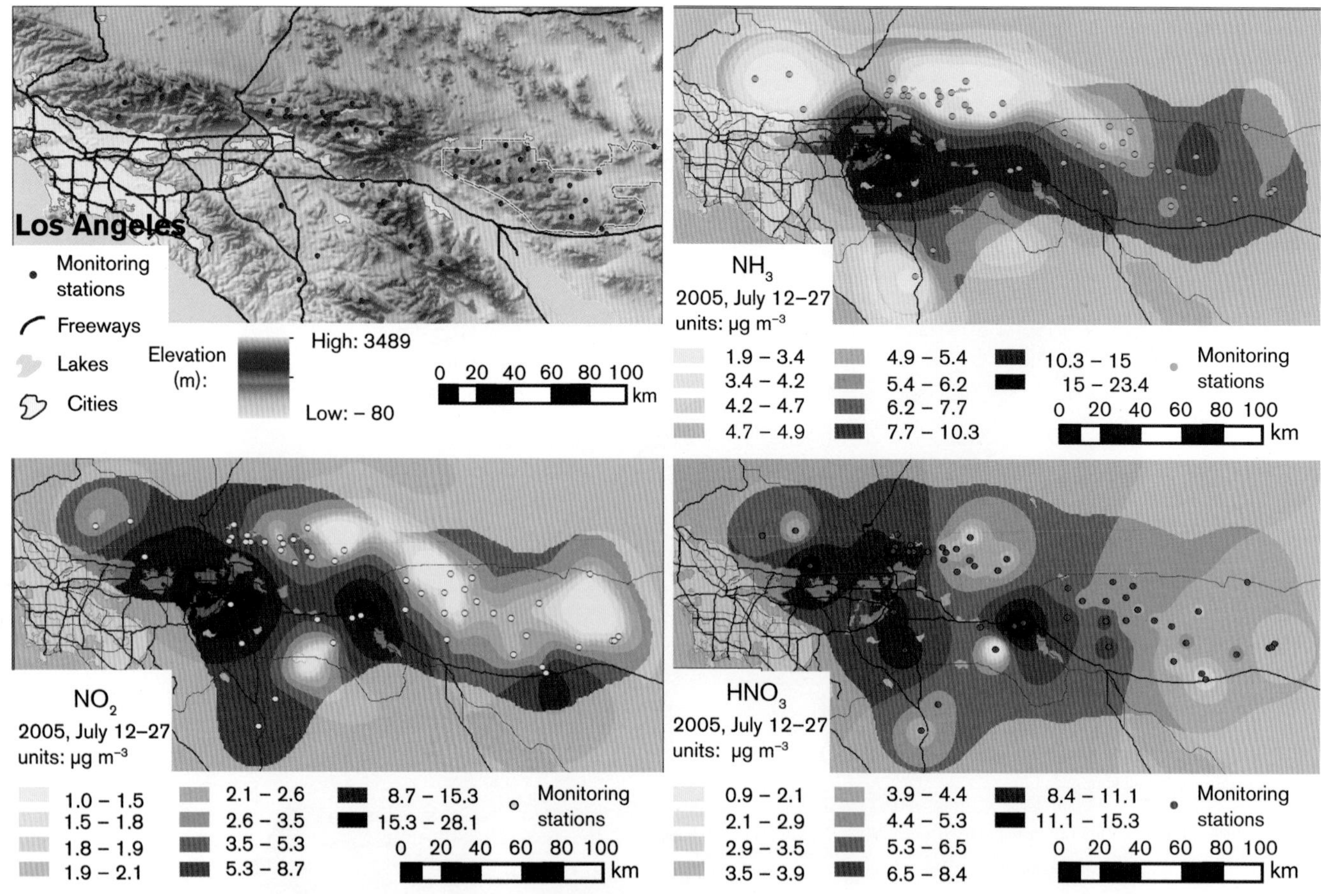

FIGURE 7.9 Nitrogenous air pollutants in southern California, summer 2005. Source: A. Bytnerowicz, unpublished.

pollutants that drive atmospheric nitrogen deposition across the landscape (Bytnerowicz et al. 2002).

High levels of ammonia and nitric acid vapor also occur on the western slopes of the Sierra Nevada Mountains near the California Central Valley (Figure 7.10). A strong gradient of both pollutants occurs across the Sierra Nevada range in the southwest-northeast direction, which coincides with the direction of prevailing winds in summer. The gradient is caused by dilution of the pollutants as they move east across the Sierras and are deposited to various surfaces and absorbed by stomatal uptake (Hanson and Lindberg 1991, Bytnerowicz and Fenn 1996). While low levels of ammonia occur in the eastern Sierra Nevada and the northern portion of the Owens Valley near Bishop and Mammoth Lakes, nitric acid vapor concentrations are elevated in the southern portion of the Owens Valley below Bishop. This may be another indication of transport of photochemical smog air masses from southern California, as with ozone (see Figure 7.7).

Ecological Effects of Nitrogen Deposition

With the possible exception of unique habitats characterized by nitrogen-bearing soil minerals (Dahlgren 1994), the natural condition of aquatic and terrestrial ecosystems in California is one of limited nitrogen availability. Chronic nitrogen deposition leads to the opposite condition: nitrogen excess. As in the case of overfertilization of crop fields, this results in leaching losses of excess nitrogen and increased emissions of nitrogenous trace gases to the atmosphere. The cardinal symptom of a forest, woodland, or chaparral ecosystem overloaded with nitrogen is elevated nitrate concentrations in surface or subsurface runoff (Fenn and Poth 1999, Fenn et al. 2008).

Nitrogen deposition can cause acidification and EUTROPHICATION effects in terrestrial and aquatic ecosystems. In California, nitrogen fertilization effects have been documented over wide areas of the state (Fenn et al. 2010), while acidification effects in terrestrial and aquatic ecosystems are of secondary importance (Shaw et al. 2014). Soils in forests and chaparral ecosystems in the Los Angeles Basin have acidified considerably since the 1970s (Fenn et al. 2011), but ecological effects of this depression in pH have not been demonstrated. This could be because these soils are high in BASE CATIONS compared to acidic and highly leached soils in the eastern U.S. and Europe, where base cation depletion has resulted from chronic atmospheric acidic deposition and leachate losses of base cations (Fenn et al. 2006).

The most widespread effects of nitrogen deposition observed in California are shifts in communities of EPIPHYTIC LICHENS in forests and chaparral/oak woodlands. OLIGOTROPHIC species are highly sensitive to atmospheric nitrogen, with initial declines in occurrence observed at nitrogen deposition levels as low as 3 kg ha^{-1} yr^{1} (Fenn et al. 2008), a level that occurs over much of California. Biodiversity impacts to plant communities can also occur at relatively low levels of long-term nitrogen deposition. In low productivity ecosystems such as grasslands, coastal sage scrub, and desert scrub,

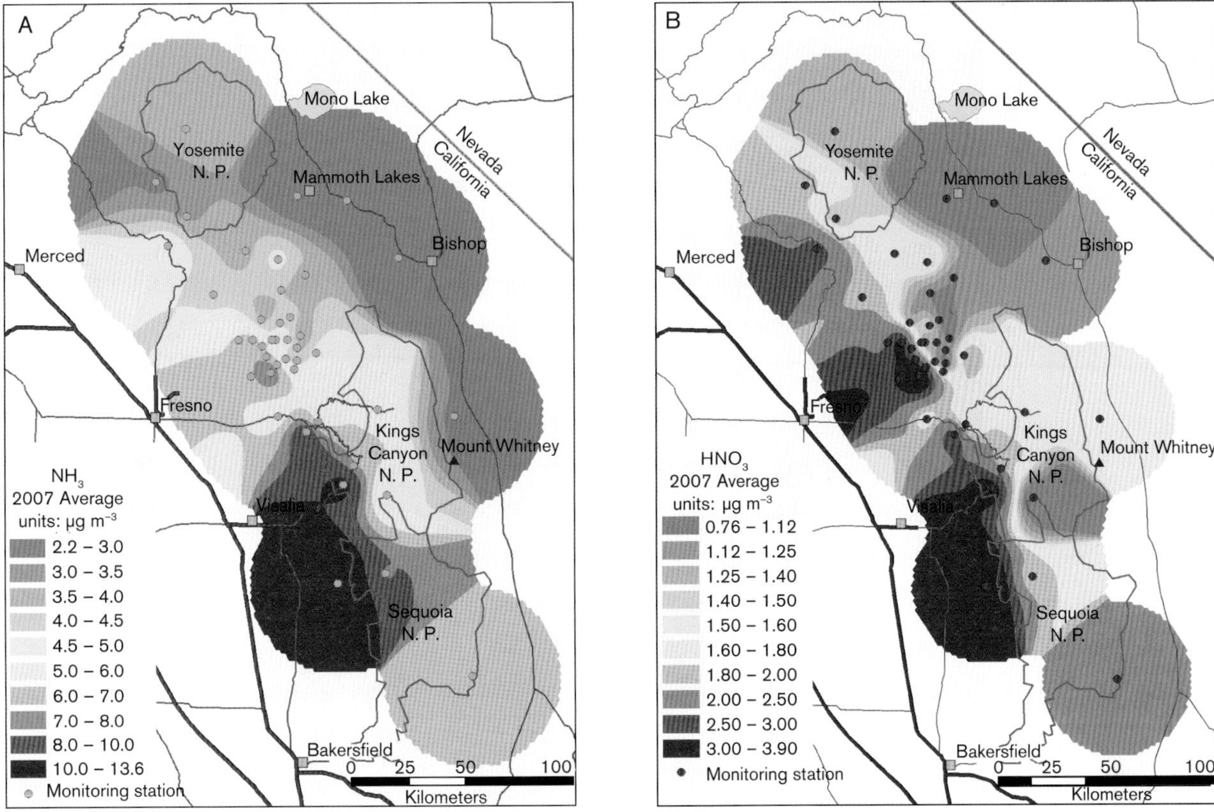

FIGURE 7.10 (A) Ammonia and (B) nitric acid vapor distribution in the southern Sierra Nevada in summer 2007. Source: A. Bytnerowicz, unpublished.

nitrogen deposition enhances the growth of invasive species, often resulting in loss of diversity and vegetation type change—sometimes as a result of increased fuel accumulation and fire occurrence (Weiss 1999, Allen et al. 2007, Fenn et al. 2010, Rao et al. 2010). Biodiversity impacts are also likely in forest understory communities subjected to elevated nitrogen deposition, though an investigation along an air pollution gradient in the San Bernardino Mountains was inconclusive due to confounding factors such as precipitation, ozone, and local disturbances (Allen et al. 2007). Effects on communities of symbiotic mycorrhizal fungi have also been shown in response to nitrogen deposition in mixed conifer forests, chaparral and coastal sage scrub vegetation of California (Egerton-Warburton and Allen 2000, Fenn et al. 2011).

In California forests exposed to elevated levels of air pollution, ozone and nitrogen deposition interact with other stressors, such as long-term fire suppression, climate change, drought stress, and bark beetle outbreaks, to affect the vigor, resilience, and sustainability of these forests. Effects are particularly acute in ponderosa and Jeffrey pine because of their sensitivity to ozone. The phytotoxic effects of ozone in combination with nitrogen enrichment result in dramatic physiological changes and increased sensitivity to bark beetle outbreaks and mortality (Jones et al. 2004, Grulke et al. 2009). Nitrogen deposition and nitrate concentrations in alpine lakes in the Sierra Nevada of California are generally lower than in the Colorado Front Range (Sickman et al. 2002, Baron et al. 2011). Nitrate concentrations in Sierran lakes begin to increase noticeably as total nitrogen deposition increases above 2 kg ha^{-1} yr^{-1} (Baron et al. 2011). Changes in DIATOMS in the sediments of two lakes in the eastern Sierra Nevada accompanied nitrogen enrichment that began in the early 1960s (Saros et al. 2011). This response has been observed with wet nitrogen deposition levels as low as 1.4 kg ha^{-1} yr^{-1}.

In a study of seven major vegetation types in California, an estimated 35% of the land area was in exceedance of CRITICAL LOADS, threshold nitrogen deposition at which harmful effects are expected to occur (Figure 7.11; Table 7.2; Fenn et al. 2010). For grasslands, coastal sage scrub, desert scrub, and pinyon-juniper woodland vegetation types, the most widespread effect of nitrogen deposition was an increase in exotic annual grasses. In grasslands and coastal sage scrub, this results in loss of native diversity and cover. In desert scrub and pinyon-juniper habitats, exotic biomass accumulation becomes sufficient to sustain fire. The most widespread effect of nitrogen deposition in forests, chaparral, and oak woodlands in California is increased nitrogen concentration in epiphytic lichens and a shift to lichen communities dominated by eutrophic species (Fenn et al. 2010). Elevated nitrate concentrations in streamwater and groundwater also occur in the chaparral, woodland, and forested watersheds most exposed to nitrogen deposition, impacting water quality in areas where the nitrogen critical load is exceeded (Fenn et al. 2010).

Other Pollutants

Atmospheric deposition of mercury (Hg) is low in California compared to the eastern U.S. (Prestbo and Gay 2009), although sampling sites are few. Localized hotspots of atmospheric mercury occur in disturbed, natural source areas, including geothermal or volcanically active regions (Nacht et al. 2004). Some studies have shown that long-range transport of pollutants from Asia contributes to mercury deposition on

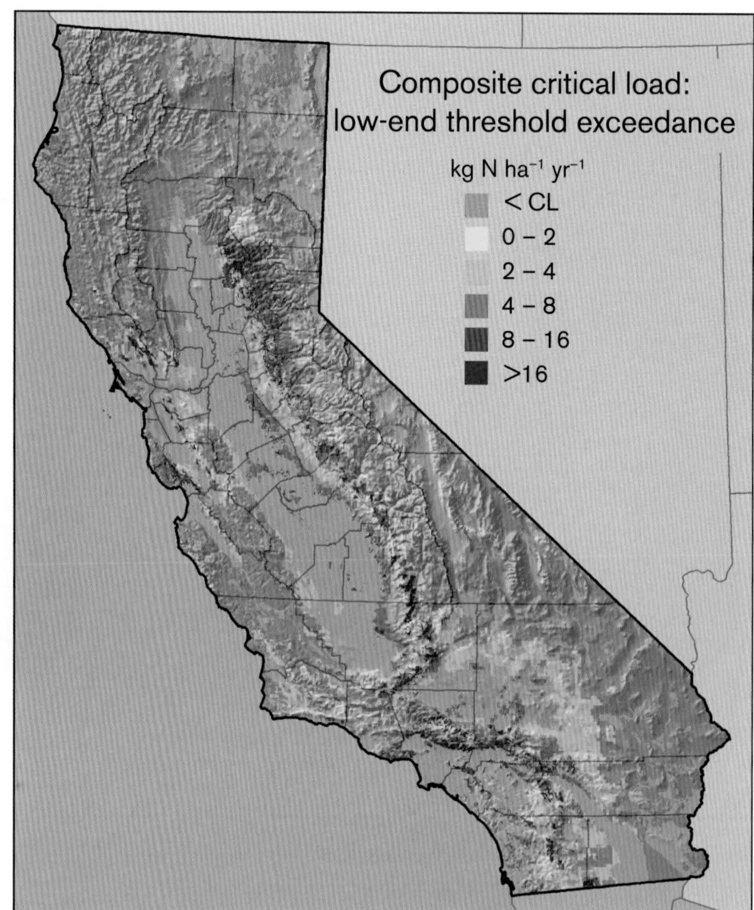

FIGURE 7.11 Exceedance values for critical loads (CL) of N deposition in California. Source: Fenn et al. 2010.

the U.S. West Coast (Weiss-Penzias et al. 2007). However, this does not result in high concentrations of atmospheric mercury in California (Prestbo and Gay 2009), so serious, widespread ecological effects caused by this pollutant are unlikely.

Sulfur dioxide emissions have been low in California because relatively little coal is used as an energy source in the state. Primary emissions of sulfur dioxide are from ships docked in ports, mobile sources, and oil refineries, but they are low and generate only local impacts. Consequently, sulfur deposition in California has historically been of little ecological significance (Cox et al. 2009). Lead (Pb) emissions to the atmosphere, from the use of leaded gasoline, increased steadily in California from the 1950s, peaked around 1970, and declined to below 1950 levels by 1982 (Mielke et al. 2010). As a result of lead phase-out regulations for gasoline, concentrations of lead in runoff from highways in California in the mid-1990s and 2000s was as much as eleven times lower than during the 1980s (Kayhanian 2012). No serious ecological impacts of lead emissions have been recently reported in California.

Long-range transport of semivolatile organic compounds (SOCs)—such as various types of pesticides, fire retardants such as polybrominated diphenyl ethers (PBDEs), polychlorinated biphenyls (PCBs), and polycyclic aromatic hydrocarbons (PAHs)—potentially have important ecological effects on high-elevation aquatic and terrestrial ecosystems of the Sierra Nevada. Measurements at the Emerald Lake and Pearl Lake area of Sequoia and Kings Canyon National Park showed significant contamination of snowpack, lake sediments, vegetation, and fish. That study also showed that Sequoia and Kings Canyon National Park had the highest concentrations of currently used pesticides among western national parks because of its proximity to agricultural sources in the Central Valley. These compounds move up the food chain, affecting health of wildlife and humans (Landers et al. 2010).

Dust, Aerosols, and Black Carbon

Dust aerosols, or particulate matter, of both natural and anthropogenic origins, play an important role in cloud formation, fertilization of oceans, supply of reaction surfaces for atmospheric chemical processes, degradation of visibility and reducing sunlight at the surface, thus affecting climate and biota as well as human health (VanCuren and Cahill 2002, Frank et al. 2007). Although many uncertainties exist in estimates of global-scale RADIATIVE FORCINGS, contribution of dust is comparable with sulfate aerosols created by industrial pollution (Tegen and Fung 1994). Aerosols of diameters between about 0.08 and 1 micrometer are the most relevant to radiative forcing of climate because of their efficiency in scattering solar radiation and their role as CLOUD CONDENSATION NUCLEI (Murphy et al. 1998). Roughly half of current global dust emissions are estimated to be of anthropogenic origin, resulting from soil degradation from activities such as agriculture, deforestation, and overgrazing (Tegen and Fung

1995, Miller and Tegen 1998). Particulate matter, in both its fine and coarse fractions, is a CRITERIA POLLUTANT with established air quality standards under the Clean Air Act.

In the California Mojave Desert the amount of dust and other particulate matter has been increasing because of anthropogenic inputs created by various land use practices (Frank et al. 2007). Dust storms occurring in the Owens Valley east of the Sierra Nevada as a result of many decades of pumping water from that aquifer to Los Angeles lead to violations of the coarse particulate matter air quality standard. The Owens Valley is one of the most turbulent valleys in the U.S. and one of the largest coarse particulate matter sources in the Western Hemisphere (Reid et al. 1994). Coarse particulate matter is generated during wind events by sandblasting of the EFFLORESCENT CRUST with saltation particles created from lakebed sediment and sand from the shoreline (Reid et al. 1994). Atmospheric coarse particulate concentrations in the Owens Valley area during windstorms can exceed 1,000 $\mu g\ m^{-3}$ (compared to the federal health standard of 150 $\mu g\ m^{-3}$), with plumes reaching above 2,000 meters in height (Reid et al. 1994).

Marine aerosols also play an important role in atmospheric processes and affect radiative forcing and climate directly by scattering and absorbing radiation and indirectly by influencing droplet-size distribution and ALBEDO of clouds in the marine boundary layer (Fitzgerald 1991). Long-range transport of polluted air masses from Asia and other remote areas also could be contributing to recent changes in mountain snow cover and related water shortages in California. Atmospheric aerosols from Asia are a regular component of the troposphere over California, particularly in spring, and a significant contributor to aerosol loading at high altitude (500–3,000 meter) remote sites across western North America. Twenty-four-hour fine particulate matter concentrations contributed from Asian aerosols range between 0.2 to 3 $\mu g\ m^{-3}$, and those of coarse particulate matter are about 5 $\mu g\ m^{-3}$ (VanCuren and Cahill 2002, VanCuren 2003). Long-rage transport of desert dust fine particles and sea salt aerosols have positive effects on the formation of cloud ice and precipitation, as documented in the northern Sierra Nevada (Rosenfeld and Givati 2006, Rosenfeld et al. 2008). Dust and biological aerosols (such as bacteria) can be transported from as far as Saharan and Asian deserts and be present in high-altitude clouds, serving as ice-formation nuclei and increasing winter snow precipitation in the Sierra Nevada (Creamean et al. 2013). In contrast, fine air pollution aerosols from densely industrialized/urbanized areas such as the San Francisco Bay and California Central Valley can reduce cloud drop effective radii and suppress downwind precipitation in the southern and central Sierra Nevada (Rosenfeld et al. 2008). Similar negative effects on cloud condensation nuclei formation and precipitation may occur downwind of emissions from wildland fires (Rosenfeld and Givati 2006).

Darkening of snow and ice by BLACK CARBON deposition is one of the main factors causing early melting of the snow pack in the Sierra Nevada. In winter, with prevailing winds from the northwest, black carbon transported from as far as Asia can contribute one-quarter to one-third of its deposition (Hadley et al. 2010). However, most black carbon deposition results from shorter-range transport of polluted air masses from California sources, such as diesel engine emissions or wood burning (Chow et al. 2010, 2011). In addition to black carbon, emissions from forest fires also contain various organic carbon molecules that contribute to the formation of haze, blocking sunlight and cooling the atmosphere (Goldammer et al. 2009). From the perspective of potential climate change effects, emissions of black and organic carbon from wildland fires counteract each other, suggesting that controlling diesel and coal-burning emissions should be the top priorities for efforts to control emissions of C compounds that contribute to climate change (Zimmer 2013).

Fire Effects on Air Quality

Fire plays a key role in the health and structure of California ecosystems (see Chapter 3, "Fire as an Ecosystem Process"). Patterns of forest fire frequency, intensity, and severity have been gradually altered by the use of fire suppression; this has contributed to conditions that favor high-intensity, destructive fires (USDA Forest Service 2001, Radke et al. 2001, Syphard et al. 2007). Wildland fires, both wild and prescribed, emit large quantities of aerosols and greenhouse gases into the atmosphere, significantly impacting climate and air quality (Zhang and Kondragunta 2008). Air pollution impacts from wildfires have been growing due to their increased size and number during the past decade (Jaffe et al. 2008), a trend expected to continue in the future (IPCC 2001).

Wildland fires involve complex combustion processes dependent on fuel loading, fire behavior, and weather conditions. Smoke from fire is composed of hundreds of chemicals in gaseous, liquid, and solid forms (Ottmar and Reinhardt 2000, Urbanski et al. 2009). Wildland fires emit substantial amounts of volatile organic compounds, carbon and nitrogen oxides, as well as directly and secondarily formed particulate matter and ozone (Cheng et al. 1998, Andreae and Merlet 2001, Pfister et al. 2008) and to a lesser extent ammonia, methane, sulfur oxides (Ward and Smith 2001, Koppmann et al. 2005), and other organic species and trace elements. Wildfire smoke can be transported for thousands of kilometers across counties, states, countries, and continents (Wotawa and Trainer 2000, Foster et al. 2001, Damoah et al. 2004, DeBell et al. 2004, Sapkota et al. 2005, Morris et al. 2006).

Forest fires impact tropospheric chemistry (Andreae and Merlet 2001) and are the dominant source of organic carbon aerosol emissions, twice as high as those resulting from the combustion of fossil fuels (DeBell et al. 2004). Forest fires also produce black carbon, which has significant human health and climate impacts, in amounts comparable to those from the burning of fossil fuels (IPCC 2001). Burning of forests also impacts global processes by releasing various greenhouse gases that affect the radiation budget as well as by emitting other scattering and absorbing aerosols (IPCC 2001). Finally, smoke from forest fires can affect the regional shortwave radiation budget and change atmospheric thermodynamics. All of these effects depend on size and intensity of the fires (Liu 2005). Particulate matter produced during catastrophic fire events is of great concern because it can adversely impact public health and be a principal cause of reduced visibility (Park et al. 2007). Smoke from wildfires can significantly increase fine particulate matter concentrations (Chandra et al. 2002, McMeeking et al. 2002, DeBell et al. 2004, Linping et al. 2006, Pfister et al. 2008) and exacerbate the already polluted air found in southern California and the California Central Valley.

While the number of forest fires and area burned have been increasing in the U.S., including California and the western states (see Chapter 3, "Fire as an Ecosystem Process"), particulate matter concentrations in selected California sites have been decreasing over the past decade. Locations in the San Francisco Bay area and mountain locations experience lower particulate matter concentrations than those in southern California and the California Central Valley. In 2008 northern California experienced a high incidence of forest fires; increased fine particulate matter concentrations in Sacramento and the southern Sierra Nevada were most likely caused by these forest fires. For particulate matter, sites closest to and downwind of the fire are the most affected. If wildfires in California continue to increase in frequency, size, and severity, fine particulate matter concentrations will likely affect both regions experiencing recent air quality improvements and areas remaining out of compliance with ambient air quality standards.

Interactive Effects of Air Pollution and Climate Change and Projections for the Future

More than one hundred years of effective fire prevention have resulted in widespread densification of forest stands, predisposing western forests to drought. Warming climates and less predictable precipitation add to soil moisture stress in California forests. In some areas, elevated ozone and nitrogen deposition levels have exacerbated drought stress and predisposed forests to bark beetle attacks (Takemoto et al. 2001), making them highly susceptible to catastrophic fires (McKenzie et al. 2009). Mixed conifer forests of the San Bernardino Mountains are a case study of such effects (Grulke et al. 2009). Although air pollution effects have been less severe in the Sierra Nevada than in the San Bernardino Mountains of southern California, the interactive effects of various abiotic and biotic stressors have affected the Sierras, particularly the southern areas. (Fenn et al. 2003, Takemoto et al. 2001). Interactive effects of air pollutants have been demonstrated for forests in the southwestern Sierra Nevada, where negative effects of ozone on tree growth (Peterson et al. 1987) have been partially offset by nitrogen deposition (Fenn et al. 2003). However, the combined effects of chronically elevated ozone concentrations and nitrogen deposition may also lead to severe perturbation of the physiology of key tree species and decreased ecosystem sustainability (Bytnerowicz et al. 2007, Fenn et al. 2003, Grulke et al. 2009).

In mixed conifer forests of southern California, where ozone effects on forests have historically been severe, recent decreases in ozone concentrations are likely to continue (Bytnerowicz, Fenn et al. 2013; Oltmans et al. 2013). Ozone will likely interact with climate change to strongly influence important ecosystem functions such as carbon sequestration and the quantity and quality of streamwater. Forest nutritional status, especially of nitrogen, can have major effects on forest responses to ozone. Simulation of future changes in these forests suggest that ozone impacts on forest growth will be closely associated with nitrogen deposition in these nitrogen-limited ecosystems. If the current trend of decreases in ozone continues, simulations indicate that tree biomass would not change significantly even under climate warming at high nitrogen deposition sites, while at low nitrogen deposition sites forest trees would recover from biomass loss in the late twenty-first century. Under scenarios of increasing ozone in the San Bernardino Mountains, tree biomass would decrease under two different nitrogen deposition projections, but much more under the medium-high emissions climate warming projection (A2) than under the low emissions (B1) projection (Bytnerowicz, Fenn et al. 2013). Similar changes can also be expected for the mixed conifer forests of the Sierra Nevada Mountains.

Human Health Effects of Key Pollutants

The Clean Air Act (CAA), a federal law passed in 1963 and last amended in 1990 (42 U.S.C. §7401 et seq.), forms the basis for national control of air pollution. The CAA was designed to "protect and enhance" the quality of the nation's air resources. Basic elements of the Clean Air Act include national ambient air quality standards (NAAQS) for criteria air pollutants (Table 7.3). In California, with regard to human health, the criteria pollutants of most importance are fine and coarse particulate matter, ozone, nitrogen dioxide, and carbon monoxide.

Long-term exposure to particulate matter causes serious human health effects (Koelemeijer et al. 2006), resulting in lower life expectancy for people living in areas with high particulate matter levels (Houthuijs et al. 2001). Negative health effects are mainly associated with fine particulate matter (WHO 2003). The adverse health effects of particulate matter include increased mortality and morbidity, reduced lung function, increased respiratory symptoms (such as chronic cough or bronchitis), aggravated respiratory and cardiovascular disease, eye and throat irritation, coughing, breathlessness, blocked and runny noses, skin rashes, and lung cancer (Radojevic and Hassan 1998, Houthuijs et al. 2001). Strong evidence suggests that fine particulate matter is more hazardous to human health because smaller particles induce more inflammation than larger particles on a mass basis. Thus epidemiological studies over the past decade have emphasized fine particulate matter (Querol et al. 2007).

Ozone is also a serious health risk. The adverse health effects associated with exposure to elevated levels of ground-level ozone include lung function decrements, airway hyper-reactivity, epithelial cell damage, and bronchoalveolar inflammation (Hayes et al. 1993). Even at relatively low levels, ozone may cause inflammation and irritation of the respiratory tract, particularly during physical activity, causing coughing, throat irritation, and difficulty breathing (EPA 2008). Ozone can increase the susceptibility of the lungs to infections, allergens, and other air pollutants, and aggravate chronic lung diseases, such as asthma, emphysema, and bronchitis. It can also reduce the immune system's ability to fight bacterial infection in the respiratory system and increase the frequency of asthma attacks (EPA 2008).

Nitrogen dioxide is a strong oxidizing agent that reacts in the air to form corrosive nitric acid vapor as well as toxic organic nitrates. It plays a major role in the atmospheric reactions that produce ground-level ozone. Nitrogen dioxide can irritate the lungs and lower resistance to respiratory infections such as influenza and enhance the effects of other environmental pollutants including allergens (WHO 2003). The effects of short-term exposure are still unclear, but long-term exposure may impair lung function and increase the risk of respiratory symptoms, and includingacute respiratory illness in children (WHO 2003). Carbon monoxide causes tissue hypoxia by preventing the blood from carrying sufficient oxygen. At low to moderate concentrations, health effects may include headache, dizziness upon exertion, fatigue, palpitations, nausea, vomiting, difficulty breath-

TABLE 7.2

Summary of critical loads (CL) and methods used to determine empirical critical loads for seven major vegetation types in California

Vegetation type	Area of vegetation cover (km^2)	Response variables for CL determination	CL values (kg N ha^{-1} yr^{-1})	References
Mixed conifer forest	106,663	Exceedance of peak streamwater NO_3^- concentration threshold (0.2 mg NO_3-N L^{-1})	17	Fenn et al. 2008
Mixed conifer forest		Enriched N in tissue of the lichen *L. vulpina* (above 1.0% N)	3.1	Fenn et al. 2008
Mixed conifer forest		Epiphytic lichen community shift away from acidophyte (oligotroph) dominance	5.2	Fenn et al. 2008
Mixed conifer forest		Extirpation of acidophytic (oligotrophic) lichens	10.2	Fenn et al. 2008
Mixed conifer forest		Fine root biomass reduction (26%) in ponderosa pine trees	17	Fenn et al. 2008
Chaparral	27,045	Exceedance of peak streamwater NO_3^- concentration threshold	10–14	Fenn et al. 2011
Chaparral and oak woodlands	59,704	Epiphytic lichen community shift to eutrophic lichen species dominance	5.5	Fenn et al. 2011, Jovan 2008, Jovan and McCune 2005
Coastal sage scrub	6,328	Decrease in native plant species and forb richness	7.8–10	Fenn et al. 2011
Coastal sage scrub		Decrease in arbuscular-mycorrhizal spore density, richness, and percentage of root infection	10	Fenn et al. 2011
Annual grassland	28,634	Exotic grass invasion	6	Weiss 1999, Fenn et al. 2010
Desert scrub	75,007	Exotic grass biomass accumulation sufficient to sustain fire	3.2–9.3	Rao et al. 2010
Pinyon-juniper	6,602	Exotic grass biomass accumulation sufficient to sustain fire	3.0–6.3	Rao et al. 2010 Fenn et al. 2010

SOURCE: Fenn et al. 2010.

ing upon exertion, impaired thinking and perception, rapid heartbeat, visual disturbance, and slow reflexes (Fierro et al. 2001). However, not all symptoms always appear and tend to become more severe as exposure and concentration increase—from a mild headache to nausea progressing to more severe cases. At very high carbon monoxide levels, unconsciousness and eventually death may result, though these levels generally can occur only in confined spaces (Fierro et al. 2001).

Although air pollution levels have decreased significantly in California, one out of three Californians lives with unhealthy air. Federal standards for ozone and fine particulate matter are still exceeded in major urban areas of the South Coast (Los Angeles), San Joaquin Valley, Sacramento, and San Diego Air Basins. While in the South Coast Air Basin 60% of the population live in areas in compliance with federal air standards, in the San Joaquin Valley Air Basin only 25% enjoy air quality that meets federal standards (Barboza 2014). Additional reductions of smog-forming air pollutants, especially nitrogen oxides and volatile organic compounds, clearly are needed to improve air quality in the unhealthiest areas in California (Table 7.3).

Conservation, Adaptation, and Mitigation

Strict and efficiently enforced air quality regulations in California have reduced risks to forests caused by ozone exposures. However, overstocked forest stands, as a result of long-term fire suppression, are highly susceptible to interactive stressors, such as elevated levels of ozone and nitrogen deposition, diseases and pests, and increasing temperatures and drought (Grulke et al. 2009). Therefore effective forest thinning, mechanical biomass removal, and carefully applied prescribed fires are important management strategies for improved resilience of California forest ecosystems. There are serious limitations in using these strategies, because of their high costs and various possible environmental risks. Prominent among these is the possibility of exceeding federal and state air pollution standards during application of prescribed fires, especially for fine and coarse particulate matter.

For some ecological effects caused by atmospheric nitrogen deposition (e.g., alteration of epiphytic lichen communities, biodiversity impacts of plant communities, enhancement of invasive species), reductions in nitrogen emissions from fossil fuel burning and agricultural activities are usu-

TABLE 7.3
California and national ambient air quality standards

Pollutant	Averaging time	Federal standards	California standards
Ozone	1-hour	None	0.07 ppm
	8-hour	0.075 ppm[A]	0.07 ppm
Inhalable particulate matter (PM_{10})	24-hour	150 μg/m³	50 μg/m³
Nitrogen dioxide (NO_2)	1-hour	0.100 ppm	0.180 ppm
	Annual arithmetic mean	0.053 ppm	0.030 ppm
Fine particulate matter ($PM_{2.5}$)	24-hour	35 μg/m³	Same as federal
	Annual arithmetic mean	12 μg/m³	Same as federal
Carbon monoxide (CO)	1-hour	35 ppm	20
	8-hour	9 ppm	Same as federal
Sulfur dioxide (SO_2)	1-hour	0.075 ppm	0.25 ppm
Lead	Rolling 3-month	0.15 μg/m³	None
	30-day	None	1.5 μg/m³

SOURCE: EPA 2008 and California Air Resources Board.
A. Calculated as the fourth highest concentration over a 3-year period.

ally the only effective strategy over the long term (Fenn et al. 2010). In forests and woodlands the overall strategy to manage the harmful effects of excess nitrogen is to reduce the levels of nitrogen accumulated in soil, litter, and biomass by releasing nitrogen from the ecosystem, and to use silvicultural treatments to enhance forest growth and nitrogen retention. This can be done by biomass removal, stand thinning, or by prescribed fire (Gimeno et al. 2009) and would primarily be applied in acutely impacted sites. In low-biomass scrub or grassland ecosystems in which nitrogen deposition has contributed to the establishment of exotic species invasions, mowing, herbicide treatments, or strategic application of prescribed fire are approaches that can be used to favor the recovery of native species (Cione et al. 2002, Gillespie and Allen 2004, Cox and Allen 2008, Fenn et al. 2010). Cattle grazing has been effectively used in serpentine grasslands in the San Francisco/San Jose area to manage the impacts of non-native invasive annual grasses (Weiss 1999, Fenn et al. 2010). However, the best restoration strategy will be to reduce nitrogen emissions below critical loads for negative ecosystem impacts (Pardo et al. 2011).

Chronic atmospheric nitrogen deposition to forest, woodland, or chaparral catchments leads to elevated concentrations of nitrogen in surface and subsurface runoff, primarily as nitrate, potentially affecting water quality (Fenn and Poth 1999, Fenn et al. 2003). In catchments with elevated nitrogen deposition, excess nitrogen accumulates in the system, primarily in biomass or NECROMASS. When such catchments burn, large amounts of the stored nitrogen are released; increased postfire nitrification rates result in very high nitrate concentrations in runoff (Riggan et al. 1994). Fire can be used as a management strategy for releasing a portion of the excess nitrogen accumulated from atmospheric nitrogen deposition, although water quality may be affected in the process. The capacity of prescribed fire to remove excess nitrogen is limited, however (Meixner et al. 2006), because 65% to 80% of the site nitrogen capital is stored belowground in California forests, and little belowground nitrogen is released by fire (Johnson et al. 2009, Wan et al. 2001). This emphasizes once again that the preferred and most effective long-term management strategy is to reduce emissions of reactive nitrogen to the atmosphere. In practice, reduced nitrogen deposition combined with periodic prescribed fire may be the best management approach for nitrogen-saturated catchments (Gimeno et al. 2009). Notwithstanding the sharp declines in nitrogen oxides emissions in California, nitrogen deposition in some forested regions of California remains high, underscoring the need for further reductions in emissions of ammonia and nitrogen oxides.

As described earlier, air quality in many areas of California has improved even as population has increased in the past thirty years, a result of regulatory emissions policies. Measures in California Assembly Bill 32 (Global Warming Solutions Act of 2006, AB 32) are expected to result in a substantial reduction in 2020 greenhouse gas emissions from all economic sectors through energy efficiency, renewable energy, and other technological measures. Emissions of other pollutants are predicted to also decline as a result of these measures, reinforcing downward trends in ozone, nitrogen oxides, and particulate matter (Zapata et al. 2013).

Summary

At present, negative impacts of air pollution on California ecosystems are caused mainly by elevated levels of ozone and nitrogen deposition. We emphasized air pollution effects on mixed conifer forests because the best available knowledge exists for these ecosystems. Generally, ozone air pollution in California has been improving significantly since the 1970s;

however, it still causes serious ecological and human health effects. The most serious ecological effects occur in mixed conifer forests of southern California and on the southwestern slopes of the Sierra Nevada. Ozone can be transported long distances, affecting remote areas such as Joshua Tree National Park in the Mojave Desert or the eastern Sierra Nevada.

Effects of nitrogen deposition on other ecosystems have been intensively studied in California for the past two decades. Nitrogen deposition to California ecosystems is dominated by dry deposition of ammonia and nitric acid vapor, although nitrogen deposition in fog water can also be important in montane regions. Movement of ammonia and nitric acid vapor in complex terrain, and therefore nitrogen deposition, are much more spatially restricted than ozone distribution due to the high deposition velocity of these pollutants. Consequently, steep landscape gradients of nitrogen deposition occur in California mountain ranges, with the highest potential for negative effects near emission source areas (such as the western side of the Sierra Nevada and near population centers) while remote areas remain relatively unaffected. The most sensitive indicators of harmful nitrogen deposition effects on California ecosystems include shifts in epiphytic lichen communities and lichen-tissue nitrogen in mixed conifer forests, oak woodlands, or chaparral ecosystems; and enhanced biomass of exotic grasses to levels capable of causing biodiversity changes and sustaining wildland fires in desert scrub, pinyon-juniper, and coastal sage scrub ecosystems. Increased nitrate concentrations in streamwater and groundwater from montane catchments can also result from nitrogen deposition, but the land area thus affected in California is much less than that experiencing biodiversity effects. Approximately 35% of California's land area exceeds critical loads of nitrogen deposition for these impacts in seven major vegetation types in California. Urgent need exists for large-scale evaluation of California forest health in light of the interactive effects of elevated ozone concentrations, nitrogen deposition, climate change, insects, and diseases.

Finally, particulate matter pollution is a serious health threat in California, especially in urban areas affected by emissions from mobile sources such as the Los Angeles Basin, San Francisco Bay Area, and California Central Valley. The Central Valley is also affected by particulate matter emissions from intensive agricultural activities, while vast arid areas, such as the Owens Valley, suffer from suspended dust during high wind events. Potential exceedances of the national and California particulate matter air quality standards can hinder the use of prescribed fire as a management tool in forests.

Acknowledgments

The authors thank Karen Magliano, of the California Air Resources Board, for providing maps for Figure 7.6 and data for Figures 7.1 and 7.5, as well as Susan Schilling, of the USDA Forest Service Pacific Southwest Research Station, and Witold Frączek, of Environmental Systems Research Institute, for help in preparing other figures and maps for the chapter.

Recommended Reading

Bytnerowicz, A., and M. Fenn. 1996. Nitrogen deposition in California forests: A review. Environmental Pollution 92:127–146.

Bytnerowicz, A., M. J. Arbaugh, and R. Alonso, editors. 2003. Ozone air pollution in the Sierra Nevada: Distribution and effects on forests. Developments in Environmental Science, volume 2. Elsevier, Amsterdam, The Netherlands.

Bytnerowicz, A., M. J. Arbaugh, A. R. Riebau, and C. Andersen, editors. 2009. Wildland fires and air pollution. Developments in Environmental Science, volume 8. Elsevier, Amsterdam, The Netherlands.

Carle, D. 2006. Introduction to air in California. California Natural History Guides. University of California Press, Berkeley, California.

Fenn, M. E., S. Jovan, F. Yuan, L. Geiser, T. Meixner, and B. S. Gimeno. 2008. Empirical and simulated critical loads for nitrogen deposition in California mixed conifer forests. Environmental Pollution 155:492–511.

Fenn, M. E., K. F. Lambert, T. F. Blett, D. A. Burns, L. H. Pardo, G. M. Lovett, R. A. Haeuber, D. C. Evers, C. T. Driscoll, and D. S. Jeffries. 2011. Setting limits: Using air pollution thresholds to protect and restore U.S. ecosystems. Issues in Ecology, Report Number 14. J. S. Baron, editor-in-chief. Ecological Society of America, Washington, D.C.

Finlayson-Pitts, B., and J. N. Pitts Jr. 2000. Chemistry of the upper and lower atmosphere. Academic Press, San Diego, California.

Pardo, L. H., M. E. Fenn, C. L. Goodale, L. H. Geiser, C. T. Driscoll, E. B. Allen, J. S. Baron, R. Bobbink, W. D. Bowman, C. M. Clark, B. Emmett, F. S. Gilliam, T. L. Greaver, S. J. Hall, E. A. Lilleskov, L. Liu, J. A. Lynch, K. J. Nadelhoffer, S. S. Perakis, M. J. Robin-Abbott, J. L. Stoddard, K. C. Weathers, and R. L. Dennis. 2011. Effects of nitrogen deposition and empirical nitrogen critical loads for ecoregions of the United States. Ecological Applications 21:3049–3082.

Seinfeld, J. H., and S. N. Pandis. 2006. Atmospheric chemistry and physics: From air pollution to climate change. Second edition. John Wiley & Sons, Inc., Hoboken, New Jersey.

Glossary

ADIABATIC HEATING Occurs when the pressure on the parcel of air moving downhill increases and the parcel's volume decreases; as the volume decreases, the temperature increases and its internal energy increases.

AEROSOLS Fine solid or liquid droplets dispersed in air.

ALBEDO Fraction of solar energy (shortwave radiation) reflected from Earth back into space.

AMMONIA (NH_3) A colorless gas with a characteristic pungent smell. Due to its high deposition velocity, ammonia is a major contributor to atmospheric N dry deposition.

ANABATIC WINDS Upslope winds moving up on a mountainslope facing the Sun.

ANTICYCLONE A large-scale circulation of winds around a central region of high atmospheric pressure—clockwise in the Northern Hemisphere, counterclockwise in the Southern Hemisphere.

BASE CATIONS Nonacid forming cations (positively charged ions—i.e., Ca^{+2}, Mg^{+2}, K^+, and Na^+). The higher the amount of exchangeable base cations in soil, the more acidity can be neutralized.

BLACK CARBON Compound consisting of pure carbon emitted during incomplete combustion of fossil fuels, biofuels, and biomass. It is also known as soot.

CHLOROTIC MOTTLE The minute chlorotic flecks developing on foliar surface of sensitive leaves as chloroplasts become disrupted by exposure to elevated O_3 concentrations.

CLEAN AIR ACT A U.S. federal law aimed at controlling air pollution on a national level. The original 1963 law was amended in 1970, 1977, and 1990.

CLOUD CONDENSATION NUCLEI Aerosols or small particles that act as the initial sites for condensation of water vapor into cloud droplets or cloud ice particles.

CONTINENTAL BACKGROUND (OF OZONE) The surface O_3 concentration that would be present over the U.S. in the absence of North American anthropogenic emissions.

CRITERIA POLLUTANTS Air pollutants harmful to public health and the environment regulated by the Clean Air Act with limits set by the National Ambient Air Quality Standards (O_3, CO, NO_2, SO_2, PM_{10}, $PM_{2.5}$, and Pb).

CRITICAL LOAD The quantitative estimate of atmospheric deposition (of nutritional nitrogen or acidifying compounds) below which significant harmful effects on specified sensitive elements of the environment do not occur according to present knowledge.

DIATOMS Major group of algae among the most common types of phytoplankton. A unique feature of diatom cells is that they are enclosed within a cell wall made of silica called a frustule.

EFFLORESCENT CRUST The whitish layer consisting of several minerals produced as an encrustation on the surface of soil or rock in arid regions.

EPIPHYTIC LICHENS Lichens growing on trees, which obtain necessary nutrients and moisture exclusively from the atmosphere.

EUTROPHICATION The process by which ecosystems become enriched in dissolved nutrients such as nitrogen or phosphorus that stimulate the growth of plants.

GEOSTROPHIC BALANCE The condition of winds produced when the forces of Earth's rotation and of pressure gradients are balanced. (In the Northern Hemisphere, Earth's rotation deflects winds in a clockwise direction as they blow from areas of high pressure towards areas of low pressure).

INSOLATION The rate of delivery of solar radiation per unit of horizontal surface.

LONG-RANGE TRANSPORT (OF POLLUTANTS) Atmospheric transport of air pollutants within a moving air mass for a distance greater than 100 kilometers.

NECROMASS Dead parts of living organisms—for example, the bark and heartwood of trees, litter, and the hair and claws of animals.

NITRIC ACID VAPOR Gaseous form of HNO_3 with strong phytotoxic properties; a major contributor to dry atmospheric nitrogen deposition.

NITROGEN DEPOSITION The transfer of nitrogen pollutants from the atmosphere to Earth's surface. Deposition occurs as wet (e.g., rainfall, fog, or snow) and dry (e.g., gaseous or particulate deposition).

NITROGEN OXIDES (NO_X) A sum of nitric oxide (NO) and nitrogen dioxide (NO_2).

OLIGOTROPHIC Environments or organisms (e.g., lichens) characterized by low levels of nutrients. For example, oligotrophic lichens are highly sensitive to increased levels of nitrogen deposition.

OZONE (O_3) Powerful oxidant formed from dioxygen during photochemical reactions of its precursors, NOx and VOCs. Due to its high oxidizing potential, at elevated concentrations it causes damage of mucus and respiratory tissues in mammals and plant tissues.

PARTICULATE MATTER ($PM_{2.5}$ AND PM_{10}) A complex mixture of extremely small particles (<2.5μm in diameter and <10μm) that are harmful to humans. Components include inorganic and organic chemicals, metals, and soil or dust particles.

PASSIVE SAMPLERS Devices for diffusive sampling of air that rely on diffusion of gaseous pollutants through a diffusive surface onto an adsorbent.

PESTICIDES Any substance or mixture of substances intended for preventing, destroying, or controlling any pest, including unwanted species of plants (herbicides) or insects (insecticides).

PHOTOCHEMICAL Relating to or resulting from the chemical action of radiant energy and especially light.

PHYTOTOXIC INDICES Various exposure matrixes based on concentration or a dose of pollutants to determine their potential toxicity to plants (phytotoxic potential).

RADIATIVE FORCING The difference between radiant energy received by Earth and energy radiated back to space.

SANTA ANA WINDS Strong, extremely dry downslope winds that originate inland and affect coastal southern California and northern Baja California. Santa Ana winds blow mostly in autumn and winter. They can range from hot to cold, depending on the prevailing temperatures in the source regions—the Great Basin and the upper Mojave Desert.

SCAVENGING The washout or removal of air pollutants (gases and particles) from the atmosphere by precipitation, resulting in wet deposition of the scavenged pollutants.

STOMATAL UPTAKE Cumulative stomatal flux or uptake rate (of ozone or other gas) over a period of time (e.g., day, season, year); that is, the amount of ozone molecules (moles) passing through the stomata into leaves during a specific time period.

SUBSIDENCE INVERSION A temperature inversion produced by the adiabatic warming of a layer of subsiding air.

THERMAL INVERSION Occurs when a layer of warm air settles over a layer of cooler air that lies near the ground. The warm air holds down the cool air and prevents pollutants from rising and scattering, causing severe cases of photochemical smog.

TROPOSPHERIC Occurring in the troposphere, the lowest portion of Earth's atmospheric layer, with an average depth of approximately 17 kilometers (11 miles) in the middle latitudes.

VOLATILE ORGANIC COMPOUNDS (VOCS) Organic chemical compounds whose composition makes it possible for them to evaporate under normal indoor atmospheric conditions of temperature and pressure (also referred to as "reactive organic gases").

References

Allen, E. B., P. J. Temple, A. Bytnerowicz, M. J. Arbaugh, A. G. Sirulnik, and L. E. Rao. 2007. Patterns of understory diversity in mixed coniferous forests of southern California impacted by air pollution. Scientific World Journal 7(S1):247–263. <doi:10.1100/tsw.2007.72>.

American Lung Association. 2013. Most polluted cities. <http://www.stateoftheair.org/2013/city-rankings/most-polluted-cities.html>. Accessed June 9, 2015.

Andreae, M. O., and P. Merlet. 2001. Emission of trace gases and aerosols from biomass burning. Global Biogeochemical Cycles 15:955–966.

Arbaugh, M. J., and A. Bytnerowicz. 2003. Introduction to a regional passive sampler ozone sampler network in the Sierra Nevada. Pages 157–164 in A. Bytnerowicz, M. Arbaugh, and R. Alonso, editors. Ozone Air Pollution in the Sierra Nevada: Distribution and Effects on Forests. Developments in Environmental Science, volume 2. Elsevier, Amsterdam, The Netherlands.

Aschmann, H. 1973. Distribution and peculiarity of Mediterranean ecosystems. Pages 11–19 in F. di Castri and H. A. Mooney, editors. Mediterranean Type Ecosystems: Origin and Structure. Springer-Verlag, Berlin, Germany.

Asher, J. E. 1956. Observation and theory on X-Disease or Needle Dieback. USDA Forest Service unpublished report, Arrowhead Ranger District, San Bernardino National Forest. California.

Austin, J., S. Gouze, J. Johnson, R. Ramalingam, and B. Tuter. 2001. Ozone transport: 2001 review. California Environmental Protection Agency, Air Resources Board, Sacramento, California.

Barboza, Tony. 2014. Exceptional dryness brings the hazy days of winter. Los Angeles Times. January 19, 2014. <http://articles.latimes.com/2014/jan/19/local/la-me-winter-air-20140120>. Accessed June 9, 2015.

Baron, J. S., C. T. Driscoll, J. L. Stoddard, and E. E. River. 2011. Empirical critical loads of atmospheric nitrogen deposition for nutrient enrichment and acidification of sensitive U.S. Lakes. BioScience 61:602–613.

Bishop, G. A., A. M. Peddle, and D. H. Stedman. 2010. On-road emission measurements of reactive nitrogen compounds from three California cities. Environmental Science and Technology 44:3616–3620.

Bognar, J. A., and J. W. Birks. 1996. Miniaturized ultraviolet ozonesonde for atmospheric measurements. Analytical Chemistry 68:3059–3062.

Burley, J. D., and J. D. Ray. 2007. Surface ozone in Yosemite National Park. Atmospheric Environment 41:6048–6062.

Burley, J. D., A. Bytnerowicz, J. D. Ray, S. Schilling, and E. B. Allen. 2014. Surface ozone in Joshua Tree National Park. Atmospheric Environment 87:95–107.

Bytnerowicz, A., and M. Fenn 1996. Nitrogen deposition in California forests: A review. Environmental Pollution 92:127–146.

Bytnerowicz, A., and N. E. Grulke. 1992. Physiological effects of air pollutants on western trees. Pages 183–233 in D. Binkley, R. Olson, and M. Bohm, editors. The Response of Western Forests to Air Pollution. Springer Verlag, Berlin, Germany.

Bytnerowicz, A., J. D. Burley, R. Cisneros, H. K. Preisler, S. Schilling, D. Schweizer, J. Ray, D. Dullen, C. Beck, and B. Auble. 2013. Surface ozone at the Devils Postpile National Monument receptor site during low and high wildland fire years. Atmospheric Environment 65:129–141.

Bytnerowicz, A., K. Omasa, and E. Paoletti, E. 2007. Integrated effects of air pollution and climate change on forests: A Northern Hemisphere perspective. Environmental Pollution 147:438–445.

Bytnerowicz, A., M. Arbaugh, S. Schilling, W. Frączek, and D. Alexander. 2008. Ozone distribution and phytotoxic potential in mixed conifer forests of the San Bernardino Mountains, southern California. Environmental Pollution 155:398–408.

Bytnerowicz, A., M. Fenn, S. McNulty, F. Yuan, A. Pourmokhtarian, C. Driscoll, and T. Meixner. 2013. Interactive effects of air pollution and climate change on forest ecosystems in the United States—Current understanding and future scenarios. Pages 333–369 in R. Matyssek, N. Clarke, P. Cudlin, T. N. Mikkelsen, J.-P. Tuovinen, G. Wieser, E. Paoletti, editors. Climate Change, Air Pollution, and Global Challenges: Understanding and Perspectives from Forest Research. Developments in Environmental Science, Volume 13. Elsevier, Amsterdam, The Netherlands.

Bytnerowicz, A., M. Tausz, R. Alonso, D. Jones, R. Johnson, and N. Grulke. 2002. Summer-time distribution of air pollutants in Sequoia National Park, California. Environmental Pollution 118:187–203.

Bytnerowicz, A., T. Dueck, and S. Godzik. 1998. Nitrogen oxides, nitric acid vapor, and ammonia. Pages 5–1 through 5–17 in R. B. Flagler, editor. Recognition of Air Pollution Injury by Vegetation: A Pictorial Atlas. Air & Waste Management Association, Pittsburg, Pennsylvania.

California Air Resources Board. http://www.arb.ca.gov/aqd/almanac/almanac.htm.

Carle, D. 2006. Introduction to air in California. California Natural History Guides, University of California Press, Berkeley, California.

Carroll, J. J., P. R. Miller, and J. Pronos. 2003. Historical perspectives on ambient ozone and its effects on the Sierra Nevada. Pages 33–54 in A. Bytnerowicz, M. J. Arbaugh, and R. Alonso, editors. Ozone Air Pollution in the Sierra Nevada: Distribution and Effects on Forests. Developments in Environmental Science, Volume 2. Elsevier, Amsterdam, The Netherlands.

Chandra, S., J. R. Ziemke, P. K. Bhartia, and R. V. Martin. 2002. Tropical tropospheric ozone: Implications for dynamics and biomass burning. Journal of Geophysical Research 107(D14, 4188). <doi:10.1029/2001JD000447>.

Chapin, F. S., P. A. Matson, and P. M. Vitousek. 2011. Principles of terrestrial ecosystem ecology. Springer, New York, New York.

Cheng, L., K. McDonald, R. Angle, and H. Sandhu. 1998. Forest fire enhanced photochemical air pollution. A case study. Atmospheric Environment 32:673–681.

Chow, J. C., J. G. Watson, D. H. Lowenthal, L-W. A. Chen, and N. Motallebi. 2010. Black and organic carbon emissions: Review and applications for California. Journal of Air and Waste Management Association 60:497–507.

———. 2011. PM2.5 source profiles for black and organic carbon emission inventories. Atmospheric Environment 45:5407–5414.

Cione, N. C., P. E. Padgett, and E. B. Allen. 2002. Restoration of a native shrubland impacted by exotic grasses, frequent fire, and nitrogen deposition in southern California. Restoration Ecology 10:376–384.

Cisneros, R., A. Bytnerowicz, D. Schweizer, S. Zhong, S. Traina, and D. H. Bennett. 2010. Ozone, nitric acid, and ammonia air pollution is unhealthy for people and ecosystems in southern Sierra Nevada, California. Environmental Pollution 158:3261–3271.

City Hunting for Source of Gas Attack. 1943. Los Angeles Times. July 27.

Clean Air Status and Trends Network (CASTNET). 2013. 2011 annual report. Prepared by AMEC Environment and Structure, Inc., for U.S. Environmental Protection Agency, EPA Contract No. EP-W-09-028.

Collett, J., Jr., B. Daube, J. W. Munger, and M. R. Hoffmann. 1989. Cloudwater chemistry in Sequoia National Park. Atmospheric Environment 23:999–1007.

Collett, J. L., Jr., B. C. Daube Jr., and M. R. Hoffmann. 1990. The chemical composition of intercepted cloudwater in the Sierra Nevada. Atmospheric Environment 24A:959–972.

Cox, P., A. Delao, A. Komorniczak, and R. Weller. 2009. The California almanac of emissions and air quality, 2009 edition. California Environmental Protection Agency, Air Resources Board. Sacramento, California.

Cox, R. D., and E. B. Allen. 2008. Stability of exotic annual grasses following restoration efforts in southern California coastal sage scrub. Journal of Applied Ecology 45:495–504.

Creamean, J. M., K. J. Suski, D. Rosenfeld, A. Cazorla, P. J. DeMott, R. C. Sullivan, A. B. White, F. M. Ralph, P. Minnis, J. M. Comstock, J. M. Tomlinson, and K. A. Prather. 2013. Dust and biological aerosols from the Sahara and Asia influence precipitation in the western U.S. Science 339:1572–1578.

Dahlgren, R. A. 1994. Soil acidification and nitrogen saturation from weathering of ammonium-bearing rock. Nature 368:838–841.

Damoah, R., N. Spichtinger, C. Forster, P. James, I. Mattis, U. Wandinger, S. Beirle, T. Wagner, and A. Stohl. 2004. Around the world in seventeen days: Hemispheric-scale transport of forest fire smoke from Russia in May 2003. Atmospheric Chemistry and Physics 4:1311–1321.

DeBell, L. J., R. W. Talbot, and J. E. Dibb. 2004. A major air pollution event in the northeastern United States caused by extensive forest fires in Quebec, Canada. Journal of Geophysical Research 109(D19305). <doi:10.1020/2004JD004840>.

Egerton-Warburton, L., and E. B. Allen. 2000. Shifts in arbuscular mycorrhizal communities along an anthropogenic nitrogen deposition gradient. Ecological Applications 10:484–496.

Environmental Protection Agency (EPA). 2008. Air quality guide for ozone. Environmental Protection Agency. http://www.epa.gov/airnow/ozone/air-quality-guide_ozone_2015.pdf. Accessed June 2015.

Farrell, C. 2005. Mega-dairies and agricultural air pollution. Pages 27–28 in M. V. Sluis and I. Douglas, editors. Everyday Heroes Protect the Air We Breathe, the Water We Drink, and the Natural Areas We Prize: Thirty-Five Years of the California Environmental Quality Act. The Planning and Conservation League Foundation and the California League of Conservation Voters. Sacramento and Oakland, California.

Fenn, M. E., and A. Bytnerowicz. 1997. Summer throughfall and winter deposition in the San Bernardino Mountains in southern California. Atmospheric Environment 31:673–683.

Fenn, M. E., A. Bytnerowicz, and D. Liptzin, D. 2012. Nationwide maps of atmospheric deposition are highly skewed when based solely on wet deposition. BioScience 62:621.

Fenn, M. E., M. A. Poth, A. Bytnerowicz, J. O. Sickman, and B. K. Takemoto. 2003. Effects of ozone, nitrogen deposition, and other stressors on montane ecosystems in the Sierra Nevada. Pages 111–155 in A. Bytnerowicz, M. J. Arbaugh, and R. Alonso, editors. Developments in Environmental Science, Volume 2: Ozone Air Pollution in the Sierra Nevada: Distribution and Effects on Forests. Elsevier, Amsterdam, The Netherlands.

Fenn, M. E., M. A. Poth, S. L. Schilling, and D. B. Grainger. 2000. Throughfall and fog deposition of nitrogen and sulfur at an N-limited and N-saturated site in the San Bernardino Mountains, southern California. Canadian Journal of Forest Research 30:1476–1488.

Fenn, M. E., and M. A. Poth. 2004. Monitoring nitrogen deposition in throughfall using ion exchange resin columns: A field test in the San Bernardino Mountains. Journal of Environmental Quality 33:2007–2014.

———. 1999. Nitrogen deposition and cycling in Mediterranean forests: The new paradigm of nitrogen excess. Pages 353–372 in P. R. Miller and J. R. McBride, editors. Oxidant Air Pollution Impacts in the Montane Forests of Southern California: A Case Study of the San Bernardino Mountains. Ecological Studies, volume 134. Springer-Verlag. New York.

Fenn, M. E., E. B. Allen, and L. H. Geiser. 2011. Mediterranean California. Pages 143–169 in L. H. Pardo, M. J. Robin-Abbott, and C. T. Driscoll, editors. Assessment of nitrogen deposition effects and empirical critical loads of nitrogen for ecoregions of the United States. Gen. Tech. Rep. NRS-80. U.S. Department of Agriculture, Forest Service, Northern Research Station, Newtown Square, Pennsylvania.

Fenn, M. E., E. B. Allen, S. B. Weiss, S. Jovan, L. Geiser, G. S. Tonnesen, R. F. Johnson, L. E. Rao, B. S. Gimeno, F. Yuan, T. Meixner, and A. Bytnerowicz. 2010. Nitrogen critical loads and management alternatives for N-impacted ecosystems in California. Journal of Environmental Management 91:2404–2423.

Fenn, M. E., S. Jovan, F. Yuan, L. Geiser, T. Meixner, and B. S. Gimeno. 2008. Empirical and simulated critical loads for nitrogen deposition in California mixed conifer forests. Environmental Pollution 155:492–511.

Fenn, M. E., T. G. Huntington, S. B. McLaughlin, C. Eagar, A. Gomez, and R. B. Cook. 2006. Status of soil acidification in North America. Journal of Forest Science (Prague) 52:3–13.

Fierro, M. A., M. K. O'Rourke, and J. L. Burgess. 2001. Adverse health effects of exposure to ambient carbon monoxide. University of Arizona, College of Public Health. <http://www.airinfonow.org/pdf/carbon%20monoxid2.pdf>. Accessed June 9, 2015.

Finlayson-Pitts, B. J., and J. N. Pitts Jr. 2000. Chemistry of the upper and lower atmosphere. Academic Press, San Diego, California.

Fitzgerald, J. W. 1991. Marine aerosols: A review. Atmospheric Environment 25A:533–545.

Foster, C., U. Wandinger, G. Wotawa, P. James, I. Mattis, D. Althausen, P. Simmonds, S. O'Doherty, S. G. Jennings, C. Kleefeld, J. Schneider, T. Trickl, S. Kreipl, H. Jager, and A. Stohl. 2001. Transport of boreal forest fire emissions from Canada to Europe. Journal of Geophysical Research 106:22887–22906.

Frank, T. D., L. D. Girolamo, and S. Geegan. 2007. The spatial and temporal variability of aerosol optical depths in the Mojave Desert of southern California. Remote Sensing of the Environment 107:54–64.

Frączek, W., A. Bytnerowicz, and M. J. Arbaugh. 2003. Use of geostatistics to estimate surface ozone patterns. Pages 215–247 in A. Bytnerowicz, M. Arbaugh, R. Alonso, editors. Ozone Air Pollution in the Sierra Nevada: Distribution and Effects on Forests, Developments in Environmental Science, volume 2. Elsevier, Amsterdam, The Netherlands.

Fujioka, F. M., J. O. Roads, and S.-C. Chen. 1999. Climatology. Pages 28–43 in P. R. Miller and J. R. McBride, editors. Oxidant Air Pollution Impacts in the Montane Forests of Southern California. Ecological Studies, volume 134. Springer-Verlag, New York.

Gertler, A., A. Bytnerowicz, T. A. Cahill, M. Arbaugh, S. Cliff, J. Kahyaoğlu-Koračin, L. Tarnay, R. Alonso, and W. Frączek. 2006. Local air quality threatens Lake Tahoe's clarity. California Agriculture 60:53–58.

Gillespie, I. G., and E. B. Allen. 2004. Fire and competition in a southern California grassland: Impacts on the rare forb *Erodium macrophyllum*. Journal of Applied Ecology 41:643–652.

Gimeno, B. S., F. Yuan, M. E. Fenn, and T. Meixner. 2009. Management options for mitigating nitrogen (N) losses from N saturated mixed conifer forests in California. Pages 425–455 in A. Bytnerowicz, M. J. Arbaugh, A. R. Riebau, and C. Andersen, editors. Wildland Fires and Air Pollution. Developments in Environmental Science, volume 8. Elsevier. Amsterdam, The Netherlands.

Goldammer, J. G., M. Statheropoulos, and M. O. Andeae. 2009. Impacts of vegetation fire emissions on the environment, human health, and security: A global perspective. Pages 3–36 in A. Bytnerowicz, M. Arbaugh, C. Andersen and A. Riebau, editors. Wildland Fires and Air Pollution. Developments in Environmental Science, volume 8. Elsevier. Amsterdam, The Netherlands.

Greaver, T. L., T. J. Sullivan, J. D. Herrick, M. C. Barber, J. S. Baron, B. J. Cosby, M. E. Deerhake et al. 2012. Ecological effects of nitrogen and sulfur air pollution in the U.S.: What do we know? Frontiers in Ecology 10:365–372.

Grulke, N. E. 2003. The physiological basis of ozone injury assessment attributes in Sierran conifers. Pages 55–81 in A. Bytnerowicz, M. Arbaugh, and R. Alonso, editors. Assessment of ozone distribution and its effects on Sierra Nevada ecosystems. Developments in Environmental Science, volume 2. Elsevier, Amsterdam, The Netherlands.

Grulke, N. E., R. A. Minnich, T. D. Paine, S. J. Seybold, D. J. Chavez, M. E. Fenn, P. J. Riggan, and A. Dunn. 2009. Air pollution increases forest susceptibility to wildfires: A case study in the San Bernardino Mountains in Southern California. Pages 365–403 in A. Bytnerowicz, M. Arbaugh, C. Andersen, and A. Riebau, editors. Wildland Fires and Air Pollution. Developments in Environmental Science, volume 8. Elsevier, Amsterdam, The Netherlands.

Haagen-Smit, A. J., and M. M. Fox. 1954. Photochemical ozone formation with hydrocarbons and automobile exhaust. Journal of the Air Pollution Control Association 4:105–108,136.

Hadley, O. L., C. E. Corrigan, T. W. Kirchstetter, S. S. Cliff, and V. Ramanathan. 2010. Measured black carbon deposition on the Sierra Nevada snow pack and implications for snow pack retreat. Atmospheric Chemistry and Physics 10:7505–7513.

Hanson, P. J., and S. E. Lindberg. 1991. Dry deposition of reactive nitrogen compounds: A review of leaf, canopy, and non-foliar measurements. Atmospheric Environment 25A:1615–1634.

Hayes, C., W. McDonnell, and H. Zenick. 1993. U.S. Environmental Protection Agency's Ozone Epidemiology Research Program: A strategy for assessing the effects of ambient ozone exposure upon morbidity in exposed populations. Journal of Air and Waste Management Association 43:950–954.

Hayes, T. P., J. J. R. Kinney, and N. J. M Wheeler. 1992. California surface wind climatology. State of California, Air Resources Board, Aerometric Data Division. Sacramento, California.

Houthuijs, D., O. Breugelmans, G. Hoek, E. Vaskovi, E. Mihalikova, J. S. Pastuszka, V. Jirik, S. Sachelarescu, D. Lolova, K. Meliefste, E. Uzunova, C. Marinescu, J. Volf, F. De leeuw, H. Van de Wiel, T. Fletcher, E. Lebret, and B. Brunekref. 2001. PM_{10} and $PM_{2.5}$ concentration in Central and Eastern Europe: Results from the Cesar study. Atmospheric Environment 35:2757–2771.

Intergovernmental Panel on Climate Change (IPCC). 2001. Climate change 2001: The scientific basis. J. T. Houghton et al., editors. Cambridge University Press, New York, New York.

Jacobs, C., and W. J. Kelly. 2008. Smogtown: The lung-burning history of pollution in Los Angeles. The Overlook Press, Peter Mayer Publishers, Inc., Woodstock and New York, New York.

Jaffe, D. A., D. Chang, W. Hafner, A. Westerling, and D. Spracklen. 2008. Influence of fires on O_3 concentrations in the western U. S. Environmental Science and Technology 42:5885–5891.

Johnson, D. W., M. E. Fenn, W. W. Miller, and C. F. Hunsaker. 2009. Fire effects on carbon and nitrogen cycling in forests of the Sierra Nevada. Pages 405–423 in A. Bytnerowicz, M. J. Arbaugh, A. R. Riebau, and C. Andersen, editors. Wildland Fires and Air Pollution. Developments in Environmental Science, volume 8. Elsevier, Amsterdam, The Netherlands.

Jones, M. E., T. D. Paine, M. E. Fenn, and M. A. Poth. 2004. Influence of ozone and nitrogen deposition on bark beetle activity under drought conditions. Forest Ecology and Management 200:67–76.

Jovan, S. 2008. Lichen bioindication of biodiversity, air quality, and climate: Baseline results from monitoring in Washington, Oregon, and California. Gen. Tech. Rep. PNW-GTR-737. U.S. Department of Agriculture, Forest Service, Pacific Northwest Research Station, Portland, Oregon.

Jovan, S., and B. McCune. 2005. Air-quality bioindication in the greater Central Valley of California, with epiphytic macrolichen communities. Ecological Applications 15:1712–1726.

Kayhanian, M. 2012. Trend and concentrations of legacy lead (Pb) in highway runoff. Environmental Pollution 160:169–177.

Kean, A. J., R. A. Harley, D. Littlejohn, and G. R. Kendall. 2000. On-road measurement of ammonia and other motor vehicle exhaust emissions. Environmental Science and Technology 34:3535–3539.

Koelemeijer, R. B. A., C. D. Homan, and J. Matthijsen. 2006. Comparison of spatial and temporal variations of aerosol optical thickness and particulate matter over Europe. Atmospheric Environment 40:5304–5315.

Koppmann, R., K. von Czapiewski, and J. S. Reid. 2005. A review of biomass burning emissions. Part 1: Gaseous emissions of carbon monoxide, methane, volatile organic compounds, and nitrogen containing compounds. Atmospheric Chemistry and Physics Discussions 5:10455–10516.

Landers, D. H., S. M. Simonich, D. Jaffe, L. Geiser, D. H. Campbell, A. Schwindt, C. Schreck, M. Kent, W. Hafner, H. E. Taylor, K. Hageman, S. Usenko, L. Ackerman, J. Schrlau, N. Rose, T. Blett, and M. M. Erway. 2010. The western airborne contaminant assessment project (WACAP): An interdisciplinary evaluation of the impacts of airborne contaminants in western U.S. National Parks. Environmental Science and Technology 44:855–859.

Linping, C., V. Kenneth, and T. Shilu. 2006. Air particulate pollution due to bushfires and respiratory hospital admissions in Brisbane, Australia. International Journal of Environmental Health Research 16:181–191.

Little, C. E. 1992. The California X-disease. American Forests 98:32–34,55–56.

Liu, Y. 2005. Atmospheric response and feedback to radiative forcing from biomass burning in tropical South America. Agricultural and Forest Meteorology 133:40–53.

McKenzie, D., D. L. Peterson, and J. J. Littell. 2009. Global warming and stress complexes in forests of western North America. Pages 319–337 in A. Bytnerowicz, M. J. Arbaugh, A. R. Riebau, and C. Andersen, editors. Wildland Fires and Air Pollution. Developments in Environmental Science, volume 8. Elsevier, Amsterdam, The Netherlands.

McMeeking, G. R., S. M. Kreidenweis, M. Lunden, J. Carrillo, C. M. Carrico, T. Lee, P. Herckes, G. Engling, D. E. Day, J. Hand, N. Brown, W. C. Malm, and J. L. Collett Jr. 2002. Smoke-impacted regional haze in California during the summer of 2002. Agricultural and Forest Meteorology 137:25–42.

Meixner, T., M. E. Fenn, P. Wohlgemuth, M. Oxford, and P. Riggan. 2006. N saturation symptoms in chaparral catchments are not reversed by prescribed fire. Environmental Science and Technology 40:2887–2894.

Middleton, J. T., J. B. Kendrick Jr., and H. W. Schwalm. 1950. Injury to herbaceous plants by smog or air pollution. Plant Disease Reporter 34:245–252.

Mielke, H. W., M. A. S. Laidlaw, and C. Gonzales. 2010. Lead (Pb) legacy from vehicle traffic in eight California urbanized areas: Continuing influence of lead dust on children's health. Science of the Total Environment 408:3965–3975.

Miller, C. 2011. Breathe deep (and then thank the EPA that you can): KCET, commentary. <http://www.kcet.org/updaily/socal_focus/commentary/breathe-deep-thank-the-epa-31265.html>. Accessed June 9, 2015.

Miller, P. R. 1992. Mixed conifer forests of the San Bernardino Mountains, California. Pages 461–497 in R. K. Olson, D. Binkley, and M. Böhm, editors. The Response of Western Forests to Air Pollution. Springer-Verlag, New York, New York.

Miller, P. R., and A. A. Millecan. 1971. Extent of oxidant air pollution damage to some pines and other conifers in California. Plant Disease Reporter 55:555–559.

Miller, P. R., J. R. McBride, S. L. Schilling, and A. P. Gomez. 1989. Trend of ozone damage to conifer forests between 1974 and 1988 in the San Bernardino Mountains of southern California. Pages 309–323 in R. K. Olson and A. S. Lefohn, editors. Effects of Air Pollution on Western Forests. Air and Waste Management Association, Pittsburg, Pennsylvania.

Miller, P. R., J. R. Parmeter Jr., O. C. Taylor, and E. A. Cardiff. 1963. Ozone injury to the foliage of *Pinus ponderosa*. Phytopathology 53:1072–1076.

Miller, R. L., and I. Tegen. 1998. Climate response to soil dust aerosols. Journal of Climate 11:3247–3267.

Minnich, R. A. 2008. California's fading wildflowers: Lost legacy and biological invasions. University of California Press, Berkeley, California.

Minnich, R. A., and P. E. Padgett. 2003. Geology, climate, and vegetation of the Sierra Nevada and the mixed-conifer zone: An introduction to the ecosystem. Pages 1–31 in A. Bytnerowicz, M. J. Arbaugh, and R. Alonso, editors. Ozone Air Pollution in the Sierra Nevada: Distribution and Effects on Forests, Developments in Environmental Science, volume 2. Elsevier, Amsterdam, The Netherlands.

Morris, G. A., S. Hersey, A. M. Thompson, S. Pawson, J. E. Nielsen, P. R. Colarco, W. W. McMillan, A. Stohl, S. Turquety, J. Warner, B. J. Johnson, T. L. Kucsera, D. E. Larko, S. J. Oltmans, and J. C. Witte. 2006. Alaskan and Canadian fires exacerbate ozone pollution over Houston, Texas, on 19 and 20 July 2004. Journal of Geophysical Research 111:D24S03.

Murphy, D. M., J. R. Anderson, P. K. Quinn, L. M. McInees, F. J. Brechtel, S. M. Kreidenweis, A. M. Middlebrook, M. Posfai, D. S. Thomson, and P. R. Buseck. 1998. Influence of sea-salt on aerosol radiative properties in the Southern Ocean marine boundary layer. Nature 392:62–65.

Nacht, D. M., M. S. Gustin, M. A. Engle, R. E. Zehner, and A. D. Giglini. 2004. Atmospheric mercury emissions and speciation at the sulphur bank mercury mine superfund site, northern California. Environmental Science and Technology 38:1977–1983.

Ohmart, C. 1980. Effects of photochemical oxidants on tree growth in the San Bernardino National Forest. Pages 65–76 in O. C. Taylor, editor. Photochemical Oxidant Air Pollution Effects on a Mixed Conifer Forest Ecosystem. Final Report. U.S. EPA, EPA-600/3-80-002. Corvallis Environment Research Laboratory, Corvallis, Oregon.

Oltmans, S. J., A. S. Lefohn, D. Shadwick, J. M. Harris, H. E. Scheel, I. Galbally, D. W. Tarasick, B. J. Johnson, E.-G. Brunke, H. Claude, G. Zeng, S. Nichol, F. Schmidlin, J. Davies, E. Cuevas, A. Redondas, H. Naoe, T. Nakano, and T. Kawasato. 2013. Recent tropospheric ozone changes: A pattern dominated by slow or no growth. Atmospheric Environment 67:331–351.

Ottmar, R., and T. Reinhardt. 2000. Smoke exposure at western wildfires. Pacific Northwest Research Station Research Paper PNW-RP-525. U.S. Department of Agriculture Forest Service, Seattle, Washington.

Panek, J., D. Saah, A. Esperanza, A. Bytnerowicz, W. Frączek, and R. Cisneros. 2013. Ozone distribution in remote ecologically vulnerable terrain of the southern Sierra Nevada, CA. Environmental Pollution 182:343–356.

Pardo, L. H., M. E. Fenn, C. L. Goodale, L. H. Geiser, C. T. Driscoll, E. B. Allen, J. S. Baron, R. Bobbink, W. D. Bowman, C. M. Clark, B. Emmett, F. S. Gilliam, T. L. Greaver, S. J. Hall, E. A. Lilleskov, L. Liu, J. A. Lynch, K. J. Nadelhoffer, S. S. Perakis, M. J. Robin-Abbott, J. L. Stoddard, K. C. Weathers, and R. L. Dennis. 2011. Effects of nitrogen deposition and empirical nitrogen critical loads for ecoregions of the United States. Ecological Applications 21:3049–3082.

Park, R., D. J. Jacob, and J. A. Logan. 2007. Fire and biofuel contributions to annual mean aerosol mass concentrations in the United States. Atmospheric Environment 41:7389–7400.

Parmeter, J. R., Jr., R. V. Bega, and T. Neff. 1962. A chlorotic decline of ponderosa pine in southern California. Plant Disease Reporter 46:269–273.

Peterson, D., M. Arbaugh, V. Wakefield, and P. Miller. 1987. Evidence of growth reduction in ozone-injured Jeffrey pines (*Pinus jeffreyi* Grev. and Balf.) in Sequoia and Kings Canyon National Parks. Journal of the Air Pollution Control Association 37:906–912.

Pfister, G. G., C. Wiedinmyer, and L. K. Emmons. 2008. Impacts of the fall 2007 California wildfires on surface ozone: Integrating local observations with global model simulations. Geophysical Research Letters 35, L19814. <doi:10.1029/2008GL034747>.

Pollack, I. B., T. B. Ryerson, M. Trainer, J. A. Neuman, J. M. Roberts, and D. D. Parrish. 2013. Trends in ozone, its precursors, and related secondary oxidation products in Los Angeles, California: A synthesis of measurements from 1960 to 2010. Journal of Geophysical Research-Atmospheres 118:5893–5911.

Prestbo, E. M., and D. A. Gay. 2009. Wet deposition of mercury in the U.S. and Canada, 1996–2005: Results and analysis of the NADP mercury deposition network (MDN). Atmospheric Environment 43:4223–4233.

Querol, X., A. Alastuey, T. Moreno, M. M. Viana, S. Castillo, J. Pey, S. Rodríguez, B. Artinano, P. Salvador, M. Sanchez, S. Garcia Dos Santos, M. D. Herce Garraleta, R. Fernandez-Patier, S. Moreno-Graue, L. Negral, M. C. Minguillon, E. Monfort, M. J. Sanz, R. Palomo-Marin, E. Pinilla-Gil, E. Cuevas, J. de la Rosa, and A. Sanchez de la Campa. 2007. Spatial and temporal variations in airborne particulate matter (PM_{10} and $PM_{2.5}$) across Spain 1999–2005. Atmospheric Environment 42:2964–3979.

Radke, L. F., D. E. Ward, and P. J. Riggan. 2001. A prescription for controlling the air pollution resulting from the use of prescribed biomass fire: Clouds. International Journal of Wildland Fire 10:103–111.

Radojevic, M., and H. Hassan. 1998. Air quality in Brunei Darussalam during the 1998 haze episode. Atmospheric Environment 30:3651–3658.

Rao, L. E., E. B. Allen, and T. Meixner. 2010. Risk-based determination of critical nitrogen deposition loads for fire spread in southern California deserts. Ecological Applications 20:1320–1335.

Reid, J. S., R. G. Flocchini, T. A. Cahill, R. S. Ruth, and D. P. Salgado. 1994. Local meteorological, transport, and source aerosol characteristics of late autumn Owens Lake (dry) dust storms. Atmospheric Environment 28:1699–1706.

Richards, B. L., O. C. Taylor, and G. F. Edmunds Jr. 1968. Ozone needle mottle of pine in southern California. Journal of the Air Pollution Control Association 18:73–77.

Riggan, P. J., R. N. Lockwood, P. M. Jacks, C. G. Colver, F. Weirich, L. F. DeBano, and J. A. Brass. 1994. Effects of fire severity on nitrate mobilization in watersheds subject to chronic atmospheric deposition. Environmental Science and Technology 28:369–375.

Rosenfeld, D., and A. Givati. 2006. Evidence of orographic precipitation suppression by air pollution-induced aerosol in the western United States. Journal of Applied Meteorology and Climatology 45:893–911.

Rosenfeld, D., W. L. Woddley, D. Axisa, E. Freud, J. G. Hudson, and A. Givati. 2008. Aircraft measurements of the impacts of pollution aerosols on clouds and precipitation over the Sierra Nevada. Journal Geophysical Research 113:D215203. <doi:10.1029/2007/JD009544, 2008>.

Sapkota, A., J. M. Symons, J. Klwissl, L. Wang, M. B. Parlange, J. Ondov, P. N. Breysse, G. B. Diette, P. A. Eggleston, and T. J. Buckley. 2005. Impact of the 2002 Canadian forest fires on particulate matter air quality in Baltimore City. Environmental Science and Technology 39:24–32.

Saros, J. E., D. W. Clow, T. Blett, and A. P. Wolfe. 2011. Critical nitrogen deposition loads in high-elevation lakes of the western US inferred from paleolimnological records. Water, Air, and Soil Pollution 216:193–202.

SCAQMD (South Coast Air Quality Management District). 1997. The Southland's war on smog: Fifty years of progress toward clean air. Diamond Bar, California, USA. <http://www.aqmd.gov/home/library/public-information/publications/50-years-of-progress> Accessed June 8, 2015.

Seinfeld, J. H., and S. N. Pandis. 1998. Atmospheric chemistry and physics. John Wiley & Sons, Inc., New York, New York.

Shaw, G. D., R. Cisneros, D. Schweizer, J. O. Sickman, and M. E. Fenn. 2014. Critical loads of acid deposition for wilderness lakes in the Sierra Nevada (California) estimated by the steady state water chemistry model. Water, Air, and Soil Pollution 225:1804; 15p. DOI: 10.1007/s11270-013-1804-x.

Sickman, J. O., J. M. Melack, and J. L. Stoddard. 2002. Regional analysis of nitrogen yield and retention in high-elevation ecosystems of the Sierra Nevada and Rocky Mountains. Biogeochemistry 57:341–374.

Stephens, S. L., R. E. Martin, and N. E. Clinton. 2007. Prehistoric fire area and emissions from California's forests, woodlands, shrublands, and grasslands. Forest Ecology and Management 251:205–216.

Syphard, A. D., V. C. Radeloff, J. E. Keeley, T. J. Hawbaker, M. K. Clayton, S. I. Stewart, and R. B. Hammer. 2007. Human influence on California fire regimes. Ecological Applications 17:1388–1402.

Takemoto, B. K., A. Bytnerowicz, and M. E. Fenn. 2001. Current and future effects of ozone and atmospheric nitrogen deposition on California's mixed conifer forests. Forest Ecology and Management 144:159–173.

Tegen, I., and I. Fung. 1995. Contribution to the atmospheric mineral aerosol load from land surface modification. Journal of Geophysical Research 100(D9):18707–18726.

———. 1994. Modeling of mineral dust in the atmosphere: Sources, transport, and optical thickness. Journal of Geophysical Research 99(D11):22897–22914.

Urbanski, S. P., W. M. Hao, and S. Baker. 2009. Chemical composition of wildland fire emissions. Pages 79–107 in A. Bytnerowicz, M. Arbaugh, C. Andersen, and A. Riebau, editors. Wildland Fires and Air Pollution. Developments in Environmental Science, volume 8. Elsevier, Amsterdam, The Netherlands.

USDA Forest Service. 2001. Record of decision: Sierra Nevada Forest Plan Amendment Environmental Impact Statement. <www.fs.usda.gov/Internet/FSE_DOCUMENTS/fsbdev3_046095.pdf>. Accessed June 8, 2015.

VanCuren, R. A. 2003. Asian aerosols in North America: Extracting the chemical composition and mass concentration of the Asian continental aerosol plume from long-term aerosol records in the western United States. Journal of Geophysical Research 108(D20):4623–4635.

VanCuren, R. A., and T. A. Cahill. 2002. Asian aerosols in North America: Frequency and concentration of fine dust. Journal of Geophysical Research 107(D24):4804–4820.

Vingarzan, R. 2004. A review of surface ozone background levels and trends. Atmospheric Environment 38:3431–3442.

Vollenweider, P., M. E. Fenn, T. Menard, and A. Bytnerowicz. 2013. Structural injury underlying mottling in ponderosa pine needles exposed to ambient ozone concentrations in the San Bernardino Mountains near Los Angeles, California. Trees: Structure and Function. 27:895–911.

Wan, S., D. Hui, and Y. Luo. 2001. Fire effects on nitrogen pools and dynamics in terrestrial ecosystems: A meta-analysis. Ecological Applications 11:1349–1365.

Wang, H., D. J. Jacob, P. Le Sager, D. G. Streets, R. J. Park, A. B. Gilliland, and A. van Donkelaar. 2009. Surface ozone background in the United States: Canadian and Mexican influences. Atmospheric Environment 43:1310–1319.

Ward, T. J., and G. C. Smith. 2001. Air sampling study of the 2000 Montana Wildfire Season. Paper No. 1131. In Proceedings of the Air and Waste Management Association, 94th Annual Conference and Exhibition, Orlando, FL, 11 pp, (CD-ROM Proceedings).

Weiss, S. B. 1999. Cars, cows, and checkerspot butterflies: Nitrogen deposition and management of nutrient-poor grasslands for a threatened species. Conservation Biology 13:1476–1486.

Weiss-Penzias, P., D. Jaffe, P. Swartzendruber, W. Hafner, D. Chand, and E. Prestbo. 2007. Quantifying Asian and biomass burning sources of mercury using the Hg/CO ratio in pollution plumes observed at the Mount Bachelor observatory. Atmospheric Environment 41:4366–4379.

WHO (World Health Organization). 2003. Health aspects of air pollution with particulate matter, ozone and nitrogen dioxide. Report on a WHO Working Group. Bonn, Germany.

Williams, W. T., M. Brady, and S. C. Willison. 1977. Air pollution damage to the forests of the Sierra Nevada Mountains of California. Journal of the Air Pollution Control Association 27:230–236.

Wotawa, G., and M. Trainer. 2000. The influence of Canadian forest fires on pollutant concentrations in the United States. Science 288:324–327.

Zapata, C., N. Muller, and M. J. Kleeman. 2013. $PM_{2.5}$ co-benefits of climate change legislation Part 1: California's AB 32. Climatic Change 117:377–397.

Zhang, X., and S. Kondragunta. 2008. Temporal and spatial variability in biomass burned areas across the USA derived from the GOES fire product. Remote Sensing of Environment 112:2886–2897.

Zimmer, C. 2013. Black carbon and warming: It's worse than we thought. Yale Environment 360. January 17, 2013. <http://e360.yale.edu/feature/carl_zimmer_black_carbon_and_global_warming_worse_than_thought/2611/>. Accessed June 9, 2015.

PART TWO

HISTORY

EIGHT

Ecosystems Past

Vegetation Prehistory

CONSTANCE I. MILLAR and WALLACE B. WOOLFENDEN

Introduction

Historical accounts are usually rendered as narratives that chronicle a sequence of events over time and space. While the story is important, history is as much about process (how things came to be) as pattern (the story). Understanding processes of change is one important way we can learn from the past and, in the context of vegetation and ecosystems, benefit conservation and stewardship. Over long expanses of time, three primary forces have influenced the development of terrestrial ecosystems across California's landscape. The first is geologic, with processes that affect vegetation at long and short time scales. Geologic settings are the stage on which regional ecosystems and vegetation develop. Over millions of years and through complex tectonic processes, landforms such as continental margins, inland seas, mountain ranges, upland plateaus, valleys, and basins were created and destroyed. In contrast to long, slow geologic processes, for example, volcanic eruptions, earthquakes, and tsunamis occur in geologic instants, exerting significant and long-lasting effects on vegetation. Geologic processes strongly affect the second primary force of historical ecosystem change: climate. If geology is the stage for vegetation development, climate is the director. The latitude of continents dictates atmospheric conditions; proximity to oceans and the configuration of continents relative to oceans confer distinct regional climates; high elevations are cooler than low elevations; and mountains focus cloud formation while creating rain shadows along their lee slopes.

Less well understood are the diverse forces and relentless nature of climate change. In that climate can be described as the average of weather variations, this average is wholly dependent on a particular time frame. As the time frame is shifted back or lengthened, climates are significantly different from present. While public awareness of anthropogenic climate change in the twentieth and twenty-first century has increased, understanding of the role of natural climate change over a longer (prehistoric) period of time has not. A widespread perception remains that climates started to change only in the late twentieth century. To the contrary, climates have been changing continually over historical time. The natural condition is for climates to be expressed at multiple, hierarchic levels, with interannual regimes (e.g., El Niño/

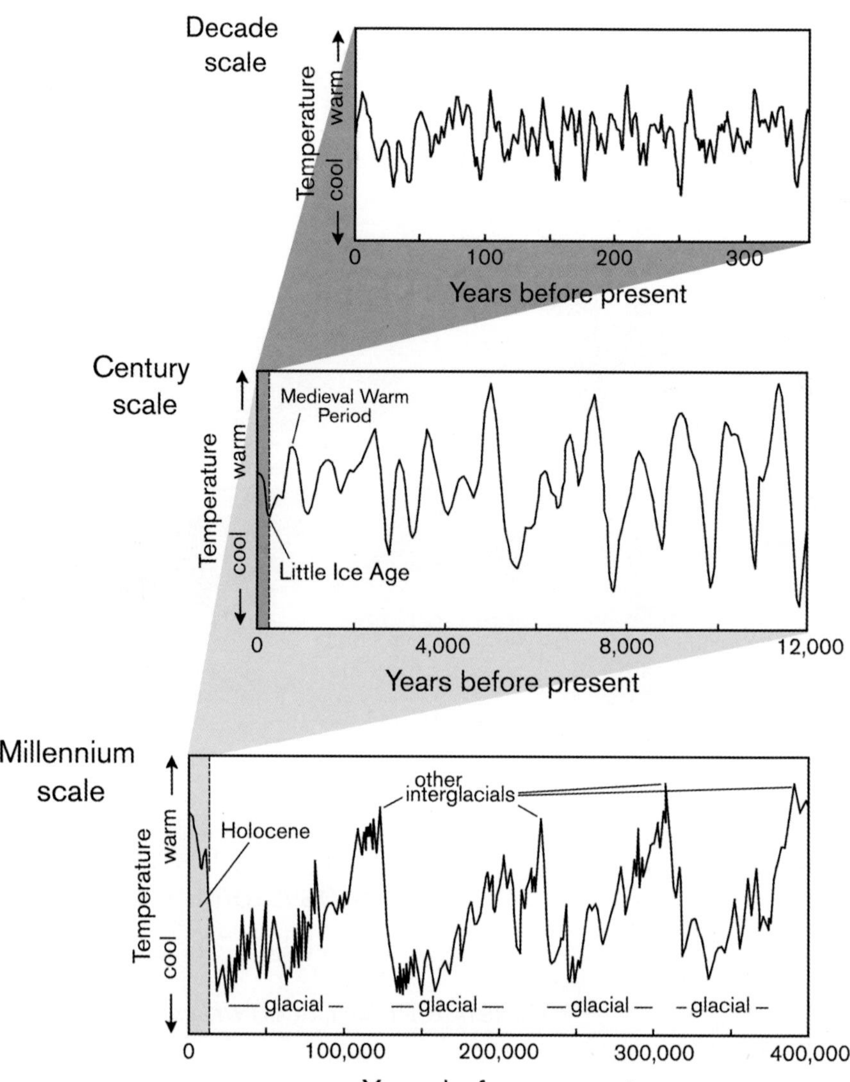

FIGURE 8.1 Global temperature cycles showing the nested nature of climate modes at different temporal scales.

TOP: Decadal cycles driven by ocean circulation and sea surface temperatures. Source: Biondi et al. 2001.

MIDDLE: Centennial cycles driven by solar variability. Source: Bond et al. 2001.

BOTTOM: Millennial cycles driven by changes in earth's orbit relative to the sun. These and other cycles interact continually and, in combination, result in ongoing changes in earth's natural climate system. Source: Petit et al. 1999.

La Niña) nested in decadal modes (e.g., Pacific Decadal Oscillation), these nested within multicentury modes (e.g., Bond cycles that influenced the Medieval Climatic Anomaly and the Little Ice Age) (Mann et al. 2009), and these nested within even longer-term multimillennial cycles (e.g., glacial and Milankovitch cycles; Figure 8.1).

Diverse physical mechanisms called "forcing factors" drive these cycles at different scales. For instance, variations in ocean-circulation and sea-surface temperatures drive interdecadal and multidecadal changes; shifts in solar activity force centennial climate modes; and variability in Earth's orbit and relationship to the Sun control the long glacial-to-interglacial cycles of the past two million years. While these are quasi-independent, the drivers interact, and climate at any one moment is expressed as the cumulative effect of all modes acting together. This results in changes that can be gradual and directional, episodic or reversible, characterized by abrupt changes and extreme events, and/or chaotic patterns. Ecosystems respond to climate changes at all of these scales, varying in extent with the magnitude and nature of change. Greenhouse gas emissions and other human influences on climate are superimposed on the ongoing natural forces of climate change.

Genetic adaptation is the third great force of change on vegetation over time. If geologic and climatic conditions provide the stage and direction for species to play out ecological dramas, evolutionary forces alter the inherent nature of the biota. Forced by geologic setting and climate, determinate processes such as natural selection drive adaptive evolution, wherein populations change in their genetic capacity to

Photo on previous page: The current landscape of the high Sierra Nevada bears witness to the cumulative effects of past geologic, climatic, and vegetation epochs. Here along the eastern escarpment of Rock Creek Canyon, pastels reveal glacial cirques, horns, and arêtes that were etched by long-gone Pleistocene glaciers along the range crest south of Mono Pass. Tiny, late Holocene glaciers, sharing no relation to their Pleistocene forebears, perch tenuously on the highest cirque headwalls as remnants from the recent Little Ice Age. Similarly, Marsh Lake in the foreground reflects wetlands and wetland vegetation relictual from the cooler, relatively wetter Little Ice Age. Subalpine forests of whitebark pine and occasional mountain hemlock fringe Marsh Lake in high density relative to their sparser woodland condition during recent centuries past. Deeper in the past, more than eleven thousand years ago, no forests—or vegetation at all—were present in this high canyon. Instead, hundreds-of-meters-deep ice formed a massive ice cap over the high Sierra Nevada during the coldest part of the last glacial period. Painting by Wallace Woolfenden.

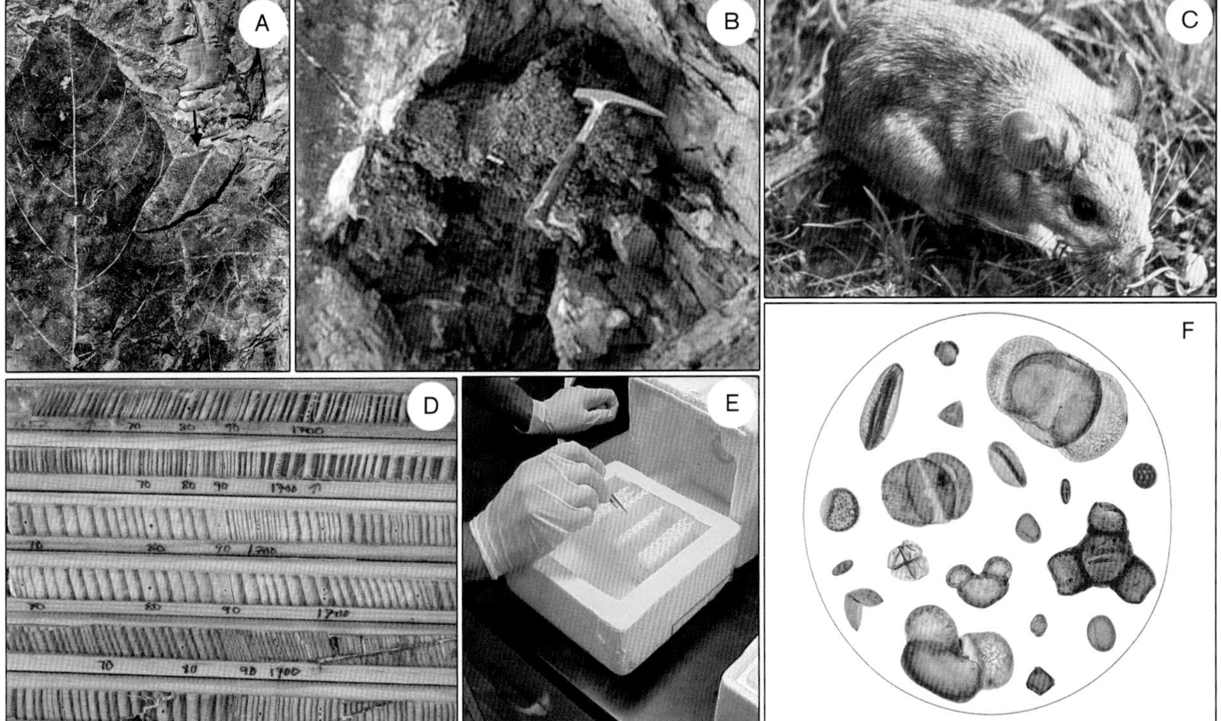

FIGURE 8.2 Diversity of proxies used for reconstructing historical vegetation.
Photos: (A) Diane Erwin, (B) U.S. Geological Survey, (C) from U.S. Geological Survey National Research Program, (D) Henri Grissino-Mayer, <http://web.utk.edu/~grissino/treering-gallery1>, (E) Paul Hodgskiss, and (F) modified from Mehringer 1967.

A Impression fossil of buckeye (*Aesculus* spp.) from Paleogene Chalk Bluffs Flora, western Sierra Nevada.

B Indurated midden constructed by bushy-tailed packrats (*Neotoma cinerea*).

C Desert packrat (*Neotoma lepida*).

D Increment cores from tree-ring extraction of ponderosa pine (*Pinus ponderosa*) stems in Arizona.

E DNA extracts from fresh foliar tissues for phylogenetic reconstruction.

F Pollen grains from a composite plate of Pleistocene age, Las Vegas Valley, Nevada.

survive and thrive in given locations and climates through reproductive and survival advantages conferred on fitter individuals. Stochastic processes, by contrast, of mutation, gene flow, and genetic drift create and alter the raw material of genetic diversity on which natural selection acts. Over long and short time spans, new life is formed as populations diverge into races, and races evolve into species. Individual mortality, population extirpation, and species extinction play significant roles by removing genotypes in determinate and stochastic ways. Geologic and climatic events, such as uplift of mountains, retreat of seas, and abrupt cold or warm periods, further drive divergence among taxa, forcing the evolution of remarkable biodiversity we inherit on Earth now.

Why does it matter in the study of California ecosystems to understand history and the forces of change that underlie vegetation development? Similar to understanding family ancestry, there is the sheer delight at knowing our regional history. For its role in revealing and explaining current conditions, history informs and clarifies. For fixing what might be broken (ecological restoration), and for anticipating and managing the future (climate projections and adaptation), the chronicles of history comprise essential course materials. History reminds us that California's diverse ecosystems today are just the leading edge of a long chain of species and ecosystems that has flowed across the region's shifting landscapes under constantly changing climates.

Reconstructing the Past: Methods of Historical Ecology

The methods of historical studies differ fundamentally from those focused on modern issues because the past cannot be repeated and experimentation is impossible (Bradley 1999). More akin to detective work, interpretation of historical process is by inference based on traces and relicts that remain, and by comparing effects of historical events across different places and times. Reconstructing historical conditions is the central task of paleoecology, whether to write the narrative for a region or to interpret the forces of change. Many sources of evidence for reconstructing terrestrial vegetation and ecosystem processes are available, depending on the environmental context and time period of interest, including molecular, organic geochemical, pollen, spores, algae, invertebrate remains ("microfossils," e.g., insects, freshwater/marine organisms, foraminifera, and dinoflagellates), charcoal from meadow, bog, or lake sediments; plant parts (micro and macrofossils) from woodrat middens; annual growth rings and fire scars from perennial woody trees and shrubs; permineralized and impression plant fossils; plant remains in archeological sites; and archival records, including ethnographic and recent historical documents, oral histories, sketches, and photographs (Figure 8.2). Each proxy has biases (TAPHONOMY, preservation, etc.), and the most robust reconstructions integrate multiple lines of evidence.

In addition to identifying and describing former plant species, including their biogeography and assemblages, historical ecologists seek information about past forces of change, geology, climate, and evolution. Thus reconstruction of environmental and genetic contexts commonly is also attempted. Many archives that reflect historical processes ("proxies") of climate and geology exist, including sediment and chemistry analysis from lake and bog cores; assessment of bedrock and overburden exposures and orientations; ash and tephra deposits; surface fluvial remains; glacial moraine orientations; and ice archives from glacial cores (Bradley 1999). Indirect reconstruction of climate is also made from assessment of plants and animals living at a historical time, basing inferences on correlations of modern taxa and climate ("climate analogs") or through analysis of plant physiognomy (Wolfe 1995).

Methods for assessing evolutionary forces traditionally focused on interpreting changes in plant parts (morphology) and their inferred function over time. These methods particularly emphasized reproductive structures, which tend to be under strong natural selection, thus conservatively representing phylogeny. Macrofossils have been especially important for understanding evolution prior to the Quaternary, where more continuous samples of microfossils are available for evolutionary assessment. The advent of biochemical and molecular techniques during recent decades, however, has revolutionized interpretation of evolutionary history in plants and animals, both through phylogenetic reconstructions of DNA and direct assessment of ancient DNA from fossil material. Recent literature on California plant and animal evolution contains many revisions from molecular analyses of phylogenetic relationships and times of divergence (Calsbeek et al. 2003). This chapter focuses on California's geologic and climatic history, highlighting the shifts in climate, landscape, and the concomitant rise and fall of California's diverse assemblages over deep geologic to recent times.

Misty Origins: Mesozoic Ecosystems (252–66 Ma)

Over multimillennia prior to the Cenozoic (>66 million years ago, Ma; Figure 8.3) and including the Mesozoic Era (252 Ma–66 Ma), the western margin of what is now North America constituted a long coastline abutting major oceans. The location of that shoreline, the presence and absence of offshore land masses (island arc volcanoes), the transgression and regression of a great inland seaway in midcontinent, and uplands that are now California changed greatly over time (Figure 8.4; Blakey 2008). However, California was under water much of this time. Exceptions to this are island relicts that are now land components mostly in northwestern California, and a varying width of land along the California–Nevada border region. Thus the early history of plants in California has to do with their origins elsewhere, their occasional appearance on fragmentary land masses, and their expansion throughout the California region with the emergence of greater amounts of land in the early Cenozoic.

Movements of the southwestern regions of the continent in this period are important to the climate and environmental context for plants. These regions passed first through latitudes lower than present earlier in time, then later through latitudes higher than present (in the mid-Cretaceous), arriving near their present latitudes by the end of the Mesozoic (Blakey 2008). Major mountain-building episodes (the Nevadan and Sevier orogenies) between 200 Ma and 70 Ma resulted in extensive north-south volcanic chains, with exposures in the Klamath Ranges, Sierra Nevada, Basin and Range Province, Mojave Desert, and Peninsula Ranges, as well as intrusion of magma, mostly granitic, far underground in batholiths (later uplifted as the Sierra Nevada) (Harden 2004). Much of the exposed portions of eastern California and the region of today's Great Basin became elevated plateaus (steppe) built by this volcanic activity (DeCourten 2003, Mix et al. 2011). Reflecting the changing latitudinal and altitudinal situations over time, early climates during this period ranged from tropical (annual temperatures 10°C warmer than present) to cool temperate, although humidities were relatively high and rain shadows mostly lacking (Figure 8.5). Although subalpine and possibly alpine conditions existed, hot arid desert did not.

Several ancient GYMNOSPERM lineages, such as cycads (Cycadaceae), redwoods (Taxodiaceae), and ginkgos (Ginkgoaceae), had their heyday during the Mesozoic (Miller 1977). Many members of the latter two families extended across the Northern Hemisphere, including western North America. Taxodiaceous taxa appeared ~245 Ma, with redwood (*Sequoia*) and relatives dating to ~200 Ma. Giant sequoia (*Sequoiadendron*) is not known from the Mesozoic, although the diversity of forms appearing after 66 Ma suggests that it had earlier origins. By ~200 Ma, modern conifer families are recognizable. Pinaceous conifers underwent an extensive radiation during the early Cretaceous (~145 Ma), lagging behind other conifer families (Miller 1976). To date, among extant genera of the pine family (Pinaceae), only pines (*Pinus*) are recognized in the Cretaceous, the other genera appearing later in the Paleogene (Smith and Stockey 2001). Early forms of Pinaceae appeared by 150 Ma, although their radiation lagged those of other conifers (Miller 1976). *Pityostrobus*, a group of Pinaceae taxa that disappeared by 33–30 Ma, and pines are among the oldest records for this family. In addition to gymnosperms, ferns (including horsetail, *Equisetum*) radiated and expanded worldwide starting ~150 Ma.

Rapid diversification of ANGIOSPERM taxa began ~110 Ma, with almost exponential increase in taxonomic diversity (Crane et al. 2000). By this time, angiosperms were abundant on a worldwide basis, and by 66 Ma they had become the most diverse and floristically dominant group of plants, as evidenced by the composition of numerous MACROFOSSIL and pollen floras (Rettalack and Dilcher 1986). In North America the Cretaceous Western Interior Seaway separated two principal floristic provinces. The western province was distinguished by the abundance of *Aquilapollenites*, an early angiosperm pollen taxon resembling grains of modern sandalwood (Santalales) but likely representing a broad polyphyletic clade (Graham 1999). Closed-canopy forests of broadleaved evergreen angiosperms and conifer forests dominated in the warm humid environments, suggesting little seasonality and annual mean temperatures of 20°C to 25°C (Tiffney 1985). Middle latitude west-coast forests contained araucarian (monkey puzzle tree), rosid (rose), plantanoid (plane-tree), hamamelid (witch hazel) elements as well as species of birch (Betulaceae), elm (Ulmaceae), basswood (Tiliaceae), walnut (Juglandaceae), and sandalwood (Santalales) families. There is also evidence for a distinct continental margin floristic province based in part on pollen samples from California. This province is recognized by absence or low abundance of *Aquilapollenites*. Indications are that angiosperms first spread to California between 120 Ma and 100 Ma. During this and sub-

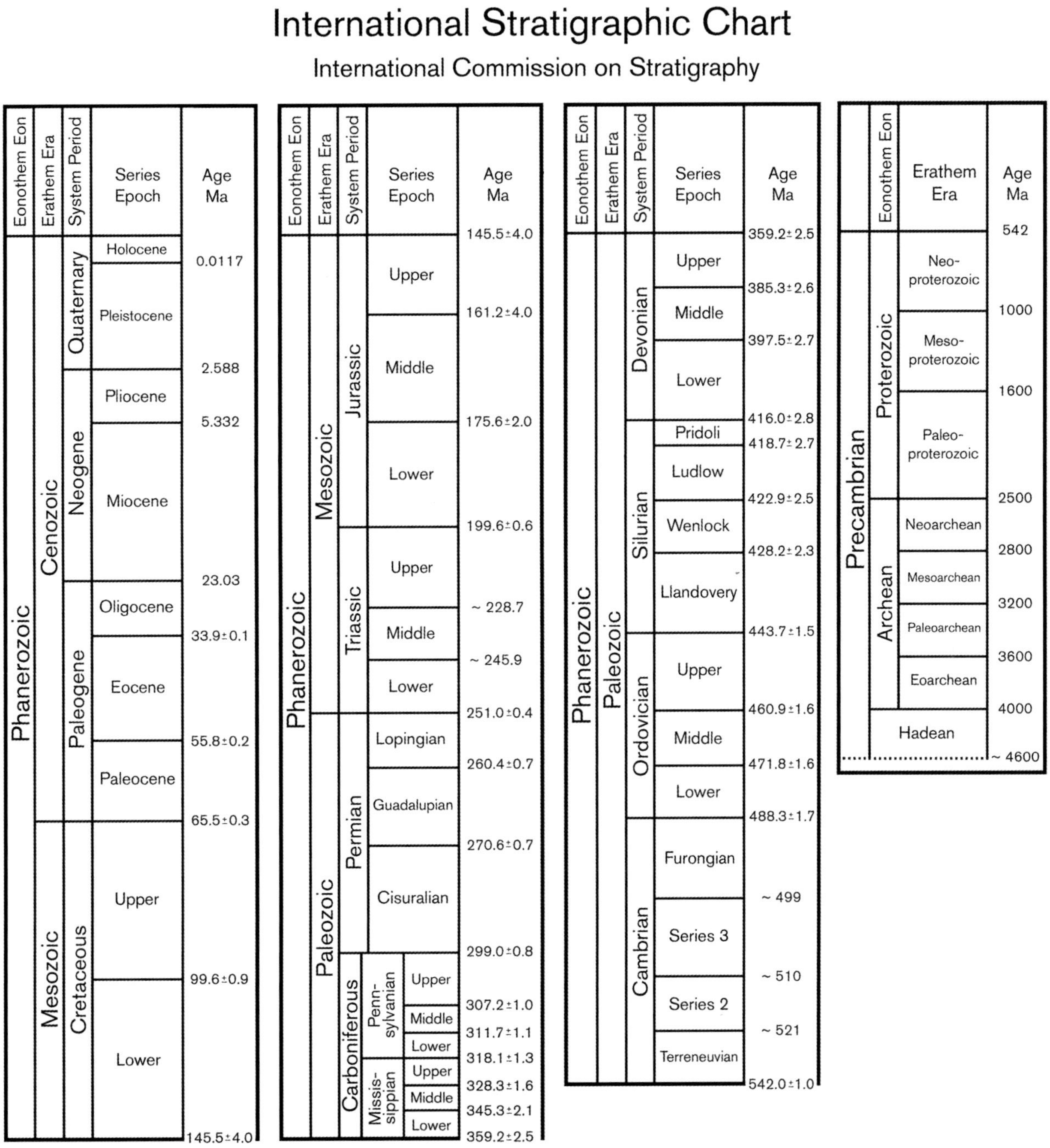

International Stratigraphic Chart

International Commission on Stratigraphy

Eonothem Eon	Erathem Era	System Period	Series Epoch	Age Ma
Phanerozoic	Cenozoic	Quaternary	Holocene	0.0117
			Pleistocene	2.588
		Neogene	Pliocene	5.332
			Miocene	23.03
		Paleogene	Oligocene	33.9±0.1
			Eocene	55.8±0.2
			Paleocene	65.5±0.3
	Mesozoic	Cretaceous	Upper	99.6±0.9
			Lower	145.5±4.0

Eonothem Eon	Erathem Era	System Period	Series Epoch	Age Ma
				145.5±4.0
Phanerozoic	Mesozoic	Jurassic	Upper	161.2±4.0
			Middle	175.6±2.0
			Lower	199.6±0.6
		Triassic	Upper	~ 228.7
			Middle	~ 245.9
			Lower	251.0±0.4
	Paleozoic	Permian	Lopingian	260.4±0.7
			Guadalupian	270.6±0.7
			Cisuralian	299.0±0.8
		Carboniferous: Penn-sylvanian	Upper	307.2±1.0
			Middle	311.7±1.1
			Lower	318.1±1.3
		Carboniferous: Missis-sippian	Upper	328.3±1.6
			Middle	345.3±2.1
			Lower	359.2±2.5

Eonothem Eon	Erathem Era	System Period	Series Epoch	Age Ma
				359.2±2.5
Phanerozoic	Paleozoic	Devonian	Upper	385.3±2.6
			Middle	397.5±2.7
			Lower	416.0±2.8
		Silurian	Pridoli	418.7±2.7
			Ludlow	422.9±2.5
			Wenlock	428.2±2.3
			Llandovery	443.7±1.5
		Ordovician	Upper	460.9±1.6
			Middle	471.8±1.6
			Lower	488.3±1.7
		Cambrian	Furongian	~ 499
			Series 3	~ 510
			Series 2	~ 521
			Terreneuvian	542.0±1.0

Eonothem Eon		Erathem Era	Age Ma
			542
Precambrian	Proterozoic	Neo-proterozoic	1000
		Meso-proterozoic	1600
		Paleo-proterozoic	2500
	Archean	Neoarchean	2800
		Mesoarchean	3200
		Paleoarchean	3600
		Eoarchean	4000
	Hadean		~ 4600

FIGURE 8.3 International stratigraphic time chart. Source: Cohen et al. 2013. Reproduced by permission © ICS International Commission on Stratigraphy, 2014.

sequent tens of millions of years, angiosperms in California appear to have been most extensive and abundant in coastal and fluvial environments, while conifers remained dominant in well-drained and upland areas (Upchurch and Wolfe 1993, Graham 1999).

The Cretaceous-Paleogene extinction at ~66 Ma marks one of the major extinction events (Pope et al. 1994, Schulte et al. 2010), with an estimated 40% loss of genera and 76% loss of species (Barnosky et al. 2011). This event has been attributed to the Chicxulub asteroid impact with Earth, but recent evidence suggests that the asteroid impact dealt only the final blow on ecosystems already under near-critical stress from climatic variability (Renne et al. 2013). During the one million years prior to asteroid impact, six abrupt shifts of >2°C in continental mean annual temperatures occurred, with the most dramatic oscillation involving a drop of 6°C to –8°C within one hundred thousand years prior to the impact. These alternated with two hot greenhouse events of about equal duration (Nordt et al. 2003; see Figure 8.5). In addition to nonavian dinosaurs and other animal lineages, many plant genera went extinct in this event, especially at locations near the impact site in Mexico (Wolfe and Upchurch 1986). Broad-leaved evergreen trees were at higher risk of extinction, whereas taxa with dormancy adaptations (e.g., deciduous leaves) fared better during the "impact winter" that followed (Wolfe 1991). Although California was relatively near the

FIGURE 8.4 Paleogeography of North and South America, circa 90 Ma. An oblique Western Hemisphere view showing the Cretaceous Western Interior Seaway of midcontinent and the extensive mountain regions of western North America. Source: Blakey 2008.

impact site and would thus have been severely affected, no records from that time are firmly documented in the region. The best records are in western interior North America, in a zone from New Mexico north into Canada. Sites in this belt clearly indicate mass plant kills, with estimates of 50% to 75% extinction of earlier taxa.

Recognizable Taxa with Nonanalog Associations: Paleogene and Neogene (66–2.6 Ma)

During the early Paleogene the region at the eastern margin of California (now the Great Basin) was an elevated upland that drained to the west via rivers that flowed through California to the Pacific Ocean (DeCelles 2004; Cassel, Graham et al. 2009; Henry and Faulds 2010). A steep gradient existed along what is now the west slope of the Sierra Nevada, but the Sierra Nevada was not the major hydrologic divide that it is today. The uplands of what is now the Sierra Nevada were the western edge of a generally mountainous region that extended eastward and had summits reaching more than 2,750 meters (Henry and Faulds 2010, Mix et al. 2011). This region has been called the Nevadaplano as it reflects similar character to South America's Altiplano (DeCelles 2004).

About 40 Ma, through incompletely understood tectonic processes, changes in plate angles at the Pacific margin exposed the bottom of the continent to the underlying mantle's heat. Partial melting of the deep crust led to massive volcanic eruptions regionally. Exposure to deep heat also caused the continent to become less rigid and to thin and stretch. As this occurred, the entire Nevadaplano region subsided, like the domed top of a cake sinking as it comes from the oven. This subsidence and stretching marked the beginning of the evolution of internal drainage and the birth of the hydrologic Great Basin (DeCourten 2003). These events set the stage for a new era of mountain building. Continuous stretching caused blocks of the continental crust to tilt along faults, giving rise to fault-block topography that characterizes the present Basin and Range province, including the Sierra Nevada. Continued extension over the past thirty million years has more than doubled the amount of land between the western (Sierra Nevada) and eastern (Wasatch Mountains, Colorado Plateau) edges of the province, adding 400 kilometers of new landscape in the process (Thatcher et al. 1999). At about the same time, a major change occurred along the western margin of the continent that allowed the North American and Pacific plates to come into direct contact for the first time. Meeting of these two plates fundamentally changed the nature of the contact along western California, converting the boundary from one of subduction to lateral shear. This shear zone was the ancestral San Andreas fault system, which developed about 25–20 Ma (DeCourten 2003).

The history of the Sierra Nevada is closely linked to these tectonic events. Although mountains are known to have existed in the late Mesozoic where the present day Sierra Nevada lie, the prevailing view had been that this ancient range never gained elevation above ~2,000 meters and eroded to lowlands by the late Paleogene. Fault-block tilting of the past 10–5 Ma is believed to have created the high elevation of the modern Sierra Nevada. An increasing body of research, ranging from the composition of regional flora (Wolfe et al. 1998) to analysis of tectonics (Small and Anderson 1995, Mix et al. 2011), isotopic analysis of volcanic glass (Cassel, Graham et al. 2009), and age and distribution of Cenozoic lava flows (Cassel, Calvert et al. 2009; Henry and Faulds 2010), however, suggests that the Sierra Nevada achieved heights over 3,000 meters in the Paleogene and remained high through subsequent millennia to the present. This evidence does not suggest that the Sierra Nevada was exempt from effects of the extensional and faulting processes. The form, topography, and specific elevation of the modern Sierra Nevada were strongly influenced by those events, which appear to have taken place over the past three million years (Small and Anderson 1995).

Extensional forces that thinned the crust and generated basin and range topography also influenced topography in interior California. Especially in the Mojave Desert, faults formed as the crust stretched starting ~35 Ma. In many desert locations so much crust was displaced that older rocks below were exposed. The creation of faults via extension facilitated volcanic activity in the Mojave province, and many eruption centers arose around fault zones starting ~20 Ma. The Transverse Ranges derive their origin and orientation from lateral shear action along the Pacific and North American plates. The current Coast Ranges are geologically young and owe their origin to diverse and still poorly understood activities of plate contact as the lateral shear zone has increased (Harden 2004). Extension, fault-block tilting, and uplift contributed relief to this region, as did volcanic activity along the newly propagating San Andreas fault zone. Elsewhere at this time, in the interior mountains, forces remained that derived from subduction and included compression forces, bends in regional faults, and thrust uplifting. Between the ancient Sierra Nevada and the Coast Ranges lay the San Pablo Sea, a shallow inland water body, which dried at its north end ~9 Ma. A shallow sea persisted in the San Joaquin Valley to ~2 Ma (Harden 2004).

Climate of the Paleogene and Neogene paralleled the evolving landscape (Zachos et al. 2001). The interval began with

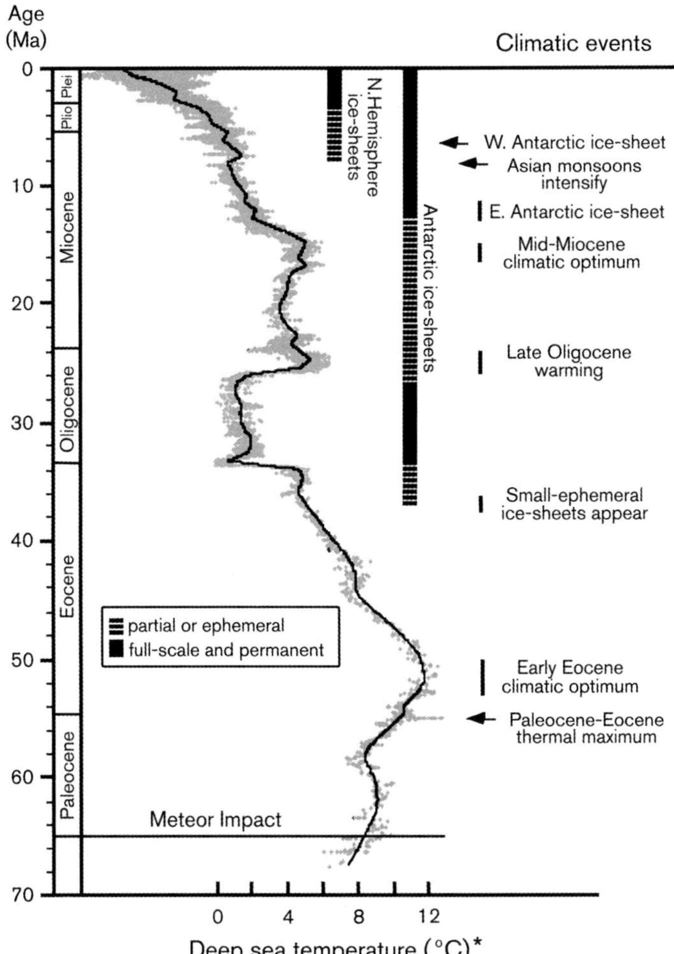

FIGURE 8.5 Major historical trends in global temperature and climatic, tectonic, and major biotic events over the past sixty-five million years. Temperature scale applies only to time before 35 Ma; deep sea values approximate sea-surface temperatures for high latitudes. Source: Modified with permission from Zachos et al. 2001.

a greenhouse climate regime, which had dominated the late Mesozoic. Two warm peaks included a hot spike at 65.5 Ma, attributed to asteroid impact, and a short hot pulse centered at 55.8 Ma, the Paleocene-Eocene Thermal Maximum (PETM), which lasted 170,000 years (see Figure 8.5; Zachos et al. 2008). During the PETM, global temperatures increased by 5°C to 10°C in fewer than twenty thousand years (20 ka). The cause of the PETM is still being debated but is widely attributed to spontaneous release of massive stores of methane hydrates from the ocean floor (Jenkyns 2003). A slight cooling trend followed that terminated with an abrupt and defining global cooling at 33.5 Ma, the Eocene-Oligocene event (Liu et al. 2009). A deep, 400,000-year-long glaciation followed, and temperatures at California latitudes during this period dropped by 6°C to 8°C. The Eocene-Oligocene event marked the return of a global icehouse regime that continues to present (see Figure 8.5). Ice-cap development began in Antarctica and only much later extended into the Northern Hemisphere. Global sea levels dropped by 70 meters, reflecting the buildup of polar ice. Two global warming periods interrupted the background icehouse conditions. Peaking at 17 to 15 Ma was the middle Miocene climatic optimum, after which global temperatures gradually declined and Northern Hemisphere glaciations began. A brief warming period, the early Pliocene climatic optimum, occurred from 4.5 to 3.5 Ma. At that time, Northern Hemisphere ice melted and temperatures were an estimated 2°C–4°C warmer than present in the western U.S. (Haywood et al. 2001) and as much as 19°C warmer in the Arctic (Ballantyne et al. 2010) with less seasonal, wetter climates characterized by less freezing conditions. This warm period was followed by the fluctuations of the ensuing ice ages, which started about 2.6 Ma.

By all indications, Paleogene warm, humid lowlands and the cooler uplands alike in the California region were characterized by precipitation distributed throughout the year; persistent drought was uncommon (Wolfe 1975). Even late in the Neogene, during the Pliocene, climates generally were characterized by mild seasonality, high humidity, and equable climates in western North America (Thompson 1991). Truly arid climates and dry environments did not develop until late in the Neogene, and seasonality began to appear regionally only after the Eocene-Oligocene event. The California Current, an ocean circulation pattern that exists at present, began to evolve about 15 Ma (Lyle et al. 2000). This current is a primary driver of Mediterranean climates in the California region and also regulates the steep summer thermal gradient from the coast to the interior. Loss of summer rain as a result and extension of a long summer drought became important influences on the evolution of the modern California flora. Significant regional rain shadows developed with evolution of Sierra Nevada and Basin and Range topography, marking initiation of summer-dry climates and the first appearance of desert environments. A Mediterranean climate pattern appears to have evolved in California by 7 to 4 Ma as the California Current strengthened, although some regions retained a pattern of summer precipitation (Hickey 1979, Axelrod 1988).

FIGURE 8.6 Eocene fossils of the northern Sierra Nevada, California. Photos: Diane M. Erwin.

A At the late Eocene LaPorte flora south of Quincy, California, sediments are exposed of a paleochannel that was part of the ancestral Yuba River system. These preserve a diversity of fossils of warm-humid tropical and subtropical plant species that were characteristic of California in the early Tertiary.

B Impression leaf fossil from another Eocene site, the Chalk Bluffs flora east of Nevada City, California, of the extinct genus *Macginitiea* (Platanaceae).

During the Paleogene and especially the Neogene, we can trace the roots of California's modern flora with satisfying detail (Millar 1996, Edwards 2004). The story of this development mirrors events in the geologic and climatic history of the interval (Wolfe and Upchurch 1986). Early in the period, species and community assemblages reflected adaptations similar to the late Mesozoic. Specifically, angiosperm and gymnosperm taxa had adaptations to conditions warmer than present and with precipitation distributed year-round (Wolfe 1985). Records from Wyoming during the PETM indicate that this hot episode created a global floristic upheaval likely experienced in California as well (Wing et al. 2005). Evidence points to massive plant species range shifts of 1,500 kilometers that occurred in less than ten thousand years in response to rapid warming. These dynamics were highly individualistic: some taxa persisted in place while others underwent significant displacement.

In California, angiosperm diversity appears to have been relatively low before 55 Ma. Fossil taxa bear scant affinity to modern lineages but show warm-temperate and some subtropical adaptations (Wolfe 1985, Axelrod 1988). Increasing temperatures and humidity ~50–52 Ma triggered significant floristic shifts toward species adapted to tropical conditions and resembling taxa now in rain forests of eastern Asia, southern Mexico, and Amazonia (Wolfe 1975, Axelrod 1988). The Chalk Bluffs fossil flora near Colfax in Nevada County, California, contains one of the richest floras in the west from this climatic period (MacGinite 1941; Figure 8.6). In it, many species belong to families long extinct in California. More than seventy-one taxa are identified, including many evergreen angiosperms and deciduous species. Few taxa overlap current native species. Five genera of laurels (including avocado, *Persea*), a palm, and a viburnum (*Viburnum*) are included, as well as now-exotic genera such as *Perminalia, Phytocrene,* magnolia (*Magnolia*), Spanish-cedar (*Cedrela*), *Hyperbaena,* jackfruit (*Artocarpus*), figs (*Ficus*), and *Meliosma*. Only one gymnosperm, a cycad, is present as a leaf fossil, although temperate conifers including pines, firs (*Abies*), and spruces (*Picea*) are represented by pollen. Such conifers are not recorded in other floras of this age in California. These and other taxa recorded only as pollen in these fossil beds (Leopold 1984), such as *Platycarya,* walnut (*Juglans*), hickory (*Carya*), and sweetgum (*Liquidambar*), have pollen widely dispersed by wind that may have drifted from uplands either in the Klamath or proto–Sierra Nevada ranges to the east. Warm-humid tropical adaptations are reflected in floras elsewhere in California, which had multistoried rain forests containing, for example, cinnamon (*Cinnamomum*), bay laurel (*Laurus*), walnut, magnolia, and cootie (*Zamia*), as well as rich understories and diverse ground layers (Axelrod 1988).

Whereas western California was blanketed by rich subtropical plant communities prior to about 33.5 Ma (Wolfe 1975, 1985), upland regions to the east in the Great Basin high plateau harbored refugial populations of temperate-adapted species, including many conifers and associates now present in the modern flora (Axelrod and Raven 1985, Axelrod 1988, Millar 1993, Millar 1996). These upland populations were important not only as sources for colonizing California following climatic cooling but also as sites of significant conifer evolution. Following the climatic deterioration at about 33.5 Ma, abrupt changes in floristic composition and structure took place in California. Tropical-adapted woody angiosperm species disappeared within two million years (Wolfe 1975, Wolfe 1985, Axelrod 1988). Throughout California, temperate-adapted species reappeared, especially cool-adapted, broad-leaved deciduous species and conifers (Axelrod and Raven 1985, Millar 1993), although in many cases the taxa differed from those previously present in California. These new plant communities had affinities to modern communities and high diversity, reflecting the heterogeneous climate and environmental conditions at that time. Taxa such as dawn redwood (*Metasequoia*), giant sequoia, pine, sweetgum, hickory, walnut, mountain ash (*Sorbus*), sycamore (*Platanus*), maple (*Acer*), hawthorne (*Crataegus*), elm, *Zelkova*, sumac (*Rhus*), and basswood (*Tilia*) appeared (Raven and Axelrod 1978, Edwards 2004). Notable for the first time in western records are terrestrial herb groups. Pollen records in particular document the expansion and widespread diversification of the aster family (Asteraceae) in the Oligocene. Increasing winter cold was likely a trigger for herb expansion.

Floras younger than 23 Ma include highly diverse assemblages with taxa present in California today as well as many native to climates warmer and milder than California and having year-round rainfall (Raven and Axelrod 1978). They indicate distinctions between upland vegetation and coastal communities, and reveal earliest adaptations to summer drying. During the warm climatic optimum at 17 to 15 Ma, global temperatures rose to the highest levels reached during the past twenty-three million years. Floras throughout the West from this period reflect adaptations and range shifts in response to these conditions, with increasing latitudinal gradients in composition as one moves from coastal environments to inland mountains (Raven and Axelrod 1978). Associations of taxa unknown at present persisted in many locations such as in the Tehachapi Mountains, where dry-adapted species occurred together, including Arizona cypress (*Cupressus arizonica*), Mexican pinyon pine (*Pinus cembroides*), manzanita (*Arctostaphylos*), madrone (*Arbutus*), California bay laurel (*Umbellularia*), mountain mahogany (*Cercocarpus*), several shrubby oaks, viburnum, and flannel bush (*Fremontodendron*) alongside now-exotic taxa such as figs, avocados, hopbush (*Dodonaea viscosa*), and Spanish-cedar (Axelrod 1988, Edwards 2004).

Inland, in the higher ranges of western Nevada and northeast California, fossil assemblages contained diverse conifers, including false-cypress (*Chamaecyparis*), ginkgo, fir, pine, nutmeg (*Torreya*), and hardwoods such as chestnut (*Castanea*), *Cedrella*, beech (*Fagus*), oaks, hickory, California bay laurel, redbud (*Cercis*), ash (*Fraxinus*), sycamore, cherry (*Prunus*), mountain ash, basswood, and elm in the Upper Cedarville Flora (16–15.5 Ma) (Chaney 1959); the conifers including fir, pine, false-cypress, and Brewer spruce (*Picea breweriana*), and hardwoods hickory, oak, alder (*Alnus*), birch (*Betula*), maple, sycamore, elm, and *Zelkova* in the Fingerrock Flora (15.5 Ma) (Wolfe 1964); and Arborvitae (*Thuja*), fir, spruce, pine, and giant sequoia, along with maple, barberry (*Berberis*), madrone (*Arbutus*), oak, avocado, black locust (*Robinia*), sycamore, mountain mahogany, and snowbell (*Styrax*) in the Middlegate Flora (15.5 Ma) (Axelrod 1985).

Intensification of the Mediterranean climate with decreased summer rainfall is reflected in younger floras (<7 Ma) of the California region, which have increasing representation of taxa adapted to mild and cooling temperatures with dry summers (Raven and Axelrod 1978, Axelrod 1988). These floras also show spatial partitioning of ecological communities. Increasing abundance of now-extinct horses corroborate the evolution and spread of California grasslands. A flora of this age in Contra Costa County, for example, is dominated by evergreen oaks, with abundant sycamore, cottonwood (*Populus*), willow (*Salix*), and understory taxa allied to tree poppy (*Dendromecon*), redbud, barberry, mountain mahogany, cherry, ironwood (*Lyonothamnus*), manzanita (*Arctostaphylos*), California lilac, flannel bush, sumac, and many grasses (Edwards 2004). Pollen analyzed from several long sediment cores taken at opposite ends of California corroborates these late Neogene dynamics.

Tree species no longer extant in North America remained present in the late Miocene (6 Ma) of northwest coastal California, indicating the more equable climates than modern with reduced seasonality in precipitation and temperature (Heusser 2000). After 5 Ma, arboreal hardwood and conifer species now native to the area appeared in the record, with oaks, alder, hemlock (*Tsuga*), and coast redwood dominating, and spruce at low levels (Heusser 2000). Increases in pine relative to cool, MESIC coastal forests reflected the gradual drying and warming of the continent to a thermal maximum in the mid-Pliocene (3.5–4.0 Ma). A similar pattern is documented in the latest Pliocene of Modoc Plateau (1,100 meters) in northeast California, where a long record includes pine, oak, sagebrush (*Artemisia*), cypresses (Cupressaceae), and asters at 3 Ma and is interpreted to indicate extensive forests that expanded and contracted following warm-dry and cool-wet fluctuations (Adam et al. 1989, Adam et al. 1990). Both the northwest coastal and the Modoc Plateau records document an increase in high-frequency oscillations of vegetation starting in the late Pliocene. By the close of the Neogene (~2.6 Ma), many species and vegetation elements of modern California and recognizable species affinities were in place. Here and there remained species that are exotic to the modern flora, and many locations of native species were different than at present.

The Ice Age Rollercoaster: Quaternary Environments (<2.6 Ma)

During the past 2.6 million years, tectonic changes had greatest OROGENIC impacts in eastern and southern California. Continuing Great Basin expansion and dynamics along the California Shear Zone contributed to the present topography of the southern Sierra Nevada, White Mountains, and Carson Range ESCARPMENTS. They also catalyzed development of adjacent deep and sharp-bordered basins, such as the Owens and Carson Valleys, as well as deepening of the Lake Tahoe Basin. Major volcanic events continued in California throughout the Quaternary, centered along extensive fault zones of the Sierra Nevada, Cascades, and Coast Ranges. A globally significant example is the Long Valley eruption of eastern California. Basaltic eruptions began around Long Valley about 4 Ma, coinciding with fault subsidence of Panamint Valley, Death Valley, Owens Valley, Saline Valley, and many other valleys in southeastern California.

Volcanism began in the Glass Mountains about 2 Ma and peaked in a cataclysmic eruption of 600 km^3 of high-silica rhyolite at 760 ka (Miller 1985). This massive eruption resulted in ash clouds extending as far as Nebraska and widespread deposition in California of the Bishop Tuff. Simultaneous 2–3 kilometer subsidence of the magma chamber roof formed the present Long Valley Caldera, the westernmost portion of which approaches the modern Sierra Nevada crest near Mammoth Lakes. Subsequent volcanism in this region shaped much of the current landscape, including, for example, Mammoth Mountain, which erupted as a series of small extrusions over a period from 110 ka to 50 ka. Volcanism shifted north, first forming the Mono–Inyo Craters chain (50 ka to 650 years before present) and then further northward to form the islands of Mono Lake, where volcanism continued to just before the historic period (about two hundred years ago) and is still active, as attested to by hot springs on the lake's islands.

The Quaternary Period is delineated mainly by climatic patterns. The general background trend starting prior to the Quaternary was toward global cooling as well as development of regions of aridity (see Figures 8.2 and 8.5). In California the Mediterranean climatic regime, with dominance of winter precipitation and dry summers, had evolved by the early Quaternary and persisted throughout the subsequent glacial and interglacial periods, although the length and intensity of the respective wet and dry seasons varied. As Earth cooled over the past four million years, and its orbital relationships intensified icehouse conditions, climate variability began to change discernibly around 2.6 Ma. Modern, high-resolution methods to detect past temperatures from stratified ice in polar ice caps and deep-ocean sediments reveal more than forty cycles of long glacial (cold) and interglacial (warm) intervals beginning about 2.6 Ma, each lasting 40,000 to 100,000 years. California appears to have experienced temperature differences as much as 7–8°C between the last glacial maximum (LGM, 20–18 ka) and present (Adam and West 1983). High-resolution analysis of ice and sediment core sections reveals that nested within these major glacial and interglacial phases were shorter repeating patterns of variability. For instance, during the last glacial interval, extreme cold periods (stadials) were regularly interrupted by shorter warmer periods (interstadials) as well as by very short reversals (fewer than a thousand years) between extreme cold and relatively warm conditions (see Figure 8.1). The cumulative effect is a sawtooth pattern typical of Quaternary climate records from around the world. An important insight from this view of the Quaternary is the overall similarity of the Holocene (formally designated as starting 11,700 years before present) to interglacial periods throughout the mid-late Pleistocene.

During glacial periods of the Quaternary, polar ice sheets expanded in Greenland and Antarctica. Continental ice sheets developed across northern North America and parts of northern Eurasia, and glaciers formed on continental mountains to the south of the ice sheets. In California glaciers formed in the Trinity Alps, Salmon Mountains, Cascade Ranges (Mount Shasta, Mount Lassen, Medicine Lake), Warner Mountains, Sweetwater Range, White Mountains, Sierra Nevada, and San Bernardino Mountains. By far the most extensive glaciations occurred in the Sierra Nevada, where during the coldest parts of glacial periods an ice cap extended over most high parts of the range. During the LGM, the Sierra Nevada ice cap was 125 kilometers long, 65 kilometers wide, and extended downslope to about 2,600 meters in elevation (Gillespie and Zehfuss 2004). Valley glaciers, fed by the ice cap, extended 65 kilometers down the west slope canyons of the Sierra Nevada and at most 30 kilometers down the shorter but steeper eastern escarpment canyons (Figure 8.7). As the mountain ranges acquired their modern geometry, glacial action in turn carved the landscape in new ways. The Quaternary glaciers of California deposited prominent MORAINES, etched glacial CIRQUES and valleys, and sculpted ARÊTES and MATTERHORN topography (see chapter lead image).

As glacial intervals waned, and the Sierra Nevada continued to be influenced by tectonic processes of tilting and subsidence, large rivers ran off both slopes, eroding deep incisions and charting new courses (Wakabayashi and Sawyer 2001). An example of the combined effect of river and glacier forces is Yosemite Valley. Deepening of the valley is attributed equally to the forces of glacial and river erosion. Widening of the valley, by contrast, is considered primarily the work of glaciers. High winter precipitation, runoff from glaciers and snow, and lower evaporative pressure from cool temperatures led to development of large lakes in the Central Valley (e.g., Lake Clyde, which filled the San Joaquin Valley 700–600 ka) (Sarna-Wojcicki 1995) and in the Great Basin (e.g., large Pleistocene versions of Mono and Owens Lakes) (Smith and Street-Perrott 1983). Feedback effects might have amplified wet conditions. For instance, water evaporating off Lake Clyde would have recharged Pacific air masses that lost water as they passed over the Coast Ranges. Additional water likely increased snowpack in the Sierra Nevada and potentially contributed to maintaining the western Great Basin PLUVIAL LAKES as well (Sarna-Wojcicki 1995, Reheis 1999).

As a result of ice buildup on land during glacial periods, global ocean levels fluctuated throughout the Quaternary, declining as much as 120 meters relative to the present during the last two glacial maxima (140 ka and 20 ka) (Inman et al. 2005, Lambeck et al. 2002). Declines of 60 meters in sea level characterized less severe stadial periods during the last two glacial cycles. Along the Pacific margin, maximum California coastline retreat at 20 ka was about 80 kilometers to a position west of the Farallon Islands that converted San Francisco Bay, Eureka Bay, and other low basins into dry land.

The present-day California Current system, which is responsible for maintaining the region's dry Mediterranean climate as well as the cool coastal fog belt, wavered in its intensity through the Quaternary (Herbert et al. 2001). When strong, as now, the California Current brought cool, relatively fresh water from the Oregon coast south along the California margin to just south of the U.S.–Mexico border. This current promotes favorable conditions for upwelling of cold water during much of the year, particularly in the summer months. During the peaks of glacial periods, however, continental ice sheets reached a large enough size to reorganize the wind systems over the North Pacific Ocean. These perturbations to wind fields caused the California Current to weaken, triggering large differences in ocean-surface temperatures relative to those of interglacial times. Collapse of the California Current during these millennia translated to weakening of the Mediterranean climate regime over California, reducing thermal gradients from coast to inland and diminishing fog belts along the California coastal zone as warmer waters came near the coast.

During interglacial periods most of these patterns reversed. As global ice melted, ocean-levels rose, coastlines moved eastward forming bays and inlets, and inland water levels lowered or dried. The oldest evidence for the San Francisco Bay estuary system is about 600 ka. At 10 ka, rising water began to fill the San Francisco Bay, which retreated partially during the middle Holocene dry and warm period, then reached a maximum extent about 4 ka (Harden 2004). The modern Sac-

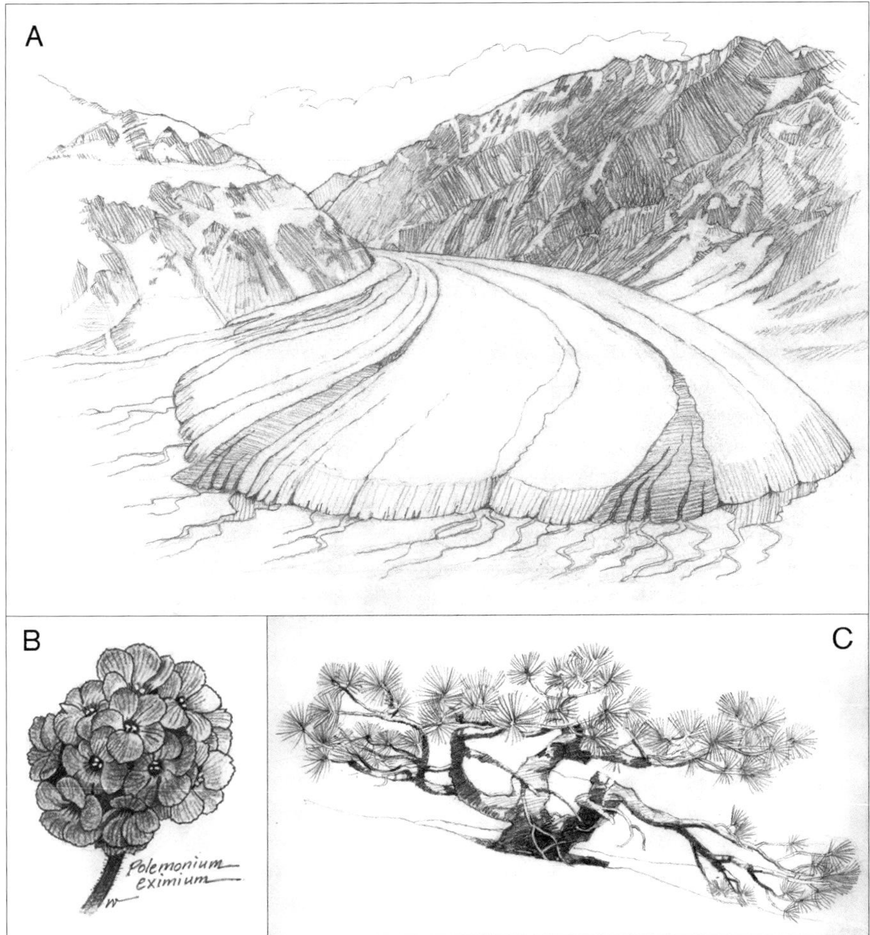

FIGURE 8.7 Pine Creek Canyon glacier at Last Glacial Maximum (20 ka), Sierra Nevada (A), and associated alpine plants skypilot (*Polemonium eximium*) (B), and whitebark pine (*Pinus albicaulis*) (C). Both species are cold-adapted and persisted in California during cold periods of the Quaternary in montane or alpine refugia, then subsequently expanded as temperatures warmed in the Holocene. Source: Artwork by Wally Woolfenden.

ramento–San Joaquin Delta formed as a consequence of postglacial sea level rise and transgression of estuarine water into the Central Valley. The California Current, with correlated summer coastal fog belt, thermal gradients, and long summer droughts, developed most strongly during peak interglacial times. The modern pattern of the current evolved about 3 ka (Herbert et al. 2001).

California plant species and communities were significantly influenced by climatic and geologic events of the Quaternary, and they responded to major and minor climate cycles. No distinct speciation or extinction events have been documented during this time in California, in contrast to abundant animal extinctions. Similarly, the major ecoregions of the state maintained species diversity throughout the Quaternary, with a few exceptions such as the extirpation of *Picea* from the Sierra Nevada, which occurred in Tahoe Basin records at 1.9 Ma (Adam 1973). Within ecoregions, however, species shifted greatly and community assemblages reflected movements of individual species across the landscape. Significant genetic adaptations at the population level occurred. Several general categories of vegetation response to Quaternary glacial-interglacial climatic change occurred in the greater California region, described here in overview and with more detail in the next section.

Latitudinal Shifts of Distribution Ranges in Low-Relief Areas

An example of latitudinal redistribution in low-relief landscapes is single-leaf pinyon pine (*Pinus monophylla*) during the last glacial cycle. Pollen and woodrat-midden records document that single-leaf pinyon pine distribution was widespread in the late Pleistocene at the southern end of its current range, mostly south of the current Mojave and Sonoran Deserts (van Devender 1990). As climates warmed during the early Holocene, single-leaf pinyon pine migrated gradually northward and upslope in the Great Basin, reaching the northern White Mountains about 8.8 ka, the Bodies Hills north of Mono Lake about 5.0 ka, Slinkyard Valley south of Lake Tahoe at 1.4 ka, the Reno area four hundred years ago, and its current northern range limit on the west side of the Great Basin near Pyramid Lake in western Nevada three hundred years ago (Figure 8.8). In much of the Mojave Desert, late glacial woodland and shrub communities—composed of such species as Utah juniper (*Juniperus osteosperma*), single-leaf pinyon, giant sagebrush (*Artemisia tridentata*), rabbitbrush (*Ericameria* spp.), and shadscale (*Atriplex confertifolia*)—shifted in composition as a result of immigration of species at different times as the climate warmed. Cool desert species were replaced by more arid

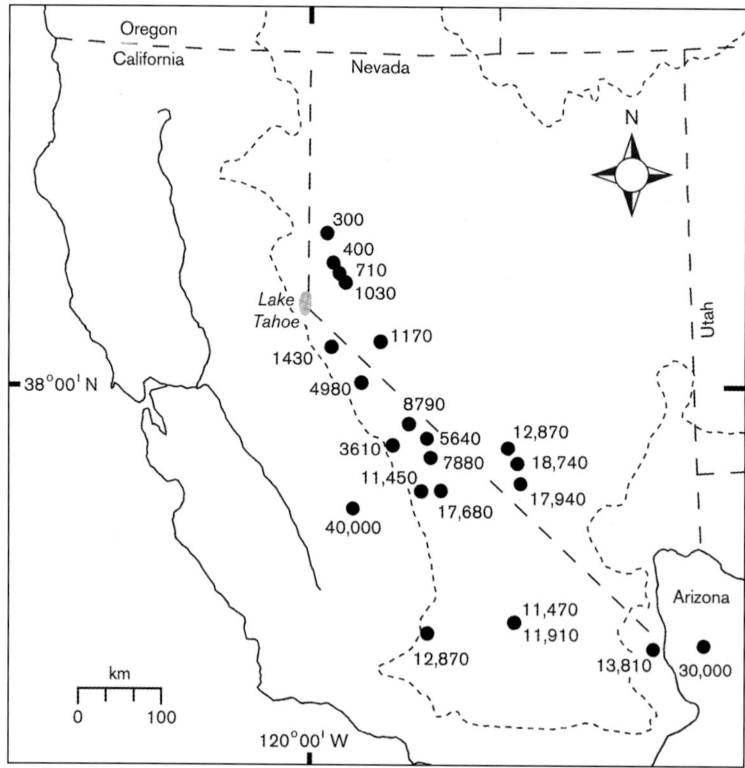

FIGURE 8.8 Movement of pinyon pine (*Pinus monophylla*) northward and upward along the western Great Basin and in southern California and western Arizona as temperatures warmed from the last glacial maximum (refugial regions in the current Mojave and Sonoran Desert regions) to its current distribution limit north of Reno near Pyramid Lake. Values indicate dates in years before present by which pinyon pine reached each point. The dotted line shows the boundary of the hydrologic Great Basin. Sites from the central and eastern Great Basin are not shown. Source: Modified with permission from Grayson 2011.

adapted species such as desert thorn (*Lycium andersonii*), rayless brittlebush (*Encelia virginenses*), and cactuses. Finally, current hot-desert adapted taxa of the present, including white bursage (*Ambrosia dumosa*) and creosote bush (*Larrea tridentata*), appeared (Spaulding 1990).

Altitudinal Shifts in Mountainous Areas

Mountains create a different kind of topographic context for species responding to climate change than do regions of low relief. Paleorecords in California document shifts in elevation that correspond to the magnitude of climatic effects of respective glacial-interglacial phases, stadial-interstadial oscillations, and centennial- to millennial-scale reversals. In the Siskiyou Mountains, for example, a record over the past fifty thousand years shows elevation shifts of 500 meters to 700 meters for tree species, with cold periods recording respective downslope movement of species in subalpine communities, mixed evergreen forests, and pine woodlands (Wanket 2002). Similarly in the southern Sierra Nevada, during coldest glacial periods when an ice cap covered the range, subalpine and montane conifer ranges shifted downslope by as much as 1,000 meters relative to their present elevations, along with similar responses by other Sierra Nevada taxa (Figure 8.9). Responses in most cases were highly individualistic and depend on the life histories and ecology of the species. Giant sequoia, for instance, appeared in packrat middens during full glacial times 700 meters below its current low elevation (1,700 meters) (Cole 1983) and might have approached as much as a 1,600 meter shift downslope (Davis 1999a). By contrast, species limited by extreme warmth and aridity during interglacials were able to expand upslope during cool stadial periods (Thompson 1988). Although major changes in species' elevation ranges occurred across climatic boundaries of the Quaternary, the changes commonly occurred at different times depending on latitude, longitude, and general elevation.

Population Contractions (Refugia and Extirpations) and Expansions (Colonizations)

Contractions and expansions were common for many California plant species in response to glacial-interglacial climate dynamics of the Quaternary. These shifts occurred sometimes with little significant change in elevational distributions. For example, coast redwood, (Poore et al. 2000, Heusser et al. 2000), the California closed-cone pines (*Pinus radiata, P. muricata*, and *P. attenuata*), coastal cypresses (*Cupressus* spp.) (Heusser and Sirocko 1997, Millar 1999), and many of California's oak species (Adam 1988, Anderson and Smith 1994) followed this pattern, contracting to fewer populations of smaller size during unfavorable periods (Figure 8.10). Such

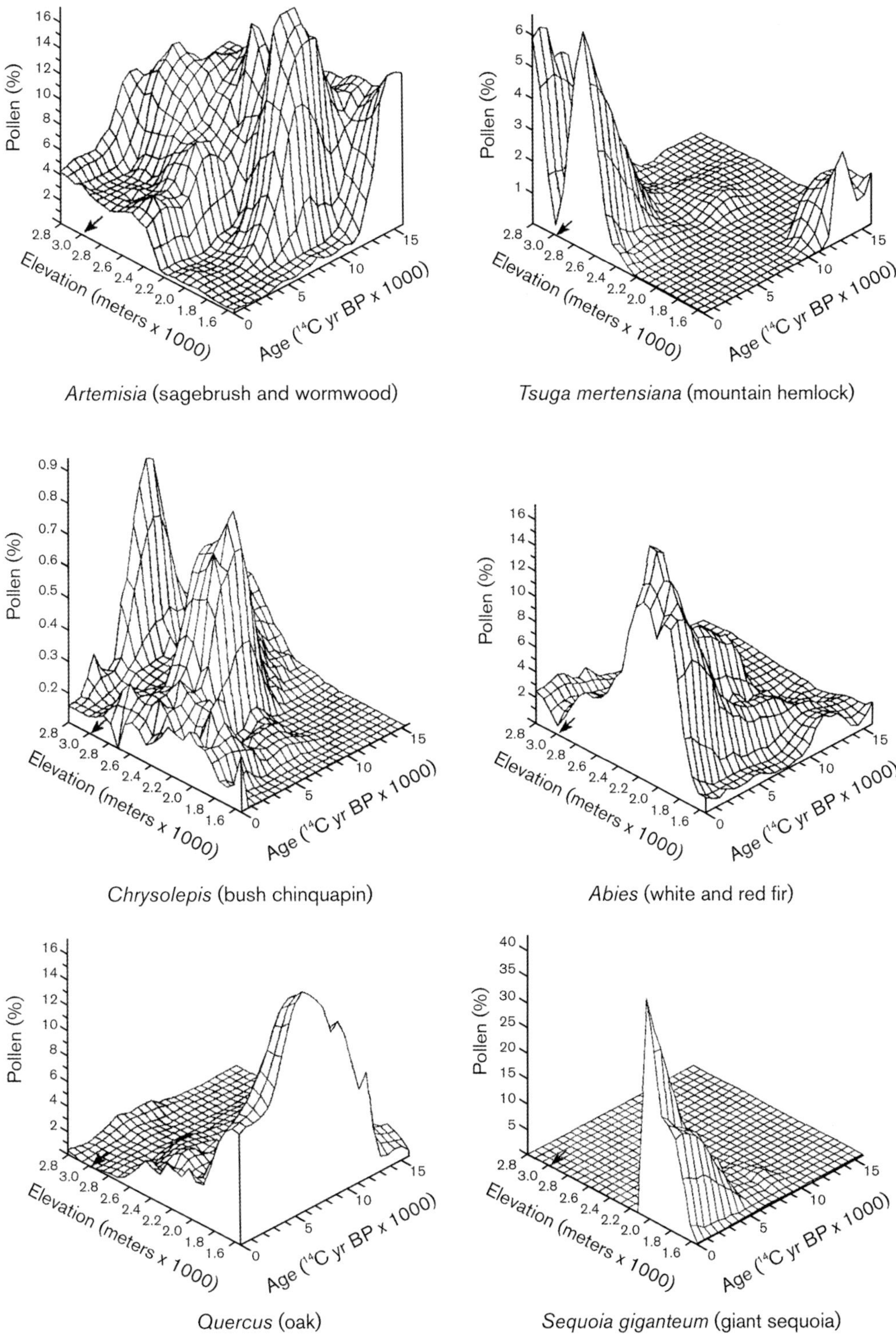

FIGURE 8.9 Schematic representation of vegetation shifts since the last glacial maximum (18 ka) in the Sierra Nevada, showing altitudinal changes as well as transmontane shifts. Values represent abundance of pollen from sediment cores at seven locations west and east of the Sierra Nevada crest (indicated by arrow). The elevation axis is from the east side (left) of the crest to the west side (right) of the range. Age is given in uncalibrated years before present (radiocarbon dates). Significant vegetation changes over time are apparent, for example, in the pattern of oak abundance, which parallels the temperature trend over the Holocene, the recent (<4,500 years) appearance and rise of giant sequoia in the western Sierra Nevada, and the recent (<5,000 years) reappearance of mountain hemlock on the west and east slopes of the range. Source: Modified from Anderson and Smith 1994.

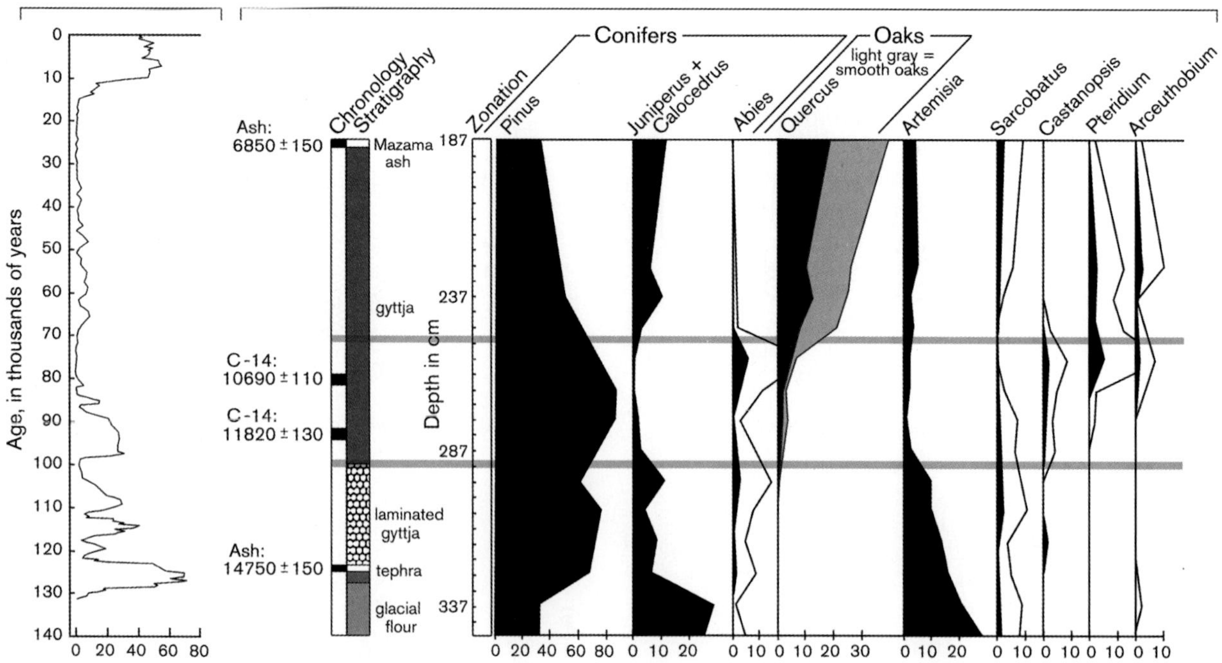

FIGURE 8.10 Pollen diagrams from Quaternary sediment cores retrieved in California.

A Percentages of oak (*Quercus*) pollen over the past 120,000 years from a Clear Lake core, Lake County. The strong correspondence (expansion/contraction) of oak abundance and temperature is shown by high pollen percentages in the Holocene, last interglacial, and interstadials of the last glacial, contrasting with low percentages during cold periods. Source: Modified from Adam 1988.

B Percentages of diverse taxa over the past 15,000 years or so from a Burgson Lake core, Sierra Nevada, showing the rapid transition at the Pleistocene-Holocene boundary. Juniper (*Juniperus*), incense-cedar (*Calocedrus*), and sagebrush (*Artemisia*) dominate in the late glacial and are replaced by oaks. The pulse of pines (*Pinus*) and fir (*Abies*) at the transition is seen in many California locations. Source: Modified from Bryne et al. 1993.

contractions rarely amounted to significant directional shift in the overall species range; rather, they caused fragmentation, loss of connectivity, and smaller population sizes. For example, California's oak populations were highly sensitive to temperature and expanded extensively during interglacials, becoming more connected and covering large areas of the California landscape. During unfavorable (glacial) climate periods, populations contracted into disjunct, isolated locations, with many population extirpations (Adam 1988, West 1993, West 1997, Mackey and Sullivan 1991, Byrne et al. 1993, Anderson and Smith 1994, Edlund 1994, Heusser 1995, Davis 1999a). Similarly, during interglacials when the California Current was strongest and coastal fog belts extensive, coast redwood expanded; the converse occurred during glacial periods (Poore et al. 2000, Heusser et al. 2000). Records in central California document rapid contractions then expansions of pines, firs, cypresses, and incense cedar (*Calocedrus decurrens*) in response to the abrupt centennial- to millennial-length reversals that occurred at the transition from Pleistocene to Holocene (West 2001).

The scattered distributions resulting from such contractions became important refugial populations for many species during unfavorable climatic periods. These were not only sources for rapid recolonization following return to favorable conditions but also critical for conservation of population-level genetic diversity. Such refugial populations also existed throughout mountainous areas, where habitat heterogeneity provided opportunities for the maintenance of small populations.

Changes in Community Composition, Including Development of Nonanalog Assemblages

Plant communities at any time and place on the California landscape reflect to varying degrees the interaction of climate with individual species' ecologies. Equilibrium with climate is rarely reached, and each species in some degree migrates toward regions of preference as climate shifts but lags relative to its ecological niche and capacity to move. In some situations, especially for broadly adapted taxa, species with similar ecologies responded synchronously to Quaternary climatic changes, such that community compositions remained relatively consistent as species shifted. For example, species of oaks, asters, and goosefoot (Chenopodiaceae) showed rapid and consistent oscillations following millennial cold-wet reversals in the southern California coast region during the last glacial and last interglacial periods (Heusser 2000). In other cases, however, species responded individualistically, and community compositions changed over time. Unusual assemblages, called nonanalog communities and created by co-occurrences of species not found together at present, resulted from unique combinations of climate, environmental conditions, species adaptation, differential migration, and chance events. One example is a glacial (31.5 ka) assemblage north of Owens Lake in eastern California where Utah juniper and Joshua tree (*Yucca brevifolia*) grew together with an understory of giant sagebrush, bitterbrush (*Purshia tridentata*), and shadscale (Koehler and Anderson 1995). On the west side of the southern Sierra Nevada in lower Kings Canyon, a unique community comprising Utah juniper, red fir (*Abies magnifica*), incense cedar, sugar pine (*Pinus lambertiana*), and ponderosa pine (*P. ponderosa*) grew during the last glaciation (Cole 1983).

Zooming In: Retreat from the Last Ice Age (~20 ka to present)

The final development of contemporary California ecosystems traces through events that occurred over the past twenty thousand years—that is, since the LGM. Modern plant taxa were in the California region by that time, entrenched by LGM conditions into favorable ice-age environments, and poised to respond to the warmth of the new interglacial (the Holocene) that was about to ensue. From the vantage of the Holocene, and from the perspective of humans in the New World, the warm and generally ice-free environment that we know seems like "preferred" habitat for plants, rather than the colder and more arid conditions of the glacial intervals. This is a biased view, of course, for conditions of many cooler periods were more optimal for plant expansion than at present, whereas many conditions of the Holocene in California exert severe climatic stress, such as extreme aridity of the low deserts and the long drought of Mediterranean summers. Ultimately it depends on the adaptations of individual taxa, their capacities to move and to adapt genetically, that determines range distributions and community types at any one time. As summarized in the last section, transitions between glacial and interglacial periods, and the climates of interglacials themselves, were anything but gradual, directional, or stable. Rather, this time period was characterized by reversals, step changes, and low-to-high frequency variability.

Next we describe general trends of vegetation history by geographic sections of California in three times slices since the LGM. For each time period, we sweep through the state from the northwest coastal and mountain regions, southward along the coast and coast ranges, then to the Central Valley, on through the low deserts, and finally to the Sierra Nevada/southern Cascades and western Great Basin/Modoc Plateau. We generalize the vegetation stories based on the number and locations of paleo-sites available to characterize them.

Late Pleistocene (20–11 ka)

Throughout California, late Pleistocene environments were conditioned by climates that were as much as 8–10°C cooler relative to modern and confronted with warming that included a number of reversals to near-full glacial conditions. In northwest California, mountains at the current upper elevation of the mixed evergreen forest (1,200 meters), forests grew that were typical of the northern Cascades Mountains, comprising mountain hemlock, western hemlock (*Tsuga heterophylla*), spruce, pine, and fir. No records of the current forest taxa, such as Douglas-fir, oak, and tanoak (*Lithocarpus densiflorus*), were evident. Early vegetation was typical of conditions much colder and drier than currently exist. At 1,600 meters, vegetation was dominated by sagebrush, pine, spruce, and cedar likely with low fire frequencies, becoming more temperate with the arrival of Douglas-fir (*Pseudotsuga menziesii*) and firs more than five thousand years later (Briles et al. 2005). Above 1,800 meters, sagebrush and grasses composed open subalpine parklands (Daniels et al. 2005, Mohr et al. 2000).

Farther south in the lowland interior of the north Coast Range (e.g., Clear Lake at 400 meters), dense LGM forests were coniferous and comprised pines, firs, cypress, and incense cedar (Adam 1988, West 2001). The high-resolution record from this region suggests a pattern that likely occurred elsewhere, namely of high frequency replacements of the cold coniferous forest with oak-dominated woodlands and vice versa (West 2001). These are interpreted as responses to the abrupt climatic oscillations of the late Pleistocene, such the Younger Dryas cold interval, which lasted for only about eight hundred years. Evidence coastward from this region and north of the San Francisco Bay (the Point Reyes area) indicate late Pleistocene forests were more typical of modern forests about 30 kilometers north of the site, dominated by Douglas-fir and fir species (Generaux et al. 2003) and possibly with spruce (Bergquist 1977, 1978).

In the southern coastal region, LGM pollen records indicate forests that were characterized by conifers and included pine and juniper-cypress, with small amounts of oak or chaparral taxa (Heusser 1995, 1998). Similar but drier ecosystems are recorded for the LGM in the interior south coast ranges. For instance, at Carrizo Plain, pine, sagebrush, juniper, and shadscale grew (Negrini et al. 2007). Charcoal evidence also suggests fire was present in these ecosystems. During the late Pleistocene (14 ka to 11 ka) abrupt transitions along the coast occurred, starting with extreme reduction in junipers and increase in oak and chaparral taxa. During this transition, short two-hundred- to five-hundred-year periods of pine dominance occurred, which have been linked to global cold events (Heinrich events) (Heusser and Sirocko 1997). The pine component likely was dominated by one or more species of the California closed-cone pine group, which are interpreted to have expanded locally elsewhere across the California coast during the cool intervals and contracted when conditions warmed, both between the cold stadials and as Holocene conditions prevailed (Axelrod 1980, Millar 1999).

The late glacial period in the Central Valley was cold and mostly wet. Pines, firs, junipers, and alders spread in the Sacramento region, as well as members of the rose (Rosaceae) and grass (Poaceae) families, while oaks were at very low levels (West 1997). Some wetland or riparian taxa including sedges (Cyperaceae) and willows were present, likely along the major water courses. Along the southern San Joaquin Valley at Tulare Lake, records show late glacial vegetation to include tree taxa that had retreated downslope from the western Sierra Nevada in response to cold and drying climates. Cupressaceous taxa, most likely juniper, grew in the region, along with pines, oaks, sagebrush, and greasewood (*Sacrobatus*), suggesting that a pinyon-juniper woodland with halophytes grew along shallow water bodies (Davis 1999a). The presence of giant sequoia pollen through the late glacial in Tulare Lake records was originally interpreted to indicate occurrence of that conifer at 54 meter elevation in the San Joaquin Valley. More likely, giant sequoia grew in riparian forests of the low western Sierra Nevada, and pollen was washed into Tulare Lake.

For the southern deserts, between 18–12 ka, the present Mojave Desert region supported much more cool-mesic and woodland vegetation. Below 1,000 meters, Utah juniper extended through the lowlands, grading to pinyon-juniper woodlands on the fans above (Spaulding 1990). Limber pine and bristlecone pine forests expanded during the cool LGM climates across uplands of the Mojave region. In adjacent regions now the Sonoran Desert, late glacial vegetation was very different from present, with pinyon pine on the upper slopes, while at lower elevations (<350 meters) California juniper (*Juniperus californica*), Joshua tree, whipple yucca (*Yucca whipplei*), bigelow beargrass (*Nolina bigelovii*), and Mojave sage (*Salvia mohavensis*) grew abundantly, with traces of big sagebrush, shadscale, and blackbrush (*Coleogyne ramosissima*) also present (van Devender 1990).

The late glacial vegetation of the mountains and steppelands of eastern California (Sierra Nevada, southern Cascades, Modoc Plateau, and western Great Basin) was affected by the extensive ice cap on the Sierra Nevada. This not only displaced vegetation to exposed land below the ice but also enforced cold-arid conditions, likely with dry winds emanating from the ice cap. Around the southern Owens Valley, Utah juniper was expansive, with pinyon pine also co-occurring, all at levels as much as 600 meters below their present lower treelines. Pollen in a highly resolved pollen core from Owens Lake suggests that subalpine limber pine and bristlecone pines were more extensive on the slopes of the White Mountains and Sierra Nevada than at present, and other montane and subalpine species such as foxtail pine (*Pinus balfouriana*), western white pine (*P. monticola*), and whitebark pine (*P. albicaulis*) also grew, likely in warmer niches along the mid-lower slopes (Woolfenden 2003).

On the western slopes of the southern to central Sierra Nevada, records similarly indicate reduced forest elevation ranges during the late glacial interval. At 920–1,270 meters in Kings Canyon, for instance, Utah juniper grew with red fir, incense cedar, sugar pine, and ponderosa pine (Cole 1983). Sagebrush was dominant in this region at locations around the edges of the ice cap, reflecting the cool, dry climate. Giant sequoias were more extensive in the late glacial period than present, growing at least as low at 920 meters (Cole 1983, Koehler and Anderson 1994). Extending north on the west slope to the Tahoe Basin, cold, dry climates supported open conifer woodlands with pine, juniper, and sagebrush-grass associations (Davis et al. 1985, Byrne et al. 1993, Mackey and Sullivan 1991, Koehler and Anderson 1994, Power 1998). On the east side of the range in central latitudes, the few available records suggest that newly deglaciated areas presently in the upper montane mixed forest zone (e.g., at 2,800 meters above Mammoth Lakes) supported cold-adapted colonizers and were mostly treeless but included sagebrush and limber pine in warmer niches (Anderson 1990). A pollen core taken from Mono Lake includes high enough percentages of giant sequoia pollen to suggest that the species was growing nearby in the late glacial period (Davis 1999b). The limited records from the southern Cascades and Modoc regions show trends similar to the Sierra Nevada for late glacial vegetation. Within what is now Lassen Volcanic National Park, sagebrush steppe grew in areas now supporting montane mixed conifer forest (West 2004). The cold continental climates of late glacial Modoc Plateau supported extensive juniper forests, scant oaks, and sagebrush steppe (Adam et al. 1989, Adam et al. 1990).

Early Holocene (11–6ka)

Dramatic shifts in climate that marked the global transition at the Pleistocene-Holocene boundary drove abrupt changes in California vegetation. Rapid warming spread after 11 ka, with short reversals in temperature back to cool climes in the latest Pleistocene/early Holocene, then rewarming to reach maximum Holocene warmth and associated drying by about 8 ka to 6 ka. In the northwest California mountains the early Holocene transition was marked by late Pleistocene subalpine forests being replaced within a few hundred years by dense pine and fir forests, which then disappeared a thousand years later (Wanket 2002). This period coincides with the globally recognized cool interval known as the Younger Dryas. As climates rewarmed at the end of the Younger Dryas in northwest California, pine, cedar, Douglas-fir, oaks, and tanoak forests spread in the uplands (Wanket 2002, Briles et al. 2005). Throughout this region charcoal evidence suggested increase in fire events as forests closed and became denser in the early Holocene. Dry-adapted chaparral shrublands expanded from northwest California north into Washington (Detling 1961). Warming and drying toward the middle Holocene drove the expansion of pines, oaks, and dry-adapted herbs, while along the coastal regions, redwood and western red cedar (*Thuja plicata*) declined (Heusser and Barron 2002). Summer drought and low annual precipitation were established by 8 ka, and with this, high fire frequencies in ecosystems dominated by pine, cedar (likely incense-cedar), oaks, and grasses. Similar pine-oak dominated forests appear in records from other northwest California sites, pointing to warm-adapted ecosystems. Farther south at Clear Lake, temperature proxies confirm that mean mid-Holocene temperatures were as much as 1–2°C warmer than today (Adam and West 1983) with surrounding vegetation dominated by warm-adapted chaparral species.

Similar vegetation shifts at the Pleistocene-Holocene boundary appear along the central and southern California coasts, with rapid declines in conifers and increases in oak woodlands, chaparral, and coastal sage scrub ecosystems (Heusser 1995, 1998). No evidence for western hemlock or coast redwood appears along the south coast during any interval of this time, suggesting that these taxa had late Quaternary southern limits on the coast at about 35°N (Heusser and Sirocko 1997). On the Channel Islands, pine and cypress forests that had characterized the island uplands during the late glacial declined dramatically and were replaced by about 11,800 years ago almost completely by coastal sage scrub and grassland (Anderson et al. 2010). As climates became warmer and drier, especially after about 9,150 years ago, sage scrub expanded and members of the rose and sunflower family became more abundant in the record (Erlandson et al. 1996).

In the Central Valley, warming global temperatures with sea level rise caused transgression of estuarine water into the Sacramento–San Joaquin Delta area (Malamud-Roam et al. 2007). This no doubt affected the nature of ecosystems, favoring aquatic and marsh species and reducing upland species as much or more than direct climate effects did. In the southern San Joaquin Valley, the cold-adapted and coniferous late glacial forests and woodlands were replaced by pine and oak species by about 8 ka (Davis 1999a). As sagebrush declined, taxa in the goosefoot and aster families increased. High charcoal values also suggest increases in wildfires during the early to middle Holocene. The southern desert records show successive stages of transition during the end of the Pleistocene indicative of cool species moving upslope and warm-arid desert taxa moving in. The Mojave Desert ecosystem shifted, depending on location, first with pinyon decline, then retreat of juniper, to desert scrub communities that variably included shadscale, bitterbrush, indigo bush (*Psorothamnus*), white bursage, and goldenbush (*Ericameria linearifolia*) by about 8 ka (Wells and Woodcock 1985, Woodcock 1986, Spaulding 1990, Koehler et al. 2005). In the Sonoran Desert regions, vegetation shifted stepwise from extensive cool late glacial woodlands and shrublands of pinyon pine–California juniper through cool desert shrubs such as sagebrush, rabbitbrush, and shadscale to more arid-adapted Mormon tea, Joshua tree, desert thorn, creosote bush, and cactus by about 7 ka (Spaulding 1990).

Many changes characterized the complex topography of the eastern California mountains during the early to middle Holocene. In the eastern Sierra Nevada/Owens Valley/White Mountains region, postglacial vegetation changed rapidly from juniper-dominated basins with subalpine conifers on the low slopes to warm-dry adapted woody shrubs including mountain mahogany and pine and fir forests above (Woolfenden 2003, Koehler and Anderson 1994, Koehler and Anderson 1995, Jennings and Elliott-Fisk 1993). Xeric species of winterfat (*Krascheninnikovia lanata*), rabbitbrush, spiny hopsage (*Grayia spinosa*), and wolfberry spread into the basins by 8.7 ka. Subalpine conifers (e.g., limber and bristlecone pines, *Pinus flexilis* and *Pinus longaeva*, respectively) retreated upslope with warming, as did the pinyon-juniper woodland belt, attaining treelines near and above present locations by 6 ka (Jennings and Elliot-Fisk 1993, La Marche 1973).

At higher elevations in the central eastern Sierra Nevada, warming temperatures and the retreating ice cap exposed abundant flat and low-gradient environments that supported the widespread development of wet meadows, dominated by wetland-adapted taxa and surrounded, varying with location, by alpine shrubs or by limber and lodgepole pine forests (*Pinus contorta*) (Byrne et al. 1979, Anderson 1990). Cold-dry ecosystems, such as sagebrush steppe, were replaced by coniferous forests; hemlock appeared and rose in abundance for a short period around 9 ka. At more mesic locations, subalpine tree species currently growing in the high Sierra appeared, including western white pine, western juniper (*Juniperus occidentalis*), red fir, mountain hemlock, and whitebark pine, although by 6 ka both upper and lower treelines were higher than at present (Anderson 1990, Power 1998).

On the Sierra Nevada west slope, early and middle Holocene ecosystems developed in response to background climatic transitions from cold-dry, continental glacial conditions to warm-dry environments by 6 ka (see Figures 8.9 and 8.10). As sagebrush steppe declined and closed, mixed coniferous forests expanded in response to warming and increased effective moisture (Smith and Anderson 1992), and a pulse of high fir abundance occurred in many records. This is interpreted as a transitional effect from cold and dry environments to more open and xeric ecosystems common in the mid-Holocene. High fire frequencies also characterized this interval (Edlund and Byrne 1991, Edlund 1994, Anderson and Smith 1994). The condition of dense forests with abundant fir and incense cedar and high fire frequencies of the early and middle Holocene has been compared to the late-twentieth-century situation in California forests. In the latter case, dense forests with high fir and incense cedar and high fire occurrence have developed in response to warming and anthropogenic fire suppression. By the middle Holocene, records from the west slope montane and subalpine elevations show loss of mesic and cold-adapted species. With warming and drying, montane and subalpine meadows that had developed in the late Pleistocene and early Holocene dried and were converted to forest, mostly lodgepole pine (Wood 1975, Anderson 1990, Koehler and Anderson 1995). This situation also is reminiscent of the succession from meadow to forest that is ongoing at present in response to late-twentieth-century warming.

In the northern mountains of the California Cascades and the Modoc Plateau, cold glacial steppe ecosystems converted to forest during the early Holocene. Abrupt transitions in fewer than five hundred years occurred from steppe to fir forest in the southern Cascades (West 2004). Increases of pine, more open, parklike forests, and higher upper treeline by the middle Holocene reflect generally warm and dry climates, even at higher elevations (Starratt et al. 2003, West et al. 2007). Fire rose in importance in the Modoc region in the early and middle Holocene, as indicated by frequent fire events recorded at wetland marshes (West and McGuire 2004).

Late Holocene (<6 ka)

The long-term warming trend of the early Holocene culminated during the middle millennia (8–6 ka) with maximum heat and aridity. Across California, ecosystems shifted in diversity and composition in response to these conditions. After about 6 ka, changes in insolation contributed to the reversal of early Holocene temperatures trends and, as elsewhere, the California region began to cool. As in the early Holocene, this was not a monotonic trend. Rather, cooling was interrupted by decade- to century-scale warm intervals as well as by variability at multiple scales in precipitation and soil-moisture relations. Starting about 4 ka, a widespread cool and wet period known as the Neoglacial developed, which drove return of glaciers in the high mountains and high lake levels throughout the region. These cooling trends—interrupted by warm intervals—triggered pervasive changes in California ecosystems, culminating in the development of modern floristic diversity.

Along the northwestern California coast and mountains, cooling after 6 ka influenced the resurgence of maritime conifers forests, including expansion of redwood, fir, spruce, and alder along the coast (Heusser and Barron 2002). At mid-montane elevations inland, pine and oak decreased in extent while Douglas-fir, tanoak, and oaks increased (Briles et al. 2005, Wanket 2002). At higher elevations, oak declined while fir, hemlock, and pine increased (West 1989, West 1990, Mohr et al. 2000, Wanket 2002, Daniels et al. 2005). Decreasing oak abundance in the Clear Lake region reflects response to declines of 1°C to 2°C after the middle Holocene (Adam and West 1983). Recorded along the southern coast are indications that high-frequency variability developed during the late Holocene, with an increase in extreme El Niño events alternating with droughts (Heusser and Sirocko 1997, Anderson 2002). On the Channel Islands, grasslands replaced sage scrub after 6,900 years ago, and wetland plants became prominent after 4,500 years ago, suggesting transition toward a cooler, wetter climate (Anderson et al. 2010).

Records are slim for the late Holocene in the Central Valley. Tree-ring and diatom reconstructions of streamflow provide evidence for regional trends toward cooling and mesic conditions over the past four thousand years (Malamud-Roam et al. 2007). Especially in the early portion of this interval, these led overall to higher flows and pulses of greater freshwater than modern values (Meko 2001, Meko et al. 2001, Stahle et al. 2001, Byrne et al. 2001, Starratt 2002). These records also show periods of drought, in some intervals correlating with hemispheric warm periods and others not (e.g., the Medieval period). In the southern San Joaquin Valley, cool and moist conditions developed after 4 ka, triggering declines of xerophytic shrub communities and taxa such as greasewood (Davis 1999a) and raising lake levels during the thirteenth through the eighteenth centuries (Negrini 2013). Higher fire frequencies relative to the mid-Holocene suggest that valley woodlands and shrublands developed sufficient fuel and cover to carry range fires.

The cool and moist conditions of the Neopluvial, a cold and wet episode 2–4 ka, correlated with expansion in the southern deserts of California of relatively mesic species such as blackbrush, Mojave sage (*Salvia mohavensis*), and goldenbush (Enzel et al. 1992, van Devender 1990). In other parts of the Mojave and Sonoran Deserts, modern desert taxa such as creosote bush, ironwood, ocotillo (*Fouquieria splendens*), and white bursage expanded after 6 ka, in some situations arriving only in the last millennium (van Devender 1990, Spaulding 1990). During the cool and wet Little Ice Age (1450–1920 CE [common era, equivalent to AD]) (Mann et al. 2009), shallow lakes filled currently dry desert playas, and desert montane shrub communities shifted downslope into zones now occupied by creosote bush communities (Cole and Webb 1985, Spaulding 1995, Koehler et al. 2005).

The warmth of the middle Holocene drove upslope movement of elevationally zoned vegetation in the mountains of eastern California. Bristlecone pine in the White Mountains reached its highest Holocene elevation 150 meters above mid-twentieth-century altitude at 6–4 ka, with corresponding upward shifts of the pinyon-juniper woodland (LaMarche 1973, Jennings and Elliott-Fisk 1993). Subsequently, these montane forest ecosystems retreated downslope in response to long-term cooling trends. At lower elevations in the White/Inyo Mountains, modern vegetation appears to have become established between 4–2 ka (Jennings and Elliott-Fisk 1993, Koehler and Anderson 1995, Reynolds 1996). In the uplands of the central Sierra Nevada, regional cooling and increased moisture triggered expansion of closed conifer forests that included fir, pine, and hemlock, and drove upward shifts of altitudinal ranges (see Figure 8.9; Anderson 1987 and 1990, Dull and Edlund 1997). Declines of conifer abundance in this region coincided with the warm dry Medieval Climatic Anomaly. At Whitewing Mountain (3,100 meters) north of Mammoth Lakes, a diverse conifer forest containing lodgepole pine, western white pine, sugar pine (*Pinus lambertiana*), Jeffrey pine, whitebark pine, and mountain hemlock grew in contexts currently above local treeline between 900 and 1350 CE (Millar et al. 2006), reflecting warm-dry conditions of that interval. This forest was unusual for having species not currently present in the eastern Sierra of this region. Similar altitudinal trends occurred in the southern Sierra Nevada (Graumlich and Lloyd 1996).

On the west slope of the Sierra Nevada, late Holocene records widely document declines in oak and increases in fir and incense-cedar throughout middle montane locations. Fire frequencies, which had peaked in the warm-dry mid-Holocene, also declined. Meadows expanded (Koehler and Anderson 1994), and downslope shifts appear to have occurred for fir, incense cedar, and oak forests (Davis et al. 1985). Giant sequoia groves expanded to their present abundance only within the last 4.5 ka (see Figure 8.9; Anderson and Smith 1994). Congruent records in the southern Cascades document cooling temperatures and increased effective moisture after 4–6 ka and expansion of mesic- and snow-adapted forests that included higher percentages of fir (Mohr et al. 2000). Similar trends occurred in the Modoc Plateau region, where fir pollen increased after 6 ka in the Medicine Lake area (Starratt et al. 2003), while at Tule Lake, juniper and sagebrush increased in response to inferred cool-dry conditions (Adam et al. 1989).

A significant new factor influencing vegetation patterns in California during the past ten thousand years was the presence of humans (see Chapter 10, "Indigenous California"). In the California region, Native American activity likely had its greatest effect on vegetation from 6–4 ka, as expansive migrations of people throughout California took place, populations grew, and sophisticated methods of plant use and vegetation control developed. Invasion of modern Eurasians starting in the 1700s and increasing greatly from the mid-1800s on vastly altered the scope, rate, and nature of vegetation change in the region (see Chapter 5, "Population and Land Use").

Lessons from the Past for the Future

An important message from the study of historical vegetation for resource managers, conservationists, and climate-adaptation planners is that dynamism, not ECOSYSTEM STATIONARITY (Milly et al. 2008), is the norm. Perspectives that assume static conditions as a baseline derive implicitly or explicitly from a specific time interval, usually unspecified and often too short for the processes under consideration (Lovejoy 2013). Embracing and understanding the nature of environmental change, and of interacting forces over time and at multiple scales, provides a more effective framework from which to sustain dynamic nature, protect biodiversity, and deliver ecosystem goods into the future (Jackson 1997, Willis and Birks 2006, Millar et al. 2007).

Teaching about historical dynamics and the fluidity of ecosystem change should not be mistaken as an admission that "anything goes." To the contrary, there is no question of the need to mitigate stressors such as greenhouse pollution. In the meantime, climate adaptation strategies must be actively implemented for wildland and urban ecosystems. We can benefit in these efforts by learning from stories of past ecosystems (Willis and Birks 2006). Incorporating knowledge of historical change into effective adaptive management and resilient conservation frameworks implies working with natural processes rather than against them (Jackson 1997, Millar and Woolfenden 1999, Millar and Brubaker 2006). An example of the past informing current conservation perspectives is the recognition that species often respond to natural climate change adaptively by moving geographically. Past dynamics illustrate that population extirpation on the one hand, and recruitment and spread on the other, are not necessarily ecological problems but can be the leading and trailing edges of adaptive migration. Landscape-level mortality events such as forest dieback can swiftly advance the genetic fitness of a population so as to make ecosystems more adapted to climatic (and other) conditions of the future (Rocca and Romme 2009, Kuparinen et al. 2010, Millar et al. 2012). Fragmentation of species into isolated populations as a result of changing climates can lead to extinction vortices. However, long-term adaptive resilience under rapidly changing climatic conditions of the past has often depended on the existence of disjunct refugial populations, the consequent genetic diversity that evolves in isolation, and the key role of refugia in recolonization and restoration (Araujo 2009). A climate-savvy adaptation approach encourages managers to assess historical conditions against the contemporary situation and to consider among the array of possibilities maintaining species in environmentally appropriate refugia. The broader challenges that depart from past circumstances involve facilitating these kinds of ecological and evolutionary dynamism in the context of new stresses, like invasive species and landscape fragmentation, that can hinder adaptive ecosystem responses.

Another example of historically informed conservation is in the context of assisted migration. This climate adaptation practice remains controversial (McLachlan et al. 2007), primarily in discussion over ethical and legal issues of moving species intentionally outside currently native ranges. A long-term perspective, however, not only challenges the concept of a static current range (rather, ranges shift with time) but more importantly can provide useful information on how species migrated under specific climatic conditions of the past. This then can inform development of modern climate-adaptation plans (Millar 1998, 1999) that help overcome new barriers to movement.

A long-term (century-scale) view can also help to frame management objectives effectively. Biotic response to change over time is a "variable chasing a variable, not a constant" (Jackson 1997), so management strategies based on historical variability as a proxy for ecological sustainability can benefit from longer temporal perspectives than usually employed (Millar 2014). In ecological restoration, for instance, setting targets by reference to historical conditions is likely to lead to failure when the historical reference conditions do not resemble future regimes. Rather, aligning restoration goals with anticipated future projections is more likely to lead to success. In western North America, for example, presettlement conditions (e.g., the mid-nineteenth century) have often been used as targets for forest restoration (Morgan et al. 1994). This time period, however, was the coldest interval of the Little Ice Age; forests that established then are poor models for forests that would flourish under future warm environments.

The obstacles and impediments of the human-built landscape lack any historical analogs and are primary drivers of novel impacts to California ecosystems. While climate, with its natural and increasingly human-dominated components, interacts significantly with other stressors, the truly new threats to ecological sustainability and ecosystem services include widespread disturbances such as land use and development; greatly accelerated fragmentation of ecosystems and waterways; land, water, and air (including greenhouse gases) pollution; invasive species; and highly altered fire regimes. Conservation attention can best focus on these elements as we also assist and mimic the natural capacities of species to adapt to ongoing climate changes.

Summary

In the same way that learning details of one's family history—the environments, traditions, and lifeways of our ancestors—helps us to understand and appreciate the modern human condition, knowledge of the historical contexts of landscapes helps us to deeply understand the diversity and ecology of modern flora and fauna. This chapter narrates a story of the geologic and climatic origins of the California region, from the emergence of land out of ancient seas, through mountain-building phases, to the ongoing drama of modern geologic forces. Regional and global geologic dynamics interacted with, and influenced, the climate of the California region. Together, sequences of geologic and climatic variability influenced the rise of modern flora. Included among the lessons in this narrative is the important role of past climatic change in shaping California's vegetation, including both individual species and community associations. Past climate changes have been continuous and included many, interacting quasicyclic patterns with nested time scales (decadal to multimillennial). Because California's native flora developed in the presence of dramatic climate change, many adaptations have evolved within species to cope with these pressures. Conservation and management efforts can be most successful when they work in concert with these natural adaptive mechanisms.

Acknowledgments

The authors thank Diane Erwin, of the University of California, Museum of Paleontology, in Berkeley, California, for review of the chapter; and Diane Delany, of the USDA Forest Service, Pacific Southwest Research Station, in Albany, California, for rendering the figures.

Recommended Reading

Baldwin, D. H. Goldman, D. J. Keil, R. Patterson, and T. J. Rosatti, editors. The Jepson manual: Vascular plants of California. Second edition. University of California Press, Berkeley, California.

———. 1996. Tertiary vegetation history. Chapter 5. Pages 71–122 in Sierra Nevada ecosystem project: Final report to Congress. Volume 2, Assessments and scientific basis for management options. Report No. 37. Centers for Water and Wildland Resources, University of California, Davis, California.

Edwards, S. W. 2004. Paleobotany of California. The Four Seasons 4:3–75.

Grayson, D. K. 2011. The Great Basin: A natural prehistory. University of California Press, Berkeley, California.

Millar, C. I. 2012. Geologic, climatic, and vegetation history of California. Pages 49–68 in B.G. Baldwin, D. Goldman, D.J. Keil, R. Patterson, T.J. Rosatti, and D. Wilken, editors. The Jepson Manual: Higher plants of California. Second edition. University of California Press, Berkeley, California.

West, G. J., W. Woolfenden, J. A. Wanket, and R. S. Anderson. 2007. Late Pleistocene and Holocene environments. Pages 11–34 in T. L. Jones and K. A. Klar, editors. California prehistory. Altamira Press, New York, New York.

Woolfenden, W. B. 1996. Quaternary vegetation history. Pages 47–70 in Sierra Nevada ecosystem project: Final report to Congress. Volume 2, Assessments and scientific basis for management options. Report No. 37. Centers for Water and Wildland Resources, University of California, Davis, California. <http://pubs.usgs.gov/dds/dds-43/VOL_II/VII_C04.PDF>.

Glossary

ANGIOSPERMS Flowering plants that (in contrast to gymnosperms) have seeds (ovules) enclosed in an ovary.

ARÊTE A thin ridge of rock formed between adjacent, presently, or previously glaciated valleys.

ASSISTED MIGRATION A climate-adaptation strategy wherein individuals from an actually or potentially impacted species are moved to locations projected to be climatically favorable for them in the future.

BOND CYCLES Approximately 1,000- to 1,500-year global climate cycles that alternate between warm and cool conditions and are influenced by cycles in solar activity.

CIRQUE A concave valley head bounded by steep slopes on three sides and formed by glacial activity and subsequent erosion.

ECOSYSTEM STATIONARITY An outmoded concept that ecosystems, including their components, structures, and functions, remain static over time.

EL NIÑO/LA NIÑA Also known as the El Niño Southern Oscillation (ENSO), this is a short-lived (interannual), equatorial Pacific Ocean–mediated climate regime that alternates at periods of two to seven years between winters of warm/dry and cool/wet. In California, strong El Niño years are associated with warm, wet winter whereas La Niña years are drier and often cooler.

ESCARPMENT A steep slope separating two relatively level areas and formed from fault activity and subsequent erosion.

GYMNOSPERMS A group of seed–producing plants that include conifers, cycads, and ginkgoes and are characterized by unenclosed seeds (ovules), in contrast to the enclosed seeds of flowering plants (Angiosperms).

LITTLE ICE AGE (LIA) A multicentury, late Holocene cold interval experienced widely around the world. Times varied for different regions. In California the LIA has been documented to have extended from about 1450 to 1920 CE. During the LIA, glaciers grew and advanced to their largest Holocene values. The LIA is one of several anomalous climate periods attributed to Bond cycles.

MACROFOSSIL A fossil sufficiently large to be studied and identified without a microscope.

MATTERHORN Pyramidal, in reference to a mountain shaped by glacial activity and subsequent erosion.

MEDIEVAL CLIMATIC ANOMALY (MCA) A multicentury, late Holocene anomalous climate interval experienced with varying effects in different regions of the world (some regions do not show it). In California the MCA is considered to have extended from 900 to 1350 CE, which included two long periods (200 years and 150 years) of intense drought. Some regions of California show evidence for above background mean temperatures also.

MESIC Characterized by moist conditions.

MORAINE An accumulation of soil and rock formed by glacial activity, typically along the lateral and/or lower margins of an extant or past glacier.

NONANALOG ASSEMBLAGES Historical vegetation communities that comprise species not found co-occurring at present.

OROGENIC Resulting from a mountain–building episode (an orogeny).

PACIFIC DECADAL OSCILLATION (PDO) A quasi–decade climate cycle mediated by conditions in the North Pacific Ocean that causes background climates along the Pacific coast to alternate between warm/dry and cool/moist. In California multiyear periods of so-called positive-phase PDO intensify El Niño–type weather (wet and warm), while negative-phase PDO has the opposite effect.

PLUVIAL LAKE A lake formed in a landlocked basin during times of high precipitation in glacial periods.

TAPHONOMY The study of decaying organisms over time and how they become fossilized. Also refers to conditions that affect decaying organisms as they become fossilized, especially those that alter the structure and morphology from the original (living) condition.

References

Adam, D. P. 1988. Palynology of two Upper Quaternary cores from Clear Lake, Lake County, California. U.S. Geological Survey Professional Paper 1363.

———. 1973. Early Pleistocene pollen spectra near Lake Tahoe, California. Journal of Research of the U.S. Geological Survey 1:691–693.

Adam, D. P., and G. J. West. 1983. Temperature and precipitation estimates through the last glacial cycle from Clear Lake, California. Pollen data. Science 219:168–170.

Adam, D. P., A. M. Sarna-Wojcicki, H. J. Rieck, J. P. Bradbury, W. E. Dean, and R. M. Forester. 1989. Tulelake, California: The last three million years. Palaeogeography, Palaeoclimatology, and Palaeoecology 72:89–103.

Adam, D. P., J. P. Bradbury, H. J. Rieck, and A. M. Sarna-Wojcicki. 1990. Environmental changes in the Tule Lake Basin, Siskiyou and Modoc Counties, California from three to two million years before present. U.S. Geological Survey Bulletin 1933:1–13.

Anderson R. S. 2002. Fire and vegetation history of Santa Rosa Island, Channel Islands National Park. Final report for a cooperative agreement between Channel Islands National Park and Northern Arizona University.

———. 1990. Holocene forest development and paleoclimates within the central Sierra Nevada. Journal of Ecology 78:470–489.

———. 1987. Late-Quaternary environments of the Sierra Nevada, California. PhD dissertation, University of Arizona, Tucson, Arizona.

Anderson, R. S., and S. J. Smith 1994. Paleoclimatic interpretations of meadow sediment and pollen stratigraphies from California. Geology 22:723–726.

Anderson, R. S., S. Starratt, R.M.B. Jass, and N. Pinter. 2010. Fire and vegetation history on Santa Rosa Island, Channel Islands, and long-term environmental change in southern California. Journal of Quaternary Science 25:782–797.

Araujo, M. B. 2009. Climate change and spatial conservation planning. Chapter 13 in A. Moilanen, K. A. Wilson, and H. P. Possingham, editors. Spatial conservation prioritization: Quantitative methods and computational tools. Oxford University Press, London, UK.

Axelrod, D. I. 1988. Outline history of California vegetation. Pages 139–194 in M. G. Barbour and J. Major, editors. Terrestrial vegetation of California, expanded edition. California Native Plant Society, Special Publication Number 9, Sacramento, CA.

———. 1985. Miocene floras from the Middlegate Basin, west-central Nevada. Geological Sciences. Volume 129. University of California Press, Berkeley, California.

———. 1980. History of the maritime closed-cone pines, Alta and Baja California. Geological Sciences. Volume 120. University of California Press, Berkeley, California.

Axelrod, D. I., and P. H. Raven. 1985. Origins of the Cordilleran flora. Journal of Biogeography 12:21–47.

Ballantyne, A. P., D. R. Greenwood, J. S. Sinninghe Damst, A. Z. Csank, J. J. Eberle, and N. Rybczynski. 2010. Significantly warmer Arctic surface temperatures during the Pliocene indicated by multiple independent proxies. Geology 38:603–606.

Barnosky, A. D., N. Matzke, S. Tomiya, G. U. Wogan, B. Swartz, T. B. Quental, C. Marshall, J. L. McGuire, E. L. Lindsey, K. C. Maguire, B. Mersey, and E. A. Ferrer. 2011. Has the Earth's sixth mass extinction already arrived? Nature 471:51–57.

Bergquist, J. R. 1978. Depositional history and fault-related studies, Bolinas Lagoon, California. U.S. Geological Survey Open-File Reports 78–802:164.

———. 1977. Depositional history and fault-related studies, Bolinas Lagoon, California. PhD dissertation. Department of Geology, Stanford University, Palo Alto, California.

Biondi, R., A. Gershunov, and D. R. Cayan. 2001. North Pacific decadal climate variability since 1661. Journal of Climate 14:5–10.

Blakey, R. C. 2008. Gondwana paleogeography from assembly to breakup—A 500 m.y. odyssey. Geological Society of America Special Paper 441:1–40.

Bond, G. B., B. Kromer, J. Beer, R. Muscheler, M. N. Evans, W. Showers, S. Hoffmann, R. Lotti-Bond, I. Hajdas, and G. Bonani. 2001. Persistent solar influence on North Atlantic climate during the Holocene. Science 294:2130–2136.

Bradley, R. S. 1999. Paleoclimatology, reconstructing climates of the Quaternary. Second edition. Harcourt Academic Press, Burlington, Massachusetts.

Briles, C., C. Whitlock, and P. Bartlein. 2005. Postglacial vegetation, fire, and climate history of the Siskiyou Mountains, Oregon, USA. Quaternary Research 64:44–56.

Byrne, R., B. L. Ingram, S. Starratt, F. Malamud-Roam, J. N. Collins, and M. E. Conrad. 2001. Carbon-isotope, diatom, and pollen evidence for late Holocene salinity change in a brackish marsh in the San Francisco Estuary. Quaternary Research 55:66–76.

Byrne, R., D. Araki, and S. Peterson. 1979. Report on pollen analysis of the core from Tule Lake, Mono County, California. Report on file, Geography Department, University of California, Berkeley, California.

Byrne, R., S. A. Mensing, and E. G. Edlund. 1993. Long-term changes in the structure and extent of California oaks. Final report to the Integrated Hardwood Range Management Program. University of California, Berkeley, California.

Calsbeek, R., J. N. Thompson, and J. E. Richardson. 2003. Patterns of molecular evolution and diversification in a biodiversity hotspot: The California Floristic Province. Molecular Ecology 12:1021–1029.

Cassel, E. J., A. T. Calvert, and S. A. Graham. 2009. Age, geochemical composition, and distribution of Oligocene ignimbrites in the northern Sierra Nevada, California: Implications for landscape morphology, elevation, and drainage divide geography of the Nevadaplano. Geology Review 51:723–742.

Cassel, E. J., S. A. Graham, and C. P. Chamberlain. 2009. Cenozoic tectonic and topographic evolution of the northern Sierra Nevada, California through stable isotope paleoaltimetry in volcanic glass. Geology 37:547–550.

Chaney, R. W. 1959. Miocene floras of the Columbia Basin. Publication 617, Part 1. Carnegie Institute of Washington, Washington, D.C.

Cohen, K. M., S. M. Finney, P. L. Gibbard, and J.-X. Fan. 2013. The ICS international chronostratigraphic chart. Episodes 36:199–204.

Cole, K. L. 1983. Late Pleistocene vegetation of the Kings Canyon, Sierra Nevada, California. Quaternary Research 19:117–127.

Cole, K. L., and R. H. Webb. 1985. Late Holocene vegetation changes in Greenwater Valley, Mojave Desert, California. Quaternary Research 23:227–235.

Crane, P. R., E. S. Fries, and K. R. Pedersen. 2000. The origin and early diversification of angiosperms. Nature 374:27–33.

Daniels, M. L., R. S. Anderson, and C. Whitlock. 2005. Vegetation and fire history since the late Pleistocene from the Trinity Mountains, northwestern California, USA. Holocene 15:1062–1071.

Davis, O. K. 1999a. Pollen analysis of Tulare Lake, California: Great Basin-like vegetation in Central California during the Full-Glacial and early Holocene. Review of Palaeobotany and Palynology 107:249–157.

———. 1999b. Pollen analysis of a Holocene–late Glacial sediment core from Mono Lake, Mono County. Quaternary Research 52:243–249.

Davis, O. K., R. S. Anderson, P. L. Falls, M. K. O'Rourke, and R. S. Thompson. 1985. Palynological evidence for early Holocene aridity in the southern Sierra Nevada, California. Quaternary Research 24:322–332.

DeCelles, P. G. 2004. Late Jurassic to Eocene evolution of the Cordilleran thrust belt and foreland basin system, western U.S. American Journal of Science 304:105–168.

DeCourten, F. L. 2003. The broken land. University of Utah Press, Salt Lake City, Utah.

Detling, L. E. 1961. The chaparral formation of southwestern Oregon, with considerations of its postglacial history. Ecology 42:348–357.

Dull, R., and E. Edlund. 1997. Paleoenvironmental analysis of Waugh Lake and Lower Rush Meadow. Investigations of CA-MNO-2440/H, Mono-2459, MNO-2460, MNO-2461, and MNO-2463. Appendix 1. Pages 1–20 in T. L. Jackson, editor. Archaeological data recovery program—Rush Meadow. Pacific Legacy, Aptos, California. Report on file, Supervisor's Office. USDA Inyo National Forest, Bishop, California.

Edlund, E. G. 1994. Bunker Lake paleoecological analysis. Pages 1–23 in R. J. Jackson, editor. Framework for archaeological research and management: National forests of north central Sierra Nevada. USDA Forest Service, Placerville, California.

Edlund, E. G., and R. Byrne. 1991. Climate, fire, and late Quaternary vegetation change in the central Sierra Nevada. Pages 390–396 in S. S. Nodvin and T. Waldrop, editors. Fire and the environment: Ecological and cultural perspectives. General Technical Report SE-69. USDA Forest Service, Southeastern Research Station, Asheville, North Carolina.

Edwards, S. W. 2004. Paleobotany of California. The Four Seasons 4:3–75.

Enzel, Y., W. J. Brown, R. Y. Anderson, L. D. McFadden, and S. G. Wells. 1992. Short-duration Holocene lakes in the Mojave River drainage basin, southern California. Quaternary Research 38:60–73.

Erlandson, J. M., D. J. Dennett, B. L. Ingram, D. A. Guthrie, D. P. Morris, M. A. Tveskov, G. J. West, and P. L. Walker. 1996. An archaeological and paleontological chronology from Daisy Cave (CA-SMI-261), San Miguel Island, California. Radiocarbon 38:355–373.

Generaux, S. T., M. Niemi, and R. Burns. 2003. Evidence for the Pleistocene-Holocene transition from a 20.8 m core obtained from Vedanta Marsh, Olema, California (abstract). North-central meeting of the Geological Society of America, Kansas City, Missouri. GSA Abstract with Program:25:53.

Gillespie, A. R., and P. H. Zehfuss. 2004. Glaciations of the Sierra Nevada, California, USA. Pages 51–62 in J. Ehiers and P. L. Gibbard, editors. Quaternary glaciations: Extent and chronology. Part II, North America. Elsevier, Oxford, UK.

Graham, A. 1999. Late Cretaceous and Cenozoic history of North American vegetation. Oxford University Press, New York.

Graumlich, L. J., and A. H. Lloyd. 1996. Dendroclimatic, ecological, and geomorphological evidence for long-term climatic change in the Sierra Nevada, USA. Pages 51–59 in J. S. Dean, D. M. Meko, and T. W. Swetnam, editors. Radiocarbon.

Grayson, D. K. 2011. The Great Basin: A natural prehistory. University of California Press, Berkeley, California.

Harden, D. R. 2004. California geology. Second edition. Pearson Prentice Hall, Upper Saddle River, New Jersey.

Haywood, A. M., P. J. Valdes, B. W. Sellwood, J. O. Kaplan, and H. J. Dowsett. 2001. Modelling middle Pliocene warm climates of the USA. Palaeontolia Electronica Article 5 4:1–21.

Henry, C. D., and J. E. Faulds. 2010. Ash-flow tuffs in the Nine Hill, Nevada, paleovalley and implications for tectonism and volcanism of the western Great Basin, USA. Geosphere 6:339–369.

Herbert, T. D., J. D. Schuffert, D. Andreasen, L. Heusser, M. Lyle, A. Mix, C. Ravelo, L. D. Stott, and J. C. Herguera. 2001. Collapse of the California Current during glacial maxima linked to climate change on land. Science 293:71–76.

Heusser, L. E. 2000. Data report. Initial results of pollen analyses from ODP sites 1018, 1020, 1021, and 1022. Pages 239–245 in M. Lyle, I. Koizumi, C. Richter, and T. C. Moore Jr., editors. Proceedings of the Ocean Drilling Project (scientific results). Volume 167. College Station, TX.

———. 1998. Direct correlation of millennial-scale changes in western North American vegetation and climate with changes in the California Current System over the past ~60 kyr. Paleoceanography 13:252–262.

———. 1995. Pollen stratigraphy and paleoecologic interpretation of the 160-ky. Pages 265–277 in J. P. Kennett, J. G. Balduaf, and M. Lyle, editors. Proceedings of the Ocean Drilling Program (scientific results). Volume 146. College Station, TX.

Heusser, L. E., and F. Sirocko. 1997. Millennial pulsing of environmental change in southern California from the past 24 k.y: A record of Indo-Pacific ENSO events? Geology 25:243–246.

Heusser, L. E., and J. A. Barron. 2002. Holocene patterns of climate change in coastal northern California. Page 157 in G. J. West and L. D. Buffaloe, editors. Proceedings of the 18th annual Pacific Climate Workshop. Technical Report 69. California Department of Water Resources, Sacramento, CA.

Heusser, L. E., M. Lyle, and A. Mix. 2000. Vegetation and climate of the northwest coast of North America during the last 500 k.y.: High resolution pollen evidence from the northern California margin. Pages 217–226 in in M. Lyle, I. Koizumi, C. Richter, and T. C. Moore Jr., editors. Proceedings of the Ocean Drilling Project (scientific results). Volume 167. College Station, TX.

Hickey, B. M. 1979. The California Current system: Hypotheses and facts. Progress in Oceanography 8:191–279.

Inman, D. L., P. M. Masters, and S. A. Jenkins. 2005. Facing the coastal challenge: Modeling coastal erosion in southern California. Pages 38–52 in O. T. Magoon, editor. California and the World Ocean '02. American Society of Civil Engineers, New York, New York.

Jackson, S. T. 1997. Documenting natural and human-caused plant invasions using paleoecological methods. Pages 37–55 in J. O. Luken and J. W. Thieret, editors. Assessment and management of plant invasions. Spring-Verlag, New York, New York.

Jenkyns, H. C. 2003. Evidence for rapid climate change in the Mesozoic-Palaeogene greenhouse world. Philosphical Trans. Royal Society of London 361:1885–1916.

Jennings, S. A., and D. L. Elliot-Fisk.1993. Packrat midden evidence of late Quaternary vegetation change in the White Mountains, California-Nevada. Quaternary Research 39:214–221.

Koehler, P. A., and R. S. Anderson. 1995. Thirty thousand years of vegetation changes in the Alabama Hills, Owens Valley, California. Quaternary Research 43:238–248.

———. 1994. The paleoecology and stratigraphy of Nichols Meadow, Sierra Nevada National Forest, California, USA. Palaeogeography, Palaeoclimatology, and Palaeoecology 112:1–17.

Koehler, P. S., R. S. Anderson, and W. G. Spaulding. 2005. Development of vegetation in the central Mojave Desert of California during the late Quaternary. Palaeogeography, Palaeoclimatology, and Palaeoecology 215:297–311.

Kuparinen, A., O. Savolainen, and F. M. Schurr. 2010. Increased mortality can promote evolutionary adaptation of forest trees to climate change. Forest Ecology and Management 259:1003–1008.

LaMarche, V.C., Jr. 1973. Holocene climatic variations inferred from treeline fluctuations in the White Mountains, California. Quaternary Research 3:632–660.

Lambeck, K., T. M. East, and E. K. Porter. 2002. Links between climate and sea levels for the past three million years. Nature 419:199–206.

Leopold, E. G. 1984. Pollen identifications from the Eocene Chalk Bluffs flora, California. Palynology 8:8.

Liu, Z., M. Pagani, D. Zinniker, R. DeConto, M. Huber, H. Brinkhuis, S. R. Shah, R. M. Leckie, and A. Pearson. 2009. Global cooling during the Eocene-Oligocene climate transition. Science 323:1187–1190.

Lovejoy, S. 2013. What is climate? EOS 94:1–2.

Lyle, M., I. Koizumi, M. L. Delany, and J. A. Barron. 2000. Sedimentary record of the California Current system, middle Miocene to Holocene: A synthesis of leg 167 results. Pages 341–276 in M. Lyle, I. Koizumi, C. Richter, and T. C. Moore, editors. Proceedings of the Ocean Drilling Program (scientific results). Volume 167. College Station, TX.

MacGinitie, H. D. 1941. A middle Eocene flora from the central Sierra Nevada. Publication 534. Carnegie Institute of Washington, Washington, D.C.

Mackey, E. M., and D. G. Sullivan. 1991. Revised final report. Results of palynological investigations at Gabbott Meadow Lake, Alpine County, California. Pages 473–499 in A. S. Peak and N. J. Neuenschwander, editors. Cultural Resource Studies, North Fork Staislaus River Hydroelectric Development Project. Peak and Associates, Sacramento, California.

Malamud-Roam, F., M. Dettinger, B. L. Ingram, M. K. Hughes, and J. L. Florsheim. 2007. Holocene climates and connections between the San Francisco Bay Estuary and its watershed: A review. San Francisco Estuary and Watershed Science Article 3 5:1–28.

Mann, M. E., Z. Zhang, S. Rutherford, R. S. Bradley, M. K. Hughes, D. Shindell, C. Ammann, G. Faluvegi, and F. Ni. 2009. Global signatures and dynamical origins of the Little Ice Age and Medieval Climate Anomaly. Science 326:1256–1259.

McLachlan, J. S., J. J. Hellmann, and M. W. Schwartz. 2007. A framework for debate of assisted migration in an era of climate change. Conservation Biology 21:297–302.

Mehringer, P. J., Jr. 1967. Pollen analysis of the Tule Springs area, Nevada. Pages 129–200 in H. M. Wormington and D. Ellis, editors. Pleistocene studies in southern Nevada. Nevada State Museum of Anthropology Paper No. 13. Carson City, Nevada.

Meko, D. M. 2001. Reconstructed Sacramento River system runoff from tree rings. Report prepared for the California Department of Water Resources. Laboratory of Tree-Ring Research. University of Arizona, Tucson, Arizona.

Meko, D. M., M. D. Therrell, C. H. Paisan, and M. K. Hughes. 2001. Sacramento River flow reconstructed to A.D. 869 from tree rings. Journal of American River Water Resources Association 37:1029–1039.

Millar, C. I. 2014. Historic variability: Informing restoration strategies, not prescribing targets. Journal of Sustainable Forestry. 33 sup 1: S28–S42.

———. 1999. Evolution and biogeography of *Pinus radiata* with a proposed revision of its Quaternary history. New Zealand Journal of Forest Science 29:335–365.

———. 1998. Reconsidering the conservation of Monterey pine. Fremontia 26:12–16.

———. 1996. Tertiary vegetation history. Chapter 5. Pages 71–122 in Sierra Nevada ecosystem project: Final report to Congress. Volume 2, Assessments and scientific basis for management options. Report No. 37. Centers for Water and Wildland Resources, University of California, Davis.

———. 1993. Impact of the Eocene on the evolution of *Pinus* L. Annals of the Missouri Botanical Garden 80:471–498.

Millar, C. I., and L. B. Brubaker. 2006. Climate change and paleoecology: New contexts for

restoration ecology. Chapter 15. Pages 315–340 in M. Palmer, D. Falk, and J. Zedler, editors. Restoration Science. Island Press, Washington, D.C.

Millar, C. I., and W. B. Woolfenden. 1999. The role of climatic change in interpreting historic variability. Ecological Applications 9:1207–1216.

Millar, C. I., J. C. King, R. D. Westfall, H. A. Alden, and D. L. Delany. 2006. Late Holocene forest dynamics, volcanism, and climate change at Whitewing Mountain and San Joaquin Ridge, Mono County, Sierra Nevada, CA, USA. Quaternary Research 66:273–287.

Millar, C. I., N. L. Stephenson, and S. L. Stephens. 2007. Climate change and forests of the future: Managing in the face of uncertainty. Ecological Applications 17:2145–2151.

Millar, C., R. D. Westfall, D. Delany, M. Bokach, A. Flint, and L. Flint. 2012. Forest mortality in high-elevation whitebark pine (*Pinus albicaulis*) forests of eastern California, USA: Influence of environmental context, bark-beetles, climatic water deficit, and warming. Canadian Journal of Forest Research 42:749–765.

Miller, C. G. 1985. Holocene eruptions at the Inyo volcanic chain, California: Implications for possible eruptions in Long Valley caldera. Geology 13:14–17.

Miller, C. N. 1977. Mesozoic conifers. Botanical Review 43:217–280.

———. 1976. Early evolution in the Pinaceae. Reviews in Palaeobotany Palynology 21:101–117.

Milly, P.C.D., J. Betancourt, M. Falkenmark, R. M. Hirsch, A. W. Kundzewicz, D. P. Lettenmier, and R. J. Stouffer. 2008. Stationarity is dead: Whither water management? Science 319:573–574.

Mix, H. T., A. Mulch, J. L. Kent-Corson, and C. P. Chamberlain. 2011. Cenozoic migration of topography in the North American cordillera. Geology 39:87–90.

Mohr, J. A., C. Whitelock, and C. Skinner. 2000. Postglacial vegetation and fire history, eastern Klamath Mountains, California, USA. Holocene 10:587–601.

Morgan, P., G. H. Aplet, J. B. Haufler, H. C. Humphries, M. M. Moore, and W. D. Wilson. 1994. Historical range of variability: A useful tool for evaluating ecosystem change. Journal of Sustainable Forestry 2:87–111.

Negrini, R. 2013. Holocene lake-level history of Tulare Lake, California as input for Sierra.

Nevada river discharge forecasts: Progress report. Pacific Climate Workshop, Asilomar State Park, Pacific Grove California, March 3–6, 2013.

Negrini, R., T. Miller, R. Stephenson, R. Ramirez, J. Leiran, D. Baron, P. Wigand, D. Rhodes, and T. Algeo. 2007. A 200 kyr record of lake-level change from the Carrizo Plain, Central Coastal California. Paper presented at 2009 Pacific Climate Workshop. Pacific Grove, CA. http://www.fs.fed.us/psw/cirmount/meetings/paclim/pdf2009/Negrini.pdf.

Nordt, L., S. Atchley, and S. Dworkin. 2003. Terrestrial evidence for two greenhouse events in the latest Cretaceous. GSA Today 13:4–9.

Petit, J. R., J. Jouzel, D. Raynaud, N. I. Barkov, N.I., J.-M. Barnola, I. Basile, M. Bender, J. Chappellaz, M. Davis, G. Delaygue, M. Delmotte, V. M. Kotlyakov, M. Legrand, V. Y. Lipenkov, C. Lorius,

L. Pepin, C. Ritz, E. Saltzmann, and M. Stievenard. 1999. Climate and atmospheric history of the past 420,000 years from the Vostok ice core, Antarctica. Nature 399:429–436.

Poore, R. Z., H. J. Dowsett, J. A. Barron, L. Heusser, A. C. Ravelo, and A. Mix. 2000. Mulitproxy record of the last interglacial (MIS 5e) off central and northern California, USA, from Ocean Drilling Program sites 1018 and 1020. U.S. Geological Survey professional paper 1632(2000): 1–19.

Pope, K. O., K. H. Baines, A. C. Ocampo, and B. A. Ivanov. 1994. Impact winter and the Cretaceous/Tertiary extinctions: Results of a Chicxulub asteroid impact model. Earth and Planetary Science Letters 128:719–725.

Power, M. J. 1998. Paleoclimatic interpretation of an alpine lake in south-central Sierra Nevada, California: Multiple proxy evidence. MA thesis. Quaternary Studies Program, Northern Arizona University, Flagstaff, Arizona.

Raven, P. H., and D. I. Axelrod. 1978. Origin and relationships of the California flora. University of California Publications in Botany 72:1–134.

Reheis, M. 1999. Highest pluvial-lake shorelines and Pleistocene climate of the western Great Basin. Quaternary Research 52:196–205.

Renne, P. R., A. L. Deino, F. J. Hilgen, K. F. Kuiper, D. F. Mark, W. S. Mitchell, L. E. Morgan, R. Mundil, and J. Smith. 2013. Time scales of critical events around the Cretaceous-Paleogene boundary. Science 339:684–686.

Retallack, G. J., and D. L. Dilcher. 1986. Cretaceous angiosperm invasion of North America. Cretaceous Research 7:227–252.

Reynolds, L. A. 1996. In the dwelling place of a great spirit: The prehistory of the pinon-juniper woodland of the Inyo-White Mountain Range, eastern California. PhD dissertation. University of Nevada, Reno, Department of Anthropology.

Rocca, M. E., and W. H. Romme. 2009. Beetle-infested forests are not "destroyed." Frontiers in Ecology and the Environment 7:71–72.

Sarna-Wojcicki, A. M. 1995. Age, areal extent, and paleoclimatic effects of "Lake Clyde," a mid-Pleistocene lake that formed the Corcoran Clay, Great Valley, California. Abstracts for glacial history of the Sierra Nevada, California—a symposium in memorial to Clyde Wahrhaftig, September 20–22. White Mountain Research Station, Bishop, California.

Schulte, P., L. Alegret, I. Arenillas, J. A. Arz, P. J. Barton, P. R. Brown, et al. 2010. The Chicxulub asteroid impact and mass extinction at the Cretaceous-Paleogene boundary. Science 327:1214–1218.

Small, E. E., and R. S. Anderson. 1995. Geomorphically driven late Cenozoic rock uplift in the Sierra Nevada, California. Science 270:277–280.

Smith, G. I., and F. A. Street-Perrott. 1983. Pluvial lakes of the western United States. Pages 190–212 in H. E. Wright Jr., editor. Late Quaternary environments of the United States. Volume 1. University of Minnesota Press, Minneapolis.

Smith, S. A., and R. S. Anderson. 1992. Late Wisconsin paleoecological record from Swamp Lake, Yosemite National Park. Quaternary Research 38:91–102.

Smith, S. Y., and R. A. Stockey. 2001. A new species of *Pityostrobus* from the Lower Cretaceous of California and its bearing on the evolution of Pinaceae. International Journal of Plant Sciences 162:669–681.

Spaulding, W. G. 1995. Environmental change, ecosystem responses, and the late Quaternary development of the Mojave Desert. Pages 139–164 in D. W. Steadman and J. I. Mead, editors. Late Quaternary environments and deep history: A tribute to Paul Martin. Scientific Papers. Volume 3, The Mammoth Site of Hot Springs. Larry Agenbroad, Hot Springs, South Dakota.

———. 1990. Vegetational and climatic development of the Mojave Desert: The last glacial maximum to present. Pages 166–199 in J. L. Betancourt, T. R. van Devender, and P. S. Martin, editors. Packrat middens: The last 40,000 years of biotic change. University of Arizona Press, Tucson, Arizona.

Stahle, D. W., J. D. Therrell, M. K. Cleaveland, D. R. Cyan, M. D. Dettinger, and N. Knowles. 2001. Ancient blue oaks reveal human impact on San Francisco salinity. EOS 82:141, 144–145.

Starratt, S. 2002. Diatoms as indicators of freshwater flow variation in central California. Pages 129–144 in G. J. West and L. D. Buffaloe, editors. Proceedings of the 18th Annual Pacific Climate Workshop, March 18–21, 2001. Technical Report 69. State of California, Department of Water Resources, Sacramento, California.

Starratt, S., J. A. Barron, T. Kneeshaw, R. L. Phillipps, J. Bischoff, J. B. Lowenstern, and J. A. Wanket. 2003. A Holocene record from Medicine Lake, Siskiyou County, California: Preliminary diatom, pollen, geochemical, and sedimentological data. Pages 131–148 in G. J. West and L. D. Buffaloe. Proceedings of the 19th Annual Pacific Climate Workshop, March 18–21, 2001. Technical Report 71. State of California, Department of Water Resources, Sacramento, California.

Thatcher, W., G. R. Foulger, B. R. Julian, J. Svarc, E. Quilty, and G. W. Bawden. 1999. Present-day deformation across the Basin and Range province, western United States. Science 283:1714–1718.

Thompson, R. S. 1991. Pliocene environments and climates. Quaternary Science Reviews 10:115–132.

———. 1988. Western North America. Pages 415–458 in B. Huntley and T. Webb III, editors. Vegetation history. Kluwer Academic Publishers, London, UK.

Tiffney, B. M. 1985. Perspectives on the origin of the floristic similarity between eastern Asia and eastern North America. Journal of the Arnold Arboretum 66:73–94.

Upchurch, G. R., and J. A. Wolfe. 1993. Cretaceous vegetation of the western interior and adjacent regions of North America. Pages 243–281 in W.G.E. Caldwell and E. G. Kauffman, editors. Evolution of the western interior basin. Geological Association of Canada Special Paper 39. Geological Association of Canada, St. Johns, Newfoundland, CA.

Van Devender, T. R. 1990. Late Quaternary vegetation and climate of the Sonoran Desert, United States and Mexico. Pages 134–165 in J. L. Betancourt, T. R. van Devender, and P. S. Martin, editors. Packrat middens: The last 40,000 years of biotic change. University of Arizona Press, Tucson, Arizona.

Wakabayashi, J., and T. L. Sawyer. 2001. Stream incision, tectonics, uplift, and evolution of topography of the Sierra Nevada, California. Journal of Geology 109:539–562.

Wanket, J. 2002. Late Quaternary vegetation and climate of the Klamath Mountains. PhD dissertation. Department of Geography, University of California, Berkeley, California.

Wells, S. G., and D. Woodcock 1985. Full-glacial vegetation of Death Valley, California: Juniper woodland opening to Yucca semidesert. Madroño 32:11–23.

West, G. J. 2004. A pollen record of late Pleistocene-Holocene vegetation and climate history, Lassen Volcanic National Park, California. Pages 65–80 in S. W. Starratt and J. L. Blomquist, editors. Proceedings of the 20th Annual Pacific Climate Workshop, April 6–9, 2003. Technical Report 72. State of California, Department of Water Resources, Sacramento, California.

———. 2001. Pollen analysis of late Pleistocene-Holocene sediments from core CL-73-5, Clear Lake, Lake County, California: A terrestrial record of California's cismontane vegetation and climate change inclusive of the Younger Dryas event. Pages 91–106 in G. J. West and L. D. Buffaloe, editors. Proceedings of the 17th Annual Pacific Climate Workshop, May 22–25, 2000. Technical Report 67. State of California, Department of Water Resources, Sacramento, California.

———. 1997. A late glacial age biozone for central California. Pages 23–35 in R. C. Wilson and V. L. Sharp, editors. Proceedings of the 14th Annual Pacific Climate Workshop, April –9, 1997. Technical Report 57. State of California, Department of Water Resources, Sacramento, California.

———. 1993. The late Pleistocene-Holocene pollen record and prehistory of California's North Coast Ranges. Pages 219–236 in. Editors: G. White, P. Mikkelsen, W. R. Hildebrandt, and M. E. Basgall. There grows a green tree: Papers in honor of David A. Fredrickson. Center for Archaeological Research at Davis. Publication no. 11. University of California, Davis, California.

———. 1990. Holocene fossil pollen records of Douglas-firs in northwestern California. Pages 119–122 in J. L. Betancourt and A. M. Mackay, editors. Proceedings of the 6th Annual Pacific Climate Workshop, March 18–21, 2001. Technical Report 23. State of California, Department of Water Resources, Sacramento, California.

———. 1989. Late Pleistocene/Holocene vegetation and climate. Pages 36–50 in M. E. Basgall and W. R. Hildebrandt, editors. Prehistory of the Sacramento River Canyon, Shasta County, California. Center for Archaeological Research at Davis, Publication no. 9. University of California, Davis, California.

West, G. J., and K. R. McGuire. 2002. 9,500 years of burning is recorded in a high desert Marsh. In Spring-fed wetlands: Important scientific and cultural resources of the intermountain region.

(Conference proceedings). http://www. dri.edu/images/stories/conferences_and_workshops/spring-fedwetlands/spring-fed-wet lands-west-mcguire.pdf. Accessed June 1, 2011.

West, G. J., W. Woolfenden, J. A. Wanket, and R. S. Anderson. 2007. Late Pleistocene and

Holocene environments. Pages 11–34 in T. L. Jones and K. A. Klar, editors. California prehistory. Altamira Press, New York, New York.

Willis, K. J., and H.J.B. Birks. 2006. What is natural? The need for a long-term perspective in biodiversity conservation. Science 314:1261–1265.

Wing, S. L., G. J. Harrington, F. A. Smith, J. I. Bloch, D. M. Boyer, and K. H. Freeman. 2005. Transient floral change and rapid global warming at the Paleocene-Eocene boundary. Science 310:993-996.

Wolfe, J. A. 1995. Paleoclimatic estimates from Tertiary leaf assemblages. Annual Review of Earth and Planetary Sciences 23:119–142.

———. 1991. Paleobotanical evidence for a June "impact winter" at the Cretaceous/Tertiary boundary. Science 352:420–423.

———. 1985. Distribution of major vegetational types during the Tertiary. Pages 357–375 in E. T. Sundquist and W. S. Broecker, editors. The carbon cycle and atmospheric CO_2: Natural variations Archean to present. Geophysical Monograph, Issue 32. American Geophysical Union, Washington, D.C.

———. 1975. Some aspects of plant geography of the Northern Hemisphere during the late Cretaceous and Tertiary. Annals of the Missouri Botanical Garden 62:264–279.

———. 1964. Miocene floras from Fingerrock Wash, southwestern Nevada. U.S. Geological Survey Professional Paper 454-N. Washington, D.C.

Wolfe, J. A., and G. R. Upchurch. 1986. Vegetation, climatic, and floral changes at the Cretaceous-Tertiary boundary. Nature 134:148–152.

Wolfe, J. A., C. E. Forest, and P. Molnar. 1998. Paleobotanical evidence of Eocene and Oligocene paleoaltitudes in midlatitude western North America. GSA Bulletin 110:664–678.

Wood, S. H. 1975. Holocene stratigraphy and chronology of mountain meadows, Sierra Nevada, California. Earth Resources Monograph 4. USDA Forest Service, Pacific Southwest Region, San Francisco, California.

Woodcock, D. 1986. The late Pleistocene of Death Valley: A climatic reconstruction based on macrofossil data. Palaeogeography, Palaeoclimatology, and Palaeoecology 57:273–283.

Woolfenden, W. B. 2003. A 180,000-year pollen record from Owens Lake, California: Terrestrial vegetation change on orbital scales. Quaternary Research 59:430–444.

———. 1996. Quaternary vegetation history. Pages 47–70 in Sierra Nevada ecosystem project: Final report to Congress. Volume 2, Assessments and scientific basis for management options. Report No. 37. Centers for Water and Wildland Resources, University of California, Davis, California.

Zachos, J., M. Pagaini, L. Sloan, E. Thomas, and K. Billups. 2001. Trends, rhythms, and aberrations in global climate 65 Ma to present. Science 292:686–693.

Zachos, J. C., G. R. Dikens, and R. E. Zeebe. 2008. An early Cenozoic perspective on greenhouse warming and carbon-cycle dynamics. Nature 45:279–283.

NINE

Paleovertebrate Communities

ELIZABETH A. HADLY and ROBERT S. FERANEC

Introduction

California's latitudinal placement along the Pacific coast, its vast geographic area, tectonic history, and climate during the past seventy million years combined to shape its unique and diverse fauna (see Chapter 8, "Ecosystems Past: Vegetation Prehistory). California's species diversity of fish, amphibians, reptiles, birds, and mammals is the highest in the United States, and it also has more endemics (species found nowhere else) than in any other state (see Chapter 12, "Vegetation"). The assembly of this animal diversity in California is due primarily to a combination of its unique climate and topography, but it is also shaped by its long history of isolation and geologic dynamism. The fossil record of this tumultuous history, for both land and sea, is also recorded in the state. Because the fossil record preserves larger, harder elements best, mammals with their relatively large size and enamel-coated teeth tend to be more frequently recovered than other animal groups. Mammals are also key shapers of terrestrial ecosystems due to their roles as plant and animal consumers, and they have coevolved with plants over their long history. While fossil nonmammalian fauna, including birds, reptiles, and amphibians, are known as far back as the Eocene (at 50 Ma) (Brattstrom 1953, Brattstrom 1955, Campbell and Tonni 1981, Chandler 1990, Clark 1985, DeMay 1941, Guthrie 2009, Howard 1930, Howard 1978, Norell 1986), their record is much rarer than the mammal fossil record, thus this chapter focuses on the prehistory of the better-known mammalian fauna of California.

California ranks first in the United States for mammalian species richness with 223 mammalian species, including 181 terrestrial and 40 marine species (CDFG 2003). Approximately 10% of the mammalian fauna present in California are endemic to the state, more than any other state (Stein et al. 2000, NatureServe), and 25% of the North American mammalian species have at least part of their range in the state (NatureServe). The goals of this chapter are to explore the dynamics of diversity in California and to hypothesize how environments of the past, present, and future may affect diversity patterns in California animals. Because mammals regulate their own metabolism, they have different energetic and environmental needs than do other terrestrial animals—the reptiles and amphibians. Responses of reptiles and amphibians to the climatic changes of the past are less understood than those of mammals, and their ability to disperse across large distances is constrained. This chapter uses data from the fossil record to investigate the assembly of the unique California mammalian community.

California spans dramatic elevational extremes from below sea level to over 4,000 meters. This relief is squeezed into a 155-kilometer width, resulting in complex environmental replacement over very small spatial scales. This is reflected in biotic turnover between species and genetic divisions within species, creating a plethora of NEOENDEMIC hotspots in the state (Davis et al. 2008). California lies between the Pacific Northwest, with its abundant moisture preserving ancient lineages of temperate rainforest species, and the xeric Southwest, with its desert-adapted fauna. The high-elevation Sierra Mountains to the east and the cold, maritime influence in the west bound the unique Mediterranean climatic region of central California, found nowhere else in North America. Animals living in this area experience equable year-round temperatures but face summers without rain. Thus they encounter a mismatch between high moisture and plant productivity and the typical mammalian seasons of growth and reproduction. This mismatch means that animals in California must face unique evolutionary pressures for their survival and growth, including earlier estivation in hibernating animals such as squirrels, seasonal migration out of extremely dry regions, or creation of year-round residents in areas with enough summer moisture.

Mammals are important and charismatic elements of modern global ecosystems, and they play significant ecological roles in them. Mammals help to structure and determine the flow of energy through ecological communities by predation, seed dispersal, herbivory, and scavenging (Brown and Heske 1990, Johnson 1996). Their contribution to each of these is a function of their body size, local population abundance, and seasonal behavior. The particular influence of past climate on the mammals in general, including evolutionary forces that act over variable spatial and temporal scales, has been detailed elsewhere (Blois et al. 2010). This chapter focuses on the unique attributes of Californian geologic and geographic history and the myriad paleontological sites containing mammalian fossils in California to investigate the forces and dynamics behind the modern diversity patterns.

Fossil History of Mammals

Although mammals arose approximately two hundred million years ago (during the late Triassic Period), the California record of fossil mammals spans only the last eighty million years (Figure 9.1). Because most of California was underwater during the Cretaceous and early part of the Tertiary (100–20 Ma) (Figure 9.2), many of the earliest California fossil localities preserved mammals from nearshore marine deposits. Indeed, California preserves mostly marine deposits until about thirty-five million years ago, when the coastal shoreline was sprinkled with offshore islands and the edge of the continent was close to the present Nevada border. The dynamic tectonic activity of California has resulted in accretion of novel geologic substrates, basins of sediment accumulation, and uplifted ranges. This dynamism stores, and reveals, its fossil history as well.

Extensive preservation of fossiliferous deposits is particularly prevalent in the southern part of the state and almost completely absent in northern California, with only scattered cave and beach deposits preserving mammalian fossils (Figure 9.3). The difference in the number and diversity of exposed fossil-bearing deposits between northern and southern California is a result of a disparity in the abundance and age of sedimentary and tectonic environments of the two regions. Southern California is more tectonically active, and the eons of sediments stripped from the Grand Canyon by the Colorado River have buried millions of years of plant and animal paleocommunities. This record was buried by over 2,500 meters of continuous sediments, but subsequent more recent tectonic movements uplifted these basins into higher relief areas. These areas then eroded, exposing their fossils to paleontologists (e.g., Jefferson and Lindsay 2006, Lofgren et al. 2008, McKenna 1955, Woodburne et al. 1990, Wilson et al. 2003, Walsh 2013). Advancing and retreating shorelines in southern California have also led to burial of coastal mammalian communities and their exhumation. Northern California has much older (500–60 Ma) marine sediments and Cenozoic (66 Ma to present) volcanic rocks, unlikely to preserve terrestrial mammals (Parrish 2006), but sporadically pockmarked by stream deposits and caves containing sediments with fossils.

Paleocene (66–56 Ma)

Following the late Cretaceous extinction event of dinosaurs, pterosaurs, and marine reptiles, mammals rose as the dominant vertebrate animal on all the continental landmasses. North American mammalian diversity began at approximately twenty genera at the beginning of the Paleocene and within the next two million years, it rose to approximately seventy genera. Continents were mostly isolated from each other, although toward the end of the Paleocene migration of animals from Europe to North America and Asia was possible, demonstrated by a shared primate (*Teilhardina*), ARTIODACTYL (*Diacodexis*), and an extinct carnivore-like CREODONT (*Arfia*) (Smith et al. 2006). The Paleocene witnessed the close of the intercontinental sea that covered today's Great Plains during the Cretaceous (145–66 Ma), opening corridors of dispersal between eastern and western North America and permitting the mixing of faunas and floras.

Globally, a paucity of fossil localities preserve Paleocene mammals, although several important locales are known from South America and Europe. In North America rich Paleocene faunas are found in basins draining the nascent Rocky Mountains from Alberta to New Mexico. Paleocene mammal sites from the western coast are missing, except for a few localities: the Goler Formation (Lofgren et al. 2008) and Butte County (Wilson et al. 2003) in California, and sediments in Baja California (Lillegraven 1976) (see Figure 9.2). The Goler Formation near Garlock in southern California preserves the oldest and temporally the most diverse vertebrate assemblage from the last sixty-six million years in western North America. It contains the oldest (~60 Ma) identifiable mammalian fossils from the state (Lofgren et al. 2008; but see Wilson et al. 2003). The Chico Formation in Butte County, California (Wilson et al. 2003), preserves only frag-

Photo on previous page: Early excavations of the important Pleistocene California locality at Rancho La Brea, Los Angeles County, California. Standing in the foreground on the right, holding the hat, is Reginald C. Stoner, Merriam's field supervisor for the UC Berkeley excavations at La Brea from August 1912 to March 1913. Names of the six others in the photograph are unknown. Photo: John C. Merriam, originally published in Stoner 1913.

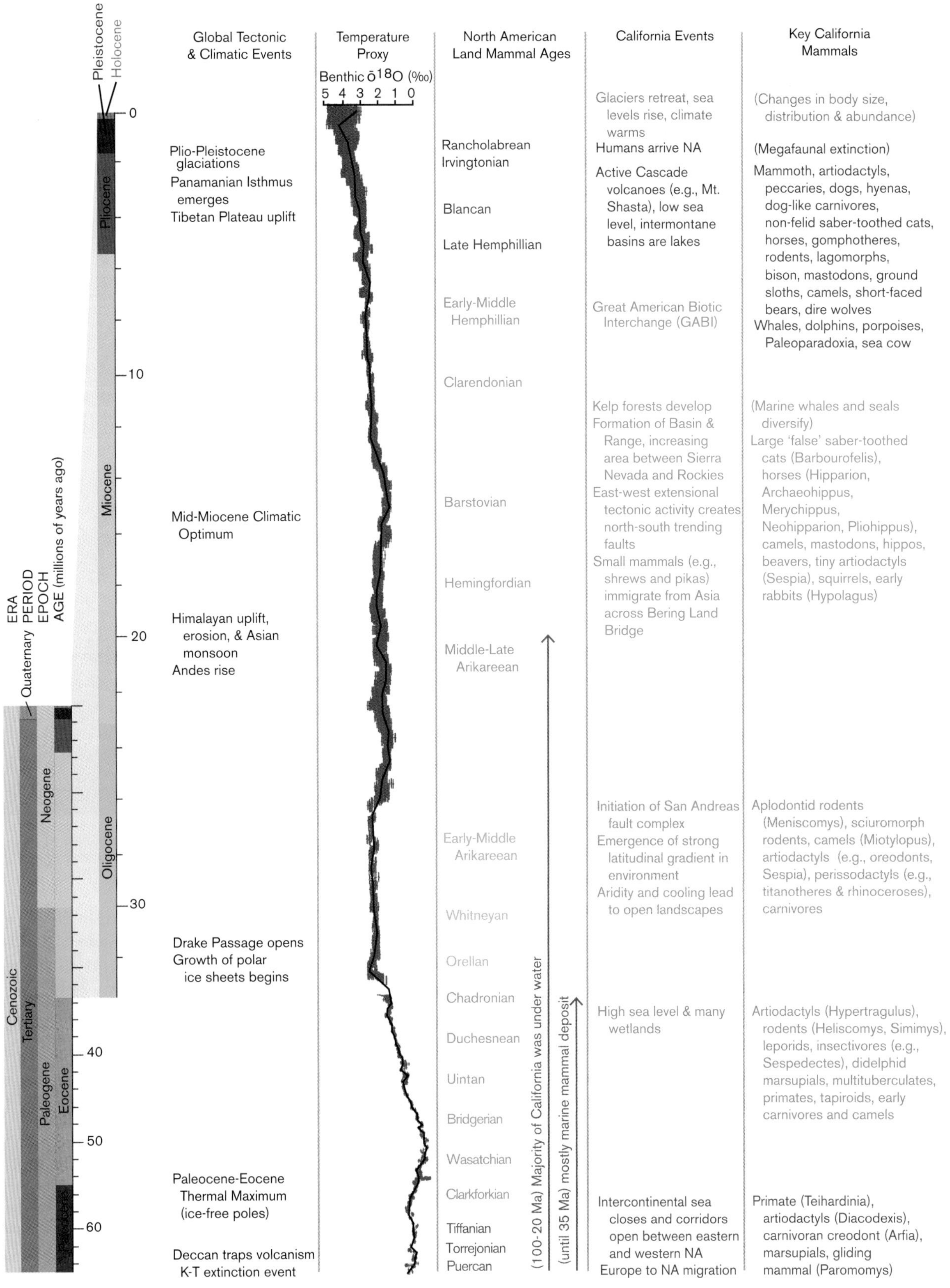

FIGURE 9.1 Timeline of global events relevant for the history of mammals in California. Source: Temperature data from Zachos et al. 2008.

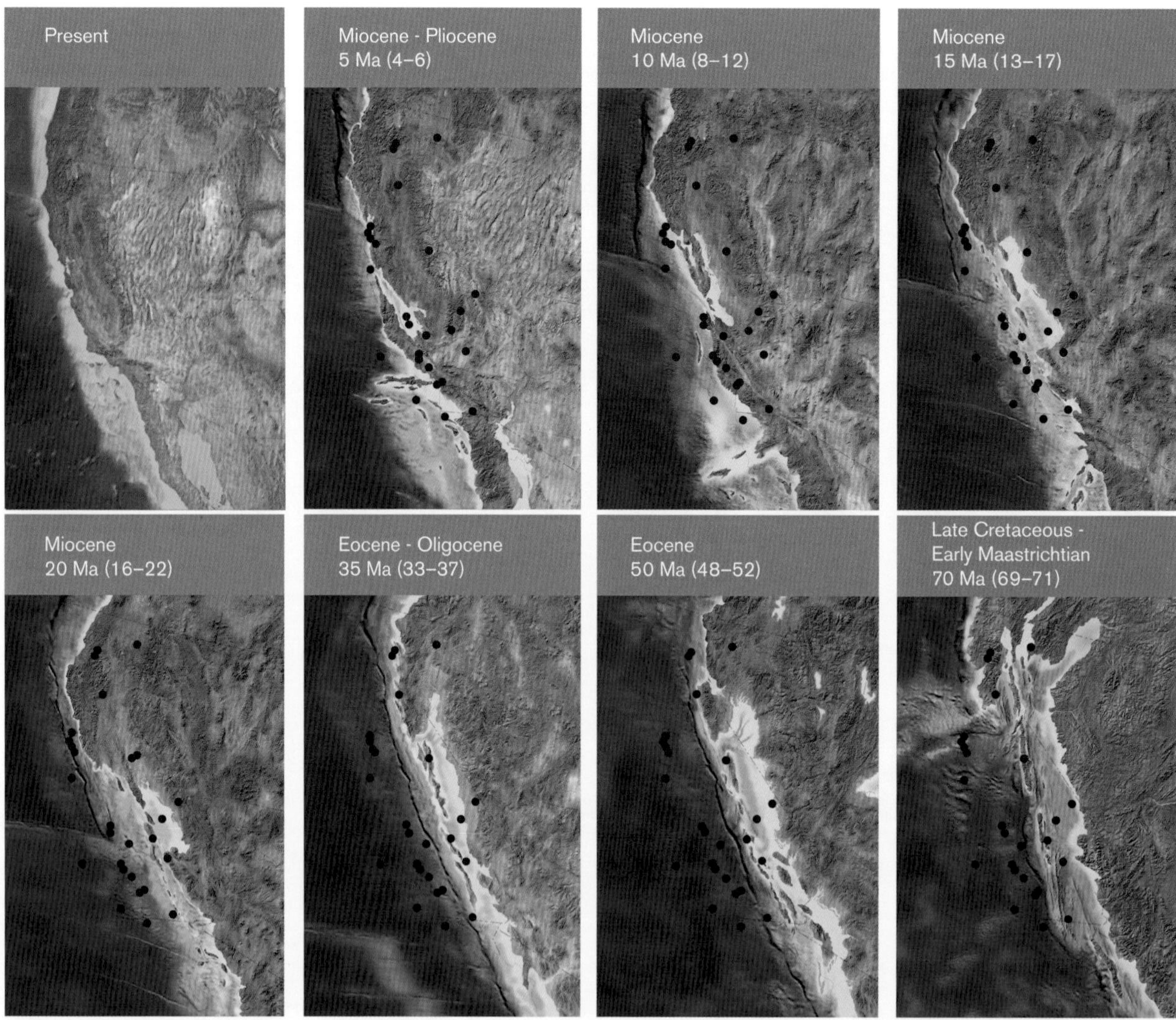

FIGURE 9.2 Western North America, with a focus on California, through the past seventy million years (Blakey 2011). Pleistocene and Holocene paleontological sites are labeled with black dots. Source: Maps modified with permission of R. Blakey (http://cpgeosystems.com). Localities compiled using MioMap (http://www.ucmp.berkeley.edu/miomap/). <http://cpgeosystems.com/>.

mentary and isolated mammalian remains. The depositional setting of the Goler Formation and its fossil assemblage represents the interfingering of marine and/or stream units with a terrestrial environment. The presence of fossil logs, some up to a few meters long, suggest a coastal wooded environment. This is also supported by evidence of mammals that include early arboreal primates, carnivores, marsupials, small ungulates, and an early gliding mammal, *Paromomys*. Fossil remains of these relatively small-bodied mammalian species and their relatives are also found in similarly aged deposits in the Rocky Mountain region, suggesting that there were few dispersal barriers during the Paleocene (66–56 Ma), unlike the mountains and desert borders of California today.

Paleocene mammals in California as elsewhere were relatively small and most had similar body forms, resembling but not related to modern squirrels. These early small mammals did have specialized cheek teeth, suggesting that they were already taking advantage of the myriad angiosperm plant tissues, including leaves, seeds, and fruits. Paleocene mammals included bizarre, highly specialized MULTITUBERCULATES, which possessed sawlike rounded cheek teeth specialized for eating seeds and left no living descendants. The multituberculates died out millions of years later (by the early Oligocene, about 30 Ma) as true rodents increased in diversity. Although the majority of Paleocene mammals were small herbivores, some were carnivorous and some were insectivorous. Insectivorous mammals included the marsupials, which radiated into the Southern Hemisphere, eventually going extinct in North America only to be recolonized during the Great American Interchange, about seven million years ago. Larger mammals from the early Paleocene had generalized herbivorous DENTITION, implying that they were less selective in their food; highly specialized browsers had not yet diversified.

The parallel increase in the sizes of angiosperm fruits and seeds and the increased specialization of the dentition of mammals suggests the beginning of the long, coevolutionary relationship between plants and mammals that continues today, especially in the tropics, where plants provide cover, habitat, and nutrition for mammals, and mammals disperse, pollinate, and fertilize plants. In some tropical plant communities, up to 98% of trees and shrubs rely on vertebrate dispersers, and most of these mammalian communities depend on fruits and seeds (Stoner and Henry 2007). Although the Paleocene encompassed a tremendous rise in mammalian diversity, few of these mammals would be recognizable to us today. Instead, the Paleocene might be viewed as a period

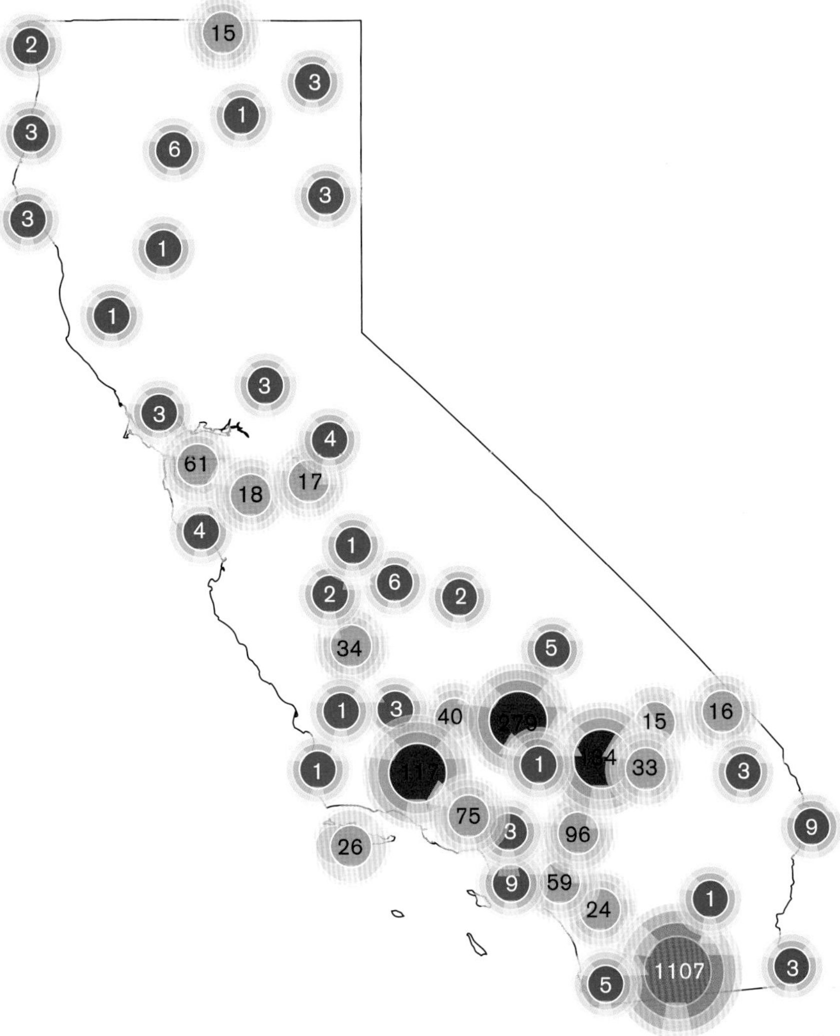

FIGURE 9.3 Map of paleontological localities in California from seventy million years ago to the present. Numbers in center of circles denote numbers of localities: 1–10 shown in blue, 11–100 shown in orange, 101–1000 shown in red, >1001 shown in purple. Note the much larger frequency of fossil localities in southern California compared with the northern part of the state. Source: miomap.berkeley.edu/neomap/search.html. Accessed June 9, 2015.

of experimentation for mammals. The end of the Paleocene was marked by the most extreme climatic change in the past sixty-six million years, the Paleocene-Eocene Thermal Maximum (PETM) (Zachos et al. 2005). During this short period of approximately ten thousand years, temperatures rose 5°C (Zachos et al. 2001), likely leading to the extinction of deep ocean foraminifera and further diversification of terrestrial mammals (Gingerich 2003).

Eocene (56–33.9 Ma)

The Eocene (see Figure 9.2) began with the extreme warmth of the PETM and ended with an abrupt cooling of global climate that resulted in growth of polar ice sheets at about 34 Ma. The Eocene was MESIC, with extensive terrestrial wetlands, forests, and high sea-level stands. Eocene frost-intolerant species of North America such as crocodiles, turtles and palm trees were found much further poleward than similar species are today. The western interior of North America to the east of present California had subtropical rainforests covering much of what are arid badlands today. Animals in these forests included diminutive early bats, horses, primates, ungulates, tapiroids, and rhinoceroses. In Oregon, figs, palms, and avocados thrived, with the few Eocene faunas preserving titanotheres, which were browsing giant rhino relatives; a horned rodent (*Epigaulus*); and creodonts, large carnivore-like predators that died out as true carnivores increased over the next tens of millions of years (Orr and Orr 1981). Californian faunas of the Eocene share more with faunas to the south and east (New Mexico, Colorado, and Wyoming) than with faunas to the north (Oregon), suggesting that barriers extended along an east-west axis in northern California, isolating the northern from the southern faunas. In Baja California, Mexico, the early Eocene fauna is very similar in composition to the same-age faunas of the western interior (Alberta to New Mexico), suggesting high dispersal between these areas (Novacek et al. 1991) that are almost 20 degrees of latitude apart.

In California, Eocene fossil localities are confined to the southern part of the state. Localities in San Diego County preserve evidence of diverse subtropical mammal communities comprised of artiodactyls (*Hypertragulus*), extinct rodents (*Heliscomys*, *Simimys*), leporids (rabbits and hares), insectivores including a hedgehog-like animal (*Sespedectes*), didelphid marsupials (ancestors of today's opossums), multituberculates, numerous primate species, tapiroids (tapir-like relatives), early carnivores, and camels (Robinson et al. 2004, Stock 1934, Walsh 1991, Walsh 1996). Eocene sites in northern California are absent. Earlier Eocene (~46 Ma) faunas of California are very similar to those of the Rocky Mountain region, but by 42 Ma, California faunas are remarkably distinct, suggesting new limitations to dispersal between these areas (Walsh 1991). Rocks from this time are preserved in the Sespe Formation from the southern part of the state (Robinson et al. 2004), which interfingers with marine deposits and is thought to represent a gradual westward retreat of the sea from southern California.

Mammals through the Eocene show expansion into a multiplicity of habitats, with early artiodactyls and perissodactyls (relatives of horses, rhinos, and tapirs) and carnivores increasing in size and species diversity. Rates of diversification in mammals were high and the faunal exchanges between Eurasia and North America led to opportunities for increasing local ecosystem complexity, while homogenizing continental faunas. Large terrestrial crocodilians were fearsome predators, and their presence demonstrated that even as far north as Wyoming and Oregon, freezing temperatures were absent. By the close of the Eocene, the subtropical climate began cooling, and the formerly closed forests opened, fostering—and possibly in part fostered by—increasing diversity of large, more specialized herbivores. The end of the Eocene is marked by a prolonged set of extinctions among some mammalian groups, with those adapted to tropical, less seasonal conditions dying out in California as in elsewhere.

Oligocene (34–24 Ma)

The Oligocene (see Figure 9.2) was a time period of active continental movement that dramatically influenced global climate. Antarctica, which had been drifting from South America for millions of years, finally separated at Drake Passage, enough to allow deep-water circulation to form around the continent by about 30 Ma (Zachos et al. 2001). This isolated the waters around Antarctica and catalyzed glaciation there. Initiation of Atlantic deep-water circulation, which characterizes the beginning of modern ocean circulation patterns also began in the early Oligocene. Volcanism and tectonics intensified in the western Americas, and global climates became considerably cooler and more arid. Major plate movements along the western coast of the North American continent caused initiation of the San Andreas fault complex—a geologic feature that remains significant for geographic variation in California to this day (Powell and Weldon 1992). A strong latitudinal gradient was established as grasslands began to increase globally, with a contraction of broadleaf forests toward the equator. Increased aridity and cooling led to the opening of landscapes, which is marked by an overall increase in the size of mammals during this time, when giant herbivores (BRONTOTHERES, UINTATHERES, and INDRICOTHERES) wandered the continents. Faunal similarity between Europe and North America suggests an Oligocene land bridge between continents, caused mostly by lowered sea levels.

Oligocene fossils are very rare in California, and all are from the coastal south or Death Valley. Mammalian diversity during the Oligocene in California appears low, mostly because of the small sample size of fossils due to the rarity of sites. Oligocene mammals of California include insectivores, APLODONTID rodents (*Meniscomys*), ancient squirrel relatives, camels (*Miotylopus*), artiodactyls including OREODONTS (*Sespia*), perissodactyls including TITANOTHERES, and rhinoceroses, carnivores, and camels (Deméré 1988, Lubar 2012, Stock and Bode 1935). Mammalian paleofaunas of the Oligocene indicate increasing complexity of habitats across the continent. Rapid morphological diversification suggests increasing predator-prey interactions and evolutionary escalation (Potts and Behrensmeyer 1992). This type of escalation means that herbivores evolved to extremely large size and specialized more in grazing and browsing dentition. Carnivores, including dogs and true cats, also got larger and both evolved heightened running abilities that are an advantage in open habitats. Other carnivores such as the catlike NIMRAVIDS, true bears, and dogs diversified. Seasonal climate dominated North America and, combined with a decrease in tree roots, served to develop soils that fostered a diversity of burrowing mammals, including mice, ground-dwelling squirrels, gophers, and rabbits. Open habitats were home to strange animals such as huge entelodonts, which were ferocious animals that looked like a cross between a pig and a rhino, and calicotheres, which had long thick necks, clawed front feet, and were about the size of a bear. Calicotheres probably used their claws to reach up into the canopy to forage on leaves, or they may have used their claws to dig open ant nests. Mixed forests housed oaks and the tree squirrels that ate them. The open grasslands of the Oligocene stimulated one of the most famous radiations of all time—that of the native North American horses, which progressed through the late Cenozoic.

Miocene (23.03–5.332 Ma)

The Miocene (see Figure 9.2) was a period of major tectonic uplift of the Himalayas, a consequence of the continental collision of India with Asia. Himalayan uplift eventually resulted in sequestering of the Asian monsoon, which is a critical catalyst in modern global climate and, by the terminal Pliocene, had resulted in initiation of glacial cycles characteristic of the latest Cenozoic (Raymo and Ruddiman 1992). The Andes also rose dramatically, with volcanic ash and the extreme rain shadow, leading to development of very xeric steppe and deserts. In North America mid-Miocene tectonics established the Basin and Range province, essentially doubling the land area between the Sierra Nevada and the Rockies. This is also the period of temporary global temperature increase, known as the mid-Miocene Climatic Optimum (14.8–14.5 Ma). Globally, rainforests contracted and grasslands continued to expand. Continental positioning was similar to the modern, and the present ocean circulation pattern was established. Kelp forests developed in nearshore environments, stimulating the evolution of marine faunas, including many marine mammals (Potts and Behrensmeyer 1992).

Globally, as in California, the Miocene mammalian fauna was similar to the modern fauna, except in South America and Australia, where evolutionarily divergent, unique lineages flourished. Marine whales and seals began to diversify. Many mammalian taxa that we see today diversified during early Miocene, such as dogs, cats, horses, raccoons, beaver, deer, camels, pocket gophers, rabbits, and mice. They coexisted with now-extinct taxa, including proboscideans (animals related to and including mammoths and mastodons), nimravids (false saber-tooth cats), entelodonts (giant piglike omnivores), camels, and a diversity of horned and hornless rhinos. About 20 Ma, small mammals including shrews and pikas immigrated from Asia across the Bering Land Bridge. By the end of the Miocene, evidence of the early phase of "waif immigrants" presaging the Great American Biotic Interchange (GABI) include the first appearance of giant ground sloths in North America (Lindsay et al. 1984).

About twenty million years ago, east-west extensional tectonic activity in North America began to dominate the environments of the western part of the continent, including California. Stretching of the continental crust lead to north-south trending faults and associated basins and ranges as the landscape increased in land surface area—as much as doubling—to accommodate the uplift. The increase in elevational relief in turn led to erosional deposition in the basins, preserving fossils. In California, areas dominated by this type of tectonic activity harbor more than a thousand Miocene fossil localities (Carrasco et al. 2005) preserving a rich record of both land and marine mammals from the time. Most of these localities are in the southern part of the state. The Barstow Formation, for which the Barstovian Land Mammal Age is named (Box 9.1), captured life between about 16 to 13 Ma in southern California. It contains one of the largest fossil assemblages in North America from the last 66 Ma (Dibblee 1968). Mammals roaming California then included large extinct false saber-tooth cats (*Barbourofelis*), a diversity of horses (*Hipparion, Archaeohippus, Merychippus, Neohipparion, Scaphohippus, Pliohippus*), camels, mastodons, hippos, beavers, tiny artiodactyls (*Sespia*), squirrels, and early rabbits (*Hypolagus*) (Creely et al. 1982, Lindsay 1972, Pagnac 2006, Pagnac 2009, Tedford et al. 2004, Woodburne et al. 1990).

For the middle Miocene the fossil record of California not only provides insights into mammalian evolution but also details into floral evolution and the development of modern ecosystems, specifically the origin and spread of the C_4 photosynthetic pathway. C_4 plants, characteristically found in warm-growing-season grasses and sedges (Ehleringer et al. 1991), play a significant role in modern ecosystems. This pathway, while found in only about 5% of plants (Ehleringer et al. 1991), accounts for about one-quarter of terrestrial photosynthesis and is used in many staple food crops (e.g., corn, millet) (Edwards et al. 2010). Even though molecular clock estimates imply an earlier origin, possibly to the late Oligocene, the earliest discovered fossil C_4 grass specimen is from the middle Miocene Dove Spring Formation of central California, dated to between 12.15 and 8.5 Ma (Nambudiri et al. 1978, Tidwell and Nambudiri 1989). However, C_4 plants were not globally abundant until the rapid increase in C_4 ecosystems event (known as the RICE) (Kohn and Cerling 2002) in the late Miocene (about 7 Ma).

Although the abundance of C_4 plants is considered negligible before the RICE, stable carbon isotope values of fossil tooth enamel, which originated from the ingested food (MacFadden and Cerling 1996) of Barstovian-aged herbivorous mammals, such as horses and pronghorn, imply a measureable abundance of C_4 plants (up to about 20%) in southern California well before the RICE (Feranec and Pagnac 2013). This abundance is similar to that suggested for the Neogene of the Great Plains (Fox and Koch 2003, 2004). Outside of southern California and the Great Plains, the abundance of this pathway does not appear geographically widespread during the middle Miocene, even in California (Feranec and MacFadden 2006). Local or regional abundance of C_4 plants may imply the greater importance of local or regional factors (e.g., local aridity) as opposed to global factors (e.g., atmospheric CO_2), controlling its abundance in particular geographic areas before the RICE.

In general, ecosystems of the Miocene became more spatially heterogeneous because of the isolation of basins and mountain-building that dominated western North America. Animals were found in all habitats, burrowing deep in soils, living high in the canopy, and grazing the increasingly grassy plains. The opening of basins not only stimulated opportunities for grasses to diversify but also permitted concentration of windborne ash to accumulate. This combination of high amounts of abrasive silica in both the glass phytoliths of grasses and the ashes deposited by the active volcanism led to

BOX 9.1 NORTH AMERICAN LAND MAMMAL AGES (NALMA)

The North American Land Mammal Ages are biochronological units defined by the presence and absence, especially the first appearance and last appearance, of particular mammal taxa in North America. The NALMA provide an additional technique to identify the ages of fossil mammals particularly when other techniques, such as radiometric dating, are not available. The different NALMA were originally based on mammal taxa from particular localities or regions or within a particular rock formation (Woodburne 2004). Currently, there are twenty NALMA for the Cenozoic (last sixty-six million years) of North America, and of these twenty, three are named and based on faunas that occurred in California, including the Barstovian, Irvingtonian, and Rancholabrean.

The Barstovian NALMA occurs within the middle Miocene between about 16 Ma to 13.3 Ma (Tedford et al. 2004) and was originally based on the faunas of the Barstow Formation of San Bernardino County, California. The beginning of the Barstovian is defined notably by the first appearance of *Plithocyon*, an extinct genus within the Hemicyoninae, a subfamily commonly referred to as "dog-bears" within the bear family (Ursidae). More recently, the Irvingtonian NALMA occurs from the early Pleistocene to the late middle Pleistocene between about 1.35 Ma to <0.27 Ma (Bell et al. 2004). It was based on the fauna occurring within the Irvington Gravels, a locality near San Francisco, California, and is defined by the first appearance of *Mammuthus* (mammoth) in North America below 55°N. The most recent NALMA, the Rancholabrean, occurs from the late middle Pleistocene to the end of the Pleistocene between about <270 ka to 11.7 ka and was originally based on the fauna from the Rancho La Brea tar pits in Los Angeles, California. The Rancholabrean is defined by the presence of *Bison*. The associations of mammals in these faunas thus provide not only information about ecology but also the opportunity to use the presence and absence of taxa and their association with other taxa as a means to date faunas and/or particular specimens.

an evolutionary response of herbivores. Across many groups of mammals (horses, rodents, camels, and artiodactyls), the shorter-statured browsing forms were augmented by groups of longer-limbed larger-sized animals with higher-crowned teeth. Their tall, sometimes ever-growing teeth favored these animal groups over browsers in the open gritty grasslands over time. Carnivores were also getting faster. Dogs, cats, and bears all had longer limbs and more specialized dentition for predation and scavenging in open country. Herding behavior likely developed in many large mammalian groups as a way to ensure survival in open habitats. Browsers also continued to specialize in patchy, wooded environments. Many groups in these habitats, including horses, dwarfed in size and developed more pointy snouts useful for targeting particular plant parts in thicker vegetation. Some proboscideans (elephant relatives) developed shovel-like lower teeth to root around in woodland soils. Western basins also drained into inland lakes, which hosted a rich diversity of aquatic life, including beavers, turtles, snakes, birds, and amphibians. It is from these lakeside habitats that many western Miocene fossils are derived (Potts and Behrensmeyer 1992).

Although specialization of local communities was high, many mammalian families had radiated into both forests and savannas, and diversity between localities was usually at the species and genus levels, not at the family level. But by the end of the Miocene, many of the browsing animals were gone, leaving a rich diversity of savanna species and a landscape in North America that looks very much like that of today, except along the California coastline, which still had several million years of evolution in store. Large inland embayments mostly separated northern from southern California and much of southwestern California had yet to form as land (see Figure 9.2). Miocene fossils from California include a diversity of dogs, cats, weasels, horses, camels, and rodents such as gophers, squirrels, and mice. In the southern part of the state, the high diversity of small mammals such as kangaroo mice and the running adaptations of larger animals indicated increasing arid and open savanna-like environments. Over nine genera of horses are found in California during this time, demonstrating the diversity of habitats and the prevalence of open landscapes (MIOMAP). The teeth of herbivorous mammals also indicate that their diet was increasingly abrasive through this time, a sign of the abundance of grasses and grit in the open environments (Janis et al. 2008).

Pliocene (5.332–2.588 Ma)

The Pliocene (see Figure 9.2) witnessed the emergence of the Isthmus of Panama (Zachos et al. 2001), a tectonically formed land bridge that led to the mixing of continental faunas of the Americas. Intercontinental migration via the Panamanian Isthmus and the Bering Land Bridge profoundly homogenized continental faunas, particularly for large mammals but also for key small mammal taxa. These events influenced the diversity of the California mammal community from both the south and north, respectively. The diverse cool temperate specialist vole lineage marks evolutionary and dispersal events in the northern high latitudes of Europe, Asia, and North America. Voles are characteristic of cool, grassy environments and, counter to most mammalian groups, their diversity is highest in the northern poleward latitudes. They are global index fossils for onset of Plio-Pleistocene cooling. In North America the vole, *Mimomys*, an Asia immigrant, first appeared in California about 4.8 Ma. This species marks the beginning of the Pliocene (Blancan) (Bell et al. 2004). Despite intercontinental sharing of faunas, however, most small mammal faunas of North America demonstrated extreme provinciality (Bell et al. 2004) over the last five million years, suggestive of increasing in situ local evolution and limited dispersal between biotic regions. Climates of the Pliocene began as warmer than today and sea levels were also higher, but at the close of the Pliocene (approximately 3 Ma) an abrupt global climatic cooling due to the uplift of the Tibetan Plateau led to the beginning of the Pleistocene Ice Ages (Raymo and Ruddiman 1992).

In California the Sierra Nevada and Cascade Mountain ranges formed and the southern San Andreas fault was activated, displacing some landscapes over 150 kilometers northward (Powell and Weldon 1992). The Pliocene record of mammalian community change is captured by an incredible fossil sequence from southern California. Indeed, the seven million years of fossil history in southern California, extending from the end of the Miocene through the present, is the most complete continuous record of biotic communities from that time period anywhere in the world (Jefferson and Lindsay 2006). The moving picture of the past there yields appreciation for the dynamics of biotic assemblages, the waxing and waning of species, and the roles that environment and isolation play in the generation and maintenance of diversity. The Colorado Delta, in particular the Anza-Borrego Desert, captured over 2,500 meters of sediments, which buried ancient riparian forests and vertebrate communities and is interfingered with volcanic ashes that help to accurately date the deposits. Over two hundred fossil localities from the Pliocene are found in California, most from southern California and the Bay Area. Pliocene mammal assemblages of California are well represented by a diversity of insectivores, bats, lagomorphs, rodents, carnivores, artiodactyls including deer, and now-extinct horses (*Nannipus*), bear-dogs (*Borophagus*), peccaries (*Platygonus*), shrub-ox (*Euceratherium*), camels (*Hemiauchenia*), rhinos (*Teleoceras*), and proboscideans (elephant relatives). Extinct forms of modern species in California mammal communities include the horse (*Equus*), pocket gophers (*Thomomys*), kangaroo rats (*Prodipodomys*), voles (*Mimomys, Pliopotamomys, Ondatra, Microtus*), cotton rat (*Sigmodon*), wood rats (*Neotoma*), gophers (*Geomys*), deer mice (*Peromyscus*), and hares (*Sylvilagus*). South American immigrants entering California during this time include the now-extinct ground sloths (*Glossotherium, Nothrotheriops*), extinct armadillo-like GLYPTODONTS (*Glyptotherium*), and porcupines (*Erethizon*).

The warmer then cooler Pliocene stimulated the further evolution of horses. Not only did the diversity of horses continue to remain high, the emergence of the direct ancestor of today's modern horse (*Pliohippus*) was marked by even longer limbs, with fewer digits. Indeed, *Pliohippus* maneuvered on a single toe (hoof), with a vestigial digit alongside it. Modern *Equus* would lose this extra toe. In California, as in the western continent, with the abundance of herbivores came an abundance and diversity of predators such as dogs, hyenas, weasels, bears, and saber-toothed cats (Carrasco et al. 2005).

Pleistocene (2.588 Ma–11,700 ybp)

The Pleistocene (see Figure 9.2) spans a series of major glacial cycles. As many as eleven major glaciations, with many more minor events, covered vast areas of high latitudes and high elevations with ice (Richmond and Fullerton 1986). Up to 30% of Earth's land mass was covered by ice at the peak of late Pleistocene glaciation, resulting in a compression of area occupied by a diverse mammalian fauna. Pleistocene mammalian community richness in North America was higher than it is today (Carrasco et al. 2009), in part due to the compression of species ranges into the smaller unglaciated land area that was then available and also because of the many large animal species then extant that are now extinct. California's Pleistocene landscape was similar to that of today, although lakes, rivers, and vegetation were configured differently. Many of today's dry intermontane basins, including the San Joaquin Valley, were lakes. The San Francisco Bay was an expansive grassland, and the Sacramento River flowed westward through the Golden Gate to the Farallon Islands (Keller 2009, Wells 1995; see Figure 9.2). The California coastline was exposed by sea level that was 120 meters lower than present day, extending the coast by as much as 80 kilometers. Cascade volcanoes such as Mount Shasta were actively erupting, and the high elevations of the Sierras were covered by ice hundreds of meters thick (Brocklehurst et al. 2008).

Because animals have evolved particular life histories, or ways of moving, eating, and reproducing, they are often confined to select regions that share similar environmental conditions. Indeed, some suites of mammals, particularly small mammals such as those from montane regions including the Sierra Nevada, have been found together since the Middle Pleistocene (Hadly et al. 2009, McGill et al. 2005). Similarly small mammal communities of arid lands—such as ground squirrels, kangaroo mice, kangaroo rats, hares, and rabbits—coexisted in the Pleistocene of California much as they do today. Small mammal communities over the past million years time show evolutionary replacement of species within genera instead of exchange of genera between different environments, suggesting stable and long-term coevolutionary relationships within these environments.

Over a thousand mammalian fossil localities distributed across California document the rich Pleistocene fauna in California (Carrasco et al. 2005). So important are the California localities that two Pleistocene land mammal ages are named after assemblages found there. In the San Francisco Bay area the Irvington gravel beds preserved a mammalian community of the earlier Pleistocene; the Irvingtonian Land Mammal Age (1.35–<0.27 Ma) is named for this assemblage (Bell et al. 2004). It is defined by presence of mammoth in California—the first in North America—and absence of bison, which first appear more recently than 270,000 years ago. This fauna includes artiodactyls, peccaries, bone-crushing dogs, hyenas, doglike carnivores, nonfelid saber-toothed cats, a diversity of horses, and GOMPHOTHERES. Extinct rodents, including giant marmots, and rabbit, hare, and pika relatives are also present, although it appears that the abundance of common small mammals during the Pleistocene may not have been as high as it is today (Blois et al. 2010). California's Pleistocene deposits are also rich in marine mammals, including ancestors of whales, dolphins, and porpoises (Janis et al. 2008). Marine mammals include the large herbivorous aquatic mammal *Paleoparadoxia*, which ranged in coastal waters from Baja California to Alaska to Japan. During the early Pleistocene (2.5–0.75 Ma), relatives of the now-extinct Stellar's sea cow were found in southern California waters (Graham and Lundelius 2010); extant members of the family Sirenidae now are confined to the Indo-Pacific region.

The Rancholabrean Land Mammal Age (Bell et al. 2004) (<0.27 Ma–0.011 Ma), named after the fauna recovered from the tar pits from Rancho La Brea, California, captured an enormous assemblage of animals and is perhaps the most famous of all Pleistocene localities in the world. Defined by first appearance of bison in North America, Rancholabrean fossil assemblages are often associated with extinct Pleistocene forms such as mammoths, mastodons, horses, ground sloths, camels, short-faced bears, saber-toothed cat (California's state fossil), and dire wolf. Although the majority of fossils from Rancho La Brea are carnivores, the sheer magnitude of fossil specimens (millions of identified bones) ensures an excellent sampling of the diversity of herbivores, including small mammals, birds, reptiles, amphibians, and fish. Isotopic evidence from the teeth of horses and bison from Rancho La Brea shows that these two animal species responded differently to seasonality (Feranec et al. 2009). Bison from the area used the local plants only during the late spring, while horses appear to have remained in the Los Angeles Basin year-round. This evidence supports an annual spring-summer migration out of the basin by bison, which fed on grasses with different isotopic signatures than are present in the basin, probably closer to the coast. Migration of bison may have been catalyzed by extreme seasonal variation in rainfall, characteristic of today's Mediterranean climate or by differences in ecological interactions between bison and other herbivores or their predators.

The end of the Pleistocene corresponds with the Late Glacial Maximum ice extent, arrival of humans to the North American continent, and extinction of a diversity of megafaunal mammals with body mass greater than 45 kilograms (100 pounds). Another megafaunal species, humans (an immigrant from Asia by way of the Bering Land Bridge), arrived to California by about 12,900 ybp to the Channel Islands (Johnson et al. 2002, Rick et al. 2012), concurrent with climatic warming and the disappearance of large mammals. The correspondence of these events in North America has provoked a century of hypotheses as to the cause of the late Pleistocene extinction event (Koch and Barnosky 2006) (see Chapter 10, "Indigenous California"). Most agree that the combination of human arrival, environmental disruption, and climatic change led to the demise of the megafauna, and data from northern California show that even small mammal communities were affected by these events (Blois et al. 2010). Although small mammals did not suffer extinctions at the terminal Pleistocene, their communities were reorganized, with a shift from very even Pleistocene small mammal abundances to the much more uneven abundances characteristic of the Holocene.

Holocene (11,700 ybp–Present)

The Holocene is the interglacial period that immediately followed the last glaciation, and the period in which we are living today. The Holocene is but one of many interglacial cycles that follow glaciations of the Pleistocene, and together the Pleistocene and Holocene make up the Quaternary (see Figure 9.1). During the Holocene the glaciers retreated; sea levels rose, submerging much of the California coastline; the climate warmed; and deserts formed in many North American basins that were formerly filled with lakes fed by the wetter, cooler glacial climate.

Globally, no new species of mammal evolved during the Holocene, and many of today's modern species are represented in the fossil record. These specimens document that the climatic change associated with the Pleistocene-Holocene transition and human activities have profoundly altered their abundance and distribution. In California several paleontological sites document the transition of the late Pleistocene through the Holocene (Akersten et al. 1983, Bell et al. 2004, Blois et al. 2010, Schultz 1937), although very few focus on the Holocene dynamics of mammals. Archaeological sites that span the Holocene focus on changes in the faunal assemblages as a function of cultural dynamics and climatic change (see Chapter 10, "Indigenous California"). Animals clearly have responded to changing climates as well. Body-size change coincident with climatic warming has been documented in ground squirrels (*Spermophilus*) of northern California, where squirrels of the Pleistocene were smaller than squirrels today (Blois et al. 2008).

Although mammals typically decrease in size with warming, the environments of northern California were hypothesized to have become locally wetter, leading to an increase in forage quality and thus body size. Small mammal community change and species turnover has been associated with the rise of generalist small mammal species such as deer mice (*Peromyscus*) (Blois et al. 2010). Changing abundances of small mammal specialists such as pocket gophers (*Thomomys* spp.) (Marcy et al. 2013) have been hypothesized as due to differences in seasonal temperature and moisture. Arguably, the increase in abundance of more "weedy" small mammals, mostly rodents, could have been due to the reduction in abundance of the diversity and abundance of megaherbivores at the end of the Pleistocene. Certainly the sculpting of the vegetation in both open country and along the margins of forests was influenced profoundly by large mammals, and the loss of these large animals opened opportunities for the expansion of small mammals into all habitats. Human-caused fire, directly or indirectly, could also have led to a disruption of habitats, further favoring weedy small mammals.

Climatic warming over the past century has also impacted the distribution of small montane mammals (Moritz et al. 2008). Resurveys of the areas occupied by small mammals in the Sierra Nevada have shown that high-elevation species such as the alpine chipmunk (*Tamias alpinus*) has contracted its lower-elevational limit upward by almost 600 meters (from 2,300 to 2,900 meters). Pikas (*Ochotona princeps*) have also been extirpated at lower elevations where they were present a century ago and are now found only at about 2,500 meters in the Yosemite area (Moritz et al. 2008).

The Holocene is marked by the dominance of evolutionarily modern humans (*Homo sapiens*) and our influence on every ecosystem on the planet. Human civilizations developed around the world throughout the Holocene, and human agriculture and domestication of livestock, urbanization, and the Industrial Revolution began to profoundly affect world climates. The Industrial Revolution corresponded with humanity's increasing use of natural resources and our exploitation of animals and their habitats. Human activities have resulted in a rise in greenhouse gases that are beginning to alter climate even further, increasing global temperatures (Solomon et al. 2007), decreasing habitats and poisoning the habitat remaining (Barnosky et al. 2012). The extinction of animal species has been escalating in the past century, and now, in addition to globally threatened reptiles, amphibians, and birds, so many global mammals are threatened (almost one out of four), that we are poised on the brink of the sixth mass extinction event in Earth's history (Barnosky et al. 2011).

Arrival to California of Europeans during the past few centuries corresponded with dramatic reduction in population sizes of large herbivores such as deer and Tule elk (Lidicker 1991). Deliberate predator control efforts caused the extirpation of the jaguar (by 1826), gray wolf (by 1924), and grizzly bear (by 1931). Similarly, the whaling and sealing industry of the late 1700s resulted in the extirpation of most of the marine mammal populations along the west coast (Newsome et al. 2007). Loss of these top predators resulted in cascading impacts through the ecosystem (Estes et al. 2011). For example, top predators such as wolves hold numbers of medium-sized canids such as coyotes down, allowing for smaller canids such as foxes to flourish. These small canids help to hold rodent numbers in check. Without the top predators, large herbivores can increase in abundance, heavily impacting their forage and spreading, and succumbing to, diseases. Urbanization, land clearing, and agriculture all have influenced extant mammal distributions in California. Indeed, habitat loss due to human population growth is the largest threat to mammalian diversity in California. The density of humans in California is now tenth in the U.S., with average density of 109.1 /km^2, although most of that density is confined to urban areas to the southern coastal and central California. Indeed, much of northern and eastern California is very lightly populated at 5.4 persons/km^2 (U.S. Census Bureau 2011). Introductions of non-native mammals (e.g., red fox, feral cats), and deliberate redistribution of native species have also changed native Californian mammalian communities (Lidicker 1991).

Summary

The long seventy-million-year history of mammals in California demonstrates how the waxing and waning of landscapes have enhanced the connectivity of California diversity with faunas across North America and contributed to its own unique evolution of faunas within it by creation of habitat, topographic barriers, and climate. The extraordinary and unique present mammalian diversity, a result of this long history, is now threatened by human activities locally and around the globe. We will certainly see extinction of many of our prized mammals in our lifetimes, as climates and environments change faster than evolution can adapt. Grasslands, once the birthplace of a plethora of uniquely North American mammals, are being lost as humans plow them into agricultural lands incapable of supporting grazing. Forests, home to the arboreal and terrestrial creatures that consume and disperse seeds and fruits, are also being lost, replaced frequently by monocultures of non-native trees void of understory and incapable of supporting the diverse seed-eating mammal communities long-evolved with forests. Surely the future will hold immigration of new species capable of dealing with these rapidly expanding human-dominated habitats, but we will see fewer and fewer of the animals characteristic of the long, diverse history of California.

Acknowledgments

We appreciate especially the invitation of Hal Mooney and Erika Zavaleta to write this chapter. Their suggestions very much improved the chapter. Thanks also to Cheng (Lily) Li for help with the figures and for her suggestions in the document. We are grateful also to Tony Barnosky for his valuable feedback and to Ron Blakey for permission to use his beautiful maps for Figure 9.2.

Recommended Reading

Bishop, E. M. 2003. In search of ancient Oregon. Timber Press, Portland, Oregon.

Harris, J. M., editor. 2001. Rancho La Brea: Death trap and treasure trove. Natural History Museum of Los Angeles County. Los Angeles, California. 56 pp.

Jefferson, G.T., and L. Lindsay, editors. 2006. Fossil treasures of the Anza-Borrego Desert. California State Parks. Sunbelt Publications, El Cajon, CA.

Schoenherr, A. A. 1995. Natural history of California. University of California Press, Berkeley, California.

Sinclair, W. J. 1907. The exploration of the Potter Creek Cave. University of California Publications in American Archaeology and Ethnology 2:1–27.

Stirton, R. A. 1939. Cenozoic mammal remains from the San Francisco Bay region. University of California Press Publications in Geological Sciences 24:339–410.

Stock, C. 1972. Rancho La Brea: A record of Pleistocene life in California. Los Angeles County Museum. Los Angeles, California.

Glossary

APLODONTIDAE A family of rodents that first evolved in the Oligocene. One species, *Aplodontia rufa*, commonly called the "mountain beaver," is extant, although the family is not closely related to modern beavers. Aplodontids show primitive features for rodents, particularly in the attachment of the masseter muscles.

ARTIODACTYL Members of the mammalian order Artiodactyla, commonly referred to as the "even-toed ungulates." Within this order, the middle of the foot passes between the third and fourth digits. The order includes animals such as pigs, cows, deer, and camels.

BRONTOTHERES An extinct family of mammals within the order Perissodactyla ("odd-toed ungulates") that existed in the Eocene. Typically large-sized and resembling a rhinoceros, the family is more closely related to horses than to rhinos. Many of the species are recognized by their unique nasal horns, which were composed of bone rather than the keratin horns of rhinos.

CREODONT An extinct order of carnivorous mammals that existed from the Paleocene to the Miocene. This group is closely related to the Carnivora. Like the Carnivora, many creodont species evolved a carnassial (shearing) tooth. But unlike the Carnivora, the upper carnassial was either the first or second molar, not the upper premolar.

DENTITION Generally referring to the type, characteristics, and arrangement of the teeth in the skull and jaw. For example, horses have a high-crowned (tall) dentition.

GLYPTODONT Members of an extinct family within the order Xenarthra. This family is composed of species that appear similar but much larger than (over 1800 kg) modern armadillos. Glyptodonts first evolved in the Miocene and went extinct during the late Pleistocene megafaunal extinction event at the end of the last Ice Age, about 11,700 years ago. The armor of glyptodonts and armadillos consists of scutes (osteoderms), which are connected pieces of dermal bone.

GOMPHOTHERES Members of an extinct family of Proboscidea, species within this group looked similar to modern elephants. Gomphotheres originate in the Miocene and may have existed until the early Holocene. This group can be distinguished from modern elephants by their teeth, which had cusps. Many species also had four tusks, two originating in the skull and two in the jaw.

INDRICOTHERES An extinct subfamily of mammals within the order Perissodactyla that existed from the Eocene into the Miocene. Exemplified by *Paraceratherium* (*Indricotherium*), the Indricotheres evolved to become the largest terrestrial mammal ever, having a weight of about 36,000 pounds (18 tons).

MESIC Typically associated with a type of habitat, "mesic" refers to a moderate amount of moisture input to that habitat. A mesic habitat is wetter than a xeric (dry) habitat, but drier than a hydric (wet) habitat.

MULTITUBERCULATES An extinct order of rodent-like mammals that existed from the Cretaceous (about 120 Ma) to the Oligocene. Similar to rodents, multituberculates had chisel-like incisors separated from the other teeth by a gap (diastema). This group of mammals is closely related to, but not within the clade of, modern placental and marsupial mammals (Theria).

NEOENDEMIC A reproductively isolated population that is generally restricted to a particular geographic range.

NIMRAVIDS Also known as the false saber-toothed cats, this extinct family of carnivorous mammals existed from the Eocene to the Miocene. Although it was likely closely related, it is not considered to be within the modern cat lineage (Felidae). For Nimravids, the saber-toothed canine evolved convergently with other saber-toothed taxa, such as the felid *Smilodon fatalis*.

OREODONTS A highly diverse group of herbivorous mammals of the extinct superfamily Merycoidodontoidea within the Artiodactyla. This group existed from the Eocene to the Pliocene. Many oreodont species were about the size of modern sheep but were more closely related to camels.

TITANOTHERES See Brontotheres.

UINTATHERES An extinct family of mammals that existed from the Paleocene to the middle Eocene. Although unrelated to modern artiodactyls and perissodactyls, these massive rhino-like animals had had bony bumps on their head and saber tooth–like canines.

References

Akersten, W. A., C. A. Shaw, and G. T. Jefferson. 1983. Rancho La Brea: Status and future. Paleobiology 9:211–217.

Insert: Barnosky, A. D., E. A. Hadly, J. Bascompte, E. L. Berlow, J. H. Brown, M. Fortelius, W. M. Getz, J. Harte, A. Hastings, P. A. Marquet, N. D. Martinez, A. Mooers, P. Roopnarine, G. Vermeij, J. W. Williams, R. G. Gillespie, J. Kitzes, C. Marshall, N. Matzke, D. P. Mindell, E. Revilla, and A. B. Smith. 2012. Approaching a state shift in Earth's biosphere. Nature. 486:52–58.

Barnosky, A. D., N. Matzke, S. Tomiya, G. Wogan, B. Swartz, T. Quental, C. Marshall, J. L. McGuire, E. L. Lindsey, K. C. Maguire, B. Mersey, and E. A. Ferrer. 2011. Has the Earth's sixth mass extinction already arrived? Nature 471:51–57.

Bell, C. J., E. L. Lundelius Jr., A. D. Barnosky, and R. W. Graham, E. H. Lindsay, D. R. Ruez, H. A. Semkem Jr., S. D. Webb, and R. J. Zakrzewski. 2004. The Blancan, Irvingtonian, and Rancholabrean mammal ages. Pages 232–314 in M. O. Woodburne, editors. Late Cretaceous and Cenozoic Mammals of North America: Biostratigraphy and Geochronology. Columbia University Press, New York, New York.

Blakey, R. 2011. Paleogeographic and tectonic history of southwestern North America: Colorado Plateau, Southern, and Central Rocky Mountains, Basin and Range, Pacific Margin. Colorado Plateau Geosystems, Inc. <http://cpgeosystems.com/index.html>. Accessed June 9, 2015.

Blois, J. L., R. S. Feranec, and E. A. Hadly. 2008. Environmental influences on spatial and temporal patterns of body-size variation in

California ground squirrels (*Spermophilus beecheyi*). Journal of Biogeography 35:602–613.
Blois, J. L., J. L. McGuire, and E. A. Hadly. 2010. Small mammal diversity loss in response to late-Pleistocene climatic change. Nature 465:771–774.
Brattstrom, B. H. 1955. New snakes and lizards from the Eocene of California. Journal of Paleontology 29:145–149.
———. 1953. Records of Pleistocene reptiles from California. Copeia 1953:174–179.
Brocklehurst, S. H., K. X. Whipple, and D. Foster. 2008. Ice thickness and topographic relief in glaciated landscapes of the western USA. Geomorphology 97:35–51.
Brown, J. H., and E. J. Heske. 1990: Control of a desert-grassland transition by a keystone rodent guild. Science 250:1705–1707.
California Department of Fish and Game (CDFG). 2008a. Complete List of amphibian, reptile, bird, and mammal species in California. September. https://www.dfg.ca.gov/biogeodata/cwhr/pdfs/species_list.pdf. Accessed August 8, 2012.
———. 2008b. Mammal species of special concern. http://www.dfg.ca.gov/wildlife/nongame/ssc/. Accessed August 8, 2012.
———. 2003. Atlas of the biodiversity of California. State of California. The Resources Agency, Department of Fish and Game. Sacramento, California.
Campbell, K. E., Jr., and E. P. Tonni. 1981. Preliminary observations on the paleobiology and evolution of teratorns (Aves: Teratornithidae). Journal of Vertebrate Paleontology 1:265–272.
Carrasco, M. A., A. D. Barnosky, and R. W. Graham. 2009. Quantifying the extent of North American mammal extinction relative to the pre-anthropogenic baseline. Public Library of Science One 4:e8331. <doi:10.1371/journal.pone.0008331>.
Carrasco, M. A., B. P. Kraatz, E. B. Davis, and A. D. Barnosky. 2005. Miocene Mammal Mapping Project (MIOMAP). University of California Museum of Paleontology. <http://www.ucmp.berkeley.edu/miomap/>. Accessed June 9, 2015.
Chandler, R. M. 1990. Part II: Fossil birds of the San Diego Formation, late Pliocene, Blancan, San Diego County, California. Ornithological Monographs 44:73–161.
Clark, J. M. 1985. Fossil plethodontid salamanders from the latest Miocene of California. Journal of Herpetology 19:41–47.
Creely, S., D. E. Savage, and B. A. Ogle. 1982. Stratigraphy of Upper Tertiary nonmarine rocks of central Contra Costa Basin, California. Pages 11–22 in Ingersoll, R. V., and M. O. Woodburne, editors. Cenozoic nonmarine deposits of California and Arizona. Pacific Section, Society of Economic Paleontologists and Mineralogists. Tulsa, OK.
Davis, E.B., M. S. Koo, C. Conroy, J. L. Patton, and C. Moritz. 2008. The California hotspots project: Identifying regions of rapid diversification of mammals. Molecular Ecology 17:120–138.
DeMay, I. S. 1941. Quaternary bird life of the McKittrick asphalt, California. Carnegie Institution of Washington, Publication 530:35–60.
Deméré, T. A. 1988. Early Arikareean (late Oligocene) vertebrate fossils and biostratigraphic correlations of the Otay Formation at Eastlake, San Diego County, California. Pages 35–44 in M. V. Filewicz and R. L. Squires, editors. Paleogene stratigraphy, West Coast of North America, Pacific Section SEPM. West Coast Paleogene Symposium, 58:251–263. Tulsa, OK.
Dibblee, T. W., Jr. 1968. Geology of the Fremont Peak and Opal Mountain Quadrangles, California. California Division of Mines and Geology, San Francisco, California.
Edwards, E. J., C. P. Osborne, C.A.E. Stromberg, S. A. Smith, and C4 grass consortium. 2010. The origins of C4 grasslands: Integrating evolutionary and ecosystem science. Science 328:587–591.
Ehleringer, J. R., R. F. Sage, L. B. Flanagan, and R. W. Pearcy. 1991. Climate change and the evolution of C_4 photosynthesis. Trends in Ecology and Evolution 6:95–99.
Estes, J. A., J. Terborgh, J. S. Brashares, M. E. Power, J. Berger, W. J. Bond, S. R. Carpenter, T. E. Essington, R. D. Holt, J. B. C. Jackson, R. J. Marquis, L. Oksanen, T. Oksanen, R. T. Paine, E. K. Pikitch, W. J. Ripple, S. A. Sandin, M. Scheffer, T. W. Schoener, J. B. Shurin, A. R. E. Sinclair, M. E. Soulé, R. Virtanen, and D. A. Wardle. 2011. Trophic downgrading of planet Earth. Science 333:301–306.
Feranec, R. S., E. A. Hadly, and A. Paytan. 2009. Stable isotopes reveal seasonal competition for resources between late Pleistocene bison (*Bison*) and horse (*Equus*) from Rancho La Brea, southern California. Palaeogeography, Palaeoclimatology, Palaeoecology 271:153–160.
Feranec, R. S., and B. J. MacFadden. 2006. Isotopic discrimination of resource partitioning among ungulates in C_3–dominated communities from the Miocene of Florida and California. Paleobiology 32:191–205.
Feranec, R. S., and D. Pagnac. 2013. Stable carbon isotope evidence for the abundance of C4 plants in the middle Miocene of southern California. Palaeogeography, Palaeoclimatology, Palaeoecology 388:42–47.
Fox, D. L., and P. L. Koch. 2004. Carbon and oxygen isotopic variability in Neogene paleosol carbonates: Constraints on the evolution of the C_4-grasslands of the Great Plains, USA. Palaeogeography, Palaeoclimatology, Palaeoecology 207:305–330.
———. 2003. Tertiary history of C_4 biomass in the Great Plains, USA. Geology 31:809–812.
Gingerich, P. D. 2003. Mammalian responses to climate change at the Paleocene-Eocene boundary: Polecat Bench record in the northern Bighorn Basin, Wyoming. Pages 463–78 in S. L. Wing, editor. Causes and consequences of globally warm climates in the early Paleogene. Geological Society of America 369. <doi:10.1130/0-8137-2369-8.463. ISBN 978-0-8137-2369-3>.
Graham, R. W., and E. L. Lundelius. 2010. FAUNMAP II: New data for North America with a temporal extension for the Blancan, Irvingtonian, and early Rancholabrean. FAUNMAP II Database, version 1.0. <http://www.ucmp.berkeley.edu/faunmap/about/citation.html>. Accessed June 9, 2015.
Guthrie, D. A. 2009. An updated catalogue of the birds from the Carpinteria Asphalt, Pleistocene of California. Bulletin of the Southern California Academy of Sciences 108:52–62.
Hadly, E. A., P. A. Spaeth, and C. Li. 2009. Niche conservatism above the species level. Proceedings of the National Academy of Sciences 106:19707–19714.
Howard, H. 1978. Late Miocene marine birds from Orange County, California. Natural History Museum of Los Angeles County 290:1–26.
———. 1930. A census of the Pleistocene birds of Rancho La Brea from the collections of the Los Angeles Museum. Condor 32:81–88.
Janis, C. M., G. F. Gunnell, and M. D. Uhen, editors. 2008. Evolution of tertiary mammals of North America. Volume 2, Small Mammals, Xenarthrans, and Marine Mammals. Cambridge University Press, Cambridge. 795 pp.
Jefferson, G. T., and L. Lindsay. 2006. Fossil treasures of the Anza-Borrego Desert. Sunbelt Publications, El Cajon, California. 394 pp.
Johnson, C. N. 1996. Interactions between mammals and ectomychorrhizal fungi. Trends in Ecology and Evolution 11:503–507.
Johnson, J. R., T. W. Stafford Jr., H. O. Ajie, and D. P. Morris. 2002. Arlington Springs Revisited. Pages 541–545 in D. Browne, K. Mitchell, and H. Chaney, editors. Proceedings of the Fifth California Islands Symposium. USDI Minerals Management Service and The Santa Barbara Museum of Natural History, Santa Barbara, CA.
Keller, B. R. 2009. Literature review of unconsolidated sediment in San Francisco Bay and nearby Pacific Ocean coast. San Francisco Estuary and Watershed Science 7. <http://repositories cdlib.org/jmie/sfews/vol7/iss1/art2>. Accessed June 9, 2015.
Koch, P. L., and A. D. Barnosky. 2006. Late Quaternary extinctions: State of the debate. Annual Review of Ecology, Evolution, and Systematics 37:215–250.
Kohn, M. J., and T. E. Cerling. 2002. Stable isotope compositions of biological apatite. Reviews in Mineralogy and Geochemistry 48:455–488.
Lidicker, W. A. 1991. Introduced mammals in California. Pages 263–272 in R. H. Groves and F. Di Castri, editors. Biogeography of Mediterranean Invasions. Cambridge University Press, Cambridge UK.
Lillegraven, J. A. 1976. A new genus of therian mammal from the late Cretaceous "El Gallo Formation," Baja California, Mexico. Journal of Paleontology 50:437–443.
Lindsay, E. H., N. D. Opdyke, and N. M. Johnson. 1984. Blancan-Hemphillian land mammal ages and late Cenozoic mammal dispersal events. Annual Review of Earth and Planetary Sciences 12:445–488.
———. 1972. Small mammal fossils from the Barstow Formation, California. University of California Publications in Geologi-

cal Sciences Volume 93. University of California Press, Berkeley, California.
Lofgren, D. L., J. G. Honey, M. C. McKenna, R. L. Zondervan, and E. E. Smith. 2008. Paleocene primates from the Goler Formation of the Mojave Desert in California. Natural History Museum of Los Angeles County. Science Series 41:11–28.
Lubar, C. A. 2012. Fossil camels from the late Oligocene Eastlake local fauna, Otay Formation, San Diego County, California. GSA Annual Meeting, Paper No. 27-27. <https://gsa.confex.com/gsa/2012AM/finalprogram/abstract_208427.htm>. Accessed June 9, 2015.
MacFadden, B. J., and T. E. Cerling. 1996. Mammalian herbivore communities, ancient feeding ecology, and carbon isotopes; a 10 million-year sequence from the Neogene of Florida. Journal of Vertebrate Paleontology 16:103–115.
Marcy, A. E., S. Fendorf, J. L. Patton, and E. A. Hadly. 2013. Morphological adaptations for digging and climate-impacted soil properties define pocket gopher (*Thomomys* spp.) distributions. PLoS One e64935.
McGill, B. J., E. A. Hadly, and B. A. Maurer. 2005. Community inertia of Quaternary small mammal assemblages in North America. Proceedings of the National Academy of Sciences 102:16701–16706.
McKenna, M. C. 1955. Paleocene mammal, Goler Formation, Mojave Desert, California. Bulletin of the American Association of Petroleum Geologists 39:512–515.
Moritz, C., J. L. Patton, C. J. Conroy, J. L. Parra, G. C. White, and S. R. Bessigner. 2008. Impact of a century of climate change on small-mammal communities in Yosemite National Park, USA. Science 322:261–264.
Nambudiri, E.M.V., W. D. Tidwell, B. N. Smith, and N. P. Hebbert. 1978. A C_4 plant from the Pliocene. Nature 276:816–817.
NatureServe. <www.natureserve.org>. Accessed June 9, 2015.
Newsome, S. D., M. A. Etnier, D. Gifford-Gonzalez, et al. 2007. The shifting baseline of northern fur seal ecology in the northeast Pacific Ocean. Proceedings of the National Academy of Sciences, USA 104:9709–9714.
Norell, M. A. 1986. Late Pleistocene lizards from Kokoweef Cave, San Bernardino County, California. Copeia 10:244–246.
Novacek, M. J., I. Ferrusquia-Villafranca, J. J. Flynn, A. R. Wyss, and M. A. Norell. 1991. Wasatchian (early Eocene) mammals and other vertebrates from Baja California, Mexico: The Lomas Las Tetas de Cabra fauna. Bulletin of the American Museum of Natural History 208:1–88.
Orr, W. N., and E. L. Orr. 1981. Handbook of Oregon plants and animal fossils. William N. and Elizabeth L. Orr, Eugene, OR.
Pagnac, D. 2009. Revised large mammal biostratigraphy and biochronology of the Barstow Formation (middle Miocene), California. PaleoBios 29:48–59.
———. 2006. *Scaphohippus*, a new genus of horse (Mammalia: Equidae) from the Barstow Formation of California. Journal of Mammalian Evolution 13:37–61.
Parrish, J. G. 2006. Geologic map of California, Map Sheet 57. California Department of Conservation, California Geological Survey. http://www.conservation.ca.gov/cgs/information/publications/ms/Documents/MS057.pdf. Accessed July 29, 2015.
Potts, R., and A. K. Behrensemeyer. 1992. Late Cenozoic terrestrial ecosystems. Pages 418–541 in A. K. Behrensmeyer, J. D. Damuth, W. A. DiMichele, R. Potts, H.-D. Sues, and S. L. Wing, editors. Terrestrial Ecosystems through Time, University of Chicago Press, Chicago, IL.
Powell, R. E., and R. J. Weldon. 1992. Evolution of the San Andreas fault. Annual Reviews of Earth and Planetary Science 20: 431–468.
Raymo, M. E., and W. F. Ruddiman. 1992. Tectonic forcing of late Cenozoic climate. Nature 359:117–122.
Richmond, G.M., and D. S. Fullerton. 1986. Summation of Quaternary glaciations in the United States of America. Quaternary Science Reviews 5:183–196.
Rick, R.C., C. A. Hofman, T. J. Braje, J. E. Maldonado, T. S. Sillett, K. Danchisko, and J. M. Erlandson. 2012. Flightless ducks, giant mice, and pygmy mammoths: Late Quaternary extinctions on California's Channel Islands. World Archaeology 44:3–20.
Riddle, B. R., D. J. Hafner, L. F. Alexander, and J. R. Jaeger. 2000. Cryptic vicariance in the historical assembly of a Baja California Peninsular Desert biota. Proceedings of the National Academy of Sciences 97:14438–14443.
Robinson, P., G. F. Gunnell, S. L. Walsh, W. C. Clyde, J. E. Storer, R. K. Stucky, D. J. Froehlich, I. Ferrusquia-Villafranca, and M. C. McKenna. 2004. Wasatchian through Duchesnean biochronology. Pages 106–155 in M. O. Woodburne, editor. Late Cretaceous and Cenozoic Mammals of North America. Columbia University Press, New York.
Savage, D. E. 1951. Late Cenozoic vertebrates of the San Francisco Bay region. University of California Publications Bulletin of the Department of Geological Sciences 28:215–314.
Smith, T., K. S. Rose, and P. D. Gingerich. 2006. Rapid Asia-Europe-North America geographic dispersal of earliest Eocene primate *Teilhardina* during the Paleocene-Eocene Thermal Maximum. Proceedings of the National Academy of Sciences 103:11223–11227.
Solomon, S., M. Qin, M. Manning, Z. Chen, M. Marquis, K. B. Averyt, M. Tignor, and H. L. Miller, editors. 2007. Contribution of working group I to the fourth assessment report of the Intergovernmental Panel on Climate Change, Cambridge University Press, Cambridge, UK and New York.
Stein, B. A., L. S. Kutner, and J. S. Adams. 2000. Precious heritage: The status of biodiversity in the United States. The Nature Conservancy and Association for Biodiversity Information. Oxford University Press, New York, New York.
Stock, C. 1934. A hypertragulid from the Sespe uppermost Eocene, California. Proceedings of the National Academy of Sciences 20:625–629.
Stock, C., and F. D. Bode. 1935. Occurrence of lower Oligocene mammal-bearing beds near Death Valley, California. Proceedings of the National Academy of Sciences 21:571–579.
Stoner K. E., and M. Henry. 2007. Seed dispersal and frugivory in tropical ecosystems. Encyclopedia of life support systems. UNESCO-EOLSS, Paris, France.
Stoner, R. 1913. Recent observations on the mode of accumulation of the Pleistocene bone deposits of Rancho La Brea. University of California Publications. Bulletin of the Department of Geology 7(20):387–396.
Tedford, R. H., L. B. Albright III, A. D. Barnosky, I. Ferrusquia-Villafranca, R. M. Hunt Jr., J. E. Storer, C. C. Swisher III, M. R. Voorhies, S. D. Webb, and D. P. Whistler. 2004. Mammalian biochronology of the Arikareean through Hemphillian interval (late Oligocene through early Pliocene epochs). Pages 169–231 in M. O. Woodburne, editor. Late Cretaceous and Cenozoic Mammals of North America: Biostratigraphy and Geochronology. Columbia University Press, New York, New York.
Tidwell, W. D., and E.M.V. Nambudiri. 1989. *Tomlinsonia thomassonii*, gen. et sp. nov., a permineralized grass from the upper Miocene Ricardo Formation, California. Review of Palaeobotany and Palynology 60:165–177.
U.S. Census. 2010. State Area Measurements and Internal Point Coordinates. United States Census Bureau. February 11, 2011. https://www.census.gov/geo/reference/state-area.html. Accessed December 21, 2011.
Walsh, S. L. 2013. New myomorph rodents from the Eocene of southern California. Journal of Vertebrate Paleontology 30(5):1610–1621.
———. 1996. Middle Eocene mammal faunas of San Diego County, California. Pages 74–114 in Prothero, D.R. and R. J. Emry, editors. The terrestrial Eocene-Oligocene transition in North America. Cambridge University Press, Cambridge, UK.
———. 1991. Eocene mammal faunas of San Diego County. Pages 161–178 in P. L. Abbott and J. A. May, editors. Eocene Geologic History San Diego Region. Pacific Section SEPM 68, Tulsa, Oklahoma.
Wells, L. E. 1995. Environmental setting and Quaternary history of the San Francisco Estuary. Pages 237–250 in E. M. Sanginfis, D. W. Andersen, and A. B. Buising, editors. Recent Geologic Studies in the San Francisco Bay Area. Pacific Section SEPM 76, Tulsa, Oklahoma.
Wilson, G. P., R. P. Hilton, and E. C. Göhre. 2003. The first Mesozoic mammal from California. PaleoBios 23:20–23.
Woodburne, M. O. 2004. Principles and procedures. Pages 1–20 in M. O. Woodburne, editor. Late Cretaceous and Cenozoic mammals of North America: Biostratigraphy and geochronology. Columbia University Press, New York, New York.
Woodburne, M. O., and C. C. Swisher. 1995. Land mammal high-resolution geochronology, intercontinental overland dispersals,

sea level, climate, and vicariance. Geochronology Time Scales and Global Stratigraphic Correlation, SEPM Special Publication No. 54:335–364.

Zachos, J.C., G. R. Dickens, and R. E. Zeebe. 2008. An early Cenozoic perspective on greenhouse warming and carbon-cycle dynamics. Nature 451:279–283. <doi:10.1038/nature06588>.

Zachos, J. C., U. Röhl, S. A. Schellenberg, A. Sluijs, D. A. Hodell, D. C. Kelly, E. Thomas, M. Nicolo, I. Raffi, L. J. Lourens, H. McCarren, and D. Kroon. 2005. Rapid acidification of the ocean during the Paleocene-Eocene thermal maximum. Science 308:1611–1615.

Zachos, J., M. Pagani, L. Sloan, E. Thomas, and K. Billups. 2001. Trends, rhythms, and aberrations in global climate 65 Ma to present. Science 292:686–693.

TEN

Indigenous California

TERRY L. JONES and KACEY HADICK

Introduction

In 1769, when Spanish padres first set foot in what is San Diego today, California was home to at least 340,000 and possibly more Native people whose occupancy extended back 13,000 years (Baumhoff 1963; Cook 1978). Not only was California populous but at the time of the arrival of Europeans it was also marked by both a startling degree of cultural diversity—reflected by a complex linguistic mosaic (Figure 10.1)—and relatively small-scale political organization. The speakers of no fewer than seventy-eight distinct languages (Golla 2011) resided in sedentary and semisedentary villages organized into four hundred to five hundred microtribes or "tribelets," each with populations between two hundred and six hundred individuals. All of these people made their living by hunting and trapping wild game and collecting a multitude of shellfish, herbs, seeds, nuts, and fruits—without farming. Tribelets in different areas focused on different suites of resources, including salmon and elk in the northwest, deer and acorns in central California, marine fish in the Channel Islands, and agave and mesquite in the southern deserts. Indeed, the remarkable variety of its natural habitats was one factor that contributed to the diversity of California's prehistoric cultures, the other being its position along the Pacific gateway into the New World from northeast Asia.

The linguistic record suggests that over the course of more than 13,000 years a great number of different groups moved into the state, some of whom remained and settled in, while others continued on to other parts of North and South America. Those who stayed developed extensive knowledge of the California environment, discovering and exploiting nearly every possible edible commodity including some foods like the acorn (a primary dietary staple in all of Native California) (Heizer 1978) that required sophisticated, labor-intensive handling (Basgall 1987, Gifford 1971). They also developed knowledge that allowed them to skillfully modify the landscape through controlled burning (Anderson 2005, Lewis 1973). Such salient facts notwithstanding, the exact role that indigenous peoples played in the evolution of California's ecosystems over the long term of their residence remains a matter of uncertainty and debate. Over the past several centuries opinions have evolved toward two alternative positions: one that views indigenous peoples as powerful but benevolent conservators and another that attributes to them certain

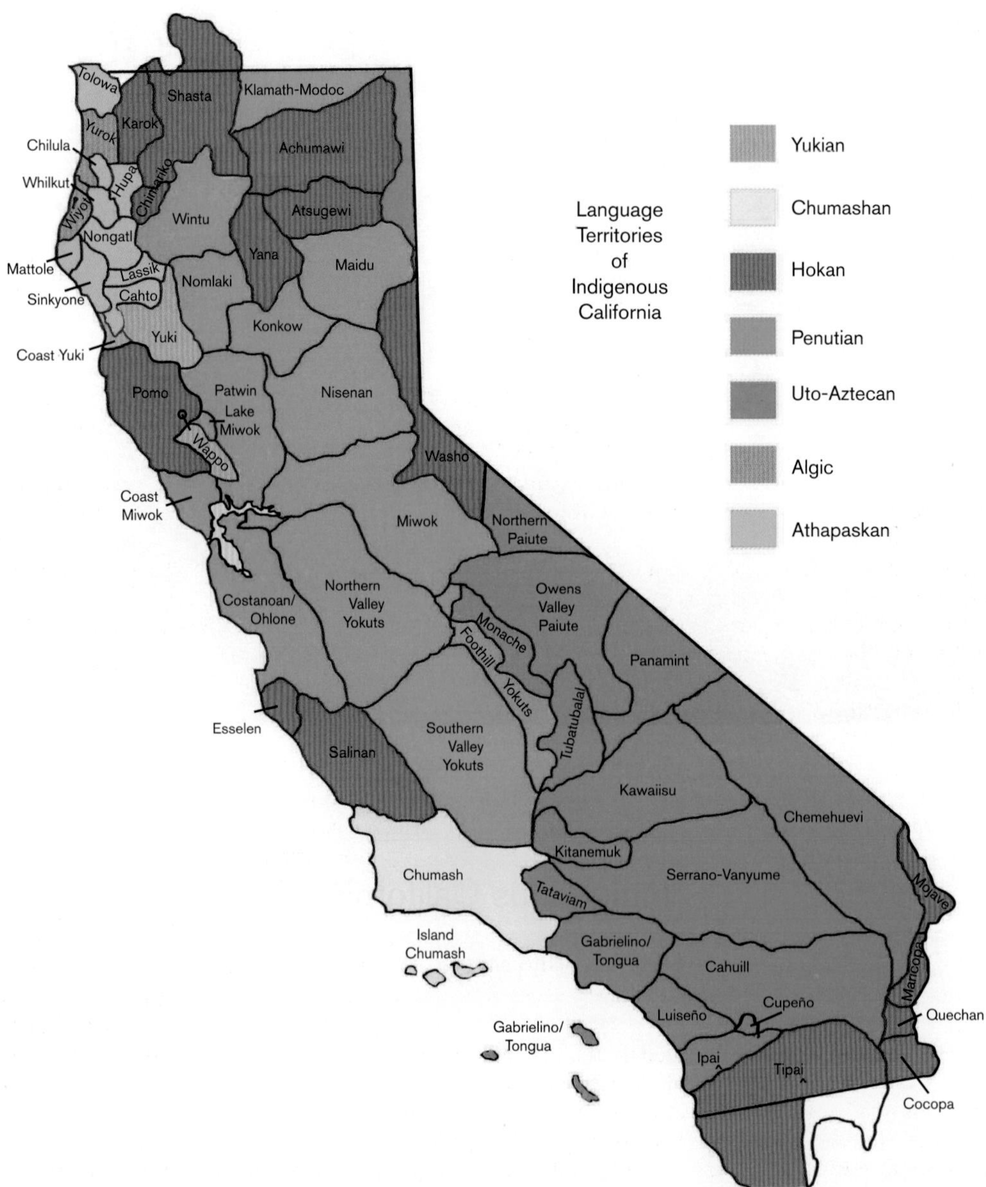

FIGURE 10.1 Language territories of indigenous California. Based on Golla (2011) and Heizer (1978).

impacts on California's native fauna due to growing populations, overhunting, and intensive foraging. This chapter explores how indigenous Californians might have shaped the landscape we see today and how scholars have arrived at and framed evolving and competing perspectives on this question over the many decades that it has been asked.

History of Research

The emergence of divergent views on the relationship between indigenous Californians and their environment is partly related to the prevailing worldviews and theoretical perspectives of the people who have constructed the anthropological record of what is now the state of California. As these views have changed over time, they have influenced the accuracy and quantity of information accumulated on pre–Euro-American human-environment relations. The earliest written accounts come from encounters between Europeans and Native Californians from the sixteenth through the nineteenth centuries. While these descriptions constitute a major part of the record of precontact indigenous California, they are limited in scope and in many cases highly biased. Typical is this description recorded by the Portolá expedition in 1769, near today's Morro Bay: "A small-sized wretched heathen village scarcely amounting to sixty souls, living in the open without house or hearth. They came over to visit us, offering us a sort of gruel (pinole) made out of parched seeds which we all thought tasted well, with a flavor of almonds" (from the diary of Gaspar de Portola, Boneu Companys 1983:206).

The ethnocentrism in this observation is repeated in doz-

Photo on previous page: Bighorn Sheep Petroglyph, Little Petroglyph Canyon, Coso Range, southeastern California. Thousands of similar rock art images are known from southeastern California and testify to the hunting of this species over a wide area at least as long as fifteen hundred years ago. Photo: Courtesy of Kit Tyler.

ens of accounts of the earliest contacts between the coastal peoples of Native California and the early explorers from the Old World. These provide some basic description of certain technologies and foods, but no detailed information about the surrounding environment or ecological interrelations. Later, the Spanish, who established twenty-one missions, three presidios, and seven pueblos between 1769 and 1825, as well as the Russians, who built an outpost at Fort Ross in northern California (1812–1842), recorded more detailed observations emphasizing population numbers and, in some cases, village names and locations. These accounts were followed by harsher, more racist descriptions from the American era (Heizer and Almquist 1971), especially during the Gold Rush, when Native Californians were trying to survive what some have described as essentially attempts at genocide (Castillo 1978, Lindsay 2012, Norton 1979). As disturbing as some of the accounts from the eighteenth and nineteenth centuries can be, they still provide the basis for many of the historical facts about Native California.

Attempts to record California Indian cultures systematically and nonjudgmentally began in earnest only in 1901 with the establishment of the Department of Anthropology at the University of California–Berkeley, where Alfred Kroeber, his students, and colleagues worked tirelessly for more than six decades collecting information on nearly all of the state's Native groups. The resulting salvage ethnographic record provides a more thorough accounting of the floral and faunal species exploited by Native people, the technologies used to capture and collect them, and—with varying levels of detail—their knowledge about distribution, seasonality, and edibility. However, while a tremendous amount of information was still known and available from Native consultants in the first half of the twentieth century, this record is also incomplete and uneven, and is most applicable to the period during and immediately following contact with Europeans.

The salvage ethnography effort culminated with a major summarizing publication by R. F. Heizer in 1978, after which anthropological research became more politically conscious. Where the salvage ethnographers had attempted to collect facts as quickly as possible and steer clear of politics of advocacy for Native peoples, a new generation of ethnographers that arose in the 1960s and 1970s put the political and social goals of achieving greater recognition and influence for Native Californians at the top of the anthropological research agenda. Influenced by the burgeoning ecology movement, the new ethnographies also provided much more detail on the resources exploited by Native peoples (e.g., Bean 1972, 1978) and pointed to the degradation that California lands had suffered following the arrival of Euro-Americans. They also consciously attempted to portray Native Californians in only the most positive light.

At this same time, archaeologists were becoming increasingly aware of widespread destruction of prehistoric sites in California due to underregulated land development. In response, California archaeologists also became more politically active and began to increasingly emphasize conservation and (when necessary) salvage. They sought to collaborate more closely with Native Californians. Aided by the passage of preservation laws in the 1960s and 1970s, these efforts quickly transformed into a sophisticated resource stewardship program known today as cultural resources management (CRM). From the 1970s on, CRM archaeology became widespread in California, and massive quantities of information about the state's prehistoric past began to accumulate. Thanks to the pervasive influence of ecological theory, this new effort included attempts to collect the types of information that can inform about the roles that prehistoric Californians played in the environment. Often overlooked prior to the 1960s, bones and shells that reflected past interactions with the environment began to be collected systematically and thoroughly analyzed for the first time. Paleoenvironmental studies were conducted as archaeologists sought to better understand the contexts of cultural changes in the past. Some archaeologists (e.g., King 1976) also attempted to align the new ecologically oriented archaeology with the emerging political goals of cultural anthropology, but it was not until decades later that sufficient bodies of archaeological faunal and floral data had been collected to support solid statements about the relationships between Native people and California's past biota. When that point was eventually reached, the stage had been set for an intellectual conflict between more empirically grounded archaeologists and those for whom interpreting the past with political sensitivity was of paramount importance. This debate continues today, and at its heart lie alternative views on the role of Native Californians in California's ecosystems.

The Peopling of California: A Framework

Any attempt to understand the role of prehistoric people in California's ecosystems needs to incorporate basic information about the numbers of people present, their time on the land, the environments they favored, and the technologies that they had at their disposal to exploit resources and influence local ecology. Over the past half century, archaeology has established some reasonably secure facts about the timing of the arrival of humans into California, the growth of their populations, the emergence of regional specializations, and the environmental trends that affected them. Before considering the alternative views on their overall role in ecosystems, it is important to establish the basic framework of California's prehistory as currently understood.

At present, a growing consensus exists that California was initially populated by culturally distinct groups that arrived via two entry routes: big-game hunting Clovis Paleoindians who entered overland from the interior of the continent, and shoreline-oriented Paleocoastal people who arrived via boats moving southward along the coast from Alaska. Of these two, Clovis is thought to be slightly older, dating circa 13,400 to 13,200 years ago (Waters and Stafford 2007), while a series of Paleocoastal sites on the northern Channel Islands date between 12,800 and 12,000 years B.P. (Erlandson et al. 2011, Johnson et al. 2002). Hints of occupation as early as 14,000 years ago exist in central Oregon, just across the California border (Gilbert et al. 2008). In truth, however, the dating of Clovis is imprecise in California due to a dearth of radiocarbon-dated finds, and the chronology used here is based on dates obtained from outside of the state. Likewise, the association between Clovis and the hunting of Pleistocene big game in California can only be asserted from faunal associations made elsewhere in the country. Nonetheless, it is reasonable to continue to assume that a megafauna-hunting adaptation is reflected by the many Clovis-like points discovered in California (Rondeau et al. 2007) (Figure 10.2).

Regional specializations apparent at the time of first Euro-American contact in the 1500s were not necessarily present at

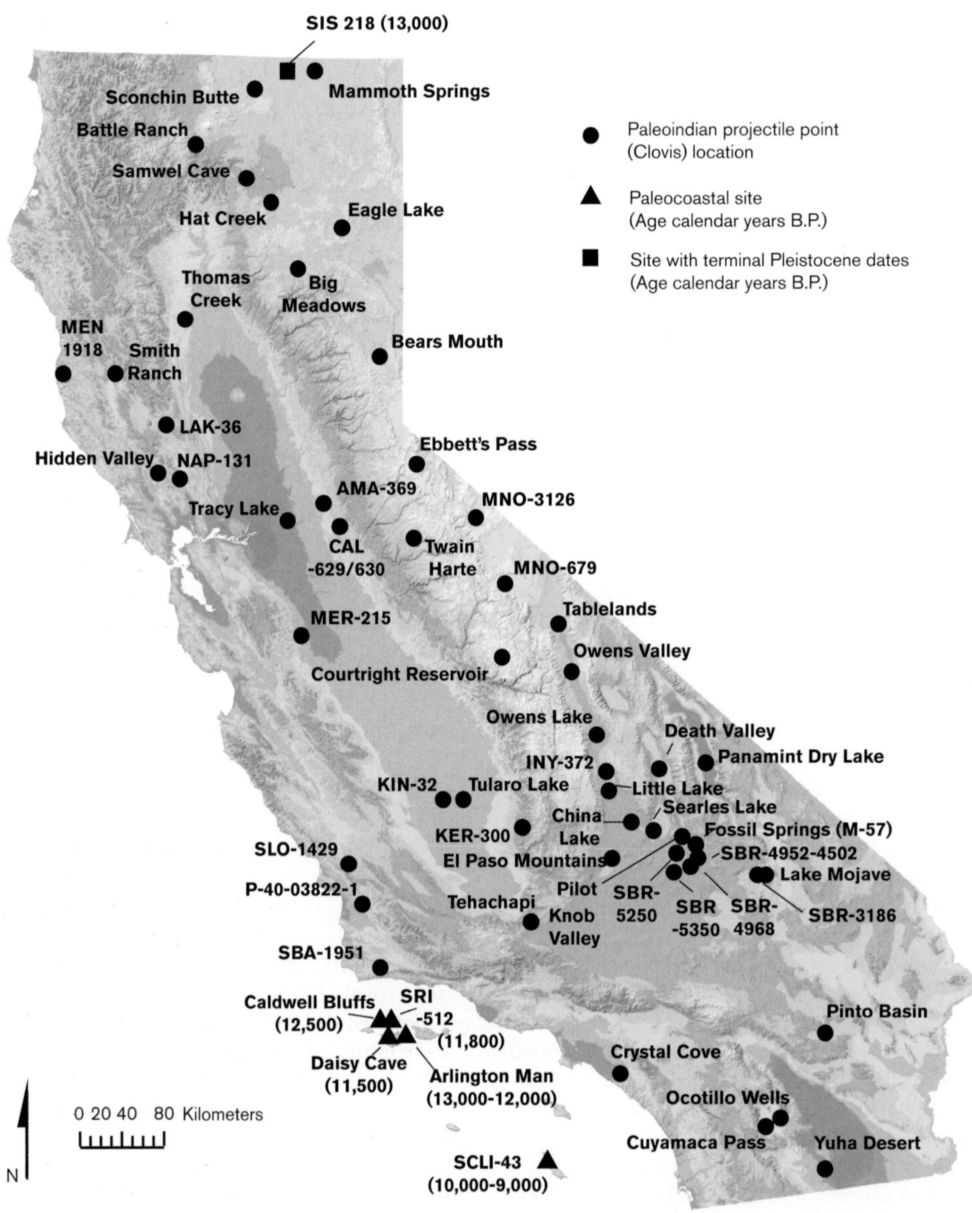

FIGURE 10.2 Terminal Pleistocene/early Holocene archaeological sites and isolated finds in California. These locations have produced limited evidence (surface finds of Clovis-like fluted projectile points) of human presence thirteen thousand years ago. Numbers outside of parentheses are parts of individual site names, with dates (years before present, B.P.) in parentheses. Based on Rondeau et al. 2007.

the end of the Pleistocene. Incoming Paleocoastal and Paleoindian populations initially employed subsistence strategies that they brought with them from afar, while the lifeways observed at the time of Euro-American contact evolved over the Holocene in California. Following the end of the Pleistocene and the disappearance of Clovis, indigenous people experienced changes in climate and related transitions in vegetation along with rising sea levels and transformation of coastal habitats. We can assume that their knowledge of California environments continued to accumulate while their populations increased. We cannot assume, however, that population growth was gradual and incremental over time, because California experienced a series of in-migrations from new ethnolinguistic groups during the Holocene that effected episodic population growth in many regions. Summarized below are key climatic trends that affected prehistoric Californians as well as the history of group migrations that influenced population trends in different regions during different periods.

Paleoenvironmental Trends

Changes in vegetation that reflect climate flux from the late Pleistocene through the Holocene are described in more detail in Chapter 8, "Ecosystems Past: Vegetation Prehistory" (see also West et al. 2007). With respect to human adaptations, six trends/events were especially important: (1) long-term, gradual warming associated with the transition from Pleistocene to Holocene; (2) the Younger Dryas event, which interrupted terminal Pleistocene warming via a rapid return to a near-glacial, cool, dry climate for circa 1,000 to 1,500 years beginning 12,900 years ago; (3) the early to mid-Holocene warm period at the beginning of the Holocene, when climate was warmer than today; (4) the gradual return to cooler, wetter conditions following the end of the early to mid-Holocene optimum (sometimes referred to as the Neoglacial); (5) the Medieval Climatic Anomaly between about 1,200 and 650 years ago, when sea surface temperatures were cool and California experienced unusually prolonged droughts; and (6) the Little Ice Age between 600 and 150 years ago, when climate was cooler.

At the end of the Pleistocene, when people first entered the state, California was perhaps 8–10°C cooler than today and vegetation complexes were different. Sea level at the Last Glacial Maximum (LGM, about twenty thousand years ago) was 120 meters lower than present, putting shorelines as much as 30 kilometers west of their current locations and exposing broad, flat coastal terraces as potentially ideal locations for settlement by early coastal explorers. Unfortunately, sea level rise subsequent to the LGM would have destroyed most records of such early coastal occupations. Other distinctive features of late Pleistocene California relevant to the lifeways of early humans included deeply incised river valleys in what are now the San Francisco Bay and the Sacramento/San Joaquin Delta (the deep sediments that fill the bay did not start to accumulate until the Holocene), pluvial (glacial-era) lakes in what are now the arid deserts of southeastern California, and a glacial cap along the crest of the Sierra Nevada that would have restricted some human movements.

Also during the Pleistocene, California animal populations were dominated by large species, including mammoths, horses, camels, and ground sloths that would have been attractive prey for the earliest human hunters. All of these animals went extinct by 12,900 years ago, and the cause of their disappearance remains a contentious issue. These animals and Native Californians both were affected by the Younger Dryas event, when climate suddenly returned to near-glacial, cold, dry conditions 12,900 years ago, only to rapidly return to warmer conditions 1,000 to 1,500 years later. Following this oscillation, climate continued a gradual warming from 11,000 to 6,000 years ago that culminated in the early Holocene peak between about 8,000 and 6,000 years ago. Glaciers were then gone from the Sierra, and many pluvial lakes disappeared from the southern deserts, making human occupation more challenging in those settings. Along the coast, sea level rose to within 30 meters of its present location by about 10,000 years ago, and sediments began to accumulate in some smaller estuarine systems, providing new habitat for mud flat–adapted clams and cockles. Radiocarbon dates from shell middens in San Diego (Masters and Gallegos 1997), Santa Barbara (Erlandson 1985), San Luis Obispo County (Jones et al. 2002), Monterey County (Jones and Jones 1992), and Sonoma County (Schwaderer 1992) testify to the presence of these incipient estuaries by 10,000 to 7,000 years ago.

The return of cooler, wetter climate following the early Holocene warm period was marked by a dramatic slowdown in the rate of sea level rise, with seas reaching within 5 to 7 meters of present levels between 6,000 and 4,000 years ago. This precipitated maturation of the youngest and largest estuarine embayment in California, San Francisco Bay. Archaeological evidence shows that people did not start exploiting oysters and clams from the bay until about 5,000 years ago (Ingram 1998). After this, evidence points to a rapid buildup of human populations on the bay shore. Human populations become much more apparent in the Central Valley after 5,000 years ago due partially to greater visibility of the archaeological record, but also probably to improved conditions and increased rainfall during the Neoglacial. Elsewhere along the southern and central coasts, smaller estuaries accumulated sediments suitable for clams and cockles as early as 10,000 years ago. Some of the smaller of these were drowned completely by sea level rise by the mid-Holocene (Erlandson 1985, Jones et al. 2002).

In the late Holocene (post 3,000 years B.P.), the indigenous peopling of California was finalized, with populations establishing in the last unoccupied environments. Sites in Riverside County testify to the exploitation of prehistoric Lake Cahuilla in the Colorado desert around 3,000 years ago (Schaefer and Laylander 2007), while radiocarbon dates from shell middens show initial occupation of the coasts of Mendocino and Humboldt Counties about 2,000 to 1,500 years ago. Likewise, alpine villages were established at elevations between 3,130 meters and 3,854 meters in the White Mountains for the first time during this same millennium. Settlement of this extremely challenging environment is thought to reflect the demands of population growth in the more accessible parts of California (Bettinger 1991). After about 1,500 years ago, migrations into lower-ranked, underutilized habitats were no longer an option for people in California, as virtually every available habitat had by then been settled.

Of the late Holocene climatic events, the Medieval Climate Anomaly (MCA), marked by two intervals of prolonged drought (circa A.D. 1020–1100 and 1200–1350) has been the subject of most research and debate (e.g., Arnold 1992, Bettinger 1999, Jones et al. 1999, Gamble 2005, Schwitalla 2013). Kennett and Kennett (2000) demonstrated that the period was associated with unusually cold and productive sea surface temperatures off southern California. They and others (Lambert 1994, Raab and Larson 1997) have argued that violence increased in southern California during this time due to reduced terrestrial productivity associated with droughts. This is consistent with evidence for declines in obsidian trade in some parts of California (Gilreath and Hildebrandt 1997, Jones et al. 1999) although island-mainland trade in shell beads seems to have increased at the same time (Arnold 1992). The MCA concluded with the onset of the Little Ice Age, during which sea surface temperatures increased (Kennett and Kennett 2000), climate became cooler and wetter, and shallow, intermittent lakes appeared in the Mojave and Colorado Deserts, providing improved subsistence opportunities in these otherwise arid settings. The renewed growth of glaciers may have impeded travel across the Sierra Nevada. Nevertheless, few archaeologists suggest that the Little Ice Age caused significant problems for indigenous Californians, though some estuaries on the southern coast declined in productivity due to sedimentation (Gallegos 2002).

Migrations, Population Trends, and Regional Specializations

To approach any understanding of the complex relationship between California's Native people and their environment also requires some knowledge of the dynamics of human migrations, population trends, and intergroup relations. The diverse linguistic mosaic apparent at the time of European contact in

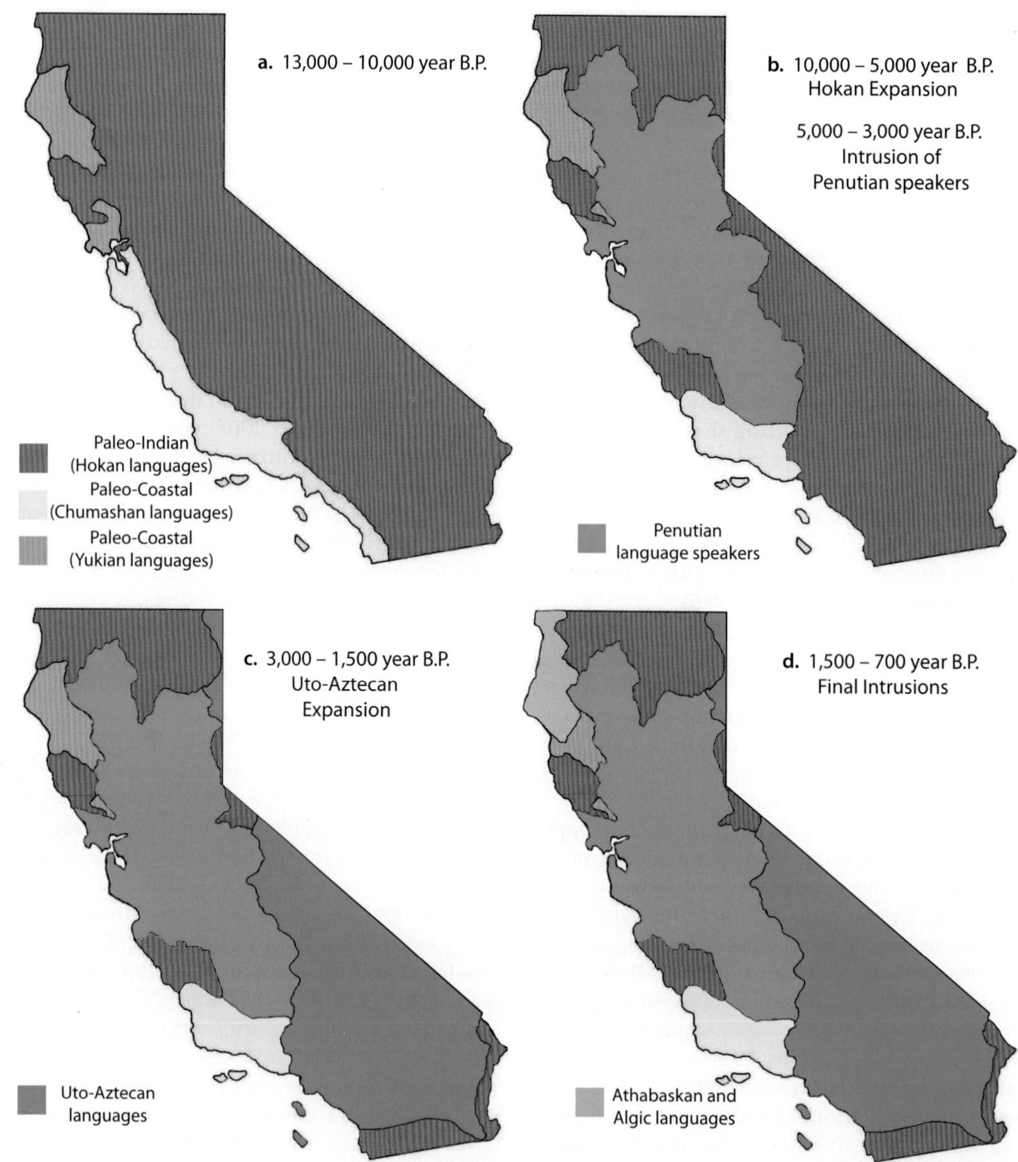

FIGURE 10.3 Hypothetical reconstruction of language group migrations into California over the late Pleistocene and Holocene. Source: T. L. Jones with input from Moratto (1984) and Golla (2007).

California (see Figure 10.1) has long been thought to be the end-product of a series of in-migrations by groups who spoke languages from different linguistic families (Figure 10.3). Archaeologists, linguists, and most recently geneticists (see Johnson et al. 2012) have struggled to reconstruct the history of these population movements for much of the past century, and their understanding remains imperfect and debated.

The presence of languages at the tip of the Baja Peninsula that are unrelated to any other in the New World suggests that some of the earliest groups to enter California stayed only temporarily, eventually moving further south to be replaced in Alta California by later groups entering from the north (Golla 2007, 2011). The Chumashan and Yukian language isolates spoken along the coast may reflect the earliest arrival of groups via the coastal entry route into California (see Figure 10.3a). The dearth of fluted projectile points on the Channel Islands and the occurrence instead of other points that seem associated with a marine-oriented subsistence focus (Erlandson 2013, Glassow et al. 2013) suggest these were not Clovis big-game hunters.

Languages spoken by Paleoindians who entered California from the interior is unclear, but those in the Hokan language stock were almost certainly being spoken throughout most of interior California by perhaps 10,000 years ago (Moratto 1984), occupying lands slightly less productive than the coastal territories staked out by the early Paleocoastal migrants (Codding and Jones 2013). The latter date is an important one because people become much more recognizable in the archaeological record after that time, reflecting an apparent threshold of sorts. Prior to 10,000 years ago, human populations do not seem to have been large enough to leave an easily detectable footprint in the archaeological record. Archaeological findings hint at occupation of river shores and uplands of the Klamath and North Coast ranges perhaps by as early as 9,000 to 8,000 years ago (Fitzgerald and Hildebrandt 2002, Tushingham 2009). Even Death Valley, today a seemingly daunting environment, had much greater effective moisture in the early Holocene and was inhabited as early as 9,000 years ago (Moratto 1984). These early Holocene populations were undoubtedly affected by reduced terrestrial productivity during the early to mid-Holocene warm period, which probably kept a check on population growth for a while.

The next wave of migrants into California were speakers of the Penutian language stock (Wintu, Maidu, Konkow, Nisenan, Miwok, Costanoan, and Yokuts), who entered the Central Valley (see Figure 10.3b) from the north between 5,000 and 3,000 years ago (Golla 2007:76). Some of the first waves of these migrants may have been people vacating the more arid parts of western North America during the latter stages of the early to mid-Holocene warm period. Their entry into California is reflected by an increase in archaeological sites dated to 3000–1000 B.C. in the San Francisco Bay area and Central Valley. A concomitant increase in certain types of violence apparent in in the skeletal record (Andrushko et al. 2010, Schwitalla et al. 2014) further suggests that this intrusion was not entirely peaceful. Hints of regional specializations begin to appear in various parts of California at this time, although these would become much more sophisticated later. These include the first murmurs of acorn economies in the Central Valley, increased fishing in the Santa Barbara Channel, and small-game plant-based adaptations in the southern deserts. Increasing numbers of mortars and pestles after 500 B.C. in the Central Valley suggest gradual economic intensification focused on the acorn (Basgall 1987). By the time of Euro-American contact, acorn granaries were visible features in villages (Figure 10.4), and isotopic studies of human bone show that acorn use increased over time (Bartelink 2009).

FIGURE 10.4 Acorn caches and Dance House, Railroad Flat (Sierra Miwok). Photo: Samuel A. Barrett, 1906, courtesy of the UC Berkeley, Phoebe A. Hearst Museum of Anthropology, Photograph 15-2749.

FIGURE 10.5 Storage basket for mesquite, Cahuilla, near Indio. Photo: Alfred Kroeber, 1907, courtesy of the UC Berkeley, Phoebe A. Hearst Museum of Anthropology, Photograph 15-4198.

Speakers of languages in the Uto-Aztecan family (which occupied much of southeastern California at the time of Euro-American contact) seem to have made their way into the southeastern deserts by 3,000 to 2,000 years ago (see Figure 10.3c) and eventually to the southern Channel Islands (replacing earlier peoples). Desert subsistence focused heavily on a variety of plant staples, including agave and mesquite (Figure 10.5), along with small animals (Golla 2007). The last migrants into California were speakers of Athabaskan (Tolowa, Hupa) and Algic (Yurok and Wiyot) languages after 2,000 years ago, who usurped coastal lands previously settled by descendants of Paleocoastal colonists (see Figure 10.3d). B. F. Codding and T. L. Jones (2013) suggest that this last intrusion was more aggressive in nature than earlier movements into California, reflecting the fact that by then there were no longer any unoccupied portions of California to settle. Ethnographic accounts document a sophisticated material culture associated with the sedentary salmon-acorn-marine economies that became established in northwestern California at this time.

Exploitation of the salmon resource was one of the more remarkable subsistence activities in indigenous California (Figure 10.6). The largest rivers benefitted from two seasonal salmon runs: one in the spring and another in the fall. The Sacramento River had four Chinook salmon runs, while the Klamath and Eel had two plus Coho salmon runs. In the Sacramento, salmon were in the river almost all months of the year. Construction of fish weirs along the Klamath and Eel Rivers (Figure 10.7) was strictly controlled by rituals that limited the number of days any given community could use their dam. This restriction ensured that some fish continued further upriver to spawn or to be captured by similarly time-restricted fish dams built by other communities. Accounts of the fish taken at any given weir indicate substantial numbers, but equally large were the numbers of fish that passed through each community before and after weirs were constructed. While there was certainly much bickering among groups, this system of ritually restricted catches allowed a great number of communities to exploit the salmon resource sustainably up and down the major rivers of northern California (Swezey and Heizer 1977).

Most of the hallmarks of indigenous Californian culture are recognizable in the archaeological record by the end of the Middle Period (circa A.D. 500–1000), including the widespread intensive reliance on acorns. The last major technological change that had significant sociopolitical and environmental repercussions was the introduction of the bow and arrow (Figure 10.8), apparently arriving first in eastern California from a point of origin further to the interior of North America (Bettinger 2013) and making its way to the Santa Barbara Channel by perhaps A.D. 900–1000 (Kennett et al. 2013) and central California by A.D. 1000–1200 (Groza et al. 2011).

FIGURE 10.6 Karuk dip net for salmon circa 1910. Photo: Alfred Kroeber, courtesy of the UC Berkeley, Phoebe A. Hearst Museum of Anthropology, Photograph 15-1384.

FIGURE 10.7 Hupa salmon weir circa 1906, below Mill Creek. Photo: Pliny E. Goddard, 1906, courtesy of the UC Berkeley, Phoebe A. Hearst Museum of Anthropology, Photograph 15-3301.

FIGURE 10.8 Ishi shooting bow and arrow, kneeling, Deer Creek, Tehama. Photo: Alfred Kroeber, 1914, courtesy of the UC Berkeley, Phoebe A. Hearst Museum of Anthropology, Photograph 15-5697.

The bow revolutionized hunting strategies and, in concert with increased reliance on acorns, fostered the emergence of relatively small-scale political organization that dominated nearly all of indigenous California at the time of Euro-American contact (Bettinger 2013).

Alternate Views on Indigenous Ecology

While archaeology and ethnography have established a basic outline for California's prehistory and have identified ways in which human populations were affected by climate and other environmental factors, the role that humans in turn played in shaping precontact ecosystems is today characterized by two alternative perspectives mentioned earlier: one that views indigenous peoples as conservators, and another that attributes to them certain impacts on California's native fauna. Historically these extreme views have been sustained largely in the face of empirical evidence insufficient to refute either one. However, it is increasingly possible to critically evaluate at least some aspects of both working hypotheses. These conflicting perspectives are perhaps best understood through a brief summary of their historical development.

Emergent Hypermanagement

For the most part, the pre-anthropological accounts from the eighteenth and nineteenth centuries tended to envision California Indians as essentially less than human and, as such, more parts of nature than masters of it (as the Europeans believed themselves to be). Many, if not all, of the earliest European accounts also describe California as a land of almost inconceivable bounty. In 1579, for example, Sir Francis Drake described the area north of San Francisco Bay as "a goodly country and fruitful soil, stored with many blessings fit for the use of man: infinite was the company of large fat deer, which there we saw by the thousands as we suppose in a herd" (Broughton 1994a:371). In 1785, sixteen years after the establishment of the first permanent Spanish settlements in California, Jean Francois La Perouse (1968:441) wrote, "No country is more abundant in fish and game of every sort . . . partridges alone are found in covies of three or four hundred." Even later in the 1830s, Wilkes (1845:113) noted in central California: "The variety of game in this country almost exceeds belief." Euro-Americans before 1900 viewed California as a land of abundant wildlife that included its Native people. California Indians were seen as essentially part of the "wilderness" that Euro-Americans sought to tame (Heizer 1974:vii).

Kroeber and the other early anthropologists certainly did not share these views and sought to undermine them through scientific collection of ethnographic facts. If any overarching conclusion about indigenous ecology emerged from the early salvage ethnographic work, it was that California Indians had benefitted from a tremendously rich and diverse resource base:

> The food resources of California were bountiful in their variety rather than in their overwhelming abundance. . . . If one supply failed, there were hundreds of others to fall back upon. If a drought withered the corn shoots, if the buffalo unaccountably shifted, or if the salmon failed to run, the very existence of people in other rewgions was shaken to its foundations. But the manifold distribution of available food in California and the working out of corresponding means of reclaiming them prevented a failure of the acorn crop from producing similar effects. It might produce short rations and racking hunger, but scarcely starvation. (Kroeber 1925:524)

Later, Kroeber (1948:811) expanded further on this relationship, suggesting that "in most of California, the climate was easy, food reasonably abundant, and the human population relatively dense for a non-farming one. If cultural progress was quiet, it was not because of nature's adversity but rather because, in Toynbeean concept, challenge was feeble and response mild."

Edwin Walker, a contemporary of Kroeber, wrote in regard to the Native people of southern California: "Many of these Indians . . . who had penetrated the country unknown centuries ago . . . once having secured a foothold . . . , seemed to have settled down to enjoy in peace the climate and abundant food supply. At the time of discovery they probably were as inoffensive, contented, and happy as any Indians in America" (Walker n.d.:2). Simplistic, naïve, and/or patronizing comments like these gave way in the 1970s to attempts to establish Native Californians as not merely the beneficiaries of a bountiful California but the architects of it. At the heart of this reconceptualization was an influential paper by Henry Lewis (1973) on controlled burning that portrayed Native use of fire as a masterful form that increased the diversity and productivity of California landscapes. The robust game populations and expansive, productive oak forests and grasslands of precontact California were seen according to this new perspective as the results of thousands of years of skillful management by Native people. California Indians were now seen as no more a part of nature than Europeans, and were able to alter it just as readily—albeit only in positive ways. In reference to Lewis's work, L. J. Bean and H. Lawton (1976:39) wrote: "Lewis has demonstrated that fire was a major factor in a system of aboriginal environmental relationships and functioned in a number of ways to increase both animal and plant resources in California. . . . Burning the woodlands grassbelt, particularly in areas near villages, would have concentrated game in specific locations for ready accessibility in hunting, since browse in burned-over areas would have been richer. Thus we suggest burning may have constituted a form of game management or incipient herding."

In another highly influential book from this era, *The Ohlone Way*, M. Margolin (1978:12) stated that "their knowledge of animals did not lead to conquest, nor did familiarity breed contempt. The Ohlones lived in a world where people were few, and animals were many, where the bow and arrow were the height of technology . . . they lived in a world where the animal kingdom had not yet fallen under the domination of the human race." This new perspective, which L. M. Rabb and T. Jones (2004) subsequently dubbed "ecofunctionalism," seemed to promote so many positives both for living California Indians and the environmental movement that it quickly became the dominant view among academics and the general public. This occurred despite the fact that there remained many unanswered questions about exactly how management was accomplished, when it was initiated, and why.

Megafaunal Extinctions

At the same time that anthropologists and historians were promoting the image of Native Americans as benevolent managers, a starkly different role in the continent's prehistoric ecology was proposed for Native Americans by Paul S.

Martin, in the form of what is sometimes referred to as the "overkill hypothesis." Martin (1967) argued that the initial peopling of North America by big-game hunters from Siberia brought with it the extinction of Pleistocene mammals. He suggested that skilled hunters representing the Clovis culture could have populated the entire New World in a period of about a thousand years, during which time previously isolated and unwary Pleistocene mammals were overhunted into extinction. The contrast between this hypothesis and the ecofunctionalist model of benign landscape management could not be greater, and the distinction between the competing hypotheses ultimately embodies the divergent contemporary views on indigenous ecology.

The potential for the type of destructive, nonconservative hunting proposed by Martin is well attested elsewhere in the world, particularly by the history and archaeology of bird hunting and extinction by early Polynesians (Steadman 1995). However, the degree to which Martin's model successfully accounts for the disappearance of Pleistocene megafauna on a continentwide basis is questionable, especially in California, where there are no dated associations between Clovis projectile points and the bones of extinct megafauna. Martin's model had seemingly reasonable empirical support when it was first put forward in the 1960s, but time has not been kind to the hypothesis (Grayson and Meltzer 2003, Meltzer 2009). Forty years of additional research have added little in the way of additional supporting evidence, and it is now clear that of the thirty-six genera of mostly large animals that went extinct at the end of the Pleistocene, only two (mammoths and bison) have been recovered in substantial numbers from archaeological sites (all from outside California). With no archaeological record of human exploitation for the vast majority of animals that disappeared, the argument that humans caused all Pleistocene megafaunal extinctions is not strong. Still, some researchers continue to pursue this hypothesis; for example, with a recent suggestion that elimination of megafauna began the development of an essentially anthropogenic landscape in western North America (Nowacki et al. 2012).

A strong but still controversial alternative to overkill is the Younger Dryas extraterrestrial impact hypothesis first advanced by R. B. Firestone et al. (2007) and subsequently debated by a host of researchers (see Jones and Kennett 2012, Kerr 2010). Under this scenario a cosmic impact (comet) about 12,900 years ago caused both the Younger Dryas climatic oscillation and the disappearance of Pleistocene megafauna. Evidence for impact-related destruction is particularly strong in southern California, where findings from Santa Rosa Island include both a distinctive black stratum dating 12,900 B.P. that produced carbon spherules indicative of intense fires (which D. J. Kennett et al. [2008] interpret as evidence of widespread wildfires), and hexagonal nanodiamonds, which are known on Earth only in meteorites and impact craters. If this hypothesis continues to be supported, it suggests that humans were severely affected by the same event that rendered the megafauna extinct, suggesting that the earliest human colonizers of California were far from in control of the landscape around them.

Tempered Overkill: Reactionary Archaeology and Resource Depression

Martin's overkill model—which argued for rapid, severe, and dramatic overhunting—has never been well supported in California. However, the ecofunctionalist perspective initiated by Lewis that emerged from the 1970s (and that envisions Native Californians as benevolent conservators who skillfully managed and shaped California landscapes) was not supported in any substantive way by archaeological evidence, either. The most compelling piece of the ecofunctionalist case involved a weak correlation between robust game populations and controlled burning. Solid, empirical evidence showing that the former were truly the result of the latter, however, has proven particularly difficult to come by. In light of this missing support and the extreme position advocated by the ecofunctionalists, archaeologists in the 1990s began to challenge this scenario with a more muted version of overkill—as did historians and others elsewhere in the country (e.g., Kay and Simmons 2002, Krech 1999). Foremost among the California critics was J. M. Broughton (1994a, 1994b, 1997, 1999), who suggested that far from managing the environment, Native people actually overexploited many highly desirable resources (such as big game), reducing their populations.

Numbers of Native people living in California were argued to have grown so high in the prehistoric past that sustaining them on diets containing deer, elk, and sea lions inevitably led to depression of these game populations. From the 1990s through the early 2000s, archaeologists argued that Native Californians overexploited everything from deer (Broughton 1999) to sea lions (Hildebrandt and Jones 1992) to fish (Broughton 1994b, Broughton 1997, Salls 1992), birds (Broughton 2004, Broughton et al. 2007, Jones et al. 2008, Whitaker 2010), and shellfish (Erlandson et al. 2008, Jones 1996). That Broughton's research in particular was undertaken in direct response to the extreme environmental management views that emerged from the 1970s is clear:

> Insofar as my analyses have shown that Native American foragers had profound impacts on the fish, mammal, and bird species of the San Francisco Bay area, they call into question the widely held belief that native peoples maintained a harmonious relationship with the animal populations with whom they shared the land. This belief has led to a "logical alliance" between Native cultures and conservation organizations. Indeed the government of Colombia has relinquished over 18 million hectares of rain forest to native peoples with the belief that they are best suited to manage it. . . . Perceived harmony is almost surely a function of limited technologies and low population densities. . . .
>
> There is no compelling reason to think that Native Americans will provide better stewardship of our threatened habitats than any other peoples. (Broughton 1999:72)

Many subsequent faunal analyses, however, have failed to confirm the early claims of overexploitation models. Larger, more recent studies have in many cases produced less dramatic findings that demonstrate persistence of game populations rather than depletion (e.g., Campbell and Butler 2010, Etnier 2002, Jones et al. 2011, Lyman 2003, Whitaker 2008b). Some studies have demonstrated that the dominant taxa existing prehistorically were different in certain regions and habitats from those of today (Rick et al. 2011), and others have shown that some animal populations (e.g., sea lions) were lower in the past at some locations (Walker et al. 2002), but these studies cannot demonstrate that this variation was caused by overhunting. A. Whitaker's (2009) research shows that deer populations would have been able to readily withstand Native exploitation. An important early study by M. A. Baumhoff (1963) also showed that Californian Indians were living well below the carrying capacity of the environment, suggesting there might have been little need to overexploit anything. On the other hand, an important paper by M. E. Basgall (1987) suggested that the heavy labor expenditures associated with acorns meant that people were probably forced to rely on them as a food source rather than simply benefitting from their ubiquity. A few key studies have also demonstrated unequivocal wildlife impacts from prehistoric human foraging in California. Salient among these is the archaeological case for the extinction of the highly vulnerable flightless duck (*Chendytes lawi*) due to overhunting (Jones et al. 2008), along with a number of studies that demonstrate human impact on shellfish populations (e.g., Erlandson et al. 2008).

Furthering Ecomanagement

Recent research in California has also sought to further the ecomanagement perspective first expressed by Lewis with renewed studies of controlled burning and plant exploitation. T. C. Blackburn and K. Anderson published a series of papers in a 1993 volume titled *Before the Wilderness: Environmental Management by Native Californians*. Much of this volume simply repeated previous assertions about Native burning, but several papers within it attempted to advance the perspective further. D. W. Peri and S. M. Patterson (1993) made a strong case that Pomo weavers encouraged growth of sedges (*Carex* spp.) used for baskets by loosening the ground around their roots, and removing weeds and rocks. Tending tracts of sedges in this manner was referred to as "cultivation" (Peri and Patterson 1993:175). This term was also used to describe pine nut exploitation in northern California by G. Farris (1993:239), who argued that the act of collecting nuts for consumption would have increased the range of pine species because some nuts lost in the food-making process would take root outside of the pine's natural range.

M. K. Anderson argued that harvest of most important plants was consciously undertaken in a sustainable way: "An important rule for most cultural groups was 'do not take.' Therefore harvesting rates were not much in excess of tribal yearly needs, and whole plants were left to insure next year's harvest. . . . The implication seems to be that prehistoric native people harvested the most important plants on a sustained-yield basis" (Anderson 1993:152). Also in this volume, H. McCarthy (1993) argued that knocking ripe acorns from trees constituted a form of "pruning" that would increase crop production in subsequent years—even though the activity affected some oak species negatively. Unquestionably, these papers and subsequent research (e.g., Anderson 1997, 2005) make strong points about indigenous knowledge of plants in California and demonstrate that some floral species were encouraged by a variety of means. However, many of these recent attempts rely solely on ethnographic information (most of it collected relatively recently). These studies assert, without archaeological support, that these seemingly modest activities carried out over the last 13,000 to 12,000 years produced an essentially gardenlike California environment.

Several archaeologists have also attempted to corroborate the ecomanagement perspective with empirical findings. C. King (1993) suggested that it was at least hypothetically possible to recognize management of firewood in the archaeological record of charcoal associated with roasting-related rock oven features, but this idea has never been systematically tested, let alone substantiated. In a study of California sea mussel (*Mytilus californianus*) remains from an archaeological site in northwestern California, A. R. Whitaker (2008a) concluded that harvesting strategies approximated "incipient aquaculture." The collection technique that he identified involved total stripping of patches of mussel beds down to bare rock that were apparently allowed to lay fallow for two years, during which time uniformly sized, relatively small mussels would recolonize the patch, only to again be harvested via the stripping method. Since this regular, intensive harvest and fallowing maintained a uniform size of shells over time, Whitaker concluded that this technique maintained long-term propagation of mussels at the expense of short-term gains. Elsewhere on the central coast, however, multiple sites have also shown that stripping was the dominant technique for mussel harvest and that it caused diminution over time in the mean size of collected individuals (Jones 1996, 2003). Whitaker's conclusions, which suggest a conscious management-oriented approach, are not consistent with biological studies showing that limited harvest of larger individuals from beds provides the greatest benefits for mussel populations (Yamada and Peters 1988). In a similar study on San Miguel Island, J. M. Erlandson et al. (2008) noted that as Native populations grew over the course of the Holocene, harvest of shellfish increased in quantity and frequency to the point that it diminished mean shell size. Despite these impacts, Erlandson et al. (2008:2144) suggested that long-term harvests were ultimately sustained by an early emphasis on fishing at lower trophic levels (shellfish), periodically shifting village locations, and intensifying the use of finfish and sea mammals through time. This approach was described as "fishing up the food web," but in other contexts it is referred to simply as economic intensification.

Controlled Burning

Among the polarized views on indigenous involvement with California landscapes, the role of intentionally set fires has received the greatest attention and remains an important subset of the overarching debate. Since Lewis (1973), several researchers have sought to elaborate and expand on the controlled-burning hypothesis. One view, which recognizes that controlled burning was done by indigenous people the world over (Stewart 2002), suggests that burning began with the initial colonization of the New World (e.g., Nowacki et al. 2012). According to this idea, the transformation of California from a purely "natural" to anthropogenic landscape began in earnest at least 13,000 years ago, when fires were set by incoming Clovis big-game hunters. Incorporating acceptance of human overhunting as the cause of megafauna extinctions, this theory is at least partially supported by temporal trends in megafauna dung spores, charcoal, and arboreal pollen in stratified lake deposits from midcontinent. Using spores as a proxy for mammoth population, J. L. Gill et al. (2009) argued that megafauna declined precipitously between about 14,800 to 13,700 years ago, preceding an increase in evidence of fires that began around 14,100 years ago. Gill et al. (2009:1102) suggest the possibility that the latter date marks of the arrival of humans who overhunted already declining megaherbivores into extinction. The authors, however, do not rule out the likelihood that all or most of these trends observed in the lake strata reflect Pleistocene-Holocene climate change. G. J. Nowacki et al. (2012) subsequently put humans at the center of these transitions, arguing that after wiping out megafauna, they established human-mediated fire regimes that encouraged certain types of new vegetation at the expense of archaic types.

These studies raise questions that continue to plague research on this issue in California and elsewhere: how can the signatures of natural fires and climate change be distinguished from human-induced fires, and what amount of charcoal or flux in pollen frequencies in paleoenvironmental records reflects the influence of humans? Most recently, a well-funded, multidisciplinary investigation of indigenous burning near Año Nuevo in central California (Cuthrell et al. 2012, Lightfoot and Lopez 2013) encountered this same problem. In summarizing the results of their analysis of charcoal and pollen, A. Cowart and R. Byrne (2013:348–349) stated: "The microscopic charcoal record . . . provides evidence of regular fires from the fifteenth century to the present. . . . We propose that at least some of these fires were ignited by humans because of the evidence of large settlements in the area. However, due to the limitations of low-resolution data and without fire scar evidence to calibrate the charcoal record, we cannot conclusively state whether the increase in charcoal from the fifteenth century to the present can be attributed to frequent low-severity fires ignited by humans or perhaps more frequent or more severe natural fires."

Given this seemingly unresolvable problem, many researchers have simply continued to assert the ethnographic record, including Anderson (1993, 1997), O. C. Stewart (2002), and K. G. Lightfoot and O. Parrish (2009). These last authors suggest that California Indians fostered microdiversity in California habitats by burning, while J. E. Keeley (2002) speculates that Native Californians type-converted shrubland to grassland in the Coast Ranges. These studies have been countered by researchers clamoring for more substantive empirical evidence. Both A. J. Parker (1997) and J. Bendix (1997) have raised serious objections to the broad assertions in many of the controlled-burning papers. For instance, it has been generally assumed that frequent but small, controlled burns by Native people kept the type of large wild fires that occur today in check. In one recent study that attempted to evaluate the frequency, intensity, and effects of Native burning via the paleo-charcoal record, S. A. Mensing et al. (1999) found clear evidence for occasional, major conflagrations in pre-European southern California, which suggests that controlled burning did not give Native people full control of the landscape.

Recent work by Lightfoot and colleagues (2013) near Año Nuevo represents the most comprehensive effort yet to bolster the empirical evidence for prehistoric indigenous burning in California. They combined archaeological research (Hylkema and Cuthrell 2013) with analyses of phytoliths (silica-based plant remains) (Evett and Cuthrell 2013), along with the noted pollen and charcoal studies (Cowart and Byrne 2013), to reach the conclusion that grasslands were more expansive along this stretch of coast between circa A.D. 1000 and 1300 as a result of frequent controlled burning. However, the A.D. 1000–1300 period is associated with prolonged droughts of the Medieval Climatic Anomaly (Stine 1994, Jones et al. 1999), which have been implicated as the cause of higher fire frequency in the Sierra Nevada during this same time (Swetnam 1993). This same inability to distinguish climatically induced vegetation change from anthropogenic change has plagued earlier estimates for when burning was initiated in California (or at least when its effects can first be recognized). While it stands to reason that the earliest human colonists could have used fire to help settle California, as suggested by Nowacki et al. (2012), charcoal is also evident in the paleoenvironmental record before humans arrived. L. Wiegel (1993) suggested that an increase in charcoal in stratified deposits in northwestern California about 5,000 years ago marks the initiation of burning and the establishment of grassy meadows in the heavily forested mountains, but this date corresponds with the peak of early to mid-Holocene warming, which provides an equally (if not more) likely cause for the appearance of these meadows. Parker (1997) suggested that burning began 2,000 years ago in the Sierra Nevada, and preliminary assessment of stratified charcoal records from the Santa Barbara Channel suggested initiation of the practice 2,000 to 3,000 years ago (Byrne et al. 1977).

Nearly all of these chronological estimates represent little more than informed speculation because of the pervasive difficulty of distinguishing human-induced change from the effects of natural climatic variation. Because burning was so widespread among hunter-gatherers globally, and within California in particular, it seems highly unlikely that this practice was independently invented here or that it has a short history. Rather, it seems most likely that it was brought in from the Old World with the initial human colonists as Nowacki et al. (2012) suggest. When its effects can be decisively recognized, and how widespread they were, has simply not been established.

Summary

After more than one hundred years of study by ethnographers, historians, paleoenvironmental specialists, and archaeologists, it remains a challenge to generalize about the relationship between indigenous Californians and their environment. Much of the past fifty years of research has been marked by a debate between two extreme views. One envisions the pre-European California landscape as the end result of a more than 13,000-year program of stewardship that featured, among other things, sophisticated knowledge of the environment and the use of controlled burning as a management tool to encourage habitat diversity and the growth of certain desired species. The other view envisions a long history of human overexploitation of resources that began with anthropogenic extinction of Pleistocene megafauna and continued with population suppression of remaining large, highly desirable species such as deer, elk, and sturgeon. As others have noted (e.g., Parker 1997, Whitaker 2008b), there is little reason to suggest that the truth about these relationships can be found in any of the views on either extreme of this debate. Few accept either the role that Anderson (1993, 1997, 2005) assigns to humans as the ultimate architects of California's landscape or the extreme arguments of Broughton (1994a, 1994b, 1999) and others for overexploitation.

Acceptance of the most solidly supported ethnographic and archaeological evidence suggests a complex relationship between indigenous Californians and their surroundings. On the one hand, Native Californians undoubtedly developed remarkable knowledge of the state's flora and fauna over their more than 13,000 years of residency. The ethnographic record also documents unequivocally that controlled burning was undertaken in most parts of the state to encourage certain species and to aid in hunting. Burning almost certainly enhanced habitat diversity within a certain radius of communities. The effects of burning, however, were probably less extensive than many have asserted (Mensing et al. 1999). The remarkable ritual system that regulated salmon fishing along the Klamath River, which limited catches and effectively ensured sustainability of the fishery among dozens of riverine fishing communities, speaks to indigenous Californians' abilities to share and manage a critical resource. Accounts of the volume of salmon harvested along this river are also consistent with the earliest European descriptions of almost unthinkably high game populations throughout California. On some level, Kroeber's (1925) assessment that California Indians benefitted from an incredibly rich resource base cannot be overlooked, nor can Baumhoff's (1963) assessment that Native peoples were living below the carrying capacity of the resource environment.

While most claims for extreme overexploitation of faunal resources are poorly substantiated, a few key facts illustrate that self-interest also guided subsistence pursuits in indigenous California as it does among all human societies. While no convincing evidence from the California archaeological record suggests that Native people brought about extinction of Pleistocene megafauna, they did render the flightless duck (*Chendytes lawi*) extinct over the course of 8,000 years of hunting. The use of fire to drive game also seems to be an example not of conservation in action but rather of a highly effective strategy for procurement of food. Erlandson et al. (2008) show unequivocally that more and more frequent harvest of abalones over the course of the Holocene led to diminution, though not extirpation. Island inhabitants and other Native Californians were also able to move settlements to allow exploited faunal resource patches to recover. Overexploitation was not pervasive, but human populations did grow over the course of the Holocene, and in the case of flightless duck and abalones, the effects of overly intensive foraging are apparent. Increasingly intensive use of plant foods, a major factor underlying population growth, had no demonstrated effect on the vegetative landscape comparable to the ones on these two animal species. Indigenous Californians accumulated great knowledge of the land, used that knowledge to manipulate certain habitats, and shared bounteous resources effectively, but self-interest, competition, population growth, climate-induced cultural changes, and resource overexploitation were also part of the highly complex, precontact human ecology.

Acknowledgments

We thank the manuscript reviewers and graphic artist for their contributions to this chapter.

All dates referred to in text are based on calibrated radiocarbon dates and refer to the calendric time scale.

Recommended Reading

Arnold, J. E., and M. R. Walsh. 2010. California's ancient past: From the Pacific to the Range of Light. SAA Press, Washington, D.C.

Chase-Dunn, C., and K. M. Mann. 1998. The Wintu and their neighbors: A very small world system in northern California. University of Arizona Press, Tucson, Arizona.

Fagan, B. M. 2003. Before California. Altamira Press, New York, New York.

Gamble, L. 2008. The Chumash world at European contact: Power, trade, and feasting among complex hunter-gatherers. University of California Press, Berkeley, California.

Jones, T. L., and K. A. Klar, editors. 2007. California prehistory: Colonization, culture, and complexity. Altamira Press, New York, New York.

McCawley, W. 1996. The first Angelinos: The Gabrielino Indians of Los Angeles. Malki Museum Press, Banning, California.

References

Anderson, M. K. 2005. Tending the wild. University of California Press, Berkeley, California.

———. 1997. California's endangered peoples and endangered ecosystems. American Indian Culture and Research Journal 21:7–31.

———. 1993. Native Californians as ancient and contemporary cultivators. Pages 151–174 in T. C. Blackburn and K. Anderson, editors. Before the wilderness: Environmental management by Native Californians. Ballena Press, Menlo Park, California.

Andrushko, V. A., A. W. Schwitalla, and P. L. Walker. 2010 Trophy-taking and dismemberment as warfare strategies in prehistoric central California. American Journal of Physical Anthropology 141:83–96.

Arnold, J. E. 1992. Complex hunter-gatherer-fishers of prehistoric California: Chiefs, specialists, and maritime adaptations of the Channel Islands. American Antiquity 57:60–84.

Bartelink, E. 2009. Late Holocene dietary change in San Francisco Bay: Stable isotope evidence for an expansion in diet breadth. California Archaeology 1:227–252.

Basgall, M. E. 1987. Resource intensification among hunter-gatherers: Acorn economies in prehistoric California. Research in Economic Anthropology 9:21–52.

Baumhoff, M. A. 1963. Ecological determinants of aboriginal California populations. University of California Publications in American Archaeology and Ethnology 49:155–336.

Bean, L. J. 1978. Cahuilla. Pages 575–587 in R. F. Heizer, editor. Volume 8, California. Handbook of North American Indians. Smithsonian Institution Press, Washington, D.C.

———. 1972. Mukat's people: The Cahuilla Indians of southern California. University of California Press, Berkeley, California.

Bean, L. J., and H. Lawton, H. 1976. Some explanations for the rise of cultural complexity in Native California with comments on proto-agriculture and agriculture. Pages 19–48 in L. J. Bean and H. Lawton, editors. Native Californians: A theoretical retrospective. Ballena Press, Menlo Park, California.

Bendix, J. 1997. Pre-European fire in California chaparral. Pages 269–294 in T. R. Vale, editor. Fire, native peoples, and the natural landscape. Island Press, Covelo, California.

Bettinger, R. L. 2013. Effects of the bow on social organization in western North America. Evolutionary Anthropology 22:118–123.

———. 1999. Comment on environmental imperatives reconsidered: Demographic crises in western North America during the medieval climatic anomaly. Current Anthropology 40:158–159.

———. 1991. Aboriginal occupation at high altitude: Alpine villages in the White Mountains of eastern California. American Anthropologist 93:656–679.

Blackburn, T. C., and K. Anderson. 1993. Before the wilderness: Environmental management by Native Californians. Ballena Press, Menlo Park, California.

Boneu Companys, F. 1983. Gaspar de Portolá, explorer and founder of California. Instituto de Estudios Ilerdenses, Lerida, Spain.

Broughton, J. M. 2004. Prehistoric human impact on California birds: Evidence from the Emeryville shellmound avifauna. Ornithological Monographs 56. American Ornithologists' Union, University of Arkansas Fayetteville.

———. 1999. Resource depression and intensification during the late Holocene, San Francisco Bay: Evidence from the Emeryville shellmound vertebrate fauna. University of California Anthropological Records 32. American Ornithologists' Union, University of Arkansas Fayetteville.

———. 1997. Widening diet breadth, declining foraging efficiency, and prehistoric harvest pressure: Ichthyofaunal evidence from the Emeryville shellmound, California. Antiquity 71:845–862.

———. 1994a. Declines in mammalian foraging efficiency during the late Holocene, San Francisco Bay. Journal of Anthropological Archaeology 13:371–401.

———. 1994b. Late Holocene resource intensification in the Sacramento River valley, California: The vertebrate evidence. Journal of Archaeological Science 21:501–514.

Broughton, J. M., D. Mullins, and T. Ekker. 2007. Avian resource depression or intertaxonomic variation in bone density? A test with San Francisco Bay avifaunas. Journal of Archaeological Science 34:374–391.

Byrne, R., J. Michaelsen, and A. Soutar. 1977. Fossil charcoal as a measure of wildfire frequency in southern California: A preliminary analysis. Symposium on the Environmental Consequences of Fire and Fuel Management in Mediterranean Ecosystems. General Technical Report WO-3. Forest Service/US Department of Agriculture (USDA), Washington DC/Palo Alto, CA.

Campbell, S. K., and V. L. Butler. 2010. Archaeological evidence for resilience of Pacific Northwest salmon populations and the socio-ecological system over the last ~7,500 years. Ecology and Society 15:17. <http://www.ecologyandsociety.org/vol15/iss1/art17/>. Accessed February 4, 2013.

Castillo, E. D. 1978. The impact of Euro-American exploration and settlement. Pages 99–127 in R. F. Heizer, editor. Volume 8, California. Handbook of North American Indians. Smithsonian Institution Press, Washington, D.C.

Codding, B. F., and T. L. Jones. 2013. Environmental productivity predicts colonization, migration, and demographic patterns in prehistoric California. Proceedings of the National Academy of Science 110:14569–14573.

Cook, S. F. 1978. Historical Demography. Pages 91–98 in R. F. Heizer, editor. California. Handbook of North American Indians, Vol. 8, Smithsonian Institution, Washington, D.C.

Cowart, A., and R. Byrne. 2013. A paleolimnological record of late Holocene vegetation change from the central California coast. California Archaeology 5:334–349.

Cuthrell, R., C. Striplen, M. Hylkema, and K. G. Lightfoot. 2012. A land of fire: Anthropogenic burning on the central coast of California. Pages 153–174 in T. L. Jones and J. E. Perry, editors. Contemporary issues in California archaeology. Left Coast Press, Walnut Creek, California.

Erlandson, J. M. 2013. Channel Island Amol Points: A stemmed paleocoastal point type from Santarosae Island, California. California Archaeology 5:105–121.

———. 1985. Early Holocene settlement and subsistence in relation to coastal paleogeography: Evidence from CA-SBA-1807. Journal of California and Great Basin Anthropology 7:103–109.

Erlandson, J. M., T. C. Rick, T. J. Braje, A. Steinberg, and R. L. Vellanoweth. 2008. Human impacts on ancient shellfish: A 10,000 year record from San Miguel Island, California. Journal of Archaeological Science 35:2144–2152.

Erlandson, J. M., T. C. Rick, T. J. Braje, M. Casperson, B. Culleton, B. Fulfrost, T. Garcia, D. Guthrie, N. Jew, D. J. Kennett, M. L. Moss, L. A. Reeder, C. Skinner, J. Watts, and L. Willis. 2011. Paleoindian seafaring, maritime technologies, and coastal foraging on California's Channel Islands. Science 441:1181–1185.

Etnier, M. A. 2002. The effects of human hunting on northern fur seal (*Callorhinus ursinus*) migration and breeding distributions in the late Holocene. PhD dissertation, University of Washington, Washington.

Evett, R. R., and R. Q. Cuthrell. 2013. Phytolith evidence for a grass-dominated prairie landscape at Quiroste Valley on the central coast of California. California Archaeology 5:317–333.

Farris, G. 1993. Quality food: The quest for pine nuts in northern California. Pages 229–240 in T. C. Blackburn and K. Anderson, editors. Before the wilderness: Environmental management by Native Californians. Ballena Press, Menlo Park, California.

Firestone, R. B., A. West, J. P. Kennett, L. Becker, T. E. Bunch, Z. S. Revay, P. H. Schultz, T. Belgya, D. J. Kennett, J. M. Erlandson, O. J. Dickenson, A. C. Goodyear, R. S. Harris, G. A. Howard, J. B. Kloosterman, P. Lechler, P. A. Mayewski, J. Montgomery, R. Poreda, T. Darrah, S. S. Que Hee, A. R. Smith, A. Stich, W. Topping, J. H. Wittke, and W. S. Wolbach. 2007. Evidence for an extraterrestrial impact 12,900 years ago that contributed to the megafaunal extinctions and Younger Dryas cooling. Proceedings of the National Academy of Science 104:16016–16021.

Fitzgerald, R. T., and W. R. Hildebrandt. 2002. Early Holocene adaptations of the North Coast Ranges: New perspectives on old ideas. Proceedings of the Society for California Archaeology 15:1–7.

Gallegos, D. 2002. Southern California in transition: Late Holocene occupation of southern San Diego County. Pages 27–40 in J. M. Erlandson and T. L. Jones, editors. Catalysts to complexity: Late Holocene societies of the California coast. Cotsen Institute of Archaeology, University of California, Los Angeles, California.

Gamble, L. H. 2005. Culture and Climate: Reconsidering the Effect of Palaeoclimatic variability among southern California hunter-gatherer societies. World Archaeology 37:92–108.

Gifford, E. W. 1971. California balanophagy. Pages 301–305 in R. F. Heizer and M. A. Whipple, editors. The California Indians: A source book. University of California Press, Berkeley, California.

Gilbert, M. T. P., D. L. Jenkins, A. Götherstrom, N. Naveran, J. J. Sanchez, M. Hofreiter, P. F. Thomsen, J. Binladen, T. F. G. Higham, R. M. Yohe II, R. Parr, L. R. S. Cummings, and E. Willerslev. 2008. DNA from pre-Clovis human coprolites in Oregon, North America. Science 320:786–789.

Gill, J. L., J. W. Williams, S. T. Jackson, K. B. Lininger, and G. S. Robinson. 2009. Pleistocene megafaunal collapse, novel plant communities, and enhanced fire regimes in North America. Science 326:1100–1103.

Gilreath, A. J., and W. R. Hildebrandt. 1997. Prehistoric use of the Coso volcanic field. Contributions of the University of California Archaeological Research Facility No. 56, Berkeley, California.

Glassow, M. A., J. M. Erlandson, and T. J. Braje. 2013. A typology of Channel Islands barbed points. Journal of California and Great Basin Anthropology 33:185–196.

Golla, V. 2011. California Indian languages. University of California Press, Berkeley, California.

———. 2007. Linguistic prehistory. Pages 71–82 in T. L. Jones and K. A. Klar, editors. California prehistory: Colonization, culture, and complexity. Altamira, New York, New York.

Grayson, D., and D. Meltzer. 2003. Requiem for North American overkill. Journal of Archaeological Science 30:585–593.

Groza, R., J. Rosenthal, J. Southon, and R. Milliken. 2011. A refined shell bead chronology for central California. Journal of California and Great Basin Anthropology 31:135–155.

Heizer, R. F., editor. 1978. Handbook of North American Indians. Volume 8, California. Smithsonian Institution Press. Washington, D.C..

———. 1974. The destruction of California Indians. Peregrine Smith, Inc., Santa Barbara, California.

Heizer, R. F., and A. F. Almquist, 1971. The other Californians. University of California Press, Berkeley, California.

Hildebrandt, W. R., and T. L. Jones. 1992. Evolution of marine mammal hunting: A view from the California and Oregon coasts. Journal of Anthropological Archaeology 11:360–401.

Hylkema, M. G., and R. Q. Cuthrell. 2013. An archaeological and historical view of Quiroste tribal genesis. California Archaeology 5:224–244.

Ingram, B. L. 1998. Differences in radiocarbon age between shell and charcoal from a Holocene shellmound in northern California. Quaternary Research 49:102–110.

Johnson, J. R., B. M. Kemp, C. Monroe, and J. G. Lorenz. 2012. A land of diversity: Genetic insights into ancestral origins. Pages 49–72 in T. L. Jones and J. E. Perry, editors. Contemporary issues in California archaeology. Left Coast Press, Walnut Creek, California.

Johnson, J. R., T. W. Stafford Jr., H. O. Ajie, and D. P. Morris. 2002. Arlington Springs revisited. Pages 541–545 in D. R. Browne, K. L. Mitchell, and H. W. Chaney, editors. Proceedings of the Fifth California Islands Symposium. Santa Barbara Museum of Natural History, Santa Barbara, California.

Jones, T. L. 2003. Prehistoric human ecology of the Big Sur coast, California. Contributions of the University of California Archaeological Research Facility No. 61. University of California, Berkeley, California.

———. 1996. Mortars, pestles, and division of labor in prehistoric California: A view from Big Sur. American Antiquity 61:243–264.

Jones, T. L., and D. J. Kennett. 2012. A land impacted? The Younger-Dryas boundary event in California. Pages 37–48 in T. L. Jones and J. E. Perry, editors. Contemporary issues in California archaeology. Left Coast Press, Walnut Creek, California.

Jones, T. L., and D. Jones. 1992 Elkhorn Slough revisited: Reassessing the chronology of CA-MNT-229. Journal of California and Great Basin Anthropology 10:163–186.

Jones, T. L., B. J. Culleton, S. Larson, S. Mellinger, and J. F. Porcasi. 2011. Toward a prehistory of the southern sea otter (*Enhydra lutris nereis*). Pages 243–272 in T. Rick and T. Braje, editors. Humans and marine ecosystems: Archaeology and historical ecology of northeastern Pacific seals, sea lions, and sea otters. University of California Press, Berkeley, California.

Jones, T. L., G. Brown, L. M. Raab, J. McVicar, G. Spaulding, D. J. Kennett, A. York, and P. L. Walker. 1999. Environmental imperatives reconsidered: Demographic crises in western North America during the Medieval Climatic Anomaly. Current Anthropology 40:137–156.

Jones, T. L., J. F. Porcasi, J. M. Erlandson, H. Dallas Jr., T. A. Wake, and R. Schwaderer. 2008. The protracted Holocene extinction of California's flightless sea duck (*Chendytes lawi*) and its implications for the Pleistocene overkill hypothesis. Proceedings of the National Academy of Science 105:4105–4108.

Jones, T. L., R. T. Fitzgerald, D. J. Kennett, C. H. Miksicek, J. L. Fagan, J. Sharp, and J. M. Erlandson. 2002. The Cross Creek Site (CA-SLO-1797) and its implications for New World colonization. American Antiquity 67:213–230.

Kay, C. E., and R. T. Simmons, editors. 2002. Wilderness and political ecology: Aboriginal influences and the original state of nature. University of Utah Press, Salt Lake City, Utah.

Keeley J. E. 2002. Native American impacts on fire regimes of the California coastal ranges. Journal of Biogeography 29:303–320.

Kennett, D. J., and J. P. Kennett. 2000. Competitive and cooperative responses to climate instability in coastal southern California. American Antiquity 65:379–395.

Kennett, D.J., J. P. Kennett, G. J. West, J. M. Erlandson, J. R. Johnson, I. L. Hendy, A. West, B. J. Culleton, T. L. Jones, and T. W. Stafford Jr. 2008. Wildfire and abrupt ecosystem disruption on California's Northern Channel Islands at the Ållerød-Younger Dryas Boundary (13.0–12.9 ka). Quaternary Science Review 27:2528–2543.

Kennett, D. J., P. M. Lambert, J. R. Johnson, and B. J. Culleton. 2013. Sociopolitical effects of bow and arrow technology in prehistoric coastal California. Evolutionary Anthropology 22:124–132.

Kerr, R. A. 2010. Mammoth-killer impact flunks out. Science 329:1140–1141.

King, C. 1993. Fuel use and resource management: Implications for a study of land management in prehistoric California and recommendations for a research program. Pages 279–298 in T. C. Blackburn and K. Anderson, editors. Before the wilderness: Environmental management by Native Californians. Ballena Press, Menlo Park, California.

———. 1976. Chumash intervillage economic exchange. Pages 289–318 in L. J. Bean and T. C. Blackburn, editors. Native Californians: A theoretical retrospective. Ballena Press, Ramona, California.

Krech, S. 1999. The ecological Indian. W. W. Norton and Company, New York, New York.

Kroeber, A. L. 1948. Anthropology. Harcourt Brace, New York, New York.

———. 1925. Handbook of the Indians of California. Bureau of American Ethnology Bulletin 78. Smithsonian Institution Press. Washington, D.C.

Lambert, P. M. 1994. War and peace on the western front: A study of violent conflict and its correlates in prehistoric hunter-gatherer societies of coastal southern California. PhD dissertation. Department of Anthropology, University of California, Santa Barbara, California.

La Perouse, J. F. G. 1968. A voyage round the world performed in the years 1785, 1786, 1787, and 1788 by the Boussole and Astrolabe, volume 1. Da Capo Press, New York, New York.

Lewis, H. 1973. Patterns of burning in California: Ecology and ethnohistory. Ballena Press, Menlo Park, California.

Lightfoot, K. G., and O. Parrish. 2009. California Indians and their environment. University of California Press, Berkeley, California.

Lightfoot, K. G., and V. Lopez. 2013. The study of indigenous landscape management practices in California: An introduction. California Archaeology 5:1–12.

Lightfoot K. G., R. Q. Cuthrell, C. M. Boone, R. Byrne, A. B. Chavez, L. Collins, A. Cowart, R. R. Evett, P. V. A. Fine, D. Gifford-Gonzalez, M. G. Hylkema, V. Lopez, T. M. Misiewicz, R. E. B. Reid, and C. J. Striplen. 2013. Anthropogenic burning on the central California coast in late Holocene and early historical times: Findings, implications, and future directions. California Archaeology 5:368–388.

Lindsay, B. C. 2012. Murder state: California's Native American genocide, 1846–1873. University of Nebraska Press, Lincoln, Nebraska.

Lyman, L. R. 2003. Pinniped behavior, foraging theory, and the depression of metapopulations and nondepression of a local population on the southern Northwest Coast of North America. Journal of Anthropological Archaeology 22:376–388.

Margolin, M. 1978. The Ohlone way. Hey Day Books, Berkeley, California.

Martin, P. S. 1967. Pleistocene overkill. Natural History 76:32–38.

Masters, P. M., and D. Gallegos. 1997. Environmental change and coastal adaptations in San Diego county during the middle Holocene. Pages 11–21 in J. M. Erlandson and M. A. Glassow, editors. Archaeology of the California Coast during the Middle Holocene. Cotsen Institute of Archaeology, University of California, Los Angeles, California.

McCarthy, H. 1993. Managing oaks and the acorn crop. Pages 213–228 in T. C. Blackburn and K. Anderson, editors. Before the wilderness: Environmental management by Native Californians. Ballena Press, Menlo Park, California.

Meltzer, D. J. 2009. First peoples in a new world. University of California Press, Berkeley, California.

Mensing, S. A., J. Michaelsen, and R. Byrne. 1999. A 560-year record of Santa Ana fires reconstructed from charcoal deposited in the Santa Barbara Basin, California. Quaternary Research 51:295–305.

Moratto, M. J. 1984. California archaeology. Academic Press, Orlando, Florida.

Norton, J. 1979. Genocide in northwestern California. Indian Historian Press, San Francisco, California.

Nowacki, G. J., D. W. MacClerry, and F. K. Lake. 2012. Native Americans, ecosystem development, and historical range of variation. Pages 76–91. in J. A. Wiens, G. D. Hayward, H. D. Stafford, and C. M. Giffen, editors. Historical environmental variation in conservation and natural resource management. Wiley-Blackwell, Hoboken, New Jersey.

Parker, A. J. 1997. Fire in Sierra Nevada forests: Evaluating the ecological impact of burning by Native Americans. Pages 233–268 in T. R. Vale, editor. Fire, Native Peoples, and the Natural Landscape. Island Press, Covelo, California.

Peri, D. W., and S. M. Patterson. 1993. The basket is in the roots, that's where it begins. Pages 175–195 in T. C. Blackburn and K. Anderson, editors. Before the wilderness: Environmental management by Native Californians. Ballena Press, Menlo Park, California.

Raab, L. M., and D. O. Larson. 1997. Medieval Climatic Anomaly and punctuated cultural evolution in coastal southern California. American Antiquity 62:319–336.

Raab, L. M., and T. L. Jones. 2004. The rediscovery of California prehistory. Pages 1–10 in L. M. Raab and T. L. Jones, editors. Prehistoric California: Archaeology and the myth of paradise. University of Utah Press, Salt Lake City, Utah.

Rick, T., J. M. Erlandson, W. R. Hildebrandt, R. DeLong, and T. L. Jones. 2011. Where were the northern elephant seals? Holocene archaeology and biogeography of *Mirounga angustirostris*. The Holocene 21:1159–1166.

Rondeau, M. F., J. Cassidy, and T. L. Jones. 2007. Colonization technologies: Fluted projectile points and the San Clemente Island woodworking/microblade complex. Pages 63–70 in T. L. Jones and K. A. Klar, editors. California prehistory: Colonization, culture, and complexity. Altamira Press, New York, New York.

Salls, R. A. 1992. Prehistoric subsistence change on California's Channel Islands: Environmental or cultural? Pages 157–172 in T. L. Jones, editor. Essays on the prehistory of maritime California. Center for Archaeological Research at Davis Publication 10. University of California, Davis, California.

Schaefer, J., and D. Laylander. 2007. The Colorado Desert: Ancient adaptations to wetlands and wastelands. Pages 247–257 in T. L. Jones and K . A. Klar, editors. California prehistory: Colonization, culture, and complexity. Altamira Press, New York, New York.

Schwaderer, R. 1992. Archaeological test excavation at the Duncans Point Cave, CA-SON-348/H. Pages 55–71 in T. L. Jones, editor. Essays on the prehistory of maritime California. Center for Archaeological Research at Davis Publication 10. University of California, Davis, California.

Schwitalla, A. W. 2013. Global warming in California: A lesson from the medieval climatic anomaly (A.D. 800–1350). Center for Archaeological Research at Davis Publication 17. Department of Anthropology, University of California, Davis, California.
Schwitalla, A. W., T. L. Jones, M. A. Pilloud, B. F. Codding, and R. S. Wiberg. 2014. Violence among foragers: The bioarchaeological record from central California. Journal of Anthropological Archaeology 33:66–83.
Steadman, D.W. 1995. Prehistoric extinctions of Pacific island birds: Biodiversity meets zooarchaeology. Science 267:1123–1131.
Stewart, O. C. 2002. Forgotten fires: Native Americans and the transient wilderness. University of Oklahoma Press, Norman, Oklahoma.
Stine, S. 1994. Extreme and persistent drought in California and Patagonia during mediaeval time. Nature 369:546–549.
Swetnam, T. W. 1993. Fire history and climate change in giant Sequoia groves. Science
262:885–89.
Swezey, S. L., and R. F. Heizer. 1977. Ritual management of salmonid fish resources in California. Journal of California and Great Basin Anthropology 4:6–29.
Tushingham, S. 2009. The development of intensive foraging systems in northwestern California. PhD dissertation. Department of Anthropology, University of California, Davis, California.
Walker, E. F. N.d. Indians of southern California. Leaflet. Southwest Museum, Los Angeles, California.
Walker, P. L, D. J. Kennett, T. L. Jones, and R. DeLong. 2002. Archaeological investigations at the Point Bennett pinniped rookery on San Miguel Island, California. Pages 628–632 in D. Browne, K. Mitchell, and H. Chaney, editors. Proceedings of the Fifth California Islands Symposium. Santa Barbara Museum of Natural History, Santa Barbara, California.
Waters, M. R, and T. W. Stafford. 2007. Redefining the age of Clovis: Implications for the peopling of the Americas. Science 315:122–1126.
West, G. J., W. Woolfenden, J. A. Wanket, and R. Scott Anderson. 2007. Late Pleistocene and Holocene environments. Pages 11–34 in T. L. Jones and K. A. Klar, editors. California prehistory: Colonization, culture, and complexity. Altamira Press, New York, New York.
Whitaker, A. R. 2010. Prehistoric behavioral depression of cormorant (*Phalacrocorax* spp.) on the northern California coast. Journal of Archaeological Science 37:2562–2571.
———. 2009. Are deer really susceptible to resource depression? Modeling deer (*Odocoileus hemionus*) populations under human predation. California Archaeology 1:93–108.
———. 2008a. Incipient aquaculture in prehistoric California? Long-term productivity and sustainability vs. immediate returns for the harvest of marine invertebrates. Journal of Archaeological Science 35:1114–1123.
———. 2008b. The role of human predation in the structuring of prehistoric prey populations in northwestern California. PhD dissertation. University of California, Davis, California.
Wiegel, L. 1993. Prehistoric burning in northwestern California. Pages 213–216 in G. White, P. Mikkelsen, W. R. Hildebrandt, and M. E. Basgall, editors. There grows a green tree: Papers in honor of David A. Fredrickson. Center for Archaeological Research at Davis no. 11. University of California, Davis, California.
Wilkes, C. 1845. Narrative of the United States exploring expedition during years 1838, 1839, 1840, 1841, 1842. Lea and Blanchard, Philadelphia, Pennsylvania.
Yamada, S. B., and E. E. Peters. 1988. Harvest management and the growth and condition of submarket size mussels, *Mytilus californianus*. Aquaculture 74:293–299.

PART THREE

BIOTA

ELEVEN

Biodiversity

BERNIE TERSHY, SUSAN HARRISON, ABRAHAM BORKER, BARRY SINERVO, TARA CORNELISSE, CHENG LI, DENA SPATZ, DONALD CROLL, and ERIKA ZAVALETA

Introduction

If California were a country, it would be among the largest of global economies, most important innovators of popular culture, leaders of technological advancement, producers of food crops, and generators of groundbreaking science. But surrounding Hollywood and Silicon Valley is a more ancient and irreplaceable wealth: California's biodiversity. Compared to the world's countries, California ranks about seventeenth in breeding bird richness and thirty-ninth in mammal richness. Compared to the rest of the United States, California ranks first in plant and animal species richness as well as single-state endemic species richness. Although it comprises only 3% of U.S. land area, California houses more than 30% of all plant and vertebrate species in the U.S. and ranks in the top five states for richness of every group of vertebrates except freshwater fishes (Figures 11.1 and 11.2).

This remarkable biodiversity was once matched by California's indigenous cultural diversity. Before the arrival of Europeans, California was one of the most culturally diverse places on earth, with more languages than any other U.S. state and an estimated 35% of all languages spoken in what is now the U.S. and Canada (Hinton 1998). California's remarkable biodiversity and former linguistic diversity are closely linked to the state's physical diversity. It has the greatest range of latitude and elevation of any state in the continental U.S., the greatest diversity of soils in the U.S. (Amundson et al. 2003), and the greatest range of mean annual rainfall (from >255 centimeters in Humboldt County to <5 centimeters in Death Valley) and temperature (from <0°C in the high Sierras to >21°C in the southeast desert) of any state in the U.S. (NOAA 2005). The range of California's microclimates is so great that several times each year California registers both the nation's highest and lowest daily temperatures on the same day (NOAA 2005). The interaction between microclimate and soil types makes for a spectacular mosaic of habitats, resulting in high levels of beta diversity and endemism. Finally, much of California is included in one of the world's five Mediterranean-climate regions, all of which are recognized for their exceptionally high plant diversity (Cody 1986).

California's spectacular biodiversity took millions of years to evolve and assemble, but its future is uncertain. California

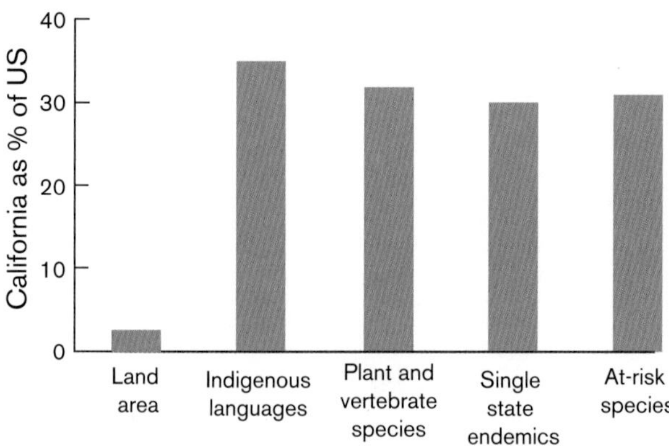

FIGURE 11.1 California's current biodiversity measures and historical cultural diversity as a percentage of U.S. totals (bars). California is the third largest state in the U.S. but ranks first in number of indigenous languages, number of plant species, number of vertebrate species, number of single state endemic species, and number of at-risk species. Sources: Biodiversity data: Parasi 2003. Language data: Hinton 1988.

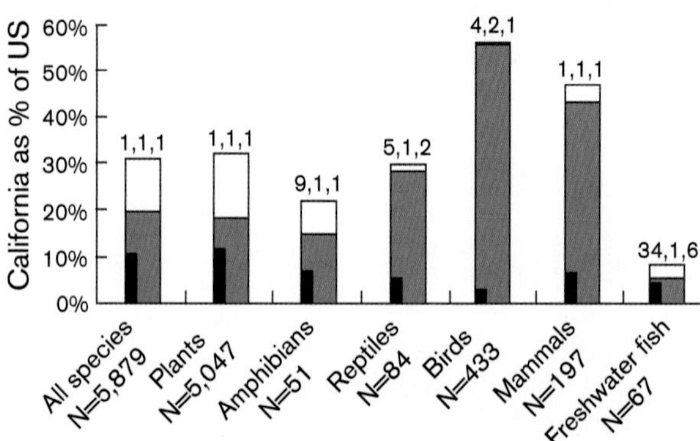

FIGURE 11.2 California's species richness as a percentage of U.S. totals for all plant and vertebrate species and by taxonomic group. Total bar is for all species in the state; the filled portion represents nonendemic species and the open portion represents state endemic species. The black line in each bar indicates percentage of federally endangered or threatened species. Numbers above the bars are national ranks for richness of species, number of endemic species, and number of threatened species, respectively. Values for freshwater fish endemism differ from those in Chapter 33, "Rivers," which reports California as having 63% endemic freshwater fishes and 19% shared with one other state. This is because we use only full species data, while the authors of Chapter 33 use data for evolutionary significant units (ESUs) and distinct population segments, some of which have yet to receive full species status. Invertebrate numbers are less well known and not included in the figure. The estimated thirty-four thousand California invertebrates are thought to make up 30% of U.S. invertebrates, ranking California first in richness. California's thirty-two endangered invertebrates make up over half of the U.S. total.

Photo on previous page: Winter storm clearing at Rancho Del Oso, Big Basin State Park, with Waddell Creek flowing near flood stage after two days of heavy rains. Visible in this one scene are redwood forest, Monterey pine forest, coastal estuary, willow/alder riparian forest, oak woodland, maritime chaparral, and coastal scrub. Photo: Ed Dickie (eddickie.com).

has more threatened species (1,822) than any other U.S. state and a higher percentage of species threatened (31%) than any other state except Hawaii (see Figure 11.1). In California, as elsewhere, the two largest threats to biodiversity are habitat loss and invasive species (responsible for 63% and 38% of California extinctions, respectively) (Table 11.1; see Chapter 13, "Biological Invasions"). Most (72%) of California's extinct species have been terrestrial mainland species, while 19% and 9% of California's extinctions have been in freshwater systems and on marine islands, respectively. However, scaled to area, freshwater systems have extinction densities six times greater than the terrestrial mainland, and marine islands have extinction densities ninety times greater than the terrestrial mainland. There have been no recorded marine extinctions in the state, and no species extinctions in California have clearly been attributed to pollution or overexploitation to date.

Fortunately, California has experienced very little permanent biodiversity loss; only about thirty-two California species, fewer than 0.1%, are known to have gone extinct in the past two hundred years (see Table 11.1). Furthermore, well-established and effective conservation actions exist that can protect the majority of the state's threatened species and assist in the successful reintroduction of extinct California species persisting outside the state. For example, the successful eradication of damaging invasive mammals from California's islands is a globally significant conservation victory that has protected many of the state's most vulnerable terrestrial species (Keitt et al. 2011; see Chapter 34, "Managed Island Ecosystems"). The successful eradication of pike (*Esox lucius*) from Lake Davis and invasive trout (Salmonidae) from many high Sierra lakes (Knapp et al. 2007) show that invasive species eradication can be an effective tool for the conservation of California's freshwater systems (see Chapter 13, "Biological Invasions"). California's network of terrestrial protected areas covers a remarkable 46% of the state (Calands 2013), and our understanding of protected area design and management for biodiversity conservation is steadily improving. Although many areas critical for the survival of threatened species remain unprotected, tools are available to identify and prioritize those lands, as are innovative approaches to protecting them (Leverington et al. 2010, Apronen et al. 2012, Bull et al. 2013, Spatz et al. 2014).

California's global leadership in the development of effective environmental protection strategies has led to significant pollution reductions in the past twenty-five years (Parrish et al. 2011). Although damaging toxins continue to be identified (e.g., atrazine, brodifacoum), a 2013 ban on lead ammunition, to help protect critically endangered species (California Assembly Bill number 711), demonstrates California's continued leadership in effective environmental regulation. Finally, the successful reintroduction of locally extinct marsh sandwort (*Arenaria paludicola*), Owens pupfish (*Cyprinodon radiosus*), Roosevelt (*Cervis canadensis roosevelti*) and tule elk (*Cervis canadensis nannodes*), bald eagles (*Haliaeetus leucocephalus*), island fox (*Urocyon littoralis*), and California condors (*Gymnogyps califonianus*) to the wild demonstrates that even the most endangered of California's species can be saved.

This chapter provides an overview of five major groups of California's biological diversity. We begin with plants and go on to the state's diversity of invertebrates, HERPETOFAUNA (reptiles and amphibians), birds, and mammals. We summarize the evolutionary diversification, biogeography, and conservation context for each taxonomic assemblage. Nonvascu-

TABLE 11.1

California species globally extinct in the past hundred years, the ecosystem in which each occurred, and the driver of each extinction

Note: H = Habitat loss; I = Invasive species; U = Unknown

Taxa[A]	Common name	Family	Species	Ecosystem[B]	Driver[C]		
					H	I	U
Fish (2)	Thicktail chub	Cyprinidae	*Gila crassicauda*	freshwater	1	1	
	Clear lake splittail	Cyprinidae	*Pogonichthys ciscoides*	freshwater	1	1	
Invertabrates (10)	Sooty crayfish	Astacidae	*Pacifastacus nigrescens*	freshwater		1	
	Pasadena freshwater shrimp	Atyidae	*Syncaris nigrescens*	freshwater	1		
	Central valley grasshopper	Acrididae	*Conozoa hyalina*	terrestrial continental	1		
	Xerces blue butterfly	Lycaenidae	*Glaucopsyche xerces*	terrestrial continental	1	1	
	Mono lake diving beetle	Dytiscidae	*Hygrotus artus*	freshwater	1		
	Antioch dunes shieldback katydid	Tettigoniidae	*Neduba extincta*	terrestrial continental	1		
	Voluntina Stonemyia fly	Tababanidae	*Stonemyia volutina*	terrestrial continental			1
	Castle lake caddis fly	Rhyacophilidae	*Rhyacophila amabilis*	freshwater		1	
	Yorba Linda weevil	Curculionidae	*Trigonoscuta yorbalindae*	terrestrial continental			1
	Fort Ross weevil	Curculionidae	*Trigonoscuta rossi*	terrestrial continental			1
Plants (20)	Bakersfield smallscale	Chenopodiaceae	*Atriplex tularensis*	terrestrial continental	1		
	Single-flowered mariposa lily	Liliaceae	*Calochortus monanthus*	terrestrial continental			1
	Point Reyes paintbrush	Orobanchaceae	*Castilleja leschkeana*	terrestrial continental			1
	Pitkin Marsh paintbrush	Orobanchaceae	*Castilleja uliginosa*	terrestrial continental			1
	Lost thistle	Asteraceae	*Cirsium praeteriens*	terrestrial continental	1		
	Hoover's cryptantha	Boraginaceae	*Cryptantha hooveri*	terrestrial continental			1
	Mariposa daisy	Asteraceae	*Erigeron mariposanus*	terrestrial continental			1
	San Nicolas Island desert-thorn	Solanaceae	*Lycium verrucosum*	terrestrial island		1	
	Mendocino bush-mallow	Malvaceae	*Malacothamnus mendocinensis*	terrestrial continental			1
	Parish's bush-mallow	Malvaceae	*Malacothamnus parishii*	terrestrial continental	1		
	Santa Cruz Island monkeyflower	Phrymaceae	*Mimulus brandegeei*	terrestrial island		1	

(continued)

TABLE 11.1 *(continued)*
Note: H = Habitat; I = Invasive; U = Unknown

Taxa[A]	Common name	Family	Species	Ecosystem[B]	Driver[C] H	I	U
	Santa Catalina Island monkeyflower	Phrymaceae	*Mimulus traskiae*	terrestrial island		1	
	Whipple's monkeyflower	Phrymaceae	*Mimulus whipplei*	terrestrial continental			1
	Merced monardella	Lamiaceae	*Monardella leucocephala*	terrestrial continental	1		
	Pringle's monardella	Lamiaceae	*Monardella pringlei*	terrestrial continental	1		
	Hairless popcorn-flower	Boraginaceae	*Plagiobothrys glaber*	terrestrial continental			1
	Mayacamas popcorn-flower	Boraginaceae	*Plagiobothrys lithocaryus*	terrestrial continental			1
	Ballona cinquefoil	Rosaceae	*Potentilla multijuga*	terrestrial continental	1		
	Cunningham Marsh cinquefoil	Rosaceae	*Potentilla uliginosa*	terrestrial continental	1		
	Parish's gooseberry	Grossulariaceae	*Ribes divaricatum*	terrestrial continental	1	1	

SOURCE: Data from International Union for the Conservation of Nature (IUCN) Redlist, Natureserve, Wikipedia, and CDFW websites (accessed April 2014).

A. Known extinction in past one hundred years/number of species in California: plants 20/5,879; invertebrates 10/34,000; fish 2/67; reptiles, amphibians, birds, and mammals = 0.

B. Ecosystems from which species have gone extinct: terrestrial continental = 23, freshwater = 6, terrestrial island = 3, marine water = 0.

C. Proximate drivers of California global extinctions: habitat destruction = 15, invasive species = 9, overexploitation and pollution = 0, unknown = 12 (multiple causes can contribute to extinction of one species).

lar plants, algae, fungi, and other taxa are not covered in this chapter, but their relative richness could also be quite high in California and linked to the state's physical diversity (e.g., Moeller et al. 2014). California's diversity of freshwater fishes is explored in detail in Chapter 33, "Rivers," rather than here. Marine diversity is described in the context of the several distinct marine ecosystem types occurring at and off the California coast (Chapter 16, "The Offshore Ecosystem"; Chapter 17, "Shallow Rocky Reefs and Kelp Forests"; Chapter 18, "Intertidal"; and Chapter 19, "Estuaries: Life on the Edge"). Finally, the importance of California's biological diversity to the functioning of California's ecosystems, including their services to its human populace, is explored in Chapter 15, "Introduction to Concepts of Biodiversity, Ecosystem Functioning, Ecosystem Services, and Natural Capital."

California has been subdivided somewhat differently for different taxa in ways that reflect both the state of knowledge and the characteristic scales and patterns of diversity and turnover in the state. The taxonomic sections that follow in this chapter describe the biogeographic distribution of species following conventions most common for that taxon. We elected this approach rather than a common ecoregional subdivision across all sections so that the reader can easily move between this volume and taxon-specific resources organized according to taxon-specific conventions. Thus the six regions used here to describe invertebrates differ slightly from the five ecoregions around which mammal biogeography is organized, and so on. Furthermore, the number of species and their relationships to each other change over time. Molecular techniques make it possible to more easily and clearly separate subspecies into full species and to identify cryptic species that are morphologically similar but genetically distinct. Molecular techniques have also made it possible to more accurately reconstruct evolutionary relationships and moved taxonomy into the framework of phylogenetic systematics. For plants, for example, the newest flora for California—*The Jepson Manual*, second edition (Baldwin et al. 2012)—has followed this framework and radically changed Californian plant taxonomy. Species definitions have changed as well, for a variety of reasons, so that even when old names persist they may have new meanings. For example, the annual herb hillside collinsia (*Collinsia sparsiflora* var. *collina*) is now a Californian endemic because its Oregonian relatives are no longer considered to belong to the same species.

Flora

California has long been recognized as the botanically richest part of the United States, as well as one of the world's most significant regions for plant diversity. Together with its sheer numbers of plant species and varieties, California is outstanding for its plant endemism—its wealth of species and varieties found nowhere else. Indeed, the majority of the state—everything but its deserts—is considered, together with small parts of adjoining Oregon and Baja California, a globally unique Floristic Province united by the shared evolutionary histories of its plant lineages. Many of the plant lineages centered in California appear to be relatively young and rapidly evolving, and since the advent of modern evolutionary biology in the mid-twentieth century, these lineages have attracted considerable attention from biosystematists interested in plant adaptation and speciation. California has thus been considered a "model system" for studying plant diversity.

In many ways, however, our understanding remains far from complete. California's large size and its rugged, climatically and geologically diverse landscape might seem obvious explanations for its botanical richness. Curiously, though, many of the diverse Californian plant lineages show only modest ecological differentiation, suggesting that something besides the state's variety of climates and soils must have given rise to their diversification. Interestingly, California is not nearly as rich in endemic animal species, except in a few groups notable for their low mobility and (again) lack of strong ecological or morphological divergence. Today, California's climate most resembles the other four Mediterranean-climate regions, with distinct wet winters and long dry summers and high interannual variability in rainfall (Cody and Mooney 1978, Cowling et al. 1996 see Chapter 2, "Climate"). Recent molecular and paleontological evidence suggests that the origins of high plant diversity arose before the onset of the modern Mediterranean-climatic pattern, 1.8 million years ago.

In the section we review plant species richness and endemism in California, including comparisons of the state with other states, the state with the Floristic Province, and the Floristic Province with the other Mediterranean-climate regions of the world. We briefly explore patterns of plant diversity within California, which are provided in more detail in Chapter 12, "Vegetation," and we review old and new evidence on the causes of California's plant diversity.

Evolutionary Diversification

Overall, 4,266 full species of plants are now considered native to the state of California, including approximately 1,307 that are endemic to the state (Baldwin et al. 2012) (see Figure 11.1). In the past, splitting of taxa was more common and numbers were thus higher (e.g., Raven and Axelrod 1978). Because the new revisions are so recent, this chapter will often draw on older figures (e.g., see Figures 11.1 and 11.2), except where noted. We are unaware of any cases in which the broad patterns of plant diversity in California have been altered by these recent taxonomic changes. In a comprehensive assessment of plant and animal diversity within the United States (that did not incorporate more recent taxonomic revisions and so has slightly different numbers than above) no other state approached California's botanical richness, with an estimated 4,839 native plant species, of which 1,416 or 30% are endemic to the state (Stein et al. 2000; see Figure 11.2). The next highest states are Texas with 4,458 species, of which 251 (6%) are endemic; Florida with 2,995 species, of which 155 (5%) are endemic; and Hawaii with 1,207 species, of which, unsurprisingly given its isolation as an ocean island, 1,048 (87%) are endemic.

Californian endemism is also high in freshwater fish (29%) and amphibians (34%) as well as in a few animal families: for example, the often flightless Acridid grasshoppers (51%), nest-building Megachilid bees (53%), and tiny Phalangogid harvestmen (60%) (Harrison 2013). However, overall endemism rates are much lower in most major group of animals (mammals, 9%; birds, 0.5%; reptiles, 6%; insects, an estimated 15%) (see Figure 11.2; Stein et al. 2000). These numbers do not change greatly if endemism to the Floristic Province is considered. In a comprehensive new analysis, Burge et al. (2016) listed 1,884 (33%) endemic plant species out of 5,782 total native plant species in the California Floristic Province (CFP), as compared with 1,736 CFP endemics among the 5,332 total plant species in the state of California. Thus, while the state's deserts add numerous species to the flora, nearly all of these are also found outside the state. These authors also found that southwestern Oregon added 90 total species and 40 endemics to the Province, while northwestern Baja added 227 total species and 107 endemics. An analysis taking into account the recent taxonomic changes (Baldwin et al. 2012) revised the earlier estimates downward slightly to approximately 4,500 total species of native plants including 1,931 (42%) endemics in the Floristic Province. Of these, now higher totals are contributed by Baja California of 969 plant species including 338 endemics, and by Oregon of 220 total species including 14 endemics (Harrison 2013).

The farewell-to-spring genus (*Clarkia*) and the monkey-flowers (*Mimulus*) illustrate radiations that took place in California in response to multiple, interacting forces. Clarkias radiated in the time of pre-Mediterranean climate and include forty-two species, of which thirty-six are found only in the California Floristic Province. Evolutionary studies on narrowly endemic *Clarkia* species initially focused on the role of nonadaptive changes, such as random chromosomal rearrangements, that could occur in small populations and lead them to become new species. Newer studies suggest that not only chromosomal rearrangements but also natural selection, spatial isolation, and breeding system changes all play roles whose relative importance is not yet clear (Gottlieb 2003). The monkey-flower genus is one of the most ecologically diverse groups of Californian neoendemics, with species occupying not only Mediterranean but also desert and alpine climates, and species restricted to wetlands, serpentine, dunes, peat bogs, geyser margins, and other unusual substrates. Diversity in flower color and shape, seasonality, growth form, and breeding systems is also high. Ecological speciation plays an undeniable role in *Mimulus*, and the genus is a model system for examining how environmental challenges (drought stress, extreme soils) interact with genetic mechanisms (e.g., chromosome duplication, allelic incompatibility, linkage structure) and reproductive strategies (e.g., seasonality, pollinators, mating system) to facilitate speciation (Beardsley et al. 2004, Hall et al. 2010, Wu et al. 2007).

Biogeography

Biogeographers divide the world based not on current climate, vegetation, or species, but rather on the shared ancestry and biogeographic history that are believed to unite the plant lineages within a region; the most widely used system recognizes Floristic Kingdoms, Regions, and Provinces (e.g., Takhtajan 1986). The California Floristic Province broadly coincides with where Mediterranean-type climate occurs in North America. It extends from south-central Oregon through the nondesert parts of California to northwestern Baja California

(Raven and Axelrod 1978, Conservation International 2011, Baldwin et al. 2012; see Figure 11.1).

All five of the world's Mediterranean-climate regions fall among the planet's top twenty-five hotspots of diversity and endangerment, defined by having >1,500 endemic plant species as well as >75% loss of native vegetation (Myers et al. 2000). Strikingly, these Mediterranean-climate regions are almost the only such hotspots outside of the tropics, as well as among the few not similarly rich in animal endemism. After adjusting for differences in area, by far the richest flora among the Mediterranean-climate regions of the world belongs to the Cape region of South Africa, which is so evolutionarily distinctive that it is considered its own Floristic Kingdom—the top level in the biogeographic classification hierarchy. Next is southwestern Australia, followed by the Mediterranean Basin; California lies fourth, ahead of only Central Chile (Cowling et al. 1996, Harrison 2013). These patterns are almost exactly opposite of what might be predicted based on topographic and geologic heterogeneity.

Patterns of Plant Diversity and Endemism in California

In a now classic analysis, G. Ledyard Stebbins and Jack Major (1965) asked what gave rise to California's botanical uniqueness by determining where in the state the greatest numbers of endemics (species found nowhere else) were found. These authors pioneered the distinction between "paleoendemics" (taxonomically isolated species thought to belong to ancient lineages that are RELICTS of past wetter climates) and "neoendemics" (species with many close relatives nearby, thought to belong to young and rapidly evolving lineages). Paleoendemics include redwoods (*Sequoia sempervirens*), giant sequoias (*Sequoiadendron giganteum*), and many other trees, shrubs, and herbs with their closest relatives often occurring in the southeastern U.S. or temperate Asian forests. These occur mainly in the wetter parts of the state, including the Klamath and North Coast regions and the coastal fog belt. Neoendemics include the species-rich plant genera most strongly centered in California and most often studied by those interested in plant speciation—shrubs such as manzanitas (*Arctostaphylos*) and California-lilac (*Ceanothus*) and herbs such as *Madia*, *Clarkia*, *Limnanthes*, and *Navarretia*. Neoendemics are most common in the Mediterranean-type climates of the central Coast Ranges, mid-elevation Sierran foothills, and southern Californian coast, and least abundant in the deserts and Central Valley. Rapid plant evolution, these authors concluded, was promoted by a fluctuating climate and a rugged landscape where short distances separated dramatically different plant habitats.

Recent, comprehensive analyses also find that the Coast Ranges are the richest part of the state for endemic plants (Thorne et al. 2009, Kraft et al. 2010). The highest concentrations of neoendemics are found in the Central Coast (particularly the San Francisco Bay area), the southern part of the North Coast region, and the Sierra Nevadan foothills. The neoendemics with the smallest ranges are found at low elevations in the Coast Ranges and at higher elevations in the Sierra and Transverse Ranges. The youngest neoendemics, as judged by molecular evidence, occur in the deserts. However, neither the means nor the heterogeneity in topography or climate variables—the drivers of plant diversification hypothesized by Stebbins and Major—are good predictors of endemic diversity (Kraft et al. 2010).

Clearly, new evidence about California's floristic history continues to come from not only molecular genetics but also paleobotany; there has been a steady growth in the quality of evidence from traditional macrofossils, fossil pollen in marine sediment cores, radiometric dating techniques, and global and regional climate reconstructions using isotope ratios. In particular, the details of how California's vegetation changed during Pleistocene glacial-interglacial cycles are now much better known (Millar 1996; see Chapter 8, "Ecosystems Past: Vegetation Prehistory"). In striking contrast to animals, the timing of genetic divergence in plants appears inconsistent both among lineages and with the timing of emergence of montane and water barriers that could provide geographic isolation leading to speciation (Calsbeek et al. 2003). For example, the well-studied tarweed lineage (Asteraceae, Madiinae) contains many neoendemics, mostly summer-flowering annuals with sticky foliage. Relationships among the fifteen species of *Calycadenia*, as well as among the six species in one subgroup of *Layia*, indicate gradual speciation in response to geographic isolation. But the patterns in other *Layia*, as well as within the genus *Holocarpha*, are more suggestive of ecological speciation, in which adaptation to a novel environment leads to isolation from the ancestor. Serpentine-restricted *Layia discoidea* is closely related to, but highly differentiated from, widespread *L. glandulosa*; the sand dune endemic *L. carnosa* is likewise differentiated from its widespread ancestor *L. gaillardiodes*.

Serpentine is the most distinctive and widespread special substrate for plants in California. Derived from oceanic crustal rocks, serpentine is excessively rich in magnesium and poor in calcium and nutrients compared with most continental rocks and soils. Long, discontinuous strings of serpentine outcrops wind from the Klamath Mountains down through the Coast Ranges and along the Sierran foothills. About two hundred plant species are confined to serpentine in California, the majority in the Klamath-Siskiyou and North Coast Ranges (Safford et al. 2005). Californian serpentine plants have often served as model subjects for studying plant ecology, adaptation, and speciation (Huenneke et al. 1990, Brady et al. 2005, Kay et al. 2011, O'Dell and Rajakaruna 2011). The jewelflower (*Streptanthus*), dwarf wild flax (*Hesperolinon*), and wild onion (*Allium*) genera are among those richest in serpentine endemics in California. Elsewhere in the world, rich floras in serpentine are found in Cuba, New Caledonia, southeast Asia, and the eastern Mediterranean region. Other edaphic (soil) environments that support unique plant species and varieties in California (albeit to a lesser extent than serpentine) are gabbro in the Sierra Nevadan foothills and Peninsular Ranges, limestone in the Klamath-Siskiyou region and central Sierra Nevada, gypsum and alkali soils in the deserts, and granite talus in the Sierras.

Vernal pools are another significant habitat for Californian endemic plants (as well as their animal associates). These winter-wet, summer-dry wetlands are found in flat or gentle terrain where drainage is impeded by bedrock, fine clays, or chemical precipitates. More than one hundred plant species and varieties are strongly associated with vernal pools, and over thirty of these are strict vernal pool endemics. Some of the typical vernal pool genera, like calicoflowers (*Downingia*), meadowfoam (*Limnanthes*), goldfields (*Lasthenia*), and stickyseeds (*Blennosperma*), are pollinated by specialized solitary bees in the family Andrenidae. Since the vernal pool habitat is so closely tied to the young Mediterranean climate, the evolutionary radiation of these genera is thought to be relatively recent (Meyers et al. 2010).

Conservation Context

Although California has an estimated 612 globally threatened plant species, only 20 California plant species are globally extinct (CNPS 2014). Causes of extinction were attributed to 12 species (8 land conversion and 4 invasive species). Three of the 19 species were Channel Island endemics, although the Channel Islands make up only 0.2% of California land area. California and the larger California Floristic Province have benefited from a number of plant conservation successes. For example, the Eureka Valley evening primrose (*Oenothera avita eurekensis*) and the Eureka dune grass (*Swallenia alexandrae*) were listed as endangered species in the 1970s due to habitat destruction caused by off-road vehicle recreation and camping on and around their dune habitat. Protection of the dunes first by the Bureau of Land Management and later by the Death Valley National Park allowed both species to recover, and they were proposed for de-listing in 2014.

Another spectacular example is the recovery of native flora on Guadalupe Island, Mexico (part of the California Floristic Province), after invasive goats were eradicated. Prior to goat eradication, there were fewer than two hundred individuals of the Guadalupe Island Pines (*Pinus radiata* var. *binata*), fewer than two thousand Guadalupe Island Cypress (*Cupressus guadalupensis guadalupensis*), and fewer than one thousand Guadalupe Island palms (*Brahea edulis*). More significant than the low numbers was the complete absence of seedlings. Within just a few years of goat eradiation, the number of all three species increased tenfold as, for the first time in over one hundred years, all seedlings weren't consumed by goats. Moreover, seven endemic species thought to be extinct were rediscovered: the western tansymustard (*Descurainia pinnata*), coyote tobacco (*Nicotiana attenuata*), dense false gilia (*Allophyllum gilioides*), Guadalupe savroy (*Satureja palmeri*), redflower currant (*Ribes sanguineum*), buckbush (*Ceanothus crassifolius*), and common woolly sunflower (*Eriophyllum lanatum* var. *grandiflorum*) (Aguirre-Muñoz et al. 2011). The hard and thoughtful work of the California Native Plant Society has laid the groundwork for many more plant conservation successes.

Invertebrates

California has an estimated thirty thousand insect species, the focus of this section, and approximately four thousand species of noninsect invertebrates, nearly 30% of all invertebrate species in the United States and Canada combined (Powell and Hogue 1980, Ballmer 1995, Carlton 2007). Over 95% of all described animal species and over 80% of all species on Earth are invertebrates, 85% to 90% of those invertebrates are insects, and many more are yet to be discovered (Price 1997, Cardoso et al. 2011) (Figure 11.3). Beetles alone make up 25% of all global biodiversity and comprise ten times more species than all vertebrates combined (Cardoso et al. 2011). California's diverse ecosystems, from snow-capped mountains to arid deserts to kelp forests, each harbor a unique set of invertebrates. California contains thirty-two listed threatened and endangered invertebrate species, which make up more than half of the federally listed insects in the United States (Connor et al. 2002). Ten California invertebrate species are known to be globally extinct, but knowledge gaps almost certainly make this an underestimate.

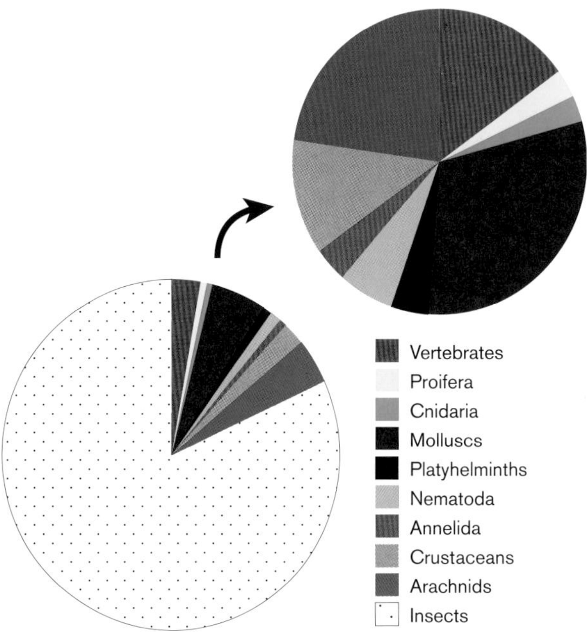

FIGURE 11.3 Invertebrates make up 95% of all animals globally, and insects are 85–90% of all invertebrates.

Evolutionary Diversification

Invertebrates are found in every ecological niche imaginable in California: on land, in freshwater, in the sea, and in between. At each location different invertebrates play roles of scavengers, predators, herbivores, detritivores, and parasites. While some are generalists and opportunists, other species are strict specialists that have evolved to consume one particular host or prey item. Invertebrate diversity stems from the variety of invertebrate forms and functions as well as habitat specializations within ecosystems, allowing them to exploit all available microhabitats. For example, nearly 50% of insects are herbivores, and a single plant can host a variety of species that feed on roots, stems, trunks, flowers, phloem, fruits, and leaves—both externally and internally—such as leaf miners, gall-makers, and root borers (Ballmer 1995).

This fine division of niches and correspondingly high diversity are possible because of several features of invertebrates. Most invertebrates are size-limited for physiological reasons; for instance, insect growth is limited by their tracheal method of gas exchange (Gullan and Cranston 2010). In addition, invertebrates have both complex sensory systems and faster generation times than vertebrates, allowing them to quickly adapt to heterogeneous habitats (Gullan and Cranston 2010). Finally, because of their high levels of diversity and niche specialization, invertebrates exhibit intricate relationships with other species that act to further diversify species through coevolution. For example, an adaptive radiation occurred in one of the largest insect superfamilies, the Scarabaeoidea (scarab beetles), following the radiation of angiosperm plants fifty million years ago. This radiation resulted in one of the largest phytophagous (plant-eating) Scarab subfamilies, the Melolonthinae (June beetles), comprised of ten thousand species (Price 1997).

California's high invertebrate diversity relative to the rest of the U.S. is linked to the climatic and topographic heterogeneity of the state. The combination of California's long dry

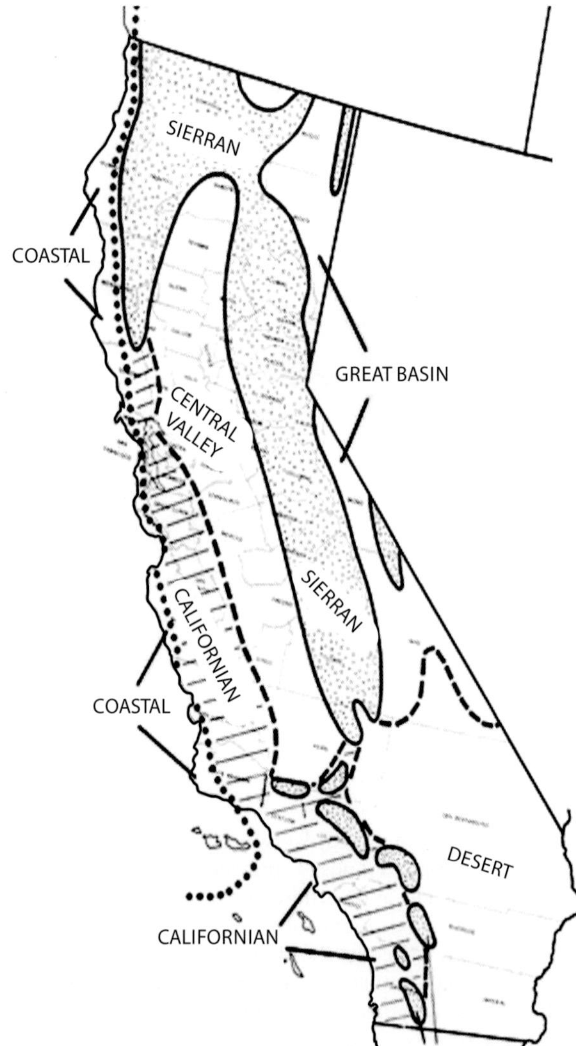

FIGURE 11.4 The six invertebrate faunal zones in California. Source: Powell and Hogue 1980.

season and varying topography creates a strong selective force on plants and animals, including invertebrates. California's climate has fluctuated from subtropical to glacial over geological time (Ballmer 1995), and as the climate fluctuated, invertebrates repeatedly either adapted, survived in refugia, or became extinct, resulting in local adaptations and in the great beta-diversity seen today throughout California.

As a result of California's long dry season from May to October, most invertebrate activity occurs in the wet winter and spring during the annual period of plant productivity (Powell and Hogue 1980). This pattern deviates from most states, where the majority of invertebrate activity occurs during the warm, humid summers. However, to grasp the entirety of California's invertebrate diversity, all seasons and locations must be examined. For example, insect activity in the Sierras peaks in the foothills in May, at intermediate elevations in June, and at the highest elevations in July and August (Powell and Hogue 1980). For insects, Powell and Hogue (1980) delineated six major faunal divisions in California: Great Basin, Sierran, Desert, Central Valley, Coastal, and Californian (Figure 11.4). The last of these contains the highest number of endemic species. These six major areas can also be used to describe overall invertebrate diversity. For each of these major invertebrate faunal divisions in the state, we highlight selected invertebrate diversity, species interactions, and conservation issues. We also describe geographic concentrations and distinct assemblages of invertebrate diversity for each, and introduce key controllers of these patterns.

Biogeography

The Great Basin high desert reaches into California at the eastern and northeastern edge of the state and is composed mainly of sagebrush scrub. Although the Great Basin is species-rich, it contains almost no endemic California insects (Powell and Hogue 1980). However, the California Great Basin is home to Mono Lake, a unique and productive ecosystem supported by halophile invertebrates (see Chapter 32, "Lakes"). Mono Lake is extremely alkaline because of high evaporation and no ocean outflow. Thus Mono Lake is tolerable only to a few species of algae and algal feeders, including the endemic brine shrimp (*Artemia monica*) and alkali flies (*Ephydra hians*). The brine shrimp and alkali flies thrive in Mono Lake due to lack of aquatic predators and competition, and the two species form the basis of the food chain for millions of migratory birds each year. Unfortunately, both upstream water diversion and climate change threatened this unique ecosystem (Ficklin et al. 2013). Water diversion and increased evaporation due to rises in temperatures raises the salinity of Mono Lake to levels lethal to even the endemic brine shrimp (Dana and Lenz 1986) and alkali fly (Herbst et al. 1988), in turn threatening the birds that depend on them (Rubega and Inouye 1994). The lake was also home to the now-extinct Mono Lake diving beetle (*Hygrotus artus*).

The standing and running waters of the Sierra Nevada support a rich diversity of dragon and damselflies (Odonates), stoneflies (Plecoptera), mayflies (Ephemeroptera), and caddisflies (Trichoptera). The alpine meadows of the Sierras are also home to numerous butterfly species. However, in the conifer forests of the Sierra Nevada, fire is a primary controller of arthropod biodiversity. In particular, fire and fire management greatly impacts leaf litter arthropods, which are responsible for forest health via nutrient cycling in Sierra mixed-conifer forests (Apigian et al. 2006). Studies investigating the changes in litter-dwelling arthropods after fire found that while the abundance of arthropods was negatively affected, species richness and diversity increased—by thirty-two species in one case—as a result of increased postfire habitat heterogeneity (Apigian et al. 2006, Ferrenberg et al. 2006). Species that increased after fire included bark and other wood-boring beetles, saproxylic (feeding on dead or decaying wood) insects, phytophagous (plant-eating) insects, and parasitic arthropods (ticks and parasitic insects). Thus frequent, low-intensity fires, common in the Sierras prior to European settlement, likely acted to sustain Sierra invertebrate diversity (Apigian et al. 2006, Ferrenberg et al. 2006). The role of large, high-intensity fires, such as the 2013 Rim Fire in the Yosemite National Park vicinity, could be less beneficial to insect diversity, as this type of fire has been facilitated by fire suppression and climate change (see Chapter 3, "Fire as an Ecosystem Process").

California's Mojave and Colorado Deserts are thriving with invertebrate life and host a prime example of the effects of coevolutionary forces on invertebrate diversity: yucca moths and their hosts. Yucca moths include several species of the

Lepidopteran family Prodoxidae that are obligate pollinators and herbivores of Yucca plants (*Yucca* spp.). Yucca moths have evolved specialized mouthparts that allow them to insert pollen directly into Yucca flowers and their own eggs directly onto the plant's ovary (Pellmyr et al. 1996). When the Yucca moth larvae hatch, they eat only some of the developing Yucca seeds, leaving the rest to propagate their host plant and continue the cycle. This has led to the radiation of at least twenty species of Yucca moths and an equal number of Yucca species (Pellmyr 2003).

California deserts are also well known for their charismatic species of Arachnids that have adapted to long, hot desert days by burrowing in the cool ground. For example, the Coachella Valley is home to the Giant Red velvet mites (*Dinothrombium pandorae*), which at 1 centimeter are orders of magnitude larger than average mites. Giant mites burrow in the desert sand to emerge only after rains that bring their target prey, swarming termites (Tevis and Newell 1962). The California deserts are also home to numerous species of scorpions, tarantulas, and the ever-strange Solifugae, or wind scorpion. California is home to sixteen hundred species of native bees, about half the number of native bees in all of the United States and Canada (Frankie et al. 2009). The exotic European honey bee (*Apis mellifera*) is by far the largest pollinator in in the U.S., with estimated value of $15 billion annually, most of which is generated in California and especially in its Central Valley; for example, California almond pollination by European honey bees alone is estimated to be worth $2 billion annually (Ratnieks and Carreck 2010). However, if the European honey bee continues to decline due to colony collapse disorder, the native bees that they outcompete are expected to take over some pollination services (Goulson 2003). Native bee pollination will only be successful with restoration and protection of natural areas in and surrounding agricultural fields, as native bees require these areas for nesting sites and floral resources (Kremen et al. 2004). For example, Kremen et al. (2002) found that native bees could provide full pollination services for watermelon when provided natural habitat.

California coastal terrestrial systems are teeming with invertebrate life, from the banana slugs under the fog-draped coastal redwoods (*Sequoia sempervirens*) to the migrating Monarch butterflies (*Danaus plexippus*) in coastal woodlands. The San Francisco Bay Area, which compromises nine counties surrounding the San Francisco and San Pablo Bays, has a topographic, climatic, edaphic (soil type), and geologic heterogeneity unparalleled in any other urban area. This diversity of habitats has led to the discovery of nearly four thousand insect species per county, including 142 butterfly species, with a high degree of endemism (Connor et al. 2002). This extraordinary habitat heterogeneity and corresponding great insect diversity has, in the context of over a century of rapid urbanization, spelled disaster for many species and has led to many species threatened with extinction (Connor et al. 2002). The urbanization of the Bay Area resulted in the first recorded extinction of an insect in the United States, the Satyr butterfly (*Cercyonis sthenele sthenele*), during the nineteenth century. As urbanization increased, sand dunes that once dominated the San Francisco Bay were destroyed and two more butterflies, the Xerces blue (*Glaucopsyche xerces*) and the Pheres blue (*Icaricia icariodes pheres*), went extinct. The remaining dune habitat at Antioch Dunes was once home to the extinct Antioch Dunes shieldback katydid (*Neduba extincta*) and is now home to another critically endangered butterfly, the Lange's metalmark (*Apodemia mormo langei*).

Conservation Context

Invertebrates perform myriad ecosystem functions, from decomposition and soil aeration to pollination and seed dispersal, that are essential in the provisioning of regulatory, supportive, and cultural ecosystem services worth billions of dollars (McIntyre 2000, Losey and Vaughan 2006, Cardoso et al. 2011). As research continues to examine human dependence on ecosystem services and the vital roles of invertebrate diversity in performing those services, invertebrate conservation can no longer be ignored (Cardoso et al. 2011, Cardinale et al. 2012). At present, thirty-two California invertebrates are on the state threatened and endangered species list due to land conversion, invasive species, and overexploitation (CDFW 2013). Of the thirty-two invertebrates listed by the state of California (CDFW 2013), three (9%) are gastropods, eight (25%) are crustaceans, and twenty-one (66%) are insects. The listed insects include fourteen butterflies, one moth, four beetles, one fly, and one grasshopper; the crustaceans include seven shrimp (five fairy shrimp) and one crayfish; and the gastropods include two species of snails and the white abalone. Invertebrate habitats are often fine-grained such that local scale, within-region characteristics are central to population persistence (e.g., Thomas et al. 2001, Fleishman et al. 2002, Collinge et al. 2003, Poyry et al. 2009, Beyer and Schultz 2010). Conservation of threatened invertebrates is greatly facilitated by understanding their habitat requirements so suitable habitat can be protected or restored (New 2007).

The endangered Ohlone tiger beetle (*Cicindela ohlone*) (Figure 11.5) is a prime example of the threats to and status of endangered insects in California. The Ohlone tiger beetle is endemic to the coastal prairies of Santa Cruz County, where it is found in five remnant patches. Adult tiger beetles are visual predators on small arthropods and require bare ground to both forage and oviposit. Larvae are sit-and-wait predators that generally require bare ground to capture prey from the mouths of their burrows in the soil (Pearson and Vogler 2001). The California coastal prairie evolved with disturbances that created conditions for bare ground, such as natural and anthropogenic fire by Native Americans, grazing and soil disturbance by native ungulates and burrowing animals, and periodic drought (Anderson 2007, Wigand et al. 2007). After European settlement, grazing regimes changed, time between fires increased, and annual exotic plants replaced perennial bunch grasses, decreasing bare ground (Hayes and Holl 2003, D'Antonio et al. 2007). Today, the remaining Ohlone tiger beetle populations depend on habitat protection and creation via grazing and vegetation removal (Cornelisse et al. 2013) and on managed mountain biking and hiking trails (Cornelisse and Duane 2013) to maintain bare ground habitat. Some Ohlone tiger beetle habitat is managed because landowners hold Incidental Take Permits under the federal Endangered Species Act (ESA) that subject them to Habitat Conservation Plans, in which they agreed to maintain habitat as mitigation for destruction elsewhere.

California is home to the rare butterflies that sparked the original Habitat Conservation Plan provision in the ESA: the Mission blue (*Icaricia icariodes missionensis*), Callippe silverspot (*Speyeria callippe callippe*), Edith's Bay checkerspot (*Euphydryas editha bayensis*), and San Bruno elfin (*Callophrys mossii bayensis*) (Beatley 1994). Today, California is home to numerous Habitat Conservation Plans for threatened invertebrates the provide habitat protections and management. Hab-

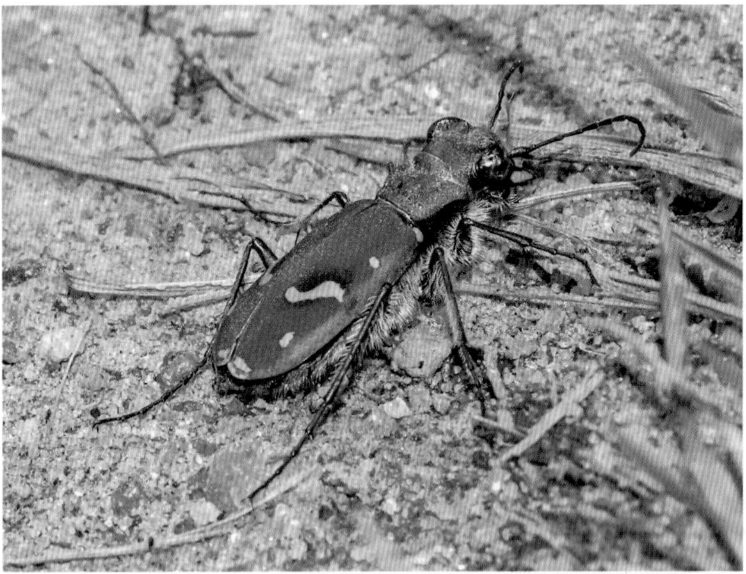

FIGURE 11.5 Ohlone tiger beetle (*Cicindela ohlone*). Photo: John Hafernik.

itat protection is key to both conservation of native pollinators and to natural enemies that provide biological control of herbivorous arthropods (Pickett and Bugg 1998). Conservation biological control that includes habitat protection and management is a key component of sustainable agroecosystems and maintenance of invertebrate biodiversity in California. For example, natural areas including hedgerows, roadside vegetation, and riparian corridors can provide nesting sites and overwintering sites for beneficial arthropods, such as parasitic wasps and predacious beetles, which can then control outbreaks of herbivores in agricultural fields (Ballmer 1995, Pickett and Bugg 1998).

Although in this chapter we focus on terrestrial biodiversity, habitat protections for rare species, including invertebrates, are not limited to the land. One of the most critically endangered invertebrate species is found in the ocean off the southern California coast: the white abalone (*Haliotis sorenseni*). The white abalone was the first marine invertebrate listed under the federal Endangered Species Act after years of overexploitation. The white abalone reproduces by broadcast spawning, and despite the federal ban on white abalone fishing in 1996, historical exploitation reduced adult densities to below those required to effectively reproduce (Hobday et al. 2001). Conservation efforts have been under way since 2001 and now include the White Abalone Restoration Consortium of scientists, fisherman, NGOs, and agencies that have developed a four-step restoration plan that includes surveying current populations, collecting brood stock, captive breeding, and establishing refugia of self-sustaining brood stocks in the wild—all in hopes to bring back the white abalone from the brink of extinction (NMFS 2008) (see Chapter 35, "Marine Fisheries").

California's expanding human population will cause further habitat loss (see Chapter 5, "Population and Land Use"). With climate change further altering species' physical and ecological habitats, protecting invertebrate species and their ecosystem functions will require comprehensive science, adaptive management, and a committed public. The Ohlone tiger beetle and white abalone are examples of how California contains the scientific and regulatory capacity and the political will needed to protect even the most critically endangered invertebrates.

Reptiles and Amphibians

As of October 2013, California harbors 171 species of reptiles and amphibians of which forty-seven (27%) are endemic: twenty-eight species of frogs of which three are endemic to the state, forty-two salamander species of which twenty-nine are endemic, forty-eight lizard species of which twelve are endemic, forty-four snake species of which only two are endemic, and nine turtle species (marine, freshwater, or terrestrial) of which only one is endemic. These calculations are date-stamped because four new species of legless lizards were added in September 2013. In addition, not all of the widespread reptile and amphibian species have undergone thorough diversity assessments with modern molecular methods, so their recognized diversity could increase, even in the well-studied herpetofaunal hotspot of the California Biogeographic Province. Here we discuss the biogeographic origins of this herpetofauna, factors influencing endemism, and their current conservation status and future prospects in the face of urbanization, climate warming, and other threats.

Evolutionary Diversification

California's extraordinary amphibian and reptile diversity is concentrated in the south (Figure 11.6), largely at the meeting points of the Sonoran and Mojave Deserts. This diversity is the by-product of the barrier formed by the Transverse Ranges, which have bisected southern Californian herpetofauna into those with northern affinities and those with southern affinities, though other breakpoints can be found to the north in the Sierras (Calsbeek et al. 2003). The origins of California's herpetological diversity can be traced directly to very old geological processes that gave rise to the entire state and, for some taxa, to even older global tectonic processes. Because the biogeography of salamander diversity is by far

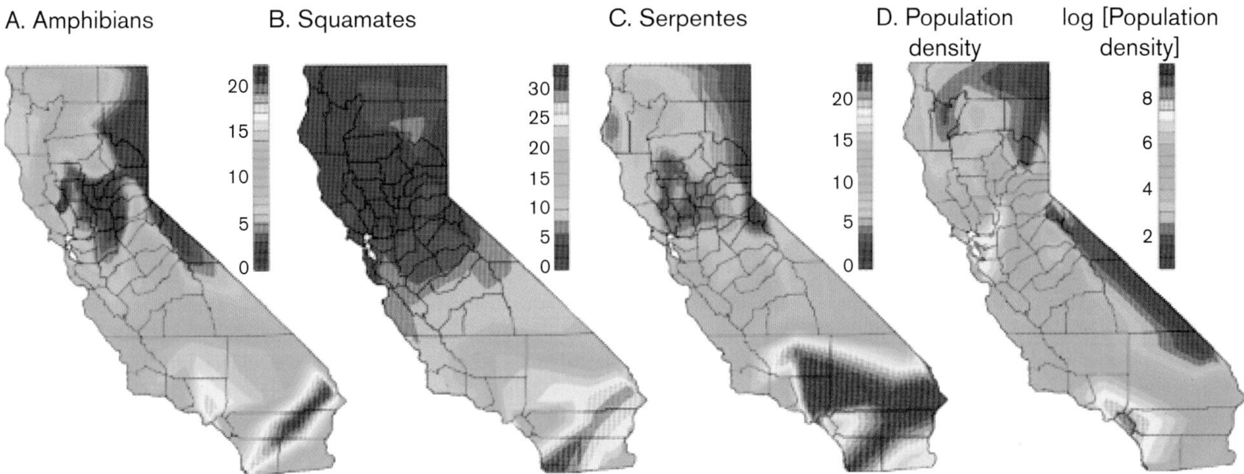

FIGURE 11.6 Plots of Amphibian, Squamates, and Serpentes species diversity and of human population density, estimated by county. Biodiversity for each group is based on museum records in Herpnet.org, which were summed by species and by county and then plotted (using the *Akima* package in [R]) by the average county location of those that were georeferenced in the Herpnet records. County population records are from the most recent census.

the best understood, we begin with the history of processes important in their speciation.

Biogeography

During the Eocene, California was underwater, with the first of the accreted TERRANES having slammed into the coast during the mid-Mesozoic and created the northern Siskiyou Mountain Range (Ernst et al. 2008). Thereafter, during the Oligocene and Miocene, more terranes accreted onto California's evolving coastline further to the south (McWilliams and Howell 1982), giving rise to the present-day Coast Range. During much of the mid-Miocene the Coast Ranges sat offshore like islands, with an inland sea in the place of the modern-day Central Valley. These offshore islands gave rise to considerable biodiversity in modern PLETHODONTID salamander lineages, as the lineages became isolated and evolved into distinct species.

During this Cenozoic Era of island biogeography, many radiations of endemic species in the family Plenthodontidae originated in situ in California, with at least seventeen California endemics in the genus *Batrachoseps*. Thus, more than half of all of California's endemic herpetofauna are in this single family of salamander. Thereafter, the Central Valley was uplifted as dry land. A major geographic break in herpetological diversity is present at the Pajaro River (Jockusch and Wake 2002, Kuchta et al. 2009), the ancient outlet of a marine embayment in the Central Valley two million years ago. Eventually this marine embayment drained, but an enormous freshwater lake still drained out of the Central Valley from this same outlet until it was rerouted to the current drainage of the Sacramento River in more geologically recent times (six hundred thousand years ago). The spectacular number of California salamanders, 70% of which are endemic, is in large part due to these plethodontid speciations in the context of these geologic events. A lack of aquatic larval stages (their eggs develop directly on land into crawl-away juveniles) also contributes to their endemism: they have often become restricted to isolated locations due to both plate tectonic activity and mountain building along the western margin of the North American plate (Jockusch and Wake 2002). Many endemic *Batrachoseps* salamanders are found as relicts at desert oases and seeps in and around the Saline and Death Valleys and other Desert Ranges, separated from other evolving lineages by a drying climate since the Pleistocene.

Other plethodontid groups have a more complex global biogeographic history. All plethodontid salamanders originated in the Jurassic in the Appalachians and then moved west to California and also to Asia, where the genus *Hydromantes* originated. Ancestors of *Hydromantes* then subsequently spread back to North America and over to Europe (Vieites et al. 2007). This reinvasion of *Hydromantes* from Asia to North America occurred over the Eocene Bering Strait land bridge, during the warmest time in the last sixty-five million years, when the Arctic supported luxuriant temperate forests. Three species of *Hydromantes* are endemic to California and restricted to the high elevations of the Sierra Nevada Range.

Another radiation of speciose (sensu the definition "beautifully lovely" [Hart 2008] as well as its more recent usage as species-rich) salamanders in the genus *Ensatina* comprises, in our view, a single "RING SPECIES complex" of related subspecies that spread from the north and radiated in a bewildering array of color and pattern POLYMORPHISM recognized as serving antipredator functions. These *Ensatina* mimic other, harmful species as a means of defense against predators. The species that various members of the *Ensatina* complex mimic include members of the family Salamandridae and western newts (*Taricha* sp.). Both the *Ensatina* and *Taricha* speciated and diversified along parallel biogeographic routes and timeframes (Kuchta and Tan 2006), indicative of the coevolutionary processes expected for a model (the species mimicked) and its mimic (Sinervo and Calsbeek 2006). Other researchers might separate the *Ensatina* complex into as many as eight biological species. If we were to count these, the number of California endemic salamanders would increase to thirty-six out of forty-eight (75%) of plethodontid species.

Many frogs are more recent (Cenozoic) in their invasion of California, but the tailed frog (*Ascaphus truei*) is in the most basal frog family, Ascaphidae. Its nearest extant relative (*Leiopelma* sp.) is in New Zealand, implying an even more ancient invasion of North America than the *Hydromantes* salamanders, or in another alternative biogeographic scenario, range extinction across Gondwana and Laurasia as they split some two hundred million years ago. The split between California's tailed frog (*Ascaphus truei*) and its New Zealand relative *Leiopelma* is dated at 180 mya based on this biogeographic event (Waters and Craw 2006), but upwards of 260 mya (Permian) based on a molecular clock (San Mauro et al. 2005).

The California state reptile, the endemic desert tortoise (*Gopherus agassizii*) also derives from an Eocene invasion across the Bering land bridge from Asia to North America, as evidenced by a clear trail of fossil remains (Eberle and Greenwood 2012). Despite their great antiquity in North America, ancestors of the modern desert tortoise only reached California in the Pleistocene (Morafka and Berry 2002). The Californian legless lizards (Annielidae) invaded North America from Asia during this same Eocene warming period (Macey et al. 1999). The single species in the genus *Anniella* was recently divided into five species (Parham and Papenfuss 2009). Their species status is too recent to have been formerly evaluated for protected status, but it is quite likely that one or more of these species should be considered for federal and state listing.

The Anguidae include California's alligator lizards in the genus *Elgaria*, of which one (*E. panimantina*) is a California endemic restricted to the mountains around Death Valley. They are closely related to the Annielidae and have basal members in Morocco and a large diversification in North America. Other nonendemic reptiles in California derive from South America, such as the whiptail lizards (Teiidae). Other families like the Xantusidae that harbor many California endemic lizard species were derived from Mexico and Caribbean ancestors (Noonan et al. 2013). The Helodermatidae, with only two species in the family, are restricted to North America and include the only venomous lizard in the United States, the Gila monster (*Heloderma suspectum*). In California, Gila monsters are now restricted to the Providence Mountains, and although only slightly more widespread in the past, they are now thought to be nearly extirpated from several other isolated historical locations in the state (Lovich and Beaman 2007). Others groups of purely North American origin include the diverse Phrynosomatidae, consisting of widespread species in the genera *Uta, Sceloporus, Urosaurus, Petrosaurus*; the species-poor Crotophytidae (including collared and leopard lizards); and the horned and sand lizards in the genera *Phrynosoma* (now in three new genera *Tapaja, Anota*, and *Doliosaurus*) (Leaché and McGuire 2006) and *Callisaurus* (Pyron et al. 2013), respectively. Other families of lizards found in California, such as the Iguanidae (with three California species), are global in their biogeographic distributions.

The Serpentes (snakes) are originally derived from Asian radiations. California harbors both ancient and globally distributed Boid snakes like the rubber and rosy boas, as well as members in the cosmopolitan family Colubridae, which includes most of California's snakes. Sea snakes (*Pleamis platurus*) are occasionally found swimming off the shores of San Diego. Rattlesnakes (Viperidae) are entirely of New World origin. California also harbors ancient basal members of the Serpentes including those in Leptotyphlopidae such as the western blind snake (*Rena humilis*). This short review cannot do justice to all the diversity of Serpentes, which is tremendous in southern California and penetrates deeply up into the more northern San Joaquin Desert. North of the limit of the San Joaquin Desert ecosystem (Germano et al. 2011), snake diversity falls off rapidly (see Figure 11.6).

Conservation Context

To date, no California herpetofauna have gone extinct. However, twenty species are federally listed as threatened or endangered or proposed for listing, including three salamanders, six frogs and toads, five turtles and tortoises, two lizards, and three snakes. The isolated San Joaquin Desert (Germano et al. 2011), distinct from California's other two desert ecosystems, harbors the Californian endemic blunt-nosed leopard lizard (*Gambelia sila*), one of the two terrestrial reptiles listed as federally endangered. The other is the San Francisco garter snake (*Thamnophis sirtalis tetrataenia*), restricted to the San Francisco peninsula north of Rancho Del Oso. The Alameda whipsnake (*Masticophis lateralis euryxanthus*) is on the federal and state threatened species list because its range is largely restricted to the rapidly developing Bay Area counties. The giant garter snake of the San Joaquin Valley (*Thamnophis gigas*) is likewise listed as threatened because of urban and agricultural development of wetlands, critical habitat for this endemic.

More California amphibian species are endemic than reptiles; this has likely contributed to the large number of amphibians currently listed or proposed as federally threatened or endangered. Besides greater levels of endemism, the greater vulnerability of amphibians reflects a combination of classic anthropogenic development pressure and the more recent, emerging threats of anthropogenic climate change and the linked, rapid spread of the fungal chytrid disease (Rohr and Raffel 2010). These two causes are driving rapid extinctions worldwide, including many extinctions of local populations in the state of California (Vrendenburg et al. 2007).

Diverse factors underlie the listed status of other California salamanders. Introduction of the invasive barred tiger salamander (*Ambystoma mavortium*) from the U.S. central plains (Johnson et al. 2011) is driving the endemic California tiger salamander (*A. californiense*) to the brink of extinction through hybridization. The invader is thought to have rapidly spread from bait shops south of Hollister, California, across the Salinas Valley (Fitzpatrick and Shaffer 2007) and across the Coast Range to "infect" Central Valley populations of California tiger salamander. Genetic assimilation of these endemic genotypes into a synthesized hybrid species may be unstoppable, as the hybrids appear to have higher fitness than the pure species (Fitzpatrick and Shaffer 2007). The other Californian endemic salamander in the family Ambistomatidae is the federally endangered Santa Cruz long-toed salamander (*A. macrodactylum croceum*). Most of its habitat has been lost to coastal development (see Figure 11.6), but its number of breeding sites has increased from two to seven thanks to a Habitat Conservation Plan involving successful collaboration between conservation organizations, local land owners, and federal, state, and county agencies. The desert slender salamander (*Batrachoseps major aridus*) is a classic microendemic only known from two localities in the Santa Rosa Mountains (Hidden Palm Canyon and Guadalupe Canyon), making it the amphibian with the most restricted distribution in North America. Several other salamanders in the same family are listed as state threatened largely because of their microendemic status, including two other slender salamanders (*B. stebbinsi* restricted to the Tehachapis and *B. simatus* restricted to Kern Canyon), web-toed salamanders (*Hydromantes brunus* restricted to two drainages in the Sierra Range and the eponymous *H. shastae*), and woodland salamander species (*Plethodon stormi* and *P. asupak*).

Of all the herpetofauna, frogs are undergoing the most

severe extinction crisis. In California, frogs at several locations have been extirpated by an introduced disease, the fungal chytrid (*Batrachochytrium dendrobatidis*); introduced vertebrates, including a number of fish species and the bull frog (*Lithobates catesbeianus*); pesticide and herbicide impacts (Hayes et al. 2002); and habitat degradation. Notable among extirpations in the frog genus *Rana* are most historical sites of mountain yellow-legged frog (*R. muscosa*) in the Sierra Nevada Range and their near extirpation from almost all historical locations in the Transverse Ranges. Fungal chytrid has been strongly implicated in local extinctions of mountain yellow-legged and Sierra Nevada yellow-legged (*R. sierra*) frogs (Vredenburg et al. 2007, 2010), although introduced trout have also played a major role given that trout removal has stabilized population declines (Vredenburg 2004). The California red-legged frog (*Rana draytonii*) is all but extinct in the Sierra foothills, now restricted to only six known breeding populations there (Barry and Fellers 2013). It is extinct from all but two locations in the Transverse Ranges of California (south of Santa Barbara and on the Santa Rosa plateau) (Federal Register 2008). One of its last strongholds in California appears to be Central Coast Range, where it is still common but still faces impacts from invasive species—males preferentially mate with female bullfrogs that are larger than females of their own species (D'Amore et al. 2009). The cause of extirpation of the closely related Cascades frog (*Rana cascadae*) from over 50% of its California range is even more enigmatic. Nevertheless, climate change is a likely cause given that it went extinct from over 99% of its Mount Lassen sites, near the southern end of its Pacific Northwest distribution, during a long-term drought (Fellers and Drost 1993).

The challenge of protecting California's herpetofauna is complicated by the striking correlation of amphibian, lizard, and snake biodiversity with the human footprint of development (population density, see Figure 11.6) and further exacerbated by the impacts climate change (Rohr and Raffel 2010). The potential impact of urban sprawl has an enormous reach beyond the urban landscape, given its hunger for energy. Wind and solar power installations have recently begun to proliferate across California desert ecosystems, with potentially huge impacts on reptiles (Lovich and Ennen 2013) from the footprint of energy installations, increased incidence of fire, and urban heat island effects (Millstein and Menon 2011). Particularly vulnerable species are the endangered Blunt-nosed leopard lizard, whose two best remaining refuges, Carrizo Plain and Panoche Valley, are slated for adjacent solar development; and the threatened desert tortoise, which faces a similar threat from climate change and planned solar development in the core parts of its Mojave Range.

Around the world, contemporary extinctions of local reptile populations are linked to rising temperatures (Sinervo et al. 2010). Even small changes of 0.5C° in maximum daily air temperatures have started to drive local extinctions in those taxa near the edges of their physiological high-temperature range limits. In the past four decades the Mojave and Sonoran Deserts have warmed considerably, and precipitation has decreased in both fall-winter and spring-summer periods. This overall drying trend may have been a significant driver of extinction for one population of the threatened Coachella Valley fringe-toed lizard (Barrows et al. 2010) and could drive other species toward extinction. Despite the challenges, there are remarkable herpetofauna conservation successes. Two excellent examples are recovery of the endangered green sea turtle (*Chelonia mydas*) through effective regulations that eliminated overharvestings in Mexico and Hawaii and the threatened island night lizard (*Xantusia riversiana*), which was protected by eradicating invasive cats (*Felis catus*) and herbivores from most of the Channel Islands (USFWS 2013a). These and other successes demonstrate the ability of California's endangered species to rapidly recover from overexploitation or invasive species following effective regulation, enforcement, or restoration, as long as suitable habitat is still available.

Birds

California has the most species-rich avifauna in the United States and the second highest levels of bird endemism besides Hawaii (see Figure 11.2). California boasts over three hundred breeding species, from boreal great gray owls (*Strix nebulosa*) in the high Sierra Nevada to desert species such as Le Conte's thrasher (*Toxostoma lecontei*). California contains globally important bird areas and spectacular migrations such as through the Central Valley wetlands, Monterey Bay Marine Sanctuary, and Salton Sea. Perhaps because of its high bird diversity and levels of endemism, California has a rich legacy of field ornithology and a highly active community of birdwatchers, making it one of the most studied avifaunas in North America.

William Dawson's three-volume tome, *The Birds of California* (1923), was the first thorough inventory of the Californian avifauna. Joseph Grinnell greatly expanded our knowledge of California birds and their finer-scale distributions during his tenure as the founding director of the Museum of Vertebrate Zoology at UC–Berkeley (1908–1939). He published the first comprehensive checklist of California birds (1902) and started the landmark text "The Distribution of the Birds of California" (Grinnell and Miller 1944). His biodiversity transects are still being used to examine how birds in the Sierra Nevada have tracked their climate niches over the past hundred years (Tingley et al. 2009). Beginning in the 1960s, a growing bird-watching community of field ornithologists such as Guy McCaskie and Rich Stallcup greatly improved our knowledge about species ranges, patterns of vagrancy, and rare species in California. The California Rare Bird Committee (CRBC), established in 1970, continues to maintain the California state list of birds (CRBC 2013) and has made significant contributions to the knowledge of California birds through the journal *Western Birds* and the publication of *Rare Birds of California* (Hamilton et al. 2007).

Evolutionary Diversification

Fossil evidence suggests that bird diversity suffered a major extinction event at the Cretaceous-Tertiary boundary, now associated with the Chicxulub crater impact approximately 65 mya. Major bird orders then likely radiated rapidly in the early Tertiary, but controversy exists as phylogenetic approaches estimate the radiation of passerine birds as far back as the mid-Cretaceous (120–90 mya) (Cracraft 2001, Feduccia 2003). The geographic and physiographic diversity of California have surely aided in the evolution of birds in the state, and over a hundred species have been found in the fossil record from more than one hundred thousand specimens excavated across a swath of California habitats (Miller and DeMay 1942). Fossils of extinct Mesozoic toothed birds such as *Alexornis*, a genus of primitive Enantiornithines, and *Ichthyornis*, a genus of fish-eating seabird similar to modern-day Charadriiformes, have been found in California's Great Central Valley (Hilton 2003). A single bone of a Neognath has also been unearthed, but this tells us very little about how this subclass diversified into the ten thousand species that are known globally today. For other taxonomic groups it is well established that much of California's genetic diversity arises from the region's geographic complexity, whereby most phylogeographic patterns are due to population genetic breaks between the Sierra Nevada, Coast, and Transverse Mountain Ranges (Calsbeek et al. 2003). However, the origin and diversification of California bird populations is less clear given their highly mobile and migratory habits (Calsbeek et al. 2003).

A total of 653 species have been documented in California (CRBC 2013), more than any other state. For example, Texas has 639 species, Florida 514 species, and New York 480 species. Of those 653 species documented in California, 464 are "regularly occurring" (CRBC nonreview species) and 313 likely breed within the state (USGS Patuxent Wildlife Research Center 2013). Ten non-native species have established breeding populations in the state, of which 7 are widespread and likely affect native species. The California native avifauna represents 72 of the world's 231 families of birds from 19 of the 27 orders (CRBC 2013, Clements 2013).

California boasts more endemic species and subspecies than any other state except Hawaii. BirdLife International recognizes California as one of the largest Endemic Bird Areas including southwest Oregon and northwestern Baja from the coastline up to 2,000 meters and mirroring the boundaries of the California Floristic Province (Birdlife International 2013). Many endemic and range-limited taxa in California fall into three broad categories: Channel Island endemics, Maritime Chaparral and Scrub specialists, and Oak Woodland specialists. California harbors three species-level endemics: the California condor (*Gymnogyps californianus*) (once extirpated from their wider range and eventually the wild but now being reintroduced around central California and outside the state), the island scrub-jay (*Aphelocoma insularis*), and the yellow-billed magpie (*Pica nuttalli*). An additional sixty-one subspecies are endemic to California, many of which are from the Channel Islands. Nine species and forty-five subspecies are near-endemic (>80% of their range in California) (Shuford and Gardali 2008).

The California condor is perhaps the best-known endemic species, after being once far more widespread across the western United States but restricted to California by 1937 (Wilbur and Kiff 1980), and their conservation is discussed later on. Condors are large scavengers that likely suffered with the collapse of North American megafauna. They have the largest wingspan of any North American bird (2.8 meters) and are one of the heaviest at about 8.5 kilograms (Snyder and Schmitt 2002). The island scrub-jay is a Channel Islands endemic within the scrub jay complex that also includes the range-restricted Florida scrub jay (*A. coerulescens*). Island scrub jays have been separated from mainland populations for at least one hundred thousand years (Delaney and Wayne 2005) and have a heavier bill and bolder plumage than coastal Western scrub jays (*A. c. californica*). They number fewer than three thousand individuals and are found only on Santa Cruz Island, where they use a large variety of habitats from oak woodlands to Bishop Pine forest (*Pinus muricata*). Fossil evidence shows that scrub jays were once present on neighboring Santa Rosa Island and may have disappeared as late as the nineteenth century (Collins 2009). The yellow-billed magpie is a particularly range-limited, but locally abundant, endemic species in California that inhabits open oak woodlands, riparian zones, and even suburban areas of the interior valleys and coast. They are highly social, nesting in loose colonies and roosting in large flocks. They are generally smaller and longer-winged than black-billed magpies, which are found in a nonoverlapping northeast area of the state. Recently yellow-billed magpie populations declined by as much as 49% within two years coinciding with the arrival of the avian disease West Nile virus (Crosbie et al. 2008).

Biogeography

Because of California's large latitudinal gradient, it contains the transition from bird species that generally inhabit the Pacific Northwest south to species of the arid Southwest (Olson et al. 2001). We break down the state into the same ecoregions used by Shuford and Gardali (2008) adapted from the Jepson geographic subdivisions of California (Hickman 1993). Here we briefly describe each region and its notable species, and notable Important Bird Areas (IBAs) as designated by California Audubon (Cooper 2004). The biogeography of California's birds reflect the state's great mosaic of habitat types. Bird communities are more species rich as one moves from north to south, and from inland to the coast, with the highest species diversity in the southwest part of the state.

NORTHWESTERN CALIFORNIA, CASCADE RANGE, AND SIERRA NEVADA

The northwest California coastal region holds the largest and least impacted rivers in the state (e.g., Klamath River) along with relatively pristine wetlands and coastal dunes, all of which contribute to bird diversity (Cooper 2004). Lakes, ponds, and other standing water provides important habitat for many wildlife in northwestern California (PRBO Conservation Science 2011). Bird taxa generally restricted to this region include Aleutian cackling goose (*Branta hutchinsii leucopareia*), ruffed grouse (*Bonasa umbellus*), barred owl (*Strix varia*), gray jay (*Perisoreus canadensis*), black-capped chickadee (*Poecile atricapillus*), and breeding individuals of the American restart (*Setophaga uticilla*). One of the most significant Important Bird Areas in this region is the Del Norte Coast IBA, which includes Castle Rock, the most structurally diverse island off the California coast and home to the largest common murre (*Uria aalge*) colony in the California Current, eleven nesting seabird species, and over 121,000 birds including roost sites for the Aleutian cackling goose and brown pelican (*Pelecanus occidentalis*). This IBA contains the entire global population of Aleutian cackling goose, which stages in the area during the spring and fall; the entire California breeding population of the Oregon vesper sparrow (*Pooecetes gramineus affinins*); and the majority of the California population of the fork-tailed storm-petrel (*Oceanodroma furcata*).

To the east, the Cascade Range is the southernmost portion of a volcanic mountain range that stretches north through Oregon and Washington, ending in British Columbia, Canada. This area is notable for its large populations of breeding willow flycatchers (*Empidonax traillii*), possibly representing the state's nesting population of the *brewsteri* (Sierra-Cascade) race. The IBAs in the region, such as the Lake Almanor Area and Big Valley/Ash Creek, support over five thousand waterfowl including over 10% of the California population of the greater sandhill crane (*Grus canadensis tabida*) and between eight and twelve sensitive species (Cooper 2004; National Audubon Society 2013b).

The Sierra Nevada range supports a diverse range of bird species due to its extreme altitudinal gradients and montane forests. It houses species found nowhere else in California, such as the great gray owl (*Strix nebulosa*) and gray-crowned rosy-finch (*Leucosticte tephrocotis*), pine grosbeak (*Pinicola enucleator*), and breeding American pipits (*Anthus rubescens*). Important bird areas include the northern and southern Sierra Meadow IBAs, which are home to California spotted owl (*Strix occidentalis occidentalis*) and a total of nine sensitive species including the endangered willow flycatcher. The northern IBA has six distinct meadow systems and distinct bird communities that depend on willow thicket habitat (e.g. Lincoln's sparrow [*Melospiza lincolnii*], Wilson's warbler [*Wilsonia pusilla*], willow flycatcher) or that concentrate at the meadow-forest interface (e.g., pine grosbeak and multiple species of owls, woodpeckers, flycatchers, and sapsuckers). The southern IBA also contains the extremely high-altitude peaks of the region and is home to great gray owls and almost the entire global populations of Mount Pinos blue grouse (*Dendragapus fuliginosus howardi*), an endemic subspecies (Cooper 2004, Bunn et al. 2007).

SACRAMENTO AND SAN JOAQUIN VALLEYS

The Sacramento Valley subregion is the cooler and wetter end of the Central Valley and contains the salt marshes and rice fields between Red Bluff and Suisun Slough, bisecting the delta area of the Sacramento and San Joaquin Rivers where it meets with the southerly San Joaquin subregion (Jepson Flora Project 2013). While 95% of the Central Valley's historic wetlands, riparian areas, and grasslands have been destroyed or modified, the area still supports important migratory waterfowl and raptor habitat. The Sacramento National Wildlife Refuge complex is comprised of five refuges and three wildlife management areas, which makes up 70,000 acres of wetland, upland, and riparian habitats that are intensively managed for wintering and breeding waterbirds (Cooper 2004, USFWS 2013b). Some agricultural lands are also managed to mimic grasslands and wetlands to attract migratory shorebirds. Arguably, the most significant bird habitat in the region is in the Cosumnes River Preserve, adjoining the only major river that drains from the western Sierra Nevada and maintains more or less natural flow regimes that allow flooding of lowland areas in spring (Cooper 2004). The preserve provides habitat to over fifty thousand migratory waterfowl and thirteen sensitive bird species, including long-billed curlew (*Numenius americanus*) and thousands of greater and lesser sandhill cranes (*G.c. tabida* and *G.c. canadensis*, respectively) (Pogson and Lindstedt 1991, Cooper 2004, Cosumnes River Preserve 2014).

The southern portion of the Great Central Valley, the San Joaquin subregion, is larger and drier than its northern counterpart with desert elements in the far south. Despite pervasive agricultural development, remnants of grasslands, vernal pools, and alkali sinks (e.g., the Carrizo Plain) as well as a few marshes and riparian woodlands along major rivers remain intact and sustain critical stopover habitat for migratory birds (Jepson Flora Project 2013). The extensive Sacramento–San Joaquin Delta, once a vast tule marsh, contains only small islets of native riparian and tidal marsh habitats and is a critical IBA for migratory shorebirds and waterfowl including long-billed curlews, sandhill cranes, rarer species such as the short-eared owl (*Asio flammeus*) and black rail (*Laterallus jamaicensis*), and breeding colonies of double-crested cormorant (*Phalacrocorax auritus*) along restored marshland habitats (Cooper 2004).

CENTRAL WESTERN AND SOUTHWESTERN CALIFORNIA

The central portion of California's north-south running Coast Range has relatively diverse habitats and avifauna due to its extensive riparian habitat, coastal marshes and estuaries (although 90% of the San Francisco Bay Area's wetlands have been developed), chaparral, oak savanna and coniferous woodlands, including enclaves of redwood forests, deep canyons, rugged headlands, sandy beaches, and pastureland. This region is home to familiar California species such as the wrentit (*Chamaea fasciata*), endemic and locally abundant yellow-billed magpie, greater roadrunner (*Geococcyx californianus*), California thrasher (*Toxostoma redivivum*), sage sparrow (*Artemisiospiza belli*), and California towhee (*Melozone crissalis*), among many others. The most famous bird species in the region is the California condor, which can be found in low numbers in the wild throughout the Big Sur Area (also a recognized global IBA) and in parts of the Los Padres National Forest. This region contains a variety of important bird areas. South San Francisco Bay contains extensive waterbird and shorebird habitats in its tidal marshes, creeks, and leveed evaporation ponds and is home to the endangered California Ridgeway's rail (*rallus obsoletus obsoletus*) and California least tern (*Sterna antillarum browni*), the endemic saltmarsh common yellowthroat (*Geothlypis trichas sinuosa*), and the endangered western snowy plover (*Charadrius nivosus nivosus*). Vandenberg Air Force Base is the farthest-south site on the mainland for many breeding marine birds, also supporting California least terns and over 10% of the coastal-breeding population of the western snowy plover.

Southwestern California, the most species-rich of California's ecoregions, overlaps the southern range edges of many northern species and the northern range edges of more southern coastal specialties such as California gnatcatcher (*Polioptila californica*). The Tijuana River Reserve IBA contains the California least tern, the light-footed Ridgeway's rail (*Rallus obsoletus levipes*); the population-size second only to Upper Newport Bay), and least Bell's vireo (*Vireo bellii pusillus*). Another IBA, the San Jacinto Valley, hosts nearly all of southern California's raptor species and is one of the few remaining areas in southern California that still supports winter flocks of shorebirds such as the long-billed curlew and white-faced ibis (*Plegadis chihi*). The mountain plover (*Charadrius montanus*) and sandhill crane once wintered here but appear locally extirpated (Cooper 2004, National Audubon Society 2013b).

No discussion of the avian biogeography of California can be complete without the Channel Islands. Together these eight islands host seventeen endemic subspecies and one endemic species, the island scrub jay (Johnson 1972). Most of these taxa are characterized by darker/drabber plumage, longer and/or heavier legs, bills and/or toes than their continental counterparts. At least some of the taxa appear to be Pleistocene relicts that have since changed in their island setting, such as the horned lark (*Eremophila alpestris insularis*) (Johnson 1972). The Channel Islands also harbor at least fourteen species of breeding seabirds. IBAs on and around these islands contain the entire U.S. breeding population of Scripps' murrelet (*Synthliboramphus scrippsi*), over 10% of the global population of black storm petrel (*Oceanodroma melania*), Cassin's auklets and California's breeding brown pelicans, and nearly half the global population of ashy storm-petrels (Cooper 2004, National Audubon Society 2013b).

CALIFORNIA DESERTS

The Mojave Desert contains the lowest and hottest areas in North America (e.g., Death Valley). The region also contains striking granitic mountains, such as the Cima Dome and Granite Mountains, with underground water seeps that feed springs and provide food and refuge for many bird species (e.g., Butterbredt Spring). Along the eastern border of this region is East Mojave Peaks, an Important Bird Area that contains over 10% of the California populations of gilded flicker (*Colaptes chrysoides*), gray vireo (*Vireo vicinior*), and Bendire's thrasher (*Toxostoma bendire*). Also within this IBA are large populations of other desert birds found in the Joshua Tree woodlands and pinyon chaparral along steep-sloped canyons. Hepatic tanager (*Piranga flava*) and Mexican whip-poor-will (*Caprimulgus arizonae*) are known to occur in California only on top of the mountain peaks in this desert.

The Sonoran Desert region occupies the southeastern corner of the state and includes the Colorado Desert. The area is arid but contains woodland habitat located along the flight path of migrant songbirds moving between California and Mexico. The Colorado Desert Microphyll Woodland IBA is one of the few important migratory habitats in this area and the only area in California with elf owls (*Micrathene whitneyi*) and northern cardinals (*Cardinalis cardinalis*). The Anza-Borrego Riparian IBA (the largest state park in the U.S.) contains least Bell's vireo (*Vireo bellii pusillus*), important populations of vermilion flycatcher (*Pyrocephalus rubinus*), and summer tanager (*Piranga rubra*). The Salton Sea, formed in 1905 after a break in a canal from the Colorado River, might be the most important body of water for birds in the interior of California. This IBA is home to the Yuma Ridgeway's rail (*R. obsoletus yumanensis*) and other birds found nowhere else in the western U.S., such as wood stork (*Mycteria Americana*), yellow-footed gull (*Larus livens*), breeding laughing gulls (*Leucophaeus atricilla*), stilt sandpiper (*Calidris himantopus*), black terns (*Chlidonias niger*), and the rare *Gelochelidon nilotica vanrossemi* race of gull-billed tern (Cooper 2004, National Audubon Society 2013b).

The Great Basin in California includes the Modoc Plateau in the northeast corner of the state and Mono Lake south to the Owen's River Valley along the central-eastern border. The Modoc Plateau IBA supports a total of fourteen sensitive species (e.g., redhead [*Aythya americana*], purple martin [*Progne subis*], and yellow-headed blackbird [*Xanthocephalus xanthocephalus*]). It also supports the highest diversity of breeding waterfowl in the state due to its location on the Pacific flyway and its dozens of reservoirs and artificial wetlands. Mono Lake supports millions of migratory birds each year and provides important habitat for western snowy plover (over 10% of California's interior breeding population), California gull (*Larus californicus*), Western and least sandpipers (*Calidris mauri* and *C. minutilla*), and American avocet (*Recurvirostra americana*).

MARINE REGIONS

The nutrient-rich waters of the California Current, which flow from Alaska, support abundant and diverse marine plants and animals, including 163 bird species (Bunn et al. 2007). The northern coastal section of California's northern marine region is arguably the most productive nearshore area due to its steep, deep-water canyons and nutrient-rich waters. This area contains important bird areas and "hot zones" such as the Cordell Bank, Bodega Canyon, and Monterey Canyon, supporting large seabird colonies on the Farallon Islands and Año Nuevo Island (Sydeman et al. 2013). The waters of this northern region move away from the coast at Point Conception, where the California coastline turns abruptly east and the cool water moving south is diverted offshore. In Monterey Bay incredible numbers of visiting seabird species have been documented; for example, a global record of eight shearwater species have three times been observed in single day (Shearwater 2013). From Point Conception south, in the Southern Bight Marine Region, exist many of the same northern marine species with the addition of more tropical species such as red-billed tropicbird (*Phaethon aethereus*), brown booby (*Sula leucogaster*), Scripps murrelet, black-vented shearwater, and Leach's storm-petrels (*Oceanodroma leucorhoa*).

Conservation Context

Many species of birds are vulnerable to extinction in California because they are range-restricted, are habitat specialists, or have relatively small population sizes. In addition to preserving rare species, California has a global responsibility to provide safe harbor for more abundant taxa that chiefly reside within the state boundaries, and to provide safe passage and quality stopover habitat for migrating birds in the Western Flyway and in the California Current. No California native bird species have gone globally extinct in the past hundred years. However, California has nine federally endangered and six threatened bird species or subspecies, and coastal California has been identified as one of two hotspots of endangered bird diversity in the continental U.S. (Godown and Peterson 2000). Shuford and Gardali (2008) conducted an exhaustive quantitative review of 238 bird taxa and found that 74 species and subspecies warrant official status as "California Bird Species of Special Concern." Habitat loss and fragmentation are the most pervasive threats to threatened California birds, affecting 97% of the Species of Special Concern, followed by non-native species (43%), pollution (24%), overexploitation (13%), and disease (5%). Wetlands harbored twenty-seven listed species, followed by thirteen in scrub habitats and twelve in grasslands; at the other end, only one species of concern was found in mixed evergreen forests.

The southwest California ecoregion contains the greatest number of listed species at thirty-seven, including six Channel Island endemic taxa. Central-western California contains thirty listed taxa, with other regions containing between eighteen and twenty-one listed species (Shuford and Gardali 2008). Despite high levels of endangerment, only two species have been extirpated from the state in modern times: the California condor (now reintroduced) and the sharp-tailed grouse (*Tympanuchus phasianellus columbianus*) (formerly in the northeast corner of the state). Conservation efforts have helped recover several declining species including the marbled murrelet (Peery et al. 2004, Peery and Henry 2010) and brown pelican (Anderson et al. 1975). The California gnatcatcher (*Polioptila californica*), whose northernmost subspecies (*P. c. californica*) in southern California was listed as threatened in 1993 (USFWS 2009), has been conserved relatively recently with the protection of 60,000 hectares through the State of California Natural Communities Conservation Program (NCCP). The Scripp's murrelet, a small crevice-nesting seabird, has benefited from the removal of most invasive mammals from its known current or suspected historical island nesting sites in the U.S. and Mexico (McChesney and Tershy 1998, Whitworth et al. 2013, Aguirre-Munoz et al. 2008). Bans on fishing and other extractive uses have been made within important areas of the Channel Islands National Marine Sanctuary; light pollution in important nearshore murrelet staging areas has been reduced; and the bird has received additional legal protections of Mexican breeding islands by the Mexican Natural Protected Areas Commission (CONANP 2014).

The ongoing recovery of the formerly extirpated California condor is perhaps the most well-known reversal of a declining bird in California. The condor was widespread before the late Pleistocene megafaunal extinctions (Emslie 1987) but by the 1950s was restricted to a small portion of southern California (Koford 1953). The condor was a charter species of the Endangered Species Act in 1972 and the subject of the nation's first endangered species recovery plan in 1975. Early conservation efforts were unsuccessful, and by 1982 only twenty-two condors remained in the wild. In 1986 the decision was made to capture the last three wild individuals for the captive breeding program. By the late 1990s the program produced twenty chicks per year (Walters et al. 2010). The captive breeding program then developed successful approaches to behaviorally condition birds for the wild, including puppet and parent rearing (Meretsky et al. 2000) and power line aversion training (Mee and Snyder 2007). Captive condor breeding programs now return birds to release sites in southern California (since 1992), Arizona (1996), Big Sur (1997), Baja California, Mexico (2002), and Pinnacles National Park (2003). Reintroduced birds first fledged a wild-born chick in California in 2004 (Walters et al. 2010). Lead poisoning, a major proximate cause of the historical population decline, continues to be the major obstacle to recovery (Cade 2007, Finkelstein and Doak 2012). However, in 2013, California became the first state to ban all lead ammunition. This is expected to greatly aid condor recovery and to protect other species of wildlife as well as human health (Bellinger et al. 2013).

The future management of California's bird biodiversity will confront two accelerating challenges: growing habitat loss and an increasingly volatile climate. The highest projected rates of human population growth are in the coastal southwest region, home to the highest number of threatened birds in the state (Shuford and Gardali 2008, CDF 2013). Growing human populations affect birds directly by destroying habitat or corridors that connect isolated foraging or nesting areas, and indirectly by altering the numbers of native and introduced species, often resulting in higher numbers of predators, nest parasites, and non-native competitors. Although the details about how California's climate will change are uncertain, abundant, connected bird populations will surely be better able to cope with climate change. Thus improved and expanded conservation efforts are the best protection for California's birds. Not all species have similar threats; Jongosmidt et al. (2012) used species distribution models to measure potential impacts from housing development and climate change and found oak woodland species suffering 80% of their losses from development, whereas birds associated with coniferous forests see the greatest losses due to climate. Across the board, 32% of species range reductions were attributed to housing development. Attempts at modeling future bird distributions under climate change scenarios suggests shifting ranges and novel communities of birds, highlighting uncertainty about how birds may respond (Stralberg 2009). Fortunately, one does not have to look far in California to see avian conservation success stories involving broad partnerships between industry, stakeholders, and scientists. Hopefully the future will remain bright for California's birds.

Mammals

Since the end of the age of the dinosaurs about sixty-six million years ago, mammals have diversified and thrived as one of the most successful animal lineages on Earth. Mammals are found in every California landscape; more than other vertebrate lineages (e.g., birds and fish), mammals have diverse modes of locomotion that allow them to flourish in air, sea, and land. They play essential roles in all California ecosystems, acting as seed hoarders and dispersers (e.g., kangaroo rats [*Dipodomys* sp.] and tree squirrels [*Sciurus* sp.]), grazers (e.g., deer [*Odocoileus* sp.]), pollinators (e.g., bats [Chiroptera]), ecosystem engineers (e.g., beavers [*Castor canadensis*]), insectivores (e.g., shrews [Soricidae]), and large predators (e.g., killer whales [*Orcinus orca*] and mountain lions [*Puma concolor*]). Consequently, their distributions are often closely tied to biotic community composition and environmental changes (see Blois et al. 2010), and their conservation is a crucial component of maintaining ecological dynamics.

California has the highest mammal diversity in the United States (NatureServe 2002). Depending on the definition of species, it has approximately 227 mammal species (including 38 marine species, about 163 native terrestrial species, and around 26 introduced terrestrial species; CDFW 2008), ranging from the diminutive Preble's shrew (*Sorex preblei*, 2.1–4.1 grams) to the largest known animal, the blue whale (*Balaenoptera musculus*, 170,000 kilograms). California's native wildlife hail from seven mammalian orders: Artiodactyla (even-toed ungulates such as deer and sheep), Carnivora (carnivores), Cetacea (dolphins and whales), Chiroptera (bats), Lagomorpha (rabbits, hares, and pika), Rodentia (rodents), and Sorimorpha (e.g., shrews and moles). Two additional mammalian orders were introduced to California: Perissodactyla (horse and donkey) by Spanish explorers and the marsupial Didelphimorpha (Virginia opossum) during the Great Depression in the early twentieth century (Lidicker 1991). About half of the terrestrial mammals in California are rodents.

Biogeography

Like plants and other animals, mammal diversity varies among California's ecoregions. The highest native mammal species richness is in the northern portion of the state (ecoregions 1 and 3 in Figure 11.7; Figure 11.8); "rare" species with limited distributions, small populations, and threatened status are most common in the southern portion of the state and the San Francisco Bay Area (mostly ecoregion 5 in Figure 11.7; CDFW 2003). This pattern reflects the fact that southern California and San Francisco Bay Area landscapes are more fragmented than those in northern California, leaving little suitable habitat for the mammal species that are now rare or restricted in the former regions. It may also suggest

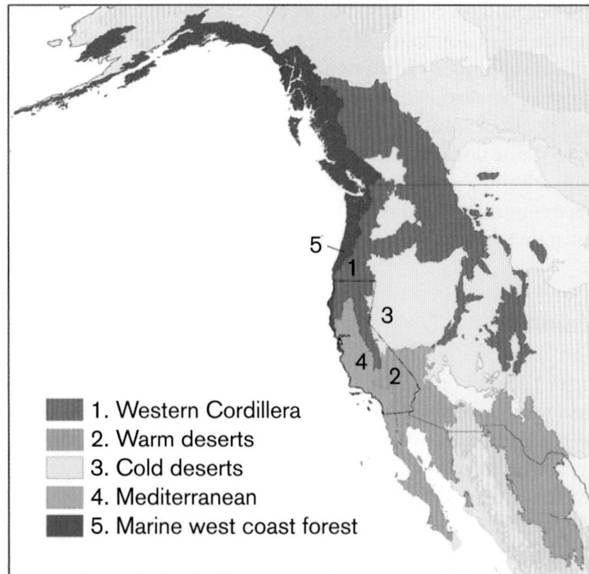

FIGURE 11.7 In this ecoregion map based on definitions of the Commission for Environmental Cooperation's Ecoregion Level II, five ecoregions overlap with California. They are (1) the Western Cordillera mountain chain, (2) warm deserts, (3) cold deserts, (4) Mediterranean region, and (5) marine west coast forest.

that northern California served as a refugium over a longer period of time than did southern California. Areas with rapid and recent intraspecies diversification occur along the California coast and southern portion of Sierra Nevada (Davis et al. 2008), which may indicate recent fragmentation of species geographic ranges, recent colonization, or both. When looking at the full range of native mammal species present in California, most of the diversity comes from northern forests, the Great Basin, and the northern coasts.

When examining California mammal species ranges, including portions that are outside of the state (see Figure 11.8a), rodents and lagomorphs show high diversity in the Great Basin and Sierra Nevada. Since rodents are the most numerous mammalian order, comprising about half of the mammal species in California, their distributions play an important role in the overall diversity pattern. Bats are the second most speciose mammalian order in California. As the only flying mammal, they have large species and individual ranges compared to other mammals of their size. The center of diversity for bats in California is the southeastern part of the state, near Mexico. Most shrews and moles are found along the Pacific Northwest coast, where rainfall is plentiful (see Figure 11.8b).

Twenty-five mammal species have more than 75% of their ranges in California (Davis et al. 2008). Among them, seventeen species (about 9%) are unique to the state; hence California has the highest mammal endemism among all the states (Table 11.2; CDFW 2003, Stein et al. 2000). With the exception of the island fox (*Urocyon littoralis*) in the Channel Islands, all of these endemics are small mammals: fifteen species of rodents and one species of shrew. These endemic species share small body size and/or small species range. In addition, California has endemic subspecies such as the Tule elk (*Cervus canadensis nannodes*), the smallest elk subspecies in North America. Many endemic mammal species are found within the unique Mediterranean landscape in the southwestern portion of the state or in other geographically complex and isolated regions (Figure 11.9). While it is not surprising that the Mediterranean environment fosters diversity unique to California, isolation and recent diversification might also contribute to this pattern. For example, approximately four thousand to eight thousand years ago dry climatic conditions allowed desert species from east of the Sierra Nevada, including several species of kangaroo rats, to expand into the San Joaquin Valley, where they became isolated when moist conditions returned.

Conservation Context

California had a diverse megafauna, animals with body mass greater than 45 kilograms (100 pounds) such as saber tooth cats (Felidae) and pygmy mammoths (*Mammuthus* sp.), until about thirteen thousand years ago (Johnson et al. 2011). Concurrent with climate change and human arrival in the Americas, many megafauna disappeared from North America (see Chapter 9, "Paleovertebrate Communities"). More recently, breeding colonies of northern fur seals (*Callorhinus ursinus*) became extinct along the coast of California eight hundred to two hundred years ago, partly due to overexploitation and disturbance. Following restrictions to commercial sealing in 1911, breeding fur seals returned to California, but the populations that recolonized from the Pribilof Island lacked the unique behavior of weaning pups at an older age that characterized California's former fur seal population (Newsome et al. 2007).

Today, nineteen species and eighteen subspecies of mammals in California are listed as endangered or threatened by either the state or federal government (California Nature Resources Agency 2013). Unlike the list of endemic species that consists predominantly of small mammals, the threatened and endangered list includes many medium- to large-sized species such as the Sierra Nevada red fox (*Vulpes vulpes necator*), two subspecies of bighorn sheep (*Ovis canadensis californiana* and *O. c. cremnobates*), and seven species of whales. Fortunately, no California mammal species are globally extinct. However, four mammal species have been extirpated (driven locally extinct) from California in the past century: the bison (*Bison bison*), gray wolf (*Canis lupus*), jaguar (*Panthera onca*), and grizzly bear (*Ursus arctos*)—the official state animal featured on the California flag.

Many furred animals were hunted to near extinction by the early twentieth century. Before the gold rush, harvesting pelts of sea otters (*Enhydra lutris*), martins (*Martes americana*), and fishers (*M. pennant*) was a major incentive for many people to explore California. In just eighty-two years between 1786 and 1868, two hundred thousand sea otters along California's coast were killed (Grinnell et al. 1937), reducing the populations to one thousand to two thousand individuals occupying a fraction of their range before the fur trade (Riedman and Estes 1990). Improved regulation of hunting and trapping, including outright bans on hunting of sea otters (such as a 1911 International Protection Treaty), halted declines and allowed most species to rebound as long as suitable habitat was available. The absence of sea otters resulted in an overabundance of sea urchins, which overgrazed the kelp forests that are habitats for many marine species. Recovery of sea otters, aided by reintroductions, helped restore kelp forests. We know less about the ecosystem impacts of reducing populations of other mustelids, wolverines, fishers, river otters, and badgers, but they were likely significant.

Anthropogenic landscape modifications (e.g., agricul-

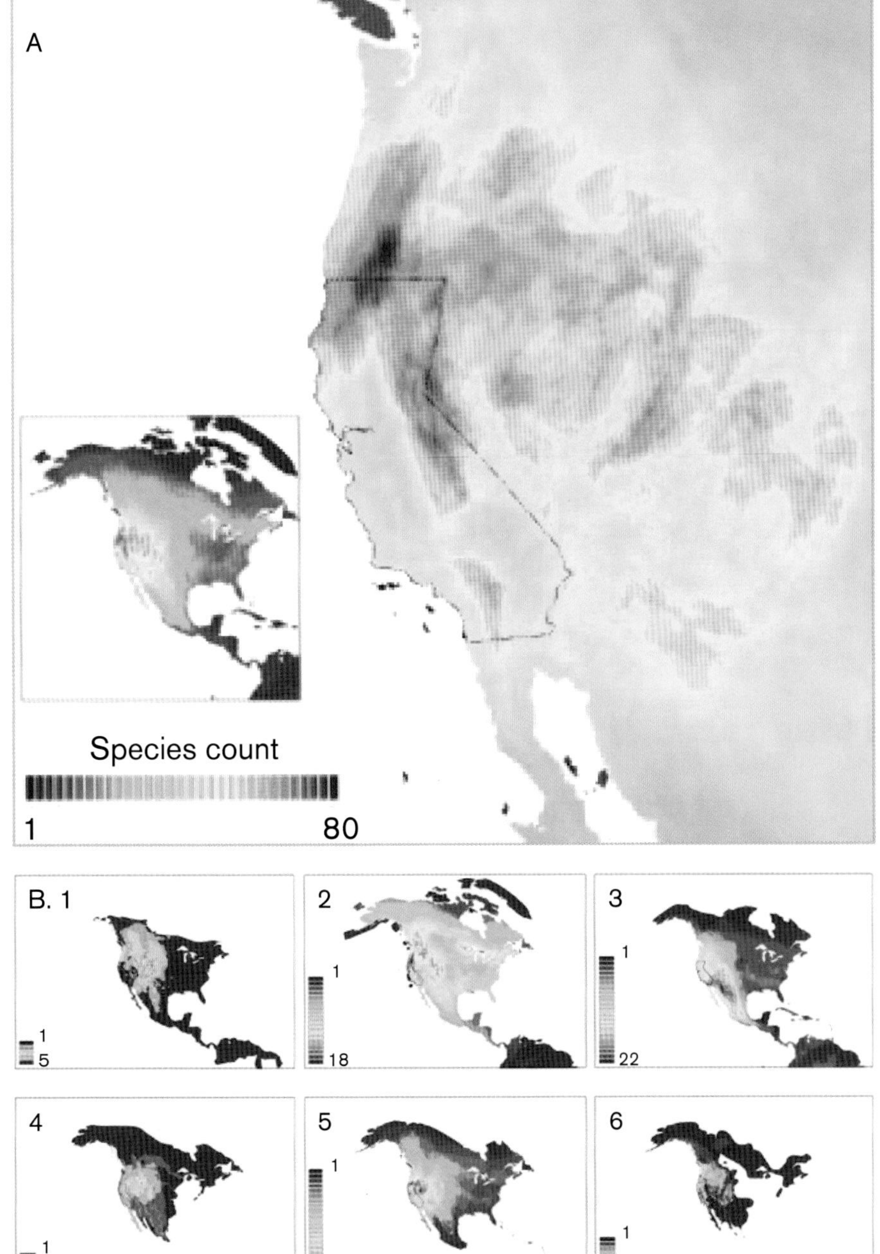

FIGURE 11.8 Diversity hotspots of terrestrial mammalian wildlife present in California, excluding species introduced to California after 1900. These maps are constructed by overlapping full species ranges (IUCN 2013) for (A) overall diversity and (B) diversity by order. From left to right, the mammalian orders are: (1) Artiodactyla, (2) Carnivore, (3) Chiroptera, (4) Lagomorpha, (5) Rodentia, and (6) Soricimorpha. Source: C. Li and E. Hadly, unpublished data.

ture and urbanization) also continue to reduce natural habitats. For example, about 43% of California was converted to agriculture land throughout the twentieth century (Kuminoff et al. 2001). The salt marsh harvest mouse (*Reithrodontomys raviventris*) is threatened by development of San Francisco Bay marshland as well as by pollution and declines in native plants. Humans have also introduced twenty-six species of terrestrial mammals, some of which are invasive and affect native mammals through predation (especially red fox, cats, and rats), overgrazing (especially sheep, goats, pigs, cattle), disease transmission, and competition for food and water. Humans have also introduced approximately a thousand nonnative plant species (including about 140 aggressive invasive species such as giant reed [*Arundo donax*] and yellow starthistle [*Centaurea solititialis*]) that alter habitat available for native mammals) (CDFW 2003). Moreover, temperature increases and unusual rainfall patterns associated with global climate change are affecting California mammals. For instance, in the span of a hundred years at least twenty-eight species of small mammals in Yosemite National Park have moved to higher elevations as temperatures have increased (Moritz et al. 2008).

Mammals with different body sizes and life history strategies face different challenges. Small mammals with small species ranges are easily impacted by local changes. For example, many kangaroo rats (e.g., *Dipodomys nitratoides nitratoides* and *D. nitratoides exilis*) in the Central Valley are threatened by habitat destruction. Compared to small mammals, large mammals typically require larger individual home ranges; increasing urbanization fragments reduces available habitat to them. Larger mammals also tend to have longer gestation periods, fewer offspring per litter, more time required to reach

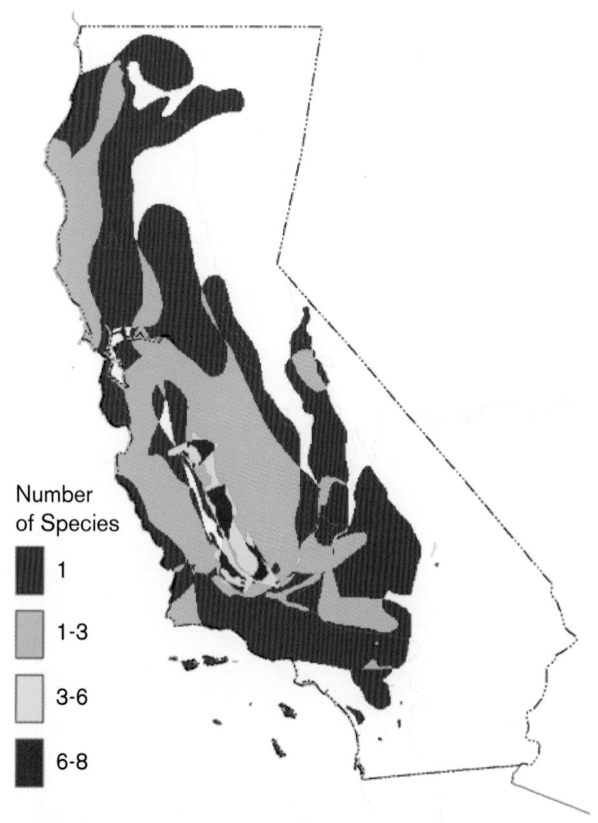

FIGURE 11.9 Diversity hotspots of mammal species endemic to California. Source: Li and Hadly unpublished data.

TABLE 11.2
Mammals endemic to California

Order	Family	Scientific name	Common name
Carnivora	Canidae	*Urocyon littoralis*	Island gray fox
Rodentia	Cricetidae	*Arborimus pomo*	California red tree vole
		Reithrodontomys raviventris	Salt-marsh harvest mouse
	Heteromyidae	*Dipodomys agilis*	Pacific kangaroo rat
		Dipodomys heermanni	Heermann's kangaroo rat
		Dipodomys ingens	Giant kangaroo rat
		Dipodomys nitratoides	Fresno kangaroo rat
		Dipodomys stephensi	Stephen's kangaroo rat
		Dipodomys venustus	Narrow-faced kangaroo rat
		Perognathus alticolus	White-eared pocket mouse
		Perognathus inornatus	San Joaquin pocket mouse
	Sciuridae	*Ammospermophilus nelsoni*	San Joaquin antelope squirrel
		Spermophilus mohavensis	Mohave ground squirrel
		Tamias alpinus	Alpine chipmunk
		Tamias ochrogenys	Yellow-cheeked chipmunk
		Tamias sonomae	Sonoma chipmunk
Soricomorpha	Soricidae	*Sorex lyelli*	Mount Lyell Shrew

SOURCE: IUCN 2013.

sexual maturity, and longer generation times. Therefore they typically recover more slowly than small mammals when populations are reduced. Whales, as the largest of all animals, are particularly at risk due to their low reproductive rate. Specialist species with particular habitat requirements are especially vulnerable to certain global environmental changes. For example, as temperature increases, suitable habitats for montane mammal species such as American pika (*Ochotona princeps*) become smaller, and these cold-adapted montane specialists can only move so high before they have nowhere to go.

State and federal hunting and fishing regulations combined with enforcement efforts have helped to protect California mammals from overharvesting, and further protections have come from state and federal laws on pollution, development, and agriculture (e.g., California Endangered Species Act, California Environmental Quality Act, and California Department of Fish and Wildlife). Today, approximately 200,000 km^2 of California (46% of the state) is protected, though much of this is desert and high mountain habitat lacking lowland species (CDPA 2013). The increasing number of protected areas has facilitated successful reintroductions of threatened mammal species in California such as the Perdido Key beach mouse (*Peromyscus polionotus trissyllepsis*) (Holler et al. 1989) and Stephen's kangaroo rat (*Dipodomys stephensi*) (Shier and Swaisgood 2012). About 90% of the mammal species present in California have at least part of their range outside the state. While conservation at state level is imperative to the survival of many species, especially because California has the highest mammal diversity (NatureServe 2002) and human population in the United States (U.S. Census Bureau 2013), many conservation challenges need to be addressed at regional, national, and international levels. Effective collaborations between California and other states are necessary for the protection and recovery of most large mammals, including the sea otter and elk. Still others, such as the gray whale and jaguar, require collaboration with Mexico, Canada, or both countries.

Summary

By almost all measures, California is the most biodiverse state in the U.S. and one of the most biodiverse regions of the world outside the tropics. California's high levels of endemism and species richness are related to its physical diversity, its Mediterranean climate, and perhaps its unique evolutionary history. Over 30% of California's species are threatened with extinction. However, fewer than 0.3% of California's native species have been driven to global extinction in the past two hundred years (see Table 11.1). This is remarkable considering the sheer scale and magnitude of California's agricultural development, suburban sprawl, water diversion, resource extraction, and pollution combined with the intentional and unintentional introduction of over fifteen hundred species and a history of overhunting and overfishing. Somehow, to paraphrase Aldo Leopold, we have managed to save almost all the pieces and, remarkably, now have a second chance to move into the future with thriving populations of nearly the full complement of California's flora and fauna. California is a wealthy state with a long history of environmental leadership and one of the world's most innovative societies. More than any high-biodiversity region in the world, California has the economic, cultural, and intellectual resources needed to have both thriving human communities and thriving ecosystems with their full diversity of species.

Although imperfect and heavily concentrated in desert and high mountain areas, the state's systems of protected areas cover 46% of its land area, offering the raw material for habitat in which species can persist and recover. With increasingly effective environmental regulation of wildlife harvest and pollution and the creation of new protected areas and smarter development, overharvest, pollution, and even habitat loss could become less significant drivers of new declines and extinctions. If this happens, then the most acute remaining challenges will be the damaging impacts of invasive species within natural and protected areas and the inability of protected areas to meet the needs of all their current species as California's climate changes. In California the days of government agencies casually introducing new species are long gone, and smarter policies govern invasive species prevention and management. Climate change will stress existing reserves and wildlife populations but may also provide new conservation opportunities. Just as California has been a national and global leader in a range of other social and economic areas, California can be a global leader in biodiversity conservation.

Acknowledgments

Bernie Tershy and Donald Croll were supported by a grant from the David and Lucile Packard Foundation. Barry Sinervo was supported by a grant from Emerging Frontiers at the National Science Foundation.

Recommended Reading

Moyle, Peter B. 2002. Inland fishes of California. University of California Press, Oakland, California.

Parisi, M. 2003. Atlas of the biodiversity of California. California Department of Fish and Game, Sacramento, California.

Thelander, C. G., and D. C. Pearson. 1994. Life on the edge: A guide to California's endangered natural resources: Wildlife. BioSystems Books, Santa Cruz, CA.

Glossary

HERPETOFAUNA A collective term referring to all reptiles and amphibians that comprise the ectothermic (cold-blooded) tetrapods (four-limbed animals).

PLETHODONTID Referring to lungless salamanders, which make up the family Plethodontidae.

POLYMORPHISM The occurrence of more than one distinct type or "morph" in a single, interbreeding population.

RELICT In biology, a naturally restricted population whose distribution was much broader in an earlier period, typically on geological time scales.

RING SPECIES A series of populations geographically arranged in a ring, such that neighboring populations along the ring can interbreed but more distant populations cannot; and such that the "end" populations (where the ring historically closed) cannot interbreed even though they occur near each other. The *Ensatina* ring complex, which some argue is actually a series of distinct species, occurs in the ring of mountains surrounding the Central Valley.

TERRANES Mini-continents floating on oceanic crustal plates.

References

Aguirre-Muñoz, A., D. A. Croll, C. J. Donlan, R. W. Henry, M. A. Hermosillo, G. R. Howald, B. S. Keitt, L. Luna-Mendoza, M. Rodríguez-Malagón, L. M. Salas-Flores, A. Samaniego-Herrera, J. A. Sanchez-Pacheco, J. Sheppard, B. R. Tershy, J. Toro-Benito, S. Wolf, and B. Wood. 2008. High-impact conservation: Invasive mammal eradications from the islands of western México. Ambio 37:10–17.

Aguirre-Muñoz, A., L. Luna-Mendoza, A. Samaniego-Herrera, M. Félix-Lizárraga, A. Ortiz-Alcaraz, M. Rodríguez-Malagón, F. Méndez-Sánchez, et al. 2011. Island restoration in Mexico: Ecological outcomes after systematic eradications of invasive mammals. Pages 250–258 in C. R. Veitch, M. N. Clout, and D. R. Towns, editors. Island Invasives: Eradication and Management. IUCN, Gland, Switzerland.

Amundson, R., Y. Guo, and P. Gong. 2003. Soil diversity and land use in the United States. Ecosystems 6:470–482.

Anderson, D., J. Jehl, and R. Risebrough. 1975. Brown pelicans: Improved reproduction off the southern California coast. Science 190(4216):806–808.

Anderson, M. K. 2007. Native American uses and management of California's grasslands. Pages 57–67 in M. R. Stromberg, J. D. Corbin, and C. M. D'Antonio, editors. California Grasslands Ecology and Management. University of California Press, Berkeley, California.

Apigian, K. O., D. L. Dahlsten, and S. L. Stephens. 2006. Fire and fire surrogate treatment effects of lead litter arthropods in a western Sierra Nevada mixed-conifer forest. Forest Ecology and Management 221:110–122.

Arponen, A., J. Lehtomäki, J. Leppänen, E. Tomppo, and A. Moilanen. 2012. Effects of connectivity and spatial resolution of analyses on conservation prioritization across large extents. Conservation Biology 26:294–304.

Baldwin, B. G., D. H. Goldman, D. J. Keil, R. Patterson, T. J. Rosatti, and D. H. Wilken, editors. 2012. The Jepson manual: Vascular plants of California. Second edition. University of California Press, Berkeley, California.

Ballmer, G. R. 1995. Nation's richest insect diversity in California. California Agriculture 49:51–52.

Barrows, C. W., J. T. Rotenberry, and M. F. Allen. 2010. Assessing sensitivity to climate change and drought variability of a sand dune endemic lizard. Biological Conservation 143:731–736.

Barry, S. J., and G. M. Fellers. 2013. History and status of the California red-legged frog (*Rana draytonii*) in the Sierra Nevada, California, USA. Herpetological Conservation Biology 8:456–502.

Beardsley, P. M., S. E. Schoenig, J. B. Whittall, and R. G. Olmstead 2004. Patterns of evolution in western North American mimulus (Phrymaceae). American Journal of Botany 91:474–489.

Beatley, T. 1994. Habitat conservation planning: Endangered species and urban growth. University of Texas Press, Austin, Texas.

Bellinger, D. C., A. Bradman, J. Burger, T. J. Cade, D. A. Cory-Slechta, M. Finkelstein, et al. 2013. Lead-free hunting rifle ammunition: Product availability, price, effectiveness, and role in global wildlife conservation. Environmental Health Perspectives 42:737–745.

Beyer, L. J., and C. B. Schultz. 2010. Oviposition selection by a rare grass skipper *Polites mardon* in montane habitats: Advancing ecological understanding to develop conservation strategies. Biological Conservation 143:862–872.

BirdLife International. 2013. Endemic Bird Area factsheet: California. <www.birdlife.org>. Accessed July 17, 2015.

Blois J. L., J. L. McGuire, and E. A. Hadly. 2010. Small mammal diversity loss in response to late-Pleistocene climatic change. Nature 465:771–775.

Brady, K. U., A. R. Kruckeberg, and H. D. Bradshaw 2005. Evolutionary ecology of plant adaptation to serpentine soils. Annual Review of Ecology Evolution and Systematics 36:243–266.

Bull, J. W., K. B. Suttle, N. J. Singh, and E. J. Milner-Gulland 2013. Conservation when nothing stands still: Moving targets and biodiversity offsets. Frontiers in Ecology and the Environment 11:203–210.

Bunn, D., A. Mummert, M. Hoshovsky, K. Gilardi, and S. Shanks. 2007. California wildlife: Conservation Challenges. California Department of Fish and Game, Sacramento, California.

Burge, D. O., E. Alverson, L. Hardison, S. Harrison, B. O'Brien, J. Rebman, J. Shevock, amd J. Thorne. In press. Plant diversity and endemism in the California Floristic Province. Madroño.

Burge, D. O., D. M. Erwin, M. B. Islam, J. Kellermann, S. W. Kembel, D. H. Wilken, and P. S. Manos. 2011. Diversification of Ceanothus (Rhamnaceae) in the California Floristic Province. International Journal of Plant Sciences 172:1137–1164.

Cade, T. J. 2007. Exposure of California condors to lead from spent ammunition. Journal of Wildlife Management 71:2125–2133.

California Native Plant Society (CNPS). 2014. Rare plant program. Inventory of rare and endangered plants (online edition, v8-02). California Native Plant Society, Sacramento, California. <http://www.rareplants.cnps.org>. Accessed March 27, 2014.

———. 2001. Inventory of rare and endangered plants of California. Sixth edition. CNPS, Sacramento, California.

California Nature Resources Agency (CNRA). 2013. <www.Resourcesca.gov>. Accessed October 2013.

California Rare Birds Committee (CRBC). 2013. Official California checklist. <http://californiabirds.org/c a_list.asp>. Accessed July 17, 2015.

Calands. 2013. California Protected Areas data portal. <www.calands.org>. Accessed April 2014.

Calsbeek, R. G., J. N. Thompson, and J. E. Richardson. 2003. Patterns of molecular evolution and diversification in a biodiversity hotspot: The California Floristic Province. Molecular ecology 12:1021–1029.

Cardinale, B. J., J. E. Duffy, A. Gonzalez, D. U. Hooper, C. Perrings, P. Venail, A. Narwani, G. M. Mace, D. Tilman, D. A. Wardle, A. P. Kinzig, G. C. Daily, M. Loreau, J. B. Grace, A. Larigauderie, D. S. Srivastava, and S. Naeem. 2012. Biodiversity loss and its impact on humanity. Nature 486:59–67.

Cardoso, P., T. L. Erwin, P. A. V. Borges, and T. R. New. 2011. The seven impediments in invertebrate conservation and how to overcome them. Biological Conservation 144:2647–2655.

Carlton, J. T., editor. 2007. Intertidal invertebrates from central California to Oregon. University of California Press, Berkeley, California.

CDF (California Department of Finance). 2013. New population projections. <www.dof.ca.gov>. Accessed September 1, 2013.

CDFW (California Department of Fish and Wildlife). 2013. State and federally listed endangered and threatened animals of California. California Department of Fish and Wildlife, Sacramento, California.

———. 2008. Complete list of amphibian, reptile, bird, and mammal species in California. <http://www.dfg.ca.gov/biogeodata/cwhr/pdfs/species_list.pdf>. Accessed September 28, 2013.

———. 2003. Atlas of the biodiversity of California. California Department of Fish and Wildlife, Sacramento.

CDPA (California Department of Parks and Recreation). 2013. <http://www.parks.ca.gov/>. Accessed October 20, 2013.

CEC (Commission for Environmental Cooperation). 2006. Ecological regions of North America. Toward a common perspective. CEC, Montreal, Quebec, Canada.

Clements, J. F., T. S. Schulenberg, M. J. Iliff, D. Roberson, T. A. Fredericks, B. L. Sullivan, and C. L. Wood. 2014. The eBird/Clements checklist of birds of the world: Version 6.9. Downloaded from <http://www.birds.cornell.edu/clementschecklist/download/>. Accessed July 17, 2015.

Cody, M. L. 1986. Diversity, rarity, and conservation in Mediterranean-climate regions. Pages 122—152 in M. E. Soulé, editor. Conservation biology: The science of scarcity and diversity. Island Press, Sunderland, Massachusetts.

Cody, M. L., and H. A. Mooney 1978. Convergence versus nonconvergence in Mediterranean-climate ecosystems. Annual Review of Ecology and Systematics 9:265–321.

Collinge, S. K., K. L. Prudic, and J. C. Oliver. 2003. Effects of local habitat characteristics and landscape context on grassland butterfly diversity. Conservation Biology 17:178–187.

Collins, P. W. 2009. Historic and prehistoric record for the occurrence of island scrub-jays (*Aphelocoma insularis*) on the Northern Channel Islands, Santa Barbara County, California. Technical Report no. 5. Santa Barbara Museum of Natural History. Santa Barbara, California.

Comisión Nacional de Áreas Naturales Protegidas (CONANP). 2014. <http://islaguadalupe.conanp.gob.mx/>. Accessed April 1, 2014.

Connor, E. F., J. Hafernik, J. Levy, V. L. Moore, and J. K. Rickman. 2002. Insect conservation in an urban biodiversity hotspot: The San Francisco Bay Area. Journal of Insect Conservation 6:247–259.

Conservation International. 2011. Biodiversity hotspots. California Floristic Province. <www.biodiversityhotspots.org/xp/Hotspots/california_floristic/>. Accessed November 1, 2011.

Cooper, D. 2004. Important bird areas of California. Audubon California, <http://iba.audubon.org/iba/stateIndex.do?state=US-CA>. Accessed July 17, 2015.

Cornelisse, T. M., and T. P. Duane. 2013. Effects of knowledge of an endangered species on recreationists' attitudes and stated behaviors and the significance of management compliance for ohlone tiger beetle conservation. Conservation Biology 27:1449–1457.

Cornelisse, T. M., M. C. Vasey, K. D. Holl, and D. K. Letourneau. 2013. Artificial bare patches increase habitat for the endangered Ohlone tiger beetle (*Cicindela ohlone*). Journal of Insect Conservation 17:17–22.

Cosumnes River Preserve. 2013. Flora and fauna. < http://www.cosumnes.org/>. Accessed April 1, 2014.

Cowling, R. M., P. W. Rundel, B. B. Lamont, M. K. Arroyo, and M. Arianotsou. 1996. Plant diversity in Mediterranean-climate regions. Trends in Ecology and Evolution 11:362–366.

CPAD (California's Protected Area Database). 2013. Data Statistics. September 2013. <http://www.calands.org/data/statistics>. Accessed October 5, 2013.

Cracraft, J. 2001. Avian evolution, Gondwana biogeography and the Cretaceous-Tertiary mass extinction event. Proceedings of the Royal Society of London Ser.B268:459–469.

CRBC (California Rare Birds Committee). 2013. <http://californiabirds.org/ca_list.asp>. Accessed September 1, 2013.

Crooks, K., and M. Soule. 1999. Mesopredator release and avifaunal extinction in a fragmented system. Nature 563–566.

Crosbie, S. P., W. D. Koenig, W. K. Reisen, V. L. Kramer, L. Marcus, R. Carney, and H. B. Ernest. 2008. Early impact of West Nile virus on the yellow-billed magpie (*Pica nuttalli*). The Auk 125(3):542–550.

Cunha, M. J., and R. T. Golightly, E. T. Nelson, and G. J. McChesney. 2008. Development of seabird monitoring methods on Castle Rock NWR. Report to the Coastal Program at Humboldt Bay, U.S. Fish and Wildlife Service, and Cooperative Fisheries Unit, Humboldt State University, USGS. 27 pages.

D'Amore, A., E. Kirby, and V. Hemingway. 2009. Reproductive interference by an invasive species: An evolutionary trap? Herpetological Conservation Biology 4:325–330.

Dana, G. L., and P. H. Lenz. 1986. Effects of increasing salinity on an Artemia population from Mono Lake, California. Oecologia 68(3):428–436.

D'Antonio, C. M., C. Malmstrom, S. A. Reynolds, and J. Gerlach. 2007. Ecology of invasive non-native species in California grassland. Pages 67–86 in M. R. Stromberg, J. D. Corbin, and C. M. D'Antonio, editors. California Grasslands Ecology and Management. University of California Press, Berkeley, California.

Davis, E. B., M. S. Koo, C. Conroy, J. L. Patton, and C. Moritz. 2008. The California Hotspots Project: Identifying regions of rapid diversification of mammals. Molecular Ecology 17:120–138.

Dawson, W. L. 1923. The birds of California: A complete, scientific and popular account of the 580 species and subspecies of birds found in the state. South Moulton Co., San Diego, California.

Delaney, K. S., and R. K. Wayne. 2005. Adaptive units for conservation: Population distinction and historic extinctions in the island scrub-jay. Conservation Biology 19(2):523–533.

Eberle, J. J., and D. R. Greenwood. 2012. Life at the top of the greenhouse Eocene world: A review of the Eocene flora and vertebrate fauna from Canada's High Arctic. Geological Society of America Bulletin 124:3–23.

Emslie, S. D. 1987. Age and diet of fossil California condors in Grand Canyon, Arizona. Science 237:768–70.

Ernst, W. G., C. A. Snow, and H. H. Scherer. 2008. Contrasting early and late Mesozoic petrotectonic evolution of northern California. Geological Society of America Bulletin 120:179–194.

Federal Register. 2014. Endangered and threatened wildlife and plants: Removing *Oenothera avita* ssp. *eurekensis* and *Swallenia alexandrae* from the federal list of endangered and threatened plants. <https://www.federalregister.gov/articles/2014/02/27/2014-04232/endangered-and-threatened-wildlife-and-plants-removing-oenothera-avita-ssp-eurekensis-and-swallenia>. Accessed March 14, 2014.

———. 2008. Endangered and threatened wildlife and plants; revised critical habitat for the California red-legged frog (*Rana aurora draytonii*) <https://www.federalregister.gov/articles/2008/09/16/E8-20473/endangered-and-threatened-wildlife-and-plants-revised-critical-habitat-for-the-california-red-legged>. Accessed July 17, 2015.

Feduccia, A. 2003. "Big bang" for tertiary birds? Trends in Ecology and Evolution 18:172–176.

Fellers, G. M., and C. A. Drost. 1993. Disappearance of the Cascades frog Rana cascadae at the southern end of its range, California, USA. Biological Conservation 65:177–181.

Ferrenberg, S. M., D. W. Schwilk, E. E. Knapp, E. Groth, and J. E. Keeley. 2006. Fire decreases arthropod abundance but increases diversity: Early and late season prescribed fire effects in a Sierra Nevada mixed-conifer forest. Fire Ecology 2:79–102.

Ficklin, D. L., I. T. Stewart, and E. P. Maurer. 2013. Effects of projected climate change on the hydrology in the Mono Lake Basin, California. Climatic Change 116(1):111–131.

Finkelstein, M., and D. Doak. 2012. Lead poisoning and the deceptive recovery of the critically endangered California condor. Proceedings of the National Academy of Sciences 109:11449–11454.

Fitzpatrick, B. M., and H. B. Shaffer. 2007. Hybrid vigor between native and introduced salamanders raises new challenges for conservation. Proceedings of the National Academy of Sciences 104:15793–15798.

Fleishman, E., C. Ray, P. Sjogren-Gulve, C. L. Boggs, and D. D. Murphy. 2002. Assessing the roles of patch quality, area, and isolation in predicting metapopulation dynamics. Conservation Biology 16:706–716.

Frankie, G. W., R. W. Thorp, J. Hernandez, M. Rizzardi, B. Ertter, J. C. Pawelek, S. L. Witt, M. Schindler, R. Coville, and V. A. Wojcik. 2009. Native bees are a rich natural resource in urban California gardens. California Agriculture 63:113–120.

Germano, D. J., G. B. Rathbun, L. R. Saslaw, B. L. Cypher, E. A. Cypher, and L. M. Vredenburgh. 2011. The San Joaquin Desert of California: Ecologically misunderstood and overlooked. Natural Areas Journal 31:138–147.

Godown, M. E., and A. T. Peterson. 2000. Preliminary distributional analysis of U.S. endangered bird species. Biodiversity and Conservation 9:1313–1322.

Gottlieb, L. D. 2003. Rethinking classic examples of recent speciation in plants. New Phytologist 161:71–82.

Goulson, D. 2003. Effects of introduced bees on native ecosystems. Annual Review of Ecology and Systematics 34:1–26.

Grinnell, J. 1902. Check-list of California birds. Pacific Coast Avifauna 3:99.

Grinnell, J., and A. Miller. 1944. The distribution of the birds of California. No. 27. Pacific Coast Avifauna 27. 610 pages.

Grinnell, J., J. S. Dixon, and J. M. Linsdale. 1937. Fur-bearing mammals of California. University of California Press, Berkeley, California.

Gullan, P. J., and P. S. Cranston. 2010. The insects: An outline of entomology. Wiley-Blackwell, Oxford, UK.

Hall, M., J. Grantham, R. Posey, and A. Mee. 2007. Lead exposure among reintroduced California Condors in southern California. Pages 139–162 in A. Mee and L. S. Hall, editors. Volume 2, California Condors in the Twenty-first Century. Series in Ornithology, American Ornithologists Union. Nuttall Ornithological Club, Washington, D.C., and Cambridge, Massachusetts.

Hall, M. C., D. B. Lowry, and J. H. Willis. 2010. Is local adaptation in *Mimulus guttatus* caused by trade-offs at individual loci? Molecular Ecology 19:2739–2753.

Hamilton, R. A., M. A. Patten, and R. A. Erickson, editors. 2007. Rare birds of California. Western Field Ornithologists. Camarillo, California.

Harrison, S. P. 2013. Plant and animal endemism in California. University of California Press, Berkeley, California.

Hart, M. W. 2008. Speciose versus species-rich. Tree 23:660–661.

Hayes, G. F., and K. D. Holl. 2003. Site-specific responses of native and exotic species to disturbances in a mesic grassland community. Applied Vegetation Science 6:235–244.

Hayes, T. B., A. Collins, M. Lee, N. Mendoza, N. Noriega, A. A. Stuart, and A. Vonk. 2002. Hermaphroditic, demasculinized frogs after exposure to the herbicide atrazine at low ecologically relevant doses. Proceedings of the National Academy of Sciences 99:5476–5480.

Herbst, D. B., F. P. Conte, and V. J. Brookes. 1988. Osmoregulation in an alkaline salt lake insect, Ephydra (Hydropyrus) hians, Say (Diptera: Ephydridae) in relation to water chemistry. Journal of Insect Physiology 34(10):903–909.

Hilton, R. P. 2003. Dinosaurs and other Mesozoic reptiles of California. University of California Press, Berkeley, California.

Hinton, L. 1998. Language loss and revitalization in California: Overview. International Journal of the Sociology of Language 132:83–94.

Hobday, A. J., M. J. Tegner, and P. L. Haaker. 2001. Over-exploitation of a broadcast spawning marine invertebrate: Decline of the white abalone. Reviews in Fish Biology and Fisheries 10:493–514.

Holler, N. R., D. W. Mason, R. M. Dawson, T. Simon, and M. C. Wooten. 1989. Reestablishment of the Perdido Key beach mouse (*Peromyscus polionotus trissyllepsis*) on Gulf Islands National Seashore. Conservation Biology 3:397–404.

Howard, H. 1937. A Pleistocene record of the passenger pigeon in California. The Condor 39:12–14.

Huenneke, L. F., S. P. Hamburg, R. Koide, H. A. Mooney, and P. M. Vitousek. 1990. Effects of soil resources on plant invasion and community structure in Californian serpentine grassland. Ecology 71:478–491.

IUCN (International Union for the Conservation of Nature). 2013. The IUCN red list of threatened species. <www.iucnredlist.org>. Accessed April 1, 2014.

Jepson Flora Project. 2013. Jepson eFlora. University of California Press, Berkeley, California. <http://ucjeps.berkeley.edu/IJM.html>. Accessed July 17, 2015.

Jockusch, E. L., and D. B. Wake. 2002. Falling apart and merging: Diversification of slender salamanders (Plethodontidae: *Batrachoseps*) in the American West. Biology Journal of Linnean Society 76:261–291.

Johnson, J. R., R. G. Thomson, S. J. Micheletti, and H. B. Shaffer. 2011. The origin of tiger salamander (*Ambystoma tigrinum*) populations in California, Oregon, and Nevada: Introductions or relicts? Conservation Genetics 12:355–370.

Johnson, N. K. 1972. Origin and differentiation of the avifauna of the Channel Islands, California. The Condor 74:295–315.

Jongsomjit, D. Stralberg, T. Gardali, L. Salas, J. A. Wiens. 2012. Between a rock and a hard place: The impacts of climate change and housing development on breeding birds in California. Landscape Ecology 28:187–200.

Kay, K. M., K. L. Ward, L. R. Watt, and D. W. Schemske. 2011. Plant speciation. Pages 71–97 in S. Harrison and N. Rajakaruna, editors. Serpentine: The evolution and ecology of a model system. University of California Press, Berkeley, California.

Keitt, B., K. Campbell, A. Saunders, M. Clout, Y. Want, R. Heinz, K. Newton, and B. Tershy. 2011. The Global Islands invasive vertebrate eradication database: A tool to improve and facilitate restoration of island ecosystems. Pages 74–77 C. R. Veitch, M. N. Clout, and D. R. Towns, editors. Island invasives: Eradication and management. IUCN, Gland, Switzerland.

Knapp, R. A., D. M. Boiano, and V. T. Vredenburg. 2007. Removal of nonnative fish results in population expansion of a declining amphibian (mountain yellow-legged frog, *Rana muscosa*). Biological Conservation 135:11–20.

Koford, C. B. 1953. The California condor. National Audubon Society. Research Report. Washington, D.C.

Kraft, N. J. B., B. G. Baldwin, and D. D. Ackerly 2010. Range size, taxon age, and hotspots of neoendemism in the California flora. Diversity and Distributions 16:403–413.

Kremen, C., N. M. Williams, and R. W. Thorp. 2002. Crop pollination from native bees at risk from agricultural intensification. Proceedings of the National Academy of Sciences 99:16812–16816.

Kremen, C., N. M. Williams, R. L. Bugg, J. P. Fay, and R. W. Thorp. 2004. The area requirements of an ecosystem service: Crop pollination by native bee communities. Ecology Letters 7:1109–1119.

Kuchta, S. R., and A. M. Tan. 2006. Lineage diversification on an evolving landscape: Phylogeography of the California newt, *Taricha torosa* (Caudata: Salamandridae). Biology Journal of the Linnean Society 89:213–239.

Kuchta, S. R., D. S. Parks, R. Lockridge Mueller, and D. B. Wake. 2009. Closing the ring: Historical biogeography of the salamander ring species *Ensatina eschscholtzii*. Journal of Biogeography 36:982–995.

Kuminoff, N., A. Sokolow, and D. Sumner. 2001. Farmland conversion: Perceptions and realities. AIC Issues Brief #16. University of California Agriculture Issues Center, Davis, California.

Lancaster, L. T., and K. M. Kay 2013. Origin and diversification of the California flora: re-examining classic hypotheses with molecular phylogenies. Evolution 67:1041–1054.

Leaché, A. D., and J. A. McGuire. 2006. Phylogenetic relationships of horned lizards (*Phrynosoma*) based on nuclear and mitochondrial data: Evidence for a misleading mitochondrial gene tree. Molecular Phylogenetics Evolution 39:628–644.

Leverington, Fiona, et al. 2010. A global analysis of protected area management effectiveness. Environmental Management 46(5):685–698.

Li, C., and E. Hadly, unpublished data.

Lidicker, W. A. 1991. Introduced mammals in California. Pages 263–272 in R. H. Groves and F. Di Castri, editors. Biogeography of Mediterranean Invasions. Cambridge University Press, New York, New York.

Losey, J. E., and M. Vaughan. 2006. The economic value of ecological services provided by insects. BioScience 56:311–323.

Lovich, J. E., and J. R. Ennen. 2013. Assessing the state of knowledge of utility-scale wind energy development and operation on non-volant terrestrial and marine wildlife. Applied Energy 103:52–60.

Lovich, J. E., and K. R. Beaman. 2007. A history of gila monster (*Heloderma suspectum cinctum*) records from California with comments on factors affecting their distribution. Southern California Academy of Sciences Bulletin 106:39–58.

Macey, J. R., J. A. Schulte Ii, A. Larson, B. S. Tuniyev, N. Orlov, and T. J. Papenfuss. 1999. Molecular phylogenetics, tRNA evolution, and historical biogeography in Anguid lizards and related taxonomic families. Molecular Phylogenetics and Evolution 12:250–272.

McChesney, G. J., and B. R. Tershy. 1998. History and status of introduced mammals and impacts to breeding seabirds on the California channel and northwestern Baja California islands. Colonial Waterbirds 21:335–347.

McIntyre, N. E. 2000. Ecology of urban Arthropods: A review and a call to action. Annals of the Entomological Society of America 93:825–835.

McWilliams, M. O., and D. G. Howell. 1982. Exotic terranes of western California. Nature 297:215–217.

Mee, A. and N. F. R. Snyder. 2007. California condors in the twenty-first century—Conservation problems and solutions. Pages 243–279 in A. Mee and L. S. Hall, editors. Series in Ornithology, volume 2. American Ornithologists Union. Nuttall Ornithological Club, Washington, D.C., and Cambridge, Massachusetts.

Mee, A., B. A. Rideout, J. A. Hamber, J. N. Todd, G. Austin, M. Clark, and M. P. Wallace. 2007. Junk ingestion and nestling mortality in a reintroduced population of California condors *Gymnogyps californianus*. Bird Conservation International 17:119–139.

Meretsky, V. J., N. F. R. Snyder, S. R. Beissinger, D. A. Clendenen, and J. W. Wiley. 2000. Demography of the California condor: Implications for reestablishment. Conservation Biology 14:957–967.

Meyers, S. C., A. Liston, and R. Meinke. 2010. A molecular phylogeny of Limnanthes (Limnanthaceae) and investigation of an anomalous Limnanthes population from California, U.S.A. Systematic Botany 35:552–558.

Millar, C. I. 2012. Geologic, climatic, and vegetation history of California. Pages 49–67 in B. G. Baldwin, D. H. Goldman, D. J. Keil, R. Patterson, T. J. Rosatti, and D. H. Wilken, editors. The Jepson manual: Vascular plants of California. Second edition. University of California Press, Berkeley, California.

———. 1996. Tertiary vegetation history. Pages 71–122 in Sierra Nevada Ecosystem Project: Final report to Congress. Volume II: Assessments and scientific basis for management options. University of California, Davis, Centers for Water and Wildlands Resources.

Miller, L., and I. DeMay. 1942. The fossil birds of California: Anavifauna and bibliography with annotations. University of California Press, Berkeley, California.

Millstein, D., and S. Menon. 2011. Regional climate consequences of large-scale cool roof and photovoltaic array deployment. Environmental Research Letters 6:1–9.

Moeller, H. V., K. G. Peay, and T. Fukami. 2014. Ectomycorrhizal fungal traits reflect environmental conditions along a coastal Cali-

fornia edaphic gradient. Federation of European Microbiological Societies Microbiology Ecology 87:797–806.
Morafka, D. J., and K. H. Berry. 2002. Is *Gopherus agassizii* a desert-adapted tortoise, or an exaptive opportunist? Implications for tortoise conservation. Chelonian Conservation Biology 4:263–287.
Myers, N., R. A. Mittermeier, C. G. Mittermeier, G. A. B. da Fonseca, and J. Kent. 2000. Biodiversity hotspots for conservation priorities. Nature 403:853–858.
National Audubon Society. 2013a. California gnatcatcher. <http://birds.audubon.org/species/calgna>. Accessed October 9, 2013.
———. 2013b. Important bird areas: Site profile reports. <http://netapp.audubon.org/iba/Reports>. Accessed August 22, 2013.
NatureServe. 2013. NatureServe Explorer: An online encyclopedia of life. Version 7.1. NatureServe, Arlington, Virginia. <http://www.natureserve.org/explorer>. Accessed October 9, 2013.
———. 2002. States of the Union: Ranking America's biodiversity. <http://www.natureserve.org/library/stateofunions.pdf>. Accessed August 25, 2013.
New, T. R. 2007. Understanding the requirements of the insects we seek to conserve. Journal of Insect Conservation 11:95–97.
Newsome, S. D., M. A. Etnier, D. Gifford-Gonzalez, D. L. Phillips, M. van Tuinen, E. A. Hadly, D. P. Costa, J. D. Kennett, T. L. Guilderson, and P. L. Koch. 2007. The shifting baseline of northern fur seal ecology in the northeast Pacific Ocean. Proceedings of the National Academy of Sciences of the United States of America 104(23):9709–9714.
Newton, K., M. McKown, C. Wolf, H. Gellerman, T. Coonan, D. Richards, L. Harvey, N. Holmes, G. Howald, K. Faulkner, B. Tershy, and D. Croll. Submitted. Ecological change ten years after rat eradication on Anacapa Island, California.
NMFS (National Marine Fisheries Service). 2008. Final white abalone recovery plan (*Haliotis sorenseni*). National Oceanic and Atmospheric Administration, National Marine Fisheries Service, Long Beach, California.
NOAA. 2015. National Climatic Data Center. Climate maps of the United States. <http://cdo.ncdc.noaa.gov/cgi-bin/climaps/climaps.pl>. Accessed August 5, 2014.
Noonan, B. P., J. B. Pramuk, R. L. Bezy, E. A. Sinclair, K. de Queiroz, and J. W. Sites Jr. 2013. Phylogenetic relationships within the lizard clade Xantusiidae: Using trees and divergence times to address evolutionary questions at multiple levels. Molecular Phylogenetics and Evolution 69:109–122.
O'Dell, R. E., and N. Rajakaruna. 2011. Intraspecific variation, adaptation, and evolution. Pages 97–137 in S. P. Harrison and N. Rajakaruna, editors. Serpentine: Evolution and ecology in a model system. University of California Press, Berkeley, California.
Olson, D. M., E. Dinerstein, E. D. Wikramanayake, N. D. Burgess, G. V. N. Powell, E. C. Underwood, and K. R. Kassem. 2001. Terrestrial ecoregions of the world: A new map of life on Earth. BioScience 51(11):933–938.
Parisi, M. 2003. Atlas of the biodiversity of California. California Department of Fish and Game, Sacramento, California.
Parham, J. F., and T. J. Papenfuss. 2009. High genetic diversity among fossorial lizard populations (*Anniella pulchra*) in a rapidly developing landscape (central California). Conservation Genetics 10:169–176.
Parrish, D. D., B. S. Hanwant, L. Molina, and S. Madronich. 2011. Air quality progress in North American megacities: A review. Atmospheric Environment 45:7015–7025.
Pearson, D. L., and A. P. Vogler. 2001. Tiger beetles. Cornell University Press, Ithaca, New York.
Peery, M. Z., and R. W. Henry. 2010. Recovering marbled murrelets via corvid management: A population viability analysis approach. Biological Conservation 143(11):2414–2424.
Peery, M. Z., S. R. Beissinger, S. H., Newman, E. B. Burkett, and T. D. Williams. 2004. Applying the declining population paradigm: Diagnosing causes of poor reproduction in the marbled murrelet. Conservation Biology 18(4):1088–1098.
Pellmyr, O. 2003. Yuccas, yucca moths, and coevolution: A review. Annals of the Missouri Botanical Garden 90:35–55.
Pellmyr, O., J. N. Thompson, J. M. Brown, and R. G. Harrison. 1996. Evolution of pollination and mutualism in the Yucca moth lineage. American Naturalist 148:827–847.
Peregrine Fund. 2013. <http://www.peregrinefund.org/docs/pdf/project-data/2013-12-31-condor-population.pdf>. Accessed April 15, 2014.
Pickett, C. H., and R. L. Bugg, editors. 1998. Enhancing biological control: Habitat management to promote natural enemies of agricultural pests. University of California Press, Berkeley, California.
Pogson, T. H., and S. M. Lindstedt. 1991. Distribution and abundance of large sandhill cranes, *Grus canadensis*, wintering in California's Central Valley. Condor 93(2):266–278.
Point Reyes Bird Observatory (PRBO) Conservation Science. 2011. Projected effects of climate change in California: Ecoregional summaries emphasizing consequences for wildlife. Version 1.0. <http://data.prbo.org/apps/bssc/uploads/Ecoregional021011.pdf>. Accessed July 17, 2015.
Powell, J. A., and C. L. Hogue. 1980. California insects. University of California Press, Berkeley, California.
Poyry, J., J. Paukkunen, J. Heliola, and M. Kuussaari. 2009. Relative contributions of local and regional factors to species richness and total density of butterflies and moths in semi-natural grasslands. Oecologia 160:577–587.
Price, P. W. 1997. Insect ecology. John Wiley and Sons, Inc., New York, New York.
Pyron, R. A., F. T. Burbrink, and J. J. Wiens. 2013. A phylogeny and revised classification of Squamata, including 4161 species of lizards and snakes. BMC Evolutionary Biology 13:93.
Ratnieks, F. L. W., and N. L. Carreck. 2010. Clarity on honey bee collapse? Science 327:152–153.
Raven, P. J., and D. I. Axelrod. 1978. Origin and relationships of the California flora. University of California Press, Berkeley, California.
Riedman, M. L., and J. A. Estes. 1990. The sea otter (*Enhydra lutris*): Behavior, ecology, and natural history. U.S. Fish and Wildlife Service Biological Report. U.S. Fish and Wildlife Service, Washington, D.C.
Rohr, J. R., and T. R. Raffel. 2010. Linking global climate and temperature variability to widespread amphibian declines putatively caused by disease. Proceedings of the National Academy of Sciences 107:8269–8274.
Rubega, M., and C. Inouye. 1994. Prey switching in red-necked phalaropes (*Phalaropus lobatus*): Feeding limitations, the functional response, and water management at Mono Lake, California, USA. Biological Conservation 70(3):205–210.
Safford, H. D., J. H. Viers, and S. Harrison. 2005. Serpentine endemism in the California flora: A database of serpentine affinity. Madroño 52:222–257.
San Mauro, D., M. Vences, M. Alcobendas, R. Zardoya, and A. Meyer. 2005. Initial diversification of living amphibians predated the breakup of Pangaea. American Naturalist 165:590–599.
Shearwater, Debra. Personal communication, September 21, 2013.
Shier, D. M., and R. R. Swaisgood. 2012. Fitness costs of neighborhood disruption in translocations of a solitary mammal. Conservation Biology 26:116–123.
Shuford, D. W., and T. Gardali. 2008. California bird species of special concern: A ranked assessment of species, subspecies, and distinct populations of birds of immediate conservation concern in California. Studies of Western Birds 1:1–78.
Sinervo, B., and R. G. Calsbeek. 2006. The developmental, physiological, neural, and genetical causes and consequences of frequency-dependent selection in the wild. Annual review of ecology, evolution, and systematics 37:581–610.
Sinervo, B., F. Méndez-de-la-Cruz, D. B. Miles, B. Heulin, E. Bastiaans, M. Villagran-Santa Cruz, R. Lara-Resendiz, N. Martínez-Méndez, M. L. Calderón-Espinosa, R. N. Meza-Lázaro, H. Gadsden, L. J. Avila, M. Morando, I. J. De la Riva, P. Victoriano Sepulveda, C. F. Duarte Rocha, N. Ibargüengoytía, C. A. Puntriano, M. Massot, V. Lepetz, T. A. Oksanen, D. G. Chapple, A. M. Bauer, W. R. Branch, J. Clobert, and J. W. Sites Jr. 2010. Erosion of lizard diversity by climate change and altered thermal niches. Science 328:894–899.
Snyder, N. F., and N. J. Schmitt. 2002. California condor (*Gymnogyps californianus*). In A. Poole, editor. The Birds of North America Online. Cornell Lab of Ornithology, Ithaca, New York.
Soule, M. E., D. T. Bolger, A. C. Alberts, M. Sorice, and S. Hill. 1988. Reconstructed dynamics of rapid extinctions of chaparral-requiring birds in urban habitat islands. Conservation Biology 2(1):75–92.
Spatz, D. R., K. M. Newton, R. Heinz, B. R. Tershy, N. D. Holmes, S.H.M. Butchart, and D. A. Croll. 2014. The biogeography of glob-

ally threatened seabirds and island conservation opportunities. Conservation Biology 28:1282–1290.
Stebbins, G. L., and J. Major 1965. Endemism and speciation in the California flora. Ecological Monographs 35:1–35.
Stein, B. A., L. S. Kutnerm, and J. S. Adams, editors. 2000. Precious heritage: The status of biodiversity in the United States. Oxford University Press, New York, New York.
Stralberg, D., D. Jongsomjit, C. A. Howell, M. A. Snyder, J. D. Alexander, J. A. Wiens, and T. L. Root. 2009. Re-shuffling of species with climate disruption: A no-analog future for California birds? PLoS ONE 4: e6825.
Sydeman, W. J., M. Losekoot, J. A. Santora, S. A. Thompson, T. Distler, A. Weinstein, M. A. Smith, N. Walker, and K. H. Morgan. 2013. Hotspots of seabird abundance in the California Current: Implications for important bird areas. Audubon California, San Francisco, California.
Takhtajan, A. 1986. Floristic regions of the world. Translated by T. J. Crovello and A. Cronquist. University of California Press, Berkeley, California.
Tevis, L., and I. M. Newell. 1962. Studies on the biology and seasonal cycle of the giant red velvet mite, *Dinothrombium pandorae* (Acari, Thrombidiidae). Ecology 43:497–505.
Thomas, J. A., N.A.D. Bourn, R. T. Clarke, K. E. Stewart, D. J. Simcox, G. S. Pearman, R. Curtis, and B. Goodger. 2001. The quality and isolation of habitat patches both determine where butterflies persist in fragmented landscapes. Proceedings: Biological Sciences 268:1791–1796.
Thorne, J. H., J. H. Viers, J. Price, and D. M. Stoms. 2009. Spatial patterns of endemic plants in California. Natural Areas Journal 29:344–366.
Tingley, M. W., W. B. Monahan, S. R. Beissinger, and C. Moritz. 2009. Birds track their Grinnellian niche through a century of climate change. Proceedings of the National Academy of Sciences of the United States of America (106 Suppl.): 19637–19643.
U.S. Census Bureau. 2013. State and County QuickFacts. Data derived from population estimates, American community survey, census of population and housing, state and county housing unit estimates, county business patterns, nonemployer statistics, economic census, survey of business owners, building permits. <http://quickfacts.census.gov/>. Accessed September 8, 2013.
USFWS (U.S. Fish and Wildlife Service). 2013a. Proposal to remove island night lizard from its current listing as threatened. <http://www.endangeredspecieslawandpolicy.com/2013/03/articles/fish-wildlife-service/u-s-fish-and-wildlife-service-proposes-removal-of-island-night-lizard/>. Accessed July 17, 2015.
———. 2013b. Sacramento NWR complex habitats. <http://www.fws.gov/refuge/Sacramento/habitats.html> Accessed 9/21/2013.
———. 2009. Spotlight species action plan (2010–2014). <http://www.fws.gov/ecos/ajax/docs/action_plans/doc3165.pdf> Accessed July 17, 2015.
USGS Patuxent Wildlife Research Center. 2013. North American breeding bird survey internet data set. <http://www.pwrc.usgs.gov/bbs/retrieval/>. Accessed September 18, 2013.
Vieites, D. R., M.-S. Min, and D. B. Wake. 2007. Rapid diversification and dispersal during periods of global warming by plethodontid salamanders. Proceedings of National Academy of Sciences 104:19903–19907.
Vredenburg, V. T. 2004. Reversing introduced species effects: Experimental removal of introduced fish leads to rapid recovery of a declining frog. Proceedings of National Academy of Sciences 101:7646–7650.
Vredenburg, V. T., R. Bingham, R. Knapp, J. A. T. Morgan, C. Moritz, and D. Wake. 2007. Concordant molecular and phenotypic data delineate new taxonomy and conservation priorities for the endangered mountain yellow-legged frog. Journal of Zoology 271:361–374.
Vredenburg, V. T., R. A. Knapp, T. S. Tunstall, and C. J. Briggs. 2010. Dynamics of an emerging disease drive large-scale amphibian population extinctions. Proceedings of the National Academy of Sciences 107: 9689–9694.
Walters, J. R., S. R. Derrickson, and D. M. Fry. 2010. Status of the California condor (*Gymnogyps californianus*) and efforts to achieve its recovery. The Auk 127:969–1001.
Waters, J. M., and D. Craw. 2006. Goodbye Gondwana? New Zealand biogeography, geology, and the problem of circularity. Systematic Biology 55:351–356.
Wigand, P. E., S. W. Edwards, and P. M. Schiffman. 2007. Pleistocene and pre-European grassland ecosystems. Pages 37–56 in M. R. Stromberg, J. D. Corbin, and C. M. D'Antonio, editors. California Grasslands Ecology and Management. University of California Press, Berkeley, California.
Wilbur, S. R., and L. F. Kiff. 1980. The California condor in Baja California, Mexico. American Birds 34:856–859.
Wu, C. A., D. B. Lowry, A. M. Cooley, Y. W. Lee, and J. H. Willis 2007. Mimulus is an emerging model system for integration of ecological and genomic studies. Heredity 100:1–11.

TWELVE

Vegetation

CHRISTOPHER R. DOLANC, TODD KEELER-WOLF,
and MICHAEL G. BARBOUR

Introduction

California harbors an extraordinarily rich diversity of vegetation types, ranging from desert scrub to some of the tallest and most productive forests in world. VEGETATION can vary over remarkably short distances in California (Figure 12.1). Examples of most of the major biomes in North America (Breckle 2002) can be found in California, including conifer forest, deciduous forest, grassland, tundra, and desert scrub. Roughly 38% (16 million hectares) of the state is dominated by FOREST OR WOODLAND vegetation, and 41% (17 million hectares) is dominated by scrub types such as chaparral, creosote bush, and sagebrush steppe. The iconic oak woodland type found throughout much of the state covers approximately 9% (3.8 million hectares); herbaceous types occupy about 16% (6.7 million hectares) of the land area (Barbour et al. 2007).

The term *vegetation* refers to all plant species of a given area and their arrangement, both vertically and horizontally, across the landscape. The term *plant community* is often used interchangeably with vegetation but tends to be used more in the context of species composition (all the different species that make up the community). Also sometimes used interchangeably with vegetation is *habitat*, which generally refers to vegetation as used by a particular animal species or community. Vegetation can be thought of as the plant (botanic or floristic) component of an ecosystem and is often used when describing different kinds of vegetation, as we do in this chapter. Many ecosystems, such as coast redwood forest, are named after the vegetation of the ecosystem, because it is the most prevalent aspect of that ecosystem. Other ecosystems are defined by a combination of vegetation and other features, such as alpine ecosystems defined by a combination of climate and certain vegetation features. See Sawyer et al. (2009) for a more detailed description and discussion of the concept of vegetation.

In this chapter we discuss the diversity of vegetation in California and how it relates to climatic diversity. We first discuss the main gradients in climate encountered when changing latitude, elevation, and distance from the sea. We then discuss the most current methods of classification and mapping used to quantify and describe vegetation in California. Finally, we summarize the major vegetation types of the state by running a virtual transect from its cool, wet northwest corner to its hot, dry southeast corner (Figure 12.2a). Given

FIGURE 12.1 Gradient from the alpine zone on Dana Plateau (circa 3,566 meters) east across dry subalpine, montane conifer forest, pinyon-juniper woodland, and sagebrush zones to alkaline Mono Lake and the Great Basin cool desert. Photo: Todd Keeler-Wolf.

our limited space, and the state's extraordinary richness, this survey must be limited to major vegetation types. Absent are accounts of azonal vegetation—vegetation types restricted to particular geologic substrates and soils, such as closed-cone conifer stands (e.g., bolander pine [*Pinus contorta* ssp. *bolanderi*]), wetland, and riparian areas. In contrast, most of the vegetation types we discuss are restricted by regional climatic (zonal) gradients. Azonal types tend to cover less of the landscape than zonal types because they are embedded as localities within an otherwise homogeneous zonal matrix. Also missing are some important but more narrowly restricted vegetation types, such as coastal scrub, and beach and dune vegetation. Many of the vegetation types not discussed in this chapter are considered as part of ecosystems in chapters that follow. For a more complete discussion of all vegetation types in California, see Barbour et al. (2007) and Sawyer et al (2009).

Climatic and Environmental Gradients

Underlying this great diversity of vegetation are gradients of climate that follow geographic and topographic features. Indeed, the distribution of vegetation in California closely resembles the distribution of climates (Figure 12.2b). A gradient of decreasing precipitation, and increasing summer drought, runs from north to south along the coast from Crescent City to Los Angeles and along the Central Valley axis from Redding to Bakersfield (Chapter 2). The distribution of coast redwood (*Sequoia sempervirens*) forest along the California coast reflects the pattern of decreasing summer moisture from north to south, with high abundance near Crescent City, trailing off to the southern end of its distribution south of Monterey (Barbour et al. 2001).

When moving from the coast inward, a gradient of increasing CONTINENTALITY (i.e., temperature range) can be found at just about any latitude in California (see Chapter 2, "Climate"). In Fort Ross, located on the coast north of San Francisco, the difference between mean January and July temperatures is 4.4°C; in Sacramento, approximately 140 kilometers straight east and inland, the difference is 16.6°C (Minnich 2007); differences between daily highs and lows follow a similar pattern. Close proximity to the ocean buffers coastal vegetation against climatic extremes: most coastal areas in California seldom freeze, alleviating the need for strong cold-tolerance adaptations; lower temperatures reduce POTENTIAL EVAPOTRANSPIRATION (PET), and thus drought stress; and summer fog adds moisture during the drier summer months, further reducing drought stress. On the coast, some plants growing in fog-shrouded redwood forest can get more than half of their water from fog in summer (Dawson 1998). In California in general, PET and summer water deficit increase with increasing continentality (see Chapter 3, "Fire as an Ecosystem Process"). The relationship of forests and woodlands to annual rainfall is best seen in the North Coast Ranges, where a west-to-east transect situated at a constant elevation of around 700 meters would show the following pattern of vegetation: the outer ranges (closest to the coast) are dominated by coast redwood forest, the middle ranges by mixed-evergreen forest, and the inner ranges (farthest inland from

Photo on previous page: Variation in vegetation related to soil depth and texture, and disturbance in an inland California coastal landscape (Santa Ynez Valley, Santa Barbara County), typical of the Mediterranean heart of the state. Valley oak woodlands occur on deeper, fine-textured soils; coast live oak woodland on cooler exposures; chaparral and coastal scrub on steep slopes; and open grasslands where fires or local soil texture have precluded the oak woodlands. The largely summer-dry Santa Ynez River is lined with Fremont cottonwoods and California sycamores, which tap into the subsurface flow of water. Photo: Todd Keeler-Wolf.

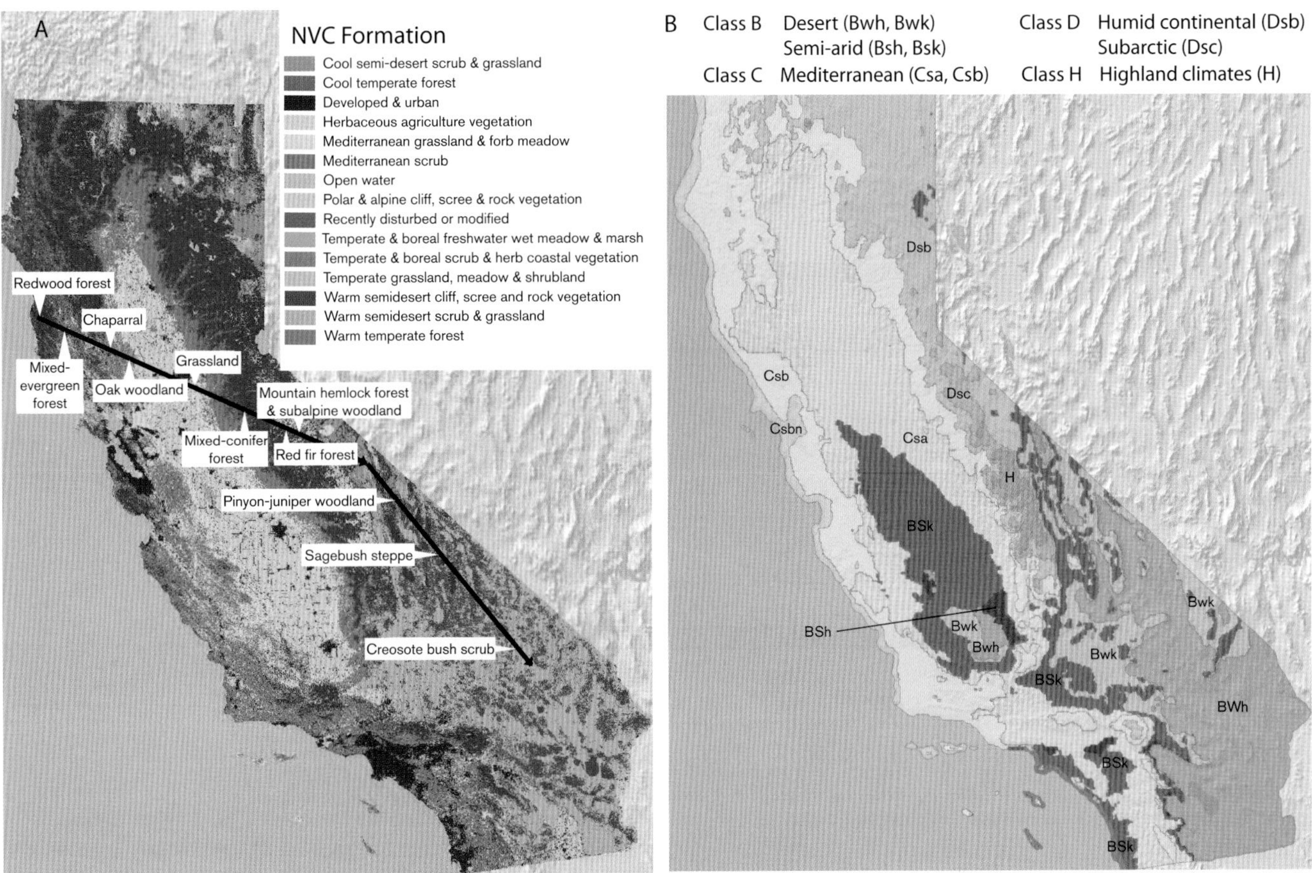

FIGURE 12.2 Map is based on the Köppen 1936 system of climate zones. Class B: Desert (Bwh, Bwk), Semiarid (Bsh, Bsk); Class C: Mediterranean (Csa, Csb); Class D: Humid continental (Dsb), Subarctic (Dsc); Class H: Highland climates.

A Distribution of vegetation types in California using the National Vegetation Classification (NVC) system at the level of the "formation," which is analogous to many of California's well-known vegetation types (highlighted by boxes on the map). Note the presence of forest types in the mountains and northwest part of the state, where precipitation is high, and dominance by scrub types in the southern, drier part of the state. The black line represents the northwest to southeast virtual transect used to "sample" major vegetation types throughout much of this chapter, including labels of many of the types described. Ecosystem types as defined in this book often coincide with boundaries of vegetation types. They sometimes encompass more than one (as in deserts, which includes desert steppe, scrub, and grassland) or only part of one (as in redwood forests, which make up a subset of the Warm Temperate Forest NVC category).

B Climate zones of California. Note the similarity between the distribution of climate in this figure and the vegetation types in (A).

the coast) by oak woodland—thus we move from tall, dense forest to progressively shorter, more open forest as precipitation declines.

The patchy coastal distributions of numerous tree species such as bishop pine (*Pinus muricata*), Torrey pine (*Pinus torreyana*), Monterey pine (*P. radiata*), Monterey cypress (*Hesperocyparis macrocarpa*), Santa Cruz cypress (*H. abramsiana*), and coast redwood are believed to be relicts of wider distributions that existed in more MESIC paleoclimates. The mild climate of modern coastal California has allowed these species to persist (Axelrod 1990). Coast redwood, which was once widely distributed throughout North America, is now relegated to a narrow strip of forest that reaches no more than about 60 kilometers inland (Barbour et al. 2001).

Strong patterns of both temperature and precipitation follow montane topography in California due to the northwest-southeast orientation of many mountain ranges and the resulting orographic lift created by large Pacific storms (see Chapter 2, "Climate," for more detail). These gradients set up zones of vegetation in elevation bands that can be seen in multiple mountain ranges in California (Küchler 1990). Figure 12.3 shows hypothetical distributions for major vegetation types along axes of elevation and moisture for the central Sierra Nevada. Differences along the moisture axis are driven by site conditions such as slope aspect and soil depth, which could be considered additional gradients (of microenvironment) operating at a finer scale than those discussed here. Thus, using elevation and a minimum amount of site information, one can predict fairly confidently the broad vegetation types that should occur at a given point on the landscape. Similar, elevation-dependent zonation patterns can be found in the mountains of northwest California (Sawyer 2007). These elevational vegetation zones rise in elevation to the south and lower to the north. The mean elevational displacement of vegetation zones is –172 meters for every increasing degree of north latitude, which is uniquely higher than the displacement in other North American mountain chains (Parker 1994). The underlying climate also drives patterns of forest structure in the central Sierra Nevada: very tall forests with nearly closed canopies (100% cover) occur around 2,000 meters, where precipitation is high and growing season long but forests become progressively shorter and sparser (often <25% cover) with increasing elevation (Rundel et al. 1990).

Continentality, combined with the decreasing frequency

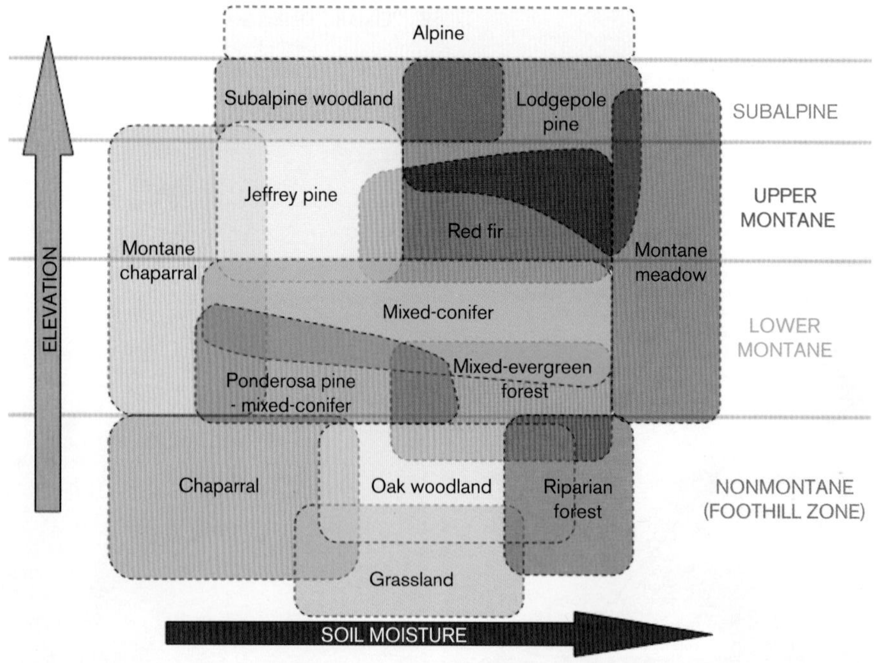

FIGURE 12.3 Hypothetical distribution of common vegetation types of the central Sierra Nevada arrayed on gradients of elevation (y-axis) and soil moisture (x-axis). The x-axis could be considered a gradient from xeric to mesic sites, caused by such factors as aspect, steepness, soil type, and bedrock depth. This diagram does not consider disturbance, which also affects the position of most vegetation types. For example, frequent disturbance of chaparral causes it to convert to grassland. Source: Dolanc, unpublished data.

of large winter storms, sets up a broad pattern whereby mean temperature increases and annual precipitation decreases (and thus increasing PET) from the northwest to the southeast in California, as well as inland valley areas in the rain shadow. A glance at a map of vegetation patterns across the state reflects this distribution, with forests in the northwest and mountains; desert and grassland in the southeast and valleys; and intermediate types in between (see Figure 12.2a). In addition to more broad, MACROCLIMATIC patterns, California is replete with MICROCLIMATIC and EDAPHIC gradients. The fine-scale effects of slope, aspect, and substrate are impossible to demonstrate on small-scale maps but add enormous complexity to the state's vegetation patterns (Figure 12.4). They can vary sharply across slope boundaries (e.g., northeast-facing is cool, shady; and opposite southwest-facing is hot, sunny) and can strongly influence vegetation patterns based on their relative position: for example, steep ridgetop stand versus shaded canyon bottom. Because the interactive factors of slope, position, and aspect alter the moisture retention capabilities of microsites (Stephenson 1998), a very steep north-facing slope in the central Coast Range might have adjacent mixed stands of redwood, tanoak, and maples; while a hundred meters away on the opposite southwest steep slope grows a matrix of grassland and oak woodland (see Figure 12.4).

Coupled with the remarkable topographic diversity of California is its geologic diversity. Soil texture and chemistry gradients associated with the variety of geological and depositional environments in hilly areas also vary at the scale of the watershed or subregional landscape (see also Chapter 4, "Geomorphology and Soils"). These gradients can produce sharp ecological boundaries in what would be more gradual in simpler, gentle terrain (see chapter lead photo). The geochemical effects of SERPENTINE and other ULTRAMAFIC rocks on vegetation in California are well-known (Kruckeberg 1984, Alexander et al. 2007). However, there are many other sharp vegetation juxtapositions due to abrupt, geologically driven shifts in soil texture, salinity, alkalinity, and moisture in most of the state outside of the relatively flat Great Valley.

Vegetation Classification

A vegetation classification develops a single, commonly accepted terminology to describe kinds of vegetation. As with all classification, it is useful to be able to refer to certain types of vegetation, and classification can help us understand what drives differences between and within types. The practice of classifying vegetation involves quantitative analysis of species composition collected from representative sample plots within uniform stands of vegetation (Peet and Roberts 2012). Vegetation classification of any large region is an iterative exercise. We gain improved understanding of relationships between all types of vegetation as more samples are analyzed and compared from a wider, representative sample universe. Now, with over forty years of systematic sampling throughout California, a breadth of quantitative understanding has been attained, backed by similar efforts in many other parts of North America and much of the world.

Any vegetation classification imposes a particular level of detail or scale. Wall maps of the vegetation of California (e.g., Küchler 1990) show broad patterns of vegetation but are not accurate at a fine, local, or regional scale. In contrast, a vegetation classification and map produced for a small nature preserve or a state park exhibit detail at a very fine scale. The concept of hierarchy in the organization of vegetation classification has been useful in much the same way that hierarchy

FIGURE 12.4 Local variation in vegetation: locally compressed but regionally broad vegetation categories occur in canyons of the Santa Lucia Mountains, Monterey County. Bottom and lower slope redwood forest (red outline) occurs adjacent to mixed-evergreen forest (blue outline) and oak woodland (yellow outline), which in turn are adjacent to grassland (orange outline). These are representative of three different broad formations, each of which have their ecological and evolutionary origins in different parts of North America but are regularly juxtaposed at local scales in central California. The coastal summer inversion layer associated with cool marine fog at lower elevations and hot cloudless summers at upper levels is largely responsible for this pattern. Photo: Todd Keeler-Wolf.

has been used by biologists to express relationships among plant or animal taxa from species, to genera, to families and beyond. The global perspective of a hierarchical vegetation classification has improved substantially with cooperation through the International Association for Vegetation Science, the Ecological Society of America's Vegetation Panel, and the establishment of state and federal vegetation standards for government agencies. At the national level vegetation ecologists have collaborated to develop a major revision of the U.S. National Vegetation Classification (NVC) system (Jennings et al. 2009, Franklin et al. 2012).

The current NVC uses an eight-level hierarchy to describe all types of vegetation on Earth. The system is subdivided into higher, mid-, and lower levels. All levels are driven principally by global, continental, and local effects of climate. The higher levels of the classification are not important if we are specifically interested in the vegetation of California. However, an inspection of the third level, the formation class, reveals how California's diverse vegetation is climatically driven. This level is represented in the map of California vegetation (see Figure 12.2a). California types from this level include warm and cool temperate forests and wetlands, warm (subtropical) and cool desert, marine, freshwater, and alpine vegetation. Of the other types described globally for this level, only tropical, polar, and boreal vegetation formations are missing or poorly developed in California. Thus, using this classification system, we are better able to understand where California's vegetation falls in a global context. Even the most unique and endemic vegetation to the state, the Mediterranean scrub, grassland and meadow, and warm temperate forests and woodlands occur in other Mediterranean climates around the world, such as the Mediterranean Basin, western and south Australia, South Africa, and central Chile. This is an example of how similar climates beget similar vegetation types. In this case, vegetation "similarity" at the continental level reflects life forms based on morphological and physiological convergence (such as SCLEROPHYLL or DROUGHT-DECIDUOUS leaves) driven by limiting climatic factors, rather than similarity of species taxonomic composition.

As we move further down the hierarchy to the mid- and finer levels, the ecological and taxonomic relationships are unveiled within and between vegetation categories. However, the broader hierarchical perspective is important to retain. It is very difficult to perceive broad relationships in vegetation patterns from a single location with a diversity of environments compounded by steep elevation, slope direction, and a myriad of soil textures and substrate chemistry (see Figure 12.4; see chapter lead photo). This is one of the principal reasons that it has been difficult to understand and synthesize the relationships among different types of California vegetation. A detailed comparison of local vegetation plots, which in turn is comparatively analyzed with similar data from other adjacent states and ecoregions, is needed to arrive at a complete understanding of ecological similarities among different groups of vegetation. Throughout the remainder of this chapter we summarize major vegetation types of California, referring to their more commonly known names but organized according to the NVC to show the relationship between these common-usage types and the NVC. This approach helps situate California's diverse vegetation within its broader context.

Summary of Major Vegetation Types

Starting on the northwest coast and proceeding southeast, we run a virtual transect across the state, across the Coast Ranges, through the Great Central Valley, up and over the great Sierra Nevada, and then south across the cold and warm deserts in the southeast part of California (see Figure 12.2a). Due to the state's complex topography and its effects on climate, this transect will take us in and out of cool temperate and warm temperate forest, in and out of Mediterranean scrub and grassland, in and out of the cool temperate and montane zones, and finally into cold and warm deserts.

Cool Temperate Coastal Vegetation

REDWOOD FOREST

We begin our virtual transect near the coast of northern California, where annual precipitation can be as high as in tropical rainforest (≥ 2,500 millimeters per year). Coast redwood forest dominates two different habitats here: a riparian floodplain near sea level and upland slopes below 350 meters. Floodplain stands tend to be monospecific, with only coast redwood (*Sequoia sempervirens*) in the OVERSTORY. Trees are massive, and UNDERSTORY trees and shrubs contribute very little COVER (Figure 12.5). On slopes, Douglas-fir (*Pseudotsuga menziesii*) shares dominance, and the cover of shrubs is much greater than on floodplains (Sawyer 2007).

Redwood forest is at the southern end of a long coastal temperate rainforest that extends north into southeast Alaska. The NVC shows that redwood forests are related to the great cool temperate rainforests of the Pacific Northwest, through shared species such as western hemlock (*Tsuga heterophylla*), grand fir (*Abies grandis*), sword fern (*Polystichum munitum*), and many others. Redwood is able to extend the boundaries of the northwestern forests farther south into central coastal California because the coast redwood is able to take advantage of extra moisture in the form of summer fog (Dawson 1998). Unlike all other northwestern rainforest conifers, redwood is also able to regenerate following fire, and fire is a significant aspect of the dry summers of California's Mediterranean climate. Thus redwood forest is the "California version" of the northwestern temperate rainforests (see Chapter 26, "Coast Redwood Forests").

In the absence of fire, redwood may be at a competitive disadvantage with Sitka spruce (*Picea sitchensis*), western hemlock, and several other conifers of the cool temperate Pacific Northwest (called Vancouverian in the NVC) rainforest. Sitka spruce and hemlock have very thin bark and are easily killed by fires of moderate to low intensity, whereas coast redwood has a thick, resistant bark and is capable of resprouting. Survival of redwood trees is thus high even after high-intensity fire. Historical FIRE RETURN INTERVALS in redwood forest were likely much lower than in much of the Pacific Northwest, and it is unclear how much of a role fire plays in redwood stand dynamics and distribution (Lorimer et al. 2009). At the southern end of its distribution, where annual precipitation is much lower, redwood reproduction comes mostly via resprouting, as moisture is too low for successful seedling germination (Stuart and Stephens 2006). Flooding may favor redwoods over other species because redwoods are able to produce new roots that extend up to the forest floor and provide a temporary source of oxygen while the tree produces more permanent roots (Stone and Vasey 1968). However, as with fire history, the degree to which flooding shapes redwood distribution is unclear. In general, redwood has a complex life history and is a very old species; many of its life-history traits could have evolved in a very different environment than it experiences today (Lorimer et al. 2009).

Other vegetation types common in the cool-temperate forest BIOCLIMATE in northwestern California include coastal scrub and grassland, dune scrub, beach and dune vegetation, and some closed-cone conifer stands. For more information on these types, see Barbour et al. (2007) and the respective ecosystem chapters in this volume. We will encounter other types of cool, temperate forests as we cross the Sierra Nevada later in our virtual transect in this chapter.

Warm Temperate Forests and Woodlands of Mediterranean California

MIXED-EVERGREEN FOREST

As we move inland on our transect, and up across the higher elevations of the Coast Ranges, we are more likely to encounter mixed-evergreen forest (Figure 12.6). Here, Douglas-fir becomes dominant, and redwoods are reduced to sporadic individuals. Many evergreen hardwoods are associated with Douglas-fir: tanbark oak (*Notholithocarpus densiflorus*), madrone (*Arbutus menziesii*), canyon live oak (*Quercus chrysolepis*), California bay (*Umbellularia californica*), and giant chinquapin (*Chrysolepis chrysophylla*), among others. This forest has long been called mixed-evergreen forest, and variants of it are found in the Big Sur Mountains, the Klamath Mountains, the North Coast Ranges, the northern Sierra Nevada (where it is sometimes called "montane hardwood"), and the Transverse and Peninsular Ranges of southern California. This forest is rich in tree species, which typically form two canopy layers: an overstory of large, widely spaced conifers (usually Douglas-fir in the north and may include big cone Douglas-fir [*P. macrocarpa*] and coulter pine [*P. coulteri*] further south) and a more closed canopy of hardwoods below (Allen-Diaz et al. 2007). The increased likelihood of repeated fire southward from the moist Northwest, coupled with reduced precipitation, tends to eliminate Douglas-fir and other conifers. By the time we get to central California, this forest has become a mixture of madrone, tanoak, chinquapin, and several oak species.

Mixed-evergreen forest is considered a warm-temperate forest in the NVC, less related to the cool temperate redwood forests than to the California foothill woodlands of oaks (*Quercus* spp.), buckeye (*Aesculus californica*), and gray pines (*Pinus sabiana*) of central California. However, the component species tend to require more moisture and tolerate less summer drought than foothill woodland species.

CHAPARRAL

As we continue east on our transect, we pass through the drier, inland portions of the Coast Ranges, where we encounter a matrix of grassland, chaparral, and oak woodland, sometimes dotted with stands of closed-cone conifers. This matrix of grassland, oak woodland, and chaparral also occurs on the other side of the Great Valley, in the Sierra Nevada foothills. Climatic attributes of regional precipitation and temperature overlap for all three vegetation types (see Figure 12.3). Instead, these types are often separated by slope position, soil characteristics, and disturbance. (Keeley and Davis 2007; see Figure 12.4, chapter lead photo.)

Chaparral is a type of scrub vegetation (dominated by shrubs) and covers 8.5% of California, making it the fifth most abundant vegetation type in terms of percentage of California's total area (see Chapter 24, "Chaparral"). The other four are creosote bush desert scrub (21.6%), mixed-conifer forest (13.6%), grassland (13.2%), and oak woodland (9.6%) (Barbour et al. 2007). Chaparral typically occupies southwest-facing slopes on skeletal, droughty, coarse-textured soils. The NVC considers the majority of the California chaparral (outside of the cooler mountains) to reside within the California chaparral macrogroup. It is broken up into several types of chaparral at the group level. These include xeric chaparral, on hotter, well-drained slopes; mesic chaparral, on shady, cooler slopes; maritime chaparral, on nutrient-poor substrates within the maritime belt adjacent to the coast; pre-montane chaparral, occurring at the interface with cool temperate montane forests; and serpentine chaparral, with numerous endemic shrubs adapted to the chemically harsh substrate wherever it outcrops.

Throughout all of these variants, chaparral is always a one-layered vegetation type, but it can be quite diverse

FIGURE 12.5 Old-growth redwood forest in Humboldt Redwoods State Park, Humboldt, County. Photo: Christopher Dolanc.

FIGURE 12.6 A two-story old-growth mixed-evergreen forest in Wooley Creek Drainage, Siskiyou County. Photo: Todd Keeler-Wolf.

FIGURE 12.7 A chaparral landscape in the San Gabriel Mountains, Los Angeles County. Stands vary with exposure, substrate, and fire history. Photo: Todd Keeler-Wolf.

(Figure 12.7). Twenty-four percent of the state's vascular plant species grow in chaparral, and nearly five hundred of these are endemic there. A very open, emergent layer of trees (e.g., gray pine, knobcone pine) may be present, with canopy cover <10%. The shrub layer usually reaches 100% cover, except in those types limited to very rocky or chemically harsh substrates, and typically the understory herb layer is very patchy and contributes <15% cover. The most common shrubs in chaparral include chamise (*Adenostoma fasciculatum*) and species of manzanita (*Arctostaphylos*), *Ceanothus*, silk tassle (*Garrya*), scrub oak (*Quercus* spp.), *Rhus*, and *Rhamnus*. Annuals seem to be underrepresented but occur in seed banks, some of which germinate only after fire. The shrubs are almost all sclerophyllous (leaves are evergreen, small, tough, and thick). Shrub branches tend to be rigid and interlocking. Average shrub height is 2 to 3 meters but shorter where the vegetation grows on chemically difficult substrates such as serpentine (Keeley and Davis 2007, Sawyer et al. 2009).

In southern California, and along the inner and middle-central Coast Ranges, is a vegetation type often associated with chaparral called coastal scrub or more commonly coastal sage scrub (Rundel 2007; see Chapter 22, "Coastal Sage Scrub"). This scrub generally grows at elevations below chaparral, and in the same landscape it tends to occupy soils of finer texture and recovers more quickly following fire. Compared with chaparral, coastal scrub is shorter, more open, and made up of species with softer leaves. Most coastal scrub species respond to the strong summer drought by dropping most leaves, and several species may produce smaller, thicker, summer leaves. Unlike chaparral, coastal scrub tends to share some species and many genera with the warm deserts of inland southern California and the coastal deserts of Baja California, Mexico, including species of cactus and other stem or leaf succulents. The NVC places coastal scrub into its own macrogroup, but along with chaparral it belongs to the same California scrub division.

OAK WOODLANDS (CALIFORNIA BROADLEAF FOREST AND WOODLAND)

Oak woodlands in California are diverse in both composition and PHYSIOGNOMY, and they cover the full range of density between open savanna and forest (see Chapter 25, "Oak Woodlands"). Where a given stand falls along this gradient appears to be largely driven by soil moisture, with greater moisture leading to higher tree density (Griffin 1990). Oak woodlands have been classified multiple ways, ranging from single-species stands to more regional descriptions (Allen-Diaz et al. 2007). The NVC considers all woodlands and forests within the Mediterranean bioclimate to be part of the warm temperate forest and woodland formation. Most oak woodlands of the state are placed within the single group: California broadleaf woodland and forest.

Most oak woodland is essentially two-layered. The overstory tree canopy is 5 to 20 meters tall and 10% to 60% closed with an understory layer of herbs below. Occasional tall, emergent, gray or ponderosa pines (*Pinus ponderosa*) tower over the oak canopy. Shrub cover is scattered, generally <5%, but an understory herb layer is almost continuous except where denser stands of live oaks (coast: *Quercus agrofolia*; canyon: *Q. chrysolepsis*) provide most of the litter (because the slow leaf decomposition and year-round shade restrict herb cover) (Griffin 1990). Dominant tree species vary by region and include seven species of evergreen and deciduous oaks (*Quercus* spp.), as well as a few other hardwood species and conifers such as gray pine. Blue oak (*Q. douglasii*) is the most widespread and prevalent dominant oak of these systems.

The understory herbs in oak woodland are often similar to those of California grassland: a mix of introduced, naturalized annual grasses and forbs, with a half-dozen associated native perennial bunch grass species and numerous native annual forbs. However, oaks can alter the hydrology and nutrient availability in their vicinity, creating differences in the composition of the herbaceous community directly beneath their canopies (Allen-Diaz et al. 2007). Though there is little evidence to inform about the history of fire patterns in oak woodlands, it seems likely that fires of anthropogenic origin were historically frequent and of low intensity (Wills 2006).

GRASSLANDS

As we head down into the Great Central Valley of California on our transect, we enter a region that historically was likely a vast expanse of prairie or grassland. Today, most of the Central Valley grassland has been converted to agriculture, and what remains has been heavily affected by invasive species. Prior to European colonization, grassland probably occupied more of California's area than any other vegetation type. The combination of valley grassland plus foothill oak woodland (because the understory is very similar to interior grassland at lower elevations) would have totaled more than 21% of the state (Barbour et al. 2007). The current distribution remains as a ring around the Central Valley and into the foothills. It also occurs along the coast in central and southern California as well as in numerous other pockets throughout the state (Bartolome et al. 2007; see Chapter 23, "Grasslands").

Grasslands typically are dominated by annual or perennial grasses in cover and biomass. Species diversity in broadleaf forbs is high and may contribute four times the richness of grasses. Grasslands may exist without any woody overstory cover, but steppe-grassland or SAVANNA grassland can have shrubs or trees regularly present with cover <25% (Bartolome et al. 2007). Plant species diversity has a tendency to be temporally based on individual species responses to timing and amount of rainfall and fluctuations in temperature (Elmendorf and Harrison 2009).

The NVC treats the California grassland as a division: California grassland and meadow. It is broken up into two groups: California annual and California perennial grasslands. The perennial grasslands are composed primarily of bunchgrasses in the genus *Stipa* (formerly *Nassella*). Purple needlegrass (*Stipa pulchra*) has long been considered the most emblematic of the California grasslands. However, it could be simply the most resistant native perennial to unnatural disturbance patterns and replacement by numerous introduced, Eurasian exotic grasses and forbs (see Stromberg et al. 2007). Mounting evidence from historical records and from more recent studies of native California Mediterranean herbaceous species' ecological tolerances indicates that much of the California "grassland" was comprised not of perennial bunchgrasses but of a much more variable pallet of annual flowering forbs.

There has been much confusion in the past about the classification of California grassland, primarily because it was little studied floristically and its vegetation has not received much comparative study with other North American grasslands. This is beginning to change. Currently under the NVC, the grasslands of California are not all members of the Mediterranean scrub and grassland formation. Other grasslands, such as the "California Coastal Prairie" of the North Coast are cool temperate grasslands, are part of the temperate grassland, meadow, and shrubland formation. Many of California's cool temperate grasslands are in even more trouble ecologically. Along the north coast, the traditional practice of Native American burning may have maintained relatively large grassland patches. However, once traditional land practices were curtailed and exotic Eurasian perennial pasture grasses became established, the species of these prairies were shaded out by successional shrublands of coyotebrush (*Baccharis pilularis*) or by forests of mixed-evergreen tree species.

Cool Temperate Forests and Woodlands of California Mountains

As we move east and up over the great Sierra Nevada, we cross through several zones used to differentiate bioclimatic zones in mountains worldwide: the foothill zone, lower montane, upper montane, subalpine, and alpine. The Sierra Nevada is a great place to experience the gradual transition from one zone to another because of its gently yet consistently rising western slope, from near sea level to >4,000 meters, accompanied by strong gradients in precipitation and temperature. The foothill zone of the Sierra Nevada is dominated by a matrix of grassland, chaparral, and oak woodland, like much of the inner Coast Ranges. The other zones are dominated largely by forest. Only the alpine zone, with its very short growing season, lacks trees. Currently the NVC classifies the forests of the middle and upper elevations of the Sierra Nevada and most other mountains of the state as components of the Vancouverian cool temperate forest division.

The lower montane zone occupies the middle elevations of the Sierra Nevada (from 600 to 800 meters to about 2,100 to 2,300 meter elevation at a latitude near Sacramento [38.5°N]). This is the zone of maximum annual precipitation, with totals of 1,800 millimeters per year in some locations. Here, snowpack can be deep, although it may be seasonally inconsistent, determined by the fluctuating temperatures of winter weather fronts. Summer thunderstorms are not nearly as frequent as at higher elevations or in the Great Basin mountain ranges to the east of California. The high precipitation and moderate winter temperatures combine to support tall forests throughout most of the lower montane zone. The vegetation type most characteristic of this zone is mixed-conifer forest (see Chapter 27, "Montane Forests").

The upper montane zone extends from the top of the lower montane to 2,600 to 2,800 meters, around 38.5°N. This zone has the deepest snowpack; 80% of precipitation falls as snow, with snow depths sometimes reaching 4 meters (Barbour et al. 1993). As in lower montane, the upper montane zone is mostly dominated by forest, but it also includes meadows and montane chaparral (Rundel et al. 1990, Fites-Kaufman et al. 2007). Red fir (*Abies magnifica*) forest dominates most of the upper montane in California. The subalpine zone ranges from the top of upper montane up to treeline (3,000–3,200 meters at this latitude; see Chapter 28, "Subalpine Forests"). Nearly all precipitation falls as snow, and the growing season lasts for only six to nine weeks (Fites-Kaufman et al. 2007). The vegetation in subalpine may best be described as woodland, with shorter, more sparsely spaced trees than the montane zone, punctuated with open areas of exposed bedrock and snow fields (Rundel et al. 1990, Sawyer et al. 2009).

Forests of the upper montane and subalpine zone fall within the Vancouverian subalpine forest macrogroup of the NVC. In most of the higher mountains of the state, they can be divided into three distinct groups: red fir forest, mountain hemlock forest, and subalpine woodland. Together, the upper montane and subalpine zones are the California analogs of the extensive subalpine forests and parklands of the high mountains of the Pacific Northwest, which share the trait of having the highest snow accumulation of any North American forests. Unlike the mixed-conifer forests, the structuring of these forests tends to be less the result of fire history and more the result of favorable colonization sites. Regeneration of trees is strongly driven by microclimatic patterns based on the topographic accumulation or deflation of the winter snowpack, and the patchy accumulation of deeper soils and skeletal, recently glacially scoured substrates (Peterson 1998). The alpine zone lies above treeline and extends to the tops of mountains (see Chapter 29, "Alpine Ecosystems"). Climate is quite harsh and vegetation is dominated by low-lying shrubs and herbaceous perennials (Sawyer and Keeler-Wolf 2007).

MIXED-CONIFER FOREST

A third of the way up the western slope of the Sierra Nevada, we begin to encounter mixed-conifer forest on our transect (Figure 12.8). Mixed-conifer forest is one of the five leading vegetation types in the state in terms of area, covering approximately 13% (5.5 million hectares) of the state. Due to its extent and the size and growth rates of its trees, it is also one of the most reliable timber-producing zones of the state. It can be found in nearly all high mountain ranges in the state, including southern California (Barbour et al. 2007).

These forests are dominated by conifers, but stands are heterogeneous and diverse. Dominant species include ponderosa pine, sugar pine (*P. lambertiana*), Jeffrey pine (*P. jeffreyi*), white fir (*Abies concolor*), Douglas-fir (*Pseudotsuga menziesii*), and incense-cedar (*Calocedrus decurrens*) as well as hardwood species such as California black oak (*Quercus kelloggii*). Many classifications subdivide mixed-conifer forest into multiple forest types (Sawyer et al. 2009), but these forests are widely known as mixed-conifer and can be bioclimatically organized into a single group: the California montane conifer forest and woodland. The complex composition and shifting structure in these forests is based on local precipitation, soil depth, and fire history of the vegetation within the broad group and can be best understood at the "alliance" level of the NVC. In general, lower-elevation portions tend to have ponderosa pine and incense-cedar as the principal conifers. These forests are called the ponderosa pine–incense cedar alliance in the NVC hierarchy. With increasing elevation, cooler annual temperatures ameliorate the summer drought and enable more moisture-loving trees such as white fir and sugar pine to have higher regeneration rates, leading to the white fir–sugar pine alliance. Shallow or chemically harsh soils throughout the California mountains tend to support Jeffrey pine woodland.

Variants of mixed-conifer forest occur in southern California's mountains and the higher central Coast Ranges, where additional endemic conifers such as Santa Lucia fir (*Abies bracteata*), Coulter pine (*Pinus coulteri*), and big-cone Douglas-fir (*Pseudotsuga macrocarpa*) occur. Another notable member of the mixed-conifer forest is the iconic giant sequoia (*Sequoiadendron gigantea*), which enriches stands from the central to southern Sierra (see Figure 12.8). Its presence and its genetic kinship with the coast redwood remind us of the ecological relationships with the bioclimate of the cool temperate coastal forests.

Mixed-conifer forests have a strong relationship with historical, natural fire return intervals of less than fifteen years. Fire suppression has markedly increased the fire return interval in many locations, facilitating infill by small trees and a shift in dominance toward shade-tolerant species such as white fir (van Wagtendonk and Fites-Kaufman 2006). Unfortunately, few places in California exist where the FIRE REGIME has been left unaltered and the forest has not been harvested for timber. The best examples occur in national and state parks and wilderness areas. Following crown fires and logging operations, montane chaparral and deciduous shrubs of bitter-cherry (*Prunus emarginata*) and deer-brush (*Ceanothus integetrrimus*) often form successional patchworks between more mature forest stands. Intervening mountain streams support riparian forest and scrub, and basin and seepage areas support meadows in patches throughout (Rundel et al. 1990, Fites-Kaufman et al. 2007).

RED FIR FOREST

We continue moving up in elevation, up the western slope of the Sierra Nevada and into the part of the range with the deepest snowpack and associated red fir forest (Figure 12.9). Red fir forest is the most common vegetation type in the upper montane zone of the Sierra Nevada–Cascade axis, and the mountains of northwest California, but does not exist in southern California. The physiognomy of red fir forest is different than the more complex and fine-scale patchiness of mixed-conifer forest. Stands tend to be larger and simpler with a one-layered canopy dominated overwhelmingly by red fir. Western white pine (*Pinus monticola*) is found in more open, rocky sites with mountain hemlock (*Tsuga mertensiana*) or lodgepole pine (*Pinus contorta*) at higher elevations. Elements of mixed-conifer forest (e.g., white fir, Jeffrey pine) occur at the lower margins. In the Klamath Mountains, noble fir (*Abies procera*) sometimes replaces red fir. Dense shading and thick LITTER accumulation make understory shrubs uncommon. Cover by shrubs and herbs usually totals less than 5%, especially in dense, continuous stands. Tree regeneration is strikingly patchy. For more information on species and physiognomy, see Rundel et al. (1990), Potter (1998), and Fites-Kaufman et al. (2007).

Fire in red fir forest is generally less frequent and of lower intensity than in mixed-conifer forest because of the former's compact fuel beds and cooler, wetter conditions (van Wagtendonk and Fites-Kaufman 2006). Fire, windthrow, and avalanches add to the complexity of the red fir forest structure, but these tend to create small openings (Scholl and Taylor 2006). One of the main climatic differences between mixed-conifer forest and red fir forest is deep and long-lasting snow. This is the bioclimatic difference that causes the NVC to place red fir forest into the subalpine forest of California group and segregates it from the lower elevation mixed-conifer group and other types of cool temperate forests in the NVC. The lack of this persistent and reliable snowpack is probably the principal reason we do not find this forest in the southern California mountains, where white fir and sugar pine forest rise up to higher elevations before giving way directly to XERIC subalpine woodlands. Snowpack appears to have a negative effect on the regeneration of white fir and other species of the mixed-conifer group (Barbour et al. 1991).

MOUNTAIN HEMLOCK FOREST

We continue up into the subalpine zone of the Sierra Nevada, where forests become increasingly short-statured until they gradually disappear at treeline. California mountains generally have broad treelines; the transition from forest to alpine is gradual instead of an abrupt line, as in mountains of other regions (Sawyer and Keeler-Wolf 2007). The vegetation of the subalpine zone is often considered together as one, but the NVC splits the zone into mesic and xeric vegetation types. Mountain hemlock forest is found above the red fir forest and often mixed with its upper edge, and it can extend up to treeline. Various combinations of mountain hemlock, lodgepole pine, western white pine, and red fir are found in the canopy, which often approaches 100% cover. In California, these stands are found usually only on protected sites, with long-lasting snowpack (Rundel et al. 1990, Fites-Kaufman et al. 2007). A few, isolated stands occur in the Klamath Mountains, where these forests are augmented with other trees characteristic of even colder conditions that exist mostly north of the California border, including subalpine fir (*Abies lasiocarpa*), Engelmann spruce (*Picea engelmannii*), and Alaska yellow cedar (*Chanmacyparis nootkaensis*). These snowy subalpine stands occur in California only where snowpack lasts long enough to ameliorate the summer drought. The Warner Mountains and the High Transverse and Peninsular Ranges of southern California are both too dry to support mountain hemlock. However, both of these mountain ranges support subalpine woodland, a xeric variant of subalpine forest.

SUBALPINE WOODLAND

Xeric subalpine woodland in California is characterized by sparse, usually short-statured trees, often mixed with extensive rock outcrops (Figure 12.10; Fites-Kaufman et al. 2007). As opposed to mountain hemlock forest, this type usually exists where snow accumulation is low and soil development is poor. Stands can be mixed or singly dominated and occur in a wide variety of combinations (Sawyer et al. 2009). Canopy cover is usually low (30%–50%) and dominated by pines such as whitebark pine (*Pinus albicaulis*), Sierra lodgepole pine (*P. contorta murrayana*), and Sierra juniper (*Juniperus grandis*). Foxtail pine (*Pinus balfouriana*) grows in the high southern Sierra and in the Klamath Mountains and adjacent North Coast ranges. Shrub cover is often lacking or made up of prostrate species. The thin fuel beds, sparse tree spacing, and cool, short growing season keep fires small and infrequent (van Wagtendonk and Fites-Kaufman 2006).

Most subalpine tree species are slow-growing and very long-lived (sometimes older than 1,000 years) because of the harsh climate of the subalpine zone. Trees growing near treeline begin to take on unusual growth forms such as multiple stems, flagging, and KRUMMHOLZ (also known as elfinwood), which likely reflect of the intense wind and cold temperatures near treeline (Major and Taylor 1990). Most subalpine species

FIGURE 12.8 Old-growth mixed-conifer forest with giant sequoia in Merced Grove, Mariposa County. Photo: Christopher Dolanc.

FIGURE 12.9 Old-growth red fir forest in Desolation Wilderness, El Dorado County. Photo: Christopher Dolanc.

FIGURE 12.10 Subalpine woodland, south side of Cathedral Peak, Yosemite National Park, Tuolumne County. Photo: Christopher Dolanc.

FIGURE 12.11 Pinyon-juniper woodland in the White Mountains, Inyo County, with the Sierra Nevada in the background. Sagebrush, which is ubiquitous throughout the Great Basin and forms its own vegetation type, usually forms an understory in this vegetation type. Photo: Christopher Dolanc.

in California have the capacity to form krummholz, but foxtail pine and bristlecone pine (*Pinus longaeva*) do not.

A closely related group of cold, dry subalpine woodland occurs in the White, Inyo, and Panamint Mountains of eastern California. These woodlands are characterized by Great Basin bristlecone pine and limber pine (*Pinus flexilis*) (Thorne et al. 2007). The dry subalpine of the Transverse and Peninsular Ranges in southern California is intermediate between the Great Basin Mountains and the Sierra and other high California mountains. It lacks mountain hemlock, whitebark, and foxtail pine, which are replaced by Sierra lodgepole pine and limber pine as the principal species.

PINYON-JUNIPER WOODLAND

After heading up and over the Sierra Nevada crest, and through the subalpine and alpine zones, we now head down the steeper and drier east slope. We move through Jeffrey pine forest and eventually come to a lower timberline, beyond which spreads the vast shrub land of the Great Basin. Located just above the lower timberline is pinyon-juniper woodland (Figure 12.11), and its distribution in the eastern parts of California (2.5% of the state) is actually the western edge of its vast distribution in the Great Basin and Colorado Plateau (Thorne et al. 2007). Pinyon-juniper woodland is characterized by short trees (5–10 meters, 20% cover) with an understory of mixed montane/desert shrubs (40%) and an open understory of perennial grasses and forbs (5%, seasonal). The dominant trees are species of pinyon pine (e.g., *Pinus monophylla*) and multiple species of juniper (e.g., *Juniperus osteosperma*). Stands may be mixed or singly dominated by pine or juniper species. Sometimes, scattered Jeffrey pine trees coexist with the pinyons and junipers (Vasek and Thorne 1990, Thorne et al. 2007).

The NVC considers pinyon-juniper woodland to be a type of cool temperate forest, technically receiving higher precipitation and lower summer temperatures than true cold desert shrublands. The relationships of these woodlands to other cool temperate forests can be observed in the southeastern Sierra Nevada and the northern Transverse Ranges of southern California, where species of the cool temperate mixed-conifer forests such as Jeffrey pine and white fir commonly intermingle with pinyon and juniper. The extent and architecture of pinyon-juniper stands have changed over the past century or more. The understory used to have more grass cover, which provided enough fuel for more frequent surface fires. Livestock grazing has degraded the amount of grass fuel, so the fire return interval has lengthened and the type of fire has changed from cool-burning surface fires to hot and intense crown fires. Pinyon pine has thin bark and is often killed in even cool, surface fires (Brooks and Minnich 2006).

COOL SEMIDESERT SCRUB AND GRASSLAND

As we reach the eastern base of the Sierra Nevada, we come into the Great Basin. We will spend the rest of our transect in the desert region of California, first passing through the cold desert and ending in the warm desert (see Figure 12.2a; see Chapter 30, "Deserts"). The Intermountain or Great Basin region of California is sometimes called the "cold desert" because its winters are cold and often have snow. In fact, these are the coldest climates in California outside of the highest mountains. Summer temperatures can be as warm as those in the Mojave and Sonoran Deserts. Annual precipitation ranges from 50 millimeters (Death Valley) to 300 millimeters at elevations higher than 1,500 meters (Major 1990, Minnich 2007). The cold desert region of California lies just east of the Sierra-Cascade axis, over to the border with Nevada, up to the northeastern corner of the state, and south to around Bishop (37.5°N).

SAGEBRUSH STEPPE

In California, vegetation types dominated by sagebrush (*Artemisia* spp.), collectively called sagebrush steppe, total 985,000 hectares (2.3% of the state). However, sagebrush also forms the dominant understory in many xeric forests and WOODLANDS in California (see Figure 12.11). The extent of sagebrush in California, though large, is just the western edge of its distribution, which covers most of the Great Basin—all of the land between the Sierra Nevada–Cascade axis and the Rocky Mountains (Barbour et al. 2007, Young et al. 2007). The cover and spacing of sagebrush varies (10%–80% cover), with shrub

FIGURE 12.12 Desert scrub vegetation in Anza-Borrego Desert State Park, San Diego County. Photo: Todd Keeler-Wolf.

heights usually 0.5–1.0 meter tall. An herbaceous layer up to 30–140 centimeters tall (5%–10% cover) is present in some types. As the name suggests, sagebrush dominates but associated shrub taxa include *Purshia, Ribes, Symphoricarpos, Chrysothamnus, Ephedra,* and *Tetradymia*. Perennial bunchgrasses are common in some types and include wild rye (*Elymus elymoides*), Idaho fescue (*Festuca idahoensis*), and bluebunch wheatgrass (*Pseudoregnia spicata*) (Young et al. 2007).

Observations over the past century document that livestock prefer to forage on grasses rather than on the much more abundant sagebrush. Consequently, overgrazing in the 1800s quickly produced a decline in grasses and an increase in nonedible shrubs. (Native browsers do, however, eat sagebrush: sage grouse, pronghorn, and mule deer). Cheat grass (*Bromus tectorum*), an introduced annual grass, has had negative impacts on sagebrush communities by outcompeting native perennials and filling in space between shrubs and grasses to create continuous fuel to carry fire, altering the fire regime (Young et al. 2007).

Warm Desert and Semidesert Scrub and Grassland

The warm desert in California lies south of the cold desert, extending south from the Owens Valley then down through most of the inland region of southern California. It includes the Mojave Desert in the north and the Sonoran Desert to the south and southeast. Most of the California Sonoran Desert abuts the lower reaches of the Colorado River and is sometimes called the Colorado Desert. Annual precipitation there generally totals less than 100 millimeters per year and is very episodic. The Mojave Desert gets most of its precipitation in winter but eastward and southward, summer rainfall increases; the Sonoran Desert has roughly equal summer and winter precipitation. Mean January temperatures are warm (>10°C) and mean July temperatures are extremely hot (>32°C) (Major 1990, Minnich 2007).

Vegetation of the warm desert is extremely diverse and includes creosote (*Larrea tridentata*), saltbush (*Extriplex californica*), shadscale, blackbush (*Coleogyne ramosissima*), psammophytic (sand-adapted), and cactus scrub types, Joshua tree (*Yucca brevifolia*) woodland, MICROPHYLL woodland, and palm (*Washingtonia filifera*) oases (Keeler-Wolf 2007, Schoenherr and Burk 2007). The Mojave Desert is much richer than the cold desert in terms of the diversity of landscapes, habitats, VEGETATION TYPES, and the flora. Of all the Californian ecoregions, the Mojave may be the most systematically studied, mapped, and understood (Keeler-Wolf 2007). However, the subtropical Sonoran Desert is structurally more diverse, including arborescent cacti, leaf succulents, and "pachycaulous" (thick, water-storing, woody stemmed) life forms (Figure 12.12). Parts of the Sonoran Desert in adjacent Mexico and Arizona have higher growth rates and standing biomass than most other deserts on Earth. Their high diversity of species and growth forms may be related to the multiple evolutionary pathways plants have taken in adapting to a very dry, high-radiation environment (Schoenherr and Burk 2007).

CREOSOTE BUSH SCRUB (SONORAN-MOJAVE CREOSOTE BUSH–WHITE BURSAGE DESERT SCRUB)

Our last stop on the California transect is in creosote bush scrub. Numerous and varied other desert vegetation types exist beyond this point (see Figure 12.12) (Keeler-Wolf 2007, Schoenherr and Burk 2007). Although the Mojave and Sonoran Deserts have their differences, the common thread between them is the huge expanse of lower slopes and alluvial fans covered by creosote bush. Creosote bush scrub vegetation covers over two-thirds of the area of the state's warm deserts, more than 8.6 million hectares (21% of the state's total area), making it the single most abundant vegetation type in California. Despite its abundance, it varies greatly in its component species and physiognomy depending on precipitation, soil, topography, and community age (Vasek and Barbour 1990). Over much of this area, creosote is accompanied by the sub-shrub burro bush (*Ambrosia dumosa*). In the southern Mojave Desert and on into the Sonoran Desert, the drought-deciduous sub-shrub *Encelia farinosa* replaces burro bush on some sites. Total cover in most creosote bush communities is usually less than 20%, with creosote bush itself usually totaling less than 8%. Creosote bush forms clonal rings, slowly growing out from the center, and may reach ages of more than a thousand years (Vasek and Barbour 1990).

Summary

Vegetation comprises all plant species of a region and their pattern across the landscape. Wide gradients of climate and topography drive tremendous diversity of vegetation types in California, ranging from tall redwood forest with >2,000 millimeters per year of rain to warm desert scrub with <50 millimeters per year. Soil and microclimate heterogeneity across the state further increase vegetation diversity. The classification of vegetation is the arrangement of plant communities into categories that share common characteristics. The National Vegetation Classification system relates vegetation to climatic data and helps demonstrate how California vegetation types are related to other vegetation types around North America and the world. California has examples of most of the major vegetation types found on Earth, lacking only tropical, polar, and boreal types. Forested vegetation types can be found in the northwest and mountainous parts of the state, where annual precipitation is high. Scrub and grassland types predominate where annual precipitation is low and where evaporative demand is higher and/or soils thinner. This chapter reviewed twelve of the most abundant vegetation types of California by running a virtual transect (see Figure 12.2a) from the northwestern corner of the state, east across the Central Valley and Sierra Nevada, and down through the deserts into the southeastern part of the state.

Acknowledgments

Thanks to Aicha Ougzin for preparing the maps of California precipitation, bioclimate, and vegetation. Thanks to M. Peinado for a timely summary of the bioclimate of California.

Recommended Reading

Barbour, M. G., T. Keeler-Wolf, and A. A. Schoenherr. 2007. Terrestrial vegetation of California. Third edition. University of California Press, Berkeley, Los Angeles, London.

Peet, R. K., and D. W. Roberts. 2012. Classification of natural and semi-natural vegetation. Pages 28–70 in J. Franklin and E. van der Maarel, editors. Vegetation Ecology. Oxford University Press, New York, New York.

Sawyer, J. O., T. Keeler-Wolf, and J. Evens. 2009. A manual of California vegetation. Second edition. California Native Plant Society, Sacramento, California.

Glossary

BIOCLIMATE A climate and its influences on and by the biological organisms within the climate.

CONTINENTALITY Degree to which climate is influenced by land versus water.

COVER A measure of areal space occupied by a species, collection of species, or vegetation type, usually expressed as a percentage of a defined unit.

DROUGHT-DECIDUOUS Describes plants that drop their leaves during dry periods.

EDAPHIC Of or related to the soil.

FIRE REGIME The long-term pattern of wildfire characteristic for a given vegetation or region. Fire frequency, severity, intensity, complexity, size, and seasonality are all components of a fire regime.

FIRE RETURN INTERVAL Number of years between fires for a given location, usually calculated as an average, or mean fire return interval.

FOREST Vegetation dominated by trees that, when combined, cover 30% to 60% of the landscape.

KRUMMHOLZ A growth form common near treeline characterized by stunted, often matted, densely spaced trees with multiple horizontal branches. Also known as elfinwood.

LITTER Plant material that has fallen and accumulated on the soil surface.

MACROCLIMATE The regional climate, driven by atmospheric factors.

MESIC Refers to sites with a moderate moisture supply.

MICROCLIMATE The climate of a localized area driven by site-specific factors that cause the climate to differ from the regional climate (macroclimate).

MICROPHYLL Characterized by leaves with very small surface area.

OVERSTORY The upper part or canopy of vegetation structure. In forests, overstory generally refers to mature trees, as opposed to small trees, shrubs, or herbs growing near the forest floor.

PHYSIOGNOMY The architecture or structure (outer appearance) of vegetation.

POTENTIAL EVAPOTRANSPIRATION (PET) Hypothetical amount of moisture returned to the atmosphere as a result of plant transpiration with unlimited moisture supply. PET is largely a function of temperature at a given site.

SAVANNA Vegetation characterized by a grassland understory with sparse trees that combine for no more than 5% to 10% of the landscape.

SCLEROPHYLL Vegetation with hard, evergreen leaves that function to reduce moisture loss.

SCRUB Vegetation dominated by shrubs.

SERPENTINE A mineral that, when found in high concentration in the bedrock and soil, causes unique vegetation characteristics due to its high concentration of heavy metals and low levels of calcium; this combination generally inhibits plant growth relative to other soil conditions.

ULTRAMAFIC Soil type dominated by minerals, such as serpentine, with high levels of heavy metals and low levels of calcium.

UNDERSTORY The lower layer of a vegetation type, usually referring to plants growing underneath a canopy of trees or shrubs.

VEGETATION All of the plant species in a region (the flora) and the manner in which those species are arranged in time and space (both vertical and horizontal). "Vegetation" is often used synonymously with "plant community."

VEGETATION TYPE A particular kind of vegetation, often formally recognized by classification systems. Coast redwood forest is a vegetation type.

WOODLAND Vegetation dominated by widely spaced trees that combine to cover greater than 5% to 10% but less than 30% of the landscape. Vegetation with less cover is savanna; vegetation with greater cover is forest.

XERIC Refers to sites with low available moisture, often used interchangeably with "dry."

References

Alexander, E. B., R. G. Coleman, T. Keeler-Wolf, and S. Harrison. 2007. Serpentine geoecology of western North America: Geol-

ogy, soils, and vegetation. Oxford University Press, New York, New York.
Allen-Diaz, B., R. Standiford, and R. D. Jackson. 2007. Oak woodlands and forests. Pages 313–338 in M. G. Barbour, T. Keeler-Wolf, and A. A. Schoenherr, editors. Terrestrial Vegetation of California. University of California Press, Berkeley, Los Angeles, London.
Axelrod, D. 1990. Outline history of California vegetation. Pages 139–193 in M. Barbour and J. Major, editors. Terrestrial Vegetation of California. California Native Plant Society, Sacramento, California.
Barbour, M., S. Lydon, M. Borchert, M. Popper, V. Whitworth, and J. Evarts. 2001. Coast redwood: A natural and cultural history. Cachuma Press, Los Olivos, California.
Barbour, M. G., B. Pavlik, F. Drysdale, and S. Lindstrom. 1993. California's changing landscapes: Diversity and conservation of California vegetation. California Native Plant Society, Sacramento, California.
Barbour, M. G., N. H. Berg, T. G. F. Kittel, and M. E. Kunz. 1991. Snowpack and the distribution of a major vegetation ecotone in the Sierra-Nevada of California. Journal of Biogeography 18:141–149.
Barbour, M. G., T. Keeler-Wolf, and A. A. Schoenherr. 2007. Terrestrial vegetation of California. Third edition. University of California, Berkeley, Los Angeles, London.
Bartolome, J. W., W. J. Barry, T. Griggs, and P. Hopkinson. 2007. Valley grassland. Pages 367–393 in M. G. Barbour, T. Keeler-Wolf, and A. A. Schoenherr, editors. Terrestrial Vegetation of California. University of California Press, Berkeley, Los Angeles, London.
Breckle, J. W. 2002. Walter's vegetation of the Earth. Nordic Journal of Botany 22, 6:712.
Brooks, M. L., and R. A. Minnich. 2006. Southeastern deserts bioregion. Pages 391–414 in N. G. Sugihara, J. W. Van Wagtendonk, K. E. Shaffer, J. A. Fites-Kaufman, and A. E. Thode, editors. Fire in California's Ecosystems. University of California Press, Berkeley, Los Angeles, London.
Dawson, T. E. 1998. Fog in the California redwood forest: Ecosystem inputs and use by plants. Oecologia 117:476–485.
Elmendorf, S. C., and S. P. Harrison. 2009. Temporal variability and nestedness in California grassland species composition. Ecology 90:1492–1497.
Fites-Kaufman, J. A., P. Rundel, N. L. Stephenson, and D. A. Weixelman. 2007. Montane and subalpine vegetation of the Sierra Nevada and Cascade Ranges. Pages 456–501 in M. G. Barbour, T. Keeler-Wolf, and A. A. Schoenherr, editors. Terrestrial Vegetation of California. University of California Press, Berkeley, Los Angeles, London.
Franklin, S., D. Faber-Langendoen, M. D. Jennings, T. Keeler-Wolf, O. L. Loucks, R. K. Peet, and A. McKerrow. 2012. Building the United States national vegetation classification. Annali di Botanica 2:1–9.
Griffin, J. R. 1990. Oak woodland. Pages 383–415 in M. Barbour and J. Major, editors. Terrestrial Vegetation of California. California Native Plant Society, Sacramento, California.
Jennings, M. D., D. Faber-Langendoen, O. L. Loucks, R. K. Peet, and D. Roberts. 2009. Standards for associations and alliances of the U.S. national vegetation classification. Ecological Monographs 79:173–199.
Keeler-Wolf, T. 2007. Mojave desert scrub vegetation. Pages 609–656 in M. G. Barbour, T. Keeler-Wolf, and A. A. Schoenherr, editors. Terrestrial Vegetation of California. University of California Press, Berkeley, Los Angeles, London.
Keeley, J., and F. W. Davis. 2007. Chapparal. Pages 339–366 in M. G. Barbour, T. Keeler-Wolf, and A. A. Schoenherr, editors. Terrestrial Vegetation of California. University of California Press, Berkeley, Los Angeles, London.
Köppen, W. 1936. Das geographische System der Klimate. Pages 1–44 in W. Köppen and R. Geiger, editors. Handbuch der Klimatologie. Gebrüder Borntraeger, Berlin.
Kruckeberg, A. R. 1984. California serpentines: Flora, vegetation, geology, soils, and management problems. University of California Publications in Botany, Berkeley, California.
Küchler, A. W. 1990. The map of the natural vegetation of California. Pages 909–938 in M. Barbour and J. Major, editors. Terrestrial Vegetation of California. California Native Plant Society, Sacramento, California.
Lorimer, C. G., D. J. Porter, M. A. Madej, J. D. Stuart, S. D. Veirs Jr., S. P. Norman, K. L. O'Hara, and W. J. Libby. 2009. Presettlement and modern disturbance regimes in coast redwood forests: Implications for the conservation of old-growth stands. Forest Ecology and Management 258:1038–1054.
Major, J. 1990. California climate in relation to vegetation. Pages 11–74 in M. Barbour and J. Major, editors. Terrestrial Vegetation of California. California Native Plant Society, Sacramento, California.
Major, J., and A. H. Taylor. 1990. Alpine. Pages 601–675 in M. Barbour and J. Major, editors. Terrestrial Vegetation of California. California Native Plant Society, Sacramento, California.
Minnich, R. A. 2007. Climate, paleoclimate, and paleovegetation. Pages 43–70 in M. G. Barbour, T. Keeler-Wolf, and A. A. Schoenherr, editors. Terrestrial Vegetation of California. University of California Press, Berkely, Los Angeles, London.
Parker, A. J. 1994. Latitudinal gradients of coniferous tree species, vegetation, and climate in the sierran-cascade axis of northern California. Vegetatio 115:145–155.
Peet, R. K., and D. W. Roberts. 2012. Classification of natural and semi-natural vegetation. Pages 28–70 in J. Franklin and E. van der Maarel, editors. Vegetation Ecology. Oxford University Press, New York, New York.
Peterson, D. H. 1998. Climate, limiting factors, and environmental change in high-altitude forests of western North America. Pages 191–208 in Beniston, M., and J. Innes, editors. The Impacts of Climate Variability on Forests. Springer, Berlin, Heidelberg, Germany.
Potter, D. A. 1998. Forested communities of the upper montane in the central and southern Sierra Nevada. Gen. Tech. Rep. PSW-GTR-169. USDA Forest Service, Pacific Southwest Forest and Range Experiment Station, Albany, California.
Rundel, P. 2007. Sage scrub. Pages 208–228 in M. G. Barbour, T. Keeler-Wolf, and A. A. Schoenherr, editors. Terrestrial Vegetation of California. University of California Press, Berkeley, Los Angeles, London.
Rundel, P., D. J. Parsons, and D. T. Gordon. 1990. Montane and subalpine vegetation of the Sierra Nevada and Cascade Ranges. Pages 559–599 in M. Barbour and J. Major, editors. Terrestrial Vegetation of California. California Native Plant Society, Sacramento, California.
Sawyer, J. O. 2007. Forests of northwestern California. Pages 253–295 in M. G. Barbour, T. Keeler-Wolf, and A. A. Schoenherr, editors. Terrestrial Vegetation of California. University of California Press, Berkeley, Los Angeles, London.
Sawyer, J. O., and T. Keeler-Wolf. 2007. Alpine vegetation. Pages 539–573 in M. G. Barbour, T. Keeler-Wolf, and A. A. Schoenherr, editors. Terrestrial Vegetation of California. University of California Press, Berkeley, Los Angeles, London.
Sawyer, J. O., T. Keeler-Wolf, and J. Evens. 2009. A manual of California vegetation. Second edition. California Native Plant Society, Sacramento, California.
Schoenherr, A. A., and J. H. Burk. 2007. Colorado desert vegetation. Pages 657–682 in M. G. Barbour, T. Keeler-Wolf, and A. A. Schoenherr, editors. Terrestrial Vegetation of California. University of California Press, Berkeley, Los Angeles, London.
Scholl, A. E., and A. H. Taylor. 2006. Regeneration patterns in old-growth red fir-western white pine forests in the northern Sierra Nevada, Lake Tahoe, USA. Forest Ecology and Management 235:143–154.
Stephenson, N. L. 1998. Actual evapotranspiration and deficit: Biologically meaningful correlates of vegetation distribution across spatial scales. Journal of Biogeography 25:855–870.
Stone, E. C., and R. B. Vasey. 1968. Preservation of coast redwood on alluvial flats—because man has altered environment active management is now required. Science 159:157–161.
Stromberg, M. R., J. D. Corbin, and C. M. D'Antonio. 2007. California grasslands ecology and management. University of California Press, Berkeley, California.
Stuart, J. D., and S. L. Stephens. 2006. North coast bioregion. Pages 147–169 in N. G. Sugihara, J. W. Van Wagtendonk, K. E. Shaffer, J. A. Fites-Kaufman, and A. E. Thode, editors. Fire in California's Ecosystems. University of California Press, Berkeley, Los Angeles, London.
Thorne, R. F., A. A. Schoenherr, C. D. Clements, and J. A. Young. 2007. Transmontane coniferous vegetation. Pages 574–586 in

M. G. Barbour, T. Keeler-Wolf, and A. A. Schoenherr, editors. Terrestrial Vegetation of California. University of California Press, Berkeley, Los Angeles, London.
van Wagtendonk, J. W., and J. A. Fites-Kaufman. 2006. Sierra Nevada bioregion. Pages 264–294 in N. G. Sugihara, J. W. Van Wagtendonk, K. E. Shaffer, J. A. Fites-Kaufman, and A. E. Thode, editors. Fire in California's Ecosystems. University of California Press, Berkeley, Los Angeles, London.
Vasek, F. C., and M. Barbour. 1990. Mojave Desert scrub vegetation. Pages 835–867 in M. Barbour and J. Major, editors. Terrestrial Vegetation of California. California Native Plant Society, Sacramento, California.
Vasek, F. C., and R. F. Thorne. 1990. Transmontane coniferous vegetation. Pages 797–832 in M. Barbour and J. Major, editors. Terrestrial Vegetation of California. California Native Plant Society, Sacramento, California.
Wills, R. 2006. Central Valley bioregion. Pages 295–320 in N. G. Sugihara, J. W. Van Wagtendonk, K. E. Shaffer, J. A. Fites-Kaufman, and A. E. Thode, editors. Fire in California's Ecosystems. University of California Press, Berkeley, Los Angeles, London.
Young, J. A., C. D. Clements, and H. C. Jansen. 2007. Sagebrush steppe. Pages 587–608 in M. G. Barbour, T. Keeler-Wolf, and A. A. Schoenherr, editors. Terrestrial Vegetation of California. University of California Press, Berkeley, Los Angeles, London.

THIRTEEN

Biological Invasions

ERIKA ZAVALETA, ELISSA M. OLIMPI, AMELIA A. WOLF, BRONWEN STANFORD, JAE R. PASARI, SARAH A. SKIKNE, PAULO QUADRI BARBA, KATHERINE K. ENNIS, and FLAVIA C. DE OLIVEIRA

Introduction

Human-caused biological invasions—the spread of species introduced into regions or continents outside of their natural distributions—are as old as human travel (Elton 1958, Davis 2009). When early Polynesians moved east across Oceania, species such as the Polynesian rat (*Rattus exulans*) and pigs (*Sus scrofa*) spread with them. Over the past five hundred years, ever-increasing transport, trade, travel, and tourism across ecological boundaries have increased the pace, reach, and impacts of invasive species (Mack et al. 2000, Davis 2009, Standards and Trade Development Facility 2013). INVASIVE species are the most common contributor to past human-caused species extinctions worldwide, and are now possibly second only to land use and cover change in their negative effects on species designated endangered and critically endangered by the International Union for the Conservation of Nature (Tershy et al. 2015, Dirzo and Raven 2003). Harmful invasive species cause billions of dollars of damage annually, ranging from crop losses to fouling of ships (Pimentel et al. 2005). Although many NON-NATIVE (also *exotic* or *alien*) species are not invasive and enhance human well-being, and although gradual species range shifts and occasional cross-continent and transoceanic natural colonizations have always occurred, anthropogenic biological invasions have become a significant global source of environmental change and degradation.

In California both the diversity of invasive species (Table 13.1), mirroring patterns of native diversity, and their ecological and societal impacts are unusually high. This reflects several features of California:

1. It is coastal, densely populated, and economically active, with high climatic, soil, and topographic diversity, so there are many INTRODUCTIONS and a huge range of potential habitats.
2. Like islands, which are especially susceptible to invaders, California is isolated from other terrestrial areas by ocean, mountains, and desert (Dowell and Gill 1989, Bakker and Slack 1971).
3. California's climate might facilitate, at least in southern coastal California, the establishment and spread of species imported from the world's other Mediterra-

nean climate regions, especially from Europe, whose flora and fauna have had much longer periods of time to adapt to agriculture and other human land uses (Figure 13.1).

4. Finally, California has the highest vascular plant, mammal, and insect diversity and the highest number of ENDEMIC vascular plant species in the U.S. (Stein 2002, Ballmer 1995, Baldwin et al. 2012, Rejmánek et al. 1991; see Chapter 11, "Biodiversity"), so it has a lot to lose.

This chapter describes the history of biological invasions in California and explores factors that contribute to the unusual diversity, extent, and impacts of invasive species across all taxonomic groups in the state. It goes on to describe past successes and potential options for managing harmful invasive species in California as well as future scenarios for invasions in the state. Throughout, it highlights examples from across California's diversity of ecosystems and details representative cases of ongoing invasions by species from a range of taxa and geographic regions with varying histories.

Invasion Ecology

Invasive species are those that spread outside of their native range; some restrict this term to invaders that negatively impact native species, economic activity, human health, or other ecological or social values (U.S. Fish and Wildlife Service 2013), but we distinguish these as *harmful* invasive species. The terminology used to describe non-native species, whether invasive or not, varies widely in the literature (Richardson et al. 2000, Lockwood et al. 2013, Davis 2009, U.S. Fish and Wildlife Service 2013). Terms including (but not limited to) ALIEN, NONINDIGENOUS, and EXOTIC are used to refer to species that are not native to a given location (Lockwood et al. 2013, U.S. Fish and Wildlife Service 2013, Richardson et al. 2011). Although the term NATURALIZED is sometimes used in the same way, it properly refers to those exotic species that have reached unmanaged habitats and/or established self-sustaining populations. Most non-native species do not become invasive because they are unable to establish and spread beyond their initial points of introduction. Richardson et al. (2011) provide a useful, integrative summary of current terminology in the field of invasion ecology.

The invasion process can be divided into three main stages—introduction, establishment, and spread (Lockwood et al. 2013, Davis 2009). Following transport from its native range, a species or taxon is introduced when it is released, either accidentally or intentionally, into a new area. Establishment occurs when a species creates a self-sustaining population through successful reproduction. Spread occurs if an established species expands its range in its new environment (Lockwood et al. 2013, Davis 2009). When introduced to a new environment, non-native species often escape constraining ecological forces such as predators, pathogens, or competitors that were present in their native range (Davis 2009, Mack et al. 2000). This "release" from previous constraints can allow INTRODUCED SPECIES to become invasive

Photo on previous page: Jubata grass (*Cortaderia jubata*), native to South America, invading coastal scrub in Santa Cruz County, California. Photo: Ed Dickie (eddickie.com).

TABLE 13.1

Total numbers of California species, naturalized species, and their proportion by taxonomic group

Taxonomic group	Number of species	Number of naturalized species	Percentage of naturalized species
Vascular plants[A]	5,967	991	16.6
Invertebrates[B]	27,000[E]	1,288	4.8
Mammals[C]	227	26	11.5
Birds[C]	654	27	4.1
Reptiles[C]	94	6	6.4
Amphibians[C]	70	5	7.1
Fish[D]	97	45	46.4

A. From Rejmánek 2012.
B. From Dowell 2002.
C. From California Department of Fish and Game 2008.
D. From Moyle 2002 and Marchetti et al. 2004.
E. Estimate taken from Ballmer 1995.

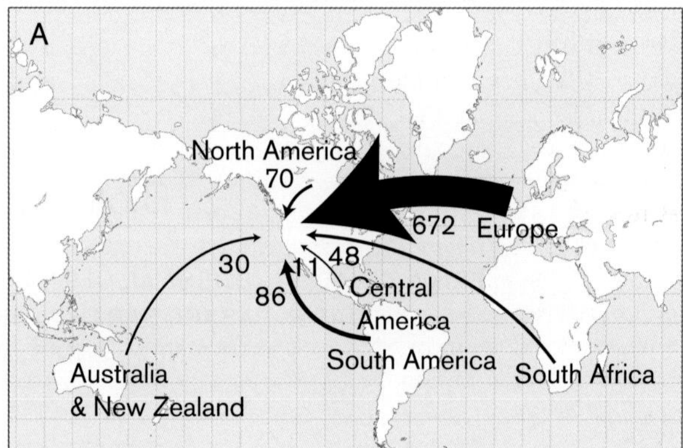

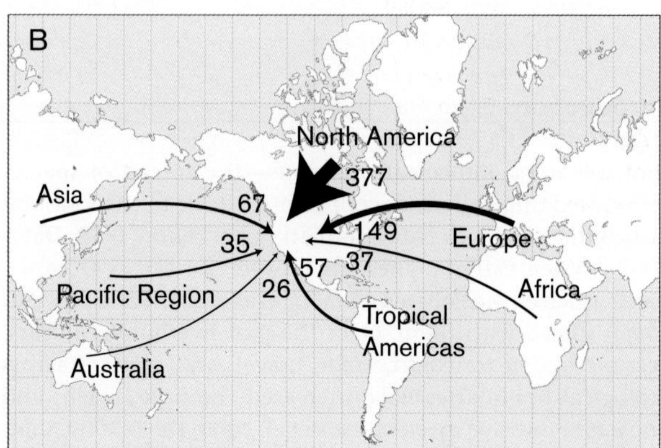

FIGURE 13.1 Origins of introduced (A) vascular plant and (B) invertebrate species (from 1955 to 1980) to California by proportion. Source: Rejmánek et al. 1991 and Dowell 2002.

as they outcompete, prey on, or parasitize native species that are disadvantaged because they have not been released from local pathogens and predators and/or lack coevolved defenses against the invader (but see Chun et al. 2010). Resource availability and fluctuations are also an important factor regulating biological invasions, particularly in plants (Vitousek and Walker 1987; Davis et al. 2000). Establishment of successful invading populations is facilitated by increases in resource availability, which can happen because of either an atypical influx of resources in a given area or reduced use of resources by the resident biotic community. For instance, unusually rainy winters, fires, and reduction of resource uptake due to disease or herbivory can all facilitate biological invasions (Lockwood et al. 2013). Human activity often increases these fluctuations through activities like timber harvest, fertilizer use, and road building.

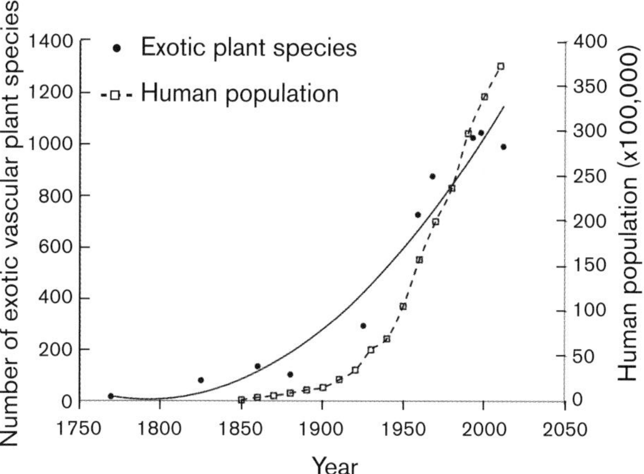

FIGURE 13.2 Number of exotic vascular plants recorded in California since the arrival of the first Spanish mission in 1769 (solid circles, smooth line; Randall et al. 1998 and Rejmánek 2012) and California's human population from 1850 through 2010 (open squares, dashed lines; Forstall 1996, U.S. Census Bureau 2010).

California's Invasion History

California's history with biological invasions is long and varied. Because the vast majority of exotic species were introduced after the first European settlements in the 1700s (Randall et al. 1998, Connor et al. 2002) (Figure 13.2), species introductions prior to European settlement are often overlooked but might have been significant. Indigenous peoples of northern California created trading networks with Spanish settlements in Mexico (Stott et al. 1998, Randall et al. 1998), suggesting that species introductions to California from both Europe and Central America may have preceded European settlement. Moreover, although Europeans did not settle in California until the mid-eighteenth century, European explorers first arrived on the coasts of California in 1579 (Bicknell and Mackey 1998, Connor et al. 2002). Human diseases introduced to North America by early European explorers also most likely reached California ahead of European settlers (Preston 1996; see Chapter 10, "Indigenous Californians").

Terrestrial introductions to California after European settlement are often divided into four relatively distinct periods defined by shifts in land use and accompanying introductions of non-native plants. The first Spanish missionaries who landed near San Diego in 1769 expanded five hundred miles north to Sonoma by 1823 and helped to establish at least sixteen non-native plant species (Hendry 1931, Frenkel 1970, Raven 1988). After the Spanish colonial period, Mexican explorers settled in California from 1825 through 1848 and added sixty-three new, non-native plant species. This was followed by the Gold Rush period from 1849 through 1860, when U.S. pioneers started settlements in California and introduced another fifty-five new, non-native plant species. This period also saw an influx of secondary plant introductions of Mediterranean European origin from Chile. These exotics, including yellow starthistle (Box 13.1), had become established in Chile at least a century earlier and were exported to California with cattle feed such as alfalfa during the Gold Rush. In a period lasting through 1880, the U.S. pioneers who settled in California for gold began shifting away from gold exploration towards agricultural development. This agricultural expansion greatly altered the landscape and the total extent of land occupied by humans. Jepson (1925) reported at least 292 non-native, NATURALIZED SPECIES found in California in 1925, following extensive road and railway infrastructure development that facilitated the movement of exotic species around the country.

The history of vascular plant arrivals illustrates the impact of European settlement on biological invasions into California. More than 69% of all naturalized, non-native plant species in California can be traced to Europe (Mack et al. 2000) (see Figure 13.1a). Many of these were brought and introduced intentionally. However, given the total number of naturalized, non-native species in California, it is likely that many more plant introductions were accidental.

The data for invertebrate introductions to California are far less complete for early settlement periods. While many recent (1955–1980) invertebrate introductions arrived to California from within North America (see Figure 13.1b) (Dowell and Gill 1989), the majority of established, non-native invertebrates prior to 1950 also arrived from Europe. Most established, non-native mammals and fishes now in California were introduced intentionally for food, transportation, or sport (Lidicker 1991, Moyle and Marchetti 2006). Half of California's established, non-native mammals are domesticated species that later established FERAL populations. Likewise, more than 68% of exotic, established inland fish species are thought to originate from INTENTIONAL INTRODUCTIONS as a result of fishery or forage stocking, water transfers, biocontrol release, shipment transport, or aquarium release (Moyle 2002, Marchetti et al. 2004). While some of these species came from Europe, such as feral pigs and fallow deer (*Dama dama*), many of the state's established, non-native mammals, such as the Virginia opossum (*Didelphis virginiana*) and the eastern gray squirrel (*Sciurus carolinensis*), are from other regions of the U.S.

While species introductions have been occurring for centuries, California's rates of introductions are still increasing and in some cases may be accelerating (see Figure 13.2). These increasing rates appear correlated with growing human populations, but precisely how human populations affect introduction (and establishment and spread) rates remains unclear. Increasingly modified landscapes for agriculture and urban uses contribute to increased rates of exotic species introduc-

BOX 13.1 YELLOW STARTHISTLE

Invasive yellow starthistle (*Centaurea solstitialis*) (Box 13.1 Figure 1) is considered the most common weed (Parkinson 2011) and one of the most economically and ecologically damaging plants in California (CDFA 2013d). It also occurs in forty-one of fifty U.S. states and four Canadian provinces (Zouhar 2002). The plant has spread throughout an estimated 5.7 million hectares of California. It is most widespread in the northern portion of state (Pitcairn et al. 2006) and widely distributed in the Central Valley and adjacent foothills (Zouhar 2002). A detailed assessment of the spread and occurrence of yellow starthistle statewide through 2002 showed that it occurs in 3,010 of the 6,389 California townships and in all its counties, with the exception of Orange and Imperial Counties (Box 13.1 Figure 2) (Pitcairn et al. 2006). Currently, its range is expanding into mountainous regions of the state (below 2,200 meters), including the Coast Ranges (DiTomaso et al. 2006). In California, yellow starthistle can grow either as a winter annual or, more rarely, as a short-lived perennial. It is usually found in full sunlight and in disturbed areas (e.g., pastures, along roadsides and walking trails) in grassland and woodland ecosystems, whereas it is not as common in desert, high mountain, and moist coastal sites (DiTomaso et al. 2006; Parkinson and Mangold 2011; California Invasive Plant Council 2013b; Zouhar 2002). Once established, yellow starthistle populations can spread and displace native plant and animal species (Parkinson and Mangold 2011).

Yellow starthistle was first documented in California in 1851, and its introduction is believed to have occurred through shipments of contaminated alfafa coming from South America and Asia as well as directly from Europe, where the plant is native (Pitcairn et al. 2006; CDFA 2013d). The spread of yellow starthistle's populations throughtout the state was facilitated by human activities such as road construction, suburban development, and ranching expansion. Seeds with stiff bristles can attach to the undercarriage of cars, allowing long-distance dispersal and establishment of satellite populations (CDFA 2013d). Starthistle's rate of spread in California rapidly increased after 1960 following a long period of slow increase in abundance, a phenomenon that has been attributed to the species having overcome an initial stage of genetic adaptation and to the successful establishment of multiple popu-

BOX 13.1 FIGURE 1 The flower of a yellow starthistle (*Centaurea solstitialis*) with its sharp spines extending from the flower head base. Photo: Joseph M. DiTomaso.

tion and establishment, as do increased interstate and international travel and trade.

Ecological and Anthropogenic Drivers of Invasions in California

The prevalence of biological invaders in California compared to other states and regions is driven by a mix of ecological and societal dynamics. California's ecology is in some ways conducive to non-native species establishment and spread. Human influence is also a key part of the story, and patterns of invasion in California have generally followed patterns of human trade and settlement. In this section we explore physical, biotic, and social dynamics that contribute to high rates of invasion in California.

In the biophysical realm, both abiotic and biotic factors govern many of California's invasion dynamics (Table 13.2) (Rejmánek et al. 1991). Two overarching ecological features of California enhance its INVASIBILITY and vulnerability to invader impacts relative to most other parts of North America. First, the same ecological diversity, both within and across ecosystem types, that fosters high native biodiversity also offers an array of potential invasion niches for introduced species (Hastings et al. 2005). Second, California's high rates of endemism statewide at very fine scales mean that it has many restricted species vulnerable to human impacts in general, including those of invasions. For example, invasive barred tiger salamanders (*Ambystoma mavortium*) threaten the endemic California tiger salamander (*A. californiense*) with extinction, in part, because of the limited distribution of the latter species and the ability of the two species to hybridize (Fitzpatrick et al. 2010) (see Chapter 11, "Biodiversity"). Ecosystem invasibility can also be affected by biotic interactions through competition from the resident community; in this sense, California's dominance by invaders may beget more invasions. For example, when the native tarweed (*Hemizonia congesta*) is present in California grasslands, the invasive yellow starthistle (*Centaurea solstitialis*) is effectively suppressed due to competition for water with the tarweed (see Box 13.1; Dukes 2002, Hulvey and Zavaleta 2012). However, widespread dominance by invasive alien annual plants in California's grasslands has likely reduced abundances of native tarweeds. Invasive plants species also can increase nitrogen fixation rates, produce litter that undergoes higher decomposition rates, or increase biomass production (Ehrenfeld 2003) and

lations that could further spread. It has also been suggested that starthistle's invasion occurred as a multistage process involving several separate introductions and subsequent spreading events, with the latter relying on both new founder populations and expansion of small, existing populations (Pitcairn et al. 2006).

Ecological and economic impacts in California associated with the invasion of yellow starthistle range from habitat fragmentation to contamination of agricultural fields and depletion of groundwater reserves to livestock deaths and disrupted military training (DiTomaso et al. 2006). Its overall economic impacts include the cost of statewide management of the plant, reduced access to recreational areas, reduced yield and quality of pastures and consequent impacts on livestock production, reduced land value, and water loss resulting from the plant's consumption of groundwater (DiTomaso et al. 2003, DiTomaso et al. 2006, Zouhar 2002). Horses poisoned by yellow starthistle are affected by a neurological disorder called chewing disease (named for symptomatic involuntary chewing), which causes severe brain damage and can cause death (DiTomaso et al. 2006; Parkinson 2011). Interestingly, the plant is also associated with substantial economic benefits to the California bee industry, as it is an important late-season source of pollen and nectar for bees (DiTomaso et al. 2006).

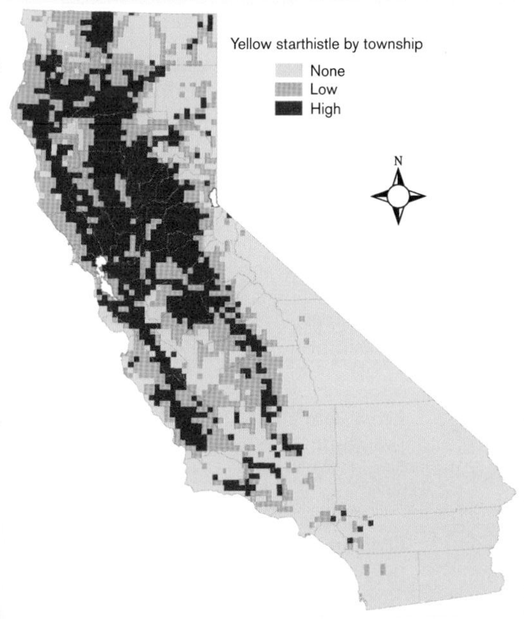

BOX 13.1 FIGURE 2 Distribution of yellow starthistle in California. Image: Pitcairn et al. 2006, copyright Regents of the University of California.

Current management strategies for yellow starthistle include a range of chemical, biological, and cultural practices to control current populations, prevent the establishment and spread of new popualtions, and actively restore control areas with desirable vegetation. Biocontrols including two weevil species, two fly species, and a rust disease potentially all help to control populations but have not been overwhelmingly successful. The weevils (*Bangasternus orientalis, Eustenopus villosus*) and flies (*Urophora sirunaseva* and *Chaetorellia succinea*) attack flower heads and can reduce seed set by 50%. Use of the rust (*Puccinea jaceae* var. *solstitialis*) has been approved for testing. Mowing, grazing, burning, hand-pulling, and timed cultivation also contribute to yellow starthistle control, but complete control has not been achieved (DiTomaso et al. 2007). Yellow starthistle has served as a model species for several studies of invasion dynamics in California (e.g., Dukes 2002, Zavaleta and Hulvey 2004, Gelbard and Harrison 2005).

the abundance of soil biota (Reinhart and Callaway 2006). These effects can make new resources available, promoting further invasion.

Introduced species must be able to exploit unused abiotic resources in their new environments to establish and spread. Often, introduced species succeed because they are better adapted than native species to exploit resources released by disturbance. For example, *Bromus tectorum*, an invasive grass in California's high-elevation deserts, benefits from increased nutrient, light, and water resources left after fires, to which native species are poorly adapted. Once established, *B. tectorum* can abruptly change the fire regime, creating ecological feedbacks that accelerate its spread (Brooks et al. 2004). Species traits conducive to rapid exploitation of pulsed or episodic resource availability are thus sometimes correlated with species invasiveness (the ability to invade) (Van Kleunen et al. 2010). For example, successful invasive pines have a short juvenile period and short intervals between large seed crops, produce a large number of small seeds with high germination rates, and have high relative growth rates as seedlings (Rejmánek and Richardson 1996, Burns and Sauer 1992).

High interannual climate variability (see Chapter 2, "Climate") and a diversity of disturbance agents prominent in California, ranging from fire to soil turnover by burrowing mammals, accentuate variation in resource availability that can facilitate the establishment and spread of introduced species. Fire, for example, is a widespread natural disturbance across California that has shaped many of its ecosystems (Keeley and Fotheringham 2003). The typical long, hot summers of the central and southern portions of the state can cause extended fire seasons, especially during low rainfall years. Likewise, less frequent but intense and destructive flooding episodes can occur during winter. Both fires and floods can increase resources available to potential invaders. For example, the invasion of the pathogen that causes sudden oak death (*Phytopthora ramorum*) benefited from a series of extended rainy seasons that boosted the sporulation process needed for successful reproduction (Rizzo and Garbelotto 2003; Box 13.2).

Key Anthropogenic Drivers and Pathways

In the century and a half since European settlers arrived in California, human transformation of the landscape has encouraged the establishment of introduced species. When

TABLE 13.2
Major hypothesized mechanisms governing species invasiveness and ecosystem invasibility

Hypothesis name	Definition	Effects mediated through	References
Natural enemies	Exotics are released from natural enemies that control their population growth.	Ecosystem invasibility	Darwin 1859, Williams 1954, Elton 1958
Evolution of invasiveness, of increased competitive ability	Exotics experience rapid genetic changes linked to new selection pressures in the novel environment.	Species invasiveness	Blossey and Nötzold 1995, Lee 2002, Stockwell et al. 2003
Empty niche	Exotics utilize resources unused by natives.	Ecosystem invasibility	Elton 1958, MacArthur 1970
Novel weapons	Exotics bring novel ways of biochemical interaction to recipient communities.	Species invasiveness	Callaway and Aschehoug 2000, Bais et al. 2003
Disturbance	Exotics are adapted to disturbance type and intensity that are novel to natives.	Species invasiveness	Gray 1879, Baker 1974
Species richness	Species-rich communities are more resistant to invasion than species-poor communities.	Ecosystem invasibility	Elton 1958, MacArthur 1970
Propagule pressure	Variations in levels of invasion among recipient communities are due to differences in the number of exotics arriving in the community.	Ecosystem invasibility	di Castri 1989, Williamson and Fitter 1996, Lonsdale 1999
Highly evolved competition	Habitats in which competition has been intense over evolutionary time may have low invasibility because natives have been selected for high competitive ability and are likely to outcompete potential invasives.	Ecosystem invasibility	Blossey and Nötzold 1995, Callaway et al. 2004

SOURCE: Adapted from Hierro et al. 2005.

Euro-American settlers arrived in the late 1700s and 1800s, they quickly began to transform the landscape through intensive grazing and conversion of grasslands and oak savannas to agriculture (Minnich 2008). Old-world species that had evolved mechanisms to cope with tilling and grazing pressure over millennia of intensive human occupation may have gained a competitive advantage over native Californian species in these rapidly changing conditions. Since settlement, human land use has progressively altered DISTURBANCE REGIMES (e.g., flooding, fires), patterns of connectivity (e.g., fragmentation, canals), and abiotic conditions (e.g., nitrogen deposition, temperature, increased freshwater inputs) throughout California and worldwide (Vitousek 1994, Mack et al. 2000, Marchetti and Moyle 2001, Bunn and Arthington 2002). High-density human presence has altered fire regimes, increasing fire frequency in some places through accidental ignitions and decreasing it in others through fire suppression (Syphard et al. 2007).

Human regulation of rivers and streams through dams, diversions, and channelization has altered flooding patterns, channel form, connectivity between aquatic and RIPARIAN habitats, and water temperatures (Kondolf 1997, Poff et al. 2007). Agriculture has replaced many native habitats, increased fragmentation of the landscape, and increased nutrients in waterways through fertilizer inputs (Mack et al. 2000). Industrial and vehicular emissions result in increased levels of nitrogen deposition, which can encourage the establishment of introduced species in low-nutrient soils (Vitousek et al. 1997). For example, California's serpentine soils host a diverse native and endemic flora that have adapted to tolerate low nutrient levels (Kruckeberg 1986, Huenneke et al. 1990). Serpentine soils also provide a refuge to native flora and fauna from exotic species (particularly European grasses) that have invaded most of California's more nutrient-rich grasslands. Human-caused nitrogen deposition has fertilized these low-nutrient soils and facilitated exotic grass invasions, leading to a decline in the abundances of native plants and of the highly endemic bay checkerspot butterfly (*Euphydryas editha bayensis*) that depends on its now serpentine-restricted native host plant (Weiss 2001, Fenn et al. 2010, Vallano et al. 2012).

Large-scale patterns of human settlement in California have shaped large-scale patterns of invasion (Mooney et al. 1984). As the most populous state in the U.S., California ranks eleventh in overall population density, with an average of ninety-three inhabitants km^{-2} (U.S. Census Bureau 2010). However, this masks a much higher density in coastal California and particularly in the two metropolitan regions extending from San Francisco Bay and Los Angeles–San Diego, where population densities range from 770 to 6,500 people km^{-2} (U.S. Census Bureau 2010). High-density coastal populations contribute to invasion both by increasing travel and traffic (affecting the number of introductions) and increasing disturbance (affecting invader establishment and spread). In addition, the human population concentration along the coastlines has created a highly connected coastal corridor for invasive species.

People have intentionally introduced exotic species for a variety of purposes. Many plants have been introduced as forage for domestic animals, and both invasive plants and animals have been introduced for human consumption. Medicinal plants, game species, and fishes for food and bait have been introduced to California waters from the eastern U.S. and around the world (Fuller 2003). Intentional species introductions also occur for environmental enhancement (such as soil or marsh stabilization, horticulture, and pets) and for biocontrol of pests (Mack 2003, Lockwood et al. 2013). For example, cape ivy (*Delairea odorata*), iceplants (e.g., *Carpobrotus edulis, Mesembryanthemum crystallinum*), and eucalyptus species (e.g., Tasmanian blue gum, *Eucalyptus globulus*) were all intentionally introduced to stabilize or beautify aspects of California's environment.

Introductions also usually accompany the movement of some desired good. These include exotic species that are carried between ports on ship hulls, in ballast, and in shipping containers (Figure 13.3); contaminants within commercial products such as straw, wood, seeds, or shellfish; transport on vehicle tires along freeways; and transport along with water through canals (Lockwood et al. 2013). The high volume of traffic through California's two major ports (San Francisco Bay and Los Angeles), as well as the state's well-developed network of highways, railroads, and airports, results in many opportunities for such introductions. Although these introductions are not intentional in the sense of having been selected and imported for a particular purpose, they are now both expected and preventable.

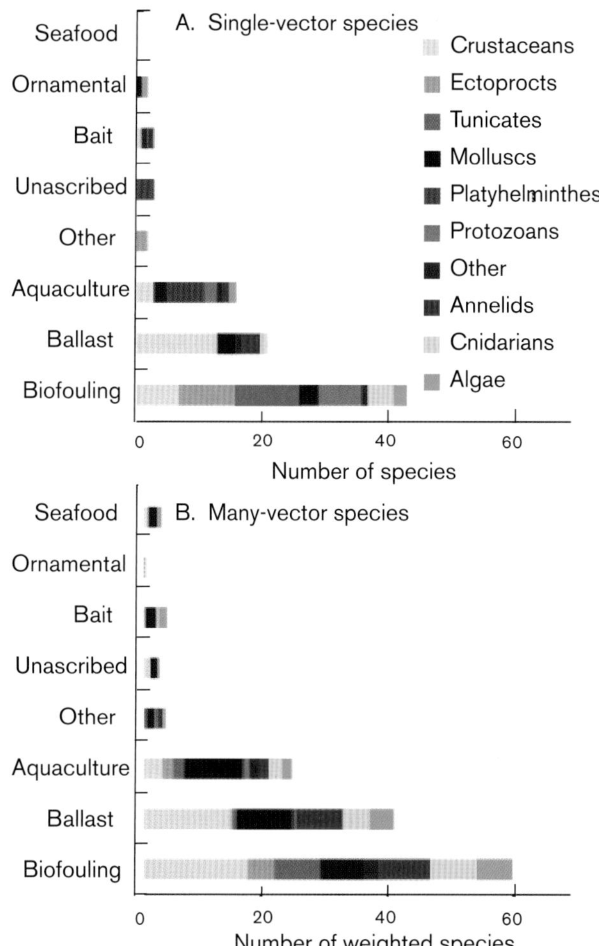

FIGURE 13.3 Vectors for introduction of invasive species (A and B) into California. Ship ballast was originally rubble, gravel, and soil, which was emptied onto shores (Mack 2003), carrying with it a potentially diverse array of species. Today, ballast consists of water but can still carry a range of exotic species from port to port. In B, species associated with >1 vector were apportioned among categories based on relative contributions of each vector to introductions.

Degree of Invasion in California's Ecosystems

As a result of differences in the numbers of introductions and the characteristics of receiving environments, some ecosystems and regions in California have many invasive species while others have relatively few. In California, marine, alpine, and forest ecosystems tend to have fewer exotic alien species, while freshwater and grassland ecosystems are frequently highly invaded (Mooney et al. 1984). These differences likely reflect a combination of ecosystem characteristics, human land use intensity and history, and patterns of introductions. In particular, the number of introductions (or PROPAGULE pressure), and especially the number of intentional introductions, is increasingly identified as an important predictor of the number of established invaders (Leprieur et al. 2008, Keller et al. 2011, Kempel et al. 2013).

Marine ecosystems generally have fewer invasive species than many other ecosystems in California, a pattern that is true for marine systems worldwide (Lockwood et al. 2013). This may be due to a relative lack of introductions or limited human ability to alter natural conditions. Early detection of an invasion of the Mediterranean marine weed *Caulerpa taxifolia* in nearshore southern California sea-bottom environments, most likely from improper aquarium dumping, allowed it to be successfully eradicated in 2006. Compared to other ecosystems, there also have been few intentional introductions of marine fishes (Schroeter and Moyle 2006). The unconfined nature of most marine ecosystems limits the ability of invaders or people to strongly alter conditions in marine environments to favor invasive species (Schroeter and Moyle 2006, Lockwood et al. 2013). A critical exception is San Francisco Bay—a relatively confined, estuarine system that by some measures is the most invaded ecosystem in the world (see Chapter 19, "Estuaries: Life on the Edge").

In contrast, freshwater fish communities in California are highly invaded. This is likely due to a long history of fish stocking, high volumes of traffic in systems such as the Sacramento–San Joaquin River Delta, and other sources of introductions such as release from aquaria and dispersal through canals (Fuller 2003, Leprieur et al. 2008). In addition, people have widely altered conditions in freshwater ecosystems, including temperature, water quality, and hydrologic regime. In California almost two-thirds of non-native freshwater fishes (both established and not) are from within the U.S.—either from another state or from another part of California (Fuller 2003).

Finally, California grasslands are highly invaded (Minnich

2008). Of the eleven hundred established non-native plant species in California, three hundred occur in grasslands, and their dominance is nearly complete in many areas (D'Antonio et al. 2007). Much research has attempted to establish why grasslands became so invaded so soon after European arrival in California. Likely this was due to a combination of disturbance through intensive grazing and cultivation (Stromberg and Griffin 1996, Minnich 2008), severe drought at a critical time early in the invasion process, and many intentional and unintentional introductions of exotic grasses for sheep and cattle forage (D'Antonio et al. 2007). Grassland invaders extend into oak savannas and woodlands and into the highly invaded coastal sage scrub and somewhat less invaded chaparral ecosystems at lower elevations and at the coast.

Despite marked variation in the degree of exotic species dominance and impact across California's diverse ecosystem types, no ecosystem type entirely escapes the effects of biological invasions. Every ecosystem chapter in this volume describes a broad range of introduced species, ranging from pathogens such as the fungus responsible for sudden oak death (SOD) that affects redwood forests and oaks (see Box 13.2; Chapter 25, "Oak Woodlands") to introduced trout in high alpine lakes (see Chapter 32, "Lakes") to introduced mammals offshore in the Channel Islands (see Chapter 34, "Managed Island Ecosystems") and exotic insect pests in agricultural areas (see Chapter 38, "Agriculture"). Although these introduced species vary widely in their effects and are welcomed in some human-dominated systems (Coates 2006; see Chapter 39, "Urban Ecosystems"), many exotic invaders have negative or undesirable effects on California's biological diversity and on ecosystem functions and services valued by California's human communities.

Impacts of Invasive Species in California

Impacts of invasive species on their co-occurring native species and host ecosystems are far ranging—from genetic impacts on individuals, to extinctions from a community, to altered nutrient cycles and disturbance regimes at an ecosystem scale, sometimes with direct impacts on human well-being (Perrings 2011, Schierenbeck 2011, Lockwood et

BOX 13.2 SUDDEN OAK DEATH

In the mid-1990s, forest managers and scientists across California were alerted to damaged and dying tanoaks (*Lithocarpus densiflorus*) and coast live oaks (*Quercus agrifolia*) infected by an unknown pathogen. The first cases appeared in 1994, in tanoaks in Marin and Santa Cruz Counties. Shortly thereafter, the pathogen was identified as *Phytophthora ramorum*, which had also been recently found in rhododendron (*Rhododendron* sp.) and viburnum (*Viburnum* sp.) in Western Europe (Lane et al. 2003, Rizzo et al. 2002). *P. ramorum* soon acquired widespread, epidemic proportions along a 300 kilometer strip of the central California coast (Garbelotto et al. 2001), infecting a large number of trees in redwood and oak woodland ecosystems. Because of its unexpected appearance and aggressiveness, the disease came to be known as sudden oak death (SOD).

BOX 13.2 FIGURE 1 Die-off of tanbark oak (*Lithocarpus densiflorus*) resulting from the spread of sudden oak death (SOD) syndrome through coastal California forests. Photo: U.S. Forest Service.

Phytophthora ramorum is an oomycete, which are commonly known as wet molds due to their similarity with fungi. As pathogens, oomycetes can have both ecologically and socially devastating impacts. For example, the potato blight that contributed to the mid-nineteenth-century Irish famine was caused by the aggressive oomycete *Phytophtora infestans* (Haas et al. 2011). Until very recently, details about the origins of *P. ramorum* invasion in California were mostly unknown. However, new computational and genetic techniques, with intensive efforts in spatial sampling coverage, have allowed the precise reconstruction of SOD history and pathways of invasion in California. Croucher et al. (2013) conclude that the pathogen arrived into California through infected nursery plants starting in Santa Cruz and Marin Counties, and that the epidemic in California stems from only three or four individuals that evolved from a single genotype. In addition, Croucher and his colleagues found initial evidence that some of the evolved genotypes identified in California seem better adapted to forest environments than others. Further research on this particular topic might inform forest management strategies against the spread of the pathogen. As for its global historical distribution, specific differences in the mating types between European and North American populations, along with a single dominant genotype and a clonal population structure, have led to the conclusion that it originated in a previous, third location. China has been suggested as the most likely origin because of its native abundance of *Phytophthora* species, particularly in Yunnan province (Goheen et al. 2005).

SOD is able to infect a wide array of species and to use some of them as reservoirs (Grünwald et al. 2008, Garbelotto et al. 2003); soon after the first cases of affected tanoaks and coast live oaks were detected, it was found that *P. ramorum* was in fact able to infect many of the dominant trees of the northern and cenal. 2013). At the smallest scale, researchers are beginning to examine the impacts of invasive species on the genetics of native populations. When introduced species spread into an area, there may be some exchange of genetic material between native and invasive populations. This often happens via HYBRIDIZATION, as is the case with the highly invasive smooth cordgrass (*Spartina alterniflora*), originally introduced to salt marshes along the San Francisco Bay. Smooth cordgrass can hybridize with its native CONGENER, California cordgrass (*Spartina foliosa*), and the resulting hybrid has spread to colonize previously open mudflats (Daehler and Strong 1997). Similarly, rainbow trout (*Oncorhynchus mykiss*), a California native introduced as a game fish to many of California's lakes and streams, can hybridize with locally endemic trout subspecies in California (California golden trout [*O. mykiss aguabonita*] and Paiute cutthroat trout [*O. clarki seleniris*]), substantially altering the genetic structure of the native populations (Busack and Gall 1986, Cordes et al. 2006).

At the population scale, native species can be influenced by invasive species in a wide variety of ways, and many native populations in California are threatened by invasive species. Data for plant invasions are especially good. Over one thousand naturalized plant species are thought to occur in California (Rejmánek and Randall 1994, Rejmánek 2003, Stohlgren et al. 2003). According to some analyses, these exotic species have already contributed to the extinctions of 14 plant species and to declines in another 709 plant species that are either listed or proposed for listing as endangered by the threat of invasive species (Seabloom et al. 2006, Stein et al. 2000). The highest numbers of invasive plant species in California occur in coastal areas, which also harbor the highest number of threatened native plant species (Seabloom et al. 2006). In other taxonomic groups, several introduced diseases have had major impacts on their host populations. These include sudden oak death, which is decimating populations of susceptible oak trees around the state (Rizzo and Garbelotto 2003); chytrid, a fungal disease that targets amphibians (Briggs et al. 2010); and the relatively newly arrived West Nile virus, which has caused population declines in corvids (crows and jays) in addition to presenting a threat to human health (Koenig et al. 2007). Invasive animals also often displace native species; for example, the invasive bullfrog (*Litho-*

tral California coast. Despite its name, the disease also infects coastal redwoods (*Sequoia sempervirens*), big leaf maple (*Acer macrophylla*), bay laurel (*Umbellularia californica*), Douglas-fir (*Pseudotsuga menziesii*), and Pacific madrone (*Arbutus menziesii*) (Grünwald et al. 2008). Infected species differ in their susceptibility to SOD, influencing the spread of the disease. For example, bay laurel seems to be almost unaffected by infection. This allows *P. ramorum* to persist in bay laurel throughout the dry summer until the wet season, when the pathogen can spread and infect other individuals and species. Thus bay laurel appears to serve as a reservoir for transmission, facilitating the infectious cycle. This was demonstrated in an eight-year study by McPherson et al. (2010), which found that tanoak and coast live oak infection and mortality rates increased with the presence and abundance of bay laurel.

SOD's transport and dispersal mechanisms provide it with high mobility. Once spores are produced, they are easily splashed or carried down to the soil by rain or water from sprinklers. If spores reach streams or agricultural runoff, they can potentially be carried over long distances. Human shoes, bicycle wheels, and the use of outdoor or camping equipment may also facilitate transmission among distant sites (Davidson and Shaw 2003, Fisher et al. 2012). Specific native and introduced beetle species also facilitate the spread and impacts of SOD. Beetles such as the oak ambrosia beetle (*Monarthrum scutellare*) and oak bark beetles (*Pseudityophthorus pubipennis*) predispose coast live oak and black oak (*Quercus kelloggii*) to infection by attacking and wounding trees, increasing wood decay, and interrupting sap flow (Švihra and Kelly 2004). Moreover, beetle species that have symbiotic relationships with specific tree fungal pathogens (e.g., *Monarthrum dentigerum*, *Xyleborinus saxeseni*, and *Xyleborus californicus*) can colonize bleeding cankers caused by SOD, further infecting trees with their associated fungal pathogens and speeding mortality by up to 65%.

At the community and ecosystem scales, changes in the composition of several coastal forests in California are already occurring due to SOD-caused mortality (Box 13.2 Figure 1). These changes in turn cause alterations in fire regimes, chiefly by increasing fuel material at different forest strata (Metz et al. 2012). Alterations of nutrient dynamics occurs through changes in forest composition, which in turn affect litterfall quality and quantity (Cobb et al. 2013) as well as the ectomycorrhizal fungi associated with tanoaks (Bergemann et al. 2013).

Although SOD is causing tremendous damage to California's coastal forests, some ecophysiological and management mechanisms are emerging as options to fight the epidemic. Scientists have found that some coast live oaks naturally produce high concentrations of phenolic compounds and tyrosols in their phloem. These biochemical defenses against the pathogen can be effective at preventing infection or inhibiting it once the tree is infected (Nagle et al. 2011). Management efforts have been growing based on new understanding of the disease and its hosts. Since there is no known cure once a tree is infected, most management strategies are aimed at preventing the spread of the disease to new areas and protecting susceptible individuals. These include inspections of nursery plants prior to purchases, removal of infected oaks, removal of nonoak host trees, disposal of plant debris, and monitoring activities (Alexander and Lee 2010). More recently, application of phosphonate, an environmentally benign, narrow-spectrum fungicide, has been shown to temporarily deter SOD infection and spread within an individual. Forest managers and scientists are looking for ways to improve and expand the use of phosphonates as an effective management tool (Garbelotto et al. 2013, Schmidt and Garbelotto 2010).

bates catesbeianus) reduces populations of native frogs, such as the mountain yellow-legged frog (*Rana muscosa*) and the California red-legged frog (*R. draytonii*) (Kupferberg 1997).

California harbors many dramatic examples of invasive species altering the areas they invade at the community scale (the composition and relative abundances of constituent species). In many cases, even if individual native species are not directly threatened with extirpation by the arrival of an exotic species, native species abundances plummet such that previously common species become rare. Invasive grasses (including *Avena barbata*, *A. fatua*, *Bromus diandrus*, *B. hordeaceous*, and *Hordeum murinum*) have replaced native (and largely perennial) grasses in over 9 million hectares of California grasslands. Cape ivy (*Delairea odorata*) invasion in California coastal areas can cause a 30% reduction in native species diversity (Alvarez and Cushman 2002). Invasive Argentine ants (*Linepithema humile*) displace most native ant species, leading to the homogenization of ant communities in invaded areas (Box 13.3; Holway and Suarez 2006). The composition of the aquatic flora and fauna of the San Francisco Bay has been transformed by invasive species, such that the majority of species as well as over 90% of the biomass within the Bay are non-native (Cohen and Carlton 1998). Islands are particularly invasible, and because of their often-endemic species communities, the impacts of invaders on island communities can be especially strong. Feral sheep and pigs on Santa Cruz Island, for example, consumed large amounts of native vegetation before their removal, causing the near-extinction of several endemic species, transforming forests and shrublands into invasive-dominated grasslands and leaving behind so much bare ground that they significantly increased the frequency and size of landslides (Van Vuren and Coblentz 1987).

In many cases, invasive species can also have large-scale impacts on ecosystem properties. These include influences on nutrient cycling (Ehrenfeld 2003), hydrology (Levine et al. 2003), and disturbance regimes (Mack and D'Antonio 1998). Generalities about the influence of invasive species on ecosystem properties have been hard to come by—impacts tend to be related to traits of the individual invasive species and can be variable and unpredictable. Salt cedar (*Tamarix* spp.), intentionally introduced in the intermountain West, now grows along arid rivers and waterways in parts of California, transpiring at a higher rate than native vegetation in the upland areas that it invades. By doing so, salt cedar can reduce streamflow, dry ephemeral desert pools, and increase aridity in areas it has invaded (Zavaleta 2000). Disturbance regimes with which native species have coevolved, including fire frequency, erosion, and biotic disturbances, can also be influenced by invaders. For instance, Great Basin desert areas dominated by annual invasive grasses are prone to increased fire frequency, while areas of coastal California with invasive pigs (*Sus scrofa*) have increased levels of soil turnover and disturbance (Mack and D'Antonio 1998).

In addition to the many ecological effects of invasive species are their great economic costs and impacts on ecosystem services. Environmental, economic, and health costs of invasive species are associated with increased wildfire potential, reduced water resources, erosion, flooding, threats to wildlife, losses in crops, forests, fisheries, and grazing capacities, diminished outdoor recreation opportunities and spread of diseases, among other costs (Elton 1958, Mack et al. 2000, Puth and Post 2005, Perrings 2011). Invasive plants can cause problems as weeds in agricultural fields or can be toxic to domestic and stock animals; invasive pathogens cause diseases in citrus crops; and a variety of aquatic invaders can cause ship fouling.

While it is often very difficult to attach specific values to the impacts of invasive species, a few efforts have been made to understand the true economic impact of various invaders (Duncan et al. 2004, Pimentel et al. 2005). Approximately six hundred species of introduced insect and mite pests affect crops in California; these species collectively account for about two-thirds of crop losses in California (Dowell and Krass 1992). The value of field crops in California in 2010 was approximately $5.5 billion (CDFAb), so losses due to invasive pests are likely on the order of hundreds of millions of dollars annually. For example, to avoid potential yearly losses of $228 million in food crops to the establishment of exotic fruit flies in the state, the California Department of Food and Agriculture has spent approximately $3.9 million in projects aimed at the eradication of fruit fly outbreaks (CDFA 2009). Each feral pig is conservatively estimated to cause $200 in crop and environmental damage yearly, though this estimate does not include many of the indirect effects caused by feral pigs (Pimentel et al. 2005).

Unifying ideas for predicting the impacts, and thus the environmental and economic costs, of invasive species have been hard to come by. However, on a case-by-case basis, the risk posed by a single invasive species can be conceptualized as a function of both the probabilities of introduction, establishment, and spread of a species and the magnitude of potential impacts of that species. Some researchers have argued that non-native species should be judged problematic and removed or prevented from spreading only if harmful impacts are apparent (Davis et al. 2011). Others argue that given the great difficulty in predicting potential impacts, especially as both climate and the distributions of other species change, the precautionary principle should guide our approach to invasive species (Simberloff et al. 2005).

Invader Management: Challenges and Success Stories

Prevention

Prevention is both the most successful and cost-effective strategy for the management of potential invasive species, but it is only possible when exotic species are prevented from entering a pathway or when transported organisms are prevented from release or escape (Lodge et al. 2006). Prevention policies vary in their geographic scale of focus, with a number of local, state, and federal agencies, NGOs, business interests and research institutions working together to prevent exotic species introductions in California. Because many of the worst invasive species arrive via international transport, many policies addressing introductions are in the form of international agreements. For example, in 2005 the International Maritime Organization passed guidelines for preventing introductions via ship ballast water and sediments. A challenge to preventive policies is that the World Trade Organization, which promotes international trade, does not allow member nations to block entry of trade items without a strong case that they are harmful.

At the national level, U.S. policy towards introductions has been mostly ad hoc; for example, the 1900 Lacey Act allows the federal government to prevent importation of blacklisted animal species but does not specify how animals should be

BOX 13.3 THE ARGENTINE ANT IN CALIFORNIA

First documented in the United States in 1891, the Argentine ant (*Linepithema humile*) made its way to California in 1907 (Woodworth 1910) and continues to spread (Holway 1995, Sanders et al. 2003). Many people living in coastal California are familiar with the Argentine ant as a pest that can swarm homes during the wet months of the year. The ant is native to northern Argentina, southern Brazil, Uruguay, and Paraguay. While its introduced distribution is global, the Argentine ant most commonly occurs in areas similar to its Mediterranean-climate region of origin (Roura-Pascual et al. 2006). Human-mediated dispersal, via cargo shipments and other forms of transportation, is largely responsible for the spread of the Argentine ant (Holway 1995). Without human interference these ants disperse slowly overland; along with transportation, high colony fertility and an ability to nest in a wide variety of environments have facilitated their spread (Holway 1995, Suarez et al. 2001, Silverman and Brightwell 2008).

Behavioral changes within their introduced range have also allowed Argentine ants to succeed as invaders (Buczkowski et al. 2004). In their native range, Argentine ants coexist with other ant species and compete with other colonies of Argentine ants (Tsutsui and Suarez 2003). However, in California these ants behave as supercolonies; competition among Argentine ant colonies disappears. The high level of cooperation observed within the introduced range of this species is likely due to high levels of genetic similarity in the invasive population (Tsutsui and Suarez 2003). Low genetic variation prevents ants from distinguishing close kin (Tsutsui et al. 2001, Tsutsui and Suarez 2003). In turn, cooperation allows Argentine ants to reach very high densities and competitively displace native ants (Holway 1999, Tsutsui et al. 2000), leading to a host of ecological problems.

Argentine ants are used as a model system to study the mechanisms behind community disassembly and other community processes because of the frequently disruptive effect they have on native communities (e.g., Sanders et al. 2003). In habitats invaded by Argentine ants, native ants decline in both abundance and diversity (Human and Gordon 1997). Argentine ants appear to have a high tolerance for fragmented and disturbed landscapes and tend to be more abundant near development and exotic vegetation (Suarez et al. 1998, Laakkonen et al. 2001), making these habitats even more hostile for native ant species. Argentine ants have also been implicated in the declines of both coast horned lizards (*Phrynosoma coronatum*) and shrews (*Notiosorex crawfordi*) in southern California. These declines appear to be caused by the invader's displacement of native harvester ants, which are an important food source for both declining species (Laakkonen et al. 2001). Non-ant invertebrates also show marked declines in diversity and abundances in the presence of Argentine ants (Human and Gordon 1997).

In agricultural settings the Argentine ant contributes to high densities of insect pests such as the California red scale (*Aonidiella aurantii*), mealybugs (e.g., *Pseudococcus viburni*, *P. mauritimus*), and aphids (*Aphis gossypii*) (Lach 2003, Daane et al. 2007, Powell and Silverman 2010) (Box 13.3 Figure 1). These small insect pests suck phloem from crop plants and secrete a sugary, honeydew substance, which is then collected by the ants. In exchange, the ants defend these insects from predation and parasitism. The net effect of the Argentine ant on crops is unknown. Although the ants protect the small sap-sucker pests from predators, they also inadvertently protect the plant from other, potentially more damaging insect herbivores (Lach 2003).

BOX 13.3 FIGURE 1 The Argentine ant (*L. humile*) tending aphids on a coyotebrush (*Baccharis pilularis* var. *consanguinea*). Photo: Dan Quinn, Jasper Ridge Docent.

Management of the Argentine ant has proven extremely difficult, and early detection and prevention of spread are critical. The ant is particularly difficult to manage because it has no known natural enemies (Orr et al. 2001). As a result, the primary control method is poisonous chemical baits, but even these are frequently ineffective because the ant can typically draw from other food resources. To date the only documented country eradication has occurred in New Zealand (Harris et al. 2002). Field experiments indicate that several integrated pest management (IPM) strategies might be successful in controlling these ants if their access to habitat, resources, and/or nesting sites is limited (Silverman and Brightwell 2008).

TABLE 13.3
California codes and agencies involved in the prevention of exotic species introductions.

State code	State agency	Invasive species managed
California Food and Agriculture Code	Department of Food and Agriculture	Animal pests, plant diseases, noxious weeds
California Fish and Game Code	Department of Fish and Wildlife	Live wild animals and plants, aquaculture
California Water Code	State Water Resources Control Board Regional Water Quality Control Boards	Biological pollutants in water
California Harbors and Navigation Code	Department of Boating and Waterways	Aquatic weeds
California Public Resources Code	State Lands Commission Department of Fish and Wildlife	Marine organisms in ballast water from commercial vessels

assessed for blacklisting. Federal agencies involved in preventing introductions include the U.S. Department of Agriculture (USDA) and its Marketing Service, Animal Plant Health Inspection Service, the U.S. Fish and Wildlife Service, the U.S. Department of Commerce, and the U.S. Coast Guard (CDFG Invasive Species Program 2008). At the state level, the California legislature has passed more specific regulatory controls under the Fish and Game, Food and Agriculture, and Public Resources Codes, while the California Water and Harbors and Navigation Codes also address aquatic invasion management (CDFG Invasive Species Program 2008) (Table 13.3). Many state agencies in California are involved in the detection and management of invasive species. Codes established by the state legislature give state agencies regulatory power to manage different categories of invasive species. California's Department of Food and Agriculture is primarily responsible for operating agricultural inspection stations set up at entry points throughout the state to prevent introductions of exotic agricultural pests.

Prevention policies vary as to whether they focus on deliberate versus inadvertent introductions (Simberloff et al. 2005) and whether they target particular species versus introduction PATHWAYS based on enforcement at entry points such as ports and state boundaries (CDFG Invasive Species Program 2008). While deliberate introductions account for the naturalization of more than half of all invasive plants (Mack and Erneberg 2002), conflicting interests and unpredictability of invasions impedes stricter limitations, such as on the importation of ornamental plants. Importers and retailers who directly facilitate the transfer of species across borders lack economic incentives to limit introductions, and federal policy does not lay out a coherent approach to limiting introductions. While the impacts of species introductions are inherently unpredictable, current legislation reflects more of an "innocent until proven guilty" approach to invasion prevention. Moreover, even with quantitative risk analysis calculations, risk estimates lack confidence limits and can give a false sense of safety (Simberloff et al. 2005).

Early Detection, Rapid Response, and Eradication

Some species will inevitably go undetected at their points of entry despite efforts to monitor potential introduction pathways. When prevention is ineffective, a small portion of introduced species will establish populations, at which point eradication may be a potential management strategy. The success of eradication efforts in most areas hinges on detection during the early stages of invasion, which can be accomplished with standardized monitoring programs, active surveillance, and cooperation with information networks (Lodge et al. 2006, CDFG Invasive Species Program 2008). In the early stages of invasion, introduced species occupy a limited range and may be functionally innocuous. For example, eradication of exotic weeds in California is usually successful when infestations are smaller than one hectare but is often unrealistic when infestations are greater than 1,000 hectares (Rejmánek and Pitcairn 2002). An incipient population may persist in this way for a variable amount of time (weeks to years) (Lodge et al. 2006) before it experiences rapid growth and range expansion. This lag time provides the best window of opportunity to take management action. Eradication is often feasible when incipient invasions are identified early and have a limited range, and response is rapid (Simberloff et al. 2005).

Island invasions are especially good candidates for eradication efforts due to their smaller typical size and their isolation. Eradication of mammals from islands is a powerful conservation tool that is gaining popularity as success stories are documented in the literature (Donlan et al. 2003), although eradication of one invasive may facilitate the invasion of other species. The eradication of black rats (*Rattus rattus*) on Anacapa Island, part of Channel Islands National Park, in 2001–2002 is a story of success through meticulous planning and collaboration. The presence of the endemic Anacapa deer mouse (*Peromyscus maniculatus anacapae*) and other protected seabirds required careful planning, anticipation, and mitigation of nontarget effects. Follow-up monitoring suggests that negative impacts were short-lived, but that the benefits to native seabirds resulting from the removal of rats from the island are ongoing (Whitworth et al. 2005, 2013).

Like islands, freshwater systems have been devastated by invasive species and are relatively isolated and well delineated, often making eradication of invasive species feasible. The eradication of invasive pike from Lake Davis and of invasive trout from many high Sierra lakes to protect threatened salmon, other native fishes, and frogs are the best known freshwater eradication successes (see Chapter 11, "Biodiversity"). A host of opportunities persist to prevent species extinctions and protect ecosystem properties through well-designed freshwater invasive species eradications in California. Successful eradications have also taken place outside of the confines of islands and fresh water systems in California. "Killer alga" (*Caulerpa taxifolia*), a fast-growing marine alga listed as one of the world's one hundred worst invaders by the International Union for the Conservation of Nature, was introduced at two sites in southern California in 2001–2002. The San Diego Regional Water Quality Control Board recognized the potential cost of the invasion without immediate action, comparing the infestation to an oil spill, and was able to mobilize emergency funding to begin eradication efforts in just seventeen days (L.W.J. Anderson 2005). The eradication was declared successful in 2005. Although federal regulations prohibit the importation, interstate sale, or transport of the aquarium strain of *Caulerpa taxifolia* (Southern California Caulerpa Action Team 2003), many species of *Caulerpa*, including *C. taxifolia*, are available online (Walters et al. 2006). After successful eradication, preventing new infestations is an important way to ensure long-term success.

Cost-effective management must include monitoring for early detection, which should be weighed against the estimated costs of eradication and the even more costly alternatives of long-term control. Surveys to detect small populations are expensive, but if a small invasive population goes undetected, eradication can quickly become more costly (Lodge et al. 2006). Similarly, post-eradication monitoring is important to ensure that eradication has been achieved or to identify the need for additional control before the invasion re-expands significantly and inflates follow-up costs. Eradication of most invasive species requires a combination of culling and follow-up control methods (Parkes et al. 2010). The initial (one- to several-year) cost of aggressive eradication programs can be high, but the alternative—long-term (but incomplete) control of invasive species—requires ongoing effort, expense, and an indefinite amount of time and resources (Zavaleta et al. 2001, Ewel et al. 1999).

Long-term Control and Management

Ongoing control efforts for harmful invasive species require coordination across scales and reassessment over time to consider population changes and to incorporate learning about exotic species effects and their responses to implemented controls. In general, long-term control strategies are costly and appropriate mainly for established species with significant impacts on biodiversity, human health, infrastructure, and other values. Other established species with less severe impacts are in practice accepted and managed as ecosystem components, in some cases even incorporated into providing services such as habitat for native species (e.g., Shapiro 2002). At the state level, the California Department of Fish and Wildlife's (CDFW) Invasive Species Program uses specific criteria and expert input to determine whether or not to take action to control an invasive species (CDFG Invasive Species Program 2008). At the county level, Cooperative Weed Management Areas (CWMAs) typically organized by agricultural commissioners' offices and consisting of local stakeholder groups, work together on weed management. Such organizations have increased from fewer than twenty in the state in 2000 to over forty today, covering all counties (California Invasive Plant Council 2014). CWMAs can foster coordination among managers, increasing effectiveness and reducing costs of invasive control (Epanchin-Niell et al. 2009). A more recent trend has led to increased multicounty, landscape-scale coordination of invader mapping and prioritization efforts. Both county- and multicounty-scale efforts can ultimately lead to more successful and cost-effective control and eradication than ad hoc, local activities, which are more likely to lead to reinvasion (Doug Johnson, pers. comm.).

Effective control should limit the dispersal and reduce densities or extents of invasive species as well as consider effects of control activities on native species and ecosystems of special concern and on human health and well-being. Many different tactics can be used in long-term control, such as hunting to control feral pigs, timed grazing to control invasive grassland weeds, and large-scale efforts to disrupt the mating of exotic agricultural pests. Wild pigs were intentionally introduced as livestock and for hunting and are now found throughout most of California (Waithman 2001). While most pigs in California are managed through hunting, pigs on Santa Cruz Island were eradicated in 2006 using a combination of pig-proof fencing, aerial and on-the-ground hunting, and Judas pigs (sterilized, radio-collared females) tracked to locate remaining individuals (Parkes et al. 2010). The invasive northern pike (*Esox lucius*) was similarly introduced illegally in California to improve recreational fishing. In a series of attempts to eradicate pike in northern California, lakes and tributaries were treated with piscicides to kill all fish then restocked with rainbow trout (Lee 2001, Vasquez et al. 2012). Northern pike reintroductions are prohibited in California, but illicit fish stocking is responsible for the introduction of many exotic fish species (CDFW 2015). Strategic education and interagency coordination can reduce reintroduction risks (Johnson et al. 2009).

Both control and eradication can, and often must, be complemented with additional restoration measures to successfully recover target ecological values and reduce the likelihood of reinvasion (Zavaleta et al. 2001) and to ensure that the removal of one invasive does not facilitate invasion of another species (Erskine Ogden and Rejmánek, 2005). Moreover, restoration efforts themselves can reduce invasion, such as when replanting and vegetation restoration reduce the availability of open, disturbed sites for reinvasion. Various state and national government agencies manage the spread of some invasive species through restoration. Restoration of invaded areas often involves the removal of invasive species and replanting with native species but can also involve measures such as restoration of flood flows in rivers, temporary erosion prevention structures, and reintroduction of animals such as seabirds. Ongoing control and restoration efforts can be labor-intensive and often rely on large numbers of community volunteers. This underscores the value of prioritization focused on harmful invaders and incorporating the feasibility of successful removal and restoration, especially when underlying changes that facilitate invasion (such as altered flows in dammed and diverted streams and rivers) cannot be remedied.

Biocontrol

BIOCONTROL is a special type of long-term management in which natural predators, parasites, pathogens, or competitors of invasive species are intentionally introduced as control agents (UC IPM 2007). Classical biological control relies on the introduction of one or more additional exotic species when the benefit of introducing the control agent is expected to outweigh the inherent risk of introducing additional exotic species. Effective biocontrol species are generally invertebrates or pathogens that have tightly coevolved with an invasive species in its native range and that play a significant role in regulating its population there. Generalist vertebrates are poor biocontrol agents because of their propensity to switch to native prey species. The U.S. Department of Agriculture's Animal and Plant Health Inspection Service, Plant Protection and Quarantine must authorize any import of a new biological control agent into the country (Scoles et al. 2012), and in California the state Department of Agriculture maintains guidelines for biocontrol introductions (CDFA 2013a, Aslan et al. 2014). International organizations also provide standards and guidelines for biological control (Tanaka and Larson 2006). Biocontrol introductions should use cost-benefit analyses that incorporate both economic and ecological consequences, weighing ecological damage against the consequences of inaction. An evolutionary and landscape perspective would also improve cost-benefit analysis, as introduced species can acquire new hosts, adapt to new environmental conditions, and disperse to new areas. Ecological damage has probably occurred more often than recorded due to minimal monitoring of post-introduction, nontarget effects of biocontrol efforts (Simberloff and Stiling 1996).

Biocontrol has rarely been used to manage invasive species that impact primarily natural ecosystems. However, it has been widely and successfully used in agricultural systems to manage crop pests and noxious weeds in pasture lands. A classic example of biological control that originated in California is the control of the cottony cushion scale (*Icerya purchasi*). The scale insect was established in the Los Angeles area and developed as a major citrus pest, causing massive destruction of citrus trees. In its native range in Australia, the scale insect was not known to be a pest as populations were controlled by the Australian vedalia ladybeetle (*Rodalia cardinalis*) and a parasitic fly (*Cryptochaetum iceryae*). Vedalia beetlesand the parasitic fly were captured in Australia and released in California in 1888. Within a year and a half, control was achieved and has been maintained with the establishment of wild populations of both biocontrol agents (Pedigo and Rice 2009).

Biocontrol has also been a successful strategy for controlling some noxious weeds in California grasslands. St. John's wort, or Klamath weed (*Hypericum perforatum*), was first identified in California near the Klamath River and became an invasive weed by the 1920s (DeBach 1974). Klamath weed, which is toxic to cattle, invaded grasslands and became the target of control efforts. Klamath weed was successfully controlled by the introduction of *Chrysolina* beetles that suppress the weed in its native range (Huffaker and Kennett 1959). In contrast to the successful control of Klamath weed, numerous biocontrol efforts have not successfully controlled yellow starthistle, one of the most economically and ecologically damaging exotic invasive plants in California (see Box 13.1; CDFA 2013d).

The Future of Biological Invasions in California

The future of invasions in California will be determined by both environmental changes and changes in how we respond to invasive species. The interacting effects of international trade, land use change, atmospheric pollution, and climate change will alter the suite of new species introduced, identities of new and formerly benign non-native species that become invasive, habitat susceptibility to invasion, and invader impacts. However, changes in public understanding of the problems posed by invasive species, prioritization by managers of invasive species removal as both critical and possible, and capitalization on past successes and new techniques and technologies could dramatically reduce the future impacts of harmful invasions on California's ecology and society.

Increasing transport, maritime trade, international air travel, and online commerce have the potential to increase the number of species introduced to California and the likelihood and rates of establishment and spread (Perrings et al. 2009). For example, the top ten U.S. container ports—which include both Los Angeles and Oakland in California—experienced a 54% increase in container movements from 2001 to 2006, and projections indicate that U.S. port container traffic will double by 2020 and triple by 2030 (U.S. Maritime Administration 2009); all else being equal, the arrival of potentially invasive species in California is expected to increase. The conditions that determine whether newly or previously introduced exotic species will establish, spread, and become problematic are also changing due to atmospheric pollution, global climate change, and land use change in California. Specific impacts are often difficult to predict. For example, elevated concentrations of CO_2 (due to increasing greenhouse gas emissions) can preferentially benefit some introduced species, but its impacts are less clear in the context of responses by other native species and of other, ongoing global changes (Dukes and Mooney 1999).

Nevertheless, some average trends indicate likely directions for biological invasions under changing conditions. The traits that make many species successful invaders, such as high plasticity (Davidson et al. 2011), rapid dispersal, and generalist habit (Dukes and Mooney 1999), will also likely serve them well under changing conditions in California. In general, disturbances from fire to land use change are expected to increase in California and to continue to facilitate invasions as climate change continues and the state's population approaches fifteen million by midcentury (California Department of Finance Demographic Research Unit 2013; see Chapters 5, "Population and Land Use," and 14, "Climate Change Impacts"). Extreme events such as floods, droughts, and heat waves are also expected to increase in magnitude and frequency, which could increase invasions and their impacts through a variety of mechanisms (Diez et al. 2012). For example, when the marine epibenthic fouling community of Bodega Harbor was exposed to a simulated heat wave, nonnative species were better able to tolerate the initial disturbance than native species and to maintain their dominance in the months following the event (Sorte et al. 2010). Where invasive species are currently limited by cool temperatures, warming could facilitate spread. For example, winter frosts currently limit the pink bollworm (*Pectinophora gossypiella*), a major cotton pest, to southern California's desert valleys. As winter frosts decrease in the San Joaquin Valley, the survival and spread of the pink bollworm is expected to increase (Gutierrez et al. 2006). In aquatic systems non-native animal species have, on average, a performance advantage over native species associated with increases in temperatures and CO_2 levels (Sorte et al. 2013). Warming temperatures could also favor the expansion of warm-water freshwater species native to the eastern portion of the U.S., such as largemouth bass, green sunfish, and bluegill that were originally introduced for sport fishing (Moyle et al. 2013).

Though several factors point to a worsening biological invasions problem in California, innovative policies and responses to prevent introductions and control spread have the potential to counter this scenario. Invasive species management efforts in California increasingly include formal prioritization: evaluating which invasive species are worth aggressively managing versus tolerating or embracing, balancing negative impacts with limited resources, and recognizing that some invasive species could provide ecosystem services that partially compensate for the damage they cause (Doug Johnson, pers. comm.). Technology innovations could also aid with prevention and detection of invasive species in the future. For example, smartphone apps allow an increasingly connected public to submit geo-tagged photos of suspected weeds and pests, facilitating early detection and control. Higher-resolution remote sensing and imaging spectrometers (Simberloff 2013) offer promising approaches to detecting and monitoring invasions, providing repeated cover over wide and less-accessible areas (Vitousek et al. 2011). Improvements in DNA sequencing will enable better detection of introduced species, allowing quick species identification as well as detection of particular species at very low densities, thereby aiding in prevention efforts (Simberloff 2013, Cross et al. 2011).

Beyond techniques and technological innovations, the potential exists for attitudes towards invasions among both the public and decision makers to shift. Increased attention to invasive species management successes, ranging from eradications in freshwater and island systems to successful biocontrol efforts in agricultural systems, could supplant a sense of hopelessness about highly invaded systems in the state and could encourage more use of successful approaches towards a wider range of targets. A continued trend towards distinguishing clearly harmful invaders, of which there are many, from relatively innocuous and even positively valued nonnatives (e.g., Coates 2006), allows both managers and the public to concentrate effort and attention on the highest priorities for action.

Finally, our responses to global change and invasions interact, meaning that priorities, policies, and management practices will need to be revised to take advantage of synergies and avoid unintended consequences of management practices. For example, climate change may undermine the assumptions used in established risk-assessment protocols for preventing introductions based on climate matching (Pyke et al. 2008), or could cause biocontrol organisms to become less effective (Gutierrez et al. 2008) or to become invasive themselves (Pyke et al. 2008). On the other hand, land use policies intended to reduce greenhouse gas emissions might also reduce rates of landscape fragmentation that accelerate invasions (Pyke et al. 2008); California's Sustainable Communities and Climate Protection Act of 2008, SB 375, could play such as role. Invasive species might even deliberately be used to maintain key ecosystem functions in the face of threats like sea level rise to coastal ecosystems (Hershner and Havens 2008). Exotic biological invaders have dramatically influenced California's ecosystems. However, California has also been—and hopefully will continue to be—an important global stage for continual innovations and evolving understanding about how to both harness established exotics for good and effectively prevent and reverse harmful invasions.

Summary

Invasive species have had tremendous impacts on the ecosystems and economy of California. Both ecological and human factors govern the dynamics of invasions in California. California's equable Mediterranean climate, diversity of geologic and climatic conditions, and widespread natural disturbances such as fires and floods contribute to surplus resources and favorable habitats for potential invaders. But patterns of invasions in California are most strongly dictated by both historical and modern human impacts on the introduction, establishment, and spread of invasive species. Major phases of terrestrial biological invasions in California have been defined by shifts in human land use following the first European settlements and exacerbated by an increasing human population and improvements in transportation infrastructure. California's unique human history has driven patterns of both intentional introductions for food, pets, sport, and horticulture as well as unintentional (though preventable) introductions via high international and interstate trade and traffic. Humans have also increased the process of establishment and spread for invasive species by altering existing disturbance regimes, patterns of connectivity, and abiotic conditions.

In general, densely populated areas of California, especially along the coast, harbor the highest numbers and associated impacts of introduced species. California's open ocean, alpine, and forest ecosystems tend to have fewer invaders, while its freshwater, grassland, and estuarine ecosystems are generally highly invaded. Documented impacts of invasive species on native species in California include genetic impacts, local or species-level extinctions via disease and displacement, changes in community composition and native species diversity, and altered ecosystem processes such as nutrient cycling and disturbance regimes. Economic costs include direct losses to crops or managed resources and investments in management and control efforts. Costs also accrue from decreased ecosystem services, such as decreased climate and flood regulation and reduced water resources.

Preventing introductions of potentially invasive species in the first place is the most successful and cost-effective management strategy. For species that establish populations in California, management options include eradication targeted at high-priority, early-stage invaders; long-term control efforts such as weeding, hunting, timed grazing, and mating disruption; and biological control, which has been used to manage invasive agricultural pests and noxious weeds. The future of invasions in California will be shaped by increases in international trade and transport, the state's population, climate change and disturbances, and innovations and investments in management. A great many successful eradication and control efforts illustrate that invaded areas can be restored, while a great many invasions have also become irreversible parts of California's diversity and ecological dynamics.

Acknowledgments

We thank Peter Moyle, Marcel Rejmánek, and Richard Hobbs for greatly improving the chapter.

Recommended Reading

Bossard, C. C., J. M. Randall, and M. C. Hoshovsky. 2000. Invasive plants of California wildlands. University of California Press, Berkeley, California.

Minnich, R. A. 2008. California's fading wildflowers: Lost legacy and biological invasions. University of California Press, Berkeley, California.

Richardson, D. M., editor. 2011. Fifty years of invasion ecology: The legacy of Charles Elton. Wiley-Blackwell, Hoboken, New Jersey.

Thompson, L., G. A. Guisti, K. L. Weber, and R. G. Keiffer. 2013. The native and introduced fishes of Clear Lake: A review of the past to assist with decisions of the future. California Fish and Game 99:7–41.

Walters, L. J., K. R. Brown, W. T. Stam, and J. L. Olsen. 2006. E-commerce and *Caulerpa*: Unregulated dispersal of invasive species. Frontiers in Ecology and the Environment 4:75–79.

Glossary

ALIEN A species or taxon that is not native to a given location (i.e., that has been introduced by human activity). Alien taxa include beneficial (e.g., domestic), benign, and harmful species and also include both naturalized and unestablished taxa. Synonyms include exotic, non-native, nonindigenous, and introduced.

BIOCONTROL A special type of long-term management in which natural predators, parasites, pathogens, or competitors of invasive species are intentionally introduced as control agents (UC IPM 2007). Also known as biological control.

CONGENER A species within the same genus as another species.

DISTURBANCE REGIME This concept describes the dominant patterns and sources of biophysical change in a given ecosystem that trigger processes of ecological succession at different spatial and temporal scales; or the pattern of disturbance (for example, fire or flooding) that shapes an ecosystem over time.

ENDEMIC Describes a taxon that occurs only in a particular geographic region.

EXOTIC See ALIEN.

FERAL Describes an organism or taxon that has escaped or been released from captivity or domestication.

HYBRIDIZATION The spread of genes of one species into the genes of a different species.

INTENTIONAL INTRODUCTION Purposeful introduction of an exotic species to a new environment by people. Intentional introductions include introductions of ornamental plants, fish and game species, and biocontrol agents.

INTRODUCED SPECIES See ALIEN; however, "introduced" can refer to that subset of alien species that reach unconfined habitats—for example, captive pets can be considered alien but not introduced unless they are released from captivity.

INTRODUCTION The process of introducing an alien species into a new environment or locale.

INVASIBILITY A characteristic of an ecological community describing the ease with which exotic species can become established and invasive in that community.

INVASIVE Describes a non-native species that establishes self-sustaining populations and spreads outside of its native range; a subset, *harmful* invasive species cause environmental and/or economic harm in their introduced ranges.

NATURALIZED SPECIES The term has been applied to describe a variety of non-native species conditions. It is considered an imprecise terminology but most recently refers to established, consistently reproducing species outside their native range, whether or not they are harmful or spreading (Richardson et al. 2011).

NONINDIGENOUS See ALIEN.

NON-NATIVE See ALIEN.

OOMYCETE A relatively large taxon of eukaryotic organisms belonging to Heterokontophyta phylum along with brown and golden algae. They resemble fungi by presenting mycelial growth and in their nutrition habits.

PATHWAY The route through which an exotic species arrives in a new location, such as a particular shipping route.

PROPAGULE A seed, a spore, or any part of an organism that is capable of producing a new individual.

RIPARIAN The zone surrounding a river or stream on either side that is strongly influenced by the presence of the river. The riparian zone also directly influences the river through shading or inputs of organic material.

References

Alexander, J., and C. A. Lee. 2010. Lessons learned from a decade of sudden oak death in California: Evaluating local management. Environmental Management 46:315–328.

Alvarez M. E., and J. H. Cushman. 2002. Community-level consequences of a plant invasion: Effects on three habitats in coastal California. Ecological Applications 12:1434–1444.

Anderson, L. W. J. 2005. California's reaction to *Caulerpa taxifolia*: A model for invasive species rapid response. Biological Invasions 7:1003–1016.

Aslan, C. E., A. Aslan, D. Croll, B. Tershy, and E. Zavaleta. 2014. Building taxon substitution guidelines on a biological control foundation. Restoration Ecology 22(4):437–441.

Bais, H. P., R. Vepachedu, S. Gilroy, R. M. Callaway, and J. M. Vivanco. 2003. Allelopathy and exotic plants: From genes to invasion. Science 301:1377–1380.

Baker, H. G. 1974. The evolution of weeds. Annual Review of Ecology and Systematics 5:1–24.

Baker, W. L. 1992. The landscape ecology of large disturbances in the design and management of nature reserves. Landscape Ecology 7:181–194.

Bakker, E., and G. Slack. 1971. An island called California: An ecological introduction to its natural communities. University of California Press, Berkeley, California.

Baldwin, B. G., D. Goldman, D. J. Keil, R. Patterson, T. J. Rosatti, and D. Wilken, editors. 2012. The Jepson manual: Vascular plants of California. Second edition. University of California Press, Berkeley, California.

Ballmer, G. 1995. Sidebar: Nation's richest insect diversity in California. California Agriculture 49:51–52.

Bergemann, S. E., N. C. Kordesch, W. VanSant-Glass, M. Garbelotto, and T. A. Metz. 2013. Implications of tanoak decline in forests impacted by *Phytophthora ramorum*: Girdling decreases the soil hyphal abundance of ectomycorrhizal fungi associated with *Notholithocarpus densiflorus*. Madroño 60:95–106.

Bicknell, S. H., and E. M. Mackey. 1998. Mysterious nativity of California's sea fig. Fremontia 26:3–11.

Blossey, B., and R. Nötzold. 1995. Evolution of increased competitive ability in invasive nonindigenous plants: A hypothesis. Journal of Ecology 83:887–889.

Briggs, C. J., R. A. Knapp, and V. T. Vredenburg. 2010. Enzootic and epizootic dynamics of the chytrid fungal pathogen of amphibians. Proceedings of the National Academy of Sciences 107:9695–9700.

Brooks, M. L., C. M. D'Antonio, D. M. Richardson, J. B. Grace, J. E. Keeley, J. M. DiTomaso, R. J. Hobbs, M. Pellant, and D. Pyke. 2004. Effects of invasive alien plants on fire regimes. BioScience 54:677–688.

Buczkowski, G., E. L. Vargo, and J. Silverman. 2004. The diminutive supercolony: The Argentine ants of the southeastern United States. Molecular Ecology 13:2235–2242.

Bunn, S. E., and A. H. Arthington. 2002. Basic principles and ecological consequences of altered flow regimes for aquatic biodiversity. Environmental Management 30:492–507.

Burns, C., and J. Sauer. 1992. Resistance by natural vegetation in the San Gabriel Mountains of California to invasion by introduced conifers. Global Ecology and Biogeography Letters 2:46–51.

Busack, C. A., and G. A. E Gall. 1981. Introgressive hybridization in populations of Paiute cutthroat trout (*Salmo clarki seleniris*). Canadian Journal of Fisheries and Aquatic Sciences 38:939–951.

California Department of Finance Demographic Research Unit. 2013. New population projections: California to surpass 50 million in 2049. Press release. Sacramento, California.

California Department of Fish and Game (CDFG) Invasive Species Program. 2008. California aquatic invasive species management plan. California Resources Agency and CDFG, Scaramento, California.

California Department of Fish and Wildlife (CDFW). 2015. California's invaders: Northern pike. <https://www.wildlife.ca.gov/Conservation/Invasives/Species/Northern-Pike>. Accessed June 1, 2015.

California Department of Food and Agriculture (CDFA). 2013a. Biocontrol. California Department of Food and Agriculture, Plant Health, and Pest Prevention Services, Integrated Pest Control Branch. <http://www.cdfa.ca.gov/plant/ipc/biocontrol/bc_whoweare.htm>. Accessed October 22, 2013.

———. 2013b. California agricultural production statistics. <http://www.cdfa.ca.gov/statistics/>. Accessed November 12, 2013.

———. 2013c. Hydrilla: Program details. <http://www.cdfa.ca.gov/plant/ipc/hydrilla/hydrilla_hp.htm>. Accessed November 8, 2013.

———. 2013d. Yellow Starthistle leading edge project: Program details. <http://www.cdfa.ca.gov/plant/ipc/ystmapping/ystmapping_hp.htm>. Accessed October 22, 2013.

———. 2009. Protecting California from biological pollution. Report. <http://www.cdfa.ca.gov/plant/publications.html>. Accessed November 8, 2013.

California Invasive Plant Council. 2014. About weed management Areas. <http://www.cal-ipc.org/policy/state/wma.php>. Accessed October 14, 2014.

———. 2013a. Don't plant a pest!—Alternatives to invasive garden plants. <http://www.cal-ipc.org/landscaping/dpp/index.php>. Accessed November 8, 2013.

———. 2013b. Invasive plants of California's wildland. <http://www.cal-ipc.org/ip/management/ipcw/>. Accessed November 8, 2013.

Callaway, R. M., and E. T. Aschehoug. 2000. Invasive plants versus their new and old neighbors: A mechanism for exotic invasion. Science 290:521–523.

Callaway, R. M., G. Thelen, A. Rodriguez, and W. E. Holben. 2004. Release from inhibitory soil biota in Europe and positive plant-soil feedbacks in North America promote invasion. Nature 427:731–733.

Chun, Y. J., M. van Kleunen, and W. Dawson. 2010. The role of enemy release, tolerance, and resistance in plant invasions: Linking damage to performance. Ecology Letters 13: 947–946.

Coates, P. 2006. American perceptions of immigrant and invasive species: Strangers on the land. University of California Press, Berkeley, California.

Cobb, R. C., D. M. Rizzo, K. J. Hayden, M. Garbelotto, J. A. N. Filipe, C. A. Gilligan, W. W. Dillon, R. K. Meentemeyer, Y. S. Valachovic, and E. Goheen. 2013. Biodiversity conservation in the face of dramatic forest disease: An integrated conservation strategy for tanoak (*Notholithocarpus densiflorus*) threatened by sudden oak death. Madroño 60:151–164.

Cohen A. N., and J. T. Carlton. 1998. Accelerating invasion rate in a highly invaded estuary. Science 279:555–558.

Connor, E. F., J. Hafernik, J. Levy, V. L. Moore, and J. K. Rickman. 2002. Insect conservation in an urban biodiversity hotspot: The San Francisco Bay Area. Journal of Insect Conservation 6:247–259.

Convention on Biological Diversity. 2013a. Text of the CBD. <http://www.cbd.int/convention/text/default.shtml>. Accessed October 19, 2013.

———. 2013b. What are invasive alien species? <http://www.cbd.int/invasive/WhatareIAS.shtml>. Accessed October 19, 2013.

Cordes, J. F., M. R. Stephens, M. A. Blumberg, and B. May. 2006. Identifying introgressive hybridization in native populations of California golden trout based on molecular markers. Transactions of the American Fisheries Society 135:110–128.

Cross, H. B., A. J. Lowe, and F. D. Gurgel. 2011. DNA barcoding of invasive species. Pages 289–299 in D. M. Richardson, editor. Fifty years of invasion ecology: The legacy of Charles Elton. Wiley-Blackwell, Hoboken, New Jersey.

Croucher, P. J. P., S. Mascheratti, and M. Garbeletto. 2013. Combining field epidemiological information and genetic data to comprehensively reconstruct the invasion history and the microevolution of the sudden oak death agent *Phytophthora ramorum* (Stramenopila: Oomycetes) in California. Biological Invasions 15:2281–2297.

Daane, K. M., K. R. Sime, J. Fallon, and M. L. Cooper. 2007. Impacts of Argentine ants on mealybugs and their natural enemies in California's coastal vineyards. Ecological Entomology 32:583–596.

Daehler, C., and D. Strong. 1997. Hybridization between introduced smooth cordgrass (*Spartina alterniflora*; Poaceae) and native California cordgrass (*S. foliosa*) in San Francisco Bay, California, USA. American Journal of Botany 84:607–611.

D'Antonio, C., C. Malmstrom, S. Reynolds, and J. Gerlach. 2007. Ecology of invasive non-native species in California grassland. Pages 67–83 in M. R. Stromberg, J. D. Corbin, and C. D'Antonio, editors. California grasslands: Ecology and management. University of California Press, Berkeley, California.

Darwin, C. 1859. On the origin of species by means of natural selection, or the preservation of favoured races in the struggle for life. John Murray, London, UK.

Davidson, A. M., M. Jennions, and A. B. Nicotra. 2011. Do invasive species show higher phenotypic plasticity than native species and, if so, is it adaptive? A meta-analysis. Ecology Letters 14:419–431.

Davidson, J. M., and C. G. Shaw. 2003. Pathways of movement for *Phytophthora ramorum*, the causal agent of sudden oak death. Sudden Oak Death Online Symposium. <http://www.apsnet.org/online/proceedings/sod/Papers/Shaw_Davidson/default.htm>. Accessed November 2013.

Davis, M. A. 2011. Invasion biology. Pages 364–369 in D. Simberloff and M. Rejmánek, editors. Encyclopedia of biological invasions. University of California Press, Berkeley, California.

———. 2009. Invasion biology. Oxford University Press, Oxford, UK.

Davis, M. A., and K. Thompson. 2000. Eight ways to be a colonizer; two ways to be an invader. Bulletin of the Ecological Society of America 81:226–230.

Davis, M. A., J. P. Grime, and K. Thompson. 2000. Fluctuating resources in plant communities: A general theory of invasibility. Journal of Ecology 88:528–534.

Davis, M. A., M. K. Chew, R. J. Hobbs et al. 2011. Don't judge species on their origins. Nature 474:153–154.

DeBach, P. 1974. Biological control by natural enemies. Cambridge University Press, London and New York.

Diez, J. M., C. M. D'Antonio, J. S. Dukes, E. D. Grosholz, J. D. Olden, C. J. Sorte, D. M. Blumenthal, B. A. Bradley, R. Early, I. Ibáñez, S. J. Jones, J. J. Lawler, and L. P. Miller. 2012. Will extreme climatic events facilitate biological invasions? Frontiers in Ecology and the Environment 10:249–257.

DiTomaso, J., G. B. Kyser, W. T. Lanini, C. D. Thomsen, and T. S. Prather. 2007. Pest notes: Yellow Starthistle UC ANR Publication 7402. IPM Education and Publications, University of California Statewide IPM Program, Davis, California.

DiTomaso, J. M., G. B. Kyser, and C. B. Pirosko. 2003. Effect of light and density on yellow starthistle (*Centaurea solstitialis*) root growth and soil moisture use. Weed Science 51:334–341.

DiTomaso, J. M., G. B. Kyser, and M. J. Pitcairn. 2006. Yellow starthistle management guide. Cal-IPC Publication 2006-03. Page 78. California Invasive Plant Council, Berkeley, California.

Donlan, C. J., B. R. Tershy, K. Campbell, and F. Cruz. 2003. Research for requiems: The need for more collaborative action in eradication of invasive species. Conservation Biology 17(6):1850–1851.

Dowell, R. V. 2002. Exotic invaders and biological control in California. Pages 47–50 in M. S. Hoddle, editor. California Conference on Biological Control III, Davis, California, August 15–16, 2012. University of California, Riverside, California.

Dowell, R.V., and C. J. Krass. 1992. On the California border, exotic pests pose growing problem for California. California Agriculture 46:6–12.

Dowell, R. V., and R. Gill. 1989. Exotic invertebrates and their effects on California. Pan-Pacific Entomologist 65:132–145.

Dukes, J. S. 2002. Species composition and diversity affect grassland susceptibility and response to invasion. Ecological Applications 12:602–617.

Dukes, J. S., and H. A. Mooney. 1999. Does global change increase the success of biological invaders? Trends in Ecology and Evolution 14:135–139.

Duncan C. A., J. J. Jachetta, M. L. Brown, V. F. Carrithers, J. K. Clark, J. M. DiTomaso, R. G. Lym, K. C. McDaniel, M. J. Renz, and P. M. Rice. 2004. Assessing the economic, environmental, and societal losses from invasive plants on rangeland and wildlands. Weed Technology 18:1411–1416.

Ehrenfeld, J. G. 2003. Effects of exotic plant invasions on soil nutrient cycling processes. Ecosystems 6:503–523.

Elton, C. 1958. The ecology of invasions by animals and plants. Chapman and Hall, London, UK.

Epanchin-Niell, R. S., M. B. Hufford, C. E. Aslan, J. P. Sexton, J. D. Port, and T. M. Waring. Controlling invasive-species in complex social landscapes. Frontiers in Ecology and the Environment 8.4(2009):210–216.

Erskine Ogden, J. A., and M. Rejmánek. 2005. Recovery of native plant communities after the control of a dominant invasive plant species, *Foeniculum vulgare*: Implications for management. Biological Conservation 125(4):427–439.

Ewel, J. J., D. J. O. Dowd, J. Bergelson, C. C. Daehler, M. Carla, D. Antonio, L. D. Gomez, D. R. Gordon, R. J. Hobbs, A. Holt, K. R. Hopper, C. E. Hughes, M. LaHart, R. R. B. Leakey, W. G. Lee, L. L. Loope, D. H. Lorence, S. M. Louda, A. E. Lougo, P. B. McEvoy, D. M. Richardson, and P. M. Vitousek. 1999. Deliberate introductions of species: Research needs. BioScience 49(8):619–630.

Fenn, M. E., E. B. Allen, S. B. Weiss, S. Jovan, L. H. Geiser, G. S. Tonnesen, R. F. Johnson, L. E. Rao, B. S. Gimeno, and F. Yuan. 2010. Nitrogen critical loads and management alternatives for N-impacted ecosystems in California. Journal of Environmental Management 91:2404–2423.

Fisher, M. C., D. A. Henk, C. J. Briggs, J. S. Brownstein, L. C. Madoff, S. L. McCraw, and S. J. Gurr. 2012. Emerging fungal threats to animal, plant, and ecosystem health. Nature 484:186–194.

Fitzpatrick, B. M., J. R. Johnson, D. K. Kump, J. J. Smith, S. R. Voss, and H. B. Shaffer. 2010. Rapid spread of invasive genes into a threatened native species. Proceedings of the National Academy of Sciences 107:3606–3610.

Forstall, Richard L. 1996. Population of states and counties of the United States: 1790 to 1990. U.S. Bureau of the Census. U.S. Government Printing Office, Washington, D.C.

Frenkel, R. E. 1970. Ruderal vegetation along some California roadsides. University of California Publications in Geography 20:1–163.

Fuller, P. L. 2003. Freshwater aquatic vertebrates: Patterns and pathways. Pages 123–151 in G. M. Ruiz and J. T. Carlton, editors. Invasive species: Vectors and management strategies. Island Press, Washington, D.C.

Garbelotto, M., and D. Schmidt. 2013. Effect of phosphonate treatments for sudden oak death on tanoaks in naturally infested forests. Page 120 in S. J. Frankel, J. T. Kliejunas, K. M. Palmieri, and J. M. Alexander, technical coordinators. Proceedings of the Sudden Oak Death Fifth Science Symposium. Gen. Tech. Rep. PSW-GTR-243. U.S. Department of Agriculture, Forest Service, Pacific Southwest Research Station, Albany, California.

———. 2009. Phosphonate controls sudden oak death pathogen for up to two years. California Agriculture 63(1):10–17.

Garbelotto, M., J. Davidson, K. Ivors, P. Maloney, D. Hüberli, S. Koike, and D. Rizzo. 2003. Non-oak native plants are main hosts for sudden oak death pathogen in California. California Agriculture 57:18–23.

Garbelotto, M., P. Svihra, and D. Rizzo. 2001. New pests and diseases: Sudden oak death syndrome fells three oak species. California Agriculture 55:9–19.

Gray, A. 1879. The predominance and pertinacity of weeds. American Journal of Science and Arts 118: 161–167.

Gelbard, J. L., and S. Harrison. 2005. Invasibility of roadless grasslands: An experimental study of yellow starthistle. Ecological Applications 15:1570–1580.

Goheen, E. M., T. L. Kubisiak, and W. Zhao. 2005. The search for the origin of *Phytophthora ramorum*: A first look in Yunnan Province, People's Republic of China. Pages 113–115 in S. J. Frankel, P. J. Shea, and M. I. Haverty, technical coordinators. Gen. Tech. Rep. PSW-GTR-196. U.S. Department of Agriculture, Forest Service, Pacific Southwest Research Station, Albany, California.

Grünwald, N. J., E. M. Goss, and C. M. Press. 2008. *Phytophthora ramorum*: A pathogen with a remarkably wide host range causing sudden oak death on oaks and ramorum blight on woody ornamentals. Molecular Plant Pathology 9:729–740.

Gutierrez, A. P., L. Ponti, T. D'Oultremont, and C. K. Ellis. 2008. Climate change effects on poikilotherm tritrophic interactions. Climatic Change 87:S167–192.

Gutierrez, A. P., T. D'Oultremont, C. K. Ellis, and L. Ponti. 2006. Climatic limits of pink bollworm in Arizona and California: Effects of climate warming. Acta Oecologica 30:353–364.

Haas, S. E., M. B. Hooten, D. M. Rizzo, and R. K. Meentemeyer. 2011. Forest species diversity reduces disease risk in a generalist plant pathogen invasion. Ecology Letters 14:1108–1116.

Harris R. J, J. S. Rees, and R. J. Toft. 2002. Trials to eradicate infestation of the Argentine ant *Linepithema humile* (Hymenoptera: Formicidae) in New Zealand. Pages 67–74 in S. C. Jones, J. Zhai, and Wm. H. Robinson, editors. Proceedings of the Fourth International Conference on Urban Pests. Pocahontas Press, Blacksburg, Virginia.

Hastings, A., K. Cuddington, K. F. Davies, C. J. Dugaw, S. Elmendorf, A. Freestone, S. Harrison, M. Holland, J. Lambrinos, U. Malvadkar, B. A. Melbourne, K. Moore, C. Taylor, and D. Thomson. 2005. The spatial spread of invasions: New developments in theory and evidence. Ecology Letters 8:91–101.

Hendry, G. W. 1931. The adobe brick as a historical source: Reporting further studies in adobe brick analysis. Agricultural History 5:110–127.

Hershner, C., and K. J. Havens. 2008. Managing invasive aquatic plants in a changing system: Strategic consideration of ecosystem services. Conservation Biology 22:544–550.

Hierro, J. L., J. L. Maron, and R. M. Callaway. 2005. A biogeographical approach to plant invasions: The importance of studying exotics in their introduced and native range. Journal of Ecology 93:5–15.

Holway, D. A. 1999. Competitive mechanisms underlying the displacement of native ants by the invasive Argentine ant. Ecology 80:238–251.

———. 1995. Distribution of the Argentine ant (*Linepithema humile*) in northern California. Conservation Biology 9:1634–1637.

Holway D. A., and A. V. Suarez. 2006. Homogenization of ant communities in Mediterranean California: The effects of urbanization and invasion. Biological Conservation 127:319–326.

Huenneke, L. F., S. P. Hamburg, R. Koide, H. A. Mooney, and P. M. Vitousek. 1990. Effects of soil resources on plant invasion and community structure in Californian serpentine grassland. Ecology 71:478–491.

Huffaker, C. B., and C. E. Kennett. 1959. A ten-year study of vegetation changes associated with biological control of Klamath weed. Journal of Rangeland Management 12:69–82.

Hulvey, K., and E. S. Zavaleta. 2012. Abundance declines of a native forb have nonlinear impacts on grassland invasion resistance. Ecology 93:378–388.

Human, K. G., and D. M. Gordon. 1997. Effects of Argentine ants on invertebrate biodiversity in northern California. Conservation Biology 11:1242–1248.

Jepson, W. L. 1925. A manual of the flowering plants of California. University of California Press, Berkeley, California.

Johnson, B. M., R. Arlinghaus, and P. J. Martinez. 2009. Are we doing all we can to stem the tide of illegal fish stocking? Fisheries 34(8):389–394.

Keeley, J., and C. J. Fotheringham. 2003. Impact of past, present, and future fire regimes on North American Mediterranean shrublands. Pages 218–262 in T. Veblen, W. Baker, G. Montenegro, and T. Swetnam, editors. Fire and climatic change in temperate ecosystems of the Western Americas. SE - 8. Springer, New York, New York.

Keller, R. P., J. Geist, J. M. Jeschke, and I. Kühn. 2011. Invasive species in Europe: Ecology, status, and policy. Environmental Sciences Europe 23:23.

Kempel, A., T. Chrobock, M. Fischer, R. P. Rohr, and M. van Kleunen. 2013. Determinants of plant establishment success in a multispecies introduction experiment with native and alien species. Proceedings of the National Academy of Sciences 110:12727–32.

Koenig, W. D., L. Marcus, T. W. Scott, and J. L. Dickinson. 2007. West Nile virus and California breeding bird declines. EcoHealth 4:18–24.

Kondolf, G. 1997. PROFILE: Hungry water: Effects of dams and gravel mining on river channels. Environmental Management 21:533–551.

Kruckeberg, A. R. 1986. The stimulus of unusual geologies for plant speciation—an essay. Systematic Botany 11(3):455–463.

Kupferberg, S. J. 1997. Bullfrog (*Rana catesbeiana*) invasion of a California river: The role of larval competition. Ecology 78:1736–1751.

Laakkonen, J., R. N. Fisher, and T. J. Case. 2001. Effect of land cover, habitat fragmentation, and ant colonies on the distribution and abundance of shrews in southern California. Journal of Animal Ecology 70:776–788.

Lach, L. 2003. Invasive ants: Unwanted partners in ant-plant interactions? Annals of the Missouri Botanical Garden 90:91–108.

Lane, C. R., P. A. Beales, K. J. D. Hughes, R. L. Griffin, D. Munro, C. M. Brasier, and J. F. Webber. 2003. First outbreak of *Phytophthora ramorum* in England, on *Viburnum tinus*. Plant Pathology 52:414.

Lee, D. P. 2001. Northern pike control at Lake Davis, California. Pages 55–61 in R. Cailteux, L. DeMong, B. J. Finlayson, W. Horton, W. McClay, R. A. Schnick, and C. Thompson, editors. Rotenone in fisheries: Are the rewards worth the risk? Trends in Fisheries Science and Management. American Fisheries Society, Bethesda, Maryland.

Lee, C. E. 2002. Evolutionary genetics of invasive species. Trends in Ecology and Evolution 17:386–391.

Leprieur, F., O. Beauchard, S. Blanchet, T. Oberdorff, and S. Brosse. 2008. Fish invasions in the world's river systems: When natural processes are blurred by human activities. PLoS Biology 6:e28.

Levine J. M., M. Vilà, C. M. D'Antonio, J. S. Dukes, K. Grigulis, and S. Lavorel. 2003. Mechanisms underlying the impacts of exotic plant invasions. Proceedings of the Royal Society of London. Series B: Biological Sciences 270.1517(2003):775–781.

Lidicker, W. Z., Jr. 1991. Introduced mammals in California. Pages 263–271 in R. H. Groves and F. Di Castri, editors. Biogeography of Mediterranean invasions. Cambridge University Press, New York, New York.

Lockwood, J. L., M. F. Hoopes, and M. P. Marchetti. 2013. Invasion ecology. Second edition. Wiley-Blackwell, Hoboken, New Jersey.

Lodge, D. M., S. Williams, H. J. MacIsaac, K. R. Hayes, B. Leung, S. Reichard, R. N. Mack, P. B. Moyle, M. Smith, D. A. Andow, J. T. Carlton, and A. McMichael. 2006. Biological invasions: Recommendations for U.S. policy and management. Ecological Applications 16:2035–2054.

Lonsdale, W. M. 1999. Global patterns of plant invasions and the concept of invasibility. Ecology 80:1522–1536.

MacArthur, R. H. 1972. Geographical ecology: Patterns in the distribution of species. Harper & Row, New York, New York.

———. 1970. Species packing and competitive equilibrium for many species. Theoretical Population Biology 1:1–11.

Mack, M. C., and C. M. D'Antonio. 1998. Impacts of biological invasions on disturbance regimes. Trends in Ecology and Evolution 13:195–198.

Mack, R. N. 2003. Global plant dispersal, naturalization, and invasion: pathways, modes and circumstances. Pages 3–30 in G. M. Ruiz and J. T. Carlton, editors. Invasive species: Vectors and management strategies. Island Press, Washington, D.C.

Mack, R. N., and M. Erneberg. 2002. The United States naturalized flora: Largely the product of deliberate introductions. Annals of the Missouri Botanical Garden 89(2):176–189.

Mack, R. N., D. Simberloff, W. M. Lonsdale, H. Evans, M. Clout, and F. A. Bazzaz. 2000. Biotic invasions: Causes, epidemiology, global consequences, and control. Ecological Applications 10:689–710.

Marchetti, M. P., and P. B. Moyle. 2001. Effects of flow regime on fish assemblages in a regulated California stream. Ecological Applications 11:530–539.

Marchetti, M. P., T. Light, P. B. Moyle, and J. H. Viers. 2004. Fish invasions in California watersheds: Testing hypotheses using landscape patterns. Ecological Applications 14:1507–1525.

McPherson, B. A., S. R. Mori, D. L. Wood, M. Kelly, A. J. Storer, P. Svihra, and R. B. Standiford. 2010. Responses of oaks and tanoaks to the sudden oak death pathogen after 8y of monitoring in two coastal California forests. Forest Ecology and Management 259:2248–2255.

Metz, M. R., K. M. Frangioso, A. C. Wickland, R. K. Meentemeyer, and D. M. Rizzo. 2012. An emergent disease causes directional changes in forest species composition in coastal California. Ecosphere 3(10):art86.

Minnich, R. A. 2008. California's fading wildflowers: Lost legacy and biological invasions. University of California Press, Berkeley, California.

Mooney, H. A., S. P. Hamburg, and J. A. Drake. 1984. The invasions of plants and animals into California. Pages 250–272 in H. A. Mooney and J. A. Drake, editors. Ecology of biological invasions of North America and Hawaii. Springer-Verlag, New York, New York.

Moyle, P. B. 2002. Inland fishes of California. Second edition. University of California Press, Berkeley, California.

Moyle, P. B., and M. P. Marchetti. 2006. Predicting invasion success: Freshwater fishes in California as a model. Bioscience 56:515–524.

Moyle, P. B., J. D. Kiernan, P. K. Crain, and R. M. Quiñones. 2013. Climate change vulnerability of native and alien freshwater fishes of California: A systematic assessment approach. PLoS One. <http://journals.plos.org/plosone/article?id=10.1371/journal.pone.0063883>. Accessed February 24, 2015.

Nagle, A. M., B. A. McPherson, D. L. Wood, M. Garbelotto, and P. Bonello. 2011. Relationship between field resistance to *Phytophthora ramorum* and constitutive phenolic chemistry of coast live oak. Forest Pathology 41(6):464–469.

Orr, M. R., S. H. Seike, W. W. Benson, and D. L. Dahlsten. 2001. Host specificity of *Pseudacteon* (Diptera: Phoridae) parasitoids that attack *Linepithema* (Hymenoptera: Formicidae) in South America. Environmental Entomology 30:742–747.

Parkes, J. P., D. S. L. Ramsey, N. Macdonald, K. Walker, S. McKnight, B. S. Cohen, and S. Morrison. 2010. Rapid eradication of feral pigs (*Sus scrofa*) from Santa Cruz Island, California. Biological Conservation 143(3):634–641.

Parkinson, H., and J. Mangold. 2011. Yellow starthistle: Identification, biology, and integrated management. MT201101AG. Montana State University Extension, Bozeman, Montana.

Pedigo, L. P., and M. E. Rice. 2009. Entomology and integrated pest management. Sixth edition. Pearson Prentice Hall, Upper Saddle River, New Jersey, and Columbus, Ohio.

Perrings, C. 2011. Invasion economics. Pages 375–378 in D. Simberloff and M. Rejmánek, editors. Encyclopedia of biological invasions. University of California Press, Berkeley, California.

Perrings, C., E. Fenichel, and A. Kinzig. 2009. Globalization and invasive alien species: Trade, pests, and pathogens. Pages 42–55 in C. Perrings, H. Mooney, and M. Williamson, editors. Bioinvasions and globalization: Ecology, economics, management, and policy. Oxford University Press, Oxford, UK.

Pimentel, D., R. Zuniga, and D. Morrison. 2005. Update on the environmental and economic costs associated with alien-invasive species in the United States. Ecological Economics 52:273–288

Pitcairn, M. J., S. Schoenig, R. Yacoub, and J. Gendron. 2006. Yellow starthistle continues its spread in California. California Agriculture 60:83–90.

Poff, N. L., J. D. Olden, D. M. Merritt, and D. M. Pepin. 2007. Homogenization of regional river dynamics by dams and global biodiversity implications. Proceedings of the National Academy of Sciences 104:5732–5737.

Powell, B. E., and J. Silverman. 2010. Impact of *Linepithema humile* and *Tapinoma sessile* (Hymenoptera: Formicidae) on three natural enemies of *Aphis gossypii* (Hemiptera: Aphididae). Biological Control 54:285–291.

Preston, W. 1996. Serpent in Eden: Dispersal of foreign diseases into pre-mission California. Journal of California and Great Basin Archaeology 18:2–37.

Puth, L. M., and D. M. Post. 2005. Studying invasion: Have we missed the boat? Ecology Letters 8:715–721.

Pyke, C. R., R. Thomas, R. D. Porter, J. J. Hellmann, J. S. Dukes, D. M. Lodge, and G. Chavarria. 2008. Current practices and future opportunities for policy on climate change and invasive species. Conservation Biology 22:585–592.

Randall, J. M., M. Rejmánek, and J. C. Hunter. 1998. Characteristics of the exotic flora of California. Fremontia 26:3–12.

Raven, P. H. 1988. The California flora. Pages 109–137 in M. G. Barbour and J. Major, editors. Terrestrial vegetation of California. Second edition. California Native Plant Society, Sacramento, California.

Reinhart, K. O., and R. M. Callaway. 2006. Soil biota and invasive plants. New Phytologist 170:445–457.

Rejmánek, M. 2012. Review of The Jepson manual: Vascular plants of California. Second edition. Plant Science Bulletin 58(3):139–142.

———. 2003. The rich get richer—responses. Frontiers in Ecology and the Environment 1:122–123.

Rejmánek, M., and D. M. Richardson. 1996. What attributes make some plant species more invasive? Ecology 77:1655–1661.

Rejmánek, M., and J. Randall. 1994. Invasive alien plants in California: 1993 summary and comparison with other areas in North America. Madrono 41:161–177.

Rejmánek, M., and M. J. Pitcairn. 2002. When is eradication of exotic pest plants a realistic goal? Pages 249–253 in C. R. Veitch and M. N. Clout, editors. Turning the tide: The eradication of invasive species. IUCN SSC Invasive Species Specialist Group. IUCN, Gland, Switzerland, and Cambridge, UK.

Rejmánek, M., C. D. Thomsen, and I. D. Peters. 1991. Invasive vascular plants of California. Pages 81–101 in R. H. Groves and F. Di Castri, editors. Biogeography of Mediterrean invasions. Cambridge University Press, Cambridge, UK.

Richardson, D. M., editor. 2011. Fifty years of invasion ecology: The legacy of Charles Elton. Wiley-Blackwell, Hoboken, New Jersey.

Richardson, D. M., P. Pyšek, and J. Carlton. 2011. A compendium of essential concepts and terminology in invasion ecology. Pages 409–420 in D. M. Richardson, editor. Fifty years of invasion ecology: The legacy of Charles Elton. Wiley-Blackwell, Hoboken, New Jersey.

Richardson D. M., P. Pyšek, D. Simberloff, M. Rejmánek, and A. D. Mader. 2008. Biological invasions—the widening debate: A response to Charles Warren. Progress in Human Geography 32(2):295–298.

Richardson D. M., P. Pyšek, M. Rejmánek, M. G. Barbour, F. D. Panetta, and C. J. West. 2000. Naturalization and invasion of alien plants: Concepts and definitions. Diversity and Distributions 6:93–107.

Rizzo, D. M., and M. Garbelotto. 2003. Sudden oak death: Endangering California and Oregon forest ecosystems. Frontiers in Ecology and the Environment 1:197–204.

Rizzo, D. M., M. Garbelotto, J. M. Davidson, G. W. Slaughter, and S. T. Koike. 2002. *Phytophthora ramorum* and sudden oak death in California: I. Host relationships. Fifth Symposium on California Oak Woodlands, San Diego, California. General Technical Report PSW-GTR-184. Pacific Southwest Research Station, Forest Service, U.S. Department of Agriculture, Albany, California.

Roura-Pascual, N., A. V. Suarez, K. McNyset et al. 2006. Niche differentiation and fine-scale projections for Argentine ants based on remotely sensed data. Ecological Applications 16:1832–1841.

Sanders, N. J., N. J. Gotelli, N. E. Heller, and D. M. Gordon. 2003. Community disassembly by an invasive species. Proceedings of the National Academy of Sciences 100:2474–2477.

Schierenbeck, K. A. 2011. Hybridization and introgression. Pages 342–346 in D. Simberloff and M. Rejmánek, editors. Encyclopedia of biological invasions. University of California Press, Berkeley, California.

Schmidt, D., and M. Garbelotto. 2010. Efficacy of phosphonate treatments against sudden oak death in tanoaks. Phytopathology 100(6):S115–S115.

Schroeter, R., and P. B. Moyle. 2006. Alien fishes in California's marine environments. Pages 611–620 in L. G. Allen, D. J. Pondella II, and M. H. Horn, editors. Ecology of marine fishes: California and adjacent waters. University of California Press, Berkeley, California.

Scoles, J., J. P. Cuda, and W. A. Overholt. 2012. How scientists obtain approval to release organisms for classical biological control of invasive weeds. Technical Report ENY-828. Institute of Food and Agricultural Sciences. University of Florida, Gainesville, Florida.

Seabloom, E. W., J. W. Williams, D. Slayback, D. M. Stoms, J. H. Viers, and A. P. Dobson. 2006. Human impacts, plant invasion, and imperiled plant species in California. Ecological Applications 16:1338–1350.

Shapiro, A. M. 2002. The Californian urban butterfly fauna is dependent on alien plants. Diversity and Distributions 8:31–40.

Silverman, J., and R. J. Brightwell. 2008. The Argentine ant: Challenges in managing an invasive unicolonial pest. Annual Review of Entomology 53:231–252.

Simberloff, D. 2013. Invasive species: What everyone needs to know. Oxford University Press, New York, New York.

Simberloff, D., and P. Stiling. 1996. How risky is biological control? Ecology 77(7):1965–1974.

Simberloff, D., I. M. Parker, and P. N. Windle. 2005. Introduced species policy, management, and future research needs. Frontiers in Ecology and the Environment 3(1):12–20.

Sorte, C. J. B., A. Fuller, and M. E. S. Bracken. 2010. Impacts of a simulated heat wave on composition of a marine community. Oikos 119:1909–1918.

Sorte, C. J. B., I. Ibáñez, D. M. Blumenthal, N. A. Molinari, L. P. Miller, E. D. Grosholz, J. M. Diez, C. M. D'Antonio, J. D. Olden, S. J. Jones, and J. S. Dukes. 2013. Poised to prosper? A cross-system comparison of climate change effects on native and non-native species performance. Ecology Letters 16:261–70.

Southern California Caulerpa Action Team. 2003. *Caulerpa taxifolia* survey and identification information package. California Department of Fish and Game and NOAA Fisheries, San Diego and Long Beach, California.

Standards and Trade Development Facility. 2013. International trade and invasive alien species. <http://www.phytosanitary.info/information/international-trade-and-invasive-alien-species>. Accessed October 19, 2013.

Stein, B. A. 2002. States of the union: Ranking America's biodiversity. NatureServe, Arlington, Virginia.

Stein, B. A., L. S. Kutner, and J. S. Adams. 2000. Precious heritage: The status of biodiversity in the United States. Oxford University Press, New York, New York.

Stockwell, C. A., A. P. Hendry, and M. T. Kinnison. 2003. Contemporary evolution meets conservation biology. Trends in Ecology and Evolution 18:94–101.

Stohlgren, T. J., D. T. Barnett, and J. T. Kartesz. 2003. The rich get richer: Patterns of plant invasions in the United States. Frontiers in Ecology and the Environment 1:11–14.

Stott, P., S. Mensing, and R. Byrne. 1998. Pre-mission invasion of *Erodium cicutarium* in California. Journal of Biogeography 25:757–762.

Stromberg, M. R., and J. R. Griffin. 1996. Long-term patterns in coastal California grasslands in relation to cultivation, gophers, and grazing. Ecological Applications 6:1189–1211.

Suarez, A. V, D. A. Holway, and T. J. Case. 2001. Patterns of spread in biological invasions dominated by long-distance jump dispersal: Insights from Argentine ants. Proceedings of the National Academy of Sciences 98:1095–1100.

Suarez, A. V, D. T. Bolger, and T. J. Case. 1998. Effects of fragmentation and invasion on native ant communities in coastal southern California. Ecology 79:2041–2056.

Švihra, P., and M. Kelly. 2004. Importance of oak ambrosia beetles in predisposing coast live oak trees to wood decay. Journal of Arboriculture 30:371–375.

Syphard, A. D., V. C. Radeloff, J. E. Keeley, T. J. Hawbaker, M. K. Clayton, S. I. Stewart, and R. B. Hammer. 2007. Human influence on California fire regimes. Ecological Applications 17:1388–1402.

Tanaka, H., and B. Larson. 2006. The role of the International Plant Protection Convention in the prevention and management of invasive alien species. Pages 56–62 in F. Koike, M. N. Clout, M. Kawamichi, M. de Poorter, and K. Iwatsuki, editors. Assessment and control of biological invasion risks. IUCN, Gland, Switzerland.

Tershy, B. R., K. Shen, K. M. Newton, N. Holmes, D.A. Croll. 2015. The importance of islands for the protection of biological and linguistic diversity. Bioscience 20:1–6.

Tsutsui, N. D., and A. V. Suarez. 2003. The colony structure and population biology of invasive ants. Conservation Biology 17:48–58.

Tsutsui, N. D., A. V Suarez, D. A. Holway, and T. J. Case. 2001. Relationships among native and introduced populations of the Argentine ant (*Linepithema humile*) and the source of introduced populations. Molecular Ecology 10:2151–2161.

Tsutsui, N. D., V. Suarez, D. Holway, and T. J. Case. 2000. Reduced genetic variation and the success of an invasive species. Proceedings of the National Academy of Sciences 97:5948–5953.

University of California Integrated Pest Management (UC IPM). 2007. Biological control and natural enemies. <http://www.ipm.ucdavis.edu/PMG/PESTNOTES/pn74140.html>. Accessed October 22, 2013.

U.S. Census Bureau. 2010. State and County QuickFacts. <http://quickfacts.census.gov/qfd/>. Accessed October 21, 2013.

U.S. Fish and Wildlife Service. 2013. Invasive plants defined: What they are and what they are not. <http://www.fws.gov/invasives/volunteerstrainingmodule/bigpicture/invasives.html>. Accessed November 8, 2013.

U.S. Maritime Administration. 2009. America's ports and intermodal transportation system. Washington, D.C.

Vallano, D., P. Selmants, and E. S. Zavaleta. 2012. Simulated nitrogen deposition enhances the performance of an exotic grass relative to native serpentine grassland competitors. Plant Ecology 213:1015–1026.

Van Kleunen, M., E. Weber, and M. Fischer. 2010. A meta-analysis of trait differences between invasive and non-invasive plant species. Ecology Letters 13:235–245.

Van Vuren D., and B. E. Coblentz. 1987. Some ecological effects of feral sheep on Santa Cruz Island, California, USA. Biological Conservation 41:253–268.

Vasquez, M. E., J. Rinderneck, J. Newman, S. McMillin, B. Finlayson, A. Mekebri, D. Crane, and R. S. Tjeerdema. 2012. Rotenone formulation fate in Lake Davis following the 2007 treatment. Environmental Toxicology and Chemistry 31:1032–1041.

Vitousek, P. M. 1994. Beyond global warming: Ecology and global change. Ecology 75:1861–1876.

Vitousek, P. M., and L. R. Walker. 1987. Colonization, succession, and resource availability; ecosystem-level interactions. Pages 207–223 in A. Gray, M. Crawley, and P. J. Edwards, editors. Colonization, succession, and stability. Blackwell Scientific, Oxford, UK.

Vitousek, P. M., C. M. D'Antonio, and G. P. Asner. 2011. Invasions and ecosystems: Vulnerabilities and the contribution of new technologies. Pages 277–288 in D. M. Richardson, editor. Fifty years of invasion ecology: The legacy of Charles Elton. Wiley-Blackwell, Hoboken, New Jersey.

Vitousek, P. M., C. M. D'Antonio, L. L. Loope, M. Rejmánek, and R. Westbrooks. 1997. Introduced species: A significant component of human-caused global environmental change. New Zealand Journal of Ecology 21:1–16.

Waithman, J. 2001. Guide to hunting wild pigs in California. California Department of Fish and Wildlife. Sacramento, California.

Walters, L. J., K. R. Brown, W. T. Stam, and J. L. Olsen. 2006. E-commerce and *Caulerpa:* Unregulated dispersal of invasive species. Frontiers in Ecology and the Environment 4(2):75–79.

Weiss, S. 2001. Cars, cows, and Checkerspot butterflies: Nitrogen deposition and management of nutrient-poor grasslands for a threatened species. Conservation Biology 13:1476–1486.

Whitworth, D. L., H. R. Carter, and F. Gress. 2013. Recovery of a threatened seabird after eradication of an introduced predator: Eight years of progress for Scripps's murrelet at Anacapa Island, California. Biological Conservation 162:52–59.

Whitworth, D. L., H. R. Carter, R. J. Young, J. S. Koepke, F. Gress, and S. Fangman. 2005. Initial recovery of Xantus's murrelets following rat eradication on Anacapa Island, California. Marine Ornithology 33:131–137.

Williams, J. R. 1954. The biological control of weeds. Pages 94–98 in Report of the Sixth Commonwealth Entomological Congress, London, UK.

Williams, S. L., I. C. Davidson, J. R. Pasari, G. V. Ashton, J. T. Carlton, R. E. Crafton, R. E. Fontana, E. D. Grosholz, A. Miller, A. Whitman, G. M. Ruiz, and C. J. Zabin. 2013. Managing multiple vectors for marine invasion in an increasingly connected world. Bioscience 63: 952–966.

Williamson, M., and A. Fitter. 1996. The varying success of invaders. Ecology 77:1661–1666.

Woodworth, C. 1910. The control of the Argentine ant. University of California Agricultural Experimental Station Circulation 207:53–82.

Zavaleta, E. 2000. Valuing ecosystem services lost to *Tamarix* invasion in the United States. Pages 261–300 in H. A. Mooney and R. J. Hobbs, editors. Invasive species in a changing world. Island Press, Washington, D.C.

Zavaleta, E. S., and K. B. Hulvey. 2004. Realistic species losses disproportionately reduce resistance to biological invaders. Science 306:1175–1177.

Zavaleta, E. S., R. J. Hobbs, and H. A Mooney. 2001. Viewing invasive species removal in a whole-ecosystem context. Trends in Ecology and Evolution 16(8):454–459.

Zouhar, K. 2002. *Centaurea solstitialis.* <http://www.fs.fed.us/database/feis/plants/forb/censol/all.html>. Accessed November 8, 2013.

FOURTEEN

Climate Change Impacts

CHRISTOPHER B. FIELD, NONA R. CHIARIELLO,
and NOAH S. DIFFENBAUGH

Introduction

Throughout this volume, climate emerges as a fundamental force shaping the distribution and dynamics of every ecosystem type in California. Climate changes thus implicitly are expected to affect all of California's ecosystems, and indeed they are identified in many chapters of this book as central forces of change in the present and future. While ecosystem-specific effects and projected changes are elaborated by chapter, we provide an overview of expected climate changes and their general impacts in California. We highlight examples from throughout the state of the types of direct and indirect climate change effects that now influence biodiversity and processes within and across ecosystem types.

This chapter explores the possible trajectories and consequences of continued climate change during the coming century. Projections of future impacts depend on a variety of unknowns and assumptions, foremost what trajectory of ongoing greenhouse emissions the world pursues in the coming century. For this reason, impact projections are generally referenced to specific, future emissions scenarios that range from no mitigation (continuation of recent trends in emissions growth) to ambitious mitigation. Future impacts are almost universally far greater under scenarios of no mitigation and smaller under aggressive mitigation scenarios. However, past emissions already ensure a degree of committed climate changes that will continue to unfold over the coming centuries regardless of future emissions changes.

Climate Change in California

Since the beginning of the twentieth century, California has warmed by approximately 0.9°C, close to the global average. The pattern across most of the state was one of rapid warming from about 1910 to 1935, cooling through the 1940s and 1950s, and rapid warming since about 1970 (Kadir et al. 2013). All regions of the state have warmed, though warming over the past forty years has been smaller in the North Coast region than in the rest of the state (Kadir et al. 2013), perhaps as a result of increased persistence of summer fog in the most coastal stations (Cordero et al. 2011).

Annual average precipitation over California has not changed consistently over the past century (Kadir et al. 2013), but the warmer temperatures tend to increase the fraction of precipitation falling as rain rather than snow. This is reflected in a decreasing fraction of annual flow that occurs during the spring snowmelt season in most of the rivers that drain the Sierra Nevada range and in decreased spring snowpack in the Northern Sierra. In the Southern Sierra, where elevations are higher, spring snowpack has increased by about 10% over the past sixty years, approximately the same magnitude as the decrease in the Northern Sierra.

Sea level along much of California's coast has risen by 15 to 20 centimeters, approximately the global mean increase, over the past century. At the upper end of this range is the Golden Gate in San Francisco, which has the longest continuous sea level record for North America (Flick et al. 1999). Due to land subsidence, uplift, and other processes that change the land surface elevation, sea level change as recorded by long-term tide gauges has varied from +2.08 mm yr^{1} at La Jolla to –0.73 mm yr^{1} (decreasing sea level) at Crescent City (National Research Council 2012).

Over the twenty-first century, climate change can be characterized as falling into two eras. The next few decades will be an era of mostly committed climate changes that are largely independent of investments in mitigation, including near-term investments. During this era, mitigation will be important, but its consequences will emerge only gradually. This is largely because cumulative emissions, which control the magnitude of climate change (IPCC 2013), separate gradually over time among even sharply contrasting emissions scenarios (Figure 14.1). In the latter decades of the twenty-first century, investments in mitigation become dominant influences on climate, leading to an era of climate options. Substantial inertia in both physical and socioeconomic aspects of the climate system means that the set of achievable options in the future depends on mitigation efforts to reduce greenhouse gas emissions soon, during the era of near-term committed climate change, as well as during the era of climate options.

By midcentury (2041–2060), California will begin to emerge from the era of committed climate change, with warming in the range of 1°C to 2°C above the late twentieth century for a scenario with aggressive mitigation and warming of 2°C to 3°C for one that continues recent trends in emissions growth (Figure 14.2). By the end of the century (2081–2100), this difference is dramatic, with warming of 1°C to 2°C above the late twentieth century in a scenario with aggressive mitigation and 4°C to 5°C in a scenario that continues recent trends. For many kinds of climate change impacts, the difference between a world that is approximately 2°C warmer than in preindustrial times and one that is more than 4°C warmer is likely to be dramatic, underscoring the importance of considering a range of possible futures. Nonetheless, even with 1°C warming, the occurrence of hot extremes is projected to increase over much of California (Diffenbaugh and Ashfaq 2010, Scherer and Diffenbaugh 2014).

In contrast to the clear trends in temperatures, projected California precipitation does not change consistently. The global projections, with generally wetter polar regions and drier subtropics, especially for scenarios with large amounts of warming, place California in a zone on the border between wetter and drier. Without clear changes in projected annual precipitation, other aspects of the water cycle—including changes in snow versus rain, snowpack melting date, interannual variability and extremes—could be very important (Diffenbaugh et al. 2015). Warmer temperatures in California's future will have a range of direct impacts on California ecosystems. Some of these are described in this chapter. Many of the impacts of a changing climate will be indirect. Some of these are physical. For example, warmer temperatures in the Sierra Nevada will increase the fraction of precipitation that falls as rain, further decreasing spring snowpack and probably lengthening the period during summer when mountain ecosystems experience drought. Climate model simulations indicate that Sierra Nevada spring snowpack at the end of the twenty-first century could be in the range of 27% of current values for a scenario with little warming to 11% of current levels in a high-emissions, business-as-usual scenario (Hayhoe et al. 2004). Other examples of physical indirect effects could include changes in coastal fog (Snyder et al. 2003) and risk of wildfire (Westerling et al. 2011).

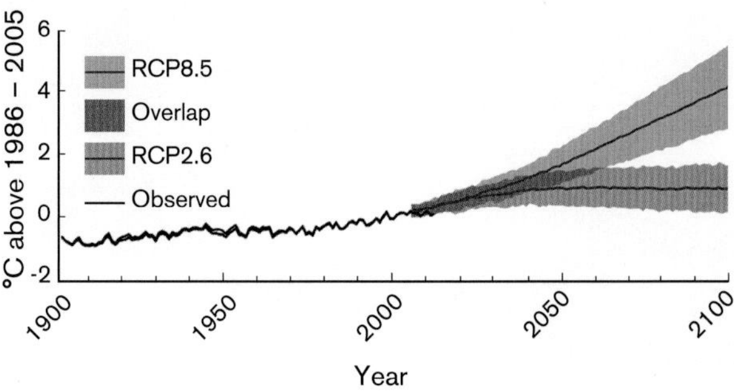

FIGURE 14.1 Time trend of observed and projected global annual temperature relative to 1986–2005. Projections and a measure of uncertainty (shading, representing ± 1.64 standard deviations) are for two scenarios or Representative Concentration Pathways (RCPs) with anthropogenic radiative forcing in year 2100 of 2.6 W m^{-2} (RCP2.6) or 8.5 W m^{-2} (RCP8.5). Projections for the two scenarios are from Phase 5 of the Coupled Model Intercomparison Project (CMIP5) of the World Climate Research Programme, representing two dozen modeling centers. Source: IPCC 2013.

Climate Change in a Multistressor Context

Another class of potential indirect effects is biologically mediated. Changes in the abundance or distribution of competitors, herbivores, pathogens, pollinators (Gilman et al. 2010, Aslan et al. 2013), and invasive species (Clements et al. 2004, Hellmann et al. 2008, Sandel and Dangremond 2012, Bellard et al. 2013) can have profound effects on the success of individual species and the functioning of ecosystems. In general, impacts of direct effects are better understood than are impacts of indirect effects, but a large body of literature documents the potential importance of indirect effects. Some of this comes from research focused on climate change. Much more comes from basic research in population, community, and ecosystem ecology.

In most parts of the world, but especially in California, climate change impacts on ecosystems occur in the context of a wide range of interacting anthropogenic impacts. The most important of these for ecosystems currently are changes in the composition of the atmosphere, extensive changes in

Photo on previous page: The south fork of the Feather River feeding Lake Oroville, a reservoir formed by the Oroville Dam, on September 5, 2014. Photo: Kelly M. Grow, California Department of Water Resources.

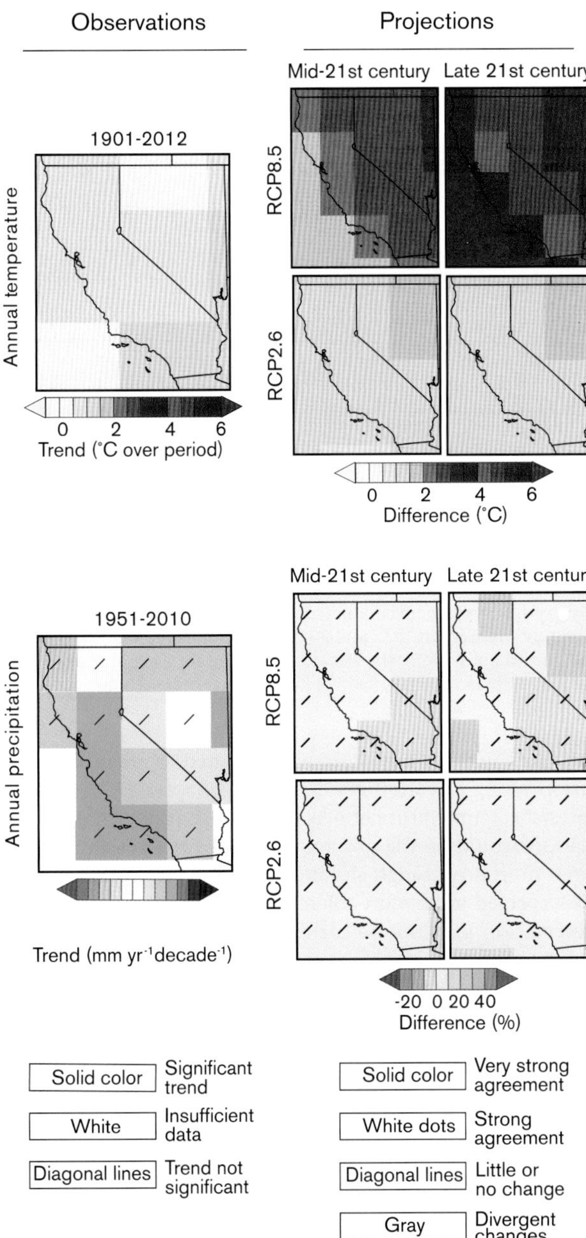

FIGURE 14.2 Observed changes in annual temperature and precipitation in California during the twentieth century and projections for the twenty-first century. Projections are for two scenarios: a low greenhouse gas emissions scenario ("peak and decline"), RCP2.6, and a high greenhouse gas emissions scenario, RCP8.5. Projections show differences in the mid-twenty-first-century period of the CMIP5 RCP8.5 model ensemble, calculated as 2046–2065 minus 1986–2005, as well as differences in the late-twenty-first-century period of the CMIP5 RCP8.5 ensemble, calculated as 2081–2100 minus 1986–2005. Colors represent multimodel means. Source: Diffenbaugh et al. 2014.

land cover and land use, and the presence of large numbers of non-native plants and animals. All these factors can have profound effects on biodiversity (Sala et al. 2000) and ecosystem function (see Chapters 11, "Biodiversity," and 15, "Introduction to Concepts of Biodiversity, Ecosystem Functioning, Ecosystem Services, and Natural Capital"). Over the next few decades, effects of these other factors may well be more important than effects of climate change (Settele et al. 2014). But over coming decades, the relative roles of direct impacts of climate change, indirect impacts of climate change, non-climate anthropogenic factors, and interactions among all of these will shift toward an increasing role for climate change, especially in a high-emissions world with large amounts of warming. The relative roles of climate change and other factors could also vary among ecosystem types.

Observed Impacts of Climate Change to Date

Climate change impacts on California ecosystems are evident from many case studies, most of which have focused on species or species ASSEMBLAGES whose historical distribution, abundance, or other properties are well documented in surveys or collections. The historical material provides baseline information for comparison with contemporary conditions. Through careful resurveys, matched as closely as possible to the original measurements and sites, these studies generally have examined ecological changes in relation to recorded climate change in circumstances where other causal explanations could be ruled out. In some cases, the ecological history is embedded in the current environment in forms such as plant architecture, tree stumps, or ocean sediment, providing site constancy and a continuous or near-continuous record of ecological change.

A study of twentieth-century climate warming and expansion of subalpine conifers in the central Sierra Nevada exemplifies this approach (Millar et al. 2004). At treeline sites across eastern Yosemite National Park and National Forest lands, KRUMMHOLZ whitebark pine (*Pinus albicaulis*) doubled its yearly branch elongation during the twentieth century and the flat-topped krummholz developed a more conical treelike form due to release of vertical branches. On north-facing slopes on the eastern slope of the Sierra Nevada, historically barren snowfields below treeline were invaded by lodgepole pine (*Pinus contorta*), western white pine (*Pinus monticola*), and whitebark pine from surrounding closed forest. Invasion of subalpine meadows by lodgepole pine changed meadows from sharply defined communities dominated by grasses, sedges, and forbs to mixed herbaceous-tree communities. All four of these trends—branch elongation, vertical branch release, snowfield invasion, and subalpine meadow invasion—were derived from field measurements and correlate with the regional minimum monthly temperature, which rose by 3.7°C during the twentieth century (Millar et al. 2004).

This study illustrates the rigor with which ecosystem change can be attributed to climate change. First, the four ecological indicators were examined in separate sites over an extensive area, yielding four independent correlations with regional temperature change. Second, the ecological responses are consistent with the role of severe climate in the spatial distribution of subalpine communities (see Chapter 28, "Subalpine Forests"). Third, other potential explanations such as land-use history and substrate type could be ruled out. Fourth, both the temperature record and the temporal detail in the ecological indicators showed a multidecadal signal that aligned with phases of the Pacific Decadal Oscillation (PDO), strengthening a climate-based explanation (Millar et al. 2004). By far the best explanation for the observed changes is that trees began to establish and change growth form in areas that previously were too cold or had snowpack for too much of the growing season.

Elevation Shifts

In mountain regions a species' distribution can be expected to shift upslope to where the amount of climate warming is compensated by the LAPSE RATE—that is, the elevation-driven temperature decrease—which on average is 6.5°C for each kilometer of elevation increase (Lundquist and Cayan 2007). By this reasoning, each 1°C of warming should lead to about 154 meters of upward shift in elevation. Initially, distributional changes might be more subtle than a range shift. One example comes from the Deep Canyon Transect, a 2,314 meter elevation gradient in the Santa Rosa Mountains that was surveyed in 1977 and again in 2007 (Kelly and Goulden 2008). Ten dominant species characterize the transect as it rises from desert scrub through pinyon-juniper woodland, chaparral shrubland, and conifer forest. Comparing the two surveys, no shifts occurred in range limits during the intervening thirty years, but for every species except desert agave (*Agave deserti*), cover increased toward the upper range limit and decreased toward the lower (Figure 14.3). In 2007 the cover-weighted distribution of each species was centered 65 meters higher on average than in 1977, an amount consistent with the lapse rate and observed increases in mean and minimum temperature (Kelly and Goulden 2008).

Lower range limits can be set by high-temperature stress or by interactions between temperature and other factors. Increased aridity is generally expected as climate warms, primarily due to greater warming of land than oceans and, consequently, greater evaporative demand (Sherwood and Fu 2014). In mountain regions this effect is compounded by reduced snowpack, which not only lengthens the snow-free season but also reduces the water bank available to meet the more prolonged and intensified evaporative demand of a warming climate.

In the Sierra Nevada, evidence is mounting that warming-mediated drought stress is pervasive in forests at lower elevations and is driving upslope retreat of ponderosa pine (*Pinus ponderosa*). Over a period of six decades, its lower range limit has moved upslope by about 180 meters, retreating from areas where monthly minimum temperatures in winter previously dropped below freezing but now stay consistently above freezing. The finding is based on a comparison between historical vegetation maps from the 1928–1940 Wieslander Vegetation Type Map (VTM) Survey and a 1996 survey by the U.S. Forest Service (Thorne et al. 2006). Although the loss of mature pines in the area of retreat was due primarily to timber harvest or other disturbances, new ponderosa pine stands failed to recruit even where fire, urbanization, and conversion to grassland could be ruled out as causal factors. Ponderosa pine forest has been replaced mostly by montane hardwood forest and annual grasslands (Thorne et al. 2006). Although there are geographic uncertainties associated with the VTM Survey (Keeley 2004, Kelly et al. 2007), the retreat of ponderosa pine is on a scale much greater than these spatial uncertainties (Kadir et al. 2013).

Mechanisms that drive plant mortality have tremendous leverage on ecosystem structure and function in a time of climate change, but they remain poorly understood (Anderegg et al. 2012). Mortality in old-growth forest stands in Sequoia and Yosemite National Parks has been analyzed with physically based models to determine whether temperature or water deficit plays a bigger role (Das et al. 2013). In low-elevation forests, mortality is best accounted for by water deficit, whereas at higher elevations, temperature alone can account. The results suggest that climate change can be viewed as

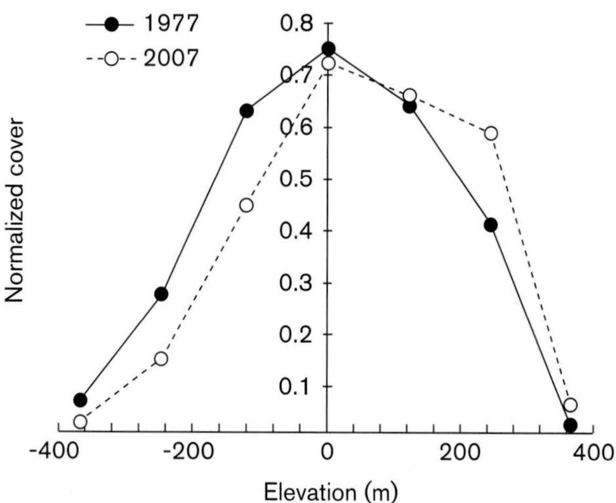

FIGURE 14.3 Asymmetrical shift to greater upslope cover of dominant plant species along the Deep Canyon Transect in southern California's Santa Rosa Mountains. Points represent the mean total normalized vegetation cover for the ten most widespread species surveyed. Surveys were conducted at fixed elevation intervals along the transect in 1977 and 2008. Elevation is referenced to the central point along the elevation gradient for each of the ten most widespread species. Source: Kelly and Goulden 2008.

shifting the transition from water-limited to energy-limited forests along elevation gradients (see Chapter 27, "Montane Forests"). Temperature effects on pathogens and insect populations could be the proximate causes for warming-driven forest mortality at high elevation (Das et al. 2013). Large trees are expected to be more tolerant of climate change, but this expectation may not be correct. In Yosemite National Park the density of large-diameter trees in plots surveyed during the 1990s was three-fourths of what the Wieslander surveys recorded in the 1930s (Lutz et al. 2009).

Sierran shifts have also occurred in butterflies and small mammals. Of twenty-eight species of small mammals surveyed by Joseph Grinnell in Yosemite National Park between 1911 and 1921, half showed an increase in the midpoint of their elevation range a century later (Moritz et al. 2008). Species at lower elevations expanded their range upward, and species of higher elevations showed an upward retreat of their lower limit (Figure 14.4). Between the two surveys, mean minimum temperature increased approximately 3°C (Moritz et al. 2008). Among 127 species of butterflies surveyed for three decades across an elevation range of 25 meters to 2,775 meters, mean elevation shifted upward by 93 meters (see Figure 14.4) (Forister et al. 2010). Extensive population surveys of Edith's checkerspot butterfly (*Euphydryas editha*) by Parmesan (1996) throughout its documented historical range found that the butterfly's range had shifted not only upward in elevation and but also northward, consistent with observed warming.

Marine Latitudinal Shifts

Sedimentary assemblages of PLANKTONIC FORAMINIFERA provide one example of climate-related latitudinal shifts in marine communities. Carried by ocean currents, these protozoans have shells (tests) that are preserved when the organisms die and sink to the seafloor. Layered sediments in the Santa Barbara Basin provide a fourteen-hundred-year record of climate-related conditions in the California Current

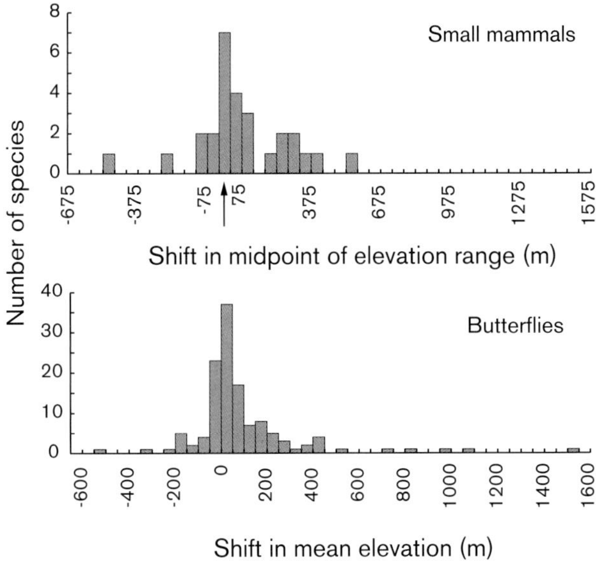

FIGURE 14.4 Histograms of elevation change for species on the west slope of the Sierra Nevada.

TOP: Shifts in the midpoint of the elevation range for 28 species of small mammals in Yosemite National Park based on a repeat of the Grinnell survey a century later. Survey sites range in elevation from 57 meters to 3871 meters. Seven species showed no change (column marked by an arrow). Source: Moritz et al. 2008, Table 1.

BOTTOM: Shifts in mean elevation for 127 species of butterflies based on surveys during 1998–2007 as compared with surveys two decades earlier. Survey sites ranged from 25 meters to 2775 meters. Source: Forister et al. 2010.

because the shells provide a timeline of species with known temperature affinity. As the ocean warmed during the twentieth century, temperate and subpolar species became less abundant in deposited sediments and tropical and subtropical species increased, forming a modern foraminiferan assemblage unlike any found earlier in the record (Field et al. 2006). North Pacific ecosystems have witnessed temperature-related changes in other sea life as well, but the sedimentary foraminifera provide a long enough time series to separate the signal of twentieth-century warming from those of natural climate oscillations.

Invertebrates of the rocky intertidal in Monterey Bay also show a northward latitudinal shift in community composition. Repetition of a 1930s survey of invertebrates, six decades later but in precisely the original plots, revealed an increase in abundance for eight of nine southern species and a decrease in five of eight northern species as shoreline ocean temperature increased by 0.75°C (Barry et al. 1995). The pattern was sustained and expanded in an enlarged survey, which also identified some southern species that were unreported in the original study, including a gastropod and the solitary form of an anemone (Sagarin et al. 1999). Natural climate oscillations occurred with similar timing relative to the studies and so could be discounted as an explanation for the changed assemblage.

Edaphic Endemics

For species that have very narrow habitat requirements, the odds of successful migration from a climatically unsuitable habitat to a better one are reduced if the habitat is discontinuous. EDAPHIC ENDEMICS are a special case because their substrates often occur as outcrops or "islands" that are small in size, with intervening substrates that disadvantage endemics in competition with soil generalists (Damschen et al. 2012). The fate of edaphically restricted species in a changing climate is especially consequential for California because its degree of edaphic specialization likely exceeds that of any other floristic province in the world (Harrison 2013).

Serpentine endemics are associated with the ultramafic rocks serpentinite and peridotite, which weather to form soils that are chemically distinctive, shallow, rocky, and less productive than more typical soils. In the context of climate change, serpentine species are a pivotal case. On the one hand, their response to climate change may serve as a general model for interactions between climate change and highly fragmented habitats. On the other hand, the ability to tolerate serpentine soils may inherently confer greater tolerance of water stress, suggesting that a warmer, drier environment might affect serpentine endemics less than it would soil-generalist species, or might even shift the competitive balance in their favor (Damschen et al. 2012).

Evidence to date on serpentine endemics conforms more to the first possibility—greater risk from climate change. In the diverse and endemically rich Klamath-Siskiyou Mountains straddling the California-Oregon border, an increase in mean summer temperature of about 2°C has affected serpentine communities even more than plant communities of more normal soils (Damschen et al. 2010). The finding is based on a repeat of a classic study in ecology, Robert Whittaker's 1949–1950 survey of the Siskiyou vegetation in relation to natural variation in soil type, elevation, and a topographic moisture gradient. In a resurvey six decades later, losses in diversity and cover occurred on both soil types but impacts were greater on serpentine soils and disproportionately affected more endemic species (Damschen et al. 2010).

Migration Timing

Migratory species depend on climate and resources across areas as large as entire hemispheres. Migration timing, such as the spring arrival of migratory songbirds, is an example of PHENOLOGY that is fundamental to species persistence. Using arrival dates recorded by long-term bird observatories and banding stations together with weather data, it is possible to ask whether arrival dates have changed, whether temperatures have changed during the arrival window, and whether any changes in arrival and temperature occur in concert. The answer to all three is yes for some species in northern and central California (MacMynowski et al. 2007). Arrival dates for ten of twenty-one songbird species have trended earlier over the past two to three decades. For eight of them, there is a significant association with temperature and with a large-scale climate index such as the El Niño-Southern Oscillation (Table 14.1). Correlations with a climate index could reflect climate changes in the wintering range or migration route (MacMynowski et al. 2007).

Collectively, these case studies form a coherent picture. The link between climate change in California and changes in the persistence, distribution, abundance, or activity of species is discernable. At the cold-limited end of their distribution, many species are expanding upward in elevation or north in latitude as climate warms. At lower elevations and lower latitudes, many species are retreating, most likely because of interactions between temperature and other factors. In many,

TABLE 14.1
Trends in spring arrival timing of migratory songbird species in central and northern California

Degree of association with climate	Arriving earlier	Arriving later	No change
Very likely climate-associated	Barn swallow Black-headed grosbeak Warbling vireo Western kingbird Wilson's warbler		
Likely climate-associated	Black-throated gray warbler Orange-crowned warbler Vaux's swift	Cliff swallow Swainson's thrush	Nashville warbler Olive-sided flycatcher Western wood-pewee
Possibly climate-associated	Lazuli bunting Northern rough-winged swallow	House wren	MacGillivray's warbler Pacific slope flycatcher
No climate association			Blue-gray gnatcatcher Western tanager Yellow warbler

SOURCE: MacMynowski et al. 2007.

if not most cases, range contractions and upslope retreat entail extinction of local populations that might be uncompensated by expansion upslope or northward, resulting in a net loss of populations. At the community level some species are responding more than others, some not at all. This could reflect differences in sensitivity to climate change or differences in response timing. In either case, differential species responses will reshape community assemblages, altering a multitude of biotic interactions. The focus on settings where climate change impacts could be evaluated in isolation from other factors can sharpen awareness of climate change but profoundly constrains a realistic picture of climate interactions that will increasingly alter ecosystems and their services and functions. Many of these case studies correlate ecological change not with mean annual temperature but with seasonal or monthly minima or maxima, consistent with the stresses that establish range limits. This adds urgency to the need for an improved understanding of the consequences of projected increases in extreme events, especially hot extremes.

Impacts of Future Climate Changes

Over the next few decades, the era of committed climate changes, the climate change impacts that California will experience will be largely independent of action to address the climate challenge, making it reasonable to pinpoint a suite of impacts. The actual trajectory of climate has some uncertainty, even over the next few decades, because of uncertainty about climate sensitivity to greenhouse gases, background variability, and changes in the frequency or severity of damaging extreme events (IPCC 2012). In the last part of the twenty-first century, the era of climate options, possible futures range from those where climate is still similar to midcentury to those where the difference from preindustrial times approaches that between GLACIALS AND INTERGLACIALS in the past (Diffenbaugh and Field 2013). For the era of climate options, it is useful to think about a broad range of possible ecosystem futures rather than about generic climate change impacts.

The situation is the same for California as for every other part of the world. A late twenty-first century with climate change stabilized at a global average warming of approximately 2°C over preindustrial levels will have ecosystems that look different and function differently from those in the world of the twentieth century. The impacts on California of climate changes to date are already widespread and consequential, and those in a 2°C world will be much larger. But a future with continuing business-as-usual emissions and global average temperatures in 2100 on the order of 4°C over preindustrial levels would be so different that the tools for projecting and describing the conditions become completely inadequate. Many studies, overviewed earlier in this chapter, address ecosystem impacts of the climate changes to date. For these, the traditional research tools of observation, analysis, modeling, and experimentation are appropriate, though with some important limitations, especially related to nonequilibrium conditions. For the +2°C world, the toolkit narrows and becomes more a sketch of possibilities than a generator of predictions. For the +4°C world, all bets are off. Many courageous investigators have conducted studies of ecosystems in +4°C worlds, and the results of those studies provide important insights. These insights need to be understood, however, as barely scratching the surface of the interacting processes that will shape the rapidly changing +4°C world.

Most of the literature on climate change and climate change impacts is not this blunt about the limitations of our knowledge. That is appropriate, because most studies are focused on identifying contributions to knowledge rather than gaps. But this is a setting where it is important that we not overinterpret based on the results available. The paucity of information about the future, especially about the +4°C world, is heavily shaped by our almost total lack of even rudimentary ability to characterize effects of exceedingly rapid temporal changes or a wide range of interacting ecological and anthropogenic effects. Is it a waste of time to even consider California ecosystems in a +4°C world? Certainly not. But we should remember that the science to date is in its infancy and could well be missing or misjudging many of the most important processes.

The Velocity of Climate Change

We usually think about the rate of climate change as the change in temperature per unit of time, typically in units of degrees per century or degrees per decade. For organisms that can make physiological adjustments (Cleland et al. 2012), for managers contemplating engineered changes in ecosystems (Hobbs et al. 2009, Suding 2011), and for organisms with short enough generation times for evolution to play a role (Parmesan 2006), degrees per unit time might be a reasonable measure. But for most organisms the challenge of adjusting to a changing climate is the challenge of moving to a new location when climate in the original habitat moves outside the acceptable range. As a starting point for understanding the challenge of moving in response to a changing climate, it is useful to think about how fast an organism would need to move to stay in its original climate. This defines a second kind of velocity of climate change, with units of distance per unit of time (Loarie et al. 2009).

The spatial velocity of climate change has been calculated two different ways (Diffenbaugh and Field 2013). One method compares climate model output for the present and future and calculates, in the modeled output, the shortest distance at some future time to a model grid cell with the same annual average temperature (or some other climate parameter). The second method starts with the modeled temperature difference but calculates the distance to a location with the original temperature based on a high-resolution view of current spatial gradients of temperature. The first (modeled trend) method (Figure 14.5) provides a coarse-grained picture that is especially meaningful over large temperature changes and distances. The second (current gradient) method captures the important role of topography but tends to be insensitive to potentially important effects like organisms becoming squeezed off the tops of mountains. For California, both approaches reveal important aspects of the challenge of moving in response to climate change.

Across most of the U.S., ISOTHERMS of temperature run basically east-west, with annual average temperature decreasing roughly 1°C per 100 kilometers northward movement. In areas with little topography, required movement velocities for staying in a climate with a constant annual average temperature are about 2 kilometers yr^{1} for a +2°C world and 4 kilometers yr^{1} for a +4°C world. In California, however, isotherms run basically north-south, with much steeper gradients (see Chapter 2, "Climate"). This reorientation of isotherms is a result partly of regional atmospheric circulation and partly of the strong effect of elevation on temperature. Roughly speaking, annual average temperature cools about 6.5°C for every 1 kilometer elevation with important local and weather-related variability (Lundquist and Cayan 2007). Because of the state's generally steep gradients in existing temperature, the velocity of climate change in California will be less than in many other regions. Especially in the Sierras, shifting roughly 300 meters higher (for a +2°C world) or 600 metes higher (for a +4°C world) over the twenty-first century might require moving only a few tens of kilometers instead of a few hundred (Figure 14.6). Because warming on land is likely to be greater than the global average warming, the necessary velocity vertically or poleward will likely be greater than what is calculated based on global mean warming.

California's topographic relief increases the probability that some species will be able to track climate change. While it is likely that many species will be able to capitalize on this topographic opportunity, many others probably will not, for four main reasons. First, maximum movement rates vary dramatically across taxa, with many rarely moving at rates as rapid as a few kilometers per decade (Settele et al. 2014). Second, many California ecosystems are structured around long-lived plants that do not reach maturity for a century or more. The concept of an ecosystem shifting is not meaningful in a time frame so compressed that the dominants do not provide the structure on which other members of the ecosystem depend. Third, the surface area in the state decreases rapidly with elevation, with suitable habitat for many species decreasing even more rapidly because the highest sites are often rocky and/or steep. Fourth, climate change might literally squeeze many species off the tops of the highest local mountains, especially in a +4°C world. The American pika (*Ochotona princeps*) is emblematic of the challenges faced by high-elevation species (Moritz et al. 2008). But in addition to the high-elevation specialists, California has many important ecosystems for which a big upward shift, especially a shift of 500 meters or more in a +4°C world, would push them either off the tops of the mountains or into a zone with little or no soil. This includes most places in the Coast Ranges, where total relief is on the order of 1,000 meters or less, as well as many iconic locations in the Sierras.

While the velocity of climate change can say a lot about the rates of movement necessary for an organism to remain in a constant climate, it does not speak directly to the question of how far a species needs to move to persist. To answer that question, one needs to consider niche breadth, especially the extent to which species can persist in warmer habitats. Niche breadth can be addressed at the scale of the species, the plant functional type, or the BIOME. Based on pollen records, vegetation changes have generally tracked rates of climate change. Many studies have addressed this for the period following the last glacial maximum (LGM) (Pitelka et al. 1997). Even when climate zones shifted over thousands of kilometers, biomes tended to keep up. Still, historical velocities of climate change, since the LGM and at other periods in the last fifty-five million years of Earth's history, have all been very slow in comparison to velocities over the past century and projected for the next (Diffenbaugh and Field 2013). In comparison to past periods at the global scale, anthropogenic warming is one to two orders of magnitude more rapid. Historical rates of range shift do not provide the necessary information to ask whether modern biomes may be able to track future changes in climate, particularly in the modern context of landscapes fragmented by human activity.

Species Ranges

A large body of work on present and potential species ranges is based on statistical approaches that define a species niche based on relationships between presence/absence observations and a number of bioclimatic variables. BIOCLIM (Booth et al. 2013) and MaxEnt (Elith et al. 2011) are widely used examples of these bioclimate envelope models (BEMs). When combined with climate model output, these models can be used to estimate the velocity of climate change, the extent of overlap between current and future suitable habitats, or change in the size of suitable area for a species. All of these metrics are relevant not only to the presence/absence of individual species but also to future biodiversity (McGill 2010) and risk of extinction (Thomas et al. 2004).

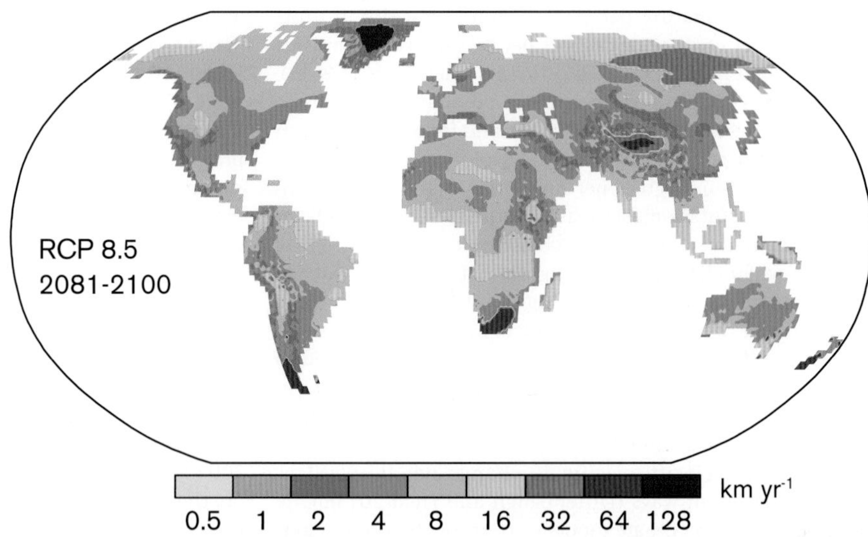

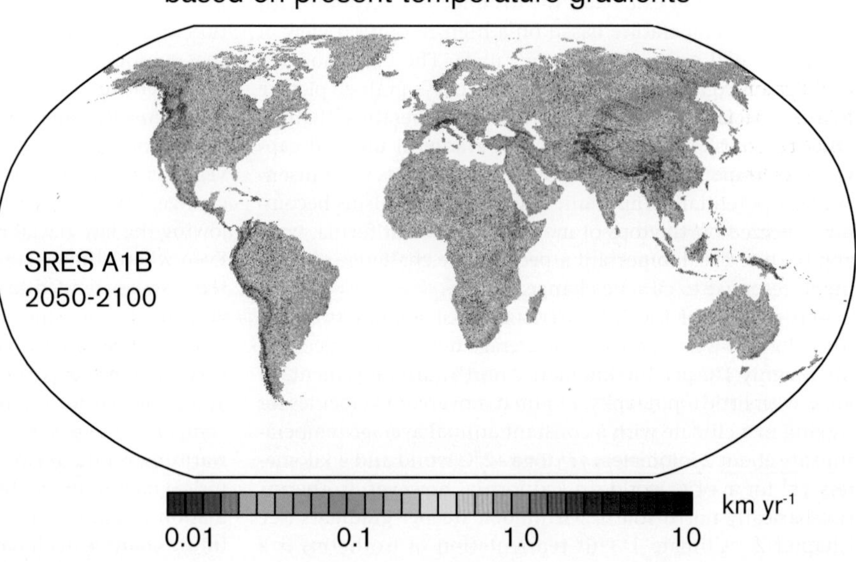

FIGURE 14.5 The velocity of climate change (km yr^{-1}) as determined by two methods. Color scales are different in the two panels.

TOP: Climate change velocity calculated by identifying for each grid point the closest location with a future annual temperature similar to the grid point's baseline annual temperature, based on the CMIP5 RCP8.5 model ensemble and accounting for baseline-period noise. Source: Diffenbaugh and Field 2013.

BOTTOM: Climate change velocity calculated from the ratio of the projected temporal gradient in temperature (from the CMIP3 ensemble in scenario A1B of the Special Report on Emissions Scenarios) and the present spatial gradient in temperature at each location, °C yr^{-1} ÷ °C km^{-1} = km yr^{-1}. Source: Loarie et al. 2009.

Loarie at al. (2008) combined climate envelope models with global climate model simulations to explore possible changes in the diversity, range size, and movement required of California endemic plants, a group that includes 2,387 taxa. Their conclusions about diversity depend critically on whether taxa can move with climate change. With a +4°C world and species that cannot move, plant biodiversity decreases by 27%. In a +2°C world where species can move, biodiversity increases, especially along the northern coasts. For all scenarios, biodiversity tends to decrease in the foothills of the southern Sierra and to increase toward the north and the coast. Changes in range size also depend on assumptions about whether species can move. In a scenario with a +4°C world and no movement, over 66% of endemics experienced range reductions of 80% or more. With the assumption that species can move, the center of the distribution shifts by an average of up to 151 kilometers, depending on the climate scenario. While most of the shifts are projected to be higher in elevation and northward, many of the range expansions are southward, reflecting the strong influence of elevation.

Biome Boundaries/Species Ranges

Modern tools for predicting biome boundaries as a function of climate trace from at least the observations of von Humboldt and Bonpland (1807), who noted consistent relationships between climate and vegetation structure, even for areas separated by large distances with vegetation of distinct evolutionary histories and in similar climates even when they occurred at different elevations. Von Humboldt's insights about rule-based biome maps directly support modern biome

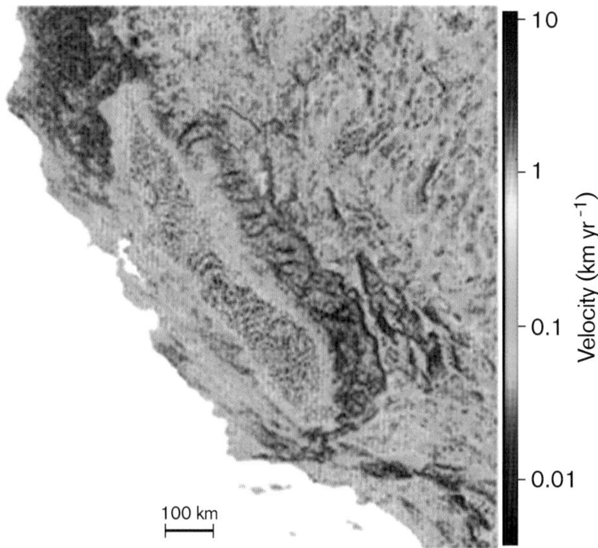

FIGURE 14.6 The velocity of climate change across California, in an enlarged view of the bottom panel of Figure 14.5. Keeping pace with changing temperature entails greater velocities in more level areas such as the Central Valley and lower velocities on mountain slopes. For this region the temporal gradient in mean annual temperature increases with distance from the coast, whereas the spatial gradient is strongly affected by topography. Source: Loarie et al. 2009.

and dynamic global vegetation models (DGVMs), which have added gradually to the core of von Humboldt's discovery. Most recent biome models add constraints based on carbon or water balance to the basic rules that set vegetation type as a function of climate. DGVMs are conceptually similar but performance is evaluated separately for several plant functional types, such that biomes are emergent results not specified in advance. All these approaches can produce reasonably accurate maps of the large-scale distribution of the world's biomes, especially for potential natural vegetation, or ecosystems not shaped by human activities.

All these approaches can also reproduce biomes of the past, especially the period since the last glacial maximum. For this period, modeled biomes can be validated by comparison with biomes reconstructed from PALYNOLOGICAL records. One consistent result from these validations is that biomes in the first few millennia following the LGM were similar to modern biomes in some respects but different in others. The biomes from the past tended to have now-absent species combinations that make them "no-analog" ecosystems in the modern biogeography (Williams and Jackson 2007). All these approaches, however, require additional information to generate reasonable biomes for some regions. The best-known example is the prairie peninsula (in the upper midwest of the U.S.), where climate conditions point to forest dominance but the pre-European vegetation was prairie. For these areas the inclusion of a process like grazing or wildfire in the model is critical for generating realistic biomes.

California biomes in a +4°C world of the late twenty-first century, simulated with the MAPSS-CENTURY 1 model (MC1), maintain surprising consistency with the present distribution (Figure 14.7). The simulation indicates substantial losses in alpine/subalpine forests, mixed evergreen woodlands, shrublands and deserts, with increases in mixed evergreen forest and grassland (Figure 14.8). The finding that high-elevation ecosystems tend to be pushed off the tops of the mountains is very widespread. It is one of the reasons that alpine habitats and species tend to be among the state's and the world's most endangered. In the simulation of Lenihan et al. (2003), the decrease in shrublands and mixed evergreen forests is compensated largely by an increase in grasslands, mainly as a consequence of greater water limitation in the coastal mountains and Sierra foothills. The replacement of conifer-dominated forest by broadleaved-dominated forest over much of the northern part of the state is a feature of the simulations with wetter climates.

MC1 simulates the locations of biomes as units, without considering the role of climate change in shaping the particular species composition. Empirical data from Kelly and Goulden (2008) indicate that this is likely not the general pattern, but that species mixtures change individualistically, with some species adjusting quickly to climate signals while other adjust slowly. Biome models that generate biomes from a mixture of plant functional types potentially have the ability to track some kinds of compositional changes, especially when these changes are regulated by environmental and not biotic controls. A few DGVMs (e.g., Moorcroft et al. 2001) simulate some aspects of biotic interactions but mainly those related to competition for light, water, and nutrients.

Interacting Factors: Climate Change as a Threat Multiplier

In general, the tools for estimating the boundaries of biomes or species distributions account for climate and atmospheric CO_2. They sometimes account for soil characteristics and atmospheric pollution. They also typically assume (1) universal availability of all potentially viable taxa, (2) lack of complication from pests and pathogens, and (3) a crisp partitioning of the landscape into human-dominated and natural units. Calibrations and validations are grounded in current or past patterns, where the role of interacting factors including other environmental changes and human impacts is either minimal or poorly known. In a world that is increasingly dominated by these interacting factors, how should approaches to defining biome or species boundaries change?

Sala et al. (2000) attempted to account for impacts on biodiversity in 2100 due to land use, atmospheric CO_2, nitrogen deposition, and biological invasions in addition to climate change. They concluded that the role of each factor varies among ecosystems, with land use the most important at the global scale. In Mediterranean-climate regions they identified land use and biotic exchange (invasions) as equally important. In general, implications of interacting factors are not accounted in projections of future biome or species distributions under climate changes. For a number of reasons, we feel that for the ecosystems of California through the twenty-first century, interacting factors are likely to be the core story and not just minor complications. We envision the process of creating new distribution boundaries as functioning like a series of environmental sieves. In the past, changes in climate were slow enough that migration distances or broken mutualistic relationships were generally not problems (see MUTUALISM). But in the future that will not be the case.

As with most processes in ecology, species responses to interacting factors will likely play out with individualistic differences among species. Some species will be relatively good at

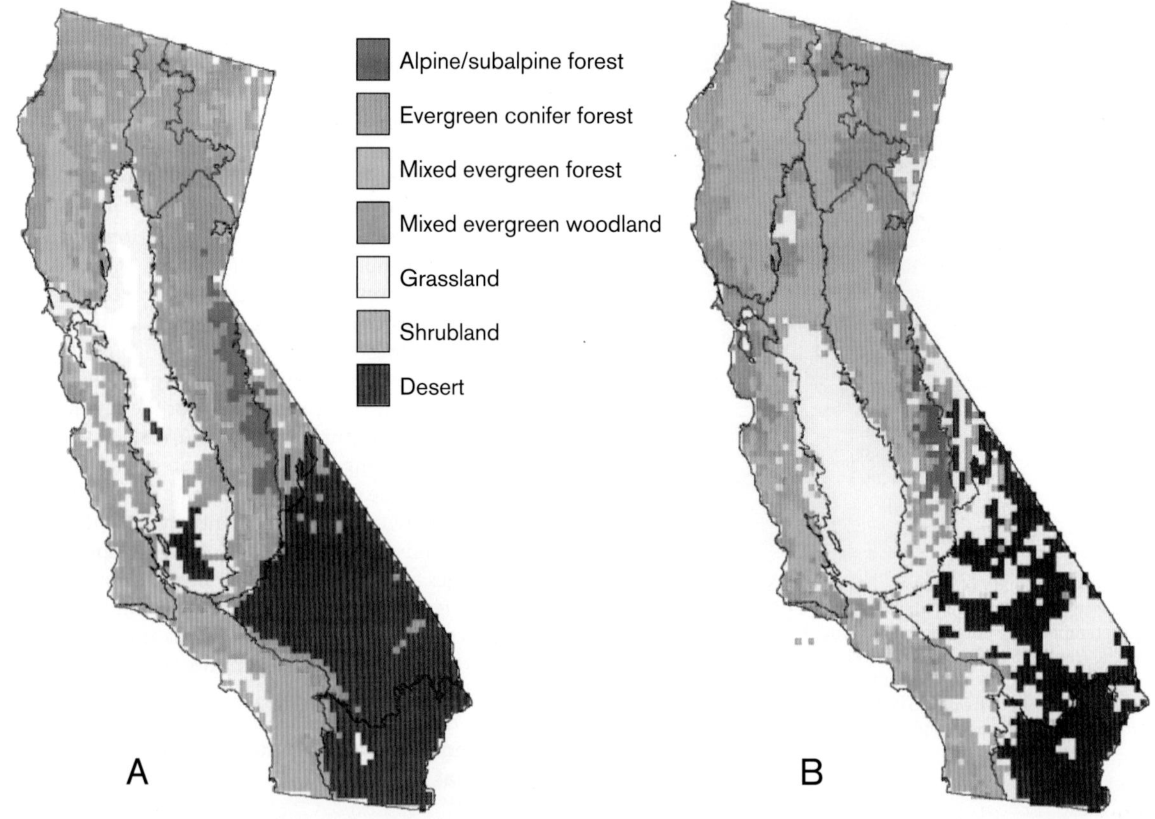

FIGURE 14.7 Vegetation distribution in California during the late twentieth century and projected for the future. Source: Lenihan et al. 2003.

A 1961–1990 baseline period map in which twenty-eight California vegetation types mapped by Küchler (1975) have been aggregated into the seven vegetation classes simulated by a dynamic vegetation model, MAPSS-CENTURY 1 (MC1).

B 2070–2099 projection for the vegetation using MC1 with the Hadley Climate Center HADCM2 climate predictions.

capitalizing on the ecological opportunities of the ANTHROPOCENE, and others will be relatively bad. In general, we anticipate that the characteristics that best suit species for success in the rapidly changing context of California's next century will be the characteristics that make plants successful as weeds. Facile long-distance dispersal, ability to colonize disturbed areas, lack of dependence on coevolved mutualists, and ability to spring back after extreme events will be the most essential characteristics of successful species. In addition, characteristics that make plants friendly to assisted management from humans might play a big role in future success.

Biotic Interactions

Biotic interactions are among the crowning glories of evolution. Natural selection has shaped myriad actors in diverse interactions that range from competition for light and water to pollination, herbivory, predation, nitrogen fixation, PATHOGENESIS, and many more. The defining feature of a biotic interaction is that more than one species is involved. In real ecosystems, biotic interactions link all species to some degree. Decreased growth in one plant might increase availability of light, facilitating growth in another. Establishment of a new disease in an insect or vertebrate predator could increase the abundance of herbivores, decreasing the abundance of their food plants. Increased temperature might stimulate biological nitrogen fixation, facilitating the invasion of more nitrogen-demanding species. These and other indirect effects might unfold over very different time periods (Van der Putten et al. 2010).

Climate change and biotic interactions is an area of expanding work on specific interactions, but the search for general principles is still in its early stages. The potential importance of understanding this area is profound, but research is challenging. Integrative studies to date have focused mainly on opening doors to understanding possibilities. For example, Aslan and colleagues (2013) combined information on at-risk vertebrates and plants pollinated or dispersed by vertebrates to estimate the global threat to plant diversity from future losses of vertebrate species. Their study, while addressing important issues, did not look at herbivory or effects of altered competition from other plants. For trout in North America, future changes in distribution appear sensitive to temperature but also to competition with other trout, changes in the flow regime, and changes in food availability (Wenger et al. 2011).

Invasive Species

Invasive species are major components of the flora and fauna of California (see Chapter 13, "Biological Invasions"). Characteristics of successful invaders have been difficult to define with any precision, but they are relatively simple to define

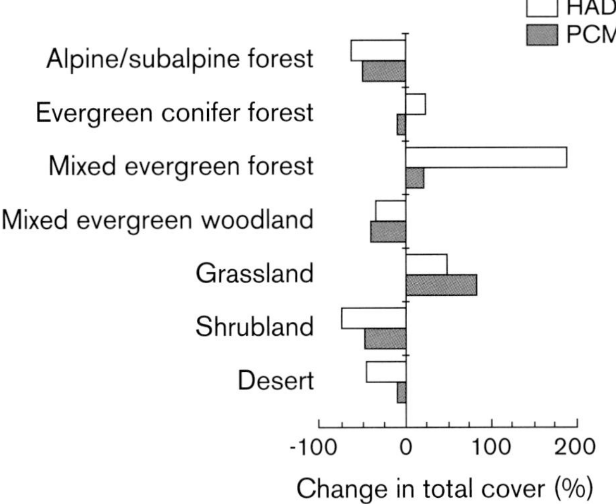

FIGURE 14.8 Comparison of percentage changes in the total cover of vegetation classes from the 1961–1990 baseline period to the 2070–2099 period as projected by the MC1 vegetation model under climate scenarios by the Hadley Climate Center HADCM2 model (HAD) and the National Center for Atmospheric Research's Parallel Climate Model (PCM). Source: Lenihan et al. 2003.

in terms of outcomes. Invaders tend to be good at getting to new locations, establishing quickly—especially in disturbed sites—and persisting in the face of environmental variation once established. Under any scenario of future climate change, California will see myriad instances of extant species stressed by novel conditions. This stress could lead to decreased vigor, decreased abundance or mortality, creating opportunities for other species. Though knowledge is far from complete, it is hard to imagine that invaders will not be common among the plants and animals most likely to capitalize on these opportunities. The juxtaposition of stress from climate change and the existence of a large pool of species good at moving to and establishing in new places seems like a recipe for creating a future "Homogenocene" (Samways 1999), with fewer and fewer species that are narrowly restricted or poor at relocating and greater abundances of generalist species that are good at moving.

Many examples document invasions mediated by climate change (Walther et al. 2009). In some examples, climate-mediated pressure to move blurs the distinction between a range shift and an invasion. In others, the winners are cosmopolitan invaders. For California, which is already so well-endowed with invaders, it will be surprising if climate change does not eventually yield ecosystems more weedy and more dominated by cosmopolitan invaders. The species that are already problem weeds are likely to be among the winners, but climate change could expand opportunities for other exotic species as well. In general, species rearrangements in a changing climate are likely to unfold like a massive game of musical chairs. When the music stops, it could be all about which species are best at scrambling for the remaining chairs.

Biodiversity

Estimating impacts of climate change on biological diversity is one of the key research challenges of the twenty-first century. The topic is central for understanding the consequences of climate change, but it is also incredibly difficult because it involves the interaction of many different kinds of factors beyond climate change, the potential for important roles of a wide suite of both direct and indirect effects, and a strong likelihood that processes will differ in importance on a range of time scales. Efforts to estimate the number or fraction of species at risk have taken a number of approaches (Bellard et al. 2012). Bioclimatic envelope models (BEMs), dynamic global vegetation models (DGVMs), and species area relationships (SARs) all define new ranges based on a new climate and work from the new ranges to estimate biodiversity. Approaches based on IUCN status or dose-response relationships attempt to characterize the level of local threat (Bellard et al. 2012). All these approaches provide important insights, but they fail to account for a broad range of potentially important factors, especially factors like the breaking of pollinator and disperser relationships (Aslan et al. 2013).

Barnosky and colleagues (2011) discuss current and potential future extinctions in the context of the five mass extinctions in Earth's history, times when the planet lost more than 75% of its species. While the list of known extinctions since the start of the anthropogenic era is still seemingly short, many species are already threatened. Comparing past mass extinctions with the cast of threatened species leads to the sobering conclusion that the loss of only species that are already "critically endangered" could make the Anthropocene a sixth mass extinction. Losses of species that are "endangered" or "vulnerable" could precipitate this outcome in only a few hundred years. None of the existing methods for estimating future changes in biodiversity produces a result that should appropriately be called a conclusion. Each method provides a way to think through the implications of a particular mechanism or set of interactions. But the actual trajectory of biodiversity will be determined by a much broader set of interacting mechanisms, with the potential for many unique aspects of each local setting. Vertical relief and REFUGIA could serve as effective buffers against biodiversity loss. Habitat destruction, air and water pollution, and large numbers of invasions could accelerate losses. The net outcome for a region like California is far from clear. Still, it is difficult not to sense the risk of a major disruption arising from these multifactor interactions. As a stress multiplier, climate change has the potential to push a challenging situation into crisis.

The temporal pattern of future changes in biodiversity is exceedingly difficult to predict. During a reshuffling, species diversity could move smoothly to a new steady state, but it could also overshoot, lag, or move initially in the opposite direction from the long-term pattern. In addition, the concept of anything approaching a steady-state could be irrelevant in the future, where changes in climate, land use, sea level, atmospheric composition, and invasions could continue well beyond the end of the twenty-first century. Even if these exogenous factors stop changing, internal ecosystem processes could lead to changes that continue to unfold over many centuries.

Managing California Ecosystems in the Changing Future

For both the era of committed climate changes and the longer-term era of climate options, climate change is a challenge of managing risks. A range of outcomes is possible, with consequences that depend on the outcome. Even for a particular mean temperature the distribution of actual conditions around that mean, including extreme events, is difficult to predict. Response uncertainties, interactions, and modulation by other anthropogenic factors all add to the range of possible ecosystem outcomes. Effective approaches to managing risks need to consider the full range of possible outcomes as well as the probability of each outcome. In general, risk scales approximately with the product of consequence and probability, meaning that a low-probability, high-consequence outcome can present risk that is comparable to a modest-probability, modest-consequence outcome.

California has warmed substantially over the past century, a period in which rapid changes in land use and other human activities were almost certainly the dominant drivers of ecosystem change. Over the twenty-first century, ongoing effects of land use change will doubtless continue to be important. If climate change is managed such that we stabilize temperatures in the range of 2°C above preindustrial levels, then climate change will have pervasive impacts on ecosystems. But there is a realistic chance that biome boundaries, biodiversity, and ecosystem function will change gradually and incrementally, likely toward a weedier world. If greenhouse gas emissions continue to grow rapidly and warming in the twenty-first century is on the order of 4°C, then the picture looks very different. The +4°C world is so far outside Earth's geologically recent, normal operating parameters that the main message from the science is that all bets are off. We could get lucky, with incremental changes, but we could also see massive, discontinuous impacts. As risk managers, avoiding this +4°C world is a top priority.

Summary

Climate change has had and will continue to have a wide range of direct and indirect effects on California's diverse ecosystems. This chapter focused on the ecological effects of climate change in the state to date and in the future. California has experienced an increase in mean annual temperature since the beginning of the twentieth century of approximately 0.9°C, close to the global average. Many cases exist of well-documented responses to this past warming. These cases most often compare current species phenologies, distributions, abundances, and physiologies with historical data. Collectively they show a discernable pattern of ecological response to climate change across the state including elevational and latitudinal shifts in terrestrial and marine environments as well as changes in migration timing, species performance, and other biotic responses. Studies of the interactions of climate change and other stressors including atmospheric and land use change and biological invasions remain relatively scarce, as do studies focused on the effects of climate extremes rather than means.

Future climate change impacts in the state depend on many unknowns, especially on what emissions trajectory the world follows in the next century. Even with ambitious MITIGATION, the world at the end of the twenty-first century will be about +2°C warmer than preindustrial levels, with widespread ecological impacts. Continuing high emissions could yield a +4°C future for California by the end of the twenty-first century. At this level, all bets are off as to how ecological systems will respond. Rates of change are one to two orders of magnitude higher than in past periods of climate change, raising the question of whether and how species can respond effectively. California's strong topographic relief and climate gradients from coast to inland mean that species can track shifting climate spaces over relatively short distances. However, varying mobility across taxa, long lags to maturity in many plants, declining available area and soil development with increasing elevation, and local limits to upslope movement such as in the Coast Ranges could all pose barriers to effective responses by native biota. Moreover, many of the species best equipped to respond rapidly to change are California's weedy invasive species, which could benefit from rapid climate changes at the expense of native biodiversity. Biodiversity changes in California in response to climate change are difficult to predict, but climate change will likely emerge as an increasingly strong threat multiplier for species already stressed by forces like land use change and invasions. The highest priority for managing risks to California's ecosystems in the long term is to reduce emissions and avoid a +4°C future.

Acknowledgments

Thanks to Mike Goulden, Anne Kelly, Ron Neilson, Terry Root, and Matthew Forister for checking our interpretation of their published datasets. Thanks to Leslie White and Geert Jan von Oldenburgh for help with Figure 14.2. We acknowledge support from the National Science Foundation program in Ecosystem Studies (Award # 0918617) and the NSF CAREER program via the Division of Atmospheric and Geospace Sciences (Award # 0955283). We acknowledge the World Climate Research Programme's Working Group on Coupled Modelling, which is responsible for CMIP, and we thank the climate modeling groups for producing and making available their model output. For CMIP the U.S. Department of Energy's Program for Climate Model Diagnosis and Intercomparison provides coordinating support and led development of software infrastructure in partnership with the Global Organization for Earth System Science Portals.

Recommended Reading

IPCC. 2014. Climate change 2014: Impacts, adaptation, and vulnerability. Contribution of Working Group II to the Fifth Assessment Report of the Intergovernmental Panel on Climate Change. Cambridge University Press, Cambridge, UK, and New York, New York.

Kadir, T., L. Mazur, C. Milanes, and K. Randles. 2013. Indicators of climate change in California. California Environmental Protection Agency, Sacramento, California. 258 pp.

National Research Council. 2010. Advancing the science of climate change. National Academies Press, Washington, D.C.

Glossary

ANTHROPOCENE A proposed term for a geological epoch extending to the present from the beginning of the period of significant human impact on the world's ecosystems.

ASSEMBLAGE A group of fossil organisms found together, indicating co-occurrence during a given period of prehistory.

BIOMES The world's major ecological communities, defined by major vegetation type (such as forest, desert) and by organismal adaptations to a particular climate and environmental setting.

EDAPHIC ENDEMIC An organism restricted in distribution to a particular, restricted soil type.

GLACIALS (VERSUS INTERGLACIALS) A geologic period of colder temperatures that alternated with warmer, or interglacial, periods during an ice age.

ISOTHERM A contour line on a map indicating areas with similar temperature.

KRUMMHOLZ Describes a stunted form of trees at high elevations exposed to strong winds and freezing temperatures.

LAPSE RATE The rate at which atmospheric temperature declines with increasing altitude.

MITIGATION Here, action to reduce the rate of increase of atmospheric greenhouse gas concentrations, through reduced emissions and/or increased sequestration of greenhouse gases.

MUTUALISM A relationship between two organisms of different species in which each benefits from the other.

PALYNOLOGICAL Based on the study of pollen or pollen records.

PATHOGENESIS The biological mechanisms underlying the development of disease.

PHENOLOGY The timing of periodic life events in organisms, such as leaf drop and budburst in deciduous trees.

PLANKTONIC FORAMINIFERA (IN SEDIMENTARY ASSEMBLAGES) Single-celled organisms in the water column belonging to a particular class, which accumulate in bottom sediments as they rain down over time.

REFUGIA A location where an isolated population of a once-widespread taxon persists.

References

Anderegg, W. R. L., J. A. Berry, and C. B. Field. 2012. Linking definitions, mechanisms, and modeling of drought-induced tree death. Trends in Plant Science 17:693–700.

Aslan, C. E., E. S. Zavaleta, B. Tershy, and D. Croll. 2013. Mutualism disruption threatens global plant biodiversity: A systematic review. PLoS ONE 8:e66993. doi.org/10.1371/journal.pone.0066993.

Barnosky, A. D., N. Matzke, S. Tomiya, G. O. Wogan, B. Swartz, T. B. Quental, C. Marshall, J. L. McGuire, E. L. Lindsey, and K. C. Maguire. 2011. Has the Earth's sixth mass extinction already arrived? Nature 471:51–57.

Barry, J. P., C. H. Baxter, R. D. Sagarin, and S. E. Gilman. 1995. Climate-related, long-term faunal changes in a California rocky intertidal community. Science 267:672–675.

Bellard, C., C. Bertelsmeier, P. Leadley, W. Thuiller, and F. Courchamp. 2012. Impacts of climate change on the future of biodiversity. Ecology Letters 15:365–377.

Bellard, C., W. Thuiller, B. Leroy, P. Genovesi, M. Bakkenes, and F. Courchamp. 2013. Will climate change promote future invasions? Global Change Biology 19:3740–3748.

Booth, T. H., H. A. Nix, J. R. Busby, and M. F. Hutchinson. 2013. BIOCLIM: The first species distribution modelling package, its early applications, and relevance to most current MaxEnt studies. Diversity and Distributions 20: 1–9.

Cleland, E. E., J. M. Allen, T. M. Crimmins, J. A. Dunne, S. Pau, S. E. Travers, E. S. Zavaleta, and E. M. Wolkovich. 2012. Phenological tracking enables positive species responses to climate change. Ecology 93:1765–1771.

Clements, D. R., A. DiTommaso, N. Jordan, B. D. Booth, J. Cardina, D. Doohan, C. L. Mohler, S. D. Murphy, and C. J. Swanton. 2004. Adaptability of plants invading North American cropland. Agriculture, ecosystems, and environment 104:379–398.

Cordero, E. C., W. Kessomkiat, J. Abatzoglou, and S. A. Mauget. 2011. The identification of distinct patterns in California temperature trends. Climatic Change 108:357–382.

Damschen, E. I., S. Harrison, D. D. Ackerly, B. M. Fernandez-Going, and B. L. Anacker. 2012. Endemic plant communities on special soils: early victims or hardy survivors of climate change? Journal of Ecology 100:1122–1130.

Damschen, E. I., S. Harrison, and J. B. Grace. 2010. Climate change effects on an endemic-rich edaphic flora: resurveying Robert H. Whittaker's Siskiyou sites (Oregon, USA). Ecology 91:3609–3619.

Das, A. J., N. L. Stephenson, A. Flint, T. Das, and P. J. van Mantgem. 2013. Climatic correlates of tree mortality in water- and energy-limited forests. PLoS One 8:e69917.

Diffenbaugh, N. S., and C. B. Field. 2013. Changes in ecologically critical terrestrial climate conditions. Science 341:486–492.

Diffenbaugh, N. S., and M. Ashfaq. 2010. Intensification of hot extremes in the United States. Geophysical Research Letters 37:doi.org/10.1029/2010GL043888.

Diffenbaugh, N. S., D. A. Stone, P. Thorne, F. Giorgi, B. C. Hewitson, R. G. Jones, and G. J. van Oldenborgh. 2014. Cross-chapter box on the regional climate summary figures. Pages 137–144 in C. B. Field, V. R. Barros, D. J. Dokken, K. J. Mach, M. D. Mastrandrea, T. E. Bilir, M. Chatterjee, K. L. Ebi, Y. O. Estrada, R. C. Genova, B. Girma, E. S., Kissel, A. N. Levy, S. MacCracken, P. R. Mastrandrea, and L. L. White, editors. Climate Change 2014: Impacts, Adaptation, and Vulnerability. Part A: Global and Sectoral Aspects. Contribution of Working Group II to the Fifth Assessment Report of the Intergovernmental Panel on Climate Change. Cambridge University Press, Cambridge, UK.

Diffenbaugh, N. S., D. L. Swain, and D. Touma. 2015. Anthropogenic warming has increased drought risk in California. Proceedings of the National Academy of Sciences 112:3931–3936.

Elith, J., S. J. Phillips, T. Hastie, M. Dudík, Y. E. Chee, and C. J. Yates. 2011. A statistical explanation of MaxEnt for ecologists. Diversity and Distributions 17:43–57.

Field, D. B., T. R. Baumgartner, C. D. Charles, V. Ferreira-Bartrina, and M. D. Ohman. 2006. Planktonic foraminifera of the California Current reflect twentieth-century warming. Science 311:63–66.

Flick, R. E., J. F. Murray, L. Ewing, and C. C. Commission. 1999. Trends in US tidal datum statistics and tide range: A data report atlas. Center for Coastal Studies, Scripps Institution of Oceanography, La Jolla, California. 214 pp.

Forister, M. L., A. C. McCall, N. J. Sanders, J. A. Fordyce, J. H. Thorne, J. O'Brien, D. P. Waetjen, and A. M. Shapiro. 2010. Compounded effects of climate change and habitat alteration shift patterns of butterfly diversity. Proceedings of the National Academy of Sciences of the United States of America 107:2088–2092.

Gilman, S. E., M. C. Urban, J. Tewksbury, G. W. Gilchrist, and R. D. Holt. 2010. A framework for community interactions under climate change. Trends in Ecology and Evolution 25:325–331.

Harrison, S. 2013. Plant and Animal Endemism in California. University of California Press, Berkeley, California.

Hayhoe, K., D. Cayan, C. B. Field, P. C. Frumhoff, E. P. Maurer, N. L. Miller, S. C. Moser, S. H. Schneider, K. N. Cahill, E. E. Cleland, L. Dale, R. Drapek, R. M. Hanemann, L. S. Kalkstein, J. Lenihan, C. K. Lunch, R. P. Neilson, S. C. Sheridan, and J. H. Verville. 2004. Emissions pathways, climate change, and impacts on California. Proceedings of the National Academy of Sciences of the United States of America 101:12422–12427.

Hellmann, J. J., J. E. Byers, B. G. Bierwagen, and J. S. Dukes. 2008. Five potential consequences of climate change for invasive species. Conservation Biology 22:534–543.

Hobbs, R. J., E. Higgs, and J. A. Harris. 2009. Novel ecosystems: Implications for conservation and restoration. Trends in Ecology and Evolution 24:599–605.

IPCC. 2013. Climate Change 2013: The physical science basis. Contribution of Working Group I to the Fifth Assessment Report of the Intergovernmental Panel on Climate Change. Cambridge University Press, Cambridge, UK, and New York, New York.

———. 2012. Managing the risks of extreme events and disasters to advance climate change adaptation. Cambridge University Press, Cambridge, UK, and New York, New York.

Kadir, T., L. Mazur, C. Milanes, and K. Randles. 2013. Indicators of climate change in California, August 2013. California Environmental Protection Agency, Sacramento, California.

Keeley, J. E. 2004. VTM plots as evidence of historical change: Goldmine or landmine? Madrono 51:372–378.

Kelly, A., and M. Goulden. 2008. Rapid shifts in plant distribution with recent climate change. Proceedings of the National Academy of Sciences 105:11823–11826.

Kelly, M., K.-i. Ueda, and B. Allen-Diaz. 2007. Considerations for ecological reconstruction of historic vegetation: Analysis of the spatial uncertainties in the California Vegetation Type Map dataset. Plant Ecology 194:37–49.
Küchler, A. W. 1975. Potential natural vegetation of the United States. Second edition. American Geographic Society, New York, New York.
Lenihan, J. M., R. Drapek, D. Bachelet, and R. P. Neilson. 2003. Climate change effects on vegetation distribution, carbon, and fire in California. Ecological Applications 13:1667–1681.
Loarie, S. R., B. E. Carter, K. Hayhoe, S. McMahon, R. Moe, C. A. Knight, and D. D. Ackerly. 2008. Climate change and the future of California's endemic flora. PLoS ONE 3:e2502.
Loarie, S. R., P. B. Duffy, H. Hamilton, G. P. Asner, C. B. Field, and D. D. Ackerly. 2009. The velocity of climate change. Nature 462:1052–1055.
Lundquist, J. D., and D. R. Cayan. 2007. Surface temperature patterns in complex terrain: Daily variations and long-term change in the central Sierra Nevada, California. Journal of Geophysical Research 112:D11124. online: doi:10.1029/2006JD007561
Lutz, J. A., J. W. van Wagtendonk, and J. F. Franklin. 2009. Twentieth-century decline of large-diameter trees in Yosemite National Park, California, USA. Forest Ecology and Management 257:2296–2307.
MacMynowski, D. P., T. L. Root, G. Ballard, and G. R. Geupel. 2007. Changes in spring arrival of Nearctic-Neotropical migrants attributed to multiscalar climate. Global Change Biology 13:2239–2251.
McGill, B. J. 2010. Towards a unification of unified theories of biodiversity. Ecology Letters 13:627–642.
Millar, C. I., R. D. Westfall, D. L. Delany, J. C. King, and L. J. Graumlich. 2004. Response of subalpine conifers in the Sierra Nevada, California, USA, to 20thcentury warming and decadal climate variability. Arctic, Antarctic, and Alpine Research 36:181–200.
Moorcroft, P., G. Hurtt, and S. Pacala. 2001. A method for scaling vegetation dynamics: The ecosystem demography model (ED). Ecological Monographs 71:557–586.
Moritz, C., J. L. Patton, C. J. Conroy, J. L. Parra, G. C. White, and S. R. Beissinger. 2008. Impact of a century of climate change on small-mammal communities in Yosemite National Park, USA. Science 322:261–264.
National Research Council. 2012. Sea-Level Rise for the Coasts of California, Oregon, and Washington: Past, Present, and Future National Academies Press, Washington, D.C. 200 pp.
Parmesan, C. 1996. Cimate and species' range. Nature 382:765–766.
Parmesan, C. 2006. Ecological and evolutionary responses to recent climate change. Annual Review of Ecology Evolution and Systematics 37:637–669.
Pitelka, L. F., R. H. Gardner, J. Ash, S. Berry, H. Gitay, I. R. Noble, A. Saunders, R. H. W. Bradshaw, L. Brubaker, J. S. Clark, and M. B. Davis. 1997. Plant migration and climate-change. American Scientist 85:464–473.
Sagarin, R. D., J. P. Barry, S. E. Gilman, and C. H. Baxter. 1999. Climaterelated change in an intertidal community over short and long time scales. Ecological Monographs 69:465–490.
Sala, O. E., F. S. Chapin III, J. J. Armesto, E. Berlow, J. Bloomfield, R. Dirzo, E. Huber-Sanwald, L. F. Huenneke, R. B. Jackson, A. Kinzig, R. Leemans, D. M. Lodge, H. A. Mooney, M. Oesterheld, N. L. Poff, M. T. Sykes, B. H.Walker, M. Walker, and D. H. Wall. 2000. Global biodiversity scenarios for the year 2100. Science 287:1770–1774.
Samways, M. J. 1999. Translocating fauna to foreign lands: Here comes the Homogenocene. Journal of Insect Conservation 3:65–66.
Sandel, B., and E. M. Dangremond. 2012. Climate change and the invasion of California by grasses. Global Change Biology 18:277–289.
Scherer, M., and N. S. Diffenbaugh. 2014. Transient twenty-first century changes in daily-scale temperature extremes in the United States. Climate dynamics 42:1383–1404.
Settele, J., R. Scholes, R. Betts, S. Bunn, P. Leadley, D. Nepstad, J. T. Overpeck, and M. A. Taboada, 2014: Terrestrial and inland water systems. Pages 271–359 in C. B. Field, V. R. Barros, D. J. Dokken, K. J. Mach, M. D. Mastrandrea, T. E. Bilir, M. Chatterjee, K. L. Ebi, Y. O. Estrada, R. C. Genova, B. Girma, E. S. Kissel, A. N. Levy, S. MacCracken, P. R. Mastrandrea, and L. L. White, editors. Climate Change 2014: Impacts, Adaptation, and Vulnerability. Part A: Global and Sectoral Aspects. Contribution of Working Group II to the Fifth Assessment Report of the Intergovernmental Panel on Climate Change Cambridge University Press, Cambridge, UK.
Sherwood, S., and Q. Fu. 2014. A drier future? Science 343:737–739.
Snyder, M. A., L. C. Sloan, N. S. Diffenbaugh, and J. L. Bell. 2003. Future climate change and upwelling in the California Current. Geophysical Research Letters 30:1823.
Suding, K. N. 2011. Toward an era of restoration in ecology: Successes, failures, and opportunities ahead. Annual Review of Ecology, Evolution, and Systematics 42:465–487.
Thomas, C. D., A. Cameron, R. E. Green, M. Bakkenes, L. J. Beaumont, Y. C. Collingham, B. F. N. Erasmus, M. F. d. Siqueira, A. Grainger, L. Hannah, L. Hughes, B. Huntley, A. S. v. Jaarsveld, G. F. Midgley, L. Miles, M. A. Ortega-Huerta, A. T. Peterson, O. L. Phillips, and S. E. Williams. 2004. Extinction risk from climate change. Nature 427:145–148.
Thorne, J. H., R. Kelsey, J. Honig, and B. Morgan. 2006. The development of seventy-year-old Wieslander Vegetation Type maps and an assessment of landscape change in the central Sierra Nevada. PIER Energy-Related Environmental Program. California Energy Commission. CEC-500-2006-10.
Van der Putten, W. H., M. Macel, and M. E. Visser. 2010. Predicting species distribution and abundance responses to climate change: Why it is essential to include biotic interactions across trophic levels. Philosophical Transactions of the Royal Society B: Biological Sciences 365:2025–2034.
von Humboldt, A., and A. Bonpland. 1807. Essay on the geography of plants. University of Chicago Press, Chicago, Illinois.
Walther, G.-R., A. Roques, P. E. Hulme, M. T. Sykes, P. Pyšek, I. Kühn, M. Zobel, S. Bacher, Z. Botta-Dukát, H. Bugmann, B. Czúcz, J. Dauber, T. Hickler, V. Jarošík, M. Kenis, S. Klotz, D. Minchin, M. Moora, W. Nentwig, J. Ott, V. E. Panov, B. Reineking, C. Robinet, V. Semenchenko, W. Solarz, W. Thuiller, M. Vilà, K. Vohland, and J. Settele. 2009. Alien species in a warmer world: Risks and opportunities. Trends in Ecology and Evolution 24:686–693.
Wenger, S. J., D. J. Isaak, C. H. Luce, H. M. Neville, K. D. Fausch, J. B. Dunham, D. C. Dauwalter, M. K. Young, M. M. Elsner, B. E. Rieman, A. F. Hamlet, and J. E. Williams. 2011. Flow regime, temperature, and biotic interactions drive differential declines of trout species under climate change. Proceedings of the National Academy of Sciences 108:14175–14180.
Westerling, A. L., B. P. Bryant, H. K. Preisler, T. P. Holmes, H. G. Hidalgo, T. Das, and S. R. Shrestha. 2011. Climate change and growth scenarios for California wildfire. Climatic Change 109:445–463.
Williams, J. W., and S. T. Jackson. 2007. Novel climates, no-analog communities, and ecological surprises. Frontiers in Ecology and the Environment 5:475–482.

FIFTEEN

Introduction to Concepts of Biodiversity, Ecosystem Functioning, Ecosystem Services, and Natural Capital

REBECCA CHAPLIN-KRAMER, LISA MANDLE, ELIZABETH RAUER, and SUZANNE LANGRIDGE

Introduction

Ecosystems, the diversity of life within them, and their basic ecological processes support and enhance human life. We explore the relationship between humans and nature from basic principles of the ecology underlying that relationship to their implications for societal decisions. We hope this chapter provides the reader with a sense of the interconnectedness between human and natural systems, and of why it is important to understand nature's benefits to people from a variety of angles.

Biodiversity: The Variety of Life on Earth

Facets of Biodiversity

Biological diversity—or biodiversity—is the variety of life across all ecological levels, from genes to species to ecosystems. Biodiversity includes everything from the vast array of life on land and in the seas to the foods we eat and the landscapes in which we live and visit. With so many dimensions to biodiversity (see, for example, Gaston 1996, Wilson 2010), scientists have recognized several aspects, including taxonomic, genetic, phylogenetic, and functional diversity. The spatial partitioning of diversity across heterogeneous landscapes is another important dimension of biodiversity.

SPECIES RICHNESS, a simple measure of the number of species in a given area, is one of the most common metrics for biodiversity, and part of the basis for the biodiversity hotspot concept that highlights highly altered regions with the highest numbers of unique species (Myers et al. 2000). Species richness provides one measure of taxonomic diversity, or the diversity of taxonomic units, which can also include genera, families, and orders. A variety of diversity indices have been developed to incorporate the numbers of species as well as their relative abundances within a community, in order to differentiate between communities with the same number of species but differences across dominance or evenness of the species within them. However, despite its ease of application, taxonomic diversity alone provides an incomplete picture of the multidimensional nature of the world's biodiversity.

Genetic diversity, the genetic variation within and between species, is critical to a species' ability to withstand and adapt to change and thus underpins all other forms of biodiversity. Species with low genetic diversity may have greater vulnerability to parasites and infectious diseases (O'Brien and Evermann 1988), and low adaptive potential, which means greater vulnerability to a changing environment. The California condor (*Gymnogyps californianus*) was reduced to fewer than twenty-five individuals left in the wild, mainly due to habitat loss and poisoning (Kiff et al. 1996). Today, nearly four hundred condors exist, with over two hundred in the wild (California Condor Recovery Program 2013). However, because they all descended from the same small group of individuals, genetic diversity is low, contributing to the continued threat of extinction for this species (Ralls and Ballou 2004).

Phylogenetic diversity is a measure of the difference in evolutionary history across species. Phylogenetic diversity is often used in cases where taxonomic units are not well-defined or described, such as in the case of bacteria. However, even where taxonomic diversity is easy to measure, phylogenetic diversity can provide additional useful information. Measures of species diversity treat any two species as equally different from each other, while phylogenetic diversity provides a measure of the evolutionary distance between species. A correlation between species diversity and phylogenetic diversity has been demonstrated across California grassland plant communities, but a particular community's rank in diversity depends on which characteristic is used (Cadotte et al. 2010). The difference between phylogenetic and genetic diversity is that phylogenetic diversity excludes shared genetic differences among species. Phylogenetic diversity therefore emphasizes clades and species that have relatively more unique diversity and underemphasizes species in clades that are species rich and radiating rapidly. These differing definitions of biodiversity have important implications for priority-setting in conservation and the designation of protected areas (Devictor et al. 2010).

Functional diversity is the range of functional traits, characteristics that influence ecological functions, and processes present in a system. Functional traits of an organism can include everything from seed or egg size, to metabolic and photosynthetic rates, to trophic level (e.g., McGill et al. 2006). Functional traits are often divided into two categories: effect traits, which determine an organism's effect on ecosystem processes such as nutrient cycling, and response traits, which govern an organism's response to environmental conditions, such as resource availability or disturbance (Lavorel and Garnier 2002). Some traits, such as an animal's body size or a plant's leaf nitrogen content, may relate to both an organism's effect on and response to its environment. Ultimately, an ecosystem's response to environmental change will be influenced by how the composition of the ecological community responds to change and what the effect of the resulting community is on ecological processes.

Photo on previous page: Laguna Creek, California wetland in first light. Coastal marshes like this one can protect surrounding areas from flooding and erosion caused by storm surge and act as filters of agricultural and industrial run-off to the sea, securing and enhancing services like recreation and fishing provided by healthy coastal habitats. California's size and diversity of ecosystems allow the provisioning of many different ecosystem services, including the supply and purification of water from the mountains to cities downstream, forest carbon sequestration and timber production, a wide array of agricultural systems and the services like pollination and pest control that support them, and myriad recreational opportunities. Photo by Ed Dickie.

Some conservation efforts have undergone a recent shift in focus from taxonomic diversity towards functional diversity, in part because functional diversity can provide a mechanistic link between biodiversity and ecological processes (Cadotte et al. 2011). There is frequently a lack of correspondence between changes in functional diversity and changes in species richness, as drivers of environmental change can affect the two different aspects of biodiversity independently (Mayfield et al. 2010). However, a continuing practical challenge when measuring functional diversity is identifying the functional traits that are truly important to ecological processes. Phylogenetic diversity is sometimes assumed to be a proxy for functional diversity and can potentially be a better predictor of ecosystem function than metrics of functional diversity, because it may capture variation in traits that has not yet been recognized or measured (Cadotte et al. 2009). On the other hand, phylogenetic distances are not always well correlated with functional differences, so reductions in phylogenetic diversity may underestimate losses in functional diversity (Prinzing et al. 2008, Fritz and Purvis 2010).

Another important aspect of biodiversity is its spatial partitioning across the landscape (see, for example, Magurran 1988). The diversity found in a particular ecosystem—which can be quantified in terms of species richness, functional diversity, or any of the other previously described measures of diversity—is called alpha diversity. Landscapes can include a diversity of ecosystem types or habitats, and the total species diversity found across this larger region is referred to as GAMMA DIVERSITY. Beta diversity is the difference in composition across ecosystems within a region and provides the link between alpha diversity at the local and gamma diversity at the regional scale. Landscapes with high turnover in species composition or diversity across ecosystem types have high levels of beta diversity, while more homogeneous landscapes have low beta diversity.

Levels and Losses of Biodiversity

Taxonomists have already identified nearly two million species (Chapman 2009), but we know this represents only a fraction of the total biodiversity on the planet. There are substantial biases in the kinds of organisms that have been cataloged so far; conspicuous and easily accessible organisms like mammals and plants are far better studied and understood than those that are harder to see and find, such as fungi, insects, and other invertebrates (Scheffers et al. 2012). The rate of discovery of new species remains high, at approximately 15,000 species per year (May 2011). Recent estimates of global biodiversity suggest that the planet currently supports 5 million to 10 million eukaryotic species (Mora et al. 2011), although the figure could be substantially higher.

Within the United States, California leads in species richness, with more than 5,500 vascular plant, vertebrate animal, and freshwater mussel and crayfish species (Stein et al. 2000). Other taxa such as insects, ferns, or fungi have not been cataloged thoroughly enough to allow for a comparison across states. California also leads in number of species unique to this state, with 1,500 endemic species described. As of 2013, 281 plant and 157 animal species were state or federally listed as rare, threatened, or endangered in California (CDFW 2013a, 2013b). By one estimate, 78% of California's 129 native freshwater fishes are at risk of becoming extinct, with 5% (7 species) already extinct (Moyle et al. 2011).

Why is the risk of species extinctions of such concern? The fossil record makes clear that extinction is a natural process that has been occurring since long before humans arrived on the scene. Today's rates of extinction, however, are a hundred to a thousand times higher than background natural rates (Millennium Ecosystem Assessment 2005). At five previous times in geologic history, more than 75% of species in existence went extinct (Jablonski 1994)—these have been dubbed the "Big Five" mass extinction events. By some estimates, current rates of extinction are at the extreme high end of the range of extinction rates in the "Big Five" (Barnosky et al. 2011). If the present pace of extinction continues, we could reach a sixth mass extinction event in the coming centuries. Even before species become globally extinct, their disappearance locally can have important consequences for ecosystem processes and the ecosystem services that are critical to our own well-being. The consequences of biodiversity loss for ecosystem functioning—both generally and within California—are explored next, while further discussions of biodiversity loss and its relationship to other forms of environmental change in California's ecosystems can be found in other chapters in this volume.

Ecosystem Functions

Introduction to Ecosystem Ecology

Ecosystem structure is the temporal and spatial patterns in the diversity and composition of the elements (both living organisms and abiotic environment) of an ecosystem and the relationships between them (Odum 1971). This structure influences and is influenced by individual species traits such as resource use, trophic dynamics, and contribution to disturbance (Chapin et al. 1997) and can also be described by each species' relative contribution to ecosystem function (Balvanera et al. 2005). The relationship between ecosystem structure and function is thus complex and bidirectional, with functional processes feeding back onto the structural elements of an ecosystem, but ecosystem function itself is determined by the identity, relative abundance, diversity of and relationships between the species that comprise the ecosystem. Ecosystem functions are ecological processes, such as primary production, nutrient cycling, and decomposition, that control the flows of energy, nutrients, and organic matter through an environment (Cardinale et al. 2012). While ecosystem function has also been used to refer to the subset of ecological processes that can directly or indirectly fulfill human needs (De Groot 1987, De Groot et al. 2002), we use the more encompassing definition to differentiate between ecosystem functions and ecosystem services.

Biodiversity and Ecosystem Functions

Determining how biodiversity affects ecosystem functions is critical to understanding the consequences of local and global species extinctions for humanity. The relationship between biodiversity and ecosystem functions emerged as a focus of ecological inquiry in the 1990s, but it is only within the past decade that enough information has been amassed to begin to determine general relationships between biodiversity and ecosystem function (Hooper et al. 2005, Balvanera et al. 2006, Cardinale et al. 2012, Naeem et al. 2012). To date, our understanding of the biodiversity-ecosystem function relationship comes primarily from studies in temperate grassland systems, as the relatively short lifespans of the plants and the moderate levels of diversity found at small scales make these systems particularly suitable for experimental studies. Several well-studied California ecosystems have contributed to this understanding, particularly the state's serpentine grasslands and annual-dominated grasslands (Hooper and Vitousek 1997, Dukes 2001, Lyons and Schwartz 2001, Zavaleta and Hulvey 2004, Selmants et al. 2012). California's kelp forests and rocky intertidal zones have also provided a model system for deepening our understanding of the role of biodiversity in the marine realm (Dayton and Tegner 1992, Sala and Knowlton 2006).

In experimental studies, increasing species richness generally increases several key ecosystem functions, including biomass production, resource capture, and nutrient cycling efficiency (Cardinale et al. 2012). The mechanisms by which this occurs have been termed the "selection effect" and "complementarity effect" (Loreau and Hector 2001). The selection effect occurs when the species pool from which communities are assembled contains some species that outperform others in terms of a particular ecosystem function. When communities are assembled by randomly drawing species from a pool, the more species that are included in the community, the higher the likelihood that the community will contain and become dominated by a top performer, resulting in a positive biodiversity-ecosystem function relationship. The complementarity effect can produce the same pattern through an entirely different process. When species in a community facilitate each other or draw on different resources, this complementarity among species can lead species-rich communities to outperform species-poor communities. Both the selection effect and complementarity effect contribute to the observed increases in ecosystem functioning with increasing biodiversity.

Biodiversity also promotes the stability and RESILIENCE of ecosystem functions in the face of environmental change in both terrestrial and aquatic systems (Cardinale et al. 2012, 2013). For example, in California's Sierra Nevada, conifer forests show greater resilience to drought with increasing species richness, returning more quickly to pre-drought levels of stand productivity (DeClerck et al. 2006). Variation in the magnitude and timing of individual species' responses to environmental change can promote stability of community- and ecosystem-level properties. Ecological theory points to a number of possible mechanisms at the root of this pattern. Statistical averaging, also called PORTFOLIO EFFECT, results increased stability with increasing diversity when fluctuations in species abundances through time are not perfectly correlated (Doak et al. 1998). Stability can also result from compensatory dynamics, which occurs when declines in abundance of some species are coupled with increases in other functionally similar species, such as through competitive release (Tilman 1996). As communities increase in diversity, there is a greater likelihood that sets of functionally similar species will be present. OVERYIELDING is a third mechanism that can increase stability. When complementarity among species increases a community property such as biomass, the relative amount of variation in the system decreases, leading to greater stability with higher diversity (Lehman and Tilman 2000). More research is needed to understand the relative importance of these mechanisms (Cardinale et al. 2012).

The positive relationship between levels of biodiversity and

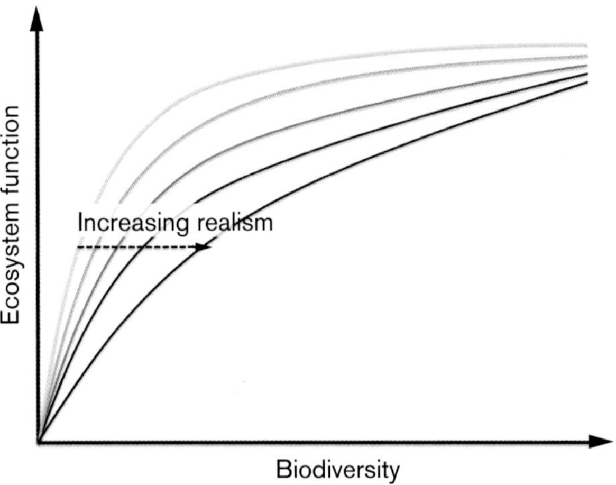

FIGURE 15.1 Ecosystem function (e.g., net primary production, nutrient cycling, decomposition) typically increases with biodiversity (e.g., species richness, number of functional types) in a saturating relationship, where at a certain point additional biodiversity does not continue to increased ecosystem function. The saturation point depends on the level of realism incorporated into studies of this relationship; as observations are made over longer time scales, at larger spatial scales, and for multiple ecosystem functions, the observed relationship between biodiversity and ecosystem function will shift from a steeper, more immediately saturating curve (represented by lighter gray lines) to a more gradual increase saturating at higher levels of biodiversity (represented by darker gray lines).

an ecosystem function is frequently not linear but instead shows saturating effects (Cardinale et al. 2006). Starting from low levels of biodiversity, increasing diversity often increases a particular ecosystem function only up to a point. Beyond that, additional biodiversity may do little to increase a given function. This pattern can result from FUNCTIONAL REDUNDANCY within a community: multiple species may contribute to a particular ecosystem function in similar ways, so the addition or loss of another functionally similar species may have little effect (Lawton and Brown 1993). Saturating effects of increasing biodiversity suggest that a low level of species losses will have only minimal consequences for an ecosystem function, if those species that are extirpated are functionally redundant (Cardinale et al. 2011). However, recent studies provide evidence that the saturating relationship between biodiversity and ecosystem function diminishes as ecosystem function is observed over longer time scales, at larger spatial scales, and when considering multiple ecosystem functions (Figure 15.1; Hector and Bagchi 2007, Zavaleta et al. 2010, Isbell et al. 2011, Reich et al. 2012, Pasari et al. 2013).

Although these studies focus exclusively on temperate grassland ecosystems, some studies of seagrass systems (Gamfeldt et al. 2008) suggest that these patterns may apply more generally, both in terrestrial and marine systems. Species that appear functionally similar in their effect on a single ecosystem function and under one set of environmental conditions may not perform similarly for all functions and under all conditions. Maintaining a suite of ecological functions, especially in the face of environmental change, requires greater levels of biodiversity than would be concluded from considering only a single function over short time scales, which unfortunately has been the scope of most ecological studies investigating the biodiversity-ecosystem function relationship. High-intensity agriculture illustrates this principle well—in selecting crops that maximize a single function (e.g., biomass production of a particular crop), we have created systems that often require high inputs of fertilizers and pesticides, and are susceptible to disease, pests, and drought.

The short-term, smaller-scale studies demonstrating saturating effects often assume that species losses will occur randomly. In reality, extinction is not a random process and functionally similar species are likely to disappear from a community at the same time (Zavaleta et al. 2009). Studies of the effects of land use intensification on animal diversity—including birds, mammals, amphibians, and arthropods—have found that functional diversity often declines more rapidly than species richness, indicating that land use change did not cause random extinctions but instead eliminated functionally similar species (Ernst et al. 2006, Schweiger et al. 2007, Flynn et al. 2009). In California's native-dominated serpentine grasslands where early-season annuals were most likely to be extirpated, and in its annual-dominated grasslands where perennials and late-season annuals were most at risk, both communities became more susceptible to invasion by exotic plant species when species losses followed realistic patterns (Zavaleta and Hulvey 2004, Selmants et al. 2012). A recent synthesis of approximately two hundred studies found that the effects of species losses on productivity and decomposition are as significant as the effects of climate warming, increased CO_2, nutrient pollution, and other drivers of global change (Hooper et al. 2012). Conservation of biodiversity is therefore important for maintaining the diversity of ecological processes on which human welfare depends through time and in the face of environmental change.

Ecological Interactions

Ecosystem functions depend not just on the identity and diversity of species within an ecosystem but also on interactions among species. Within communities, the presence or absence of some species have large effects on community structure, composition, and community; these species have been termed STRONG INTERACTORS (MacArthur 1972). Keystone species and ECOSYSTEM ENGINEERS are two types of strong interactors. KEYSTONE SPECIES are those species that have a large effect on community structure and function, compared to their biomass within the system. The keystone species concept was put forth by Paine (1969), based in part on his observations of the role of starfish (*Pisaster ochraceus*) in structuring the Pacific rocky intertidal community. Sea otters (*Enhydra lutris*) along the Pacific coast are another classic example of a keystone species. They regulate the structure of kelp forest (*Macrocystis* sp.) communities through a TROPHIC CASCADE: by preying on sea urchins (*Strongylocentrotus* sp.), which in turn graze kelp, sea otters maintain the diversity and structural complexity of kelp forest communities (Estes and Palmisano 1974). When sea otters are eliminated—as occurred in throughout much of their range in the eighteenth and nineteenth centuries due to overhunting for the fur trade—urchin populations increase, leading to overgrazing of algae and even shifts from kelp forest to urchin barrens.

While keystone species shape ecosystem functioning through trophic cascades, ecosystem engineers exert their influence on ecosystem structure and functions through the physical formation or modification of habitat (Jones et al. 1994). In California, both the native and invasive cordgrass

(*Spartina* spp.) act as ecosystem engineers by trapping sediment and providing structure (Brusati and Grosholz 2006). However, native cordgrass (*S. foliosa*) increases benthic invertebrate densities relative to uncolonized mudflats, whereas the invasive cordgrass (a hybrid, *S. alterniflora* × *S. foliosa*) reaches such high densities aboveground and belowground that it excludes invertebrates.

Strong interactors such as keystone species and ecosystem engineers were an early focus of ecological research. However, the majority of species in a given community are considered weak interactors, with their presence or absence in a community usually having small effects. This does not mean that weak interactions are without ecological importance. Weak interactions have been found to promote stability in productivity and community composition (e.g., McCann et al. 1998, Neutel et al. 2002). In addition, a species' status as a weak interactor is not fixed—species that have little effect on average or under certain conditions can play a large role in structuring communities under other circumstances (Berlow 1999). Finally, although weak interactors may have small effects on a per capita basis, at high densities their population-level effects may be substantial. Returning to California's kelp forests, relative to sea urchins, amphipods (*Ampithoe humeralis*) have weak per capita interactions with kelp, in part due to their small individual size (Sala and Graham 2002). However, during El Niño events, amphipods can reach high densities and in these circumstances play a significant role in structuring kelp communities (Sala and Sugihara 2005).

Ecosystem Services

Ecosystem Services and Natural Capital

The Millennium Ecosystem Assessment (MA 2003, 2005) succinctly defined ECOSYSTEM SERVICES as the benefits people obtain from ecosystems, combining two prior definitions focused on including both natural and human-modified ecosystems as sources of ecosystem services (Costanza et al. 1997) and both the tangible and intangible benefits that comprise ecosystem services (Daily 1997) to highlight how ecosystems sustain and fulfill human life. The value of ecosystem services can be considered a flow of benefits from nature to people. The stock of these benefits is what we call NATURAL CAPITAL (Tallis, Polasky et al. 2012). The difference between these two is akin to the difference become income and wealth—they are often positively correlated, and while poor management of a capital asset may produce short-term gains in income, long-term degradation of that asset will ultimately erode the benefits it can provide. Natural capital, as part of a broader economic framework including four other types of capital (manufactured, human, social, and financial), has gained more traction than ecosystem services in certain applications, particularly in national accounting and inclusive wealth accounting (Tallis, Polasky et al. 2012). However, recent polling has determined that the terms "natural capital" and "ecosystem services" are unpreferred by and unfamiliar to the U.S. populace, especially in comparison to more straightforward terms like "nature's benefits" or "nature's value" (Fairbank et al. 2010).

Regardless of the terms chosen, these stocks and flows of ecosystem assets are often related to biodiversity for many of the same reasons as for ecosystem function. Research on the relationships between biodiversity and ecosystem function and biodiversity and ecosystem services, respectively, has involved quite different methods of inquiry, with the former employing manipulative (often small-scale) experiments and mathematical theory, and the latter consisting of mostly correlative, landscape-scale studies comparing major habitat modifications (Cardinale et al. 2012). In the smaller-scale controlled studies, a mixed or negative association has been shown between biodiversity and certain ecosystem services, especially for food production and disease control, where more species richness can detrimental to the ecosystem service over the short term. Still, mutually beneficial or win-win outcomes have been documented for biodiversity and many ecosystem services over the longer-term, especially in cases where the stock of natural capital is more valuable than the consumption or extraction of the flow of ecosystem services from that stock (Reyers et al. 2012).

Distinction between Ecosystem Function and Ecosystem Services

Ecosystem functions support ecosystem services, and in common parlance these two terms are often used interchangeably, but they are not the same thing. The MA framework includes four types of services: provisioning (such as food, fuel, and fiber), regulating (such as air and water purification, climate stabilization, and hazard mitigation), cultural (such as spiritual, aesthetic, and educational enjoyment of nature), and supporting (such as soil formation, primary production, and nutrient cycling). By these definitions ecosystem functions can be considered supporting services, the processes necessary for the production of all other services, and indeed the MA suggests that supporting services differ from the other services in that "their impact on people are either indirect or occur over a very long time."

This definition can lead to confusion or misinterpretation of the ways that we measure and communicate nature's value to people. For example, according to this framework, pollination is defined as a regulating service and soil formation as a supporting service, though both can be thought of as contributing to crop production and therefore to human nutrition and food security. Furthermore, it is acknowledged that some processes could be classified as either a supporting or a regulating service, depending on the time scale and immediacy of their impact on people. To address this confusion, and to make a clearer distinction between supporting ecosystem functions and ecosystem services, we consider the flow of benefits from ecosystems to humans as a supply chain: the supply of ecosystem services, the ecosystem services themselves, and the value of those services to people (Tallis, Lester et al. 2012; Tallis, Mooney et al. 2012).

Supply, Service, and Value

Tracing ecosystem services along the chain of supply, service, and value helps clearly delineate the ecological and social processes that intersect in human experience of and dependence on nature. The supply of an ecosystem service is the ecosystem function that supports the service, the total potentially available to society, irrespective of actual consumption of or demand for that supply. The ecosystem service is the intersection of the supply of a service with the demand for or use of that service, as determined by location or action of the bene-

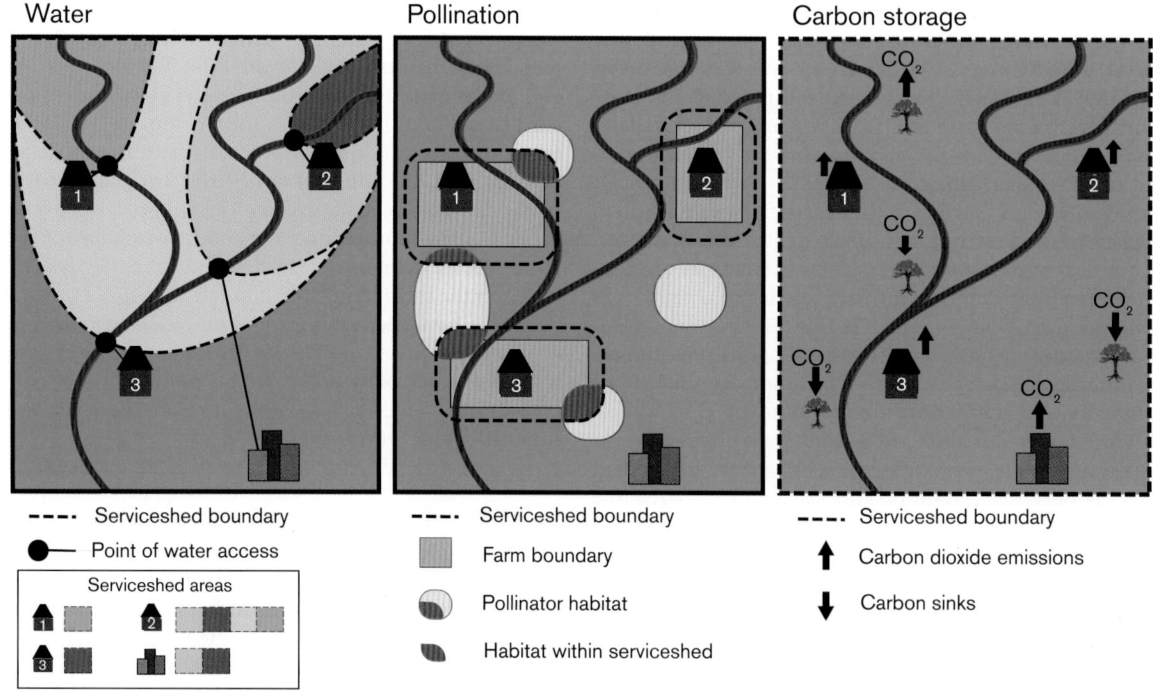

FIGURE 15.2 A serviceshed is the area that provides a specific service to a specific beneficiary. A serviceshed's location and extent depend on the biophysical processes that determine the supply of a particular service as well as on the ability of people to access those benefits. This figure shows how servicesheds differ across three services—water provision, crop pollination, and carbon storage—for four beneficiaries, specifically three farms and a city.

LEFT: For water provisioning services, the serviceshed is the area upstream of a beneficiary's point of water access, as the quantity and quality of water will depend on the state of upstream ecosystems. Some servicesheds overlap: the servicesheds of Farm 1 and Farm 2 fall entirely within Farm 3's serviceshed because Farm 3 takes water from further downstream. Because the city pipes water across a distance, its water provision serviceshed is also located far from the city itself.

MIDDLE: Servicesheds for crop pollination depend on pollinators' flight ranges. The current provision of pollination services occurs where pollinator habitat overlaps with a farm's serviceshed, as indicated in red. In some cases a pollinator habitat is too far away from a farm for that habitat to provide crop pollination services, as is the case of the habitat located below Farm 2.

RIGHT: In the case of carbon storage, all beneficiaries share a global serviceshed. Because the Earth's atmosphere is well mixed, everyone is affected by carbon sequestration and carbon emissions that occur anywhere else in the world.

ficiaries. The value of an ecosystem service encompasses the economic and/or social impacts of the service provided, the contribution of the service to human well-being, and can be assessed by combining the magnitude of the ecosystem service provided with social preference (including both needs and desires). Another popular method of ecosystem service assessment, benefits transfer, skips over ecosystem function to apply economic value estimates from one location to a similar site in another location. Benefits transfer treats all units of a given landscape type as identical, which makes resolving the specificity of the landscape type and deciding what constitutes "similar enough" particularly important and notably challenging (Plummer 2009). The supply chain approach, in contrast, connects ecological processes to social outcomes, without any intervening assumptions.

The supply of an ecosystem service can be thought of as an ecological production function, the outputs of ecosystem processes that are relevant to supporting and sustaining human life (Tallis and Polasky 2009). In this sense, the biotic structure of ecosystems and environmental conditions interact in processes that regulate and regenerate the natural capital upon which we depend. Societal decisions about land and marine management and natural resource use affect the structure of ecosystems and therefore the functions they perform. Many efforts have modeled the structural and functional responses of ecosystems to human-induced change in order to better inform decisions (reviewed by Waage et al. 2008, Nemec and Raudsepp-Hearne 2012).

Moving beyond the biophysical supply of an ecosystem service, which is where many ecosystem service assessments stop, requires a consideration of a SERVICESHED—the area that provides a specific service to a specific beneficiary (Tallis, Polasky et al. 2012). Servicesheds can operate over vastly different scales, depending on the nature of the service (Figure 15.2). Carbon sequestration and its contribution to climate regulation benefits all humans on the planet, which suggests its serviceshed would be global. In contrast, the serviceshed for water production or purification would in nonengineered systems be the watershed upstream from a particular city's extraction point. Modern proclivity for pumping and delivering water from watersheds far removed from consumption points (such as is the case throughout much of California) can create distant and noncontiguous servicesheds for these services. Some services cannot be transported, and their benefits will be experienced much more locally; the servicesheds of pollination and pest control services provided by naturally occurring insects (rather than managed honeybees or biocontrol agents) will be constrained by the foraging distance of those insects from a particular farm. Selecting the appropriate scale over which to delineate these servicesheds is necessary to connect the supply of the ecosystem service to the value accruing to the people who benefit from it.

Valuation of ecosystem services can take many different forms and produce different metrics, both monetary and nonmonetary. Monetary valuation has focused on distinguishing between market and nonmarket values of different services and various methods for assessing nonmarket values (Mendelsohn and Olmstead 2009). Market-based valuation is applied for ecosystem services that are already traded—primarily the "provisioning" services, such as crop, livestock, fish, and timber production, but also potentially "regulating" services, if a cap-and-trade program or similar regulatory framework is in effect, such as the Clean Air Act for air quality or California's AB 32 for carbon sequestration. Nonmarket valuation includes stated preference methods, what people say they are willing to pay for an ecosystem service or willing to accept when losing access to a service, and revealed preference methods, which use proxies of related consumer behavior, such as the cost to travel to a place where ecosystem services are consumed or a comparison of property values that differ only in their access to a particular ecosystem service (Freeman 2003).

Avoidance or replacement costs can also fall under this category of revealed preference; the water-filtering capacity of a wetland, for instance, may be valued as the cost of building and maintaining a water treatment plant that would be necessary if the wetland were not providing that service. Approaches for valuing marginal changes in ecosystem services are important in the consideration of trade-offs between different decisions, and the value of such marginal changes can be dramatically different depending upon where they fall on the ecosystem service supply curve (Fisher et al. 2008). Marginal values of services can increase exponentially as they grow scarcer, especially those services responsible for critical life-support functions and without an adequate or sustainable technological substitute (Heal 2000). These vastly different approaches to monetary valuation can produce substantially different estimates of value, and their appropriateness should be considered carefully for the services and decision in question.

There are many aspects of human well-being that can be captured through monetary valuation, but it is not always desirable to express ecosystem service values in such currencies to inform decisions. For example, human health risk metrics already are widely adopted and accepted by public and private decision-making bodies. Thus the contribution of water quality to human health can be valued as the reduced risk of mortality or morbidity (Keeler et al. 2012), or can also be valued in terms of the percentage of population with access to clean drinking water and/or resulting reduction in disease burden that may be set through national or international goals. Likewise, crop production, fisheries landings, or nontimber forest products could be assessed at their market value, or by their contribution to alleviating malnutrition (Tallis, Mooney et al. 2012). Cultural services span a particularly wide range of values, from market-based values of visitation rates for recreation, to religious values for sacred sites or plants, to nonuse values of inspiration and wonder; new approaches to integrating such disparate values are necessary to include them in environmental assessment (Satz et al. 2013). A new branch of cultural services is emerging in the realm of PSYCHOLOGICAL ECOSYSTEM SERVICES, the benefits of human experience of nature to cognitive function, including concentration, impulse inhibition, short-term and working memory, and mood (Bratman et al. 2012). Expanding beyond our traditional notions of "value" will help more thoroughly capture the full benefits of ecosystem services to people.

Examples of Ecosystem Functions and Services in Californian Ecosystems

Agricultural Production

California supplies a diverse mix of agricultural products, producing $43 billion in revenues in 2011 across more than eighty crop and animal products (USDA National Agricultural Statistics Service 2012) (see also Chapter 38, "Agriculture"). Crop production is an ecosystem service in and of itself and is also supported by pollination and pest control services provided by beneficial insects that inhabit the farm and surrounding areas. Livestock that graze on California pastures, grasslands, and open woodlands represent another important ecosystem service in the agricultural system. As provisioning services with a direct market value, service valuation is fairly well advanced, even for the partial contributions to the production value of supporting services like pollination and pest control. The ecosystem function or biophysical supply (crop or grassland productivity, delivery of pollen to crops, or suppression of pests) is well-documented in the literature, the service to people (available food for livelihood generation and consumption) is readily understood, and its value (revenues from crop or livestock production and the contribution of pollination and pest control to generating those revenues) is easily accounted for in economic analysis. Less well explored is the full value of agricultural production and supporting services to human nutritional health and overall food security, which do not always align with economic returns from farming. While growing cash crops provides an economic resource base from which to buy other goods, including a more diverse selection of food, this can leave growers vulnerable to environmental and economic shocks and ultimately less food secure. California's high diversity in agricultural production allows for an unusual degree of localized food and nutritional security in the modern globalized food economy.

Supporting Agricultural Services: Pollination and Pest Control

Pollination by wild bee populations enhances production of many high-value crops in California, including watermelon (Kremen et al. 2004), almond (Brittain et al. 2013), sunflowers (Greenleaf and Kremen 2006b), and tomatoes (Greenleaf and Kremen 2006a). Seminal work in watermelons has illustrated a general trend found in California and throughout the world: crop pollination services provided by native bee communities strongly depends on the proportion of noncrop or unmanaged habitat around the farm site. Kremen and colleagues (2004) found that native bee populations could fully support watermelon yields (without managed honeybees) in farms situated in areas containing more than 40% of natural habitat within a 2.4 kilometer radius. This supporting service is becoming increasingly important as colony collapse disorder and other threats posed to honeybee colonies compromise their availability for crop pollination on many farms. Furthermore, wild bees can enhance production in certain crops that honeybees cannot. Tomatoes are self-pollinating to a certain degree, but bumblebees in California have been shown to pollinate with a particular vibration frequency that releases more pollen than would otherwise be achieved, increasing yields accordingly (Greenleaf and Kremen 2006a).

Wild bees can also enhance the efficiency or productivity of honeybees through their direct and indirect interactions with this managed species. Wild bees have been shown to increase bee movement between male and female flowers by disrupting honeybee visits to sunflowers in the Central Valley of California, where 90% of U.S. hybrid sunflower seed production occurs (Greenleaf and Kremen 2006b). This enhanced pollination is worth an estimated $10.4 million annually, which nearly doubles the value for direct pollination by honeybees. Such bee movement between male and female flowers is critical in all crops with separate male and female flowers, such as melons, pumpkins, and kiwis, or with self-incompatibility, such as apples, sweet cherries, and almonds. Wild bees have similarly been shown to enhance honeybee efficiency in California almonds—a crop so high in value that even the modest gain in efficiency of a 5 percent yield increase would augment economic returns to the farmer by $591 per hectare (Brittain et al. 2013), or $182 million across 307,560 hectares of almond in California (USDA National Agricultural Statistics Service 2012).

Pest control services can also be enhanced by natural or unmanaged perennial habitat surrounding the farm, which concentrates or sustains populations of predators and parasitic insects, natural enemies of agricultural pests. Diversity and abundance of natural enemies has been found to increase with the proportion of noncrop habitat in the landscape (Chaplin-Kramer, O'Rourke et al. 2011), and this trend has been linked to pest suppression in many systems in California. Insect populations in tomatoes in the Central Valley responded more strongly to landscape features than to on-farm management (conventional or organic), with higher natural enemy populations and lower pest populations on farms located in more natural landscapes (Letourneau and Goldstein 2001). Lepidopteran pests in the Central Coast region of California were better contained by parasitism in landscapes with less annual cropland (Letourneau et al. 2012), and aphid pests in the same system showed suppressed population growth by natural enemies in landscapes with more natural habitat (Chaplin-Kramer and Kremen 2012). Vertebrate predators can play important roles in maintaining pest control on farms as well; conservation practices that benefited the western bluebird in vineyards in the Russian River Valley doubled to tripled the removal rate of important grape pests (Jedlicka et al. 2011).

It is important to recognize that natural or unmanaged habitat in agricultural landscapes could provide ecosystem disservices as well, by providing resources for pests and pathogens in addition to natural enemies. For example, the non-native brassicas that dot many Californian roadsides and fallow fields or pastures provide an enemy-free refuge for aphids that can then spill over onto vegetable crops (Chaplin-Kramer, Kliebenstein et al. 2011). Non-native predator species can also outcompete more specialized native predators, reducing effective pest control, as has been shown for spiders in Napa Valley vineyards (Hogg and Daane 2011). Recently, concern over food safety emerging from a 2006 disease outbreak of *Escherichia coli* in California spinach has added to the perception that unmanaged habitat adjacent to farms harbors harmful and undesirable species. New protocols put in place in the Salinas Valley in response to this outbreak have resulted in the loss of 13.3% of remaining riparian habitat in the region, and if these practices were implemented statewide, it is estimated that up to 40% of riparian habitat and 45% of wetlands in some counties would be impacted (Gennet et al. 2013). This "sterilization" of farm landscapes to reduce the risk of microbial food contamination events should be weighed against the value of possible pollination, pest control, and other ecosystem services that would be lost in the process. In many cases, the types or qualities of habitat that contribute either ecosystem services or disservices are very different, and it may be possible to manage to promote the services and constrain the disservices (Chaplin-Kramer, Kliebenstein et al. 2011).

Valuation of pollination and pest control could take several forms. Pollination services have been valued in terms of the replacement costs (of renting honeybees or hand-pollinating) to perform the same service provided by wild pollinators (De Groot et al. 2002). The replacement cost for pest control services could be considered the amount spent on pesticides, although it is somewhat controversial whether the two methods provide equivalent levels of control (Pimentel et al. 1992). A more commonly used approach for valuing pollination services estimates the value of crop production attributable to pollination. Crop yield reduction in the absence of pollinators has been approximated for all major crop types (Klein et al. 2007), and this yield reduction is then multiplied by the market value of production (Morse and Calderone 2000). The analogous approach in pest control is to quantify the amount that yield is reduced by pest damage in the absence of natural enemies, and value the avoided damage (Losey and Vaughan 2006). Recently a new approach to valuing these supporting services in agriculture has been developed, called the attributable net income method, which subtracts the cost of inputs to crop production from the value of the ecosystem service and does not attribute value to the service in excess of the plants' requirements (Winfree et al. 2011).

Forage Production

The rangelands that account for about half the land area (approximately 24 million hectares) of California (Brown et al. 2004) produce grass and hay for livestock forage but also provide many other ecosystem services, including pollination (Chaplin-Kramer, Tuxen-Bettman et al. 2011) and carbon sequestration (Silver et al. 2010; see below; see also Chapter 37, "Range Ecosystems"). Unlike many industrialized cropland systems, rangelands can provide habitat for wildlife and support an aesthetic and a quality of life cherished by many Californians. Over half of oak woodlands landowners in California are estimated to produce livestock, though this figure has been declining steadily since 1985 as productive land is converted to vacation homes (Huntsinger et al. 2010). Most valuation in these systems, however, focuses on the forage production supporting a livestock industry that constitutes a major component of California's economy. By rough estimates, California produces 13 Teragrams (1 million Megagrams or metric tons) of forage annually, which could support an average of 1.5 million cows without any supplemental feed (according to simple approximations assuming 4,300 kilograms of dry matter per year per cow with 50% consumption to account for trampling; Shaw et al. 2011), which is approximately a third of all livestock produced in California (USDA National Agricultural Statistics Service 2012).

This 13 Tg of forage production can be valued as $165

million in profits from livestock or $555 million in cost of replacement for hay (Shaw et al. 2011). More local-scale assessments suggest high spatial heterogeneity in the supply and value of this service, with much higher capacity for production in the wetter northern than the drier southern portions of the San Francisco Bay Area (Chaplin-Kramer and George 2013) and much higher values for production in Kern County than in neighboring San Luis Obispo County due to proximity to feedlots, slaughterhouses, and transportation routes (Chan et al. 2006).

Timber and Nontimber Forest Products

California's 16.1 million hectares of forest covers almost 40% of the state, 6.9 million hectares of which are classified as timber lands, supporting a large timber industry (Shih 1998, Laaksonen-Craig et al. 2003; see also Chapter 36, "Forestry"). Although timber does not play as large a role in the state's economy as in other west coast states, 3.04 million cubic meters (1.29 billion board feet) of timber was harvested in California in 2011, worth $272 million (California State Board of Equalization 2012). Including what the Forest Service calls "multiplier effects," the additional economic activities from processing the timber into final products, yields a much higher estimate—over $12 billion for the 5.0 million cubic meters (2.1 billion board feet) produced in 1999 (Laaksonen-Craig et al. 2003). This forest products industry and related economic sectors support more than 220,000 jobs in California, which is only 1% of the state's total employment, but comprises a vital livelihood for many people living in rural areas (Laaksonen-Craig et al. 2003). Managed timber forests also provide a complex web of ecosystem services that contribute to human well-being, along with the state's 9.3 million hectares of nonproduction forest. California forests provide nontimber forest products such as mushrooms, floral greens, a variety of edible and medicinal plant species, and wildlife for hunting (Krieger 2001). As reviewed in other sections, forests also sequester carbon, provide recreational opportunities, support pest control and pollination services to nearby farmland, and regulate water supplies to people.

Fisheries and Aquaculture

The California commercial fishing industry landed over 181 million kilograms of fish and shellfish in 2011, worth over $200 million of landed value (CDFG 2012a) (see also Chapter 35, "Marine Fisheries"). Like farming and ranching, fishing provides not only revenues but a livelihood and a way of life; the seafood industry employs over 122,000 people in California, more than in any other state (National Marine Fisheries Service 2013). Meanwhile, aquaculture is growing rapidly in California and around the world. It is the fastest growing animal food production sector, and within a few years is expected to produce half of the fish we eat (Klinger and Naylor 2012). The income gained from commercial fishing and marine aquaculture operations reached $4.3 billion in 2011, adding a total of $7.2 billion to California's economy in direct and related revenues (National Marine Fisheries Service 2013).

The supply of California's seafood is supported by healthy marine ecosystems and the water quality of streams feeding into the ocean. Many commercially important species rely on offshore habitat, such as rockfish on rocky reefs, and tuna in pelagic ecosystems, but some of the highest value species, such as farmed oysters and salmon, are particularly sensitive to nutrient and sediment loadings, freshwater inputs, and other services provided by upland and coastal ecosystems. Low streamflows contributed to the rapid decline of California's salmon populations, and the complete closure of California's commercial salmon fishery in 2008 and then again in 2009, resulting in the loss of 1,823 jobs and $118.4 million in income (Macfarlane et al. 2008, Business Forecasting Center 2010). In addition to supporting commercial fishing and aquaculture, healthy coastal and marine ecosystems also support a recreational fishing industry in California, providing recreational opportunities to over 1.6 million anglers, supporting over 7,700 full- and part-time jobs in the state, and generating $1 billion of value added to the local economy in 2011 (National Marine Fisheries Service 2013).

Water Production and Regulation

The relationship between water production and vegetation is complex, with dynamic processes operating across multiple spatial and temporal scales. Supply of this service, the total water-yielding capacity of a watershed, can be more difficult to measure and understand than the service provided to people, in the form of water available for human uses such as irrigation, drinking water consumption, and hydropower. Monetary valuation of these uses is based on market values of streamflow, which range from $0.21 per 1,000 cubic meters ($0.26 per acre foot) for electricity generation to as much as $40 per 1,000 cubic meters ($50 per acre foot) for irrigation and municipal uses (Krieger 2001). Nonmarket values of water include supplying natural systems for biodiversity, aesthetic value, and recreation. Southern California residents were willing to pay $115 per household to raise the water level in Mono Lake (Brown 1992).

However, the pathways by which water is captured and delivered to people and ecosystems are often uncertain, especially the interplay between surface water and groundwater resources, making it difficult to assign value to particular ecosystems providing the service. In general, greater evapotranspiration rates from increased vegetative growth can reduce overall water supply downstream, although the biophysical mediation of hydrologic processes results in more regular and reliable flows of water (as opposed to long dry periods punctuated by flash flooding during rain events) (Brauman et al. 2007). Some habitats create their own microclimates to capture more water from the air than would otherwise be possible. The coastal redwood forest of California provides more intercepting surfaces to capture moisture in its tall vegetation, storing twice as much water from fog as treeless sites (Brauman et al. 2007).

Water Purification

Water filtration or purification through the trapping of sediments and nutrients by vegetation is a regulating service that is the basis for many PAYMENTS FOR ECOSYSTEM SERVICES (PES) programs (Long Tom Watershed Council 2008, Goldman-Benner et al. 2012), but very often the assessment of this ecosystem service stops at the ecosystem function or supply of the service (biophysical nutrient retention, or reduction in nutrient loadings in streams), without consideration of service to people (water quality at intake points for drinking water) or the value of that service (avoided cost of building or maintaining a treatment plant). One of the most famous examples of a valuation of water quality services is New York City's $2 billion investment in restoration of the Catskills to avoid spending $8 billion to build a water treatment plants plus $300 million annually in operating costs (Turner and Daily 2007). In California there has not yet been the same level of economic analysis, but the biophysical supply of the service is well documented throughout the state. In the San Diego region restoration of the 8 hectare Famosa Slough reduced nitrogen loading and resulting algal blooms in Mission Bay, with co-benefits including enhanced mudflat habitat to support better wildlife viewing opportunities for residents (Zedler and Kercher 2005). Such coastal wetlands have been shown to be effective nutrient traps across California, including Elkhorn Slough in the Monterey Bay region, where this function is not saturated despite high background nitrogen inputs from intensive upstream agriculture in the Salinas Valley (Nelson and Zavaleta 2012).

Quantitative analysis of area requirements to perform this ecosystem service indicates less than 3 percent of the land in agricultural watersheds in the San Joaquin Valley would need to be in wetlands in order to reduce nitrate concentrations below a required threshold of 0.5 mg L^{-1} (Karpuzcu and Stringfellow 2012). Similar analyses have shown that the current wetland area enrolled in the USDA Wetlands Reserve Program in the Central Valley could denitrify nitrate loads to the delta in as little as eighteen days (Duffy and Kahara 2011). Riparian buffers can provide similar services to wetlands over much smaller areas, and valuation of the incremental impact of changes in water quality is simpler over this finer scale; a net benefit of vegetated buffer strips to farmers has been demonstrated in California, with improvements in water quality and reductions in soil loss outweighing the opportunity cost of land taken out of production (Brauman et al. 2007).

Carbon Sequestration and Storage

A key component of climate regulation is reducing the greenhouse gases responsible for global warming through carbon sequestration. In this case, the supply is the same as the service, in that all people on the planet benefit from lower concentrations of carbon dioxide in a globally mixed atmosphere. The value may be different for different populations, depending on their vulnerability to climate change, with low-lying coastal areas more sensitive to sea level rise and certain areas at higher risk of losing agricultural, forest, or water production than others (Mimura et al. 2007). California's varied ecosystems store carbon to different degrees, and the total live aboveground carbon stored in California is estimated at 1025 Tg, which, with a social cost of carbon between $23 and $185 per metric ton, could be valued in the range of $23.5 billion and $190 billion (Shaw et al. 2011). The abundant biomass of forests make them especially important carbon sinks, and California has some of the most carbon-rich forests on the planet; the living aboveground biomass in the California coastal redwoods alone is thought to contain five times more carbon than any other forest (Sillett et al. 2010). Freshwater and tidal wetlands are also critically important in terms of carbon storage in California (Trulio et al. 2007). However, there is a difference between the stock of stored carbon, for which value should be considered from the perspective of avoided loss, and the flow of carbon sequestration, for which value can be thought of as the contribution to reducing total global greenhouse gas emissions (Tallis, Polasky et al. 2012).

California's working landscapes are in constant flux of growth and harvest, and thus there is important potential for greater carbon sequestration through improved management of these lands (Ackerly et al. 2012). Managed forests are considered to be at only 50% of their carbon carrying capacity and could considerably increase sequestration through selective logging that increases the stocking rate of large (>110 cm diameter at breast height) trees (Roxburgh et al. 2006). Similarly, rangeland and cropping systems could sequester more carbon through grazing management, pasture improvement, no-till agriculture, and conversion to perennial crops. Soil carbon pools in California rangelands are already higher than in the rest of the U.S., likely due to the prevalence of woody plants, which must be balanced against forage production needs for livestock (Silver et al. 2010). Improved grazing practices such as moderate stocking rates can significantly increase rates of soil carbon sequestration (Conant et al. 2001), and a high degree of variability in soil carbon pools in California's rangelands across similar soil types and climate suggests there is a considerable role for management to increase soil carbon (Silver et al. 2010). Meanwhile, California's agriculture sequesters an average of 19 grams carbon per meter per year, which is equivalent to 0.7% of the state's fossil fuel emissions, and this amount could be doubled if conservation tillage and improved orchard pruning and waste management practices were implemented (Kroodsma and Field 2006).

Hazard Prevention: Flood Mitigation and Coastal Protection

Many California ecosystems have the capacity to moderate extreme events such as floods and coastal storms. Maintaining wetland or riparian habitat that is part of a natural flood regime can reduce the risk of catastrophic flooding by retaining in soils and vegetation high volumes of water that would run off of impervious surfaces in a watershed. Similarly, maintaining benthic habitat such as mangrove or eelgrass along shorelines can provide coastal protection from erosion and flooding by attenuating storm surge. The water retention or wave attenuation resulting in reduced flooding or coastal erosion is the biophysical supply of this regulating service; intersecting this ecosystem function with the location and activities of people yields the service itself, in the form of reduced damage to property. The value of this service is therefore typically measured by avoided damage costs, although consideration of the distributional impacts of this value is particularly important in this case, as poorer populations with low property values may be disproportionately situated in high-risk areas (Arkema et al. 2013).

Restoration of 150 hectares on floodplain in Napa Valley has provided flood mitigation along a 10 kilometer stretch of the Napa River, as well as a host of co-benefits such as recreation and tourism activities (Turner and Daily 2007). Flood mitigation services are often correlated with recreation, whether in floodplain or narrower riparian habitats, and has also been shown to overlap with pollination in the Salinas Valley and forage production in the San Jose area (Chan et al. 2006) and nutrient retention in the Central Valley (Duffy and Kahara 2011). Coastal habitats providing protection from erosion and coastal flooding are important as well; in fact, a nationwide assessment of coastal hazards found California's coastal ecosystems to provide protection for the greatest number of total people, socially vulnerable populations, and properties in the country (Arkema et al. 2013).

Recreation

California's open space and coastal areas provide significant economic and social benefits. The supply of this service is determined by the existence and quality of habitat in which recreation activities could occur, while the service itself depends on access to the recreation area, such that aesthetically pleasing areas nearer to urban centers will have higher service values for recreation. Recreation can be valued a variety of ways: in market terms, through visitation fees and other revenue generated by tourism; nonmarket methods include stated willingness to pay or revealed preference methods such as travel cost to recreation areas or property values near these areas. Outdoor recreation in California generates revenues of approximately $46 billion annually and supports 408,000 jobs (Outdoor Industry Foundation 2006). Beaches are a particularly important recreational resource in California, both to residents and to tourists. Over 15 million people a year use California's beaches, making over 150 million trips a year (Pendleton and Kildow 2006). California residents spend over $4 billion a year on beach recreation (Pendleton et al. 2011). On top of this, California's beaches generate $14 billion a year in related revenues from beachgoers spending money on amenities such as food, parking, and beach-related activities, making California's state beaches a multibillion-dollar natural resource (Pendleton et al. 2011).

Biodiversity, Ecosystem Functioning, and Ecosystem Services in Decision Making

Parts of the conservation field have broadened in scope in recent years to include goals to maintain and enhance human well-being in addition to preserving biodiversity (Kareiva and Marvier 2012). This has created some tensions within the conservation community, amid concerns from many conservation scientists and advocates that ecosystem services and "valuing nature" will distract from and dilute efforts to conserve biodiversity (Soule 2013, Doak et al. 2014). It has been shown that integrating ecosystem services into decisions can expand the potential partners and funders for conservation rather than detracting from funding available for biodiversity-focused conservation (Goldman et al. 2009, Reyers et al. 2012). However, it is true and worth considering that win-wins between biodiversity and human well-being are not always possible; in some cases, nature provides disservices or comes into direct conflict with people (McCauley 2006).

Integrating ecosystem service information into decisions can expand the potential partners that support environmental protection and restoration beyond those within the traditional conservation community (Reyers et al. 2012) and can help make explicit the conflicts and synergies among stakeholders with different goals (Guerry et al. 2012). Recognizing the value of multiple ecosystem services for human well-being is a first step in connecting ecosystem service value to land and ocean management decisions, but it is also necessary to have a clear understanding of the needs and expectations of different institutions involved in decision making (Daily et al. 2009). Creating this type of institutional change in natural resource decisions requires a clear accounting of the condition of the ecosystem (supply metrics), the amount of natural resources used by people (service metrics), and the people's preference for that level of service (value metrics) (Tallis, Lester et al. 2012; Tallis, Mooney et al. 2012). Information about biodiversity, ecosystem function, and ecosystem services will guide decisions in different ways, and if considered as separate approaches, they will often result in different visions of what our world should look like. However, there is often room for compromise and finding complementarities among biodiversity and ecosystem services in these approaches. Three specific decision contexts are reviewed here (conservation planning, climate adaptation, and impacts assessment), and biodiversity- and ecosystem services–based approaches are compared for each.

Conservation Planning

Maintaining biodiversity, ecosystem function, and ecosystem services in the face of humanity's increasing dominance of Earth's ecosystems requires landscape-level decisions about where to manage for production of food, materials, and other benefits to people, and where to limit human activities. Conservation planning involves identifying the location and configuration of areas that, if properly managed, can promote the persistence of biodiversity and other natural values (Pressey et al. 2007). An unavoidable reality is that human activities very often threaten biodiversity. While wildlife-friendly forms of management can lessen the severity of such threats, successful conservation requires an explicit recognition of their existence, and guiding activities that pose a threat away from the most sensitive or most diverse or unique places will generally benefit biodiversity. Conservation planning is thus critical to effectively balancing human needs with the preservation of nature, but when framed in terms of biodiversity only, conservation decisions are viewed as inherently in conflict with development. From this perspective, setting aside areas for protection of biodiversity requires forgoing uses that might otherwise benefit people. This can cause misunderstanding and resentment, and the perception that conservation prioritizes endangered species over livelihoods, other species over humans. Ecosystem-service approaches to conservation planning can reduce this apparent conflict, by considering a wider range of nature's values to people and better capturing both trade-offs and synergies that emerge from conservation.

An ecosystem services–based framework can illuminate the ways in which conservation in specific places might purify water, enhance fish stocks, provide recreational opportunities, mitigate hazards like flooding, or buffer against extreme heat events in cities. For example, marine protected areas designed to reduce degradation of coastal ecosystems also provided an estimated $2.5 million per kilometer of coastline in recreational benefits to beach visitors in southern California (Hall et al. 2002). Furthermore, ecosystem services approaches can create opportunities for conservation that would not exist with a biodiversity-only approach. Napa County restored 250 hectares of floodplain that would never have been undertaken for preserving biodiversity alone; this massive conservation investment was viable due to the perceived win-win outcomes for flood mitigation as well as enhancement of fish and wildlife populations, scenic beauty, and the accompanying recreation and tourism benefits (Turner and Daily 2007). Residents were willing to pay an additional $50 million to implement this ecosystem services approach to flood control over the traditional infrastructure approach because of the anticipated value of those additional benefits.

While biodiversity- and ecosystem services–based approaches to conservation planning can often be employed together, the two approaches are not necessarily substitutable, especially with services that are negatively correlated with biodiversity. This is often the case with provisioning services that are maximized by more intensive management of the land. In the Central Coast region of California, reserve design that maximized forage production and pollination services would only protect 44% of the biodiversity targets achieved by a reserve system based solely on biodiversity goals; however, more strategic targeting of biodiversity and only the services with which it was positively correlated (water production, carbon storage, flood control, and recreation) achieved nearly the same biodiversity outcomes as when targeting biodiversity alone, with many additional benefits (Chan et al. 2006).

In practice, the complementarity of ecosystem services–based and biodiversity-based approaches will depend upon how well the scales over which the services are produced match the habitat requirements of the species of interest. Flows of some services (e.g., climate regulation, water-related services) can originate at great distances from the ultimate beneficiaries, but many services are provided at more local scales (e.g., agriculture-related services, coastal protection), requiring conservation of smaller areas close to people and embedded within human-dominated landscapes. Such configuration may be difficult to reconcile with a biodiversity-based approach that prioritizes large contiguous areas removed from anthropogenic impacts. Merging the two approaches will be most successful when connectivity between protected areas can also establish connectivity between ecosystems and people and the flows of benefits.

For example, large coastal no-take marine protected areas can severely reduce the ability of small, nearshore fleets to access fish stocks, thereby reducing the provision of fishing services (Roberts et al. 2005). In some cases, smaller but more numerous no-take areas could better provide benefits to the nearshore fleets by maintaining access to fishing grounds, while still protecting fish stocks and associated biodiversity. In contrast to marine systems, grassland ecosystems in California are largely privately owned and managed as rangelands for livestock production, making large protected areas unfeasible. However, integrated management of California rangelands can provide many benefits both for species and people, including livestock production, recreation opportunities, carbon sequestration, and improved water supply (Kroeger et al. 2010). Protecting public land targeted to maximize conservation of species while promoting incentives for best management practices on private rangelands in these regions can connect biodiversity- and ecosystem services–based approaches (Community Foundation Sonoma County 2010).

Despite some incompatibilities between certain services and at certain scales, biodiversity and ecosystem services approaches to conservation have much in common (Reyers et al. 2012). Many argue that integrating the two objectives in landscape-scale conservation planning decisions can increase the range of people in support of conservation while achieving better outcomes for both nature and society than if either objective is considered alone (Goldman and Tallis 2009; Ruckelshaus, McKenzie et al. 2013). However, integrating biodiversity and ecosystem service approaches will not eliminate trade-offs, and ultimately conservation planners will need to decide what to prioritize

Climate Adaptation

Climate change impacts individual species, the ecosystems they comprise, the processes or functions of those ecosystems, and ultimately the ecosystem services provided to people. The effects of climate change on species and ecosystems include range shifts, asynchronies in phenology, altered food web dynamics and community interactions like pollination, and disruption of key functions such as seasonal water flows upon which other ecosystems rely (Moritz et al. 2008, Mawdsley et al. 2009, Hoegh-Guldberg and Bruno 2010, Walther 2010, Null and Viers 2012, National Climate Assessment 2013). Climate adaptation planning addresses these impacts, though the approaches taken and results of these efforts differ depending on whether biodiversity or ecosystem services are the focus.

With a biodiversity-based approach, the focal unit is species or ecosystems, and adaptive measures may include increasing the number or area of reserves, improving management within reserves, and maintaining and enhancing connectivity (Heller and Zavaleta 2009, Mawdsley et al. 2009). Species-specific adaptation strategies tend to focus on managing and restoring reserves and corridors specifically for the focal species' needs or reintroducing or relocating species at risk (Rahel et al. 2008, Grewell et al. 2013). However, such species-specific climate adaptation does not address resilience of the system in the face of novel species and interactions that may occur with climate change (Seastedt et al. 2008, West et al. 2009, Bernhardt and Leslie 2013). Uncertainty associated with projections of climate change and species' range shifts could also lead to adaptation efforts that do not provide an appropriate range of conditions for species' persistence. Climate adaptation planning can also focus on maintaining biodiversity at the ecosystem level—for example, prioritizing conservation and restoration of marshes for a diversity of habitat types (Stralberg et al. 2011) or managing river flows to support aquatic systems (Palmer et al. 2008).

An ecosystem services approach to climate adaptation will consider changes in the provision of services rather than tracking movement of species or even habitats across landscapes. A serviceshed depends upon the location and activity of beneficiaries of the service as well as the scale at which they can benefit from it, and its delineation will change primarily in response to demographic changes. Thus, while the magnitude of service provided will certainly change with the structure of the ecosystem responding to climate change, servicesheds will tend to be more stationary than species and habitats in the face of climate change. It is therefore important in an ecosystem services approach to adaptation to anticipate changes in the structure of ecosystems within the serviceshed that will lead to changes in function that will impact people. Impacted services may be species-specific, such as pollination and pest control of crops (Luedeling et al. 2011, Vanbergen and Initiative 2013), and fisheries (Brander 2010; Doney et al. 2012; Ruckelshaus, Doney et al. 2013), or at the whole habitat level, as with coastal protection from storms and sea level rise (Hayhoe et al. 2004, Heberger et al. 2009, Doney et al. 2012) or recreation on beaches and in the mountains (Hayhoe et al. 2004, King et al. 2010).

Understanding and adapting to climate impacts on species-specific services will require much of the same research as biodiversity-based adaptation, particularly with regards to shifts in resource availability and the timing of community interactions (Brander 2010). However, a higher degree of substitutability exists when conserving species-specific services than when conserving specific species; pollinators or commercially important fish that respond more positively to climate change could potentially compensate for the loss of function of species harmed by climate change. Habitat-specific services may be less substitutable in many cases, such as sea level rise causing inundation of marsh or beach habitat when there is no space for the habitat to migrate upshore (Heberger et al. 2009; Hanak and Moreno 2011; Committee on Sea Level Rise in California, Oregon, and Washington et al. 2012). In these cases, the service of coastal protection or recreation will be lost, with no option for replacing it. Other services, such as carbon sequestration and water provision, are produced by many different habitats, though to different degrees. Woody encroachment throughout much of California's grasslands and the retreat of many of the state's oak woodlands expected in response to climate change (Cornwell et al. 2012) will alter the patterns of carbon and water cycling, resulting in changes to climate-regulating carbon sequestration and to water supply in certain regions.

An ecosystem services approach to climate adaptation prioritizes the best locations for protection and restoration of habitats within the same region or serviceshed, to produce optimal outcomes for the people who remain there, in contrast to the biodiversity-based approach of planning reserve networks to follow species or habitats. These two approaches will often not be complementary and in some cases may conflict with each other. For example, in the San Francisco Bay two endangered estuarine plants are less successful at upslope colonization when they are closer to anthropogenic activity, while coastal protection services provided by estuaries are of greatest benefit in areas of high population density, where they will protect the most people (Grewell et al. 2013). It is therefore important for climate adaptation projects to have very clear and specific goals, whether conserving biodiversity or ecosystem services or both, and identify where and how to meet each goal, separately, if needed.

Environmental Impact Assessment and Mitigation

Development can create new jobs, increase food production, improve transportation and communication, and provide cheaper energy. However, these benefits need to be weighed against the environmental costs, which often include water and air pollution, loss of recreation opportunities, and threats to species and habitats. Development in California is governed by a suite of federal and state legislation (e.g., the California Environmental Quality Act, the California Endangered Species Act, the National Environmental Policy Act, the Clean Water Act, and the Endangered Species Act) that requires developers to identify significant environmental impacts of proposed activities and determine how to avoid, minimize, and mitigate these impacts, where feasible. MITIGATION OFFSETS in the United States primarily require restoration of habitat or ecosystem functions, though sometimes protection that prevents future losses can also count as mitigation. Mitigation decisions—how much mitigation is needed and where—depends to a large degree on whether environmental impact is viewed through the lens of biodiversity, ecosystem function, or ecosystem services.

In California, mitigation requirements have been established for the functions (water storage and transport; nutrient retention and cycling) and habitats (maintenance of native vegetation and wildlife) provided by wetlands as well as for endangered species. This mitigation for wetlands was traditionally undertaken on a project-by-project basis, with each developer held responsible for restoring or creating a replacement wetland to compensate for unavoidable impacts. However, this approach proved to be inadequate—by some estimates, one-third of the required wetlands were never built, and those that were successfully created or restored tended to be small and fragmented (Rolband et al. 2000). Wetland mitigation banks—consolidated areas of restored, enhanced, constructed, or preserved wetlands—emerged in the 1980s and 1990s as a response to this problem (CDFG 2012b). Banks sell credits based on the area and quality of wetland the bank possesses to those in need of mitigation within the bank's "service areas" (often watersheds) (Ruhl and Salzman 2006). In California as of 2012, thirty-three banks across more than 1090 hectares sell or have sold wetland mitigation credits (CDFG 2012b). In addition to wetland mitigation banking, California pioneered conservation banking, which, instead of providing credits for wetlands, provides credits for particular (often endangered) species or habitats. To date, California has approved credits for thirty-four species of animals and plants as well as twenty-seven habitat types (CDFG 2012b). Thirty-two conservation banks have been approved by the California Department of Fish and Game, covering over 11,300 hectares of habitat (CDFG 2012b).

While mitigation banking represents an improvement on the previous, piecemeal approach, there are still limitations to mitigation banking's effectiveness at biodiversity conservation. Mitigation credits are calculated using simple metrics of habitat or ecosystem quality. Given the many facets of biodiversity and ways to measure it, as discussed earlier in this chapter, these simple approaches can obscure important aspects of biodiversity, such as genetic diversity or connectivity between populations, making it difficult to establish whether a mitigation credit adequately offsets the biodiversity lost with development (Burgin 2008, Walker et al. 2009). Finding robust yet practical ways to assess equivalence between damage to biodiversity from development and benefits to biodiversity from mitigation remains a challenge. However, even if mitigation successfully maintains certain aspects of biodiversity or ecosystem function, it does not necessarily restore ecosystem services at the same time. When mitigation redistributes biodiversity and ecosystems/ecosystem function across the landscape, ecosystem services can be transferred across servicesheds, altering who receives the benefits from biodiversity and ecosystem functions.

In other words, mitigation that does not explicitly account for the link between the landscape and people can reduce ecosystem service benefits even when the total supply of the service stays the same (Tallis and Polasky 2011, Mandle et al. in prep). This redistribution of ecosystem services can create inequities. Mitigation banks, though they are likely to be more effective at achieving mitigation targets than the conventional, project-by-project, piecemeal approach, may also lead to the concentration of ecosystem services in areas near mitigation banks. Wetland mitigation banking is leading to the redistribution of ecosystems services, taking services such as pollution control, flood mitigation, and recreational opportunities away from urban populations and concentrating them in rural areas (Ruhl and Salzman 2006,

BenDor et al. 2008). Furthermore, biodiversity and some ecosystem services may be restored more slowly than habitat, and such time lags may lead to temporary inequity that needs to be addressed (Bullock et al. 2011). Explicitly incorporating ecosystem services into mitigation requirements would help provide a more complete picture of the environmental impacts of development and ensure that the benefits and costs of development are distributed equitably within society.

Although there is growing interest from governments, business, and multilateral organizations in including ecosystem services in impact assessments and mitigation requirements (Council on Environmental Quality 2009, Landsberg et al. 2011, IFC 2012), the development of standardized approaches to determining suitable offsets for ecosystem services lags behind those that have been developed for wetlands and for particular species. This is an issue for institutions like the California Coastal Commission, which is mandated by the Coastal Act to protect biodiversity, such as environmentally sensitive habitats and species, as well as to ensure the continued provision of several ecosystem services including recreational opportunities, fisheries, aesthetics, and ocean access. When coastal development is permitted, the California Coastal Commission may levy mitigation fees to compensate for environmental losses, but there is currently not a comprehensive, systematic approach for determining mitigation requirements or fees. For example, the mitigation fee for development of a seawall in Monterey County only took into account the loss of recreational services, not other services such as coastal protection provided by the beach (Caldwell and Segall 2007). A holistic impact assessment and mitigation framework that simultaneously assesses impacts on biodiversity, ecosystem function, and ecosystem services would better guide development and mitigation decisions in the diverse decision contexts facing California.

Conclusion

Ecosystem services can illuminate the many different benefits that functioning ecosystems can provide, rather than just benefits for a single species or single function, and relate those benefits to the people receiving them. Biodiversity has intrinsic value, and many conservation efforts do not require a broader approach to consider ecosystem function or ecosystem services to successfully preserve biodiversity. However, ecosystem functions are both affected by and can affect biodiversity, and therefore the functions underpinning ecosystem services can be correlated with biodiversity (Cardinale et al. 2012). This is not always the case, especially for sensitive species or habitats that are threatened by proximity to human impact and services that must be produced and received locally. Making such trade-offs explicit is better than not understanding or appreciating the consequences of natural resource decisions for multiple objectives. Where synergies do exist, considering biodiversity and ecosystem services together can create a stronger approach to conserving all aspects of nature that humans care about. An integrated framework for biodiversity and ecosystem services allows for scientific measurement of nature's diverse benefits to assist policy makers in defining goals and provides managers with tools to track progress toward these goals, with improved outcomes for humans and the ecosystems they rely upon.

Summary

This chapter introduces the concepts of biodiversity, ecosystem functions, ecosystem services, and their relationships to human well-being. The many facets of biodiversity are examined, along with current levels and losses of biodiversity in California in particular, and the consequences of those losses to ecosystem functioning. Ecosystem functioning is first presented within the framework of ecosystem ecology and ecological interactions and then extended as a foundation for the concepts of ecosystem services and natural capital. The socio-ecological systems thinking that defines ecosystem services and natural capital is described to help differentiate among ecosystem functioning, ecosystem services, natural capital, and the value of these numerous benefits of nature to people. Examples from Californian ecosystems illustrate a diverse set of ecosystem services provided by natural and managed systems. These include agricultural production, pest control, pollination, forage production for livestock, timber and non-timber forest products, fisheries and aquaculture, water production and regulation, water purification, carbon sequestration, hazard mitigation (from coastal and inland flooding), and recreation. The chapter closes with an examination of how information about biodiversity, ecosystem functioning, and ecosystem services can help inform decisions in different ways and for different policy contexts, such as conservation planning, climate adaptation, and permitting and mitigation. These three contexts give a brief but diverse view of the many ways to value nature, and of how using science to reveal these values can translate into actionable policy.

Acknowledgments

The authors wish to thank the Gordon and Betty Moore Foundation, which supported their work during the researching and writing of this chapter, and Heather Tallis and Mary Ruckelshaus for valuable insight to inform its discussion.

Recommended Reading

Daily, G., and K. Ellison. 2002. The new economy of nature: The quest to make conservation profitable. Island Press, Washington, D.C.

Gaston, K., and J. Spicer. 2004. Biodiversity: An introduction. Second edition. Blackwell Publishing, Oxford, UK.

Kareiva, P., H. Tallis, T. H. Ricketts, G. C. Daily, and S. Polasky. 2011. Natural capital: Theory and practice of mapping ecosystem services. Oxford University Press, Oxford, UK.

Naeem, S., D. E. Bunker, A. Hector, M. Loreau, and C. Perrings. 2009. Biodiversity, ecosystem functioning, and human wellbeing. An ecological and economic perspective. Oxford University Press, Oxford, UK.

National Research Council. 2004. Valuing ecosystem services: Toward better environmental decision-making. National Academies Press, Washington, D.C.

Solan, M., R. J. Aspden, and D. M. Paterson. 2012. Marine biodiversity and ecosystem functioning: Frameworks, methodologies, and integration. Oxford University Press, Oxford, UK.

Glossary

ECOSYSTEM ENGINEERS Species that exert their influence on ecosystem structure and functions through the physical formation or modification of habitat.

ECOSYSTEM SERVICES The benefits people receive from ecosystems. The value of ecosystem services can be considered a flow of benefits from nature to people. The four main types of ecosystem services are provisioning services (such as food, fuel, and fiber), regulating services (such as air and water purification, climate stabilization, and hazard mitigation), cultural services (such as spiritual, aesthetic and educational enjoyment of nature), and supporting services (such as soil formation, primary production, and nutrient cycling).

FUNCTIONAL REDUNDANCY When multiple species contribute to a particular ecosystem function in similar ways, so the addition or loss of another functionally similar species may have little effect.

GAMMA DIVERSITY The total species diversity found across a landscape.

KEYSTONE SPECIES Species that have a very large effect on community structure and function, compared to their biomass within the system.

MITIGATION OFFSETS The restoration of habitat or ecosystem functions to compensate for habitat or ecosystem services lost due to development.

NATURAL CAPITAL The stock of ecosystem services.

OVERYIELDING When complementarity among species increases a community property such as biomass, the relative amount of variation in the system decreases, leading to greater stability with higher diversity.

PAYMENTS FOR ECOSYSTEM SERVICES (PES) A financial arrangement where beneficiaries of an ecosystem service pay landowners to manage their land in a way that will provide them with an ecological service.

PORTFOLIO EFFECT When ecosystem stability increases with diversity because fluctuations in species abundances through time are not perfectly correlated.

PSYCHOLOGICAL ECOSYSTEM SERVICES The benefits of human experience of nature to cognitive function, including concentration, impulse inhibition, short-term and working memory, and mood.

RESILIENCE The ability of an ecosystem to bounce back from a stressor or disturbance.

SERVICESHED The area that provides a specific ecosystem service to specific beneficiaries.

SPECIES RICHNESS The number of species in a given area.

STRONG INTERACTORS A species whose presence or absence has large effects on community structure, composition and community.

TROPHIC CASCADE When predators in a food web greatly reduce the abundance of their prey, minimizing predation on their prey's prey.

References

Ackerly, D. D., R. A. Ryals, W. K. Cornwell, S. R. Loarie, S. Veloz, K. D. Higgason, W. L. Silver, and T. E. Dawson. 2012. Potential impacts of climate change on biodiversity and ecosystem services in the San Francisco Bay Area. Publication number: CEC-500-2012-037. California Energy Commission. Sacramento, California.

Arkema, K. K., G. Guannel, G. Verutes, S. A. Wood, A. Guerry, M. Ruckelshaus, P. Kareiva, M. Lacayo, and J. M. Silver. 2013. Coastal habitats shield people and property from sea-level rise and storms. Nature Climate Change <doi:10.1038/nclimate1944>.

Balvanera, P., A. B. Pfisterer, N. Buchmann, J.-S. He, T. Nakashizuka, D. Raffaelli, and B. Schmid. 2006. Quantifying the evidence for biodiversity effects on ecosystem functioning and services. Ecology Letters 9:1146–1156.

Balvanera, P., C. Kremen, and M. Martínez-Ramos. 2005. Applying community structure analysis to ecosystem function: Examples from pollination and carbon storage. Ecological Applications 15:360–375.

Barnosky, A. D., N. Matzke, S. Tomiya, G.O.U. Wogan, B. Swartz, T. B. Quental, C. Marshall, J. L. McGuire, E. L. Lindsey, K. C. Maguire, B. Mersey, and E. A. Ferrer. 2011. Has the Earth's sixth mass extinction already arrived? Nature 471:51–57.

BenDor, T., N. Brozovic, and V. G. Pallathucheril. 2008. The social impacts of wetland mitigation policies in the United States. Journal of Planning Literature 22:341–357.

Berlow, E. L. 1999. Strong effects of weak interactions in ecological communities. Nature 398:330–334.

Bernhardt, J. R., and H. M. Leslie. 2013. Resilience to climate change in coastal marine ecosystems. Annual Review of Marine Science 5:371–92.

Brander, K. 2010. Impacts of climate change on fisheries. Journal of Marine Systems 79:389–402.

Bratman, G. N., J. P. Hamilton, and G. C. Daily. 2012. The impacts of nature experience on human cognitive function and mental health. Annals of the New York Academy of Sciences 1249:118–136.

Brauman, K. A., G. C. Daily, T. K. Duarte, and H. A. Mooney. 2007. The nature and value of ecosystem services: An overview highlighting hydrologic services. Annual Review of Environment and Resources 32:67–98.

Brittain, C., N. Williams, C. Kremen, and A.-M. Klein. 2013. Synergistic effects of non-Apis bees and honey bees for pollination services. Proceedings of the Royal Society B-Biological Sciences 280:20122767.

Brown, S., A. Dushku, T. Pearson, D. Shoch, J. Winsten, S. Sweet, and J. Kadyszewski. 2004. Carbon supply from changes in management of forest, range, and agricultural lands Winrock International, for the California Energy Commission, PIER Energy-Related Environmental Research. 500-04-068F.

Brown, T. C. 1992. Streamflow needs and protection in wilderness areas. General technical report SE-US Department of Agriculture, Forest Service, Southeastern Forest Experiment Station (USA). U.S. Department of Agriculture, Forest Service, Southeastern Forest Experiment Station, Asheville, North Carolina.

Brusati, E. D., and E. D. Grosholz. 2006. Native and introduced ecosystem engineers produce contrasting effects on estuarine infaunal communities. Biological Invasions 8:683–695.

Bullock, J. M., J. Aronson, A. C. Newton, R. F. Pywell, and J. M. Rey-Benayas. 2011. Restoration of ecosystem services and biodiversity: Conflicts and opportunities. Trends in Ecology and Evolution 26(10):541–549.

Business Forecasting Center. 2010. Employment impacts of California salmon fishery closures in 2008 and 2009. Pages 1–6. Business Forecasting Center, Stockton, California.

Burgin, S. 2008. BioBanking: An environmental scientist's view of the role of biodiversity in banking offsets in conservation. Biodiversity Conservation 17:807–816.

Cadotte, M. W., J. Cavender-Bares, D. Tilman, and T. H. Oakley. 2009. Using phylogenetic, functional, and trait diversity to understand patterns of plant community productivity. PloS One 4:e5695.

Cadotte, M. W., K. Carscadden, and N. Mirotchnick. 2011. Beyond species: Functional diversity and the maintenance of ecological processes and services. Journal of Applied Ecology 48:1079–1087.

Cadotte, M. W., T. Jonathan Davies, J. Regetz, S. W. Kembel, E. Cleland, and T. H. Oakley. 2010. Phylogenetic diversity metrics for ecological communities: Integrating species richness, abundance, and evolutionary history. Ecology Letters 13:96–105.

Caldwell, M., and C. Segall. 2007. No day at the beach: Sea level rise, ecosystem loss, and public access along the California coast. Ecology Law Quarterly 9:534–578.

California Condor Recovery Program. 2013. Condor program monthly status report and locations: Population size and distribution February 28, 2013. Sacramento, California.

California Department of Fish and Game (CDFG). 2012a. Final California commercial landings for 2011. Sacramento, California.

———. 2012b. Report to the legislature: California wetland mitigation banking. Page 100. Sacramento, California.

California Department of Fish and Wildlife (CDFW). 2013a. State

and federally listed endangered, threatened, and rare plants of California. Sacramento, California.
———. 2013b. State and federally listed endangered and threatened animals of California. Sacramento, California.
California State Board of Equalization. 2012. California timber harvest statistics. Sacramento, California.
Cardinale, B. J., D. S. Srivastava, J. E. Duffy, J. P. Wright, A. L. Downing, M. Sankaran, and C. Jouseau. 2006. Effects of biodiversity on the functioning of trophic groups and ecosystems. Nature 443:989–992.
Cardinale, B. J., J. E. Duffy, A. Gonzalez, D. U. Hooper, C. Perrings, P. Venail, A. Narwani, G. M. Mace, D. Tilman, D. A. Wardle, A. P. Kinzig, G. C. Daily, M. Loreau, J. B. Grace, A. Larigauderie, D. S. Srivastava, and S. Naeem. 2012. Biodiversity loss and its impact on humanity. Nature 486:59–67.
Cardinale, B. J., K. Gross, K. Fritschie, P. Flombaum, J. Fox, C. Rixan, J. van Ruijven, P. Reich, M. Scherer-Lorenzen, and B. J. Wilsey. 2013. Biodiversity simultaneously enhances the production and stability of community biomass, but the effects are independent. Ecology. Vol. 94, 8:1697–1707.
Cardinale, B. J., K. L. Matulich, D. U. Hooper, J. E. Byrnes, E. Duffy, L. Gamfeldt, P. Balvanera, M. I. O'Connor, and A. Gonzalez. 2011. The functional role of producer diversity in ecosystems. American Journal of Botany 98:572–592.
Chan, K. M., M. R. Shaw, D. R. Cameron, E. C. Underwood, and G. C. Daily. 2006. Conservation planning for ecosystem services. PLoS Biology 4:e379.
Chapin, F. S., B. H. Walker, R. J. Hobbs, D. U. Hooper, J. H. Lawton, O. E. Sala, and D. Tilman. 1997. Biotic control over the functioning of ecosystems. Science 277:500–504.
Chaplin-Kramer, R., and C. Kremen. 2012. Pest control experiments show benefits of complexity at landscape and local scales. Ecological Applications 22:1936–1948.
Chaplin-Kramer, R., and M. R. George. 2013. Effects of climate change on range forage production in the San Francisco Bay Area. PLoS One 8:e57723.
Chaplin-Kramer, R., D. J. Kliebenstein, A. Chiem, E. Morrill, N. J. Mills, and C. Kremen. 2011. Chemically-mediated tritrophic interactions: Opposing effects of glucosinolates on a specialist herbivore and its predators. Journal of Applied Ecology 48:880–887.
Chaplin-Kramer, R., K. Tuxen-Bettman, and C. Kremen. 2011. Value of wildland habitat for supplying pollination services to Californian agriculture. Rangelands 33:33–41.
Chaplin-Kramer, R., M. E. O'Rourke, E. J. Blitzer, and C. Kremen. 2011. A meta-analysis of crop pest and natural enemy response to landscape complexity. Ecology Letters 14:922–932.
Chapman, A. D. 2009. Numbers of living species in Australia and the world. Australian Biological Resources Study, Canberra, Australia.
Community Foundation Sonoma County. 2010. Biodiversity action plan: Priority actions to preserve biodiversity in Sonoma County. Page 89. Sonoma County, California.
Conant, R., K. Paustian, and E. Elliott. 2001. Grassland management and conversion into grassland: Effects on soil carbon. Ecological Applications 11:343–355.
Cornwell, W., S. Stuart, A. Ramirez, and D. Ackerly. 2012. Climate change impacts on California vegetation: Physiology, life history, and ecosystem change. Publication number: CEC-500-2012-023. California Energy Commission, Sacramento, California.
Costanza, R., R. Arge, R. De Groot, S. Farberk, M. Grasso, B. Hannon, K. Limburg, S. Naeem, R. V. O. Neill, J. Paruelo, R. G. Raskin, and P. Suttonkk. 1997. The value of the world's ecosystem services and natural capital. Nature 387:253–260.
Council on Environmental Quality. 2009. Proposed national objectives, principles, and standards for water and related resources implementation studies. Page 27. Washington, D.C.
Daily, G. C. 1997. Nature's services: Societal dependence on natural ecosystems. Island Press, Washington, D.C.
Daily, G. C., S. Polasky, J. Goldstein, P. M. Kareiva, H. A. Mooney, L. Pejchar, T. H. Ricketts, J. Salzman, and R. Shallenberger. 2009. Ecosystem services in decision making: Time to deliver. Frontiers in Ecology and the Environment 7:21–28.
Dayton, P., and M. Tegner. 1992. Temporal and spatial patterns of disturbance and recovery in a kelp forest community. Ecological Monographs 62:421–445.
DeClerck, F. A. J., M. G. Barbour, and J. O. Sawyer. 2006. Species richness and stand stability in conifer forests of the Sierra Nevada. Ecology 87:2787–2799.
De Groot, R. S. 1987. Environmental functions as a unifying concept for ecology and economics. The Environmentalist 7:105–109.
De Groot, R. S., M. A. Wilson, and R.M.J. Boumans. 2002. A typology for the classification, description, and valuation of ecosystem functions, goods, and services. Ecological Economics 41:393–408.
Devictor, V., D. Mouillot, C. Meynard, F. Jiguet, W. Thuiller, and N. Mouquet. 2010. Spatial mismatch and congruence between taxonomic, phylogenetic, and functional diversity: The need for integrative conservation strategies in a changing world. Ecology Letters 13:1030–1040.
Doak, D. F., D. Bigger, and E. K. Harding. 1998. The statistical inevitability of stability-diversity relationships in community ecology. American Naturalist 151:264–276.
Doak, D. F., V. J. Bakker, B. E. Goldstein, and B. Hale. 2014. Moving forward with effective goals and methods for conservation: A reply to Marvier and Kareiva. Trends in Ecology and Evolution. <http://dx.doi.org.ezproxy.stanford.edu/10.1016/j.tree.2014.01.008>.
Doney, S. C., M. Ruckelshaus, J. Emmett Duffy, J. P. Barry, F. Chan, C. A. English, H. M. Galindo, J. M. Grebmeier, A. B. Hollowed, N. Knowlton, J. Polovina, N. N. Rabalais, W. J. Sydeman, and L. D. Talley. 2012. Climate change impacts on marine ecosystems. Annual Review of Marine Science 4:11–37.
Duffy, W. G., and S. N. Kahara. 2011. Wetland ecosystem services in California's Central Valley and implications for the Wetland Reserve Program. Ecological Applications 21:18–30.
Dukes, J. S. 2001. Productivity and complementarity in grassland microcosms of varying diversity. Oikos 94:468–480.
Ernst, R., K. E. Linsenmair, and M.-O. Rödel. 2006. Diversity erosion beyond the species level: Dramatic loss of functional diversity after selective logging in two tropical amphibian communities. Biological Conservation 133:143–155.
Estes, J. A., and J. F. Palmisano. 1974. Sea otters: Their role in structuring nearshore communities. Science 185:1058–1060.
Fairbank, Maslin, Maullin, Metz & Associates, 2010. Key findings from recent national opinion research on "Ecosystem Services": A report to The Nature Conservancy. Washington, D.C.
Fisher, B., K. Turner, M. Zylstra, R. Brouwer, R. de Groot, S. Farber, P. Ferraro, R. Green, D. Hadley, J. Harlow, P. Jefferiss, C. Kirkby, P. Morling, S. Mowatt, R. Naidoo, J. Paavola, B. Strassburg, D. Yu, and A. Balmford 2008. Ecosystem services and economic theory: Integration for policy-relevant research. Ecological Applications 18:2050–2067.
Flynn, D. F. B., M. Gogol-Prokurat, T. Nogeire, N. Molinari, B. T. Richers, B. B. Lin, N. Simpson, M. M. Mayfield, and F. DeClerck. 2009. Loss of functional diversity under land use intensification across multiple taxa. Ecology Letters 12:22–33.
Freeman, A. M., J. A. Herriges, and C. L. Kling. 2003. The Measurements of Environmental and Resource Values: Theory and Methods. Resources for the Future, Washington, D.C.
Fritz, S. A., and A. Purvis. 2010. Phylogenetic diversity does not capture body size variation at risk in the world's mammals. Proceedings of the Royal Society B: Biological Sciences 277:2435–2441.
Gamfeldt, L., H. Hillebrand, and P. R. Jonsson. 2008. Multiple functions increase the importance of biodiversity for overall ecosystem functioning. Ecology 89:1223–1231.
Garfin, G., G. Franco, H. Blanco, A. Comrie, P. Gonzalez, T. Piechota, R. Smyth, and R. Waskom, 2014: Ch. 20: Southwest. Climate Change Impacts in the United States: The Third National Climate Assessment, J. M. Melillo, Terese (T.C.) Richmond, and G. W. Yohe, Eds., U.S. Global Change Research Program, 462-486. doi:10.7930/J08G8HMN.
Gaston, K. J., editor. 1996. Biodiversity: A biology of numbers and difference. Blackwell Science, Oxford, UK.
Gennet, S., J. Howard, J. Langholz, K. Andrews, M. D. Reynolds, and S. A. Morrison. 2013. Farm practices for food safety: An emerging threat to floodplain and riparian ecosystems. Frontiers in Ecology and the Environment 11:236–242.
Goldman, R. L., and H. Tallis. 2009. A critical analysis of ecosystem services as a tool in conservation projects: The possible perils, the promises, and the partnerships. Annals of the New York Academy of Sciences 1162:63–78. <doi:10.1111/j.1749-6632.2009.04151.x>.
Goldman-Benner, R. L., S. Benitez, T. Boucher, A. Calvache, G. Daily, P. Kareiva, T. Kroeger, and A. Ramos. 2012. Water funds and pay-

ments for ecosystem services: Practice learns from theory and theory can learn from practice. Oryx 46:55–63.

Greenleaf, S. S., and C. Kremen. 2006a. Wild bee species increase tomato production and respond differently to surrounding land use in northern California. Biological Conservation 133:81–87.

———. 2006b. Wild bees enhance honey bees' pollination of hybrid sunflower. Proceedings of the National Academy of Sciences 103:13890–13895.

Grewell, B. J., E. K. Espeland, and P. L. Fiedler. 2013. Sea change under climate change: Case studies in rare plant conservation from the dynamic San Francisco Estuary 1(318):309–318.

Guerry, A. D., M. H. Ruckelshaus, K. K. Arkema, J. R. Bernhardt, G. Guannel, C.-K. Kim, M. Marsik, M. Papenfus, J. E. Toft, G. Verutes, S. A. Wood, M. Beck, F. Chan, K. M. A. Chan, G. Gelfenbaum, B. D. Gold, B. S. Halpern, W. B. Labiosa, S. E. Lester, P. S. Levin, M. McField, M. L. Pinsky, M. Plummer, S. Polasky, P. Ruggiero, D. A. Sutherland, H. Tallis, A. Day, and J. Spencer. 2012. Modeling benefits from nature: Using ecosystem services to inform coastal and marine spatial planning. International Journal of Biodiversity Science, Ecosystem Services, and Management 8:107–121.

Hall, D., J. Hall, and S. Murray. 2002. Contingent valuation of marine protected areas: Southern California rocky intertidal ecosystems. Natural Resource Modeling 15:335–368.

Hanak, E., and G. Moreno. 2011. California coastal management with a changing climate. Climatic Change 111:45–73.

Hayhoe, K., D. Cayan, C. B. Field, P. C. Frumhoff, E. P. Maurer, N. L. Miller, S. C. Moser, S. H. Schneider, K. N. Cahill, E. E. Cleland, L. Dale, R. Drapek, R. M. Hanemann, L. S. Kalkstein, J. Lenihan, C. K. Lunch, R. P. Neilson, S. C. Sheridan, and J. H. Verville. 2004. Emissions pathways, climate change, and impacts on California. Proceedings of the National Academy of Sciences of the United States of America 101:12422–12427.

Heal, G. 2000. Valuing Ecosystem Services. Ecosystems 3:24–30.

Heberger, M., H. Cooley, P. Herrera, P. Gleick, and E. Moore. 2009. The impacts of sea-level rise on the California coast. California Energy Commission. Publication number: CEC-500-2009-024-F. Sacramento, California.

Hector, A., and R. Bagchi. 2007. Biodiversity and ecosystem multifunctionality. Nature 448:188–190.

Heller, N., and E. Zavaleta. 2009. Biodiversity management in the face of climate change: A review of twenty-two years of recommendations. Biological Conservation 142:14–32.

Hoegh-Guldberg, O., and J. F. Bruno. 2010. The impact of climate change on the world's marine ecosystems. Science 328:1523–1528.

Hogg, B. N., and K. M. Daane. 2011. Ecosystem services in the face of invasion: The persistence of native and nonnative spiders in an agricultural landscape. Ecological Applications: A publication of the Ecological Society of America 21:565–576.

Hooper, D. U., E. C. Adair, B. J. Cardinale, J. E. K. Byrnes, B. A. Hungate, K. L. Matulich, A. Gonzalez, J. E. Duffy, L. Gamfeldt, and M. I. O'Connor. 2012. A global synthesis reveals biodiversity loss as a major driver of ecosystem change. Nature 486:105–108.

Hooper, D. U., F. S. Chapin III, J. J. Ewel, A. Hector, P. Inchausti, S. Lavorel, J. H. Lawton, D. M. Lodge, M. Loreau, S. Naeem, B. Schmid, H. Setala, A. J. Symstad, J. Vandermeer, and D. A. Wardle. 2005. Effects of biodiversity on ecosystem functioning: A consensus of current knowledge. Ecological Monographs 75:3–35.

Hooper, D. U., and P. M. Vitousek. 1997. The effects of plant composition and diversity on ecosystem processes. Science 277:1302–1305.

Huntsinger, L., M. Johnson, M. Stafford, and J. Fried. 2010. Hardwood rangeland landowners in California from 1985 to 2004: Production, ecosystem services, and permanence. Rangeland Ecology and Management 63:324–334.

International Finance Corporation (IFC). 2012. IFC performance standards on environmental and social sustainability. Page 66. Washington, D.C.

Isbell, F., V. Calcagno, A. Hector, J. Connolly, W. S. Harpole, P. B. Reich, M. Scherer-Lorenzen, B. Schmid, D. Tilman, J. van Ruijven, A. Weigelt, B. J. Wilsey, E. S. Zavaleta, and M. Loreau. 2011. High plant diversity is needed to maintain ecosystem services. Nature 477:199–202.

Jablonski, D. 1994. Extinctions in the fossil record. Philosophical Transactions of the Royal Society B: Biological Sciences 344:11–16.

Jedlicka, J. A., R. Greenberg, and D. K. Letourneau. 2011. Avian conservation practices strengthen ecosystem services in California vineyards. PloS One 6:e27347.

Jones, C. G., J. H. Lawton, and M. Shachak. 1994. Organisms as ecosystem engineers. Oikos 69:373–386.

Kareiva, P. and M. Marvier. 2012. What is conservation science? BioScience 62:962–969.

Karpuzcu, M. E., and W. T. Stringfellow. 2012. Kinetics of nitrate removal in wetlands receiving agricultural drainage. Ecological Engineering 42:295–303.

Keeler, B. L., S. Polasky, K. A. Brauman, K. A. Johnson, J. C. Finlay, A. O'Neill, K. Kovacs, and B. Dalzell. 2012. Linking water quality and well-being for improved assessment and valuation of ecosystem services. Proceedings of the National Academy of Sciences of the United States of America 109:18619–18624.

Kiff, L. F., R. I. Mesta, and M. P. Wallace. 1996. Recovery plan for the California condor. U.S. Fish and Wildlife Service. Portland, Oregon.

King, P. G., A. R. McGregor, and J. D. Whittet. 2010. The economic costs of sea-level rise to California beach communities. Report to California Department of Boating and Waterways. Fresno, California.

Klein, A.-M., B. E. Vaissière, J. H. Cane, I. Steffan-Dewenter, S. A. Cunningham, C. Kremen, and T. Tscharntke. 2007. Importance of pollinators in changing landscapes for world crops. Proceedings of the Royal Society B-Biological Sciences 274:303–313.

Klinger, D., and R. Naylor. 2012. Searching for solutions in aquaculture: Charting a sustainable course. Annual Review of Environment and Resources 37:247–276.

Kremen, C., N. M. Williams, R. L. Bugg, J. P. Fay, and R. W. Thorp. 2004. The area requirements of an ecosystem service: Crop pollination by native bee communities in California. Ecology Letters 7:1109–1119.

Krieger, D. 2001. The economic value of forest ecosystem services: a review. Report delivered to the Wilderness Society. Washington, D.C.

Kroeger, T., F. Casey, P. Alvarez, M. Cheatum, and L. Tavassoli. 2010. An Economic Analysis of the Benefits of Habitat Conservation on California Rangelands. Conservation Economics Program, Defenders of Wildlife. Washington, D.C.

Kroodsma, D. A., and C. B. Field. 2006. Carbon sequestration in California agriculture, 1980–2000. Ecological applications: A publication of the Ecological Society of America 16:1975–1985.

Laaksonen-Craig, S., G. Goldman, and W. McKillop. 2003. Forestry, forest industry, and forest products consumption in California. University of California, Oakland, California.

Landsberg, F., S. Ozment, and M. Stickler. 2011. Ecosystem services review for impact assessment: Introduction and guide to scoping. World Resources Institute. Washington, D.C.

Lavorel, S., and E. Garnier 2002. Predicting changes in community composition and ecosystem functioning from plant traits: Revisiting the Holy Grail. Functional Ecology 16:545–556.

Lawton, J. H. , and V. K. Brown. 1993. Redundancy in ecosystems. Pages 255–270 *in* E.-D. Schulze and H. A. Mooney, editors. Biodiversity and ecosystem function. Springer-Verlag, Berlin, Germany.

Lehman, C. L., and D. Tilman. 2000. Biodiversity, stability, and productivity in competitive communities. The American Naturalist 156:534–552.

Letourneau, D. K., and B. Goldstein. 2001. Pest damage and arthropod community structure in organic vs. conventional tomato production in California. Journal of Applied Ecology 38:557–570.

Letourneau, D. K., S. G. Bothwell Allen, and J. O. Stireman. 2012. Perennial habitat fragments, parasitoid diversity, and parasitism in ephemeral crops. Journal of Applied Ecology 49:1405–1416.

Long Tom Watershed Council. 2008. Ecosystem restoration in the Long Tom River Basin for water quality improvement in the Willamette River. Eugene, Oregon.

Loreau, M., and A. Hector. 2001. Partitioning selection and complementarity in biodiversity experiments. Nature 412:72–76.

Losey, J. E., and M. Vaughan. 2006. The economic value of ecological services provided by insects. Bioscience 56:311–323.

Luedeling, E., K. P. Steinmann, M. Zhang, P. H. Brown, J. Grant, and E. H. Girvetz. 2011. Climate change effects on walnut pests in California. Global Change Biology 17:228–238.

Lyons, K. G., and M. W. Schwartz. 2001. Rare species loss alters ecosystem function–invasion resistance. Ecology Letters 4:358–365.

MacArthur, R. H. 1972. Strong, or weak, interactions. Transactions of the Connecticut Academy of Arts and Sciences 44:177–188.

Macfarlane, R. B., S. Hayes, and B. Wells. 2008. Coho and Chinook salmon decline in California during the spawning seasons of 2007/08. Pages 8–11. Fisheries Service. Southwest Region. Santa Cruz and La Jolla, California.

Magurran, A. E. 1988. Ecological diversity and its measurement. Princeton University Press, Princeton, New Jersey.

Mandle, L., H. Tallis, L. Sotomayor, and A. L. Vogl. (in press) Who loses? Tracking ecosystem service redistribution from road development and mitigation in the Peruvian Amazon. Frontiers in Ecology and the Environment. Washington, D.C.

Mawdsley, J. R., R. O'Malley, and D. S. Ojima. 2009. A review of climate-change adaptation strategies for wildlife management and biodiversity conservation. Conservation Biology 23:1080–1089.

May, R. M. 2011. Why worry about how many species and their loss? PLoS Biology 9:e1001130.

Mayfield, M. M., S. P. Bonser, J. W. Morgan, I. Aubin, S. McNamara, and P. A. Vesk. 2010. What does species richness tell us about functional trait diversity? Predictions and evidence for responses of species and functional trait diversity to land-use change. Global Ecology and Biogeography 19:423–431.

McCann, K., A. Hastings, and G. Huxel. 1998. Weak trophic interactions and the balance of nature. Nature 395:794–798.

McCauley, D. J. 2006. Selling out on nature. Nature 443:27–8.

McGill, B. J., B. J. Enquist, E. Weiher, and M. Westoby. 2006. Rebuilding community ecology from functional traits. Trends in Ecology and Evolution 21:178–185.

Mendelsohn, R., and S. Olmstead. 2009. The economic valuation of environmental amenities and disamenities: Methods and applications. Annual Review of Environment and Resources 34:325–347.

Millennium Ecosystem Assessment (MA). 2005. Ecosystems and human well-being: Biodiversity synthesis. World Resources Institute, Washington, D.C.

———. 2003. Ecosystems and their services. Pages 49–70 in Ecosystems and Human Well-Being: A Framework for Assessment. World Resources Institute, Washington, D.C.

Mimura, N., L. Nurse, R. McLean, and J. Agard. 2007. Small islands. Pages 687–716 in M.L. Parry, O. F. Canziani, J. P. Palutikof, P. J. van der Linden, and C. E. Hanson, editors. Climate Change 2007: Impacts, Adaptation and Vulnerability. Contribution of Working Group II to the Fourth Assessment Report of the Intergovernmental Panel on Climate Change. Cambridge University Press, Cambridge, UK.

Mora, C., D. P. Tittensor, S. Adl, A. G. B. Simpson, and B. Worm. 2011. How many species are there on Earth and in the ocean? PLoS Biology 9:e1001127.

Moritz, C., J. L. Patton, C. J. Conroy, J. L. Parra, G. C. White, and S. R. Beissinger. 2008. Impact of a century of climate change on small-mammal communities in Yosemite National Park, USA. Science 322:261–264.

Morse, R. A., and N. W. Calderone. 2000. The Value of Honey Bees as Pollinators of U.S. Crops in 2000. Bee Culture Magazine 128:2–15.

Moyle, P. B., J.V.E. Katz, and R. M. Quiñones. 2011. Rapid decline of California's native inland fishes: A status assessment. Biological Conservation 144:2414–2423.

Myers, N., R. A. Mittermeier, C. G. Mittermeier, G.A.B. da Fonseca, and J. Kent. 2000. Biodiversity hotspots for conservation priorities. Nature 403:853–858.

Naeem, S., J. E. Duffy, and E. Zavaleta. 2012. The functions of biological diversity in an age of extinction. Science 336:1401–1406.

National Marine Fisheries Service. 2012. Fisheries Economics of the United States, 2011. U.S. Dept. Commerce, NOAA Tech. Memo. NMFS-F/SPO-118, 175p. <https://www.st.nmfs.noaa.gov/st5/publication/index.html>.

National Research Council. 2012. Sea-Level Rise for the Coasts of California, Oregon, and Washington: Past, Present, and Future. National Academies Press, Washington, D.C.

Nelson, J. L., and E. S. Zavaleta. 2012. Salt marsh as a coastal filter for the oceans: Changes in function with experimental increases in nitrogen loading and sea-level rise. PloS One 7:e38558.

Nemec, K. T., and C. Raudsepp-Hearne. 2012. The use of geographic information systems to map and assess ecosystem services. Biodiversity and Conservation 22:1–15.

Neutel, A.-M., J.A.P. Heesterbeek, and P. C. De Ruiter. 2002. Stability in real food webs: Weak links in long loops. Science 296:1120–1123.

Null, S., and J. Viers. 2012. Water-Energy Sector Vulnerability to Climate Warming in the Sierra Nevada: Water Year Classification in Non-Stationary Climates. Public Interest Energy Research (PIER) Program White Paper. Prepared for the California Energy Commission. Sacramento, California.

O'Brien, S. J., and J. F. Evermann. 1988. Interactive influence of infectious disease and genetic diversity in natural populations. Trends in Ecology and Evolution 3:254–259.

Odum, E. P., H. T. Odum, and J. Andrews. 1971. Fundamentals of Ecology. Volume 3. Saunders: Philadelphia, Pennsylvania.

Outdoor Industry Foundation. 2006. The active outdoor recreation economy. Page 20. <https://outdoorindustry.org/pdf/OIA_Recreation_Economy_State_2006.pdf>. Boulder, Colorado.

Paine, R. T. 1969. A note on trophic complexity and community stability. American Naturalist 103:91–93.

Palmer, M. A., C. A. Reidy Liermann, C. Nilsson, M. Flörke, J. Alcamo, P. S. Lake, and N. Bond. 2008. Climate change and the world's river basins: Anticipating management options. Frontiers in Ecology and the Environment 6:81–89.

Pasari, J. R., T. Levi, E. S. Zavaleta, and D. Tilman. 2013. Several scales of biodiversity affect ecosystem multifunctionality. Proceedings of the National Academy of Sciences. 110:10219–10222.

Pendleton, L., and J. Kildow. 2006. The non-market value of beach recreation in California. Shore Beach 74:34–37.

Pendleton, L., P. King, C. Mohn, D. G. Webster, R. Vaughn, and P. N. Adams. 2011. Estimating the potential economic impacts of climate change on Southern California beaches. Climatic Change 109:277–298.

Pimentel, D., H. Acquay, M. Biltonen, and P. Rice. 1992. Environmental and economic costs of pesticide use. BioScience 42:750–760.

Plummer, M. L. 2009. Assessing benefit transfer for the valuation of ecosystem services. Frontiers in Ecology and the Environment 7:38–45.

Pressey, R., M. Cabeza, and M. Watts. 2007. Conservation planning in a changing world. Trends in Ecology and Environment 22:583–592.

Prinzing, A., R. Reiffers, W. G. Braakhekke, S. M. Hennekens, O. Tackenberg, W. A. Ozinga, J. H. J. Schaminée, and J. M. van Groenendael. 2008. Less lineages—more trait variation: Phylogenetically clustered plant communities are functionally more diverse. Ecology Letters 11:809–819.

Rahel, F. J., B. Bierwagen, and Y. Taniguchi. 2008. Managing aquatic species of conservation concern in the face of climate change and invasive species. Conservation Biology: The Journal of the Society for Conservation Biology 22:551–561.

Ralls, K., and J. D. Ballou. 2004. Genetic status and management of California condors. The Condor 106:215–228.

Reich, P. B., D. Tilman, F. Isbell, K. Mueller, S. E. Hobbie, D. F. B. Flynn, and N. Eisenhauer. 2012. Impacts of biodiversity loss escalate through time as redundancy fades. Science 336:589–592.

Reyers, B., S. Polasky, H. Tallis, H. A. Mooney, and A. Larigauderie. 2012. Finding common ground for biodiversity and ecosystem services. Bioscience. 62:503–507.

Roberts, C. M., J. P. Hawkins, and F. R. Gell. 2005. The role of marine reserves in achieving sustainable fisheries. Philosophical Transactions of the Royal Society of London. Series B, Biological Sciences 360:123–132.

Rolband, M. S., A. Redmon, and T. Kelsch. 2000. Wetland mitigation banking. Pages 181–214 in D. M. Kent, editor. Applied Wetlands Science and Technology. Second edition. Lewis Publishers, Boca Raton, Florida.

Roxburgh, S. H., S. W. Wood, B. G. Mackey, G. Woldendorp, and P. Gibbons. 2006. Assessing the carbon sequestration potential of managed forests: A case study from temperate Australia. Journal of Applied Ecology 43:1149–1159.

Ruckelshaus, M., E. McKenzie, H. Tallis, A. Guerry, G. Daily, P. Kareiva, S. Polasky, T. Ricketts, N. Bhagabati, S. A. Wood, and J. Bernhardt. 2013. Notes from the field: Lessons learned from using ecosystem service approaches to inform real-world decisions. Ecological Economics. <doi:10.1016/j.ecolecon.2013.07.009>.

Ruckelshaus, M., S. Doney, and H. Galindo. 2013. Securing ocean benefits for society in the face of climate change. Marine Policy 40:154–159.

Ruhl, J., and J. Salzman. 2006. The effects of wetland mitigation banking on people. National Wetlands Newsletter 28(2):1–13.

Sala, E., and G. Sugihara. 2005. Food-web theory provides guidelines for marine conservation. Pages 170–183 in A. Belgrano, U. M. Scharler, J. Dunne, and R. E. Ulanowicz, editors. Aquatic Food

Webs: An Ecosystem Approach. Oxford University Press, New York, New York.
Sala, E., and M. H. Graham. 2002. Community-wide distribution of predator-prey interaction strength in kelp forests. Proceedings of the National Academy of Sciences of the USA 99:3678–3683.
Sala, E., and N. Knowlton. 2006. Global marine biodiversity trends. Annual Review of Environment and Resources 31:93–122.
Satz, D., R. K. Gould, K. M. A. Chan, A. Guerry, B. Norton, T. Satterfield, B. S. Halpern, J. Levine, U. Woodside, N. Hannahs, X. Basurto, and S. Klain. 2013. The Challenges of Incorporating Cultural Ecosystem Services into Environmental Assessment. Ambio 42:675–684.
Scheffers, B. R., L. N. Joppa, S. L. Pimm, and W. F. Laurance. 2012. What we know and don't know about Earth's missing biodiversity. Trends 27:501–510.
Schweiger, O., M. Musche, D. Bailey, R. Billeter, T. Diekötter, F. Hendrickx, F. Herzog, J. Liira, J.-P. Maelfait, M. Speelmans, and F. Dziock. 2007. Functional richness of local hoverfly communities (Diptera, Syrphidae) in response to land use across temperate Europe. Oikos 116:461–472.
Seastedt, T., R. Hobbs, and K. Suding. 2008. Management of novel ecosystems: Are novel approaches required? Frontiers in Ecology and the Environment 6:547–553.
Selmants, P. C., E. S. Zavaleta, J. R. Pasari, and D. L. Hernandez. 2012. Realistic plant species losses reduce invasion resistance in a California serpentine grassland. Journal of Ecology 100:723–731.
Shaw, M. R., L. Pendleton, D. R. Cameron, B. Morris, D. Bachelet, K. Klausmeyer, J. MacKenzie, D. R. Conklin, G. N. Bratman, J. Lenihan, E. Haunreiter, C. Daly, and P. R. Roehrdanz. 2011. The impact of climate change on California's ecosystem services. Climatic Change 109:465–484.
Shih, T. 1998. The Land Base of California's Forests. California Department of Forestry and Fire Protection, Fire and Resource Assessment Program. Sacramento, California.
Sillett, S. C., R. Van Pelt, G. W. Koch, A. R. Ambrose, A. L. Carroll, M. E. Antoine, and B. M. Mifsud. 2010. Increasing wood production through old age in tall trees. Forest Ecology and Management 259:976–994.
Silver, W. L., R. Ryals, and V. Eviner. 2010. Soil carbon pools in California's annual grassland ecosystems. Rangeland Ecology and Management 63:128–136.
Soule, M. 2013. The "New Conservation." Conservation Biology 27:895–897.
Stein, B. A., L. S. Kutner, G. A. Hammerson, L. L. Master, and L. E. Morse. 2000. State of the States: Geographic patterns of diversity, rarity, and endemism. Pages 146–185 in B. A. Stein, L. S. Kutner, and J. S. Adams, editors. Precious Heritage: The Status of Biodiversity in the United States. Oxford University Press, New York, New York.
Stralberg, D., M. Brennan, J. C. Callaway, J. K. Wood, L. M. Schile, D. Jongsomjit, M. Kelly, V. T. Parker, and S. Crooks. 2011. Evaluating tidal marsh sustainability in the face of sea-level rise: A hybrid modeling approach applied to San Francisco Bay. PloS One 6:e27388.
Tallis, H., and S. Polasky. 2009. Mapping and valuing ecosystem services as an approach for conservation and natural-resource management. Annals of the New York Academy of Sciences 1162:265–283.
Tallis, H., H. Mooney, S. Andelman, P. Balvanera, W. Cramer, D. Karp, S. Polasky, B. Reyers, T. Ricketts, S. Running, K. Thonicke, B. Tietjen, and A. Walz. 2012. A global system for monitoring ecosystem service change. BioScience 62:977–986.
Tallis, H., S. E. Lester, M. Ruckelshaus, M. Plummer, K. McLeod, A. Guerry, S. Andelman, M. R. Caldwell, M. Conte, S. Copps, D. Fox, R. Fujita, S. D. Gaines, G. Gelfenbaum, B. Gold, P. Kareiva, C. Kim, K. Lee, M. Papenfus, S. Redman, B. Silliman, L. Wainger, and C. White. 2012. New metrics for managing and sustaining the ocean's bounty. Marine Policy 36:303–306.
Tallis, H., S. Polasky, J. S. Lozano, and S. Wolny. 2012. Inclusive wealth accounting for regulating ecosystem services. Pages 195–214 in UNEP and UNU-IHDP, editors. Inclusive Wealth Report 2012. Measuring progress toward sustainability. Cambridge University Press. Cambridge, UK.
Tilman, D. 1996. Biodiversity: Population versus ecosystem stability. Ecology Vol 77, issue 2:350–363.
Trulio, L., J. Callaway, and S. Crooks. 2007. White paper on carbon sequestration and tidal salt marsh restoration. South Bay Salt Pond Restoration Project. San Jose, California.
Turner, R. K., and G. C. Daily. 2007. The Ecosystem Services Framework and natural capital conservation. Environmental and Resource Economics 39:25–35.
USDA National Agricultural Statistics Service. 2012. California agricultural statistics 2011 crop year. Page 97. Sacramento, California.
Vanbergen, A. J., and the Insect Pollinators Initiative. 2013. Threats to an ecosystem service: pressures on pollinators. Frontiers in Ecology and the Environment 11:251–259.
Waage, B. S., E. Stewart, and K. Armstrong. 2008. Measuring Corporate Impact on Ecosystems: A Comprehensive Review of New Tools. Business for Social Responsibility. San Francisco, California.
Walker, S., A. L. Brower. R. T. Theo Stephens and W. G. Lee. 2009. Why bartering biodiversity fails. Conservation Letters 2:149–157.
Walther, G.-R. 2010. Community and ecosystem responses to recent climate change. Philosophical transactions of the Royal Society of London. Series B, Biological sciences 365:2019–24.
West, J. M., S. H. Julius, P. Kareiva, C. Enquist, J. J. Lawler, B. Petersen, A. E. Johnson, and M. R. Shaw. 2009. U.S. natural resources and climate change: Concepts and approaches for management adaptation. Environmental Management 44:1001–1021.
Wilson, E. O. 2010. The diversity of life. Harvard University Press, Cambridge, Massachusetts.
Winfree, R., B. J. Gross, and C. Kremen. 2011. Valuing pollination services to agriculture. Ecological Economics 71:80–88.
Zavaleta, E. S., and K. B. Hulvey. 2004. Realistic species losses disproportionately reduce grassland resistance to biological invaders. Science 306:1175–1177.
Zavaleta, E. S., J. Pasari, J. Moore, D. Hernández, K. B. Suttle, and C. C. Wilmers. 2009. Ecosystem responses to community disassembly. Annals of the New York Academy of Sciences 1162:311–333.
Zavaleta, E. S., J. R. Pasari, K. B. Hulvey, and G. D. Tilman. 2010. Sustaining multiple ecosystem functions in grassland communities requires higher biodiversity. Proceedings of the National Academy of Sciences of the USA 107:1443–1446.
Zedler, J. B., and S. Kercher. 2005. Wetland resources: Status, trends, ecosystem services, and restorability. Annual Review of Environment and Resources 30:39–74.

PART FOUR

ECOSYSTEMS

SIXTEEN

The Offshore Ecosystem

STEVEN J. BOGRAD, ELLIOTT L. HAZEN, SARA M. MAXWELL,
ANDREW W. LEISING, HELEN BAILEY, and RICHARD D. BRODEUR

Introduction

The California Current System (CCS) is one of the world's four eastern boundary upwelling systems, which are among the most productive ecosystems in the ocean. Prevailing northwesterly winds at the California coast drive a southward-flowing current that moves cold water to lower latitudes. These winds also drive surface water offshore, causing upwelling of colder, nutrient-rich subsurface water to replace it. This seasonal abundance of nutrients results in phytoplankton blooms at the base of a food web that supports an abundance of animal species from zooplankton to small fish (e.g., anchovy and sardines) up to large predators such as tuna, sharks, and whales. This rich marine ecosystem sustains California's many important fisheries and contributes to its value for ecotourism.

The highly dynamic nature of the CCS makes it difficult to strictly define its boundaries. In general, the CCS extends from the Transition Zone near 50°N, separating the Alaskan Gyre and North Pacific Subtropical Gyre, south to the subtropical waters off Baja California, Mexico (20°N–25°N). Distinct biogeographical domains within the CCS have been proposed, with divisions at Cape Mendocino (40.4°N) and Point Conception (34.4°N) (Parrish et al. 1981, Allen et al. 2006, Longhurst 1998). In the cross-shore direction, the CCS extends from the intertidal and coastal zones (see Chapters 17, "Shallow Rocky Reefs and Kelp Forests," and 18, "Intertidal") to hundreds of kilometers offshore into the North Pacific Subtropical Gyre. For this chapter we define the offshore region of the CCS as the area from 4.8 kilometers (3 miles) offshore, the outer boundary of state jurisdiction, to 200 kilometers offshore, which represents the western boundary of the federal Exclusive Economic Zone (Figure 16.1). We further focus on the waters offshore of the state of California.

The CCS is one of the most thoroughly monitored and studied oceanic regions in the world (Bograd et al. 2003, Peña and Bograd 2007, Checkley and Barth 2009). One key research program in this area is the California Cooperative Oceanic Fisheries Investigations (CalCOFI), which has provided consistent monitoring of the physics, chemistry, and lower-trophic biology of the CCS (primarily the southern component) since 1949 (McClatchie 2014). Numerous other monitoring programs and process studies have been conducted by academic, federal, and state government scientists over the past

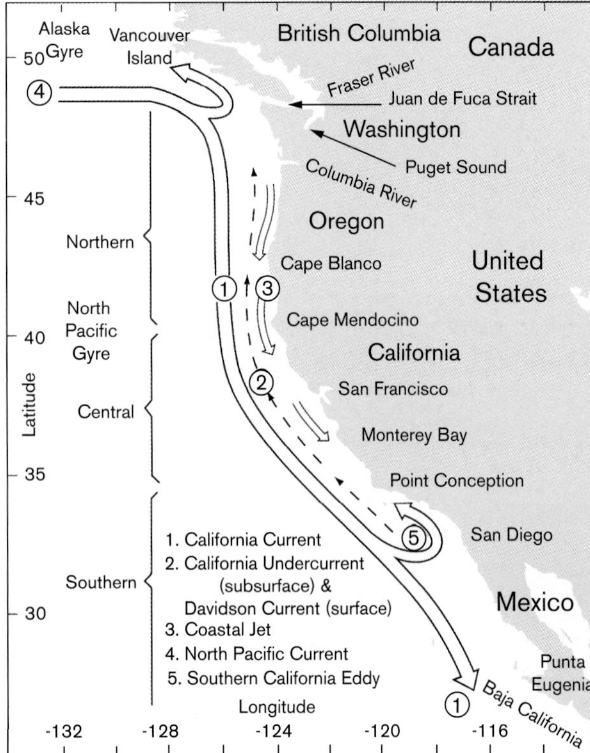

FIGURE 16.1 Map of California Current Ecosystem (CCE) showing dominant currents and oceanographic features.

several decades (see summary in Checkley and Barth 2009). We begin with a review of the key taxa and species that compose the offshore component of the CCS ecosystem, from primary producers to top predators. We also describe some of the dominant processes of TROPHIC INTERACTIONS and ecosystem functioning within the offshore CCS. We then move to the human dimensions of the CCS, focusing on ecosystem services, conservation issues, and management structures. We conclude with a brief discussion of the future of the CCS offshore ecosystem and highlight potential climate-driven changes that could occur.

Offshore Ecosystems and Food Webs of the California Current System

The oceanography of the CCS is characterized by strong physical forcing across multiple time scales and drives high biological productivity and a complex ecosystem structure (see Chapter 6, "Oceanography"). Its seasonal pulses of productivity lead to a high biomass of PELAGIC species that in turn support a diversity of top predators and economically important marine fisheries (see Chapter 35, "Marine Fisheries"). Many mobile species migrate seasonally over the latitudinal extent of the CCS (Horne and Smith 1997, Agostini et al. 2008, Checkley and Barth 2009, Block et al. 2011), while others migrate long distances across the Pacific to the CCS to exploit seasonally recurrent resources (Block et al. 2011). Geographic and bathymetric features (e.g., capes, islands, and submarine canyons) and oceanographic features (e.g., eddies and fronts) affect the distribution of many species (Checkley and Barth 2009). Vertically, pelagic habitat is defined as below the surface and above the bottom, but more specifically as the epipelagic (0–200 meters, EUPHOTIC), MESOPELAGIC (200–1,000 meters), and bathypelagic (>1,000 meters bottom depth). In this section we describe the diversity of species occurring in the CCS from primary producers to top predators, their trophic interactions, and hotspots, focusing on the epipelagic and mesopelagic.

Photo on previous page: Offshore hotspot of shearwaters, common dolphins, and minke whales at sunset, southern California. Photo: Elliott L. Hazen.

Primary Producers

The base of the offshore food web is primary production by unicellular algae—the phytoplankton (Kudela et al. 2008; Figure 16.2). The predominant phytoplankton groups within the California Current include three classes:

- Diatoms—eukaryotic cells with hard silica-based shells, dominant in strong coastal upwelling areas, occasionally forming a harmful algal bloom.
- Dinoflagellates—eukaryotic cells, many slightly motile, often dominant in stratified regions and more commonly forming harmful algal blooms than diatoms.
- Cyanobacteria—prokaryotic cells, predominant in further offshore regions but still abundant in nearshore regions (about 20% of phytoplankton productivity).

Diatoms, which range in size from a few microns to chains of cells several hundred microns long, are probably the most critical phytoplankton contributors to overall productivity and as a food resource for higher trophic levels. Diatoms grow rapidly in nearshore regions where upwelling provides cool, nutrient-rich water. Diatoms thus typically dominate the phytoplankton biomass during strong upwelling. In turn, diatoms are grazed by secondary producers (i.e., the microzooplankton and mesozooplankton, described below, and certain small and larval fish). Occasionally, certain species of diatoms may form harmful algal blooms. Specifically, the diatom *Pseudo-nitzschia multiseries* produces the powerful neurotoxin domoic acid, which can bioaccumulate in the tissues of fish and potentially harm humans, marine mammals, and possibly seabirds (Kudela et al. 2005). Although diatoms are important prey for copepods, their protective silica casings (known as frustules) and larger size provide some protection from smaller microzooplankton, another factor allowing them to form large blooms.

Dinoflagellates can outcompete diatoms under certain conditions when silica is limiting, because dinoflagellates do not require silica for growth. Many dinoflagellates are also somewhat motile and can swim to deeper waters at night to obtain nutrients when the water column is stratified and surface nutrient levels are low. Dinoflagellates, with their relatively enriched nutrient content and lack of hard silica encasements, are typically preferred over diatoms as a food source by other microzooplankton and small crustacean zooplankton (Kleppel 1993, Leising et al. 2005). Because of this, when dinoflagellates predominate, a longer chain of organisms often exists between phytoplankton and higher predators, reducing total energy transfer to higher trophic levels (only about 30% to 35% of energy is transferred upwards from each trophic level) (Paffenhofer 1976, Fenchel 1987). In

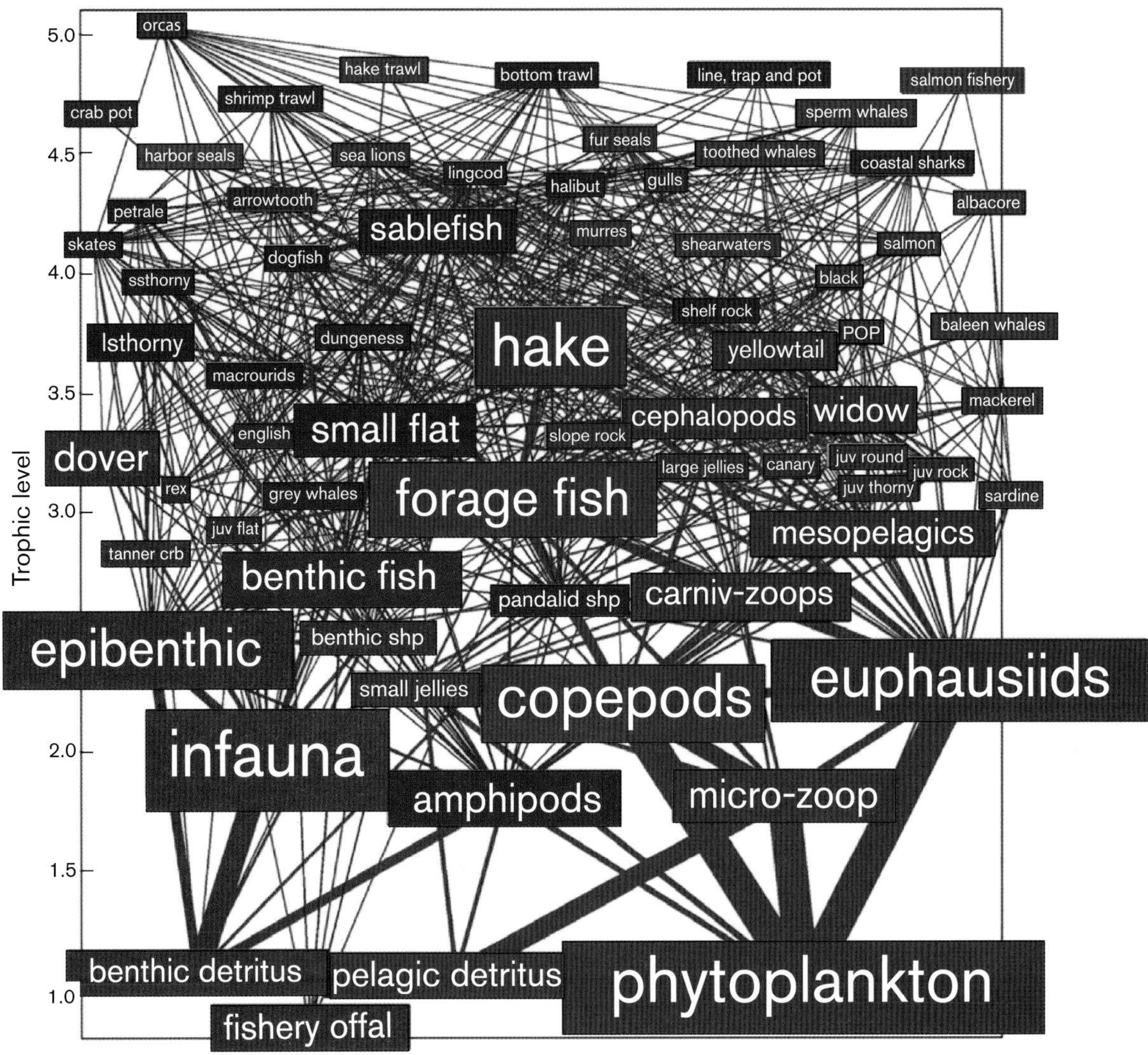

FIGURE 16.2 Food web diagram for the California Current Ecosystem. Red represents the benthic ecosystem while blue represents the pelagic. The estimated trophic level is on the y-axis and the size of each box represents its relative biomass in the food web. Width of lines represents biomass flux of prey to predator. Source: Field et al. 2006.

contrast, in diatom-dominated systems the diatoms may be directly consumed by krill, copepods, and other zooplankton, which in turn are eaten by small fish and some fish larvae.

Cyanobacteria are more important in offshore regions where, although they do not have a high biomass, they can have high growth rates, causing rapid nutrient turnover (Sherr et al. 2005). Cyanobacteria are consumed primarily by unicellular microzooplankton that may be prey for other microzooplankton. Thus far offshore food webs dominated by cyanobacteria, which already have low total productivity due to lower biomass compared to the nearshore, tend to have an even greater reduction of biomass at higher trophic levels due to the relatively large number of trophic links (see Figure 16.2).

Primary Consumers

Primary consumers are species that feed either primarily or partially on the primary producers (phytoplankton). They include the following groups ordered approximately from smallest to largest by individual body size:

- Microzooplankton—unicellular zooplankton that feed at high rates on phytoplankton, other microzooplankton, and bacteria.
- Copepods—smaller crustacean zooplankton, often the numerically dominant multicellular organism in many areas of the CCS that feed on phytoplankton, other zooplankton, and microzooplankton.
- Other crustacean zooplankton—this group includes shrimps, mysids, and other less numerically dominant but important organisms that consume phytoplankton, other zooplankton, and microzooplankton.
- Gelatinous zooplankton—soft-bodied zooplankton, such as jellyfish, ctenophores, PELAGIC gastropods (primarily pteropods), salps, doliolids, and appendicularians; chaetognaths can be important in some areas.
- Euphausiids—also known as krill, relatively large, often swarm- or school-forming crustacean zoo-

plankton that feed on both phytoplankton and zooplankton.

- Ichthyoplankton—small larval stages of fish that feed on both phytoplankton and zooplankton, including the larvae of the small pelagic fish, plus the larval stages of large pelagic fish and groundfish, such as Pacific hake, jack mackerel, and rockfish.
- Small pelagic fish—includes baitfish and other forage fish, such as sardine, anchovy, and smelts, which are relatively small as adults and feed on phytoplankton and/or zooplankton.

Unicellular microzooplankton include a diverse array of organisms, such as heterotrophic dinoflagellates, ciliates, and choanoflagellates. These organisms primarily eat other microzooplankton, phytoplankton, cyanobacteria, and bacteria. The CCE biomass of unicellular microzooplankton is usually low; however, their grazing rates are comparable to the growth rates of phytoplankton (Li et al. 2011). Thus, contrary to common belief, it is these unicellular microzooplankton, not crustaceans or fish, that consume the majority of phytoplankton standing stock and production within many areas of the CCE (Calbet and Landry 2004).

Particularly in the regions offshore of the main wind-driven upwelling front, a large portion of the energy that flows into microzooplankton does not reach higher trophic levels but is returned to detrital pools or recycled within the microzooplankton trophic level (see Figure 16.2). This retention of energy within the unicellular microzooplankton trophic level is known as the "microbial loop" and, when prevalent, decreases the overall productivity of higher trophic levels (see review in Fenchel 2008). Unicellular microzooplankton are a key prey source for copepods, gelatinous zooplankton, and other small crustacean zooplankton due to their enriched nitrogen content compared to similarly sized phytoplankton.

Copepods and other small crustacean zooplankton have similar roles to krill within the CCE (Figure 16.3). Unlike krill, copepods and small crustacean zooplankton do not tend to form large, dense schools, although for brief periods (a few hours to days) they can occur at locally higher densities when they aggregate near physical (e.g., horizontally along physical fronts or vertically near the main thermocline) or biological discontinuities (e.g., phytoplankton "thin layers"). Copepods, which often dominate the zooplankton numerically, eat phytoplankton, microzooplankton, and other smaller crustacean zooplankton, and in turn are food for krill, fish larvae, and small pelagic fish. Many of the larger, crustacean zooplankton undergo daily vertical migrations from as deep as several hundred meters during the day to near the surface at night, mainly to avoid visual predators such as fish (Enright and Hamner 1967, Hays 2003).

This vertical migration could contribute significantly to carbon export from surface layers to depth, as copepods feed near the surface and then can die, be eaten, or produce fecal pellets while at depth (Stukel et al. 2013). Unlike many other zooplankton, several dominant species of copepods, those of the genera *Calanus* and *Neocalanus* in particular, undergo a wintertime dormant period wherein they descend to great depths (around 400 to 1,000 meters) for four to eight months of the year (Dahms 1995). They then emerge in the spring to reproduce. Copepods thus have marked seasonal variation in their availability to higher trophic levels, often leading to timing mismatch problems critical to the overall phenology of the CCE and potentially sensitive to climate change. Other

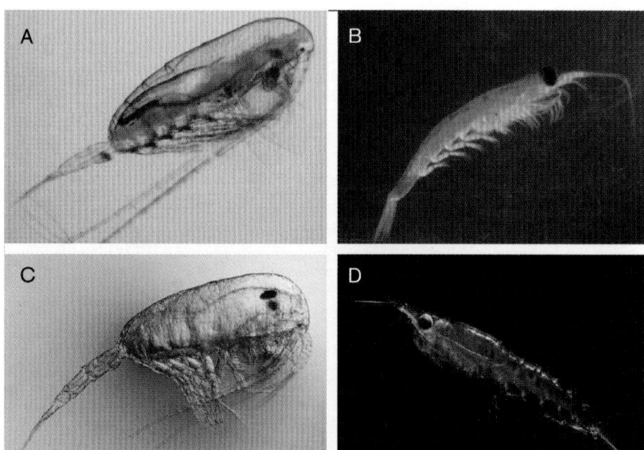

FIGURE 16.3 Photographs of dominant zooplankton species in the California Current. Photos: (A) NOAA Fisheries; (B) Moira Galbraith, Fisheries and Oceans Canada; (C) Russ Hopcroft, University of Alaska, Fairbanks; (D) Steve Haddock, Monterey Bay Aquarium Research Institute.

A *Calanus pacificus*

B *Euphausia pacifica*

C *Metridia pacifica*

D *Thysanoessa spinifera*

small crustaceans, such as shrimps and mysids, tend to be less abundant but can be important in some areas. Mysids often form swarms in shallow nearshore waters and can be an important food source for outmigrating smolts (Brodeur 1990). Crab larvae can also be seasonally important during their larval PLANKTONIC phase.

When prevalent, gelatinous zooplankton provide an alternate pathway for energy flow that might or might not lead to production in higher trophic levels (Brodeur et al. 2011). Gelatinous zooplankton include a variety of forms, from free-floating jellyfish that passively ambush zooplankton and small larval fish prey, to appendicularians that build large gelatinous "houses" used to filter large quantities of the smallest phytoplankton from the water column. While gelatinous zooplankton grow and feed at high rates, their bodies are composed mostly of water. As a result, they are not typically a good food source for larger organisms, with the exception of certain turtles (e.g., leatherbacks, *Dermochelys coriacea*) and fishes (e.g., ocean sunfish, *Mola mola*) that specialize in gelatinous prey. Systems dominated by gelatinous zooplankton as the primary predators of phytoplankton tend to have limited fish production and are generally considered "dead-end." An exception are pteropods—pelagic gastropods that form large, gelatinous nets much larger than their body size, used to capture falling detritus in the water column. Unlike the other taxa in this group, pteropods are known to be an important food source for some salmon (Brodeur 1990) and possibly other fish species. Gelatinous zooplankton blooms (especially salps, a type of planktonic tunicate) can be found offshore in OLIGOTROPHIC regions, while medusae and ctenophore blooms can be important nearshore during warmer periods.

Euphausiids, primarily the species *Euphausia pacifica* and *Thysanoessa spinifera*, are another key link in the trophic web of the CCE (Brinton and Townsend 2003; see Figure 16.2, Figure 16.3). These species eat primarily phytoplankton (diatoms) and small zooplankton, and in turn provide food for many fishes, birds, and marine mammals. Euphausiids can form large, conspicuous schools and swarms that attract larger predators, including baleen whales. Due to their high feeding and growth rates and key prey status for many species, euphausiids play a critical role in the overall flow of energy through the CCE.

Ichthyoplankton, the larvae of larger fish and small pelagics, are a key resource for larger fish and other marine predators. Although only within the water column for a short period of time, from weeks to a few months, ichthyoplankton abundance may at times dominate the total abundance of secondary consumers, making them important grazers on phytoplankton and smaller zooplankton classes. Finally, small pelagic fish, such as sardine and anchovy, comprise an integral part of the CCE, feeding nearly exclusively on phytoplankton (typically diatoms), small pelagic crustaceans, and copepods (Emmett et al. 2005; Figure 16.4). This group, often termed the "forage" fish (discussed in more detail elsewhere in this chapter), functions as the main pathway of energy flow in the CCE from phytoplankton to larger fish and to the young life stages of larger predators (Crawford 1987, Cury et al. 2000; see Figure 16.2).

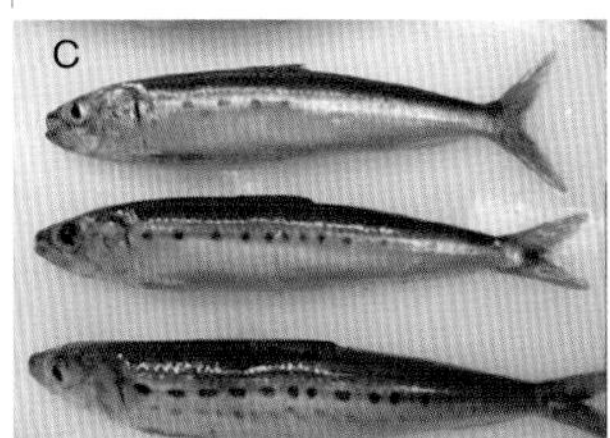

FIGURE 16.4 Key forage and mid-trophic fish species in the California Current. Photos: (A) NOAA Oceanic and Atmospheric Research/ National Undersea Research Program; (B, C) NOAA Southwest Fisheries Science Center; (D) California Academy of Sciences.

A Northern anchovy (*Engraulis mordax*)

B Chilipepper rockfish (*Sebastes goodei*)

C Pacific sardine (*Sardinops sagax*)

D Coho salmon (*Oncorhynchus kisutch*)

The Small Pelagics

Small pelagic fishes such as northern anchovy (*Engraulis mordax*), Pacific sardine (*Sardinops sagax*), Pacific mackerel (*Scomber japonicus*), and jack mackerel (*Trachurus symmetricus*) dominate the fish fauna of the epipelagic California Current. These schooling planktivores supported major fisheries in the past and in some cases still do (Allen and Cross 2006; see Chapter 35, "Marine Fisheries"). Their abundances vary dramatically over time, often peaking asynchronously with each other. These species spawn primarily in the Southern California Bight but are distributed along the entire California shelf region as juveniles and adults (Zwolinski et al. 2012). As in other upwelling ecosystems, they consume primarily smaller planktonic prey including phytoplankton, copepods, pteropods, decapod larvae, and small larval and juvenile euphausiids (van der Lingen et al. 2009), although larger mackerel can eat adult euphausiids and small fishes and squids. The ability of sardines and anchovies to filter feed places them at a relatively low trophic level and allows them to pass production on to higher trophic levels relatively efficiently.

In addition to these dominant forage species, other regionally important fishes include Pacific pompano (*Peprilus simillimus*), Pacific bonito (*Sarda chiliensis*), and yellowtail (*Seriola lalandi*) in southern California, Pacific saury (*Cololabis saira*) in offshore waters, and Pacific herring (*Clupea pallasi*) and smelts (family Osmeridae) off central and northern California (Brodeur et al. 2003, Allen and Cross 2006, Harding et al. 2011). Another dominant species in terms of biomass and fishery harvest levels in the California Current is the Pacific hake (*Merluccius productus*), which is distributed widely along the coast of California and undergoes seasonal migrations from spawning grounds off southern California to feeding grounds off the Pacific Northwest and Canada (Ressler et al. 2007). This species inhabits midwater regions along the shelf and is important as prey (mainly in the larval and juvenile stage) and predator throughout the year (Livingston and Bailey 1985).

A number of small squid species occur in the CCE, but off central and southern California the most important species by far is the market squid (*Doryteuthis* [formerly *Loligo*] *opalescens*). Although this species is relatively short-lived (lifespan about one year), it is the mainstay of a pelagic fishery for several California ports (Zeidberg et al. 2006). Market squid feed mainly on copepods early in life, switching to euphausiids, small fish, and other squid as adults (Karpov and Cailliet 1978). They in turn become an important component in the diets of many fishes, seabirds, and marine mammals in coastal waters (Morejohn et al. 1978).

The Mesopelagics

MESOPELAGIC species occur primarily at 200–1,000 meter depth and are present in all of the world's oceans, but the difficulty of sampling them has led to uncertainty about their abundances and ecological roles (Brodeur and Yamamura 2005). Mesopelagic fish in particular are an important component of the DEEP SCATTERING LAYER, and their sheer biomass make them important components of the open ocean food web globally. They inhabit depths below the photic zone (200–1,000 meters) by day but exhibit diel vertical migration to the surface to feed at night, presumably to minimize predation risk while maximizing foraging capabilities (Robison 2004).

Mesopelagic fish in the CCS include over twenty genera (Ahlstrom 1969), making them an extremely diverse component of the CCE. From the limited diet studies available, they are consumers primarily of zooplankton including mainly copepods and euphausiids but also some species of amphipods, ostracods, molluscs, and larvaceans (Mauchline and Gordon 1991, Suntsov and Brodeur 2008). They serve as important prey species for many large fishes, sharks, seabirds, Humboldt squid (*Dosidicus gigas*), and marine mammals (Pearcy et al. 1988; Fiedler, Barlow et al. 1998; Arizmendi-Rodriguez et al. 2006; Barlow et al. 2008; Field et al. 2012; Preti et al. 2012). Over the past fifty years, mesopelagic fish abundance in the CCS has been in decline, with a hypothesis that links it to the shoaling (movement to shallowed depths) of the OXYGEN MINIMUM ZONE (OMZ) over the same time period (Bograd et al. 2008, Koslow et al. 2011). Given the sheer abundance of these organisms in the CCS, perhaps an order of magnitude greater than currently estimated (Kaartvedt et al. 2012), and their repeated presence in predator stomach contents, they are likely an integral but poorly understood part of the CCS food web and nutrient cycle (Davison et al. 2013).

Top Predators

The California Current is a hotspot for a high diversity and abundance of top predators because of the abundant prey supported by its seasonal upwelling and nutrient-rich waters (Figure 16.5). A number of top predators reside in the CCS year round, while even more travel vast distances to forage seasonally in the CCS (Block et al. 2011; Figure 16.6). Large pelagic fishes are abundant and support a number of fisheries, including salmon, rockfish, billfish, sharks, and a few species of tuna (Field et al. 2010, Block et al. 2011, Glaser 2011, Preti et al. 2012, Wells et al. 2012). Seabird species include local breeders and oceanic migrants, both of which rely on the CCS as their foraging grounds (Shaffer et al. 2006, Yen et al. 2006, Mills et al. 2007, Kappes et al. 2010). Six pinniped species breed on the coast of California, with many of these animals foraging in offshore waters (Antonelis and Fiscus 1980). A high diversity of cetacean species also occur in the region (Barlow and Forney 2007). These predators have all evolved strategies to benefit from the seasonal productivity of the CCS while minimizing interspecific competition.

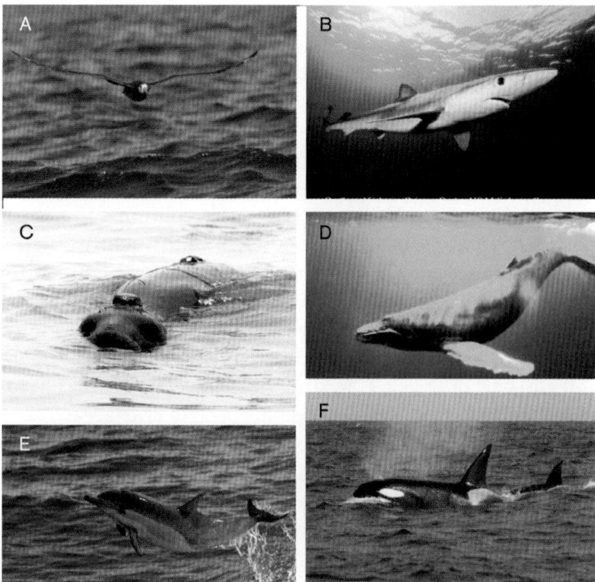

FIGURE 16.5 Key top predators in the California Current. Photos: (A, E, F) Elliott Hazen, NOAA; (B) Mark Conlin, NOAA Southwest Fisheries Science Center; (C) Dan Costa, UC Santa Cruz; (D) NOAA.

A Black-footed albatross (*Phoebastria nigripes*)

B Blue shark (*Prionace glauca*)

C Northern elephant seal with electronic tag (*Mirounga angustirostris*)

D Humpback whale (*Megaptera novaeangliae*)

E Short-beaked common dolphin (*Delphinus delphis*)

F Transient killer whales (*Orcinus orca*)

FISHES

Salmon species in California include coho (*Oncorhynchus kisutch*) and Chinook salmon (*Oncorhynchus tshawytscha*), both populations federally endangered (see Chapter 35, "Marine Fisheries"). Adult salmon serve as important predators in the pelagic ecosystem (Thayer et al. 2014) and support economically valuable fisheries. Juvenile salmon are important predators of euphausiids and small fish. The largest Chinook runs are in the Central Valley (Sacramento–San Joaquin River system) and Klamath River. Chinook salmon inhabit a relatively narrow temperature range in the CCS. This may underlie observed connections between ocean conditions and salmon survival (Hinke et al. 2005). The first year at sea for Chinook salmon is thought to be the most sensitive, with surviving individuals returning to spawn as adults four to seven years after hatching (MacFarlane 2010, Wells et al. 2012). Because of their ties to ocean conditions, both salmon species are often used as indicators of ecosystem status, with spawning returns (escapement) providing a time series of salmon abundance in the CCS back to 1970 (Lindley et al. 2009, Levin and Schwing 2011). A 2009 collapse in Central Valley Chinook was attributed to a combination of a historical reduction in the population's diversity of run timings and life history strategies caused by water competition with human uses, and poor ocean conditions for the yearling stage in 2004 and 2005 (Lindley et al. 2009). This event illustrated how salmon are intimately tied to both land and sea conditions and vulnerable to changes in both.

Adult rockfishes are a complex of over seventy species, many of which are late maturing and extremely long-lived (Love et al. 2002, Mills et al. 2007, Field et al. 2010). They support important fisheries, both recreational and commercial (see Chapter 35, "Marine Fisheries"). The deep-water rockfishes found in offshore environments are particularly sensitive because they are the longest-lived and suffer the greatest proportional mortality when brought to the surface (Love et al. 2008). Long-term fishing pressure appears to have resulted in changes in community composition (Love et al. 2008) and decreases in fish size (Mason 1998). Similar to salmon survival, rockfish growth has been correlated with winter upwelling, indicating that some rockfish species are highly dependent on the early physical processes in the CCS (Black et al. 2011). Their role as predators given fishery depletion is less clearly quantified but could be important, as they feed primarily on pelagic forage fish. Both juvenile salmon and rockfish serve as important forage fishes in the CCS and are found in the diets of many larger fish, seabirds, marine mammals, and even Humboldt squid (Mills et al. 2007, Field et al. 2010, Wells et al. 2012).

A number of species of tuna, billfish, and sharks use the CCS as a seasonal foraging ground, relying on the upwelling dynamics to provide an abundance of food. Albacore (*Thunnus alalunga*), yellowfin (*T. albacares*), skipjack (*Euthynnus pelamis*), and Pacific bluefin tuna (*T. orientalis*) are all found off the coast of California. Albacore and skipjack use the entire U.S. West Coast, while bluefin and yellowfin occur primarily in the central and southern CCS, respectively (Block and Stevens 2001). Tuna specialize on forage fishes such as anchovy, Pacific sardine, Pacific saury, and squids as adults (Pinkas 1971, Bernard et al. 1985, Glaser 2011). North Pacific albacore could provide significant top-down pressure on anchovy populations previously believed to be largely regulated by the physical forcing and upwelling dynamics (Glaser 2011). Swordfish (*Xiphias gladius*) and striped marlin (*Kajikia audax*) are the two main billfish species in the CCS and are ocean migrants (Bed-

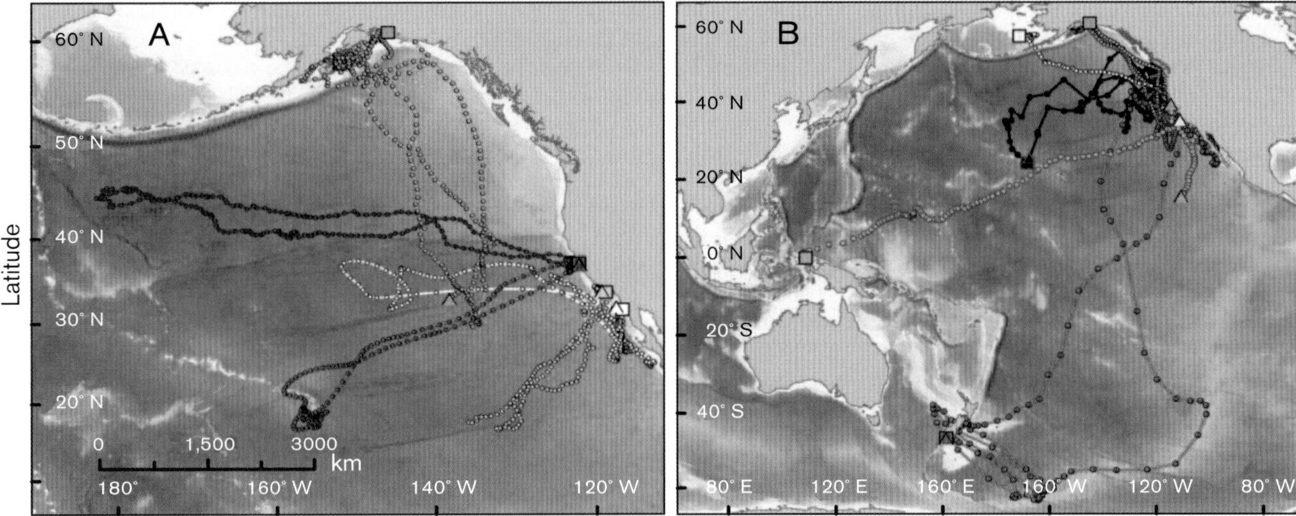

FIGURE 16.6 Fidelity and attraction to the California Current Ecosystem (CCE). Source: Block et al. 2011.

A Examples of pelagic predators released and electronically tracked in the CCE that show fidelity to deployment locations and the CCE. We show the release locations (square), pop-up satellite end-point locations (triangle), and daily mean positions (circles) of the following species: yellowfin tuna (yellow), bluefin tuna (white), white shark (red), elephant seal (blue), and salmon shark (orange).

B Individual tracks of pelagic animals released 2,000 kilometers away from the CCE indicate cross-basin or ecosystem attraction to, and temporary residency within, the eastern North Pacific. Symbols as in (A); for leatherback sea turtles (green), sooty shearwaters (pink), fur seals (pale yellow), black-footed albatrosses (black), and salmon sharks (orange).

ford and Hagerman 1983). Swordfish and striped marlin are both known to target forage fishes and cephalopods, based on diet studies in the tropical Pacific (Markaida and Hochberg 2005). The high energetic demand of these pelagic predators has made them susceptible to the OMZ in the tropical Atlantic (Stramma et al. 2011), and it is plausible that the shoaling OMZ in the CCS may also compress their pelagic habitat (Bograd et al. 2008, Koslow et al. 2011). Tagging data from bluefin, albacore, and yellowfin tuna show high site fidelity to the CCS with seasonal migrations from the southern CCS northward as temperatures increase (Block et al. 2011).

Shark species occupy a range of foraging niches in the CCS, from planktivore to scavenger to top predator. Much research on sharks has stemmed from fisheries bycatch or directed tagging studies. Basking sharks (*Cetorhinus maximus*) that feed on zooplankton aggregations were once abundant in the CCS, but fisheries harvest and directed mortality has reduced them to a remnant population with little remaining ecological impact (Ebert 2003). Blue (*Prionace glauca*), salmon (*Lamna ditropis*), shortfin mako (*Isurus oxyrinchus*), and white sharks (*Carcharodon carcharias*) show significant niche partitioning in the CCS. Blue, mako, and white sharks primarily forage in the CCS, while salmon sharks likely use it mostly as a pupping ground (Block et al. 2011). Salmon sharks migrate throughout the eastern North Pacific, seasonally taking advantage of salmon, pollock, and herring in the northern Gulf of Alaska in the summer through the winter and giving birth in the spring off the California coast (Weng et al. 2008, Carlisle et al. 2011).

Thresher (*Alopias vulpinus*), mako, and blue sharks are commonly caught by fisheries, providing insights into their distribution and diet. Thresher sharks feed primarily on pelagic forage fish including anchovy, sardine, and hake, with a smaller contribution from squid species. Mako and blue sharks feed on Humboldt squid (*Dosidicus gigas*), particularly when they are abundant in the CCS (Vetter et al. 2008, Camhi et al. 2008, Preti et al. 2012). Blue sharks consume both pelagic fish and cephalopods. White sharks use the CCS most heavily during the pinniped pupping season, then move offshore to an area nicknamed the "White Shark Café," where they exhibit very different diving behaviors than in the CCS and may be foraging and/or mating (Camhi et al. 2008, Jorgensen et al. 2010, Jorgensen et al. 2012). When farthest offshore, many of the shark species likely supplement their diet with deep scattering layer organisms, such as mesopelagic fishes and squid (Jorgensen et al. 2012).

SEABIRDS

Nearly 150 seabird species occur in the CCS. These include locally breeding species, such as auklets and murres, and long distance migrants, such as albatrosses and shearwaters. These species all use the CCS as a foraging ground. A number of local species have become key indicators of climate variability because their breeding success is closely tied to CCS upwelling regimes (Black et al. 2011). A late start to the upwelling season in 2005 led to unprecedented and complete breeding failure in Cassin's auklet (*Ptychoramphus aleuticus*) that was also apparent but less extreme in other top predator taxa (Sydeman, Bradley et al. 2006). Further research has confirmed that upwelling is critical for these seabirds' reproductive success and, more specifically, that winter conditions and early season upwelling are most important (Schroeder et al. 2009, Black et al. 2011).

Weak upwelling combined with less stratified waters than usual can provide nutrients to jump start the food web at critical times in seabird life histories (Schroeder et al. 2009). Summer upwelling was closely correlated with Cassin's auklet fledgling success, while common murre (*Uria aalge*) fledging success and both species' egg laying dates were associated with the anomalous winter upwelling mode (Black et al. 2011). Prey availability near seabird colonies is the proximate cause of local seabird breeding success, with changes in key prey species such as juvenile rockfish and krill directly influencing breeding success in a number of bird species (Ainley et al. 1995, Sydeman et al. 2001). The proportions of juvenile rockfish found in the diets of three species—common murre, pigeon guillemot (*Cepphus columba*), and rhinoceros auklet (*Cerorhinca monocerata*)—have been directly related to their reproductive success, highlighting their importance as forage fish in the system (Ainley et al. 1995, Mills et al. 2007). In more recent studies, however, prey switching and conservative life history strategies (laying at most a single egg per clutch) seem to have buffered these three species from the effects of juvenile rockfish declines of 50% to 75% (Field et al. 2010). Cassin's auklet breeds later, with lower fledging success, in warmer years such as during El Niño events, indicating that long-term climate change could result in later breeding and reduced recruitment for a number of these indicator species (Sydeman et al. 2009).

Many highly migratory bird species, including sooty shearwaters (*Puffinus griseus*), blackfooted albatross (*Phoebastria nigripes*), and Laysan albatross (*Phoebastria immutabilis*), depend upon the CCS as primary foraging grounds. These migrants depend highly on wind patterns to reach their foraging grounds but can spend over half of the year in the CCS. Sooty shearwaters are one of the world's greatest migrants, traveling from New Zealand breeding grounds to the CCS foraging grounds in April through October (Shaffer et al. 2006) where they feed on an abundance of fish, squid, and krill. They can also migrate to other foraging grounds as productivity wanes in the CCS or depart early when the CCS is affected by anomalous conditions such as delayed upwelling or El Niño events. The two albatross species breed in the northwest Hawaiian Islands, with an additional Laysan albatross colony on Guadalupe Island off Baja California, Mexico (Pitman et al. 2004, Kappes et al. 2010). During the incubation period, both species migrate to the CCS, although Laysan albatross use the western Pacific more heavily and are less common in the CCS (Kappes et al. 2010). Both species are largely diurnal scavengers on fish and squid, and their migration patterns are less constrained during the incubation period than during chick-rearing. This allows them to better adapt to both interannual and decadal variability (Pitman et al. 2004, Kappes et al. 2010). Several seabird species, including the blackfooted albatross, red pharalope (*Phalaropus fulicaria*), and Leach's storm petrel (*Oceanodroma leucorhoa*), are associated with mesoscale features in the CCS, such as topographic or upwelling fronts, that could be a response to enhanced local productivity (Yen et al. 2006).

SEA TURTLES

No sea turtles nest in California, although leatherback turtles (*Dermochelys coriacea*), a small population of green turtles (*Chelonia mydas*), and occasionally loggerhead turtles (*Caretta caretta*) forage in the CCS. The green turtles occur only in San Diego Bay and breed in Mexico (MacDonald et al. 2012). Loggerheads are common off the Baja California peninsula and present in low numbers off California during El Niño years (Carretta et al. 2004, Wingfield et al. 2011). Leatherback turtles migrate to the CCS foraging grounds from their breeding grounds in the tropical western Pacific (Benson et al. 2011, Block et al. 2011, Bailey et al. 2012). They will also return in multiple years to these CCS foraging grounds for the summer and autumn, then migrate to low-latitude, eastern tropical Pacific wintering areas without returning to their nesting beaches.

Three main high-use areas in the CCS have been identified for leatherbacks (Benson et al. 2011). The first is off central California, where relatively cool water over the coastal shelf is characterized by high levels of chlorophyll-*a* concentration, indicative of high productivity. The second is in offshore waters off central and northern California, where sea surface temperature fronts occur in early summer. Finally, the third is on the continental shelf and slope off Oregon and Washington, particularly in the area surrounding the Columbia River Plume, which supports seasonally high abundances of the turtles' gelatinous zooplankton prey (Benson et al. 2011). Leatherback turtles are critically endangered and have recently been named California's marine reptile due to their dependence on CCS resources. Beach development at nesting grounds outside the CCS and bycatch in fisheries could both be hindering its recovery (Carretta et al. 2004, Benson et al. 2011, Tapilatu et al. 2013).

CETACEANS

Twenty-one species of cetaceans, including odontocetes and baleen whales, have been sighted off the California coast during marine mammal surveys since 1991 (Barlow and Forney 2007). The development of species-habitat models from these survey sightings and environmental data have revealed that the distribution of many cetacean species can be explained by both temporally dynamic variables, such as sea surface temperature and its variance, and more static variables, such as water depth and seabed slope (Becker et al. 2010, Forney et al. 2012).

Odontocete species (toothed whales) include warm water, cool water, and cosmopolitan species, and their sighting rates vary based on the oceanographic regime, such that during El Niño conditions warm water species are much more common in the CCS (Barlow and Forney 2007). Some of the rarest and deepest diving species, beaked whales, have declined in abundance in the CCS since 1991, which could reflect increased anthropogenic use of the offshore environment or broader-scale ecosystem changes (Moore and Barlow 2013). Beaked whales are known to forage on mesopelagic fish and squid (Moore and Barlow 2013). Another deep diver that also forages on squid, the sperm whale (*Physeter macrocephalus*), did not show an abundance decline over the 1991–2005 survey period (Barlow and Forney 2007).

Baleen whales, characterized by baleen plates for filtering their food, feed on pelagic forage fish and krill (Croll et al. 2005, Barlow et al. 2008, Burrows et al. 2012). Although baleen whales have a 2.5-fold greater biomass than odontocetes, their primary production requirement in the CCS is only 13% of that required by odontocetes because they feed at a lower trophic level (Barlow et al. 2008). Occurrences of baleen whales in the CCS are affected by the distribution and abundance of dense prey aggregations that they target (Croll et al. 1998; Fiedler, Reilly et al. 1998). Sightings data have revealed important patterns in interannual variability, such as decreased presence of blue whales (*Balaenoptera musculus*) in the CCS following the anomalous upwelling year of

2005, presumably due to poor krill recruitment (Barlow and Forney 2007). Integrative studies in central California have shown that increased krill density lags seasonal upwelling and increased productivity by three to four months and that blue whales target the densest patches of krill in the California vicinity before moving to other foraging hotspots in the northeast Pacific (Croll et al. 2005, Bailey et al. 2009, Calambokidis et al. 2009). Marine mammals in Monterey Bay generally moved nearshore in El Niño conditions to more productive waters, while anomalous upwelling conditions led to migration to other, less-affected foraging areas (Burrows et al. 2012). Many large whale populations are still recovering from harvest, suggesting they might have played a greater role in the ecosystem before the historical whaling era. Recent research suggests that Blue whales (*Balaenoptera musculus*) have recovered to their carrying capacity since the cessation of whaling (Monnahan et al. 2015), although human impacts including noise and ship strikes may still affect the Eastern Pacific population (Goldbogen et al. 2013, Irvine et al. 2014).

PINNIPEDS

Six species of pinnipeds breed on the California coast, many of which use the CCS as their foraging grounds (Antonelis and Fiscus 1980). Two of the most abundant offshore visitors are the California sea lion (*Zalophus californianus*) and the northern elephant seal (*Mirounga angustirostris*). California sea lions are extremely abundant in the CCS, and typically forage opportunistically on fish, decapods, and cephalopods on the continental shelf (Weise et al. 2006). Their plasticity in foraging strategy is apparent in anomalous years. For example, they foraged up to 600 kilometers offshore in 2005 during a delayed upwelling event compared to 100- kilometer migrations in normal years. Sea lion pup mortality has been directly linked to productivity, with higher mortality during El Niño regimes (Sydeman and Allen 1999). Northern elephant seals have one of the richest tagging histories of any top predator and are central place foragers returning to California beaches to breed and molt (Robinson et al. 2012). Most female northern elephant seals move far offshore to the transition zone to feed, but a significant portion exhibit a distinct and more nearshore strategy (Robinson et al. 2012). Males tend to migrate northward, foraging along the continental margin from Oregon to the western Aleutian Islands (Le Boeuf et al. 2000).

Trophic Interactions and Ecosystem Functioning

The CCS food web is driven by variability in upwelling-driven, bottom-up processes (Checkley and Barth 2009). Once upwelling has kick-started primary production, nutrients drive a pelagic food web highly dependent on the phytoplankton base, with copepods, euphausiids, forage fish, and hake serving as key pathways of biomass to higher trophic levels in the northern California Current (Checkley and Barth 2009; see Figure 16.2). The importance of forage fish in the pelagic food web suggests potential wasp-waist dynamics, in which the food web is strongly controlled both up and down by these midtrophic organisms. Similar food web structure occurs in other eastern Pacific boundary currents (Cury et al. 2000). However, recent studies have challenged the wasp-waist hypothesis. For example, recent food web models suggest that alternative trophic pathways are available in the CCS when a key forage species is depleted (Fréon et al. 2009). Stable isotopes have also shown that many top predators are more plastic than once believed and can switch prey types and even trophic levels based on what is available (Madigan et al. 2012).

The diversity in midtrophic species in the CCS may also buffer the ecosystem from wasp-waist dynamics compared to systems where a single species of forage fish dominates. While fishing impacts have had an effect on forage fish in the CCS (Essington et al. 2015), the variability in seasonal upwelling is equally, if not more, important in regulating forage fish and the ultimate dynamics of the system (Fréon et al. 2005). The fact that juveniles of a high trophic level species can serve as an important forage fish could also provide alternate food web pathways when other forage fish are less prevalent (Field et al. 2010). As in other eastern Pacific boundary currents, the large biomass of lower trophic level species supports a high diversity of large predators, including fishes, seabirds, and marine mammals (Checkley and Barth 2009).

The strong influence of bottom-up forcing through climate variability in the CCS (Ware and Thomson 2005) is highlighted by the range expansion of Humboldt squid (Field et al. 2007). Following the 1997–1998 El Niño, Humboldt squid were observed in unprecedented numbers from central California up to British Columbia, Canada (Zeidberg and Robison 2007, Field et al. 2007, Field et al. 2012). Initial hypotheses included a combination of environmental changes, including shoaling low oxygen and warming temperatures, and population release following overfishing of sharks and tuna that could have reduced predation pressure on this species (Zeidberg and Robison 2007). However, the timing mismatch between fisheries pressure and the expansion indicate that environmental mechanisms, combined with a fast migration by the squid into the CCS, was the more likely driver (Watters et al. 2008, Stewart et al. 2012). Humboldt squid are important predators of mesopelagics and forage fish as well as a large portion of the diet of many top predators in the CCS (Field et al. 2012, Preti et al. 2012). A concurrent decline of Pacific hake during Humboldt squid expansion could indicate competition with or predation of this species (Zeidberg and Robison 2007). The shoaling OMZ, which has compressed the habitats of numerous top predators with high energetic demand, could also provide a new ecological niche for expansion of the hypoxia-tolerant Humboldt squid (Stramma et al. 2010, Hoving et al. 2013).

The dynamics of these diverse trophic groups underscore how both the timing and strength of upwelling can have large effects on the CCS (Bograd et al. 2009). The drastic effects of the spring transition's timing on CCE food webs and production are highlighted by the events of the 2005 upwelling season. In that year, upwelling was delayed by up to several months, producing warmer waters, lower nutrients, fewer lipid-rich copepods, and failed recruitment of fish and seabird species (Brodeur et al. 2006; Mackas et al. 2006; Sydeman, Bradley et al. 2006). Anomalous wintertime upwelling can lead to greater recruitment of seabird species and rockfish growth and higher salmon ocean survival, while strong summer events are important for other seabird species and for salmon returns (Wells et al. 2008, Black et al. 2011, Schroeder et al. 2013). These differential responses to upwelling highlight the complexity of marine species interactions and dynamics and offer insight into potential long-term changes as the North Pacific warms.

Broad-scale climate variability including ENSO (El Niño) events, the NPGO (North Pacific Gyre Oscillation), and the PDO (Pacific Decadal Oscillation) also drive major responses in the CCE, arguably including some irreversible regime shifts (Ohman et al. 2013). During El Niño events, warmer surface waters and deeper thermoclines result in lower CCS productivity. Two key forage fish (anchovy and sardine) exhibit strong, decadal-scale variation in ecosystem dominance, total abundance, and recruitment (Barange et al. 2009, Checkley and Barth 2009). In warm years, sardine dominate the CCS in both surveys and top predator diet, while anchovy are more dominant in cooler years (Barange et al. 2009). Debate persists about the relative roles of climate and fishing effects on suppressing forage fish populations, but fished species exhibit greater sensitivity to climatic variability than their unfished counterparts (Hsieh et al. 2008, Barange et al. 2009, Essington et al. 2015). Highly migratory predators can often shift their behavior and distribution during El Niño years in response to lower trophic level processes, but extreme events can result in poor recruitment or juvenile survival among these migratory predators (Sydeman and Allen 1999, Benson et al. 2002, Weise et al. 2006). Since the early 1970s, variance in broad-scale indices like the PDO and ENSO has remained constant, but the NPGO has shown increasing variance since 1985 (Sydeman, Santora et al. 2013).

This increased variance may propagate through the CCE, particularly for climate-sensitive indicator species (Sydeman, Santora et al. 2013). Some extreme events, such as the 1998 El Niño, may have led to a shift in climate forcing from a warm, low productivity regime to a cool, highly productive regime (Peterson and Schwing 2003). Concurrent changes occurred in species communities and perhaps even ecosystem functioning, but it is difficult to determine mechanistically whether these constitute a cycle or a regime shift (Peterson and Schwing 2003, Overland et al. 2008). The differential responses of marine species to CCS processes highlight the need for multiple indicators of ecosystem state, as well as composite indicators that combine physical forcing and species, to ensure effective management of the CCE that incorporates both anthropogenic use and climate variability and change (Levin and Schwing 2011).

Spatial Distributions

Spatial features and temporal processes can generate MARINE HOTSPOTS—predictable and persistent areas of productivity or aggregation of lower trophic level organisms with greatly increased trophic flow and ecosystem importance (Sydeman, Brodeur et al. 2006; Hazen et al. 2013). Here we discuss processes that can create marine hotspots and identify recurrent hotspots in the CCS. Bathymetric features such as seamounts, shelf breaks, or islands can generate increased upwelling of nutrients and retention of forage species (Reese and Brodeur 2006). A high diversity of top predators relies on the seasonal variability and productivity of the CCS. These top predators aggregate based on specific oceanographic and bathymetric features to forage (Block et al. 2011). Based on a decade of tracking data, many top predator species use the entire CCS as a regional hotspot, with use patterns seasonally shifting northward with increasing productivity as temperature rises in the Southern California Bight (Block et al. 2011).

Mesoscale features such as eddies and fronts can result in marine hotspots when increased productivity is entrained in an eddy or the mixing of two water masses increases productivity and aggregation (Logerwell and Smith 2001, Palacios et al. 2006, Yen et al. 2006). For example, mesoscale eddies created from meanders of the California Current form important hotspots for top predators including blackfooted albatross, red phalaropes, Leach's storm petrel, and elephant seals (Yen et al. 2006, Robinson et al. 2012). Upwelling can directly produce hotspots, particularly when particular locations have persistent and/or stronger upwelling than surrounding areas (Palacios et al. 2006 and references within). In the CCS, Palacios et al. (2006) identified three coastal hotspots driven by upwelling: Cape Mendocino to Point Arena, Bodega Head to Point Sur, and Cape San Martin to Point Arguello. Chlorophyll-*a* persistence indices corroborated these locations as productive for a large portion of the year (Suryan et al. 2012). Additional work in the upwelling region off Point Conception in southern California showed that the high chlorophyll-*a* concentrations in turn supported krill (Santora et al. 2011) and that the same areas are important for foraging by seabirds (Yen et al. 2006) and blue whales (Bailey et al. 2009).

Krill hotspots generally are also located near known upwelling centers, but krill avoid the regions of strongest Ekman transport where they would be advected offshore and instead are more strongly associated with areas of retention (Santora et al. 2011). Two critical forage species, the euphausiids (krill) *E. pacifica* and *T. spinifera*, are distributed throughout California waters but form patchy aggregations where they serve as important food resources for top predators (Croll et al. 2005, Santora et al. 2011). Blue whale foraging hotspots closely overlap with krill hotspots, particularly in these regions (Croll et al. 1998; Fiedler, Reilly et al. 1998; Bailey et al. 2009; Santora et al. 2011). One of the best studies decomposing a seasonal hotspot examined upwelling, phytoplankton blooms, krill aggregations, and blue whale foraging in Monterey Bay (Croll et al. 2005). After the start of the upwelling season, when wind-driven upwelling provides nutrients to the photic zone, phytoplankton blooms occurred six to ten days after upwelling events. Densities of both *T. spinifera* and *E. pacifica* adults were greatest in late summer a few months after the peak upwelling. Blue whales tended to exploit the late-season patches of krill found along the edge of the canyon in Monterey Bay, taking advantage of the increased productivity from submarine upwelling but also using the shelf break as a buffer from currents to minimize energetic costs (Croll et al. 2005). These hotspots recur seasonally, with some interannual variability (Croll et al. 2005, Bailey et al. 2009).

The Gulf of the Farallones and the waters surrounding the Channel Islands are two important foraging areas for marine predators, particularly seabirds and pinnipeds. Both areas provide terrestrial haul-out and nesting habitats near a shelf break and corresponding area of increased productivity (Ainley and Lewis 1974, Sydeman et al. 2001, Hyrenbach and Veit 2003, Carretta et al. 2009). Finally, areas of curl-driven upwelling, higher salinity, and sea surface temperature values between 12°C and 16°C were important in defining regional hotspots for sardine spawning aggregations, while finer-scale hotspots important for foraging predators are less well understood (Weber and McClatchie 2010, Zwolinski et al. 2011). Finally, spawning anchovy regional hotspots were best predicted using depth of the chlorophyll maximum and geostrophic flow (Weber and McClatchie 2010). Both of these species exhibit seasonal migrations along the coast with patchy aggregations, making their distributions potential mobile hotspots for foraging predators. These concentrations of high trophic transfer indicate important hotspots and potentially conservation areas, yet they can move or wane with seasonal, interannual, and even long-term changes in ecosystem dynamics, making adaptive and dynamic approaches critical for long-term management of these hotspots in the CCS

(Palacios et al. 2006, Žydelis et al. 2011, Hazen et al. 2013, Scales et al. 2014, Maxwell et al. 2015).

Ecosystem Services, Threats, and Management Structure in the Offshore California Current

In the CCE, ecosystem services include provisioning services, such as food and water; regulating services, including regulation of climate, wastes, and water quality; and additional services such as transportation via shipping and oil and gas extraction. Habitats that provide nursery areas and foraging grounds support commercial and recreational fisheries. Finally, the CCE provides important cultural services, such as ecotourism. Although the CCE provides many ecosystem services, human activities pose threats to these marine resources through stresses that include pollution and habitat degradation. We focus here on three major services in the offshore California Current: carbon sequestration, shipping, and oil and gas production. We also discuss threats from the shipping and oil and gas industries and their potential impact to the offshore ecosystem.

Services Provided by Offshore Ecosystems

CARBON SEQUESTRATION

The offshore ecosystem plays a large part in modulating a number of atmospheric processes. Key among these is regulating the amount of carbon dioxide in the atmosphere. Through the "biological organic carbon pump," photosynthetic organisms in the upper layers of the ocean intake carbon. As they die, this carbon is sequestered in the deep ocean as the photosynthetic organisms sink toward the ocean floor. The ocean is responsible for removing approximately 48% of human carbon emissions (Sabine et al. 2004) and is the second largest sink for anthropogenic carbon after the atmosphere itself (Riebesell et al. 2007). Given increasing anthropogenic production of carbon dioxide and resulting climate change, this ecosystem service is of increasing importance. Oceanic carbon sequestration is not, however, without consequences (see the "Ocean Acidification" section later in this chapter).

SHIPPING AND CRUISE LINERS

California waters are a major economic driver of California and the entire U.S. Shipping and cruise industries provide millions of U.S. jobs for millions of people, billions of dollars in tax revenue, and billions of dollars to the U.S. economy. Transportation via container ships is one of the largest services provided by the CCE, facilitating massive domestic and, particularly, international trade. California is home to some of the largest ports in the U.S., including the ports of Long Beach, Los Angeles, and Richmond—all in the top fifty U.S. ports by total trade volume for 2011 (AAPA 2012). Shipping is considered a more environmentally sound means of transporting goods than road, train, and air (Butt 2007). The cruise industry in the U.S. is another major economic driver and employed over 350,000 people in the U.S. in 2011, including many at the ports of San Francisco, Los Angeles, Long Beach, and San Diego.

OIL AND GAS PRODUCTION

Oil and gas production has a long cultural history in terrestrial systems in California, but 16% of the state's extraction occurs offshore of California. California was the location of the world's first offshore oil development, with the first well placed offshore of Santa Barbara in 1896. Production quickly climbed, with over 180 wells placed offshore of Santa Barbara County by 1902, and with quick expansion south to Orange, Los Angeles, and Ventura Counties. Regulation of the industry followed in 1921 (McCrary et al. 2003).

Despite its long history in California, offshore oil and gas activity in the state contribute a small proportion of the country's production. The Bureau of Ocean Energy Management (BOEM) reports that in the Pacific region, which includes the offshore regions of Washington, Oregon, and California, 43 of the 49 active leases were actively producing an average of 61,113 barrels of oil and 113 million cubic feet of gas per day in 2009 (BOEM 2013). This amounts to 1.24 billion barrels of gas and 1.67 trillion cubic feet of gas per year, which is less than 1% of the total daily production of oil and gas in the U.S. (U.S. Energy Information Administration 2013, BOEM 2013). Six companies operate the twenty-three oil and gas platforms along the U.S. West Coast, nine of which are active in California, in the southern California region between Santa Barbara and San Pedro Bay/Long Beach Harbor (BOEM 2013). By comparison, the Gulf of Mexico has over four thousand active offshore platforms (McCrary et al. 2003).

Ecosystem Threats

The scale and continued rise of the shipping and cruising industries along the U.S. West Coast, particularly in California, pose a number of threats to the larger ecosystem. Key among those affecting the offshore ecosystem are noise emitted by the oil and gas industry and military, discharge of pollutants (such as oil), risk of collisions, transport of invasive species from distant regions, and pollution from trash and sewage discards.

NOISE

Understanding of noise impacts on marine organisms remains poor, and noise threats to cetaceans has been of particular concern (Nowacek et al. 2007). Sound is the primary sense used by cetaceans for a number of life functions, and many cetaceans in the CCE use low-frequency sounds to communicate (Nowacek et al. 2007, Weilgart 2007, Clark et al. 2009). The baleen whales such as blue, fin, humpback, and gray whales, communicate over long distances of approximately 100 kilometers (Payne and Webb 1971, Payne and McVay 1971). Although much about the significance of these sounds is unclear, we know that some of the sounds, also known as "songs," play critical roles in socialization and mating (Darling and Berube 2001, Simon et al. 2010). While mysticete whales do not echolocate like dolphins, they may still use these low-frequency sounds for navigation, as evidenced by the wide berth they take around ice floes even when the floes are out of visual range (George et al. 1989).

Ship traffic in California has increased exponentially over the past sixty years (McDonald et al. 2006). Commercial vessels emit loud (180–195 dB re 1μPa), low-frequency (10–500 Hz) underwater sound. This noise can impair cetaceans' ability to detect relevant noises ("masking"), affecting the hearing threshold or behavior of the animals (Nowacek et al. 2007). This in turn can impair their ability to navigate, detect prey, and communicate with conspecifics (Clark et al. 2009). Some noise impacts are acute, with behavioral or physiological impacts. For example, an animal's hearing might be damaged, or individuals might leave an area that may be important for feeding or breeding (Weilgart 2007). Chronic impacts, often in the form of masking, can cause stress and lead to effects on individual or reproductive fitness (Weilgart 2007, Clark et al. 2009). Animals might attempt to change vocalization patterns in response to masking by changing vocalization frequencies, volume, and timing (Weilgart 2007, Parks et al. 2011, Castellote et al. 2012, Rolland et al. 2012). The effects of chronic noise impacts are particularly hard to detect at a population level, although reduction in noise levels has been shown to significantly decrease stress levels in North Atlantic right whales (Rolland et al. 2012).

Similar noise impacts are likely to occur to other marine taxa such as diving birds, fish, reptiles, and invertebrates that use sound, either passively or directly, to communicate, detect prey, or navigate (Wysocki and Ladich 2005, Codarin et al. 2009, Popper and Hastings 2009, Simpson et al. 2010). For example, some fishes respond to increased noise by increasing vocalization rates, with unknown consequences on fitness (Picciulin et al. 2012). Brown shrimp (*Crangon crangon*) exposed to sound levels 30 dB above ambient noise had decreased growth and reproductive rates (Lagardere 1982). Very few studies have investigated the impacts of chronic noise on species beyond cetaceans.

Sounds produced by the oil and gas industry, such as during geological and geophysical surveys used to identify new potential hydrocarbon resources, tend to be loud (>200 dB re 1μPa) and to include mid- to high frequencies (>1 kHz) and acute noises. This is in contrast to commercial vessels, which produce low-frequency chronic noise (Nowacek et al. 2007). In particular, seismic surveys for oil and gas fields often produce loud (220–255 dB re 1μPa) sounds that expand across a range of frequencies (>300 Hz to over 2 kHz). Baleen whales are considered the most sensitive to seismic surveys. Effects from these acute noises fall into behavioral, acoustic, and physiological categories (Nowacek et al. 2007). Mitigation measures, such as soft starts to operations that gradually increase the sound, should help to reduce the likelihood of physiological impacts such as hearing damage and threshold shifts. Most observed responses have been behavioral, with animals displaced from previous habitat more than 30 kilometers away and sometimes rapidly changing course to avoid survey areas (Richardson et al. 1995, Nowacek et al. 2007). Odontocetes have also been observed to change vocalization patterns in response to air guns (Goold and Fish 1998).

Noise impacts from military sonar can be similar to those from seismic surveys, with displacement of animals in the range of sonar activities. Active sonar produces loud (>210 dB re 1μPa) sounds across a range of frequencies, including those over 10 kHz. Changes in vocalization may also result. For example, humpback whales lengthened or delayed songs during playbacks of sonar (Miller et al. 2000, Fristrup et al. 2003). Military sonar has also been suggested as a cause of marine mammal strandings (Cox et al. 2006). While the link between sonar and strandings is not confirmed, a probable hypotheses is that decompression-like symptoms (e.g., "the bends") can occur when whales surface quickly in response to the loud sounds (Jepson et al. 2003). Additional research into noise effects, particularly to understand stress thresholds, behavioral responses, and population impacts, are warranted (Southall et al. 2012).

SHIP STRIKES

The shipping industry also affects offshore ecosystems through collisions with large marine species. Most studies on ship strikes have focused on cetaceans because they are struck frequently relative to their small numbers (Clapham et al. 1999, Kraus et al. 2005). Ship strikes have been of concern for cetacean populations only since the early 1950s, when ship engines gained the power to travel at speeds sufficient to injure whales (Laist et al. 2001). Ships of any size can strike whales; however, those over 80 meters and traveling faster than 14 knots are most likely to have lethal effects (Laist et al. 2001). The commercial shipping industry is the primary concern due to vessel size as well as the volume of vessel traffic in California waters.

Along the California coast, the large whales most susceptible to ship strikes include blue, humpback, fin, and gray whales (Redfern et al. 2013, McKenna et al. 2015). Between 1988 and 2007, twenty-one blue whale strandings attributed to ship strikes were recorded (Berman-Kowalewski et al. 2010). Recent data indicate that two humpback whale, four gray whale, one sperm whale, and four blue whale deaths were caused by ship strikes between 2004 and 2008, with additional historical records of a strike on a minke whale (Carretta et al. 2010). These numbers undoubtedly underestimate mortality caused by ship strikes, as many animals do not strand on land following injury or death, and many strikes are not reported or even detected by large container ships (Kraus et al. 2005). Other offshore marine species undoubtedly are victims of ship strikes, but these species have been less studied or strikes are less easily detected. Boat strikes to leatherback sea turtles are known to occur but are not considered a major source of mortality (Turtle Expert Working Group 2007). Seabirds are attracted to the lights of ships at night and may become disoriented, striking hard surfaces on the boats and suffering injury or mortality; this has not be studied in the CCS (Black 2005).

POLLUTION

Assessments of ship discharge effects have focused on oil and have been studied primarily for individual taxa, such as seabirds and marine mammals, rather than for the entire offshore ecosystem. Seabirds exposed to even small amounts of oil can lose flight capability and experience wasting fat and muscle tissues and abnormal conditions in the lungs, kidneys, and other organs (Clark 1984, Henkel et al. 2012). Strandings of seabirds occur regularly in areas of heavy vessel traffic because of exposure to oils associated with many commercial vessels. The number of stranded birds is likely a gross underestimate, as approximately 95% of bird carcasses sink within several days (Wiese and Robertson 2004). In the Monterey Bay region, seabird strandings are regularly attributed to oiling in the absence of large-scale spills and include offshore species such as sooty shearwaters (Newton et al. 2009). Chronic exposure to oil might have larger impacts on seabird populations than occasional, large oil spills often considered more catastrophic (Wiese and Robertson 2004). Overall impacts of chronic, low-level oil exposure on marine mammals and sea turtles are less than on seabirds. Moderate exposure to oil can affect these organisms' skin, blood, digestive systems and salt glands, behavior, and thermoregulatory abilities. However, acute impacts from low-level exposure are considered minimal, and recovery occurs within several weeks (Engelhardt 1983, Lutcavage et al. 1995, Milton et al. 2003).

Oil spills can affect many offshore ecosystem components, such as deep-water corals, seabirds, sea turtles, pinnipeds, and cetaceans. Oil spill impacts on fish stocks extend from ecological to economic as people reduce fish consumption out of fear of contamination (Engelhardt 1983, Clark 1984, McCrea-Strub et al. 2011, Henkel et al. 2012, White et al. 2012). Our knowledge of oil pollution effects on offshore marine ecosystems is increasing rapidly following the Deepwater Horizon spill in the Gulf of Mexico, from an oil well approximately 80 kilometers from shore in waters 1,500 meters deep (Lubchenco et al. 2012). Large oil spills have occurred in the CCS, including the famous 1969 Santa Barbara oil spill that resulted from oil seeping from a well in the Santa Barbara channel. Approximately 13,000 to 16,000 m^3 of crude oil spilled into the channel and surrounding area, causing large-scale environmental damage. The Santa Barbara oil spill, despite its devastation, impelled a number of marine protective measures including the creation of the National Marine Sanctuaries.

OCEAN ACIDIFICATION

While carbon uptake helps to regulate Earth's climate, increased oceanic carbon uptake due to increases in fossil fuel emissions are causing changes in ocean chemistry. Ocean acidification—a decrease in the pH of the ocean—influences the ability of animals with carbonate skeletons to uptake carbonate for skeletal structures. It could pose greater risks in coastal upwelling areas such as the CCE because upwelling brings more acidic waters to the surface waters (Harris et al. 2013, Hauri et al. 2012, 2013). Ocean acidification has affected a number of species common in the CCE including deep-sea corals, krill, fish, mollusks, and gelatinous zooplankton (Attrill et al. 2007, Fabry et al. 2008, Guinotte and Fabry 2008). Changes in ocean chemistry may also change the way that sound travels, particularly by decreasing sound absorption (Hester et al. 2008, Sehgal et al. 2010). This could affect species such as whales that use long-distance calls to communicate (McDonald et al. 2009). Changes to the CCE resulting from ocean acidification will be compounded by other climate change impacts (e.g., ocean warming, ocean deoxygenation) and are expected to include range shifts in many CCE species, reduced fishery landings, and potentially reduced prey availability for apex marine predators (Ainsworth et al. 2011).

OTHER ISSUES AND RISKS

Other risks associated with commercial shipping include transportation of invasive species and pollution resulting from direct trash and sewage discards. Through ballast water, marine species ranging from crabs to fish to microorganisms may be transported across entire ocean basins. Measures are in place to reduce invasions. For example, the International Maritime Organization recommends ballast water be exchanged at-sea (known as "reballasting") to reduce potential invasions of species from ports of origin; however, the impacts on offshore ecosystems are unknown (Tsolaki and Diamadopoulos 2010). The shipping industry, particularly cruise ships, also generates large amounts of waste. It is estimated that while cruise ships account for only a small fraction of the commercial vessels, they produce over a quarter of all merchant vessel waste (Butt 2007).

International laws allow the discharge of raw, untreated sewage on the high seas beyond 12 miles from land; however, the U.S. Clean Cruise Ships Act of 2005 prohibits the discharge of gray water, sewage, or bilge waters within U.S. waters. Under the International Convention for the Prevention of Pollution from Ships (MARPOL 73/78), there is a complete ban on dumping of plastics at sea; these must be incinerated or disposed of at ports. Despite these restrictions, a large amount of waste is disposed of at-sea, particularly offshore, and while little is known of its environmental impact at the ecosystem level, the Pacific Garbage Patch illustrates the long-term effects of regular dumping at sea (Howell et al. 2012). This highlights the importance of reducing waste and increasing the ability to better handle and treat waste onboard vessels (Johnson 2002, Butt 2007).

Conservation Issues and Management Structure

Management of the offshore ecosystem is complex because it is highly dynamic and, in many regards, a poorly understood system. In addition, there are multiple impacts on this system, occurring simultaneously and resulting in cumulative impacts with complex interactions. Effectively managing the offshore ecosystem requires being able to effectively characterize the threats, impacts, and management needs of the system, as well as developing appropriate management tools. Here we describe some of the potential cumulative impacts on the offshore ecosystem, current management tools, and an example of where science and management have worked together in an effort to improve protection of whales in the offshore ecosystem.

CUMULATIVE IMPACTS ON THE OFFSHORE ECOSYSTEM

Despite our still limited knowledge, the CCS is one of the best-studied ecosystems in the world, and a number of studies have characterized cumulative impacts on this system. Building on a global assessment of human impacts on marine ecosystems (Halpern et al. 2008), Halpern and colleagues (Halpern et al. 2009) conducted an assessment of human impacts on the CCS. Looking across twenty-five human activities, they ranked the threats and their impacts on nineteen different marine ecosystems within the CCS including surface (>30 meters) and deep (>200 meters) pelagic ecosystems, and the hard and soft substrates found in deep waters including canyons and seamounts. Climate change impacts, particularly ocean acidification, and activities that affect the benthic surfaces, such as oil rigs and destructive demersal fishing practices, were identified as being the greatest threat to offshore ecosystems. The spatial pattern of impact showed an increase in cumulative impacts moving further north, largely due to the affect of climate change.

Another assessment (Maxwell et al. 2013) considered the impacts specifically on pelagic predators. Using similar threats and weighting methods as Halpern et al. (2009), they found that the continental shelf was the region most impacted by human activities across the eight pelagic predator species studied. The impact of climate change stressors were again rated highest, along with various forms of pollution (Figure 16.7).

MANAGEMENT OF THE CALIFORNIA OFFSHORE ECOSYSTEM

MARINE PROTECTED AREAS (MPAs) are management tools that have been utilized extensively in California waters, particularly nearshore via the California Marine Life Protection Act (see Chapter 37, "Range Ecosystems") and through the U.S. National Marine Sanctuaries. Five National Marine Sanctuaries have been designated along the U.S. West Coast. These five sanctuaries are the Olympic Coast, Cordell Bank, Gulf of the Farallones, Monterey Bay, and Channel Islands National Marine Sanctuaries, totally over 31,263 km² in the CCS (Table 16.1, see Figure 16.1). The newest addition to the sanctuaries was an extension of the Monterey Bay Sanctuary to include Davidson Seamount in 2009. Davidson Seamount is 129 kilometers southwest of Monterey, California, 42 kilometers long, 13 kilometers wide, and 2,280 meters tall but still 1,250 meters from the water's surface. It hosts a dense and diverse array of deep-water corals and sponges, particularly along the flanks of the seamount (Clague et al. 2010). Due to its depth, the benthic ecosystem is still pristine, and restrictions on bottom fishing have been put in place to maintain the benthic habitat. Expansion of the Cordell Bank and Gulf of Farallones Sanctuaries north to Point Arena is also currently under consideration (NOAA 2013).

The Sanctuary Program was created primarily in response to concerns over pollution through dumping of waste and oil spills in coastal regions. The sanctuaries began with grand intentions, and some of its early backers originally envisioned the sanctuaries to be akin to the National Parks System on land, with protections at the level of those afforded under the Wilderness Act (Owen 2003, Chandler and Gillehan 2004). Over time, however, Congress has defined the primary purpose of National Marine Sanctuaries as multiple-use regions, often with little restrictions on uses within their boundaries, and the act as a whole is considered to be weakly structured with little ability to afford significant protection to marine ecosystems (Chandler and Gillehan 2004). While many activities, such as fishing, are allowed throughout many of the sanctuaries, dumping of waste is prohibited in all sanctuaries, with some minor exceptions, and oil and gas development is prohibited in all of the sanctuaries in the CCS (Owen 2003). Furthermore, the sanctuaries have played an important role in scientific research and education in the regions where they have been designated.

The highly dynamic and integrated system of the CCS has resulted in calls for management that is as dynamic as the marine system (Dunn et al. 2011, Hazen et al. 2013, Maxwell et al. 2013). Dynamic management can be put into place through large-scale protection for species or ecosystems (e.g., mobile marine protected areas [Game et al. 2009]), or through managing multiple or individual sectors using management measures that move and shift with the changing ecosystem (e.g., TurtleWatch, a tool that highlights probable bycatch regions of endangered loggerhead sea turtles within pelagic longline fishing grounds off Hawaii [Howell et al. 2008]). While there is still a need to develop the legal and ecological frameworks to ensure feasibility of DYNAMIC OCEAN MANAGEMENT, incorporating the dynamic nature of marine ecosystems into management strategies will undoubtedly be the future of marine management (Lewison et al. 2015, Maxwell et al. 2015).

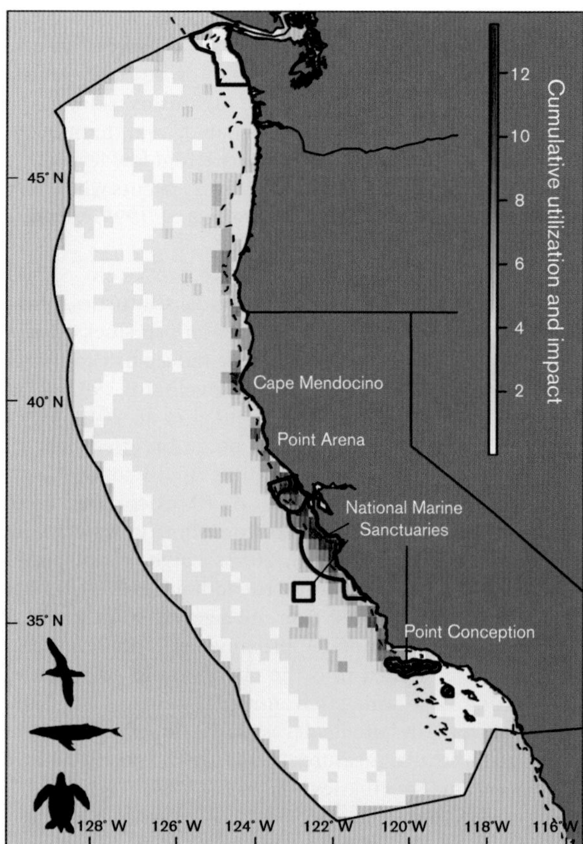

FIGURE 16.7 Cumulative utilization and impacts (CUI) that combines tracking data and impact data for eight marine predators in the U.S. exclusive economic zone. Outer solid line represents the U.S. exclusive economic zone; solid inner lines represent the U.S. National Marine Sanctuaries; hashed lines represent the 200 meter depth contour. Source: Maxwell et al. 2013.

Integrating Science and Management

CASE STUDY: MODIFYING SHIPPING LANES TO AVOID WHALE STRIKES

The region around San Francisco Bay is known as a hotspot for marine mammals, particularly whales (Keiper et al. 2005). San Francisco Bay is also home to a number of the largest ports on the U.S. West Coast, with approximately twenty tankers, container ships, or barges entering and exiting the port everyday via the predesignated shipping lanes. As a result of this traffic, from 1988 to 2011 there have been thirty documented whale strikes within the Gulf of the Farallones and Cordell Bank National Marine Sanctuaries, with the real number likely much higher (Joint Working Group on Vessel Strikes and Acoustic Impacts 2012). The species affected by ship strikes include blue, humpback, fin, and gray whales, and in some cases, the mortality caused by ship strikes greatly

TABLE 16.1
U.S. West Coast National Marine Sanctuaries (NMS)

Sanctuary name (designation year)	Area	Area fully protected (no-take) designated as part of the National Marine Sanctuaries	Key activities restricted or prohibited
Channel Islands NMS (1980)	4,294 km^2	2,344 km^2	Alteration or construction on the seafloor Oil and gas exploration or production Removal/damage of cultural or historical resources Depositing or discharging material
Cordell Bank NMS (1989)	1,362 km^2	None	Oil and gas exploration or production Exploration or production of other minerals Depositing or discharging material Depositing or discharging material outside the NMS that may injure NMS resources
Gulf of the Farallones NMS (1981)	3,250 km^2	None	Alteration or construction on the seafloor Oil and gas exploration or production Removal/damage of cultural or historical resources Depositing or discharging material Use of motorized watercraft
Monterey Bay NMS (1992)	13,784 km^2	None	Alteration or construction on the seafloor Oil and gas exploration or production Removal of natural resources Removal/damage of cultural or historical resources Depositing or discharging material Depositing or discharging material outside the NMS that may injure NMS resources
Olympic Coast NMS (1994)	8,573 km^2	None	Alteration or construction on the seafloor Oil and gas exploration or production Exploration or production of other minerals Removal of natural resources Removal/damage of cultural or historical resources Depositing or discharging material Depositing or discharging material outside the NMS that may injure NMS resources

SOURCE: Adapted from Marine Conservation Institute National Marine Sanctuaries Fact Sheets, 2006, http://www.marine-conservation.org/what-we-do/program-areas/mpas/national-marine-sanctuaries.

exceeds the sustainable human-caused mortality (also known as "potential biological removal," or PBR) populations can withstand without negatively impacting populations. For example, the PBR for blue whales in the eastern North Pacific is 3.1 animals; documented ship strikes can be as high as 4 annually, and this number is likely an underestimate (Joint Working Group on Vessel Strikes and Acoustic Impacts 2012; Redfern et al. 2013).

In an effort to reduce ship strike mortality in the San Francisco Bay Area, a joint working group (JWG) was convened by the Gulf of the Farallones and Cordell Bank National Marine Sanctuaries. This JWG included representatives from NOAA, the agency responsible for managing and protecting whales under the Marine Mammal Protection Act and Endangered Species Act, and the U.S. Coast Guard, which is responsible for implementing the Ports and Waterways Safety Act, which promotes navigation, safety, and protection of the marine environment. The fine-scale patterns of whale habitat use in the region were identified across seasons, and this was compared with shipping vessel traffic patterns to identify the areas of greatest risk to whales (Keiper et al. 2012).

Using this scientific assessment, and combining it with

available management measures, the JWG came up with three key recommendations to reduce whale strikes (Joint Working Group on Vessel Strikes and Acoustic Impacts 2012). Carbon emissions and economic impacts on the shipping industry were considered at all stages, with the goal of maximizing whale protection while minimizing economic and emission impacts. First, the JWG recommended modifying the shipping lanes, extending them to three nautical miles beyond the continental shelf edge to minimize shipping activity within the most sensitive areas. The shelf-break region is a key area for whales because of the high productivity associated with upwelling along the shelf edge. Second, the JWG recommended the implementation of dynamic management areas (DMAs). Vessels would have to choose alternate shipping lanes or reduce speeds when concentrations of whales are present, with DMAs designated using data from real-time sightings of whales. DMAs have been applied to reduce ship strikes on the U.S. East Coast with variable success (Silber et al. 2012) and are considered to be a better option economically for the shipping industry than semipermanent restrictions that would go into effect seasonally. Finally, the JWG recommended a real-time whale sighting/monitoring network with participation from the shipping industry to support the DMAs. The Joint Working Group recommendations have been approved by both the National Marine Sanctuaries and the International Maritime Organization (IMO), and extension of the shipping lanes was implemented in June 2013. This demonstrates how science and management can interact to inform how anthropogenic impacts on marine ecosystems can be reduced while maintaining sustainable human uses. A similar process is under way to reduce ship strikes in the Santa Barbara Channel shipping lanes, which are the gateway to the ports of Los Angeles and Long Beach (Abramsom et al. 2009, DeAngelis et al. 2010, Betz et al. 2011). The inbound lane was shifted northward in June 2013 to move traffic away from known whale concentrations.

Summary

The California Current System is a dynamic eastern boundary current system, driven by seasonal coastal upwelling that transports nutrients into the photic zone and supports a diverse and productive ecosystem. As a result, the offshore ecosystem is driven by phytoplankton blooms that support a diverse food web from zooplankton and forage fish to top predators. Copepods, euphausiids, and forage fish (e.g., sardine, anchovy) serve as critical prey resources for a suite of predators from seabirds to large whales. Intermittent gelatinous zooplankton blooms can alter the energy flow through the food web, although the forcing and trophic impact of these blooms are not well understood. Many mobile species migrate seasonally within the CCS following patterns of productivity, while the predictable prey resources bring other species from across the Pacific. Mesoscale features such as eddies, fronts, and upwelling shadows can be considered marine hotspots in the CCS, which are associated with increased trophic exchange (predation hotspots) and are often of increased ecosystem importance (biodiversity hotspots).

Historically, forage fish provided livelihood for coastal communities throughout the region, although collapses have resulted in increased economic importance from bottom fish, salmon, highly migratory fish, and squid fisheries, to name a few. Population centers along the California coast use the offshore ecosystem for fishing, oil exploration, military activities, ecotourism, and shipping, although increased use also results in increased risk to resident species, including pollution, oil spills, ship strikes, gear entanglements, bycatch, and ocean noise. Given the strong bottom-up forcing of the CCS, the impacts of climate-driven changes in the system could be profound. These impacts include changes in the timing and strength of upwelling, which may lead to mismatches between prey availability and predator distribution, and increased hypoxia and ocean acidification, which may reduce viable habitat for many species and alter community structure. Understanding the interplay between natural climate variability and ecosystem services is critical for effective management of the CCS into the future.

Acknowledgments

The authors thank the external reviewers for useful comments on earlier drafts of the chapter. We thank John Field for permission to use Figure 16.2. The authors also thank Hal Mooney and Erika Zavaleta for providing editorial support and leadership in developing this book.

Recommended Reading

Allen, L. G., and M. H. Horn, editors. 2006. The ecology of marine fishes: California and adjacent waters. University of California Press, Berkeley, California.

Block, B. A., I. D. Jonsen, S. J. Jorgensen, A. J. Winship, S. A. Shaffer, S. J. Bograd, E. L. Hazen, D. G. Foley, G. A. Breed, A. L. Harrison, J. E. Ganong, A. Swithenbank, M. Castleton, H. Dewar, B. R. Mate, G. L. Shillinger, K. M. Schaefer, S. R. Benson, M. J. Weise, R. W. Henry, and D. P. Costa. 2011. Tracking apex marine predator movements in a dynamic ocean. Nature 475:86–90.

Bograd, S. J., W. J. Sydeman et al. 2010. The California Current, 2003–08. Pages 106–141 in S. M. McKinnell and M. Dagg, editors. Marine Ecosystems of the North Pacific Ocean, 2003–2008. PICES Special Publication 4. North Pacific Marine Science Organization, Sidney, BC, Canada.

Checkley, D. M., Jr., and J. A. Barth. 2009. Patterns and processes in the California Current System. Progress in Oceanography 83:49–64.

Mann, K. H., and J.R.N. Lazier. 2006. Dynamics of marine ecosystems: Biological-physical interactions in the oceans. Third edition. Blackwell Publishing, Oxford, UK.

McClatchie, S. 2014. Regional fisheries oceanography of the California Current System: The CalCOFI program. Springer Press, Dordrecht, Netherlands.

Norse, E., and L. B. Crowder. 2005. Marine conservation biology. Island Press, Washington, D.C.

Glossary

DEEP SCATTERING LAYER A horizontal zone of organisms at mid-depths that tend to rise toward the surface at dusk and descend again at dawn.

DYNAMIC OCEAN MANAGEMENT Measures that manage ocean resources by taking into account the dynamic nature of marine organisms and processes.

EUPHOTIC At depths exposed to sufficient sunlight for photosynthesis to occur.

MARINE HOTSPOTS In marine systems, these are defined by (1) important life history areas for a particular species, (2) areas of high biodiversity or abundance of individuals, and (3) areas of important productivity, trophic transfer, and biophysical coupling.

MARINE PROTECTED AREAS (MPAS) Special areas established and managed for conserving marine resources, often allowing specific recreational and commercial uses.

MESOPELAGICS Species that primarily occur in the mesopelagic zone, which extends from 200 to 1,000 meter depth.

OLIGOTROPHIC Describes an environment with very low nutrient availability.

PELAGIC Refers to the open ocean rather than nearshore waters, and vertically above seafloor habitats that are considered benthic.

PLANKTON Organisms that live in the water column and are incapable of swimming against a current. These include phytoplankton (plants) and zooplankton (animals).

TROPHIC INTERACTIONS Interactions between the producers and consumers in an ecosystem (i.e., a food web).

References

American Association of Port Authorities. 2012. World Port Rankings 2011. <http://aapa.files.cms-plus.com/PDFs>.

Abramsom, L., S. Polefka, S. Hastings, and K. Bor. 2009. Reducing the threat of ship strikes on large cetaceans in the Santa Barbara Channel Region and Channel Islands National Marine Sanctuary: Recommendations and case studies. Channel Islands National Marine Sanctuary Advisory Council, Santa Barbara, California.

Agostini, V. N., A. N. Hendrix, A. B. Hollowed, C. D. Wilson, S. D. Pierce, and R. C. Francis. 2008. Climate-ocean variability and Pacific hake: A geostatistical modeling approach. Journal of Marine Systems 71:237–248.

Ahlstrom, E. H. 1969. Mesopelagic and bathypelagic fishes in the California Current region. CalCOFI Reports 13:39–44.

Ainley, D. G., and T. J. Lewis. 1974. The history of Farallon Island marine bird populations, 1854–1972. Condor 76:432–446.

Ainley, D. G., W. J. Sydeman, and J. Norton. 1995. Upper trophic level predators indicate interannual negative and positive anomalies in the California Current food web. Marine Ecology Progress Series 118:69–79.

Ainsworth C. H., J. F. Samhouri, D. S. Busch, W.W.L. Cheung, J. Dunne, and T. A. Okey. 2011. Potential impacts of climate change on northeast Pacific marine foodwebs and fisheries. ICES Journal of Marine Science 68:1217–1229.

Allen, L. G., and J. N. Cross. 2006. Surface waters. Pages 320–341 in L. G. Allen, D. J. Pondella, and M. H. Horn, editors. Ecology of Marine Fishes: California and Adjacent Waters. University of California Press, Berkeley, California.

Allen, L. G., D. J. Pondella, and M. H. Horn. 2006. Ecology of marine fishes: California and adjacent waters. University of California Press, Berkeley, California.

Antonelis, G.,A., Jr., and C. H. Fiscus. 1980. The pinnipeds of the California Current. CalCOFI Reports 21:68–78.

Arizmendi-Rodriguez, D. I., L. A. Abitia-Cardenas, F. Galvan-Magana, and I. Trejo-Escamilla. 2006. Food habits of sailfish *Istiophorus platypterus* off Mazatlan, Sinaloa, Mexico. Bulletin of Marine Science 79:777–791.

Attrill M. J., J. Wright, and M. Edwards. 2007. Climate-related increases in jellyfish frequency suggest a more gelatinous future for the North Sea. Limnology and Oceanography 52:480–485.

Bailey, H., B. R. Mate, D. M. Palacios, L. Irvine, S. J. Bograd, and D. P. Costa. 2009. Behavioural estimation of blue whale movements in the Northeast Pacific from state-space model analysis of satellite tracks. Endangered Species Research 10:93–106.

Bailey, H., S. R. Benson, G. L. Shillinger, S. J. Bograd, P. H. Dutton, S. A. Eckert, S. J. Morreale, F. V. Paladino, T. Eguchi, D. G. Foley, B. A. Block, R. Piedra, C. Hitipeuw, R. F. Tapilatu, and J. R. Spotila. 2012. Identification of distinct movement patterns in Pacific leatherback turtle populations influenced by ocean conditions. Ecological Applications 22:735–747.

Barange, M., M. Bernal, M. Cercole, L. Cubillos, C. Cunningham, G. Daskalov, J. De Oliveira, M. Dickey-Collas, K. Hill, and L. Jacobson. 2009. Current trends in the assessment and management of small pelagic fish stocks. Pages 191–255 in D. M. Checkley et al., editors. Climate Change and Small Pelagic Fish. Cambridge University Press, New York, New York.

Barlow, J., and K. A. Forney. 2007. Abundance and population density of cetaceans in the California Current ecosystem. Fishery Bulletin 105:509–526.

Barlow, J., M. Kahru, and B. Mitchell. 2008. Cetacean biomass, prey consumption, and primary production requirements in the California Current ecosystem. Marine Ecology Progress Series 371:285–295.

Becker, E. A., K. A. Forney, M. C. Ferguson, D. G. Foley, R. C. Smith, J. Barlow, and J. V. Redfern. 2010. Comparing California Current cetacean-habitat models developed using in situ and remotely sensed sea surface temperature data. Marine Ecology Progress Series 413:163–183.

Bedford, D. W., and F. B. Hagerman. 1983. The billfish fishery resource of the California Current. CalCOFI Reports 24:70–78.

Benson, S. R., D. A. Croll, B. B. Marinovic, F. P. Chavez, and J. T. Harvey. 2002. Changes in the cetacean assemblage of a coastal upwelling ecosystem during El Niño 1997–98 and La Niña 1999. Progress in Oceanography 54:279–291.

Benson, S. R., T. Eguchi, D. G. Foley, K. A. Forney, H. Bailey, C. Hitipeuw, B. P. Samber, R. F. Tapilatu, V. Rei, P. Ramohia, J. Pita, and P. H. Dutton. 2011. Large-scale movements and high-use areas of western Pacific leatherback turtles, *Dermochelys coriacea*. Ecosphere 2(7):art84. <doi:10.1890/ES11-00053.1>.

Berman-Kowalewski, M., F.M.D. Gulland, S. Wilkin, J. Calambokidis, B. Mate, J. Cordaro, D. Rotstein, J. S. Leger, P. Collins, K. Fahy, and S. Dover. 2010. Association between blue whale (*Balaenoptera musculus*) mortality and ship strikes along the California Coast. Aquatic Mammals 36:59–66.

Bernard, H. J., J. B. Hedgepeth, and S. B. Reilly. 1985. Stomach contents of albacore, skipjack, and bonito caught off southern California during summer 1983. CalCOFI Reports 26:175–183.

Betz, S., K. Bohnsack, A. Callahan, L. Campbell, S. E. Green, and K. M. Labrum. 2011. Reducing the risk of vessel strikes to endangered whales in the Santa Barbara Channel: An economic analysis and risk assessment of potential management scenarios. Bren School of Environmental Science and Management, University of California, Santa Barbara, Santa Barbara, California.

Black, A. 2005. Light induced seabird mortality on vessels operating in the Southern Ocean: Incidents and mitigation measures. Antarctic Science 17:67–68.

Black, B. A., I. D. Schroeder, W. J. Sydeman, S. J. Bograd, B. Wells, and F. B. Schwing. 2011. Winter and summer upwelling modes and their biological importance in the California Current Ecosystem. Global Change Biology 17:2536–2545. <doi:10.1111/j.1365-2486.2011.02422.x>.

Block, B. A., and E. D. Stevens. 2001. Tuna: Physiology, ecology, and evolution. Academic Press, San Diego.

Block, B. A., I. D. Jonsen, S. J. Jorgensen, A. J. Winship, S. A. Shaffer, S. J. Bograd, E. L. Hazen, D. G. Foley, G. A. Breed, A. L. Harrison, J. E. Ganong, A. Swithenbank, M. Castleton, H. Dewar, B. R. Mate, G. L. Shillinger, K. M. Schaefer, S. R. Benson, M. J. Weise, R. W. Henry, and D. P. Costa. 2011. Tracking apex marine predator movements in a dynamic ocean. Nature 475:86–90.

Bograd, S. J., C. G. Castro, E. Di Lorenzo, D. M. Palacios, H. Bailey, W. Gilly, and F. P. Chavez. 2008. Oxygen declines and the shoaling of the hypoxic boundary in the California current. Geophysical Research Letters 35(12). <doi:10.1029/ 2008GL034185>.

Bograd, S. J., D. M. Checkley, and W. S. Wooster. 2003. CalCOFI: A half century of physical, chemical, and biological research in the California Current System. Deep-Sea Research II 50(14–16):2349–2353.

Bograd, S. J., I. Schroeder, N. Sarkar, X. Qiu, W. J. Sydeman, and F. B. Schwing. 2009. The phenology of coastal upwelling in the California Current. Geophysical Research Letters 36, L01602. <doi:10.1029/2008GL035933>.

Brinton, E., and A. Townsend. 2003. Decadal variability in abundances of the dominant euphausiid species in southern sectors of the California Current. Deep-Sea Research II 50(14–16):2449–2472.

Brodeur, R. D. 1990. A synthesis of the food habits and feeding ecology of salmonids in marine waters of the North Pacific. FRI-UW-9016. Fisheries Research Institute, University of Washington, Seattle, Washington.

Brodeur, R., and O. Yamamura, editors. 2005. Micronekton of the North Pacific. PICES Scientific Report No. 30. North Pacific Marine Science Organization, Sidney, BC, Canada.

Brodeur, R. D., J. J. Ruzicka, and J. H. Steele. 2011. Investigating alternate trophic pathways through gelatinous zooplankton and planktivorous fishes in an upwelling ecosystem using end-to-end models interdisciplinary studies on environmental chemistry. Pages 57–63 in K. Omori, X. Guo, N. Yoshie, N. Fujii, I. C. Handoh, A. Isobe and S. Tanabe, editors. Marine Environmental Modeling and Analysis, TERRAPUB, Tokyo, Japan.

Brodeur, R. D., S. Ralston, R. L. Emmett, M. Trudel, T. D. Auth, and A. J. Phillips. 2006. Anomalous pelagic nekton abundance, distribution, and apparent recruitment in the northern California Current in 2004 and 2005. Geophysical Research Letters 33, L22S08. <doi:10.1029/2006GL026614>.

Brodeur, R. D., W. G. Pearcy, and S. Ralston. 2003. Abundance and distribution patterns of nekton and micronekton in the Northern California Current Transition Zone. Journal of Oceanography 59:515–534.

Bureau of Ocean Energy Management. 2013. Pacific Region Facts and Figures. <http://www.boem.gov/BOEM-Newsroom/Offshore-Stats-and-Facts/Pacific-Facts-and-Figures.aspx>.

Burrows, J., J. Harvey, K. Newton, D. Croll, and S. Benson. 2012. Marine mammal response to interannual variability in Monterey Bay, California. Marine Ecology Progress Series 461:257–271.

Butt, N. 2007. The impact of cruise ship generated waste on home ports and ports of call: A study of Southampton. Marine Policy 31:591–598.

Calambokidis, J., J. Barlow, J.K.B. Ford, T. E. Chandler, and A. B. Douglas. 2009. Insights into the population structure of blue whales in the Eastern North Pacific from recent sightings and photographic identification. Marine Mammal Science 25:816–832.

Calbet, A., and M. R. Landry. 2004. Phytoplankton growth, microzooplankton grazing, and carbon cycling in marine systems. Limnology and Oceanography 49:51–57.

Camhi, M. D., E. K. Pikitch, and E. A. Babcock. 2008. Sharks of the open ocean: Biology, fisheries, and conservation. Wiley-Blackwell, Oxford, UK.

Carlisle, A. B., C. R. Perle, K. J. Goldman, B. A. Block, and J. M. Jech. 2011. Seasonal changes in depth distribution of salmon sharks (*Lamna ditropis*) in Alaskan waters: Implications for foraging ecology. Canadian Journal of Fisheries and Aquatic Sciences 68:1905–1921.

Carretta, J. V., K. A. Forney, E. Oleson, K. Martien, M. M. Muto, M. S. Lowry, J. Barlow, J. Baker, B. Hanson, D. Lynch, L. Carswell, R. L. Brownell, J. Robbins, D. K. Mattila, K. Ralls, and M. C. Hill. 2010. U.S. Pacific Marine Mammal Stock Assessments: 2010. NOAA Technical Memorandum NMFS-SWFSC-476. La Jolla, California.

Carretta, J. V., K. A. Forney, M. S. Lowry, J. Barlow, J. Baker, D. Johnston, B. Hanson, R. L. Brownell, J. Robbins, D. K. Mattila, K. Ralls, M. M. Muto, D. Lynch, and L. Carswell. 2009. US Pacific Marine Mammal Stock Assessments: 2009. NOAA Technical Memorandum NMFS-SWFSC-453. La Jolla, California.

Carretta, J. V., T. Price, D. Petersen, and R. Read. 2004. Estimates of marine mammal, sea turtle, and seabird mortality in the California drift gillnet fishery for swordfish and thresher shark, 1996–2002. Marine Fisheries Review 66:21–30.

Castellote, M., C. W. Clark, and M. O. Lammers. 2012. Acoustic and behavioural changes by fin whales (*Balaenoptera physalus*) in response to shipping and airgun noise. Biological Conservation 147:115–122.

Chandler, W. J., and H. Gillelan. 2004. The history and evolution of the National Marine Sanctuaries Act. Environmental Law Reporter 34:10505–10565.

Checkley, D. M., Jr., and J. A. Barth. 2009. Patterns and processes in the California Current System. Progress in Oceanography 83:49–64.

Clague, D., L. Lundsten, J. Hein, J. Paduan, and A. Davis. 2010. Davidson Seamount. Oceanography 23:126–126.

Clapham, P. J., S. B. Young, and R. L. Brownell. 1999. Baleen whales: Conservation issues and the status of the most endangered populations. Mammal Review 29:35–60.

Clark, C. W., W. T. Ellison, B. L. Southall, L. Hatch, S. M. Van Parijs, A. Frankel, and D. Ponirakis. 2009. Acoustic masking in marine ecosystems: Intuitions, analysis, and implication. Marine Ecology Progress Series 395:201–222.

Clark, R. B. 1984. Impact of oil pollution on seabirds. Environmental Pollution Series a-Ecological and Biological 33:1–22.

Codarin, A., L. E. Wysocki, F. Ladich, and M. Picciulin. 2009. Effects of ambient and boat noise on hearing and communication in three fish species living in a marine protected area (Miramare, Italy). Marine Pollution Bulletin 58:1880–1887.

Cox, T. M., T. J. Ragen, A. J. Read, E. Vos, R. W. Baird, K. Balcomb, J. Barlow, J. Caldwell, T. Cranford, L. Crum, A. D'Amico, G. D'Spain, A. Fernandez, J. Finneran, R. Gentry, W. Gerth, F. Gulland, J. Hildebrand, D. Houser, T. Hullar, P. D. Jepson, D. Ketten, C. D. MacLeod, P. Miller, S. Moore, D. Mountain, D. Palka, P. Ponganis, S. Rommel, T. Rowles, B. Taylor, P. Tyack, D. Warzok, R. Gisiner, J. Mead, and L. Benner. 2006. Understanding the impacts of anthropogenic sound on beaked whales. Journal of Cetacean Research and Management 7:177–187.

Crawford, R.J.M. 1987. Food and population variability in five regions supporting large stocks of anchovy, sardines, and horse mackerel. South African Journal of Marine Science 5:735–757.

Croll, D. A., B. Marinovic, S. Benson, F. P. Chavez, N. Black, R. Ternullo, and B. R. Tershy. 2005. From wind to whales: Trophic links in a coastal upwelling system. Marine Ecology Progress Series 289:117–130.

Croll, D., B. Tershy, R. Hewitt, and D. Demer. 1998. An integrated approach to the foraging ecology of marine birds and mammals. Deep-Sea Research II 45:1353–1371.

Cury, P., A. Bakun, R.J.M. Crawford, A. Jarre, R. A. Quiñones, L. J. Shannon, and H. M. Verheye. 2000. Small pelagics in upwelling systems: Patterns of interaction and structural changes in "wasp-waist" ecosystems. ICES Journal of Marine Science 57:603–618.

Dahms, H. U. 1995. Dormancy in the copepod—an overview. Hydrobiologia 306:199–211.

Darling, J. D., and M. Berube. 2001. Interactions of singing humpback whales with other males. Marine Mammal Science 17:570–584.

Davison, P. C., D. M. Checkley Jr., J. A. Koslow, and J. Barlow. 2013. Carbon export mediated by mesopelagic fishes in the northeast Pacific Ocean. Progress in Oceanography 116:14–30.

DeAngelis, M., C. Fahy, and J. Cordaro. 2010. Reducing vessel strikes of large whales in California: Report from a workshop held in Long Beach, California. NOAA/NMFS Southwest Regional Office, Long Beach, California.

Dunn, D. C., A. M. Boustany, and P. N. Halpin. 2011. Spatio-temporal management of fisheries to reduce by-catch and increase fishing selectivity. Fish and Fisheries 12:110–119.

Ebert, D. A. 2003. Sharks, rays, and chimaeras of California. University of California Press, Berkeley, California.

Emmett, R. L., R. D. Brodeur, T. W. Miller, S. S. Pool, P. J. Bentley, G. K. Krutzikowsky, and J. McCrae. 2005. Pacific sardine (*Sardinops sagax*) abundance, distribution, and ecological relationships in the Pacific Northwest. CalCOFI Reports 46:122–143.

Engelhardt, F. R. 1983. Petroleum effects on marine mammals. Aquatic Toxicology 4:199–217.

Enright, J. T., and W. M. Hammer. 1967. Vertical diurnal migration and endogenous rhythmicity. Science 157(3791):937–941.

Essington, T.E., P. E. Moriarty, H. E. Froehlich, E. E. Hodgson, L. E. Koehn, K. L. Oken, M. C. Siple, and C. C. Stawitz. 2015. Fishing amplifies forage fish population collapses. Proceedings of the National Academy of Sciences 112(21):6648–6652.

Fabry, V. J., B. A. Seibel, R. A. Feely, and J. C. Orr. 2008. Impacts of ocean acidification on marine fauna and ecosystem processes. ICES Journal of Marine Science 65:414–432.

Fenchel, T. 2008. The microbial loop—25 years later. Journal of Experimental Marine Biology and Ecology 366(1–2):99–103.

———. 1987. Ecology of protozoa: The biology of free living phagotrophic protists. Springer-Verlag, Berlin.

Fiedler, P. C., J. Barlow, and T. Gerrodette. 1998. Dolphin prey abundance determined from acoustic backscatter data in eastern Pacific surveys. Fishery Bulletin 96:237–247.

Fiedler, P. C., S. B. Reilly, R. P. Hewitt, D. Demer, V. A. Philbrick, S. Smith, W. Armstrong, D. A. Croll, B. R. Tershy, and B. R. Mate. 1998. Blue whale habitat and prey in the California Channel Islands. Deep-Sea Research II 45:1781–1801.

Field, J. C., A. D. MacCall, R. W. Bradley, and W. J. Sydeman. 2010.

Estimating the impacts of fishing on dependent predators: A case study in the California Current. Ecological Applications 20:2223–2236.

Field, J. C., C. Elliger, K. Baltz, G. E. Gillespie, W. F. Gilly, R. I . Ruiz-Cooley, D. Pearse, J. S. Stewart, W. Matsubu, and W. A. Walker. 2012. Foraging ecology and movement patterns of jumbo squid (*Dosidicus gigas*) in the California Current System. Deep Sea Research II. <doi:10.1016/j.dsr2.2012.09.006>.

Field, J. C., K. Baltz, A. J. Phillips, and W. A. Walker. 2007. Range expansion and trophic interactions of the jumbo squid, *Dosidicus gigas*, in the California Current. California Cooperative Oceanic Fisheries Investigations Reports 48:131–146.

Field, J. C., R. C. Francis, and K. Aydin. 2006. Top-down modeling and bottom-up dynamics: Linking a fisheries-based ecosystem model with climate hypotheses in the Northern California Current. Progress in Oceanography 68:238–270.

Forney, K. A., M. C. Ferguson, E. A. Becker, P. C. Fiedler, J. V. Redfern, J. Barlow, I. L. Vilchis, and L. T. Balance. 2012. Habitat-based spatial models of cetacean density in the eastern Pacific Ocean. Endangered Species Research 16:113–133.

Fréon, P., J. Arístegui, A. Bertrand, R.J.M. Crawford, J. C. Field, M. J. Gibbons, J. Tam, L. Hutchings, H. Masski, C. Mullon, M. Ramdani, B. Seret, and M. Simier. 2009. Functional group biodiversity in Eastern Boundary Upwelling Ecosystems questions the wasp-waist trophic structure. Progress in Oceanography 83:97–106.

Fréon, P., P. Cury, L. Shannon, and C. Roy. 2005. Sustainable exploitation of small pelagic fish stocks challenged by environmental and ecosystem changes: A review. Bulletin of Marine Science 76:385–462.

Fristrup, K. M., L. T. Hatch, and C. W. Clark. 2003. Variation in humpback whale (*Megaptera novaeangliae*) song length in relation to low-frequency sound broadcasts. Journal of the Acoustical Society of America 113:3411–3424.

Game, E. T., H. S. Grantham, A. J. Hobday, R. L. Pressey, A. T. Lombard, L. E. Beckley, K. Gjerde, R. Bustamante, H. P. Possingham, and A. J. Richardson. 2009. Pelagic protected areas: The missing dimension in ocean conservation. Trends in Ecology and Evolution 24:360–369.

George, J. C., C. Clark, G. M. Carroll, and W. T. Ellison. 1989. Observations on the ice-breaking and ice navigation behavior of migrating bowhead whales (*Baleana mysticetus*) near Point Barrow, Alaska, spring 1985. Arctic 42:24–30.

Glaser, S. M. 2011. Do albacore exert top-down pressure on northern anchovy? Estimating anchovy mortality as a result of predation by juvenile north pacific albacore in the California Current System. Fisheries Oceanography 20:242–257.

Goldbogen, J. A., B. L. Southall, S. L. DeRuiter, J. Calambokidis, A. S. Friedlaender, E. L. Hazen, E. A. Falcone, G. S. Schorr, A. Douglas, D. J. Moretti, C. Kyburg, M. F. McKenna, P. L. Tyack. 2013. Proceedings of the Royal Society B 280:1–8.

Goold, J. C., and P. J. Fish. 1998. Broadband spectra of seismic survey air-gun emissions, with reference to dolphin auditory thresholds. Journal of the Acoustical Society of America 103:2177–2184.

Guinotte, J. M., and V. J. Fabry. 2008. Ocean acidification and its potential effects on marine ecosystems. Pages 320–342 in R. S. Ostfeld, editor. Year in Ecology and Conservation Biology. Volume 1134. Wiley-Blackwell, Hoboken, New Jersey.

Halpern, B. S., C. V. Kappel, K. A. Selkoe, F. Micheli, C. M. Ebert, C. Kontgis, C. M. Crain, R. G. Martone, C. Shearer, and S. J. Teck. 2009. Mapping cumulative human impacts to California Current marine ecosystems. Conservation Letters 2:138–148.

Halpern, B. S., S. Walbridge, K. A. Selkoe, C. V. Kappel, F. Micheli, C. D'Agrosa, J. F. Bruno, K. S. Casey, C. Ebert, H. E. Fox, R. Fujita, D. Heinemann, H. S. Lenihan, E.M.P. Madin, M. T. Perry, E. R. Selig, M. Spalding, R. Steneck, and R. Watson. 2008. A global map of human impact on marine ecosystems. Science 319:948–952.

Harding, J. A., A. J. Ammann, and R. B. MacFarlane. 2011. Regional and seasonal patterns of epipelagic fish assemblages from the central California Current. Fishery Bulletin 109:261–281.

Harris, K. E., M. D. DeGrandpre, and B. Hales 2013. Aragonite saturation state dynamics in a coastal upwelling zone. Geophysical Research Letters 40: 2720–2725.

Hauri, C., N. Gruber, M. Vogt, S. C. Doney, R. A. Feely, Z. Lachkar, A. Leinweber, A. M. P. McDonnell, M. Munnich, and G.-K. Plattner. 2012. Spatiotemporal variability and long-term trends of ocean acidification in the California Current System. Biogeosciences Discussions 9: 10371–10428.

Hauri, C., N. Gruber, G.-K. Plattner, S. Alin, R. A. Feely, B. Hales, and P. A. Wheeler. 2013. Ocean acidification in the California Current System. Oceanography 22(4):60–71.

Hays, G. C. 2003. A review of the adaptive significance and ecosystem consequences of zooplankton diel vertical migrations. Hydrobiologia 503:163–170.

Hazen, E. L., S. Jorgensen, R. R. Rykaczewski, S. J. Bograd, D. G. Foley, I. D. Jonsen, S. A. Shaffer, J. P. Dunne, D. P. Costa, L. B. Crowder, and B. A. Block. 2013. Predicted habitat shifts of Pacific top predators in a changing climate. Nature Climate Change 3:234–238. <doi:10.1038/NCLIMATE1686>.

Henkel, J. R., B. J. Sigel, and C. M. Taylor. 2012. Large-scale impacts of the Deepwater Horizon oil spill: Can local disturbance affect distant ecosystems through migratory shorebirds? Bioscience 62:676–685.

Hester, K. C., E. T. Peltzer, W.J . Kirkwood, and P. G. Brewer. 2008. Unanticipated consequences of ocean acidification: A noisier ocean at lower pH. Geophysical Research Letters 35. <doi:10.1029/2008GL034913>.

Hinke, J., G. Watters, G. Boehlert, and P. Zedonis. 2005. Ocean habitat use in autumn by Chinook salmon in coastal waters of Oregon and California. Marine Ecology Progress Series 285:181–192.

Horne, J. K., and P. E. Smith. 1997. Space and time scales in Pacific hake recruitment processes: Latitudinal variation over annual cycles. California Cooperative Oceanic Fisheries Investigations Reports 38:90–102.

Hoving, H.-J., W. F. Gilly, U. Markaida, K. J. Benoit-Bird, Z. W. Brown, P. Daniel, J. C. Field, L. Parassenti, B. Liu, and B. Campos. 2013. Extreme plasticity in life-history strategy allows a migratory predator (jumbo squid) to cope with a changing climate. Global Change Biology. <doi:10.1111/gcb.12198>.

Howell, E., D. Kobayashi, D. Parker, and G. Balazs. 2008. TurtleWatch: A tool to aid in the bycatch reduction of loggerhead turtles *Caretta caretta* in the Hawaii-based pelagic longline fishery. Endangered Species Research 5:267–278.

Howell, E. A., S. J. Bograd, C. Morishige, M. P. Seki, and J. J. Polovina. 2012. On North Pacific circulation and associated marine debris concentration. Marine Pollution Bulletin 65:16–22.

Hsieh, C.-h., C. S. Reiss, R. P. Hewitt, and G. Sugihara. 2008. Spatial analysis shows that fishing enhances the climatic sensitivity of marine fishes. Canadian Journal of Fisheries and Aquatic Sciences 65:947–961.

Hyrenbach, K. D., and R. R. Veit. 2003. Ocean warming and seabird communities of the southern California Current System (1987–98): Response at multiple temporal scales. Deep Sea Research II 50:2537–2565.

Irvine, L. M., B. R. Mate, M. H. Winsor, D. M. Palacios, S. J. Bograd, D. P. Costa, and H. Bailey. 2014. Spatial and temporal occurrence of blue whales (*Balaenoptera musculus*) off the U.S. West Coast with implications for conservation. PLoS ONE, 9(7): e102959. doi:10.1371/journal.pone.0102959.

Jepson, P. D., M. Arbelo, R. Deaville, I.A.P. Patterson, P. Castro, J. R. Baker, E. Degollada, H. M. Ross, P. Herraez, A. M. Pocknell, F. Rodriguez, F. E. Howie, A. Espinosa, R. J. Reid, J. R. Jaber, V. Martin, A. A. Cunningham, and A. Fernandez. 2003. Gas-bubble lesions in stranded cetaceans—was sonar responsible for a spate of whale deaths after an Atlantic military exercise? Nature 425:575–576.

Johnson, D. 2002. Environmentally sustainable cruise tourism: A reality check. Marine Policy 26:261–270.

Joint Working Group on Vessel Strikes and Acoustic Impacts. 2012. Vessel Strikes and Acoustic Impacts. Report of a Joint Working Group of Gulf of the Farallones and Cordell Bank National Marine Sanctuaries Advisory Councils. U.S. National Marine Sanctuaries, San Francisco California.

Jorgensen, S. J., C. A. Reeb, T. K. Chapple, S. Anderson, C. Perle, S. R. Van Sommeran, C. Fritz-Cope, A. C. Brown, A. P. Klimley, and B. A. Block. 2010. Philopatry and migration of Pacific white sharks. Proceedings of the Royal Society B 277:679–688.

Jorgensen, S. J., N. S. Arnoldi, E. E. Estess, T. K. Chapple, M. Rückert, S. D. Anderson, and B. A. Block. 2012. Eating or meeting? Cluster analysis reveals intricacies of white shark (*Carcharodon carcharias*) migration and offshore behavior. PloS One 7:e47819.

Kaartvedt, S., A. Staby, and D. L. Aksnes. 2012. Efficient trawl avoid-

ance by mesopelagic fishes causes large underestimation of their biomass. Marine Ecology Progress Series 456:1–6.
Kappes, M., S. A. Shaffer, Y. Tremblay, D. G. Foley, D. M. Palacios, P. W. Robinson, S. J. Bograd, and D. P. Costa, 2010. Hawaiian albatrosses track interannual variability of marine habitats in the North Pacific. Progress in Oceanography 86:246–260.
Karpov, K. A., and G. M. Cailliet. 1978. Feeding dynamics of *Loligo opalescens*. California Department of Fish and Game Fish Bulletin 169:45–65.
Keiper, C. A., D. G. Ainley, S. G. Allen, and J. T. Harvey. 2005. Marine mammal occurrence and ocean climate off central California, 1986 to 1994 and 1997 to 1999. Marine Ecology-Progress Series 289:285–306.
Keiper, C., J. Calambokidis, G. Ford, J. Casey, C. Miller, and T. R. Kieckhefer. 2012. Risk assessment of vessel traffic on endangered blue and humpback whales in the Gulf of the Farallones and Cordell Bank National Marine Sanctuaries: Summary of research results. Oikonos, Benicia, California.
Kleppel, G. S. 1993. On the diets of calanoid copepods. Marine Ecology Progress Series 99:183–195.
Koslow, J. A., R. Goericke, A. Lara-Lopez, and W. Watson. 2011. Impact of declining intermediate-water oxygen on deepwater fishes in the California Current. Marine Ecology Progress Series 436:207–218.
Kraus, S. D., M. W. Brown, H. Caswell, C. W. Clark, M. Fujiwara, P. K. Hamilton, R. D. Kenney, A. R. Knowlton, S. Landry, C. A. Mayo, W. A. McLellan, M. J. Moore, D. P. Nowacek, D. A. Pabst, A. J. Read, and R. M. Rolland. 2005. North Atlantic right whales in crisis. Science 309:561–562.
Kudela, R., G. Pitcher, T. Probyn, F. Figueiras, T. Moita, and V. Trainer. 2005. Harmful algal blooms in coastal upwelling systems. Oceanography 18(2):184–197.
Kudela, R. M., N. S. Banas, J. A. Barth, E. R. Frame, D. A. Jay, J. L. Largier, E. J. Lessard, T. D. Peterson, and A.J.V. Woude. 2008. New insights into the controls and mechanisms of plankton productivity in coastal upwelling waters of the northern California Current System. Oceanography 21(4):46–59.
Lagardere, J. P. 1982. Effects of noise on growth and reproduction of Crangon-Crangon in rearing tanks. Marine Biology 71:177–185.
Laist, D. W., A. R. Knowlton, J. G. Mead, A. S. Collet, and M. Podesta. 2001. Collisions between ships and whales. Marine Mammal Science 17:35–75.
Le Boeuf, B. J., D. E. Crocker, D. P. Costa, S. B. Blackwell, P. M. Webb, and D. S. Houser. 2000. Foraging ecology of northern elephant seals. Ecological Monographs 70: 353–382.
Leising, A. W., J. J. Pierson, C. Halsband-Lenk, R. A. Horner, and J. R. Postel. 2005. Copepod grazing during spring blooms: Does *Calanus pacificus* avoid harmful diatoms? Progress in Oceanography 67:384–405.
Levin, P. S., and F. B. Schwing, editors. 2011. Technical background for an integrated ecosystem assessment of the California Current: Groundfish, salmon, green sturgeon, and ecosystem health. U.S. Dept. of Commerce, NOAA Tech. Memo., NMFS-NWFSC-109. La Jolla, California.
Lewison, R., A. J. Hobday, S. M. Maxwell, E. L. Hazen, J. R. Hartog, D. C. Dunn, D. Briscoe, S. Fossette, C. E. O'Keefe, M. Barnes-Mauthe, M. Abecassis, S. J. Bograd, N. D. Bethoney, H. Bailey, D. Wiley, S. Andrews, E, Howell, L. J. Hazen, and L. B. Crowder. 2015. Dynamic ocean management: 21st century approaches for marine resource management and conservation. BioScience 65(5):486–498.
Lindley, S. T., C. B. Grimes, M. S. Mohr, W. T. Peterson, J. E. Stein, J. J. Anderson, L. W. Botsford, D. L. Bottom, C. A. Busack, and T. K. Collier. 2009. What caused the Sacramento River fall Chinook stock collapse? Pre-publication report to the Pacific Fishery Management Council, U.S. Department of Commerce, NOAA-NMFS, Southwest Fisheries Science Center, Fisheries Ecology Division, Santa Cruz, California.
Li, Q. P., P.J.S. Franks, and M. R. Landry. 2011. Microzooplankton grazing dynamics: Parameterizing grazing models with dilution experiment data from the California Current ecosystem. Marine Ecology Progress Series 438:59–69.
Livingston, P. A., and K. M. Bailey. 1985. Trophic role of the Pacific whiting, *Merluccius productus*. Marine Fisheries Review 47:16–22.
Logerwell, E. A., and P. E. Smith. 2001. Mesoscale eddies and survival of late stage Pacific sardine (*Sardinops sagax*) larvae. Fisheries Oceanography 10:13–25.
Longhurst, A. R. 1998. Ecological geography of the sea. Academic Press, San Diego, California.
Love, M. S., M. Yoklavich, and D. M. Schroeder. 2008. Demersal fish assemblages in the Southern California Bight based on visual surveys in deep water. Environmental Biology of Fishes 84:55–68.
Love, M., M. Yoklavich, and L. Thorsteinson. 2002. The rockfishes of the northeast Pacific. University of California Press, Berkeley, California.
Lubchenco, J., M. K. McNutt, G. Dreyfus, S. A. Murawski, D. M. Kennedy, P. T. Anastas, S. Chu, and T. Hunter. 2012. Science in support of the Deepwater Horizon response. Proceedings of the National Academy of Sciences of the USA 109:20212–20221.
Lutcavage, M. E., P. L. Lutz, G. D. Bossart, and D. M. Hudson. 1995. Physiological and cliniopathological effects of crude-oil on loggerhead sea turtles. Archives of Environmental Contamination and Toxicology 28:417–422.
MacDonald, B. D., R. L. Lewison, S. V. Madrak, J. A. Seminoff, and T. Eguchi. 2012. Home ranges of East Pacific green turtles *Chelonia mydas* in a highly urbanized temperate foraging ground. Marine Ecology Progress Series 461:211–221.
MacFarlane, R. B. 2010. Energy dynamics and growth of Chinook salmon (*Oncorhynchus tshawytscha*) from the Central Valley of California during the estuarine phase and first ocean year. Canadian Journal of Fisheries and Aquatic Sciences 67:1549–1565.
Mackas, D. L., W. T. Peterson, M. D. Ohman, and B. E. Lavaniegos. 2006. Zooplankton anomalies in the California Current system before and during the warm ocean conditions of 2005. Geophysical Research Letters 33, L22S07. <doi:10.1029/2006GL027930>.
Madigan, D. J., A. B. Carlisle, H. Dewar, O. E. Snodgrass, S. Y. Litvin, F. Micheli, and B. A. Block. 2012. Stable isotope analysis challenges wasp-waist food web assumptions in an upwelling pelagic ecosystem. Scientific Reports 2:654. <doi:10.1038/srep00654>.
Markaida, U., and F. G. Hochberg. 2005. Cephalopods in the diet of swordfish (*Xiphias gladius*) caught off the west coast of Baja California, Mexico. Pacific Science 59:25–41.
Mason, J. E. 1998. Declining rockfish lengths in the Monterey Bay, California, recreational fishery, 1959–94. Marine Fisheries Review 60:15–28.
Mauchline, J., and J. D. Gordon. 1991. Oceanic pelagic prey of benthopelagic fish in the benthic boundary layer of a marginal oceanic region. Marine Ecology Progress Series 74:109–115.
Maxwell, S. M., E. L. Hazen, S. J. Bograd, B. S. Halpern, G. A. Breed, B. Nickel, N. M. Teutschel, S. Benson, H. Bailey, M. A. Kappes, C. Kuhn, M. J. Weise, B. Mate, S. A. Shaffer, J. Hassrick, R. W. Henry, L. Irvine, B. I. McDonald, P. W. Robinson, B. A. Block, and D. P. Costa. 2013. Cumulative human impacts on marine predators. Nature Communications. <doi:10.1038/ncomms3688>.
Maxwell, S. M, E. L. Hazen, R. Lewison, D. C. Dunn, H. Bailey, S. J. Bograd, D. K. Briscoe, S. Fossette, A. J. Hobday, M. Bennett, S. Benson, M. R. Caldwell, D. P. Costa, H. Dewar, T. Eguchi, L. Hazen, S. Kohin, T. Sippel, and L. B. Crowder. 2015. Dynamic ocean management for a dynamic marine environment. Marine Policy 58:42–50.
McClatchie, S. 2014. Regional fisheries oceanography of the California Current System: The CalCOFI program. Springer Press, Dordrecht, Netherlands.
McCrary, M. D., D. E. Panzer, and M. O. Pierson. 2003. Oil and gas operations offshore California: Status, risks, and safety. Marine Ornithology 31:43–49.
McCrea-Strub, A., K. Kleisner, U. R. Sumaila, W. Swartz, R. Watson, D. Zeller, and D. Pauly. 2011. Potential impact of the Deepwater Horizon oil spill on commercial fisheries in the Gulf of Mexico. Fisheries 36:332–336.
McDonald, M. A., J. A. Hildebrand, and S. Mesnick. 2009. Worldwide decline in tonal frequencies of blue whale songs. Endangered Species Research 9:13–21.
McDonald, M. A., J. A. Hildebrand, and S. M. Wiggins. 2006. Increases in deep ocean ambient noise in the northeast Pacific west of San Nicolas Island, California. Journal of the Acoustical Society of America 120:711–718.
McKenna, M. F., J. Calambokidis, E. M. Oleson, D. W. Laist, and J. A. Goldbogen. 2015. Simultaneous tracking of blue whales and large

ships demonstrates limited behavioral responses to avoiding collision. Endangered Species Research 27(3):219–232.

Miller, P.J.O., N. Biassoni, A. Samuels, and P. L. Tyack. 2000. Whale songs lengthen in response to sonar. Nature 405:903–903.

Mills, K. L., T. Laidig, S. Ralston, and W. J. Sydeman. 2007. Diets of top predators indicate pelagic juvenile rockfish (*Sebastes* spp.) abundance in the California Current System. Fisheries Oceanography 16:273–283.

Milton, S., P. Lutz, and G. Shigenaka. 2003. Oil toxicity and impacts on sea turtles. Pages 35–48 in Oil spills and sea turtles: Biology, planning and response. National Oceanic and Atmospheric Administration, Silver Spring, Maryland.

Monnahan, C. C., T. A. Branch, and A. E. Punt. 2015. Do ship strikes threaten the recovery of endangered eastern North Pacific blue whales? Marine Mammal Science 31.1:279–297.

Moore, J. E., and J. P. Barlow. 2013. Declining abundance of beaked whales (Family Ziphiidae) in the California Current large marine ecosystem. PloS One 8:e52770.

Morejohn, G. V., J. T. Harvey, and L. T. Krasnow. 1978. The importance of *Loligo opalescens* in the food web of marine vertebrates in Monterey Bay, California. California Department of Fish and Game Fish Bulletin 169:67–98.

National Oceanic and Atmospheric Administration (NOAA). 2013. Boundary expansion of Cordell Bank and Gulf of the Farallones National Marine Sanctuaries; intent to prepare draft environmental impact statement; scoping meetings. Federal Register 78:1178–1179.

Newton, K. M., D. A. Croll, H. M. Nevins, S. R. Benson, J. T. Harvey, and B. R. Tershy. 2009. At-sea mortality of seabirds based on beachcast and offshore surveys. Marine Ecology Progress Series 392:295–305.

Nowacek, D. P., L. H. Thorne, D. W. Johnston, and P. L. Tyack. 2007. Responses of cetaceans to anthropogenic noise. Mammal Review 37:81–115.

Ohman, M. D., K. Barbeau, P.J.S. Franks, R. Goericke, M. R. Landry, and A. J. Miller. 2013. Ecological transitions in a coastal upwelling ecosystem. Oceanography 26(3):210–219.

Overland, J., S. Rodionov, S. Minobe, and N. Bond. 2008. North Pacific regime shifts: Definitions, issues, and recent transitions. Progress in Oceanography 77:92–102.

Owen, D. 2003. The disappointing history of the National Marine Sanctuaries Act. NYU Environmental Law Journal 11:711–758.

Paffenhofer, G. A. 1976. Feeding, growth, and food conversion of the marine planktonic copepod *Calanus helgolandicus*. Limnology and Oceanography 21:39–50.

Palacios, D. M., S. J. Bograd, D. G. Foley, and F. B. Schwing. 2006. Oceanographic characteristics of biological hot spots in the North Pacific: A remote sensing perspective. Deep-Sea Research II 53:250–269.

Parks, S. E., M. Johnson, D. Nowacek, and P. L. Tyack. 2011. Individual right whales call louder in increased environmental noise. Biology Letters 7:33–35.

Parrish, R. H., C. S. Nelson, and A. Bakun. 1981. Transport mechanisms and reproductive success of fishes in the California Current. Biological Oceanography 2:175–203.

Payne, R., and D. Webb. 1971. Orientation by means of long range acoustic signaling in baleen whales. Annals of the New York Academy of Sciences 188:110–141.

Payne, R. S., and S. McVay. 1971. Songs of humpback whales. Science 173:585–597.

Pearcy, W. G., R. D. Brodeur, J. M. Shenker, W. W. Smoker, and Y. Endo. 1988. Food habits of Pacific salmon and steelhead trout, midwater trawl catches, and oceanographic conditions in the Gulf of Alaska, 1980–1985. Bulletin of the Ocean Research Institute, University of Tokyo 26(2):29–78.

Peña, M. A., and S. J. Bograd. 2007. Time series of the northeast Pacific. Progress in Oceanography 75(2):115–119.

Peterson, W. T., and F. B. Schwing. 2003. A new climate regime in northeast Pacific ecosystems. Geophysical Research Letters 30(17). <doi:10.1029/ 2003GL017528>.

Picciulin, M., L. Sebastianutto, A. Codarin, G. Calcagno, and E. A. Ferrero. 2012. Brown meagre vocalization rate increases during repetitive boat noise exposures: A possible case of vocal compensation. Journal of the Acoustical Society of America 132:3118–3124.

Pinkas, L. 1971. Food habits of albacore, bluefin tuna, and bonito in California waters. Fishery Bulletin 152:5–10.

Pitman, R. L., W. A. Walker, W. T. Everett, and J. P. Gallo-Reynoso. 2004. Population status, foods, and foraging of Laysan albatrosses, *Phoebastria immutabilis*, nesting on Guadalupe Island, Mexico. Marine Ornithology 32:159–165.

Popper, A. N., and M. C. Hastings. 2009. The effects of anthropogenic sources of sound on fishes. Journal of Fish Biology 75:455–489.

Preti, A., C. U. Soykan, H. Dewar, R.J.D. Wells, N. Spear, and S. Kohin. 2012. Comparative feeding ecology of shortfin mako, blue, and thresher sharks in the California Current. Environmental Biology of Fishes 95:127–146.

Redfern, J. V., M. F. McKenna, T. J. Moore, J. Calambokidis, M. L. DeAngelis, E. A., Becker, J. Barlow, K. A. Forney, P. C. Fiedler, and S. J. Chivers. 2013. Assessing the risk of ships striking large whales in marine spatial planning. Conservation Biology 27:292–302.

Reese, D. C., and R. D. Brodeur. 2006. Identifying and characterizing biological hotspots in the northern California Current. Deep-Sea Research II 53:291–314.

Ressler, P. H., J. A. Holmes, G. W. Fleischer, R. E. Thomas, and K. D. Cooke. 2007. Pacific hake (*Merluccius productus*) autecology: A timely review. Marine Fisheries Review 69:1–24.

Richardson, W. J., C. R. Greene, C. I. Malme, and D. H. Thomson. 1995. Marine mammals and noise. Academic Press, San Diego California.

Riebesell, U., K. G. Schulz, R.G.J. Bellerby, M. Botros, P. Fritsche, M. Meyerhofer, C. Neill, G. Nondal, A. Oschlies, J. Wohlers, and E. Zollner. 2007. Enhanced biological carbon consumption in a high CO_2 ocean. Nature 450:545–548.

Robinson, P. W., D. P. Costa, D. E. Crocker, J. P. Gallo-Reynoso, C. D. Champagne, M. A. Fowler, C. Goetsch, K. T. Goetz, J. L. Hassrick, L. A. Hückstädt, C. E. Kuhn, J. L. Maresh, S. M. Maxwell, B. I. McDonald, S. H. Peterson, S. E. Simmons, N. M. Teutschel, S. Villegas-Amtmann, and K. Yoda. 2012. Foraging behavior and success of a mesopelagic predator in the northeast Pacific Ocean: Insights from a data-rich species, the northern elephant seal. PloS One 7:e36728.

Robison, B. H. 2004. Deep pelagic biology. Journal of Experimental Marine Biology and Ecology 300:253–272.

Rolland, R. M., S. E. Parks, K. E. Hunt, M. Castellote, P. J . Corkeron, D. P. Nowacek, S. K. Wasser, and S. D. Kraus. 2012. Evidence that ship noise increases stress in right whales. Proceedings of the Royal Society B-Biological Sciences 279:2363–2368.

Sabine, C. L., R. A. Feely, N. Gruber, R. M. Key, K. Lee, J. L. Bullister, and A. F. Rios. 2004. The oceanic sink for anthropogenic CO_2. Science 305:367–371.

Santora, J. A., W. J. Sydeman, I. D. Schroeder, B. K. Wells, and J. C. Field. 2011. Mesoscale structure and oceanographic determinants of krill hotspots in the California Current: Implications for trophic transfer and conservation. Progress in Oceanography 91:397–409.

Scales, K. L., P. I. Miller, L. A. Hawkes, S. N. Ingram, D. W. Sims, and S. C. Votier. 2014. On the front line: Frontal zones as priority at-sea conservation areas for mobile marine vertebrates. Journal of Applied Ecology 51(6):1575–1583.

Schroeder, I. D., B. A. Black, W. J. Sydeman, S. J. Bograd, E. L. Hazen, J. A. Santora, and B. K. Wells. 2013. The North Pacific High and wintertime pre-conditioning of California Current productivity. Geophysical Research Letters 40. <doi:10.1002/grl.50100>.

Schroeder, I. D., W. J. Sydeman, N. Sarkar, S. A. Thompson, S. J. Bograd, and F. B. Schwing. 2009. Winter pre-conditioning of seabird phenology in the California Current. Marine Ecology Progress Series 393:211–223.

Sehgal, A., I. Tumar, and J. Schonwalder. 2010. Effects of climate change and anthropogenic ocean acidification on underwater acoustic communications. OCEANS 2010 Institute of Electrical and Electronics Engineers–Sydney.

Shaffer, S. A., Y. Tremblay, H. Weimerskirch, D. Scott, D. R. Thompson, P. M. Sagar, H. Moller, G. A. Taylor, D. G. Foley, and B. A. Block. 2006. Migratory shearwaters integrate oceanic resources across the Pacific Ocean in an endless summer. Proceedings of the National Academy of Sciences of the USA 103:12799–12802.

Sherr, E., B. Sherr, and P. Wheeler. 2005. Distribution of coccoid cyanobacteria and small eukaryotic phytoplankton in the upwelling system off the Oregon coast during 2001 and 2002. Deep-Sea Research II 52:317–330.

Silber, G. K., A.S.M. Vanderlaan, A. T. Arceredillo, L. Johnson, C. T. Taggart, M. W. Brown, S. Bettridge, and R. Sagarminaga. 2012. The role of the International Maritime Organization in reducing vessel threat to whales: Process, options, action, and effectiveness. Marine Policy 36:1221–1233.

Simon, M., K. M. Stafford, K. Beedholm, C. M. Lee, and P. T. Madsen. 2010. Singing behavior of fin whales in the Davis Strait with implications for mating, migration, and foraging. Journal of the Acoustical Society of America 128:3200–3210.

Simpson, S. D., M. G. Meekan, N. J. Larsen, R. D. McCauley, and A. Jeffs. 2010. Behavioral plasticity in larval reef fish: Orientation is influenced by recent acoustic experiences. Behavioral Ecology 21:1098–1105.

Southall, B. L., D. Moretti, B. Abraham, J. Calambokidis, S. L. DeRuiter, and P. L. Tyack. 2012. Marine mammal behavioral response studies in Southern California: Advances in technology and experimental methods. Marine Technology Society Journal 46:46–59.

Stewart, J. S., E. L. Hazen, D. G. Foley, S. J. Bograd, and W. F. Gilly. 2012. Marine predator migration during range expansion: Humboldt squid (*Dosidicus gigas*) in the northern California Current System. Marine Ecology Progress Series 471:135–150.

Stramma, L., E. D. Prince, S. Schmidtko, J. Luo, J. P. Hoolihan, M. Visbeck, D.W.R. Wallace, P. Brandt, and A. Körtzinger. 2011. Expansion of oxygen minimum zones may reduce available habitat for tropical pelagic fishes. Nature Climate Change 2:33–37.

Stramma, L., S. Schmidtko, L. A. Levin, and G. C. Johnson. 2010. Ocean oxygen minima expansions and their biological impacts. Deep-Sea Research I 57:1–9.

Stukel, M. R., M. D. Ohman, C. R. Benitez-Nelson, and M. R. Landry. 2013. Contributions of mesozooplankton to vertical carbon export in a coastal upwelling system. Marine Ecology Progress Series 491:47–65.

Suntsov, A. V., and R. D. Brodeur. 2008. Trophic ecology of three dominant myctophid species in the northern California Current region. Marine Ecology Progress Series 373:81–96.

Suryan, R. M., J. A. Santora, and W. J. Sydeman. 2012. New approach for using remotely sensed chlorophyll *a* to identify seabird hotspots. Marine Ecology Progress Series 451:213–225.

Sydeman, W. J., and S. G. Allen. 1999. Pinniped population dynamics in central California: Correlations with sea surface temperature and upwelling indices. Marine Mammal Science 15:446–461.

Sydeman, W. J., M. M. Hester, J. A. Thayer, F. Gress, P. Martin, and J. Buffa. 2001. Climate change, reproductive performance, and diet composition of marine birds in the southern California Current system, 1969–1997. Progress in Oceanography 49:309–329.

Sydeman, W. J., R. W. Bradley, P. Warzybok, C. L. Abraham, J. Jahncke, K. D. Hyrenbach, V. Kousky, J. M. Hipfner, and M. D. Ohman. 2006. Planktivorous auklet *Ptychoramphus aleuticus* responses to ocean climate, 2005: Unusual atmospheric blocking? Geophysical Research Letters 33. <doi:10.1029/2006GL026736>.

Sydeman, W. J., J. A. Santora, S. A. Thompson, B. Marinovic, and E. D. Lorenzo. 2013. Increasing variance in North Pacific climate relates to unprecedented pelagic ecosystem variability off California. Global Change Biology. <doi:10.1111/gcb.12165>.

Sydeman, W. J., K. L. Mills, J. A. Santora, S. A. Thompson, D. F. Bertram, K. H. Morgan, M. A. Hipfner, B. K. Wells, and S. G. Wolf. 2009. Seabirds and climate in the California Current-a synthesis of change. CalCOFI Reports 50:82–104.

Sydeman, W., R. Brodeur, C. Grimes, A. Bychkov, and S. McKinnell. 2006. Marine habitat "hotspots" and their use by migratory species and top predators in the North Pacific Ocean: Introduction. Deep Sea Research II 53:247–249.

Tapilatu, R. F., P. H. Dutton, M. Tiwari, T. Wibbels, H. V. Ferdinandus, W. G. Iwanggin, and B. H. Nugroho. 2013. Long-term decline of the western Pacific leatherback, *Dermochelys coriacea*: A globally important sea turtle population. Ecosphere 4:art25.

Thayer, J. A., J. C. Field, and W. J. Sydeman. 2014. Changes in California Chinook salmon diet over the past fifty years: Relevance to the recent population crash. Marine Ecology Progress Series 498:249–261.

Tsolaki, E., and E. Diamadopoulos. 2010. Technologies for ballast water treatment: A review. Journal of Chemical Technology and Biotechnology 85:19–32.

Turtle Expert Working Group. 2007. An assessment of the leatherback turtle population in the Atlantic Ocean. NOAA Technical Memorandum NMFS-SEFSC-555. NOAA, Miami, Florida.

U.S. Energy Information Administration. 2013. How much of the oil produced in the United States is consumed in the United States? <http://www.eia.gov/tools/faqs/faq.cfm?id=268&t=6>. Accessed March 23, 2013.

van der Lingen, C. D., A. Bertrand, A. Bode, R. Brodeur, L. Cubillos, P. Espinoza, K. Friedland, S. Garrido, X. Irigoien, T. Miller, C. Möllman, R. Rodriguez-Sanchez, H. Tanaka, and A. Temming. 2009. Trophic dynamics. Pages 112–157 in D. M. Checkley, C. Roy, J. Alheit, and Y. Oozeki, editors. Climate Change and Small Pelagic Fish. Cambridge University Press, Cambridge, UK.

Vetter, R., S. Kohin, A. Preti, S. McClatchie, and H. Dewar. 2008. Predatory interactions and niche overlap between mako shark, *Isurus oxyrinchus*, and jumbo squid, *Dosidicus gigas*, in the California Current. CalCOFI Reports 49:142–156.

Ware, D. M., and R. E. Thomson. 2005. Bottom-up ecosystem trophic dynamics determine fish production in the Northeast Pacific. Science 308:1280–1284.

Watters, G. M., R. J. Olson, J. C. Field, and T. E. Essington. 2008. Range expansion of the Humboldt squid was not caused by tuna fishing. Proceedings of the National Academy of Sciences of the USA 105(3):E5.

Weber, E. D., and S. McClatchie. 2010. Predictive models of northern anchovy, *Engraulis mordax*, and Pacific sardine, *Sardinops sagax*, spawning habitat in the California Current. Marine Ecology Progress Series 406:251–263.

Weilgart, L. S. 2007. The impacts of anthropogenic ocean noise on cetaceans and implications for management. Canadian Journal of Zoology 85:1091–1116.

Weise, M. J., D. P. Costa, and R. M. Kudela. 2006. Movement and diving behavior of male California sea lion (Zalophus californianus) during anomalous oceanographic conditions of 2005 compared to those of 2004. Geophysical Research Letters 33, L22S10. <doi:10.1029/2006GL027113>.

Wells, B., J. Santora, J. Field, R. MacFarlane, B. Marinovic, and W. Sydeman. 2012. Population dynamics of Chinook salmon, *Oncorhynchus tshawytscha*, relative to prey availability in the central California coastal region. Marine Ecology Progress Series 457:125–137.

Wells, B. K., J. C. Field, J. A. Thayer, C. B. Grimes, S. Bograd, W. J. Sydeman, F. B. Schwing, and R. Hewitt. 2008. Untangling the relationships among climate, prey, and top predators in an ocean ecosystem. Marine Ecology Progress Series 364:15–29.

Weng, K. C., D. G. Foley, J. E. Ganong, C. Perle, G. L. Shillinger, and B. A. Block. 2008. Migration of an upper trophic level predator, the salmon shark *Lamna ditropis*, between distant ecoregions. Marine Ecology Progress Series 372:253–264.

White, H. K., P. Y. Hsing, W. Cho, T. M. Shank, E. E. Cordes, A. M. Quattrini, R. K. Nelson, R. Camilli, A.W.J. Demopoulos, C. R. German, J. M. Brooks, H. H. Roberts, W. Shedd, C. M. Reddy, and C. R. Fisher. 2012. Impact of the Deepwater Horizon oil spill on a deep-water coral community in the Gulf of Mexico. Proceedings of the National Academy of Sciences of the USA 109:20303–20308.

Wiese, F. K., and G. J. Robertson. 2004. Assessing seabird mortality from chronic oil discharges at sea. Journal of Wildlife Management 68:627–638.

Wingfield, D. K., S. H. Peckham, D. G. Foley, D. M. Palacios, B. E. Lavaniegos, R. Durazo, W. J. Nichols, D. A. Croll, and S. J. Bograd. 2011. The making of a productivity hotspot in the Coastal Ocean. PloS One 6(11):e27874. <doi:10.1371/journal.pone.0027874>.

Wysocki, L. E., and F. Ladich. 2005. Hearing in fishes under noise conditions. Journal of the Association for Research in Otolaryngology 6:28–36.

Yen, P.P.W., W. J. Sydeman, S. J. Bograd, and K. D. Hyrenbach. 2006. Spring-time distributions of migratory marine birds in the southern California Current: Oceanic eddy associations and coastal habitat hotspots over seventeen years. Deep-Sea Research II 53:399–418.

Zeidberg, L. D., and B. H. Robison. 2007. Invasive range expansion by the Humboldt squid, *Dosidicus gigas*, in the eastern North Pacific.

Proceedings of the National Academy of Sciences of the USA 104:12948–12950.
Zeidberg, L., W. Hamner, N. Nezlin, and A. Henry. 2006. The fishery for California Market squid (*Loligo opalescens*) (Cephalopoda: Myopsida), from1981 through 2003. Fishery Bulletin 104:46–59.
Zwolinski, J. P., D. A. Demer, K. A Byers, G. R. Cutter, J. S. Renfree, T. S. Sessions, and B. J. Macewicz. 2012. Distributions and abundances of Pacific sardine (*Sardinops sagax*) and other pelagic fishes in the California Current Ecosystem during spring 2006, 2008, and 2010, estimated from acoustic-trawl surveys. Fishery Bulletin 110:110–122.
Zwolinski, J. P., R. L. Emmett, and D. A. Demer. 2011. Predicting habitat to optimize sampling of Pacific sardine (*Sardinops sagax*). ICES Journal of Marine Science 68:867–879.
Žydelis, R., R. L. Lewison, S. A. Shaffer, J. E. Moore, A. M. Boustany, J. J. Roberts, M. Sims, D. C. Dunn, B. D. Best, Y. Tremblay, M. A. Kappes, P. N. Halpin, D. P. Costa, and L. B. Crowder. 2011. Dynamic habitat models: Using telemetry data to project fisheries bycatch. Proceedings of the Royal Society B 278: 3191–3200.

SEVENTEEN

Shallow Rocky Reefs and Kelp Forests

MARK H. CARR and DANIEL C. REED

Introduction

KELP forests are among the iconic ecosystems of California despite most people having experienced them only remotely. From shore, viewers are captivated by the forest canopy formed at the ocean surface and the associated marine birds and mammals. Some observers have experienced kelp forests in public aquaria, but most are familiar with these ecosystems only through photographs and video. Nonetheless, these glimpses impress one with the extraordinary three-dimensional structure and biodiversity characteristic of kelp forest ecosystems. These impressions are captured in Charles Darwin's exuberant description of the forests of giant kelp (*Macrocystis pyrifera*) around the coast of Tierra del Fuego, even though his observations were largely limited to the surface and samples brought to him aboard the RV *Beagle*:

> The number of living creatures of all Orders, whose existence intimately depends on the kelp, is wonderful. A great volume might be written, describing the inhabitants of one of these beds of sea-weed. . . . Innumerable crustacea frequent every part of the plant. On shaking the great entangled roots, a pile of small fish, shells, cuttle-fish, crabs of all orders, sea-eggs, star-fish, beautiful Holuthuriae, Planariae, and crawling nereidous animals of a multitude of forms, all fall out together. Often as I recurred to a branch of the kelp, I never failed to discover animals of new and curious structures. . . . I can only compare these great aquatic forests of the southern hemisphere with the terrestrial ones in the intertropical regions. Yet if in any country a forest was destroyed, I do not believe nearly so many species of animals would perish as would here, from the destruction of the kelp. Amidst the leaves of this plant numerous species of fish live, which nowhere else could find food or shelter; with their destruction the many cormorants and other fishing birds, the otters, seals, and porpoises, would soon perish also.
> (C. Darwin, 1839)

Globally, a variety of species of kelp establish forests along margins of continents and islands in the temperate oceans of both the southern and northern hemispheres. Kelp forests also develop in some subtropical areas that experience considerable COASTAL UPWELLING. The distribution of these kelp forests is generally limited to areas where rocky reefs occur at shallow depths (generally <40 meters) and are consistently or intermittently bathed in cool, relatively nutrient-rich waters. Along the west coast of North America are five canopy-forming kelp species that extend from the rocky bot-

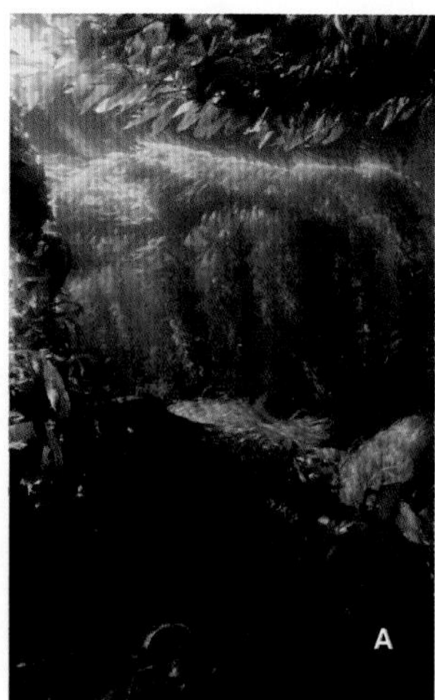

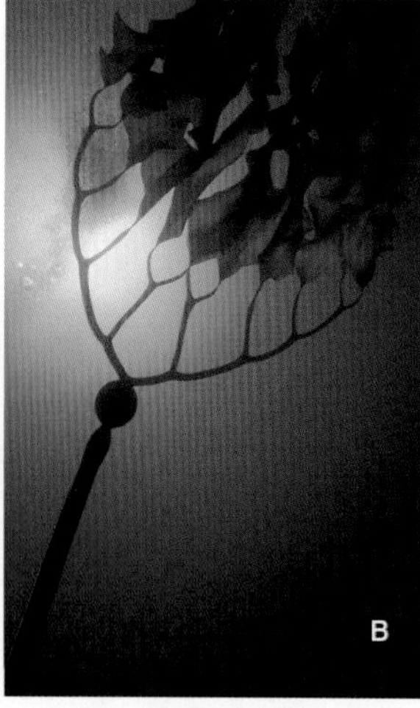

FIGURE 17.1 Images of the various species of kelps (family Laminariales) that form surface canopies in kelp forests along the coast of California. Photos: (A–D) Ronald McPeak.

A Giant kelp (*Macrocystis pyrifera*)

B Southern elk kelp (*Pelagophycus porra*)

C Bull kelp (*Nereocystis luetkeana*)

D Feather boa kelp (*Egregia menziesii*)

tom to the ocean surface, including the giant kelp (*Macrocystis pyrifera*), bull kelp (*Nereocystis luetkeana*), elk kelp (*Pelagophycus porra*), and the feather boa kelp (*Egregia menziesii*) (Figure 17.1). The dragon kelp (*Eualaria fistulosa*; formerly *Alaria* and *Druehlia*) is limited to waters along Alaska (Figure 17.2). Of these, several are limited to colder, deeper, or shallower waters; thus giant kelp and bull kelp are the primary species that form surface canopies along the coast of California.

Canopy-forming kelps exhibit markedly high rates of productivity, which reflect the combined effects of both the unique conditions in which they grow and the evolution of a form and physiology that enable kelps to capitalize on their aqueous environment. Attached firmly to the reef substrate by a tenacious HOLDFAST, canopy-forming species of kelp extend to the sea surface to access sunlight and translocate the products of photosynthesis to deeper parts of the plant that can be in near darkness. Buoyed by seawater and, for several species, gas-filled structures referred to as PNEUMATOCYSTS, most kelp biomass is allocated to leaflike BLADES rather than the structural trunks, limbs, and leaves of terrestrial plants. The large surface area of these blades serves as the primary tissue for photosynthesis and nutrient absorption. The numerous blades and upright structure of these massive algae create habitat used by the myriad invertebrates and fishes that Darwin described. The biodiversity attained in kelp forests rivals that of any marine or terrestrial ecosystem in temperate latitudes. For example, counts by divers of conspicuous species in three kelp forests along the mainland of southern California produced an average of 53, 191, and 44 species of macroalgae, invertebrates, and fishes, respectively (Reed, personal observation). But these counts only included the larger more conspicuous species typically recorded by kelp forest ecologists, and not the great diversity of smaller cryptic taxa (e.g., mesocrustaceans and microcrustaceans, polychaetes, and mollusks) that seek refuge in kelp forest ecosystems. One especially thorough examination of giant kelp forests in southern California and northern Baja California, Mexico, listed 130 species of algae and almost 800 species of animals (introduction in North 1971).

Photo on previous page: The great diversity of flora and fauna commonly portrayed by underwater photographs of California kelp forests. Photo: Chad King.

Because kelp forests are highly productive, species-rich, and close to shore, they provide a variety of ECOSYSTEM SERVICES to California's coastal communities and beyond. Commercial and recreational fishing and kelp harvesting are economically and culturally important consumptive services provided by kelp forests. Nonconsumptive services include ecotourism such as scuba diving, kayaking, and wildlife watching from shore as well as a variety of spiritual and cultural experiences. But the proximity of kelp forests to shore also exposes these ecosystems to a variety of anthropogenic impacts. These include overfishing, sediment from runoff, and a variety of pollutants and contaminants including shore-borne diseases.

Several excellent and comprehensive reviews exist of the ecology of giant kelp (North 1971, Graham et al. 2007), the ecosystems these kelp forests support (North 1971, Dayton 1985, Schiel and Foster 2015, Schiel and Foster 1986, Schiel and Foster 2006, Graham et al. 2008, Foster et al. 2013), and the ecosystems associated with bull kelp forests (Springer et al. 2010). In this chapter we draw from these reviews and more recent literature to provide an overview of kelp forest ecosystems along the coast of California and the biotic and abiotic processes that influence them. We discuss how regional variation in species composition and ecosystem function translates into regional differences in the services kelp forests provide and the anthropogenic threats they face. We close with a discussion of future challenges and opportunities for ensuring the sustainability of services generated by these highly productive and species-rich ecosystems in the face of growing coastal human populations and a changing global climate.

Geographic Distribution of Kelp Forests

The distribution of kelp in California is limited to a narrow coastal band, whose width is determined largely by the combined effects of depth, water clarity, wave action, and availability of the rocky bottom to which kelps attach. In clearer water, light penetrates deeper, allowing the forest to extend to greater depths. Likewise, an ocean floor that slopes gradually away from shore provides shallower habitat in which kelp can flourish. Within the typically narrow band along the shore that supports kelp forests, the presence of individual kelp species varies along a latitudinal gradient, corresponding to changes in abiotic and biotic conditions that determine their range limits. In this section we describe the geographic ranges of surface and subsurface, canopy-forming kelps in California, and the latitudinal differences in forest species composition that result from them. Where the various species of surface, canopy-forming kelps and upright and prostrate subcanopy-forming kelps co-occur, they create multiple layers of forest canopies above the rocky reef.

Surface Canopy–forming Kelps

Giant kelp occurs in both the southern and northern hemispheres but is restricted to cool, temperate latitudes and some subtropical areas that experience considerable coastal upwelling. In the northern hemisphere along the west coast of North America, giant kelp extends across California and from Mexico to Alaska (Table 17.1, see Figure 17.2). In northern California, however, giant kelp forests are sparse and restricted to sites well-protected from ocean waves (Schiel and Foster 2015, Seymour et al. 1989, Graham 1997, Graham et al. 2007). The southern extent of giant kelp forests is thought to be limited by both low nutrient availability, especially of nitrogen, and increasing water temperature (Ladah et al. 1999, Hernández-Carmona et al. 2000, Hernández-Carmona et al. 2001, Edwards 2004, Graham et al. 2007) or competition with warm-tolerant species (Edwards and Hernández-Carmona 2005). Historically, three species of *Macrocystis* were recognized in California—*M. pyrifera, angustifolia*, and *integrifolia*—with *angustifolia* at a few subtidal locations in southern California and *integrifolia* in the low intertidal and subtidal from central California to Alaska. More comprehensive morphological and genetic comparisons now indicate these are ecotypes of one species, the giant kelp *M. pyrifera* (Demes et al. 2009).

The latitudinal range of bull kelp extends from Point Conception, California, to Alaska. Where the southern range of bull kelp overlaps with giant kelp, giant kelp appears to outcompete bull kelp, restricting it to either the outer, deeper edge of the giant kelp forest or the shallow inshore where water turbulence prevents the retention of giant kelp (Foster and Schiel 1985, Graham 1997, Graham et al. 2007). Along the more exposed coastline north of Santa Cruz, California, bull kelp becomes the predominant surface canopy–forming kelp throughout the open and protected coast where shallow rocky reefs occur (Figure 17.2; Springer et al. 2010).

The geographic range of elk kelp extends from Mexico to the California Channel Islands. Because some stands of elk kelp do not form surface canopies, its distribution within its range is not well-known. Like bull kelp, elk kelp is limited to the deeper offshore edges of giant kelp forests where they co-occur. The shallow depth limit of elk kelp could be influenced

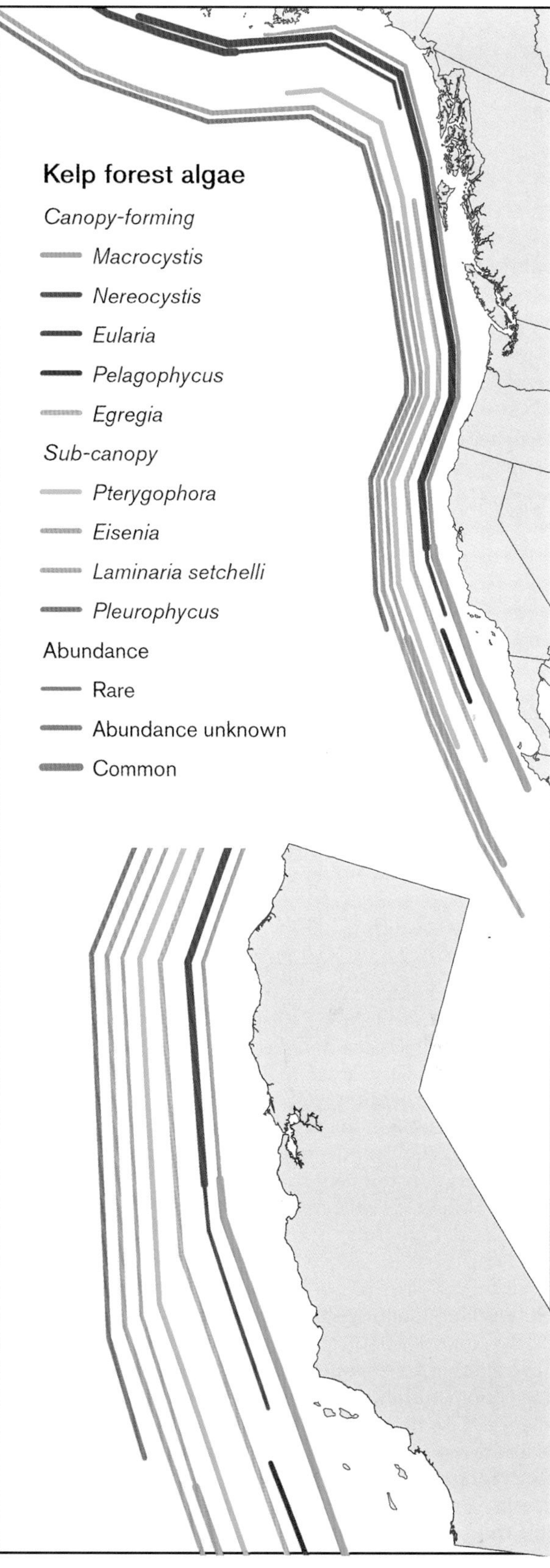

FIGURE 17.2 Geographic range of the canopy and subsurface canopy-forming macroalgae that constitute the vertical structure of kelp forests along the coast of North America. The thickness of each line reflects the relative abundance of a species across its geographic range. This figure illustrates how the species composition and relative abundance of structure-forming macroalgae vary along the coast. Source: Illustration by Emily Saarman.

TABLE 17.1
Geographic range of canopy forming and subsurface canopy-forming kelp species along the west coast of North America

Species	Southern limit	Northern limit	Most abundant	References
Macrocystis pyrifera	Punta San Hipolito, Baja California, Mexico	Kodiak Island, Alaska	South of Santa Cruz, California	Foster and Schiel 1985, Schiel and Foster 1986, Seymour et al. 1989, Graham 1997, Edwards and Hernández-Carmona 2005, Graham et al. 2007, B. Konar pers. comm.
Nereocystis luetkeana	Point Conception, California	Unimak Island, Alaska	North of Santa Cruz, California	Druehl 1970, Abbott and Hollenberg 1976, Miller and Estes 1989, Springer et al. 2010
Eularia fistulosa	British Columbia	Aleutian Islands	Aleutian Islands	Citations reviewed in Springer et al. 2010
Pelagophycus porra	Isla San Benito and San Quintin, Baja California, Mexico	Santa Cruz Island, California Channel Islands, California		Abbott and Hollenberg 1976, Miller and Dorr 1994, Miller et al. 2000, M. Edwards pers. comm.
Egregia menziesii	Punta Eugenia, Baja California, Mexico	Queen Charlotte Islands, British Columbia, Canada		Abbott and Hollenberg 1976, Henkel and Murray 2007
Pterygophora californica	Bahia Rosario, Baja California, Mexico	Cook Inlet, Alaska		Abbott and Hollenberg 1976, Matson and Edwards 2007
Eisenia arborea	Bahia Magdalena, Baja California, Mexico	Graham Island, British Columbia, Canada	South of Point Conception, California	Edwards and Hernández-Carmona 2005, Matson and Edwards 2007
Laminaria setchelli	Baja California, Mexico	Attu Island, Alaska		Abbott and Hollenberg 1976, Lindeberg and Lindstrom 2012
Pleurophycus gardneri	Piedras Blancas, San Luis Obispo County, California	Aleutian Islands, Alaska		Abbott and Hollenberg 1976, VanBlaricom et al. 1986, Lindeberg and Lindstrom 2012

by exposure to ocean waves, competition for light with giant kelp, or the low light-tolerance of microscopic stages (Fejtek et al. 2011). In contrast, the feather boa kelp is tolerant to great wave energy in the very shallow subtidal and is therefore almost ubiquitous wherever shallow rocky reef occurs along the coast of California.

Subsurface Canopy–forming Kelps

Several other kelp species reach heights of <3 meters above the bottom, forming a subsurface canopy a few meters above the reef. Like those species that form surface canopies, these kelps are restricted to shallow rocky reefs, establishing subsurface canopies either in the presence or absence of taller kelp species. Four of these kelps stand upright with a stiff but flexible trunk-like STIPE. Of these, the northern sea palm (*Pterygophora californica*) (see Figure 17.3a) and southern stiff-blade kelp (*Laminaria setchelli*; see Figure 17.3c) are broadly distributed across California from Mexico to Alaska. The southern sea palm (*Eisenia arborea*) (see Figure 17.3b), is prominent on rocky reefs from Mexico to Point Conception, California, though it occurs in low abundance on reefs across California and as far north as British Columbia, Canada. The fourth species, *Pleurophycus gardneri* (see Figure 17.3d), ranges from the Point Conception, California, to Alaska. In central California it occurs in deeper water, usually below the lower limit of giant kelp (Spalding et al. 2003). Many other kelp species common to California kelp forests are characterized by a very short stipe that supports a long, wide blade that drapes over the rocky reef. These more prostrate species include *Laminaria farlowii*, *Agarum fimbriatum*, *Costaria costata*, and *Dictyoneurum californicum* (Figure 17.4).

Environmental Determinants of Kelp Distributions within Their Geographic Range

The kelp species introduced in the preceding section share common key environmental drivers of distribution within their geographic ranges. However, the relative influence of these drivers differs among species due to their markedly different growth forms and physiologies. These differences in turn determine the upper and lower depth distributions and relative vulnerability of these species to removal by wave action. For example, light is the primary constraint on the maximum depth of kelps, and differences in minimum and maximum light tolerances can explain differences in the rel-

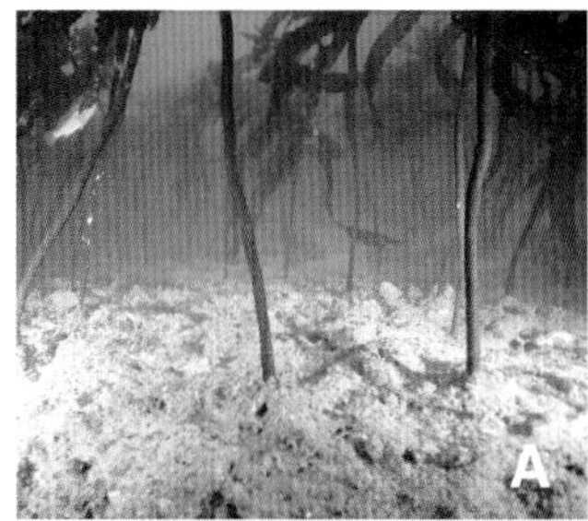

FIGURE 17.3 Images of the common species of macroalgae that form subcanopies 1 to 2 meters above the reef surface and contribute to vertical structure of forests along the coast of California. Photos: (A, B) Ronald McPeak, (C, D) Steven Lonhart.

A Northern sea palm (*Pterygophora californica*)

B Southern sea palm (*Eisenia arborea*)

C Southern stiff-blade kelp (*Laminaria setchelli*)

D Broad-ribbed kelp (*Pleurophycus gardneri*)

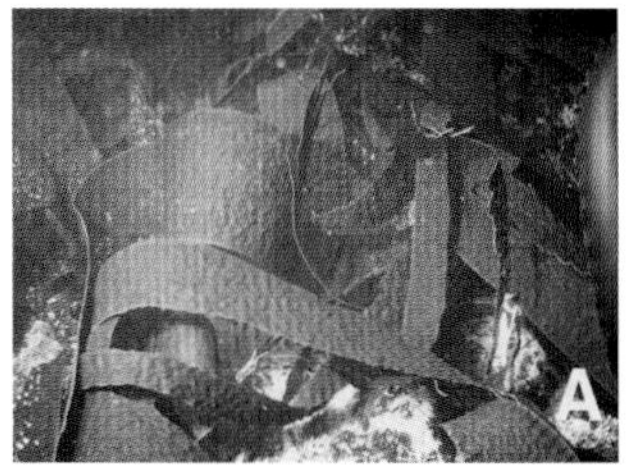

FIGURE 17.4 Images of the common prostrate species of kelp whose blades lie across the surface of the rocky reef, forming habitat for fishes and invertebrates. Photos: (A, B) Ronald McPeak, (C, D) Steven Lonhart.

A (*Laminaria farlowii*)

B Fringed sieve kelp (*Agarum fimbriatum*)

C Seersucker kelp (*Costaria costata*)

D (*Dictyoneurum californicum*)

ative depth range of species (Schiel and Foster 2015, Schiel and Foster 2006). However, somewhat like the seedling stages of terrestrial plants, it is the light requirements of the microscopic GAMETOPHYTE life stages and the young SPOROPHYTE stages that determine their successful germination and early growth under low light conditions (reviewed by Schiel and Foster 2006, Matson and Edwards 2007). The growth form of giant kelp (i.e., multiple FRONDS each possessing multiple blades distributed through the water column) greatly enhances the acquisition of light as compared to kelp species possessing a single stipe and fewer blades (e.g., bull kelp and several shorter upright species such as northern sea palm, southern sea palm, and *Laminaria* spp.). However, the growth form of giant kelp greatly increases its drag and susceptibility to being torn from the reef by wave action. Thus the single stipe species occur in more exposed sites while giant kelp is generally restricted to more protected sites (Foster and Schiel 1985).

Physical factors such as topography, substrate geology, and wave exposure can interact in ways that greatly increase their individual effects on the distribution of kelp species. For example, kelps attached to more friable sedimentary reefs are more likely to be detached by wave action than individuals of similar size attached to harder granitic or basaltic reefs. Similarly, the erosion of sedimentary reefs increases turbidity and reduces light penetration, which can limit the depth range and abundance of kelps (Spalding et al. 2003, Shepard et al. 2009). Rocky reefs with low vertical relief, surrounded by or interspersed with sand, are also more likely to experience scouring by ocean waves and thus are characterized by lower densities of perennial kelps and relatively high densities of more ephemeral and rapidly colonizing algae (e.g., *Desmarestia*, many species of foliose red algae).

Another example of a strong interaction between geologic and oceanographic factors is the rare exception where kelps establish on sandy substrata rather than on rocky reef. Historically, an extensive giant kelp forest persisted for decades on sandy seafloor along the mainland just south of Point Conception, in an area protected from waves by the Northern Channel Islands (Thompson 1959). The existence of this forest illustrates how the restriction of kelps to areas of rocky substrate results from their susceptibility to removal by waves. The upper depth range of many macroalgal species can be determined by their tolerance for high wave action (e.g., for bull kelp) (Graham 1997), desiccation, ultraviolet energy (Swanson and Druehl 2000), grazing, and competition (Graham 1997). One key trait of shallow-dwelling species is a thick, flexible stipe and blades resistant to tearing and abrading against the rocky reef. Kelps that occur at shallow depths often extend into the low intertidal zone, and their thick blades are also more tolerant to desiccation (see Chapter 18, "Intertidal").

Other factors that influence the distribution and abundance of kelp forests are nutrient availability and water temperature, which are both linked to large-scale oceanographic forcing (e.g., Pacific Decadal Oscillation [PDO], El Niño Southern Oscillation [ENSO]) and more local-scale oceanographic processes (e.g., COASTAL UPWELLING, currents, thermal stratification of the water column), some of which are influenced by the geomorphology of the coastline. For example, the profound influence of the 1976 PDO that altered oceanographic productivity in southern California (Roemmich and McGowan 1995) was manifest in reduced productivity in surf perch populations, which Holbrook et al. (1997) attributed to reduced production of invertebrate prey and the benthic algae that supported those prey. More episodic climatic events such as El Niño and La Niña can also have profound effects on regional patterns of distribution and abundance of kelps that persist for multiple years (see the "Disturbance, Forest Dynamics, and Shifts in Community Structure" section later in this chapter). At regional scales, Broitman and Kinlan (2006) used an archive of aerial surveys to identify the spatial correlation between kelp forest biomass and upwelling associated with coastal headlands. Similarly, chronic increased water temperature in a bull kelp forest due to discharge from an adjacent nuclear power plant in central California led to a decline in bull kelp and a concomitant increase in giant kelp. A wholesale change in community structure took place, including dramatic changes in understory algae (Schiel et al. 2004). A strong east-west geographic gradient in the structure of kelp forest communities, including the algal assemblage, in the Northern Channel Islands corresponds with a marked cline in water temperature (Hamilton et al. 2010).

Kelp Forest Phenology

Kelp forest phenology is shaped by the typically brief lifespan of the species that constitute the forest; its annual cycles of spore production, recruitment, and growth; and the loss of adults during winter storms (Figure 17.5). Some California kelp forest species are annuals, such as *Nereocystis luetkeana* (Amsler and Neushul 1989), but most are perennials, including most *Laminaria* species (Kain 1963), northern sea palm (Hymanson et al. 1990), and giant kelp (Neushul 1963). Graham et al. (2007) describe how the predictable seasonality of giant kelp growth at higher latitudes is influenced by seasonal variation in sunlight availability and wave exposure (Foster 1982, Harrold et al. 1998, Graham et al. 1997). At lower latitudes like southern California, seasonal growth rates correspond with variability in ambient nitrate concentrations, such that frond growth was greatest during winter-spring upwelling periods and reduced during summer-fall nonupwelling periods (Zimmerman and Kremer 1986).

Thus the phenology of giant kelp forests varies across its geographic range. More recently, by comparing net annual primary production of giant kelp forests in southern and central California, Reed et al. (2011) found that productivity of the southern forests was greater because of their reduced wave disturbance and prolonged growing season, despite their lower nutrient availability and greater abundance of grazers. The importance of insulation and wave exposure on seasonality of forest production at higher latitudes is also reflected by bull kelp, whose sporophytes can grow at extremely high rates, up to 6 cm day^{-1} (Scagel 1947). Maximum photosynthesis occurs in summer and early fall, and mortality of bull kelp sporophytes reaches a maximum in winter, primarily due to dislodgement by winter storms. This phenology of giant kelp and bull kelp contributes to and is embedded in a complex suite of drivers of forest dynamics that markedly influences ecosystem dynamics.

FIGURE 17.5 Giant kelp (*Macrocystis pyrifera*) that has been torn from offshore reefs by storm waves and deposited on a sandy beach near Santa Barbara, California. Photo: Shane Anderson.

Trophic Structure and Functional Attributes of Kelp Forest Ecosystems

Kelp forest communities are characterized by a trophic structure unique to shallow reef ecosystems in that the primary space holders (i.e., macroalgae and SESSILE suspension feeding invertebrates) occupy different trophic levels. Macroalgae are primary producers that derive their nutrition from sunlight and dissolved nutrients, whereas sessile invertebrates are consumers nourished by filtering plankton and other organic matter from the water column. This trophic structure leads to two different pathways in the kelp forest food web: one derived from primary production of benthic algae and the other from primary production of phytoplankton in the water column. These different trophic pathways contribute to complex trophic interactions within kelp forests that includes omnivory and carnivory across multiple trophic levels. The prey composition of many kelp forest species changes as they grow, resulting in individuals occupying multiple trophic levels over their lifetime. Taken together, trophic webs and interaction networks in kelp forests are very complicated and difficult to characterize accurately within the simplified categories generally used to describe the structural and functional relationships in communities. While we are aware of this complexity, we nonetheless present the structural and functional relationships among species in a simplified organization to illustrate qualitative differences in the species composition of trophic groups along the coast of California.

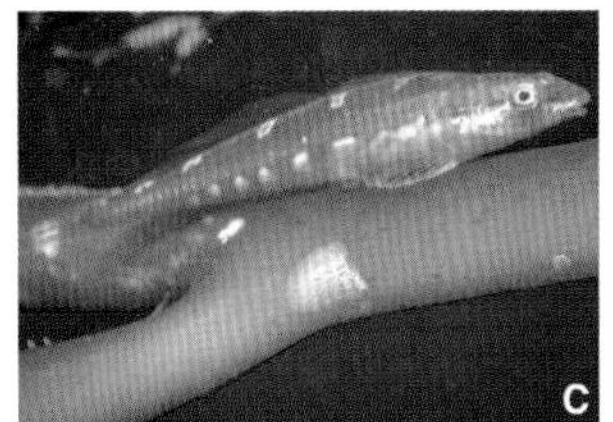

FIGURE 17.6 Examples of the cryptic coloration of kelp forest fishes, reflecting their strong association with algal habitats. Cryptic coloration enhances the ability of these species to avoid predation or ambush their prey. Photos: (A–D) Steven Lonhart.

A Coralline sculpin (*Artedius corallines*)

B Giant kelpfish (*Heterostichus rostratus*) and kelp perch (*Brachyistius frenatus*)

C Manacled sculpin (*Synchirus gilli*)

D Onespot fringehead (*Neoclinus uninotatus*)

Primary Producers

Much like the trees of forests on land, canopy-forming kelps serve as the structural species of submarine forests in the ocean. Their fast-growing, three-dimensional structure extends from the ocean floor to the sea surface and provides food and shelter for a diverse array of species (Graham 2004, Graham et al. 2008, Byrnes et al. 2011). As such, kelps are important AUTOGENIC ECOSYSTEM ENGINEERS of shallow rocky reef ecosystems. Beneath the overlying surface canopy, multiple vegetation layers of different algal forms occur in a patchwork mosaic competing for light and space on the bottom. Short-statured kelps with nonbuoyant, rigid stipes (e.g., southern sea palm, southern stiff-blade kelp, and northern sea palm) often grow in dense patches, forming a subsurface canopy 1–2 meters above the bottom (Dayton et al. 1984, Reed and Foster 1984, Reed 1990a). Smaller foliose, branching and filamentous forms of red, brown, and green algae produce a low-growing, bushy understory that attains its greatest biomass in areas where the surface and subsurface canopy kelps are less dense (Pearse and Hines 1979, Kastendiek 1982, Reed and Foster 1984, Miller et al. 2011). Canopies in competitive equilibrium can persist for many years by resisting invasion from other species (Dayton et al. 1984, Reed and Foster 1984) because once established, the adult plants are dominant competitors for light and space and provide the nearest source of spores when small disturbances thin their ranks (Tegner and Dayton 1987).

The geographic distribution of kelp species described in the previous section sets the stage for geographic variation in the species composition of the key primary producers within kelp forests. South of Point Conception, giant kelp is the dominant surface canopy–forming kelp with elk kelp forming subsurface canopies in some areas (Figure 17.7c). The subcanopy is composed primarily of the cosmopolitan northern sea palm and the more restricted southern sea palm and *Laminaria farlowi* (Figure 17.3). In this region major contributors to the understory layer of the forest are brown algae in the genera *Desmarestia* and *Dictyota*, *Sargassum* on the offshore islands, and various species of filamentous, branching, and foliose red algae. Crustose CORALLINE ALGAE are particularly abundant, especially in association with URCHIN BARRENS. In central California, *Macrocystis* and *Nereocystis* both contribute to the surface canopy, with *Nereocystis* typically confined to wave-exposed sites and the offshore and inshore edges of *Macrocystis* forests (see Figures 17.2 and 17.7B). The subsurface canopy–forming kelps include northern sea palm and *Laminaria setchelli*, and the understory algae are dominated by extensive assemblages of foliose red algae and erect articulated corallines. The articulated corallines are particularly abundant where water motion is moderate to high.

In northern California, bull kelp is by far the predominant surface canopy–forming species, whereas giant kelp only forms small stands at protected, shallow water sites. In addition, *Egregia* and *Stephanocystis* (formerly *Cystoseira*) can form a surface canopy in very shallow (<5 meters) depths (see Figure 17.1d). Like central California, subsurface canopy species are primarily northern sea palm and *Laminaria setchelli*, with an increased abundance of *Pleurophycus gardneri* (see Figures 17.3a, b, d and 17.7a). Because of the great exposure of reefs to ocean waves and the increased numbers of sea urchins, the understory algae on these reefs is largely erect and crustose coralline algae. These geographic patterns reflect both temperature differences and the strong species interactions described below.

Annual rates of net primary production (NPP) for giant kelp vary regionally, from 2.15 kg dry mass m^{-2} yr^{1} in southern California to 1.05 kg dry mass m^{-2} yr^{1} in central California (Reed et al. 2011). While other algae within forests add to this annual productivity, giant kelp is by far the major source of production where it occurs. Much like terrestrial forests, the fate of primary production in kelp forests follows two principal pathways: grazing of live kelp and other macroalgae by herbivores, and consumption of kelp litter by detritivores. However, in contrast to terrestrial forests, a much greater portion of the primary production generated by kelps is also exuded into the water column in the form of dissolved or particulate organic matter. Kelp-derived dissolved organic matter (DOM) and particulate organic matter (POM) can be consumed directly by many species of planktivores, which have evolved to feed on dissolved substances or minute particles suspended in the water.

Another critical difference between these forests and terrestrial forests is the high degree to which kelp forest primary production is exported to other ecosystems (e.g., Gerard 1976). Algal fragments, whole algae, and even entire forests can be exported from their natal rocky reefs and transported shoreward by currents and waves to rocky intertidal and sandy beach ecosystems (see Figure 17.5), where they supply nutrients (Dugan et al. 2011) and fuel detrital pathways just as they do within kelp forests (Dugan et al. 2003, Revell et al. 2011, Robles 1987). On sandy beaches shorebirds feed on amphipods that consume kelp detritus, or "wrack," and the abundances of shorebirds and their prey are correlated with the abundance of wrack delivered from offshore forests (Dugan et al. 2003). Alternatively, detached macroalgae (also referred to as "drift" or "litter") can be swept offshore along the bottom, where it eventually collects on deeper rocky reefs, depressions in deep sandy bottoms, and especially in deep submarine canyons where it can account for up to 80% of the particulate carbon reaching the sea floor (Harrold et al. 1998, Vetter and Dayton 1998). Kelp litter provides an important source of dietary carbon for many consumers in these deep habitats as well as structure within which small animals such as crustaceans, snails, and young fish can find shelter.

Yet another fate of detached kelp plants is to float for long periods (several months) at the ocean surface, potentially transported great distances by ocean currents (Hobday 2000a). These "kelp rafts" form habitat structure, attracting small fishes and invertebrates. These in turn attract larger fishes and marine mammals, creating floating islands or localities of intensified feeding interactions. When many of these rafts are ultimately transported back inshore, they carry with them small fishes, including the opaleye (*Girella nigricans*) and juveniles of many species of rockfishes. Thus, during these excursions, kelp rafts become vectors of transport and delivery of young to their nearshore adult habitats (Kingsford 1993 and 1995, Hobday 2000b). This "ecosystem connectivity" whereby nearshore kelps contribute various functional roles to other coastal ecosystems underscores the broader importance of kelp forests in California's coastal ecosystems.

Kelps and other forest algae create habitat structure that is used by other species in various ways. The BIOGENIC HABITAT (biologically created) formed by macroalgae adds enormous amounts of structurally complex surface area upon which other algae (EPIPHYTES), microbes, fungi, and invertebrates (EPIBIONTS) attach. Epibionts on kelp represent a variety of trophic guilds, including grazers that feed upon the kelp (e.g., amphipod crustaceans, gastropod mollusks), sessile invertebrates that feed on plankton swept near the kelp throughout the water column (e.g., caprellid amphipods, nudibranchs, and the very common encrusting bryozoan, *Membranipora*), and mobile invertebrate (e.g., crabs) and fish predators that feed on the epibionts. The structural complexity of the algae provides refuge from predation for juvenile fishes and adults of small species. The strength and importance of these associations is reflected in the cryptic coloration that fish species of a wide variety of families have to match algal habitats (Figure 17.6), the strong relationships between the relative abundances and composition of fishes and algae in a forest (Carr 1989), and the correspondence of interannual dynamics of recruitment of young fishes with year-to-year variation in abundance of species like the giant kelp (Anderson 1994, Carr 1994, others reviewed in Carr and Syms 2006, White and Caselle 2008).

Foliose and articulated coralline algae (see Figures 17.6A and 17.7A, B) form important and structurally complex habitat inhabited by a myriad of small invertebrate species (see Kenner 1992 and Dean and Connell 1987 for an intertidal example). Many small, mobile invertebrates including a diverse array of crustaceans, polychaetes, mollusks, and echinoderms seek food and shelter in the understory assemblage and in turn serve as prey for fish. Coralline algae are longer-lived and more predictable in occurrence through time, and they produce chemical cues that induce settlement and metamorphosis in the larvae of many invertebrate species such as abalone (Morse and Morse 1984). Similar to the way coral erosion leads to the formation of sand habitats in tropical latitudes, the calcium carbonate structures of articulated coralline algae within kelp forests contribute to the physical structure of adjacent, soft-bottom seafloors.

Grazers

The great productivity and diversity of forms of kelp forest algae support an abundant and taxonomically diverse group of herbivores and omnivores. Among the most important are sea urchins, which depending on the abundance of kelps and production of litter are more typically relegated to roles as detritivores. However, when the supply of litter is reduced, sea urchins can switch from passive drift feeding to active foraging on attached algae. They can form dense aggregations or "fronts" that move across rocky reefs consuming all algae they encounter, including kelp holdfasts (Dean et al. 1984, Ebeling et al. 1985, Harrold and Reed 1985, Harrold and Pearse 1987). Four species of sea urchins inhabit kelp forests of California, and their relative abundance varies geographically. Kelp forests in southern California are inhabited by the highest diversity and numbers of sea urchins: red (*Strongylocentrotus franciscanus*), purple (*S. purpuratus*), white (*Lytechinus anamesus*), and the more tropical-associated crowned (*Centrostephanus coronatus*; see Figure 17.7c). Neither the crowned nor the white urchin occurs north of Point Conception. Along the central coast, with large numbers of sea otters, the abundance of sea urchins is greatly diminished; the numbers of red and purple sea urchins do not increase again until north of Santa Cruz, coinciding with the northern extent of sea otters (see Figure 17.7b). In northern California, both red and purple sea urchins are abundant in the absence of sea otters.

A diversity of herbivorous mollusks, including snails, limpets, and chitons, graze on the kelps, and red and green algae; and the relative abundances of these grazers vary along the coast. In southern California forests four species are of notable occurrence, including the smooth turban snail (*Norrisia norrisii*), wavy turban snail (*Megastrea undosa*), giant keyhole limpet (*Megathura crenulata*), and California sea hare (*Aplysia californica*) (see Figure 17.7c). The smooth turban is particularly abundant on giant kelp in southern California but rare north of Point Conception (Lonhart and Tupen 2001). The large California sea hare grazes on red algae throughout reefs of southern California but is far less abundant north of Point Conception. In central California other turban and top snails (genera *Tegula* and omnivorous species of *Calliostoma*) become very abundant and are distributed broadly throughout kelp forests (Watanabe 1984; see Figure 17.6b). Also more abundant in central and northern California forests is the large gumboot chiton (*Cryptochiton stelleri*) (see Figure 17.7a,b), an important grazer of turf algae. Throughout southern, central, and northern California kelp forests, crustaceans ranging in size from small amphipods to larger crabs graze directly on kelps and understory algae (Davenport and Anderson 2007). Especially in central and northern California, spider crabs (family Majidae) are particularly abundant and distributed up and down kelps and among the understory algae (e.g., the northern kelp crab, *Pugettia producta*) (Hines 1982).

The many species of snails and small crabs that graze on kelps and understory algae have been shown to compete with one another for this food resource. For example, two species of small turban snails, *Tegula aureotincta* and *T. eiseni*, exhibit

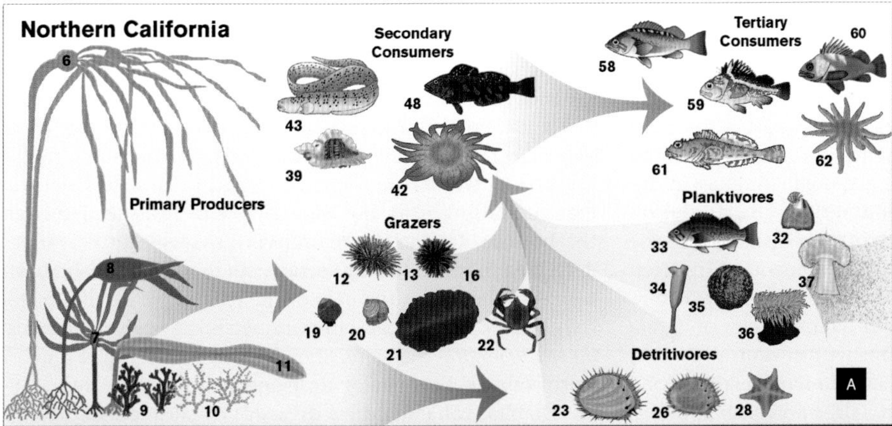

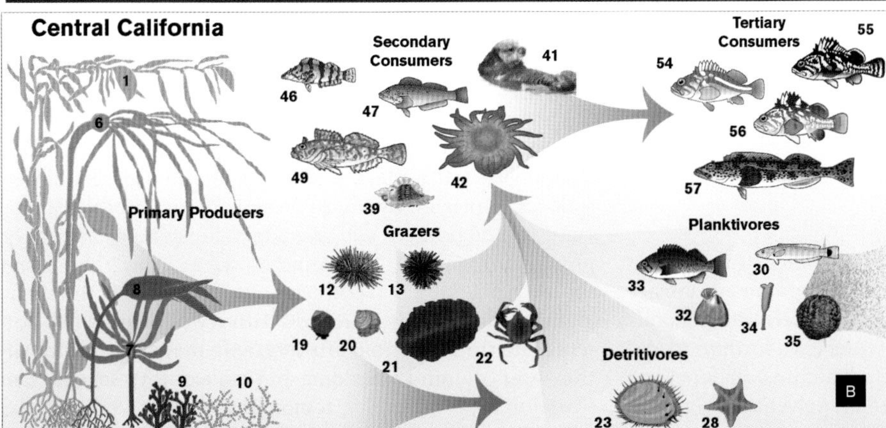

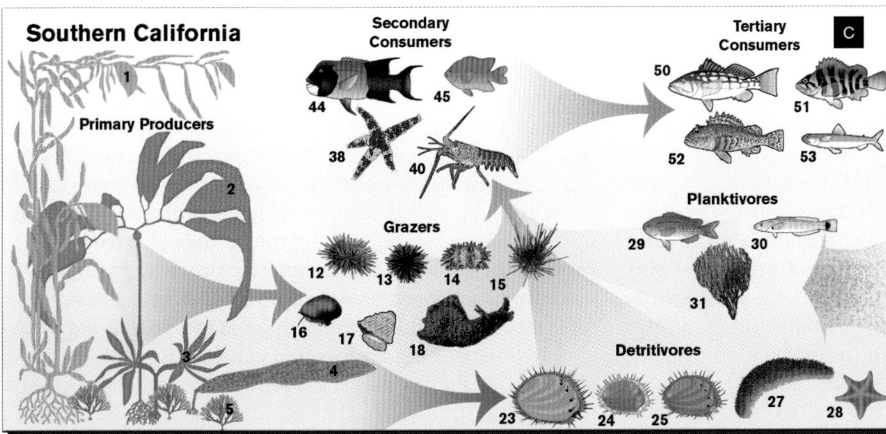

FIGURE 17.7 Geographic variation in species composition of trophic groups that constitute kelp forest communities and trophic pathways in kelp forests of California. Shown are the abundant and distinctive species that constitute each trophic group in (A) northern California (the mouth of San Francisco Bay to the Oregon border), (B) central California (Point Conception to the mouth of San Francisco Bay, and (C) southern California (the Mexican border to Point Conception) kelp forests. Artwork by Emily Saarman, Claire Saarman, Larry Allen, and Rodrigo Beas.

KEY

PRIMARY PRODUCERS
1. *Macrocystis*
2. *Pelagophycus*
3. *Eisenia*
4. *Laminaria farlowi*
5. *Dictyota*
6. *Nereocystis*
7. *Pterygophora*
8. *Laminaria setchelli*
9. *Foliose red algae*
10. *Erect coralline algae*
11. *Pleurophycus*

GRAZERS
12. *Strongylocentrotus franciscanus*
13. *S. purpuratus*
14. *Lytechinus*
15. *Centrostephanus*
16. *Norrisia*
17. *Megastrea*
18. *Aplysia*
19. *Tegula*
20. *Calliostoma*
21. *Cryptochiton*
22. *Pugettia*

DETRITIVORES
23. *Haliotis rufescens*
24. *H. sorensoni*
25. *H. fulgens*
26. *H. kamschatkana*
27. *Parastichopus parvemensis*
28. *Patiria*

PLANKTIVORES
29. *Chromis*
30. *Oxyjulis*
31. *Lophogorgia*
32. *Balanus nobilis*
33. *Sebastes mystinus*
34. *Styela*
35. *Tethya*
36. *Urticina*
37. *Metridium*

SECONDARY CONSUMERS
38. *Kellitia*
39. *Ceratostoma*
40. *Panularis*
41. *Enhydra*
42. *Pycnopodia*
43. *Anarrhichthys*
44. *Semicossyphus*
45. *Hypsypops*
46. *Oxylebius*
47. *Hexagrammos decagrammus*
48. *H. superciliosus*
49. *Scorpaenichthys*

TERTIARY CONSUMERS
50. *Paralabrax*
51. *Sebastes serriceps*
52. *Sebastes guttata*
53. *Synodus*
54. *Sebastes caurinus*
55. *Sebastes chrysomelas*
56. *Sebastes carnatus*
57. *Ophiodon*
58. *Sebastes melanops*
59. *Sebastes nebulosus*
60. *Sebastes maliger*
61. *Hemilepidotus*
62. *Solaster*

exploitative competition for the fine microalgae they graze from rock surfaces in southern California forests (Schmitt 1985, 1996). This competition is intensified by their co-occurrence in cobble habitat that provides the two species a refuge from their shared predators (sea stars, lobster, and octopi) (see Schmitt 1982, 1987). Their coexistence in this refuge habitat reflects trade-offs in their different grazing techniques at different densities of the algae (Schmitt 1996). The studies on these two snails have generated fascinating insights into the complex interactions of predation and competition in determining the distributions and coexistence of these two competitors (Schmitt 1987). Similarly, different species of *Tegula* exhibit different habitat associations within central California kelp forests: some distributed at different heights along kelp plants, others in the understory algae and each at different depth strata (Watanabe 1984). These spatial patterns of the snails (Watanabe 1984) and crabs (Hines 1982) are considered examples of resource partitioning by which the species use algal resources in different areas so as to avoid competitive exclusion by one another.

Detritivores

The great production of litter by kelps and other algae supports a diverse, abundant, and economically important assemblage of detritivores. Detritivores are divided between those mobile species that actively forage for algal litter (e.g., shrimps, crabs, sea stars) and those less mobile (e.g. sea urchins, abalone) and immobile, sessile species (e.g., hydroids, polychaete worms in calcareous tubes) that depend on water movement to deliver detritus to them. The latter are referred to as sessile suspension feeders. The several species of sea urchins described as grazers also consume vast amounts of kelp litter. Of the snails that consume kelp litter, the seven species of abalone are particularly important. Southern California forests have historically harbored large numbers of red (*Haliotis rufescens*), black (*H. cracherodii*), pink (*H. corrugata*), and green (*H. fulgens*) abalone (see Figure 17.7c). Pink, green, and black abalone extend south into Mexico, but black and red abalone are the only large abalone species that typically occur north of Point Conception.

Decades of overfishing, diseases, and expanding sea otter populations have not only resulted in termination of commercial fisheries for all abalone species in California but also restricted recreational take to red abalone (and this only north of San Francisco Bay) and placed the white abalone on the endangered species list. A bacterial disease referred to as the "withering foot syndrome" has caused severe declines of black abalone across its range in southern and central California, leading to its recent listing as an endangered species. Abalone are now far less abundant and restricted to cracks and crevices in the presence of sea otters in central California forests. Here and to the north, two other smaller abalone occur: the flat (*H. walallensis*) and pinto (*H. kamschatkana*) abalone (see Figure 17.7a).

Other important, mobile detritivores include three species of sea cucumbers (*Eupentacta* and two *Apostichopus* spp.); a host of crustaceans including amphipods, crabs, and shrimps; and some sea stars (Asteroidea) and brittle stars (Ophioroidea). Many of these species, such as the warty sea cucumber (*Apostichopus parvimensis*), are referred to as deposit feeders, collecting small bits of organic matter off the bottom (see Figure 17.6a). The most predominant detritivorous sea star is the bat star (*Patiria miniata*), distributed throughout California but in greatest numbers north of Point Conception (Figure 17.7a–c). This species everts the five folds of its stomach directly onto the rocky bottom, digesting detritus in place.

A wide variety of sessile species wait for kelp litter to be delivered to them, including many species of tube-forming polychaete worms that extend tentacles to collect detrital material falling from the water above or resuspended from the bottom. Unlike the planktivorous sessile invertebrates described in the following section, these species inhabit horizontal surfaces near the base of the reef where detrital material collects. Of particular importance is the polychaete worm (*Diopatra ornata*) that consumes drift algae and whose mats of worm tubes collect bits of algae and shells that create a complex habitat inhabited by a diversity of crustaceans, worms, snails, and small fishes (Kim 1992).

Planktivores

Like detritivores, planktivores can be sedentary (e.g., sea cucumbers, brittle stars, anemones), sessile (e.g., barnacles, sponges, tunicates, hydroids) or mobile (e.g., fishes). Planktivores can be primary and secondary consumers, feeding on phytoplankton and zooplankton, respectively. The major source of plankton is ALLOCTHONOUS, from outside the forest, and planktivores rely largely on delivery of plankton by currents into the forest from offshore. Kelp that extends through the water column causes drag and reduces the movement of plankton into the forest (Jackson and Winant 1983, Jackson 1998). Thus planktivores tend to be more abundant where currents are strongest, where kelp is less dense, and at the up-current end of forests (Bernstein and Jung 1979). In fact, planktivorous fishes like the blacksmith (*Chromis punctipinnis*) in southern California forests will move from one end of a forest to the other as the up-current and down-current end of forests alternate with the ebb and flow of tidal currents (Bray 1981).

The reef substrate used by kelp and algae also serves as substrate for sessile filter feeders, which stay fixed in place and rely on currents to bring plankton to them for feeding. The diversity of strategies and adaptations to filter plankton out of the water column is astounding. Most kelp forest sessile filter feeders rely on extended appendages (e.g., arms, tentacles) with large surface areas that can trap the tiny species of plankton. In many cases, these sessile filter feeders are passive (e.g., brittle stars, polychaete worms, hydrocorals, hydroids, bryozoans), extending these structures into the water column and waiting for plankton to drift into them, then capturing the plankton with slimy surfaces or tiny barbs and hairs. In contrast, some sessile filter feeders are active (e.g., barnacles, *Melibe* nudibranch), actively sweeping their feeding structures through the water. In addition, other filter feeders (e.g., tunicates, sponges, bivalves [boring clams and scallops]) have internal structures to capture plankton and actively draw in plankton-rich water by generating their own currents, pumping the water through internal filtering structures. The many sessile invertebrates mentioned above such as anemones, sponges, bryozoans, hydroids, and tunicates are particularly abundant on the vertical surfaces of high-relief rocks, where they find refuge from competition with algae and can better position themselves to collect particles as currents sweep by. Their abundance is reduced in the presence of subcanopy kelps that reduce the rate of water movement near the surface of the rocky reef (Eckman et al. 1989). A particularly important planktivore is the colonial polychaete *Phragmatopoma californica*. This tubeworm creates massive reefs of their sand-impregnated tubes that provide habitat for boring clams and other species.

Fishes can be very important planktivores in kelp forest ecosystems, particularly by collecting plankton from the water column and delivering that energy and nutrients to organisms on the reef surface. For example, blacksmith (*Chromis punctipinnis*) feed on plankton in large aggregations above the reef throughout the day, and shelter in cracks and crevices at night where they urinate, defecate, and provide nitrogen that enhances algal production on the reef (Bray et al. 1981). The señorita (*Oxyjulis californica*) also forms large aggregations and feeds on plankton throughout the kelp forest (Hobson and Chess 1976). Kelp perch live mostly up in the surface canopy of kelp forests and feed both on planktonic crustaceans and those associated with the forest canopy (Anderson 1994). Juveniles of some species of rockfishes (genus *Sebastes*) form large aggregations throughout the water column (e.g., blue, black, olive, and yellowtail) and, like blacksmith, seek shelter on the reef at night. Others associate with the forest canopy (copper, gopher, kelp, black, and yellow) and feed on plankton throughout the day and shelter there throughout the night (Singer 1985, Carr 1991, Love et al. 1991). Aggregations of juvenile rockfishes in central California create a "wall of mouths" that likely reduces the delivery of larvae of nearshore species like barnacles to habitats inshore (Gaines and Roughgarden 1987). Aggregations of juvenile and adult blue rockfish (*Sebastes mystinus*) are the most abundant fish in central and northern California forests, where they feed on plankton throughout the water column. Other schooling planktivorous fishes are more ephemeral, passing through kelp forests as they move along shore (e.g., salema, anchovy, topsmelt, jack mackerel).

As with other trophic groups, the species composition of the predominant planktivores in kelp forests varies geographically. Southern California forests support much greater abundances of particular planktivorous reef fishes, including the blacksmith and the señorita, and sessile and sedentary planktivores including five species of gorgonians (only one of which extends north of Point Conception), particular bryozoans (e.g., *Bugula*, *Crisia*), sea cucumbers (*Pachythyone*), and brittle stars (*Ophiothrix*). In central California forests the señorita is joined by huge schools of the blue rockfish (*Sebastes mystinus*) (Figure 17.8), which is also the predominant planktivorous fish in northern California forests. Central California forests support much greater abundances of barnacles (e.g., *Balanus nubilus*, *B. crenatus*), compound and solitary tunicates (e.g., *Didemnum* and *Styela*, respectively), bryozoans (*Hippodiplosia*), sponges (e.g., the orange puffball sponge, *Tethya*), and anemones (e.g., four species of *Urticina* and the strawberry anemone, *Corynactis californica*). Sessile planktivores in northern California are similar to central California, with exceptions of greater abundances of the sea cucumber *Cucumaria minitata*, and some anemones (e.g., *Urticina* and the large white anemone, *Metridium farcimen*). The greater productivity of plankton associated with coastal upwelling north of Point Conception may explain the greater abundances of sessile planktivores in central and northern California kelp forests.

Secondary Consumers

The tremendous production of grazers, detritivores, and planktivores in California kelp forests fuels a highly diverse assemblage of secondary consumers. These predators are almost all mobile species that forage across spatial mosaics of algae and sessile invertebrates. Key among these are the great diversity of sea stars that digest their prey externally by everting their stomachs. One of the most important and voracious sea stars in central and northern California is the large sunflower star (*Pycnopodia helianthoides*), which uses its more than twenty rays and hundreds of tube feet to dislodge prey from the reef surface (e.g., turban snails, abalone) or chase down mobile prey (e.g., sea urchins, many species of snails, other sea stars) (Moitoza and Phillips 1979, Duggins 1983, Harrold and Pearse 1987, Pearse and Hines 1987, Byrnes et al. 2006). Unlike other sea stars, the sunflower star ingests its prey. Although *Pycnopodia* is also a tertiary consumer, we mention it here because of the prevalence of sea urchins and other primary consumers in its diet.

FIGURE 17.8 Clouds of planktivorous blue rockfishes (*Sebastes mystinus*) that are characteristic of central and northern California kelp forests. Photo: Steven Lonhart.

The mollusks have several adaptations that facilitate consumption of both sessile filter feeders and mobile herbivores and grazers. For example, the leafy hornmouth (*Ceratostoma foliatum*) uses a spine on its shell to pry open barnacles or puncture a hole through the shells of newly settled barnacles. Kellet's whelk (*Kelletia kelletii*) has a highly extensible and prehensile proboscis that moves into the tubes of filter-feeding polychaete worms and shreds soft tissue with a radula full of rasping teeth at the tip of the proboscis. The California cone snail (e.g., *Conus californicus*) uses its proboscis to subdue its prey with a venomous protein, and other predatory snails subdue small mobile prey by enveloping them in their large, fleshy foot. Many dorid nudibranchs specialize on feeding on particular sponges, matching the color of their prey as insects do on terrestrial plants. In southern California, secondary consumers include predatory snails like *Kellettia*, *Ceratostoma nuttalli*, and other muricids. In central and northern California, *C. nuttalli* is replaced by *C. foliatum*. Octopi are also abundant, mobile, voracious predators that feed at night on snails, crabs, and other mobile organisms in kelp forests (Ambrose 1986) throughout California.

In contrast to mollusks, crabs and other crustaceans can attack sessile filter feeders and mobile prey with powerful claws, and either tear or crush the external defenses to access the internal organs and soft tissue. In southern California forests the California spiny lobster (*Panuliris interruptus*) can be an important predator on purple and red sea urchins (Behrens and Lafferty 2004, Lafferty 2004). The extent, distribution, and spatial scales at which spiny lobster limit or control urchin abundance is unclear, with studies in the Northern Channel Islands suggesting that spiny lobster control urchin populations and their distributions (Behrens and Lafferty 2004, Lafferty 2004), whereas other studies along the mainland suggest they do not (Foster and Schiel 2010, Guenther et al. 2012).

California sheephead (*Semicossyphus pulcher*) are also well-known urchin predators in southern California forests (Cowen 1983, Cowen 1986, Hamilton et al. 2011, Hamilton et al. 2014), and urchin density or foraging rates can be inversely related to sheephead density (Cowen 1983, Harrold and Reed 1985, Hamilton et al. 2011). In central California, southern sea otters (*Enhydra lutris nereis*) are important predators of sea urchins (Tinker et al. 2008), and the almost ubiquitous low densities of sea urchins there is thought to reflect the presence of sea otters (McLean 1962, Riedman and Estes 1988, Reed et al. 2011), though examples of changes in urchin abundance independent of otters also exist (e.g., Pearse and Hines 1979, Pearse and Hines 1987, Watanabe and Harrold 1991). The voracious otter consumes 25% to 33% of its body weight per day, and individuals specialize on crabs, abalone, sea urchins, and clams (Costa and Kooyman 1982, Yeates et al. 2007). Sea otters are such effective predators on red sea urchins and abalone that their current numbers have negated commercial and recreational fisheries for these species within their range.

In northern California kelp forests, *Pycnopodia helianthoides* and the wolf eel (*Anarrhichthys ocellatus*) are voracious predators of adult sea urchins, but their influence on sea urchin density or foraging behavior has not been assessed in that region. In central California urchin barrens are rare, whereas in southern California, barrens vary spatially from localized patches to entire reefs and temporally from several months to many years (Dayton et al. 1984, Dayton et al. 1992, Dayton et al. 1999, Dayton and Tegner 1984, Harrold and Reed 1985, Graham 2004). Urchin barrens are also more common in northern California than central California (L. Rogers-Bennett pers. comm.). How strongly the effects of any one of these predators on sea urchins cascade to the spatial and temporal variation in kelp abundance continues to be debated among kelp forest ecologists. Interestingly, Byrnes et al. (2006) found positive correlations between predator diversity and kelp abundance, but not predator abundance and kelp abundance, in kelp forests in the Northern Channel islands. These correlations were supported by manipulations of predator diversity and kelp abundance in small experimental MESOCOSMS. That study and others (e.g., Cowen 1983) indicate that altered foraging behavior of kelp grazers in the presence of predators could contribute to possible cascading effects.

Predators in kelp forests can influence the structure of communities in adjacent ecosystems as well. For example, both California sheephead and California spiny lobster feed on intertidal mussels. Researchers have shown that lobster foraging on mussels can greatly reduce the abundance of this competitive dominant and alter the community structure of rocky intertidal ecosystems (Robles 1987, Robles and Robb 1993). This example illustrates how predation can enhance the connectivity of kelp forests with adjacent coastal marine ecosystems. Myriad species of reef fishes feed on grazers and detritivores, especially on the great production of small crustaceans (amphipods, mysids) and snails that feed on or associate with macroalgae. Many of these fishes are small cryptic species of an amazing diversity of families, including the clingfishes (Gobiesocidae), eelpouts (Zoarcidae), blennies (Blenniidae), clinids (Clinidae), pipefishes (Syngnathidae), poachers (Agonidae), snailfishes (Liparididae), pricklebacks (Stichaeidae), gunnels (Pholididae), gobies (Gobiidae), and sculpins (Cottidae), which in turn are all consumed by larger fishes. These small fishes are akin to the lizards and amphibians that consume insects in terrestrial forests. Because of their small size (usually <10 centimeters long), they are vulnerable to predation by larger fishes and are therefore well camouflaged to match their algal habitats (see Figure 17.6). In addition to these small fishes, larger reef fishes feed on small crustaceans, crabs, and snails, including many species of surfperches (family Embiotocidae) distributed throughout the coast of California.

In southern California small wrasses (*Halichoeres semicinctus*) and California's state marine fish, the bright orange Garibaldi (*Hypsypops rubicundus*), add to the diversity of reef fishes that depend on the great production of herbivorous and detritivorous crustaceans. In central California the painted (*Oxylebius pictus*) and kelp (*Hexagrammos decagrammus*) greenling also feed on small crustaceans, crabs, and snails. In northern California the rock greenling (*Hexagrammos superciliosus*) and grunt sculpin (*Rhamphocottus richardsonii*) become more abundant. Fishes that target larger invertebrates include the horn shark (*Heterodontus francisci*) and the swell shark (*Cephaloscyllium ventriosum*) in southern California and the bat ray (*Myliobatis californica*). Also more abundant in central California and northern California is the cabezon (*Scorpaenichthys marmoratus*), which yanks abalone from the rock surface, ingests shell and all, and regurgitates the shell after digesting the meat from it.

The high abundances of many of these secondary consumers provide excellent examples of both intraspecific and interspecific competition as a key mechanism structuring kelp forest communities (reviewed by Hixon 2006). Competition for nesting territories among Garibaldi was one of the earlier documented examples of intraspecific competition in regulating the density of reef fishes (Clarke 1970). Intraspecific and interspecific competition within and between the black and striped surfperches has generated some of the most thorough field studies of competition in fishes (reviewed by Hixon 2006). Similarly, the species of small blennies (Stephens et al. 1970) that exhibit distinct depth and habitat associations are thought to reflect more examples of resource partitioning and niche diversification as a means of species coexistence and the maintenance of diversity.

Tertiary Consumers

The great diversity of primary and secondary consumers are fed upon by a diverse assemblage of tertiary consumers, most of which are larger, piscivorous fishes of ecological and economic importance. As mentioned earlier, many of these tertiary predators are opportunistic and feed on a combination of larger invertebrates (e.g., carnivorous gastropods, octopus, sea stars, crabs) and the many smaller fishes described above as secondary consumers. In southern California the most abundant tertiary consumer is the kelp or calico bass (*Paralabrax clathratus*), which feeds on a wide variety of smaller fishes. Additional predatory fishes characteristic of southern California forests are the treefish (*Sebastes serriceps*), the scorpion fish (*Scorpaena guttata*), and the California lizardfish (*Synodus lucioceps*). Forests located in areas of cooler, upwelled water such as Palos Verdes and the western Channel Islands support species more common to central California, including several species of rockfishes of the genus *Sebastes* (Holbrook et al. 1997, Hamilton et al. 2010).

In central California no fewer than nine species of rockfishes inhabit kelp forests (Miller and Giebel 1973, Hallacher and Roberts 1985, Love et al. 2002), including species that form aggregations in the water column (e.g., blue, black, olive, yellowtail) and more solitary species that lie on the rocky reef (e.g., grass, black and yellow, gopher, copper, vermillion, China) or up in the water column among fronds of giant kelp (kelp rockfish). A particularly voracious predator of other fishes in both central and northern California forests is the lingcod (*Ophiodon elongates*). Although this species and the cabezon also inhabit rocky reefs beyond depths of kelp forests, both species mate on shallow rocky reefs where the male guards nests of eggs. In northern California three species of rockfishes—the black (*S. melanops*), China (*S. nebulosus*), and quillback (*S. maliger*)—are more abundant and major constituents of the kelp forest fish assemblage. In addition, three large (circa 40 centimeters long) sculpins, including the buffalo sculpin (*Enophrys bison*) and the brown and red Irish lord (*Hemilepidotus spinosus* and *H. hemilepidotus*, respectively), are tertiary consumers distinctive to northern California and further north.

In addition to fishes, some invertebrates are tertiary consumers, feeding on the predators of detritivores, planktivores, and herbivores. In southern and central California forests the moon snail (*Euspira*, formally *Polinices*) feeds in the sand adjacent to rocky reefs on reef-associated predatory snails. Several species of crustaceans also consume predatory snails. In southern California crustaceans that feed on predatory snails include the spiny lobster (*Panulirus interruptus*) and rock crabs of the genus *Metacarcinus* (formally *Cancer*). In central California forests the rock crabs *M. antennarius* and *M. productus* prey upon predatory snails, peeling away the aperture of the shell to access the soft tissue within. In northern California forests, *M. magister* is more common in shallow waters and is joined by the voracious morning sun star (*Solaster dawsoni*), which feeds on other sea stars, other echinoderms, and predatory snails. Several species of octopi occur up and down the coast of California, but diversity and abundance is particularly high in southern California forests.

Like the many species of primary and secondary consumers, tertiary consumers exhibit distinctive habitat associations thought to reflect habitat and resource partitioning. The rockfishes, in particular, exhibit distributions stratified throughout the water column and by depth (Hallacher and Roberts 1985). Elegant experimental removals of the shallower- and deeper-dwelling black and yellow (*Sebastes chrysomelas*) and gopher (*S. carnatus*) rockfishes, respectively, have revealed that their depth stratification is a result of asymmetric competition by which the superior black and yellow rockfish excludes the subordinate gopher rockfish from the preferred highly productive shallow reef habitats (Larson 1980a, 1980b).

Apex Predators

Apex predators are species that tend to occupy higher trophic levels; have few, if any, predators of their own; and strongly influence the abundance of an important prey species or trophic level, such that the loss of an apex predator can cause cascading effects across lower trophic levels. The complex food webs of kelp forests, with many trophic pathways, can support a diversity of potential apex predators such as fishes, invertebrates, marine birds, mammals, and of course human beings. For many of these species, however, the extent to which they actually limit or control the abundance of their prey is unclear. We focus on species that are resident to kelp forests, because the extent to which more transient predators such as the great white shark (*Carcharodon carcharias*), California barracuda (*Sphyraena argentea*), white seabass (*Cynoscion nobilis*), and the Pacific electric ray (*Torpedo californica*) determine the numbers of kelp forest fishes is unknown.

Even for the resident predators, such as harbor seals (*Phoca vitulina*), diving Brandt's cormorants (*Phalacrocorax penicillatus*), snowy egrets (*Egretta thula*), and great blue herons (*Ardea Herodias*), which feed on juvenile and adult kelp forest fishes throughout California, the extent to which they control prey populations has not been assessed. Distinctive resident apex predators in southern California kelp forests include the highly evasive California moray eel (*Gymnothorax mordax*) and the now rarely encountered giant seabass (*Stenolepis gigas*). Because of the nocturnal and cave-dwelling behavior of California morays and the paucity of giant seabass as a result of historical overfishing, our understanding of the ecological significance of these species to kelp forest ecosystems is also poorly understood. In central California harbor seals are joined by the sunflower star and the southern sea otter. The primary predator of both harbor seals and the sea otter is the transient white shark. Apex predators in northern California forests include the sunflower star, the morning sunstar, and harbor seals. Although these species of sea stars and the sea otter are notable predators of sea urchins, they also consume a variety of carnivorous gastropods and sea stars. Our lack of knowledge of the ecological significance of many of these potential apex predators in structuring kelp forest communities underscores the need for research on their functional roles.

Determinants of Community Structure

Abiotic Determinants of Community Structure

The many abiotic drivers of species distributions described in the previous section also determine the species composition of kelp forest communities. Large-scale differences in oceanographic conditions driven by interactions among the California Current, nearshore wind fields, and the configuration of the coastline drive regional differences in the prevalence of coastal upwelling and wave exposure. Regional differences in these oceanographic drivers generally correspond with major headlands and create the foundation for the regional differences in macroalgae, invertebrate, and fish assemblages described earlier. Most conspicuous are the biogeographic differences between the Oregonian and San Diegan provinces north and south of Point Conception, respectively (e.g., Briggs 1974). North of Point Conception, notable differences in community structure occur north and south of Point Reyes and the mouth of San Francisco Bay, with additional differences north and south of Monterey Bay (e.g., the transition between prevalence of giant kelp and bull kelp). Between and within each region the topography of the seafloor (reef slope, rock type, size, and vertical relief) interacts with water movement to shape species composition. In particular, the relative prevalence of sand and sedimentary reefs greatly influences water clarity, which collectively can affect the species composition of algae and sessile invertebrates. These geomorphological and oceanographic conditions set the stage upon which species interactions further shape the structure of kelp forest ecosystems.

Biotic Determinants of Trophic Structure

Because macroalgae and sessile invertebrates occupy different trophic levels, they do not compete for resources other than space. However, competition *within* the two space-holder groups for other resources may indirectly affect the strength of competition for space *between* them. For example, different species of macroalgae compete with one another for available sunlight. Although large, canopy-forming kelps (e.g., giant kelp and bull kelp) occupy relatively little space on the bottom (typically less than 10%), they can monopolize available sunlight and reduce the amount reaching the bottom by more than 90% (Pearse and Hines 1979, Reed and Foster 1984). The large reduction in light caused by the surface canopy suppresses understory macroalgae (Reed and Foster 1984, Dayton et al. 1984, Edwards 1998, Clark et al. 2004), which can have indirect positive effects on the abundance of sessile invertebrates via reduced competition for space (Arkema et al. 2009). Indeed, stands of these subcanopy-forming and low-lying algae can reduce delivery rates of invertebrate larvae and the planktonic prey on which sessile planktivores depend (Eckman et al. 1989). As described earlier, such interactions have implications for higher trophic levels as the composition of understory algae alters the abundance of habitat structure and prey for reef fishes (Schmitt and Holbrook 1990, Holbrook and Schmitt 1984, 1988), which in turn determines the production and survival of young fish (Okamoto et al. 2012) as well as the abundance and species composition of small, cryptic benthic fishes (Carr 1989).

Perhaps the most striking difference between kelp forests and adjacent areas occurs in the mid- and surface waters where canopy-forming kelps can provide the only physical structure above featureless seafloors (Larson and DeMartini 1984, DeMartini and Roberts 1990). Kelp blades provide habitat for a variety of sessile invertebrates, including hydroids and bryozoans, as well as a myriad of mobile crustaceans and gastropods (Bernstein and Jung 1979, Coyer 1985, 1987, Davenport and Anderson 2007). In addition to the many sessile and mobile invertebrates attached directly to the kelp, numerous species of fish associate closely with kelp structure. Adults of several species, such as the kelp perch (Anderson 1994) and manacled sculpin, feed on the invertebrates associated with the algae but also find refuge from predators in the dense forest canopy (Larson and DeMartini 1984, Anderson 2001, Deza and Anderson 2010, Stephens et al. 2006, Steele and Anderson 2006). The distribution, dynamics, and survival of juvenile fishes and the overall patterns of population replenishment of a number of reef fish species can be strongly influenced by the distribution and dynamics of the density of plants and blades that constitute forest structure. A number of experiments demonstrate the influence of the kelp density and forest area on recruitment and population dynamics of kelp forest fishes (reviewed in Carr and Syms 2006, Steele and Anderson 2006, Stephens et al. 2006).

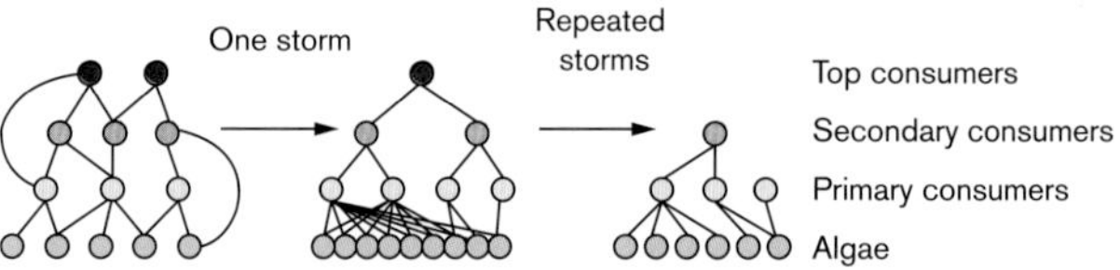

FIGURE 17.9 Model simulations and experiments show that repeated storm disturbance simplifies kelp forest food webs. Species richness goes up following a single storm as increases in the number of species of algae exceed decreases in top consumers. This leads to increases in the average number of feeding links per species. Repeated disturbance leads to less diverse and less complex food webs with fewer trophic levels and fewer feeding links per species. Source: Byrnes et al. 2011.

Interactions between Abiotic and Biotic Processes

The ecological importance of canopy-forming kelps extends far beyond their role as provider of food and shelter. Their mere physical presence dramatically alters the physical conditions of the nearshore environment and creates a habitat very distinct from adjacent waters. In this way, canopy-forming kelps function as classic autogenic ecosystem engineers (sensu Jones et al. 1994) that dramatically reduce the amount of light reaching the bottom (Foster 1975, Heine 1983, Gerard 1984, Reed and Foster 1984, Dean 1985), attenuate and redirect currents and internal waves (Jackson and Winant 1983, Jackson 1984, Jackson 1998, Gaylord et al. 2007, Rosman et al. 2007, 2010, Fram et al. 2008) and enhance mixing and turbulent flow (Rosman et al. 2010, Gaylord et al. 2012). Such modifications of the physical environment can have far-reaching biological consequences for inhabitants of the kelp forest community by affecting nutrient uptake (Wheeler 1980, Fram et al. 2008), morphology and chemical composition (Stewart et al. 2009), primary production (Miller et al. 2011), propagule dispersal (Gaines and Roughgarden 1987, Graham 2003, Gaylord et al. 2004, Morton and Anderson 2013), food supply and growth (Bernstein and Jung 1979, Arkema 2009), foraging behavior (e.g., Bray 1981), and competition (Reed and Foster 1984, Dayton et al. 1984, Clarke et al. 2004). Separately and in combination, these effects influence the productivity and spatial distribution of species, which in turn influence the composition and strength of interactions among species in the forest.

Competition among the different vegetation layers for light (and hence its indirect effects on sessile invertebrates) is very much influenced by storm-induced wave disturbance because an alga's probability of being removed by waves tends to be positively related to its stature in the water column (and hence its ability to compete for light). Unlike the giant kelp, which is dislodged by waves quite easily (Gaylord et al. 2008), many low-lying species of understory algae are able to resist removal by all but the largest of waves (Dayton and Tegner 1984, Ebeling et al. 1985, Seymour et al. 1989). Moderate wave events that remove only the surface canopy of kelp may tip the scale of space competition in favor of understory algae, which flourish in the high-light environment created by loss of the kelp canopy (Cowen et al. 1982, Foster 1982, Miller et al. 2011). Such changes can cascade throughout the entire kelp forest community, as wave disturbance has been linked to measured changes in the structure and complexity of kelp forest food webs. The periodic removal of giant kelp by wave disturbance was shown to increase local species richness and the density of feeding links of food webs by both direct and indirect pathways (Byrnes et al. 2011). Predictions from statistical simulations of time series data, and results from a multiyear kelp removal experiment designed to simulate frequent large storms, suggested that periodic storms help maintain the complexity of kelp forest food webs. However, if large storms occur year after year, then kelp forest food webs become less diverse and complex as species go locally extinct. The loss of complexity occurs primarily due to decreases in the diversity of higher trophic levels (Figure 17.9).

Disturbance, Forest Dynamics, and Shifts in Community Structure

Kelp forests in California are very dynamic systems that fluctuate greatly in response to a complex of predictable (seasonal) and unpredictable (aseasonal and human-induced) events (reviewed in Dayton 1985, Schiel and Foster 1986, Reed et al. 2011). Frequent disturbance coupled with the relatively short lifespans of the dominant vegetation species thwart progress toward a state of equilibrium and result in a preponderance of postdisturbance succession. Off central California, for example, the thinning of mature plants by large waves associated with winter storms, along with spring upwelling of nutrients and the recruitment of new plants, leads to predictable, seasonal regeneration of kelp forests (Foster 1982, Graham et al. 1997, Harrold et al. 1988). Sea otters and strong wave action control populations of sea urchins that otherwise might graze back new plant growth (McLean 1962, Lowry and Pearse 1974, Pearse and Hines 1979, Hines and Pearse 1982, Cowen et al. 1982), contributing to seasonally lush kelp forests throughout central California.

Off southern California, seasonal fluctuations in kelp forests are less predictable. Although generally weaker, storm disturbance varies greatly from year to year (Ebeling et al. 1985, Tegner and Dayton 1987, Dayton et al. 1989, Seymour et al. 1989, Reed et al. 2011), nutrient regeneration from upwelling is less dependable (Jackson 1977, Gerard 1982, Zimmerman and Kremer 1986, Zimmerman and Robertson 1985), and recruitment events occur more sporadically (Deysher and Dean 1986, Dayton et al. 1984, Dayton et al. 1992, Reed 1990b). The absence of sea otters and the insufficient numbers of other predators of macroinvertebrates make regenerating forests more vulnerable to deforestation by grazing sea urchins (Leighton et al. 1966, Leighton 1971, Dean et al. 1984, Ebeling et al. 1985, Harrold and Reed 1985) or displacement by dense aggregations of suspension-feeding invertebrates (Carroll et al. 2000, Rassweiler et al. 2010). In addition, abundant species of subtropical fishes (kyphosids and labrids), which are rare or absent in central and northern California forests, browse the kelp and under certain circumstances can inhibit forest regeneration (Rosenthal et al. 1974, North 1976, Bernstein and Jung 1979, Harris et al. 1984).

Both the 1982–1984 and the 1997–1998 El Niño Southern Oscillation (ENSO) events demonstrated the large and widespread impact that episodic climatic changes can have on nearshore kelp communities (Gerard 1984, Dayton and Tegner 1984, Zimmerman and Robertson 1985, Ebeling et al. 1985, Cowen 1985, Dayton et al. 1999, Edwards 2004, Edwards and Estes 2006). For example, the 1997–1998 El Niño resulted in the near-complete loss of all giant kelp throughout one-half of the species' range in the northeast Pacific Ocean (Edwards 2004, Edwards and Estes 2006). The effects of ENSO are usually stronger and last longer in southern California than in regions farther north (Paine 1986, Tegner and Dayton 1987, Edwards 2004, Edwards and Estes 2006). These erratic or episodic disturbances in kelp forests can contribute to the formation of barren areas (Figure 17.10) of variable size that persist for indeterminate periods in southern California (Leighton et al. 1966, Leighton 1971, Dean et al. 1984, Harrold and Reed 1985, Ebeling et al. 1985). The regeneration of the forested state in barren areas depends on a fortuitous combination of oceanographic events and biological processes (Harrold and Reed 1985, Rassweiler et al. 2010, Bestelmeyer et al. 2011). For example, Ebeling et al. 1985 chronicled the loss and reforestation of kelp forests off Santa Barbara. Strong storms removed much of the giant kelp on a reef, triggering sea urchins to vacate cracks and crevices and remove much of the algae across the reef. The area remained an "urchin barrens" until a subsequent storm caused mass mortality of the exposed sea urchins, allowing the giant kelp to recolonize and reforest the reef.

FIGURE 17.10 A barren area in southern California caused by physical disturbance and urchin predation is characterized by an absence of macroalgae and high cover of encrusting coralline algae. Photo: Ron McPeak.

Kelp Forest Ecosystem Services

Because of their great productivity, biodiversity, and close proximity to shore, California's kelp forests have a long and diverse history of human use. Kelp forest ecosystems provide humans with a diversity of consumptive and nonconsumptive services, including kelp harvesting for several products, recreational and commercial fisheries, ecotourism (e.g., kayaking, wildlife viewing, scuba diving), shoreline protection, and spiritual and cultural values.

Kelp Harvesting

Kelp beds were favorite fishing grounds of Native Americans living near the coast of California, providing fish and shellfish as important sources of protein in their diets (Landberg 1965). Kelp itself was used by Native Americans to make fishing line (Swan 1870); bottles for storing bait, food, and freshwater (Driver 1939); seasoning for food (Leachman 1921); and medicines (Mead 1976). By the turn of the twentieth century, the United States had become the world's largest consumer and importer of potash, an organic compound found in plants and used to manufacture fertilizers and black gunpowder. World War I created enormous demands for potash as well as for acetone, a solvent used to manufacture smokeless gunpowder (Neushul 1987, 1989). Enterprising American businessmen developed a new industry designed to extract both potash and acetone from California's giant kelp (Haynes 1954). Although short-lived, California's World War I kelp industry was the largest ever created in the United States for the processing of marine plants (Neushul 1987).

Kelps are also an important natural source of alginate, a PHYCOCOLLOID used in a wide variety of pharmaceutical, household, and food products. The commercial harvesting of kelp for the production of alginates began in San Diego in 1929 and reached its peak in the 1970s, when annual harvests of giant kelp in California averaged nearly 142,000 metric tons (Leet et al. 1992). The productivity and sustainability of this industry was enhanced by limiting kelp removal to the upper 2 meters of the surface canopy. Specialized vessels with rotating cutting blades literally "mowed the lawn" of the surface canopy of giant kelp forests (Figure 17.11), which allowed young fronds from the same plants to rapidly replace the removed canopy. The kelp alginate industry in California continued until 2006, when International Specialty Products (formerly Kelco), the nation's largest and oldest kelp harvesting company, moved its manufacturing operations to Scotland. Since the termination of California's large-scale commercial harvest of kelp, human harvest has consisted primarily of a small industry that harvests giant kelp to support the abalone mariculture industry along the coast of California. Kelp harvest for this industry involves smaller mechanized vessels and harvest by hand.

The California Department of Fish and Wildlife manages the harvest of giant kelp by leasing beds for commercial harvest. Aerial photographic surveys have been used to assess the state of the resource, and this time series of the spatial extent of the giant kelp forests along the coast has provided a valuable time series of forest dynamics.

FIGURE 17.11 A kelp harvester designed with a mower on the bow of the vessel to remove the surface canopy of a giant kelp forest. Photo: Kendra Karr.

Fisheries

California kelp forests have long supported economically and culturally significant recreational and commercial fisheries (see also Chapter 35, "Marine Fisheries"). In southern California invertebrates including several species of abalone (genus *Haliotus*) and the spiny lobster (*Panulirus interruptus*) have been primary targets of recreational fisheries. Private and commercial passenger fishing vessels have supported a highly active hook-and-line recreational fishery (e.g., Love et al. 1998). Several species of abalone also supported a commercial fishery in southern California for several decades until it was realized that stocks of all abalone species were greatly depleted. Consequently, both the recreational and commercial take of abalone have been terminated there since 1997 (Karpov et al. 2000). Now, the only abalone fishery is the recreational fishery confined to the coastline north of the mouth of San Francisco Bay. The commercial and recreational spiny lobster fisheries in southern California continue to today. In addition, a fishery for the warty sea cucumber occurs in southern California kelp forests.

Historically, nearshore shallow (<30 meter depth) rocky reef and kelp forest ecosystems were fished for finfishes more heavily by recreational than commercial fisheries along the California coast (Starr et al. 2002). Nearshore rocky areas became more important to commercial finfish fisheries in the early 1980s and later as a result of the more lucrative live-fish fishery (CDFW 2002a). Rockfishes are the predominant component of commercial catches in nearshore rocky reef and kelp habitats; about fifteen rockfish species are commonly caught in these shallow areas, especially in central California. Annual commercial landings of fishes from shallow rocky habitats averaged about 330,000 kg yr^{-1} from 1991 to 1998, almost twice that of the annual landings in the 1980s. Declines in catch rates in shallow kelp and reef habitats during the 1990s suggest that fishing rates were not sustainable. In the late 1990s commercial landings declined in rocky nearshore habitats, due to a decrease in fish abundance and more restrictive fishery regulations (Figure 17.12). Increased landings of many species, especially cabezon, kelp greenling, and grass rockfish, in the early 1990s have been attributed to the increase in the live-fish fishery. Since 1998, however, more rigorous fishing regulations have reduced landings of several nearshore fishes.

The commercial live-fish fishery began in southern California as a trap fishery primarily for California sheephead but quickly spread up the California coast. In the early 1990s the fishery expanded to central California, and in 1995 the region recorded the highest catches in California, with the majority caught using various hook-and-line and trap methods. The fishery is comanaged, depending on species, by the federal Pacific Fishery Management Council (PFMC) and the California Department of Fish and Wildlife. As of this writing, the fishery is considered "data poor" based on the paucity of stock assessments and difficulty in assessing catch (CDFW 2002b).

Human Impacts to Kelp Forests and Management Responses

Restoration

Kelp forests are potentially at risk from a number of human activities in the nearshore coastal zone. Land uses that alter the amount and constituents of runoff and the coastal discharge of municipal, agricultural and industrial wastes can negatively impact kelp forests by degrading the physical, chemical and biological environment in which they occur (North et al. 1964, Meistrell and Montagne 1983,

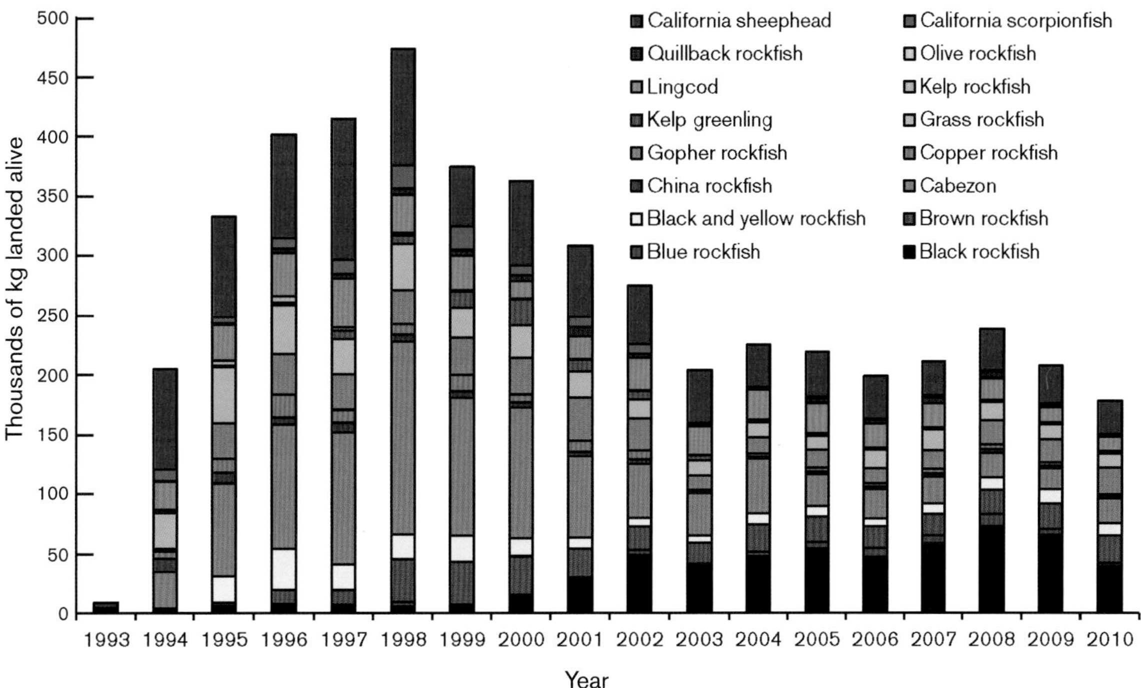

FIGURE 17.12 The trend in commercial landings of fish species targeted by the live-fish fishery in nearshore waters, especially kelp forests. The trend reflects the rapid growth of the fishery in the early 1990s and the subsequent decline due to greater restrictions. Source: Data from PacFIN (Pacific Fisheries Information Network) database.

Ambrose et al. 1996, Airoldi and Beck 2007, Gorman et al. 2009). The most severe effects appear to result from increased turbidity and sedimentation, which cause a reduction in bottom irradiance and loss of suitable rocky substrata needed for kelp attachment (Schiel and Foster 1992). The natural recovery of kelp often proceeds rapidly once human-induced stressors have been removed and the nearshore environment has been returned to its natural state.

The damaging effects of sewage discharge, coastal development, and sedimentation were realized between 1950 and 1970 in kelp forests at Palos Verdes and Point Loma near the rapidly growing cities of Los Angeles and San Diego. Discharge of domestic and industrial wastes and pollutants from the cities of Los Angeles and San Diego increased more than tenfold during this period (Foster and Schiel 2010). Sedimentation from coastal development and harbor expansion further reduced water quality in both areas. Such heightened activities in the coastal zone can adversely affect the reproduction, growth, and survival of microscopic stages of kelp by reducing availability of exposed hard substrate and light on the bottom and increasing concentrations of toxic chemicals (Devinny and Volse 1978, Deysher and Dean 1986, Schiff et al. 2000). Not surprisingly, dramatic declines in the canopy area of giant kelp occurred at Palos Verdes and Point Loma during this time. Recovery of the kelp canopies at both sites coincided with increases in water quality that resulted from improvements in sewage treatment and extension of the sewage outfall into deeper water (Foster and Schiel 2010).

The construction of artificial reefs has been used to mitigate for the loss of kelp forest habitat in the case where the stressors causing degradation were allowed to continue. The most prominent example of this is a large, artificial reef near San Clemente, California, that was constructed to compensate for the loss of kelp forest habitat caused by the operation of the San Onofre Nuclear Generating Station (Reed et al. 2006a; Elwany et al. 2011). This artificial reef was rapidly colonized by giant kelp and reef fish (Reed et al. 2004, Reed et al. 2006b) and supports populations of many kelp forest species similar to natural reefs in the region. Artificial reefs have also been used to transform soft-bottom habitats into hard-bottom areas in efforts to expand kelp habitat beyond its natural occurrence (Turner et al. 1969, Lewis and McKee 1989). The depth, topography, and bottom coverage of an artificial reef as well as its proximity to existing kelp forests are important determinants of the timing and extent of colonization by kelp and its ability to persist (Reed et al. 2004; Reed et al. 2006a). Although the technology for building artificial reefs that support kelp is largely developed, the large-scale transformation of soft-bottom habitats into hard-bottom kelp forests is expensive and involves trading resources associated with one habitat type for those associated with another. For these reasons, the pros and cons of using artificial reefs for habitat transformation should be carefully weighed and considered.

Invasive Species

Invasive (i.e., introduced) species are a much greater concern in coastal embayments with concentrated vessel traffic, like San Francisco Bay, than in ecosystems along the open coast. Nonetheless, a handful of more prominent algae and invertebrates have successfully invaded kelp forests and shallow rocky reef habitats along the coast of California (Page et al. 2006, Maloney et al. 2007, Williams and Smith 2007, Miller et al. 2011). The brown alga (*Sargassum muticum*) inhabits shallow (<10 meter) depths and ranges from British Columbia, Canada, the likely site of introduction, south to Baja California, Mexico. This species can inhibit the reestablishment of giant kelp where it has invaded after removal of giant kelp

(Ambrose and Nelson 1982). It also invaded former giant kelp forests at some sites after the 1982–1983 El Niño removed giant kelp, but the invader died out over four years as giant kelp recovered (Foster and Schiel 1993).

A more recently introduced congener, *Sargassum horneri* (formally *filicinum*), was first found in Long Beach Harbor on the southern California mainland and now occurs in kelp forests across several islands off southern California (Miller et al. 2011). Another recent invasive alga is *Undaria pinnatifida*, which was restricted to harbors until its recent discovery in kelp forests off Santa Catalina Island in southern California (Aguilar-Rosas et al. 2004, Thornber et al. 2004). Other less conspicuous invasive algae are more abundant in southern California than to the north (Miller et al. 2011 and Miller pers. comm.).

Most of the invasive invertebrates found in kelp forests tend to be inconspicuous species, including the bryzoan *Bugula neritina*, the colonial tunicate *Botryllus schlosseri*, a polychaete worm *Branchiosyllis exilis*, the tube-forming serpulid worm *Hydroides elegans*, and the amphipod *Monocorophium insidiosum*—all of which have been detected on natural reefs (Maloney et al. 2007). One conspicuous bryozoan invader in the genus *Watersipora* is likely a species complex (Mackie et al. 2012) and is growing increasingly abundant in at least one central California kelp forest adjacent to the Hopkins Marine Station in Monterey Bay. Although the invasive algae are starting to receive greater attention, the invertebrates are not, and the geographic distribution and rate of spread of all of these invaders is not being systematically monitored in kelp forests. Only in the case of *Sargassum muticum* have the ecological consequences of invasion in giant kelp forests been assessed.

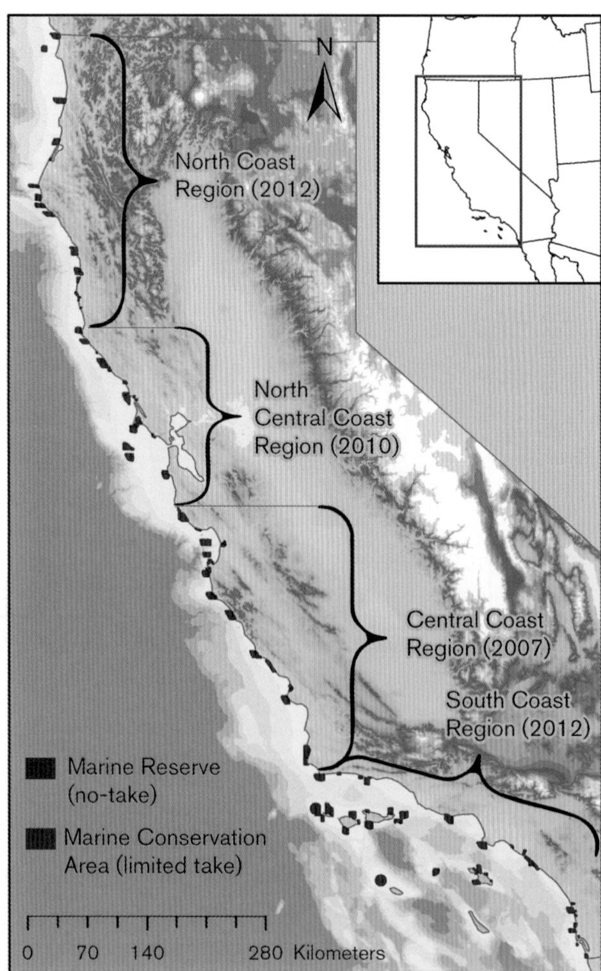

FIGURE 17.13 Map of the statewide network of marine protected areas along the coast of California. Red polygons indicate "no-take" marine reserves and blue polygons indicate marine conservation areas that allow take of some species (e.g., recreational fishing). Source: Illustration by Emily Saarman.

Ecosystem-based Management and Marine Protected Areas

The recent interest in more ecosystem-based approaches to fisheries management has become more tangible in kelp forest ecosystems in recent years. This is evidenced by the growing number of studies of oceanographic drivers of replenishment and dynamics of species fished from kelp forests (reviewed in Carr and Syms 2006, Caselle et al. 2010); the identification of critical habitat components, including giant kelp and bull kelp forests, for fished species; and a slowly growing understanding of the ecological function of fished species and the potential ecosystem-wide consequences of their removal (Tegner and Levin 1983, Dayton and Tegner 1998, Tegner and Dayton 2000, Steneck et al. 2002, Behrens and Lafferty 2004, Lafferty 2004). In the near future the ecosystem-based approach will turn more attention to better understanding the human dimensions of these nearshore fisheries and the factors sustaining these coupled social-ecological systems, especially in the face of a changing climate.

Because the surface canopy of giant kelp forests creates habitat for a community of invertebrates (Coyer 1985 and 1987, Bernstein and Jung 1979) and fish populations (Anderson 1994) and provides nursery habitat for juvenile fishes (Carr 1989, 1991, 1994, Singer 1985, Johnson 2006a, 2006b, Deza and Anderson 2010), a more ecosystem-based approach to managing kelp harvest considers these potential ecosystem-wide consequences (Springer et al. 2010). The sustainability of giant kelp harvest is based on its growth form; new fronds are propagated from the base of the plant, allowing rapid replacement of the harvested canopy. Moreover, the reproductive blades (SPOROPHYLLS) are located at the base of giant kelp plants, protecting them from harvest. Such is not the case for bull kelp. Removal of the surface canopy of bull kelp essentially removes the entire plant, including the reproductive blades, reducing the ability of a harvested forest to replenish itself (reviewed by Springer et al. 2010).

One of the most notable efforts toward ecosystem-based management of kelp forest ecosystems is the recent establishment of a statewide network of marine protected areas (MPAs) (Figure 17.13). Goals of the MPAs created by the Marine Life Protection Act include: (1) to protect of the natural diversity and abundance of marine life, and the structure, function, and integrity of marine ecosystems; (2) to help sustain, conserve, and protect marine life populations, including those of economic value, and rebuild those that are depleted; (3) to improve recreational, educational, and study opportunities provided by marine ecosystems that are subject to minimal human disturbance, and to manage these uses in a manner consistent with protecting biodiversity; (4) to protect marine natural heritage, including protection of representative and unique marine life habitats in California waters for their intrinsic value; and (5) to ensure that the state's MPAs are designed and managed, to the extent possible, as a network.

Because of the greater dispersal potential of young organisms, populations in MPAs are more connected to populations outside of protected areas than are populations in terrestrial reserves (Carr et al. 2003). Kelp forests are one of thirteen ecosystems specified for protection by MPAs in California, and the network includes kelp forests distributed across state waters (Saarman et al. 2013). The proportion of kelp forests in each of four regions of the coast in no-take reserves and all MPAs combined varies from 5% and 8% on the North Coast to 28% and 44% on the Central Coast, respectively (Table 17.2; Gleason et al. 2013). Not only are these MPAs likely to contribute to ecosystem-wide conservation (e.g., the functional roles of harvested species and curtailing habitat impacts associated with some fishing methods), but in combination with coupled ecological and oceanographic monitoring programs they also serve as valuable tools for fisheries management (e.g., Schroeter et al. 2001, Babcock and MacCall 2011) and for assessing the combined effects of fishing and climate change on kelp forest ecosystems (Carr et al. 2011). In addition, a federally designated MPA, the Monterey Bay National Marine Sanctuary, contributes to the protection of reef habitats that support kelp forests along the coast of central California. Separate from these management roles, reserves contribute to the aesthetic values of coastal marine ecosystems like their terrestrial counterparts (e.g., national parks and wildlife refuges).

TABLE 17.2

Proportion of kelp forests within no-take state marine reserves and all marine protected areas (MPAs) combined

Includes both reserves and conservation areas that allow limited take of specified species

Regions	Proportion of kelp forests in no-take reserves	Proportion of kelp forests in all MPAs
North Coast	5.0%	8.4%
North Central Coast	15.4%	39.4%
Central Coast	27.7%	44.1%
South Coast	9.4%	13.2%
Statewide	13.3%	21.9%

SOURCE: Modified from Gleason et al. 2013.

Impending Challenges

California's kelp forest ecosystems face three overarching challenges, each of which is a consequence of ever-growing coastal human populations and a changing global climate. Growing coastal populations and global demands on California's highly productive coastal agriculture look to the ocean as a substantial means of replacing or augmenting dwindling freshwater sources. As coastal power stations close or shift to onshore cooling systems, growing numbers of desalination facilities will continue to extract seawater and the larvae of marine organisms that occupy those waters, though likely at lower rates than historically observed for power stations. Simultaneously, agricultural and urban runoff and wastewater discharge continue to threaten coastal water quality in various ways including eutrophication. Careful management of water withdrawals from and discharge into the coastal ocean so as not to impair the productivity of coastal marine ecosystems will be paramount. Likewise, growing demands for protein will increase pressure on the many existing and emerging fisheries associated with kelp forests.

Simultaneously, climate models predict changes in the magnitude, timing, and distribution of coastal upwelling, which fuels kelp forest productivity (e.g., Snyder et al. 2003, Diffenbaugh et al. 2004). Predicted increases in surface ocean temperatures and associated low nutrients have the potential to shift the southern limit of giant kelp along the mainland from central Pacific Baja to somewhere between Santa Barbara and Los Angeles. Giant kelp might even disappear from the southern islands, from Santa Catalina Island south, that are little-influenced by the cooler California Current. Other coastal manifestations of climate and atmospheric change include hypoxia and ocean acidification, both of which are directly linked to upwelling processes (Grantham et al. 2004). How anthropogenic impacts interact with a changing coastal ocean will influence the ability of kelp forests, like other coastal marine ecosystems, to generate the services we have come to rely upon and expect. The great challenge is to innovate new approaches to understanding and managing the social and ecological relationships that underpin the sustainability and resilience of California's remarkable kelp forest ecosystems and the coastal communities that benefit so much from them.

Summary

Kelp forests are among the most productive and species-rich ecosystems in temperate latitudes. Much like terrestrial forests, kelp forests are often layered with tall, canopy-forming kelps extending from the seafloor to the water's surface (as much as 40 meters) and a variety of shorter algal species that constitute a layered understory. Their complex physical structure creates habitat, food, and refuge for a diverse array of organisms, including a number of commercially and recreationally important fish and invertebrate species. Like terrestrial forests, kelp forests modify the physical environment by reducing light penetration to the seafloor and reducing wave action and current velocity.

The species of kelp, other algae, fishes, and invertebrates that constitute kelp forest communities vary latitudinally, with marked differences among southern, central, and northern California. Within each of these regions the distribution of kelp forests is patchy and determined by the availability of rocky substratum, light, water temperature, exposure to waves, and grazers. The extent and density of kelp forests varies among years, influenced by oceanographic conditions such as El Niños and La Niñas. The magnitude and duration of effects of these disturbances vary geographically and are most pronounced in southern California.

Complex kelp forest food webs are fueled by the great primary and detrital production of the kelps and other algae as well as by a continuous influx of plankton. These sources of production support a phenomenal diversity of invertebrates including herbivores, detritivores, planktivores, and carnivores. In turn, these species are consumed by a great variety of carnivorous invertebrates and fishes. In strong contrast to terrestrial forest ecosystems, the primary producers (algae) and consumers (sessile invertebrates) compete directly for limited space on the rocky substratum. The strength of these various species interactions (competition, predation, mutualisms) varies geographically with change in the species composition of the forest community. Notably, sea urchins, important grazers of structure-forming kelps, show dramatically different patterns of abundance in southern, central, and northern California. In southern and northern California, intense grazing by large numbers of urchins can eliminate kelp from localized areas. In central California, where greater numbers of sea otters occur, these voracious predators greatly diminish urchin abundance and their impact on kelp.

The great diversity and productivity of species associated with shallow rocky reefs and kelp forests support a variety of human activities and ecosystem services. Nonconsumptive services include tourism, shoreline protection, and spiritual and cultural values that extend back to the period of indigenous Californians. Consumptive services include economically and culturally significant recreational and commercial fisheries and, historically, the harvest of kelp for a variety of uses. Because of their close proximity to shore, kelp forest ecosystems are vulnerable to a number of anthropogenic threats including diminished water quality (e.g., sedimentation, turbidity, contaminants, shore-based water intake and discharge), direct and indirect effects of fishing, invasive species, and a changing global atmosphere and climate. Climate change is manifest in kelp forests in a variety of ways, including changes in the magnitude and frequency of major storm events, sea surface temperature, and the magnitude and location of coastal upwelling—all of which determine nutrient availability and the productivity of the forests. Additional climate-related impacts also associated with coastal upwelling include hypoxia and ocean acidification.

While the climate-related threats to kelp forests are relatively intractable to local management, California is taking bold steps to address threats posed by fisheries and water quality. Examples include a recently established statewide network of marine protected areas and more stringent water-quality regulations. It is hoped that these management actions will protect the structural and functional integrity of kelp forest ecosystems, enhancing their resistance and resilience to the multitude of potential perturbations associated with a changing global climate.

Acknowledgments

We thank Emily Saarman and Rodrigo Beas for support on graphics and valuable comments on this chapter. Michael Foster and Steven Lonhart provided valuable comments and suggested edits. Many of the photographic images were provided to us by the Ronald H. McPeak, Underwater and Coastal California Photographs, 1965–1999 (Mss 292) Department of Special Collections, Davidson Library, University of California–Santa Barbara. Additional photographic images were provided by Steven Lonhart and Chad King of the Monterey Bay National Marine Sanctuary. Financial support was provided by the National Science Foundation's Long-Term Ecological Research Program (OCE-1232779) to DCR and by NSF-NOAA NMFS Comparative Assessment of Marine Ecosystem Organization (CAMEO-1041454) to MHC. This is contribution number 445 by the Partnership for Interdisciplinary Studies of Coastal Oceans (PISCO), a Long-Term Ecological Consortium funded by the David and Lucile Packard Foundation.

Recommended Reading

Dayton, P. K. 1985. Ecology of kelp communities. Annual Review of Ecology and Systematics 16:215–246.

Graham, M. H., B. S. Halpern, and M. H. Carr. 2008. Diversity and dynamics of California subtidal kelp forests. Pages 103–134 in T. R. McClanahan and G. M. Branch, editors. Food Webs and the Dynamics of Marine Reefs. Oxford University Press, New York, New York.

Graham, M. H., J. A. Vasquez, and A. H. Buschmann. 2007. Global ecology of the giant kelp Macrocystis: From ecotypes to ecosystems. Oceanography and Marine Biology: An Annual Review 45:39–88.

North, W. J. 1971. The biology of giant kelp beds (*Macrocystis*) in California. Nova Hedwegia 32:1–600.

Schiel, D. R., and Foster, M.S. 2015. The biology and ecology of giant kelp forests. University of California Press, Berkeley, California.

———. 2006. The population biology of large brown seaweeds: Ecological consequences of multiphase life histories in dynamic coastal environments. Annual Review of Ecology, Evolution, and Systematics 37:343–72.

———. 1986. The structure of subtidal algal stands in temperate waters. Oceanography and Marine Biology: An Annual Review 24:265–307.

Springer, Y. P., C. G. Hays, M. H. Carr, and M. R. Mackey. 2010. Towards ecosystem-based management of marine macroalgae: The bull kelp, *Nereocystis luetkeana*. Oceanography and Marine Biology: An Annual Review 48:1–42.

Glossary

ALLOCTHONOUS Input of material to a system or place that originated elsewhere. For example, the influx of plankton to a forest or reef, the influx of drift kelp to a submarine canyon or sandy beach.

AUTOGENIC ECOSYSTEM ENGINEER An organism that modifies the environment by its presence and growth. For example, the presence of kelp creates habitat for other organisms, attenuates light, and alters water flow on a reef.

BIOGENIC HABITAT Physical habitat structure created by living organisms such as algae, corals, sponges, and the shells of sessile invertebrates (e.g., large barnacles, scallops).

BLADE A flat or leaflike multicellular, photosynthetic structure attached to the stipe of an alga.

COASTAL UPWELLING The coupled atmospheric and oceanographic process by which coastal winds cause surface waters to move offshore and are replaced by deeper, cooler, nutrient-rich waters from offshore.

CORALLINE ALGAE Red algae that are hardened by calcareous (containing calcium carbonate) deposits. They can be articulated (branched) or crustose (thin crusts attached to hard surfaces).

ECOSYSTEM SERVICES The benefits obtained by people from ecosystems, such as provisioning resources for consumption (e.g., fish), regulating systems (e.g., control of climate), supporting systems (e.g., nutrient cycling), and cultural benefits (e.g., recreation).

EPIBIONT An organism that lives on the surface of another organism and is generally harmless to the host.

EPIPHYTES A plant that grows on another plant and is not parasitic.

FROND The photosynthetic structure of an alga comprised of a stipe and one or more blades.

GAMETOPHYTE The multicellular, independently-living stage in the life cycle of an alga with alternating generations that produces gametes (haploid eggs or sperm). For kelps, this stage is often microscopic.

HOLDFAST The structure that anchors an alga to rock, sand, or other substratum. It can be rootlike or disc-shaped in appearance.

KELP Marine algae generally of the order Laminariales, although sometimes considered to include another order of large brown algae, the Fucales).

MESOCOSM An experimental setup that mimics a portion of an ecosystem to allow testing of mechanistic hypotheses.

PHYCOCOLLOID Algal colloids (chemically modified sugar molecules) in the cell walls of many seaweeds. The three major phycocolloids are alginates, agars, and carrageenans.

PNEUMATOCYSTS Gas-filled organs on algae that provide the alga with buoyancy to enable it to extend vertically through the water column.

SESSILE An organism that is fixed in one place (nonmobile), such as a barnacle.

SPOROPHYLL The specialized reproductive blades on the sporophyte stage of an alga where spores are produced.

SPOROPHYTE The multicellular, independently-living stage in the life cycle of an alga that is diploid and produces haploid spores. For kelps, this is the macroscopic that creates forests.

STIPE A thickened, stemlike structure bearing other structures such as blades. The stipe of subcanopy species is short, but stipes of surface canopy–forming species are very long.

URCHIN BARRENS An area largely devoid of fleshy red and brown algae caused by extensive grazing by sea urchins. Such areas are characterized by high cover of coralline algae.

References

Abbott, I. A., and G. J. Hollenberg. 1976. Marine algae of California. Stanford University Press, Stanford, California.

Aguilar-Rosas R., L. Aguilar-Rosas, G. Avila-Serrano, and R. Marcos-Ramirez. 2004. First record of *Undaria pinnatifida* (Harvey) Suringar (Laminariales, Phaeophyta) on the Pacific coast of Mexico. Botanica Marina 47:255–258.

Airoldi, L., and M. W. Beck. 2007. Loss, status, and trends for coastal marine habitats of Europe. Oceanography and Marine Biology: An Annual Review 45:345–405.

Ambrose, R. F. 1986. Effects of octopus predation on motile invertebrates in a rocky subtidal community. Marine Ecology Progress Series 30:261–273.

Ambrose, R. F., and B.V. Nelson. 1982. Inhibition of giant kelp recruitment by an introduced alga. Botanica Marina 25:265–267.

Ambrose, R. F., R. J. Schmitt, and C. W. Osenberg. 1996. Predicted and observed environmental impacts: Can we foretell ecological change? Pages 345–369 in R. J. Schmitt and C. W. Osenberg. Detecting ecological impacts: Concepts and applications in coastal habitats. Academic Press, San Diego, California.

Amsler, C. D., and M. Neushul. 1989. Diel periodicity of spore release from the kelp *Nereocystis luetkeana* (Mertens) Postels et Ruprecht. Journal of Experimental Marine Biology and Ecology 134:117–127.

Anderson, T. W. 2001. Predator responses, prey refuges, and density dependent mortality of a marine fish. Ecology 82:245–257.

———. 1994. Role of macroalgal structure in the distribution and abundance of a temperate reef fish. Marine Ecology Progress Series 113:279–290.

Arkema, K. K. 2009. Flow-mediated feeding in the field: Consequences for the performance and abundance of a sessile marine invertebrate. Marine Ecology Progress Series 388: 207–220.

Arkema, K. K., D. C. Reed, and S. C. Schroeter. 2009. Direct and indirect effects of giant kelp determine benthic community structure and dynamics. Ecology 90:3126–3137.

Babcock, E. A., and A. D. MacCall. 2011. How useful is the ratio of fish density outside versus inside marine reserves as a metric for fishery management control rules? Canadian Journal of Fisheries and Aquatic Sciences 68:343–359.

Behrens, M., and K. Lafferty. 2004. Effects of marine reserves and urchin disease on southern Californian rocky reef communities. Marine Ecology Progress Series 279:129–139.

Bernstein, B. B., and N. Jung. 1979. Selective processes and coevolution in a kelp canopy community in southern California. Ecological Monographs 49:335–355.

Bestelmeyer, B. T., A. M. Ellison, W. R. Fraser, K. B. Gorman, S. J. Holbrook, C. M. Laney, M. D. Ohman, D. P. C. Peters, F. C. Pillsbury, A. Rassweiler, R. J. Schmitt, and S. Sharma. 2011. Analysis of abrupt transitions in ecological systems. Ecosphere 2:1–26.

Bray, R. N. 1981. Influence of water currents and zooplankton densities on daily foraging movements of blacksmith, *Chromis punctipinnis*, a planktivorous reef fish. U.S. Fishery Bulletin 78:829–841.

Bray, R. N., A. C. Miller, and G. G. Geesey. 1981. The fish connection: A trophic link between planktonic and rocky reef communities. Science 214:204–205.

Briggs, J. C. 1974. Marine zoogeography. McGraw Hill, New York, New York.

Broitman, B. R., and B. P. Kinlan. 2006. Spatial scales of benthic and pelagic producer biomass in a coastal upwelling ecosystem. Marine Ecology Progress Series 327:15–25.

Byrnes, J. E., D. C. Reed, B. J. Cardinale, K. C. Cavanaugh, S. J. Holbrook, and R. J. Schmitt. 2011. Climate driven increases in storm frequency simplify kelp forest food webs. Global Change Biology 17: 2513–2524.

Byrnes, J., J. J. Stachowicz, K. M. Hultgren, Randall Hughes, S. V Olyarnik, and C. S. Thornber. 2006. Predator diversity strengthens trophic cascades in kelp forests by modifying herbivore behaviour. Ecology Letters 9:61–71.

California Department of Fish and Wildlife (CDFW). 2002a. Nearshore Fisheries Management Plan. Chapter 2: Background. <http://www.dfg.ca.gov/marine/nfmp/>. Accessed April 15, 2012.

———. 2002b. Nearshore Fisheries Management Plan. Chapter 3: Management Measures for Sustainable Nearshore Fisheries. <http://www.dfg.ca.gov/marine/nfmp//>. Accessed April 15, 2012.

Carr, M. H. 1994. Effects of macroalgal dynamics on recruitment of a temperate reef fish. Ecology 75:1320–1333.

———. 1991. Habitat selection and recruitment of an assemblage of temperate zone reef fishes. Journal of Experimental Marine Biology and Ecology 146:113–137.

———. 1989. Effects of macroalgal assemblages on the recruitment of temperate zone reef fishes. Journal of Experimental Marine Biology and Ecology 126:59–76.

Carr, M. H., and C. Syms. 2006. Recruitment. Pages 411–427 in L. G. Allen, D. J. Pondella II, and M. H. Horn, editors. The Ecology of Marine Fishes: California and Adjacent Waters. University of California Press, Berkeley, and Los Angeles, California.

Carr, M. H., C. B. Woodson, O. M. Cheriton, D. Malone, M. A. McManus, and P. T. Raimondi. 2011. Knowledge through partnerships: Integrating marine protected area monitoring and ocean observing systems. Frontiers in Ecology and the Environment 9:342–350.

Carr, M. H., J. E. Neigel, J. A. Estes, S. J. Andelman, R. R. Warner, and J. L. Largier. 2003. Comparing marine and terrestrial ecosystems: Implications for the design of coastal marine reserves. Ecological Applications 13:S90–S107.

Carroll, J. C., J. M. Engle, J. A. Coyer, and R. F. Ambrose. 2000. Long-term changes and species interactions in a sea urchin-dominated community at Anacapa Island, California. D. R. Browne, K. L. Mitchell, and H. W. Chaney, editors. Pages 370–378 in Proceedings of the Fifth California Islands symposium.

Caselle, J. E., M. H. Carr, D. Malone, J. R. Wilson, and D. E. Wendt. 2010. Can we predict interannual and regional variation in delivery of pelagic juveniles to nearshore populations of rockfishes (genus *Sebastes*) using simple proxies of ocean conditions? California Cooperative Fisheries Investigations Reports 51:91–105.

Clarke, T. A. 1970. Territorial behavior and population dynamics of a pomacentrid fish, the Garibaldi, *Hypsypops rubicunda*. Ecological Monographs 40:189–212.

Clark R. P., M. S. Edwards, and M. S. Foster. 2004. Effects of shade from multiple kelp canopies on an understory algal assemblage. Marine Ecology Progress Series 267:107–119.

Costa, D. P., and G. L. Kooyman. 1982. Oxygen consumption, thermoregulation, and the effect of fur oiling and washing on the sea otter, *Enhydra lutris*. Canadian Journal of Zoology 60:2761–2767.

Cowen, R. K. 1986. Site-specific differences in the feeding ecology of the California sheephead, *Semicossyphus pulche* (Labridae). Environmental Biology of Fishes 16:193–203.

———. 1985. Large scale pattern of recruitment by the labrid, *Semicossyphus pulcher*: Causes and implications. Journal of Marine Research 43:719–742.

———. 1983. The effect of sheephead (*Semicossyphus pulcher*) predation on red sea urchin (*Strongylocentrotus franciscanus*) populations: An experimental analysis. Oecologia 58:249–255.

Cowen R. K., C. R. Agegian, and M.S. Foster. 1982. The maintenance of community structure in a central California giant kelp forest. Journal of Experimental Marine Biology and Ecology 64: 189–201.

Coyer, J. A. 1987. The mollusk assemblage associated with the fronds of giant kelp *Macrocystis pyrifera* at Santa Catalina Island, California, USA. Bulletin of the Southern California Academy of Sciences 85:129–138.

———. 1985. The invertebrate assemblage associated with the giant kelp *Macrocystis pyrifera* at Santa Catalina Island, California, USA: A general description with emphasis on amphipods, copepods, mysids, and shrimps. U.S. Fishery Bulletin 82:55–66.

Darwin, C. R. 1839. Journal of researches into the geology and natural history of the various countries visited by the H.M.S. *Beagle*. Henry Colburn, England.

Davenport, A. C., and T. W. Anderson. 2007. Positive indirect effects of reef fishes on kelp performance: The importance of mesograzers. Ecology 88:1548–1561.

Dayton, P. K. 1985. The ecology of kelp communities. Annual Review of Ecology, Evolution, and Systematics 16:215–245.

Dayton P. K. and M. J. Tegner. 1998. Sliding baselines, ghosts, and reduced expectations in kelp forest communities. Ecological Applications 8:309–322.

———. 1984. Catastrophic storms, El Niño, and patch stability in a southern California kelp community. Science 224:283–285.

———. 1989. Bottoms beneath troubled waters: Benthic impacts of the 1982-1984 El Niño in the temperate zone. Pages 433–472 in P. W. Glynn, editor. Global ecological consequences of the 1982–1983 El Niño Southern Oscillation. Elsevier Oceanography Series, No. 52. Amsterdam, The Netherlands.

Dayton, P. K, M. J. Tegner, P. E. Parnell, and P. B. Edwards. 1992. Temporal and spatial patterns of disturbance and recovery in a kelp forest community. Ecological Monographs 62:421–445.

Dayton, P. K., M. J. Tegner, P. B. Edwards, and K. L. Riser. 1999. Temporal and spatial scales of kelp demography: The role of oceanographic climate. Ecological Monographs 69:219–250.

Dayton, P. K., V. Currie, T. Gerrodette, B. D. Keller, R. Rosenthal, and D. Ven Tresca. 1984. Patch dynamics and stability of some California kelp communities. Ecological Monographs 54:253–289.

Dean, R. L., and J. H. Connell. 1987. Marine invertebrates in an algal succession. III. Mechanisms linking habitat complexity with diversity. Journal of Experimental Marine Biology and Ecology 109:249–273.

Dean, T. A. 1985. The temporal and spatial distribution of underwater quantum irradiation in a southern California kelp forest. Estuarine Coastal Shelf Science 21:835–844.

Dean, T. A., S. C. Schroeter, and J. D. Dixon. 1984. Effects of grazing by two species of sea urchins (*Strongylocentrotus franciscanus* and *Lytechinus anamesus*) on recruitment and survival of two species of kelp (*Macrocystis pyrifera* and *Pterygophora californica*). Marine Biology 78:301–313.

DeMartini, E. E., and D. A. Roberts. 1990. Effects of giant kelp (*Macrocystis*) on the density and abundance of fishes in a cobble-bottom kelp forest. Bulletin of Marine Science 46:287–300.

Demes, K. W., M. H. Graham, and T. S. Suskiewicz. 2009. Phenotypic plasticity reconciles incongruous molecular and morphological taxonomies: The giant kelp, *Macrocystis* (Laminariales, Phaeophyceae), is a monospecific genus. Journal of Phycology 45:1266–1269.

Devinny, J. S., and L. A. Volse. 1978. Effects of sediments on the development of *Macrocystis pyrifera* gametophytes. Marine Biology 48:343–348.

Deysher, L. E., and T. A. Dean. 1986. In situ recruitment of sporophytes of giant kelp Macrocystis pyrifera (L.) C.A. Agardh: Effects of physical factors. Journal of Experimental Marine Biology and Ecology 103:41–63.

Deza, A. A., and T. W. Anderson. 2010. Habitat fragmentation, patch size, and the recruitment and abundance of kelp forest fishes. Marine Ecology Progress Series 416:229–240.

Diffenbaugh, N. S., M. A. Snyder, and L. C. Sloan. 2004. Could CO_2-induced land-cover feedbacks alter near-shore upwelling regimes? Proceedings of the National Academy of Sciences 101:27–32.

Driver, H. E. 1939 Culture element distributions, northwest California. Volume 10. University of California Press, Berkeley, California.

Druehl, L. D. 1970. The pattern of Laminariales distribution in the northeast Pacific. Phycologia 9:237–247.

Dugan, J., D. Hubbard, H. Page, and J. Schimel. 2011. Marine macrophyte wrack inputs and dissolved nutrients in beach sands. Estuaries and Coasts 34: 839–850.

Dugan, J. E., D. M. Hubbard, M. McCrary, and M. Pierson. 2003. The response of macrofauna communities and shorebirds to macrophyte wrack subsidies on exposed beaches of southern California. Estuarine, Coastal, and Shelf Science 58S:133–148.

Duggins, D. O. 1983. Starfish predation and the creation of mosaic patterns in a kelp-dominated community. Ecology 64:1610–1619.

Ebeling, A. W., D. R. Laur, and R. J. Rowley. 1985. Severe storm disturbances and reversal of community structure in a southern California kelp forest. Marine Biology 84:287–294.

Eckman, J. E., D. O. Duggins, and A. T. Sewell. 1989. Ecology of understory kelp environments. I. Effects of kelp on flow and particle transport near the bottom. Journal of Experimental Marine Biology and Ecology 129:173–187.

Edwards, M. S. 2004. Estimating scale-dependency in disturbance impacts: El Niños and giant kelp forests in the northeast Pacific. Oecologia 138:436–447.

———. 1998. Effects of long-term kelp canopy exclusion on the abundance of the annual alga *Desmarestia ligulata* (Light F). Journal of Experimental Marine Biology and Ecology 228:309–326.

Edwards, M. S., and G. Hernández-Carmona. 2005. Delayed recovery of giant kelp near its southern range limit in the North Pacific following El Niño. Marine Biology 147:273–279.

Edwards, M. S., and J. A. Estes 2006. Catastrophe, recovery, and range limitation in NE Pacific kelp forests: A large-scale perspective. Marine Ecology Progress Series 320:79–87.

Elwany, M.H.S, C. Eaker, R. S. Grove, and J. Peeler. 2011. Construction of Wheeler North Reef at San Clemente, California. Journal of Coastal Research 59:266–272.

Fejtek, S. M., M. S. Edwards, and K. Y. Kim. 2011. Elk kelp, *Pelagophycus porra*, distribution limited due to susceptibility of microscopic stages to high light. Journal of Experimental Marine Biology and Ecology 396:194–201.

Foster, M. 1975. Algal succession in a *Macrocystis pyrifera* forest. Marine Biology 329:313–329.

Foster, M. S. 1982. The regulation of macroalgal associations in kelp forests. Pages 185–205 in L. M. Srivastava, editor. Synthetic and Degradative Processes in Marine Macrophytes. Walter de Gruyter & Co., Berlin, Germany.

Foster, M. S., and D. R. Schiel. 2010. Loss of predators and the collapse of southern California kelp forests: Alternatives, explanations and generalizations. Journal of Experimental Marine Biology and Ecology 393: 59–70.

———. 1993. Zonation, El Niño disturbance, and the dynamics of subtidal vegetation along a 30 m depth gradient in two giant kelp forests. Pages 151–162 in C. N. Battershill, D. R. Schiel, G. P. Jones, R. G. Creese, and A. B. MacDiarmid, editors. Proceedings of the Second International Temperate Reef Symposium. NIWA Marine, Wellington.

———. 1985. The ecology of giant kelp forests in California: A community profile. Biological Report, 85 (7.2). U.S. Fish and Wildlife Service, Washington, D.C.

Foster, M. S., D. C. Reed, M. H. Carr, P. K. Dayton, D. P. Malone, and J. S. Pearse. 2013. Kelp forests of California. Pages 115–132, M. A. Lang, R. L. Marinelli, S. Roberts and P. Taylor, editors. Research and Discoveries: The Revolution of Science through Scuba Proceedings. Smithsonian Contributions to the Marine Sciences, No. 39. Smithsonian Institution Scholarly Press, Washington, D.C.

Fram, J. P., H. L. Stewart, M. A. Brzezinski, B. Gaylord, D. C. Reed, S. L. Williams et al. 2008. Physical pathways and utilization of nitrate supply to the giant kelp, *Macrocystis pyrifera*. Limnology and Oceanography 53(4):1589–1603.

Gaines, S. D., and J. Roughgarden. 1987. Fish in offshore kelp forests affect recruitment to intertidal barnacle populations. Science 235:479–481.

Gaylord, B., D. C. Reed, L. Washburn, and P. T. Raimondi. 2004.

Physical-biological coupling in spore dispersal of kelp forest macroalgae. Journal of Marine Systems 49:19–39.

Gaylord, B., J. Rosman, D. Reed, and J. Koseff. 2007. Spatial patterns of flow and their modification within and around a giant kelp forest. Limnology and Oceanography 52:1838–1852.

Gaylord, B., K. J. Nickols, and L. Jurgens. 2012. Roles of transport and mixing processes in kelp forest ecology. Journal of Experimental Biology 215:997–1007.

Gaylord, B., M. W. Denny, and M. A. R. Koehl. 2008. Flow forces on seaweeds: Field evidence for roles of wave impingement and organism inertia. Biological Bulletin 215:295–308.

Gerard, V. A. 1984. The light environment in a giant kelp forest: Influence of *Macrocystis pyrifera* on spatial and temporal variability. Marine Biology 84:189–195.

———. 1982. Growth and utilization of internal nitrogen reserves by the giant kelp *Macrocystis pyrifera* in a low nitrogen environment. Marine Biology 66:27–35.

———. 1976. Some aspects of material dynamics and energy flow in a kelp forest in Monterey Bay, California. PhD dissertation. University of California, Santa Cruz.

Gleason, M., E. Fox, J. Vasques, E. Whiteman, S. Ashcraft, A. Frimodig, P. Serpa, E. T. Saarman, M. Caldwell, M. Miller-Henson, J. Kirlin, B. Ota, E. Pope, M. Weber, and K. Wiseman. 2013. Designing a statewide network of marine protected areas in California: Achievements, costs, lessons learned, and challenges ahead. Ocean and Coastal Management 74:90–101.

Gorman, D., B. D. Russell, and S. D. Connell. 2009. Land-to-sea connectivity: Linking human-derived terrestrial subsidies to subtidal habitat change on open rocky coasts. Ecological Applications 19:1114–1126.

Graham, M. H. 2004. Effects of local deforestation on the diversity and structure of southern California giant kelp forest food webs. Ecosystems 7:341–357.

———. 2003. Coupling propagule output to supply at the edge and interior of a giant kelp forest. Ecology 84:1250–1264.

———. 1997. Factors determining the upper limit of giant kelp, *Macrocystis pyrifera Agardh*, along the Monterey Peninsula, central California, U.S.A. Journal of Experimental Marine Biology and Ecology 218:127–149.

Graham, M. H., B. S. Halpern, and M. H. Carr. 2008. Diversity and dynamics of California subtidal kelp forests. Pages 103–134 in T. R. McClanahan and G. M. Branch, editors. Food Webs and the Dynamics of Marine Reefs. Oxford University Press, New York, New York.

Graham, M. H., C. Harrold, S. Lisin, K. Light, J. Watanabe, and M. S. Foster. 1997. Population dynamics of *Macrocystis pyrifera* along a wave exposure gradient. Marine Ecology Progress Series 148:269–279.

Graham, M. H., J. A. Vasquez, and A. H. Buschmann. 2007. Global ecology of the giant kelp *Macrocystis*: From ecotypes to ecosystems. Oceanography and Marine Biology: An Annual Review 45:39–88.

Grantham, B. A., F. Chan, K. J. Nielsen, D. S. Fox, J. A. Barth, A. Huyer, J. Lubchenco, and B. A. Menge. 2004. Upwelling-driven nearshore hypoxia signals ecosystem and oceanographic changes in the northeast Pacific. Nature 429:749–754.

Guenther, C. M., H. S. Lenihan, L. E. Grant, D. Lopez-Carr, and D. C. Reed. 2012. Trophic cascades induced by lobster fishing are not ubiquitous in southern California kelp forests. PloS One 7:e49396.

Hallacher, L. E., and D. A. Roberts. 1985. Differential utilization of space and food by the inshore rockfishes (Scorpaenidae: *Sebastes*) of Carmel Bay, California. Environmental Biology of Fishes 12:91–110.

Hamilton, S. L., J. E. Caselle, C. A. Lantz, T. L. Egloff, E. Kondo, S. D. Newsome, K. Loke-Smith, D. J. Pondella, K. A. Young, and C. G. Lowe. 2011. Extensive geographic and ontogenetic variation characterizes the trophic ecology of a temperate reef fish on southern California (USA) rocky reefs. Marine Ecology Progress Series 429:227–244.

Hamilton, S. L. , J. E. Caselle, D. Malone, and M. H. Carr. 2010. Incorporating biogeography into evaluations of the Channel Islands marine reserve network. Proceedings of the National Academy of Sciences 107:18272–1827.

Hamilton, S. L., S. D. Newsome, and J. E. Caselle. 2014. Niche expansion of a kelp forest predator recovering from intense commercial exploitation. Ecology. 95:164–172.

Harris, L. G., A. W. Ebeling, D. R. Laur, and R. J. Rowley. 1984. Community recovery after storm damage: A case of facilitation in primary succession. Science 224:1339–1338.

Harrold, C., and D. C. Reed. 1985. Food availability, sea urchin grazing, and kelp forest community structure. Ecology 66:1160–1169.

Harrold, C., and J. S. Pearse. 1987. The ecological role of echinoderms in kelp forests. Pages 137–233 in M. Jangoux and J. M. Lawrence, editors. Echinoderm studies, Volume 2. A. A. Balkema Press, Rotterdam, The Netherlands.

Harrold, C., J. Watanabe, and S. Lisin. 1988. Spatial variation in the structure of kelp forest communities along a wave exposure gradient. Marine Ecology 9:131–156.

Harrold, C., K. Light, and S. Lisin. 1998. Organic enrichment of submarine-canyon and continental-shelf benthic communities by macroalgal drift imported from nearshore kelp forests. Limnology and Oceanography 43:669–678.

Haynes W. W. 1954. American chemical industry, a history. D. Van Nostrand Co., New York, New York.

Heine, J. 1983. Seasonal productivity of two red algae in a central California kelp forest. Journal of Phycology 19:146–152.

Henkel, S. K., and S. N. Murray. 2007. Reproduction and morphological variation in southern California populations of the lower intertidal kelp *Egregia menziesii* (O. Laminariales). Journal of Phycology 43:242–255.

Hernández-Carmona, G., O. Garcia, D. Robledo, and M. Foster. 2000. Restoration techniques for *Macrocystis pyrifera* populations at the southern limit of their distribution in Mexico. Botanica Marina 43: 273–284.

Hernández-Carmona G., D. Robledo, and E. Serviere-Zaragoza. 2001. Effect of nutrient availability on *Macrocystis pyrifera* recruitment and survival near its southern limit off Baja California. Botanica Marina 44:221–229.

Hines, A. H. 1982. Coexistence in a kelp forest: Size, population dynamics, and resource partitioning in a guild of spider crabs (Brachyura, Majidae). Ecological Monographs 52:179–198.

Hines, A. H. and J. S. Pearse. 1982. Abalones, shells, and sea otters: Dynamics of prey populations in central California. Ecology 63:1547–1560.

Hixon, M. A. 2006. Competition. Pages 449–465 in L. G. Allen, D. J. Pondella II, and M. H. Horn, editors. The Ecology of Marine Fishes: California and Adjacent Waters. University of California Press, Berkeley, and Los Angeles, California.

Hobday, A. J. 2000a. Age of drifting *Macrocystis pyrifera* (L.) C. Agardh rafts in the Southern California Bight. Journal of Experimental Marine Biology and Ecology 253:97–114.

———. 2000b. Persistence and transport of fauna on drifting kelp (*Macrocystis pyrifera* (L.) C. Agardh) rafts in the Southern California Bight. Journal of Experimental Marine Biology and Ecology 253:75–96.

Hobson, E. S., and J. R. Chess. 1976. Trophic interactions among fishes and zooplankters near shore at Santa Catalina Island, California. Fishery Bulletin 74:567–598.

Holbrook, S. J., and R. J. Schmitt. 1988. The combined effects of predation risk and food reward on patch selection. Ecology 69:125–134.

———. 1984. Experimental analyses of patch selection by foraging black surfperch (*Embiotoca jacksoni* Agazzi). Journal of Experimental Marine Biology and Ecology 79:39–64.

Holbrook, S. J, R. J. Schmitt, and J. S. Stephens Jr. 1997. Changes in an assemblage of temperate reef fishes associated with a climate shift. Ecological Applications 7:1299–1310.

Hymanson, Z. P., D. C. Reed, M. S. Foster, and J. W. Carter. 1990. The validity of using morphological characteristics as predictors of age in the kelp *Pterygophora californica* (Laminariales, Phaeophyta). Marine Ecology Progress Series 59:295–304.

Jackson, G. A. 1998. Currents in the high drag environment of a coastal kelp stand off California. Continental Shelf Research 17:1913–28.

———. 1984. Internal wave attenuation by coastal kelp stands. Journal of Physical Oceanography 14:1300–1306.

———. 1977. Nutrients and production of giant kelp, *Macrocystis pyrifera*, off southern California. Limnology and Oceanography 22: 979–995.

Jackson G. A, and C. D. Winant. 1983. Effect of a kelp forest on coastal currents. Continental Shelf Research 20:75–80.

Jones, C. G., J. H. Lawton, and M. Shachak. 1994. Organisms as ecosystem engineers. Oikos 69:373–386.
Johnson, D. W. 2006a. Density dependence in marine fish revealed at small and large spatial scales. Ecology 87:319–325.
———. 2006b. Predation, habitat complexity, and variation in density-dependent mortality of temperate reef fishes. Ecology 87:1179–1188.
Kain (Jones), J. M. 1963. Aspects of the biology of *Laminaria hyperborea* II. Age, weight, and length. Journal of the Marine Biological Association of the United Kingdom 43:129–151.
Karpov, K., P. L. Haaker, I. Taniguchi, and L. Rogers-Bennett. 2000. Serial depletion and the collapse of the California abalone fishery. Canadian Special Publication Fisheries and Aquatic Sciences 130:11–24.
Kastendiek, J. E. 1982. Factors determining the distribution of the sea pansy *Renilla kollikeri*, in a subtidal sand-bottom habitat. Oecologia 52:340–347.
Kenner, M. C. 1992. Population dynamics of the sea urchin *Strongylocentrotus purpuratus* in a central California kelp forest: Recruitment, mortality, growth, and diet. Marine Biology 112:107–118.
Kingsford, M. J. 1995. Drift algae: A contribution to near-shore habitat complexity in the pelagic environment and an attractant for fish. Marine Ecology Progress Series 116:297–301.
———. 1993. Biotic and abiotic structure in the pelagic environment: Importance to small fishes. Bulletin of Marine Science 53:393–415.
Kim, S. L. 1992. The role of drift kelp in the population ecology of a *Diopatra ornata* Moore (Polychaeta: Onuphidae) ecotone. Journal of Experimental Marine Biology and Ecology. 156:253–272.
Ladah, L. B., J. A. Zertuche-Gonzalez, and G. Hernandez-Carmona. 1999. Giant kelp (*Macrocystis pyrifera*, Phaeophyceae) recruitment near its southern limit in Baja California after mass disappearance during ENSO 1997–1998. Journal of Phycology 35:1106–1112.
Lafferty, K. D. 2004. Fishing for lobsters indirectly increases epidemics in sea urchins. Ecological Applications 14:1566–1573.
Landberg, L. 1965. The Chumash Indians of southern California. No. 19. Southwest Museum, Los Angeles, California.
Larson, R. J. 1980a. Competition, habitat selection, and the bathymetric segregation of two rockfish (*Sebastes*) species. Ecological Monograph 50:221–239.
———. 1980b. Influence of territoriality on adult density in two rockfishes of the genus *Sebastes*. Marine Biology 58:123–132.
Larson, R. J., and E. E. DeMartini. 1984. Abundance and vertical distribution of fishes in a cobble-bottom kelp forest off San Onofre, California. U.S. Fishery Bulletin 82:37–53.
Leachman, J. C. 1921. Indian uses of kelp. Scientific American Monthly 212:137–140.
Leet, W. S., C. M. Dewees, and C. W. Haugen. 1992. California's living marine resources and their utilization. Sea Grant Extension Publication UCSGEP-92-12. Davis, California.
Leighton, D. L. 1971. Grazing activities of benthic invertebrates in southern California kelp beds. Nova Hedwigia 32:421–453.
———. 1966. Studies of food preference in algivorous invertebrates of southern California kelp beds. Pacific Science 20:104–113.
Leighton, D. L., L. G. Jones, and W. J. North. 1966. Ecological relationships between giant kelp and sea urchins in southern California. Pages 141–153 in E. G. Young and J. L. McLachlan, editors. Proceedings of the Fifth International Seaweed Symposium. Pergamon Press: New York.
Lewis, R. D., and K. K. McKee. 1989. A guide to the artificial reefs of southern California. State of California Resources Agency. Department of Fish and Game, Sacramento, California.
Lindeberg, M. R., and S. C. Lindstrom. 2012. Field guide to seaweeds of Alaska. University of Chicago Press, Chicago, Illinois.
Lonhart, S. I., and J. W. Tupen. 2001. Recent range extensions of twelve marine invertebrates: The role of El Niño and other mechanisms in southern and central California. Bulletin of the Southern California Academy of Sciences 100:238–248.
Love, M. S., J. E. Caselle, and W. Van Buskirk. 1998. A severe decline in the commercial passenger fishing vessel rockfish (*Sebastes spp.*) catch in the Southern California Bight, 1980–1996. California Cooperative Fisheries Reports 39:180–195.
Love, M. S., M. H. Carr, and L. J. Haldorson. 1991. The ecology of substrate-associated juveniles of the genus *Sebastes*. Environmental Biology of Fishes 30:225–243.
Love, M. S., M. Yoklavich, and L. Thorsteinson. 2002. The rockfishes of the northeast Pacific. University of California Press, Berkeley, California.
Lowry, L. F., and J. S. Pearse 1974. Abalones and sea urchins in an area inhabited by sea otters. Marine Biology 23:213–219.
Mackie, J. A., J. A. Darling, and J. B. Geller. 2012. Ecology of cryptic invasions: Latitudinal segregation among Watersipora (Bryozoa) species. Scientific Reports 2(871):1–10.
Maloney, E., R. Fairey, A. Lyman, Z. Walton, and M. Sigala. 2007. Introduced aquatic species in California's open coastal waters—2007. Final Report. California Department of Fish and Game, Sacramento, California.
Matson, P. G., and M. S. Edwards. 2007. Effects of ocean temperature on the southern range limits of two understory kelps, *Pterygophora californica* and *Eisenia arborea*, at multiple life-stages. Marine Biology 151:1941–1949.
McLean, J. H. 1962. Sublittoral ecology of kelp beds of the open coast near Carmel, California. Biological Bulletin (Woods Hole) 122:95–114.
Mead, G. R. 1976. The ethnobotany of the California Indians, a compendium of the plants, their uses. University of Northern Colorado, Greeley, Colorado.
Meistrell, J. C., and D. E. Montague. 1983. Waste disposal in southern California and its effects on the rocky subtidal habitat. Pages 84–102 in W. Bascom, editor. The effects of waste disposal on kelp communities. Southern California Coastal Water Research Project, Long Beach, California.
Miller, D. J., and J. J. Geibel. 1973. Summary of blue rockfish and lingcod life histories; a reef ecology study; and giant kelp, *Macrocystis pyrifera*, experiments in Monterey Bay, California. California Department of Fish and Game, Sacramento, California.
Miller, K. A., and H. A. Dorr. 1994. Natural history of mainland and island populations of the deep water elk kelp Pelagophycus (Laminariales, Phaeophyta): How many species? Pages 59–70 in W. L. Halvorson and G. J. Maender, editors. Fourth California Islands Symposium: Update on the Status of Resources. Santa Barbara Museum of Natural History, Santa Barbara, California.
Miller, K. A., and J. A. Estes. 1989. Western range extension for *Nereocystis luetkeana* in the North Pacific Ocean. Botanica Marina 32:535–538.
Miller, K. A., E. Alar-Rosas, and F. F. Pedroche. 2011. Review of non-native seaweeds from California, USA, and Baja California, Mexico. Hydrobiológica 21:365–379.
Miller, K. A., J. L. Olsen, and W. T. Stam. 2000. Genetic divergence correlates with morphological and ecological subdivision in the deep-water elk kelp, *Pelagophycus porra* (Phaeophyceae). Journal of Phycology 36:862–870.
Moitoza, D. J., and D. W. Phillips. 1979. Prey defense, predator preference, and nonrandom diet: The interactions between *Pycnopodia helianthoides* and two species of sea urchins. Marine Biology 53:299–304.
Morse, A.N.C., and D. E. Morse. 1984. Recruitment and metamorphosis of Haliotis larvae are induced by molecules uniquely available at the surfaces of crustose red algae. Journal of Experimental Marine Biology and Ecology 75:191–215.
Morton, D. N., and T. W. Anderson. 2013. Spatial patterns of invertebrate settlement in giant kelp forests. Marine Ecology Progress Series 485:75–89.
Neushul, P. 1987. Energy from marine biomass: The historical record. Pages 1–37 in K. T. Bird and P. H. Benson, editors. Seaweed Cultivation for Renewable Resources. Elsevier Science Publishers B. V., Amsterdam.
Neushul, P. 1989. Seaweed for war: California's World War I kelp industry. Technology and Culture 30:561–583.
Neushel, M. 1963. Studies on the giant kelp, *Macrocystis*. 2. Reproduction. American Journal of Botany 50:354–359.
North, W. J. 1976. Aquacultural techniques for creating and restoring beds of giant kelp, *Macrocystis* spp. Journal of the Fisheries Research Board of Canada 33:1015–1023.
———, editor. 1971. The biology of giant kelp beds (*Macrocystis*) in California. Nova Hedwegia 32:1–600.
North, W. J., M. Neushul, and K. A. Clendenning. 1964. Successive biological changes observed in a marine cove exposed to a large

spillage of mineral oil. Pages 335–354 in Pollution marines par les produits petroliers. Symposium de Monaco, Monaco.

Okamoto, D. K., R. J. Schmitt, S. J. Holbrook, and D. C. Reed. 2012. Fluctuations in food supply drive recruitment variation in a marine fish. Proceedings of the Royal Society Biological Sciences 279:4542–4550.

Page, H. M., J. E. Dugan, C. S. Culver, and J. C. Hoesterey. 2006. Exotic invertebrate species on offshore oil platforms. Marine Ecology Progress Series 325:101–107.

Paine, R. 1986. Benthic community-water column coupling during the 1982–1983 El Niño. Are community changes at high latitudes attributable to cause or coincidence? Limnology and Oceanography 31:351–360.

Pearse, J. S., and A. H. Hines. 1987. Long-term population dynamics of sea urchins in a central California kelp forest: Rare recruitment and rapid decline. Marine Ecology Progress Series 39:275–283.

———. 1979. Expansion of a central California kelp forest following mass mortality of sea urchins. Marine Biology 51:83–91.

Rassweiler, A. R., R. J. Schmitt, and S. J. Holbrook. 2010. Triggers and maintenance of multiple shifts in the state of a natural community. Oecologia 164:489–498.

Riedman, M. L., and J. A. Estes. 1990. The sea otter *Enhydra lutris*: Behavior, ecology, and natural history. U.S. Fish and Wildlife Service Biological Report 90:1–126.

Reed, D. C. 1990a. An experimental evaluation of density dependence in a subtidal algal population. Ecology 71:2286–2296.

———. 1990b. The effects of variable settlement and early competition on patterns of kelp recruitment. Ecology 71:776–87.

Reed, D. C., and M. S. Foster. 1984. The effects of canopy shading on algal recruitment and growth in a giant kelp (*Macrocystis pyrifera*) forest. Ecology 65:937–948.

Reed, D. C., A. Rassweiler, M. H. Carr, K. C., Cavanaugh, D. P. Malone, and D. A. Siegel. 2011. Wave disturbance overwhelms top-down and bottom-up control of primary production in California kelp forests. Ecology 92:2108–2116.

Reed, D. C., S. C. Schroeter, and D. Huang. 2006a. An experimental investigation of the use of artificial reefs to mitigate the loss of giant kelp forest habitat. A case study of the San Onofre Nuclear Generating Station's artificial reef project. California Sea Grant College Program Publication No. T-058. San Diego, California.

Reed, D.C, S. C. Schroeter, D. Huang, T. W. Anderson, and R. F. Ambrose. 2006b. Quantitative assessment of different artificial reef designs in mitigating losses to kelp forest fishes. Bulletin of Marine Science 78:133–150.

Reed, D. C., S. C. Schroeter, and P. T. Raimondi. 2004. Spore supply and habitat availability as sources of recruitment limitation in giant kelp. Journal of Phycology 40:275–284.

Revell, D. L., J. E. Dugan, and D. M. Hubbard. 2011. Physical and ecological responses of sandy beaches to the 1997–98 El Niño. Journal of Coastal Research 27:718–730.

Riedman, M. L., and J. A. Estes. 1988. A review of the history, distribution, and foraging ecology of sea otters. Pages 4–21in G. R. VanBlaricom and J. A. Estes, editors. The community ecology of sea otters. Springer-Verlag, Berlin, Germany.

Robles, C. 1987. Predator foraging characteristics and prey population structure on a sheltered shore. Ecology 68:1502–1514.

Robles, C., and J. Robb. 1993. Varied carnivore effects and the prevalence of intertidal algal turfs. Journal of Experimental Marine Biology and Ecology 166:65–91.

Roemmich, D., and J. McGowan. 1995. Climatic warming and the decline of zooplankton in the California Current. Science 267:1324–1326.

Rosenthal, R. J., W. D. Clarke, and P. K. Dayton. 1974. Ecology and natural history of a stand of giant kelp, *Macrocystis pyrifera*, off Del-Mar, California. U.S. Fishery Bulletin 72:670–684.

Rosman, J. H., J. R. Koseff, S. G. Monismith, and J. Grover. 2007. A field investigation into the effects of a kelp forest (*Macrocystis pyrifera*) on coastal hydrodynamics and transport. Journal of Geophysical Research: Oceans 112(C2):1–16. Rosman, J. H., S. G. Monismith, M. W. Denny, and J. R. Koseff. 2010. Currents and turbulence within a kelp forest (*Macrocystis pyrifera*): Insights from a dynamically scaled laboratory model. Limnology and Oceanography 55:1145–1158.

Saarman, E. T., M. Gleason, J. Ugoretz, S. Airamé, M. H. Carr, E. Fox, A. Frimodig, T. Mason, and J. Vasques. 2013. The role of science in supporting marine protected area network planning and design in California. Ocean and Coastal Management 74:45–56.

Scagel, R. F. 1947. An investigation on marine plants near Hardy Bay, B.C. Provincial Department of Fisheries. Report 1, Victoria, British Columbia, Canada.

Schiel, D. R., and M. S. Foster. 2015. The biology and ecology of giant kelp forests. University of California Press, Berkeley, California.

———. 2006. The population biology of large brown seaweeds: Ecological consequences of multiphase life histories in dynamic coastal environments. Annual Review of Ecology, Evolution, and Systematics. 37:343–372.

———. 1992. Restoring kelp forests. Pages 279–342 in G. W. Thayer, editors. Restoring the Nation's Marine Environment. Maryland Sea Grant, College Park, Maryland.

———. 1986. The structure of subtidal algal stands in temperate waters. Oceanography and Marine Biology: An Annual Review 24:265–307.

Schiel, D. R., J. R. Steinbeck, and M. S. Foster. 2004. Ten years of induced ocean warming causes comprehensive changes in marine benthic communities. Ecology 85:1833–1839.

Schiff, K. C., M. J. Allen, E. Y. Zeng, and S. M. Bay. 2000. Southern California Marine Pollution Bulletin 1:76–93.

Schmitt, R. J. 1996. Exploitation competition in mobile grazers: Tradeoffs in use of a limited resource. Ecology 77:408–425.

———. 1987. Indirect interactions between prey: Apparent competition, predator aggregation, and habitat segregation. Ecology 68:1887–1897.

———. 1985. Competitive interactions of two mobile prey species in a patchy environment. Ecology 66:950–958.

———. 1982. Consequences of dissimilar defenses against predation in a subtidal marine community. Ecology 63:1588–1601.

Schmitt, R. J., and S. J. Holbrook. 1990. Contrasting effects of giant kelp on dynamics of surfperch populations. Oecologia 84:419–429.

Schroeter, S. C., D. C. Reed, D. J. Kushner, J. A. Estes, and D. S. Ono. 2001. The use of marine reserves in evaluating the dive fishery for the warty sea cucumber (*Prastichopus parvimensis*) in California, U.S.A. Canadian Journal of Fisheries and Aquatic Sciences 58:1773–1781.

Seymour, R. J., M. J. Tegner, P. K. Dayton, and P. E. Parnell. 1989. Storm wave induced mortality of giant kelp, *Macrocystis pyrifera*, in southern California. Estuarine, Coastal and Shelf Science 28:277–292.

Shepherd, S. A., J. E. Watson, H.B.S. Womersley, and J. M. Carey. 2009. Long-term changes in macroalgal assemblages after increased sedimentation and turbidity in Western Port, Victoria, Australia. Botanica Marina 52:195–206.

Singer, M. M. 1985. Food habits of juvenile rockfishes (*Sebastes*) in a central California kelp forest. U.S. Fishery Bulletin 83:531–541.

Snyder, M. A., L. C. Sloan, N. S. Diffenbaugh, and J. L. Bell. 2003. Future climate change and upwelling in the California Current. Geophysical Research Letters 1823. <doi:10.1029/2003GL017647>.

Spalding, H., M. S. Foster, and J. N. Heine. 2003. Composition, distribution, and abundance of deep-water (>30 m) macroalgae in central California. Journal of Phycology 39:273–284.

Springer, Y. P., C. G. Hays, M. H. Carr, and M. R. Mackey. 2010. Towards ecosystem-based management of marine macroalgae: The bull kelp, *Nereocystis luetkeana*. Oceanography and Marine Biology: An Annual Review 48:1–42.

Starr, R. M., J. M. Cope, and L. A. Kerr. 2002. Trends in fisheries and fishery resources associated with the Monterey Bay National Marine Sanctuary from 1981–2000. California Sea Grant College Program University of California, San Diego, La Jolla, California. <http://www.montereybay.noaa.gov/research/techreports/fishery trends.pdf>. Accessed May 20, 2012.

Steele, M. A., and T. W. Anderson. 2006. The role of predation in the ecology of California's marine fishes. Pages 428–448 in L. G. Allen, D. J. Pondella II, and M. H. Horn, editors. The Ecology of Marine Fishes: California and Adjacent Waters. University of California Press, Berkeley, and Los Angeles, California.

Steneck, R. S., M. H. Graham, B. J. Bourque, D. Corbett, J. M. Erlandson, J. A. Estes, and M. J. Tegner. 2002. Kelp forest ecosystems: Biodiversity, stability, resilience, and future. Environmental Conservation 29:436–459.

Stephens, J. S., R. K. Johnson, G. S. Key, and J. E. McCosker. 1970. The comparative ecology of three sympatric species of California

blennies of the genus *Hypsoblennius* gill (Teleostomi, Blennidae). Ecological Monographs 40:213–233.
Stephens J. S., R. J. Larson, and D. J. Pondella. 2006. Rocky reefs and kelp beds. Pages 227–252 In L. G. Allen, D. J. Pondella II, and M. H. Horn, editors. The Ecology of Marine Fishes: California and Adjacent Waters. University of California Press, Berkeley, and Los Angeles, California.
Stewart, H. L., J. P. Fram, D. C. Reed, S. L. Williams, M. A. Brzezinski, S. MacIntyre, and B. P. Gaylord. 2009. Differences in growth, morphology, tissue carbon, and nitrogen of *Macrocystis pyrifera* within and at the outer edge of a giant kelp forest in California, USA. Marine Ecology Progress Series 375:101–112.
Swan, J. G. 1870. The Indians of Cape Flattery, at the entrance to the strait of Fuca, Washington Territory. Smithsonian Institution, Washington, D.C.
Swanson, A. K., and L. D. Druehl. 2000. Differential meiospore size and tolerance of ultraviolet light stress within and among kelp species along a depth gradient. Marine Biology 136:657–664.
Tegner, M. J., and L. A. Levin. 1983. Spiny lobsters and sea urchins: Analysis of a predator-prey interaction. Journal of Experimental Marine Biology and Ecology 73:125–150.
Tegner, M. J., and P. K. Dayton. 2000. Ecosystem effects of fishing in kelp forest communities. Ices Journal of Marine Science 57:579–589.
———. 1987. El Niño effects on southern California kelp forest communities. Advances in Ecological Research 17:243–279.
Thompson, W. G. 1959. Attachment of the giant kelp, *Macrocystis pyrifera,* in fine sediment and its biological and geological significance. Page 596 in Proceedings of the International Oceanographic Congress, American Association for the Advancement of Science, Washington, D.C.
Thornber, C. S., B. P. Kinlan, M. H. Graham, and J. J. Stachowicz. 2004. Population ecology of the invasive kelp *Undaria pinnatifida* in California: Environmental and biological controls on demography. Marine Ecology Progress Series 268:69–80.
Tinker, M. T., G. Bentall, and J. A. Estes. 2008. Food limitation leads to behavioral diversification and dietary specialization in sea otters. Proceedings of the National Academy of Sciences 105:560–565.
Turner, C. H., E. E. Ebert, and R. R. Given. 1969. Manmade reef ecology. Fish Bulletin 146. State of California Resources Agency, Department of Fish and Game, Sacramento, California.
VanBlaricom, G. R., D. C. Reed, C. Harrold, and J. Bodkin. 1986. A sublittoral population of *Pleurophycus gardneri* Schell and Saunders 1900 (Phaeophyceae: Laminariaceae) in central California. Southern California Academy of Science 85:120–122.
Vetter, E. W., and P. K. Dayton. 1998. Macrofaunal communities within and adjacent to a detritus-rich submarine canyon system. Deep-Sea Research 45:25–54.
Watanabe, J. M. 1984. The influence of recruitment, competition, and benthic predation on spatial distributions of three species of kelp forest gastropods. Ecology 65:920–936.
Watanabe, J. M., and C. Harrold. 1991. Destructive grazing by sea urchins *Strongylocentrotus* spp. in a central California kelp forest: Potential roles of recruitment, depth, and predation. Marine Ecology Progress Series 71:125–141.
Wheeler, W. N. 1980. Effect of boundary layer transport on the fixation of carbon by the giant kelp *Macrocystis pyrifera*. Marine Biology 56:103–110.
White, J. W., and J. E. Caselle. 2008. Scale-dependent changes in the importance of larval supply and habitat to abundance of a temperate reef fish. Ecology 89:1323–1333.
Williams, S. L., and J. E. Smith. 2007. A global review of the distribution, taxonomy, and impacts of introduced seaweeds. Annual Review of Ecology, Evolution, and Systematics 38:327–359.
Yeates, L. C., T. M. Williams, and T. L. Fink. 2007. Diving and foraging energetics of the smallest marine mammal, the sea otter (*Enhydra lutris*). Journal of Experimental Biology 210:1960–1970.
Zimmerman R. C., and D. L. Robertson. 1985. Effects of El Niño on local hydrography and growth of the giant kelp, *Macrocystis pyrifera*, at Santa Catalina Island, California. Limnology and Oceanography 30:1298–1302.
Zimmerman, R. C., and J. N. Kremer. 1986. In situ growth and chemical composition of the giant kelp, *Macrocystis pyrifera*: Response to temporal changes in ambient nutrient availability. Marine Ecology Progress Series 27:277–285.

EIGHTEEN

Intertidal

CAROL A. BLANCHETTE, MARK W. DENNY, JOHN M. ENGLE, BRIAN HELMUTH, LUKE P. MILLER, KARINA J. NIELSEN, and JAYSON SMITH

Introduction

Intertidal ecosystems exist at the interface between land and ocean, occupying the thin strip of shoreline that is regularly covered and uncovered by tides. At the highest of tides these ecosystems are covered or regularly splashed by water, and on the lowest of tides they are fully uncovered and exposed to air. Because intertidal organisms endure regular periods of immersion and EMERSION, they essentially live both underwater and on land and are adapted to a large range of conditions. Since most intertidal organisms are primarily marine in evolutionary origin, they benefit greatly from immersion in seawater during high tide, which moderates temperature, delivers food and nutrients, and facilitates reproduction by mixing gametes and transporting larvae. During low-tide periods, when organisms are uncovered, they can experience large changes in temperature, ultraviolet and solar radiation, desiccation, and even salinity from freshwater inputs or evaporation. Intertidal ecosystems also occur where wave forces and impacts are greatest. The high hydrodynamic forces imposed by intense wave action can crush, break, and dislodge intertidal organisms. Given the severity and challenges of this environment, the intertidal ecosystems of rocky shores in California are home to a surprising, incredibly high diversity of species. As John Steinbeck famously noted in *The Log from the Sea of Cortez,* "The exposed rocks had looked rich with life under the lowering tide, but they were more than that: they were ferocious with life. . . . Mussels, sculpins, kelps, and urchins; anemones and sea stars of all sizes and colors; barnacles, worms, limpets, and abalone; algae that look like corals; others that look like tar—the diversity of rocky shores rivals that of tropical rainforests."

Intertidal habitats can have either soft-bottom or hard-bottom substrates. Soft-sediment habitats include sandy beaches and intertidal wetlands such as mudflats and salt marshes. Soft-bottom habitats are generally protected from large waves but tend to have more variable salinity levels. They also offer a third habitable dimension—depth; many soft-sediment inhabitants are adapted for burrowing. Hard-bottom intertidal habitat can consist of either human-made (e.g., jetties, pilings, and seawalls) or natural rock surfaces. Natural rocky shores are found along exposed headlands as well as in more wave-protected habitats. They range from consolidated rocky benches to cobble beaches. Many of the organisms found on rocky shores are SESSILE and live attached to the rock, although a wealth of mobile predators and grazers of these sessile organisms inhabit the shore as well. Because other chapters in this book examine sandy beaches and wetlands, this chapter focuses on the intertidal ecosystems of rocky shores.

Rocky intertidal habitats provide a range of ecosystem services such as shoreline stabilization and protection of upland areas from the wave erosion and the impacts of storm surges and sea level rise. They provide haul-out areas for seals and support the diets of foraging birds as well as other diverse organisms vital to the base of the food web (UNEP 2006, Arkema et al. 2013). Rocky intertidal ecosystems also support valuable recreational and commercial fisheries for invertebrates such as mussels and limpets and for edible seaweeds. They provide for subsistence, ceremonial, sport, and commercial gathering and hunting of a diversity of intertidal organisms. Finally, rocky shores are greatly valued for their aesthetic qualities and offer easily accessible coastal areas for recreation, education, and research. In an attempt to quantify these values, Hall et al. (2002) estimated a mean of $7 per family per visit that users would be willing to pay to prevent reductions in the status of southern California's rocky intertidal zone.

Rocky intertidal shores occur along the entire length of the California coastline. In some regions, long stretches of rocky habitat dominate the shoreline, while in others (southern California, in particular) small rocky outcroppings are separated by long expanses of sandy beaches. Approximately 800 miles of rocky habitat occur along the California coast, comprising about 35% of the entire shoreline of California's outer coast. Rocky shores support an array of intertidal species living on rock faces, crevices, undersides, and tide pools. Some coastal areas, particularly rocky headlands and exposed outer coasts, experience tremendous wave action; here only the most tenacious organisms survive. Sheltered embayments and coastal areas protected by offshore rocks, reefs, or islands receive considerably less wave shock and support a variety of more delicate forms. The ability to withstand desiccation and overheating while exposed to air by low tides is an important factor in determining where marine organisms occur in the intertidal. Organisms living in tide pools of many rocky shores avoid some of the problems associated with desiccation but must still contend with elevated temperatures and rapidly changing salinities and oxygen levels.

Significance and History of Rocky Intertidal Research

We cannot begin a discussion about California's rocky intertidal ecosystems without reference to Ed Ricketts. Ricketts was a scientist and careful observer of nature who opened a biological supply company in Pacific Grove, California, in 1923. He collected and observed organisms and became one of the first marine biologists to describe them in an ecological context. His classic book *Between Pacific Tides*, coauthored with Jack Calvin and J. Hedgpeth and published in 1939, is widely regarded as the authoritative text on intertidal ecology. It continues to be revised and expanded and remains as an important point of reference for marine biologists. Ricketts elegantly described the seashore as "probably the most prolific zone in the world, a belt so thickly populated that often not only is every square inch of the area utilized by some plant or animal, but the competition for attachment sites is so keen that animals settle upon each other—plants grow upon animals, and animals upon plants" (quoted in Tamm 2004:86).

Until the early part of the twentieth century, much of marine biology and ecology was descriptive and followed in the traditions of early plant ecologists (Benson 2002). Ricketts was one of the key marine scientists of the 1930s to pioneer the modern approach to community ecology of rocky shores. Community ecologists investigate patterns, processes, and mechanisms that describe or explain the composition and dynamics of populations interacting and persisting in a particular habitat. Huge advances in intertidal community ecology in the 1930s and 1940s were facilitated by marine laboratories, primarily on the California coast. The Hopkins Marine Station (Stanford University), the Kerckhoff Laboratory (Caltech), and the Scripps Institution of Oceanography (UC San Diego) operated year-round with full-time research staffs by 1930. George MacGintie, the founder of the Kerckhoff laboratory, known for his studies of Elkhorn Slough (Mac Ginitie 1935), argued strongly for more long-term field studies. Willis G. Hewatt of Hopkins Marine Station adopted Mac Ginitie's recommendation for long-term study but also incorporated field experiments to investigate community dynamics (Hewatt 1937). Their work catalyzed a new approach to the study of the dynamics of intertidal communities. From these humble beginnings, scientists studying rocky intertidal ecosystems have steadily continued to expand the science of ecology, developing new theories and insights about community and ecosystem dynamics both in the intertidal and more broadly.

Photo on previous page: A diverse community of intertidal algae and animals from the wave-swept shores of Monterey Bay. Photo: Luke P. Miller.

The California Coast

Coastal Geology and Topography

California is one of the most biologically and geologically diverse regions in North America. The current geological configuration of the California shoreline arises from tectonic activity over millions of years (Hayes and Michel 2010). The majority of California's coast, from the southern border with Baja north to Mendocino, sits on the Pacific plate. Many of the rock formations that make up this coastline (those of the FRANCISCAN COMPLEX) were accreted onto the edge of the North American plate starting about 150 million to 130 million years ago as the Farallon plate and later the Pacific plate were subducted beneath the North American plate. Between 10 million and 30 million years ago, the Pacific plate stopped subducting and instead began to travel northwest relative to the North American plate. This shift gave rise to the San Andreas fault, which turns offshore near Mendocino toward the north. Both the accreted marine sediments of the Franciscan complex and granite formations originally from the southern Sierra Nevada mountains have been carried to their current locations by the northwest movement of the Pacific plate (Harden 2004).

In places where sedimentary rock (e.g., sandstone, mudstone, or shale) makes up the shore, erosion often forms broad, intertidal benches (Figure 18.1). By contrast, erosion-resistant igneous and metamorphic rocks (e.g., granite, basalt, schists) are typically cut into steep, topographically complex

FIGURE 18.1 Examples of an easily eroded sedimentary intertidal bench (above) and an erosion-resistant granite shoreline with high topographic relief (below). Photos: Jayson Smith (above), Luke P. Miller (below).

shapes (Griggs and Trenhaile 1997). The resulting interspersion of erosion-prone and erosion-resistant rocks determines the overall pattern of alternating headlands and beaches along the southern and central California coasts. North of Mendocino, the shoreline is a product of recent SUBDUCTION, volcanic activity, and other OROGENIC processes. The vertical location of wave-induced erosion depends on sea level, which has fluctuated through geological time in conjunction with the coming and going of ice ages. Currently, sea level is 120 meters higher than at the peak of the last ice age, and it is rising at a rate of at least 22 to 44 centimeters per century as Earth warms (Harden 2004).

The large-scale pattern of California coastal topography is modified by small-scale geological processes: folding, terrestrial erosion, and local uplift or subsidence. The most obvious results of some of these processes are the MARINE TERRACES found along much the coast. Marine terraces are formed by (1) the erosive activity of waves, which sculpts wide benches in the intertidal zone, followed by (2) sea level declines during glacial maxima, and (3) subsequent tectonic uplift of the shoreline out of reach of the waves when sea level rises again during glacial minima. Several periods of sea level change and continued tectonic uplift have created multiple, stepped marine terraces throughout San Diego, Orange, Los Angeles, San Luis Obispo, Santa Cruz, San Mateo, Mendocino, Humboldt, and Del Norte Counties. These areas are often flanked by present-day rocky intertidal benches (Griggs et al 2005).

Biogeographic Patterns

BIOGEOGRAPHIC patterns of California's rocky intertidal communities have strong spatial structure and correlate closely with both geography and sea surface temperature patterns (Blanchette et al. 2008, 2009). Temperature is a useful proxy for tracking the movement of oceanic water masses. Temperature can also directly affect critical biological functions including growth, survival, and reproduction. Biogeographic

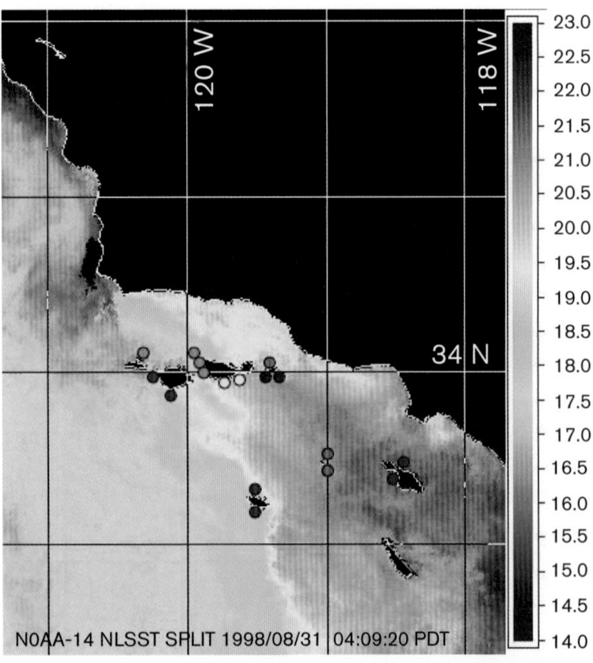

FIGURE 18.2 Biogeographic patterns of rocky intertidal community structure at the California Channel Islands. Sites with dots of the same color are most similar to one another in their species composition. Community similarity is strongly influenced by sea surface temperature. Source: Blanchette et al. 2009.

patterns of community similarity along the west coast of North America largely involve shifts in relative abundances of taxa rather than wholesale changes in species assemblages among regions. Many of the most abundant species characterizing particular biogeographic regions are not absent from any region, but differ consistently and substantially in abundance among regions. However, several exceptions to these general grouping patterns occur, suggesting that while similar processes shape species distributions and abundances across taxa and life histories, important local features such as topography, geology, and wave exposure, as well as species interactions, can also be important drivers of rocky intertidal community composition (Blanchette et al. 2008).

All major California rocky intertidal biogeographic regions are delimited by coastal features associated with transitions in oceanographic conditions, and/or changes in geomorphology and substrate type (such as long stretches of sandy beaches or changes in coastline orientation) (Blanchette et al. 2008). Point Conception is one of the most notable transition regions on the California coastline and the most important biogeographic and oceanographic discontinuities on the west coast of North America (Figure 18.2; Valentine 1966, Doyle 1985, Burton 1998). Two major water masses meet here—the southward-flowing California current and the westward-flowing southern California countercurrent (Hickey 1993). The northern region experiences consistent, strong, coastal upwelling that brings cold, nutrient-rich waters to the surface, resulting in both cold coastal sea surface temperatures and high nutrient concentrations. The Santa Barbara Channel, immediately southeast of Point Conception, experiences weak seasonal upwelling, which tends to occur in the winter months (Blanchette et al. 2002, Winant et al. 2003). The California Channel Islands, located just offshore from Point Conception, lie within this highly diverse oceanographic region. They experience variable mixing between the cold waters of the California current and the warm, nearshore waters of the southern California countercurrent (Huyer 1983, Hickey et al. 2003). As on the mainland, temperature strongly determines the composition of Channel Island intertidal communities (Figure 18.3).

The Physical Environment

The effects of the exceptionally severe intertidal environment on population and community dynamics appear at many different scales, from regional-scale variation in the timing and amplitude of tidal fluctuations to local topographic effects on exposure of individuals to stressful hydrodynamic forces and temperatures. The alternating exposure of intertidal organisms to aerial and marine conditions is controlled largely by the cycle of the tides. As the moon orbits Earth, and Earth orbits the sun, gravity and celestial motion interact with the ocean to create the a periodic fluctuation in sea level—the tides—that determines how often and for how long shoreline organisms are exposed to terrestrial conditions. The temporal and spatial variation of the tides underlies all other aspects of the intertidal physical environment.

Two high tides and two low tides occur in the course of each tidal day (24 hours, 50 minutes). On the coast of California the two high tides have different heights, as do the low tides—a pattern know as mixed semidiurnal tides (Figure 18.4). The inequality of high tides and low tides means that organisms low in the intertidal zone (below the higher low tide) are emersed only once a day. Similarly, organisms high in the intertidal zone (above the lower high tide) are immersed only once a day. In contrast, organisms in the middle of the zone make the transition from air to water and back twice a day. These patterns of immersion and emersion strongly influence the stress to which the physiology of intertidal plants and animals must adapt.

The amplitude of the tides (the difference between higher high tide and lower low tide) is typically 1–3 meters but varies with the moon's phase and the seasons. Tidal amplitude is greatest when the moon is new or full (spring tides) and least at the first-quarter and third-quarter moons (neap tides). The disparity of the tides (the difference between higher and lower high tides and between higher and lower low tides) is typically greatest near the summer and winter solstices and least near the spring and fall equinoxes. Spring tides are most notable because they emerse organisms lower on the shore than other tides do in the remainder of the tidal cycle.

A variety of secondary factors modulates these general patterns. Because the moon's orbit is elliptical, the distance between Earth and the moon varies. The moon's gravitational effect on the ocean therefore fluctuates by almost 40% over the 27.3 days of its orbital period. When the moon's closest approach to Earth coincides with new or full moon, tidal amplitude increases, exposing plants and animals that otherwise would not be emersed. The reverse occurs when the moon is farthest from Earth. Similarly, tidal amplitudes increase when Earth is nearest the sun (early January) and diminished when Earth is farthest away (early July). The angle between the plane of the moon's orbit and Earth's equatorial plane varies with a period of 18.6 years, which can also affect the amplitude and disparity of the tides (Denny and Paine 1998).

FIGURE 18.3 Rocky intertidal community buried by sand in July. Photo: Carol Blanchette.

Because the tidal day is slightly longer than the solar day (24 hours), the timing of the tides shifts. For example, lower low tide tomorrow is (on average) 50 minutes later than it was today, although the precise timing is affected by the amplitude fluctuations discussed earlier. The timing of tides on the California coast also varies with latitude—the farther north, the later the tide. An 8:00 low tide in San Diego does not reach Point Reyes until 9:30 and Humboldt Bay until 10:15. Summertime spring low tides in California typically occur in the morning, so this latitudinal shift in the time of the tide means that the farther north a site, the more time it is exposed to potentially stressful midday terrestrial conditions. Both the timing and amplitude of tides can be affected by seafloor topography. Tides inside the San Francisco Bay have much lower amplitude and occur nearly an hour later than tides just outside, for instance. For an accurate prediction of the tides at any particular location, it is best to consult the site-specific predictions provided by the National Oceanographic and Atmospheric Administration (http://www.tidesandcurrents.noaa.gov/). Even then, one can expect some deviation of actual tides from those predicted—as much as 10–20 centimeters—due to weather-driven changes in barometric pressure. For more detailed explanation of the tides, consult Brown et al. (1999) or Cartwright (1999).

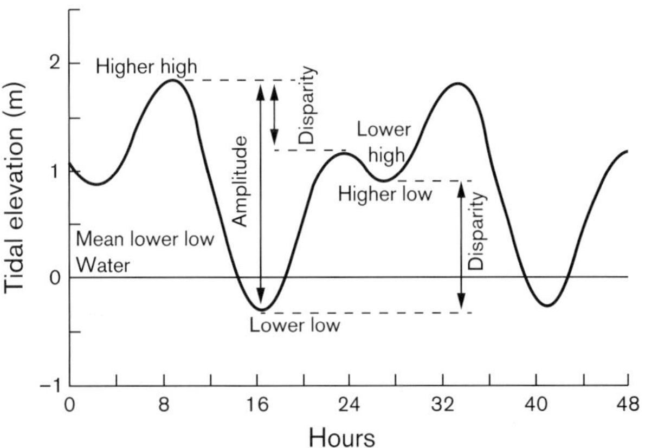

FIGURE 18.4 Example of mixed semidiurnal tides, in which there are two high tides and two low tides differing in amplitude every lunar day. Source: Denny 1988.

THE CONTRAST BETWEEN TERRESTRIAL AND AQUATIC ENVIRONMENTS

The physical differences between seawater and air have profound effects on individual physiology and community structure (Denny 1994). Many of these effects are tied to temperature and therefore to the specific heat capacities of these two media. Specific heat capacity is the amount of heat energy required to raise the temperature of 1 kilogram of a substance 1°C. Water has an unusually high specific heat capacity, more than four times that of air. As a result, water temperature varies much less than air temperature. In Monterey, for instance, annual maximum sea surface temperature is 16°C, only 6°C warmer than the annual minimum. By contrast, the low specific heat of air allows for rapid changes in temperature; air temperature can vary by more than 20°C in a single day.

Air and water temperature variations contribute to variation in the body temperatures of intertidal organisms. During submersion at high tide, the water's high thermal conductivity ensures that the temperature of an organism is the same as the water around it. Thus submerged body temperature can vary by at most a few degrees Celsius in a day as the sun heats surface waters or upwelling delivers cold subsurface water. During aerial exposure at low tide, body temperatures of intertidal organisms are affected by air temperature but also by the multiple, interacting environmental factors (e.g., solar heating, conduction of heat to or from the rock, evaporative cooling). As a result, on sunny days, the body temperature of intertidal organisms can be considerably warmer (10–15°C) than the surrounding air and can vary over very fine spatial scales; animals on south-facing sides of rocks can be many degrees hotter than nearby animals on shaded surfaces

(Helmuth and Hofmann 2001, Denny et al. 2011). Emersed body temperature can also be colder than the surrounding air, especially at night, as organisms lose heat by infrared radiation to the sky.

The temperature of an organism's body affects most physiological processes, such as metabolic rate (Jansen et al. 2007) and efficiency of enzyme functioning (Somero 2011). Increases in metabolic demand, and thus oxygen demand, in turn can lead to oxygen deficiency at the cellular level (Pörtner and Farrell 2008). While the relative importance of intertidal body temperatures in water and in air remains unclear, and varies between species, both can have significant effects on rates of mortality, growth, and reproduction (Blanchette et al. 2007, Somero 2011). Experiments show that these impacts can be due to both rare but extreme events (Harley and Paine 2009, Denny et al. 2009) and chronic exposure to suboptimal temperatures (Petes et al. 2008, Sará et al. 2011 and 2012). For example, Harley (2008) reported mortality of mussels and limpets in March and April 2004 in Bodega Bay, California, following exposures to a series of sunny, warm days when low tide exposed animals to the air during the mid-day.

Evaporative cooling allows organisms to avoid (or at least postpone) high temperature stress. Each gram of water evaporated removes 2,500 joules of heat energy from the organism. Excessive water loss can be lethal, however. Thus a trade-off exists between desiccation and thermal stress. Many mobile organisms seek refuge from potentially desiccating conditions underneath algal canopies or in crevices and tide pools. Some intertidal animals (e.g., littorine snails [*Littorina* spp.]) retreat into their shells at low tide, sealing in water and relying instead on their ability to cope with subsequent high temperatures. Lacking shells or waxy cuticles, seaweeds readily lose water, allowing them to stay cool for a time. Seaweeds have also evolved physiological mechanisms to cope with the resulting desiccation.

In addition to temperature and desiccation stress, intertidal organisms must contend with broad variation in salinity, sand burial, and other conditions. Variability in salinity is typically low during high-tide submersion but can increase dramatically at low tide during rain events or from exposure to freshwater runoff from streams or storm drains. Movement of sand along the coast can bury intertidal organisms in seasons of limited wave scouring, typically in summer (see Figure 18.3). Sand movement and tolerance of sandy conditions is especially important for rocky intertidal communities in southern California, where rocky benches are typically interspersed with long stretches of sandy beach.

WAVE EXPOSURE

As winds blow, they transfer energy to the ocean surface, producing waves (Denny 1988). In the area directly affected by wind, waves—known as *seas*—are steep and disorganized, with periods of 4 to 6 seconds. But waves can travel great distances; as they move away from the winds that generated them, their character gradually changes. Waves that arrive from a distant storm—known as *swell*—oscillate with periods of 8 to 20 seconds. On a typical day the waves impinging on a shore are a complex combination of seas and swell. The interaction of intertidal organisms with ocean waves—their *wave exposure*—is mediated by the slope of the seafloor. As waves progress from deep to shallow water, accompanying water motion changes from a nearly circular orbit confined to the upper portion of the water column to a shoreward-seaward oscillation extending all the way to the seafloor. An increase in velocity accompanies this shift in flow pattern. In deep water a wave with a period of 10 seconds and a trough-to-crest height of 1 meter causes a maximum water velocity of 0.3 meter per second. When the same wave has SHOALED to a depth of 2 meters, velocity increases tenfold. As waves shoal even further—to a depth approximately equal to their height—they break. Breaking sets the maximum velocity waves can produce before reaching shore. Velocity at the crest of a breaking wave is approximately 4.4 times the square root of wave height, more than 4 meters per second for a 1 meter high wave and more than 6 meters per second for a 2 meter high wave.

Whether these high velocities are imposed on BENTHIC organisms depends in large part on the slope of the seafloor. If the slope is gradual, waves break seaward of the intertidal zone and lose energy (and velocity) to VISCOUS turbulent processes as they move up the shore. In this case the intertidal community is relatively protected. By contrast, if the shore slopes steeply, waves break directly on the intertidal zone, where crest velocity can be amplified by the water's interaction with the rock's small-scale topography. When this occurs, velocities of 10 meters per second are common, and storm waves can cause speeds in excess of 30 meters per second (approximately 67 miles per hour). Where shoreline topography is complex, water velocity can vary substantially over short distances. While the seaward faces of rocks might see extremely high water velocities, the leeward sides of the same rocks can be relatively sheltered, allowing a different suite of animals and plants to survive. The exposure of a site also depends on the direction from which waves arrive. Waves that approach on a path perpendicular to shore lose the least energy before reaching the intertidal zone and therefore have the greatest impact. Those approaching on a path more parallel to shore have a smaller effect.

Wave-induced water velocities have both detrimental and beneficial effects. Hydrodynamic forces (drag and lift) are proportional to the square of velocity (Vogel 1994), and—given the extreme velocities associated with waves—can pose challenges for intertidal organisms. Many organisms found on wave-swept shores, such as limpets (e.g., *Lottia* spp.) and chitons (e.g., *Leptochiton* spp.), have evolved unique, low-profile shapes to reduce the forces imposed on them by waves and to reduce their likelihood of becoming dislodged by wave action. Wave-induced disturbance (when organisms are torn from the rock by wave action) has important ecological consequences for the diversity and function of rocky shore communities. For example, the California mussel *Mytilus californianus* is the competitive dominant for space on exposed shores in California, but forces imposed by breaking waves can rip them from the rock. Although this disturbance harms mussels, the dislodged animals are food for sea anemones, and the open space they leave behind makes room for fugitive species such as the sea palm, *Postelsia palmaeformis* (Dayton 1973, Paine 1988, Blanchette 1996). Hydrodynamic forces can also constrain movement by predators and herbivores, which is bad for the consumers but good for their prey. The same forces that cause disturbance also splash water high on the shore, transporting food to barnacles (Cirripedia) and keeping both plants and animals moist and cool. The dynamics of intertidal communities vary in predictable fashion along gradients of wave exposure at least in part in response to wave-induced water motion. These patterns are discussed later in the chapter in the context of intertidal ecology.

Organisms of California's Rocky Intertidal Ecosystems

The narrow ribbon of California's marine coast hosts an extraordinary diversity of flora and fauna. Terrestrial life resistant to saltwater encroaches from inland; subtidal species able to survive limited air exposure or dynamic tide pool conditions extend up the shore; and other organisms thrive solely within the rocky intertidal ecosystem. No exact enumeration of California shore species exists, even if tiny organisms are not considered. At least 669 species of intertidal and subtidal seaweeds are known in California (Abbott and Hollenberg 1976), while over 3,700 rocky and sandy coast invertebrates have been identified from central California to Oregon (Carlton 2007). A major intertidal survey throughout southern California found 213 seaweed species (Murray and Littler 1989) and 349 invertebrate species (Seapy and Littler 1993); however, a contemporary, intensive inventory within mussel beds "conservatively" discovered 141 algae and 610 invertebrate species (Kanter 1980). Adding to coastal diversity are tide pool and migratory intertidal fishes along with visiting shorebirds and a few mammals.

Rocky intertidal organisms belong to a broad range of evolutionary (phylogenetic) groups that include seaweeds and flowering plants (Chromista and Plantae); sponges (Porifera); hydroids and sea anemones (Cnidaria); flatworms (Platyhelminthes); peanut worms (Sipuncula); segmented worms (Annelida); barnacles, isopods, amphipods, shrimps, crabs, and insects (Arthropoda); octopus, chitons, snails, sea slugs, and bivalves (Mollusca); sea urchins, sea stars, brittle stars, and sea cucumbers (Echinodermata); and tunicates, fishes, birds, and mammals (Chordata). An ecologically useful way to characterize intertidal life forms is by how they acquire energy to sustain life. Common groupings include primary producers (that acquire energy from sunlight), suspension feeders (that filter or trap drifting microbiota and detritus), grazers (that consume seaweeds), and carnivores (that capture animals). Species within and among these trophic groupings interact in intricate food webs. From a resource management perspective, another set of groupings includes those harvested or impacted by humans, those designated for special protection, and those introduced from faraway shores.

Primary Producers

Photosynthetic seaweeds provide a productive nutritional base for intertidal food webs, compete for limited shore space, and often create structural habitat for other organisms. California's diverse sun-lovers range from tiny blue-green bacteria (cyanobacteria) through commonly categorized green (Chlorophyta), brown (Heterokonta), and red (Rhodophyta) seaweeds, to true flowering surfgrass (Tracheophyta). Reds are the most species-rich, followed by browns, greens, and the two species of surfgrass. Seaweed structural forms adapted to intertidal lifestyles include wave-resistant films or crusts; leathery, desiccation-resistant rockweeds; filamentous turfs with high surface area for nutrient and light uptake; stony coralline algae; and larger, bushy growths and fleshy blades that rise above the substrate when submerged.

Dominant primary producers on California shores often create intricate structural habitats, hosting rich floral and faunal assemblages that shelter within or attach as epiphytes. Key dominant producer types include erect corallines (e.g., *Corallina*) and soft turfs (e.g., *Endocladia*, *Gelidium*), tough rockweeds (e.g., *Silvetia*, *Fucus*), fleshy blades (e.g., *Ulva*, *Chondracanthus*, *Mazaella*), branching bushes (e.g., *Stephanocystis*, *Sargassum*), large bladed or bladdered kelps (e.g., *Laminaria*, *Eisenia*, *Egregia*), and meadowy surfgrass (*Phyllospadix*) (Figure 18.5).

Suspension Feeders

As adults, many rocky intertidal invertebrates are sessile, an adaptation to hold space and minimize wave dislodgement. Their food arrives primarily as phytoplankton, zooplankton, or detritus particles suspended in rushing seawater. Some species use active mechanisms for straining this tiny food during submerged periods; these include sweeping sieve-like legs (e.g., barnacles) and pumping water through comb-like filters (e.g., sponges, bivalves, tunicates). Others feed more passively by extending sticky or filtering appendages for longer periods of time. Tube snails (e.g., *Serpulorbis*) employ mucous nets; sea anemones (Anthozoa) have stinging tentacles; crevice-dwelling sea cucumbers (e.g., *Cucumaria*) and peanut worms (e.g., *Themiste*) have sticky, branched tentacles; and plume worms (e.g., *Spirobranchus*) and colonial moss animals (Bryozoa) extend feathery filters.

Suspension feeders such as acorn (e.g., *Chthamalus*, *Balanus*) and stalked (e.g., *Pollicipes*) barnacles, and anemones (e.g., *Anthopleura*), can dominate intertidal reefs through sheer numbers. Other filter feeders are important habitat-forming bioengineers; these include sand-castle worms (e.g., *Phragmatopoma*) that fill in crevices with sandy tube colonies, mussels (e.g., *Mytilus*) that form dense thickened beds with interstitial microhabitats, and pholad bivalves (e.g., *Penitella*) that bore holes in sedimentary reefs. These holes then host numerous small organisms.

Grazers

California's intertidal seaweed consumers (herbivores) can be relatively sedentary if they trap drift seaweeds (e.g., abalone, sea urchins) or graze algal films within a small area (e.g., many limpets and chitons); however, others, such as top snails, sea hares, and shore crabs, forage more widely. Herbivorous mollusks have file-like radulas, urchins use beak-like jaws, and shore crabs employ claws to scrape seaweed films or larger plants. Grazers such as periwinkles (e.g., *Littorina*), limpets (e.g., *Lottia*), turban snails (e.g., *Chlorostoma*), chitons (e.g., *Nuttalina*), shore crabs (e.g., *Pachygrapsus*), and sea urchins (e.g., *Strongylocentrotus*) can occur in great numbers where conditions are suitable. Hermit crabs (e.g., *Pagurus*) may be abundant in tide pools, scavenging plant and animal materials. Owl limpets (*Lottia gigantea*) can dominate upper intertidal rocks, where they maintain grazing territories by removing most other organisms.

Carnivores

Diverse predators are ecologically important in upper levels of intertidal food webs. Some like crabs and octopus are active crevice or tide pool residents, while other mobile predators are migratory—lobsters and fishes moving inshore to forage at higher tides and seabirds arriving to hunt at lower tides. Some

FIGURE 18.5 A broad meadow of surfgrass (*Phyllospadix torreyi*) covers the low shore. Photo: Carol Blanchette.

carnivores are slow-moving (e.g., predatory snails, sea slugs, and sea stars). Sedentary sea anemones snare creatures that wander or drift onto them. Intertidal adaptations for capture of prey include drilling (e.g., snails like *Ceratostoma* and *Acanthinucella*), poisoning (e.g., *Octopus* and the cone snail *Conus*), rasping or piercing (e.g., nudibranchs), prying or engulfing (e.g., sea stars, such as *Pisaster* spp.), stabbing or hammering (e.g., black oystercatchers, *Haematopus bachmani*), and picking at or swallowing whole (e.g., most fishes and shorebirds).

The ochre sea star (*Pisaster ochraceus*) is well known as a keystone predator that can greatly affect ecological conditions in communities of its mussel prey. Ochre sea star populations have declined due to disease outbreaks associated with warm water conditions in the 1970s and the recent El Niño periods of 1982–1983 and 1997–1998 (Eckert et al. 2000). A massive sea star wasting disease epidemic that has not been associated with warm water, and has affected all species of sea stars, began in summer 2013 and has extended as far north as Alaska (Stockstad 2014). Shorebirds commonly can be seen foraging at low tide on intertidal reefs; more elusive terrestrial mammals (including rats, cats, raccoons, and foxes) may hunt for shore crabs and other invertebrates at night.

Species of Special Concern

Surfgrass (*Phyllospadix*) and sea palms (*Postelsia palmaeformis*), recognized as important but susceptible habitat-forming plants, are specifically protected from disturbance and sport harvest (although sea palms are not protected from commercial harvest in California). The black abalone (*Haliotis cracherodii*), once abundant and extensively gathered for food, suffered such catastrophic declines, particularly in southern California, during the 1980s (due to overfishing and withering syndrome disease) that it was listed as a federally endangered species in 2009. Species introduced to California marine waters by hitchhiking on ships or other means present ecological threats to native species. Most introduced species are known from sheltered bays and harbors, with relatively few discovered on the open coast. Maloney et al. (2006) found 16 non-native species in representative outer-coast intertidal reefs (667 species were native and 59 others were of unknown origin). The most widespread invaders were two seaweeds: a large brown bladderweed (*Sargassum muticum*) and a small red turf (*Caulacanthus ustulatus*).

Benthic-pelagic Coupling

Rocky intertidal ecosystems are inextricably linked to the oceanic environment through the delivery of food, nutrients, and propagules (both larval invertebrates and algal spores). The oceanographic processes driving the delivery of these constituents span large spatial scales and thereby connect distant communities (see Chapter 6, "Oceanography"). Rocky intertidal organisms may also alter the amounts and kinds of materials in the waters that pass over, among, and through them, and transform the PELAGIC (offshore) waters arriving to benthic (bottom-dwelling) organisms further upshore or along the shoreline. The exchange of essential materials between the two ecosystems is referred to as benthic-pelagic coupling (Figure 18.6). The nature and degree of coupling can strongly influence the rate and extent of recovery from natural or anthropogenic disturbances, productivity, and the relative abundances and diversity of species that make up rocky intertidal communities (Menge et al. 2003, Blanchette et al. 2008).

Sessile animals and plants that live attached to the rocks rely on ocean currents to deliver food and nutrients. Much of the food of suspension-feeding invertebrates such as mussels and barnacles consists of phytoplankton, single-celled photosynthetic organisms (e.g., diatoms and dinoflagellates) common to coastal waters. Microscopic zooplankton, including meroplankton (larval forms of nonplanktonic adults) and mixotrophic plankton (plankton that depend on a variety of carbon sources), that feed on smaller planktonic forms (including phytoplankton) are also ingested by sessile, suspension-feeding invertebrates. Some suspension feeders feed on even smaller planktonic forms, such as the bacteria, ciliates, and flagellates that form the microbial food webs of pelagic waters. In addition to the living components of their diets, many of these animals consume small detrital particles derived from the breakdown and decay of seaweeds and other marine plants (collectively referred to as macrophytes) from nearby algal beds, kelp forests, and seagrass meadows.

Macrophytes of rocky shores all depend on the flow of water over their THALLI or leaves to deliver nitrogen, phosphorus, and other nutrients for use in essential metabolic pathways (such as photosynthesis, protein synthesis, respiration, Adenosine Triphosphate (ATP) synthesis, DNA replication, RNA transcription) supporting growth and reproduction. Nitrogen and phosphorous in seawater can be present in several inorganic and organic forms, but the inorganic forms nitrate (NO_3^-), ammonium (NH_4^+), and (ortho-) phosphates (HPO_4^{2-} and PO_4^{-3}) are most readily available to macrophytes. Although both phosphorus and nitrogen can limit macrophyte growth, nitrogen is generally more limiting along California's coast. The most important source of new nutrients (as opposed to nutrients remineralized and recycled through microbial food webs) for macrophyte growth is from the process of coastal upwelling.

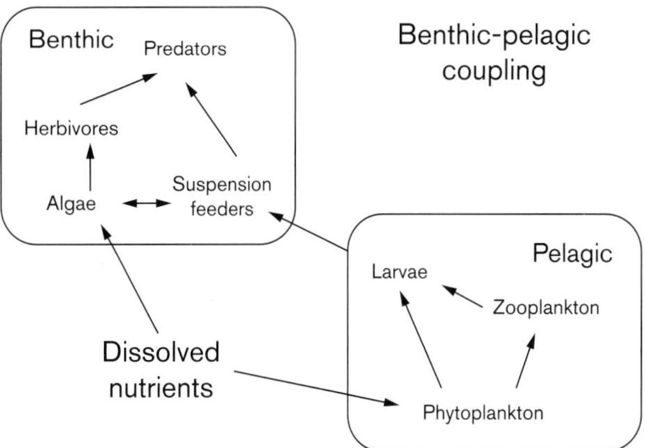

FIGURE 18.6 Conceptual diagram of coupling between the benthic marine intertidal ecosystem and the pelagic marine ecosystem. Dissolved nutrients fuel the growth of phytoplankton as well as macroalgae. Larvae from the pelagic environment settle in the benthic intertidal environment. Source: Carol Blanchette.

Coastal Upwelling

Although upwelling regions are only about 1% of the ocean's surface, they are the source of approximately 50% of the seafood humans harvest from the oceans each year. The high primary productivity of phytoplankton in these regions propagates upward to support a diverse and productive ocean food web. Both intertidal macrophytes and suspension-feeding invertebrates can benefit from the nutrient-rich waters delivered by coastal upwelling (see Chapter 6, "Oceanography"). Upwelled waters fuel the growth of macrophytes, phytoplankton, and, indirectly, the rest of the planktonic food web that supports suspension-feeding invertebrates. Since both macrophytes and phytoplankton can strip nutrients from the water column, this productive boost fuels competitive interactions between these two groups. The dense blooms of phytoplankton that can form in response to upwelled nutrients reduce light reaching benthic-dwelling macrophytes by preemptively intercepting it for their own use (Kavanaugh et al. 2009). Clearer, colder, nutrient-rich waters conducive to lush growth of macrophytes tends to prevail near and just to the south of coastal upwelling centers (which often coincide with headlands) (Broitman and Kinlan 2006).

As newly upwelled waters move away from where they were shoaled, they bring along an initial inoculum of phytoplankton that will eventually proliferate and grow in the sunlit surface waters, but this occurs over a period of several days. Thus older, warmer, phytoplankton-rich waters tend to occur further downstream and/or offshore of upwelling centers. Depending on the prevailing trajectory of newly upwelled waters and the strength and duration of upwelling favorable winds, the locations of "downstream" or "aged" waters with abundant phytoplankton can vary. Local topography and bathymetry, including offshore banks and canyons, help create relatively predictable nearshore circulation patterns (Woodson et al. 2012). This results in a mosaic of shoreline habitats with qualitative and quantitative differences in the degree of benthic-pelagic coupling with respect to inorganic nutrients for macrophytes and organic nutrition for invertebrates (Blanchette et al. 2009, Krenz et al. 2011, Watson et al. 2011). Locations closer to upwelling centers are more conducive to lush growth of macrophytes, while those receiving more aged waters that deliver a rich suspension of planktonic foods, or occurring just downshore from upwelling centers that receive detrital macrophytes and drift-algae, will tend to favor the growth of invertebrates the feed on suspensions of organic particulates and larger drift-algae (Broitman and Kinlan 2006, Lester et al. 2007).

Complex Life Histories

Many, but not all, intertidal animals have complex life histories that include indirect development and dispersal of pelagic larval forms. Some invertebrates such as mussels have a plankton-feeding (planktotrophic) larval stage coupled with a suspension-feeding adult stage and thus experience strong, direct benthic-pelagic coupling throughout their life cycles. Invertebrates such as urchins (Echinoderms in the class Echonoidea) without suspension-feeding as adults are still influenced by their larval transit through the pelagic realm and may experience indirect coupling with the pelagic environment later in life through the availability of drift seaweed. Invertebrates such as predatory whelks (e.g., *Kelletia kelletii*) with direct developing, crawl-away larvae (no pelagic phase) can still be influenced by benthic-pelagic coupling because their prey have pelagic larvae (Wieters et al. 2011). Not all rocky intertidal invertebrates are strongly influenced by benthic-pelagic coupling. Chitons (molluscs in the class Polyplacophora), for example, have short-lived, nonfeeding (lecithotrophic) larvae and as adults depend primarily on in situ algal resources.

The influence of the pelagic phase of life on intertidal invertebrate populations varies strongly and depends in part on larval characteristics. Larval stages may be short-lived or long-lived. They may need to encounter and capture their own planktonic food or be accompanied by a maternally sourced, lipid-rich nutritional package instead, or sometimes a combination of the two (Denny and Gaines 2007). In feeding larvae, such as the VELIGERS of mussels (bivalve molluscs), planktonic food availability can affect juvenile survivorship and growth on the shore (Phillips 2002). Thus timing of lar-

FIGURE 18.7 Examples of distinct bands of organisms (zonation) in the rocky intertidal. Photo: Jayson Smith.

val release to match the availability of phytoplankton is probably an important influence on survivorship of feeding larval forms (Phillips 2004). Planktonic larvae are also subject to predation while in the pelagic zone. Fishes can markedly reduce the survivorship of a well-fed cohort of larval barnacles previously destined to arrive on the rocky shores just beyond a kelp forest (Gaines and Roughgarden 1987). Despite their microscopic size, dispersing larvae are not always at the mercy of the currents; larvae can effect changes in their horizontal position within the water column and thus move themselves into onshore- or offshore-flowing waters. In the end, most larvae do not make it back to shore. The realized dispersal, metamorphosis, and settlement of invertebrates to the intertidal zone depends on a highly favorable convergence of the timing of release and duration of the larval stage, larval behavioral tactics, the nearshore circulation dynamics that generate currents, waves, fronts, and eddies, and conditions on the shore that permit or prevent survival of settling larvae.

Intertidal Ecology

Rocky intertidal ecosystems have long served as a proving ground for developing and testing ecological theory. Their alternating exposure to marine and terrestrial conditions creates steep environmental gradients that help to explain the striking patterns of distribution and abundance seen on most rocky shores. Several features combine to make rocky shores ideal outdoor laboratories, including variable physical conditions over short distances and the presence of small organisms that are mostly sessile or sedentary, often reach high densities, have short generation times, and are readily experimentally manipulated.

Patterns on the Shore

Zonation is the characteristic pattern of distribution and abundance observable as successive bands of organisms as one moves from the low shore to the high shore (Figure 18.7). Zonation is perhaps the best-known pattern in rocky intertidal communities. It occurs universally in rocky intertidal regions (Lewis 1964, Stephenson and Stephenson 1972) even where tidal range is only a few tens of centimeters. A typical rocky shore can be divided into a spray zone or splash zone above the mean high-tide line and covered by water only during storms and an intertidal zone that lies between the high and low tidal extremes (Figure 18.8). Along most shores, the intertidal zone can be clearly separated into high, middle, and low intertidal subzones with characteristic assemblages and patterns of zonation. Along the California coast, barnacles (*Chthamalus* and *Balanus*) characterize the high zone, rockweeds (*Silvetia, Fucus*) the upper-mid zone, mussels (*Mytilus*) the lower-mid zone, and an assemblage of macrophytes, typically red algae, kelps, and surfgrass, the low zone.

Gradients in wave exposure provide an important backdrop against which community structure varies horizontally in space (Lewis 1964). Even over short distances, patterns of distribution and species composition can shift dramatically from wave-exposed headlands to nearby wave-sheltered coves while still displaying sharp vertical zonation (e.g., Dayton 1971, Menge 1976). Exposure to sun as well as waves can also influence species composition, with entirely different assemblages occurring on north-facing and south-facing rocky surfaces. At smaller scales within zones, organisms can also be patchily distributed. Patchiness can be generated by wave-borne disturbance, which removes clumps of organisms from the rocks. The gaps formed in mussel beds are a classic example of patchiness (Dayton 1971, Paine and Levin 1981). Disturbance due to wave action can, in some cases, determine the structure of the entire intertidal community. This can happen through a process of ecological succession, when species replace one another through time following a disturbance. A classic experiment examining the effects of disturbance and succession on community structure took place in an intertidal boulder field on the southern California coast (Sousa 1979). The frequency with which boulders are overturned, and therefore disturb the communities of organisms living on them, depends on a combination of wave action strength and the sizes of the boulders themselves. Sousa (1979) found the greatest diversity of organisms on medium-sized boulders that were overturned occasionally, providing an intermediate level of disturbance. Boulders that were overturned constantly could only support ephemeral assemblages, and those rarely overturned were dominated by competitively superior species. Sousa's study and others in rocky intertidal ecosystem have supported the general hypothesis that a moderate level of disturbance is important to the maintenance of diversity in these ecosystems.

Community Dynamics

For many years marine ecologists assumed that the structure of rocky intertidal communities was under largely physical control (e.g., Lewis 1964). Explanations for species distributions, for example, were sought through study of species' tolerances of waves, thermal stress, and desiccation. Many thought that species could not live in particular zones because they could not tolerate the physical conditions there. We now know that while physical factors are important, they are only part of the story. In 1961, Joe Connell published two papers that elegantly and convincingly demonstrated that the lower limits of two zone-forming barnacles were set by species interactions. At Millport, Scotland, he found that interspecific competition for space determined the lower limit of

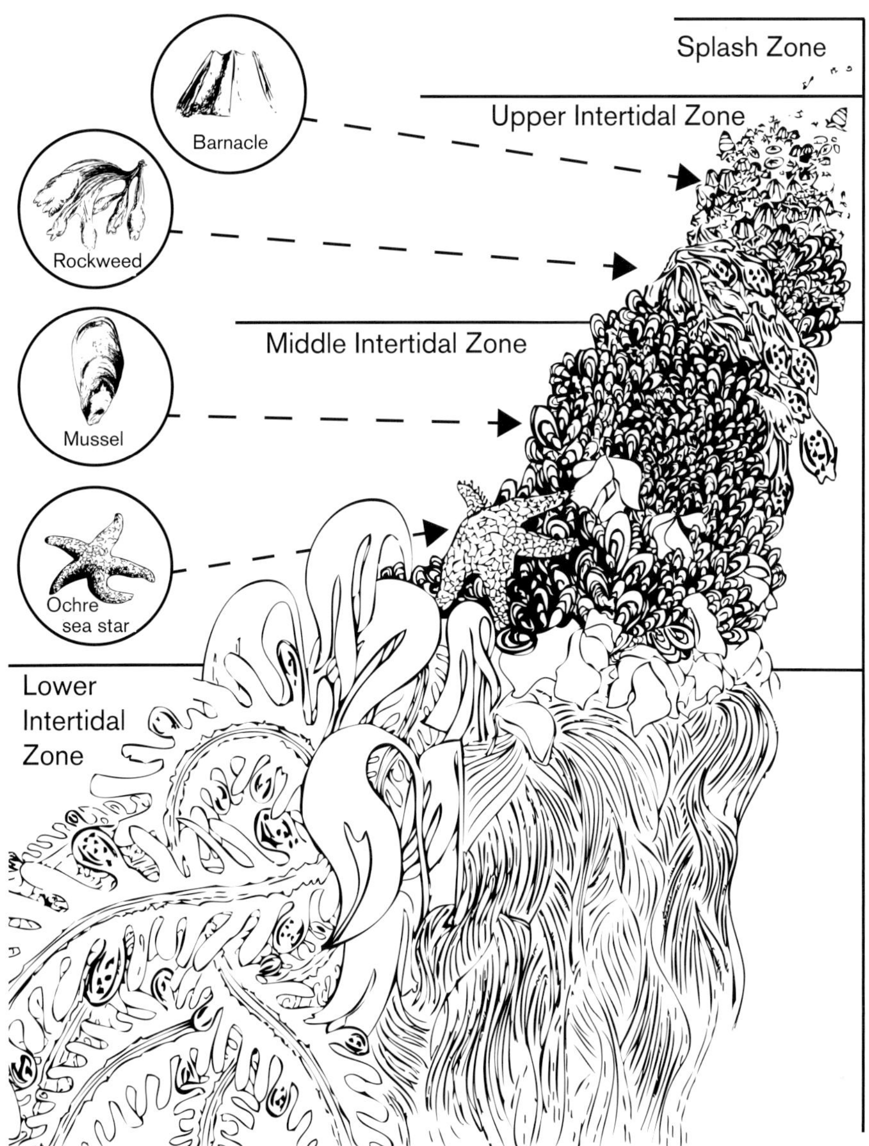

FIGURE 18.8 Conceptual diagram of zonation depicting the intertidal zones. Source: Illustration by Aeon Brady.

the upper-shore barnacle, and that both intraspecific competition and predation by whelks determined the lower limit of the lower-shore barnacle (Connell 1961a, Connell 1961b).

While biotic drivers set the lower limits for both species, physical factors set the upper limits. Although upper-shore barnacles were outcompeted by lower-shore barnacles, the inability of lower-shore barnacles to persist in the high zone due to desiccation stress provided refuge for upper-intertidal barnacles to exist, as they were more tolerant to long periods of emersion. Five years later, Paine (1966) published the early results of a study on the Washington coast clearly demonstrating that predation by a sea star (*Pisaster ochraceus*) maintained the lower limits of midshore mussel beds (Figure 18.9). Because the upper limit of sea stars typically reaches only the lower intertidal zone, mussels can persist in the middle intertidal zone because of release of predation. Due largely to these two influential studies, attention shifted dramatically in the 1960s toward the view that community patterns can be controlled by biotic factors as well. Both studies provided evidence for the ecological paradigm in rocky intertidal habitats that the lower limits of species are set by biotic interactions while the upper limits are driven by physical factors.

Paine's work not only demonstrated that predation could determine the lower distributional limit of a competitively dominant intertidal organism but also made important conceptual advances. His study was one of the earliest experimental demonstrations of the predation hypothesis, which states that predation can control the diversity of species in a community (Paine 1966). By selectively feeding on a dominant competitor, thereby preventing COMPETITIVE EXCLUSION, predators can facilitate the coexistence of many species of both dominant and subordinate competitors. In this case, sea star (*Pisaster*) predation mediated the abundance of the competitive dominant mussel (*Mytilus*), allowing for a myriad of competitively inferior species, such as barnacles and seaweeds, to persist. Paine's study established the concept of "keystone species"—species that have disproportionately large effects on their communities relative to their abundances (Paine 1969, Power et al. 1996). Finally, Paine's study was one of the first clear demonstrations of indirect effects.

FIGURE 18.9 The keystone predator, sea star (*Pisaster ochraceus*), feeding on its prey, the California mussel (*Mytilus californianus*). Photo: Jayson Smith.

Indirect effects are the effects of one species on a second, mediated through a third. In the *Mytilus-Pisaster* example, *Pisaster* has large, positive indirect effects on many subordinate competitors of *Mytilus*. The existence of indirect effects was first noted through the unexpected or surprising outcomes of experiments investigating species interactions (e.g., Paine 1966 and 1974, Dayton 1971). The broader significance of indirect effects was underappreciated, however, until theorists (e.g., Holt 1977, Bender et al. 1984) helped spur research to explicitly quantify their impact on community structure (see, e.g., Dungan 1986, Schmitt 1987, Wootton 1994).

Recruitment Dynamics

In rocky shore ecosystems two aspects of larval biology powerfully influence population dynamics and community structure. The first is the behavior of larvae in selecting settlement sites; the second relates to the quantities of larvae that recruit to the shore. A considerable body of work has shown that barnacle larvae have very specific requirements when they settle. The position of larvae in the water column (Grosberg 1982), the texture of the rock face (Crisp and Barnes 1954), the presence of CONSPECIFICS (gregarious settlement) (Knight-Jones 1955, Minchinton and Scheibling 1993), and chemical cues from coexisting species (Raimondi 1988) are among many factors that influence recruitment success.

The effect of a variable supply of new individuals on benthic populations has also long been of interest in marine ecology (see reviews by Underwood and Denley 1984, Young 1987 and 1990, Grosberg and Levitan 1992) and has been dubbed "supply-side ecology" (Lewin 1986). However, ecologists have only recently focused explicitly on the relative degree to which community structure is affected by settlement (the act of colonization and metamorphosis by propagules; Connell 1985) and recruitment (survival of settlers for some longer but usually arbitrary period of time Connell 1985) versus postrecruitment factors, such as predation and competition. Most early research on the influence of recruitment dealt with barnacle populations and the impact of variable recruitment or settlement densities on adult density (e.g., Gaines and Roughgarden 1985, Connell 1985, Raimondi 1990). In central California, for instance, abundances of adult *Balanus glandula* in the high zone vary from nearly complete coverage of the available rock surface at wave-exposed sites to low cover on more wave-sheltered sites (Gaines and Roughgarden 1985). Rates of recruitment were up to twenty times higher at wave-exposed sites compared to wave-sheltered sites. These and other studies also strongly suggest that when recruitment is low, patterns of abundance and community structure may be more strongly influenced by the supply rate of new individuals than by agents of postrecruitment mortality. For example, the negative relationship between an index of upwelling intensity and the recruitment of barnacle larvae (Roughgarden et al. 1988) is a strong indicator that offshore transport dictates barnacle densities via negative effects on recruitment.

Community Regulation

Whether and when biological communities are regulated by consumers (top-down) or primary productivity (bottom-up) remains a fundamental question in all of ecology (Oksanen et al. 1981, Fretwell 1987, Polis et al. 2000, Schmitz et al. 2000, White 2001). Some recent research in marine ecosystems has provided evidence for both top-down and bottom-up controls on communities (Burkepile and Hay 2006). A unique aspect of rocky shores is the occupation of primary space by two distinctly different groups of competing organisms: algae and filter-feeding invertebrates. Marine ecologists have spent considerable effort to understand the factors that contribute to the community pattern resulting from differences in the relative proportion of these two groups. One major mechanistic hypothesis linking nearshore oceanography to community pattern relates to the spatial and temporal variability in coastal upwelling. Latitudinal variation in upwelling intensity has been suggested as an important factor in the recruitment of benthic invertebrates along the U.S. West Coast.

The upwelling/relaxation model asserts that planktonic larvae are swept offshore by Ekman transport, where they accumulate along coastal fronts and are occasionally returned to shore when upwelling-favorable winds relax (Roughgarden et al. 1988, Shanks et al. 2000). Consistently strong upwelling along much of the California coast has been proposed to limit invertebrate recruitment (Gaines et al. 1985, Gaines and Roughgarden 1985, Roughgarden et al. 1988, Strub and James 1995), resulting in communities dominated by macrophytes in areas of strong upwelling. Regions of strong coastal upwelling may also influence community structure through positive direct effects on macroalgae, which compete for space with mussels and barnacles (Schiel 2004, Blanchette et al. 2006). Coastal upwelling delivers cold, nutrient-rich water to shore, and locations of strong upwelling are characterized by high nutrient concentrations, which have been shown to have positive effects on the abundance (Bustamante et al. 1995, Broitman et al. 2001) and growth rates (Blanchette et al. 2002, Nielsen and Navarrete 2004) of benthic macroalgae. Strong coastal upwelling is predicted to favor macroalgal dominated communities through both direct positive effects of nutrients on algae and indirect effects of reduced competition with recruitment-limited invertebrates for space. However, the relative importance of these two mechanisms is still not well understood.

Human Impacts

With approximately 68% of Californians living near the shoreline in 2008 (Wilson and Fischetti 2010), coastal ecosystems experience multiple threats from human activities. High urbanization can affect coastal ecosystems through air and water pollution, land development, habitat destruction, commercial and recreational harvest, recreational use, and introduction of non-native species, among other human-induced environmental changes. Rocky intertidal ecosystems are especially under threat because they lie at the land-ocean interface and thus receive direct runoff of terrestrial pollutants, coincide with settling locations for oceanic oil spills, and can be easily accessed during low tides for exploitation. Over the past several decades, many changes in species abundances have been observed in the rocky intertidal, including large declines in black abalone populations in southern and central California (Miller and Lawrenz-Miller 1993, Richards and Davis 1993, Altstatt et al. 1996); shifts in southern California macroalgal community structure from large fleshy species to more disturbance tolerant, turf-forming seaweeds (Widdowson 1971, Thom and Widdowson 1978, Goodson 2004, Gerrard 2005); declines in mussels in southern California (Smith, Ambrose, and Fong 2006) and mussel bed–associated macroinvertebrate diversity statewide (Smith, Fong, and Ambrose 2006); regional extinction of the dorid nudibranch (*Felimare californiensis*) (Goddard et al. 2013); shifts in species range limits (Sagarin et al. 2007, Zacherl et al. 2003), and increases in non-native species (Cohen and Carlton 1995, Murray et al. 2005).

Water Pollution

Water pollution includes manufactured chemicals such as DDT, elevated levels of naturally occurring chemicals such as heavy metals and nutrients, altered natural temperature regimes, and modified biota such as the introduction of non-native species. Water pollution in the rocky intertidal can be linked to terrestrial runoff, storm drain flow, aerial deposition, sewage effluent, wastewater discharges, and oil spills, and can involve chronic or pulse disturbances from either point or nonpoint sources. The impacts of water pollution on rocky intertidal species' health and normal ecosystem functioning are highly variable but are relatively understudied (Crowe et al. 2000, Thompson et al. 2002).

Although chronic input of oil washed into storm drains far exceeds oil spills (Foster et al. 1988, Suchanek 1993), the low rate of input as well as quick dilution has made it difficult to measure direct effects of the former. Pulse disturbances of large quantities of oil have received more attention. The combined impacts of oil coating, direct lethal toxicity, sublethal impacts on health, and clean-up efforts using chemical dispersants and physical removal can harm many rocky intertidal populations. Mass mortality of macroalgae and benthic invertebrates can result from chemical toxicity and smothering by oil, while high-pressure, hot-water clean-up efforts can have equally devastating, if not worse, effects including lengthened recovery time (Paine et al. 1996, Peterson et al. 2003). Sublethal impacts include physiological, carcinogenic, and cytogenic effects, resulting in population-level and community changes (Suchanek 1993, Peterson et al. 2003).

The largest oil spill in California and the third largest in the United States occurred near Santa Barbara in 1969, dumping about 4 million gallons of crude oil (Clarke and Hemphill 2002). Notable short-term impacts included marked losses of rocky intertidal barnacles and macrophytes (Foster et al. 1971, Straughan 1973); understanding of the spill's long-term effects, however, remains poor. Also near Santa Barbara, the 1997 Torch/Platform Irene Oil pipeline rupture spilled 6,846 gallons of petroleum, oiling approximately 17 miles of coastline. In 2007 the container ship *Cosco Busan* struck a San Francisco bridge, spilling 53,569 gallons of fuel, which oiled 200 miles of wave-protected and wave-exposed coastline. In 2009 the tank vessel *T/V Dubai Star* spilled 400 gallons of oil, reaching 10 miles of San Francisco Bay shoreline. Oil from these more recent spills coated portions of the rocky intertidal zone and its inhabitants, but their impacts were complex to measure, complicated by natural temporal variation and a lack of baseline information (Torch/Platform Irene Trustee Council 2007, Raimondi et al. 2009 and 2011). Some generalized effects of the spills included declines in barnacles, mussels, and rockweeds and increases in opportunistic algae.

In addition to oil, surface runoff from urban and agricultural sources discharges high amounts of fresh water, nutrients, heavy metals, pesticides, and other substances into California coastal waters (Schiff et al. 2000). Influxes of nutrients can cause declines in PERENNIAL seaweeds and increases in opportunistic seaweeds that use the nutrients to grow and bloom. For example, the addition of nutrients, in this case sewage-based, on San Clemente Island led to a decrease in slowly growing brown algae and seagrasses and an increase in opportunistic green algae and cyanobacteria (Littler and Murray 1975). Little work has examined the field effects of even single heavy metals on rocky intertidal ecosystems (Crowe et al. 2000), let alone of synergistic effects of multiple contaminants. Effects of sublethal levels of heavy metals and other contaminants can include opportunistic algal blooms (Castilla 1996) and impacts on larval development of benthic invertebrates (Fichet et al. 1998).

Recreational Human Visitation and Exploitation

Rocky intertidal habitats during low tide provide a glimpse of the natural marine world without the need for specialized underwater equipment and training. In heavily urbanized areas of California, visitation to some rocky intertidal locations can reach fifty thousand to seventy-five thousand visitors per year (Ambrose and Smith 2005, Ware 2009, Laguna Ocean Foundation 2012). People visit these habitats for recreation, education, and subsistence harvesting and engage in activities such as collecting, rock turning, handling, and trampling. Through both experimental manipulations and observational comparisons of high- and low-use locations, some detrimental impacts of these activities have been documented. These effects include locally depleted floral and faunal populations, reduced biodiversity, shifts in the size and age structure of populations, and altered ecological processes (e.g., Castilla and Bustamante 1989, Duran and Castilla 1989, Brown and Taylor 1999, Espinosa et al. 2009).

Harvesting of rocky intertidal organisms is relatively common in California and extends back thousands of years (Braje et al. 2007). People engage in legal harvesting as well as illegal poaching of protected species. Commercial harvesting of intertidal seaweeds is a growing cottage industry, especially in northern California (Thompson et al. 2010). Subsistence and ceremonial harvesting of intertidal mussels, seaweeds, and other intertidal organisms remains an important practice for the members of California's many Native American tribes. Organisms are harvested for food, fish bait, and souvenirs, with mussels, octopuses (*Octopus*), abalone (*Haliotis*), limpets (*Lottia*), urchins (*Strongylocentrotus*), snails (e.g., *Chlorostoma*), crabs (*Pachygrapsus*), seaweeds (e.g., *Postelsia*), and sea stars (*Pisaster*) often targeted.

Local declines in the abundances of many of these species have been attributed to overharvesting. For example, mussels (Smith et al. 2008), large conspicuous invertebrates such as keyhole limpets and sea hares (Ambrose and Smith 2005), and various echinoderms and gastropods (Addessi 1994) occur in lower abundances at heavily visited sites. Recreational harvest of red abalone virtually eliminates it from the intertidal zone, although it can be found intertidally in locations well protected from both legal harvest and poaching (Rogers-Bennett et al. 2013). Overharvesting can shift the size structures of intertidal populations (e.g., owl limpets) toward smaller and younger individuals, as humans tend to be size-selective predators (Fenberg and Roy 2008, Kido and Murray 2003, Ambrose and Smith 2005, Sagarin et al. 2007).

Management

Along the California coast, especially adjacent to heavily urbanized centers, a clear need exists to manage and protect rocky intertidal ecosystems. Conservation of rocky shores currently focuses on designations such as areas of special biological significance (ASBS) and/or marine protected areas (MPAs). The ASBS designation focuses on water quality, with thirty-four locations (32% of the California coast) managed by the State Water Resources Control Board. Within ASBS boundaries, state policy prevents discharge of any wastes in order to maintain natural water quality (SWRCB 2005). MPAs focus on the protection of marine organisms. As a result of the California Marine Life Protection Act passed in 1999, a network of 124 MPAs and 15 special closures (covering 16% of coastal waters) are now under the jurisdiction of the California Department of Fish and Wildlife. Within reserves, marine life is protected through limitations or bans on harvesting. MPAs in northern California also explicitly protect tribal rights to ceremonial and subsistence harvest of intertidal organisms. MPAs are very effective in protecting subtidal marine life (Halpern 2003), but their effectiveness in protecting rocky intertidal habitats needs to improve. Collecting in rocky intertidal MPAs continues to occur despite regulations (Murray 1997, Murray et al. 1999, Ambrose and Smith 2005). In addition, management is solely focused on collecting while other impacts are not clearly addressed (Smith et al. 2008).

While current management practices are strong and successful, improved conservation requires adaptive management and supplemental strategies. Publicly owned treatment works (POTWs) are well regulated, but storm water runoff management is still in its early stages, as is understanding of the singular and synergistic effects of pollutants. Continued and expanded long-term monitoring of rocky intertidal resources, such as that conducted by the Multi-Agency Rocky Intertidal Network (MARINe), provides vital baseline information to document impacts from oil spills and other anthropogenic disturbances. Increased support is needed for local organizations that help fill some management gaps. Groups such as numerous regional Baykeepers organizations, the Orange County MPA Council, Heal the Bay, and others provided essential local oversight, monitoring and research, and educational and outreach services. Restoration of rocky intertidal habitats is still nascent but could aid species recovery, as shown through the successful reestablishment of rockweeds (Whitaker et al. 2010) and surfgrass (Bull et al. 2004) following localized extirpation. Finally, conservation efforts of the future can be expanded by promoting public understanding of the economic and other values of rocky intertidal shores (e.g., Hall et al. 2002).

Climate Change

Global climate change is the backdrop against which all ecological and socioeconomic interactions now occur. The rocky intertidal zone has long served as a model system for examining the effects of the physical environment on the physiology and ecology of organisms, and as such has emerged as a natural laboratory for exploring the effects of environmental change (Connell 1972, Paine 1994). Impacts of climate change on patterns of distribution, abundance, and the provision of ecosystem services have been reported worldwide (Helmuth, Broitman et al. 2006), with numerous examples in California (e.g., Barry et al. 1995, Zacherl et al. 2003, Smith et al. 2006, Hilbish et al. 2010). While the exploration of the complex and often nonlinear effects of environmental change on intertidal ecosystems remains an active and growing area of research, several key themes—as well as knowledge gaps— have emerged in the search to understand and potentially forecast likely impacts (Howard et al. 2013).

Future Scenarios

Coastal habitats face myriad threats from global change, including increases in temperature, increased rates of coastal erosion, sea level rise, decreases in ocean pH, and altered circulation patterns (Howard et al. 2013). Globally, ocean acidity has increased by 30% (from an average pH value of 8.2 to 8.1) over the past century (Feely et al. 2004) with a further decline of 0.3 to 0.4 pH units expected by 2100 (Orr et al. 2005). The average temperature of the upper layers of the ocean has increased 0.2°C since 1955 (Bindhoff et al. 2007) and is expected to increase by 0.4°C to 1.1°C in the next few decades. Projections of future climate, which depend significantly on greenhouse gas emissions, suggest an increase in mean air temperature of 2°C to 5°C by 2100 in California, with the greatest amount of change occurring in summer (Cayan et al. 2009).

Notably, these global averages mask much higher levels of variability in environmental change (Hoegh-Guldberg and Bruno 2010), and coastal environments are likely being altered more quickly than offshore waters. Measurements of pH in Monterey Bay show a decrease about 8.1 to 8.05 from 1993 to 2009, although this is one of the few longer-term measurements from the region (Monterey Bay Aquarium Research Institute 2010 Annual Report. 2011). Hofmann et al. (2011) describe the results of a one-month time series of continuous pH measurement at seven sites along the coast of California and report high variability from site to site, with fluctuations of 1 pH unit (i.e., an order of magnitude variability) at sites such as Elkhorn Slough and levels at some sites approaching those predicted for the open ocean in 2100. California's coastal upwelling waters are typically very acidic, with pH values as low as 7.5 (Feeley et al. 2008, Gruber et al. 2012). Models predict a continuing decline in pH in these waters over time (Hauri et al. 2009) (Figure 18.10). Recent work has shown a mosaic of pH along the California coast, with persistent spatial variation in the cumulative frequency of exposure to relatively corrosive (pH <7.7) conditions (Hofmann et al. 2014).

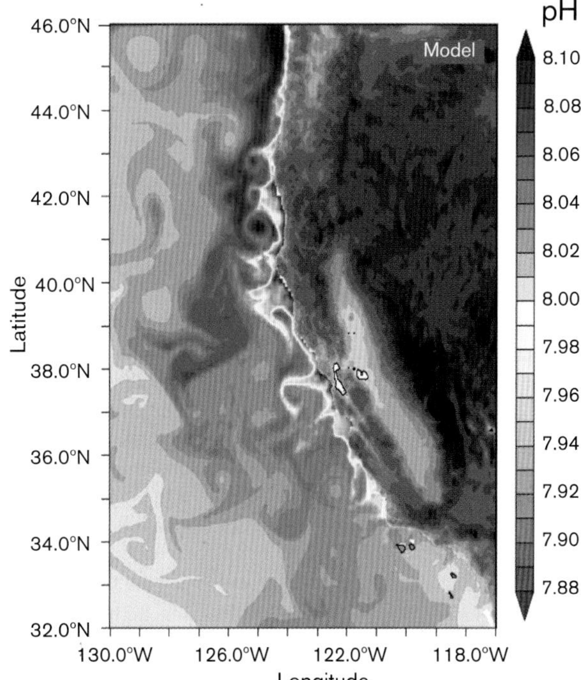

FIGURE 18.10 Model simulated snapshot of surface pH for the month of August. Low-pH waters in nearshore areas are the result of seasonal upwelling in summer, while the elevated pH in offshore waters reflects the photosynthetic removal of CO_2 from the water as it is transported offshore. Source: Hauri et al. 2009.

Nearshore water temperatures vary considerably from northern to southern California. Water temperatures in northern California are fairly homogeneous across latitude (31.5–40.5°N) with a mean temperature of 13.5°C and a mean annual range of 3.4°C (Payne et al. 2011). South of Point Conception in the Southern California Bight, waters are considerably warmer (17.8°C) and more variable (annual range of 5.6°C) (Payne et al. 2011). Geographic patterns of intertidal (aerial) temperature are even more complex, exhibiting a mosaic pattern in which extremes in temperature do not necessarily increase with decreasing latitude (Helmuth, Mieszkowska et al. 2006).

In general, the impacts of climate and related change in the intertidal can be categorized as direct physiological effects—the influence of environmental change on the survival, growth, reproduction, and physiological performance of individual organisms—and indirect effects, the cascading influence of altered behavior and physiological performance on species interactions, including predation, competition, and facilitation (Harley et al. 2006, Blanchette et al. 2008). Direct effects are better understood. Sanford (2002) showed that increased water temperatures enhanced feeding rates by the keystone sea star on mussel prey in central California. In contrast, increased sea star temperatures in air reduced feeding by 40% at the same site (Pincebourde et al. 2008). Competitive ability between barnacles in experiments depends on their relative physiological tolerances to thermal stress (Wethey 1984), and field collections in San Francisco Bay showed that small-scale distributions of native and invasive species of mussels were linked to aerial body temperature (Schneider and Helmuth 2007). Although understanding of emergent impacts on species assemblages remains incomplete, shifts in species phenology and ranges, increases in rates of species invasions and disease spread, and changes in the abundance of ecologically and economic important species have been reported worldwide, including on the coast of California (Harley et al. 2006, Howard et al. 2013).

Interactions between Stressors

Climate change is often "the trigger that fires the bullet," delivering the coup de grace on organisms already impacted by other stressors such as overharvesting and eutrophication (Harley and Rogers-Bennett 2004, Crain et al. 2008, Firth and Williams 2009). As such, the impacts of environmental stressors are best considered in the context of other climatic and nonclimatic drivers of physiology and ecology. Crain et al. (2008) conducted a meta-analysis of marine studies that examined multiple stressors and found that cumulative effects were more or less evenly divided among additive (sum of individual stressors), synergistic (overall impact more than the sum of the individual stressors), and antagonistic (impact less than the sum of the individual effects) types. Overharvesting, for example, predisposes populations of fish to collapse when exposed to stressors such as pollution and climate change (Hsieh et al. 2008, Sumaila et al. 2011). Taken in sum, these studies signal a need to understand the processes by which climate change impacts intertidal organisms, at scales ranging from subcellular to ecosystem (Helmuth 2009).

Summary

Intertidal ecosystems exist at the interface between land and ocean and occupy a narrow band of the coast that is above water at low tide and under water at high tide. Organisms occupying intertidal areas have evolved unique adaptations to withstand the wide variation in physical conditions (temperature, salinity, desiccation) characteristic of these environments. Although intertidal habitats can have either soft (sand, mud) or hard (rocky) bottom substrates, we have focused this chapter on rocky intertidal ecosystems, which occur along the entire California coast. Rocky intertidal ecosystems of the Pacific coast support a high diversity of invertebrate and algal species and have served as a model ecosystem for experimental marine ecology.

The organisms inhabiting rocky intertidal ecosystems tend to occur in characteristic bands or zones determined in part by time of submergence (underwater) and emergence (above water). Along the coast of California the high intertidal zone, which is inundated only during high tides, has species including rockweed, acorn barnacles, turban snails, and lined shore crabs. The middle intertidal zone, exposed to the air at least once a day, is home to creatures such as sea lettuce, aggregating anemones, chitons, gooseneck barnacles, mussels, and ochre stars. The low intertidal zone, exposed only during very low tides, is inhabited by kelps, coralline algae, surfgrass, giant green anemones, purple sea urchins, and bat stars. Ecological processes, such as competition, predation, and recruitment, play an important role in determining the species composition of intertidal assemblages. Many invertebrate and algal species that occupy the shoreline as adults have early life history stages such as spores and larvae that may spend days to months drifting in the ocean before settlement on the shore. These early life history stages are one important connection between the benthic (rocky bottom) habitat of the intertidal and the pelagic (open ocean) realm. Intertidal organisms also depend on water movement for delivery of food and nutrients as well as reproduction and dispersal.

People use intertidal ecosystems for food and recreation; however, these ecosystems are also sensitive to anthropogenic impacts from water pollution, oil spills, harvesting, and trampling. Following the California Marine Life Protection Act (1999) a statewide network of marine protected areas has been established along the California coast, and many of these reserves include significant portions of rocky intertidal habitat. Climate change likely poses the most serious threat to intertidal ecosystems, where many species are already living close to their physiological tolerance limits. Increases in temperature, coastal erosion rates, and sea level rise; decreases in ocean pH; and altered circulation patterns resulting from changing climate conditions all could significantly impact intertidal ecosystems in the coming decades.

Acknowledgments

The authors thank the U.S. Department of the Interior Bureau of Ocean Energy Management, the Multi-Agency Rocky Intertidal Network, the Partnership for Interdisciplinary Studies of Coastal Oceans (PISCO), the Tatman Foundation, and Aeon N. Brady.

Recommended Reading

Abbott, I., and G. Hollenberg. 1976. Marine algae of California. Stanford University Press, Stanford, California.

Denny, M. W. 1988. Biology and the mechanics of the wave-swept environment. Princeton University Press, Princeton, New Jersey.

Denny, M. W., and S. D. Gaines, editors. 2007. Encyclopedia of tidepools and rocky shores. University of California, Press, Berkeley, California.

Morris, R. H., D. P. Abbott, and E. C. Haderlie. 1980. Intertidal invertebrates of California. First edition. Stanford University Press, Stanford, California.

Ricketts, E. F., J. Calvin, and J. Hedgpeth. 1939. Between Pacific tides. Fifth edition. Stanford University Press, Stanford, California.

Glossary

BENTHIC This refers generally to organisms that live in close relationship with the substrate bottom and many that are permanently attached to the bottom.

BIOGEOGRAPHIC Refers to the distribution of organisms in the context of geographical space.

COMPETITIVE EXCLUSION The proposition that states that two species competing for the same resources cannot coexist if other ecological factors are constant. When one species has even the slightest advantage or edge over another, then the one with the advantage will dominate in the long term.

CONSPECIFIC Members of the same species.

EMERSION Refers to the time that organisms spend out of or uncovered by water.

FRANCISCAN COMPLEX An assemblage of sandstone, shale, chert, and mildly metamorphosed basalts derived from ocean floor material accreted onto the California coast by subduction. These rocks comprise large portions of the California coast and Coast Range mountains.

MARINE TERRACE Broad, flat expanses of coastal land originally created by erosion of waves when the land was at sea level. Multiple sea level changes and tectonic uplift later raise the flat terraces above sea level, leaving characteristic stepped hills.

OROGENIC Any geological process that leads to the formation of mountains. Often caused by the pressures of colliding and subducting tectonic plates or volcanic activity.

PELAGIC This refers to organisms that are not associated with the bottom and occur in the water column or in the open sea.

PERENNIAL These are plants and seaweeds that live for more than two years and is generally a term used to differentiate from annuals, which complete their life cycle in one year.

SESSILE This refers to organisms that are directly attached to the bottom or substrate.

SHOAL This term refers to when water becomes more shallow.

SUBDUCTION The geologic process by which the edge of an oceanic tectonic plate is forced beneath another plate. Subduction can create coastal mountains due to pressure lifting land behind the subduction zone.

THALLI These are the undifferentiated vegetative tissues of macroalgae, and generally refer to the entire individual seaweed organisms in the case of macroaglae.

VELIGER The planktonic larva of many kinds of gastropod and bivalve molluscs.

VISCOUS Refers to the properties of fluid that resist deformation to stress. Viscous fluids are generally thought of as being more "thick" (e.g., honey).

References

Abbott, I. A., and G. J. Hollenberg. 1976. Marine algae of California. Stanford University Press, Stanford, California.

Addessi, L. 1994. Human disturbance and long-term changes on a rocky intertidal community. Ecological Applications 4:786–797.
Altstatt, J. M., R. F. Ambrose, J. M. Engle, P. L. Haaker, K. D. Lafferty, and P. T. Raimondi. 1996. Recent declines of black abalone *Haliotis cracherodii* on the mainland coast of central California. Marine Ecology Progress Series 142:185–192.
Ambrose, R. F., and J. R. Smith. 2005. Restoring rocky intertidal habitats in Santa Monica Bay. Technical Report for the Santa Monica Bay Restoration Commission, Los Angeles, California.
Arkema, K, G. Guannel, G. Verutes, S. A. Wood, A. Guerry, M. Ruckelshaus, P. Kareiva, M. Lacayo, and J. M. Silver. 2013. Coastal habitats shield people and property from sea-level rise and storms. Nature Climate Change 3:913–918.
Barry, J. P., C. H. Baxter, R. D. Sagarin, and S. E. Gilman. 1995. Climate-related, long-term faunal changes in a California rocky intertidal community. Science 267:672–675.
Bender, E. A., T. J. Case, and M. E. Gilpin. 1984. Perturbation experiments in community ecology: Theory and practice. Ecology 65:1–13.
Benson, K. R. 2002. The study of vertical zonation on rocky shores—A historical perspective. Integrative and Comparative Biology 42:776–779.
Bindoff, N. L., J. Willebrand, V. Artale, A. Cazenave, J. M. Gregory, S. Gulev, K. Hanawa, C. Le Quéré, S. Levitus, Y. Nojiri et al. 2007. Observations: Oceanic climate change and sea level. Pages 385–432 in S.E.A. Soloman, editor. Climate Change 2007: The Physical Science Basis: Contribution of Working Group I to the Fourth Assessment Report of the Intergovernmental Panel on Climate Change. Cambridge University Press, Cambridge, UK, and New York, New York.
Blanchette, C. A. 1996. Seasonal patterns of disturbance influence recruitment of the sea palm, *Postelsia palmaeformis*. Journal of Experimental Marine Biology and Ecology 197:1–14.
Blanchette C. A., B. G. Miner, and S. D. Gaines. 2002. Geographic variability in form, size, and survival of *Egregia menziesii* around Point Conception, California. Marine Ecology Progress Series 239:69–82.
Blanchette, C. A., B. Helmuth, and S. D. Gaines. 2007. Spatial patterns of growth in the mussel, *Mytilus californianus*, across a major oceanographic and biogeographic boundary at Point Conception, California, USA. Journal of Experimental Marine Biology and Ecology 340:126–148.
Blanchette C. A., B. R. Broitman, and S. D. Gaines. 2006. Intertidal community structure and oceanographic patterns around Santa Cruz Island, CA, USA. Marine Biology 149:689–701.
Blanchette, C. A., C. M. Miner, P. T. Raimondi, D. Lohse, K. E. K. Heady, and B. R. Broitman. 2008. Biogeographical patterns of rocky intertidal communities along the Pacific coast of North America. Journal of Biogeography 35:1593–1607.
Blanchette, C. A., P.T. Raimondi, and B. R. Broitman. 2009. Spatial patterns of intertidal community structure across the California Channel Islands and links to ocean temperature. Pages 161–173 in C. C. Damiani and D. K. Garcelon, editors. Proceedings of the 7th California Islands Symposium. Institute for Wildlife Studies, Arcata, California.
Braje, T. J., D. J. Kennett, J. M. Erlandon, and B. J. Culleton. 2007. Human impacts on nearshore shellfish taxa: A 7,000 year record from Santa Rosa Island, California. American Antiquity 72:735–756.
Broitman, B. R., and B. P. Kinlan. 2006. Spatial scales of benthic and pelagic producer biomass in a coastal upwelling ecosystem. Marine Ecology Progress Series 327:15–25.
Broitman B. R., S. A. Navarrete, F. Smith, and S. D. Gaines. 2001. Geographic variation of southeastern Pacific intertidal communities. Marine Ecology Progress Series 224:21–34.
Brown, E., A. Colling, D. Park, J. Phillips, D. Rothery, and J. Wright. 1999. Waves, tides, and shallow-water processes. Second edition. Butterworth-Heineman, Milton Keynes, UK.
Brown, P. J., and R. B. Taylor. 1999. Effects of trampling by humans on animals inhabiting coralline algal turf in the rocky intertidal. Journal of Experimental Marine Biology and Ecology 235:45–53.
Bull, J. S., D. C. Reed, and S. J. Holbrook. 2004. An experimental evaluation of different methods of restoring *Phyllospadix torreyi* (Surfgrass). Restoration Ecology 12:70–79.
Burkepile, D. E. and M. E. Hay. 2006. Herbivore vs. nutrient control of marine primary producers: Context-dependent effects. Ecology 87:3128–3139.
Burton, R. S. 1998. Intraspecific phylogeography across the Point Conception biogeographic boundary. Evolution 52:734–745.
Bustamante R. H., G. M. Branch, and S. Eekhout. 1995. Maintenance of an exceptional intertidal grazer biomass in South Africa: Subsidy by subtidal kelps. Ecology 76:2314–2329.
Carlton, J. T., editor. 2007. The Light and Smith manual: Intertidal invertebrates from central California to Oregon. University of California Press, Berkeley, California.
Cartwright, D. E. 1999. Tides: A scientific history. Cambridge University Press, New York, New York.
Castilla, J. C. 1996. Copper mine tailing disposal in northern Chile rocky shores: *Enteromorpha compressa* (Cholorphyta) as a sentinel species. Environmental Monitoring and Assessment 40:171–184.
Castilla, J. C., and R. H. Bustamante. 1989. Human exclusion from rocky intertidal of Las Cruces, central Chile: Effects on *Durvillaea antarctica* (Phaeophyta, Durvilleales). Marine Ecology Progress Series 50:203–214.
Cayan, D., M. Tyree, M. Dettinger, H. Hidalgo, T. Das, E. Maurer, P. Bromirski, N. Graham, and R. Flick. 2009. Climate change scenarios and sea level rise estimates for the California 2009 Climate Change Scenarios Assessment: California Climate Change Center. Washington, D.C.
Clarke, K. C., and J. J. Hemphill. 2002. The Santa Barbara oil spill, a retrospective. Pages 157–162 in D. Danta, editor. Yearbook of the Association of Pacific Coast Geographers. University of Hawai'i Press, Honolulu, Hawaii.
Cohen, A. N., and J. T. Carlton. 1995. Nonindigenous aquatic species in a United State estuary: A case study of the biological invasions of the San Francisco Bay and Delta. Report for the U.S. Fish and Wildlife Service and National Sea Grant College Program. U.S. Fish and Wildlife Service, Washington, D.C.
Connell, J. H. 1985. The consequences of variation in initial settlement vs. post settlement mortality in rocky intertidal communities. Journal of Experimental Marine Biology and Ecology 93:11–45.
———. 1972. Community interactions on marine rocky intertidal shores. Annual Review of Ecology and Systematics 3:169–192.
———. 1961a. Effects of competition, predation by *Thais lapillus,* and other factors on natural populations of the barnacle *Balanus balanoides*. Ecological Monographs 31: 61–104.
———. 1961b. The influence of interspecific competition and other factors on the distribution of the barnacle *Chthamalus stellatus*. Ecology 42: 710–723.
Crain, C. M., K. Kroeker, and B. S. Halpern. 2008. Interactive and cumulative effects of multiple human stressors in marine systems. Ecology Letters 11:1304–1315.
Crisp, D. J., and H. Barnes. 1954. The orientation and distribution of barnacles at settlement with particular reference to surface contour. Journal of Animal Ecology 23:142–162.
Crowe, T. P., R. C. Thompson, S. Bray, and S. J. Hawkins. 2000. Impacts of anthropogenic stress on rocky intertidal communities. Journal of Aquatic Ecosystem Stress and Recover 7:273–297.
Dayton, P. K. 1973. Dispersion, dispersal, and persistence of the annual intertidal alga, *Postelsia palmaeformis* Ruprecht. Ecology 54:433–438.
———. 1971. Competition, disturbance, and community organization: The provision and subsequent utilization of space in a rocky intertidal community. Ecological Monographs 41:351–389.
Denny, M. W. 1994. Air and water: The physics of life's media. Princeton University Press, Princeton, New Jersey.
———. 1988. Biology and the mechanics of the wave-swept environment. Princeton University Press, Princeton, New Jersey.
Denny, M. W., and R. T. Paine. 1998. Celestial mechanics, sea-level changes, and intertidal ecology. Biological Bulletin 194:108–115.
Denny, M. W., S. D. Gaines, editors. 2007. Encyclopedia of tidepools and rocky shores. University of California, Press, Berkeley, California.
Denny, M. W., L. J. Hunt, L. P. Miller, and C. D. G. Harley. 2009. On the prediction of extreme ecological events. Ecological Monographs 79:397–421.
Denny, M. W., W. W. Dowd, L. Bilir, and K. J. Mach. 2011. Spreading the risk: Small-scale body temperature variation among intertidal organisms and its implications for species persistence. Journal of Experimental Marine Biology and Ecology 400:175–190.

Doyle, R. F. 1985. Biogeographical studies of rocky shores near Point Conception, California. University of California, Santa Barbara, California.

Dungan, M. L. 1986. Three-way interactions: Barnacles, limpets, and algae in a Sonoran Desert rocky intertidal zone. American Naturalist 127: 292–316.

Duran, L. R., and J. C. Castilla. 1989. Variation and persistence of the middle rocky intertidal community of central Chile, with and without human harvesting. Marine Biology 103:555–562.

Eckert, G. L., J. M. Engle, and D. J. Kushner. 2000. Sea star disease and population declines at the Channel Islands. Pages 390–393 in Proceedings of the Fifth California Islands Symposium. Minerals Management Service 99-0038.

Espinosa, F., G. A. Rivera-Ingraham, D. Fa, and J. C. Garcia-Gomez. 2009. Effect of human pressure on population size structures of the endangered Ferruginean limpet: Toward future management measures. Journal of Coastal Research 25:857–863.

Feely, R. A., C. L. Sabine, J. M. Hernandez-Ayon, D. Ianson, and B. Hales. 2008. Evidence for upwelling of corrosive "acidified" water onto the continental shelf. Science 320:1490–1492.

Feely, R. A., C. L. Sabine, K. Lee, W. Berelson, J. Kleypas, V. J. Fabry, and F. J. Millero. 2004. Impact of anthropogenic CO_2 on the $CaCO_3$ system in the oceans. Science 305:362–366.

Fenberg, P. B., and K. Roy. 2008. Ecological and evolutionary consequences of size-selective harvesting: How much do we know? Molecular Ecology 17:209–220.

Fichet, D., G. Radenac, and P. Miramand. 1998. Experimental studies of impacts of harbor sediments resuspension to marine invertebrate larvae: Bioavailability of Cd, Cu, Pb and Zn and toxicity. Marine Pollution Bulletin 36:7–12.

Firth, L. B., and G. A. Williams. 2009. The influence of multiple environmental stressors on the limpet *Cellana toreuma* during the summer monsoon season in Hong Kong. Journal of Experimental Marine Biology and Ecology 375:70–75.

Foster, M. S., A. P. DeVogelaere, C. Harrold, J. S. Pearse, and A. B. Thum. 1988. Causes of spatial and temporal patterns in rocky intertidal communities in central and northern California. Memoirs of the California Academy of Sciences 9:1–45.

Foster, M. S., M. Neushul, and R. Zingmark. 1971. The Santa Barbara oil spill, part 2: Initial effects on intertidal and kelp organisms. Environmental Pollution 2:115–134.

Fretwell, S. D. 1987. Food chain dynamics: The central theory of ecology? Oikos 50:291–301.

Gaines, S. D., and J. Roughgarden. 1987. Fish in offshore kelp forests affect recruitment to intertidal barnacle populations. Science 235:479–481.

———. 1985. Larval settlement rate—a leading determinant of structure in an ecological community of the marine intertidal zone. Proceedings of the National Academy of Sciences of the United States of America 82:3707–3711.

Gaines, S., S. Brown, and J. Roughgarden. 1985. Spatial variation in larval concentrations as a cause of spatial variation in settlement for the barnacle, *Balanus glandula*. Oecologia 67:267–272.

Gerrard, A. L. 2005. Changes in rocky intertidal floras along the Palos Verdes Peninsula (Los Angeles County) since E. Y. Dawson's surveys in the late 1950s. MS thesis. California State University, Fullerton.

Goddard, J. H. R., M. C. Schaefer, C. Hoover, and A. Valdes. 2013. Regional extinction of a conspicuous dorid nudibranch (Mollusca: Gastropoda) in California. Marine Biology 160:1497–1510.

Goodson, J. 2004. Long-term changes in rocky intertidal populations and communities at Little Corona del Mar, California: A synthesis using traditional and non-traditional data. MS thesis. California State University, Fullerton.

Griggs, G. B., and A. S. Trenhaile. 1997. Coastal cliffs and platforms. Pages 425–450 in R.W.G. Carter and C. D. Woodroffe, editors. Coastal evolution: Late quaternary shoreline morphodynamics. Cambridge University Press, Cambridge, UK.

Griggs, G., K. Patsch, and L. Savoy. 2005. Living with the changing California coast. University of California Press, Berkeley, California.

Grosberg, R. K. 1982. Intertidal zonation of barnacles: The influence of planktonic zonation of larvae on vertical distribution of adults. Ecology 63:894–899.

Grosberg, R. K., and D. Levitan. 1992. For adults only? Supply-side ecology and the history of larval biology. Trends in Ecology and Evolution 7:130–133.

Gruber, N., C. Hauri, Z. Lachkar, D. Loher, T. L. Frolicher, and G. K. Plattner. 2012. Rapid progression of ocean acidification in the California Current System. Science 337:220–223.

Hall, D. C., J. V. Hall, and S. N. Murray. 2002. Contingent valuation of Marine Protected Areas: Southern California rocky intertidal ecosystems. Natural Resource Modeling 15:335–368.

Halpern, B. S. 2003. The impact of marine reserves: Do reserves work and does reserve size matter? Ecological Applications 13:117–137.

Harden, D. R. 2004. California geology. Pearson Prentice Hall, Upper Saddle River, New Jersey.

Harley, C.D.G. 2008. Tidal dynamics, topographic orientation, and temperature-mediated mass mortalities on rocky shores. Marine Ecology Progress Series 371:37–46.

Harley, C.D.G., and L. Rogers-Bennett. 2004. The potential synergistic effects of climate change and fishing pressure on exploited invertebrates on rocky intertidal shores. California Cooperative Oceanic Fisheries Investigations Reports 45:98–110.

Harley, C.D.G., and R. T. Paine. 2009. Contingencies and compounded rare perturbations dictate sudden distributional shifts during periods of gradual climate change. Proceedings of the National Academy of Sciences 106:11172–11176.

Harley, C.D.G., A. R. Hughes, K. A. Hultgren, B. G. Miner, C. J. B. Sorte, C. S. Thornber, L. F. Rodriguez, L. Tomanek, and S. L. Williams. 2006. The impacts of climate change in coastal marine systems. Ecology Letters 9:228–241.

Hauri, C., N. Gruber, G. K. Plattner, S. Alin, R. A. Feely, B. Hales, and P. Wheeler. 2009. Ocean acidification in the California Current System. Oceanography 22:60–71.

Hayes, M. O., and J. Michel. 2010. A coast to explore. Coastal geology and ecology of central California. Pandion Books, Columbia, South Carolina.

Helmuth, B. 2009. From cells to coastlines: How can we use physiology to forecast the impacts of climate change? Journal of Experimental Biology 212:753–760.

Helmuth, B., B. R. Broitman, C. A. Blanchette, S. Gilman, P. Halpin, C. D. G. Harley, M. J. O'Donnell, G. E. Hofmann, B. Menge, and D. Strickland. 2006. Mosaic patterns of thermal stress in the rocky intertidal zone: Implications for climate change. Ecological Monographs 76:461–479.

Helmuth, B., N. Mieszkowska, P. Moore, and S. J. Hawkins. 2006. Living on the edge of two changing worlds: Forecasting the responses of rocky intertidal ecosystems to climate change. Annual Review of Ecology Evolution and Systematics 37:373–404.

Helmuth, B. S. T., and G. E. Hofmann. 2001. Microhabitats, thermal heterogeneity, and patterns of physiological stress in the rocky intertidal zone. Biological Bulletin 201:374–384.

Hewatt, W. G. 1937. Ecological studies on selected marine intertidal communities of Monterey Bay, California. American Midland Naturalist 18:161–206.

Hickey, B. 1993. Physical oceanography. Page 926 in M. D. Dailey, D. J. Reisch, and J. W. Anderson, editors. Ecology of the Southern California Bight. University of California Press, Berkeley, California.

Hickey, B., E. L. Dobbins, and S. E. Allen. 2003. Local and remote forcing of currents and temperature in the central Southern California Bight. Journal of Geophysical Research: Oceans 108:no. C3.

Hilbish, T. J., P. M. Brannock, K. R. Jones, A. B. Smith, B. N. Bullock, and D. S. Wethey. 2010. Historical changes in the distributions of invasive and endemic marine invertebrates are contrary to global warming predictions: The effects of decadal climate oscillations. Journal of Biogeography 37:423–431.

Hoegh-Guldberg, O., and J. F. Bruno. 2010. The impact of climate change on the world's marine ecosystems. Science 328:1523–1528.

Hofmann, G. E., J. E. Smith, K. S. Johnson, U. Send, L. A. Levin, F. Micheli, A. Paytan, N. N. Price, B. Peterson, Y. Takeshita et al. 2011. High-frequency dynamics of ocean pH: A multi-ecosystem approach. PLoS One 6:e28983.

Hofmann, G. E., T. G. Evans, M. W. Kelly, J. L. Padilla-Gamiño, C. A. Blanchette, L. Washburn, F. Chan, M. A. McManus, B. A. Menge, B. Gaylord, T. M. Hill, E. Sanford, M. LaVigne, J. M. Rose, L. Kapsenberg, and J. M. Dutton. 2014. Exploring local adaptation and the ocean acidification seascape—studies in the California Current Large Marine Ecosystem. Biogeosciences 11:1–13.

Holt, R. D. 1977. Predation, apparent competition, and the structure of prey communities. Theoretical Population Biology 12: 197–229.

Howard, J. E. et al. 2013. Oceans and marine resources in a changing climate. Oceanography and Marine Biology 51:71–192.
Hsieh, C., C. S. Reiss, R. P. Hewitt, and G. Sugihara. 2008. Spatial analysis shows that fishing enhances the climatic sensitivity of marine fishes. Canadian Journal of Fisheries and Aquatic Sciences 65:947–961.
Huyer, A. 1983. Coastal upwelling in the California current system. Progress in Oceanography 12:259–284.
Jansen, J. M., A. E. Pronker, S. Kube, A. Sokolowski, J. C. Sola, M. A. Marquiegui, D. Schiedek, S. W. Bonga, M. Wolowicz, and H. Hummel. 2007. Geographic and seasonal patterns and limits on the adaptive response to temperature of European *Mytilus* spp. and *Macoma balthica* populations. Oecologia 154:23–34.
Kanter, R. G. 1980. Biogeographic patterns in mussel community distribution from the southern California Bight. Pages 341–355 in D. M. Power, editor. The California Islands: Proceedings of a multidisciplinary symposium. Santa Barbara Museum of Natural History, Santa Barbara, California.
Kavanaugh, M. T., K. J. Nielsen, F. T. Chan, B. A. Menge, R. M. Letelier, and L. M. Goodrich. 2009. Experimental assessment of the effects of shade on an intertidal kelp: Do phytoplankton blooms inhibit growth of open coast macroalgae? Limnology and Oceanography 54: 276–288.
Kido, J. S., and S. N. Murray. 2003. Variation in owl limpet *Lottia gigantea* population structures, growth rates, and gonadal production on Southern California rocky shores. Marine Ecology Progress Series 257:111–124.
Knight-Jones, E. W. 1955. The gregarious setting reaction of barnacles as a measure of systematic affinity Nature 174: 266.
Krenz, C., B. A. Menge, T. L. Freidenberg, J. Lubchenco, F. Chan, M. Foley, and K. J. Nielsen. 2011. Ecological subsidies to rocky intertidal communities: Linear or non-linear changes along a consistent geographic upwelling transition? Journal of Experimental Biology and Ecology 409:361–370.
Kroeker, K., R. L. Kordas, R. N. Crim, and G. G. Singh. 2010. Meta-analysis reveals negative yet variable effects of ocean acidification on marine organisms. Ecology Letters 13:1419–1434.
Laguna Ocean Foundation. 2012. Tidepool interpretive program at the Treasure Island seashore, 2011–2012 Annual Report. Technical Report submitted by J. Bonus to the Montage Resort and Spa. Laguna Beach, California.
Lester, S. E., S. D. Gaines, and B. P. Kinlan. 2007. Reproduction on the edge: Large scale patterns of individual performance in a marine invertebrate. Ecology 88:2229– 2239.
Lewin, R. 1986. Supply-side ecology. Science 234:25–27.
Lewis, J. R. 1964. The ecology of rocky shores. English Universities Press, London, UK.
Littler, M. M., and S. N. Murray. 1975. Impact of sewage on the distribution, abundance, and community structure of rocky intertidal macro-organisms. Marine Biology 30:277–291.
MacGintie, G. E. 1935. Ecological aspects of a California marine estuary. American Midland Naturalist 16:629–765.
Maloney, E., R. Fairy, A. Lyman, K. Reynolds, and M. Sigala. 2006. Introduced aquatic species in California open coastal waters. Technical Report. Office of Spill Prevention and Response. California Department of Fish and Game, Sacramento, California.
Menge, B. A. 1976. Organization of the New England rocky intertidal community: Role of predation, competition and environmental heterogeneity. Ecological Monographs 46:355–393.
Menge, B. A., J. Lubchenco, M.E.S. Bracken, F. Chan, M. M. Foley, T. L. Freidenburg, S. D. Gaines, G. Hudson, C. Krenz, H. Leslie, D.N.L. Menge, R. Russell, and M .S. Webster. 2003. Coastal oceanography sets the pace of rocky intertidal community dynamics. Proceedings of the National Academy of Sciences of the United States of America 21:12229–12234.
Miller, A. C., and S. E. Lawrenz-Miller. 1993. Long-term trends in black abalone, *Haliotis cracherodii* Leach, 1814, populations along the Palos Verdes Peninsula, California. Journal of Shellfish Research 12:195–200.
Minchinton, T. E., and R. E. Scheibling. 1993. Free space availability and larval substratum selection as determinants of barnacle population structure in a developing rocky intertidal community. Marine Ecology Progress Series 95: 233–244.
Monterey Bay Aquarium Research Institute 2010 Annual Report. 2011. <http://www.mbari.org/news/publications/pubs.html>.
Murray, S. N. 1997. Effectiveness of marine life refuges on southern California shores. Proceedings of the Conference of the American Society of Engineers, San Diego, California.
Murray, S. N., and M. M. Littler. 1989. Seaweeds and seagrasses of southern California: Distributional lists for twenty-one rocky intertidal sites. Bulletin of the Southern California Academy of Sciences 88:61–79.
Murray, S. N., L. Fernandez, and J. A. Zertuche-Gonzalez. 2005. Status, environmental threats, and policy considerations for invasive seaweeds for the Pacific Coast of North America. Report for the Commission on Environmental Cooperation. Montreal, Canada.
Murray, S. N., T. G. Denis, J. S. Kido, and J. R. Smith. 1999. Human visitation and the frequency and potential effects of collecting on rocky intertidal populations in southern California marine reserves. California Cooperative Oceanic Fisheries Investigations Reports 40:100–106.
Nielsen K. J., and S. A. Navarrete. 2004. Mesoscale regulation comes from the bottom-up: Intertidal interactions between consumers and upwelling. Ecology Letters 7:31–41.
Oksanen L., S. D. Fretwell, J. Arruda, and P. Niemela. 1981. Exploitation ecosystems in gradients of primary productivity. American Naturalist 118:240–261.
Orr, J. C., V. J. Fabry, O. Aumont, L. Bopp, S. C. Doney, R. A. Feely, A. Gnanadesikan, N. Gruber, A. Ishida, F. Joos et al. 2005. Anthropogenic ocean acidification over the twenty-first century and its impact on calcifying organisms. Nature 437:681–686.
Paine, R. T. 1994. Marine rocky shores and community ecology: An experimentalist's perspective. Ecology Institute, Oldendorf/Luhe, Germany.
———. 1988. Habitat suitability and local population persistence of the sea palm *Postelsia palmaeformis*. Ecology 69:1787–1794.
———. 1974. Intertidal community structure: Experimental studies on the relationship between a dominant competitor and its principal predator. Oecologia 15:93–120.
———. 1969. A note on trophic complexity and community stability. American Naturalist 103:91–93.
———. 1966. Food web complexity and species diversity. American Naturalist 100: 65–75.
Paine, R. T., and S. A. Levin. 1981. Intertidal landscapes: Disturbance and the dynamics of pattern. Ecological Monographs 51: 145–178.
Paine, R. T., J. L. Ruesink, A. Sun, E. L. Soulanille, M. J. Wonham, C.D.G. Harley, D. R. Brumbaugh, and D. L. Secord. 1996. Trouble on oiled waters: Lessons from the Exxon Valdez oil spill. Annual Review of Ecology and Systematics 27:197–235.
Payne, M. C., C. A. Brown, D. A. Reusser, and H. Lee II. 2011. Ecoregional analysis of nearshore sea-surface temperature in the North Pacific. PLoS ONE 7:e30105.
Peterson, C. H., S. D. Rice, J. W. Short, D. Esler, J. L. Bodkin, B. E. Ballachey, and D. B. Irons. 2003. Long-term ecosystem response to the Exxon Valdez oil spill. Science 302:2082–2086.
Petes, L. E., B. A. Menge, and A. L. Harris. 2008. Intertidal mussels exhibit energetic trade-offs between reproduction and stress resistance. Ecological Monographs 78:387–402.
Phillips, N. E. 2004. Variable timing of larval food has consequences for early juvenile performance in a marine mussel. Ecology 85:2341–2346.
———. 2002. Effects of nutrition-mediated larval condition on juvenile performance in a marine mussel. Ecology 83:2562–2574.
Pincebourde, S., E. Sanford, and B. Helmuth. 2008. Body temperature during low tide alters the feeding performance of a top intertidal predator. Limnology and Oceanography 53:1562–1573.
Polis G. A., A.L.W. Sears, G. R. Huxel, D. R. Strong, and J. Maron. 2000. When is a trophic cascade a trophic cascade? Trends in Ecology and Evolution 15:473–475.
Pörtner, H. O., and A. P. Farrell. 2008. Physiology and climate change. Nature 322:690–692.
Power, M. E., D. Tilman, J. A. Estes, B. A. Menge, W. J. Bond, L. S. Mills, G. Daily, J. C. Castilla, J. Lubchenco, and R. T. Paine. 1996. Challenges in the quest for keystones. BioScience 46: 609–620.
Raimondi, P. T. 1990. Patterns, mechanisms, and consequences of variability in settlement and recruitment of an intertidal barnacle. Ecological Monographs 60: 283–309.
———. 1988. Settlement cues and determination of the vertical limit of an intertidal barnacle. Ecology 69:400–407.
Raimondi, P., D. Orr, C. Bell, M. George, S. Worden, M. Redfield, R. Gaddam, L. Anderson, and D. Lohse. 2009. Determination of the extent and type of injury to rocky intertidal algae and animals

one year after the initial spill (Cosco Busan): A report prepared for Office of Spill Prevention and Response (OSPR). California Department of Fish and Game, Sacramento, California.
Raimondi, P., M. Miner, D. Orr, C. Bell, M. George, S. Worden, M. Redfield, R. Gaddam, L. Aunderson, and D. Lohse. 2011. Determination of the extent and type of injury to rocky intertidal algae and animals during and after the initial spill (Dubai Star): A report prepared for Office of Spill Prevention and Response (DFG-OSPR). California Department of Fish and Game, Sacramento, California.
Richards, D. V., and G. E. Davis. 1993. Early warnings of modern population collapse in black abalone *Haliotis cracherodii*, Leach, 1814 at the California Channel Islands. Journal of Shellfish Research 12:189–194.
Rogers-Bennett, L., K. E. Hubbard, and C. I. Juhasza. 2013. Dramatic declines in red abalone populations after opening a "de facto" marine reserve to fishing: Testing temporal reserves. Biological Conservation 157:423–431.
Roughgarden J., S. Gaines, and H. Possingham. 1988. Recruitment dynamics in complex life cycles. Science 241:1460–1466.
Sagarin, R. D., R. F. Ambrose, B. J. Becker, J. M. Engle, J. Kido, S. F. Lee, C. M. Miner, S. N. Murray, P. T. Raimondi, D. Richards, and C. Roe. 2007. Ecological impacts on the limpet *Lottia gigantea* populations: Human pressures over a broad scale on island and mainland intertidal zones. Marine Biology 150:399–713.
Sanford, E. 2002. Water temperature, predation, and the neglected role of physiological rate effects in rocky intertidal communities. Integrative and Comparative Biology 42:881–891.
Sará, G., M. Kearney, and B. Helmuth. 2011. Combining heat-transfer and energy budget models to predict thermal stress in Mediterranean intertidal mussels. Chemistry and Ecology 27:135–145.
Sará, G., G. K. Reid, A. Rinaldi, V. Palmeri, M. Troell, and S. Kooijman. 2012. Growth and reproductive simulation of candidate shellfish species at fish cages in the Southern Mediterranean: Dynamic Energy Budget (DEB) modelling for integrated multi-trophic aquaculture. Aquaculture 324:259–266.
Schiel, D. R. 2004. The structure and replenishment of rocky shore intertidal communities and biogeographic comparisons. Journal of Experimental Marine Biology and Ecology 300:309–342.
Schiff, K. C., M. J. Allen, E. Y. Zeng, and S. M. Bay. 2000. Southern California. Marine Pollution Bulletin 41:76–93.
Schmitt, R. J. 1987. Indirect interactions between prey: Apparent competition, predator aggregation, and habitat segregation. Ecology 68:1887–1897.
Schmitz, O. J., P. A. Hambäck, and A. P. Beckerman. 2000. Trophic cascades in terrestrial systems: A review of the effects of carnivore removals on plants. American Naturalist 155:141–153.
Schneider, K. R., and B. Helmuth. 2007. Spatial variability in habitat temperature may drive patterns of selection between an invasive and native mussel species. Marine Ecology Progress Series 339:157–167.
Seapy, R. R., and M. M. Littler. 1993. Rocky intertidal macroinvertebrates of the southern California Bight: An overview and checklist. Pages 293–322 in F. G. Hochberg, editor. Third Channel Islands Symposium: Recent advances in research on the Channel Islands. Santa Barbara Museum of Natural History, Santa Barbara, California.
Shanks A. L., J. Largier, L. Brink, J. Brubaker, and R. Hooff. 2000. Demonstration of the onshore transport of larval invertebrates by the shoreward movement of an upwelling front. Limnology and Oceanography 45:230–236.
Smith, J. R., P. Fong, and R. F. Ambrose. 2008. The impacts of human visitation on mussel bed communities along the California coast: Are regulatory marine reserves effective in protecting these communities? Environmental Management 41:599–612.
———. 2006. Dramatic declines in mussel bed community diversity: Response to climate change? Ecology 87:1153–1161.
Smith, J. R., R. F. Ambrose, and P. Fong. 2006. Long-term change in mussel (*Mytilus californianus* Conrad) populations along the wave-exposed coast of California. Marine Biology 149:537–545.
Somero, G. N. 2011. Comparative physiology: A "crystal ball" for predicting consequences of global change. American Journal of Physiology—Regulatory integrative and comparative physiology 301:R1–R14.
Sousa, W. P. 1979. Experimental investigations of disturbance and ecological succession in a rocky intertidal community. Ecological Monographs 49:227–254.
State Water Resource Control Board (SWRCB). 2005. California ocean plan. SWRCB, Sacramento, California.
Stephenson, T. A., and A. Stephenson. 1972. Life between tidemarks on rocky shores. Freeman, San Francisco, California.
Stokstad, E. 2014. Death of the Stars. Science. 344:464–467.
Straughan, D. 1973. Biological studies of the Santa Barbara oil spill. Pages 4–16 in Proceedings of the American Association of Petroleum Geologists 1973 Annual Meeting. University of Southern California, Los Angeles, California.
Strub, P. T., C. James. 1995. The large-scale summer circulation of the California current. Geophysical Research Letters 22, 207–210.
Suchanek, T. H. 1993. Oil impacts on marine invertebrate populations and communities. American Zoologist 33:510–523.
Sumaila, U. R., W. W. L. Cheung, V. W. Y. Lam, D. Pauly, and S. Herrick. 2011. Climate change impacts on the biophysics and economics of the world fisheries. Nature Climate Change 1:449–456.
Tamm, E. E. 2004. Beyond the outer shores. Four Walls Eight Windows. New York. New York.
Thom, R. M., and T. B. Widdowson. 1978. A resurvey of E. Yale Dawson's forty-two intertidal algal transects on the southern California mainland after fifteen years. Bulletin of the Southern California Academy of Sciences 77:1–13.
Thompson, R. C., T. P. Crowe, and S. J. Hawkins. 2002. Rocky intertidal communities: Past environmental changes, present status, and predictions for the next twenty-five years. Environmental Conservation 29:168–191.
Thompson, S. A., H. Knoll, C. A. Blanchette, and K. J. Nielsen. 2010. Population consequences of biomass loss due to commercial collection of the wild seaweed *Postelsia palmaeformis*. Marine Ecology Progress Series 413:17–31.
Torch/Platform Irene Trustee Council. 2007. Torch/Platform Irene Oil spill final restoration plan and environmental assessment. San Luis Obispo, California.
Underwood, A. J., and E. J. Denley. 1984. Paradigms, explanations, and generalisations in models for the structure of intertidal communities on rocky shores. Pages 151–180 in D. R. Strong Jr., D. Simberloff, L. G. Abele and A B. Thistle, editors. Ecological communities: Conceptual issues and the evidence. Princeton University Press, Princeton, New Jersey.
UN Environment Program (UNEP). 2006. Marine and coastal ecosystems and human well-being: A synthesis report based on the findings of the Millennium Ecosystem Assessment. UNEP. Nairobi, Kenya.
Valentine, J. W. 1966. Numerical analysis of marine molluscan ranges on the extratropical northeastern Pacific shelf. Limnology and Oceanography 11:198–211.
Vogel, S. 1994. Life in moving fluids. Princeton University Press, Princeton, New Jersey.
Ware, R. 2009. Central Orange County Areas of Special Biological Significance public use monitoring program. Prepared for the City of Newport Beach Public Works. Newport Beach, California.
Watson, J. R., C. G. Hays, P. T. Raimondi, S. Mitarai, C. Dong, J. C. McWilliams, C. A. Blanchette, J. E Caselle, and D. A. Siegal. 2011. Currents connecting communities: Nearshore community similarity and ocean circulation. Ecology 92:1193–1200.
Wethey, D. S. 1984. Sun and shade mediate competition in the barnacles *Chthamalus* and *Semibalanus*: A field experiment. Biological Bulletin 167:176–185.
Whitaker, S. G., J. R. Smith, and S. N. Murray. 2010 Reestablishment of the southern California rocky intertidal brown alga, *Silvetia compressa*: An experimental investigation of the techniques and abiotic and biotic factors that affect restoration success. Restoration Ecology 18:18–26.
White T. C. R. 2001. Opposing paradigms: Regulation or limitation of populations? Oikos 93:148–152.
Widdowson, T. B. 1971. Changes in the intertidal algal flora of the Los Angeles area since the survey by E. Yale Dawson in 1956–1959. Bulletin of the Southern California Academy of Sciences 70:2–16.
Wieters, E. A., S. D. Gaines, S. A. Navarrete, C. A. Blanchette, and B. A. Menge. 2008. Scales of dispersal and the biogeography of marine predator-prey interactions. American Naturalist 171:405–417.
Wilson, S. G., and T. R. Fischetti. 2010. Coastline population trends

in the United States: 1960–2008. U.S. Department of Commerce, U.S. Census Bureau, Washington, D.C.

Winant, C. D., E. P. Dever, and M. C. Hendershott. 2003. Characteristic patterns of shelf circulation at the boundary between central and southern California. Journal of Geophysical Research: Oceans 108:1–13.

Woodson, C. B., M. A. McManus, J. A. Tyburczy, J. A. Barth, M. H. Carr, D. P. Malone, P. T. Raimondi, B. A. Menge, and S. R. Palumbi. 2012. Coastal fronts set recruitment and connectivity patterns across multiple taxa. Limnology and Oceanography 57:582–596.

Wootton, J. T. 1994. Predicting direct and indirect effects: An integrated approach using experiments and path analysis. Ecology 75:151–165.

Young, C. M. 1990. Larval ecology of marine invertebrates: A sesquicentennial history. Ophelia 32:1–48.

———. 1987. Novelty of "supply-side" ecology. Science 235:415–416.

Zacherl, D., S. D. Gaines, and S. I. Lonhart. 2003. The limits to biogeographical distributions: Insights from the northward range extension of the marine snail, *Kelletia kelletii* (Forbes, 1852). Journal of Biogeography 30:913–924.

NINETEEN

Estuaries

Life on the Edge

JAMES E. CLOERN, PATRICK L. BARNARD, ERIN BELLER, JOHN C. CALLAWAY, J. LETITIA GRENIER, EDWIN D. GROSHOLZ, ROBIN GROSSINGER, KATHRYN HIEB, JAMES T. HOLLIBAUGH, NOAH KNOWLES, MARTHA SUTULA, SAMUEL VELOZ, KERSTIN WASSON, and ALISON WHIPPLE

Introduction

On May 14, 1769, Friar Juan Crespí described his happiness upon arriving at the "splendid Harbor of San Diego," a vast bay "plentiful in very large sardines, rays, and many other fish, and a great many mussels" (Crespí and Brown 2001). Over the following months, Crespí traversed the California coastline, encountering an abundance and variety of estuaries. He observed "a great deal of glitter where salt must be collecting" in a seasonally dry lagoon, the sand-dammed Santa Ynez River where "the sea has been putting a height of sand in front of it," and finally a bay so large "that all the navies of Spain could fit in it"—California's largest estuary, the San Francisco Bay-Delta. Crespí's journal is part of a rich collection of observations detailing the physical and ecological diversity of California's estuaries before modern modifications, ranging from large tidal bays to intermittently closed lagoons at the mouths of small creeks (Grossinger et al. 2011). In estuaries across this spectrum early records show heterogeneous mosaics of habitat types reflecting California's geologic, topographic, and climatic diversity.

This diversity can be illustrated by comparing two very different estuary types: California's largest estuary and some of its smallest (Figure 19.1). The San Francisco Bay-Delta historically drained 40% of the state's area, with flows coalescing in the Sacramento and San Joaquin Rivers and meeting the tides within the estuary's inland delta. Consequently, a large portion of the estuary was tidal yet fresh: 66% of the estuary's 2,240 square kilometers of wetlands occurred in the freshwater Delta (Whipple et al. 2012). Though portions of these wetlands appeared to be "covered with nothing but TULE" (Abella and Cook 1960), the landscape was also composed of 2,600 kilometers of winding tidal channels, willow-fern communities (Atwater 1980), sand mounds, and riparian forests along major river channels. This heterogeneity contributed to the higher observed plant diversity in the Delta as compared to other regions of the Bay-Delta estuary (Atwater et al. 1979, Vasey et al. 2012). Downstream, the estuary opened into a series of large bays with extensive fringing tidal flats and marshes. Open-water habitats at the seaward end of the estuarine gradient were bordered by broad tidal flats and pickleweed-dominated salt marshes with a dense network of tidal channels.

In contrast to the Bay-Delta, the Santa Clara River mouth and associated estuaries in southern California had only seasonal freshwater input (Beller et al. 2011), with more limited tidal influence because the river mouth was "blocked up by sandhills" during summer (Cooper 1887) and connected to the ocean only "after the rains of winter" (Johnson 1855). A series of backbarrier lagoons marked former river mouths, separated from the ocean by sand dunes that effectively blocked the tides (Reed 1871). Instead of the Delta's tules and extensive forests, many of these small estuaries were dominated by shallow hypersaline open-water areas, pickleweed-dominated salt marsh, and extensive salt PANNES (Bard 1869). However, local springs brought more freshwater to other, neighboring lagoons to maintain permanent open-water areas with a compressed salinity gradient and fringing stands of tules, creating very different conditions even among adjacent systems.

These examples drawn from reconstructions of early 1800s conditions illustrate the substantial seasonal variability and diversity of forms, physical characteristics, and biological communities of these coastal ecosystems. In this chapter we describe the diversity of California's estuaries today, the processes that generate the complex patterns of variability characteristic of estuaries, the biological communities they support, the services they provide, their fast-paced transformations by human actions, and how future transformations will be influenced by choices we make. We begin with descriptions of the geographic and climatic settings of coastal California to provide the physical context for understanding why its estuaries exhibit the diversity of forms first documented in the eighteenth century and still expressed to varying extent today.

Physical Features of the California Coast

Estuaries are transitional ecosystems at the land-sea interface, and unlike terrestrial and freshwater ecosystems they are strongly influenced by connectivity to both land and ocean. The morphology (size, form) and dynamics of estuaries are shaped by physical features of the land-ocean transition. California's 1,766-kilometer-long coast is situated along the active tectonic boundary between the North American and Pacific plates (dashed line in Figure 19.2). The geologic complexity and active uplift associated with this setting created a mountainous terrain with deeply incised stream channels intersecting a plunging coastline (shown as a narrow band between the +100 meter and –100 meter contour lines on Figure 19.2); exceptions are the coastal plains bordering Monterey Bay and the Los Angeles Basin. Over 70% of the shoreline comprises sea cliffs, bluffs, and coastal mountains; and the high-relief cliffs, headlands, and points are most common in the northern half of the state, where more erosion-resistant rocks predominate (Griggs et al. 2005, Hapke et al. 2009). California's coast is fronted by a narrow continental shelf.

The rugged coastline, proximity of mountains to the ocean, irregular shoreline, and narrow continental shelf create a physical setting that distinguishes California's estuaries from those situated in the coastal plains of the U.S. Atlantic coast. Many California estuaries form along the lower reaches of stream valleys fronted by small beaches and barrier spits adjacent to headlands or behind barrier beaches, and they are typically backed by a narrow coastal plain (San Francisco Bay and the smaller estuaries in the Los Angeles basin are notable exceptions). Those situated in narrow coastal plains (e.g., Noyo, see Figure 19.2) drain WATERSHEDS of only a few hundred square kilometers—much smaller than watersheds characteristic of East Coast estuaries. High relief along the coast also isolates California's estuaries topographically, both alongshore and cross-shore, so they have a wide diversity of forms and sizes. Lastly, the narrow continental shelf implies that California's estuaries are closely connected to a high-productivity coastal upwelling system that is a source of PHYTOPLANKTON biomass; larval and juvenile stages of marine fish and invertebrates that rear in estuaries; and nutrient-rich, low-oxygen, low-pH, deep ocean water.

Three other coastal features influence the morphology and seasonal dynamics of California's estuaries: sediment transport, waves, and tides. Alongshore transport is important because it carries away sediment from coastal erosion or streams that can otherwise seal off the mouths of smaller estuaries when energy from streamflow, waves, or tides is not sufficient to keep the inlets open. Sediment transport is controlled by geologic features that constrain alongshore flows, including submarine canyons that incise the continental shelf and transport sediment to the deep-sea floor. Several of these canyons extend nearly to the shoreline (e.g., Mugu and Monterey Canyons) and define the boundaries of coastal sediment transport ("littoral cells"). Rocky headlands also define the limits of littoral cells as well as the alongshore extent of numerous small beaches and longer expanses of uninterrupted sandy beaches.

Waves are an important source of energy that shape estuaries through their influence on sediment erosion, suspension, and transport. Wave energy off the California coast is dominated by long-period, westerly ocean swell. Wave energy increases from south to north along the coast, with average wave heights in central California of approximately 2.5 meters and a few tens of centimeters lower and higher in southern and northern California, respectively. Variability in the strength of ocean swell is strongly seasonal, with the largest waves arriving from November through April. Annual wave height in deep water exceeds 6 meters and reaches up to about 9 meters during extreme events (Wingfield and Storlazzi 2007). However, depending on direction of the swell relative to the coastline and the degree of topographic sheltering, which is prevalent in southern California, nearshore wave heights can be a fraction of those in deep water (Adams et al. 2008).

Waves interact with changes in sea level. Warmer coastal waters and lowered atmospheric pressure during El Niño winters raise sea level along the California coast up to 30 centimeters, with an additional 5–10 centimeters of

Photo on previous page: *Mt. Tamalpais from Napa Slough* by William Marple. This 1869 painting of Napa Valley's tidal marshlands provides a rare view of a California estuary before reclamation. A steamer winds through the tall tules on its way to the port of Napa; small islands covered in willows can be seen at right. Courtesy of the California Historical Society.

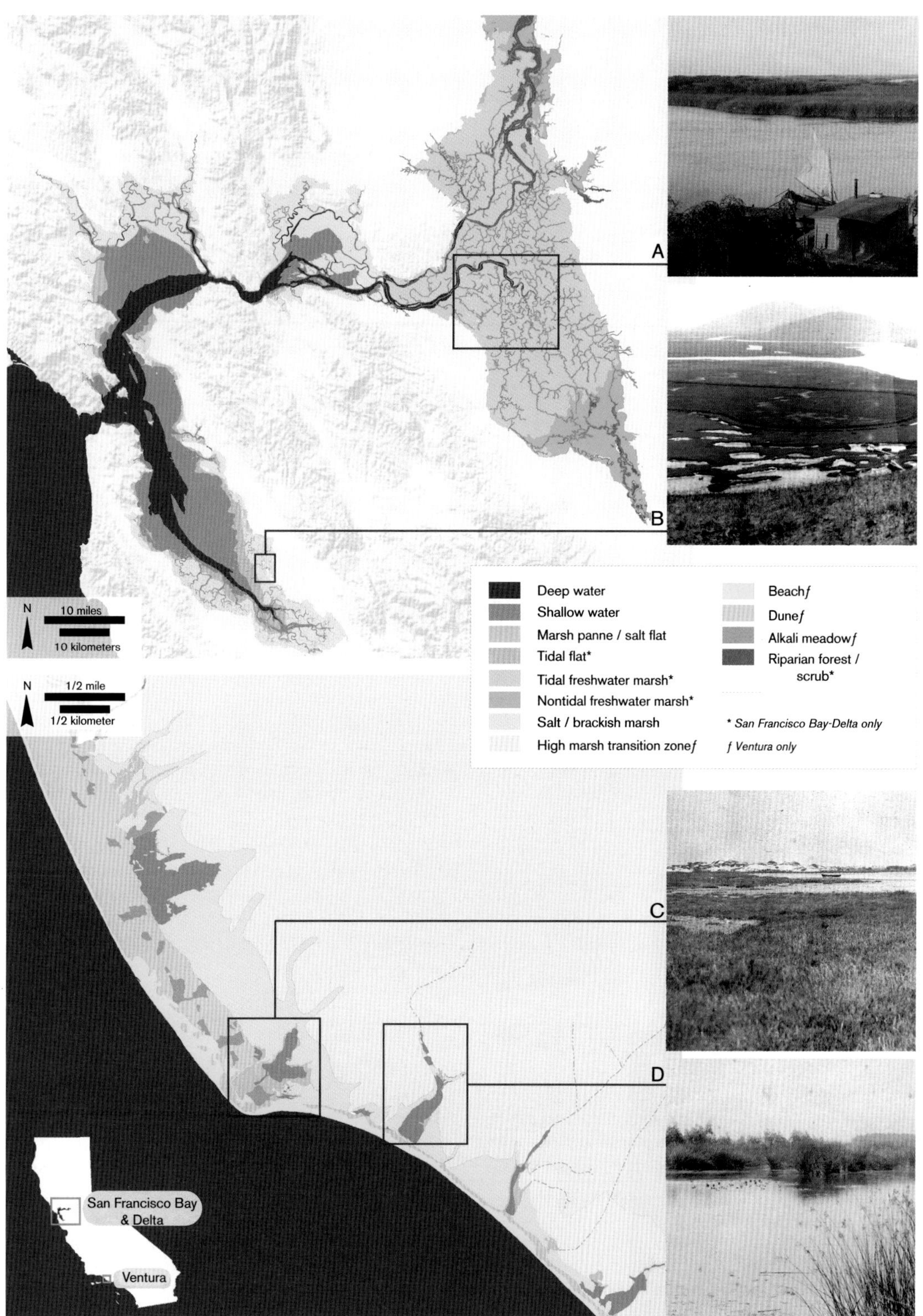

FIGURE 19.1 Reconstructions of early 1800s landscapes for California's largest estuary and some of its smallest, illustrating the substantial physical complexity and biodiversity formerly exhibited by California estuaries. In the San Francisco Bay–Delta estuary's 2,240 square kilometers of wetlands (top), a diversity of ecological communities existed along the estuarine gradient. These included willow-fern complexes and dense riparian forest within the tule-dominated freshwater wetlands of the Delta (A), with the subtidal bays, broad tidal flats, and pickleweed-dominated tidal marshes of San Francisco Bay (B) further downstream. In comparison, a series of small, backbarrier lagoons associated with relict mouths of the Santa Clara River in Ventura County (bottom) experienced extremely limited tidal influence and freshwater input. High sand dunes blocked tidal access, creating shallow, hypersaline open-water areas, seasonally flooded salt flats, and pickleweed plains (C). At some lagoons local springs created fresher conditions, supporting fringing tule (D). Historical mapping courtesy of the San Francisco Estuary Institute. Photo credits: (A) artist unknown n.d. [LB67-712-41], courtesy of the Haggin Museum, Stockton, California; (B) artist unknown 1916 [A-1005], courtesy of the San Francisco Public Utilities Commission; (C) photograph by John Peabody Harrington 1913 [neg. 91-30700], courtesy of the National Anthropological Archives, Smithsonian Institution; (D) Brewster ca. 1889, courtesy of the Museum of Ventura County.

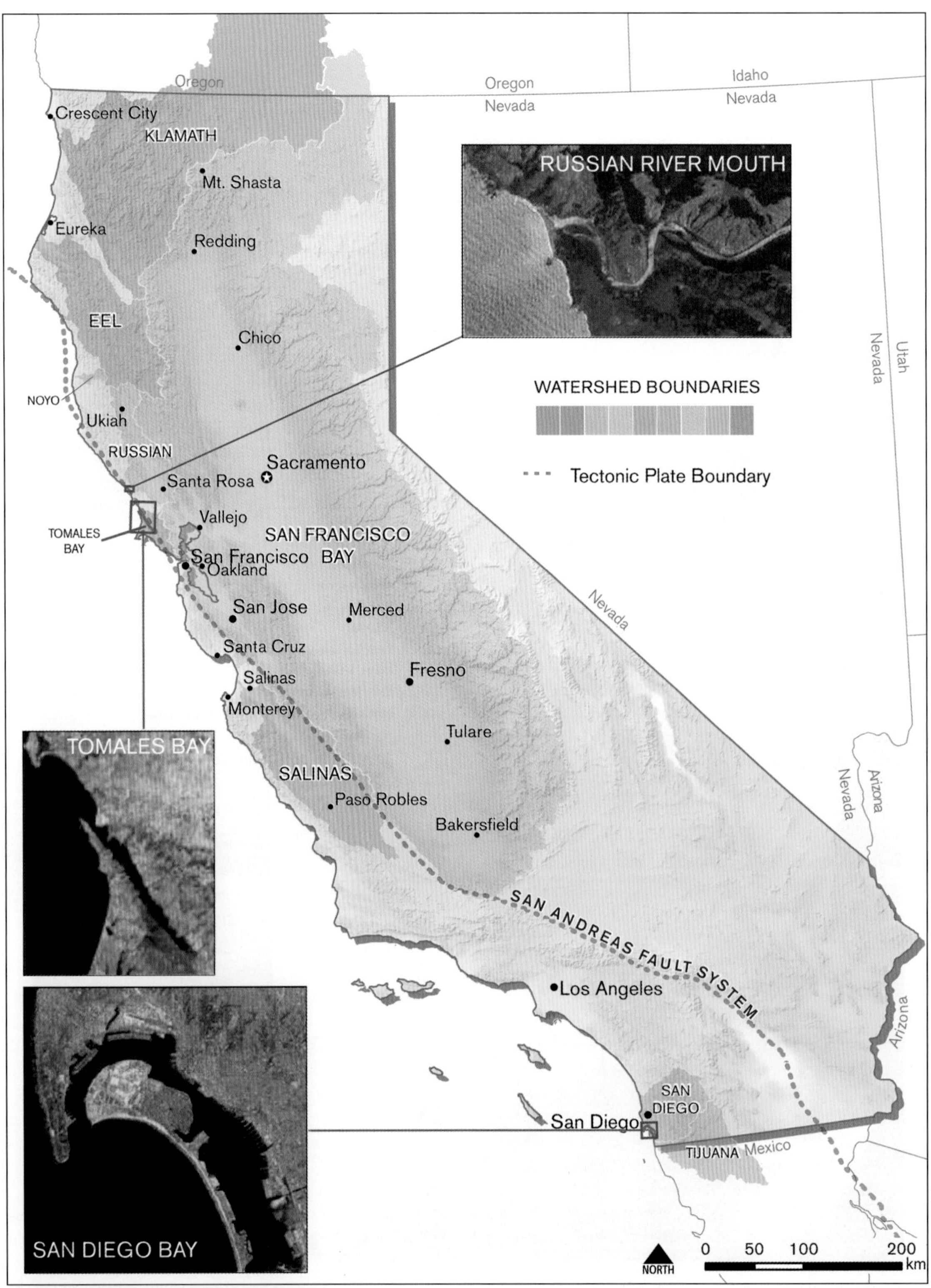

FIGURE 19.2 Topography of the California coast, including tectonic plate boundaries (dashed red line) and selected watersheds (names capitalized in black). Three common types of estuaries are highlighted: drowned river mouth (Russian River mouth), tectonic (Tomales Bay), and barrier spit (San Diego Bay). Not shown: Pajaro River watershed, located immediately east of the Salinas watershed. Source: Data from U.S. Geological Survey, National Hydrography Dataset (NHD). Map: Parker Welch, Center for Integrated Spatial Research (CISR).

TABLE 19.1

Watersheds of California's estuaries have diverse sizes, degrees of water management, and runoff

This table summarizes data for estuaries shown in Figure 19.3.

Estuarine watershed	Area (km²)	Reservoir storage ($\times 10^6$ m³)	1970–2010 mean average outflow (m³/s)	Runoff ratio
Klamath	40,609	3,951	470	0.44
Eel	9,529	96	243	0.51
Noyo	293	0	6	0.49
Russian	3,843	405	62	0.51
San Francisco Bay	164,655	73,122	762	0.20
Pajaro	3,368	44	4	0.10
Salinas	11,084	897	13	0.07
Tijuana	4,490	286	5	0.04

SOURCES: U.S. Army Corps of Engineers 2013, U.S. Geological Survey 2013, CDWR 2011, International Boundary and Water Commission 2013, Watershed Boundary Dataset 2013.

NOTE: Outflow and runoff are based on water-year (WY, beginning October 1) statistics.

decadal variability possibly associated with the Pacific Decadal Oscillation (Bromirski et al. 2003). The narrow shelf and absence of hurricanes to generate extreme winds and low atmospheric pressure result in small surge elevations during severe storms along the Pacific coast compared to Atlantic and Gulf coast settings. Nevertheless, storm surges force water-level fluctuations as high as 70 centimeters in protected embayments of central California. In estuaries connected to large rivers, these water-level extremes are amplified further when the ocean surge coincides with high river inflow (Cayan et al. 2008). During extreme events waves are the dominant factor that elevates water levels along the exposed outer coast and are capable of increasing water levels by several meters. Therefore, overtopping and breaching of beaches and barrier spits that protect and/or close off estuary mouths are often associated with large waves.

Tides are important because they drive hourly changes in water level and currents that transport ocean water into estuaries and are the most important source of energy to vertically mix estuaries. Tides of the Pacific coast are mixed, with both diurnal and semidiurnal periods of oscillation. Similar to the gradient of wave energy, the range of the tides increases from south to north, with an average diurnal range of 1.6 meters along the open coast in San Diego and up to 2.1 meters in Crescent City. The tidal range inside estuaries can be damped or amplified, depending on bathymetry and basin configuration. For example, the tidal range in lower South San Francisco Bay exceeds the range at the entrance by about 1 meter. Tides also oscillate over the fortnightly neap-spring cycle; the energetic spring tidal ranges can exceed neap tidal ranges by 1 meter or more.

The Climate System: Precipitation and Runoff

As mixing zones between seawater and freshwater, estuaries are dynamic ecosystems where variability of HYDRODYNAMICS, water chemistry, sediment transport, habitats, and biological communities are strongly influenced by variability of freshwater inflows from upstream watersheds. Patterns of freshwater inflow to California's estuaries are shaped by the state's geographic and land-use diversity as well as its meteorological patterns. Differences across estuaries in watershed size, hydrologic response, reservoir storage, and level of development result in a wide range of flow characteristics. Here we use eight estuarine watersheds (summarized in Table 19.1 and shown in Figure 19.3) to illustrate this diversity, and in the following section we show how variability of flow generates complex patterns of chemical and biological variability within estuaries.

MEAN ANNUAL PATTERNS

Annual cycles of estuarine freshwater inflows are driven primarily by the seasonality of watershed outflows, which is determined largely by California's climate of wet winters and prolonged summer dry seasons (see Figure 19.3a). The seasonal patterns of atmospheric variability over the eastern North Pacific that produce this seasonality of runoff also produce the annual cycle of wind-driven coastal upwelling that is strongest in summer and relaxes during autumn-winter. The timing and magnitude of freshwater inflows to California's estuaries are also affected by human activities in the watersheds. Dams delay and reduce annual runoff to varying degrees depending on reservoir size and the ultimate uses of the captured water. Groundwater pumping and recharge and water transfers between watersheds also affect annual cycles of estuarine inflow.

The combination of atmospheric forcing, human activities, and watershed hydrology produce a variety of estuarine inflow patterns throughout California. Rugged terrain generates intense precipitation over watersheds draining to rivers along the northern coast such as the Eel, Noyo, and Russian Rivers (see Figure 19.3b). These basins have relatively little artificial storage or in-basin losses (e.g., EVAPOTRANSPIRATION), resulting in high runoff ratios (outflow/precipita-

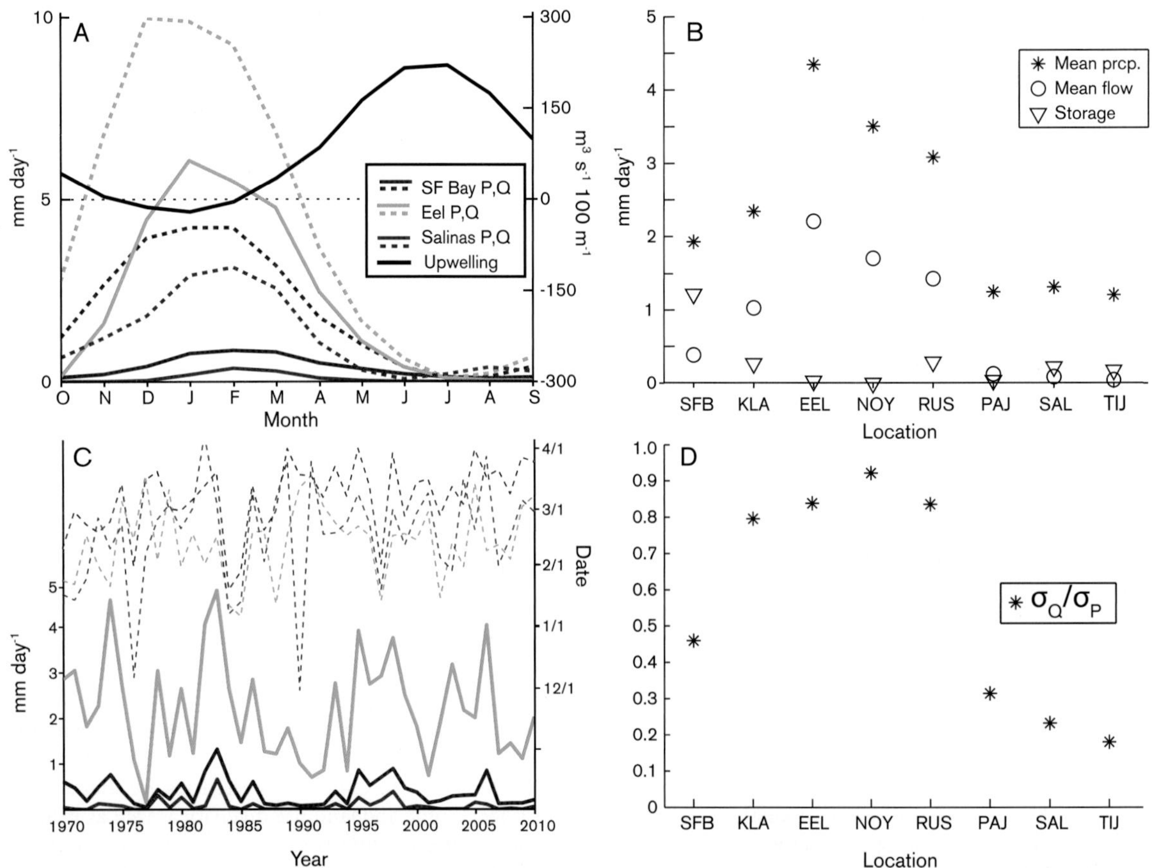

FIGURE 19.3 California's estuaries have diverse patterns of climate-driven variability in their watersheds and in the adjacent coastal ocean. See Table 19.1 for additional data sources. The x-axis labels in panels B and D correspond to the watersheds listed in Table 19.1.

A Mean annual cycles for water years (October–September) 1970–2010; area-averaged daily precipitation (P) and outflow (Q, from watershed to estuary) in three watersheds (Maurer et al. 2002) and of upwelling (black line, right y-axis) near the Central Coast (Pacific Fisheries Environmental Laboratory 2013).

B Mean area-averaged precipitation, outflow, and reservoir storage in major California watersheds in 2000. SFB: San Francisco Bay; from north to south: KLA: Klamath River; EEL: Eel River; NOY: Noyo River; RUS: Russian River; PAJ: Pajaro River; SAL: Salinas River; TIJ: Tijuana River.

C Mean annual flow magnitude (solid lines) and timing (dashed lines, right y-axis). Timing is computed as the weighted average of dates in a given water year, where each date is weighted by that day's flow magnitude. An early (e.g., December 1) date indicates a concentration of flow early in the rainy season for that year and conversely for later dates. Watershed color-coding follows panel A.

D Ratio of standard deviations (σ) of mean annual flow (Q) and precipitation (P). This ratio is a measure of the damping effect of watershed processes on interannual precipitation variability. Abbreviations follow panel B.

tion, see Table 19.1). The larger watersheds of the Klamath River and San Francisco Bay-Delta have more diverse topography and include substantial areas of moderate-to-low precipitation and significant in-basin losses. The Bay-Delta watershed in particular has agricultural regions with high losses to evapotranspiration and a massive freshwater management infrastructure, so its runoff ratio is low as a result of human activities. Rivers draining watersheds of the central coast (Pajaro, Salinas) receive less precipitation, and although they have little artificial storage, most flows are used for groundwater recharge (California Department of Water Resources 2009), resulting in low runoff ratios. The Tijuana basin follows a similar pattern, though urban consumption in an arid climate is the main in-basin loss. Historically, wastewater has been a major component of inflow to the Tijuana estuary (Zedler et al. 1984).

INTERANNUAL PATTERNS

Annual estuarine inflows are highly correlated throughout the state (see Figure 19.3c), but the timing of runoff is more dependent on the effects of artificial and natural water storage within basins. Storage and in-basin losses also reduce flow variability relative to precipitation variability (see Figure 19.3d). In particular, in-basin agricultural and urban losses strongly reduce interannual variability in the central coast (e.g., Pajaro, Salinas basins) and Tijuana basins, and freshwater management in the watershed reduces variability of inflow to the San Francisco Bay-Delta. Interannual outflow variability in the less developed northern coastal basins (e.g., Klamath, Eel, Noyo, Russian basins) is only slightly less than precipitation variability. Even in the more highly managed basins, however, meteorological forcing (air temperature, precipitation) remains the dominant mechanism of interannual variability in the timing and magnitude of outflow (Knowles 2002). Another aspect of interannual variability that impacts all estuaries is drought—a natural and recurring feature of California's climate that leads to increased salinity intrusion and longer residence times (slower flushing). Recent examples include the 1976–1977 and 1987–1992 droughts (see Figure 19.3c) and the record drought of 2013–2015.

El Niño and La Niña events are important drivers of California's interannual climate variability associated with opposing patterns of sea surface temperature in the equatorial Pacific that cycle roughly every three to seven years (Diaz and Markgraf 1992) (see Chapter 2, "Climate"). El Niño events tend to dampen coastal upwelling (Schwing et al. 2005). They also tend to cause wet years in southern California with milder impacts in the rest of the state, although impacts vary greatly among El Niño years. La Niña events tend toward the opposite weather pattern across California but with more consistent impacts across different La Niña events (Redmond and Koch 1991, Cayan et al. 1999).

MULTIDECADAL PATTERNS

The Pacific Decadal Oscillation (PDO) has a similar north-south pattern of impacts on precipitation as the El Niño/La Niña cycle (Mantua et al. 1997, Cayan et al. 1998), but its cycles have a longer period of forty to sixty years. The PDO and, to a greater extent the NORTH PACIFIC GYRE OSCILLATION (NPGO), modulate the annual cycle of coastal upwelling and its associated physical and biological impacts (Di Lorenzo et al. 2008). The NPGO in particular has important impacts on biological communities through its influence on populations of marine species that migrate into estuaries (Cloern et al. 2010). Finally, clear evidence from records contained in tree-rings (Stine 1994) and estuarine sediment cores (Ingram et al. 1996) indicates that California's climate has included droughts lasting from decades to centuries. Multidecadal droughts must have restructured biological communities across all California ecosystems, including in its estuaries.

EXTREME FLOWS

Peak flow events associated with storms play a critical role, flushing contaminants and supplying sediment while perturbing or altering estuaries through processes such as bottom scouring and precipitous drops in salinity that lead to displacement or wholesale mortality of marine organisms. El Niño years can bring such high-flow events, especially in the southern California watersheds (Cayan et al. 1999). Recent discoveries have revealed that long streams of water vapor originating in the tropics, termed "atmospheric rivers" (AR), are responsible for most major precipitation events in the western U.S. (Dettinger and Ingram 2013) (see Chapter 2, "Climate"). Concentrated in an average of about ten days each year, ARs cause more than 80% of flooding in California rivers. Approximately every one hundred to two hundred years an AR persists for a month or longer. The last such "megaflood" occurred in 1862, when sustained extreme precipitation swelled rivers along the California coast, transformed San Francisco Bay into a freshwater lake, reversed coastal currents, and amplified an associated ocean surge that cut a new channel into San Diego Bay (Engstrom 1996).

The Diversity of California Estuaries

California's coastline has over four hundred bays, lagoons, and river mouths that we collectively refer to as estuaries. Based on their positions within the gradients of coastal geomorphology, runoff, and oceanography described earlier, California estuaries can be classified into three broad (and overlapping) classes.

CLASSIC ESTUARIES

The classic estuary has adequate freshwater inflow and tidal exchange to maintain a broad salinity gradient year-round (Pritchard 1967). The only estuarine system in California with these properties is northern San Francisco Bay, although others—such as Humboldt, Tomales, and San Diego Bays—function as classic estuaries during the wet season. A key feature of this estuary type is estuarine circulation, where fresher water at the surface flows out of the estuary and saltier coastal water flows into the estuary along the bottom. Strong spring tides disrupt this circulation pattern by causing rapid vertical mixing. Thus, rather than being persistently layered with lower salinity near the surface and higher salinity near the bottom (characteristic of East Coast estuaries such as Chesapeake Bay), the salinity gradient in California estuaries tends to appear as a series of increasingly saltier cells from land to sea.

LAGOONS

Lagoonal estuaries are marine-dominated most of the year, have an open connection to the ocean, and thus are tidally influenced; a related type occurs at stream mouths (see next in chapter). They are often formed by the development of a sand spit that encloses a coastal embayment in the lee of an island or headland. By this definition lagoons are not formed directly in stream channels, so their relief is flat enough to support extensive tidal marshes and mudflats or sandflats. Examples of these lagoonal systems are Bodega Harbor, Bolinas Lagoon, and Morro and San Diego Bays. South San Francisco and Tomales Bays are lagoons formed primarily by tectonic processes. During summer or when lagoons are closed, freshwater inflow is less than evaporative water loss so salinity increases, in some cases above seawater salinity. Some lagoonal estuaries become extremely hypersaline when they are isolated from tidal exchange with the coastal ocean after formation of a sand barrier. Examples are Agua Hediondia and Batiquitos Lagoons in southern California and the Estero de Americano in central California. With increased freshwater inflow during winter, these estuaries freshen dramatically until the sand barrier breaches and tidal exchange of water is restored.

Some of California's shallow lagoons flush completely every tidal cycle and tend to be fully marine year-round (e.g., Bodega Harbor, Bolinas Lagoon, Morro Bay). Larger lagoonal estuaries are deeper and have longer water residence times. Warming of lagoon water during summer compensates for the increased density caused by high salinity. These opposing factors slow the density-driven estuarine circulation, so during summer lagoons such as Tomales Bay, South San Francisco Bay, and San Diego Bay retain water trapped at their head with an essentially infinite residence time. Long water retention isolates estuarine populations and alters water chemistry as the

FIGURE 19.4 Typical habitat types in California estuaries. Photos: (A, C, D, E, F) Kerstin Wasson, (B) John Callaway

A Brackish marsh, with a mix of freshwater and salt-tolerant vegetation.

B Salt marsh, which dominates in the high intertidal of saline portions of estuaries.

C Mudflat habitat dominates the intertidal zone below mean high water.

D Oyster beds provide structured habitat on low intertidal or shallow subtidal mudflats.

E Eelgrass beds provide structured habitat on low intertidal or shallow subtidal mudflats.

F Open water provides water column habitat; below that, the subtidal bottom habitat is dominated by soft sediments.

effects of biogeochemical processes, such as denitrification (Smith et al. 1996), accumulate during the dry season. Cooling and freshwater inflow during the wet season trigger rapid exchange of estuarine water with the ocean, leading to redistributions of salinity, organisms, and chemical constituents.

RIVER MOUTH ESTUARIES

These are the most common estuarine type in California, ranging from rivers and streams large enough to maintain freshwater inflow in midsummer to those with no summer inflow. The estuary is confined to a river channel, which is often steep-sided and supports only limited areas of intertidal mudflats or salt marshes. A critical factor in the hydrodynamics and ecology of these systems is whether they remain open to tidal exchange year-round. Although saline during summer, river-dominated systems in northern California do not become hypersaline and they may become completely fresh following high runoff events. Some of these estuaries, such as the Russian, Gualala, Noyo, and Navarro Rivers, are important migratory corridors for ANADROMOUS fishes such as salmon and steelhead. Stream mouth estuaries that drain smaller watersheds or watersheds receiving little rainfall (typical of southern California) have little or no freshwater inflow by midsummer and can become hypersaline, particularly if ocean exchange is limited by formation of a sand barrier across the mouth. Winter runoff retained behind the sand bar freshens the estuary and may cause upstream flooding until the bar is overtopped and washed out. These seasonal changes in hydrology also lead to variable inundation of bordering wetlands. Examples of this estuary type include Pescadero Creek, Pajaro River, Salinas River, Estero de San Antonio, and Estero Americano.

HABITAT DIVERSITY WITHIN ESTUARIES

Estuarine ecosystems include a mosaic of interconnected habitat types (Figure 19.4) commonly classified by their salinity and elevation. From river to the sea, *tidal freshwater habitats* are not salty, but their water levels rise and fall with the tides. *Brackish habitats* are also affected by tides but have a larger saltwater component and salinity ranging up to about 18 (i.e., approximately half seawater and half freshwater). *Marine habitats* have salinity above 18. Another categorization defines habitats by their position along the elevational gradient from the intertidal to subtidal zone. Vegetated marsh often occupies the upper intertidal zone from the highest reach of the tide down to mean tide level or, in freshwater systems, as low as mean lower low water (Atwater et al. 1979). Riparian trees and shrubs can occur within intertidal elevations, especially under fresher conditions. Tidal fresh, brackish, and salt marsh ecosystems include a mosaic of habitat types including tidal creeks and bare pannes as well as areas of dense marsh vegetation. Below marshes, the lower intertidal and subtidal zones can be further distinguished by pelagic (water column) and benthic (bottom) habitats. Mudflats and sandflats are the dominant habitat type in the intertidal zone, although there may also be rocky areas or oyster or seagrass beds. Soft bottom sediments dominate the benthos in the subtidal zone but again can be interrupted by patches of rocky areas, BIVALVE reefs, or seagrass.

Complex Patterns of Ecosystem Variability

As transitional ecosystems between rivers and oceans, estuaries are characterized by sharp spatial gradients and large variability measured at times scales ranging from hours to decades. We illustrate examples of chemical and biological variability in the SUBTIDAL HABITATS of Tomales Bay and San Francisco Bay.

Spatial Patterns

A prominent feature of spatial variability in estuaries is the longitudinal salinity gradient, a result of mixing between ocean water (salinity about 35) and riverine freshwater, seen in lagoonal estuaries such as Tomales Bay during the wet season (Figure 19.5a). In this state estuaries have a low-salinity or freshwater landward domain, a marine seaward domain, and transitional brackish habitats between the two. Each salinity domain has its own characteristic chemistry, biological communities, and biogeochemical and ecological processes (Smith and Hollibaugh 1997). California's estuaries shift to a different state during the dry season, when freshwater inflow is reduced or absent, salinity increases, and the salinity gradient can reverse as a result of salt concentration by evaporation. In this state estuaries function as shallow marine ecosystems or evaporative salt flats depending on climate and closure patterns. Therefore the seasonal input of freshwater is an essential process of estuarine dynamics that alters the mixture of ocean and river water within estuaries and drives fast seaward flows that transform estuaries from long-retention systems to flow-through systems with short residence times (days to weeks).

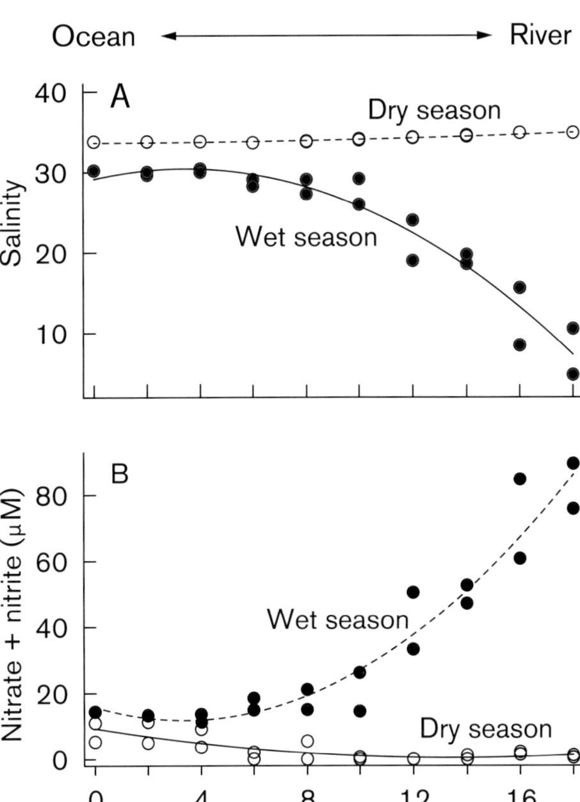

FIGURE 19.5 Estuaries are characterized by large spatial gradients. Source: http://lmer.marsci.uga.edu/tomales/tb_diss_metadata.html, accessed June 10, 2015.

A Distribution of surface salinity (practical salinity scale, unitless) along the ocean-river continuum of Tomales Bay, from its mouth toward the head of the bay, during the dry season (September 5–7, 1991) and the wet season (March 5–7, 1991).

B Distributions of nitrate + nitrite concentration along Tomales Bay during the dry season and wet season.

Rivers and oceans have distinct chemical compositions, so estuarine chemistry also varies along the salinity gradient. Relative to ocean water, rivers generally have elevated concentrations of nutrients, organic carbon, trace elements, and toxic contaminants, so a common spatial pattern is progressive seaward dilution of river-derived constituents, illustrated by the gradient of nitrate+nitrite (key forms of nitrogen used by primary producers) along Tomales Bay during the wet season (see Figure 19.5b). However, we see that nitrate+nitrite concentrations fall in Tomales Bay during the dry season when the river supply is lost. Moreover, the spatial gradient reverses because residence time in the upper estuary is long enough for denitrification to remove nitrate faster than it is supplied by land runoff. Therefore complex patterns in estuaries are manifested as seasonally varying spatial gradients that result from fluctuating river flow, mixing of water sources having distinct compositions, and fast biogeochemical transformations.

Patterns of Variability over Time

Biological variability in estuaries is driven by many processes including human disturbances, seasonal and interannual flow variability, and tidal oscillations. This variability

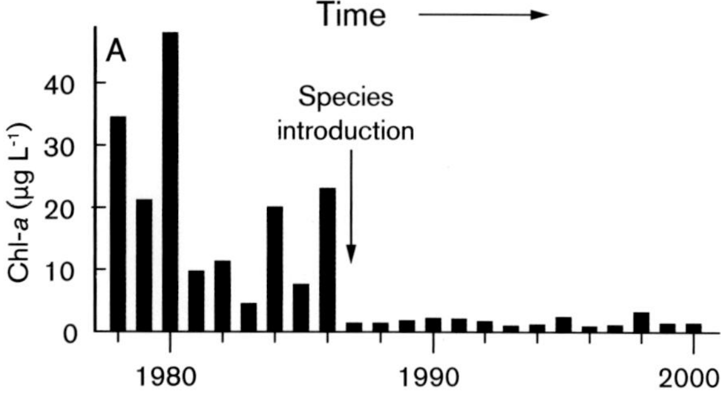

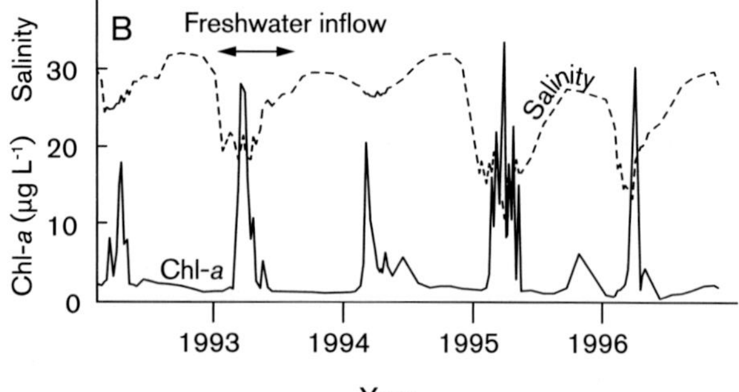

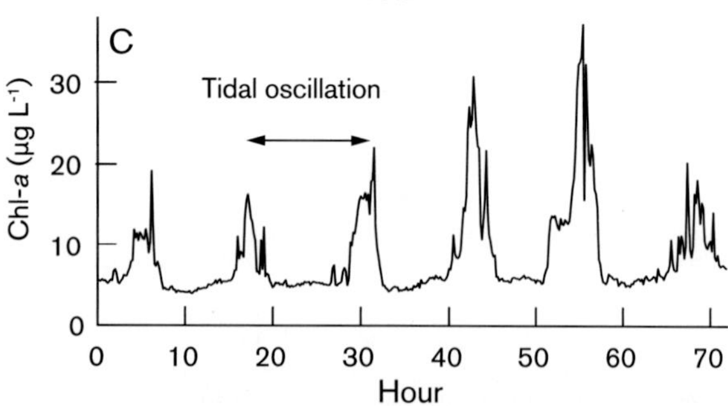

FIGURE 19.6 Estuaries are characterized by variability over a spectrum of time scales. Data sources: (A, B) <http://lmer.marsci.uga.edu/tomales/>; (C) <http://www.water.ca.gov/bdma/meta/Discrete/data.cfm>.

A Variability at time scales of years and decades (chlorophyll-*a* in northern San Francisco Bay, Interagency Ecological Program Station D7).

B Months and years (surface chlorophyll-*a* [solid line] and salinity [dashed line] in South San Francisco Bay, USGS Station 27, timing of peak annual freshwater inflow indicated).

C Hours (chlorophyll fluorescence at the Dumbarton Bridge, South San Francisco Bay, January 25–27, 2003, cycle of tidal oscillation indicated).

includes ecological regime shifts, such as the abrupt decrease of phytoplankton biomass (measured as CHLOROPHYLL-*a*) in northern San Francisco Bay after introduction of the filter-feeding clam *Corbula (Potamocorbula) amurensis* in 1986 (Figure 19.6a). This fivefold reduction in the phytoplankton food supply was followed by population crashes of ZOOPLANKTON species and native fishes that rely on these zooplankton as a food resource. Many estuaries have recurring seasonal patterns of biological variability, and a common pattern is peak chlorophyll-*a* during spring when the water column is stratified. STRATIFICATION develops when the input of buoyant freshwater overcomes the mixing power of tides and wind so the water column becomes partitioned into a low-salinity surface layer and a higher-salinity bottom layer.

This establishment of a shallow, sunlit surface layer promotes fast phytoplankton growth, so a prominent seasonal pattern in South San Francisco Bay is the spring bloom (high surface chlorophyll-*a*) when river inflow is high and salinity is low (Figure 19.6b). Years of low river flow, such as 1994, are years of weak salinity stratification and damped spring blooms; years of high river flow and strong salinity stratification, such as 1995, are years of large, prolonged spring blooms. Blooms have transformative effects on water chemistry caused by rapid phytoplankton uptake of nutrients, trace elements, and CO_2 (causing pH shifts), and they are followed by bursts of population growth by bacteria, CILIATES, COPEPODS, AMPHIPODS, and bivalves as their phytoplankton food supply increases (Cloern 1996). Therefore, complex patterns are also manifested in estuaries as linked biogeochemical and biological variability tied to seasonal and interannual fluctuations of river flow and its influence on vertical mixing. Seasonal salinity variations are also pronounced in California salt marshes. Soil salinity in *Spartina*-dominated areas regularly inundated by tides fluctuates with salinity variability in adjacent estuarine waters, while seasonal salinity fluctuations in the upper, less frequently flooded marsh areas are more influenced by evapotranspiration and rainfall. These seasonal salinity shifts affect plant distributions because seed germination in tidal marshes is restricted to periods of low salinity (Noe and Zedler 2001).

Estuaries also have pronounced variability at time scales of hours to days, and some of this variability reflects the strong oceanic influence on California's estuaries. For example, episodic occurrences of low dissolved oxygen in bottom waters of San Francisco Bay are caused by intrusions of low-oxygen deep ocean water brought to the surface by wind-driven upwelling and then transported into the estuary. Tides generate hourly variability as horizontal gradients of constituents such as chlorophyll-*a* oscillate over a fixed location (Figure 19.6c). The amplitude of these oscillations is comparable to that of annual phytoplankton cycles in lakes and oceans, but these estuarine cycles repeat twice daily. This example illustrates the challenge of understanding estuarine plankton dynamics based on sampling from a fixed position where variability results from the combination of fast water motions (tidal oscillatory transport) and biological processes such as growth and grazing.

Biota and Their Roles in the Ecosystem

The Biological Communities

The spatial gradients and temporal variability of estuaries result in varied assemblages of plant and animal species that are key components of California's rich biological diversity. Studies of biological communities reveal distinctive patterns of diversity and variability, and they illustrate eight *principles* (labeled in the text that follows) of how estuaries function as ecosystems (Box 19.1).

PRIMARY PRODUCERS

Estuaries have five major primary producer groups—phytoplankton, BENTHIC MICROALGAE, macroalgae such as *Ulva* spp., seagrass such as *Zostera marina*, and tidal marsh vascular plants. Unlike terrestrial ecosystems where most primary pro-

BOX 19.1 EIGHT PRINCIPLES OF ESTUARINE ECOLOGY

Estuaries have properties distinct from other ecosystems because of their geographic setting at the land-sea interface. We highlight eight principles of estuarine ecology:

1. *Fate of primary production.* Much of the primary production in estuaries is contributed by fast-growing algae; unlike vascular plants, most of that production is consumed rather than stored in structural biomass.
2. *Plant distributions.* Estuarine plant communities vary systematically along the gradients of habitat type between open water and marsh plains, and between saline and freshwater.
3. *Seasonal patterns.* California's estuaries do not share one common community or seasonal pattern of primary producers because their habitat mosaics are spatially diverse and seasonally dynamic.
4. *Roles of microbes.* Estuaries receive external inputs of organic matter, are fast-running biogeochemical reactors, and prokaryotes are the key agents of biogeochemical transformations.
5. *The salinity gradient.* Biological communities vary along the estuarine salinity gradient, and pelagic biota (plankton, fish) are continually redistributed as the salinity gradient oscillates with seasonal fluctuations of freshwater inflow.
6. *Habitat connectivity.* Chemical and biological variability in estuaries are strongly influenced by vertical exchanges between water and bottom sediments and horizontal exchanges between subtidal and intertidal habitats.
7. *Estuaries are open ecosystems.* For example, fish communities are structured by immigrations of marine species whose population abundances track annual climate variability across ocean basins.
8. *Biota as agents of element transport.* Migratory fish and invertebrates transfer carbon and nutrients from tidal marshes and other shallow-water habitats to the open estuary and to the ocean, while salmon transfer carbon and nutrients from the ocean to rivers.

duction is from photosynthesis of vascular plants, algal photosynthesis is a large component of estuarine primary production (Jassby et al. 1993). This is important because algae grow rapidly, and most of their production goes into energy-rich biochemicals that are a high-quality food resource consumed as fast as it is produced. The biomass of algal producers in estuaries turns over rapidly (up to one thousand times faster than vascular-plant producers) (Cebrian 1999), and most is consumed instead of stored in structural biomass (*Principle 1*).

The relative importance of the five producer groups varies with habitat attributes such as water depth and light availability, substrate stability, and nutrient concentrations. Phytoplankton tend to be the dominant primary producers in deep water and codominant with benthic microalgae in shallow subtidal habitats. As depths decrease toward the shore, light reaches the bottom and subtidal habitats can then be colonized by attached forms—seagrasses, benthic microalgae, and macroalgae. Benthic microalgae and macroalgae are generally the dominant primary producers on mudflats and sandflats where seagrasses are limited by desiccation and temperature stress. Freshwater, brackish, and salt marsh dominates the higher intertidal zone, with flood-tolerant riparian shrubs and trees at the upper edge of the ecotone from the aquatic to terrestrial habitat. The composition of estuarine plant communities varies systematically along the gradients of habitat type, from open water to marsh plains and from saltwater to freshwater (*Principle 2*). This principle applies across California's estuarine ecosystems. Primary production in muddy, TURBID estuaries like San Francisco Bay is dominated by phytoplankton photosynthesis (Jassby et al. 1993), although the historical loss of tidal marsh habitat within San Francisco Bay and elsewhere has greatly reduced the contribution of vascular plants to overall estuarine productivity. Shallow lagoons with clearer water (such as Tomales, Humboldt, Morro, and San Diego Bays) provide ideal habitats for seagrasses and attached algal forms. River mouth estuaries (such as the Santa Clara River and Eel River) have limited seagrass extent due to instability of bottom sediments, variable salinity, and high turbidity. In these types of estuaries phytoplankton and benthic microalgae typically dominate the shallow, unvegetated subtidal habitat of the main channel, while macroalgae and marsh plants dominate in side channels and adjacent FLOODPLAINS. Vascular plant productivity is also strongly affected by the estuarine salinity gradient, with productivity reduced at higher salinities (Callaway et al. 2012a).

A synoptic study across twenty-three southern California lagoon and river mouth estuaries illustrates seasonal changes in the biomass of three components: phytoplankton, benthic algae, and submerged aquatic vegetation (*Ruppia* spp.; McLaughlin et al. 2013). Macroalgae are ubiquitous throughout the year, with peak biomass in the summer and fall (Figure 19.7). Benthic microalgae and phytoplankton biomass peak in spring, and *Ruppia* biomass is ephemeral. Summer biomass accumulates to high levels in estuaries where tidal inlets are restricted by a sand bar, illustrating how biological communities respond to physical processes that alter rates of estuary-ocean exchange. California's estuaries do not share one common community or seasonal pattern of primary producers because their habitat mosaics are spatially diverse and seasonally dynamic (*Principle 3*).

MICROBES

The most abundant organisms in estuaries are the Bacteria and Archaea—the microbial community of prokaryotes. A liter of estuarine water contains one billion to ten billion bacterioplankton; abundance is about a thousand times higher (per unit volume) in sediments. This biomass doubles every few days (Hollibaugh and Wong 1996), and it is consumed at a comparable rate by flagellates, ciliates, and filter-feeding invertebrates such as bivalve MOLLUSCS, so bacterial production is an important supply of energy, carbon, and nutrients to estuarine consumers. The microbial community is extremely rich, with estimates of thousands to tens of thousands of taxa per liter of water and even greater diversity in sediments.

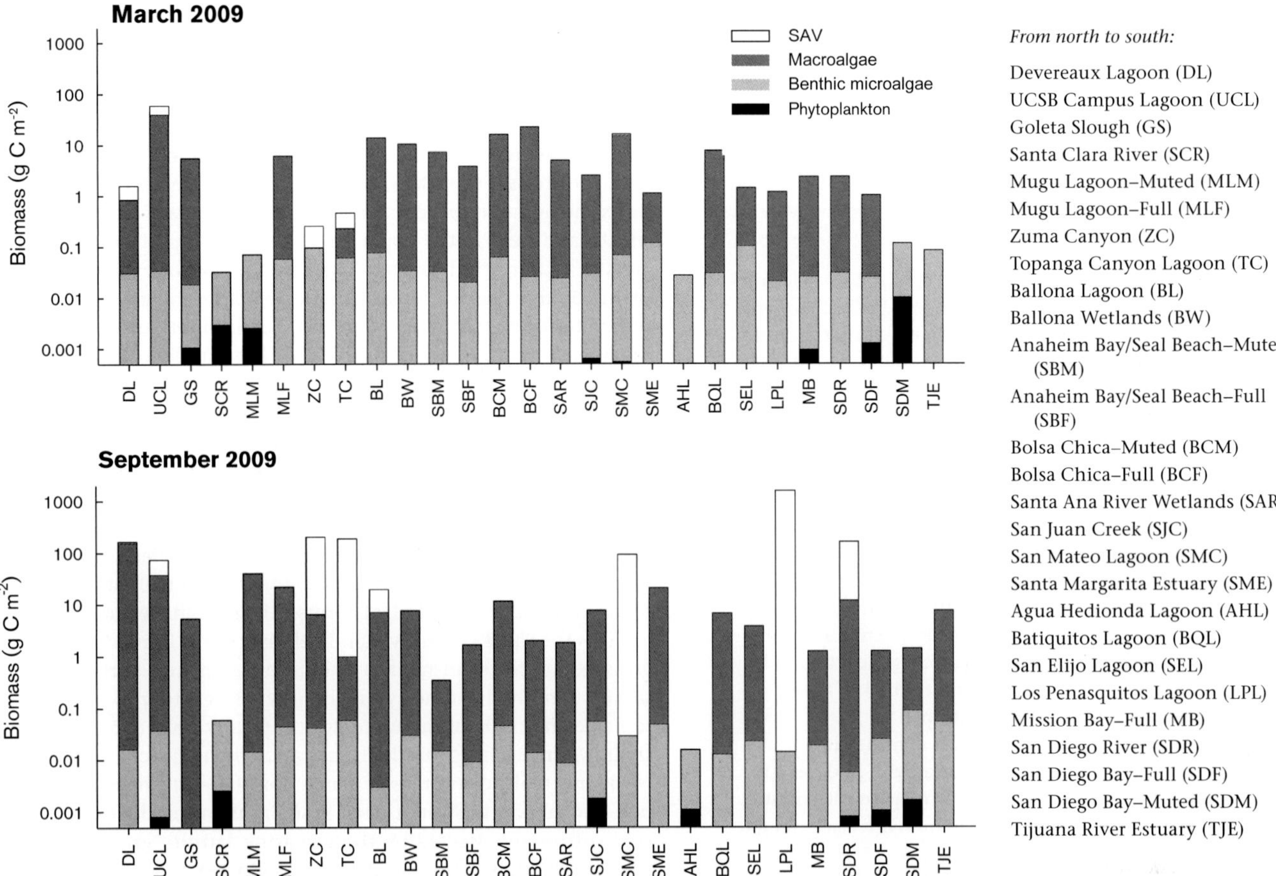

FIGURE 19.7 No single community or seasonal pattern exists that governs all of California's estuarine primary producers, because their habitat mosaics are spatially diverse and seasonally dynamic. This concept is illustrated in plots of biomass (g C m^{-2}) of phytoplankton, macroalgae, benthic microalgae, and submerged aquatic vegetation (SAV) in twenty-three southern California estuaries during March 2009 (top panel) and September 2009 (bottom panel). Note log scale on y-axis. Source: McLaughlin et al. 2013.

Estuaries receive ALLOCTHONOUS inputs of organic matter as plant biomass and detritus from oceans and rivers and autochthonous inputs from primary production. The prokaryotes play essential roles in the metabolism of this organic matter and the cycling of reactive elements. Microbial activity helps break down toxic organic contaminants such as pesticides or spilled hydrocarbons, and it transforms detrital organic matter having low food value into nutritious prokaryote biomass that can reenter the food web. Microbial oxidation of organic matter releases carbon dioxide, typically at a rate faster than carbon fixation by photosynthesis, so many estuaries are HETEROTROPHIC ECOSYSTEMS, reflecting the importance of external supplies of organic carbon.

In aerobic waters the prokaryotes use oxygen for respiration as they metabolize organic compounds; this is a key process of oxygen consumption in estuaries. In the absence of oxygen, either in ANOXIC waters or in bottom sediments, specialized prokaryotes respire other compounds—sulfate, nitrate, and oxidized metals such as iron, selenium, and arsenic. The product of prokaryotic sulfate respiration is sulfide, which binds and precipitates many heavy metals but is also toxic to fish and invertebrates. Another is reduced iron, which is soluble and diffuses into the overlying oxygenated water where it precipitates to scrub the water column of heavy metals and phosphorus. Other anaerobic processes include methylation of mercury that makes this toxic element more bioavailable and mobile, and reduction of selenate and selenite to elemental selenium that is precipitated in sediments. Microbial respiration of nitrate removes a large fraction of the nitrogen pollution delivered from land runoff or wastewater. Although prokaryotes are small in size, their biochemical reactions have large-scale significance to the water quality and life support functions of estuarine ecosystems. Estuaries are fast-running biogeochemical reactors, and prokaryotes are the key agents of these processes (*Principle 4*).

INVERTEBRATES

Estuarine invertebrates are a taxonomically diverse group of (mostly small) animals that consume detritus, microbes, algae, or other invertebrates and are an essential food resource for many vertebrates. They comprise two distinct communities: benthic species that live on or in the bottom sediments, and pelagic species that are components of the plankton. The pelagic community is dominated by mesozooplankton including copepods. Low-salinity regions of San Francisco

Bay include copepods, such as *Eurytemora affinis*, that have largely been replaced by non-native species, including *Pseudodiaptomus forbesi, Limnoithona tetraspina,* and *Acartiella sinensis*. Higher-salinity zones include native *Acartia* spp. as well as non-native *Tortanus dextrilobatus, Pseudodiaptomus marinus,* and *Oithonia davisae* (Kimmerer 2004). These spatial patterns illustrate *Principle 5*: biological communities vary along the salinity gradient; the pelagic forms (plankton, fish) are translocated along the estuary as the salinity gradient moves with changes in freshwater inflow (see Figure 19.5a). Larger zooplankton in upper San Francisco Bay include native (e.g., *Neomysis mercedis*) and introduced (*Hyperacanthomysis longirostris*, formerly *Acanthomysis bowmanii*) mysid shrimp as well as and native and introduced (e.g., *Gammarus daiberi*) amphipods. Abundances of gelatinous zooplankton such as jellyfish appear to be expanding, and population outbursts of *Aurelia* spp. are common in central and northern California estuaries (e.g., Tomales Bay, Bolinas Lagoon). Heavily invaded estuaries like San Francisco Bay now have annual blooms of several non-native species, including HYDROZOANS *Maeotias marginata, Moerisia* sp., and *Blackfordia virginica*.

The benthic invertebrates are dominated by molluscs, CRUSTACEANS, and POLYCHAETES, many of which are non-native (Cohen and Carlton 1995). Common molluscs include GASTROPODS such as the native mudsnail (*Cerithidea californica*), non-native mudsnails (*Batillaria attramentaria* and *Ilyanassa obsoleta*), and non-native oyster drills (*Urosalpinx cinerea*). Bivalve molluscs include several widely distributed invaders like the Manila clam (*Venerupsis philippinarum*), soft-shell clam (*Mya arenaria*), and two species—the mussel (*Geukensia demissa*) and clam (*Corbula [Potamocorbula] amurensis*)—which have transformed their environments. Native clams include harvestable species such as the geoduck (*Panopeus generosa*), Washington clams (*Saxidomus gigantea*), and horse clams (*Tresus* spp.), which have declined substantially. Common estuarine crustaceans include Bay shrimp, especially of the genus *Crangon*, small shore crabs such as *Hemigrapsus oregonensis* in higher tidal elevations in northern and central California and fiddler crabs (*Uca crenulata*) common in southern California. Lower tidal elevations support native rock crabs (*Cancer productus, C. antennarius*), Dungeness crabs (*Metacarcinus magister*), and non-native green crabs (*Carcinus maenas*). Dozens of amphipod species include many introduced species such as the highly invasive *Grandidierella japonica* and *Ampithoe valida*. There are also burrowing shrimp (*Neotrypaea californiensis* and *Upogebia pugettensis*) and in southern California spiny lobsters (*Panulirus interruptus*). The few structured habitats in California estuaries include beds of the native oyster (*Ostrea lurida*) and bay mussels (*Mytilus trossulus/galloprovincialis*) as well as eelgrass (*Zostera marina*). These limited habitats support species such as HYDROIDS, colonial botryllid TUNICATES, caprellid shrimp, isopods, and several shrimp species not found in the majority of estuarine habitats.

The invertebrate communities illustrate *Principle 6*: estuaries have distinct vertical components, a water column overlaying bottom sediments, and lateral components organized along the transition from subtidal to INTERTIDAL HABITATS. These components are tightly coupled: for example, many benthic invertebrates have life stages that enter the plankton, microbial respiration in sediments removes oxygen, and filtration by benthic invertebrates removes phytoplankton from the overlying water.

FISH

The fish communities of California's estuaries range from resident species dominating small lagoons in southern California to anadromous species dominating river-mouth estuaries in northern California (Allen et al. 2006). Some species are permanent estuarine residents, including delta smelt (*Hypomesus transpacificus*), splittail (*Pogonichthys macrolepidotus*), topsmelt (*Atherinop affinis*), California killifish (*Fundulus parvipinnis*), several species of gobies, and spotted sand bass (*Paralabrax maculatofasciatus*). Marine migrants reproduce or rear in estuaries, anadromous species migrate from the ocean to spawn in freshwater, CATADROMOUS species migrate from freshwater to spawn in the ocean, and some freshwater and marine species move into estuarine habitats seasonally. Some species use estuaries in the north and south differently because of California's latitudinal gradients of freshwater inflow and temperature. For example, Pacific staghorn sculpin (*Leptocottus armatus*) is a resident species in southern California lagoons but a marine migrant in northern California estuaries that receive high winter-spring freshwater inflow. Like the invertebrates, fish communities include two groups: demersal (bottom-living) species such as flatfish, sturgeon and rays, and pelagic species such as anchovies, herring, and smelt.

Estuarine fish populations often have large annual fluctuations. Three different patterns are illustrated from long-term studies of San Francisco Bay (Figure 19.8): (1) an abrupt increase of English sole (*Parophrys vetulus*) abundance after 1999; (2) episodic appearances of California halibut (*Paralichthys californicus*); and (3) long-term decline of delta smelt (*Hypomesus transpacificus*). These patterns reflect different life histories and susceptibilities to human disturbance. English sole is a demersal marine fish that migrates into estuaries as juveniles to rear. It is a cold-temperate species affiliated with the northern biogeographic Oregon Province (Briggs and Bowen 2012). Its abrupt population increase followed a 1999 transition of the northeast Pacific Ocean from its warm to its cool phase (see below). California halibut is a warm-temperate demersal marine fish that rears in estuaries and is affiliated with the southern California Province. Its episodic appearances in San Francisco Bay occurred during or immediately after El Niño events. Estuaries are open ecosystems, and their fish communities are structured by the immigration of marine species whose population abundances track large-scale climate patterns (*Principle 7*).

BIRDS

A great diversity of bird taxa exploit the wide range of habitat types available in estuarine ecosystems (Takekawa et al. 2011). Dabbling ducks feed in shallow subtidal habitats, but individual species exploit different food resources: northern pintails (*Anas acuta*) feed primarily on small seeds filtered from bottom sediments, while northern shovelers (*Anas clypeata*) primarily feed on invertebrates and seeds suspended in water. Diving ducks and PISCIVOROUS birds use a greater diversity of subtidal habitats. Ruddy duck (*Oxyura jamaicensis*) dive to feed on benthic organisms in shellfish beds, plant beds and in the water, and species such as the great egret (*Ardea alba*) feed primarily on fish. Piscivorous birds forage in most subtidal habitat types. For example, Brandt's cormorant (*Phalacrocorax penicillatus*) in San Francisco Bay forages in the benthos,

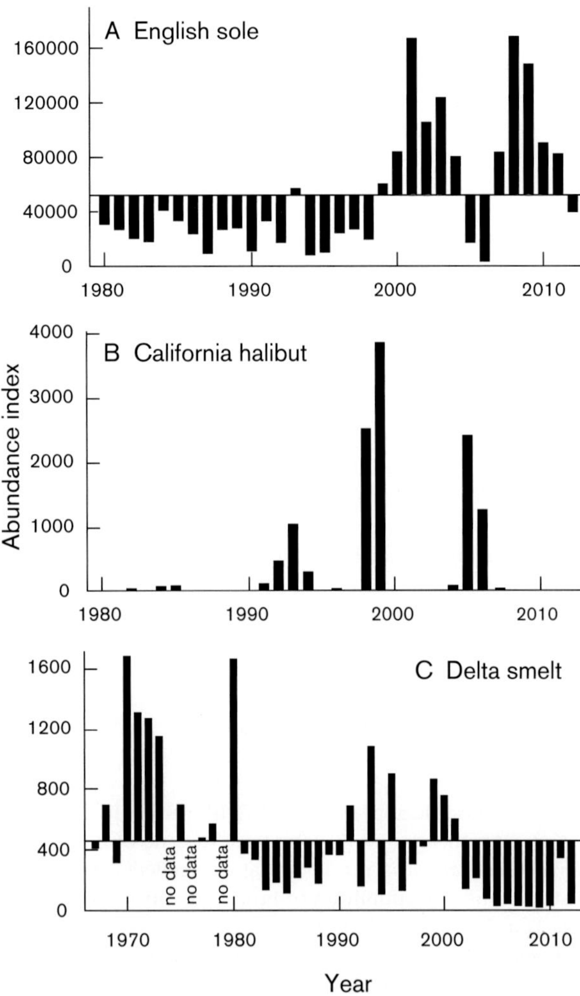

FIGURE 19.8 Three patterns of annual fish abundance in the San Francisco Bay–Delta: (A) decadal-scale shift from low to high abundance, in juvenile English sole (*Parophrys vetulus*); (B) episodic year classes, in juvenile California halibut (*Paralichthys californicus*); and (C) a long-term decline, in delta smelt (*Hypomesus transpacificus*). Sources: English sole and California halibut data from the San Francisco Bay Study of the California Department of Fish and Wildlife (CDFW) (1980–2012); delta smelt data from CDFW Fall Midwater Trawl Survey (1967–2012). Panels A and C are centered around long-term mean abundances.

over hard bottom substrate and in the water column while the brown pelican (*Pelecanus occidentalis*) and Clark's grebe (*Aechmorphous clarkia*) only forage within the water column.

Intertidal mudflats support large numbers of shorebirds that feed primarily on invertebrates. At least forty-three species of shorebirds coexist within California estuaries because of evolutionary adaptations of bill shapes and body sizes allowing species to exploit food resources at different water and mud depths (Page et al. 1999). For example, the short bill of the least sandpiper (*Calidris minutilla*) restricts its foraging to shallow depths on the upper edge of mudflats while long-billed curlew (*Numenius americanus*) can probe deeper into mudflats for food (Figure 19.9). Tidal marsh habitat is important for songbirds, shorebirds, rails, herons, egrets, and ducks. Some species are tidal marsh obligates such as the Ridgway's rail (*Rallus obsoletus obsoletus*), which uses cordgrass for cover as it moves along tidal channels to forage on invertebrates. Many marsh species are gleaners, foraging on the marsh surface for invertebrates and seeds.

Many species of shorebirds, waterfowl, and seabirds migrate between wintering and breeding habitat along the Pacific coast from Alaska and eastern Siberia to South America following the Pacific Flyway. Along the way these birds require wetland habitats to rest and forage to build energy to complete their journey. Estuaries along the Pacific Flyway provide some of the most important stopover locations because of the abundance and diversity of food resources available. Four California estuaries are listed as sites of importance by the Western Hemisphere Shorebird Reserve Network (Table 19.2). At least forty-three species of shorebirds are found in wetlands along the Pacific coast, with the largest numbers found in San Francisco Bay. An average 66.7% of the total numbers of thirteen focal shorebird species surveyed in fifty-six wetlands along the Pacific coast between 1988 and 1995 were found in San Francisco Bay during the fall (Page et al. 1999). Thus California's estuaries have global significance for sustaining populations and biodiversity of migratory birds.

INTERACTIONS BETWEEN COMMUNITIES

The PRIMARY PRODUCERS, decomposers, grazers, and predators of estuaries are tightly connected through trophic (feeding) linkages. These linkages are revealed when abundances of predators increase or decrease abruptly, with effects that cascade to change abundances of their prey and organisms at lower trophic levels. Such a trophic cascade occurred in San Francisco Bay after 1999 when large numbers of marine predators—bottom-feeding fish (e.g., English sole, see Figure 19.8a), crabs (e.g., Dungeness crab), and shrimp—migrated from the coastal Pacific into the bay. Heavy predation by these marine immigrants reduced the abundance of clams in the estuary, releasing grazing pressure on phytoplankton and allowing its biomass to grow (Cloern et al. 2010). This restructuring of biological communities followed a shift in the climate system across the North Pacific as the NPGO became positive and coastal upwelling intensified (Figure 19.10), signaling an increase in coastal productivity and strong recruitment of marine predators that migrate into estuaries to feed. A four-level trophic cascade was triggered in Elkhorn Slough by population recovery of an apex predator (sea otter [*Enhydra lutris*]) leading to declines of its prey (*Cancer* crabs), increases of grazers preyed upon by crabs (the isopod *Idotea resecata* and sea slug [*Phyllaplysia taylori*]), and biomass decrease of microalgae scraped off surfaces by the grazers (Hughes et al. 2013). Microalgae grow on leaves of vascular plants and inhibit their growth, so an unanticipated outcome of the otter recovery in Elkhorn Slough was synchronous recovery of seagrass (*Zostera marina*) as microalgal growth was removed from its leaves by the abundant grazers. In both estuaries changing abundance of crabs that prey upon grazers led to changing biomass of microalgae, either phytoplankton or attached forms.

Services Provided by Estuarine Biota and Their Habitats

Coasts attract human settlement, and many of the world's great cities such as London, Rio de Janeiro, Tokyo, New York, and San Francisco were built on estuaries because of the resources and services they provide. Although estuaries

FIGURE 19.9 Shorebirds illustrate dramatic morphological adaptations allowing many species to coexist within the same locations. Long-billed curlew (A) have a long bill that allows them to probe deep into mudflats for food. The black-necked stilt (B) uses its delicate, slightly recurved bill to capture prey by pecking or sweeping its bill at or near the water surface. The long-billed curlew and black-neck stilt are tall, allowing them to forage in deeper waters, while dowitcher (C) and willet (D) are medium-sized shorebirds, which forage in shallower depths. In contrast, least sandpiper (E) are one of the smallest shorebirds, and their foraging is restricted to shallow water on the upper edges of mudflats. Photos: Tom Grey.

TABLE 19.2
California estuaries recognized as important for shorebird conservation by the Western Hemisphere Shorebird Reserve Network (WHSRN)

Estuary	WHSRN Class	Description
Elkhorn Slough	Site of Regional Importance	At least 20,000 shorebirds annually
South San Diego Bay	Site of Regional Importance	At least 20,000 shorebirds annually
Humboldt Bay Complex	Site of International Importance	At least 100,000 shorebirds annually
San Francisco Bay	Site of Hemispheric Importance	At least 500,000 shorebirds annually

NOTE: Classes of importance are based on the observed number of shorebirds at each site within a year.

occupy only 0.3% of Earth's surface, they provide goods and services valued highest per unit area (\$22,832 ha^{-1} yr^{-1}) among all the world's biomes (Costanza et al. 1997). Beyond the dollar value, estuaries are beautiful and fascinating places where people boat, swim, bird, hunt, walk, take photographs, view wildlife, and conduct research.

FISH NURSERY AND MIGRATION CORRIDORS

Ecologically and commercially important fish and invertebrates rear in warm estuarine waters over soft bottoms rich with small invertebrates. Many of these species reproduce in the ocean, the small juveniles migrate into estuaries to rear, and the larger juveniles migrate back to the ocean. This group includes Dungeness crab, Bay shrimp (*Crangon* spp.), brown rockfish, English sole, speckled sanddab, and starry flounder in northern California. Other species—such as leopard shark, Pacific herring, and the surfperches in northern California and yellowfin croaker, California halibut, and diamond turbot in southern California (Allen et al. 2006)—migrate from the ocean to estuaries to reproduce, where the young rear. California estuaries also serve as migration corridors for anadromous salmon, steelhead, sturgeon, striped bass, and American shad. Salmon and steelhead transfer carbon and nitrogen from the coastal ocean to rivers and adjacent terrestrial systems when consumed by predators and scavengers and their carcasses decay (Gende et al. 2002, Merz and Moyle 2006). Fish and invertebrates that rear in estuaries transfer carbon and nutrients from tidal marshes and other shallow-water habitats to the open estuary and to the ocean, while salmon transfer carbon and nutrients from the ocean to the rivers (*Principle 8*).

ORGANIC CARBON PRODUCTION, EXPORT, AND STORAGE

The vascular plants of estuarine marshes have very high rates of primary production. For example, annual production of pickleweed (*Sarcocornia pacifica*, formerly *Salicornia virginica*) ranges up to 690 g C m^{-2} in San Francisco Bay, 2,860 g C m^{-2} in Los Peñasquitos Lagoon, and 1,050 g C m^{-2} in Tijuana Estuary (Grewell et al. 2007). This carbon supply becomes part of a detrital pool that fuels benthic food webs in estuaries and is exported to oceanic deep water as a food and energy source. The rate of organic carbon production in tidal marshes exceeds the rate of ANAEROBIC DECOMPOSITION, so these habitats are efficient at storing carbon belowground. Annual rates

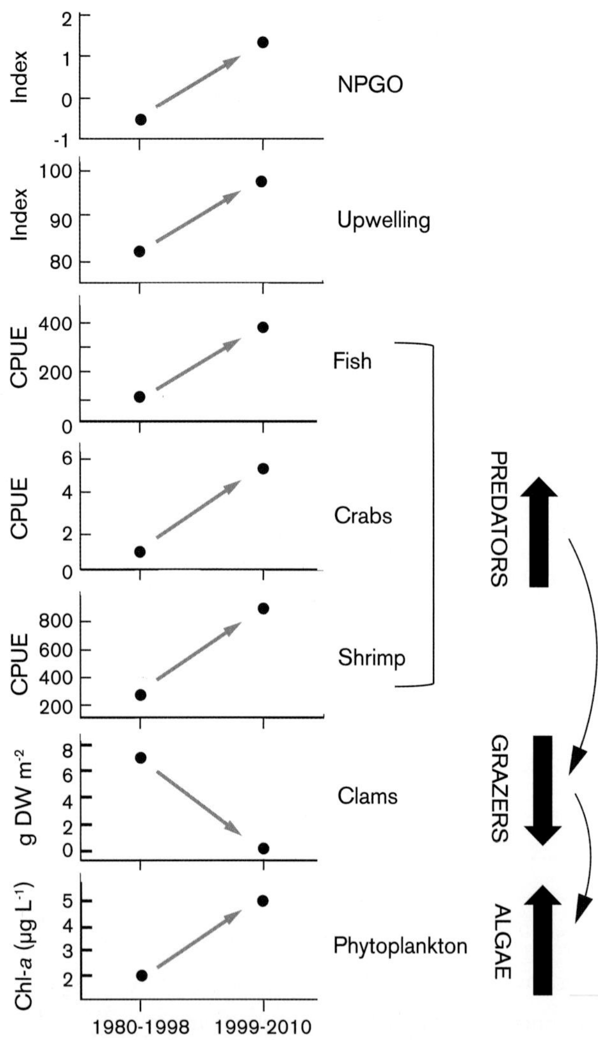

FIGURE 19.10 Biological communities in San Francisco Bay were restructured after a 1999 climate shift when the North Pacific Gyre Oscillation (NPGO) shifted from negative to positive; coastal upwelling (and biological productivity) intensified; and predator (ten species of bottom-feeding fish, crabs, and shrimp) abundances increased, leading to decreased abundance of grazers (clams) and then to increased phytoplankton biomass. Dark circles show medians (climatic indices, abundances [CPUE, catch per unit effort] or biomass) for the periods 1980–1998 and 1999–2010. Source: Redrawn from Figure 17 in Cloern and Jassby 2012.

of soil CARBON SEQUESTRATION in salt and brackish marshes of San Francisco Bay average about 80 g C m^{-2} (Callaway et al. 2012b). Managed freshwater marshes in the Sacramento–San Joaquin Delta are very productive (1,300 to 3,200 g C m^{-2} yr^{-1}) and can accrete approximately 4 cm yr^{1} of organic-rich sediment (Miller and Fuji 2010). As a result, creation of "farmed" wetlands is now being considered to sequester carbon to mitigate atmospheric CO_2 emissions.

FOOD PRODUCTION

Half of U.S. commercial fish harvest is of estuarine-dependent species. Fish production is strongly correlated with phytoplankton primary production (Houde and Rutherford 1993) because phytoplankton photosynthesis provides much of the energy that fuels production of organisms we harvest. Phytoplankton primary production ranges from 70 to 810 g C m^{-2} yr^{1} in Tomales Bay (Cole 1989) and from 30 to >400 g C m^{-2} yr^{1} in San Francisco Bay (Alpine and Cloern 1992, Cloern and Jassby 2012). These measures imply a thirtyfold range of potential fish production, and this large variability implies comparable variability of consumer production in California's estuaries. We harvest some of this production in the form of cultured oysters, a practice that began in San Francisco Bay during the nineteenth century and was colorfully chronicled in Jack London's *Tales of the Fish Patrol* (Asprey 2010). Oyster culture in San Francisco Bay was doomed by declining water quality, but introduced Pacific oysters (*Crassostrea gigas*), mussels, clams, scallops, abalone, and brine shrimp are cultured in Humboldt Bay, Tomales Bay, Drakes Estero, Morro Bay, and Agua Hedionda. We once harvested another component of estuarine production through commercial fishing, an important source of food that has disappeared from California estuaries (see below).

FLOOD BUFFERING

Aquatic plants dampen currents and waves to protect shorelines, and marsh vegetation attenuates storm and flood impacts. While hurricane-force storms are unlikely in California, erosion and flooding are still major coastal concerns (Hanak and Moreno 2011). As sea level continues to rise, tidal marshes will play an increasingly valuable role in buffering adjacent terrestrial systems from flooding and storm impact, although their sustainability is uncertain in the face of rapidly accelerating sea level rise (Stralberg et al. 2011).

WASTE ASSIMILATION

Microbes provide a suite of ecosystem services such as NITRIFICATION-DENITRIFICATION, which converts organic nitrogen into nitrogen gas (Figure 19.11) and regulates accumulation of nitrogen delivered to estuaries from agricultural runoff and sewage. Without this service nitrogen pollution would accumulate unchecked in estuaries to levels that degrade water quality, and costly actions would be required to reduce human inputs of nitrogen. These kinds of biological processes are unseen and their values are not recognized, but we can estimate the monetary value of processes such as microbial removal of nitrogen pollution. The mean denitrification rate in estuaries is 5,600 kg N km^{-2} yr^{1} (Seitzinger et al. 2006). The area of California's estuaries and coastal wetlands is approximately 3,300 km^2 (Larson 2001, Gleason et al. 2011), so these habitats potentially remove about 2 x 10^7 kg N annually. The average cost of nitrogen removal in sewage treatment plants is \$275 kg^{-1} N (CBP 2002), so the nitrogen-removal service provided by California's estuaries has an annual value exceeding \$5 billion in 2002 dollars. Tidal marshes and their microbial communities also trap and sequester nutrients and contaminants, thereby improving water quality and buffering coastal waters from contaminants carried by urban runoff.

OPPORTUNITIES TO UNDERSTAND PROCESSES OF EVOLUTION

Tidal marshes in California are hot spots of bird and mammal biodiversity and habitat for nineteen ENDEMIC subspe-

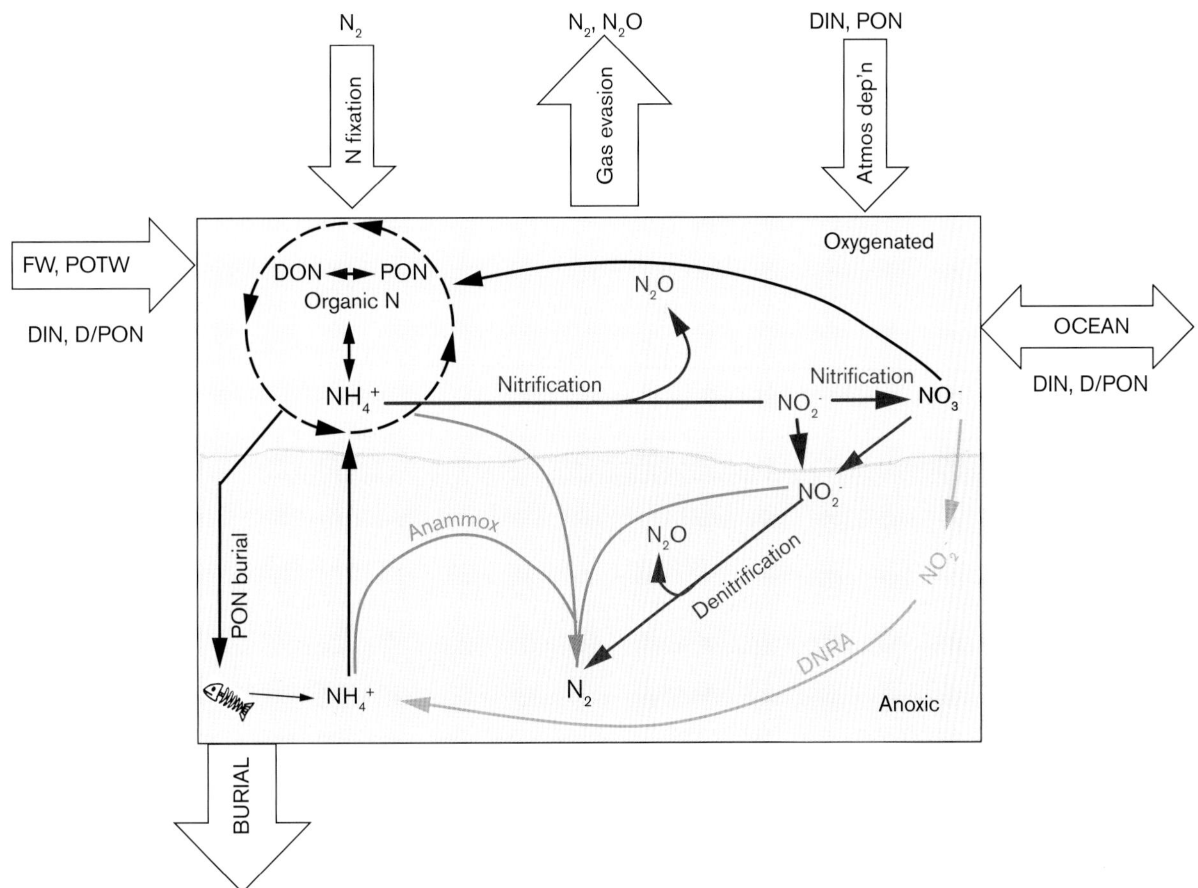

FIGURE 19.11 Diagram of nitrogen (N) cycling in estuaries. N sources and sinks are shown in block arrows around a box that encloses within-estuary transformations. The box is divided into water column (light blue, generally oxygenated) and sediment (light brown, typically anoxic below a depth of a few millimeters).

On left, N enters the estuary as dissolved inorganic nitrogen (DIN) and either dissolved or particulate organic nitrogen (DON and PON, or "D/PON"). DIN is assimilated by biota in the estuary to cycle between organic and inorganic forms (such as ammonium, NH_4^+). FW: freshwater (riverine inflow and groundwater); POTW: publicly owned treatment works (discharges from municipal and industrial treatment works).

N fixation and atmospheric N deposition, indicating nitrogen deposited in the estuary as dust or in precipitation, are two additional input sources. OCEAN indicates two-way tidal exchange of N with the coastal ocean. Gas evasion is the loss of fixed nitrogen that has been converted to gaseous forms (N_2, nitrogen gas; and N_2O, nitrous oxide) by microbial processes (ammonia oxidation, denitrification [blue] and the microbial process of anammox [anaerobic ammonium oxidation, green]).

BURIAL indicates permanent burial in sediments. Fixed N cycles between NH_4^+ regenerated by microbial degradation or excretion by animals and D/PON in biomass and detritus. PON can be buried temporarily in surface sediments, where it can undergo degradation or be buried permanently. Aerobic microbes oxidize NH_4^+ to nitrite (NO_2^-) and then to nitrate (NO_3^-), with some production of N_2O as a by-product (nitrification, red), while NO_2^- and NH_4^+can be combined in anammox to yield N_2. NO_3^- can be taken up by phytoplankton to reenter the internal cycle of assimilation and regeneration shown on the left. Nitrate is converted to N_2 by denitrification (blue), which also yields some N_2O, or is converted to NH_4^+ by another microbial respiratory process called dissimilatory reduction of nitrate to ammonia or DNRA (orange). Illustration by James T. Hollibaugh.

cies (Table 19.3). Tidal marsh populations tend to be grayer or darker than their more terrestrial analogs (Greenberg and Maldonado 2006), and tidal marsh bird races often have longer, thinner bills (Grenier and Greenberg 2005). The benefits of these differences and the mechanisms that maintain them are not known, but two interesting possibilities for advancing evolutionary biology are evident. First, new information about bird bill size diversity is opening the door to reconsidering seminal work in evolutionary biology. Greenberg et al. (2012) showed that sparrow bill size varies with maximum summer temperature in tidal marshes, and they hypothesize that bills diffuse heat and thus help conserve water—key adaptations in saline habitats with little shade. Therefore, heat regulation as well as feeding ecology must be considered when studying adaptations in bill morphology—a fundamental system from which Darwin developed the theory of evolution via natural selection (Darwin 1845). Second, tidal marshes may be sites of incipient ecological speciation, which has been identified rarely in terrestrial vertebrates and almost never in birds. Most examples of speciation are thought to occur when populations become geographically isolated. ECOLOGICAL SPECIATION, on the other hand, arises from DIVERGENT SELECTION across ecological gradients within connected populations. Three California tidal marsh song sparrow subspecies are morphologically distinct despite geographic contact with SUBSPECIES occupying terrestrial habitats (Chan and Arcese 2003). Ecological gradients between terrestrial habitats and tidal marsh are steep (including large changes in HYDROLOGY, salinity, and vegetative structure) and likely require concomitant adaptation to successfully exploit tidal marsh resources. These gradients provide opportunities to learn whether and how such adaptations lead to REPRODUCTIVE ISOLATION.

TABLE 19.3
Mammals and birds endemic to California tidal marshes

Common name	Scientific name (with subspecies)	Distribution
Ridgway's rail	*Rallus obsoletus obsoletus*	San Francisco Bay
	R. l. levipes	Southern California
Common yellowthroat	*Geothlypis trichas sinuosa*	San Francisco Bay
Song sparrow	*Melospiza melodia samuelis*	San Pablo Bay
	M. m. pusillula	San Francisco Bay
	M. m. maxillaris	Suisun Bay
Savanna sparrow	*Passerculus sandwichensis beldingi*	Southern California
Ornate shrew	*Sorex ornatus sinuosus*	San Pablo Bay
	S. o. salaries	Monterey Bay
	S. o. salicornicus	Los Angeles Bay
Wandering shrew	*Sorex vagrans halicoetes*	South San Francisco Bay
Salt marsh harvest mouse	*Reithrodontomys raviventris raviventris*	San Francisco Bay
	R. r. halicoetes	San Pablo and Suisun Bays
Western harvest mouse	*Reithrodontomys megalotis distichlis*	Monterey Bay
	R. m. limicola	Los Angeles Bay
California vole	*Microtus californicus paludicola*	San Francisco Bay
	M. c. sanpabloensis	San Pablo Bay
	M. c. halophilus	Monterey Bay
	M. c. stephensi	Los Angeles coast

SOURCE: Greenberg and Maldonado 2006.

The Human Dimension

In their undisturbed state, estuaries have the capacity to support animal abundances and diversity that are difficult for us to imagine today, but the living resources of California's estuaries have been greatly altered as the human population has grown (see Chapter 8, "Ecosystems Past: Vegetation Prehistory"). Reports from San Francisco Bay by eighteenth-century explorers described: "countless fowl, ducks, geese, cranes, and other kinds" (Crespí and Brown 2001), "the spouting of whales, a shoal of dolphins or tunny fish, sea otter, and sea lions" near the Golden Gate, and "great piles of fresh-water mussels" and "very fine salmon in abundance" being fished by native residents (Bolton 1933). John E. Skinner's (1962) remarkable history of fish and wildlife resources tells that this biological richness persisted into the late nineteenth century: "No other area in California can match the rich fisheries potential of this region. This potential lies in the wealth of marine life found within its bays and adjacent coastal waters"; "sardines are reported so abundant in San Francisco Bay that they literally obstruct the passage of boats"; and Dungeness crabs "are taken in immense numbers in seines, together with many shoal water species of fish, yet the supply seems to be undiminished" (Skinner 1962). It turns out that these supplies did have bounds because an era of rapid declines of waterfowl, fish, and shellfish populations began in the early twentieth century. These losses reflect a deep and broad human footprint on California's estuaries.

The Many Forms of Human Disturbance

LANDSCAPE TRANSFORMATION

In the 250 years since Crespí's journey, California's estuaries have been dredged to create ports or harbors, or leveed, filled, or drained (see Figure 19.1), contributing to a loss of over 91% of the state's wetlands (Dahl 1990, Goodwin et al. 2001). Through filling and excavation we have disproportionately eliminated tidal flats, tidal marshes, and salt flats, and many estuaries now have a much higher proportion of open-water habitat than they did historically. For example, nearly half of San Francisco Bay was exposed at low tide in the 1850s compared to less than a quarter today (Goals Project 1999). In the Sacramento–San Joaquin Delta, wetland area was historically fourteen times greater than open-water area; today open- water area is five times greater than wetland area (Whipple et al. 2012). These kinds of changes have resulted in an overall homogenization of California's estuarine landscapes—in other words, a loss of habitat diversity. In particular, freshwater and HYPERSALINE estuarine habitat mosaics are rare or even unrecognized today. Though extensive salt flats were once dominant features of many northern San Diego County estuaries, almost none remain today (Beller et al. 2014). Most traces of the Santa Clara River's dune-dammed lagoon complexes have been completely erased (Beller et al. 2011). The early and nearly complete loss of freshwater tidal marshes in the Bay-Delta estuary has dramatically changed the landscape and reduced the estuary's habitat and biological diversity (Vasey et al. 2012, Whipple et al. 2012).

A related landscape transformation is the alteration of tidal circulation within estuaries, in particular the restriction of tidal exchange by dikes, berms, and operations of water-control structures that reduce tidal range. The stagnant conditions in areas of tidal restriction can amplify the effects of nutrient enrichment, leading to accumulation of high algal biomass (Hughes et al. 2011); and they lead to reduced diversity of estuarine communities (Ritter et al. 2008). Conversely, some historically intermittently closing systems have experienced enhancement of tidal circulation—for example, through the construction of jetties.

Another ubiquitous landscape transformation is river damming that facilitates water storage, consumption, and interbasin transfers that have greatly altered the timing and magnitude of freshwater inflow to many California estuaries. The median inflow to San Francisco Bay is only 60% of the inflow that would occur from an unimpaired watershed. Inflow reductions result from water storage during the wet season and exports during the dry season (Cloern and Jassby 2012). Conversely, importation of water from the Bay-Delta watershed has increased summer river discharge in urban watersheds of southern California by 250% or more (Townsend-Small et al. 2013). Human modification of freshwater inflow has wide-reaching effects on estuaries through changes in transport processes, sediment input, water quality, and salinity—changes that have degraded habitat quality for some native fishes (Feyrer et al. 2011), facilitated invasions by non-native species (Winder et al. 2011), and altered plant distributions in salt marshes (Watson and Byrne 2009).

SPECIES INTRODUCTIONS

Human introductions of non-native plants and animals are also major disturbances to natural communities and their habitats (see Chapter 13, "Biological Invasions"). California estuaries are some of the most highly invaded coastal systems on the planet (Ruiz et al. 2000), with upwards of 235 introduced species of invertebrates and algae and 20 species of marine/estuarine fishes (Schroeter and Moyle 2005). San Francisco Bay is the most invaded (217 non-native species), followed by Los Angeles/Long Beach (95), Elkhorn Slough (80), San Diego (78), and Humboldt Bay (77) (Figure 19.12a). Vectors for invasive species include discharge of ship ballast water, hull fouling, sales of live bait and seafood, aquarium/ornamental species trade, and transport via aquaculture (Figure 19.12b). Many of these vectors are poorly understood and largely unregulated. For instance, thousands of non-native plants and animals are imported into the U.S. annually through the aquarium/ornamental trade (Williams et al. 2013), but the likelihood of release and probability of their survival in California estuaries is often not known (Chang et al. 2009). Introductions of plant species have also profoundly changed California's marsh communities, particularly in the high marsh and ECOTONE between marsh and uplands where plant diversity peaks (Traut 2005, Wasson and Woolfolk 2011).

Two case studies from San Francisco Bay illustrate the power of disturbance from species introductions. Following intentional introduction of the non-native marsh plant *Spartina alterniflora* from the U.S. Atlantic coast in 1974, this species hybridized with the native *Spartina foliosa,* creating a hybrid that spread throughout most of central and south San Francisco Bay (Hogle, 2010). Hybrid *Spartina* dramatically altered ecosystem function by colonizing previously unvegetated mudflats and reducing water flow, significantly increasing deposition of fine sediments and reducing biomass of benthic invertebrates by 90% (Neira et al. 2006). This invasion eliminated mudflat habitats that previously supported shorebirds, fishes, and crabs, and it was followed by local EXTIRPATION of the native *Spartina.*

Another invasion with ecosystem-wide impacts was introduction of the clam *Corbula (Potamocorbula) amurensis* from the west Pacific, likely from ballast water. Within a year of its 1986 introduction, this clam carpeted the bottom sediments of the upper estuary. Water filtration by the clam population led to a fivefold drop of phytoplankton biomass and primary production and elimination of the summer phytoplankton bloom (Figure 19.12c). This transformed the estuary to a state of chronic food limitation of zooplankton, and populations of native copepods, mysid shrimp, and rotifers fell abruptly. These zooplankton taxa are key food resources for some indigenous fish, such as delta smelt, and they were replaced by smaller copepods having lower food value (Winder and Jassby 2011). This loss of pelagic production is a contributing factor to population declines of planktivorous fish now designated as threatened or endangered species. The *Corbula* introduction is an iconic example of how non-native species can reorganize biological communities and significantly alter ecosystem processes such as primary production.

POLLUTION

Some California estuaries are contaminated by pollutants at levels that threaten ecosystem or human health. Sediments in half of southern California estuaries have high concentrations of toxic metals such as zinc and organic pollutants such as polynuclear aromatic hydrocarbons, pesticides, and polybrominated diphenyl ethers (PBDEs) (SCB [Southern California Bight 2008 Regional Monitoring Program Coastal Ecology Committee] 2012). The California mussel and the California sea lion have PBDE concentrations among the highest measured in the U.S., a concern because these contaminants disrupt nervous system development and hormone regulation (Kimbrough et al. 2009, Meng et al. 2009). Many California estuaries also receive high nitrogen loadings from wastewater treatment plants and urban and agricultural runoff, leading to poor water and habitat quality from excess production of phytoplankton biomass in Elkhorn Slough and Santa Clara River Estuary, MACROALGAE in Newport Bay and Morro Bay, and hypoxia (low dissolved oxygen levels) in Elkhorn Slough, Newport Bay, and Tijuana Estuary (Bricker et al. 1999, Hughes et al. 2011, McLaughlin et al. 2013). Hypoxia in intermittently tidal estuaries such as San Elijo and Los Penasquitos Lagoon has forced actions to maintain a permanently open inlet to increase tidal flushing, causing the extirpation of brackish water species such as the endangered tidewater goby. In response to these water quality issues, the U.S. Environmental Protection Agency and the state of California have developed sediment quality objectives and are developing nutrient

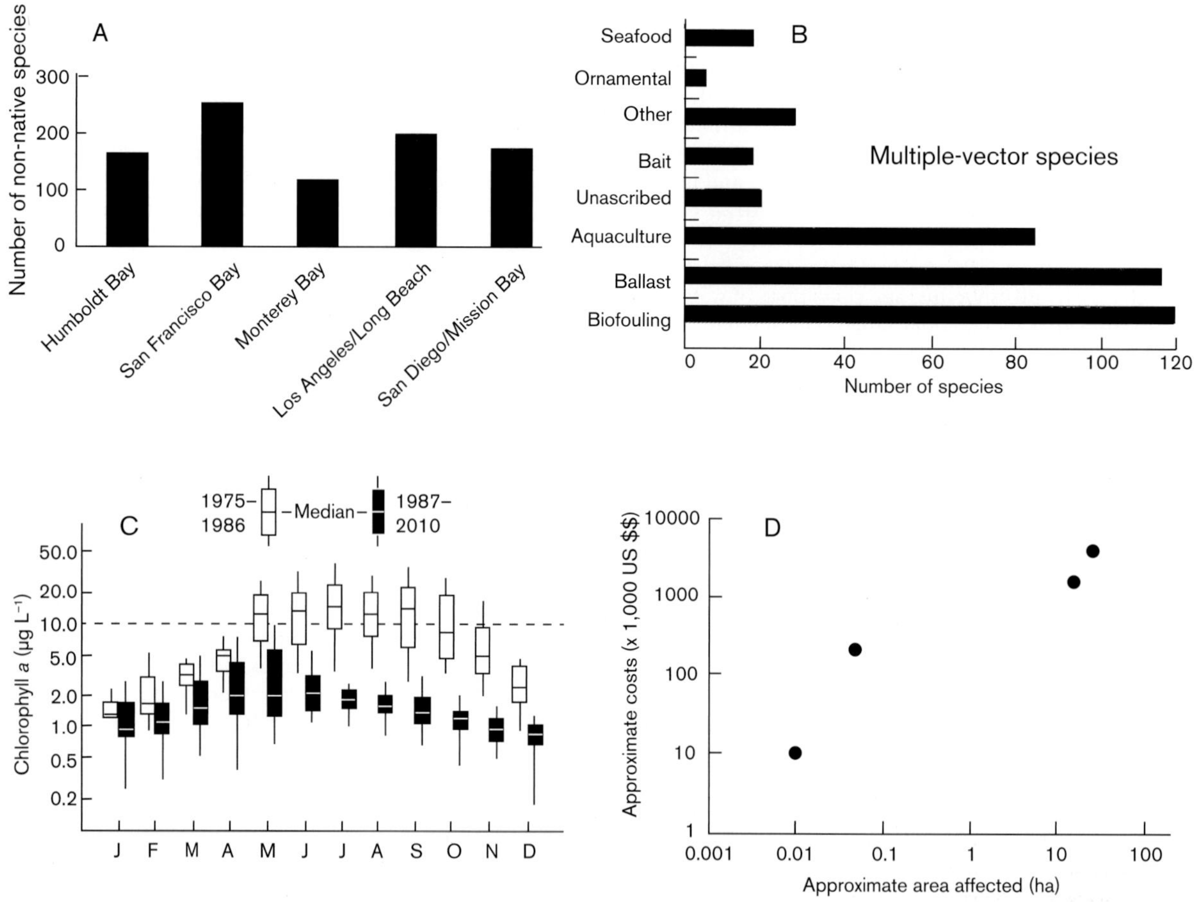

FIGURE 19.12 Hundreds of non-native species have been introduced into California waters via ship-based vectors including ballast water and hull fouling as well as via aquaculture, live bait, and ornamental trades. These introductions have had numerous negative consequences for ecosystem function and human economies.

A Numbers of established non-native species of invertebrates and algae in major California embayments ordered from north to south showing total number for each bay. Source: Fofonoff et al. 2011.

B Contributions of vectors to introductions of 145 non-native marine species that have each been brought into California via multiple vectors (N=389 vector × species combinations). Source: Williams et al. 2013.

C Box plot of monthly mean chlorophyll-*a* values in Suisun Bay before and after the introduction of *Corbula (Potamocorbula) amurensis* in 1986. The dashed line represents phytoplankton concentrations below which zooplankton populations may be food limited. Source: Cloern and Jassby 2012.

D Plot of approximate eradication costs as a function of the area invaded for recent successful eradication programs for estuarine invasions, including *Caulerpa taxifolia* (uppermost point). Note the log scale for both invaded area and eradication costs. Source: Edwin D. Grosholz, unpublished data.

criteria to ensure that beneficial uses provided by California estuaries (e.g., fish spawning, shellfish harvest, and water contact) are not impaired by contaminants (Sutula et al. 2007).

What Has Been Lost? What Is at Risk?

HUMAN HEALTH ADVISORIES

Inputs of toxic metals have been reduced dramatically in some estuaries, such as San Francisco Bay, through source controls and advanced wastewater treatment. But nonpoint sources (urban runoff, atmospheric deposition) and legacy pollutants that persist in sediments remain challenging problems. As a result, state advisories limit human consumption of some fish and shellfish because of high levels of mercury, PCBs, or pathogens.

HABITAT LOSSES

California estuaries have lost vast areas of their historic marshes, including salt marshes, brackish marshes, and tidal freshwater marshes (Goals Project 1999, Van Dyke and Wasson 2005). Eelgrass and oyster beds, which provide important structured habitat, have also been negatively impacted by anthropogenic activities such as introduction of non-native species (Wasson 2010) and eutrophication (Hughes et al. 2013).

SPECIES LOSSES

The cumulative effects of habitat loss, pollution, introduced species, and other disturbances such as dredging, water diversions, and river damming have taken a large toll on Califor-

TABLE 19.4
California's threatened or endangered species that require or use estuarine and tidal marsh habitats

Class	Common name	Scientific name	Status
Mammal	Southern sea otter	*Enhydra lutris nereis*	FT
	Salt-marsh harvest mouse	*Reithrodontomys raviventris*	SE FE
Bird	California least tern	*Sterna antillarum browni*	SE FE
	Western snowy plover	*Charadrius alexandrinus nivosus*	FT
	Ridgway's Rail	*Rallus obsoletus obsoletus*	SE FE
	California black rail	*Laterallus jamaicensis coturniculus*	ST
	Light-footed clapper rail	*Rallus longirostris levipes*	SE FE
	Belding's savannah sparrow	*Passerculus sandwichensis beldingi*	SE
Fish	Tidewater goby	*Eucyclogobius newberryi*	FE
	Chinook salmon spring run	*Oncorhynchus tshawytscha*	ST FT
	Chinook salmon winter run	*Oncorhynchus tshawytscha*	SE FE
	Steelhead	*Oncorhynchus mykiss*	FE or FT by region
	Coho salmon	*Oncorhynchus kisutch*	SE FE
	Longfin smelt	*Spirinchus thaleichthys*	ST
	Delta smelt	*Hypomesus transpacificus*	SE FT
	Green sturgeon	*Acipenser medirostris*	FT
	Pacific eulachon, southern DPS	*Thaleichthys pacificus*	FT

SOURCE: California Department of Fish and Wildlife 2013.
NOTE: Populations of these species are listed as either threatened (T) or endangered (E) under criteria of the California state (S) or U.S. federal (F) Endangered Species Acts.

nia's estuarine biota. Population declines of seventeen species of birds, fish, and mammals have reached levels so low that these are now designated as threatened or endangered species (Table 19.4). Many other animals and plants are species of concern because their populations have fallen to levels that might not be sustainable. Others have been locally extirpated, such as the tidewater goby from San Francisco Bay.

LOSS OF ESTUARINE FISHERIES

Perhaps the most compelling indicator of the power of human disturbance is the loss of commercial fishing from California's largest estuary. San Francisco was once a leading fishing center of the U.S. Today, other than a small herring fishery and several bait fisheries, not a single remaining commercial fishery for shellfish or finfish remains in this great estuary. At its peak, commercial fishing on San Francisco Bay employed forty-four hundred fishermen who sailed a thousand vessels and annually caught over a thousand tons each of oysters (once the most valuable fishery on the U.S. Pacific coast), clams, shrimp, salmon, shad, striped bass, and flatfish (Skinner 1962). Commercial hunting provided 250,000 ducks yearly to San Francisco markets, and more were taken for the table. But within decades stocks of all harvested species plummeted, and one by one commercial fisheries for these estuarine species were closed, permanently. These indicators of human disturbance now motivate policies to protect, restore, and sustain California's estuaries and the species they support.

Plans for Recovery and Protection

PUBLIC POLICIES

Tidal marshes and other estuarine habitats have received significant conservation and restoration attention because of their regulatory protection under the federal Clean Water Act (CWA) and Endangered Species Act (ESA). Listing of endemic fishes as threatened or endangered (see Table 19.4) has been the major impetus for the BAY DELTA CONSERVATION PLAN (BDCP), and intermittently tidal estuaries are now managed to protect the endangered tidewater goby (Lafferty et al. 1999). California's 1965 McAtter-Petris Act was a landmark step in protection of estuarine and coastal habitats, creating the San Francisco Bay Conservation and Development Commission for the protection of the bay. State and federal laws require mitigation of human impacts, including habitat restoration to offset unavoidable wetland impacts, and these laws have led to substantial restoration of estuarine wetlands (Environmental Law Institute 2007).

HABITAT RESTORATION

Projects are under way in many California estuaries to restore lost or degraded habitats. Dikes and water control structures are being removed to restore more natural tidal exchange. Sediment addition projects are increasing elevation in estuarine habitats that subsided due to diking, thus enabling restoration of salt marsh. Native oyster and eelgrass restoration projects are enhancing populations of these estuarine endemics and the structured habitat they create. Debate exists about the effectiveness of mitigation-based restoration, and movement has begun toward more pro-active, large-scale planning to protect ecosystems rather than the project-by-project, mitigation-based approach typical under CWA and ESA. For example, the Southern California Wetlands Recovery Project established regional goals for coastal and estuarine restoration in southern California. Similarly the Habitat Goals Project (Goals Project 1999) integrated large-scale habitat management within San Francisco Bay.

The scope of many projects is now so large that they have regional effects. For example, the South Bay Salt Pond Restoration Project is the largest program of tidal marsh restoration in the western U.S., restoring 6,100 hectares of former salt ponds to promote recovery of special-status species that depend on estuarine-marsh habitats (SBSPRP 2012). In addition, the state of California has put substantial effort into planning through MARINE PROTECTED AREAS that include about 12% of available estuarine habitat (Gleason et al. 2012). Goals of the BDCP include restoration of at least 26,000 hectares of tidal habitat in the Sacramento–San Joaquin Delta (BDCP 2013). The plan also addresses water management as a stressor on estuarine biota—a critical issue for California estuaries that is likely to become more challenging as the climate system and freshwater demand continue to change.

CONTROLLING SPECIES INTRODUCTIONS

Managing vectors for invasive species includes the regulation of ship ballast water under the 2003 CALIFORNIA MARINE INVASIVE SPECIES ACT. Large ships are now required to manage ballast through—for example, midocean ballast exchange to minimize likelihood of ship-based introductions to estuaries. Invasive species management also includes large-scale eradication programs (Figure 19.12d). The most successful has been eradication of the Mediterranean alga *Caulerpa taxifolia* from Aqua Hedionda Lagoon and Huntington Harbor. This effort cost more than $6 million over several years and involved intensive treatment methods. An equally large program to eradicate hybrid *Spartina* from San Francisco Bay has cost several million dollars over a six-year period and, to date, has removed 90% of the *Spartina* hybrid.

There have also been many small-scale programs to remove recently introduced species having limited distribution, such as the Japanese kelp *Undaria pinnatifida* that was first found in southern California in 2000 and arrived in Monterey Bay shortly thereafter. This rapidly growing species can profoundly change estuaries because of its large size (>2 meters). It also fouls docks, ship hulls, and moorings. Since 2010, small populations have been found in San Francisco Bay and Half Moon Bay. Other small-scale efforts have been successful at manually removing the snail *Littorina littorea* in Orange County and the alga *Ascophyllum nodosum* in San Francisco Bay. Other efforts remain unsuccessful or incomplete at control of snails (*Batillaria attramentaria* and *Undaria pinnatifida*) in Monterey Bay and San Francisco Bay and Japanese eelgrass (*Zostera japonica*) in Humboldt Bay (Williams and Grosholz 2008).

A Long View of California's Estuaries

The landscapes and biological communities of California estuaries have been transformed, some beyond recognition, from those viewed by Spanish explorers in the eighteenth century. These ecosystems will continue to evolve, but the pace and trajectories of future changes are uncertain. Three central questions emerge as we develop long views to anticipate future pressures that will further change California's ecosystems and plan strategies for adapting to them.

What Will Drive Future Changes?

Continued growth of California's population, projected to exceed fifty million by 2050 (CDF 2012), implies intensification of commerce, agriculture, urbanization, waste production, energy and water consumption, land development, and continued translocations of plants and animals—the human pressures that transformed coastal landscapes during the past century. Estuarine ecosystems will also continue to respond to multidecadal climate oscillations that restructure biological communities. We can anticipate intense disruption of coastal ecosystems by the next megaflood, the last of which filled San Francisco Bay with freshwater in 1862 (Dettinger and Ingram 2013). These drivers of change will interact with regional manifestations of global climate change—accelerating sea level rise, altered timing and magnitude of runoff, ACIDIFICATION of seawater, warming of air and water, and growing frequency of extreme events such as storms, heat waves, and extended droughts (Cloern et al. 2011).

What Is at Risk?

If unchecked, these growing pressures will drive further changes in the freshwater inflow, sediment supply, GEOMORPHOLOGY, habitat composition and connectivity, water quality, productivity, and biological communities of California's estuaries. Tidal marshes and mudflat habitats are not sustainable if sea level rises faster than sediment accretion (Stralberg et al. 2011), a likely scenario in estuaries such as San Francisco Bay where sediment input has been reduced by river damming and channelization (Schoellhamer 2011). Populations of dozens of plant and animal species native to California estuaries have fallen to levels so low they might not be sustainable as human pressures intensify. Extinctions of native species will likely occur in synchrony with continued population expansions of non-native species, particularly those adapted to warming waters, salinity regimes created by highly managed freshwater inflows, and further homogenization and fragmentation of coastal habitats. Extirpation of rare species can be triggered by extreme events (Zedler 2010), so sustainability of California's at-risk estuarine species will become increasingly challenged if projections of more frequent and intense heat waves, droughts, and storms are realized.

The uncertain future of estuarine habitats and biological communities also implies uncertain provision of the myriad benefits we derive from them. Susceptibility of human populations and infrastructure to inundation by storm surges grows as tidal marshes are lost, and so does the capacity of estuarine systems to sequester carbon (Canuel et al. 2012) and of tidal marshes to filter contaminants from urban runoff. Warming will promote faster growth of algae, so habitat quality will potentially degrade as macroalgae proliferate further in nutrient-rich estuaries (Lotze and Worm 2002). Warming will accelerate ecosystem respiration and decrease oxygen solubility, leading to growing potential for hypoxia of estuarine waters. We can anticipate significant cumulative effects of these kinds of changes on populations of migratory birds that rely on California's estuaries; on marine fish and invertebrates that use estuaries as nursery or migratory habitat; on our culture and harvest of food from coastal waters including the potential to restore commercial fishing in estuaries; and on opportunities for future generations to glimpse the natural beauty, diversity, and living resources of California's estuaries that awed early Spanish explorers.

What Steps Can We Take?

The future of California's estuaries will be determined by the choices we make as a society and the way those choices are manifested through policies, such as those described in the previous section to restore, rehabilitate, and sustain estuarine ecosystems. We suggest seven general actions, grounded in contemporary scientific understanding of how estuaries function as ecosystems, to anticipate and lessen the threats to these vital California ecosystems:

- Use modeling tools to develop future scenarios (e.g., Cloern et al. 2011, Stralberg et al. 2011, Veloz et al. 2013) so that flexible plans of conservation and restoration anticipate environmental changes and have contingencies to accommodate them.
- Consider the habitat requirements of estuarine species when developing new strategies of freshwater management such as adaptations to changing climate and water demand.
- Take steps to conserve resources, such as water recycling and recovery of sewage nutrients, to dampen the pressures from a growing human population.
- Evaluate the overall costs and benefits of different policies by taking into account the economic and social value of goods and services provided by estuaries.
- Monitor and analyze environmental changes as they unfold so that adaptive policies can be implemented efficiently and their outcomes can be measured.
- Take bold steps, such as creating new kinds of partnerships between scientists and policy makers to identify those actions most likely to increase resilience and sustain biodiversity of California's estuaries (Cloern and Hanak 2013).
- Teach Californians and visitors about the unique habitats, plant and animal communities of California's estuaries, how they have changed in the past, and implications of the choices Californians and visitors make to shape the future evolution of these ecosystems in a fast-changing world.

Summary

California's 1,766-kilometer coast has more than four hundred lagoons, inlets, stream valleys, and bays—transitional ecosystems at the land's edge that we collectively refer to as "estuaries." California's estuaries have a diversity of sizes, forms, and habitat mosaics shaped by climate, coastal topography, and oceanography. Estuaries are strongly influenced by their connectivity to the Pacific Ocean through landward propagation of tides and waves and immigration of marine organisms, and by their connectivity to watersheds that deliver freshwater, sediments, nutrients, and contaminants from runoff. Estuaries are dynamic ecosystems with significant physical, chemical, and biological variability at time scales ranging from hours (tidal oscillations) to months (wet and dry seasons) to decades (shifts in the climate system) to centuries (changes in sea level, river flow, water quality, habitats, and biological communities).

Organisms occupying the unique habitats of estuaries are important components of California's rich biological diversity. They include a distinctive mix of algal and plant species and hundreds of species of invertebrates, fish, birds, and marine mammals. Some are "estuarine endemics," limited in their distribution mostly or entirely to estuaries; others are coastal generalists that rely on estuaries for critical foraging, resting, or breeding habitat. For instance, some marine fish, crab, and shrimp use estuaries as nursery habitat, while other fishes including salmon, sturgeon, and shad migrate from ocean to rivers to spawn and return as juveniles, and many shorebirds, waterfowl, and seabirds rest and forage in California estuaries as residents or during annual migrations along the Pacific Flyway.

Estuaries and their biota provide invaluable services to people. Commercial ocean fisheries include estuarine-dependent species such as Dungeness crab, English sole, and California halibut. Tidal marshes sequester substantial carbon, protect shorelines from storm surges and floods, and filter urban contaminants. We use estuaries to culture shellfish. Estuarine microbes assimilate human wastes and degrade many organic pollutants. The natural harbors of California provide ports for commercial transport. We are strongly attracted to coastal settings because of their breathtaking beauty and the many opportunities they provide for recreation.

However, the landscapes and biological communities of California estuaries (and services they provide) have been transformed, some beyond recognition, from those viewed by Spanish explorers in the eighteenth century. Degradation has occurred through overfishing, dredging new channels, filling mudflats and tidal marshes for urban and agricultural uses, sewage disposal, introductions of hundreds of non-native plant and animal species, damming and diverting rivers, and contaminant inputs. As a consequence over 90% of California's tidal marshes have been lost and fifteen species of mammals, birds, and fish are at risk of extinction, while non-native species dominate many estuarine communities. San Francisco Bay was once a major U.S. fishing center, but commercial fishing for most species was closed decades ago. An active sports fishery persists, but some fish remain contaminated with unsafe levels of mercury and PCBs. Concern over these changes motivates policies to reverse the effects of human disturbance, and large-scale programs are ongoing to restore estuarine ecosystems, curtail the introduction of non-native species, and improve water quality. Sustainability of California's estuaries, their native species, and the services they provide is uncertain in the face of a growing human population and accelerating global change. Success will be determined largely by actions we take today.

Acknowledgments

Thanks to Ruth Askevold for production of Figure 19.1.

Recommended Reading

Barnhart, R. A., M. J. Boyd, and J. E. Pequegnat. 1992. The ecology of Humboldt Bay, California: An estuarine profile. U.S. Fish and Wildlife Service. Biological Report 1. <http://www.nwrc.usgs.gov/techrpt/92-1.pdf> Accessed June 10, 2015.

Caffrey, J. M., M. Brown, and B. Tyler, editors. 2002. Changes in a California estuary: An ecosystem profile of Elkhorn Slough. Elkhorn Slough Foundation, Moss Landing, California.

Hollibaugh, J. T., editor. 1996. San Francisco Bay; the ecosystem. Pacific Division, American Association for the Advancement of Science, San Francisco, California.

Morro Bay National Estuary Program. 2010. Estuary tidings. A Report on the Health of Morro Bay Estuary. Morro Bay, California. <http://www.mbnep.org/wp-content/uploads/2014/12/Tidings_2010.pdf> Accessed June 10, 2015.

Rubissow Okamoto, A., and K. M. Wong. 2011. Natural history of San Francisco Bay. University of California Press, Berkeley, California.

Zedler, J. B., C. S. Nordby, and B. E. Kus. 1992. The ecology of Tijuana Estuary, California: A national estuarine research reserve. NOAA Office of Coastal Resource Management, Sanctuaries and Reserves Division, Washington, D.C.

Glossary

ACIDIFICATION A downward shift in the pH of water making it more acidic. For example, carbon dioxide dissolved in water produces an acidic solution and ocean waters are becoming more acidic as atmospheric CO_2 concentrations increase. This is a threat to calcified marine organisms such as corals, clams, mussels, and oysters.

ALLOCHTHONOUS Material (organic carbon, nutrients, etc.) that originates outside of the system of interest, in contrast to *autochthonous,* which indicates material that is generated within the system. Allochthonous material thus represents a subsidy to the system, whereas autochthonous material is generated in the system at a direct cost to the system in terms of material and energy.

AMPHIPODS Members of the diverse crustacean order Amphipoda and are generally small consumers that are a large portion of organismal abundance and diversity in benthic habitats.

ANADROMOUS Fish that migrate from saltwater to freshwater to reproduce and the juveniles migrate back to saltwater to rear, sometimes over very long distances. For example, adult Chinook salmon migrate from the ocean to the rivers where they were born; the juvenile salmon migrate from the rivers to the ocean, where they rear for several years.

ANAEROBIC DECOMPOSITION Decomposition (or respiration) that takes place in anoxic environments. Since oxygen is not available to support respiration and the oxidation of organic matter, alternative respiration pathways are used. These may involve using oxidized compounds such as nitrate, iron oxyhydroxide (rust), arsenate, or sulfate as the terminal electron acceptor in place of oxygen.

ANOXIC Indicates environments devoid of oxygen, such as the deeper layers of water-saturated sediments.

BAY DELTA CONSERVATION PLAN (BDCP) A conservation strategy aiming to improve ecological function of the delta and protect water supplies provided by the State Water Project and Central Valley Project. The BDCP was initiated in 2006 and incorporates input from a wide range of state and federal agencies, public water agencies, environmental groups, and other interested parties. The BDCP is intended to serve as a joint Habitat Conservation Plan (HCP) and Natural Community Conservation Plan (NCCP), providing protection for listed species, including a number of fish species within the delta, while also regulating permitted incidental take of these species. With the passage of the Delta Reform Act in 2009, the BDCP has been incorporated into a broader package of state and federal programs with similar goals of protecting delta ecosystems while managing water use and withdrawals from the delta.

BENTHIC MICROALGAE Microscopic single-celled algae (diatoms and dinoflagellates) and cyanobacteria that inhabit the surface layers (0–4 centimeters) of aquatic sediments. Benthic microalgae are ecologically significant in many freshwater and marine environments, including estuaries. They are a major food source for benthic feeders such as crustaceans, bivalves, and polychaete worms. Benthic microalgal communities also modify exchange of nitrogen and phosphorus between the water column and sediments and therefore play an important role in regulating water quality.

BIVALVES Members of the molluscan class Bivalvia and include what are commonly referred to as clams.

CALIFORNIA MARINE INVASIVE SPECIES ACT A California law that was passed in 2003 and aims to reduce the import and impact of nonindigenous species within the state's estuaries and coasts. The act regulates the discharge and treatment of ballast water in California ports and the removal of fouling organisms from hulls for large ships (over 300 tons) in order to reduce the importation and establishment of invasive marine species.

CARBON SEQUESTRATION The uptake of atmospheric carbon by plants or other photosynthetic organisms and the storage of this carbon in biomass or soil organic matter. *Net carbon sequestration* includes the consideration of counteracting emissions of greenhouse gases, converted into CO_2 equivalents, primarily methane (CH_4) and nitrous oxide (N_2O). While methane is not commonly produced at salinities close to seawater, it can be produced in anaerobic, low-salinity environments, such as tidal freshwater or low-salinity brackish wetlands.

CATADROMOUS Fish that migrate from freshwater to saltwater to reproduce; the juveniles migrate back to freshwater to rear.

CHLOROPHYLL-*A* The primary light-harvesting pigment of plants; used as a measure of phytoplankton biomass in lakes, rivers, estuaries, and oceans.

CILIATES Members of the protozoan phylum Ciliophora and are typically characterized by the presence of slender hairlike organelles called cilia.

COPEPODS Members of the crustacean subclass Copepoda, which includes small, generally planktonic species that are among the most abundant grazers of phytoplankton.

CRUSTACEANS Members of the well-known class Crustacea within the larger phylum Arthropoda, which also includes insects. Crustaceans include many common groups including shrimps, crabs, and lobsters as well as many planktonic species including copepods.

DIVERGENT SELECTION A process that results in the increased survival and reproductive success within a population of two groups of individuals that have different characteristics from one another. Darwin's finches are an example of divergent selection, where birds with deep bills typical of seed eaters and birds with narrow bills typical of insectivores evolved from a common ancestor.

ECOLOGICAL SPECIATION The evolution of reproductive isolation between populations as a result of ecologically based divergent natural selection.

ECOTONE A transition zone between two ecological habitats or community types (e.g., aquatic to terrestrial habitat; intertidal to subtidal habitat). It may be narrow or wide, appearing as a gradual blending of the two communities across a broad area, or it may manifest itself as a sharp boundary line.

ENDEMIC Found only in a defined geographic location, such as an island, continent, or other defined range. Organisms that are native to a place are not endemic to it if they are also found elsewhere.

EVAPOTRANSPIRATION The transfer of water from land to atmosphere through the combined effects of direct evaporation from water and soil surfaces and of transpiration (the loss of water through leaf pores) in plants.

EXTIRPATION Local extinction. Ceasing to exist in a given area, though still present elsewhere. Local extinctions are contrasted with global extinctions. Local extinctions may be followed by a replacement of the species taken from other locations; wolf reintroduction is an example of this.

FLOODPLAIN A floodplain is a relatively level area adjacent to a stream channel that is formed and maintained by the stream and periodically overflowed during flood events.

GASTROPODS A class within the Molluscs, which typically (but not exclusively) have a calcified shell and include grazing herbivores, scavengers, and predators. Gastropods include common groups such as snails, chitons, and abalone.

GEOMORPHOLOGY The study of landforms. The discipline is concerned with understanding not only the physical form of landscapes but also their origin, evolution, and the physical processes and dynamics that shape them. In estuaries, geomorphology can be used to both classify different types of systems (such as lagoons, bays, or river-mouth estuaries) and to characterize the distinct physical settings (e.g., bathymetry, topography) and processes (e.g., tidal currents and range, wave dynamics, sediment delivery, and transport through fluvial and tidal inputs) experienced by each system, as well as how these vary with time and space.

HETEROTROPHIC ECOSYSTEMS Ecosystems, such as many estuaries, where total system respiration exceeds total system photosynthesis; this implies external inputs of organic carbon. These ecosystems are net consumers of organic carbon and net producers of carbon dioxide.

HYDRODYNAMICS The study of the dynamics of fluids in motion. In an estuary, this applies to the response of water levels and currents to multiple forcings, including tides, storm surges, barometric pressure changes, and freshwater inflows. Also, the hydrodynamical processes and patterns characteristic of a particular area—for example, "the hydrodynamics of Tomales Bay."

HYDROIDS A common name referring to species in the class Hydrozoa but typically referring to the polyp stage (attached, with arborescent feeding tentacles) of the life cycle.

HYDROLOGY The study of processes affecting the movement of water, usually in relation to land. These processes can include precipitation, snowpack accumulation and melt, surface flows, soil water movement, and percolation to aquifers. Also, the hydrological processes and patterns characteristic of a particular area—for example, "the hydrology of the Klamath basin."

HYDROZOANS Members of the class Hydrozoa in the phylum Cnidaria. These sessile animals are generally attached to hard substrate and feed with tentacles and defend themselves with specialized stinging structures.

HYPERSALINE Conditions where salinity regularly exceeds that of seawater (about 35 parts per thousand). Hypersalinity is common in Mediterranean-climate estuaries with relatively small watersheds and limited tidal exchange due to seasonal inlet closure, where evaporation can greatly exceed freshwater inflow during the dry season. Extreme hypersalinity can exclude the growth of marsh vegetation; as a result, a salt flat or salt panne is an extreme expression of hypersaline conditions. The salinity of these estuaries can often fluctuate widely by season, with hypersaline summer conditions replaced by saline or even fresh-brackish conditions during the winter.

INTERTIDAL HABITAT Areas between high and low tides. During high tides these areas are submerged; during low tides these areas are exposed.

MACROALGAE A group of single to multicellular primary producers found in all aquatic ecosystems. Members of this functional group (including red, green, and brown algae and cyanobacteria) include such diverse forms as simple chains of prokaryotic cells, multinucleate single cells over 1 meter in length, and giant kelps over 45 meters in length with complex internal structures analogous to vascular plants. They provide the same ecological functions as vascular plants in terrestrial ecosystems but lack the structural tissues characteristic of plants. They are important primary producers in intertidal and shallow subtidal estuaries, providing food and refuge for invertebrates, juvenile fish, crabs, and other species. Some species of macroalgae thrive in nutrient-enriched waters to create extensive blooms, outcompeting other primary producers.

MARINE PROTECTED AREAS (MPAS) Areas along the California coast and estuaries that receive special protection under the Marine Life Protection Act, passed in 1999; MPAs were initiated to improve protection of marine ecosystems within the state. Four MPA regions have been established along the California coast as well as one within San Francisco Bay. MPAs include reserves (all harvesting excluded, including commercial, recreational, and geologic), parks (recreational harvesting allowed), conservation areas (select commercial and recreational harvest can be allowed), and recreational management areas (subtidal protection but waterfowl hunting allowed).

MOLLUSCS Members of the very common phylum Mollusca. Members typically have a hard calcified shell and include many familiar groups including snails, clams, mussels, squids, and octopods.

NITRIFICATION-DENITRIFICATION The stepwise process whereby reduced nitrogen, present in water as an equilibrium mixture of ammonia (NH_3) and ammonium (NH_4^+), is converted to dinitrogen gas. Ammonia is first oxidized to nitrite (NO_2^-) by one functional guild of prokaryotes. Some of this nitrite may be oxidized further by another functional guild of prokaryotes to yield nitrate (NO_3^-). These steps require oxygen and this two-step process constitutes nitrification. Some of the nitrite produced as an intermediate of nitrification may be used by another group of prokaryotes to oxidize ammonia via the anaerobic ammonia oxidation, or "anammox," reaction, resulting in the production of dinitrogen (N_2) gas. The organisms that mediate these steps are autotrophs, using the energy obtained from oxidizing ammonia to reduce carbon dioxide to organic carbon. Both nitrite and nitrate can be used by some heterotrophic prokaryotes to oxidize organic matter anaerobically, producing dinitrogen gas and carbon dioxide. The reactions that yield dinitrogen gas are referred to as autotrophic and heterotrophic denitrification, respectively.

NORTH PACIFIC GYRE OSCILLATION (NPGO) A climate pattern that is the secondary mode of sea surface height variability in the northeast Pacific (the primary mode is the Pacific Decadal Oscillation). The NPGO is significantly correlated with fluctuations of salinity, nutrients, and chlorophyll-*a* measured in long-term observations in the California Current and Gulf of Alaska (modified from http://www.o3d.org/npgo/).

PANNE Also known as salt panne, pan, marsh pond, or *salina*, panne is a type of shallow, natural depression that forms on poorly drained areas of tidal marsh plains, such as areas between drainage networks or along the upland-tidal marsh boundary. Pannes receive water during very high tides and lose water through evaporation and are usually unvegetated or sparsely vegetated. Some pannes can become encrusted with sea salt that precipitate as the tidal water evaporates. In some marshlands salts were historically harvested from pannes by native Californians and early settlers.

PHYTOPLANKTON Microscopic algae suspended in water; an important component of the primary-producer community of lakes, rivers, and estuaries.

PISCIVOROUS Any animal that primarily consumes fish as part of its diet.

POLYCHAETES Members of the most species rich class (Polychaeta) of worms in the phylum Annelida; these include species with a broad range of feeding modes and life histories and are among the most abundant and diverse benthic invertebrates in most estuaries.

PRIMARY PRODUCERS Organisms in an ecosystem that produce biomass from inorganic compounds (autotrophs). In most cases these are photosynthetically active organisms (plants, cyanobacteria, and a number of other unicellular organisms). However, some unicellular organisms exist that that produce biomass from the oxidation of inorganic chemical compounds (chemoautotrophs). Because primary producers produce carbon from energy, they form the foundation for the food chain. In terrestrial ecoregions these are mainly vascular plants, while in aquatic ecosystems algae are the dominant primary producers (see "macroalgae," "benthic microalgae," "phytoplankton").

PROKARYOTES The group of organisms that do not have membrane-bound nuclei. Nearly all are microscopic, though they may form colonies, mats, or other structures that are visible to the naked eye. They include members of the kingdoms Archaea and Bacteria but are distinct from microscopic members of the kingdom Eukarya, such as yeasts or unicellular plants. Familiar examples include *Lactobacillus* and *Escherichia coli* (*E. coli*).

REPRODUCTIVE ISOLATION The inability of two different species to produce fertile offspring due to behavioral or physiological mechanisms. These barriers maintain the differences between species over time by preventing genetic mixing of the species.

STRATIFICATION Vertical layering of water in a lake or estuary as low-density (warmer, fresher) surface water overlays higher-density (cooler, saltier) bottom water. Stratification impedes vertical mixing and allows for the establishment of vertical gradients of biota (e.g., phytoplankton) and chemical constituents (e.g., dissolved oxygen).

SUBSPECIES A category in biological classification that ranks immediately below a species. Subspecies are morphologically or genetically distinguishable from one another. Organisms that belong to different subspecies of the same species are capable of interbreeding and producing fertile offspring, but they often do not interbreed in nature due to geographic isolation or other factor.

SUBTIDAL HABITAT Any habitat adjacent to the coast that is submerged below sea level except during extremely low tides. These areas include mud, sand, rocks, artificial structures, submerged aquatic vegetation, and macroalgal beds.

TULE A commonly used term for bulrush species native to California, including but not limited to hardstem bulrush (*Schoenoplectus acutus*), California bulrush (*S. californicus*), and Olney's bulrush (*S. americanus*). Tule is dominant in freshwater and brackish marshes across the state.

TUNICATES Members of the chordate subphylum Tunicata, which include both planktonic and sessile species known as sea squirts that can be important filter feeders in both planktonic and benthic habitats.

TURBID Adjective describing rivers, lakes, or estuaries having large concentrations of suspended particles (e.g., sediments or phytoplankton) or dissolved constituents that cloud water and restrict light penetration to a shallow depth. Photosynthesis is confined to a thin surface layer in turbid waters.

WATERSHED An area of land, usually defined by topography, from which all surface-water flows exit the at the same outflow point.

ZOOPLANKTON Small animals suspended in water; most feed on phytoplankton, detritus, or single-celled organisms (ciliates, flagellates) and are a key food resource for early life stages of fish and adult plankton-feeding fish such as smelt, anchovies, and herring.

References

Abella, R., and S. F. Cook. 1960. Colonial expeditions to the interior of California Central Valley, 1800–1820. University of California Press, Berkeley, California.

Adams, P. N., D. L. Imnan, and N. E. Graham. 2008. Southern California deep-water wave climate: Characterization and application to coastal processes. Journal of Coastal Research 24:1022–1035.

Allen, L. G., M. M. Yoklavich, G. M. Cailliet, and M. H. Horn. 2006. Bays and estuaries. Pages 119–148 in L. G. Allen, D. J. P. II, and M. H. Horn, editors. The Ecology of Marine Fishes: California and Adjacent Waters. University of California Press, Berkeley, California.

Alpine, A. E., and J. E. Cloern. 1992. Trophic interactions and direct physical effects control phytoplankton biomass and production in an estuary. Limnology and Oceanography 37:946–955.

Asprey, M., editor. 2010. Jack London's San Francisco stories. CreateSpace Independent Publishing Platform.

Atwater, B. F. 1980. Distribution of vascular-plant species in six remnants of intertidal wetland of the Sacramento–San Joaquin Delta, California. U.S. Geological Survey. Open-File Report 80-883.

Atwater, B. F., S. G. Conard, J. N. Dowden et al. 1979. History, landforms, and vegetation of the estuary's tidal marshes. Pages 347–386 in T. J. Conomos, editor. San Francisco Bay, the urbanized estuary. American Association for the Advancement of Science, Pacific Division, San Francisco, California.

Bard, T. R. 1869. U.S. v. Valentin Cota et al., Land Case No. 231 SD [Rio de Santa Clara]. Docket 418 part 1, U.S. District Court, Southern District. Courtesy of the Bancroft Library, UC Berkeley, California.

Bay Delta Conservation Plan (BDCP). 2013. Bay Delta Conservation Plan highlights. <http://baydeltaconservationplan.com/Libraries/Dynamic_Document_Library/Draft_BDCP_Highlights_12-9-13.sflb.ashx>. Accessed June 10, 2015.

Beller, E. E., R. M. Grossinger, M. N. Salomon et al. 2011. Historical ecology of the lower Santa Clara River, Ventura River, and Oxnard Plain: An analysis of terrestrial, riverine, and coastal habitats. SFEI contribution #641. San Francisco Estuary Institute, Oakland, California.

Beller, E. E., S. Baumgarten, and R. M. Grossinger. 2014. Northern San Diego County lagoons historical ecology investigation: Regional patterns, local diversity, and landscape trajectories. San Francisco Estuary Institute, Oakland, California.

Bolton, H. E. 1933. Font's complete diary: A chronicle of the founding of San Francisco. University of California Press, Berkeley, California.

Bricker, S. B., C. G. Clement, D. E. Pirhalla, S. P. Orlando, and D. R. G. Farrow. 1999. National estuarine eutrophication assessment: Effects of nutrient enrichment in the nation's estuaries. U.S. National Oceanographic and Atmospheric Administration, National Ocean Service, Special Projects Office and the National Center for Coastal Ocean Science, Silver Spring Maryland.

Briggs, J. C. and B. W. Bowen. 2012. A realignment of marine biogeographic provinces with particular reference to fish distributions. Journal of Biogeography 39:12–30.

Bromirski, P. D., R. E. Flick, and D. R. Cayan. 2003. Storminess variability along the California coast: 1858–2000. Journal of Climate 16:982–993.

California Department of Finance (CDF). 2012. Interim population projections for California and its counties, 2010–2050. <http://www.dof.ca.gov/research/demographic/reports/projections/interim/view.php>. Accessed June 10, 2015.

California Department of Fish and Wildlife (CDFW). 2013. State and federally listed endangered and threatended animals of California, October 2013. <http://www.dfg.ca.gov/biogeodata/cnddb/pdfs/TEAnimals.pdf> Accessed June 10, 2015.

California Department of Water Resources (CDWR). 2011. Dayflow: Determining historical Delta boundary hydrology. <http://www.water.ca.gov/dayflow/output/Output.cfm>. Accessed January 7, 2013.

———. 2009. California water plan update (Bulletin 160-09). Volume 3, Central Coast Report. <http://www.waterplan.water.ca.gov/docs/cwpu2009/0310final/v3_centralcoast_cwp2009.pdf> Accessed June 10, 2015.

Callaway, J. C., A. B. Borde, H. L. Diefenderfer, V. T. Parker, J. M. Rybcyzk, and R. M. Thom. 2012a. Pacific Coast tidal wetlands. Pages 103–116 in D. P. Batzer and A. H. Baldwin, editors. Wetland Habitats of North America: Ecology and Conservation Concerns. University of California Press, Berkeley, California.

Callaway, J. C., E. L. Borgnis, R. E. Turner, and C. S. Milan. 2012b. Carbon sequestration and sediment accretion in San Francisco Bay tidal wetlands. Estuaries and Coasts 35:1163–1181.

Canuel, E. A., S. S. Cammer, H. A. McIntosh, and C. R. Pondell. 2012. Climate change impacts on the organic carbon cycle at the land-ocean interface. Annual Review of Earth and Planetary Sciences 40:685–711.

Cayan, D. R., K. T. Redmond, and L. G. Riddle. 1999. ENSO and hydrologic extremes in the western United States. Journal of Climate 12:2881–2893.

Cayan, D. R., M. D. Dettinger, H. F. Diaz, and N. E. Graham. 1998. Decadal variability of precipitation over western North America. Journal of Climate 11:3148–3166.

Cayan, D. R., P. D. Bromirski, K. Hayhoe, M. Tyree, M. D. Dettinger, and R. E. Flick. 2008. Climate change projections of sea level extremes along the California coast. Climatic Change 87:S57–S73.

Cebrian, J. 1999. Patterns in the fate of production in plant communities. American Naturalist 154:449–468.

Chan, Y., and P. Arcese. 2003. Morphological and microsatellite differentiation in Melospiza melodia (Aves) at a microgeographic scale. Journal of Evolutionary Biology 16:939–947.

Chang, A. L., J. D. Grossman, T. S. Spezio, H. W. Weiskel, J. C. Blum, J. W. Burt, A. A. Muir, J. Piovia-Scott, K. E. Veblen, and E. D. Grosholz. 2009. Tackling aquatic invasions: Risks and opportunities for the aquarium fish industry. Biological Invasions 11:773–785.

Chesapeake Bay Program. 2002. Nutrient reduction technology cost estimations for point sources in the Chesapeake Bay Watershed. <http://www.chesapeakebay.net/content/publications/cbp_13136.pdf> Accessed June 10, 2015.

Cloern, J. E. 1996. Phytoplankton bloom dynamics in coastal ecosystems: A review with some general lessons from sustained investigation of San Francisco Bay, California. Reviews of Geophysics 34:127–168.

Cloern, J. E., and A. D. Jassby. 2012. Drivers of change in estuarine-coastal ecosystems: Discoveries from four decades of study in San Francisco Bay. Reviews of Geophysics. <doi:10.1029/2012RG000397>.

Cloern, J. E., and E. Hanak. 2013. It's time for bold new approaches to link Delta science and policymaking. San Francisco Estuary and Watershed Science 11(3). <http://escholarship.org/uc/item/4px547r2>. Accessed June 10, 2015.

Cloern, J. E., K. A. Hieb, T. Jacobson, B. Sanso, E. Di Lorenzo, M. T. Stacey, J. L. Largier, W. Meiring, W. T. Peterson, T. M. Powell, M. Winder, and A. D. Jassby. 2010. Biological communities in San Francisco Bay track large-scale climate forcing over the North Pacific. Geophysical Research Letters 37:L21602.

Cloern, J. E., N. Knowles, L. R. Brown, D. Cayan, M. D. Dettinger, T. L. Morgan, D. H. Schoellhamer, M. T. Stacey, M. van der Wegen, R. W. Wagner, and A. D. Jassby. 2011. Projected evolution of California's San Francisco Bay-Delta-River System in a century of climate change. PLoS One 6(9): e24465.

Cohen, A. N., and J. T. Carlton. 1995. Biological study. Nonindigenous aquatic species in a United States estuary: A case study of the biological invasions of the San Francisco Bay and Delta. U.S. Fisheries and Wildlife and National Sea Grant College Program Report, NTIS Number PB96-166525, Springfield, Virginia.

Cole, B. E. 1989. Temporal and spatial patterns of phytoplankton production in Tomales Bay, California, U.S.A. Estuarine, Coastal, and Shelf Science 28:103–115.

Cooper, J. G. 1887. Additions to the birds of Ventura County, California. Auk 4(2):85–94.

Costanza, R., R. d'Arge, R. deGroot, S. Farber, M. Grasso, B. Hannon, K. Limburg, S. Naeem, R. V. Oneill, J. Paruelo, R. G. Raskin, P. Sutton, and M. vandenBelt. 1997. The value of the world's ecosystem services and natural capital. Nature 387:253–260.

Crespí, J., and A. K. Brown. 2001. A description of distant roads: Original journals of the first expedition into California, 1769–1770. San Diego State University Press, San Diego, California.

Dahl, T. E. 1990. Wetlands losses in the United States, 1780's to 1980's. Report to the Congress. U.S. Department of the Interior, Fish and Wildlife Service, Washington, D.C.

Darwin, C. 1845. Journal of researches into the natural history and geology of the countries visited during the voyage of H.M.S. Beagle round the world, under the Command of Capt. Fitz Roy, R.N. Second edition. John Murray, London, UK.

Dettinger, M. D., and B. L. Ingram. 2013. The coming megafloods. Scientific American January 2013:65–71.

Diaz, H. F., and V. Markgraf. 1992. El Niño—Historical and paleoclimatic aspects of the Southern Oscillation. Cambridge University Press, Cambridge, UK.

Di Lorenzo, E., N. Schneider, K. M. Cobb, P. J. S. Franks, K. Chhak, A. J. Miller, J. C. McWilliams, S. J. Bograd, H. Arango, E. Curchitser, T. M. Powell, and P. Rivière. 2008. North Pacific Gyre Oscillation links ocean climate and ecosystem change. Geophysical Research Letters 35. L08607, pages 1–6.

Engstrom, W. N. 1996. The California storm of January 1862. Quaternary Research 46:141–148.

Environmental Law Institute. 2007. The Clean Water Act jurisdictional handbook. Environmental Law Institute, Washington, D.C.

Feyrer, F., K. Newman, M. Nobriga, and T. Sommer. 2011. Modeling the effects of future outflow on the abiotic habitat of an imperiled estuarine fish. Estuaries and Coasts 34:120–128.

Fofonoff, P., R. GM, S. B, and J. Carlton. 2011. National Exotic Marine and Estuarine Species Information System (NEMESIS). <http://invasions.si.edu/nemesis/index.html>. Accessed March 18, 2012.

Gende, S. M., R. T. Edwards, M. F. Willson, and M. S. Wipfli. 2002. Pacific salmon in aquatic and terrestrial ecosystems. Bioscience 52:917–928.

Gleason, M., E. Fox, S. Ashcraft, J. Vasques, E. Whiteman, P. Serpa, E. Saarman, M. Caldwell, A. Frimodig, M. Miller-Henson, J. Kirlin, B. Ota, E. Pope, M. Weber, and K. Wiseman. 2012. Designing a network of marine protected areas in California: Achievements, costs, lessons learned, and challenges ahead. Ocean and Coastal Management. 74:90–101.

Gleason, M. G., S. Newkirk, M. S. Merrifield, J. Howard, R. Cox, M. Webb, J. Koepcke, B. Stranko, B. Taylor, M. W. Beck, R. Fuller, P. Dye, D. Vander Schaaf, and J. Carter. 2011. A conservation assessment of West Coast (USA) estuaries. The Nature Conservancy. Arlington, Virginia.

Goals Project. 1999. Baylands ecosystem habitat goals. A report of habitat recommendations prepared by the San Francisco Bay Area Wetlands Ecosystem Goals Project. U.S. Environmental Protection Agency, San Francisco, California; San Francisco Bay Regional Water Quality Control Board, Oakland, California.

Goodwin, P., A. J. Mehta, and J. B. Zedler. 2001. Tidal wetland restoration: An introduction. Journal of Coastal Research. Special Issue No. 27:1–6.

Greenberg, R., R. Danner, B. Olsen, and D. Luther. 2012. High summer temperature explains bill size variation in salt marsh sparrows. Ecography 35:146–152.

Greenberg, R. S., and J. E. Maldonado. 2006. Diversity and endemism in tidal-marsh vertebrates. Pages 32–53 in R. S. Greenberg, J. E. Maldonado, S. Droege, and M. V. McDonald, editors. Terrestrial Vertebrates of Tidal Marshes: Evolution, Ecology, and Conservation. Studies in Avian Biology No. 32. Cooper Ornithological Society, Camarillo, California.

Grenier, J. L., and R. Greenberg. 2005. A biogeographic pattern in sparrow bill morphology: Parallel adaptation to tidal marshes. Evolution 59:1588–1595.

Grewell, B. J., J. C. Callaway, and W. R. Ferren Jr. 2007. Estuarine wetlands. Pages 124–154 in M. G. Barbour, T. Keeler-Wolf, and A. A. Schoenherr, editors. Terrestrial Vegetation of California. University of California Press, Berkeley, California.

Griggs, G., K. Patsch, and L. Savoy. 2005. Living with the changing California Coast. University of California Press, Berkeley, California.

Grossinger, R. M., E. D. Stein, K. Cayce et al. 2011. Historical wetlands of the southern California coast: An atlas of U.S. Coast Survey T-sheets, 1851–1889. SFEI contribution #586, SCCWRP technical report #589. San Francisco Estuary Institute, Oakland, California.

Hanak, E., and G. Moreno. 2011. California coastal management with a changing climate. Climatic Change 111:45–73.

Hapke, C. J., D. Reid, and B. Richmond. 2009. Rates and trends of coastal change in California and the regional behavior of the beach and cliff system. Journal of Coastal Research 25:603–615.

Hogle, I. 2010. San Francisco Estuary Invasive Spartina 2010 Monitoring Report. Report to the California State Coastal Conservancy. San Francisco Estuary Invasive Spartina Project, Oakland, California.

Hollibaugh, J. T., and P. S. Wong. 1996. Distribution and activity of bacterioplankton in San Francisco Bay. Pages 263–288 in J. T. Hollibaugh, editor. San Francisco Bay: The Ecosystem. Pacific Division, American Association for the Advancement of Science, San Francisco, California.

Houde, E. D., and E. S. Rutherford. 1993. Recent trends in estuarine fisheries—predictions of fish production and yield. Estuaries 16:161–176.

Hughes, B. B., J. C. Haskins, K. Wasson, and E. Watson. 2011. Identifying factors that influence expression of eutrophication in a central California estuary. Marine Ecology Progress Series 439:31–43.

Hughes, B. B., R. Eby, E. Van Dyke, M. T. Tinker, C. I. Marks, K. S. Johnson, and K. Wasson. 2013. Recovery of a top predator mediates negative eutrophic effects on seagrass. Proceedings of the National Academy of Sciences of the United States of America. 110: 15313–15318.

Ingram, B. L., J. C. Ingle, and M. E. Conrad. 1996. A 2000 year record of Sacramento San Joaquin river inflow to San Francisco Bay estuary, California. Geology 24:331–334.

International Boundary and Water Commission. 2013. Tijuana River gage at the international boundary data. <http://www.ibwc.state.gov/wad/DDQTJRIB.HTM>. Accessed January 5, 2013.

Jassby, A. D., J. E. Cloern, and T. M. Powell. 1993. Organic-carbon sources and sinks in San-Francisco Bay—variability induced by river flow. Marine Ecology-Progress Series 95:39–54.

Johnson, W. M. 1855. Appendix No. 28. Extracts from the report of Sub-Assistant W. M. Johnson, relative to the features of Santa Cruz island, the valley of San Buenaventura, and the coast north of Santa Barbara channel. In Report of the superintendent of the Coast Survey, showing the progress of the survey during the year 1855 (1856), ed. A.O.P. Nicholson, Printer, Washington, D.C.

Kimbrough, K. L., W. E. Johnson, G. G. Lauenstein, J. D. Christensen, and D. A. Apeti. 2009. An assessment of polybrominated diphenyl ethers (pbdes) in sediments and bivalves of the U.S. coastal zone. NOAA Technical Memorandum NOS NCCOS 94. NOAA, Silver Spring, Maryland.

Kimmerer, W. 2004. Open water processes of the San Francisco Estuary: From physical forcing to biological responses. San Francisco Estuary and Watershed Science 2(1). <http://escholarship.org/uc/item/9bp499mv>. Accessed June 10, 2015.

Knowles, N. 2002. Natural and management influences on freshwater inflows and salinity in the San Francisco Estuary at monthly to interannual scales. Water Resources Research 38:1289. <doi:1210.1029/2001WR000360>.

Lafferty, K. D., C. C. Swift, and R. F. Ambrose. 1999. Extirpation and recolonization in a metapopulation of an endangered fish, the tidewater goby. Conservation Biology 13:1447–1453.

Larson, E. J. 2001. Coastal wetlands–emergent marshes. Pages 483–486 in California's Living Resources: A status report. <https://nrm.dfg.ca.gov/FileHandler.ashx?DocumentID=34366&inline=true> Accessed June 10, 2015.

Lotze, H. K., and B. Worm. 2002. Complex interactions of climatic and ecological controls on macroalgal recruitment. Limnology and Oceanography 47:1734–1741.

Mantua, N. J., S. R. Hare, Y. Zhang, J. M. Wallace, and R. C. Francis. 1997. A Pacific interdecadal climate oscillation with impacts on salmon production. Bulletin of the American Meteorological Society 78:1069–1079.

Maurer, E. P., A. W. Wood, J. C. Adam, D. P. Lettenmaier, and B. Nijssen. 2002. A long-term hydrologically-based data set of land surface fluxes and states for the conterminous United States. Journal of Climate 15:3237–3251.

McLaughlin, K., M. Sutula, L. Busse, S. Anderson, J. Crooks, R. Dagit, D. Gibson, K. Johnston, N. Nezlin, and L. Stratton. 2013. Southern California Bight 2008 Regional Monitoring Program. Volume 8, Estuarine Eutrophication. Southern California Coastal Water Research Project, Costa Mesa, CA, Technical Report 711. <www.sccwrp.org>

Meng, X.-Z., M. E. Blasius, R. W. Gossett, and K. A. Maruya. 2009. Polybrominated diphenyl ethers in pinnipeds stranded along the southern California coast. Environmental Pollution 157:2731–2736.

Merz, J. E., and P. B. Moyle. 2006. Salmon, wildlife, and wine: Marine-derived nutrients in human-dominated ecosystems of central California. Ecological Applications 16:999–1009.

Miller, R. L., and R. Fuji. 2010. Plant community, primary productivity, and environmental conditions following wetland re-establishment in the Sacramento–San Joaquin Delta, California. Wetlands Ecology and Management 18:1–16.

Neira, C., E. D. Grosholz, L. A. Levin, and R. Blake. 2006. Mechanisms generating modification of benthos following tidal flat invasion by a Spartina hybrid. Ecological Applications 16:1391–1404.

Noe, G. B., and J. B. Zedler. 2001. Variable rainfall limits the germination of upper intertidal marsh plants in southern California. Estuaries 24:30–40.

Pacific Fisheries Environmental Laboratory. 2013. Upwelling index data. <http://www.pfeg.noaa.gov/products/PFEL/modeled/indices/upwelling/NA>. Accessed June 10, 2015.

Page, G. W., L. Stenzel, and J. E. Kjelmyr. 1999. Overview of shorebird abundance and distribution in wetlands of the Pacific coast of the contiguous United States. The Condor 101:461–471.

Pritchard, D. W. 1967. What is an estuary: Physical viewpoint. Pages 3–5 in Estuaries. American Association for the Advancement of Science, Washington, D.C.

Redmond, K. T., and R. W. Koch. 1991. Surface climate and streamflow variability in the western United States and their relationship to large-scale circulation indexes. Water Resources Research 27:2381–2399.

Reed, S. 1871. U.S. v. Valentine Cota et al., Land Case No. 231 SD [Rio de Santa Clara]. Docket 418 part 1, U.S. District Court, Southern District. p. 1–17, 79–101. Courtesy of the Bancroft Library, University of California–Berkeley, California.

Ritter, A. F., K. Wasson, S. I. Lonhart, R. K. Preisler, A. Woolfolk, K. A. Griffith, S. Connors, and K. W. Heiman. 2008. Ecological signatures of anthropogenically altered tidal exchange in estuarine ecosystems. Estuaries and Coasts 31:554–571.

Ruiz, G. M., P. W. Fofonoff, J. T. Carlton, M. J. Wonham, and A. H. Hines. 2000. Invasion of coastal marine communities in North America: Apparent patterns, processes, and biases. Annual Review of Ecology and Systematics 31:481–531.

SCB (Southern California Bight 2008 Regional Monitoring Program Coastal Ecology Committee). 2012. Coastal ecology synthesis report. Southern California Coastal Water Research Project. <ftp://ftp.sccwrp.org/pub/download/documents/Bight08_CE_Synthesis_web.pdf>. Accessed June 10, 2015.

Schoellhamer, D. H. 2011. Sudden clearing of estuarine waters upon crossing the threshold from transport to supply—regulation of sediment transport as an erodible sediment pool is depleted: San Francisco Bay, 1999. Estuaries and Coasts 34:885–899.

Schroeter, R. E. and P. B. Moyle. 2006. Alien fishes. Pages 611–620 in L. G. Allen, D. J. Pondella and M. H. Horn, editors. Ecology of Marine Fishes: California and Adjacent Waters. University of California Press, Berkeley, California.

Schwing, F., D. Palacios, and S. Bograd. 2005. El Niño impacts on the California Current Ecosystem. CLIVAR Variations 3(2). <http://www.usclivar.org/sites/default/files/Variations-V3N2.pdf> Accessed June 10, 2015.

Seitzinger, S., J. A. Harrison, J. K. Bohlke, A. F. Bouwman, R. Lowrance, B. Peterson, C. Tobias, and G. Van Drecht. 2006. Denitrific-

aiton across landscapes and waterscapes: A synthesis. Ecological Applications 16:2064–2090.
Skinner, J. E. 1962. An historical review of the fish and wildlife resources of the San Francisco Bay Area. California Department of Fish and Game, Water Project's Branch Report No. 1. <http://downloads.ice.ucdavis.edu/sfestuary/skinner/>.
Smith, S. V., and J. T. Hollibaugh. 1997. Annual cycle and interannual variability of ecosystem metabolism in a temperate climate embayment. Ecological Monographs 67:509–533.
Smith, S. V., R. M. Chambers, and J. T. Hollibaugh. 1996. Dissolved and particulate nutrient transport through a coastal watershed-estuary system. Journal of Hydrology 176:181–203.
South Bay Salt Pond Restoration Project (SBSPRP). 2012. South Bay Salt Pond Restoration Project, 2012 Annual Report. <http://www.southbayrestoration.org/documents/technical/2012sbspannualreport.FINAL.pdf> Accessed June 10, 2015.
Stine, S. 1994. Extreme and persistent drought in California and Patagonia during medieval time. Nature 369:546–549.
Stralberg, D., M. Brennan, J. C. Callaway, J. K. Wood, L. M. Schile, D. Jongsomjit, M. Kelly, V. T. Parker, and S. Crooks. 2011. Evaluating tidal marsh sustainability in the face of sea-level rise: A hybrid modeling approach applied to San Francisco Bay. PloS One 6:e27388.
Sutula, M., C. Creager, and G. Wortham. 2007. Technical approach to develop nutrient numeric endpoints for California estuaries. Southern California Coastal Water Research Project, Costa Mesa California, Technical Report 516. <www.sccwrp.org>
Takekawa, J. Y., I. Woo, R. Gardiner, M. Casazza, J. T. Ackerman, N. Nur, L. Liu, and H. Spautz. 2011. Avian communities in tidal salt marshes of San Francisco Bay: A review of functional groups by foraging guild and habitat associations. San Francisco Estuary and Watershed Science 9(3). <https://escholarship.org/uc/item/3tg4f18n>. Accessed August 31, 2015.
Townsend-Small, A., D. E. Pataki, L. Hongxing, L. Zhaofu, W. Qiusheng, and B. Thomas. 2013. Increasing summer river discharge in southern California, USA, linked to urbanization. Geophysical Research Letters 40. <doi:10.1002/grl.50921>.
Traut, B. H. 2005. The role of coastal ecotones: A case study of the salt marsh/upland transition zone in California. Journal of Ecology 93:279–290.
U.S. Army Corps of Engineers. 2013. National inventory of dams. Federal Emergency Management Agency, Washington, D.C. <http://nid.usace.army.mil>. Accessed January 4, 2013.
U.S. Geological Survey. 2013. National water information system data (water data for the nation). <http://waterdata.usgs.gov/nwis>. Accessed March 2, 2013.
Van Dyke, E., and K. Wasson. 2005. Historical ecology of a central California estuary: 150 years of habitat change. Estuaries 28:173–189.
Vasey, M. C., V. T. Parker, J. C. Callaway, E. R. Herbert, and L. M. Schile. 2012. Tidal wetland vegetation in the San Francisco Bay-Delta Estuary. San Francisco Estuary and Watershed Science 10(2) <http://escholarship.org/uc/item/44z5v7xf>. Accessed August 31, 2015.
Veloz, S. D., N. Nur, L. Salas, D. Jongsomjit, J. K. Wood, D. Stralberg, and G. Ballard. 2013. Modeling climate change impacts on tidal marsh birds: Restoration and conservation planning in the face of uncertainty. Ecosphere 4:art4.
Wasson, K. 2010. Informing Olympia oyster restoration: Evaluation of factors that limit populations in a California estuary. Wetlands 30:449–459.
Wasson, K., and A. Woolfolk. 2011. Salt marsh-upland ecotones in central California: vulnerability to invasions and anthropogenic stressors. Wetlands 31:1–14.
Watershed Boundary Dataset. 2013. Coordinated effort between the United States Department of Agriculture-Natural Resources Conservation Service (USDA-NRCS), the United States Geological Survey (USGS), and the Environmental Protection Agency (EPA). <http://nhd.usgs.gov/wbd.html>. Accessed January 1, 2013.
Watson, E. B., and R. Byrne. 2009. Abundance and diversity of tidal marsh plants along the salinity gradient of the San Francisco Estuary: Implications for global change ecology. Plant Ecology 205:113–128.
Whipple, A. A., R. M. Grossinger, D. Rankin, B. Stanford, and R. A. Askevold. 2012. Sacramento–San Joaquin Delta historical ecology investigation: Exploring pattern and process. Prepared for the California Department of Fish and Game and Ecosystem Restoration Program. A Report of SFEI-ASC's Historical Ecology Program, SFEI-ASC Publication #672. San Francisco Estuary Institute–Aquatic Science Center, Richmond, California.
Williams, S. L., and E. D. Grosholz. 2008. The invasive species challenge in estuarine and coastal environments: Marrying management and science. Estuaries and Coasts 31:3–20.
Williams, S. L., I. C. Davidson, J. R. Pasari, G. V. Ashton, J. T. Carlton, R. E. Crafton, R. E. Fontana, E. D. Grosholz, A. W. Miller, G. M. Ruiz, and C. J. Zabin. 2013. Managing multiple vectors for marine invasions in an increasingly connected world. Bioscience 63:952–966.
Winder, M., and A. D. Jassby. 2011. Shifts in zooplankton community structure: Implications for food-web processes in the upper San Francisco Estuary. Estuaries and Coasts 34:675–690.
Winder, M., A. D. Jassby, and R. Mac Nally. 2011. Synergies between climate anomalies and hydrological modifications facilitate estuarine biotic invasions. Ecology Letters 14:749–757.
Wingfield, D. K., and C. D. Storlazzi. 2007. Spatial and temporal variability in oceanographic and meteorologic forcing along central California and its implications on nearshore processes. Journal of Marine Systems 68:457–472.
Zedler, J. B. 2010. How frequent storms affect wetland vegetation: A preview of climate-change impacts. Frontiers in Ecology and the Environment 8:540–547.
Zedler, J. B., R. Koenigs, and W. P. Magdych. 1984. Freshwater release and southern California coastal wetlands: Streamflow for the San Diego and Tijuana Rivers. San Diego Association of Governments, San Diego, California.

TWENTY

Sandy Beaches

JENIFER E. DUGAN and DAVID M. HUBBARD

Introduction

Sandy beach ecosystems are perched at the dynamic boundary of land and sea with important functional links to both. Beach ecosystems are strongly influenced by marine and terrestrial processes and make up part of a larger system comprised of surf zone, beach, and backshore. The sand in this linked system is constantly moved by the forces of winds, waves, currents, and tides. Although restricted to a narrow strip running along the coast, sandy beaches are iconic assets highly valued by society for recreation, aesthetics, and cultural identity. Beaches sit high on the list of desirable places to visit, support vibrant coastal towns and cities, and annually contribute billions of dollars to the California economy.

However, compared with their high socioeconomic values, the unique biodiversity and ecological functions and resources supported by sandy beach ecosystems are often underappreciated (Schlacher et al. 2007, 2014). Intrinsic ecological roles and functions of sandy beach ecosystems in California include rich invertebrate communities that serve as prey for birds and fish, buffering and absorption of wave energy by stored sand, filtration of large volumes of seawater, extensive detrital and wrack processing and nutrient recycling, and provision of critical habitat and resources for declining and endangered wildlife, such as SHOREBIRDS and PINNIPEDS.

Geomorphic Properties and Characteristics

Formed by mobile sediments and shaped by wave, wind, and tide regimes, beaches come in all shapes and sizes along the California coast. Sandy beaches also intersperse with rocky shore habitats in a wide range of settings, creating mixed rock/sand habitats. Some ocean beaches are composed of gravel, shingles, cobbles, or boulders. This chapter focuses on the distinctive habitat and ecology of open coast beaches that are primarily sandy. Beach morphologies are strongly influenced by landscape, topography, wave climate, and the presence of streams and rivers (Habel and Armstrong 1977, Griggs et al. 2005). On predominantly rocky coasts, sandy beaches are often limited to small, isolated pocket beaches of 100 meters to 1 kilometer in shoreline length located in coves bounded by rocky headlands. Examples include Horseshoe Cove on Bodega Head, Natural Bridges State Beach north of Santa Cruz, Whaler's Cove south of Carmel, and Big Dume Cove on Santa Monica Bay (Figure 20.1).

Longer beaches and terminal spits form at the deltas of large rivers that flow over broad, shallow floodplains, and these are often stabilized between rocky headlands. Primarily found in the northern part of the state, examples of these delta beaches and spits are found at the mouths of the Smith River, Redwood Creek, the Bear River, the Mattole River, and

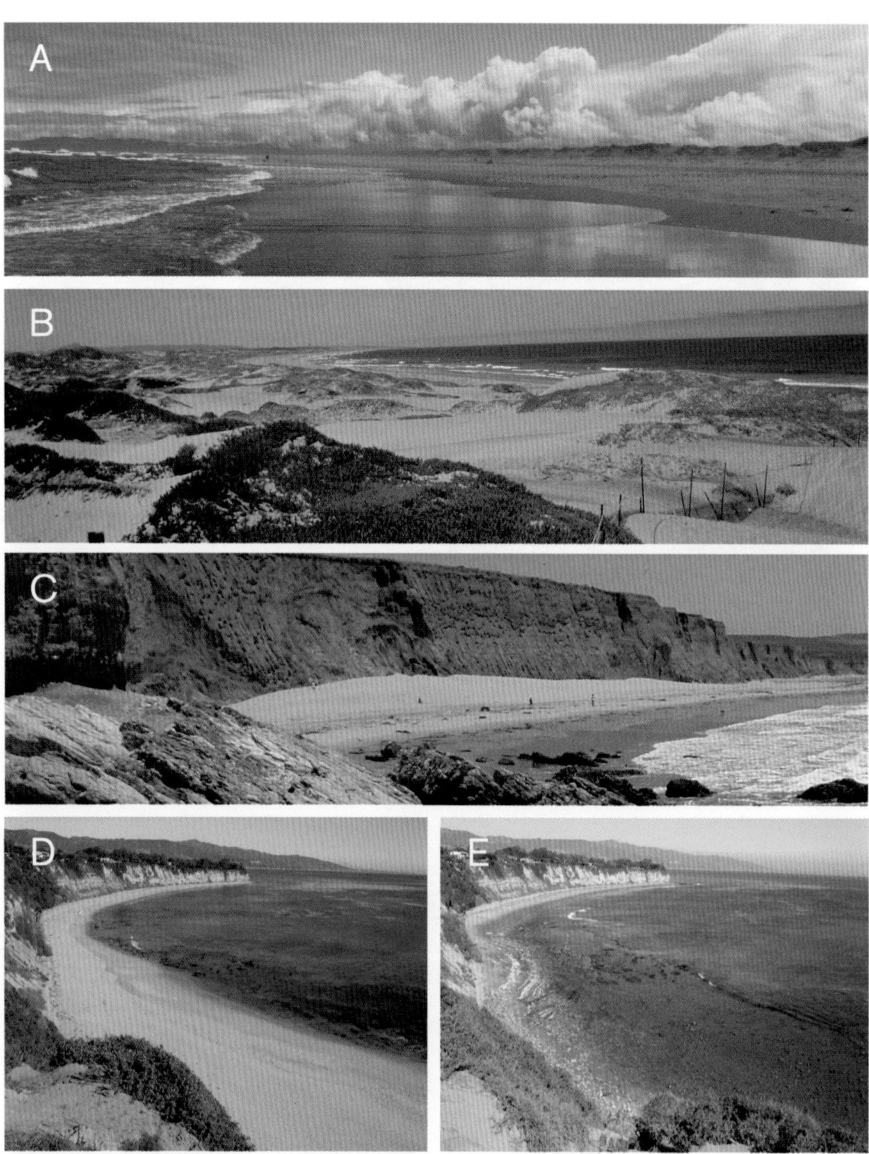

FIGURE 20.1 California beaches come in a wide variety of forms ranging from short pocket beaches in rocky coasts to long stretches of dune-backed coastline. All of them change constantly in response to shifting tide and wave energy conditions. Photos: David Hubbard.

(A) a wide flat dissipative beach at Malel Dunes in Humboldt County, (B) a dune-backed beach in northern Santa Barbara County, (C) a narrow bluff-backed beach at Jalama County Park in Santa Barbara County, and (D) and (E) a pocket beach in a cove east of Point Dume in Los Angeles County showing the dramatic seasonal variation in the cover of sand typical of many bluff-backed beaches exposed by wave action.

Ten Mile River (Habel and Armstrong 1977). In the south, the Santa Clara River mouth forms a large spit; at the San Diego River the beach and river delta have been altered and stabilized by channelization and jetties.

DOWNCOAST of resistant rocky points, crescent or crenulate bays with relatively stable, curving coastlines that conform to a LOG SPIRAL shape can support the formation of extensive beaches. Examples of these occur in Shelter Cove, Half Moon Bay, and San Luis Bay (Habel and Armstrong 1977). Where tidal marshes or lagoons are located inshore of these curved coasts, sand spits can form that enclose the embayment (Wright and Short 1980). Bodega and Bolinas and Drake's Bays are striking California examples of CRENULATE SPITS. Upcoast of major rocky points, straight, stable beaches aligned with the dominant wave direction can develop. On these coasts, wide beaches, often backed by extensive dune fields, form in the vicinity of rivers that provide sufficient sediment supply. Manchester State Beach north of Point Arena, Ten Mile River Beach, Pelican Bay north of Point Saint George, Salmon Creek Beach north of Bodega Head, Oceano Dunes, Guadalupe Dunes north of Point Sal, and the Vandenberg Air Force Base beach and dune complexes north of Purisima Point and

Photo on previous page: Many shorebirds, like this dense flock of sanderlings running with the waves on a winter morning, spend as much as eight months a year feeding on the abundant intertidal invertebrates inhabiting California's sandy beaches. Photo: David Hubbard.

Point Arguello, respectively, exemplify the types of beaches and associated dune fields found in these parallel alignments (Habel and Armstrong 1977) (see Figure 20.1).

Along much of California's coast, the dominant wave energy coming from the north Pacific hits the shoreline at an angle generating LITTORAL CURRENTS and LONGSHORE sediment transport that is generally towards the south and east (Griggs et al. 2005). The wave-driven transport of sand by longshore or littoral currents forms a "river of sand" that moves along the shoreline in shallow water, strongly affecting sediment supply and beach morphology. LITTORAL TRANSPORT-dominated beach systems bounded upcoast by a barrier and sand sources and downcoast by sinks for sand make up most of the California coast, particularly in the most developed and urbanized regions. Estimated annual rates of littoral sand transport past any single point can be enormous, ranging from 38,000 to 765,000 cubic meters (Griggs et al. 2005). In some areas, pulses of sand have been shown to move along the shore as erosion and accretion waves that can be hundreds or thousands of meters long (Barnard et al. 2012).

The California coastline can be divided into beach compartments known as littoral cells. A littoral cell is a geographically distinct section of coastline that contains a complete SEDIMENT BUDGET including sources of supply, alongshore transport, and loss of sand (Inman and Frautschy 1966). Littoral cells feature a series of sand sources (streams, rivers, bluffs) and the generally unidirectional longshore transport of sand that ends at a sink, such as a submarine canyon or a dune field, removing the sand from the cell (Patsch and Griggs 2006, Habel and Armstrong 1977). Twenty-five major littoral cells have been identified in the state (Patsch and Griggs 2006, Habel and Armstrong 1977). Examples of major littoral cells that end in submarine canyons (often demarcated by a rocky headland) include San Pedro Point, Santa Cruz to Monterey Canyon, Pinos Point to Monterey Canyon, Point Conception to Hueneme and Mugu Canyons, Point Dume to Redondo Canyon, Point Fermin to Newport Canyon, and Dana Point to La Jolla Canyon (Habel and Armstrong 1977, Patsch and Griggs 2006). Examples of major littoral cells that end in coastal dune fields include the Ten Mile River cell, the Navarro River cell, and the Morro Bay cell (Habel and Armstrong 1977). Many beaches in the littoral cells of southern California are backed by bluffs and cliffs, some of which also serve as sources of beach sand as they erode (Patsch and Griggs 2006, Young and Ashford 2006) (see Figure 20.1). Clearly important as elements of beach and sediment dynamics, littoral cells may also help delineate regions that have a higher degree of ecological connectivity, not only of sediment characteristics and sources but also among populations of organisms, especially animals with DIRECT DEVELOPMENT and limited dispersal.

Within the landscape types just described, beaches can be classified along a MORPHODYNAMIC SCALE that describes the effects of the surf regime interacting with the characteristics of the available sand (Short and Wright 1983, Short 1996). At one end of this scale are DISSIPATIVE beaches, which have wide (hundreds of meters), high-energy surf zones that dissipate large amounts of incoming wave energy before it reaches the intertidal zone. These wide, flat beaches have very fine sand and LAMINAR, long-period SWASH CLIMATES (McArdle and McLachlan 1992). Examples of dissipative beaches in California include Pismo Beach in San Luis Obispo County and Clam Beach in Humboldt County. At the other end of the spectrum are REFLECTIVE beaches with very narrow (or no) surf zones, where waves break near or directly on the shore and some wave energy is reflected seaward. Reflective beaches generally have coarse sediments, steep slopes, and short-period, turbulent swash climates. Most pocket beaches can be considered reflective beaches.

The majority of beaches in California and across the globe are intermediate beaches that span the broad spectrum between dissipative and reflective types and represent a wide range of sizes and shapes as well as sand grain sizes. Intermediate beaches also show strong temporal variation in size and shape compared to either dissipative or reflective beaches (Wright and Short 1980). Many intermediate beaches shift to a more dissipative state during storms and a more reflective state during calm periods. RIP CURRENTS influence shoreline shape on intermediate sandy beaches exposed to strong surf. Greater erosion in the lee of the rip current creates MEGA-CUSP embayment features that can span 100–300 meters of shoreline (Short and Hesp 1982, Thornton et al. 2007). Beach width varies from narrow in the mega-cusp embayments to wider in the intervening horns, creating a deeply scalloped shoreline, such as the beaches lining southern Monterey Bay and Vandenberg AFB.

Beach Profiles and Features

A typical cross-section or beach profile of an idealized, intermediate-type beach at low tide provides an overview of beach features, particularly those that are ecologically relevant (Figure 20.2). Ocean swells steepen as they enter shallower water near the shoreline. Once waves steepen beyond a critical point, they become unstable and break, creating the SURF ZONE and moving water and sediment onto the beach in complex patterns near the shoreline. At high tide the surf zone covers the intertidal beach. During extreme storms, waves can run across the entire beach and may erode the beach as well as dunes and bluffs backing the beach. The lowest area of the beach during any tide is the swash zone, where the remaining wave energy that has passed through the surf zone runs up onto the beach face, stops, and then retreats as backwash. Swashes are generally most turbulent and loaded with sediment at the start of the wave's upwash. Swash movement slows and becomes more laminar until the maximum upwash is achieved, then the motion stops and reverses into a backwash. The wet sand in the swash zone tends to move readily both in suspension and as BEDLOAD, where it rolls and slides along the bottom. The swash zone moves with the tidal cycle, shifting landward during the rising tide and seaward on the falling tide.

At low tide the zone of shiny, fully saturated sand exposed by the swash can also extend well above the swash zone, reflecting the sky like a mirror. The upper edge of this zone of fully saturated sand is termed the WATER TABLE OUTCROP (or the effluent line). This feature marks where the subsurface beach WATER TABLE (OR AQUIFER) reaches the sand surface, and water pumped into the beach by waves and tides drains across the open beach face toward the sea. During high tides waves and tides charge and fill the beach aquifer with seawater, which then drains at low tide. The beach water table has a sloping surface that tilts upward toward the land. This water table can be connected to terrestrial aquifers, making the beach a location where freshwater, nutrients, and contaminants may enter the ocean. On some bluff-backed beaches, the beach aquifer can be 100% seawater that is perched on a bedrock platform beneath the sand. The breakdown and

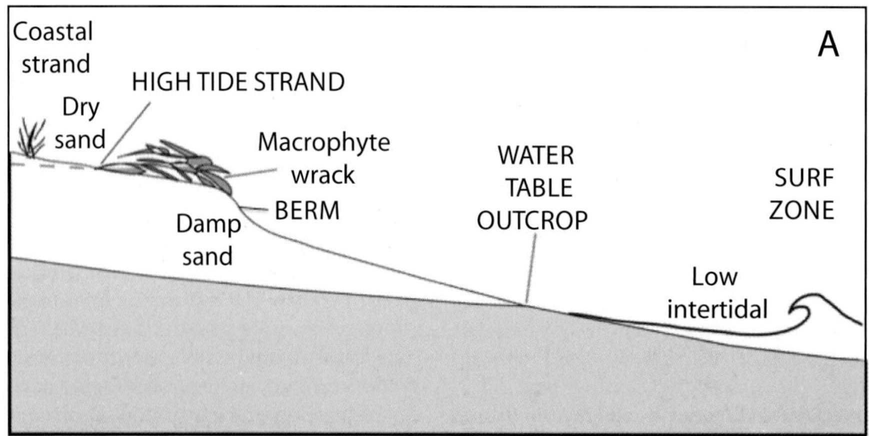

FIGURE 20.2 The physical conditions experienced by beach animals range from dry, sun-baked, and wind-blown at the top of the beach to wet and wave-pounded on the lower shore.

A Diagram depicting a California beach at low tide, showing habitat zones from low to high: surf zone, saturated sand, damp sand, dry sand, and coastal strand vegetation. Illustration by David Hubbard.

B Arroyo Burro Beach in Santa Barbara County, a bluff-backed beach with the same features as shown in the diagram. Photo: Jenifer Dugan.

remineralization of kelps and other macroalgal wrack on the beach can be associated with high concentrations of nutrients in the beach aquifer (Dugan et al. 2011).

The slope of the beach face can be relatively uniform from the high tide line to the swash zone at times. Alternatively, the beach face can be punctuated by alongshore features such as BERMS and runnels. Berms are shore-parallel ridges that represent erosional or accretional events. When an intertidal berm is present, the lower beach rises with increasing slope to the BERM CREST or SCARP near the mean high tide line. NEAP high tides often fall short of the berm crest, while spring high tides can frequently wash over the berm crest. Landward of the active intertidal berm crest, there may be a variety of topographic features. These can include a relatively flat terrace, a backslope from the berm crest to a low RUNNEL, or a series of older berms and runnels. Some beaches support a zone of COASTAL STRAND VEGETATION just above the reach of average waves and tides. At their landwardmost edges, beaches are bounded by natural features, such as a FOREDUNES, bluffs, floodplains, estuaries, river mouths, or by human-made structures and developments such as armoring, buildings, roads, and parking lots. On narrow beaches where high tides regularly reach cliffs or human-made structures, berms, coastal strand vegetation, and dunes are usually absent.

The HIGH TIDE STRAND line (HTS), or driftline, marks the highest reach of the tides in a twenty-four-hour period (see Figure 20.2). The high tide strand line is the zone where the primary deposition of buoyant material from the ocean and rivers occurs. This flotsam includes MACROPHYTE wrack (kelps, red and green macroalgae, and seagrasses), driftwood, carrion, and other marine and terrestrial debris including leaf litter and trash. Sand below the high tide strand line and above the water table outcrop holds moisture from the waves and tides and is generally somewhat firm and cohesive, although not saturated.

Above the high tide strand line is an upper beach zone (sometimes referred to as the SUPRALITTORAL zone) that varies in width with tide phases and across the seasons. The landwardmost edge of this upper beach zone can support the establishment of coastal strand vegetation, at least during periods of accretion when the beach is wide (Barbour et al. 1976, Barbour et al. 1985, Barbour and Johnson 1988, Dugan and Hubbard 2010). This colonizing vegetation, although composed of perennial plant species, can be functionally annual on many beaches because of strong seasonal erosion cycles. When present for sufficient time, coastal strand vegetation traps windblown sand to form hummocks and embryonic dunes. During periods with sufficient sand supplies and relatively low wave energy, these features may build into primary foredunes.

Key Drivers, Processes, and Patterns

Waves and tides are considered the major drivers of beach ecosystem dynamics and characteristics (McLachlan and Brown 2006). Waves drive both the longshore (parallel to the coastline) and the CROSS-SHORE (perpendicular to the coastline) transport of sand on beaches. Varying tide levels also have direct effects on beach processes but are much more predictable than waves (see Chapter 18, "Intertidal"). The combination of these two factors along with others that influence local sea level produce a "total water level" that can differ by more than a meter from levels listed in a simple tide table. Much of this difference is due to the ability of the energy in waves entering the swash zone to carry them up the sloping ramp of the beach face.

The overall shape of a sandy beach is affected by the type and grain size of sand, the typical wave energy regime, and the influence of nearby rocky reefs, headlands, and human-made structures on wave exposure and water circulation (Loureiro et al. 2013, Orme et al. 2011, Short and Wright 1983). The stability of a beach's shape depends on variability of forcing factors and processes such as wave climate and direction, sand supply, and variation in sea level. Dune-backed beaches are generally more stable because of buffering provided by the sand stored in the dunes. The dunes feed sand to the beach during storms and protect inland areas from storm-generated waves. Beach shapes also respond to modification of nearshore or onshore wave energy patterns by human-made rigid structures (seawalls, revetments, GROINS, jetties, BREAKWATERS) (e.g., Griggs 2005b, Orme et al. 2011) or of sediment volumes, size structure, or water depth during dredge and fill operations.

The sand on California's beaches comes mainly from erosion of inland watersheds. An estimated 80% to 95% of the sand on California's beaches is delivered to the coast by streams or rivers (Griggs et al. 2005), with smaller contributions from erosion of bluffs and dunes (e.g., Young and Ashford 2006). Sediment delivered to the coast by rivers and streams includes size classes both coarser and finer than beach sand (Warwick 2013). Sorting by wave action in the swash and surf zones separates the different size fractions. Finer sediment is exported offshore (Warwick 2013). Larger materials, such as cobbles and boulders, are most commonly found near stream mouths, often buried under the sand. However, these can be exposed when sand is eroded off beaches during winter storm events.

The sand that makes up beaches is constantly in motion. After sand moves onto beaches from upland sources, it is transported along the coast by longshore currents, stored on the shoreline for a while, and eventually lost from the littoral cell. These losses can include offshore transport of sand to deeper waters where waves can no longer move it back to the shore, loss to SUBMARINE CANYONS, onshore transport to coastal dune fields by wind, and entrapment and storage behind artificial barriers. The balance of sand inputs and losses to a littoral cell is termed the sediment budget. Over time, this balance determines the width of the beaches within a littoral cell.

Regional sediment budgets have been constructed using harbor dredging records as a proxy for littoral sediment transport along the coast of California (Patsch and Griggs 2006). Using these records, the reduction in sand supply caused by the impoundment of sand behind dams in the Santa Barbara littoral cell has been estimated to be about 40% and 55% in San Diego (Willis and Griggs 2003). Mining of beach sand can also affect the sediment budget of entire littoral cells (Thornton et al. 2006), although only a single beach sand mine remains in operation in California. Reduced regional sand supply can strongly affect beach width and the quality and quantity of sandy beach ecosystems. Despite concerns about the loss of beaches in southern California due to reduced sand supply, a multidecadal evaluation of beach width changes in the major littoral cells of southern California by Orme et al. (2011) detected little long-term beach narrowing. They suggested instead that beach widths in the region have fluctuated historically in response to other factors such as large-scale climate changes, littoral obstructions, and beach nourishment.

In southern California, sediment budget analyses are complicated by the addition of massive volumes of imported sand (tens of millions of cubic meters per beach) to beaches by large, coastal construction projects beginning in the 1930s (see Flick 1993, Orme et al. 2011). These projects include bypassing and clearing navigation channels, dredging new marinas, and filling or nourishing beaches to maintain beach widths for recreation and tourism (Flick 1993, Patsch and Griggs 2006, Orme et al. 2011). As a result of such projects, beaches in some littoral cells, such as Santa Monica Bay and Silver Strand, are now much wider than they were historically (Flick 1993, Patsch and Griggs 2006). Where frequently applied, large-scale beach fill projects can alter regional sand budgets and damp variation in beach widths, as exemplified by the beaches of Santa Monica and Venice (Orme et al. 2011). Despite frequent, large fill projects, significant oscillation in beach width persists in some areas of southern California (Orme et al. 2011).

Beaches undergo major EROSION and ACCRETION cycles on a variety of time scales. Many beaches in California and elsewhere show strong seasonal accretion and erosion cycles (e.g., Bascom 1980, Barnard et al. 2009, Griggs et al. 2005) (Figure 20.3). Wave energy reaching the coast drives these distinct cycles of accretion and erosion, sometimes with considerable time lags (Griggs et al. 2005, Barnard et al. 2012). Large, winter waves tend to remove sand from the beach face and move it into sand bars in the nearshore zone. Sandy beaches can retreat up to 30 meters in a few hours and can virtually disappear in a single storm event. During calmer, summer wave conditions, sand moves back onto the beach face and the beach widens (Winant et al. 1975, Barnard et al. 2012). As overall beach width changes, all of the zones of the beach shift across the shore (Dugan et al. 2013).

Coastal erosion is a physical expression of a deficit in the sediment budget, when the transport of sediment exceeds the sediment supply. Coastal erosion can be a seasonal, chronic, or episodic process. Long-term reductions in sand supply caused by disruption of sediment transport and delivery by rivers and streams, shoreline armoring, and sand mining can lead to chronic beach erosion. Although average annual erosion rates are often reported, these rates are extremely variable in time and space with episodic large storm events causing the bulk of coastal erosion (Revell et al. 2011, Storlazzi and Griggs 1998, Storlazzi and Griggs 2000). As beaches narrow from erosion, they provide less protection for adjoining

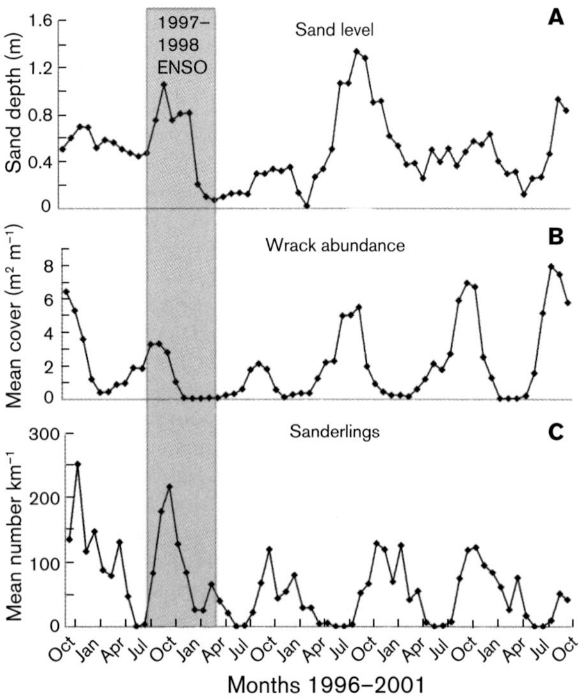

FIGURE 20.3 The complex responses and recoveries of California beaches to a strong El Niño Southern Oscillation (ENSO) event are illustrated by time series of the monthly mean values of (A) beach condition indicated by sand level, (B) subsidies from kelp forests indicated by marine wrack abundance, and (C) the abundance of higher trophic levels indicated by a shorebird, sanderlings (*Calidris alba*), from 1996 to 2001 on beaches in Isla Vista, California. Adapted from Revell et al. 2011.

terrestrial habitats, and the shoreline tends to retreat inland. When retreat of the coastline from erosion approaches residences, businesses, agricultural areas, or other resources or infrastructure, societal responses often include building barriers to halt further retreat but generally do not address the erosion of the beach itself. The majority of California's sandy coasts are classified as eroding (Hapke et al. 2006, Hapke et al. 2009, Hapke and Reid 2007, Patsch and Griggs 2007, 2008), much of which can be linked to human-induced changes in sediment supply and transport (Komar 1998).

Beach ecosystems respond strongly to a variety of climatic drivers. Although overall beach widths have not decreased over time in southern California (Orme et al. 2011), variation in beach widths related to different phases of the PACIFIC DECADAL OSCILLATION (PDO, an approximately thirty-year climate index of sea surface temperature) have been detected using historical beach width analyses based on aerial photography (Revell and Griggs 2006). Beach width responses to the PDO were most apparent for beaches in Santa Barbara and Zuma littoral cells, with a pattern of wider beaches during the cool phase of the PDO. Episodic storm events, often associated with El Niño Southern Oscillation (ENSO) conditions, can have significant, catastrophic, and long-lasting effects on beaches (e.g., Storlazzi and Griggs 1998, 2000). During these extreme events increased precipitation and ocean temperatures raise water levels, making the shoreline more susceptible to erosion from large waves (McGowan 1984). Major beach and dune erosion can result in shrinkage of beach widths by >50% during EL NIÑO storms (Revell and Griggs 2006, 2007). The formation of erosion hotspots during El Niño years appears related to a pattern of beach rotations resulting from a southwesterly shift in wave direction (Revell and Griggs 2006, 2007). High wave energy associated with El Niño events erodes shorelines and can leave beaches sand-starved and narrow for more than a year (Barnard et al. 2011, 2012). These events also affect the distribution of beach zones, nearshore kelp beds and wrack inputs, the survival of intertidal invertebrates, and habitat and prey resources for birds requiring recovery periods stretching from months to years (Revell et al. 2011) (see Figure 20.3). The ecological consequences of storm-related erosion on sandy coastal habitats operate on different time scales according to proximity to sand supply, persistence of beach rotations and hotspots, metapopulation and community dynamics, and plant and animal life histories (Arntz et al. 1987, Revell et al. 2011).

Paradoxically, large, episodic storm events can also have positive effects on the sediment budget of the shoreline (Kniskern et al. 2011). Intense precipitation and runoff events can transport massive amounts of sediment to the coast, as exemplified in January 2005 when the Santa Clara River (Ventura County) delivered 5,000,000 cubic meters of sediment to the coast (ten times the annual average) and built the shoreline more than 170 meters seaward at the river delta (Barnard and Warrick 2010) (see Figure 20.1). The immediate effects of erosion are obvious and receive a great deal of media attention, while new sediment supplied to the coast is not generally widely noticed. In fact, the sand delivered from large storms may be deposited primarily in the nearshore zone and appreciated mostly by surfers. However, beaches are often observed to be wider following major storm, rainfall, and runoff years (Griggs et al. 2005).

Finally, sea level rise is likely to exacerbate coastal erosion by raising mean water levels and consequently increasing exposure of backshores, including the toes of dunes and bluffs to wave attack. If sea levels rise high enough dunes may be breached, allowing seawater to flood behind the dune. Dune breaching can reduce the extent of coastal strand and dune habitat, increase salinity levels, and increase exposure to inundation.

Ecosystem Attributes and Food Webs

To a casual visitor, the wave-swept sands of California's beaches might appear relatively empty of life. No plants can take hold on the shifting sand of open beaches, and most characteristic animals are highly mobile and nocturnal, burrowing deeply into the sand during the day. However, sandy beaches in California support a unique and rich animal diversity that includes resident animals; fish and invertebrates that depend on beaches for a key part of their life cycle; and birds and pinnipeds that winter, forage, breed, or nest on beaches and dunes.

California's sandy beaches support some of the most diverse intertidal invertebrate communities ever reported for beach ecosystems (McLachlan 1994, McLachlan and Dorvlo 2005), with more than 45 species found in single surveys on a variety of beaches and more than 105 species recorded in southern and central regions (Straughan 1983; Dugan, Hubbard, Engle et al. 2000; Dugan et al. 2003; Schooler, Dugan and Hubbard 2014; Schooler et al. in prep.). Crustaceans, polychaete worms, and mollusks are major intertidal invertebrate

FIGURE 20.4 Connectivity between beaches and kelp forests is an important driver of beach ecosystems in California. Wrack, in the form of beach-cast macroalgae and seagrass, exported from kelp forests and reefs is a prominent feature and key ecological resource on California beaches. Imported wrack supports a major component of the beach food web and a high diversity of endemic intertidal animals. Beach-cast giant kelp (*Macrocystis pyrifera*), feather boa kelp (*Egregia menziesii*), and surfgrass (*Phyllospadix scouleri*) on a beach near Isla Vista, California. Photo: David Hubbard.

groups on California beaches and elsewhere. Endemic insects, including a number of flightless beetles, form an important element of the diversity of California's beaches. Many additional species are likely present on California beaches, but identification of several important taxa including INFAUNAL polychaete worms and wrack-associated insects is limited by current taxonomic knowledge.

Zonation

The distinctive mobility of beach intertidal animals and of the sand itself limit the applicability of many classic tenets of intertidal zonation useful for exposed rocky shore biota (Peterson 1991). On rocky intertidal shores, many characteristic plants and animals survive wave and tidal action by strongly resisting movement (see Chapter 18, "Intertidal"). On sheltered muddy shores, many animals build and inhabit relatively permanent burrows in consolidated sediments or attach to plants (see Chapter 19, "Estuaries: Life on the Edge"). On sandy beaches, intertidal animals must move; although they can occupy burrows for minutes to a few days, they do not inhabit permanent burrows or locations on the beach profile. Most regularly move up and down the beach profile in response to tide height and phase (e.g., Dugan et al. 2013). Over the course of larger seasonal or event-driven erosion and accretion, these animals also move much greater distances across the shore. The remarkably high mobility of beach animals thus underpins many of the major differences in intertidal ecology observed among sandy beaches and other more stable shore types.

Three relatively distinct zones of intertidal beach animals can be often be identified for a given day or tide condition (McLachlan and Jaramillo 1995). These zones generally correspond to (1) the relatively dry sand around and above the high tide strand line, (2) the damp sand of the middle intertidal, and (3) the saturated sand of the lower and swash intertidal zone (see Figure 20.2). The locations of these zones and of their characteristic inhabitants move up and down (as well as along) the beach in response to tides and water motion, shifting dramatically in just hours. As the tide floods after a low tide, animals burrowed in the swash and low zone of a beach, such as sand crabs, emerge from the sand to migrate up the shore. On the ebb (receding) tide, they move down the shore again and reburrow. The positions of many beach animals on the profile also respond distinctly to the lunar tide cycle, burrowing higher on the beach during SPRING TIDES and occupying lower strata during neap tides (Dugan et al. 2013). Although overall abundance remains the same, these semilunar movements create changes in the density of animals burrowed in a particular zone. These shifts in density can affect the intensity of biotic interactions and must be accounted for in the design of quantitative surveys. The positions of these mobile burrowing animals also react strongly to wave energy, beach erosion, and accretion. Annual shifts in position defined as the ecological envelopes of these animals generally extend across greater than 60% of the overall beach width (Dugan et al. 2013).

Beach Food Webs

Because beaches lack attached plants, they have very low in situ primary production. Primary production is limited mostly to DIATOMS in the surf and lower intertidal zones. Thus beach food webs depend mainly on imported organic matter from other marine ecosystems. In California the main sources are phytoplankton from nearshore pelagic ecosystems and macrophytes (algae and seagrass) from nearby kelp forests, rocky shores, and estuaries (Figure 20.4). These two major marine inputs support distinct components (or subwebs) of the intertidal invertebrate community. Drift algae and seagrasses stranded on beaches as macrophyte wrack (see Figure 20.3) represent an important link between reef and kelp forest ecosystems and beaches in many regions, with estimated annual inputs exceeding 500 kg m^{-1} (ZoBell 1971, Dugan et al. 2011).

Intertidal consumers consist of (1) SUSPENSION-FEEDING clams, hippid crabs, MYSIDS, and amphipods that filter PLANKTON from the wave wash, (2) wrack-feeding amphipods, isopods, and insects that feed on drift macrophytes deposited by waves on the beach, and (3) burrowing deposit feeders that feed on both wrack particles and phytoplankton pumped into the sand by waves and tides. The dependence of beach food

FIGURE 20.5 On the lower beach and in the swash zone many of the invertebrates are suspension feeders that sieve or filter plankton from the surf and swash water. Photos: (A–C, F) David Hubbard; (D) Dan Ayres, Washington Department of Fish and Wildlife; (E) Shane Anderson.

- A Sand crabs (*Emerita analoga*) on surface including females carrying clutches of orange eggs.
- B Backwash of a wave showing texture of sand crab feeding aggregation.
- C Bean clams (*Donax gouldii*) exposed at low tide at La Jolla with inset of an individual clam.
- D Pacific razor clams (*Siliqua patula*), found only in the northern part of the state.
- E A Pismo clam (*Tivela stultorum*) underwater with siphons extended (the large frilly intake siphon helps to filter sandy water, the smaller open siphon is for outflow).
- F Legally harvestable Pismo clams from an intertidal beach.

webs on ALLOCHTHONOUS marine resources results in strong BOTTOM-UP EFFECTS that propagate up to avian and other predators (Dugan et al. 2003).

Suspension Feeders

Sand crabs, clams, and other suspension feeders make up most of the biomass (80%–98%) of invertebrate communities on California beaches (Figure 20.5). They can be extremely abundant in the swash zone, exceeding 100,000 individuals m^{-1} of shoreline and providing important prey for shorebirds, seabirds, fish, pinnipeds, and even sea otters. The growth and population biology of these animals are closely coupled to ocean processes such as UPWELLING that stimulates growth of nearshore phytoplankton and currents that carry their pelagic larvae away from and back to beaches (see Chapter 16, "The Offshore Ecosystem").

The most widespread and often the most abundant suspension-feeding beach invertebrate is the sand crab (*Emerita analoga*), which can occur on almost every type and length of exposed sandy beach in California (Efford 1970, 1976). This hippid crab is a rapidly burrowing sediment generalist (sensu Alexander et al. 1993) with excellent orientation and swimming abilities that can colonize the full spectrum of exposed sandy beaches, from fully reflective to dissipative (Dugan, Hubbard, and Lastra 2000). These highly mobile crabs generally aggregate in the active swash zone and follow this zone up and down the beach with the tides (see Figure 20.5). The sand crab uses its plumose (feathery) second antennae to sieve fine particles, primarily phytoplankton, from the turbulent moving water in the swash zone (Efford 1966). Its growth is correlated with surf zone CHLOROPHYLL-*a* concentrations (an indicator of phytoplankton abundance) along the California coast (Dugan et al. 1994) indicating coupling of its population biology with upwelling and productivity gradients. Sand crab larvae spend three to four months as ZOEA in the PLANKTON before settling on beaches as MEGALOPA/POSTLARVAE (Efford 1970, 1976). Populations in the northeastern Pacific appear well mixed with high gene flow (Dawson et al. 2011). Sand crabs have sensitive and plastic life history responses to environmental variation (Fusaro 1978, Dugan et al. 1991, Dugan et al. 1994, Dugan and Hubbard 1996). Size and age at maturity, growth rate, maximum male and female crab size, and survival all increase significantly from south to north across its geographic range in California (Dugan et al. 1991, Dugan et al. 1994, Wenner et al. 1993). This strong geographic pattern appears to be related to the gradient of increasingly productive yet colder waters from southern to northern California (Dugan 1990, Dugan et al. 1994).

Sand crab populations have been successfully used as bioindicators (Siegel and Wenner 1984, Wenner 1988) as they readily bioaccumulate metals, hydrocarbons, pesticides (e.g., Burnett 1971, Rossi et al. 1978, Wenner 1988) and harmful algal toxins such as Paralytic Shellfish Poisoning and domoic acid (Bretz et al. 2002, Ferdin et al. 2002). Tissue loadings of DDT in sand crabs were a key factor used to describe the coastal distribution of this now-banned pesticide associated with the White's Point Outfall on Palos Verdes in the Southern California Bight (Burnett 1971). This major Los Angeles sewage outfall discharged tons of DDT from the nation's largest manufacturer of this pesticide, Montrose Chemical Corporation, into the ocean on the Palos Verdes shelf from the 1950s through 1971.

Intertidal clams of California beaches have more limited distributions than sand crabs, preferring beaches with flatter slopes and finer sand. Species include the bean clam (*Donax gouldii*), the Pismo clam (*Tivela stultorum*), and the razor clam (*Siliqua patula*, as well as *S. lucida*) (see Figure 20.5). Colorful bean clams are a southern species most abundant and most commonly encountered on intermediate beaches south of Point Conception, where they can cover the beach like gravel at times (Coe 1953, 1955). Thick-shelled, slow-burrowing Pismo clams inhabit intermediate to dissipative beach types from Half Moon Bay south; their distribution can extend from the intertidal into subtidal sands (Fitch 1950, McLachlan et al. 1995, 1996). Thin-shelled, rapidly burrowing razor clams are restricted to dissipative or nearly dissipative beaches in the northernmost part of the state (McLachlan et al. 1995, 1996).

Both razor clams and Pismo clams are fished recreationally in California. Fishing of all types has impacted beach clams around the world, but long-lived, large intertidal species appear to be particularly vulnerable (McLachlan et al.

FIGURE 20.6 Higher on the beach, much of the food web is fueled by beach cast wrack, particularly kelps. The major consumers of wrack resources are beach hoppers (*Megalorchestia* spp.) that burrow in damp sand during the day and emerge at night to locate and feed on freshly deposited kelp. Photos: David Hubbard.

A Raylike stripes on the surface mark burrows of *Megalorchestia californiana* (inset shows a mature male perched on a stranded pneumatocyst of giant kelp).

B Burrows of other species are marked by irregular mounds, the inset shows two male *Megalorchestia corniculata* competing for a burrow that contains a female.

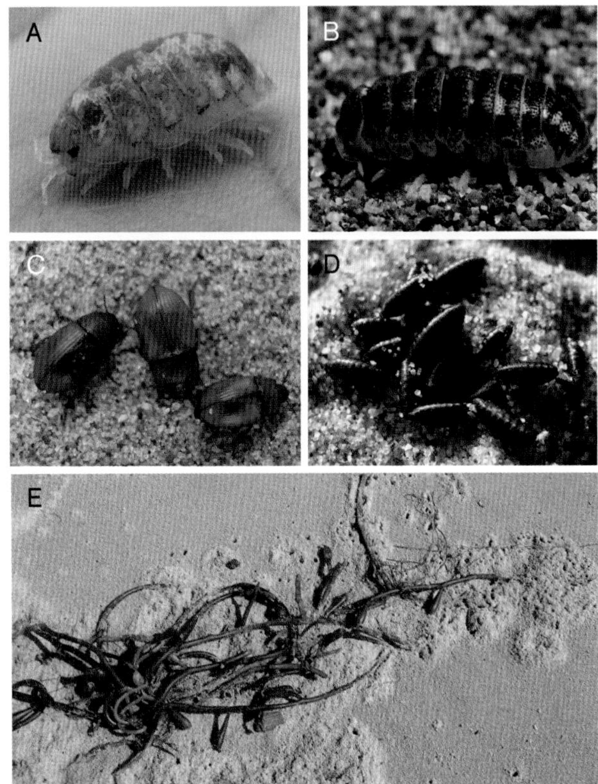

FIGURE 20.7 Kelp wrack inputs are rapidly processed by a wide variety of species found only on beaches. Photos: (A-C) David Hubbard, (D-E) Jenifer Dugan.

These include two species of oniscid isopods, (A) *Alloniscus perconvexus* and (B) *Tylos punctatus,* that burrow in damp sand above the twenty-four-hour high-tide line during daylight, emerging at night to feed on kelp and other organic material; (C) herbivorous tenebrionid beetles (*Phaleria rotundata*); (D) pupal cases of kelp flies (*Fucellia*) that feed on and develop in piles of kelp wrack with the timing of emergence related to spring lunar tides; and (E) only stipes (stems) of giant kelp (*Macrocystis pyrifera*), surrounded by the burrows of beach hoppers remain on the beach after all the kelp blades (leaves) on this frond were consumed overnight.

1996). The Pismo clam, which can live for more than fifty years and reach shell lengths of greater than six inches (Fitch 1950), is a classic example of this problem. This large, slow-moving BROADCAST SPAWNING clam might be considered the "abalone of the beach," although its decline preceded that of the abalone fishery by decades. In the face of declining landings, the commercial fishery for Pismo clams was closed in the state in 1948. Despite rolling closures, transplants, and changes in regulations on size and bag limits (Fitch 1950), populations of this highly desirable clam have never recovered to commercially harvestable levels.

Suspension-feeding mysids (*Archeomysis, Acanthomysis* spp.) can be extremely abundant in the swash zone, particularly in the northern region of the state (Nielsen et al. 2013). These swimming and burrowing crustaceans provide a major prey resource for fishes. In the midbeach zone, polychaetes in the family Spionidae that capture suspended particles with their long PALPS can be very abundant (Dauer 1985).

Wrack Feeders

In California more than 40% of the intertidal invertebrate species on a beach are directly associated with WRACK (Dugan et al. 2003). Intertidal invertebrate species richness is strongly correlated with wrack abundance on beaches that are relatively unmanipulated (Dugan et al. 2003). Strong spatial and temporal variation in wrack inputs (see Figure 20.3) affect intertidal community and food web structure and dynamics (e.g., Revell et al. 2011). Wrack-dependent invertebrates are typically most abundant and diverse where marine macroalgae, particularly kelps and kelp forests, grow on nearshore reefs (see Chapter 17, "Shallow Rocky Reefs and Kelp Forests"). Although kelps are greatly preferred as food sources for intertidal consumers, macrophyte wrack of all types (brown, red and green macroalgae, surfgrass, and eelgrass) functions as habitat for many of these invertebrates (Figures 20.6, 20.7).

FIGURE 20.8 Detritus that is pumped into the sand by waves and tides supports a number of burrowing deposit-feeders. The red polychaete (*Thoracophelia mucronata*), seen here excavated in a shovelful of sand at Scripps Beach, California, from the mid-beach at low tide, feeds like an earthworm, ingesting sand as it burrows through it and digesting organic material from on and between the sand grains. Photo: Nicholas Schooler.

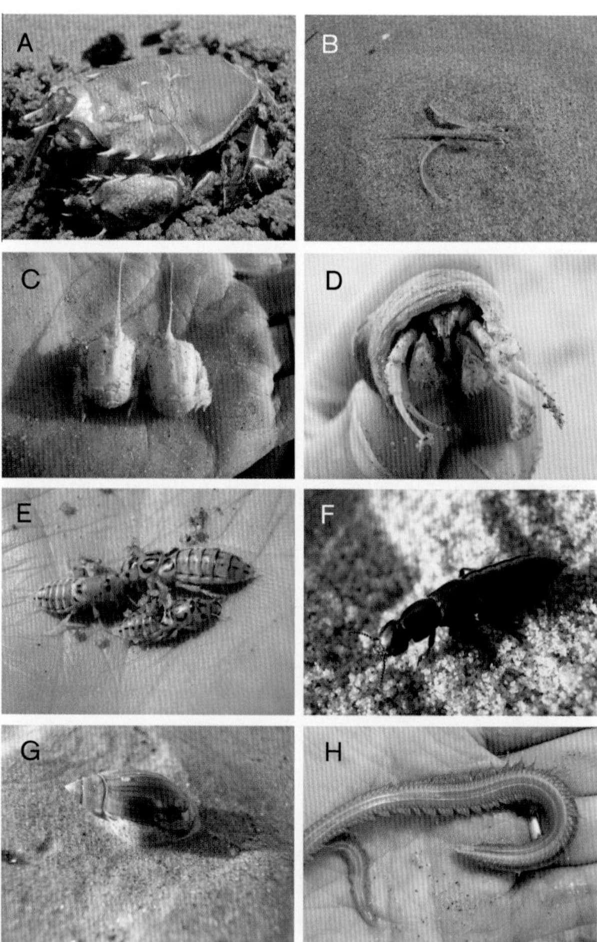

FIGURE 20.9 Invertebrate predators and scavengers feed on the abundant lower-beach suspension feeders and the wrack-dependent upper-beach species as well as carrion delivered by waves. Photos: (A–E, G–H) David Hubbard, (F) Jenifer Dugan.

(A) Spiny sand crabs (*Blepharipoda occidentalis*) on the surface and (B) in typical burrowed position with only eyes and antennae above sand, (C) porcelain sand crabs (*Lepidopa californica*), (D) the hermit crab (*Isocheles pilosus*), (E) pictured rove beetles (*Thinopinus pictus*), (F) black rove beetle (*Hadrotes crassus*), (G) the purple olive snail (*Callianax biplicata*), and (H) a predatory polychaete worm (*Nephtys californicus*).

The damp sand near the high tide strand line is preferred by many wrack consumers, such as beach hoppers, isopods, and some beetles that build temporary burrows in this zone during the day and emerge at night to feed on freshly deposited kelp wrack. Amphipods or beach hoppers (Talitridae *Megalorchestia spp.*) are dominant wrack consumers, greatly preferring kelps (e.g., *Macrocystis pyrifera, Egregia menziesii, Nereocystis luetkeana*) over other macrophytes (Lastra et al. 2008). These widespread, nocturnal amphipods can reach abundances of greater than 90,000 individuals m^{-1} on kelp-strewn beaches (Lastra et al. 2008). *Megalorchestia* is represented by six species in California, and individual beaches can support up to four species at a time (Schooler et al. in prep). Isopods (e.g., *Alloniscus perconvexus* and *Tylos punctatus*) build distinctive burrows in the vicinity of the high wrack line and can reach high abundance on some beaches (Hubbard et al. 2014). Other important wrack consumers include a great variety of intertidal insects, such as kelp and seaweed flies (*Fucellia* and *Coelopa* spp.), whose larvae feed on and develop in moist, aging piles of kelp wrack. Herbivorous beetles (*Phalaria rotundata, Epantius obscurus*, Tenebrionidae) and larvae of the intertidal weevil (*Emphyastes fucicola*) also feed on kelp wrack, while adult weevils are considered SAPROPHAGOUS.

As stranded wrack ages on the beach, it is colonized and fed on by a successional sequence of invertebrates starting with amphipods (Talitridae), followed by flies and specialized beetles (Yaninek 1980). Piles of wrack provide both food and essential microhabitat for beach invertebrates from the first night stranded on the beach until they disappear. Beaches with high wrack inputs support dense populations of these invertebrate consumers that provide prey to a high diversity and abundance of wintering and migratory shorebirds even during high tides (Dugan et al. 2003, Hubbard and Dugan 2003). Wrack-associated invertebrates and insects appear to be particularly important for short-billed shorebirds that search for prey visually, such as black-bellied plovers (*Pluvialis squatarola*) and snowy plovers (*Charadrius nivosus*) (Dugan et al. 2003). Snowy plovers are federally listed as a threatened species and are one of the few shorebirds that nest and rear chicks on sandy beaches in California.

Wrack consumers lack planktonic larvae and are direct-developing species that depend on the reproduction of resident populations. In addition, many important wrack consumers are flightless and do not swim. The disappearance of populations of two species of upper intertidal isopods (*Tylos punctatus* and *Alloniscus perconvexus*) along much of the coast of southern California during the past century illustrates the vulnerability of these types of animals to habitat alteration, loss and fragmentation from coastal development, and anthropogenic disturbance (Hubbard et al. 2014). The remaining populations are largely restricted to bluff-backed beaches where vehicle access is limited (Hubbard et al. 2014).

Deposit Feeders

The polychaete worm (*Thoracophelia*, formerly known as *Euzonus*) feeds on detrital particles flushed into the sand by waves

FIGURE 20.10 Birds feed on beach invertebrates from all levels of the food web across the entire intertidal zone. Shorebirds are particularly abundant on California beaches between fall migration (September) and spring migration (April), but the summer is the time when a rare shorebird, the threatened western snowy plover, nests on California beaches. Photos: (A–B) David Hubbard, (C) Callie Bowdish.

On a typical winter morning, (A) a southern California beach is covered by feeding birds including sanderlings (*Calidris alba*), marbled godwits (*Limosa fedoa*), willets (*Tringa semipalmata*), black-bellied plovers (*Pluvialis squatarola*), snowy egrets (*Egretta thula*), and ring-billed gulls (*Larus delawarensis*) (Isla Vista, California); (B) long-billed dowitchers (*Limnodromus scolopaceus*) feed on beach hoppers burrowed near kelp wrack (Isla Vista, California); and (C) a precocial snowy plover chick (*Charadrius nivosus*) feeds on a beach hopper (Sands Beach, California).

FIGURE 20.11 Beach-nesting fishes. Photos: (A) Karen Martin, (B) Doug Martin, (C) California Fish Bulletin.

In southern and central California, (A) California grunion (*Leuresthes tenuis*) surf in to shore to spawn near the high-tide mark during spring tides. (B) Close view of a male grunion approaching a female grunion burrowed in wet sand. In northern California, (C) a Native Californian using a dip net to catch surf smelt (*Hypomesus pretiosus*) in the 1930s at a beach in Humboldt County, California.

and tides. It can be extremely abundant in the midbeach zone (up to 40,000 individuals m^{-2}, McConnaughey and Fox 1949) (Figure 20.8). It is found in distinct beds marked by small, irregular holes on the surface of damp, cohesive sand (see Figure 20.7). *Thoracophelia* is represented by three congeners in California (*T. mucronata, T. dillonensis*, and *T. williamsi*) that can be found living together on some beaches (Law et al. 2013).

Carnivores

A diversity of predatory invertebrates along with predatory fish and birds occupy the upper trophic levels of beach food webs. Commonly encountered predatory invertebrates on beaches include crustaceans such as swimming crabs (*Portunus xantusii xantusii*), graceful Cancer crabs (*Cancer gracilis*), hermit crabs (*Isocheles pilosus*), and shrimp (*Lissocrangon stylirostris, Crangon nigricauda*) that prey on mysids in the surf zones; and scavenging crabs, such as the spiny sand crab (*Blepharipoda occidentalis*) and the porcelain sand crab (*Lepidopa californica*) in the surf and swash zones (Figure 20.9). Active, carnivorous polychaete worms, such as *Nephtys* spp. and the strong-jawed *Glycera* and *Hemipodia* spp., are found in the mid- and low intertidal zones. Fast-swimming scavenging isopods (*Excirolana* spp.) can be very abundant in the mid-intertidal, often preying on sand crab eggs as well as carrion and nipping the occasional human ankle. Around the wrack and high tide line and above, a variety of predatory beetles prowl the beach including tiger beetles (*Cicindela* spp., Carabidae), predaceous ground beetles (*Dyschirius marinus*), and many species of rove beetles (Staphylinidae, e.g., *Cafius* spp., *Aleochara* spp.) that prey on or parasitize kelp flies. The endemic intertidal rove beetles of California beaches include two large, flightless species (*Thinopinus pictus, Hadrotes crassus*) that prey exclusively on talitrid amphipods.

SHOREBIRDS are top predators that feed on all the types of intertidal invertebrates living on beaches and respond strongly to prey availability (Figure 20.10). Species richness and abundance of shorebirds are positively correlated with the availability of wrack and the diversity, biomass, and abundance of invertebrate prey, as well as tide, beach type, and width (Connors et al. 1981, Dugan et al. 2003, Dugan et al. 2008, Dugan and Hubbard in prep., Neumann et al. 2008, Nielsen et al. 2013). Beaches in developed regions, such as southern California, can provide birds with needed prey resources that are no longer available in coastal wetlands (Hubbard and Dugan 2003). Some SEABIRDS dive in the surf zone or swash to catch beach invertebrates. Sand crabs and spiny sand crabs are important prey for surf scoters. Gulls regularly feed on sand crabs, either by catching them on their own or stealing them from foraging shorebirds. Gulls also feed on Pismo clams, dropping them from great heights to smash their thick shells.

Nearshore fishes such as barred surfperch, redtail surfperch, yellowfin and spotfin croaker, and corbina feed on swash zone invertebrates including sand crabs and mysids (Love 1991) (Figure 20.11). These fish support important recreational and artisanal surf fisheries in the state (Fritzsche and Collier 2001, Valle and Oliphant 2001a and 2001b, O'Brien and Oliphant 2001), though population information for these fish is limited (see Chapter 35, "Marine Fisheries").

Sea otters and sea lions regularly prey on spiny and common sand crabs. Young sea otters may feed largely on spiny and common sand crabs as they learn to catch their own food. Pismo clams are also a favored prey of sea otters. A number of terrestrial vertebrates, including birds, mammals, and reptiles, feed on intertidal invertebrates in both the wrack line and the swash zone. Terrestrial birds that regularly feed on beaches include passerines such as barn swallows (*Hirundo rustica*) and cliff swallows (*Petrochelidon* spp.), black and Say's phoebes (*Sayornis* spp.), American pipits (*Anthus rubescens*), kingbirds (*Tyrannus* spp.), savannah sparrows (*Passerculus* spp., including Belding's savannah sparrow, *P. rostratus/sandwichensis beldingi*, an endangered songbird), and Brewer's blackbirds (*Euphagus cyanocephalus*). Raptors including peregrine falcons (*Falco peregrinus*) hunt shorebirds on beaches, while scavengers such as turkey vultures (*Cathartes aura*), crows and ravens (*Corvus* spp.), as well as a variety of gulls and now a few reintroduced California condors (*Gymnogyps californianus*) regularly feed on the carcasses of marine mammals washed up on beaches. Mallard ducks (*Anas platyrhynchos*) have recently been observed dabbling in the swash zone for sand crabs in central and southern California (Lafferty et al. 2013). Mammals such as California ground squirrels (*Otospermophilus beecheyi*), raccoons (*Procyon lotor*), feral pigs (*Sus scrofa*), gray foxes (*Urycyon cinereoargenteus*), and the endangered dwarf island fox (*Urocyon littoralis*) prey on a variety of the intertidal invertebrates inhabiting California beaches.

Ecosystem Functions

Along with their unique biodiversity and productive food webs, beaches provide ecological functions and services not supplied other open coast ecosystems (Schlacher et al. 2007). These include filtering large volumes of seawater, accumulating and storing sand, wave dissipation and buffering, processing of organic matter, recycling of imported nutrients, support for coastal fisheries, and pupping, nesting, and foraging habitat for endangered wildlife species. Beaches can filter large volumes of seawater (~10 m^3 $m^{-1}d^{-1}$ for intermediate type beaches) pumped into the porous beach by the action of waves and tides trapping particulates in the sand (McLachlan 1989, McLachlan and Turner 1994, McLachlan and Brown 2006). Particles trapped in the sand matrix include detritus, phytoplankton, wrack particles, microorganisms, pollutants, and other particular organic matter. These organic materials become available for biogeochemical processing and transformation in the beach sand.

Beaches are energy sinks that function as buffers between waves and the coastline. Stored sand on beaches, in sand bars, and in dunes plays an important role in absorbing and dissipating wave energy, even during extreme events (e.g., storms, tsunamis). Wide beaches with high volumes of sand can reduce wave energy more effectively than narrow sand-starved beaches. During storms, sand eroded from the beach is also carried off the shore to form sand bars in the shallow nearshore zone. As waves break on these nearshore sand bars, they lose wave energy and arrive at the beach with less power, mediating further erosion.

Processing of imported organic matter, such as phytoplankton and marine macrophyte wrack, by intertidal consumers and microbial communities is an important ecosystem function of beach ecosystems that contributes to nearshore nutrient cycling (Dugan et al. 2011). Beaches were described as "great digestive and incubating systems" (Pearse et al. 1942). Wrack inputs and processing represent an important nutrient and energetic linkage between the marine and intertidal beach and dune environments (Dugan et al. 2011, Dugan and Hubbard 2010) with implications for conservation and management of adjacent coastal ecosystems. Nutrient cycling through the processing of wrack on beaches is mediated by intertidal invertebrates that quickly consume stranded drift macrophytes, breaking them down to particles (Lastra et al. 2008) that are then available to interstitial meiofaunal and microbial communities where turnover and remineralization are rapid (Griffiths et al. 1983, Koop et al. 1982, Koop and Lucas 1983, Dugan et al. 2011). Dense populations of amphipods are estimated to consume approximately 50% of the 42 kg m^{-1} $month^{-1}$ of fresh kelp wrack (*Macrocystis*) deposited on a southern California beach during the summer (Lastra et al. 2008). Recent results suggest that processing and subsequent mineralization of wrack on beaches may be a source of nutrients to nearshore primary producers such as seagrasses and kelps (Dugan et al. 2011). Wrack also traps wind-blown sand and can promote the formation of hummocks and embryo dunes and provides nutrients that support the colonization of native dune plants (Dugan and Hubbard 2010, Nordstrom 2012).

Shorebirds exemplify wildlife that use California beaches as wintering and migration habitat. The abundant intertidal invertebrates of beaches provide prey for a remarkably rich and abundant assemblage of wintering and migratory shorebirds, with more than thirty species observed at a single beach in southern California (Hubbard and Dugan 2003) (see Figure 20.10). Many species spend the majority of each year (about eight months) on California beaches, particularly in the south and central regions, leaving to migrate to breeding grounds for a few months in spring and returning by late summer or early fall. Sanderlings (*Calidris alba*) make up the majority of shorebirds (more than 50%) on many California beaches (e.g., Hubbard and Dugan 2003, Neumann et al. 2008, Nielsen et al. 2013) and can often be seen in large flocks running back and forth in the swash zone (see Chapter 20 cover figure and Figure 20.10). A variety of other shorebird species are commonly encountered on California beaches (Hubbard and Dugan 2003, Neumann et al. 2008, Nielsen et al. 2013). Although only a few species are resident breeders (Western snowy plover, killdeer [*Charadrius vociferous*], and American black oystercatcher [*Haematopus bachmani*]), annual means exceeding 100 birds km^{-1} have been observed on southern and central California beaches (Hubbard and Dugan 2003, Dugan and Hubbard in prep.). These values are among the highest ever reported globally for shorebirds on temperate beaches (Hubbard and Dugan 2003). Shorebird use of beaches is characterized by high spatial and temporal variability, including strong seasonal patterns (see Figure 20.3). Peak values for single censuses can exceed 1,000 birds km^{-1}, but the abundance of shorebirds on California beaches can vary by over an order of magnitude among beaches and across seasons and years (see Figure 20.3) (Hubbard and Dugan 2003, Revell et al. 2011, Colwell and Sundeen 2000, Shuford et al. 1989, Neumann et al. 2008, Dugan and Hubbard in prep.). Collectively, the role of beach ecosystems in supporting wintering shorebirds on the California coast may be more important than is generally appreciated. The fact that populations of many species of shorebirds are declining in North America (Bart et al. 2007, Morrison et al. 2001, 2006) highlights the need to conserve coastal habitat and resources required by these wildlife, including sandy beach ecosystems.

The uppermost zones of beaches located between the average reach of high tides and the toe of the vegetated foredune are particularly important for wildlife that breed on beaches. Nesting birds and mammal rookeries require beach and/or dune habitat relatively undisturbed by human activity, sparsely vegetated, and not regularly swept by waves during the nesting or pupping season. The threatened Western snowy plover and California least tern (*Sterna antillarum browni*) nest on open coast and sheltered beaches (Lehman 1994, Page et al. 1995) using distinctly different strategies to protect their shallow nests and chicks. Least terns nest in colonies on beaches and protect their nests and chicks by mobbing predators. In contrast, snowy plovers (and killdeer) depend on CRYPSIS to hide their shallow nest scrapes and chicks (see Figure 20.10). Within a few hours of hatching, the precocial chicks of snowy plovers (and killdeer) permanently leave the nest to follow their parents, finding their own food (Page et al. 1995). These tiny chicks are particularly dependent on wrack-associated amphipods, isopods, and insects.

The uppermost intertidal zones of open sandy beaches represent critical spawning habitat for beach-nesting fish, such as the California grunion (*Leuresthes tenuis*) and day and night smelt species (Figure 20.11). These fish surf up the beach to bury their eggs in the sand near the high tide line during spring high tides. After incubating in the moist, warm sand for two weeks or more, the eggs hatch as the waves hit the nests during subsequent spring high tides (e.g., Thompson 1919, Smyder et al. 2002, Martin 2015).

A diversity of pinnipeds, including northern elephant seals, California sea lions, northern fur seals, and harbor seals, pup and raise their young on sandy beaches in rookeries throughout the state (LeBoeuf and Bonnell 1980). Northern elephant seals breed in sizable colonies on the mainland beaches at Año Nuevo and Piedras Blancas and on many beaches of the northern Channel Islands. Small harbor seal rookeries are also present on the mainland coast and islands. California sea lions and northern fur seals breed in large beach colonies on San Miguel Island at the mouth of the Santa Barbara Channel (northern Channel Islands). Finally, fish and invertebrates of sandy surf zones and the low intertidal zones of beaches provide prey resources for a wealth of seabirds. For many of these seabirds, beaches also serve as roosting habitat—a function that is important and underappreciated in seabird conservation. Safe roosting areas on isolated beaches may be particularly essential for coastal diving birds, such as cormorants and pelicans, that need to dry their feathers regularly.

Human Impacts and Influences

A number of widespread human activities, including watershed and coastal structures and management practices and recreation, can significantly affect habitat and community structure, biodiversity, and function of beach ecosystems (Defeo et al. 2009). In southern California the large-scale human alteration of beaches includes a 50% reduction in sediment supply from damming rivers (Orme et al. 2011, Griggs 2005a), armoring of 27% of the coastline (Griggs 1998, 2005b), beach filling totaling more than 200 million cubic meters of sand (Orme et al. 2011), and grooming of 45% of the beaches (Dugan et al. 2003) (Figure 20.12). Recreational use of California beaches is intense; for example, in the Santa Monica Bay area and the nearby coastline of north Los Angeles County, between 50 million and 60 million visits to beaches are made annually (Dwight et al. 2007). Driving in the intertidal zone, including the recreational use of ORVs (off-road vehicles) at designated beaches and the widespread use of public safety vehicles, crushes and kills beach invertebrates (Schooler et al. in prep) and wildlife.

The ecological disturbance of sandy beach ecosystems by coastal management practices can be remarkably intense in urban areas of southern California. For example, mechanical beach grooming and raking with heavy equipment—a practice that removes all wrack and disturbs the sand of the beach to a depth of more than 6 inches—is conducted as often as twice a day on beaches of Santa Monica Bay in Los Angeles, making beaches the most frequently disturbed ecosystem in the state. Some beaches have been groomed regularly for more than forty years. The loss of wrack subsidies from beach grooming is associated with substantial and widespread alteration in macrofauna community structure of sandy beach ecosystems in southern California (Dugan et al. 2003). This has resulted in a significant reduction in prey resources available to shorebirds over more than 160 kilometers of the California coast (Dugan et al. 2003). The mechanical disturbance of beach grooming also kills grunion eggs as they incubate in the sand near the high tide line (Martin et al. 2006). Beach grooming is also associated with loss of dune vegetation and habitats and their buffering function in southern California (Dugan and Hubbard 2010).

Beach ecosystems are strongly affected by active interventions or coastal defense efforts that attempt to prevent shoreline retreat or change. Approaches to coastal defense can be soft (beach fills or nourishment) or hard (armoring) (Komar 1998), both with substantial ecological and physical consequences for beach ecosystems (e.g., Griggs 2005, Peterson et al. 2006 and 2014, Dugan and Hubbard 2006, Dugan et al. 2008). Societal responses to beach erosion and shoreline retreat have relied heavily on coastal armoring for centuries (Charlier et al. 2005, Nordstrom 2000). During the past century approximately 130 miles of California's coast were armored, and coastal armoring increased 400% between 1971 and 1992 (Griggs 1998), a trend expected to accelerate. These shoreline alterations have reduced the width of the beach over large stretches of coastline in California (Revell and Griggs 2007). Shoreline retreat and erosion coupled with coastal armoring causes a disproportionate reduction (and in many cases the complete loss) of dry upper beach and high tide line habitat relative to wet and saturated lower beach habitats (Dugan and Hubbard 2006, Dugan et al. 2008 and 2012). This directly eliminates the zone of wrack deposition and retention, removing habitat and food for wrack-associated species (Dugan et al. 2008, Jaramillo et al. 2012). Lower species richness and abundance of shorebirds (2 and 3.7 times lower, respectively) have been reported on armored beaches by Dugan and Hubbard (2006) and Dugan et al. (2008). The abundance of roosting seabirds also declined strongly in front of armoring structures (gulls 4.8 times, seabirds 3.3 times lower) (Dugan et al. 2008, 2012).

Soft coastal defense in the form of beach filling has been conducted on a massive regional scale for years in south-

FIGURE 20.12 Human impacts to beach ecosystems are many and occur on a variety of scales, frequencies, and intensities. Photos: (A) Eduardo Jaramillo, (B, F) Jenifer Dugan, (C–E) David Hubbard.

Widespread habitat loss is caused by coastal armoring with engineered seawalls and revetments, including (A) seawalls in the intertidal zone (Summerland, California) and (B) revetment/seawall combinations such as this large structure in Pacifica, California.

(C) Beach filling or nourishment can provide beach space for recreation, but this intensive disturbance defaunates the intertidal zone, reducing prey resources for birds and fish for extended periods (Goleta Beach, California).

(D) Likewise, mortality of intertidal animals caused by seasonal scraping of the intertidal zone to create winter sand berms seaward of homes and infrastructure can be substantial (Carpinteria, California).

(E) The widespread practice of beach grooming, raking, and sifting with heavy equipment to remove trash and wrack is conducted weekly on many beaches and up to twice a day on popular beaches in Santa Monica Bay, disturbing beach ecosystems more frequently than any agricultural activity (Carpinteria, California).

(F) Vehicle driving in the intertidal zone, including the recreational use of ORVs, occurs at selected beaches, and the widespread use of public safety vehicles, crushes and kills beach invertebrates and wildlife (Oceano Dunes, California).

ern California (Flick 1993, Orme et al. 2011) with little to no scientific evaluation of the direct or cumulative ecological effects on beach ecosystems (Peterson and Bishop 2005). Despite a dearth of information from California, the ecological impacts of beach filling on beach biota are severe, often resulting in 100% mortality of resident fauna (Speybroek et al. 2006) with lasting effects propagating up the food web to shorebirds (Peterson et al. 2006). Recovery of important invertebrate species can take years (Peterson et al. 2000, 2006, 2014). Use of fill sediments finer or coarser than the native beach sand causes even greater and longer lasting ecological impacts to biota (Peterson et al. 2006 and 2014, Speybroek et al. 2006, Viola et al. 2014).

Sea level rise and other predicted effects of climate change, including increased storminess, are expected to intensify pressures on beach ecosystems by increasing rates of shoreline erosion and retreat and degrading habitat (Nordstrom 2000, Slott et al. 2006), especially where coastal land uses and development constrain shoreline evolution and retreat. The direction of responses of beach ecosystems to sea level rise may be similar to that observed in episodic El Niño Southern Oscillation (ENSO) events (Revell et al. 2011) although the time scale will differ greatly. The habitat loss, fragmentation, and alteration resulting from climate change carry profound ecological implications, as beaches become narrower, steeper, and coarser and as once continuous stretches of sandy beach are interrupted by submerged coast or drowned beaches. Although beaches are often assumed to be robust, disturbance-adapted ecosystems, strong and lasting negative responses suggest that beaches are in fact sensitive to anthropogenic pressures and impacts and sometimes slow to recover (McLachlan et al. 1996, Hubbard et al. 2014, Peterson et al. 2014). Bounded by land and sea, sandy beach ecosystems are increasingly squeezed between the impacts of coastal development and the manifestations of climate change in the sea (Schlacher et al. 2007, Nordstrom 2000, Defeo et al. 2009, Dugan et al. 2010). Human alterations limit the ability of beach ecosystems to adjust to changes in shoreline stability (Clark 1996), sea level rise, and erosion caused by climate change.

Conservation and Restoration Strategies

Conserving beaches first requires recognizing beaches as ecosystems in coastal policy and management. The fact that a number of sandy beaches are now included as part of a broad network of marine protected areas (MPAs) across the state, protecting harvested species, such as clams and fish, in many regions is a major step forward. However, the majority of these MPAs extend only up to the MEAN HIGH TIDE line, meaning many of the highly mobile beach biota, including a wide range of intertidal invertebrates as well as nesting California grunion, regularly use areas that are outside the MPA boundaries. The lack of restrictions on impacts, such as beach grooming, vehicle use, or beach filling, in current MPA regulations is also of concern for some beaches. Nonetheless, the beaches now in MPAs could be used to evaluate responses of beach ecosystems to increased protection from disturbance.

Changes in disturbance directly linked to management practices and recreation, such as beach grooming practices and vehicle use, offer low-cost opportunities for conservation in California and elsewhere in the world. For example, an approach that designates beach areas to be left undisturbed by grooming from their landward boundaries to the sea could provide much needed restoration opportunities on developed coastlines. This approach, if interspersed with groomed areas, could conserve biodiversity in designated areas while allowing traditional recreational and tourism to continue in others.

As sea level rises, beaches with enough space to evolve and retreat landward combined with a sufficient sand supply will be able to adjust to changing water levels and maintain ecosystem integrity. Where retreat is constrained by resistant cliffs or armoring and infrastructure, beach ecosystems and their biota and functions will disappear as sea level rises. This is of particular concern for endemic biota already restricted to bluff-backed beaches in some littoral cells (Hubbard et al. 2014). Promoting the use of ample setbacks for new coastal development and identifying locations and opportunities where infrastructure can be removed as part of "managed retreat" to allow beaches to evolve and migrate landward can increase opportunities to maintain and conserve the diversity and ecosystem function of beaches as sea level rises. Moving or abandoning infrastructure to allow room for coastal retreat is already part of the management strategy for California State Parks. One of the best California examples of the use of managed retreat to restore open coast beach and dune ecosystems is a 2010 project at Surfer's Point near the mouth of the Ventura River, in Ventura County (http://surferspoint.org/). The Surfer's Point project removed a rock revetment and relocated a parking lot and bike path to give the beach 20 meters of space to migrate landward. The project also restored dunes and coastal strand vegetation in the area where the parking lot was removed.

Summary

Composed of sand and biota that are constantly moving across and along the shoreline, sandy beaches are among the most dynamic ecosystems in the world. Dominating open coastlines of California, beaches are iconic assets highly prized for recreation and coastal economies. Less appreciated is the fact that beaches are ecosystems that harbor unique biodiversity, support productive food webs, and provide irreplaceable ecosystem functions and services to society. These include filtering vast volumes of seawater and buffering the land from storm waves. Although their characteristic, highly mobile burrowing animals are often invisible to a casual visitor, California beaches can be hotspots of intertidal biodiversity. Subsidies of kelp and phytoplankton from other marine ecosystems to beach food webs fuel intense biological productivity capable of supporting a high abundance of wildlife, rapid processing of organic inputs, and high rates of nutrient remineralization. However, ongoing disturbance and escalating threats to beach ecosystems pose formidable challenges in California and elsewhere.

Groomed beaches in urban areas are subject to the most intense disturbance regime of any ecosystem in the state. Beaches are increasingly trapped in a "coastal squeeze" between urbanization and effects of sea level rise from climate change. Societal responses to beach erosion and retreat rely largely on "soft" (beach filling) or "hard" (shoreline armoring) engineering that both affect the biodiversity, food webs, and functioning of beaches as ecosystems. The widespread but unsupported assumption that beach ecosystems recover very rapidly from all forms of disturbance is used to justify numerous management actions. Increased recognition and understanding of sandy beaches as vulnerable and threatened ecosystems are needed to promote the conservation and protection of these dynamic ecosystems on the edge of a warming and rising sea.

Acknowledgments

We dedicate this chapter to Betsy Hubbard for decades of inspiration and encouragement. We thank Karina Nielsen and an anonymous reviewer for their helpful comments on the manuscript. We are grateful to Karen and Doug Martin of Pepperdine University, Shane Anderson, Callie Bowdish and Nicholas Schooler of the University of California at Santa Barbara, and Dan Ayres of the Washington Department of Fish and Wildlife for allowing us to use their photographs in this chapter. Financial support was provided by the National Science Foundation's Long-Term Ecological Research program (OCE-1232779) (JED) and by the California Sea Grant Project R/MPA-24 through the California Ocean Protection Council.

Recommended Reading

Griggs, G., K. Patsch, and L. Savoy. 2005. Living with the changing California coast. University of California Press, Berkeley, California.

McLachlan, A., and A. C. Brown. 2006. The ecology of sandy shores. Academic Press, Elsevier, London, UK.

Nordstrom, K. F. 2000. Beaches and dunes of developed coasts. Cambridge University Press, Cambridge, UK.

Pilkey, O. H., W. J. Neal, J. T. Kelley, and J.A.G. Cooper. 2011. The world's beaches: A global guide to the science of the shoreline. University of California Press, Berkeley, California.

Pilkey, O.H, and J. A. G. Cooper. 2014. The Last Beach. Duke University Press. Durham, North Carolina.

Glossary

ALLOCHTHONOUS Originating from outside the system.

BEDLOAD The portion of the total sediment in transport that is carried by intermittent contact with the seabed by rolling, sliding, and bouncing.

BERM A raised ridge of sand found at high tide, or storm tide marks on a beach.

BERM CREST The highest portion of the ridge of sand near the high tide line on a beach.

BOTTOM-UP EFFECTS In reference to food webs, influences on the system that are driven by nutrient supply or productivity rather than top-down such as predators.

BREAKWATER A human-made armoring structure designed to absorb the energy of the waves before they reach the shoreline.

BROADCAST SPAWNING Releasing of gametes (sperm and eggs) into open water for external fertilization with no subsequent parental care.

CHLOROPHYLL-*a* A pigment that is essential for photosynthesis; extracts of chlorophyll-*a* from water samples can be used as estimates of phytoplankton quantities and productivity.

COASTAL STRAND VEGETATION The plant community between the high tide line and the foredune.

CRENULATE SPIT The term describing a spit that forms at the end of a beach with a wavy or scalloped shoreline form.

CROSS-SHORE In a direction perpendicular to the shoreline; also termed "shore-normal."

CRYPSIS The ability of an organism to avoid observation or detection by other organisms using methods including camouflage, nocturnal or subterranean lifestyle, transparency, and mimicry.

CUSPS Rhythmic alongshore features of soft sandy shorelines that consist of repeated arc-shaped patterns of horns pointing seaward alternating with concave bays. Cusps represent a combination of constructive and destructive coastal processes. The spacing of bays and horns in cusps is related to wave energy and is often fairly uniform with intervals of 20 to 60 meters. Megacusps associated with strong waves and rip circulation with spacing of >200 meters can form on some beaches. A cusp horn is the pointed seaward projections of sand on the shoreline that separate cusp bays (the concavity in the shoreline between cusp horns).

DIATOM Unicellular phytoplankton that are enclosed within a cell wall made of silica (hydrated silicon dioxide) called a frustule. Diatoms are among the most common types of phytoplankton and are important primary producers within the food chain.

DIRECT DEVELOPMENT Lacking any planktonic larval stages, direct developing species have very low dispersal potential during larval development. The reproduction of resident individuals is thus important in maintaining populations at a given location. These larvae are also known as "crawl-away larvae," since forms with this type of development may have larvae crawl away from the brooding female or the egg mass.

DISSIPATIVE Refers to surf zones and beach systems with waves that break far from the intertidal zone and dissipate their force progressively along wide surf zones that are flat in profile. Dissipative beaches tend to be wide and have fine sediments and flat slopes.

DOWNCOAST OR UPCOAST Refers to the location of a beach with respect to the prevailing littoral current and a feature that affects sand transport and supply. These features can include a rocky point, a sand source or sink, or a barrier, such as a harbor or a groin.

EL NIÑO Also termed the El Niño Southern Oscillation or ENSO, this is expressed as a band of anomalously warm ocean water temperatures and atmospheric anomalies that periodically develop off the Pacific coast of South America at intervals of two to seven years. Its effects often extend to North America and can be associated with strong climatic effects in California, including altered storm tracks, increased storm intensities, higher sea levels, and increased precipitation.

FOREDUNE A dune ridge that runs parallel to the shore of an ocean, lake, bay, or estuary. In active dune systems the foredunes are located closest to the sea or other body of water.

GROIN A human-made armoring structure that is placed perpendicular to the shoreline to retain sand by stopping or slowing the littoral transport of sand along the shoreline.

HIGH TIDE STRAND The driftline or tidal high water mark, a shoreline feature where the deposition of buoyant debris and the boundary of damp sand marks the highest extent of tides and wave run-up.

INFAUNA Organisms that live within the sediments rather than on the surface.

JETTY A human-made armoring structure that extends across the beach from the mouth of a harbor, lagoon, or river into deeper water. Jetties are often placed in parallel pairs and stabilize entrance channels needed for shipping.

LAMINAR Describes flow in which fluid moves in parallel layers, without disruption among the layers; typically this occurs at lower velocities than more turbulent flow patterns.

LITTORAL CURRENT A current located in the littoral zone (an indefinite zone extending seaward from the shoreline to just beyond the surf zone) that generally moves parallel to the shoreline. This current is generated by waves breaking at an angle to the shoreline and is also called the longshore current.

LITTORAL TRANSPORT The movement of sedimentary material by waves and currents in the littoral zone. Commonly used as synonymous with longshore transport. Often expressed as a rate of volume per year.

LOG SPIRAL A type of beach that develops in the shelter of a prominent headland. These logarithmic spiral shapes in map view may also be called "half heart" or "crenulate" or "headland bays."

LONGSHORE In a direction parallel to the coast.

MACROPHYTE Aquatic plant large enough to be seen without magnification that grows in or near water.

MEAN HIGH TIDE The average elevation of the high tides.

MEGA-CUSP Embayments in the shoreline (usually several hundred meters long) associated with rip currents.

MEGALOPA/POSTLARVAE The final developmental stage of a decapod crab before it becomes a juvenile crab. This stage follows the larval stages.

MORPHODYNAMIC SCALE A description of the shape of a beach resulting from the interaction of the wave regime with the available sand. This scale encompasses beach states across the spectrum from fully dissipative to fully reflective conditions.

MYSID Shrimplike crustaceans in the superorder Peracarida that brood their young.

NEAP Designating a tide that occurs just after the first and third quarters of the moon, when there is least difference between high tide and low tide levels.

PACIFIC DECADAL OSCILLATION A long-lived El Niño–like pattern of Pacific climate variability with cycles extending over twenty to thirty years that is detected as warm or cool surface waters in the Pacific Ocean, north of 20°N.

PALP An oral appendage in some invertebrates that plays roles in sensory perception, feeding, and locomotion.

PINNIPEDS Semiaquatic marine mammals including seals, sea lions, fur seals, and walrus.

PLANKTON A diverse group of organisms that live in the water column and cannot swim against a current. Phytoplankton refers to photosynthetic organisms; zooplankton refers to animals that live in the plankton for all or part of their lives.

REFLECTIVE Refers to beaches with narrow, shoaling surf zones, steep slopes, and coarse sand, with waves break abruptly on the intertidal zone.

RIP CURRENT A seaward flow of water from near the shore, typically through the surf line. Rip currents are usually generated by the energy of breaking waves and develop through gaps in sand bars in the surf zone.

RUNNEL A shallow trough or low point in the beach that runs parallel to the shoreline where water can pool temporarily. On wide flat beaches with moderate wave energy, runnels can form in a series separated by ridges. Runnels can also develop landward of a berm that has a backslope from its crest.

SAPROPHAGOUS Feeding on dead or decaying organic matter.

SCARP A steep abrupt feature on the beach face that is caused by erosion.

SEABIRD Birds that have adapted to life within the marine environment, including gulls, terns, cormorants, pelicans, and petrels.

SEDIMENT BUDGET The balance between sediment inputs and losses from the coastal littoral system.

SHOREBIRD Birds that are members of the order Charadriiformes. These include plovers, stilts, avocets, oystercatchers, and sandpipers. These birds feed by wading in shallow waters or at waterlines and probing into the water or sand for insects, polychaetes, mollusks, and crustaceans. Shorebirds are found frequently on beaches, marshes, wetlands, mudflats, rocky, and inland shores. However, shorebirds are not confined to these areas and many can also be found in open fields and agricultural areas near water sources.

SPRING TIDES Designating a tide that occurs near full or new moons, when there is maximum difference between high tide and low tide levels. These tides occur when the moon and sun are in alignment.

SUBMARINE CANYON A steep-sided valley cut into the sea floor of the continental slope, sometimes extending well onto the continental shelf.

SUPRALITTORAL Coastal zone above the reach of the tides.

SURF ZONE The region of breaking waves that forms near the shoreline.

SUSPENSION-FEEDING Describing animals that obtain their food from material carried in the water column, often by filter-feeding.

SWASH CLIMATE The characteristics of a beach's swash zone in which a turbulent layer of water washes up on a beach after a wave has broken, such as length, period, and speed.

UPWELLING An oceanographic phenomenon that involves the wind-driven movement of dense, cooler, and usually nutrient-rich water from deeper depths to the ocean surface, replacing the warmer, usually nutrient-depleted surface water. This nutrient-rich upwelled water stimulates the growth and reproduction of primary producers such as phytoplankton. Due to the biomass of phytoplankton and presence of cool water in these regions, upwelling zones can be identified by cool sea surface temperatures (SST) and high concentrations of chlorophyll-*a*.

WATER TABLE (OR AQUIFER) The underground layer of water-bearing unconsolidated sediments (gravel, sand, or silt).

WATER TABLE OUTCROP The location where the water table emerges on the beach face; also called the effluent line.

WRACK Floating material, such as macroalgae and seagrass, that is deposited on the beach.

References

Alexander, R. R., R. J. Stanton, and J. R. Dodd. 1993. Influence of sediment grain size on the burrowing of bivalves: Correlation with distribution and stratigraphic persistence of selected Neogene clams. Palaios 8:289–303.

Arntz, W. E., T. Brey, J. Tarazona, and A Robles. 1987. Changes in the structure of a shallow sandy-beach community in Peru during an El Niño event. South African Journal of Marine Science 5:645–658.

Barbour, M. G., and A. F. Johnson. 1988. Beach and dune. Pages 223–261 in M. G. Barbour and J. Major, editors. Terrestrial vegetation of California. California Native Plant Society Special Publication 9. Sacramento, California.

Barbour, M. G., T. M. DeJong, and A. F. Johnson. 1976. Synecology of beach vegetation along the Pacific Coast of the United States of America: A first approximation. Journal of Biogeography 3:55–69.

Barbour, M. G., T. M. DeJong, and B. M. Pavlik 1985. Marine beach and dune plant communities. Pages 296–322. B. F. Chabot and H.A. Mooney, editors. Physiological ecology of North American plant communities. Chapman and Hall, New York, New York.

Barnard, P. L., and J. A. Warrick. 2010. Dramatic beach and nearshore morphological changes due to extreme flooding at a wave-dominated river mouth. Marine Geology 271:131–148.

Barnard, P. L., D. L. Revell, D. Hoover, J. Warrick, J. Brocatus, A. E. Draut, P. Dartnell, E. Elias, N. Mustain, P. E. Hart, and H. F. Ryan. 2009. Coastal processes study of Santa Barbara and Ventura County, California. U.S. Geological Survey Open-File Report 2009–1029. <http://pubs.usgs.gov/of/2009/1029/>. Accessed January 2014.

Barnard, P. L., D. M. Hubbard, and J. E. Dugan. 2012. Sand dynamics on an alongshore-dominated littoral cell: Correlating a seventeen-year single-point time series with regional patterns, Santa Barbara, California, USA. Geomorphology 139–140:588–598.

Barnard, P. L., J. Allan, J. E. Hansen, G. M. Kaminsky, P. Ruggiero, and A. Doria. 2011. The impact of the 2009–10 El Niño Modoki on U.S. West Coast beaches. Geophysical Research Letters 38 (L13604).

Bart, J., S. Brown, B. Harrington, and R.I.G. Morrison. 2007. Survey trends of North American shorebirds: Population declines or shifting distributions. Journal of Avian Biology 38: 73–82.

Bascom, W. 1980. Waves and beaches. Anchor Books, Garden City, New York.

Bretz, C. K., T. J. Manouki, and R. G. Kvitek. 2002. *Emerita analoga* (Stimpson) as an indicator species for paralytic shellfish poisoning toxicity along the California coast. Toxicon 40:1189–1196.

Burnett, R. 1971. DDT Residues: Distribution of concentrations in *Emerita analoga* (Stimpson) along coastal California. Science 74:606–608.

Charlier, R. H., M.C.P. Chaineux, and S. Morcos. 2005. Panorama of the history of coastal protection. Journal of Coastal Research 21:79–111.

Clark, J. R. 1996. Coastal zone management handbook. CRC Press, Boca Raton, Florida.

Coe, W. C. 1955. Ecology of the bean clam, *Donax gouldii* on the coast of southern California. Ecology 36: 512–514.

———. 1953. Resurgent populations of littoral marine invertebrates and their dependence on ocean currents and tidal currents. Ecology 34:225–229.

Colwell, M. A., and K. D. Sundeen. 2000. Shorebird distributions on ocean beaches of northern California. Journal of Field Ornithology 71:1–14.

Connors, P. G., J. P. Myers, C.S.W. Connors, and F. A. Pitelka. 1981. Interhabitat movements by sanderlings in relation to foraging profitability and the tidal cycle. Auk 98:49–64.

Dauer, D. M. 1983. Functional morphology and feeding behavior of *Scolelepis squamata* (Polychaeta: Spionidae). Marine Biology 77:279–285.

Dawson, M. N., P. H. Barber, L. I. Gonzales, R. J. Toonen, J. E. Dugan, R. K. Grosberg. 2011. Phylogeography of *Emerita analoga* (Crustacea, Decapoda, Hippidae), an eastern Pacific Ocean sand crab with long-lived pelagic larvae. Journal of Biogeography 38:1600–1612.

Defeo, O., A. McLachlan, D. Schoeman, T. Schlacher, J. E. Dugan, A. Jones, M. Lastra, and F. Scapini. 2009. Threats to sandy beach ecosystems: A review. Estuarine Coastal and Shelf Science 81:1–12.

Dugan J. E. 1990. Geographic and temporal variation in the life history, growth, and reproductive biology of the sand crab, Emerita analoga (Stimpson). Ph.D. dissertation. University of California, Santa Barbara. 329 pp.

Dugan J. E., and D. M. Hubbard. 2010. Loss of coastal strand habitat in southern California: The role of beach grooming. Estuaries and Coasts 33:67–77.

———. 2006. Ecological responses to coastal armoring on exposed sandy beaches. Shore and Beach 74(1):10–16.

———. 1996. Local variation in populations of the sand crab, *Emerita analoga* on sandy beaches in southern California. Revista Chilena de Historia Natural 69:579–588.

———. In prep. Shorebirds as indicators of beach ecosystem diversity and function.

Dugan, J. E., A. M. Wenner, and D. M. Hubbard. 1991. Geographic variation in the reproductive biology of the sand crab, *Emerita analoga* (Stimpson), on the California coast. Journal of Experimental Marine Biology and Ecology 150:63–81.

Dugan, J. E., D. M. Hubbard, and A. M. Wenner. 1994. Geographic variation in life history in populations of the sand crab, *Emerita analoga* Stimpson, on the California coast: Relationships to environmental variables. Journal of Experimental Marine Biology and Ecology 181:255–278.

Dugan, J. E., D. M. Hubbard, and B. J. Quigley. 2013. Beyond beach width: Steps toward identifying and integrating ecological envelopes with geomorphic features and datums for sandy beach ecosystems. Geomorphology 199:95–105.

Dugan J. E., D. M. Hubbard, and M. Lastra. 2000. Burrowing abilities and swash behavior of three crabs, *Emerita analoga* Stimpson, *Blepharipoda occidentalis* Randall and *Lepidopa californica* Efford (Anomura, Hippoidea), of exposed sandy beaches. Journal of Experimental Marine Biology and Ecology 255:229–245.

Dugan, J. E., D. M. Hubbard, H. M. Page, and J. Schimel. 2011. Marine macrophyte wrack inputs and dissolved nutrients in beach sands. Estuaries and Coasts 34(4):839–850.

Dugan, J. E., D. M. Hubbard, I. F. Rodil, D. L. Revell, and S. Schroeter. 2008. Ecological effects of coastal armoring on sandy beaches. Marine Ecology 29:160–170.

Dugan, J. E., D. M. Hubbard, J. M. Engle, D. L. Martin, D. M. Richards, G. E. Davis, K. D. Lafferty, and R. F. Ambrose. 2000. Macrofauna communities of exposed sandy beaches on the southern California mainland and Channel Islands. Pages 339–346 in D. R. Brown, K. L. Mitchell, and H. W. Chang, editors. Proceedings of the Fifth California Islands Symposium, OCS Study, Minerals Management Service Publication 99–0038. Camarillo, California.

Dugan, J. E., D. M. Hubbard, M. McCrary, and M. Pierson. 2003. The response of macrofauna communities and shorebirds to macrophyte wrack subsidies on exposed sandy beaches of southern California. Estuarine, Coastal, and Shelf Science 58S:25–40.

Dugan, J. E., L. Airoldi, M. G. Chapman, S. Walker, and T. A. Schlacher. 2012. Estuarine and coastal structures: Environmental effects: A focus on shore and nearshore structures. Pages 17–41 M. Kennish and M. Elliot, editors. Chapter 2, "Estuaries and Coasts." Treatise on Estuarine and Coastal Science. Volume 8, Human-induced Problems (Uses and Abuses). <doi:10.1016/B978-0-12-374711-2.00802-0>.

Dugan, J. E., O. Defeo, E. Jaramillo, A. R. Jones, M. Lastra, R. Nel, C. H. Peterson, F. Scapini, T. Schlacher, and D. S. Schoeman. 2010. Give beach ecosystems their day in the sun. Science 329:1146.

Dwight, R. H., M. V. Brinks, G. SharavanaKumar, and J. C. Semenza. 2007. Beach attendance and bathing rates for Southern California beaches. Ocean and Coastal Management 50(10): 847–858.

Efford, I. 1976. Distribution of the sand crabs in the genus Emerita (Decapoda, Hippidae). Crustaceana 30:169–183.

———. 1970. Recruitment to sedentary marine populations as exemplified by the sand crab, *Emerita analoga* (Decapoda, Hippidae). Crustaceana 18:293–308.

———. 1966. Feeding in the sand crab, *Emerita analoga* (Stimpson) (Decapoda, Anomura). Crustaceana 10:167–182.

Ferdin, M. E., R. G. Kvitek, C. K. Bretz, C. L. Powell, G. J. Doucetter, K. A. Lefebvre, S. Coale, and M. W. Silver. 2002. *Emerita analoga* (Stimpson)—possible new indicator species for the phycotoxin domoic acid in California coastal waters. Toxicon 40:259–265.

Flick, R. E. 1993. The myth and reality of southern California beaches. Shore and Beach 61(3):3–13.

Fitch, J. E. 1950. The Pismo clam. California Fish and Game 36:285–312.

Fritzsche, R. A., and P. Collier. 2001. Surfperch. Pages 236–240 in W. S. Leet, C. M. Dewees, R. Klingbeil, and E. J. Larson, editors. California's living marine resources: A status report. California Department of Fish and Game. <www.dfg.ca.gov/mrd>.

Fusaro, C. 1978. Growth rate of the sand crab, *Emerita analoga* (Hippidae), in two different environments. Fisheries Bulletin 76:369–375.

Griffiths, C. L., J.M.E. Stenton-Dozey, and K. Koop. 1983. Kelp wrack and the flow of energy through a sandy beach ecosystem. Pages 547–556 in A. McLachlan and T. Erasmus, editors. Sandy Beaches as Ecosystems. Developments in Hydrobiology 19. Junk, The Hague, the Netherlands.

Griggs, G. B. 2005a. California's retreating coastline: Where do we go from here? Pages 121–125 in O. T. Magoon, H. Converse, B. Baird, and M. Miller-Henson, editors. California and the World Ocean, Conference Proceedings, October 2002, Santa Barbara, California. American Society of Civil Engineers, Reston, Virginia.

———. 2005b. The impacts of coastal armoring. Shore and Beach 73(1):13–22.

———. 1998. The armoring of California's coast. Pages 515–526 in O. T. Magoon, H. Converse, B. Baird, and M. Miller-Henson, editors. California and the World Ocean '97. Conference Proceedings. American Society of Civil Engineers, Reston, Virginia.

Griggs, G. B., K. Patsch, and L. E. Savoy 2005. Living with the changing California coast. University of California Press, Berkeley, California.

Habel, J. S., and G. A. Armstrong. 1977. Assessment and atlas of shoreline erosion along the California coast. California Department of Navigation and Ocean Development. Sacramento, California.

Hapke, C. J., and D. Reid 2007. National assessment of shoreline change. Part 4: Historical coastal cliff retreat along the California Coast. USGS Open File Report 2007–1133. <http://pubs.usgs.gov/of/2007/1133>. Accessed October 2013.

Hapke, C. J., D. Reid, and B. Richmond. 2009. Rates and trends of coastal change in California and the regional behavior of the beach and cliff systems. Journal of Coastal Research 25:603–615.

Hapke, C. J., J. List, D. Reid, B. M. Richmond, and P. Ruggiero. 2006. National assessment of shoreline change. Part 3: Historical shoreline change and associated coastal land loss along sandy shorelines of the California coast. U.S. Geological Survey Open File Report 2006-1219. <http://pubs.usgs.gov/of/2006/1219/>. Accessed March 27, 2014.

Hubbard, D. M., and J. E. Dugan. 2003. Shorebird use of an exposed sandy beach in southern California. Estuarine, Coastal, and Shelf Science 58S:41–54.

Hubbard, D. M., J. E. Dugan, N. K. Schooler, and S. M. Viola. 2014. Local extirpations and regional declines of endemic upper beach invertebrates in southern California. Estuarine, Coastal, and Shelf Science 150:67–75. <http://dx.doi.org/10.1016/j.ecss.2013.06.017>.

Inman, D. L., and J. D. Frautschy. 1966. Littoral processes and the development of shorelines. Pages 511–536 in T. Saville, Santa Barbara Specialty Conference on Coastal Engineering 1965, New York, New York.

Jaramillo, E., J. E. Dugan, D. M. Hubbard, D. Melnick, M. Manzano, C. Duarte, C. Campos, and R. Sanchez. 2012. Ecological implications of extreme events: Footprints of the 2010 earthquake along the Chilean coast. PloS One 7(5), e35348.

Kniskern, T. A., J. A. Warrick, K. L. Farnsworth, R. A. Wheatcroft, and M. A. Goñi. 2011. Coherence of river and ocean conditions along the U.S. West Coast during storms. Continental Shelf Research 31:789–805.

Koop, K., and M. I. Lucas. 1983. Carbon flow and nutrient regeneration from the decomposition of macrophyte debris in a sandy beach microcosm. Pages 249–262 in A. McLachlan and T. Erasmus, editors. Sandy Beaches as Ecosystems. Developments in Hydrobiology 19. Junk, The Hague, the Netherlands.

Koop, K., R. C. Newell, and M. I. Lucas. 1982. Microbial regeneration of nutrients from the decomposition of macrophyte debris on the shore. Marine Ecology Progress Series 9:91–96.

Komar, P. 1998. Beach processes and sedimentation. Prentice Hall, Upper Saddle River, New Jersey.

Lafferty, K. D., J. P. McLaughlin, and J. E. Dugan. 2103. Novel foraging in the swash zone on sand crabs (*Emerita analoga*, Hippidae) by mallards. Wilson Journal of Ornithology 125(2):423–426.

Lastra, M., H. M. Page, J. E. Dugan, D. M. Hubbard, and I. F. Rodil. 2008. Processing of allochthonous macrophyte subsidies by sandy beach consumers: Estimates of feeding rates and impacts on food resources. Marine Biology 154:163–174.

Law, C. J., K. M. Dorgan, and G. W. Rouse. 2013. Validation of three sympatric *Thoracophelia* species (Annelida: Opheliidae) from Dillon Beach, California, using mitochrondrial and nuclear DNA sequence data. Zootaxa 3608:67–74.

LeBoeuf, B. J., and M. L. Bonnell. 1980. Pinnipeds of the California Islands: Abundance and distribution. Pages 475–493 in D. Power, editor. The California Islands: Proceedings of a Multidisciplinary Symposium. Santa Barbara Museum of Natural History, Santa Barbara, California.

Lehman, P. E. 1994. Birds of Santa Barbara County, California. First edition. Vertebrate Museum, University of California. Santa Barbara, California.

Loureiro, C., O. Ferreira, and J.A.G. Cooper. 2013. Applicability of parametric beach morphodynamic state classification on embayed beaches. Marine Geology 346:153–164.

Love, R. M. 1991. Probably more than you want to know about the fishes of the Pacific coast. Really Big Press, Santa Barbara, California.

Martin, K. L. M. 2015. Beach-spawning fishes: reproduction in an endangered ecosystem. CRC Press. Taylor and Francis Group. Boca Raton, Florida.

Martin, K., T. Speer-Blank, R. Pommerening, J. Flannery, and K. Carpenter. 2006. Does beach grooming harm grunion eggs? Shore and Beach 74:17–22.

McArdle, S. B., and A. McLachlan. 1992. Sand beach ecology: Swash features relevant to the macrofauna. Journal of Coastal Research 8:398–407.

McConnaughey, B. H., and D. L. Fox. 1949. The anatomy and biology of the marine polychaete, *Thoracophelia mucronata* (Treadwell), Opheliidae. University of California Publications in Zoology 47:319–340.

McGowan, J. A., 1984. The California El Niño, 1983. Oceanus 27:48–51.

McLachlan, A. 1990. Dissipative beaches and macrofauna communities on exposed intertidal sands. Journal of Coastal Research 6:57–71.

McLachlan, A. 1989. Water filtration by dissipative beaches. Limnology and Oceanography 34:774–780.

McLachlan, A., and A. C. Brown. 2006. The ecology of sandy shores. Academic Press, Elsevier, London, UK.

McLachlan, A., and A. Dorvlo. 2005. Global patterns in sandy beach macrobenthic communities. Journal of Coastal Research 21:674–687.

McLachlan, A., and E. Jaramillo. 1995. Zonation on sandy beaches. Oceanography and Marine Biology Annual Review 33:301–335.

McLachlan, A. and I. Turner 1994. The interstitial environment of sandy beaches. Marine Ecology 15:177–212.

McLachlan, A., E. Jaramillo, O. Defeo, J. E. Dugan, A. de Ruyck, and P. Coetzee. 1995. Adaptations of bivalves to different beach types. Journal of Experimental Marine Biology and Ecology 187:147–160.

McLachlan, A., J. Dugan, O. Defeo, A. Ansell, D. Hubbard, E. Jaramillo, and P. Penchaszadeh. 1996. Beach clam fisheries. Oceanography and Marine Biology Annual Review 34:163–232.

Morrison, R.I.G., B. J. McCafferey, R. E. Gill, S. K. Skagen, S. L. Jones, G. W. Page, C. L. Gratto-Trevor, and B. A. Andres. 2006. Population estimates of North American shorebirds 2006. Wader Study Group Bulletin 111:67–85.

Morrison R.I.G., Y. Augry, R. W. Butler, G. W. Beyersbergen, G. M. Donaldson, C. L. Gratto-Trevor, P. Wicklin, V. H. Johnston, and R. K. Ross. 2001. Declines in North American shorebird populations. Wader Study Group Bulletin 94:34–38.

Neumann, K. K., L. A. Henkel, and G. W. Page 2008. Shorebird use of sandy beaches in central California. Waterbirds 31(1):115–121.

Nielsen, K., S. Morgan, and J. E. Dugan 2013. Baseline characterization of sandy beach ecosystems in California's north central coast region. Final Report to Ocean Science Trust. <http://www.csgc.ucsd.edu/RESEARCH/RESEARCH_PDF/NCCMPA/Final/RMPA-14_Nielsen_Morgan_Dugan_FinalReport.pdf>. Accessed September 2013.

Nordstrom, K. F. 2000. Beaches and dunes of developed coasts. Cambridge University Press. Cambridge, UK.

Nordstrom, K. F., N. L. Jackson, L. Nancy, A. L. Freestone, K. H. Koroticy, and J. A. Puleo. 2012. Effects of beach raking and sand fences on dune dimensions and morphology. Geomorphology 179:106–115.

O'Brien, J. W., and M. S. Oliphant. 2001. Yellowfin croaker. Pages 232–233 in W. S. Leet, C. M. Dewees, R. Klingbeil, and E. J. Larson, editors. California's living marine resources: A status report. California Department of Fish and Game. <www.dfg.ca.gov/mrd>. Accessed January 2014.

Orme, A. R, J. G. Zoulas, G. B. Griggs, C. C. Grandy, D. L. Revell, and H. Koo. 2011. Beach changes along the southern California coast during the twentieth century: A comparison of natural and human forcing factors. Shore and Beach 79:38–50.

Page, G. W., J. S. Warriner, J. C. Warriner, and P. W. Paton. 1995. Snowy plover (*Charadrius alexandrinus*). Retrieved from the Birds of North America Online: <http://bna.birds.cornell.edu/bna/species/154> in A. Poole and F. Gill, editors. The Birds of North America, No. 154. The Birds of North America, Inc., Philadelphia, Pennsylvania.

Patsch, K., and G. B. Griggs 2008. A sand budget for the Santa Barbara littoral cell, California. Marine Geology 252:50–61.

Patsch and Griggs. 2007. Development of Sand Budgets for California's Major Littoral Cells: Eureka, Santa Cruz, Southern Monterey Bay, Santa Barbara, Santa Monica (including Zuma), San Pedro, Laguna, Oceanside, Mission Bay, and Silver Strand Littoral Cells. Institute of Marine Sciences, University of California, Santa Cruz, California Department of Boating and Waterways, California Coastal Sediment Management Work Group, January 2007.

———. 2006. Littoral cells, sand budgets, and beaches: Understanding California's shoreline. <http://www.dbaw.ca.gov/csmw/PDF/LittoralDrift.pdf>. Accessed March 2014.

Pearse, A. S., H. J. Humm, and G. W. Wharton. 1942. Ecology of sand beaches at Beaufort, N. C. Ecological Monographs 12(2):135–190.

Peterson, C. H. 1991. Intertidal zonation of marine invertebrates in sand and mud. American Scientist 79(3):236–249.

Peterson, C. H., and M. J. Bishop. 2005. Assessing the environmental impacts of beach nourishment. BioScience 55:887–896.

Peterson, C. H., D.H.M. Hickerson, and G. G. Johnson. 2000. Short-term consequences of nourishment and bulldozing on the dominant large invertebrates of a sandy beach. Journal of Coastal Research 16(2):368–378.

Peterson, C. H., M. J. Bishop, G. A. Johnson, L. M. D'Anna, and L. M. Manning. 2006. Exploiting beach filling as an unaffordable experiment: Benthic intertidal impacts propagating upwards to shorebirds. Journal of Experimental Marine Biology and Ecology 338:205–221.

Peterson, C. H., M. J. Bishop, L. M. D'Anna, and G. A. Johnson. 2014. Multi-year persistence of beach habitat degradation from nourishment using coarse shelly sediments. Science of the Total Environment 487:481–492.

Revell, D. L., and G. B. Griggs. 2007. Regional shoreline and beach changes in the Santa Barbara sandshed. Pages 1740–1753 in N. C. Kraus and J. D. Rosati, editors. Coastal Sediments 2007. Proceedings of the Sixth International Symposium on Coastal Engineering and Science of Coastal Sediment Processes, Volume 3. American Society of Civil Engineers, New Orleans, Louisiana.

———. 2006. Beach width and climate oscillations in Isla Vista, Santa Barbara, California. Shore and Beach 74:8–16.

Revell, D. L., J. E. Dugan, and D. M. Hubbard. 2011. Physical and ecological responses of sandy beaches to the 1997–98 El Niño. Journal of Coastal Research 27:718–730.

Rossi, S. S., G. W. Rommel, and A. A. Benson. 1978. Hydrocarbons in sand crabs (*Emerita analoga*) from southern California (USA). Chemosphere 2:131–141.

Schlacher, T., D. S Schoeman, A. R. Jones, J. E. Dugan, D. M. Hubbard, O. Defeo, C. H. Peterson, M. A. Weston, B. Maslo, A. D. Olds, F. Scapini, R. Nel, L. R. Harris, S. Lucrezi, M. Lastra, C. M. Huijbers, M. Chantal, and R. M. Connolly. 2014. Metrics to assess ecological condition, change, and impacts in sandy beach ecosystems. Journal of Environmental Management 144:322–335.

Schlacher, T., J. E. Dugan, D. S. Schoeman, M. Lastra, A. Jones, F. Scapini, A. McLachlan, and O. Defeo. 2007. Sandy beaches at the brink. Diversity and Distributions 13:556–560.

Schooler, N. K., J. E. Dugan and D. M. Hubbard. 2014. Detecting change in intertidal species richness on sandy beaches: Calibrating across sampling designs. Estuarine, Coastal, and Shelf Science 150:58–66.

Schooler, N. K., J. E. Dugan, D. M. Hubbard, and D. L. Straughan. In prep. Changing sandy beach ecosystems in California: Comparisons of intertidal biodiversity three decades apart.

Short, A. D. 1996. The role of wave height, period, slope, tide range, and embaymentization in beach classifications: A review. Revista Chilena de Historia Natural 69:589–604.

Short, A. D., and L. D. Wright. 1983. Physical variability of sandy beaches. Pages 133–144 in A. McLachlan and T. Erasmus, editors. Sandy Beaches as Ecosystems. Developments in Hydrobiology 19. Junk, The Hague, the Netherlands.

Short, A. D., and P. A. Hesp. 1982. Wave, beach, and dune interactions in southeastern Australia. Marine Geology 48:259–284.

Shuford, W. D., G. W. Page, J. G. Evens, and L. E. Stenzel. 1989 Sea-

sonal abundance of waterbirds at Point Reyes: A coastal California perspective. Western Birds 20:137–265.
Siegel, P. R., and A. M. Wenner, 1984. Abnormal reproduction of the sand crab (*Emerita analoga*) in the vicinity of a nuclear generating station in southern California. Marine Biology 80:341–345.
Slott, J. M., A. B. Murray, A. D. Ashton, and T. J. Crowley. 2006. Coastline responses to changing storm patterns. Geophysical Research Letters 33:L18404.
Smyder, E. A., K.L.M. Martin, and R. E. Gatten Jr. 2002. Temperature effects on egg survival and hatching during the extended incubation period of California grunion, *Leuresthes tenuis*. Copeia 2002:313–320.
Speybroeck, J., D. Bonte, W. Courtens, T. Gheskiere, P. Grootaert, J.-P. Maelfait, M. Mathys, S. Provoost, K. Sabbe, W.M. Stienen, V. Van Lancker, M. Vincx, and S. Degraer. 2006. Beach nourishment: An ecologically sound coastal defence alternative? A review. Aquatic Conservation: Marine and Freshwater Ecosystems 16:419–435.
Storlazzi, C. D., and G. B. Griggs. 2000. The influence of El Niño-Southern Oscillation (ENSO) events on the evolution of central California's shoreline. Geological Society of America Bulletin 112:2:236–249.
———. 1998. The 1997–98 El Niño and erosion processes along the central coast of California. Shore and Beach 66(3):12–17.
Straughan, D. 1983. Ecological characteristics of beaches in the southern California Bight. Pages 441–447 in A. McLachlan and T. Erasmus, editors. Sandy Beaches as Ecosystems. Developments in Hydrobiology 19. Junk, The Hague, the Netherlands.
Thompson, W. F. 1919. The spawning of the grunion (*Leuresthes tenuis*). California Fish and Game 3:1–27.
Thornton, E. B., A. Sallenger, J. C. Sesto, L. Egley, T. McGee, and R. Parsons. 2006. Sand mining impacts on long-term dune erosion in southern Monterey Bay. Marine Geology 229:45–58.
Thornton, E. B., J. MacMahan, and A. H. Sallenger Jr. 2007. Rip currents, mega-cusps, and eroding dunes. Marine Geology 240:151–167.
Valle, C. F., and M. S. Oliphant. 2001a. California corbina. Pages 228–229 in W. S. Leet, C. M. Dewees, R. Klingbeil, and E. J. Larson, editors. California's living marine resources: A status report. California Department of Fish and Game. <http://www.dfg.ca.gov/marine/status/status2001.asp>. Accessed February 2014.
———. 2001b. Spotfin croaker. Pages 230–231 in W. S. Leet, C. M. Dewees, R. Klingbeil, and E. J. Larson, editors. California's living marine resources: A status report. <http://www.dfg.ca.gov/marine/status/status2001.asp> Accessed February 2014.
Viola, S. M., D. M. Hubbard, and J. E. Dugan. 2014. Burrowing inhibition by fine textured beach fill: Implications for recovery of beach ecosystems. Estuarine, Coastal, and Shelf Science 150:142–148.
Warrick, J. 2013. Dispersal of fine sediment in nearshore coastal waters. Journal of Coastal Research 29:579–596.
Wenner, A. M. 1988. Crustaceans and other invertebrates as indicators of beach pollution. Pages 199–229 in D. F. Soule and G. S. Kleppel, editors. Marine Organisms as Indicators. Springer-Verlag, New York, New York.
Wenner, A. M., J. E. Dugan, and D. Hubbard. 1993. Sand crab population biology on the California Islands and mainland. Pages 335–348 in F. G. Hochberg, editor. Third California Islands Symposium, Recent Advances in Research on the California Islands. Santa Barbara Museum of Natural History, Santa Barbara, California.
Willis, C. M., and G. B. Griggs. 2003. Reductions in fluvial sediment discharge by coastal dams in California and implications for beach sustainability. Journal of Geology 111(2):167–182.
Winant, C. D., D. L. Inman, and C. E. Nordstrom. 1975. Description of seasonal beach changes using empirical eigenfunctions. Journal of Geophysical Research 80:1979–86. <doi:10.1029/JC080i015p01979>.
Wright, L. D., and A. D. Short.1980. Morphodynamic variability of surf zones and beaches: A synthesis. Marine Geology 70:251–285.
Yaninek, J. S. 1980. Beach wrack: Phenology of a limiting resource and utilization by macroinvertebrates of sandy beaches. MA thesis. University of California, Berkeley, California.
Young, A.P., and S. A. Ashford. 2006. Application of airborne LIDAR for seacliff volumetric change and beach-sediment budget contributions. Journal of Coastal Research 22(2):307–318.
ZoBell, C. E. 1971. Drift seaweeds on San Diego County beaches. Nova Hedwigia 32:269–314.

TWENTY-ONE

Coastal Dunes

PETER ALPERT

Introduction

One of the great attractions of California is its ocean coast, a strip approximately 1,800 kilometers long of terraces and headlands punctuated by coves, bays, estuaries, and accompanying beaches and sand dunes (Griggs et al. 2005, Griggs 2010, California Coastal Commission publications at www.coastal.ca.gov, aerial photographs at www.californiacoastline.org). About 13% of this strip consists of cliffs over 100 meters tall that are relatively resistant to erosion, and another 59% is lower, more erodible cliffs (Runyan and Griggs 2003). Most of the rest is beaches backed by dunes (Cooper 1967; see Chapter 20, "Sandy Beaches"). This chapter focuses on these coastal dunes—lands a few tens of meters to several kilometers across, made of sand blown inland from the beach, colonized by distinctive communities of plants and animals, and visited for pleasure by people. Other chapters cover the ocean beaches (Chapter 20, "Sandy Beaches") and rocky intertidal systems (Chapter 18) that lie just seaward of dunes; the estuaries (Chapter 19, "Estuaries: Life on the Edge"), wetlands (Chapter 31), forests (Chapter 26, "Coast Redwood Forests"), grasslands (Chapter 23), shrublands (Chapter 22, "Coastal Sage Scrub," and Chapter 24, "Chaparral"), farmlands (Chapter 38, "Agriculture"), and cities (Chapter 39, "Urban Ecosystems") that adjoin dunes on their inland edge; and the dunes on the islands off the coast of California (Chapter 34, "Managed Island Ecosystems") and in the interior deserts (Chapter 30).

Among California's terrestrial ecosystems, coastal dunes are particularly dynamic. As long as they are partly bare, they move in the wind and shift underfoot. This creates opportunities and problems for organisms, including humans. Plants and animals find open sites to colonize but suffer from burial or excavation. Humans find recreation, but moving dunes can cover homes, roads, and harbors. Both plants and humans respond by stabilizing dunes. In California, people have introduced plants from other continents to hold down dunes, and some of these introduced species have spread so abundantly that coastal dune ecosystems dominated by native species have shrunk to a few.

Geography

Dunes occur along the Californian coast in disjunct patches that range in size from less than 1 hectare to over 100 square kilometers (Figure 21.1; Zedler 1962, Cooper 1967). The California Coastal Commission (1987) listed twenty-seven dune fields. The two largest were at Monterey Bay, covering about 105 square kilometers; and at Nipomo, covering 47 square kilometers. Barbour and Johnson (1988) named thirteen major dune localities:

1. Crescent City (likely corresponding mainly to dunes at the mouth of the Smith River and Lakes Earl and Tolowa in Tolowa Dunes State Park).
2. Humboldt Bay (the North and South Spits, including the Lanphere and Ma-le'l Dunes in Humboldt Bay National Wildlife Refuge).
3. Fort Bragg (south of the mouth of Ten-Mile River, largely in MacKerricher State Park).
4. Point Arena (Manchester Beach, including Manchester Beach State Park).
5. Bodega Beach (from the mouth of Salmon Creek south to Bodega Head).
6. Dillon Beach east of the mouth of Tomales Bay.
7. Point Reyes (Kehoe Beach south to North Beach, notably near Abbotts Lagoon, plus low dunes on Limantour Spit).
8. San Francisco (once very extensive, then almost entirely built or planted over, now restored in areas at Bakers Beach and south of Ocean Beach).
9. Monterey (mostly built or planted over but with remnants at the mouth of the Salinas River [Bluestone 1981] and at Marina and Asilomar State Beaches).
10. Morro Bay.
11. The Santa Maria River complex (likely the area between San Luis Obispo Bay and Point Conception, including dunes at Oceano, Oso Flaco, Guadalupe, Nipomo, Pismo Beach, the Santa Maria River, Vandenberg Air Force Base, and the Santa Ynes River).
12. Los Angeles (almost entirely built or planted over, including former low dunes on barrier spits [Engstrom 2006] and remnant areas at El Segundo Dunes).
13. San Diego Bay (almost entirely built or planted over).

Additional, smaller areas of relatively intact dunes include those on Gold Bluff Beach north of Prairie Creek in Prairie Creek State Park (a narrow zone of low dunes between beach and tall cliffs), at the mouth of the Little River (a narrow zone), at the mouth of the Mattole River, in Año Nuevo State Reserve at Franklin and North Points, at Coal Oil Point Reserve in Santa Barbara, and at the mouth of the Santa Margarita River in Camp Pendleton Marine Base north of Oceanside (a narrow zone).

Most of California's coastal dunes have been highly transformed by human use and introduced plants. Barbour and Johnson (1988) cited Humboldt Bay and Point Reyes as the least altered of the major dune localities north of Big Sur (see Figure 21.1). Areas at Lanphere and Male'l Dunes at Humboldt Bay and near Abbotts Lagoon on Point Reyes, plus a smaller area at Franklin Point in Año Nuevo State Reserve, probably now support the best remnants of native dune vegetation in northern California (Figure 21.2), followed by the dunes at the mouths of the Ten-Mile and Salinas Rivers and at Asilomar. Of the major dune localities south of Big Sur, Barbour and Johnson (1988) cited Morro Bay and parts of the Santa Maria complex as the least altered. Peinado et al. (2007) identified these parts as the dunes at Guadalupe, Nipomo, Pismo Beach, and Oso Flaco. However, considerable portions of these dunes have been heavily affected by off-road driving and introduced plants.

Along with the rest of the immediate coast of California, coastal dunes enjoy moderate temperatures (see Chapter 2, "Climate"). Mean monthly air temperature at a given site varies by 9°C or less during the year, and mean annual air temperature rises from north to south by only a few degrees, from 11°C to 17°C (Barbour and Johnson 1988). A few nights of frost per year occur on average along the northern and central coast; snow is virtually unknown. This moderation stems in part from relatively low seasonal change in the surface temperature of the ocean near the coast (see Chapter 16, "The Offshore Ecosystem") and a related prevalence of convection fog in the summer, when the daily maximum temperature can be 15°C higher 10 kilometers inland than at the coastline.

Precipitation on coastal dunes does vary greatly with both season and latitude. The entire coast receives much more rain in the winter than in the summer, and the southern coast is much drier than the north. The dry season in summer increases from two months with less than 1.5 centimeters of rain each in Crescent City to five months with less than 0.5 centimeter each in San Diego. Mean total annual precipitation decreases from approximately 165 to 25 centimeters north to south. The central and southern coastal dunes have a Mediterranean-type climate. Finally, wind speed is often high at the coast, particularly in fair weather in spring. Areas of low air pressure over the Pacific in the rainy season cause winds to tend to come from the south and southwest, while high pressure in the dry season causes north and northwesterly winds to predominate. In sum, the climate features wet and dry seasons rather than cold and warm ones, potentially permits year-round activity of many organisms except as limited by drought, and is relatively windy.

Dune Formation and Shape

Coastal dunes in California (Wiedemann and Pickart 2004, Griggs et al. 2005) and in general (Nordstrom 2000, McLachlan and Brown 2006, Maun 2009) are formed by sand blown inland from an adjoining beach. Measurements and models of wind-driven transport of sand indicate that grain size, surface moisture, microtopography, and a variety of aspects of air movement are important (e.g., Namikas 2003, Sherman and Li 2012). Brief, high-velocity movements account for a considerable amount of transport (Craig 2000). In California the movement of sand from beach to dunes is just the last step in a long chain of supply. This begins with the erosion of lands in watersheds as far east as the crest of the Sierra Nevada and continues with transport of sediments to the coast in rivers and then along the coast by currents within littoral cells, followed by deposition onto beaches by waves (Peterson et al. 2010; see also Chapter 20, "Sandy Beaches"). Erosion of coastal bluffs also provides some of the sediments that become dunes. However, Runyan and Griggs (2003) estimated that the contribution of bluffs to deposition of sand on beaches at various sites in the state ranged from less than 1% to at least 12%. Soils on

Photo on previous page: Native vegetation on partly stabilized dunes at Point Reyes National Seashore. In the foreground are seaside daisy (*Erigeron glaucus*, in flower), yellow sand verbena (*Abronia latifolia*, with green, succulent leaves), and Tidestrom's lupine (*Lupinus tidestromii*, with silvery leaves, a federally and state endangered species). Photo: Sarah Minnick, courtesy of the National Park Service.

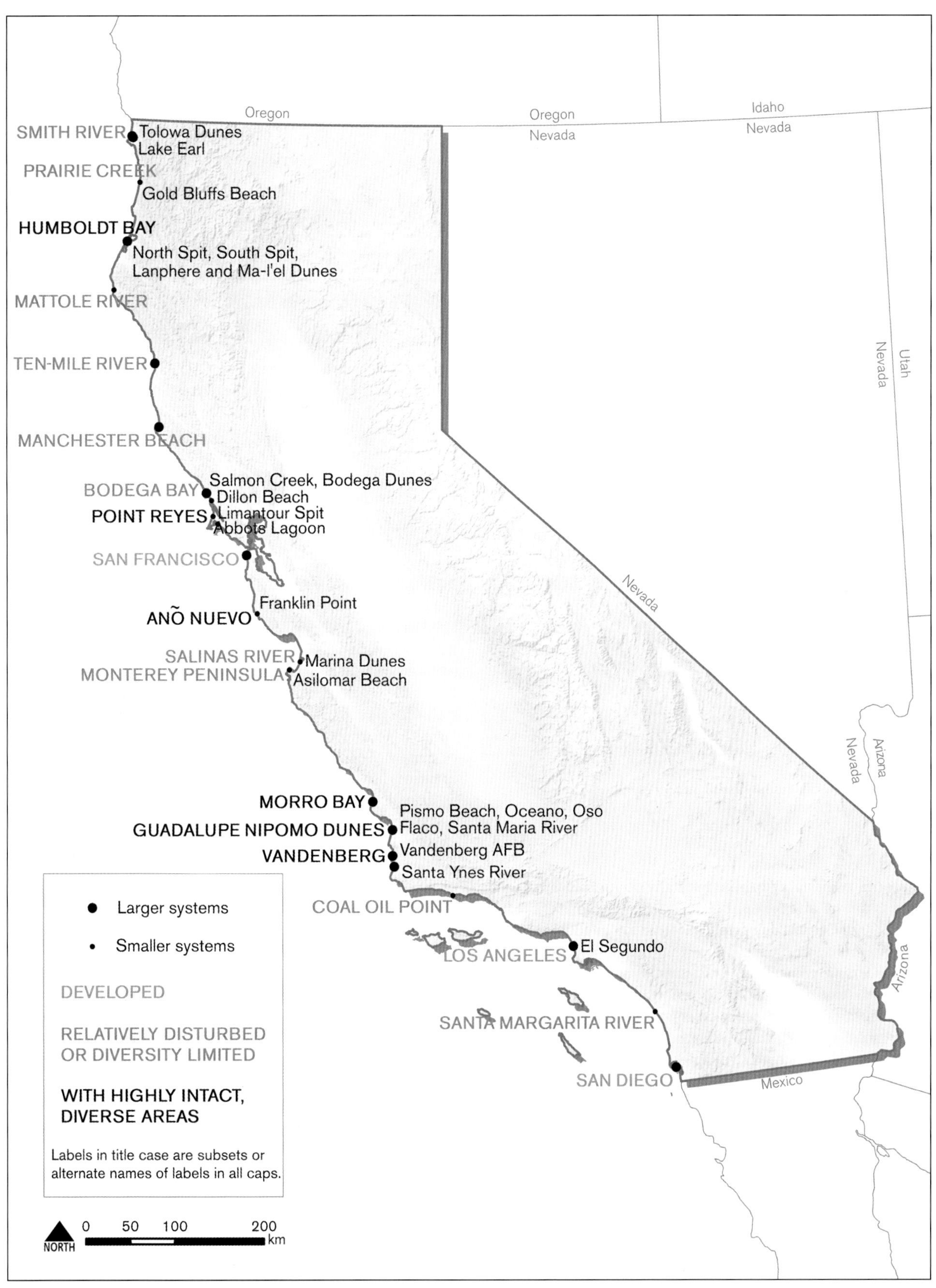

FIGURE 21.1 Locations of systems of coastal dunes in California. Data from U.S. Geological Survey and ESRI. Map: P. Welch, Center for Integrated Spatial Research (CISR).

FIGURE 21.2 Native vegetation on dunes at (A) Lanphere and Ma-le'l Dunes, and (B) Abbotts Lagoon, Point Reyes National Seashore. Photos: (A) Andrea Pickart, (B) Peter Baye.

FIGURE 21.3 Coastal dune system at Vandenberg Air Force Base. Photo: Andrea Pickart.

Californian coastal dunes are generally dominated by silicates such as quartz and feldspar derived from inland areas (Muhs et al. 2009). Coastal dunes in California are in good part recycled mountains and hills.

Californian coastal dunes date from the Pleistocene and Holocene (Cooper 1967, Barbour and Johnson 1988, Pickart and Barbour 2007). The Pleistocene dunes have largely lost their mobility and dune-like features, and it is the Holocene dunes that are generally considered in treatments of dune ecology and that account for the dune systems treated here. These Holocene dunes often overlie other formations. For instance, some dunes in the Guadalupe-Nipomo system were laid atop estuarine deposits approximately 4,300 to 3,500 years ago (Knott and Eley 2006). In other cases, sand has blown up onto low coastal terraces, creating perched dunes as at Franklin Point. Peterson (2006) provides dating and morphostratigraphy of dune sheets in northern and central California, and Peterson et al. (2007) date dunes in central and southern Oregon.

Especially in northern and central California, dune systems have a ridge, or FOREDUNE, that runs along the inland edge of the beach. If there is a large enough area of wind-driven sand, a system may form numerous TRANSVERSE DUNES, ridges that run perpendicular to the prevailing wind; or PARABOLIC DUNES, curved ridges whose arms point upwind. Sets of ridges can move downwind more or less in unison, creating a mobile landscape or DUNE SHEET (Figure 21.3) of relatively sheltered and sometimes moist troughs, windward faces where objects are excavated, relatively wind-blown and dry ridge tops, and lee faces where objects are buried.

Especially in the wetter climates of northern California, sizable areas upwind of dunes can be eroded down to the water table, forming DEFLATION PLAINS or basins. Small seasonal wetlands, some of which are termed dune swales or SLACKS, and even small permanent lakes occur in dune systems in California, such as Fen Lake at Ten-Mile Dunes and Oso Flaco Lake at Oceano Dunes. Wind may also hollow out portions of dune ridges, forming BLOWOUTS (Hesp 2002). Various sets of terms distinguish dunes at different distances inland, such as nearshore dunes, moving dunes, and back dunes (Pickart and Barbour 2007). Hesp (2007) and Barchyn and Hugenholtz (2012) discuss classification and formation of dunes.

Plants modify the shapes and movement of dunes both by holding sand down and by intercepting blowing sand. Worldwide, the most complex dunes may occur where disturbance by wind and stabilization by plants are roughly equal (Doing 1985). One dramatic demonstration of the influence of plants on dune morphology in California has been the remodeling of the foredunes by the introduced European beach grass (*Ammophila arenaria*) (Figure 21.4). Before this grass was introduced, the backs of beaches in southern California were generally colonized by taprooted, perennial forbs that formed a zone of large mounds of sand. The backs of beaches and foredunes in northern California were colonized by forbs and grasses including the native, rhizomatous American dune grass (*Elymus mollis*), which formed a low, gradual, partly open ridge (Barbour and Johnson 1988). European beach grass has now replaced American dune grass on foredunes just about everywhere in unrestored areas in California except near Abbotts Lagoon at Point Reyes and on the Lanphere and Ma-l'el Dunes at Humboldt Bay (Wiedemann and Pickart 2004). Concurrently, the gradual foredunes in northern California have been replaced by steeper, taller, more densely vegetated ones that are more effective at trapping sand (Zarnetske et al. 2012). This tends to truncate the back of the beach and cut off sand supply to more

FIGURE 21.4 Foredunes dominated by (A) European beach grass (*Ammophila arenaria*) at Bodega Marine Reserve (B) native plants such as American dune grass (*Elymus mollis*) at Abbotts Lagoon. Photos: (A) Jackie Sones, (B) Peter Baye.

inland dunes, which then become more densely vegetated and stable.

This change in the shape of foredunes appears due largely to the contrasting responses of European beach grass and American dune grass to burial. European beach grass produces dense, vertical rhizomes and tillers when buried, whereas American dune grass increases lateral spread. The growth response of European beach grass sets up a positive feedback, trapping more sand that induces further vertical growth. Where European beach grass grows on dunes behind the foredune, it can also raise their height; at Bodega Bay the height of dunes with European beach grass increased 4 centimeters per year during the 1900s, while the height of nonvegetated areas decreased at about the same rate (Danin et al. 1998). In Oregon, where European beach grass had spread over all foredunes by 1983 except on one island at the mouth of the Columbia River, a new phase of remodeling has begun (Hacker et al. 2012): another introduced grass, American beach grass (*Ammophila breviligulata*), is replacing European beach grass. American beach grass has a growth form somewhat intermediate between those of European beach grass and American dune grass, and the foredunes are getting lower again.

Physical Conditions for Organisms

Physical factors likely to limit the performance of organisms on dunes in California include burial or excavation by movement of sand, low soil nutrient availability, low water availability, desiccation by wind, high solar radiation, and high salinity in soil and aerosols (e.g., Fink and Zedler 1990, Wilson and Sykes 1999, Pickart and Barbour 2007, Cornelisse and Hafernik 2009). Little work seems to have been done to characterize these factors since about 1990. Pickart and Barbour (2007) reviewed the literature and concluded that many of these factors are important. They note that burial may be particularly so, although burial can have positive effects on some species and negative effects on others (e.g., Zedler et al. 1983, Zhang and Maun 1992, Bonte et al. 2006).

Availability of nitrogen on bare dune soils is very low. Cushman et al. (2010) found a mean concentration of 5–7 µg inorganic nitrogen (N) per gram dry mass of soil and a net MINERALIZATION rate of 2 µg N per gram soil per month at 0–5 centimeters below the soil surface during February on a stabilized dune at Bodega Bay. Since nutrient levels are generally higher on older dunes and nearer the soil surface, and highest in winter at this site, these values are likely to be maximal. For instance, Alpert and Mooney (1996) reported a mean concentration of 0.5–1.2 µg inorganic N per gram dry mass of soil and net mineralization of 0.06 µg N per gram per month at 0–15 centimeters depth in summer on partly stabilized dunes at Franklin Point; concentrations were no more than 0.2 µg per gram at 15–60 centimeters depth. By comparison, Maron and Jefferies (1999) measured net mineralization rates of about 4 and 10 µg N per gram soil per month at 5–10 centimeters depth away from and under nitrogen-fixing shrubs, respectively, in grassland adjacent to dunes at Bodega Bay.

Availability of water may not be as low as is sometimes assumed. The upper 20–100 centimeters of the soil on dunes can be very dry when deeper soil is very moist, forming surprisingly distinct layers. Measurement of the predawn water potential of American dune grass on foredunes in Oregon suggested that soil WATER POTENTIAL in its rooting zone never fell below –0.2 MPa during the driest part of the year (Pavlik 1985), a value unlikely to limit growth of terrestrial plants. However, plants did display evidence of midday water stress such as partial closure of STOMATA, suggesting that high solar radiation or wind made the habitat effectively dry at certain hours. Rapid drainage and evaporation from the coarsely textured soils on dunes can dry the upper soil quickly and likely makes drought a limiting factor in the establishment of seedlings and the performance of shallowly rooted plants. The dry upper layer of sand can bar movement of water upwards from deeper sand, resulting in dry and wet layers. Recent measurements on dunes in Korea emphasize the high variability between levels of both soil moisture and nutrients at different distances from the sea and in different topographic positions (Kim et al. 2008).

On beaches, salt spray and overwash can strongly affect plants (Pickart and Barbour 2007). However, negative effects of high salinity on dunes may be largely limited to the seaward edges of areas of dunes and the times when unusually strong winds blow spray inland or unusually high waves overtop foredunes. Marine aerosols transfer sodium (Na) and other cations to the leaves of shrubs on dunes and thence potentially to soil (Clayton 1972), but inputs of Na, potassium (K), magnesium (Mg), and calcium (Ca) in salt spray can roughly equal losses from leaching at 1 to 2 meters in depth in the soil. There appear to be no published studies on the intensity or frequency of fire on coastal dunes.

Macroorganisms

Species

Most of California's dunes are dominated by perennial, herbaceous to shrubby plants. Trees dominate some stabilized dunes from Mendocino County north and near Monterey. The fully resident animals on dunes are mostly invertebrates, a few rodents, and possibly rabbits. However, dune forests have additional vertebrate residents, vertebrates from adjacent habitats seek food on dunes, and dunes and beaches serve mammals as relatively open avenues of travel (Moore 2002). A few species of birds such as the western snowy plover (*Charadrius nivosus nivosus*) nest, and some marine mammals such as northern elephant seal (*Mirounga angustirostris*) rest where dunes meet beaches. One photogenic mammalian use of coastal dunes in California is by Roosevelt elk (*Cervus canadensis roosevelti*) that travel between inland meadows and the ocean at Prairie Creek State Park. Dunes also support annual plants, bryophytes, lichens, and macrofungi, including some distinctive species of mosses and lichens (Danin et al. 1998, Glavich 2003, Cushman et al. 2010). The first species of plant described from California was the beach and dune species pink sand verbena (*Abronia umbellata*), collected in 1786 at Monterey Bay and named a few years later by a British botanist based on plants grown in a garden in Paris (Beidleman 2006).

Many species of herbaceous plants and some species of shrubs and insects and other invertebrates live only on dunes. The natural communities on dunes thus are very different from those in the adjacent coastal forests, grasslands, and shrublands. Plant traits associated with growth on dunes include succulence, trailing stems, clonal growth via rhizomes or STOLONS, large taproots, and pale color of leaves or stems due to dense hair or thick wax (see Figure 21.5). The distinctiveness of the natural communities on dunes generally diminishes with distance from the ocean and with the length of time that dunes have been covered and stabilized by plants—that is, with the degree to which a dune habitat has become more like the adjacent habitat. Several semipopular guides to the dune plants of California (e.g., Munz 1964, Dawson and Foster 1982), and many scientific publications on dune vegetation at individual sites and along the coast (e.g., as reviewed in Barbour and Johnson 1988 and Pickart and Barbour 2007) are available.

Listings of endangered, threatened, and rare species by the California Natural Diversity Database (CNDDB, dfs.ca.gov/biogeodata/cnddb) and the California Native Plant Society (CNPS, rareplants.cnps.org) suggest that a number of plant species of conservation concern are essentially limited to coastal dunes in California. Federally endangered or threatened species are Menzies's wallflower (*Erysimum menziesii*, family Brassicaceae), beach layia (*Layia carnosa*, Asteraceae), Nipomo Mesa lupine (*Lupinus nipomensis*, Fabaceae), and Tidestrom's lupine (*Lupinus tidestromii*, Fabaceae). Additional, state-listed endangered or threatened plant species are surf thistle (*Cirsium rhothophilum*, Asteraceae, also found in coastal bluff scrub [Zedler et al. 1983]) and beach spectacle pod (*Dithyrea maritima*, Brassicaceae [Aigner 2004]). Additional species listed by CNPS as endangered, threatened, or rare include Nuttall's acmispon (*Acmispon prostratus*, Fabaceae, formerly *Lotus nuttallii*), coastal goosefoot (*Chenopodium littoreum* Chenopodiaceae), round-headed Chinese houses (*Collinsia corymbosa*, Scrophulariaceae), and sand-loving wallflower (*Erysimum ammophilum*, Asteraceae). These do not include subspecific taxa, species that are rare in California

FIGURE 21.5 Some distinctive dune plant species. Photos: (A, E) Jackie Sones, (B–C) Andrea Pickart, (D, F–H) Peter Baye.

A Yellow sand verbena (*Abronia latifolia*) at Bodega Marine Reserve.

B Beach bur (*Ambrosia chamissonis*) at Lanphere and Ma-l'el Dunes.

C Beach morning glory (*Calystegia soldanella*) at Ten-Mile Dunes.

D Menzies' wallflower (*Erysimum menziesii*) at Abbotts Lagoon.

E Silky beach pea (*Lathyrus littoralis*) at Wrights Beach, Sonoma County.

F Beach layia (*Layia carnosa*) at Abbotts Lagoon.

G Tidestrom's lupine (*Lupinus tidestromii*) at Abbotts Lagoon.

H Douglas' bluegrass (*Poa douglasii*) at Abbotts Lagoon.

but common in Oregon, or species that appear to have primary habitats besides dunes.

At least two species of moths are known only from coastal dunes in California. Powell (1976) found a new, flightless species (*Areniscythris brachypteris*, Scythrididae) on dunes at Oso Flaco (Powell 1976) and a new, winged species in the genus *Lithariapteryx* (Heliodinidae) on other dunes (Powell 1991). The globose dune beetle (*Coelus globosus*, Tenebrionidae) occurs only on foredunes from northern California to Baja California. Subspecies of insects confined to California coastal dunes include a hairy tiger beetle (*Cicindela hirticollis gravida*, Cicindelidae; Nagano 1980), a satyrid butterfly (*Coenonympha tullia*, Nymphalidae; Porter and Mattoon 1989) Belkin's dune tabanid fly (*Brennania belkini*, Tabanidae), the El Segundo flower-loving fly (*Rhaphiomidas terminatus terminatus*, Mydidae), and the El Segundo blue butterfly (*Euphilotes battoides allyni*, Lycaenidae; Arnold 1983). The last is known only from the El Segundo Dunes and is federally listed as endangered. The California coastal dune beetle (*Hyperaspis annexa*, Coccinellidae; Gordon 1985) is confined to California but not to the coast. Two other unusual groups of animals found on Californian coastal dunes are the stiletto flies (Therevidae; Holston 2005) and the legless lizards (*Anniella* spp., Anniellidae; Kuhnz et al. 2005, Papenfuss and Parham 2013), but neither group appears to contain any taxa restricted to dunes.

Patterns of Vegetation

The vegetation of coastal dunes in California tends to vary on three scales. First, over hundreds of kilometers from north to south, the vegetation of foredunes shifts from dominance by grasses to dominance by FORBS; and the vegetation of more inland, stabilized dunes shifts from forest to shrubland. These patterns are likely tied to climate. Recent, extensive studies of dune vegetation types along the Pacific Coast from Alaska to Baja California (Peinado et al. 2007, 2011) suggest two main latitudinal transitions. Between about Cape Mendocino (40°N) and the Chetco River (42°N) in southern Oregon, a southward transition from temperate to Mediterranean vegetation is marked by the disappearance of dune forests. At about 37°N, near Santa Cruz, there is a second southward transition marked partly by a shift from herbaceous to shrubby species. This transition was also noted by Barbour et al. (1976).

On a second scale, over hundreds of meters, vegetation changes from dominance by herbs near the beach to dominance by woody species inland. For example, foredunes at the mouth of the Salinas River are dominated by trailing, herbaceous perennials and subshrubs, whereas rear dunes are dominated by shrubs (Bluestone 1981). This pattern is likely tied both to levels of stress and disturbance and to SUCCESSION. Using ORDINATIONS, Holton and Johnson (1979) found that dune scrub plant communities at Point Reyes correlated with distance inland and with soil organic matter, nitrogen content, and particle diameter, suggesting that drought and nutrient stress affected community composition. Over a decade, Williams and Williams (1984) observed changes in the vegetation of dunes at Morro Bay that included the replacement of some non-nitrogen-fixing species by legumes. The occurrence of mosses on the soils of some stabilized dunes (e.g., Danin et al. 1998, Cushman et al. 2010) probably depends on earlier colonization by plants that better tolerate unstabilized sand. The restriction of certain species to the more sheltered parts of dunes is observed on other continents and seems more pronounced where climate is harsher (Doing 1985).

On a third scale, plant community composition differs over meters from the crests to the hollows of individual dunes. For instance, plant species composition differs between the windward slope, the top, and the lee side of dunes at Morro Bay (Williams and Potter 1972, Williams 1974). Total numbers of individuals and species there are highest on the lee side, but some individual species are most abundant on the windward slopes or tops of dunes. These patterns are likely associated with differences in stress and disturbance. The various scales of patterns in Californian coastal dune vegetation have been reviewed by Barbour and Johnson (1988) and Pickart and Barbour (2007) and incorporated into the treatment of the plant communities of California by Sawyer et al. (2009) and into treatments of dune vegetation of the Pacific Coast and North America (Barbour et al. 1976, 1981, 1983).

Population and Evolutionary Ecology

The relative geological and climatic similarity of coastal dunes in California combine with their high disturbance levels, disjunct distribution, and sharp environmental differences from adjacent habitats to create a distinctive landscape for population dynamics and microevolution. This landscape is not unlike a very long, linear archipelago of numerous, small to tiny islands. One likely consequence is that the degree of genetic differentiation among populations of a dune-restricted species will be determined largely by the ability of the species to disperse between dune systems. Accordingly, two dune species likely to have low long-distance dispersal rates, the flightless beetle *Coelus ciliatus* (Chatzimanolis and Caterino 2008a) and the trapdoor spider *Aptostichus simus* (Bond et al. 2001), show strong genetic differentiation between central and southern California populations. The dune beetle *Cercyon fimbriatus* shows high genetic diversity within populations yet very little effect of distance on genetic diversity between populations (Chatzimanolis and Caterino 2008b). This suggests high rates of long-distance dispersal, though the rates appear not to have been independently measured.

Capacity for long-distance dispersal also seems to vary greatly among plant species on dunes. A few dune plants appear to have dispersed between California and Chile. Coast strawberry (*Fragaria chiloensis*) is considered native to both California and Chile but not to areas in between; the species is also considered native to Hawaii. Long-distance dispersal from California to South America followed by speciation is the likely origin of two Chilean species of *Gilia* (Morrell et al. 2000). On the other hand, the fitness of experimentally planted populations of a widespread beach and dune herb, beach evening primrose (*Camissoniopsis cheiranthifolia*), did not change across the current northern range limit, suggesting that other factors such as dispersal may limit its range (Samis and Eckert 2009). Some of the populations of this species have small flowers and predominant self-pollination (Dart and Eckert 2013), a DERIVED characteristic associated with insular populations with little incoming dispersal.

A second likely consequence of the sharp and relatively consistent environmental differences between dunes and inland habitats is selection for coastal races of inland species. For example, plants of common monkey flower (*Mimulus guttatus*) tend to be perennials on the coast and annuals inland, and the coastal plants tolerate salt spray better (Lowry et al. 2009). The QUANTITATIVE TRAIT LOCI (~genes) involved in this salt tolerance affect fitness at the coast but not inland, suggesting local adaptation to coastal conditions without a trade-off against fitness in inland habitats. Coastal and inland populations are reproductively isolated from each other by selection against immigrants and by differences in time of flowering (Lowry et al. 2008). Selection appears driven by seasonal drought inland and by salt spray on the coast, and limited gene flow might prevent the evolution of races adapted to both types of habitat (Hall et al. 2010). A different genetic mechanism, POLYPLOIDY, appears associated with spread of the native herb, yarrow (*Achillea millefolium*) onto dunes (Ramsey 2011). Differences between tolerance of salinity by coastal dune and freshwater lakeshore subspecies of American searocket (*Cakile edentula*) are consistent with selection for salt tolerance on beaches and foredunes (Boyd and Barbour 1986). California poppies (*Eschscholzia californica*) show genetically-based differences between native coastal and inland populations in California and similar differences between introduced coastal and inland populations in Chile (Leger and Rice 2007).

Published studies on the population dynamics of dune organisms appear very few. Herbarium records indicate that the ranges of two common dune and beach plants, beach evening primrose and pink sand verbena, have been stable over the past hundred years (Samis and Eckert 2007). The density of plants within populations was not greater nearer the centers of their ranges, but beach evening primrose showed higher seed production nearer the center. In the MONOCARPIC surf thistle, mortality on dunes in Santa Barbara County was 41% over two years, but mean lifespan appeared to be about five years and population size was fairly stable (Zedler et al. 1983). Population size can fluctuate greatly and rapidly in yellow bush lupine (*Lupinus arboreus*), a large shrub of coastal dune and grassland (Strong et al. 1995).

Dune habitat might indirectly affect the population dynamics and structure of plants via selection for clonal growth, reproduction by means of vegetative offspring that remain attached to the parent. Connected plants within a clone can often share resources such as water, photosynthates and nutrients (e.g., Alpert and Mooney 1986), enabling a parent plant to support an offspring if it is buried or while its roots reach down to sand that remains moist. In some clonal dune plants such as coast strawberry, successful reproduction from seeds is rarely observed while rates of vegetative reproduction are often high. This can lead to a population of intermingled clones (Alpert et al. 1993). In outcrossing (versus self-pollinating) species, clonal structure can limit seed production. For example, clonal diversity within a 10 square meter area strongly predicted seed set in beach spectacle pod (Aigner 2004).

Community Ecology

EFFECTS OF PLANTS

Two salient physical features of coastal dunes are their instability and low soil nitrogen content. Two major effects of plants on dunes are to stabilize the soil and increase nitrogen availability. As an example of the second effect (Alpert and Mooney 1996), concentrations of total nitrogen in the soil at a depth of 0–15 centimeters on a partly stabilized dune at Franklin Point were three to four times higher under shrubs of yellow bush lupine and coastal sagewort (*Artemisia pycnocephala*) than in open areas adjacent to shrubs; concentrations at a depth of 15–45 centimeters were about two times higher under shrubs than in the open. As in other systems, nitrogen-fixing plants such as species in the Fabaceae, the pea family, can have relatively large effects. Concentrations of inorganic nitrogen (most of the nitrogen available for uptake by plants) and net rates of mineralization of nitrogen to inorganic form were approximately two to three times higher under yellow bush lupine, which fixes nitrogen, than under coastal sagewort, which does not (Alpert and Mooney 1996). Neither species of shrub affected total soil phosphorus. Effects may be smaller on older, stabilized dunes where plants have already raised overall nitrogen availability. In soil at a depth of 0–5 centimeters on a stabilized dune at Bodega Bay (Cushman et al. 2010), concentrations of inorganic nitrogen were approximately two times higher under shrubs of chamisso bush lupine (*Lupinus chamissonis*) and mock heather (*Ericameria ericoides*) than away from shrubs. Net nitrogen mineralization rate was about four times higher under the nitrogen-fixing chamisso bush lupine and two times higher under the non-nitrogen-fixing mock heather than away from shrubs.

Some dune plants strongly reduce light availability for other plants. Light availability for photosynthesis near the soil surface was 70% lower 20 centimeters inside the edge of the canopies of shrubs of yellow bush lupine than in the open, and 90% lower 20 centimeters under shrubs of coastal sagewort than in the open at Franklin Point (Alpert and Mooney 1996). Shrubs of yellow bush lupine thus created reciprocal patchiness of light and nitrogen availability, with low-light, high-nitrogen patches under shrubs and high-light, low-nitrogen patches between shrubs.

Plants can have multiple, opposing effects on availability of water on dunes. At Franklin Point during the summer dry season (Alpert and Mooney 1996), soil water content was approximately 30% higher under shrubs than in the open at a soil depth of 0–15 centimeters. In contrast, water content at 15–45 centimeter depths was about 20–40% lower under shrubs than in the open. Shrubs likely caused this pattern by decreasing evaporation from the soil surface and taking up water in their rooting zones below the surface. After a century, soils on dunes forested with trees in Golden Gate Park in San Francisco had 40–80 Mg ha^{-1} organic carbon whereas an unstabilized dune had 5 Mg ha^{-1} (Amundson and Tremback 1989), suggesting that forestation greatly increased water-holding capacity. However, water repellency was high on the planted dunes and absent on the unstabilized one, suggesting that availability of water in the soil after a small amount of precipitation might be higher on the unstabilized dune. McBride and Stone (1976) likewise correlated concentration of organic carbon and water-holding capacity with apparent time since stabilization by plants on dunes on the Monterey Peninsula.

Environmental patchiness created by plants can in turn affect establishment and growth of other plant species. Here again, net effects are often composed of positive and negative

FIGURE 21.6 Coast strawberry (*Fragaria chiloensis*): (A) a population of clones on the North Spit of Humboldt Bay; (B) clones growing between open sand, where light availability is high but nitrogen is low; and underneath yellow bush lupine (*Lupinus arboreus*), which creates complementary, low-light and high-nitrogen patches at Franklin Point, Año Nuevo State Reserve. Photos: (A) Andrea Pickart; (B) Peter Alpert.

components. For instance, embryo dunes formed by sea sandwort (*Honckenya peploides*), a common species at the inland edge of beaches in Oregon, promote emergence of seedlings of American dune grass. However, seedling growth is lower on than off these dunes, possibly due to burial by accumulating sand and relatively high salinity (Gagné and Houle 2001). Net effects depend on the species or even the form of species causing the effects and the species responding to them. The prostrate but not the erect form of coyote bush (*Baccharis pilularis*) facilitates establishment of yellow bush lupine at Bodega Bay (Rudgers and Maron 2003). However, areas under prostrate shrubs have lower richness and abundance of other plants than areas under erect shrubs, possibly due to low light or differences in soil surface temperature or litter depth (Crutsinger et al. 2010). On a stabilized dune at Bodega Bay, density and aboveground dry mass of different herbaceous species were variously higher, lower, or no different under than away from shrubs (Cushman et al. 2010).

The clonal herb, coast strawberry, can reciprocally transport photosynthates and nitrogen between connected plants through stolons (Friedman and Alpert 1991). Plants appear able to mine the low-light, high-nutrient patches created by yellow bush lupine by first sending photosynthates along stolons from plants in the open to connected plants under shrubs. These shaded plants can then grow, take up nitrogen, and transport it to plants in the open (Figure 21.6). Resource-sharing capacity was higher in clones from dunes than in clones from grasslands, suggesting selection for sharing on dunes in response to high resource patchiness (Alpert 1999, Roiloa et al. 2007).

Interactions between plants and the physical environment on dunes generate a diversity of habitats for animals. The nine species of stiletto flies at the Nipomo Dunes occur in three plant assemblages—one each on active dunes, in dunes stabilized by shrubs, and in shrubby wetland areas (Holston 2005). Nesting of a native leafcutter bee is associated with certain plants on some dunes in northern California and appears to depend upon persistence of intermediate successional states of vegetation (Gordon 2000). At Point Reyes, shading by vegetation promotes abundance of the burrows used for reproduction by two species of tiger beetle (*Cicindela*; Cornelisse and Hafernik 2009). The two different species are associated with different grain sizes and ranges of soil moisture, pH, or salinity. Dense stands of European beach grass or dune rush (*Juncus lescurii*) on dunes at Point Reyes provide nesting sites for the deer mouse (*Peromyscus maniculatus*); at one site the mouse concentrated its activities in these stands even though abundance of its food plants was relatively low there (Pitts and Barbour 1979). In contrast, European beach grass appears to shelter the introduced purple veldtgrass (*Ehrharta calycina*) from a different herbivore, the black-tailed jackrabbit (*Lepus californicus*; Cushman et al. 2011).

INTERACTIONS BETWEEN PLANTS AND ANIMALS AND MICROBES

Herbivory can substantially reduce plant growth and reproduction on dunes. Rodents consumed approximately 65–85% of yellow bush lupine seeds placed on dunes at Bodega Bay, compared to 5–55% in adjacent grassland (Maron and Simms 1997). The seed bank of the species on dunes was only about 3% as large as in grassland. Excluding rodents from dunes increased emergence and establishment of adults from sown seeds several-fold over three years (Maron and Simms 2001). Predation on seeds after dispersal had no effect on seedling recruitment of cobweb thistle (*Cirsium occidentale*) on dunes at Bodega Bay, but herbivory on flowers by specialized insects reduced seed production and recruitment by more than 50% (Maron et al. 2002). At a different site, insect damage to seeds of cobweb thistle was low and fungi instead reduced seed production by around 30% in one of two years (Palmisano and Fox 1997), while rabbits reduced growth and delayed the reproduction of established plants. Zedler et al. (1983) estimated that insects destroy approximately 25% of the achenes (fruits) of surf thistle on sand dunes at two sites in Santa Barbara County.

Herbivory can modify effects of plants on resource availability and on other dune organisms. Exclosures at Bodega Bay showed that black-tailed deer (*Odocoileus hemionus columbianus*) decreased seedling growth and adult seed production of chamisso bush lupine. Deer sometimes increased net mineralization of nitrogen or decreased inorganic nitrogen concentrations under the shrub, presumably through effects on the concentration of nitrogen in litter (Warner and Cushman 2002, McNeil and Cushman 2005). These exclosures also showed that presence of black-tailed jackrabbit decreased flowering of grass and abundances of forbs, shrubs, and the four most visible invertebrate herbivores: two snails, a grasshopper, and the tiger moth caterpillar (Huntzinger et al. 2008). The effect on snails appeared due to the decrease in shade that accompanied herbivory by the jackrabbits (Huntzinger et al. 2011). Some herbivores can actually decrease total herbivory. Branches of the willow *Salix hookeriana* containing the aphid-tending ant *Formica obscuripes* had more arthropods per leaf shelter but less herbivory than branches without ants (Crutsinger and Sanders 2005).

There appear to be almost no published studies of pollination on coastal dunes in California. Vilà et al. (1998) reported a number of generalist pollinators on highway iceplant (*Carpobrotus edulis*). Removal of highway iceplant and sea rocket flowers did not affect seed set of beach spectacle pod, providing no evidence for competition among these plants for pollinators (Aigner 2004). However, seed set of beach spectacle pod was very low at a site with almost no pollinators, suggesting that pollination can sometimes limit reproduction of dune plants. Published research on soil microbes on Californian coastal dunes also appears scarce. Studies from dunes elsewhere indicate that microbe abundance increases as plants colonize and stabilize dunes. Near Ensenada in Baja California, Siguenza et al. (1996) found less than 1% colonization by mycorrhizal fungi of red sand verbena (*Abronia maritima*) in mobile dunes but up to 80% colonization of six species in fixed dunes. Analysis of phospholipid fatty acids in soil along transects from the shoreline to inland shrubland in Australia suggested that total microbial biomass and proportional abundance of fungi were highest in the shrubland (Yoshitake and Nakatsubo 2008). Near the sea, microbial biomass increased with soil organic matter and was not correlated with soil salinity. Some dune plants on Cape Cod in Massachusetts depend on mycorrhizae to survive (Gemma and Koske 1997). Even though unvegetated dune sites there appear to lack spores of mycorrhizal fungi, uninoculated plantings of native species can eventually be infected, presumably by dispersal of spores from outside a site.

Ecosystem Services

Coastal sand dunes around the world provide a variety of products and functions that contribute to human well-being and can in theory be sustainably used (Barbier et al. 2011). The main products, or social and economic goods, that humans extract from coastal dunes are probably sand and its component minerals such as silica and feldspar, followed by fodder for livestock and then by wild foods such as fruits and mushrooms. The two main functions, or social and economic services, of coastal dunes are likely protection of property and structures from damage by waves and soil erosion; and recreation in the forms of walking, sunbathing, off-road driving, playing, swimming or wading in dune ponds, photography, horseback riding, solitude, and viewing of animals and plants. In addition, dunes catch and purify water for human use, maintain biodiversity that underlies various goods and services, provide opportunities for education and research, and sequester carbon. The quantitative values to humans of most of these goods and services of dunes have been little studied, but estimates of people's willingness to pay for erosion control and recreation suggest that they are substantial ecosystem services (Barbier et al. 2011).

Despite the apparent unavailability of published studies of the values of the ecosystem services of Californian coastal dunes, one can reasonably hypothesize about their relative importance. Recreation, both for day use and for overnight camping, is very likely the most highly valued service. Many dunes are easily accessible from cities, and the mild climate of the immediate coast makes recreation attractive year-round and offers escape from inland summer heat. Mining of sand and grazing on dunes are probably now very limited in California. Dunes likely protect estuaries, harbors, and some built-up areas near river mouths from storms. However, cities have largely eliminated the dunes that might protect them.

Effects of Humans

Humans have had major effects on the ecology and probably on the ecosystem services provided by nearly all of California's coastal dunes. Major causes have been conversion to residential, industrial, and other land uses; and intentional introduction of plant species to stabilize the sand. Land use has largely eliminated dunes near major cities including San Francisco, Los Angeles, and San Diego; about one-third of the city of San Francisco sits atop a Holocene dune system that was once one of the largest in the state. Effects of introduced species are reviewed below.

Other effects of humans on dunes include vegetation loss and destabilization by foot traffic and off-road vehicles. Disturbance by recreational use can have measurable effects on plants and animal communities and is locally important. For example, 5–20% of variation in the community compositions of arthropods on the El Segundo Dunes was explained by level of disturbance (Mattoni et al. 2000). Abundance of the burrowing legless lizard *Anniella pulchra* was lower in more disturbed soils on central coast dunes (Kuhnz et al. 2005). However, total plant cover did not differ between sites with unrestricted and restricted foot traffic in a study of seventeen sites in California (Tobias 2013), and restriction of visitor use for two years had only slight effects on the abundance and diversity of native plants and animals at Fort Funston in San Francisco (Russell et al. 2009). Driving on dunes can clearly denude them. Effects of driving on beaches are less clear; at Assateague National Seashore in Virginia and Padre Inland in Texas, beach driving did not appear to cause net loss of sediment from the beach and dune system but did reduce the size of dunes (Houser et al. 2013). Beach grooming can inhibit the formation of dunes in southern California even though it increases transport of sand by wind (Dugan and Hubbard 2010; see also Chapter 20, "Sandy Beaches").

Livestock grazing can have strong effects on dunes (Moore 2002). The introduction of sheep to San Miguel Island contributed to dune destabilization; dunes there have begun to restabilize following the removal of sheep and other introduced animals (Erlandson et al. 2005; see also Chapter 34, "Managed Island Ecosystems"). Published studies of grazing on dunes along the mainland California coast appear lacking, but studies from northern Europe suggest that livestock can have mixed effects on dunes in cool, moist climates like those of northern California. Autocorrelation of trampling by cattle and humans on Flemish dunes has led to local extinction of specialized arthropods (Bonte and Maes 2008). Reintroduction of livestock to dunes in North Wales after decades of exclusion increased plant diversity on dune ridges but not in slacks (Plassmann et al. 2010).

Introduced and Invasive Species

INTRODUCED species are those brought into a new region intentionally or incidentally by humans; INVASIVE species are those that have spread into a new habitat and that have had negative effects on species already there (see Chapter 13, "Biological Invasions"). Gaertner et al. (2009) concluded that introduced plant species are generally associated with lower numbers of native species on dunes in Mediterranean-type climates. In California, a few intentionally introduced, perennial plants have become highly invasive on coastal dunes. Foremost are European beach grass, introduced from Europe to stabilize dunes; and highway iceplant, a succulent introduced from southern Africa as a horticultural plant and to stabilize dunes and roadsides (Figure 21.7). These introduced, invasive species contrast with a number of introduced plant species that have become widespread on dunes in California but appear so far to have had no substantial effects on existing species or ecological processes. Examples include the succulent, perennial American sea rocket (*Cakile edentula*).

European beach grass was first introduced to the Pacific Coast of the U.S. in 1868 to stabilize dunes in San Francisco for the future Golden Gate Park (Lamb 1898 as cited in Pickart and Barbour 2007). It has since occupied nearly all the foredunes and much of the rest of the dunes from central California to the mouth of the Columbia River. On the North Spit of Humboldt Bay, cover of European beach grass increased more than fivefold over fifty years ending in 1989; spread on inland dunes was mainly due to plantings, whereas spread on foredunes was less dependent on planting (Buell et al. 1995), perhaps partly due to the ability of rhizome fragments to survive for several days in saltwater (Baye 1990 as cited in Pickart and Barbour 2007) and thus disperse via the ocean. Although not widespread in southern California so far, European beach grass can survive along the entire Californian coast and has become abundant at some southern sites (Pickart and Barbour 2007).

Invasiveness of European beach grass on California dunes appears linked to having a growth form unlike that of native species and possibly to having a relatively high tolerance of stress. No native plant species forms such dense stands on foredunes. Rhizomes of European beach grass show more vertical and less lateral growth than rhizomes of the common native large grass of foredunes, American beach grass, especially when nitrogen availability is low, as well as greater survivorship and capacity for vegetative reproduction (Pavlik 1983). In one field study European beach grass maintained higher midday water potential, turgor pressure, and stomatal conductance than American beach grass despite showing less seasonal adjustment of solute accumulation and osmotic pressure (Pavlik 1985). Invasiveness of European beach grass does not appear to depend on interactions with soil microbes (Kowalchuk et al. 2002, Beckstead and Parker 2003).

The direct negative effects of European beach grass on other dune plants are likely mediated largely by competition for light. One indirect negative effect is mediated by a positive effect of European beach grass on the deer mouse (*Peromyscus maniculatus*); the mouse nests and shelters in stands of European beach grass and preys on the seeds of other plants such as European sea rocket (Boyd 1988) and Tidestrom's lupine (Dangremond et al. 2010). The latter is an endangered dune endemic at increased risk of extinction because of APPARENT COMPETITION with the invader. European beach grass directly affects the federally threatened western snowy plover by reducing the extent of its nesting habitat at the backs of beaches (Zarnetske et al. 2010). European beach grass has negative effects on various dune invertebrates, either due to

FIGURE 21.7 Three of the most highly invasive introduced species on coastal dunes in California. Photos: (A) courtesy of Lorraine Parsons, National Park Service; (B–C) Andrea Pickart.

A European beach grass (*Ammophila arenaria*) near Abbotts Lagoon.

B Highway iceplant (*Carpobrotus edulis*) at Samoa Dunes National Recreation Area.

C Purple veldtgrass (*Ehrharta calycina*) at Guadalupe-Nipomo Dunes.

direct effects or by displacing native plants. Dunes dominated by European beach grass lack stiletto flies at Nipomo Dunes (Holston 2005). Whereas diversity of dune arthropods increases with cover of native plant species at sites from Sonoma to San Luis Obispo Counties, it declines with cover of European beach grass (Slobodchikoff and Doyen 1977).

Invasiveness of highway iceplant likewise appears linked to its ability to form very dense stands, high tolerance of stress, and effective dispersal. Comparison of highway iceplant with a dune native in Europe suggests that drought tolerance of seedlings, dispersal by rabbits, and allelopathy all increase the ability of highway iceplant to spread on dunes (Novoa et al. 2012). Highway iceplant spreads much more than another introduced species in the same genus, Chilean sea fig (*Carpobrotus chiloensis*); dispersal of the former's seeds by native mammals that eat the fruits could be partly responsible. Proportions of the two species' seeds in scat of mule deer (*Odocoileus hemionus*) and black-tailed jackrabbit suggest preferential consumption of highway iceplant fruits, and passage through animals increased germination of seeds of highway iceplant but decreased germination in Chilean sea fig (Vilá and D'Antonio 1998). Dispersal of highway iceplant seeds by deer and rabbits likely aids its spread (D'Antonio 1990) even though herbivory limits its establishment (D'Antonio 1993). Hybridization can sometimes promote invasiveness; data from chloroplast DNA, ALLOZYMES, and plant morphology all indicate that hybridization results in gene flow from Chilean sea fig to highway iceplant (Schierenbeck et al. 2005).

In southern Europe, plant-soil interactions inhibit initial establishment of highway iceplant (de la Pena et al. 2011); however, once established, the species alters soils so as to be more favorable to its own growth and less favorable to at least some native plants. Even after removal, highway iceplant can inhibit colonization by native plants through persistent effects on soil chemistry (Conser and Connor 2009). Over a decade, Williams and Williams (1984) observed changes in dune vegetation at Morro Bay that included displacement of natives by spread of highway iceplant or Chilean sea fig. Competition with highway iceplant for water decreases water potential and shoot growth in native mock heather and leads it to root more deeply (D'Antonio and Mahall 1991). Molinari et al. (2007) review the multiple, strong effects of highway iceplant on dunes.

Two other intentionally introduced, highly invasive perennials on dunes along parts of the coast are purple veldtgrass (Figure 21.7) and yellow bush lupine. Purple veldtgrass was introduced from southern Africa to control erosion and provide forage. The grass is said to be very abundant on dunes at Vandenberg Air Force Base and could prove a major invasive species on dunes in southern California. No work on its invasion ecology in California seems to have been published yet. Yellow bush lupine is a nitrogen-fixing shrub native to coastal dunes in central California. It was intentionally introduced to northern California to increase soil fertility and stabilize dunes and has become locally abundant (Pickart et al. 1998b). Dunes are also subject to invasion by the introduced, European annual grasses that have spread widely in California's coastal grasslands (see Chapter 23, "Grasslands"). On a stabilized dune at Bodega Bay, the most abundant introduced species was the invasive annual grass known as ripgut brome (*Bromus diandrus*; Lortie and Cushman 2007). Abundance of these grasses is positively associated with nitrogen availability, and introduction of yellow bush lupine to Humboldt Bay has facilitated the spread of introduced annual grasses on dunes there (Pickart et al. 1998b) .

Management Strategies

Strategies for managing coastal dunes worldwide include (Doody 2013):

- regulation of development, such as housing, that obliterates dunes
- decisions about which areas to maintain in a seminatural state for agricultural uses such as forestry and grazing
- encouragement or restriction of recreational uses of natural areas
- compensation for erosion through addition of sand
- stopping sand from moving onto adjacent areas such as roads and harbors
- restoring dunes that have been devegetated by human use or covered by the spread of introduced species
- maintaining populations of rare or endangered species

All of these are of some importance in California except perhaps allocation of lands to forestry and grazing, which seem little practiced on coastal dunes in the state. Since two main effects of humans on coastal dunes in California have been development and plant introductions, two logical main areas of management are protection of remaining dunes from development and removal of introduced plants.

A key law governing development on coastal dunes in California is the California Coastal Act of 1976 (Division 20 of the California Public Resources Code, www.coastal.ca.gov), established pursuant to the Federal Coastal Zone Management Act of 1972 (Title 16 U.S.C. 1451-1454). The California Coastal Act designates a coastal zone whose terrestrial portion generally extends 1,000 yards (914 meters) inland from the mean high tide line. The extent is less in developed urban areas and more, up to five miles (8 kilometers) or to the first major ridgeline, in "significant coastal estuarine, habitat, and recreational areas." The act thus applies to nearly all of the state's remaining dunes.

The act declares that "it is necessary to protect the ecological balance of the coastal zone and prevent its deterioration and destruction." Furthermore, "existing developed uses, and future developments that are carefully planned and developed consistent with the policies of this division, are essential." Among the basic goals of the act are to ensure public access to the coast, to maintain prime agricultural land in production, and to protect "environmentally sensitive habitat" and "scenic and visual qualities." The act creates a California Coastal Commission to implement it as the designated state planning and management agency for the coastal zone. The commission exercises this charge in large part by evaluating, and either granting or denying permission for, any activity in the coastal zone covered by the act. The act provides in a general way for the use of science to inform management, in part by instructing the commission to consult with social, physical and natural scientists on a wide variety of coastal issues, especially "coastal erosion and geology, marine biodiversity, wetland restoration, the question of sea level rise, desalination plants, and the cumulative impact of coastal zone developments." The act does not refer specifically to dunes, but one of its stated aims is to reduce the risk of beach erosion, and the commission has included dunes in areas designated as environmentally sensitive habitat.

Whether as a result of the act or by elimination through development of the dunes outside preserves, the relatively intact portions of major dune systems along the California coast now mostly lie within federal, state, or local preserves of some kind. This moots purely commercial development and emphasizes the issue of how to balance recreational use and ecological conservation. In some cases, such as the use of dunes by animals of special conservation concern, human use and ecological conservation may be mutually exclusive. For instance, Lafferty (2001) concluded based on work near Santa Barbara that protection of nesting by western snowy plovers requires that all access be prohibited to stretches of beach where birds are nesting and that dogs in adjacent stretches be on leash during the nesting season. These recommendations are being followed at a number of locations including the Coal Oil Point Reserve of the University of California at Santa Barbara, where populations of plovers have increased (Snowy Plover Program 2014).

In other cases, management can help reconcile use and conservation. Addition of sand to beaches, also known as beach nourishment or replenishment, is common around the world and in some places in California (Clayton 1991, Speybroeck et al. 2006). Nordstrom et al. (2011) suggest promoting natural features on heavily used shores by adapting techniques such as beach nourishment to more closely mimic natural landforms and by restricting some activities such as driving and raking. Removing wrack from the seaward slope of the foredune can reduce scouring of the foredune and increase transport of sand inland (Jackson and Nordstrom 2013). Fencing at the seaward base of the foredune can also reduce scouring but tends to decrease transport of sand. In a survey of beaches and dunes on three continents, McLachlan et al. (2013) suggested using one index of conservation value and another of recreation potential to guide management for conservation, recreation, or both. While some of the net effects of management can probably be judged by informal inspection, others—such as effects on populations of endangered species—are better measured with quantitative monitoring (Pickart et al. 2000).

Restoration

Like some other habitats where frequent natural disturbance maintains early successional stages with minimal soil development, the unstabilized and partly stabilized portions of coastal dunes appear relatively amenable to restoration of native vegetation. Essential steps appear to include curtailment of driving or other human uses that remove plants, and restoration of a natural regime of sand movement. If native plants remain at a site, they sometimes spread by themselves. If not or to speed restoration, native plants can be grown in a local nursery and transplanted (Trent et al. 1983). Since areas without plants may lack mycorrhizal fungi, transplants already infected with fungi may grow better than uninfected transplants (Gemma and Koske 1997).

On dunes along California's northern and central coasts, restoring the physical environment for native vegetation now generally begins with removal of introduced plants (Pickart and Sawyer 1998). These are most often European beach grass and highway iceplant. One notably successful set of restorations of dunes covered by European beach grass has taken place at Humboldt Bay using only manual pulling and digging (Pickart 2013). For instance, one project used intensive, paid labor in each of three years followed by annual maintenance mainly by volunteers; topography and vegetation twenty-five years later were similar to conditions on nearby, intact dunes. These projects also provide a nice example of cooperation between agencies and nongovernmental organizations (Deblinger and Jenkins 1991).

Alternative methods of removing European beach grass and highway iceplant are to use heavy equipment to uproot and bury plants or to spray them with herbicides such as glyphosate or imazapyr. An ongoing series of projects near Abbotts Lagoon in Point Reyes National Seashore has yielded promising results with either mechanical removal or herbicides, sometimes abetted by hand pulling, removal of dead plants, or transplanting natives (Abbotts Lagoon Coastal Dune Restoration Project 2014). Mechanical removal of European beach grass in this work was relatively expensive and required digging up to 3 meters deep. Mechanical burial has also been used to eradicate rugosa rose (*Rosa rugosa*) from dunes in Denmark (Kollmann et al. 2011).

Removal of introduced plants from dunes can help restore communities of native animals as well as of native plants. At Fort Funston in the Golden Gate National Recreation Area, active dune restoration has increased the cover and number of species of native plants and the abundance and diversity of native animals (Russell et al. 2009). Removal of European beach grass in Oregon and Washington has increased abundance of both the western snowy plover and native dune plants (Zarnetske et al. 2010). Sampling at six sites in northern and central California showed higher abundance and diversity of arthropods on foredunes from which European beach grass had been removed than on foredunes dominated by the grass (Doudna and Connor 2012).

Restoration of dunes occupied by introduced shrubs of yellow bush lupine at Humboldt Bay requires not just removing the shrubs but also reversing their effects on the soil and other plants (Pickart et al. 1998a). Yellow bush lupine increases nitrogen availability and amount of plant litter and favors the spread of introduced, annual grasses. Pickart et al. (1998b) were finally able to remove and decrease reestablishment of this suite of introduced plants by clearing yellow bush lupine with a brush rake, removing litter and duff with a plow blade, and laying down weed mats for two years. Research in Italy indicates that the numbers of introduced and of native plant species on dunes can be controlled by different natural and human factors (Carboni et al. 2010), which might suggest further strategies for restoration.

Future Scenarios

The remaining coastal dunes in California are largely protected from development, since they lie mostly within reserves, recreational areas, or military bases. Their most immediate threat is probably the continued spread of introduced invasive plants. Even though the most far-spreading invasives are no longer intentionally planted within reserves and are widely agreed to be undesirable on natural dunes, eradicating these species is difficult and controlling them requires continuing effort. A key conservation measure would be to focus this effort on the roughly ten areas in California where native communities of dune plants and animals are well developed and fairly intact.

In the longer term, loss of coastal dunes to climate change appears likely. The National Research Council (2012) has projected a rise in sea level of about 0.9 meter by 2100 along the coast of California south of Cape Mendocino.

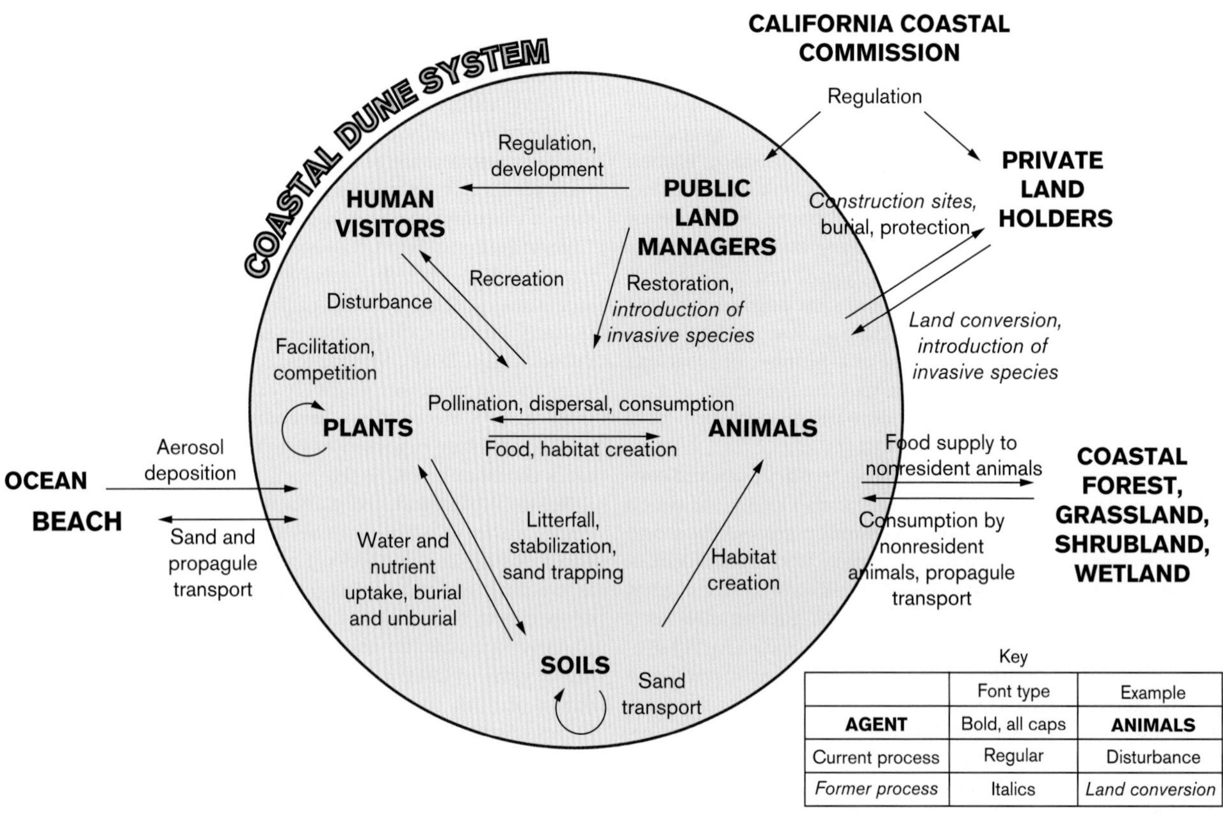

	Font type	Example
AGENT	Bold, all caps	**ANIMALS**
Current process	Regular	Disturbance
Former process	Italics	*Land conversion*

FIGURE 21.8 Key components of coastal dune systems in California.

Revell et al. (2011) used a downscaled regional global climate model, statewide data on coastal geology, and two methods of estimating flood elevations to predict erosion distances of 170 to 600 meters on coasts backed by dunes in California given a 1.4 meter rise in sea level. Although effects of climate change on the frequency or intensity of storms along the California coast are uncertain (National Research Council 2012), wave height has increased along the Pacific Coast of the U.S. over the past twenty-four years, consistent with increases in the North Pacific and Multivariate ENSO Indices over the past century that may reflect climate change (Seymour 2011; see Chapter 2, "Climate"). Increases in sea level and wave height could interact with effects of introduced species on dune morphology to flood large areas of dunes with saltwater. A model of dune overtopping as a function of storm intensity and sea level rise showed that the reduction in foredune heights associated with replacement of European beach grass by American beach grass in Oregon could triple the area subject to flooding by saltwater washing over the foredune (Seabloom et al. 2013). A model of succession on dunes in Texas suggests that sea level rise would particularly lead to losses of late-successional plants (Feagin et al. 2005).

Because beaches supply the sand for dunes, changes in beach erosion will also influence the future of dunes. Hapke et al. (2009) showed a recent increase in net beach erosion, finding that only 40% of beaches along approximately 750 kilometers of the California coast had undergone net erosion over the past 120 years, but that 66% had shrunk over the past 25 years. This could be caused by an increase in gross erosion associated with climate change or by a decrease in gross deposition caused by engineering. Slagel and Griggs (2008) estimated that dams have reduced the transport of sand down rivers to the ocean by 5%, 31%, and 50% respectively in northern, central, and southern California. Human construction can also erect barriers to longshore transport of sand (see Chapter 20, "Sandy Beaches"). For example, erosion of Ocean Beach in San Francisco is associated with both reduced sediment supply from San Francisco Bay and an exposed sewage outflow pipe (Barnard et al. 2012).

Other potential effects of climate change are more speculative. Higher temperatures throughout the state might increase visitation to beaches but shift use to activities with relatively low impact such as bathing (Coombes and Jones 2010). Although no clear expectations have emerged about effects of climate change on ocean currents, changes to the southerly, longshore flow that characterizes the northern and central California coast could reduce fog and increase temperatures. Where space exists on their inland edge, dune systems might respond to higher seas by migrating inland rather than disappearing. Psuty and Silveira (2010) offer a conceptual model of accretion and transport of sand based on observations of dunes on Fire Island in New York that suggests that sea level rise can sometimes lead to more positive sediment budgets and the displacement of dune systems inland without net loss of the system. However, development on the inland side of dunes could cause a "coastal squeeze" (Schlacher et al. 2007), with dunes caught between a rising, stormier sea and homes or businesses.

To adapt management of dunes to climate change in California, one could thus avoid development where shorelines are retreating (Defeo et al. 2009). One could also counter erosion with appropriate beach nourishment (Brown and McLachlan 2002) and by avoiding the reduction of inputs of sand to beaches, such as by dams along rivers (Slagel and Griggs

2008). The coastal dunes of California are a geologically ephemeral fringe. However, they embody natural dynamics that cover most of the state, from erosion in the Sierra Nevada and coastal mountains to currents and storms in the ocean; and social dynamics that involve most of the state's people, through coastal development, engineering of rivers, recreation, and concern for other species. For both research and management, the coastal dune ecosystem should be viewed as comprising open, dynamic, coupled natural and human systems (Figure 21.8).

Summary

Coastal sand dunes are recycled land—washed down from inland mountains in rivers, carried alongshore by currents, washed ashore by waves, and blown in from beaches to form a moving landscape of ridges and hollows. Dunes have distinctive plants and invertebrates, some rare or confined to the state. Plants that colonize bare dunes stabilize them, at which point other plants appear and the main factors controlling vegetation shift from movement of sand to availability of resources such as water, nitrogen, and light.

Coastal dunes offer the people of California recreation, scenery, and attractive sites for construction. However, the movement of sand dunes can also damage property and infrastructure. People have responded by protecting some dunes, building over many of the dunes close to cities, and stabilizing dunes with introduced plants. Dunes in northern California now are largely covered with introduced plants; dunes in southern California have been mostly built over; and most of the state's relatively intact dunes lie within public reserves. Further development of coastal dunes in most of the state is regulated by the California Coastal Commission, created by the California Coastal Act of 1976. Management of remaining dunes requires a balance of human use and conservation, restoration of dunes laid bare by use or covered with introduced plants, and control of introduced plants where communities of native plants and animals persist. Restorations have been notably successful at several sites in northern California. In the long term, the future of dunes is linked to climate change. Rising sea level is expected to displace dunes inland, likely causing net loss.

Acknowledgments

I thank the California Department of Parks and Recreation and the U.S. Park Service, particularly the staffs of Point Reyes National Seashore and Año Nuevo State Reserve as well as the University of California Bodega Marine Laboratory and Reserve for facilitating the research that gave me familiarity with the coastal dunes of California. Peter Baye, Carla D'Antonio, Lorraine Parsons, Andrea Pickart, and Jackie Sones kindly provided photographs; and Carla D'Antonio contributed helpful comments on an earlier version of the chapter. I am also very grateful to Hal Mooney and Erika Zavaleta for their editorial leadership, guidance, and patience.

Recommended Reading

California Coastal Commission. 2003. California coastal access guide. University of California Press, Berkeley, California.

Doody, J. P. 2013. Sand dune conservation, management, and restoration. Springer Verlag, New York, New York.

Griggs, G., K. Patsch, and L. Savoy, editors. 2005. Living with the changing California coast. University of California Press, Berkeley, California.

Pickart, A. J., and M. G. Barbour. 2007. Beach and dune. Pages 155–173 in M. G. Barbour, T. Keeler-Wolf, and A. A. Schoenherr, editors. Terrestrial vegetation of California. Third edition. University of California Press, Berkeley, California.

Glossary

ALLOZYMES Enzymes that occur in organisms in variant or alternate forms as a result of coding by different alleles (versions or alternative forms of a gene).

APPARENT COMPETITION A mutual though often asymmetrical negative effect of two species on each other caused, not by direct interaction or consumption of a common resource, but instead by an increase in a predator or parasite.

BLOWOUT A portion of a dune ridge hollowed out by wind.

DEFLATION PLAIN An area upwind of a dune that wind has eroded down to the water table.

DERIVED Of a trait of an organism, present in some taxa but not in their common ancestor.

DUNE SHEET A set of dune ridges that form a continuous area of sand.

FORBS Plants that are herbaceous and not grasses or like grasses; includes plants commonly called wildflowers.

FOREDUNE The most seaward dune of a dune system, adjacent to and paralleling the beach.

INTRODUCED Of a species, brought into a new region by human action.

INVASIVE Of a species, entering into a habitat where it was not previously present and having negative effects on species already there.

MINERALIZATION Conversion from organic to inorganic form, as of nitrogen from amino acids to ammonium or nitrate, the main forms in which nitrogen is taken up by plants.

MONOCARPIC Refers to plants that reproduce (fruit) only once and then die, without necessarily having a short lifespan.

ORDINATION Any of various statistical methods for arranging items in an abstract space such that more similar items are nearer each other.

PARABOLIC DUNE A curved dune ridge whose ends point upwind.

POLYPLOIDY The condition of containing more than two paired sets of chromosomes. When polyploidy occurs in plants, it can yield a new species if the polyploid individuals cannot reproduce with their diploid ancestors and counterparts.

QUANTITATIVE TRAIT LOCI The regions of DNA that are associated with the genes for a particular trait.

SLACK A seasonal wetland in a dune system.

STOLON A horizontal stem that grows at or just below the soil surface and that can form new shoots and roots at stem nodes; distinguished from rhizomes mainly by the location of rhizomes well below the soil surface.

STOMATA A pore in the epidermis of a plant that can be opened and closed, controlling movement of gasses in and out of the plant.

SUCCESSION A progressive change in species composition in a place over time.

TRANSVERSE DUNE A dune ridge oriented perpendicular to prevailing winds.

WATER POTENTIAL A measure of the free energy of water; water tends to moves from where water potential is higher to where it is lower, so the water potential in the roots of a plant must be lower than in the adjacent soil for the plant to take up water.

References

Abbotts Lagoon Coastal Dune Restoration Project. 2014. <http://www.nps.gov/pore/parkmgmt/planning_dunerestoration_abbottslagoon.htm>. Accessed March 3, 2014.

Aigner, P. A. 2004. Ecological and genetic effects on demographic processes: Pollination, clonality, and seed production in *Dithyrea maritima*. Biological Conservation 116:27–34.

Alpert, P. 1999. Clonal integration in *Fragaria chiloensis* differs between populations: Ramets from grassland are selfish. Oecologia 120:69–76.

Alpert, P., and H. A. Mooney. 1996. Resource heterogeneity generated by shrubs and topography on coastal sand dunes. Vegetatio 122:83–93.

———. 1986. Resource sharing among ramets in the clonal herb, *Fragaria chiloensis*. Oecologia 70:227–233.

Alpert, P., R. Lumaret, and F. Digiusto. 1993. Population structure inferred from allozyme analysis in the clonal herb *Fragaria chiloensis* (Rosaceae). American Journal of Botany 80:1002–1006.

Amundson, R. G., and B. Tremback. 1989. Soil development on stabilized dunes in Golden Gate Park, San Francisco. Soil Science Society of America Journal 53:1798–1806.

Arnold, R. A. 1983. Ecological studies of six endangered butterflies (Lepidoptera: Lycaenidae): Island biogeography, patch dynamics, and design of habitat preserves. University of California Publications in Entomology 99:1–161.

Barbier, E. B., S. D. Hacker, C. Kennedy, E. W. Koch, A. C. Stier, and B. R. Silliman. 2011. The value of estuarine and coastal ecosystem services. Ecological Monographs 81:169–193.

Barbour, M. G., and A. F. Johnson. 1988. Beach and dune. Pages 223–261 in M. G. Barbour and J. Major, editors. Terrestrial vegetation of California. California Native Plant Society, Sacramento, California.

Barbour, M. G., A. Shmida, A. F. Johnson, and B. Holton. 1981. Comparison of coastal dune scrub in Israel and California—physiognomy, association patterns, species richness, phytogeography. Israel Journal of Botany 30:181–198.

Barbour, M. G., T. M. de Jong, and A. F. Johnson. 1976. Synecology of beach vegetation along the Pacific Coast of the United States of America: A first approximation. Journal of Biogeography 3:55–69.

Barbour, M. G., T. M. De Jong, and B. M. Pavlik. 1983. Marine beach and dune plant communities. Pages 296–322 in B. F. Chabot and H. A. Mooney, editors. Physiological ecology of North American plant communities. Chapman and Hall, New York, New York.

Barchyn, T. E., and C. H. Hugenholtz. 2012. A process-based hypothesis for the barchan-parabolic transformation and implications for dune activity modelling. Earth Surface Processes and Landforms 37:1456–1462.

Barnard, P. L., J. E. Hansen, and L. H. Erikson. 2012. Synthesis study of an erosion hot spot, Ocean Beach, California. Journal of Coastal Research 28:903–922.

Baye, P. R. 1990. Comparative growth responses and population ecology of European and American beachgrasses (*Ammophila* spp.) in relation to sand accretion and salinity. University of Western Ontario, London, Ontario.

Beckstead, J., and I. M. Parker. 2003. Invasiveness of *Ammophila arenaria*: Release from soil-borne pathogens? Ecology 84:2824–2831.

Beidleman, R. G. 2006. California's frontier naturalists. University of California Press, Berkeley, California.

Bluestone, V. 1981. Strand and dune vegetation at Salinas River State Beach, California. Madroño 28:49–60.

Bond, J. E., M. C. Hedin, M. G. Ramirez, and B. D. Opell. 2001. Deep molecular divergence in the absence of morphological and ecological change in the Californian coastal dune endemic trapdoor spider *Aptostichus simus*. Molecular Ecology 10:899–910.

Bonte, D., and D. Maes. 2008. Trampling affects the distribution of specialised coastal dune arthropods. Basic and Applied Ecology 9:726–734.

Bonte, D., L. Lens, and J.-P. Maelfait. 2006. Sand dynamics in coastal dune landscapes constrain diversity and life-history characteristics of spiders. Journal of Applied Ecology 43:735–747.

Boyd, R. S. 1988. Microdistribution of the beach plant *Cakile maritima* (Brassicaceae) as influenced by a rodent herbivore. American Journal of Botany 75:1540–1548.

Boyd, R. S., and M. G. Barbour. 1986. Relative salt tolerance of *Cakile edentula* (Brassicaceae) from lacustrine and marine beaches. American Journal of Botany 73:236–241.

Brown, A. C., and A. McLachlan. 2002. Sandy shore ecosystems and the threats facing them: Some predictions for the year 2015. Environmental Conservation 29:62–77.

Buell, A. C., A. J. Pickart, and J. D. Stuart. 1995. Introduction history and invasion patterns of *Ammophila arenaria* on the north coast of California. Conservation Biology 9:1587–1593.

California Coastal Commission. 1987. The California coastal resource guide. University of California Press, Berkeley, California.

Carboni, M., W. Thuiller, F. Izzi, and A. Acosta. 2010. Disentangling the relative effects of environmental versus human factors on the abundance of native and alien plant species in Mediterranean sandy shores. Diversity and Distributions 16:537–546.

Chatzimanolis, S., and M. S. Caterino. 2008a. Phylogeography and conservation genetics of Californian coastal terrestrial communities: A comparative study using three beetles. Insect Conservation and Diversity 1:222–232.

Chatzimanolis, S., and M. S. Caterino. 2008b. Phylogeography of the darkling beetle *Coelus ciliatus* in California. Annals of the Entomological Society of America 101:939–949.

Clayton, J. L. 1972. Salt spray and mineral cycling in two California coastal ecosystems. Ecology 53:74–81.

Clayton, T. D. 1991. Beach replenishment activities on the U.S. continental Pacific coast. Journal of Coastal Research 7:1195–1210.

Conser, C., and E. F. Connor. 2009. Assessing the residual effects of *Carpobrotus edulis* invasion: Implications for restoration. Biological Invasions 11:349–358.

Coombes, E. G., and A. P. Jones. 2010. Assessing the impact of climate change on visitor behaviour and habitat use at the coast: A UK case study. Global Environmental Change 20:303–313.

Cooper, W. S. 1967. Coastal dunes of California. Memoir of the Geological Society of America 104:1–131.

Cornelisse, T. M., and J. E. Hafernik. 2009. Effects of soil characteristics and human disturbance on tiger beetle oviposition. Ecological Entomology 34:495–503.

Craig, M. S. 2000. Aeolian sand transport at the Lanphere Dunes, northern California. Earth Surface Processes and Landforms 25:239–253.

Crutsinger, G. M., and N. J. Sanders. 2005. Aphid-tending ants affect secondary users in leaf shelters and rates of herbivory on *Salix hookeriana* in a coastal dune habitat. American Midland Naturalist 154:296–304.

Crutsinger, G. M., S. Y. Strauss, and J. A. Rudgers. 2010. Genetic variation within a dominant shrub species determines plant species colonization in a coastal dune ecosystem. Ecology 91:1237–1243.

Cushman, J. H., C. J. Lortie, and C. E. Christian. 2011. Native herbivores and plant facilitation mediate the performance and distribution of an invasive exotic grass. Journal of Ecology 99:524–531.

Cushman, J. H., J. C. Waller, and D. R. Hoak. 2010. Shrubs as ecosystem engineers in a coastal dune: Influences on plant populations, communities, and ecosystems. Journal of Vegetation Science 21:821–831.

Dangremond, E. M., E. A. Pardini, and T. M. Knight. 2010. Apparent competition with an invasive plant hastens the extinction of an endangered lupine. Ecology 91:2261–2271.

Danin, A., S. Rae, M. G. Barbour, N. Jurjavcic, P. Connors, and E. Uhlinger. 1998. Early primary succession on dunes at Bodega Head, California. Madroño 45:101–109.

D'Antonio, C. M. 1993. Mechanisms controlling invasion of coastal plant communities by the alien succulent *Carpobrotus edulis*. Ecology 74:83–95.

———. 1990. Seed production and dispersal in the non-native, invasive succulent *Carpobrotus edulis* (Aizoaceae) in coastal strand communities of central California. Journal of Applied Ecology 27:693–702.

D'Antonio, C. M., and B. E. Mahall. 1991. Root profiles and competition between the invasive, exotic perennial, *Carpobrotus edulis*, and two native shrub species in California coastal scrub. American Journal of Botany 78:885–894.

Dart, S., and C. G. Eckert. 2013. Experimental and genetic analyses reveal that inbreeding depression declines with increased self-fertilization among populations of a coastal dune plant. Journal of Evolutionary Biology 26:587–599.

Dawson, E., and M. Foster. 1982. Seashore plants of California. University of California Press, Berkeley, California.

Deblinger, R. D., and R. E. Jenkins. 1991. Preserving coastal biodiversity—the private, nonprofit approach. Coastal Management 19:103–112.

Defeo, O., A. McLachlan, D. S. Schoeman, T. A. Schlacher, J. Dugan, A. Jones, M. Lastra, and F. Scapini. 2009. Threats to sandy beach ecosystems: A review. Estuarine, Coastal, and Shelf Science 81:1–12.

de la Peña, E., N. de Clercq, D. Bonte, S. Roiloa, S. Rodriguez-Echeverria, and H. Freitas. 2011. Plant-soil feedback as a mechanism of invasion by *Carpobrotus edulis*. Biological Invasions 12:3637–3648.

Doing, H. 1985. Coastal fore-dune zonation and succession in various parts of the world. Vegetatio 61:65–75.

Doody, J. P. 2013. Sand dune conservation, management, and restoration. Springer Verlag, New York, New York.

Doudna, J. W., and E. F. Connor. 2012. Response of terrestrial arthropod assemblages to coastal dune restoration. Ecological Restoration 30:20–26.

Dugan, J. E., and D. M. Hubbard. 2010. Loss of coastal strand habitat in southern California: The role of beach grooming. Estuaries and Coasts 33:67–77.

Engstrom, W. N. 2006. Nineteenth century coastal geomorphology of southern California. Journal of Coastal Research 22:847–861.

Erlandson, J. M., T. C. Rick, and C. Peterson. 2005. A geoarchaeological chronology of Holocene dune building on San Miguel Island, California. Holocene 15:1227–1235.

Feagin, R. A., D. J. Sherman, and W. E. Grant. 2005. Coastal erosion, global sea-level rise, and the loss of sand dune plant habitats. Frontiers in Ecology and the Environment 3:359–364.

Fink, B. H., and J. B. Zedler. 1990. Maritime stress tolerance studies of California dune perennials. Madroño 37:200–213.

Friedman, D., and P. Alpert. 1991. Reciprocal transport between ramets increases growth of *Fragaria chiloensis* when light and nitrogen occur in separate patches but only if patches are rich. Oecologia 86:76–80.

Gaertner, M., A. Den Breeyen, C. Hui, and D. M. Richardson. 2009. Impacts of alien plant invasions on species richness in Mediterranean-type ecosystems: A meta-analysis. Progress in Physical Geography 33:319–338.

Gagné, J.-M., and G. Houle. 2001. Facilitation of *Leymus mollis* by *Honckenya peploides* on coastal dunes in subarctic Québec, Canada. Canadian Journal of Botany 79:1327–1331.

Gemma, J. N., and R. E. Koske. 1997. Arbuscular mycorrhizae in sand dune plants of the North Atlantic coast of the U.S.: Field and greenhouse inoculation and presence of mycorrhizae in planting stock. Journal of Environmental Management 50:251–264.

Glavich, D. A. 2003. The distribution, ecology, and taxonomy of *Bryoria spiralifera* and *B. pseudocapillaris* on the Samoa Peninsula, Humboldt Co., coastal northern California. Bryologist 106:588–595.

Gordon, D. M. 2000. Plants as indicators of leafcutter bee (Hymenoptera: Megachilidae) nest habitat in coastal dunes. Pan-Pacific Entomologist 76:219–233.

Gordon, R. D. 1985. The Coccinellidae (Coleoptera) of America north of Mexico. Journal of the New York Entomological Society 93:1–912.

Griggs, G. B. 2010. Introduction to California's beaches and coast. University of California Press, Berkeley, California.

Griggs, G., K. Patsch, and L. Savoy, editors. 2005. Living with the changing California coast. University of California Press, Berkeley, California.

Hacker, S. D., P. Zarnetske, E. Seabloom, P. Ruggiero, J. Mull, S. Gerrity, and C. Jones. 2012. Subtle differences in two non-native congeneric beach grasses significantly affect their colonization, spread, and impact. Oikos 121:138–148.

Hall, M. C., D. B. Lowry, and J. H. Willis. 2010. Is local adaptation in *Mimulus guttatus* caused by trade-offs at individual loci? Molecular Ecology 19:2739–2753.

Hapke, C. J., D. Reid, and B. Richmond. 2009. Rates and trends of coastal change in California and the regional behavior of the beach and cliff system. Journal of Coastal Research 25:603–615.

Hesp, P. A. 2007. Coastal dunes in the tropics and temperate regions: location, formation, morphology and vegetation processes. Pages 29–52 in M. L. Martinez and N. P. Psuty, editors. Coastal dunes: Ecology and conservation. Springer-Verlag, Berlin, Germany.

———. 2002. Foredunes and blowouts: Initiation, geomorphology, and dynamics. Geomorphology 48:245–268.

Holston, K. C. 2005. Evidence for community structure and habitat partitioning in coastal dune stiletto flies at the Guadalupe-Nipomo dunes system, California. Journal of Insect Science 5:paper 42.

Holton, B., Jr., and A. F. Johnson. 1979. Dune scrub communities and their correlation with environmental factors at Point Reyes National Seashore, California. Journal of Biogeography 6:317–328.

Houser, C., B. Labude, L. Haider, and B. Weymer. 2013. Impacts of driving on the beach: Case studies from Assateague Island and Padre Island National Seashores. Ocean and Coastal Management 71:33–45.

Huntzinger, M., R. Karban, and J. H. Cushman. 2008. Negative effects of vertebrate herbivores on invertebrates in a coastal dune community. Ecology 89:1972–1980.

Huntzinger, M., R. Karban, and J. L. Maron. 2011. Small mammals cause non-trophic effects on habitat and associated snails in a native system. Oecologia 167:1085–1091.

Jackson, N. L., and K. F. Nordstrom. 2013. Aeolian sediment transport and morphologic change on a managed and an unmanaged foredune. Earth Surface Processes and Landforms 38:413–420.

Kim, D., K. B. Yu, and S. J. Park. 2008. Identification and visualization of complex spatial pattern of coastal dune soil properties using GIS-based terrain analysis and geostatistics. Journal of Coastal Research 24:50–60.

Knott, J. R., and D. S. Eley. 2006. Early to middle Holocene coastal dune and estuarine deposition, Santa Maria Valley, California. Physical Geography 27:127–136.

Kollmann, J., K. Brink-Jensen, S. I. Frandsen, and M. K. Hansen. 2011. Uprooting and burial of invasive alien plants: A new tool in coastal restoration? Restoration Ecology 19:371–378.

Kowalchuk, G. A., F. A. De Souza, and J. A. Van Veen. 2002. Community analysis of arbuscular mycorrhizal fungi associated with *Ammophila arenaria* in Dutch coastal sand dunes. Molecular Ecology 11:571–581.

Kuhnz, L. A., R. K. Burton, P. N. Slattery, and J. M. Oakden. 2005. Microhabitats and population densities of California legless lizards, with comments on effectiveness of various techniques for estimating numbers of fossorial reptiles. Journal of Herpetology 39:395–402.

Lafferty, K. D. 2001. Disturbance to wintering western snowy plovers. Biological Conservation 101:315–325.

Lamb, F. H. 1898. Sand dune reclamation on the Pacific coast. The Forester 4:141–142.

Leger, E. A., and K. J. Rice. 2007. Assessing the speed and predictability of local adaptation in invasive California poppies (*Eschscholzia californica*). Journal of Evolutionary Biology 3:1090–1103.

Lortie, C. J., and J. H. Cushman. 2007. Effects of a directional abiotic gradient on plant community dynamics and invasion in a coastal dune system. Journal of Ecology 95:468–481.

Lowry, D. B., C. R. Rockwood, J. H. Willis, and D. Schoen. 2008. Ecological reproductive isolation of coast and inland races of *Mimulus guttatus*. Evolution 62:2196–2214.

Lowry, D. B., M. C. Hall, D. E. Salt, and J. H. Willis. 2009. Genetic and physiological basis of adaptive salt tolerance divergence between coastal and inland *Mimulus guttatus*. New Phytologist 183:776–788.

Maron, J. L., and E. L. Simms. 2001. Rodent-limited establishment of bush lupine: Field experiments on the cumulative effect of granivory. Journal of Ecology 89:578–588.

———. 1997. Effect of seed predation on seed bank size and seedling recruitment of bush lupine (*Lupinus arboreus*). Oecologia 111:76–83.

Maron, J. L., and R. L. Jefferies. 1999. Bush lupine mortality, altered resource availability, and alternative vegetation states. Ecology 80:443–454.

Maron, J. L., J. K. Combs, and S. M. Louda. 2002. Convergent demographic effects of insect attack on related thistles in coastal vs. continental dunes. Ecology 83:3382–3392.

Mattoni, R., T. Longcore, and V. Novotny. 2000. Arthropod monitoring for fine-scale habitat analysis: A case study of the El Segundo sand dunes. Environmental Management 25:445–452.

Maun, M. A. 2009. The biology of coastal sand dunes. Oxford University Press, Oxford, UK.

McBride, J. R., and E. C. Stone. 1976. Plant succession on the sand dunes of the Monterey Peninsula, California. American Midland Naturalist 96:118–132.

McLachlan, A., and A. C. Brown. 2006. The ecology of sandy shores. Academic Press, Burlington, Massachusetts.

McLachlan, A., O. Defeo, E. Jaramillo, and A. D. Short. 2013. Sandy beach conservation and recreation: Guidelines for optimising management strategies for multi-purpose use. Ocean and Coastal Management 71:256–268.

McNeil, S. G., and J. H. Cushman. 2005. Indirect effects of deer herbivory on local nitrogen availability in a coastal dune ecosystem. Oikos 110:124–132.

Molinari, N., C. D'Antonio, and G. Thompson. 2007. *Carpobrotus* as a case study of the complexities of species impacts. Pages 139–162 in K. Cuddington, J. E. Byers, W. G. Wilson, and A. Hastings, editors. Ecosystem engineers: Plants to protists. Elsevier Academic Press, San Diego, California.

Moore, P. G. 2002. Mammals in intertidal and maritime ecosystems: Interactions, impacts, and implications. Oceanography and Marine Biology 40:491–608.

Morrell, P. L., J. M. Porter, and E. A. Friar. 2000. Intercontinental dispersal: The origin of the widespread South American plant species *Gilia laciniata* (Polemoniaceae) from a rare California and Oregon coastal endemic. Plant Systematics and Evolution 224:13–32.

Muhs, D. R., G. Skipp, R. R. Schumann, D. L. Johnson, J. P. McGeehin, J. Beann, J. Freeman, T. A. Pearce, and Z. M. Rowland. 2009. The origin and paleoclimatic significance of carbonate sand dunes deposited on the California Channel Islands during the last glacial period. Pages 3–14 in C. C. Damiani and D. K. Garcelon, editors. Proceedings of the Seventh California Islands Symposium. Institute for Wildlife Studies, Arcata, California.

Munz, P. 1964. Shore wildflowers of California, Oregon, and Washington. University of California Press, Berkeley, California.

Nagano, C. D. 1980. Population status of the tiger beetles of the genus *Cicindela* (Coleoptera: Cicindelidae) inhabiting the marine shoreline of southern California. Atala 8:33–42.

National Research Council. 2012. Sea-level rise for the coasts of California, Oregon and Washington: past, present and future. National Academy Press, Washington, D.C.

Namikas, S. L. 2003. Field measurement and numerical modelling of aeolian mass flux distributions on a sandy beach. Sedimentology 50:303–326.

Nordstrom, K. F. 2000. Beaches and dunes on developed coasts. Cambridge University Press, Cambridge, UK.

Nordstrom, K. F., N. L. Jackson, N. C. Kraus, T. W. Kana, R. Bearce, L. M. Bocamazo, D. R. Young, and H. A. De Butts. 2011. Enhancing geomorphic and biologic functions and values on backshores and dunes of developed shores: A review of opportunities and constraints. Environmental Conservation 38:288–302.

Novoa, A., L. Gonzalez, L. Moravcova, and P. Pysek. 2012. Effects of soil characteristics, allelopathy, and frugivory on establishment of the invasive plant *Carpobrotus edulis* and a co-occurring native, *Malcolmia littorea*. PloS One 7(12): e53166.

Palmisano, S., and L. R. Fox. 1997. Effects of mammal and insect herbivory on population dynamics of a native Californian thistle, *Cirsium occidentale*. Oecologia 111:413–421.

Papenfuss, T. J., and J. F. Parham. 2013. Four new species of California legless lizards (*Anniella*). Breviora 536:1–17.

Pavlik, B. M. 1985. Water relations of the dune grasses *Ammophila arenaria* and *Elymus mollis* on the coast of Oregon, USA. Oikos 45:197–205.

———. 1983. Nutrient and productivity relations of the dune grasses *Ammophila arenaria* and *Elymus mollis*. 3. Spatial aspects of clonal expansion with reference to rhizome growth and the dispersal of buds. Bulletin of the Torrey Botanical Club 110:271–279.

Peinado, M., F. M. Ocaña-Peinado, J. L. Aguirre, J. Delgadillo, M. A. Macías, and G. Díaz-Santiago. 2011. A phytosociological and phytogeographical survey of the coastal vegetation of western North America: Beach and dune vegetation from Baja California to Alaska. Applied Vegetation Science 14:464–484.

Peinado, M., J. L. Aguirre, J. Delgadillo, and M. A. Macias. 2007. Zonobiomes, zonoecotones, and azonal vegetation along the Pacific coast of North America. Plant Ecology 191:221–252.

Peterson, C. D. 2006. Dating and morphostratigraphy of coastal dune sheets. Oregon Sea Grant, Corvallis, Oregon.

Peterson, C. D., E. Stock, D. M. Price, R. Hart, F. Reckendorf, J. M. Erlandson, and S. W. Hostetler. 2007. Ages, distributions, and origins of upland coastal dune sheets in Oregon, USA. Geomorphology 91:80–102.

Peterson, C. D., E. Stock, R. Hart, D. Percy, S. W. Hostetler, and J. R. Knott. 2010. Holocene coastal dune fields used as indicators of net littoral transport: West Coast, USA. Geomorphology 116:115–134.

Pickart, A. J. 2013. Dune restoration over two decades at the Lanphere and Ma-le'l Dunes in northern California. Pages 159–172 in M. L. Martínez, J. B. Gallego-Fernández, and P. A. Hesp, editors. Restoration of coastal dunes. Springer-Verlag, Berlin, Germany.

Pickart, A. J., and J. O. Sawyer. 1998. Ecology and restoration of northern California coastal dunes. California Native Plant Society, Sacramento, California.

Pickart, A. J., and M. G. Barbour. 2007. Beach and dune. Pages 155–173 in M. G. Barbour, T. Keeler-Wolf, and A. A. Schoenherr, editors. Terrestrial vegetation of California. Third edition. University of California Press, Berkeley, California.

Pickart, A. J., A. L. Eicher, M. M. Bivin, and K. F. Hayler. 2000. Changes in a metapopulation of the endangered Humboldt Bay wallflower (*Erysimum menziesii* [Hook.] Wettst. ssp *eurekense* R.A. Price) in relation to disease incidence and management. Natural Areas Journal 20:234–242.

Pickart, A. J., L. M. Miller, and T. E. Duebendorfer. 1998a. Yellow bush lupine invasion in northern California coastal dunes. I. Ecological impacts and manual restoration techniques. Restoration Ecology 6:59–68.

Pickart, A. J., K. C. Theiss, H. B. Stauffer, and G. T. Olsen. 1998b. Yellow bush lupine invasion in northern California coastal dunes. II. Mechanical restoration techniques. Restoration Ecology 6:69–74.

Pitts, W. D., and M. G. Barbour. 1979. Microdistribution and feeding preferences of *Peromyscus maniculatus* in the strand at Point Reyes National Seashore, California. American Midland Naturalist 101:38–48.

Plassmann, K., M.L.M. Jones, and G. Edwards-Jones. 2010. Effects of long-term grazing management on sand dune vegetation of high conservation interest. Applied Vegetation Science 13:100–112.

Porter, A. H., and S. O. Mattoon. 1989. A new subspecies of *Coenonympha tullia* (Muller) (Nymphalidae: Satyrinae) confined to the coastal dunes of northern California. Journal of the Lepidopterists' Society 43:229–238.

Powell, J. A. 1991. A review of *Lithariapteryx* (Heliodinidae), with description of an elegant new species from coastal sand dunes in California. Journal of the Lepidopterists' Society 45:89–104.

———. 1976. A remarkable new genus of brachypterous moth from coastal sand dunes in California (Lepidoptera: Gelechioidea, Scythrididae). Annals of the Entomological Society of America 69:325–339.

Psuty, N. P., and T. M. Silveira. 2010. Global climate change: An opportunity for coastal dunes? Journal of Coastal Conservation 14:153–160.

Ramsey, J. 2011. Polyploidy and ecological adaptation in wild yarrow. Proceedings of the National Academy of Sciences of the United States of America 108:7096–7101.

Revell, D. L., R. Battalio, B. Spear, P. Ruggiero, and J. Vandever. 2011. A methodology for predicting future coastal hazards due to sea-level rise on the California Coast. Climatic Change 109:251–276.

Roiloa, S. R., P. Alpert, N. Tharayil, G. Hancock, and P. Bhowmik. 2007. Greater capacity for division of labour in clones of *Fragaria chiloensis* from patchier habitats. Journal of Ecology 95:397–405.

Rudgers, J. A., and J. L. Maron. 2003. Facilitation between coastal dune shrubs: A non-nitrogen fixing shrub facilitates establishment of a nitrogen-fixer. Oikos 102:75–84.

Runyan, K., and G. B. Griggs. 2003. The effects of armoring seacliffs on the natural sand supply to the beaches of California. Journal of Coastal Research 19:336–347.

Russell, W., J. Shulzitski, and A. Setty. 2009. Evaluating wildlife response to coastal dune habitat restoration in San Francisco, California. Ecological Restoration 27:439–448.

Samis, K. E., and C. G. Eckert. 2009. Ecological correlates of fitness across the northern geographic range limit of a Pacific Coast dune plant. Ecology 90:3051–3061.

———. 2007. Testing the abundant center model using range-wide demographic surveys of two coastal dune plants Ecology 88:1747–1758.

Sawyer, J. O., T. Keeler-Wolf, and J. Evens. 2009. A manual of California vegetation. California Native Plant Society, Sacramento, California.

Schierenbeck, K. A., V. V. Symonds, K. G. Gallagher, and J. Bell. 2005. Genetic variation and phylogeographic analyses of two species of *Carpobrotus* and their hybrids in California. Molecular Ecology 14:539–547.

Schlacher, T. A., J. Dugan, D. S. Schoeman, M. Lastra, A. Jones, F. Scapini, A. McLachlan, and O. Defeo. 2007. Sandy beaches at the brink. Diversity and Distributions 13:556–560.

Seabloom, E. W., P. Ruggiero, S. D. Hacker, J. Mull, and P. Zarnetske. 2013. Invasive grasses, climate change, and exposure to storm-wave overtopping in coastal dune ecosystems. Global Change Biology 19:824–832.

Seymour, R. J. 2011. Evidence for changes to the northeast Pacific wave climate. Journal of Coastal Research 27:194–201.

Sherman, D. J., and B. Li. 2012. Predicting aeolian sand transport rates: A reevaluation of models. Aeolian Research 3:371–378.

Siguenza, C., I. Espejel, and E. B. Allen. 1996. Seasonality of mycorrhizae in coastal sand dunes of Baja California. Mycorrhiza 6:151–157.

Slagel, M. J., and G. B. Griggs. 2008. Cumulative losses of sand to the California coast by dam impoundment. Journal of Coastal Research 24:571–584.

Slobodchikoff, C. N., and J. T. Doyen. 1977. Effects of *Ammophila arenaria* on sand dune arthropod communities. Ecology 58:1171–1175.

Snowy Plover Program. 2014. <www.coaloilpoint.ucnrs.org/SnowyPloverProgram.html>. Accessed May 20, 2014.

Speybroeck, J., D. Bonte, W. Courtens, T. Gheskiere, P. Grootaert, J.-P. Maelfait, M. Mathys, S. Provoost, K. Sabbe, E. W. M. Stienen, V. V. Lancker, M. Vincx, and S. Degraer. 2006. Beach nourishment: An ecologically sound coastal defense alternative? A review. Aquatic Conservation: Marine and Freshwater Ecosystems 16:419–435.

Strong, D. R., J. L. Maron, P. G. Connors, A. Whipple, S. Harrison, and R. L. Jefferies. 1995. High mortality, fluctuation in numbers, and heavy subterranean insect herbivory in bush lupine, *Lupinus arboreus*. Oecologia 104:85–92.

Tobias, M. M. 2013. Effect of trampling on *Ambrosia chamissonis* and *Cakile maritima* cover on California beaches. Madroño 60:4–10.

Trent, S. A., K. Sellery, and T. Gordinier. 1983. The revegetation potential of California coastal sand dunes using containerized native plant species. Hortscience 18:622.

Vilà, M., and C. M. D'Antonio. 1998. Fruit choice and seed dispersal of invasive vs. noninvasive *Carpobrotus* (Aizoaceae) in coastal California. Ecology 79:1053–1060.

Vilà, M., E. Weber, and C. M. D'Antonio. 1998. Flowering and mating system in hybridizing *Carpobrotus* (Aizoaceae) in coastal California. Canadian Journal of Botany 76:1–6.

Warner, P. J., and J. H. Cushman. 2002. Influence of herbivores on a perennial plant: Variation with life history stage and herbivore species. Oecologia 132:77–85.

Wiedemann, A. M., and A. J. Pickart. 2004. Temperate zone coastal dunes. Pages 53–65 in M. L. Martinez and N. P. Psuty, editors. Coastal dunes—ecology and conservation. Springer Verlag, New York, New York.

Williams, W. T. 1974. Species dynamism in the coastal strand plant community at Morro Bay, California. Bulletin of the Torrey Botanical Club 101:83–89.

Williams, W. T., and J. R. Potter. 1972. The coastal strand community at Morro Bay State Park, California. Bulletin of the Torrey Botanical Club 99:163–171.

Williams, W. T., and J. A. Williams. 1984. Ten years of vegetation change on the coastal strand at Morro Bay, California. Bulletin of the Torrey Botanical Club 111:145–152.

Wilson, J. B., and M. T. Sykes. 1999. Is zonation on coastal sand dunes determined primarily by sand burial or by salt spray? A test in New Zealand dunes. Ecology Letters 2:233–236.

Yoshitake, S., and T. Nakatsubo. 2008. Changes in soil microbial biomass and community composition along vegetation zonation in a coastal sand dune. Australian Journal of Soil Research 46:390–396.

Zarnetske, P. L., E. W. Seabloom, and S. D. Hacker. 2010. Non-target effects of invasive species management: Beachgrass, birds, and bulldozers in coastal dunes. Ecosphere 1:art13.

Zarnetske, P. L., S. D. Hacker, E. W. Seabloom, P. Ruggiero, J. R. Killian, T. B. Maddux, and D. Cox. 2012. Biophysical feedback mediates effects of invasive grasses on coastal dune shape. Ecology 93:1439–1450.

Zedler, R. P. 1962. A general reconnaissance of coastal dunes of California. U.S. Army Corps of Engineers Beach Erosion Board, Washington, D.C.

Zedler, P. H., C. R. Gautier, C. Scheidlinger, and K. Guehlstorff. 1983. The population ecology of a dune thistle, *Cirsium rhothophilum* (Asteraceae). American Journal of Botany 70:1516–1527.

Zhang, J., and M. A. Maun. 1992. Effects of burial in sand on the growth and reproduction of *Cakile edentula*. Ecography 15:296–302.

TWENTY-TWO

Coastal Sage Scrub

ELSA E. CLELAND, JENNIFER L. FUNK, and EDITH B. ALLEN

Introduction

From a distance, coastal sage scrub might not appear the most compelling of California ecosystems; short in stature, it lacks the majesty of a redwood forest—but up close, coastal sage scrub is a feast for the senses. This ecosystem is known for its fragrance; it is often (though not necessarily) dominated by shrubs in the genera *Artemisia* and *Salvia*, and visitors are frequently overwhelmed by the heady scent of sage in the air. Coastal sage scrub is also renowned for both its beauty—the texture and colors when in bloom are reminiscent of a coral reef—as well as its spectacular diversity. Coastal sage scrub includes some two hundred species of forbs throughout its range (Skinner and Pavlik 1994) as well as a diverse array of associated animal species of conservation concern (Diffendorfer et al. 2007). The Mediterranean climate region of California is considered one of the global biodiversity hotspots (Myers et al. 2000), and coastal sage scrub with its interspersed forblands and riparian areas has a greater concentration of rare species than any other California ecosystem type. This has made coastal sage scrub one of the most endangered ecosystems in the U.S. (Rubinoff 2001); hence, restoration and conservation are important aspects of this chapter.

Coastal sage scrub is found in coastal zones between San Francisco and Baja California and, despite its name, extends up to 100 kilometers inland in some areas (Figure 22.1). DROUGHT-DECIDUOUS shrubs tend to dominate coastal sage scrub, while evergreen shrubs are more common in adjacent chaparral communities; this distinction has led to the colloquial description of coastal sage scrub as "soft chaparral" (Mooney and Dunn 1970, Harrison et al. 1971). In the northern range coastal sage scrub occurs at low elevations often intermixed with grassland, chaparral, and/or oak woodland (Kirkpatrick and Hutchinson 1980; Figure 22.2). At the southern extent of its range coastal sage scrub is found both at the coast and at higher elevations, between zones of desert scrub and higher-elevation chaparral (Mooney and Harrison 1972). The complexity of this mosaic suggests that disturbance, soils, and/or topographic effects play a major role in determining distributions, as opposed to purely climate.

Major Ecosystem Services Provided by This System

FOOD AND FORAGE

Historically, coastal sage scrub and interspersed forblands provided food for indigenous native Californians as documented by 1770s Spanish explorers who were invited to consume seeds of native wildflowers such as *Salvia columbariae* that occurred in great abundance (Minnich 2008). European settlers grazed cattle and sheep in coastal sage scrub, but dense shrublands were not prized grazing lands. Rather, interspersed forblands and the occasional perennial grasslands of southern California were the most productive grazed areas in lowlands. Coastal sage shrubs could be easily removed mechanically or by burning, and shrublands were thus converted to exotic annual grassland to improve forage (Burcham 1957, Robinson et al. 1993). Nevertheless, the short growing season and semiarid climate proved too harsh for a sustained grazing industry, and most large-scale grazing operations ended by the 1930s (Robinson et al. 1993). The recent decline of coastal sage scrub has been postulated by some researchers as failure to recover from grazing, but many sites that were mapped as annual grassland in the 1930s have been able to recover native shrub cover (Minnich and Dezzani 1998).

By the time these early botanical surveys were conducted, most land that could be cultivated for agriculture had been converted. The vegetation type map (VTM) survey of the 1930s (Wieslander, http://vtm.berkeley.edu/about/) showed that most level valley bottoms in coastal sage scrub landscapes had been planted to annual grains or were grazed and converted to exotic grassland, while slopes remained occupied mainly by shrubs. Today much abandoned agricultural land is undergoing conversion to urban development (Chen et al. 2010), but other areas are being restored to coastal sage scrub for biodiversity protection (Allen et al. 2005, Marushia and Allen 2011).

URBAN RECREATION AND BIODIVERSITY SERVICES

Because of its location in coastal areas with a desirable climate and low topographic relief (relative to chaparral, which is often found on steeper slopes), the major modern-day use of coastal sage scrub land is urban development. Some 25% of California's coastal sage scrub has been converted to urban and suburban development (Figure 22.3). Shrubs provide important erosion control on slopes adjacent to urban development; following heavy winter rain events, slopes occupied by exotic grasses are more susceptible to erosion than slopes occupied by shrubs (Gabet and Dunne 2002). Current important ecosystem services of coastal sage scrub include "natural beauty" (Huntsinger and Oviedo 2014) and recreational opportunities for nearby urban dwellers as well as biodiversity maintenance in this highly diverse ecosystem type. Some one hundred listed and sensitive animal species occur in southern California coastal sage scrub, including more than thirty bird species, thirty-plus mammals, over twenty-five herptiles, and several invertebrates (Riverside County Transportation and Land Management Agency 2015, San Diego Multispecies Conservation Plan 2015). Conserving the lands in which these species occur requires major efforts by local and federal agencies, including land acquisition to increase the extent of reserves, land management for invasive species control, wildfire control, recreation management, and maintenance of rare species populations (Scott et al. 2006, Barrows et al. 2005).

Photo on previous page: Santa Monica Mountains National Recreation Area, off of Deer Creek Road. Photo: Jessica D. Pratt.

Major Physical Features and Controls over Distribution

The coastal zones where coastal sage scrub occurs have a Mediterranean-type climate with a winter rainy season and a prolonged summer drought. Rainfall across the range averages 250–450 mm yr^1, and while found on a range of aspects, coastal sage scrub is most common on steep, south-facing slopes (Kirkpatrick and Hutchinson 1980). Coastal sage scrub soils tend to be relatively nutrient-rich; Westman (1981b) surveyed soils in sixty-seven coastal sage scrub sites and found total nitrogen of 0.15%, two to three times greater than measurements taken in California chaparral. Other major nutrients also tend to be relatively abundant, with 24–28 mg/g extractable phosphorus and 141–246 mg/g potassium in Venturan and Riversidean sage scrub (Westman 1981b, Padgett et al. 1999). It is unclear whether high soil nutrients result from high nutrient turnover rates by quickly decomposing deciduous litter, or whether coastal sage scrub species have high nutrient requirements and hence soil nutrient availability is an underlying predictor of their distribution. However, coastal sage scrub tends to be found more commonly on argillaceous soils with high clay content as compared with shallow siliceous soils where chaparral may be more common (Kirkpatrick and Hutchinson 1980). This suggests that inherently high cation exchange capacity could explain some of the higher soil nutrient availability in coastal sage scrub. In Mediterranean-climate regions such as this, fine-textured soils can retain moisture closer to the surface during the rainy season, promoting drought-deciduous shrubs with shallow root systems. Correspondingly, roots of coastal sage scrub shrubs are concentrated in shallow soil layers to 1.5 meters, whereas chaparral has species with the potential for roots to extend to several meters depth (Hellmers et al. 1955, Harrison et al. 1971, Wood et al. 2006).

The current distribution of coastal sage scrub is limited most by urbanization and land-use change. An estimated 10–15% of original coastal sage scrub remains intact (Westman 1981a). These figures are based on an estimated 1 million hectares covered by coastal sage scrub before European-American settlement (Küchler 1977), although more recent estimates suggest that coastal sage scrub covered less area (632,800 hectares in Fenn et al. 2010). The original extent of coastal sage scrub is uncertain based on Minnich's (2008) reanalysis of vegetation descriptions from the travel diaries of mid-eighteenth-century Spanish explorers. In areas where Küchler mapped coastal sage scrub in the Los Angeles and Riverside–Perris Plains, explorers described extensive fields of wildflowers rather than shrubs. Minnich interprets these as a vegetation type that has been little recognized in California, annual forblands, which occur throughout California in areas with low precipitation (less than 30 centimeters). Coastal sage scrub occurred on hillsides but less on valley bottoms, according to reinterpreted descriptions. Bottomlands were extensively converted to agriculture or intensive grazing before the 1930s VTM survey (Wieslander 1935), so few modern-day accounts of annual forblands exist. The hydrologic characteristics of soils and plant water relations that would limit coastal sage scrub from colonizing finer-textured, deeper soils of valley bottoms still need to be explored. Altered fire regimes, nitrogen deposition and subsequent conversion to exotic annual grassland threaten the integrity of coastal sage scrub (Talluto and Suding 2008, Keeley et al. 2005, Eliason and Allen 1997, Minnich and Dezzani 1998). The impacts of these human activi-

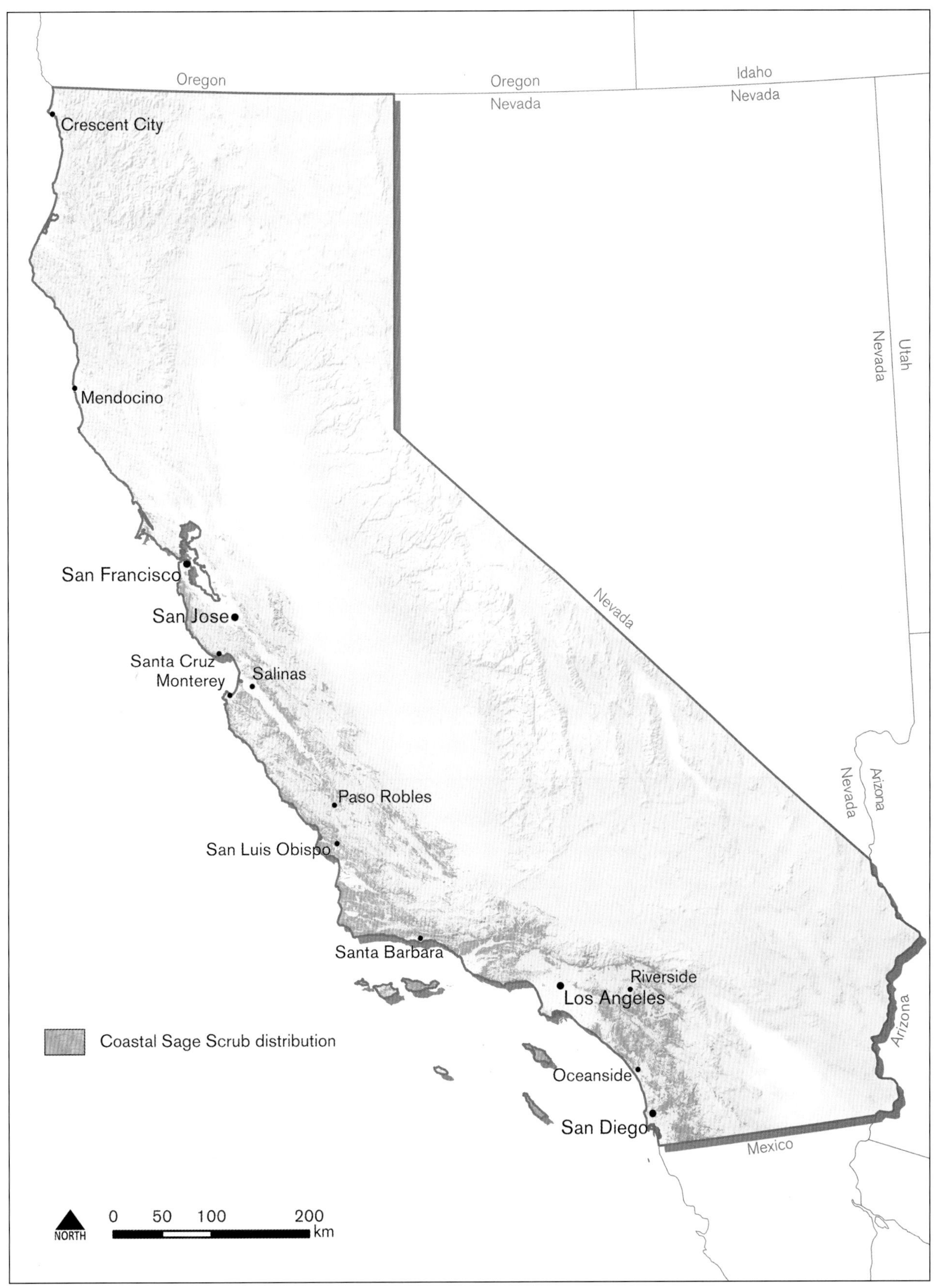

FIGURE 22.1 Distribution of coastal sage scrub in California. Data from U.S. Geological Survey, Gap Analysis Program (GAP). Map: Parker Welch, Center for Integrated Spatial Research (CISR).

FIGURE 22.2 *(Above)* Coastal sage scrub is a diverse plant community dominated by short-statured shrubs but with significant variation in species composition across its range. Photos: (A) Todd Keeler-Wolf, (B) Justin Valliere, (C) E. B. Allen, (D) Elizabeth Wolkovich. From north to south, four major variants of coastal sage scrub occur:

A Diablan (January 2007 in eastern Alameda County); plants include *Artemisia california* and *Salvia mellifera* interfacing with *Quercus douglasii* woodland in background.

B Venturan (December 2012 at Deer Creek); plants include *Salvia apiana, Artemisia californica, Hazardia squarosa, Opuntia littoralis*, and *Avena fatua*, with the evergreen shrub *Malosma laurina* in background.

C Riversidian (Lake Skinner); plants include *Keckiella antirrhinoides* and *Malacothamnus fasciculatus* in foreground, *Eschscholzia californica* in open spaces between shrubs, and exotic annual grasses in areas with shrubs historically cleared for grazing; in background, upper slopes of Black Mountain covered by mixed chaparral.

D Diegan (April 2007, facing east in the Sweetwater area of San Diego National Wildlife Refuge); plants include *Eriogonum fasciculatum, Artemisia californica*, and *Malosma laurina*.

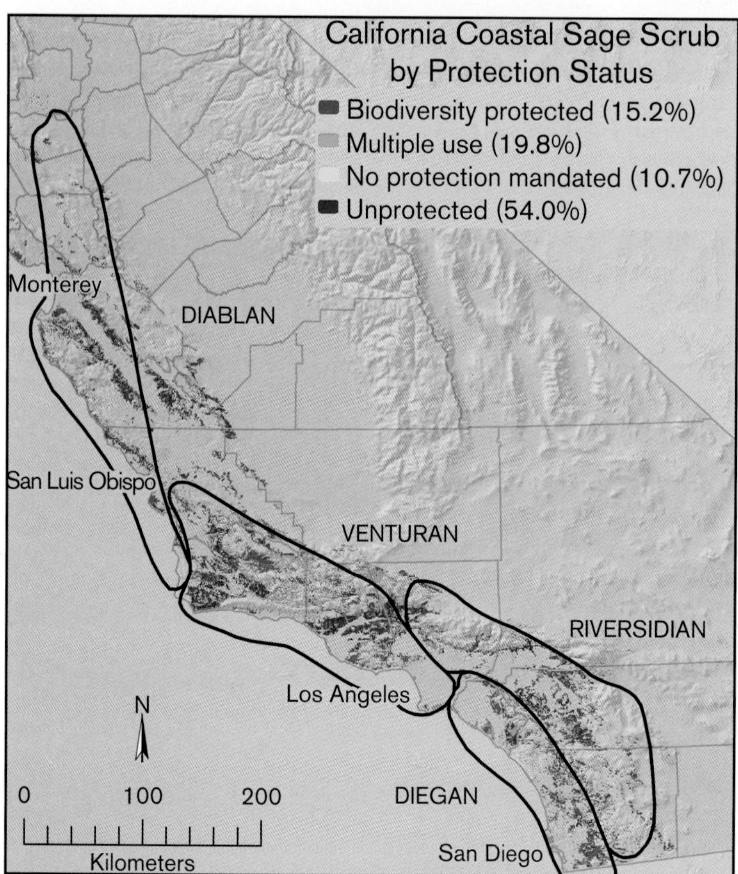

FIGURE 22.3 *(Left)* Protected area status of coastal sage scrub in California (data from U.S. Geological Survey 2013, <http://gapanalysis.usgs.gov/padus/>), with the four major variants of coastal sage scrub outlined in black (after Westman 1983).

ties on coastal sage scrub is the focus of later sections in this chapter.

Principal Organisms

The shrubs that comprise the majority of coastal sage scrub community biomass include many drought-deciduous or semievergreen species (Table 22.1). These shrubs are typically less than 2 meters in height with relatively shallow root systems, soft stems, and often thin, deciduous leaves (Holland and Keil 1995). A few common evergreen species occur, which survive in dry coastal environments via deep roots. In the understory and in open areas between shrubs is a great diversity of annual and perennial forb species as well as several common, native, perennial grass species. Several species of cactus occur in the southern areas of coastal sage scrub; the most common is *Opuntia littoralis*. At a local level, community composition is influenced by aspect, soil texture, and soil depth; south-facing slopes, coarser-textured soils, and shallower soils create more xeric conditions and favor drought-tolerant shrubs like *Eriogonum fasciculatum, Artemisia californica,* and *Salvia apiana* along with higher abundance of *Opuntia* species (DeSimone and Burk 1992). Because community composition and species dominants can change during succession following a disturbance, these factors do not consistently pre-

TABLE 22.1
Common coastal sage scrub native and exotic plant species, and their responses to fire

Scientific name	Common name	Origin	Functional type	Response to fire
Amsinckia menziesii	Common fiddleneck	Native	Annual forb	Reseeder
Cryptantha intermedia	Common cryptantha	Native	Annual forb	Reseeder
Artemisia californica	California sage	Native	Deciduous shrub	Reseeder
Encelia californica	California brittlebush	Native	Deciduous shrub	Reseeder
Eriogonum fasciculatum	California buckwheat	Native	Deciduous shrub	Reseeder
Salvia apiana	White sage	Native	Deciduous shrub	Resprouter
Salvia leucophylla	Purple sage	Native	Deciduous shrub	Reseeder
Salvia mellifera	Black sage	Native	Deciduous shrub	Reseeder
Heteromeles arbutifolia	Toyon	Native	Evergreen shrub/tree	Resprouter
Malosma laurina	Laurel sumac	Native	Evergreen shrub/tree	Resprouter
Rhamnus californica	California buckthorn	Native	Evergreen shrub/tree	Resprouter
Rhus integrifolia	Lemonadeberry	Native	Evergreen shrub/tree	Resprouter
Acmispon glaber	Deer weed	Native	N-fixing subshrub	Reseeder
Eschscholzia californica	California poppy	Native	Perennial forb	Reseeder
Dichelostemma capitatum	Blue dicks	Native	Perennial forb (corm)	Resprouter
Opuntia littoralis	Coastal prickly pear	Native	Succulent	Resprouter
Marah macrocarpus	Wild cucumber	Native	Vine	Resprouter
Brassica nigra	Black mustard	Exotic	Annual forb	Generally positive
Centaurea melitensis	Maltese star-thistle	Exotic	Annual forb	Generally positive
Erodium cicutarium	Redstem filaree	Exotic	Annual forb	Generally positive
Avena fatua	Wild oat	Exotic	Annual grass	Generally positive
Bromus hordeaceus	Soft brome	Exotic	Annual grass	Generally positive
Bromus madritensus spp rubens	Red brome	Exotic	Annual grass	Generally positive
Vulpia myuros	Rat tail fescue	Exotic	Annual grass	Generally positive
Medicago polymorpha	Bur clover	Exotic	Annual n-fixing forb	Generally positive
Cynara cardunculus	Artichoke thistle	Exotic	Perennial forb	Generally positive
Hirschfeldia incana	Short-podded mustard	Exotic	Perennial forb (short-lived)	Generally positive

SOURCE: Malanson and O'Leary 1982.
NOTE: Reseeders may be weak resprouters if not burned to ground level; strong resprouters can also reseed.

FIGURE 22.4 Exotic annual grasses that have senesced late in the growing season on a previously burned hillside in Orange County, surrounded by mature coastal sage scrub. Exotic grass litter is highly flammable and helps spread fire, fueled by Santa Ana winds in many parts of southern California. Photo: Jennifer Funk.

dict species presence or absence within particular coastal sage scrub habitats.

Four regional associations of coastal sage scrub are often described based on differences in community dominants: Diablan, Venturan, Riversidian, and Diegan (c.f. Westman 1983, building on Kirkpatrick and Hutchinson 1977, Axelrod 1978; see Figure 22.2, spatial distribution in Figure 22.3). Diablan coastal sage scrub extends from Mount Diablo in the north to just south of San Luis Obispo and is sometimes termed "northern coastal scrub" (Ford and Hayes 2007). Venturan and Diegan types include coastal areas extending from Santa Barbara to San Diego and San Diego to Baja California, respectively. Riversidian sage scrub includes inland areas from Ventura south to Baja California and is also called inland sage scrub. Within these types many authors have proposed sage scrub associations based on geographic boundaries, community composition, or dominant species (Westman 1983, Sawyer and Keeler-Wolf 1995). One type that is consistent across these variants is alluvial sage scrub that occurs wherever rivers flow through coastal sage scrub and contains some shrub and forb species not found in other coastal sage scrub variants (Sawyer and Keeler-Wolf 1995).

Coastal sage scrub communities across this range exhibit high beta-diversity; while only two to five shrub species usually dominate any given locality (Minnich and Dezzani 1998), strong regional variation yields different dominant species dominating in each zone. Describing this regional variation in vegetation composition has been the focus of excellent prior reviews (e.g., Rundel 2007). Variation in community dominants might be driven partly by environmental gradients. For example, an analysis of forty-three habitat variables found summer evaporative stress—in particular, the temperature of the warmest month as opposed to total or seasonal rainfall—to be the best predictor of species distributions across sixty-seven coastal sage scrub sites (Westman 1981b). Species richness also varies regionally within coastal sage scrub. Richness is positively correlated with distance inland and soil pH, and negatively correlated with soil nutrient content (Keeley et al. 2005b).

Community composition changes following fire as some shrubs and cactus resprout and a diverse mix of herbaceous annual and perennial species appear (see Table 22.1; O'Leary and Westman 1988). One of the most dominant species following fire is *Acmispon glaber* (previously *Lotus scoparius*), a keystone nitrogen-fixing shrub that replenishes nitrogen lost in the fire and provides nutrient-rich leaves for herbivores (Rundel 2007). *Yucca whipplei* is also common in areas characterized by frequent fire, as its fibrous main stem makes it particularly fire-resistant (Rundel 2007). Invasive species can be common in coastal sage scrub, particularly following disturbances such as fire (Figure 22.4). Most invasive species are annual grasses and forbs introduced from other Mediterranean-climate ecosystems. These species germinate early in the growing season, have shallow, fibrous root systems, and produce a thick layer of LITTER that persists until the next growing season (Bartolome 1979, Eliason and Allen 1997, Wainwright et al. 2012).

Several animal species that occur in coastal sage scrub habitat are listed as threatened, endangered, or of conservation concern by state and federal agencies (CDFG 2013). For example, the California gnatcatcher (*Polioptila californica*) is a federally threatened species and requires coastal sage scrub habitat. Modeling studies show that this species is particularly threatened by climate change due to projected shifts in the future range and extent of coastal sage scrub (Preston et al. 2008). As discussed later in this chapter, the abundance and diversity of animal species is strongly linked to vegetation dynamics and their responses to fire and human disturbance.

Ecosystem Characteristics: Coastal Sage Scrub versus Chaparral

Many researchers have quantified ecosystem characteristics of coastal sage scrub for the purpose of comparing them to chaparral, as a way of contrasting communities dominated by similar life forms (shrubs) but differing patterns of growth and leaf longevity (drought-deciduous versus evergreen). Primary production in coastal sage is generally lower than evergreen chaparral and varies among sites—255 g m^{-2} yr^{1} at one site (Gray and Schlesinger 1981), 355 g m^{-2} yr^{1} at another (Gray 1982)—and also among years with varying precipitation (e.g., from 250–600 g m^{-2} yr^{1}) (Vourlitis et al. 2009). The lower productivity of coastal sage scrub compared with chaparral is partially explained by lower precipitation and the shorter growing season of drought-deciduous shrubs (Gray 1982). However, consistent with their location closer to the high-return end of the leaf economic spectrum (Wright et al. 2004), deciduous coastal sage scrub shrubs can produce two to three times more biomass during the peak spring growing season than co-occurring evergreen species (Gray and Schlesinger 1983).

The lower production of coastal sage scrub relative to chaparral has been investigated in relation to a number of physiological differences, particularly nutrient-use efficiency (NUE) and drought tolerance. The short-lived leaves of drought-deciduous shrubs tend to have higher N content but lower NUE than leaves of evergreen chaparral shrubs (Gray 1983). This is likely a key difference given that fertilization experiments suggest the production of coastal sage shrubs is nitrogen-limited (Padgett and Allen 1999, Vourlitis 2012). Drought tolerance and overall water relations in coastal sage scrub are strongly influenced by rooting depths. Roots of coastal sage scrub species are often shallower than chaparral species (e.g., Harrison et al. 1971, Poole and Miller 1975). Poole and Miller (1975) found drought-deciduous species had shallower roots, higher rates of transpiration, and earlier onset of summer water stress than evergreen species characteristic of chaparral. While co-occurring *S. mellifera* (coastal sage) and *Ceanothus megacarpus* (chaparral) reached similarly low seasonal water potential (Gill and Mahall 1986), *S. mellifera* suffered greater embolism and loss of conductivity from drought stress (Kolb and Davis 1994). Similarly, Jacobsen et al. (2008) found that stem xylem was more resistant to cavitation in a suite of chaparral shrubs than in coastal sage shrubs; consequently, chaparral shrubs maintained physiological processes at lower water potentials relative to coastal sage shrubs (Jacobsen et al. 2008).

The Mediterranean-type climate results in a distinct phenology of coastal sage scrub, where most growth and nutrient dynamics are constrained by the prolonged summer drought. While most shoot and leaf production occurs during the winter rainy season, *A. californica* and other common drought-deciduous coastal sage scrub dominants (*S. leucophylla* and *S. mellifera*) have seasonally dimorphic leaves: following leaf drop of the larger leaves, smaller leaves are produced on auxiliary shoots that persist through the summer (Westman 1981c, Gray and Schlesinger 1981). Subsequently, *A. californica* flowers between April and December, with more northern populations flowering thirty to fifty days earlier than southern populations (Pratt and Mooney 2013).

Soil nitrate availability in coastal sage scrub is also influenced by the timing of rainfall and subsequent plant uptake. Soils generally have low soil nitrate levels during the wet season, presumably due to plant uptake (Padgett et al. 1999, Liu and Crowley 2009), and higher levels during the summer dry season, with a peak of availability following the first winter rains (Padgett et al. 1999, Vourlitis et al. 2009) when accumulated N from mineralization and dry deposition is flushed into the soil. Similarly, organic nitrogen and carbon at three coastal sage scrub sites were lower during the wet season and higher during the dry season, reflecting soil moisture limitation of microbial activity (Liu and Crowley 2009).

Biogeochemical cycles in coastal sage scrub can also be strongly influenced by invasion into these systems. For instance, Wolkovich et al. (2010) found that experimental addition of exotic annual grass litter increased carbon and nitrogen pools in coastal sage scrub by approximately 20%, due to both increased production and decreased rates of litter decomposition. The increase in production likely resulted from increased soil water availability under the exotic litter layer (Wolkovich et al. 2009b), although invasive grasses can also accelerate water loss from soils via high transpiration rates (Wood et al. 2006). The decreased decomposition rates observed with litter addition might have resulted from reduced UV photodegradation; this abiotic avenue for decomposition is important in other areas of California and declines in magnitude with increased shading under deeper litter layers (Henry et al. 2008). As already noted, the phenology of common invaders is distinct from that of native coastal sage scrub species (Cleland et al. 2013), with potentially important implications for the timing of ecosystem carbon uptake. A comparison of NDVI (normalized difference vegetation index, a measure of canopy greenness) shows a longer and less pronounced period of growth for plots dominated by native *S. mellifera* versus a shorter period of rapid growth for plots dominated by herbaceous exotic species (Figure 22.5; Ellen Esch unpublished data).

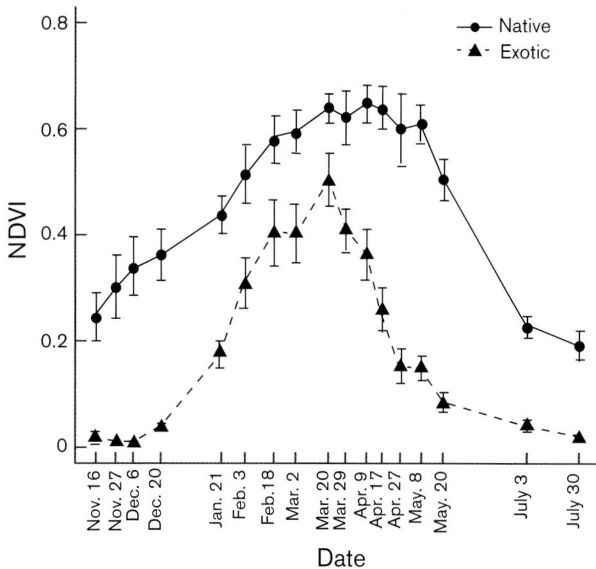

FIGURE 22.5 Normalized Difference Vegetation Index (NDVI), a measure of canopy greenness, collected during the 2012–2013 growing season at the Santa Margarita Ecological Reserve. Data were collected over plots dominated by native shrubs (*Salvia mellifera*) or exotic herbaceous species (*Hirschfeldia incana, Centauria melitensis,* and several exotic annual grasses). Source: Ellen Esch, unpublished data.

Key Community Interactions

Native and Exotic Species Interactions

Disturbances such as fire, grazing, and nitrogen deposition facilitate invasion by exotic species, and once established, exotic species can outcompete native coastal sage scrub shrub species for limiting resources (Schultz et al. 1955, Davis and Mooney 1985, Eliason and Allen 1997, Cione et al. 2002, Yelenik and Levine 2010). Roots of exotic annual grasses and native shrub seedlings occupy the same soil region (Figure 22.6); thus annual grasses have the strongest competitive effects on native shrubs at the seedling stage both via water and through their effects on shading (Figure 22.7; Eliason and Allen 1997, Yelenik and Levine 2010). Competition for water can be alleviated in larger native shrubs by deeper roots; however, shallow-rooted exotic grass species can preferentially use precipitation before it reaches deeper roots of native coastal sage scrub shrubs (Eliason and Allen 1997, Wood et al. 2006).

While exotic grasses compete effectively for light and water, competition for nutrients appears to be more even between native and exotic species. For instance, Padgett and Allen (1999) found that exotic grasses and native shrub seedlings displayed similar positive responses to nitrogen fertilization, and native species can outcompete annual exotic species for nitrogen under low-nutrient conditions (Zink and Allen 1998, Yoshida and Allen 2001). Some shrubs appear to compete particularly well with exotic species (*Eriogonum fasciculatum, Hazardia squarrosa, Baccharis pilularis*); how these species outperform exotic species is an open and interesting question (Rundel 2007). In a new twist on the invasion process, commercial cultivars of *Pinus radiata* (an endangered species native to the California central coast) have invaded northern coastal sage scrub and are associated with reduced species richness and cover in areas they invade (Steers et al. 2013).

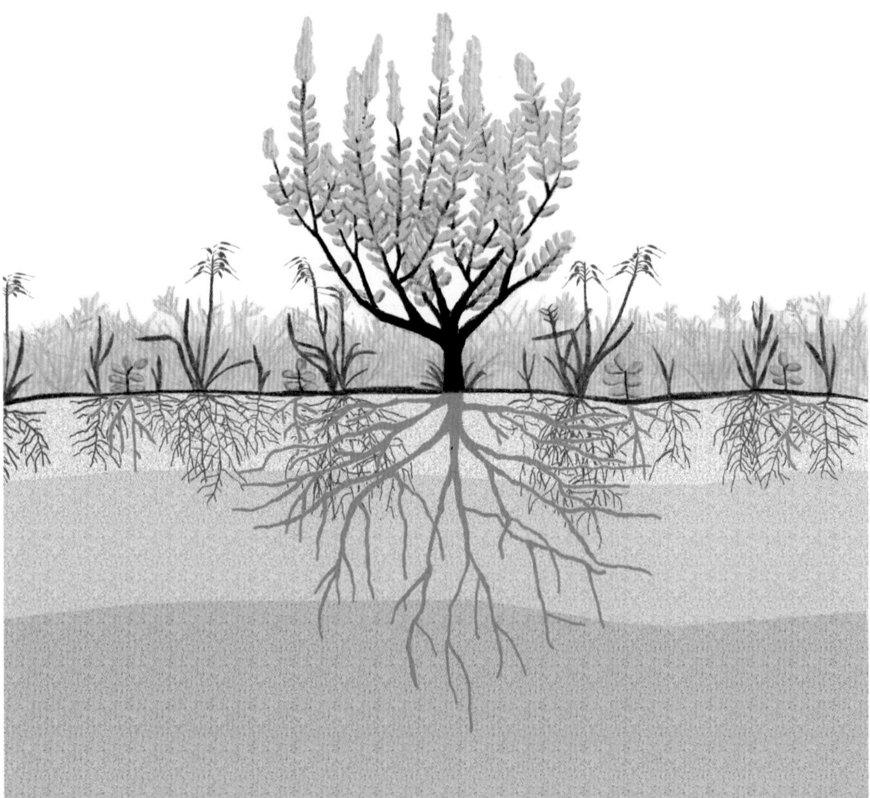

FIGURE 22.6 Root profiles of native shrubs (light brown) and exotic annual grasses (darker brown). Roots of establishing shrubs occupy the same shallow layers as roots of exotic annual grasses and place them in direct competition for water and nutrients. Exotic annual grasses also contribute to a significant litter layer aboveground, with multiple potential effects on establishing shrub seedlings including shading of shrub seedlings and greater soil moisture retention for deeper-rooted, mature shrubs. Illustration: Julie E. Larson.

In addition to competition, exotic grasses affect native shrubs through modification of the abiotic environment. By decreasing evaporation and consequently increasing soil moisture, invasive grass litter increased growth of the native shrub *A. californica* (Wolkovich et al. 2009b). Such beneficial effects of exotic grass litter might be restricted to adult shrubs, as other studies have found that exotic grass litter suppresses native shrub seedling establishment through competition for light (Eliason and Allen 1997, DeSimone and Zedler 1999; see Figure 22.7). Exotic grasses can alter abiotic factors in other ways that benefit native plant growth in coastal sage scrub habitat. Yelenik and Levine (2011) found that *A. californica* displayed higher growth on soils influenced by the exotic grass *Avena barbata*. However, *A. californica* failed to colonize grassland during the four-year study period, leading the authors to conclude that processes other than plant-soil feedbacks, such as competition, were more important in native species recovery. The mechanism for the positive plant-soil feedback observed in this study was not investigated and could involve effects of *A. barbata* on soil nutrients, structure, or biota.

Plant-Animal Interactions

Biotic disturbances created by small mammals influence shrub seedling recruitment during interfire periods (DeSimone and Zedler 1999). Specifically, herbivores and pocket gophers create gaps between plants within coastal sage scrub stands and in adjacent grasslands, and these gaps facilitate seedling establishment. More rodents are found in coastal sage scrub than neighboring grassland because shrubs provide better shelter, and rodents increase native seedling survival by grazing on herbaceous species under shrubs (Bartholomew 1970). Seed predation has a stronger impact on native seedling recruitment than seedling herbivory, although this varies among shrub species because species with large or multiple-seeded propagules are more attractive to granivores (DeSimone and Zedler 1999).

Changes in plant community composition can influence shrub- and ground-dwelling arthropods in coastal sage scrub habitat. Higher productivity in invaded coastal sage scrub increased the abundances of shrub-dwelling arthropod herbivores and predators associated with the grazing food web but reduced the abundance of ground-dwelling arthropods associated with the detrital food web (Wolkovich et al. 2009a; Wolkovich 2010). The positive effect of invasion on shrub-dwelling arthropods was linked to overall increases in shrub biomass, while the decline in ground-dwelling arthropods was likely caused by decreased temperatures and reduced foraging ability under the dense litter accumulated by exotic annual grasses.

Soil Biota

Soil fungal communities in coastal sage scrub habitats are taxonomically and functionally diverse—roughly twenty times more taxonomically diverse than coastal sage scrub plant communities (Karst et al. 2013). Fungi can be beneficial, neutral, or detrimental to plant growth. Mordecai (2012) found that soil moisture negatively influenced seed germination rate in both coastal sage scrub and grassland systems, likely through positive effects of soil moisture on fungal growth. Seed germination rate was lower in coastal sage scrub than in grassland and was unaffected by the presence of exotic grass

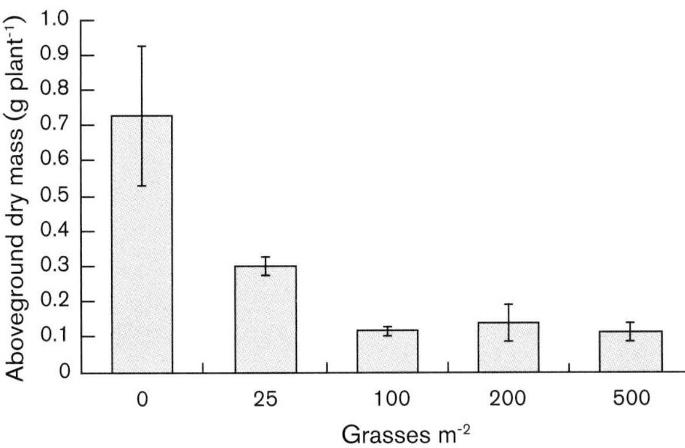

FIGURE 22.7 Mean dry mass of California sagebrush (*A. californica*) seedlings grown in competition with exotic annual grasses planted at varying densities. Source: Redrawn from Eliason and Allen 1997.

thatch, suggesting that exotic grass invasion into coastal sage scrub might not reduce seed survival by promoting fungal growth.

Working across nine sites that varied in nitrogen deposition, Egerton-Warburton and Allen (2000) found that the richness and diversity of ARBUSCULAR MYCORRHIZAL (AM) FUNGI declined as nitrogen deposition increased. This increase was accompanied by shifts in AM community composition with important ramifications for plant community composition and performance. In a study of the fungal communities associated with native (*A. californica*) and exotic (*B. rubens*) components of coastal sage scrub, Sigüenza et al. (2006) found that while native species were colonized primarily by AM fungi, with reductions in colonization under high nitrogen availability, exotic species were instead associated primarily with a fine AM ENDOPHYTE that promoted growth regardless of nitrogen availability.

Pink-pigmented FACULTATIVE methylotrophic (PPFM) bacteria are thought to benefit plants by excreting growth hormones that positively influence seed germination and root growth and by excreting osmoprotectants that protect plants from desiccation. In return, PPFM bacteria use simple carbon compounds, such as methanol, generated by plants. In a survey of annual and perennial coastal sage scrub species, Irvine et al. (2012) found that PPFM bacteria are more abundant in the root zones of annual plants, likely due to greater carbon production rates by actively growing roots. As many of the most aggressive invaders in coastal sage scrub are annual species, PPFM bacteria might benefit invasive species over native species in coastal sage scrub and adjacent grassland systems.

Variation of the System in Time and Space

Temporal Variation in Plant Community Composition

Temporal variation in coastal sage scrub plant diversity is strongly tied to fire cycles, with diversity peaking in the first two years following a fire, particularly on south-facing slopes (O'Leary 1990). Historically, fire is more common in coastal sage scrub than in neighboring chaparral communities. As natural sources of ignition are rare in coastal areas, fire-return intervals likely were on the order of thirty to one hundred years (Rundel 2007). The drought-deciduous shrubs that dominate coastal sage scrub communities are less fire-resistant than shrubs in chaparral communities because they lack woody root crowns or BURLS. The ability of shrubs to resprout following fire depends on plant age and fire intensity. Older stands can burn more intensely than younger stands, and few coastal sage scrub shrub species resprout following intense fire (Westman et al. 1981, Malanson and O'Leary 1982), particularly older plants (Keeley et al. 2005a). However, two SUFFRUTESCENT species (*A. glaber* and *Helianthemum scoparium*) are favored by high-intensity fire (Keeley et al. 2005a), which triggers the germination of their dormant seeds.

Postfire succession involves a shift in composition among three regeneration modes: OBLIGATE resprouters, facultative seeders, and obligate seeders (Keeley et al. 2006). Obligate resprouters regenerate vegetatively, have deep roots that tap into groundwater, are drought sensitive, lack a dormant seed bank, and have low seedling recruitment, especially in low precipitation years. Facultative seeders are capable of both vegetative regeneration and postfire germination of dormant seed banks. Obligate seeders do not regenerate vegetatively following fire and instead rely on dormant seed banks in the soil. In the first five years following fire, facultative seeders are most abundant (60–70% cover), while obligate resprouters (20–25% cover) and obligate seeders (0–5 % cover) comprise a smaller fraction of the community (Keeley et al. 2006). Seedlings of obligate seeders (e.g., annual and perennial herbaceous species) are most abundant the first year following fire and can disappear if intervals between fires are long (Keeley et al. 2005b, 2006). Many coastal sage scrub shrubs produce copious seeds in the first few years following fire, but this levels off after the canopy closes (Keeley et al. 2005). Closing the canopy can ameliorate drought stress and promote seedling establishment of obligate resprouters, which take longer to establish following fire (Keeley 1992).

Several obligate resprouting subshrubs such as *Encelia californica* and *Hazardia squarrosa* are not subject to these limitations and often display numerous seedlings resulting from seeding of resprouted plants in the second year following fire (Keeley et al. 2006). For many other shrub species, few seedlings might establish in the first year following fire because of limited seed dispersal from neighboring, unburned areas (Minnich and Dezzani 1998, Rundel 2007). In larger burned areas with no adjacent unburned area, the introduction of seed will come primarily from resprouted individuals (Keeley et al. 2005b). This can open a window of opportunity for exotic species with superior dispersal traits to establish and preempt resources prior to native species establishment (Keeley et al. 2005; Keeley and Brennan 2012), initiating a type-conversion from shrubland to grassland.

Fire can affect the structure of animal communities (Figure 22.8); species that require open habitat often increase in abundance following fire, at the expense of species that require mature, shrub-dominated habitat (small mammals [Brehme et al. 2011], birds [Mendelsohn et al. 2008], herpetofauna [Rochester et al. 2010]). Furthermore, Diffendorfer et al. (2012) found that mammal species composition following fire was more strongly influenced by habitat heterogeneity and vegetation composition than by fire intensity or distance to adjacent unburned areas. Fire can also lead to declines in species diversity (herpetofauna [Rochester et al. 2010], ants [Matsuda et al. 2011]), although for some groups the shift in community composition following fire is not accompanied by changes in diversity (e.g., small mammals [Brehme et al. 2011, Diffendorfer et al. 2012]).

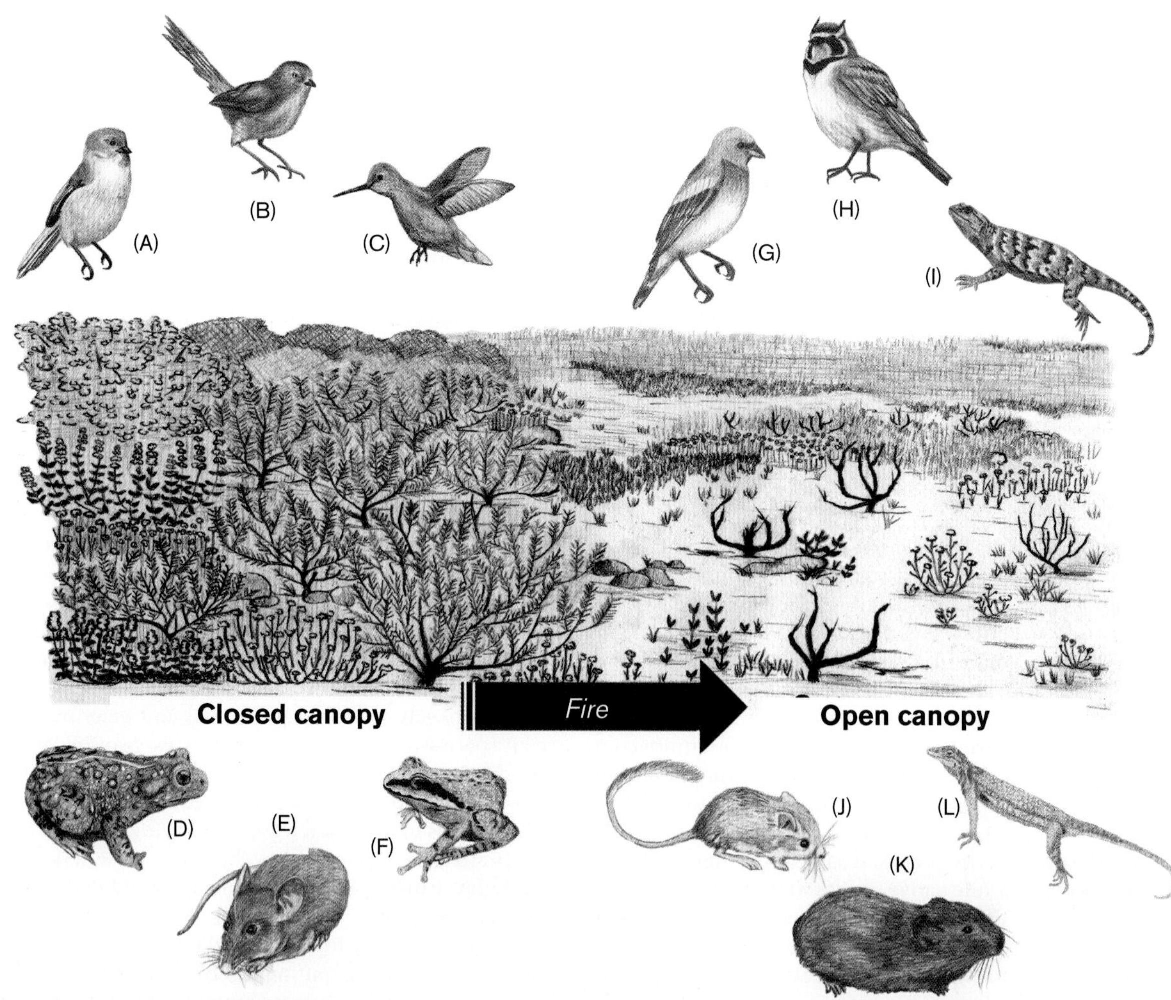

FIGURE 22.8 Composition of the animal community in coastal sage scrub shifts following fire with the loss of shrub cover. Closed canopies provide habitat for (A) bushtit (*Psaltriparus minimus*), (B) wrentit (*Chamaea fasciata*), (C) Anna's hummingbird (*Calypte anna*), (D) western toad (*Bufo boreas*), (E) California mouse (*Peromyscus californicus*), and (F) pacific treefrog (*Pseudacris regilla*). Postfire, open canopies favor a different suite of species, including (G) lazuli bunting (*Passerina amoena*), (H) horned lark (*Eremophila alpestris*), (I) western fence lizard (*Scheloporus occidentalis*), (J) kangaroo rat (*Dipodomys* sp.), (K) California vole (*Microtus californicus*), and (L) common side-blotched lizard (*Uta stansburiana*). Illustration: Julie E. Larson.

Transitions between Coastal Sage Scrub and Grassland

Although coastal sage scrub can transition between grassland and chaparral or oak woodland as part of a "shifting landscape mosaic" (Callaway and Davis 1993), coastal sage scrub is not generally thought of as simply a successional stage on a trajectory to another vegetation type. Using aerial photographs and vegetation maps, researchers have documented transitions between coastal sage scrub and grassland over multiple decades. Historical records are unclear about how much land was occupied by shrubland, grassland, or forbland prior to the arrival of Franciscan missionaries in the late 1700s (Minnich 2008). However, in the last century, conversions of coastal sage scrub to exotic annual grassland and vice versa have been influenced by fire frequency, grazing pressure, and nitrogen deposition. For example, Talluto and Suding (2008) resampled 232 plots established in the VTM survey in the early 1930s and found that exotic grasses were more dominant in plots with increased fire frequency. While nitrogen availability is widely understood to promote invasion (Huenneke et al. 1990, Davis et al. 2000), Talluto and Suding (2008) found that nitrogen deposition was positively correlated with grass cover only in plots with low fire frequency in Diegan sage scrub. However, a higher proportion of Riversidean sage scrub was converted to exotic grassland in areas with high nitrogen deposition (Minnich and Dezzani 1998, Fenn et al. 2010).

Once exotic annual grasses establish, they can promote increased fire frequency, which maintains their dominance (see Figure 22.5). Annual grasses can increase the fuel load within ecosystems as their dry biomass accumulates (D'Antonio and Vitousek 1992, Keeley et al. 2005a). Repeated, low-intensity fires favor exotic annual grasses for two reasons. First, exotic seed bank survivorship is high when fire intensity is low; and second, a short fire-return interval can inhibit the regeneration of native woody species, particularly obligate seeding shrubs (Keeley and Brennan 2012). Shrub colonization into grassland can also be limited by a depleted seed bank, low dispersal from neighboring areas, and competition from grasses (Stylinski and Allen 1999, Cione et al. 2002).

Cases have been documented of conversion from grassland

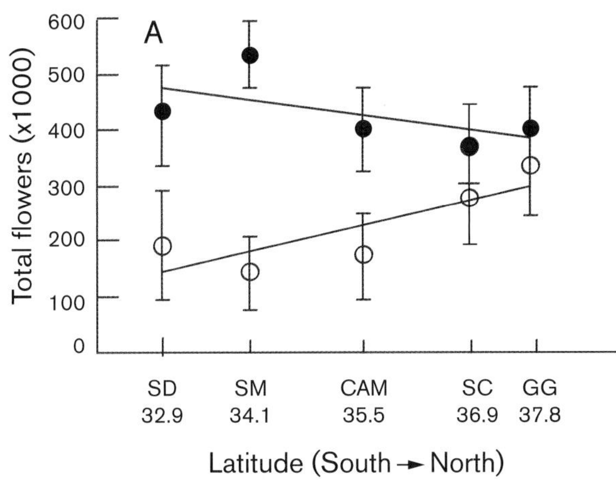

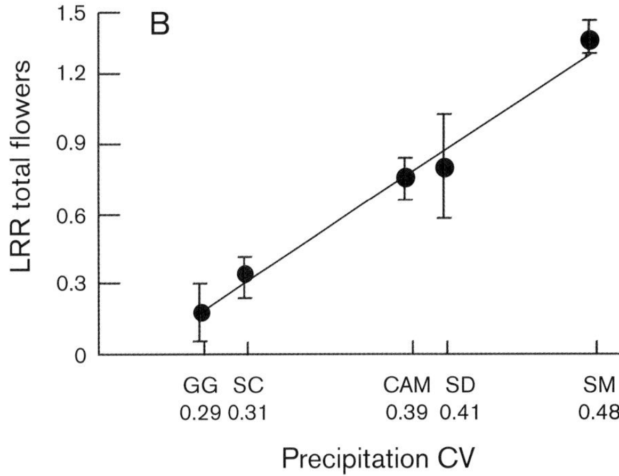

FIGURE 22.9 (A) Number of flowers per shrub grown under high (closed symbols) or low (open symbols) rainfall, for California sagebrush (*A. californica*) collected at five locations. From south to north: SD=San Diego, SM=Santa Monica, CAM=Cambria, SC=Santa Cruz, GG=Golden Gate National Recreation Area. (B) The log response ratio (LRR) of the flowering response to increased water availability is strongly predicted by the coefficient of variation (CV) of annual precipitation at these five sites. Source: Based on Figures 2c and 3c in Pratt and Mooney 2013.

to shrubland (Freudenberger et al. 1987, Callaway and Davis 1993, DeSimone and Zedler 2001). For example, an analysis of vegetation from 1946 to 1955 at Starr Ranch in south Orange County, California, found a shift from native perennial grassland to shrubland (DeSimone and Zedler 2001). These authors found that four woody species (*A. californica, A. glaber, E. fasciculatum*, and *S. apiana*) colonized grassland by producing large seed crops, recruiting in gaps (particularly those created by pocket gophers), and displaying rapid seedling growth and low susceptibility of seedlings to herbivory. In contrast, in northern coastal scrub, *Baccharis pilularis* (coyote brush) invades adjacent grasslands in the absence of gaps created by disturbance (Hobbs and Mooney 1986). Shrub establishment in these northern coastal scrub systems tends to be episodic, associated with high rainfall years (Williams et al. 1987), while in southern coastal sage scrub DeSimone and Zedler (2001) found that woody species establishment was relatively insensitive to annual precipitation. Thus the drivers of coastal sage scrub and grassland transitions vary across the range of this vegetation type.

Human Impacts from the Postcolonial Era to Present

Climate Change

Southern California will likely be a hotspot of future climate change (Diffenbaugh et al. 2008), experiencing both drier and more variable conditions (Cayan 2008, Schubert et al. 2008, see Chapter 2, "Climate"). Dynamic vegetation models predict that shrublands in southern California (including both coastal sage scrub and chaparral) will decline in extent in response to drier conditions and greater fire frequency and will be replaced by grasslands (Lenihan et al. 2003, 2008). Models predicting the shift in vulnerable species across the landscape with future climate change illustrate the additional challenge of the highly fragmented nature of coastal sage scrub habitat. For instance Hannah et al. (2012) identified four areas of California requiring additional land protection to create corridors to facilitate range shifts of vulnerable species. One of these sites spans Santa Barbara and Ventura Counties where *Salvia leucophylla*, a key coastal sage scrub shrub species, will likely decline without these additional protections.

Animal populations in coastal sage scrub will likely be strongly affected by climate change via shifts in the abundances of food sources and nesting habitat. Two federally listed coastal sage scrub animals, the Quino checkerspot butterfly and the California gnatcatcher, were predicted to have smaller suitable habitat areas under higher temperature and diminished areal extent of coastal sage scrub (Preston et al. 2008). New populations of Quino checkerspot butterflies have been observed in higher-elevation (cooler and moister) chaparral, with interspersed forblands supporting larval host plants as predicted by global warming models (Preston et al. 2012). Variation in rainfall associated with El Niño cycles might also play a role; Morrison and Bolger (2002) found that rufous-crowned sparrows (*Aimophila ruficeps*) had higher reproductive success in high rainfall (El Niño) years due to both higher food abundance and reduced nest predation by snakes.

Relatively little experimental work has evaluated coastal sage scrub responses to climate change. A recent common garden study collected cuttings of *A. californica* (California sage, one of the key foundational species of coastal sage scrub) from populations across its range and found that populations from more variable climates also showed the greatest growth responses to high versus low rainfall (Figure 22.9; Pratt and Mooney 2013). Local adaptation among populations thus could play a key role in coastal sage scrub responses to climate change. In contrast to the dearth of experimental work on coastal sage scrub responses to climate change, a great deal of research has addressed the roles of urbanization and agriculture, increasing fire frequency and atmospheric nitrogen deposition on coastal sage scrub loss and decline.

Urbanization and Agriculture

The greatest impacts on coastal sage scrub both historically and today are urbanization and agriculture. Valley bottoms in much of California have rich, deep soils suited to irrigated agriculture and/or some dryland small-grain production. Historically, irrigated citrus and avocado orchards and vineyards were planted both in valleys and on hillsides. However, agriculture is in decline as urbanization increases (Chen et al. 2010). Urban development is expanding into abandoned agricultural fields (e.g., Orange County, which was notable for its citrus industry in former coastal sage scrub habitat, no longer produces commercial citrus), and some previously pristine coastal sage scrub areas are also being developed for housing. A statewide analysis comparing the original 1930s VTM (Wieslander 1935) coastal sage scrub acreage to the 2006 vegetation map (Hollander 2007) shows a loss of 6.1% of coastal sage scrub to agriculture and 19.4% to urban development in that period (Table 22.2).

The area of coastal sage scrub converted to agriculture prior to the 1930s is unknown. Of the remaining, undeveloped land previously occupied by coastal sage scrub, 15.3% has converted to exotic annual grassland and 44% remains shrubland (33% coastal sage scrub plus 11% chaparral). In Riverside County, 71% of remaining undeveloped coastal sage scrub has converted to exotic annual grassland based on a more detailed California Department of Fish and Wildlife 2006 vegetation map (Evens and Klein 2006). Type conversion could be related to abandonment from agriculture, but Riversidean sage scrub could be more highly invaded than other coastal sage scrub subassociations because it has lower shrub cover, providing larger interspaces for invasion. It also has hotter summers that cause greater shrub leaf fall, further reducing canopy cover and enabling invasion at the onset of fall rains. As described below, it also has greater levels of nitrogen deposition.

Most commercial grazing in coastal sage scrub declined greatly by the 1930s (Robinson et al. 1993); these lands were used for agriculture, abandoned and allowed to recover, or eventually urbanized. Grazing has persisted to the present in some areas, and recent grazing was related to local extirpation of Quino checkerspot butterflies (Preston et al. 2012). Native forbs declined relative to exotic grasses and forbs under domestic grazing in annual forblands (Kimball and Schiffman 2003). Grazing has also been blamed for the spread of invasive species. Fecal analyses have demonstrated that domestic grazing animals move seeds (Malo and Suarez 1995), but seeds also move along roadsides and other corridors (Zink et al. 1995). Domestic grazing might have hastened dispersal, but with widespread human disturbances in coastal sage scrub and possibly native animal dispersers, these seeds would have arrived eventually (Minnich and Dezzani 1998, Minnich 2008). By whatever means invasive species arrive, their productivity is assured in relatively nutrient-rich coastal sage scrub soils, and atmospheric nitrogen inputs further stimulate productivity.

TABLE 22.2

Remaining coastal sage scrub vegetation and conversion to agriculture and urban development in 2006 relative to the 1930s vegetation type mapping (VTM) survey

Map year	Cover type	Hectares	Percentage of original VTM
1930s VTM	Original VTM coastal sage scrub	715,132	100.0
2006	Converted to agriculture	43,401	6.1
	Converted to urban	138,914	19.4
	Converted to exotic grassland	109,350	15.3
	Remaining coastal sage scrub	234,494	32.8
	Classified as chaparral	81,457	11.4
	Classified as woodland, forest	81,256	11.4
	Classified as other types	26,260	3.7

SOURCE: Hollander 2007. The 1930s VTM survey is at http://vtm.berkeley.edu.

NOTE: Areas that were classified as chaparral, woodland, or forest in 2006 may have experienced vegetation shifts since the 1930s; or differences may be due to map scaling errors, as in the case of classification to other types (barren, desert, or water). Analysis does not include the Channel Islands, which have approximately 30,000 hectares of coastal sage scrub.

Nitrogen Deposition

The critical load of anthropogenic nitrogen deposition of 10 kg N ha^{-1} yr^{-1} is exceeded in 33% of coastal sage scrub land area, a higher proportion than any other California ecosystem type (Figure 22.10; Fenn et al. 2010). A critical load is the value of a pollutant input rate above which negative ecosystem consequences occur. In coastal sage scrub, negative impacts of elevated nitrogen include increased exotic grass productivity causing increased fine fuels for fire (Fenn et al. 2010). The amount of nitrogen added increased exotic grass biomass to the fire threshold value of greater than 1 ton ha^{-1} in all but the driest years, while unfertilized plots had lower productivity (Fenn et al. 2003). By contrast, forbs disarticulate in the dry season and are relatively poor carriers of fire across the landscape (Brooks et al. 2004). Elevated nitrogen also reduced richness of native forbs along a nitrogen deposition gradient from 6 to 20 kg N ha^{-1} yr^{-1}, with a steep drop from sixty-seven to thirty-seven species per site at 10 kg N ha^{-1} yr^{-1} and a further drop to sixteen species at 20 kg N ha^{-1} yr^{-1} (Fenn et al. 2010). Reduced richness and percent infection of AM fungi occurred along the same gradient, although with a gradual decline rather than a threshold (Egerton-Warburton and Allen 2000). The shift in AM species composition promoted reduced mutualism for the native shrub *A. californica*, but inoculum from a high-nitrogen-deposition soil was still beneficial for the exotic grass *Bromus rubens* (Sigüenza et al. 2006). This implies that the poor establishment of *A. californica* seedlings observed in mixtures with exotic grasses is exacerbated by less effective mycorrhizal inoculum of soils experiencing high nitrogen deposition.

An eight-year nitrogen fertilization experiment in coastal sage scrub showed that nitrogen addition increased shrub production only in years when rainfall exceeded 45 cm yr^{-1} (Vourlitis 2012), but shrub relative abundance shifted to greater dominance by *A. californica* within five years (Vourlitis et al. 2009). Other changes to the nitrogen cycle under elevated nitrogen include increased plant, soil, and microbial nitrogen levels (Sirulnik et al. 2007b, Vourlitis and Fernan-

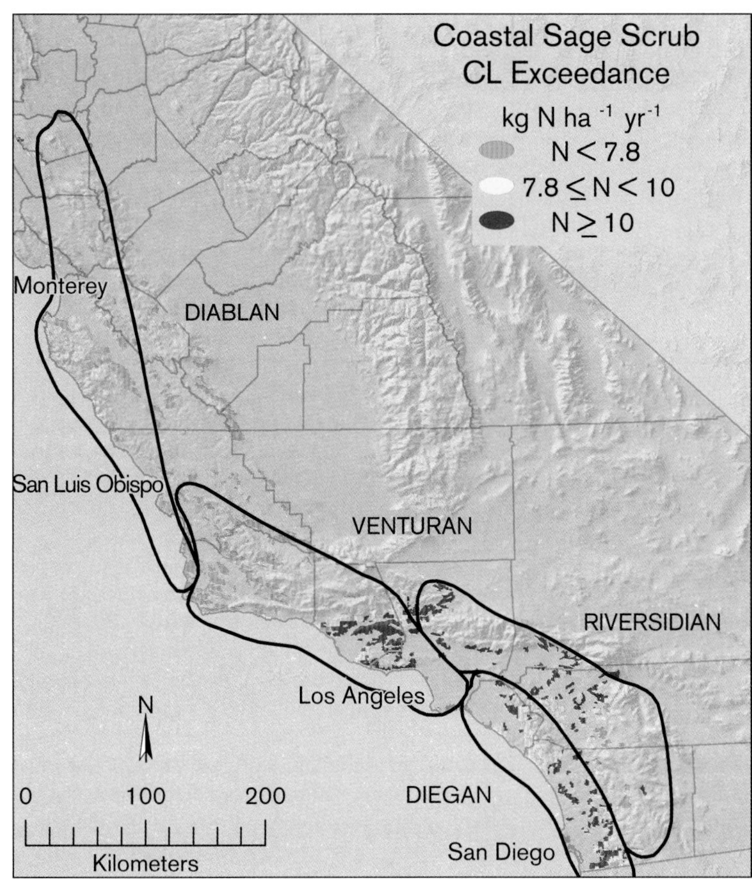

FIGURE 22.10 Critical loads (CL) of anthropogenic nitrogen (N) deposition in coastal sage scrub, which increase exotic grass productivity and reduce richness of native forb and arbuscular mycorrhizal species. The higher value of 10 kg N ha^{-1} yr^{-1} is based on modeled CMAQ (Congestion Monitoring and Air Quality) data; the lower level of 7.8 is based on empirical data (data from Fenn et al. 2010).

dez 2012), and increased rate of nitrogen but not carbon mineralization (Sirulnik et al. 2007a, Vourlitis and Zorba 2007, Vourlitis et al. 2007). The implication of the latter is that increased nitrogen absorbed by plants will cycle back to the soil as mineral nitrogen, but there will be no change in soil carbon, resulting in decreased soil C:N. Overall, legislative efforts to curb nitrogen deposition below critical loads should be encouraged. Those areas below critical loads of 10 kg N ha^{-1} yr^{-1} will be the best candidates for conservation reserves to maintain current diversity and ecosystem functioning.

Change in Fire Frequency

Estimating the historic change in fire frequency in coastal sage scrub is difficult because historical fire frequencies are unknown and estimates of current frequencies are sparse. Native Californians might have used fire as a tool to convert coastal sage scrub to forb- and grasslands (Keeley 2002). Spanish explorers of the mid-1700s reported extensive and frequent, sometimes annual, Indian burns in the Los Angeles Basin (Minnich 2008). One reason for this could have been that fire promoted the dominance of native annual forbs, as seeds of some species were a staple food. Estimates of mid- to late-twentieth-century fire return intervals are twenty years in Venturan sage scrub of the Santa Monica Mountains (Westman and O'Leary 1986) and twenty-five years in Riversidean sage scrub of the Box Springs Mountains (based on aerial photography, Minnich unpublished). Currently, the fire return interval in the Box Springs Mountains in Riverside is only about ten years (Minnich unpublished), possibly a result of increased exotic grass productivity from nitrogen deposition (Fenn et al. 2010) and anthropogenic ignitions from local development. At the military reserve Camp Pendleton, many coastal sage scrub sites had two to eight fires in a twenty-six-year period in the late twentieth century (Fleming et al. 2009). A recent analysis shows that fire frequency has increased throughout coastal sage scrub vegetation (see Chapter 3, "Fire as an Ecosystem Process"). The difficulty with determining fire return interval in coastal sage scrub is that it is commonly interspersed with chaparral, such that landscape-scale analyses easily confound the two vegetation types. Focused analyses of larger-scale coastal sage scrub landscapes are needed to determine fire return interval.

Fire has direct effects on biogeochemistry as well as indirect effects from altered plant-soil feedbacks of invasive species that colonize after fire. While we are not aware of studies that examine how frequent fire affects soil nutrients in coastal sage scrub, a southern California perennial grassland (in a matrix of coastal sage scrub) that was burned at seven-year intervals showed no changes in soil carbon or in total or extractable nitrogen (Allen et al. 2011). Vegetation with low fuel loads such as coastal sage scrub burn at relatively low temperatures, thus preserving soil nutrients (Allen et al. 2011). While stocks of nitrogen and carbon in plant tissue are depleted by fire, soil nitrogen and carbon can remain little changed, although soil mineral nitrogen is often ephemerally increased immediately postfire because of deposited mineralized plant nitrogen. This pattern was observed in burned chaparral that experienced no long-term impacts of fire on soil nutrient cycling (Fenn et al. 1993). Stocks of nitrogen and carbon in vegetation typically recover rapidly during succession following fire in semiarid shrublands (Allen et al. 2011). However, when coastal sage scrub has been type-converted to annual grassland under frequent fire, long-term and persistent impacts to soils can be expected such as elevated soil nitrogen and increased rates of nitrogen cycling (Dickens et al. 2013). These can be restored once shrubs have reestablished. Soil total nitrogen and carbon are not changed by exotic grass invasion into coastal sage scrub, although their spatial distribution is more homogeneous (Dickens et al. 2013).

Fragmentation: Impacts on Plants and Animals

Fragmentation of coastal sage scrub by urban development has caused declines in both plant and animal species. The number of native plant species decreased and exotic species increased in coastal sage scrub patches isolated up to eighty-six years ago in San Diego County (Alberts et al. 1993). While size was the major determinant of species richness, average native species loss over all patch sizes was approximately 43%. The overall richness of native coastal sage scrub plant species was higher than exotic invasive species richness, but native and exotic species richness were positively correlated at all scales of observation from 1 to 400 m^2 in the Santa Monica Mountains (Sax 2002). Conversely, cover of exotic species can be much higher than of native species in some coastal sage scrub fragments, impacting habitat quality for wildlife.

Crooks and Soulé (1999) proposed that habitat fragmentation reduces the abundance of top-level predators like coyotes (*Canis latrans*), leading to an increase in mesopredators (e.g., gray fox [*Urocyon cinereoargenteus*], Virginia opossum [*Didelphis virginianus*], domestic cat [*Felis sylvestris catus*]) and a consequent decrease in bird diversity. However, Patten and Bolger (2003) argued that trophic cascades are more complex in coastal sage scrub habitat. Animals other than mesopredators, such as avian predators and snakes, contribute to nest predation. Additionally, raptors and snakes can consume mesopredators. Thus interactions among predatory groups complicate our understanding of how fragmentation affects food webs and, consequently, bird diversity.

Coastal sage scrub habitat loss to exotic species or development has negatively affected dozens of mammal, bird, and reptile species (reviewed in Keeley and Swift 1995). Working across a gradient of exotic plant cover, Diffendorfer et al. (2007) found that animal species richness decreased with increasing exotic plant cover only for some groups (e.g., small mammals and birds) in some years. Overall, species richness did not change along the exotic plant gradient. Instead, animal taxa favoring native woody shrubs were replaced with those favoring grassy, exotic-dominated habitat. Urban development over the past decade has drastically reduced the population of San Diego cactus wren in Los Angeles County, even in protected wildlife areas on the Palos Verdes Peninsula (Cooper et al. 2012). In contrast, habitat fragmentation increases the abundance of native and non-native spiders with corresponding increases in taxonomic diversity of non-native spiders (Bolger et al. 2008). Increased spider density in smaller fragments may arise because of higher primary productivity, as increased edge area results in higher water flow into fragments, or because of more favorable microsites due to shading of non-native tree species. Edge effects also impact birds and mammals of coastal sage scrub, because of either poor habitat quality caused by dominance of invasive plants at edges or other impacts that reduced their abundance at edges (Kristan et al. 2003).

Management and Restoration

The major management issues for coastal sage scrub arise from exotic species invasions that have caused vegetation-type conversion, frequent fire that prevents natural successional processes from recovery of invaded coastal sage scrub, fragmentation of coastal sage scrub habitat from urban development (Soulé et al. 1988, Bolger et al. 1997), and accompanying declines of rare and listed plant and animal species. The direct loss of habitat to urbanization has prompted development of habitat conservation plans (HCPs) mandated under the Endangered Species Act to identify and protect remaining critical habitat and is reviewed below. In this section we focus on restoration of protected habitat fragments that have been degraded by invasive species, the most pervasive conservation problem for coastal sage scrub. Some abandoned agricultural lands are also being restored to coastal sage scrub, and these have the combined challenges of invasive species and lack of a native seed bank.

Invasive species affect soil chemical and microbial properties, but these feedbacks have not been the major factor limiting restoration. Negative feedbacks of soils conditioned by invasive grasses did not limit field establishment of coastal sage scrub shrubs (Yelenik and Levine 2011). Conversely, native shrubs can have different effects on mineralization rates, promoting or inhibiting exotic grass colonization (Yelenik and Levine 2010). Phenologies of native shrub and invasive grass were major determinants of soil microbial activity and rates of nitrogen mineralization, but invaded soils recovered once native shrubs were reestablished (Dickens et al. 2013). The low impact of exotic grasses on biogeochemical processes is surprising given the many decades they have dominated some areas of coastal sage scrub. In fact, soil total nitrogen and carbon did not change with invasion, indicating that soil chemical and biological properties are resilient to invasion (Dickens et al. 2013). Conversely, invaded vegetation is itself resilient and requires active restoration including invasive plant control and, often, seeding or planting of native species.

Control of abundant exotic annuals requires seed bank reduction, as annual plants require seed banks to persist. The exotic soil seed bank in historically grazed Riversidean sage scrub was greater than 10,000 seeds m^{-2}, while native species had only 400 seeds m^{-2} (Cox and Allen 2008a). In an area of high nitrogen deposition and frequent fire, no native seed bank was left at all (Cione et al. 2002). Similarly, areas abandoned from agriculture have little or no native seed bank (Allen et al. 2005). Methods for exotic seed bank control include fire both before and after seed dispersal (Gillespie and Allen 2004, Cox and Allen 2008a, Cox and Allen 2008b), solarization (soil heating with plastic) (Marushia and Allen 2010), herbicides and dethatching (Cione et al. 2002, Allen et al. 2005), and mowing and mechanical control (DeSimone 2006). Timed grazing to remove plants before they go to seed appears to be an obvious technique but is seldom used in coastal sage scrub both because it is difficult to time grazing during a short growing season and because of public and agency perceptions that domestic grazing animals are undesirable on public lands (Sulak and Huntsinger 2007).

Drought is part of the natural cycle of coastal sage scrub and can deplete the seed banks of exotic invasives with short-lived seed banks. For instance, the exotic annual grass *Bromus rubens* is subject to local seed bank extirpation following several dry years in the desert (Salo 2004), and seed bank depletion has been observed in coastal sage scrub (Minnich 2008). Restoration ecologists might be able to take advantage of natural fluctuations in exotic seed banks to restore native plants, but considerable work is needed to understand seed bank longevity and susceptibility to drought and other factors.

While passive restoration has resulted in stable, native-dominated coastal sage scrub communities in some cases (DeSimone 2013), active restoration might be required in severely disturbed or invaded coastal sage scrub soils, where natural succession might not effectively restore native vegetation (Stylinski and Allen 1999). Revegetation success after exotic species control has been variable. Removal of invasive grass species led to an increase of exotic forb species, especially *Erodium* spp., rather than of seeded native shrub species, although native forb species increased somewhat (Cox and Allen 2008b). This suggests that shrubs are part of a competitive hierarchy in order of decreasing aggressiveness from exotic annual grasses to exotic forbs, native forbs, and native shrub seedlings (Cox and Allen 2011), and that exotic forbs as well as grasses might need to be controlled for successful restoration. Managers might take advantage of the early establishment phenology of invasive forbs and grasses and control them early in the season, before they can negatively impact native species (Wainwright et al. 2012).

Mulch addition and litter removal have both been used to control exotic species and establish native species, with variable outcomes. Mulch immobilizes excess soil nitrogen and has been used for experimental restoration of nitrogen-impacted coastal sage scrub (Zink and Allen 1998, Cione et al. 2002). High litter cover from exotic grasses increased growth of mature native shrubs through increased soil moisture (Wolkovich et al. 2010), while litter reduction either improved or had no significant effect on establishment of native plants from seed (Allen et al. 2005, Cox et al. 2008b, McCullough and Endress 2012). A more impractical aspect of mulch addition or removal is that it can only be used for relatively small-scale restorations and not for extensive invaded landscapes. Fire, herbicides, grazing, and mowing to reduce exotic grass cover are more useful for large-scale restoration.

Restored as well as natural coastal sage scrub vegetation might be unstable under the constant threat of invasion from exotic species (Allen et al. 2005, Cox and Allen 2008b), although the long-term success of coastal sage scrub restoration efforts varies considerably. An experimental removal study showed that exotics return to pretreatment levels within four to five years without continued management (Allen et al. 2005). A factor that promotes invasion resistance is the closed shrub canopy in Venturan and Diegan sage scrub, compared to the more invasible open canopy of Riversidean sage scrub (Westman 1983). Once invasive grasses dominate shrub interspaces, the threat of fire can increase, making imperative the need for grass control. The real test of coastal sage scrub restoration will come when a restored site has burned and is able to recover naturally by succession (Bowler 2000). Restored, burned Riversidean sage scrub reverted to exotic grassland (Cione et al. 2002, Allen unpublished), while burned, restored Diegan sage scrub recovered (Margot Griswold unpublished). Passive restoration was successful after invasive plant control in more mesic Diegan sage scrub (DeSimone 2013).

Given the high degree of invasion and continual efforts to restore coastal sage scrub in some parts of its range, this vegetation can be considered a highly managed, hybrid ecosystem (as defined by Hobbs et al. 2009, maintaining some native species but also having persistent novel components). The major plant diversity lies in the native forbs—as many as two hundred species throughout the range of coastal sage scrub (Skinner and Pavlik 1994), but these are the most difficult to restore. In many areas today, particularly those close to human population centers, coastal sage scrub has an overstory of native shrubs with an understory dominated by exotic annuals. Managers often apply site-specific treatments to increase populations of sensitive and listed plant and animal species. These include mowing grass and even removing shrubs to maintain Stephen's kangaroo rat (*Dipodomys stephensi*) habitat (Price et al. 1994, Kelt et al. 2005), restoration plus artificial burrows for burrowing owls (*Athene cunicularia*), and exotic plant control coupled with seeding host plants (especially *Plantago erecta*) for Quino checkerspot butterfly habitat (Marushia and Allen 2011). The resulting habitat often is not pristine and is continually invaded by existing and even new invasive species; but with concerted management, rare species can be maintained.

Future Scenarios

Because of its location on the coast and relatively gentle terrain, coastal sage scrub vegetation has been converted to a greater extent than most other vegetation types in California. The maximum potential development scenario for southern California shows conversion of most coastal sage scrub vegetation except for on steep slopes (Landis 2006). However, these scenarios are likely to be ameliorated due to coastal sage scrub's high concentrations of endangered, threatened, and sensitive species, which render many areas subject to HCPs under the federal Endangered Species Act (ESA) or natural communities conservation plans (NCCP) under State of California regulations. Figure 22.3 summarizes the conservation status of coastal sage scrub to date: 15.5% is protected under HCPs, NCCPs, or other conservation reserves; another 19.8% is multiple use such as BLM and Forest Service; 10.7 % is designated as "no protection mandated," lands such as military or Indian reservations that are primarily wildlands and can be developed but are subject to some protections under the ESA; and 54% is unprotected. Conservation programs are expanding and will acquire lands currently in the unprotected category.

Two of the counties with both the fastest rate of urban development and the most coastal sage scrub, San Diego and Riverside Counties, have active HCPs that are acquiring habitat for listed species. For instance, western Riverside County has only 12% coastal sage scrub by land area, but of the approximately 200,000 hectares designated for HCP protection, a disproportionately large share (more than 24,000 hectares) will likely be coastal sage scrub because of the large number of listed species relying on that habitat type. These lands are still being purchased, so the proportion of coastal sage scrub they will eventually contain is unknown (www.rctlma.org/mshcp). The urbanization of agricultural lands and their loss as buffers with coastal sage scrub has increased the amount of urban-wildland interface (Scott et al. 2006), further necessitating large coastal sage scrub preserves. The Orange County NCCP requires conservation protection of15,000 hectares, a large proportion of which is coastal sage scrub (www.dfg.ca.gov/habcon/). Counties with coastal sage scrub vegetation but without HCPs either have lower development rates and therefore reduced threats to coastal sage scrub species or are under negotiation to develop plans for habitat conservation.

Habitat connectivity is a major concern for movement, genetic diversity, and protection of coastal sage scrub species and ecosystem functioning (Crooks and Sanjayan 2006), especially because coastal sage scrub is naturally patchy. Undeveloped coastal sage scrub landscapes include a matrix of other vegetation types such as chaparral, native or exotic annual grasslands, and riparian corridors. Planning efforts are under way statewide to maintain corridors between conserved habitat patches, with notable efforts such as the "Tenaja Corridor" linking coastal sage scrub as well as other vegetation types between Riverside and San Diego Counties (Morrison and Reynolds 2006). Emphasis is also on maintaining large patches of coastal sage scrub to reduce edge effects, but success in this effort will depend on which currently unprotected areas can be maintained as conservation reserves.

Beyond conservation efforts, the future hope for coastal sage scrub diversity and functioning lies in the large number of restoration efforts. Information on websites and published literature has expanded greatly for coastal sage scrub restoration in the past two decades; these activities are in part supported by legally mandated mitigation funds for off-site development (Bowler 2000). Efforts to improve air quality (see Chapter 7, "Atmospheric Chemistry") will reduce the long-distance impacts of pollutants such as nitrogen and ozone on this sensitive vegetation type. While restoration efforts do not always result in predisturbance conditions (DeSimone 2013), mitigation has given rise to conservation reserves that are open to public scrutiny and to improved potential for future improvement of diversity and functioning.

Summary

Coastal sage scrub is a taxonomically and functionally diverse plant community. The dominant native shrub species tend to be drought-deciduous and more shallowly rooted than the evergreen species in neighboring chaparral communities; as a result, a long history of ecophysiological studies has compared the life-history strategies of species that sometimes co-occur at the ecotones between these two ecosystem types (see Chapter 24, "Chaparral"). Coastal sage scrub is also among the most threatened ecosystems, facing numerous challenges for land management and conservation. Its inherently coastal distribution means that this ecosystem faces some of the greatest pressures associated with anthropogenic land-use change in California as well as other environmental changes associated with large human population centers—in particular, nitrogen deposition from fossil fuel production, accelerated fire regimes, and invasion by exotic species. Exotic annual grasses are especially problematic and often defy attempts at restoration. Recent research in coastal sage scrub has focused on environmental conditions that favor native shrub establishment over the growth of exotic annual grasses, opening windows into our understanding of how factors such as fire, seasonality (phenology), and interactions with soil microbial communities structure species interactions in Mediterranean-type ecosystems.

Acknowledgments

We thank Sandra DeSimone and Elizabeth Wolkovich for valuable comments on this chapter. We are very grateful to Robert Johnson of the Center for Conservation Biology at the University of California at Riverside for analysis of spatial data and assistance with maps.

Recommended Reading

Ford, L. D., and G. F. Hayes. 2007. Northern coastal scrub and coastal prairie. Pages 180–207 in M. G. Barbour, T. Keeler-Wolf, and A. A. Schoenherr, editors. Terrestrial vegetation of California. Third edition. University of California Press, Berkeley, California.

Minnich, R. A. 2008. California's fading wildflowers: Lost legacy and biological invasions. University of California Press, Berkeley, California.

Rundel, P. W. 2007. Sage scrub. Pages 208–228 in M. G. Barbour, T. Keeler-Wolf, and A. A. Schoenherr, editors. Terrestrial vegetation of California. Third edition. University of California Press, Berkeley, California.

Glossary

ARBUSCULAR MYCORRHIZAL (AM) FUNGI A mutualistic association between certain species of fungi and roots of land plants, whereby the fungus penetrates the root cortical cells, allowing the plant to transfer carbohydrates to the fungus, and in turn soil nutrients and water are supplied to the plant.

BURL A widening of the base of a shrub just at or below the soil surface where resources can be stored and largely used to fuel regrowth following biomass loss due to fire.

DROUGHT-DECIDUOUS Having short-lived leaves that are shed annually during the summer drought.

ENDOPHYTE A microbe (bacteria or fungus) that lives in an endosymbiotic relationship with a plant without causing harm and often having benefit to the plant.

FACULTATIVE Meaning that the phenomenon is capable of occurring but is not required, often referring to plant regeneration capacity: the opposite of "obligate."

LITTER The accumulation of dead plant material on the soil surface, "litter" can refer to either herbaceous material or woody debris.

OBLIGATE Equivalent to "required" or "necessary." Often referring to regeneration capacity of plants, the opposite of "facultative."

SUFFRUTESCENT Being slightly woody at the base but not having woody tissue throughout the support structure of a plant. Generally refers to the woody base of subshrubs, which have otherwise nonwoody stems.

References

Alberts, A. C., Richman, A. D., Tran, R. Sauvajot, C. McCalvin, and D. T. Bolger. 1993. Effects of habitat fragmentation on native and exotic plants in southern California coastal scrub. Pages 103–110 in J. E. Keeley, editor. Interface between ecology and land development in California. Southern California Academy of Sciences.

Allen, E. B., R. J. Steers, and S. J. M. Dickens. 2011. Impacts of fire and invasive species on desert soil ecology. Rangeland Ecology and Management 64:450–462.

Allen, E. B., R. D. Cox, T. Tennant, S. N. Kee, and D. H. Deutschman. 2005. Landscape restoration in southern California forblands: Response of abandoned farmland to invasive annual grass control. Israel Journal of Plant Sciences 53:237–245.

Axelrod, D. I. 1978. The origin of coastal sage vegetation, Alta and Baja California. American Journal of Botany 65:1117–1131.

Barrows, C. W., M. B. Swartz, W. L. Hodges, M. F. Allen, J. T. Rotenberry, B.-L. Li, T. A. Scott, and X. Chen. 2005. A framework for

monitoring multiple-species conservation plans. Journal of Wildlife Management 69: 333–1345.
Bartholomew, B. 1970. Bare zone between California shrub and grassland communities: The role of animals. Science 170:1210–1212.
Bartolome, J. W. 1979. Germination and seedling establishment in California annual grassland. Journal of Ecology 67:273–281.
Bolger, D. T., A. C. Alberts, R. M. Sauvajot, P. Potenza, C. McCalvin, D. Tran, S. Mazzoni, and M. E. Soule. 1997. Response of rodents to habitat fragmentation in coastal southern California. Ecological Applications 7:552–563.
Bolger, D. T., K. H. Beard, A. V. Suarez, and T. J. Case. 2008. Increased abundance of native and non–native spiders with habitat fragmentation. Diversity and Distributions 14:655–665.
Bowler, P. A. 2000. Ecological restoration of coastal sage scrub and its potential role in habitat conservation plans. Environmental Management 26:S85–S96.
Brehme, C. S., D. R. Clark, C. J. Rochester, and R. N. Fisher. 2011. Wildfires alter rodent community structure across four vegetation types in southern California, USA. Fire Ecology 7:81–98.
Brooks, M. L., C. M. D'antonio, D. M. Richardson, J. B. Grace, J. E. Keeley, J. M. DiTomaso, R. J. Hobbs, M. Pellant, and D. Pyke. 2004. Effects of invasive alien plants on fire regimes. BioScience 54:677–688.
Burcham, L. T. 1957. California range land: an historico-ecological study of the range resource of California. Division of Forestry, Department of Natural Resources, Sacramento, California.
California Department of Fish and Game (CDFG). 2013. State and federally listed endangered and threatened animals of California. <http://www.dfg.ca.gov>. Accessed 2014.
Callaway, R. M., and F. W. Davis. 1993. Vegetation dynamics, fire, and the physical environment in coastal central California. Ecology 74:1567–1578.
Cayan, D. R. 2008. Climate change scenarios for the California region. Climatic Change 87:S21–S42.
Chen, X., B.-L. Li, and M. F. Allen. 2010. Characterizing urbanization, and agricultural and conservation land-use change in Riverside County, California, USA. Ecological Complexity and Sustainability 1195:E164–E176.
Cione, N., P. Padgett, and E. Allen. 2002. Restoration of a native shrubland impacted by exotic grasses, frequent fire, and nitrogen deposition in southern California. Restoration Ecology 10:376–384.
Cleland, E. E., L. Larios and K. N. Suding. 2013. Strengthening invasion filters to reassemble native plant communities: Soil resources and phenological overlap. Restoration Ecology 21:390–398.
Cooper, C. B., K.A.T. Loyd, T. Murante, M. Savoca, and J. Dickinson. 2012. Natural history traits associated with detecting mortality within residential bird communities: Can citizen science provide insights? Environmental Management 50:11–20.
Cox, R. D., and E. B. Allen. 2011. The roles of exotic grasses and forbs when restoring native species to highly invaded southern California annual grassland. Plant Ecology 212:1699–1707.
———. 2008a. Composition of soil seed banks in southern California coastal sage scrub and adjacent exotic grassland. Plant Ecology 198:37–46.
———. 2008b. Stability of exotic annual grasses following restoration efforts in southern California coastal sage scrub. Journal of Applied Ecology 45:495–504.
Crooks, K. R., and M. A. Sanjayan, editors 2006. Connectivity conservation. Cambridge University Press, Cambridge, UK.
Crooks, K. R., and M. E. Soulé. 1999. Mesopredator release and avifaunal extinctions in a fragmented system. Nature 400:563–566.
D'Antonio, C. M., and P. M. Vitousek. 1992. Biological invasions by exotic grasses, the grass/fire cycle, and global change. Annual Review of Ecology and Systematics 23:63–87.
Davis, M. A., J. P. Grime, and K. Thompson. 2000. Fluctuating resources in plant communities: A general theory of invasibility. Journal of Ecology 88:528–534.
Davis, S. D., and H. A. Mooney. 1985. Comparative water relations of adjacent California shrub and grassland communities. Oecologia 66:522–529.
DeSimone, S. A. 2013. Restoration and science: A practitioner/scientist's view from rare habitat restoration at a southern California preserve. Restoration Ecology 21:149–152.
———. 2006. Non-chemical restoration of coastal sage scrub in artichoke thistle-infested grasslands (California). Ecological Restoration 24:278–279.
DeSimone, S. A., and P. H. Zedler. 2001. Do shrub colonizers of southern Californian grassland fit generalities for other woody colonizers? Ecological Applications 11:1101–1111.
———. 1999. Shrub seedling recruitment in unburned Californian coastal sage scrub and adjacent grassland. Ecology 80:2018–2032.
DeSimone, S. A., and J. H. Burk. 1992. Local variation in floristics and distributional factors in Californian coastal sage scrub. Madroño 39:170–188.
Dickens, S.J.M., E. B. Allen, L. S. Santiago, and D. Crowley. 2013. Exotic annuals alter the variation in coastal sage scrub soil chemical and biological characteristics. Soil Biology and Biochemistry 58: 70–81.
Diffenbaugh, N. S., F. Giorgi, and J. S. Pal. 2008. Climate change hotspots in the United States. Geophysical Research Letters 35:L16709.
Diffendorfer, J. E., G. M. Fleming, Duggan, R. E. Chapman, M. E. Rahn, M. J. Mitrovich, and R. N. Fisher. 2007. Developing terrestrial, multi-taxon indices of biological integrity: An example from coastal sage scrub. Biological Conservation 140:130–141.
Diffendorfer, J., G. M. Fleming, S. Tremor, W. Spencer, and J. L. Beyers. 2012. The role of fire severity, distance from fire perimeter, and vegetation on post-fire recovery of small-mammal communities in chaparral. International Journal of Wildland Fire 21:436–448.
Egerton-Warburton, L. M., and E. B. Allen. 2000. Shifts in arbuscular mycorrhizal communities along an anthropogenic nitrogen deposition gradient. Ecological Applications 10:484–496.
Eliason, S. A., and E. B. Allen. 1997. Exotic grass competition in suppressing native shrubland re-establishment. Restoration Ecology 5:245–255.
Evens, J. M. and A. N. Klein. 2006. A new model for conservation planning: vegetation mapping in western Riverside County. Fremontia 34:11–18.
Fenn, M. E., E. B. Allen, S. B. Weiss, S. Jovan, L. H. Geiser, G. S. Tonnesen, R. F. Johnson, L. E. Rao, B. S. Gimeno, F. Yuan, T. Meixner, and A. Bytnerowicz. 2010. Nitrogen critical loads and management alternatives for N-impacted ecosystems in California. Journal of Environmental Management 91:2404–2423.
Fenn, M. E., J. S. Baron, E. B. Allen, H. M. Rueth, K. R. Nydick, L. Geiser, W. D. Bowman, J. O. Sickman, T. Meixner, D. W. Johnson, and P. Neitlich. 2003. Ecological effects of nitrogen deposition in the western United States. BioScience 53:404–420.
Fenn, M. E., M. A. Poth, P. H. Dunn, and S. C. Barro. 1993. Microbial N and biomass, respiration and N mineralization in soils beneath two chaparral species along a fire-induced age gradient. Soil Biology and Biochemistry 25:457–466.
Fleming, G. M., J. E. Diffendorfer, and P. H. Zedler. 2009. The relative importance of disturbance and exotic-plant abundance in California coastal sage scrub. Ecological Applications 19:2210–2227.
Freudenberger, D. O., B. E. Fish, and J. E. Keeley. 1987. Distribution and stability of grasslands in the Los Angeles Basin. Bulletin of the Southern California Academy of Sciences 86:13–26.
Ford, L. D., and G. F. Hayes. 2007. Northern coastal scrub and coastal prairie. Pages 180–207 in M. G. Barbour, T. Keeler-Wolf, and A. A. Schoenherr, editors. Terrestrial Vegetation of California. Third Edition. University of California Press, Berkeley, California.
Gabet, E. J., and T. Dunne. 2002. Landslides on coastal sage-scrub and grassland hillslopes in a severe El Niño winter: The effects of vegetation conversion on sediment delivery. Geological Society of America Bulletin 114:983–990.
Gill, D. S., and B. E. Mahall. 1986. Quantitative phenology and water relations of an evergreen and a deciduous chaparral shrub. Ecological Monographs 56:127–143.
Gillespie, I. G., and E. B. Allen. 2004. Fire and competition in a southern California grassland: impacts on the rare forb *Erodium macrophyllum*. Journal of Applied Ecology 41:643–652.
Gray, J. T. 1983. Nutrient use by evergreen and deciduous shrubs in Southern California: I. Community nutrient cycling and nutrient-use efficiency. Journal of Ecology 71:21–41.
———. 1982. Community structure and productivity in *Ceanothus* chaparral and coastal sage scrub of southern California. Ecological Monographs 52:415–435.
Gray J. T., and W. H. Schlesinger. 1983. Nutrient use by evergreen and deciduous shrubs in southern California. II. Experimen-

tal investigations of the relationship between growth, nitrogen uptake, and nitrogen availability. Journal of Ecology 71:43–56.

———. 1981. Biomass, production, and litterfall in the coastal sage scrub of southern California. American Journal of Botany 68:24–33.

Hannah, L., M. R. Shaw, M. Ikegami, P. R. Roehrdanz, O. Soong, and J. Thorne. 2012. Consequences of climate change for native plants and conservation. Publication number: CEC-500-2012-024. California Energy Commission.

Harrison, A. T., E. Small, and H. A. Mooney. 1971. Drought relationships and distribution of two Mediterranean-climate California plant communities. Ecology 52:869–875.

Hellmers, H., J. S. Horton, G. Junren, and J. O'Keefe. 1955. Root systems of some chaparral plants in southern California. Ecology 36:667–678.

Henry H.A.L., K. Brizgys, and C. B. Field. 2008. Litter decomposition in a California annual grassland: Interactions between photodegradation and litter layer thickness. Ecosystems 11:545–554.

Hobbs, R. J., E. Higgs, and J. A. Harris. 2009. Novel ecosystems: Implications for conservation and restoration. Trends in Ecology and Evolution 24:599–605.

Hobbs, R. J., and H. A. Mooney. 1986. Community changes following shrub invasion of grassland. Oecologia 70:508–513.

Holland, V. L., and D. J. Keil. 1995. California vegetation. Kendall/Hunt, Dubuque, Iowa.

Hollander, A. D. 2007. California augmented multisource landcover map version 1. Information Center for the Environment, University of California, Davis. <http://climate.calcommons.org/dataset/california-augmented-multisource-landcover-map-caml-2010>.

Huenneke, L. F., S. P. Hamburg, R. Koide, H. A. Mooney, and P. M. Vitousek. 1990. Effects of soil resources on plant invasion and community structure in California serpentine grassland. Ecology 71:478–491.

Huntsinger, L., and J. L. Oviedo. 2014. Ecosystem services are social-ecological services in a traditional pastoral system: The case of California's Mediterranean rangelands. Ecology and Society 19: 8–20.

Irvine, I. C., C. A. Brigham, K. N. Suding, and J.B.H. Martiny. 2012. The abundance of pink-pigmented facultative methylotrophs in the root zone of plant species in invaded coastal sage scrub habitat. PLoS One 7:e31026. <doi:31010.31371/journal.pone.0031026>.

Jacobsen, A. L., R. B. Pratt, S. D. Davis, and F. W. Ewers. 2008. Comparative community physiology: Nonconvergence in water relations among three semi-arid shrub communities. New Phytologist 180:100–113.

Karst, J., B. Piculell, C. Brigham, M. Booth, and J. D. Hoeksema. 2013. Fungal communities in soils along a vegetative ecotone. Mycologia 105:61–70.

Keeley, J.E. 2002. American Indian influence on fire regimes in California's coastal ranges. Journal of Biogeography 29: 303–320.

——— 1992. Demographic structure of California chaparral in the long-term absence of fire. Journal of Vegetation Science 3:79–90.

Keeley, J. E., and C. C. Swift. 1995. Biodiversity and ecosystem functioning in Mediterranean-climate California. Pages 121–183 in G. W. Davis and D. M. Richardson, editors. Mediterranean-Type Ecosystems: The Function of Biodiversity Springer-Verlag, Berlin and Heidelberg, Germany.

Keeley, J. E., and T. J. Brennan. 2012. Fire-driven alien invasion in a fire-adapted ecosystem. Oecologia 16:1043–1052.

Keeley, J. E., C. J. Fotheringham, and M. Baer-Keeley. 2006. Demographic patterns of postfire regeneration in Mediterranean-climate shrublands of California. Ecological Monographs 76:235–255.

———. 2005a. Determinants of postfire recovery and succession in Mediterranean-climate shrublands of California. Ecological Applications 15:1515–1534.

———. 2005b. Factors affecting plant diversity during post fire recovery and succession of Mediterranean-climate shrublands in California, USA. Diversity and Distributions 11:525–537.

Keeley, J. E., M. Baer-Keeley, and C. J. Fotheringham. 2005. Alien plant dynamics following fire in Mediterranean-climate California shrublands. Ecological Applications 15:2109–2125.

Kelt, D. A., E. S. Konno, and J. A. Wilson. 2005. Habitat management for the endangered Stephens' kangaroo rat: The effect of mowing and grazing. Journal of Wildlife Management 69:424–429.

Kimball, S., and P. M. Schiffman. 2003. Differing effects of cattle grazing on native and alien plants. Conservation Biology 17:1681–1693.

Kirkpatrick, J. B., and C. F. Hutchinson. 1980. The environmental relationships of Californian coastal sage scrub and some of its component communities and species. Journal of Biogeography 7:23–38.

——— 1977. The community composition of Californian coastal sage scrub. Vegetatio 35: 21–33.

Kolb, K. J., and S. D. Davis. 1994. Drought tolerance and xylem embolism in co-occurring species of coastal sage and chaparral. Ecology 75:648–659.

Kristan III, W. B., A. J. Lynam, M. V. Price, and J. T. Rotenberry. 2003. Alternative causes of edge-abundance relationships in birds and small mammals of California coastal sage scrub. Ecography 26:29–44.

Küchler, A. W. 1997. The map of the natural vegetation of California. John Wiley and Sons, New York, NY.

Landis, J. D., H. Hood, G. Li, T. Rogers, and C. Warren. 2006. The future of infill housing in California: Opportunities, potential, and feasibility. Housing Policy Debate 17:681–725.

Lenihan, J. M., D. Bachelet, R. P. Neilson, and R. Drapek. 2008. Response of vegetation distribution, ecosystem productivity, and fire to climate change scenarios for California. Climatic Change 87:215–230.

Lenihan, J. M., R. Drapek, D. Bachelet, and R. P. Neilson. 2003. Climate change effects on vegetation distribution, carbon, and fire in California. Ecological Applications 13:1667–1681.

Liu, K., and D. Crowley. 2009. Nitrogen deposition effects on carbon storage and fungal: Bacterial ratios in coastal sage scrub soils of southern California. Journal of Environmental Quality 38:2267–2272.

Malanson, G. P., and J. F. O'Leary. 1982. Post-fire regeneration strategies of Californian coastal sage shrubs. Oecologia 53:355–358.

Malo, J. E., and F. Suárez. 1995. Herbivorous mammals as seed dispersers in a Mediterranean dehesa. Oecologia, 104:246–255.

Marushia, R. G., and E. B. Allen. 2011. Control of exotic annual grasses to restore native forbs in abandoned agricultural land. Restoration Ecology 19:45–54.

Matsuda, T., G. Turschak, C. Brehme, C. Rochester, M. Mitrovich, and R. Fisher. 2011. Effects of large-scale wildfires on ground foraging ants (Hymenoptera: Formicidae) in southern California. Environmental Entomology 40:204–216.

McCullough, S. A., and B. A. Endress. 2012. Do postfire mulching treatments affect plant community recovery in California coastal sage scrub lands? Environmental Management 49: 142–150.

Mendelsohn, M. B., C. S. Brehme, C. J. Rochester, D. C. Stokes, S. A. Hathaway, and R. N. Fisher. 2008. Responses in bird communities to wildland fires in southern California. Fire Ecology 4:63–82.

Minnich, R. A. 2008. California's fading wildflowers: Lost legacy and biological invasions. University of California Press, Berkeley, California.

Minnich, R. A., and R. J. Dezzani. 1998. Historical decline of coastal sage scrub in the Riverside–Perris Plain, California. Western Birds 29:366–391.

Mooney, H. A., and A. T. Harrison. 1972. The vegetational gradient on the lower slopes of the Sierra San Pedro Martir in northwest Baja California. Madroño 21:439–445.

Mooney, H., and E. Dunn. 1970. Photosynthetic systems of Mediterranean climate shrubs and trees of California and Chile. American Naturalist 104:447–453.

Mordecai, E. A. 2012. Soil moisture and fungi affect seed survival in California grassland annual plants. PloS One 7(6):e39083.

Morrison, S. A., and D. T. Bolger. 2002. Variation in a sparrow's reproductive success with rainfall: Food and predator-mediated processes. Oecologia 133:315–324.

Morrison, S. A., and M. D. Reynolds. 2006. Where to draw the line: Integrating feasibility into connectivity planning. Pages 536–554 in K. R. Crooks and M. A. Sanjayan, editors. Connectivity Conservation. Cambridge University Press, Cambridge, UK.

Myers, N. A., A. Mittermeier, C. G. Mittermeier, G. A. B. Da Fonseca, and J. Kent. 2000. Biodiversity hotspots for conservation priorities. Nature 403: 853–858.

O'Leary, J. F. 1990. Post-fire diversity patterns in two subassociations of Californian coastal sage scrub. Journal of Vegetation Science 1:173–180.

O'Leary, J. F., and W. E. Westman. 1988. Regional disturbance effects on herb succession patterns in coastal sage scrub. Journal of Biogeography 15:775–786.

Padgett, P. E., and E. B. Allen. 1999. Differential responses to nitrogen fertilization in native shrubs and exotic annuals common to Mediterranean coastal sage scrub of California. Plant Ecology 144:93–101.

Padgett, P. E., E. B. Allen, A. Bytnerowicz, and R. A. Minnich. 1999. Changes in soil inorganic nitrogen as related to atmospheric nitrogenous pollutants in southern California. Atmospheric Environment 33:769–781.

Patten, M. A., and D. T. Bolger. 2003. Variation in top-down control of avian reproductive success across a fragmentation gradient. Oikos 101:479–488.

Poole, D. K., and P. C. Miller. 1975. Water relations of selected species of chaparral and coastal sage communities. Ecology 56:1118–1128.

Pratt, J. D., and K. A. Mooney 2013. Clinal adaptation and adaptive plasticity in Artemisia californica: Implications for the response of a foundation species to predicted climate change. Global Change Biology 19:2454–2466.

Preston, K. L., R. A. Redak, M. F. Allen, and J. T. Rotenberry. 2012. Changing distribution patterns of an endangered butterfly: linking local extinction patterns and variable habitat relationships. Biological Conservation 152: 280–290.

Preston, K. L., J. T. Rotenberry, R. A. Redak, and M. F. Allen. 2008. Habitat shifts of endangered species under altered climate conditions: Importance of biotic interactions. Global Change Biology 14(11):2501–2515.

Price, M. V., R. L. Goldingay, L. S. Szychowski, and N. M. Waser. 1994. Managing habitat for the endangered Stephens kangaroo rat (*Dipodomys-stephensi*)—effects of shrub removal. American Midland Naturalist 131:9–16. Riverside County Transportation and Land Management Agency. Western Riverside County Multispecies Habitat Conservation Plan, Volume 1. <http://rctlma.org/Portals/0/mshcp/volume1/index.html>. Accessed June 19, 2015.

Robinson, J. W., B. D. Risher and E. S. Bakker. 1993. The San Jacintos: The mountain country from Banning to Borrego Valley. Big Santa Anita Historical Society. Arcadia, California.

Rochester, C. J., C. S. Brehme, D. R. Clark, D. C. Stokes, S. A. Hathaway, and R. N. Fisher. 2010. Reptile and amphibian responses to large-scale wildfires in southern California. Journal of Herpetology 44:333–351.

Rubinoff, D. 2001. Evaluating the California gnatcatcher as an umbrella species for conservation of southern California coastal sage scrub. Conservation Biology 15:1374–1383.

Rundel, P. W. 2007. Sage scrub. Pages 208–228 in M. G. Barbour, T. Keeler-Wolf, and A. A. Schoenherr, editors. Terrestrial Vegetation of California. Third edition. University of California Press, Berkeley and Los Angeles, California.

Salo, L. F. 2004. Population dynamics of red brome (*Bromus madritensis subsp. rubens*): Times for concern, opportunities for management. Journal of Arid Environments 57:291–296.

San Diego County Multispecies Conservation Plan. MSCP Biology. http://www.sdcounty.ca.gov/pds/mscp/biology. Accessed June 19, 2015.

Sawyer, J. O., and T. Keeler-Wolf. 1995. A manual of California vegetation. California Native Plant Society, Sacramento, California.

Sax, D. F. 2002. Native and naturalized plant diversity are positively correlated in scrub communities of California and Chile. Diversity and Distributions 8:193–210.

Schubert, S. D., Y. Chang, M. J. Suarez, and P. J. Pegion. 2008. ENSO and wintertime extreme precipitation events over the contiguous United States. Journal of Climate 21:22–39.

Schultz, A. M., J. L. Launchbaugh, and H. H. Biswell. 1955. Relationship between grass density and brush seedling survival. Ecology 36:226–238.

Scott, T. A., L. Fernandez, and M. F. Allen. 2006. Land use planning. Pages 206–217 in J. A. Scott, D. D. Goble, and F. W. Davis, editors. The Endangered Species Act at Thirty. Volume 2. Conserving Biodiversity in Human-Dominated Landscapes. Island Press, Washington, D.C.

Sigüenza, C., D. E. Crowley, and E. B Allen. 2006. Soil microorganisms of a native shrub and exotic grasses along a nitrogen deposition gradient in southern California. Applied Soil Ecology 32:3–26.

Sirulnik, A. G., E. B. Allen, T. Meixner, and M. F. Allen. 2007a. Impacts of anthropogenic N additions on nitrogen mineralization from plant litter in exotic annual grasslands. Soil Biology and Biochemistry 39:24–32.

Sirulnik, A. G., E. B. Allen, T. Meixner, M. E. Fenn, and M. F. Allen. 2007b. Changes in N cycling and microbial N with elevated N in exotic annual grasslands of southern California. Applied Soil Ecology 36:1–9.

Skinner, M.W., and B. M. Pavlik. 1994. CNPS inventory of rare and endangered vascular plants of California. California Native Plant Society, Sacramento, California.

Soulé, M. D., D. T. Bolger, A. C. Alberts, R. Sauvajot, J. Wright, M. Sorice, and S. Hill. 1988. Reconstructed dynamics of rapid extinctions of chaparral-requiring birds in urban habitat islands. Conservation Biology 2:75–92.

Steers, R. J., S. L. Fritzke, J. J. Rogers, J. Cartan, and K. Hacker. 2013. Invasive pine tree effects on northern coastal scrub structure and composition. Invasive Plant Science and Management 6:231–242.

Stylinski, C. D., and E. B. Allen. 1999. Lack of native species recovery following severe exotic disturbance in southern Californian shrublands. Journal of Applied Ecology 36:544–554.

Sulak, A., and L. Huntsinger. 2007. Public land grazing in California: Untapped conservation potential for private lands? Working landscapes may be linked to public lands. Rangelands 29:9–12.

Talluto, M. V., and K. N. Suding. 2008. Historical change in coastal sage scrub in southern California, USA, in relation to fire frequency and air pollution. Landscape Ecology 23:803–815.

USGS GAP Analysis Program. 2013. Protected areas database of the United States. <www.protectedlands.net/>. Accessed July 2013.

Vourlitis, G. L. 2012. Aboveground net primary production response of semi-arid shrublands to chronic experimental dry-season N input. Ecosphere 3:art22.

Vourlitis, G. L., and J. S. Fernandez. 2012. Changes in the soil, litter, and vegetation nitrogen and carbon concentrations of semiarid shrublands in response to chronic dry season nitrogen input. Journal of Arid Environments 82:115–122.

Vourlitis, G. L., and G. Zorba. 2007. Nitrogen and carbon mineralization of semi-arid shrubland soil exposed to long-term atmospheric nitrogen deposition. Biology and Fertility of Soils 43:611–615.

Vourlitis, G. L., S. C. Pasquini, and R. Mustard. 2009. Effects of dry-season N input on the productivity and N storage of Mediterranean-type shrublands. Ecosystems 12:473–488.

Vourlitis, G. L., G. Zorba, S. C. Pasquini, and R. Mustard. 2007. Chronic nitrogen deposition enhances nitrogen mineralization potential of semiarid shrubland soils. Soil Science Society of America Journal 71: 836–842.

Wainwright, C. E., E. M. Wolkovich, and E. E. Cleland. 2012. Seasonal priority effects: Implications for invasion and restoration in a semi-arid system. Journal of Applied Ecology 49:234–241.

Westman, W. E. 1983. Xeric Mediterranean-type shrubland associations of Alta and Baja California and the community/continuum debate. Vegetatio 52:3–19.

———. 1981a. Diversity relations and succession in Californian coastal sage scrub. Ecology 62:170–184.

———. 1981b. Factors influencing the distribution of species of Californian coastal sage scrub. Ecology 62:439–455.

———. 1981c. Seasonal dimorphism of foliage in Californian coastal sage scrub. Oecologia 51:385–388.

Westman, W. E. and J. F. O'Leary. 1986. Measures of resilience: the response of coastal sage scrub to fire. Vegetatio 65:179–189.

Westman, W. E., J. F. O'Leary, and G. P. Malanson. 1981. The effects of fire intensity, aspect, and substrate on postfire growth of Californian coastal sage scrub. Pages 151–179 in N. S. Margaris and H. A. Mooney, editors. Components of Productivity of Mediterranean Regions, The Hague, The Netherlands.

Wieslander, A. E. 1935. A vegetation type map of California. Madroño 3:140–144.

Williams, K., R. J. Hobbs, and S. P. Hamburg. 1987. Invasion of an annual grassland in northern California by *Baccharis pilularis* ssp. *consanguinea*. Oecologia 72:461–465.

Wolkovich, E. M. 2010. Nonnative grass litter enhances grazing arthropod assemblages by increasing native shrub growth. Ecology 91:756–766.

Wolkovich, E. M., D. A. Lipson, R. A. Virginia, K. L. Cottingham, and D. T. Bolger. 2010. Grass invasion causes rapid increases in ecosystem carbon and nitrogen storage in a semiarid shrubland. Global Change Biology 16:1351–1365.

Wolkovich, E. M., D. T. Bolger, and D. A. Holway. 2009a. Complex responses to invasive grass litter by ground arthropods in a Mediterranean scrub ecosystem. Oecologia 161:697–708.
Wolkovich, E. M., D. T. Bolger, and K. L. Cottingham. 2009b. Invasive grass litter facilitates native shrubs through abiotic effects. Journal of Vegetation Science 20:121–1132.
Wood, Y. A., T. Meixner, P. J. Shouse, and E. B. Allen. 2006. Altered ecohydrologic response drives native shrub loss under conditions of elevated nitrogen deposition. Journal of Environmental Quality 35:76–92.
Wright, I. J., P. B. Reich, M. Westoby, D. D. Ackerly, Z. Baruch, F. Bongers, J. Cavender-Bares, T. Chapin, J.H.C. Cornelissen, M. Diemer, J. Flexas, E. Garnier, P. K. Groom, J. Gulias, K. Hikosaka, B. B. Lamont, T. Lee, W. Lee, C. Lusk, J. J. Midgley, M. L. Navas, U. Niinemets, J. Oleksyn, N. Osada, H. Poorter, P. Poot, L. D. Prior, V. I. Pyankov, C. Roumet, S. C. Thomas, M. G. Tjoelker, E. J. Veneklaas, and R. Villar. 2004. The worldwide leaf economics spectrum. Nature 428:821–827.
Yelenik, S. G., and J. M. Levine. 2011. The role of plant-soil feedbacks in driving native-species recovery. Ecology 92:66–74.
———. 2010. Processes limiting native shrub recovery in exotic grasslands after non-native herbivore removal. Restoration Ecology 18:418–425.
Yoshida, L. C., and E. B. Allen. 2001. Response to ammonium and nitrate by a mycorrhizal annual invasive grass and native shrub in southern California. American Journal of Botany 88:1430–1436.
Zink, T., and M. Allen. 1998. The effects of organic amendments on the restoration of a disturbed coastal sage scrub habitat. Restoration Ecology 6:52–58.
Zink, T. A., M. F. Allen, B. Heindl-Tenhunen, and E. B. Allen. 1995. The effect of a disturbance corridor on an ecological reserve. Restoration Ecology 3:304–310.

TWENTY-THREE

Grasslands

VALERIE T. EVINER

Introduction

Much of California's original grassland habitat has been lost to both changes in hydrology and in urban and agricultural development. Even with this extensive habitat loss, more than 10% of California's land area remains covered by grasslands today (Corbin et al. 2007a, Barbour et al. 2007). These remaining grasslands are among California's most altered ecosystems (Corbin et al. 2007a, Jantz et al. 2007). Non-native plant species comprise more than 90% of plant cover in most grassland areas, with many sites below 1% native cover (Bartolome et al. 2007). Even in their non-native dominated state, California's grasslands are a tremendous diversity hotspot, averaging more than fifty plant species per 30 x 30 meter area (Heady et al. 1992) and providing habitat for nearly 90% of state-listed rare and endangered species (Skinner and Pavlik 1994) and seventy-five federally listed plants and animals (Jantz et al. 2007).

These grasslands provide many ecosystem services critical for adjacent agricultural and suburban/urban areas. Almost all of California's surface water passes through grasslands and oak woodlands (Tate et al. 1999). The grasslands provide high INFILTRATION rates that attenuate storm events, leading to gradual release of storm water to streams (Lewis 1968, Dahlgren et al. 2001). This reduces flood risk while also maintaining streamflow into the dry season. Grasslands can also improve water quality by filtering pathogens, nutrients, and sediments, serving as effective buffer strips between agricultural and urban uplands and streams (Tate et al. 2006, Atwill et al. 2006). California's grasslands contribute significantly to regional carbon storage through their large spatial extent and high quantity of carbon storage per unit area (Silver et al. 2010). Grasslands also support many of the pollinators needed in California's crop systems (Chaplin-Kramer et al. 2011). Direct economic benefits of these grasslands include their provisioning of 75% of the state's livestock forage (Corbin et al. 2007a, CCCC 2009, Cheatum et al. 2011). Because 88% of California grasslands are privately owned (Jantz et al. 2007), their conservation and restoration depend largely on private land owners and the ways they balance management for livestock production, biotic diversity, and ecosystem services (SRDC 2006, Barry et al. 2006, FRAP 2010, Ferranto et al. 2011).

Managing California's grasslands can be challenging because their structure and function are influenced by multiple, interacting controllers. This produces heterogeneous community and ecosystem dynamics across space and time (Huenneke and Mooney 1989). Grasslands are distributed across a broad range of precipitation regimes; from the high-rainfall coasts to drier inland valleys (Figure 23.1). Grassland structure and function vary across this precipitation gradient and with high temporal variability in weather across seasons and years (see Chapter 2, "Climate"). While precipitation patterns are the strongest controller of California grassland dynamics, within the confines of weather patterns grassland structure and function also respond to human management and interactions with soil type, topography, non-native plants, small mammals, insects, microbes, livestock, wild herbivores, and disturbance regimes (Figure 23.2) (Bartolome et al. 2007).

California's Mediterranean climate makes its grasslands distinct from other North American grasslands, which are exposed to a temperate climate where temperature drives the seasonality of plant growth (Corbin et al. 2007b). In contrast, seasonality of precipitation largely governs ecosystem processes in California's Mediterranean climate, with most plant production occurring during the cool, wet winters and with little plant activity during the hot, dry summers (Corbin et al. 2007b). California's grasslands differ from other Mediterranean grasslands across the globe because of the stable long-term dominance of annual species in most areas of California. While annual species play an important role in other Mediterranean grasslands shortly after disturbances, successional dynamics eventually lead to domination by perennial species (Rice 1989). Domination of annuals likely makes California's grasslands more sensitive to fluctuations in abiotic and biotic controllers and is likely the reason behind the need for persistent management to meet many conservation and production goals (Bartolome et al. 2007, Malmstrom et al. 2009).

California's grasslands are experiencing further changes due to shifts in management and the environment, including nitrogen deposition, altered weather patterns, non-native species introductions, and altered grazing and fire regimes. California's grasslands are also threatened by further land use change. Successful management of these grasslands, particularly in a changing environment, will require site- and region-specific approaches (Bartolome et al. 2007) because sites from different climate regimes and soil types respond differently to weather variability (George et al. 1988) and management (Bartolome et al. 2007).

Primary Factors Controlling the Distribution of California's Grasslands

California's 5,640,400 hectares of grassland (Bartolome et al. 2007) are most commonly found in well-drained areas below 1,200 meter elevation (Heady 1977), across a wide diversity of soils (Jackson et al. 2007) and across a broad precipitation gradient ranging from 12 to 200 centimeters per year (Bartolome et al. 2007). Many of the herbaceous species that dominate open grasslands are also key components of other California ecosystems (Bartolome et al. 2007), including oak savannas (Chapter 25, "Oak Woodlands"), shrublands (Chapters 22, "Coastal Sage Scrub," and 24, "Chaparral") and deserts (Chapter 30, "Deserts"). California's grasslands experience a Mediterranean climate with a mismatch in the timing of ideal temperature versus moisture conditions for plant growth (Figure 23.3). Moisture limits plant growth in the hot and dry summers, while temperature and light limit growth during the cool, wet winters. Ideal periods for plant growth are thus restricted to short periods in the fall and spring (Evans and Young 1989, Bartolome et al. 2007). The growing season begins with the first significant rains (greater than 1.5 centimeters within a week) (Chiariello 1989) and continues until soil moisture declines in the spring (exact timing depends on amount and timing of precipitation as well as the water-holding capacity of soil).

When the system dries in the spring, most early- to mid-PHENOLOGY annuals set seed and SENESCE, avoiding the hot, dry summer conditions. Some summer annual species (e.g., tarweeds [*Hemizonia, Madia*] and wild lettuce [*Lactuca*]) do grow through the hot, dry summer, using their deep taproots to access moisture (Chiariello 1989, Bartolome et al. 2007). Native perennial grasses often begin growth early in the fall, sometimes even before the rains begin, and can grow later into the summer than most annuals. However, most native perennial grasses do experience aboveground senescence in the summer (Bartolome et al. 2007). This highly seasonal climate, with soil moisture limiting plant growth for four to eight months out of the year (Bartolome et al. 2007), results in stable grasslands even at total annual precipitation levels that, if evenly distributed through the year, would support woody-dominated species in temperate climates. In areas with precipitation patterns that can support either herbaceous or woody species, soils that are fine-textured tend to be dominated by grasslands (Tyler et al. 2007). While environmental conditions shape the distribution of many grasslands, some of California's grasslands were formerly woody-dominated and were converted through burning, cutting, and herbicide applications (Tyler et al. 2007). The distribution of grasslands across broad precipitation gradients and soils leads to three key subtypes: interior, coastal, and more localized soil-specific grasslands (Keeler-Wolf et al. 2007) (Figure 23.4).

Interior Grassland

The most widespread grassland type is interior grassland (also known as valley grassland, south coastal grassland) (see Figure 23.4a). Interior grasslands tend to be distributed in the Central Valley as well as up to 700 meters into the foothills and coastal hills (particularly in the South Coastal hills and in the interior valleys of the Northern Coast Range) (Keeler-Wolf et al. 2007). Since the early nineteenth century, non-native grasses and FORBS have dominated these grasslands (Keeler-Wolf et al. 2007). Grass cover dominates, but forb species richness is four times greater than grass richness (Sims and Risser 2000). Some native perennial grasses persist in this system (e.g., purple needle grass [*Stipa pulchra*], valley wild rye [*Elymus triticoides*], blue wild rye [*Elymus glaucus*], and California brome [*Bromus carinatus*]), but their growth, survival, and seed establishment are limited in the interior grasslands by the fast growth, high density, shading effect, and high water use of the highly competitive non-native species (Corbin et al. 2007a). Interior grasslands extend across a wide mean annual precipitation gradient, producing variations in plant

Photo on previous page: California wildflowers in bloom at the North Table Mountain Ecological Reserve, Butte County. Photo: Valerie Eviner.

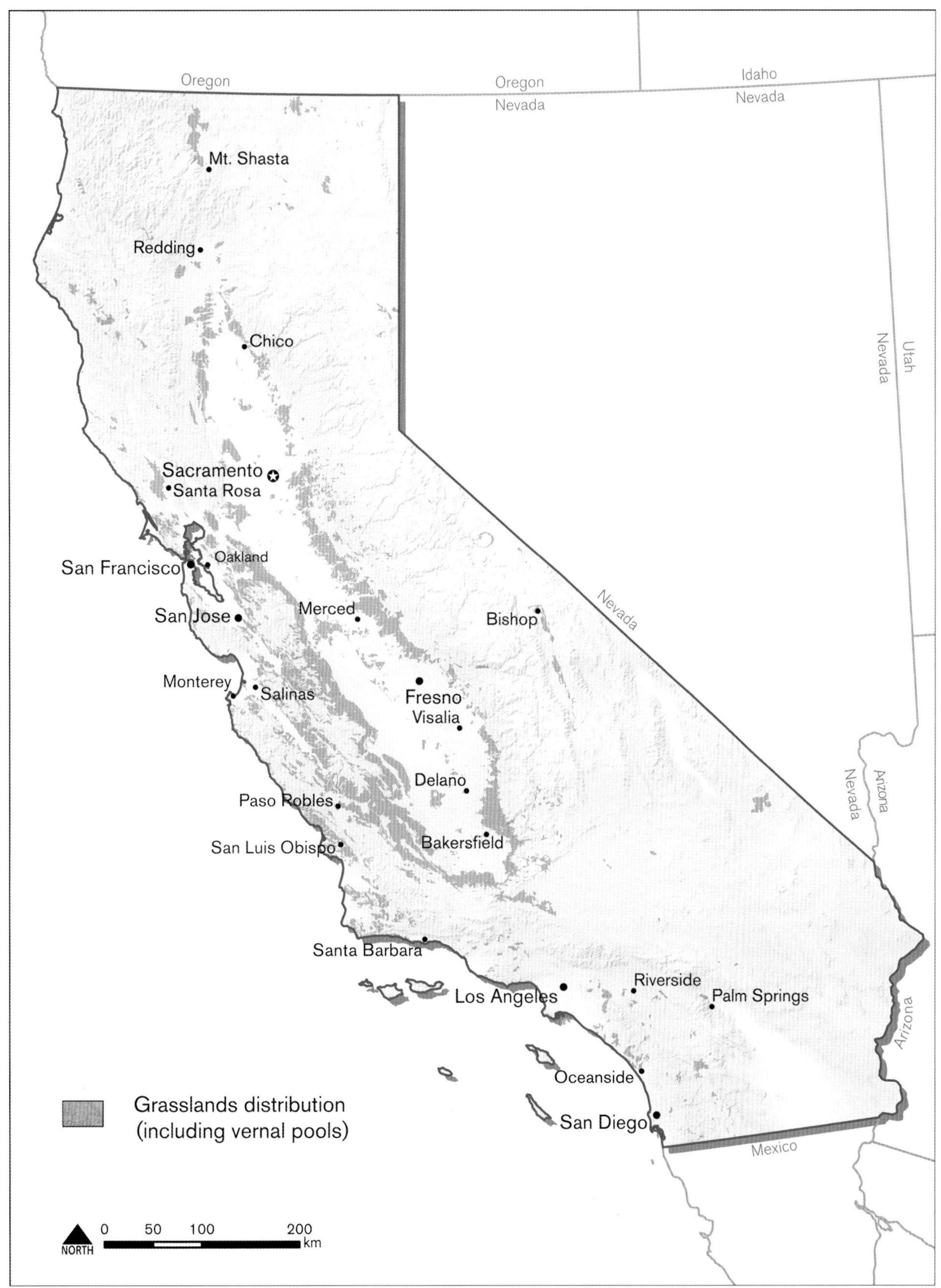

FIGURE 23.1 Distribution of grasslands in California. Additional grassland not shown here occurs in the understory of oak savannas and woodlands in much of the state (see Chapter 25, "Oak Woodlands"). Data from U.S. Geological Survey, Gap Analysis Program (GAP). Map: P. Welch, Center for Integrated Spatial Research (CISR).

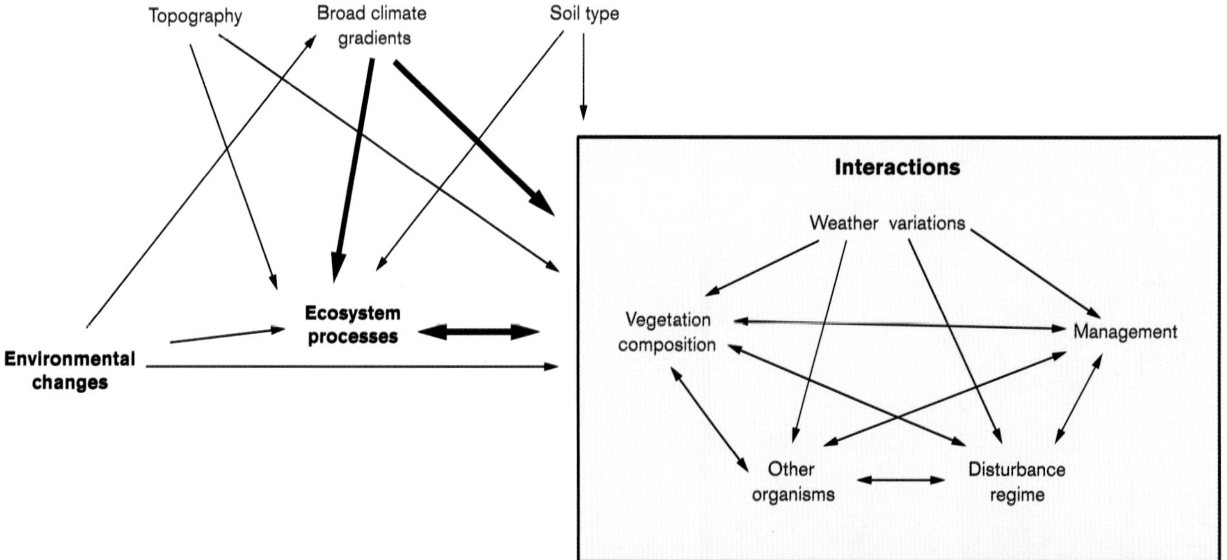

FIGURE 23.2 Controls over the structure and function of California's grasslands. Broad climate gradients are the primary controller of structure and function, while soil type and topography have impacts within the confines of climate conditions. All three of these state factors affect how weather variations influence affect how weather variations influence interactions among vegetation composition, other organisms (e.g., small mammals, large herbivores, microbes, insects), disturbance regimes, and human management. These interactions determine ecosystem processes (C cycling, N cycling, water dynamics), which feed back to affect these interactive factors. Environmental changes (e.g., climate change, nitrogen deposition) can lead to unique interactions that influence grassland structure and function. Illustration by Valerie Eviner.

community composition. Species such as foxtail brome (*Bromus madritensis*) and red-stemmed filaree (*Erodium cicutarium*), both exotic, tend to be common in dry sites (less than 25 centimeter mean annual precipitation), while exotic species such as soft chess (*Bromus hordeaceus*), wild oats (*Avena barbata*), and broad leaf filaree (*Erodium botrys*) tend to be more common on wetter sites (65–100 centimeter mean annual precipitation) (Bartolome et al. 1980).

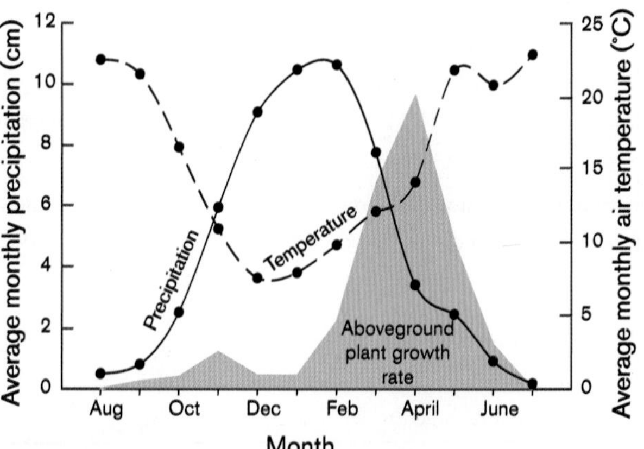

FIGURE 23.3 Seasonal variations in temperature (dashed line) and precipitation (solid line) drive plant growth rate (gray shaded area), with most production occurring when both moisture and ideal growing temperatures are present. Temperature and moisture data are from the California Irrigation Management Information System (CIMIS), averaged across 1985 through 2005 and across grassland sites, including: Sierra Foothills, San Joaquin Valley, Bay Area, Sacramento Valley, North Coast Valley, South Coast Valley, and Central Coast Valley. The left-side y-axis provides the precipitation scale, while the right-side y-axis represents the temperature scale. Aboveground growth rate is not present on either y-axis, but scales from 0 to 200 g/m²/month. Growth rate data is a seasonal average across experimental sites in the Central Valley and North Coast (Eviner, unpublished data). Source: Figure updated from Biswell 1956.

Coastal Grassland

Grasslands (also called prairies) along California's central and north coasts (ranging from San Luis Obispo to southern Oregon) tend to experience longer, wetter growing seasons than inland areas (Ford and Hayes 2007, Keeler-Wolf et al. 2007) (see Figure 23.4b). In addition, fog inputs mitigate summer moisture limitation and can account for 28% to 66% of root water uptake by perennial grasses in summer (Corbin et al. 2005). These wetter conditions (especially when precipitation is greater than 100 centimeters per year) lead to dominance by native and non-native perennial herbaceous and woody species. Common woody invaders include Scotch broom (*Cytisus scopartus*), French broom (*Genista monspessulana*), and gorse (*Ulex europeus*) (Heady et al. 1992, Ford and Hayes 2007). Overall, native cover is higher in coastal than interior grasslands. The annual non-natives that are common in the interior grasslands are often only minor components of the coastal grasslands or restricted to disturbed areas (Corbin et al. 2007a). While some of these coastal grasslands are stable as grasslands, particularly in the drier sites, others are maintained by disturbance regimes such as burning, livestock grazing, and deer browsing that impede the persistence of woody plants (Ford and Hayes 2007).

FIGURE 23.4 Diversity of California grassland types. Photos: Valerie Eviner.

A Annual grassland with a mix of grasses, forbs, and legumes (Interior Coast Range, Mendocino County).

B Native perennial grassland (Coast Range, Marin County).

C More recent invasion of late-season non-native grasses (goatgrass, medusa head) in the foreground (green), invading into naturalized annual non-native grassland (background, senesced) (Interior Coast Range, Mendocino County).

D Alkali grassland (Sacramento Valley floor, Glenn County).

E Vernal pool (Sacramento Valley floor, Solano County).

F Serpentine grassland (Interior Coast Range, Mendocino County).

Subtypes of Grasslands Determined by Unique Soils

Unique soil conditions in both interior and coastal grasslands create relatively small patches of distinctive grassland types, including serpentine, alkali sinks, and vernal pools. Serpentine soils are derived from rock from the earth's mantle. They tend to be nutrient-poor, with low calcium to magnesium ratios, high levels of heavy metals (particularly nickel), and low water availability. These stressful soil conditions lead to a low-productivity system with sparse, short plants and a high degree of endemism (species that are unique to particular locations). Serpentine sites are usually dominated by diverse native forbs, with less than 10% grass cover (see Figure 23.4f). While serpentine grasslands typically have far fewer non-native species than surrounding grasslands on nonserpentine soils, invasion from surrounding grasslands does occur, particularly in areas receiving high amounts of nitrogen deposition (Harrison and Viers 2007).

Vernal pools are shallow, seasonal wetlands within a grassland matrix, usually found in shallow depressions with an impermeable soil layer (see Figure 23.4e). While the edges of vernal pools may be dominated by upland grassland species, the pools themselves contain a rich diversity of native and introduced grasses and forbs with composition strongly influenced by depth and duration of flooding (Solomeshch et al. 2007). Alkali sinks (see Figure 23.4d) are also seasonal wetlands but with a high pH and high salinity. These foster a rich community of native and introduced grasses and forbs including a number of endemic, threatened, and endangered plants (Heady 1977, Dawson et al. 2007).

Variations within Grassland Types: Local Controls over Structure and Function

While broad precipitation gradients and soil types can determine the distribution of distinct grassland types, each grassland type also contains considerable spatial and temporal variation within it. Interactions of multiple biotic and abiotic controllers mediate heterogeneity in community and ecosystem dynamics (Huenneke and Mooney 1989) (see Figure 23.1), as described in the following sections.

TOPOGRAPHY AND SOILS

California's grasslands occur on diverse soil types, including five of the twelve SOIL ORDERS. Even at a local scale, soil can be highly heterogeneous, affecting vegetation composition and growth through differences in soil fertility and water infiltration and storage (Jackson et al. 2007). Species such as soft chess are common on many soil types, but soil type limits the distribution of many other species, including wild oats, medusa head (*Taeniatherum caput-medusae*), and filaree (Evans and Young 1989). Clay soils have higher water-holding capacity and thus tend to increase plant production. Similarly, deep soils increase plant production by providing water to deep-rooted plants (Reever Morghan et al. 2007). Other soil characteristics, such as pH, nutrient content, soil organic matter and texture, can also influence community composition (Hoopes and Hall 2002).

Topography also has strong impacts on local heterogeneity in vegetation composition and production, largely through its impacts on microenvironment (McNaughton 1968, Evans and Young 1989, Heady et al. 1992). For example, south-facing slopes are so much drier and hotter than north-facing slopes that the growing season can be one month shorter on south-facing slopes (Hufstader 1978). North-facing slopes tend to favor species with deeper roots, greater water use and later phenology (Ng and Miller 1980). Thus native perennials and late-season invaders such as goatgrass (*Aegilops triuncialis*) are more common on north-facing than south-facing slopes (personal observation). Germination rates tend to be higher on north-facing slopes (Evans et al. 1975), but it is not clear whether this is due to environmental conditions at germination or variation in seed characteristics determined by environmental conditions during seed production the previous spring. Topography can also alter the impacts of grazing (Huntsinger et al. 2007) and elevation (Bartolome et al. 2007) on community and ecosystem dynamics.

VARIATIONS IN WEATHER

As discussed previously, the amount and seasonality of moisture and temperature determine the presence of grasslands, while precipitation gradients structure the distribution of grassland types. Variations in grassland structure and function within a given site are strongly driven by fluctuations in weather patterns within a growing season and across years (Heady et al. 1992, Bartolome et al. 2007, Keeler-Wolf et al. 2007). At a given site, annual precipitation can vary as much as 50 centimeters to 100 centimeters from its long-term mean (Pitt and Heady 1978, Reever Morghan et al. 2007), with high variation particularly associated with El Niño–Southern Oscillation events (Reever Morghan et al. 2007). Lower rainfall years tend to produce lower plant diversity (Bartolome et al. 1980), but total rainfall does not reliably predict plant production and community composition—the timing of rainfall is far more important than the annual total (Figure 23.5) (Pitt and Heady 1978, George et al. 2001, Reever Morghan et al. 2007, Suttle et al. 2007).

Early fall weather conditions can have large impacts on vegetation composition, mediated through plant germination characteristics. The timing and temperature of initial fall rains can influence the germination of rare plants (Levine et al. 2011) as well as the identity of dominant plants (Pitt and Heady 1979). Alternating dominance among grasses, forbs, and legumes has been frequently observed across years in California's grasslands (Pitt and Heady 1979, Keeler-Wolf et al. 2007) and has been attributed to variations in weather conditions. An initial flush of germinating rains (at least 1.5 centimeters with a week) stimulates rapid germination of the annual grasses, depleting most of their seedbank (Young and Evans 1989, Chiariello et al. 1989, Bartolome et al. 2007). If precipitation continues throughout the fall, grasses dominate the vegetation throughout the growing season. However, when a germinating rain is followed by a dry fall, the germinated grasses are likely to die. In these years grasslands are dominated by forbs (e.g., filaree) that can survive the fall drought or forbs and legumes that germinate with later rains (Young and Evans 1989, Bartolome et al. 2007, Keeler-Wolf et al. 2007). The response of vegetation composition to rainfall patterns can vary greatly across sites, so that the conditions for a "forb year" are likely to result in more frequent patches of forbs across the landscape, among diverse vegetation patches (Jackson and Bartolome 2002).

Precipitation patterns in the winter and spring also affect community dynamics. Extended winter or spring drought enhances clovers (*Castilleja, Medicago, Melilotus, Orthocarpus, Trifolium*) (Corbin et al. 2007a) and alters seed production (Ewing and Menke 1983). Midwinter droughts are common in California's grasslands, averaging nineteen days without rain in December through January (Reever Morghan et al. 2007). These midwinter droughts favor perennials over annuals, which are less tolerant of dry conditions during the growing season (Corbin et al. 2007a). Spring precipitation strongly impacts the amount and timing of seed production, but the effects vary by species and ecotype. For example, during dry springs some species flower earlier while others have a later but shorter flowering period (Chiariello 1989). Late-spring and early summer rains can enhance the growth and FECUNDITY of late-season species, such as the non-native yellow starthistle (*Centaurea solstitialis*) and native tarweeds. These late-spring rains are unlikely to affect most annual grasses (Pitt and Heady 1978), which are hard-wired to senesce by early summer even in the presence of ample moisture (Jackson and Roy 1986, Chiariello 1989). However, later-season noxious annual grasses, such as medusa head and goatgrass, do benefit from late-season rains (Eviner, Rice and Malmstrom in prep.). In addition to shaping community composition, this temperature and moisture variability strongly regulates the amount and timing of net primary production (discussed later in the chapter, under "Ecosystem Functioning").

FIRE

Fire can have strong impacts on grassland structure and function, with effects depending on the timing, intensity, and frequency of burning (D'Antonio et al. 2006). The effects of any individual fire are generally limited to less than three years (Bartolome et al. 2007) and include decreased soil moisture (Henry et al. 2006), increased soil available nitrogen and phosphorus, and increased rates of nitrogen mineralization and nitrogen fixation (D'Antonio et al. 2006, Reiner 2007). Fire also has short-term effects on soil microbial community composition, with decreased gram negative and positive bacteria (Docherty et al. 2012) and a slight decrease in extracellular enzyme activity (Gutknecht et al. 2010). Over the long term, frequent fires can decrease soil nitrogen and sulfur due to repeated volatilization losses (D'Antonio et al. 2006).

Impacts of fire on plant communities are varied (D'Antonio et al. 2006) and depend on the dominant vegetation prior to burns. Fires increase species richness of non-natives in areas dominated by non-natives before the burns and increase natives in native-dominated areas (Harrison et al. 2003). In general, fires increase the prevalence of forbs and legumes by removing thatch, thus increasing light and soil temperature. Sustained increases in forbs require annual burns, but particularly for native forbs, this is only true in ungrazed areas (D'Antonio et al. 2006). This is likely because grazing, like burning, removes thatch, thus increasing legumes and forbs. Spring burns favor native over non-native forbs, although the effects are weak and depend on burn frequency and grazing regimes (D'Antonio et al. 2006). Fires are often timed to control non-native species. For example, to control late-season noxious weeds such as medusa head and goatgrass, prescribed burns are targeted in the late spring, after most other annuals have senesced but before weed seeds have matured and dropped. The senesced annuals are dry enough to support a moderately intense fire, which can kill the seeds of late-season weeds. This can decrease weeds over the short-term but must be repeated to maintain weed control (Reiner 2007).

Fire regimes have been greatly altered by human activity. Native Americans frequently burned to enhance grassland production, alter grassland communities, and convert shrublands to grasslands (Bartolome et al. 2007). In the nineteenth century, fire frequency in the Central Coast was one to five years, but it now has decreased to twenty to thirty years (Greenlee and Langenheim 1980). Near urban areas, however, fire frequency has increased (Bartolome et al. 2007). These changes in fire regime have strong potential effects on ecosystem and community dynamics (D'Antonio et al. 2006, Bartolome et al. 2007).

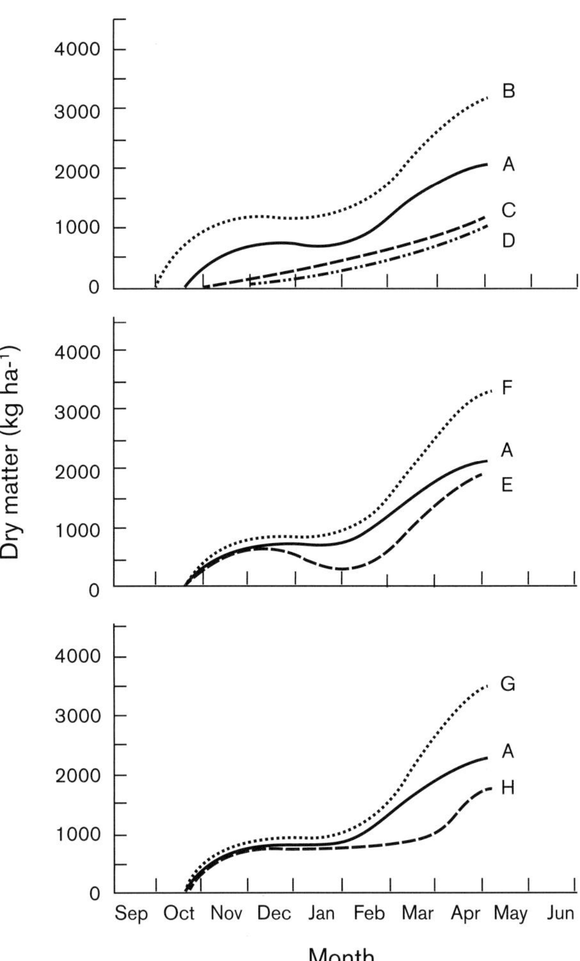

FIGURE 23.5 Seasonal forage production, as affected by seasonal weather patterns, at the San Joaquin Experimental Station (data from 1935 through 1984). Curves are associated with the following weather conditions: (A) average fall, winter and spring; (B) warm, wet fall, average winter and spring; (C) cold, wet fall, average winter and spring; (D) dry fall, average winter and spring; (E) average fall, cold winter, average spring; (F) average fall, mild winter, average spring; (G) average fall, short winter, early onset of warm spring temperatures; (H) average fall, long winter, late onset of warm spring temperatures. Source: George et al. 2001.

Biota

Diverse biota rely on California's grasslands for habitat and actively shape grassland structure and function through their interactions (see Figure 23.1).

LARGE HERBIVORES

Herbivory is a critical controller of most of the world's grassland ecosystems, many of which have evolved under grazing pressure. The extent of adaptation to grazing in California's native flora is unclear. California's native grassland flora was exposed to grazing and browsing by the rich megafauna present during the Rancholabrean (150,000 years before present [YBP] to 11,700 YBP), including bison, elk, deer, mammoth, pronghorns, horses, and camels. (Edwards 2007). These megafauna were largely absent during the Holocene (11,700 YBP to the present), leaving a significant time period when plants could have adapted to the absence of megafauna. Even in the absence of megafauna, California grasslands continued to experience high rates of herbivory by rodents, rabbits, hares, birds, and elk (Edwards 2007). While deer and pronghorn have been prevalent for part of the Holocene, they are mostly browsers, so their main effect is likely exclusion of woody species with more modest impacts on herbaceous community composition (Edwards 2007). Herbivore identity has large impacts on vegetation composition. Cows and horses preferentially consume grass, while sheep and deer preferentially consume forbs. Antelopes consume grasses, forbs, and shrubs, changing preference with season (Edwards 2007). Similarly, tule elk consume forbs in the spring and summer and consume grasses in the fall and winter (Johnson and Cushman 2007). Removing elk from coastal grasslands decreased annual plant cover and increased some non-native perennial grasses but did not affect other perennials (Johnson and Cushman 2007).

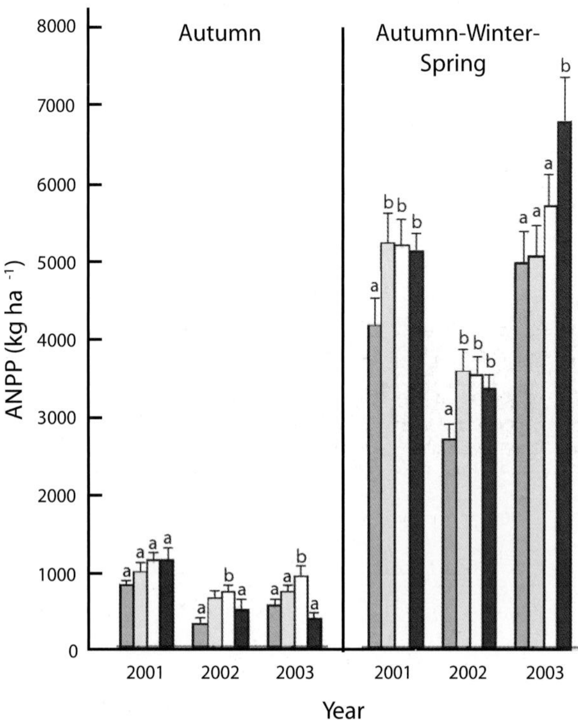

FIGURE 23.6 Effects of residual dry matter (RDM) on aboveground net primary production (ANPP) at Sierra Foothills Research and Extension Center from 2001 through 2003. From left to right within each year, gray bars are 225 kg/ha RDM, dotted bars are 560 kg/ha RDM, white bars are 900 kg/ha RDM, and black bars are 5,000 kg/ha RDM. Within each year, bars labeled with different lowercase letters differ significantly from each other. Source: Bartolome et al. 2007.

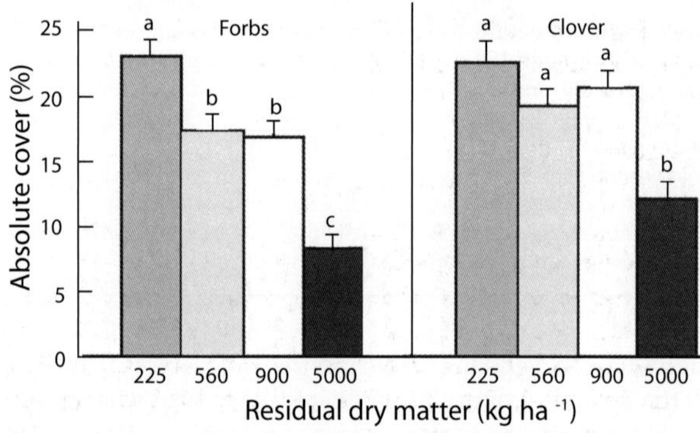

FIGURE 23.7 Impacts of residual dry matter (RDM) treatments on cover of forbs (left) and clovers (right) across five years at Sierra Foothills Research and Extension Center. Source: Bartolome et al. 2007.

Domesticated livestock have been significant controllers of California's grassland dynamics and economics since the 1770s on the coast and the 1820s inland (Jackson and Bartolome 2007; see Chapter 37, "Range Ecosystems"). While most livestock in California are cattle (approximately 5 million), they also include sheep (0.5 million), goats, pigs, and horses (Jackson and Bartolome 2007). Livestock impact grasslands in a number of ways. The first is consumption of live plant material. Precise timing of grazing has been used to control weeds, with livestock consuming the weedy species before it is able to produce viable seeds (Huntsinger et al. 2007). A second mechanism driving grazing impacts is the accumulation of thatch or residual dry matter (RDM), the amount of senesced material remaining before the start of a new growing season (Bartolome et al. 2007). High RDM causes shading and lower temperatures, which can suppress new plants by decreasing seed germination and seedling growth (Figure 23.6, Autumn). Increasing RDM can decrease species richness, forbs, and legumes (Figure 23.7); and increase tall grasses such as wild oats and ripgut brome (*Bromus diandrus*) and other large-seeded species (Bartolome et al. 2007, Corbin et al. 2007a, Amatangelo et al. 2008). High RDM also decreases root to shoot allocation (Betts 2003), potentially affecting ecosystem processes such as erosion control, water dynamics, and carbon and nitrogen cycling. However, some amount of RDM benefits grasslands by increasing germination and production (see Figure 23.6) and controlling erosion (Bartolome et al. 2002, Corbin et al. 2007a). In sites with more than 38 centimeters of rainfall per year, RDM affects biomass production (Bartolome et al. 2002), with aboveground production generally highest at intermediate amounts of RDM (Amatangelo et al. 2008). The ideal amount of RDM varies by climate and topography, with higher RDM levels recommended at wetter sites and on steeper slopes (Bartolome et al. 2002). RDM levels are achieved through consumption of live plant tissue but also through consumption and trampling of senesced tissues, so early fall grazing can mitigate initially high RDM.

Grazing effects depend on livestock species as well as grazing timing, intensity, duration, and frequency (see Figure 23.1) (see Chapter 37, "Range Ecosystems"). Grazer impacts also vary through interactions with environmental conditions (climate, soil, elevation, slope/aspect, land use history) and initial plant community composition (Huntsinger et al. 2007). A meta-analysis of grazing impacts across diverse soils and precipitation conditions in California emphasized the context-dependent effects of grazing on plant communities (Stahlheber and D'Antonio 2013). For example, grazing effects on non-native forbs vary across a precipitation gradient (but could not be separated by interior versus coastal grasslands), strongly increasing non-native forb cover in dry sites and decreasing it at wetter sites. Grazing increased native forb cover in interior grasslands but reduced it in coastal grasslands (Stahlheber and D'Antonio 2013). Relative cover of non-native and native grasses more strongly reflects season of grazing and more weakly responds to site conditions. Wet-season grazing enhances native grasses (particularly at dry sites) while decreasing non-native grasses.

On average, grazing in California's grasslands increases non-native forb cover (but not richness), increases native forb richness (with little change in cover), increases non-native grass richness (with little change in cover), and increases native grass cover (Figure 23.8) (Stahlheber and D'Antonio 2013). The prevalence of case studies that contradict these trends, however, highlights the need for site-specific management guidance (see Chapter 37, "Range Ecosystems"). For example, in one coastal grassland, grazing increased native forb prevalence (Hayes and Holl 2003). In another case study, grazing decreased grass cover, increased forb cover, and had no effect on species richness and little effect on natives (Skaer et al. 2013). While grazing exclosures have been suggested as a tool to increase native vegetation, decades of livestock exclosure have inconsistent effects across sites (D'Antonio et al. 2006).

Grazing also alters soil properties. Moderate to high grazing (especially in the wet season) can increase soil BULK

DENSITY, which can in turn reduce water infiltration (Jackson and Bartolome 2007). Consumption of plant material can short-circuit the decomposition cycle, increasing the speed of nutrient release from plants and often concentrating nutrients in areas where animals congregate (e.g., under shade trees) (Jackson and Bartolome 2007). While the grazing effects on soil nutrients vary, grazing in California's grasslands generally increases soil nitrogen availability but decreases phosphorus and sulfur (Vaughn et al. 1986, Stromberg and Griffin 1996). Feral pigs, formerly domesticated livestock, can strongly influence grassland dynamics, especially as their populations increase rapidly. They disturb large soil areas at 5 to 15 centimeter depths in search of bulbs, roots, fungi, and invertebrates. This disturbance leads to short-term decreases in plant diversity and long-term increases in non-native plants and decreases in oak seedlings (Cushman 2007). Coastal studies have shown that native perennials can reestablish in pig exclosures, but also that pigs tend to avoid disturbing established native bunchgrasses (Cushman 2007). While feral pig disturbance can alter soil processes in other systems, effects on soil nutrient availability and cycling rates have not been shown in California's coastal grasslands (Cushman 2007).

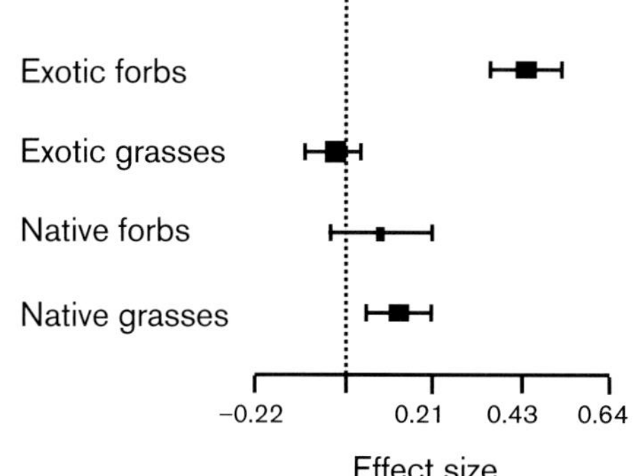

FIGURE 23.8 Effects of grazing on percentage of cover of exotic forbs, exotic grasses, native forbs, and native grasses, as determined by meta-analysis. Positive effect sizes indicate positive effects of grazing, and negative effect sizes indicate negative effects of grazing. Error bars indicate 95% confidence intervals. Source: Stahlheber and D'Antonio 2013.

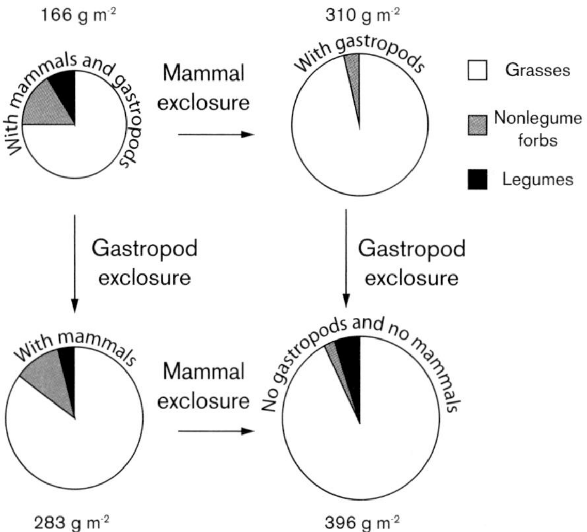

FIGURE 23.9 Effects of mammals and gastropods on aboveground biomass and composition during the 2001–2 growing season. Source: Peters 2007.

SMALL MAMMALS

Small mammals are generally abundant in California's grasslands (Lidicker 1989), with varying population numbers and community dominance across sites and years (Pearson 1963, Lidicker 1989, Hobbs and Mooney 1985). Key small mammals include pocket gophers (*Thomomys bottae*), ground squirrels (*Spermophilus beecheyi*), mice (*Reithrodontomys megalotis, Peromyscus maniculatus, Mus musculus*), voles (*Microtus californicus*), moles (*Scapanus* spp.), rabbits (*Sylvilagus* spp., *Lepus californicus*), and in some regions kangaroo rats (*Dipodomys heermannii*) (Lidicker 1989, Schiffman 2007). Small mammals act as herbivores, granivores, and seed dispersers. Some species also cause significant soil disturbance (Schiffman 2007). Small mammals can reduce plant biomass through substantial herbivory and granivory (Bartolome et al. 2007). For example, in the San Joaquin Experimental Range, gophers, squirrels, and kangaroo rats consumed at least 33% of annual aboveground production (Fitch and Bentley 1949). In a grassland in the coastal hills, removal of small mammals increased aboveground biomass by 40% to 87%, partly by increasing grass abundance (Figure 23.9) (Peters 2007). During population peaks small mammals can consume up to 93% of the annual seed crop (Pearson 1964), and herbivory of live plants can decrease seed production by up to 70% (Batzli and Pitelka 1970).

Small mammals can strongly alter plant community composition (Hobbs and Mooney 1991, Bartolome et al. 2007, Cushman 2007, Keeler-Wolf 2007). Seed predation can range from 0% to 75% of seed production of preferred species (e.g., wild oats) (Marshall and Jain 1970, Borchert and Jain 1978), substantially shifting plant dominance. Density of preferred seed species can decline by 30% to 62%; the resulting competitive release can increase growth and fecundity of non-preferred plant species (Borchert and Jain 1978). Voles and mice decrease purple needle grass density, likely through granivory (Orrock et al. 2008). Similarly, squirrels and rabbits decrease purple needle grass establishment by 52%, recruitment by 30%, and reproduction by 43%. These effects are greatest when purple needle grass is located near patches of black mustard (*Brassica nigra*) (Orrock et al. 2008, Orrock and Witter 2010).

Pocket gopher populations can range from 26.6 to 100.8 ha^{-1} (Lidicker 1989), with larger populations in ungrazed than grazed sites (Stromberg and Griffin 1996). Gophers consume approximately 8% of aboveground biomass (Lidicker 1989) and likely more belowground, since they specialize on roots and bulbs (Lidicker 1989). They preferentially feed on patches of legumes, forbs (Hunt 1992, Eviner and Chapin 2005), and geophytes (plants with storage organs that are underground) (Seabloom and Richards 2003, Schiffman 2007) when these are available. Despite these preferences, their diets often mirror dominant plant species composition such as annual non-native grasses and forbs (Hobbs and Mooney 1985, Schiffman 2007). Gophers disturb 1% to 30% of the soil surface each year, and on average any given soil surface turns over every three to fifteen years (Hobbs and Mooney 1985, Bartolome et al. 2007). Mounds are preferentially built in patches with high SOIL SHEAR STRENGTH, usually in grass patches with high root surface area (Eviner and Chapin 2005). This soil disturbance can strongly alter the plant community, but which plant species colonize mounds can vary year to year (Hobbs and Mooney 1985). In general, gophers increase the prevalence of forbs (Tyler et al. 2007) and annual grasses while reducing perennial grasses (Bartolome et al. 2007).

Burrowing is also a significant activity of ground squirrels, kangaroo rats, mice, voles, and moles. This burrowing can increase plant diversity, especially of native forbs, and can increase prevalence of non-native species adapted to disturbance. Native perennial grasses often decrease (Schiffman 2007). Burrowing can reduce soil bulk density and increase soil temperatures and short-term pools of soil nitrogen (Eviner and Chapin 2005, Canals et al. 2003, Bartolome et al. 2007). Ground squirrel densities can range from 4.2 to 45.2 ha^{-1} (Lidicker 1989) and tend to increase with livestock grazing (see Chapter 37, "Range Ecosystems"). Ground squirrels form extensive burrows (Bartolome et al. 2007). They directly consume 3–7% of net primary production and harvest (but do not consume) up to an additional 16.8% of standing biomass (Lidicker 1989). Their most important food items include several forbs (filaree, tarweed, buckwheat (*Eriogonum* spp.), popcorn flower (*Plagiobothrys* spp.), ripgut brome seeds, and acorns (Fitch 1948). Their extensive burrows provide habitat for burrowing owls and many other animals (Lidicker 1989).

Like ground squirrels, kangaroo rats also tend to increase in population size under grazed conditions (see Chapter 37, "Range Ecosystems"). Their burrows increase non-native annuals and decrease natives (Schiffman 1994), and they can cache high quantities of seeds (Lidicker 1989). Kangaroo rats remove up to 16% of standing biomass (Fitch and Bentley 1949), although much of this plant harvest is associated with building runways and nests and not direct consumption. They are primarily granivores (Schiffman 2007) and can consume up to 95% of their preferred seed species, red stemmed filaree (Soholt 1973).

Voles have dramatic population variation, with densities ranging from 0.25 to 1,110 ha^{-1} (Lidicker 1989). Their densities tend to decline with increased grazing (Bartolome et al. 2007), and they can be absent from heavily grazed sites (Lidicker 1989). At high densities they can harvest 61.4% of grassland productivity (Lidicker 1989), resulting in 50% to 85% decreased cover of their preferred food species (wild oats, ripgut brome, Italian ryegrass [*Festuca perennis*]) and 70% decreased seed fall (Batzli and Pitelka 1970, Batzli and Pitelka 1971). Their activity can both increase (Fehmi and Bartolome 2002, Bartolome et al. 2007) and decrease (Lidicker 1989) plant species richness. Voles selectively feed on legumes, some grasses, and some forbs (e.g., filaree [Rice 1987], yarrow [*Achillea*], figwort [*Scrophularia*], wild lettuce, clover [*Medicago*], dock [*Rumex*]), and some of these species are absent from areas with vole activity (Lidicker 1989). Their selective granivory can alter plant community composition (Cockburn and Lidicker 1983), decreasing wild oats while increasing other annuals such as ripgut brome, Italian ryegrass, and foxtail barley (*Hordeum murinum*) (Borchert and Jain 1978).

Rabbits are abundant in California's grasslands and intensively use this system (Zedler and Black 1992). Like other small mammals, during population outbreaks they can consume great quantities of biomass and alter community composition (Vivrette and Muller 1977).

INSECTS, ANNELIDS, AND GASTROPODS

California's grasslands host a diverse and abundant insect fauna. Arthropod biomass has been measured at 126 g m^{-2} belowground and 1.2g/m^{-2} aboveground (Burdic et al. 1979, Heady et al. 1992). The roles of many insects have not been studied in this system, but some are known to impact structure and function. Ants are seed consumers and dispersers. Most studies on their effects have taken place in serpentine grasslands, where they have a density of one ant mound per 100 m^2 with feeding paths 10–12 meters long (Hobbs and Mooney 1985). Some studies have shown that ant foraging alters the spatial distribution (Peters et al. 2005) and composition (Hobbs 1985) of plants (Hobbs 1985), but others studies have seen no impact of ant seed dispersal on plant communities (Brown and Human 1997). The selectivity of ants likely varies by year, with low selectivity in dry years with low food availability (Peters et al. 2005). Ant preference for certain plants also changes throughout the season as initially preferred plant seeds are consumed (Hobbs 1985). Ant mounds, though they make up a small area of grassland (approximately 0.6% [Hobbs 1985]), consistently have been found to increase legumes and non-native annual grasses (Peters et al. 2005), while decreasing forbs and enhancing seed production of other species (e.g., peppergrass [*Lepidium nitidum*]) (Brown and Human 1997). Ant mounds also increase soil bacteria, fungi, microarthropods, and nematodes (Boulton et al. 2003) as well as soil organic matter and nutrients such as phosphorus, potassium, and nitrogen (Beattie 1989, Boulton et al. 2003).

Grasshoppers in California's grasslands, though little studied, strongly affect vegetation composition and standing biomass in other grasslands, consuming as much as 25–92% of standing vegetation (Joern 1989). California hosts almost two hundred species of grasshoppers that feed on grasses and forbs, making it highly likely that they are key players in this system. In a native California perennial bunchgrass stand, grasshopper density averaged 2.3 m^{-2} (June through August) with an annual consumption rate of 140 kg ha^{-1}, large enough to cause economic forage losses (Porter et al. 1996). Most grasshoppers in California reach maturity in late spring and summer, so they have little effect on annual grasses, which have largely senesced by this time (Porter et al. 1996, Joern 1989). Thus grasshoppers in California consume more native than non-native grasses, although their most abundant food item is forbs (Porter and Redak 1997). Care must be taken in generalizing the impacts of these few studies, since they focus on one grasshopper species, and different grasshopper species are frequently associated with different plant species (Stroehecker et al. 1968).

Gastropods (e.g., slugs, snails) can consume high amounts of aboveground biomass, and their exclusion can increase aboveground biomass 28–71% (see Figure 23.9) (Peters 2007). They strongly prefer certain plant species and can affect seedling survival (Peters et al. 2006, Strauss et al. 2009, Motheral and Orrock 2010). Their selectivity varies by season, with higher consumption of grasses in fall (leading to higher legume and forb cover) but higher forb consumption in winter (leading to higher grass cover). By spring, gastropod presence increases grass cover at the expense of forbs (Peters 2007). The impacts of gastropods on the plant community can be so great that their feeding behavior mediates about half of the changes in plant community composition seen in response to experimental global changes (Peters et al. 2006).

Earthworms are also important players in California's grasslands. Earthworms stimulate litter mass loss rates by breaking up litter and incorporating it into the soil. Earthworm burrowing and casting also increase water infiltration and aeration by increasing macropores (Standiford et al. 2013). Both native and non-native earthworms occur in California grasslands, with non-native earthworms dominating disturbed and fertile environments and natives dominating relatively undisturbed grasslands (Winsome et al. 2006). The non-native earthworms are more active than natives, leading to greater physical disturbance of the soil. Through this increased activity, non-native earthworms increase plant growth and uptake, enhance N turnover through litter decomposition, and decrease microbial biomass (Winsome 2003).

BIRDS

California's grasslands are primary habitat for some bird species and provide feeding and/or nesting grounds for other species. Their use can be seasonal or year-long (reviewed in Lidicker 1989, CPIF 2000, Shuford and Gardali 2008). While few studies document the ecological impacts of these birds on California's grasslands, there are some critical roles played by grassland birds in general. Birds can have substantial impacts on plant populations and species composition through seed dispersal and granivory, with effects that are distinct from those of granivorous small mammals (reviewed in Espeland et al. 2005). Many of the same bird species are also important insectivores, controlling populations of grasshoppers and other potential pest insects, and sometimes also disturbing soil to feed on insects, grubs, and worms (Fix and Bezener 2000, Sekercioglu 2006). Examples of birds in California's grasslands that are both granivores and insectivores include savannah sparrow (*Passerculus sandwhichensis*), grasshopper sparrow (*Ammondramus savannarum*), horned lark (*Eremophila alpestris*), western meadowlark (*Sturnella neglecta*), vesper sparrow (*Pooecetes gramineus*), and lark sparrow (*Chondestes grammacus*) (Lidicker 1989, Fix and Bezener 2000, see both references for a more extensive list). The relative importance of seeds versus insects in bird diets often vary by season and by species (Shuford and Gardali 2008). Many of these birds nest on the ground from early spring through July, so their breeding can be disrupted by mowing, grazing, disking, or burning during the spring (CPIF 2000). Their populations have been steadily declining, at least partly due to loss of continuous grassland habitat (CPIF 2000, Rao et al. 2008).

Predaceous birds can have significant effects on grassland structure and function through their controls over the populations of small mammals. In order to avoid predation, in the presence of birds, small mammals alter their behavior and habitat use, leading to less use of areas with short or sparse vegetation (Sekercioglu 2006). Most predatory birds also feed on smaller birds, amphibians, reptiles, large insects, and sometimes carrion (Fix and Bezener 2000). Key avian predators in California's grassland include hawks (red-tailed [*Buteo jamaicensis*], ferrunginous [*Buteo regalis*], Swainson's [*Buteo swainsoni*], northern harrier [*Circus cyaneus*]), owls (burrowing [*Athene* cunicularia], short-eared [*Asio flammeus*]), and the white-tailed kite (*Elanus leucurus*) (Lidicker 1989, CPIF 2000, Shuford and Gardali 2008).

NONAVIAN PREDATORS

Since small mammals and insects can have such large effects on California grassland structure and function, regulation of these groups by predation has significant impacts on these grasslands (Schiffman 2007). Predatory animals are diverse, including birds, snakes, coyote (*Canis latrans*), fox (*Vulpes fulva, Urocyon cinereoargenteus*), badger (*Taxidea taxus*), alligator lizards (*Elgaria* spp.), and the domesticated/feral cats (*Felis domesticus*) (Lidicker 1989). These species can have diverse diets, including insects, birds, bird eggs, small mammals, and in some cases, one another (Fix and Bezener 2000, Jameson and Peeters 2004, Stebbins and McGinnis 2012). Important insectivores include the Pacific tree frog (*Pseudacris regilla*), tiger salamander (*Ambystoma* spp.), skinks (*Eumeces* spp.), and a variety of lizards (western fence lizard [*Sceloporus occidentalis*], coast horned lizard [*Phrynosoma blainvillii*]) (Stebbins and McGinnis 2012). Omnivores are also common, eating a wide variety of plant species and tissues, as well as insects, earthworms, amphibians, reptiles, and small mammals (e.g., skunk [*Mephitis mephitis*], raccoon [*Procyon lotor*]) (Lidicker 1989, Jameson and Peeters 2004).

As described earlier, the small mammals with the largest impacts on grasslands include ground squirrels, gophers, and voles. The primary predators of ground squirrels include raptors (e.g., red-tailed hawk) and the western rattlesnake (*Crotalus viridis*). White-tailed kites, gopher snakes (*Pituophis melanoleucus*), and garter snakes (*Thamnophis sp.*) are considered the most important predators of voles. Key predators of gophers include gopher snakes, western rattlesnake, red-tailed hawk, barn owl (*Tyto alba*), great-horned owl (*Bubo virginianus*), and coyote (Lidicker 1989).

MICROBES

California's grasslands have high soil microbial biomass and richness (Sanchez-Moreno et al. 2011), with a dynamic microbial community that changes in response to plant communities (Hawkes et al. 2005, Batten et al. 2006), temperature, and moisture (Waldrop and Firestone 2006). Microbial community shifts can have important effects on plant communities and ecosystem processes. Seasonal shifts in microbial communities due to temperature and moisture lead to shifts in the soil enzymes that mediate decomposition and nutrient cycling, with many enzymes peaking in the early spring and/or winter and least active in the summer (Waldrop and Firestone 2006). Dry conditions can decrease bacterial biomass and can decrease (Alster et al. 2013) or increase enzyme activity (Henry et al. 2005). Higher spring precipitation reduces the abundance and diversity of fungi and increases decomposition rates (Hawkes et al. 2011). Microbial communities can directly affect plant performance, altering plant growth rate and root-to-shoot allocation, with effects varying by plant species (Brandt et al. 2009). Plant communities also can shape microbial communities. For example, non-native grasses have increased the population size and altered the composition of the ammonium oxidizer community, leading to more than doubled rates of nitrification over native grass soils (Hawkes et al. 2005). Increased nitrification can have strong effects on plant nitrogen availability, nitrogen retention, and water quality.

Arbuscular mycorrhizae (AM) are fungal symbionts with plants, exchanging plant carbon for various resources including nitrogen, phosphorus, and/or water. Most grassland plants are mutualistic with these fungi (Hopkins 1987, Harrison and Viers 2007), and the composition of the AM community can alter plant growth and seed production, nutrient uptake, root-to-shoot allocation, and drought stress tolerance (Allen and Allen 1990, Nelson and Allen 1993, Harrison and Viers 2007). AM also strongly enhance soil aggregate formation, which can affect carbon and nutrient dynamics, soil water infiltration and storage, and erosion control (Rillig et al. 2002). AM in California's grasslands play a particularly important role in plant phosphorus uptake. In the presence of AM, plant production is nitrogen-limited, but without the AM symbiosis, plants are limited by phosphorus (Grogan and Chapin 2000). AM hyphal networks can associate with many individual plants simultaneously, leading to transfers of phosphorus (and possibly other resources) among diverse plant species. For example, when radioactive phosphorus was added to a given plant, that phosphorus was transferred to 20% of the plant's close neighbors through the AM network (Chiariello et al. 1982). This AM network among plant species can influence dynamics between native and non-native plants. For example, in the presence of the AM community the non-native Napa star thistle (*Centaurea melitensis*) dominated over native purple needle grass. However, when AM biomass was reduced, the non-native plant was much less competitive (Callaway et al. 2003), suggesting that the AM network provided the non-native plant with resources from the native plants.

AM communities change in response to environmental conditions, with much change not in direct response to environmental changes but mediated through vegetation changes (Rillig et al. 1998). Because AM species have plant species-specific effects, vegetation-induced changes in AM community composition can alter plant competitive outcomes (Allen and Allen 1990). A number of studies have shown that the AM community differs under native and non-native plants (Hawkes et al. 2006, Nelson and Allen 1993, Vogelsang and Bever 2009), with non-native plants exerting stronger effects on AM than native plants do (Vogelsang and Bever 2009). Non-native plants alter not only the soil AM community but also that associated with native plants. For example, when wild oats and purple needle grass grow as neighbors, the AM associated with wild oats dominated purple needle grass roots but purple needle grass did not affect the AM on wild oat roots (Hausmann and Hawkes 2009). This effect was particularly strong when wild oats established before purple needle grass (Hausmann and Hawkes 2010). In another study non-natives and natives both grew best associated with their own AM communities (Vogelsang and Bever 2009). Finally, non-native plant effects on the AM community increased the seed production of non-native plants but not native plants (Nelson and Allen 1993).

Dynamics between non-native and native plant species can also be mediated by microbial and viral pathogens. Crown rust can decrease wild oats while increasing purple needle grass (Carsten et al. 2001). In contrast, barley yellow dwarf virus and cereal dwarf virus can negatively affect both native and non-native grasses, but they have a stronger negative effect on natives, particularly because the non-native annual grasses enhance transmission of the viruses to natives (Malmstrom 1998). When exposed to these viruses and to competition with non-native annuals, first-year survivorship of natives can be halved (Malmstrom et al. 2006), with other studies showing the viruses can decrease native survival 0–80% and fecundity 30–70% (Borer et al. 2007). Grazing can interact with these viruses, but overall impacts are not unclear, with studies showing that vertebrate herbivores can increase plant infection by viruses (Borer et al. 2009) but that survivorship of the infected plants can increase (Malmstrom et al. 2006). The soil food web is an important mediator of biogeochemical processes. While only a limited number of studies have addressed it in California's grasslands, we know that abundance and richness of groups such as protozoa and nematodes are high but vary greatly across sites, seasons, and years (Freckman et al. 1979, Heady et al. 1992, Sanchez-Moreno et al. 2011, Baty 2012). Processes such as litter decomposition are strongly controlled by the size and composition of the food web, which is in turn controlled by both resource availability and predation (Barstow 2011).

Interacting Factors: Transition of California's Grasslands to a Non-Native-Dominated State

Frequent interactions among biotic and abiotic factors determine the structure and function of California's grasslands (see Figure 23.1). For example, the effects of gopher mounds on plant composition differ with precipitation (Hobbs and Mooney 1991), as the effects of burning on plant communities vary with grazing regime (D'Antonio et al. 2006). The interplay of multiple factors is perhaps best demonstrated by a suite of hypotheses about the causes of non-native plant domination in California's grasslands.

The composition of California's grasslands at the time of European settlement is not well documented (Wigand et al. 2007); it is unclear whether the currently common native species were previous dominants or were historically unusual species able to survive changing conditions. There has been substantial debate about the pre-European composition of this system, with theories ranging from: (1) it was dominated by native perennial bunchgrasses interspersed with native forbs, and replacement by exotic annuals was due to overgrazing and drought; versus (2) it was dominated by wildflowers (both annual and perennial forbs), which declined due to the competitive nature of the newly introduced exotic grasses and forbs (reviewed in Minnich 2008). While there are strong advocates for both of these alternatives, it is generally accepted that native systems likely contained perennial bunchgrasses and forbs, rhizomatous grasses, and annual forbs and grasses, with different plant groups dominating different regions (Bartolome et al. 2007). Perennial grasses likely dominated wetter areas, such as those adjacent to the coast, the windward aspect of the coast range, and wetter areas of the Central Valley. Annual forbs likely were present in all of California's grasslands but dominated in drier areas, including the foothills, the interior coast ranges, and in the drier areas of the Central Valley (D'Antonio et al. 2007). The abundance of forbs on most sites were likely to annually vary from rare to abundant, depending on weather and disturbance regimes (Schiffman 2007). Using the term "grasslands" to describe this diverse group of communities can underplay the current and historical importance and prevalence of forbs, and many advocate returning to the term "prairie," which was historically used to describe these diverse systems in California (Holstein 2011).

While we can only speculate about the composition of historical plant communities, we know that non-native species replaced the dominant native vegetation during the 1700s and 1800s (Bartolome et al. 2007, D'Antonio et al. 2007). Non-native species invasions occurred in a number of waves (Heady et al. 1992, D'Antonio et al. 2007, Bossard and Randall 2007, Minnich 2008). Species such as wild oats, filaree, and mustard (*Brassica*) were found in adobe bricks of early Spanish missions, indicating their prevalence even before the mid-1800s, when European settlements and livestock expanded. Bromes (*Bromus* spp.) and barleys/foxtails (*Hordeum* spp.) spread in the 1860s and 1870s. In the late 1800s hairgrass (*Aira*), foxtail brome, and Napa starthistle invaded. Species currently invading California's grasslands include barbed goatgrass, medusa head, and yellow starthistle (*Centaurea solstitialis*) (Heady et al. 1992, D'Antonio et al. 2006, D'Antonio et al. 2007, Keeler-Wolf et al. 2007) (see Figure 23.4c); coastal grasslands are also currently being invaded by non-native perennial grasses, including velvet grass (*Holcus lanatus*), tall fescue (*Festuca arundinacea*), Harding grass (*Phalaris aquatica*), and orchard grass (*Dactylis glomerata*) (Corbin and D'Antonio 2010). California's grasslands now contain four hundred non-native plant species (Bartolome et al. 2007), amounting to 37% of California's invasive flora—the largest of any ecosystem in the state (Bossard and Randall 2007).

A number of hypotheses, all with strong experimental support, address what caused the widespread invasion of non-native species. Most of these hypotheses focus on transition from native perennial bunchgrasses (Bartolome et al. 2007, D'Antonio et al. 2007), which will be the focus of the next discussion. In areas that were not dominated by native perennial grasses, other mechanisms (e.g., superior competitor ability of invaders) may have driven the transition from native to exotic domination (Minnich 2008). Many have argued that the domination of non-native species resulted primarily from the competitive superiority of non-natives due to their rapid early-season growth, drought tolerance, high seed production, and earlier seed establishment (Bartolome and Gemmill 1981, D'Antonio et al. 2007). However, competition on its own was likely not enough to drive such dramatic shifts from native perennial bunchgrasses. Well-established stands of native perennial bunchgrasses resist invasion. Even though newly established native grasses can be initially invaded by non-natives, in a number of cases natives persisted in these invaded patches and eventually suppressed non-native grasses (Corbin and D'Antonio 2004, D'Antonio et al. 2007, Eviner et al. 2013). Thus the extensive transition from native to non-native domination that took place likely also required a stressor that decreased the performance or cover of natives if the previous dominants were perennial grasses.

Drought and overgrazing are the most commonly hypothesized such stressors driving the native to non-native transition (D'Antonio et al. 2007). While native grasses might have evolved under seasonal grazing and browsing, in the 1700s they were exposed to heavy, year-round livestock grazing. This could have exceeded the grazing tolerance of natives, while Mediterranean non-natives could tolerate it (Bartolome et al. 2007, Hille Ris Lambers et al. 2010). Overgrazing also decreased productivity through erosion and loss of soil fertility (Allen-Diaz et al. 2007). Moreover, the native grassland plants had evolved under wetter, longer growing seasons (Dyer 2007), and were likely particularly hard hit by severe, multiyear droughts in 1850–1851 and 1862–1864. Annuals cope with the prolonged dry season by producing seeds at the onset of summer and dying. This strategy might have allowed them to establish under low-rainfall conditions and to be poised to spread when the droughts ended (Reever Morghan et al. 2007).

In addition to drought and overgrazing, a number of other well-supported mechanisms might have contributed to invasion by non-native species. Increased settlement by Europeans across California wrought major changes to hydrology and fire regimes. River damming and levees destroyed many fertile, moist floodplains, decreasing the water and silt deposition that supported rich vegetation (Dyer 2007). Native Americans also managed grasslands through high-frequency burns, and the cessation of these burns may have increased non-natives (Dyer 2007, Bartolome et al. 2007). Another key land management change was the rise of crop agriculture, with extensive tilling that the native perennials could not survive (D'Antonio et al. 2007). In addition to land use changes, extensive biotic interactions could have contributed to the vegetation transition. In the late 1800s to early 1900s, increased hunting pressure on predators led to extremely high abundance of small mammals. Their extensive soil disturbance might have favored annuals, with their high seed production and ability to establish quickly on disturbed areas (Schiffman 2007). An already stressed native community could have been further decimated by grasshopper outbreaks. Because these outbreaks occur during summer, they would negatively affect perennials but have no effect on non-native annuals, which are already dead at this time of year (Joern 1989).

Once the transition to annual non-natives occurred, a number of mechanisms could have maintained the invaded state. Barley and cereal yellow dwarf viruses decrease native grass growth, survivorship, and fecundity (Malmstrom et al. 2005a, 2005b). The presence of non-native grasses more than doubles infection of native grasses by these viruses (Malmstrom et al. 2005a, 2005b), partly by increasing abundance of aphid—the vector of these pathogens (Borer et al. 2009). Non-native grasses also alter soil chemistry and microbial communities, which can feed back to favor non-natives over native plants (Grmn and Suding 2010, Hausmann and Hawkes 2010). Finally, the decline of native grasses might have caused widespread seed limitation, preventing natives from reestablishing on their own (Hamilton et al. 1999, Seabloom et al. 2003).

Ecosystem Functioning

This review of ecosystem function focuses mostly on the annual grassland, since it is the dominant type in California. As discussed earlier, in most of the world's grasslands dominance of annual species is limited to early successional stages. Most paradigms for understanding and managing grasslands thus focus on perennial grasslands. These frameworks are not adequate for understanding annual-dominated systems, where the annual growth habit, coupled with high interannual variability in precipitation, strongly influence functioning and management needs (Heady et al. 1992, Bartolome et al. 2007).

Net Primary Production (NPP)

Timing of plant production is driven by seasonality of temperature and moisture (see Figure 23.3), with an initial pulse of production early in the season when temperature and moisture are both ideal. When the first rains occur during colder periods, lower temperatures do not inhibit stand establishment but can limit growth (Evans and Young 1989). In the winter, low temperatures inhibit aboveground biomass growth but root growth continues, reaching its peak before mid-March (Evans and Young 1989, Heady et al. 1992). When midwinter droughts occur, water can limit growth during the rainy season (Corbin et al. 2007a). As temperatures rise in mid- to late February, aboveground NPP increases, with peak biomass often occurring in mid-April to late May, just before the soil dries and plants begin to senesce (Evans and Young 1989, Heady et al. 1992).

The high variability in annual weather coupled with the annual growth form of the dominant plants renders NPP in California's grasslands extremely variable, with typical annual variations of at least 50% of mean NPP (Bartolome et al. 2007). For example, from 1935 through 1999 at the San Joaquin Experimental Range, aboveground NPP ranged from 1,008 to 5,040 kg ha^{-1}, while at Hopland Research and Extension Center, aboveground production ranged from 1,008 to 3,920 kg ha^{-1} from 1953 through 1999 (George et al. 2001). Although California grasslands have been studied intensively for decades, limited ability persists to explain this variability in production using the conventional predictors of climate, soil type and residual dry matter (RDM) (George et al. 2001). NPP only weakly relates to total annual precipitation and is much more strongly affected by timing of rainfall during adequate temperatures for growth (see Figure 23.5) (Pitt and Heady 1978, George et al. 2001, Reever Morghan et al. 2007, Suttle et al. 2007).

In general, NPP tends to be highest in years with high and steady rainfall in November through February (Murphy 1970, Pitt and Heady 1978, Reever Morghan et al. 2007, Chou et al. 2008), particularly when temperatures are higher in this period (Pitt and Heady 1978, George et al. 2001). However, this generalization does not always hold—even in long-term datasets, the timing and total amount of precipitation do not always correlate with production (Pitt 1975, Duncan and Woodmansee 1975). Moreover, different sites respond uniquely to timing of rainfall. Sites in northern California's coastal range and foothills have their highest NPP when fall and winter are warm and wet. In contrast, a drier southern California site has its highest NPP in years with high spring precipitation (George et al. 2001). Plant community composition can strongly shape the impacts of spring rains on NPP. When vegetation at a site is dominated by species that senesce early to midspring, spring rains (March, April) either have no effect or decrease NPP (Pitt and Heady 1978, Reever Morghan et al. 2007, Chou et al. 2008). However, late-season rains increase NPP at sites with late-season species, particularly in sites with summer annuals, which can produce up to 10% of a site's NPP. In these cases, the duration of the rainy season can determine the duration of the growing season (Hooper and Heady 1970, Chiariello 1989). In perennial-dominated grasslands along the coast, the duration of the growing season is also extended by moisture supplied through fog inputs (Corbin et al. 2005).

While weather conditions are likely the strongest controls over production (Corbin et al. 2007a, Bartolome et al. 2007), there are a number of other factors that also play an important role, within the constraints of weather patterns. When moisture is not limiting to growth, soil nutrients are the next-most limiting factor (Pitt and Heady 1979, Harpole et al. 2007). Nitrogen is the most commonly limiting nutrient to plant growth in this system, but NPP can also be limited by phosphorus or sulfur, depending on the site and the vegetation community. Some sites can respond equally to nitrogen additions versus sulfur and phosphorus additions. Nitrogen additions will enhance grass production, while sulfur and phosphorus will stimulate legume production, if they are present (Jones et al. 1970; Jones and Martin 1964; Jones et al. 1983). Fertilization in the fall is particularly effective in increasing NPP (Jones 1974). Plant production from the previous year can also impact NPP. In sites with greater than 400 millimeters of rainfall per year, maximum production is associated with intermediate residual dry matter (RDM) levels of 840 kilograms per hectare. Too much RDM can suppress production the following year through shading, and too little can decrease production, presumably due to the loss of RDM's roles in microclimate mitigation, nutrient provision, and water infiltration (Bartolome et al. 2007).

Seed production from the previous year, and seedling dynamics also have strong impacts on NPP. Annual plants in California translocate 63–77% of their aboveground nitrogen to seeds (Woodmansee and Duncan 1980), over 90% of these seeds germinate at the start of the growing season, and up to 50% of germinated seedlings can die within the first six to eight weeks of the growing season. After this initial pulse of thinning, seedling death proceeds steadily throughout the growing season, so that 75–90% of seedlings die throughout the growing season (Bartolome 1979, Young et al. 1981). Seedling thinning results in inputs of very labile litter with low structural material, leading to rapid availability of seedling nitrogen to other plants. Self-thinning acts as a perfectly timed slow-release fertilizer, with release of highly labile nutrients at the time of peak plant competition (Eviner and Firestone 2007). Manipulations of seed density show that seedling thinning can double the NPP compared to planting at seed densities that are too low for thinning to occur (Eviner et al. in prep.). Similarly, increased seed density enhances aboveground productivity in other grasslands (Turnbull et al. 2000, Moles and Westoby 2006).

In fact, productivity is often so enhanced in high-density stands, that fertilizer additions cause little if any increase in productivity (while fertilizer does increase growth at low density) (Bolland 1995, Thompson and Stout 1996, Eviner et al. in prep.). Seedling thinning likely plays a role in regulating the annual variability in NPP, since these grasslands experience dramatic variations in seed production (four- to one-hundred-fold variation), seedling numbers (two- to sixfold variation), and self-thinning (one- to fivefold variation) from year to year at a given site and across sites within a given year (Heady 1958, Bartolome 1979, Young et al. 1981). Through effects on seed production, weather patterns in a given growing season may impact productivity of the following growing season. For example, winter droughts and low spring precipitation can greatly decrease seed production (Heady et al. 1992), which may lead to lower production the following growing season.

Decomposition

Breakdown of litter is critical for nutrient recycling, and for regulating excess thatch accumulation. In California grasslands, root litter typically decomposes within a year, while aboveground litter takes two to two and a half years to turn over (Savelle 1977). There are a number of key controllers of decomposition rates in grasslands. Plant senescence creates litter in the late spring, when moisture conditions are not conducive to microbial activity. Despite this, grassland litter tends to lose 8–10% of its mass and 20% of its lignin during the first summer, due to PHOTODEGRADATION. After one year, litter exposed to sunlight in the summer has double the mass loss compared with litter that is shaded (Henry et al. 2008). As litter layers thicken, due to increased production, photodegradation effects on mass loss remain constant, but lignin breakdown decreases substantially (Henry et al. 2008). This photodegradation can have significant impacts on ecosystem carbon dynamics in the early fall. The first significant rains usually induce a 5% litter mass loss through leaching (Savelle 1977) and a respiration pulse that can be responsible for up to 10% of ecosystem carbon loss a year. These losses likely depend on photodegradation (Ma et al. 2012).

Once the rainy season begins, soil temperature and moisture determine microbial activity and decomposition rates. The peak timing of microbial decomposition roughly coincides with that of plant growth but is a bit more buffered from low temperatures (Savelle 1977, Heady et al. 1992, Eviner and Firestone 2007). Microbial activity can also persist under lower moisture conditions than plants, because they can exploit moist microsites within the soil. Because of their short generation times, microbes can respond more readily to late-season rains than plants, leading to pulses of decomposition after these rains (Chou et al. 2008). Drought conditions can decrease decomposition through moisture limitation but also through shifts in the microbial community that persist even when moisture conditions become ideal (Allison et al. 2013).

Litter chemistry is an important determinant of the rate of mass loss and nutrient release. As in other systems, higher nitrogen content of litter leads to faster decomposition rates. An important exception to this is some of the litter from forbs, which can contain defensive compounds, such as alkaloids that can inhibit decomposition (Eviner 2001). Litter structure is another key controller of decomposition rates. Standing litter that is not in contact with the soil surface decomposes more slowly than litter in contact with the surface, while buried litter is the most quickly decomposed (Dukes and Field 2000). The more litter buildup there is, the less contact there is with the soil, leading to greater inhibition of decomposition and faster buildup of litter. However, wind and rain, as well as trampling by herbivores can drive standing litter down, enhancing decomposition. Decomposition can be accelerated when litter is incorporated into the soil through gopher activity, which can decrease standing litter by two- to eightfold (Stromberg and Griffin 1996). Macrofauna, which break up litter and incorporate it into the soil, can cause 20% mass loss (Savelle 1977, Heady et al. 1992).

Nitrogen Cycling

Nitrogen is the most commonly limiting nutrient to plant growth in California's grasslands, so its cycling can be a critical controller of NPP, as well as vegetation composition (Corbin et al. 2007a, Harpole et al. 2007). Soil organic nitrogen represents 94% of the system's nitrogen pool (Eviner and Firestone 2007), but much of this is not readily available to plants and microbes, due to physical and chemical protection. Nitrogen becomes available to plants through litter decomposition, soil organic matter mineralization, atmospheric deposition, and nitrogen fixation by legumes (Woodmansee and Duncan 1980, Pendelton et al. 1983, Vaughn et al. 1986, Center et al. 1989, Heady et al. 1992). Additionally, 37% to 63% of annual internal nitrogen cycling is mediated through seedling thinning, essentially acting as a slow-release fertilizer, providing nitrogen at peak times of plant nitrogen demand (Eviner and Firestone 2007). This is a key example of a driver of ecosystem processes that is unique to annual grasslands.

Like other processes, nitrogen cycling, uptake, and loss have strong seasonal trends. At plant senescence, approximately 70% of aboveground nitrogen is stored as seeds, with the remaining as litter. A range of 1% to 75% of seeds may be consumed by granivores during the summer (Heady et al. 1992), leading to potentially high nitrogen release through granivory. Summer dynamics of aboveground litter nitrogen are variable, with some studies showing loss of 25% of aboveground litter nitrogen (and 35% of root litter nitrogen) (Jackson et al. 1988), while others show nitrogen accumulation during the summer, even as mass loss occurs through photodegradation (Henry et al. 2008). This accumulation is due to microbial immobilization of nitrogen, leading to a buildup in soil microbial biomass through the summer, with its annual peak at the end of the summer (Jackson et al. 1988). Rates of nitrogen cycling can be low after spring dry-down and before the first fall rains (Herman et al. 2003, Eviner et al. 2006), but surprisingly, microbial populations and enzyme activity can be maintained through the summer (Treseder et al. 2010, Parker and Schimel 2011), leading to sustained cycling of nitrogen and accumulation of inorganic nitrogen in the soil (Parker and Schimel 2011). Part of the reason for high inorganic nitrogen accumulation is lack of moisture to facilitate gaseous and leaching losses (Eviner and Firestone 2007) as well as generally low plant uptake during the summer, because most annual plants are senesced. However, in grasslands with high biomass of summer annuals, summer uptake can be up to 10 kg N/ha, approximately 8% of the total taken up between October and June, the typical growing season (Chiariello 1989).

Fall rains stimulate nitrogen mineralization rates but have an even greater stimulatory effect on microbial immobilization and microbial biomass (Herman et al. 2003). Repeated wet-dry cycles, which are typical between fall rains, further stimulate nitrogen mineralization, microbial biomass, and microbial activity (Xiang et al. 2008). High immobilization does not prevent some nitrogen leaching loss, which is often at its peak within a few weeks after wet up (Figure 23.10) (Jones et al. 1977, Vaughn et al. 1986, Jackson et al. 1988, Davidson et al. 1990, Maron and Jeffries 2001, Lewis et al. 2006). In the winter, low temperatures cause nitrogen cycling rates to decrease, with immobilization decreasing to a greater extent than mineralization, leading to net mineralization occurring in the winter (as opposed to net immobilization in the fall) (Jones and Woodmansee 1979, Schimel et al. 1989, Davidson et al. 1990, Maron and Jeffries 2001, Herman et al. 2003, Eviner et al. 2006). Low temperatures limit plant uptake as well, leading to an increase in soil inorganic nitrogen levels (Vaughn et al. 1986, Jackson et al. 1988). Warming in early spring increases nitrogen cycling rates as well as plant and microbial uptake of nitrogen, and 82% of plant nitrogen uptake is completed by this time, even though only 45% of plant production has occurred. As the soil dries out in the spring, nitrogen cycling rates decrease (Eviner and Firestone 2007), and plant nitrogen availability may be restricted by lack of soil moisture (Everard et al. 2010). While the general seasonal trends are presented above, these seasonal patterns can vary year to year (Herman et al. 2003).

Nitrogen cycling rates also vary depending on which plant species are dominant (Eviner et al. 2006, Eviner and Fires-

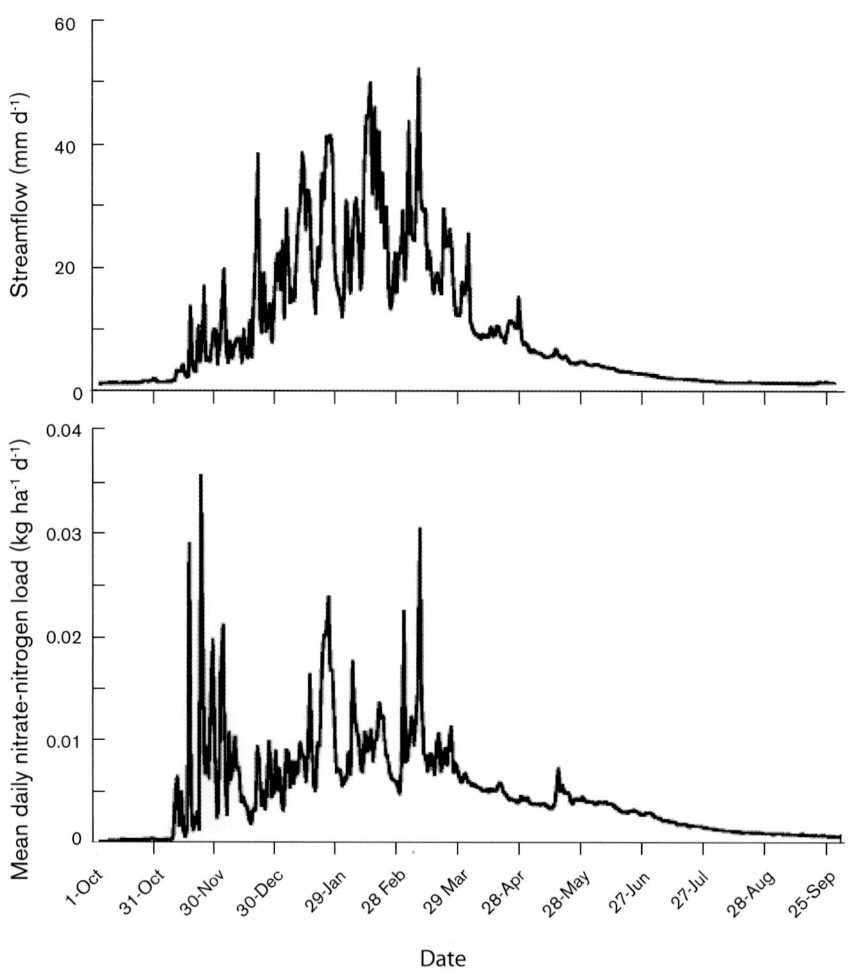

FIGURE 23.10 Seasonal fluxes of streamflow (upper) and stream nitrogen load (lower) at Sierra Foothills Research and Extension Center, by water year (October–September) from 1981 to 2000. Source: Lewis et al. 2006.

tone 2007, Corbin and D'Antonio 2011). Soil disturbance by gophers and feral pigs have the potential to increase nitrogen availability over the short term (Canals et al. 2003, Eviner and Chapin 2005), but this is not always the case (Cushman et al. 2004, Tierney and Cushman 2006, Eviner and Firestone 2007). Grazing can vary in its effects on nutrient availability, but a number of studies have indicated that grazing California's grasslands can increase soil nitrogen and sulfur but lower phosphorus (Jackson et al. 2007).

Water Balance

Water availability is the key driver of this system's structure and function, so that water inputs, infiltration, storage, and losses determine water supply for plants, animals, and humans (Parton and Jackson 1989, Reever Morghan et al. 2007, Salve and Torn 2011, Salve et al. 2011). While water availability partly depends on precipitation inputs, the ability of the system to capture and store water is critical to support annual peak evapotranspiration in the spring, when precipitation is low and infrequent (Ryu et al. 2008). Water capture is determined by infiltration into the soil versus runoff over the surface. Early in the season, when soils are dry, water infiltration is largely determined by soil type and porosity (determined by soil texture, soil channels from roots and soil fauna, and soil disturbance from organisms such as gophers). Standing vegetation and litter can decrease physical compaction of the soil by decreasing the impact of raindrops, and vegetation and litter also slow runoff, allowing more time for water to infiltrate into the soil. Early season rains wet up the soil surface, and with increasing rain, the soil gradually wets up deeper, creating a "wetting front." The depth and speed of this wetting front depend on the magnitude and frequency of early season rains, as well as soil channels from roots and macrofauna (Salve and Torn 2011). When small precipitation events occur, with a week or more between them, the initial soil moisture at the surface is lost due to evapotranspiration, and the next rains recharge surface soil, rather than increase the depth of the wetting front. In order to recharge soil moisture below a 0.2 meter depth, substantial rainfall over successive days is needed (e.g., 66 millimeters or more), and deep soil (1.5 meter depth) is not saturated until later in the growing season, when successive storms have occurred (Salve and Tokunaga 2000). In low rainfall years, deep soil may not be recharged (Reever Morghan et al. 2007).

Once the soil is recharged, water storage is determined by water-holding capacity of the soil, which is determined by soil texture, organic matter, and depth. Precipitation beyond this water-holding capacity leads to a mix of surface runoff (due to lack of infiltration) and leaching through the soil column and into the groundwater and/or streams. Because much of the rain falls at a time of low plant growth and evapotranspiration, 19–76% of precipitation can be lost through streamflow (Nixon and Lawless 1960, Parton and Jackson 1989, Lewis et al. 2006, Reever Morghan et al. 2007). Initial rains tend to have lower loss to streamflow, since they are still wetting up the soil column. Once the soil column has wet up (estimated at 15 to 25 centimeters of accumulated rainfall), 70% of additional rainfall is lost to the system (Dahlgren et al. 2001, Lewis et al. 2006). Most of this is lost in limited pulses throughout the growing season (see Figure 23.10). For example, in one study, moisture moved below the top 0.5 meter of soil only during five significant rain periods, amounting to the twenty-one days of the growing season that received 71% of that year's precipitation (Salve and Tokunaga 2000). This can lead to highly variable streamflow from grasslands.

Annual evapotranspiration rates are less variable than streamflow, because most evapotranspiration occurs in the spring, when precipitation is low or has stopped for the season, and thus much of the annual evapotranspiration is derived from water stored in the soil (Ryu et al. 2008, Salve et al. 2011). Plant traits can influence the timing and amount of evapotranspiration, due to their different phenologies and rooting depths. Those with deeper roots can access soil water that is unavailable to many other grassland species and tend to be active later into the dry season (Enloe et al. 2004, Reever Morghan et al. 2007).

Management practices can impact water dynamics. For example, in a study of long-term (thirty to forty years) grazing treatments, compared to ungrazed sites, heavy grazing increased soil compaction and bulk density, decreasing infiltration. This led to heavily grazed plots having two- to fivefold higher runoff and a twofold reduction in water storage. The effects of light grazing were more similar to ungrazed than heavily grazed treatments (Liacos 1962). Conversion of woody systems (oak woodlands, chaparral, coastal sage scrub) to grasslands also has large impacts on water dynamics, increasing streamflow by an average of 60%, due to lower evapotranspiration rates. However, grasslands have higher infiltration rates than woody systems, leading to more gradual release of water into streams. This results in lower maximum volume of peak storm streamflow (e.g., can minimize flooding) but longer periods of stormflow (Lewis 1968, Dahlgren et al. 2001). However, there are exceptions to these patterns, with removal of woody vegetation on some sites increasing deep water storage but not affecting runoff (Veihmeyer 1953).

Ecology and Management of Ecosystem Services

California grasslands have the potential to provide a number of key ecosystem services, including forage and livestock production, weed control, pollination, carbon sequestration, water supply and purification (including erosion control), fire control, recreation, and scenic vistas (FRAP 2010, Cheatum et al. 2011, Ferranto et al. 2011). In addition, maintenance and enhancement of plant and wildlife diversity is a key management goal in many restoration and conservation efforts and is important in enhancing the delivery and resilience of most ecosystem services. This section highlights successful management strategies for ecosystem services, although it is important to keep in mind that the effects of management are constrained by environmental factors, which can have a strong impact on any of these ecosystem services (see Figure 23.1) (Jackson and Bartolome 2007). This results in strong site-specific and year-specific effects of management, requiring adaptive management approaches (see Chapter 37, "Range Ecosystems"). Another considerable challenge is balancing management for multiple goals, since all ecosystem services are desirable but rarely achievable simultaneously.

Focal ecosystem service goals depend on who owns the land. Eighty-eight percent of California's grasslands are under private ownership (FRAP 2003, Jantz et al. 2007), with 53% designated as agricultural (for grazing), 20% as open space, 22% as residential (at very low to low density), and 5% as "other" (Jantz et al. 2007). Fortunately, many private landowners manage for services other than forage production, with 50% or more managing for each of the following services: fire control, wildlife habitat, water quality, and erosion control. In addition, approximately 40% of private landowners actively remove non-native species and 40% plant native species (Ferranto et al. 2011).

Biodiversity

Biodiversity is a key controller of ecosystem services and is a focal goal of many conservation and restoration efforts. Even in their invaded state, California grasslands are species rich, averaging greater than fifty plant species per 30 x 30 meter area (Heady et al. 1992). California grasslands also contain a number of rare and unique habitats, including vernal pools, serpentine grasslands, and riparian systems, which are hotspots of native diversity. California's grasslands are critical habitat for diverse plants and animals, including many endemic, threatened, and endangered species. These grasslands provide habitat for nearly 90% of species in the Inventory of Rare and Endangered Species in California (Skinner and Pavlik 1994), and seventy-five federally listed threatened or endangered species, including: fifty-one plants, fourteen invertebrates, and ten vertebrates (Jantz et al. 2007). Examples of key species of concern include the San Joaquin kit fox (*Vulpes macrotis mutica*), burrowing owl (*Athene cunicularia*), bay checkerspot butterfly (*Euphydruas editha bayensis*), Swainson's hawk (*Buteo swainsoni*), California tiger salamander (*Ambystoma californiense*), and California quail (*Callipepla californica*) (Barry et al. 2006, Cheatum et al. 2011).

Because 88% of California grasslands are privately owned (Jantz et al. 2007), conservation and restoration of diversity largely depends on private land owners. Large ranches are critical for wildlife conservation, providing habitat and connectivity between habitats (FRAP 2010). Wildlife are a priority for many landowners, with more than 50% managing for wildlife habitat (Ferranto et al. 2011), and many employing management strategies for specific species (SRDC 2006, Barry et al. 2006). For example, moderate grazing can benefit kit foxes, which prefer grasslands with aboveground biomass less than 560 kilogram per hectare. Mixed grazing patterns benefit burrowing owls, which prefer heavily grazed areas for nesting but require areas with tall grass cover to provide habitat for voles, their preferred prey (Barry et al. 2006). The checkerspot butterfly requires the native forb, California plantain (*Plantago erecta*), which increases in prevalence under moderate to high grazing by cattle (which prefer grasses over forbs) (Weiss 1999).

The plant community is another key focus of conservation and restoration efforts, with 40% of landowners employing management practices to decrease non-native plants and increase natives (Ferranto et al. 2011). At present, large-scale, complete eradication of non-natives is not feasible. Many restoration efforts have failed to achieve long-term self-sustaining native communities due to high rates of reinvasion of non-natives (Malmstrom et al. 2009). However, some restoration sites have been successful, particularly with repeated, long-term management of non-natives through burning, mowing, and grazing (Bossard and Randall 2007). Because of this, current restoration goals focus on decreasing weeds, while maintaining or enhancing native grasses and forbs (Stromberg et al. 2007). These restoration efforts focus on three stages: reducing non-natives, restoring natives, and controlling reinvasion (Bartolome et al. 2007). Reducing non-natives is achieved as just described, with a combination of carefully timed grazing or burning, herbicide applications, thatch removal, and sometimes tillage (Bossard and Randall 2007, D'Antonio et al. 2007). Natives are then planted, either as drilled seeds or plugs (Stromberg et al. 2007). The use of local genotypes in restoration can be important, because they are best-suited for local environmental conditions (e.g., coastal versus inland, soil type), plant competitors, and management regimes (Knapp and Rice 1998, McKay et al. 2005, Bartolome et al. 2007).

Once the natives are planted, aggressive management of weeds is typical for the first two to three years (Bartolome et al. 2007). However, a number of studies have shown that the natives can be competitive with the weeds (Seabloom et al. 2003), and that annual non-natives may dominate native restoration plots for the first few years, but then natives become dominant over the long-term, even without weed management (Corbin and D'Antonio 2004, Eviner et al. 2013). While native suppression of non-natives has been documented in a few cases, this level of successful restoration is still rare and is likely limited to key environmental conditions (e.g., moist coastal sites, valley bottoms with deep soils, and access to groundwater). Most successful restoration projects require long-term, aggressive management of annual non-natives (Bartolome et al. 2007, Malmstrom et al. 2009).

Forage Production

The largest direct economic benefit of California's grasslands comes from providing forage for livestock. Grasslands annually provide 75% of California's livestock forage (Corbin et al. 2007a, CCCC 2009, Cheatum et al. 2011). Forage availability depends on aboveground plant production and the palatability of plant biomass. Palatability is strongly influenced by plant species composition, with species differing in tissue quality and in how long they remain green into the spring and summer (green forage is much more nutritious than senesced litter). High-quality forage species include legumes such as clovers and lupines, forbs such as filaree, and some grasses with longer green forage periods (e.g., Italian ryegrass) (George et al. 2001). Low-quality species include recent invaders such as yellow starthistle, medusa head, and barbed goatgrass, which have lower production and lower forage quality than the naturalized invaders and can decrease livestock productivity 50–75% (Jacobsen 1929, Pitcairn et al. 1998, Gerlach and Rice 2003, Malmstrom et al. 2009).

While environmental factors have the strongest impacts on both production and plant composition (see Figure 23.1), short-term improvements in forage production and composition can be achieved through planting legumes and fertilizing with nitrogen, and in some areas, fertilizing with phosphorus and sulfur (Heady et al. 1992). Forage quality and production can also be increased by controlling low-quality plants (particularly invasive noxious weeds) through the use of herbicides and carefully timed grazing or burning (Heady et al. 1992, Jackson and Bartolome 2007). Grazing management is one of the most effective and flexible tools for managing vegetation composition and production (Huntsinger et al. 2007). For example, grazing to maintain threshold levels of residual dry matter (RDM) can have a positive effect on production (Jackson and Bartolome 2002). Conversely, overuse of forage in one year can reduce production in the following year. To restore forage production in degraded grasslands, ranchers have moved away from continuous, season-long grazing, and are resting pastures and employing grazing rotations during key seasons, depending on the management goal (FRAP 2003). Because of these changes in grazing management, grassland conditions have been static or improving over the past few decades (FRAP 2003).

Pollination

Many plant species in California grasslands are wind-pollinated or can self-polinate and thus do not require pollinators (Moldenke 1976). However, this is not the case for all species, and interactions between pollinators and many forb species can be critically important for gene flow (Chiariello 1989). These grasslands support high pollinator diversity and abundance (Wood et al. 2005, Colteaux et al. 2013) and are critical for providing pollen sources for both native bees and the honey bee during seasons when surrounding crops are not flowering (Moldenke 1976). Pollination of agricultural crops relies on the proximity of wildlands (Kremen et al. 2004), and since grasslands are often adjacent to agricultural crops, grasslands support a large portion of the pollinators for California's agriculture (Chaplin-Kramer et al. 2011). The main threats to pollinators in California's grasslands are habitat loss and invasion of non-native grasses, which decrease the abundance of forbs (Black et al. 2009).

Pollinators require a diverse community of forbs, containing species that differ in phenology and morphological traits, so that collectively they bloom throughout the season and support diverse pollinator morphologies (Black et al. 2009). Diversity of forbs is particularly critical because many grassland forbs have short flowering times and vary in timing of flowering, depending on rainfall (Moldenke 1976). Restoration efforts to increase the prevalence of native forbs in California's grasslands have successfully enhanced native pollinator populations and diversity (Black et al. 2009). Forb patches should be at least 0.2 hectares but are more effective when containing a core habitat of at least 0.8 hectares, surrounded by multiple smaller patches. These forb patches should be within 150 meters to 600 meters of nesting sites and crops that need to be pollinated, given the typical flight range of bees (Black et al. 2009). Grassland management practices that are typically used to enhance forbs (grazing, burning, and mowing) can have mixed effects on pollinators. While these management practices maintain forb cover and diversity, they can also disrupt pollinators by ruining nesting sites and interfering with immediate food supply (Black et al. 2009). To the extent possible, mowing and burning should be timed to avoid flowering, and should avoid any summer blooms, when flowers are rare (and thus more crucial to pollinators) (Black et al. 2009). For both mowing and fire, these treatments should occur on no more than 33% of the habitat per year. This is particularly critical for fire, which can cause longer-term decreases in bee populations than mowing (Black et al. 2009). Livestock can destroy nests and trample bees and consume pollinator food (particularly livestock such as sheep, which prefer forbs) (Sugden 1985). Like mowing or fire, grazing management should be timed to minimize impacts on forbs during flowering times. When this is not possible, due to the need to control for noxious grasses, grazing should occur in small areas on any given year (Black et al. 2009).

Water Quality and Supply

Almost all of California's surface water passes through grasslands and oak woodlands (Tate et al. 1999). Thus grasslands can have strong impacts on water flow and quality. As discussed with water balance, grasslands have lower evapotranspiration than woody systems, so a higher proportion of rainfall flows into streams. In addition, because grassland soils have high infiltration, they attenuate any given storm event, leading to gradual release of the storm water to the streams (Lewis 1968, Dahlgren et al. 2001). This both reduces flood risk but also allows for continued streamflow into the dry season. Since these grasslands are naturally effective in water provision and flood control, management practices should focus on not compromising water infiltration and storage. For example, minimizing high densities of livestock during the wet season can prevent soil compaction, allowing for water infiltration.

Water quality can be a key concern, since grasslands are susceptible to erosion due to typically thin soils and prevalence of steep topography (FRAP 2003). Grasslands can also be a source of nitrogen early in the growing season, when leaching rates are high (Jackson et al. 2007). However, grasslands can also serve as important filters of pathogens, nutrients, and sediments, and are effective buffer strips between agricultural and urban uplands and streams (Tate et al. 2006, Atwill et al. 2006). However, the ability of these grasslands to filter pollutants can be overwhelmed during large storms, so not surprisingly, nitrogen and sediment inputs into streams tend to be associated with high precipitation periods (Lewis et al. 2006). Grazing can be associated with impaired water quality, particularly on the North coast (FRAP 2003), but light grazing can also enhance water quality (Barry et al. 2006).

Carbon Sequestration

California's grasslands contribute significantly to regional carbon storage due to their large spatial extent, as well as high quantity of carbon storage per unit area (similar in quantity to temperate perennial grasslands, which are well known for their high carbon storage) (Silver et al. 2010). High root allocation contributes to soil organic matter storage, and rooting depth can impact the depth distribution of soil carbon. Deeper soil carbon tends to be more stable than surface carbon, as it is less likely to undergo disturbances such as gopher or earthworm activity, and decomposer activity is lower due to fewer resources (Silver et al. 2010). Across sites, soil carbon tends to increase with increasing soil clay content and is highest in grasslands with intermediate aboveground net primary production (Silver et al. 2010).

On average, California's grasslands are carbon neutral, varying between being a weak source and a weak sink, depending on annual weather patterns (Xu and Baldocchi 2004, Ma et al. 2007, Kroeger et al. 2009). As with other ecosystem processes, carbon dynamics are more strongly affected by the seasonality of precipitation than the total annual precipitation (Ma et al. 2007, Chou et al. 2008). When late-phenology plants are present, longer growing seasons with wetter springs increase net primary production to a greater extent than decomposition (Berhe et al. 2012), resulting in net storage of soil carbon (Ma et al. 2007). However, when late-phenology plants are absent, late-season rains stimulate soil respiration but do not alter net primary production (Chou et al. 2008), leading to carbon loss. Higher rains during the winter can increase loss of soil organic matter, despite increases in net primary production, possibly due to decreased roles of iron and aluminum oxides in stabilizing soil carbon (Berhe et al. 2012).

Despite the annual source-sink fluctuations, there is potential to increase carbon sequestration in some California grassland sites, although these protocols have not been approved for carbon credits (FRAP 2010), and important trade-offs may exist. Woody species increase soil carbon storage in California's grasslands (Silver et al. 2010) but may also decrease water supply, as has happened in other semiarid regions (Mark and Dickinson 2008). It is assumed that native perennial grasses increase soil carbon storage, and observational studies have shown that soil carbon is higher under native perennials than under non-natives annuals (Koteen et al. 2011). However, in the Koteen study it is not clear whether natives preferentially establish on soils with higher soil carbon, or if they promote higher carbon in soils where they are present. Whether perennial grasses can enhance soil carbon can be more reliably determined through experimental plantings of native versus non-native plants on the same soil types, or by comparing restored versus adjacent unrestored areas that are on the same soil. Such studies have not detected a difference in total soil carbon between natives versus non-natives (Potthoff et al. 2005) but have found that the distribution of soil carbon changes. Soils associated with perennial grasses have deeper soil carbon than soils associated with annuals (Eviner et al. in prep.) and thus could lead to longer-term sequestration.

Legumes can increase soil organic matter and microbial biomass carbon (Eviner et al. 2006, Potthoff et al. 2009) but may also enhance nitrous oxide emissions, a more potent greenhouse gas than carbon dioxide. Addition of inorganic nitrogen fertilizer has mixed impacts on soil carbon, sometimes increasing soil carbon storage through increased net primary production and litter quality, but other times decreasing it through decreasing root allocation and stimulating microbial breakdown of organic matter (Conant et al. 2001). Similar to legumes, fertilizer additions have the likely trade-off of increasing nitrous oxide production. In general, grazing has mixed effects on soil carbon storage (Conant et al. 2001, Derner and Schuman 2007), and broad comparisons of grazed versus ungrazed sites in California show no consistent effects of grazing on soil carbon (Silver et al. 2010). Light grazing does not tend to impact soil organic matter in California grasslands (Jackson et al. 2007), although overgrazing that results in high erosion has the potential to greatly decrease soil carbon. Carbon sequestration will be particularly vulnerable to wildfires and droughts, so is likely to decrease in response to climate change (FRAP 2010).

Fire Control

While fires can be harmful to human infrastructure and air quality, they tend to be less of a threat in grasslands than in woodlands and shrublands (FRAP 2010). Fire control in grasslands is primarily managed through decreasing fuel load through grazing, prescribed fire, and/or mowing (FRAP 2010). The level to which thatch is removed has great impacts on fire severity. For example, a fuel load of 2,242 kilograms per hectare can lead to fires with 15-meter-long flames, while grazing to half that fuel load can limit flames to 1–3 meters long. Grazing down to 560 kilograms per hectare leaves a fuel load that cannot support a continuous fire, so only isolated patches will burn (Barry et al. 2006).

Impacts of Humans on Grasslands

As reviewed above, California's grasslands greatly changed with European settlement, largely through the introductions of non-native plants (Bossard and Randall 2007) and domesticated livestock (Allen-Diaz et al. 2007) as well as conversion of grasslands to cropping systems. Several million hectares of California's grasslands have been cultivated, with a peak of grassland conversion occurring in the late 1800s (Heady et al. 1992). More recent land use changes also strongly affect grassland structure and function. Extensive areas of grasslands were created from woody-dominated systems, particularly in the 1950s to 1960s, in an attempt to increase forage production (Standiford and Tinnin 1996). Currently in California, grasslands are the ecosystem most at risk from development (FRAP 2010). On average, over the past few decades, more than 190 square kilometers of grassland per year have been lost to vineyards, orchards, dispersed housing, and urban development, and this loss of grassland will continue in the future, particularly with losses to vineyards and urban areas (Jackson et al. 2007, FRAP 2010). Many large ranches are being subdivided, and these smaller parcels receive less management for species conservation and ecosystem services (Ferranto et al. 2011). In fact, many grassland areas are now experiencing undergrazing, where lack of fire or grazing leads to thatch buildup, domination by species such as ripgut brome, and declines in key services such as productivity, wildlife habitat, pollination, and plant diversity (Biswell 1956, Bartolome et al. 2007).

Many shifts in disturbance regimes have occurred in California's grasslands. Over the past few centuries, the hydrology of the Central and San Joaquin Valleys has been drastically altered by dams and levees, altering the types of grassland habitats supported, and preventing the flooding regimes that regularly maintained soil fertility (Corbin et al. 2007a). There have also been substantial changes in the fire regime. On the Central Coast, fires occurred every three to five years before 1880 and now occur every twenty to thirty years (Reiner 2007). In the Sierra foothills the fire return internal was twenty-five years before European settlement, then changed to seven years after settlement, and since the 1950s, fire suppression has led to rare fires (McClaran and Bartolome 1989). Particularly in areas that have reductions in both grazing and fire, these grasslands are susceptible to increased thatch buildup, higher fuel loads, and lower diversity (particularly of forbs and legumes).

Nitrogen deposition is increasingly affecting California's grasslands, but its effects are patchily distributed. Approximately 30% of California grasslands have at least 5 kg N/ha/yr deposition, with levels up to 45 kg/ha/yr in southern California and 16 kg/ha/yr in northern California (Weiss 2006, Dukes and Shaw 2007). This nitrogen deposition can increase production (Dukes et al. 2005), decrease diversity (especially of forbs), and stimulate decomposition rates (Allison et al. 2013). Nitrogen additions tend to increase non-native grasses (Dukes and Shaw 2007), and nitrogen deposition rates are high enough to enhance non-native grasses on 44% of California's grassland area (Fenn et al. 2010).

Climate change is likely to have significant impacts on the structure and function of California's grasslands. In this century, temperature rises are expected of 1.7°C to 3°C under low emissions, and 3.8°C to 5.8°C under high emission scenarios (Dukes and Shaw 2007, Cayan et al. 2008), with more warming inland than on the coast (Pierce et al. 2013). Summer temperatures will become markedly hotter. A modestly cool July in 2060 will be the same temperature as our hottest July temperatures to date. Mean temperatures in the winter will also increase, but the coolest days will be as cool or cooler than they are now (Pierce et al. 2013). Warming in the winter is expected to increase production and accelerate flowering and senescence of many species (Dukes and Shaw 2007), but cooler days may make plants more susceptible to frost kill. Annual changes in precipitation are likely to be modest, but there will be marked trends in seasonal patterns (Figure 23.11). For example, in northern California, winters will be 1–10% wetter, but times of peak plant growth will be drier, with spring precipitation decreasing by 11–18% and fall precipitation decreasing 3–8% (Pierce et al. 2013). Southern California is also likely to have drier springs and falls, but unlike northern California, its winters will also be drier (1–5%) and its summers will be wetter (46–59%) due to monsoons (Pierce et al. 2013). While projections of precipitation changes are mixed (Dukes and Shaw 2007), all precipitation projections agree that there will be increased variability in precipitation across years, with increased frequency of El Niño events and a projected 1.5–2.5-fold increase in drought frequency (Reever Morghan et al. 2007, Dukes and Shaw 2007). In addition, extreme rain events are likely to increase in frequency and magnitude, with a 10–50% increase in large three-day rain events by 2060 (Pierce et al. 2013).

The effects of these changes on precipitation will depend on when the precipitation falls. Increased precipitation during the rainy season will have little impact on overall production and species composition but can increase shoot production and decrease root production (Zavaleta et al. 2003, Dukes et al. 2005). Late-season rains have variable effects, depending on the study, but responses include increased perennials (Suttle et al. 2007), increased non-natives (Suttle and Thomsen 2007), increased abundance and diversity of forbs, and increased diversity of grasses (Zavaleta et al. 2003). Warmer and drier conditions are expected to increase shrubland area at the expense of grasslands, resulting in a 14–58% decrease in forage production by the late 2000s (CCCC 2009). However, other climate scenarios predict an increase in the extent of grasslands at the expense of woody vegetation, as increased temperatures and increased frequency of droughts significantly enhance the frequency, intensity, and extent of fires, which woody species cannot tolerate (Dukes and Shaw 2007).

Elevated carbon dioxide is another change that California's grasslands are experiencing, which can lead to shifts in plant and microbial communities, independent of the changes in temperature that they can induce. The impacts of elevated CO_2 will partially offset decreases in precipitation, since elevated CO_2 increases water use efficiency of most plants, which

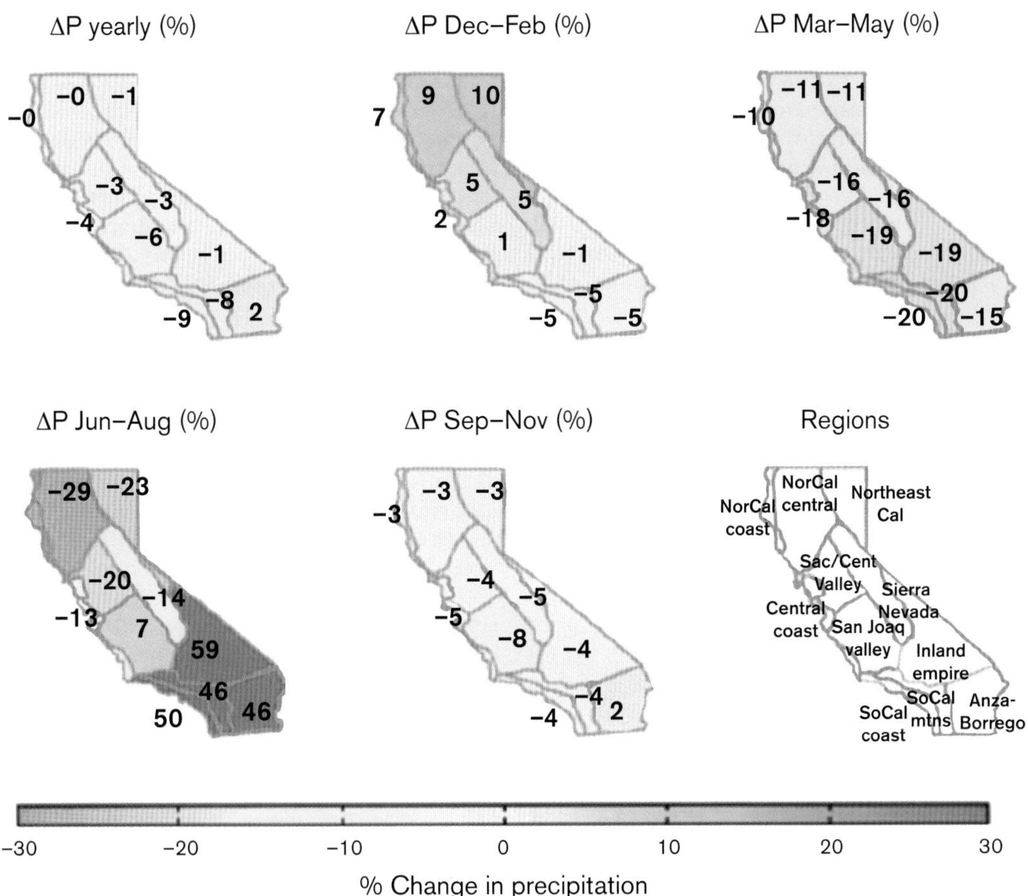

FIGURE 23.11 Predicted percentage change in precipitation (ΔP) during the period 2060–2069, compared with the period 1985–1994. Precipitation changes vary by region and by month. *Top left:* annual percentage change in precipitation. *Top center:* percentage change in precipitation over December, January, and February. *Top right:* percentage change in precipitation over March, April, and May. *Bottom left:* percentage change in precipitation over June, July, and August. *Bottom center:* percentage change in precipitation over September, October, and November. *Bottom right:* regional splits, as designated on all maps. Source: Modified from Pierce et al. 2013.

then increases spring soil moisture. This prolongs the growing season (Harpole et al. 2007) and accelerates nitrogen cycling (Dukes and Shaw 2007).

Management under Future Conditions

Managing California's grasslands under multiple environmental changes will be challenging, particularly when considering the need to balance management for multiple organisms and ecosystem services. Despite the complexity of the controls and responses of these grasslands, there are some clear challenges that lay ahead, and some relatively simple principles to consider for managing these challenges. While presented as discrete challenges, grassland managers will need integrated approaches to address all of these, simultaneously.

Management Challenge 1: The Interaction of Changing Precipitation Patterns and Non-Native versus Native Plants

While predictions of future precipitation patterns are uncertain, all climate predictions emphasize that the annual variation of precipitation will be high. There will be an increased frequency in years with shorter and drier growing seasons as well as more frequent years with longer and wetter growing seasons (CCCC 2009). Vegetation composition will vary strongly along with precipitation. Late-season rainfall benefits the most recent grassland invaders, which are noxious weeds (e.g., goatgrass, medusa head, yellow starthistle). These are a management priority for both conservation and rangeland managers because these weeds decrease plant diversity, production, and forage quality (Pitcairn et al. 1998, Gerlach and Rice 2003, Malmstrom et al. 2009). These late-season noxious weeds decline during shorter, drier growing seasons, particularly when competing with other species that can use soil moisture early in the season (Eviner et al. in prep.). Fluctuating precipitation may allow for noxious weed control through restoration of native perennial grasses. Many native grasses overlap in phenology with the late-season noxious weeds, and once established, natives can suppress these weeds by up to 90% (Eviner et al. 2013). These natives are resilient to short-term droughts but also benefit from late-season rains (Reever Morghan et al. 2007), so are likely to establish and persist under these fluctuating conditions, providing control of the late-season noxious weeds during the years that receive late rainfall.

Management Challenge 2: Managing Fragmented Grasslands for Diversity

Much of our current grassland area is under ranching, but many ranchers are uncertain if they, or future generations, will continue ranching, putting grasslands at risk for subdivision and development (Ferranto et al. 2011, Cheatum et al. 2011). As working ranches convert to dispersed housing with large properties, much less management for ecosystem services occurs, and grazing is often absent (Ferranto et al. 2011). Without grazing, thatch can build up to high levels, which can become a fire hazard, lower abundance and diversity of forbs and grasses, and decrease habitat for animals that are conservation targets, such as ground nesting birds (Barry et al. 2006). In addition, high thatch (5,000 kilograms per hectare) can increase the prevalence of noxious non-native weeds such as goatgrass and medusa head (Bartolome et al. 2007). The consequences of removal of grazers, without substituting controlled burns or mowing, has already been well acknowledged in many grassland reserves and parks, which are increasingly using short-term livestock rotations to remove fire fuel, manage non-native species, enhance plant diversity, and improve wildlife habitat (Weiss 1999, CCWD 2005, SRDC 2006). Conservation professionals will need to work with owners of small grassland parcels to implement some type of thatch removal, through controlled burns, grazing, or mowing.

Management Challenge 3: Managing for Grassland Resilience in the Face of Multiple Environmental Changes

Since California grasslands are experiencing many types of environmental changes, it is critical to consider the simultaneous impacts of these multiple changes, which can interact in important and unexpected ways (Dukes and Shaw 2007). Predicting and managing the impacts of these multiple environmental changes is challenging, particularly considering the strong spatial and temporal variation in these environmental conditions (Bartolome et al. 2007, Hobbs et al. 2007). Long-term studies have demonstrated that California's grasslands are RESILIENT to fluctuating environmental conditions due to high plant diversity. Different plant species respond to unique suites of environmental conditions, so that rare species under some conditions become common in other conditions (Hobbs et al. 2007).

Clearly, functional diversity of species is critical, but under changing conditions, there may be a loss of species with certain strategies. For example, nitrogen deposition tends to favor species with higher aboveground biomass allocation, which may lead to loss of species with higher root allocation that can withstand low soil moisture (Tilman and Downing 1994, Suding et al. 2005, Pan et al. 2011). Areas that lose these deep-rooted plants will lose a key strategy for drought resilience. To deal with these types of functional losses, managers should focus on maintaining biodiversity, while policy makers need to prioritize reversing certain environmental changes. For example, control over precipitation is much harder to achieve than reductions in nitrogen deposition, so while continued efforts should be made to mitigate climate change, we particularly need to push to decrease nitrogen emissions.

Summary

California's grasslands are distributed across a wide precipitation gradient, ranging from 12 to 200 centimeters per year (Bartolome et al. 2007). The drier interior grasslands tend to be dominated by non-native annuals, while the wetter coastal grasslands tend to be dominated by a mix of native and non-native perennials. Unique soil conditions (e.g., poor drainage, salinity, heavy metal toxicity) also define distinctive grassland types such as vernal pools, alkali sinks, and serpentine grasslands. Even within each of these grassland types, there is considerable variation in ecosystem structure and function, due to spatial and temporal variability in seasonal and annual weather patterns, topography, soil, disturbance regimes, and interactions among large herbivores, small mammals, insects, microbes, and plant communities. The predominance of annual species likely makes California's grasslands particularly sensitive to intra-annual and interannual fluctuations in abiotic and biotic controllers.

The high variability in multiple controlling factors leads to both challenges and opportunities in land management. Successful management and policy will have to shift away from a one-size-fits-all approach and embrace the reality that different techniques and guiding principles are needed from site to site, due to variations in soil, topography, and weather. In addition, at a given site, management recommendations may vary from year to year, due to high weather fluctuations (see Chapter 37, "Range Ecosystems"). Managers and scientists will need to collaborate on adaptive management approaches to understand how multiple environmental conditions interact to impact a given goal, while exploring the synergies and trade-offs associated with suites of species and ecosystem services needed from grasslands. The dominance of annuals over large areas of grasslands will require sustained management for many different goals but also provides a relative flexibility in "resetting" the system through adaptive management approaches.

Grasslands are one of the most altered ecosystems in California (Corbin et al 2007a, Janzen et al. 2007), with non-native plant species comprising over 90% of plant cover in most areas (Bartolome et al. 2007). Despite this, California's grasslands are a diversity hotspot, averaging greater than fifty plant species per 30 x 30 meter area (Heady et al. 1992) and providing habitat for nearly 90% of state-listed rare and endangered species (Skinner and Pavlik 1994), and seventy-five federally listed plants and animals (Jantz et al. 2007). They also provide 75% of the state's livestock forage, the main direct economic benefit from these systems (Corbin et al. 2007a, CCCC 2009, Cheatum et al. 2011). These grasslands are critical in regulating water flow (e.g., flood prevention, maintaining streamflow into the dry seasons) (Lewis 1968, Dahlgren et al. 2001) and water quality (Tate et al. 2006, Atwill et al. 2006), and contribute significantly to regional soil carbon storage (Silver et al. 2010). Grasslands also support a large portion of the pollinators needed in California's cropping systems (Chaplin-Kramer et al. 2011). Because 88% of California grasslands are privately owned (Jantz et al. 2007), conservation and restoration of these grasslands largely depends on private land owners and how they balance management for livestock production, biotic diversity, and ecosystem services (SRDC 2006, Barry et al. 2006, FRAP 2010, Ferranto et al. 2011). Currently, many ranchers actively manage to improve wildlife habitat, decrease noxious weeds, and enhance water quality (Ferranto et al. 2011).

However, as working ranches convert to dispersed housing with large properties, management for ecosystem services declines (Ferranto et al. 2011), and the lack of grazing can increase fires and lower diversity of forbs and grasses (Barry et al. 2006). Other threats to grasslands include conversion to agriculture (particularly vineyards and orchards) and urban areas, and high nitrogen deposition. Climate change is likely to increase the variability in precipitation, making it more challenging to reliably manage for suites of ecosystem services. High species diversity is critical for maintaining resilience of these grasslands to changes in the means and variability of biotic and abiotic controlling factors. Rare species under one set of conditions become the dominants under other conditions, so that the species that maintain ecosystem production vary greatly across time and space in this annual grassland (Hobbs et al. 2007).

Acknowledgments

I am grateful to Jeff Corbin, Hall Cushman, Erika Zavaleta, and Hal Mooney for feedback on earlier versions, which improved this chapter. Thanks to Melissa Chapin for improving the figures and her attention to detail. This chapter is based on work supported by the University of California's Division of Agriculture and Natural Resources competitive grants, the Western Sustainable Agriculture, Research and Education Program, and the U.S. Department of Agriculture's Agriculture and Food Research Initiative's Managed Ecosystems and Weedy and Invasive Species programs.

Recommended Reading

Bartolome, J. W., J. Barry, T. Griggs, and P. Hopkinson. 2007. Valley grassland. Pages 367–393 in M. G. Barbour, T. Keeler-Wolf, and A. A. Schoenherr, editors. Terrestrial vegetation of California. University of California Press, Berkeley, California.

Heady, H. F., J. W. Bartolome, M. D. Pitt, G. D. Savelle, and M. C. Stroud. 1992. California Prairie. Pages 313–335 in R. T. Coupland, editor. Natural grasslands: Introduction and Western Hemisphere. Elsevier, Amsterdam, The Netherlands.

Huenneke, L. F., and H. A. Mooney. 1989. Grassland structure and function: California annual grassland. Kluwer Academic Publishers, Dordrecht, The Netherlands.

Stromberg, M. R., J. D. Corbin, and C. M. D'Antonio. 2007. California grasslands: Ecology and Management. University of California Press, Berkeley, California

Glossary

BULK DENSITY The dry mass of soil divided by its volume, used as an indicator of soil compaction.

FECUNDITY Reproductive capacity or output.

FORB A flowering plant that is herbaceous but not a graminoid (grass, sedge, rush). When the term is used in contrast with grasses, this group often includes both legume and nonlegume plants. When the term is used in contrast with grasses and legumes, it is used to denote the herbaceous species that are neither graminoids nor legumes.

INFILTRATION The entry of water into the soil.

PHENOLOGY The timing of periodic events in the life cycles of organisms, often related to climate patterns (such as seasonality). In California's grasslands the timing of plant death in the dry spring is often categorized as early-, mid-, or late-season phenology.

PHOTODEGRADATION The degradation of molecules by the absorption of light.

RESILIENCE The ability of an ecosystem to recover from a disturbance.

SENESCENCE Programmed breakdown and death of plant tissues. In annual species this allows plants to resorb nutrients from leaves that will die and allocate those nutrients to seeds.

SOIL ORDERS The broadest classification of soils, on a global level.

SOIL SHEAR STRENGTH The ability of soil to remain intact despite force applied against it.

References

Allen-Diaz, B., R. Standiford, and R. D. Jackson. 2007. Pages 313–338 in M. G. Barbour, T. Keeler-Wolf, and A. A. Schoenherr, editors. Terrestrial vegetation of California. Third edition. University of California Press, Berkeley, California.

Allen, E. B., and M. F. Allen. 1990. The mediation of competition by mycorrhizae in successional and patchy environments. Pages 367–390 in J. B. Grace and D. Tilman, editors. Perspectives on plant competition. Academic Press, San Diego, California.

Allison, S. D., Y. Lu, C. Weihe, M. L. Goulden, A. C. Martiny, K. K. Treseder, and J.B.H. Martiny. 2013. Microbial abundance and composition influence litter decomposition response to environmental change. Ecology 94:714–725.

Alster, C. J., D. P. German, Y. Lu, and S. D. Allison. 2013. Microbial enzymatic responses to drought and to nitrogen addition in a southern California grassland. Soil Biology and Biochemistry 64:68–79.

Amatangelo, K. L., J. S. Dukes, and C. B. Field. 2008. Responses of a California annual grassland to litter manipulation. Journal of Vegetation Science 19:605–612.

Atwill, E. R., K. W. Tate, M. Das Gracas, C. Pereira, J. W. Bartolome, and G. A. Nader. 2006. Efficacy of natural grass buffers for removal of Cryptosporidium parvum in rangeland runoff. Journal of Food Protection. 69:177–184.

Barbour, M., T. Keeler-Wolf, and A. A. Schoenherr, editors. 2007. Terrestrial vegetation of California. Third edition. University of California Press, Berkeley, California.

Barry, S., R. Larson, G. Nader, and M. Doran. 2006. Understanding livestock grazing impacts: Strategies for the California annual grassland and oak woodland vegetation series. Publication 21626. University of California, Division of Agriculture and Natural Resources, Oakland, California.

Barstow, J. L. 2011. Facilitation and predation structure a grassland detrital food web: The responses of soil nematodes to isopod processing of litter. Journal of Animal Ecology 80:947–957.

Bartolome, J. 1979. Germination and seedling establishment in California annual grassland. Journal of Ecology 67:273–281.

Bartolome, J. W., and B. Gemmill. 1981. The ecological status of *Stipa pulchra* (Poaceae) in California. Madroño 28:172–184.

Bartolome, J. W., J. Barry, T. Griggs, and P. Hopkinson. 2007. Valley grassland. Pages 367–393 in M. G. Barbour, T. Keeler-Wolf, and A. A. Schoenherr, editors. Terrestrial vegetation of California. Third edition. University of California Press, Berkeley, California.

Bartolome, J. W., M. C. Stroud, and H. F. Heady. 1980. Influence of natural mulch on forage production on differing California annual range sites. Journal of Range Management 33:4–8.

Bartolome, J. W., W. E. Frost, N. K. McDougald, and J. M. Connor. 2002. California guidelines for residual dry matter (RDM) management on coastal and foothill annual rangelands. Rangeland Management Series 8092. University of California Division of Agriculture and Natural Resources, Oakland, California.

Batten, K. M., K. M. Scow, K. F. Davies, and S. P. Harrison. 2006. Two invasive plants alter soil microbial community composition in serpentine grasslands. Biological Invasions 8:217–230.

Baty, J. H. 2012. Changes to the seasonality of plant-soil systems

by three phenologically distinct groups of California grassland plants. MA thesis. University of California, Davis, California.
Batzli, G., and F. A. Pitelka. 1970. Influence of meadow mouse populations on California grassland. Ecology 51:1027–1039.
Batzli, G. O., and F. A. Pitelka. 1971. Condition and diet of cycling populations of California vole, *Microtus-Californicus*. Journal of Mammology 52:141–163.
Beattie, A. J. 1989. The effects of ants on grasslands. Pages 105–116 in L. F. Huenneke and H. A. Mooney, editors. Grassland structure and function: California annual grassland. Kluwer Academic Publishers, Dordrecht, The Netherlands.
Berhe, A. A., B. Suttle, S. D. Burton, and J. F. Banfield. 2012. Contingency in the direction and mechanics of soil organic matter responses to increased rainfall. Plant and Soil 358:371–383.
Betts, A.D.K. 2003. Ecology and control of goatgrass (*Aegilopstriuncialis*) and medusahead (*Taeniatherum caput-medusae*) in California annual grasslands. PhD dissertation. University of California, Berkeley, California.
Biswell, H. H. 1956. Ecology of California grasslands. Journal of Range Management 9:19–24.
Black, S. H., M. Shepard, M. Vaughan, C. LaBar, and N. Hodges. 2009. Pollinator conservation strategy. Report to Yolo Natural Heritage Program. The Xerces Society for Invertebrate Conservation, Sacramento, California.
Bolland, M. 1995. Effect of sowing density and flooding on the comparative phosphorus requirement of *Trifolium balansae* and *Trifolium subterraneum*. Journal of Plant Nutrition 18:1825–1843.
Borchert, M. I., and S. K. Jain. 1978. The effect of rodent seed predation on four species of California annual grasses. Oecologia 33:101–113.
Borer, E. T., C. E. Mitchell, A. G. Power, and E. W. Seabloom. 2009. Consumers indirectly increase infection risk in grassland food webs. Proceedings of the National Academy of Sciences USA 106:503–506.
Borer, E. T., P. R. Hosseini, E. W. Seabloom, and A. P. Dobson. 2007. Pathogen-induced reversal of native dominance in a grassland community. Proceedings of the National Academy of Sciences USA 104:5473–5478.
Bossard, C. C., and J. M. Randall. 2007. Nonnative plants of California. Pages 107–123 in M. G. Barbour, T. Keeler-Wolf, and A. A. Schoenherr, editors. Terrestrial vegetation of California. Third edition. University of California Press, Berkeley, California.
Boulton, A. M., B. A. Jaffee, and K. M. Scow. 2003. Effects of a common harvester ant (*Messor andrei*) on richness and abundance of soil biota. Applied Soil Ecology 23:257–265.
Brandt, A. J., E. W. Seabloom, and P. R. Hosseini. 2009. Phylogeny and provenance affect plant-soil feedbacks in invaded California grasslands. Ecology 90:1063–1072.
Brown, M. J. F., and K. G. Human. 1997. Effects of harvester ants on plant species distribution and abundance in a serpentine grasslands. Oecologia 112:237–243.
Burdic, D. J., D. A. Duncan, J. R. Larson, and M. Robinson. 1979. Arthropod inventories for two seasons in an annual grassland ecosystem. Page 52 in Abstracts 32nd annual meeting of the Society for Range Management, Littleton, Colorado.
Callaway, R. M., B. E. Mahall, C. Wicks, J. Pankey, and C. Zabinski. 2003. Soil fungi and the effects of an invasive forb on grasses: Neighbor identity matters. Ecology 84:129–135.
Canals, R. M., D. J. Herman, and M. K. Firestone. 2003. How disturbance by fossorial mammals alters N cycling in a California annual grassland. Ecology 84:875–881.
Carsten, L. D., B. Maxwell, M. R. Johnston, and D. C. Sands. 2001. Impact of crown rust (*Puccinia coronate* f. sp. *avenae*) on competitive interactions between wild oats (*Avena fatua*) and stipa (*Nassella pulchra*). Biological Control 22:207–218.
Cayan, D. R., E. P. Maurer, M. D. Dettinger, M. Tyree, and K. Hayhoe. 2008. Climate change scenarios for the California region. Climatic Change 87:S21–S42.
CCCC (California Climate Change Center). 2009. The impact of climate change on California's ecosystem services. CEC-500-2009-025-F. California Energy Commission PIER program, Sacramento, California.
CCWD (Contra Costa Water District). 2005. Using livestock grazing as a resource management tool in California. Contra Costa Water District, Concord, California.
Center, D. M., C. E. Vaughn, and M. B. Jones. 1989. Effects of management on plant production and nutrient cycling on two annual grassland sites. Hilgardia 57:1–40.
Chaplin-Kramer, R., K. Tuxen-Bettman, and C. Kremen. 2011. Value of wildlife habitat for supplying pollination services to Californian agriculture. Rangelands 33: 33–41.
Cheatum, M., F. Casey, P. Alvarez, and B. Parkhurst. 2011. Payments for ecosystem services: A California rancher perspective. Conservation Economics White Paper. Conservation economics and finance program. Defenders of Wildlife, Washington, D.C.
Chiariello, N. R. 1989. Phenology of California grasslands. Pages 47–58 in L. F. Huenneke and H. A. Mooney, editors. Grassland structure and function: California annual grassland. Kluwer Academic Publishers, Dordrecht, The Netherlands.
Chiariello, N., J. C. Hickman, and H. A. Mooney. 1982. Endomycorrhizal role for interspecific transfer of phosphorus in a community of annual plants. Science 217:941–943.
Chou, W. W., W. L. Silver, R. D. Jackson, A. W. Thompson, and B. Allen-Diaz. 2008. The sensitivity of annual grassland carbon cycling to the quantity and timing of rainfall. Global Change Biology 14:1382–1394.
Cockburn, A., and W. Z. Lidicker. 1983. Microhabitat heterogeneity and population ecology of an herbivorous rodent, *Microtus californicus*. Oecologia 59:167–177.
Colteaux, B. C., C. McDonald, M. Kolipinski, J. B. Cunningham, and S. Ghosh. 2013. A survey of pollinator and plant interactions in meadow and grassland habitats of Marin County, CA. BIOS 84:1–7.
Conant, R. T., K. Paustian, and E. T. Elliot. 2001. Grassland management and conversion into grassland: Effects on soil carbon. Ecological Applications 11:343–355.
Corbin, J. D., and C. M. D'Antonio. 2011. Abundance and productivity mediate invader effects on nitrogen dynamics in a California grassland. Ecosphere 2:art32.
———. 2010. Not novel, just better: Competition between native and non-native plants that share species traits. Plant Ecology 209:71–81.
———. 2004. Competition between native perennial and exotic annual grasses: Implications for an historical invasion. Ecology 85:1273–1283.
Corbin, J. D., A. R. Dyer, and E. W. Seabloom. 2007a. Competitive interactions. Pages 156–168 in M. R. Stromberg, J. D. Corbin, and C. D'Antonio, editors. California grasslands: Ecology and management. University of California Press, Berkeley, California.
Corbin, J. D., C. M. D'Antonio, A. R. Dyer, and M. R. Stromberg. 2007b. Introduction. Pages 1–4 in M. R. Stromberg, J. D. Corbin, and C. D'Antonio, editors. California grasslands: Ecology and management. University of California Press, Berkeley, California.
Corbin, J. D., M. A. Thomsen, T. E. Dawson, and C. M. D'Antonio. 2005. Summer water use by California coastal prairie grasses: Fog, drought, and community composition. Oecologia 145:511–521.
CPIF (California Partners in Flight). 2000. The draft grassland bird conservation plan: A strategy for protecting and managing grassland habitats and associated birds in California. Point Reyes Bird Observatory, Stinson Beach, California.
Cushman, J. H. 2007. History and ecology of feral pig invasions in California grasslands. Pages 191–196 in M. R. Stromberg, J. D. Corbin, and C. D'Antonio, editors. California grasslands: Ecology and management. University of California Press, Berkeley, California.
Cushman, J. H., T. A. Tierney, and J. M. Hinds. 2004. Variable effects of feral pig disturbances on native and exotic plants in a California grassland. Ecological Applications 14:1746–1756.
Dahlgren, R. A., K. W. Tate, D. Lewis, E. R. Atwill, J. M. Harper, and B. Allen–Diaz. 2001. Watershed research examines rangeland management effects on water quality. California Agriculture 55:64–71.
D'Antonio, C. M., C. Malmstrom, S. A. Reynolds, and J. Gerlach. 2007. Ecology of invasive non–native species in California grassland. Pages 67–86 in M. R. Stromberg, J. D. Corbin, and C. D'Antonio, editors. California grasslands: Ecology and management. University of California Press, Berkeley, California.
D'Antonio, C., S. Bainbridge, C. Kennedy, J. Bartolome, and S. Reynolds. 2006. Ecology and restoration of California grasslands with special emphasis on the influence of fire and grazing on native grassland species. A report to the David and Lucille Packard Foundation. University of California, Santa Barbara, California.
Davidson, E. A., J. M. Stark, and M. K. Firestone. 1990. Microbial pro-

duction and consumption of nitrate in an annual grassland. Ecology 71:1968–1975.

Dawson, K., K. E. Veblen, and T. P. Young. 2007. Experimental evidence for an alkali ecosystem of *Lolium multiflorum* in the Central Valley, CA, USA. Biological Invasions 9:327–334.

Derner, J. D., and G. E. Schuman. 2007. Carbon sequestration and rangelands: A synthesis of land management and precipitation effects. Journal of Soil and Water Conservation 62:77–85.

Docherty, K. M., T. C. Balser, B. J. M. Bohannan, and J. L. M. Gutknecht. 2012. Soil microbial responses to fire and interacting global change factors in a California annual grassland. Biogeochemistry 109:63–83.

Dukes, J. S., and C. B. Field. 2000. Diverse mechanisms for CO_2 effects on grassland litter decomposition. Global Change Biology 6:145–154.

Dukes, J. S., and M. R. Shaw. 2007. Responses to changing atmosphere and climate. Pages 218–232 in M. R. Stromberg, J. D. Corbin, and C. D'Antonio, editors. California grasslands: Ecology and management. University of California Press, Berkeley, California.

Dukes, J. S., N. R. Chiariello, E. E. Cleland, L. A. Moore, M. R. Shaw, S. Thayer, T. Tobeck, H. A. Mooney, and C. B. Field. 2005. Responses of grassland production to single and multiple global environmental changes. Public Library of Science Biology 3:1829–1837.

Duncan, D. A., and R. G. Woodmansee. 1975. Forecasting forage yield from precipitation in California's annual rangeland. Journal of Range Management 28:327–329.

Dyer, A. 2007. Historical factors that influence interpretation of grassland ecology. Pages 2–3 in M. R. Stromberg, J. D. Corbin, and C. D'Antonio, editors. California grasslands: Ecology and management. University of California Press, Berkeley, California.

Edwards, S. W. 2007. Rancholabrean mammals of California and their relevance for understanding modern plant ecology. Pages 48–56 in M. R. Stromberg, J. D. Corbin, and C. D'Antonio, editors. California grasslands: Ecology and management. University of California Press, Berkeley, California.

Enloe, S. F., J. M. DiTomaso, S. B. Orloff, and D. J. Drake. 2004. Soil water dynamics differ among rangeland plant communities dominated by yellow starthistle (*Centaurea solstitialis*) annual grasses, or perennial grasses. Weed Science 52:929–935.

Espeland, E. K., T. M. Carlsen, and D. Macqueen. 2005. Fire and dynamics of granivory on a California grassland forb. Biodiversity and Conservation 14:267–280.

Evans, R. A., and J. A. Young. 1989. Characterization and analysis of abiotic factors and their influence on vegetation. Pages 13–28 in L. F. Huenneke and H. A. Mooney, editors. Grassland structure and function: California annual grassland. Kluwer Academic Publishers, Dordrecht, The Netherlands.

Evans, R. A., B. L. Kay, and J. A. Young. 1975. Microenvironment of a dynamic annual community in relation to range improvement. Hilgardia 43:78–102.

Everard, K., E. W. Seabloom, W. S. Harpole, and C. de Mazancourt. 2010. Plant water use affects competition for nitrogen: Why drought favors invasive species in California. American Naturalist 175:85–97.

Eviner, V. T. 2001. Linking plant community composition and ecosystem dynamics: Interactions of plant traits determine the ecosystem effects of plant species and plant species mixtures. PhD dissertation. University of California, Berkeley, California.

Eviner, V. T., and F. S. Chapin. 2005. Selective gopher disturbance influences plant species effects on nitrogen cycling. Oikos 109:154–166.

Eviner, V. T., and M. K. Firestone. 2007. Mechanisms determining patterns of nutrient dynamics. Pages 94–106 in M. R. Stromberg, J. D. Corbin, and C. D'Antonio, editors. California grasslands: Ecology and management. University of California Press, Berkeley, California.

Eviner, V. T., F. S. Chapin, and C. E. Vaughn. 2006. Seasonal variations in species effects on N and P cycling. Ecology 87:974–986.

Eviner, V. T., J. Heraty, J. Baty, C. Malmstrom, and K. J. Rice. 2013. Impacts of native vs. exotic vegetation. California Invasive Plant Council News 21:13–14.

Eviner, V. T., C. M. Malmstrom, and K. J. Rice. In preparation. Timing and amount of precipitation impacts community composition in California's grasslands.

Eviner, V.T., C. Vaughn, and J. M. Heraty. In preparation. Impacts of seed density on seasonal grassland population dynamics, nutrient availability, and plant production.

Eviner, V. T., K. J. Rice, and C. M. Malmstrom. In preparation. Tradeoffs in multiple ecosystem services between California's native vs. naturalized vs. invasive grasses.

Ewing, A. L., and J. W. Menke. 1983. Reproductive potential of *Bromus mollis* and *Avena barbata* under drought conditions. Madroño 30:159–167.

Fehmi, J. S., and J. W. Bartolome. 2002. Species richness, cattle grazing, and the effect of Microtus californicus in coastal California grasslands. Western North American Naturalist. 62:73–81.

Fenn, M. E., E. B. Allen, S. B. Weiss, S. Jovan, L. H. Geiser, G. S. Tonnesen, R. F. Johnson, L. E. Rao, B. S. Gimeno, F. Yuan, T. Meixner, and A. Bytnerowicz. 2010. Nitrogen critical loads and management alternatives for N-impacted ecosystems in California. Journal of Environmental Management 91:2404–2423.

Ferranto, S., L. Huntsinger, C. Getz, G. Nakamura, W. Stewart, S. Drill, Y. Valachovic, M. DeLasaux, and M. Kelly. 2011. Forest and rangeland owners value land for natural amenities and as financial investment. California Agriculture 65:184–191.

Fitch, H. S. 1948. Ecology of the California ground squirrel on grazing lands. American Midland Naturalist 39:513–597.

Fitch, H. S., and J. R. Bentley. 1949. Uses of California annual plant forage by range rodents. Ecology 30:306–321.

Fix, D., and A. Bezener. 2000. Birds of northern California. Lone Pine Publishing, Auburn, Washington.

Ford, L. D., and G. F. Hayes. 2007. Northern coastal scrub and coastal prairie. Pages 180–208 in M. G. Barbour, T. Keeler-Wolf, and A. A. Schoenherr, editors. Terrestrial vegetation of California. Third edition. University of California Press, Berkeley, California.

FRAP (Fire and Resource Assessment Program). 2010. California's forests and rangelands: 2010 assessment. California Department of Forestry and Fire Protection. Sacramento, California.

———. 2003. California's forests and rangelands: 2003 assessment. California Department of Forestry and Fire Protection, Sacramento, California.

Freckman, D. W., D. A. Duncan, and J. R. Larson. 1979. Nematode density and biomass in an annual grassland ecosystem. Journal of Range Management 32:418–422.

George, M., J. Bartolome, N. McDougald, M. Connor, C. Vaughn, and G. Markegard. 2001. Annual range forage production. Publication 8018. University of California Agriculture and Natural Resources, Oakland, California.

George, M., C. Raguse, W. Clawson, C. Wilson, R. Willoughby, N. McDougald, D. Duncan, and A. Murphy. 1988. Correlation of degree-days with annual herbage yields and livestock gains. Journal of Range Management 41:193–196.

Gerlach, J. D., and K. J. Rice. 2003. Testing life history correlates of invasiveness using congeneric plant species. Ecological Applications 13:167–179.

Greenlee, J. M., and J. H. Langenheim. 1980. The history of wildfires in the region of Monterey Bay. California Department of Parks and Recreation, Sacramento, California.

Grmn, E., and K. N. Suding. 2010. Within-year soil legacies contribute to strong priority effects of exotics on native California grassland communities. Restoration Ecology 18: 664–670.

Grogan, P., and F. S. Chapin. 2000. Nitrogen limitation of production in a Californian annual grassland: The contribution of arbuscular mycorrhizae. Biogeochemistry 49:37–51.

Gutknecht, J.L.M., H. A. Henry, and T. C. Balser. 2010. Inter-annual variation in soil extra-cellular enzyme activity in response to simulated global change and fire disturbance. Pedobiologia 53:283–293.

Hamilton, J. G., C. Holzapfel, and B. E. Mahall. 1999. Coexistence and interference between a native perennial grass and nonnative annual grasses in California. Oecologia 121:518–526.

Harpole, W. S., L. Goldstein, and R. J. Aicher. 2007. Resource limitation. Pages 119–130 in M. R. Stromberg, J. D. Corbin, and C. D'Antonio, editors. California grasslands: Ecology and management. University of California Press, Berkeley, California.

Harrison, S. P., and J. H. Viers. 2007. Serpentine grasslands. Pages 145–155 in M. R. Stromberg, J. D. Corbin, and C. D'Antonio, editors. California grasslands: Ecology and management. University of California Press, Berkeley, California.

Harrison, S., B. D. Inouye, and H. D. Safford. 2003. Ecological heterogeneity in the effects of grazing and fire on grassland diversity. Conservation Biology 17:837–845.

Hausmann, N. T., and C. V. Hawkes. 2010. Order of plant host establishment alters the composition of arbuscular mycorrhizal communities. Ecology 91:2333–2343.

———. 2009. Plant neighborhood control of Arbuscular mycorrhizal community composition. New Phytologist 183:1188–1200.

Hawkes, C. V., I. F. Wren, D. J. Herman, and M. K. Firestone. 2005. Plant invasion alters nitrogen cycling by modifying the soil nitrifying community. Ecology Letters 8:976–985.

Hawkes, C. V., J. Belnap, C. M. D'Antonio, and M. K. Firestone. 2006. Arbuscular mycorrhizal assemblages in native plant roots change in the presence of exotic grasses. Plant and Soil 281:369–380.

Hawkes, C. V., K. N. Kivlin, J. D. Rocca, V. Hugue, M. A. Thomsen, and K. B. Suttle. 2011. Fungal community responses to precipitation. Global Change Biology 17:1637–1645.

Hayes, G. F., and K. D. Holl. 2003. Cattle grazing impacts on annual forbs and vegetation composition of mesic grasslands in California. Conservation Biology 17:1694–1702.

Heady, H. 1958. Vegetational changes in the California annual type. Ecology 39:402–416.

Heady, H. F. 1977. Valley grassland. Pages 491–514 in M. G. Barbour and J. Major, editors. Terrestrial vegetation of California. Special Publication Number 9. California Native Plant Society, Sacramento, California.

Heady, H. F., J. W. Bartolome, M. D. Pitt, G. D. Savelle, and M. C. Stroud. 1992. California prairie. Pages 313–335 in R. T. Coupland, editor. Natural grasslands. Ecosystems of the World 8A. Elsevier, New York, New York.

Henry, H.A.L., J. D. Juarez, C. B. Field, and P. M. Vitousek. 2005. Interactive effects of elevated CO_2, N deposition, and climate change on extracellular enzyme activity and soil density fractionation in a California annual grassland. Global Change Biology 11:1808–1815.

Henry, H.A.L., K. Brizgys, and C. B. Field. 2008. Litter decomposition in a California annual grassland: Interactions between photodegradation and litter layer thickness. Ecosystems 11:545–554.

Henry, H.A.L., N. R. Chiariello, P. M. Vitousek, H. A. Mooney, and C. B. Field. 2006. Interactive effects of fire, elevated carbon dioxide, nitrogen deposition, and precipitation on a California annual grassland. Ecosystems 9:1066–1075.

Herman, D. J., L. J. Halverson, and M. K. Firestone. 2003. Nitrogen dynamics in an annual grassland: Oak canopy, climate, and microbial population effects. Ecological Applications 13:593–604.

HilleRisLambers, J., S. G. Yelenik, B. P. Colman, and J. M. Levine. 2010. California annual grass invaders: The drivers or passengers of change? Journal of Ecology 98:1147–1156.

Hobbs, R. J. 1985. Harvester ant foraging and plant species distribution in annual grassland. Oecologia 67:519–523.

Hobbs. R. J., and H. A. Mooney. 1991. Effects of rainfall variability and gopher disturbance on serpentine annual grassland dynamics. Ecology 72:59–68.

———. 1985. Community and population dynamics of serpentine grassland annuals in relation to gopher disturbance. Oecologia 67:342–351.

Hobbs, R. J., S. Yates, and H. A. Mooney. 2007. Long-term data reveal complex dynamics in relation to climate and disturbance. Ecological Monographs 77:545–568.

Holstein, G. 2011. Prairies and grasslands: What's in a name? Fremontia 39:2–5.

Hooper, J. F., and H. F. Heady. 1970. An economic analysis of optimum rates of grazing in California annual-type grassland. Journal of Range Management 23:307–311.

Hoopes, M., and L. Hall. 2002. Edaphic factors and competition affect pattern formation and invasion in a California grassland. Ecological Applications 12:24–39.

Hopkins, N. A. 1987. Mycorrhizae in a California serpentine grassland community. Canadian Journal of Botany/Revue canadienne de botanique 65:484–487.

Huenneke, L. F., and H. A. Mooney. 1989. Grassland structure and function: California annual grassland. Kluwer Academic Publishers, Dordrecht, The Netherlands.

Hufstader, R. W. 1978. Growth rates and phenology of some southern California grassland species. Journal of Range Management 31:465–466.

Hunt, J. 1992. Feeding ecology of valley pocket gophers (*Thomomys bottae* sanctidiegi) on a California coastal grassland. American Midland Naturalist 127:41–51.

Huntsinger, L., J. W. Bartolome, and C.M.D'Antonio. 2007. Grazing management on California's Mediterranean grasslands. Pages 233–253 in M. R. Stromberg, J. D. Corbin, and C. D'Antonio, editors. California grasslands: Ecology and management. University of California Press, Berkeley, California.

Jackson, L. E., and J. Roy. 1986. Growth patterns of Mediterranean annual and perennial grasses under simulated rainfall regimes of southern France and California. Acta Oecologia/Oecologia Plantarum 7:191–212.

Jackson, L. E., M. Potthoff, K. L. Steenwerth, A. T. O'Geen, M. R. Stromberg, and K. M. Scow. 2007. Soil biology and carbon sequestration in grasslands. Pages 107–118 in M. R. Stromberg, J. D. Corbin, and C. D'Antonio, editors. California grasslands: Ecology and management. University of California Press, Berkeley, California.

Jackson, L. E., R. Strauss, M. K. Firestone, and J. Bartolome. 1988. Plant and soil nitrogen dynamics in California annual grassland. Plant and Soil 110:9–17.

Jackson, R. D., and J. W. Bartolome. 2007. Grazing ecology of California grasslands. Pages 197–206 in M. R. Stromberg, J. D. Corbin, and C. D'Antonio, editors. California grasslands: Ecology and management. University of California Press, Berkeley, California.

———. 2002. A state-transition approach to understanding nonequilibrium plant community dynamics in Californian grasslands. Plant Ecology 162:49–65.

Jacobsen, W. 1929. Goatgrass—a wee pest of the range. The monthly bulletin: Department of Agriculture, State of California 18:37–41.

Jameson, E. W., Jr, and H. J. Peeters 2004. Mammals of California. University of California Press, Berkeley, California.

Jantz, P. A., B.F.L. Preusser, J. K. Fujikawa, J. A. Kuhn, C. J. Bersbach, J. L. Gelbard, and F. W. Davis. 2007. Regulatory protection and conservation. Pages 297–318 in M. R. Stromberg, J. D. Corbin, and C. D'Antonio, editors. California grasslands: Ecology and management. University of California Press, Berkeley, California.

Joern, A. 1989. Insect herbivory in the transition to California annual grasslands: Did grasshoppers deliver the coup de grass? Pages 117–134 in L. F. Huenneke and H. A. Mooney, editors. Grassland structure and function: California annual grassland. Kluwer Academic, Dordrecht, The Netherlands.

Johnson, B. E., and J. H. Cushman. 2007. Influence of a large herbivore reintroduction on plant invasions and community composition in a California grassland. Conservation Biology 21:515–526.

Jones, M. B. Fertilisation of annual grasslands of California and Oregon. 1974. Pages 255–275 in D. A. Mays, editor. Forage Fertilization. American Society of Agronomy and Soil Science Society of America, Madison, Wisconsin.

Jones, M. B., and R. G. Woodmansee. 1979. Biogeochemical cycling in annual grassland ecosystems. Botanical Review 45:111–144.

Jones, M. B., C. C. Delwiche, and W. A. Williams. 1977. Uptake and losses of 15N applied to annual grass and clover in lysimeters. Agronomy Journal 69:1019–1023.

Jones, M., and W. Martin. 1964. Sulfate-sulfur concentration as an indicator of sulfur status in various California dryland pasture species. Soil Science Society of America Proceedings 28:539–541.

Jones, M., P. Lawler, and J. Ruckman. 1970. Differences in annual clover response to phosphorus and sulfur. Agronomy Journal 62: 439–442.

Jones, M., W. Williams, and C. Vaughn. 1983. Soil characteristics related to production on subclover-grass range. Journal of Range Management 36:444–446.

Keeler-Wolf, T., J. M. Evens, A. I. Solomeshch, V. I. Holland, and M. G. Barbour. 2007. Community classification and nomenclature. Pages 21–36 in M. R. Stromberg, J. D. Corbin, and C. D'Antonio, editors. California grasslands: Ecology and management. University of California Press, Berkeley, California.

Knapp, E. E., and K. J. Rice. 1998, Comparison of isozymes and quantitative traits for evaluating patterns of genetic variation in purple needlegrass. Conservation Biology 12:1031–1041.

Koteen, L. E., D. D. Baldocchi, and J. Harte. 2011. Invasion of nonnative grasses causes a drop in soil carbon storage in California grasslands. Environmental Research Letters 6:044001.

Kremen, C., N. M. Williams, R. L. Bugg, J. P. Fay, and R. W. Thorp. 2004. The area requirements of an ecosystem service: Crop pollination by native bee communities in California. Ecology Letters 7:1109–1119.

Kroeger, T., F. Casey, P. Alvarez, M. Cheatum, and L. Tavassoli. 2009. An economic analysis of the benefits of habitat conservation on California rangelands. Conservation Economics White Paper. Conservation Economics Program. Defenders of Wildlife, Washington, D.C.

Levine, J. M., K. A. McEachern, and C. Cowan. 2011. Seasonal timing of first rain storm affects rare plant population dynamics. Ecology 92:2236–2247.

Lewis, D., M. J. Singer, R. A. Dahlgren, and K. W. Tate. 2006. Nitrate sediment fluxes from a California rangeland watershed. Journal of Environmental Quality 35:2202–2211.

Lewis, D. C. 1968. Annual hydrologic response to watershed conversion from oak woodland to annual grassland. Water resources research 4:59–72.

Liacos, L. G. 1962. Water yield as influenced by degree of grazing in the California winter grasslands. Journal of Range Management 15:34–42.

Lidicker, W. Z. 1989. Impacts of non-domesticated vertebrates on California grasslands. Pages 135–150 in L. Huenneke and H. A. Mooney, editors. Grassland structure and function: California annual grassland. Kluwer Academic Publishers, Boston, Massachusetts.

Ma, S., D. D. Baldocchi, J. A. Hatala, M. Detto, and J. C. Yuste. 2012. Are rain-induced ecosystem respiration pulses enhanced by legacies of antecedent photodegradation in semi-arid environments? Agricultural and Forest Meteorology 154–155:203–213.

Ma, S., D. D. Baldocchi, L. Xu, and T. Hehn. 2007. Inter-annual variability in carbon dioxide exchange of an oak/grass savanna and open grassland in California. Agricultural and Forest Meteorology 147:157–171.

Malmstrom, C. M. 1998. Barley yellow dwarf virus in native California grasses. Grasslands 8:6–10.

Malmstrom, C. M., A. J. McCullough, H. A. Johnson, L. A. Newton, and E. T. Borer. 2005a. Invasive annual grasses indirectly increase virus incidence in California native perennial bunchgrasses. Oecologia 145:153–164.

Malmstrom, C. M., C. C. Hughes, L. A. Newton, and C. J. Stoner. 2005b. Virus infection in remnant native bunchgrasses from invaded California grasslands. New Phytologist 168:217–230.

Malmstrom, C. M., C. J. Stoner, S. Brandenburg, and L. A. Newton. 2006. Virus infection and grazing exert counteracting influences on survivorship of native bunchgrass seedlings competing with invasive exotics. Journal of Ecology 94:264–275.

Malmstrom, C. M., H. S. Butterfield, C. Barber, B. Dieter, R. Harrison, J.Q. Qi, D. Riano, A. Schrotenboer, S. Stone, C. J. Stoner, and J. Wirka. 2009. Using remote sensing to evaluate the influence of grassland restoration activities on ecosystem forage provisioning services. Restoration Ecology 17:526–538.

Mark, A. F., and K. J. M. Dickinson. 2008. Maximizing water yield with indigenous non-forest vegetation: A New Zealand perspective. Frontiers in Ecology and the Environment 6:25–34.

Maron, J. L. and R. L. Jeffries. 2001. Restoring enriched grasslands: effects of mowing on species richness, productivity, and nitrogen retention. Ecological Applications 11:1088–1100.

Marshall, D. R., and S. K. Jain. 1970. Seed predation and dormancy in the population dynamics of *Avena fatua* and *A. barbata*. Ecology 51:886–891.

McClaran, M., and J. Bartolome. 1989. Fire-related recruitment in stagnant *Quercus douglasii* populations. Canadian Journal of Forest Research 19:580–585.

McKay, J., C. E. Christian, S. H. Harrison, K. J. Rice, and J. Thompson. 2005. How local is local? Practical and conceptual issues in the genetics of restoration. Restoration Ecology 13:432–440.

McNaughton, S. J. 1968. Structure and function in California grasslands. Ecology 49:962–972.

Minnich, R. A. 2008. California's fading wildflowers: Lost legacy and biological invasions. University of California Press, Berkeley, California.

Moldenke, A. R. 1976. California USA pollination ecology and vegetation types. Phytologia 34:305–361.

Moles, A. T., and M. Westoby. 2006. Seed size and plant strategy across the whole life cycle. Oikos 113:91–105.

Motheral, S. M., and J. L. Orrock. 2010. Gastropod herbivore preference for seedlings of two native and two exotic grass species. American Midland Naturalist 163:106–114.

Murphy, A. H. 1970. Predicted forage yield based on fall precipitation in California annual grasslands. Journal of Range Management 23:363–365.

Nelson, L. L., and E. B. Allen. 1993. Restoration of *Stipa pulchra* grasslands: Effects of mycorrhizae and competition from *Avena barbata*. Restoration Ecology 1:40–50.

Ng, E., and P. C. Miller. 1980. Soil moisture relations in Southern California chaparral. Ecology 61:98–107.

Nixon, P. R., and G. P. Lawless. 1960. Translocation of moisture with time in unsaturated soil profiles. Journal of Geophysical Research 65:655–661.

Orrock, J. L., and M. S. Witter 2010. Multiple drivers of apparent competition reduce re-establishment of a native plant in invaded habitats. Oikos 119:101–108.

Orrock, J. L., M. S. Witter, and O. J. Reichman. 2008. Apparent competition with an exotic plant reduces native plant establishment. Ecology 89:1168–1174.

Pan, Q., Y. Bai, J. Wu, and X. Han. 2011. Hierarchical plant responses and diversity loss after nitrogen addition: Testing three functionally-based hypotheses in the Inner Mongolia grassland. PLOS One 6:e20078.

Parker, S. S., and J. P. Schimel. 2011. Soil nitrogen availability and transformations differ between the summer and the growing season in a California grassland. Applied Soil Ecology 48:185–192.

Parton, W. J., and L. Jackson. 1989. Simulated water budgets for an annual grassland site in the Sierra foothills. Pages 163–172 in L. F. Huenneke and H. A. Mooney, editors. Grassland structure and function: California annual grassland. Kluwer Academic Press, Dordrecht, The Netherlands.

Pearson, O. P. 1964. Carnivore-mouse predation: An example of its intensity and bioenergetics. Journal of Mammalogy 45:177–188.

———. 1963. History of two local outbreaks of feral house mice. Ecology 44: 540–549.

Pendelton, D. F., J. W. Menke, W. A. Williams, and R. G. Woodmansee. 1983. Annual grassland ecosystem model. Hilgardia 5:1–44.

Peters, H. A. 2007. The significance of small herbivores in structuring annual grassland. Journal of Vegetation Science 18:175–182.

Peters, H. A., E. E. Cleland, H. A. Mooney, and C. B. Field. 2006. Herbivore control of annual grassland composition in current and future environments. Ecology Letters 9:86–94.

Peters, H. A., N. R. Chiariello, H. A. Mooney, S. A. Levin and A. E. Hartley. 2005. Native harvester ants threatened with widespread displacement exert localized effects on serpentine grassland plant community composition. Oikos 109: 351–359.

Pierce, D. W., T. Das, D. R. Cayan, E. P. Maurer, N. L. Miller, Y. Bao, M. Kanamitsu, K. Yoshimura, M. A. Snyder, L. C. Sloan, G. Franco, and M. Turee. 2013. Probablistic estimates of future changes in California temperature and precipitation using statistical and dynamical downscaling. Climate Dynamics 40:839–856.

Pitcairn, M. J. , R. A. O'Connell, and J. M. Gendron. 1998. Yellow starthistle: Survey of statewide distribution. Pages 64–66 in D. M. Woods, editor. Biological control program annual summary, 1997. Plant health and pest prevention services. California Department of Food and Agriculture, Sacramento, California.

Pitt, M. C. 1975. The effects of site, season, weather patterns, grazing and brush conversion on annual vegetation, watershed II, Hopland field station. PhD dissertation. University of California, Berkeley, California.

Pitt, M. D., and H. F. Heady. 1978. Responses of annual vegetation to temperature and rainfall patterns in northern California. Ecology 59:336–350.

Porter, E. E., and R. A. Redak. 1997. Diet of migratory grasshopper (Orthoptera: Acrididae) in a California native grassland and the effect of prescribed spring burning. Environmental Entomology 26:234–240.

Porter, E. E., R. A. Redak, and H. E. Braker. 1996. Density, biomass, and diversity of grasshoppers (Orthoptera: Acrididae) in a California native grassland. Great Basin Naturalist 56:172–176.

Potthoff, M., L. E. Jackson, K. L. Steenwerth, I. Ramirez, M. R. Stromberg, and D. E. Rolston. 2005. Soil biological and chemical properties in restored perennial grassland in California. Restoration Ecology 13:61–73.

Potthoff, M., L. E. Jackson, S. Sokolow, and R. G. Joergensen. 2009. Below and aboveground responses to lupines and litter mulch in a California grassland restored with native bunchgrasses. Applied Soil Ecology 42:124–133.

Rao D., S. Gennet, M. Hammond, P. Hopkinson, and J. Bartolome. 2008. A landscape analysis of grassland birds in a valley grassland-oak woodland mosaic. General Technical Report PSW-GTR-217. U.S. Forest Service.

Reever Morghan, K. J., J. D. Corbin, and J. Gerlach. 2007. Water relations. Pages 87–93 in M. R. Stromberg, J. D. Corbin, and C. D'Antonio, editors. California grasslands: Ecology and management. University of California Press, Berkeley, California.

Reiner, R. J. 2007. Fire in California grasslands. Pages 207–217 in M. R. Stromberg, J. D. Corbin, and C. D'Antonio, editors. California grasslands: Ecology and management. University of California Press, Berkeley, California.

Rice, K. J. 1989. Competitive interactions in California annual grasslands. Pages 59–71 in L. F. Huenneke and H. A. Mooney, editors. Grassland structure and function: California annual grassland. Kluwer Academic Press, Dordrecht, The Netherlands.

Rice, K. J. 1987. Interaction of disturbance patch size and herbivory in Erodium colonization. Ecology 68:1113–1115.

Rillig, M. C., M. F. Allen, J. N. Klironomos, N. R. Chiariello, and C. B. Field. 1998. Plant species-specific changes in root inhabiting fungi in a California annual grassland: Responses to elevated CO_2 and nutrients. Oecologia 113:252–259.

Rillig, M. C., S. F. Wright, M. R. Shaw, and C. B. Field. 2002. Artificial climate warming positively affects arbuscular mycorrhizae but decreases soil aggregate water stability in an annual grassland. Oikos 97:52–58.

Ryu, Y., D. D. Baldocchi, S. Ma, and T. Hehn. 2008. Interannual variability of evapotranspiration and energy exchange over an annual grassland in California. Journal of Geophysical Research 13:D09104.

Salve, R., and M. Torn. 2011. Precipitation and soil impacts on partitioning of subsurface moisture in *Avena barbata*. Vadose Zone Journal 10:437–449.

Salve, R., and T. K. Tokunaga. 2000. Processes in a rangeland catchment in California. Journal of Range Management 53:489–498.

Salve, R., E. A. Sudderth, S. B. St. Clair, and M. S. Torn. 2011. Effect of grassland vegetation type on the responses of hydrological processes to seasonal precipitation patterns. Journal of Hydrology 410:51–61.

Sanchez-Moreno, S., H. Ferris, A. Young-Matthews, S. W. Culman, and L. E. Jackson. 2011. Abundance, diversity, and connectance of soil food web channels along environmental gradients in an agricultural landscape. Soil Biology and Biogeochemistry 43:2374–2383.

Savelle, G. 1977. Comparative structure and function in a California annual and native bunchgrass community. PhD dissertation. University of California, Berkeley, California.

Schiffman, P. M. 2007. Ecology of native animals in California grasslands. Pages 180–190 in M. R. Stromberg, J. D. Corbin, and C. D'Antonio, editors. California grasslands: Ecology and management. University of California Press, Berkeley, California.

Schiffman, P. M. 1994. Promotion of exotic weed establishment by endangered giant kangaroo rats (*Dipodomys ingens*) in a California grassland. Biodiversity and Conservation 3:524–537.

Schimel, J. P., L. E. Jackson, and M. K. Firestone. 1989. Spatial and temporal effects of plant-microbial competition for inorganic nitrogen in a California annual grassland. Soil Biology and Biochemistry 21:1059–1066.

Seabloom, E. W., W. S. Harpole, O. J. Reichman, and D. Tilman. 2003. Invasion, competitive dominance, and resource use by exotic and native California grassland species. Proceedings of the National Academy of Sciences USA 100:13384–13389.

Seabloom, E. W., and S. A. Richards. 2003. Multiple stable equilibria in grasslands mediated by herbivore population dynamics and foraging behavior. Ecology 84:2891–2904.

Sekercioglu, C. H. 2006. Increasing awareness of avian ecological function. TRENDS in Ecology and Evolution 21:464–469.

Shuford, W. D., and T. Gardali. 2008. California bird species of special concern: A ranked assessment of species, subspecies, and distinct populations of birds of immediate conservation concern in California. Pages 393–399 in Studies of Western Birds 1. Western Field Ornithologists, Camarillo, California, and California Department of Fish and Game, Sacramento.

Silver, W., B. Ryles and V. T. Eviner. 2010. Soil carbon pools in California's annual grassland ecosystems. Rangeland Ecology and Management 63:128–136.

Sims, P. L., and P. G. Risser. 2000. Grasslands. Pages 323–356 in M. G. Barbour and W. D. Billings, editors. North American terrestrial vegetation. Cambridge University Press, New York, New York.

Skaer, M. J., D. J. Graydon, and J. H. Cushman. 2013. Community-level consequences of cattle grazing for an invaded grassland: Variable responses of native and exotic vegetation. Journal of Vegetation Science 24:332–343.

Skinner, M. W., and B. M. Pavlik. 1994. Inventory of rare and endangered vascular plants of California. Fifth edition. California Native Plant Society, Sacramento, California.

Soholt, L. F. 1973. Consumption of primary production by a population of kangaroo rats (*Dipodomys Merriami*) in the Mojave Desert. Ecological Monographs 43:357–376.

Solomeshch, A. I., M. G. Barbour, and R. F. Holland. 2007. Vernal pools. Pages 394–424 in M. G. Barbour, T. Keeler-Wolf, and A. A. Schoenherr, editors. Terrestrial vegetation of California. Third edition. University of California Press, Berkeley, California.

SRDC (Sotoyome Resource Conservation District). 2006. Grazing handbook: A guide for natural resource managers in Coastal California. Santa Rosa, California.

Stahlheber, K. A., and C.M.D'Antonio. 2013. Using livestock to manage plant composition: A meta-analysis of grazing in California Mediterranean grasslands. Biological Conservation 157:300–308.

Standiford, R. B., and P. Tinnin. 1996. Guidelines for managing California's hardwood rangelands. Publication 3368. Division of Agriculture and Natural Resources, University of California, Berkeley, California.

Standiford, R. B., J. Vreeland, and W. Tietje. 2013. Earthworm ecology in California. <http://ucanr.edu/sites/oak_range/Oak_Articles_On_Line/Oak_Woodland_Ecology_and_Monitoring/Earthworm_Ecology_in_California/>. Accessed October 10, 2013.

Stebbins, R. C., and S. M. McGinnis. 2012. Field guide to amphibians and reptiles of California. University of California Press, Berkeley, California.

Strauss, S. Y., M. L. Stanton, N. C. Emery, C. A. Bradley, A. Carleton, D. R. Ditrich-Reed, O. A. Ervin, L. N. Gray, A. M. Hamilton, J. H. Rogge, S. D. Harper, K. C. Law, V. Q. Pham, M. E. Putnam, T. M. Roth, J. H. Theil, L. M. Wells, and E. M. Yoshizuka. 2009. Cryptic seedling herbivory by nocturnal introduced generalists impacts survival, performance of native and exotic plants. Ecology 90: 419–429.

Strohecker, H. F., W. W. Middlekauff, and D. C. Rentz. 1968. The grasshoppers of California (Orthoptera: Acridoidea). Bulletin of the California Insect Survey. Volume 10. University of California Press, Berkeley, California.

Stromberg, M. R., and J. R. Griffin. 1996. Long-term patterns in coastal California grasslands in relation to cultivation, gophers and grazing. Ecological Applications 6:1189–1211.

Stromberg, M. R., C. M. D'Antonio, T. P. Young, J. Wirka, and P. R. Kephart. 2007. California grassland restoration. Pages 254–280 in M. R. Stromberg, J. D. Corbin, and C. D'Antonio, editors. California grasslands: Ecology and management. University of California Press, Berkeley, California.

Suding, K. N., S. L. Collins, L. Gough, C. Clark, E. E. Cleland, K. L. Gross, D. G. Milchunas, and S. Pennings. 2005. Functional- and abundance-based mechanisms explain diversity loss due to N fertilization. Proceedings of the National Academy of Sciences USA 102:4387–4392.

Sugden E. A. 1985. Pollinators of *Astragalus monoensis* Barneby (Fabaceae): New host records; potential impact of sheep grazing. Great Basin Naturalist 45:299–312.

Suttle, K. B., and M. A. Thomsen. 2007. Climate change and grassland restoration in California: Lessons from six years of rainfall manipulation in a northern grassland. Madroño 54:225–233.

Suttle, K. B., M. A. Thomsen, and M. E. Power. 2007. Species interactions reverse species responses to climate change. Science 315:640–642.

Tate, K. W., E. R. Atwill, J. W. Bartolome, and G. Nader. 2006. Significant *Escherichia coli* attenuation by vegetative buffers on annual grasslands. Journal of Environmental Quality 35:795–805.

Tate, K. W., R. A. Dahlgren, M. J. Singer, B. Allen-Diaz, and E. R. Atwill. 1999. On California rangeland watersheds: Timing, frequency of sampling affect accuracy of water quality monitoring. California Agriculture 53:44–48.

Thompson, D. J., and D. G. Stout. 1996. Influence of sowing rate on dry matter yield, plant density and survival of Lucerne (*Medicago sativa*) under dryland and irrigated conditions. Journal of Agricultural Science 126:301–306.

Tierney, T., and J. H. Cushman. 2006. Temporal changes in native and exotic vegetation and soil characteristics following disturbances by feral pigs in a California grassland. Biological Invasions 8:1073–1089.

Tilman, D., and J. A. Downing. 1994. Biodiversity and stability in grasslands. Nature 367:363–365.

Treseder, K. K., J. P. Schimel, M. Garcia, M. D. Whiteside. 2010. Slow turnover and production of fungal hyphae during a California dry season. Soil Biology and Biochemistry 42:1657–1660.

Turnbull, L. A., M. J. Crawley, and M. Rees. 2000. Are plant populations seed-limited? A review of seed sowing experiments. Oikos 88:225–238.

Tyler, C. M., D. C. Odion, and R. M. Callaway. 2007. Dynamics of woody species in the California grasslands. Pages 169–179 in M. R. Stromberg, J. D. Corbin, and C. D'Antonio, editors. California grasslands: Ecology and management. University of California Press, Berkeley, California.

Vaughn, C. E., D. M. Center, and M. B. Jones. 1986. Seasonal fluctuations in nutrient availability in some northern California annual range soils. Soil Science 141:43–51.

Veihmeyer, F. J. 1953. Use of water by native vegetation versus grasses and forbes in watersheds. American Geophysical Union Transactions. 34:201–212.

Vivrette, N., and C. H. Miller. 1977. Mechanisms of invasion and dominance of coastal grasslands by *Mesembryanthemum crystallinum*. Ecological Monographs 47:301–318.

Vogelsang, K. M., and J. D. Bever. 2009. Mycorrhizal densities decline in association with nonnative plants and contribute to plant invasion. Ecology 90:399–407.

Waldrop, M. P., and M. K. Firestone. 2006. Seasonal dynamics of microbial community composition and function in oak canopy and open grassland soils. Microbial Ecology 52:470–479.

Weiss, S. B. 2006. Impacts of nitrogen deposition on California ecosystems and biodiversity. CEC-500-2005-165. PIER Energy-Related Environmental Research. California Energy Commission, Sacramento, California.

———. 1999. Cars, cows, and checkerspot butterflies: Nitrogen deposition and management of nutrient-poor grasslands for a threatened species. Conservation Biology 13:1478–1486.

Wigand, P. 2007. Late quaternary paleoecology of grasslands and other grassy habitats. Pages 37–48 in M. R. Stromberg, J. D. Corbin, and C. D'Antonio, editors. California grasslands: Ecology and management. University of California Press, Berkeley, California.

Winsome, T. 2003. Native and exotic earthworms in California oak savanna. Dissertation. University of Georgia, Athens, Georgia.

Winsome, T., L. Epstein, P. F. Hendrix, and W. R. Horwath. 2006. Competitive interactions between native and exotic earthworm species as influenced by habitat quality in a California grassland. Applied Soil Ecology 32:38–53.

Wood, H., V. Moore, C. Fenter, M. Culpepper, J. Nicolloff, and J. Hafernick. 2005. Bee diversity in restored habitats in the Presidio San Francisco. Presidio Trust, San Francisco, California.

Woodmansee, R., and D. Duncan. 1980. Nitrogen and phosphorus dynamics and budgets in annual grasslands. Ecology 61:893–904.

Xiang, S., A. Doyle, P. A. Holden, J. P. Schimel. 2008. Drying and rewetting effects on C and N mineralization and microbial activity in surface and subsurface California grassland soils. Soil Biology and Biochemistry 40:2281–2289.

Xu, L., and D. D. Baldocchi. 2004. Seasonal variation in carbon dioxide over a Mediterranean annual grassland in California. Agriculture and Forest Meteorology 1232:79–96.

Young, J. A., and R. A. Evans. 1989. Seed production and germination dynamics in California annual grasslands. Pages 39–45 in L. F. Huenneke and H. A. Mooney, editors. Grassland structure and function: California annual grassland. Kluwer Academic Publishers, Dordrecht, The Netherlands.

Young, J., R. Evans, C. Raguse, and J. Larson. 1981. Germinable seeds and periodicity of germination in annual grasslands. Hilgardia 49:1–37.

Zavaleta, E. S., M. R. Shaw, N. R. Chiariello, B. D. Thomas, E. E. Cleland, C. B. Field, and H. A. Mooney. 2003. Grassland responses to three years of elevated temperature, CO_2, precipitation, and N deposition. Ecological Monographs 73:585–604.

Zedler, P. H., and C. Black. 1992. Seed dispersal by a generalized herbivore: Rabbits as dispersal vectors in a semiarid California vernal pool landscape. American Midland Naturalist 128:1–10.

TWENTY-FOUR

Chaparral

V. THOMAS PARKER, R. BRANDON PRATT, and JON E. KEELEY

Introduction

One of the most dynamic California ecosystems is chaparral. Dominated by evergreen, SCLEROPHYLLOUS shrubs and small trees, chaparral is the most extensive vegetation type in the state (Figure 24.1). The nearly impenetrable tangle of stiff branches of this unusual vegetation inhibits exploration, and as a consequence the public know little about its natural history and unique characteristics. This undervalued ecosystem is recognized instead by the threat of its extensive, high-intensity canopy-burning wildfires that characterize the dry summer and fall seasons of the state. Because urban areas frequently share borders or intermix with chaparral, societal interests often conflict with conservation of this ecosystem, and understanding its history and dynamics are key to appreciating its importance.

Chaparral contains numerous plants and animals found in no other habitat, and many of them are rare and threatened. A large number of environmental and biotic influences drive this diversity, but three primary ones are the protracted summer rainless period of California's Mediterranean-type climate, low-nutrient, and often shallow and rocky soils, and a fire regime that completely burns the vegetation one or more times a century. Within the widespread distribution of chaparral, different combinations of these processes produce locally unique combinations of species, including more than one hundred evergreen shrub species across this range (Wells 1962, Keeley and Keeley 1988, Sawyer and Keeler-Wolf 1995). Many associations are named based on the dominant species, such as manzanita chaparral (*Arctostaphylos* sp.), chamise-redshank chaparral (*Adenostoma* sp.), or mixed chaparral (Sawyer and Keeler-Wolf 1995). Others are named based on the soils, such as serpentine and dune chaparral, or based on the climatic location, such as maritime chaparral (Griffin 1978) and montane chaparral (Hanes 1977) (Figure 24.2). In all these variations the overall character and dynamics of the vegetation are directly related to strong summer droughts, low-nutrient soils, and wildfire.

The extensive spatial distribution of chaparral means that stands reflect different climatic extremes and interact with different plant assemblages. At lower elevations, for example, the vegetation includes not only the dominant shrubs, but also a postfire flora that persists only a few years after fire. These annuals and short-lived perennials arise phoenix-like after wildfires, blanketing the landscape in colorful displays and subsequently remaining dormant as seeds in soil until the next fire. In more northerly distributions in the coast ranges, chaparral intergrades with mixed evergreen and conifer forests, sometimes as a patchwork, often as successional vegetation. Cold temperatures become important at higher elevations and in cold-air drainage basins (Ewers et al. 2003). For example, chamise drops out at high elevations in interior Sierra Nevada drainages (Westman 1991) and in Arizona chaparral (Mooney and Miller 1985). At higher elevations, especially in the Sierra Nevada and Cascades, a variant referred to as montane chaparral dominates in patches in areas above the winter snowline. While sharing dominant genera and other dynamics with chaparral of lower elevation, this mountain chaparral contains unique species and lacks familiar components like the diverse, postfire herbaceous plant response.

Besides the characteristic plants, chaparral contains numerous other organisms of which some are restricted or nearly so to chaparral. These include small rodents like woodrats (*Neotoma* sp.) and mice (e.g., *Peromyscus californicus*) as well as birds (e.g., wrentit and Bewick's wren). Animals are involved in a variety of interactions, from dispersal of seed by scatter-hoarding rodents and birds to herbivory and seed predation. Animal activity can be critical for the success of some plants (e.g., Parker 2010) or shift the plant composition of areas (Quinn 1994, Moreno and Oechel 1993, Ramirez et al. 2012). Less studied are other vertebrates and insects (Andres and Connor 2003, Miller 2005) and the soil biota, even though soil nutrients are often limiting to primary production and MYCORRHIZAE influence vegetation dynamics (Horton et al. 1999, Dunne and Parker 1999, Treseder and Allen 2000, Egerton-Warburton et al. 2007).

In this chapter we emphasize the principal structure and dynamics of this important ecosystem. The long, summer rainless period has strong impacts on all organisms and on the fire regime that characterizes chaparral. These features make significant impacts from climate change very likely. Attempts to suppress fire also affect chaparral dynamics. Because of its dominance at lower elevations, chaparral also frequently occurs at or near the boundaries of urban developments and metropolitan centers. Conflicts between the impacts of chaparral wildfire and human activities and structures have occurred throughout California's history but have increased as development encroaches ever more into chaparral regions. Consequently, understanding of chaparral ecology is important not only because of its significance in understanding ecological evolution and ecological services provided by chaparral but also because of its direct impacts on human communities.

Geography of Chaparral

Chaparral covers much of the Peninsular, Transverse, and Coastal Ranges and portions of the Sierra Nevada and Cascade Ranges. This represents over 9% of the wildland vegetation in California, with most of it below 2,000 meters in elevation (see recent reviews by Keeley 2000, Davis, Stoms, et al. 1998, Keeley and Davis 2007) (see Figure 24.1). Chaparral is particularly abundant in the mountains of southern California, which contain over a third of all chaparral found in that region (Davis, Stoms, et al. 1998), especially on the slopes of the Peninsular and Transverse Ranges (Cooper 1922, Epling and Lewis 1942). Chaparral extends south into northwest Baja California, with disjunct populations on mountainslopes as far south as 28°. Coastal mountain ranges are dominated by chaparral at most elevations in southern California but form mosaics with oak woodlands and conifer forest from central California northward.

Throughout its range, chaparral is often replaced by localized patches of grassland. This is sometimes due to moisture and edaphic characteristics but more often due to disturbance (Wells 1962) (see Figure 24.2). North of the San Francisco Bay region, chaparral dominance shifts inland and progressively diminishes to widely scattered patches on interior slopes as far north as Washington State. The foothills of the Sierra Nevada and the southern Cascades similarly are covered by chaparral at elevations generally above 300 meters, giving way to forest with increasing precipitation at higher elevations (Keeley, Baer-Keeley et al. 2005). Within the upper-elevation forest regions, chaparral appears on serpentine or other low-nutrient or shallow soils or after wildfires (Cooper 1922) (see Figure 24.2) and may persist as a consequence of self-reinforcing, high-intensity wildfires. Eastward, chaparral forms disjunct patches in mountainous areas in Arizona with particularly large chaparral landscapes above the Mogollan Rim in the middle of the state (Knipe et al. 1979). Some chaparral species form stands in areas of Arizona and Mexico with a summer rainfall regime (Vankat 1989; Bhaskar et al. 2007; Keeley, Fotheringham et al. 2012).

Stands dominated by chamise (*Adenostoma fasciculatum*) are the most abundant type of chaparral in California (Hanes 1977). Chamise often forms nearly pure stands on hot and dry slopes that are generally equatorial-facing with shallow soils. In chamise stands, other common subdominant species are manzanitas (*Arctostaphylos* spp.) and ceanothus (or California lilac; *Ceanothus* spp.) along with various sage scrub species (e.g. *Salvia* spp. and *Artemisia californica*). Coastal and montane areas may also be dominated by nearly pure stands of ceanothus or manzanita species. On more mesic slopes and in deeper soils within a site, chaparral can contain a broader range of dominant evergreen species (Hanes 1971).

Chaparral gives way to other plant associations based on water availability, temperature, soil, aspect, and elevation. At drier, low-elevation sites in nondesert areas, chaparral is replaced by sage scrub species (see Chapter 22, "Coastal Sage Scrub"). In valley bottoms with deeper soils, chaparral is replaced by oak savannas. In some cases, this transition can also be related to cold air drainage and freezing temperatures (Ewers et al. 2003, Pratt et al. 2005), animal activity (e.g., pocket gophers), or fire regime. Replacement by oak woodlands also occurs at higher elevations throughout the range of chaparral, which is generally attributed to greater rainfall. On more mesic sites, in the northern part of the state, chaparral gives way to an evergreen sclerophyllous woodland dominated by species such as tan-bark oak (*Notholithocarpus densiflorus*; formerly *Lithocarpus d.*), California bay laurel (*Umbellularia californica*), oaks, and madrone (*Arbutus menziesii*) (Cooper 1922). On desert-facing slopes, chaparral forms ecotones with Mojave desert scrub communities in the Transverse and Coast Ranges and with Sonoran desert shrub communities in the Peninsular Range and is replaced by these desert communities at more arid, lower elevations.

Photo on previous page: Santa Monica Mountains (Los Angeles County); chamise and redshank (*Adenostoma fasciculatum* and *A. sparsifolium*) with big-pod ceanothus in bloom (*Ceanothus megacarpus*). Photo: R. Brandon Pratt.

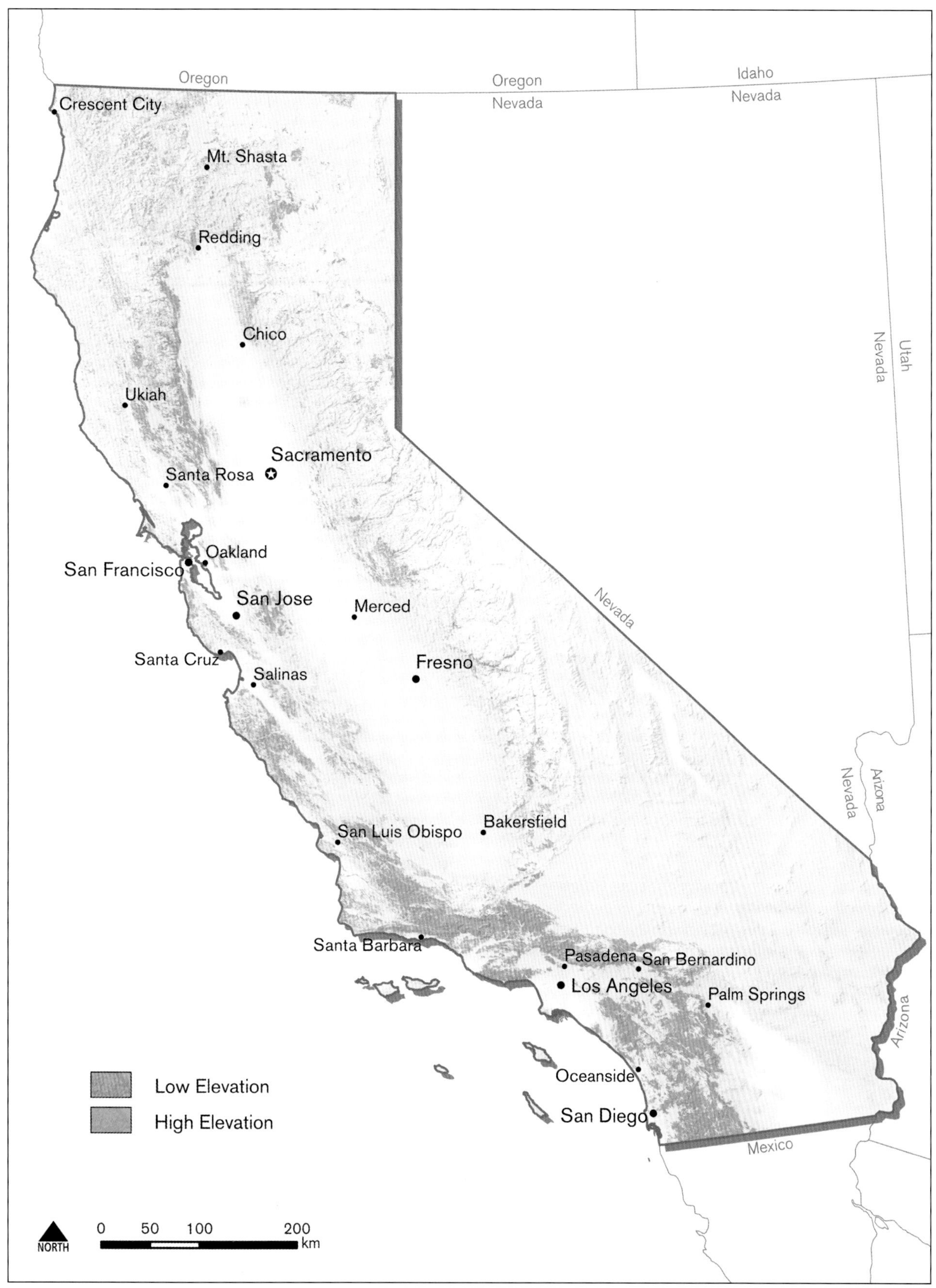

FIGURE 24.1 Distribution of chaparral vegetation in California. Data from Cal Fire, Fire Resource and Assessment Program (FRAP). Map: P. Welch, Center for Integrated Spatial Research (CISR).

FIGURE 24.2 Examples of variation in chaparral vegetation. Photos: V. Thomas Parker.

A Chamise-dominated chaparral (*Adenostoma fasciculatum*) with big-berry manzanita (*Arctostaphylos glauca*) as a co-dominant (Santa Lucia Mountains).

B Maritime chaparral in the Santa Cruz Mountains dominated by *Arctostaphylos crustacea, A. andersonii, A. sensitiva, Ceanothus thyrsiflorus,* and *C. papillosus.*

C Chaparral occurs on unusual soils, in this case *A. myrtifolia* and *A. viscida* on Oxisols near Ione, California.

D Montane chaparral patches in the northern Sierra Nevada dominated by *Quercus vaccinifolia, Arctostaphylos patula, A. nevadensis, Chrysolepis sempervirens, Ceanothus cordulatus, C. integerrimus, Prunus emarginata,* and *Spiraea splendens* alternating with *Abies*-dominated forest.

Origins

Most dominant chaparral taxa date to the early Tertiary, with origins in the Eocene (Keeley, Bond et al. 2012). Assemblages with similarities to contemporary chaparral appear to have been present by the early Miocene, although the center of distribution was likely in the interior reaches of the southwestern corner of North America (Ackerly 2009; Keeley, Bond et al. 2012). By the mid-Miocene, chaparral dominants were evident in fossil floras from western Nevada and California, but the extent to which these communities resembled contemporary California chaparral is unknown. For example, contemporary chaparral in Mediterranean-climate California is markedly different from communities in summer-rain Arizona (Keeley, Fotheringham et al. 2012). Although these two different communities share many of the same shrub dominants, these climates have selected for very different postfire herbaceous assemblages. In the Mediterranean-type climate winter annuals dominate the community, whereas in the summer rain region the herbaceous community is dominated by perennials with a substantial contribution of C_4 grasses. Thus, while shrub dominants appear to have very early Tertiary origins, the origin of contemporary California chaparral assemblages is likely tied to the origin of the Mediterranean-type climate. The timing of this event is a matter of some debate. Axelrod (1973) has long contended that the Mediterranean-type climate was late in development, dating from the Pliocene or early Pleistocene. Others argue that this summer-drought climate originated much earlier and was in place in western Nevada and south-central California by mid-Miocene (Keeley, Bond et al. 2012; see Chapter 2, "Climate").

Evergreen sclerophyllous leaves occurred in lineages before the onset of the Mediterranean-type climate, suggesting that this feature of Mediterranean-type shrubs was not an adaptive response to that climate per se (Axelrod 1989, Verdú et al. 2003, Ackerly 2004a). Some have interpreted these sclerophyll taxa as relicts of Tertiary origins present today merely by chance avoidance of random extinctions rather than because they are adapted to contemporary environments (Herrera 1992, Valiente-Banuet et al. 2006). Others see a clear adaptive role for these taxa in the current landscape (Keeley, Pausas et al. 2012). Adaptive traits, however, are not necessarily adaptations, which are traits that have arisen via natural selection in response to a particular environmental factor such as the Mediterranean-type climate (Gould and Lewontin 1979). One view is that physiological and morphological traits in evergreen sclerophylls are adaptations to both water deficits and nutrient-poor soils, conditions present both before and after the widespread development of a Mediterranean-type climate (Keeley, Bond et al. 2012). In this model, the primary influence of the Mediterranean-type climate has not been through selection on these traits but rather has contributed to a massive expansion of suitable sites for these drought-adapted shrubs. Thus, in this view, many traits in contemporary chaparral shrubs are adaptations to contemporary conditions of periodic soil drought and nutrient-poor soils, but chaparral assemblages reflect sorting processes beginning with the origin of the Mediterranean-type climate (Ackerly 2004a).

Shrublands that resemble chaparral are also widely distributed in four other global regions: the Mediterranean basin, the Cape Region of South Africa, western and southern Australia, and central Chile—all of which share a similar Mediterranean-type climate (however, see Cowling et al. 2005). The geographical and phylogenetic distances of species inhabiting these shrublands, coupled with their similar structure, led early biogeographers to postulate that the common Mediterranean-type climate of these regions spurred convergent evolution of the evergreen sclerophyllous shrub growth form (Schimper 1903). Mooney and Dunn (1970a) extended this conclusion by providing an ecophysiological model to explain the advantage of evergreen sclerophyllous leaves in Mediterranean-type environments. Following this, extensive comparisons between chaparral and the Chilean Mediterranean-type shrublands called *matorral* generally supported the convergence hypothesis (di Castri and Mooney 1973, Miller 1981). More recent fossil evidence showing that many of the ancestral evergreen sclerophyllous species predated the Mediterranean-type climate has been interpreted to mean that the convergence hypothesis is not supported by the widespread presence of evergreen sclerophyllous species in these regions (Axelrod 1989).

Much of this debate is tied to an inordinate emphasis on similarities in the general climatic parameters of winter rain and summer drought evident across the five Mediterranean-type climate regions, rather than on differences among the regions. Evolutionary convergence is predicted when taxa evolve in similar "environments," but each Mediterranean-type climate region exhibits subtle differences in rainfall patterns and not-so-subtle differences in soils and fire regimes that all would be expected to contribute to differences in plant traits and community assemblages (Keeley, Bond et al. 2012). Recent studies of water relations, particularly XYLEM structure and function, have found California chaparral shrubs to be convergent with South African fynbos shrubs when sites were matched (Jacobsen et al. 2009). However, shrubs from the two regions also differ in life history characteristics (Pratt et al. 2012).

Principal Organisms Found in Chaparral

Plants

While many plant species can be found in chaparral, the dominant shrubs that structure of the ecosystem represent a few genera common to most sites throughout the state. Climatic patterns and soil heterogeneity sort local shrub dominance, which in turn modifies ecosystem processes like hydrology and biogeochemistry as well as animal communities. Genera with multiple species, including rare species, include manzanita, ceanothus, shrub oak, and silk tassel bush (*Garrya*) (Table 24.1). Chamise occurs throughout the range of chaparral. California red-shank, a sister taxon (*Adenostoma sparsifolium*), sporadically joins chamise from Santa Barbara County south, mostly away from the coast. Other important genera that are monotypic or have only a few species include mountain mahogany (*Cercocarpus*), cherry (*Prunus*), coffee berry (*Frangula*), sugar or lemonade bush (*Rhus*), toyon (*Heteromeles arbutifolia*), chaparral pea (*Pickeringia montana*), and laurel sumac (*Malosma laurina*).

Trees commonly associated with chaparral in some areas are usually species of pine (*Pinus*), cypress (*Hesperocyparis*), oaks, and big-cone Douglas-fir (*Pseudotsuga macrocarpa*). The species of pines and cypress in chaparral are generally SEROTINOUS (e.g., knobcone pine, Sargent's cypress) or semiserotinous, with slow-dispersing, heavy, thick cones (e.g., ghost, Coulter, or torrey pine). Stands of these trees are open with a dense chaparral understory or mosaic. In more mesic regions other tree species also found in adjacent mixed evergreen or coniferous forests can intergrade with chaparral. In southern California big-cone Douglas-fir is commonly found in chaparral from Santa Barbara County to San Diego County. Coast live oak (*Quercus agrifolia*) and sometimes other oaks can also invade chaparral; in some maritime associations coast live oak is a co-dominant of the chaparral.

While chaparral contains a highly diverse component of annuals and herbaceous perennials, with few exceptions older stands of chaparral lack significant herbaceous cover (Hanes 1981). This is generally because most of these species have deep seed dormancy that requires stimulation from wildfire (Sweeney 1956). For other annuals and many herbaceous perennials lacking this dormancy, growth is limited by significant herbivory from chaparral animals or by limited resources (Mooney and Dunn 1970a, Christensen and Muller 1975, Swanck and Oechel 1991). Nevertheless, postfire stands of chaparral are often dominated by diverse herbaceous annuals and perennials for several years before shrubs regain dominance (Table 24.2).

Chaparral also contains a number of SUFFRUTESCENT shrubs whose presence or absence depends upon a number of factors. They are common in postfire stands because some or all of their SEED BANKS are responsive to wildfire. However, these plants may persist long afterwards in more open conditions, such as in rockier habitats, along trails, in poor soil conditions such as in serpentine, or along the edges of drier systems like deserts or coastal scrub. While frequent or common in chaparral systems, these shrubs sometimes dominate adjacent plant communities.

Mycota and Other Microbiota

Chaparral harbors considerable diversity of fungi and microbes, but little is known about individual species or their overall ecological impacts. These organisms play key roles in decomposition, nitrogen fixation, and mineral cycling, and some are pathogens of dominant plants. Experiments indicate that they are critical in many ecosystem processes and can be affected by wildfire (Horton et al. 1998, Stoll 1998, Baar et al. 1999, Peay et al. 2009) and increased atmospheric CO_2 (Allen et al. 2005).

Surveys of MYCOTA and DNA fingerprinting indicate that chaparral stands can have a high diversity of mycota (Bradford 1998, Blair 1999). Over 134 taxa of fungi in 33 families and 17 orders were found beneath stands of manzanita (Blair 1999); 5 fungal families had the highest representation, including 2 familiar as boletes or amanitas. Almost all of these species are thought to form mycorrhizal relationships with plant hosts. In another study that sampled manzanita root tips, diversity of mycorrhizal fungi was extremely high (Bradford 1998). Within chaparral, species of pines, manzanitas, and shrub oaks all associate with ECTOMYCORRHIZAE and as a consequence might facilitate successional dynamics from shrub- to forest-dominated sites (Amaranthus and Perry 1994, Horton et al. 1999, Dunne and Parker 1999, Bode 1999). Other plant genera associate with ARBUSCULAR MYCORRHIZAE, usually with taxa in the

TABLE 24.1
Common plants in California chaparral

Species	Common name	Notes	Occurrence and distribution	Life history
TREES				
Pinus	Pine	Especially *P. attenuata, P. radiata, P. muricata, P. sabiniana*		Serotinous or slow seed dispersal (semiserotinous)
Hesperocyparis (formerly *Cupressus*)	Cypress	Especially *H. sargentii, H. macnabiana*		Serotinous
Quercus agrifolia	Coast live oak	Most common oak found in chaparral	Coast ranges from San Francisco Bay region south	Obligate sprouter
Pseudotsuga macrocarpa	Big-cone Douglas-fir		Occasional in southern California mountains	Obligate sprouter
SHRUBS				
Adenostoma sp.	Chamise	Especially *A. fasciculatum*	Common and widespread	Facultative seeder
Arctostaphylos sp.	Manzanita	96 taxa in California; many rare	Common and widespread, especially in more mesic ranges	Facultative seeder or obligate seeder
Ceanothus sp.	California lilac; buckbrush; etc.	60 taxa in California; many rare	Common and widespread, mostly chaparral	Facultative seeder or obligate seeder
Quercus sp.	Scrub oak	Especially *Q. berberidifolia, Q. durata, Q. vaccinifolia, Q. wislizenii var. frutescens*	Common and widespread	Obligate sprouter
Heteromeles arbutifolia	Toyon		Common and widespread	Obligate sprouter
Pickeringia montana	Chaparral pea			Obligate sprouter
Garrya sp.	Silk tassel	Especially *G. elliptica, G. fremontii, G. veatchii*	Frequent	Obligate sprouter
Prunus sp.	Holly-leaved cherry	Especially *P. ilicifolia, P. emarginata, P. subcordata*	Frequent, southern California to southern North Coast ranges, deciduous species at high elevation	Obligate sprouter
Frangula sp. (formerly *Rhamnus*)	Coffee berry	Especially *F. californica, F. rubra*	Widespread and frequent	Obligate sprouter
Cercocarpus sp.	Mountain mahogany	Especially *C. betuloides*	Widespread	Obligate sprouter
Rhus sp.	Sugar berry, Lemonade bush	Especially *R. ovata, R. integrifolia*	Mostly southern California	Obligate sprouter or facultative seeder
Malosma laurina			Southern California	Obligate sprouter

SOURCE: Sweeney 1956, Keeley and Keeley 1988, Soule et al. 1988, Keeley, Fotherington, and Baer-Keeley 2005.

fungal genera *Acaulospora*, *Glomus*, *Gigaspora*, or *Scutellospora* (Allen et al. 1999). Chamise, in the rose family, appears to associate with mycorrhizae that are usually arbuscular; it has also been observed associating with ectomycorrhizae that include seven different mushrooms or cup fungi (Allen et al. 1999). Other members of the rose family appear to also produce both types of mycorrhizae (Smith and Read 1997).

The roles of microbes in chaparral, though relatively poorly understood, undoubtedly play a critical role in a number of ecosystem functions. For example, mycorrhizae can produce extensive hyphal networks that can link multiple individual plants. While mycorrhizae generally are the principal pathway for mineral uptake, these networks also have been implicated in the survival of seedlings through summer drought (Horton et al. 1999, Dunne and Parker 1999, Egerton-Warburton et al. 2003, Egerton-Warburton et al. 2007, Plamboeck et al. 2007). Nitrogen cycling within vegetation is regulated largely by microbial communities, both bacterial and fungal

TABLE 24.2
Representative plants found in postfire chaparral areas in California

Species	Family	Range
COMMON POSTFIRE ANNUALS		
Chaenactis artemisiifolia	Asteraceae	Common, southern California
Emmenanthe penduliflora	Boraginaceae	Common
Phacelia brachyloba	Boraginaceae	Frequent
Phacelia parryi	Boraginaceae	Common, southern California
Phacelia grandiflora	Boraginaceae	Common, southern California
Phacelia cicutaria	Boraginaceae	Common, southern California
Phacelia minor	Boraginaceae	Common, southern California
Phacelia suaveolens	Boraginaceae	Common, northern California
Eucrypta chrysanthemifolia	Boraginaceae	Frequent
Cryptantha microstachys	Boraginaceae	Common
Silene coniflora	Caryophyllaceae	Frequent
Lupinus succulentus	Fabaceae	Occasional
Lupinus bicolor	Fabaceae	Common
Acmispon maritimus	Fabaceae	Occasional
Salvia apiana	Lamiaceae	Frequent, central, southern California
Salvia columbariae	Lamiaceae	Common
Calandrinia ciliata	Montiaceae	Common
Calyptridium monandrum	Montiaceae	Common, central, southern California
Eulobus californicus (Camissonia)	Onagraceae	Common, central, southern California
Ehrendorferia chrysantha (Dicentra)	Papaveraceae	Common, northern California
Ehrendorferia ochraleuca (Dicentra)	Papaveraceae	Common, southern California
Papaver californicum	Papaveraceae	Occasional
Romneya coutleri	Papaveraceae	Occasional, southern California
Antirrhinum coulterianum	Plantaginaceae	Common, southern California
Allophyllum glutinosum	Polemoniaceae	Frequent, central, southern California
Gilia capitata	Polemoniaceae	Common
Saltugilia australis (Gilia)	Polemoniaceae	Frequent, southern California
Chorizanthe fimbriata	Polygonaceae	Frequent, southern California
COMMON SUFFRUTESCENTS		
Artemisia californicum	Asteraceae	Common
Baccharis pilularis	Asteraceae	Common, esp. northern California
Ericameria arborescens	Asteraceae	Common, northern California
Eriodictyon californicum	Boraginaceae	Common, central, northern California
Eriodictyon crassifolium	Boraginaceae	Common, southern California
Helianthemum scoparium	Cistaceae	Common
Acmispon glaber (Lotus scoparius)	Fabaceae	Common
Lepichinia calycina	Lamiaceae	Common, northern California

(continued)

TABLE 24.2 *(continued)*

Species	Family	Range
COMMON SUFFRUTESCENTS		
Salvia mellifera	Lamiaceae	Common, southern California
Mimulus aurantiacus	Phyrmaceae	Common
Eriogonum fasciculatum	Polygonaceae	Common, southern California

SOURCES: Sweeney 1956, Keeley and Keeley 1988, Soule et al. 1988, Keeley, Fotherington, and Baer-Keeley 2005.

(Grogan et al. 2000). Increases in atmospheric CO_2 concentrations appear to increase the importance of microbial regulation of nitrogen (Allen et al. 2005), as elevated CO_2 increases nitrogen deficiency in chaparral soils.

Chaparral Animals

Invertebrate diversity in chaparral is thought to be considerable, but relatively few studies have been conducted at the community level. Invertebrates are a key component of ecosystem processes of mineral and energy flow as DETRITIVORES and FOLIVORES. Also, most chaparral plants are pollinated by a diversity of insects (Mosquin 1971, Fulton and Carpenter 1979). Other invertebrates are key members of food webs as parasitoids and predators and in other trophic roles. One study of a single montane chaparral species, green-leaf manzanita, found over 500 arthropod taxa from 169 different families in 19 orders (Valenti et al. 1997). About 80% of these species were herbivores, predators, or parasitoids. Another study investigated insects associated with leaves and branches of 26 coastal manzanita species and found over 209 insect taxa, with over 85% of them folivores (Andres and Connor 2003). They found a density of approximately 350 individuals m^{-2} for just leaf miners, leaf gallers, sap-suckers, and chewing insects. These studies indicate the importance of small insects and other arthropods in energy and mineral cycling of chaparral food webs. Chaparral also is a habitat in which many insect lineages have evolved (Miller and Crespi 2003). For example, one aphid genus (*Tamallia*) has radiated on species of manzanita (Miller 1998a, 1998b).

Chaparral also harbors a large number of vertebrates, from mammals like woodrats, chipmunks, and harvest mice (Table 24.3) and birds (Table 24.4) like Bewick's wren and the wrentit to a variety of common reptiles like the western fence lizard (*Scleroporus occidentalis*) and the Pacific rattlesnake (*Crotalus viridis*). These animals are generally granivores (seed eaters), herbivores, insectivores, or other types of predators that modify and extend the food web found within chaparral. Because of their size and density, such animals can significantly influence the dominance and frequency of certain plants (Quinn 1994, Mills 1983, Frazer and Davis 1988). For example, grazing by deer or rodents in the first several years after fire tends to differentially impact certain plant species, shifting their dominance (Mills 1983, Quinn 1994, Frazer and Davis 1988, Ramirez et al. 2012). Seed predators can limit seed input to seed banks (Keeley and Hays 1976, Kelly and Parker 1990, Quinn 1994, O'Neil and Parker 2005, Warzecha and Parker 2014). On the other hand, scatter-hoarding rodents may be critical in the burial of seed for many PERSISTENT SEED BANK species, burying them deep enough to permit survival of high temperature wildfires (Parker 2010).

Life Histories and Wildfire

Fires are a natural and critical ecosystem process in chaparral. Chaparral dynamics correspond to cycles of wildfire, postfire recovery, and stand maturation. Chaparral is resilient to fires at 30 to 150+ year intervals, and within this range communities quickly return to prefire conditions. This occurs because all components of the prefire state are present after fire and because colonization plays a limited role in reestablishing vegetation (Hanes 1971). Of critical importance is that chaparral is adapted to a particular fire regime of a range of frequency, intensity, and timing (see Chapter 3, "Fire as an Ecosystem Process"). A departure from the natural fire regime, either by excluding fire or adding too much fire, reduces the sustainability of this ecosystem (Zedler et al. 1983, Parker 1990, Zedler 1995, Parker and Pickett 1998, Jacobsen et al. 2004, Keeley et al. 2005a, Keeley et al. 2005b).

Postfire plant regeneration involves dormant seed banks that germinate after fire and resprouting from persistent stem bases and lignotubers (Parker and Kelly 1989). Consequently, fire size often does not affect community recovery. Rather, an appropriate fire regime that allows stands to recover and begin reproduction is critical. Because canopy fires typify chaparral, intensity and heat penetration into the soil vary with temperature, wind, soil, and fuel moisture prior to the fire, as well as aspect, exposure, and other characteristics. Heat penetration into the soil critically influences outcomes because many plant species recover from seed in the soil that must survive heat pulses (e.g., Odion and Davis 2000, Odion and Tyler 2002).

Different types of seed banks can be found among chaparral plants. They illustrate a range of adaptations based on the type and degree of seed dormancy. Species with seeds that lack any type of long-term dormancy and germinate within a year are described as having TRANSIENT SEED BANKS. For these species a period of time exists when no seed reserve is found in the soil. Should a wildfire occur during that time period, the population will be eliminated unless some other life history stage can survive the fire. Species with more extensive seed dormancy, barring predation, always have seeds present in the soil. These are referred to as having persistent seed banks, whose crucial characteristic is that a reserve of seed is typically available. Trees found in chaparral often have serotinous cones, considered a persistent canopy or aerial seed bank.

TABLE 24.3
Common mammals found in chaparral areas in California

Species	Common name	Taxonomic subgroups	Occurrence in chaparral
LARGE MAMMALS			
Puma concolor	Mountain lion		Occasional
Lynx rufus	Bobcat		Common
Odocoileus hemionus	Mule deer		Common, esp. postfire
Canis latrans	Coyote		Common
Taxidea taxus	Badger		Occasional postfire
Procyron lotor	Raccoon		Occasional postfire
Urocyron cineroargenteus	Gray fox		Occasional
SMALL MAMMALS			
Tamias sp.	Chipmunks	Especially *T. merriami, T. sonomae T. quadrimaculatus,*	Frequent, common at higher elevations
Spermophilus sp.	Ground squirrel	Especially *S. lateralis, S. beecheyi*	
Sylvilagus sp.	Brush rabbit	Especially *S. bachmanii and S. audobonii*	Common
Lepus sp.	Jackrabbit	*L. californicus*	Common
Chaetodipus sp.	Pocket mouse	Especially *C. californicus and C. fallax*	Frequent, especially in southern California
Dipodomys sp.	Kangaroo rat	*D. venustus, D. agilis, D. heermanni*	Coastal Ranges
Neotoma sp.	Woodrats	Especially *N. fuscipes, N. lepida*	Common
Peromycus sp.	Deer mouse	Especially. *P. maniculatus, P. boylii, P. californicus*	Common
Reithrodontomys sp.	Harvest mouse	Especially *R. megalotis*	Frequent
Perognathus californicus			
Microtus sp.	Vole	Especially *M. californicus*	Frequent postfire

SOURCES: Based on Lawrence 1966, Fellers 1994, Price et al. 1995, Schwilk and Keeley 1998, Laakkonen 2003.

Characteristic postfire annuals (or PYRO-ENDEMICS) and suffrutescents usually produce a wholly or partially dormant, persistent soil seed bank that responds to wildfire by losing dormancy and germinating in the next growing season (Sweeney 1956, Hanes 1977, Keeley 1991). Dormant seed banks of these species are triggered by either intense heat shock or combustion products from smoke or charred wood (e.g., Keeley 1991, Keeley and Fotheringham 2000). Their relative dominance depends on site history and the rainfall and temperature pattern of the initial postfire year, but generally their cover is significant and they continue to expand their populations into the second year. Consequently, chaparral typically has the highest plant diversity in the first and second years after fire (Sweeney 1956, Keeley et al. 2005a). Plant diversity declines in later years, although this trend may be reversed by very high rainfall in early seral stages (Keeley et al. 2005b). While annuals decline, suffrutescents remain until overtopped by reestablishing sclerophyllous shrubs or trees. Within chaparral, some annuals and suffrutescents typically establish in gaps and tolerate drought and other environmental conditions found in postfire habitats. The substantial restriction of these widespread native annuals and suffrutescents to postfire stands evinces the long history of wildfire shaping plant community dynamics in the Mediterranean-type climate.

Woody plants can be grouped into three general, postfire life history categories based on combinations of seed dormancy and postfire resprouting (Keeley 1987; Keeley, Bond et al. 2012; Parker and Kelly 1989). One cluster of species survives fire as adults; their aboveground stems are killed, but they resprout from stem or root crowns afterwards. Because of their transient seed banks, these species have no postfire seedling recruitment; consequently these types of plants are considered OBLIGATE RESPROUTERS. The seeds and seedling establishment patterns of obligate resprouters reflect no specific response to fire and are similar in reproductive characteristics and patterns to close relatives in other vegetation types. Two groups of plants, however, produce seeds that are dormant at maturity and create persistent soil or aerial canopy seed banks. Their seeds are wholly or principally stimu-

TABLE 24.4
Common birds found in chaparral areas in California

Species	Common name	Occurrence in chaparral
COMMON CHAPARRAL BIRDS		
Callipepla californica	California quail	Common
Thryomanes bewickii	Bewick's wren	Common
Chamaea fasciata	Wrentit	Common
Toxostoma redivivum	California thrasher	Common
Psaltriparus minimus	Bushtit	Frequent
Aphelocoma californica	Western scrub jay	Common
Piplio maculatus	Spotted towhee	Common
Passerina amoena	Lazuli bunting	Occasional
Melozone crissalis	California towhee	Common
Melozone fuscus	Canyon towhee	Frequent
Polioptila californica	California gnatcatcher	Occasional in southern California
Geococcyx californianus	Road runner	Occasional
Calypte costae	Costa's hummingbird	Occasional
Calypte anna	Anna's hummingbird	Occasional
Artemisiospiza belli	Sage sparrow	Occasional
Aimophila ruficeps	Rufous-crowned sparrow	Occasional
Spizella atrogularis	Black-chinned sparrow	Occasional
Zenada macroura	Mourning-dove	Occasional, especially postfire
Columba livia	Rock dove	Occasional, especially postfire
COMMON POSTFIRE PREDATORS		
Buteo jamaicensis	Red-tailed hawk	Occasional postfire
Accipiter cooperii	Cooper's hawk	Occasional postfire
Accipiter striatus	Sharp-shinned hawk	Occasional postfire
Falco sparverius	American kestrel	Occasional postfire
Bubo virginianus	Great horned owl	Occasional postfire
Corvus corax	Raven	Occasional postfire

SOURCES: Based on Lawrence 1966, Soule et al. 1988.

lated by wildfire and they germinate and establish in postfire stands. Of these plants, many can also resprout after fire and are considered FACULTATIVE SEEDERS, reflecting the survival of the adults and the postfire potential for a flush of new recruits. Finally, a third group of species does not resprout after fire, and their adults are killed by fire. Their populations persist exclusively through seed banks and seedling recruitment to reestablish their populations. These types of plants are called OBLIGATE SEEDERS and in California are made up primarily by manzanitas and ceanothus among the shrubs and by pines and cypresses among the trees.

Common obligate resprouters are toyon and shrub oak species (see Table 24.1). Toyon produces fleshy, bright-red, bird-dispersed fruit that mature in early winter. Once deposited in the droppings of birds, toyon seeds generally germinate quickly. The seedlings tolerate the shaded conditions in the understory of a mature chaparral canopy. Similarly, oak acorns mature in the fall and are dispersed by scatter-hoarding birds or rodents; acorns not buried shortly after falling from shrubs dry out and lose viability over a few weeks. The seeds lack complex dormancy mechanisms and germinate following initial fall rains or after STRATIFICATION, resulting in yearly germination under chaparral canopies. Obligate resprouters thus build up small to extensive seedling banks in the understory of older-growth chaparral (e.g., Keeley 1992) and to some extent depend on longer fire-free intervals in chaparral to provide the occasional and necessary canopy gap for seedling emergence.

Facultative and obligate seeders both produce persistent soil seed banks. Such seed banks derive from PHYSIOLOGICAL DORMANCY mechanisms (manzanitas), have thick seed coats that prevent the entry of water until modified by heat pulses (PHYSICAL DORMANCY; ceanothus species), have combinations of physical and physiological dormancy mechanisms (chamise), or retain seeds in thick woody cones that remained closed until opened by age or wildfire (pines and cypresses). In each of these ways, recruitment is restricted to the first year following wildfire. Fire opens canopies, increasing available light energy and soil surface temperature; ashes organic matter, making minerals available; and limits leaf area, reducing overall water loss from the soil by transpiration. These conditions are relatively ideal for seedling establishment in these genera, although the overall success of establishment then depends on survival of summer drought and herbivory.

Woody plants that fall into these seed bank categories predictably reflect other sets of adaptive characteristics. Surveys of chaparral over large regions indicate that chaparral is dominated by species with persistent soil seed banks (facultative and obligate seeders) (Parker and Kelly 1989). Shrubs with persistent seed banks average over 80% cover across both coastal and interior conditions (Vasey et al. 2014). Patterns are occur within sites. Obligate resprouters, for example, are often more mesophytic (moisture loving) and tend to dominate more mesic sites like north-facing slopes or ravines. Obligate seeders and some facultative seeders are more xerophytic (adapted to dry conditions) in structure and dominate drier sites such as ridgelines and south-facing aspects. These persistent seed bank species might also be seen as occupying a gradient of population dynamic responses to fire, from species with adults surviving most wildfires, to species losing a considerable number of adults in fires, to obligate seeders that lose all adults that burn. The trade-offs in retaining some adults vegetatively versus sexually reproducing a cohort of seedlings after a fire lead reflect complex combinations of allocational trade-offs, history, site productivity, spatial and temporal environmental variability at a site, and the frequency with which fire returns.

Organisms besides plants also have to survive wildfire. Wildfires undoubtedly have substantial impacts on microbial communities (Kaminsky 1981), but soils tend to buffer them except in the uppermost levels (Taylor and Bruns 1999). Like many chaparral plants, microbes have resistant stages. For example, fungi build up spore banks containing dormant spores and sclerotia in the soil (Taylor and Bruns 1999, Baar et al. 1999). The heat and ash from wildfires can influence the dominance of particular microbial species in postfire stands, sometimes favoring particular groups of fungi (e.g., Ascomycetes, Stoll 1998) but differentially sorting microbial species based on their ability to tolerate heat and ash (Baar et al. 1999, Izzo et al. 2006, Peay et al. 2009, 2010). Reviews of the roles of soil microbes in ecosystem processes and the influence of wildfire on those soil communities can be found in Neary et al. (1999) and Cairney and Bastias (2007). Animal recovery following fire differs profoundly from plant responses. Most plant taxa regenerate endogenously from dormant seed banks and/or resprouting and are relatively insensitive to fire intensity and fire size (Keeley et al. 2005a). In contrast, many chaparral fauna are far more sensitive to fire behavior characteristics, including fire severity and fire size, as well as the extent to which land management practices have fragmented metapopulations and altered corridors (see Chapter 3, "Fire as an Ecosystem Process").

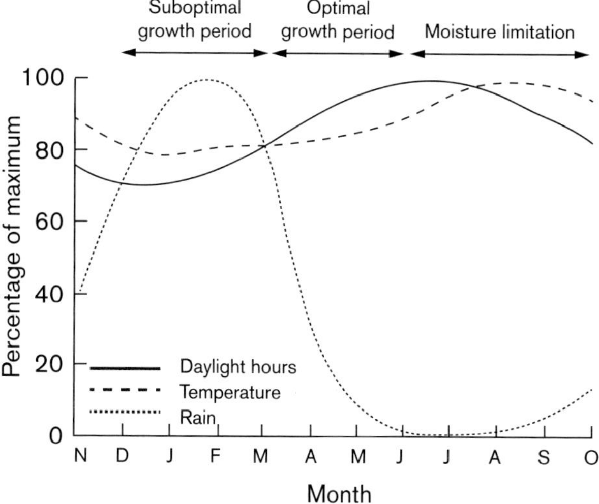

FIGURE 24.3 Seasonality of the Mediterranean-type climate. Seasonal maxima of three key factors are illustrated: daylight hours, temperature, and rain. At top, suboptimal and optimal growth periods for plant growth are represented, followed by the season in which moisture limitation restricts growth potential. Source: Data calculated from long-term average monthly means at the Los Angeles Civic Center (NOAA).

Physiology of Chaparral Shrubs

In the past fifty years, the physiology of evergreen chaparral shrubs has been more intensively studied than that of perhaps any other plant community. Many excellent reviews have been written of chaparral shrub physiology (Mooney and Parsons 1973, Mooney et al. 1977, Miller and Hajek 1981, Mooney and Miller 1985, Carlquist 1989, Field and Davis 1989, Davis, Kolb, and Barton 1988, Keeley 2000). Chaparral shrub physiology is strongly shaped by the seasonality of the Mediterranean-type climate. Winter and spring rains recharge soil moisture, with most of the rain falling when temperatures are cool and days are short. This is the time when growth and photosynthesis of shrubs and ecosystem processes are most active (Figure 24.3). The evolutionary implications of this have not been well explored. Much of the interest in evolution of chaparral taxa has focused on the summer dry season, but many traits (particularly reproductive ones) are tied to winter rains, which likely have been present far longer than dry summers (Keeley, Bond et al. 2012). A second factor affecting chaparral physiology is the recurrent crown fires that occur during the summer or fall. These fires open space for seedlings of obligate seeders, gap specialists with a suite of life history and physiological characters linked to the postfire regeneration niche, to recruit (Figure 24.4). Obligate resprouters, in contrast, recruit seedlings during fire-free intervals and resprout after fire, and their physiology and life history traits diverge from the obligate seeders.

FIGURE 24.4 Abundant seedlings of (left) *Ceanothus megacarpus*, a postfire obligate seeder, and (right) resprouts of chamise (*Adenostoma fasciculatum*). Photos: R. Brandon Pratt.

Growth and Photosynthesis

Vegetative growth of chaparral shrubs is affected by temperature, by photoperiod, and most strongly by available soil moisture (Miller and Hajek 1981, Miller 1983). During the wettest winter months, temperatures and photoperiod are at their lowest, producing suboptimal growth conditions (see Figure 24.3). The peak growing season for most shrubs is in spring, when temperatures and photoperiod rise and soils are still moist (Mooney et al. 1975, Mooney et al. 1977). During the dry summer and autumn months, growth is limited by low soil moisture availability (Davis and Mooney 1986). Timing of flowering diverges among shrubs, with some species flowering in the winter (e.g., big-berry manzanita and big-pod ceanothus), some in the spring (e.g., sugar bush and scrub oak), and still others during the summer and autumn (e.g., chamise and toyon) (Bauer 1936). Winter- and spring-flowering species tend to produce flower buds in the prior year and thus flower on old growth prior to current-year leaf production, whereas summer-flowering species flower on new growth following leaf production.

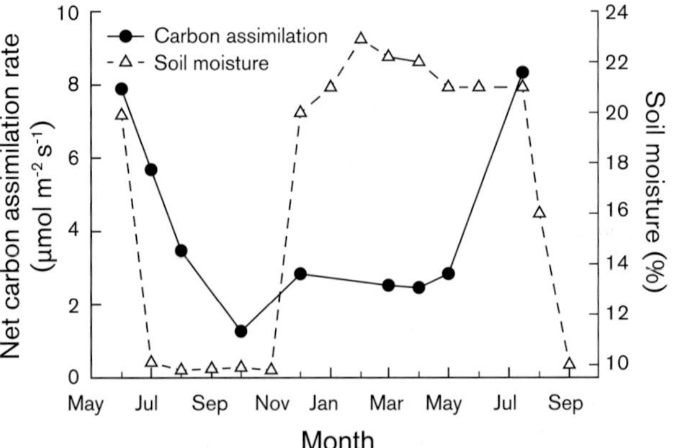

FIGURE 24.5 Seasonal patterns of soil moisture and maximum photosynthesis (carbon assimilation) for a typical chaparral shrub. Unpublished data from a southern California site are for *Rhus ovata* and soil moisture content at 2 meter depth. Source: Modified from Mooney and Dunn 1970b.

The evergreen leaves of chaparral shrubs can photosynthesize year-round, but rates are moderate in the winter and early spring and increase in early summer (Figure 24.5). The chief factors affecting photosynthesis, ordered from most to least important, are available soil moisture, photoperiod, and temperature (Mooney et al. 1975). During the winter-growing season, chaparral species are able to photosynthesize at near-maximum rates over a broad range of temperatures (85% of maximum rates can be achieved between approximately 10°C and 30°C) (Mooney et al. 1975, Oechel et al. 1981). This broad temperature response is adaptive because daily and seasonally temperatures can fluctuate broadly. During the summer and autumn months, shrubs restrict stomatal apertures to conserve water and avoid desiccation, which limits diffusion of CO_2 to chloroplasts. The cool and short days during growing season favor C3 photosynthesis and C4 species virtually absent from chaparral communities (Sage et al. 1999).

Evergreen and deciduous leaf habits represent two different strategies for photosynthetic carbon assimilation. Longer-lived evergreen leaves have lower maximum photosynthetic rates than shorter-lived deciduous ones (Table 24.5). For evergreen chaparral leaves, net carbon gain accrues more slowly over a longer period, whereas deciduous leaves have a faster return rate over a shorter period (Mooney and Dunn 1970b, Harrison et al. 1971, Orians and Solbrig 1977, Field et al. 1983, Field and Mooney 1986, Ackerly 2004b, Wright et al. 2004). Evergreen leaves have lower SPECIFIC LEAF AREA (SLA) and are more sclerophyllous and mechanically stronger and stiffer, providing a more protected and durable leaf with greater longevity than deciduous leaves (Mooney and Dunn 1970b, Balsamo et al. 2003, Wright et al. 2004). In addition, deciduous leaves tend to have higher nitrogen levels and greater SLA (because they are less sclerophyllous) than evergreen leaves.

In more arid sites evergreen chaparral gives way to sage scrub and desert scrub communities dominated by deciduous species. This pattern has been explained in the context of leaf economics (Mooney and Dunn 1970b, Mooney 1989). Because stomatal closure limits evergreen photosynthesis during the dry season, the costs of long-lived evergreen leaves exceed the return they can achieve at sites with more protracted dry seasons such as desert ecotones and coastal areas (Poole and Miller 1981, Mooney 1989). In these more arid sites the net carbon gain of deciduous leaves exceeds evergreens, giving the former a competitive advantage.

TABLE 24.5

Leaf function of deciduous (n=6) and evergreen (n=6) chaparral shrubs grown in a common garden

Leaf habit	Anet area (μmol m^{-2} s^{-1})	Anet mass (μmol kg^{-1} s^{-1})	Nitrogen (%)	Specific leaf area (m^2/kg)	Tensile strength[A] (N/mm^2)
Deciduous	31.5 (3.6)	414.1 (69.1)	4.16 (0.40)	12.71 (0.80)	0.72 (0.15)
Evergreen	23.6 (4.1)	191.5 (3.5)	2.61 (0.16)	8.88 (1.30)	1.45 (0.24)

SOURCE: Pratt, unpublished data.
NOTE: Data are means with 1SE in parentheses.
A. This is the modulus of rupture, or maximum force before breaking per unit leaf cross-sectional area of leaf.

TABLE 24.6

Leaf stress traits: Adaptive leaf traits for coping with the stressful summer and autumn dry season typical of a Mediterranean-type climate

Leaf traits	Function	References
Sclerophyllous leaves	Structural support when turgor is lost and prevention of cell implosion; durability	Oertli et al. 1990, Brodribb and Holbrook 2005, Balsamo et al. 2003
Xeromorphic leaves	Aid in water retention	Cooper 1992
Stomatal response to drying soils	Reduce transpiration	Poole and Miller 1975, Jacobsen et al. 2008
Leaf angling during dry season	Reduce interception of solar radiation; thermal balance; reduced transpiration and photoinhibition	Comstock and Mahall 1985, Ehleringer and Comstock 1989, Valladares and Pearcy 1997, Valiente-Banuet et al. 2010
Heat shock proteins	Aid in stress tolerance	Knight 2010
Xanthophyll cycling and carotenoid accumulation	Protect photosynthetic pigments	Stylinski et al. 2002

Water Stress

The protracted summer/fall rainless season creates hot, dry, and stressful conditions. South-facing slopes are often more arid and dominated by drought-tolerant species such as ceanothus, manzanitas, and chamise. North-facing slopes experience lower evaporation; however, north-facing slopes may dry out more rapidly and to a greater degree than south-facing slopes in mature stands because of a higher leaf area index and stand transpiration (Ng and Miller 1980). The effect of aspect may be especially important after fire when sensitive seedlings and resprouts are in the early establishment stage. Fog along the coast can help to mitigate the summer dry season (Vasey et al. 2012) because fog reduces evapotranspiration, and in some coastal areas because fog drip can lead to significant soil inputs of precipitation (Corbin et al. 2005). In southern California's coastal areas fog inputs to the soil apparently do not provide a significant water source for shrubs (Evola and Sandquist 2010). Chaparral shrubs must cope during the protracted summer and fall rainless season with water stress, high temperature stress, and solar radiation that exceeds photosynthetic needs. The leaves of chaparral shrubs have a host of traits that equip them to manage these stressful conditions (Table 24.6).

Shrubs can be categorized along a continuum by the degree of water stress they experience during an average dry season, which is measured as the minimum seasonal WATER POTENTIAL (Bhaskar and Ackerly 2006). At one end of the continuum are water stress tolerators that experience low water potentials during the dry season because they are relatively shallowly rooted (e.g., some ceanothus and manzanita species) (Hellmers, Horton et al. 1955; Poole and Miller 1975; Miller and Poole 1979; Poole and Miller 1981; Thomas and Davis 1989; Ackerly 2004b; Jacobsen et al. 2007a). At the other end of the continuum are deeply rooted water stress avoiders that experience a narrower range of water potential declines seasonally. This group is exemplified by Anacardiaceae including laurel sumac, sugar bush, lemonade bush (Miller and Poole 1979, Poole and Miller 1981, Thomas and Davis 1989, Jacobsen et al. 2007a). Most species experience water potentials in between the tolerators and avoiders, indicating that they have intermediate rooting depths or those varying from intermediate to deep depending on local edaphic conditions (e.g., chamise, ceanothus, toyon, scrub oak). Even water stress avoiders with deep roots experience a drop in water potential during the dry season, because all shrubs have some roots in shallow soil layers to acquire nutrients (Kummerow, Krause et al. 1978; Marion and Black 1988).

TABLE 24.7
Tolerator/avoider strategies for coping with water stress

Traits	Stress tolerators: *Ceanothus* spp. subgenus Cerastes[A]	Intermediate: *Heteromeles arbutifolia*	Stress avoiders: *Malosma laurina*	References
Maximum rooting depth (m)	2.4	n/a	>13.2	1
Minimum seasonal water potential (MPa)	-6.9	-4.3	-1.8	2, 3
Stem cavitation resistance (MPa)[B]	-9.1	-6.2	-1.6	2, 3
Water potential at stomatal closure (MPa)	-5.5	-3.5	-2.2	4
Turgor loss point (MPa)	-5.6	-4.0	-2.3	5, 6, 7
Density of stem xylem (kg/m3)	674	611	462	2, 8
Stem mechanical Strength (N mm^{-2})	251	238	168	2, 3
Stem xylem starch storage (%)	2.9	3.0	4.8	9
Vessel implosion resistance $(t/b)_h^2$	0.041	0.035	0.019	2, 8
Vessel density (#/mm^2)	244	182	129	10
Vessel diameter (µm)	25	26	53	2, 8
Stem hydraulic efficiency[C]	1.5	2.3	5.7	2

SOURCES: 1. Thomas and Davis 1989; 2. Jacobsen, Pratt, Ewers et al. 2007; 3. Pratt, Jacobsen, Ewers et al. 2007; 4. Poole and Miller 1975; 5. Pratt et al. 2005; 6. Roberts 1982; 7. Calkin and Pearcy 1984; 8. Pratt et al. 2008; 9. Pratt, unpublished data; 10. Anna Jacobsen, unpublished data.

A. Data are from *Ceanothus crassifolius, C. cuneatus, C. gregii,* or *C. megacarpus.* Data taken from references 2, 3, and 8 reported multiple species and data reported here are means.

B. This is water stress–induced cavitation estimated as the water potential causing 50% loss in hydraulic conductivity.

C. This is the maximum stem hydraulic conductivity (in the absence of emboli) divided by the sapwood area (xylem specific conductivity).

Stress tolerators diverge from the avoiders in a suite of traits that allow them to maintain a broader range of physiological function at more negative water potentials (Table 24.7). Key among these is greater resistance to water stress–induced xylem CAVITATION (Kolb and Davis 1994, Davis, Kolb, and Barton 1988, Davis et al. 2002). Cavitation describes the process by which air is pulled into xylem conduits and displaces water with air EMBOLI (Tyree and Sperry 1989). When this happens, emboli reduce flow (hydraulic conductivity) through the vascular system. If emboli occur in many conduits, a positive feedback loop can ensue, leading to runaway cavitation and desiccation of leaves, dieback of branches, or whole plant mortality (Davis et al. 2002, Paddock et al. 2013, Pratt et al. 2008). Species that experience more negative minimum seasonal water potentials have greater cavitation resistance (Davis, Kolb, and Barton 1988; Davis, Ewers et al. 1999; Bhaskar et al. 2007; Jacobsen et al. 2007a; Pratt, Jacobsen, Ewers et al. 2007) (Figure 24.6). Moreover, greater cavitation resistance is correlated with greater survival of drought in chaparral seedlings (Pratt et al. 2008) In mixed stands, co-occurring species often have widely divergent cavitation resistances that reflect differences in access to soil moisture during the dry season and selection that occurs at the seedling stage and during episodic drought (Thomas and Davis 1989, Davis, Kolb, and Barton 1988, Jacobsen et al. 2008).

The only way for plants to recover hydraulic conductivity following cavitation is to refill conduits or regrow new xylem, both of which cannot occur during the protracted dry season when water potentials are low (Kolb and Davis 1994, Williams et al. 1997). Thus, avoiding cavitation by resisting it is the most effective strategy for evergreen shrubs whose leaves require a sustained water supply. Evergreen chaparral shrubs do have greater cavitation resistance of stems than deciduous shrubs that occur in the chaparral community (Figure 24.7). However, deciduous species are not necessarily strict drought avoiders (Gill and Mahall 1986, Jacobsen et al. 2008).

Cavitation and reduced hydraulic conductivity can occur in roots, stems, or leaves, and a process similar to xylem cavitation can occur in the rhizosphere. Among stress tolerators, the rhizosphere's hydraulic conductivity may be most limiting during the dry season because of the high resistance of stems and roots (Davis et al. 2002; Pratt, Jacobsen, Golgotiu et al. 2007). This allows stress tolerators to extract the maximum amount of water from a limited volume of drying soil and also to rapidly resume water and nutrient uptake when winter rain falls (Poole and Miller 1975; Mooney and Rundel 1979; Gill and Mahall 1986; Pratt, Jacobsen, Golgotiu et al. 2007). At least two other traits are important for stress tolerators to maintain physiological function. The leaves of stress tolerators close their stomata at more negative water potentials than the stress avoiders, allowing them to continue to photosynthesize at greater water deficits (Poole and Miller 1975, Miller and Poole 1979, Oechel et al. 1981, Jacobsen et al. 2008). They also have lower turgor loss points than stress avoiders (Roberts 1982). In spite of a lower turgor loss point, stress tolerators lose turgor during the dry season, so it is not avoidance of turgor loss that is important but maintenance of turgor at more negative water potentials and tolerance of turgor loss (Saruwatari and Davis 1989).

Additional traits are associated with the stress-tolerator strategy (see Table 24.7). Stem vascular tissue is denser and mechanically stronger (Wagner et al. 1998, Jacobsen et al.

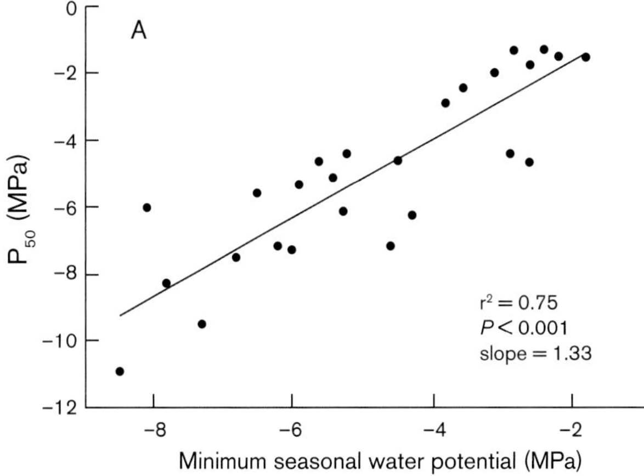

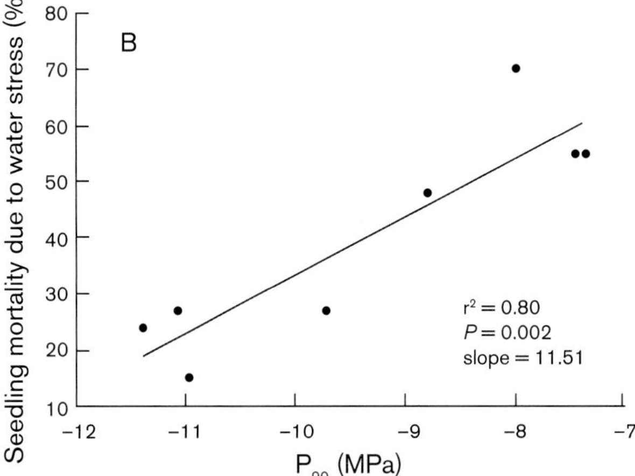

FIGURE 24.6 Species that experience more negative minimum seasonal water potentials have greater cavitation resistance. Source: Data modified from Jacobsen et al. 2007a and Pratt et al. 2008.

A Stem xylem cavitation resistance estimated as the water potential at 50% loss of hydraulic conductivity (P50) plotted against the seasonal low in water potential measured during the peak of the summer rainless period for adult chaparral shrubs.

B Greater cavitation resistance is associated with lower levels of mortality due to water stress for seedlings.

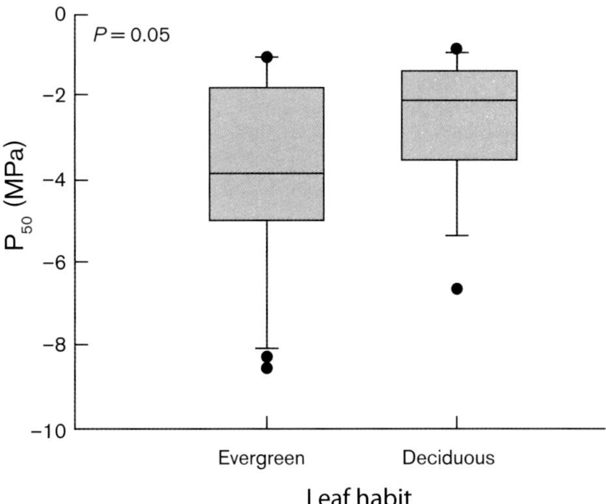

FIGURE 24.7 Stem resistance to cavitation estimated as the water potential at which 50% of conductivity is lost (P50, n=16 for deciduous and n=18 for evergreen). Data are from chaparral shrubs growing at four field sites located in the San Gabriel, Santa Monica, San Bernardino, and the San Jacinto Mountains. Source: R. Brandon Pratt, unpublished data.

2005, Jacobsen et al. 2007a). The vessels of stress tolerators are more resistant to implosion when the xylem is under tension (Jacobsen et al. 2007a; Pratt, Jacobsen, Ewers et al. 2007) and have narrower diameter vessels (Jacobsen et al. 2007a). Shoots of tolerators have lower leaf area per unit sapwood area of their branches (Ackerly 2004b). Finally, the stem xylem of stress tolerators store less carbohydrate than the stress avoiders during the dry season (see Table 24.7). This is hypothesized to be due to the ability of stress tolerators to photosynthesize at more negative water potentials and rely less on stored carbohydrates than stress avoiders (McDowell et al. 2008).

Species dominating the more arid sage scrub and Mojave Desert communities are less resistant to water stress–induced xylem cavitation than chaparral communities (Jacobsen et al. 2007b), even though species in these communities do not differ in minimum seasonal water potential they experience (Jacobsen et al. 2008). The costs associated with greater cavitation resistance may limit cavitation resistance in these species (Pratt, Jacobsen, Ewers et al. 2007). Leaf shedding during dry periods, common among species in the more arid communities, may mitigate water stress compared to evergreen chaparral. However, drought-deciduous species are not necessarily water stress avoiders (Gill and Mahall 1986, Kolb and Davis 1994, Jacobsen et al. 2008). At a Sonoran Desert/chaparral ecotone, some desert species—for example, jujube (*Ziziphus parryi*)—are fully deciduous, quite vulnerable to cavitation, have low water-storage capacity, and experience highly negative water potentials during the dry season, suggesting that their roots remain in contact with dry soils. Perhaps species with this trait combination are able respond to seasonal rains or rain pulses by rapidly refilling xylem conduits and growing new high SLA leaves.

Freezing and Distribution

Freezing temperatures can limit the distribution of frost-sensitive species at higher elevations and at low-elevation basins that fill with cold air. The coldest air temperatures are commonly caused by radiation frosts on calm and clear nights in the months of December and January (Davis et al. 2007). At freezing ecotones, species turnover can be abrupt and the turnover occurs where the minimum air temperatures drop to levels that cause damage to sensitive species (Ewers et al. 2003, Davis et al. 2007). In the Santa Monica Mountains of southern California, laurel sumac and ceanothus species dominate on coastal exposures and warmer sites outside cold air drainage zones. On the lower slopes and the valley floors these species are replaced by other more frost-tolerant species: sugar bush and other species of ceanothus (Davis et al. 2007).

Some cold-sensitive species like laurel sumac suffer direct damage to their living leaf cells by freezing temperatures (Boorse et al. 1998, Pratt et al. 2005) and suffer freeze/thaw-induced cavitation (Langan et al. 1997). The mechanism of cavitation caused by freeze/thaw-induced cavitation is different from that caused by water stress (Jarbeau et al. 1995), but they both result in emboli that reduce xylem hydraulic conductivity. The emboli typically form in the distal branches and can lead to desiccation of leaves in the days and weeks that follow the frost (Langan et al. 1997, Pratt et al. 2005, Davis et al. 2007). Overnight freezing temperatures are frequently followed by warm sunny days, thus the combination of evergreen leaves and a highly embolized vascular system can lead to dieback of branches even during the moist winter (Davis et al. 2005). For a plant under water stress, freeze/thaw-induced cavitation leads to more extensive formation of emboli, dieback, and plant mortality (Langan et al. 1997, Davis et al. 2005, Davis et al. 2007). Species with larger-diameter vessels are more vulnerable to freeze/thaw-induced embolism (Davis, Sperry et al. 1999).

The Link between Life History Type and Physiology

Recurring crown fires are important for understanding the physiology of chaparral shrubs, particularly at the critical seedling stage. An important framework for understanding the nexus between fire and physiology is to consider the different chaparral life history types. The three different life history types recruit seedlings in different environments, and that recruitment environment selects for different physiologies (Keeley 1998, Pratt et al. 2012). This coupled with physiological and allocation trade-offs leads to divergence in the suite of functional traits of the different life history types. Obligate seeders recruit seedlings in the most arid and open canopy microsites. Consistent with this, obligate seeders are more water stress tolerant and the least shade tolerant than the other life history types (Pratt et al. 2008). Facultative seeders recruit seedlings in open environments, but have greater survival in shadier or moister microsites where stress is ameliorated (Pratt et al. 2008). Accordingly, these facultative seeders have lower water stress tolerance and greater mortality of seedlings during the first dry season following fire (Thomas and Davis 1989). Obligate resprouter seedlings recruit during fire-free intervals in the shady understory of mature chaparral canopies (Keeley 1992). These species have the highest degree of shade tolerance, and they are of similar or greater water stress tolerance to the facultative seeders, which may be related to competition for water in a mature chaparral stand (Pratt et al. 2008).

This divergence in seedling recruitment environments (Figure 24.8) is linked to other characteristics as well, such as differences in rooting patterns (Thomas and Davis 1989, Keeley 1998). Obligate seeders are commonly shallow-rooted, whereas facultative seeders are variable and some are relatively shallow-rooted (e.g., some populations of chamise and manzanita), yet others are among the most deeply rooted (e.g., laurel sumac). Instructively, the more shallowly rooted facultative seeders tend to be the ones that recruit more seedlings after fire and often resprout more weakly (e.g., some chamise populations)—that is, they trend towards the obligate seeder end of the spectrum. Successful seedling recruitment in gaps after fire is achieved by both the ability to rapidly acquire resources when they are abundant after fire and by greater levels of stress tolerance when water is limiting. Evolving this ability and the associated necessary traits appears to compromise resprouting ability (Pratt et al. 2014).

Stress tolerators have trait combinations that include both stress-tolerance traits and rapid-resource acquisition traits such as high net carbon assimilation rates per unit leaf area (Ackerly 2004b, Pratt et al. 2012), transpiration rates (Parker 1984), and hydraulic efficiency at the whole plant level (Pratt

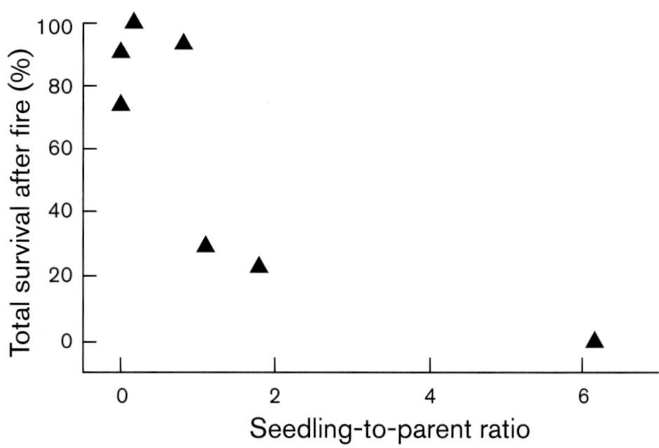

FIGURE 24.8 Greater seedling production (seedling-to-parent ratio) is significantly associated with lower levels of resprout survival two years after fire (r= −0.81; P=0.03). All species co-occurred at a Santa Monica Mountains site. Source: Pratt et al. 2014.

et al. 2010). This is likely because during the wet season in the postfire environment, water and nutrients are readily available and seedlings must compete for these resources with other seedlings, including those of herbaceous fire-followers, and resprouting shrubs (McPherson and Muller 1967). At this time, they also must grow fast enough to establish a root system that will prevent them from desiccating during the hot and dry summer and fall. Once the summer and fall season arrives, seedlings experience considerable stress and mortality is often high at this time (Thomas and Davis 1989). These circumstances select for seedlings to rapidly grow and acquire resources when they are available and also to tolerate low levels of resources as they become scarce (Keeley 1998).

Chaparral in the Long Absence of Fire

Because chaparral ranges from arid southern California to more mesic maritime regions and northern California mountain ranges, chaparral dynamics similarly can vary. Thus the phrase "the long absence of fire" has to be defined in the local climatic context. We can reiterate that climate, topography, soils, and wildfire are the principal determinants of the distribution of chaparral across the California landscape. As these principal influences vary among sites and when the between-fire period increases, chaparral dynamics might be expected to change. Earlier studies of chaparral in southern California led to a paradigm that little succession occurred in chaparral and that stands older than sixty years were decadent (Hanes 1971). The idea was that stands reached some age at which plants began to senesce, productivity dropped, and no seedling establishment occurred (Hanes 1971, Hanes 1977, Vogl 1977, Reid and Oechel 1984). *Ceanothus* species, especially from subsection Cerastes, were thought to live only thirty-five to fifty years at best. Succession was seen as the eclipsing of coastal sage scrub species by evergreen sclerophyllous species in the first few decades. While some thought that woodland might eventually invade and convert the site if fire was excluded (Horton and Kraebel 1955, Horton 1960, Wells 1962), others thought no further succession would occur (Hanes 1971).

More detailed studies shifted the concepts of chaparral dynamics in the long absence of fire. Old-growth stands of big-pod ceanothus were found to have dead individuals within them, but the larger living plants were still growing and mortality patterns suggested little change in the stand as it aged (Montygierd-Loyba and Keeley 1987). When a large number of sites were compared along an age gradient, species diversity was found to be stable although some composition change occurs as stands age (Keeley 1992). The greatest mortality rates were among species that fail to grow tall fast enough as they age, such as nonsprouting ceanothus species; other evergreen species showed almost no mortality across a diverse latitudinal and elevation gradient (Keeley 1992). One significant difference between these studies and the earlier paradigm was the evidence that obligate resprouters were establishing seedling banks in the understory of these older stands at fairly high densities (0.1-3.7 m^{-2}). This work confirmed and extended earlier studies reporting the establishment of obligate resprouter seedlings in chaparral understory (P. H. Zedler 1981, P. A. Zedler 1982, Parker and Kelly 1989, Lloret and Zedler 1991).

These seedling patterns in southern California chaparral tend to reinforce the life history categories found among the woody plants, those with persistent seed banks recruiting new individuals in the year or two after fire (obligate seeders, facultative seeders), while obligate resprouters require longer time intervals for their shade-adapted seedlings to establish in the understory of chaparral. Succession beyond these demographic shifts depends upon the proximity of other vegetation to old-growth chaparral. Conifers have limited dispersal ranges, and if chaparral stands are quite extensive, initially they have little ability to invade beyond the edges. Similarly, oaks and other hardwoods may benefit from animal dispersal in terms of farther potential dispersal distances, but establishment patterns remain low because of the low productivity and resource limitations of chaparral in this part of the state.

Moving toward central and northern California or shifting to higher elevations into montane chaparral yields a different pattern. In these regions chaparral forms mosaics with forests with the sizes of each type of vegetation patch depending on local climate, topography, soils, and wildfire history. In areas near urban sites or where forest timber is economically critical, fire suppression has generally been the practice for the past century. As a consequence, chaparral stands often are invaded by conifers or other trees and the extent of chaparral may be quite reduced (Vankat and Major 1978, Conard and Radosevich 1982, Nagel and Taylor 2005, Collins and Stephens 2010, van Wagtendonk et al. 2012). One study in the Sierra reported that over the past sixty to seventy years, comparisons of aerial photographs reveal a loss of chaparral spatial coverage by over 60% (Nagel and Taylor 2005). Conifer invasion of chaparral does not always require long-term lack of fire in northern California, however, where, if conditions are appropriate, conifers may invade immediately after fire (Sparling 1994, Horton et al. 1998). For example, following a 1945 wildfire, one chaparral stand adjacent to a forest was invaded the first growing season after the fire, followed by pulses of invasion over the next thirty years (Sparling 1994, Horton et al. 1998).

The conifer forest–montane chaparral mosaics have received considerable attention because of the economic importance of the forests. Studies indicate that forest and chaparral burn at different time intervals and at substantially different fire intensities; forests burn at relatively low intensities while chaparral fires are high intensity. Early researchers considered forest and chaparral patches as alternative vegetation states across the landscape, each maintaining itself due to their different interactions with fire (Leiberg 1902, Show and Kotok 1924, Wilken 1967). Similar patterns are found in other Mediterranean-climate systems (Mount 1964, Jackson 1968). The differential distribution of these two vegetation types contributes to the self-reinforcing nature of their interaction with fire. High-intensity wildfires tend to occur on steeper or more south-facing aspects in the northern part of the state (Weatherspoon and Skinner 1995, Taylor and Skinner 1998, Alexander et al. 2006). The abiotic conditions combined with further resource limitations imposed by chaparral reduce the rate of conifer invasion and productivity. The cumulative effects of multiple high-intensity fires reduces soil carbon and site productivity, further slowing tree growth rates (Waring and Schlesinger 1985).

Such differential impacts by chaparral and forest were modeled by Odion et al. (2010) to test the concept of alternative vegetation states. Their models supported co-occurring but different stands of vegetation due to different self-reinforcing relationships with fire. Chaparral vegetation burned at higher intensity, particularly on steep or equatorial-facing slopes, and its fire regime kept soil productivity from increasing through time. Forests maintain themselves in sites with gentler slopes and greater soil depth and tend to dominate polar-facing slopes. Their conclusion was that conifer invasion of chaparral sites resulted in conifers being in a "fire trap." Chaparral sites burned at high enough intensity to remove conifers that had established since the last fire. This pattern has been found frequently in the western United States (e.g., Thompson et al. 2007, Holden et al. 2010). Focusing on the central Sierra Nevada, van Wagtendonk et al. (2012) found that these different vegetation patches were maintained as long as fire intensities were low to moderate; high fire intensities resulted in dominance of montane chaparral regardless of the prior vegetation.

Another aspect to the dynamics between chaparral and forest patches is that some types of chaparral create conditions favorable to the facilitation of forest establishment. For example, most conifer seedlings benefit from chaparral canopies providing shade and higher levels of moisture, even though their growth rates may be restricted by resource competition (Conard and Radosevich 1982, Dunne and Parker 1999). Coast live oak, for example, is facilitated by chaparral and coastal scrub (Callaway and D'Antonio 1991) and populations differentially expand within shrub-dominated areas in central California (Callaway and Davis 1998). Furthermore, in the more mesic regions of chaparral distributions in which chaparral exists in mosaics with forests, the dominants of chaparral tend to be species of manzanita or shrub oak, both of which have mycorrhizal mutualisms with fungal species that are shared with conifers in the Pinaceae (Horton et al. 1998). The mycelial networks of fungal mutualists facilitate the establishment of conifer seedlings in conditions that otherwise prevent establishment (Dunne and Parker 1999, Horton et al. 1998). A study testing this idea randomly sampled chaparral stands from northern and central California that were adjacent to forests; chaparral was invaded by conifers in those stands at a rate and density proportional to the percentage of ectomycorrhizal species in the chaparral stand (Bode 1999).

In the long absence of fire, chaparral begins to shift demographically; early successional species including those that may be prominent in coastal or sage scrub vegetation tend to disappear in the first few years to the first decade. As individuals increase in size, compositional shifts or proportions

TABLE 24.8
Adaptive traits for nutrient-poor soils

Traits	Function	References
Root nodules[A]	Symbioses with bacteria that fix atmospheric nitrogen	Pratt, Jacobsen, Ewers, et al. 2007 Kummerow, Alexander, et al. 1978
Long-lived leaves	Greater nitrogen use efficiency	Aerts and Van der Peijl 1993
Evergreen sclerophyllous leaves	Storae compartment for nutrients captured during nutrient pulse following first fall rains	Mooney and Rundel 1979, Shaver 1981
Luxury consumption	Consume nutrients beyond immediate need and store for later use	Rundel and Parsons 1980, Gray 1983
Mychorrizae	Aid in phosphorous extraction and uptake	Allen et al. 1999

A. Examples include *Ceanothus* spp., *Cercocarpus betuloides*, and legumes such as *Acmispon glaber* (formerly *Lotus scoparius*).

of dominance also change. In the southern ranges of chaparral, fire usually returns prior to any further shifts; however, in more mesic regions, chaparral dynamics involve adjacent vegetation. Some chaparral species, for example, may facilitate forest invasion because of their shared mutualisms with mycorrhizal fungi and the modification of environmental extremes that chaparral canopies may provide. Wildfires balance this process. Chaparral sites burn at an intensity too high for conifers or most forest species to survive, creating fire traps that provide maintenance of chaparral stands over the long term. These changes in chaparral result from differences among chaparral species in their rates of growth, height, or other aspects. While shared mutualisms with forest species may facilitate invasion of chaparral, wildfire, climate, topography, and soil conditions generate the conditions that retain chaparral as a dominant vegetation type in California.

Biogeochemical and Hydrological Dynamics

Carbon Exchange

Community productivity indicates the amount of energy captured and converted to biomass and has important implications for trophic interactions and biotic diversity. At the community scale, chaparral stands can be quite productive annually. For example, stands dominated by big-pod ceanothus have productivity rates of 850 g m^{-2} yr^{1} (Schlesinger and Gill 1980) and have been reported to be as high as 1,056 g m^{-2} yr^{1} (Gray 1982). The higher value is comparable to some temperate forest communities and is generally higher than nearby coastal sage communities (Schlesinger and Gill 1980, Gray 1982). Other studies have documented productivity values somewhat lower to much lower at more arid chaparral sites where chamise is abundant (Rundel and Parsons 1979, Vourlitis et al. 2009). Productivity broadly varies on an annual basis depending on temperature and seasonal rainfall (Hellmers, Bonner et al. 1955; Li et al. 2006; Vourlitis et al. 2009).

The net ecosystem exchange of CO_2 of old-growth chaparral stands indicates that they can be substantial carbon sinks (Luo et al. 2007). This suggests that gross primary productivity can remain high in these communities and does not support the idea that the productivity of chaparral stands declines as they age (Hanes 1971). The amount of CO_2 that old-growth stands accumulate or give off annually depends on current and previous year precipitation and environmental conditions (Luo et al. 2007) and the interaction between the time since the last fire and available nutrients (see "Mineral Nutrition," below).

Mineral Nutrition

Unburned chaparral soils are poor in available nutrients, and chaparral shrubs have a host of traits that are adaptive in this context (Table 24.8). Nitrogen, and in some cases phosphorous, are in limiting supply, leading to reduced levels of productivity, whereas exchangeable CATIONS are of secondary importance (Rundel 1983). When long unburned plots are fertilized with nitrogen, growth of plants is generally stimulated, which demonstrates the influence of nitrogen on productivity (Hellmers, Bonner et al. 1955; McMaster et al. 1982; Vourlitis 2012). At the system level, most of the nitrogen exists in unavailable standing biomass and litter (Rundel 1983). This reservoir is converted by periodic crown fires and results in a pulse of available nitrogen to the soil (Christensen 1973, Christensen and Muller 1975, Rundel and Parsons 1980, Vourlitis et al. 2009). Immediately after fire, the ammonium significantly increases in the upper soil layers, whereas nitrate is little affected (DeBano, Eberlein et al. 1979; Rundel 1983; Fenn et al. 1993). In the months after fire, the soil pH increases towards neutral and this stimulates NITRIFICATION, leading to an increase in soil nitrate (Dunn et al. 1979, Rundel 1983).

Although fires greatly increase available forms of nitrogen in the soil, nitrogen is volatilized by fire, resulting in significant losses from the system (DeBano and Conrad 1978; DeBano, Eberlein et al. 1979; Rundel 1983). The intensity of the fire is an important determinant of how much nitrogen is volatilized (DeBano, Rice et al. 1979; Marion et al. 1991). Other postfire losses include leaching, surface runoff, dry erosion, and biogenic emissions (Christensen 1973, DeBano and Conrad 1978, Rundel and Parsons 1980, Gray and Schlesinger 1981, DeBano and Dunn 1982, Rundel 1983, Mooney et al. 1987). Losses would be greater if nutrients were not immobilized by a dense growth of fire-following annual herbs and short-lived shrubs such as deer weed (*Acmispon glaber*, formerly *Lotus scoparius*) (Nilsen and Schlesinger 1981).

After successive fires, chaparral soils would eventually be depleted of nitrogen without new inputs. Atmospheric nitrogen fixation by microorganisms that are free-living and symbiotic with plants are an important new nitrogen input that offsets some losses (Kummerow, Alexander et al. 1978; Dunn et al. 1979; Ellis and Kummerow 1989; Ulery et al. 1995). Other smaller nitrogen inputs come from precipitation and dry deposition of nutrients on leaves, which reach the soil in solution as a pulse following the first fall rains (Christensen 1973, Schlesinger and Hasey 1980). These atmospheric inputs have increased due to pollution caused by the burning of fossil fuels (see below).

Decomposition converts complex organic substances into simpler forms, and it affects nitrogen availability in between fires. Decomposition by soil animals and microorganisms occurs primarily during the wet season and at a much lower level during the summer dry season (Quideau et al. 2005, Li et al. 2006). Rates are also affected by local conditions such as soil texture and type, slope, and elevation, and rates differ under different evergreen species (Quideau et al. 1998, Quideau et al. 2005). The chief litter input is from leaves, thus their nutrient content and turnover rate are dominant factors in nutrient cycling and are key reasons why the litter of a given species affects decomposition. Much of the nitrogen and phosphorous of leaves are reabsorbed prior to abscission, thus the nutrient quality of the litter in chaparral stands is poor (Mooney and Rundel 1979, Schlesinger 1985, Quideau et al. 2005). The poor quality of the litter (high C:N and C:P ratios) slows decomposition (Schlesinger 1985). Moreover, decomposition is slowed by the high levels of carbon forms that are resistant to decomposition, such as lignin, cutin, and phenolics, which are typically higher in evergreen sclerophylls than deciduous species (Schlesinger 1985, Aerts 1997).

Decomposition of leaves occurs in three phases: first is the leaching of soluble components (K, Mg, carbohydrates, phenolics) during rainstorms (Schlesinger and Hasey 1981). This phase is rapid (greater than one year) and is determined by the amount of soluble components in the litter. The second phase is slower (approximately one to five years) and results from litter fragmentation and slow release initially of nonsoluble components (e.g., N, P, Ca, and lignin) upon breakdown by soil microbes. Turnover rates of litter organic matter during this phase ranges from 2.8 to 7.7 years, with litter bag studies tending to yield higher values than mass balance methods (Schlesinger 1985). A three-year study found that the nitrogen and phosphorous becomes immobilized in the litter layer, making it unavailable over this time period (Schlesinger 1985). A third, slower decomposition phase occurs when organic matter is mixed with mineral soil and chemically altered and breakdown products are leached (Chapin et al. 2002). Studies of this phase are lacking, but there have been studies of nutrients across chronosequences that provide some insight. Total nitrogen and potentially mineralizable nitrogen decline in stands older than fifty years (Marion and Black 1988). In some systems, nitrogen is immobilized in microbial products; however, this does not appear to be the case in chaparral topsoil (Fenn et al. 1993). The decline of available soil nitrogen as stands age occurs because the amount sequestered into biomass and recalcitrant soil compounds is greater than inputs. The tendency for stands to become nutrient poor in the decades following fire, particularly in nitrogen, has been suggested to lead to declines in productivity and senescence of plants in old stands (Rundel and Parsons 1980, Marion and Black 1988; however, see Fenn et al. 1993) (Figure 24.9).

Many aspects of decomposition are poorly understood in the chaparral. One in particular is phase three dynamics

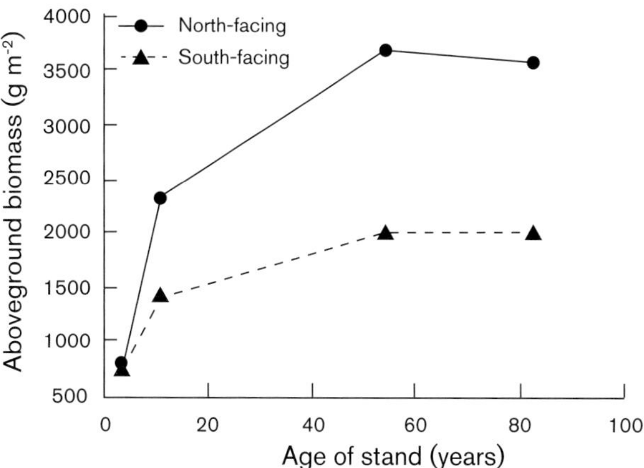

FIGURE 24.9 Relationship between aboveground biomass of shrubs on north- and south-facing slopes and age of chaparral. Source: Data modified from Table 24.1 in Marion and Black 1988. To simplify chronosequence, same-age sites are averaged.

and the controls over longer-term decomposition processes. Another area that is little studied is decomposition in the rhizosphere. Fine root mass has significant turnover in the top 10 to 20 centimeters of soil on a seasonal basis (Kummerow, Krause et al. 1978). Many fine roots in these shallow soil layers die during the summer dry season and then presumably decompose during the following wet season (Kummerow, Krause et al. 1978).

Phosphorous may be a limiting nutrient for some species in long unburned stands as suggested by fertilization studies (Hellmers, Bonner et al. 1955; McMaster et al. 1982). In particular, species that form symbioses with nitrogen-fixing bacteria may have adequate nitrogen but may become phosphorous-limited (Schlesinger and Gill 1980, McMaster et al. 1982, Schlesinger 1985). The majority of phosphorous in chaparral systems is in unavailable forms in the soil (DeBano and Conrad 1978, Rundel 1983). Like nitrogen, but to a lesser degree, available phosphorous increases following fire (Christensen and Muller 1975, Marion and Black 1988). Unlike nitrogen, little phosphorous is lost from the system after fire (DeBano and Conrad 1978, Marion and Black 1988). Phosphorous inputs are from weathering, inorganic solutes in precipitation, dry deposition, and, to a lesser degree, decomposition (Marion and Black 1988). Available phosphorous in older stands (older than fifty years since the last fire) is low and availability is determined by absorption and desorption reactions between soluble phosphorous and soil surfaces (Marion and Black 1988). Chaparral species form associations with mycorrhizal fungi that likely aids in extraction of phosphorous from soils (Allen et al. 1999).

Burning of fossil fuels has led to the production of numerous air pollutants that contain nitrogen (Bytnerowicz and Fenn 1996). Some of these pollutants are dry deposited on chaparral canopies and are then leached to the soil during rains. Areas that have fog may also experience significant wet deposits of nitrogen. An area especially affected is the Los Angeles Air Basin. Because chaparral communities are nitrogen-limited, deposition can lead to higher rates of net productivity (Vourlitis 2012). In areas of high and chronic deposition, the system may become nitrogen-saturated, as has been documented in the portions of the San Gabriel and San Bernardino Mountains (Fenn et al. 1998). Compared to unsaturated systems, nitrogen-saturated systems have elevated leaf and tissue nitrogen content, nitrate losses from streams, NO loss from the soil, N mineralization and litter decomposition, and lowered pH and base saturation of soils (Fenn et al. 1996, Vourlitis and Fernandez 2012).

Hydrology

Studies have examined the precipitation inputs and losses of chaparral watersheds at the San Dimas Experimental forest in the San Gabriel Mountains in Los Angeles County and at Echo Valley in San Diego (Hamilton and Rowe 1949, Rowe and Colman 1951, Poole et al. 1981). The chief input of precipitation is about seven to fifteen rainstorms during the winter wet season (Cowling et al. 2005). About 78% to 80% of precipitation reaches the soil as throughfall, which falls directly to the soil or drips off the canopy to the soil (Hamilton and Rowe 1949, Poole et al. 1981), and another fraction of water reaches the soil by flowing down stems (Poole et al. 1981). Stemflow is affected by canopy architecture, and species with erect branches and smooth bark have greater stemflow (Hamilton and Rowe 1949). In one study, chamise had greater stemflows than other co-occurring chaparral shrubs (Poole et al. 1981).

Losses of precipitation occur via canopy interception, surface runoff, evaporation from the soil, and TRANSPIRATION. Water may be lost through subsurface drainage into fractures in the soil depending on site, and such losses are greater in heavier rainfall years (Rowe and Colman 1951, Hill 1963, Ng and Miller 1980, Poole et al. 1981). Some precipitation intercepted by the canopy evaporates from plant surfaces. The amount of loss from the canopy is determined by the number of rainfall events, the intensity of storms, and the canopy architecture (Poole et al. 1981). Previous studies have found that 5–41% of precipitation is lost due to canopy interception with average losses higher in southern California (Hill 1963, Hill and Rice 1963, Poole et al. 1981). Greater losses may occur when a storm occurs in the warm summer, when canopies have higher levels of leaf area, and when precipitation falls as snow (Poole et al. 1981). Greater numbers of smaller storms leads to greater losses from the canopy (Hamilton and Rowe 1949). With needle leaves and erect branches, chamise has low levels of canopy interception (Poole et al. 1981), whereas species with more leaf surface area incept more precipitation (Poole et al. 1981).

Surface runoff is the difference between precipitation inputs, soil storage, and EVAPOTRANSPIRATION. The amount of precipitation that makes it into the soil storage is dependent on frequency and size of rainfall events, slope, postfire factors, as well as soil structure and chemistry. Soil structure is partially affected by species composition, as is stemflow, thus species-level effects can influence infiltration of precipitation. Surface runoff is generally low but can be high during high rainfall years (Rowe and Colman 1951, Meixner and Wohlgemuth 2003). At a site in San Diego County, surface runoff in average and low rainfall years was low (0–4%) with the greater runoff on north-facing slopes (Ng and Miller 1980, Poole et al. 1981). Farther north in Los Angeles County, runoff of a chaparral watershed has been estimated by streamflow, and the fifteen-year average of streamflow yield was 11% of the total rainfall input (Hill and Rice 1963). During the wettest year, streamflow yield was higher at 21% and during the driest year streamflow yield was trace. More direct smaller-scale measurements of runoff have been made at this site in large LYSIMETER studies (Patric 1961), which found about 14.5% of precipitation inputs was lost as runoff averaged across five consecutive dry years, and 40% was lost during a wet year (Hill and Rice 1963). Over the short-term, crown fire leads to large increases in surface runoff and streamflow (Meixner and Wohlgemuth 2003). This effect is due to a decline in evapotranspiration and the formation of hydrophobic soils after fire (DeBano et al. 1977, Valeron and Meixner 2010).

The chief loss of water is due to evapotranspiration. In lysimeter studies virtually all of the water that enters the soil is lost to evapotranspiration during below-average rainfall years, and more than 80% of it is lost during years when rainfall is substantially above average (Patric 1961). A chamise-dominated south-facing slope can show 80% loss due to evapotranspiration, whereas a north-facing slope of mixed chaparral with greater leaf area can lose virtually all of the precipitation input to evapotranspiration (Ng and Miller 1980). Estimates of the separate contribution of evaporation and transpiration have been made in a chamise-dominated stand, in which the amount of water transpired is about equal to the amount evaporated (Poole et al. 1981). However, in mixed chaparral stands with greater canopy cover, transpiration is about three times greater than evaporation (Poole et al. 1981). Hydraulic redistribution refers to the movement of water by plant roots from one soil compartment to another down a water potential gradient. Such water fluxes may be an important factor affecting the hydrology of chaparral sites, particularly in its effects on evapotranspiration. Studies of hydraulic redistribution are currently lacking for chaparral sites.

Ecosystem Services

Ecosystem services describe the ways that ecosystems benefit people. Such services can be categorized as regulating (e.g., climate, flooding), provisioning (e.g., food, fuel, fresh water), supporting (e.g., nutrient cycling and carbon sequestration), and cultural (e.g., aesthetic, educational, recreation) (Millennium Ecosystem Assessment 2005). Chaparral provides services in each of these categories. For regulating services, chaparral vegetation absorbs sunlight and transpires water—both of which help to regulate temperature during the hot summer months compared to highly urbanized areas that experience the "heat island effect" (LaDochy et al. 2007). The growth of shrublands on steep hillsides helps to reduce flooding, erosion, and mudslides that can occur during heavy rains that commonly occur each winter (Gabet and Dunne 2002). This service is especially apparent after chaparral has been removed by fire, and heavy winter rains cause costly and lethal mudslides (Ren et al. 2011).

Provisioning services of chaparral includes filtration of rainwater, which helps to maintain fresh drinking water in aquifers and reduce EUTROPHICATION in the ocean and reservoirs that receive runoff. This is important in some areas where nitrogen deposition is high and nitrogen pollutants such as nitrate might be more prone to leach into groundwater supplies and collect in downstream bodies of water. Areas that were formerly chaparral that have been converted to grassland are not as effective at filtering water and they yield greater nitrate runoff (Riggan et al. 1985). In areas where nitrogen pollution is the most severe, such as some watersheds in the San Bernardino and San Gabriel Mountains northeast of Los Angeles, runoff of nitrate is among the highest in the United States (Fenn and Poth 1999).

Supporting services include carbon sequestration with stands of chaparral, even very old ones, acting as carbon sinks (Luo et al. 2007). The pollination services provided by native bees are associated with the amount of nearby natural habitat (including chaparral) where these bees reside (Kremen et al. 2004). As discussed already, chaparral vegetation has a substantial impact on the hydrology of a watershed. Studies conducted in the Transverse mountain range at the San Dimas Experimental Station manipulated the vegetation in an effort to increase usable water. Chaparral and riparian vegetation was removed from a portion of the watershed and this increased water yield from the watershed (Hill and Rice 1963, Meixner and Wohlgemuth 2003). This result confirms many studies that removing chaparral or any vegetation type that is deeply rooted reduces transpiration of the system. Increases in water yield by removing chaparral are likely to come at the expense of water quality, a reduction in temperature regulation services, and a loss in cultural services.

Cultural services provided by chaparral systems are high. Chaparral systems are located in some of the largest metropolitan areas in North America such as Los Angeles. This ensures that there are many millions of visitors to these shrublands for recreation activities such as hiking, biking, horse riding, and camping. The presence of chaparral on the low-elevation slopes beautifies the landscape. The educational impact of chaparral is high due to the large numbers of parks, colleges and universities, and organizations that operate near chaparral systems. For example, the Santa Monica Mountains National Recreation Area is a park in southern California that receives about thirty-five million visitors annually with outreach and educational programs that target people of all ages.

The Future of Chaparral

Predictions are that the climate in California will be increasingly warmer and drier in the coming decades (Hayhoe et al. 2004); however, there is uncertainty in this prediction because rainfall may increase in some regions of California (Neelin et al. 2013). The water deficits for chaparral shrublands will depend on interplay between temperature, the amount and timing of rainfall, and local soil water storage dynamics. Of paramount importance will be how the changing climate affects extreme weather patterns (maximum and minimum temperatures and drought intensity) and wildfire (Westerling et al. 2006). Extreme events such as the record droughts since 2012 and heat waves will likely have direct impacts on chaparral communities. These effects are already evident at the arid ecotones where chaparral mixes with desert scrub communities and some adult chaparral species have experienced significant levels of mortality (Paddock et al. 2013). Increases in minimum nighttime temperature (Crimmins et al. 2011) will affect species whose current distributions are limited by subzero temperatures (Ewers et al. 2003, Davis et al. 2005, Davis et al. 2007). Higher nighttime temperatures may lead to greater rates of respiration with implications for carbon balance. Climate will likely interact with fire to drive change. For example, a recent study found that postfire resprouts of some species suffered high levels of mortality in the first year after a fire during an intense drought, whereas adjacent unburned plants did not suffer mortality (Pratt et al. 2014).

One of the most immediate and devastating affects to chaparral communities is alteration of the fire regime. Chaparral stands are generally not resilient to short fire-return intervals less than about fifteen to twenty years (Zedler et al. 1983, Jacobsen et al. 2004, Keeley et al. 2005b). Such short return intervals have become more common due to anthropogenic ignitions and the abundant fine fuels produced by annual alien grasses in disturbed areas (Brooks et al. 2004). If short fire-return interval fires continue or increase in the future, increasing areas of chaparral communities will be converted into homogenous savannahs where only the most vigorous resprouters persist (e.g., laurel sumac in southern California).

Other aspects of climate change, such as increasing CO_2, may increase water-use efficiency and alter patterns of fuel moisture in ways that potentially could offset increasing fire ignition hazard due to warmer temperatures (Oechel et al. 1995); however, CO_2 may also stimulate biomass accumulation and lead to an increase in fuels and high-intensity fires. Increased CO_2 will also subtly shift the importance of the less well-known microbial communities as already low levels of nutrients may become more limiting and cascade along food webs (Oechel et al. 1995). Because of its presence at or near the boundaries of urban developments and metropolitan centers, conflicts between the impacts of chaparral wildfire and human life and structures likely will increase without intelligent regional development policies. Historically the primary management focus on chaparral has been one of fuels and fire hazard (Parker 1987, 1990; see Chapter 3, "Fire as an Ecosystem Process"); indeed that was the primary motivation for the development of the vegetation-type mapping project begun in the late 1920s (Keeley 2004). Today fire hazard and watershed hydrology are the primary foci of management, and the maintenance of chaparral cover for its critical role in hydrology will increase in importance in a future with potentially less precipitation and warmer temperatures.

Summary

Chaparral shrublands are biotically diverse and the most abundant vegetation type in the state. These shrublands are dominated by evergreen species and occur in areas with hot, dry summers and cool, moist winters. The species that inhabit the chaparral are adapted to a Mediterranean-type climate. Chaparral is a dynamic ecosystem, and wildfires (see Chapter 3, "Fire as an Ecosystem Process") facilitated by the summer rainless period are more predictable than in many other fire-prone landscapes; this is reflected in many evolutionary responses to fire. While diverse in microbes and animals, the dominant plants exhibit characteristics explicitly selected by wildfire in their development of persistent soil or canopy seed banks. Chaparral ecosystems provide many services, such as the stabilization of steep slopes, filtration of drinking water, and myriad recreational opportunities. They also beautify the landscape for many millions of California inhabitants and visitors. Increasingly, chaparral is being managed for its intrinsic value to resource conservation and even community restoration programs. There are many threats to chaparral ecosystems from climate change, altered fire regimes, development, nonindigenous invasive species, and poor management practices.

Acknowledgments

V. Thomas Parker was supported by the San Francisco State University Office of Research and Sponsored Programs;

R. Brandon Pratt by a National Science Foundation CAREER grant (IOS-0845125); and Jon E. Keeley by the U.S. Geological Survey Fire Risk Scenario Project.

Recommended Reading

Keeley, J. E. 1989. A chaparral family shrub—A genealogy of chaparral ecologists. Pages 3-6 in S. Keeley, editor. California Chaparral: Paradigms Re-examined. Natural History Museum of Los Angeles, Science Series No. 34, Los Angeles, California.

Keeley, J. E. 1993. Proceedings of the symposium interface between ecology and land development in California. International Journal of Wildland Fire, Fairfield, Washington.

Pincetl, S. S. 2003. Transforming California: A political history of land use and development. Johns Hopkins University Press, Baltimore, Maryland.

Stephenson, J. R., and G. M. Calcarone. 1999. Southern California mountains and foothills assessment: Habitat and species conservation issues. General Technical Report, PSW-GTR-172. USDA Forest Service, Pacific Southwest Research Station, Albany, California.

Tenhunen, J. D., F. M. Catarino, O. L. Lange, and W. C. Oechel. 1987. Plant response to stress. Functional analysis in Mediterranean ecosystems. Springer, New York, New York.

Glossary

ARBUSCULAR MYCORRHIZAE Mycorrhizae are mutualistic associations between higher fungi and vascular plants. In arbuscular mycorrhizae the fungus forms hyphae that penetrate the cell walls of plant roots, where they form structures (arbuscules) with large surface areas that facilitate the exchange of minerals and carbohydrates. The fungi involved in arbuscular mycorrhizae are from a lineage in the Zygomycetes.

CATIONS A positively charged atom or molecule such as potassium and calcium.

CAVITATION The breaking of the water column in vessels or tracheids whereupon liquid water changes to water vapor ultimately leading to emboli. Plants differ in their susceptibility to cavitation, but it is common in the vascular tissues when water content of the soil is low or during episodes of freezing and thawing.

DETRITIVORES These heterotrophic organisms consume detritus (which is decomposing plant and animal parts) to obtain energy and minerals, and consequently they contribute to decomposition and the nutrient cycles.

ECTOMYCORRHIZAE These mycorrhizae (mutualistic associations between higher fungi and vascular plants) are characterized by the presence of a fungal mantle covering the plant host roots with some fungal hyphae penetrating between root cells (called a Hartig net). The fungi are usually from two fungal groups, Basidiomycetes and Ascomycetes.

EMBOLI (SING. EMBOLUS) These gas bubbles form following cavitation in the water and transport cells (vessels or tracheids) within plant vascular tissue.

EUTROPHICATION The response of an aquatic system to pollutants contained in runoff. In the case of nitrogen pollutants, this response is often a bloom of algal growth that can choke waterways and lead to the reduction in oxygen levels to levels lethal to some species.

EVAPOTRANSPIRATION The sum of the water lost via evaporation and transpiration.

FACULTATIVE SEEDERS Shrubs or trees that survive wildfire and sprout new shoots after the fire. These types of plants also have persistent soil seed banks that fire stimulates, and they recruit new individuals from seedlings that successfully establish in the postfire environment.

FOLIVORE An herbivore that specializes in eating leaves.

LYSIMETER A device used to measure the evapotranspiration from plant/soil systems as the difference between precipitation inputs and water lost through the soil.

MYCORRHIZA (PL.: MYCORRHIZAE) A symbiotic, mutualistic (but occasionally weakly pathogenic) association between a fungus and the roots of a vascular plant. Mycorrhizae are critical in bringing water and minerals to their host plant, which in turn provides carbon energy to the fungus.

MYCOTA Refers to species from the kingdom Fungi.

NITRIFICATION The oxidation of ammonia into nitrate by microorganisms.

OBLIGATE RESPROUTER Shrubs or trees that can survive wildfire and sprout new shoots after the fire. Generally no seedlings are recruited in the postfire environment.

OBLIGATE SEEDERS Shrubs or trees that are killed by wildfire and persist in the habitat because they have persistent soil seed banks that fire stimulates. Obligate seeders recruit new individuals after wildfire from the seed bank and establish new populations in the postfire environment.

PERSISTENT SEED BANK Refers to viable seed constantly being found in the soil unless stimulated by a strong environmental event such as a wildfire.

PHYSICAL DORMANCY When referring to seeds, this generally means that there is a thick seed coat or other structure that does not allow water or gasses to enter a seed, keeping the seed in a dormant state.

PHYSIOLOGICAL DORMANCY When referring to seeds, this generally means that there are physiological processes that have to be met before normal metabolism will stimulate germination; examples are light, temperatures, and chemicals from smoke.

PYRO-ENDEMICS Refers to annual or short-lived plants that are only found in postfire stands of vegetation.

SCLEROPHYLLOUS Refers to plants or to a vegetation indicating plants have generally small tough leaves with thick cuticles; usually an adaptation to low water availability and nutrient-poor soils.

SEED BANK Viable plant seed stored in the soil or in serotinous cones or woody fruit in the canopy of a tree or shrub.

SEROTINOUS Having seed held in woody cones or fruit rather than releasing at seed maturation. Release occurs in response to an environmental trigger, usually fire, or death of the stem.

SPECIFIC LEAF AREA (SLA) The fresh leaf area divided by the oven-dry mass; SLA is an index of sclerophylly with lower values being more sclerophyllous.

STRATIFICATION Some seeds require a chilling period (generally several degrees above freezing) that lasts a minimum time period (weeks to months) before dormancy is broken and germination can occur; the chilling is called stratification.

SUFFRUTESCENT A small shrub having a stem that is woody only at the base or some of the main stems; generally the wood is light.

TRANSIENT SEED BANK Refers to all seed germinating or losing viability within a year such that there is a fraction of the year with no seed stored in the soil.

TRANSPIRATION Loss of water through the tiny pores (stomata) of plant leaves.

WATER POTENTIAL The potential energy of water relative to pure water. It is used as a measure of plant water status with more negative values indicating that tissues are more dehydrated.

XYLEM The vascular system of plants that conducts water. Cells are usually dead and hollow at maturity.

References

Ackerly, D. D. 2009. Evolution, origin, and age of lineages in the Californian and Mediterranean floras. Journal of Biogeography 36:1221–1233.

———. 2004a. Adaptation, niche conservatism, and convergence: Comparative studies of leaf evolution in the California chaparral. American Naturalist 163:654–671.

———. 2004b. Functional strategies of chaparral shrubs in relation to seasonal water deficit and disturbance. Ecological Monographs 74:25–44.

Aerts, R. 1997. Climate, leaf litter chemistry, and leaf litter decomposition in terrestrial ecosystems: A triangular relationship. Oikos:439–449.

Aerts, R., and M. Van der Peijl. 1993. A simple model to explain the dominance of low-productive perennials in nutrient-poor habitats. Oikos:144–147.

Alexander, J. D., N. E. Seavy, C. J. Ralph, and B. Hogoboom. 2006. Vegetation and topographical correlates of fire severity from two fires in the Klamath-Siskiyou region of Oregon and California. International Journal of Wildland Fire 15:237–245.

Allen, M. F, J. N. Klironomos, K. K. Treseder, and W. C. Oechel. 2005. Responses of soil biota to elevated CO_2 in a chaparral ecosystem. Ecological Applications 15:1701–1711.

Allen, M. F., L. M. Egerton-Warburton, E. B. Allen, and O. Kårén. 1999. Mycorrhizae in *Adenostoma fasciculatum* Hook. & Arn.: A combination of unusual ecto- and endo-forms. Mycorrhiza 8:225–228.

Amaranthus, M. P., and D. A. Perry. 1994. The functioning of mycorrhizal fungi in the field: Linkages in space and time. Plant and Soil 189:133–140.

Andres, M. R., and E. F. Connor. 2003. The community-wide and guild-specific effects of pubescence on the folivorous insects on manzanitas (*Arctostaphylos* spp.). Ecological Entomology 28:383–396.

Axelrod, D. I. 1989. Age and origin of chaparral. Pages 7–19 in S. C. Keeley, editor. The California chaparral: Paradigms reexamined. Natural History Museum of Los Angeles County, Los Angeles, California.

——— 1973. History of the Mediterranean ecosystem in California. Pages 225–277 in F. di Castri & H.A. Mooney, editors. Mediterranean ecosystems: Origin and structure. Springer, New York.

Baar, J., T. R. Horton, A. Kretzer, and T. D. Bruns. 1999. Mycorrhizal recolonization of *Pinus muricata* from resistant propagules after a stand-replacing wildfire. New Phytologist 143:409–418.

Balsamo, R. A., A. M. Bauer, S. D. Davis, and B. M. Rice. 2003. Leaf biomechanics, morphology, and anatomy of the deciduous mesophyte *Prunus serrulata* (Rosaceae) and the evergreen sclerophyllous shrub *Heteromeles arbutifolia* (Rosaceae). American Journal of Botany 90:72–77.

Bauer, H. L. 1936. Moisture relations in the chaparral of the Santa Monica Mountains, California. Ecological Monographs 6:409–454.

Bhaskar, R., and D. D. Ackerly. 2006. Ecological relevance of minimum seasonal water potentials. Physiologia Plantarum 127:353–359.

Bhaskar, R., A. Valiente-Banuet, and D. D. Ackerly. 2007. Evolution of hydraulic traits in closely related species pairs from Mediterranean and nonmediterranean environments of North America. New Phytologist 176:718–726.

Blair, J. R. 1999. Fungi associated with Arctostaphylos in central California. MA thesis Department of Biology, San Francisco State University, California.

Bode, K. 1999. Patterns of association among shrubs and conifers, a test of mycorrhizal association. MA thesis. Department of Biology, San Francisco State University, California.

Boorse, G. C., F. W. Ewers, and S. D. Davis. 1998. Response of chaparral shrubs to below-freezing temperatures: Acclimation, ecotypes, seedlings vs. adults. American Journal of Botany 85:1224–1230.

Bradford, K. A. 1998. Mycorrhizal funga species composition and abundance in mature *Arctostaphylos glandulosa* stands. MA thesis. Department of Biology, San Francisco State University, California.

Brodribb, T. J., and N. M. Holbrook. 2005. Water stress deforms tracheids peripheral to the leaf vein of a tropical conifer. Plant Physiology 137:1139–1146.

Brooks, M. L., C. M. D'Antonio, D. M. Richardson, J. M. DiTomaso, J. B. Grace, R. J. Hobbs, J. E. Keeley, M. Pellant, and D. Pyke. 2004. Effects of invasive alien plants on fire regimes. Bioscience 54:677–688.

Bytnerowicz, A., and M. E. Fenn. 1996. Nitrogen deposition in California forests: A review. Environmental Pollution 92:127–146.

Cairney, J.W.G., and B. A. Bastias. 2007. Influences of fire on forest soil fungal communities. Canadian Journal of Forest Research 37:207–215.

Calkin, H. W., and R. W. Pearcy. 1984. Seasonal progressions of tissue and cell water relations parameters in evergreen and deciduous perennials. Plant, Cell, and Environment 7:347–352.

Callaway, R. M., and C. M. D'Antonio. 1991. Shrub facilitation of coast live oak establishment in central California. Madroño 38:158–169.

Callaway, R. M., and F. W. Davis. 1998. Recruitment of *Quercus agrifolia* in central California: The importance of shrub-dominated patches. Journal of Vegetation Science 9:647–656.

Carlquist, S. 1989. Adaptive wood anatomy of chaparral shrubs. Pages 25–35 in S. C. Keeley, editor. The California chaparral: Paradigms reexamined. Natural History Museum of Los Angeles County, Los Angeles, California.

Chapin, F. S., III, P. A. Matson, and P. M. Vitousek. 2002. Principles of terrestrial ecosystem ecology. Springer-Verlag, New York, New York.

Christensen, N. L. 1973. Fire and the nitrogen cycle in California chaparral. Science 181:66–68.

Christensen, N. L., and C. H. Muller. 1975. Effects of fire on factors controlling plant growth in *Adenostoma* chaparral. Ecological Monographs 45:29–55.

Collins, B. M., and S. L. Stephens. 2010. Stand-replacing patches within a "mixed severity" fire regime: Quantitative characterization using recent fires in a long-established natural fire area. Landscape Ecology 25:927–939.

Comstock, J. P., and B. E. Mahall. 1985. Drought and changes in leaf orientation for two California chaparral shrubs: *Ceanothus megacarpus* and *Ceanothus crassifolius*. Oecologia 65:531–535.

Conard, S. G., and S. R. Radosevich. 1982. Post-fire succession in white fir (*Abies concolor*) vegetation of the northern Sierra Nevada. Madroño 29:42–56.

Cooper, W. S. 1922. The broad-sclerophyll vegetation of California. An ecological study of the chaparral and its related communities. Publication No. 319. Carnegie Institution of Washington, Washington, D.C.

Corbin, J. D., M. A. Thomsen, T. E. Dawson, and C. M. D'Antonio. 2005. Summer water use by California coastal prairie grasses: Fog, drought, and community composition. Oecologia 145:511–521.

Cowling, R. M., F. Ojeda, B. Lamont, P. W. Rundel, and R. Lechmere-Oertel. 2005. Rainfall reliability, a neglected factor in explaining convergence and divergence of plant traits in fire-prone Mediterranean-climate ecosystems. Global Ecology and Biogeography 14:509–519.

Crimmins, S. M., S. Z. Dobrowski, J. A. Greenberg, J. T. Abatzoglou, A. R. Mynsberge 2011. Changes in climatic water balance drive downhill shifts in plant species' optimum elevations. Science 331:324–327. DOI: 10.1126/science.1199040.

Davis, F. W., D. M. Stoms, A. D. Hollander, K. A. Thomas, P. A. Stine, D. Odion, M. I. Borchert, J. H. Thorne, M. V. Gray, R. E. Walker, K. Warner, and J. Graae. 1998. The California Gap Analysis Project—Final Report. University of California, Santa Barbara, California. <http://www.biogeog.ucsb.edu/projects/gap/gap_rep.html>. Accessed January 22, 2013.

Davis, S. D., A. M. Helms, M. S. Heffner, A. R. Shaver, A. C. Deroulet, N. L. Stasiak, S. M. Vaughn, C. B. Leake, H. D. Lee, and E. T. Sayegh. 2007. Chaparral zonation in the Santa Monica Mountains: The influence of freezing temperatures. Fremontia 35(4):12–15.

Davis, S. D., and H. A. Mooney. 1986. Water use patterns of four co-occurring chaparral shrubs. Oecologia 70:172–177.

Davis, S. D., F. W. Ewers, J. S. Sperry, K. A. Portwood, M. C. Crocker, and G. C. Adams. 2002. Shoot dieback during prolonged drought in *Ceanothus* (Rhamnaceae) chaparral of California: A possible case of hydraulic failure. American Journal of Botany 89:820–828.
Davis, S. D., F. W. Ewers, J. Wood, J. J. Reeves, and K. J. Kolb. 1999. Differential susceptibility to xylem cavitation among three pairs of *Ceanothus* species in the Transverse Mountain Ranges of southern California. Ecoscience 6:180–186.
Davis, S. D., F. W. Ewers, R. B. Pratt, P. L. Brown, and T. J. Bowen. 2005. Interactive effects of freezing and drought on long distance transport: A case study for chaparral shrubs of California. Pages 425–435 in N. M. Holbrook and M. A. Zwieniecki, editors. Vascular Transport in Plants. , Elsevier/AP, Oxford, UK.
Davis, S. D., J. S. Sperry, and U. G. Hacke. 1999. The relationship between xylem conduit diameter and cavitation caused by freezing. American Journal of Botany 86:1367–1372.
Davis, S. D., K. J. Kolb, and K. P. Barton. 1998. Ecophysiological processes and demographic patterns in the structuring of California chaparral. Pages 297–310 in P. W. Rundel, G. Montenegro, and F. Jaksic, editors. Landscape degradation and biodiversity. Springer-Verlag, Berlin, Germany.
DeBano, L. F., and C. E. Conrad. 1978. The effect of fire on nutrients in a chaparral ecosystem. Ecology 59:489–497.
DeBano, L. F., and P. H. Dunn. 1982. Soil and nutrient cycling in Mediterranean-type ecosystems: A summary and synthesis. Pages 358–364 in C. E. Conrad and W. C. Oechel, editors. Proceedings of the symposium on dynamics and management of Mediterranean-type ecosystems. USDA Forest Service, Pacific Southwest Forest and Range Experiment Station, Berkeley, California.
DeBano, L. F., G. E. Eberlein, and P. H. Dunn. 1979. Effects of burning on chaparral soils. I. Soil nitrogen. Soil Science Society of America Journal 43:504–509.
DeBano, L. F., P. H. Dunn, and C. E. Conrad. 1977. Fire's effect on physical and chemical properties of chaparral soils. Pages 65–74 in H. A. Mooney and C. E. Conrad, editors. Proceedings of the symposium on environmental consequences of fire and fuel management in Mediterranean ecosystems. General Technical Report WO-3. USDA Forest Service, Washington, D.C.
DeBano, L. F., R. M. Rice, and C. E. Conrad. 1979. Soil heating in chaparral fires: Effects on soil properties, plant nutrients, erosion, and runoff. Research Paper PSW-145. USDA Forest Service, Pacific Southwest Forest and Range Experiment Station, Albany, California.
di Castri, F., and H. A. Mooney, editors. 1973. Mediterranean ecosystems: Origin and structure. Springer-Verlag, New York, New York.
Dunn, P. H., L. F. DeBano, and G. E. Eberlein. 1979. Effect of burning on chaparral soils: II. Soil microbes and nitrogen mineralization. Soil Science Society of America Journal 43:509–514.
Dunne, J. A., and V. T. Parker. 1999. Seasonal soil water potential patterns and establishment of *Pseudotsuga menziesii* seedlings in chaparral. Oecologia 119:36–45.
Egerton-Warburton, L. M., J. I. Querejetam, and M. F. Allen. 2007. Common mycorrhizal networks provide a potential pathway for the transfer of hydraulically lifted water between plants. Journal of Experimental Botany 58:1473–1483.
Egerton-Warburton, L. M., R. C. Graham, and K. R. Hubbert. 2003. Spatial variability in mycorrhizal hyphae and nutrient and water availability in a soil-weathered bedrock profile. Plant and Soil 249:331–342.
Ehleringer, J. R., and J. Comstock. 1989. Stress tolerance and adaptive variation in leaf absorptance and leaf angle. Pages 21–24 in S. C. Keeley, editor. The California chaparral: Paradigms reexamined. Natural History Museum of Los Angeles County, Los Angeles, California.
Ellis, B. A., and J. Kummerow. 1989. The importance of N_2 fixation in *Ceanothus* seedlings in early and postfire chaparral. Pages 115–116 in S. C. Keeley, editor. The California chaparral: Paradigms reexamined. Natural History Museum of Los Angeles County, Los Angeles, California.
Epling, C., and H. Lewis. 1942. The centers of distribution of the chaparral and coastal sage. American Midland Naturalist 27:445–462.
Evola, S., and D. R. Sandquist. 2010. Quantification of fog input and use by *Quercus pacifica* on Santa Catalina Island. Proceedings of an on-island workshop, February 2–4, 2007. Catalina Island Conservancy, Avalon, California.
Ewers, F. W., M. C. Lawson, T. J. Bowen, and S. D. Davis. 2003. Freeze/thaw stress in *Ceanothus* of southern California chaparral. Oecologia 136:213–219.
Fellers, G. M. 1994. Species diversity, selectivity, and habitat associations of small mammals from coastal California. Southwestern Naturalist 39:128–136.
Fenn, M. E. and M. A. Poth. 1999. Temporal and spatial trends in streamwater nitrate concentrations in the San Bernardino Mountains, southern California. Journal of Environmental Quality 28:822–836.
Fenn, M. E., M. A. Poth, and D. W. Johnson. 1996. Evidence for nitrogen saturation in the San Bernardino Mountains in southern California. Forest Ecology and Management 82:211–230.
Fenn, M. E., M. A. Poth, J. D. Aber, J. S. Baron, B. T. Bormann, D. W. Johnson, A. D. Lemly, S. G. McNulty, D. F. Ryan, and R. Stottlemyer. 1998. Nitrogen excess in North American ecosystems: Predisposing factors, ecosystem responses, and management strategies. Ecological Applications 8:706–733.
Fenn, M. E., M. A. Poth, P. H. Dunn, and S. C. Barro. 1993. Microbial N and biomass, respiration and N mineralization in soils beneath two chaparral species along a fire-induced age gradient. Soil Biology and Biochemistry 25:457–466.
Field, C. B., and S. D. Davis. 1989. Physiological ecology. Pages 154–164 in S. C. Keeley, editor. The California chaparral: Paradigms reexamined. Natural History Museum of Los Angeles County, Los Angeles, California.
Field, C., and H. A. Mooney. 1986. The photosynthesis—nitrogen relationship in wild plants. Pages 25–55 in T. J. Givnish, editor. On the economy of plant form and function. Cambridge University Press, Cambridge, UK.
Field, C., J. Merino, and H. A. Mooney. 1983. Compromises between water-use efficiency and nitrogen-use efficiency in five species of California evergreens. Oecologia 60:384–389.
Frazer, J. M., and S. D. Davis. 1988. Differential survival of chaparral seedlings during the first summer drought after wildfire. Oecologia 76:215–221.
Fulton, R. E., and F. L. Carpenter. 1979. Pollination, reproduction, and fire in California *Arctostaphylos*. Oecologia 38:147–157.
Gabet, E. J., and T. Dunne. 2002. Landslides on coastal sage-scrub and grassland hillslopes in a severe El Niño winter: The effects of vegetation conversion on sediment delivery. Geological Society of America Bulletin 114:983–990.
Gill, D. S., and B. E. Mahall. 1986. Quantitative phenology and water relations of an evergreen and a deciduous chaparral shrub. Ecological Monographs 56:127–143.
Gould, S. J., and R. C. Lewontin. 1979. The spandrels of San Marco and the Panglossian paradigm: A critique of the adaptationist programme. Proceedings of the Royal Society of London. Series B. Biological Sciences 205:581–598.
Gray, J. T. 1983. Nutrient use by evergreen and deciduous shrubs in southern California. I. Community nutrient cycling and nutrient-use efficiency. Journal of Ecology 71:21–41.
———. 1982. Community structure and productivity in *Ceanothus* chaparral and coastal sage scrub of southern California. Ecological Monographs 52:415–435.
Gray, J. T., and W. H. Schlesinger. 1981. Nutrient cycling in Mediterranean type ecosystems. Pages 259–285 in P. C. Miller, editor. Resource use by chaparral and matorral. Springer-Verlag, New York, New York.
Griffin, J. R. 1978. Maritime chaparral and endemic shrubs of the Monterey Bay region, California. Madroño 25:65–81.
Grogan, P., T. D. Bruns, and F. S. Chapin. 2000. Fire effects on ecosystem nitrogen cycling in a Californian bishop pine forest. Oecologia 122:537–544.
Hamilton, E. L., and P. B. Rowe. 1949. Rainfall interception by chaparral in California. USDA Forest Service, California Forest and Range Experiment Station, Berkeley, California.
Hanes, T. L. 1981. California chaparral. Pages 139–174 in F. di Castri, D. W. Goodall, and R. L. Specht, editors. Ecosystems of the World. 11. Mediterranean-type shrublands. Elsevier Scientific, New York, New York.
———. 1977. California chaparral. Pages 417–470 in M. G. Barbour and J. Major, editors. Terrestrial vegetation of California. John Wiley & Sons, New York, New York.
———. 1971. Succession after fire in the chaparral of southern California. Ecological Monographs 41:27–52.

Harrison, A. T., E. Small, and H. A. Mooney. 1971. Drought relationships and distribution of two Mediterranean-climate California plant communities. Ecology 52:869–875.

Hayhoe, K., D. Cayan, C. B. Field, P. C. Frumhoff, E. P. Maurer, N. L. Miller, S. C. Moser, S. H. Schneider, K. N. Cahill, E. E. Cleland, L. Dale, R. Drapek, R. M. Hanemann, L. S. Kalkstein, J. Lenihan, C. K. Lunch, R. P. Neilson, S. C. Sheridan, J. H. Verville. 2004. Emissions pathways, climate change, and impacts on California. Proceedings of the National Academy of Sciences (USA) 101(34):12422–12427.

Hellmers, H., J. F. Bonner, and J. M. Kelleher. 1955. Soil fertility: A watershed management problem in the San Gabriel Mountains of southern California. Soil Science 80:189–197.

Hellmers, H., J. S. Horton, G. Juhren, and J. O'Keefe. 1955. Root systems of some chaparral plants in southern California. Ecology 36:667–678.

Herrera, C. M. 1992. Historical effects and sorting processes as explanations of contemporary ecological patterns: character syndromes in Mediterranean woody plants. American Naturalist 140: 421–446.

Hill, L. W. 1963. The San Dimas Experimental Forest. Pacific Southwest Forest and Range Experiment Station, USDA Forest Service, Albany, California.

Hill, L. W., and R. M. Rice. 1963. Converting from brush to grass increases water yield in southern California. Journal of Range Management 16:300–305.

Holden, Z. A., P. Morgan, A. M. S. Smith, and L. Vierling. 2010. Beyond Landsat: A comparison of four satellite sensors for detecting burn severity in ponderosa pine forests of the Gila Wilderness, NM, USA. International Journal of Wildland Fire 19:449–458.

Horton, J. S. 1960. Vegetation types of the San Bernardino Mountains. Technical Paper No. 44. USDA Forest Service, Pacific Southwest Forest and Range Experiment Station, Albany, California.

Horton, J. S., and C. J. Kraebel. 1955. Development of vegetation after fire in the chamise chaparral of southern California. Ecology 36:244–262.

Horton, T. R., E. Cázares, and T. D. Bruns. 1998. Ectomycorrhizal, vesicular-arbuscular, and dark septat fungal colonization of bishop pine (*Pinus muricata*) seedlings in the first 5 months of growth after wildfire. Mycorrhiza 8:11–18.

Horton, T. R., T. Bruns, and V. T. Parker. 1999. Ectomycorrhizal fungi in *Arctostaphylos* patches contribute to the establishment of *Pseudotsuga menziesii*. Canadian Journal of Botany 77:93–102.

Izzo, A. D., M. Canright, and T. D. Bruns. 2006. The effects of heat treatments on ectomycorrhizal resistant propagules and their ability to colonize bioassay seedlings. Mycological Research 110:196–202.

Jackson, W. D. 1968. Fire, air, water, and earth—an elemental ecology of Tasmania. Proceedings of the Ecological Society of Australia 3:9–16.

Jacobsen, A. L., F. W. Ewers, R. B. Pratt, W. A. Paddock III, and S. D. Davis. 2005. Do xylem fibers affect vessel cavitation resistance? Plant Physiology 139:546–556.

Jacobsen, A. L., K. J. Esler, R. B. Pratt, and F. W. Ewers. 2009. Water stress tolerance of shrubs in Mediterranean-type climate regions: Convergence of fynbos and succulent karoo communities with California shrub communities. American Journal of Botany 96:1445–1453.

Jacobsen, A. L., R. B. Pratt, F. W. Ewers, and S. D. Davis. 2007a. Cavitation resistance among twenty-six chaparral species of southern California. Ecological Monographs 77:99–115.

Jacobsen, A. L., R. B. Pratt, S. D. Davis, and F. W. Ewers. 2007b. Cavitation resistance and seasonal hydraulics differ among three arid Californian plant communities. Plant Cell and Environment 30:1599–1609.

Jacobsen, A. L., R. B. Pratt, S. D. Davis, and F. W. Ewers. 2008. Comparative community physiology: Nonconvergence in water relations among three semi-arid shrub communities. New Phytologist 180:100–113.

Jacobsen, A. L., S. D. Davis, and S. L. Babritus. 2004. Fire frequency impacts non-sprouting chaparral shrubs in the Santa Monica Mountains of southern California. M. Arianoutsou and V. P. Panastasis, editors. Ecology and conservation of Mediterranean climate ecosystems. Millpress, Rotterdam, the Netherlands.

Jarbeau, J. A., F. W. Ewers, and S. D. Davis. 1995. The mechanism of water-stress-induced embolism in two species of chaparral shrubs. Plant, Cell, and Environment 18:189–196.

Kaminsky, R. 1981. The microbial origin of the allelopathic potential of *Adenostoma fasciculatum* H. & A. Ecological Monographs 51:365–382.

Keeley, J. E. 2004. VTM plots as evidence of historical change: Goldmine or landmine? Madroño 51:372–378.

———. 2000. Chaparral. Pages 203–253 in M. G. Barbour and W. D. Billings, editors. North American terrestrial vegetation. Cambridge University Press, Cambridge, UK.

———. 1998. Coupling demography, physiology, and evolution in chaparral shrubs. Pages 257–264 in P. W. Rundel, G. Montenegro, and F. Jaksic, editors. Landscape Degradation and Biodiversity in Mediterranean-type Ecosystems. Springer-Verlag, Berlin and Heidelberg, Germany.

———. 1992. Demographic structure of California chaparral in the long-term absence of fire. Journal of Vegetation Science 3:79–90.

———. 1991. Seed germination and life history syndromes in the California chaparral. Botanical Review 57:81–116.

———. 1987. Ten years of change in seed banks of the chaparral shrubs, *Arctostaphylos glauca* and *A. glandulosa*. American Midland Naturalist 117:446–448.

Keeley, J. E., and C. J. Fotheringham. 2000. Role of fire in regeneration from seed. Pages 311–330 in M. Fenner, editor. Seeds: The ecology of regeneration in plant communities. Second edition. CAB International, Oxon, UK.

Keeley, J. E., and F. W. Davis. 2007. Chaparral. Pages 339–366 in M. G. Barbour, T. Keeler-Wolf and A. A. Schoenherr, editors. Terrestrial vegetation of California. Third edition. University of California Press, Los Angeles, California.

Keeley, J. E., and R. L. Hays. 1976. Differential seed predation on two species of *Arctostaphylos* (Ericaceae). Oecologia 24:71–81.

Keeley, J. E. and S. C. Keeley. 1988. Chaparral. Pages 165–207 in M. G. Barbour and W. D. Billings, editors. North American terrestrial vegetation. Cambridge University Press, Cambridge, U.K.

Keeley, J. E., C. J. Fotheringham, and M. Baer-Keeley. 2005a. Determinants of postfire recovery and succession in Mediterranean-climate shrublands of California. Ecological Applications 15:1515–1534.

———. 2005b. Factors affecting plant diversity during postfire recovery and succession of Mediterranean-climate shrublands in California, USA. Diversity and Distributions 11:535–537.

Keeley, J. E., C. J. Fotheringham, and P.W. Rundel. 2012. Postfire regeneration of chaparral under Mediterranean and non-Mediterranean climates. Madroño 59:109–127.

Keeley, J. E., J. G. Pausas, P. W. Rundel, W. J. Bond, and R. A. Bradstock. 2012. Fire as an evolutionary pressure shaping plant traits. Trends in Plant Science 16:406–411.

Keeley, J. E., M. Baer-Keeley, and C. J. Fotheringham. 2005. Alien plant dynamics following fire in Mediterranean-climate California shrublands. Ecological Applications 15:2109–2125.

Keeley, J. E., W. J. Bond, R. A. Bradstock, J. G. Pausas, and P. W. Rundel. 2012. Fire in Mediterranean ecosystems: Ecology, evolution, and management. Cambridge University Press, Cambridge, UK.

Kelly, V. R., and V. T. Parker. 1990. Seed bank survival in sprouting and nonsprouting *Arctostaphylos* species. American Midland Naturalist 124:114–123.

Knight, C. A. 2010. Small heats protein responses differ between chaparral shrubs from contrasting microclimates. Journal of Botany. <doi:10.1155/2010/171435>.

Knipe, O., C. Pase, and R. Carmichael. 1979. Plants of the Arizona chaparral. General Technical Report RM 54. USDA Forest Service, Rocky Mountain Forest and Range Experiment Station, Fort Collins, Colorado.

Kolb, K. J., and S. D. Davis. 1994. Drought tolerance and xylem embolism in co-occurring species of coastal sage and chaparral. Ecology 75:648–659.

Kremen, C., N. M. Williams, R. L. Bugg, J. P. Fay, and R. W. Thorp. 2004. The area requirements of an ecosystem service: Crop pollination by native bee communities in California. Ecology Letters 7:1109–1119.

Kummerow, J., D. Krause, and W. Jow. 1978. Seasonal changes of fine root density in the southern California chaparral. Oecologia 37:201–212.

Kummerow, J., J. V. Alexander, J. W. Neel, and K. Fishbeck. 1978.

Symbiotic nitrogen fixation in *Ceanothus* roots. American Journal of Botany 65:63–69.

Laakkonen, J. 2003. Effect of arboreal activity on species composition and abundance estimates of rodents in a chaparral habitat in southern California. American Midland Naturalist 150:348–351.

LaDochy, S., R. Medina, and W. Patzert. 2007. Recent California climate variability: Spatial and temporal patterns in temperature trends. Climate Research 33:159–169.

Langan, S. J., F. W. Ewers, and S. D. Davis. 1997. Xylem dysfunction caused by water stress and freezing in two species of co-occurring chaparral shrubs. Plant, Cell, and Environment 20:425–437.

Lawrence, G. 1966. Ecology of vertebrate animals in relation to chaparral fire in the Sierra Nevada foothills. Ecology 47:278–291.

Leiberg, J. B. 1902. Forest conditions in the northern Sierra Nevada, California. U.S. Geological Survey Professional Paper No. 8. Series H. Forestry, No. 5. U.S. Government Printing Office, Washington, D.C.

Li, X., T. Meixner, J. O. Sickman, A. E. Miller, J. P. Schimel, and J. M. Melack. 2006. Decadal-scale dynamics of water, carbon, and nitrogen in a California chaparral ecosystem: DAYCENT modeling results. Biogeochemistry 77:217–245.

Lloret, F., and P. H. Zedler. 1991. Recruitment patterns of *Rhus integrifolia* populations in periods between fire in chaparral. Journal of Vegetation Science 2:217–230.

Luo, H., W. C. Oechel, S. J. Hastings, R. Zulueta, Y. Qian, and H. Kwon. 2007. Mature semiarid chaparral ecosystems can be a significant sink for atmospheric carbon dioxide. Global Change Biology 13:386–396.

Marion, G. M., and C. H. Black. 1988. Potentially available nitrogen and phosphorous along a chaparral fire cycle chronosequence. Soil Science Society of American Journal 52:1155–1162.

Marion, G., J. Moreno, and W. Oechel. 1991. Fire severity, ash deposition, and clipping effects on soil nutrients in chaparral. Soil Science Society of America Journal 55:235–240.

McDowell, N., W. T. Pockman, C. D. Allen, D. D. Breshears, N. Cobb, T. Kolb, J. Plaut, J. S. Sperry, A. West, D. G. Williams, and E. A. Yepez. 2008. Mechanisms of plant survival and mortality during drought: Why do some plants survive while others succumb to drought? New Phytologist 178:719–739.

McMaster, G., W. Jow, and J. Kummerow. 1982. Response of *Adenostoma fasciculatum* and *Ceanothus greggii* chaparral to nutrient additions. Journal of Ecology 70:745–756.

McPherson, J. K., and C. H. Muller. 1967. Light competition between *Ceanothus* and *Salvia* shrubs. Bulletin of the Torrey Botanical Club 94:41–55.

Meixner, T. and P. M. Wohlgemuth. 2003. Climate variability, fire, vegetation recovery, and watershed hydrology. Pages 651–656 in K. G. Renard, S. A. McElroy, W. J. Gburek, H. E. Canfield, R. L. Scott, editors. Proceedings of the First Interagency Conference on Research in the Watersheds, Benson, Arizona. October 28–30, 2003.

Millenium Ecosystem Assessment. 2005. Ecosystems and Human Well-Being. World Resources Institute, Washington, D.C.

Miller, D. G., III. 2005. Ecology and radiation of galling aphids (*Tamalia*; Hemiptera: Aphididae) on their host plants (Ericaceae). Basic and Applied Ecology 6:463–469.

Miller, D. G. 1998a. Consequences of communal gall occupation and a test for kin discrimination in the aphid *Tamalia coweni*. Behavioral Ecology and Sociobiology 43:95–103.

———. 1998b. Life history, ecology, and communal gall occupation in the manzanita leaf-gall aphid, *Tamalia coweni* (Cockerell) (Homoptera: Aphididae). Journal of Natural History 32:351–366.

Miller, D. G., and B. Crespi. 2003. The evolution of inquilinism, host-plant use, and mitochondrial substitution rates in *Tamalia* gall aphids. Journal of Evolutionary Biology 16:731–743.

Miller, P. C. 1983. Canopy structure of Mediterranean-type shrubs in relation to heat and moisture. Pages 133–166 in F. J. Kruger, D. T. Mitchell, and J. Jarvis, editors. Mediterranean-type ecosystems. The role of nutrients. Springer-Verlag, New York, New York.

———, editor. 1981. Resource use by chaparral and matorral. Springer-Verlag, New York, New York.

Miller, P. C., and D. K. Poole. 1979. Patterns of water use by shrubs in southern California. Forest Science 25:84–98.

Miller, P. C., and E. Hajek. 1981. Resource availability and environmental characteristics of Mediterranean type ecosystems. Pages 17–41 in P. C. Miller, editor. Resource use by chaparral and matorral. Springer-Verlag, New York, New York.

Mills, J. N. 1983. Herbivory and seedling establishment in post-fire southern California chaparral. Oecologia 60:267–270.

Montygierd-Loyba, T. M., and J. E. Keeley. 1987. Demographic structure of *Ceanothus megacarpus* chaparral in the long absence of fire. Ecology 68:211–213.

Mooney, H. A. 1989. Chaparral physiological ecology—paradigms revisited. Pages 85–90 in S. C. Keeley, editor. The California chaparral: Paradigms reexamined. Natural History Museum of Los Angeles County, Los Angeles, California.

Mooney, H. A., and D. J. Parsons. 1973. Structure and function of the California chaparral: An example from San Dimas. Pages 83–112 in F. di Castri and H. A. Mooney, editors. Mediterranean type ecosystems: Origin and structure. Springer-Verlag, New York, New York.

Mooney, H. A., and E. L. Dunn. 1970a. Convergent evolution of Mediterranean climate evergreen sclerophyll shrubs. Evolution 24:292–303.

———. 1970b. Photosynthetic systems of Mediterranean climate shrubs and trees in California and Chile. American Naturalist 104:447–453.

Mooney, H. A., and P. C. Miller. 1985. Chaparral. Pages 213–231 in B. F. Chabot and H. A. Mooney, editors. Physiological ecology of North American plant communities. Chapman and Hall, New York, New York.

Mooney, H. A., and P. W. Rundel. 1979. Nutrient relations of the evergreen shrub, *Adenostoma fasciculatum*, in the California chaparral. Botanical Gazette 140:109–113.

Mooney, H. A., A. T. Harrison, and P. A. Morrow. 1975. Environmental limitations of photosynthesis on a California evergreen shrub. Oecologia 19:293–301.

Mooney, H. A., J. Kummerow, A. W. Johnson, D. J. Parson, S. Keeley, A. Hoffman, R. I. Hayes, J. Giliberto, and C. Chu. 1977. The producers—their resources and adaptive responses. Pages 85–143 in H. A. Mooney, editor. Convergent evolution of Chile and California Mediterranean climate ecosystems. Dowden, Hutchinson and Ross, Stroudsburg, Pennsylvania.

Mooney, H. A., P. M. Vitousek, and P. A. Matson. 1987. Exchange of materials between terrestrial ecosystems and the atmosphere. Science 238:926.

Moreno, J. M., and W. C. Oechel. 1993. Demography of *Adenostoma fasciculatum* after fires of different intensities in southern California chaparral. Oecologia 96:95–101.

Mosquin, T. 1971. Competition for pollinators as a stimulus for the evolution of flowering time. Oikos 22:398–402.

Mount, A. B. 1964. The interdependence of the eucalypts and forest fires in southern Australia. Australian Forestry 30: 231–242.

Nagel, T. A., and A. H. Taylor. 2005. Fire and persistence of montane chaparral in mixed conifer forest landscapes in the northern Sierra Nevada, Lake Tahoe Basin, California, USA. Journal of the Torrey Botanical Society 132:442–457.

Neary, D. G., C. C. Klopatek, L. F. DeBano, P. F. Folliot. 1999. Fire effects on belowground sustainability: A review and synthesis. Forest Ecology and Management 122:51–71.

Neelin, J. D., B. Langenbrunner, J. S. Meyerson, A. Hall, and N. Berg. 2013. California winter precipitation change under global warming in the coupled model intercomparison project phase 5 ensemble. Journal of Climate 26:6238–6256.

Ng, E., and P. C. Miller. 1980. Soil moisture relations in the southern California chaparral. Ecology 61:98–107.

Nilsen, E. T., and W. H. Schlesinger. 1981. The influence of the Mediterranean climate on nutrients, particularly nitrogen in an even aged stand of the summer deciduous, fire response shrub *Lotus scoparius*. Oecologia 50:217–224.

Odion, D. C., and F. W. Davis. 2000. Fire, soil heating, and the formation of vegetation patterns in chaparral. Ecological Monographs 70:149–169.

Odion, D., and C. Tyler. 2002. Are long fire-free periods needed to maintain the endangered fire-recruiting shrub *Arctostaphylos morroensis* (Ericaceae)? Conservation Ecology 6(2):4. <http://www.consecol.org/vol6/iss2/art4>. Accessed October 13, 2009.

Odion, D. C., M. A. Moritz, and D. A. DellaSala. 2010. Alternative community states maintained by fire in the Klamath Mountains, USA. Journal of Ecology 98:96–105.

Oechel, W. C., S. J. Hastings, G. L. Vourlitis, M. A. Jenkins, and C. L.

Hinkson. 1995. Direct effects of elevated CO_2 in chaparral and Mediterranean-type ecosystems. Pages 58–75 in J. M. Moreno and W. C. Oechel, editors. Global Change and Mediterranean-Type Ecosystems. Springer-Verlag, New York, New York.

Oechel, W. C., W. T. Lawrence, J. Mustafa, and J. Martinez. 1981. Energy and carbon acquisition. Pages 151–183 in P. C. Miller, editor. Resource use by chaparral and matorral. Springer-Verlag, New York, New York.

Oertli, J., S. Lips, and M. Agami. 1990. The strength of sclerophyllous cells to resist collapse due to negative turgor pressure. Acta oecologica 11:281–289.

O'Neil, S. E., and V. T. Parker. 2005. Factors contributing to the seed bank size of two obligate seeding *Ceanothus* species in northern California. Madroño 52:182–190.

Orians, G. H., and O. T. Solbrig. 1977. A cost-income model of leaves and roots with special reference to arid and semiarid areas. American Naturalist 111:677–690.

Paddock, W. A. S., III, S. D. Davis, R. B. Pratt, A. L. Jacobsen, M. F. Tobin, J. Lopez-Portillo, and F. W. Ewers. 2013. Factors determining mortality of adult chaparral shrubs in an extreme drought year in California. Aliso 31:49–57.

Parker, V. T. 2010. How will obligate seeders survive climate change: Persistent seed banks, immaturity risk, and rodent-caching in *Arctostaphylos* (Ericaceae). Presentation and abstract, Ecological Society of America, 2010 Annual Meeting, Pittsburg, Pennsylvania.

———. 1990. Problems encountered while mimicking nature in vegetation management: An example from a fire-prone vegetation. Pages 231–234 in R. S. Mitchell, C. J. Sheviak and D. J. Leopold, editors. Ecosystem Management: Rare species and significant habitats. Proceedings of the 15th Annual Natural Areas Conference. New York State Museum Bulletin 471.

———. 1987. Effect of wet-season management burns on chaparral regeneration: Implications for rare species. Pages 233–237 in T. E. Elias, editor. Conservation and Management of Rare and Endangered Plants. California Native Plant Society, Sacramento, California.

———. 1984. Correlation of physiological divergence with reproductive mode in chaparral shrubs. Madroño 31:231–242.

Parker, V. T., and S. T. A. Pickett. 1998. Historical contingency and multiple scales of dynamics in plant communities. Pages 171–191 in D. L. Peterson and V. T. Parker, editors. Ecological Scale: Theory and applications. Columbia University Press, New York.

Parker, V. T., and V. R. Kelly. 1989. Seed banks in California chaparral and other Mediterranean climate shrublands. Pages 231–255 in M. A. Leck, V. T. Parker, and R. L. Simpson, editors. Ecology of soil seed banks. Academic Press, San Diego, California.

Patric, J. H. 1961. The San Dimas large lysimeters. Journal of Soil and Water Conservation 16:13–17.

Peay, K. G., M. Garbelotto, and T. D. Bruns. 2009. Spore heat resistance plays an important role in disturbance-mediated assemblage shift of ectomycorrhizal fungi colonizing seedlings. Journal of Ecology 97:537–547.

Peay, K. G., T. D. Bruns, and M. Garbelotto. 2010. Testing the ecological stability of ectomycorrhizal symbiosis: Effects of heat, ash, and mycorrhizal colonization on *Pinus muricata* seedling performance. Plant and Soil 330:291–302.

Plamboeck, A. H., T. E. Dawson, L. M. Egerton-Warburton, M. North, T. D. Bruns, and J. I. Querejeta. 2007. Water transfer via ectomycorrhizal fungal hyphae to conifer seedlings. Mycorrhiza 17:439–447.

Poole, D. K., and P. C. Miller. 1981. The distribution of plant water stress and vegetation characteristics in southern California chaparral. American Midland Naturalist 105:32–43.

———. 1975. Water relations of selected species of chaparral and coastal sage communities. Ecology 56:1118–1128.

Poole, D. K., S. W. Roberts, and P. C. Miller. 1981. Water utilization. Pages 123–149 in P. C. Miller, editor. Resource use by chaparral and matorral. Springer-Verlag, New York, New York.

Pratt, R. B., A. L. Jacobsen, A. R. Ramirez, A. M. Helms, C. A. Traugh, M. F. Tobin, M. S. Heffner, and S. D. Davis. 2014. Mortality of resprouting chaparral shrubs after a fire and during a record drought: Physiological mechanisms and demographic consequences. Global Change Biology 20:893–907.

Pratt, R. B., A. L. Jacobsen, F. W. Ewers, and S. D. Davis. 2007. Relationships among xylem transport, biomechanics, and storage in stems and roots of nine Rhamnaceae species of the California chaparral. New Phytologist 174:787–798.

Pratt, R. B., A. L. Jacobsen, J. Hernandez, F. W. Ewers, G. B. North, and S. D. Davis. 2012. Allocation tradeoffs among chaparral shrub seedlings with different life history types (Rhamnaceae). American Journal of Botany 99:1464–1476.

Pratt, R. B., A. L. Jacobsen, K. A. Golgotiu, J. S. Sperry, F. W. Ewers, and S. D. Davis. 2007. Life history type and water stress tolerance in nine California chaparral species (Rhamnaceae). Ecological Monographs 77:239–253.

Pratt, R. B., A. L. Jacobsen, R. Mohla, F. W. Ewers, and S. D. Davis. 2008. Linkage between water stress tolerance and life history type in seedlings of nine chaparral species (Rhamnaceae) Journal of Ecology 96:1252–1265.

Pratt, R. B., F. W. Ewers, M. C. Lawson, A. L. Jacobsen, M. M. Brediger, and S. D. Davis. 2005. Mechanisms for tolerating freeze-thaw stress of two evergreen chaparral species: *Rhus ovata* and *Malosma laurina* (Anacardiaceae). American Journal of Botany 92:1102–1113.

Pratt, R. B., G. B. North, A. L. Jacobsen, F. W. Ewers, and S. D. Davis. 2010. Xylem root and shoot hydraulics is linked to life history type in chaparral seedlings. Functional Ecology 24:70–81.

Pratt, S. D., A. S. Konopka, M. A. Murry, F. W. Ewers, and S. D. Davis. 1997. Influence of soil moisture on the nodulation of post fire seedlings of *Ceanothus* spp. growing in the Santa Monica Mountains of southern California. Physiologia Plantarum 99:673–679.

Price, M. V., N. M. Waser, K. E. Taylor, and K. L. Pluff. 1995. Fire as a management tool for Stephen's kangaroo rat and other small mammal species. Pages 51–61 in J. E. Keeley and T. Scott, editors. Brushfire in California: Ecology and resource management. International Association of Wildland Fire, Fairfield, Washington.

Quideau, S., R. Graham, O. Chadwick, and H. Wood. 1998. Organic carbon sequestration under chaparral and pine after four decades of soil development. Geoderma 83:227–242.

Quideau, S., R. Graham, S.-W. Oh, P. Hendrix, and R. Wasylishen. 2005. Leaf litter decomposition in a chaparral ecosystem, southern California. Soil Biology and Biochemistry 37:1988–1998.

Quinn. R. D. 1994. Animals, fire, and vertebrate herbivory in Californian chaparral and other Mediterranean-type ecosystems. Pages 46–78 in J. M. Moreno and W. C. Oechel, editors. The role of fire in Mediterranean-type ecosystems. Springer-Verlag, New York, New York.

Ramirez, A. R., R. B. Pratt, A. L. Jacobsen, and S. D. Davis. 2012. Exotic deer diminish post-fire resilience of native shrub communities on Santa Catalina Island, southern California. Plant Ecology 213:1037–1047.

Reid, C., and W. Oechel. 1984. Effects of shrubland management on vegetation. Pages 25–41 in J. J. DeVries, editor. Shrublands in California: Literature review and research needed for management. University of California, Davis, California.

Ren, D., R. Fu, L. M. Leslie, and R. E. Dickinson. 2011. Modeling the mudslide aftermath of the 2007 southern California wildfires. Natural Hazards 57:327–343.

Riggan, P. J., S. Franklin, and J. A. Brass. 1985. Fire and chaparral management at the chaparral/urban interface. Fremontia 14:28–30.

Roberts, S. W. 1982. Some recent aspects and problems of chaparral plant water relations. Pages 351–357 in C. E. Conrad and W. C. Oechel, editors. Proceedings of the symposium on dynamics and management of Mediterranean-type ecosystems. USDA Forest Service, Pacific Southwest Forest and Range Experiment Station, Albany, California.

Rowe, R. B., and E. A. Colman. 1951. Disposition of rainfall in two mountain areas of California. Agriculture Technical Bulletin 1018. USDA.

Rundel, P. W. 1983. Impact of fire on nutrient cycles in Mediterranean-type ecosystems with reference to chaparral. Pages 192–207 in F. J. Kruger, D. T. Mitchell, and J. Jarvis, editors. Mediterranean-type ecosystems. The role of nutrients. Springer-Verlag, New York, New York.

Rundel, P. W., and D. J. Parsons. 1980. Nutrient changes in two chaparral shrubs along a fire-induced age gradient. American Journal of Botany 67:51–58.

———. 1979. Structural changes in chamise (*Adenostoma fasciculatum*) along a fire induced age gradient. Journal of Range Management 32:462–466.

Sage, R. F., D. A. Wedin, and M. Li. 1999. The biogeography of C4 photosynthesis: Patterns and controlling factors. Pages 313–373 in R. F. Sage and R. K. Monson, editors. C4 plant biology. Academic Press, New York, New York.

Saruwatari, M. W., and S. D. Davis. 1989. Tissue water relations of three chaparral shrub species after wildfire. Oecologia 80:303–308.

Sawyer, J. O., and T. Keeler-Wolf. 1995. A manual of California vegetation. California Native Plant Society, Sacramento, California.

Schimper, A. F. W. 1903. Plant-geography upon a physiological basis. Clarendon Press, Oxford, UK.

Schlesinger, W. H. 1985. Decomposition of chaparral shrub foliage. Ecology 66:1353–1359.

Schlesinger, W. H., and D. S. Gill. 1980. Biomass, production, and changes in the availability of light, water, and nutrients during development of pure stands of the chaparral shrub, *Ceanothus megacarpus*, after fire. Ecology 61:781–789.

Schlesinger, W. H., and M. M. Hasey. 1981. Decomposition of chaparral shrub foliage losses of organic and inorganic constituents from deciduous and evergreen leaves. Ecology 62:762–774.

———. 1980. The nutrient content of precipitation, dry fallout, and intercepted aerosols in the chaparral of southern California. American Midland Naturalist 103:114–122.

Schwilk, D. W., and J. E. Keeley. 1998. Rodent populations after a large wildfire in California chaparral and coastal sage scrub. Southwestern Naturalist 43:480–483.

Shaver, G. R. 1981. Mineral nutrient and nonstructural carbon utilization. Pages 237–257 in P. C. Miller, ed. Resource use by chaparral and matorral. Springer-Verlag, New York, New York.

Show, S. B., and E. I. Kotok. 1924. The role of fire in California pine forests. U.S. Department of Agriculture Bulletin 1294. USDA, Washington, D.C.

Smith, S. E., and D. J. Read. 1997. Mycorrhizal symbiosis. Second edition. Academic Press, San Diego, California.

Soulé, M. E., D. T. Bolger, A. C. Alberts, J. Wrights, M. Sorice, and S. Hill. 1988. Reconstructed dynamics of rapid extinctions of chaparral-requiring birds in urban habitat islands. Conservation Biology, 2:75–92. doi: 10.1111/j.1523-1739.1988.tb00337.x

Sparling, P. M. 1994. Invasion of *Pseudotsuga menziesii* into chaparral: Analysis of spatial and temporal patterns. MA thesis. San Francisco State University, San Francisco, California.

Stoll, W. 1998. Diversity and composition of mycorrhizal fungal community following fire in lodgepole pine. MA thesis. Department of Biology, San Francisco State University, California.

Stylinski, C., J. Gamon, and W. Oechel. 2002. Seasonal patterns of reflectance indices, carotenoid pigments, and photosynthesis of evergreen chaparral species. Oecologia 131:366–374.

Swank, S. E., and W. C. Oechel. 1991. Interactions among the effects of herbivory, competition, and resource limitation on chaparral herbs. Ecology 72:104–115.

Sweeney, R. 1956. Responses of vegetation to fire: A study of the herbaceous vegetation following chaparral fires. University of California Publications in Botany 29:143–216.

Taylor, A. H., and C. N. Skinner. 1998. Fire history and landscape dynamics in a late-successional reserve, Klamath Mountains, California, USA. Forest Ecology and Management 111:285–301.

Taylor, D. L., and T. D. Bruns. 1999. Community structure of ectomycorrhizal fungi in a *Pinus muricata* forest: Minimal overlap between the mature forest and resistant propagule communities. Molecular Ecology 8:1837–1850.

Thomas, C. M., and S. D. Davis. 1989. Recovery patterns of three chaparral shrub species after wildfire. Oecologia 80:309–320.

Thompson, J. R., T. A. Spies, and L. M. Ganio. 2007. Reburn severity in managed and unmanaged vegetation in a large wildfire. Proceedings of the National Academy of Sciences 104:10743–10748.

Treseder, K. K., and M. F. Allen. 2000. Mycorrhizal fungi have a potential role in soil carbon storage under elevated CO_2 and nitrogen deposition. New Phytologist 147:189–200.

Tyree, M. T., and J. S. Sperry. 1989. Vulnerability of xylem to cavitation and embolism. Annual Review of Plant Physiology and Molecular Biology 40:19–38.

Ulery, A., R. Graham, O. Chadwick, and H. Wood. 1995. Decade-scale changes of soil carbon, nitrogen, and exchangeable cations under chaparral and pine. Geoderma 65:121–134.

Valenti, M. A., G. T. Ferrell, and A. A. Berryman. 1997. Insects and related arthropods associated with greenleaf manzanita in montane chaparral communities of northeastern California. USDA Forest Service, Pacific Southwest Research Station, Forest Service Gen. Tech. Rep. PSW-GTR-167. Albany, California.

Valeron, B., and T. Meixner. 2010. Overland flow generation in chaparral ecosystems: Temporal and spatial variability. Hydrological Processes 24:65–75.

Valiente-Banuet, A., A. Vital, M. Verdú, R. Callaway. 2006. Modern Quaternary plant lineages promote diversity through facilitation of ancient Tertiary lineages. Proceedings National Academy of Sciences USA 103:16812–16817.

Valiente-Banuet, A., M. Verdú, F. Valladares, and P. Garcia-Fayos. 2010. Functional and evolutionary correlations of steep leaf angles in the mexical shrubland. Oecologia 163:25–33.

Valladares, F., and R. W. Pearcy. 1997. Interactions between water stress, sun-shade acclimation, heat tolerance, and photoinhibition in the sclerophyll *Heteromeles arbutifolia*. Plant, Cell, and Environment 20:25–36.

van Wagtendonk, J. W., K. A. van Wagtendonk, and A. E. Thode. 2012. Factors associated with the severity of intersecting fires in Yosemite National Park, California, USA. Fire Ecology 8:11–31. <doi:10.4996/fireecology.0801011>.

Vankat, J. 1989. Water stress in chaparral shrubs in summer rain versus summer drought climates. Whither the Mediterranean type climate paradigm. Pages 117–124 in S. C. Keeley, editor. The California chaparral: Paradigms reexamined. Natural History Museum of Los Angeles County, Los Angeles, California.

Vankat, J. L., and J. Major. 1978. Vegetation changes in Sequoia National Park, California. Journal of Biogeography 5:377–402.

Vasey, M. C., M. E. Loik, and V. T. Parker. 2012. Influence of summer marine fog and low cloud stratus on water relations of evergreen woody shrubs (*Arctostaphylos*: Ericaceae) in the chaparral of central California. Oecologia 170 (2):1–13

Vasey, M. C., V. T. Parker, K. D. Holl, M. E. Loik and S. Hiatt. 2014. Maritime climate influence on chaparral composition and diversity in the coast range of central California. Ecology and Evolution 4(18):3662–3674.

Verdú, M., P. Dávila, P. García-Fayos, N. Flores-Hernández, and A. Valiente-Banuet. 2003. "Convergent" traits of Mediterranean woody plants belong to pre-Mediterranean lineages. Biological Journal of the Linnean Society 78:415–427.

Vogl, R. J. 1977. Fire frequency and site degradation. Pages 151–162 in H. A. Mooney and C. E. Conrad, editors. Proceedings of the symposium on environmental consequences of fire and fuel management in Mediterranean ecosystems. USDA Forest Service, General Technical Report WO-3, Washington, D.C.

Vourlitis, G. L. 2012. Aboveground net primary production response of semi-arid shrublands to chronic experimental dry-season N input. Ecosphere 3. art22. <http://dx.doi.org/10.1890/ES11-00339.1>.

Vourlitis, G. L, and J. Fernandez. 2012. Changes in the soil, litter, and vegetation nitrogen and carbon concentrations of semiarid shrublands in response to chronic dry season nitrogen input. Journal of Arid Environments 82:115–122.

Vourlitis, G. L., S. C. Pasquini, and R. Mustard. 2009. Effects of dry-season N input on the productivity and N storage of Mediterranean-type shrublands. Ecosystems 12:473–488.

Wagner, K. R., F. W. Ewers, and S. D. Davis. 1998. Tradeoffs between hydraulic efficiency and mechanical strength in the stems of four co-occurring species of chaparral shrubs. Oecologia 117:53–62.

Waring, R. H., and W. H. Schlesinger. 1985. Forest ecosystems: Concepts and management. Academic Press, Oxford, UK.

Warzecha, B., and V. T. Parker. 2014. Differential post-dispersal seed predation drives chaparral seed bank dynamics. Plant Ecology 215:1313–1322.

Weatherspoon, C. P., and C. N. Skinner. 1995. An assessment of factors associated with damage to tree crowns from 1987 wildfires in northern California. Forest Science 41:430–451.

Wells, P. V. 1962. Vegetation in relation to geological substratum and fire in the San Luis Obispo quadrangle, California. Ecological Monographs 32:79–103.

Westerling, A. L., H. G. Hidalgo, D. R. Cayan, and T. W. Swetnam. 2006. Warming and earlier spring increase western U.S. forest wildfire activity. Science 313:940–943.

Westman, W. E. 1991. Measuring realized niche spaces: Climatic response of chaparral and coastal sage scrub. Ecology 72:1678–1684.

Wilken, G. C. 1967. History and fire record of a timberland brush field in the Sierra Nevada of California. Ecology 48:302–304.

Williams, J. E., S. D. Davis, and K. A. Portwood. 1997. Xylem embolism in seedlings and resprouts of *Adenostoma fasciculatum* after fire. Australian Journal of Botany 45:291–300.

Wright, I. J., P. B. Reich, M. Westoby, D. D. Ackerly, Z. Baruch, F. Bongers, J. Cavender-Bares, T. Chapin, J. H. Cornelissen, M. Diemer, J. Flexas, E. Garnier, P. K. Groom, J. Gulias, K. Hikosaka, B. B. Lamont, T. Lee, W. Lee, C. Lusk, J. J. Midgley, M. L. Navas, U. Niinemets, J. Oleksyn, N. Osada, H. Poorter, P. Poot, L. Prior, V. I. Pyankov, C. Roumet, S. C. Thomas, M. G. Tjoelker, E. J. Veneklaas, and R. Villar. 2004. The worldwide leaf economics spectrum. Nature 428:821–827.

Zedler, P. A. 1982. Demography and chaparral management in southern California. Pages 123–127 in C. E. Conrad and W. C. Oechel, editors. Proceedings of the symposium on environmental consequences of fire and fuel management in Mediterranean ecosystems. General Technical Report WO-3. USDA Forest Service, Washington, D.C.

Zedler, P.H. 1995. Fire frequency in southern California shrublands: Biological effects and management options. Pages 101–112 in J. E. Keeley and T. Scott, editors. Brushfires in California: Ecology and resource management. International Association of Wildland Fire Publisher, Fairfield, Washington.

———. 1981. Vegetation change in chaparral and desert communities in San Diego County, California. Pages 406–430 in D. C. West, H. H. Shugart, and D. Botkin, editors. Forest succession: Concepts and applications Springer-Verlag, New York, New York.

Zedler, P. H., C. R. Gautier, and G. S. McMaster. 1983. Vegetation change in response to extreme events: The effect of a short interval between fires in California chaparral and coastal scrub. Ecology 64:809–818.

TWENTY-FIVE

Oak Woodlands

FRANK W. DAVIS, DENNIS D. BALDOCCHI, and CLAUDIA M. TYLER

Introduction

For thousands of years California's oak woodland and savanna ecosystems have provided a bounty of ecological goods and services to human societies. Oak woodlands harbor high plant and animal diversity and supply livestock forage and firewood. They occur in climates and on soils that can produce many valuable crops, including some of the world's finest wine grapes. They are also among the state's most iconic and attractive landscapes and are prized for rural residential housing (Pavlik et al. 1993). In the 250 years since European settlement, as human values and socioeconomic systems changed and population growth increased pressure on these systems, oak woodlands have undergone significant changes in human use and associated landscape and ecosystem structure, composition, and function. Some KEYSTONE SPECIES, like the California grizzly bear, have been eliminated. Domestic livestock, exotic diseases, and invasive plants and animals have transformed natural communities. Fire, once a dominant force, is now suppressed. Climate, watershed hydrology, and nutrient inputs have changed rapidly over the past century. Today some large tracts of oak woodland still retain their rural character and ranching economy, but many others are fragmented and degraded by residential development, agricultural conversion, and dense road networks.

In this chapter we summarize current knowledge about the distribution, structure, and ecosystem ecology of California oak woodlands and savannas. Another recent review covers the distribution, composition, and general ecology and management of oak woodlands (Allen-Diaz et al. 2007). We focus on biodiversity and ecosystem processes in foothill oak woodlands and particularly blue oak (*Quercus douglasii*) woodlands, where ecosystem processes have been studied in more detail. We discuss historical trends and current patterns of human use of foothill oak woodlands and some ecosystem services they provide. We conclude by considering the future of oak woodlands under projected climate and land use change.

Distribution

By modern convention, "woodland" is defined as vegetation with 20% to 60% tree cover (Sawyer et al. 1995, 2009; Anderson et al. 1998), but California inventories and wildlife habitat assessments have tended to also include vegetation with

10% to 20% tree cover, pooling oak "savannas" and "woodlands" into a single type (Mayer and Laundenslayer 1988, Gaman and Firman 2006). We will broadly define oak woodlands as vegetation with 10% to 60% tree canopy cover, dominated by one to several deciduous or evergreen ARBORESCENT oaks, and with an herbaceous understory often dominated by exotic annual grasses, native and exotic forbs, and scattered shrubs. For some oak woodland types, the understory can alternatively be comprised of a dense layer of shrubs associated with chaparral or coastal sage scrub.

Oak woodlands extend across coastal, foothill, and montane environments, but foothill woodlands are most extensive (Figure 25.1). Southern coastal oak woodlands are dominated by coast live oak (*Q. agrifolia*) or the more geographically restricted Engelmann oak (*Q. engelmannii*). Interior foothill woodlands that occupy the periphery of the Central Valley and Interior Coast Ranges are dominated by blue oak, interior live oak (*Q.wislizenii* var. *wislizenii*), and valley oak (*Q. lobata*). Foothill pine (*Pinus sabiniana*) often co-dominates the tree layer with blue oak in interior foothill woodlands. Oregon white oak (*Q. garryana*) woodlands increase in importance in the northwestern part of state, whereas canyon live oak (*Q. chrysolepis*) and black oak (*Q. kelloggii*) dominate montane oak woodland and forest vegetation across large areas of the Sierra Nevada and Coast Ranges. According to a recent statewide inventory, oak woodlands occupy roughly 3.5 million hectares (8.6 million acres) or 8–9% of the California land area. Foothill oak woodlands account for slightly over 2 million hectares (5.1 million acres), or 60% of the woodland acreage. Blue oak woodland is by far the most widespread type, comprising 37% of all oak woodlands and 62% of foothill oak woodland area (Table 25.1).

Oak Woodland Climate

Oak woodlands experience a Mediterranean-type climate with cool wet winters and hot dry summers. Foothill woodland types develop in locations experiencing 400–800 millimeters (mm) of winter rainfall and mean annual temperatures of 14°C to 17°C (Figure 25.2). Montane woodland and forest types typically receive 1,200–1,400 mm of precipitation as rain and snow and experience mean annual temperatures of 10°C to 11.5°C. Chaparral vegetation is widespread in the lower montane settings between these foothill and montane zones (see Chapter 24, "Chaparral").

Foothill woodland climates combine extreme precipitation and temperature seasonality. Over 90% of precipitation falls between December and March when days are cool and nighttime frosts are common. During the period 1911–2000, winter daily minimum air temperatures at 3,273 sample plot locations supporting blue oak averaged 1.4 ± 1.4°C with over one hundred frost days per year. Summer maximum daily temperatures at these same sites averaged 32.9 ± 3.4°C. High year-to-year variation in precipitation occurs in relation to three- to seven-year El Niño and La Niña climate oscillations and other atmospheric dynamics (Haston and Michaelsen 1994, Jones 2000).

Soil moisture in oak woodlands is highest between January and March and lowest in late summer or early autumn, depending on local rainfall inputs, soil water storage capacity, and losses to actual evapotranspiration (AET), surface runoff, and groundwater. This means that for deciduous oaks like blue oak, valley oak, and Oregon oak, soil water supply is greatest several months before the tree canopy has fully developed. While many understory plants, notably now-dominant non-native annual grasses, have winter-spring growing seasons to exploit the early pulse of shallow soil moisture, foothill oaks must be adapted to withstand hot and dry summer-growing seasons. The asynchrony between water supply and demand in oak woodlands is illustrated by trajectories of cumulative CLIMATE WATER DEFICIT (CWD) between December and November (Figure 25.3). This deficit is the difference between potential evapotranspiration (PET), which is the amount of water that would have been lost had it been available, and actual evapotranspiration (AET) as limited by available soil water (Stephenson 1998). Given a soil's water-holding capacity and wilting point, soil water available for evapotranspiration (AW) can be estimated as (Flint and Flint 2007):

$$AW = P + S_m - PET - S_a + S_s \qquad \text{(Eq 25.1)}$$

Where,

P = precipitation
S_m = snowmelt
PET = potential evapotranspiration, estimated based on modeled hourly solar radiation and air temperature (the Priestley-Taylor equation)
S_a = snow accumulation and snow storage carried over from previous time period
S_s = soil water storage carried over from the previous time period

When CWD is positive, evaporative demand exceeds available soil water. In blue oak and coast live oak woodlands, modeled cumulative CWD is close to zero between November and April but increases rapidly thereafter (see Figure 25.3). Averaged across the ranges of the species, cumulative CWD for coast live oak and blue oak totals over 800 mm by the end of the year. Cumulative CWD is less than 500 mm for black oak, which occupies wetter and cooler environments. The CWD trajectories suggest that readily available soil water, at least as modeled using mapped soil water-holding capacity and climate grids, is depleted by late spring, during or shortly after the production of new foliage. This implies that oaks must also be tapping deeper groundwater or water in rock fractures to remain active throughout the hot summer months, a conclusion supported by tracer studies (Lewis and Burgy 1964), water balance models, and observed water table fluctuations (Miller et al. 2010, Gou and Miller 2013). In summary, the various oak woodland ecosystems in California occur across a fairly wide range of temperature and rainfall regimes. Additional variation is created by local topography and soil properties that exert a strong control on radiation and temperature, evapotranspiration, and available soil water supply. The resulting local environments exert strict and multiple constraints on oak woodland function, structure, and metabolism, as is discussed below.

Biodiversity and Characteristic Species

The rich flora and fauna of California's oak woodlands contribute considerably to the designation of the California

Photo on previous page: Blue oaks at the University of California Sedgwick Reserve near Los Olivos covered with the epiphytic lichen, *Ramalina menziesii*. Photo: C. Tyler.

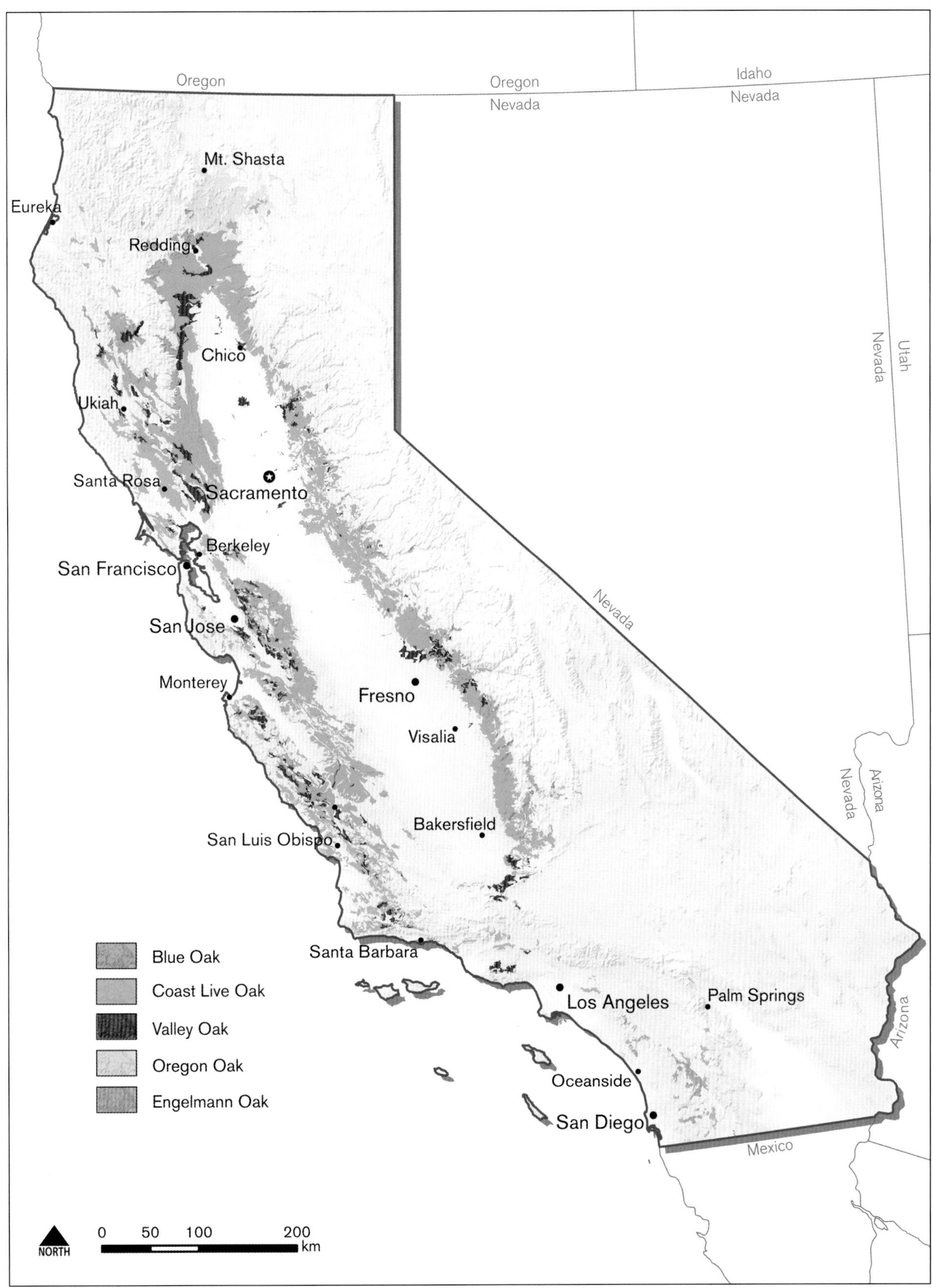

FIGURE 25.1 Generalized distributions of foothill oak woodlands in California. Montane oak woodlands are not mapped. Data from U.S. Geological Survey, Gap Analysis Program (GAP). Map: Parker Welch, Center for Integrated Spatial Research (CISR).

TABLE 25.1
Areal extent of oak woodlands in California, circa 2003, based on 30-meter satellite imagery and ancillary sources.

Woodland type	Acres	Hectares	Phenology	General distribution
FOOTHILL WOODLANDS				
Engelman oak* *Quercus engelmannii*	20,367	8,246	Semideciduous	Narrowly distributed endemic, Peninsular Ranges, mainly San Diego and Riverside Counties
Coast live oak *Q. agrifolia*	930,534	376,734	Evergreen	Coastal plain, valleys, and foothills of the Central Coast Ranges, Transverse Ranges and Peninsular Ranges
Valley oak* *Q. lobata*	85,882	34,770	Deciduous	Interior valleys, foothills, and riparian zones, Santa Monica Mountains north to Oregon
Blue oak* *Q. douglasii*	3,184,018	1,289,076	Deciduous	Interior foothills of the Central Coast Ranges and foothills surrounding the Central Valley
Interior live oak* *Q. wislizeni var. wislizeni*	869,380	351,976	Evergreen	Foothill to lower montane zones surrounding the Central Valley and in southern ranges, from the upper Sacramento Valley to northern Baja California
MONTANE AND NORTHERN WOODLANDS				
Black oak *Q. kelloggii*	692,507	280,367	Deciduous	Lower to mid-montane zone, widespread throughout mountain ranges west of and including the Sierra Nevada
Oregon oak *Q. garryana*	639,449	258,886	Deciduous	Valleys and foothills, western Sierra Nevada, Cascades, and North Coast Ranges north to British Columbia
Canyon live oak* *Q. chrysolepis*	1,016,373	411,487	Evergreen	Lower and mid-montane zones throughout California
Tanoak *Notholithocarpus densiflorus*	388,695	157,366	Evergreen	Coastal and lower montane, mainly Coast Ranges with scattered population in Cascades and northern Sierra Nevada
Mixed oak	738,455	298,970	Mixed	Foothill and montane zones, especially upper Sacramento Valley, North Coast Ranges, and Central Coast Ranges
TOTAL	**8,565,660**	**3,467,879**		

SOURCE: Gaman and Firman 2006.
* Indicates species whose native ranges are restricted or nearly so to California.

Floristic Province as a "biodiversity hotspot" (Myers et al. 2000). Only a handful of tree species define and shape these communities, but this relatively simple structure belies the diversity within. Oak woodlands support thousands of understory plant species, over three hundred species of vertebrates, and thousands of invertebrate species. This diversity creates complex networks of species interactions and interdependence that have yet to be extensively studied. Here we focus on some of the principal organisms and interactions that play key roles in these communities.

Plants

Blue oaks can be the only overstory species over large areas of blue oak woodland. Other tree species present in these woodlands can include foothill pine, California buckeye (*Aesculus californica*), valley oak, interior live oak, and coast live oak (Pavlik et al. 1993, Sawyer et al. 2009). Co-dominant tree species in valley oak woodlands include trees common to riparian habitats such as box elder (*Acer negundo*), white alder (*Alnus rhombifolia*), Oregon ash (*Fraxinus latifolia*), western sycamore (*Platanus racemosa*), Fremont cottonwood (*Populus fremontii*), and California walnut (*Juglans californica*). In drier upland habitats, valley oaks can co-occur with coast live oak, interior live oak, or blue oak (Pavlik et al. 1993, Sawyer et al. 2009).

Coast live oaks often occur in monospecific woodland and forest stands. Other tree species present can include bigleaf maple (*Acer macrophyllum*), box elder, madrone (*Arbutus menziesii*), California walnut, western sycamore, Fremont cottonwood, blue oak, valley oak, and bay laurel (*Umbellularia californica*) (Pavlik et al. 1993, Sawyer et al. 2009). The herbaceous understory is the locus of oak woodland plant diver-

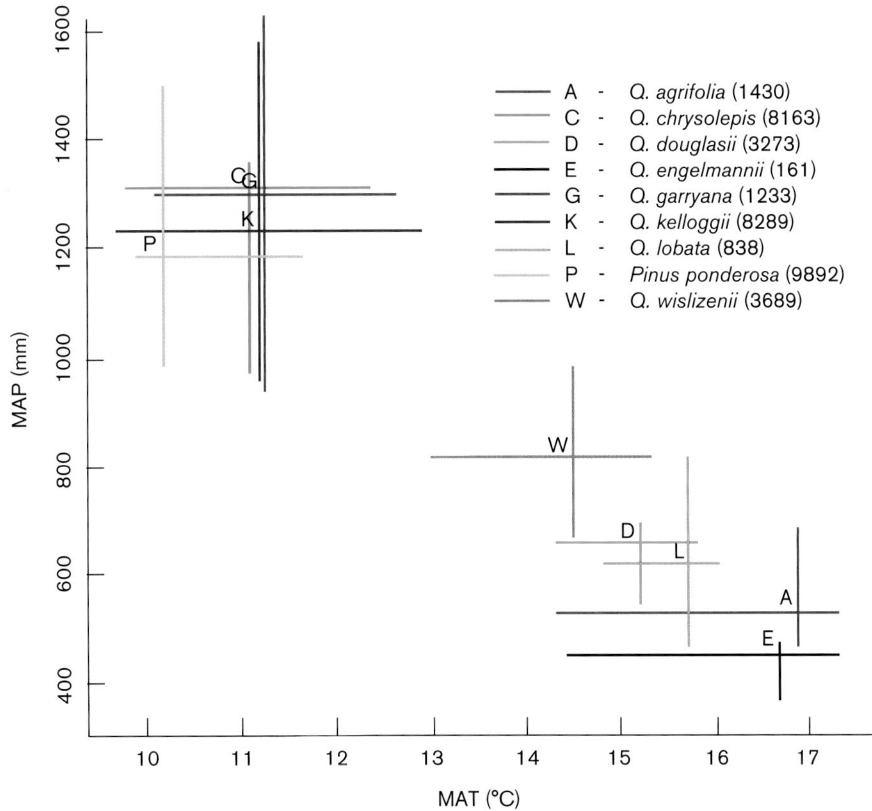

FIGURE 25.2 Modeled median annual temperature (MAT) and median annual precipitation (MAP), 1971–2000, at locations supporting eight dominant species of California oaks. Ponderosa pine is included for comparison. The 270 meter climate grids are produced as described in Flint and Flint 2012 and downloaded from <http://climate.calcommons.org>. Climate values extracted for species localities in the database as described by Viers et al. 2006. Numbers in parentheses indicate the number of sample localities for each species. Lines intersect at the median MAT and MAP values for species identified by a letter code (placed to the upper left of median values). They span the first to third quartiles of the observed distribution. Foothill woodland species cluster in the lower right portion of the figure, and montane woodland species cluster in the upper left. Illustration created by Frank W. Davis.

sity. Although relative cover is dominated by a few non-native annual grasses (e.g., *Avena barbata, A. fatua, Bromus diandrus, B. hordeaceous, B. madritensis*, or *Hordeum murinum*), the herb layer can support high species richness. Many species are native, including annual grasses (e.g., *Bromus carinatus, Vulpia microstachys*), perennial grasses (e.g., *Elymus glaucus, Stipa* sp., *Poa secunda, Koeleria macrantha*), and numerous perennial and annual forbs. The annual forbs are particularly diverse, accounting for the preponderance of rare and threatened plant species associated with oak woodlands. The herb layer also includes many non-native forb species, some of which are invasive and undesirable (e.g., yellow starthistle [*Centaurea solstitialis*], tocalote [*Centaurea melitensis*]). Others non-natives are ubiquitous but less noxious (e.g., *Cerastium glomeratum, Erodium cicutarium, Stellaria media*).

The species composition of the herbaceous understory vegetation is influenced by a variety of factors that have been investigated either in oak habitats or adjacent grasslands. These factors include climate, tree cover (Parker and Muller 1982, Borchert et al. 1991, Maranon and Bartolome 1993, Rice and Nagy 2000, Roche et al. 2012), insolation (Borchert et al. 1991), present and historical land use (Stromberg and Griffin 1996, Knapp et al. 2002, Keeley et al. 2003), and annual variation in rainfall (Knapp et al. 2002, Suttle et al. 2007), fire, and disease (Brown 2007). Oak woodlands support many moss and lichen species. A distinctive constituent of relatively cool and humid oak woodlands, especially stands of blue oak near the coast, is the epiphytic lichen, *Ramalina menziesii* (see Lead Photo). This lichen plays an important role in biomass turnover and nutrient cycling in these ecosystems, as it captures rainfall and dry deposition of atmospheric nitrogen and phosphorus (Boucher and Nash 1990, Knops et al. 1996). Experiments conducted at the University of California's Hastings Reserve demonstrated that trees with lichens present had higher nutrient levels (e.g., N, Ca) in the throughfall beneath the canopy as well as slower decomposition rates of oak leaf litter (Knops et al. 1996)—factors that could affect abundance or composition of understory species.

Shrubs and woody sub-shrubs can be present in oak woodland or savanna but are generally at low density and cover. Frequent species include poison oak (*Toxicodendron diversilobum*), California coffeeberry (*Rhamnus californica*), coyote bush (*Baccharis pilularis*), and various species of *Ceanothus, Arctostaphylos, Ribes*, and *Eriogonum*. The shrub species represented in a particular oak habitat are governed by soil moisture and texture, amount of canopy cover, and climate. However, the cover or relative abundance of woody understory species is often a function of disturbance (Tyler et al. 2007).

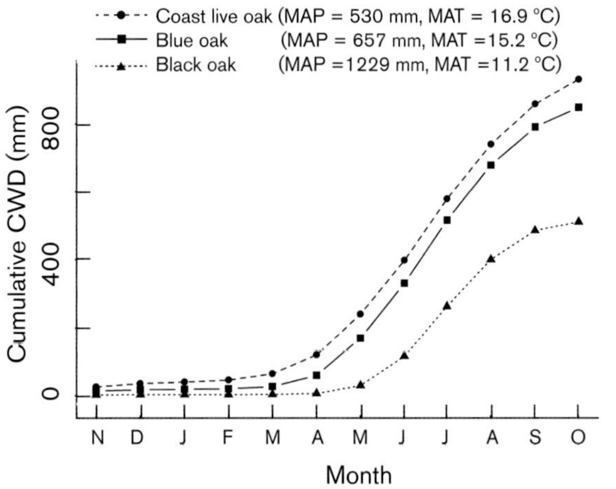

FIGURE 25.3 Modeled trajectories of cumulative climate water deficit (CWD) for the period 1971–2000 for the ranges of two foothill oak species (coast live oak, blue oak) and a montane oak species (black oak). Values are averages of modeled CWD (270 meter resolution) at the same vegetation plot locations used to produce Figure 25.2. Grids of CWD produced by L. and A. Flint using methods detailed in Flint and Flint 2007, Flint and Flint 2012. These data downloaded January 2013 from <http://climate.calcommons.org>. Also shown are estimated median annual precipitation (MAP) and median annual temperatures (MAT) across all localities for each species. Illustration created by Frank W. Davis.

Common Vertebrates and Invertebrates

The native fauna within California's oak woodland habitats is remarkably diverse, with over three hundred species of vertebrates (Guisti et al. 1996, CDFW 2008) and thousands of invertebrates (Swiecki et al. 1997). Some are species of conservation concern with special status designation by the California Department of Fish and Game and/or the U.S. Fish and Wildlife Service. The overwhelming majority of animal species present depends directly or indirectly on the food or shelter that oaks provide (CDFW 2008). The diversity of fauna reflects the abundance and diversity of those resources: acorns, leaves, twigs, sap, leaf litter, and a complex physical structure including canopy, shaded and open branches, cavities, bark, and standing, dead, or downed logs. Acorns are a nutrient-rich food resource for many species. The acorn crop varies greatly from year to year, especially white and red oak species like blue oak, valley oak, and coast live oak, whose acorns mature in one year (Koenig et al. 1994, Koenig and Knops 2013). As in other temperate and Mediterranean oak woodlands and forests, oak MASTING can drive population dynamics of animals dependent on them and throughout the food webs (Koenig and Knops 2005, Ostfeld et al. 2006, Koenig et al. 2009).

VERTEBRATES

Mammal species using oak woodland habitats include carnivores such as cougar (*Puma concolor*), bobcat (*Lynx rufus*), American badger (*Taxidea taxus*), coyote (*Canis latrans*), gray fox (*Urocyon cinereoargenteus*), and long-tailed weasel (*Mustela frenata*), as well as large omnivores and browsers such as American black bear (*Ursus americanus*) and mule deer (*Odocoileus hemionus*). Insect, seed, or herb consumers include tree and ground squirrels, Botta's pocket gopher (*Thomomys bottae*) and other rodents, brush rabbit (*Sylvilagus bachmani*), and bats. Grizzly bears (*Ursus arctos californicus*) were historically abundant and may have been important not only as predators but also through their extensive digging for food resources in the ground layer (Pavlik et al. 1993). Now nonnative wild pigs (*Sus scrofa*) are an important agent of soil disturbance in many oak woodlands and grasslands, but their activities are associated with increases in exotic plant species that recover from pig disturbance faster than native species (Tierney and Cushman 2006). A few of the mammal species commonly found today significantly reduce the rate of acorn, seedling, and sapling survival, especially gophers and California ground squirrel (*Otospermophilus beecheyi*), which limit seedling emergence and survival, and deer, which can limit sapling establishment (Tyler et al. 2006, Davis et al. 2011). Relative abundances of rodent species are correlated with microhabitat such as shrub and downed wood cover. Dusky-footed woodrats (*Neotoma fuscipes*), for example, are more abundant where there is shrub cover, whereas a sparsely vegetated ground cover is associated with higher numbers of deer mice (*Peromyscus* spp.) (Tietje and Vreeland 1997).

Birds are the most diverse group of vertebrates in these habitats, with over one hundred species represented. Some of these rely on acorns as a primary food source, notably the acorn woodpecker (*Melanerpes formicivorus*), western scrub-jay (*Aphelocoma californica*), yellow-billed magpie (*Pica nuttalli*), oak titmouse (*Baeolophus inornatus*), Nuttall's woodpecker (*Picoides nuttallii*), and band-tailed pigeon (*Patagioenas fasciata*). Others, such as phainopepla (*Phainopepla nitens*) and western bluebird (*Sialia Mexicana*), rely on food sources associated with oaks, feeding seasonally on the fruits of the epiphytic oak parasite, mistletoe (*Phoradendron* spp.). Many birds that breed in oak habitats are cavity-nesting species and thus benefit from the matrix of living and dead branches in old large oak trees, as well as downed or standing dead trees (Tietje et al. 1997). Raptors such as red-tailed hawk, red-shouldered hawk, Cooper's hawk, great horned owl, and golden eagle, though not restricted to oak habitats, nest in these woodlands and can play a major role in the community trophic structure as predators on small mammal populations (Tietje et al. 1997). Turkey vultures (*Cathartes aura*) are an important carrion feeder in these ecosystems.

Reptiles and amphibians benefit from shelter provided by leaf litter, downed wood, or hollows in oak trunks, as well as abundant food sources—especially insects and small mammals (Tietje and Vreeland 1997, Tietje et al. 1997, Block and Morrison 1998). Lizards and snakes are important predators in oak communities and include skinks (*Plestiodon* spp.), western fence lizard (*Sceloporus occidentalis*), California legless lizard (*Anniella pulchra*), alligator lizards (*Elgeria* spp.), racers (*Coluber* spp.), common kingsnake (*Lampropeltis getula*), gopher snake (*Pituophis catenifer*), and western rattlesnake (*Crotalus oreganus*). Gopher snakes and western rattlesnakes, though not always apparent, may significantly impact small mammal populations. For example, research indicates they can remove 14–35% of juvenile ground squirrels annually (Fitch 1948, Diller and Johnson 1988). Amphibian abundance and diversity vary considerably with site conditions and associated microhabitats. Salamanders and frogs are among the most common amphibian species, notably slender salamanders (*Batrachoseps* spp.), ensatina (*Ensatina* spp.), and chorus frogs (*Pseudacris* spp.) (Tietje and Vreeland 1997, Block and Morrison 1998). Most species depend on moist microsites under downed logs and brush piles or in litter, riparian elements, or vernal pools (Block and Morrison 1998).

INVERTEBRATES

Thousands of invertebrate species are associated with California's oak woodland habitats, including an estimated five thousand arthropod species, mainly insects (Swiecki et al. 1997). Some depend on and affect oaks directly. Nearly all parts of an oak provide food for some insect, which can be classified based on its niche: acorn feeder; foliar feeder; INSECT GALL former; sap feeder; or twig, bark, and wood borers (Swiecki and Bernhardt 2006). While some of these insect species are significant pests (e.g., the introduced goldspotted oak borer), most native species seldom inflict severe or fatal damage to the host tree, even those that have conspicuous impacts (Swiecki and Bernhardt 2006).

One species with dramatic though rarely fatal impact on oaks is the California oak worm (*Phryganidia californica*), which is the larval stage of the California oak moth. Outbreaks of the oak moth fluctuate annually, with up to three generations per year. At high population densities the larvae can defoliate one to many trees within a stand. Following an outbreak, the oak moth population may collapse due to predation and larval parasites (Swiecki and Bernhardt 2006). Both environmental and density-dependent factors contribute to population limitation (Milstead et al. 1987). Interactions between oaks and oak moth larvae strongly affect cycling of macronutrients such as nitrogen and phosphorus because input via leaf litter is reduced, while input from insect fecal material is increased, during outbreaks (Hollinger 1986).

Filbert weevils (moth larva, *Curculio* sp.) and filbertworm (beetle larva, *Cydia latiferreana*) are the most common invertebrate consumers of acorns. Levels of infestation vary annually and among and within trees (Lewis 1992). Reported infestation levels range from 38% to 62% on coast live oak acorns (Lewis 1992, Dunning et al. 2002) but can be as high as 75% to 80% (Swiecki and Bernhardt 2006). In spite of these high rates, it is not clear that infestation results in loss of germinability in the acorns affected. Dunning et al. (2002) found that most infested acorns suffered less than 20% damage, which might not prevent germination if tissue is intact at the growing tip (Swiecki and Bernhardt 2006). However, in valley oak, over an eight-year period Griffin (1979) estimated that 20% of viable acorns dropped were lost to insect damage.

Among the noticeable, but relatively harmless, impacts of insects on their oak hosts are insect galls, induced most often by wasps in the family Cynipidae. California oaks support more than two hundred species of gall wasps, which each specialize on either the white oak or black oak group (Russo 2006). The large "oak apple," produced by the wasp *Andricus quercuscalifornicus*, can reach a diameter of 8 centimeters (cm) and is one of the most commonly recognized galls, though a great diversity of shapes, colors, and sizes of these intriguing structures exists, reflecting the diversity of gall-making species. Perhaps even more fascinating are the complex associated food webs, as the galls themselves and developing larvae attract a myriad of predators, parasites, competitors, and mutualists (Russo 2006). Finally, not as well understood or described but of great importance to the oak woodland ecosystem is the invertebrate community residing in the litter layer and soil. In addition to serving as a prey base for small vertebrate consumers, many organisms here play vital roles in production and maintenance of soil and in nutrient flow, including microfauna (nemotodes), mesofauna (mites, springtails, larval insects), and macrofauna (earthworms, beetles, flies, ants, snails).

Oak Diseases

A diverse and still poorly understood array of disease organisms variously afflict oak acorns, leaves and twigs, branches and trunks, or root systems (Swiecki and Bernhardt 2006). Most of these are of minor importance, but a few have serious ecological and economic impacts. Canker rot fungi, notably *Inonotus andersonii* and *I. dryophilus*, cause widespread mortality among oak. Sulfur fungus (*Laetiporus gilbertsonii*) is also a major cause of tree failure (Swiecki and Bernhardt 2006).

Since its discovery in the San Francisco Bay Area of California in the mid-1990s, *Phytophthora ramorum*, the causal agent of the forest disease known as sudden oak death (SOD), has killed millions of tanoaks (*Notholithocarpus densiflorus*) and oaks in the mixed broadleaf evergreen forests and redwood forests of coastal California (Meentemeyer et al. 2008). *P. ramorum* is now established in coastal forests from the Big Sur coast northward to southern Mendocino County; disjunct introductions have also been detected in southern Humboldt County and Curry County, Oregon. This introduced disease infects at least thirty native California woody and herbaceous host species, causing nonlethal foliar and twig damage in some species (e.g., the important host and carrier California bay laurel, *Umbellularia californica*) and lethal twig and stem cankers in others. Not all oaks are affected. Red and black oaks, which are placed into the *Erythrobalanus* ("red oak") section of the genus and include coast live oak, Shreve's oak (*Quercus parvula* var. *shrevei*), and black oak, are especially vulnerable (Rizzo and Garbelotto 2003). The disease does not affect white oaks (section *Quercus*), like valley oak and blue oak, and is mainly associated with forest climates rather than drier foothill woodlands. However, where the disease occurs, it has significantly impacted coast live oak woodlands and forests (Davis et al. 2010). Annual mortality rates for coast live oak of 4.5% to 5.5% (an order of magnitude higher than background rates) have been reported in infested areas of Big Sur and the San Francisco Bay region (Brown and Allen-Diaz 2009).

Functional Roles: Foundation Species, Keystones, and Ecosystem Engineers

To truly portray the role a species plays in its community requires an understanding of the complex web of direct and indirect interactions within that system. For California oak woodlands this level of understanding has not yet been achieved. Many of the "pieces" required to build models of these complex interactions are available: lists of species (as sketched earlier), and both population- and community-level studies of some key organisms. However, most of the latter focus on interactions involving pairs of or several species. Some notable exceptions in North American oak woodland research include the studies conducted in eastern oak forests illuminating the complex web linking acorn production to gypsy moth outbreaks to Lyme disease risk (Ostfeld et al. 1996, Jones et al. 1998).

In spite of our limited knowledge of interaction webs, certain species do appear to play particularly important roles in the function of California's oak woodlands. Next we propose terms that describe some of these key roles and suggest that this is an area of oak woodland ecology with great potential for future research. A better understanding of the functional roles played by various species in these systems may improve our ability to predict consequences of species losses and potential extinction cascades (Zavaleta et al. 2009, Colwell et al. 2012).

OAKS AS FOUNDATION SPECIES

Obviously, without oaks there is no oak woodland. They define the structure of the community both literally and functionally, and the vast majority of animal species in these systems depend directly or indirectly on the resources that oaks provide. Although it has not been calculated or even estimated, the "community importance" value (sensu Power et al. 1996) of oaks is clearly greater than any other species in this ecosystem. We propose that the term "FOUNDATION SPECIES" best describes the role of oaks in California. As discussed by Ellison et al. (2005), a foundation species is one that "controls population and community dynamics and modulates ecosystem processes," whose loss "acutely and chronically impacts fluxes of energy and nutrients, hydrology, food webs, and biodiversity" (Ellison et al. 2005, p. 479). Oaks act as foundation species whether they are "dominant" in terms of biomass or abundance (oak forests and dense woodlands) or less common (oak savanna).

MUTUALIST SEED-DISPERSERS

Oaks do not require seed dispersal by animals, as evidenced by the cohorts of young seedling that establish in some years under the tree canopy or at the drip-line. However, most acorns that drop under adult trees are consumed by animals, and those that remain on the soil surface succumb to desiccation or heat stress. Acorns that are shallowly buried have a higher probability of producing emergent seedlings (Borchert et al. 1989, Nives and Weitkamp 1991), and while some may be buried naturally (e.g., by falling into deep leaf litter), acorn-caching animals likely play an important role in dispersing acorns to microsites that promote their survival and germination. Of singular importance is the western scrub-jay (*Aphelocoma californica*), described by Grinnell (1936) as the "uphill planter" responsible for the distribution of black oak seedlings upslope from adult trees. The western scrub-jay may cache, or "plant," up to five thousand acorns in a season but only recover and consume half (Carmen 1988), leaving thousands of buried acorns across the landscape. Other acorn-caching animals include the yellow-billed magpie (*Pica nuttalli*) and the California ground squirrel.

KEYSTONE PREDATORS

The concept of a keystone species has been broadly applied and debated in the ecological literature (Paine 1969, Mills et al. 1993, Power et al. 1996, Cottee-Jones and Whittaker 2012). Here we use the term to refer to a species high in the food web that has large effects on the community that far exceed its abundance (Power et al. 1996). Accordingly, the removal of such a species from the community is expected to have considerable impacts, such as reduced species diversity (Mills et al. 1993). In oak woodlands, large carnivores such as cougars (*Puma concolor*) may function as keystone predators by reducing herbivore populations that limit oak establishment. For example, mule deer (*Odocoileus hemionus*) have been found to limit establishment of oak saplings (Ripple and Beschta 2008, Tyler et al. 2008, Davis et al. 2011), but their impacts are reduced where cougars are active (Ripple and Beschta 2008). A review of large predators and trophic cascades in five national parks in the western United States supports the hypothesis of top-down control in oak woodlands (Beschta and Ripple 2009). The authors report that where large predators have been displaced or locally extirpated, ungulates have had major impacts on dominant woody species (e.g., black oaks in Yosemite) and ecological processes.

Similarly, medium-sized carnivores such as the bobcat (*Lynx rufus*), American badger (*Taxidea taxus*), and coyote (*Canis latrans*) may function as keystone predators by reducing populations of pocket gophers and ground squirrels—small mammal species that significantly limit oak establishment at the seedling stages (Tyler et al. 2006, Tyler et al. 2008). The importance of these carnivores in structuring oak woodland communities has not been studied, and impacts of their removal on oak populations may be difficult to discern given the long life span of oaks.

ECOSYSTEM ENGINEERS

Several groups of oak woodland species function as ECOSYSTEM ENGINEERS as defined by Jones et al. (1994). These organisms impact the availability of resources to other species by causing physical changes to the environment and thereby influence biodiversity within the community. "Soil engineers" include pocket gophers and California ground squirrels as well as non-native pigs and badgers. These species influence the composition of soil biota, herbaceous vegetation, and potentially the establishment of oaks by moving or removing acorns. The work of ecosystem engineers in the oaks is also evident, as they modify the tissue of the trees. Some of the most apparent ecosystem engineers include woodpeckers (e.g., acorn woodpecker, Nuttall's woodpecker) and gall-forming insects (e.g., cynipid wasps). With the exception of feral pigs, the aforementioned "engineers" most likely enhance biodiversity in these systems.

Ecosystem Structure and Processes

The ecosystem ecology of Mediterranean-climate oak woodlands is distinctly different from that of temperate oak woodlands (Baldocchi and Xu 2005, 2007). In this section we describe the structure and function of the woodlands and their metabolism in terms of energy capture, water use, carbon assimilation, and respiration.

Stand Structure

Tree crowns in woodlands are typically isolated and nonoverlapping, but the vegetation structure of oak woodlands varies widely depending on environmental setting (climate, topography, and soils), tree composition, and history of tree cutting and burning. The tree canopy usually consists of a single layer

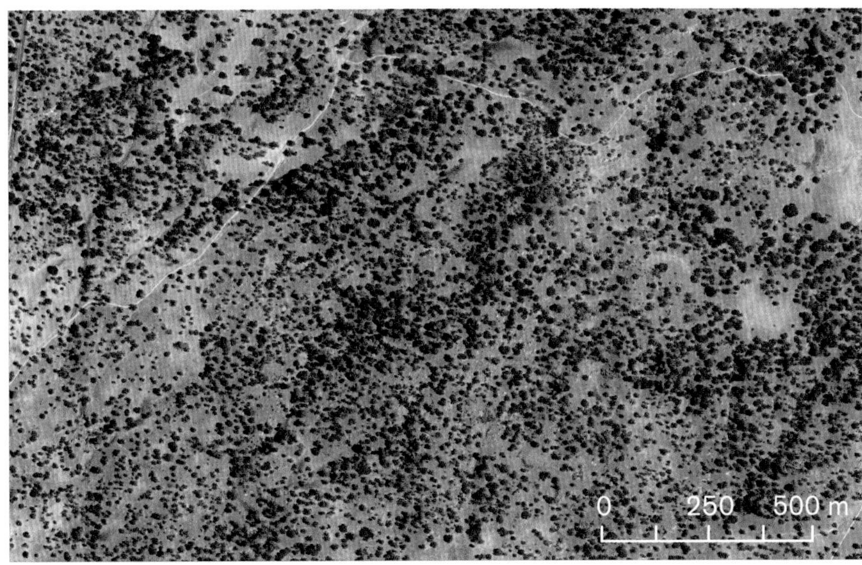

FIGURE 25.4 August 2012 orthophoto of the San Joaquin Experimental Range near Fresno, California. Dark dots are individual tree crowns and are mainly blue oaks with scattered foothill pines. The ground layer is predominantly residual thatch from annual grasses that senesced several months earlier. This landscape illustrates the open nature of blue oak woodlands and the tendency for trees to cluster at multiple scales. Source: Google Earth, image date August 26, 2012.

TABLE 25.2
Structural characteristics of widespread foothill woodland types
Numbers generalized from multiple sources

Woodland type	Typical canopy height [max] (m)	Representative adult tree density (number per hectare)	Total tree basal area (m^2/hectare)	
			Average	Range
Coast live oak	6–12 [24]	20–50	9–23	4–59
Valley oak	12–18 [36]	15–100	11–17	6–59
Blue oak	6–18 [28]	100–500	8–12	4–30
Blue oak / Foothill pine	6–18 [35]	100–500	11–14	5–30
Interior live oak	6–18 [28]	10–50	8–14	5–24

SOURCE: Allen-Diaz et al. 2007, Bolsinger 1988, Holzman and Allen-Diaz 1991, Kertis et al. 1993, Whipple et al. 2011.

6–18 meters (m) in height (Table 25.2); pines, when present, create a second layer 20–30 m in height. The isolated oak canopies create understory light, temperature, soil moisture, and nutrient conditions that can contrast strongly with those in the surrounding grassland.

Part of the challenge in neatly summarizing oak woodland structure is that trees are usually clustered at multiple scales so that properties such as stand composition, tree canopy closure, and leaf area are highly sensitive to the scale of spatial sampling (Figure 25.4). This scale-dependence affects any conclusions drawn from monitoring as well as spatially explicit modeling of ecosystem status and processes based on remotely sensed imagery.

Aboveground woody biomass has not been reported for California oak woodlands, so we rely here on published estimates of tree BASAL AREA in mature stands (see Table 25.2) and relate those to basal area and aboveground biomass estimates for other temperate and Mediterranean-climate oak woodlands. Basal area in mature foothill oak woodland ecosystems averages 20–30 m^2 ha^{-1} but can range from less than 10 m^2 ha^{-1} to greater than 40 m^2 ha^{-1} or higher for coast live oak, valley oak, and black oak woodlands. These values are comparable to or slightly lower than those reported for oak woodlands of the Mediterranean Basin, where basal areas average 25–30 m^2 ha^{-1} and associated aboveground biomass estimates generally range between 150–250 t ha^{-1} (Ibanez et al. 1999, Salvador 2000, Johnson et al. 2002). By comparison, basal area for mature temperate oak forests of eastern North America is typically 25–30 m^2 ha^{-1} with an associated aboveground biomass of 120–140 t ha^{-1} (Held and Winstead 1975, Keddy and Drummond 1996, Johnson et al. 2002). Thus despite growing in a semiarid climate, foothill oak woodlands can support woody biomass comparable to that reported from wetter, second-growth temperate forested systems, although the biomass in California oak woodlands tends to be concentrated in fewer, larger trees.

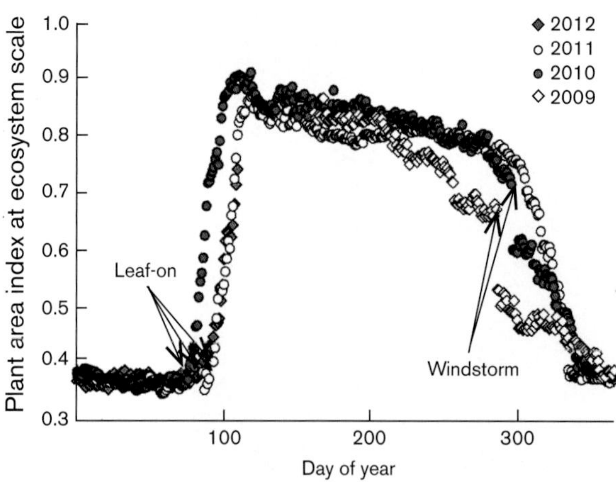

FIGURE 25.5 Seasonal variation in plant area index (PAI) of deciduous blue oak woodland. The dynamics of canopy structure and PAI were measured using the probability of light transmission, as detected with a network of digital cameras. PAI is almost identical to leaf area index (LAI) but derived from different measurements (Ryu et al. 2012). In two of the four years, windstorms accelerated leaf drop.

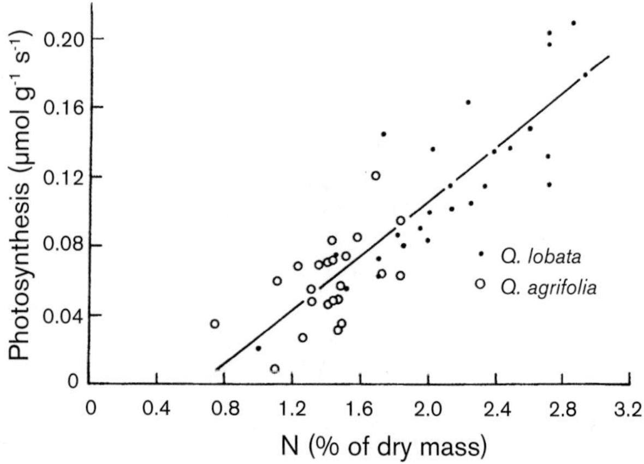

FIGURE 25.6 Relationship between leaf nitrogen (N) and leaf photosynthesis on a mass basis for the evergreen coast live oak (*Q. agrifolia*) and the deciduous valley oak (*Q. lobata*), r^2=0.77. Source: Figure copied from Hollinger 1992.

Canopy Architecture and Phenology

California oaks range from broadleaved evergreen and deciduous trees to small-leaved desert and subalpine shrubs, with species' canopy architecture and phenology adapted to particular light, temperature, and moisture regimes. In foothill oak woodlands, evergreen sclerophyllous, and broad-leaved deciduous trees often co-occur, although where they do, the evergreen live oaks tend to occur in more mesic sites such as north-facing slopes, lower slopes, and swales. By comparison, large-leaved deciduous valley oaks associate with alluvial soils close to the water table, and smaller-leaved deciduous blue oaks increase in importance on upper slopes, spurs, and hilltops (White 1966, Griffin 1973, Hollinger 1992, Robinson et al. 2010).

The deciduous blue oaks and valley oaks exhibit similar phenology. Leaf budburst occurs between late February and early April, and leaves develop while trees are producing male and then female flowers (Koenig et al. 2012). Leaves are dropped during October through November, although early leaf abscission can occur under severe drought (Callaway and Nadkarni 1991). The time course of the development of LEAF AREA INDEX (LAI) of deciduous oaks is very dynamic (Ryu et al. 2012), and the start and end of the growing season may vary by thirty days from year to year (Figure 25.5).

Leaf area index (LAI) and SPECIFIC LEAF AREA (SLA) are important ecosystem variables related to energy and nutrient exchange, light absorption, and photosynthesis. Leaf area index, which is defined as the one-sided area of green leaf surface per unit of ground area, is a dimensionless quantity often used to predict primary production and evapotranspiration. Specific leaf area is the ratio of leaf area to leaf dry weight (e.g., mm^2 mg^{-1}) and is an important plant functional trait related to photosynthesis, leaf longevity, nutrient retention, and water use. Neither LAI nor SLA has been systematically analyzed across a range of oak woodland sites. However, the potential leaf mass of individual oaks can be estimated with allometric relationships between diameter at breast height (dbh) and tree leaf area (Karlik and McKay 2002). Because leaf mass scales with specific leaf area, one can estimate leaf area per tree and the leaf area index of the stand. One set of data indicates that blue oak trees hold about 4 m^2 of leaves per m^2 of ground. By inference, taking into consideration the spatial extent among trees, oak woodlands support tree canopy LAI on the order of 0.9 (Karlik and McKay 2002, Ryu et al. 2010).

Oak Physiology

Plants face trade-offs and compromises in adopting either an evergreen or deciduous leaf habit. Ecological scaling theory predicts that evergreen life forms are associated with leaves possessing lower nitrogen levels and lower PHOTOSYNTHETIC CAPACITY compared to deciduous forms of similar genera (Hollinger 1992, Reich et al. 1997). For example, the deciduous valley oak attains greater rates of photosynthesis by acquiring more nitrogen than the co-occurring evergreen coast live oak (Figure 25.6). Mahall et al. (2009) also documented higher rates of photosynthesis in valley oak than coast live oak.

The habit of an oak leaf and its fate of enduring a long, dry summer have a marked impact on the dynamics and capacity of STOMATAL CONDUCTANCE (the rate of carbon dioxide or water vapor exchange between the leaf and the atmosphere), leaf photosynthesis, and transpiration (Goulden 1996, Xu and Baldocchi 2003). For example, the maximum photosynthetic rate (A_{max}) experiences great seasonal variability in blue oak, peaking at approximately 25 mmol m^{-2} s^{-1} just after full leaf expansion during the spring when soils are wet and declining thereafter as stomata close gradually with a depleted soil reservoir (Xu and Baldocchi 2003). It is noteworthy that deciduous blue oaks attain very high A_{max} values compared to evergreen oaks (Goulden 1996), eastern deciduous oaks (Wilson et al. 2000), and fertilized crops (Wullschleger 1993); the evergreen coast live oak, for example, attains peak rates near 10 mmol m^{-2} s^{-1} in the spring and drops to below 2 mmol m^{-2} s^{-1} in September. The ability for blue oaks to achieve very high rates of photosynthesis rapidly in the spring is probably highly adaptive given their need to acquire enough carbon to sustain the foliar canopy during the short/wet and long/dry periods of the spring and summer, respectively.

Carbon, Water, and Energy Exchange

Ecophysiological research on plants occurs across multiple organizational levels and scales from individual leaves to whole plants to multiple plants at the site or ecosystem scale. Knowledge of carbon, water, and energy exchange of California oak woodlands at the ecosystem scale has been produced by three methods. One uses long-term and continuous EDDY COVARIANCE flux measurements; a second is based on water balance of gauged catchments; and the third uses models driven with remote sensing.

Two sets of direct, eddy covariance flux measurements have been made over oak woodlands during the past decade. One set is near Ione, California, in the central foothills of the Sierra Nevada (Baldocchi, Chen, et al. 2011). At this site blue oak woodlands receive about 565 mm yr^{-1} of rain and evaporate about 390 mm yr^{-1} of water vapor against a demand of 1,429 mm yr^{-1} by potential evaporation. On the basis of this water balance, woodlands assimilate 1007 +/- 193 gC m^{-2} yr^{-1} of carbon and respire 907 +/- 189 gC m^{-2} yr^{-1} (Baldocchi, Chen, et al. 2011). Thus, on average and over many years, this blue oak woodland is a net carbon sink, taking up about 100 gC m^{-2} yr^{-1}. Another set of carbon and water flux data has been collected along the foothills of the southern Sierra Nevada (Goulden et al. 2012). At this site, at an elevation of 400 m, oak woodlands receive about 500 mm y^{-1} of rain, evapotranspire about 500 mm yr^{-1}, and assimilate about 1,100 gC m^{-2} yr^{-1}. Although it is not possible from the eddy covariance measurements to partition water loss from the tree layer versus the understory grasses, evapotranspiration decreases from roughly 3 mm per day in May to 2 mm per day in midsummer to less than 1 mm per day in September, suggesting that the tree layer is responsible for around two-thirds of springtime evapotranspiration.

These direct measurements of evapotranspiration from oak woodlands are consistent with water balance studies. In one study the conversion from an oak woodland watershed to grassland found evaporation to decrease from 513 to 378 mm yr^{-1} (Lewis 1968). Evaporation rates deduced using the Thornthwaite equation (Thornthwaite 1948) and soil moisture accounting range between 280 and 382 mm yr^{-1} across the oak woodlands of California (Major 1988). Based on a seventeen-year watershed study at the Sierra Foothill field station in the northern portion of the foothill woodland distribution, mean annual evaporation was estimated to be 368 mm +/- 89 mm yr^{-1} from 708 mm yr^{-1} of rainfall (Lewis et al. 2000). In a two-year study at Sierra Field station catchment evapotranspiration was found to vary from 296 to 498 mm yr^{-1} as rainfall ranged between 498 and 610 mm (Swarowsky et al. 2011). A study in Sonoma County of water balance before and after the conversion of oak woodlands (40–60% canopy cover) to irrigated vineyards concluded that oaks used about 270 mm of water and the grapes used about 300 mm of water per year (Grismer and Asato 2012).

The carbon balance of foothill woodlands is the net result of uptake of atmospheric carbon dioxide through photosynthesis and carbon dioxide loss to the atmosphere through ecosystem respiration. These fluxes are difficult to measure at the whole ecosystem level over large areas. Data assimilation modeling using flux measurements, satellite remote sensing information, and statistical analysis indicates that blue oak woodlands collectively take up 53.8 teragrams of carbon per year (TgC yr^{-1}), lose 45.2 TgC yr^{-1} through respiration, and thus accumulate 8.6 TgC yr^{-1}. On an area basis the annual sum of carbon assimilation is 932 gC m^{-2} y^{-1} and the net carbon exchange is -150 gC m^{-2} y^{-1} (Baldocchi, Chen, et al. 2010). On a unit land area basis, evergreen oak woodland, with its lower photosynthetic capacity, tends to acquire similar amounts of carbon and use similar amounts of water to a more productive deciduous stand with a similar LAI (Hollinger 1992, Baldocchi, Ma, et al. 2010). In other words, the longer the growing season for the species, the lower the photosynthetic capacity.

Ecosystem Processes in Oak Woodlands: Synthesis

Ultimately, oak woodland ecosystems must regulate water use such that carbon gain at least offsets respiratory needs and evaporative demand. How does oak woodland achieve a balance between function, structure, and metabolism given these distinct climatic constraints? We attempt to answer this question for a deciduous oak woodland site by inspecting a set of figures showing links between the fluxes of carbon and water and their dependence on rainfall, soil moisture, and the leaf area index of the canopy (Figure 25.7). First and foremost, the oak woodland must assimilate more carbon through photosynthesis than it loses through respiration (see Figure 25.7a). This is not as trivial as it may seem given the annual asynchrony between the periods of water supply and water demand. The period of highest photosynthetic capacity is relatively short (see Figure 25.7b); peak photosynthesis of deciduous oaks is generally constrained to a hundred-day period between late spring (approximately day 80) and early summer (approximately day 180). The soil water reservoir is depleted during the long summer drought period (see Figure 25.3), which induces stomatal closure and down-regulates transpiration and photosynthesis (Goulden 1996, Xu and Baldocchi 2003). Respiration, on the other hand, persists year-round and has the potential to be elevated during hotter periods unless it is also down-regulated by reduced photosynthesis (Atkin et al. 2005).

This brings us to the next question: How much carbon assimilation is potentially possible? Sunlight is not a limiting factor in California. The oak woodlands receive about 6.5 gigajoules (GJ) m^{-2} y^{-1} of sunlight (Ryu et al. 2008). If this energy was converted to carbon assimilation, we would expect annual carbon assimilation to reach about 1,400 gC m^{-2} y^{-1}. This computation is based on the assumption that the PHOTOSYNTHETIC EFFICIENCY of an ecosystem is 2%, that half of sunlight is available to photosynthesis, and that the energy content of photosynthetic fixation is 496 kilojoule (kj) $mole^{-1}$ CO_2. The actual amount of woodland photosynthesis is one-half to three-quarters of the potential amount based on available sunlight (Ma et al. 2007). The key limiting factor on the annual sum of carbon assimilation by oak woodland is the amount of available water. Consequently, annual photosynthesis, or gross primary productivity (GPP), scales with annual evaporation (see Figure 25.7c). For a deciduous oak woodland, annual photosynthesis (GPP) increases from about 700 to 1,100 gC m^{-2} y^{-1} as evaporation increases from about 350 to 520 mm yr^{-1}.

Oak woodlands do not achieve much higher rates of carbon assimilation as rainfall increases. During dry years, annual evapotranspiration of oak woodland approaches and is proportional to total rainfall. In wet years evapotranspiration falls well below total rainfall and appears to level out at rainfall levels greater than 600 mm (see Figure 25.7d). It appears that the trees are unable to exploit the surplus rainfall, especially early season rainfall. While it is more convenient to relate

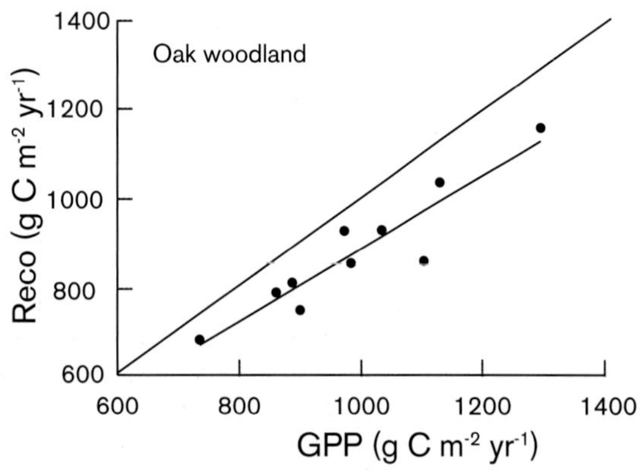

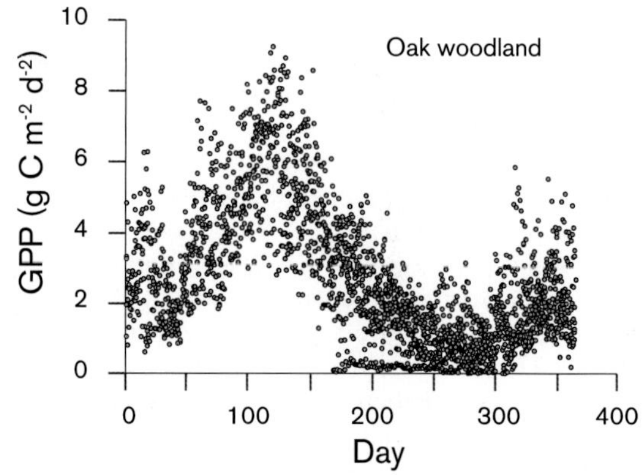

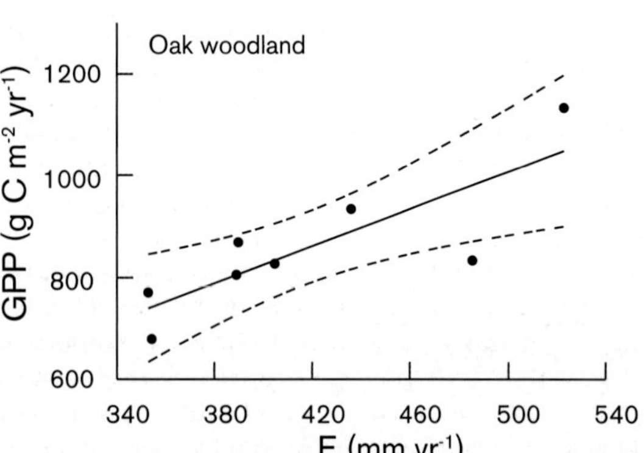

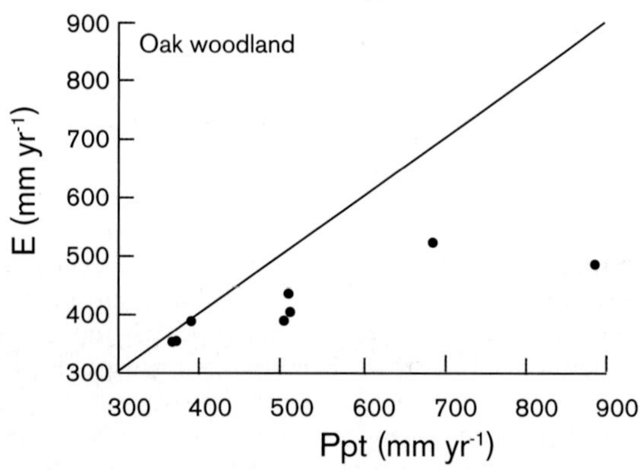

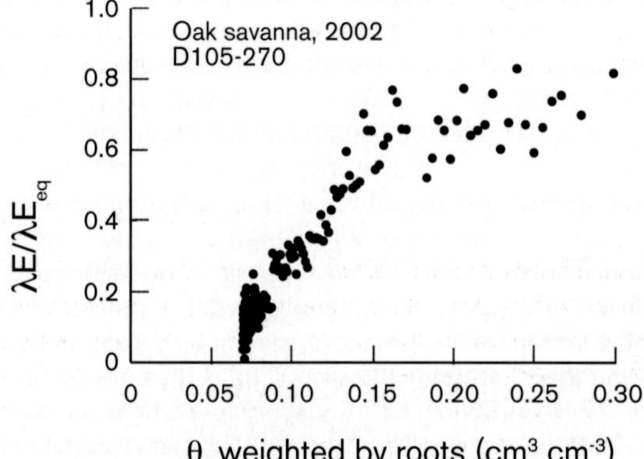

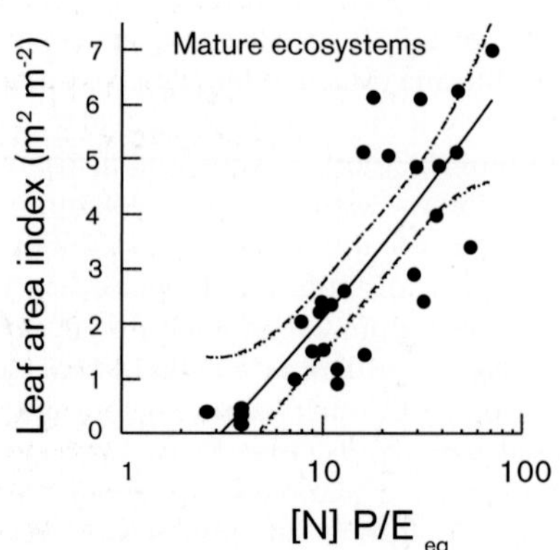

FIGURE 25.7 Summary of key relationships that govern carbon and water use in oak woodland ecosystems. See chapter for detailed explanation. Data are annual averages. Sources: (A, B, E) Baldocchi, Chen et al. 2010; (C) Baldocchi et al. 2004; (D) Baldocchi, Ma et al. 2010; (F) Baldocchi and Meyers 1998.

A Relationship between gross primary productivity (GPP) and respiration (R_{eco}, ecosystem respiration).

B Annual variation in GPP, from January 1 (Julian day=1).

C Relationship between evaporation (E, from ecosystem, estimated from net radiation measurements) and GPP.

D Relationship between annual precipitation (ppt, mm yr^{-1}) and evaporation (E).

E Relationship between soil moisture deficits and transpiration.

F Relationship between ecosystem water balance and woodland-scale leaf area index (LAI, m leaves/m soil), r^2=0.67.

annual carbon and water fluxes to annual sums of rainfall, researchers in California and the Mediterranean Basin find that carbon assimilation (GPP) is better correlated with total spring (March–May) rainfall (Ma et al. 2007, Allard et al. 2008).

Oak trees must overcome severe moisture deficit stresses during the hot dry summer—volumetric soil moisture is often below 5% by volume, causing oak trees to experience predawn water potentials as low as –7.0 megapascals (MPa) (Baldocchi et al. 2004). They accomplish this in two ways. First, soil moisture deficits induce gradual stomatal closure, yielding a marked reduction in transpiration (see Figure 25.7e). But stomatal closure is not enough. To survive the hottest and driest portion of the summer, oak trees must tap into the groundwater (Lewis and Burgy 1964), where they can extract up to 50% of the water they need to survive during that dry period (Miller et al. 2010). On annual to decadal time scales, the water balance of the system limits the leaf area index of the woodland (see Figure 25.7f). A prominent feature of oak woodlands is its savanna nature, with open canopies and leaf area indices below 2 (Ryu et al. 2010). This openness reduces the amount of energy absorbed by the vegetation and used to drive evaporation.

Disturbance and Ecosystem Resilience

Ecologists define a disturbance as a relatively discrete event that disrupts ecosystem, community, or population structure and changes resources, substrate availability, and/or the physical environment (Davis and Moritz 2001). Disturbances tend to free up limiting resources such as space, light, and nutrients, triggering successional processes of ecosystem and community recovery. Resilience is a measure of an ecosystem's ability to recover to its original state when subjected to disturbance. Here we focus on important disturbance processes that operate over stand-to-landscape scales in oak woodlands, including fire, woodcutting, and livestock grazing. Other disturbances such as flooding (notably for valley oak), extreme wind events, snow and ice storms, and local landslides can have important local effects but are not as pervasive in oak woodlands and are not discussed here. We discuss ecosystem conversion to cropland and residential and urban development in a later section.

Fire

Lightning is uncommon in foothill woodlands; humans set most fires. This generalization probably applies to prehistoric as well as modern fire regimes. Lighting is more common in montane black oak woodlands, and fire suppression now exerts a strong influence on fire regime in those systems. In both foothill and montane woodlands, fires readily ignite in the dry grass layer during hot dry summer months and tend to be fast moving and of low intensity, with 0.5–1 m flame lengths (Skinner and Chang 1996). We have scant information from a few analyses of fire scars, pollen cores, and early historical narratives on prehistoric fire regimes in foothill woodlands. Available evidence suggests that some blue oak woodlands were regularly burned by native Californians. Estimates of mean fire return intervals range from seven to fourteen years (McClaran and Bartolome 1989, Mensing 2006, Standiford et al. 2012). Coast live oak and mixed oak woodlands in the Coast Ranges may have been burned as frequently as every one to two years in some areas (Greenlee and Langenheim 1990), although much longer intervals of twenty to thirty years have also been reported (Mensing et al. 1999). Native American burning was probably also responsible for the relatively short three- to seven-year fire return intervals reported for black oak woodlands, where fire was used to promote oaks over pines and perhaps to control acorn pests such as Tilbert worm and Filbert weevil (Mensing 2006; see Chapter 10, "Indigenous California").

The modern fire regime in foothill woodlands is controlled by active suppression and indirectly by livestock grazing that reduces fuel loads. Frequent human ignitions result in numerous small wildfires that are quickly extinguished, especially along busy roads. Long fire-free periods in coastal woodlands can allow the development of shrub understories so that when fires do occur, they tend to be much more severe (Davis and Borchert 2006). Fire suppression in black oak woodlands has dramatically reduced fire frequency and may be leading to an increase in conifers over oaks as well as to an increase in fire severity when fires occur (Mensing 2006, Miller et al. 2009).

Oak woodlands are relatively resilient to burning, with coast live oaks the most fire-tolerant and interior live oak the least fire-tolerant species (Lathrop and Osborne 1991). In coast live oak, most large trees can produce new canopies after burning, and most saplings and even some seedlings resprout after being top-killed by fire (Holmes et al. 2008). Blue oak trees will survive low-moderate fires but can be killed in more severe burns. A high proportion of blue oak seedlings and saplings are top-killed but resprout, so that the main effect of burning is to retard progression of saplings to the tree layer (Swiecki and Bernhardt 2002, Allen-Diaz et al. 2007). In montane woodlands, black oaks can survive fires once they attain a 16 cm stem diameter, and top-killed trees usually resprout vigorously after burning. Oak woodland herb communities also appear to be quite resilient to fires. The non-native annual grasses that now dominate the understory produce enormous quantities of seed, enough of which survive low-severity grass fires to provide full recovery in the growing seasons that follow. Native perennial grasses and bulbs resprout after burning, and populations of native annuals may be relatively neutral, responding more to postfire temperature, rainfall variation, and livestock grazing than to fire occurrence (Wills 2006).

Tree Cutting for Firewood and Range Management

Because acorns of foothill oaks were a food staple for many native Californian groups, deliberate tree removal seems unlikely prior to European settlement (Rossi 1980, Mensing 2006). During the Spanish Mission era (1770–1830) and Mexican rancho era (1830–1850), oak was occasionally cut locally for fuelwood and fencing, but no evidence suggests any major effects on oak distribution or abundance (Mensing 2006). Rather, the main impact of Europeans prior to 1850 was to dramatically reduce the size of native Californian populations who for millennia had occupied and, through burning, influenced oak woodlands and specific plant and animal resources in them. The second major impact of early Europeans was the introduction of domesticated livestock. These impacts registered more strongly on the understories than on the tree layer of oak woodlands.

After the Gold Rush of 1849, the rapid increase in the number of towns and agricultural expansion probably claimed large tracts of oak woodlands near major rivers and on arable valley soils. None of the California oaks has much value for lumber, especially compared to native pines such as ponderosa pine (*Pinus ponderosa*) or sugar pine (*P. lambertiana*), but oaks were harvested for fuelwood and charcoal and cleared for cropland. Agricultural clearing was especially widespread in the Central Valley and San Francisco Bay region, where large tracts of valley oaks and live oaks were felled. Further south on the coastal plain and the inland valleys of the Coast, Transverse, and Peninsular Ranges, coast live oaks, valley oaks, and blue oaks were thinned or cleared for row crops and orchards (Kelly et al. 2005, Mensing 2006, Whipple et al. 2011).

No evidence of widespread oak cutting in foothill woodlands for fuelwood or range improvement appears until the twentieth century. Beginning around 1930 and continuing for at least another fifty years, a deliberate campaign of woody plant removal in California rangelands, largely conceived and promoted by University of California rangeland specialists, resulted in controlled burning for shrub removal and tree cutting to increase forage production and water yield over millions of acres. The extent of tree removal for range improvement is poorly documented, but between 1950 and 1973 perhaps 900,000 acres of foothill woodlands were cleared (Alagona 2008). The policy of oak clearing has since been reversed on both scientific grounds, as evidence mounted that oaks can improve soil fertility and forage production and as a result of public pressure to protect oaks for wildlife habitat and other amenity values. Oak clearing for range improvement is now discouraged, especially in areas receiving less than 50 cm annual precipitation (Allen-Diaz et al. 2007). Oak cutting for firewood continues but is highly localized. A four-year statewide survey conducted between 1988 and 1992 documented firewood harvesting on roughly 25,000 acres per year, only 0.11% of woodland acreage (Standiford et al. 1996).

Intensive COPPICE MANAGEMENT of oak woodlands for fuelwood production has long been practiced in the Mediterranean Basin but is uncommon in California. California oaks appear to be moderately resilient to tree cutting. Most trees including blue oak and interior live oak, which are the primary sources of firewood for commercial harvest, produce basal sprouts after cutting. The rate of resprouting in blue oak declines with tree size, from nearly 70% for trees less than 10 cm dbh to under 20% for trees greater than 50 cm dbh (Allen-Diaz et al. 2007, Standiford et al. 2011). Pillsbury et al. (2002) reported 30–45% resprouting from cut stumps in experimentally thinned stands of coast live oak. Because browsing by livestock and deer promotes multistemmed "hedged" shrub morphology and slows sprout extension to the tree canopy, some form of protection may be needed to promote recovery of the tree layer.

Low recruitment of new oaks in most oak woodlands and savannas means that these systems are not very resilient to mechanical tree removal or to tree cutting with herbicide treatment to prevent resprouting. Many areas where trees were deliberately cleared more than a half-century ago remain grasslands today (Brooks and Merenlender 2001). Stand thinning may have a more subtle effect on oak demography by increasing the distance between trees, thereby reducing gene flow by pollination as well as acorn production. Sork et al. (2002) documented short-range pollen dispersal and small effective population sizes in open stands of valley oak. Knapp et al. (2001) reported lower acorn production by more isolated blue oaks.

Tree removal can strongly affect local climate, hydrology, and ecosystem processes. Trees absorb more sunlight than annual grassland, exert a greater effect on air flow and sensible heat transfer, and evaporate considerably more water (Baldocchi, Chen, et al. 2010). Isolated trees in oak woodlands and savannas create microenvironments distinctly different than the surrounding grasslands. The tree canopy reduces light reaching the understory by 25% to 90% and can intercept 5% to 50% of rainfall (Maranon et al. 2009). Conversely, areas of grassland adjacent to oak woodland can produce edge effects in oak woodland microclimates that extend tens of meters into the woodland and affect woodland wildlife communities (Sisk et al. 1997). Tree removal can also have significant effects on soils and nutrient cycling. Soil nutrient levels, soil organic matter, and nitrogen cycling are considerably higher in oak understories than in surrounding grassland, especially in deeper soils where tree roots are able to access deeper pools of water and nutrients than are more shallow-rooted herb species (Callaway et al. 1991). Tree understories also support higher microbial activity, higher canopy dry deposition and animal deposition (perching birds, shade-seeking cattle, deer, and other animals), and reduced nutrient losses from leaching and soil erosion (Callaway and Nadkarni 1991, Knops et al. 1996, Dahlgren et al. 1997, Herman et al. 2003, Maranon et al. 2009).

Livestock Grazing

Grazing animals have been part of California grasslands and woodlands for several million years (Jackson and Bartolome 2007), although many large grazers of the late Pleistocene such as bison, llamas, and horses went extinct near the close of the last Ice Age more than ten thousand years ago. Immediately prior to European settlement, the main grazers were pronghorn antelope (*Antilocapra americana*) and tule elk (*Cervus canadensis nannodes*). Those species have been eliminated over most of their former California range and now play a negligible role in oak woodlands except in a few areas.

Cattle grazing has been the dominant use of oak woodlands since European settlement (Huntsinger et al. 2010). Since that time, cattle operations have depended on natural forage production and thus have been highly sensitive to interannual variability in rainfall and, to a lesser degree, temperature. During the Mission Era, the number of cattle in California rose to approximately 400,000 head. The first major boom in livestock grazing accompanied the Gold Rush and lasted from 1849 to 1868, when the number approached 1,000,000 animals (Olmstead and Rhode 2004). Livestock numbers statewide plummeted between 1868 and 1871 due to severe drought and then partially recovered over the next several decades to a statewide herd of about 470,000 animals. The livestock industry boomed again after World War II to a peak of 3.2 million head in 1976 (Alagona 2008). Numbers have continued to decline, and only 710,000 beef cows and heifers grazed California rangelands in 2011, down from 920,000 in 2001 (see Chapter 37, "Range Ecosystems"). Though commercial ranching has declined in recent decades, more than 80% of oak woodland properties larger than 80 hectares continue to be grazed by livestock, and roughly 90% of those properties practice year-round cattle grazing (Huntsinger et al. 2010).

In many ways, today's oak woodlands are structurally, compositionally, and functionally a legacy of two centuries of continuous livestock grazing. The advent of cattle (and sheep) grazing in the eighteenth century initiated large changes to oak woodland ecosystems due to a combination of factors including the introduction of invasive exotic grasses, reduction in fire frequency, and introduction of new ungulate herds. Cattle trampling increases bulk density of the topsoil, affecting both water infiltration and root penetration (Dahlgren et al. 1997, Herman et al. 2003, Allen-Diaz et al. 2007); cattle also concentrate and redistribute nutrients and increase nutrient fluxes by promoting more rapid turnover of organic matter (Herman et al. 2003).

CATTLE GRAZING AND OAKS

Structurally, livestock grazing promotes a more open tree layer by reducing seedling and sapling recruitment and, through repeated browsing, delaying the development of established saplings into the tree layer (Borchert et al. 1989, Tyler et al. 2006, Davis et al. 2011). Grazing impacts on seedlings depend on seasonal grazing patterns and, at least for blue oaks, are especially pronounced during spring and summer (Hall 1992). Over many decades, grazing can lead to declining tree densities if the rate of new tree recruitment is less than adult tree mortality (Callaway and Davis 1993, Davis et al. 2011).

GRAZING AND WOODLAND UNDERSTORY VEGETATION

Grazing disturbance can suppress shrub recruitment and maintain an understory of annual herbs (Callaway 1992, Huntsinger and Bartolome 1992, Callaway and Davis 1993). Shrubs can facilitate recruitment of some foothill oak species, notably blue oak and coast live oak; over time the suppression of a shrub layer could thus also contribute to declining tree densities (Callaway 1992, Callaway and Davis 1998). Given sufficient time and lack of fire and grazing, shrubs or woody sub-shrubs commonly establish in the grasslands between oaks in savanna or under oaks where canopy cover is incomplete. This has been observed as rapid colonization by coyote brush (*Baccharis pilularis*) in moist northern California sites where cattle have been excluded (McBride and Heady 1968, Williams et al. 1987, Williams and Hobbs 1989). Grazing exerts a strong influence on the height and cover of both the growing and senesced herb layer, with associated effects on surface energy exchanges and water balances. Contrary to reports from other savanna and grassland ecosystems, grazing does not appear to increase plant growth. Furthermore, current year herbage production declines when grazing pressure (measured as residual dry matter) is higher in the previous year, especially in areas of higher rainfall (Jackson and Bartolome 2007).

Contemporary herb communities in oak woodlands and grasslands are relatively resilient to continued light-to-moderate livestock grazing. Grazing can have species-specific effects on understory species and resulting plant community composition and richness, but these effects are hard to disentangle from the effects of large year-to-year weather variation (Jackson and Bartolome 2007). Studies in California grasslands suggest that moderate grazing can increase plant diversity compared to nongrazed or heavily-grazed areas (Bartolome et al. 1994). Native annual forbs may be favored by grazing that reduces competition with taller introduced annual grasses (Safford and Harrison 2001, Gelbard and Harrison 2003, Hayes and Holl 2003). Livestock grazing can be a viable method for reducing some noxious weeds (Reiner and Craig 2011) as well as potential fire severity.

Land Use Conversion and Ecosystem Fragmentation

Agricultural Conversion

As described earlier, large-scale woodland conversion to cropland and orchards began in the latter half of the nineteenth century but was mainly limited to arable valley and floodplain soils. By 1900, 6 million to 7 million acres were already in cultivation—a number that increased to 8 million acres by 1950 and has ranged between 7 million and 8.5 million acres since that time (Olmstead and Rhode 2004). Thus most lowland oak woodland conversion to cropland occurred over a century ago. Rapid growth of California's wine industry during the last quarter of the twentieth century produced a second wave of agricultural conversion that mainly affected foothill oak woodlands. For example, between 1976 and 2010 vineyard acreage jumped from 52,609 hectares to 198,296 hectares (USDA NASS n.d.). Large-scale vineyard expansion into oak woodlands occurred in many coastal counties, notably Sonoma, Mendocino, San Luis Obispo, and Santa Barbara Counties. Merenlender (2000) estimated that 2,925 hectares of oak woodland were converted to vineyard between 1990 and 1997 in Sonoma County alone.

Urban and Residential Development

Since 1950, suburban and rural residential development has transformed many oak woodland landscapes, notably in the San Francisco Bay region, the "Gold Country" of Nevada, Placer and Eldorado Counties, coastal counties from San Luis Obispo to San Diego, and parts of western Inyo and Riverside Counties. Perhaps two-thirds of the new housing development has occurred at urban and suburban densities (0.2–2 hectare lots) on agricultural lands, many that were formerly oak woodlands (FRPP 2010). However, large-lot suburban and rural residential housing (2–8 hectare lots) pervades many oak woodland landscapes. Most coast live oak woodlands and forests in coastal foothills from Santa Barbara County to San Diego County have been transformed by residential development (Davis et al. 1995). Rural housing development has been imprinted on foothill oak woodlands of the central Sierra Nevada in what Duane (1999, p. 200) characterized as "low-density, land-intensive, large-lot exurban sprawl" that has altered "both the ecological and the social landscape." This same exurban sprawl increasingly affects montane oak woodland communities as well.

Spero (2001) analyzed census data from 1950 through 1990 to document historical residential development in oak woodlands. Based on population projections, he then modeled future development to 2040 (see Figure 25.7). Recent trends in rural residential development are consistent with or exceed his projections. For example, Gaman and Firman (2006) estimated that by 2006 more than 400,000 hectares of oak woodland habitat had been developed. Stewart et al. (2008) estimated that 84% of new residential development in oak woodlands between 1990 and 2000 occurred in lot sizes between 2 and 8 hectares. The woodlands in and around these dispersed residences can be additionally fragmented by roads and fencing, degraded by heavy modification of understory vegetation associated with rural ranchettes, and impacted by domestic pets, impaired air quality, altered surface and groundwater hydrology, and water quality. Fire is half as frequent in rural residential areas as in undeveloped areas (Spero 2001). These and other factors lead to systematic shifts in the bird, mammal, and plant communities of rural residential areas compared to extensive woodlands (Maestas et al. 2001, 2003; Merenlender et al. 2009)

Ecosystem Services

The Millennium Ecosystem Assessment (2005) distinguished four types of ecosystem services including provisioning, regulating, supporting, and cultural services. We have already described the importance of oak woodlands for provisioning services such as livestock production, firewood, and game species as well as oak contribution to soil fertility, a supporting service. Here we focus on the role of oaks in climate regulation (carbon storage, hydrology, local energy balance), and on cultural services such as nongame wildlife and aesthetic values (Millenium Ecosystem Assessment 2005, Kroeger et al. 2010, Plieninger et al. 2012).

Carbon Storage, Hydrology, and Climate Regulation

Badocchi, Chen, et al. (2010) calculate that blue oak woodlands serve as a small net carbon sink (-92 ± 48 gC m^{-2} yr^{-1}). This is roughly half the average net carbon uptake reported for other ecosystems in the U.S. and reflects a close balance between carbon uptake via photosynthesis (1,031 gC m^{-2} $year^{-1}$) and loss through respiration (939 gC m^{-2} yr^{-1}). These values are only approximate and vary considerably between years as a function of spring rainfall and seasonal water balance (Ma et al. 2007, Baldocchi, Chen, et al. 2010). Though small on a per area basis, this uptake becomes tangible when integrated over the extent of blue oak woodlands (1.19 Tg yr^{1}, or about 0.2% of California's total greenhouse emissions in 2006). Kroeger et al. (2010) suggest that reforestation of cleared oak woodlands could sequester up to 1% of the state's current emissions annually when averaged over a seventy-five-year period. Other activities with relatively large carbon benefits include restoration of riparian vegetation in oak woodland landscapes and restoration of perennial grasses (Kroeger et al. 2010).

As described earlier, oaks can exert a significant effect on site hydrology by intercepting rainfall lost by evaporation from the canopy and by using soil and groundwater below the rooting depths of herbaceous understory plants. For example, Miller et al. (2010) estimated summer groundwater uptake by blue oaks of 15 mm to 23 mm per month. To the extent that soil water, local groundwater, and associated streamflows are desired for other purposes, oaks could be seen as reducing local hydrological services. This could depend on how much groundwater taken up by deep roots is transported to shallow soil layers through hydraulic redistribution during the dry summer season (Gou and Miller 2014). Oaks have complex effects on local climate that could offset their positive effects on the climate system through carbon uptake. Oak canopies absorb more sunlight than open grasslands and reduce the rate of airflow by increasing surface roughness, thereby reducing heat sensible heat exchange between the surface and the atmosphere. As a result, average air temperature in blue oak woodland is about 0.84°C warmer than surrounding grasslands, despite the fact that oak canopies provide cool microsites (Baldocchi, Chen, et al. 2010).

Cultural Services

In recent decades oak woodlands have been increasingly valued for their environmental amenities such as aesthetic views, nonharvested plant and animal diversity, and the peace and quiet associated with rural rangelands. As documented by Huntsinger et al. (2010) based on surveys conducted between 1985 and 2004, oak woodlands have attracted a new generation of landowners with different values and land management practices than traditional ranching families. Over that period, the percentage of owners that relied on livestock ranching as a major source of income declined from 27% to 14%, and the number of landowners citing "living near natural beauty" as an important factor influencing their decision to live in oak woodlands increased from 46% to 71% of respondents. Furthermore, owners in 2004 reported more reasons to value and plant oaks than in previous surveys, and a lower proportion reported cutting oaks. These trends were especially pronounced among owners with properties less than 80 hectares.

Huntsinger et al. (2010) point out that owners on small properties may be satisfied with cultural ecosystem services such as natural beauty, but that these small lots cannot support other kinds of ecosystem services such as maintaining viable populations of harvested and nonharvested wildlife, regulating water quality, or sequestering carbon. Owners of large properties tend to be interested in undertaking environmental improvements that increase ecosystem services at a meaningful scale, but these same owners typically lack financial resources to do so. Compared to other ecosystems, oak woodlands on large ranches appear to allow fuller bundling of (rather than trading off between) provisioning, regulating, and amenity services (Plieninger et al. 2012). However, many of these benefits from extensive woodlands such as water quality, wildlife habitat, and scenic quality accrue off-site rather than to the landowners. As a result, ranchers have not had much incentive to invest in management actions such as oak restoration or riparian protection where private costs may exceed private benefits (Kroeger et al. 2010). Increased private market prices for carbon sequestration and water quality could induce ranchers to supply more of these public benefits.

Both Kroeger et al. (2010) and Huntsinger et al. (2010) emphasize that maintaining and managing large properties for provisioning and regulating services will require new funding sources and programs that incentivize conservation. To support such policy formulation, research is needed to better assess the market value of ecosystem services on oak woodlands. Amenity values are challenging to estimate, especially given the diffuse nature of benefits such as nonharvestable biodiversity, viewshed quality, and open space. Standiford and Huntsinger (2012) present several analytical approaches for doing this, including contingent valuation and hedonic regression. Standiford and Scott (2008) used hedonic regression to analyze the effect of oak woodland open space on urban property values in southern California and showed that both land and home value decreased significantly as the distance from open space boundaries, trailheads, and local stands of native oak habitat increased. These studies indicate the tangible value of oak woodlands to property owners but do not necessarily translate into public funding for new oak woodland conservation. To the contrary, available empirical studies of public willingness to pay indicate that large areas of oak woodland cannot be protected by land acquisition with public funds (Thompson et al. 2002).

Scenarios of Oak Woodlands in the Mid-twentieth Century

Changing land use and climate are likely to be the most important drivers of ecosystem change in oak woodlands. These primary drivers could bring other kinds of changes, such as new fire regimes associated with increased population density and longer fire seasons, or local extinctions of species from habitat loss and fragmentation that affect nutrient cycling and ecosystem services. While such changes cannot be forecasted with any certainty, it is possible to construct plausible scenarios for oak woodlands over the next several decades. In this section we focus on the two primary drivers: climate change and land use change.

Climate Change

Since 1950, the most significant trend in the climate of the California foothills has been an increase in minimum nighttime temperatures (ca. +0.4°C decade^{-1}) and to a lesser extent in mean annual temperature (ca. +0.3°C decade^{-1}) (Christy et al. 2006, LaDochy et al. 2007, Crimmins et al. 2011). This warming trend is due to both regional land use change, including the expansion of urban areas and irrigated agriculture, and global climate change. Precipitation has also increased slightly during this time at a rate of 3 mm to 4 mm decade^{-1} (Crimmins et al. 2011), with considerable spatial variation in trends. Interannual climate variability has also increased.

These changes in climate have been accompanied by detectable trends in many ecological processes and species dynamics such as increasing wildfire activity (Westerling et al. 2006), changes in plant phenology (Cayan et al. 2001), higher tree mortality rates related to warm drought (Van Mantgem and Stephenson 2007, Van Mantgem et al. 2009), and elevational shifts in species distributions (Kelly and Goulden 2008, Moritz et al. 2008). Few studies have focused on the direct effects of climate change on oak woodlands. McLaughlin and Zavaleta (2012) surveyed sapling and adult valley oak populations across the southwestern part of the species range and found, in a pattern consistent with changing climate, that sapling recruitment was more constricted around surface water than were adult populations.

Global climate models all predict that California will continue to warm over the next century, with increases in mid-century mean annual temperatures of 1°C to 3°C compared to the second half of the twentieth century (Hayhoe et al. 2004, Cayan et al. 2008). End-of-century increases range from 2°C to almost 6°C depending on the climate model and emissions scenario used. Precipitation projections have varied considerably among the climate models, although the most recent Coupled Model Intercomparison results (CMIP5) show much higher agreement than previous model intercomparisons (Neelin et al. 2013). Depending on the region, at least eleven and as many as fifteen out of fifteen CMIP5 models currently project increased precipitation over areas now occupied by oak woodlands (Neelin et al. 2013). Whether this increase translates into lower climate water deficits has not been evaluated.

Climate exerts multiple, interacting controls in oak woodlands. Winter temperatures control seed survival, germination, and seedling development. Early spring temperature and humidity affect pollen production and transport. Air temperatures near the ground may become lethally hot for new seedlings. Rainfall timing and amount exert a strong control on seasonal soil moisture availability, plant community composition, net primary production, and nutrient cycling. Many of these climate factors vary at the microclimate scale of centimeters to meters as a function of topography and soils, and are regulated by the vegetation canopy so as to create feedbacks between local climate and vegetation. The combination of very fine-scale controls on climate near the ground and vegetation-climate coupling pose a great challenge to predicting how modern climate change will affect species distributions and associated ecosystem processes.

A variety of approaches have been used to investigate how climate change could affect the distributions of ecosystems and species in California. For example, Lenihan et al. (2008) used a dynamic general vegetation model (DGVM) to model coupled climate, vegetation, carbon dioxide, and fire scenarios under warmer/wetter and warmer/drier scenarios. Mixed evergreen forest and grassland increased by 40% to 80% in these scenarios, and mixed evergreen woodland decreased by 10% to 35%. These changes were partly driven by increased wildfire in all scenarios.

Kueppers et al. (2005) produced climate envelope models for valley oak and blue oak and projected them forward to late-twenty-first-century climate scenarios using both a regional climate model and a downscaled global climate model. Based on the regional climate model, suitable habitat for both species shrank to less than 60% of current potential habitat, with contraction of the southern range and some expansion into northwestern California and higher elevations of the Sierra Nevada. Sork et al. (2010) sampled genetic variation in valley oak across the range of the species and found a strong association between nuclear multilocus genetic structure and climate gradients. They also showed that regional populations of valley oak occupy significantly different climatic conditions across the species' range. McLaughlin and Zavaleta (2012) explored differences in modeled species distributions based on current climate envelopes of valley oak saplings versus adults and highlighted the potential significance of drought-mediating microrefugia for local persistence of the species under climate change. These examples all highlight the need for continued study and model improvement to assess the potential vulnerability of oak species (and plant species in general) to ongoing climate change (Morin and Thuiller 2009, Dawson et al. 2011).

Projected changes in the distribution and composition of oak woodlands under the stress of future climate must be considered in the context of the variability that these woodlands have experienced historically (Klausmeyer et al. 2011). Stress could vary across the range of a species or ecosystem

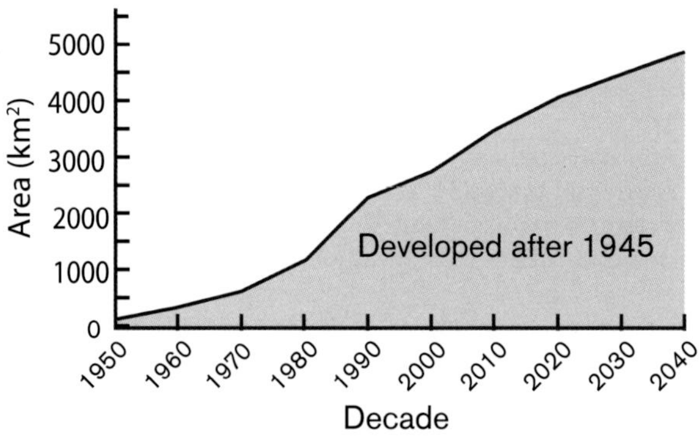

FIGURE 25.8 Historical and projected development of private hardwood lands in California, 1950–2040. Undeveloped acres in 1945: 7,472,979 (3,042,027 ha). Source: Spero 2001.

partly because climate change will vary across the area, but also because of geographic differences in the historical range of climate variability, which could influence both community composition and the amount of adaptive variation within populations of a species (e.g., Davis and Shaw 2001, Sork et al 2010). Unusual drought years and wet years could also play an important role in determining oak persistence and redistribution. Critical climate thresholds or triggers associated with oak woodlands are poorly understood, but evidence from other forest and woodland systems suggests they could be significant (e.g., Reyer et al. 2013, Knapp et al. 2008).

Land Use Change

California's Department of Finance projects that over the next thirty years, the state's population will increase 27%, from thirty-seven million in 2010 to forty-seven million in 2040. Demand for new housing, continued demand from current urban residents for primary- and second-home rural housing, and associated economic pressure to subdivide large ranches all pose significant threats to oak woodland ecosystems. According to Gaman and Firman (2006), roughly 303,500 hectares of oak woodland are at high risk of development by 2040. A recent assessment by the Department of Forestry and Fire Protection classified 506,500 hectares of foothill oak woodland types at medium to high risk of development by 2040 (Figure 25.8). Woodlands at highest risk are in the Sierra Nevada foothills northeast of Sacramento, in Nevada, Placer and El Dorado Counties, foothills of Madera and Fresno Counties, and south of San Francisco Bay in Santa Clara, Contra Costa, and Alameda Counties. The ongoing fragmentation of oak woodlands, climate change, fire regime shifts, and changes in owner preferences and land management make the long-term sustainability of oak woodlands in these areas highly uncertain.

Management and Adaptation Strategies

Since 1980, oak woodlands have been priority conservation targets for both state and county agencies and nongovernmental organizations like The Nature Conservancy, the Audubon Society, the California Oaks Foundation, the California Cattleman's Association, and numerous county land trusts. The California Legislature passed the Oak Woodland Conservation Act in 2001, and at least forty-one counties have now adopted policies focused on conservation and sustainable development of oak woodlands (http://ucanr.edu/sites/oak_range/Description_of_County_Oak_Conservation_Policies/). Public bond funds have been used to acquire high-profile sites such as the Ahmanson Ranch, a 1,200 hectare property purchased in 2003 for $135 million. Some large tracts of oak woodlands have been protected from development by conservation easements and others by multispecies habitat conservation plans and Natural Community Conservation Plans engendered by the federal Endangered Species Act and the California Endangered Species Act. A noteworthy recent example is the 57,870 hectares Tehachapi Uplands Multispecies Habitat Conservation Plan, which encompasses thousands of hectares of diverse oak woodlands on the Tejon Ranch in the western Tehachapi Mountains.

Despite some high-profile successes, conservation through land purchases can be contentious and difficult to achieve due to lack of funding or political support. In addition, lack of interest or economic incentive to maintain cattle ranching on large family ranches is leading to subdivision of large ranches, due in part to estate taxes encumbered during intergenerational transfers (Giusti et al. 2004). Easement purchase of development rights has now become the conservation tool of choice for protecting oak woodlands on large working ranches, although easements are not a panacea (Merenlender et al. 2004, Reiner and Craig 2011). Payments for ecosystem services such as carbon sequestration or watershed protection are of intense interest to conservation organizations, but they have had limited application to date, in part for reasons just discussed. Furthermore, many undeveloped oak woodland landscapes have already been subdivided into 20 to 40 acre lots, making large-scale conservation through acquisition, purchase of development rights, or ecosystem service payments infeasible or undesirable. In those areas the best course of action may be educating small-lot landowners about sustainable land management practices (Brussard et al. 2004).

Though many techniques have been designed and management practices identified to help sustain or restore oak woodland ecosystems (McCreary 2004), we only touch on a few examples here. Low-cost shelters can be used to protect seedlings and sapling oaks from cattle and other large ungulates. Reduced livestock grazing during summer months also improves survival of young oaks. Progressive livestock ranching techniques such as fencing riparian areas, distribution of water troughs to allow better dispersion of grazing pressure, and retaining adequate end-of-season residual dry matter to conserve soil and promote grassland productivity (mentioned earlier) have all been shown to promote increased biodiversity and ecosystem sustainability (Huntsinger et al. 2007).

This is not to say that sustaining oak woodlands is simple or without real costs. For example, control of invasive noxious weeds, feral pigs, and other nuisance species can be extremely expensive and challenging. Furthermore, management outcomes are increasingly uncertain when climate change, air pollution, and fragmentation associated with rural residential development are considered. In principle, the best strategy for managing under such uncertainty engages adaptive ecosystem-based management (Huntsinger et al. 2007, Millar et al. 2007). This requires explicit management goals, formal monitoring of management outcomes compared to control

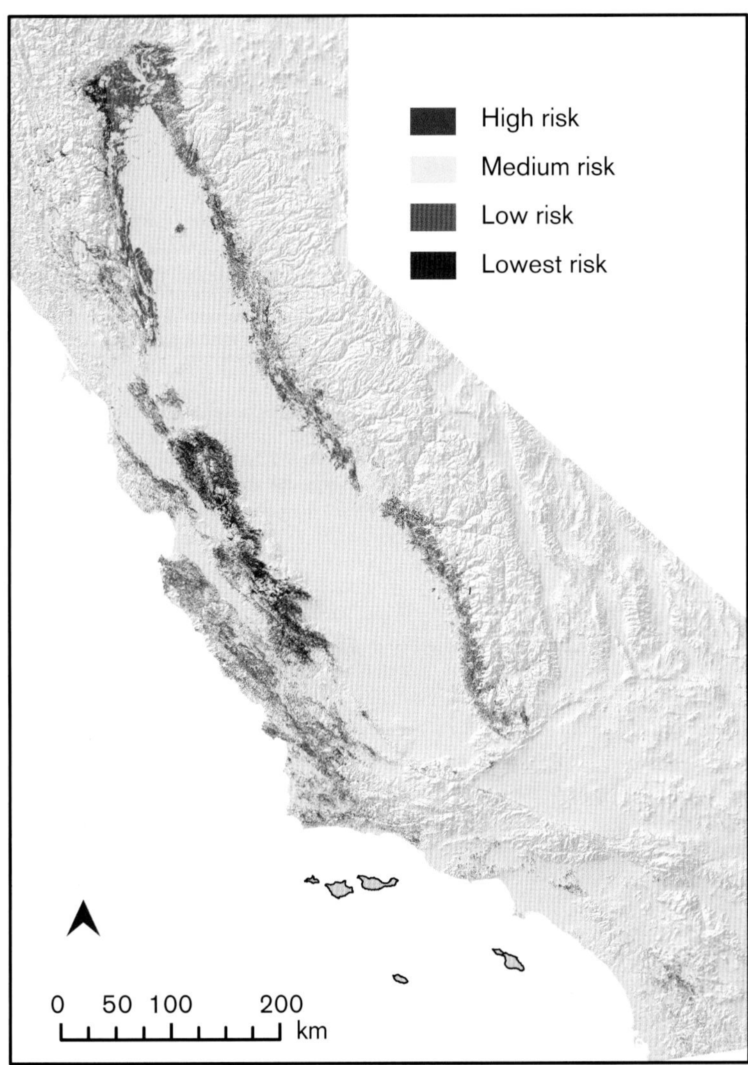

FIGURE 25.9 Projected threat of development to current oak woodlands. The map was produced by combining a map of foothill woodland habitats (extracted from California Department of Forestry and Fire Protection multisource land cover data, 2006) with a map of localized and landscape development threat based on projected population growth, land ownership, current land use, roads, and county general plans.

areas under a different management practice, and the adjustment of management as learning occurs over time. Such management is scientifically challenging. Time lags in ecosystem responses to management changes, interacting with larger-scale changes in ecosystem drivers such as climate and air quality, create complexities that make it difficult to pin management practices to ecological outcomes. Furthermore, while attractive in theory, adaptive management in practice faces hurdles including lack of landowner training, added expense of design and implementation, and limited landowner ability or willingness to change practices (Lee 1999, Aslan et al. 2009).

Research Needs and Priorities

Much is known about the ecology and management of California oak woodland, but the body of research is still relatively shallow compared to that for other California ecosystems such as mixed conifer forests or wetlands, or compared to other oak woodland ecosystems such as midwestern and eastern North American deciduous woodlands and forests (Johnson et al. 2002). We conclude by listing a few research areas that, based on our review of the scientific literature, are particularly in need of additional research.

Oak management and restoration require better knowledge of key demographic parameters including acorn dispersal distances and rates, species-specific age- and size-based sapling survival and growth rates, and adult tree acorn production and mortality rates. To improve climate change adaptation strategies for oak woodlands, research is needed on species-specific ecophysiology, microclimate factors controlling seedling establishment and early growth, climate controls on oak mortality, and patterns and scales of genetic climate adaptation. Managing water resources and oak woodland ecosystem services can be improved by ecohydrologic research on shrub-tree-grass interactions and associated spatio-temporal patterns of water availability, and on associated spatio-temporal variation in soil moisture in woodlands in complex rugged terrain. Biodiversity conservation planning and wildlife management lack community-level research on food webs and species interactions—for example, the role of herbivores versus site physical factors in regulating oak regeneration as a function of climate and soils; the role of top predators such as mountain lions, bobcats, and coyotes on community composition and dynamics; impacts of invasive plants on animal community composition; and mechanisms and controls on community invasibility.

For land use planning, fire management, and ecosystem services management, landscape and ecosystem models need continued development and refinement to clarify the relationships between fire regime and woodland pattern, composition, and dynamics; effects of low-density residential housing on community composition and ecosystem processes; and the relationships among climate, vegetation structure and dynamics, and transfers of energy, water, carbon, and other nutrients. Finally, to devise effective policy for ecosystem services, socioeconomic research is needed on valuation of regulating, supporting, and amenity services associated with oak woodlands as a function of woodland location, structure, and composition; and on policy design to incentivize private landowners to conserve or increase provision of ecosystem services on their properties.

Summary

California's oak woodlands occupy a wide range of foothill and montane environments and harbor exceptional plant and animal diversity. The open canopy of scattered trees over grass or shrub understories creates high local variation in microclimates and soils associated with tree understories and canopy gaps. The acorn crop is an important food resource for many animal species, and the trees also supply important habitat elements such as trunk cavities and downed wood. Oaks serve as foundation species in these ecosystems in that they exert inordinate control on community and ecosystem processes.

This chapter focuses on foothill oak woodlands in general and on blue oak woodlands in particular. The foothill climate combines high temperature seasonality, low winter and early spring rainfall, and summer and autumn drought. Both evergreen and deciduous oaks in these woodlands must cope with extreme summer heat and moisture stress. They do so by gradually reducing gas and water exchange between leaves and the atmosphere over the course of the summer and by tapping deep soil water and/or groundwater. Net primary production is largely controlled by the amount of available water, and in general uptake of carbon dioxide by photosynthesis is only slightly higher than loss of carbon dioxide through ecosystem respiration. Because oak woodlands occupy such a large area (roughly 3.5 million hectares), this small per-area carbon gain translates into significant carbon storage across the entire system. For example, blue oak woodlands are estimated to store around 8.6 teragrams of carbon annually on a statewide basis.

Oak woodlands have been significantly reduced in extent by agricultural and residential development. Ongoing suburban and rural residential development poses the greatest immediate threat to remaining oak woodlands, but climate change is also a serious concern. Both land development and climate change threaten to diminish the many ecosystem services provided by oak woodlands such as forage for livestock, important habitat for game and nongame wildlife species, and highly valued scenery. These services are mutually compatible, allowing for bundling of multiple services when designing conservation strategies such as payments for ecosystem services or purchasing of development rights.

Acknowledgments

Frank W. Davis was supported in part by the National Science Foundation Macrosystems Biology Program, NSF #EF-1065864. Dennis D. Baldocchi was supported in part by the U.S. Department of Energy Terrestrial Ecosystem Science Program.

Recommended Reading

Baldocchi D., Q. Chen, X. Chen, S. Ma, G. Miller, Y. Ryu, J. Xiao, R. Wenk, and J. Battles. 2010. The dynamics of energy, water, and carbon fluxes in a blue oak (Quercus douglasii) savanna in California. Pages 135–154 in M. J. Hill and N. P. Hannan, editors. Ecosystem Function in Savannas: Measurement and Modeling at Landscape to Global Scales. CRC Press, Boca Raton, Florida.

Keator, G. 1998. The life of an oak. Heyday Books, Berkeley, California.

Pavlik, B. M., P. C. Muick, S. G. Johnson, and M. Popper. 1991. Oaks of California. Cachuma Press, Los Olivos, California.

Tyler, C. M., B. Kuhn, and F. W. Davis. 2006. Demography and recruitment limitations of three oak species in California. Quarterly Review of Biology 81(2):127–152.

Glossary

ARBORESCENT Used to describe a woody plant that at maturity assumes a tree growth form, typically one or a few stems and greater than 5 meters in height.

BASAL AREA The total cross-sectional area of tree stems in a given land area, usually measured 1.3 meters above the ground surface, and often expressed in square feet per acre (ft^2/ac) or in square meters per hectare (m^2/ha).

CLIMATE WATER DEFICIT (CWD) An important bioclimatic variable, CWD is the difference between potential evapotranspiration (PET), which is the amount of water that would have been lost, had it been available, and actual evapotranspiration (AET) as limited by available soil water (Stephenson 1998).

COPPICE MANAGEMENT A method of woodland management in which trees are cut and allowed to resprout from the stumps for future reharvest.

ECOSYSTEM ENGINEER A species that directly or indirectly controls the availability of resources to other organisms by causing physical state changes in biotic or abiotic materials (Jones et al. 1994).

EDDY COVARIANCE Often referred to as the eddy flux method, eddy covariance is an important technique for measuring vertical turbulent fluxes in the lower atmosphere. Knowing rates of vertical and horizontal air movement as well as properties such as gas concentrations, temperature, pressure, and humidity, it is possible to estimate important ecosystem processes such as the exchange of water vapor and carbon dioxide between vegetated land surfaces and the atmosphere.

FOUNDATION SPECIES A species that by virtue of its structural and/or functional properties plays a defining role in the biotic composition and ecosystem processes associated with an ecological community (Ellison et al. 2005).

INSECT GALL Abnormal plant growth induced by insects through injection of chemicals, usually into leaf or twig tissues, by larvae or adults.

KEYSTONE SPECIES A species that is high in the food web and whose large effects on the community are highly disproportionate to its abundance.

LEAF AREA INDEX (LAI) An important descriptor of ecosystem structure and predictor of ecosystem function, LAI is the one-sided area of green leaf surface per unit of ground area and is a dimensionless quantity that ranges from less than 1 to greater than 7 for some forest types.

MASTING Used to describe the more or less synchronous production of large quantities of seeds by members of a plant population preceded by a long period of time without high production. Many oaks exhibit masting every few years.

PHOTOSYNTHETIC CAPACITY ($_{AMAX}$) The maximum rate at which leaves are able to fix carbon from atmospheric carbon dioxide during photosynthesis, typically expressed as $\mu mol\ m^{-2}\ s^{-1}$.

PHOTOSYNTHETIC EFFICIENCY The percentage of incoming light energy that is converted into chemical energy by photosynthesis. Typical values for plant canopies range from 0.1% to 2%.

SPECIFIC LEAF AREA (SLA) The ratio of leaf area to leaf dry weight (e.g., square millimeters per milligram [mm^2 per mg]). SLA is an important plant functional trait related to photosynthesis, leaf longevity, nutrient retention, and water use.

STOMATAL CONDUCTANCE The rate of exchange of either water vapor or carbon dioxide between a plant and the atmosphere through the stomata, or small pores of the plant. Usually expressed in $mm\ s^{-1}$ or $mmol\ m^{-2}\ s^{-1}$.

References

Alagona, P. S. 2008. Homes on the range: Cooperative conservation and environmental change on California's privately owned hardwood rangelands. Environmental History 13:325–349.

Allard, V., J. M. Ourcival, S. Rambal, R. Joffre, and A. Rocheteau. 2008. Seasonal and annual variation of carbon exchange in an evergreen Mediterranean forest in southern France. Global Change Biology 14:714–725.

Allen-Diaz, B., R. Standiford, and R. D. Jackson. 2007. Oak woodlands and forests. Pages 313–338 in M. G. Barbour, T. Keeler-Wolf, and A. A. Schoenherr, editors. Terrestrial Vegetation of California. University of California Press, Berkeley, California.

Anderson, M., P. Bourgeron, M. T. Bryer, R. Crawford, L. Engelking, D. Faber-Langendoen, M. Gallyoun, K. Goodin, D. H. Grossman, and S. Landaal. 1998. International classification of ecological communities: Terrestrial vegetation of the United States. Volume 2. The National Vegetation Classification System: List of types. The Nature Conservancy, Arlington, Virginia.

Aslan, C. E., M. B. Hufford, R. S. Epanchin-Niell, J. D. Port, J. P. Sexton, and T. M. Waring. 2009. Practical challenges in private stewardship of rangeland ecosystems: Yellow starthistle control in Sierra Nevadan foothills. Rangeland Ecology and Management 62:28–37.

Atkin, O., D. Bruhn, V. Hurry, and M. Tjoelker. 2005. Evans Review No. 2: The hot and the cold: Unravelling the variable response of plant respiration to temperature. Functional Plant Biology 32:87–105.

Baldocchi, D. D., and L. Xu. 2005. Carbon exchange of deciduous broadleaved forests in temperate and Mediterranean regions. Pages 187–216 in H. Griffiths and P. Jarvis, editors. The Carbon Balance of Forest Biomes. Taylor Francis, Trowbridge, UK.

———. 2007. What limits evaporation from Mediterranean oak woodlands—The supply of moisture in the soil, physiological control by plants, or the demand by the atmosphere? Advances in Water Resources 30:2113–2122.

Baldocchi, D. D., and T. Meyers. 1998. On using eco-physiological, micrometeorological, and biogeochemical theory to evaluate carbon dioxide, water vapor, and trace gas fluxes over vegetation: A perspective. Agricultural and Forest Meteorology 90:1–25.

Baldocchi, D. D., L. Xu, and N. Kiang. 2004. How plant functional-type, weather, seasonal drought, and soil physical properties alter water and energy fluxes of an oak-grass savanna and an annual grassland. Agricultural and Forest Meteorology 123:13–39.

Baldocchi, D., Q. Chen, X. Chen, S. Ma, G. Miller, Y. Ryu, J. Xiao, R. Wenk, and J. Battles. 2010. The dynamics of energy, water, and carbon fluxes in a blue oak (Quercus douglasii) savanna in California. Pages 135–154 in M. J. Hill and N. P. Hannan, editors. Ecosystem Function in Savannas: Measurement and Modeling at Landscape to Global Scales. CRC Press, Boca Raton, Florida.

Baldocchi, D. D., S. Y. Ma, S. Rambal, L. Misson, J. M. Ourcival, J. M. Limousin, J. Pereira, and D. Papale. 2010. On the differential advantages of evergreenness and deciduousness in Mediterranean oak woodlands: A flux perspective. Ecological Applications 20:1583–1597.

Bartolome, J. W., B. H. Allen-Diaz, and W. D. Tietje. 1994. The effect of *Quercus douglasii* removal on understory yield and composition. Journal of Range Management 47:151–154.

Beschta, R. L., and W. J. Ripple. 2009. Large predators and trophic cascades in terrestrial ecosystems of the western United States. Biological Conservation 142:2401–2414.

Block, W. M., and M. L. Morrison. 1998. Habitat relationships of amphibians and reptiles in California oak woodlands. Journal of Herpetology 32:51–60.

Bolsinger, C. L. 1988. The hardwoods of California's timberlands, woodlands, and savannas. USDA Forest Service, Pacific Northwest Research Station, Portland, Oregon.

Borchert, M., F. W. Davis, and B. Allen-Diaz. 1991. Environmental relationships of herbs in blue oak (*Quercus douglasii*) woodlands of central coastal California. Madroño 38:249–266.

Borchert, M. I., F. W. Davis, J. Michaelsen, and L. D. Oyler. 1989. Interactions of factors affecting seedling recruitment of Blue oak (*Quercus douglasii*) in California. Ecology 70:389–404.

Boucher, V. L., and T. H. Nash. 1990. The role of the fruticose lichen *Ramalina menziesii* in the annual turnover of biomass and macronutrients in a blue oak woodland. Botanical Gazette 151:114–118.

Brooks, C. N., and A. M. Merenlender. 2001. Determining the pattern of oak woodland regeneration for a cleared watershed in northwest California: A necessary first step for restoration. Restoration Ecology 9:1–12.

Brown, L. B. 2007. Consequences of sudden oak death: Overstory and understory dynamics across a gradient of Phytophthora ramorum-infected coast live oak/bay laurel forests. University of California at Berkeley, Berkeley, California.

Brown, L. B., and B. Allen-Diaz. 2009. Forest stand dynamics and sudden oak death: Mortality in mixed-evergreen forests dominated by coast live oak. Forest Ecology and Management 257:1271–1280.

Brussard, P., F. Davis, J. Medieros, B. Pavlik, and D. Sada. 2004. Report of the science advisors: Planning principles, uncertainties, and management recommendations for the Placer County Natural Communities Conservation Plan and Habitat Conservation Plan. Placerville, California.

California Department of Fish and Wildlife (CDFW). 2008. California wildlife habitat relationships system (Version 8.2). <https://www.dfg.ca.gov/biogeodata/cwhr>.

Callaway, R. M. 1992. Effect of shrubs on recruitment of *Quercus-Douglasii* and *Quercus-Lobata* in California. Ecology 73:2118–2128.

Callaway, R., and F. Davis. 1998. Recruitment of *Quercus agrifolia* in central California: The importance of shrub-dominated patches. Journal of Vegetation Science 9:647–656.

———. 1993. Vegetation dynamics, fire, and the physical environment in coastal central California. Ecology 74:1567–1578.

Callaway, R. M., and N. M. Nadkarni. 1991. Seasonal patterns of nutrient deposition in a *Quercus douglasii* woodland in central California. Plant and Soil 137:209–222.

Callaway, R. M., N. M. Nadkarni, and B. E. Mahall. 1991. Facilitation and interference of *Quercus douglasii* on understory productivity in central California. Ecology 72:1484–1499.

Carmen, W. J. 1988. Behavioral ecology of the California scrub jay (*Aphelocoma coerulescens Californica*): A non-cooperative breeder with close cooperative relatives. University of California, Berkeley, California.

Cayan, D. R., E. P. Maurer, M. D. Dettinger, M. Tyree, and K. Hayhoe. 2008. Climate change scenarios for the California region. Climatic Change 87:S21–S42.

Cayan, D. R., S. A. Kammerdiener, M. D. Dettinger, J. M. Caprio, and D. H. Peterson. 2001. Changes in the onset of spring in the western United States. Bulletin-American Meteorological Society 82:399–416.

Christy, J. R., W. B. Norris, K. Redmond, and K. P. Gallo. 2006. Methodology and results of calculating central California surface temperature trends: Evidence of human-induced climate change? Journal of Climate 19:548–563.

Colwell, R. K., R. R. Dunn, and N. C. Harris. 2012. Coextinction and persistence of dependent species in a changing world. D. J.

Futuyma, editor. Annual Review of Ecology, Evolution, and Systematics 43:183–203.
Cottee-Jones, H. E. W., and R. J. Whittaker. 2012. The keystone species concept: A critical appraisal. Frontiers of Biogeography 4:117–127.
Crimmins, S. M., S. Z. Dobrowski, J. A. Greenberg, J. T. Abatzoglou, and A. R. Mynsberge. 2011. Changes in climatic water balance drive downhill shifts in plant species' optimum elevations. Science 331:324–327.
Dahlgren, R. A., M. J. Singer, and X. Huang. 1997. Oak tree and grazing impacts on soil properties and nutrients in a California oak woodland. Biogeochemistry 39:45–64.
Davis, M. B. and R. G. Shaw. 2001. Range shifts and adaptive responses to Quaternary climate change. Science 292: 673–679.
Davis, F. W., and M. A. Moritz. 2001. Mechanisms of disturbance. Pages 153–160 in S. A. Levin, editor. Encyclopedia of Biodiversity. Academic Press, New York, New York.
Davis, F. W., and M. Borchert. 2006. Central coast bioregion. Pages 321–349 in N. G. Sugihara, J. W. van Wagtendonk, K. E. Shaffer, J. Fites-Kaufman, and A. E. Thode, editors. Fire in California's Ecosystems. University of California Press, Berkeley, California.
Davis, F. W., C. M. Tyler, and B. E. Mahall. 2011. Consumer control of oak demography in a Mediterranean-climate savanna. Ecosphere 2:art108.
Davis, F. W., M. Borchert, R. K. Meentemeyer, A. Flint, and D. M. Rizzo. 2010. Pre-impact forest composition and ongoing tree mortality associated with sudden oak death in the Big Sur region; California. Forest Ecology and Management 259:2342–2354.
Davis, F. W., P. A. Stine, D. M. Stoms, M. I. Borchert, and A. D. Hollander. 1995. Gap analysis of the actual vegetation of California: 1. The Southwestern Region. Madrono 42:40–78.
Dawson, T. P., S. T. Jackson, J. I. House, I. C. Prentice, and G. M. Mace. 2011. Beyond predictions: Biodiversity conservation in a changing climate. Science 332:53–58.
Diamond, N. K., R. B. Standiford, P. C. Passof, and J. LeBlanc. 1987. Oak trees have varied effect on land values. California Agriculture 41:4–6.
Diller, L. V., and D. R. Johnson. 1988. Food-habits, consumption rates, and predation rates of western rattlesnakes and gopher snakes in southwestern Idaho. Herpetologica 44:228–233.
Duane, T. P. 1999. Shaping the Sierra: Nature, culture, and conflict in the changing West. University of California Press, Berkeley, California.
Dunning, C. E., T. D. Paine, and R. A. Redak. 2002. Insect-oak interactions with coast live oak (*Quercus agrifolia*) and Engelmann oak (*Q. engelmannii*) at the acorn and seedling stage. Pages 205–218 in R. B. Standiford et al., technical editors. Proceedings of the Fifth Symposium on Oak Woodlands: Oaks in California"s Challenging Landscape. USDA Forest Service, Pacific Southwest Research Station, Albany,California.
Ellison, A. M., M. S. Bank, B. D. Clinton, E. A. Colburn, K. Elliott, C. R. Ford, D. R. Foster, B. D. Kloeppel, J. D. Knoepp, G. M. Lovett, J. Mohan, D. A. Orwig, N. L. Rodenhouse, W. V. Sobczak, K. A. Stinson, J. K. Stone, C. M. Swan, J. Thompson, B. Von Holle, and J. R. Webster. 2005. Loss of foundation species: Consequences for the structure and dynamics of forested ecosystems. Frontiers in Ecology and the Environment 3:479–486.
Fire and Resource Protection Program (FRPP). 2010. California's forests and rangelands: 2010 assessment. California Department of Forestry and Fire Protection, Sacramento, California.
Fitch, H. S. 1948. Ecology of the California ground squirrel on grazing lands. American Midland Naturalist 39:513–596.
Flint, L. E. and A. L. Flint. 2012. Downscaling future climate scenarios to fine scales for hydrologic and ecological modeling and analysis. Ecological Processes 1:1–15.
Flint, A. L., and L. E. Flint. 2007. Application of the basin characterization model to estimate in-place recharge and runoff potential in the Basin and Range carbonate-rock aquifer system, White Pine County, Nevada, and adjacent areas in Nevada and Utah. U.S. Geological Survey. Reston, Virginia.
Gaman, T., and J. Firman. 2006. Oaks 2040: The status and future of oaks in California. California Oak Foundation, Oakland,California.
Gelbard, J. L. and S. Harrison. 2003. Roadless habitats as refuges for native grasslands: interactions with soil, aspect and grazing. Ecological Applications 13:404–415.
Giusti, G. A., T. A. Scott, and B. A. Garrtison. 1996. Oak woodland wildlife ecology and habitat relationships. Pages 34–50 in R. B. Standiford and P. Tinnin, editors. Guidelines for managing California's hardwood rangelands. University of California Division of Agriculture and Natural Resources, Berkeley, California.
Giusti, G. A., R. B. Standiford, D. D. McCreary, A. Merenlender, T. Scott. 2004. Oak Woodland Conservation in California's Changing Landscape. A White Paper. Integrated Hardwood Range Management Program publication. University of California, Berkeley. 6 pp. <http://danr.ucop.edu/ihrmp>.
Goulden, M. L. 1996. Carbon assimilation and water-use efficiency by neighboring Mediterranean-climate oaks that differ in water access. Tree Physiology 16:417–424.
Goulden, M. L., R. G. Anderson, R. C. Bales, A. E. Kelly, M. Meadows, and G. C. Winston. 2012. Evapotranspiration along an elevation gradient in California's Sierra Nevada. Journal of Geophysical Research-Biogeosciences 117:1–13. doi:10.1029/2012JG002027.
Gou, S. and G. Miller. 2014. A groundwater–soil–plant–atmosphere continuum approach for modelling water stress, uptake, and hydraulic redistribution in phreatophytic vegetation. Ecohydrology 7:1029–1041.
Greenlee, J. M., and J. H. Langenheim. 1990. Historic fire regimes and their relation to vegetation patterns in the Monterey Bay area of California. American Midland Naturalist 124:239–253.
Griffin, J. R. 1979. Animal damage to valley oak acorns and seedlings, Carmel Valley, California. Pages 26–28 in T. R. Plumb, technical coordinator and editor. Proceedings of the symposium on the ecology, management, and utilization of California oaks. USDA Forest Service Pacific Southwest Research Station, Albany, California.
———. 1973. Xylem sap tension in 3 woodland oaks of central California. Ecology 54:153–159.
Grinnell, J. 1936. Up-hill planters. The Condor 38:80–82.
Grismer, M., and C. Asato. 2012. Converting oak woodland or savanna to vineyards may stress groundwater supply in summer. California Agriculture 66:144–152.
Hall, L. M., M. R. George, D. D. McCreary, and T. E. Adams. 1992. Effects of cattle grazing on blue oak seedling damage and survival. Journal of Range Mangement 45:503–506.
Haston, L., and J. Michaelsen. 1994. Long-term central coastal California precipitation variability and relationships to El Nino southern oscillation. Journal of Climate 7:1373–1387.
Hayhoe, K., D. Cayan, C. B. Field, P. C. Frumhoff, E. P. Maurer, N. L. Miller, S. C. Moser, S. H. Schneider, K. N. Cahill, E. E. Cleland, L. Dale, R. Drapek, R. M. Hanemann, L. S. Kalkstein, J. Lenihan, C. K. Lunch, R. P. Neilson, S. C. Sheridan, and J. H. Verville. 2004. Emissions pathways, climate change, and impacts on California. Proceedings of the National Academy of Sciences of the United States of America 101:12422–12427.
Hayes, G. F. and K. D. Holl. 2003. Cattle grazing impacts on annual forbs and vegetation composition of mesic grasslands in California. Conservation Biology 17:1694–1702.
Held, M. E., and J. E. Winstead. 1975. Basal area and climax status in mesic forest systems. Annals of Botany 39:1147–1148.
Herman, D. J., L. J. Halverson, and M. K. Firestone. 2003. Nitrogen dynamics in an annual grassland: Oak canopy, climate, and microbial population effects. Ecological Applications 13:593–604.
Holling, C. S. 1973. Resilience and stability of ecological systems. Annual Review of Ecology and Systematics 4:1–23.
Hollinger, D. Y. 1992. Leaf and simulated whole-canopy photosynthesis in 2 cooccurring tree species. Ecology 73:1–14.
———. 1986. Herbivory and the cycling of nitrogen and phosphorus in isolated California oak trees. Oecologia 70:291–297.
Holmes, K. A., K. E. Veblen, T. P. Young, and A. M. Berry. 2008. California oaks and fire: A review and case study. Pages 551–565 in A. Merenlender, D. McCreary, and K. L. Purcell, editors. Proceedings of the Sixth California Oak Symposium: Today's Challenges, Tomorrow's Opportunities. Redding, California. Gen. Tech. Rep. PSW-GTR-217. U.S. Department of Agriculture, Forest Service, Pacific Southwest Research Station, Albany, California.
Holzman, B. A., and B. H. Allen-Diaz. 1991. Vegetation change in blue oak woodlands in California. General Technical Report PSW-126. USDA Forest Service. Pages 189–193 in R. B. Standiford, technical coordinator. Proceedings of the symposium on oak woodlands and hardwood rangeland management; October

31–November 2, 1990; Davis, California. Gen. Tech. Rep. PSW-GTR-126. USDA Forest Service Pacific Southwest Research Station, Berkeley, California.
Huntsinger, L., and J. W. Bartolome. 1992. Ecological dynamics of *Quercus* dominated woodlands in California and southern Spain—a state-transition model. Vegetatio 100:299–305.
Huntsinger, L., J. W. Bartolome, and C. M. D'Antonio. 2007. Grazing management on California's Mediterranean grasslands. California grasslands. Pages 233–253 in M. R. Stromberg, J. D. Corbin and C. M. D'Antonio, editors. California Grasslands: Ecology and Management. University of California Press, Berkeley, California.
Huntsinger, L., M. Johnson, M. Stafford, and J. Fried. 2010. Hardwood rangeland landowners in California from 1985 to 2004: Production, ecosystem services, and permanence. Rangeland Ecology and Management 63:324–334.
Ibanez, J. J., M. J. Lledo, J. R. Sanchez, and F. Roda. 1999. Stand structure, above-ground biomass and production. Pages 31–43 in A. F. Roda, editor. Ecology of Mediterranean Evergreen Oak Forests. Springer-Verlag, Berlin, Germany.
Jackson, R. D., and J. W. Bartolome. 2007. Grazing ecology of California grasslands. Pages 197–206 in M. R. Stromberg, J. D. Corbin, and C. M. D'Antonia, editors. California Grasslands: Ecology and Management. University of California, Berkeley, California.
Jackson and Bartholome 2003. cited in chapter--confirm spelling of Bartholome (see above) and flesh out rest of cite
Johnson, P. S., S. R. Shifley, and R. Rogers. 2002. The ecology and silviculture of oaks. CABI, Wallington, UK.
Jones, C. 2000. Occurrence of extreme precipitation events in California and relationships with the Madden-Julian oscillation. Journal of Climate 13:3576–3587.
Jones, C. G., J. H. Lawton, and M. Shachak. 1994. Organisms as ecosystem engineers. Oikos 69:373–386.
Jones, C. G., R. S. Ostfeld, M. P. Richard, E. M. Schauber, and J. O. Wolff. 1998. Chain reactions linking acorns to gypsy moth outbreaks and Lyme disease risk. Science 279:1023–1026.
Karlik, J. F., and A. H. McKay. 2002. Leaf area index, leaf mass density, and allometric relationships derived from harvest of blue oaks in a California oak savanna. Pages 719–729 in R. B. Standiford, D. McCreary, and K. L. Purcell, editors. Proceedings of the Fifth Symposium on Oak Woodlands: Oaks in California's Challenging Landscape. Pacific Southwest Research Station, Forest Service, U.S. Department of Agriculture, Albany,California.
Keddy, P. A., and C. G. Drummond. 1996. Ecological properties for the evaluation, management, and restoration of temperate deciduous forest ecosystems. Ecological Applications 6:748–762.
Keeley, J. E., D. Lubin, and C. J. Fotheringham. 2003. Fire and grazing impacts on plant diversity and alien plant invasions in the southern Sierra Nevada. Ecological Applications 13:1355–1374.
Kelly, A. E., and M. L. Goulden. 2008. Rapid shifts in plant distribution with recent climate change. Proceedings of the National Academy of Sciences 105:11823–11826.
Kelly, P. A., S. E. Phillips, and D. F. Williams. 2005. Documenting ecological change in time and space: The San Joaquin Valley of California. Pages 57–78 in E. A. Lacey and P. Myers, editors. Mammalian Diversification: From Chromosomes to Phylogeography (A Celebration of the Career of James L. Patton). University of California Publications in Zoology, Berkeley, California.
Kertis, J. A., R. Gross, D. L. Peterson, M. J. Arbaugh, R. B. Standiford, and D. D. McCreary. 1993. Growth trends of blue oak (*Quercus douglasii*) in California. Canadian Journal of Forest Research/Revue Canadienne De Recherche Forestiere 23:1720–1724.
Klausmeyer, K. R., M. R. Shaw, J. B. MacKenzie, and D. R. Cameron. 2011. Landscape-scale indicators of biodiversity's vulnerability to climate change. Ecosphere 2:art88. <http://dx.doi.org/10.1890/ES11-00044.1>.
Knapp, A. K., C. Beier, D. D. Briske, A. T. Classen, Y. Luo, M. Reichstein, M. D. Smith, S. D. Smith, J. E. Bell, P. A. Fay, J. L. Heisler, S. W. Leavitt, R. Sherry, B. Smith, and E. Weng. 2008. Consequences of more extreme precipitation regimes for terrestrial ecosystems. Bioscience 58:811–821.
Knapp, A. K., P. A. Fay, J. M. Blair, S. L. Collins, M. D. Smith, J. D. Carlisle, C. W. Harper, B. T. Danner, M. S. Lett, and J. K. McCarron. 2002. Rainfall variability, carbon cycling, and plant species diversity in a mesic grassland. Science 298:2202–2205.
Knapp, E. E., M. A. Goedde, and K. J. Rice. 2001. Pollen-limited reproduction in blue oak: Implications for wind pollination in fragmented populations. Oecologia 128:48–55.
Knops, J. M. H., T. H. Nash, and W. H. Schlesinger. 1996. The influence of epiphytic lichens on the nutrient cycling of an oak woodland. Ecological Monographs 66:159–179.
Koenig, W. D., A. H. Krakauer, W. B. Monahan, J. Haydock, J. M. H. Knops, and W. J. Carmen. 2009. Mast-producing trees and the geographical ecology of western scrub-jays. Ecography 32:561–570.
Koenig, W. D., and J. M. Knops. 2013. Large scale spatial synchrony and cross-synchrony in acorn production by two California oaks. Ecology 94:83–93.
Koenig, W. D., and J. M. H. Knops. 2005. The mystery of masting in trees. American Scientist 93:340–347.
Koenig, W. D., K. A. Funk, T. S. Kraft, W. J. Carmen, B. C. Barringer, and J. M. H. Knops. 2012. Stabilizing selection for within-season flowering phenology confirms pollen limitation in a wind-pollinated tree. Journal of Ecology 100:758–763.
Koenig, W. D., R. L. Mumme, W. J. Carmen, and M. T. Stanback. 1994. Acorn production by oaks in central coastal California—Variation within and among years. Ecology 75:99–109.
Kroeger, T., F. Casey, P. Alvarez, M. Cheatum, and L. Tavassoli. 2010. An economic analysis of the benefits of habitat conservation on California rangelands. Conservation Economics White Paper. Conservation Economics Program, Defenders of Wildlife, Washington, D.C.
Kueppers, L. M., M. A. Snyder, L. C. Sloan, E. S. Zavaleta, and B. Fulfrost. 2005. Modeled regional climate change and California endemic oak ranges. Proceedings of the National Academy of Sciences of the United States of America 102:16281–16286.
LaDochy, S., R. Medina, and W. Patzert. 2007. Recent California climate variability: Spatial and temporal patterns in temperature trends. Climate Research 33:159–169.
Lathrop, E.W. and C.D. Osborne. 1991. Influence of Fire on Oak Seedlings and Saplings in Southern Oak Woodland on the Santa Rosa Plateau Preserve, Riverside County, California. Pages 366–370 in R. B. Standiford, technical coordinator. Proceedings of the symposium on oak woodlands and hardwood rangeland management; October 31–November 2, 1990; Davis, California. Gen. Tech. Rep. PSW-GTR-126. Berkeley, CA: Pacific Southwest Research Station, Forest Service, U.S. Department of Agriculture.
Lee, K. N. 1999. Appraising adaptive management. Conservation Ecology 3(2):3. <http://www.consecol.org/vol3/iss2/art3/>.
Lenihan, J. M., D. Bachelet, R. P. Neilson, and R. Drapek. 2008. Response of vegetation distribution, ecosystem productivity, and fire to climate change scenarios for California. Climatic Change 87:215–230.
Lewis, D. C. 1968. Annual hydrologic response to watershed conversion from oak woodland to annual grassland. Water Resources Research 4:59–72.
Lewis, D. C., and R. H. Burgy. 1964. Relationship between oak tree roots and groundwater in fractured rock as determined by tritium tracing. Journal of Geophysical Research 69:2579–2587.
Lewis, D., M. J. Singer, R. A. Dahlgren, and K. W. Tate. 2000. Hydrology in a California oak woodland watershed: A seventeen-year study. Journal of Hydrology 240:106–117.
Lewis, V. R. 1992. Wiithin-tree distribution of acorns infested by *Curculio occidentis* (Coleoptera, Curculionidae) and *Cydia latiferreana* (Lepidoptera, Tortricidae) on the coast live oak. Environmental Entomology 21:975–982.
Ma, S. Y., D. D. Baldocchi, L. K. Xu, and T. Hehn. 2007. Inter-annual variability in carbon dioxide exchange of an oak/grass savanna and open grassland in California. Agricultural and Forest Meteorology 147:157–171.
Maestas, J. D., R. L. Knight, and W. C. Gilgert. 2003. Biodiversity across a rural land-use gradient. Conservation Biology 17:1425–1434.
———. 2001. Biodiversity and land-use change in the American Mountain West. Geographical Review 91:509–524.
Mahall, B. E., C. M. Tyler, E. S. Cole, and C. Mata. 2009. A comparative study of oak (Quercus, FAGACEAE) seedling physiology during summer drought in southern California. American Journal of Botany 96:751–761.
Major, J. 1988. California climate in relation to vegetation. Pages 11–74 in M. Barbour and J. Major, editors. Terrestrial

Vegetation of California. Native Plant Society of California, Sacramento,California.
Maranon, T., and J. W. Bartolome. 1993. Reciprocal transplants of herbaceous communities between *Quercus agrifolia* woodland and adjacent grassland. Journal of Ecology 81:673–682.
Maranon, T., F. I. Pugnaire, and R. M. Callaway. 2009. Mediterranean-climate oak savannas: The interplay between abiotic environment and species interactions. Web Ecology 9:30–43.
Mayer, K. E., and W. F. Laundenslayer, editors. 1988. A guide to wildlife habitats of California. State of California Resources Agency, Department of Fish and Game, Sacramento, California.
McBride, J. and H. F. Headey. 1968. Invasion of grassland by *Baccharis pilularis* DC. Journal of Range Management 21:106–108.
McClaran, M. P., and J. W. Bartolome. 1989. Fire-related recruitment in stagnant *Quercus douglasii*. Canadian Journal of Forest Research/Revue Canadienne de Recherche Forestiere 19:580–585.
McCreary, D. 2004. Managing and restoring California's oak woodlands. Natural Areas Journal 24:269–275.
Mclaughlin, B. C., and E. S. Zavaleta. 2012. Predicting species responses to climate change: Demography and climate microrefugia in California valley oak (Quercus lobata). Global Change Biology 18:2301–2312.
Meentemeyer, R. K., N. E. Rank, D. A. Shoemaker, C. B. Oneal, A. C. Wickland, K. M. Frangioso, and D. M. Rizzo. 2008. Impact of sudden oak death on tree mortality in the Big Sur ecoregion of California. Biological Invasions 10:1243–1255.
Mensing, S. 2006. The history of oak woodlands in California, Part II: The Native American and historic period. The California Geographer 46:1–31.
Mensing, S. A., J. Michaelsen, and R. Byrne. 1999. A 560-year record of Santa Ana fires reconstructed from charcoal deposited in the Santa Barbara Basin, California. Quaternary Research 51:295–305.
Merenlender, A. 2000. Mapping vineyard expansion provides information on agriculture and the environment. California Agriculture 54:7–12.
Merenlender, A. M., L. Huntsinger, G. Guthey, and S. K. Fairfax. 2004. Land trusts and conservation easements: Who is conserving what for whom? Conservation Biology 18:65–75.
Merenlender, A. M., S. E. Reed, and K. L. Heise. 2009. Exurban development influences woodland bird composition. Landscape and Urban Planning 92:255–263.
Millar, C. I., N. L. Stephenson, and S. L. Stephens. 2007. Climate change and forests of the future: Managing in the face of uncertainty. Ecological Applications 17:2145–2151.
Millenium Ecosystem Assessment. 2005. Ecosystems and human well-being: Synthesis. Island Press, Washington, D.C.
Miller, G. R., X. Chen, Y. Rubin, S. Ma, and D. D. Baldocchi. 2010. Groundwater uptake by woody vegetation in a semiarid oak savanna, Water Resour. Res. 46. W10503. doi:10.1029/2009WR008902.
Miller, J. D., H. D. Safford, M. Crimmins, and A. E. Thode. 2009. Quantitative evidence for increasing forest fire severity in the Sierra Nevada and southern Cascade Mountains, California and Nevada, USA. Ecosystems 12:16–32.
Mills, L. S., M. E. Soule, and D. F. Doak. 1993. The keystone-species concept in ecology and conservation. Bioscience 43:219–224.
Milstead, J. E., J. A. Volney, and V. R. Lewis. 1987. Environmental factors influencing California oakworm feeding on California Live Oak1. General Technical Report PSW-United States. USDA Forest Service, Pacific Southwest Forest and Range Experiment Station. Berkeley, California.
Morin, X., and W. Thuiller. 2009. Comparing niche- and process-based models to reduce prediction uncertainty in species range shifts under climate change. Ecology 90:1301–1313.
Moritz, C., J. L. Patton, C. J. Conroy, J. L. Parra, G. C. White, and S. R. Beissinger. 2008. Impact of a century of climate change on small-mammal communities in Yosemite National Park, USA. Science 322:261–264.
Myers, N., R. A. Mittermeier, C. G. Mittermeier, G. A. B. da Fonseca, and J. Kent. 2000. Biodiversity hotspots for conservation priorities. Nature (London) 403:853–858.
Neelin, J. D., B. Langenbrunner, J. E. Meyerson, A. Hall, and N. Berg. 2013. California winter precipitation change under global warming in the Coupled Model Intercomparison Project 5 ensemble. Journal of Climate 26:6238–6256.
Olmstead, A. L., and P. W. Rhode. 2004. The evolution of California agriculture, 1850–2000. Pages 1–29 in J. B. Siebert, editor. California Agriculture: Dimensions and Issues. University of California Press, Berkeley,California.
Ostfeld, R. S., C. D. Canham, K. Oggenfuss, R. J. Winchcombe, and F. Keesing. 2006. Climate, deer, rodents, and acorns as determinants of variation in Lyme-disease risk. PloS Biology 4:1058–1068.
Ostfeld, R. S., C. G. Jones, and J. O. Wolff. 1996. Of mice and mast. Bioscience 46:323–330.
Paine, R. T. 1969. A note on trophic complexity and community stability. American Naturalist 103:91–93.
Parker, V. T., and C. H. Muller. 1982. Vegetational and environmental changes beneath isolated live oak trees (*Quercus agrifolia*) in a California annual grasslands. American Midland Naturalist 107:69–81.
Pavlik, B., P. C. Muick, and S. Johnson. 1993. Oaks of California. Cachuma Press, Los Olivos,California.
Pillsbury, N. H., L. E. Bonner, and R. P. Thompson. 2002. Coast live oak long-term thinning study—Twelve-year results. Pages 22–25 in R. B. Standiford, D. McCreary, and K. L. Purcell, editors. Proceedings of the fifth symposium on oak woodlands: Oaks in California's changing landscape. Pacific Southwest Research Station, Albany,California.
Plieninger, T., S. Ferranto, L. Huntsinger, M. Kelly, and C. Getz. 2012. Appreciation, use, and management of biodiversity and ecosystem services in California's working landscapes. Environmental Management 50:427–440.
Power, M. E., D. Tilman, J. A. Estes, B. A. Menge, W. J. Bond, L. S. Mills, G. Daily, J. C. Castilla, J. Lubchenco, and R. T. Paine. 1996. Challenges in the quest for keystones. Bioscience 46:609–620.
Reich, P. B., M. B. Walters, and D. S. Ellsworth. 1997. From tropics to tundra: Global convergence in plant functioning. Proceedings of the National Academy of Sciences 94:13730–13734.
Reiner, R., and A. Craig. 2011. Conservation easements in California blue oak woodlands: Testing the assumption of livestock grazing as a compatible use. Natural Areas Journal 31:408–413.
Reyer, C. P., S. Leuzinger, A. Rammig, A. Wolf, R. P. Bartholomeus, A. Bonfante, F. de Lorenzi, M. Dury, P. Gloning, R. A. Jaoudé, T. Klein, M. Kuster, M. Martins, G. Niedrist, M. Riccardi, G. Wohlfahrt, P. de Angelis, G. de Dato, L. François, A. Menzel and M. Pereira. 2013. A plant's perspective of extremes: Terrestrial plant responses to changing climatic variability. Global Change Biology 19:75–89.
Rice, K. J., and E. S. Nagy. 2000. Oak canopy effects on the distribution patterns of two annual grasses: The role of competition and soil nutrients. American Journal of Botany 87:1699–1706.
Ripple, W. J., and R. L. Beschta. 2008. Trophic cascades involving cougar, mule deer, and black oaks in Yosemite National Park. Biological Conservation 141:1249–1256.
Rizzo, D. M., and M. Garbelotto. 2003. Sudden oak death: Endangering California and Oregon forest ecosystems. Frontiers in Ecology and the Environment 1:197–204.
Robinson, D. A., I. Lebron, and J. I. Querejeta. 2010. Determining soil-tree-grass relationships in a California oak savanna using ecogeophysics. Vadose Zone Journal 9:528–536.
Roche, L. M., K. J. Rice, and K. W. Tate. 2012. Oak conservation maintains native grass stands in an oak woodland-annual grassland system. Biodiversity and Conservation 21:2555–2568.
Rossi, R. S. 1980. History of cultural influences on the distribution and reproduction of oaks in California. Pages 7–18 in T. R. Plumb, editor. Proceedings of a Symposium on the Ecology, Management, and Utilization of California Oaks. Pacific Southwest Forest and Range Experiment Station, Berkeley,California.
Russo, R. A. 2006. Field guide to plant galls of California and other western states. University of California Press, Berkeley, California.
Ryu, Y., D. D. Baldocchi, S. Ma, and T. Hehn (2008), Interannual variability of evapotranspiration and energy exchange over an annual grassland in California, J. Geophys. Res., 113, D09104, doi:10.1029/2007JD009263.
Ryu, Y., J. Verfaillie, C. Macfarlane, H. Kobayashi, O. Sonnentag, R. Vargas, S. Ma, and D. D. Baldocchi. 2012. Continuous observation of tree leaf area index at ecosystem scale using upward-pointing digital cameras. Remote Sensing of Environment 126:116–125.
Ryu, Y., O. Sonnentag, T. Nilson, R. Vargas, H. Kobayashi, R. Wenk, and D. D. Baldocchi. 2010. How to quantify tree leaf area index in an open savanna ecosystem: A multi-instrument and multi-model approach. Agricultural and Forest Meteorology 150:63–76.

Safford, H. D. and S. P. Harrison. 2001. Grazing and substrate interact to affect native vs. exotic diversity in roadside grasslands. Ecological Applications 11:1112–1122.

Salvador, R. 2000. An assessment of the spatial variability of basal area in a terrain covered by Mediterranean woodlands. Agriculture Ecosystems and Environment 81:17–28.

Sawyer, J., T. Keeler-Wolf, and J. Evens. 2009. A manual of California vegetation. Second edition. California Native Plant Society, Sacramento, California.

———. 1995. A manual of California vegetation. California Native Plant Society, Sacramento, California.

Sisk, T. D., N. M. Haddad, and P. R. Ehrlich. 1997. Bird assemblages in patchy woodlands: Modeling the effects of edge and matrix habitats. Ecological Applications 7:1170–1180.

Skinner, C. N., and C. Chang. 1996. Fire regimes, past and present. Pages 1041–1069. Sierra Nevada ecosystem project: Final report to congress. University of California Centers for Water and Wildlands Resources, Davis, California.

Sork, V., F. Davis, P. Smouse, V. Apsit, R. Dyer, J. Fernandez, and B. Kuhn. 2002. Pollen movement in declining populations of California Valley oak, *Quercus lobata*: Where have all the fathers gone? Molecular Ecology 11:1657–1668.

Sork, V. L., F. W. Davis, R. Westfall, A. Flint, M. Ikegami, H. F. Wang, and D. Grivet. 2010. Gene movement and genetic association with regional climate gradients in California valley oak (*Quercus lobata Nee*) in the face of climate change. Molecular Ecology 19:3806–3823.

Spero, J. G. 2002. Development and fire trends in oak woodlands of the northwestern Sierra Nevada foothills. Pages 287–301 in R. B. Standiford, D. McCreary, and K. L. Purcell, editors. Proceedings of the Fifth Symposium on Oak Woodlands: Oaks in California's Changing Landscape. Southwest Research Station, Forest Service, U.S. Department of Agriculture, Pacific Southwest Research Station, Albany, California.

Standiford, R. B., and T. Scott. 2008. Value of oak woodlands and open space on private property values in southern California. Forest Systems 10:137–152.

Standiford, R. B., D. McCreary, S. Barry, and L. Forero. 2011. Blue oak stump sprouting evaluated after firewood harvest in northern Sacramento Valley. California Agriculture 65:148–154.

Standiford, R. B., R. L. Phillips, and N. K. McDougald. 2012. Fire history in California's southern Sierra Nevada blue oak woodlands. Fire Ecology 8:163–164.

Standiford, R., D. McCreary, S. Barry, L. Forero, and R. Knight. 1996. Impact of firewood harvesting on hardwood rangelands varies with region. California Agriculture 50:7–12.

Stephenson, N. L. 1998. Actual evapotranspiration and deficit: Biologically meaningful correlates of vegetation distribution across spatial scales. Journal of Biogeography 25:855–870.

Stewart, W., J. Spero, and S. Saving. 2008. The economic drivers behind residential conversion in the oak woodlands. Pages 165–172 in A. Merenlender, D. McCreary, and K. L. Purcell, editors. Proceedings of the Sixth California Oak Symposium: Today's Challenges, Tomorrow's Opportunities. U.S. Department of Agriculture, Forest Service, Pacific Southwest Research Station, Albany,California.

Stromberg, M. R., and J. R. Griffin. 1996. Long-term patterns in coastal California grasslands in relation to cultivation, gophers, and grazing. Ecological Applications 6:1189–1211.

Suttle, K. B., M. A. Thomsen, and M. E. Power. 2007. Species interactions reverse grassland responses to changing climate. Science 315:640–642.

Swarowsky, A., R. A. Dahlgren, K. W. Tate, J. W. Hopmans, and A. T. O'Geen. 2011. Catchment-scale soil water dynamics in a Mediterranean-type oak woodland. Vadose Zone Journal 10:800–815.

Swiecki, T. J., and E. A. Bernhardt. 2006. A field guide to insects and diseases of California oaks. U.S. Department of Agricultutre, Washington, D.C.

Swiecki, T. J., and E. Bernhardt. 2002. Effects of fire on naturally occurring blue oak (*Quercus douglasii*) saplings. Pages 251–259 in R. B. Standiford, D. McCreary, and K. L. Purcell, editors. Proceedings of the Fifth Symposium Oak Woodlands: Oaks in California's Changing Landscape. Pacific Southwest Research Station, Albany, California.

Swiecki, T. J., E. A. Bernhardt, and R. A. Arnold. 1997. The California oak disease and arthropod (CODA) database. Pages 19–22 in N. H. Pillsbury, J. Verner, and W. D. Tietje, editors. Proceedings of the Symposium on Oak Woodlands: Ecology, Management, and Urban Interface Issues. Pacific Southwest Research Station, Albany, California.

Thompson, R. P., J. E. Noel, and S. P. Cross. 2002. Oak woodland economics: A contingent valuation of conversion alternatives. General Technical Report: PSW-GTR-184:501. USDA Forest Service, Albany, California.

Thornthwaite, C. W. 1948. An approach toward a rational classification of climate. Geophysical Review 38:55. Geophysical Review 38:55–94.

Tierney, T. A., and J. H. Cushman. 2006. Temporal changes in native and exotic vegetation and soil characteristics following disturbances by feral pigs in a California grassland. Biological Invasions 8:1073–1089.

Tietje, W. D., and J. K. Vreeland. 1997. Vertebrates diverse and abundant in well structured oak woodland. California Agriculture 51:8–11.

Tietje, W. D., J. K. Vreeland, N. R. Siepel, and J. L. Dockter. 1997. Relative abundance and habitat associations of vertebrates in oak woodlands in coastal-central California. Pages 543–552 in N. H. Pillsbury, J. Verner, and W. D. Tietje, editors. Proceedings of the Symposium on Oak Woodlands: Ecology, Management, and Urban Interface Issues. Pacific Southwest Research Station, USDA Forest Service, San Luis Obispo, California.

Tietje, W. D., S. L. Nives, J. A. Honig, and W. H. Weitkamp. 1991. Effect of acorn planting depth on depredation, emergence, and survival of valley and blue oak. Pages 14–20 in R. B. Standiford, Technical Coordinator. Proceedings of the Symposium on Oak Woodlands and Hardwood Rangeland Management, October 31–November 2, 1990, Davis, California. U.S. Department of Agriculture, Pacific Southwest Research Station, Berkeley, California.

Tyler, C. M., B. Kuhn, and F. W. Davis. 2006. Demography and recruitment limitations of three oak species in California. Quarterly Review of Biology 81:127–152.

Tyler, C. M., D. C. Odion, and R. M. Callaway. 2007. Dynamics of woody species in the California grassland. Pages 169–179 in M. R. Stromberg, J. D. Corbin, and C. M. D'Antonio, editors. California Grasslands Ecology and Management. University of California Press, Berkeley, California.

Tyler, C. M., F. W. Davis, and B. E. Mahall. 2008. The relative importance of factors affecting age-specific seedling survival of two cooccurring oak species in southern California. Forest Ecology and Management 255:3063–3074.

U.S. Department of Agriculture National Agricultural Statistics Service ((USDA NASS). N.d. California: Historical data. U.S. Department of Agriculture. <http://www.nass.usda.gov/Statistics_by_State/California/Historical_Data/index.asp>. Accessed March 28, 2014.

Van Mantgem, P. J., and N. L. Stephenson. 2007. Apparent climatically induced increase of tree mortality rates in a temperate forest. Ecology Letters 10:909–916.

Van Mantgem, P. J., N. L. Stephenson, J. C. Byrne, L. D. Daniels, J. F. Franklin, P. Z. Fulé, M. E. Harmon, A. J. Larson, J. M. Smith, and A. H. Taylor. 2009. Widespread increase of tree mortality rates in the western United States. Science 323:521–524.

Viers, J. H., J. H. Thorne, and J. F. Quinn. 2006. CalJep: A spatial distribution database of CalFlora and Jepson plant species. San Francisco Estuary and Watershed Science 4:1–18.

Westerling, A. L., H. G. Hidalgo, D. R. Cayan, and T. W. Swetnam. 2006. Warming and earlier spring increase western U.S. forest wildfire activity. Science 313:940–943.

Whipple, A., R. Grossinger, and F. Davis. 2011. Shifting baselines in a California oak savanna: Nineteenth century data to inform restoration scenarios. Restoration Ecology 19:88–101.

White, K. L. 1966. Structure and composition of foothill woodland in central coastal California. Ecology 47:229–237.

Williams, K. and R. J. Hobbs. Control of shrub establishment by springtime soil water availability in an annual grassland. Oecologia 81:62–66.

Williams, K., R. J. Hobbs, and S.P. Hamburg. 1987. Invasion of an annual grassland in Northern California by *Baccharis pilularis* ssp. *consanguinea*. Oecologia 72:461–465.

Wills, R. 2006. Central Valley bioregion. Pages 321–349 in N. G. Sugihara, J. W. Van Wagtendtonk, K. E. Schaffer, J. Fites-Kaufman, and

A. E. Thode, editors. Fire in California's Ecosystems. University of California Press, Berkeley, California.

Wilson, K. B., D. D. Baldocchi, and P. J. Hanson. 2000. Spatial and seasonal variability of photosynthesis parameters and their relationship to leaf nitrogen in a deciduous forest. Tree Physiology 20:565–587.

Wullschleger, S. 1993. Biochemical limitations to carbon assimilation in C3 plants—a retrospective analysis of the A/Ci curves from 109 species. Journal of Experimental Botany 44:907–920.

Xu, L., and D. D. Baldocchi. 2003. Seasonal trend of photosynthetic parameters and stomatal conductance of blue oak (*Quercus douglasii*) under prolonged summer drought and high temperature. Tree Physiology 23:865–877.

Zavaleta, E., J. Pasari, J. Moore, D. Hernandez, K. B. Suttle, and C. C. Wilmers. 2009. Ecosystem responses to community disassembly. Year in Ecology and Conservation Biology 2009 1162:311–333.

TWENTY-SIX

Coast Redwood Forests

HAROLD MOONEY and TODD E. DAWSON

Introduction

The coast redwood forest of California is a major component of the state's northern forest region, which extends northward from about 150 kilometers south of Big Sur into southern Oregon. As an ecosystem type, the coast redwood forest is both globally unique and historically fascinating. Blanketing the northwest corner of the state, it dominates the western faces of the Coast Ranges, the coastal marine terraces, and the alluvial plains that drain some of the most pristine watersheds in the region. Redwood forest is also found in the most southern and immediately coastal sections of the Klamath Mountains.

In this chapter we do not cover in detail the variants of the redwood forest forest type that occur in drier sites away from strong coastal influences. We further cannot cover the remarkable and unusually diverse vegetation of the Klamath Mountains, which lie mostly between the immediate coastal region and the Cascade Range to the east. We point those interested to learning of the exceptional diversity of the vegetation of the Klamath Mountains to John Sawyer's *Northwest California: A Natural History* (2006) and to the classic vegetation study of this region by Robert Whittaker (1960) as well as the recent resampling of Whittaker's original analysis by J. Grace et al. (2011). The montane and subalpine forests even further to the east, in the Cascade Range, are a continuation of the vegetation found in the Sierra Nevada to the south and are not included here but are reviewed in Chapters 27, "Montane Forests," and 28, "Subalpine Forests."

Physiographic Setting

Geological History and Features

The coastal zone of northwestern California has a diverse and complex geological history characterized by a legacy of tectonic and some volcanic activity and a predominantly sedimentary geomorphological influence (see Chapter 4, "Geomorphology and Soils"). These features have shaped the existing topography, watershed diversity and hydrology, and vegetation composition. Many abrupt boundaries between vegetation types of the region are clearly linked to its complex geology and soil development. Tectonic and volcanic activity first set the stage for the region's diverse rock and soil types. However, sedimentary processes, marked metamorphic events, and the current moist climatic regime have largely created patterns of erosion and associated landscape features, such as landslide-associated river systems.

SOILS AND SOME UNIQUE PLANT ASSOCIATIONS

The region's unique coastal zone geology has also left a distinctive mark on the soils and soil development of the region (see Chapter 4, "Geomorphology and Soils"). Soils are generally quite shallow in the steeper topographic settings but become deeper and well developed in valley bottoms and even on some of the coastal marine terraces. Soils that have developed on serpentine and peridotite have low fertility but do support a diverse assemblage of coniferous tree species (including some endemics) such as Sargent's cypress (*Hesperocyparis sargentii*), Macnab's cypress (*Hesperocyparis macnabiana*), and knobcone pine (*Pinus attenuata*). Some montane conifers—Jeffrey pine (*P. jeffreyi*), sugar pine (*P. lambertiana*), ponderosa pine (*P. ponderosa*), and incense-cedar (*Calocedrus decurrens*)—also can be found, but no hardwoods inhabit these infertile soils.

Marine terraces of diverse ages caused by changes in sea level, just adjacent to the coast, provide a remarkable illustration of the impact of time on the development of soils. Growing on these soils is a diversity of vegetation types that are closely associated with specific soil properties that are derived from the same substrates and under the same climate regime. The time of origin of each marine terrace is the sole variable in the development of the vegetation types that are found. These range from grasslands on the youngest soils, to redwood–Douglas-fir forests on more mature soils, to stunted trees like Pygmy cypress (*Hesperocyparis pygmaea*) and a subspecies of lodgepole pine, Bolander's beach pine (*Pinus contorta* ssp. *bolanderi*), on the oldest soils. Over hundreds of thousands of years, accumulated nutrients are leached out of the soil and the clay minerals are moved downward, forming a hardpan that leads to very poor drainage and thus an unsuitable environment for normal tree growth (Jenny et al. 1969). This unique topographical setting, or "ecological staircase," is found in coastal Mendocino County near the village of Caspar. Because of its uniqueness, it is now largely protected as the Jug Handle State Natural Reserve.

At the extreme northern end of the California coast, the forest takes on a physiognomy that more closely resembles the great temperate rainforests of the Pacific Northwest, with vast, alluvial deposits along river courses supporting the tallest forests on the planet. Tree diversity is low and dominated by a mixture of the widespread conifers Douglas-fir (*Pseudotsuga menziesii*) and coast redwood (*Sequoia sempervirens*) with some Sitka spruce (*Picea sitchensis*), western hemlock (*Tsuga mertensiana*), Port Orford–cedar (*Chameacyparis lawsoniana*), and even (at or on serpentine soil contacts) western white pine (*Pinus monticola*).

General Vegetation Extent and History of the Pacific Coastal Forest

Northern coastal forests are part of a rich evergreen coniferous forest belt found running along the western edge of North America and the Pacific coast. It begins as patchy forests along stream channels of the Santa Lucia Mountains in south-central California about 200 kilometers south of San Francisco, then becomes more continuous over the land surface beginning in the Santa Cruz Mountains and extending northward through the coast ranges into the states of Oregon and Washington and finally into western Canada. In past geological times, this forest type possessed even greater species richness than today because it also included many more deciduous tree species closely related to those found today (e.g., *Acer, Fraxinus, Salix,* etc.). These taxa had the greatest alliance to trees from along the eastern coast of North America as well to many taxa still found in Japan and China.

By the late Pliocene, however, deciduous tree diversity had been significantly reduced. This was probably associated with intensification of a winter-wet, summer-dry Mediterranean-type climate (MTC) (see Chapter 8, "Ecosystems Past: Vegetation Prehistory"). As in the other MTC regions of the world, evergreen plant life forms dominate the vegetation and thrive under the drought- and fire-prone conditions that prevail today. Coniferous trees dominate the forests, with a rich flora of other woody evergreen species—often shrubs—in the understory that are able to maintain positive carbon gain and necessary nutrient levels throughout the year. Even during the cool winter months when soil moisture is highest, nutrients are available and temperatures are above freezing. Because deciduous trees have no leaves during the winter months (November through March or April) when metabolism would be favorable, they experience a shorter carbon gain period than the rich evergreen elements in the flora. Further, the needle-shaped leaves of conifers track air temperatures more closely than do larger, deciduous leaves, allowing the former to maintain a more favorable energy balance. Moreover, when deciduous-leaved taxa experience water deficit, because of their generally larger leaf size, their leaf temperatures can rise above ambient temperatures by 3°C to 10+°C due to poor convective heat loss, resulting in tissue damage (Waring and Franklin 1979).

One remarkable feature of the vast majority of conifers that dominate the Pacific coastal forest is the great age and size they attain (Table 26.1). Western red cedar, redwood, and Douglas-fir can all exceed twelve hundred years of age, and redwood and Douglas-fir grow to 75 meters to 110+ meters in height. In 2013 the redwood named Hyperion, which is the tallest known tree in the world and is found in Redwood National Park, was measured to be 115.8 meters (380 feet) tall, or 22 meters (72 feet) taller than the Statue of Liberty (S. Sillett, personal communication). These same coniferous species also can accumulate standing aboveground biomass that rivals or exceeds the great angiosperm-dominated forests of the Amazon, the Congo Basin, and Southeast Asia.

Within the Californian northwest coastal region, in addition to the unusual forest types found on specialized soils noted earlier, are a variety of other ecosystem types including communities that contain a significant fraction of the companion species to redwood, Douglas-fir or tanoak (also called tan-bark oak) (*Notholithocarpus densiflorus*), or other coastal conifers such as Sitka spruce, Port Orford–cedar, and grand fir (*Abies grandis*). At the southerly end of these great forests one can even find them intergrading with chaparral, northern coastal scrub, grassland, and oak woodlands and savannas (see Chapters 22, "Coastal Sage Scrub"; 23, "Grasslands"; 24, "Chaparral"; and 25, "Oak Woodlands"). In general, redwood-dominated forests give way to Douglas-fir and tanoak to the immediate interior and further to the east, where con-

Photo on previous page: Coastal redwood forest in northwestern California near Humboldt Redwoods State Park. Photo: Anthony Ambrose.

TABLE 26.1
Age and dimensions of some conifers of California northwest forests

Species	Typical			Maximum	
	Age (years)	Diameter (cm)	Height (m)	Age (years)	Diameter (cm)
Silver fir *Abies amabilis*	> 400	90 to 110	44 to 55	590	206
Port Orford-cedar *Chamaecyparis lawsoniana*	> 500	120 to 180	60		359
Incense-cedar *Calocedrus decurrens*	> 500	90 to 120	45	> 542	368
Engelman spruce *Picea engelmannii*	> 400	> 100	45 to 50	> 500	231
Sitka spruce *Picea sitchensis*	> 500	180 to 230	70 to 75	> 750	525
Sugar pine *Pinus lambertiana*	> 400	100 to 125	45 to 55		306
Western white pine *Pines rnonticola*	> 400	110	60	615	197
Ponderosa pine *Pines ponderosa*	> 600	75 to 125	30 to 50	726	267
Douglas-fir *Pseudotsuga menziesii*	> 750	150 to 220	70 to 80	1,200	434
Coast redwood *Sequoia sempervirens*	> 1,250	150 to 380	75 to 100	2,200	501
Western red cedar *Thuja plicata*	> 1,000	150 to 300	> 60	> 1200	631
Western hemlock *Tsuga heterophylla*	> 400	90 to 120	50 to 65	> 500	260
Mountain hemlock *Tsuga mertensiana*	> 400	75 to 100	> 35	> 800	221

SOURCE: Waring and Franklin 1979.

ditions are much less mesic. At the eastern edge of the more lush coastal forest belt one finds Douglas-fir and ponderosa pine with increasing dominance. With increasing elevation in the Coastal Ranges, one encounters white fir (*Abies concolor*) and Shasta red fir (*Abies magnifica* var. *shastensis*) in the montane regions. Further upward in elevation, mountain hemlock (*Tsuga mertensiana*) is an important dominant in the subalpine zone (Sawyer 2006) (see Chapter 28, "Subalpine Forests").

The Redwood Forest

Because of its iconic beauty, recreational and economic value, and biological uniqueness, the redwood forest has attracted considerable attention by the general public, biologists, conservationists, and the forest industry (Noss 2000) (see Chapter 36, "Forestry"). Despite global recognition of the unique properties of the coastal redwood forest, information on the physiology, ecology, and forest-scale processes that characterize the dynamics of this system is not extensive. In recent decades our fundamental understanding about redwoods and the forest ecosystem has increased, especially in light of environmental pressures such as land use, urbanization, and climate change that pose real threats to the long-term viability of redwoods. Our focus in this chapter is on the nature and dynamics of the remnants of the pristine redwood forest.

Redwood forests are distributed in a narrow coastal strip of central and northern California extending from the southwest corner of Oregon at latitude 42°09′N southward to southern Monterey County at 35°41′N (Olson et al. 1990) (Figure 26.1). This extensive latitudinal range includes areas with a mean annual rainfall from approximately 600 millimeters in the south to well over 3,000 millimeters (Olson et al. 1990). This fact along with its paleo-distribution, encompassing former summer rainfall climates, poses somewhat of an enigma. However, because of their great stature, redwood trees create their own local climate and favorable microcli-

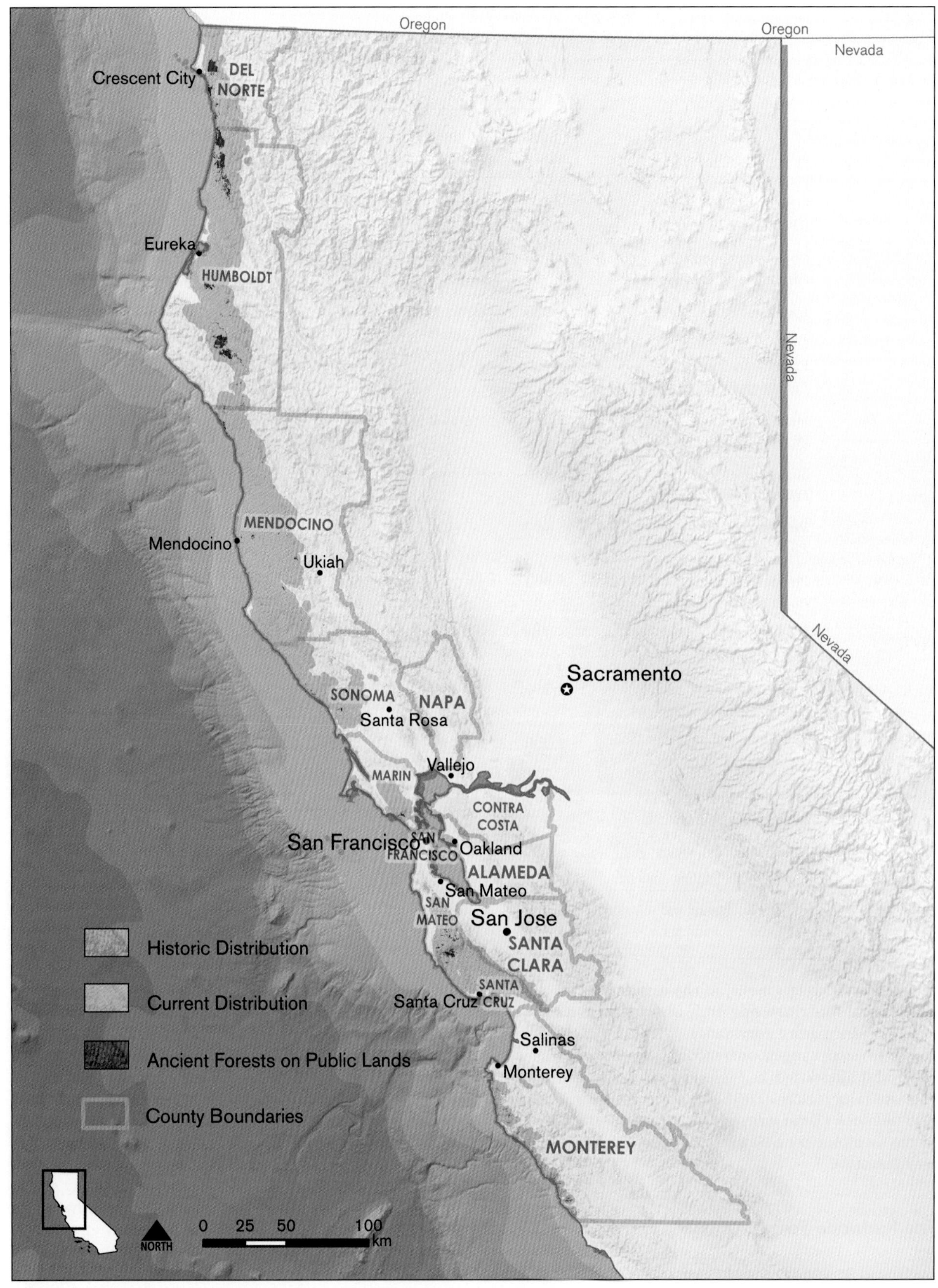

FIGURE 26.1. Distribution of redwood (*Sequoia sempervirens*) indicating locations of remaining old-growth stands. Data courtesy of the Save the Redwoods League and Cal Fire, Fire Resource and Assessment Program (FRAP). Map: Parker Welch, Center for Integrated Spatial Research (CISR).

mates that are more constant than the variability of rainfall received throughout its range would indicate. In the redwood forest mean annual temperatures are relatively cool all year and mild compared to other forest ecosystems in the state, with temperatures that range between 5°C to 25°C. Frost or snow is very rare and patchy in winter. Sumer heat waves that exceed 30°C are also very rare, though these have been more common since the mid-1980s (Fernandez et al. 2012; Johnstone and Dawson 2010).

Principal Organisms

PLANTS

The redwood forest is dominated by its namesake. This forest does, however, include a set of commonly associated tree species that are generally more broadly distributed than redwood itself. Among these tree taxa are California bay (*Umbellularia californica*), tanoak, and Douglas-fir. The distributions of these trees overlap redwood's range but are not coincident (Figure 26.2). Douglas-fir has quite a wide distribution and is an important component of the Pacific Coastal Forest. California bay and tanoak are predominately Californian and extend into many drier regions of the state than does redwood. Pacific madrone (*Arbutus menzeisii*) is most abundant from central coastal California north through Washington and British Columbia, with scattered populations in the Sierra Nevada as well as the mountains of Baja California in the south.

This discordance in distributions is also apparent in the understory plants. For example, the very prominent and characteristic herbaceous perennial redwood sorrel (*Oxalis oregana*) is found not only with the coastal redwood but also throughout coastal Oregon and into Washington. The characteristic evergreen huckleberry (*Vaccinium ovatum*) occurs in the redwood forest as well as in fir-spruce, Douglas-fir, and lodgepole pine forests and is found north into British Columbia as well as in the Sierra Nevada.

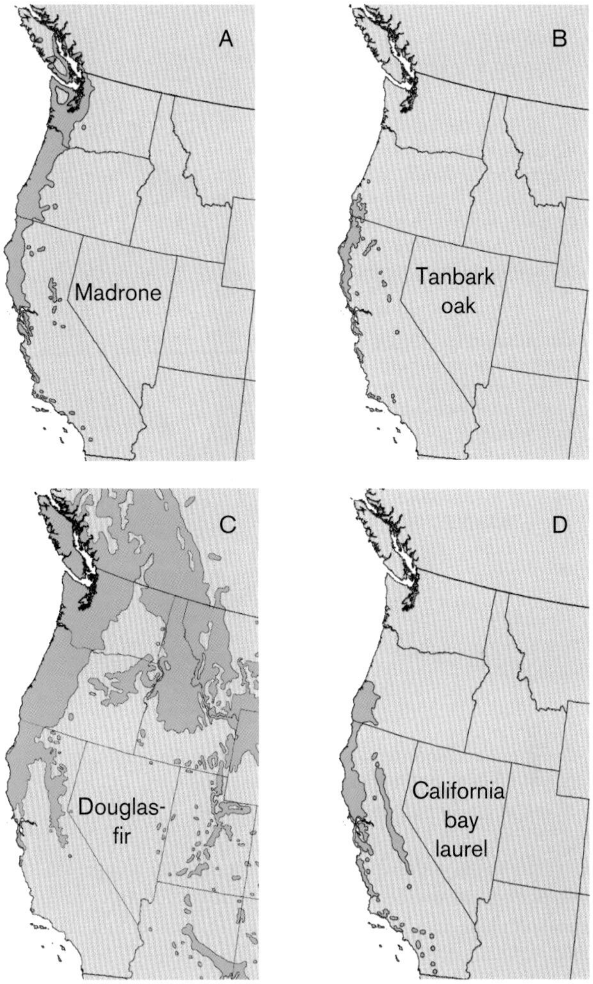

FIGURE 26.2. Distribution of some of the major co-occurring tree species found in the redwood forest. (U.S. Geological Survey 1999). Note the disparate ranges of key "members" of the redwood forest.

EPIPHYTES AND ENDOPHYTES: UP IN THE CANOPY

Although the diversity of higher organisms is relatively low in redwood canopies, a dramatic diversity of epiphytic species (organisms growing with no direct connection to the ground) (Williams and Sillett 2007) occurs at these heights. The complex structure that reiterated trunks can provide can result in large catchments for leaves and canopy debris that develop into soils able to support a wide range of epiphytic plants. These canopy or arboreal soils have a high water-holding capacity (Ambrose 2004, Sillett and Van Pelt 2007). and can be colonized by leather fern (*Polypodium scouleri*) and the evergreen California huckleberry as well as a rich community of fungi, invertebrates, and even a salamander (*Aneides vagrans*) (Figure 26.3). In a study of 9 ancient redwood trees, Williams and Sillett (2007) found 256 species of EPIPHYTES that included 100 species of microlichens, 69 macrolichens, 17 CYANOLICHENS, 45 bryophytes, 19 liverworts, and 26 mosses. They attributed this richness to the great diversity of microhabitat types that these plants favor within these tree crowns. For example, some of these species were found associated principally with burned bark, others on burned wood. Although the species diversity of epiphytes was high, their biomass was low compared to that found in other tree species of the coastal forests. Further, an ecologically important epiphytic form, the nitrogen-fixing cyanolichens, are scarce in redwoods although they are abundant in old-growth Douglas-fir forest and serve as in important nitrogen input to that system (Denison 1973, Pike et al. 1977). One possibility is that herbivore-deterring toxins, commonly associated with redwoods, could inhibit biomass growth of epiphytes as well as perhaps of such specialists as the cyanolichens (Williams and Sillett 2007).

A class of microbes, endophytes, is also associated with the canopy of redwoods and is as species-diverse as in other coniferous forests. Some of these species could be endemic to redwood foliage. Fungi associated with the exterior and interior of redwood leaves are numerous but also show a very patchy distribution. These endophytes might play diverse roles in the redwood canopy; many have been found to be mutualists or latent pathogens (Espinosa-Garcia and Langenheim 1990). A recent investigation also shows that these leaf endophytes likely play a role in the absorption of water that accumulates on the leaf surfaces of redwood trees (see Burgess and Dawson 2004). Ongoing investigations are showing

FORESTS IN THE AIR
Hundreds of feet above the ground, the crowns of ancient redwoods shelter another forest. Thickets of berry bushes, ferns, and other conifers--some large enough to bear cones--rise from dense mats of soil on broad limbs or in trunk forks
The soil, as thick as three feet, forms from decayed leatherleaf ferns and redwood leaves and bark, nourishing an aerial ecosystem unknown until the 1990s, when scientists first climbed into the canopy.
STELLER'S JAY
REDWOOD TRUNK GROWING FROM LIMB
RED HUCKLEBERRY
YELLOW CHEEKED CHIPMUNK
COPEPODS
FUNGI
CANOPY SOIL
EVERGREEN HUCKLEBERRY
MARBLED MURRELET
SALAMANDER

FIGURE 26.3. A complete ecosystem high above the ground in the canopy of a mature redwood. Source: Boume 2009. Reprinted with permission from National Geographic.

that the fungi obtain a small fraction of carbon from the tree leaves themselves; this represents a new and undocumented type of plant-fungal mutualism (K. M. Lader, T. E. Dawson and C. D. Specht, unpublished data).

BELOW THE GROUND: MYCORRHIZAE

In addition to free-living microbes inhabiting soils is a very large number of mycorrhizae—fungi intimately associated with the roots of higher plants and able to form a symbiotic relationship with them. Mycorrhizal hyphae (very thin strands of the fungi that colonize a large volume of soil) mine and transport mineral nutrients and water from the soil into the plant in exchange for energy in the form of carbon (sugars) that the host plant produces. Three major types of the fungi have this type of relationship with plants: ECOTOMYCORRHIZAE, arbuscular mycorrhizae, and ERICOID MYCORRHIZAE (Molina 1994).

ECTOMYCORRHIZAE (ECM): These consist of a fungal sheath, or mantle, formed on the short, fine-feeder roots of plants. The mantle serves as a storage body for nutrients transported from the soil. These fungi, generally basidiomycetes and occasionally ascomycetes, penetrate plant roots between the cortical cells and have hyphae that connect to the soil and extend outward from the root into the soil. These fungi often produce fruiting bodies, mushrooms—many of which are prized as edible. Ectomycorrhizae are found in Douglas-fir as well as tanoak. Bergemann and Garbelotto (2006) estimated that eighty-three species of fungi species provided mycorrhizal associations in tanoak. Similarly, Kennedy et al. (2003) found many of species of fungi forming ECM connections with Douglas-fir and further showed that some of these species are the same as found on tanoak.

ARBUSCULAR MYCORRHIZAE (AM): These do not form a fungal sheath around the roots but penetrate the roots and move into cortical cells, forming finely branched hyphae that proliferate each single cortical cell. The hyphae also penetrate the soil but do not produce aboveground fruiting bodies; rather, they form numerous spores and some fruiting bodies beneath the ground. They, like the ecotomycorrhizae, transport soil nutrients, especially phosphorus and nitrogen, into the host plant in return for carbon from the host plant. The coast redwood has AM fungi associated with its fine roots.

ERICOID MYCORRHIZAE: These are restricted to species of the family Ericaceae. In the redwood forest they are associated with very abundant understory shrubs *Gaultheria, Rhododendron,* and *Vaccinium*. These mycorrhizal fungi are associated with young roots and occupy the epidermal cells of these roots. This mycorrhizal type is unique in that it can mobilize nitrogen directly from organic sources, bypassing the longer path of decomposition to a more reduced form of nitrogen. Pacific madrone, although a member of the Ericaceae, does not have standard ericoid mycorrhizae; rather, it has an intermediate type that shares morphological features of ecotomycorrhiza and ericoid mycorrhizas and has been termed "arbutoid mycorrhizas." Like tanoak, Pacific madrone may share mycorrhizal networks with Douglas-fir. Kennedy et al. (2012) suggest based on shared species of mycorrhizae with Douglas-fir that Pacific madrone, which vigorously resprouts after disturbance including fire, serves as a reservoir of beneficial fungi to the nonsprouting Douglas-fir as it regenerates from seed.

Wildlife

The fauna of the coastal redwood forest shows its strongest alliance to the vast coniferous forests in the Pacific Northwest. At first glance many biologists have incorrectly concluded that redwood and other coastal forests are depauperate of animals. Upon closer inspection, and if both vertebrates and invertebrates are tallied, their wildlife diversity rivals many other ecosystem types in the state. One reason the redwood forest seems like a "zoological desert" is that so much of its diversity is harbored in the forest canopy, well out of sight to most observers. Additionally, a sizable fraction of the wildlife is cryptic, nocturnal, or rare. Some animals are federally listed as threatened or endangered; the most notable are the marbled murrelet (*Brachyramphus marmoratus*) and the northern spotted owl (*Strix occidentalis caurina*).

INVERTEBRATES

The vast majority of species found in the redwood forest, and particularly in old-growth redwood, are invertebrates. Snails and slugs are common in this forest type and include the second largest slug in the world, the Pacific banana slug (*Ariolimax columbianus*). In contrast, ants, butterflies, and bees are uncommon. Pollination is commonly performed by flies, moths, and beetles. Ancient redwood, Douglas-fir, and Sitka spruce trees offer a wide variety of habitats for insects. Many canopy invertebrates have very specialized habitats, preferring to live in very old trees with narrowly restricted distributions. Moreover, enough canopy invertebrates occur in the large moss mats found in and on old-growth trees to support the dietary needs of resident clouded salamanders (*Aneides ferreus*), which may live their entire lives in the tree crowns. For this reason concern exists that there has been considerable loss of species with the loss of the old-growth forests (Cooperrider et al. 2000).

Although many insects are found in the redwoods, most do not get their food directly from the tree itself. No insect is apparently capable of killing a redwood tree—a record not matched by any other tree species in North America. The co-occurring Douglas-fir has thirty or more species of bark beetles that attack it, whereas the redwood has only four. Redwood does not produce much resin, a common insect deterrent, so protection against pests or pathogens likely comes from other chemical defense compounds. Thus, remarkably for such a long-lived tree inhabited by short life-span insects, evolution by insects in breaching defensive compounds does not appear very successful (Snyder 1992).

VERTEBRATES

The redwood forest is comparatively depauperate in birds, with only six nesting species. However, approximately one hundred species of birds can be found in the redwood forest at one time or another. The remainder of the vertebrate fauna inhabiting redwood stands is not generally distinctive from that found in the coastal forests along the entire western edge of North America and has no apparent endemic full species (but see below). As might be expected for a moist, cool, and high-humidity environment, redwood and Douglas-fir forests are rich in amphibian species numbers and overall abundance. During the breeding season, as many as ten different species co-occur in the same general habitat. The most abundant amphibians are salamanders. Reptiles, due to their relatively high heat requirements, are uncommon and found mostly in open habitats such as forest edges and sunny river courses.

Although the redwood forests have been in existence for a very long time, their fauna has changed significantly through the ages except for their herpetofauna, which has relatively ancient members (or taxa that have evolved from them). The mammals of the coastal coniferous forests have had a complex history—with waves of species colonizations, particularly from Eurasia, occurring through time. Many of the mammals seen today have only been residents since the post-Pleistocene. Eighteen mammalian carnivores have historically inhabited the redwood region, most with wide distributions. One of these, the grizzly bear (*Ursus arctos*), has been extirpated in all of California. Another, the Humboldt marten (*Martes americana* spp. *humboldtensis*), is found only in mature redwood forests and was thought to be extinct but is now quite rare and in danger of extinction. This subspecies is genetically distinct from the marten found in the Sierra Nevada. Similarly, the Pacific fisher (*Martes pennanti*), once with a wide distribution, has one population in coastal redwood forest in addition to the Sierras, where they are thought to be in danger of "imminent extinction." A number of individual fishers have been transplanted from the coast population to the Sierra (Cooperrider et al. 2000).

Mazurek and Zielinski (2004) compared the vertebrate denizens of "legacy" old-growth trees left in harvested stands to young redwoods in these stands that were matched for habitat. The LEGACY TREES were characteristically "battle-scarred"—that is, with at least some of the features of old-growth trees such as cavities, deeply furrowed bark, reiterated crowns, and basal hollows (often called "goose pens" for the function they served early foresters as cages for their geese and other livestock inside of the massive, burned-out hollows at the bases of previously burned old-growth redwood trees). Mazurek and Zielinski (2004) found a significantly larger number of bird and bat species associated with the legacy trees. In general, except for bats, only a few small mammals showed a higher association with legacy trees: the wood rat and two insectivores. In total, thirty-eight vertebrate species were associated with legacy trees and twenty-four with young trees. The study concluded that legacy trees represent a "lifeboat" of assemblages for regenerating stands.

Forest Structure

In many ways the northernmost temperate redwood forests are comparable to the rain forests of the tropics. While they lack the biotic diversity tropical forests harbor, they share a degree of structural complexity. The redwood forest is layered with plant species of differing heights and light requirements. The composition of these layers varies with site and particularly with latitude. In the well-studied old-growth redwood forest of Muir Woods, McBride and Jacobs (1977) reported that the upper tree layer is composed principally of redwood and some Douglas-fir. A second tree layer consists of shorter-statured trees that also have shorter life spans, including California bay, tanoak, coast live oak (*Quercus agrifolia*), bigleaf maple (*Acer macrophyllum*), and red alder (*Alnus rubra*). Still lower is a rich layer of shrubs consisting of western azalea (*Rhododendron occidentale*), California hazel (*Corylus cornuta*

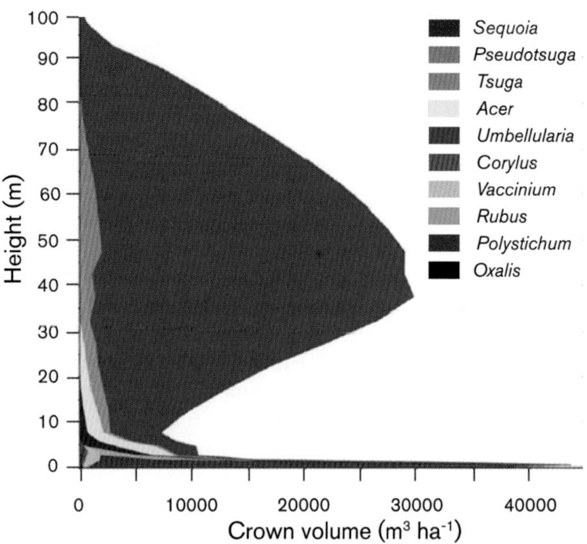

FIGURE 26.4. Vertical distribution of crown volume (5-meter-deep slices for volume) in an old-growth redwood forest on a well-developed, low-elevation site in Humboldt County. Small and low-density species not shown. Source: Sillett and Van Pelt 2007.

FIGURE 26.5. Forest floor at the Humboldt Redwood State Park, with researchers at the base of the tree preparing instruments for measuring canopy light climate. Note the more typical forest floor of this forest with considerable dead wood on the floor of differing ages. Photo: Anthony Ambrose.

californica, thimbleberry (*Rubus parviflorus*), sword fern (*Polystichum munitum*), and California huckleberry. Below that, a relatively species-rich herb layer is composed of perennial species such as redwood sorrel, redwood violet (*Viola sempervirens*), wild ginger (*Asarum caudatum*), fairy lantern (*Disporum smithii*), western trillium (*Trillium ovatum*), California fetid adder's tongue (*Scoliopus bigelovii*), miner's lettuce (*Montia perfoliata*), and Andrew's clintonia (*Clintonia andrewsiana*). Finally there is a moss layer characterized by the Oregon eurhynchium moss (*Eurhynchium oreganum*). Although there can be considerable structural complexity from the top to the bottom of the old-growth forest, the vast majority of the forest biomass is redwood (Figure 26.4).

On the forest floor of unmanaged forests is a considerable amount of fallen dead wood of varying ages. This common feature is quite different from that observed in secondary forests and even some of California's state parks (Figure 26.5). The explorations of Jedediah Smith in 1828 indicate the difficulty of traversing mature redwood forests on deep soils: when the massive trees fall, "they often take other trees with them, leaving jackstraws of massive logs over older piles of rot-resistant logs. Often the forest floor was such a tangled mass that the men could not see the ground. They scrambled over the logs, but horses had to be led around them." They estimated that it would take a month to traverse 65 kilometers through such country (Sawyer 2006).

Forest Dynamics

Redwood trees of the coastal forests commonly grow taller (over 100 meters) and live longer (more than two thousand years) than any other tree species in North America. In a word, redwood forests are truly unique, so it is not surprising that they violate common rules of forest succession. For example, in many forests one expects the seeds of a late successional species to be relatively large and able to establish in the shady understory that they have created. However, redwood seeds are very small and rarely establish in nature without the aid of disturbances caused by flooding, fire, or tree falls that create bare mineral soil able to support new seedling germination. Lorimer et al. (2009) reconstructed the history of fire, flooding, and landslides in redwood forests and their role in forest regeneration. They concluded that episodic establishment within the forest on micro-disturbances, such tree-fall root mounds or on decaying logs was sufficient to maintain the redwood dominants, particularly coupled with their vegetative resprouting characteristics and their great longevity. In light of these features, yearly or even decadal seedling input is not required for maintenance.

An ongoing and novel perturbation in the structure of redwood forests is occurring due to the invasion of the pathogen sudden oak death (SOD) since the mid-1990s. This pathogen has resulted in death or severe dieback of tanoak in many regions (see Chapter 13, "Biological Invasions"). The cause of this disease, a relative of the one that caused the Irish potato famine, is a new species of the fungus-like protist microorganism *Phytophthora ramorum*. It was simultaneously found infecting *Rhododendron* shrubs in the Netherlands and most likely was exchanged between continents by the nursery trade (Garbelotto and Rizzo 2005). SOD has been found to infect a wide number of plant species in the redwoods. An associate of tanoak in redwood forests, California bay, is in part responsible for the epidemic movement of this pathogen because it can become infected and lead to high spore production and relatively long-distance spore dispersal without itself dying. The loss or impairment of tanoak by SOD most likely will have ecosystem-level impacts due to tanoaks' extensive mycorrhizal networks (Bergemann et al. 2013). The rapidity of change will be determined in part by the abundance of California bay in individual stands (Cobb et al. 2012). Projections suggest that the redwood tree will benefit from loss of the tanoak competitor (Waring and O'Hara 2008).

Another dimension of this marked change in the forest is the impact it can have on the amount of standing dead biomass of tanoak in many forests; these dead trees represent an additional fuel source for wildfires (Kuljian and Varner 2010) that could increase the vulnerability of redwood forest to damage. Changes in the fire regime along with other critical global environmental changes (warmer and also drier future climates) are likely to alter fire regimes (intensity and duration) of and in redwood forests in the future. In a recent study of an unusual episode of fires throughout the redwood region due to dry lightning events in June 2008, although both redwood and tanoak resprout after fire damage, the BOLE survival of redwood was greater than tanoak (Ramage et al. 2010). So, while redwood clearly has survived under many different climatic and site conditions over its very long history, it might also benefit under some new and increasingly widespread conditions. This depends, however, on a continued supply of water through fog or rainfall.

REGENERATION

Old-growth redwoods can produce millions of seeds ha^{-1} of forested land (Boe 1961). However, these seeds are quite small (averaging about 2 milligrams per individual seed), and generally fewer than 10% of those dispersed are viable. Of those viable seeds produced, a high percentage will actually germinate. Seed disperses in late fall and can peak in early winter. Seed output varies though time, with periods (years) of high seed production every five to seven years in some localities, mostly in the central and southerly part of the redwood range (Sloan and Boe 2008). In northern stands little to no interannual variation in seed production occurs, and many years can pass without a single viable seed being produced. The small seeds do not disperse very far, in contrast to wind-dispersed seeds.

Viable seed that hit the forest floor are generally short-lived; redwood forests therefore have little to no seed bank. If seeds land in a moist area, they will germinate, whether on a log, on litter, or on the rare patch of bare soil. Seed will also very likely be consumed by numerous seed predators before germination—birds (juncos, towhees, and song sparrows) and mammals (deer mice [*Peromyscus maniculatis*] and brush rabbits [*Sylvilagus bachmani*]) in particular. A host of fungal pathogens can also attack both seeds and seedlings, and if they do, they can largely eliminate regeneration. Those seeds that fall on mineral soils free of pathogenic fungi have the best chance of success. Such sites are found where fire has consumed the litter layer and where bare soils are produced by tree fall and flooding that brings silt over the site (McBride and Jacobs 1977). If and when seeds do germinate, the resulting seedlings have another barrier to overcome before transitioning into saplings: herbivory. Pacific banana slugs, pack rats (*Neotoma fuscipes*), and brush rabbits are among the animals that can do the most notable damage (McBride and Jacobs 1977).

Despite the low odds of success that a redwood seed and seedling have for completing successful germination and development into a healthy sapling, survival still appears adequate to maintain viable populations and persistent forests. Redwoods are not completely dependent on sexual reproduction for long-term survival and have a remarkable capacity for stand maintenance through vegetative reproduction (i.e., resprouting from basal burls or even from the main trunk) when injured by disturbances like fire. The long lifespan of redwoods and their resistance to insects and pathogens results in forests with the potential for persistence well into the future as long as further harvesting of old growth or rapid environmental changes do not challenge them anew. If the remaining redwood forests are subject to science-based conservation and management, their future could be bright.

Although an individual redwood tree can live for millennia, its actual lifetime can be longer because it can readily respond to catastrophes by resprouting. Even in the seedling stage, it is already "preparing" for the possibility of the loss of the shoot by the formation of a lignotuber, or a swelling of the stem containing growth buds, produced at the site of the cotyledons (Del Tredici 1999). With age the lignotubers can become enormous. The rings of saplings that surround harvested mature redwood trees, so commonly seen in young redwood forests and many old-growth forests as well, are the result of resprouting from the lignotuber. On the stem, after injury, lignotuber-like structures are formed and are generally called "burls." These, like the ground lignotuber, contain suppressed buds and can sprout under certain conditions such as injury. In addition are dormant EPICORMIC BUDS beneath the bark that will sprout following fire injury. The remarkable regenerative power of redwood even extends to establishment of new "daughter" plants by layering (a partially buried stem can generate roots and new stems, and large branches that fall from old trees can regenerate an entirely new tree). When we think of regeneration, we generally look to the forest floor. In the redwood forest we also need to look up. A lot of regeneration of the canopy takes place due to storm events. One of the redwood giant trees, known as the Arco Giant, illustrates this phenomenon: a storm in January 1998 broke off the top of this tree, and a new crown regenerated at the point of breakage (Van Pelt 2001).

FIRE FREQUENCY AND RESPONSE

Fire return intervals in redwood forests predictably decrease from very wet northern coastal stands (125 to 500 years) to those in the drier, southern, and interior localities of its distribution (about 50 years). However, considerable variance has occurred around these means through history. Frequent burning of prairies adjacent to the redwoods by indigenous Californians caused some ignitions of the forests at the transition zone that did not spread to a great degree due to the cool, moist forest interiors. The thick, insulating bark of older redwood trees can protect them from ignition to some degree if it retains moisture. However, if dry, it will burn, resulting in partially hollowed trunk sections called "goose pens" at the bases of trees—hollows that can become larger through recurring, low-level fires (Stuart and Stephens 2006). If trees do burn, entry points can emerge for fungal infection into otherwise healthy sapwood. Brown and Baxter (2003) postulate that prior to human occupation of the redwoods, fires in this mesic ecosystem were not common. Fires can stimulate reproduction but are certainly not a prerequisite for the establishment of new seedlings. Disturbance gaps within the forest can also provide sites for reproduction. The uneven age structure in mature, natural forest stands is a testimony to the patchy nature of recruitment opportunities. The long lifespan and unique life history characteristics of coast redwood therefore mean that in a sense this species is a "pioneer" as well as a "climax" species in the forest that it largely defines (Lorimer et al. 2009).

Redwood Forest Energy and Carbon Balance

Redwood represents an unusual keystone species in that it is the primary controller of the microclimate essential for a host of dependent species of this forest type. Light, temperature,

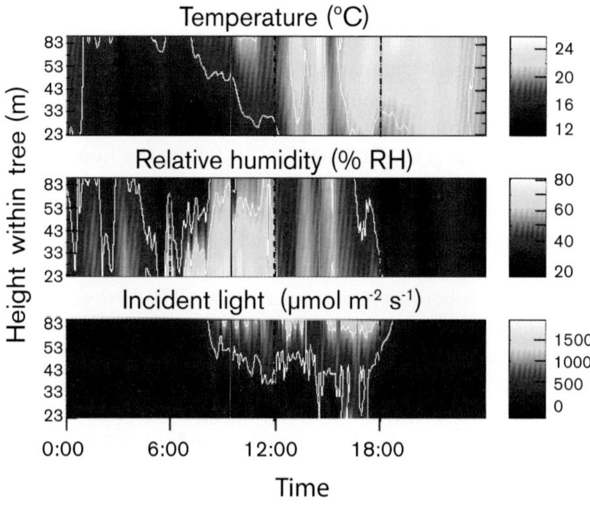

FIGURE 26.6. Temperature, relative humidity, and incident photosynthetically active radiation measured throughout the canopy of a redwood forest. Source: Tolle et al. 2005.

humidity, and the overall moisture regime are all influenced by the presence of these massive forest trees. Light levels at the forest floor are very, very low (1–3% of full sun), and sun flecks are of a short duration (Figure 26.6). Plants at the bottom of the forest floor are thought to be specialized for efficient use of the light they do receive (Santiago and Dawson 2014).

One of the most common redwood understory herbs is redwood sorrel, which survives in an environment that receives only about 0.5% of full sunlight (Bjorkman and Powles 1980). This truly shade-tolerant plant reaches 90% of its saturated photosynthetic rate at only 100 quanta m^{-2} s^{-1} of incoming radiation (1,600 quanta m^{-2} s^{-1} is full sunlight) (Powles and Bjorkman 1980). Their biochemical adaptation to these very low light levels conversely puts them under stress if full light flecks impinge upon them. When this happens, the trifoliate leaves fold up to reduce the amount of full radiation received to prevent damage to their shade-adapted photosynthetic machinery. This response happens in a matter of minutes but can fully reverse after the passing of the sun fleck, over a period of an hour or more.

The very low energy received at the forest floor throughout the year puts constraints on adaptive possibilities. Even though specialized plant species can thrive in low-light environments, once established the likelihood of receiving enough energy to go from seed to seed in one year is low. No annuals grow in the full-shade microsites. This is comparable to alpine environments, where, due not to light limitations but to temperature constraints, few annual plants occur. (In the circumpolar arctic tundra is only one annual plant species).

Redwood forests are world-class in terms of carbon accumulation and storage. Their remarkable storage is the result not of exceptional rates of carbon accumulation in any given year but rather of the longevity of the tree. Busing and Fujimori (2005) reported on the carbon stores in an old-growth stand of redwoods in Bull Creek, in Humboldt Redwoods State Park, occurring on an alluvial flat. The stand they investigated was dominated (99% by basal area) by redwoods, some exceeding 90 meters in height. California bay, tanoak, and Pacific yew were also in the stand but as subordinates. Their estimates of stem biomass ranged from 3,000 to 5,200 Mg ha^{-1} depending on how stem volume was calculated and which wood-specific gravity was used. Using stem diameter increment (growth) during the interval from a previous study of the site in 1972 (Fujimori 1977), their most accurate estimate of annual stem net primary productivity was between 4 and 5 Mg ha^{-1} yr^{-1} with total tree, aboveground net productivity of 7 to 10 Mg ha^{-1} yr^{-1}. The forest floor contained 262 Mg ha^{-1} of coarse woody debris and 5 Mg ha^{-1} of fine woody material. These values indicate a uniquely high value of standing biomass and moderate-to-high annual productivity compared to other forests of the world. In a different location, Sillett and Van Pelt (2007) measured total aboveground biomass distribution in a 1 hectare Prairie Creek stand. They calculated a static biomass value of 4,283 Mg ha^{-1} exclusive of snags and logs. Forest stands such as these represent the highest biomasses per unit ground area found anywhere in the world. The leaf area for this forest was 14.2 m^2 m^{-2} of forest floor. As of 2014, newly obtained data point to even higher biomass and carbon stores than these previously published results (Robert Van Pelt, pers. comm.).

Annual litterfall in old-growth redwood has been measured at a range of sites from 3,120 to 4,690 kg ha^{-1} yr^{-1} with decomposition rate constants of 0.177 to 0.238 yr^{-1} (decomposition rate constant = annual litterfall/total forest floor litter mass). The total litter mass in one forest ranged from 15,700 to 30,000 kg ha^{-1} (Pillers and Stuart 1993). Decomposition rates were more related to moisture availability than to temperature, which is probably representative of most California ecosystems where the warmest temperatures coincide with a lack of moisture.

Fog and Coast Redwood Forest Water Balance

Redwood trees evolved and expanded their range across many temperate zones over their 100+ million-year history (Mao et al. 2012) well before the appearance and strengthening of the Mediterranean-type climate with its long summer drought. Given the shrinkage of the past distribution of this species to the narrow (40–70 kilometers wide) and long (approximately 750 kilometers) strip along coastal California where fog is frequent, it seems reasonable to conjecture that summertime fog and the water subsidies it can provide have replaced at least some fraction of the missing summer rain redwoods once enjoyed during warmer and wetter times in the past.

The several million years that the Mediterranean-type climate has been in place in California have been marked by cool, wet winters, with generally ample rainfall and rainless summer months. During June through October each year, when the coastal upwelling of very cold, deep ocean waters along the Pacific edge strengthens, fog is most abundant (Figure 26.7). Fog banks form most nights and move onshore as the warmer air inland raises. When the fog is intercepted by vegetation, and especially the towering and deep crowns of the coast redwood trees, the water that drips from tree crowns can account for over 33% of the total annual hydrological input (precipitation + fog). Using the hydrogen-stable isotope composition of fog water, it was determined that fog was taken up by the plants and that 35% to 80% of all the water used by plants within the understory community came from fog (Dawson 1998, Limm et al. 2009).

Quantification of fog water inputs to coast redwood forests in Humboldt County, near Orick and Redwood National and State Parks, has continued since 1991 in order to quan-

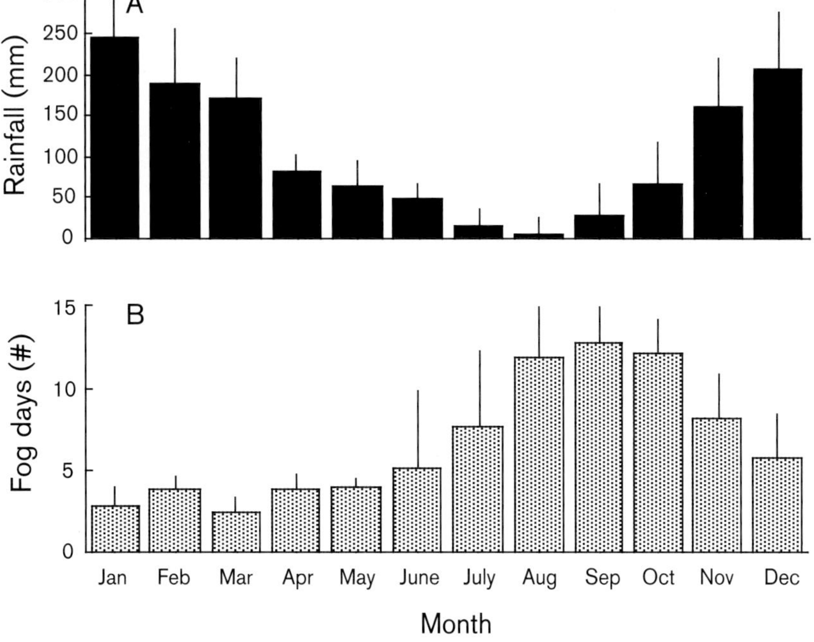

FIGURE 26.7. (A) Rainfall amount and (B) fog frequency by month in the North Coast redwood country. Source: After Dawson 1998.

tify long-term trends and variation in fog water input relative to winter rainfall and to relate trends to broad-scale climatic factors. In parallel, research focused on looking a broad-scale trends in fog along the entire California coast has shown that overall fog frequency has declined by more than 30% since 1951 and that fog inputs vary quite dramatically from year to year (Johnstone and Dawson 2010). Despite the overall decline in fog, twenty-three years of collector data show that 33% ± 7% of all water inputs to these forest ecosystems come as fog in the summer (Dawson, unpublished data). Interestingly, it is clear that not only are these summertime water inputs important but that the tree crowns themselves are providing the impaction surfaces for collections and drip to occur. This is evidenced by the fact that when trees were removed, fog inputs declined significantly (Dawson 1998). In these logged sites, overall site humidity decreased 17–36% and temperatures increased 3–5°C due to greater surface heating. These changes in local microclimate appear to affect overall rainfall inputs slightly but to reduce fog water inputs by more than 65% (Dawson, unpublished data).

Redwood needles can also directly take up a small fraction of their summer daily water requirement from fog. Using both field observations and isotope labeling of water, Burgess and Dawson (2004) showed that 6–8% of the water that condenses onto foliage each foggy night enters the leaf directly. While this input is low in comparison to fog drip into the soil from tree crowns, it is being absorbed directly into the sites where is can best be utilized. As such, its physiological impact is disproportionally high compared with fog drip that must be taken up by roots and elevated through these towering giants to leaves 50–110+ meters above the ground before it can be used.

Beyond contributing to water supplies, fog also reduces the evaporative demand from leaf surfaces, both day and night, and hence reduces overall transpiration and increased tree and forest water-use efficiency in the high, diffuse light environment that can prevail on foggy days. Foliar uptake of water has been shown to enhance photosynthesis in coast redwood up to threefold compared to plants that do not receive such wetting events (see Simonin et al. 2009). Finally, although redwood trees in any particular stand will receive the same amount of precipitation input (from vertically delivered rainfall), they differ individually in how much fog they trap as a function of location. Since fog moves horizontally from the ocean onto land, trees on the edge of a forest stand trap more fog than those in the interior (Ewing et al. 2009). The capacity of leaves to absorb fog water, as well as rain and dew, directly has also recently been found in a majority of the redwood understory species studied to date (ten to twelve species). This direct foliar uptake improves plant water balance as well as reducing nighttime transpiration (Figure 26.8).

Nutrient Dynamics

Redwood forests, not unlike other large-statured forests, contain the largest fraction of their nutrients within the long-lived, massive trees. For example, approximately 80% of the carbon and phosphorus at the old-growth site in Humboldt State Park resides in the trees (Zinke et al. 1979) (Table 26.2). This means that when the trees are harvested, a large amount of the nutrient capital is removed from the site, particularly phosphorus. Dahlgren (1998) studied the nitrogen dynamics of an eighty-year-old, secondary-growth, redwood–Douglas-fir stand at the Caspar Creek experimental watershed in the Jackson Demonstration State Forest of Mendocino County. During the eighty-year period, the forest had accumulated 1,480 kg ha^{-1} of nitrogen (N). Harvest of this forest would remove 950 kg ha^{-1} of these stores (wood plus bark) from the site. Additional site losses of nitrogen would occur by streamwater flux, particularly suspended sediment flux, due mainly to harvesting activities (80–160 kg ha^{-1}). Inputs are meager,

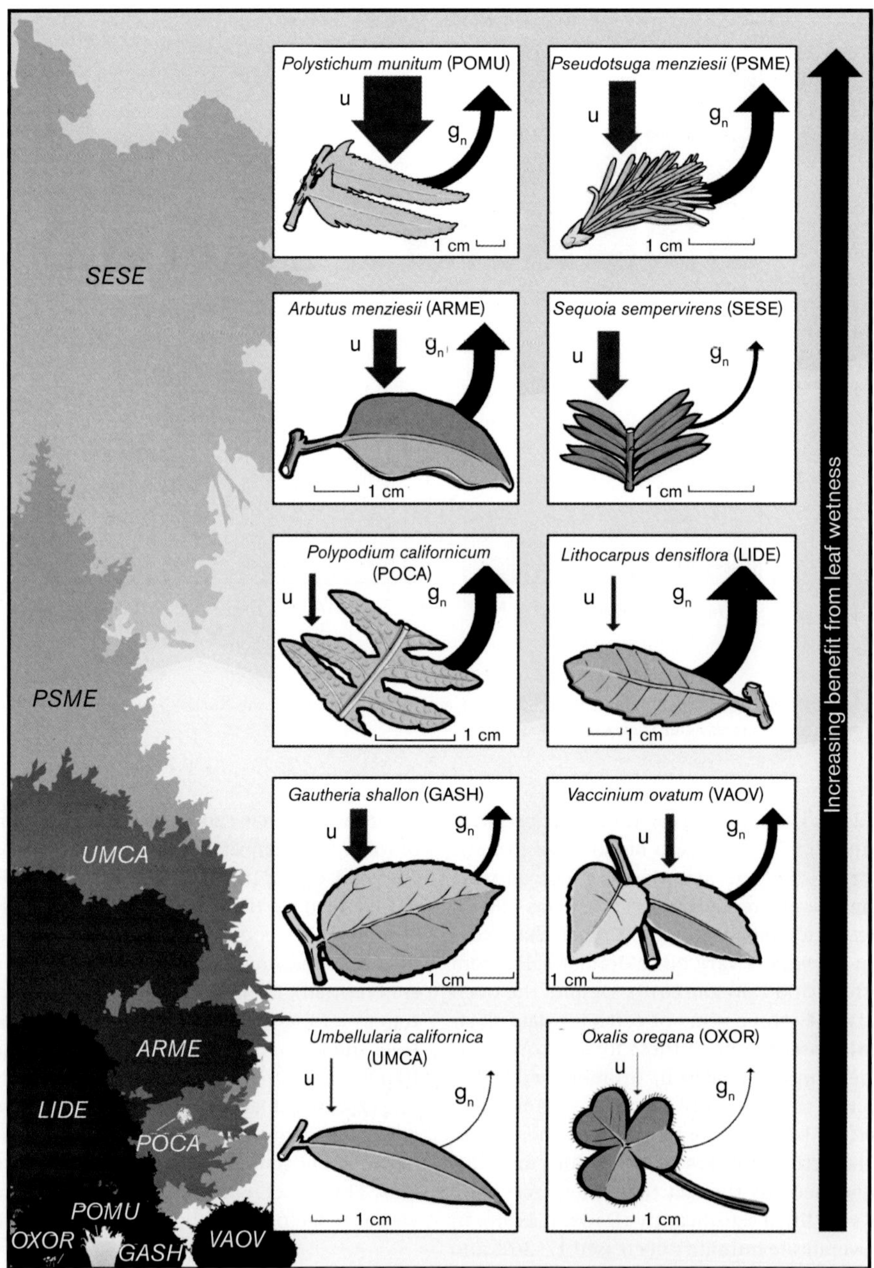

FIGURE 26.8. Proportional foliar water uptake capacity (down arrows, U) and proportional suppression of nighttime transpiration loss through stomata (up arrows, g_n) for ten redwood forest species. During leaf wetting, increased foliar hydration in many of the dominant broadleaf, coniferous, and fern species of the redwood forest ecosystem occurs. Down-arrow thickness represents the foliar uptake capacity of each species relative to the maximum capacity measured and up arrows illustrate water conservation when leaf wetting stops nocturnal water loss through stomata, with arrow thickness representing the nocturnal conductance rate of each species relative to the maximum rate measured. Species are ranked in order of how influential foliar uptake may be for leaf hydration relative to the suppression of nocturnal conductance when leaves are wet. *P. munitum* is ranked first because it demonstrated the highest ratio of foliar uptake capacity to nocturnal conductance and *U. californica* and *O. oregana* are ranked last because no foliar uptake capacity was measured. All illustrated species experience leaf wetting either in the canopy of redwood forest, where fog impaction and interception occurs first during fog exposure, or on the forest floor, where occult precipitation delivers fog water after canopy foliage saturates. Crown silhouettes on the left indicate the relative position of each species within the redwood forest profile. Source: Limm et al. 2009.

with atmospheric deposition adding 20 kg ha^{-1} during the eighty-year period by rough calculations. Using a detailed sampling array, higher deposition values were measured at a more southerly site in Sonoma County somewhat nearer to developed areas. The latter study measured a mean value over a three-year sampling period of 0.78 kg N ha^{-1} yr^{1} during the fog season (June through October) and 1.62 kg N ha^{-1} yr^{1} during the rainy months (November through May; total of 3.3 kg N $ha^{-1}yr^{1}$). Dissolved nitrogen, ammonium, and nitrate were depleted as fog and rain moved through the canopy to the forest floor (Ewing et al. 2009).

Some controversy occurred regarding nitrate availability for tree growth in mature redwood forests (Bradbury and Firestone 2007). Early studies implied a great lack of nitrate in old-growth redwood forest soils, which would have severe implications for reproduction (Florence 1965; Bollen and Wright 1961). These studies were based on the lack of nitrate accumulation when the soils were incubated. Given the earlier results, Stone and Vasey (1968) proposed that active management is needed in old-growth stands to maintain them. They specifically recommended not controlling major floods by damming, since this would restrict inputs of fresh silt to the habitat and provide more available nutrients on a fresh surface for establishment. They further noted that old redwood trees are particularly tolerant to flooding events and can generate a new root system (Figure 26.9).

TABLE 26.2

Nutrient content in trees in an old-growth redwood stand at the Humboldt State Park

About 80% of the carbon and phosphorus reside in the trees (values are in g m^{-2})

	Carbon	Nitrogen	Phosphorus
Foliage	1,234	10.4	1.09
Stem			
Wood	62,000	97.6	6.2
Bark	19,000	69.6	0.1
Total tree	82,192	177.6	7.4
(% of site total)	84	16	77
Litter	1,660	19.8	1.8
Soil (to 1m)	14,361	907	0.3
FOREST SITE TOTAL	**98,213**	**1,104**	**9.5**

SOURCE: Zinke et al. 1979.

Aquatic Systems: Land-Water Connections

Virtually all vertebrates of redwood forests have ties to estuarine habitats—most stands contain surface streams with connections to the sea. Historically, marine nutrients have also been delivered to coastal and inland forests by migrating salmon and seabirds (Merz and Moyle 2006). In turn, forests provided habitat and resources to organisms inhabiting the streams (see Chapter 33, "Rivers"). Streamside trees interact strongly with the streambed either by contributing deadwood or as rooted trees in the streamside itself. These features alter streamflow and can form a partial dam in the stream, serving as a sediment trap, or can block upward migration of fish. Large, downed redwood material can remain in place for over a century. The resulting streamflow alterations, sediment movement, and entrapment by the woody material provides habitats for diverse organisms.

Logging has also had profound and long-term residual impacts on stream dynamics and on the organisms that reside there. For example, Ashton et al. (2006) found that headwater streams located in old-growth redwood forests maintained higher numbers and densities of amphibian species than did those in successional forests thirty-seven to sixty years post-harvest. They attributed the biotic dissimilarities not to differences in thermal environments provided by the vegetation cover but rather to differences still evident in sediment loads of the streams even after a long period after perturbation.

Ecosystem Services

Redwood forests have provided benefits to societies since humans first occupied California. California's northern coastal indigenous peoples used redwood for building canoes and as timber for houses. They harvested the fruits of tanoak and hunted deer and elk common in the redwood region. However, the main food for indigenous peoples of the redwood region was obtained from the coast, salmon-filled rivers, and more open vegetation adjacent to deeply wooded areas (Lightfoot and Parrish 2009).

The redwood forest has also been considered the central resource of California's "second Gold Rush," providing lumber for the early development of the city of San Francisco. The "gold mine" of favored heartwood of these trees is no longer available. However, regrowth of these forests still provides a substantial amount of highly favored building material. Moreover, these forests sequester large amounts of carbon and might be the greatest forest biomass accumulators on Earth (Busing and Fujimori, 2005). In an era when carbon sequestration in forests can serve as a potential mitigation strategy against steady increases in anthropogenic CO_2 emissions, this service is increasingly valuable. Though the forests redwood trees inhabit are limited in geographical extent and land cover, they provide a promising sequestration vehicle, particularly if integrated with sustainable timber harvest practices where a sizable fraction of land is being actively used to grow redwood.

Redwood forests also provide a number of regulating services, including erosion control. This service is particularly critical in the redwood forest region because it is often marked by steep topography with highly erodible substrates. The visible effects of erosion caused by logging these forests in an unsustainable manner in the past motivated the establishment of Redwood National Park. The redwood canopy OVERSTORY provides other unique regulating services related to microclimate control, such as fog-water harvesting, that enhance habitats for other service-providing organisms of the forest. Finally, the cultural services provided by these unique and awesome forests inspire not only the residents of the region but also visitors from around the world. It was the threats to these forests that played an important role in building the U.S. conservation movement starting with the work of the Save the Redwoods League (see Chapter 1, "Introduction").

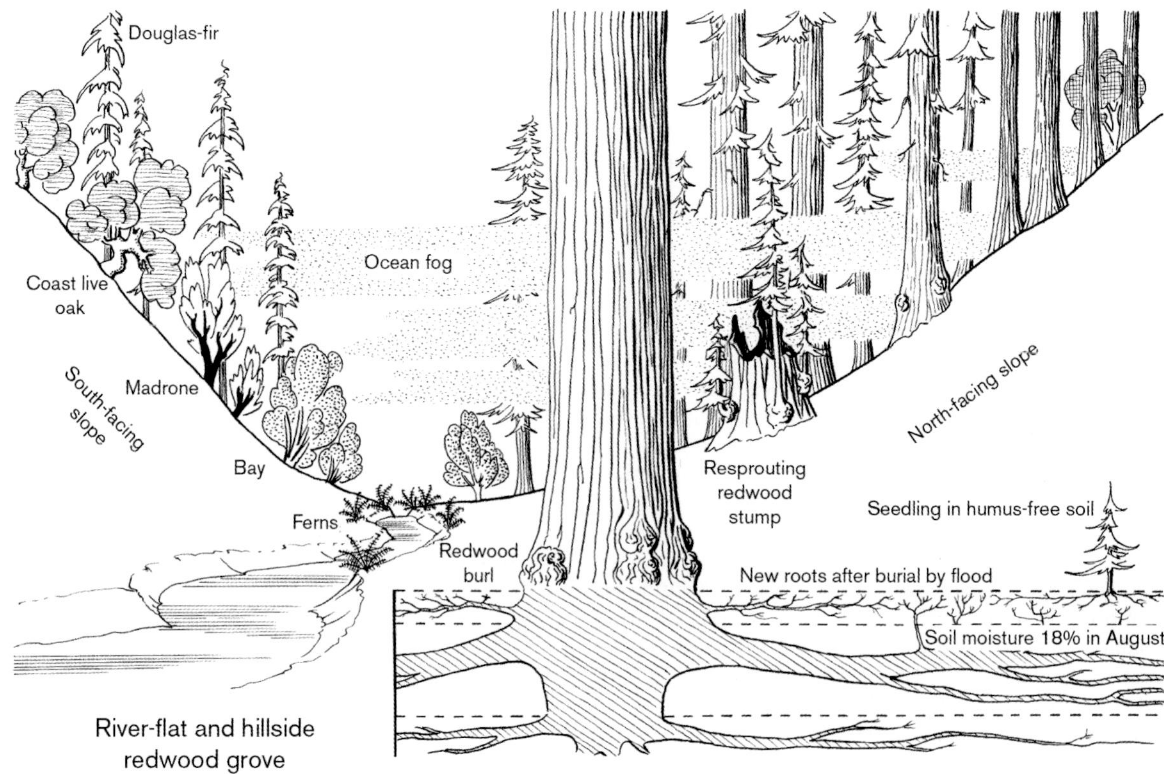

FIGURE 26.9. Regeneration of a new root system by a redwood tree subsequent to burial by silt from flooding. Source: Bakker 1985.

History of Redwood Exploitation

The remaining vast, old-growth redwood forest is only a very small fraction (4–5%) of what it once was. The first use of redwoods in construction after settlement appears to have been for construction of the Missions Santa Clara, Dolores, and Presidio of San Francisco. Subsequently, the Russian settlement at Fort Ross, starting in 1812, used local redwood for the construction of the fort and for several boats (which were unsuccessful due to lack of proper seasoning). San Francisco utilized redwood timber for construction, at first from San Mateo County but by 1820 mainly from Marin County. The first waterpower mills appeared in 1834 in Sonoma County; however, it was the advent of the steam engine–powered sawmill at Bodega, also in 1834, that changed the industry.

Sudden demand for lumber after the Gold Rush fueled a surge in the development of the forest industry. Lumbering and milling accelerated, and the opening of Humboldt Bay as a lumber source resulted in nine sawmills in operation there by 1854. As demand for lumber grew, lumber was loaded onto ships, often precariously by cable suspensions, from sixty "landings" along the north coast from Bodega to Humboldt (Figure 26.10). This era left behind stump-filled landscapes throughout the region (Figure 26.11). By 1860, Humboldt County, the second-ranking county in timber production in the state, was producing 71,000 m^3 (30 million board feet) yr^1, mostly redwood.

Caterpillar tractors first appeared at Klamath Bluff in 1925 and power saws first made their appearance in the 1930s. After World War II the lumber industry accelerated; tractors blazed roads into logging areas, and big trucks with trailers carried logs to the mills. These practices caused considerable physical damage to watersheds. Most loss of soil was not due to harvesting the trees per se but to the accompanying road building. Harvesting rates continued to climb. In Del Norte County annual timber harvest grew from 125,000 m^3 (53 million board feet) in 1946 to 710,000 m^3 (300 million board feet) in 1953 and included Douglas-fir. The latter figure was beyond replacement capacity and raised considerable alarm by conservationists (information in this section from Bearss 1965).

The Fight to Save the Redwoods

Early Conservation

The history of the efforts to conserve the coastal redwood forests is a dramatic one, and as it extends back over a century it reflects the development of conservation efforts in the country as a whole. This history also indicates that some of the strong, early conceptual battles are still with us and that a strong philosophical position can bring strength but also the danger that rigidity can work against achieving goals. The first redwood park established was Big Basin State Redwoods Park in the Santa Cruz Mountains in 1902, culminating the lobbying efforts of a group of twenty-six citizens of the local area who founded the Sempervirens Fund to accomplish this goal (Yaryan et al. 2000). The park has grown from 1,540 hectares (3,800 acres) when established (also as the first California State Park) to approximately 7,300 hectares (18,000 acres) today. In early state history the Santa Cruz Mountains were heavily logged because they were so close to the building boom occurring in San Francisco following the Gold Rush. Between 1850 to 1890 most of the area's redwood trees were harvested. An irony is that many of these old-growth trees, as lumber in buildings, went up in smoke in the fires that

FIGURE 26.10. Loading schooners with redwood logs and lumber for transport to San Francisco from Westport Landing, Mendocino County. Estimated date of picture is 1882. Photo from the Kelley House Archives, courtesy of Carolyn Zeitler and Nancy Freeze.

raged periodically in that city and culminated with the massive fires associated with the 1906 earthquake.

A state bond issue in 1909 provided resources to open up the northern riches of the redwood forests to public—and to private—interests with the construction of the Redwood Highway. Timber harvested before the construction of this overland pathway was transported overland to seagoing vessels. Actual construction of the new highway was not completed until 1923, when through traffic in Del Norte and Humboldt Counties became a reality. The state required the counties to turn over the land needed for the highway without logging it first. Thus only that logging necessary for the roadway construction took place; this was also the case in subsequent highway route relocations (Bearss 1969).

Opening the prime redwood forests to easy transportation sent a warning signal to the growing conservation community of the increasing threats to these forests. Three distinguished conservationists—Madison Grant, Henry Fairfield Osborn, and John Campbell Merriam—in 1917 traveled north to investigate the new country opening up. Grant was a founder of the New York Zoological Society and Osborn was on the staff of the New York Museum of Natural History. Merriam was a professor of paleontology at the University of California in Berkeley, later to become the director of the Carnegie Institution of Washington (Schrepfer 1983). The excursion prompted the three to establish the Save the Redwoods League in 1918. Near this time, William Kent from Marin County, a member of Congress and leader in the establishment of the U.S. National Park Service (1916), purchased the last old-growth stand of redwoods in Marin County and donated it to the U.S. government. Kent called for the formation of a Redwood National Park in 1913. Unfortunately his vision was not to become a reality until a half a century later, in 1968 (Schrepfer 1983).

A philosophical schism between the leaders of the Save the Redwoods League and those of the National Park Service and the Forest Service in the early twentieth century mirrored broader debates in conservation at the time. Both of the agencies took a more utilitarian view of wildlands than was acceptable to the leaders of the Save the Redwoods League. Gifford Pinchot, the second director of the U.S. Forest Service, promoted "wise use of natural resources based on science;" the Park Service policy of 1924 stated that National Parks must "be conserved in their natural state so that coming generations, as well as the people of our own time, may be

FIGURE 26.11. A stump-filled, deforested landscape in the 1890s. Mad River area, Humboldt County. Note resprouting. Courtesy of Humboldt State University Library.

assured their use for the purpose of recreation, education, and scientific research." In 1938 the Save the Redwoods League rejected a National Park Service proposal for a Redwood National Park on grounds that the Park Service was pandering to public desires, detracting from the inspirational and educational value of the parks, and destroying their primitive nature (Schrepfer 1983). The efforts of the Save the Redwoods League have since gone into redwood forestland acquisition in support of the development of sixty-two parks and preserves encompassing nearly 73,000 hectares.

The dramatic escalation of redwood harvesting rates in the 1950s made clear that the philosophy of solely saving patches of the biggest, old-growth trees on lower alluvial sections would lead to jeopardy. Record winter rains in 1954–1955 caused the loss of hundreds of giant redwoods at Bull Creek Flat in Humboldt Redwoods State Park. This, along with restructuring of the Redwood Highway cutting through this park that caused more loss of trees, highlighted the fragile nature of old-growth forest protection. By the end of the 1950s only 10% of the original, old-growth redwood belt remained (Noss 2000).

These events led to involvement by another conservation group, the Sierra Club, in the redwood protection movement—with a new approach. Its leadership concluded that federal involvement was needed to meet the crisis, and they revived the movement to form a Redwood National Park. They started an aggressive campaign to bring this about, which included the publication of two books. The first documented the enormous losses that were occuring (Hyde and Leydet 1963), while the second advanced a specific site proposal for the formation of a National Park (Leydet 1969). This effort introduced a new, more aggressive approach to conservation—education and publicity followed by lobbying and litigation—under the leadership of the late David Brower, whose work contributed to the enormous accomplishments in environmental legislation in the 1960s and 1970s.

The renewed battle to form Redwood National Park initially pitted the Sierra Club (which proposed a landscape-selection approach for the park—Redwood Creek, Prairie Creek Redwoods State Park) against the Save the Redwood League (which advocated saving the oldest trees at Bull Creek, Humboldt Redwoods State Park). Most of all, it was a battle between the forest industry and conservationists waged slowly in Congress, during which a great deal of additional old-growth forest was lost. In 1968 the park was finally approved at Redwood Creek (23,000 hectares, but only 4,400 hectares of old growth). A battle ensued to enlarge the park to protect the forests there from continued harvesting in the surrounding area. In 1978, Congress approved a second National Redwood Park Act that added 19,500 hectares to the park as well as an upstream protection zone of 12,000 hectares. Susan Schrepfer (1983) documents the long and dramatic saga of the formation of Redwood National Park.

What Will the Future Bring?

If the climate of today were to persist, changes to the dynamics of California's redwood forests would nevertheless ensue from pertubations such as invasive pathogens. These forests are, however, remarkably resilient ecosystems because of the capacity of many of the dominant plants to respond to damage by resprouting. Redwoods themselves are remarkably resistant to insects, disease, and even fire. While it is unfortunate that we have lost such a vast extent of old-growth redwood forests, we have protected, thanks to the intensive efforts of many individuals and groups, representive old-growth stands of trees of extrordinary heights and biomass. The bulk of redwood forests are in private hands and are managed as production forests. Because these holdings are larger than in the past, there is the opportunity for planning at the landscape level. Further, the public owns three times as much area in young-growth redwood forests than it does in old growth, presenting opportunities to develop innovative, sustainable practices for the whole forest ecosystem. California's Forest Practice Act of 1973 was passed in response to the harvest practices that led to loss of more than 90% of mature redwood forests. The act has changed forestry practices on both private and public lands, with particular attention to protecting riparian areas. Selective harvesting is becoming more common, and some private companies are managing habitat for endangered and critical wildlife (Hartley 2012) (see Chapter 36, "Forestry").

The primary threat to the future of these forests is the fate of the cool, temperate climate, including foggy summers, that favors redwoods. A critical "controller" of fog production is the cold water associated with the California Current. If the current warmed, we would lose one of the critical elements behind fog and low cloud formation along the coast (Johnstone and Dawson 2010, Schwartz et al. 2014). Fog and cloud cover have already declined over the past sixty to one hundred years; it is not clear whether this will continue (Johnstone and Dawson 2010). With global warming, climate-vegetation models predict a shift from the prevailing, moist coniferous forest species toward evergreen forest dominants currently on more xeric (e.g., south-facing) slopes (see Chapter 14, "Climate Change Impacts").

Summary

The redwood forest region of California occupies the coastal plains and mountains of northwestern California. The region is rich in its diversity of ecosystem types—a feature driven mainly by topographic and substrate diversity. North coastal forests, which extend into Oregon and Washington, are remarkable for their diversity of conifers for their longevity. This heavily forested region is relatively sparsely occupied by humans. The high rainfall of the area's uplands feeds a large number of rivers that flow into the Pacific, including some in a wild condition, a rarity for California. This chapter focuses on the iconic redwood forest ecosystem, located mainly on ocean-facing slopes and plains. This forest, in its primal state, attains world records for tree heights and biomass accumulated during the millenial lifespan of its dominants. This forest type had a vast distributional range in prehistoric times, when a summer rainfall climate existed in California. With the disappearance of summer rainfall, this ecosystem is now restricted to the cool temperatures of the north coast, where fog occurs in the summer. Redwood trees trap fog water to support their own growth and provide moisture from drip to understory plants as well as tree roots. The future of this ecosystem under ongoing climate change will depend largely on the fate of the cold California Current, which has a marked impact on patterns of winter rainfall and generates both the summer drought and the conditions leading to summer fog.

Because of the very large leaf area of these forests, and

their predominately evergreen nature, very little light falls on understory plants, particularly at ground level. The inhabitants of these areas have specialized capacity for capture and utilization of light energy. The relatively stable, cool, and moist conditions of the forest support a diversity of fungi that evidently play a key role in ecosystem nutrient balance through symbiotic relationships. Further, high atmospheric moisture and diversity of tree trunk surfaces, and soil development in tree crevices, provide habitat for a large number of epiphytic plants and animals. Unlike in the Sierra Nevada, where much land was put into forest reserves and parklands early in the history of the state, the vast majority of California's northern coastal forests remained unprotected until relatively recently. Only in the past several decades was Redwood National Park established, although earlier efforts provided some conservation areas elsewhere in the state. Today only 4–5% of old-growth redwood forests remain, virtually all of it protected. The large area of young forest, under both public and private ownership, is now being managed in a more sustainable manner with increased attention to the dynamics of the entire redwood ecosystem.

Acknowledgments

We thank George Koch, Steve Sillett, and Anthony Ambrose for advice and help on this chapter as well as the Save the Redwoods League for the years of support that made many of the redwood investigations cited in this chapter possible.

Recommended Reading

Evarts, J., and M. Popper, editors. 2001. Coast redwood: A natural and cultural history. Cachuma Press, Los Olivos, California.

Noss, R. F., editor. 2000. The redwood forest: History, ecology, and conservation of the coast redwoods. Island Press, Washington, D.C.

Sawyer, J. O. 2006. Northwest California: A natural history. University of California Press, Berkeley, California.

Schrepfer, S. R. 1983. The fight to save the redwoods. University of Wisconsin Press, Madison, Wisconsin.

Glossary

BOLE The main trunk of a tree.

CYANOLICHENS Lichens that have a blue-green algal component and can fix atmospheric nitrogen.

ECTOMYCORRHIZAE Fungi that form a sheath around the fine roots of woody plants and trade nitrogen and phosphorus from the soil in exchange for carbon of the host plant.

EPICORMIC BUDS Latent buds that can sprout from the bark in response to tree damage.

EPIPHYTES Plants that are not attached to the ground but rather are attached to branches. They acquire their water and nutrients from the atmosphere.

ERICOID MYCORRHIZAE Fungi that associate with the roots of plant members of the Ericacea family in a symbiotic relationship. Some of these fungi have the capacity to obtain nitrogen directly from decaying plant material.

LEGACY TREES Old-growth trees that remain in a forest that is predominately second-growth.

OVERSTORY The trees that form the upper canopy of a forest.

References

Ambrose, A. R. 2004. Water-holding capacity of canopy soil mats and effects on microclimates in an old-growth redwood forest: A report to Save the Redwoods League. Humboldt State University, Arcata, California.

Ashton, T.A., S. B. Marks, H. H. Welsh. 2006. Evidence of continued effects from timber harvesting on loctic amphibians in redwood forests of northwestern California. Forest Ecology and Management 221:183–193.

Bakker, E. 1985. An island called California. University of California Press, Berkeley, California.

Bearss, E. C. 1969. History basic data: Redwood National Park, Del Norte and Humboldt Counties, California. U.S. Department of Interior, National Park Service, Division of History, Washington, D.C.

Bergemann, S. E., and M. Garbelotto. 2006. High diversity of fungi recovered from the roots of mature tanoak (*Lithocarpus densiflorus*) in northern California. Canadian Journal of Botany/Revue Canadienne de Botanique 84:1380–1394.

Bergemann, S. E., N. C. Kordesch, W. VanSant-Glass, M. Garbelotto, and T. A. Metz. 2013. Implications of tanoak decline in forests impacted by Phytophthora ramorum: Girdling decreases the soil hyphal abundance of ectomycorrhizal fungi associated with *Notholithocarpus densiflorus*. Madrono 60:95–106.

Bjorkman, O., and S. B. Powles. 1980. Leaf movement in the shade species *Oxalis oregana*. I. Response to light level and light quality. Carnegie Institution Year Book 79:59–62.

Boe, K. N. 1961. Redwood seed dispersion in old-growth cutovers. Pacific Southwest Forest and Range Experiment Station. Research Note PSW-177:1–7.

Bollen, W. B., and E. Wright. 1961. Microbes and nitrates in soils from virgin and young-growth forests. Canadian Journal of Microbiology 7:785–792.

Boume, J. E., Jr. 2009. Super trees. National Geographic 216: 28+.

Bradbury, D., and M. Firestone. 2007. Environmental control of microbial N transformations in redwood forest. U.S. Department of Agriculture Forest Service, Pacific Southwest Experiment Station. Report no. Berkeley, California.

Brown, P. M., and W. T. Baxter. 2003. Fire history in coast redwood forests of the Mendocino Coast, California. Northwest Science 74:147–158.

Burgess, S.O.O., and T. E. Dawson. 2004. The contribution of fog to the water relations of Sequoia sempervirens (D. Don): Foliar uptake and prevention of dehydration. Plant, Cell, and Environment 27:1023–1034.

Busing, R. T., and T. Fujimori. 2005. Biomass, production, and woody detritus in an old coast redwood (*Sequoia sempervirens*) forest. Plant ecology 177:177–188.

Cobb, R. C., J.A.N. Filipe, R. K. Meentemeyer, C. A. Gilligan, and D. M. Rizzo. 2012. Ecosystem transformation by emerging infectious disease: Loss of large tanoak from California forests. Journal of Ecology 100:712–722.

Cooperrider, A., R. F. Noss, H. H. Welsh Jr., C. Carroll, W. Zielinski, D. Olson, S. K. Nelson, and B. G. Marcot. 2000. Terrestrial fauna of redwood forests. Pages 119–163 in R. F. Noss, editor. The Redwood Forest. Island Press, Washington, D.C.

Dahlgren, R. A. 1998. Effects of forest harvest on stream-water quality and nitrogen cycling in the Caspar Creek watershed. Pages 45–53 in R. R. Ziemer, technical coordinator and editor. Conference on Coastal Watersheds: The Caspar Creek Story. U.S. Department of Agriculture Forest Service, Ukiah, California.

Dawson, T. E. 1998. Fog in the California redwood forest: Ecosystem inputs and use by plants. Oecologia 117:476–485.

Del Tredici, P. 1999. Redwood burls: Immortality underground. Arnoldia (Jamaica Plain) 59:14–22.

Denison, W. C. 1973. Life in tall trees. Scientific American 228:74–80.

Espinosa-Garcia, F. J., and J. H. Langenheim. 1990. The endophytic fungal community in leaves of a coastal redwood population—diversity and spatial patterns. New Phytologist 116:89–97.

Ewing, H. A., K. C. Weathers, P. H. Templer, T. E. Dawson, M. K. Firestone, A. M. Elliott, and V.K.S. Boukili. 2009. Fog water and ecosystem function: Heterogeneity in a California redwood forest. Ecosystems 12:417–433.

Fernandez, M. E., J. E. Gyenge, M. M. de Urquiza, and S. Varela. 2012. Adaptability to climate change in forestry species: Drought effects on growth and wood anatomy of ponderosa pines growing at different competition levels. Forest Systems 21:162–173.

Florence, R. G. 1965. Decline of old-growth redwood forests in relation to some soil microbiological processes. Ecology 46:52–64.

Fujimori, T. 1977. Stem biomass and structure of a mature Sequoia sempervirens stand of the Pacific Coast of northern California. Journal of Japanese Forestry Society 59:431–441.

Garbelotto, M., and D. M. Rizzo. 2005. A California-based chronological review (1995–2004) of research on Phytophthora ramorum, the causal agent of sudden oak death. Phytopathologia Mediterranea 44:127–143.

Grace, J., S. Harrison, and E. Damschen. 2011. Local richness along gradients in the Siskiyou herb flora: R. H. Whittaker revisited. Ecology 92:108–120.

Hartley, R. K. 2012. Redwood forest conservation: Where do we go from here? Pages 1–10 in R. B. Standiford, T. J. Weller, D. D. Piirto, and J. D. Stuart, editors. Proceedings of Coast Redwood Forests in a Changing California: A Symposium for Scientists and Managers. General Technical Report. PSW-GTR-238. Pacific Southwest Research Station, U.S. Forest Service, Department of Agriculture, Albany, California.

Hyde, P., and F. Leydet. 1963. The last redwoods. Sierra Club, San Francisco, California.

Jenny, H., R. J. Arkley, and A. M. Schultz. 1969. The pygmy forests ecosystems and its dune associates of the Mendocino coast. Madrono 20:60–74.

Johnstone, J. A., and T. E. Dawson. 2010. Climatic context and ecological implications of summer for decline in the coast redwood region. Proceedings of the National Academy of Sciences of the United States of America 107:4533–4538.

Kennedy, P. G., A. D. Izzo, and T. D. Bruns. 2003. There is a high potential for the formation of common mycorrhizal networks between understorey and canopy trees in mixed evergreen forest. Journal of Ecology 91:1071–1080.

Kennedy, P. G., D. P. Smith, T. R. Horton, and R. Molina R. 2012. *Arbutus menziesii* (Ericaceae) facilitates regeneration dynamics in mixed evergreen forests by promoting mychorrhizal fungal diversity and host connectivity. American Journal of Botany 99:1691–1701.

Kuljian, H., and J. Varner. 2010. The effects of sudden oak death on foliar moisture content and crown fire potential in tanoak. Forest Ecology and Management 259:2103–2110.

Leydet, F. 1969. The last redwoods, and the Parkland of Redwood Creek. Sierra Club, San Francisco, California.

Lightfoot, K. G., and O. Parrish. 2009. California Indians and their environment. University of California Press, Berkeley, California.

Limm, E.B., K. A. Simonin, A. G. Bothman, and T. E. Dawson. 2009. Foliar water uptake: A common water acquisition strategy for plants of the redwood forest. Oecologia (Berlin) 161:449–459.

Lorimer, C. G., D. J. Porter, M. A. Madej, J. D. Stuart, S. D. Veirs, S. P. Norman, K. L. O'Hara, and W. J. Libby. 2009. Presettlement and modern disturbance regimes in coast redwood forests: Implications for the conservation of old-growth stands. Forest Ecology and Management 258:1038–1054.

Mao, K., R. I. Milne, L. Zhang, Y. Peng, J. Lui, P. Thomas, R. R. Mill, and S. S. Renner. 2012. Distribution of living Cupressaceae reflects the breakup of Pangea. Proceedings of the National Academy of Sciences of the United States of America 109:7793–7798.

Mazurek, M. J., and W. J. Zielinski. 2004. Individual legacy trees influence vertebrate wildlife diversity in commercial forests. Forest Ecology and Management 193:321–334.

McBride, J. R., and D. F. Jacobs. 1977. The ecology of redwood (*Sequoia sempervirens* (D. Don) Endl.) and the impact of man's use of the redwood forest as a site for recreational activities. Prepared for the United States National Park Service. Department of Forestry and Conservation, University of California, Berkeley, California.

Merz, J. E., and P. B. Moyle. 2006. Salmon, wildlife, and wine: Marine-derived nutrients in human-dominated ecosystems of central California. Ecological Applications 16:999–1009.

Molina, R. 1994. The role of mycorrhizal symbioses in the health of giant redwoods and other forest ecosystems. Pages 78–81 in Aune PS, technical coordinator, editor. Proceedings of the symposium on Giant Sequoias: Their place in the ecosystem and society. General Technical Report PSW-151. Albany, California: U.S Forest Service.

Noss, R. F., editor. 2000. The redwood forest: History, ecology, and conservation of the coast redwoods. Island Press, Washington, D.C.

Olson, D. F., D. F. Roy, and G. A. Walters. 1990. Sequoia sempervirens (D. Don) Endl. Pages 541–551 in R. M. Barnes and B. H. Konkala, editors. Silvics of North America. Volume 1. Conifers. U.S. Department of Agriculture Forest Service, Washington, D.C.

Pike, L. H., R. A. Rydell, and W. C. Denison. 1977. 400-year-old Douglas-fir tree and its epiphytes: Biomass, surface-area, and their distributions. Canadian Journal of Forest Research/Revue Canadienne de Recherche Forestiere 7:680–699.

Pillers, M. D., and J. D. Stuart. 1993. Leaf-litter accretion and decomposition in interior and coastal old-growth redwood stands. Canadian Journal of Forest Research 23:552–557.

Powles, S. B., and O. Bjorkman. 1980. Leaf movement in the shade species *Oxalis oregana*. II. Role of protection against injury by intense light. Carnegie Institution Year Book 79:63–66.

Ramage, B. S., K. L. O'Hara, and B. T. Caldwell. 2010. The role of fire in the competitive dynamics of coast redwood forests. Ecosphere 1(6):20.

Santiago, L. S. and T. E. Dawson. 2013. Light use efficiency of California redwood forest understory plants along a moisture gradient. Oecologia 174:351–363.

Sawyer, J. O. 2006. Northwest California: A natural history. University of California Press, Berkeley, California.

Schrepfer, S. R. 1983. The fight to save the redwoods. University of Wisconsin Press, Madison, Wisconsin.

Schwartz, R. E., A. Gershunov, S. F. Iacobellis, and D. R. Cayan. 2014. North American West Coast summer low cloudiness: Broadscale variability associated with sea surface temperature. Geophysical Research Letters 41:3307–3314.

Sillett, S. C., and R. Van Pelt. 2007. Trunk reiteration promotes epiphytes and water storage in an old-growth redwood forest canopy. Ecological Monographs 77:335–359.

Simonin, K. S., L. S. Santiago, and T. E. Dawson. 2009. Fog interception by *Sequoia sempervirens* (D. Don) crowns decouples physiology from soil water deficit. Plant, Cell, and Environment 32:882–892.

Sloan, J. P., and K. N. Boe. 2008. Sequoia sempervirens (Lamb. ex D. Don) Endl. Pages 1034–1036 in F. T. Bonner and R. P. Karrfalt, editors. Woody Plant Seed Manual, Agriculture Handbook 727. U.S. Department of Agriculture Forest Service, Washington, D.C.

Snyder, J. A. 1992. The ecology of Sequoia sempervirens. San Jose State University, San Jose, California.

Stone, E. C. and R. B. Vasey. 1968. Preservation of coast redwood on alluvial flats: Because man has altered environment, active management is now required. Science 159:157–161.

Stuart, J. D., and S. L. Stephens. 2006. North coast bioregion. Pages 147–169 in N. Sugihara, J. van Wagtendonk, J. Fites-Kaufmann, K. Shaffer, and A. Thode, editors. Fire in California's Ecosystems. University of California Press, Berkeley, California.

Tolle, G., et al. 2005. A macroscope in the redwoods. Third International Conference on Embedded Networked Sensor Systems. San Diego, California.

U.S. Geological Survey (USGS). 1999. Digital representations of tree species range maps from "Atlas of United States Trees" by Elbert L. Little, Jr. (and other publications).

Van Pelt, R. 2001. Forest giants of the Pacific Coast. University of Washington Press, Seattle, Washington.

Waring, K. M., and K. L. O'Hara. 2008. Redwood/tanoak stand development and response to tanoak mortality caused by Phytophthora ramorum. Forest Ecology and Management 255:2650–2658.

Waring, R. H., and J. F. Franklin. 1979. Evergreen coniferous forests of the Pacific Northwest. Science 204:1380–1386.

Whittaker, R. H. 1960. Vegetation of the Siskiyou Mountains, Oregon and California. Ecological Monographs 30:279–338.

Williams, C. B., and S. C. Sillett. 2007. Epiphyte communities on redwood (*Sequoia sempervirens*) in northwestern California. Bryologist 110:420–452.

Yaryan, W., D. Verardo, and J. Verardo. 2000. The Sempervirens Story: A Century of Preserving California's Ancient Redwood Forest 1900–2000. Los Altos, California, Sempervirens Fund.

Zinke, P. J., A. Stangenberger, and W. Colwell. 1979. Fertility of the forest. California Agriculture 33:10–11.

TWENTY-SEVEN

Montane Forests

MALCOLM NORTH, BRANDON COLLINS, HUGH SAFFORD,
and NATHAN L. STEPHENSON

Introduction

California's montane forests include some of the most productive and diverse temperate ecosystems in the world. They contain the largest single-stem tree (the 1,487 cubic meter General Sherman giant sequoia [*Sequoiadendron giganteum*]) (Van Pelt 2001) and the highest conifer diversity (thirty-plus species in the Klamath-Siskiyou mountain range) (Sawyer 2006) in the world (Table 27.1). Although these forests share some attributes with the Pacific Northwest (i.e., long-lived large trees and some common wildlife species) (North et al. 2004) and Southwest (i.e., historical forests dominated by pine and shaped by frequent fire), their combination of high productivity, strong seasonal drought, and fire dependence distinguish them ecologically from montane forests in these adjacent areas. The distribution of different forest types is strongly influenced by temperature and precipitation gradients associated with elevation and inland distance from the Pacific Ocean. Historically the forests have been logged, but interestingly for the nation's most populous state, some large areas of montane forest—especially in the central and southern Sierra Nevada—remain only lightly affected by human resource use. Management practices in these montane forests have often been controversial, and fire suppression has significantly altered forest conditions such that fires escaping containment are often large and produce extensive areas burned at high severity. Climate change, California's increasing population, and projected increases in wildfire pose challenges that will require collaborative and inventive future management.

In this chapter we focus on montane forest ecosystems in California's Sierra Nevada, Klamath, Cascade, Coastal, Traverse, and Peninsular Ranges. These forests often border, at lower elevations, warmer, drier ecosystems that include oak-savanna and chaparral (see Chapters 24, "Chaparral," and 25, "Oak Woodlands"). At upper elevations, montane forests often border colder red fir and subalpine forests characterized by deeper, more persistent snowpacks (see Chapter 28, "Subalpine Forests").

TABLE 27.1

Characteristics of mature trees for major tree species in California's montane forests at the turn of nineteenth century

Species	Elevation (m)	Height (m)	Diameter at breast height (DBH) (cm)	Mature age (years)
White fir	800–2,300 N: 1,500–2,400 S	53–58 (66)	110–170 (223)	200–300 (372)
Red fir	1,400–2,400 N; 1,700–2,700 S	51–56 (77)	100–180 (295)	250–400 (665)
Incense cedar	600–1,600 N; 800–2,100 S	24–31 (70)	150–210 (456)	250–600 (unk)
Jeffrey pine	1,500–2,400 N; 1,700–2,800 S	34–49 (61)	90–150 (250)	120–350 (813)
Sugar pine	1,000–2,000 N; 1,400–2,700 S	55–61 (82)	120–180 (352)	100–400 (unk)
Ponderosa pine	300–1,800 N; 1,200–2,100 S	45–55 (70)[B]	90–120 (277)[C]	100–350 (907)[A]
Douglas-fir	300–2,100 N; 600–2,100 S	46–53 (92)[A]	120–210 (485)[A]	120–400 (1,350)
Black oak	900–1,500 N; 1,400–2,100 S	28–34 (38)[C]	130–160 (273)[C]	120–400 (unk)
Giant sequoia	900–2,000 N; 1,600–2,700 S	50–75 (94)	400–600 (1,228)	400–1,100 (3,266)

SOURCE: According to Sudworth 1900.
NOTE: In height and DBH columns, values in parentheses are for the largest dimension on record (in van Pelt 2001) and the oldest on record (in The Gymnosperm Database), www.conifers.org.
A. Record holder in Washington State
B. Record holder in Idaho
C. Record holder in Oregon
UNK = unknown

Physiographic Setting

Climate

California's Mediterranean climate, in which 85% of annual precipitation occurs between November and May, significantly influences montane forest composition, distribution, and ecosystem functions (Minnich 2007). Unlike montane weather in much of the Rockies and the Southwest, summer thunderstorms and significant rain events are infrequent and often highly localized in California. During the growing season (generally March through July), plants rely on soil moisture stocks from winter precipitation and melting snow (Major 1977). The distribution of montane forest is influenced by site water availability and evaporative demand and roughly corresponds to an elevation zone with a mean annual temperature of 7°C to 12°C and total precipitation of 800 to 1,800 mm yr^{1} (Stephenson 1998, Goulden et al. 2012). In general, the elevation of this zone shifts upward from north to south and coast to inland. For example, mixed-conifer forests in the Klamath Mountains occur between about 1,000 to 2,100 meters in elevation, compared to 1,400 to 2,400 meters in the southern Sierra Nevada (Fites-Kaufman et al. 2007). Temperatures decrease by approximately 4°C to 6°C km^{-1} of elevation gain (Major 1977). Precipitation rises with elevation up to a point then gradually decreases. For example, maximum precipitation in the central Sierra Nevada occurs around 1,900 meters (Armstrong and Stidd 1967, Major 1977).

The percentage of annual precipitation that occurs as snow ranges from approximately 25% to 65% in lower to upper montane forests. Montane forests typically transition to red fir (*Abies magnifica*)–dominated forest types at elevations where winter and spring temperatures ensure that most of the precipitation occurs as snow (Barbour et al. 1991). A large increase in snowpack accompanies the transition from ponderosa pine (*Pinus ponderosa*)–dominated forest through mixed conifer to red fir. For example, in the Pit River basin in northern California, April 1 snow depths below 1,500 meters are minimal (13 centimeters at Burney Springs in ponderosa pine) but reach over 200 centimeters at elevations over 1,950 meters in the red fir zone. In the American River basin of the central Sierra Nevada, similar patterns occur, with 37 centimeters average April 1 snow depth at 1,600 meters eleva-

Photo on previous page: Mixed-conifer forest with a restored fire regime, containing horizontal and vertical structural diversity, in the Illilouette Basin of Yosemite National Park. Photo: Marc Meyer.

tion (pine-dominated, mixed conifer) and 215 centimeters at 2,270 meters (red fir) (WRCC). In red fir forests the deeper snowpack and cooler temperatures substantially reduce the length and magnitude of the summer drought (Royce and Barbour 2001).

On an annual basis, California experiences one of the most variable precipitation regimes in the United States. In montane forests this means snowpack depth (and available water during the growing season) can vary by more than an order of magnitude between years (Mote 2006). The El Niño/Southern Oscillation (ENSO) often drives this interannual variability, but the area affected in any annual event varies across the range of montane forests (Minnich 2007). An El Niño year may produce a deep snowpack in the southern California mountains while northern California experiences normal or below normal precipitation. Patterns vary year-to-year depending on the strength of the ENSO event. California Department of Water Resources splits its Sierra Nevada snowpack assessment into northern, central, and southern zones because winter storms tracking from the Pacific Northwest and southern California might only impact the northern and southern half, respectively, of the state (see Chapter 2, "Climate"). Long-term averages suggest Yosemite National Park might roughly be a transition zone, as montane forest precipitation significantly decreases south of the park coincident with the southern range limit of Douglas-fir (*Pseudotsuga menziesii*) in the Sierra Nevada (Burns and Honkala 1990).

Precipitation patterns within the wet season are also highly variable. A few large winter storms usually account for a third to a half of annual precipitation and can occur over a seasonal total of only five to ten wet days per year. So-called atmospheric rivers (ARs) generate 20% to 50% of the state's precipitation totals (Dettinger et al. 2011). ARs are narrow bands (typically less than 200 kilometers wide) of concentrated water vapor that develop over the oceans and direct large amounts of moisture at continental areas (see Chapter 2, "Climate"). Due to the influence of periodic ARs developing over the tropical Pacific, California experiences more extreme precipitation events than any other part of the U.S., including the hurricane-affected Gulf Coast (Dettinger et al. 2011). ARs in montane forests, such as the New Year's Day storm of 1997, can cause widespread flooding and landslides, reshaping riparian corridors and forest stands on unstable slopes.

Soils

Montane forest soils are generally relatively young and weakly developed because of the recent glaciation of most California mountain ranges (generally higher than 1,400 meters in elevation) during the Late Wisconsin glacial episode (thirty thousand to ten thousand years ago) (Atwater et al. 1986; see Chapter 4,"Geomorphology and Soils"). Soils over granitic parent material, which predominate in montane ecosystems south of the Merced River (O'Green et al. 2007), often are highly porous and well-drained because they contain a substantial fraction of decomposed granite. California's mountains also contain older, metamorphosed rocks invaded by batholithic magma and young volcanic and sedimentary postbatholithic rocks (Harden 2004). Most lower montane soils are ALFISOLS and more highly leached ULTISOLS and are moderate to strongly acidic. Organic horizons may be deep (often depending on time since last fire) due to low decomposition rates resulting from conifer's poor litter quality and from minimal topsoil mixing by soil fauna (O'Green et al. 2007).

Microbial activity and organic matter decomposition are also limited by dry conditions during California's annual summer drought. For example, the thick litter layers often found around the base of mid-elevation trees result in part from reduced decomposition rates from rapid drying produced by accelerated snowmelt from solar heating of the tree bole (Johnson et al. 2009). Soil depth varies considerably, strongly affecting water-holding capacity and in turn forest productivity. Maximum clay content may range from 30% to 55% in the lower montane zone, but a significant reduction occurs in soil development above 1,500 to 1,800 meters in elevation, with clay content often dropping to less than 15% (O'Green et al. 2007). INCEPTISOLS and ANDISOLS dominate these higher-elevation soils. Generally, such soils are shallow and rich in organic matter with large, unconsolidated fragments and limited soil moisture storage. One study examining soil change along an elevation gradient (200–2,900 meters) found decreasing pH (about two units) and base saturation (90% to 10%) and increasing organic carbon with increasing elevation (Dahlgren et al. 1997). They also found maximum chemical weathering at mid-elevations (ponderosa and mixed-conifer forest types). Aspect and slope position also influence soil development and processes, with more weathering and deeper, richer soils on mesic, northerly aspects and lower-slope positions compared to xeric, south-facing, and upper-slope conditions.

After water, nitrogen is typically the most limiting plant growth resource in temperate zones (Vitousek and Howarth 1991). In California's montane forests mineral soil holds most (65–90%) of the nitrogen (Johnson et al. 2008). Nitrogen loss from fire volatilization increases with fire intensity but is often rapidly replenished by common actinorhizal shrubs such as *Ceanothus* spp. and bear clover (*Chamaebatia foliolosa*) that are associated with nitrogen-fixing bacteria (*Frankia* spp.) (Oakley et al. 2003, 2004; Stein et al. 2010). Ultramafic soils are not widespread in Sierra Nevada montane conifer ecosystems except in the Feather River drainages, but where present they significantly limit plant productivity and species composition as they lack most macronutrients and contain various heavy metals. The Klamath-Siskiyou Mountains have extensive ultramafic soil areas that support many rare plants and plant communities unique to this region of high diversity (Alexander et al. 2007).

Montane Forest Types

Several classification schemes exist for montane forest types in California (Critchfield 1971, Davis et al. 1995, Holland and Keil 1995, Barbour et al. 2007, Sawyer et al. 2009). Although each slightly differs in the number and types of forest ecosystems, they generally concur, particularly for the most widely distributed forest types discussed in this chapter. More detailed vegetation information using finer forest-type classifications are available in Barbour et al. (2007) and Sawyer et al. (2009). We generally have used the California Wildlife Habitat Relationships System (Meyer and Laudenslayer 1988) (Figure 27.1), which builds upon the U.S. Forest Service California Vegetation (CALVEG 2013) classification based on existing vegetation (rather than potential natural vegetation). All of the forest types discussed in this chapter could be viewed as related to the mixed-conifer group because they are delineated by changes in

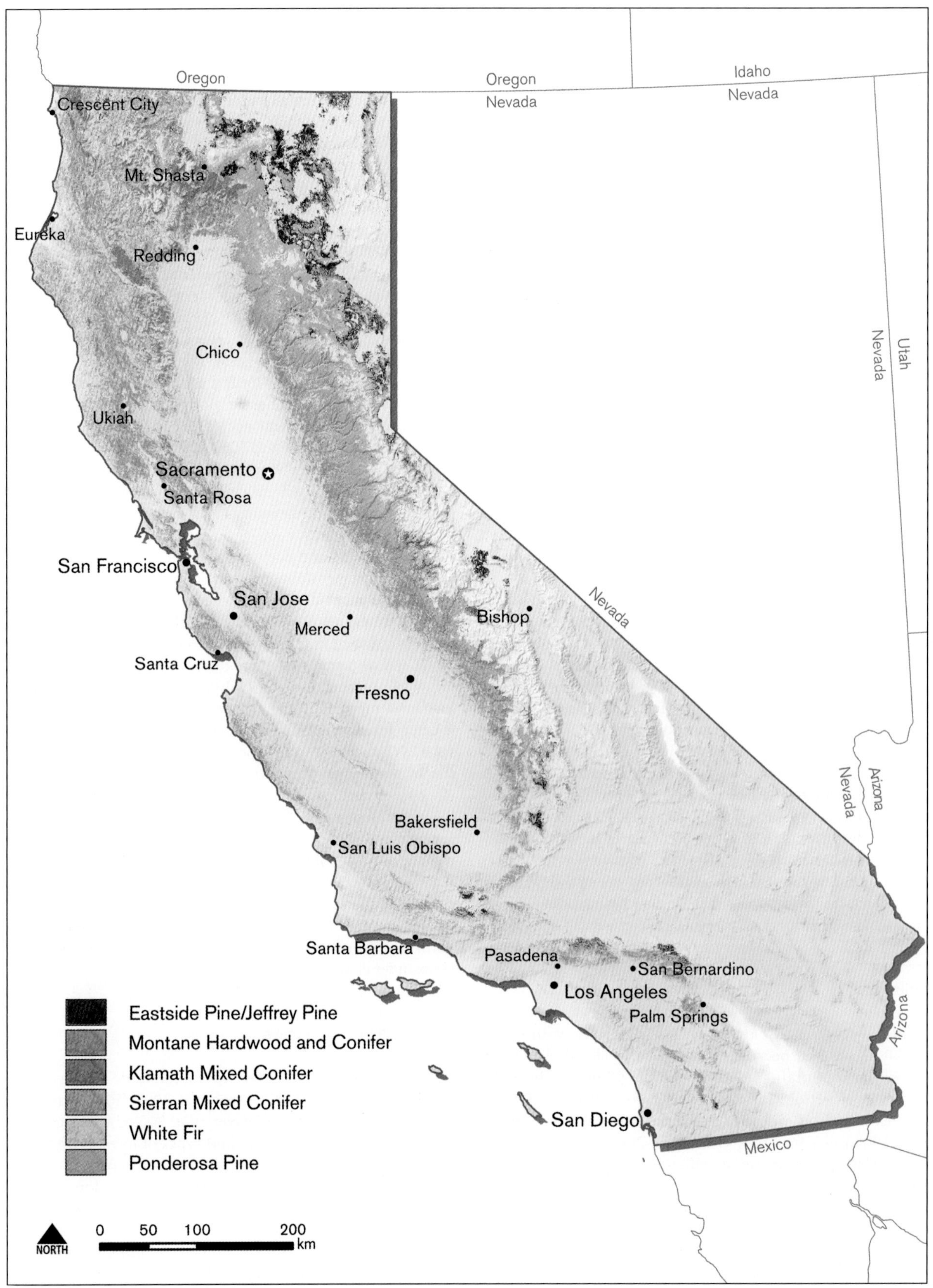

FIGURE 27.1 Distribution of montane forest types in California based on California wildlife habitat and CALVEG classifications. Giant sequoia groves not shown. Data from Cal Fire, Fire Resource and Assessment Program (FRAP). Map: Ross Gerrard, USFS PSW Research Station, and Parker Welch, Center for Integrated Spatial Research (CISR).

environmental or EDAPHIC conditions that allow one or several typical mixed-conifer species to become dominant.

Mixed Conifer

Mixed conifer (2,484,012 hectares) is one of the most common montane forest ecosystems in California and has the highest diversity among them of vertebrate species (Meyer and Laudenslayer 1988) (Figure 27.2a). Major tree species include ponderosa pine, Jeffrey pine (*Pinus jeffreyii*), sugar pine (*P. lambertiana*), white fir (*Abies concolor*), incense-cedar (*Calocedrus decurrens*), Douglas-fir, and black oak (*Quercus kelloggii*). Red fir, lodgepole pine (*Pinus contorta murrayana*), and western white pine (*Pinus monticola*)—all upper montane species—intermix with mixed conifer at higher elevations and in cold air drainages. Within mixed conifer, species composition can change over small distances, often in response to water availability (i.e., generally transitioning from fir to pine with increasing dryness) and microclimate (i.e., cold air drainages that retain snowpack are dominated by lodgepole pine, and white and red fir). Differences with aspect in temperature and insolation influence the elevations at which different forest types occur (Figure 27.3).

Considering the overwhelming importance of water availability and fire—historic mean fire return intervals (HFRI) averaged eleven to sixteen years (Van de Water and Safford 2011)—to mixed-conifer ecosystems, perhaps the most important distinction within the mixture of species concerns those that are highly tolerant of fire and drought but intolerant of shade (black oak and the yellow pines) and those that are less tolerant of fire and drought but grow relatively well in low-light conditions (white fir, incense-cedar, Douglas-fir) (Table 27.2). Historically, frequent fire kept forests generally open and exposed bare mineral soil, although conditions varied with topography and fire history (Collins, Lydersen et al. 2015, Stephens, Lydersen et al. 2015). These conditions favored pines, which could comprise up to 40–65% of the trees (McKelvey and Johnston 1992, North et al. 2007, Lydersen and North 2012). Fire suppression has significantly increased stem densities and CANOPY COVER and reduced understory light, resulting in heavy dominance by fir and incense-cedar and little shrub cover in many mixed-conifer forests today (North, Oakley et al. 2005; Collins et al. 2011; Dolanc et al. 2013; Knapp et al. 2013).

Klamath Mixed Conifer

Mixed-conifer forests in the Klamath Mountains (461,666 hectares) contain many species found in montane ranges in both California and the Pacific Northwest, contributing to high diversity and unique community assemblages (Sawyer 2006) (see Figure 27.2b). The diverse flora has developed over a long period from many biogeographic sources (Whittaker 1960, Briles et al. 2005) including migration from other regions (Stebbins and Major 1965), relictual species such as the recently identified Shasta snow-wreath (*Neviusia cliftonii*) (Lindstrand and Nelson 2006), and newly evolved taxa (Smith and Sawyer 1985). This diversity does not appear to result from the Klamath's fire regimes (HFRI seven to thirteen years) (Fry and Stephens 2006), which are similar to those in the Sierra Nevada, but instead is probably due to its ecotonal location straddling an area where different climate, geologic, and edaphic zones collide. Ultramafic, mafic, granitic, sedimentary, and metamorphic substrates are common (Waring 1969, Kruckeberg 1984), and temperature and precipitation gradients are very steep between the wet, cool western slopes and dry, hot interior areas bordering the Central Valley. Pleistocene glaciation in the Klamath Mountains was primarily confined to higher elevations (Sawyer 2007), and unlike most of the Sierra Nevada, modern streamflow is more driven by rainfall than by snowpack (Miller et al. 2003).

Populations of some conifers in this range are geographically quite distant from their distributions in other mountain ranges, and some endemic conifers occur here as well (Sawyer 2007). Examples of the former include foxtail pine (*Pinus balfouriana*; shared with the southern Sierra Nevada), Engelmann spruce (*Picea engelmannii*), and subalpine fir (*Abies lasiocarpa*—both at their southern range limit in the Klamaths); the latter is exemplified by Brewer spruce (*Picea breweriana*). In addition to thirty conifer species, Sawyer (2007) lists nineteen common hardwood tree species and more than seventy species of shrubs. The rugged topography in these mountains contributes to different fire regimes and forest types associated with aspect, slope position, and elevation (Taylor and Skinner 2003). Because the mountains are discontinuous and highly dissected, forest types tend to occur in patches rather than continuous belts. The rugged topography and lack of a dominant orientation provides many edaphic, microclimate, and disturbance regime differences over fine scales (Skinner et al. 2006). Whereas mixed conifer in the Sierra Nevada may have three to five tree species at any one site, Klamath mixed conifer typically has five to seven or more species growing together. A few sites in the Klamath Mountains apparently support the highest local diversity of conifers in the world. For example, the Sugar Creek drainage in the headwaters of the Scott River contains seventeen conifer species within an area of less than 2.6 square kilometers (Cheng 2004).

White Fir

Forests in which white fir (379,372 hectares) makes up more 60% of the relative canopy cover are often typed white fir (Sawyer et al. 2009), although other species such as incense-cedar, dogwood (*Cornus nuttallii*), ponderosa and Jeffrey pine, and Douglas-fir may also be present (see Figure 27.2c). Although white fir is more widely distributed than any other fir in California, intermixing with many species, it becomes dominant in mesic areas that have a longer fire return interval (greater than forty-five years) (Van de Water and Safford 2011), where regenerating trees can grow large enough to survive low- to moderate-intensity fire. White fir forests may be intermixed with or adjacent to mixed conifer and usually indicate an ABIOTIC shift toward cooler, wetter conditions. However, white fir is also found in drier interior ranges including the Warner Mountains (1,550–1,850 meters) in northeastern California and the Clark, Kingston, and New York Ranges (2,300–2,900 meters) (Paysen et al. 1980) in the Mojave area.

The dominance of a shade-tolerant species creates high canopy cover and multilayer stands with less fine-scale variability in microclimate, habitat, and understory conditions. Few openings and low understory light conditions reduce shrub and herbaceous cover; reduced fire frequency can produce thick litter and duff layers, higher fuel loads, and more snags and coarse woody debris than are common in mixed conifer. Heart rots are common, producing snags for cavity-

FIGURE 27.2 Forest types.

A Mixed conifer (Photo: Malcolm North)

B Klamath mixed conifer (Photo: Carl Skinner)

C White fir (Photo: Malcolm North)

D Montane hardwood-conifer (Photo: Carl Skinner)

E Giant sequoia (Photo: Nate Stephenson)

F Eastside pine (Photo: Malcolm North)

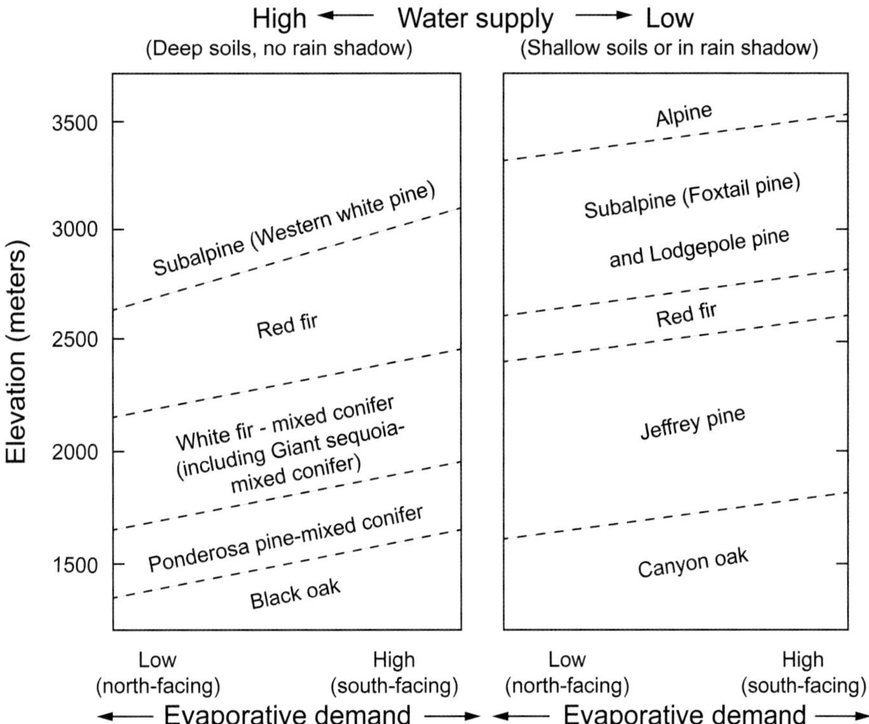

FIGURE 27.3 The approximate distribution of forest types in the southern Sierra Nevada relative to elevation (y-axis), evaporative demand (x-axis), and water supply (compare left and right panels). Source: Fites-Kaufmann et al. 2007.

dependent wildlife and large logs that can be used as runway structures for small mammals. White fir is the preferred tree species for several insect-gleaning birds, including yellow-rumped warblers (*Setophaga coronate*), western tanagers (*Piranga ludoviciana*), mountain chickadee (*Poecile gambeli*), chestnut-backed chickadee (*Parus rufescens*), golden-crowned kinglet (*Regulus satrapa*), and black-headed grosbeak (*Pheucticus melanocephalus*) (Airola and Barrett 1985).

Montane Hardwood-Conifer

There are many variations of montane hardwood-conifer (2,484,012 hectares), sometimes called mixed evergreen, which is characterized by composition including at least one-third hardwoods and one-third conifer (Anderson et al. 1976) (see Figure 27.2d). Hardwoods are usually dominated by species from the oak family, such as interior live oak (*Quercus wislizeni*), canyon live oak (*Q. chrysolepis*), tanoak (*Notholithocarpus densiflorus*), California black oak, Oregon white oak (*Q. garryana*), and golden chinquapin (*Chrysolepis chrysophylla*). Other hardwood associates include Pacific madrone (*Arbutus menziesii*) and big-leaf maple (*Acer macrophyllum*), while common conifers are Douglas-fir, ponderosa pine, white fir, incense-cedar and sugar pine, and in central coastal and southern California, bigcone Douglas-fir (*Pseudotsuga macrocarpa*) and coulter pine (*Pinus coulteri*) (Meyer and Laudenslayer 1988).

The overstory canopy (30–60 meters) is often dominated by conifers, especially where fire has been lacking for many years. Hardwoods comprise a lower layer (10–30 meters) above a shrub layer that can be sparse (in stands with high total canopy cover) to impenetrable (following fire). Although present in all of California's mountain ranges, the montane hardwood-conifer type is most extensive in the Klamath and North Coast Ranges and the northern Sierra Nevada and is often transitional between dense coniferous forests and mixed chaparral, open woodlands, or savannas. The mix of species can be highly variable, but some general patterns are apparent. Tanoak is a significant component in more mesic areas in the northern and western montane areas of California, and Douglas-fir is a local dominant in the same areas. Both species are absent in the southern Sierra Nevada and south Coast Ranges. Drier inland regions tend to have more black and canyon live oak, with the latter particularly found on steep slopes with thinner soils where sparse fuel accumulation reduces fire frequency and intensity. A recently introduced pathogen, sudden oak death (*Phytophthora ramorum*), has spread throughout many coastal montane hardwood-conifer forests within the moist fog belt, whose conditions favor the disease's dispersal. Tanoak experiences almost 100% mortality to sudden oak death. Although the pathogen rarely kills California bay (*Umbellularia californica*), research has identified it as the best predictor of the disease's presence (Rizzo and Garbelotto 2003).

Many of these hardwood species benefit from severe fire because they resprout. Warming temperatures, increasing precipitation, and increasing nutrient inputs from air pollution enhance their competitiveness with conifers. Lenihan et al. (2008) projected a notable increase in the area of hardwood forest by the end of the twenty-first century as a result of climate change. A recent study comparing forest structure between the 1930s and 2000s found that stem densities in Sierran montane hardwood forest have increased more than in any other forest type and that the proportion of plots dominated by montane hardwood species increased

TABLE 27.2

Comparative ecological tolerances of common tree species in California's montane forests

Species arranged from low tolerance (top) to high tolerance (bottom)

Shade	Frost	Temperature[A]	Drought	Fire[B]
Black oak/western juniper	Madrone	Lodgepole pine	Red fir	Lodgepole pine
Ponderosa pine/giant sequoia	Douglas-fir	Red fir	White fir	Sugar pine/white fir
Lodgepole pine	White fir	Jeffrey pine	Sugar pine/ giant sequoia	Incense cedar/ Douglas-fir
Sugar pine	Sugar pine/giant sequoia	White fir/giant sequoia	Douglas-fir	Jeffrey pine/ponderosa pine/giant sequoia
Incense cedar	Incense cedar	Douglas-fir/sugar pine/ incense cedar	Lodgepole pine/ incense cedar/ madrone	
Douglas-fir	Ponderosa pine/ Jeffrey pine/red fir	Ponderosa pine/black oak/ madrone	Ponderosa pine	
Red fir	Lodgepole pine		Jeffrey pine	
White fir			Black oak	

SOURCE: Data from Minore 1979, Burns and Honkala 1990, and the Fire Effects Information System (FEIS).

A. Least heat tolerant/most cold tolerant on top.

B. Fire tolerance of mature trees. Fir and Douglas-fir seedlings and saplings are less tolerant of fire than yellow pine and sugar pine.

by almost 100% between the two time periods (Dolanc et al. 2013).

Giant Sequoia

Giant sequoia occurs naturally in roughly seventy relatively small, scattered groves (total area of 14,600 hectares) along the western slope of the Sierra Nevada, mostly south of the Kings River (Stephenson 1996, Fites-Kaufman et al. 2007) (see Figure 27.2e). The eight groves north of the Kings River span elevations of 1,370 to 2,000 meters, while those to the south are mostly found between 1,700 and 2,250 meters in elevation. Within these groves, giant sequoia usually dominates BASAL AREA, but by stem frequency and composition the groves would be considered mixed conifer. Grove locations are usually characterized by deep, well-drained soils with relatively high water availability. Although the trees can grow rapidly, typically to 400–800 centimeters in diameter and 65–80 meters tall, they are also long-lived, reaching ages of one thousand years or older.

More than any other tree species in the Sierra Nevada, giant sequoia is a pioneer species requiring disturbance for successful regeneration (Stephenson 1994). In the past, frequent, moderate-intensity fires burned through sequoia groves, creating occasional gaps in the forest canopy in locations where these fires burned at high severity. These canopy gaps, with their greatly reduced competition for light and water, are the sites of virtually all successful sequoia regeneration (Stephenson 1994, York et al. 2011, Meyer and Safford 2011). Following Euro-American settlement, more than a century of fire exclusion led to a nearly complete failure of sequoia regeneration. Where fire has subsequently been reintroduced, sequoia regeneration has been restored (Stephenson 1996, Stephenson 1999, York et al. 2013).

Ponderosa, Jeffrey, and "Eastside" Pine

Sometimes collectively called the "yellow pines," ponderosa and Jeffrey pine are closely related (both in the subgenus Pinus, section Pinus, subsection Ponderosae) and occasionally hybridize (Baldwin et al. 2012). Ponderosa pine, one of the most widely distributed pine species in North America (327,778 hectares), is found throughout the mountainous regions of the western U.S., whereas Jeffrey pine is primarily a California tree, with a few occurrences in westernmost Nevada, southwestern Oregon, and northern Baja California, Mexico (see Figure 27.2f). Of the two species, Jeffrey pine is more stress-tolerant and replaces ponderosa pine at higher elevations, on poorer soils, and in colder and/or drier climates (Haller 1959, Stephenson 1998, Barbour and Minnich 2000). Ponderosa pine–dominated forests can occur from approximately 300 to 1,800 meters and 1,200 to 2,100 meters in northern and southern California, respectively (Fites-Kaufman et al. 2007). Jeffrey pine–dominated forests occur mostly between 1,500 and 2,400 meters and 1,700 and 2,800 meters in northern and southern California (with the highest elevations usually on the east side of the Sierra Nevada), respectively (Fites-Kaufman et al. 2007, Barbour and Minnich 2000). Both yellow pine species also occur in other forest types including mixed conifer, where they were dominant in many places before logging and fire suppression.

A large area of the northern Sierra Nevada east of the crest supports a mixed yellow pine forest, sometimes called "eastside pine," with co-dominance by ponderosa and Jeffrey pine

(782,526 hectares of Jeffrey and eastside pine area combined). Like white fir forests, forests dominated by ponderosa and Jeffrey pine are closely intermingled with mixed conifer, in this case indicating a shift toward drier, warmer (ponderosa) or drier, colder (Jeffrey) site conditions. Historically these forests had very frequent fires that supported low-density open-stand conditions characterized by shrub patches, sparse litter cover, and relatively high diversity of herbs and grasses.

Forest Structure and Function

In the nineteenth century John Muir wrote, "These forests were so open, early travelers could ride a horse or even pull wagons through [them]." An early timber survey in the northern Sierra Nevada noted the same conditions and lamented that fire kept the forest at only 30% of its potential lumber stocking (Lieberg 1902). Historically these low-density, large tree–dominated forests had an almost flat DIAMETER DISTRIBUTION (an equal abundance of all tree sizes) in contrast to the reverse J-shaped distribution (tree abundance rapidly decreases in larger-size classes) many early foresters were familiar with from forests with more infrequent disturbance regimes (North et al. 2007). Based on detailed timber surveys conducted by the Forest Service in the central Sierra Nevada in 1911, tree densities ranged from 40 to 80 trees ha^{-1} and estimated canopy cover was 17–24% (Collins et al. 2011). These open conditions were maintained by frequent surface fires that consumed surface fuels and small-diameter trees, providing a pulse of nutrients to the soil, creating patches of bare mineral soil for seed establishment, and reducing competition for soil moisture (Gray et al. 2005, Zald et al. 2008). Without fire, forest structure becomes more homogeneous, and some ecosystem functions "stall" (Ma et al. 2004, North and Rosenthal 2006) (Figure 27.4).

Frequent fire creates structural diversity at fine (stand) and coarse (landscape) scales associated with several ecosystem processes. The within-stand structure has been characterized as containing three main conditions: individual trees, clumps of trees, and openings or gaps (ICO) (Larson and Churchill 2012, Lydersen et al. 2013, Fry et al. 2014). Stand-level average canopy cover under frequent-fire conditions is typically low (20–45%) compared to modern, fire-suppressed conditions (typically 55–85%). However, within a stand, ICO conditions produce heterogeneity such that CANOPY CLOSURE (a point-level measure) (Jennings et al. 1999, North and Stine 2012) is highly variable, providing a scattering of dense areas for wildlife cover. Several studies suggest this fine-scale heterogeneity affects ecosystem conditions and functions, producing a wide range of microclimates (Rambo and North 2009, Ma et al. 2010), a diversity of understory plants (Wayman and North 2007) and soil invertebrates (Marra and Edmonds 2005), variation in soil respiration (Concilio et al. 2005, Ryu et al. 2009), and limits to pest and pathogen spread (Maloney et al. 2008). In addition, modeling efforts that have compared fire-suppressed forest conditions with two different fuel reduction treatments found higher avian richness in forests treated to create variable canopy closure and increase structural heterogeneity (White et al. 2013a, b).

At a larger scale, models suggest that fire created a mosaic of different forest SERAL conditions that diversified landscape structure (Kane et al. 2014). For example, modeling by the LANDFIRE program (Rollins and Frame 2006, Rollins 2009) predicts that under an active fire regime, 10–20% of yellow and mixed-conifer forests in California would have been in early seral stages (herbs, shrubs, seedlings/saplings) with approximately 30–40% in areas dominated by trees between 10 and 53 centimeters dbh (diameter at breast height) (5–21"), and 40–60% in areas dominated by larger trees (higher than 53 centimeters dbh). Furthermore, the models indicate that most of the landscape was under open forests of less than 50% canopy cover ("open" stages), especially in the yellow pine and drier mixed-conifer types (Rollins 2009). This is quite different than modern forest conditions where 85% of montane forests are dominated by 10–53 centimeter trees and canopy cover averages greater than 65%.

Water availability appears to be one of the strongest influences on ecosystem function. At fine scales, functions such as decomposition, nutrient cycling, and soil respiration vary strongly within forest stands by patch type (North and Chen 2005) and their different levels of available soil moisture (Erickson et al. 2005, North, Oakley et al. 2005, Concilio et al. 2006). At larger scales, forest greenness (Trujillo et al. 2012), CO_2 uptake, and evapotranspiration (Goulden et al. 2012) are correlated with elevational differences in snowpack depth and total precipitation.

Fauna

Montane forests in California support at least 355 vertebrate species (Verner and Boss 1980). The high species richness of montane forests probably stems in part from changing habitat conditions created by frequent fire and seral development. For example, a study of the avian community between a burned area and neighboring unburned forest in the Sierra Nevada found that over a third of species occurred only in the burned area (Bock and Lynch 1970). In addition, a study of breeding birds observed over a twenty-five-year period found that bird community guild structure shifted among species with different foraging strategies (i.e., foliage searching to bark gleaning) as forest succession progressed (Raphael et al. 1987).

Concern has often focused on species that might be affected by modern changes in forest conditions that differ from their historical analogs or that have become increasingly rare (North and Manley 2012, Stephens et al. 2014). For instance, some songbirds are strongly associated with shrub patches (Burnett et al. 2009) now uncommon in the low-light understory of fire-suppressed forests (Knapp et al. 2013). The most widely known sensitive species, however, are associated with old forest conditions such as the northern (*Strix occidentalis caurina*) (Moen and Gutierrez 1997, North et al. 1999) and California spotted owls (*S. o. occidentalis*) (North et al. 2000, Lee and Irwin 2005), northern goshawk (*Accipiter gentilis*) (Morrison et al. 2009), fisher and marten (*Martes pennanti* and *M. martes*) (Zielinski et al. 2004a, b), southern red-backed vole (*Clethrionomys gapperi*) (Sullivan and Sullivan 2001), and northern flying squirrel (*Glaucomys sabrinus*) (Meyer et al. 2005, 2007; Meyer, North, and Kelt 2007) (Figure 27.5). The California spotted owl and fisher have been studied more extensively than other species because both are considered threatened. Guidelines for maintaining and improving their habitats strongly affect forest management on public lands (North, Stine et al. 2009; Roberts and North 2012). Both species are associated with large, old structures that contain high levels of canopy closure to use for nesting and resting. This has often resulted in minimal or no fuels removal in these areas, which in turn makes these sites prone to burning at

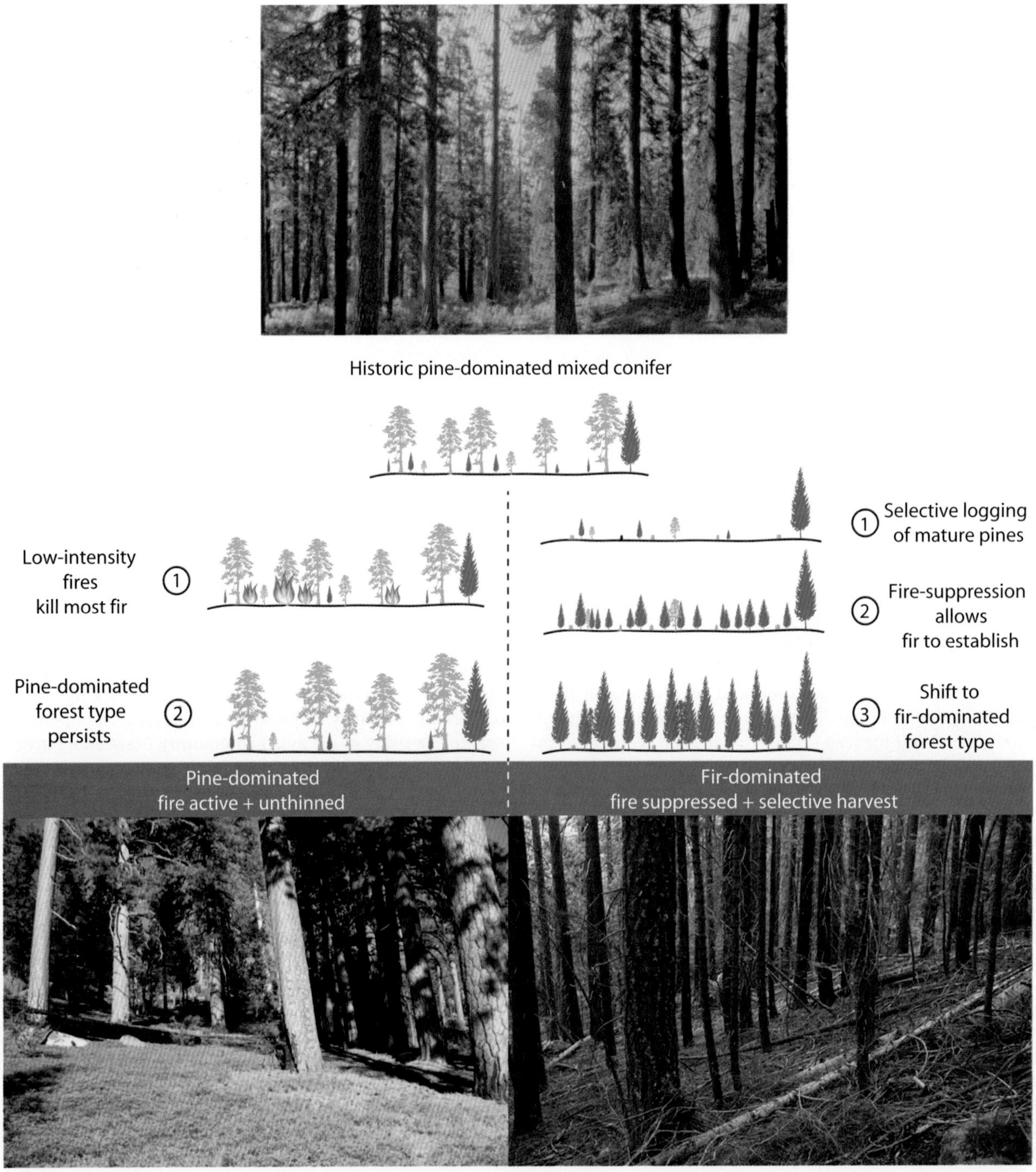

Historic pine-dominated mixed conifer
Low-intensity fires kill most fir
1
Pine-dominated forest type persists
2
1 Selective logging of mature pines
2 Fire-suppression allows fir to establish
3 Shift to fir-dominated forest type
Pine-dominated fire active + unthinned
Fir-dominated fire suppressed + selective harvest

FIGURE 27.4 Two generalized successional pathways for historic mixed-conifer forests (top). The left side shows how an active-fire regime maintains a resilient composition and structure dominated by a low density of large pine. The right side shows how past selective logging and fire suppression can lead to a high-density, white fir–dominated forest stand. This right side is a common condition in many montane forests and can be very susceptible to high-intensity fire and drought mortality. Source: Earles et al. 2014.

high severity in the event of a wildfire and to subsequent loss of nesting and resting habitat (North et al. 2010). For foraging, however, both species use a variety of habitat conditions, possibly because they have broad prey bases that include several small mammal species associated with a range of forest and shrub conditions (Innes et al. 2007, Meyer et al. 2007).

Some controversy has focused on the black-backed woodpecker (*Picoides arcticus*), a species associated with large, recently dead (four to eight years old) trees and often found foraging in "snag forests" produced by stand-replacing fires (Saab et al. 2007, Hanson and North 2008). The black-backed woodpecker might seem like an unlikely candidate for sensitive species status. With fire suppression, although the extent of wildfire has decreased, increased fire severity has kept the area of snag forests at levels consistent with estimates of historical conditions (though patch size has significantly increased) (Miller et al. 2009, Mallek et al. 2013). The concern with black-backed woodpecker habitat is not an areal decrease but a reduction in habitat suitability if many snags are removed by postfire salvage logging.

In addition to reduced old forest conditions, some special habitat elements (e.g., "defect" trees) may have declined

FIGURE 27.5 Sensitive species that affect land management in California's montane forests: (A) fisher resting on a large black oak limb, (B) a northern flying squirrel holding a truffle (its primary food source), (C) northern goshawk, (D) a California spotted owl, and (E) a black-backed woodpecker on a snag.

in abundance (Bouldin 1999). Large defect trees and snags are often rare in managed montane forests because they are removed for worker safety, and past stand "improvement" practices removed "defect" structures that did not contribute to wood production. Trees and snags selected by primary cavity nesters, woodpeckers, and nuthatches (*Sitta* spp.) could be particularly important because the cavities, once vacated, are used by other birds and mammals (Bull et al. 1997). Several studies have found that cavity availability can limit abundances of some of these species in managed forests (Carey et al. 1997, Carey 2002, Cockle et al. 2011, Wiebe 2011).

Ecosystem Characteristics

Drought, Pests, and Pathogens

Although montane forests are adapted to annual drought stress characteristic of Mediterranean climates, periods of multiple, consecutive dry years can have large impacts (e.g., see Guarin and Taylor 2005). For example, a massive die-off of conifer trees took place in the San Bernardino Mountains after the drought of the late 1990s and early 2000s. In the absence of frequent fire, increases in forest density result in greater competition for scarce water (Innes 1992, Dolph et al. 1995). Potential increases in older tree mortality are a major concern because large trees are often more prone to drought-induced mortality (Allen et al. 2010). Some studies have found higher than expected mortality rates in large trees (Smith et al. 2005, Lutz et al. 2009), suggesting that a "leave it alone" forest management approach that does not reduce stand density might actually contribute to the loss of old-growth trees.

Drought itself is usually not the proximal cause of tree mortality, however, as drought-induced stress also leads to greater insect and disease susceptibility (Savage 1994, Logan et al. 2003, Fettig et al. 2007, Allen et al. 2010). In general, open stands with a mix of species have had more localized damage and mortality, while the scale and extent of mortality have been greater in dense, single-species stands and plantations (Stephens et al. 2012). Beetles are probably the greatest source of stress and mortality. Some beetle species are specialists focused primarily on one or two species, such as western (*Dendroctonus brevicomis*) and Jeffrey pine (*D. jeffreyi*) beetles primarily affecting ponderosa and Jeffrey pines, respectively. Mountain pine beetle (*D. ponderosae*) and California five-spined ips (*Ips paraconfusus*), however, are more generalist and affect most of the conifers in California's montane ecosystems (Fettig 2012). Several pathogens also notably influence montane tree mortality. White pine blister rust (*Cronartium ribicola*) has been devastating to sugar pine since the disease entered northern California around 1930, and impacts to western white pine are also locally severe (Maloney et al. 2011). Pathologists and foresters have widely collected sugar pine seeds and conducted nursery experiments to identify blister rust–resistant individuals to help regenerate the species (Kinloch 1992). Root rot (*Heterobasidion* spp.) disease is also widespread, particularly in fir-dominated forests. Some evidence suggests that forest thinning can accelerate spread of root rot because the disease's windblown spores can colonize tree stumps (Rizzo and Slaughter 2001).

Fire

Under presettlement conditions, most of California's montane forests supported fire regimes characterized by frequent, predominantly low- to moderate-severity fires (Agee 1993, Sugihara et al. 2006, Barbour et al. 2007) (see Chapter 3, "Fire as an Ecosystem Process"). Historically these fire regimes were limited principally by the amount of available fuels rather than by fuel moisture during the summer drought. As elevation increases, the role of fuel moisture becomes more important, gradually supplanting fuel availability in red fir and higher-elevation forest types (Agee 1993, Miller and Urban 1999a, Sugihara et al. 2006, Van de Water and Safford 2011).

Historically ignitions originated with Native American burning or lightning. Oral history suggests that many groups used fire to produce more open forest conditions favorable for foraging and hunting (Anderson et al. 1997). Whether these ignitions were concentrated in a few favored places or broadly used has been debated (Parker 2002; see Chapter 10, "Indigenous California"). In contrast, areas of heavy lightning activity are more easily identified. In a statewide analysis (van Wagtendonk and Cayan 2008), strikes increased with elevation up to 2,400 meters, had the highest monthly totals from June through the end of September, and occurred most between the hours of 1400 and 1900. Fire ignitions from lightning likely varied substantially from year to year. For the period between 1985 and 2000, van Wagtendonk and Cayan (2008) found a fivefold difference between the years with the highest and lowest number of strikes.

Across the state, fire return intervals (FRIs) averaged eleven to sixteen years in yellow pine and mixed-conifer forests, with a mean minimum and maximum FRI of five and forty to eighty years, respectively (Van de Water and Safford 2011; North, Van de Water et al. 2009). Presettlement fire frequencies were higher in the drier, lower-elevation forest types (yellow pine and dry mixed conifer) and lower in moister and higher-elevation montane forests (Caprio and Swetnam 1995, Sugihara et al. 2006, Fites-Kaufman et al. 2007). Fire frequencies and patterns of fire severity were also influenced by local topographic variables. Several studies have documented longer FRIs and greater proportions of high severity on cooler, more mesic slopes (mostly north-facing), with the opposite pattern on warmer, more xeric slopes (mostly south-facing) (Kilgore and Taylor 1979, Fites-Kaufman et al. 1997, Taylor 2000, Beaty and Taylor 2001). Riparian areas also followed this pattern, with forests around smaller, headwater streams having a similar fire regime to adjacent uplands while larger streams (generally third order or greater) had longer fire return intervals (Van de Water and North 2010, 2011).

In the absence of fire, many modern forests have unusually high fuel loads with much greater potential for high-severity, crown fires (Brown et al. 2008, Taylor et al. 2013). These conditions have shifted the fire regime from "fuel-limited" to "climate-limited" or "weather-limited" (Miller and Urban 1999b, Running 2006, Morgan et al. 2008, Collins et al. 2009, Miller et al. 2009, Steel, Safford et al. 2015). Adding to this trend is a policy of fire suppression on many forested lands, causing most wildfires to occur when they escape containment during extreme weather conditions (i.e., low humidity and high temperatures and wind speeds). In most montane forests the proportion and area of stand-replacing fire area and the sizes of stand-replacing patches are increasing (Miller et al. 2009, Miller and Safford 2012; however, see Miller, Skinner et al. 2012). These increases may be problematic because most of California's montane trees species do not have direct mechanisms to regenerate following stand-replacing fire (e.g., serotiny, vegetative sprouting) (Goforth and Minnich 2008, Keeley 2012). This is particularly a concern in large stand-replacing patches, where the likelihood of wind-blown seed establishing is low (McDonald 1980). Conifer regeneration in stand-replacing patches can be highly variable. However, a recent study found that it was completely absent in nearly three-quarters of sampled high-severity patches, at least in the short term after fire (less than ten years) (Collins and Roller 2013).

Topography's Influence

Slope aspect, through its effects on insolation and hence the evaporative demand experienced by plants, has a relatively modest influence on montane forests and mostly affects the elevation at which particular forest types are found (Stephenson 1998, Fites-Kaufman et al. 2007, Lydersen and North 2012). For example, in the Sierra Nevada a given montane forest type can generally be found a few hundred meters higher on south-facing (sunward) slopes than on north-facing (shaded) slopes (see Figure 27.3). Water availability has more dramatic effects (Tague et al. 2009). For instance, firs are usually most abundant where water availability is high (such as on deep soils, with their high water-holding capaci-

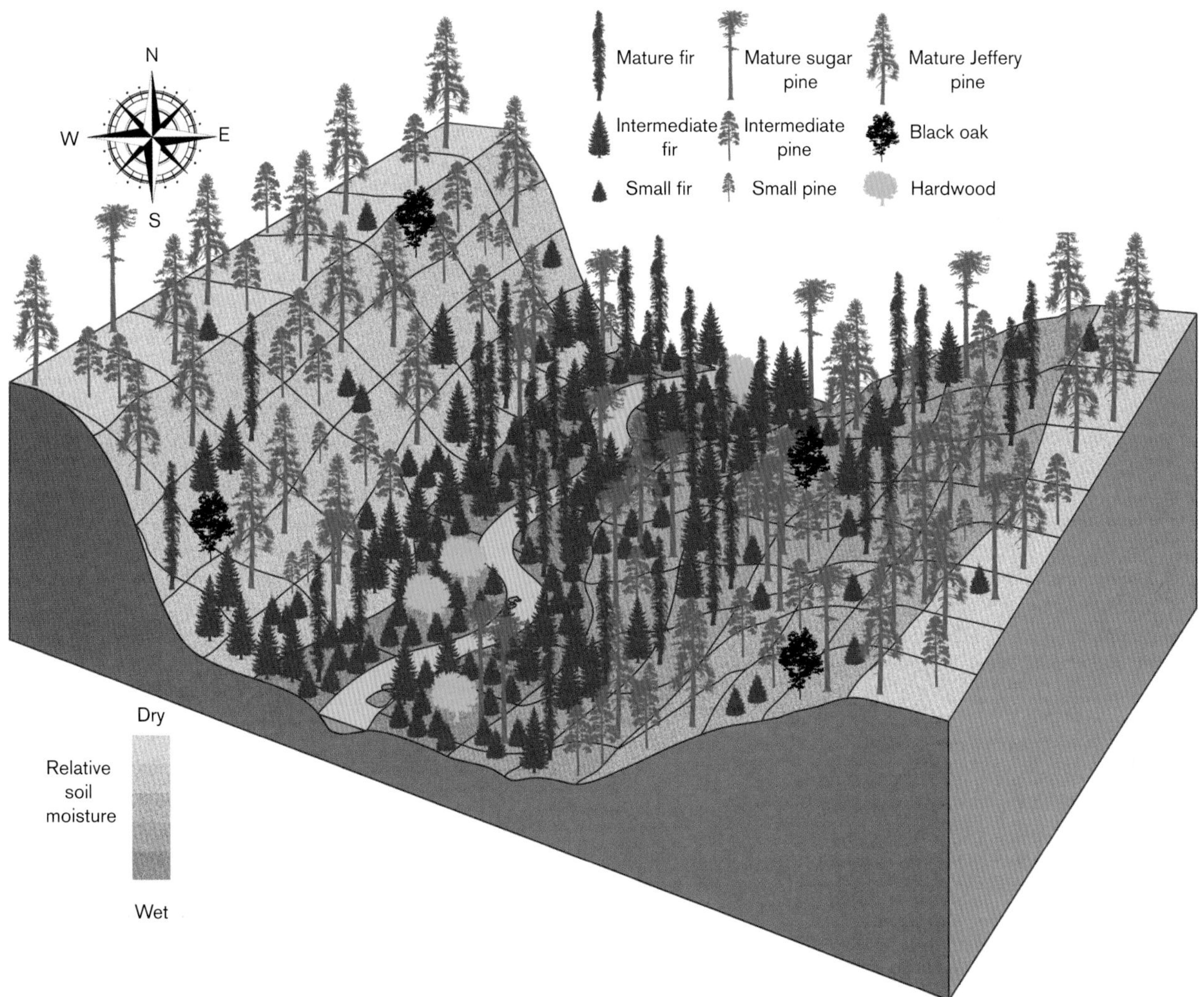

FIGURE 27.6 Landscape schematic of variable mixed-conifer conditions produced by an active fire regime. Forest density and composition vary with topographic features such as slope, aspect, and slope position. Ridgetops, with drier soils and higher fire intensity, have lower stem density and a higher percentage of pine than more mesic riparian areas with lower-intensity fire. Midslope forest density and composition vary with aspect: density and fir abundance increase on more northern aspects (right side) and flatter slope angles. Illustration by Steve Oerding.

ties), whereas pines are most abundant where water availability is low (such as on shallow soils or in rain shadows) (Stephenson 1998; Fites-Kaufman et al. 2007; Meyer, North, Gray et al. 2007). Slope steepness and slope position (e.g., ridgetop, midslope, valley bottom) also affect the reception and retention of both meteoric waters and water flowing above, within, and beneath the soil.

The influence of topography can be twofold, affecting both productivity and fire intensity (Figure 27.6) (Kane et al. 2015). Topographic locations that contain more mesic, productive sites (i.e., lower slope and riparian areas) were associated with greater densities of large, overstory trees, high total basal area and canopy cover, and an abundance of large snags and logs. This high-biomass forest structure existed in these topographic positions regardless of recent fire history. Outside of mesic sites and in forests that still have an active fire regime (i.e., no suppression), recent fire history was found to have the strongest influence on understory conditions (Lydersen and North 2012). Small tree density decreased and shrub cover increased with increased fire intensity and frequency, which in turn tended to occur on upper slope and ridgetop locations. These findings suggest that topography, fire history, and their interaction produce the heterogeneity characteristic of montane forest landscapes (Taylor and Skinner 2003, Lydersen and North 2012).

Wind

Overall, few historical accounts exist of large wind events in montane forests. In at least one study, the random direction of downed trees in old mixed conifer suggested that big wind events were not a significant driver of mortality (Innes et al. 2006). According to maps (Peterson 2000), California and neighboring states are subject to fewer major wind events like tornados and convective events ("downbursts") than any other part of the contiguous United States. However, winds can have strong local effects. Very high winds can be common when winter storms arrive at the Sierra Nevada crest, but these elevations generally support subalpine forests. One recent event in fall 2011 in Devil's Postpile National Monument in the upper San Joaquin River basin had winds exceeding 145 kilometers per hour (Hilimire et al. 2012). Thousands of mature trees were downed—mostly red fir, white fir, and lodgepole pine—but areas of Jeffrey pine were also impacted. In some areas more than 70% of live trees were downed. Large trees and snags were more susceptible to uprooting than smaller ones, and effects were distributed fairly evenly across species. This size-dependent response to wind has a very different impact on forest structure than does fire, which preferentially kills smaller trees.

Forest Turnover

Montane forests are more dynamic than forests found at higher elevations. For example, tree turnover rates (the average of tree recruitment and mortality rates) for old-growth Sierra Nevada forests are roughly three times greater in montane forests than in subalpine forests at treeline (Stephenson and van Mantgem 2005). The strong decline of forest turnover rates with increasing elevation may be related to parallel declines in forest productivity (Stephenson and van Mantgem 2005).

Background tree mortality rates in montane forests generally can be higher in fire-suppressed forests than in contemporary forests with a more intact fire regime, possibly due to reduced competition among trees in burned stands (Ansley and Battles 1998, Maloney and Rizzo 2002, Stephens and Gill 2005). Similarly, modern plantation studies show much higher annual mortality in high-density than in low-density stands. In ponderosa pine, one study found annual mortality rates of between 0% and 0.8% in thinned stands of less than 332 trees per hectare, versus rates of 0.6% to 2.3% in stands of more than 2,450 trees per hectare (Zhang et al. 2006). Recent studies (van Mantgem and Stephenson 2007, van Mantgem et al. 2009) found that tree mortality rates in western U.S. forests have roughly doubled over the past few decades—an apparent consequence of warming temperatures.

Ecosystem Services

The Millennium Ecosystem Assessment defines ecosystem services as the direct and indirect benefits people obtain from ecological systems (MEA 2005). California's montane forests contribute to quality of life for millions of people, many living at some distance from the state's mountain ranges. Ecosystem services are broadly categorized as provisioning (e.g., water, timber, fuels, food); regulating (e.g., carbon sequestration, erosion control, water quality); cultural (e.g., recreation, spiritual enrichment, educational opportunities); or supporting (biological diversity, nutrient cycling, etc.). All of these services are important, but we focus here on water, recreation, and carbon because of their particular relevance to California policies and economic development.

WATER

By one estimate, about 246,700,000,000 cubic meters (200 million acre feet [maf]) of precipitation falls annually on California, of which about 92,500,000,000 cubic meters (75 maf) is unimpaired runoff available for management and use (Energy Almanac 2014). About two-thirds of this annual runoff comes from one-fifth of California's land area—the mountains in the northern half of the state. A substantial portion of this water originates from precipitation in forested watersheds within the montane forest zone. Most of this water is eventually used by agriculture (41,900,000,000 cubic meters, or 34 maf). Furthermore, most montane rivers are highly engineered with multiple dams and impoundments that contribute to California's greater than 13,725 gigawatt hours of hydroelectric power capacity (meeting about 8% of California's electricity demand).

A recent assessment of forested watersheds found the greatest threats to water quality and fisheries were concentrated in north coast watersheds. These threats stemmed from erosion following forest management activities, development, mass wasting, and high-severity wildfire (California Department of Forest and Fire Protection 2010). The high canopy cover in these forests caused by fire suppression might reduce water runoff because less snow reaches the ground and more is caught in the canopy, where it can sublimate directly back into the atmosphere (Golding and Swanson 1986, Essery et al. 2003). Climate change is expected to increase the percentage of precipitation that occurs as rain rather than snow (Hunsaker et al. 2012). This is expected to accelerate snowmelt and to challenge current reservoir capacity.

RECREATION

Montane forests are used heavily for a wide range of recreational activities. In 2010, Yosemite National Park alone drew four million visitors and provided more than $350 million in tourism revenue. Surveys on National Forest land in California found that the most popular activities were relaxing (52%), viewing natural features (52%), hiking and walking (47%), viewing wildlife (38%), and downhill skiing (36%), with an average of one to five trips per visitor annually (U.S. Department of Agriculture, Forest Service Region 2012). For the Sierra Nevada one study estimated an average rate of fifty million to sixty million annual visitor days for public forestlands alone (Duane 1996). Giant sequoia groves are probably among the most visited forest ecosystems in the world, and their appeal was instrumental in halting logging of the groves and establishing federal protection in the 1890s.

CARBON STORAGE

Through the long-lived nature of many trees, global forests store twice as much carbon as Earth's atmosphere. Global forest growth is a significant net carbon sink, adding 2.4±1.0 Pg C year[1] to biomass storage (Pan et al. 2011) and helping to offset anthropogenic emissions of CO_2. Although developing countries often reduce their carbon stores when forestland is converted to other uses, California's forest acreage has not changed appreciably over the past fifty years. Most montane forests in the state have been net carbon sinks in the last century due to regrowth from past harvesting and ingrowth from fire suppression (Hurteau and North 2009). California forests (all types and ownerships) are estimated to store 2.3 Pg of carbon (Fried and Zhou 2008). However, loss due to fire and conversion of forests due to development could offset, or even exceed, carbon stored from tree growth (Battles et al. 2013, Gonzalez, Battles et al. 2015). Thus the long-term stability of these carbon stores in forest is a key concern.

There has been substantial debate about whether carbon loss through fuels treatment (mechanical thinning and/or prescribed fire) in fire-prone forests is offset by a reduction in later carbon emissions if the treated stand is burned by wildfire (Hurteau et al. 2008, Hurteau and North 2009, Mitchell et al. 2009, Hurteau and North 2010, North and Hurteau 2011, Campbell et al. 2012, Carlson et al. 2012). In general, treating forests leads to net carbon loss because of the low current probability of wildfire burning the treated area, the modest reduction in wildfire combustion and carbon emissions, and the need to maintain fuels reduction through periodic, additional carbon removal (Campbell et al. 2012).

The concept of carbon carrying capacity (Keith et al. 2009) could be particularly relevant to California's montane forests. Carbon carrying capacity emphasizes the level of stable carbon storage that a forest can maintain over the long term. In the absence of disturbance, a forest can "pack on" more carbon as tree density and size increase (Hurteau and North 2009, Hurteau et al. 2013). Many montane forests are in this state today. This additional biomass, however, makes the forest prone to disturbances—such as drought stress, pests, pathogens, and higher-severity wildfire—that increase tree mortality. Mortality reduces carbon stocks as dead trees decompose and much of the carbon returns to the atmosphere through efflux. Carbon carrying capacity, therefore, is lower than the maximum storage potential of a forest but represents the biomass that can be maintained in the context of disturbance and mortality agents characteristic of a particular ecosystem. In California's forests with historically frequent fire and drought events, carbon carrying capacity is the amount that a forest can store while maintaining low levels of mortality in response to periodic disturbances. In general, forests managed so that growth and carbon accumulation are concentrated in large trees will provide longer, more secure carbon storage than forests where growth is concentrated in a high density of small trees prone to pest, pathogen, and fire mortality (North, Hurteau et al. 2009; Earles et al. 2014). Recent research shows that large trees have remarkably high growth rates, giving them a more dynamic role in forest carbon storage than had been previously appreciated (Stephenson et al. 2014).

Human Impacts

Although American Indians used trees for a variety of purposes, large-scale timber harvest did not begin until after widespread Euro-American settlement (circa 1850). Most logging before the 1900s was done to support mining operations. Timber was cut to build homes and commercial buildings, tunnels, mine and ore processing infrastructure, and railroad lines. It was also the fuel for heating, railroad engines, and other machines, and the various types of mills used for processing ore. In some areas a very valuable market in sugar pine shakes (for roofing or siding) also arose (McKelvey and Johnston 1992). The majority of timber harvests before and after 1900 occurred in yellow pine and mixed-conifer forest and often selected the largest, most valuable pine trees (Sudworth 1900, Leiberg 1902).

Between the 1890s and 1920s, railroad lines were extended throughout the state's lower- and middle-elevation forests to access timber resources beyond the reach of animal-drawn transport. After the Second World War, dramatically increasing wood demand from federal lands led the Forest Service to greatly expand their sale of timber. For example, harvest on the Eldorado National Forest averaged approximately 3.8 million board feet per year between 1902 and 1940 but increased to 35.1 million board feet during the war, and to over 56 million board feet per year between the end of the war and 1959 (Beesley 1996). Harvest techniques were more industrial than before the war, and large areas of forest were clearcut. Since the 1960s, national legislation, regulations, changing economics, and environmental concerns have acted in concert to greatly reduce the amount of logging occurring on California public land, although private lands have made up some of the difference (see Chapter 36, "Forestry").

In the end, Barbour et al. (1993) estimated that half the original area of California's mixed-conifer forest had been cut at least once in the past 150 years. The Sierra Nevada Ecosystem Project executive summary (SNEP 1996) has a succinct summary of the impacts of European settlement on montane ecosystems (Figure 27.4): "The primary impact of 150 years of forestry on middle-elevation conifer forests has been to simplify structure (including large trees, snags, woody debris of large diameter, canopies of multiple heights and closures, and complex spatial mosaics of vegetation), and presumably function, of these forests. By reducing the structural complexity of forests, by homogenizing landscape mosaics of woody debris, snags, canopy layers, tree age and size diversity, and forest gaps, species diversity has also been reduced and simplified." Livestock grazing did not widely affect montane forests because, with the exception of scattered meadows, forage in these ecosystems is scarce, and most sheep and cattle concentrate their summer grazing in alpine meadows. Some areas of montane forests, however, are heavily affected by air pollution (see Chapter 7, "Atmospheric Chemistry").

Current Management Strategies

Fuels Treatment

Fuels treatment is becoming the dominant forest management activity on public lands throughout the montane forest region of California. Mechanical thinning, prescribed fire, or combinations of both are most often used to reduce fuels (Safford et al. 2009; Safford, Stevens et al. 2012). Although controversy has persisted over the ecological effects of these treatments, a recent article synthesizing published studies found "few unintended consequences, since most ecosystem components (vegetation, soils, wildlife, bark beetles, carbon sequestration) exhibit very subtle effects or no measurable effects at all" to treatments (Stephens et al. 2012). Aside from controversy, limited budgets and other regulatory constraints have significantly reduced the pace and scale of fuels treatments (North et al. 2015). First-priority actions usually treat areas near homes in the wildland-urban interface (or WUI). With increasing home construction in these areas, more fuel treatment effort has been concentrated in these areas and correspondingly less in the larger forest matrix (Theobold and Romme 2007). One study of federal forestlands in the Sierra Nevada compared current levels of all fuels reduction treatments (including wildfire) to historical levels of fuel reduction from frequent fire. The study's authors found that fewer than 20% of forests needing treatment were actually treated each year (North, Collins et al. 2012). They also calculated that at current rates more than 60% of the forest would never get treated, as maintenance of existing treatments would eventually subsume all of the fuels reduction effort.

In mechanical fuels reduction, two measures are commonly used for implementing treatments: maximum tree diameter

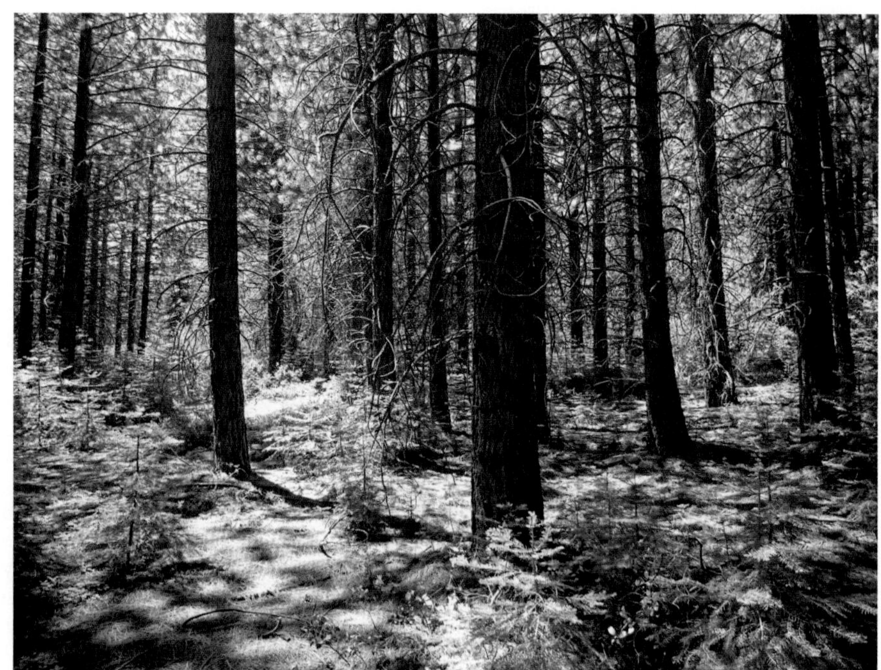

FIGURE 27.7 A pine plantation forest managed to maximize tree growth rates. A single tree species is planted at regular spacing, producing a simplified stand structure. Photo: Malcolm North.

FIGURE 27.8 A prescribed burn at Blodgett Experimental Forest burning at low intensity and effectively reducing fuel loads. Photo: Kevin Krasnow.

removed ("diameter limits") and minimum residual canopy cover. These metrics are set by the standards and guidelines in planning documents (e.g., SNFPA 2004). Diameter limits and canopy cover requirements are intended to ensure that treatments will move forest structure toward an "old forest" condition. If the diameter limit is set too high, large trees that do not substantially affect fuel conditions might be removed (Bigelow and North 2012). If the diameter limit is set too low, treatment might not produce the open conditions described by studies of historical forest structure (Beaty and Taylor 2007, 2008, Collins et al. 2011, Taylor et al., 2013) or create enough openings to regenerate shade-intolerant, fire-resistant species such as pines (Bigelow et al. 2011).

Fire, as both prescribed burning and managed wildfire, is generally underused for fuels treatment (Figure 27.8). Although ecological restoration of these forests requires fire, numerous constraints limit its use (Collins et al. 2010; North, Collins et al. 2012). These include impacts to local communities from smoke production, reduced recreation opportunities, inadequate personnel to conduct and monitor fires, liability for fire escapes, and risk-adverse policies and institutions. Many concerns about fuel treatment intensity and fire use are inherently social in nature (McCaffrey and Olsen 2012). Addressing these issues will require more focused engagement and education of local communities and the general public to balance shorter-term impacts with the potential for longer-term benefits.

Increasing Forest Heterogeneity and Resilience

Efforts to increase FOREST RESILIENCE have emphasized management strategies that work with and adapt to dynamic ecological processes at different scales (North et al. 2014). Management is now often focused on restoring heterogeneous forest conditions consistent with how productivity and historical fire intensity affected stand- and landscape-level forest conditions (North and Keeton 2008, Lydersen and North

2012) (see Figure 27.6). Forest managers use existing stand conditions and topography as a template to vary treatments in order to simultaneously achieve objectives such as fire hazard reduction, provision of wildlife habitat, and forest restoration (Knapp et al. 2012; North, Boynton et al. 2012). Within stands, thinning treatments attempt to create the ICO (individual tree, clumps of trees, and openings) structure that would have been created by frequent fire. Managers vary the proportions and sizes of these three structural conditions with small-scale changes in soil moisture and microclimate conditions (North, Stine et al. 2009, North 2012). At a larger scale, managers try to produce the forest density and composition associated with different slope positions and aspects that affect productivity and would have influenced fire severity (Underwood et al. 2010; North, Boynton et al. 2012).

Restoration Successes

Several national parks in California have recognized the importance of fire in montane forests and been able to overcome the many challenges associated with managing fire. Two of the most notable examples are the Illilouette basin in Yosemite National Park and the Sugarloaf basin in Sequoia–Kings Canyon National Park. In both areas, lightning-ignited fires have been allowed to burn relatively unimpeded since the early 1970s (see Lead Photo for this chapter). Although both areas experienced several decades of fire suppression, fire occurrence since the onset of natural fire programs in the 1970s is similar to that in the historical period (1700–1900, prior to fire suppression) (Collins and Stephens 2007). In addition, fire effects and interactions among fires in the program are consistent with our understanding of how historical fires burned in these landscapes (Collins et al. 2007, Collins et al. 2009, Collins and Stephens 2010, van Wagtendonk et al. 2012).

This suggests that fire in both areas might approximate a restored regime. This type of restoration cannot likely take place across much of the montane forest region with managed fire alone. However, the examples of Sugarloaf and Illilouette basins, as well as other areas with successful managed fire programs such as Lassen Volcanic National Park, illustrate the potential to expand fire use to meet restoration objectives. An important objective of these programs is to allow fires to burn under a range of fuel moisture and weather conditions rather than only under the fairly extreme conditions associated with "escaped" wildfires common on Forest Service land managed for fire suppression (Miller, Collins et al. 2012; North, Collins et al. 2012, Lydersen, North et al. 2014). The Forest Service and other landowners sometimes object to wider use of fire. Their reasons can include pursuit of multiple objectives, air quality restrictions, and lack of budget and personnel.

Future Scenarios

Drought and Bark Beetles

Warming temperatures will probably reduce the depth and duration of montane snowpacks, lengthening and deepening the summer drought. This will likely increase moisture stress for many forests (Safford, North et al. 2012, McDowell and Allen 2015) (Figure 27.9). Climate models currently do not agree on future precipitation patterns in California, but they all predict temperature increases and greater year-to-year variability. This will likely mean more pronounced El Niño/La Niña cycles that drive cycling between moderate snowpacks and potentially none at all for montane forests. These drought cycles could become bottlenecks for forest regeneration, killing most seedlings and saplings in dry conditions that are pronounced and/or occur in sequential years (Gray et al. 2005; North, Hurteau et al. 2005).

Climate change could also increase bark beetle populations because warming can allow extra generations to complete their life cycles each year and adult beetle emergence and flight to occur early in the season and to continue further into the fall (Fettig 2012). Mountain pine beetles will likely become especially damaging to higher-elevation conifer forests (Bentz et al. 2010). Large, warming- and drought-driven beetle outbreaks have recently occurred in the U.S. and Canadian Rockies (Kurz et al. 2008) and might occur in California's montane forests in the future. Bark beetle populations currently restricted to the southwestern U.S. and Mexico will also likely move northward as climates warm.

Fire

The combination of warmer climate and possibly increased fuel production (due to lengthened growing seasons) will likely cause more frequent and extensive fires throughout western North America (Price and Rind 1994, Flannigan et al. 2000, Committee on Stabilization Targets for Atmospheric Greenhouse Gas Concentrations et al. 2011, Yue et al. 2013). A recent study from the northern Sierra Nevada indicates noticeable increases in the occurrence of high-to-extreme fire weather since the mid-1990s (Collins 2014). These increases, which are expected to continue at least into the near future, are likely contributing to the rising incidence of large fires in the region (Collins 2014, Lydersen, North et al. 2014). Fire responds rapidly to changes in climate and could overshadow the direct effects of climate change on tree species distributions and migrations (Flannigan et al. 2000, Dale et al. 2001). Under most climate change projections, fire will increase in frequency, size, and severity (Flannigan et al. 2009). The human population of California is expected to increase to more than fifty million by 2050 with a large increase in wildland/urban interface settlements. While educational efforts can help to reduce fire ignitions and improve public safety, more people usually leads to more fire (Syphard et al. 2009). Increased frequencies and intensities of fire in coniferous forest in California will almost certainly drive abrupt changes in tree species compositions and will likely reduce the size and extent of old-growth forest conditions (McKenzie et al. 2004, Stephens et al. 2013).

Species Distribution

Projected changes in California's terrestrial avifauna and flora are likely over the next century. Stralberg et al. (2009) developed current and future species distribution models for sixty focal bird species and found that novel avian assemblages with no modern analogy could occupy over half of California. This implies a dramatic reshuffling of avian communities and altered pattern of species interactions, even in the upper elevations of the Sierra Nevada, where only a modest proportion of novel avian communities were projected. A similar study projected that 66% of California's native flora will experience greater than 80% reduction in range size within a cen-

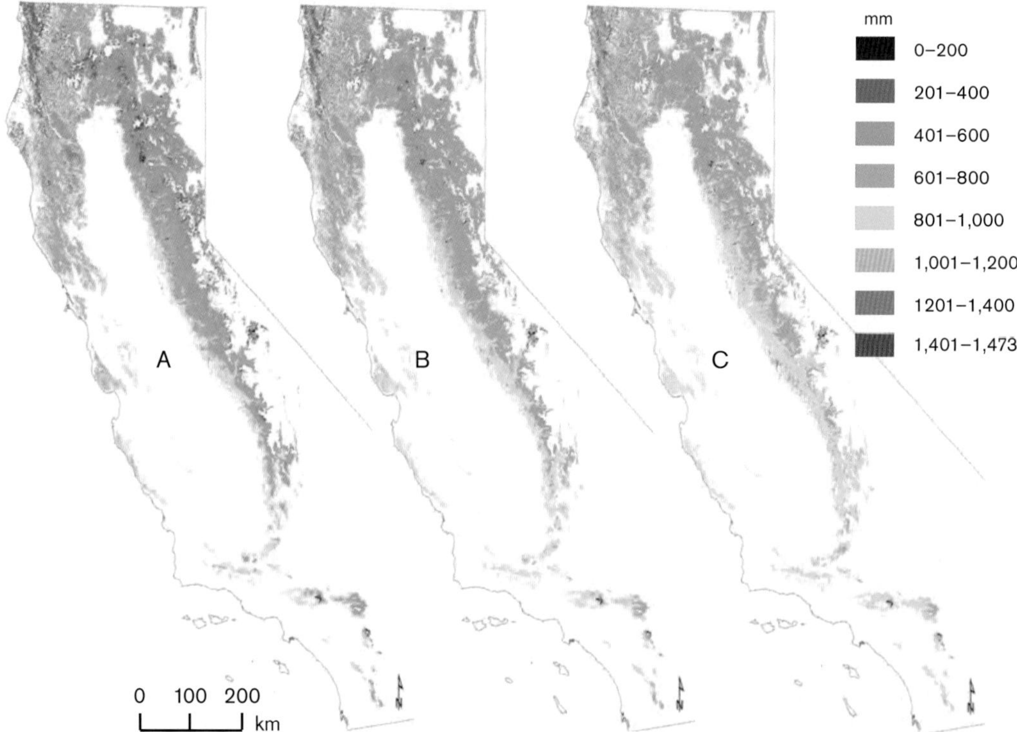

FIGURE 27.9 Current (A) and future (B, C) projections of climatic water deficit for California's montane forests. Climatic water deficit is the amount of water (scaled in millimeters [mm]) by which potential evapotranspiration exceeds actual evapotranspiration indicating relative drought stress. Projections based on (B) the Parallel Climate Model (PCM) and (C) the Geophysical Fluid Dynamics Laboratory CM 2.1 model (GFDL), using the A2 (medium-high) CO_2 emissions scenario. Illustration by Jim Thorne.

tury (Loarie et al. 2008). Their study identified the southern Sierra Nevada and the coastal mountains of northwest California as climate change refugia, defined as areas projected to harbor species with shrinking ranges (presumably retaining subsets of regional species assemblages over time). Loarie et al. (2008) recommended novel adaptive management approaches and large-scale planning efforts that promote landscape and regional habitat connectivity. They also recommended serious consideration of human-assisted dispersal of California's flora and prioritization of climate change refugia for conservation and restoration.

California's montane forests have withstood the pressures of the state's burgeoning human population, frequent droughts and the long-term, general absence of its keystone process—frequent, low-intensity fire. Yet the future promises that these stressors will persist and possibly be amplified by climatic change. The challenge to conserving California montane forests into the future is to increase their resilience while sustaining the old growth, wildlife, and ecosystem services that make them so unique among the world's temperate forests.

Summary

The strong, seasonal drought and historically frequent fire associated with a Mediterranean-type climate shape the composition and distribution of California's montane forests. Differences in fire intensity and soil moisture availability associated with small- and large-scale topographic features such as drainages, aspect, and slope position affect ecosystem productivity and processes as well as ecosystem resilience to the most common stressors: fire, drought, and bark beetles. The resulting forest is highly heterogeneous, and the range of habitats—from dry, open woodlands with understory shrubs to dense, mesic, multistory stands—supports the highest vertebrate diversity of California's forest types. Sensitive and threatened species are most associated with forest structures and habitat that have become increasingly rare after a century of logging and fire suppression.

Management of these forests on public lands tends to focus on reducing densities of trees and fuels accumulated from fire suppression and increasing frequency and extent of low-intensity burns. This type of burning has demonstrated potential to restore many ecosystem processes that have stalled in the long absence of fire and to increase forest resilience to stresses likely to increase under climate change, such as drought and pests. Montane forests provide important ecosystem services to the state's large and growing population, including much of its water, hydroelectric power, and substantial carbon storage, which can help offset human CO_2 emissions. Although many challenges confront montane forests as human population and rural home construction increase, lessons learned from past forest management and progressive use of fire by the National Parks provide future pathways for sustaining and improving the ecological resilience of these forests.

Acknowledgments

We would like to thank Ross Gerrard, who provided the montane ecosystem map, and Carl Skinner, who provide feedback and photographs—both of the U.S. Forest Service Pacific Southwest Research Station.

Recommended Reading

Fites-Kaufman, J., P. Rundel, N. L. Stephenson, and D. A. Weixelman 2007. Montane and subalpine vegetation of the Sierra Nevada and Cascade Ranges. Pages 456–501 in M. Barbour, T. Keeler–Wolf, and A. A. Schoenherr, editors. Terrestrial Vegetation of California. University of California Press, Berkeley, California.

North, M., P. Stine, K. O'Hara, W. Zielinski, and S. Stephens. 2009. An ecosystem management strategy for Sierran mixed–conifer forests. Pacific Southwest General Technical Report. PSW–GTR-220. U.S. Department of Agriculture Forest Service, Albany, California.

Safford, H. D., M. North, and M. D. Meyer. 2012. Climate change and the relevance of historical forest conditions. Pages 23–45 in M. North, editor. Managing Sierra Nevada Forests. General Technical Report PSW-GTR-237. U.S. Department of Agriculture Forest Service, Pacific Southwest Research Station, Albany, California.

Stephenson, N. L. 1998. Actual evapotranspiration and deficit: Biologically meaningful correlates of vegetation distribution across spatial scales. Journal of Biogeography 25(5):855–870.

Glossary

ABIOTIC Not associated with or derived from living organisms. Abiotic factors in an environment include factors such as sunlight, temperature, wind patterns, and precipitation.

ALFISOLS One of twelve soil orders in the U.S. Soil Taxonomy, Alfisols make up 9.6% of global soils. They are primarily in cool, moisture regions of the Northern Hemisphere and have sufficient water to support at least three consecutive months of plant growth. They have high-to-medium base saturation, are moderately weathered, and are rich in iron and aluminum.

ANDISOLS One of twelve soil orders in the U.S. Soil Taxonomy, Andisols account for only 0.7% of soils globally. They are formed from volcanic parent material, are high in organic matter content and phosphorous, and have a low bulk density.

BASAL AREA A sum of the cross-sectional area of trees stems, measured by the diameter at breast height (dbh) (1.3 meters above the ground) and standardized to a hectare or acre area. It is a commonly used forestry measure that indicates the relative amount of biomass (and by implication resource use) of different sizes and species of trees within a stand.

CANOPY CLOSURE This is a point measure of how much of the sky hemisphere is obscured by vegetation.

CANOPY COVER This is a stand-level average of how vertically porous a forest canopy is.

DIAMETER DISTRIBUTION The number of trees in different diameter-size classes. It is a widely used measure in forestry that provides insight into a stand's structure and disturbance history.

EDAPHIC Produced or influenced by the soil.

FOREST RESILIENCE The capacity of a forest to absorb disturbance and reorganize while still retaining its essential structure, composition, and ecological functions.

INCEPTISOLS One of twelve soil orders in the U.S. Soil Taxonomy, Inceptisols (9.9% globally) often lack distinctive subsurface horizons. Inceptisols are generally found in landscapes with continuously eroded conditions or areas with young deposits.

SERAL A phase in the sequential development of a community.

ULTISOLS One of twelve soil orders in the U.S. Soil Taxonomy, Ultisols (8.5% globally) have low base saturation at depth.

References

Agee, J. K. 1993. Fire ecology of Pacific Northwest forests. Island Press, Washington, D.C.

Airola, D. A., and R. H. Barrett. 1985. Foraging and habitat relationships of insect-gleaning birds in a Sierra-Nevada mixed-conifer forest. Condor 87:205–216.

Alexander, E. B., R. G. Coleman, T. Keeler-Wolf, and S. P. Harrison. 2007. Serpentine geoecology of western North America. Oxford University Press, Oxford, UK.

Allen, C. D., K. Alison, H. C. Macalady, D. Bachelet, N. G. McDowell, M. Vennetier, T. Kitzberger, A. Rigling, D. D. Breshears, E. H. Hogg, P. Gonzalez, R. J. Fensham, Z. Zhang, J. Castro, N. Demidova, J. H. Lim, A. Gillian, S. W. Running, A. Semerci, and N. Cobb. 2010. A global overview of drought and heat-induced tree mortality reveals emerging climate change risks for forests. Forest Ecology and Management 259:660–684.

Anderson, J. R., E. E. Hardy, J. T. Roach, and R. E. Witmer. 1976. A land use and land cover classification system for use with remote sensor data. Geological Survey. U.S.G.S. Circular 671. U.S. Geological Survey, Washington, D.C.

Anderson, M. K., M. G. Barbour, and V. Whitworth. 1997. A world of balance and plenty—Land, plants, animals, and humans in a pre-European California. California History 76:12–47.

Ansley, J. A. S., and J. J. Battles. 1998. Forest composition, structure, and change in an old-growth mixed conifer forest in the northern Sierra Nevada. Journal of the Torrey Botanical Society 125:297–308.

Armstrong, C. F., and C. K. Stidd. 1967. A moisture-balance profile on the Sierra Nevada. Journal of Hydrology 5:258–268.

Atwater, B. F., D. P. Adam, J. P. Bradbury, R. M. Forester, R. K. Mark, W. R. Lettis, G. R. Fisher, K. W. Gobalet, and S. W. Robinson. 1986. A fan dam for Tulare Lake, California, and implications for the Wisconsin glacial history of the Sierra-Nevada. Geological Society of America Bulletin 97:97–109.

Baldwin, B. G., D. H. Goldman, R. Patterson, and T. J. Rosatti. 2012. The Jepson manual. Second edition. Benjamin Cummings Publishing, Menlo Park, California.

Barbour, M., B. Pavlik, F. Drysdale, and S. Lindstrom. 1993. California's changing landscapes: Diversity and conservation of California vegetation. California Native Plant Society, Sacramento, California.

Barbour, M. G., and R. A. Minnich. 2000. California upland forests and woodlands. Pages 162–202 in M. G. Barbour and B. J. Billings, editors. North American Terrestrial Vegetation. Cambridge University Press, Cambridge, UK.

Barbour, M. G., N. H. Berg, T. G. F. Kittel, and M. E. Kunz. 1991. Snowpack and the distribution of a major vegetation ecotone in the Sierra-Nevada of California. Journal of Biogeography 18:141–149.

Barbour, M. G., T. Keeler-Wolf, and A. A. Schoenherr, editors. 2007. Terrestrial vegetation of California. Third edition. University of California Press, Berkeley, California.

Battles, J. J., P. Gonzalez, T. Robards, B. M. Collins, and D. S. Saah. 2013. California forest and rangeland greenhouse gas inventory development. Final Report to California Air Resources Board No. 10-778.

Beaty, R. M., and A. H. Taylor. 2008. Fire history and the structure and dynamics of a mixed conifer forest landscape in the northern Sierra Nevada, Lake Tahoe Basin, California, USA. Forest Ecology and Management 255:707–719.

———. 2007. Fire disturbance and forest structure in old-growth mixed conifer forests in the northern Sierra Nevada, California. Journal of Vegetation Science 18:879–890.

———. 2001. Spatial and temporal variation of fire regimes in a mixed conifer forest landscape, southern Cascades, California, USA. Journal of Biogeography 28:955–966.

Beesley, D. 1996. The opening of the Sierra Nevada and the beginnings of conservation in California—1827–1900. California History 75:322–337.

Bentz, B. J., J. Regniere, C. Fettig, E. M. Hansen, J. L. Hayes, J. A. Hicke, R. G. Kelsey, J. F. Negron, and S. J. Seybold. 2010. Climate change and bark beetles of the western U.S. and Canada: Direct and indirect effects. Bioscience 60:602–613.

Bigelow, S. W., and M. P. North. 2012. Microclimate effects of fuels-reduction and group-selection silviculture: Implications for fire

behavior in Sierran mixed-conifer forests. Forest Ecology and Management 264:51–59.
Bigelow, S. W., M. P. North, and C. F. Salk. 2011. Using light to predict fuels-reduction and group selection effects on succession in Sierran mixed-conifer forest. Canadian Journal of Forest Research 41:2051–2063.
Bock, C. E., and J. F. Lynch. 1970. Breeding bird populations of burned and unburned conifer forest in the Sierra Nevada. The Condor 72:182–189.
Bouldin, J. 1999. Twentieth-century changes in forests of the Sierra Nevada, California. PhD dissertation. University of California, Davis, California.
Briles, C. E., C. Whitlock, and P. J. Bartlein. 2005. Postglacial vegetation, fire, and climate history of the Siskiyou Mountains, Oregon, USA. Quaternary Research 64:44–56.
Brown, P. M., C. L. Wienk, and A. J. Symstad. 2008. Fire and forest history at Mount Rushmore. Ecological Applications 18:1984–1999.
Bull, E. L., C. G. Parks, and T. R. Torgersen. 1997. Trees and logs important to wildlife in the interior Columbia River basin. PNW-GTR-391. U.S. Department of Agriculture Forest Service. Portland, Oregon.
Burnett, R., D. Jongsomjit, and D. Stralberg. 2009. Avian monitoring in the Lassen and Plumas National Forest: 2008 Annual Report. Contribution 1684. Pages 104–186.
Burns, R. M., and B. H. Honkala. 1990. Silvics of North America. Volume 1, Conifers. Agriculture Handbook 654. U.S. Department of Agriculture Forest Service, Washington, D.C.
California Department of Forest and Fire Protection. 2010. California's forests and rangelands: 2010 Assessment. California Department of Forest and Fire Protection, Sacramento, California.
CALVEG. 2013. CALVEG mapping zones. U.S. Department of Agriculture Forest Service, Pacific Southwest Region. <http://www.fs.usda.gov/detail/r5/landmanagement/resourcemanagement/?cid=stelprdb5347192>. Accessed June 2014.
Campbell, J. L., M. E. Harmon, and S. R. Mitchell. 2012. Can fuel-reduction treatments really increase forest carbon storage in the western U.S. by reducing future fire emissions? Frontiers in Ecology and the Environment 10:83–90.
Caprio, A. C., and T. W. Swetnam. 1995. Historic fire regimes along an elevational gradient on the west slope of the Sierra Nevada, California. Pages 173–179 in J. K. Brown, R. W. Mutch, C. W. Spoon, and R. H. Wakimoto, editors. Proceedings: Symposium on fire in wilderness and park management. General Technical Report INT-GTR-320. U.S. Department of Agriculture Forest Service, Intermountain Research Station, Ogden, Utah.
Carey, A. B. 2002. Response of northern flying squirrels to supplementary dens. Wildlife Society Bulletin 30:547–556.
Carey, A. B., T. M. Wilson, C. C. Maguire, and B. L. Biswell. 1997. Dens of northern flying squirrels in the Pacific Northwest. Journal of Wildlife Management 61:684–699.
Carlson, C. H., S. Z. Dobrowksi, and H. D. Safford. 2012. Variation in tree mortality and regeneration affect forest carbon recovery following fuel treatments and wildfire in the Lake Tahoe Basin, California, USA. Carbon Balance and Management 7:7. <doi:10.1186/1750-0680-7-7>.
Cheng, S. 2004. Forest Service research natural areas in California. PSW-GTR-188. U.S. Department of Agriculture Forest Service, Albany, California.
Cockle, K. L., K. Martin, and T. Wesolowski. 2011. Woodpeckers, decays, and the future of cavity-nesting vertebrate communities worldwide. Frontiers in Ecology and the Environment 9:377–382.
Collins, B. M. 2014. Fire weather and large fire potential in the northern Sierra Nevada. Agricultural and Forest Meteorology. 189: 30–35.
Collins, B. M., J. M. Lydersen, R. G. Everett, D. L. Fry, and S. L. Stephens. 2015. Novel characterization of landscape-level variability in historical vegetation structure. Ecological Applications 25:1167–1174.
Collins, B. M., and G. B. Roller. 2013. Early forest dynamics in stand-replacing fire patches in the northern Sierra Nevada, California, USA. Landscape Ecology. <doi:10.1007/s10980-013-9923-8>.
Collins, B. M., and S. L. Stephens. 2010. Stand-replacing patches within a "mixed severity" fire regime: Quantitative characterization using recent fires in a long-established natural fire area. Landscape Ecology 25:927–939.
———. 2007. Managing natural wildfires in Sierra Nevada wilderness areas. Frontiers in Ecology and the Environment 5:523–527.
Collins, B. M., J. D. Miller, A. E. Thode, M. Kelly, J. W. van Wagtendonk, and S. L. Stephens. 2009. Interactions among wildland fires in a long-established Sierra Nevada natural fire area. Ecosystems 12:114–128.
Collins, B. M., M. Kelly, J. W. van Wagtendonk, and S. L. Stephens. 2007. Spatial patterns of large natural fires in Sierra Nevada wilderness areas. Landscape Ecology 22:545–557.
Collins, B. M., R. G. Everett, and S. L. Stephens. 2011. Impacts of fire exclusion and managed fire on forest structure in an old growth Sierra Nevada mixed-conifer forest. Ecosphere 2.
Collins, B. M., S. L. Stephens, J. M. Moghaddas, and J. Battles. 2010. Challenges and approaches in planning fuel treatments across fire-excluded forested landscapes. Journal of Forestry 108:24–31.
Committee on Stabilization Targets for Atmospheric Greenhouse Gas Concentrations, Board on Atmospheric Sciences and Climate, Division on Earth and Life Studies, and National Research Council. 2011. Climate stabilization targets: Emissions, concentrations, and impacts over decades to millennia. National Academies Press. Washington, D.C.
Concilio, A., S. Y. Ma, Q. L. Li, J. LeMoine, J. Q. Chen, M. North, D. Moorhead, and R. Jensen. 2005. Soil respiration response to prescribed burning and thinning in mixed-conifer and hardwood forests. Canadian Journal of Forest Research 35:1581–1591.
Concilio, A., S. Y. Ma, S. R. Ryu, M. North, and J. Q. Chen. 2006. Soil respiration response to experimental disturbances over three years. Forest Ecology and Management 228:82–90.
Critchfield, W. B. 1971. Profiles of California vegetation. Research Paper PSW-76. Pacific Southwest Forest and Range Experiment Station, U.S. Department of Agriculture Forest Service, Berkeley, California.
Dahlgren, R. A., J. L. Boettinger, G. L. Huntington, and R. G. Amundson. 1997. Soil development along an elevational transect in the western Sierra Nevada, California. Geoderma 78:207–236.
Dale, V. H., L. A. Joyce, S. G. McNulty, R. P. Neilson, M. P. Ayres, M. Flannigan, P. J. Hanson, L. C. Irland, A. E. Lugo, C. J. Peterson, D. Simberloff, F. J. Swanson, B. J. Stocks, and B. W. Wotton. 2001. Climate change and forest disturbances. Bioscience 51:723–734.
Davis, F. W., P. A. Stine, D. M. Stoms, M. I. Borchert, and A. D. Hollander. 1995. Gap analysis of the actual vegetation of California 1. The southwestern region. Madroño 42:40–78.
Dettinger, M. D., F. M. Ralph, T. Das, P. J. Neiman, and D. R. Cayan. 2011. Atmospheric rivers, floods, and the water resources of California. Water 3:445–478.
Dolanc, C. R., H. D. Safford, S. Z. Dobrowksi, and J. H. Thorne. 2013. Twentieth century shifts in abundance and composition of vegetation types of the Sierra Nevada, CA, USA. Applied Vegetation Science. <doi:10.1111/avsc.12079>.
Dolph, K. L., S. R. Mori, and W. W. Oliver. 1995. Long-term response of old-growth stands to varying levels of partial cutting in the eastside pine type. Western Journal of Applied Forestry 10:101–108.
Duane, T. P. 1996. Recreation in the Sierra. Pages 557–610 in Sierra Nevada Ecosystem Project. Wildland Resources Center Report No. 37. University of California, Davis, California.
Earles, M., M. North, and M. Hurteau. 2014. Wildfire and drought dynamics destabilize carbon stores of fire-suppressed forests. Ecological Applications. 24:732–740.
Energy Almanac. 2014. California Energy Commission. <http://www.energyalmanac.ca.gov/renewables/hydro/>. Accessed June 2015.
Erickson, H. E., P. Soto, D. W. Johnson, B. Roath, and C. Hunsaker. 2005. Effects of vegetation patches on soil nutrient pools and fluxes within a mixed-conifer forest. Forest Science 51:211–220.
Essery, R., J. Pomeroy, J. Parviainen, and P. Storck. 2003. Sublimation of snow from coniferous forests in a climate model. Journal of Climate 16:1855–1864.
Fettig, C. J. 2012. Forest health and bark beetles. Pages 13–22 in M. North, editor. Managing Sierra Nevada Forests. PSW-GTR-237. U.S. Department of Agriculture Forest Service, Albany, California.
Fettig, C. J., K. D. Klepzig, R. F. Billings, A. S. Munson, T. E. Nebeker, J. F. Negron, and J. T. Nowak. 2007. The effectivenss of vegetation management practices for prevention and control of bark bettle outbreaks in coniferous forests of the western and southern United States. Forest Ecology and Management 238:24–53.

Fire Effects Information System (FEIS) <http://www.fs.fed.us/database/feis/>. Accessed July 1, 2015.

Fites-Kaufman, J., P. Rundel, N. L. Stephenson, and D. A. Weixelman. 2007. Montane and subalpine vegetation of the Sierra Nevada and Cascade Ranges. Pages 456–501 in M. Barbour, T. Keeler-Wolf, and A. A. Schoenherr, editors. Terrestrial Vegetation of California. University of California Press, Berkeley, California.

Flannigan, M. D., B. J. Stocks, and B. M. Wotton. 2000. Climate change and forest fires. Science of the Total Environment 262:221–229.

Flannigan, M., M. A. Krawchuk, W. J. de Groot, B. M. Wotton, and L. M. Gowman. 2009. Implications of changing climate for global wildland fire. International Journal of Wildland Fire 18:483–507.

Fried, J. S., and X. Zhou. 2008. Forest inventory-based estimation of carbon stocks and flux in California forests in 1990. PNW-GTR-750. U.S. Department of Agriculture Forest Service, Portland, Oregon.

Fry, D. L., and S. L. Stephens. 2006. Influence of humans and climate on the fire history of a ponderosa pine-mixed conifer forest in the southeastern Klamath Mountains, California. Forest Ecology and Management 223:428–438.

Fry, D. L., S. L. Stephens, B. M. Collins, M. P. North, E. Franco-Vizcaino, and S. J. Gill. 2014. Contrasting spatial patterns in active-fire and fire-suppressed Mediterranean climate old-growth, mixed conifer forests. PLoS One. doi 10.1371/journal.pone.0088985.

Goforth, B. R., and R. A. Minnich. 2008. Densification, stand-replacement wildfire, and extirpation of mixed conifer forest in Cuyamaca Rancho State Park, southern California. Forest Ecology and Management 256:36–45.

Golding, D. L., and R. H. Swanson. 1986. Snow distribution patterns in clearings and adjacent forest. Water Resources Research 22:1931–1940.

Gonzalez, P., J. J. Battles, B. M. Collins, T. Robards, and D. S. Saah. 2015. Aboveground live carbon stock changes of California wildland ecosystems, 2001–2010. Forest Ecology and Management 348: 68–77.

Goulden, M., R. G. Anderson, R. C. Bales, A. E. Kelly, M. Meadows, and G. C. Winston. 2012. Evapotranspiration along an elevation gradient in California's Sierra Nevada. Journal of Geophysical Research—Biogeosciences 117. G03028.

Gray, A. N., H. S. J. Zald, R. A. Kern, and M. North. 2005. Stand conditions associated with tree regeneration in Sierran mixed-conifer forests. Forest Science 51:198–210.

Guarin, A., and A. H. Taylor. 2005. Drought triggered tree mortality in mixed conifer forests in Yosemite National Park, California, USA. Forest Ecology and Management 218:229–244.

Haller, J. R. 1959. Factors affecting the distribution of ponderosa and Jeffrey pines in California. Madroño 15:65–71.

Hanson, C. T., and M. P. North. 2008. Postfire woodpecker foraging in salvage-logged and unlogged forests of the Sierra Nevada. Condor 110:777–782.

Harden, D. R. 2004. California geology. Pearson/Prentice Hall, Upper Saddle River, New Jersey.

Hilimire, K., J. Nesmith, A. Caprio, R. Milne, and L. Mutch. 2012. Winds of change: Characterizing windthrown trees in a Sierra Nevada mixed conifer forest. Mountain Views 6. <http://www.fs.fed.us/psw/cirmount>. Accessed June 2015.

Holland, V. L., and D. J. Keil. 1995. California vegetation. Kendall/Hunt Publishing Company, Dubuque, Iowa.

Hunsaker, C. T., T. W. Whitaker, and R. C. Bales. 2012. Snowmelt runoff and water yield along elevation and temperature gradients in California's Southern Sierra Nevada. Journal of the American Water Resources Association 48:667–678.

Hurteau, M., and M. North. 2009. Fuel treatment effects on tree-based forest carbon storage and emissions under modeled wildfire scenarios. Frontiers in Ecology and the Environment 7:409–414.

Hurteau, M. D., and M. North. 2010. Carbon recovery rates following different wildfire risk mitigation treatments. Forest Ecology and Management 260:930–937.

Hurteau, M. D, B. A. Hungate, G. W. Koch, M. P. North and G. R. Smith. 2013. Aligning ecology and markets in the forest carbon cycle. Frontiers in Ecology and the Environment 11: 37–42.

Hurteau, M. D., G. W. Koch, and B. A. Hungate. 2008. Carbon protection and fire risk reduction: Toward a full accounting of forest carbon offsets. Frontiers in Ecology and the Environment 6:493–498.

Innes, J. C., M. P. North, and N. Williamson. 2006. Effect of thinning and prescribed fire restoration treatments on woody debris and snag dynamics in a Sierran old-growth, mixed-conifer forest. Canadian Journal of Forest Research 36:3783–3793.

Innes, J. L. 1992. Forest decline. Progress in Physical Geography 16:1–64.

Innes, R. J., D. H. Van Vuren, D. A. Kelt, M. L. Johnson, J. A. Wilson, and P. A. Stine. 2007. Habitat associations of dusky-footed woodrats (*Neotonia fuscipes*) in mixed-conifer forest of the northern Sierra Nevada. Journal of Mammalogy 88:1523–1531.

Jennings, S. B., N. D. Brown, and D. Sheil. 1999. Assessing forest canopies and understorey illumination: Canopy closure, canopy cover, and other measures. Forestry 72:59–73.

Johnson, D. W., J. D. Murphy, R. F. Walker, W. W. Miller, D. W. Glass, and D. E. Todd. 2008. The combined effects of thinning and prescribed fire on carbon and nutrient budgets in a Jeffrey pine forest. Annals of Forest Science 65:601–613.

Johnson, D. W., W. W. Miller, R. B. Susfalk, J. D. Murphy, R. A. Dahlgren, and D. W. Glass. 2009. Biogeochemical cycling in forest soils of the eastern Sierra Nevada Mountains, USA. Forest Ecology and Management 258:2249–2260.

Kane, V., M. North, J. Lutz, D. M. Churchill, S. L. Roberts, D. F. Smith, R. McGaughey, and J. Kane. 2014. Assessing fire effects on forest spatial structure using a fusion of Landsat and airborne LiDAR data in Yosemite National Park. Remote Sensing of Environment. 151:89–101.

Kane, V. R., J. A. Lutz, C. A., Cansler, N. A. Povak, D. J. Chruchill, D. F. Smith, J. T. Kane, and M. P. North. 2015. Water balance and topography predict fire and forest structure patterns. Forest Ecology and Management 338:1–13.

Keeley, J. E. 2012. Ecology and evolution of pine life histories. Annals of Forest Science 69:445–453.

Keith, H., B. G. Mackey, and D. B. Lindenmayer. 2009. Re-evaluation of forest biomass carbon stocks and lessons from the world's most carbon-dense forests. Proceedings of the National Academy of Sciences 106:11635–11640.

Kilgore, B. M., and D. Taylor. 1979. Fire history of a sequoia-mixed conifer forest. Ecology 60:129–142.

Kinloch, B. B. 1992. Distribution and frequency of a gene for resistance to white-pine blishter rust in natural populations of sugar pine. Canadian Journal of Botany 70:1319–1323.

Knapp, E. E., C. G. Skinner, M. P. North, and B. L. Estes. 2013. Long-term overstory and understory change following logging and fire exclusion a Sierra Nevada mixed-conifer forest. Forest Ecology and Management 310:903–914.

Knapp, E., M. North, M. Benech, and B. Estes. 2012. The variable-density thinning study at Stanislaus-Tuolumne Experimental Forest. Pages 127–140 in M. North, editor. Managing Sierra Nevada Forests. PSW-GTR-237 U.S. Department of Agriculture Forest Service, Albany, California.

Kruckeberg, A. R. 1984. California serpentines: Flora, vegetation, geology, soils, and management problems. University of California Publications in Botany 78:1–180.

Kurz, W. A., C. C. Dymond, G. Stinson, G. J. Rampley, E. T. Neilson, A. L. Carroll, T. Ebata, and L. Safranyik. 2008. Mountain pine beetle and forest carbon feedback to climate change. Nature 452:987–990.

Larson, A. J., and D. M. Churchill. 2012. Tree spatial patterns in fire-frequent forests of western North America, including mechanisms of pattern formation and implications for designing fuel reduction and restoration treatments. Forest Ecology and Management 267:74–92.

Lee, D. C., and L. L. Irwin. 2005. Assessing risks to spotted owls from forest thinning in fire-adapted forests of the western United States. Forest Ecology and Management 211:191–209.

Lenihan, J. M., D. Bachelet, R. P. Neilson, and R. Drapek. 2008. Response of vegetation distribution, ecosystem productivity, and fire to climate change scenarios for California. Climatic Change 87:S215–S230.

Lieberg, J. B. 1902. Forest conditions in the northern Sierra Nevada, California. Professional Paper 8. Government Printing Office, Washington, D.C.

Lindstrand, L., and J. K. Nelson. 2006. Habitat, geologic, and soil characterstics of Shasta snow-reath (*Neviusia cliftonii*) populations. Madroño 53:65–68.

Loarie, S. R., B. E. Carter, K. Hayhoe, S. McMahon, R. Moe, C. A.

Knight, and D. D. Ackerly. 2008. Climate change and the future of California's endemic flora. PLoS One 3:e2502.

Logan, J. A., J. Regniere, and J. A. Powell. 2003. Assessing the impacts of global warming on forest pest dynamics. Frontiers in Ecology and the Environment 1:130–137.

Lutz, J. A., J. W. van Wagtendonk, and J. F. Franklin. 2009. Twentieth-century decline of large-diameter trees in Yosemite National Park, California, USA. Forest Ecology and Management 257:2296–2307.

Lydersen, J., and M. North. 2012. Topographic variation in structure of mixed-conifer forests under an active-fire regime. Ecosystems 15:1134–1146.

Lydersen, J. M., M. P. North, E. E. Knapp, and B. M. Collins. 2013. Quantifying spatial patterns of tree groups and gaps in mixed-conifer forests: Reference conditions and long-term changes following fire suppression and logging. Forest Ecology and Management 304:370–382.

Lydersen, J., M. North, and B. Collins. 2014. Severity of an uncharacteristically large wildfire, the Rim Fire, in forests with relatively restored frequent fire regimes. Forest Ecology and Management 328:326–334.

Major, J. 1977. California climate in relation to vegetation. Pages 11–74 in M. G. Barbour and J. Major, editors. Terrestrial vegetation of California. John Wiley & Sons, New York, New York.

Mallek, C., H. D. Safford, J. H. Viers, and J. D. Miller. 2013. Modern departures in fire severity and area vary by forest type, Sierra Nevada and southern Cascades, California, USA. Ecosphere 4:art153.

Maloney, P. E., and D. M. Rizzo. 2002. Dwarf mistletoe-host interactions in mixed-conifer forests in the Sierra Nevada. Phytopathology 92:597–602.

Maloney, P. E., D. R. Vogler, A. J. Eckert, C. E. Jensen, and D. B. Neale. 2011. Population biology of sugar pine (*Pinus lambertiana Dougl.*) with reference to historical disturbances in the Lake Tahoe Basin: Implications for restoration. Forest Ecology and Management 262:770–779.

Maloney, P. E., T. F. Smith, C. E. Jensen, J. Innes, D. M. Rizzo, and M. P. North. 2008. Initial tree mortality and insect and pathogen response to fire and thinning restoration treatments in an old-growth mixed-conifer forest of the Sierra Nevada, California. Canadian Journal of Forest Research 38:3011–3020.

Marra, J. L., and R. L. Edmonds. 2005. Soil anthropod responses to different patch types in a mixed-conifer forest of the Sierra Nevada. Forest Science 5:255–265.

Ma, S., J. Chen, M. North, H. E. Erickson, M. Bresee, and J. Le Moine. 2004. Short-term effects of experimental burning and thinning on soil respiration in an old-growth, mixed-conifer forest. Environmental Management 33:S148–S159.

Ma, S. Y., A. Concilio, B. Oakley, M. North, and J. Q. Chen. 2010. Spatial variability in microclimate in a mixed-conifer forest before and after thinning and burning treatments. Forest Ecology and Management 259:904–915.

Mayer, K. E., and W. F. Laudenslayer. 1988. A guide to wildlife habitats of California. Department of Fish and Game, Sacramento, California, 166 pages.

McCaffrey, S. M., and C. S. Olsen. 2012. Research perspectives on the public and fire management: A synthesis of current social science on eight essential questions. NRS-GTR-104. U.S. Department of Agriculture Forest Service, Newton Square, Pennsylvania.

McDonald, P. M. 1980. Seed dissemination in small clearcuttings in north-central California. General Technical Report PSW-150. U.S. Department of Agriculture, Forest Service, Pacific Southwest Forest and Range Experiment Station, Berkeley, California.

McDowell, N.G. and C.D. Allen. 2015. Darcy's law predicts widespread forest mortality under climate warming. Nature Climate Change 5:669–672.

McKelvey, K. S., and J. D. Johnston. 1992. Historical perspectives on forest of the Sierra Nevada and the Transverse Range of southern California: Forest conditions at the turn of the century. Pages 225–246 in J. Verner, K. S. McKelvey, B. R. Noon, R. J. Gutierrez, G. I. Gould Jr., and T. W. Beck, editors. The California Spotted Owl: A Technical Assessment of Its Current Status. PSW-GTR-133 U.S. Department of Agriculture Forest Service, Pacific Southwest Research Station, Albany, California.

McKenzie, D., Z. Gedalof, D. L. Peterson, and P. Mote. 2004. Climatic change, wildfire, and conservation. Conservation Biology 18:890–902.

Meyer, M. D., and H. D. Safford. 2011. Giant sequoia regeneration in groves exposed to wildfire and retention harvest. Fire Ecology 7:2–16.

Meyer, M. D., D. A. Kelt, and M. P. North. 2005. Nest trees of northern flying squirrels in the Sierra Nevada. Journal of Mammalogy 86:275–280.

———. 2007. Microhabitat associations of northern flying squirrels in burned and thinned forest stands of the Sierra Nevada. American Midland Naturalist 157:202–211.

Meyer, M. D., M. P. North, and D. A. Kelt. 2007. Nest trees of northern flying squirrels in Yosemite National Park, California. Southwestern Naturalist 52:157–161.

Meyer, M. D., M. P. North, A. N. Gray, and H. S. J. Zald. 2007. Influence of soil thickness on stand characteristics in a Sierra Nevada mixed-conifer forest. Plant and Soil 294:113–123.

Millennium Ecosystem Assessment (MEA). 2005. Ecosystems and human wellbeing: Synthesis. Island Press, Washington, D.C.

Miller, C., and D. L. Urban. 1999a. Forest pattern, fire, and climatic change in the Sierra Nevada. Ecosystems 2:76–87.

———. 1999b. A model of surface fire, climate, and forest pattern in the Sierra Nevada, California. Ecological Modelling 114:113–135.

Miller, J. D., and H. Safford. 2012. Trends in wildfire severity: 1984 to 2010 in the Sierra Nevada, Modoc Plateau, and Southern Cascades, California. Fire Ecology 8:41–57.

Miller, J. D., B. M. Collins, J. A. Lutz, S. L. Stephens, J. W. van Wagtendonk, and D. A. Yasuda. 2012. Differences in wildfires among ecoregions and land management agencies in the Sierra Nevada region, California, USA. Ecosphere 3:art80.

Miller, J. D., C. N. Skinner, H. D. Safford, E. E. Knapp, and C. M. Ramirez. 2012. Trends and causes of severity, size, and number of fires in northwestern California, USA. Ecological Applications 22:184–203.

Miller, J. D., H. D. Safford, M. Crimmins, and A. E. Thode. 2009. Quantitative evidence for increasing forest fire severity in the Sierra Nevada and Southern Cascade Mountains, California and Nevada, USA. Ecosystems 12:16–32.

Miller, N. L., K. E. Bashford, and E. Strem. 2003. Potential impacts of climate change on California hydrology. Journal of the American Water Resources Association 39:771–784.

Minnich, R. A. 2007. Climate, paleoclimate, and paleovegetation. Pages 43–70 in M. Barbour, T. Keeler-Wolf, and A. A. Schoenherr, editors. Terrestrial Vegetation of California. University of California Press, Berkeley, California.

Minore, D. 1979. Comparative autecological characteristics of northwestern tree species—a literature review. PNW-GTR-87. U.S. Forest Service, Portland, Oregon.

Mitchell, S. R., M. E. Harmon, and K. E. B. O'Connell. 2009. Forest fuel reduction alters fire severity and long-term carbon storage in three Pacific Northwest ecosystems. Ecological Applications 19:643–655.

Moen, C. A., and R. J. Gutierrez. 1997. California spotted owl habitat selection in the central Sierra Nevada. Journal of Wildlife Management 61:1281–1287.

Morgan, P., E. K. Heyerdahl, and C. E. Gibson. 2008. Multi-season climate synchronized forest fires throughout the twentieth century, Northern Rockies, USA. Ecology 89:717–728.

Morrison, M. L., R. J. Young, J. S. Romsos, and R. Golightly. 2009. Restoring forest raptors: Influence of human disturbance and forest condition on northern goshawks. Restoration Ecology 19:273–279.

Mote, P. W. 2006. Climate-driven variability and trends in mountain snowpack in western North America. Journal of Climate 19:6209–6220.

North, M. 2012. Managing Sierra Nevada Forests. USDA Forest Service, PSW General Technical Report. PSW-GTR-273. Albany, California. 184 p.

North, M, A. Brough, J. Long, B. Collins, P. Bowden, D. Yasuda, J. Miller and N. Sugihara. 2015. Constraints on mechanized treatment significantly limit mechanical fuels reduction extent in the Sierra Nevada. Journal of Forestry 113:40–48.

North, M., and J. Chen. 2005. Introduction to the Teakettle (special issue). Forest Science 51:185–186.

North, M., B. Collins, J. Keane, J. Long, C. Skinner, and B. Zielinski. 2014. Synopsis of emergent approaches. Pages 55–70 in J. W. Long,

L. Quinn-Davidson, C. Skinner, editors. Science synthesis to promote resilience of social-ecological systems. I, the Sierra Nevada and Southern Cascades. USFS Forest Service, PSW-GTR-237.
North, M., B. M. Collins, and S. Stephens. 2012. Using fire to increase the scale, benefits, and future maintenance of fuels treatments. Journal of Forestry 110:392–401.
North, M., B. Oakley, R. Fiegener, A. Gray, and M. Barbour. 2005. Influence of light and soil moisture on Sierran mixed-conifer understory communities. Plant Ecology 177:13–24.
North, M., J. Innes, and H. Zald. 2007. Comparison of thinning and prescribed fire restoration treatments to Sierran mixed-conifer historic conditions. Canadian Journal of Forest Research 37:331–342.
North, M., J. Q. Chen, B. Oakley, B. Song, M. Rudnicki, A. Gray, and J. Innes. 2004. Forest stand structure and pattern of old-growth western hemlock/Douglas-fir and mixed-conifer forests. Forest Science 50:299–311.
North, M., K. Van de Water, S. Stephens, and B. Collins. 2009. Climate, rain shadow, and human-use influences on fire regimes in the eastern Sierra Nevada, California, USA. Fire Ecology 5:17–31.
North, M., M. Hurteau, and J. Innes. 2009. Fire suppression and fuels treatment effects on mixed-conifer carbon stocks and emissions. Ecological Applications 19:1385–1396.
North, M., M. Hurteau, R. Fiegener, and M. Barbour. 2005. Influence of fire and El Nino on tree recruitment varies by species in Sierran mixed conifer. Forest Science 51:187–197.
North, M., P. Stine, K. O'Hara, W. Zielinski, and S. Stephens. 2009. An ecosystem management strategy for Sierran mixed-conifer forests. PSW-GTR-220. U.S. Department of Agriculture Forest Service, Albany, California.
North, M., P. Stine, W. Zielinski, K. O'Hara, and S. Stephens. 2010. Harnessing fire for wildlife. The Wildlife Professional 4:30–33.
North, M., R. Boynton, P. Stine, K. Shipley, E. Underwood, N. Roth, J. Viers, and J. Quinn. 2012. Geographic information system landscape analysis using GTR 220 concepts. Pages 107–115 in M. North, editor. Managing Sierra Nevada Forests. PSW-GTR-237 U.S. Department of Agriculture Forest Service, Albany, California.
North, M. P., and A. Rosenthal. 2006. Restoring forest health: Fire and thinning effects on mixed-conifer forests. Science Perspective 7. Albany, California.
North, M. P., and M. D. Hurteau. 2011. High-severity wildfire effects on carbon stocks and emissions in fuels treated and untreated forest. Forest Ecology and Management 261:1115–1120.
North, M. P., and P. A. Stine. 2012. Clarifying concepts. Pages 149–164 in M. North, editor. Managing Sierra Nevada Forests. PSW-GTR-237. U.S. Department of Agriculture Forest Service, Albany, California.
North, M. P., and P. N. Manley. 2012. Managing forests for wildlife communities. Pages 73–80 in M. North, editor. Manaing Sierra Nevada Forests. PSW-GTR-237 U.S. Department of Agriculture Forest Service, Albany, California.
North, M. P., and W. S. Keeton. 2008. Emulating natural disturbance regimes: An emerging approach for sustainable forest management. Pages 341–372 in Patterns and Processes in Forest Landscapes: Multiple Use and Sustainable Management. Springer Science Publishing, New York, New York.
North, M. P., G. N. Steger, R. G. Denton, G. E. Eberlein, T. E. Munton, and K. Johnson. 2000. Association of weather and nest-site structure with reproductive success in California spotted owls. Journal of Wildlife Managment 64:797–807.
North, M. P., J. F. Franklin, A. B. Carey, E. D. Forsman, and T. Hamer. 1999. Forest stand structure of the northern spotted owl's foraging habitat. Forest Science 45:520–527.
Oakley, B. B., M. P. North, and J. F. Franklin. 2003. The effects of fire on soil nitrogen associated with patches of the actinorhizal shrub Ceanothus cordulatus. Plant and Soil 254:35–46.
Oakley, B., M. North, J. F. Franklin, B. P. Hedlund, and J. T. Staley. 2004. Diversity and distribution of *Frankia* strains symbiotic with *Ceanothus* in California. Applied and Environmental Microbiology 70:6444–6452.
O'Green, A. T., R. A. Dahgren, and D. Sanchez-Mata. 2007. California soils and examples of ultramafic vegetation. Pages 71–106 in M. Barbour, T. Keeler-Wolf, and A. A. Schoenherr, editors. Terrestrial Vegetation of California. University of California Press, Berkeley, California.
Pan, Y., R. A. Birdsey, J. Fang, R. Houghton, P. E. Kauppi, W. A. Kurz, O. L. Phillips, A. Shvidenko, S. L. Lewis, J. G. Canadell, P. Ciais, R. B. Jackson, S. W. Pacala, A. D. McGuire, S. Piao, A. Rautiainen, S. Sitch, and D. Hayes. 2011. A large and persistent carbon sink in the world's forests. Science 333:988–993.
Parker, A. J. 2002. Fire in Sierra Nevada forests: Evaluating the ecological impact of burning by Native Americans. Pages 233–267 in T. R. Vale, editor. Fire, native peoples, and the natural landscape. Island Press, Covelo, California.
Paysen, T. E., J. A. Derby, H. Black Jr., V. C. Bleich, and J. W. Mincks. 1980. A vegetation classification system applied to southern California. General Technical Report PSW-45. U.S. Department of Agriculture Forest Service, Pacific Southwest Forest and Range Experiment Station, Berkeley, California.
Peterson, C. J. 2000. Catastrophic wind damage to North American forests and the potential impact of climate change. Science of the Total Environment 262:287–311.
Price, C., and D. Rind. 1994. Lightning fires in a 2xCO_2 world. Pages 77–84 in proceedings of twelfth conference on fire and forest meterology, October 26–28, Jekyll Island, Georgia. Society of American Foresters, Washington, D.C.
Rambo, T. R., and M. P. North. 2009. Canopy microclimate response to pattern and density of thinning in a Sierra Nevada forest. Forest Ecology and Management 257:435–442.
Raphael, M. G., M. L. Morrison, and M. P. Yoder-Williams. 1987. Breeding bird populations during twenty-five years of postfire succession in the Sierra Nevada. Condor 89:614–626.
Rizzo, D. M., and G. W. Slaughter. 2001. Root disease and canopy gaps in developed areas of Yosemite Valley, California. Forest Ecology and Management 146:159–167.
Rizzo, D. M., and M. Garbelotto. 2003. Sudden oak death: Endangering California and Oregon forest ecosystems. Frontiers in Ecology and the Environment 1:197–204.
Roberts, S., and M. North. 2012. California spotted owls. Pages 165–175 in M. North, editor. Managing Sierra Nevada Forests. PSW-GTR-237. U.S. Department of Agriculture Forest Service, Albany, California.
Rollins, M. G. 2009. LANDFIRE: A nationally consistent vegetation, wildland fire, and fuel assessment. International Journal of Wildland Fire 18:235–249.
Rollins, M. G., and C. K. Frame. 2006. The LANDFIRE prototype project: Nationally consistent and locally relevant geospatial data for wildland fire management. RMRS-GTR-175. U.S. Department of Agriculture Forest Service, Fort Collins, Colorado.
Royce, E. B., and M. G. Barbour. 2001. Mediterranean climate effects. I. Conifer water use across a Sierra Nevada ecotone. American Journal of Botany 88:911–918.
Running, S. W. 2006. Is global warming causing more, larger wildfires? Science 313:927–928.
Ryu, S.-R., A. Concilio, J. Chen, M. North, and S. Ma. 2009. Prescribed burning and mechanical thinning effects on belowground conditions and soil respiration in a mixed-conifer forest, California. Forest Ecology and Management 257:1324–1332.
Saab, V. A., R. E. Russell, and J. G. Dudley. 2007. Nest densities of cavity-nesting birds in relation to postfire salvage logging and time since wildfire. Condor 109:97–108.
Safford, H. D., D. A. Schmidt, and C. H. Carlson. 2009. Effects of fuel treatments on fire severity in an area of wildland-urban interface, Angora Fire, Lake Tahoe Basin, California. Forest Ecology and Management 258:773–787.
Safford, H. D., J. T. Stevens, K. Merriam, M. D. Meyer, and A. M. Latimer. 2012. Fuel treatment effectiveness in California yellow pine and mixed conifer forests. Forest Ecology and Management 274:17–28.
Safford, H., M. North, and M. Meyer. 2012. Climate change and the relevance of historical forest conditions. Pages 23–45 in M. North, editor. Managing Sierra Nevada Forest. PSW-GTR-237. U.S. Department of Agriculture Forest Service, Albany, California.
Savage, M. 1994. Anthropogenic and natural disturbance and patterns of mortality in a mixed conifer forests in California. Canadian Journal of Forest Research 24:1149–1159.
Sawyer, J. O. 2007. Forests of northwestern California. Pages 253–295 in M. Barbour, T. Keeler-Wolf, and A. A. Schoenherr, editors. Terrestrial Vegetation of California. University of California Press, Berkeley, California.
———. 2006. Northwest California: A natural history. University of California Press, Berkeley, California.

Sawyer, J. O., T. Keeler-Wolf, and J. M. Evens. 2009. A manual of California Vegetation. Second edition. California Native Plant Society, Sacramento, California.

Skinner, C. N., A. H. Taylor, and J. K. Agee. 2006. Klamath Mountains bioregion. Pages 170–194 in N.G. Sugihara, J. W. van Wagtendonk, K. E. Shaffer, J. Fites-Kaufman, and A. E. Thode. Fire in California's Ecosystems. University of California Press, Berkeley, California.

Smith, J. P., and J. O. Sawyer. 1985. Endemic vascular plants of northwestern California and southwestern Oregon. Madroño 35:54–69.

Smith, T. F., D. M. Rizzo, and M. North. 2005. Patterns of mortality in an old-growth mixed-conifer forest of the southern Sierra Nevada, California. Forest Science 51:266–275.

SNEP (Sierra Nevada Ecosystem Project). 1996. Sierra Nevada Ecosystem Project. Final Report to Congress, Status of the Sierra Nevada. University of California, Davis, California.

SNFPA (Sierra Nevada Forest Plan Amendment). 2004. Sierra Nevada forest plan amendment: Final environmental impact statement. 1–6. U.S. Department of Agriculture, Forest Service, Pacific Southwest Region. Vallejo, California.

Stebbins, G. L., and J. Major. 1965. Endemism and speciation in the Californian flora. Ecological Monographs 35:1–35.

Steel, Z. L., H. D. Safford, and J. H. Viers. 2015. The fire frequency-severity relationship and the legacy of fire suppression in California forests. Ecosphere 6:8.

Stein, C. M., D. W. Johnson, W. W. Miller, R. F. Powers, D. A. Young, and D. W. Glass. 2010. Snowbrush (*Ceanothus velutinus Dougl*) effects on nitrogen availability in soils and solutions from a Sierran ecosystem. Ecohydrology 3:79–87.

Stephens, S. L., and S. J. Gill. 2005. Forest structure and mortality in an old-growth Jeffrey pine-mixed conifer forest in north-western Mexico. Forest Ecology and Management 205:15–28.

Stephens, S. L., J. D. McIver, R. E. J. Boerner, C. J. Fettig, J. B. Fontaine, B. R. Hartsough, P. L. Kennedy, and D. W. Schwilk. 2012. The effects of forest fuel-reduction treatments in the United States. Bioscience 62:549–560.

Stephens, S. L., J. K. Agee, P. Fule, M. P. North, W. H. Romme, T. W. Swetnam, and M. G. Turner. 2013. Managing forests and fire in changing climates. Science 342:41–42.

Stephens, S. L., S. W. Bigelow, R. D. Burnett, B. M. Collins, C. V. Gallagher, J. Keane, D. A. Kelt, M. P. North, S. Roberts, P. A. Stine, and D. H. Van Vuren. 2014. California spotted owl, songbird, and small mammal responses to landscape fuel treatments. Bioscience 64:893–906.

Stephens, S. L., J. M. Lydersen, B. M. Collins, D. L. Fry, and M. D. Meyer. 2015. Historical and current landscape-scale ponderosa pine and mixed conifer forest structure in the Southern Sierra Nevada. Ecosphere 6: art79.

Stephenson, N. L. 1999. Reference conditions for giant sequoia forest restoration: Structure, process, and precision. Ecological Applications 9:1253–1265.

———. 1998. Actual evapotranspiration and deficit: Biologically meaningful correlates of vegetation distribution across spatial scales. Journal of Biogeography 25:855–870.

———. 1996. Ecology and management of giant sequoia groves. Pages 1431–1467 in Sierra Nevada Ecosystem Project: Final Report to Congress. Volume 2, Assessments and scientific basis for management options. Centers for Water and Wildland Resources, University of California, Davis, California.

———. 1994. Long-term dynamics of giant sequoia populations: Implications for managing a pioneer species. Pages 56–63 in P. S. Aune, editor. Proceedings of the Symposium on Giant Sequoias: Their place in the ecosystem and society. PSW-GTR-151 U.S. Department of Agriculture Forest Service, Albany, California.

Stephenson, N. L., A. J. Das, R. Condit, S. E. Russo, P. J. Baker, N. G. Beckman, D. A. Coomes, E. R. Lines, W. K. Morris, N. Ruger, E. Alvarez, C. Blundo, S. Bunyavejchewin, G. Chuyong, S. J. Davis, A. Duque, C. N. Ewango, O. Flores, J. F. Franklin, H. R. Grau, Z. Hao, M. E. Harmon, S. P. Hubbell, D. Kenfack, Y. Lin, J.-R. Makana, A. Malizia, L. R. Malizia, R. J. Pabst, N. Pongpattananurak, S.-H. Su, I.-F. Sun, S. Tan, D. Thomas, P. J. van Mantgem, X. Wang, S. K. Wiser, and M. A. Zavala. 2014. Rate of tree carbon accumulation increases continuously with tree size. Nature. <doi:10.1038/nature12914>.

Stephenson, N. L., and P. J. van Mantgem. 2005. Forest turnover rates follow global and regional patterns of productivity. Ecology Letters 8:524–531.

Stralberg, D., D. Jongsomjit, C. A. Howell, M. A. Snyder, J. D. Alexander, J. A. Wiens, and T. L. Root. 2009. Re-shuffling of species with climate disruption: A no-analog future for California birds? PLoS One 4:e6825.

Sudworth, G. B. 1900. Stanislaus and Lake Tahoe Forest Reserves, California, and adjacent territories. Pages 505–561. Government Printing Office, Washington, D.C.

Sugihara, N. G., J. W. van Wagtendonk, and J. Fites-Kaufman. 2006. Fire as an ecological process. Pages 58–74 in N. G. Sugihara, J. W. van Wagtendonk, K. E. Shaffer, J. Fites-Kaufman, and A. E. Thode. Fire in California's Ecosystems. University of California Press, Berkeley, California.

Sullivan, T. P., and D. S. Sullivan. 2001. Influence of variable retention harvest on forest ecosystems. II. Diversity and population dynamics of small mammals. Journal of Applied Ecology 38:1234–1252.

Syphard, A. D., V. C. Radeloff, T. J. Hawbaker, and S. I. Stewart. 2009. Conservation threats due to human-caused increases in fire frequency in Mediterranean-climate ecosystems. Conservation Biology 23:758–759.

Tague, C., K. Heyn, and L. Christensen. 2009. Topographic controls on spatial patterns of conifer transpiration and net primary productivity under climate warming in mountain ecosystems. Ecohydrology 2:541–554.

Taylor, A. H. 2000. Fire regimes and forest changes in mid and upper montane forests of the southern Cascades, Lassen Volcanic National Park, California, USA. Journal of Biogeography 27:87–104.

Taylor, A. H., A. M. Vandervlugt, R. S. Maxwell, R. M. Beaty, C. Airey, and C. N. Skinner. 2013. Changes in forest structure, fuels, and potential fire behaviour since 1873 in the Lake Tahoe Basin, USA. Applied Vegetation Science. <doi:10.1111/avsc.12049>.

Taylor, A. H., and C. N. Skinner. 2003. Spatial patterns and controls on historical fire regimes and forest structure in the Klamath Mountains. Ecological Applications 13:704–719.

Thoebald, D. M., and W. H. Romme. 2007. Expansion of the U.S. wildland-urban interface. Landscape Urban Planning 83:340–354.

Trujillo, E., N. P. Molotch, M. Goulden, A. Kelly, and R. Bales. 2012. Elevation-dependent influence of snow accumulation on forest greening. Nature Geoscience 5:705–709.

Underwood, E. C., J. H. Viers, J. F. Quinn, and M. North. 2010. Using topography to meet wildlife and fuels treatment objectives in fire-suppressed landscapes. Environmental Management 46:809–819.

U.S. Department of Agriculture, Forest Service Region. 2012. Visitor use report. <http://apps.fs.usda.gov/nrm/nvum/results/ReportCache/Rnd3_R05_Master_Report.pdf>. Accessed June 2015.

Van de Water, K., and H. Safford. 2011. A summary of fire frequency estimate for California vegetation before Euro-American settlement. Fire Ecology 7:26–58.

Van de Water, K. and M. North. 2011. Stand structure, fuel loads, and fire behavior in riparian and upland forests, Sierra Nevada Mountains, USA; a comparison of current and reconstructed conditions. Forest Ecology and Management 262:215–228.

———. 2010. Fire history of coniferous riparian forests in the Sierra Nevada. Forest Ecology and Management 260:384–395.

van Mantgem, P. J., and N. L. Stephenson. 2007. Apparent climatically induced increase of tree mortality rates in a temperate forest. Ecology Letters 10:909–916.

van Mantgem, P. J., N. L. Stephenson, J. C. Byrne, L. D. Daniels, J. F. Franklin, P. Z. Fule, M. E. Harmon, A. J. Larson, J. M. Smith, A. H. Taylor, and T. T. Veblen. 2009. Widespread increase of tree mortality rates in the Western United States. Science 323:521–524.

Van Pelt, R. 2001. Forest giants of the Pacific coast. University of Washington Press, Seattle, Washington.

van Wagtendonk, J. W., and D. R. Cayan. 2008. Temporal and spatial distribution of lightning strikes in California in relation to large-scale weather patterns. Fire Ecology 4:34–56.

van Wagtendonk, J. W., K. A. van Wagtendonk, and A. E. Thode. 2012. Factors associated with the severity of intersecting fires in Yosemite National Park, California, USA. Fire Ecology 8:11–31.

Verner, J., and A. S. Boss. 1980. California wildlife and their habitats: Western Sierra Nevada. General Technical Report PSW-37. U.S.

Department of Agriculture Forest Service, Pacific Southwest Forest and Range Experiment Station, Berkeley, California.

Vitousek, P. M., and R. W. Howarth. 1991. Nitrogen limitation on land and in the sea: How can it occur? Biogeochemistry 13:87–115.

Waring, R. H. 1969. Forest plants of the eastern Siskiyous: Their environmental and vegetational distribution. Northwest Science 43:1–17.

Wayman, R. B., and M. North. 2007. Initial response of a mixed-conifer understory plant community to burning and thinning restoration treatments. Forest Ecology and Management 239:32–44.

Western Regional Climate Center (WRCC). 2014. <. http://www.wrcc.dri.edu/>. Accessed June 2014.

White, A. M., E. F. Zipkin, P. N. Manley, and M. D. Schlesinger. 2013a. Conservation of avian diversity in the Sierra Nevada: Moving beyond a single-species management focus. PLoS One 8:e63088.

———. 2013b. Simulating avian species and foraging group responses to fuel reduction treatments in coniferous forests. Forest Ecology and Management 304:261–274.

Whittaker, R. H. 1960. Vegetation of the Siskiyou Mountains, Oregon and California. Ecological Monographs 30:279–338.

Wiebe, K. L. 2011. Nest sites as limiting resources for cavity-nesting birds in mature forest ecosystems: A review of the evidence. Journal of Field Ornithology 82:239–248.

York, R. A., J. J. Battles, A. K. Eschtruth, and F. G. Schurr. 2011. Giant sequoia (*Sequoiadendron giganteum*) regeneration in experimental canopy gaps. Restoration Ecology 19:14–23.

York, R. A., N. L. Stephenson, M. Meyer, S. Hanna, T. Moody, A. Caprio, and J. Battles. 2013. A natural resource condition assessment for Sequoia and Kings Canyon National Parks: Appendix 11—Giant sequoia. U.S. Geological Survey Natural Resource Report, NPS/SEKI. Fort Collins, Colorado.

Yue, X., L. J. Mickley, J. A. Logan, and J. O. Kaplan. 2013. Ensemble projections of wildfire activity and carbonaceous aerosol concentrations over the western United States in the mid-21st century. Atmospheric Environment 77:767–780.

Zald, H. S. J., A. N. Gray, M. North, and R. A. Kern. 2008. Initial tree regeneration responses to fire and thinning treatments in a Sierra Nevada mixed-conifer forest, USA. Forest Ecology and Management 256:168–179.

Zhang, J. W., W. W. Oliver, and M. D. Busse. 2006. Growth and development of ponderosa pine on sites of contrasting productivities: Relative importance of stand density and shrub competition effects. Canadian Journal of Forest Research/Revue Canadienne de Recherche Forestiere 36:2426–2438.

Zielinski, W. J., R. L. Truex, G. A. Schmidt, F. V. Schlexer, K. N. Schmidt, and R. H. Barrett. 2004a. Home range characteristics of fishers in California. Journal of Mammalogy 85:649–657.

———. 2004b. Resting habitat selection by fishers in California. Journal of Wildlife Management 68:475–492.

TWENTY-EIGHT

Subalpine Forests

CONSTANCE I. MILLAR and PHILIP W. RUNDEL

Introduction

Subalpine forests in California, bounded by the treeline at their upper margin, are the forest zone influenced primarily by abiotic controls, including persistent snowpack, desiccating winds, acute and chronic extreme temperatures, soil moisture and evapotranspirative stresses in both summer and winter, and short growing seasons (Fites-Kaufman et al. 2007). Subalpine forest species derive their annual precipitation primarily in the form of snow. Disturbances such as fire, and biotic interactions including competition, are less important than in montane forests. Although some subalpine forests are dense and have closed canopies, most are more accurately considered woodlands, with short-statured individuals and wide spacing of young as well as old trees. Subalpine forest stands are commonly interrupted by areas of exposed bedrock, snowfields, and upland herbaceous and shrub types—the latter comprising important components of broader subalpine ecosystems (Figure 28.1; Rundel et al. 1990, Sawyer et al. 2009).

Subalpine forests comprise the highest-elevation ecosystems in California dominated by trees. Although scattered upright trees and wind-swept, shrubby individuals (KRUMMHOLZ) grow sparsely in the alpine zone, subalpine forests have their upper limit at the alpine-treeline ECOTONE. Treeline has long fascinated ecologists for its predominance worldwide, from equatorial tropical forests to polar zones. While many environmental factors mediate the exact location of regional treelines—a "devil-is-in-the-details" that also delights ecologists—a robust unifying theory has been developed to explain the treeline ecotone as the thermal contour (isotherm) on the landscape where average growing-season temperature is 6.4°C (Körner and Paulsen 2004, Körner 2012). In this context "trees" are defined as plants having upright stems that attain height ≥3 meters regardless of taxonomy, and "forest" is characterized as more-or-less continuous patches of trees whose crowns form at least a loose canopy (Körner 2007). Although not without some controversy, the hypothesized mechanism behind the global treeline isotherm relates to the fact that upright trees are more closely coupled with the atmosphere than shorter-statured vegetation types such as those found in the alpine zone. This coupling is tightly interrelated with rooting zone temperatures, tissue thermal capacities, primary production (photosynthesis and carbon allocation), water transport, canopy shade, snowfall filtering, and relationships of incoming solar radiation.

FIGURE 28.1 Typical woodland structure of California's subalpine forest ecosystems, characterized by scattered trees and abundant rocky ground. *Pinus albicaulis* forest type, Humphreys Basin, Sierra Nevada. Photo: Constance Millar.

Two corollaries follow from this treeline mechanism: that mean growing-season temperature mechanistically translates into a life-form boundary (the alpine-forest ecotone), and that treeline should not be strictly related to elevation. Nonetheless, for a particular region, elevation provides a rough proxy for the thermal treeline. The treeline isotherm logically rises where local conditions are warmer (e.g., south slopes), depresses where cooler (north slopes), and varies by latitude as well as regional climate regimes. California traverses more than nine degrees of latitude, and thermal treeline elevations also vary among the mountain regions of the state. They are lowest in the north, where they range from about 2,700 meters near Mount Shasta to 2,800 meters on Mount Lassen. At similar respective latitudes, treeline elevation is slightly lower in the Klamath Mountains to the west and slightly higher in the Warner Mountains to the east due to differing climate regimes and species compositions. In the Sierra Nevada thermal treeline ranges from 2,800 meters in the northern forests; to 3,000 meters near Donner Pass; to 3,200 meters in the Yosemite region; and to 3,500 meters in the southern Sierra Nevada (Rundel 2011). Thermal treeline in the Great Basin ranges to the east of the Sierra Nevada are slightly higher than corresponding Sierran latitudinal positions.

Treeline isotherm is the background regulator for the highest (coolest) occurrence of subalpine forests; however, local environmental factors control the specific position (including elevation) of upper subalpine forests. These include slope and aspect, substrate type and geomorphology, avalanche occurrence, and other disturbance history. This "ecological noise" can be critically important for ecosystem function and diversity and reminds us that changes in treeline position over time (or lack of change) are not necessarily indicators of climate change. Subalpine forests in California include communities dominated by whitebark pine (*Pinus albicaulis*), foxtail pine (*P. balfouriana*), limber pine (*P. flexilis*), western white pine (*P. monticola*), mountain hemlock (*Tsuga mertensiana*), or Sierra juniper (*Juniperus grandis,* formerly *J. occidentalis* var. *australis*). In addition, lodgepole pine (*Pinus contorta*) also commonly occurs in subalpine forests in California, either as the dominant species or intermixed with others. Because it extends across many more environments than subalpine, including elevations down to sea level, lodgepole pine alone is not an indicator of subalpine forests. In addition to these conifers, several very small stands of otherwise wide-ranging subalpine fir (*Abies lasiocarpa*) grow in the Trinity Alps and Marble Mountains of northwest California, and several tiny stands of Alaska yellow-cedar (*Callitropsis nootkatensis*, formerly *Chamaecyparis nootkatensis*) occur in the Siskiyou Mountains; these species are indicators of the subalpine zone at these rare locations. The hardwoods quaking aspen (*Populus tremuloides*) and curl-leaf mountain mahogany (*Cercocarpus ledifolius*) also grow commonly in subalpine environments, but because they extend abundantly to lower montane zones, they are not indicator species.

Photo on previous page: Long-lived bristlecone pines of the White Mountains are emblematic of subalpine forest ecosystems in California. Photo: Constance Millar.

Whereas the upper bounds of subalpine forests have a robust, thermal delineation and form a visible transition from forest to alpine vegetation, the lower limits of the subalpine zone are less distinct. These generally follow the elevation of snowpack dominance, which strongly influences tree species diversity. The subalpine/montane forest ecotone is also controlled by shifts in fire regimes (Caprio and Graber 2000, Minnich 2007). On the one hand, while the dense canopies and surface fires of lower-elevation red and white fir (*Abies magnifica*, *A. concolor*, respectively) limit establishment of subalpine species, high-intensity fires burning downslope from lodgepole pine or hemlock forests can create openings in the fir forests and expose mineral soils. In these cases, subalpine species can advance downslope until succession of fir regains dominance uphill. As with upper treeline, elevation only roughly defines lower limits of the subalpine zone, and these vary with latitude across the state. Lower boundaries extend to 2,200 meters in the Klamath Mountains; 2,300 meters at Mount Shasta; 2,400 meters in the northern Sierra Nevada; 2,750 meters in the southern Sierra Nevada; 2,900 meters in the southern California mountains; and 3,000 meters in the Great Basin ranges (Griffin and Critchfield 1976, Elliott-Fisk and Peterson 1991, Holland and Keil 1995).

In California today, subalpine forest ecosystems conservatively extend over 390,270 hectares of California (Figure 28.2,

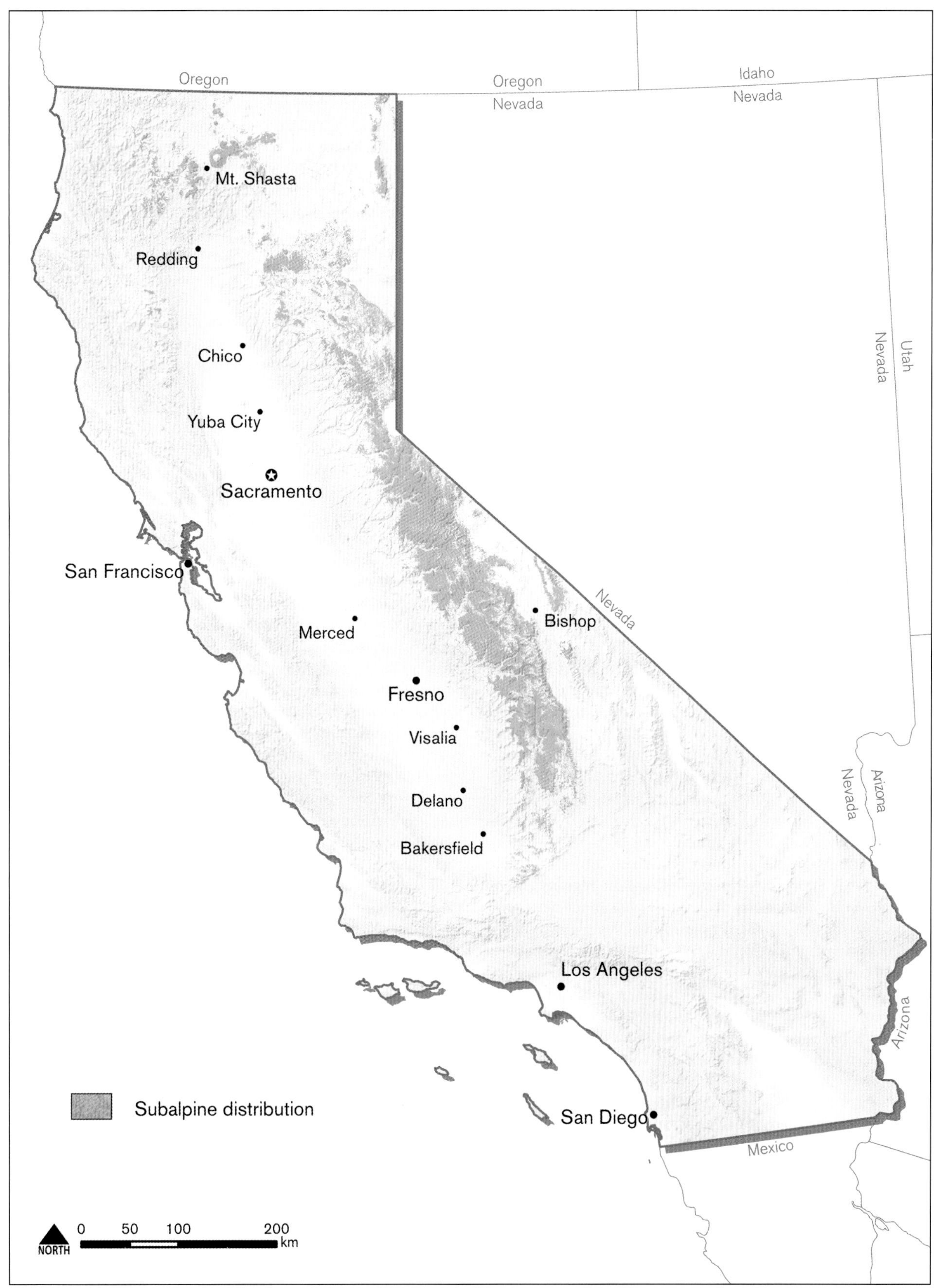

FIGURE 28.2 Distribution of subalpine forest ecosystems in California. Source: Data from U.S. Geological Survey, Gap Analysis Program (GAP). Map: P. Welch, Center for Integrated Spatial Research (CISR).

TABLE 28.1
Area and percentage of total subalpine forests in California by mountain region

Mountain region	Area (hectares)	Percentage of total
South Cascades[A]	284	0.1
Great Basin North[B]	3,494	0.1
Klamath Mountains[C]	77,920	20.1
Sierra Nevada	290,830	75.2
Great Basin, Central[D]	10,590	2.7
Great Basin, Southern[E]	376	0.1
Southern California[F]	6,777	1.7
TOTAL	**390,271**	**100**

Data from U.S. Geological Survey, Gap Analysis Program (GAP).

A. Mounts Shasta and Lassen
B. Warner Mountains
C. Marble Mountains, Trinity Alps, Salmon Mountains, Yolla Bolly Mountains
D. Sweetwater Mountains, White-Inyo Range
E. Panamint Range
F. Tehacapi Mountains, San Gabriel Mountains, San Bernardino Mountains, San Jacinto Mountains

Table 28.1; Davis et al. 1998) and occur in the Klamath Mountains, including the Marble Mountains, Trinity Alps, Mount Eddy, Salmon Mountains, and North and South Yolla Bolly Mountains; southern Cascade Range, including Mounts Shasta and Lassen; Sierra Nevada; Great Basin ranges, including the Warner Mountains, Carson Range, Zunamed Mountains (Charlet 2014), and Sweetwater Mountains; Glass Mountains, Mono Craters, White-Inyo Range, and Panamint Range; and southern California ranges, including the Tehachapi Mountains, San Gabriel Mountains, San Bernardino Mountains, and San Jacinto Mountains (Griffin and Critchfield 1976). Forests types differ across mountain regions of the state in overall tree species diversity as well as species dominance, diversity of affiliated nonarboreal vegetation, faunal relations, climate interactions, productivity, and biogeochemistry. Although subalpine forests commonly occur on all slope aspects of California mountain ranges, they are limited to wetter aspects in more arid regions such as southern California and the Great Basin. These usually include western slopes in southern California (Holland and Keil 1995) and northern slopes in the Great Basin (Elliott-Fisk and Peterson 1991).

The large majority of subalpine forest ecosystem in California occurs in the Sierra Nevada, with more than 75% of the total (see Table 28.1). Subalpine forests dominate in a broad band on the gradual west slope of the Sierras and in a narrow, less diverse and more scattered band on the steep eastern escarpment. The areas high enough to support subalpine forest in the jumbled Klamath Mountains of northwest California collectively amount to the second largest region, with 20% of the state's total. The southern Cascades support a deceptively small amount of subalpine forest (less than 1%), which results from the narrow perimeter area around Mounts Shasta and Lassen. The remaining mountain regions of the Great Basin and southern California each also contain less than 1% of the total subalpine forest in the state (see Table 28.1).

Environmental Controls

Geology, Geomorphology, and Soils

The environmental context for California's subalpine ecosystems derives from the unique sequence of historical geologic processes that gave rise to its upland regions (see Chapter 8, "Ecosystems Past: Vegetation Prehistory"). Subalpine forests have shifted greatly in diversity and geography over the past thirty million years as topography changed in the California region. Prior to that time, California was mostly under water and/or characterized by lowlands with subtropical climates. Mountain ranges of the pre-Sierra/Cascade cordillera first emerged as eruptive centers along the subduction plate boundary that defined the Pacific margin of North America more than seventy-five million years ago (Millar 2012). Tectonic action related to plate boundaries led to emplacement of magmatic batholiths (subsequently granitic rocks) deep below the continent. Plate-boundary tectonics also catalyzed extensive aboveground volcanoes that defined the Nevadan and Sevier orogenies and led to development of the extensive Nevadaplano, with high-elevation summits that extended across present-day eastern California and Nevada.

This early volcanism largely defined the stage for subsequent bedrock exposures, soil development, and geomorphic conditions supporting subalpine forests in California today. On the highest ranges and especially in the arid ranges where erosion has been minimal (e.g., the White-Inyo Range and parts of the southern Sierra Nevada), highly metamorphosed rocks called roof pendants occur and date to times when California was submerged under sea. These rocks are often characterized by complex, colorful, and tortuously folded strata, including formations of limestone, marble, and other carbonate substrates. Where they are exposed, unusual chemical compositions and pH levels constrain plant growth to species able to tolerate these conditions, with bristlecone pine on dolomite substrate as an example. Also dating to these eras are exposures of ultramafic and serpentine rocks, with patchwork soils of complex origin primarily derived from former oceanic terranes subsequently accreted into California. Soils derived from these rocks also present nutritional limitations for plant growth and exclude many taxa. Tolerant subalpine species such as foxtail pine and western white pine can be found on these soils in the few locations where they are exposed at high elevations, primarily in northwest California. In eastern California hydrothermal alteration of volcanic rocks created substrates with another type of unique chemistry limiting plant growth. Subalpine conifers such as lodgepole pine and limber pine are able to grow on these soils, and are often found on these substrates in very disjunct locations and at much lower elevations than usual, in zones otherwise dominated by montane or woodland conifers.

Far more extensive substrates underlying California subalpine forests are granitic rocks and associated soils that derive from the early magmatic plutons of subduction plate dynamics. These were exposed over subsequent eras during the processes of mountain-building and erosion by glaciers, water, and wind. Granitic rocks create soils that favor growth of many subalpine conifer species, with characteristics such as coarse grain that enable drainage yet adequate water-holding capacity, intermediate to moderate acidity, and a sufficient balance of vital plant nutrients. In some regions, such as the Great Basin ranges, southern Cascades, and eastern Sierra Nevada, geologic hot spots occur where range-front faulting is active or magmatic centers are shallow. In these locations volcanism has continued from the late Tertiary into present times. Soils that develop in these regions, especially from Quaternary eruptions such as Mounts Shasta and Lassen and the Glass Mountains in eastern California, are poorly developed and challenge plant growth.

Current Climate and Climate Variability

Although subalpine forest ecosystems in California lie within the general Mediterranean-climate regime of the state, high elevations modify its influence. For instance, as elevation increases, temperatures and evaporative demand decrease, reducing the stress of the otherwise long summer drought. The subalpine forest zone in California is characterized by short growing seasons (six to nine weeks), prolonged winter snowpack (usually deeper than 2 meters except in the Great Basin ranges), and cool summer and winter temperatures with frost possible any month (Agee 1993, Fites-Kaufmann et al. 2007). Proximity to the Pacific Ocean and dominance of prevailing storms from the west protect these high-elevation ecosystems from extreme cold, although the Great Basin ranges of eastern California experience more continental climates. These include greater extremes, especially of cold temperatures in winter, than other mountain regions in the state experience. Annual and monthly temperatures tend to be cooler as the subalpine zone rises in elevation (i.e., with decreasing latitude) and in interior ranges, regardless of latitude (Table 28.2; PRISM climate model, Daly et al. 1994).

Precipitation falls on subalpine forests mostly as winter snow. Summer precipitation derives from local convectional storms, which vary in intensity and abundance across the range of subalpine forests as well as by topographic position within ranges (Fites-Kaufman et al. 2007). Gradients of precipitation occur in both latitude and longitude. Annual precipitation, including winter snowfall, is generally highest in the northern mountains, including the Klamath Mountains and southern Cascades, which can approach conditions of the Pacific Northwest, and lowest in the semiarid regimes of the southeastern Great Basin ranges (see Table 28.2). Despite their southerly latitude, precipitation in subalpine regions of southern California is similar to locations in the central Sierra Nevada, though far less than in the southern Cascades and Klamath Mountains. Precipitation also varies strongly across heterogeneous environments within mountain ranges, so some subalpine sites receive high precipitation despite their location in a generally dry region and vice versa.

More precipitation falls in summer in California's southern subalpine forests than in northern forests due to the Gulf of California monsoon influence (see Table 28.2). In the southeastern Great Basin ranges, for instance, summer monthly precipitation is about equal to the winter amount, although annual averages are an order of magnitude lower than in northern mountains. July tends to be the driest month in the subalpine zone, with increasing precipitation in August and September. This trend reflects the various influences of summer convective activity and monsoon, especially in the southern regions; and early snowfalls, especially in northern regions. Longitudinal trends also occur in precipitation across the subalpine regions of California, with mountains nearer the Pacific Ocean (e.g., Marble Mountains, Yolla Bolly Mountains) generally receiving more annual precipitation (including winter snowpack) than progressively inland ranges at the same latitudes. This results from California's regional rain shadow (see Chapter 2, "Climate"). Rainshadow effects are also common within mountain ranges and shape subalpine forest composition and structure at local and regional scales. These result from local OROGRAPHIC EFFECTS, where moisture-laden clouds condense as rain when clouds rise on west slopes of the mountains and evaporate on the east slopes. Orographic processes, even over short distances across range crests, can translate to large differences in annual precipitation for local subalpine forests.

Snowfall and snowpack data and models are lacking for most of the state's subalpine regions. In California, SNOTEL sites (automated snow-measuring stations run by the U.S. Department of Agriculture Natural Resources Conservation Service) exist only in the Warner Mountains, central-eastern Sierra Nevada, the Carson Range, and the Sweetwater Mountains, and most stations are located in the upper montane forest zone rather than in the subalpine. The sufficiently high stations, however, provide a window into snowfall depth and interannual variation in subalpine forests across regions (Figure 28.3a). The trend of snowfall follows an expected geographic pattern, with latitude trumping orographic effects. One of the northernmost sites (Dismal Swamp), in the interior Warner Mountains, has the highest April 1 snow depth over the years of all sites. Snowpack generally decreases from north to south among the Sierra Nevada stations with the lowest depths at the southernmost station, Virginia Ridge just north of the Mono Basin. Snow depths also decrease eastward in the Great Basin, including the Carson Range (the Heavenly Valley station) and the Sweetwater Mountains (the Lobdell Lake station).

While it is common to define ecosystem envelopes by their temperature and precipitation parameters and to compare differences in these variables among regions, factors related to water availability and timing—not too much, not too little, when needed—are often more important in this region (Stephenson 1998). Temperature is important in controlling upper treeline, but evaporative stress, often measured through soil moisture interactions and CLIMATIC WATER DEFICIT (CWD), strongly influences subalpine distribution of species at lower elevations and interior dry margins. Intrinsic differences in evaporative demand and water supply regulate the ability of trees to survive and grow. Local topographic and substrate effects, interacting with rainfall and snowfall, determine the amount and retention of soil moisture and lead to differences in plant growth on soils of differing water-holding capacities, such as granitic versus metamorphic substrates. Similarly, differences in elevation of forests on different aspects reflect available growing-season soil moisture, which drives the presence of subalpine forests about 200 meters higher on steep, south-facing slopes than on steep, north-facing slopes (Fites-Kaufmann et al. 2007). In subalpine forests, CWD values are generally greater than 200 millimeters and are important in distinguishing the niche for this forest type from lower montane forests (Stephenson 1990, 1998). Variation in interannual CWD can be a key trigger, especially when combined with chronic warm summer temperatures, for subalpine forest insect outbreaks and forest mortality (Millar, Westfall et al. 2007; Millar et al. 2012).

While these summary patterns of temperature, precipitation, and available soil moisture define general boundary conditions, high interannual and interdecadal variation in California's weather exerts important controls on vegetation distribution and structure. The primary drivers of this vari-

TABLE 28.2

Climate data for subalpine forest zones in California by mountain range

					Temperature °C											
					Jan		July		Annual			Precipitation (mm)				
Location	Mountain range	Latitude (° W)	Longitude (° N)	Elevation (M)	max	min	max	min	max	min	mean	Jan	July	Aug	Sept	Annual
Kings Castle Pk	Marble Mtns	41.616	123.222	2212	1.5	-4.7	20.7	8.9	9.8	0.7	5.3	528	11	17	53	2902
Warren Peak	Warner Mtns	41.377	120.219	2820	-2.1	-10.5	18.7	3.0	6.9	-4.7	1.1	162	14	21	39	1163
Mt Shasta, Panther Mdws	S Cascades	41.357	122.195	2454	1.0	-6.5	19.9	6.5	8.8	-1.1	3.9	332	10	16	38	2030
High Lake, Russian Wild.	Salmon Mtns	41.298	122.956	2209	2.2	-4.8	20.6	9.5	9.8	1.0	5.4	249	16	23	43	1445
Caribou Lake	Trinity Alps	41.032	122.971	2133	1.9	-5.2	20.2	8.6	9.6	0.4	5.0	510	4	51	30	2134
Shadow Lake, Mt Lassen	S Cascades	40.480	121.472	2332	3.1	-6.3	21.9	6.9	11.2		5.1	488	12	36	54	2838
Lake Helen, Mt Lassen	S Cascades	40.475	121.503	2608	1.8	-7.2	19.9	5.9	9.4	-2.1	3.7	519	12	39	58	2994
S Yolly Bolly Peak	Yolla Bolly Mtns	40.037	122.863	2320	3.5	-4.6	22.1	10.0	11.5	1.5	6.5	364	6	10	25	1898
Mt Rose Saddle	Sierra Nevada	39.340	119.931	2970	0.4	-10.0	18.7	4.6	7.8	-4.3	1.8	229	21	24	44	1521
Ebbetts Pass, Highland Pk	Sierra Nevada	38.489	119.798	2754	2.5	-8.3	19.4	6.3	9.8	-2.3	3.8	234	27	40	38	1391

Ellery Lake, Tioga Pass	Sierra Nevada	37.934	119.238	2930	1.8	-9.9	19.4	5.6	9.3	-3.4	3.0	135	21	16	27	752
Arrowhead Lk, Mammoth	Sierra Nevada	37.581	118.981	3007	3.6	-8.2	20.3	6.4	10.6	-2.4	4.1	275	8	4	18	1348
Crooked Creek	White Mtns	37.506	118.170	3140	0.2	-11.8	17.8	3.8	7.8	-5.3	1.3	33	28	35	21	391
First Lake, N Palisades	Sierra Nevada	37.129	118.487	3073	1.7	-10.3	18.4	4.4	8.8	-4.0	2.4	132	10	13	39	836
Wacoba Mtn	Inyo Mtns	37.025	118.002	3105	2.4	-8.3	19.0	6.5	9.4	-2.4	3.5	33	25	29	19	346
Cottonwood Basin	Sierra Nevada	36.489	118.200	3262	1.0	-10.7	16.8	3.4	7.7	-5.0	1.4	87	7	8	18	511
Telescope Peak	Panamint Range	36.175	117.092	3150	1.9	-8.9	21.0	6.0	10.8	-2.5	4.2	39	20	39	34	362
Cucamonga Peak	San Gabriel Mtns	34.222	117.586	2700	6.7	-2.9	23.3	10.3	12.8	1.8	7.3	231	6	15	31	1142
San Gorgonio Mtn	San Bernardino Mtns	34.103	116.822	3201	1.7	-10.5	17.8	2.6	8.5	-5.3	1.6	261	17	25	34	1306
Average				**2757**	**1.9**	**-7.9**	**19.8**	**6.3**	**9.5**	**-2.1**	**3.7**	**255**	**15**	**24**	**35**	**1437**

SOURCE: Data excerpted from the PRISM climate model (Daly et al. 1994) for point locations selected as representative of the mid-upper subalpine zone for the region. PRISM data represent 1971-2000 normals, with 800 m grid.

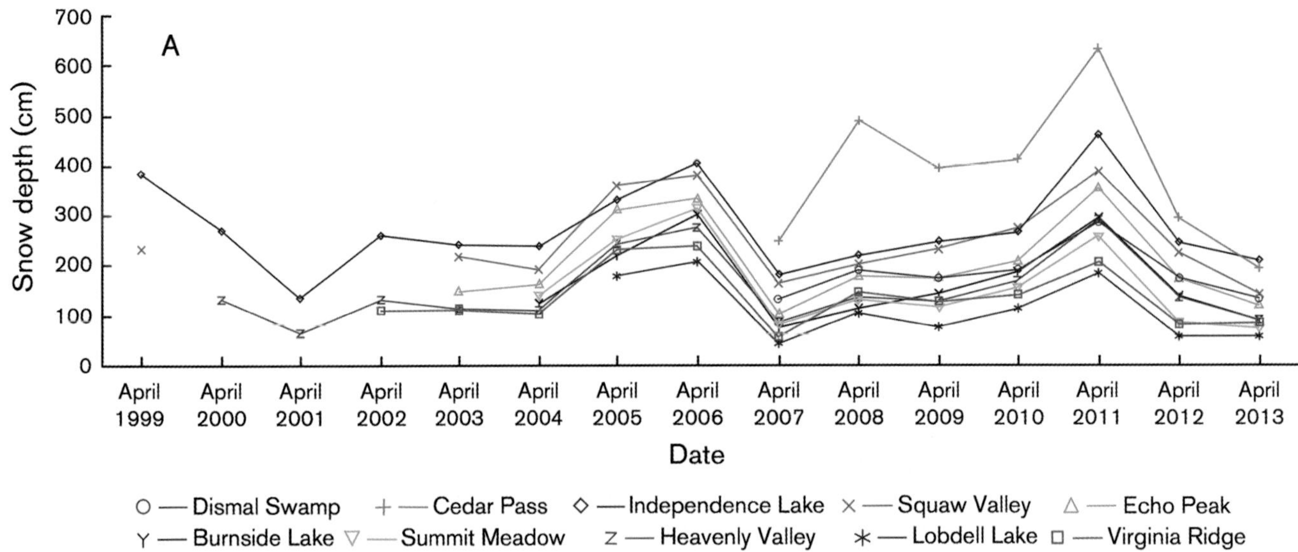

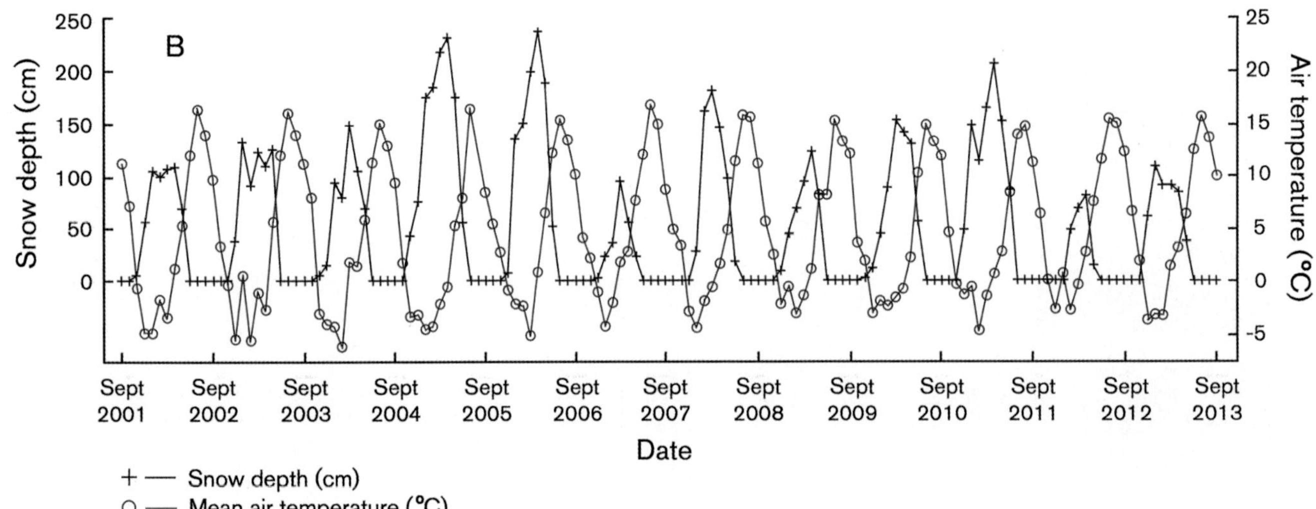

FIGURE 28.3 Snow depths from SNOTEL snow-monitoring stations in California subalpine zones. Source: Data extracted from NRCS SNOTEL station data, 2013.

A Snow-depth variation (April 1) across diverse subalpine locations in the Warner Mountains (Dismal Swamp, Cedar Pass), Sierra Nevada (Independence Lake, Squaw Valley, Echo Peak, Burnside Lake, Summit Meadow, Virginia Ridge), Carson Range (Heavenly Valley), and Sweetwater Mountains (Lobdell Lake), 1999–2013.

B Monthly snow depth and temperature variation at the Virginia Ridge SNOTEL site in the subalpine forest of the Sierra Nevada (2879 meters), 2001–2013.

ability are forcing mechanisms related to ocean circulation. Precipitation especially varies in episodic, often quasi-cyclic manners, and in patterns that vary across California (Redmond and Koch 1991, Abatzoglou et al. 2009). In particular, the El Niño–Southern Oscillation (ENSO) (Cayan et al. 1999) and multidecadal modes, including the Pacific Decadal Oscillation (PDO) and Atlantic Multidecadal Oscillation (Mantua et al. 1997, Cayan et al. 1998, McCabe et al. 2004), drive large differences in precipitation delivered to California among years and among decades (see Chapter 2, "Climate"). An example of vegetation response to these variations is the episodic response of lodgepole pine recruitment into subalpine meadows during the twentieth century, which occurred during negative phases of the PDO (Millar et al. 2004). Particularly important for biota are recurring multiyear droughts that characterize the instrumental record (Cayan et al. 1999) as well as historical reconstructions (Biondi et al. 2001, Cook et al. 2007); these droughts often trigger forest insect and pathogen infestation (e.g., limber and whitebark pine; see Millar, Westfall et al. 2007; Millar et al. 2012). Recent research is also elucidating the importance of ATMOSPHERIC RIVERS (Dettinger 2013) as a significant determinant of interannual variability in precipitation that, at elevations of subalpine forests, translates to large differences in snowpack (McCabe and Dettinger 1999) (see Figure 28.3b).

California's high wind speeds may occur anywhere within the state, with the greatest velocities at high elevations (WRCC 2013). An important controlling factor exerted by wind on subalpine forests is in combination with snowfall and topography, which together influence snowpack drifting

FIGURE 28.4 Wind-sculpted and wind-thrown whitebark pine forests near treeline. Photos: Constance Millar.

A Stunted trees and krummholz matts, Mount Dunderberg, Sierra Nevada.

B Windthrow in whitebark forests as a result of the autumn 2011 extreme downslope wind event, Tioga Crest, Sierra Nevada.

and variability in snow depth. Patches and zones of deeper, wind-influenced snowdrifts define areas that retain moisture late into the growing season (persistent snowfields) and have higher CWD. Many of these locations support subalpine forest but are surrounded by dry upland slopes with herbaceous or shrub cover. Scattered across the landscape, these support small to large "snowpocket forests," which tend to occur on north aspects and in slumps, along stepped terrain, or in depressions. In interaction with forest density, wind also influences the distribution of snow accumulation under the forest canopy. Low-moderate forest densities typical of many subalpine forests maintain the highest amount of snowpack relative to either higher or lower densities (Raleigh et al. 2013, Lundquist et al. 2014). Chronic winds in exposed areas, especially in winter when tree crowns are not protected by snow, affect crown growth and shape (e.g., krummholz and branch flagging; Figure 28.4a) and limit tree regeneration to wind-sheltered sites.

Windthrow is relatively rare in subalpine forests, given the inherent mechanical capacity of the species to accommodate and resist wind. Occasionally, however, the "perfect storm" of atmospheric conditions coincides to produce monstrous wind events. The most recent and potentially largest recorded of these was an extreme downslope wind event in the central Sierra Nevada on November 30 and December 1, 2011. This extreme event was unusual for its wind direction (north), duration (over twelve hours), and sustained high velocities, which exceeded 145 kilometers per hour for the duration of the event with gusts over 240 kilometers per hour (Hilimire et al. 2013). Montane forests on the high west slopes of Yosemite National Park and Devil's Postpile National Monument sustained massive, although localized, forest downfall, and subalpine whitebark pine forests of this region also experienced dramatic local areas of windthrow (see Figure 28.4b).

Avalanches occur throughout the snow zone of California's mountains but become more common with increasing elevation and steeper slopes. Avalanches exert locally important controls on subalpine forest ecosystems through effects on tree size, form, persistence, and species diversity. Severe avalanches uproot both mature and most young trees, and recurring avalanches maintain slopes in treeless conditions, favoring sprouting shrubs such as alder (*Alnus* spp.). Avalanches also produce a variety of geomorphic effects on subalpine environments. These include scouring soils from hillslopes, maintenance of vertical troughs, accumulation of debris in the runout zone, and creation of impact and scour pits (Davis 1962). In some canyons avalanches are common enough (≥ one per decade) to give the slopes a striped appearance, where the tracks are treeless or with young tree cohorts and are separated by protected zones where mature forests can develop (Martinelli 1974, Mears 1992). Where avalanches are separated by intervals of several decades, conifers or aspen often regrow. A thick jumble of debris can remain in avalanche runout zones for decades if undisturbed and potentially influences other disturbances such as fire, insects, and disease. Along the edges of avalanche tracks, surviving trees are often broken and twisted with bark broken off—conditions that stress trees and favor entry of insects. During heavy snowpack years, such as the record wet winter of 1985–1986, avalanches occurred in unusually high numbers in the Sierra Nevada and toppled hundreds of hectares of subalpine forest (Wilson 1986, Kattleman 1996). A large proportion of trees were 125–150 years old. Some trees destroyed near Sonora Pass were 350 years old. The effect of avalanches in that season on forest throwdown can still be seen from many transmountain passes, such as along Tioga Pass in Yosemite National Park.

Ecosystems of the Subalpine Forest Zone

Subalpine ecosystems in California are commonly dominated by open stands of conifer forest. Local areas of deciduous broadleaf trees can also occur along riparian corridors or other areas with available water. Scattered areas of wet and dry meadows, often with associated shrublands, are present; extensive montane chaparral communities dominate some regions. Through all of the subalpine forest communities in California is a general pattern of decreasing stand densities and basal areas with increasing elevation (Pinder et al. 1997). These declines are associated with a complex mix of environmental and climatic factors, including decreasing soil depth and development, lower temperature, shortening of the growing season, increased wind, and increased effects of snowmelt depth and topography on water availability. Models of site moisture availability and irradiance coupled with field measurements of stand characteristics and tree-ring records suggest strong correlations of microsite conditions with age class (Bunn et al. 2005). Finally, these declines have also been associated with lower nutrient inputs from aboveground litter (Fites-Kaufman et al. 2007).

Subalpine Adaptations to Extreme Physical Conditions

Many species of subalpine ecosystems, like those in the alpine zone, have evolved specialized adaptations to endure extreme climates and environments including rocky substrates with thin, poorly developed and often nutritionally impoverished soils; steep, unstable slopes that experience avalanches and landslides; and subfreezing temperatures, high and desiccating winds, and intense solar radiation. A case in point is Great Basin bristlecone pine, which grows in the White-Inyo and Panamint Ranges of California and many more ranges in Nevada and Utah. Throughout its distribution, bristlecone pine forests occur at the highest elevations and extreme exposures under cold, arid climates.

Evolved adaptations to these conditions are many. One that contributes to the species capacity to persist in these environments is its needle retention, which is longer than other conifer species, reaching over fifty years (Barber 2013, Ewers and Schmid 1981). This unusual capacity enables trees to retain foliage and to photosynthesize (i.e., to survive) even during multiyear periods when weather conditions in the growing season are severe enough that new needles cannot develop. Waxiness and resin buildup on needles add to their durability as well. Another attribute contributing to the species' persistence and great longevity is the capacity to form stripbark growth. This occurs when portions of the main stem (secondary cambium) die back as the tree ages. This leaves increasingly smaller strips of live stem (cambium) and bark on one side of the tree. Such stripbark trees can continue to grow for centuries and millennia—a capacity shared with only a few other, and mostly subalpine, conifers.

The stripbark habit is assumed to be an adaptation to the extreme climate conditions of the species' range, enabling trees to "cast away" branches and stem as stress increases and remain alive with only part of the vasculature and crown functional. Many bristlecone pines, especially those that have developed stripbark, also have intensely spiral grain, known to be a highly heritable trait. This leads to a corkscrew form of the main stem, which has the effect of exposing more of the crown—especially when a narrow strip as a result of stripbark—to sunlight. High fecundity of bristlecone pine is known to persist throughout the life of individuals, and even trees more than three millennia in age produce many cones with fertile seed. Because replacement is very low for long-lived individuals, this high fecundity of stands of mixed ages provides high genetic diversity for seedling generations that can be important for natural selection as climates change over the course of time (decades to millennia).

Another example of adaptation to extreme conditions of the subalpine zone is the crown plasticity of several conifer species, especially the capacity to form krummholz. This ability to tolerate nonapical-dominance and to spread laterally allows species such as whitebark pine, limber pine, and mountain hemlock to remain below the sheltering influence of winter snowpacks, where temperatures are stable at freezing temperature and protected from desiccating winds.

Whitebark Pine Forests

Whitebark pine is a wide-ranging treeline species that extends from central British Columbia east to Wyoming and south to the central Sierra Nevada (Weaver 2001). It forms the dominant treeline species in the southern Cascade Range and on the higher slopes in the Warner Mountains. Whitebark pine forests are scattered in the Klamath Mountains with populations on Mount Eddy, Thompson Peak, Russian Peak, and the Marble Mountains (Griffin and Critchfield 1976). At several locations in the Klamath Mountains, such as Crater Creek and Sugar Creek Research Natural Areas (RNAs), stands of exceptional subalpine diversity exist with high density, productivity, and basal area (Cheng 2004). In these areas, whitebark pine is one prominent subalpine forest type out of seven that commonly occur.

Whitebark pine is common in the bands of subalpine ecosystems that ring the southern Cascade volcanoes, especially Mounts Shasta and Lassen. Whitebark pine forests occur mixed with mountain hemlock as low as 2,103 meters along ridgetops of the Antelope Creek RNA, forming one of the lowest subalpine whitebark pine occurrences in this region (Cheng 2004). In the Sierra Nevada, whitebark pine ecosystems occur abundantly from the Lake Tahoe Basin south to Mount Whitney. In the central Sierra, whitebark pine typically is present in mixed stands with lodgepole pine, mountain hemlock, and Sierra juniper; while in the southern Sierra it grows with limber pine and slightly overlaps in range with foxtail pine (see Figure 28.1). A watershed study in Eastern Brook Lakes on the eastern slope of the Sierra Nevada at 3,170 to 3,780 meters found mixed dominance of lodgepole pine and whitebark pine. The mean leaf area index for canopies of whitebark pine was 4.6 m^2m^2, compared to 4.1 m^2m^{-2} for lodgepole pine (Peterson et al. 1989).

Whitebark pine forests are considered KEYSTONE ECOSYSTEMS for the subalpine zone throughout the cordillera of western North America (Tomback and Achuff 2010). Whitebark pine is highly plastic in crown and growth form and varies readily in response to severity of growing conditions. On favorable sites it can form upright, small trees 10 to 15 meters in height that live to 350 years. At higher elevations above treeline or exposed slopes below, its crown becomes stunted, often exhibiting gnarled and twisted branches in response to desiccating winds. A lower ground layer of prostrate crown is often present in these stands. In the treeline ecotone and up to 500 meters above treeline, whitebark pines readily take on a multistemmed krummholz form of growth, and finally a low mat of growth less than 1 meter in height (Fites-Kaufman et al. 2007). At these locations whitebark pine stands commonly form monotypic communities that dominate the upper treeline ecotone and play important roles in snowpack retention. Krummholz plants often root as the crowns spread across the ground, and individuals can live up to 1,700 years old (King and Graumlich 1998). Krummholz mats are often thought to be CLONAL, deriving from a single seed, but genetic studies show this is not the case, at least for krummholz trees with crowns larger than about 3 meters in diameter (Rogers et al. 1999). A single krummholz mat can comprise 2 to 12 genets, with genetic variation and genetic distance among individuals within the krummholz increasing in the downwind direction. Krummholz crowns are very dense and provide important hiding cover for small mammals, especially the white-tailed hare (*Lepus townsendii*). A remarkable coadaptation exists between whitebark pine cones and seeds and Clark's nutcracker (*Nucifraga columbiana*), a midsized bird in the crow family (Tomback 2001). Increasing density in whitebark pine ecosystems in recent decades might relate to changes in behavior of Clark's nutcracker in response to changing climates as well as to direct response by the pine.

Whitebark pine forests exemplify a trend observed for other subalpine forests in California, with the exception of limber pine. Whereas there appears to be little significant advance of whitebark pine seedlings above the twentieth-century upper treeline, density in these zones has been steadily increasing throughout the century, with a net increase in the Sierra Nevada of 30%, including a 44–91% increase in small tree densities (Dolanc et al. 2013). Correspondingly, the density of large trees has declined. These increases in small tree density are accelerating, especially above 3,000 meter elevation.

Western White Pine Forests

Western white pine (*Pinus monticola*) extends from British Columbia through the Cascade Range and Klamath Mountains, through the northern Great Basin ranges of California, and throughout the Sierra Nevada, where it reaches its limit in southern Tulare County. In the Sierra Nevada it is a minor component of upper montane forests but becomes increasingly important in subalpine habitats, although monotypic stands are rarely more than a few hectares. Most commonly, western white pine mixes with lodgepole pine, Jeffrey pine, mountain hemlock, red fir, and/or whitebark pine (Potter 1998). Although Sierran trees of this species may reach 40 meters in height and 2.5 meters in diameter, larger sizes are attained by the same species in the northern Rocky Mountains and Pacific Northwest (Van Pelt 2001). Western white pine generally maintains an upright tree form of growth nearly to treeline, where it is commonly replaced by whitebark pine or foxtail pine depending on geography. Seedlings are reported to be relatively few compared to other subalpine conifers (Parker 1988).

Foxtail Pine Forests

Foxtail pine is the dominant subalpine and treeline pine of the southern Sierra Nevada and is locally important in subalpine forests of the Klamath Mountains. It has highly disjunct populations, with the Sierran and Klamath distributions separated by hundreds of kilometers. These two groups of populations are well differentiated, with the southern Sierra Nevada taxon, subspecies *austrina*, morphologically distinct in the foliage, bark, cones, and seeds from populations of subspecies *balfouriana* in the Klamath Mountains (Mastrogiuseppe and Mastrogiuseppe 1980). The disjunction of these two populations is thought to relate to the development of summer-dry Mediterranean climates during the late Tertiary (Millar 1996) further modified by effects of glacial/interglacial cycles of the Pleistocene and drought conditions of the mid-Holocene (Eckert et al. 2008).

Foxtail pine in the Sierra Nevada is restricted to higher elevations (2,600–3,660 meters) south of the Middle Fork of the Kings River. At its lower elevational limits it often occurs in open stands with lodgepole pine, Jeffrey pine, western white pine, and red fir. At higher elevations it forms relatively pure but low-density stands, although it often mixes with limber pine. Treeline stands of foxtail pine often show a preference for cooler, north-facing slopes (Rundel and Rabenold 2014), likely related to soil moisture availability (Bunn et al. 2005). Vankat and Major (1978) sampled stands of foxtail pine from elevations of 3,170 to 3,290 meters in Sequoia National Park and reported a relatively high mean density of 418 tree ha^{-1} and a canopy cover of 26%, with a basal area of 31 m^2ha^{-1}. Tree densities and stand basal areas, however, decline with increasing elevation from foxtail pine woodlands to treeline (Lloyd 1997, 1998, Rundel and Rabenold 2014).

Foxtail pines can grow to be several thousand years old. Like bristlecone pine, foxtail pine has highly resinous wood that with the cold, arid climates in the southern Sierra Nevada can persist as remnant dead wood for millennia. Together the live and dead wood are important archives for paleoclimatic and paleoecological study. Foxtail pines have been documented to respond to warm and cold historical climate periods by, respectively, advancing upslope and retract-

FIGURE 28.5 Limber pine forests on the eastern escarpment of the Sierra Nevada, south of Mammoth Lakes. Photo: Constance Millar.

ing downslope (Scuderi 1993, Lloyd and Graumlich 1997). In the Klamath Mountains, foxtail pine plays a more diverse ecological role than in the Sierra Nevada. Habitat heterogeneity at multiple spatial scales has been found to favor persistence of foxtail pine populations in northwest California (Eckert 2010). At large spatial scales, the presence of ultramafic (low silica content, often basic) soils favors this species relative to other conifers and leads to greater ecological importance.

Limber Pine Forests

Limber pine has a wide range extending from central Alberta and South Dakota south to New Mexico in the Rocky Mountains and across the higher ranges of the Great Basin. In California limber pine is most common along the eastern escarpment of the Sierra Nevada, where it extends from scattered and disjunct stands in Buckeye Canyon near Bridgeport, California, then southward with increasing importance (Figure 28.5). The transition at the north between limber pine and whitebark pine forests appears to reflect the latter's higher tolerance of high snowloads and long, dry summers. In Tulare County of the far southern Sierra, extensive limber pine forests occur on the west slope of the crest as well as on the east slope. In its Sierran belt, limber pine has a niche similar to whitebark pine as the upper-treeline dominant species, even forming ragged krummholz in the treeline ecotone. North of Mammoth Lakes, limber pine becomes restricted to steep, north slopes, usually of decomposed or fractured granitic rocks, whereas to the south and in other mountain ranges (with the exception of the White Mountains) it grows on diverse soil types and all aspects.

In the White and Inyo Mountains limber pine is common on granitic and other noncarbonate soils of the subalpine zone. At low and middle elevations limber pine forests are often monotypic, with virtually closed canopy conditions. At higher elevations, sparse stands comprise scattered gnarled giants that can live to two thousand years. Sharp delineations generally occur between limber pine stands on granitic soils and open stands of bristlecone pine on soils of dolomite parent material. While bristlecone pines occasionally mix with limber pine, few mature limber pine stands occur on dolomite soils in these mountains, and bristlecones have higher upper- and lower-range boundaries. Curiously, however, limber pine seedlings have been recruiting 300 meters upslope in the late twentieth and early twenty-first centuries, above living bristlecone pine forests. Further, these upslope expansions are occurring on dolomite soils, at least in the White Mountains above Patriarch Grove and in the northern Cottonwood Canyon, at elevations and locations where no live bristlecone pine seedlings have yet established. Similar recruitment by limber pine seedlings (only) above current upper treeline is under way in granitic soils in the northern White Mountains.

Limber pine forests also occur in Great Basin ranges north of the White Mountains, including the Sweetwater Mountains, Bodie Hills, and Glass Mountains. In the Sweetwaters, limber pine dominates the northern peaks, which have mafic soils of Tertiary volcanic origin, whereas whitebark pine forest is more common on the felsic (more silica-rich) soils of the southern peaks. In the Bodie Hills, limber pine is highly restricted and occurs as scattered individuals on Potato Peak and Bodie Mountain and small stands on the Brawley Peaks and Mount Hicks, just across the Nevada state line. Extensive stands occur in subalpine zones on the barren soils of Quaternary volcanic origin of the Glass Mountains and Mono-Inyo Craters.

Limber pine forests form the treeline community in the higher Transverse and Peninsular Ranges of southern California, with relict populations at relatively low elevations on the crests of Mount Pinos, Brush Mountain, and Frazier Mountain near the junction of the Transverse and Central Coast Ranges. These last populations occur as scattered trees at elevations of approximately 2,600 meters within an open forest dominated by Jeffrey pine. The presence of a relict alpine FELLFIELD (slope area with plant communities influenced by abiotic frost and freeze/thaw dynamics) community on the crest of Mount Pinos suggests that seasonal drought conditions and strong winds may allow the survival of limber pine (Gibson et al. 2008).

Although similar in general appearance, limber pine is not closely related to whitebark pine. Like whitebark pine, however, limber pine has convergently evolved large pine nuts that rely heavily on Clark's nutcrackers for seed dispersal (Tombach and Kramer 1980, Carsey and Tomback 1994).

FIGURE 28.6 Mountain hemlock forests favor cool, moist, often north-facing aspects, such as in Convict Canyon of the Sierra Nevada. Photo: Jeffrey Wyneken.

Unlike whitebark pine, limber pine cones open at maturity, and the seeds have a rudimentary wing. Some seeds are no doubt dispersed by wind and gravity, albeit at relatively short distances from the mother tree.

Bristlecone Pine Forests

Great Basin bristlecone pine forms subalpine forests from Utah westward across the higher Great Basin ranges to the White Mountains, with scattered populations in the Inyo and Last Chance Mountains and on Telescope Peak in the Panamint Range. In the White Mountains bristlecone pine occurs largely on dolomite soils, although scattered trees may be present on sandstone and granitic soils with limber pine at elevations of 3,100 to 3,700 meters (Billings and Thompson 1957, Wright and Mooney 1965). It is a medium-size tree, typically 5–15 meters in height and trunk diameters up to 2.5–3.6 meters. Cones open at maturity, and the small seeds are winged and aerodynamic, although Clark's nutcrackers also disperse bristlecone pine. Some large-diameter trees have multiple stems, potentially resulting from seeds cached by Clark's nutcrackers (Carsey and Tombach 1994).

Bristlecone pines are a remarkable species in many respects. Their most well-known feature is the great age reached by individuals, making them the oldest known nonclonal organisms. In 2012 a tree in the White Mountains was found to be 5,062 years old, making it more than two centuries older than the famous Methuselah Tree, the former record holder. Tree ages vary with slope aspect in the White Mountains. North-facing slopes typically have the oldest trees, with an average of 2,000 years as compared to 1,000 years on south-facing slopes. The dry subalpine climate coupled with the durability of bristlecone wood can preserve them long after death, with dead trunks as old as 7,000 years scattered among living trees. The great longevity of trees and the long persistence of remnant dead wood combine to make bristlecone pine forests one of the most important scientific archives in the world for historical climate. Cross-dated tree-ring series, compiled from live and dead trees in overlapping fashion, have been developed for more than 9,000 continuous years of growth into the past. A short, several-century gap (no wood found) separates that archive from another well-resolved 2,000-year chronology. Climate reconstructions from this 11,000-year record provide continuous proxies for annual, interannual, decadal, and centennial climate variability over the entire Holocene.

Bristlecone pine stands on dolomite in the White Mountains are notable for their almost complete lack of woody understory plants—a striking contrast to the stands of limber pine, where a number of shrub species are present. Herbaceous perennials growing on dolomite also often differ substantially in community structure from fellfield communities a few meters away on granitic soils. Similarly sharp boundaries exist between dolomite soil communities and nearby sagebrush-dominated communities on shale substrate.

Mountain Hemlock Forests

Mountain hemlock forests have a broad distribution that extends from the coastal ranges of Alaska south through British Columbia and the Pacific Northwest into the Sierra Nevada. In the northern Sierra Nevada this species can be found in upper montane forests of red fir and lodgepole pine (Potter 1998) but is more characteristic at higher elevations up to 3,500 meters, where it is frequently the dominant tree species in mixed stands with Sierra juniper and whitebark pine. Mountain hemlock is locally abundant in the Klamath Mountains and the subalpine zones of Mounts Shasta and Lassen in the southern Cascades. Most of the extent of mountain hemlock forests in the Sierra Nevada occurs from Sierra County south through Yosemite National Park, with a few isolated stands reaching Fresno and Tulare County.

Mountain hemlock in the Sierra Nevada is most characteristic of moist but well-drained mountain soils, often showing a preference for north-facing slopes (Figure 28.6; Fites-Kaufman et al. 2007). This contrasts with stands in the southern Cascade Range, where greater summer precipitation and warmer temperatures broaden topographic distribution (Parker 1994, 1995). Expansion of mountain hemlock in Lassen Volcanic National Park has been traced to warming temperatures as the Little Ice Age terminated in the early twentieth century, a response that might indicate the species' behavior to continued warming in the future (Taylor 1995).

FIGURE 28.7 Old-growth tree on Glass Mountain. Sierra juniper forests contain trees of often massive size and growing on exposed, rocky substrates. Photo: Constance Millar.

In the central Sierra of Yosemite National Park, mountain hemlock forests can be found in extensive groves with virtually closed canopies and individual trees reaching up to 30 meters in height and 2 meters in diameter. At higher elevations mountain hemlock is more scattered and often assumes a lower, shrubby growth form (Fites-Kaufman et al. 2007). Seedlings are relatively shade-tolerant compared to other subalpine conifers and grow well under this type of canopy. South of Yosemite, mountain hemlock becomes increasingly restricted to small stands in cold moist valleys and sheltered ravines, where snowbanks remain late into the summer. Unlike pure stands of the central and northern Sierra Nevada, these scattered trees in the southern portions of the range are commonly mixed with lodgepole pine, foxtail pine, western white pine, and red fir. The southernmost occurrence of mountain hemlock is below Silliman Lake in northern Tulare County, the site of a small grove of about sixty trees with heights up to 24 meters, diameters to nearly 90 centimeters, and healthy reproduction (Parsons 1972).

Sierra Juniper

Sierra juniper is one of the most striking trees of subalpine Sierra Nevada ecosystems, with its short but massive trunk appearing to grow out of seemingly solid granite substrate (Figure 28.7). It ranges through the high Sierra Nevada from south of Susanville to Owens Peak in Kern County, with scattered trees in the Inyo, White, and Panamint Mountains (Griffin and Critchfield 1976). Disjunct populations also occur in the San Gabriel and San Bernardino Mountains. Sierra juniper typically grows on shallow soils from 2,100 to 3,000 meters elevation, often with Jeffrey pine, red fir, whitebark pine, mountain hemlock, and/or lodgepole pine. More than any other subalpine tree, Sierra juniper has a remarkable ability to colonize and become established in small fractures of granite domes that would not support other species.

Upper montane forests of lodgepole pine forest in the Tahoe Basin support mixed stands of Sierra juniper with red fir and Jeffrey pine, but these associated tree species are replaced by western white pine and mountain hemlock with increasing elevation (Fites-Kaufman et al. 2007). More typically, Sierra juniper occurs mixed in lodgepole pine stands up to treeline, where it may take on a krummholz growth form. Some Sierra junipers are reported to reach ages of over a thousand years (Graf 1999). The largest Sierra juniper—a tree 26 meters in height and 4 meters in diameter—is reported from the Stanislaus National Forest (Lanner 1999).

Lodgepole Pine Forests

Open stands of lodgepole pine form a widespread forest belt that covers the upper montane zone and extends into the subalpine over much of California's high mountains (Figure 28.8). The most common lodgepole pine taxon in subalpine forests is *Pinus contorta* subsp. *murrayana*, as distinguished from the Rocky Mountain lodgepole pine (*P. contorta* subsp. *latifolia*), the beach pine of the coastal Pacific Northwest (*P. contorta* subsp. *contorta*), and the local endemic Bolander pine of the pygmy forest area of Mendocino County (*P. contorta* subsp. *bolanderi*). Lodgepole pine forests extend over a very broad geographic and elevational range, including subalpine inclusions in the Klamath Mountains (including an unnamed Del Norte County variant), through the southern Cascades with populations as low as about 1,000 meters on Mount Shasta, in the northern Sierra Nevada to elevations of about 1,830–2,400 meters, and up to 2,440–3,350 meters in the southern Sierra Nevada. Topography strongly influences elevational distribution; lodgepole pine forests reach much lower elevations with cold air drainage down glacial canyons (Potter 1998, Fites-Kaufman et al. 2007).

Lodgepole pine forests also commonly extend up into the subalpine zone in the northern and central Great Basin ranges, including the Warner Mountains, Carson Range, Sweetwater Mountains, Bodie Hills, and Glass Mountains. Disjunct colonies grow in the White Mountains, the largest of which is a nearly pure stand of approximately 100 hectares near Cabin Creek at 3,200 meters (Critchfield 1957). Larger populations appear on the San Gabriel, San Bernardino, and San Jacinto Mountains in southern California. Lodgepole pine has broad environmental tolerances, colonizing both shallow, rocky soils and semi-saturated meadow edges in an elevational belt from sea level to subalpine habitats. Only

FIGURE 28.8 Lodgepole pine forests often have narrow crowns and relatively closed canopies in the subalpine zone, as in Molybdenite Canyon, Sierra Nevada. Photo: Constance Millar.

rarely does it comprise true treeline forest ecosystems, as it is more typically replaced by whitebark pine, foxtail pine, or limber pine. The generally low stature and open stand structure of lodgepole pine subalpine forests are a function of the short growing season, associated severe climate conditions, and the thin, nutrient-poor soils that characterize the subalpine zone. These stands commonly contain few understory shrubs and little litter accumulation. Mature lodgepole pines in the subalpine zone are generally smaller than mature individuals of the dominant treeline pines and only rarely exceed 50 centimeters in diameter.

Forests of Pacific Northwest Subalpine Tree Species

Three conifer species characteristic of subalpine communities of the Pacific Northwest and/or Rocky Mountains barely extend their range into California. Subalpine fir and Engelmann spruce (*Picea engelmannii*) are widespread in subalpine forests across western North America. The former has six known populations in the Klamath Ranges of western Siskiyou County at1,700 to 2,100 meters, while the latter is known from three populations in the lowest subalpine forests at 1,200 to 2,100 meters in the Klamath and Cascade Ranges. A third, wet-forest species from the Pacific Northwest, Alaska yellow-cedar, extends south from Alaska and barely reaches a few areas of the Klamath Mountains in Siskiyou and Del Norte Counties at elevations to 2,500 meters. While Alaska yellow-cedar is characteristically a species of cool, wet forests, its upper elevational limit extends into subalpine habitats.

Deciduous Subalpine Forests

Several deciduous, broad-leaved tree species form dense local stands of subalpine forest in moist environments such as riparian corridors, meadow fringes, and upland slopes with abundant soil moisture. The most common is quaking aspen, which commonly occurs in pure groves fringing wet or moist meadows and on slopes watered by springs or seeps with subsurface water, including talus slopes (Figure 28.9; Potter 1998, Fites-Kaufman et al. 2007). Aspen is widespread in appropriate habitats throughout subalpine areas of the Klamath Mountains, southern Cascade Range, Warner Mountains, Sierra Nevada, and the high mountains of southern California. Aspen is shade-intolerant and requires high light conditions to regenerate. It sprouts vigorously from suckers arising on an extensive lateral root system following fire, which plays an important role in perpetuating aspen stands by reducing competition for light from conifers. This sprouting results in a dense stand of trunks formerly assumed to be wholly clonal. More recent genetic studies reveal that some aspen groves comprise multiple genotypes (Tuskan et al. 1996). Health threats to aspen forests throughout the species range from native insects, pathogens, and incursions from conifer recruitment have heightened attention to this broadleaf ecosystem. Californian populations, however, have so far mostly been unaffected; areas of concern are concentrated in northeastern California and some parts of the northern Sierra Nevada. Notably, rapid mortality caused by sudden aspen decline (Shepperd 2008), first observed and studied in Rocky Mountain and intermountain populations, has not been reported in California (Morelli and Carr 2011).

Water birch (*Betula occidentalis*), a widespread multistemmed small tree 6–9 meters in height, occurs over a wide range of elevations across the western United States and Canada. In California, water birch ecosystems are common at 1,500 to 2,750 meters and grow mostly along stream corridors draining the east side of the central and southern Sierra Nevada into the Owens Valley, White Mountains, and in disjunct populations in the Klamath ranges. The species is absent from the northern Sierra Nevada and northern California. A third deciduous broadleaf tree that occasionally reaches subalpine habitats is black cottonwood (*Populus trichocarpa*). This tree is widespread on alluvial flats and streamsides across California up to 3,000 meters.

Curl-leaf mountain mahogany, a tall evergreen shrub or small tree in the rose family, extends into the subalpine zone of California, where it can form extensive and dense canopies on dry, rocky, and exposed slopes (Brayton and Mooney 1966). Mountain mahogany has a wide distribution in subalpine zones throughout California, including the Klamath Mountains, southern Cascades, Sierra Nevada, Great Basin ranges, and high ranges of southern California. It has

FIGURE 28.9 Quaking aspen stands are common along watercourses, such as in Parker Canyon of the eastern Sierra Nevada, along meadow edges, or on slopes with high soil moisture. Photo: Constance Millar.

extremely hard wood and can attain ages of least 1,350 years (Schultz et al. 1990). Mountain mahogany provides browse for deer and bighorn sheep and important hiding cover from predators for these and other midsize to large mammals. Mountain mahogany ecosystems influence subalpine conifers by fixing nitrogen through associated root nodules, thereby increasing available nitrogen in otherwise nutrient-limited high-elevation soils (Lepper and Fleschner 1977).

Subalpine Meadows

Meadows are scattered throughout the subalpine and montane forest zones of the Klamath Mountains, Cascade Range, Sierra Nevada, and high southern California mountains.

The single most important factor explaining the distribution of meadows is the presence of a shallow water table that provides high soil moisture and excludes establishment by woody plants (Wood 1975). Although the total area of meadows is small, herbaceous plant species in meadows make up a large part of the floral diversity of subalpine zones. Meadow community composition, productivity, and biomass vary widely depending on a suite of factors. Subalpine meadows can be classified into four broad types based on vegetation composition and water table depth. These broad meadow types have been further classified based on vegetation, elevation, water table, landform, hydrology, and soil characteristics (Bennett 1965, Benedict and Major 1982, Ratliffe 1985, Allen-Diaz 1991, Sawyer et al. 2009, Stevenson 2004, Rundel et al. 2009, Weixelman et al. 2001).

Wet meadows are composed predominately of perennial sedges, rushes, and grasses. Dominant species generally spread by rhizomes and often form dense sod over large areas. Soils in this type are saturated in the rooting zone for most of the growing season and are generally dark loams due to large amounts of organic material (Weixelman et al. 2001). In contrast, dry meadows are dominated by herbaceous species adapted to drier conditions, including grasses, sedges, and herbaceous dicots. Soils are not saturated within the rooting zone during the growing season, with saturation typically much deeper than the rooting zone (Allen-Diaz 1991, Weixelman et al. 2001). In shrub meadows, open areas are interspersed with clumps of shrubs, often willow (*Salix* spp.) but sometimes evergreen, ericaceous shrubs such as *Rhododendron columbianum* (formerly *Ledum glandulosum*), *Kalmia polifolia*, and *Vaccinium cespitosum* (Rundel et al. 2009). Willow stands can include any of a diverse set of *Salix* species as dominants and occur on sites with periodic flooding during the growing season. Floods allow the ongoing establishment of willow from seed. Drier shrub meadows can have scattered but significant cover of red heather (*Phyllodoce breweri*), pinemat manzanita (*Arctostaphylos nevadensis*), the winter deciduous Utah serviceberry (*Amelanchier utahensis*), bitter cherry (*Prunus emarginata*), and California mountain ash (*Sorbus californica*).

Woodland meadows are the fourth community type, typified by scattered sedges, grasses, and broadleaf herbs in open stands of lodgepole pine and/or aspen. Great diversity of herbaceous species occurs within this type, varying with elevation, water table, and geographic region, (Fites-Kaufman et al. 2007). The causes and dynamics of lodgepole pine establishment and survival in Sierra meadows appear to be a function of both existing water tables and climate cycles. Fluctuations in water table with interannual and interdecadal climate variability can result in cyclical lodgepole establishment, survival, and mortality (Bartolome et al. 1990, Millar et al. 2004).

Wildlife Diversity of Subalpine Forest Ecosystems

Fifty native mammal species commonly use California subalpine forest ecosystems as seasonal or permanent habitat (Table 28.3; Ingles 1965, Jameson and Peeters 2004). These include a range of orders and families, including shrews, bats, rabbits, many rodents, carnivores, and ungulates. Iconic species of the upper subalpine and alpine zones include yellow-bellied marmot (*Marmota flaviventris*), alpine chipmunk (*Neotamias alpinus*), Belding's ground squirrel (*Urocitellus beldingi*), American pika (*Ochotona princeps*), and both Sierra Nevada and desert bighorn sheep (*Ovis canadensis*), each of which depends on specific environments for shelter and forage. Unfortunately, all these species are challenged or thought to be at

TABLE 28.3
Mammal species that use California subalpine ecosystems as habitat (Ingles 1965; Jameson and Peeters 2004)

Order	Family	Species	
Insectivora	Soricidae	*Sorex*	*palustris*
			lyelli
			monticolus
Chiroptera	Vespertilionidae	*Myotis*	*lucifugus*
Lagomorpha	Ochotonidae	*Ochotona*	*princeps*
	Leporidae	*Lepus*	*americanus*
			californicus
			townsendii
Rodentia	Aplodontidae	*Aplodontia*	*rufa*
	Sciuridae	*Marmota*	*flaviventris*
		Tamias	*alpinus*
			amoenus
			minimus
			quadrimaculatus
			speciosus
			umbrinus
		Callospermophilus	*lateralis*
		Otospermophilus	*beecheyi*
		Urocitellus	*beldingii*
		Tamiasciurus	*douglasii*
	Geomyidae	*Thomomys*	*bottae*
			mazama
			monticola
	Cricetidae	*Reithrodontomys*	*megalotis*
	subf Cricetinae	*Neotoma*	*cinerea*
		Peromyscus	*maniculatus*
	subf Microtonae	*Clethrionomys*	*californicus*
		Microtus	*longicaudus*
			montanus
			oregoni
		Phenacomys	*intermedius*
	Zapodidae	*Zapus*	*princeps*
			trinotatus
	Erethizontidae	*Erethizon*	*dorsatum*
Carnivora	Canidae	*Canis*	*latrans*
		Vulpes	*vulpes*
	Felidae	*Felis*	*rufus*
		Puma	*concolor*

(continued)

TABLE 28.3 *(continued)*

Order	Family	Species	
	Mustelidae	*Gulo*	*gulo*
		Martes	*americana*
			pennanti
		Mephitis	*mephitis*
		Mustela	*erminea*
			frenata
		Taxidea	*taxus*
	Procyonidae	*Bassariscus*	*astutus*
		Procyon	*lotor*
	Ursidae	*Ursus*	*americanus*
Artiodactyla	Cervidae	*Odocoileus*	*hemionus*
		Ovis	*canadensis*

risk from various human stressors. Most common are declines or impacts associated with contemporary climate change (Moritz et al. 2008). Marmot, alpine chipmunk (Rubidge et al. 2012), bushy-tailed packrat (*Neotoma cinerea*; Moritz et al. 2008), and Belding's ground squirrel (Morelli et al. 2012) have experienced changes in distribution and population dynamics from warming temperatures and changing snowpacks. American pika has long been considered at risk from changing climate and appears threatened in the central Great Basin. California populations, however, appear to be more buffered against change (CDFW 2013).

Sierra Nevada bighorn sheep, a distinct subspecies in the central and southern Sierra Nevada, suffered drastic population declines over the twentieth century. The species was placed on the federal Endangered Species list in 2000 when its numbers declined to near one hundred. Implementation of formal recovery plans has led to recovery toward the goal of five hundred adults distributed throughout historical herd units (Stephenson et al. 2011).

Avian species that depend on subalpine forests include mountain bluebird (*Sialia currucoides*), red crossbill (*Loxia curvirostra*), pine grosbeak (*Pinicola enucleator*), Cassin's finch (*Carpodacus cassinii*), Williamson's sapsucker (*Sphyrapicus thyroideus*), black-backed woodpecker (*Picoides arcticus*) (Mayer and Laudenslayer 1988), and Clark's nutcracker (Meyer 2013). The dependence of whitebark pine on Clark's nutcracker for reproduction is a remarkable example of coadaptation among species in subalpine forests. Seed cones of whitebark pine are unique among the pines in having indehiscent bracts—that is, the cones do not break apart on their own when mature (Figure 28.10). Further, cones remain closed and tightly adhered to the stem even at seed maturity. Cones can only be broken open and seed released by Clark's nutcrackers, which in turn depend on whitebark pine seeds for food (Tomback 1982, 1986). The birds open the cones while on the tree, carry batches of seeds in specialized pouches under their bills, and plant seeds in caches, usually in protected locations. A single Clark's Nutcracker caches as many as ninety-eight thousand seeds per season (Hutchins and Lanner 1982). The birds have uncanny ability to relocate their caches, even under a meter of snow, and they utilize these caches to feed young birds through early growth and development. Sufficient seeds are left unrecovered by Clark's nutcrackers that whitebark pine seedlings can germinate (Lanner 1996). Clark's nutcrackers also use limber, foxtail, bristlecone, and western white pine. During migrations to lower altitudes, the birds also extensively harvest the seeds of pinyon pines.

Like Clark's nutcracker, several other bird species and small mammals serve important ecological roles for subalpine tree species. Douglas's squirrel (*Tamiasciurus douglasii*), lodgepole chipmunk (*Neotamias speciosus*), and other seed-caching wildlife species are important seed dispersers and predators of subalpine tree species in subalpine ecosystems (Tomback 1982, Van Der Wall 2008).

Origins of Subalpine Forest Species and Ecosystems

The biogeographic origins of California's present-day subalpine forest species and forest communities are highly complex given the geologic uplift and subsidence history, diversity of historical climates, and influences on vegetation of multiple periods of dramatic climate change that characterize the region (see Chapter 8, "Ecosystems Past: Vegetation Prehistory"; Millar 1996, 2012). The biogeography of most present-day species extends back more than twenty million years. However, species' locations, environmental contexts, elevations, climates, and vegetation associations have varied drastically over time. Many cool-temperate species, including subalpine conifers and other mountain-adapted plant species still in the region, found refugial habitat in the expansive Nevadaplano uplands during a long period when temperate zone climates elsewhere throughout North America were subtropical. The pre–Sierra Nevada ranges did not form a hydrologic divide as the Sierra Nevada do now, nor were they the

FIGURE 28.10 Coadaptations between (A) whitebark pine cone and (B) Clark's nutcracker ensure that the birds have sustenance and that pines are planted. Photos: Constance Millar.

highest summits of this expansive upland region. The elevations of many ranges within this Nevadaplano, including the pre-Sierran mountains, had summits estimated to extend more than 3,000 meters.

Fossil flora that date to the middle Tertiary from this region, now located mostly in Nevada but indicative of California, include a great diversity of gymnosperm and angiosperm taxa, including subalpine species with affiliations to bristlecone pine, foxtail pine, lodgepole pine, western white pine, Alaska yellow-cedar, and mountain hemlock (Millar 1996). These floras, however, do not reflect ecological stratification as do present upland communities, as they included in single associations a mix of diverse montane-adapted species as well as conifer taxa now occurring only in lower montane and coastal types. In addition, many summer/wet-adapted angiosperm species that grow now in southeast North America and even in subtropical climates co-occurred in these upland sites. The diversity and lack of zonation of these Tertiary floras is interpreted to indicate, despite the high elevations, that climates were relatively warm and wet with precipitation distributed year-round.

Subsequent changing dynamics of plate boundaries and new tectonic activity associated with the development of the San Andreas, Southern California Shear, and Walker Lane fault zones initiated massive changes to the topography and climate of the region. These in turn triggered drastic changes in the vegetation of the mountains of California and Nevada. By about ten million years ago, extensional forces led to the development of the Great Basin, with its more than three hundred fault-blocked mountains and basins and internal drainage, as well as to development of the present-day Sierra Nevada with its increasing significance as a major hydrologic divide. These tectonic changes catalyzed orographic rainshadow effects leading to vegetation zonation both in elevation, introducing modern subalpine ecosystems, and from the Pacific coast inland (i.e., longitudinally). The California Mediterranean-climate regime grew in dominance, exerting strong selection pressures for traits enhancing survival of increasingly long, dry summers. Truly arid environments (desert) and alpine ecosystems began to emerge for the first this time in the California/Nevada region as well. These changes triggered major extirpations of summer/wet-adapted species. Many montane conifers and cool/mesic-adapted plant species that had lived for millennia on the Nevadaplano persisted in the present-day Sierra Nevada and in northwest California while disappearing from inland Great Basin regions as climates dried.

The present-day diversity of subalpine conifers was in place in the California high mountain regions at the onset of the Quaternary, two million years ago (Millar and Woolfenden 1999). The roller-coaster climate changes that ensued brought as many as forty cycles of cold glacial and warm interglacial conditions to North America, with maximum temperature differences in the western mountains of as much as 8°C to 10°C (Millar 2012). Abrupt and gradual changes in climates catalyzed significant movements of subalpine conifers—downslope to 2,600 meters in the Sierra Nevada during glacials when ice caps covered the mountains and upslope during interglacials such as the present Holocene.

The maximum altitudinal response of subalpine species to glacial-interglacial cycles was approximately 1,000 meters. During the warmest intervals within interglacials, such as the mid-Holocene interval (four thousand to eight thousand years ago), treeline ascended about 100 meters higher than at present in the Sierra Nevada (Anderson 1990, Hallett and Anderson 2010) and as much as 150 meters in the White Mountains (LaMarche 1973). Compositions and associations of subalpine communities also changed between glacials and interglacials with changing taxonomic diversities, species abundances, population expansion and contractions (into important refugial areas), and changes in disturbance regimes (e.g., Mohr et al. 2000, Anderson 1990, Hallett and Anderson 2010) but with no apparent extirpations or extinctions (Millar and Woolfenden 1999). During the latter period of the last glacial period, 13,000 to 11,500 years ago, giant sequoia (*Sequiadendron giganteum*) moved far above its current range in the Sierra Nevada as recorded in a sediment core at 2,863 meters from East Lake. Its floristic associates included subalpine taxa and indicated that giant sequoia was part of the subalpine ecosystem at the time (Power 1998).

Changes in the fire regimes of mountain ecosystems across fluctuating glacials and interglacials mirrored changes in mountain climate and vegetation composition and structure (Skinner and Chang 1996). Where fire history studies have been done in the subalpine zones of California, they show increasing fire severity and extent when climate was wet enough to support dense forest growth, and reduced fire effects during dry intervals—both cold and warm—when subalpine forests became sparser. In the central Sierra Nevada near Mammoth Lakes during the end of the last glacial period, when climates were cold and dry and subalpine pine and mountain chaparral species remained sparse as they shifted upslope into deglaciated areas, fires were few and low severity (Hallett and Anderson 2010). After eight thousand years ago, as mountain hemlock moved into the region and dense forests formed, fire became more frequent and intense. During the warm and dry mid-Holocene, subalpine forests again became sparser and fire was less important. During the neoglacial dry periods starting approximately four thousand years ago, fire was also of minor importance in the subalpine forests. After about twelve hundred years ago, fires in the subalpine forests became increasingly synchronized with inferred drought, and fire activity in the high Sierra is interpreted to have been highly sensitive to dynamics of the El Niño–Southern Oscillation (Hallett and Anderson 2010).

In the Klamath Mountains fire history reconstructed over the past 15,500 years shows a slightly different pattern of changes in forest composition and density and fire relationships (Mohr et al. 2000). Before the end of the last glacial period, subalpine forests were open and parklike, dominated by scattered pines and firs and marked by low fire frequencies. Forest density increased in the latest Pleistocene and shifted to western white pine, lodgepole, and firs, yet fire frequency remained low during a period interpreted as cold and wet. During the middle Holocene, conditions became warm and dry with increasing fire frequencies. Similar, high frequencies were inferred at the onset of the neoglacial period four thousand years ago as hemlock increased in abundance, displacing pines and oaks. Elsewhere in the Klamath region, fire-scar records of the last four hundred years in the Scott Mountains show that fire return intervals ranged from one to seventy-six years with averages of about seven years (Skinner 2003). Most fires, however, scarred only one sampled tree, suggesting that although fires were frequent in subalpine forests, most were probably small and low-intensity.

In the southern Cascades, Bekker and Taylor (2001) found long fire return intervals over the past 350 years in subalpine forests of the Thousand Lake Wilderness. Fire regimes varied with forest composition, elevation, and inferred soil moisture, and fire return intervals ranged from twenty to thirty-seven years for lodgepole pine forests and twenty to forty-seven years for mountain hemlock types. Fires occurred mostly in the late growing season and dormant season (Bekker and Taylor 2001). Similar patterns marked historical western white pine subalpine forests over the last 350 years at Mount Lassen (Taylor 2001). In both regions of the southern Cascades, marked declines in fire frequency took place in the twentieth century.

Ecosystem Dynamics

Wildfire

By and large, fire is less important in subalpine forests than in forests at lower elevations. Landscape-scale fires are rare because high-elevation landscapes form a mosaic of individual trees; tree stands; upland shrub and herbaceous communities including meadows, wetlands, and riparian corridors; rock outcrops; talus; avalanche tracks; creeks; and lakes. Fuel buildup is usually slight in these extreme conditions with short growing seasons, limiting opportunities for fire to spread. In open whitebark pine woodlands and even krummholz communities, lightning ignitions can cause single trees to explode and burn, but fires that do start from these points tend to smolder at ground level and extend only to the edges of patches of fuel accumulation.

Where stand densities increase to the point of canopy closure, however, crown fires and fires of high intensity can occur in subalpine ecosystems. Even in these forests, such as lodgepole pine and mountain hemlock types, deep snowpacks and saturated soils from spring snowmelt usually restrict fires to the late growing season or dormant season (Skinner et al. 2006). On some shallow substrates with poor fertility, as in the Klamath Mountains and southern Cascade Range, fire behavior influences the persistence and dominance of montane shrub communities (e.g., *Arctostaphylos nevadensis, Chrysolepis sempervirens, Quercus vaccinifolia,* and *Ceanothus* spp.). Once trees are removed by crown fire and shrub species regenerate into burns, they can claim dominance over time because their resinous, highly flammable canopies increase fire frequencies and they sprout or seed into burned areas more successfully and rapidly than conifers (Pinder et al. 1997).

Where investigated, fire regimes in the denser subalpine forest types were characterized by long return intervals in the presettlement period (1700–1800s) (van de Water and Safford 2011). The longest fire interval reported, 133 years, is for typical subalpine forest types that include whitebark, bristlecone, limber and/or foxtail pine, and mixed stands containing those species plus western white pine, lodgepole pine, and mountain hemlock. Fire return interval for Sierra juniper forests, which almost always occur as sparse stands on rocky substrates, was eighty-three years. Western white pine and curl-leaf mountain mahogany forest fire return intervals were about fifty years, and lodgepole pine forest intervals were thirty-seven years. Somewhat unexpectedly given their high soil moistures, fire return intervals for aspen were shortest of all subalpine types at nineteen years (van de Water and Safford 2011).

Presettlement spatial patterns of fires in subalpine environments are difficult to assess and, except at the lower ecosystem border or in special conditions, mostly influence local structure and composition (Caprio and Graber 2000, Meyer 2013). Mean fire size in the southern Cascade subalpine elevations was estimated as 405 hectares for lodgepole pine forests and 140 hectares for red-fir/mountain hemlock, with mean size at Mount Lassen of 176 hectares. Studies in the Tahoe Basin indicate mostly small and patchy presettlement fires, with evidence that some areas burned severely enough to produce even-aged cohorts (Scholl and Taylor 2006). During the later twentieth and twenty-first century, observations of uncontrolled wildfires in subalpine forests of California indicate much smaller spatial extent than these presettlement estimates, with most less than 4 hectares (Meyer 2013). Even with a slight increase in fire size observed during the first decade of the twenty-first century (Miller et al. 2009), the small sizes and long return intervals of fire in subalpine forests underscore the minor and local effects that fires have on controlling ecosystem structure and function.

Insects and Pathogens

Cold temperatures, low humidities, rocky environments, and wide spacing of trees limit insects and disease-causing organisms to minor roles in subalpine forests. Although insects that damage or kill trees (e.g., defoliators and bark beetles) occur in forests at those elevations, they rarely reach outbreak conditions (but see Brunelle et al. 2008 for the Rocky Mountains). Their effects, as observed over the past century, have been to influence background mortality. In the latest twentieth and early twenty-first century, however, tree mortality related to insect and disease outbreaks appears to have vastly increased in subalpine forests of western North America. Investigation of these changes in bark beetle activities point to warming temperatures, which allow the insects to overwinter and in some locations to complete two generations each year (Logan and Powell 2001, 2007). In association with periodic drought, and in conditions where soil moisture stress is high, bark beetle outbreaks, primarily mountain pine beetle (*Dendroctonus ponderosae*) on whitebark pine, have been at record high levels.

California's subalpine forests have so far resisted landscape-scale mortality from bark beetles (Millar et al. 2012). They have experienced, however, population-scale outbreaks and mortality events in the late twentieth century and early twenty-first century on limber pine (*Pinus flexilis*) and whitebark pine (Millar, Westfall et al. 2007; Millar et al. 2012). Increasing background temperatures, multiyear drought, and low soil moisture (low CWD) are implicated in both cases. In both outbreaks only stands at low elevations for each species' range, northerly aspects, and young, dense, fast-growing stands were affected. Further, the degree of forest mortality increased latitudinally, from the southern Sierra Nevada to the Warner Mountains, reflecting improved conditions for insects as precipitation and stand densities increased (Millar et al. 2012).

Limitations to spread of beetle outbreak in California are likely related to endogenous factors (insect competitor and prey relations) but also to environmental context of the forests. California's historically warm and dry Mediterranean climate both preadapts forests to arid conditions and influences bark beetle behavior in ways quite different from situations in the Pacific Northwest and Rocky Mountains (Bentz et al. 2014). In Californian beetle populations, due to historic adaptation to warm, dry climates, the trend toward BIVOLTINISM (two generations per year) is less common, and will require greater temperature increases to evolve, than elsewhere.

The major disease-causing species in current subalpine forests of western North America is the invasive white pine blister rust (WPBR), caused by the fungus *Cronartium ribicola*. This fungus was introduced on nursery stock more than one hundred years ago and has since been spreading on five-needled pines (subgenus *Strobus*) throughout North American forests (Smith 1996). The high-elevation pine species are highly susceptible, but remote locations and unfavorable climate conditions have until recently limited effects on subalpine forests. In recent decades, WPBR has invaded subalpine forests in the Cascade Range, inland mountains, and Rocky Mountains. The rust has caused extensive mortality on whitebark pine, and in 2011 the U.S. Fish and Wildlife Service granted the species protection under the Endangered Species Act (USFWS 2011). California subalpine forests have so far experienced only localized mortality from WPBR (Maloney and Dunlap 2007, Dunlap 2012) in some parts of the western Sierra Nevada, Mount Rose, and at scattered, low levels elsewhere. WPBR has caused extensive damage to lower-elevation white pine species, especially sugar pine and western white pine.

A suite of other insects and pathogens cause minor damage and localized mortality on subalpine forests. Dwarf mistletoes (*Arceuthobium* spp.), a group of vascular plants that live aerially on conifer branches and stems, cause branch death and brooming on the subalpine pines and many other species (Hawksworth et al. 1996). Dwarf mistletoe is not common in subalpine forests but does occur on limber pine forests of the eastern Sierra Nevada (Millar, Westfall et al. 2007) and whitebark pine forests in northern California, where it appears to exacerbate outbreaks of mountain pine beetle.

In the first decade of the 2000s, occasional individual or clumps of bristlecone pine trees in the subalpine forests of the White Mountains were observed dying or experiencing branch dieback. These sporadic effects seem most likely to be caused by black stain fungus (*Leptographium wageneri*), a native species not known or expected to cause widespread damage to the bristlecone pine forests (B. Bulaon, U.S. Forest Service, pers. comm.). No mountain pine beetle incidences have been known in bristlecone pine forests of California to date. Native red turpentine beetle (*Dendroctonus valens*) has been found on bristlecone pine in the White Mountains but is mostly a secondary invader that forages on dying trees and dead wood.

Biogeochemical Cycling and Hydrology

The biologically rich subalpine and alpine basins of the Sierra Nevada have had a long history of descriptive study, with much of what is known about the hydrology and biogeochemical cycling coming from long-term studies of the subalpine Emerald Lake basin in Sequoia National Park (see Chapter 32, "Lakes"). Many of the hydrologic studies in the Sierra Nevada centered on assessing and monitoring patterns of seasonal and interannual change across large elevation gradients from subalpine and alpine watersheds to the San Joaquin Valley. Recent studies have shown that the fluctuations of selected rivers draining the Sierra Nevada and Rocky Mountains are highly correlated each spring, indicating an organized, regional-scale signal of snowmelt initiation and runoff (Cayan et al. 2001). These basins integrate the effects of broad ranges of aspect and elevation. Hydrologic studies in subalpine watersheds have focused on understanding streamflows, water balance, and the association of snowmelt and runoff with solute chemistry (Kattelmann and Elder 1991, Williams and Melack 1991 Meixner and Bales 2003, Meixner et al. 2004). Other studies have quantified the components of old water stored in the watershed from the previous year (10–20%) compared to new water from current snowmelt (80–100%) (Huth et al. 2004).

The Emerald Lake watershed provides a case study of biogeochemical cycles of nitrogen in a subalpine watershed (Tonnessen 2001). The soil pool of organic nitrogen was about ten times nitrogen storage in litter and biomass, and assimilation by vegetation was balanced by the release of nitrogen from litter decay, soil mineralization, and nitrification (Williams et al.

TABLE 28.4
Biomass of plant material in the 120 hectare Emerald Lake watershed, Sequoia National Park

Community type	Basin coverage (ha)	Aboveground biomass (kg ha-1)	Belowground biomass	Litter biomass
Willow	8.55	965	567	439
Mesic shrub	0.73	26.5	42.4	29.5
Mesic crevice	15.15	36.9	58.8	40.0
Wet meadow	4.14	130	999	47.3
Xeric crevice	13.40	6.0	33	48.7
Dry meadow	7.73	62.9	361	49.7
Fellfield	0.84	0.4	2.1	0.3
Colluvium	3.44	1.5	8.5	1.2
Trees	ND	16,000	5,630	37.7
TOTAL		**17,200**	**7710**	**694**

SOURCE: Adapted from Rundel et al. 1989. See Rundel et al. 2009 for a description of communities.

1995, Wolford et al. 1996, Wolford and Bales 1996, Meixner and Bales 2003, Sickman et al. 2001, 2003). Trees make up about 90% of the aboveground biomass and nitrogen in plant tissue in the watershed, but only about three-fourths of belowground biomass and half of belowground nitrogen (Table 28.4). As much as 90% of annual wet deposition of nitrogen was stored in the seasonal snowpack, and both nitrate and ammonium ions were released in a strong ionic pulse with the first fraction of spring snowmelt. This nitrate release was evident in a small but significant pulse in streamwater concentration with early snowmelt. However, almost all of the ammonium input from both wet and dry deposition was retained in the watershed by biological assimilation (Williams et al. 1995).

Ecosystem Services

Snowpack and Water Supply

By far the greatest ecosystem service provided by high mountain watersheds is their capacity for storage and delivery of critical water supply for downstream agricultural, industrial, urban use. Subalpine hydrologic reserves, stored primarily as winter snowpack, provide water both to the west in California and to the increasingly urbanized eastern front of the Sierra Nevada/Carson Ranges. Snowpack retention is an extremely important function of subalpine forests given the long Mediterranean summer drought regime of the California climate. Density of trees and canopy cover are important determinants in the amount of snow that develops on the forest floor and also on the retention into spring (Raleigh et al. 2013, Lundquist et al. 2014). Although many subalpine forests are sparse, those with moderate density provide the greatest snowpack retention of all forest types.

In addition to forest canopy and density, many factors affect the stability and hydrology of high-elevation environments. Subalpine ecosystems are sensitive to small changes in growing season conditions of temperature and water availability, and their stability impacts hydrological conditions of lowland ecosystems (Bales et al. 2006, Trujillo et al. 2012). Given the high interannual variability of precipitation in the California region, and corollary differences in snowpack depth, water supplies in the critical spring forecast season vary drastically (Figure 28.11). In that precipitation and snowpack vary greatly from year to year as a result of natural forcing (McCabe and Dettinger 1999), further impacts on these sensitive functions have large cascading impacts. The most significant effect on snowpack and water supply is from warming temperatures as a result of anthropogenic forcing on climate (Bonfils et al. 2008). With snowpack amount declining and snowmelt advancing, the ability to provide water to increasingly hot and arid urban users during a prolonging summer drought will be severely challenged (Stewart et al. 2005). The many skeletal and oligotrophic subalpine watersheds of the Sierra Nevada also have the potential to be strongly affected by atmospheric nitrogen deposition and acidification associated with the expanding urbanization of the San Joaquin Valley (Sickman, Leydecker et al. 2003).

Biodiversity

Subalpine ecosystems in California support important and distinct biodiversity. In addition to the tree diversity of subalpine forest ecosystems, many thousands of vascular and nonvascular plant species grow in the diverse habitats of California's high elevations. The Jepson eFlora lists taxa by floristic subprovinces, from which estimates for the number of plant taxa in several subalpine regions can be derived. Of more than 6,500 plant taxa in California as a whole, these include 1,710 species in the high North Coast Ranges, 1,860 species in the high Cascades, and 2,740 species in the Sierra Nevada (Jepson eFlora 2014). Although these numbers are only rough estimation of actual subalpine zone diversity, they

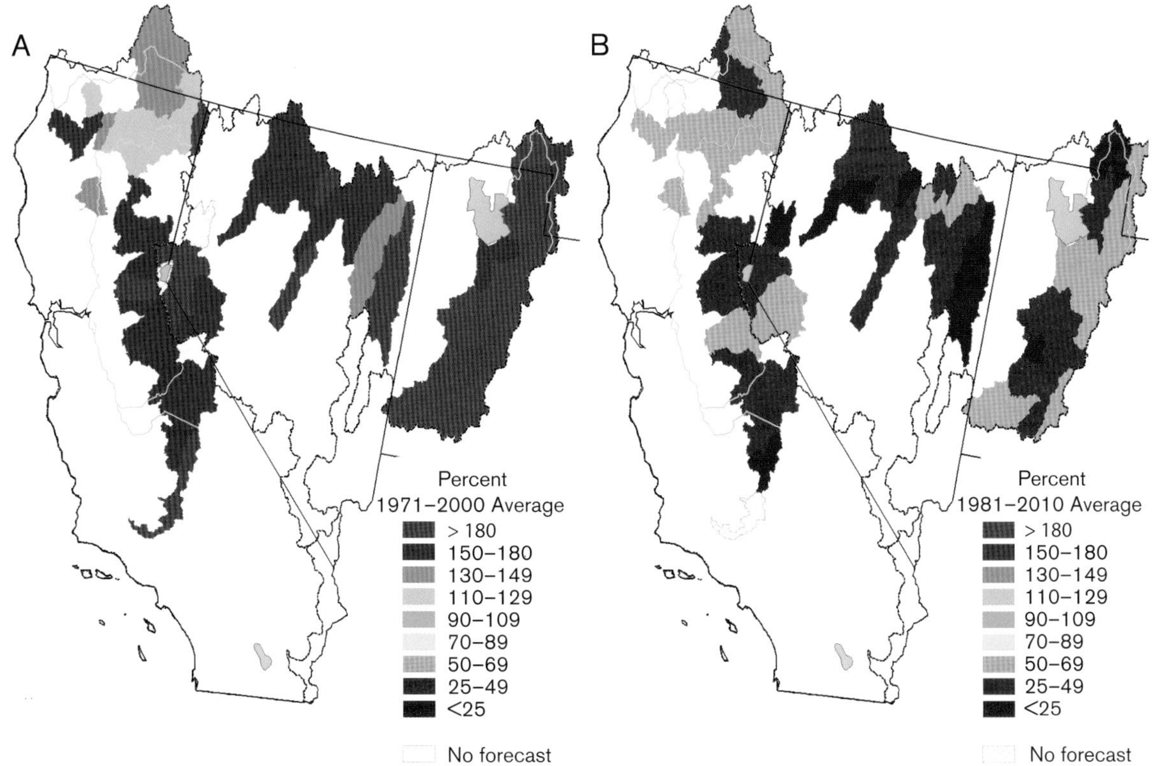

FIGURE 28.11 Great Basin and major water supply basins in California showing contrasting water years of wet (A, 2010–2011) and dry (B, 2012–2013). Source: From spring and summer streamflow forecasts by the U.S. Department of Agriculture Natural Resources Conservation Service (NRCS), National Water and Climate Center.

exemplify the high overall diversity and trend of increasing diversity southward. Wetlands and wet meadows support the highest plant biodiversity of all subalpine communities (see Chapter 31, "Wetlands"; Weixelman et al. 2011), including taxa with adaptations to high-elevation extreme temperatures, freeze-thaw conditions, extreme soil moisture variability, and heavy snow cover.

Meadows, riparian habitats, and other wetlands are especially important in the dry mountains of California's Great Basin, southern Sierra Nevada, and southern California, where harsh and arid upland environments limit plant diversity and wetlands become important hot spots for vegetation. Wetlands are critical habitat for the mammal species that use subalpine habitats. Bird diversity (Beedy and Pandolfino 2013) and arthropod diversity (Holmquist et al. 2011) of subalpine elevations also depend on and concentrate in wetlands. With diminishing snowpacks and increasingly earlier snowmelt, wet environments are likely to dry earlier, and many will convert to nonwetland types. An important exception are wetlands associated with springs resistant to warming, such as those in the forefields of rock glaciers and many talus fields (Millar, Westfall, Evenden et al. 2014).

Cool Refugia under Warming Climates

Generalized projections for future subalpine ecosystems under global warming conclude that subalpine taxa will shift continuously upslope until they run out of area at mountain summits and mostly disappear (e.g., Hayhoe et al. 2004). While this is possible in many decades to centuries, mountain environments are highly heterogeneous and present great physical diversity across small distances. This patchiness creates escape avenues other than upslope. Patchiness occurs across slope, aspect, substrate, elevation, and microclimate heterogeneity (Lundquist and Cayan 2007). Paleoecological research in mountain regions worldwide indicates that mountain environments, when and where not covered by ice caps or valley glaciers, provide refugial habitats where species persist during unfavorable climates (e.g., Ravazzi 2001, Bennett and Provan 2008, Mitton et al. 2000). As climates ameliorate, refugia become highly important sources of diversity for emigration and reestablishment of former as well as new habitats (Dobrowski 2011). Coupled environments, such as talus fields and their wetland forefields, that already support high diversities of cool-adapted plant, mammal, and arthropod species could become increasingly important in the future as refugia in California's mountains (Millar, Westfall, Evenden et al. 2014).

Recreation, Scientific, and Commodity Services

Subalpine forests throughout California are widely cherished for developed (e.g., ski areas) as well as dispersed uses (e.g., hiking, camping, hunting, fishing). Much of the subalpine forest landscape is contained in wilderness designation, which provides long-term protection of little-disturbed ecosystems for societal enjoyment. As California's population becomes increasingly urbanized (Duane 1996a), demand for access to both rustic and wild landscapes in California's mountains as retreat for personal refreshment, recreation, and exercise similarly heightens (Duane 1996b). Expansion of the urban front of the eastern Sierra Nevada and Carson Range in Nevada heightens demand for recreation in the subalpine forest ecosystems of that region.

Protected subalpine environments also provide important services as ecological archives for scientific research. In that much of California's landscapes elsewhere are highly modified by direct human development and use, subalpine ecosystems afford opportunity to study natural composition, structure, and function. The rich archives stored in long-lived trees and preserved deadwood, such as bristlecone pine, have served the international science community. Finally, with much of the subalpine zone in wilderness or other limited-use designations, little extractive and commodity services are available under present policy. Whereas mining of gold, silver, and tungsten, for example, have been important historically in many high elevations of California, and in some regions continuing into the mid-twentieth century, only limited commercial requests for mining access occur at present.

Agents of Anthropogenic Change

Climate Change

Because many lineages of subalpine forest species evolved more than thirty million years ago, taxa that live now in the California mountains have been shaped by forces of climate variation and change throughout their evolution. Mechanisms for adapting to climate change include natural selection (changes in genetic composition), migration (shifts in geography), and ecological accommodation (reassembly of abundances and species diversities) (Millar and Brubaker 2006). Subalpine forests in California over the past twenty million years have experienced drastic changes in species diversity and distribution (Millar 1996, 2012). Over the past two million years (the Quaternary period), however, the diversity of conifer species of the subalpine zone has mostly remained constant within respective mountain regions, with only one extirpation known from the early to mid-Quaternary (a species of spruce [*Picea* sp.], from Tahoe Basin and Owens Valley) (Adam 1973, Litwin et al. 1997). By contrast, the distribution and extent of subalpine species have changed drastically in response to past changes in climate (Millar and Woolfenden 1999).

Added to the list of factors that create changes in climate are anthropogenic forces—most significantly, emissions of greenhouse gases. While human controls on the climate system began millennia ago with the rise of land-clearing, forest burning, and agriculture (Ruddiman 2003), the rate of emissions has accelerated drastically in the industrial era. The impact of anthropogenic forcing is increasingly a primary control on climate; the degree to which it will interact in the future with natural forcing remains poorly understood.

In California, as elsewhere, major changes in climate have been recorded over the past hundred years. Recent climate trends indicate that the mean annual and monthly temperatures have increased in the higher elevations (more than 2,200 meters) of the Sierra Nevada, with as much about 1°C increase over the past century (Moritz et al. 2008) and accelerating rises within the past thirty years (Edwards and Redmond 2011, Moser et al. 2009). Changes in late twentieth-century temperatures in mountain regions of the western United States are attributed primarily to anthropogenic forces rather than natural climate variability (Bonfils et al. 2008). Further, the annual number of days with below-freezing temperatures at higher elevations has declined, resulting in a 40–80% decrease in spring snowpack over the last fifty years in the northern and central Sierra Nevada and onset of spring advancing by two to four days per decade (Cayan et al. 2001, Lundquist et al. 2004, Moser et al. 2009). Snowpack in the southern Sierra Nevada has increased 30–100% over the same period, due partly to the higher-elevation terrain of the region. Precipitation has remained stable or steadily increased over the past several decades in the higher elevations of the California cordillera (Edwards and Redmond 2011, Safford et al. 2012).

Significant effects on subalpine forests are anticipated as a result of future changes in climate (Hayhoe et al. 2004). Most projections anticipate upslope movements of plants with warming temperatures. For subalpine forests where diminishing land area exists at increasing elevation, these projections translate to up to 90% losses of the ecosystem under extreme scenarios (Hayhoe et a. 2004). Early observations, however, are not (yet) revealing significant upslope movement. Rather, twentieth-century changes in subalpine forests have been characterized by increases in forest density (Dolanc et al. 2013), changes in subalpine tree growth and form (Millar et al. 2004), type conversions within the subalpine zone (Millar et al. 2004), changes in forest insect outbreaks and mortality (Millar, Westfall et al. 2007, Millar et al. 2012), and even downslope movement (Crimmins 2011).

Regional Environmental Changes

Remoteness, federal ownership, and management designation limit anthropogenic effects on subalpine forest ecosystems in California. Much subalpine forest is designated as federal Wilderness Areas, which enforces roadless conditions and minimal human impact in general. Outside of federal Wilderness Areas, subalpine forests occur primarily within National Forests and National Parks, where management commonly emphasizes primitive and undeveloped uses with only localized development.

Aside from the effects of greenhouse gas emissions, the most widespread anthropogenic stressor on subalpine forests is atmospheric contamination (Burley and Bytnerowicz 2011, Bytnerowicz et al. 2013; see Chapter 7, "Atmospheric Chemistry"). In California, ozone (O_3) is the main phytotoxic air pollutant for plants at ambient levels and derives from transportation and industrial sources. While usually found near urban centers, elevated levels of ozone have been recorded in remote locations, with concentration increasing above 2,000 meters. These include subalpine ecosystem elevations in the central Sierra Nevada, from Lake Tahoe to the Mammoth Lakes area, and in the White Mountains (Burley and Bytnerowicz 2011, Bytnerowicz et al. 2013). Ozone induces a mottled condition on foliage and, more importantly, contributes to tree stress.

Although timber harvest occurred prior to current protections in a few of California's subalpine forests, logging is mostly limited now to hazard tree removal, trail or road construction and maintenance, management of recreation facilities, and fire suppression and control. Highways traverse subalpine forests in limited areas, and some dirt roads also have been built in areas outside federal Wilderness Areas. Both affect only adjacent tree stands, although in some locations where salt is used for de-icing, roadside trees are damaged or killed. Of greater impact are sediment effects to subalpine watersheds where roads occur, including impacts on aquatic biota, erosion, and downstream water quality and supply. Historical mining impacts are highly localized and mostly occur in the Great Basin ranges, although mining exploration was a widespread catalyst for road building in the early twentieth century, and many existing roads trace to mining origins.

Livestock grazing historically was a widespread and dominant agent of change in high-elevation regions of California. By the mid-1800s, millions of sheep were grazed without regulation in the high Sierra Nevada, White Mountains, and other ranges of the state. The heavy summer grazing of high Sierran meadows began when the record precipitation of 1861–1862 was followed by major droughts in 1862–1863 and 1863–1864, forcing herders to seek higher-elevation meadows. This led to the annual practice of summer grazing in the mountains, with associated overstocking and overgrazing of high mountain meadows. All of the major montane and subalpine meadows in the Sierra Nevada were heavily grazed each summer by flocks in search of pasture with significant overstocking (Ratliff 1985), and the abundance of sheep is reflected in John Muir's reference to them as "hoofed locusts." Many graphic accounts describe the damage caused by sheep herding in this era (Odion et al. 1988, Dilsaver and Tweed 1990, McKelvey and Johnston 1992, Kinney 1996). Most heavily impacted were the alpine zone and subalpine meadows, but effects on subalpine forests were likely significant as well because sheep were trailed through these forests to reach pastures. Impacts include changes in meadow and upland biodiversity, introduction of invasive species, soil compaction and resulting changes in erosion, water-table depth, and runoff. Because sheep grazing was so widespread, leaving few known ungrazed areas (i.e., control areas), legacy impacts from the early era are difficult to assess.

Sheep and cattle grazing were eliminated from the National Parks in the early to mid- twentieth century, and high-elevation livestock allotments on other federal land (primarily U.S. Forest Service) increasingly are being closed. Closures are intended to reduce disease transmission to Sierra Nevada bighorn sheep (in the case of domestic sheep allotments) and for protection of fragile upland ecosystems generally. Allotments still occur, however, in many subalpine forest ecosystems of eastern California. Damage, including plant trampling and soil disruption, is often considerable in meadows and riparian forests in areas such as the northern White Mountains (Holmquist et al. 2013).

Exotic invasive plant species exert significant local but limited landscape effects in subalpine forests. In California, as elsewhere, abundance of invasive plant species tend to decline as elevations increase (Alexander et al. 2011, Rundel and Keeley 2014). At high elevations, impacts from invasive species occur within meadows and wetlands, riparian areas, and aquatic ecosystems associated with subalpine forests. Wet meadows, for instance, have a relatively large list of high-impact invasive species (Stillwater Sciences 2012). Despite a long history of grazing, relatively few non-native species have established in subalpine forests of California, indicating that environmental stress rather than propagule dispersal has been the major limiting factor. However, species invasions are a dynamic process, and new, non-native introductions from other high mountain regions of the world present a possible future concern. On dry uplands but in limited regions cheat grass (*Bromus tectorum*) can invade the subalpine zone. This widespread Mediterranean-origin invasive grass mainly invades lower elevations in Great Basin ecosystems following grazing and fire. Once established, it is virtually impossible to control and causes significant changes in ecosystem composition, structure, and function. Regeneration of native subalpine conifers, especially lodgepole pine, into meadows is often considered an invasion, although at high elevations this appears to be primarily a response to climate change (Millar et al. 2004). In lake ecosystems of the subalpine zone, invasive species are a significant factor controlling native biodiversity and ecological functioning (see also Chapter 32, "Lakes").

Another common species, until recently considered exotic in the high elevations of California with status still uncertain, is the North American beaver (*Castor canadensis*). Known to have occurred in historical times at low elevations of the Central Valley and Owens Valley, beavers were not observed as native by the early naturalists, including the intrepid George Grinnell, above 300 meters through the early 1900s (Tappe 1942, Hensley 1946, Busher 1987). Beavers were widely introduced for fur trapping to lakes and streams of high elevations in California, where they have established and spread. Recent evidence from an excavated dam in the North Fork Feather River Watershed—60 miles north of Truckee, California, at 1,637 meters—showed radiocarbon dates prior to the historical regulation time, namely 580 CE and 1730 CE (James and Lanman 2012). Subsequent documentation from historical records and ethnography argues that beavers were native to other parts of the high Sierra as well (Lanman et al. 2012), although physical evidence has not been recovered elsewhere and their status in high elevations of the central and southern Sierra Nevada remains controversial. As environmental engineers, beavers vastly transform watersheds, damming streams, altering streamflows and water quality, creating ponds, submerging riparian and valley forests, and harvesting aspens and other hardwoods. Beavers and their effects are widespread in the high valleys of the eastern Sierra Nevada, where they episodically expand to new canyon territories. In other regions where beavers are known to be native, such as the Utah mountains, engineering capacities of beavers have been harnessed through resource management projects to maintain, restore, and augment water in increasingly dry upland watersheds (GCT 2013).

Recreation is a common use of subalpine forests in California, although it is generally limited to regions along trails, lakes, and campsites. As such, effects on forests are generally localized, and include soil trampling, fuelwood cutting, and introduction of invasive species via cars, boots, and improper hygiene. This might include the introduction to high-elevation waters of giardia bacteria (*Giardia intestinalis*), which causes intestinal disorders for humans and other mammals. Localized effects on subalpine forests occur around developed ski areas, which are almost exclusively located in the subalpine zone. At those locations tree harvest, snow-making, de-icing, road-building, groundwater pumping, and other infrastructure developments can alter both forest structure and function and also affect watershed conditions. Many ski resorts increasingly promote all-season recreation, expanding impacts on the local forests and watersheds. One Sierran ski resort, June Mountain Ski Area, was strongly affected by the 2006–2012 drought and bark beetle outbreak. The event caused high mortality in whitebark pine forests throughout the resort, decreasing snowpack retention, wind buffering, visual quality, and safety of recreationists. Dead trees are being harvested for safety and resource management.

The most widespread effect of recreation in and near California subalpine forests is as an ignition source. Wildfires left unattended and ignitions along highways cause fires in both subalpine forest and at lower elevations. The Rim Fire of 2013, for instance, was the third largest wildfire in California history and the largest recorded in the Sierra Nevada. Ignited by an illegal hunter's campfire near the south-central border of Yosemite National Park, the fire eventually spread over 1,041.31 square kilometers and consumed large areas of subalpine forest on the west slope of the Sierra Nevada.

Management Issues and Climate Adaptation

In much of the subalpine forest landscape, resource management primarily aims to minimize impacts from human use and restore and maintain natural conditions. As recreation increased in subalpine ecosystems over the twentieth century, restrictions were put in place to protect natural features (Duane 1996b). In lands with limited-use designation, these included restrictions on group sizes, type of uses, road decommissioning, trail improvement to protect resources, campsite restrictions, regulations to protect water quality and watershed conditions, and restoration of degraded habitats such as overused camps along lakeshores and streamsides. Around developments such as ski resorts, federal special-use permit conditions focus on protection of impacts from resort development and maintenance of ecosystem health on the surrounding lands. Similarly, recent evaluations of high-elevation watersheds in canyons containing reservoirs have been conducted throughout California's mountain in response to updating FERC (Federal Energy Regulatory Commission) permit conditions. Renewal of these permits included much stronger environmental protection clauses for subalpine forests than defined in the original permits, often issued early in the twentieth century, and focused on comprehensive watershed health and ecosystem restoration and sustainability.

Fire management is less of a resource focus than in lower montane forests. Fire policy in federal Wilderness Areas and similar designations aims primarily to maintain natural process and protect human lives and infrastructure. In many cases naturally ignited fires that do not threaten wilderness values are allowed to burn with minimal control or management. As mountain hemlock and lodgepole pine forests are the types most likely to burn at large scales in California's subalpine zone, fire suppression efforts most often are directed toward those forest ecosystems.

Control of invasive species has been a major focus of resource management in high-elevation habitats. Efforts have primarily addressed invasive species in aquatic environments, where projects to remove exotic fish and restore native aquatic fauna and riparian vegetation have been under way for several decades, especially in the Sierra Nevada (see Chapter 13, "Biological Invasions"). Early progress was hopeful for widespread restoration, but in recent years the spread and devastation caused by chytrid fungus on amphibian species has imposed formidable challenges (Bradford et al. 1994, Fellers et al. 2001). In subalpine meadows, restoration of meadow hydrology and biodiversity has been the focus of aggressive resource management (e.g., "plug and pond"), especially in the Tahoe Basin of the Sierra Nevada. Applying these techniques widely through high-elevation meadows, with a focus on removing invasives and restoring wetland functions, is the goal of current projects (e.g., CIPC 2014). Many of these efforts are increasingly urgent given the pressure exerted by changing climates. Innovative new approaches to increase resilience of subalpine meadows to warming climates are being developed to retain wetland condition rather than allow meadows to convert to dry or nonmeadow types (AR 2014, WCS 2014). Finally, management of pack animals in high-elevation wetlands is an ongoing concern. Federal Wilderness plans limit domestic packstock use in subalpine and alpine environments; these limits have recently been revised to better protect fragile ecosystems.

Climate Adaptation

Climate-adaptation efforts for subalpine forest ecosystems have focused to date on conducting vulnerability assessments, evaluating risks, developing priorities, and outlining climate-adaptation strategies for the near future (e.g., Morelli et al. 2012) or midterm horizon (e.g., USDA 2013). For federally administered lands, these planning efforts follow newly developed guidance for climate adaptation (Peterson et al. 2011, USDA 2008, USDI 2010) that include the following steps: (1) review basic climate change science and integrate that understanding with knowledge of local resource conditions and issues, (2) evaluate and rank sensitivity of natural resources to climate change, (3) resolve, develop, and implement options for adapting resources to climate change, and (4) observe and monitor the effectiveness of on-the-ground management and adjust as needed.

In the third step, climate-adaptation practices encompass four management strategies—resistance, resilience, response, and realignment—that encourage consideration of a wide range of possible options (Millar, Stephenson et al. 2007). Resistance includes actions that enhance the ability of species, ecosystems, or environments (including social) to resist forces of climate change and maintain values and ecosystem services in their present or desired states. A resilience strategy enhances the capacity of ecosystems to withstand or absorb increasing effects without irreversible changes in important processes and functionality. The response strategy assists transitions to future states by mitigating and minimizing undesired and disruptive outcomes. Finally, the realignment strategy uses restoration techniques to enable ecosystem processes and functions to persist through a changing climate. Processes and tools used to accomplish adaptation differ among subalpine forest types, depending on local resource conditions, management objectives, and organizational preferences. As of 2014, new resource-management plans are in process for many of the California public lands at high elevations and, when complete, these will include direction for climate adaptation and mitigation in the subalpine forest zones.

Future Climate Scenarios

Quantitative models evaluated from hemispheric to regional scales project warming of approximately 1°C to 6°C in annual temperature in California by the end of the twenty-first century (Hayhoe et al. 2004, CCCC 2006, Moser et al. 2009). Growing yet inconclusive evidence indicates rates of warming are elevation dependent and that higher elevations are changing faster than lower (i.e., are more sensitive to forcing factors) (Diaz and Bradley 1997, Rangwala and Miller 2012). To the extent this is the case—and exceptional growth rates from subalpine species such as bristlecone pine in the highest White Mountains hint that it is (Salzer et al. 2009)—subalpine forests might face rates of warming higher and/or sooner than projected for the California lowlands. Coupled with these increases are less certain projected changes in precipitation, though current models are converging on drier futures. Together these projections portend decreased snowpack in the subalpine zones, drier soils with greater climatic water deficits, earlier snowmelt, and lower streamflow volumes. Increasing variability, with extreme years of high and contrasting amplitude are also projected, with both drought and heavy precipitation years more likely (Dettinger 2013). Although some parts of the highest Sierra Nevada and other high peaks of the state such as Mount Shasta, might maintain snow depths at high elevations, recent research on changes in Pacific-origin storms counter this projection. Modeling westerly winds that normally bring rain and snow to the cordillera of western North America, Luce et al. (2013) show that declines in mountain precipitation are resulting from climate change–induced slowdown of winds.

A second general caveat regarding the subalpine zone and climate projections for the future at state and regional scales relates to the mesoscale and microscale variability that characterizes mountain environments. Mountains have enormous heterogeneity in slope, aspect, topography, relative context, landform, and other factors (Daly et al. 2007, Lundquist and Cayan 2007), affording dependent plants and animals escape opportunities more diverse than merely upslope. For instance, cold air drainage creates positive lapse rate conditions (i.e., decreasing temperature with declining elevation) widely in mountain environments. This process might actually increase in the future under forcing factors of anthropogenic climate change (Pepin and Lundquist 2008), with the net effect that canyon bottoms, basins, and swales become cooler than slopes and summits. Another example of mountain landforms at least partially decoupled from synoptic climatology are rocky environments such as talus slopes and rock glaciers. These features develop internal thermal regimes buffered from extremes and potentially resistant to rates of temperature exchange in free air above them (Millar, Westfall, and Delany 2014).

These generalities about high mountain environments and their climates lead to considerable uncertainty about future effects on subalpine forest ecosystems in California. On the one hand, models based on regional warming and assumptions that ecological habitats will shift upslope over the twenty-first century project and that 50% to 90% (depending on the model) of subalpine forest habitat in California will be lost (Hayhoe et al. 2004). On the other hand, high heterogeneity of mountain microclimates might provide refugial environments for long-term persistence of subalpine biota (e.g., Millar, Westfall, Evenden et al. 2014). Projections of plant species distributions in the White Mountains under forecasted warming climates showed near-total losses of habitat by the end of the twenty-first century for many subalpine species, including bristlecone pine (van de Ven et al. 2007). Subsequent observational studies of thermal regimes in the White Mountains, however, indicated patterns of microclimate variability and strong cold air drainage trends even on shallow slopes and basins (van de Ven and Weiss 2009). Refugial environments might therefore exist for plant species that were projected by regional models to disappear upslope of the summit of the range.

Summary

The subalpine forests of California comprise the highest-elevation ecosystems dominated by upright trees. They are influenced primarily by abiotic controls, including persistent snowpack, desiccating winds, acute and chronic extreme temperatures, soil moisture and evapotranspirative stresses, and short growing seasons. Bounded at the upper elevation by treeline, these forests persist under conditions of deep snows, exposure to severe winds, and high solar radiation. Biotic interactions and disturbances like fire are less important than in lower-elevation montane forests. Most subalpine forests in California are sparse woodlands, with short-statured individuals and wide spacing of young as well as old trees, commonly interrupted by areas of exposed rock, dry upland slopes, meadows, and lakes. Subalpine forest ecosystems extend across California in the highest mountains. In the subalpine, conifer forest types are diverse and characterized by iconic and charismatic species such as bristlecone pine, whitebark pine, mountain hemlock, foxtail pine, limber pine, western white pine, and Sierra juniper. Broadleaf subalpine ecosystems include those associated with high soil moisture, such as quaking aspen and water birch, as well as evergreen species on dry uplands such as mountain mahogany.

Subalpine forests have existed in California for more than twenty million years, although species diversity, ecosystem function, and mountain climates have changed drastically during that time. Unique adaptations have evolved among subalpine forests species to cope with extreme climates. These include individual longevity, long needle retention, strip-bark growth habit, and high fecundity. A remarkable coadaptation for seed dispersal and planting is exemplified by the mutual dependence of Clark's nutcracker and whitebark pine, whereby the indehiscent seed cones of the pine must be opened by birds, and birds in turn depend on seeds for food. By caching pine nuts for later harvest, the birds ensure pine regeneration in the thin and desiccating soils of the subalpine zone. Much of the area of these forests lies in remote locations under federal administration with limited recreational and grazing uses. However, subalpine forests in California face an uncertain future under changing climates. Some projections show very high losses if species move upslope and off mountain summits with warming, while others suggest that environmental heterogeneity could afford adequate refugia for long-term species persistence.

Acknowledgments

The authors wish to thank Diane Delany, of the U.S. Department of Agriculture Forest Service, Pacific Southwest Research Station, in Albany, California, for rendering the figures.

Recommended Reading

Cheng, S., editor. 2004. Forest Service Research Natural Areas in California. General Technical Report PSW-GTR-188. Pacific Southwest Research Station, Forest Service, U.S. Department of Agriculture, Albany, California.

Dolanc, C. R., J. H. Thorne, and H. D. Safford. 2013. Widespread shifts in the demographic structure of Sierra Nevada subalpine forests over the last 80 years. Global Ecology and Biogeography 22:264–276.

Fites-Kaufman, J. A., P. Rundel, N. Stephenson, and D. A. Weixelman. 2007. Montane and subalpine vegetation of the Sierra Nevada and Cascade regions. Pages 456–502, Chapter 17, in M. G. Barbour, T. Keeler-Wolf, and A. A. Schoenherr, editors. Terrestrial Vegetation of California. Third edition. University of California Press, Berkeley, California.

Minnich, R. 2007. Southern California conifer forests. Pages 502–538, Chapter 18, in M. G. Barbour, T. Keeler-Wolf, and A. A. Schoenherr, editors. Terrestrial Vegetation of California. Third edition. University of California Press, Berkeley, California.

Skinner, C. N. 2003. Fire history of upper montane and subalpine glacial basins in the Klamath Mountains of northern California. Pages 145–151 in K. E. M. Gally, R. C. Klinger, and N. G. Sugihara, editors. Proceedings of the Fire Conference 2000: The First National Congress on Fire Ecology, Prevention, and Management. Misc. Pub 13. Tall Timbers Research Station, Tallahassee, Florida.

Thorne, R. F., A. A. Schoenherr, C. D. Clements, and J. A. Young. 2007. Transmontane coniferous vegetation. Pages 574–586, Chapter 20, in M. G. Barbour, T. Keeler-Wolf, and A. A. Schoenherr, editors. Terrestrial Vegetation of California. Third edition. University of California Press, Berkeley, California.

Glossary

ATMOSPHERIC RIVERS Giant, episodic storms that funnel large amounts of precipitation, orographically scaled, to regions of southwestern North America and particularly California. Bivoltinism The capacity of insects—in particular, bark beetles—to successfully brood two generations per year.

CLIMATIC WATER DEFICIT Evaporative demand not met by available water—a measure of how much more water could have been evaporated or transpired from a site covered by a standard plant, had that water been available. Climatic water deficit is a meaningful measure of absolute drought that is independent of the actual vegetation of the site.

CLONAL A single individual consisting of multiple stems yet all the same genotype.

ECOTONE The transition area between two communities or biomes—for instance, the alpine treeline ecotone is the zone where forest and herbaceous or shrubby vegetation meet.

FELLFIELD Alpine habitat with shallow, stony, and poorly developed stony soils.

KEYSTONE SPECIES/ECOSYSTEMS Species, plant communities, and biomes that serve critical functions to many other species.

KRUMMHOLZ A stunted growth form, matt-like or shrub-like, developed by several subalpine conifers in response to desiccating winds and subfreezing temperatures.

OROGRAPHIC EFFECT The enhancement of precipitation in mountain regions that results as water-laden clouds rise along upwind slopes, cooling, condensing, and falling as rain as they encounter higher altitudes. Due to orographically enhanced precipitation on the windward side, the lee side of mountains are often correspondingly dry, called a rainshadow effect.

SNOTEL The automated snow-measuring stations administered by the U.S. Department of Agriculture's Natural Resources Conservation Service.

References

Abatzoglou, J. T., K. T. Redmond, and L. M. Edwards. 2009. Classification of regional climate variability in the state of California. Journal of Applied Meteorology and Climatology 48:1527–1541.

Adam, D. P. 1973. Early Pleistocene pollen spectra near Lake Tahoe, California. Journal of Research of the U.S. Geological Survey 1:691–693.

Agee, J. K. 1993. Fire ecology of Pacific Northwest forests. Island Press, Washington, D.C.

Alexander, J., C. Kueffer, C. C. Daehler, P. J. Edwards, A. Pauchard, T. Seipel, and MIREN Consortium. 2011. Assembly of non-native floras along elevational gradients explained by directional ecological filtering. Proceedings of the National Academy of Sciences 108:656–666.

Allen-Diaz, B. H. 1991. Water table and plant species relationships in Sierra Nevada meadows.

American Midland Naturalist 126:30–43.

Anderson, R. S. 1990. Holocene forest development and paleoclimates within the central Sierra Nevada. Journal of Ecology 78:470–489.

Anderson A. E. and O. C. Wallmo. 1984. *Odocoileus hemionus*. Mammalian Species 19:1–9

AR (American Rivers). 2014. Headwaters restoration projects. <http://www.americanrivers.org>. Accessed January 5, 2014.

Bales, R. C., N. P. Molotch, T. H. Painter, M. D. Dettinger, R. Rice, and J. Dozier. 2006. Mountain hydrology of the western United States. Water Resources Research 42:W08432. <doi:10.1029/2005WR00438>.

Barber, A. 2013. Physiology and early life-history associated with extreme longevity: An investigation of *Pinus longaeva* (Great Basin bristlecone pine). PhD dissertation. Department of Biology, University of California, Santa Cruz, California.

Bartolome, J. W., D. C. Erman, and C. F. Schwartz. 1990. Stability and change in minerotrophic peatlands, Sierra Nevada of California and Nevada. Research Paper PSW-RP-198. Pacific Southwest Forest and Range Experiment Station, Forest Service, U.S. Department of Agriculture, Berkeley, California.

Beedy, E., and E. Pandolfino. 2013. Birds of the Sierra Nevada—Their natural history, status,

and distribution. University of California Press, Berkeley, California.

Bekker, M. F., and A. H. Taylor. 2000. Gradient analysis of fire regimes in montane forests of the southern Cascade Range, Thousand Lakes Wilderness, California, USA. Plant Ecology 155:15–28.

Benedict, N. B., and J. Major. 1982. A physiographic classification of subalpine meadows of the Sierra Nevada, California. Madroño 29:1–12.

Bennett, K. D. 1965. An investigation of the impact of grazing on ten meadows in Sequoia and Kings Canyon National Park. MS thesis. San Jose State College, San Jose, California.

Bennett, K. D., and J. Provan. 2008. What do we mean by "refugia"? Quaternary Science Reviews 27:2449–2455.

Bentz, B., J. Vandygriff, C. Jensen, T. Coleman, P. Maloney, S. Smith, A. Grady, and G. Schen-Langenheim. 2014. Mountain pine beetle voltinism and life history characteristics across latitudinal and elevational gradients in the Western United States. Forest Science 60:434–449.

Billings, W. D., and J. H. Thompson. 1957. Composition of a stand of old bristlecone pines in the White Mountains of California. Ecology 38:158–160.

Biondi, F., A. Gershunov, and D. R. Cayan. 2001. North Pacific decadal climate variability since 1661. Journal of Climate 14:5–10.

Bonfils, C., B. D. Santer, D. W. Pierce, H. G. Hidalgo, G. Bala, T. Das, T. P. Barnett, D. R. Cayan, C. Doutriaux, A. W. Wood, A. Mirin, and T. Nozawa. 2008. Detection and attribution of temperature changes in the mountainous western United States. Journal of Climate 21:6404–6424.

Bradford, D. F., D. M. Graber, and F. Tabatabai. 1994. Population declines of the native frog, *Rana muscosa*, in Sequoia and Kings Canyon National Parks, California. Southwestern Naturalist 39:323– 327.

Brayton, R., and Mooney, H. A. 1966. Population variability of *Cercocarpus* in the White Mountains of California as related to habitat. Evolution 20:383–391.

Brunelle, A., G. E. Rehfeldt, B. Bentz, and A. S. Munson. 2008. Holocene records of *Dendroctonus* bark beetles in high elevation pine forests of Idaho and Montana, USA. Forest Ecology and Management 255:836–846.

Bunn, A. G., L. A. Waggoner, and L. J. Graumlich. 2005. Topographic mediation of growth in high elevation foxtail pine (*Pinus balfouriana* Grev. et Balf.) forests in the Sierra Nevada, USA. Global Ecology and Biogeography 14:103–114.

Burley, J. D., and A. Bytnerowicz. 2011. Surface ozone in the White Mountains of California. Atmospheric Environment 45:4591–4602.

Busher, P. E. 1987. Population parameters and family composition of beaver in California. Journal of Mammalogy 68:860–864.

Bytnerowicz, A., M. Fen, A. Gertler, H. Preisler, and B. Zielinska. 2013. Distribution of ozone, ozone precursors, and gaseous components of atmospheric nitrogen deposition in the Lake Tahoe Basin. Final Report. Contract No. P063. Report to the Southern Nevada Public Land Management Act, Contract No. P063, Riverside, California. September 2013. 86 p.

Caprio, A. C., and D. M. Graber. 2000. Returning fire to the mountains: Can we successfully restore the ecological role of pre-Euro-American fire regimes to the Sierra Nevada? Pages 233–241 in D. N. Cole, S. F. McCool, W. T. Borrie, and J. O'Loughlin, editors. Wilderness Science in a Time of Change. Volume 5, Wilderness Ecosystems, Threats, and Management, 1999 May 23–27, Missoula, Montana. RMRS-P-15-VOL-5. U.S. Department of Agriculture, Forest Service, Rocky Mountain Research Station, Ogden, Utah.

Carsey, K. S., and D. F. Tomback. 1994. Growth form distribution and genetic relationships in tree clusters of *Pinus flexilis*, a bird-dispersed pine. Oecologia 98:401–411.

Cayan, D. R., K. T. Redmond, and L. G. Riddle. 1999. ENSO and hydrologic extremes in the western United States. Journal of Climate 12:2881–2893.

Cayan, D. R., M. D. Dettinger, H. F. Diaz, and N. E. Graham. 1998. Decadal variability of precipitation over western North America. Journal of Climate 11:3148–3166.

Cayan, D. R., S. A. Kammerdiener, M. D. Dettinger, J. M. Caprio, and D. H. Peterson. 2001. Changes in the onset of spring in the western United States. Bulletin of the American Meteorological Society 82:399–415.

CCCC (California Climate Change Center). 2006. Our changing climate: Assessing the risks to California. CEC-500-2006-077. California Energy Commission. Sacramento, California.

CDFW (California Department of Fish and Wildlife). 2013. Status review of the American pika (*Ochotona princeps*) in California. Final report of the California Fish and Game Commission.

Charlet, D. A. 2014. Atlas of Nevada conifers. Second edition. University of Nevada Press, Reno, Nevada.

Cheng, S., editor. 2004. Forest Service Research Natural Areas in California. General Technical Report PSW-GTR-188. Pacific Southwest Research Station, Forest Service, U.S. Department of Agriculture, Albany, California.

CIPC (California Invasive Plant Council). 2014. Strengthening resiliency in Sierra Nevada meadows. Climate adaptation fund grants program reports. <http://www.wcsnorthamerica.org/ClimateAdaptationFund/>. Accessed January 5, 2014.

Cook, E. R., R. Seager, M. A. Cane, and D. W. Stahle. 2007. North American drought: Reconstructions, causes, and consequences. Earth-Science Reviews 81:93–134.

Crimmins, S. M., S. Z. Dobrowski, J. A. Greenberg, J. T. Abatzoglou, and A. R. Mynsberger. 2011. Changes in climatic water balance drive downhill shifts in plant species' optimum elevations. Science 331:324–327.

Critchfield, W. B. 1957. Geographic variation in *Pinus contorta*. Maria Moors Cabot Found. Publication 3. Harvard University, Cambridge, Massachusetts.

Daly, C., J. W. Smith, J. I. Smith, and R. B. McKane. 2007. High-resolution spatial modeling of daily weather elements for a catchment in the Oregon Cascade Mountains, United States. Journal of Applied Meteorology and Climatology 6:1565–1586.

Daly, C., R. P. Neilson, and D. L. Phillips. 1994. A statistical topographic model for mapping climatological precipitation over mountainous terrain. Journal of Applied Meteorology 33:140–158.

Davis, F. W., D. M. Stoms, A. D. Hollander, K. A. Thomas, P. A. Stine, D. Odion, M. I. Borchert, J. H. Thorne, M. V. Gray, R. E. Walker, K. Warner, and J. Graae. 1998. The California gap analysis project—final report. University of California, Santa Barbara, California. <http://legacy.biogeog.ucsb.edu/projects/gap/gap_rep.html>. Accessed January 1, 2014.

Davis, G. 1962. Erosional features of snow avalanches, Middle Fork Kings River, California. Professional Paper 450-D. U.S. Geological Survey, Washington, D.C.

Dettinger, M. D. 2013. Atmospheric rivers as drought busters on the U.S. west coast. Journal of Hydrometeorology. <doi:10.1175/JHM-D-13-02: 11721-1732>.

Diaz, H. F., and R. S. Bradley.1997. Temperature variations during the last century at high
elevation sites. Climatic Change 36:253–279.

Dilsaver, L. M., and W. C. Tweed. 1990. Challenge of the big trees. Sequoia Natural History Association, Three Rivers, California.

Dobrowski, S. Z. 2011. A climatic basis for microrefugia: The influence of terrain on climate. Global Change Biology 17:1022–1035.

Dolanc, C. R., J. H. Thorne, and H. D. Safford. 2013. Widespread shifts in the demographic structure of Sierra Nevada subalpine forests over the last 80 years. Global Ecology and Biogeography 22:264–276.

Duane, T. 1996a. Human settlement: 1850–2040. Pages 235–360, Chapter 11. Sierra Nevada Ecosystem Project. Final report to Congress, Volume II. Assessments and Scientific Basis for Management Options, Centers for Water and Wildland Resources, Report No. 37. University of California, Davis, California.

———. 1996b. Recreation in the Sierra Nevada. Pages 557–610, Chapter 19. Sierra Nevada Ecosystem Project, Final report to Congress, Volume II. Assessments and Scientific Basis for Management Options, Centers for Water and Wildland Resources, Report No. 37. University of California, Davis, California.

Dunlap, J. M. 2012. Variability in and environmental correlates to white pine blister rust incidence in five California white pine species. Northwest Science 86:248–263.

Eckert, A. J. 2010. Effects of historical demography and ecological context on spatial patterns of genetic diversity within foxtail pine (*Pinus balfouriana*; Pinaceae) stands located in the Klamath Mountains, California. American Journal of Botany 97:650–659.

Eckert, A. J., B. R. Tearse, and B. D. Hall. 2008. A phylogeographical analysis of the range disjunction for foxtail pine (*Pinus balfouriana*, Pinaceae): The role of Pleistocene glaciation. Molecular Ecology 17:1983–1997.

Edwards, L. M., and K. T. Redmond. 2011. Climate assessment for the Sierra Nevada network parks. Sequoia and Kings Canyon National Parks Natural Resource Report NPS/2011/NRR—2011/482.

Elliott-Fisk, D. L., and A. M. Peterson. 1991. Trees. Pages 87–108 in C. Hall, editor. Natural history of the White-Inyo Range, eastern California. University of California Press, Berkeley, California.

Epanchin, P. N., and A. Engilis Jr. 2009. Mount Lyell shrew (*Sorex lyelli*) in the Sierra Nevada, California, with comments on alpine records of Sorex. The Southwestern Naturalist, 543:354–357.

Ewers, F. W., and R. Schmid. 1981. Longevity of needle fascicles of *Pinus longaeva* (bristlecone pine) and other North American pines. Oecologia 51:107–15.

Fellers, G. M., D. E. Green, J. E. Longcore, and R. E. Gatten Jr. 2001. Oral chytridiomycosis in the mountain yellow-legged frog (*Rana muscosa*). Copeia 2001:945–953.

Fites-Kaufman, J. A., P. Rundel, N. Stephenson, and D. A. Weixelman. 2007. Montane and subalpine vegetation of the Sierra Nevada and Cascade Regions. Pages 456–502, Chapter 17, in M. G. Barbour, T. Keeler-Wolf, and A. A. Schoenherr, editors. Terrestrial Vegetation of California. Third edition. University of California Press, Berkeley, California.

GCT (Grand Canyon Trust). 2013. Beaver restoration project reports. <http://www.grandcanyontrust.org>. Accessed December 28, 2013.

Gibson, A. C., P. W. Rundel, and M. R. Sharifi. 2008. Ecology and ecophysiology of a subalpine fellfield community on Mount Pinos, southern California. Madroño 55:1–51.

Graf, M. 1999. Plants of the Tahoe Basin. California Native Plant Society, Sacramento, California.

Grayson, D. K., and S. D. Livingston. 1989. High-elevation records for Neotoma cinerea in the White Mountains, California. The Great Basin Naturalist 1989:392–395.

Griffin, J. R., and W. B. Critchfield. 1976. The distribution of forest trees in California. U.S. Department of Agriculture Forest Service Research Paper, PSW 82/1972/Supplement 1976. Berkeley, California.

Hallett, D. J., and R. S. Anderson. 2010. Paleofire reconstruction for high-elevation forests in the Sierra Nevada, California, with implications for wildfire synchrony and climate variability in the late Holocene. Quaternary Research 73:180–190.

Hayhoe, K., D. Cayan, C. B. Fields, P. C. Frumhoff et al. 2004. Emissions pathways, climate change, and impacts on California. Proceedings of the National Academy of Science 34:12422–12427.

Hawksworth, F. G., D. Wiens, R. Nisley, and B. W. Geils. 1996. Dwarf mistletoes: Biology, pathology, and systematics. USDA Agricultural Handbook 709. U.S. Dept. of Agriculture, Forest Service. Washington, D.C. 410 pages.

Hensley, A. L. 1946. A progress report on beaver management in California. California Fish and Game 32:87–99.

Hilimire, K., J. C. B. Nesmith, A. C. Caprio, and R. Milne. 2013. Attributes of windthrown trees in a Sierra Nevada mixed-conifer forest. Western Journal of Applied Forestry 28:85–89.

Holland, V. L., and D. J. Keil. 1995. California vegetation. Kendall/Hunt Publishing Company, Dubuque, Iowa.

Holmquist J. G., J. R. Jones, J. Schmidt-Gengenbach, L. F. Pierotti, and J. P. Love. 2011. Terrestrial and aquatic macroinvertebrate assemblages as a function of wetland type across a mountain landscape. Arctic, Antarctic, and Alpine Research 43:568–584.

Holmquist, J. G., J. Schmidt-Gengenbach, and S. A. Haultain. 2013. Equine grazing in managed subalpine wetlands: Effects on arthropods and plant structure as a function of habitat. Environmental Management 52:1474–1486.

Hutchins, H. E., and R. M. Lanner. 1982. The central role of Clark's nutcracker in the dispersal and establishment of whitebark pine. Oecologia 55:192–201.

Huth, A. K., A. Leydecker, J. O. Sickman, and R. C. Bales. 2004. A two-component hydrograph separation for three high-elevation catchments in the Sierra Nevada, California. Hydrological Processes 18:1721–1733.

Ingles, L. G. 1965. Mammals of the Pacific states. Stanford University Press, Palo Alto, California.

James, C. D., and R. B. Lanman. 2012. Novel physical evidence that beaver historically were native to the Sierra Nevada. California Fish and Game 98:129–132.

Jameson, E. W., and H. J. Peeters. 2004. Mammals of California. University of California Press, Berkeley, California.

Jepson eFlora. 2014. <http://ucjeps.berkeley.edu/UM.html>. Accessed January 22, 2014.

Kattelmann, R. 1996. Impacts of floods and avalanches. Pages 1263–1269, Chapter 49. Sierra Nevada Ecosystem Project. Final report to Congress, Volume II. Assessments and Scientific Basis for Management Options, Centers for water and Wildland Resources, Report No. 37. University of California, Davis, California.

Kattelmann, R., and Elder, K. 1991. Hydrologic characteristics and water balance of an alpine basin in the Sierra Nevada. Water Resources Research 27:1553–1562.

King, J. C., and L. J. Graumlich. 1998. Stem-layering and genet longevity in whitebark pine (*Pinus albicaulis*). Final Report on Cooperative Research with the National Park Service (CA 8000-2-9001). Laboratory of Tree-Ring Research, University of Arizona, Tucson, Arizona.

Kinney, W. C. 1996. Conditions of rangelands before 1905. Sierra Nevada ecosystem project: Final report to congress. Status of the Sierra Nevada. Volume 2, pages 31–45. Centers for Water and Wildland Resources, University of California, Davis, California.

Körner, C. 2012. Alpine treelines. Functional ecology of the global high elevation tree limits. Springer Books, Basel, Switzerland.

———. 2007. Climatic treelines: Conventions, global patterns, causes. Erdkunde 61:316–324.

Körner, C., and J. Paulsen. 2004. A world-wide study of high altitude treeline temperatures. Journal of Biogeography 31:713–732

LaMarche, V. C., Jr. 1973. Holocene climatic variations inferred from treeline fluctuations in the White Mountains, California. Quaternary Research 3:632–660.

Lanman, R. B., H. Perryman, B. Dolman, and C. D. James. 20112. The historical range of beaver in the Sierra Nevada: A review of the evidence. California Fish and Game 98:65–80.

Lanner, R. M. 1999. Conifers of California. Cachuma Press, Los Olivos, California.

———. 1996. Made for each other: A symbiosis of birds and pines. Oxford University Press, New York, New York.

Lepper, M. G., and M. Fleschner. 1977. Nitrogen fixation by *Cercocarpus ledifolius* (Rosaceae) in pioneer habitats. Oecologia 27:333–338.

Litwin, R. J., D. P. Adam, N. O. Frederiksen, and W. B. Woolfenden. 1997. An 800,000–year pollen record from Owens Lake: Preliminary analyses. Pages 127–142 in G. I. Smith and J. L. Bischoff, editors. An 800,000–year Paleoclimatic Record from core OL-92, Owens Lake, Southeast California. Special Paper 317. Geological Society of America, Washington, D.C.

Logan, J. A., and J. A. Powell. 2009. Ecological consequences of climate change altered forest insect disturbance regimes. In F. H. Wagner, editor. Climate Change in Western North America: Evidence and Environmental Effects. <http://searchworks.stanford.edu/view/8523961>. University of Utah Press, Salt Lake City, Utah.

———. 2001. Ghost forests, global warming, and the mountain pine beetle (Coleoptera: Scolytidae). American Entomologist 47:160–172.

Lloyd, A. H. 1998. Growth of foxtail pine seedlings at treeline in the southeastern Sierra Nevada, California. Ecoscience 5:250–257.

———. 1997. Response of tree-line populations of foxtail pine (*Pinus balfouriana*) to climate variation over the last 1,000 years. Canadian Journal of Forest Research 27:936–942.

Lloyd, A. H., and L. J. Graumlich. 1997. Holocene dynamics of treeline forests in the Sierra Nevada. Ecology 78:1199–1210.

Luce, C. H., J. T. Abatzoglou and A. Z. Holden. 2013. The missing mountain water: Slower westerlies decrease orographic enhancement in the Pacific Northwest USA. Science 342:1360–1364.

Lundquist, J. D., and D. R. Cayan. 2007. Surface temperature patterns in complex terrain: Daily variations and long-term change in the central Sierra Nevada, California. Journal of Geophysical Research 112, D11124. <doi:10.1029/2006JD007561>.

Lundquist, J. D., D. R. Cayan, and M. D. Dettinger. 2004. Spring onset in the Sierra Nevada: When is snowmelt independent of elevation? Journal of Hydrometeorology 5:327–342.

Lundquist, J. D., S. E. Dickerson-Lange, J. A. Lutz, and N. C. Cristea. 2014. Lower forest density enhances snow retention in regions with warmer winters: A global framework developed from plot-scale observations and modeling. Water Resources Research. 49:6356–6370.

Maloney, P., and J. Dunlap. 2007. White pine blister rust and whitebark pine ecosystems in California. U.S. Forest Service R6-NRFHP-2007-01. Pages 106–107.

Mantua, N. J., S. R. Hare, Y. Zhang, J. M. Wallace, and R. C. Francis. 1997. A Pacific interdecadal climate oscillation with impacts on salmon production. Bulletin of the American Meteorological Society 78:1069–1079.

Martinelli, M., Jr. 1974. Snow avalanche sites, their identification, and evaluation. Agriculture Information Bulletin 360.U.S. Department of Agriculture Forest Service, Washington, D.C.

Mastrogiuseppe, R. J., and J. D. Mastrogiuseppe.1980. A study of *Pinus balfouriana* Grev. and Balf. (Pinaceae). Systematic Botany 5:86–104.

Mayer, K.E. and W. F. Laudenslayer. 1988. A guide to wildlife habitats of California. California Department of Forestry and Fire Protection, Sacramento, California. 166 pp.

McCabe, G. J., and M. D. Dettinger. 1999. Decadal variations in the strength of ENSO teleconnections with precipitation in the western United States. International Journal of Climatology 19:1399–1410.

McCabe, G. J., M. A. Palecki, and J. L. Betancourt. 2004. Pacific and Atlantic Ocean influences on multidecadal drought frequency in the United States. Proceedings of the National Academy of Science 101:4136–4141.

McKelvey, K. S., and J. D. Johnston. 1992. Historical perspectives on forests of the Sierra Nevada and the Transverse Ranges of southern California: Forest conditions at the turn of the century. Pages 225–246 in J. Verner et al., technical coordinators. The California spotted owl: A technical assessment of its current status. General Technical Report PSW-GTR-133. U.S. Department of Agriculture Forest Service, Albany, California.

Mears, A. I. 1992. Snow-avalanche hazard analysis for land-use planning and engineering. Bulletin 49. Colorado Geological Survey, Denver, Colorado.

Meixner, T., and R. C. Bales. 2003. Hydrochemical modeling of coupled C and N cycling in high-elevation catchments: Importance of snow cover. Biogeochemistry 6:289–308.

Meixner, T., C. Gutmann, R. Bales, A. Leydecker, J. Sickman, J. Melack, and J. McConnell. 2004. Multidecadal hydrochemical response of a Sierra Nevada watershed: Sensitivity to weathering rate and changes in deposition year. Journal of Hydrology 285:272–285.

Meyer, M. D. 2013. Natural range of variation of subalpine forests in the bioregional assessment area. Unpublished report. U.S. Department of Agriculture Forest Service, Pacific Southwest Region, Clovis, California.

Millar, C. I. 2012. Geologic, climatic, and vegetation history of California. Pages 49–67 in B. G. Baldwin, D. H. Goldman, D. J. Deil, R. Patterson, T. J. Rosatti, and D. H. Wilken, editors. The Jepson manual: Vascular plants of California. Second edition. University of California Press, Berkeley, California.

———. 1996. Tertiary vegetation history. Pages 71–122 in Sierra

Nevada Ecosystem Project, Final report to Congress, Volume II. Assessments and Scientific Basis for Management Options. Centers for water and Wildland Resources, Report No. 37, University of California, Davis, California.

Millar, C. I., and L. B. Brubaker. 2006. Climate change and paleoecology: New contexts for restoration ecology. Pages 315–340, Chapter 15, in M. Palmer, D. Falk, and J. Zedler, editors. Restoration Science. Island Press, Washington, D.C.

Millar, C. I., and W. B. Woolfenden. 1999. Sierra Nevada forests: Where did they come from? Where are they going? What does it mean? Transactions of the North American Wildlife and Natural resources Conference 64:206–236.

Millar, C. I., N. L. Stephenson, and S. L. Stephens. 2007. Climate change and forests of the future: Managing in the face of uncertainty. Ecological Applications 17:2145–2151.

Millar, C. I., R. D. Westfall, A. Evenden, J. G. Holmquist, J. Schmidt-Gengebach, R. S. Franklin, J. Nachlinger, and D. L. Delany. 2014. Potential climatic refugia in semi-arid, temperate mountains: Plant and arthropod assemblages associated with rock glaciers, talus slopes, and their forefield wetlands, Sierra Nevada, California, USA. Quaternary International. <http://dx.doi.org/10.1016/j.quaint.2013.11.003>.

Millar, C. I., R. D. Westfall, and D. L. Delany. 2014. Thermal regimes and snowpack relations of periglacial talus slopes, Sierra Nevada, California, USA. Arctic, Antarctic, and Alpine Research.

Millar, C. I., R. D. Westfall, D. L. Delany, M. J. Bokach, A. L. Flint, and L. E. Flint. 2012. Forest mortality in high-elevation whitebark pine (*Pinus albicaulis*) forests of eastern California, USA; influence of environmental context, bark beetles, climatic water deficit, and warming. Canadian Journal Forest Research 42:749–765.

Millar, C. I., R. D. Westfall, and D. L. Delany. 2007. Response of high-elevation limber pine (*Pinus flexilis*) to multiyear droughts and twentieth-century warming, Sierra Nevada, California, USA. Canadian Journal of Forest Research 37:2508–2520.

Millar, C. I., R. D. Westfall, D. L. Delany, J. C. King, and L. Graumlich. 2004. Response of subalpine conifers in the Sierra Nevada, California, U.S.A., to 20th-century warming and decadal climate variability. Arctic, Antarctic, and Alpine Research 36:181–200.

Miller, J., H. Safford, M. Crimmins, and A. Thode. 2009. Quantitative evidence for increasing forest fire severity in the Sierra Nevada and southern Cascades, California and Nevada, USA. Ecosystems 12:16–32.

Minnich, R. 2007. Southern California conifer forests. Pages 502–538, Chapter 18, in M. G. Barbour, T. Keeler-Wolf, and A. A. Schoenherr, editors. Terrestrial Vegetation of California. Third edition. University of California Press, Berkeley, California.

Mitton, J. B., B. R. Kreiser, and R G. Latta. 2000. Glacial refugia of limber pine (*Pinus flexilis* James) inferred from the population structure of mitochondrial DNA. Molecular Ecology 9:91–97.

Mohr, J. A., C. Whitlock, and C. N. Skinner. 2000. Postglacial vegetation and fire history, eastern Klamath Mountains, California, USA. The Holocene 10:587–601.

Morelli, T. L., and S. C. Carr. 2011. Review of the potential effects of climate change on

quaking aspen (*Populus tremuloides*) in the western United States and a new tool for surveying aspen decline. General Technical Report PSW-GTR-235. U.S. Department of Agriculture, Forest Service, Pacific Southwest Research Station, Albany, California.

Morelli, T. L., S. Yeh, N. Smith, M. B. Hennessy, and C. I. Millar. 2012. Climate project screening tool: An aid for climate change adaptation. Research Paper. PSW-RP-263. U.S. Department of Agriculture, Forest Service, Pacific Southwest Research Station, Albany, California.

Moritz, C., J. L. Patton, C. J. Conroy, J. L. Parra, G. C. White, and S. R. Beissinger. 2008. Impact of a century of climate change on small-mammal communities in Yosemite National Park, USA. Science 322:261–264.

Moser, S., G. Franco, S. Pittiglio, W. Chou, and D. R. Cayan. 2009. The future is now: An update on climate change science impacts and response options for California. Special Report; California Climate Change Center, California Energy Commission Public Interest Energy Research Program. Sacramento, California.

Odion, D. C., T. L. Dudley, and C. M. D'Antonio. 1988. Cattle grazing in southeastern Sierran meadows: Ecosystem change and prospects for recovery. Pages 277–292 in C. A. Hall and V. Doyle-Jones, editors. Plant biology of eastern California. Natural history of the White-Inyo Range, Symposium Volume 2. White Mountains Research Station, University of California, Los Angeles, California.

Parker, A. J. 1995. Comparative gradient structure and forest cover types in Lassen Volcanic and Yosemite National Parks, California. Bulletin of the Torrey Botanical Club 122:58–68.

———. 1994. Latitudinal gradients of coniferous tree species, vegetation, and climate in the Sierra-Cascade axis or northern California. Vegetatio 115:145–155.

———. 1988. Stand structure of subalpine forests of Yosemite National Park, California. Forest Science 34:1047–1058.

Parsons, D. J. 1972. The southern extensions of *Tsuga mertensiana* (mountain hemlock) in the Sierra Nevada. Madroño 21:536–539.

Pepin, N. C., and J. D. Lundquist. 2008. Temperature trends at high elevations: Patterns across the globe. Geophysical Research Letters 35:L14701. <doi:10.1029/2008GL034026>.

Peterson, D. L., C. I. Millar, L. A. Joyce, M. J. Furniss, J. E. Halofsky, R. P. Neilson, and T. L. Morelli. 2011. Responding to climate change in national forests: A guidebook for developing adaptation options. PNW General Technical Report PNW-GTR-855. U.S. Department of Agriculture Forest Service, Portland, Oregon.

Peterson, D. L., M. J. Arbaugh, and M. A. Lardner. 1989. Leaf area of lodgepole pine and whitebark pine in a subalpine Sierra Nevada, California, U.S.A. Canadian Journal of Forest Research 19:401–403.

Pinder, J. E., G. C. Kroh, J. D. White, and A. M. B. May. 1997. The relationship between vegetation type and topography in Lassen Volcanic National Park. Plant Ecology 131:17–29.

Potter, D. A. 1998. Forested communities of the upper montane in the central and southern Sierra Nevada. General Technical Report PSW-GTR-169. U.S. Department of Agriculture Forest Service, Pacific Southwest Research Station, Albany, California.

Power, M. J. 1998. Paleoclimatic interpretation of an alpine lake in south-central Sierra Nevada, California: Multiple proxy evidence. MA thesis. Quaternary Studies Program, Northern Arizona University, Flagstaff, Arizona.

Raleigh, M. S., K. Rittger, C. E. Moore, B. Henn, J. A. Lutz, and J. D. Lundquist. 2013. Ground-based testing of MODIS fractional snow cover in subalpine meadows and forests of the Sierra Nevada. Remote Sensing of the Environment 128:44–57.

Rangwala, I., and J. R. Miller. 2012. Climate change in mountains: A review of elevation-dependent warming and its possible causes. Climatic Change 114:527–547.

Ratliffe, R. D. 1985. Meadows in the Sierra Nevada of California: State of knowledge. General Technical Report PSW-84. U.S. Department of Agriculture Forest Service, Berkeley, California.

Ravazzi, C. 2001. Late Quaternary history of spruce in southern Europe. Review of Palaeobotany and Palynology 120:131–177.

Redmond, K. T., and R. W. Koch. 1991. Surface climate and streamflow variability in the western United States and their relationship to large scale circulation indices. Water Resources Research 27:2381–2399.

Rogers, D., C. I. Millar, and R. D. Westfall. 1999. Fine-scale genetic structure of whitebark pine (*Pinus albicaulis*): Associations with watershed and growth form. Evolution 53:74–90.

Rubidge, E. M., J. L. Patton, M. Lim, A. C. Burton, J. S. Brashares, and C. Moritz. 2012.

Climate-induced range contraction drives genetic erosion in an alpine mammal. Nature Climate Change 2:285–288.

Ruddiman, W. F. 2003. The anthropogenic greenhouse era began thousands of years ago Climatic Change 61:261–293.

Rundel, P., D. J. Parsons, and D. T. Gordon. 1990. Montane and subalpine vegetation of the Sierra Nevada and Cascade Ranges. Pages 559–600, Chapter 17, in M. G. Barbour and J. Major, editors. Terrestrial vegetation of California. Special Publication No. 9. California Native Plant Society, Sacramento, California.

Rundel, P. W. 2011. The diversity and biogeography of the alpine flora of the Sierra Nevada, California. Madroño 58:153–184.

Rundel, P. W., and P. Rabenold. 2014. Subalpine conifer demography in the Emerald Lake Basin, Sequoia National Park, California.

Rundel, P. W., D. J. Herman, W. L. Berry, and T. V. St. John. 1989. Emerald Lake: Vegetation process studies. Final Report, Contract A6-081-32. California Air Resources Board, Sacramento, California.

Rundel, P. W., M. Neuman, M. and P. Rabenold. 2009. Plant communities and floristic diversity of the Emerald Lake Basin, Sequoia National Park, California. Madroño 56:184–198.

Safford, H. D., M. North, and M. D. Meyer. 2012. Climate change and the relevance of historical forest conditions. Pages 23–46, Chapter 3, in M. North, editor. Managing Sierra Nevada forests. General Technical Report PSW-GTR-237. U.S. Department of Agriculture Forest Service, Pacific Southwest Research Station, Albany, California.

Salzer, M. W., M. K. Hughes, A. G. Bunn, and K. F. Kipfmueller. 2009. Recent unprecedented tree-ring growth in bristlecone pine at the highest elevations and possible causes. Proceedings of the National Academy of Sciences 106:20348–20353.

Sawyer, J. O., T. Keeler-Wolf, and J. M. Evens. 2009. A manual of California vegetation. Second edition. California Native Plant Society, Sacramento, California.

Scholl, A., and A. H. Taylor. 2006. Regeneration patterns in old-growth red fir-western white pine forests in the northern Sierra Nevada, Lake Tahoe, USA. Forest Ecology and Management 235:143–154.

Schultz, B. W., P. T. Tueller, and R. J. Tausch. 1990. Ecology of curlleaf mahogany in western and central Nevada: Community and population structure. Journal of Range Management 43:13–19.

Scuderi, L. A. 1993. A 2000-year tree ring record of annual temperatures in the Sierra Nevada Mountains. Science 259:1433–1436.

Shepperd, W. D. 2008. Sudden aspen decline in the western U.S.: Introduction and background. In Sudden aspen decline (SAD) meeting. Fort Collins, Colorado. <http://www.aspensite.org/>. Accessed February 2013.

Sickman, J. O., A. Leydecker, and J. M. Melack. 2001. Nitrogen mass balances and abiotic

controls on N retention and yield in high-elevation catchments of the Sierra Nevada, California, United States. Water Resources Research 37:1445–1461.

Sickman J. O., A. C. Leydecker, C. Y. Chang, C. Kendall, J. M. Melack, D. M. Lucero, and J. Schimel. 2003. Mechanisms underlying export of N from high-elevation catchments during seasonal transitions. Biogeochemistry 64:1–24.

Sickman J. O., J. M. Melack, and D. W. Clow. 2003. Evidence for nutrient enrichment of high-elevation lakes in the Sierra Nevada, California. Limnology and Oceanography 48:1885–1892.

Skinner, C. N. 2003. Fire history of upper montane and subalpine glacial basins in the Klamath Mountains of northern California. Pages 145–151 in K. E. M. Gally, R. C. Klinger, and N. G. Sugihara, editors. Proceedings of the Fire Conference 2000: The First National Congress on Fire Ecology, Prevention, and Management. Miscellaneous Publication 13. Tall Timbers Research Station, Tallahassee, Florida.

Skinner, C. N., A. H. Taylor, and J. K. Agee. 2006. Klamath Mountains bioregion. Pages 170–194 in N. G. Sugihara, J. van Wagtendonk, J. Fites-Kaufmann, K. E. Shaffer, and A. E. Thode, editors. Fire in California's Ecosystems. University of California Press, Berkeley, California.

Skinner, C. N., and C. R. Chang. 1996. Fire regimes past and present. Pages 1041–1069 in Sierra Nevada Ecosystem Project: Final Report to Congress. Volume 2, Assessments and scientific basis for management options. Centers for Water and Wildland Resources, University of California, Davis, California.

Smith, R. S. 1996. Spread and intensification of blister rust in the range of sugar pine. Pages 112–118 in B. B. Kinloch Jr., M. Marosy, and M. Huddleston, editors. Sugar Pine: Status, Values, and Role in Ecosystems. Proceedings of a symposium presented by the California Sugar Pine Management Committee, March 30–April 1, 1992. University of California, Davis, California Publication No. 3362. Division of Agriculture and Natural Resources, University of California, Davis, California.

Stephenson, N. L. 1998. Actual evapotranspiration and deficit: Biologically meaningful correlates of vegetation distribution across spatial scales. Journal of Biogeography 25:855–870.

———. 1990. Climatic control of vegetation distribution: The role of the water balance. American Naturalist 135:649–670.

Stephenson, T. R., J. D. Wehausen, A. P. Few, D. W. German, D. F. Jensen, D. Spitz, K. Know, B. M. Pierce, J. L. Davis, J. Ostergard, and J. Fusaro. 2011. 2010–2011 Annual report of the Sierra Nevada bighorn sheep recovery program: A decade in review. Final report to the California Department of Fish and Wildlife.

Stevenson, K. M. 2004. Conservation of plant and abiotic diversity in grazed and ungrazed meadows of the Sierra Nevada. PhD dissertation. Plant Biology Graduate Group, University of California, Davis, California.

Stewart, I. T., D. R. Cayan, and M. D. Dettinger. 2005. Changes toward earlier streamflow timing across western North America. Journal of Climate 18:1136–1155.

Stillwater Sciences. 2012. A guide for restoring functionality to mountain meadows of the Sierra Nevada. Technical memorandum prepared by Stillwater Sciences, Berkeley, California for American Rivers, Nevada City, California.

Storer, T. I., R. L. Usinger, and D. Lukas. 2004. Sierra Nevada natural history. Revised edition. University of California Press, Berkeley, California.

Tappe, D. T. 1942. The status of beavers in California. Museum of Vertebrate Zoology and Division of Fish and Game, State of California.

Taylor, A. H. 2001. Fire regimes and forest changes in mid and upper montane forests of the southern Cascades, Lassen Volcanic National Park, California, USA. Journal of Biogeography 27:87–104.

———. 1995. Forest expansion and climate change in the mountain hemlock (*Tsuga mertensiana*) zone, Lassen Volcanic National Park, California, USA. Arctic, Antarctic, and Alpine Research 27:207–216.

Tomback, D. F. 2001. Clark's nutcracker: Agent of regeneration. Pages 89–104 in D. F. Tomback, S.F. Arno, and R. E. Keane, editors. Whitebark pine communities: Ecology and restoration. Island Press, Washington, D.C.

———. 1986. Post-fire regeneration of whitebark pine: A consequence of nutcracker seed caching. Madroño 33:11–110.

———. 1982. Dispersal of whitebark pine seeds by Clark's nutcracker: A mutualism hypothesis. Journal of Animal Ecology 51:435–467.

Tomback, D. F., and K. A. Kramer. 1980. Limber pine seed harvest by Clark's nutcracker (*Nucifraga columbiana*) in the Sierra Nevada, USA: Timing and foraging behavior. Condor 82:467–468.

Tomback, D. F., and P. Achuff. 2010. Blister rust and western forest biodiversity: Ecology, values, and outlook for white pines. Forest Pathology 40:186–225.

Tonnessen, K. A. 1991. The Emerald Lake watershed study: Introduction and site description. Water Resources Research 27:1537–1539.

Trujillo, E., N. P. Molotoch, M. L. Goulden, A. E. Kelly, and R. C. Bales. 2012. Elevation-dependent influence of snow accumulation on forest greening. Nature Geoscience 5. <doi:10.1038/NGE01571>.

Tuskan, G. A., K. E. Francis, S. L. Russ, W. H. Romme, and M. B. Turner. 1996. RAPD markers reveal diversity within and among clonal and seedling stands of aspen in Yellowstone National Park, U.S.A. Canadian Journal of Forest Research 26:2088–2098.

USDA (U.S. Department of Agriculture). 2013. Final Sierra-Nevada bio-regional assessment. Unpublished report. Forest Service, Pacific Southwest Regional Office. <http://www.fs.usda.gov/Internet/FSE_DOCUMENTS/stelprdb5444575.pdf>. Accessed May 2013.

USDA (U.S. Department of Agriculture, Forest Service). 2008. Forest Service strategic framework for responding to climate change: Version 1.0. <http://www.fs.fed.us/climatechange/documents/strategic-framework-climate-change-1-0.pdf>. Accessed May 2013.

USDI (U.S. Department of Interior). 2010. Climate change response strategy. National Park Service Climate Change Response Program, Fort Collins, Colorado.

USFWS (U.S. Fish and Wildlife Service). 2011. Endangered and threatened wildlife and plants; 12-month finding on a petition to list *Pinus albicaulis* as endangered or threatened with critical habitat. Federal Register. 50 CFR Part 17 Docket No. [FWS-R6-ES-2010-0047] [MO 92210-0-0008]. <http://www.regulations.gov>. Accessed May 2013.

Van der Wall, S. 2008. On the relative contributions of wind vs. animals to seed dispersal of four Sierra Nevada pines. Ecology 89:1837–1849.

Van de Ven, C., and S. B. Weiss. 2009. Downscaling to the climate near the ground: Measurements and modeling along the macro-, meso-, topo-, and microclimate hierarchy. Abstract #B33A-0373. Abstract of the American Geophysical Union, Fall Meeting, San Francisco, California.

Van de Ven, C. M., S. B. Weiss, and W. G. Ernst. 2007. Plant species distributions under present conditions and forecasted for warmer climates in an arid mountain range. Earth Interactions Paper No. 9. 11:1–33.

Van de Water, K., and H. Safford. 2011. A summary of fire frequency estimates for California vegetation before Euro-American settlement. Fire Ecology 7:26–58.

Van Pelt, R. 2001. Forest giants of the Pacific slope. Global Forest Society. University of Washington Press, Vancouver. Washington.

Vankat, J. L., and J. Major. 1978. Vegetation changes in Sequoia National Park, California Journal of Biogeography 5:377–402.

WCS (Wildlife Conservation Society). 2014. Climate adaptation fund grants program reports. <www.wcsnorthamerica.org/ClimateAdaptationFund/>. Accessed January 5, 2014.

Weaver, T. 2001. Whitebark pine and its environment. Pages 41–73 in D. F. Tomback, S. F. Arno, and R. E. Keane, editor. Whitebark pine communities: Ecology and restoration. Island Press, Washington, D.C.

Weixelman, D. A., B. Hill, D. J. Cooper, E. L. Berlow, J. H. Viers, S. E. Purdy, A. G. Merrill and A. E. Gross. 2011. Meadow hydrogeomorphic types for the Sierra Nevada and southern Cascade Ranges in California. General Technical Report R5-TP-034. U.S. Department of Agriculture Forest Service, Pacific Southwest Region.

Williams, M. W., and J. M. Melack. 1991. Solute chemistry of snowmelt and runoff in an alpine basin, Sierra Nevada. Water Resources Research 27:1575–1588.

Williams M. W., R. C. Bales, A. D. Brown, and J. M. Melack. 1995. Fluxes and transformations of nitrogen in a high-elevation catchment, Sierra Nevada. Biogeochemistry 28:1–31.

Wilson, N. 1986. A widespread cycle of unusual avalanche events. Proceedings of the International Snow Science Workshop, Squaw Valley. Pages 153–154.

Wolford, R. A., and R. C. Bales. 1996. Hydrochemical modeling of Emerald Lake watershed, Sierra Nevada, California: Sensitivity of stream chemistry to changes in fluxes and model parameters. Limnology and Oceanography 41:947–954.

Wolford, R. A., R. C. Bales, and S. Sorooshian. 1996. Development of a hydrochemical model for seasonally snow-covered alpine watersheds: Application to Emerald Lake Watershed, Sierra Nevada, California. Water Resources Research 32:1061–1074.

Wood, S. 1975. Holocene stratigraphy and chronology of mountain meadows. Sierra Nevada, California. Earth Monograph Series 4. U.S. Department of Agriculture Forest Service, Pacific Southwest Region.

Wright, R. D., and H. A. Mooney. 1965. Substrate-oriented distribution of bristlecone pine in the White Mountains of California. American Midland Naturalist 73:257–284.

WRRC (Western Regional Climate Center). 2013. Desert Research Institute, Reno, Nevada. <http://www.wrcc.dri.edu/>. Accessed December 30, 2013.

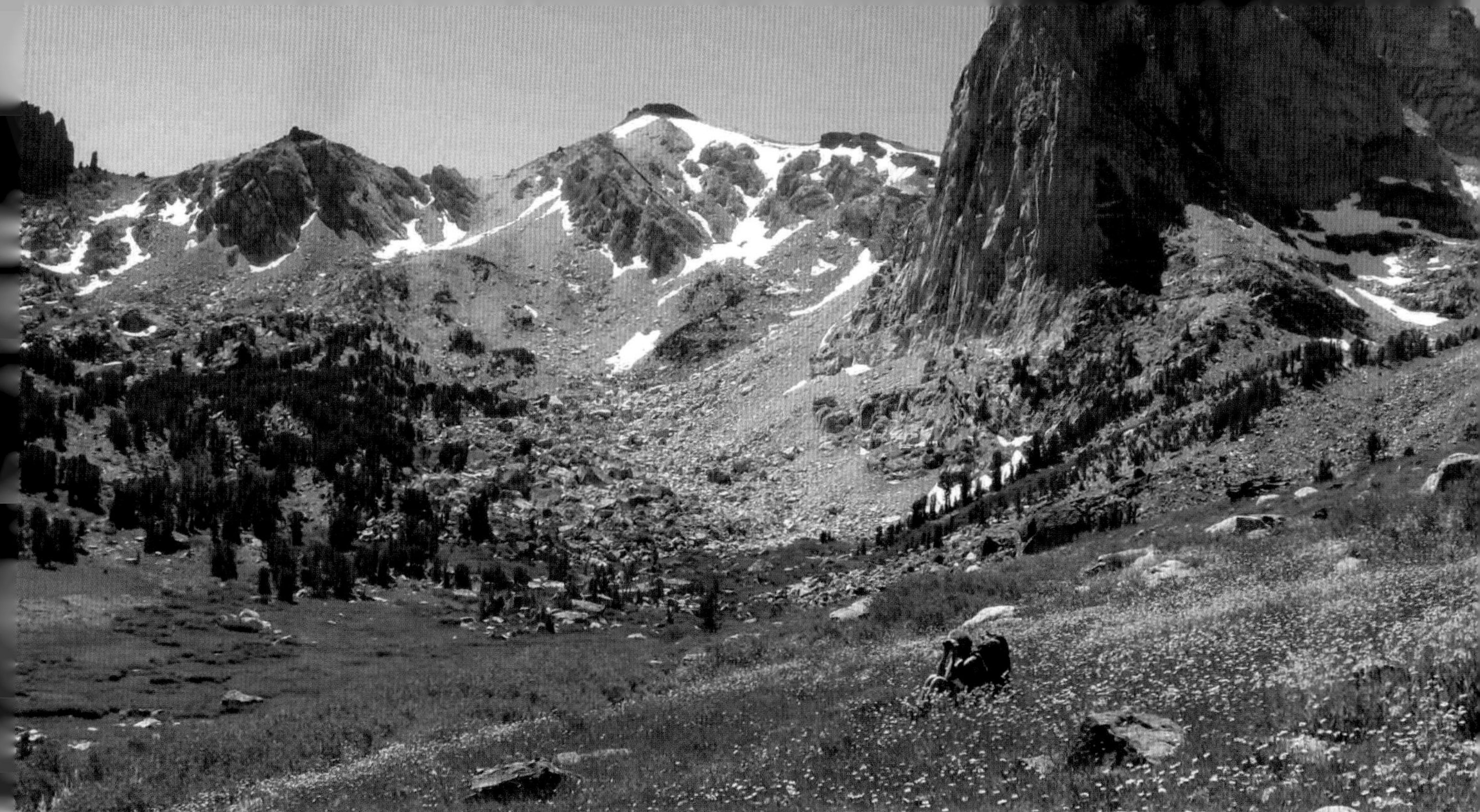

TWENTY-NINE

Alpine Ecosystems

PHILIP W. RUNDEL and CONSTANCE I. MILLAR

Introduction

Alpine ecosystems comprise some of the most intriguing habitats of the world for the stark beauty of their landscapes and for the extremes of the physical environment that their resident biota must survive. These habitats lie above the upper limit of tree growth but seasonally present spectacular floral shows of low-growing herbaceous perennial plants. Globally, alpine ecosystems cover only about 3% of the world's land area (Körner 2003). Their biomass is low compared to shrublands and woodlands, giving these ecosystems only a minor role in global biogeochemical cycling. Moreover, species diversity and local endemism of alpine ecosystems is relatively low. However, alpine areas are critical regions for influencing hydrologic flow to lowland areas from snowmelt.

The alpine ecosystems of California present a special case among alpine regions of the world. Unlike most alpine regions, including the American Rocky Mountains and the European Alps (where most research on alpine ecology has been carried out), the California alpine region has a Mediterranean-type climate regime with winter precipitation and summer drought. This condition provides an added stress quite different from other alpine areas and has contributed to the unique biota of the Sierra Nevada alpine. John Muir, in writing about the alpine meadows of the Sierra Nevada, felt his words were inadequate to describe "the exquisite beauty of these mountain carpets as they lie smoothly outspread in the savage wilderness" (Muir 1894).

Defining Alpine Ecosystems

Alpine ecosystems are classically defined as those communities occurring above the elevation of treeline. However, defining the characteristics that unambiguously characterize an alpine ecosystem is problematic. Defining alpine ecosystems based on presence of alpine-like communities of herbaceous perennials is common but subject to interpretation because such communities may occur well below treeline, while other areas well above treeline may support dense shrub or matted tree cover.

Defining alpine ecosystems on a floristic basis is also potentially flawed, as many plant species that dominate alpine communities well above treeline have ranges that extend down into subalpine or even montane forest communities (Rundel 2011; Figure 29.1). While we recognize that at the local scale

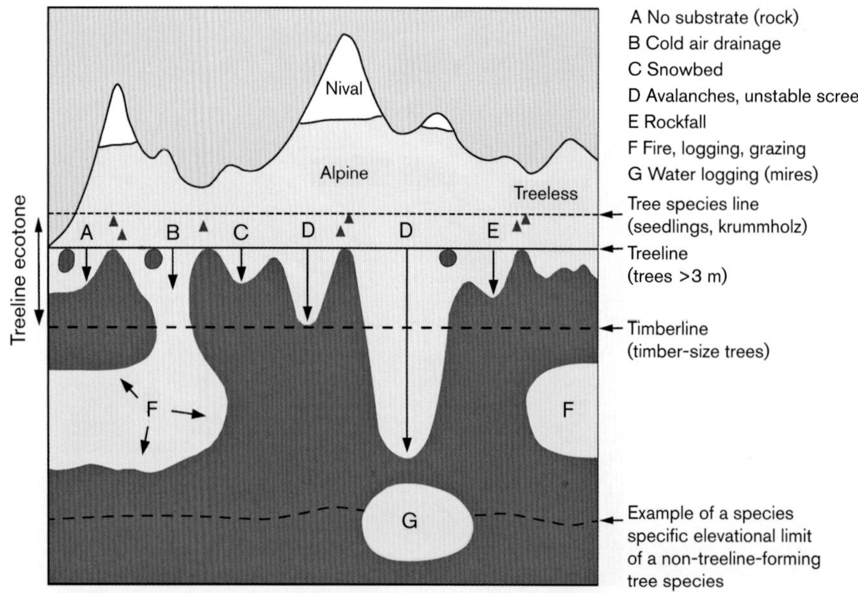

FIGURE 29.1 Schematic representation of the subalpine-alpine ecotone, showing various ways in which the thermal treeline can be displaced downslope by disturbance, snowbeds, or substrate. The alpine-nival ecotone is shown high on the peaks. Between these two ecotones is the alpine zone. Source: Modified from Körner 2012.

alpine ecosystems have excursions upward and downward for reasons including geology, geomorphology, and microclimate, to classify California alpine ecosystems at the regional scale, we adopt the global thermal limit for treeline as a convenient low-elevation baseline. Treeline has been defined as the zone on the landscape where average growing season temperature is 6.4°C or lower (Körner and Paulsen 2004). In this context, trees are defined as plants having upright stems that attain height ≥3 meters regardless of taxonomy, and the treeline community is characterized as more-or-less continuous patches of trees whose crowns form at least a loose canopy (Körner 2007).

Typically, the upper-elevational zones around treeline support mosaics of subalpine forest, dwarfed or KRUMMHOLZ trees, shrublands, and low alpine perennials, each responding to a complex mix of environmental conditions, soil, and disturbance history (Figure 29.2). Environmental stresses associated with temperate alpine ecosystems include extreme winter temperatures, short growing season, low nutrient availability, high winds, low partial pressures of CO_2, high UV irradiance, and limited water availability (Billings 2000, Bowman and Seastedt 2001, Körner 2003).

The California alpine ecosystem lies in regions colder, and usually above, this zone. For the purpose of this chapter, we allow alpine ecosystems to include also the small area of NIVAL regions that occurs in the state. The latter is defined by another globally occurring threshold: the zone where average growing season temperatures are ≤3°C, below which even plants shorter than 3 meters cannot endure freezing damage (Körner 2007). Only hardy lichens, isolated plants in protected microenvironments, snow algae, and other snow ice–dwelling invertebrates can survive these conditions. The definition of alpine we adopt differs from what is often generically called tundra. Technically, "tundra" refers to specific vegetation formations as well as regions of permanently frozen soils and usually is applied to Arctic latitudes (Billings 1973). Alpine ecosystems extend beyond the typically envisioned high-elevation open slopes and summits of cold-adapted shrubs and herbs to also include lithic environments of cliffs, TALUS FIELDS, boulder fields and ROCK GLACIERS; permanent and persistent snow and icefields, including glaciers; and various water bodies such as streams, TARNS, and large lakes.

Photo on previous page: Granitic cirque at head of Burt Canyon, Sierra Nevada, with wetlands along the creek and aster- and paintbrush-festooned upland slopes. Photo: Jeffrey Wyneken.

Geographic Distribution of Alpine Ecosystems in California

The lower (warm) limit of the alpine ecosystem, or climatic treeline, varies with latitude across California, ranging from 3,500 meters in the southern California mountains, to 3,200 meters in the Yosemite region, to 3,000 meters near Donner Pass, to 2,800 meters with somewhat higher elevations in ranges of the western Great Basin east of the Sierra Nevada (Rundel 2011) (Figure 29.3). To the north, in the Cascade Range, climatic treeline begins at approximately 2,800 meters on Lassen Peak and 2,700 meters on Mount Shasta.

Moving from south to north, high elevations with alpine communities are first encountered in the Transverse and Peninsular Ranges of southern California. These ranges support local areas of weakly developed, alpine-like communities populated by a subset of Sierran alpine species (Hall 1902, Parish 1917, Horton 1960, Hanes 1976, Major and Taylor 1977, Meyers 1978, Gibson et al. 2008). Mount San Gorgonio in the San Bernardino Mountains reaches 3,506 meters and had local glacial activity in the Pleistocene (Sharp et al. 1959). Other high points are Mount San Jacinto in the San Jacinto Mountains at 3,302 meters and Mount Baldy (San Antonio) in the San Gabriel Mountains at 3,068 meters. Alpine species

FIGURE 29.2 The forest-alpine ecotone at upper treeline is a zone on the landscape that can include krummholz whitebark pines, as here on the uplifted, metamorphic plateau of the Tamarack Crest, Sierra Nevada. Photo: Constance Millar.

are present in both xeric and mesic habitats at high elevations, but alpine communities in the form of extended areas dominated by assemblages of alpine species are only weakly developed.

The greatest area of alpine ecosystems in California occurs in the Sierra Nevada. The elevational contour of 3,500 meters, a limit that roughly corresponds to treeline in the southern Sierra Nevada, has been used as one simple parameter to delineate alpine ecosystems (Sharsmith 1940). This boundary defines a relatively continuous area from Kings Canyon and Sequoia National Parks along the crest of the central and southern Sierra Nevada extending to northern Tuolumne and Mono Counties. The alpine zone of the southern Sierra Nevada first appears on Olancha Peak (3,698 meters) on the Tulare-Inyo County line, the southernmost glaciated summit of the range (Howell 1951, Tatum 1979). Cirque Peak (3,932 meters) in Sequoia National Park forms the southern limit of an extensive and virtually contiguous alpine zone of glaciated peaks in the Sierra Nevada. Here occur extensive areas of alpine habitat and high peaks that reach above 4,000 meters, with Mount Whitney at 4,421 meters the highest point in the contiguous United States.

Alpine habitats in the central Sierra Nevada are well developed in the area of Leavitt Peak (3,527 meters) near Sonora Pass and south across Yosemite National Park, whose highest peak is Mount Lyell (3,999 meters). Further south, this belt of alpine habitat continues into Kings Canyon and Sequoia National Parks. Tioga Pass in Yosemite National Park (3,031 meters) and Mammoth Pass (Minaret Summit,2,824 meters), which is the route for California Highway 203, provide two major breaks containing subalpine elevations but not true alpine habitats. North of the Tioga Pass area, the crest of the Sierra Nevada lies at lower elevations with only scattered areas of typical alpine habitat present. Fragmented communities of alpine species are present at elevations well below 3,500 meters, particularly along exposed ridgelines and on steep, north-facing slopes that were once heavily glaciated. Alpine habitats are weakly developed in Alpine County (Sonora Peak, 3,493 meters) and eastern El Dorado County (Freel Peak, 3,318 meters), extending to their northern limit on Mount Rose (3,285 meters) in the Carson Range east of Lake Tahoe along the California-Nevada border. Nevertheless, scattered communities of alpine-like habitat exist at upper elevations in the northern Sierra Nevada, positioned above and around local, edaphically controlled treelines, and an alpine flora is well represented (Smiley 1915). The substrate north of Sonora Pass is largely volcanic and thus quite distinct from the granitic bedrock of the central and southern Sierra Nevada. Notable exceptions exist where granitic plutons are exposed in the Desolation Wilderness, Donner Pass region, and adjacent parts of the Tahoe Basin.

Several high mountain ranges lie to the east of the Sierra Nevada at the western margin of the Great Basin, and these support small but diverse areas of alpine ecosystems. The White Mountains have an extensive alpine area, with 106 square kilometers above 3,500 meters and the third highest peak in California, on White Mountain Peak, at 4,344 meters (Figure 29.4). To the south, Mount Waucoba forms the high point in the Inyo Mountains at 3,390 meters. The Panamint Mountains east of the Inyo Mountains reach a maximum elevation of 3,366 meters on Telescope Peak.

The Sweetwater Mountains, located 33 kilometers east of the north-central Sierra Nevada north of Bridgeport, reach 3,552 meters on Mount Patterson and contain a significant zone of diverse alpine ecosystems (Bell-Hunter and Johnson 1983; Figure 29.5). At the south end of the Mono Basin, volcanic Glass Mountain reaches 3,392 meters and supports a small, mostly edaphically controlled alpine zone.

To the north of the Sierra Nevada, the southern Cascade Mountains provide local areas of alpine habitat and were likely once stepping-stones for high-elevation plants and animals migrating into California with the late Neogene and Pleistocene tectonic dynamics of the Sierra Nevada (see Chapter 8, "Ecosystems Past: Vegetation Prehistory"). Mount Shasta reaches an elevation of 4,322 meters, while Lassen Peak extends to 3,187 meters (Gillett et al. 1995). Magee Peak (2,641 meters), located midway between Mounts Lassen and Shasta, supports limited areas of alpine vegetation in CIRQUES on its north face (Major and Taylor 1977). In northeast California, the Warner Mountains, another fault-block range of the Great Basin province, run 140 kilometers from south to north and attain plateau heights near 3,000 meters. Alpine ecosystems are scattered along their crest, primarily in the South Warner section.

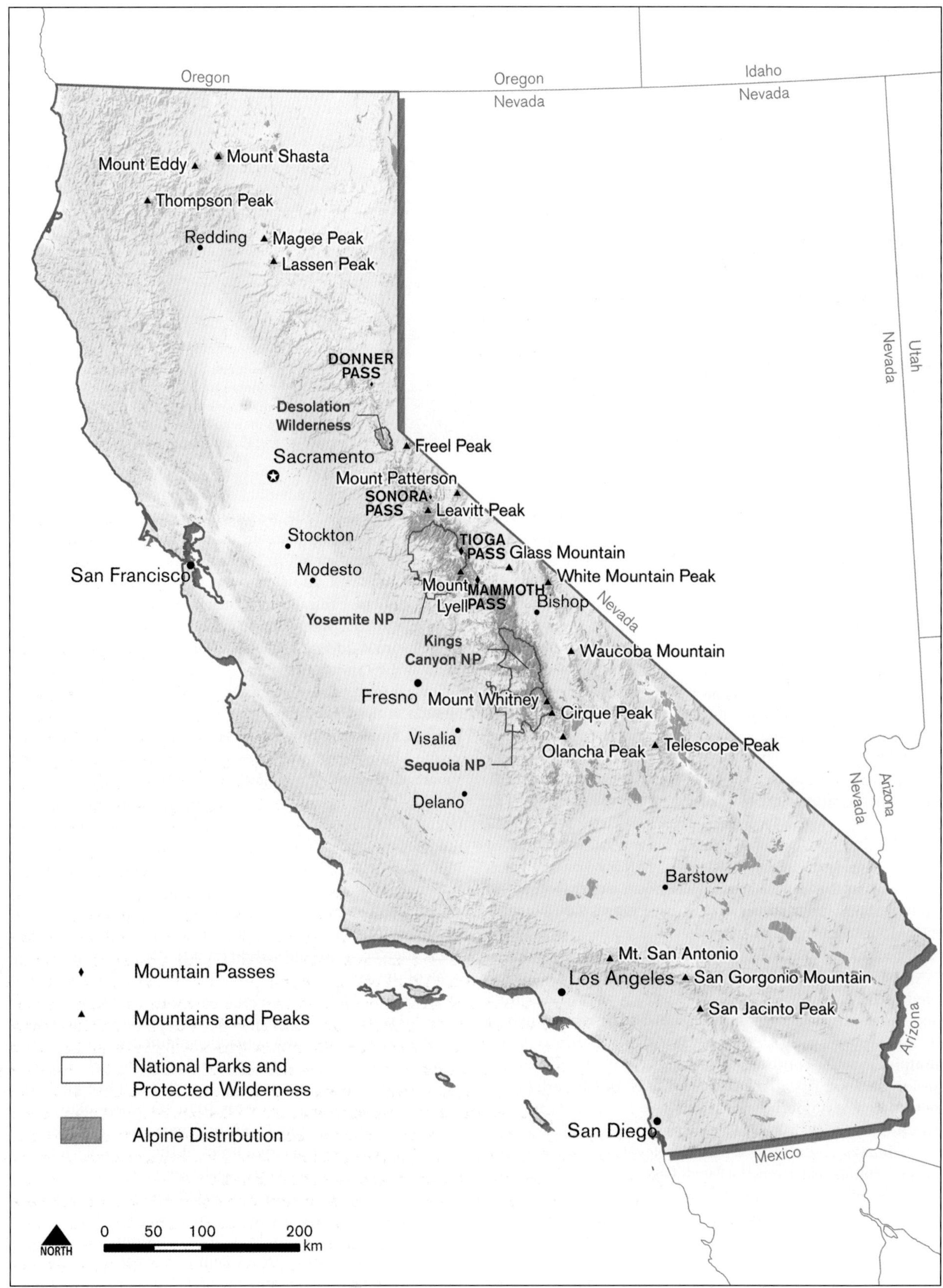

FIGURE 29.3 Distribution of alpine ecosystems in California. Source: Data from U.S. Geological Survey, Gap Analysis Program (GAP); and Cal Fire, Fire Resource and Assessment Program (FRAP). Map: Parker Welch, Center for Integrated Spatial Research (CISR).

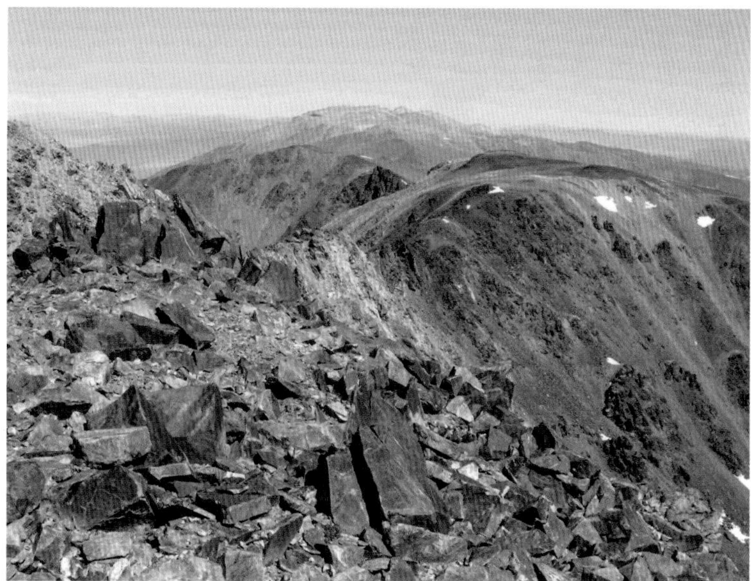

FIGURE 29.4 Extensive alpine fellfields extend across the broad alpine plateaus of the White Mountains, interrupted occasionally by inselbergs, patterned ground, and other periglacial features. Photo: Constance Millar.

FIGURE 29.5 The diverse volcanic soils of the Sweetwater Mountains in the California Great Basin appear barren from a distance but support a great number of alpine herbs, including many endemics. Photo: Constance Millar.

In northwestern California the higher peaks of the Klamath Mountains, especially in the Trinity Alps, Marble Mountains, and Scott Mountains, support alpine ecosystems and contain areas of permanent or long-lasting snowfields on north-facing slopes (Howell 1944, Major and Taylor 1977). The highest peaks are Mount Eddy (2,750 meters) in Siskiyou County, Thompson Peak (2,744 meters) in Trinity County, and Mount Ashland (2,296 meters) in Jackson County, Oregon. Major and Taylor (1977) note that alpine species distributions dip as low as 2,000 meters or less on KARST TOPOGRAPHY associated with marble substrates in the Marble Mountains, and alpine-like communities also have lower-elevation excursions onto ultramafic (e.g., serpentine) soils (Kruckeberg 1984).

Climate Regimes and Abiotic Stress

At the regional or synoptic scale, the alpine zone of the Sierra Nevada experiences a Mediterranean-type climate regime with dry summers and with precipitation heavily centered on the winter months. This regime differs significantly from that present in the more continental and monsoon-dominated regions of western and southwestern U.S. and in most of the continental alpine habitats of the world, where summer precipitation predominates. This seasonality is a significant element of the alpine environments of California and a strong factor in explaining the relatively high rate of endemism in the alpine flora. Much of the historic literature on plant and animal adaptations to high-elevation, alpine habitats has come from studies in the colder and more continental alpine ecosystems of the Rocky Mountains and the European Alps.

In alpine habitats at the upper treeline in the Sierra Nevada, about 95% of annual precipitation falls as winter snow. By contrast to the Pacific Northwest, where snowpacks accumulate during regular winter storms throughout the cold season, much snow in the California alpine zones falls during a very small number of storms separated by long, dry intervals. The absence of one or two of these storm episodes in a year can cause a dry snowpack year relative to average levels. By contrast, fortuitous landing of one or more ATMOSPHERIC RIVER storms ("pineapple express") on the California region can result in record wet years and deep snowpacks (Dettinger et al. 2011).

Deep snowpacks and cool temperatures at higher elevations mean that snowmelt extends into spring, but the length and magnitude of the summer drought period experienced by plants and animals is significant. Patterns of rainfall decline gradually from north to south in the main California cordillera, and summer drought decreases as elevation increases because of both increased levels of precipitation and cooler temperatures with lower evaporative demand at higher elevations (Stephenson 1998, Urban et al. 2000).

Very few climate stations are situated in the California alpine zone. In general, winter mean monthly low temperatures are moderate in the Sierra Nevada (Table 29.1) compared to the more continental climates of the interior Great Basin and Rocky Mountains, and in general soils rarely freeze beyond moderate depths. While the mean minimum temperature above treeline is generally below freezing for ten months of the year, nighttime lows typically reach only –3°C to –6°C, although temperature extremes can fall below –20°C on high, north slopes and in cold air sinks (Millar et

TABLE 29.1

Climate data for select alpine locations in California

Location	Mountain range	Latitude (° W)	Longitude (° N)	Elevation (M)	Temperature °C							Precipitation (mm)				
					Jan		July		Annual							
					max	min	max	min	max	min	temp	Jan	July	Aug	Sept	Annual
Mount Shasta	South Cascades	41.42997	122.19914	3261	-2.4	-10.9	15.2	0.8	4.9	-6.3	-0.7	275	17	15	43	1898
Thompson Peak	Trinity Alps	41.00065	123.04834	2717	0.9	-6.3	18.6	6.7	8.3	-1.0	3.7	436	9	56	35	1974
Mount Lassen	South Cascades	40.48916	121.50747	3130	-0.6	-9.1	18.0	3.0	7.5	-4.4	1.6	532	12	40	58	3064
Mount Rose	Sierra Nevada	39.34403	119.91807	3283	-0.4	-11.0	17.6	3.2	7.0	-5.5	0.8	229	21	23	47	1467
Barcroft Station	White Mountains	37.58281	118.23721	3790	-4.5	-12.4	12.6	2.7	2.7	-6.5	-1.9	36	23	30	22	450
Mammoth Crest	Sierra Nevada	37.55376	118.98012	3514	0.6	-10.1	16.9	4.5	7.3	-4.1	1.6	297	6	3	23	1473
Whitney N (Tulainyo Lake)	Sierra Nevada	36.60582	118.27619	3754	-1.7	-11.9	12.7	-0.5	4.1	-7.6	-1.8	114	8	10	19	697

SOURCE: Data excerpted from the PRISM climate model (Daly et al. 1994) for point locations selected as representative of the mid-upper alpine zone for the region. PRISM data represent 1971–2000 normals, with 800 m grid.

al. 2014b, and unpublished data). A cooperative climate station on the summit of Mount Warren (3,757 meters, Western Regional Climate Center) operated for six years before high winds destroyed the major infrastructure in 2011. In 2009, when data were most complete for all months, average annual temperature was –1.3°C; the lowest monthly minimum temperature (December) was –22.3°C and the highest monthly maximum temperature (August) was 20.1°C. Winds throughout 2009 were mainly westerly (cold seasons) and southwesterly (warm seasons), with gusts commonly over 54 m s^{-1} (120 mph). The maximum monthly wind gust (March) was 42 m s^{-1} (94 mph), and that month had two days with maximum gusts over 134 m s^{-1} (300 mph) including one at 171 m s^{-1} (382 mph)!

Climatic data to characterize the alpine environment of the White Mountains have been collected for many years at the Barcroft Station at 3,801 meters (Pace et al. 1974, Powell and Klieforth 1991). The mean monthly maximum temperatures at Barcroft vary from a high of 11.9°C in July to a low of –5.3°C in February. Record maximum temperatures of 22°C have been reached in July and August. Mean monthly maximum temperatures remain below freezing for six months of the year from November through April. Mean minimum temperatures range from a high of 2.4°C in July to a low of –14.0°C in March. Mean minimum temperatures drop below freezing for every month of the year except July and August (Rundel et al. 2008). Still, many winter days have midday temperatures that rise above freezing. Such temperatures, combined with soils that do not freeze below shallow surface layers, allow for diurnal water uptake by plant species.

Because of their position in the rain shadow of the Sierra Nevada, precipitation in the White Mountains is only about a third of that in the Sierra Nevada at the same elevation (see Table 29.1). A Mediterranean-climate pattern remains of winter precipitation in the White Mountains, but a strong added influence of summer convective storms from the south and east brings scattered precipitation events throughout the growing season. Mean annual precipitation at Barcroft is 478 millimeters, with all of this precipitation falling as snow except in July through September. Mean monthly precipitation ranges from a high of 56 millimeters in December to a low of 18 millimeters in September, but year-to-year variation is high. The extremes in annual precipitation over the record period have ranged from 242 to 852 millimeters (Rundel et al. 2008).

California alpine ecosystems are influenced by interannual and interdecadal climate modes, such as the El Niño/La Niña system (ENSO) (Diaz and Markgraf 2000) and the Pacific Decadal Oscillation (PDO) (Mantua et al. 1997). These ocean-mediated climate modes have alternate states that bring to the California region years of wet, warm winters (El Niño) or cool, dry winters (La Niña). Decadal oscillators such as PDO amplify the effects of one or the other condition. While extreme conditions of ENSO usually occur about every two to seven years, in California more El Niño conditions occurred during the 1980s and 1990s, while La Niña conditions have had a stronghold in the 2000s. The latter tend to modify already dry winters to be record low precipitation years, even in alpine ecosystems. The ENSO system expresses itself in opposite patterns (wet-warm versus cold-dry) in the Pacific Northwest compared to the American Southwest, and northern California lies in the zone of transition between these patterns. Thus northern California alpine ecosystems as far south as the central Sierra Nevada can experience quite different winter temperatures and snowpacks than the southern parts of the range. Other, longer-term trends that affect the alpine zone include multiyear droughts. During the twentieth century in the central Sierra Nevada, these tended to recur every fifteen years or so and persist for five to seven years (Cayan et al. 1998, Millar et al. 2007).

Geologic and Geomorphic Setting

Historical Geology of Uplift and Erosion (Subsidence)

The geologic history of the Sierra Nevada has been discussed in more detail in previous chapters (see Chapters 4, "Geomorphology and Soils," and 8, "Ecosystems Past: Vegetation Prehistory"), which have highlighted changing interpretations of the geomorphic development of the range. Traditional understanding held that the present-day Sierra Nevada was a young, uplifted mountain range resulting from Great Basin extensional forces and faulting. Although scientists have long recognized that mountains of volcanic origin existed in the late Mesozoic and early Tertiary at the site of the present-day Sierra Nevada, the prevailing view was that this ancient range had never gained elevation greater than approximately 2,000 meters and had eroded to lowlands during the early to mid-Tertiary. Fault-block tilting in the past 10–5 Ma was believed to have created the high elevation of the modern Sierra Nevada. New evidence suggests that the Sierra Nevada in fact reached heights of more than 2,800 meters in the early Tertiary and remained high through subsequent millennia (see Chapter 8, "Ecosystems Past: Vegetation Prehistory"). Nevertheless, the form, topography, and elevation of the modern Sierra Nevada were strongly influenced by effects of more recent extensional and faulting processes—processes that today continue through tectonic action along the Sierra Micro-Plate and Eastern California Shear Zones.

Glacial and Periglacial History

The major glacial activity present in California has been in the Sierra Nevada, and this history of multiple glacial advances and retreats has had a major impact on the distribution and fragmentation of the biota. During the last glacial maximum of the Pleistocene (approximately 20 ka; 1 ka = 1000 years), an ice cap 125 kilometers long and 65 kilometers wide spread over most of the high parts of the Sierra Nevada and reached downslope to an elevation of about 2,600 meters. Valley glaciers moving from the ice cap extended as far as 65 kilometers down canyons on the west slope of the range and 30 kilometers down canyons of the steeper eastern escarpment (Raub et al. 2006). Smaller areas of glaciers formed in the Trinity Alps, Salmon Mountains, Cascade Ranges (Mount Shasta, Mount Lassen, Medicine Lake), Warner Mountains, Sweetwater Range, White Mountains, and San Bernardino Mountains. Prior mountain glaciation events are evident most dramatically in the multiple MORAINES of the eastern Sierra Nevada, some of which reached greater extents than the last glacial maximum.

Evidence suggests that Pleistocene glaciers in the Sierra Nevada completely melted at the latest during the thermal optimum of the Holocene 4,000 to 6,000 years ago (Bowerman and Clark 2011). Neoglaciation began with a moderate advance, 3,200 years ago, followed by a possible glacier maxi-

FIGURE 29.6 Cirque, cliff, and valley slope environments of the eastern Sierra Nevada show erosional and depositional effects resulting from multiple Pleistocene glaciations. Small neoglacial icefields now occupy the highest of these cirque headwalls. Photo: Jeffrey Wyneken.

mum at ~2,800 years ago and four distinct glacier maxima at approximately 2,200 years, 1,600 years, 700 years, and 250 to 170 years ago, the most recent being the largest (Bowerman and Clark 2011). The advent of the global LITTLE ICE AGE about 600 years ago (Grove 1988), brought on by shifts in the solar cycle and significant volcanic eruptions, resulted in a period with the coldest conditions of the past 4,000 years. The coldest part of the Little Ice Age in California occurred during the late 1800s and into the early decades of the twentieth century and left a legacy of rock ice formations and high-elevation microclimates that continue to have a significant impact.

Geomorphic Settings and Habitats

Community composition in alpine communities is strongly influenced by geomorphic structures and their relationship to erosion, snow accumulation, and snowmelt. Such features as soil accumulation and stability, water availability, and exposure to wind are strongly shaped by these settings.

Mountain Summits and Upland Alpine Plateaus

Mountain summits in the alpine zone of California are modifications of two primary shapes. One is the classic cone shape, most symmetric in volcanic cones such as Mount Lassen and Mount Shasta, while the other is the highly irregular result of fault-block tectonics. The latter, such as Mount Whitney, often have sheer cliffs on one side (the escarpment) while the other slopes often grade to broad, often surprisingly flat, alpine plateaus. These low-relief uplands, often terraces (treads) with steep cliffs (risers), have long been recognized as important features of the Sierra Nevada (Lawson 1904).

These plateaus are interpreted as former lowland erosion surfaces brought to their high-elevation locations during the late Tertiary and Quaternary through episodic tectonic uplift and fault action (Wahrhaftig 1965). The plateaus remain broad and flat, usually with a slight gradient and mostly not incised due to lack of opportunity for snowpack accumulation and melt from higher elevations. The plateaus present a large habitat landscape for alpine communities at high elevations. Because of their elevations, the summits and high plateaus of the Sierra Nevada and White Mountains, Mount Shasta, and some regions of the Klamath Mountains experience repeated freeze-thaw action, which breaks what would in many cases be exposures of underlying plutons into extensive fields of shattered rock, known as FELSENMEER. The dynamic processes present in these habitats makes it difficult for plant communities to develop significant cover in them. Together summits and alpine plateaus experience rather unique climates for complex mountain regions. Given their extension upward to high altitudes and their relative isolation from adjacent barriers, these high points are strongly influenced by synoptic or regional climatology and more likely to "take the pulse" of changes in regional or hemispheric climate trends than are lower mountain elevations (Barry 2008).

Upland Slopes and Basins: Cirques, Cliffs, and Depositional Chutes

Below the highest mountain summits and upland plateaus of California's alpine zone are cirque, cliff, and valley slope environments (Figure 29.6). Valleys in glaciated areas head in cirques, amphitheater-shaped basins with broad, flat floors and sloping walls, whereas unglaciated valleys head in slopes that often are narrow and can have very steep walls. Glaciated valley slopes, especially near the range crests and on escarpment direction, often have steep walls above U-shaped valley floors. The "trim line" represents the upper height of glacial activity. This is often visible as a change in slope and composition of the valley wall, with steep, ice-scoured rocks below the trim line and frost-shattered slopes rising to summits, ridgetops, and upland plateaus above. As a result of differences in substrate texture, vegetation is often quite different above and below trim lines. Glaciated and unglaciated valley walls support cliffs, talus slopes, and avalanche, debris, and landslide chutes that attract lithic-adapted flora and/or those adapted to unstable substrates. Shallower-gradient slopes support stable vegetation communities.

FIGURE 29.7 Rock glaciers, such as on the east slope of Mount Gibbs in the Sierra Nevada, are common periglacial features in many alpine canyons. Photo: Constance Millar.

Broken Rock Habitats: Rock Glaciers, Scree, Fellfield, and Talus Slopes

Rock glaciers and periglacial talus slopes are widespread geomorphic features associated with cirques and high valleys of the central and southern parts of the Sierra Nevada (Figure 29.7). Although widely overlooked as important features in the past, these now are understood to play an important role in mountain hydrology (Millar and Westfall 2008, 2010). Unlike typical ice glaciers and exposed areas of snowpack, the ice and groundwater contained within rock glaciers and talus slopes are insulated from the direct effects of solar radiation by blankets of rock debris (Clark et al. 1994). Amplifying the insulation effect of rock mantling are internal thermal regimes created by air circulation within the matrix of rock (Millar et al. 2013, 2014b).

As a result, thaw of ice in rock glaciers lags behind thaw in typical ice glaciers. The former appear to be in disequilibrium with climate, especially when climates are changing rapidly such as at present. The unique thermal regimes of high and north-facing talus slopes and rock glaciers in the Sierra Nevada are cold enough to support persistent internal ice. Thus persistent cold conditions associated with rock glaciers can provide microclimates equivalent to alpine conditions 1,000 meters higher in elevation. Increasingly, these rocky environments are recognized as unique mountain ecosystems (Kubat 2000), with cold-displaced species such as the predatory rhagidiid mite (*Rhagidia gelida*) inhabiting internal matrices far below its usual elevation limits (Zacharda et al. 2005) and plant species adapted to unstable lithic environments growing on the rocky mantles (Burga et al. 2004). In California these alpine ecosystems are poorly described, but pilot studies indicate that distinct vegetation associations are found on the surfaces of talus slopes, and that the wetlands supported by talus and rock glacier springs also support distinct plant and arthropod communities (Millar, Westfall, Evenden et al. 2014). Meltwater from snow, internal ice, permafrost, and/or stable groundwater within and below these features appears to provide an important hydrologic reservoir through the summer months (Raub et al. 2006, Maurer 2007, Millar et al. 2013, Millar et al. 2014b), contributing to streamflow and downslope recharge. In this way, these features support abundant wetlands in high-elevation canyons and provide critical habitat for a host of alpine biota, of which some, like the American pika (*Ochotona princeps*), depend on wetland habitats supported by adjacent talus fields and rock glaciers (Millar and Westfall 2010). Moreover, wetlands act as sponges to retain water in upper-elevation basins in contrast to meltwaters from annual snowpacks and ice glaciers, which more typically flow out of the uplands in incised channels.

Patterned Ground

Patterned ground and related PERMAFROST features are common in arid, cold climates of the world, and permafrost dynamics can have a strong impact on the development of plant communities (Washburn 1980). However, these have been little-mentioned for the Sierra Nevada. This is because permafrost generally has not been assumed to exist in the range generally, although permafrost features now are known to exist in both rock glaciers and high, cold talus slopes (Millar et al. 2013, 2014b). Ample evidence of patterned ground, especially sorted circles and slope stripes from historical (likely Pleistocene) PERIGLACIAL action, exists in many alpine zones of the Sierra Nevada, especially upland plateaus. Some areas other than rocky slopes such as shallow edges of tarns (Figure 29.8) suggest that these processes are ongoing.

Intensive research in the adjacent White Mountains of California has demonstrated the presence of discontinuous, modern, patterned ground features and processes at 3,800 meters. Modern patterned ground processes with sorted circles, nets, and stripes become the dominant landscape phenomena above 4,150 meters (Wilkerson 1995). FREEZE-THAW CYCLES throughout the year are common in some parts of the White Mountains, with over 220 cycles per year observed (LaMarche 1968). While the larger patterned ground features in the White Mountains have been assumed to be relict (Wilkerson 1995), the presence of active permafrost processes there suggests that similar active processes may exist in the Sierra Nevada, especially on exposed plateaus and ridgetops where water collects yet wind sweeps away snow, maintaining exposure of the ground surface to freezing air (Millar and Westfall 2008, Millar et al. 2013).

Wetlands

Wetland environments, characterized by high groundwater moisture, are important generally in mountain regions of the world for the distinctive biodiversity they support. This is especially true in the California alpine zone, where Mediterranean-type and dry continental (Great Basin) climates and low latitudes combine to drive temperatures high and make water during the growing season scarce. Where wetlands occur, plant communities differ significantly from those occurring on uplands (Sawyer et al. 2009, Weixelman et al. 2011). Invertebrate assemblages also differ substantially between alpine upland and wetland habitats (Holmquist et al. 2011), with wetlands tending to be more speciose. In the California alpine zone, wetlands around springs and seeps and wet meadows derive their high soil moisture primarily from persistent subterranean groundwater sources that often are augmented by snowpack and snowmelt, especially where slope gradients are low (Figure 29.9). Snowbeds (small wetlands fed by late-lying snowfields that recur in specific locations) and glacial forefields (including rock glacier and talus slope forefields) are fed by closely adjacent water sources (melting snow and ice bodies). Riparian corridors tend to be very narrow and to track valley bottoms along streams as well as along creek drainages of valley slopes. The character of wetlands and thus the habitat they create for plants and animals varies depending on the substrate, which affects soil water-holding capacity and acidity. Some soils (e.g., volcanic) drain rapidly while others (e.g., granitic) can develop so-called Teflon basins that hold water near the surface.

Aquatic environments including the moving water of streams, creeks, and rivers and the still water of lakes, tarns, and ephemeral pools are also extremely important habitats in the otherwise relatively dry alpine zones of California (see Chapter 32, "Lakes"). In glaciated regions, TARNS, PATERNOSTER PONDS, and moraine-impounded lakes constitute the bulk of still waters, which number many in the Sierra Nevada (more than four thousand) (Knapp 1996) and Klamath Ranges and very few in the drier interior Great Basin ranges (Warner Mountains, Sweetwater Mountains, White Mountains). Snowmelt-derived streams flowing from high slopes and cirques are sources for important rivers of mid-montane and lowland reaches. Due to the presence of an extensive ice cap during the last glacial maximum in the Sierra Nevada, lakes and streams above 1,800 meters were fishless during the late Pleistocene and Holocene and prior to European settlement supported rich amphibian and invertebrate diversity (Jennings 1996, Erman 1996). Stocking of non-native fish starting in the early twentieth century, however, widely transformed these alpine waters; amphibian species have greatly declined in abundance and distribution, while aquatic invertebrate diversity has shifted drastically in response to predation by fish (Knapp 1996).

Glaciers and Permanent Snowfields

More than seventeen hundred permanent snow or ice bodies are located in California, with seventy of these larger than 0.1 square kilometers (Figure 29.10). Twenty of these glaciers have been named—seven on Mount Shasta and thirteen in the Sierra Nevada. Snow and ice bodies are also located in the Trinity Alps and near Mount Lassen. In total, permanent snow and ice bodies cover over 46 square kilometers of California (Fountain et al. 2007).

An inventory in 2006 identified 497 glaciers covering a total area of 50 square kilometers in the Sierra Nevada (Raub et al. 2006), while 421 rock glaciers and related features were inventoried from the central Sierra Nevada alone (Millar and Westfall 2008). Aside from the Sierra Nevada, the alpine zone of California supports glaciers primarily on Mount Shasta, where seven to ten glaciers were recognized as of 1987 (USGS 1986, Rhodes 1987). Despite regional warming over the past half century, the glaciers of Mount Shasta have shown a greater sensitivity to precipitation than to temperature and have continued to expand following a contraction during a prolonged drought in the early twentieth century (Howat et al. 2007). However, the strong warming trend predicted by regional climate models will be the dominant forcing with an expected near-total loss of glaciers on Mount Shasta and elsewhere in California by the end of the twenty-first century (Basagic 2008).

Processes and Ecosystem Dynamics

Alpine and subalpine watersheds in California play critical hydrologic roles for downstream agriculture and urban development in California, particularly with respect to the seasonality and amount of snowmelt (Bales et al. 2006). The hydrologic flow and biogeochemical processes of these high-mountain ecosystems are sensitive to small changes in growing-season temperature and water availability. The thin oligotrophic soils of alpine watersheds also have the potential to be significantly affected by atmospheric nitrogen deposition and acidification associated with the expanding urbanization of the San Joaquin Valley (Sickman et al. 2003). While there has been a long history of research on high-mountain hydrology and biogeochemistry of lakes and streams in the Sierra Nevada, these studies have largely focused on subalpine watersheds (see Chapters 28, "Subalpine Forests," and 32, "Lakes").

Hydrologic studies in high-elevation watersheds in the Sierra Nevada have modeled streamflows and water balance and the association of snowmelt and runoff with the solute chemistry of aquatic systems (Kattelmann and Elder 1991, Williams and Melack 1991). Climate change is expected to affect hydrology by increasing snowmelt rates, promoting earlier runoff (Wolford and Bales 1996). Acid deposition has the potential to alter streamwater pH and increase sensitivity to acidification (Sickman et al. 2001). A key factor influencing nitrogen cycling is duration of snow cover, which influences plant uptake, mineralization, and mineral nitrogen export (Meixner and Bales 2003). Because of the extreme heterogeneity of soil depth and vegetation cover in alpine watersheds, soil mineralization rates for nitrogen are highly site-specific (Miller et al. 2009).

Although data on aboveground production are available for subalpine communities in the Sierra Nevada, very little attempt has been made to collect such data in alpine habitats above treeline. Studies from the central Rocky Mountains and the European Alps have generally found aboveground production rates of approximately 100 to 400 g m^{-2} yr^{-1}, with

FIGURE 29.8 Sorted circles result from repeated freeze-thaw action when lake waters are shallow in alpine environments, as along the borders of the deep basin of Silverpine Lake, Sierra Nevada. Photo: Constance Millar.

FIGURE 29.9 Wetlands commonly surround alpine lakes, as at Greenstone Lake in the Sierra Nevada, where talus contributes persistent springs in addition to streamflow from upland glaciers. Photo: Constance Millar.

FIGURE 29.10 North Palisade Glacier, Sierra Nevada. Glaciers in the California alpine zone are remnants from the Little Ice Age, 1450–1920 CE and, except for glaciers on Mount Shasta, exist only in highest headwall cirques. Photo: Constance Millar.

typical values closer to 200 g m^{-2} yr^{1} (see Bowman and Seastedt 2001, Körner 2003). However, these mean values mask the high spatial heterogeneity in rates of aboveground net primary productivity, with plot-level values ranging from as low as 50 g m^{-2} yr^{1} to as much as 500 g m^{-2} yr^{1} or more (Bowman et al. 1993, Walker et al. 1994). This heterogeneity is strongly influenced by topographic controls on microclimate conditions as well as biotic impacts from grazers and burrowing animals (Scott and Billings 1964). Interannual variation in productivity is also typical, with summer temperatures, patterns of snowmelt, and levels of summer drought strongly influencing the length of growing season. On an ecosystem level, much of the biomass accumulation and net primary productivity of alpine communities occurs belowground. Ratios of belowground to aboveground biomass range from approximately 2.5 to 8.8 in studies carried out in alpine systems in the Rocky Mountains and European Alps (see Bowman and Seastedt 2001, Körner 2003). Studies of alpine meadows at Niwot Ridge in the Rocky Mountains have reported ratios of belowground to aboveground productivity that vary from approximately 1.0 in moist alpine meadows to 1.6 in wet meadows and 2.3 in dry meadows (Fisk et al. 1998).

Vegetation and Flora

Local distribution of individual plant habitats is determined strongly by features of the physical environment including topographic position, wind exposure, snow accumulation, and soil depth and drainage (Taylor 1977, Sawyer and Keeler-Wolf 2007). These diverse habitats include windswept ridges, snowbeds, dry meadows, basins and gentle slopes, and shrub-dominated drainage channels. The most severe conditions for plant growth occur on windswept summits and ridges. These communities may be snow-free through much of winter and typically consist of well-drained, coarse soils. Under extreme conditions, patterned soils can occur in these settings from frost heaving. FELLFIELD communities fall into this category and often exhibit a dominance of cold- and drought-tolerant mats and cushions along with low-growing herbaceous perennials.

Areas with late-lying snowbeds are characterized by a short growing season with limited water stress and typically support communities dominated by grasses and sedges. Dry meadows occur in areas with shallow soils and with little access to soil moisture once drought conditions extend into the summer. These communities are dominated by a mix of low-growing herbaceous perennials and GRAMINOIDS and typically are more limited in growth by water availability than by the length of the growing season. Broad alpine valleys and meandering streams exhibit a mix of herbaceous communities dominated by a mix of graminoids and forbs on shallower soils and shrub cover on areas with water availability and some shelter from wind exposure. Willow (*Salix*) species often form dense, low-growing stands or mats, and a diversity of low, ericaceous shrubs are often present. More arid areas of glaciated bedrock with shallow and rapidly draining sandy soils may support stands of *Artemisia*, particularly east of the Sierra crest.

A number of studies have developed relatively detailed classifications of flora and plant community alliances and associations for major habitats (Howell 1951, Klikoff 1965, Pemble 1970, Taylor 1976a, Taylor 1976b, Major and Taylor 1977, Tatum 1979, Burke 1982, Porter 1983, Constantine-Shull 2000). Alpine herbaceous and shrub alliances are described comprehensively by Sawyer et al. (2009) in the broader context of California vegetation types, although these types are often difficult to reconcile with specific stands of alpine vegetation. Ecological habitat descriptions for the alpine zone of the White Mountains have been made by Morefield (1988, 1992) with a somewhat simpler system of seven categories proposed by Rundel et al. (2008). Along a rough gradient from mesic to xeric these ecological habitats comprise aquatic sites, wet sites (areas with saturated soils and riparian habitats), moist sites (wet meadows and areas with snowmelt accumulation), fellfields with seasonal moisture availability, talus slopes, open slopes, and dry rocky slopes. Howell (1944) commented on the elements of boreal flora in the Klamath Mountains.

Plant Functional Groups and Adaptive Traits

Regardless of specific growth form, alpine plants are typically small and grow close to the ground. Spacing between plants is often wide with intervening areas of soil or rock. Such patterns illustrate the role of the physical environment in finely influencing microclimate to create favorable or nonfavorable microsites for plant establishment and growth. A few centimeters' difference in microtopography can have significant influence on air and soil temperatures, wind desiccation, and snow accumulation.

While plant life forms are commonly discussed in modern treatments of alpine vegetation (Billings 2000, Bowman and Seastedt 2001, Körner 2003), only limited attention has been given to quantifying these as plant functional groups. Herbaceous perennials of a variety of forms and architectures (i.e., broad-leaved herbaceous perennials, mats and cushions, graminoids, and more rarely geophytes) form the dominant community cover in temperate alpine ecosystems. Also present with lower species richness are shrubs, as subshrubs (chamaephytes) with a low form of woody growth. Other plant life forms such as taller woody shrubs (phanerophytes) and annuals (therophytes) are rare in most alpine habitats.

Life forms of the Sierra Nevada alpine flora, as in other temperate alpine floras, are heavily dominated by broad-leaved herbaceous perennials (48% of species) followed by graminoid perennials (22%) and mats and cushions (12%). Annuals and woody shrubs account for 6% each of the flora. Life forms are similar in the alpine flora of the White Mountains with broad-leaved herbaceous perennials dominant (53%) followed by graminoid perennials (22%), mats and cushions (11%), annuals (8%), and woody shrubs including low subshrubs less than 50 centimeters in height (6%). The proportion of annual species is relatively high in the Sierra Nevada and White Mountains compared to other continental alpine regions. Annual plants face a strong disadvantage in alpine ecosystems because of the short, cool growing season during which they must complete their entire life cycle. The relatively warm growing season temperatures of alpine habitats in California likely explains this greater success. Clear differences in root morphology exist between growth forms, suggesting functional differences in adaptive strategies. Cushion plants and subshrubs exhibit characteristic tap roots, while mat-forming cushions also have shallow, spreading, adventitious roots arising along stems to take advantage of temporary surface soil moisture (Billings and Mooney 1968). Perennial graminoids have spreading, fibrous roots. A consistent pattern across growth forms exists wherein most alpine species have stomates on both their upper and lower leaf surfaces, reflecting the high light environments in which they grow (Rundel et al. 2005). Studies of seed germination and seedling establishment across a gradient of changing soil substrate in the Sierra Nevada have shown that water might be the limiting factor for species germination and that differential nutrient availability across soil types strongly influences early seedling growth (Wenk and Dawson 2007).

Ecophysiological traits of alpine plants have been broadly reviewed (Billings and Mooney 1968, Billings 1974, Bowman and Seastedt 2001, Körner 2003) but are not well studied in California alpine plants. Rundel et al. (2005) compared ecophysiological traits of leaf structure, midday leaf temperature, mean maximum photosynthetic rate, and predawn and midday water potentials among four perennial life forms in an alpine fellfield in the White Mountains without finding consistent patterns associated with plant functional types. However, plant growth form may significantly influence diurnal leaf temperatures. The ability of some canopy architectures to promote high leaf temperatures helps explain the ability of the C_4 grass *Muhlenbergia richardsonis* to grow successfully at elevations up to nearly 4,000 meters in the White Mountains (Sage and Sage 2002). In adjacent communities the leaf temperatures of two upright species (*Chrysothamnus viscidiflorus* and *Linanthus nuttallii* subsp. *pubescens*) track ambient air temperature, while the mat-forming *Penstemon heterodoxus* has leaves that are heated significantly compared to air temperatures at midday (Rundel et al. 2005).

Floristics Diversity and Phylogenetic Breadth and Depth

The alpine zone of the Sierra Nevada, if defined as nonforested areas at or above 3,500 meters, includes 385 species of native vascular plants (Rundel 2011). If the alpine boundary were defined as at or above 3,300 meters, the alpine flora would grow to 536 species. Ninety-seven species reach elevations of 4,000 meters, and 27 species reach to 4,200 meters. Only a relatively small number of species are high-elevation specialists; 9 species have ranges restricted to elevations above 3,500 meters, and an additional 67 species (17% of the flora) are restricted to subalpine and alpine habitats. These high-elevation specialists are spread across multiple families but as a group share the feature of relatively high endemism compared to the overall Sierra Nevada flora. More than a quarter of the species in the Sierran alpine flora have elevational ranges that extend as low as foothill habitats below 1,200 meters (Rundel 2011).

Over half of the Sierran alpine species occur in just six families, led by the Asteraceae (55 species), Poaceae (39 species), Brassicaceae (34 species), and Cyperaceae (39 species). The largest genus present is *Carex* with 29 species, and 18 more species would be added by lowering the alpine boundary to 3,300 meters. Next in size are *Draba* (14 species) and *Lupinus* (11 species). The level of endemism in the Sierra Nevada alpine flora is moderate to high depending on how the geographic unit for endemism is defined. The 36 Sierran endemics present in the alpine flora compare with 205 endemic taxa for the montane areas of the range and thus compose 18% of the endemic flora of the higher Sierra Nevada (Rundel 2011). The unique Californian component of the alpine flora of the Sierra Nevada is considerably greater if one considers 31 species present in the alpine flora that are not limited to the Sierra Nevada but occur elsewhere in California or in ranges adjacent to the Sierra Nevada. Under this definition, 66 endemic taxa represent 16% of the Sierran alpine flora. This is high compared to other alpine ranges in continental North America and Europe and reflects both the environmental stress associated with the summer-dry, Mediterranean-type climate of the Sierra Nevada and the relative isolation of the range.

The alpine zone of the White Mountains, defined as nonforested areas above 3,500 meters, includes 163 native species of vascular plants. Seven families account for nearly two-thirds of the flora, led by the Asteraceae (30 species), followed by the Brassicaceae (18 species), Poaceae (17 species), Cyperaceae (15 species), Rosaceae (9 species), Caryophyllaceae (9 species), and Polygonaceae (7 species). While 31% of the alpine flora are restricted to alpine habitats, more than two-thirds of this flora extend to lower-elevation communities in the White Mountains of montane forest, pinyon-juniper woodland, or cold desert. Fellfields form the characteristic habitat for 41% of the flora, while moist meadows and open-slope habitats contain 24% and 22% of the flora, respectively. Endemism is low in the alpine zone of the White Mountains, with just three endemic species, although three more come close to being endemic. Two of these have small populations on the east slope of the Sierra Nevada, and one has a disjunct population in the Klamath Mountains.

The Sweetwater Mountains, 33 kilometers east of the Sierra Nevada, support an alpine flora of 173 species in 16 square kilometers of alpine habitat and share 94% of this flora with the Sierra Nevada (Bell-Hunter and Johnson 1983). The small alpine zone on Mount Grant to the north of the Sweetwater Mountains in western Nevada supports a flora of 70 species dominated by Sierra Nevadan elements in just 2.6 square kilometers (Bell and Johnson 1980).

Evolution of the Flora

The evolution of the alpine flora of the Sierra Nevada has involved a variety of factors including geologic history, climate history, modes of colonization, and factors promoting regional speciation (Stebbins 1982). On a biogeographic basis, there are strong indications of a north-to-south route of colonization of high mountain areas of the Sierra Nevada during the late Pliocene and Pleistocene. This evidence comes from a pattern of decreasing presence of Rocky Mountain floristic elements and an increased number of endemic alpine species as one moves from the northern to southern crest of the range where elevations are higher (Chabot and Billings 1972, Raven and Axelrod 1978, Rundel 2011). This gradient is shaped not just by geographic distance but also by steadily decreasing levels of precipitation moving to the south. Floristic elements of subalpine, subalpine wet meadows, and other moist sites typically have broad geographic ranges but become increasingly restricted to the most mesic sites as precipitation decreases southward in the Sierra Nevada (Kimball et al. 2004). Species growing in xeric rocky habitats show higher levels of endemism and smaller range sizes due to isolation and divergence from ancestral populations distributed in wetter habitats to the north. Endemism also increases in the Sierra Nevada with increasing elevation. Of species obligately occurring above 3,000 meters, fully one-third are California endemics, double the level of endemism for the entire mountain range.

A number of alpine species reach their southern occurrence limit on Mount Lassen, suggesting that some of these and other Cascade Range species might have been present in the Sierra Nevada in the late Pliocene or early Pleistocene. Although the species compositions of lower- and middle-elevation conifer forests of Lassen National Park are strongly related to those of the Sierra Nevada, the summits of the highest peaks in Lassen support an alpine flora with stronger floristic links to Mount Shasta and the Cascade Range to the north (Gillett et al. 1995). The Klamath Mountains also mark the southern distribution limit for a number of high-elevation species that do not occur in the Sierra Nevada (Howell 1944). The relative isolation of the Sierra Nevada from northern ranges and the summer drought have acted as a filter to exclude some widespread, circumpolar, arctic-alpine species such as *Dryas integrifolia* and *Silene acaulis*, which do not occur in California.

More controversy exists about the possible migration of significant components of the Sierran alpine flora from the Rocky Mountains across the Great Basin. Both geological and paleobotanical evidence exist to suggest that the mean elevation of the Great Basin was up to 1,500 meters higher in the Miocene and that the current basin and range topography is the result of subsidence rather than uplift (Wernicke et al. 1988, Wolfe et al. 1997). The presence of higher elevations in the Great Basin during the Pleistocene could have provided stepping-stones for the dispersal of alpine organisms from the east. Several notable examples exist of disjunct Rocky Mountain species with restricted distributions in the central and southern Sierra Nevada, often growing in azonal soil conditions (Major and Bamberg 1967, Taylor 1976a). Molecular evidence has shown that at least one lineage of butterflies entered the Sierra Nevada by this route (Nice and Shapiro 2001). However, other authors feel that the majority of these disjunct plant species reached the Sierra Nevada by the same dominant route via the Cascade Range (Chabot and Billings 1972). Only a preliminary understanding exists of the origins of the endemic alpine flora of the Sierra Nevada and White Mountains, and modes of speciation are clearly complex (Rundel 2011). Factors promoting endemism in the alpine flora include the recent uplift of the mountains, the relative isolation of the Sierra Nevada from other ranges, glacial restrictions on migrations, Holocene climate variability, the mixing of desert and mountain floras, and the unusual conditions of summer drought (Chabot and Billings 1972).

There are many examples of genera in the alpine flora where apomixis (emergence of asexual reproduction) has been important in speciation. These include *Boechera* (Schranz et al. 2005, Dobeš et al. 2007) and *Draba* (Jordon-Thaden and Koch 2008) (Brassicaceae), *Antennaria* (Bayer and Stebbins 1987) and *Arnica* and *Crepis* (Noyes 2007) (Asteraceae), *Poa* and *Calamagrostis* (Poaceae), and *Potentilla* (Rosaceae) (Asker and Jerling 1992). Diploid lineages of polyploid complexes often occupy unglaciated areas and resist introgression, hypothetically due to a significantly higher seed set. However, asexual apomictic populations are often more widespread than their sexually reproducing relatives in glaciated areas. The advantages of apomixis include reproductive isolation and stability of vegetative lineages in their area of distribution. Other modes of alpine speciation include population disjunction, reproductive isolation (Chase and Raven 1975), and upslope migration and colonization by arid-adapted lowland taxa at the end of the Pleistocene (Went 1948, 1953).

The White Mountains present a particularly interesting area for study of evolutionary history of the flora and fauna given their position at the interface between two major geomorphic provinces, the Sierra-Cascade Province and the arid Basin and Range Province. Despite this interface, the White range is isolated from direct contact with high elevations of these provinces. Moreover, warmer and more xeric climatic conditions of the middle Holocene climatic optimum allowed an upward movement of subalpine conifers, restricting the area available for growth of alpine communities (Jennings and Elliot-Fisk 1991, 1993). Thus the White Mountains present an example where both climate history and geographic isolation have played significant roles in the evolution of the biota.

Fauna

The alpine zone of California harbors relatively low mammal diversity. Few species are restricted to alpine habitats, while many more use the alpine environment transiently or seasonally (Table 29.2). Large herbivores such as mule deer (*Odocoileus hemionus*) (Anderson and Wallmo 1984) and desert and Sierra Nevada bighorn sheep (*Ovis canadensis nelsoni* and *O. c. sierrae*, respectively) (Wehausen et al. 2007) use the alpine zone in summers both for foraging and as retreat and escape from predators. The prime predator of these ungulates, mountain lion (*Puma concolor*), occasionally follows them to the alpine regions.

Sierra Nevada bighorn sheep (*Ovis canadensis sierrae*) makes major use of alpine areas of the Sierra Nevada during summer. Individuals range over a broad elevational distribution, with winter range as low as 1,450 meters. Individuals near the Mono Basin also migrate far to the east. Sierra Nevada bighorn sheep favor open areas where predators can be seen at a distance and steep rocky slopes can serve as refuge from attacks by mountain lions. There once were as many as a thousand bighorn sheep in the Sierra Nevada, but this number had declined to about 125 adults at the time of their listing as endangered in 1999 (Wehausen et al. 2007). By 2007 they had recovered to more than 400 individuals distributed in a metapopulation of eight subpopulations. They are approaching the target population size of 500, thanks to concerted efforts both to augment herd units and to reduce predator pressure. Threats to Sierra Nevada bighorn sheep survival include disease transfer from domestic sheep, mountain lion predation, and extreme climate conditions.

Many more small and meso-mammals occur in the alpine zone than large animals, and a few are highly restricted to that zone. Among the more charismatic of small mammals is the American pika (*Ochotona princeps*), a small rabbit relative highly restricted to talus slopes and similar broken-rock landforms (Smith and Weston 1990) (Figure 29.11). Pikas range throughout the mountains of western North America. In California they are found throughout the Sierra Nevada, White Mountains, Bodie Mountains, Sweetwater Mountains, southern Cascades, and Warner Mountains (USFWS 2010, Millar and Westfall 2010.) Like other lagomorphs, pikas do not hibernate and collect a diverse range of herbaceous and shrubby vegetation during the warm season, which they cache in stacks (referred to as "haypiles") within the talus and consume during the winter. Pikas are poor thermoregulators, tolerant of cold yet sensitive to heat, and are often assumed to be alpine-restricted and at risk from global warming. In

TABLE 29.2
Mammal species known to occur in alpine ecosystems of California

Common name	Scientific name	Elevation (m)	Citation for species' elevation
		Large mammals	
Desert bighorn sheep	*Ovis canadensis nelson*	4300	California Department of Fish and Wildlife
Sierra Nevada bighorn sheep	*Ovis canadensis sierra*	1500–4270	California Department of Fish and Wildlife
Mule deer	*Odocoileus hemionus*	< timberline	Anderson and Wallmo 1984
Black bear	*Ursus americanus*	100–3000+	California Department of Fish and Wildlife
Sierra Nevada red fox	*Vulpes vulpes necator*	1200–3600	Perrine et al. 2010
*Mountain lion	*Puma concolor*	< 4000	California Department of Fish and Wildlife
		Mesocarnivores and small predatory mammals	
*Sierra Nevada marten	*Martes americana sierra*	2300–3150	Kucera et al. 1996, Storer et al. 2004
Long-tailed weasel	*Mustela frenata*	< 3500?	Storer et al. 2004
		Small mammals	
White-tailed jackrabbit	*Lepus townsendii*	< 3650	Storer et al. 2004
Bushy-tailed woodrat	*Neotoma cinerea*	1500–4000	Grayson and Livingstone 1989; Storer et al. 2004
Golden-mantled squirrel	*Callospermophilus lateralis*	1646–3200	Moritz et al. 2008
Mount Lyell shrew	*Sorex lyelli*	2100–3630	Epanchin and Engilis 2009
Water shrew	*Sorex palustris*	1658–3535	Epanchin and Engilis 2009
	Sorex monticolus	3400	Epanchin and Engilis 2009
	Sorex vagrans	3400	Epanchin and Engilis 2009
	Sorex tenullus	4267	Epanchin and Engilis 2009
Belding ground squirrel	*Urocitellus beldingi*	2286–3287	Moritz et al. 2008
Alpine chipmunk	*Tamias alpinus*	2307–3353	Moritz et al. 2008
American pika	*Ochotona princeps*	2377–3871	Moritz et al. 2008
Deer mouse	*Peromyscus maniculatus*	57–3287	Moritz et al. 2008
Yellow-bellied marmot	*Marmota flaviventris*	2469–3353	Moritz et al. 2008

SOURCE: * indicates occasional use in the alpine zone.

fact, pikas range from sagebrush-steppe ecosystems through the montane zones to the highest summit reaches and find their optimal elevation range from the mid-subalpine to mid-alpine zone (Millar and Westfall 2010; Millar et al. 2014a). The capacity of pikas to tolerate warm ambient temperatures despite their thermal sensitivity relates both to the unique microclimates of talus and related landforms (Millar et al. 2014b) and to their behavioral adaptations. Talus thermal regimes are highly buffered from external air, remaining cool in summer and warm in winter. Pikas adapt behaviorally by using this "air-conditioned" habitat for refuge as needed in response to external air temperatures (Smith 1974).

Yellow-bellied marmots (*Marmota flaviventris*) are another important mammal species for alpine ecosystems in the White Mountains, Sierra Nevada, and higher mountain ranges to the north. Yellow-bellied marmots have a harem-polygynous social system whereby a male defends and mates with one or more females. Female daughters often do not disperse and settle around their mothers. Sons invariably disperse as yearlings and try to find and defend one or more females. Females tend to breed as two-year olds. Litter sizes average a bit over four pups, of which about half survive their first year. Yellow-bellied marmots chuck, whistle, and trill when alarmed by predators. They breed in alpine and subalpine meadows.

A number of other small mammal species have ranges extending up to elevations with alpine conditions but are more characteristic of upper montane and subalpine habitats. These include the bushy-tailed woodrat (*Neotoma cinerea*) (Grayson and Livingstone 1989), Belding's ground squirrel (*Urocitellus beldingi*), golden-mantled squirrel (*Callospermophilus lateralis*), alpine chipmunk (*Tamias alpinus*), deer mouse

FIGURE 29.11 The American pika, a typical small mammal of the alpine zone. Photo: Andrey Shcherbina.

(*Peromyscus maniculatus*), and Mount Lyell shrew (*Sorex lyelli*) (Epanchin and Engilis 2009). Recent studies resampling century-old plots in Yosemite National Park have shown that all of these species as well as pikas (although the sample size for pikas was low and the patterns not strongly significant) and yellow-bellied marmots have increased their lower elevational limit of occurrence, likely reflecting warming climatic conditions (Moritz et al. 2008, Tingley et al. 2009).

Several species of small to medium-sized carnivores have ranges that extend beyond the conifer zone into open rocky alpine areas of the Sierra Nevada and Cascade Range. These include the rare wolverine (*Gulo gulo*), which may prey on marmots, and the rare Sierra Nevada red fox (*Vulpes vulpes necator*) (Perrine et al. 2010). American martens (*Martes americana*) feed on a variety of vertebrates including chipmunks and ground squirrels and occasionally prey on pikas (Kucera et al. 1996, Jameson and Peeters 2004). While bird use of alpine habitats is largely seasonal and transitory, a notable exception is the gray-crowned rosy finch (*Leucostichte tephrocotis*), which is a common winter resident of the high Sierra Nevada, Mount Shasta, Mount Lassen, and the Sweetwater and White Mountains at elevations up to 4,000 meters. It forages on the ground, in dwarf shrub habitat, and in alpine barrens above timberline for seeds and insects. The finch breeds in talus slopes and in rock-face crevices. In their California range, these birds are nomadic rather than migratory.

Another common member of the alpine avifauna that breeds and summers in California is the water pipit (*Anthus spinoletta alticola*), which ranges from the central to southern Sierra Nevada and occasionally uses high elevations of the San Gorgonio Mountains of southern California (Miller and Green 1987). Water pipits prefer wet meadow habitat but also frequent open rocky plateaus and slopes. Sage grouse (*Centrocercus urophasianus*) inhabit high-elevation sagebrush and grassland habitat across the Great Basin and occur as high as 3,700 meters in the White Mountains. Resident birds in subalpine forests such as pine siskin (*Carduelis pinus*), dark-eyed junco (*Junco hyemalus*), mountain quail (*Oreortyx pictus*), Clark's nutcracker (*Nucifraga columbiana*), and others may extend their foraging above timberline but are not regular residents. Red-tailed hawks (*Buteo jamaicensis*), peregrine falcons (*Falco peregrinus*), and golden eagles (*Aquila chrysaetos*) are occasionally observed flying over alpine habitats but are not regular residents and breed at lower elevations (Charlet and Rust 1991).

The Sierra Nevada yellow-legged frog (*Rana muscosa*), native to high subalpine and alpine lakes in the mountains, was once the most common frog species over broad areas. Over the past century, however, this species has dramatically declined in abundance (Drost and Fellers 1996, Vredenburg et al. 2005). Although this decline was largely attributed for many years to the introduction of non-native trout and/or to pesticides, recent declines have continued even in apparently unpolluted lakes without fish. Studies have now identified pathogenic chytrid fungi (*Batrachochytrium dendrobatidis*) as an additional cause of population loss (Briggs et al. 2005). It has been suggested that the former abundance of this species made them a keystone predator and prey and a crucial agent of nutrient and energy cycling in Sierra Nevada aquatic and terrestrial ecosystems (Drost and Fellers 1996).

A second species of once-common amphibian in wet subalpine and alpine meadows that has experienced sharp drops in population numbers in recent decades is the Yosemite toad (*Anaxyrus canorus*). The species epithet references the melodic call of the male toads. A notable feature of this species is the sharp differentiation in color patterns of males and females, arguably the greatest sexual dimorphism of any anuran in North America. These are long-lived toads with upper age limits estimated from fifteen to twenty years—a life span thought to be an adaptation to their seasonal, high-elevation environment.

Human Interactions

Despite their high elevation, abundant evidence indicates that Native Americans made at least limited use of alpine ecosystems in both the Sierra Nevada and White Mountains. Early use of alpine zones in California included transient use by male hunters to track and procure large game, likely with significant impacts on desert and Sierra Nevada bighorn sheep populations (Wehausen et al. 2007). After about two thousand years, family groups started to move to alpine zones for the warm season, where they established village sites in the high White Mountains as well as in two alpine ranges of Nevada (Bettinger 1991, David Hurst Thomas, pers. comm. 2012). With entire family units residing in alpine regions, much wider use of mammal species occurred for consumption, clothing, and shelter materials, and small mammals (rodents and lagomorphs) were hunted regularly (Grayson and Livingstone 1989). It is clear also that prehistoric humans influenced the abundance and distribution of deadwood in alpine landscapes, complicating interpretations of paleotreelines (Grayson and Millar 2008).

The heavy summer grazing of high Sierran meadows by sheep was widespread up into alpine meadows in the last four decades of the nineteenth century. Several accounts describe how overstocking and overgrazing altered vegetation composition in high-elevation Sierran meadows (Ratliff 1985; see Chapter 31, "Wetlands"). A permit process to limit grazing in national park lands began in 1905, and much recovery has occurred, although cattle grazing is still permitted in some high-mountain meadows on national forest land. Grazing in high-elevation meadows of the White Mountains was halted in 1988, and recovery has been taking place (Ababneh and Woolfenden 2010).

Invasive Species

Alpine plant communities in California have remained free of any significant invasion by non-native plant species, likely due to the extreme conditions presented by the physical environment. A small number of non-native species have been collected around areas of human activity in the alpine zone of the White Mountains, but none of these appear to have become permanently established (Rundel et al. 2008). Information is lacking on significant establishment of non-native plant species in the high Sierra Nevada. Past disturbance by grazing and other human activities suggests that an absence of propagule dispersal is not the limiting factor in the rarity of non-native species. Nevertheless, aggressive species from other global regions of high-elevation habitat could become widely established in the future if introduced.

Subalpine and alpine lakes in the Sierra Nevada originally lacked fish, but the widespread introduction of non-native trout species began in the mid- to late nineteenth century and populated all watersheds. Fish stocking was completely halted in the Sierran national parks in 1991 but continues on national forest lands. Studies in high-elevation Sierran lakes and streams have shown significant impacts of introduced trout on native trout, amphibians, zooplankton, and benthic macroinvertebrates (Knapp 1996; see Chapter 32, "Lakes"). White-tailed ptarmigan (*Lagopus leucurus*) were introduced to the high Sierra Nevada in 1971–1972 by the California Fish and Wildlife Service and have become well established locally in alpine grassland and fellfield habitats. No studies to date have assessed possible impacts of this introduction.

Conservation

Alpine ecosystems in California today remain largely free of major human impacts due to their isolated locations and positions within protected areas and national parks. Some high-elevation degradation still takes place on national forest lands, but the major effects today are the scattered impacts of summer cattle grazing and recreational activities including pack trains and mountain biking. These activities are much more common in subalpine meadows rather than alpine meadows. Alpine watersheds with pack animal presence and summer cattle grazing have increased periphytic algal biomass, attached heterotrophic bacteria, and *E. coli* compared with nongrazed areas. Thus pollution from cattle grazing might be a significant cause of deteriorating water quality within some watersheds (Derlet and Carlson 2006, Derlet et al. 2012, Myers and Whited 2012).

Invasive plants have not yet become a conservation issue, but this could change in the future. Introduced trout in alpine streams and lakes have certainly had an impact on native amphibian populations. Possible impacts of introduced white-tailed ptarmigan have not been studied. Overall, the collective impacts from all of these invasions are relatively small. Of much greater concern, as described earlier, is the potential impact of climate change on alpine ecosystems.

Climate Adaptation

The significant roles of climatic variables in shaping alpine ecosystem productivity suggest that climate change impacts on alpine plant communities could be more pronounced than on lower-elevation communities (Grabherr et al. 2000). Moreover, alpine ecosystems are predicted to experience some of the highest levels of warming globally and are expected to exhibit signs of change before other terrestrial ecosystems because of their high sensitivity to disturbance. Alpine ecosystems likely also will be affected by other attendant factors such as declining snowpack, earlier spring runoff, and earlier phenology (Cayan et al. 2001, Duffy et al. 2007, Mote et al. 2005, Stewart et al. 2005).

The international program for monitoring response of alpine plants to climate change, GLORIA (Global Observation Research Initiative in Alpine Environments; see Grabherr et al. 2000, Malanson and Fagre 2013), promotes stations on mountain summits worldwide. For each "target region," standardized monitoring designs are installed on four mountain summits that span the elevational extent from upper treeline to the highest peak in the local region. Seven target regions have been established in California: the Panamint Range; the White Mountains; the Sierra Nevada; and the Sweetwater Mountains (see the North American GLORIA website at http://www.fs.fed.us/psw/cirmount/gloria/). The earliest were established in 2004, and several will undergo the second round of five-year remeasurements in 2014. Early results show no striking or significant changes in vegetation or floristics; the most obvious changes are increases in soil temperature. Data from the California GLORIA target regions document local floristic diversity of the summits and provide an excellent reference for local conditions. In addition to these standard target regions, the White Mountain Research Center (at the University of California) operates as one of two GLORIA master sites (the other is in Austria) where interdisciplinary alpine studies are conducted in addition to the multisummit protocol to monitor the impacts from and adaptation to climate change of alpine biota and ecosystems (see http://www.fs.fed.us/psw/cirmount/gloria/).

At the broad scale of environmental modeling and climate change, global change models (GCMs) predict that alpine areas will experience higher levels of temperature increase than global averages (Theurillat and Guisan 2001, Beniston 2005). Concerns about the potential impacts of higher temperatures on high-elevation communities have led to a variety of studies, including experimental warming manipulations to look at impacts of increased temperatures on alpine and subalpine plant phenology and community structure (Harte et al. 1995, Price and Waser 2000, Klein et al. 2005). As useful as GCMs can be, they operate on grid scales of kilometers along horizontal axes and tens of meters along the vertical. Thus they are most effective at heights well above the soil, excluding the plant canopy levels where alpine microclimate affects biological and local ecosystem processes. For alpine ecosystems a range of factors complicate the straightforward interpolation from macroclimate to microclimate (Wundram et al. 2010). Boundary layer dynamics at the ground surface complicate predictions because the complexity of interactive factors such as wind shear, pressure gradients, and energy balance cause the environment to become decoupled from free-air conditions above the ground surface.

The topographic heterogeneity of alpine habitats creates a fine pattern of thermal microhabitat conditions at a scale of centimeters. The magnitude of these temperature differences is greater than the range of warming scenarios over the next century in IPCC projections (Graham et al. 2012). If short dispersal and establishment is possible for alpine plants, then fellfield habitats may offer significant buffering from global warming because of the mosaic of thermal microclimates present. However, we know very little about the significance of moisture availability for plant distributions or its interactions of temperature and soil moisture (Winkler 2013). GCM models are able to make temperature predictions with far more confidence than precipitation ones, leaving open the question of moisture availability. The roles of microclimate in alpine habitats suggest that models predicting upslope movements of species under increasing temperatures might not be entirely realistic and that sufficient microclimate heterogeneity might exist to slow species range shifts.

Summary

Alpine ecosystems are typically defined as those areas occurring above treeline, but alpine ecosystems at a local scale can be found below this boundary for reasons including geology, geomorphology, and microclimate. The lower limit of alpine ecosystems, the climatic treeline, varies with latitude across California, ranging from about 3,500 meters in the southern California mountains and southern Sierra Nevada to 3,200 meters in the Yosemite region, 3,000 meters near Donner Pass, 2,800 meters at Lassen Peak, and finally 2,700 meters on Mount Shasta. Alpine ecosystems extend beyond the typically envisioned high-elevation open slopes and summits of cold-adapted shrubs and herbs to include as well lithic environments of cliffs, talus fields, boulder fields and rock glaciers; permanent and persistent snow and icefields, including glaciers; and various water bodies such as streams, tarns, and large lakes. Alpine ecosystems provide severe physiological stresses for both animal and plant populations. These environmental stresses in California include low winter temperatures, short growing season, low nutrient availability, high winds, low partial pressures of CO_2, high UV irradiance, and limited water availability under summer drought.

The alpine regions of California typically experience a Mediterranean-type climate regime with dry summers and precipitation heavily centered on the winter months. This regime differs significantly from that present in most of the continental alpine habitats of the world, where summer precipitation predominates. At the upper treeline in the Sierra Nevada about 95% of annual precipitation falls as winter snow, with much of this accumulating during regular winter during a very small number of storms separated by long, dry intervals. This pattern produces extreme interannual variability in precipitation and water availability. Alpine plant communities are dominated by herbaceous perennials (broad-leaved herbaceous perennials, mats and cushions, graminoids, and geophytes) that form the dominant community cover. Also present with lower species richness are low shrubs and semi-woody subshrubs. Other plant life forms such as taller woody shrubs and annuals are rare. Alpine ecosystems support a low diversity of resident mammal species, but many others use the alpine environment occasionally or seasonally. Notable are large herbivores such as mule deer and desert and Sierra Nevada bighorn sheep that forage in the alpine zone in summer. Many more small and midsized mammals occur in the alpine zone, with yellow-bellied marmots and pikas commonly seen in such habitats. Alpine ecosystems are predicted to experience strong levels of temperature increase from global warming globally but will likely be most impacted by indirect effects such as declining snowpack, earlier spring runoff, and earlier growth and flowering phenology.

Acknowledgments

We thank the staff of Sequoia and Kings Canyon and Yosemite National Parks for making their data available; the staff of the White Mountains Research Station for their support; and the volume editors for their guidance.

Recommended Reading

Billings, W. D. 1974. Adaptations and origins of alpine plants. Arctic and Alpine Research 6:129–142.

Bowman, W. D., and T. R. Seastedt, editors. 2001. Structure and function of an alpine ecosystem: Niwot Ridge, Colorado. Oxford University Press, Oxford, UK.

Körner, C. 2003. Alpine plant life: Functional plant ecology of high mountain ecosystems. Springer Verlag, Berlin, Germany.

Millar, C. I. 2012. Geologic, climatic, and vegetation history of California. Pages 49–68 in B. G. Baldwin, D. Goldman, D.J. Keil, R. Patterson, T.J. Rosatti, and D. Wilken, editors. The Jepson Manual: Higher plants of California. Second edition. University of California Press, Berkeley, California.

Nagy, L., and G. Grabherr. 2009. The biology of alpine habitats. Oxford University Press, Oxford, UK.

Rundel, P. 2011. The diversity and biogeography of the alpine flora of the Sierra Nevada, California. Madroño 58:153–184.

Sawyer, J. O., and T. Keeler-Wolf. 2007. Alpine vegetation. Pages 539–573 in M. Barbour, A. Schoenherr, and T. Keeler-Wolf, editors. Terrestrial vegetation of California. Second edition. University of California Press, Berkeley, California.

Glossary

ATMOSPHERIC RIVER A narrow atmospheric band of concentrated moisture that can cause extreme precipitation events at midlatitudes. Atmospheric rivers affecting the coast of western North America are informally referred to as "pineapple express" phenomena.

CIRQUE An amphitheater-shaped basin below a mountain peak carved by glacial action.

FELLFIELD Alpine habitat with shallow, stony, and poorly developed stony soils.

FELSENMEER Exposed rock surface that has been broken up by frost action so that much rock is buried under a cover of angular, shattered boulders.

FREEZE-THAW CYCLE A weathering cycle in which water seeps into cracks and then freezes and expands, promoting breakdown of the rock.

GRAMINOID Having a grasslike form of growth, as in the Poaceae, Cyperaceae, and Juncaceae.

KARST TOPOGRAPHY A region where the terrain has been impacted by the physical and chemical weathering of carbonate rocks such as dolomite and limestone.

KRUMMHOLZ A stunted and often deformed growth of trees at the treeline limit.

LITTLE ICE AGE A global period of cooling, extending from about 1550 or earlier to about 1850, marked by a significant expansion of glaciers.

MORAINE An accumulation of unconsolidated glacial debris.

NIVAL Growing with or under snow; also used to connote an upper alpine region continuously under snow or ice throughout the year.

PATERNOSTER POND A glacial pond or lake connected to multiple others in a string by a single stream or a system of linked streams.

PERIGLACIAL Describes any place where geomorphic processes related to freeze-thaw cycles of water occur.

PERMAFROST Permanently frozen subsurface layers of soil.

ROCK GLACIER Geomorphological landforms consisting of angular rock debris frozen in interstitial ice.

TALUS FIELD, TALUS SLOPE Describes a landform of jumbled rock debris lying with an inclination up to the maximum angle of repose.

TARN A small lake at the base of a cirque formed by past glacial action.

References

Ababneh, L., and W. Woolfenden. 2010. Monitoring for potential effects of climate change on the vegetation of two alpine meadows in the White Mountains of California, USA. Quaternary International 215:3–14.

Anderson, A. E., and O. C. Wallmo. 1984. *Odocoileus hemionus*. Mammalian Species Account 219:1–9.

Asker, S. E., and L. Jerling. 1992. Apomixis in plants. CRC Press, Boca Raton, Florida.

Bales, R. C., N. P. Molotch, T. H. Painter, M. D. Dettinger, R. Rice, and J. Dozier. 2006. Mountain hydrology of the western United States. Water Resources Research 42:W08432. <doi:10.1029/2005WR00438>

Barry, R. G. 2008. Mountain weather and climate. Third edition. Cambridge University Press, Cambridge, UK.

Basagic, H. 2008. Quantifying twentieth century glacier change in the Sierra Nevada, California. MS thesis in geography. Portland State University, Portland, Oregon.

Bayer, R. J., and G. L. Stebbins. 1987. Chromosome numbers, patterns of distribution, and apomixis in *Antennaria* (Asteraceae: Inuleae). Systematic Botany 12:305–319.

Bell-Hunter, K. L., and R. E. Johnson. 1983. Alpine flora of the Sweetwater Mountains, Mono County, Nevada. Madroño 30:89–105.

Bell, K. L., and R. E. Johnson. 1980. Alpine flora of the Wassuk Range, Mineral County, Nevada. Madroño 27:25–35.

Beniston, M. 2005. Climatic change and its possible impacts in the alpine region. Revue de Geographie Alpine/Journal of Alpine Research 93:25–32.

Bettinger, R. L. 1991. Aboriginal occupation at high altitude: Alpine villages in the White Mountains of eastern California. American Anthropologist 93:656–679.

Billings, W. D. 2000. Alpine vegetation. Pages 536–572 in M. G. Barbour and W. D. Billings, editors. North American terrestrial vegetation. Second edition. Cambridge University Press, Cambridge, UK.

———. 1974. Adaptations and origins of alpine plants. Arctic and Alpine Research 6:129–142.

———. 1973. Arctic and alpine vegetation similarities, differences, and susceptibility to disturbance. BioScience 23: 697–704.

Billings W. D., and H. A. Mooney. 1968. Ecology of arctic and alpine plants. Biological Reviews 43:481–529.

Bowerman, N. D., and D. H. Clark. 2011. Holocene glaciation of the central Sierra Nevada, California. Quaternary Science Reviews 30:167–185.

Bowman, W. D., and T. R. Seastedt, editors. 2001. Structure and function of an alpine ecosystem: Niwot Ridge, Colorado. Oxford University Press, Oxford, UK.

Bowman, W. D., T. A. Theodose, J. C. Schardt, and R. T. Conant. 1993. Constraints of nutrient availability on primary production in two alpine communities. Ecology 74:2085–2098.

Briggs, C. J., V. T. Vredenburg, R. A. Knapp, and L. J. Rachowicz. 2005. Investigating the population-level effects of chytridiomycosis: An emerging infectious disease of amphibians. Ecology 86:3149–3159.

Burga, C. A., R. Frauenfelder, J. Ruffet, M. Hoelzle, and A. Kääb. 2004. Vegetation on alpine rock glacier surfaces: A contribution to abundance and dynamics of extreme plant habitats. Flora 199:505–151.

Burke, M. T. 1982. The vegetation of the Rae Lakes Basin, southern Sierra Nevada. Madroño 29:164–179.

California Department of Fish and Wildlife. 2013. California wildlife habitat relationships. Life history accounts and range maps. <http://www.dfg.ca.gov/biogeodata/cwhr/cawildlife.aspx>. Accessed October 2013.

Cayan, D. R., M. D. Dettinger, H. F. Diaz, and N. E. Graham. 1998. Decadal variability of precipitation over western North America. Journal of Climate 11:3148–3166.

Cayan, D. R., S. A. Kammerdiener, M. D. Dettinger, J. M. Caprio, and D. H. Peterson. 2001. Changes in the onset of spring in the western United States. Bulletin of the American Meteorological Society 82:399–415.

Chabot, B. F., and W. D. Billings. 1972. Origins and ecology of the Sierran alpine flora and vegetation. Ecological Monographs 42:163–199.

Charlet, D. A., and R. W. Rust. 1991. Visitation of high mountain bogs by golden eagles in the northern Great Basin. Journal of Field Ornithology 62:46–52.

Chase, V. C., and P. H. Raven. 1975. Evolutionary and ecological relationships between *Aquilegia formosa* and *A. pubescens* (Ranunculaceae), two perennial plants. Evolution 29:474–486.

Clark, D. H., M. M. Clark, and A. R. Gillespie. 1994. Debris-covered glaciers in the Sierra Nevada, California, and their implications for snowline reconstruction. Quaternary Research 41:139–153.

Constantine-Shull, H. M. 2000. Floristic affinities of the San Joaquin Roadless Area, Inyo National Forest, Mono County, California. MS thesis. Humboldt State University, Arcata, California.

Daly, C., R. P. Neilson, and D. L. Phillips. 1994. A statistical topographic model for mapping climatological precipitation over mountainous terrain. Journal of Applied Meteorology 33:140–158.

Derlet, R.W., and J. R. Carlson. 2006. Coliform bacteria in Sierra Nevada wilderness lakes and streams: What is the impact of backpackers, pack animals, and cattle? Wilderness Environmental Medicine 17:15–20.

Derlet, R. W., J. R. Richards, L. L. Tanaka, C. Hayden, K. A. Ger, and C. R. Goldman. 2012. Impact of summer cattle grazing on the Sierra Nevada watershed: Aquatic algae and bacteria. Journal of Environmental and Public Health. <http://dx.doi.org/10.1155/2012/760108>.

Dettinger, M. D., R. M. Ralph, T. Das, P. J. Neiman, and D. R. Cayan. 2011. Atmospheric rivers, floods, and the water resources of California. Water 3:445–478.

Diaz, H. F., and V. Markgraf, editors. 2000. El Niño and the Southern Oscillation: Multiscale variability, global, and regional impacts. Cambridge University Press, Cambridge, UK.

Dobeš, C., T. F. Sharbel, and M. Koch. 2007. Towards understanding the dynamics of hybridization and apomixis in the evolution of the genus *Boechera* (Brassicaceae). Systematics and Biodiversity 5:321–331.

Drost, C. A., and G. M. Fellers. 1996. Collapse of a regional frog fauna in the Yosemite area of the California Sierra Nevada, USA. Conservation Biology 10:414–425.

Duffy, P. B., C. Bonfils, and D. Lobell. 2007. Interpreting recent temperature trends in California. EOS, Transactions American Geophysical Union 88:409–410.

Epanchin, P. N., and A. Engilis. 2009. Mount Lyell shrew (*Sorex lyelli*) in the Sierra Nevada, California, with comments on alpine records of *Sorex*. Southwestern Naturalist 54:354–357.

Erman, N. A. 1996. Status of aquatic invertebrates. Sierra Nevada ecosystem project: Final report to Congress. Volume II: Assessments and scientific basis for management options. Wildland Resources Center Report 37:987–1009.

Fisk, M. C., S. K. Schmidt, and T. R. Seastedt. 1998. Topographic patterns of above- and belowground production and nitrogen cycling in alpine tundra. Ecology 79:2253–2266.

Fountain, A. G., M. Hoffman, K. Jackson, H. J. Basagic, T. H. Nylen, and D. Percy. 2007. Digital outlines and topography of the glaciers of the American West. U.S. Geological Survey Open-File Report 2006-1340.

Gibson, A. C., P. W. Rundel, and M. R. Sharifi. 2008. Ecology and ecophysiology of a subalpine fellfield community on Mount Pinos, southern California. Madroño 55:41–51.

Gillett, G. W., J. T. Howell, and H. Leschke. 1995. A flora of Lassen Volcanic National Park, California. California Native Plant Society, Sacramento, California.

Grabherr, G., M. Gottfried, and H. Pauli. 2010. Climate change impacts in alpine environments. Geography Compass 4:1133–1153.

———. 2000. GLORIA: A global observation research initiative in alpine environments. Mountain Research and Development 20:190–192.
Graham, E. A., P. W. Rundel, W. Kaiser, Y. Lam, M. Stealey, and E. M. Yuen. 2012. Fine-scale patterns of soil and plant surface temperatures in an alpine fellfield habitat, White Mountains, California. Arctic, Antarctic, and Alpine Research 44:288–295.
Grayson, D. K., and C. I. Millar. 2008. Prehistoric human influence on the abundance and distribution of deadwood in alpine landscapes. Perspectives in Plant Ecology, Evolution, and Systematics 10:101–108.
Grayson, D. K., and S. D. Livingstone. 1989. High-elevational records for *Neotoma cinerea* in the White Mountains, California. Great Basin Naturalist 49:392–395.
Grove, J. M. 1988. The Little Ice Age. Methuen Publishing, London, UK.
Haines, T. L. 1976. Vegetation types of the San Gabriel Mountains. Pages 65–76 in J. Latting, editor. Plant communities of southern California. California Native Plant Society Special Publication 2. Sacramento, California.
Hall, H. M. 1902. A botanical survey of San Jacinto Mountain. University of California Publications in Botany 1:1–140.
Hanes, T. L. 1976. Vegetation types of the San Gabriel Mountains. Pages 65–76 in J. Latting, editor. Plant communities of southern California; symposium proceedings. Special Publication Number 2. California Native Plant Society, Sacramento, California.
Harte, J., M. S. Torn, F. R. Chang, B. Feifarek, A. Kinzig, R. Shaw, and K. Shen. 1995. Global warming and soil microclimate—Results from a meadow-warming experiment. Ecological Applications 5:132–150.
Holmquist, J. G., J. R. Jones, J. Schmidt-Gengenbach, L. F. Pierotti, and J. P. Love. 2011. Terrestrial and aquatic macro-invertebrate assemblages as a function of wetland type across a mountain landscape. Arctic, Antarctic, and Alpine Research 43:568–584.
Horton, J. S. 1960. Vegetation types of the San Bernardino Mountains. U.S. Department of Agriculture Forest Service, Southwest Forest and Range Experiment Station, Technical Paper 44:1–29.
Howat, I. M., S. Tulaczyk, P. Rhodes, K. Israel, and M. Snyder. 2007. A precipitation-dominated, mid-latitude glacier system: Mount Shasta, California. Climate Dynamics 28:85–98.
Howell, J. T. 1951. The arctic-alpine flora of three peaks in the Sierra Nevada. Leaflets of Western Botany 6:141–56.
———. 1944. Certain plants of the Marble Mountains in California with remarks on the boreal flora of the Klamath area. Wasmann Collector 6:13–19.
Jameson, E. W., and H. J. Peeters 2004. Mammals of California. University of California Press, Berkeley, California.
Jennings, M. R. 1996. Status of amphibians. Sierra Nevada ecosystem project: Final report to Congress. Volume II, Assessments and scientific basis for management options. Wildland Resources Center Report 37:921–945.
Jennings, S. A., and D. L. Elliot-Fisk. 1993. Packrat midden evidence of late Quaternary vegetation change in the White Mountains, California-Nevada. Quaternary Research 39:214–221.
———. 1991. Late Pleistocene and Holocene changes in plant community composition in the White Mountain region. Pages 1–17 in C. A. Hall, V. Doyle-Jones, and B. Widawski, editors. Natural History of Eastern California and High-Altitude Research. White Mountains Research Station, Symposium 3. University of California, Los Angeles, California.
Jordon-Thaden, I., and M. Koch. 2008. Species richness and polyploid patterns in the genus *Draba* (Brassicaceae): A first global perspective. Plant Ecology and Diversity 1:255–263.
Kattelmann, R., and K. Elder. 1991. Hydrologic characteristics and water balance of an alpine basin in the Sierra Nevada. Water Resources Research 27:1553–1562.
Kimball, S., P. Wilson, and J. Crowther. 2004. Local ecology and geographic ranges of plants in the Bishop Creek watershed, Sierra Nevada, California. Journal of Biogeography 31:1637–1657.
Klein, J. A., J. Harte, and X. Q. Zhao. 2005. Dynamic and complex microclimate responses to warming and grazing manipulations. Global Change Biology 11:1440–1451.
Klikoff, L. G. 1965. Microenvironmental influence on vegetational pattern near timberline in the central Sierra Nevada. Ecological Monographs 35:187–211.
Knapp, R. A. 1996. Non-native trout in natural lakes of the Sierra Nevada: An analysis of their distribution and impacts on native aquatic biota. Sierra Nevada ecosystem project: Final report to Congress. Volume III, Assessments and scientific basis for management options. University of California, Centers for Water and Wildland Resources, Davis, California Wildland Resources Center Report 38:363–409.
Körner, C. 2012. Alpine treelines. Functional ecology of the global high elevation tree limits. Springer Books, Basel, Switzerland.
———. 2007. Climatic treelines: Conventions, global patterns, causes. Erdkunde 61:316–324.
———. 2003. Alpine plant life: Functional plant ecology of high mountain ecosystems. Second edition. Springer Verlag, Berlin, Germany.
Körner, C., and J. Paulsen. 2004. A world-wide study of high altitude treeline temperatures. Journal of Biogeography 31:713–732.
Kruckeberg, A. R. 1984. California serpentines: Flora, vegetation, geology, soils, and management problems. University of California Publications in Botany. University of California, Berkeley and Los Angeles, California; London, UK.
Kubat, K., editor. 2000. Stony debris ecosystems. Studia Biologica 52. Univerzita J. E. Purkyně, Ústí nad Labem, Czech Republic.
Kucera, T. E., W. J. Zielinski, and R. H. Barrett. 1996. Current distribution of the American marten, *Martes americana,* in California. California Fish and Game 81:96–103.
LaMarche, V. C. 1968. Rates of slope degradation as determined from botanical evidence. White Mountains, California. U.S. Geographical Survey Professional Paper, 352-I.
Lawson, A. C. 1904. The geomorphogeny of the upper Kern basin. University of California, Department of Geological Science Bulletin 3:291–376.
Major, J., and D. W. Taylor. 1977. Alpine. Pages 601–675 in M. G. Barbour and J. Major, editors. Terrestrial vegetation of California. Wiley, New York, New York.
Major, J., and S. A. Bamberg. 1967. Some cordilleran plants disjunct in the Sierra Nevada of California and their bearing on Pleistocene ecological conditions. Pages 171–189 in H. E. Wright and W. H. Osburn, editors. Arctic and alpine environments. Indiana University Press, Bloomington, Indiana.
Malanson, G. P., and D. B. Fagre. 2013. Spatial contexts for temporal variability in alpine vegetation under ongoing climate change. Plant Ecology 214:1309–1319.
Mantua, N. J., S. R. Hare, Y. Zhang, J. M. Wallace, and R. C. Francis. 1997. A Pacific interdecadal climate oscillation with impacts on salmon production. Bulletin of the American Meteorological Society 78:1069–1079.
Maurer, E. 2007. Uncertainty in hydrologic impacts of climate change in the Sierra Nevada, California, under two emissions scenarios. Climatic Change 82:309–325.
Meixner, T., and R. C. Bales. 2003. Source hydrochemical modeling of coupled C and N Cycling in high-elevation catchments: Importance of snow cover. Biogeochemistry 62:289–308.
Meyers, P. A. 1978. A phytogeographic survey of the subalpine and alpine regions of southern California. PhD dissertation. University of California, Santa Barbara, California.
Millar, C. I., and R. D. Westfall. 2010. Distribution and climatic relationships of the American pika (*Ochotona princeps*) in the Sierra Nevada and Western Great Basin, U.S.A.: Periglacial landforms as refugia in warming climates. Arctic, Antarctic, and Alpine Research 42:76–88. (S. Wolf comment, AAAR 2010; C. Millar and R. Westfall reply, AAAR 2010).
———. 2008. Rock glaciers and periglacial rock-ice features in the Sierra Nevada: Classification, distribution, and climate relationships. Quaternary International 188:90–104.
Millar, C. I., R. D. Westfall and D. L. Delany. 2014a. New records of marginal sites for American pika (*Ochotona princeps*) in the Western Great Basin. Western North American Naturalist. 73:457–476.
———. 2014b. Thermal regimes and snowpack relations of periglacial talus fields, Sierra Nevada, California, USA. Arctic, Antarctic, and Alpine Research. 46:483–504.
———. 2013. Thermal and hydrologic attributes of rock glaciers and periglacial talus landforms: Sierra Nevada, California, USA. Quaternary International 310:169–180.
———. 2007. Response of high-elevation limber pine (*Pinus flexilis*) to multiyear droughts and 20th-century warming, Sierra Nevada, California, USA. Canadian Journal of Forest Research 37:2508–2520.

Millar, C. I., R. D. Westfall, A. Evenden, J. G. Holmquist, J. Schmidt-Gengenbach, R. S. Franklin, J. Nachlinger, and D. L. Delany. 2014. Potential climatic refugia in semi-arid, temperate mountains: plant and arthropod assemblages associated with rock glaciers, talus slopes, and their forefield wetlands, Sierra Nevada, USA. Quaternary International. <dx.doi.org/10.1016/j.quaint.2013.11.003>.

Miller, A. E., J. P. Schimel, J. O. Sickman, K. Skeen, T. Meixner, and J. M. Melack. 2009. Seasonal variation in nitrogen uptake and turnover in two high-elevation soils: Mineralization responses are site-dependent. Biogeochemistry 93:253–270.

Miller, J. H., and M. T. Green. 1987. Distribution, status, and origin of water pipits breeding in California. Condor 89:788–797.

Morefield, J. D. 1992. Spatial and ecologic segregation of phytogeographic elements in the White Mountains of California and Nevada. Journal of Biogeography 19:33–50.

———. 1988. Floristic habitats of the White Mountains, California and Nevada: A local approach to plant communities. Pages 1–18 in C. A. Hall and V. Doyle-Jones, editors. Plant biology of eastern California. Natural history of the White-Inyo range, Symposium. Volume 2, White Mountains Research Station. University of California, Los Angeles, California.

Moritz, C., J. L. Patton, C. J. Conroy, J. L. Parra, G. C. White, and S. R. Beissinger. 2008. Impact of a century of climate change on small-mammal communities in Yosemite National Park, USA. Science 322:261–264.

Mote, P., A. F. Hamlet, M. P. Clark, and D. P. Lettenmaier. 2005. Declining snowpack in western North America. Bulletin of the American Meteorological Society 86:39–49.

Muir, J. 1894. The mountains of California. Century, New York, New York.

Myers, L., and B. Whited. 2012. The impact of cattle grazing in high elevation Sierra Nevada mountain meadows over widely variable annual climatic conditions. Journal of Environmental Protection 3:823–837.

Nice, C. C., and A. M. Shapiro. 2001. Patterns of morphological, biochemical, and molecular evolution in the *Oeneis chryxus* complex (Lepidoptera: Satyridae): A test of historical biogeographical hypotheses. Molecular Phylogenetics and Evolution 20:11–123.

Noyes, R. D. 2007. Apomixis in the Asteraceae: Diamonds in the rough. Functional Plant Science and Biotechnology 1:208–222.

Pace, N., D. W. Kiepert, and E. M. Nissen. 1974. Climatological data summary for the Crooked Creek Laboratory, 1949–1973, and the Barcroft Laboratory, 1953–1973. White Mountain Research Station Special Publication, Bishop, California.

Parish, S. G. 1917. An enumeration of the pteridophytes and spermatophytes of the San Bernardino Mountains, California. Plant World 20:163–178, 208–223, 245–259.

Pemble, R. H. 1970. Alpine vegetation in the Sierra Nevada of California as lithosequences and in relation to local site factors. PhD dissertation. University of California, Davis, California.

Perrine, J., L. A. Campbell, and G. G. Green. 2010. Sierra Nevada red fox (*Vulpes vulpes necator*), a conservation assessment. U.S. Department of Agriculture, Forest Service Report: R5-FR-010.

Perrine, J. D., L. A. Campbell, and G. A. Green. 2010. Sierra Nevada red fox (*Vulpes vulpes necator*); A conservation assessment. USDA R5-FR-010. U.S. Forest Service. Vallejo, California. 52 pages.

Porter, B. R. 1983. A flora of the Desolation Wilderness, El Dorado County, California. MS thesis. Humboldt State University, Arcata, California.

Powell, D. R., and H. E. Klieforth. 1991. Weather and climate. Pages 3–26 in C. A. Hall, editor. Natural History of the White-Inyo Range. University of California Press, Berkeley, California.

Price, M. V., and N. M. Waser. 2000. Responses of subalpine meadow vegetation to four years of experimental warming. Ecological Applications 10:811–824.

Ratliff, R. D. 1985. Meadows in the Sierra Nevada of California: State of knowledge. General Technical Report, PSW-84. U.S. Department of Agriculture, Forest Service, Pacific Southwest Research Station, Albany, California.

Raub, W., C. S. Brown, and A. Post. 2006. Inventory of glaciers in the Sierra Nevada. U.S. Geological Survey, Open File Report 2006-1239.

Raven, P. H., and D. I. Axelrod. 1978. Origin and relationships of the California flora. University of California Publications in Botany 72:1–134.

Rhodes, P. T. 1987. Historic glacier fluctuations on Mount Shasta, Siskiyou County. California Geology 40:205–2011.

Rundel, P. 2011. The diversity and biogeography of the alpine flora of the Sierra Nevada, California. Madroño 58:153–184.

Rundel, P. W., A. C. Gibson, and M. R. Sharifi. 2008. The alpine flora of the White Mountain, California. Madroño 55:204–217.

———. 2005. Plant functional groups in alpine fellfield habitats of the White Mountains, California. Arctic, Antarctic, and Alpine Research 37:358–365.

Sage, R. F., and T. L. Sage. 2002. Microsite characteristics of *Muhlenbergia richardsonis* (Trin.) Rydb., an alpine C_4 grass from the White Mountains, California. Oecologia 132:501–508.

Sawyer, J. O., and T. Keeler-Wolf. 2007. Alpine vegetation. Pages 539–573 in M. Barbour, A. Schoenherr, and T. Keeler-Wolf, editors. Terrestrial Vegetation of California. Second edition. University of California Press, Berkeley, California.

Sawyer, J. O., T. Keeler-Wolf, and J.M. Evens. 2009. A manual of California vegetation. Second edition. California Native Plant Society, Sacramento, California.

Schranz M. E., C. Dobeš, M. A. Koch, and T. Mitchell-Olds. 2005. Sexual reproduction, hybridization, apomixis, and polyploidization in the genus *Boechera* (Brassicaceae). American Journal of Botany 92:1797–1810.

Scott, D., and W. D. Billings. 1964. Effects of environmental factors on standing crop and productivity of an alpine tundra. Ecological Monographs 34:243–270.

Sharp, R. P., C. R. Allen, and M. F. Meier. 1959. Pleistocene glaciers on southern California mountains. American Journal of Science 257:81–94.

Sharsmith, C. 1940. A contribution to the history of the alpine flora of the Sierra Nevada. PhD dissertation. University of California, Berkeley, California.

Sickman, J. O., A. Leydecker, and J. M. Melack. 2001. Nitrogen mass balance and abiotic controls of nitrogen N retention and yield in high elevation catchments of the Sierra Nevada, California, USA. Water Resources Research 37:1445–1461.

Sickman J. O., J. M. Melack, and D. W. Clow. 2003. Evidence for nutrient enrichment of high–elevation lakes in the Sierra Nevada, California. Limnology and Oceanography 48:1885–1892.

———. 1915. The alpine and subalpine vegetation of the Lake Tahoe region. Botanical Gazette 59:265–286.

Smith, A. T. 1974. Distribution and dispersal of pikas: Influence of behavior and climate. Ecology 55:1368–1376.

Smith, A. T., and M. L. Weston. 1990. Mammalian species, *Ochotona princeps*. American Society of Mammologists 352:1–8.

Stebbins, G. L. 1982. Floristic affinities of the high Sierra Nevada. Madroño 29:189–99.

Stephenson, N. L. 1998. Actual evapotranspiration and deficit: Biologically meaningful correlates of vegetation distribution across spatial scales. Journal of Biogeography 25:855–870.

Stewart, I. T., D. R. Cayan, and M. D. Dettinger. 2005. Changes toward earlier streamflow timing across western North America. Journal of Climate 18:1136–1155.

Storer, T. I., R. L. Usinger, and D. Lukas. 2004. Sierra Nevada natural history. Revised edition. University of California Press, Berkeley, California.

Tatum, J. W. 1979. The vegetation and flora of Olancha Peak, southern Sierra Nevada, California. MS thesis. University of California, Santa Barbara, California.

Taylor, D. W 1977. Floristic relationships along the Cascade-Sierran axis. American Midland Naturalist 97:333–349.

———. 1976a. Disjunction of Great Basin plants in the northern Sierra Nevada. Madroño 29:301–310.

———. 1976b. Ecology of the timberline vegetation at Carson Pass, Alpine County, California. PhD dissertation. University of California, Davis, California.

Theurillat, J. P., and A. Guisan. 2001. Potential impact of climate change on vegetation in the European Alps: A review. Climatic Change 50:77–109.

Tingley, M. W., W. B. Monahanc, S. R. Beissingera, and C. Moritz. 2009. Birds track their Grinnellian niche through a century of climate change. Proceedings of the National Academy of Science 106:19637–19643.

Urban, D. L., C. Miller, P. N. Halpin, and N. L. Stephenson. 2000. Forest gradient response in Sierran landscapes: The physical template. Landscape Ecology 15:603–620.

USFWS (U.S. Fish and Wildlife Service). 2010. Endangered and threatened wildlife and plants: 12-month finding on a petition to list the American pika as threatened or endangered. Federal Register 50 CFR Part 17 [FWS-R6-ES-2009-0021 MO 92210-0-0010].

USGS (U.S. Geological Survey). 1986. Topographic map of Mount Shasta. U.S. Geological Survey, Reston, Virginia.

Vredenburg, V. T., G. Fellers, and C. Davidson. 2005. The mountain yellow-legged frog (*Rana muscosa*). Pages 563–566 in M. J. Lannoo, editor. Status and conservation of U.S. amphibians. University of California Press, Berkeley, California.

Wahrhaftig, C. 1965. Stepped topography of the southern Sierra Nevada. Geological Society of America Bulletin 76:1165–1190.

Walker, D., R. C. Ingersoll, and P. J. Webber. 1994. Effects of interannual climate variation on aboveground phytomass in alpine vegetation. Ecology 75:393–408.

Washburn, A. L. 1980. Geocyrology: A survey of periglacial processes and environments. Wiley, New York, New York.

Wehausen, J. D., H. Johnson, and T. R. Stephenson. 2007. Sierra Nevada bighorn sheep: 2006–2007 status. California Department of Fish and Game, Sacramento, California.

Weixelman, D. A., B. Hill, D. J. Cooper, E. L. Berlow, J. H. Viers, S. E. Purdy, A. G. Merrill, and A. E. Gross. 2011. Meadow hydrogeomorphic types for the Sierra Nevada and southern Cascade Ranges in California. U.S. Forest Service General Technical Report R5-TP-034. U.S. Department of Agriculture, Forest Service, Pacific Southwest Region. Vallejo, California.

Wenk, E. H., and T. E. Dawson. 2007. Interspecific differences in seed germination, establishment, and early growth in relation to preferred soil type in an alpine community. Arctic, Antarctic, and Alpine Research 39:165–176.

Went, F. W. 1953. Annual plants at high altitudes in the Sierra Nevada, California. Madroño 12:109–114.

———. 1948. Some parallels between desert and alpine floras in California. Madroño 9:241–249.

Wernicke, B., G. J. Axen, and J. K. Snow. 1988. Basin and Range extensional tectonics at the latitude of Las Vegas, Nevada. Geological Society of America Bulletin 100:1738–1757.

Wilkerson, F. D. 1995. Rates of heave and surface rotation of periglacial frost boils in the White Mountains, California. Physical Geography 16:487–502.

Williams, M. W., and J. M. Melack. 1991. Solute chemistry of snowmelt and runoff in an alpine basin, Sierra Nevada. Water Resources Research 27:1575–1588.

Winkler, D. E. 2013. A multi-level approach to assessing alpine productivity responses to climate change. MA thesis. University of California, Merced, California.

Wolfe, J. A., H. E. Schorn, C. E. Forest, and P. Molnar. 1997. Paleobotanical evidence for high altitudes in Nevada during the Miocene. Science 276:1672–1675.

Wolford, R. A., and R. C. Bales. 1996. Hydrochemical modeling of Emerald Lake watershed, Sierra Nevada, California: Sensitivity of stream chemistry to changes in fluxes and model parameters. Limnology and Oceanography 41:947–954.

Wundram, D., R. Pape, and J. Löffler. 2010. Alpine soil temperature variability at multiple scales. Arctic, Antarctic, and Alpine Research 42:117–128.

Zacharda, M., M. Gude, S. Kraus, C. Hauck, R. Molenda, and V. Růžička. 2005. The relict mite *Rhagidia gelida* (Acari, Rhagidiidae) as a biological cryoindicator of periglacial microclimate in European highland screes. Arctic, Antarctic, and Alpine Research 37:402–408.

THIRTY

Deserts

JAYNE BELNAP, ROBERT H. WEBB, TODD C. ESQUE, MATTHEW L. BROOKS, LESLEY A. DEFALCO, and JAMES A. MACMAHON

Introduction

The deserts of California (Figure 30.1) occupy approximately 38% of the state's landscape (Table 30.1) and consist of three distinct deserts: the Great Basin Desert, the Mojave Desert, and the Colorado Desert, which is a subdivision of the Sonoran Desert (Brown and Lowe 1980). The wide range of climates and geology found within each of these deserts produce very different vegetation communities and ecosystem processes and therefore different ecosystem services. In deserts, extreme conditions such as very high and low temperatures and very low rainfall result in control by abiotic factors—climate, geology, geomorphology, and soils—of the composition and function of ecosystems, including plant and animal distributions. This situation is in contrast to ecosystems where wetter and milder temperatures occur and the dominant organizing factors are often disturbance (such as fire, landslides, and floods) and biotic interactions (such as competition, herbivory and predation) (Clark 1991).

Despite their harsh conditions, deserts are home to a surprisingly large number of plants and animals. Deserts are also places where organisms display a wide array of adaptations to the extremes they encounter, providing some of the best examples of evolution by natural selection (MacMahon and Wagner 1985, Ward 2009). Humans have also utilized these regions for thousands of years, despite the relatively low productivity and harsh climates of these landscapes. Unlike much of California, most of these desert lands have received little high-intensity use since European settlement, leaving large areas relatively undisturbed. Desert landscapes are being altered, however, by the introduction of fire following the recent invasion of Mediterranean annual grasses (D'Antonio and Vitousek 1992). As most native plants are not adapted to fire, they do not recover, whereas the non-native grasses flourish. Land uses such as energy exploration and development, recreational use, and urban development are rapidly increasing as well, and because desert lands are slow to recover, such disturbances will alter these landscapes for many years to come.

This chapter begins with a brief description of where the different deserts of California are located and their dominant vegetation communities. The abiotic factors that define these deserts, and how these factors control vegetation and thus also animal distributions, are examined next. After this

TABLE 30.1
Areas of the California desert units

Land mass	Area (km^2)	Percentage area
California	423,970	100.0
Mojave Desert	129,523	30.5
Colorado Desert	26,317	6.2
Modoc Plateau	4,000	0.9
Owens Valley	1,936	0.5
Mono Lake basin	2,030	0.5
TOTAL	**161,775.7**	**38.2**

SOURCE: Calculated by RH Webb.
NOTE: Modoc Plateau, Owens Valley and Mono Lake Basin are zones of the California Great Basin Desert.

section, ecosystem processes and iconic species of these deserts are discussed, followed by a concluding section on the future of these landscapes. This last section focuses primarily on the Mojave Desert, as it is both the largest California desert and the focus of most existing research on California deserts.

Biogeography

The smallest desert region in California is the Great Basin Desert, which occurs in two distinct subregions in California (see Figure 30.1). The southern subregion occurs east of the Sierra Nevada in the Mono Lake Basin and the Owens Valley. The northern section includes the Modoc Plateau east of the Cascade Range in northeastern California (Sawyer et al. 2009). Only the southwestern corner of the Great Basin Desert occurs within California, with the rest in Idaho, Nevada, Oregon, Utah, Washington, and Wyoming (see Table 30.1). It is dominated by big sage (*Artemisia tridentata*), single-leaf pinyon pine (*Pinus monophylla*), and one seed juniper (*Juniperus monosperma*).

The Mojave Desert borders on Utah, Arizona, and Nevada and is the largest desert in California, occupying 30.5% of the state. The Mojave Desert is unique among the North American deserts for its extensive display of winter annual plants and its many ENDEMIC plants and animals. Extreme variations in climate and topography, coupled with active geologic activity, are the fundamental ecosystem drivers associated with this high diversity of plant species and ecosystem properties. Six distinct subregions of the Mojave Desert have been defined on the basis of seasonal precipitation patterns, landscape types, and floral diversity (Figure 30.2; Webb, Heaton et al. 2009). The northern Mojave Desert, with its climatic extremes, has the highest plant species richness in the Mojave Desert (1,025 species) (Rowlands et al. 1982). The eastern Mojave Desert contains most of the high elevations in the Mojave Desert. Combined with higher summer rainfall and exposed outcrops of rock strata like those of the Colorado Plateau, this region has high soil diversity and hotspots of plant endemism. The southeastern Mojave Desert grades into the Sonoran Desert and contains, across the border in Arizona, the co-occurrence of Joshua tree (*Yucca brevifolia*) and saguaro (*Carnegiea gigantea*). The south-central Mojave Desert contains large, iconic Joshua tree forests. The central Mojave Desert encompasses the lower reaches of the internally drained Mojave River, including a series of relatively low-elevation playas (dry lakes). The separation of the central Mojave Desert from the Great Basin and Colorado Deserts, along with its relatively moderate topography, results in less ecological variability than the other subregions, including the fewest number of vascular plant species (458 species) (Rowlands et al. 1982, Bell et al. 2009, Wood et al. 2012). Lastly, the western Mojave Desert has intermediate plant species richness (663 species) (Rowlands et al. 1982).

The Colorado Desert occurs in southeastern Arizona and southwestern California, extending southward into Mexico. It is dominated by creosote (*Larrea tridentata*) and also has abundant succulent plants, notably cholla (*Cylindropuntia* spp.) (Pinkava et al. 2001) and saguaro, and leguminous trees, particularly paloverde (*Parkinsonia microphylla*) and ironwood (*Olneya tesota*). The Salton Sea and its predecessor, Lake Cahuilla (one of the last and largest Pleistocene lakes, which evaporated approximately four hundred years ago), dominate this desert, and much of its substrate is fine-grained ALLUVIUM derived from the combination of runoff from the Colorado River and the Transverse Ranges.

Drivers of Ecosystem Processes in Space and Time

Desert ecosystems are complex entities (Figure 30.3). Desert ecosystem processes are controlled mainly by the abiotic factors of climate, geology, soils, geomorphic setting, and various disturbances. These ecosystem processes in turn set the stage for the plants and animals that inhabit these landscapes.

Climate

The most defining characteristic of deserts is high spring and summer temperatures accompanied by very low and variable precipitation. These factors result in scant vegetative cover that is generally short in stature. Although climatic regimes are important in determining the structure and function of all ecosystems, they are an especially dominant force in deserts, where water availability is the ultimate determinant for plant and animal survival. The availability of soil moisture for plants and soil biota, which in turn provide food and habitat for desert animals, is determined by temperature, precipitation regimes (the overall amount of precipitation and the type and seasonality of events), and soil characteristics. Lower temperatures, which allow for longer retention of soil moisture, occur in fall and winter, at higher elevations, and on north and east slope aspects.

The type of precipitation is also important. Compared to summer convective storms, winter frontal storms are generally less spatially variable with more gentle rainfall, allowing more water to infiltrate more deeply into the soil and over a larger area. If precipitation events are too short or too small, the resulting soil moisture stays at the surface and quickly evaporates. Seasonality, or the timing of precipitation relative

Photo on previous page: A typical Mojave Desert setting, with the New York Mountains in the background. The foreground is covered with biological soil crusts. Photo: T. E. Esque.

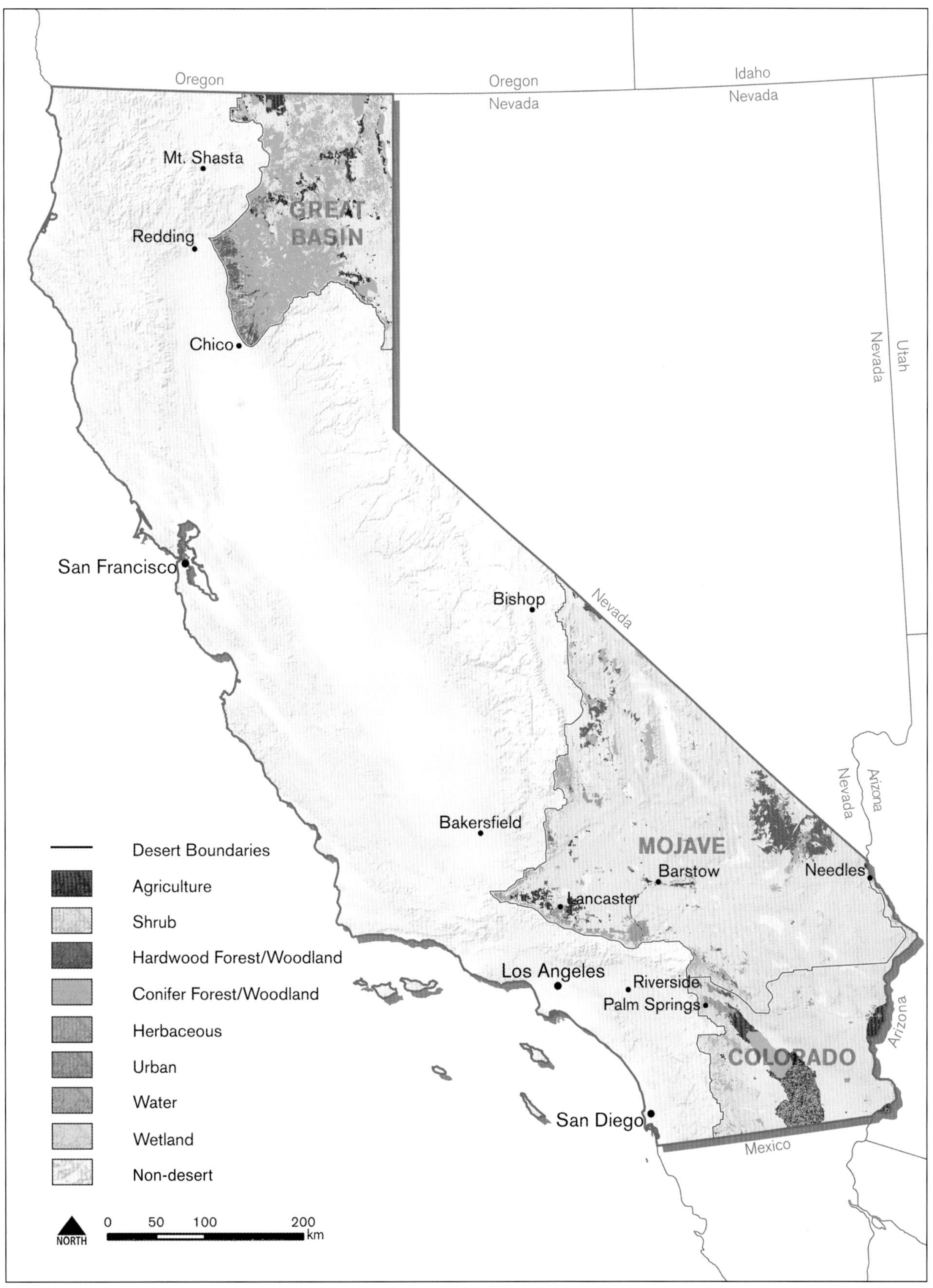

FIGURE 30.1 California's desert regions. Source: Data from Cal Fire, Fire Resource and Assessment Program (FRAP). Map: P. Welch, Center for Integrated Spatial Research (CISR).

FIGURE 30.2 Map of the Mojave Desert showing the six subregions. Source: Webb, Fenstermaker et al. 2009.

to temperature, also matters because rain falling when temperatures are high evaporates more quickly than rain or snow falling when temperatures are low. In addition, some plants can only utilize precipitation that occurs in specific seasons. For example, many perennial grasses and succulent plants only occur in high abundance where significant summer rainfall occurs (Comstock and Ehleringer 1992, Ehleringer 2001).

All three California deserts average less than 250 millimeters annual precipitation because of the rainshadow effect of the Sierra Nevada and Transverse Ranges. The Great Basin Desert has the lowest POTENTIAL EVAPOTRANSPIRATION (PET) of the three deserts due to its lower overall temperatures, which reflect its higher elevation and more northerly position in the state. Freezing temperatures occur there for four to five months a year. Because most precipitation falls during the cold winter, evaporation and transpiration are limited, allowing most of the water to infiltrate deeply into the soil. For example, at Bridgeport, northwest of Mono Lake, three-quarters of the average precipitation of 238 millimeters falls between November and March (Western Regional Climate Center 2013a).

The Mojave Desert is warmer than the Great Basin Desert and has four distinct precipitation zones: (1) low winter/low summer (average=113 mm yr^{-1}, 70% winter, October–April); (2) moderate winter/moderate summer (177 mm yr^{-1}, 64% winter); (3) high winter/low summer (153 mm yr^{-1}, 82% winter); and (4) high winter/high summer (271 mm yr^{-1}, 61% winter) (Tagestad et al. in press). Interannual variability is high and has ranged from 47 to 587 mm yr^{-1}since records have been kept (Hereford et al. 2006). Like the Great Basin, the Mojave Desert is subject to freezing temperatures, which approach –9°C in many parts of the desert, but for a shorter time period. Thus the PET of the Mojave Desert is higher than the Great Basin's.

The Colorado Desert in southern California is the warmest and driest region in North America, reflecting its generally low elevation and southerly position. This desert seldom experiences freezing temperatures, and its PET is extremely high. Rainfall is strongly biseasonal, with average winter rainfall only slightly above average summer rainfall. For example, El Centro has a mean annual precipitation of 67 millimeters, 60% of which falls in the winter months. However, summer-fall incursions of tropical moisture from the Pacific Ocean can make these averages meaningless because of extreme precipitation events associated with summer monsoonal rains. These monsoonal rains are highly intense events of short duration, resulting in high runoff and little contribution to soil moisture. The average maximum temperature in this region exceeds 38°C from June through September (Western Regional Climate Center 2013b), causing extremely high PET (greater than 2,500 mm yr^{-1}).

Given that precipitation in desert regions is highly variable in both space and time, extreme drought and wet years are important ecosystem drivers because they can result in large-scale and long-term effects on ecosystem structure through

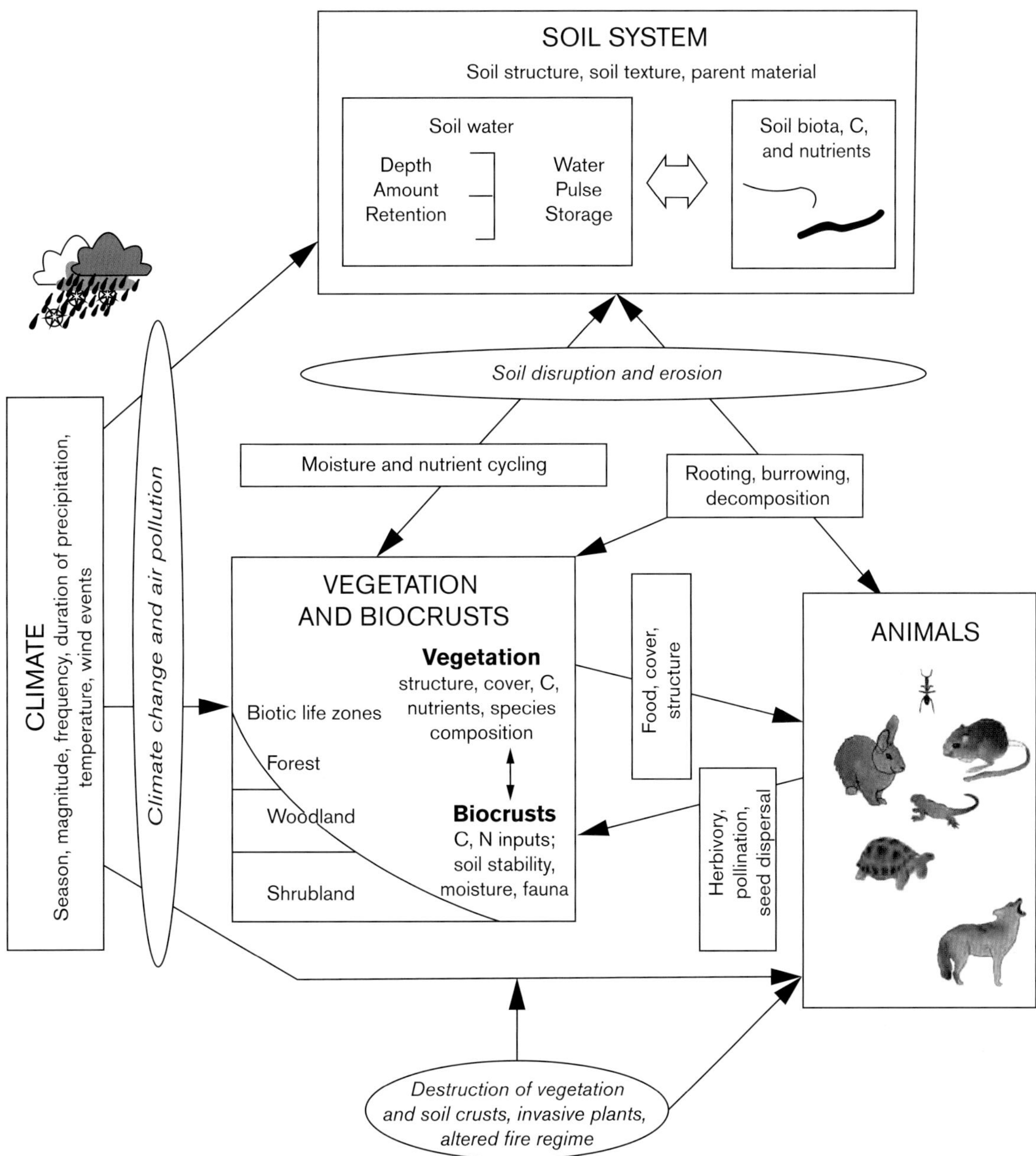

FIGURE 30.3 Conceptual model of the Mojave Desert ecosystem. Source: Modified from Chung-MacCoubrey et al. 2008.

episodes of plant death, establishment, or growth (Noy-Meir 1973, Ehleringer 2001). Therefore a great deal of effort has gone into developing a framework to understand the effects of precipitation events on various ecosystem processes. The pulse-dynamic and pulse-reserve are the most widely accepted conceptual models in use today (Noy-Meir 1973, Reynolds et al. 2004). In its simplest form, the pulse-dynamic model posits that most desert productivity (such as germination, growth, seed production) is a direct response to discrete rainfall events. The pulse-reserve model suggests that some of this productivity is carried over as reserves, such as seeds, litter, and nutrient or carbon (C) storage in roots. Recently, these models have included an emphasis on the role of nutrients as a driver of productivity, as it has been increasingly recognized that relatively infertile desert soils can quickly limit plant productivity when water is not limiting, such as in years of high precipitation or frequent precipitation pulses (Ogle and Reynolds 2004). A pulse of productivity results in an increase in consumers (animals) and their consumption rates. Animals are not only important consumers of desert productivity; they also alter ecosystem processes by redistributing resources such as seeds around the landscape, disturbing the ground through digging, and preying on other animals (Whitford 2002). They also are much better than plants at amortizing the gains and losses experienced over a series of individual pulse events (Schmitz 2009).

The pulse-dynamic and the pulse-reserve models continue to develop as other authors propose needed additions or alterations (Collins et al. 2014). For instance, Ogle and Reynolds (2004) noted that the effects of antecedent water and processes like the ability of plants to alter their rooting habits and to delay their response to rainfall need to be included in these models. Schwinning et al. (2004) and Schwinning and Sala (2004) have shown there is a hierarchy of soil moisture pulses and ecological responses to these pulses that needs consideration. Specifically, because most precipitation events in deserts are less than 5 millimeters and only stimulate activity in organisms at the soil surface (Pointing and Belnap 2012), larger pulses of precipitation that penetrate deeper into the soil can trigger a greater variety of longer-lasting events, including stimulation of plant productivity. As a result, soil and plant processes in deserts may be temporally or spatially asynchronous or synchronous. For example, small wetting events result in nutrient input and accumulation in surface soils, but these small events are often too small to translocate nutrients to vascular plant roots (asynchrony). On the other hand, large wetting events stimulate nutrient inputs and transformations at the surface at the same time as translocations of these nutrients to vascular plants occur (synchrony).

Geology, Soils, and Geomorphic Setting

After climate, other abiotic factors become important in determining the composition and function of desert ecosystems. Of these, geology, soils, and geomorphic setting are the most dominant, as they all have a strong influence on water and nutrient availability.

GEOLOGY

California's deserts are all on the western margin of the Basin and Range Province. The geologic framework of these deserts consists of numerous mountains, generally north-south trending, created by fault-driven rock displacement upwards, and separated by fault-delineated, depressed blocks of land called grabens (Hall 2007, Cooke et al. 1993). This type of regional geology promotes internal drainage into valley lakes and playas rather than the ocean. This geology also provides the elevation gradients that are so influential on these desert ecosystems. Two of California's most striking elevational gradients are found in Owens Valley of the Great Basin Desert and in Death Valley of the Mojave Desert, where desert floor to mountaintop elevation differences are the greatest in the continental United States, exceeding 3,500 meters. The northern Great Basin Desert is the least tectonically active of the California deserts. In contrast, the Mojave Desert is tectonically active with numerous active faults, and geology of the Colorado Desert is strongly controlled by the San Andreas fault system.

PARENT MATERIAL matters greatly in determining what plant communities, and therefore what animal communities, can thrive in a location. This is because parent material controls nutrient content and the infiltration and retention of water in soils derived from them. The northern Great Basin Desert in California is dominated by volcanic rocks associated with the Cascade Mountains, but the southern Great Basin is mostly granitoid and associated metamorphic rocks from the Sierra Nevada and Inyo Mountains. In the Mojave Desert, approximately 55% of the bedrock is sedimentary, and most of these rocks are Paleozoic limestones, dolomites, and shales. Many mountains in the Mojave Desert have granitoid rocks at their cores, and 34% of the exposed bedrock in the Mojave Desert is plutonic. In contrast, the Colorado Desert contains only 38% consolidated bedrock, with the remainder consisting of Lake Cahuilla sediments and alluvial fans of Quaternary age.

SOILS

As with climate and geology, desert soils have a dramatic effect on what plants and ecosystem processes occur in a given location. The wide variety of igneous, sedimentary, and metamorphic parent materials that are exposed in the California deserts results in a large range of soil types, which promotes high vegetative diversity. Desert soils possess various properties that are very different from soils in mesic regions and have a profound influence on ecosystem processes. One of the most important differences between desert soils and those in wetter regions is what is referred to as the "inverse texture hypothesis" (Sala et al. 1988). Most desert soils contain substantial amounts of sand and rocks, which when combined with low inputs of plant litter, soil biotic activity, and nutrient-holding capacity, result in coarser soils that are generally less fertile than soils containing more fine particles and organic material (Ward 2009). However, coarser soils allow water to infiltrate below the evaporative zone more rapidly than finer soil, allowing them to retain soil moisture longer. Because water is more limiting than nutrients in desert ecosystems, coarser textured soils therefore generally support higher plant and animal productivity than finer-textured soils (Sala et al. 1988). This is in contrast to wetter ecosystems, where nutrients are often more limiting than water, rendering finer, more fertile soils more productive than coarse soils.

Other features distinguish desert soils from those found in wetter regions. The low weathering rates of rocks in deserts can result in soils with physical and chemical characteristics very similar to the parent material from which they were derived (Jenny 1941). Most desert soils are very old, and older soils in deserts generally support less plant productivity and species diversity than younger soils. Several features can develop with age in these settings that have a strong negative influence on plant productivity and ecosystem processes. These features include desert varnish, vesicular horizons, desert pavement, and subsurface clay and carbonate horizons (reviewed in Belnap et al. 2008).

Dark desert varnish often covers the rocks found on the soil surfaces of hot deserts such as the Mojave and Colorado Deserts (Springer 1958). Its color comes from iron and manganese oxides. The origin of the varnish is still under debate, with the main theories being that the iron and manganese oxides are (1) deposited by wind onto wetted rocks, (2) leached out from the interior of the rocks, and/or (3) bioaccumulated by bacteria and fungi. All three processes can play a partial role in the formation of desert varnish. Vesicular horizons form in older soils when fine soil particles transported from distant sources by the wind and deposited over thousands of years create a thin layer of silt at the soil surface (McFadden and Knuepfer 1990, McDonald 1994). As air rises through moist soils, it can become trapped in the silt layer, creating layers of air pockets, or vesicles. Once formed, these vesicles restrict the ability of rainwater to infiltrate into the soil, thereby restricting the growth of vascular plants. Desert pavement also forms on very old soils, which are generally of Pleistocene age. After many studies, most researchers agree that desert pavement results from two main forces: the erosion of surface soils exposing subsurface rocks (e.g., Wainwright et al. 1995) and/or subsurface rocks rising to the surface due to wind-blown silts accumulating under them (e.g., McFadden et al. 1987).

Silt particles move down in soils in two ways. First, after the silt is deposited, the infiltration of large rain events car-

FIGURE 30.4 Geomorphic surfaces in the Mojave Desert. At the top of the photo are steep hillslopes, cut by water channels. In the middle of the photo are mid- and low- elevation alluvial fans that receive materials from above. Fire scars can be seen on a lower- and mid-elevation alluvial fan. Note the patchy aspects of the fire, and the way geomorphic surfaces (higher terraces versus washes) influenced what areas were burned. Photo: Matthew L. Brooks.

ries silt downwards into the soil. Second, the shrinking and swelling of soils accompanied by wetting and drying cycles can rearrange the soil particles. In desert pavements the rocks at the surface are closely packed together, covering the soil surface almost entirely. Because these rocks are often covered with desert varnish and extremely close together, they create very high temperatures at the soil surface. Vesicular horizons also form under these rocks (Springer 1958). The combined presence of the hot rocks and vesicular horizons restrict the entry of water. Desert pavements are therefore generally devoid of plant cover, and their microbial activity is extremely restricted. Subsurface clay or carbonate horizons also are often present in hot deserts (McFadden et al. 1998). These horizons can effectively restrict water infiltration and inhibit root penetration. The same is true for subsurface cemented carbonate layers, which can accumulate over 200 kg C m^{-3}, making them equal to peat bogs as carbon stores (Monger 2006). While carbonate layers can restrict root access to deep water, in some situations they may also store water that is then made available to plants during drought (Duniway et al. 2010).

Episodic erosional events resulting from flooding or landslides often disrupt the process of soil formation. These episodic events can move "foreign" materials that occur upslope and deposit them onto of different surface types found below. New stream channels are often cut through different aged surfaces, exposing them. For instance, coarse material moved downslope can bury finer-textured deposits or desert pavements, creating an entirely new type of soil in which different plants can germinate and grow compared to what was originally found there. As a result, multiple ages and types of soils from different parent materials can occur side by side, creating the interesting mixture of plant and animal communities found in many settings throughout the California deserts.

Important Geomorphic Settings and Associated Vegetation

In deserts, the interaction of climate, soil formation, and geomorphic processes (e.g., landslides, overland flow, eolian [wind-blown] deposition) creates a mosaic of heterogeneous geomorphic units, highly variable in space and often in time, that determine ecosystem processes and thus where plants and animals live (Figure 30.4; Webb et al. 1988, McAuliffe and McDonald 1995, Hamerlynck et al. 2002). In the California deserts, the spatially dominant geomorphic units are playas, eolian features, alluvial fans, and hillslopes. All of these units are shrub-dominated, with plant cover ranging from less than 5% to approximately 35%. Water features, while not spatially extensive, are very important to particular communities of plants and animals.

During the wet periods of the Pleistocene, extensive systems of lakes and rivers existed within the Mojave and Great Basin deserts. Most of these were internally drained, with no outlet to the sea, with the exception of the far southernmost part of the Mojave, which drained into the Colorado River. These waterways were extensive. For example, what was once Lake Manly in Death Valley was fed by the Owens River via Lakes Searles and Panamint, as well as the Amarogosa and Mojave Rivers. As the climate dried, the lakes became what are now playas. In very wet years runoff sometimes reaches these old Pleistocene salt-encrusted lake beds.

There are two fundamental types of playas: wet and dry (Reynolds et al. 2007). Wet playas have shallow groundwater levels and perennial evaporation, resulting in high salt levels at or near the surface that often completely prevent plant growth; these playas tend to be the termini of larger regional rivers or Pleistocene drainage systems and are often large dust sources. Dry playas have deep water tables and are only periodically inundated, resulting in less salt accumulation in the soils. Dry playas generally also have a hard clay surface that produces a large amount of dust when disturbed. They also often have a local source of water and sediment and can sometimes support limited plant cover by salt-tolerant species. Small, local sand dunes often form around the playa edge and can also support salt-tolerant species. These species typically include four wing saltbush (*Atriplex canescens*), shadscale (*Atriplex confertifolia*), and pickleweed (*Salicornia virginica*). Various cholla cacti occur sporadically in this and other vegetation communities and provide infrequent, but important, nesting substrate for a variety of birds. Intermittent flooding of some playas can stimulate the hatching of an invertebrate community of fairy shrimp, tadpole shrimp, and amphipods that can be extremely abundant for short periods. These hatches may attract large accumulations of water birds and, as a result, can be important for migration stopovers (Carlisle et al. 2009).

Large, eolian sand dunes are common where there is an

abundant sand supply, including areas downwind of major rivers, washes, old PLUVIAL LAKE deposition, and some playas (e.g., Clarke and Rendell 1998). Active or destabilized dunes can undergo blowouts caused by rapidly erosive winds that can allow sand migration into areas without previous eolian deposits. Dunes store water and thereby support unique plants, including deep-rooted ones such as mesquite (*Prosopis* spp.), which can anchor dunes. Large dunes in the Mojave Desert include the Eureka, Death Valley, Panamint, and Kelso Dunes. In the Colorado Desert the main eolian features are the Coachella Valley and the Algodones Dunes. All these dune systems have endemic and rare plant and animal species (e.g., Skinner and Pavlik 1994). Many dune systems are now also important recreational sites. Furthermore, many of these dune systems are important archeological sites because they were occupied by Native Americans during the Holocene, when extensive lake systems filled many of the valleys. The mesquite trees' pods were a staple food source for aboriginal people (Fowler 1999). The mesquite bosque (woodland) near Death Valley's Furnace Creek has long been highly prized for its sweet pods and is currently used by the Timbisha Shoshone Tribe (Timbisha Shoshone Tribal Elders, pers. comm.). However, the Furnace Creek mesquite stand does not appear to be reproducing, possibly due to water diversion.

Alluvial fans are by far the most common geomorphic surface in the California deserts. These units are composed of loose rock and coarse particles (e.g., sand) moved by fast-moving mountain streams and overland flow events. Loose rock and sand are transported downhill until a change in slope slows the flow, and this material is deposited in a fan-like shape. Soils farther from the mountain source are finer in texture than upslope soils because the finer, lighter particles stay suspended longer and are transported farther. Because most surface-water drainage channels and debris flows cross each other and disrupt soil formation on these fans, soils of different ages are exposed, supporting a patchwork of different plant and animal communities. Although most surfaces are of Holocene age (the last eleven thousand years), many older surfaces (e.g., Pleistocene desert pavements) are also present. Dominant shrubs and animals change with elevation and latitude (Benson and Darrow 1981, Turner 1994). In the Mojave and Colorado Deserts the majority of lower-elevation fans are dominated by creosote, with the understory vegetation changing as the age of the soil surface changes. The most common subdominant plant is white bursage (*Ambrosia dumosa*) in the Mojave Desert and triangle leaf bursage (*Ambrosia deltoidea*) in the Colorado Desert. In both deserts these dominant species can be surrounded by a relatively rich mixture of other shrubs and annual species (Turner 1994). Alluvial fans, because of their great spatial extent, support the greatest annual productivity in all three California deserts.

Hillslopes and upper alluvial fans occur as elevations rise, and the dominance of creosote gives way to that of blackbrush (*Coleogyne ramosissima*). The lower end of the blackbrush belt is where the visually dominant Joshua trees are found. Above approximately1,250 meters, various juniper (*Juniperus* spp.) and pinyon (*Pinus* spp.) trees replace the Joshua trees. These trees increase in density until the shrubland vegetation gives way to woodlands, dominated by trees with a shrub understory of species like mountain mahogany (*Cercocarpus* spp.) and buckbrush (*Ceanothus* spp.). The most northerly areas of the California desert are occupied by Great Basin sage scrub, where some of the chenopod shrubs dominate in association with several sagebrush species (*Artemisia* spp.).

Water features including lakes, springs, and rivers also occur in the California deserts. The largest is the Salton Sea, which formed in 1905 when the Colorado River was diverted into its ancestral drainage patterns that once filled Pleistocene Lake Cahuilla (see Chapter 32, "Lakes"). Once a wet playa, the Salton Sea now is sustained by agricultural drainage from the Imperial Valley. However, drought conditions threaten this supply. Water diversion to Los Angeles has changed the nature of the larger California desert lakes. Owens Lake occasionally is filled with runoff from the Owens River, but typically it is a playa due to water diversions. Mono Lake has decreased considerably in size because of similar human-made water diversions. In contrast, larger perennial lakes occur on the Modoc Plateau in the north, where water development has not significantly decreased inflows.

Springs are common in the mountain ranges and upper parts of alluvial fans in the California deserts. Most springs have small catchment areas within mountain ranges; as a result, their flows increase and decrease with changes in precipitation and snowmelt. A few larger springs occur, often the end points of large groundwater flow systems, discharging water tens of thousands of years old and therefore not responsive to climate fluctuations. Unique riparian ecosystems support many endemic herbaceous plant and invertebrate species around these isolated springs. Groundwater development, combined with the establishment of non-native species including saltcedar (*Tamarix* spp.), threaten or have already irreversibly affected many of these small ecosystems (Hultine and Bush 2011).

Several large rivers occur in the deserts of California, with the Colorado River forming the southeastern boundary of the California desert region. Before being diverted for human use, the Owens, Mojave, and Whitewater Rivers transported water and sediment into the desert, depositing fertile, fine-grained sediments on alluvial plains; raising groundwater levels; and increasing ecosystem productivity. The fine-grained sediment deposited by these rivers is also one of the largest sources for the large sand dune systems found in the Colorado and Mojave Deserts. However, because dams trap sediment, water diversion threatens sand supplies needed to maintain and form the dunes.

Surface-water dependent (riparian) vegetation and animals are concentrated along the rivers that cross the deserts, especially where groundwater levels are high as the result of perched water tables or subsurface geology that locally forces groundwater to the surface. XERO-RIPARIAN plant communities also occur along these rivers and along intermittently flowing washes. This habitat type supports more vegetation than upland desert communities, but less so than riparian areas, and contains a mixture of plants that both do and do not require surface water. Xero-riparian areas are fairly widespread in the California deserts. Because they modulate extreme environmental conditions and provide predator protection, nesting substrates, and food for many animal species, they are occupied by the greatest number and diversity of animal species in the deserts (Carlisle et al. 2009). They also provide important travel routes for migrant birds.

Ecosystem Components and Processes

All ecosystems have basic processes in common, including production, decomposition, and carbon (C) and nitrogen (N) cycling. The drivers and rates of these processes, however, are often substantially different in deserts than in mesic regions.

Biological Soil Crusts

A unique feature of desert regions is the presence of biological soils crusts (biocrusts) (Figures 30.5 and 30.6; Belnap and Lange 2003). Biocrusts are communities of micro-organisms (cyanobacteria, bacteria, fungi, and green algae), macroscopic lichens and mosses, and microarthropods that occur within the top centimeter of the soil surface. As plants are often widely spaced in deserts, biocrusts can cover up to 70% of the soil surface. The biodiversity found in biocrusts often far exceeds that of the vascular plant community in which they are embedded. There are hundreds to thousands of species in biocrusts, whereas most dryland plant communities contain fewer than one hundred species. Biocrusts play many essential roles in deserts, and their influence increases with their biomass (Housman et al. 2006), which is positively related to precipitation and also controlled by parent material. For instance, in the California deserts, biocrust development is greatest on soils derived from gruss-weathered granites (those that weather directly into grain-sized particles and silt), followed by soils derived from sedimentary, other igneous, and finally metamorphic rocks (Belnap et. al 2014). This is likely due to the differences in the texture and nutrients found in the soils weathered from these rocks. Soils with higher levels of silt also have higher biocrust development (Belnap and Lange 2003), likely because silt can increase the water-holding capacity of the soil.

Because biocrusts often completely cover the soil surface, they mediate most inputs to and from desert soils, including gases, light and heat, water, dust, plant litter, and seeds. They thus play a central role in the functioning of desert ecosystems (see Figure 30.6; Belnap et al. 2003). All biocrust organisms are integral in the formation and stabilization of soils and are believed to have played this role since they first appeared on land seven hundred million to one billion years ago. These organisms accelerate soil weathering by altering soil pH through secretion of acids, calcium, and hydroxide. Rock and soil weathering also increase because biocrust organisms retard evaporation of soil moisture, increasing the length of time these materials are wet. Biocrusts are very effective at reducing or eliminating erosion of soil particles, as cyanobacterial and fungal filaments bind soil particles together (see Figure 30.5, top photograph). This soil-binding action does not depend on the presence of living filaments; layers of abandoned sheaths build up over long periods of time and can still be found clinging to soil particles at depth in the soil. Lichens and mosses also protect the soil surface from wind and water, reducing soil erosion that in the absence of biocrusts is substantial because of the deserts' low vegetative cover.

The external morphology of biocrusts influences resource retention as well. In the Great Basin Desert and higher elevations of the Mojave Desert, biocrusts roughen the soil surface as a result of frost-heaving upwards and differential erosion downwards. This roughening enhances water infiltration and the capture of dust, seeds, and other materials crossing the soil surface. In hotter areas where soils do not freeze, however, the presence of biocrust can flatten the soil surface, leading to less water infiltration and an accelerated loss of local materials.

Biocrusts also play other critical element-cycling roles in deserts. Biocrusts darken the soil surface, warming it through

FIGURE 30.5 Biological soil crusts. Photos: Jayne Belnap (top) and Todd Esque (bottom).

A A scanning electron micrograph of a biocrust (x 90). Cyanobacterial filaments wind among the sand grains, linking them together and conferring great soil surface stability.

B A close-up of the lichen-dominated biocrusts found on grussy granite soil surfaces. Note the tarantula in the photo.

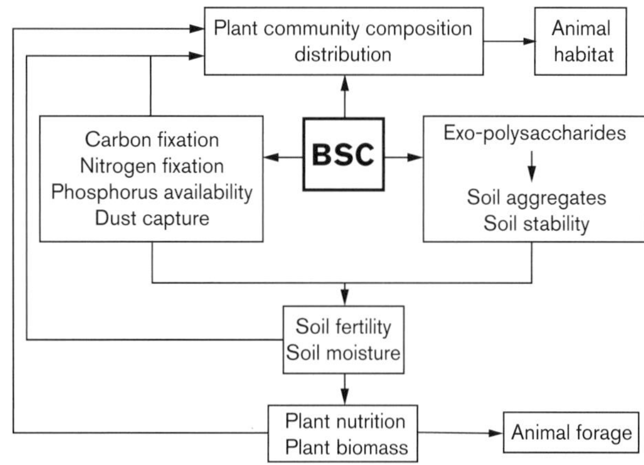

FIGURE 30.6 A conceptual model showing the many crucial roles biological soil crusts (BSC) play in the desert ecosystems of California.

increased absorption of sunlight, which increases soil nutrient transformation rates, plant growth, and soil biotic activity. Cyanobacteria, green algae, lichens, and mosses are all photosynthetic and thus contribute carbon to desert soils that are otherwise quite low in organic matter. Adequate carbon is required for microbial activity, and low levels slow decomposition and nutrient transformations. The carbon contributed by biocrusts can be substantial, often similar to the soil surface being covered by a vascular plant leaf. Biocrusts can also be the dominant source of nitrogen in deserts. As with carbon, the amount of nitrogen contributed can be large. Secretions by fungi and lichens free biologically unavailable phosphorus, another limiting nutrient, making it available to soil biota and vascular plants. Biocrust organisms can reduce the leaching of nutrients from soils, as their sticky sheaths are covered with clay particles to which essential nutrients cling. In addition, crust organisms secrete powerful metal chelators that maintain nutrients in plant-available forms—an important process in high pH desert soils (Belnap et al. 2003). As a result, vascular plants growing in biocrusted areas have higher levels of many essential nutrients than plants growing in areas without biocrusts. Although losses of carbon and nitrogen gases from soils are of great concern globally; the global significance of biocrust effects on these processes are not well understood.

The composition of the biocrust community can influence the composition of the vascular plant community. Almost all seed types, regardless of size or shape, can easily penetrate or be buried in bare soil or a thin, early successional biocrust with cracks, unless the soil is covered with a hard mineral crust. However, seeds with large appendages (e.g., exotic cheatgrass, *Bromus tectorum*) have difficulty penetrating a well-developed, late-successional lichen or moss biocrust that completely covers the soil surface. Therefore a very different vascular flora occurs where early successional cyanobacterially dominated biocrusts are prevalent compared to sites where moss-lichen biocrusts dominate. Biocrusts are highly vulnerable to compressional forces (e.g., trampling, vehicles) and are easily broken by soil surface disturbance. When this occurs, all seed types again obtain easy access to underlying soils. Plant community composition therefore reflects the tension between the successional sequence of the biocrust and disturbance. This dynamic creates a mosaic of soil, nutrient, and plant patch types that move and change through space and time and across multiple scales. There are also many direct ecosystem feedbacks with biocrusts (Schlesinger et al. 1990). For example, soil characteristics and climate influence the distribution of biocrust and vegetation types (Aguiar and Sala 1999), whereas biocrusts and vegetation type affect soil resources via water and nutrient input/uptake, litter deposition, and microclimate alteration. Once disturbed, recovery of biocrusts can be very slow. As biocrusts are only metabolically active when wet, recovery rates depend on rainfall, which is low in deserts. For instance, in the Colorado Desert a study of tank tracks showed only 3–6% recovery of lichens in the plant interspaces fifty years after disturbance (Belnap and Warren 2002).

The concept of a "critical zone," the area above and below the soil surface that is essential for supporting life, has become central in ecological thinking. In most ecosystems the belowground part of the critical zone is meters deep. In deserts, given that the majority of precipitation events are less than 5 millimeters and soil moisture is required for activity, biocrusts may define the critical zone for nutrients and many processes in deserts (Pointing and Belnap 2012). Because biocrusts influence almost all materials entering and leaving desert soils, they affect many aspects of ecosystem function and processes in these regions (Belnap et al. 2003). Thus their presence and composition influence trophic levels ranging from soil microbes to plants to the macrofauna that feed on the plants.

Decomposition

Decomposition—the breakdown of organic matter into its constituent parts—is a basic ecosystem process because much of the fertility of an ecosystem is bound up in these materials. Decomposition in deserts, like many other processes, is controlled more by abiotic factors than biotic ones (Whitford 2002, Ward 2009). Up to 85% of decomposition in deserts results from photodegradation, the process whereby ultraviolet sunlight breaks down compounds in leaves; and by wind, which breaks larger plant parts into smaller ones. Biotic decomposers include micro-organisms (bacteria, fungi, and actinomycetes) and macro-organisms (e.g., mites, collembolans nematodes, protozoa, ants, termites, and beetles). Because soil organisms depend on moisture and organic matter to fuel their activities, and because both are generally low in desert soils, the number and activity rates of soil organisms often is also low. Decomposition was thus long thought to be slow in deserts. However, more recent studies have shown that rates can be surprisingly fast, especially during wet years and periods where heat and soil moisture coincide (Ward 2009, Weatherly et al. 2003).

Soil fauna accelerate decomposition in several ways. First, macropores (or soil cavities) created by burrowing organisms allow more water to enter the soil, extending activity times for decomposers. Second, arthropods carry plant matter below the soil surface, preventing it from washing or blowing away and keeping it moist longer. Third, organic matter can be ingested, digested, and excreted by animals, both decomposing it and creating more easily degraded material. Finally, soil animals shred organic matter into smaller pieces, giving fungi and bacteria more surface area for enzymatic attack. Because fungi are able to be active at lower soil moisture, they are likely more important than bacteria in desert decomposition.

The Carbon Cycle

The role of carbon in global climate change has garnered much attention recently. This has led to the question of how much carbon is being stored in vegetation and soils relative to how much is being released to the atmosphere in different terrestrial ecosystems. As deserts have sparse vegetation and low growth rates, they are expected to have relatively low net carbon uptake compared to other ecosystems. Most studies from California and other U.S. deserts support this finding. Uptake values from creosote shrublands in the Mojave Desert were found to be 10–30 gC m^{-2} yr^{-1} (Lane et al. 1984, Rundel and Gibson 1996); in Arizona and New Mexico these values were 46–72 gC m^{-2} yr^{-1} (Chew and Chew 1965, Whittaker and Niering 1975, Huenneke and Schlesinger 2006). The carbon content of the other major pools from Mojave sites include plant tissues (25–65 gC m^{-2} [Schlesinger and Jones 1984]), with roughly similar amounts in roots. Small carbon pools are found in biocrusts (42 gC m^{-2}). This makes a total pool of ~170 gC m^{-2} in desert plants, compared to 19,300 gC m^{-2} for dry tropical forest plants (Jaramillo et al. 2003). Whereas soil organic matter pools are small (~670 gC m^{-2} in the 0–10 cm layer; Belnap, unpublished data), large pools of carbon are found in carbonates ($CaCO_3$) in hot desert soils (~30,000 g C m^{-2}; Schlesinger 1982). However, current soil carbonate accumulation is slow, ranging from 0.12 to 0.42 gC m^{-2} yr^{-1} (Schlesinger 1985, Marion et al. 2008), as it is largely constrained by the atmospheric deposition of calcium. Walvoord et al. (2005) found no evidence for substantial carbon accumulation in the deep unsaturated zone of soils in the Amargosa (Mojave) Desert and documented only a small net upward flux of CO_2 from soils to the atmosphere at that site. Other studies from nearby U.S. deserts also show desert soils to be a small net sink in spring and a small net source in fall (Bowling et al. 2011). There have been two studies from the Mojave reporting net ecosystem carbon uptake as large, but major concerns about values reported in these studies have been raised (Schlesinger et al. 2009).

The Nitrogen Cycle

Although in most years water is the limiting resource in deserts, nitrogen can be limiting in wet years. Indeed, after only a short time of above-average precipitation, nitrogen and phosphorus (P) limit plant growth. Nitrogen pools in desert soils are small compared to other ecosystems, as soils contain only ~0.02–0.12% N, compared to 1.2% in the boreal forest (Lavoie et al. 2011). In the northern Mojave, shrub nitrogen was estimated at 33 kgN ha^{-1} and total nitrogen (plants and soils) at three sites ranged from ~965–1,533 kgN ha^{-1}. Because of the relatively low vegetative biomass in deserts, 70–98% of the system's nitrogen can be found in the soils (Rundel and Gibson 1996). Wetter ecosystems receive most of their nitrogen via precipitation, but deserts have low precipitation and generally receive only ~1–2 kgN ha^{-1} yr^{-1} in nonurban areas. Nitrogen fixation by bacteria inside nodules on roots of legumes (e.g., mesquite) can be a good source at a very local scale, but the abundance of these plants is limited in California deserts, as are any contributions by free-living bacteria. Fixation by biocrusts can be a main source of nitrogen. They can contribute 4 kgN ha^{-1} yr^{-1} or more where they are exceptionally well developed; however, this value varies widely depending on lichen and cyanobacterial biomass. Dust inputs are important as well.

Nitrogen losses in these deserts have the potential to be very high. For example, McCauley and Sparks (2009) showed abiotic gaseous losses of ~3 kgN ha^{-1} yr^{-1} in the Mojave Desert. Soil erosion also can result in high levels of nitrogen loss, depending on site disturbance. For instance, losses were estimated at 2 kgN ha^{-1} yr^{-1} for one site in the Mojave ungrazed by livestock, whereas losses at nearby grazed sites were up to 24 kgN ha^{-1} yr^{-1} (Rundel and Gibson 1996). Because availability is low in desert soils, plants attempt to conserve what nitrogen they have in their tissue. Accordingly, many plants can move up to 40% of the nitrogen found in their leaves to their stems or roots before they drop their leaves. Another loss pathway can be through the death of biocrust organisms. Although data are lacking for the California deserts, data from the nearby Colorado Plateau desert showed that loss of biocrust moss substantially altered nitrogen cycles (Reed et al. 2012). In soils under dead mosses nitrate (NO_3^-) was higher and ammonium (NH_4^+) was lower than in soils beneath live mosses. Microbial nitrogen pools were also lower in soils with dead mosses. As nitrate is more easily lost from soils via leaching and gaseous losses, this switch from ammonium to nitrate could result in lowered total soil nitrogen. Also, type of nitrogen (NH_4^+ vs. NO_3^-) may be more important than quantity in regulating ecosystem function (Austin et al. 2004). Organisms can readily uptake and use ammonium, but if they are confronted with nitrate, they have to use energy to convert it to ammonium before uptake.

Nutrient Transfers and Distribution

It is generally believed that in all ecosystems, plants obtain the bulk of their nutrients from the soil via either plant roots or mycorrhizal fungi attached to their roots. Recent studies in deserts, however, have suggested that an additional mechanism may be operative in these regions. When labeled N and C were added to the top few millimeters of root-free interspace soil, both were detected in plants over 1 meter away within twenty-four hours (Green et al. 2008). The C label, but not the N label, from the plants was detected in biocrusts. Because the transfer occurred so quickly, these interspace compounds clearly bypassed bulk soils that would have resulted in a very slow transfer. As there were no roots in the soil, these compounds were most likely moved by a fungal network dominated by dark septate fungi, a type of endophytic fungi common in desert soils. Many nutrients are concentrated at the soil surface in deserts as the result of biocrust activity (e.g., C and N fixation, greater bioavailability of other nutrients such as P), dust deposition, and reduced loss via leaching because rainfall is low. This situation could favor the development of a fungal "highway" located at the soil surface that directly links biocrusts to nearby vascular plants (Collins et al. 2008, 2014).

In deserts, nutrients and organic matter are often concentrated under shrubs. These zones have been termed "islands of fertility" (e.g., Schlesinger et al. 1990, Walker et al. 2001). Because carbon, some nutrients, and soil moisture can be higher where these islands occur, the abundance and activity of soil fauna, decomposition, nutrient transformation rates, and nutrient availability are higher there as well. This concentration of nutrients and organic matter influences plant germination and growth. A variety of processes can lead to these patterns. Plants extract nutrients from the interspace soils with their roots and use them to build leaf and stem tissue. This tissue eventually dies and is dropped, enriching the soil beneath the plant. Plant canopies also provide shade so that soils retain moisture longer, which allows greater microbial activity and nutrient transformations, increasing nutrient availability.

In addition, soil and organic matter moved by wind and water from plant interspaces are intercepted by the plants (Soulard et al. 2013). This dynamic between "source" patches (where materials come from—in this case, the plant interspace) and "sinks" (where materials are deposited—in this case, under the plant canopy) can be a strong driver of ecosystem processes in deserts (Ludwig and Tongway 1997). Although the evidence is quite compelling that islands of fertility form in places where livestock grazing has heavily impacted plant interspaces (Schlesinger et al. 1990), fertile islands are less frequently observed where interspace soils are still covered by well-developed biocrusts and lack visible soil loss (Housman et al. 2007, Allington and Valone 2011). Therefore an alternative explanation for heterogeneous nutrient distributions in deserts is that heavy land use has resulted in "oceans of depletion" rather than "islands of fertility."

Primary Producers: The Vascular Plants

Adaptations to Extreme Conditions

The variable and extreme conditions found in deserts present a great challenge for plants, with the lack of water generally the most challenging condition plants face. Desert plants exhibit several strategies for surviving low levels of soil water: escape (e.g., annuals that escape as seeds), evasion (e.g., cacti that use tissue succulence or plants able to use perennial waters), endurance using deciduousness (e.g., bursage), or resistance (e.g., creosote). Some plants can combine these responses. For example, a drought resister can become drought-deciduous and drop its leaves when low soil water persists. Organisms can only work within the constraints of their evolutionary history, meaning all strategies are not possible for a given species. If, for instance, there is no genetic material orchestrating a leaf-drop response to drought, a plant will not be able to adopt this strategy. Many plants growing in deserts today did not originally evolve in a desert setting, so features seen in a given plant may be not adaptations to desert living but carryovers from some other set of conditions.

Desert plants have many structural and physiological adaptations to help them tolerate extreme conditions (Rundel and Gibson 1996). Their leaves are often fewer, small, and narrow (less than 10 millimeters wide). These leaves have a high surface-to-volume ratio that helps them stay below lethal temperatures without having to use evaporative cooling, thus conserving water. In addition, maximal photosynthetic rates often acclimatize as leaf temperatures increase (Rundel and Gibson 1996). Some plants can maintain both wide and narrow leaves, then drop the wide leaves when water is scarce. Water loss and leaf temperature can be reduced with stems and leaves that are thick and/or waxy; covered with light-colored hairs, spines, or salt crystals to reflect light; and either oriented parallel to incoming light (creosote, prickly pear) or able to track solar rays (e.g., sunflower [*Malvastrum rotundifolium*]). Pores (stomata) that allow gas exchange can occur on the underside of the leaf, where they are shaded; this reduces water loss when pores are opened.

Photosynthetic pathways can also help plants adapt to extremely dry conditions (Smith et al. 1997). All three pathways (C_3, C_4, and Crassulacean acid metabolism [CAM]) occur in desert plants. The C_3 pathway is the most common. Plants using this pathway open their stomata during the day to obtain CO_2 while ambient light allows for photosynthesis. However, these open stomata also release water from the plant's leaves, reducing water efficiency. For this reason, C_3 photosynthesis is especially abundant in winter-active plants, when water is less limiting. The C_4 pathway is thought to have evolved from the C_3 pathway, either because of, or allowing, a migration of grasses from shady forests to more open environments. The enzymes used in the C_4 pathway are more efficient at high light and temperatures found in open habitats and are also thought to have high water-use efficiency. Thus C_4 plants are most often summer annuals found in in the hottest desert locations or in very salty soils. In CAM photosynthesis, the leaf stomates remain shut during the day to reduce evapotranspiration and open at night for CO_2 uptake, making these plants much more water-use efficient than C_3 or C_4 plants. The CO_2 is stored until daytime, when it is used for photosynthethis. CAM is common in plants with succulent leaves and/or stems (e.g., cactus) and is highly correlated with aridity.

Roots of desert plants were long thought to go deeper than those of plants in other biomes to access deep water. While desert plants do not have the deepest roots of all biomes, their roots on average are deeper than most (Schwinning and Hooten 2009). However, desert plant root architecture is tremendously variable among both species and individuals within a species. Some plants have mostly surface, compact roots (e.g., grasses, prickly pear), some rely mostly on a deep taproot (e.g., mesquite), and others have roots that both spread widely and go deep (e.g., creosote). Root type is often a trade-off between the ability to transport smaller volumes of water in wetter soils (e.g., drought-deciduous shrubs) and the ability to operate in very dry soils (e.g., drought-tolerant evergreen shrubs). Multiple root types can occur in one plant (e.g., broom snakeweed [*Gutierrezia sarothrae*]). Root distributions often depend on geomorphic setting. For instance, plants along washes tend to lack lateral roots (e.g., Mormon tea [*Ephedra* spp.]), whereas many common shrubs in alluvial fan settings (e.g., creosote, bursage) have lateral roots as well as deep taproots (Rundel and Gibson 1996). Surface age, calcic horizons, soil texture, and desert pavements can all influence rooting patterns (Schwinning and Hooten 2009). On Holocene surfaces in one study, for example, creosote roots commonly penetrated to over 100 centimeters, whereas on Pleistocene surfaces, they were mostly restricted to the top 50 centimeters (Stevenson et al. 2009). Most roots are found at least 10 centimeters below the soil surface, as conditions are too hot and dry for root survival above that level. It was long believed that in the search for scarce water, desert plants should have far more roots relative to aboveground biomass than plants in wetter ecosystems. However, it turns out that the root-to-shoot ratio is very similar for perennial plants in both the Mojave Desert and temperate forests (0.5–1.0) (Rundel and Gibson 1996).

Desert roots also have a high capacity to extract water from dry soils through several strategies. First, some species like creosote can maintain turgor at much lower soil water levels than more mesic species and can therefore maintain a water potential gradient for water uptake from drying soils. Roots can appear within a day after rainfall events, follow soil moisture downward, and be shed after soils dry (Schwinning and Hooten 2009). Plants can also use hydraulic redistribution—a process whereby roots in moist soil layers absorb water and passively translocate it to roots in dry layers. This water is then exuded at night and reabsorbed the next morning, along with nutrients dissolved in the water. In this way plants can keep their entire root system active despite patchy water distribution in the soil (Caldwell et al. 1998). As released water can be taken by other plants, some plant roots such as creosote exude compounds to keep other plants' roots away, a process termed allelopathy (Mahall and Callaway 1992).

Another extreme condition desert plants often confront is salty soils. Rapid evaporation rates leave salts at the soil surface, and low rainfall prevents them from being leached downward into the soil. Salt levels can be toxic and difficult for plants to exclude. Plants have three options: (1) exclude salt-containing water at the root; (2) store salt in internal membrane-bound compartments, or vacuoles, making their leaves plump and liquid-filled, as seen in greasewood (*Sarcobatus vermiculatus*); or (3) exude salt onto their leaves (e.g., tamarisk) or into leaf hairs (e.g., saltbush). However, many plants are unable to utilize any of these techniques, which is why very salty soils support few, if any, plants. Plants that can tolerate salty soils are called halophytes.

As plants are a fundamental unit of ecosystems, both their three-dimensional shape and the pattern of their spacing are important aspects of ecosystem structure. These characteristics primarily define the habitat that animals "see" and food that is available to them. The architecture of a plant can be so important to some species of birds and spiders that they will inhabit a stick imitation of a shrub, ignoring the fact it is dead. Lizards that are "sit-and-wait" predators require shrubs with branches low enough to hide them, while sufficiently high to provide a clear line of sight and unencumbered access to prey. Many birds require perches of a certain height and select plant species accordingly.

The shape of a plant is a cost-benefit game. For instance, the shape and size of plants and individual branches can enhance water harvesting. Large, flat, spread-out canopies and horizontal branches intercept the most rain. Where the plant's shape delivers intercepted water is also important. The optimum is water delivery to where the plant's roots are concentrated, which requires inwardly sloping rather than flat branches. Shaded soils retain moisture longer, and concentrated canopies are best for creating shade. Light is not limiting in deserts, as there are wide spaces between plants, so unlike trees in a forest, desert plants generally expend energy to grow out rather than up. With so much light, desert plants can also be bushy without shading their own leaves, unlike their forest counterparts.

There are other design constraints on desert plants. For example, deserts often have extreme winds. In response, plants can be very stiff, such as blackbrush and cottonwood (*Populus fremontii*). This strategy can fail if winds are so strong the branches break. Alternatively, plants can be very limber and sway with the wind, like rabbitbrush (*Chrysothamnus* spp.), or can twist as they grow, like juniper and sagebrush. Some tall species, such as cottonwood, are able to regenerate vegetatively, and wind damage may create the possibility of new clones when fallen branches take root. Heat and water stress are also important in determining what a plant looks like: stems can act as water storage (cacti) or be arranged to maximize cooling (e.g., saltbush with vertical, reflective leaves).

Plant–Plant Interactions and Vegetation Dynamics

There are several factors that shape the spatial patterning of plants at a given site. Although light is important in determining these patterns in mesic regions, light is seldom limiting in deserts. Abiotic factors can heavily influence where plants grow at a very local scale. Biotic interactions, including rooting patterns and nurse plant interactions, can also structure plant patterns. Plants that root at the same depth may be in direct competition for water (Cody 1986)—a finding that is supported by the fact that the highest levels of plant diversity are found on coarse alluvial fans, where water can infiltrate to deeper levels. Conversely, surface-rooting plants (e.g., annuals) can intercept water before it infiltrates to depth, giving them an advantage over plants rooted below them. Allelopathic compounds secreted by creosote keep the roots of bursage and of other creosote plants at a distance, giving the creosote an evenly spaced pattern. Bursage roots, on the other hand, avoid contact with roots only of other bursage plants and are often found clumped with other species. Some desert shrubs have roots that go straight down from the plant base to a deep soil layer, turn ninety degrees, grow laterally for some distance, and then go straight back up to the surface, discouraging plants from growing in the space between the root and plant base (Gile et al. 1995, 1997). Therefore, root architecture can shape plant distributions for some species.

Nurse plants also influence plant distribution and composition patterns at a local scale. Nurse plants are larger established plants that shelter smaller plants, "nursing" them by providing shade and thus more soil moisture; cover to hide from predators; organic matter; and sometimes soil nutrients. In the Colorado Desert, ironwood may act as the nurse plant for a variety of plants. In the Mojave, Joshua trees often establish under a variety of shrubs and the desert agave (*Agave deserti*) under big galleta grass (*Pleuraphis rigida*). In many cases, the plant being nursed conveys a benefit to another species, and no harm is caused to either plant (Callaway 1995). However, in some cases the plant that is being nursed harms or eventually kills its benefactor (e.g., saguaros under paloverde; McAuliffe 1984). In an experimental study the nurse plants white bursage, creosote, and blackbrush potentially facilitated growth of other species, but their net effect was sometimes negative due to shading or root competition (Walker et al. 2001). It has been suggested that imitation of the nurse-plant phenomenon might be used to restore damaged ecosystems in harsh environments (Padilla and Pugnaire 2006).

Precipitation also has a profound influence on the composition and productivity of desert plant communities. For example, Beatley (1980) concluded that most perennial plants recorded in eastern Mojave plots in 1963 were still present in 1975, but the number of plants had increased by 20% to 30% due to a wet period in the late 1960s. Hereford et al. (2006) found that drought had resulted in a large increase in dead biomass on living plants, and Miriti et al. (2007) and McAuliffe and Hamerlynck (2010) concluded that drought had culled substantial numbers of creosote and bursage in the southeastern and eastern Mojave Deserts, with up to a 100% loss in both white bursage and triangle leaf bursage.

Because prolonged droughts and episodic wet periods characterize deserts, study results can depend on both what years are reported and the geographic location of the study area. Cody (2000) reported little change in a creosote-white bursage plot near the border of the central and eastern Mojave Deserts (see Figure 30.2) measured at an interval of twenty-five years; however, the two measures of this single plot spanned a wet period. Similarly, plots in the Colton Hills, measured periodically from 1966 to 2001 (Smith and Smith 2002), showed little change with time. Although these studies would appear to refute claims of pronounced long-term change in Mojave Desert vegetation, they were mostly conducted in wet periods and show little drought effect.

Two extensive and very long-term studies examining vegetative change have been performed in the California deserts. In the Great Basin Desert of northeastern California, sixty-eight transects measured between 1957 and 1998 showed a large increase in juniper and pinyon and a concomitant decrease in antelope bitterbrush (*Purshia tridentata*) and big sage (Schaefer et al. 2003). The transition from sage-bitterbrush shrublands to juniper-pinyon woodlands substantially reduced the shrub food base for ungulates (Schaefer et al.

2003). Another long-term study was begun at the Nevada National Security Site (NNSS, formerly Nevada Test Site) in the eastern Mojave in 1963 (Beatley 1980) and remeasured in 1975–2011 (Webb et al. 2003, R. H. Webb, unpublished data). Changes observed in these plots illustrate the tension between vegetation increases (e.g., germination, establishment, and productivity) during sustained wet periods and decreases (e.g., branch pruning and mortality) during droughts. Low-elevation sites showed the greatest changes at NNSS, with drought resulting in a high mortality of chenopods (e.g., spiny hopsage [*Grayia spinosa*], saltbushes, and winterfat [*Krascheninnikovia lanata*]). Wet years, such as those in the early 1980s, resulted in dominance by Indian ricegrass (*Achnatherum hymenoides*) (Figure 30.7). Subsequent drought reduced these grasses, leaving Anderson thornbush (*Lycium andersonii*) dominant by 2011. Extreme cold affected plants as well over the monitoring period, decreasing cover of spiny menodora (*Menodora spinescens*), brittlebush (*Encelia farinosa*), barrel cactus (*Ferocactus eastwoodii*), and prickly pear cactus (*Opuntia*; Webb et al. 2003; Webb, DeFalco et al. 2009). Overall, creosote-dominated areas increased in cover, despite fluctuations in associated subshrubs (Figure 30.8). Exceptions occurred in some lower-elevation creosote assemblages with substantial chenopod die-off. At higher elevations, blackbrush and big sage assemblages generally lost cover but had low mortality; however, pinyon and juniper trees increased in cover. Thus long-term vegetation response strongly depends on elevational gradients and species composition.

Changes observed over a half century at NNSS underscore the potential for climatically driven processes to significantly alter the structure, function, and species composition of perennial vegetation in the Mojave Desert. Shrub assemblages in this part of the Mojave Desert respond to climatic events as aggregations of individual species, not as a collective community, and directional changes can occur without immediate rebound. For some species climatically induced changes may rival the magnitude of some changes caused by land-use practices such as dispersed livestock grazing and vehicular recreation.

Finally, succession in plant communities—a process whereby early colonizing plant are replaced over time by plants considered to be late colonizers—is a central tenet in many ecosystem studies. However, succession appears less operative in deserts. Long-term transects and repeat photography indicates that a wide variety of plants can become established at a site after disturbance and, once there, can persist for extraordinary lengths of time. It may be that by garnering available nutrients and water, the initial colonizers simply keep other plants from establishing. Nevertheless, certain species that are most often found in disturbed sites, such as cheesebush (*Hymenoclea*), snakeweed, and tumbleweed (*Salsola*), and these often do eventually give way to longer-lived shrubs.

Key Consumers

Food Webs and Trophic Pyramids

Nutrients and energy are captured by plants and subsequently eaten by animals. These complex resource networks have long been described as food webs—a concept introduced nearly one hundred years ago to simplify complicated biotic interactions (Elton 1927). Food webs can be immensely complicated and multidirectional, as illustrated by the numerous connections among just a few of the predaceous arthropods living in the Coachella Valley of the Colorado Desert (Polis 1991) (Figure 30.9). These organisms then fit within an even bigger food web, as they consume and are consumed by others.

Another conceptual model used to describe the movement of resources through ecosystems, the trophic pyramid, not only describes the directional flow of nutrients through organisms but also groups organisms with similar ecosystem functions into trophic levels (e.g., producers, primary consumers, omnivores, predatory consumers). Higher trophic levels feed on those below them; the primary producers (plants) support all consumers in an ecosystem, either directly or indirectly. First-order consumers, animals that eat plants, include herbivorous insects and their larvae, some reptiles and birds, many small mammals, and ungulates. Granivores eat the seeds of plants. Many ants, birds, and small mammal species are particularly important granivores because they consume a large proportion of total seed production. Preferences for certain seed characteristics (e.g., size, shape, nutrient content) of granivores influences the composition of the seed bank, often determining the composition of the plant community and the recovery of desert landscapes after disturbance (Esque 2004). Pollinators often consume plant nectar or pollen. Whereas most pollinators are insects, some vertebrates perform this role (e.g., bats and hummingbirds). Folivores, animals that eat plant leaves and stems, include invertebrates, reptiles, amphibians, birds, and small and large mammals. Frugivores, animals that consume plant fruits, are also very common among the various animal groups.

Second- and third-order consumers feed on organisms in trophic levels below them. Complex food web interactions often make it difficult to classify species as strictly second- or third-order consumers. Position in a food web also can vary among individuals within a species, depending on resource availability. Top predators can often feed at any consumer level of the pyramid. Many animals are omnivorous consumers, eating both plant and animal materials. Omnivores are dominated by birds and mammals that adapt to food shortages by accepting a variety of foods. Decomposers complete the loop, breaking down dead plants and animal materials and enabling the nutrients and carbon contained within these materials to reenter the ecosystem.

Each time organisms are consumed, up to 90% of their resources are lost to the environment through inefficiencies such as heat transfer and physiological by-products, reducing resources available to support the abundance of individuals in each successively higher trophic level (Rundel and Gibson 1996). Therefore primary plant producers have the greatest mass, followed by primary consumers, and so on, such that top-order predators are quite rare, resulting in a pyramid of biomass, species diversity, and abundance. Limited numbers of species in the higher tropic levels especially occur in desert ecosystems, where prey are usually less abundant and more sporadically available than in mesic environments.

Animal Adaptations to Desert Life

Desert animals have many behavioral and physiological adaptations to extreme desert conditions, especially high temperatures and lack of water. Maintaining sublethal body temperatures is achieved through a combination of body size, activity

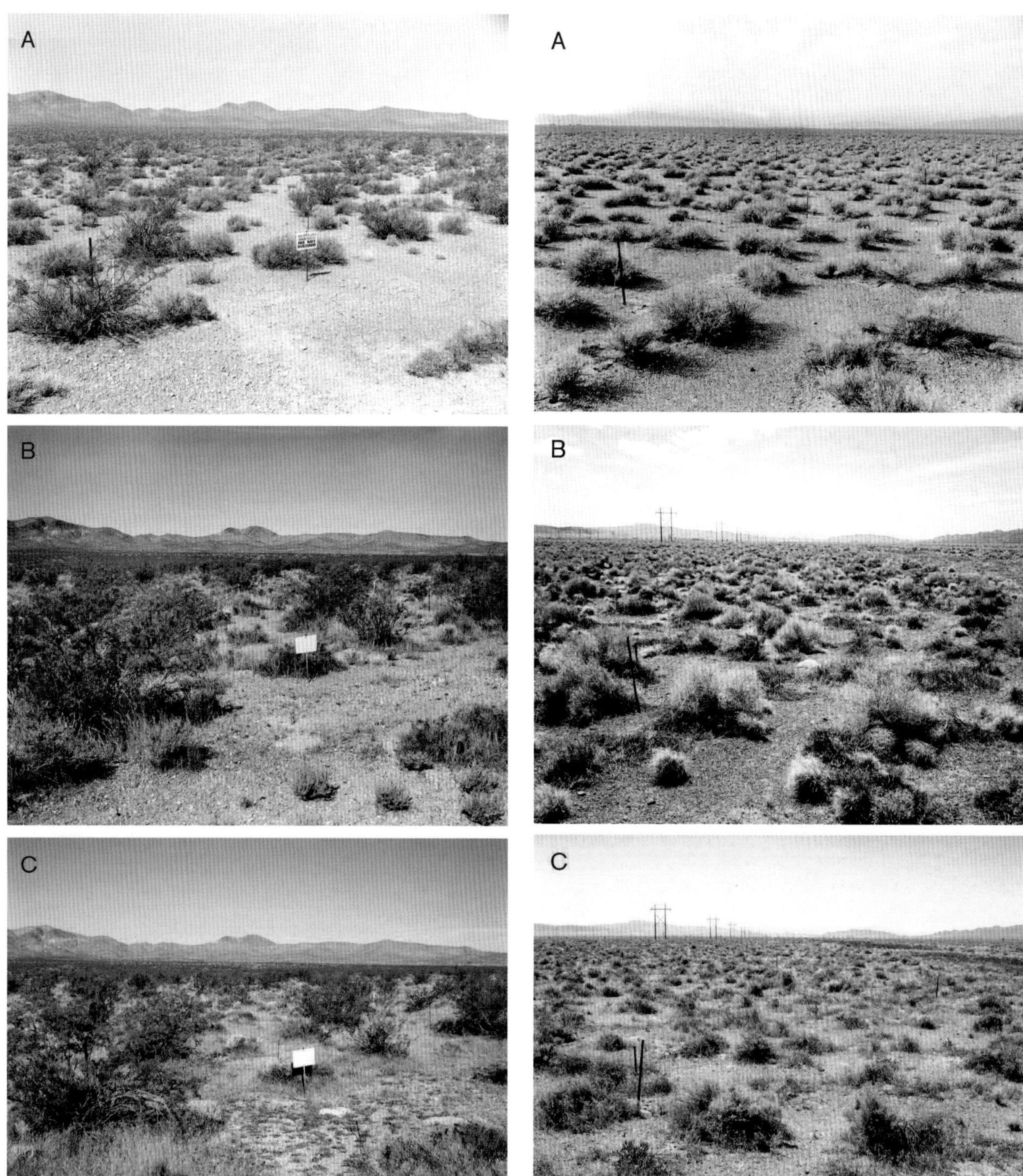

FIGURE 30.7 Photographs of Plot 2, a mixed-shrub assemblage visually dominated by creosote bush (*Larrea tridentata*), on the Nevada National Security Site (NNSS), formerly Nevada Test Site. Source: R. H. Webb et al. unpublished data.

A 1964: A mixture of shrubs is present, notably creosote bush, spiny hopsage (*Grayia spinosa*), and winterfat (*Krasheninikovia lanata*). White bursage (*Ambrosia dumosa*) is a minor component of this assemblage.

B 2000: Creosote bush now dominates this plot in terms of cover; white bursage is the co-dominant. Spiny hopsage and winterfat cover is greatly reduced because of drought effects from 1989 through 1991.

C 2011: Although reduced in cover due to the early twenty-first-century drought, creosote bush and white bursage are the co-dominants with Mormon tea (*Ephedra nevadensis*), which has increased in cover.

FIGURE 30.8 Photographs of Plot 50, Nevada National Security Site, formerly Nevada Test Site, which has been undisturbed for its forty-eight years of existence as a monitoring plot. Source: R. H. Webb et al. unpublished data.

A 1964: At this time, the plot was dominated by chenopods, primarily spiny hopsage (*Grayia spinosa*) and winterfat (*Krashinennikovia lanata*).

B 2001: Drought decimated the chenopods, resulting in an assemblage dominated by Indian rice grass (*Achnatherum hymenoides*).

C 2011: Anderson's thornbush (*Lycium andersonii*), which tends to co-occur with spiny hopsage, now dominates this plot.

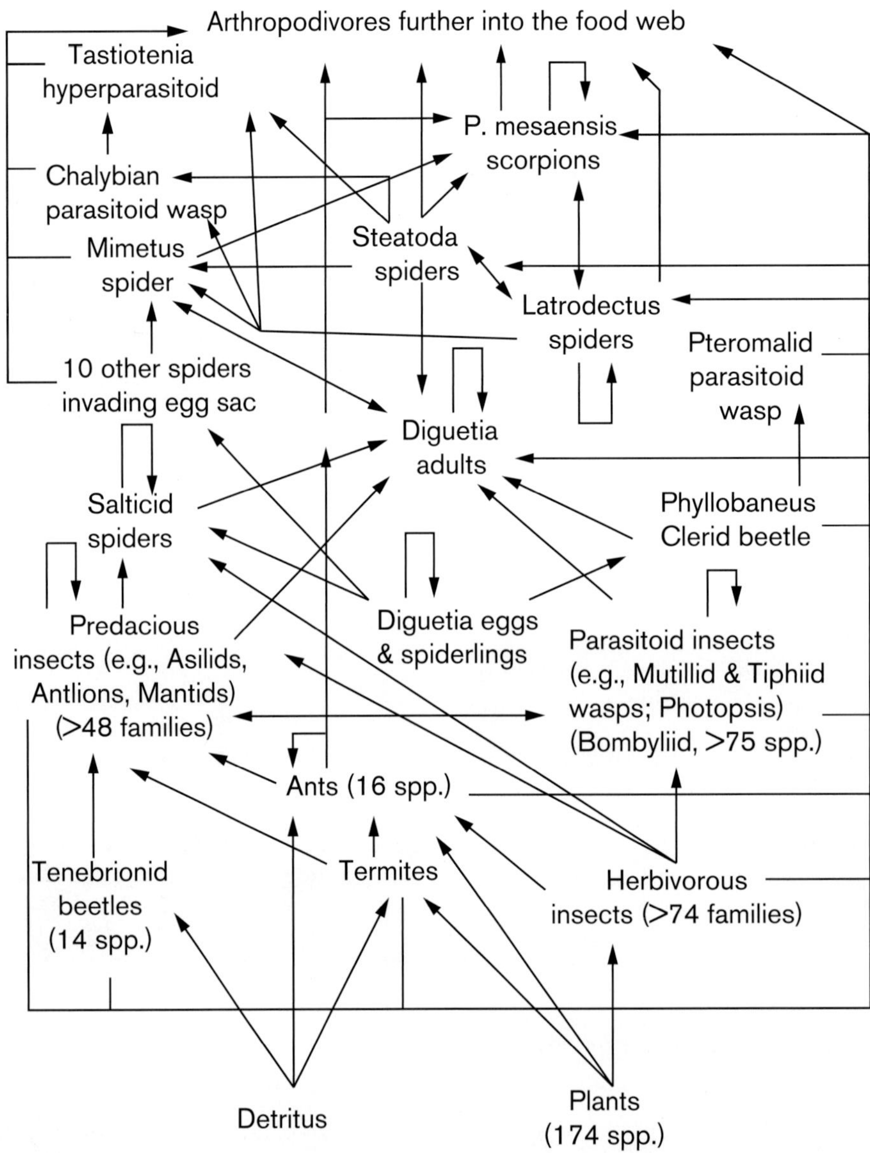

FIGURE 30.9 Trophic interactions above the soil surface involving a few of the predacious arthropods living within the Coachella Valley, Colorado Desert. This subweb is focused around the spiders *Diguetia mojavea* and *Latrodectus hesperus*. An arrow returning to a taxon indicates cannibalism. Source: Polis 1991.

patterns, microhabitat selection, coloration, metabolic rate regulation, hyperthermia (storing body heat and releasing it hours later), and countercurrent heat exchange systems (using blood). Water balance and osmoregulation are also closely regulated. As different animal groups utilize different mechanisms to regulate temperature, water, and solute concentrations, these various approaches are discussed by animal group below. There are, however, some aspects in common among all groups. Optimal body temperatures for desert animals range from 35°C to 39°C, several degrees higher than for nondesert animals (Schmidt-Nielson 1990, Rundel and Gibson 1996). Despite this, most desert animals still cannot be active on hot summer days. To avoid the heat, many animals (including invertebrates, reptiles, and small mammals) employ burrows. Soil temperatures just 30 centimeters below the surface can be a comfortable 33°C in summer, varying only 1–2°C over a twenty-four-hour period. Burrow air is also highly humid, reducing the amount of water vapor lost during respiration. Coloration may play a role in regulating heat loss and gain. However, as animals range in color from very light to black (e.g., common raven [(*Corvus coras*], tenebrionid beetles), it is not clear whether coloration serves to avoid predation, to regulate temperature, or a combination of both. Body size is important in thermoregulation, as animals with larger bodies have a lower surface-to-volume ratio and therefore gain heat more slowly.

Water loss through evaporation and respiration is a common problem for all animals but is especially acute for desert dwellers for two reasons. First, hot dry times when water losses through evaporation and respiration are the highest (e.g., summer) are also the times when water is least available as free surface water or in vegetation. Second, the potential for rapid water loss during these hot dry times, resulting in high fluid electrolyte concentrations, is extremely high in deserts and can quickly cause great stress (Schmidt-Nielson 1990). The water flux of an animal is the rate of water gain and loss per day. Water is lost via excretion (urine and feces) and evaporation from respiration and body surfaces. Water gain occurs through drinking, eating food that contains water, or body surfaces. Daily loss of water is linearly and positively correlated with the mass of an animal (Schmidt-Nielson 1990, Rundel and Gibson 1996). For example, a 10 gram bird loses twice as much water each day than a 5 gram bird. This rule of thumb is true for reptiles, birds, mammals, and arthropods, though the amount of water lost differs among the animal groups, with reptiles and arthropods by far the most water efficient, followed by mammals, then birds. A 10 gram bird loses water three times faster than a 10 gram rodent; the rodent, in turn, loses six times the water of a 10 gram reptile. In general, desert vertebrates are more water efficient than nondesert vertebrates. However, organisms in the California deserts do not have specialized internal water storage and must instead conserve it. The trade-off with body mass places animals in a conundrum: larger body size prevents excess heat gain but accelerates water loss.

INVERTEBRATES

Invertebrates are the most abundant, diverse, and highest in total biomass of desert faunal groups, making them essential to many ecosystem processes (Crawford 1981). Most invertebrates are first-order consumers and include herbivores, pollinators (especially bees, wasps, moths, and butterflies), granivores, and/or root herbivores. Some invertebrates prey on other invertebrates. Other invertebrates decompose plant (detritivores) and animal materials (coprovores eat fecal material, necrovores eat carcasses). Invertebrates also are eaten by many second- and third-order consumers as well as by top predators. Outside of their role in food pyramids, invertebrates have many important influences on plant community composition through herbivory, seed predation, and seed dispersal. Invertebrates also influence soil structure and fertility as the result of burrowing and vertebrate community structure by providing food to these animals.

Desert invertebrate communities generally involve larger body sizes, higher abundances of predatory insects, a larger predator-to-prey ratio, and increased sociality in groups with predicable food resources (e.g., ants, termites) when compared to nondesert groups (Crawford 1986). Most arthropods avoid temperature extremes to some degree (Whitford 2002), as their optimal temperature range is between 30°C and 39°C, with 46°C being lethal (Rundel and Gibson 1996). Behavioral adaptions include seeking lower temperatures in the day by burrowing into sand, leaf litter, or finding deep shade (e.g., centipedes, millipedes); being active at night, dawn, and/or dusk (e.g., tenebrionid beetles, arachnids); or moving up and down in plant canopies (e.g., grasshoppers). Some species combine these strategies. For instance, termites use deep burrows and limit their activity to times of favorable temperatures. Invertebrates also have physiological adaptations to desert conditions. Their relatively small body size means they have a large surface-to-volume ratio that can result in faster and greater heat gain.

On the other hand, that same small body size means that heat generated by activity or from the air can be quickly lost. To control water loss, many invertebrates have a cuticle, a hard outside coat. Water vapor is allowed to leave through small holes in the cuticle (spiracles), allowing some evaporative cooling. These cuticles are often covered by thick waxes with high melting points (Rundel and Gibson 1996). In one study, desert arthropods were found to be more water efficient and have lower evaporation rates than similar species from nondesert regions (Crawford 1981). Many soil invertebrates can also use anhydrobiosis, the ability to desiccate and suspend all activity until wetted, to avoid extreme conditions (Crawford 1981). Lastly, some arthropods, such as the desert cockroach (*Arenivaga investigata*), can replenish body water by absorbing it from unsaturated air in their burrows (Rundel and Gibson 1996).

Some of the more important, visible, and interesting invertebrates in deserts include ants, termites (discussed below), bees, moths, butterflies, grasshoppers, and scorpions. Ants are a vital component of most desert ecosystems, as they engineer many aspects of the environment. Ants are both first- and second-order consumers and provide food for many other animals. The diversity of ant species follows a climatic gradient in the California deserts (Figure 30.10). Harvester ants are especially important, as they move large quantities of nutrient-containing subsurface soil, seed coats, and insects (80–280 kg soil ha^{-1} yr^{-1}) to the surface when they create their mounds, increasing soil fertility (Parmenter et al. 1984, Taber 1998). Several ant species clear vegetation around their nests, affecting plant distribution patterns, and make mounds up to 5 meters wide and 1 meter high, affecting local hydrologic patterns. Colony densities range from twenty to fifty colonies per hectare. As a group, harvester ants eat more than one hundred species of seeds, but different species often show narrow seed preferences. Unlike rodents, ants usually collect seeds from the soil surface. Like rodents, ants play a role in seed dispersal because they drop many of the seeds they collect (MacMahon et al. 2000, DeFalco et al. 2010). Ant nests also provide refuge for other animal species, including beetles, orthopterans, termites, homopterans, collembollans, thysanurans, diplurans, millipedes, spiders, and mites. In a southeastern Arizona study, harvester ant mounds contained thirtyfold higher densities of microarthropods and fivefold more protozoans than plots without mounds (Wagner et al. 1997).

Native bees are one of the most diverse groups in California deserts. As pollinators, they are first-order consumers. Solitary bees, which do not live in colonies, do most of the pollination in desert ecosystems (Crawford 1986). This may result from the low quantity and unpredictability of desert flowers, making this food source too unreliable to support large bee colonies. Desert bee sizes range from tiny to some of the largest bees in California. This range in size may help partition resources so that more species can be supported in a given setting. In addition, many bees are oligolectic, meaning they specialize on one plant species.

Moths and butterflies are also important consumers of plant material. Adults deposit eggs on plant leaves; when the eggs hatch, the resulting caterpillars eat the plant leaves. Often, the adults pollinate the plant at the same time they deposit their eggs. Similar to bees, the larvae are often oligolectic. Thus, through herbivory, moths and butterflies can heavily influence plant community composition. Moths and butterflies are also important prey items for birds and reptiles. Grasshoppers consume vegetation and, as they are often quite numerous, can have a large impact on desert vegetation. While some species eat many different plant species (polyphagy), other grasshopper species eat only a specific plant (monophagy). For example, the creosotebush grasshopper (*Bootettix argentatus*) is found only on creosote. This grass-

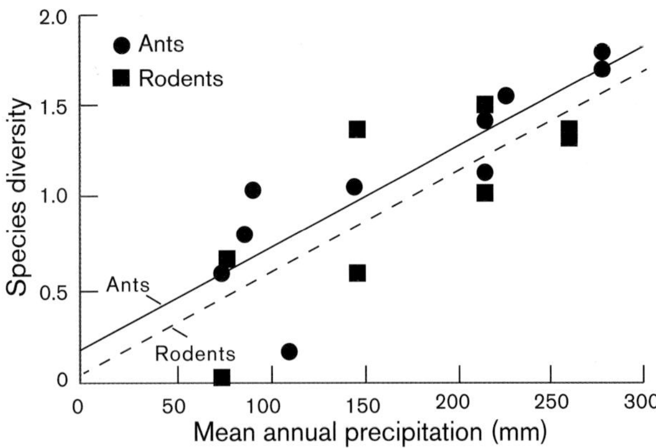

FIGURE 30.10 The effect of mean annual precipitation on desert ant and rodent species diversity in the deserts of the southwestern United States. Source: Davidson 1977.

Ants: Y=0.0054X+0.1774, r=0.93, p<0.01.

Rodents: Y+0.0057X-0.0140, r=0.87, p<0.01.

hopper is stimulated to bite the creosote leaves by the presence of nordihydroguaiaretic acid (NDGA) that can comprise up to 10% of the dry weight of the leaf. In contrast, other grasshoppers can barely tolerate NDGA. Host specificity of the creosotebush grasshopper is enhanced by its avoidance of compounds present in the surface waxes of other plant species. These tight relationships between invertebrates and their hosts can change through time, as herbivores become more tolerant of the plant's defensive compounds or the plants increase their unpalatability. These changes influence the stress placed on both parties, as making defensive compounds is an expense to the plant and digesting these compounds costs the herbivore. The outcome of such relationships can profoundly affect the structure of an ecosystem. If a plant is highly defended, decreased herbivory allows it to put more resources toward growth, while the herbivores may starve or move to other hosts. Conversely, if not defended enough, the plant may die from herbivory or other stresses.

Scorpions are important second- and third-order consumers in the California deserts, particularly the Mojave and Colorado Deserts. California possesses at least twenty-five species of desert scorpions. Several species occur almost exclusively in the Colorado Desert, and the Mojave Desert also has multiple endemics. Scorpions are nocturnal, and those seen at night are usually females that stay in the burrow entrance. Scorpions feed on a wide variety of small animals, including insects, small lizards, and small mammals. The chitinous shell of scorpions glows when illuminated by black light (Stahkne 1972). This shell is quite impervious to water loss; scorpions, as a result, have one of lowest evaporation loss rates recorded in desert animals (Rundel and Gibson 1996).

Mimicry is commonly found in desert invertebrates. In the Mojave Desert the blister beetle (*Meloe franciscanus*) gathers in large groups on plants, including the Borrego milkvetch (*Astragalus lentiginosus* var. *borreganus*), a California-listed endangered forb. On this plant blister beetle larvae aggregations mimic the outline of one species of female solitary bee (*Habropoda pallida*), which is depends on the nectar of the plant (Hafernik and Saul-Gershenz 2000). The larvae aggregations also release pheromones to attract male bees (Anderson et al. 2002). When male bees attempt to mate with what they perceive to be a female bee, the beetle larvae attach themselves to the males and are transferred to female bees during subsequent sexual contact. The female bee then inadvertently transports the beetle larvae to the bee's nest, where pollen, nectar, and the bee's eggs provide nutrition for the larvae. Both the beetle and the bee utilize and are dependent at various times on the Borrego milkvetch, which provides the link in this unusual food web.

VERTEBRATES

Vertebrates represent less than 1% of the individuals or biomass in California desert ecosystems (Chew and Chew 1965, Brown and Maurer 1986). Their low numbers mean their direct influence is limited and occurs through their consumption of prey, as prey for others, and movement and modification of objects (e.g., soil, seeds, feces, plant stems, and leaves). However, vertebrates profoundly influence ecosystems by regulating organisms (e.g., plants, invertebrates) and processes (e.g., nutrient cycling) that directly influence the ecosystem. Many of the activities of vertebrates are selective, such as when an animal preferentially eats a specific plant or burrows in a specific soil texture or on a particular geomorphic surface, influencing landscape structure and function. Although desert vertebrates have many behavioral and physiological adaptations to desert conditions, most attempt to avoid these extremes by being active, growing, and reproducing when or where moderate conditions prevail. This may be a season (e.g., spring), time of day (e.g., dawn/dusk or nighttime) or a microclimate (e.g., burrows, rock crevices, plant canopies). To survive times when conditions are extreme, vertebrates can also employ hibernation (lowered metabolism in winter) or estivation (lowered metabolism in summer).

Physiological adaptations are also important to survival. One strategy that is common to many vertebrate groups is countercurrent heat-exchange, where the heat in blood going to the brain is transferred to blood leaving the heart. This process allows the animal to function at body temperatures that would be lethal to the brain. Blood can also be moved near the skin to release heat to the air or deeper within the body to conserve the heat. In addition, most native vertebrates (e.g., reptiles, birds, rodents, and large mammals) in the California deserts do not sweat, reducing evaporative water loss through the skin. Exceptions to this include the non-native burro (*Equus asinus*) and the native desert bighorn (*Ovis canadensis nelson*), which both have sweat glands, although it is not known if they sweat. The largest source of water loss for vertebrates is the use of respiratory surfaces for evaporative cooling. For example, lizards can exhale air 7°C lower than air temperature (Schmidt-Nielson 1990). Panting is a common way to thermoregulate for reptiles and mammals, especially larger ones, and can lower body temperatures to 40°C at ambient temperatures of 50°C (Schmidt-Nielson 1990). However, if free surface water is not available, vertebrates need to use and expend the water found in certain food sources such as green vegetation, arthropods, and invertebrate larvae.

Excessive water loss can have large repercussions for all vertebrates if the electrolytes (i.e., potassium, sodium, and chloride salts) in their bodily fluids get too concentrated, a situation that negatively affects many physiological processes. Vertebrates have a fairly small range of acceptable electrolyte concentrations. When electrolyte concentrations are too dilute, water is released as urine to concentrate the salts; if salts are too concentrated, the salts are excreted. Desert vertebrates therefore need high tolerance for extended periods of dehydration and the resulting high salt concentrations. Water loss can be limited by (1) reducing water in feces and urine, (2) reducing evaporation from body surfaces, (3) utilizing nasal passages to reclaim water, and (4) using salt glands to excrete salts. As reptiles, birds, and mammals handle these challenges differently, their various approaches are discussed by group in the following sections.

REPTILES AND AMPHIBIANS: Reptiles are relatively abundant in the Mojave Desert. They can be first-, second-, and third-order consumers (eating invertebrates and other reptiles) as well as omnivores. Reptiles provide an important food base for other animals. In addition, their burrowing affects soil and hydrologic properties and creates habitat for other species. Lizards represent a large proportion of the desert vertebrate biomass. At NNSS, 123 lizard individuals weighing a total 182 grams were found per hectare (Rundel and Gibson 1996). In contrast, the most common snake, the western shovel-nosed snake (*Chionactis occipitalis*), averaged only five to ten individuals per hectare, and other snakes generally had less than one individual per hectare. Therefore, the overall contribution by snakes to animal biomass, at about 70 g ha^{-1}, can be small compared to lizards.

Reptiles are ectothermic, meaning their body temperatures vary with the external environment. However, they have a narrow range of acceptable body temperatures for activity similar to arthropods: temperatures between 30°C and 39°C are optimal, and 46°C is lethal. Thus, while the California deserts have many year-round resident reptiles, most avoid seasonal and even daily environmental extremes through behavioral adaptations. When cold, reptiles precisely orient themselves to the sun and warm surfaces (including flattening and spreading their ribs) for optimal heat gain. When optimal temperatures are exceeded, they seek protected places such as heavy shade, sand dunes, vertical rock faces, burrows, or crevices. Because of their dependency on external temperatures, the activity times of reptiles varies with the season. For example, in winter they may be active only during the middle of warm days, whereas in summer they may avoid activity during that time. Lizards often store fat in their tails, allowing them to reduce insulating fat over most of their body and facilitating efficient heat loss.

Few reptiles are known to drink free water in the wild, with the notable exception of the desert tortoise (*Gopherus agassizii*). This species has been observed to scrape out shallow depressions that fill with rainwater and then drink the water through its snout to flush uric acid from its kidneys. Some reptiles can utilize metabolic water, formed during the oxidation of carbohydrates, but no known species can rely on it alone. All reptiles need to ingest water-containing food, including insects, other invertebrates, and plants to maintain positive water balance. Reptiles can excrete uric acid and very dry fecal pellets to reduce excretory water loss. The majority of lizards also have salt glands that excrete potassium, sodium, and chloride with minimal water loss. Carnivorous lizards, however, ingest fewer salts and are less likely to use salt glands. Desert tortoises lack salt glands but accumulate high levels of electrolytes in their bladder, which they flush when surface water is available.

As ecototherms, reptiles have much lower energy requirements than mammals or birds; their metabolic rates are only 10–20% of mammals or birds at the same body temperature. Combined with long periods of inactivity when body temperatures are suboptimal, this means reptiles require only 1–5% of the energy needed by mammals or birds (Brown and Maurer 1986). A given desert environment can thus support a far greater abundance and biomass of reptiles than that of mammals or birds. A large reptilian biomass can then support a large biomass of animals dependent on them as prey. As reptile abundance and biomass increase, the impact of reptiles on the surrounding habitat as the result of burrowing, herbivory, and predation increases.

Several notable species of reptiles occur in the California deserts. The Gila monster (*Heloderma suspectum*) is the largest and only venomous lizard present in these deserts (Lovich and Beaman 2007). It feeds on small lagomorphs, ground squirrels, birds, and desert tortoise eggs. As it is carnivorous, it does not possess salt glands. The second largest lizard, the common chuckwalla (*Sauromalus ater*), is herbivorous, feeding on flowers and leaves. It lives in rocky areas, where it seeks refuge in crevices and either estivates or hibernates, depending on the time of year, when food supplies are low or it is physiologically stressed. During hibernation, its metabolic rates drop to 80% of active rates, keeping weight loss and water flux very low. The common chuckwalla appears unable to concentrate urine even when electrolyte loading is high. The desert iguana (*Dipsosaurus dorsalis*) is another large herbivore, feeding on leaves, fruit, and flowers and is limited to sandy habitats. It has salt glands through which it can excrete 43% of ingested potassium, 49% of ingested sodium, and 93% of ingested chloride (Rundel and Gibson 1996).

Most small lizards (e.g., the side-blotched lizard, *Uta stansburiana*) feed on insects or other small animals and are also prey for larger reptiles, birds, and mammals. The desert tortoise is an icon of the Mojave Desert, as both the largest native reptile in California's deserts and the California state reptile (Box 30.1). The California deserts also support six rattlesnake species. Of special interest are the Mojave rattlesnake (*C. scutulatus*), as it is unusually aggressive for a rattlesnake and possesses both a cardiotoxin and a neurotoxin; the sidewinder (*C. cerastes*), which is a small, sand-dwelling specialist; and the rare red diamond rattlesnake (*C. ruber*), found mainly on the coast and in the Colorado Desert. Several unusual snakes also have noses adapted for burrowing in sand dunes.

Amphibians are quite uncommon in deserts, as they have little tolerance for high temperatures, highly permeable skin, and very dilute urine that results in rapid water loss (Whitford 2002). Most desert amphibians are only found where standing water is available, such as at palm oases, springs, or temporary water pools (*tinajas*) present for a short time after rain events. One exception is the spadefoot toad (*Scaphiopus* sp.), which has multiple adaptations that allow it to survive desert extremes. Behaviorally, the toad digs deep burrows in the soil with its large, spade-like back feet and lies dormant in the burrow for ten to eleven months a year, waiting for an intense rainy period to emerge and lay eggs. Spadefoot toads have several physiological adaptations to desert conditions, including one of the fastest reproductive cycles known in amphibians: eggs hatch within one to two days, and froglets develop within a few weeks. These toads, like other amphibians, have highly permeable skin, which allows them to extract sufficient water from the soil during dormancy to keep them alive. When out of their burrow, however, spadefoot toads are extremely vulnerable to water stress and must lay their eggs and dig another burrow hastily to avoid drying out. Spadefoots also line their burrow with mucus to enhance water

BOX 30.1 SOME CALIFORNIA DESERT ICONS

CALIFORNIA FAN PALM: The California fan palm (*Washingtonia filifera*) is the only native palm in southwestern North America. It has disjunct distributions in the Colorado and Mojave Deserts, with many groves occurring in oases along the San Andreas fault system in the Coachella Valley and in valleys emanating from the Transverse Ranges in the Colorado Desert. These oases are very diverse: a study of the vegetation of twenty-four oases in the western Colorado Desert identified seventy-eight species of plants from thirty-four families (Vogl and McHargue 1966). Palm groves provide shelter for a number animal species, including birds, rodents, frogs, and some uncommon species such as the western yellow bat (*Lasiurus xanthinus*). Periodic fires are an important aspect of palm survival, as they are fire resistant unless fire suppression leads to a dense understory that increases fire intensity. Kamia and Cahuilla Indians chose palm groves as village sites (Parish 1907). These palms have now been introduced into many areas throughout the desert.

CALIFORNIA'S DESERT YUCCAS: In the Agavaceae family, California's desert yuccas have stiff whorls of narrow leaves ranging from 10 to 50 centimeters long that can painfully puncture the skin. The appearance of the various species can vary widely, ranging from small clumps to erect, treelike plants as tall as 10 meters. Their pallid cream-colored flowers, forming clusters on branch tips, are strongly scented. The pollination system of yuccas is highly specialized and has long been of interest to scientists (Pellmyr and Leebens-Mack 1999), including Charles Darwin (1874). Twenty of twenty-seven yucca species with known pollinators depend on a single species of moths for pollination (Smith et al. 2011). Each Joshua tree variety (also yuccas) has a mutualistic relationship with a single moth species. Variety *brevifolia* is pollinated by a small dark moth named *Tegeticula synthetic*, and variety *jaegeriana* is pollinated by *T. antithetica*. To complicate things, "cheating" moth species use the yucca resources without conferring the mutualistic benefit to the plants (Althoff et al. 2004).

For pollen collection, female yucca moths use specialized tentacles around their mouthparts that are known only in yucca moths. The pollen is carried underneath the female while she searches for an appropriate host flower. Finding an acceptable flower, she uses a blade-like ovipositor to insert the eggs. The ovipositor length for each moth species closely matches the depth of the plant ovaries, which varies by yucca species. When eggs are deposited too shallowly in the flower, the larvae never reach their seed food supply; but when eggs are deposited too close to the plant ovaries, the flower is aborted, killing both the seeds and the larvae. Thus each moth species will only pollinate its particular host species. After oviposition, the female uses her tentacles to deposit part of her pollen load to the internal surfaces of the style with bobbing movements. First-time visits to flowers usually result in egg laying and pollination, but completion of either is influenced by the amount of pheromone left by previous visitors.

Several trade-offs are apparent from the mutualistic relationship between Joshua tree flowers and moth larvae. First, these plants efficiently produce small amounts of pollen, and the obligate "prearranged" pollinators increase pollination potential with small amounts of pollen (C. Smith, Willamette University, pers. comm.). In exchange for pollination, the moth has assurance that her offspring are provided with a dependable food source during their larval development. The larvae do not eat all the seeds, but leave some for dispersal. The larvae then exit the seed pods before pod drop, finding more favorable locations to pupate.

Other invertebrate and vertebrate seed predators use Joshua trees, including squirrels, weevils, ravens, and ants; these benefit the tree by dispersing its seeds. Joshua tree seed pods do not open by themselves, and the seeds are relatively large and heavy with no physical means to increase dispersal. Rodents (probably antelope ground squirrels) harvest the seeds before they drop, clean the seeds from the pods, and cache them for later use (Waitman et al. 2012). Some seeds are eaten immediately, while others are cached up to 30 meters away from the parent tree (Vander Wall et al. 2006). Individual seeds may be stolen and recached among squirrels several times, which increases dispersal distances. Furthermore, average cache depth is 3–30 millimeters, which overlaps the range known to be most successful for germination of Joshua tree seeds (Reynolds et al. 2012).

The challenges of germination and establishment of yuccas are rife in the desert's pulse-driven environment. They include not only an array of hungry herbivores that can eat all stages of Joshua trees but also newly introduced invasive plant species that enhance wildfires lethal to large Joshua tree populations (DeFalco et al. 2010) and climate change that will likely affect Joshua tree habitat availability (Barrows and Murphy-Mariscal 2012). Cole et al. (2011) suggested that the (extinct) Shasta ground sloth (Nothrotheriops shastensis) dispersed Joshua tree seeds and the sloth's extinction has limited the Joshua tree's range. However, extant animals readily disperse the seeds (Waitman et al. 2012) and data suggests their current distribution is limited by site conditions, not dispersal (Godsoe et al. 2009). In addition, reconstructions of Joshua trees' past distribution and genetic data suggest that Joshua trees have undergone population expansion during the late Pleistocene (Smith et al. 2011).

CREOSOTE: As discussed earlier, creosote (*Larrea tridentata*) is the dominant shrub of the Mojave and Colorado Deserts and covers 14–18 million hectares across the warm deserts of North America. Creosote and bursage together make up a third of aboveground biomass and cover 70% of the area of the Mojave Desert (Schwinning and Hooten 2009). Livestock find creosote unpalatable, but native animals such as the black-tailed jackrabbits and desert woodrats (*Neotoma lepida*) eat the leaves and stems. Creosote exhibits polyploidy (most plant and animal species are diploid, meaning they have two sets of chromosomes, whereas creosote can have more than two sets) (Box Figure 30.1.1). In the late Pleistocene, creosote

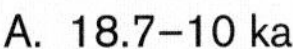

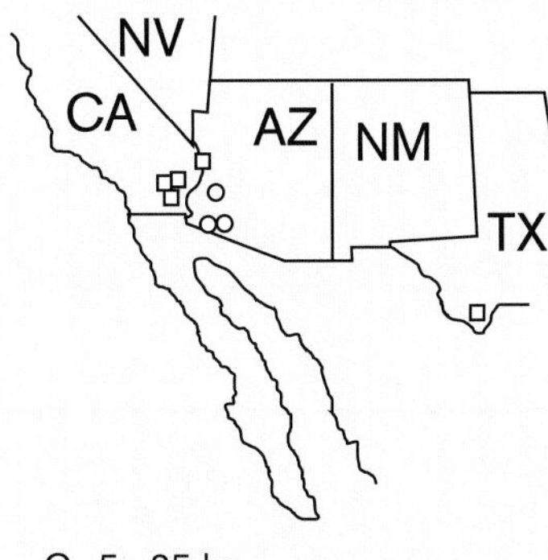

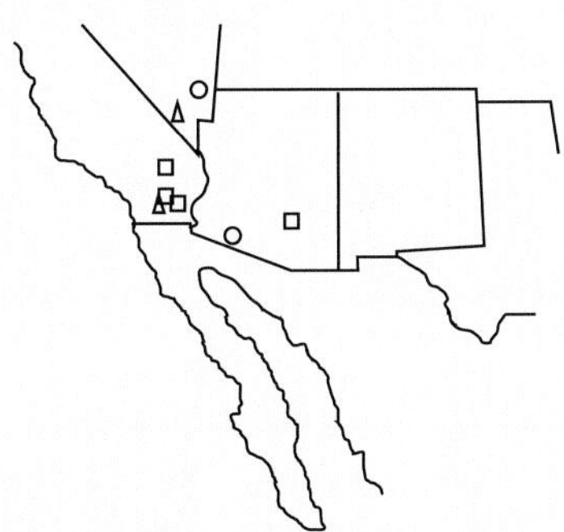

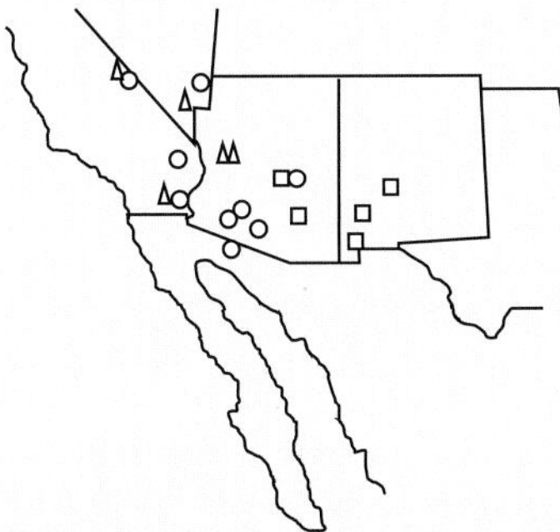

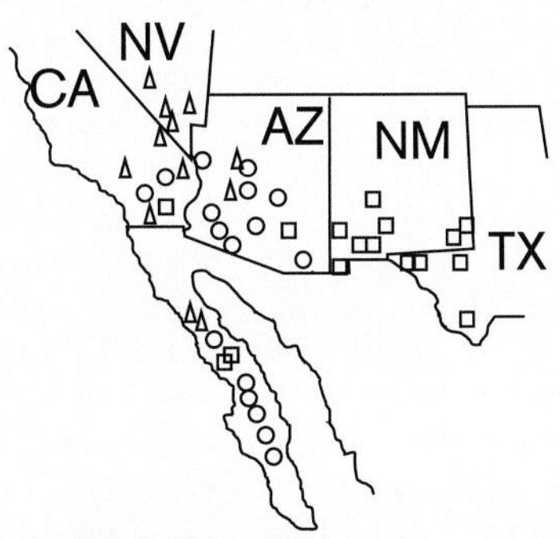

BOX FIGURE 30.1.1 Distribution of polyploids of creosote (*Larrea tridentata*) through time (Hunter et al. 2001). Squares are diploids, circles are tetraploids, and triangles are hexaploids. (A) late Pleistocene/early Holocene, (B) mid-Holocene, (C) late Holocene, and (D) modern distribution of polyploids.

occurred as a diploid species restricted to a small area of southwestern Arizona and southeastern California. Over the subsequent eighteen thousand years, it developed more ploidy levels and vastly extended its range (Hunter et al. 2001, Laport et al. 2012).

Several hypotheses persist as to how creosote came to dominate such vast regions of low- elevation land despite variation in soil types and climate: (1) multiple gene copies confer flexibility in responding to new environmental conditions; (2) it is a quintessential drought resistor, and its wide distribution could demonstrate the superiority of this strategy; and (3) the combination of flexibility, drought resistance, and creosote's many adaptive strategies (e.g., maintaining turgor at much lower water potentials than many plants, root allelopathy and distribution, and leaf waxes) have made it extremely successful. Interestingly, the NDGA compound that both attracts and repels grasshoppers (discussed in the chapter) and antioxidant ligands may have medical uses as antioxidants, antibacterials, antivirals, and anticancer drugs (Arteaga et al. 2005). Creosote was and is used by Native Americans for treatment of sexually transmitted diseases, tuberculosis, chicken pox, dysmenorrhea, and snake bite (Arteaga et al. 2005).

DESERT TORTOISES: These tortoises of the Mojave Desert eat mostly herbaceous plant material, including flowers and some shrubs (Jennings 2002) but may rely heavily on beaver-tail prickly pear cactus (*Opuntia basilaris*) during drought periods when there is little else to eat (Esque et al. in press). Required minerals may be supplemented by eating animal bones, stones, or soil (Esque and Peters 1994). Desert tortoises inhabit valley and rocky mountain slopes, and are important ecosystem engineers because of their burrowing (fossorial) habits. By excavating large underground burrows, desert tortoises provide protective sites for themselves and other species that often cohabitate with it, including kit fox, spotted skunk (*Spilogale putorius*), burrowing owl (*Athene cunicularia*), sidewinder rattlesnake, and a host of invertebrate commensals.

The tortoise is active from March through November and dormant from June through August unless it rains. Because water is scarce in the desert, the tortoise has developed physiological adaptations to aridity. For example, when rains occur, desert tortoises drink deeply and excrete metabolic wastes immediately (Medica et al. 1980). Similarly, desert tortoises are slow-growing, requiring from fifteen to eighteen years to reach reproductive maturity. Wild tortoises may live up to fifty years (Medica et al. 2012). Although tortoises almost always lay eggs in April through June, very few survive to maturity. Tortoise populations have declined severely in recent decades (USFWS 2011), despite protection under the Endangered Species Act. Several animals that prey on young tortoises are subsidized by human activities. These include transmission lines, where the common raven and the golden eagle can perch for a better view of the young animals, and food trash that allow raven and coyote populations to grow beyond natural numbers (Grover and DeFalco 1986, Kristan and Boarman 2003, Esque et al. 2010).

retention during hibernation and concentrate their urine while in the burrow to reduce water loss.

FISH: During the Pleistocene, when rivers and lakes were plentiful throughout the deserts, fish were abundant (Rinne and Minckley 1991). As these water bodies have dried with the drying climate and accelerated human use, including dams and pumping, fish populations have been accordingly reduced. At this point in time, fishes are restricted to the few rivers still remaining (e.g., Colorado and Mojave Rivers) and isolated springs and seeps. Even in these large rivers, most of the native fish are endangered. The most well known of desert fishes is the endangered desert pupfish (*Cyprinodon macularius*). It is typically less than 8 centimeters long (Dudek and ICF International 2012). These fish can tolerate extreme aquatic environments, including those of low oxygen content (as low as 0.13 parts per million) but high salinity (up to 70 parts per thousand), pH, and temperature (4°C and 45°C). This exceeds the tolerances of virtually all other freshwater fish. The desert pupfish was once common but has been lost from most of its historical range due to habitat loss through groundwater pumping and water diversion; contamination from agricultural return flows and other contaminants; and physical changes in water quality and disease and predation from nonnative species. The desert pupfish was listed as endangered in 1986 and many efforts have been aimed at its conservation. Despite this, the only remaining natural populations of the desert pupfish are located at a few sites in the Salton Sea drainage in California, and the Colorado River delta in Baja California and Sonora, Mexico.

BIRDS: A brief survey of the diet of breeding birds in California deserts shows that approximately one-half are herbivorous, one-fourth are omnivorous, and one-fourth are predators (T. Esque, U.S. Geological Survey, unpublished data). (It should be noted that regardless of what foods they specialize on later in life, most birds feed insects to their young to provide the protein needed for rapid growth.) Granivorous birds include year-round residents such as horned larks (*Eremophila alpestris*) and the communal pinyon jay (*Gymnorhinus cyanocephalus*), both well known for eating and dispersing seeds. Many seed-eating birds in the California deserts are winter migrants from Canada and the Great Basin. Some of these separate along elevational gradients and avoid interspecific competition (Repasky and Schluter 1994). Frugivorous birds are less common, but not absent, in deserts. Some bird-plant relationships are highly specialized, such as that between the silky flycatcher (*Phainopepla nitens*) and the desert mistletoe (*Phoradendron* spp.). The flycatchers nest in Colorado Desert mistletoe plants and eat the berries, dispersing the seeds when they defecate on branches of other plants. This type of relationship works well in deserts, as many host plants are patchily distributed and rely on a long-distance, faithful disperser.

Many bird species are important predators on invertebrates. Birds can feed more or less randomly on invertebrates or closely follow insects associated with the successive spring blooming of plants, such as paloverde in May, ironwood in June, and acacia in July. Hummingbirds are omnivores, as they eat insects and plant sap, and also are among the few desert avian pollinators. Up to seven species of hummingbirds may be observed in California's deserts, both as residents and migrants. Some birds eat only larger animals. Roadrunners (*Geococcyx californianus*) feed on snakes and lizards. Loggerhead shrikes (*Lanius ludovicianus*) eat large insects, lizards, snakes, rodents, and occasionally birds. Hawks and eagles prey on a variety of smaller animals. Common ravens are omnivores and eat just about anything: insects, human trash, other birds, and desert tortoise.

Bird species diversity is low in deserts relative to mesic ecosystems because of lack of free surface water, relatively low abundance of prey, and limited habitat resulting from short-statured vegetation. In U.S. deserts, only 31 species of birds are considered residents (MacMahon 1979); however, these numbers swell during spring and fall migration when as many as 220 species have been recorded at NNSS (Rundel and Gibson 1996). California desert riparian communities are particularly crucial to neotropical migrants that travel through in the spring and fall and use these zones to refuel. Because of their importance, damage to desert riparian areas can have an substantial negative influence on migrant breeding populations (Paxton et al. 2008). The highest avian diversity in deserts, as in other biomes, is found where vegetative structure is most diverse. Surveys found 92 and 83 species of birds in pinyon-juniper woodlands and creosote, respectively, compared with only 38 species in a sparse, short-statured saltbush community (Rundel and Gibson 1996).

Birds, unlike reptiles, are endothermic, as they produce and maintain their own internal heat. Desert birds require relatively high internal temperatures to support their high levels of foraging activity, typically 39°C to 41°C. This allows most birds to be diurnal, though they still need to take evasive action in the middle of a hot desert day as body temperatures of 46°C to 47°C are lethal. Maintaining such high body temperatures requires an abundant and constant food supply. One adaptation to this need is tremendous flexibility in the diet and foraging behavior of most birds. For example, a bird that is generally granivorous may switch to insects if seed supplies become low, or vice versa. A few birds, like hummingbirds and swifts, can save energy when food is low by dropping their internal temperatures at night. Birds can also fly to other locations that offer shade, lower temperatures, or water when food supplies are exhausted, water is required, or environmental conditions are not optimal. Behavioral responses also include avoiding flying during the heat of the day, as this creates high body heat; nesting off the ground in the shade and away from surface heat; and fledging young before the intense summer heat.

Many birds are also physiologically adapted to desert conditions. All birds can pant and some use gular fluttering (the flapping of throat membranes to increase evaporation) to cool themselves. Some birds use facultative hyperthermia, or the ability to tolerate very high body temperatures (up to 46°C) for short periods of time (one to two hours), after which a cool microhabitat is sought and the heat quickly released before damage occurs. Water loss is lower in desert birds than in nondesert birds (Whitford 2002). Some desert birds have a reduced metabolic rate, small clutch sizes, and reduced nestling growth rates as adaptations to their severe desert environments (Williams and Tieleman 2005). Of special note is the black-throated sparrow (*Amphispiza bilineata*), a common bird in the Mojave Desert that is truly adapted to desert living and appears to be more independent of drinking water than any passerine in North America (Rundel and Gibson 1996). Even when conditions are very dry, this sparrow is able to maintain 57% water in its nonliquid excreta, but it also can concentrate urine rapidly. Black-throated sparrows have a very flexible diet, consuming green vegetation when available and switching to termites, ants, and beetles when the vegetation dries and no longer provides sufficient water.

MAMMALS: More than fifty mammal species live in the California deserts. Most are small, such as mice, kangaroo rats, voles, and shrews, but there are many larger species as well. The high diversity of mammals in deserts is surprising, given that they lack the energy efficiency of reptiles and that smaller rodents lack the mobility of birds. All mammals, like birds, are endothermic and also require a large and constant supply of food, although many can estivate or hibernate in burrows when food is low or to escape daily extreme temperatures. Some desert mammals have specialized body parts to "dump" heat, such as the highly vascularized ears of black-tailed jackrabbits (*Lepus californicus*). The success of mammals in deserts is most likely due to their flexibility in foraging behavior and diet. As with birds, most can switch from one food source to another. Mammals that do have specialized food sources have developed ways to overcome seasonal shortages, such as caching or hoarding. Overall, mammals are much more ecologically diverse than the other animal groups in terms of diet, movement, and body size (Brown and Maurer 1986).

SMALL MAMMALS: Most desert small mammals are herbivores, and are either generalists, eating many types of plant materials (e.g, cactus mouse [*Peromyscus eremicus*]), or specialists, like the desert pocket mouse (*Chaetodipus penicillatus*) that eats only seeds. Perhaps one of the most unusual and specialized plant-feeders is the chisel-tooth kangaroo rat (*Dipodomys microps*), which uses its awl-shaped incisors to remove the salty outer layer of saltbush (*Atriplex* spp.) leaves so that it can consume the less salty part of the leaf. Small mammals can have large effects on plant community structure. A large proportion of short (less than 1 meter tall) Joshua trees may be lost to herbivores during drought periods (DeFalco et al. 2010), and similar observations have been made for immature blackbrush plants (S. Meyer, USDA Rocky Mountain Research Station, pers. comm.). Some small mammals are omnivores or second-order consumers. The southern grasshopper mouse (*Onychomys torridus*) feeds on plant material but is also a voracious predator on insects, including some tenebrionid beetles that spray repugnant compounds as defenses. Desert shrews (*Notiosorex crawfordi*) feed on insects, preferring larvae because they provide more liquid than adults.

Small mammals have many adaptations to deal with the extremes of desert living (Whitford 2002). Many small mammals are active at night rather than daytime, particularly the seed-eating specialists that obtain little water from their food. These animals must avoid daytime activity both because they have a high surface-to-volume ratio and absorb heat quickly from their surroundings and because activity creates metabolic heat. A notable exception is the antelope ground squirrel (*Ammospermophilus leucurus*), which dashes about in the middle of the day, folding its tail over its back to provide shade for its body. This species also uses facultative hyperthermia, with its body heat able to reach 43°C to 44°C before it needs to find a burrow in which to cool down. This ability to withstand high body heat enables cooling via conduction or radiation, reducing the need to rely on evaporation and saving body water. Jackrabbits employ this strategy, using both the shade of shrubs and some evaporation from respiratory surfaces for cooling.

As discussed earlier, most vertebrate water loss occurs as evaporation. Many small mammals combat this loss by having narrow, cooled nasal passages so that water vapor leaving the nostrils condenses onto the nasal lining before being lost to the air. The air in burrows is also humidified, reducing water loss during respiration. Urine is highly concentrated in the kidneys of small mammals, and their fecal pellets are very dry. To increase water intake, many rodents eat green vegetation with high water contents. Metabolic water can be important for those rodents dependent on very dry food sources such as seeds, but its importance varies widely among species. The average metabolic rate of desert rodents is much lower than that of nondesert rodents, reducing water loss through respiration. Desert rodents also have lower weight specific rates of water loss than nondesert rodents.

The number of rodents present at a site has a profound influence on the structure and function of the ecosystem because they provide prey for larger animals, create habitat and soil structure through their burrows, and are important seed predators and dispersal agents. Rodent densities in deserts show extremely wide fluctuations among years. Their numbers were long thought to be positively correlated with rainfall, as higher rain resulted in higher plant productivity and successful reproduction was thought to depend on ingestion of green vegetation (Reichman and van de Graaff 1975). However, many studies do not support this conclusion, so the cause of varying densities is not understood (reviewed in Rundel and Gibson 1996). As with ants, the species diversity of rodents increases linearly with mean annual precipitation (see Figure 30.10). Similarly, rodents, along with many desert animal groups discussed (e.g., bees, birds, and lizards), show a wide range in in size and weight, which may allow them to utilize their environment in different ways and enable more species to coexist (Brown 1973a, b).

Three families of bats are commonly found in the deserts of California, including Phyllostomidae (e.g., the California leaf-nosed bat, *Macrotis californicus*), Vespertilionidae (approximately sixteen species, with ten in the genus *Myotis*, the most common bats), and Molossidae (five species, among them the pocketed free-tailed bat [*Nyctinomops femorosaccus*]). These bats congregate in caves or near human dwellings. Many are insectivores, but some are frugivorous pollinators. Because bats fly mostly at dusk or at night, high temperatures are seldom a challenge. Consumption of insects by bats also reduces the problem of water loss.

LARGE HERBIVORES: Large desert herbivores include the native ruminants (mule deer [*Odocoileus hemionus*], desert bighorn, and the American pronghorn [*Antilocarpra Americana*]). Exotic ungulates include feral horse (*Equus caballus*) and burro. All large herbivores can affect plant productivity where they forage. In addition, they generally forage selectively, choosing some plants over others, sometimes heavily influencing plant community composition. As with all groups, these animals need to avoid extreme temperature conditions, though their large body size and mobility makes this less critical than for smaller animals. Some large herbivores are able to utilize hyperthermia and high-quality forage (i.e., with high water content) to reduce the need for free surface water. Still, these large animals need access to free surface water, which severely restricts their distribution because water sources are sparse and nonrandomly distributed. Even at water sources, native herbivores, especially pronghorn, are not abundant. In contrast, feral equids can occur locally in high numbers, causing great damage to desert ecosystems when they congregate, generally around water sources, as desert ecosystems did not evolve with high intensity or prolonged ungulate use. When these large herbivores are adults, few predators can effectively capture and kill them. However, when young, all these species are vulnerable to the top desert predators. For instance, pronghorn fawns are known to be vulnerable to eagle predation (K. Longshore, U.S. Geological Survey, pers. comm.).

MESOPREDATORS, TOP PREDATORS, AND OMNIVOROUS PREDATORS: California's deserts host a diversity of medium-sized and large carnivorous mammals. Because these animals are at the top of the trophic pyramid, they have far lower diversities, biomass, and abundance than animals below them. Medium-sized predators (mesopredators) include bobcat (*Lynx rufus*), kit and gray fox (*Urocyon cinereoargenteus*), skunk (*Mephitis* sp.), and golden eagle. Large top predators, which are limited in deserts because scarce water limits the numbers of their prey, include the cougar (*Felis concolor*), coyote, and mountain lion (*Felis concolor*). Top predators typically shift their diets to survive fluctuations in prey abundance, meaning these animals may function as top consumers or the food chain may be much longer by the time they feed on a given animal. Mesopredators and top predators have the ability to travel great distances in search of prey and may easily travel from one desert mountain range to another in a single day. These large, mobile, endothermic carnivores are much less affected by extremes of temperature and water scarcity than other desert animals. Their large body size minimizes heat gain, and their mobility enables them to seek more favorable microhabitats. Eating other animals provides them with plenty of liquid, so they can afford to utilize evaporative cooling and seldom require free water. These predators are often selective in their choice of prey, influencing the composition of the faunal community. Because prey numbers in deserts are low, desert habitats have been viewed as mostly sink habitats for larger predators compared to more productive areas (K. Longshore, U.S. Geological Survey, pers. comm.).

DETRITIVORES: Detritivores close the loop, feeding on deceased plant and animal material. As discussed earlier, microbes are important in plant matter decomposition. Invertebrates, including microarthropods (mites, collembolans, nematodes, and protozoa) and macroarthropods (isopods, millipedes, and insects) are also important, especially as shredders of plant and animal materials to create more surface area for microbial attack. Of all the invertebrates, termites are likely the most important and abundant detritivores in most deserts, including California's (Whitford 2002). Termites are also extremely influential as ecosystem engineers because, like ants, they move tremendous amounts of soil from the subsurface to the surface, increasing soil fertility for plants. Their activity creates macropores, or large spaces going downward into the soil, providing for accelerated water infiltration. Finally, turkey vultures (*Cathartes aura*) and a variety of other small animals consume fresh carcasses. Flesh and bones may last for decades and longer in the desert, with a surprising assortment of animals visiting the deteriorating bones to acquire minerals such as phosphorus, calcium, and manganese (Esque and Peters 1994).

Major Ecosystem Services

The Millennium Ecosystem Assessment (2005) established a framework within which to assess ecosystem services that includes regulating, supporting, provisioning, and cultural services. Regulating services include factors such as geomorphologic processes and biogeochemical cycling. Supporting services include processes such as primary productivity and water, which are discussed earlier in the chapter. Next we discuss provisioning and cultural services.

Provisioning Services of Water, Food, and Fiber

Provisioning services are ecosystem products that humans use directly (Millennium Ecosystem Assessment 2005). The most obvious of these services in desert regions is water, both because it directly supports plants, wildlife, and humans and because it regulates food and fiber production required for human populations. Water, food, and fiber were critical in sustaining prehistoric hunter-gatherer populations present in the California deserts for at least the past ten thousand years (Hughson 2009).

The archaeological record shows that the number and diversity of sites used by humans increased and began to show evidence of agrarian activities during the late Holocene, but the distribution of these sites were typically associated with perennial water supplies, especially the permanent ones. Provisioning services including water and game also supported the first Anglo-American settlers in the 1800s, although travel across these deserts was a challenge. Trade routes such as the Spanish Trail, and later the railroads, allowed importation of materials that helped to support a larger human population than the extant desert ecosystems would have provisioned on their own. Populations began exponential growth with construction of the Hoover Dam on the Colorado River in the 1930s, as its reservoir provided a large and predictable source of water for agricultural development, particularly in the Colorado Desert. Recently this water has been supplemented by groundwater pumping, and plans are under way to import more water from the southern Great Basin to California.

ENERGY

The California deserts, replete with cloud-free sunny days and almost constant winds, have fueled a burgeoning renewable energy industry. Electrical utility companies in California are required to generate 33% of their power from renewable sources by 2020 (California Senate Bill X1-2, 2011) and virtually all of the solar installations in the state have been built in, or are planned for, the California deserts. Between 1981 and 1992, six solar energy facilities were built in the Mojave Desert; five of these facilities are still operational (California Energy Commission 2013). Between 2008 and 2011, another six projects were approved for siting in the Mojave Desert, five more were approved for the Colorado Desert, and other projects are currently under review. Two of California's three major wind farms are located at the western edges of the Colorado and Mojave Deserts. These energy sources do not come without an environmental cost, which are discussed next.

CULTURAL SERVICES

Cultural services are characterized by nonmaterial benefits to human society and are rooted in the relationship between humans and their environments. These relationships may be recreational, such as the desire for off-highway vehicle areas, camping, rock climbing, or viewing spring wildflower displays. California deserts have a long history of meeting the religious and spiritual need of humans: Native Americans sought the deserts for vision quests or ceremonial purposes, and more recently, the desert has been visited by people who seek fulfillment in communing with the natural environment. Solitude and "untrammeled" landscapes are at the core of millions of hectares of wilderness designated by legislation such as the California Desert Protection Act of 1994 (Public Law 103-433), giving the public an invaluable opportunity to experience this service. Finally, an evolutionary argument asserts that human psyches are tangibly linked to the aesthetics of their natural environment (e.g., the biophilia hypothesis, Wilson 1984).

Impacts of Humans during the Postcolonial Period

The conversion of desert lands for housing, roads, energy development, and other purposes is a growing direct, local stressor in California's deserts. Human developments can usurp large areas of desert shrubland, leaving fragmented and isolated natural remnants within a larger sea of development. Moderate to heavy off-road vehicle use can cause vegetation loss and soil erosion, which can persist for tens to hundreds of years, especially on hillslopes. Agriculture can have similar effects, although the amount of landscape recontouring and installation of impervious surfaces in the case of agriculture is much less than with urbanization. Mining activities can have significant local impacts, altering aboveground land cover extensively in mined areas.

The California deserts have a long history of mining activity that stretches from the early explorations of the Spaniards in the mid-1500s through the mid-1900s. During the early 1900s, mining townsites located in remote areas of the northern and western Mojave Desert and southern Great Basin supported thousands of people. Although many mines have been abandoned for almost a century after the gold, silver, and other minerals were depleted, ecosystem effects—increased soil compaction and altered vegetation due to wood harvesting and vegetation removal—still persist in some areas (Webb, DeFalco et al. 2009). Similarly, many agricultural areas have been abandoned because their soils have become contaminated and/or their water supplies have been diverted to support burgeoning urban areas. If left to recover naturally, these agricultural areas can remain largely devoid of perennial vegetation for many decades (Carpenter et al. 1986).

Populated and agricultural areas, as well as roads, are also sources for many invasive species, some of which spread outward into the desert. Notable species include the Mediterranean annual grasses (*Bromus tectorum*, *B. madretensis*, *Schismus barbatus*); African mustard (*Brassica tournefortii*), which arrived in California with date tree stock planted in the Coachella Valley (Minnich and Sanders 2000); and fountain grass (*Pennisetum setaceum*), which has been reported by park staff spreading from residential neighborhoods into Joshua Tree National Park and Lake Mead National Recreation Area. Human settlement has also led to abnormally large populations of native predators such as coyotes and common ravens, which are buoyed by supplemental food and water associated with human developments. Ravens are especially abundant around human developments because of features like readily available roadkill on highways, artificial ponds, food at roadside rest stops, and garbage in landfills (Kristan and Boarman 2007). Moreover, powerlines provide nesting platforms mostly safe from terrestrial predators and useful for tracking prey, particularly young desert tortoises, on the ground. Coyotes are subsidized by the same foods as ravens and also benefit from the ready availability of human pets (Esque et al. 2010).

Domesticated and feral animals, especially dogs and cats, are anchored to human habitations for food and shelter but roam far and wide searching for prey and in response to instinctual territorial behavior. Dogs pose a known threat to the desert tortoise and likely wreak havoc on many other wildlife species as well, particularly jackrabbits and lizards. Domestic and feral cats have long been known as a threat to birds (Loss et al. 2013), but they also impact rodent and lizard populations. Feral cats, in particular, are detrimental to wildlife populations in riparian areas, where the cats benefit from cover, ready access to water, and abundant native prey.

Solar- and wind-energy installations have replaced large tracts of shrublands in valley bottoms of the Mojave and western Colorado Deserts. Solar developments completely remove vegetation and biocrusts, whereas wind development is marked by tight grids of roads connecting wind towers that fragment ecosystems (Lovich and Ennen 2011). Because both types of energy development compact soils, while solar farms also use large amounts of water, they are direct local ecosystem stressors in the California deserts. The effects of these types of renewable energy development are similar to those of agriculture, as they remove vegetation and alter soils, although they lack attendant large human populations that accompany agriculture. The size of renewable energy installations is an issue because vegetation removal and reflective mirrors increase the amount of energy reflected back into the atmosphere relative to undisturbed surfaces, and if the area is large, it can change regional weather (Pielke 2001). The pressure to increase development of renewable energy infrastructure will likely increase in the future, but the impact on desert wildlands could be minimized by focusing development on microgrid power generation within urban or abandoned agricultural footprints.

Although the large contiguous impacts associated with townsites, agricultural fields, mines, and renewable energy installations represent the most intensive land-cover conversions in California's deserts, linear utility and vehicular route corridors are clearly the most extensive. These corridors crisscross the desert and their cumulative footprint rivals that of large contiguous direct local stressors. Utility corridors include aqueducts, buried water pipelines, gas pipelines, and transmission lines. The footprint of utility and vehicular routes range in width from a few tens of meters to a hundred meters or more, and they universally include a graded maintenance road. Vehicular routes include off-highway vehicle trails and unimproved local roads, improved local roads and collector roads, and arterial road and limited-access highways

(Brooks and Lair 2009). These linear features compact soils, interrupt overland flow patterns, and alter vegetation distribution and productivity. Roads can have especially dramatic and lasting effects on ecosystem structure, processes, and services because they involve the complete removal of vegetation and alteration of soils, often overlaying soils with asphalt and concrete, as well as introducing weed seeds and altering overland flow patterns (Leu et al. 2008, Brooks and Lair 2009). Finally, unpaved roads produce large amounts of dust, even when not driven on, that negatively affects roadside vegetation, human health, and water supplies when deposited on mountain snowpacks.

Invasive Plants and Fire Regimes

One of the most influential ecosystem processes in California is related to the spatial and temporal occurrence of fire (see also Chapter 3, "Fire as an Ecosystem Process"). Three primary native vegetation fire regimes occur within California deserts: (1) in low- and middle-elevation shrublands, fires are very infrequent and typically small because of lack of fuels (see Figure 30.4); (2) in high-elevation shrublands and woodlands, fires are infrequent but sufficient fuels give them the potential to be large; and (3) in riparian shrublands and woodlands and spring/oasis sites, fires are moderately frequent and small (Brooks and Minnich 2006, Brooks et al. 2013). The general trend during the Holocene has been toward greater aridity, especially since the Little Ice Age (Brooks et al. 2013). With increased aridity has come a decline in the amount of land occupied by humans and an increase in sparse vegetative cover insufficient to carry fire, which has ultimately resulted in a decrease in fire occurrence. The shift from perennial grasses to woody shrubs in lower and middle elevations also suggests a shift toward decreased frequency and size of fires during the later Holocene (Brooks et al. 2013). By the time of Euro-American settlement in the mid-1800s, most fires were likely limited to higher-elevation shrublands and woodlands.

The invasion of non-native annual grasses into the California deserts during the late 1800s has changed this equation. Exotic annual plants can create continuous fuels between native perennial plants, especially during high rainfall years. Once dry, the grasses remain standing throughout the following year, providing fuels for fires that can become very large; in 2005 more than 1 million acres burned across the Mojave Desert (Brooks and Minnich 2006, Brooks 2009, Brooks et al. 2013). Although native annuals could have fueled such fires before the 1800s, native annuals do not persist long as standing senesced fuels, and far fewer ignition sources existed (Brooks 1999). Because non-native annual grasses tend to increase following fire and native perennials tend to decrease as fires recur, there is notable concern that a positive grass-fire cycle has established, changing communities and ecosystem properties for the foreseeable future. Although these conditions seem to have established across large expanses of deserts in surrounding states, they have occurred mainly in localized areas within California (Brooks et al. 2013).

Another contributor to plant invasions in the desert is nitrogen pollution. The high concentration of automobiles in urban areas, especially in the western regions of the California deserts and adjacent cismontane cities, results in plumes of atmospheric nitrogen extending downwind into less developed regions (Fenn et al. 2010). When deposited onto normally nutrient-poor soils, this nitrogen can further increase invasion of annual grasses (Brooks 2003), increasing fire frequencies. Recent plans to construct cogeneration facilities in California's deserts to produce electricity have been met with great resistance due to concern about the potential effects of increased nitrogen deposition rates on plant invasions and subsequent fire regimes (Fenn et al. 2010).

The invasion of the non-native saltcedar (*Tamarix* spp.) has also changed fire regimes in riparian areas (Busch and Smith 1995). Although native riparian shrubs and trees can carry fire on their own, their high fuel moisture content and fuel structure produce low- to moderate-intensity fires that typically burn only surface fuels, resulting in lower mortality rates and higher postfire recovery rates of native vegetation. The addition of saltcedar increases riparian fuel loads, decreases fuel moisture levels, adds more fine fuels that readily ignite, and promotes larger, higher-intensity fires that cause higher mortality among native species. The vigorous resprouting and postfire recovery exhibited by saltcedar, coupled with the reduced resilience of native vegetation following fire, has meant the conversion of many riparian areas to almost monocultures of saltcedar.

Increases in atmospheric CO_2 and climate change are also expected to impact these deserts. Increased CO_2 may lead to increased plant productivity and biomass as the result of improved plant water-use efficiency, especially of C_3 shrub species in desert regions (Drake et al. 1997). In the Mojave Desert this increase will likely be most pronounced during years of high rainfall (Naumburg et al. 2003). Precipitation and temperature are the primary drivers of many desert ecosystem processes, and these climate variables are predicted to directionally shift in the future. Although climate models diverge in predicted outcomes, most suggest that the southwestern United States, including the California deserts, will become increasingly dry, especially in winter, compared to the preceding century (Seager and Vecchi 2010, Dai 2011). The strongest evidence exists for increasing temperatures (Karl et al. 2009), which alone would result in greater soil moisture deficit and increasingly arid conditions. Evidence also exists that winter precipitation (Seager and Vecchi 2010) and the difference between precipitation and evaporation will both decline (Seager et al. 2007), which is consistent with increased aridity. Although potential trends in summer monsoonal precipitation are unknown, a recent study suggests that its onset could shift from early July to early August (Cook and Seager 2013).

Multiple stressors—livestock grazing, off-highway vehicle use, urbanization, and nitrogen deposition—across the landscape can have cumulative effects. These could simply be additive and threaten natural resources through "death by a thousand cuts." In some cases, multiple stressors could also result in higher-order interactions and produce emergent stressors such as altered fire regimes and altered hydrologic regimes. Because of their complexity, these stressors are hard to quantify, and their effects on ecosystems or ecological processes are difficult to predict because they may be highly context-dependent.

Future Scenarios

Environmentally stressful conditions in desert regions have often led to the evolution of adaptive strategies for stress tolerance (Grime 1979). Future increases in atmospheric CO_2 and

N could produce less stressful conditions for plant species that are good competitors for soil water and nutrients, such as non-native invasive plants and possibly native C_3 annuals, at the expense of long-lived perennial native species. This situation would increase the continuity of fuel and therefore fire frequency in the California deserts, increasing mortality of non-fire-adapted native plants (Brooks and Minnich 2006). These non-native species can also directly displace native plants. On the other hand, future projected increases in temperatures and overall aridity could also reduce effective soil moisture and increase environmental stress, potentially counterbalancing the effects of changing atmospheric chemistry. This situation may favor native plants and C_4 plants or deeper-rooted (shrubs) over shallow-rooted (e.g., grasses, cacti) plants.

Extreme highs and lows in precipitation can have significant effects on desert shrublands, even if mean precipitation remains constant. For example, although a drought may not kill perennial plants, it can increase their vulnerability to a subsequent drought or fire. Pinyon pine is highly susceptible to beetle infestation once drought-stressed. In addition, variation in resource availability is best capitalized on by species that have high relative growth rates and reproductive capacity (Grime 1979). All of this suggests that non-native invasive plants and short-lived perennials may benefit most if rainfall variation increases. Extreme spikes in precipitation may also cause massive flooding that may scour drainages and reset successional clocks.

Annual precipitation patterns follow a bimodal distribution in parts of California deserts (Hereford et al. 2006), and C_4 grasses and CAM plants tend to occur where summer precipitation is highest. These same plant groups also tend to occur where the number of frost-free days are low, which is characteristic of the monsoonal region of the eastern Mojave and Colorado Deserts. Therefore, if the monsoonal regions shift in the future or the length and/or amount of precipitation changes, then the structure and composition of desert shrublands may change as well. Increased aridity and seasonal shifts in rainfall timing could lead to possible range shifts for plant species and assemblages, although predictions are difficult because most of these desert regions will have no contemporary analogs by 2090 (Rehfeldt et al. 2006, Munson et al. 2012). Despite the inherent difficulty in making projections, scientists agree that temperatures will increase, especially nocturnal minima (Smith et al. 2009). By one estimate, the areal extent of the desert scrub envelope in California will remain relatively constant during the twenty-first century, with the different deserts' boundaries shifting northward and upward in elevation, leaving only a small vestige of Great Basin desert scrub (Rehfeldt et al. 2006). Despite the large uncertainty inherent in these projections, especially as they relate to the rates at which specific species and assemblages will respond, we know that temperature and precipitation changes will stress many plants in their current locations. These changes could also increase bioclimatic suitability of sites for species beyond their current ranges, which may differentially facilitate range extensions of invasive species that tend to have more rapid dispersal rates than noninvasive species.

In summary, the net effects of warming, decreased winter rainfall, increased human usage, and increasing pollution (with CO_2 and N) suggest a scenario of shifting vegetation communities and increasing dominance by annual invasive species in the California deserts, leading to potential increases in fire frequency. If conditions also become more arid, native perennials, especially grasses, may decline as well, causing a reduction in overall plant cover. Arid conditions could also reduce dominance of some invasive annual plants (e.g., brome grasses and mustards), although others that already occur in the most hyperarid regions would likely persist and expand due to competitive release as the abundance of other species (e.g., filaree [*Erodium cicutarium*]) wanes.

Incorporating Future Scenarios into Land Management

Most of what is known about the effects of land management actions in the California deserts, particularly for restoration strategies, is based on a climatic period of relatively high rainfall that resulted in elevated primary productivity (Belnap et al. 2008). With future projections of lower and/or more variable soil moisture, some current land management practices will likely become obsolete. It is therefore important to determine which practices are effective, and which place ecosystems at risk, under future scenarios. The concepts of resistance (resisting change to an undesirable state) and resilience (the ability to recover from a disturbance) are useful for developing robust management practices that maximize an ecosystem's capacity to withstand irreversible transformation to less desirable states (Gunderson and Holling 2002). This approach is consistent with the general approach of climate-smart conservation, which explicitly considers climate change impacts and resource vulnerabilities in the goals, objectives, and actions of natural resource management (Stein et al. 2013).

For ecosystem management under future climates and land uses to be successful, it is important to establish clear objectives. The first step in this process is to identify the stressors that contribute to ecosystem degradation. Indicators of ecosystem response to those stressors can then be identified. These metrics need to be scientifically based and feasible to implement and monitor over appropriate time intervals (Belnap 1998)—possibly years to decades in deserts (Rapport et al. 1985). Subsequent steps include conducting spatial assessment of landscape conditions, understanding ecological thresholds, and prioritizing actions for removing stressors and enhancing resilience (Brooks and Chambers 2011). Because deserts recover so slowly compared to mesic regions, it is most important to avoid creating impacts where possible, especially in landscapes with low resistance and resilience and those occupied by vulnerable species. Avoiding unnecessary impacts of management actions could be aided by mapping lands with high and low resistance and resilience and siting intentional disturbances in the least vulnerable locations. Another need is to map areas of high ecological value and designate them as ecological reserves, with corridors among them and existing reserves that reflect future climate conditions.

Many impacts can be minimized by changing the timing, type, or intensity of land use, such as by reducing how much soil surface is cleared or compacted. Restoration is extremely difficult in deserts because compacted soils are difficult to restore, surface disturbance diminishes seed reserves in the soil (DeFalco et al. 2009), ants and rodents collect and consume seeds used during restoration efforts (DeFalco et al. 2009, 2012), and reproduction and the dropping of native seed occurs only infrequently for many perennial species. Rainfall necessary for germination is generally lacking and unpredictable, limiting opportunities for plants to reestablish after disturbances. While some successes have been attained by reseeding disturbed areas with native species and transplanting greenhouse-raised seedlings, success has been highly variable (e.g., Abella and Newton 2009; Scoles-Sciulla and DeFalco 2009; Webb, Belnap et al. 2009; Weigand and Rodgers 2009), leaving scientists without a reliable prescription for rehabilitating disturbed desert sites. Creative solutions such as encapsulating seeds in soil pellets before distribution, applying herbicide in combination with seeding to suppress competitive non-native annuals, and protecting developing seedlings with mesh cages are being evaluated and are expected to enhance restoration on severely degraded desert shrublands (Steers and Allen 2010, DeFalco et al. 2012, Abella et al. 2013). Careful thought about the restoration objectives, as well as a priori determination of triggers for actions, are necessary for a broad distribution of managed disturbances before management actions are taken (Elzinga et al. 2001).

In addition to creative restoration strategies, effective monitoring of restoration efforts is needed to establish whether, and which, management actions are effective (Herrick et al. 2005).Though rarely performed, monitoring the effects of just removing stressors can help establish whether the ecosystem components that promote resilience are in place. Luckily, successful and standardized monitoring protocols have been developed for the California deserts to document disturbances and track the success of restoration actions over time (Belnap et al. 2008, DeFalco and Scoles-Sciulla 2009). If recovery does not occur, then attention to the underlying processes that have been affected may be needed.

Summary

The desert ecosystems of California stand in stark contrast to the more verdant ecosystems found in other parts of the state. Sparse vegetation gives the impression that there is little life in these deserts. In reality, these regions support a rich and complex web of microbes, plants, and animals that have specialized ways of coping with the extremes of temperature, light, and moisture found in desert environments. All life in these ecosystems revolves around water availability. For this reason rain events are followed by a frenzy of activity, with everything from tiny microbes to large predators taking advantage of temporary moisture. Where permanent surface water is found, the tempo of life is more constant and less pulsed.

Desert plants have evolved many strategies for living in arid conditions, including the ability to escape, evade, endure, or resist drought. The most abundant and widespread plant in the California deserts is creosote, a classic drought-resistor. Plant species also have many adaptive physiological features such as thickened and reflective leaves and deep roots. Despite these adaptations, many species are still highly vulnerable to drought, as illustrated by the total shift in plant community dominance sometimes seen after extreme climate events. Invertebrates are tremendously important in desert environments. They can exert a strong control on plant community composition, plant distributions, soil structure, and the distribution of higher-trophic-level animals. Invertebrates also supply vital protein to the many animals that feed on them. Vertebrates are also a critical part of the California deserts. Despite sparse, short vegetation, the deserts support a relatively large abundance and diversity of these animals. Unlike plants, animals have the advantage of being able to move into shade or burrows to avoid extreme temperatures. Accordingly, almost no animals are seen in the heat of the day. Animals have many physiological adaptations to desert conditions, including body size, panting, color, heat exchange in blood flow, and hyperthermia.

Because the California deserts have abundant mineral and energy sources, as well as warm winters, the constant threat of human development looms. Climate change will also alter plant and animal abundance and distribution. Unfortunately, these desert regions have low resistance and resilience to disturbance. Because desert ecosystems are fragile, and their restoration is difficult if not impossible, finding ways to avoid or minimize impacts from these threats is essential. Meeting societal needs while preserving the integrity of California's deserts will be a difficult but essential challenge.

Acknowledgments

Jayne Belnap, Todd C. Esque, Lesley A. DeFalco, and Matthew L. Brooks acknowledge the contribution of U.S. Geological Survey's Ecosystems and Priority Ecosystems Programs.

Recommended Reading

Barbour, M. G., T. Keeler-Wolf, and A. A. Schoenherr, editors. 2007. Terrestrial vegetation of California. Third edition. University of California Press, Berkeley, California.

Pavlik, B. M. 2008. The California deserts: An ecological rediscovery. University of California Press, Berkeley, California.

Rundel, P. W., and A. C. Gibson. 1996. Ecological communities and processes in a Mojave Desert ecosystem: Rock Valley, Nevada. Cambridge University Press, Cambridge, UK.

Sawyer, J. O., T. Keeler-Wolf, and J. M. Evens. 2009. A manual of California vegetation. Second edition. California Native Plant Society, Sacramento, California.

Schoenherr, A. A. 1992. A natural history of California. University of California Press, Berkeley, California.

Webb, R. H., L. F. Fenstermaker, J. S. Heaton, D. L. Hughson, E. V. McDonald, and D. M. Miller, editors. 2009. The Mojave Desert: Ecosystem processes and sustainability. University of Nevada Press, Reno, Nevada.

Whitford, W. G. 2002. Ecology of desert systems. Academic Press, San Diego, California.

Glossary

ALLUVIUM Loose soil or sediments deposited by water.

ENDEMIC Occurring nowhere else.

PARENT MATERIAL The underlying geological substrate from which soils form.

PLUVIAL LAKE A lake formed in a landlocked basin during times of high precipitation in glacial periods.

POTENTIAL EVAPOTRANSPIRATION (PET) The potential amount of water lost to the atmosphere due to evaporation and transpiration combined.

XERO-RIPARIAN From "xeric" (water-limited) and "riparian," which refers to the zone of shallow groundwater adjacent to a surface water feature. "Xero-riparian" refers to the riparian zone of water bodies with only intermittent surface water.

References

Abella, S. R., and A. C. Newton. 2009. A systematic review of species performance and treatment effectiveness for revegetation in the Mojave Desert, USA. Pages 45–74 in A. Fernandez-Bernal and

M. A. De La Rosa, editors. Arid environments and wind erosion. Nova Science Publishers, Inc., Hauppauge, New York.

Abella, S. R., A. A. Suazo, C. M. Norman, and A. C. Newton. 2013. Treatment alternatives and timing affect seeds of African mustard (*Brassica tournefortii*), an invasive forb in American Southwest arid lands. Invasive Plant Science and Management 6:559–567.

Aguiar, M. R., and O. E. Sala. 1999. Patch structure, dynamics, and implications for the functioning of arid ecosystems. Trends in Ecology and Evolution 14:273–277.

Allington, G. R. H., and T. J. Valone. 2011. Long-term livestock exclusion in an arid grassland alters vegetation and soil. Rangeland Ecology and Management 64:424–428.

Althoff, D. M., K. A. Segraves, and J. P. Sparks. 2004. Characterizing the interaction between the bogus yucca moth and yuccas: Do bogus yucca moths impact yucca reproductive success? Oecologia 140:321–327.

Anderson, R. S., R. Beatty, and S. Church. 2002. Insects and spiders of the world. Marshall Cavendish, Tarrytown, New York.

Arteaga, S., A. Andrade-Cetto, and R. Cardenas. 2005. *Larrea tridentata* (Creosote bush), an abundant plant of Mexican and U.S.-American deserts and its metabolite nordihydroguaiaretic acid. Journal of Ethnopharmacology 98:231–239.

Austin, A. T., L. Yahdjian, J. M. Stark, J. Belnap, A. Porporato, U. Norton, D. A. Ravetta, and S. M. Schaeffer. 2004. Water pulses and biogeochemical cycles in arid and semiarid ecosystems. Oecologia 141:221–235.

Barrows, C. W., and M. L. Murphy-Mariscal. 2012. Modeling impacts of climate change on Joshua trees at their southern boundary: How scale impacts predictions. Biological Conservation 152:29–36.

Beatley, J. C. 1980. Fluctuations and stability in climax shrub and woodland vegetation of the Mojave, Great Basin, and Transition Deserts of southern Nevada. Israel Journal of Botany 28:149–168.

Bell, K. C., D. J. Hafner, P. Leitner, and M. D. Matocq. 2009. Phylogeography of the ground squirrel subgenus *Xerospermophilus* and assembly of the Mojave Desert biota. Journal of Biogeography 37:363–378.

Belnap, J. 1998. Choosing indicators of natural resource condition: A case study in Arches National Park, Utah, USA. Environmental Management 22:635–642.

Belnap, J., and O. L. Lange. 2003. Biological soil crusts: Structure, function, and management. In I. T. Baldwin, M. M. Caldwell, G. Heldmaier, O. L. Lange, H. A. Mooney, E.-D. Schulze, and U. Sommer, editors. Ecological Studies Series 150, Volume 150. Springer-Verlag, Berlin, Germany.

Belnap, J., and S. D. Warren. 2002. Patton's tracks in the Mojave Desert, USA: An ecological legacy. Arid Land Research and Management 16:245–258.

Belnap, J., C. V. Hawkes, and M. K. Firestone. 2003. Boundaries in miniature: Two examples from soil. BioScience 53:739–749.

Belnap, J., D. M. Miller, D. R. Bedford, S. L. Phillips. 2014. Pedological and geological relationships with soil lichen and moss distribution in the eastern Mojave Desert, CA, USA. Journal of Arid Environments 106:45–57, doi: 10.1016/j.jaridenv.2014.02.007.

Belnap, J., R. H. Webb, M. E. Miller, D. M. Miller, L. A. DeFalco, P. A. Medica, M. L. Brooks, T. C. Esque, and D. Bedford. 2008. Monitoring ecosystem quality and function in arid settings of the Mojave Desert. U.S. Geological Survey Scientific Investigations Report 2009-5064. <http://pubs.usgs.gov/sir/2008/5064/>. Accessed February 9, 2014.

Benson, L. D., and R. A. Darrow. 1981. Trees and shrubs of the southwestern deserts. Third edition. University of Arizona Press, Tucson, Arizona.

Bowling, D. R., E. E. Grote, and J. Belnap. 2011. Rain pulse response of soil CO_2 exchange by biological soil crusts and grasslands of the semiarid Colorado Plateau, United States. Journal of Geophysical Research: Biogeosciences 116:1–17.

Brooks, M. L. 2009. Spatial and temporal distribution of non-native plants in upland areas of the Mojave Desert. Pages 101–124 in R. H. Webb, L. F. Fenstermaker, J. S. Heaton, D. L. Hughson, E. V. McDonald, and D. M. Miller, editors. The Mojave Desert: Ecosystem processes and sustainability. University of Nevada Press, Reno, Nevada.

———. 2003. Effects of increased soil nitrogen on the dominance of alien annual plants in the Mojave Desert. Journal of Applied Ecology 40:344–353.

———. 1999. Alien annual grasses and fire in the Mojave Desert. Madroño 46:13–19.

Brooks, M. L., and B. M. Lair. 2009. Ecological effects of vehicular routes in a desert ecosystem. Pages 168–195 in R. H. Webb, L. F. Fenstermaker, J. S. Heaton, D. L. Hughson, E. V. McDonald, and D. M. Miller, editors. The Mojave Desert: Ecosystem processes and sustainability. University of Nevada Press, Reno, Nevada.

Brooks, M. L., and J. C. Chambers. 2011. Resistance to invasion and resilience to fire in desert shrublands of North America. Rangeland Ecology and Management 64:431–438.

Brooks, M. L., and R. A. Minnich. 2006. Southeastern deserts bioregion. Pages 391–414 in N. G. Sugihara, J. W. van Wagtendonk, K. E. Shaffer, J. Fites-Kaufman, and A. E. Thode, editors. Fire in California's ecosystems. University of California Press, Berkeley, California.

Brooks, M. L., J. C. Chambers, and R. A. McKinley. 2013. Fire history, effects, and management in southern Nevada. Pages 75–96 in J. C. Chambers, M. L. Brooks, B. K. Pendleton, and C. B. Raish, editors. The Southern Nevada Agency Partnership Science and Research Synthesis: Science to support land management in Southern Nevada. General Technical Report RMRS-GTR-303, U.S. Department of Agriculture, Forest Service, Rocky Mountain Research Station, Fort Collins, Colorado.

Brown, D. E., and C. H. Lowe, 1980. Biotic communities of the southwest. General Technical Report RM-78, U.S. Department of Agriculture, Forest Service, Rocky Mountain Forest and Range Experiment Station, Fort Collins, Colorado.

Brown, J. H. and B. A. Maurer. 1986. Body size, ecological dominance and Cope's rule. Nature 324.6094:248–250.

Brown, J. H. 1973a. The role of vertebrates in desert ecosystems. Pages 51–72 in W. G. Whitford, editor. Patterns and processes in desert ecosystems. University of New Mexico Press, Albuquerque, New Mexico.

———. 1973b. Species diversity of seed-eating desert rodents in sand dune habitats. Ecology 54:775–787.

Busch, D. E., and S. D. Smith. 1995. Mechanisms associated with decline of woody species in riparian ecosystems of the southwestern U.S. Ecological Monographs 65:347–370.

Caldwell, M. M., T. E. Dawson, and J. H. Richards. 1998. Hydraulic lift: Consequences of water efflux from roots of plants. Oecologia 113:151–161.

California Energy Commission. 2013. <http://www.energy.ca.gov/>. Accessed February 13, 2014.

Callaway, R. M. 1995. Positive interactions among plants. Botanical Review 61:306–349.

Carlisle, J. D., S. K. Skagen, B. E. Kus, C. van Riper III, K. L. Paxton, and J. F. Kelly. 2009. Landbird migration in the American West: Recent progress and future research directions. Condor 111:211–225.

Carpenter, D. E., M. G. Barbour, and C. J. Bahre. 1986. Old field succession in Mojave Desert scrub. Madroño 33:111–122.

Chew, R. M., and A. E. Chew, 1965. The primary productivity of a desert-shrub (*Larrea tridentata*) community. Ecological Monographs 35:355–375.

Chung-MacCoubrey, A. L., R. E. Truitt, C. C. Caudill, T. J. Rodhouse, K. Irvine, J. R. Siderius, and V. K. Chang. 2008. Mojave Desert Network vital signs monitoring plan. Natural Resources Report NPS/MOJN/NRR-2008/057. U.S. Department of Interior, National Park Service, Natural Resource Program Center, Fort Collins, Colorado.

Clarke, M. L., and H. M. Rendell. 1998. Climate change impacts on sand supply and the formation of desert sand dunes in the southwest U.S.A. Journal of Arid Environments 39:517–531.

Clark, J. S. 1991. Disturbance and population structure on the shifting mosaic landscape. Ecology 72:1119–1137.

Cody, M. L. 2000. Slow-motion population dynamics of Mojave Desert perennial plants. Journal of Vegetation Science 11:351–358.

———. 1986. Structural niches in plant communities. Pages 381–405 in J. Diamond and T. J. Case, editors. Community Ecology. Harper and Row, New York, New York.

Cole, K. L., K. Ironside, J. Eischeid, G. Garfin, P. B. Duffy, and C. Toney. 2011. Past and ongoing shifts in Joshua tree distribution support future modeled range contraction. Ecological Applications 21:137–149.

Collins, S. L., R. L. Sinsabaugh, C. Crenshaw, L. Green, A. Porras-Alfaro, M. M. Stursova, and L. H. Zeglin. 2008. Pulse dynamics and microbial processes in aridland ecosystems. Journal of Ecology 96:413–420.

Collins S. L., J. Belnap, N.B. Grimm, J. A. Rudgers, C. N. Dahm, P. D'Odorico, M. Litvak, D. O. Natvig, D. C. Peters, W. T. Pockman, R. L. Sinsabaugh, B. O. Wolf. 2014. A multi-scale, hierarchical model of pulse dynamics in aridland ecosystems. Annual Review of Ecology, Evolution, and Systematics 45:397–419

Comstock, J. P., and J. R. Ehleringer. 1992. Plant adaptation in the Great Basin and Colorado Plateau. The Great Basin Naturalist 52:195–215.

Cook, B. I., and R. Seager. 2013. The response of the North American monsoon to increased greenhouse gas forcing. Journal of Geophysical Research: Atmospheres 118:1690–1699.

Cooke, R., A. Warren, and A. Goudie. 1993. Desert geomorphology. University of London Press, London, UK.

Crawford, C. S. 1986. The role of invertebrates in desert ecosystems. Pages 71–91 in W. G. Whitford, editor. Patterns and processes in desert ecosystems. University of New Mexico Press, Albuquerque, New Mexico.

———. 1981. Biology of desert invertebrates. Springer-Verlag, Berlin, Germany.

Dai, A. 2011. Drought under global warming: A review. Wiley Interdisciplinary Reviews: Climate Change 2:45–65.

D'Antonio, C. M., and P. M. Vitousek. 1992. Biological invasions by exotic grasses, the grass/fire cycle, and global change. Annual Review of Ecology and Systematics: 63–87.

Darwin, C. 1874. Letter to J. D. Hooker, April 7, 1874, in F. Burkhardt and S. Smith, editors. A calendar of the correspondence of Charles Darwin, 1821–1882. The Press Syndicate of the University of Cambridge, Cambridge, UK.

Davidson, D. W. 1977. Species diversity and community organization in desert seed-eating ants. Ecology 58:711–724.

DeFalco, L. A., and S. J. Scoles-Sciulla. 2009. Effectiveness of active rehabilitation of vehicle routes in the Bureau of Land Management's California Desert District. Technical report prepared for Bureau of Land Management, California State Office, Division of Natural Resources, Sacramento, California.

DeFalco, L. A., T. C. Esque, J. M. Kane, and M. B. Nicklas. 2009. Seed banks in a degraded desert shrubland: Influence of soil surface condition and harvester ant activity on seed abundance. Journal of Arid Environments 73:885–893.

DeFalco, L. A., T. C. Esque, M. B. Nicklas, and J. M. Kane. 2012. Supplementing seed banks to rehabilitate disturbed Mojave Desert shrublands: Where do all the seeds go? Restoration Ecology 20:85–94.

DeFalco, L. A., T. C. Esque, S. J. Scoles-Sciulla, and J. Rodgers. 2010. Desert wildfire and severe drought diminish survivorship of the long-lived Joshua tree (*Yucca brevifolia*; Agavaceae). American Journal of Botany 97:243–250.

Drake, B. G., M. A. Gonzàlez-Meler, and S. P. Long. 1997. More efficient plants: A consequence of rising atmospheric CO_2? Annual Review of Plant Physiology and Plant Molecular Biology 48:609–639.

Dudek and ICF International. 2012. Desert Renewable Energy Conservation Plan (DRECP) Baseline Biology Report. Prepared for the California Energy Commission, Sacramento, California.

Duniway, M. C., J. E. Herrick, and H. C. Monger. 2010. Spatial and temporal variability of plant-available water in calcium carbonate-cemented soils and consequences for arid ecosystem resilience. Oecologia 163:215–226.

Ehleringer, J. R. 2001. Productivity of deserts. Pages 345–362 in J. Roy, B. Saugier, and H. A. Mooney, editors. Terrestrial global productivity. Academic Press, San Diego, California.

Elton, C. S. 1927. Animal ecology. Macmillan Company, New York, New York.

Elzinga, C. L., D. W. Salzer, J. W. Willoughby, and J. P. Gibbs, 2001. Monitoring plant and animal populations. Blackwell Science, Inc., Malden, Massachusetts.

Esque, T. C. 2004. The role of fire, rodents, and ants in changing plant communities in the Mojave Desert. Dissertation. University of Nevada, Reno, Nevada.

Esque, T. C., and E. L. Peters. 1994. Ingestion of bones, stones and soil by desert tortoises. Pages 105–111 in R. B. Bury and D. J. Germano, editors. Biology of North American tortoises. National Biological Survey, Fish and Wildlife Research No.13. U.S. Department of the Interior, Washington, D.C..

Esque, T. C., K. E. Nussear, K. K. Drake, A. D. Walde, K. H. Berry, R. C. Averill-Murray, A. P. Woodman, W. I. Boarman, P. A. Medica, J. Mack, and J. S. Heaton. 2010. Effects of subsidized predators, resource variability, and human population density on desert tortoise populations in the Mojave Desert, USA. Endangered Species Research 12:167–177.

Esque, T. C., K. K. Drake, and K. E. Nussear. In press. Water and food acquisition and their consequences on life history and metabolism of North American tortoises. In D. Rostal, H. Mushinsky, and E. D. McCoy, editors. Ecology of North American tortoises. Johns Hopkins University Press, Baltimore, Maryland.

Fenn, M. E., E. B. Allen, S. B. Weiss, S. Jovan, L. H. Geiser, G. S. Tonnesen, R. F. Johnson, L. E. Rao, B. S. Gimeno, F. Yuan, T. Meixner, and A. Bytnerowicz. 2010. Nitrogen critical loads and management alternatives for N-impacted ecosystems in California. Journal of Environmental Management 91:2404–2423.

Fowler, C. S. 1999. The Timbisha Shoshone of Death Valley. Pages 66–70 in R. B. Lee and R. Daly, editors. The Cambridge Encyclopedia of Hunters and Gatherers. Cambridge University Press, New York, New York.

Gile, L. H., R. P. Gibbens, and J. M. Lenz. 1997. The near-ubiquitous pedogenic world of mesquite roots in an arid basin floor. Journal of Arid Environments 35:39–58.

———. 1995. Soils and sediments associated with remarkable, deeply-penetrating roots of crucifixion thorn (*Koeberlinea spinosa* Zucc.). Journal of Arid Environments 31:137–151.

Godsoe, W., E. Strand, C. I. Smith, J. B. Yoder, T. C. Esque, and O. Pelimyr. 2009. Divergence in an obligate mutualism is not explained by divergent climatic factors. New Phytologist 183:589–599.

Grime, J. P. 1979. Plant strategies and vegetation processes. John Wiley, Chichester, West Sussex, UK.

Green, L. E., A. Porras-Alfaro, and R. L. Sinsabaugh. 2008. Translocation of nitrogen and carbon integrates biotic crust and grass production in desert grassland. Journal of Ecology 96:1076–1085.

Grover, M. C., and L. A. DeFalco. 1995. Desert tortoise (*Gopherus agassizii*): Status-of-knowledge outline with references. General Technical Report INT-GTR-136. U.S. Department of Agriculture, Forest Service, Intermountain Research Station, Ogden, Utah.

Gunderson, L. H., and C. S. Holling, editors. 2002. Panarchy: Understanding transformations in human and natural systems. Island Press, Washington, D.C..

Hafernik, J., and L. Saul-Gershenz. 2000. Beetle larvae cooperate to mimic bees. Nature 405:35–36.

Hall, C. A., Jr. 2007. Introduction to the geology of southern California and its native plants. University of California Press, Berkeley and Los Angeles, California.

Hamerlynck, E. P., J. R. McAuliffe, E. V. McDonald, and S. D Smith. 2002. Ecological responses of two Mojave Desert shrubs to soil horizon development and soil water dynamics. Ecology 83:768–779.

Hereford, R., R. H. Webb, and C. Longpré. 2006. Precipitation history and ecosystem response to multidecadal precipitation variability in the Mojave Desert region, 1893–2001. Journal of Arid Environments 67:13–34.

Herrick, J. E., J. W. Van Zee, K. M. Havstad, and W. C. Whitford. 2005. Monitoring manual for grassland, shrubland, and savanna ecosystems. Agricultural Research Service Jornada Experimental Range, U.S. Department of Agriculture, Las Cruces, New Mexico.

Housman, D. C., C. M. Yeager, B. J. Darby, R. L. Sanford Jr., L. C. R. Kuske, D. A. Neher, and J. Belnap. 2007. Heterogeneity of soil nutrients and subsurface biota in a dryland ecosystem. Soil Biology and Biochemistry 39:2138–2149.

Housman, D. C., H. H. Powers, A. D. Collins, and J. Belnap. 2006. Carbon and nitrogen fixation differ between successional stages of biological soil crusts in the Colorado Plateau and Chihuahuan Desert. Journal of Arid Environments 66:620–634.

Huenneke, L. F., and W. H. Schlesinger. 2006. Patterns of net primary production in Chihuahuan desert ecosystems. Pages 232–246 in K. Havstad, L. F. Huenneke, and W. H. Schlesinger, editors. Structure and function of a Chihuahuan Desert ecosystem: The Jornada Basin long-term ecological research site. Oxford University Press, New York, New York.

Hughson, D. L. 2009. Human population in the Mojave Desert: resources and sustainability. Pages 57–77 in R. H. Webb, L. F. Fenstermaker, J. S. Heaton, D. L. Hughson, E. V. McDonald, and D. M.

Miller, editors. The Mojave Desert: Ecosystem processes and sustainability. University of Nevada Press, Reno, Nevada.
Hultine, K. R,. and S. E. Bush. 2011. Ecohydrological consequences of non-native riparian vegetation in the southwestern United States: A review from an ecophysiological perspective. Water Resources Research 47:1–13.
Hunter, K. L., J. L. Betancourt, B. R. Riddle, T. R. Van Devender, K. L. Cole, and W. G. Spaulding. 2001. Ploidy race distributions since the Last Glacial Maximum in the North American desert shrub, *Larrea tridentata.* Global Ecology and Biogeography 10:521–533.
Jaramillo, V. J., R. Ahedo-Hernández, and J. B. Kauffman. 2003. Root biomass and carbon in a tropical evergreen forest of Mexico: Changes with secondary succession and forest conversion to pasture. Journal of Tropical Ecology 19:457–464.
Jennings, W. B. 2002. Diet selection by the desert tortoise in relation to the flowering phenology of ephemeral plants. Chelonian Conservation Biology 4:353–358.
Jenny, H. 1941. Factors of soil formation: A system of quantitative pedology. McGraw-Hill Book Company, New York, New York.
Karl, T. R., J. M. Melillo, and T. C. Peterson, editors. 2009. Global climate change impacts in the United States. Cambridge University Press, New York, New York.
Kristan, W. B., III, and W. I. Boarman. 2007. Effects of anthropogenic developments on common raven nesting biology in the west Mojave Desert. Ecological Applications 17:1703–1713.
———. 2003. Spatial pattern of risk of common raven predation on desert tortoises. Ecology 84:2432–2443.
Lane, L. J., E. M. Romney, and T. E. Hakonson. 1984. Water balance calculations and net production of perennial vegetation in the northern Mojave desert. Journal of Range Management 37:12–18.
Laport, R. G., R. L. Minckley, and J. Ramsey. 2012. Phylogeny and cytogeography of the North American creosote bush (*Larrea tridentata,* Zygophyllaceae). Systematic Botany 37:153–164.
Lavoie, M., M. C. Mack, and E. A. G. Schuur. 2011. Effects of elevated nitrogen and temperature on carbon and nitrogen dynamics in Alaskan arctic and boreal soils. Journal of Geophysical Research: Biogeosciences (2005–2012) 116:1–14.
Leu, M., S. E. Hanser, and S. T. Knick. 2008. The human footprint in the west: A large-scale analysis of anthropogenic impacts. Ecological Applications 18:1119–1139.
Loss, S. R., T. Will, and P. P. Marra. 2013. The impact of free-ranging domestic cats on wildlife of the United States. Nature Communications 4:1396. <http://www.nature.com/ncomms/journal/v4/n1/abs/ncomms2380.html>. Accessed February 13, 2013.
Lovich, J. E., and J. R. Ennen. 2011. Wildlife conservation and solar energy development in the desert southwest, United States. BioScience 61:982–992.
Lovich, J. E., and K. R. Beaman. 2007. A history of Gila monster (*Heloderma suspectum cinctum*) records from California with comments on factors affecting their distribution. Bulletin, Southern California Academy of Sciences 106:39–58.
Ludwig, J. A., and D. J. Tongway. 1997. A landscape approach to rangeland ecology. Pages 1–12 in J. Ludwig, D. Tongway, K. Hodgkinson, D. Freudenberger, and J. Noble, editors. Landscape ecology, function, and management: Principles from Australia's rangelands. CSIRO Publishing, Collingwood, Victoria, Australia.
MacMahon, J. A. 1979. North American deserts: Their floral and faunal components. Pages 21–82 in D. W. Goodall, and R. A. Perry, editors. Arid-land ecosystems: Structure, function, and management. International Biological Programme Series No. 16. Volume 1. Cambridge University Press, Cambridge, UK.
MacMahon, J. A., and F. H. Wagner. 1985. The Mojave, Sonoran, and Chihuahuan Deserts of North America. Pages 105–202 in M. Evanari, I. Noy-Meir, and D. W. Goodall, editors. Ecosystems of the world. Elsevier, Amsterdam, The Netherlands.
MacMahon, J. A., J. F. Mull, and T. O. Crist. 2000. Harvester ants (*Pogonomyrmex* spp.): Their community and ecosystem influences. Annual Review of Ecology and Systematics 31:265–291.
Mahall B. E., and R. M. Callaway. 1992. Root communication mechanisms and intracommunity distributions of two Mojave Desert shrubs. Ecology 73:2145–2151.
Marion, G. M., P. S. J. Verburg, E. V. McDonald, and J. A. Arnone. 2008. Modeling salt movement through a Mojave Desert soil. Journal of Arid Environments 72:1012–1033.
McAuliffe, J. R. 1984. Sahuaro-nurse tree association in the Sonoran Desert: Competitive effects of sahuaros. Oecologia 64:319–321.
McAuliffe, J. R., and E. P. Hamerlynck. 2010. Perennial plant mortality in the Sonoran and Mojave Deserts in response to severe, multi-year drought. Journal of Arid Environments 74:885–896.
McAuliffe, J. R., and E. V. McDonald. 1995. A piedmont landscape in the eastern Mojave Desert: Examples of linkages between biotic and physical components. San Bernardino County Museum Association Quarterly 42:53–63.
McCauley, C. K., and J. P. Sparks. 2009. Abiotic gas formation drives nitrogen loss from a desert ecosystem. Science 326:837–840.
McDonald, E. V. 1994. The relative influences of climatic change, desert dust, and lithologic control on soil-geomorphic processes and soil hydrology of calcic soils formed on Quaternary alluvial-fan deposits in the Mojave Desert, California. PhD dissertation. University of New Mexico, Albuquerque, New Mexico.
McFadden, L. D., and P. L. K. Knuepfer. 1990. Soil geomorphology: The linkage of pedology and surficial processes. Geomorphology 3:197–205.
McFadden, L. D., E. V. McDonald, S. G. Wells, K. Anderson, J. Quade, and S. L. Forman. 1998. The vesicular layer and carbonate collars of desert soils and pavements: Formation, age, and relation to climate change. Geomorphology 24:101–145.
McFadden, L. D., S. G. Wells, and M. J. Jercinovich. 1987. Influences of eolian and pedogenic processes on the origin and evolution of desert pavements. Geology 15:504–508.
Medica, P. A., K. E. Nussear, T. C. Esque, and M. B. Saethre. 2012. Long-term growth of desert tortoise (*Gopherus agassizii*) in a southern Nevada population. Journal of Herpetology 46:213–220.
Medica, P. A., R. B. Bury, and R. A. Luckenbach. 1980. Drinking and construction of water catchments by the desert tortoise, *Gopherus agassizii,* in the Mojave Desert. Herpetologica 36:301–304.
Millennium Ecosystem Assessment. 2005. Ecosystems and human well-being: Biodiversity synthesis. World Resources Institute, Washington, D.C.
Minnich, R. A., and A. C. Sanders. 2000. *Brassica tournefortii* Gouan. Pages 68–71 in C. C. Bossard, J. M. Randall, and M. C. Hoshovsky, editors. Invasive plants of California's wildlands. University of California Press, Berkeley, California.
Miriti, M. N., S. Rodríguez-Buriticá, S. J. Wright, and H. F. Howe. 2007. Episodic death across species of desert shrubs. Ecology 88:32–36.
Monger, H. C. 2006. Soil development in the Jornada basin. Pages 81–106 in K. M. Havstad, L. F. Huenneke, and W. H. Schlesinger, editors. Structure and function of a Chihuahuan Desert ecosystem. Oxford University Press, New York, New York.
Munson, S. M., R. H. Webb, J. Belnap, J. A. Hubbard, D. E. Swann, and S. Rutman. 2012. Forecasting climate change impacts to plant community composition in the Sonoran Desert region. Global Change Biology 18:1083–1095.
Naumburg, E., D. C. Housman, T. E. Huxman, T. N. Charlet, M. E. Loik, and S. D. Smith. 2003. Photosynthesis responses of Mojave Desert shrubs to free air CO_2 enrichment are greatest during wet years. Global Change Biology 9:276–285.
Noy-Meir, I. 1973. Desert ecosystems: Environment and producers. Annual Review of Ecology and Systematics 4:25–51.
Ogle, K., and J. F. Reynolds. 2004. Plant responses to precipitation in desert ecosystems: Integrating functional types, pulses, thresholds, and delays. Oecologia 141:282–294.
Padilla, F. M., and F. I. Pugnaire. 2006. The role of nurse plants in the restoration of degraded environments. Frontiers in Ecology and the Environment 4:196–202.
Parish, S. B. 1907. A contribution toward a knowledge of the genus *Washingtonia.* Botanical Gazette 44:408–434.
Parmenter, R. R., J. A. MacMahon, and S. B. Vander Wall. 1984. The measurement of granivory by desert rodents, birds and ants: A comparison of an energetics approach and a seed-dish technique. Journal of Arid Environments 7:75–92.
Paxton, K. L., C. van Riper III, and C. O'Brien. 2008. Movement patterns and stopover ecology of Wilson's warblers during spring migration on the lower Colorado River in southwestern Arizona. Condor 110:672–681.
Pellmyr, O., and J. Leebens-Mack. 1999. Forty million years of mutualism: Evidence for Eocene origin of the yucca-yucca moth association. Proceedings of the National Academy of Sciences of the United States of America 96:9178–9183.
Pielke, R. A. 2001. Influence of the spatial distribution of vegeta-

tion and soils on the prediction of cumulus convective rainfall. Reviews of Geophysics 39:151–177.

Pinkava, D. J., J. P. Rebman, and M. A. Baker. 2001. Nomenclatural changes in *Cylindropuntia* and *Opuntia* (Cactaceae) and notes on interspecific hybridization. Journal of the Arizona/Nevada Academy of Sciences 33:150.

Polis, G. A, editor. 1991. The ecology of desert communities. University of Arizona Press, Tucson, Arizona.

Pointing, S. B., and J. Belnap. 2012. Microbial colonization and controls in dryland systems. Nature Reviews: Microbiology 10:551–562.

Rapport, D. J., H. A. Regier, and T. C. Hutchinson. 1985. Ecosystem behavior under stress. The American Naturalist 125:617–640.

Reed, S. C., K. K. Coe, J. P. Sparks, D. C. Housman, T. J. Zelikova, and J. Belnap. 2012. Changes to dryland rainfall result in rapid moss mortality and altered soil fertility. Nature Climate Change 2:752–755.

Rehfeldt, G. E., N. L. Crookston, M. V. Warwell, and J. S. Evans. 2006. Empirical analyses of plant-climate relationships for the western United States. International Journal of Plant Sciences 167:1123–1150.

Reichman, O. J., and K. M. van de Graaff. 1975. Association between ingestion of green vegetation and desert rodent reproduction. Journal of Mammalogy 56:503–506.

Repasky, R. R., and D. Schluter. 1994. Habitat distributions of wintering sparrows along an elevational gradient: Tests of the food, predation, and microhabitat structure hypotheses. Journal of Animal Ecology 63:569–582.

Reynolds, J. F., P. R. Kemp, K. Ogle, and R. J. Fernández. 2004. Modifying the "pulse-reserve" paradigm for deserts of North America: Precipitation pulses, soil water, and plant responses. Oecologia 141:194–210.

Reynolds, M. B. J., L. A. DeFalco, and T. C. Esque. 2012. Short seed longevity, variable germination conditions, and infrequent establishment events provide a narrow window for *Yucca brevifolia* (Agavaceae) recruitment. American Journal of Botany 99:1647–1654.

Reynolds R. L., J. C. Yount, M. Reheis, H. Goldstein, P. Chavez Jr., R. Fulton, J. Whitney, C. Fuller, and R. M. Forester. 2007. Dust Emission from Wet and Dry Playas in the Mojave Desert, USA. Earth Surface Processes and Landforms.

Rinne, John N., and W. L. Minckley. 1991. Native Fishes of Arid Lands: A Dwindling Resource of the Desert Southwest. General Technical Report RM-206. USDA Forest Service, Fort Collins, Colorado.

Rowlands, P. G., H. Johnson, E. Ritter, and A. Endo. 1982. The Mojave Desert. Pages 103–162 in G. L. Bender, editor. Reference handbook on the deserts of North America. Greenwood Press, Westport, Connecticut.

Rundel, P. W., and A. C. Gibson. 1996. Ecological communities and processes in a Mojave Desert ecosystem: Rock Valley, Nevada. Cambridge University Press, Cambridge, UK.

Sala, O. E., W. J. Parton, L. A. Joyce, and W. K. Laurenroth. 1988. Primary production of the central grassland region of the United States. Ecology 69:40–45.

Sawyer, J. O., T. Keeler-Wolf, and J. M. Evens. 2009. A manual of California vegetation. Second edition. California Native Plant Society, Sacramento, California.

Schaefer, R. J., D. J. Thayer, and T. S. Burton. 2003. Forty-one years of vegetation change on permanent transects in northeastern California: Implications for wildlife. California Fish and Game 89:55–71.

Schlesinger, W. H. 1985. The formation of caliche in soils of the Mojave desert, California. Geochimica et Cosmochimica Acta 49:57–66.

———. 1982. Carbon storage in the caliche of arid soils: A case study from Arizona. Soil Science 133:247–255.

Schlesinger, W. H., and C. S. Jones. 1984. The comparative importance of overland runoff and mean annual rainfall to shrub communities of the Mojave Desert. Botanical Gazette 145:116–124.

Schlesinger, W. H., J. Belnap, J., and G. Marion. 2009. On carbon sequestration in desert ecosystems. Global Change Biology 15:1488–1490.

Schlesinger, W. H., J. F. Reynolds, G. L. Cunningham, L. F. Huenneke, W. M. Jarrell, R. A. Virginia, and W. G. Whitford. 1990. Biological feedbacks in global desertification. Science 247:1043–1048.

Schmidt-Nielsen, K. 1990. Animal physiology: Adaptation and environment. Fifth edition. Cambridge University Press, Cambridge, UK.

Schmitz, O. J. 2009. Indirect effects in communities and ecosystems: The role of trophic and nontrophic interactions. Pages 289–295 in A. S. Levin, editor. The Princeton Guide to Ecology. Princeton University Press, Princeton, New Jersey.

Schwinning, S., and M. M. Hooten. 2009. Mojave desert root systems. Pages 279–311 in R. H. Webb, L. F. Fenstermaker, J. S. Heaton, D. L. Hughson, E. V. McDonald, and D. M. Miller, editors. The Mojave Desert: Ecosystem Processes and Sustainability. University of Nevada Press, Reno, Nevada.

Schwinning, S., and O. E. Sala. 2004. Hierarchy of responses to resource pulses in arid and semi-arid ecosystems. Oecologia 141:211–220.

Schwinning, S., O. E. Sala, M. E. Loik, and J. R. Ehleringer. 2004. Thresholds, memory, and seasonality: Understanding pulse dynamics in arid/semi-arid ecosystems. Oecologia 141:191–193.

Scoles-Sciulla, S. J., and L. A. DeFalco. 2009. Seed reserves diluted during surface soil reclamation in eastern Mojave Desert. Arid Land Research and Management 23:1–13.

Seager, R., and G. A. Vecchi. 2010. Greenhouse warming and the 21st century hydroclimate of southwestern North America. Proceedings of the National Academy of Sciences of the United States of America 107:21277–21282.

Seager, R., M. Ting, I. Held, Y. Kushnir, J. Lu, G. Vecchi, H.-P. Huang, N. Harnik, A. Leetmaa, N.-C. Lau, C. Li, J. Velez, and N. Naik. 2007. Model projections of an imminent transition to a more arid climate in southwestern North America. Science 316:1181– 1184.

Skinner, M. W., and B. M. Pavlik. 1994. California Native Plant Society's inventory of rare and endangered vascular plants of California. California Native Plant Society, Sacramento, California.

Smith, C. I., S. Tank, W. Godsoe, E. Strand, J. Levenick, T. Esque, and O. Pellmyr. 2011. Comparative phylogeography of a coevolved community: Concerted population expansions in Joshua trees and four yucca moths. PLoS One 6:e25628.

Smith, E. L., and D. Smith. 2002. Colton Hills exclosure, Mojave National Preserve. Unpublished report. Cascabel Consultants, Benson, Arizona.

Smith, S. D., R. K. Monson, and J. E. Anderson. 1997. Physiological ecology of North American desert plants. Springer-Verlag, New York, New York.

Smith, S. D., T. N. Charlet, L. F. Fenstermaker, and B. A. Newingham. 2009. Effects of global change on Mojave Desert ecosystems. Pages 31–56 in R. H. Webb, L. F. Fenstermaker, J. S. Heaton, D. L. Hughson, E. V. McDonald, and D. M. Miller, editors. The Mojave Desert: Ecosystem Processes and Sustainability. University of Nevada Press, Reno, Nevada.

Soulard, C. E., T. C. Esque, D. R. Bedford, and S. Bond. 2013. The role of fire on soil mounds and surface roughness in the Mojave Desert. Earth Surface Processes and Landforms 38:111–121.

Springer, M. E. 1958. Desert pavement and vesicular layer of some soils of the desert of the Lahontan Basin, Nevada. Soil Science Society of America Journal 22: 63–66.

Stahnke, H. L. 1972. UV light, a useful field tool. BioScience 22:604–607.

Steers, R. J., and E. B. Allen. 2010. Post-fire control of invasive plants promotes native recovery in a burned desert shrubland. Restoration Ecology 18:334–343.

Stein, B., P. Glick, N. Edelson, and A. Stadut. 2013. Quick guide to climate-smart conservation. National Wildlife Federation. Washington, D.C. <https://www.nwf.org/pdf/Climate-Smart-Conservation/Climate-Smart_Conservation_Quick_Guide.pdf>. Accessed February 13, 2014.

Stevenson, B. A., E. V. McDonald, and T. G. Caldwell. 2009. Root patterns of *Larrea tridentata* in relation to soil morphology in Mojave Desert soils of different ages. Pages 312–328 in R. H. Webb, L. F. Fenstermaker, J. S. Heaton, D. L. Hughson, E. V. McDonald, and D. M. Miller, editors. The Mojave Desert: Ecosystem Processes and Sustainability. University of Nevada Press, Reno, Nevada.

Taber, S. W. 1998. The world of the harvester ants. Texas A & M University Press, College Station, Texas.

Tagestad, J. D., M. L. Brooks, V. I. Cullinan, J. L. Downs, and R. A. Mckinley. In press. Precipitation regime classification for the Mojave Desert: Implications for fire occurrence. Journal of Arid Environments.

Turner, R. 1994. Warm-temperate-desert lands: Mojave Desert scrub.

Pages 156–168 in D. E. Brown, editor. Biotic communities: Southwest United States and northwest Mexico. Second edition. University of Utah Press, Salt Lake City, Utah.
U.S. Fish and Wildlife Service (USFWS). 2011. Revised recovery plan for the Mojave population of the desert tortoise (*Gopherus agassizii*). U.S. Fish and Wildlife Service, Pacific Southwest Region, Sacramento, California.
Vander Wall, S. B., T. C. Esque, B. A. Waitman, D. F. Haines, and M. G. Garnett. 2006. Joshua tree (*Yucca brevifolia*) seeds are dispersed by seed-caching rodents. Ecoscience 13:539–543.
Vogl, R. J., and L. T. McHargue. 1966. Vegetation of California fan palm oases on the San Andreas Fault. Ecology 47:532–540.
Wagner, D., M. J. F. Brown, and D. M. Gordon. 1997. Harvester ant nests, soil biota, and soil chemistry. Oecologia 112:232–236.
Wainwright, J., A. J. Parsons, and A. D. Abrahams. 1995. A simulation study of the role of raindrop erosion in the formation of desert pavements. Earth Surface Processes and Landforms 20:277–291.
Waitman, B. A., S. B. Vander Wall, and T. C. Esque. 2012. Seed dispersal and seed fate in Joshua tree (*Yucca brevifolia*). Journal of Arid Environments 81:1–8.
Walker, L. R., D. B. Thompson, and F. H. Landau. 2001. Experimental manipulations of fertile islands and nurse plant effects in the Mojave Desert, USA. Western North American Naturalist 61:25–35.
Walvoord, M. A., R. G. Striegl, D. E. Prudic, and D. A. Stonestrom. 2005. CO_2 dynamics in the Amargosa Desert: Fluxes and isotopic speciation in a deep unsaturated zone. Water Resources Research 41. <doi:10.1029/2004WR003599>.
Ward, D. 2009. The biology of deserts. Oxford University Press, Oxford, UK.
Weatherly, H. E., S. F. Zitzer, J. S. Coleman and, J. A. Arnone III. 2003. *In situ* litter decomposition and litter quality in a Mojave Desert ecosystem: Effects of elevated CO_2 and interannual climate variability. Global Change Biology 9:1223–1233.
Webb, R. H., J. Belnap, and K. A. Thomas. 2009. Natural recovery from severe disturbance in the Mojave Deserts. Pages 343–377 in R. H. Webb, L. F. Fenstermaker, J. S. Heaton, D. L. Hughson, E. V. McDonald, and D. M. Miller, editors. The Mojave Desert: Ecosystem processes and sustainability. University of Nevada Press, Reno, Nevada.
Webb, R. H., J. S. Heaton, M. Brooks, and D. M. Miller. 2009. Threats through time: Introduction. Pages 1–6 in R. H. Webb, L. F. Fenstermaker, J. S. Heaton, D. L. Hughson, E. V. McDonald, and D. M. Miller, editors. The Mojave Desert: Ecosystem processes and sustainability. University of Nevada Press, Reno, Nevada.
Webb, R. H., J. W. Steiger, and E. B. Newman. 1988. The response of vegetation to disturbance in Death Valley National Monument, California. U.S. Geological Survey Bulletin 1793. U.S. Government Printing Office, Denver, Colorado.
Webb, R. H., L. A. DeFalco, T. C. Esque, and P. A. Medica. 2009. A review of selected long-term ecological studies of the Mojave Desert. Pages 429–456 in R. H. Webb, L. F. Fenstermaker, J. S. Heaton, D. L. Hughson, E. V. McDonald, and D. M. Miller, editors. The Mojave Desert: Ecosystem processes and sustainability. University of Nevada Press, Reno, Nevada.
Webb, R. H., L. F. Fenstermaker, J. S. Heaton, D. L. Hughson, E. V. McDonald, and D. M. Miller, editors. 2009. The Mojave Desert: Ecosystem processes and sustainability. University of Nevada Press, Reno, Nevada.
Webb, R. H., M. B. Murov, T. C. Esque, D. E. Boyer, L. A. DeFalco, D. F. Haines, D. Oldershaw, S. J. Scoles, K. A. Thomas, J. B. Blainey, and P. A. Medica. 2003. Perennial vegetation data from permanent plots on the Nevada Test Site, Nye County, Nevada, USA. Open-File Report 03-336, U.S. Geological Survey, Tucson, Arizona.
Weigand, J., and J. Rodgers. 2009. Active restoration for the Mojave Desert. Pages 378–409 in R. H. Webb, L. F. Fenstermaker, J. S. Heaton, D. L. Hughson, E. V. McDonald, and D. M. Miller, editors. The Mojave Desert: Ecosystem processes and sustainability. University of Nevada Press, Reno, Nevada.
Western Regional Climate Center. 2013a. Bridgeport, California. <http://www.wrcc.dri.edu/cgi-bin/cliMAIN.pl?ca1072>. Accessed February 13, 2014.
Western Regional Climate Center. 2013b. El Centro 2 SSW, California. <http://www.wrcc.dri.edu/cgi-bin/cliMAIN.pl?ca2713>. Accessed February 13, 2014.
Whitford, W. G. 2002. Ecology of desert systems. Academic Press, San Diego, California.
Whittaker, R. H., and W. A. Niering. 1975. Vegetation of the Santa Catalina Mountains, Arizona. V: Biomass, production, and diversity along the elevation gradient. Ecology 56:771–790.
Williams, J. B., and B. I. Tieleman. 2005. Physiological adaptation in desert birds. BioScience 55:416–425.
Wilson, E. O. 1984. Biophilia. Harvard University Press, Cambridge, Massachusetts.
Wood, D. A., A. G. Vandergast, K. R. Barr, R. D. Inman, T. C. Esque, K. E. Nussear, and R. N. Fisher. 2012. Comparative phylogeography reveals deep lineages and regional evolutionary hotspots in the Mojave and Sonoran Deserts. Diversity and Distributions 18:1–16.

THIRTY-ONE

Wetlands

WALTER G. DUFFY, PHILIP GARONE, BRENDA J. GREWELL, SHARON KAHARA, JOSEPH FLESKES, BRENT HELM, PETER MOYLE, ROSEMARY RECORDS, and JOSEPH SILVEIRA

Introduction

Freshwater wetlands are among the most important ecosystems in California, although the area they occupy has been greatly reduced. Historically, large portions of the Central Valley and Bay-Delta Regions would have been classified as wetlands, but since European settlement, much of this area has been lost to agricultural conversion, urban development, and other uses (Water Education Foundation 2000). Wetland loss has been poorly documented in other regions of the state. Today, freshwater wetlands currently occupy about 950,000 hectares of California (Table 31.1), or about 2.3% of the surface area of the state (CNRA 2010).

Wetlands are distributed throughout the state, extending from the Colorado Desert in the south to the Modoc Plateau in the north. For many people, scattered freshwater marshes along the fringes of the BRACKISH San Francisco Bay as well as those of the Sacramento–San Joaquin Delta (Bay-Delta) and Central Valley are characteristic of wetlands in California, and this region does indeed contain 38% of the wetland surface area in the state (CNRA 2010). However, the combined area of marshes, temporary wetlands, vernal pools, mountain meadows, and fens in the Sierra Nevada and Cascades and their eastern neighboring ecoregions is comparable to the area of wetlands in the Bay-Delta and Central Valley regions. Elsewhere, freshwater marsh wetlands, although not extensive, are common in coastal regions outside the Bay-Delta region, and bogs occur rarely in the North Coast region. Perhaps counterintuitively, the surface area of freshwater wetlands in the Mojave and Colorado Basin and Range ecoregions each exceeds that in the Klamath Mountains/High North Coast ecoregion. Wetlands in these desert regions consist primarily of riparian wetlands and palustrine wetlands associated with lake and reservoir margins. Riparian and forested scrub-shrub wetlands occur along streams and rivers in all regions of the state.

During the nineteenth and well into the twentieth century, wetlands in California and elsewhere were referred to by a variety of terms, such as swamp, marsh, bog, fen, mire, and moor. These terms were used imprecisely and often interchangeably, but as wetlands came to be valued for the ecosystem services they provide, management of them required a more precise definition. The U.S. Fish and Wildlife Service (USFWS) introduced one of the first formal uses of the term "wetlands" in 1956, defining them as "lowlands covered with shallow and sometimes temporary or intermittent waters"

TABLE 31.1
Area of freshwater wetlands within ecoregions of California

	Freshwater wetlands (hectares)					
Ecoregion	Emergent	Forest / shrub	Pond	Other	Riverine	Total
Cascades	25,226	6,686	778	58	714	33,462
Central Basin Range	26,159	2,650	323	300	353	29,784
Central California Foothills	23,200	17,512	9,702	42,550	49,124	142,088
Central Valley	126,474	26,689	10,454	149,762	45,219	358,598
Coast Range	11,364	7,179	709	24	13,680	32,956
East Cascades	93,504	21,241	1,279	410	1,940	118,374
Klamath Mountains	3,959	4,207	434	9	7,015	15,623
Mojave Basin	4,774	6,121	1,018	1,954	13,658	27,525
North Basin Range	24,509	25,517	143	115	27	50,311
Sierra Nevada	47,740	26,485	3,958	175	3,819	82,178
Southern California Mountains	4,109	5,139	454	107	7,952	17,762
Southern California North Baja	5,518	16,644	3,576	700	14,887	41,325
TOTAL	**396,536**	**166,069**	**32,828**	**196,163**	**158,388**	**949,985**

SOURCE: Derived from U.S. Fish and Wildlife Service, National Wetland Inventory Program mapping data for 2012.

(Shaw and Fredine 1956). This definition included shallow lakes and ponds, which usually contain emergent vegetation, but excluded streams, reservoirs, and deep lakes. Primarily concerned at that time with the value of wetlands to the waterfowl of the four great North American flyways, the Fish and Wildlife Service identified twenty types of wetlands based on their importance for these birds. This system remained the basis of wetland classification in the United States until 1979, when the USFWS introduced a new and more comprehensive definition of wetlands as transitional between terrestrial and aquatic ecosystems. For land to be classified as a wetland, at least one of three attributes needs to be present: (1) hydrophytic vegetation; (2) a substrate of predominantly undrained HYDRIC soil; and (3) a nonsoil substrate that is saturated with water or covered by shallow water at some time during the growing season of each year (Cowardin et al. 1979).

In addition to this more precise definition, the USFWS developed a hierarchical classification scheme for wetlands and deepwater habitats, dividing the five major systems—marine, estuarine, riverine, LACUSTRINE, and palustrine—into a total of ten subsystems and fifty-six classes (Cowardin et al. 1979). All systems contain some deepwater habitats except the palustrine, which includes all shallow nontidal wetlands dominated by trees, shrubs, persistent emergent vegetation, emergent mosses or lichens, as well as tidal wetlands with a low (<0.5%) concentration of ocean-derived salts. This chapter is concerned primarily with California's freshwater wetlands—those within the riverine, lacustrine, and palustrine systems. Most freshwater wetlands in California, about 64%, can be classified as palustrine. These wetlands typically occur in low-lying areas, such as the troughs of basins within the Central Valley, or in depressions at various elevations. Other freshwater wetlands are associated primarily with the margins of lakes, bays, reservoirs, or streams.

The hydrology of wetlands is central to their value as habitats for a variety of organisms and their delivery of ecosystem services. Hydrology in interior freshwater wetlands is under the influence of hillslope and geomorphic processes that together influence wetland HYDROPERIOD or period of flooding. The hydroperiod influences wetland water quality, soil development, nutrient cycling, and biological colonization (Jackson 2006). The hydroperiod of most freshwater wetlands in California is temporary or seasonal; they are flooded from a few days or weeks to several months each year. These alternate wet and dry periods create a dynamic environment that facilitates the decomposition of organic matter, cycling of nitrogen and phosphorus, growth of plant communities, and use by animal communities. Manipulation of the hydroperiod to promote development of plant communities and attract animal communities, often birds, is a common tool in wetland management in California.

California's freshwater wetlands provide a variety of ecosystem services to citizens and visitors to the state. They have high ecological diversity (IWJV 2005) and are recognized internationally as ecosystems of importance to migratory birds. Freshwater wetlands of the Central Valley and Upper Klamath River Basin are important wintering areas for waterbirds and also provide habitat during migration and breeding periods. These freshwater marshes support more than 60% of the waterfowl populations of the Pacific flyway (CVJV 2006). In the Sierra Nevada, riparian wetlands and meadows support a high proportion of vertebrates present in the region

Photo on previous page: Ross's snow geese (*Anser rossii*) in a flooded rice field in California's Central Valley. Photo: Robert McLandress.

(Erman et al. 1996). More permanent wetlands associated with coastal lagoons, estuaries, and the lower Sacramento and San Joaquin Rivers and their delta support diverse fish communities, although these fish communities are threatened by introduced species (Brown and May 2006). California wetlands also deliver several supporting ecosystem services related to hydrologic processes. Wetlands function as filters, improving water quality by transforming (Duffy and Kahara 2011) or sequestering nutrients and pollutants in their plants and soils. They can accommodate stormwater runoff and ameliorate the impacts of flooding, contribute to recharging groundwater aquifers, stabilize shorelines, and buffer saltwater intrusion (Water Education Foundation 2000). Wetlands also provide cultural ecosystem services, such as recreational opportunities for anglers, hunters, and bird watchers valued in millions of dollars.

Historical Ecology

California has been subject to fluctuating sea levels and land-forming tectonic processes, with the result that the state's freshwater wetlands differ significantly in age. As sea levels stabilized near their current levels approximately 4,000 to 6,000 B.P., San Francisco Bay was filled and the flow of the lower reaches of the Sacramento and San Joaquin Rivers was impeded, backing the rivers out of their channels and creating the brackish and freshwater wetlands of the Bay-Delta. The freshwater wetlands of the Central Valley are also relatively young, by geological time scales, having existed in some form for approximately two million years, since a combination of uplift and erosional deposition from the Coast Ranges and the Sierra Nevada raised the floor of the valley above sea level (Whipple et al. 2012).

California's wetlands were a source of bounty to Native Americans, who exploited them for food, such as fish, waterfowl, and edible plant roots and seeds, and for raw materials, such as common tules (*Schoenoplectus acutus*), from which Central Valley tribes wove rafts for hunting on rivers and lakes, and various sedges, which they utilized for basket weaving. Waterfowl taken from freshwater wetlands were an important food source for Native Americans in various parts of the state, including the Klamath Basin and Modoc Plateau in the northeast, the Central Valley, and the Central Coast. Waterfowl were hunted in a variety of ingenious ways, including by stretching nets across tule swamps and rivers, employing snares and long-handled nets, using decoys constructed of tules or stuffed bird skins, and setting alight piles of brush to attract and kill flocks of geese. Native Americans also burned wetlands to increase productivity by removing old growth, providing space for emergent plants that served as animal forage, and stimulating the growth of new tules (Heizer 1978, Lewis 1993).

California's wetlands became associated with disease and mortality late in 1832, when malaria reached the Central Valley in the wake of British fur trappers entering California from Oregon. The epidemic that followed devastated the human population of the Central Valley, reducing it by as much as 75% by 1846, just a few years prior to the massive influx of population to California in the Gold Rush (Cook 1955). Unlike Native Americans, emigrants to California conceived of wetlands as "wastelands" that represented an obstacle to settling the land and converting it to productive agricultural enterprises. The federal government shared this view, and under the Swamp and Overflowed Lands Act of 1850 the U.S. government ultimately ceded over 886,000 hectares of the public domain to the State of California (Gates 1975). Proceeds from the state's sale of these lands were to be directed toward reclaiming (i.e., draining) them.

The earliest and most extensively drained wetlands were those of the Sacramento–San Joaquin Delta, the Sacramento Valley, and the Tulare Basin (Figure 31.1). Delta reclamation began in the 1850s and continued until about 1930 (Thompson 1957). The earliest levees on the delta's islands and low-lying tracts were constructed by hand, most often by Chinese laborers. By the 1880s mechanically powered earth-moving equipment increased the pace and scope of reclamation. By the end of World War I, more than 120,000 hectares had been converted to agricultural land; levees protected the low-lying delta from tidal—but usually fresh—and river overflows (Thompson and Dutra 1983). Vegetable crops and orchards replaced wetlands and the wildlife that they had supported.

The Sacramento Valley contains five enormous wetland basins (Colusa and Yolo to the west of the Sacramento River and Butte, Sutter, and American to the east) that historically flooded regularly as the Sacramento River overflowed from rain and snowmelt in winter and spring. These basins could remain inundated for months and contained in excess of 200,000 hectares of tule marshes (McGowan 1961). The Sacramento Flood Control Project, constructed over several decades beginning in the 1910s, protected the Sacramento Valley by channeling the valley's floodwaters through a system of weirs into leveed bypasses that run parallel to the river (Kelley 1989). The project enabled the reclamation and settlement of four of the five tule basins. Today, only the northernmost, the Butte Basin, remains as seasonal wetland; rice production and managed wetlands for duck clubs are the dominant land uses there today.

Prior to drainage, the Tulare Basin—the southern half of the San Joaquin Valley—contained several large lakes, including Tulare, Kern, and Buena Vista lakes, which were surrounded and linked by an estimated 250,000 hectares of marshland (Heitmeyer et al. 1989). The extent of the basin's lakes and wetlands varied widely, based on annual precipitation. Tulare Lake was by far the largest body of water in the basin, reaching a maximum historic size during the great flood of 1862 of nearly 200,000 hectares and a depth of more than 11 meters (Warner and Hendrix 1985). Tulare Lake and its wetlands supported populations of Sacramento perch (*Archoplites interruptus*) numerous enough to sustain a commercial fishery during the late-nineteenth century, as well as waterfowl, terrapins, and tule elk (*C. canadensis nannodes*). Flow into the Tulare Basin began to decrease as early as the mid-1850s with the first irrigation diversions along the basin's rivers, and Tulare Lake went dry for the first time in recorded history in 1898 (Preston 1981, Grunsky 1901). The drainage process was essentially completed in the 1950s and 1960s, when each of the rivers flowing into the basin—the Kings, Kaweah, Tule, and Kern—was dammed for flood control and water storage.

The San Joaquin Basin—the northern half of the San Joaquin Valley—lacked the large fluctuating, but permanent, lakes of the Tulare Basin; most of its wetlands consisted instead of riparian corridors and seasonally flooded grasslands, with the latter occurring primarily astride the San Joaquin River. This natural seasonal flooding was eliminated in the 1940s when the Central Valley Project diverted approximately 95% of the flow of the San Joaquin River to agricultural lands on

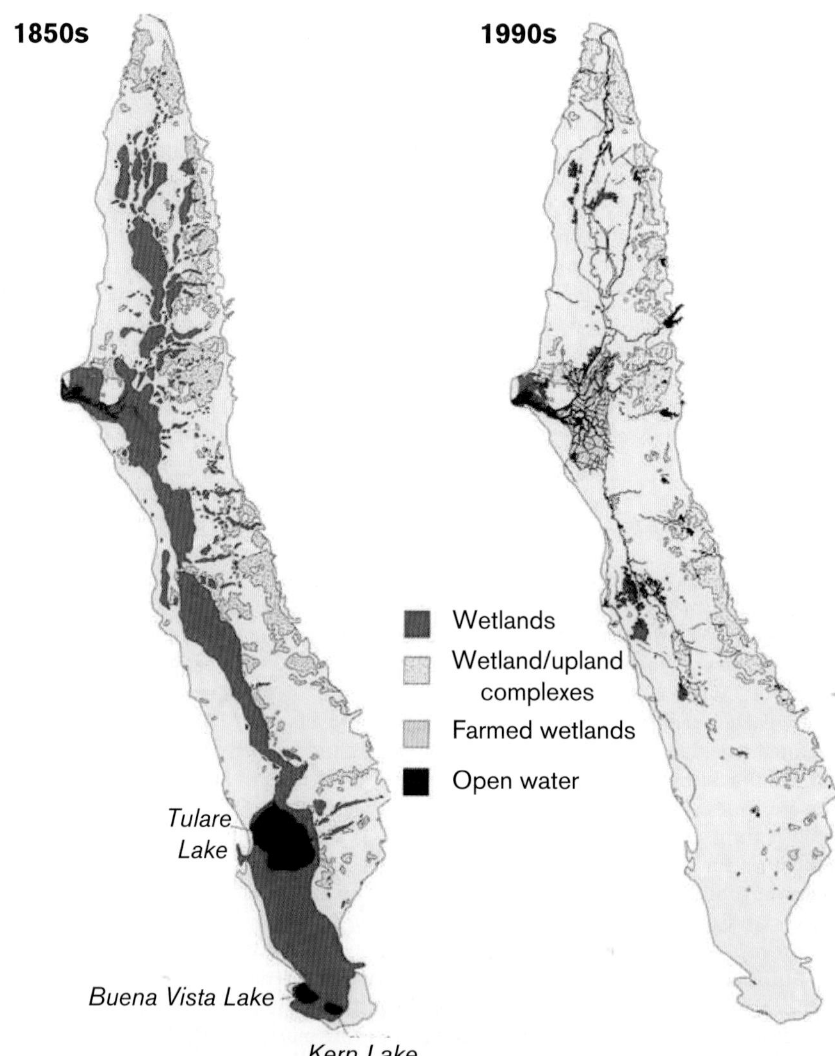

FIGURE 31.1 Distribution of wetlands in the Central Valley of California in the 1850s and 1990s. Source: Image courtesy of the U.S. Fish and Wildlife Service, Division of Habitat Conservation, Branch of Habitat Assessment.

the eastern side of the San Joaquin Valley. Since 1954, following a protracted struggle led by landowners along the dewatered portions of the San Joaquin River, the U.S. Bureau of Reclamation (USBOR) has provided "substitute" water to the lower San Joaquin Valley. This allotment, enhanced in subsequent years, has allowed for managed seasonal flooding and the preservation of extensive tracts of wetlands, primarily under the ownership of private duck clubs, national wildlife refuges, and state wildlife areas, in an approximately 75,000 hectare region known as the Grasslands Ecological Area, declared a Wetland of International Importance in 2005 under the 1971 Ramsar Convention (Garone 2011).

Between 1860 and 1900, grazing activities not only obliterated much of the Central Valley's native grasslands but also affected wetlands, particularly meadows, of the adjacent Sierra Nevada. Cattle and especially sheep—which naturalist John Muir famously referred to as "hoofed locusts" and which numbered 5.7 million in California by 1880—grazed in Sierra meadows. This activity resulted in the reduction of native perennial plants and their replacement by more aggressive introduced annual species, especially in the higher elevations of the southern Sierra Nevada (Muir 1911, Barbour et al. 1993, Beesley 2004).

In northeastern California, wetlands of the Klamath Basin have also been dramatically altered. Historically, Lower Klamath Lake was a vast expanse of open water and more than 30,000 hectares of wetlands sustained by seasonal flow from the Klamath River (Weddell 2000). In 1906 the U.S. Reclamation Service initiated a large-scale project to drain Lower Klamath Lake and convert the lake bed and marshlands to agricultural land. In later years, partial flows were restored to Lower Klamath Lake, but the basin's hydrology has been profoundly altered and is now highly managed. For decades, agricultural interests, the USFWS, and Native American tribes holding water rights remained locked in contentious battles over allocation of the basin's water resources. Adjudication of water rights was completed in March 2013, granting senior rights to tribes (Oregon Water Resources Department 2013), but controversies over Klamath River flows continue.

Hydrologic engineering has profoundly affected the wetlands of the Owens Valley on the eastern side of the Sierra Nevada. The Los Angeles Department of Water and Power began tapping the Owens River in 1913, draining its riparian wetlands and reducing Owens Lake to an alkali flat. In 1941, Los Angeles reached further north in the Owens Valley and began diversions from streams that supplied Mono Lake and transported that water more than 500 kilometers south to the city. Riverine wetlands along the streams were destroyed and lake levels dropped nearly to the point of ecosystem collapse before a 1994 decision by the California State Water Resources Control Board—following upon years of lawsuits—ordered the protection and restoration of Mono Lake, its tributary streams, and its riparian and lake-fringing wetlands (Hart 1996, CSWRCB 1994; see Chapters 30, "Deserts," and 32, "Lakes").

Most of the wetlands of the north, central, and southern coastal regions of California are marine or estuarine, but historically there were considerable freshwater wetlands on some of the inland plateaus and along river valleys, especially along the southern and central coast. In coastal southern California, Los Angeles and Orange Counties contained numerous *cienegas*, spring-fed freshwater wetlands (Hall 2011). These occurred where runoff from the mountains that had percolated underground was forced back to the surface by impermeable bedrock. Along the central coast, the Santa Clara and lower Salinas valleys contained substantial freshwater wetlands as well. Unlike the Central Valley and Klamath Basin, where wetlands were reclaimed for agricultural development, wetlands of the coastal plains and river valleys were lost primarily to urbanization, especially during the early decades of the twentieth century (Hall 2011).

Geographic Distribution

Wetland ecosystems in California include poorly known wetlands such as bogs, playas, and desert oases (Bertoldi and Swain 1996). However, the marshes of the Central Valley, coastal and riparian wetlands, vernal pools, and mountain meadow wetlands have the greatest coverage and correspondingly have received greater attention.

Marshes of the Central Valley

Hydrology of most Central Valley marshes is extensively modified and intensively managed, primarily to provide food and refuge for the millions of waterfowl and other waterbirds that winter, breed, or migrate through the region (CVJV 2006). Natural overflow flooding from snowmelt and rain has mostly been replaced by managed flooding via controlled diversions, timed reservoir releases, and pumped water delivery from ditches, rivers, sloughs, and wells. Central Valley marshes generally can be impounded by levees and classified by hydroperiod as semipermanent or seasonal. Geomorphology, climate, water availability, and management objective determine marsh type, and because seasonal wetlands can be managed to produce more waterfowl food using less water than semipermanent wetlands, they compose about 87% of the managed marshes in the Central Valley (CVJV 2006). In many cases, the lowest parts of wetland basins are semipermanent, while the shallower portions are seasonal.

Hydroperiod differs by wetland type. In wetlands managed to be semipermanent, water is usually maintained year-round in at least part of the basin to provide habitat for breeding and molting waterfowl as well as other wetland-dependent birds and other fauna. However, if emergent vegetation overtakes the basin (which commonly occurs in shallow basins after a few years), and if water levels can be manipulated, wetlands are drained and emergent vegetation disked or burned to restore the desired interspersion of open water and vegetation (Euliss and Smith 2010). Hydrology of most seasonal wetlands is designed to maximize production of waterbird food resources (primarily seeds but also aquatic invertebrates) and, on most private and many public lands, to provide opportunity for waterfowl sport harvest. Exact timing of flooding differs somewhat among regions and years to match timing of waterfowl use and hunting seasons. A small percentage (e.g., 7% in Grasslands Ecological Area; Chouinard 2000) of seasonal wetlands are managed in reverse cycle (i.e., flooded March through August and left dry during September through February) to supplement semipermanent wetlands as waterbird breeding and brood habitat.

Historically, about 40% of Central Valley's wetlands occurred in the San Joaquin Valley and 60% in the Sacramento Valley, Delta, and Suisun Marsh (USFWS 1978). The southern San Joaquin Valley had the largest block of wetlands, but most of these were lost by the 1920s with the conversion of Tulare Lake (once the largest freshwater lake west of the Mississippi River) and associated wetlands to agricultural lands (Kirk 1994). Severe wetland losses also occurred in the Sacramento Valley and Delta. However, many wetlands in the Sacramento Valley were converted to rice and in the Delta to grain fields that retain higher value for waterbirds than the cotton, orchards, and nongrain croplands that dominate the San Joaquin Valley landscape (Fleskes, Yee et al. 2005). Today, wetlands and flooded rice provide nearly contiguous waterbird habitat in the Sacramento Valley. In the San Joaquin Valley, large expanses of agriculture of relatively low waterbird value separate wetland habitats into three distinct blocks: the Grasslands Ecological Area, the Mendota Wildlife Area, and the Tulare Lake Bed and vicinity.

Coastal Wetlands

Coastal wetlands in California are diverse and include beaches, mudflats, salt flats, and similar extreme environments. However, only tidal wetlands, mostly brackish, that are dominated by vascular plants are considered here. While these wetlands are widespread and provide important habitat for a wide array of specialized animals and plants, outside of the San Francisco Estuary they are limited in area.

Coastal wetlands are characterized by distinct communities of plants, which vary with latitude, with physical factors—especially salinity, freshwater inflow, and temperature—and with geomorphic features of each estuary (Grewell et al. 2007). Relatively undisturbed tidal wetlands are threaded with DENDRITIC tidal creeks that provide fish and invertebrates access to intertidal reaches during twice-daily tides and that export nutrients and small organisms during outgoing tides. During low tides, herons, egrets, and other birds move in to prey on fish and invertebrates in the shallow channels. In northern California, Roosevelt elk (*Cervus canadensis roosevelti*) still commonly use coastal wetlands (Figure 31.2).

Tidal wetlands occur from the Tijuana Estuary on the Mexican border to Lake Earl and the Smith River on the Oregon border (see Chapter 19, "Estuaries: Life on the Edge"). Grewell et al. (2007) noted forty-nine major estuarine marshes along the coast, exclusive of those in the San Francisco Estuary. Most of the estuaries are urbanized and often confined to smaller areas than they occupied historically. The largest collection of coastal wetlands is found in the San Francisco Estuary (see also Chapter 19, "Estuaries: Life on the Edge"), although the largely freshwater tidal marshes of the Sacramento–San Joaquin Delta, more than 150 kilometers inland,

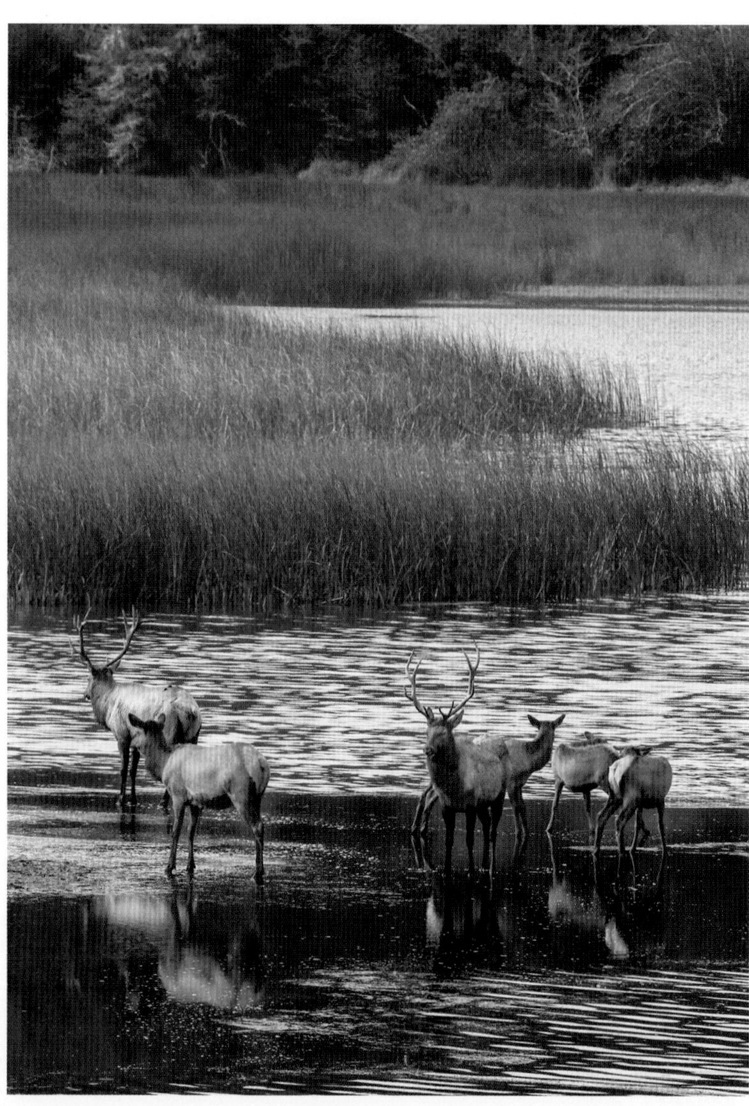

FIGURE 31.2 Roosevelt elk (*Cervus canadensis roosevelti*) in freshwater marsh fringing Dry Lagoon, Humboldt County, California. Roosevelt elk regularly feed in these coastal wetlands. Photo: Jill Duffy.

are almost entirely converted to agriculture. Just downstream from the Delta, Suisun Marsh is the largest brackish-water tidal marsh on the West Coast. Ironically, most of it is diked off and managed as nontidal marsh to support hunting for waterfowl (Moyle et al. 2013). Along San Pablo and San Francisco Bays, some substantial tidal salt marshes persist, including the marshes at the mouths of the Napa and Petaluma Rivers. Their mud-lined tidal channels and bays support wintering concentrations of wading birds and a population of Sacramento splittail (*Pogonichthys macrolepidotus*), a species of minnow endemic to the Central Valley.

Much of California's historic coastal wetland area has been affected by introduced exotic species and compromised by development. These wetland ecosystems have been highly invaded by alien species, to the detriment of native fish and birds. In some areas, the native cordgrass (*Spartina foliosa*) is being replaced by aggressive invasive forms of the same genus (*Spartina alterniflora*) that displace the rail-friendly native cordgrass and take over tidal flats needed by foraging shorebirds. Coastal wetlands are also shrinking, especially as sea level rises and coastal development prevents them from shifting inland. Their ability to support wetland-dependent species, such as the clapper rail (*Rallus longirostris*), is increasingly compromised.

Riverine Wetlands

Riverine wetlands include river and stream channels as well as the areas of interface between uplands and these channels. We emphasize the areas of interface, sometimes referred to as riparian wetlands. These may be perennially, intermittently, or ephemerally flooded by overbank flow and may also receive subsurface flow (Warner and Hendrix 1984, Mitsch and Gosselink 2007). Riparian wetlands usually form wherever soil moisture exceeds what would otherwise be available through precipitation alone, resulting in hydric soils and HYDROPHYTIC vegetation. In California, riparian wetlands receive floodwater from adjacent rivers primarily in the winter, spring, and early summer months (Katibah 1984). If river margins are exposed long enough during the growing season, hydrophytic vegetation will become established, creating lush greenbelts of riparian vegetation readily distinguished from relatively dry uplands of California south of the mid–Sacramento Valley (Roberts et al. 1980).

In the semiarid climate that characterizes much of California, riparian wetlands exhibit greater diversity of flora and fauna than adjacent uplands. Riparian vegetation provides shelter, food, and nutrients to over 225 species of birds, mammals, reptiles, and amphibians (Riparian Habitat Joint

Venture 2004). Riparian vegetation also provides shade and reduces pollutant runoff from adjacent uplands. Fish and aquatic insects also rely on in-stream habitat created by downed riparian vegetation (Jensen et al. 1993). Riparian vegetation differs widely across California by elevation and ecoregion. Deciduous broad-leaf trees, shrubs, and herbs line montane and bottomland streams, while riparian habitats of the North Coast also include evergreen species such as coast redwoods (*Sequoia sempervirens*) (Roberts et al. 1980).

The greatest losses of riparian wetlands have been in the Central Valley where, beginning in the 1800s, more than 98% of these wetlands were destroyed (Riparian Habitat Joint Venture 2004). Although historical records are incomplete, California's riparian wetlands potentially covered millions of hectares with over 965,000 kilometers of streams capable of supporting riparian habitat (Smith 1980, RHJV 2004, CVJV 2006). The Central Valley's fertile ALLUVIAL bottomlands once contained 373,100 hectares of riparian wetlands, but by 1850 this area had been reduced to about 314,000 hectares (Katibah 1984, Roberts et al. 1980, Smith 1980). Impoundments, levee construction, channelization, timber harvest, gold mining, and agriculture have all contributed to riparian wetland loss in California, particularly in the Central Valley. Riparian wetlands are currently estimated to cover 145,000 hectares, which is between 2% and 15% of their historic coverage (Katibah 1984, Dawdy 1989, CDF 2002). Losses and degradation of riparian wetlands due to logging have been reported for other areas of California (Brode and Bury 1984).

Vernal Pools

Vernal pools form in shallow depressions typically underlain by an impervious layer such as hardpan, clay, or mudflows, which causes water to pond. These seasonal wetlands are characterized by a distinctive seasonal wet and dry pattern. Vernal pools occur throughout California in seventeen geographically distinct regions (Figure 31.3), but are most abundant in and around the Central Valley, occurring at specific geologic formations associated with basin rim, young and old alluvial terraces, and mud/basalt flow landforms (Hobson and Dahlgren 1998).

A mound-swale microtopography, consisting of the interspersion of raised areas and depressions, typically characterizes most landforms containing vernal pools but some vernal pools appear as relatively large flat ponds (Thompson et al. 2010, Solomeshch et al. 2007). California's vernal pools are unique and display a remarkable natural diversity, with a relatively high degree of endemism in the indigenous flora and fauna owing to its Mediterranean climate, geologic history, landforms, and soils. Vernal pools occur in landscapes comprising a rich mosaic of vegetation, including grasslands, wildflower fields, dunelands, alkali meadow, alkali sink and desert scrubs, sagebrush, chaparral, and oak and juniper woodlands (CDFG 1998). The vegetation within a single vernal pool may comprise several associations (patches of unique collections of species), and each of these can occur in other pools where specific environmental or habitat conditions (soil characteristics, hydrology, climate) are present (Barbour et al. 2003) (Figure 31.4).

These associations can be widespread, localized, or rare. Some species occur in many associations and others are highly restricted. Rare, threatened, and endangered vernal pool plant species are found in specific associations. Floral displays of yellow carpets, goldfields, meadowfoams, and downingias are visited by pollen-foraging specialist bees. These solitary bees nest in the habitats surrounding vernal pools, so the conservation of certain vernal pool wildflowers is dependent on intact vernal pool landscapes (Thorp and Leong 1998). This is also true for the California tiger salamander (*Ambystoma californiense*) because adults spawn and young hatch and develop in vernal pools during the inundated phase; then when the pools dry out, adults aestivate in burrows in the surrounding "uplands" until onset of winter rains is sufficient to inundate pools.

Migratory waterfowl use vernal pool landscapes during late winter and spring when behavioral and physiological changes drive energetic demands for increased protein and endogenous fat storage necessary for courtship, reproduction, and spring migration (Silveira 1998). Most ducks forage for snails, crustaceans (tadpole and fairy shrimps), and insects (Bogiatto and Karnegis 2007), while geese graze on annual grasses in the surrounding upland.

Central Valley vernal pools, including the surrounding mosaic of vegetation, may have occupied 2.4 million hectares prior to European contact, but during more than 150 years of settlement have been reduced to about 370,000 hectares—an 85% decline (Holland 2011). Land use changes include dryland and irrigated agriculture (currently high value vineyards and orchards) as well as urban and suburban developments. Habitat loss and fragmentation and invasive species destroy and degrade vernal pool ecosystems. Much of the remaining vernal pool landscapes are private rangelands, primarily used for cattle ranching, which is compatible with vernal pool conservation. Cattle grazing has been demonstrated to maintain vernal pool wildflower and crustacean diversity (Marty 2005), and to improve grass forage for grazing migratory waterfowl.

A multispecies ecosystem recovery plan for federal threatened and endangered vernal pool plants and animals aims to focus recovery efforts for many, often associated, species, while it also addresses species of special concern, thus potentially preventing further population declines and petitions for listing (USFWS 2005). Solutions to vernal pool ecosystem loss include land conservation consisting of public ownership and private conservation easements as well as urban growth conservation planning. Management, restoration, monitoring and research, education, and outreach are necessary to maintain and recover species of vernal pool ecosystems.

Mountain Meadow Wetlands

Wetlands occupy substantial portions of the Sierra Nevada and southern Cascades ecoregions. These ecosystems include large wetlands that border sinks and alkali lakes at lower elevations on the slopes of the southern Cascades and in the Owens Valley. They also include large marshes such as Upper Truckee Marsh bordering Lake Tahoe and those in the Sierra Valley area. As with all wetlands, development and functioning of meadow wetlands in the Sierra Nevada is largely governed by hydrology (Cooper and Wolfe 2006), although vegetation and soils have also been used to classify these wetlands (Ratliff 1982). Hydrologically, these meadows have been classified as dry or wet meadows and peatlands or peat-forming wetlands such as fens and bogs (Cooper and Wolf 2006). Dry meadows are wetlands with hydroperiods of only a few weeks each year while hydroperiods of wet meadows extend for one

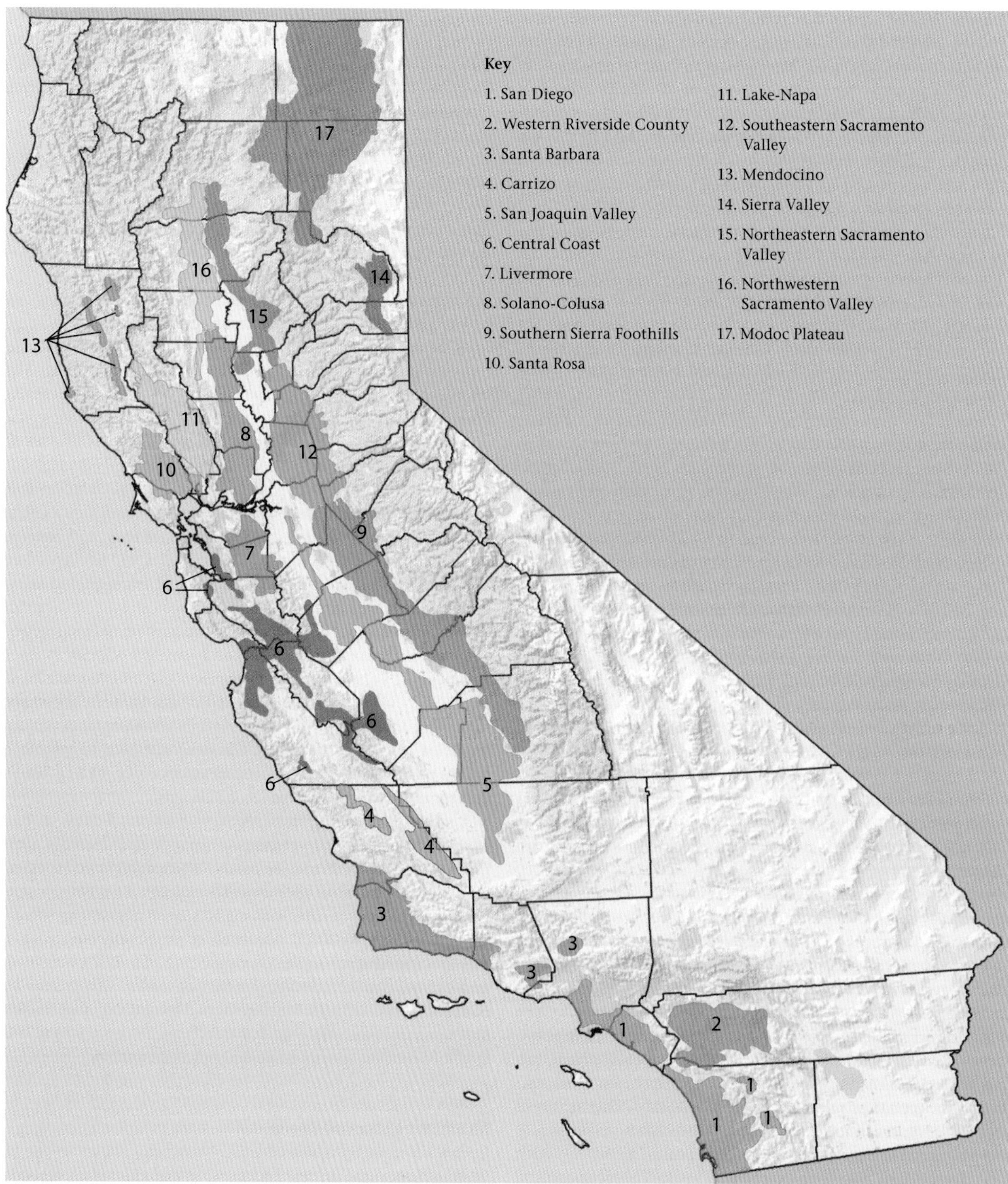

FIGURE 31.3 Distribution of vernal pool wetlands in California. Map: Todd Keeler-Wolf, California Department of Fish and Wildlife, 2013.

or two months and peatlands remain saturated throughout the summer. Fens are the most common meadow wetlands in the Sierra Nevada and Cascade regions.

Fens are wetlands with an organic soil developed from peat-forming vegetation (Cooper and Wolf 2006). Peat forms in fens because, on average, the amount of organic matter produced by plant growth annually is greater than the amount that decomposes. Anaerobic conditions created by soil saturation facilitate peat formation. Herbaceous plants such as sedges dominate fens, and fens generally have few or no trees but are surrounded by mixed coniferous forest. Most fens in the Sierra Nevada and Cascade regions are small, having an area of less than 1 hectare and have accumulated 1 meter or more of peat soil (Cooper and Wolf 2006). The age of fens in the Sagehen Basin of the Sierra Nevada ranges from a few hundred to more than eight thousand years (Bartolome et al. 1990). Fens develop where groundwater discharge occurs, typically in depressions on the landscape or at

FIGURE 31.4 A vernal pool on Sacramento National Wildlife Refuge in California's Central Valley surrounded by Fremont's goldfields (*Lasthenia fremontii*) and Hoover's downingia (*Downingia bella*). Photo: Joseph Silveira

the base of slopes. Position on the landscape is strongly influenced by groundwater resources. Elevation of fens in Lassen and Plumas National Forests of the southern Cascades averages about 1,700 meters but about 3,000 meters in the drier Inyo National Forest of the Sierra Nevada (Cooper and Wolf 2006). In Yosemite National Park they extend from about 1,000 meters to 4,000 meters. These elevation differences largely reflect differences in annual precipitation and snowpack and subsequent influences on groundwater.

Fens and mountain meadow wetlands are recognized as "hotspots" of biodiversity. Although these wetlands have been impacted by grazing and by other human activities (Ratliff 1985), the amount of these wetlands that has been lost is poorly documented or unknown. However, while meadow wetlands currently represent only 1% of the Sierra Nevada area (Davis and Stoms 1996), they are estimated to make up 3% of Yosemite National Park, and loss in this park is thought to be minimal during the past century.

Drivers and Patterns of Variability

Long dry summers and mild rainy winters generally characterize California's climate. West of the Coast Range, temperature ranges are typically moderate, but a continental climate of warmer summers, cooler winters, and greater temperature fluctuations occurs in the state's interior. Mean annual precipitation is greatest in the northern half of the state and on the western slopes of mountains. Much of the precipitation in the Sierra Nevada is in the form of snow. This snowpack provides an important source of water during the growing season (NOAA 1985, Schoenherr 1992).

Temporal and geographic variations in long-term patterns of precipitation and temperature, together with the local landscape template, drive variability in California wetlands by influencing magnitude, duration, and frequency of natural or artificial flooding; source and chemistry of wetland inflows from surfacewater or groundwater; timing and rate of drawdown and cycles of wetting and drying; OXIDATION state, dictating chemical reactions that occur and extent of organic matter accumulation; and, indirectly, sea level, occurrence, and persistence of coastal wetlands, and inundation of low-lying coastland areas, particularly the Bay-Delta (Cayan et al. 2008, Mitsch and Gosselink 2007). For example, ponding in California vernal pools is controlled primarily by the total amount of seasonal precipitation, in turn strongly influencing plant species composition, and dry summers in the Sierra Nevada restrict mountainous wet meadows to areas of shallow groundwater (Bauder 2005, Loheide et al. 2008). However, the majority of California's Central Valley and Klamath Marsh wetlands are now dependent on water delivery systems at least seasonally, and water management may substantially influence expressions of California wetland variability (CNRA 2010, Duffy et al. 2011).

Variability in Hydrology

Approximately 8% of California's wetlands are associated with streams and rivers (CNRA 2010). In addition to riverine wetlands, thousands of acres of seasonal depressional wetlands and vernal pools of the Central Valley historically received overland flooding from the Sacramento and San Joaquin Rivers. Most of these wetlands were lost when agriculture and human settlements expanded across the Central Valley, necessitating the construction of reservoirs, levees, and

FIGURE 31.5 A diverse range of vegetation types are associated with wetlands of California. Photos: Brenda Grewell.

A California cordgrass (*Spartina foliosa*) tracks bayshore and sinous tidal creeks next to pickleweed (*Sarcocornia pacifica*) plains at China Camp State Park, San Francisco Bay Estuary.

B Tall hardstem bulrush (*Schoenoplectus acutus*) backs California cordgrass along fresh brackish reaches of the Napa River.

C Yellow pond lily (*Nuphar polysepala*), a floating-leaf aquatic plant, is found at Lagoon Creek Marsh, Humboldt Redwoods National Park, and other lakes, ponds, and slow streams.

D Bands of willow scrub (*Salix* sp.), cottonwoods (*Populus fremontii*), red alder (*Alnus rubra*), and coast redwood (*Sequoia sempervirens*) are riverine wetland species along the Russian River.

dams to control the rivers' natural flooding (Scott and Marquiss 1984). The Sacramento and San Joaquin Rivers also provided fresh water to the San Francisco Bay-Delta, the largest contiguous tidal marsh system on the Pacific Coast (Josselyn 1983).

Reductions in flows resulting from construction of upstream dams and water exports have contributed to the subsidence and salinization of Bay-Delta wetlands (Ingebristen et al. 2000). In the southern Central Valley, vast tracts of littoral, or lake-fringing, wetlands were lost when water from rivers that supplied them was diverted for agriculture and municipal use in the late nineteenth century (USEPA 2007). The Kern, Tule, Kaweah, and South Fork Kings Rivers once fed Tulare, Buena Vista, and Kern Lakes and occasionally exchanged surface water with the San Joaquin River via a complex of marshes and sloughs. The dry beds once occupied by the lakes occasionally flood in high water years when precipitation or snowmelt are unusually high (USEPA 2007).

Habitats, Biological Communities, and Their Interactions

Primary Habitat Types

Most freshwater wetlands in California are classified as PALUSTRINE and are further delineated as supporting rooted vegetation (Cowardin et al. 1979). Palustrine wetlands include the marshes of the Central Valley, the delta and coastal areas, riparian wetlands, vernal pools, and mountain meadows. The biological communities of these wetlands are discussed in the section below.

Wetland Vegetation

Wetland plants play critical roles in the functioning of wetlands, providing oxygen and habitat structure for other organisms. Through photosynthetic processes, they convert energy from light and CO_2 into available forms of carbon and thereby initiate the energy flow that fuels biological food webs in wetland ecosystems. Wetland plants are distinguishing features of California wetlands (Mason 1957). Shorelines edged with California cordgrass (*Spartina foliosa*) are easily recognized as coastal salt marshes, luxuriant stands of tules bring to mind emergent marshes, and bands of Fremont cottonwood (*Populus fremontii*), red alder (*Alnus rubra*), and willow scrub are immediately identified as riverine or riparian wetlands (Figure 31.5). Wetland plants have diverse morphological and physiological adaptations to inundated conditions. Hydroperiod (the depth, duration, and frequency of flooding) varies by wetland type and is the primary factor controlling the distribution, abundance, and productivity of plants in wetlands (Casanova and Brock 2000, Fraser and Kernezis 2005). Light, CO_2, temperature, water chemistry, sediment character, available nutrients, and biological interactions combine with wetland SURFICIAL hydrology and geomorphology to drive plant growth and distribution (Lacoul and Freedman 2006). Plants also influence the water quality, hydrology, and sediment processes in wetlands through shading, evapotranspiration, modification of currents, and shoreline stabilization (Mitsch and Gosselink 2007).

Vascular wetland plants can be aggregated into functional groups based on their growth form and relationship to hydrology and sediment (Sculthorpe 1967, Cronk and Fennessy 2001). Emergent macrophytes, such as California bulrush (*Schoenoplectus californicus*), are rooted in sediment but their shoots extend above the water surface. Floating-leaved hydrophytes, such as water smartweed (*Persicaria amphibia*), are rooted in sediment but have leaves that float on the water surface. Submerged plants are underwater flowering plants such as eelgrass (*Zostera marina*), which are usually rooted but can be free-floating. Free-floating plants such as duckweed (*Lemna minor*) float on the water surface, do not have roots in sediment, and move freely with wind and water current.

The floristics of California wetlands cannot be differentiated simply by geography or climate; coastal to lowland to montane freshwater marshes, riverine wetlands, and vernal pools all have characteristic floras (Mason 1957). Generalist wetland plant species that are widespread and occur in diverse wetland types include cattails, tules and bulrushes, and pondweeds. More specialized species are typically western and local endemics that primarily occur in wetlands with intermittent flooding such as calico flower and pincushion plant species from vernal pools, and saltbush and milkvetch species from vernal alkali wetlands (Mason 1957).

Wetlands are unique because of their role as transitional ecotones between aquatic and terrestrial ecosystems, a position that conveys high biological diversity, as wetlands support both obligate and facultative wetland plant species that tolerate inundation. Wetland plants also provide habitat structure that supports other taxonomic groups of organisms (e.g., epiphytic bacteria, invertebrates, fish, birds, and mammals). Plant community composition therefore has implications for overall biological diversity within wetlands (Cronk and Fennessy 2001). Individual plant species within wetlands such as parasitic saltmarsh dodder (*Cuscuta salina*) can have disproportionate, positive effects on community diversity through a continuum of negative to positive interactions (Grewell 2008a,b). Manipulative field experiments confirm that dodder clearly suppresses otherwise dominant

FIGURE 31.6 Salt marsh dodder (the orange vine, *Cuscuta salina*) (A) suppresses its primary hosts, seaside plantain and pickleweed, and (B) improves the fitness of the rare Point Reyes bird's-beak (purple hemiparasitic plant, *Chloropyron maritimum* ssp. *palustre*) at Bodega Bay, California. Photos: Brenda Grewell.

host plants in salt marsh plant communities, such as seaside plantain (*Plantago maritima*) and pickleweed (*Sarcocornia pacifica*), but the fitness of rare plants and plant species richness and diversity in the community are enhanced through indirect positive effects when dodder is present (Grewell 2008b) (Figure 31.6). The differential influence of parasites on the FECUNDITY of dominant and rare species can change population dynamics, benefit rare species, and alter community structure. Understanding the continuum of negative to positive consequences of parasitic interactions may be key to conservation management of tidal wetlands.

The historic loss and degradation of wetland area in California has contributed to a high number of threatened and endangered wetland species. For example, 80% of historic wetlands have been lost in the San Francisco Estuary, and forty-eight plant species from the extant wetlands are threatened, endangered, or species of concern.

FIGURE 31.7 Pintail (*Anas acuta*) on an island within a wetland in California's Central Valley. Photo: Robert McLandress.

Birds

California wetlands are internationally renowned for supporting great abundance and diversity of birds. About 650 bird species are known to occur in California (CBRC 2013), and those most closely associated with wetlands can be grouped based on taxonomy and ecology into eight groups: waterfowl, shorebirds, secretive marsh birds, colonial-nesting waders, colonial-nesting seabirds, grebes, sandhill cranes, and others (Fleskes 2012). About a third of California's threatened, endangered, or special concern bird species rely on or are commonly associated with wetland habitats (CDFW 2008, 2013). These include tricolored blackbirds that are largely endemic and resident to California and nest in large colonies in the Central Valley marshes (CDFW 2008), the greater sandhill crane (*Grus canadensis tabida*) that breeds in the Klamath Basin and winter-roosts in Central Valley wetlands, and several secretive marsh birds such as the least bittern (*Lxobrychus exilis*) and black rail (*Laterallus jamaicensis*).

Birds use all wetland types in the state, with species such as the common moorhen (*Gallinula chloropus*), marsh wren (*Cistothorus palustris*), song sparrow (*Melospiza melodia*), and tricolored blackbird (*Agelaius tricolor*) found mostly in densely vegetated marshes, while others such as the pied-billed grebe (*Podilymbus podiceps*) and American coot (*Fulica americana*) also use less vegetated wetlands (USFWS 2009b). Many species breed in wetlands, including colonial-nesting birds such as American white pelicans (*Pelecanus erythrorhynchos*), cormorants, gulls, and terns that typically nest on islands in large wetlands to avoid disturbance. Migratory species use wetlands to rest and feed during migration and, in the Central Valley where wetlands rarely freeze, as wintering habitat.

The most abundant and visible wetland-dependent birds in California are waterfowl. Waterfowl breeding is substantial in the Central Valley and Klamath Basin, averaging 605,000 ducks and 1,200 pairs of western Canada geese (*Branta canadensis moffitti*) during 1990–2008 (Collins and Trost 2009). The most abundant species breeding is the mallard (*Anas platyrhynchos*), but gadwall (*A. strepera*), cinnamon teal (*A. cyanoptera*), northern shoveler (*A. clypeata*), and twelve other waterfowl species also breed in California. However, abundance and species diversity is much greater during winter in the Central Valley and during spring and fall migration in the Klamath Basin. Gilmer et al. (1982) estimated that about 10 million to 12 million waterfowl annually winter in or pass through the Central Valley. More recent (1998–2001) estimates found that peak waterfowl abundance averaged 4.8 million in California during early January and 1.1 million during fall migration in the Klamath Basin (Gilmer et al. 2004). Up to 65% of the northern pintails (*A. acuta*) in North America winter in the Central Valley, and despite continental declines, they are still the most common species (Fleskes and Yee 2007) (Figure 31.7).

California also provides critically important habitat for shorebirds; in winter and spring the Central Valley is the most important, and in fall the second-most important, inland site in western North America (Hickey et al. 2003). About 33 shorebird species migrate through the Klamath Basin and the Central Valley or winter in the Central Valley, with total abundance in the Central Valley during the early 1990s averaging 134,000 in August, 211,000 in November, 303,000 in January, and 335,000 in April (Shuford et al. 1998).

Other Vertebrates

Our understanding of how vertebrates historically used wetlands is based on observations made since the eighteenth century, after the Native peoples were greatly diminished (Whipple et al. 2012). Cunningham (2010), however, provides a view of what the wetlands of pre-Euro-American California were like when grizzly bears (*Ursus arctos horribilis*) and tule elk were an important presence. Historically, annual runs of one million to two million adult Chinook salmon (*Oncorhynchus tshawytscha*) in the Central Valley were supported, in part, by productive habitats available to juveniles when seasonal wetlands flooded in spring.

All endemic native fishes in California spawn in spring, in large part to take advantage of flooded wetlands for rearing of their young (Moyle 2002). Species such as Sacramento splittail and Sacramento perch have special adaptations for spawning and rearing in floodplains. Most native fishes, including salmon, have their life cycles tuned to seasonal flooding and possess the instinctual capacity to leave wetlands as flooding recedes to avoid stranding. The former abundance of salmon and steelhead (*Oncoryunchus mykiss*) in California (three million to four million adult fish each year) was in good part the result of the availability of extensive seasonal wetlands for rearing of young. Tidal marshes in coastal areas, including the San Francisco Estuary, have also been important rearing areas for native fishes, especially salmon and steelhead.

Amphibians are largely dependent on wetlands, especially those lacking fish. Unfortunately, one of the frog species dependent on California wetlands is the introduced American bullfrog (*Rana catesbeiana*), a predator on other amphibians as well as other vertebrates. California tiger salamanders migrate to vernal pools for breeding, while mountain yellow-legged frogs (*R. muscosa*) depend on riverine, mountain meadow, and lacustrine wetland pools for breeding. The Pacific pond turtle (*Actinemys marmorata*), a declining reptile, is found in a wide variety of wetlands. Some snake species such as the aquatic garter snake (*Thamnophis atratus*) and the giant garter snake (*T. gigas*) occur in wetlands where they feed on fish and amphibians (Fitch 1941).

Many California mammals have some degree of dependency on wetlands. Some cryptic species, such as ornate shrew (*Sorex ornatus*), Pacific shrew (*S. pacificus*), and salt marsh harvest mouse (*Reithrodontomys raviventris*), are found largely in

FIGURE 31.8 Vernal pool tadpole shrimp (*Lepidurus packardi*) from a playa vernal pool at Westervelt Ecological Service's Burke Ranch Conservation Bank, Solano County, California. This species is listed as endangered under the Federal Endangered Species Act. Photo: Brent Helm.

wetlands and are often important in local food webs. Some of California's most charismatic native mammals—river otter (*Lontra canadensis*), beaver (*Castor canadensis*), and tule elk—are wetland species. Beaver are "ecosystem engineers" and have created many meadow and riverine wetlands. Other charismatic vertebrates, including waterbirds such as herons and egrets, also can play important functional roles in wetland ecosystems and are important foci for ecotourism, which is growing in California (Palaima 2012, Moyle et al. 2013).

Invertebrates

Invertebrates inhabit the full range of wetland types, including vernal pools and freshwater marshes. Vernal pools are harsh environments, especially for resident macroscopic aquatic invertebrates. Not only must these invertebrates adjust to extreme fluctuations in water temperature, depth, volume, and chemistry (e.g., dissolved oxygen, pH) that can occur daily, but they must also avoid predators and parasites while striving to complete their life cycle before the aquatic phase of their habitat ends.

Upon flooding, invertebrates quickly emerge from their diapause (dormant) stages (e.g., eggs and larvae) after oversummering in the dry basin. Having withstood extreme temperatures and dehydration, resting PROPAGULES reactivate to essential stimuli (e.g., water temperature and dissolved oxygen) (Thorp and Covich 1991, Alekseev et al. 2006). Invertebrate phenology generally coincides with food availability (Helm 1999). Within hours to a few days after inundation, detritivores emerge. They include surface-dwelling springtails, bottom-living filtering seed shrimp, and the suspension-feeding fairy shrimp residing in the water column. Next, at the microscopic level, ROTIFERS and GASTROTRICHS appear as populations of plankton, protozoans, and prokaryotes increase. Free-living scavenging flat worms, roundworms, and water mites follow.

Arriving soon after are the omnivorous, filter-feeding crustaceans: copepods, water fleas, clam shrimp, and tadpole shrimp. At this time, the winged insects have likely invaded, consisting of detritivorous water boatman and herbivorous crawling water beetles, trailed by parasitic water mites and predatory insects: adult backswimmers, water scavenger beetles, and predacious diving beetles. By the second to third week of ponding, most of the significant invertebrate players are present, albeit many in juvenile form. Oligochaete worms and midge and mosquito larvae increase during the later part of a pool's hydrologic cycle when water temperatures increase, dissolved oxygen decreases, and the water column is choked with FILAMENTOUS ALGAE. While crustaceans dominate in terms of biomass, insects dominate in terms of species richness (Helm 1999).

As most California freshwater marshes are dry in the summer (Szalay et al. 1999), their invertebrate assemblages and phenology are similar to those of vernal pools. However, species having long life cycles such as mayflies, damselflies, dragonflies, snails, and leeches are typically absent in vernal pools. With hydroperiods commonly dictating species presence, perennial wetlands have the greatest species richness. Nevertheless, large branchiopods—fairy shrimp, clam shrimp, and tadpole shrimp—are less common in freshwater marshes than in vernal pools. Of these three groups, the fairy shrimp—named for their translucent appearance and ability to swim gracefully upside down (Eriksen and Brown 1980)—are the most diverse. California wetlands support twenty-seven species of fairy shrimp, constituting over 40% of the species found in North America (Brendonck et al. 2008). Of the nine species endemic to California (Ericksen and Belk 1999), five—vernal pool fairy shrimp (*Branchinecta lynchi*), longhorn fairy shrimp (*B. longiantenna*), Conservancy fairy shrimp (*B. conservatio*), San Diego fairy shrimp (*B. sandiegonensis*), and Riverside fairy shrimp (*Streptocephalus woottoni*)—are listed as threatened or endangered by the USFWS. Only three other freshwater invertebrates are listed in California: the Shasta crayfish (*Pacifastacus fortis*) and the California freshwater shrimp (*Syncaris pacifica*) from riverine wetlands and the vernal pool tadpole shrimp (*Lepidurus packardi*) (USFWS 2013). Vernal pools are the natural habitat of many endemic invertebrates and thereby contribute significantly to evolutionary processes and the conservation of biological and genetic diversity (Figure 31.8).

FIGURE 31.9 Invasive Uruguayan primrose-willow (*Ludwigia hexapetala*) overgrowing tules at the Colusa National Wildlife Refuge in the Sacramento Valley. Photo: Brenda Grewell.

Invasive Plant Species

Nonindigenous (i.e., exotic or alien) plant species that invade wetlands competitively displace native flora, alter nutrient cycles, and threaten biological diversity and the functioning of ecosystems (Bossard and Randall 2007; see Chapter 13, "Biological Invasions"). Many aquatic plants have been introduced purposefully as aquarium or ornamental plants and escaped into natural waterways after introduction. Others have been unintentionally introduced to new areas when they "hitchhike" in ship ballast water, on boats, or with travelers or trade goods.

Giant reed (*Arundo donax*), a tall perennial grass, and salt cedar (*Tamarix* spp.) are Eurasian invaders of riverine and other wetlands. Giant reed is especially problematic in south coastal watersheds where it has invaded entire river channels (Bell 1997). Both species have dramatically altered geomorphology, hydrology, fire frequency, biogeochemistry, and biodiversity of wetlands (Gordon 1998, Zavaleta 2000, Cushman and Gaffney 2010). Water hyacinth, Brazilian waterweed (*Egeria densa*), hydrilla (*Hydrilla verticillata*), and Eurasian watermilfoil (*Myriophyllum spicatum*) are the most destructive of the aquatic plants that have invaded a wide range of wetland types in California (Bossard and Randall 2007). They impede water flow and recreation, increase sedimentation, and reduce light, oxygen, and aquatic biodiversity (Santos et al. 2009). Over the last twenty years, more than $50 million has been spent to control water hyacinth and Brazilian waterweed in the Bay-Delta alone.

The Invasive Spartina Project, a regional effort in the San Francisco Estuary, aims to eradicate introduced species of cordgrasses that hybridize with native species and alter the physical and biological structure of tidal wetlands (Grosholz et al. 2009). Perennial pepperweed (*Lepidium latifolium*) is a major invader of alkaline and brackish tidal wetlands. Pepperweed and the highly invasive Uruguayan primrose-willow (*Ludwigia hexapetala*) have degraded the Laguna de Santa Rosa Wetland Complex, a Ramsar Convention–designated Wetland of International Importance in Sonoma County, and have become a major expense for enhancement of wildlife habitat in managed seasonal wetlands in the Sacramento Valley (Figure 31.9).

Biogeochemical Processes

Precipitation patterns associated with California's Mediterranean climate cause wetlands to fill with water during winter or after spring snowmelt and to dry during summer. These alternating wet and dry periods strongly influence nutrient processing in wetlands, as does the timing of wet periods. Wetlands flooded during spring and early summer create conditions that favor aquatic plant growth and, with this plant biomass production, the accumulation of nitrogen, phosphorus, and carbon in plant tissues. When flooded long enough, wetland sediments become ANOXIC; this condition favors the growth of anaerobic bacteria. These bacteria mediate wetland nutrient processing and can reach numbers as high as 10–100 billion per liter in wetlands (Boon 2006).

Denitrifying bacteria use nitrate (NO_3) in their metabolism and produce nitrogen gas (N_2) lost to the atmosphere. Denitrification declines greatly if wetlands are not flooded long enough to develop anoxic soils. Nitrogen can also be lost from wetlands during dry periods, through a bacterially mediated process called nitrification. Unlike nitrogen, phosphorus is not lost from wetlands through biologically mediated, gas-producing processes. However, bacteria and chemical processes do affect the processing of phosphorus in wetlands during wet and dry phases. As sediments become anoxic, chemical reactions that cause phosphorus to ADSORB to sediments are weakened, and phosphorus may be released to the water column. Bacteria also play a large role in wetland phosphorus dynamics, ingesting it and releasing it as part of normal metabolism, and accumulating it in their tissue. As wetlands dry, these aquatic bacteria die, and the phosphorus and nitrogen sequestered in their tissues is released (Boon 2006).

Wet and dry phases are also important to the decomposition of wetland plant biomass and to the generation of greenhouse gases. Most of the plant biomass produced in wetlands is not consumed by herbivores but eventually dies and begins to decay, forming detritus. This detritus forms the base of some wetland food webs, in which bacteria and fungi play an important role in conditioning detritus before larger invertebrates consume it. More recent research has reported that microalgae and methane can be important sources of carbon in wetland food webs, at least temporally (Euliss et al. 1999, Hart and Lovorn 2003, Murase and Frenzel 2007).

As wetland soils dry, the decomposition or mineralization of detritus is rapid but rarely complete. Thus organic matter gradually accumulates in most wetlands. The decomposition of organic matter releases carbon dioxide gas, from both soil organic matter and dying bacterial biomass. Furthermore, loss of soil carbon is apparently enhanced under warm, dry conditions common in Mediterranean climates (Boon 2006). Under wet conditions when wetland soils are anoxic, the end product of decomposition of organic matter is methane, although carbon dioxide, oxides of sulfur, and nitrogen may also be generated (Figure 31.10). Methane production in wetlands appears variable (Segers 1998) and dependent on temperature and duration of wetting.

Alternate wetting and drying of wetland soils contributes to the production of nitrogen gas, carbon dioxide, and methane. All three are greenhouse gases, but methane is arguably the most potent of the three. Wetlands can be important sources of these gases, and human activities, such as rice agriculture, contribute to methane production. Experiments with rice agriculture in California found that interactions between flooding and the amount of straw incorporated into paddy soils controlled the amount of methane released (Fitzgerald et al. 2000).

Wetland Ecosystem Services

The rich biotic diversity of wetlands serves as the basis for the many ecosystem services these habitats provide, including sequestering carbon, providing flood abatement and storage, and offering opportunities for recreation and aesthetic appreciation. Wetland valuation methods attempt to quantify these and other wetland ecosystem services.

Carbon Sequestration

Wetlands are very productive ecosystems that can develop deep organic soils that store carbon. Worldwide estimates of carbon storage in wetlands range from 56 to 504 g/m²/yr and average 174 g/m²/yr (Bernal and Mitsch 2012). In contrast, average carbon storage in ecosystems of the southwest United States, including California, has been estimated at 13.7 g/m²/yr (Schimel et al. 2000). However, wetlands can either store or be sources of carbon, depending on climate, location in the landscape, age, and management practices. A fraction of the carbon produced in wetlands is converted to methane, and wetlands release about one-quarter of global methane emissions annually (IPCC 2007). The influence of wetland management on carbon storage is important because most freshwater wetlands in the Central Valley are managed. Management practices such as tilling and burning promote soil oxidation and the loss of carbon stored in wetland soils. These practices have caused wetland soils in the Bay-Delta region to subside as much as 6 meters during the past 150 years (Miller et al. 2008). Seasonal wetlands intensively managed for waterfowl using similar management also store less carbon than less intensively managed seasonal wetlands (Duffy et al. 2011).

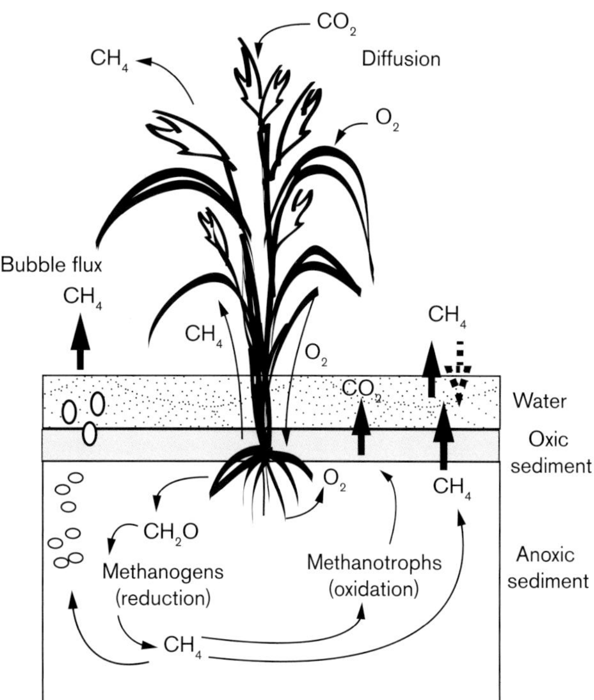

FIGURE 31.10 Methane emission from wetland soils. When wetland soils are saturated, they become anoxic, and methanogenic bacteria convert organic compounds such as methanal (CH_2O) to methane (CH_4) that can be transported to the atmosphere by emergent macrophytes, molecular diffusion, or bubble flux. When wetland soils are oxic (contain oxygen) during initial wetting or a dry phase, methanotrophic bacteria can convert methane to carbon dioxide (CO_2). Image created by Walt Duffy.

Flood Storage

Despite significant losses, wetlands are regionally important for floodwater storage. Flood risk management for the Central Valley, particularly the city of Sacramento, relies highly on the Sacramento Flood Control Project's Yolo and Sutter bypasses, 24,000 hectares and 7,300 hectares of engineered floodplains that incorporate some wetland habitat (Sommer et al. 2001). Also in the Central Valley, the unregulated Cosumnes River retains substantial connectivity with its floodplain, which floods for months at a time during the winter and is the focus of ongoing riverine wetland restoration (Sommer et al. 2001, CVJV 2006). Landowner reports of natural seasonal flooding of privately managed wetlands indicate local importance of these wetlands for floodwater storage (Duffy et al. 2011).

Nevertheless, over 95% of California's riverine wetlands have been modified or destroyed, including historically extensive freshwater wetlands of the Central Valley (CNRA 2010). Here, land conversion and subsidence from diking and draining of carbon-rich valley soils, floodplain development, levee construction, and incision and simplification of channel habitat from engineering and straightening have greatly reduced wetland floodwater storage potential (Williams et al. 2009, Lund 2012).

Recreation, Aesthetics, and Valuation

California's wetlands provide a number of recreational uses and aesthetic values that include hunting, fishing, birdwatching, hiking, photography, natural and cultural history education, and scientific research. It is difficult to quantify recreational uses specifically for freshwater wetlands—as opposed to total wetlands—but from 1999 to 2011, California averaged 49,687 waterfowl hunters who dedicated an estimated five hundred thousand days to waterfowling and harvested an average of 1,341,899 ducks and 143,063 geese annually (Olson and Trost 2012). Approximately 1.8 million anglers purchase California sport-fishing licenses annually, generating approximately $60 million in revenue from this one recreational fee alone (http://www.dfg.ca.gov/licensing/statistics). Millions of birdwatchers and photographers visit California's wetlands to view migratory waterfowl as well as other waterbirds and upland birds that rely on wetlands. One representative national wildlife refuge, the Lower Klamath National Wildlife Refuge, attracts 135,000 visitors a year (Sexton et al. 2012).

In addition to the wetland ecosystem services discussed earlier, benefits and values that wetlands provide include improved water quality, groundwater recharge, nutrient cycling, erosion control, and shoreline stabilization (CNRA 2010). Wetland valuation methods—and thus results—vary widely, but most valuations are based either on ecological (functional) or economic (monetary) evaluation (Mitsch and Gosselink 2007). Few studies of the overall value of California's wetlands have been attempted, but one frequently cited study, which quantified the values of flood control, water supply, water quality, recreation, commercial fisheries, and habitat, concluded the total annual statewide benefit of wetlands to be $10 billion, of which $160 million was attributable to recreation (Allen et al. 1992). Adjusted for inflation, the 2013 statewide benefit would be $16.6 billion and the recreational benefit would be $266 million.

Wetland Management

Wetland managers have traditionally treated wetlands as isolated habitats rather than as nested within larger, highly modified landscapes (Mensik and Paveglio 2004). Management to provide valuable ecosystem services (e.g., wildlife habitat, carbon storage, stormwater retention) within these altered watersheds is extremely challenging, and to be effective requires balancing social choices and political influences, and a dynamic process-based perspective that considers HYDROGEOMORPHIC setting and wetland science (Smith et al. 2008, Euliss et al. 2008).

Water Distribution and Allocation

California's long dry summers and spatial patterns of precipitation have important implications for all wetlands, particularly those that are managed. Most managed freshwater wetlands are located in the Central Valley and most are in private ownership. Significant exceptions in public ownership include wetlands on national wildlife refuges and state wildlife areas in the Central Valley and Klamath River Basin in far northern California. These wetlands are primarily marshes that are managed to have either seasonal or semipermanent hydroperiods. Historically, marshes in the Sacramento Basin were fed by flooding during winter precipitation, while those in the San Joaquin Basin were fed by flooding during snowmelt runoff, resulting in distinct differences in the timing of flooding. Today, water is delivered to these wetlands through a system of canals and ditches.

Delivery of water to wetlands in these areas is dependent on agreements negotiated between wetland managers and irrigation districts or the U.S. Bureau of Reclamation (USBOR). The biggest challenges to all wetland managers are identifying reliable sources of water and meeting the increasing costs of water (CVJV 2006). Water deficits in California are now nearly 200,000 hectare meters during years of normal precipitation and can exceed 600,000 hectare meters during drought. Private wetland managers are also increasingly competing with municipal water users from southern California to purchase water, making reliability of water for wetlands uncertain (CVJV 2006). Water for wetlands on national wildlife refuges in the Central Valley is delivered by the USBOR under the Central Valley Project Improvement Act, but deliveries in recent years have been less than half the volume identified as needed by waterbirds (CVJV 2006).

Vegetation Management

Vegetation management within natural wetlands (e.g., riverine, vernal pools, undiked tidal marshes) has largely been limited to selective weed control to restore diverse, native plant communities. Created or restored wetlands enclosed in human-made levees with infrastructure (e.g., canals, pumps, weirs, control gates) to control wetland hydroperiods can be intensively managed to target the precise requirements of a particular species, but most often they are managed for broad wildlife habitat goals (e.g., cover, desirable wildlife food plants), and if successful, it is assumed they also provide other ecosystem functions (Kahara et al. 2012).

Water management is the most important tool for production of desirable vegetation and also for control of undesirable weeds and mosquito production in wetlands (Mensik and Reid 1995, Kwasny et al. 2004, Jiannino and Walton 2004, Lawler et al. 2007). Management plans include deliberate hydrologic manipulations to control timing, depth, and duration of flooding, coupled with periodic soil and vegetation disturbances to direct vegetation succession toward a diverse community of desirable plant species (e.g., Smith et al. 1994, USFWS 2009a). Seasonal wetlands are the most common managed wetland type, because in fall-winter, when populations of migratory waterbirds increase in California, they provide more food than any other habitat type (USFWS 2009a).

Plant species such as smartweeds, swamp timothy (*Crypsis schoenoides*), tuberous river bulrush (e.g., *Bolboshoenus fluviatilis*), and barnyard grass/watergrass (*Echinochloa crus-galli*) are considered desirable, and diverse communities provide habitat for abundant invertebrate food sources. Management typically includes fall flooding with highly managed timing of spring drawdowns to promote germination of emergent plant species from moist soil seed banks (Strong et al. 1990). Spring or summer irrigations may be implemented to increase seed production of species such as watergrass. In brackish wetlands, leach cycles may be applied to reduce soil salinity for improved seed production (Rollins 1981). Water levels may be maintained year round to support semipermanent to permanent ponds. For weed control, managers may apply pulse applications of water timed with vulnerable periods in the life cycle of undesirable species such as cocklebur.

Prescribed burns have been used to reduce dense stands of cattails and bulrushes to maintain a balance between open-water habitats and cover for optimum wildlife use or for targeted weed control. However, recent legislation to reduce air pollution has restricted the use of burning for vegetation management (Elphick and Oring 1998), and burning can actually increase biomass and density of undesirable plant species (Flores et al. 2011). Tillage (i.e., disking), mowing, prescribed livestock grazing during the dry season, and herbicides are all tools that may be utilized but are best used in integrated management strategies to reduce dense stands of rhizomatous perennials, to control problem weeds, or to create disturbance to reset vegetation succession from moist soil seed banks (Mensik and Reid 1995, Naylor 2002).

Rice Fields as Wetlands

Flooded rice fields with relatively high wildlife value (Eadie et al. 2008) have replaced many natural wetlands in the Sacramento Valley and to some degree in the Delta and San Joaquin Valley (Fleskes 2012). Although birds heavily use both dry and flooded rice fields, flooded fields retain more of the same functions as the wetlands they replaced (Elphick 2000) and have greater bird species richness than dry fields (Day and Colwell 1998, Elphick and Oring 1998). Rice fields provide bird habitat during all seasons, with at least 118 species during winter and 140 species overall using rice fields in the Central Valley (Eadie et al. 2008). Harvested and newly seeded fields flooded in spring provide waterfowl pair habitat and foraging habitat for shorebirds, waders, and other over-water feeders (Sterling and Buttner 2011). Ducks (especially mallards) and some shorebirds nest on vegetated and bare levees, respectively (McLandress et al. 1996; Robinson et al. 1997, 1999). During late spring and summer, rice fields serve as brood habitat, although duckling survival is greater after rice plants have grown and provide dense emergent cover for concealment and escape from predators (Yarris 2008). Use of rice fields by birds is greatest during fall and winter when migratory waterfowl are most abundant, and waterfowl and other bird species feed extensively on waste rice seed after harvest (Eadie et al. 2008, Sterling and Buttner 2011) (see chapter Lead Photo).

Although some harvested rice fields were flooded for duck hunting before the late 1980s, conservation programs of the Central Valley Joint Venture that began in 1986 and the California Rice Straw Burning Reduction Act of 1991 increased flooding as a way to dispose of rice straw while increasing waterbird habitat and waterfowl hunting opportunities (Hill et al. 1999, Eadie et al. 2008). From the 1970s to 2000 winter-flooded rice in the northern Central Valley increased by nearly 150% to include 79,000 hectares; from 1988 to 2000 the total area of rice planted increased by 23%; and from 1972 to 2000 the area of harvested rice that was flooded increased by 27% (Heitmeyer et al. 1989; Fleskes, Perry et al. 2005). Managed flooding of rice fields provides habitat for waterbirds months earlier, for longer duration, and over a greater area than winter rains would otherwise produce. As a result of this increased habitat in the Sacramento Valley, many species of waterbirds have shifted their winter distribution from other Central Valley regions into the Sacramento Valley (Fleskes, Yee et al. 2005) with resulting benefits including improved body condition of seed-eating species such as northern pintails (Fleskes et al. 2009, Thomas 2009) and reduced mortality from disease and predation (Fleskes et al. 2007). However, changes in rice straw management practices that bury seeds (e.g., increased plowing) or reduce the extent of decomposition-flooding would greatly reduce the value of rice fields to waterfowl and other wetland-dependent wildlife given current land use and competition for water resources. Today, agricultural wetlands that leave a significant quantity of waste rice in fields, with a large portion of the fields flooded after harvest, are vital for sustaining the substantial populations of waterfowl and other birds that rely upon Central Valley habitats (CVJV 2006).

Toxicity and Pollution Issues

California's wetlands face threats from pollution and toxic contaminants that derive from industry, agriculture, and legacy events such as mercury releases associated with nineteenth-century placer gold mining (Conaway 2004). The wetlands of the Bay-Delta region are subject to contaminants released by local industry, including oil refineries, as well as those delivered from more distant sources via the Sacramento and San Joaquin Rivers. This contaminant load includes polychlorinated biphenyls (PCBs), polycyclic aromatic hydrocarbons (PAHs), organochlorine pesticides (such as DDT, chlordane, and dieldrin), polybrominated diphenyl ethers (PBDEs), dioxins, selenium, and mercury. Many of these contaminants have accumulated in soils and sediments of the Sacramento and San Joaquin River watersheds and are transported to the Bay-Delta, especially during large storm events. Mercury is a particular concern, as it BIOACCUMULATES in wetlands in the form of methylmercury (MeHg) from algae to the higher trophic levels of fish and wildlife. When ingested, methylmercury is readily absorbed by organisms. Concern about methylmercury's toxic effects, including neurological damage, has resulted in fish consumption advisories (David et al. 2012).

Agricultural irrigation wastewater can carry not only pesticide and fertilizer residues but also leachates including salts and trace elements such as arsenic, boron, chromium, molybdenum, and selenium (SJVDP 1990). Of these, selenium has proved to be the greatest threat to California wetlands, especially those in the Central Valley (Moore et al. 1990). When California's Central Valley Project and State Water Project brought the seleniferous soils of the San Joaquin Valley under irrigation, the agricultural wastewater that was generated proved toxic to wildlife (Hoffman et al. 1988). Selenium is an essential nutrient in small doses but is toxic when present in excess in bioavailable forms. Effects of selenium toxicity are often fatal and include teratogenesis (embryonic malformation) and organ failure in adults. During the late 1970s and early 1980s, subsurface irrigation wastewater from drainage-impaired lands on the west side of the northern San Joaquin Valley—primarily from the Westlands Water District—were transported as much as 135 kilometers northward to constructed ponds on the newly created Kesterson National Wildlife Refuge in the Grasslands. Selenium concentrations in the drainage water entering Kesterson averaged 300 µg/L, three orders of magnitude above background levels for freshwater and at least sixty times the toxicity threshold for waterborne selenium. This resulted in the death of at least one thousand waterbirds among several species, including black-necked stilts (*Himantopus mexicanus*) and American avocets (*Recurvirostra americana*), before the State Water Resources Control Board ordered the permanent drainage of the ponds at Kesterson (Ohlendorf 1989).

Problems with selenium toxicity were also found at this time elsewhere in the Grasslands, farther south in the Tulare Basin in on-site evaporation ponds on private agricultural lands, and also in other locations throughout the western United States where seleniferous soils were present in locations served by large-scale federal irrigation projects (Skorupa 1998). These disturbing events received widespread media coverage and led to a proliferation of studies of selenium remediation. However, in large part as a result of the deeply politicized nature of federally subsidized irrigation projects, satisfactory solutions have not yet been found, and selenium toxicity remains an issue in California wetlands and elsewhere (Chapman et al. 2010).

Future Scenarios

Climate Change and Likely Impacts on Wetlands

Some climate projections for the California region indicate potential mean annual warming of up to 0.8–2.3°C by the mid-twenty-first century and 1.5–4.5°C by the late twenty-first century, relative to 1961–1990 temperatures (Cayan et al. 2008). Projected warming shows both seasonal and spatial variation. Warming in some climate projections in summer and early fall exceeds that in winter and spring by the mid-twenty-first century, with potential increases of 1–4°C in winter and up to 1.5–6°C in summer for the state. Projections also suggest greater annual warming and more pronounced seasonality of warming in inland California than at the coast, and indicate heat waves becoming longer and occurring both earlier and later in the season over this century (Cayan et al. 2008, 2012).

Projections for precipitation are generally more uncertain than those for temperature (Cayan et al. 2008, Neelin et al. 2013). This is particularly the case in California, which bridges mid-to-high latitudes where precipitation is projected to increase and the subtropics where precipitation decreases are projected. Despite the lack of consensus on the magnitude and direction of projected precipitation changes, shifts in the proportion of snow to rain and associated shifts in spring snowpack and runoff appear more certain. Such changes have already been observed in the western United States and are projected to continue (Knowles and Cayan 2002). Several analyses project greater than 50% reductions in Sierra Nevada spring snow water equivalent (SWE) by the late twenty-first century, particularly in mid- to lower elevations in the northern Sierra Nevada and Cascades (Knowles and Cayan 2002, Cayan et al. 2008, 2012). Seasonal shifts such as higher runoff peaks prior to April, and decreases in the April to July fraction of total flow, are quite possible (Knowles and Cayan 2002). However, snowpack projections show large interannual variability, with SWE in some years at or above normal, and hydrologic projections remain highly uncertain (Knowles and Cayan 2002, Cayan et al. 2008).

Potential effects of future climate on California wetlands are diverse and vary substantially among wetland types and regions. Changes in precipitation, temperature, and evapotranspiration would alter wetland hydroperiod, residence times, and biogeochemical processes such as mineralization, denitrification, and carbon sequestration. Although future changes in timing of runoff could be significant, the majority of the state's managed wetlands are at least partially dependent on high-demand water from delivery systems, rather than natural flooding (CNRA 2010). Nearly 40% of California wetlands are in the Bay-Delta region, where reservoir storage already has some capacity to regulate seasonal shifts in streamflow (CNRA 2010, Hanak and Lund 2012). These wetlands could be substantially affected by future shifts in water demand and pricing, in addition to changes in timing and volume of runoff. Wetlands of the Bay-Delta may face further stressors, including saltwater intrusion and greater water depths from rising sea levels and a resulting increase in the cost of freshwater imports, as well as increased risk of failure of aging levees (Ackerly et al. 2012). For the state's coastal wetlands, projected rises in sea level may reduce wetland extent if coastal erosion is more rapid than sediment accretion, and if wetland habitat cannot migrate over time because of adjacent agriculture or development (Hanak and Lund 2012). Climate change may also affect coastal wetland salinity by altering timing and, potentially, volume of freshwater runoff (CNRA 2010).

Human Population Growth

In addition to climate change, California's rapidly expanding population will place pressure on wetlands, both in terms of intensifying competition for limited water supplies and of encroachment and conversion (Duffy and Kahara 2011). California's population in 2010 was over 37.3 million and is expected to reach nearly 52.7 million by 2060, an increase of almost 15.4 million. Southern California (the counties of San Luis Obispo, Santa Barbara, Kern, San Bernardino, Ventura, Los Angeles, Orange, Riverside, San Diego, and Imperial) is expected to lead the state's growth between 2010 and 2060, adding 8.3 million people, especially in the inland counties. Significant growth is also expected in the San Joaquin Valley (the counties of San Joaquin, Stanislaus, Merced, Madera, Fresno, Kings, and Tulare), which will double in population from 3.1 million to 6.2 million, and in the greater Sacramento area (the counties of Sacramento, Yolo, El Dorado, Placer, Yuba, and Sutter), which will increase from 2.3 million to 3.8 million people (California Department of Finance 2013).

Population growth will have significant impacts on water demand in the state. According to California Department of Water Resources (CDWR) estimates released in 2011, in 2005 California used approximately 4.96 million hectare meters of water for urban and agricultural purposes, of which 22% (or 1.1 million hectare meters) was for urban use and 78% (or 3.85 million hectare meters) was for agriculture (CDWR 2011). Under a "Current Trends" scenario that takes into account the effects of climate change, urban water demand for the years 2043–2050 is projected to increase over the 1998–2005 average by approximately 0.7 million hectare meters per year. Conversely, agricultural water demand is projected to decrease by approximately 0.4–0.6 million hectare meters, primarily because of an anticipated reduction in irrigated acreage of approximately 0.3 million hectares (CDWR 2009). Environmental water use for 1998–2005 averaged 5.1 million hectare meters, of which 0.19 million hectare meters was applied to managed wetlands (CDWR 2011). Although total environmental water is expected to increase slightly by approximately 0.12 million hectare meters, wetlands remain threatened by the direct effects of urbanization, particularly in the Central Valley, as well as continuing coastal development, especially in southern California (CDWR 2009).

Wetland Restoration

By the 1930s habitat loss and drought had combined to drastically reduce populations of migratory waterfowl. Concern for the waterfowl resource led to federal and state policies to protect and restore—rather than drain—wetlands. Over the course of the later twentieth century, wetland protection efforts intensified, eventually leading to passage of the Emergency Wetlands Resources Act of 1986, which contained several provisions to assist the U.S. in meeting international obligations to migratory bird treaties. During this same period, the U.S. adopted a policy "No Net Loss" of wetlands, having the goal of balancing wetland loss with wetlands reclamation, mitigation, and restoration, so that the total acreage of wetlands in the U.S. would not decrease.

Wetland restoration has now been undertaken in all regions of California, often with multiple agencies and interest groups sharing resources, and is best documented for the Central Valley. Wetland restoration in the Central Valley is typically supported by the U.S. Department of Agriculture's Natural Resource Conservation Service (NRCS), using the Wetlands Reserve Program (WRP)—a Farm Bill Conservation program—or by a consortium of groups under the umbrella of the Central Valley Joint Venture (CVJV). In 2012 the NRCS announced that its WRP program had restored or protected 48,562 hectares of wetlands in California that are home to almost two hundred species of birds (http://www.ca.nrcs.usda.gov/news/releases/2012/wrp_5-30-12.html). The CVJV (2006) reported restoring 3,913 hectares of Central Valley wetlands in 1986–1989 and 26,382 hectares in 1990–2003. Their goal is to restore 43,919 hectares of seasonal wetlands, 5,059 hectares of semipermanent wetlands, and 4,047 hectares of riparian wetlands. Ducks Unlimited has restored or enhanced 290,969 hectares of wetlands and associated upland habitats in California, and the California Waterfowl Association is currently restoring or enhancing 7,036 hectares of wetland and associated upland habitats. Many of the wetlands restored by waterfowl interests are located in the Central Valley but also include wetlands in other regions. In addition to marshes, the USFWS has restored or created numerous vernal pools in the Central Valley and its foothills. The California Wetlands portal lists 8,281 hectares of wetlands as having been restored in the San Francisco Bay region, 1,220 hectares on the Central Coast, and 687 hectares on the South Coast (http://www.californiawetlands.net/tracker/).

The recovery of ecosystem processes in California's restored wetlands has not been thoroughly assessed. However, in Central Valley marshes restored under the WRP, climate, intensity of management, and availability of water influenced carbon storage, biogeochemical processes, and bird use of wetlands (Duffy et al. 2011, Kahara et al. 2012). An assessment of mitigation wetlands created in California reported that only 19% were considered ecologically successful and that wetland protection programs were generating more wetlands of lower quality than the wetlands they allowed to be destroyed (Ambrose et al. 2007). Assessing recovery of restored wetlands worldwide, Moreno-Mateos et al. (2012) reported that biological structure and biochemical functions in restored wetlands remained less than in reference wetlands for decades. These authors report that recovery of ecosystem function is more rapid in large wetlands and wetlands receiving hydrologic exchange than in small depressional wetlands.

Summary

Freshwater wetlands can be found in all of California's ecoregions and cover almost 950,000 hectares, or about 2.3% of the area of the state. The most recognizable wetlands in California include marshes of the Central Valley, the Sacramento–San Joaquin Delta region, and the Klamath Basin; vernal pools scattered across southern California and the margins of the Central Valley; riparian wetlands associated with rivers throughout the state; and fens occurring at higher elevations of the Cascades and Sierra Nevada. Coastal wetlands are emblematic of San Francisco Bay but occur from Tijuana Slough near the Mexican border to Del Norte County in northernmost California.

Wetlands historically occupied a much greater portion of California than they currently do and were valued by Native Americans for the fish, waterfowl, and edible plant roots and seeds they provided as well as the raw materials used in making rafts and baskets. However, their early association with disease, and policies fostering agricultural development and flood control, led to the loss of extensive wetlands in the Tulare Lake area, Sacramento River Basin, and riparian corridors throughout the state. Other human activities, such as urban development and livestock grazing, have contributed to wetland loss or diminishment of wetland ecological functioning in some areas.

California's wetlands provide a variety of services to human society. Most freshwater wetlands in California are classified as palustrine wetlands, which support plants ranging from mosses to shrubs. Wetland plant communities contribute to biological diversity, support animal community diversity, and play a role in biogeochemical processes. Wetlands of the Central Valley and Klamath Basin are recognized for their global importance to waterfowl and shorebirds, as well as other birds, amphibians, and mammals. Vernal pools are valued for supporting a unique invertebrate community while also providing habitat for vertebrates. Riparian wetlands and fens in the Sierra Nevada support much of the biological diversity of that region. The biogeochemical functioning of wetlands can under certain conditions contribute to improving water quality by sequestering or storing nitrogen and phosphorus and by storing carbon—an increasingly important ecosystem service. Wetlands in California also store floodwater runoff and support human recreation. The latter, including hunting, fishing, wildlife viewing, and general recreation, contributes substantially to the state's economy each year.

Management of California's wetlands varies with ownership. Many wetlands under private ownership in the Central Valley and Bay-Delta regions are managed, and acquiring sufficient amounts of water to support desirable plant communities and provide bird habitat poses challenges to landowners. In these regions, flooded rice fields with relatively high wildlife value are now considered a specific type of managed wetland. Elsewhere, most wetlands are under public ownership where management is focused on protecting habitats and, in some cases, controlling introduced species. Introduced plant species that invade wetlands can displace native flora and fauna, alter nutrient cycles, and threaten the functioning of ecosystems.

In the future, a changing climate and continued human population growth will influence wetland ecology in California. Climate changes will influence evapotranspiration and have the potential to change wetland hydroperiods and biogeochemical processes. California's rapidly expanding human population will place pressure on wetlands, both by intensifying competition for limited water supplies and through encroachment and conversion. However, the services provided by wetlands to society are now more widely recognized than in the past, and the restoration of converted wetlands is under way throughout California.

Recommended Reading

California Natural Resources Agency (CNRA). 2010. State of the state's wetlands: Ten years of challenges and progress. California Natural Resources Agency, Sacramento, California.

Garone, P. 2011. The fall and rise of the wetlands of California's Great Central Valley. University of California Press, Berkeley and Los Angeles, California.

Millennium Ecosystem Assessment. 2005. Ecosystems and human well-being: Wetlands and water synthesis. World Resources Institute, Washington, D.C.

Vileisis, A. 1997. Discovering the unknown landscape: A history of America's wetlands. Island Press, Washington, D.C.

Whipple, A., R. M. Grossinger, D. Rankin, B. Stanford, and R. Askevold. 2012. Sacramento–San Joaquin Delta historical ecology investigation: Exploring pattern and process. San Francisco Estuary Institute, Richmond, California.

Glossary

ADSORB To bind as a thin film to the surfaces of a solid material.

ALLUVIAL Made up of the materials (e.g., cobble, sediments) left by river waters or floodwaters.

ANOXIC Referring to a process or setting in which oxygen is absent.

BIOACCUMULATE To become concentrated in the tissues of an organism.

BRACKISH Slightly salty, as when freshwater and ocean water mix.

DENDRITIC Having a branching form.

FECUNDITY The reproductive rate of an organism or population.

FILAMENTOUS ALGAE Aquatic algae that form filaments or mats out of single cells joined end to end.

GASTROTRICH A member of a group (phylum) of microscopic, wormlike animals also known as hairybacks or hairy-bellied worms.

HYDRIC Of soil, permanently or seasonally saturated by water, leading to anaerobic (without oxygen) conditions.

HYDROGEOMORPHIC Involving the interaction of hydrologic (involving water) and geomorphic (involving landforms or earth materials) processes.

HYDROPERIOD The depth, duration, and frequency of flooding.

HYDROPHYTIC Growing wholly or partially submerged in water.

LACUSTRINE Of lakes.

OXIDATION (STATE) An indication of degree of oxidation or reduction (deficit or surplus of electrons), which shapes the environment for plants, microbes, and other organisms and associated processes in a wetland.

PALUSTRINE Describes inland, nontidal wetlands characterized by the presence of trees, shrubs, and other emergent vegetation.

PROPAGULES (INVERTEBRATE) A structure or material that propagates an organism to the next stage in its life cycle.

ROTIFER A member of a group (phylum) of microscopic or near-microscopic aquatic animals.

SURFICIAL Relating to Earth's surface.

References

Ackerly, D. D., R. R. Ryals, W. K. Cornwell, S. R. Loarie, S. Veloz, K. D. Higgason, W. L. Silver, and T. E. Dawson. 2012. Potential impacts of climate change on biodiversity and ecosystem services in the San Francisco Bay Area. California Energy Commission. Publication no. CEC-500-2012-037. Sacramento, California.

Alekseev, V. R., J.-S. Hwang, and M.-H. Tseng. 2006. Diapause in aquatic invertebrates: What's known and what's next in research and medical application? Journal of Marine Science and Technology 14:269–286.

Allen, J., M. Cunningham, A. Greenwood, and L. Rosenthal. 1992. The value of California wetlands: An analysis of their economic benefits. The Campaign to Save California Wetlands, Oakland, California.

Ambrose, R. F., J. C. Callaway, and S. F. Lee. 2007. An evaluation of compensatory mitigation projects permitted under Clean Water Act section 401 by the California State Water Resources Control Board, 1991–2002. Report prepared for the Los Angeles Regional Water Quality Control Board. University of California, San Francisco, California.

Barbour, M., B. Pavlik, F. Drysdale, and S. Lindstrom. 1993. California's changing landscapes: Diversity and conservation of California vegetation. California Native Plant Society, Sacramento, California.

Barbour, M. G., A. Solomeshch, C. Witham, R. Holland, R. Macdonald, S. Cilliers, J. A. Molina, J. Buck, and J. Hillman. 2003. Vernal pool vegetation of California: Variations within pools. Madroño 50:129–146.

Bartolome, J. W., D. C. Erman, and C. F. Schwart. 1990. Stability and change in minerotrophic peatlands: Sierra Nevada of California and Nevada. Research Paper PSW-198. Pacific Southwest Forest and Range Experiment Station, U.S. Department of Agriculture, Forest Service, Berkeley, California.

Bauder, E. T. 2005. The effects of an unpredictable precipitation regime on vernal pool hydrology. Freshwater Biology 50: 2129–2135.

Beesley, D. 2004. Crow's range: An environmental history of the Sierra Nevada. University of Nevada Press, Reno and Las Vegas, Nevada.

Bell, G. 1997. Ecology and management of *Arundo donax* and approaches to riparian habitat restoration in southern California. Pages 103–113 in J. M. Brock, M. Wade, P. Pyšek, and D. Green, editors. Plant invasions: Studies from North America and Europe. Backhuys Publications, Leiden, Netherlands.

Bernal, B., and W. J. Mitsch. 2012. Comparing carbon sequestration in temperate freshwater wetland communities. Global Change Biology 18:1636–1647.

Bertoldi, G. L., and W. C. Swain. 1996. California wetland resources. Pages 127–134 in J. D. Fretwell, J. S. Williams, and P. J. Redman, compilers. National water summary on wetland resources. Water Supply Paper 2425. U.S. Geological Survey, Reston, Virginia.

Bogiatto, R. J., and J. D. Karnegis. 2007. Pages 111–118 in R. A. Schlising and D. G. Alexander, editors. Vernal pool landscapes. Studies from the Herbarium, No. 14. California State University, Chico, California.

Boon, P. I. 2006. Biogeochemistry and bacterial ecology of hydrologically dynamic wetlands. Pages 115–176 in D. P. Batzer and R. R. Sharitz, editors. Ecology of freshwater and estuarine wetlands. University of California Press, Berkeley, California.

Bossard, C. C., and J. M. Randall. 2007. Nonnative plants of California. Pages 107–123 in M. G. Barbour, T. Keeler-Wolf, and A. A. Schoenherr, editors. Terrestrial vegetation of California. University of California Press, Berkeley, California.

Brendonck, L., D. C. Rogers, J. Olesen, S. Weeks, and W. R. Hoeh. 2008. Global diversity of large branchiopods (Crustacea: Branchiopoda) in freshwater. Hydrobiologia 595:167–176.

Brode, J. M., and R. B. Bury. 1984. The importance of riparian systems to amphibians and reptiles. Pages 30–36 in R. E. Warner and K. M. Hendrix, editors. California riparian systems: Ecology, conservation, and productive management. University of California Press, Berkeley, California.

Brown, L., and J. May. 2006. Variation in spring nearshore resident fish species composition and life histories in the lower Sacramento–San Joaquin Watershed and Delta (California). San Francisco Estuary and Watershed Science 4(2):1–15.

California Bird Records Committee (CBRC). 2013. Official California checklist by the California Bird Records Committee. <http://www.californiabirds.org/ca_list.asp>. Accessed February 1, 2013.

California Department of Finance. 2013. New population projections: California to surpass 50 million in 2049. Sacramento, California. <http://www.dof.ca.gov/research/demographic/reports/projections/p-1/documents/Projections_Press_Release_2010-2060.pdf>. Accessed February 23, 2013.

California Department of Fish and Game (CDFG). 1998. California vernal pool assessment preliminary report. Prepared by T. Keller-Wolf, D. R. Elam, K. Lewis, and S. A. Flint. Sacramento, California. <http://www.dfg.ca.gov/biogeodata/wetlands/pdfs/VernalPoolAssessmentPreliminaryReport.pdf>. Accessed March 20, 2013.

California Department of Fish and Wildlife (CDFW). 2013. Threatened and endangered birds. <http://www.dfg.ca.gov/wildlife/nongame/t_e_spp/bird.html>. Accessed February 2013.

———. 2008. California bird species of special concern. <http://www.dfg.ca.gov/wildlife/nongame/ssc/birds.html>. Accessed February 2013.

California Department of Forestry and Fire Protection (CDF). 2002. Multi-source land cover data (2002 V2). <http://www.fire.ca.gov/php/>. Accessed March 20, 2013.

California Department of Water Resources (CDWR). 2011. Statewide water balance (1998–2005). Sacramento, California. <http://www.waterplan.water.ca.gov/docs/technical/cwpu2009/statewide_water_balance(1998-2005)04-28-11.xlsx>. Accessed February 23, 2013.

———. 2009. California Water Plan update 2009: Integrated water management. Bulletin 160-09. Sacramento, California.

California Natural Resources Agency (CNRA). 2010. State of the state's wetlands: Ten years of challenges and progress. California Natural Resources Agency, Sacramento, California.

California State Water Resources Control Board (CSWRCB). 1994. Mono Lake Basin Water Right Decision 1631. Decision and order amending water right licenses to establish fishery protection flows in streams tributary to Mono Lake and to protect public trust resources at Mono Lake and in the Mono Lake Basin. September 28, 1994. Sacramento, California.

Casanova, M. T., and M. A. Brock. 2000. How do depth, duration, and frequency of flooding influence the establishment of wetland plant communities? Plant Ecology 147:237–250.

Cayan, D. R., E. P. Maurer, M. D. Dettinger, M. Tyree, and K. Hayhoe. 2008. Climate change scenarios for the California region. Climatic Change 87:21–42.

Cayan, D., M. Tyree, D. Pierce, and T. Das. 2012. Climate change and sea level rise scenarios for California vulnerability and adaptation assessment. Prepared for California Energy Commission by Scripps Institution of Oceanography. Publication no. CEC-500-2012-008. La Jolla, California.

Central Valley Joint Venture (CVJV). 2006. Central Valley Joint Venture implementation plan—conserving bird habitat. Central Valley Joint Venture, U.S. Fish and Wildlife Service, Sacramento, California.

Chapman, P. M., W. J. Adams, M. L. Brooks, C. G. Delos, S. N. Luoma, W. A. Maher, H. M. Ohlendorf, T. S. Presser, and D. P. Shaw, editors. 2010. Ecological assessment of selenium in the aquatic environment. CRC Press, Boca Raton, Florida.

Chouinard, M. P., Jr. 2000. Survival and habitat use of mallard broods in the San Joaquin Valley, California. MS thesis. Humboldt State University, Arcata, California.

Collins, D. P., and R. E. Trost. 2009. 2009 Pacific flyway data book: Waterfowl harvests and status, hunter participation, and success in the Pacific flyway and United States. U.S. Fish and Wildlife Service, Portland, Oregon.

Conaway, C. H., E. B. Watson, J. R. Flanders, and A. R. Flegal. 2004. Mercury deposition in a tidal marsh of south San Francisco Bay downstream of the historic New Almaden mining district, California. Marine Chemistry 90:175–184.

Cook, S. F. 1955. The epidemic of 1830–1833 in California and Oregon. University of California Publications in American Archaeology and Ethnology 43:303–325.

Cooper, D. J., and E. C. Wolf. 2006. Fens of the Sierra Nevada, California. Department of Forest, Rangeland and Watershed Stewardship, Colorado State University, Fort Collins, Colorado.

Cowardin, L. M., V. Carter, F. C. Golet, and E. T. LaRoe. 1979. Classification of wetlands and deepwater habitats of the United States. FWS/OBS-79/31. U.S. Fish and Wildlife Service, Washington, D.C.

Cronk, J. K., and M. S. Fennessy. 2001. Wetland plants: Biology and ecology. Lewis Publishers, CRC Press LLC, Boca Raton, Florida.

Cunningham, L. 2010. A state of change: Forgotten landscapes of California. Heyday Press, Berkeley, California.

Cushman J. H., and K. A. Gaffney. 2010. Community-level consequences of invasion: Impacts of exotic clonal plants on riparian vegetation. Biological Invasions 12:2765–2776.

David, N., D. C. Gluchowski, J. E. Leatherbarrow, D. Yee, and L. J. McKee. 2012. Estimates of loads of mercury, selenium, PCBs, PAHs, PBDEs, dioxins, and organochlorine pesticides from the Sacramento–San Joaquin River Delta to San Francisco Bay. San Francisco Estuary Institute, Richmond, California.

Davis, F. W., and M. Stoms. 1996. Sierran vegetation: A gap analysis. Pages 671–690 in Sierra Nevada Ecosystem Project: Final Report to Congress, Volume II. Wildland Resources Center Report No. 37. University of California, Davis, California.

Dawdy, D. R. 1989. Feasibility of mapping riparian forests under natural conditions in California. Proceedings of the California Riparian Systems Conference. GTR PSW-110. Davis, California.

Day, J. H., and M. A. Colwell. 1998. Waterbird communities in rice fields subjected to different post-harvest treatments. Colonial Waterbirds 21:185–197.

Duffy, W. G., and S. N. Kahara. 2011. Freshwater wetlands in California's Central Valley: A review of ecosystem services. Ecological Applications 21(3):S21–S30.

Duffy, W. G., S. N. Kahara, and R. M. Records, editors. 2011. Conservation Effects Assessment Project—Wetlands assessment in California's Central Valley and Upper Klamath River Basin: Open-File Report 2011-1290. U.S. Geological Survey, Reston, Virginia.

Eadie, J. M., C. S. Elphick, K. J. Reinecke, and M. R. Miller. 2008. Wildlife values of North American ricelands. Pages 7–89 in S. W. Manley, editor. Conservation in ricelands of North America. The Rice Foundation, Stuggart, Arkansas.

Elphick C. S. 2000. Functional equivalency between rice fields and seminatural wetland habitats. Conservation Biology 14:181–191.

Elphick, C. S., and L. W. Oring. 1998. Winter management of California rice fields for waterbirds. Journal of Applied Ecology 35:95–108.

Eriksen, C. H., and D. Belk. 1999. Fairy shrimps of California's puddles, pools, and playas. Mad River Press, Inc., Eureka, California.

Eriksen, C. H., and R. J. Brown. 1980. Comparative respiratory physiology and ecology of phyllopod Crustacea. II. Anostraca. Crustaceana 39:11–21.

Erman, D. C., N. A. Erman, L. Costick, and S. Beckwitt. 1996. Riparian areas and wetlands. Chapter 5 in R. Kattelmann and M. Embury, editors. Sierra Nevada Ecosystem Project: Final report to Congress. Volume III, Assessments and scientific basis for management options. Center for Water and Wildland Resources, University of California, Davis, California.

Euliss, N. D., L. M. Smith, D. A. Wilcox, and B. A. Browne. 2008. Linking ecosystem processes with wetland management goals: Charting a course for a sustainable future. Wetlands 28:553–562.

Euliss, N. H., D. A. Wrubleski, and D. M. Mushet. 1999. Wetlands of the prairie pothole region: Invertebrate species composition, ecology, and management. Pages 471–514 in D. P. Batzer, R. B. Rader, and S. A. Wissinger, editors. Invertebrates in freshwater wetlands of North America: Ecology and management. Wiley, New York, New York.

Euliss, N. H., Jr., and L. M. Smith. 2010. Ecosystem processes and the hemi-marsh concept: Clarifying principles for wetland management. National Wetlands Newsletter 32:23–24.

Fitch, H. S. 1941. The feeding habits of California garter snakes. California Fish and Game 27(2):1–32.

Fitzgerald, G. J., K. M. Scow, and J. E. Hill. 2000. Fallow season straw and water management effects on methane emissions in California rice. Global Biogeochemical Cycles 14:767–776.

Fleskes, J. P. 2012. Wetlands of the Central Valley of California and Klamath Basin. Chapter 25. Pages 357–370 in D. Batzer and A. Baldwin, editors. Wetland habitats of North America: Ecology and conservation concerns. University of California Press, Berkeley, California.

Fleskes J. P., and J. L. Yee. 2007. Waterfowl distribution and abundance during spring migration in southern Oregon and northeastern California. Western North American Naturalist 67:409–428.

Fleskes J. P., J. L. Yee, G. S. Yarris, M. R. Miller, and M. L. Casazza. 2007. Pintail and mallard survival in California relative to habitat, abundance, and hunting. Journal of Wildlife Management 71:2238–2248.

Fleskes, J. P., J. L. Yee, M. L. Casazza, M. R. Miller, J. Y. Takekawa, and D. L. Orthmeyer. 2005. Waterfowl distribution, movements, and habitat use relative to recent habitat changes in the Central Valley of California: A cooperative project to investigate impacts of the Central Valley Habitat Joint Venture and changing agricultural practices on the ecology of wintering waterfowl. Published Final Report. U.S. Geological Survey-Western Ecological Research Center, Dixon Field Station, Dixon, California. <http://www.werc.usgs.gov/ProductDetails.aspx?ID=3247>. Accessed February 23, 2013.

Fleskes, J. P., M. R. Miller, G. S. Yarris, D. R. Thomas, and J. M. Eadie. 2009. Increased winter habitat improves body condition of ducks in the Central Valley of California. The Wildlife Society Annual Conference. September 2009. Monterey, California. (Abstract).

Fleskes J. P., W. M. Perry, K. L. Petrik, R. Spell, and F. Reid. 2005. Change in area of winter-flooded and dry rice in the northern Central Valley of California determined by satellite imagery. California Fish and Game 91:207–215.

Flores, C., D. L. Bounds, and D. E. Ruby. 2011. Does prescribed fire benefit wetland vegetation? Wetlands 31:35–44.

Fraser, L. H., and J. P. Kernezis. 2005. A comparative assessment of seedling survival and biomass accumulation for fourteen different wetland plant species grown under minor water depth differences. Wetlands 25:520–530.

Garone, P. 2011. The fall and rise of the wetlands of California's Great Central Valley. University of California Press, Berkeley and Los Angeles, California.

Gates, P. W. 1975. Public land disposal in California. Agricultural History 49:158–178.

Gilmer, D. S., J. L. Yee, D. M. Mauser, and J. L. Hainline. 2004. Waterfowl migration on Klamath Basin National Wildlife Refuges 1953–2001. Biological Science Report USGS/BRD/BSR-2003-0004. U.S. Geological Survey, Reston, Virginia.

Gilmer, D. S., M. R. Miller, R. D. Bauer, and J. R. LeDonne. 1982. California's Central Valley wintering waterfowl: Concerns and challenges. Transactions of the North American Wildlife and Natural Resources Conference 47:441–452.

Gordon, D. R. 1998. Effects of invasive, non-indigenous plant species on ecosystem processes: Lessons from Florida. Ecological Applications 8:975–989.

Grewell, B. J. 2008a. Hemiparasites generate environmental heterogeneity and enhance species coexistence in salt marshes. Ecological Applications 18(5):1297–1306.

———. 2008b. Parasite facilitates plant species coexistence in a coastal wetland. Ecology 89(6):1481–1488.

Grewell, B. J., J. C. Callaway, W. R. Ferren Jr. 2007. Estuarine wetlands. Pages 124–154 in M. G. Barbour, T. Keeler-Wolf, and A. A. Schoenherr. Terrestrial vegetation of California. Third edition. University of California Press, Berkeley, California.

Grosholz, E. D., L. A. Levin, A. C. Tyler, and C. Neira. 2009. Changes in community structure and ecosystem function following *Spartina alterniflora* invasion of Pacific estuaries. Pages 23–40 in B. R. Silliman, M. D. Bertness, and E. D. Grosholz, editors. Human impacts on salt marshes: A global perspective. University of California Press, Berkeley, California.

Grunsky, C. E. 1901. Water appropriation from Kings River, report of irrigation investigations in California. Bulletin No. 100. U.S. Department of Agriculture, Office of Experiment Stations, Washington, D.C.

Hall, F. A. 2011. They came to shoot: A history of California duck clubs and wetland conservation. California Waterfowl Association, Sacramento, California.

Hanak, E., and J. R. Lund. 2012. Adapting California's water management to climate change. Climatic Change 111:17–44.

Hart, E. A., and J. R. Lovorn. 2003. Algal vs. macrophyte inputs to food webs of inland saline wetlands. Ecology 84(12):3317–3326.

Hart, J. 1996. Storm over Mono: The Mono Lake battle and the California water future. University of California Press, Berkeley and Los Angeles, California.

Heitmeyer M. E., D. P. Connell, and R. L. Pederson. 1989. The Central, Imperial, and Coachella Valleys of California. Pages 475–505 in L. M. Smith, R. L. Pedersen, and R. M. Kaminski, editors. Habitat management for migrating and wintering waterfowl in North America. Texas Tech University Press, Lubbock, Texas.

Heizer, R. F., editor. 1978. Handbook of North American Indians. Volume 8, California. Smithsonian Institution, Washington, D.C.

Helm, B. P. 1999. Feeding ecology of *Linderiella occidentalis* (Dodds) (Crustacea: Anostraca). PhD dissertation. University of California, Davis, California.

Hickey, C., W. D. Shuford, G. W. Page, and S. Warnock. 2003. Version 1.1. The Southern Pacific shorebird conservation plan: A strategy for supporting California's Central Valley and coastal shorebird populations. PRBO Conservation Science, Stinson Beach California.

Hill, J. E., D. M. Brandon, and S. M. Brouder. 1999. Agronomic implications of alternative rice straw management practices. Agronomy Progress Report No. 264. University of California, Davis, California.

Hobson, W. A., and R. A. Dahlgren. 1998. Soil forming processes in vernal pools of northern California, Chico area. Pages 24–37 in C. W. Witham, E. T. Bauder, D. Belk, W. R. Ferre Jr., and R. Ornduff, editors. Ecology, Conservation, and Management of Vernal Pool Ecosystems. Proceedings from a 1996 Conference. California Native Plant Society, Sacramento, California.

Hoffman, D. J., H. M. Ohlendorf, and T. W. Aldrich. 1988. Selenium teratogenesis in natural populations of aquatic birds in Central California. Archives of Environmental Contamination and Toxicology 17:519–525.

Holland, R. F. 2011. Great Valley vernal pool distribution rephotorevised. 2005. Pages 107–122 in D. G. Alexander and R. A. Schlising, editors. Research and recovery of vernal pool landscapes. Studies from the Herbarium, No. 16. California State University, Chico, California.

Ingebritsen, S. E., M. E. Ikehara, D. L. Galloway, and D. R. Jones. 2000. Delta subsidence in California: The sinking heart of the state. U.S. Geological Survey Fact Sheet. <http://pubs.usgs.gov/fs/2000/fs00500/> Accessed September 6, 2013.

Intergovernmental Panel on Climate Change (IPCC). 2007. Climate change 2007: Synthesis report. Contribution of Working Groups I, II, and III to the Fourth Assessment Report of the Intergovernmental Panel on Climate Change. IPCC, Geneva, Switzerland.

Intermountain West Joint Venture (IWJV). 2005. Intermountain West Joint Venture, coordinated bird conservation plan, v. 1.1. <http://iwjv.org/resource/iwjv-2005-implementation-plan-archive>. Accessed February 25, 2013.

Jackson, C. R. 2006. Wetland hydrology. Pages 43–81 in D. P. Batzer and R. R. Sharitz, editors. Ecology of freshwater and estuarine wetlands. University of California Press, Berkeley, California.

Jensen, D., S. Torn, and J. Harte. 1993. In our hands: A strategy for conserving California's biological diversity. University of California Press. Berkeley, California.

Jiannino, J. A., and W. E. Walton. 2004. Evaluation of vegetation management strategies for controlling mosquitoes in a southern California constructed wetland. Journal of the American Mosquito Control Association 20:18–26.

Josselyn, M. 1983. The ecology of San Francisco Bay tidal marshes: A community profile. Washington, D.C.: U.S. Fish and Wildlife Service, Division of Biological Services.

Kahara, S. N., W. G. Duffy, R. DiGaudio and R. Records. 2012. Climate, management, and habitat associations of avian fauna in restored wetlands of California's Central Valley, USA. Diversity 4:396–418. <doi:10.3390/d4040396>.

Katibah, E. F. 1984. A brief history of riparian forests in the Central Valley of California. Pages 2–22 in R. E. Warner and K. M. Hendrix, editors. California riparian systems: Ecology, conservation, and productive management. University of California Press, Berkeley, California.

Kelley, R. 1989. Battling the inland sea: American political culture, public policy, and the Sacramento Valley, 1850–1986. University of California Press, Berkeley and Los Angeles, California.

Kirk, A. 1994. Vanished lake, vanished landscape. Pages 171–179 in C. G. Thelander, editor. Life on the edge. Biosystem Books, Santa Cruz, California.

Knowles, N., and D. R. Cayan. 2002. Potential effects of global warming on the Sacramento/San Joaquin watershed and the San Francisco estuary. Geophysical Research Letters 29:1891–1895.

Kwasny, D. C., M. Wolder, and C. R. Isola. 2004. Central Valley Joint Venture technical guide to best management practices for mosquito control in managed wetlands. California Department of Fish and Game and U.S. Fish and Wildlife Service, Sacramento, California.

Lacoul, P., and B. Freedman. 2006. Environmental influences on aquatic plants in freshwater ecosystems. Environmental Review 14:89–136.

Lawler, S. P., L. Reimer, T. Thiemann, J. Fritz, K. Parise, D. Feliz, and D. Elnaiem. 2007. Effects of vegetation control on mosquitoes in seasonal freshwater wetlands. Journal of the American Mosquito Control Association 23:66–70.

Lewis, H. T. 1993. Patterns of Indian burning in California: Ecology and ethnohistory. Pages 55–116 in T. C. Blackburn and K. Anderson, editors. Before the wilderness: Environmental management by Native Californians. Ballena Press, Menlo Park, California.

Loheide, S. P., Deitchman, R. S., Cooper, D. J., Wolf, E. C., Hammersmark, C. T., and Lundquist, J. D. 2008. A framework for understanding the hydroecology of impacted wet meadows in the Sierra Nevada and Cascade Ranges, California, USA. Hydrogeology Journal, 17, 229–246. doi:10.1007/s10040-008-0380-4.

Lund, J. R. 2012. Flood management in California. Water 4:157–169.

Marty, J. T. 2005. Effects of cattle grazing on diversity in ephemeral wetlands. Conservation Biology 19:1626–1632.

Mason, H. A. 1957. A flora of the marshes of California. University of California Press, Berkeley, California.

McGowan, J. A. 1961. A history of the Sacramento Valley. Lewis Historical Publishing Company, New York, New York.

McLandress, R. M., G. S. Yarris, A. E. H. Perkins, D. P. Connelly, and D. G. Raveling. 1996. Nesting biology of mallards in California. Journal of Wildlife Management 60:94–107.

Mensik, J. G., and F. A. Reid. 1995. Managing problem vegetation. Ducks Unlimited Valley Habitats Series, No. 7. Sacramento, California.

Mensik, J. G., and F. L. Paveglio. 2004. Biological integrity, diversity, and environmental health policy and the attainment of refuge purposes: A Sacramento National Wildlife Refuge case study. Natural Resources Journal 44:1162–1183.

Miller, R. L., M. Fram, R. Fujii, and G. Wheeler. 2008. Subsidence reversal in a re-established wetland in the Sacramento–San Joaquin Delta, California, USA. San Francisco Estuary and Watershed Science 6(3):article 1.

Mitsch, W. J., and J. G. Gosselink. 2007. Wetlands. Fourth edition. John Wiley & Sons, Inc., New York, New York.

Moore, S. B., J. Winckel, S. J. Detwiler, S. A. Klasing, P. A. Gaul, N. R. Kanim, B. E. Kesser, A. B. DeBevec, K. Beardsley, and L. K. Puckett. 1990. Fish and wildlife resources and agricultural drainage in the San Joaquin Valley, California. Two volumes. San Joaquin Valley Drainage Program, Sacramento, California.

Moreno-Mateos, D., M. E. Power, F. A. Comin, and R. Yockteng. 2012. Structural and functional loss in restored wetland ecosystems. PLoS Biology 10(1):1–8.

Moyle, P. B. 2002. Inland fishes of California. Revised and expanded. University of California Press, Berkeley, California.

Moyle, P. B., A. Manfree, and P. L. Fiedler, editors. 2013. Suisun: Ecological history and possible futures. University of California Press, Berkeley, California.

Muir, J. 1911. My first summer in the Sierra. Houghton Mifflin, New York, New York.

Murase, J., and P. Frenzel. 2007. A methane-driven microbial food web in a wetland rice soil. Environmental Microbiology 9(12):3025–3034.

National Oceanic and Atmospheric Administration. 1985. Narrative summaries, tables, and maps for each state with overview of state climatologist programs. Volume 1, Alabama–New Mexico. Third edition. Gale Research Company, Emeryville, California.

Naylor, L. W. 2002. Evaluating moist-soil seed production and management in Central Valley wetlands to determine habitat needs for waterfowl. MS thesis. University of California, Davis, California.

Neelin, J. D., B. Langenbrunner, J. E. Meyerson, A. Hall, and N. Berg. 2013. California winter precipitation change under global warming in the Coupled Model Intercomparison Project 5 ensemble. J. Climate 26:6238–6256, doi:10.1175/JCLI-D-12-00514.1.

Ohlendorf, H. M. 1989. Bioaccumulation and effects of selenium in wildlife. Pages 133–177 in L. W. Jacobs, editor. Selenium in agriculture and the environment. SSSA special publication no. 23. Soil Science Society of America, Madison, Wisconsin.

Olson, S. M., and R. E. Trost. 2012. 2012 Pacific flyway data book: Waterfowl harvests and status, hunter participation, and success in the Pacific flyway and United States. U.S. Fish and Wildlife Service, Portland, Oregon.

Oregon Water Resources Department 2013. Klamath River Basin Adjudication. http://www.oregon.gov/owrd/Pages/adj/index.aspx.

Palaima, A., editor. 2012. Ecology, conservation, and restoration of tidal marshes: The San Francisco Estuary. University of California Press, Berkeley, California.

Preston, W. L. 1981. Vanishing landscapes: Land and life in the Tulare Lake Basin. University of California Press, Berkeley, California.

Ratliff, R. D. 1985. Meadows in the Sierra Nevada, California: State of knowledge. General Technical Report PSW-84. Pacific Southwest Forest and Range Experiment Station, USDA Forest Service, Berkeley, California.

———. 1982. A meadow site classification for the Sierra Nevada, California. General Technical Report PSW-60. Pacific Southwest Forest and Range Experiment Station, USDA Forest Service, Berkeley, California.

Riparian Habitat Joint Venture (RHJV). 2004. The riparian bird conservation plan: A strategy for reversing the decline of riparian associated birds in California, Version 2.0. California Partners in Flight, Point Reyes Bird Observatory, Stinson Beach, California. <http://www.prbo.org/calpif/pdfs/riparian.v-2.pdf>. Accessed March 20, 2013.

Roberts, W. G., J. G. Howe, and J. Major. 1980. A survey of riparian forest flora and fauna in California. Pages 3–20 in A. Sands, editor. Riparian forests in California: Their ecology and conservation. Institute of Ecology Publication No. 15. University of California, Davis, California.

Robinson, J. A., J. M. Reed, J. P. Skorupa, and L. W. Oring. 1999. Black-necked stilt (*Himantopus mexicanus*). Pages 1–32 in A. Poole and F. Gill, editors. The Birds of North America, no. 449. Academy of Natural Sciences, Philadelphia, Pennsylvania, and the American Ornithologists' Union, Washington, D.C.

Robinson, J. A., L. W. Oring, J. P. Skorupa, and R. Boettcher. 1997. American avocet (*Recurvirostra americana*). Pages 1–32 in A. Poole and F. Gill, editors. The Birds of North America, no. 275. Academy of Natural Sciences, Philadelphia, Pennsylvania, and the American Ornithologists' Union, Washington, D.C.

Rollins G. L. 1981. A guide to waterfowl habitat management in Suisun Marsh. California Department of Fish and Game, Sacramento, California.

San Joaquin Valley Drainage Program (SJVDP). 1990. A management plan for agricultural subsurface drainage and related problems on the Westside San Joaquin Valley: Final report of the San Joaquin Valley Drainage Program. U.S. Department of the Interior and California Resources Agency, Sacramento, California.

Santos, M. J., S. Khanna, E. L. Hestir, M. E. Andrew, S. S. Rajapakse, J. A. Greenberg, L. W. J. Anderson, and S. L. Ustin. 2009. Use of hyperspectral remote sensing to evaluate the efficacy of aquatic plant management. Invasive Plant Science and Management 2:216–229.

Schimel, D. J. Melillo, H. Tian, A. D. McGuire, D. Kicklighter, T. Kittel, N. Rosenbloom, S. Running, P. Thornton, D. Ojima, W. Parton, R. Kelly, M. Sykes, R. Neilson, and B. Rizzo. 2000. Contribution of increasing CO2 and climate to carbon storage in ecosystems in the United States. Science 287:2004–2006.

Schoenherr, A. A. 1992. A natural history of California. University of California Press, Berkeley, California.

Scott, L. B., and S. K. Marquiss. 1984. A historical overview of the Sacramento River. Pages 46–50 in R. E. Warner and K. M. Hendrix, editors. California Riparian Systems: Ecology, Conservation, and Productive Management. University of California Press, Berkeley, California.

Sculthorpe, C. D. 1967. The biology of aquatic vascular plants. Edward Arnold Publishers, London, UK.

Segers, R. 1998. Methane production and methane consumption: A review of processes underlying wetland methane fluxes. Biogeochemistry 41:23–51.

Sexton, N. R., A. M. Dietsch, A. W. D. Carlos, L. M. Koontz, A. N. Solomon, and H. M. Miller. 2012. National wildlife refuge visitor survey 2010/2011—Individual refuge results. U.S. Geological Survey Data Series 643. <http://pubs.usgs.gov/ds/643>. Accessed February 11, 2013.

Shaw, S. P., and C. G. Fredine. 1956. Wetlands of the United States: Their extent and their value to waterfowl and other wildlife. Circular 39. U.S. Fish and Wildlife Service, Washington, D.C.

Shuford W. D., G. W. Page, and J. E. Kjelmyr. 1998. Patterns and dynamics of shorebird use of California's Central Valley. Condor 100:227–244.

Silveira, J. G. 1998. Avian uses of vernal pools and implications for conservation practice. Pages 92–106 in C. W. Witham, E. T. Bauder, D. Belk, W. R. Ferren Jr., and R. Ornduff, editors. Ecology, conservation, and management of vernal pool ecosystems: Proceedings from a 1996 conference. California Native Plant Society, Sacramento, California.

Skorupa, J. P. 1998. Selenium poisoning of fish and wildlife in nature: Lessons from twelve real-world examples. Pages 315–354 in W. T. Frankenberger Jr. and R. A. Engberg, editors. Environmental chemistry of selenium. Marcel Dekker, New York, New York.

Smith, F. E. 1980. A short review of the status of riparian forests in California. Pages 1–2 in A. Sands, editor. Riparian forests in California: Their ecology and conservation. Institute of Ecology Publication no. 15. University of California, Davis, California.

Smith, L. M, N. H. Euliss Jr., D. A. Wilcox, and M. M. Brinson. 2008. Application of a geomorphic and temporal perspective to wetland management in North America. Wetlands 28:563–577.

Smith, W. D., G. L. Rollins, and R. Shinn. 1994. A guide to wetland

habitat management in the Central Valley. California Department of Fish and Game and the California Waterfowl Association, Sacramento, California.
Solomeshch, A. I., M. G. Barbour, and R. F. Holland. 2007. Vernal pools. Pages 394–424 in M. G. Barbour, T. Keeler-Wolf, and A. A. Schoenherr, editors. Terrestrial vegetation of California. Third edition. University of California Press, Berkeley, California.
Sommer, T., B. Harrell, M. Nobriga, R. Brown, P. Moyle, and L. Schemel. 2001. California's Yolo Bypass: Evidence that flood control can be compatible with fisheries, wetlands, wildfire, and agriculture. Fisheries 26:6–16.
Sterling, J., and P. Buttner. 2011. Wildlife known to use California ricelands. <http://www.calrice.org/pdf/Species+Report.pdf>. Accessed February 23, 2013.
Strong, M. A., J. G. Mensik, and D. S. Walsworth. 1990. Converting rice fields to natural wetlands in the Sacramento Valley of California. 1990 Transactions of the Western Section of the Wildlife Society 26:29–35.
Szalay, F. A., N. H. Eulish Jr., and D. P. Batzer. 1999. Seasonal and semipermanent wetlands of California: Invertebrate community ecology and response to management methods. Pages 829–856 in D. B. Batzer, R. B. Rader, and S. C. Wissinger, editors. Invertebrates in freshwater wetlands of North America: Ecology and management. First edition. Wiley, John & Sons, Inc., New York, New York.
Thomas, D. R. 2009. Assessment of waterfowl body condition to evaluate the effectiveness of the Central Valley Joint Venture. MS thesis. University of California, Davis, California. <http://gradworks.umi.com/14/72/1472632.html>. Accessed June 15, 2012.
Thompson, J. 1957. The settlement geography of the Sacramento–San Joaquin Delta, California. PhD dissertation. Stanford University, Menlo Park, California.
Thompson, J., and E. A. Dutra. 1983. The tule breakers: The story of the California dredge. The Stockton Corral of Westerners International. University of the Pacific, Stockton, California.
Thompson, S. E., G. G. Katul, and A. Porporato. 2010. Role of microtopography in rainfall-runoff partitioning: An analysis using idealized geometry. Water Resources Research 46, W07520, doi:10.1029/2009WR008835.
Thorp, J. H., and A. P. Covich, editors. 1991. Ecology and classification of North American freshwater invertebrates. Academic Press, Inc., London, UK.
Thorp, R. W., and J. M. Leong. 1998. Specialist bee pollinators of showy vernal pool flowers. Pages 169–179 in C. W. Witham, E. T. Bauder, D. Belk, W. R. Ferren Jr., and R. Ornduff, editors. Ecology, conservation, and management of vernal pool ecosystems: Proceedings from a 1996 conference. California Native Plant Society, Sacramento, California.
U.S. Environmental Protection Agency (EPA). 2007. Tulare Lake Basin Hydrology and Hydrography: A Summary of the Movement of Water and Aquatic Species. <http://www.epa.gov/region9/water/wetlands/tulare-hydrology/tulare-summary.pdf>.
U.S. Fish and Wildlife Service (USFWS). 2013. Endangered species program. <http://www.fws.gov/endangered/species/us-species.html>. Accessed February 27, 2013.
———. 2012. National Wetland Inventory Program mapping data for 2012. http://www.fws.gov/wetlands/data/Data-Download.html.
———. 2009a. Sacramento, Delevan, Colusa and Sutter National Wildlife Refuges: Comprehensive Conservation Plan. Pacific Southwest Region, Refuge Planning Office, Sacramento, California, and Sacramento National Wildlife Refuge Complex, Willows, California.
———. 2009b. Winter waterfowl survey, Pacific flyway, January 5–9, 2009. U.S. Fish and Wildlife Service, Sacramento, California.
———. 2005. Recovery plan for vernal pool ecosystems of California and southern Oregon. Portland, Oregon. <http://ecos.fws.gov/docs/recovery_plan/060614.pdf>. Accessed February 20, 2013.
———. 1978. Concept plan for waterfowl wintering habitat preservation, Central Valley, California. U.S. Fish and Wildlife Service, Portland, Oregon.
Warner, R. E., and K. M. Hendrix. 1985. Final draft: Riparian resources of the Central Valley and California Desert. California Department of Fish and Game, Sacramento, California.
———, editors. 1984. California riparian systems: Ecology, conservation, and productive management. University of California Press, Berkeley, California.
Water Education Foundation. 2000. California's wetlands. Water Education Foundation, Sacramento, California.
Weddell, B. J. 2000. Relationship between flows in the Klamath River and Lower Klamath Lake prior to 1910. Prepared for the U.S. Department of the Interior, Fish and Wildlife Service, Klamath Basin Refuges, Tulelake, California.
Whipple, A., R. M. Grossinger, D. Rankin, B. Stanford, and R. Askevold. 2012. Sacramento–San Joaquin Delta historical ecology investigation: Exploring pattern and process. San Francisco Estuary Institute, Richmond, California.
Williams, P. B., E. Andrews, J. J. Opperman, S. Bozkurt, and P. B. Moyle. 2009. Quantifying activated floodplains on a lowland regulated river: Its application to floodplain restoration in the Sacramento Valley. San Francisco Estuary and Watershed Science 7:1–29.
Yarris, G. S. 2008. Survival of mallard ducklings in the rice-growing region of the Sacramento Valley, California. MS thesis. University of California, Davis, California.
Zavaleta, E. S. 2000. Valuing ecosystem services lost to *Tamarix* invasion in the United States. Pages 262–299 in H. A. Mooney and R. J. Hobbs, editors. Invasive species in a changing world. Island Press, Covelo, California.

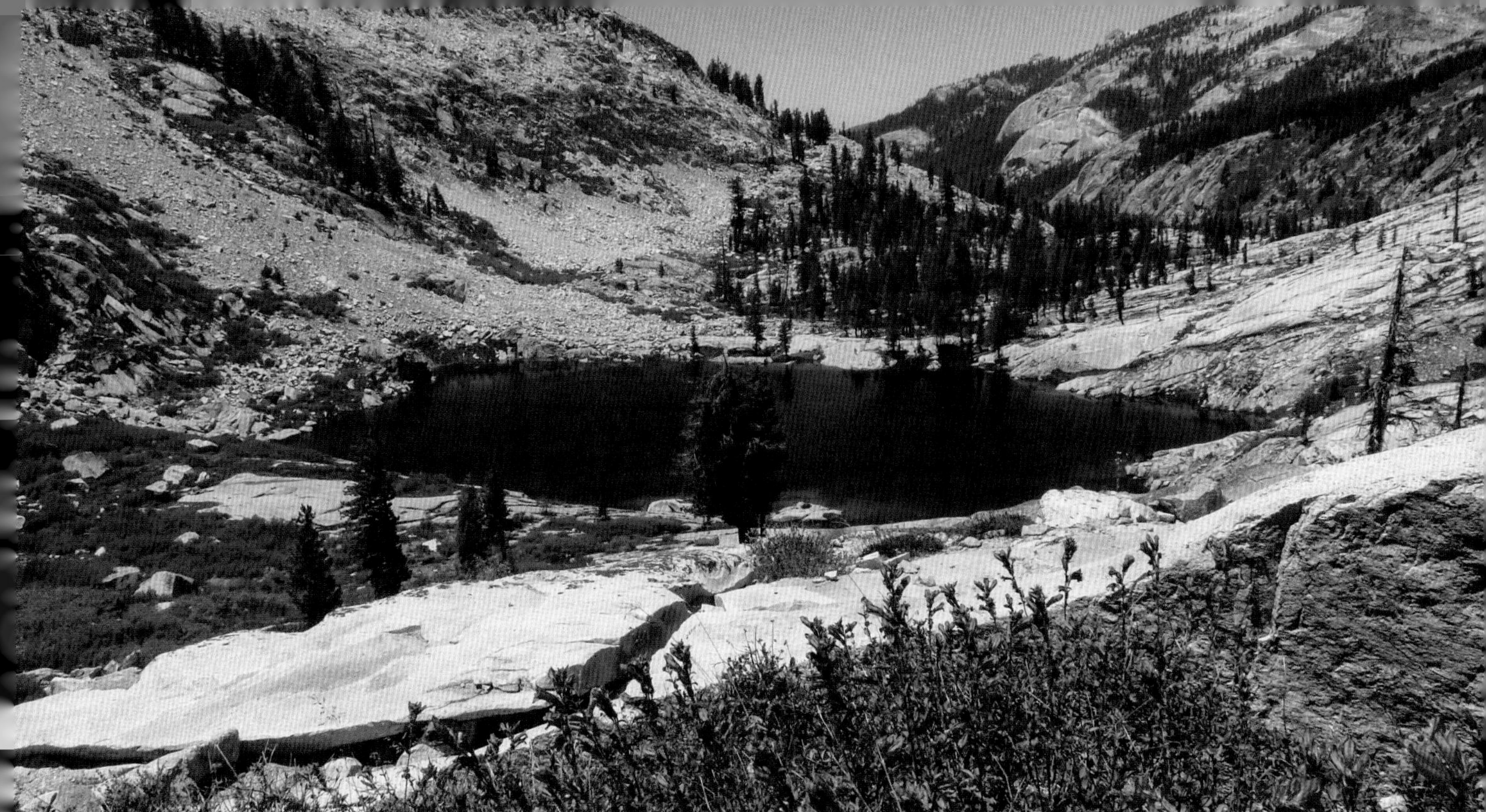

THIRTY-TWO

Lakes

JOHN MELACK AND S. GEOFFREY SCHLADOW

Introduction

Lakes occur throughout the varied landscapes of California (Figure 32.1). The Sierra Nevada is the state's most lake-rich region and includes iconic Lake Tahoe and thousands of high-elevation lakes and ponds. On the flanks of the Sierra Nevada and fed by snowmelt are saline waters, such as Mono Lake, and numerous water supply reservoirs. The coastal ranges of central and southern California have few natural lakes, though coastal ponds and lagoons are widespread and reservoirs are common. To the north, Clear Lake represents the only large, natural lake in the coastal ranges, and the Trinity Alps are sprinkled with small lakes. Saline PLAYAS are scattered across the inland deserts and rarely contain surface water under the current climate. Few lakes or wetlands remain in the Central Valley, though vernal pools can be locally abundant, and some wetlands in the Sacramento–San Joaquin Delta have lake-like features. In total, California has 2,624 named lakes and 1,382 reservoirs listed in the California gazetteer (http://california.hometownlocator.com/).

TECTONIC, volcanic, glacial, erosional, and coastal processes have formed the basins that contain lakes in California. Water inputs to these basins from rain and snowmelt range annually by a factor of 10 and are highly seasonal and often episodically intense. Average annual precipitation varies from 150 to 600 millimeters in southern and southeastern California and from 600 to 1,800 millimeters in the Sierra Nevada and northern California, though interannual variability is high (Melack et al. 1997; see Chapter 2, "Climate"). Runoff in the state is characterized as intermittent and flashy, or winter rain or snowmelt dominated (Poff and Ward 1989; see Chapter 33, "Rivers"). Vegetative cover in lake basins varies with climate, topography, and soils to include forests, chaparral, woodlands, savanna, grasslands, and deserts (Majors and Taylor 1977). Urban and agricultural development and population growth have modified portions of California, particularly in the Central Valley, Los Angeles Basin, and San Francisco Bay Area, and human influences occur everywhere to some degree (see Chapter 5, "Population and Land Use").

As a consequence of California's diverse topographic, geological, hydrological, climatic and ecological settings, and human-modified landscapes, the physical, chemical, and biological conditions in its lakes vary considerably. To examine the variety of California's lakes, we use a regional approach in which we describe lake districts and provide in-depth information about particular lakes, highlighting prominent features. General ecological understanding that has emerged from studies of these lakes addresses: (1) eutrophication and factors controlling water clarity, (2) ecological responses to invasive species, (3) ecological aspects of persistent chemical STRATIFICATION and PLANKTON DYNAMICS in low-diversity ecosystems, (4) implications of variations in snowfall, (5) mercury pollution and its ecological effects, and (6) long-term trends related to climatic and landscape changes.

Limnologists characterize lakes based on the mode of formation of their basins, land cover and use in their watersheds, stratification and mixing dynamics, major solute and nutrient concentrations in the water, and TROPHIC STATUS and other features of the biota. We begin with a brief introduction to these limnological concepts. In contrast to some countries of similar size to California, such as Sweden, no regular, statewide monitoring of lake status exists. Occasional surveys of lakes in the Sierra Nevada have been done (e.g., Melack and Stoddard 1991; Knapp and Matthews 2000; Sickman, Melack et al. 2003), and a few parameters of reservoirs are typically monitored. Fortunately, a few lakes have received sustained attention for decades, and findings from these studies provide a rich foundation for this chapter.

Studies of lakes in California generally began in the early 1900s. Lake Tahoe was an early exception, with the pioneering work of John LeConte (1883–1884) describing measurements undertaken in the 1870s. Edmondson (1963) summarized early literature on Lake Tahoe, Castle, Mono, and Convict Lakes and the Salton Sea in his review of lakes of the Pacific coast and Great Basin. Goldman and Horne (1983) include numerous examples from lakes in California in a textbook with especially interesting photographs of surface patterns and data on NITROGEN FIXATION, cyanobacteria, and POLYMIXIS in Clear Lake, and with information on nutrient conditions in Lake Tahoe and Castle and Clear Lakes. Davis (1933) described 129 specific inland waters throughout California in terms of the formation of their basins. Reports by the U.S. Geological Survey have dealt with geographical, physical, and chemical features of lakes in California for many decades (e.g., Iwatsubo et al. 1972, Rettig and Bortleson 1983; USGS Water Science Center, http://ca.water.usgs.gov/). Finally, Moyle (2002) provides a comprehensive treatment of fishes in California's inland waters (see also Chapter 35, "Marine Fisheries").

Limnological Concepts

LIMNOLOGY is the study of waters contained within terrestrial boundaries. As a synthetic science, limnology includes aspects of geology, geomorphology, hydrology, ecology, hydrodynamics, environmental chemistry, biogeochemistry, public health, and most areas of biology (Goldman and Horne 1983, Kalff 2002). Physical processes in lakes determine variations in time and space of the physical structure and properties such as temperature that in turn influence chemical and biological conditions. Occurrence of ice-cover, energy exchanges across the surface, frequency and depth of mixing and stratification all vary depending on lake depth. The frequency of vertical mixing on an annual time scale is described as polymictic, DIMICTIC, MONOMICTIC, OLIGOMICTIC, or meromictic. The depth to which solar and thermal energy of various wavelengths penetrates a lake depends on the optical properties of the water, which are determined largely by dissolved and particulate matter in the water. Concentrations of phytoplankton, dissolved organic carbon, and suspended sediments range over several orders of magnitude with pronounced influence on rates of heating, stratification, and light availability to organisms. Finally, the hydrological balance of a lake depends on inputs from precipitation, groundwater, and streams as well as losses via surface and subsurface outflows and evaporation. These hydrological pathways convey dissolved and particulate material into and out of lakes and determine mass balance of nutrients and other solutes and particles. Lakes without surface or subsurface outflows are considered HYDROLOGICALLY CLOSED BASINS or ENDORHEIC lakes and typically accumulate salts.

Many substances with a very wide range of concentrations shape the chemical composition of lakes. MAJOR SOLUTES (sodium, potassium, calcium, magnesium, chloride, bicarbonate, sulfate) are responsible for most of the SALINITY; NUTRIENTS (nitrogen, phosphorus, silicon, and some metals [iron, molybdenum]) influence biological productivity; and pollutants (e.g., pesticides, some metals [mercury, selenium], acids, nanomaterials, endocrine-disrupting pharmaceuticals) can harm organisms and endanger human uses. The nature and amounts of these substances that enter lakes depend on geological, hydrological, and geomorphological characteristics; soils; and land uses in the watersheds and AIRSHEDS of the lakes.

Interacting physical and chemical conditions play an important role in shaping the trophic status and biological diversity of lakes. Trophic status reflects the level of biological productivity and abundance of organisms and is described broadly as either OLIGOTROPHIC (low productivity and abundances) or EUTROPHIC (high productivity and abundances). In lakes with very high salinities, biological diversity is low, but most lakes have considerable numbers of species of many kinds of organisms. Modern molecular techniques have revealed a rich diversity of microbes and fungi in lakes and increased understanding of evolutionary relations among higher organisms in lakes. A long history of taxonomic and ecological work exists on phytoplankton, zooplankton, benthic algae, aquatic plants, invertebrates, amphibians, fish, and aquatic birds. Natural dispersal and human introductions continue to modify aquatic food webs.

The inland waters of California span a wide range of the possible physical and chemical conditions observed in lakes, with concomitant large variations in rates of ecological processes and biological diversity. Temporal lake mixing patterns range from polymixis to MEROMIXIS. Exceptional water clarity in lakes, such as Tahoe and smaller high-elevation lakes, contrasts with dense algal blooms that reduce transparency considerably in some eutrophic waters such as Clear Lake. Dilute waters, bordering on distilled water, are common in the snowmelt-dominated Sierra Nevada and contrast with saturated salt solutions in desert playas. Nutrient-poor lakes with low productivity contrast with highly nutrient-enriched waters marked by high biological productivity and abundant populations of aquatic organisms. Few species exist in the HYPERSALINE waters of California, while considerable biological diversity is found in many of the state's freshwater lakes.

Photo on previous page: Emerald Lake, Sequoia National Park, looking west. Photo: Steven Sadro.

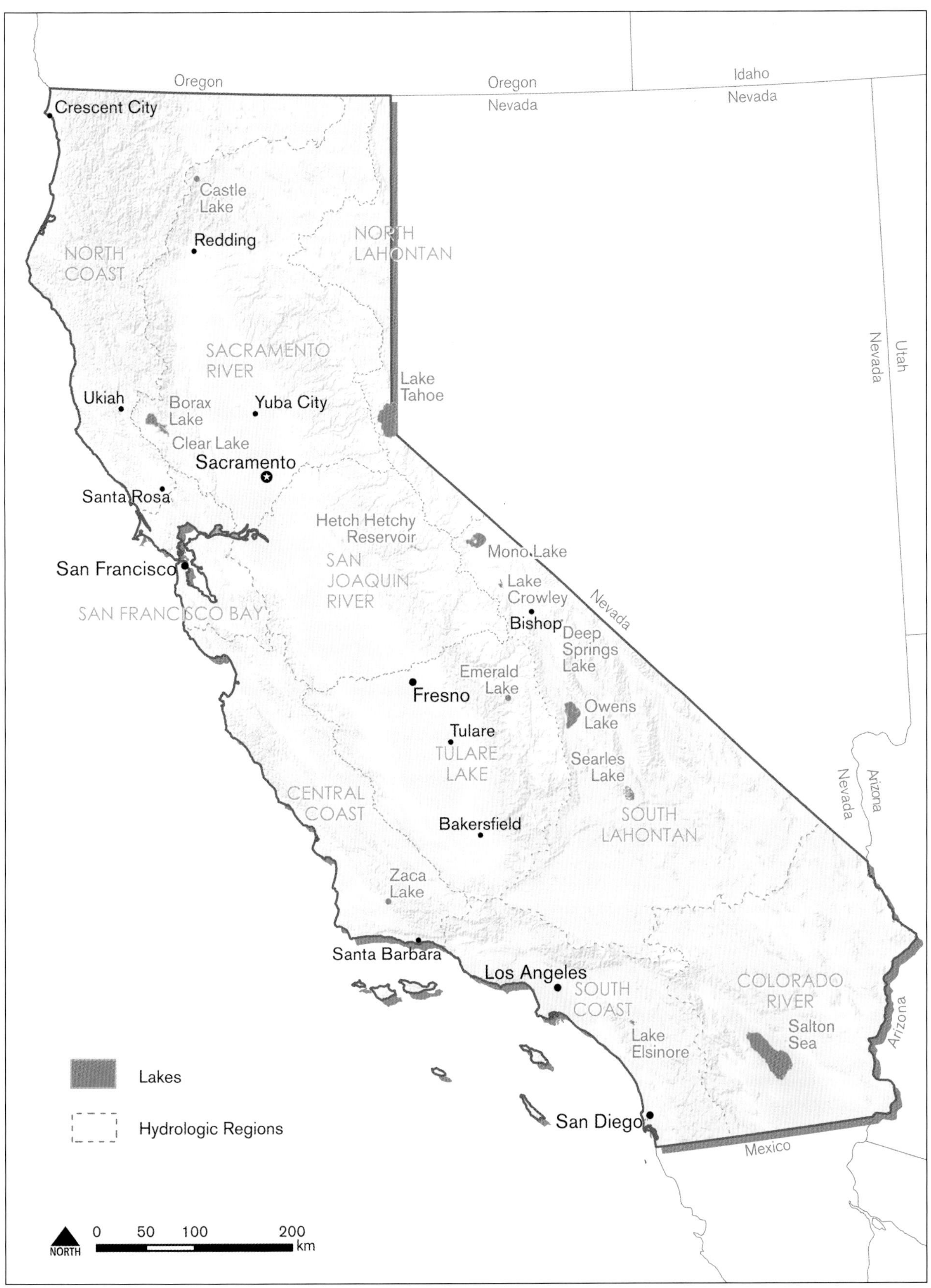

FIGURE 32.1 California lakes larger than 5 square kilometers and selected smaller lakes noted in text are highlighted. Source: Data from U.S. Geological Survey, National Hydrography Dataset (NHD). Map: P. Welch, Center for Integrated Spatial Research (CISR).

Regional Characteristics of California Lakes

This section considers geographical regions of California, providing an overview of each region along with case studies that describe limnological and ecological conditions of representative and well-studied systems.

Sierra Nevada and Western Great Basin

HIGH-ELEVATION LAKES: SNOW-DOMINATED ECOSYSTEMS

The Sierra Nevada extends about 700 kilometers (40°15′N to 35°N), reaching elevations along its crest above 4,250 meters, and is composed largely of igneous and metamorphic rocks of diverse composition and age; additional characteristics are summarized in Melack and Stoddard (1991). Approximately 11,650 lakes and ponds located above 2,280 meters have been recorded, with 27% larger than 0.5 hectare (Steven Sadro, personal communication). Early studies of the limnology of high-elevation lakes in the Sierra Nevada focused on lakes in the Convict Creek basin in the eastern Sierra and were motivated by interest in the fishery of introduced brook trout (*Salvelinus fontinalis*) (Reimers et al. 1955). Concerns about potential impacts of acidic atmospheric deposition resulted in considerable research on geochemical, hydrological, and ecological conditions in the 1980s and 1990s (e.g., Melack et al. 1985, Barmuta et al. 1990, Stoddard 1987, Melack and Stoddard 1991, Williams and Melack 1991, Melack et al. 1993, Engle and Melack 1995, Wolford and Bales 1996, Melack et al. 1998, Leydecker et al. 1999, Clow et al. 2003; http://ccb.ucr.edu/emeraldlake/index.html provides an extensive list of publications).

Here we examine ecological aspects of atmospheric deposition and watershed biogeochemistry in high-elevation lakes, primarily using results from Emerald Lake located in Sequoia National Park. We begin with the detailed watershed features and limnological characteristics of Emerald Lake because these conditions are typical of high-elevation Sierran lakes. We then discuss the preponderance of introduced species in many lakes and the case of frog-trout-fungal interactions in the Sierra Nevada.

Emerald Lake (36°35′49″N, 118°40′29″W), a GLACIAL CIRQUE LAKE located in the headwaters of the Marble Fork of the Kaweah River in the southern Sierra Nevada, is representative of high-elevation lakes throughout the Sierra Nevada (Melack and Stoddard 1991; see this chapter's Lead Photo). The geology of its watershed is dominated by igneous rocks such as granodiorite and granite. Most of the basin is composed of bedrock and talus, but areas of wet meadow soils occur in upper portions of the basin and in riparian zones. Trees, mainly lodgepole pine (*Pinus contorta*) and western white pine (*P. monticola*), are sparse (see Chapter 28, "Subalpine Forests"). Precipitation is strongly seasonal with snowfall accounting for 80% to 90% of annual totals. AEROSOL concentrations can be elevated due to long-distance transport and emissions from local and regional wildfires and can lead to significant deposition of nutrients and other materials during the prolonged dry season (Vicars and Sickman 2011). In particular, Vicars et al. (2010) found that dry deposition of atmospheric particulate matter can be a significant source of phosphorus to oligotrophic aquatic ecosystems like Emerald Lake.

Emerald Lake covers 2.7 hectares in its 120 hectare watershed and has a mean depth 6 meters. Ice, composed of alternating layers of ice and slush, covers the lake for six to nine months each year, with thickness ranging from 1 to 6 meters. As is typical of lakes with seasonal ice cover, it mixes twice a year, with spring turnover usually occurring in late May or early June and autumn turnover during September or early October. Thermal stratification is weak during the summer; INVERSE STRATIFICATION occurs under ice cover. During a twenty-three-year record, peak summer temperatures in the lake ranged from a low of 11°C in 1983 to a high of 20°C in 1990 and were related to the quantity of snowmelt runoff; higher runoff resulted in lower maximum temperatures. Surface waters in Emerald Lake are well-oxygenated year-round. Periods of low dissolved oxygen have been observed near the bottom during both winter and summer stratification and are particularly low in winters following intense summer rains (Engel and Melack 2001). The lake is oligotrophic (midsummer CHLOROPHYLL <1 μg L^{-1}, TOTAL PHOSPHORUS <10 μg L^{-1}), chemically very dilute (SPECIFIC CONDUCTANCE <5 μS cm^{-1}), and poorly buffered (ACID NEUTRALIZING CAPACITY 15–50 μeq L^{-1}), with pH ranging from 5.5 to 6.5.

Zooplankton in Emerald Lake are numerically dominated by ROTIFERS with rotifer densities averaging eight times those of crustaceans. The most common rotifer and crustacean species, respectively, are *Keratella taurocephala* and *Bosmina longirostris*. A reproducing population of brook trout (*Salvelinus fontinalis*) lives in the lake, and its presence selects for the observed zooplankton community of small-bodied species. Experimental studies conducted in large plastic cylinders suspended in Emerald Lake and designed to mimic episodic acidification potentially associated with snowmelt or rain storms indicated that several species of zooplankton decreased in abundance at pH <5.5 (e.g., *Diaptomus signicauda*, *Daphnia rosea*, and *Conochilus unicornis*), while others (e.g., *Bosmina longirostris* and *Keratella taurocephala*) increased in abundance at pHs between 5.5 and 5 (Barmuta et al. 1990).

Investigations of Emerald and other Sierran lakes have indicated how changes in annual snowfall have modified the timing and magnitude of hydrological and chemical fluxes (e.g., Williams et al. 1995; Sickman et al. 2001; Sickman, Melack et al. 2003; Sickman, Leydecker et al. 2003). Nitrogen retention is high in the soils and biota of most watersheds of the Sierra Nevada, with nitrate in streams typically below 1 μM. However, high-elevation watersheds export nitrate during early snowmelt, and the timing of snowmelt runoff influences inorganic nitrogen fluxes. Nitrate pulses were greater and nitrate retention was lower in years with deep, late-melting snowpacks (Sickman et al. 2002). Conversely, nitrate pulses had lower concentrations and watershed retention was higher in years with less snowfall. As climate warming alters the timing and magnitude of snowfall and snowmelt, this indicates potential changes in the nutrient supply to high-elevation lakes. Long-term measurements of nutrients and particulate carbon in Emerald Lake have revealed a marked decline in nitrate during the ice-free growing season during the 1980s and 1990s. Increased particulate carbon and a shift from phosphorus to nitrogen limitation of phytoplankton abundance occurred over the period (Sickman, Melack et al. 2003). Because phosphorus inputs are high in relation to nitrogen inputs, nitrogen tends to limit algal productivity.

Sickman et al. (2013) used diatoms preserved in lake sediments to examine long-term relationships between diatom assemblages and acid neutralizing capacity (ANC) of Sierran lakes. They applied these relationships to interpretation of a sediment core from Moat Lake, a subalpine lake in the eastern Sierra Nevada. During the years from ca. 600 to the early twentieth century, ANC varied from 85 to 115 μEq L^{-1}, but beginning in the 1920s a multidecadal decline occurred until the 1970s. Subsequently, ANC increased to levels observed in the early twentieth century by the early twenty-first century. The decline corresponded to a period of increased use of fossil fuels and injection of sulfur and nitrogen oxides into the atmosphere. However, climate warming also occurred, as inferred by Porinchu et al. (2007) using chironomid remains in sediment cores as a surrogate for temperatures. One consequence of warming could be earlier snowmelt, which can lead to increased summer and autumn ANC, as demonstrated by Sickman et al. (2013) for Emerald Lake. Hence, the cause or causes of the changes in ANC during the twentieth century require further analysis but could reflect interactions among older and more recent environmental changes.

Significant ecological changes are caused by infrequent but severe rainstorms, a pattern that could also indicate potential impacts of increased rainfall as the climate warms (Engle and Melack 2001, Sadro and Melack 2012). Whole-lake, depth-integrated NET ECOSYSTEM PRODUCTION (NEP) measured in Emerald Lake illustrates the effect of a large autumn rainstorm on ecosystem function (Figure 32.2). The event washed large amounts of terrestrial material into the lake; rates of whole-lake gross primary production dropped by nearly 50% after the flood, and ecosystem respiration increased by 30%. The net effect of the rainstorm was to shift net ecosystem production from typical autumn AUTOTROPHY (positive NEP) to HETEROTROPHY (negative NEP). Related changes included large increases in nitrate, dissolved organic nitrogen, particulate phosphorus, dissolved organic carbon, and light attenuation.

Most lakes above 1,800 meters in the Sierra Nevada lacked fish prior to human efforts to introduce trout starting in the nineteenth century (Moyle 1996). Government programs to plant fish were conducted throughout the region, and visitors made haphazard transfers among lakes. A ban on official stocking was introduced in Yosemite and Sequoia–Kings Canyon National Parks in 1975, though reproducing populations persist in many lakes (Armstrong and Knapp 2004). With a few exceptions, only small, shallow ponds that freeze to the bottom, develop hypoxia, or become too warm in the summer do not currently support trout.

Ecological consequences of trout introductions to high-elevation lakes include highly altered invertebrate and amphibian populations (Figure 32.3). Based on a survey of seventy-five lakes, Stoddard (1987) found that the presence of trout was a good predictor of the zooplankton species present (or absent); large, pigmented species disappeared in the presence of fish, and the phantom midge (*Chaoborus americanus*) may have been extirpated from the Sierra Nevada.

In a survey of over seventeen hundred sites, Knapp and Matthews (2000) identified a strong negative effect of introduced fishes on the mountain yellow-legged frog (*Rana muscosa*). This frog is especially vulnerable to predation by trout because it occupies the same habitat as the fish and is also affected by pesticides from lowland agricultural activities (Davidson and Knapp 2007). Furthermore, the recently discovered infectious disease chytridiomycosis, caused by a fungal pathogen (*Batrachochytrium dendrobatidis*), is implicated as the cause of high mortality in postmetamorphic yellow-legged frogs and threatens the species with extirpation at numerous sites in the Sierra Nevada (Rachowicz et al. 2006). A further

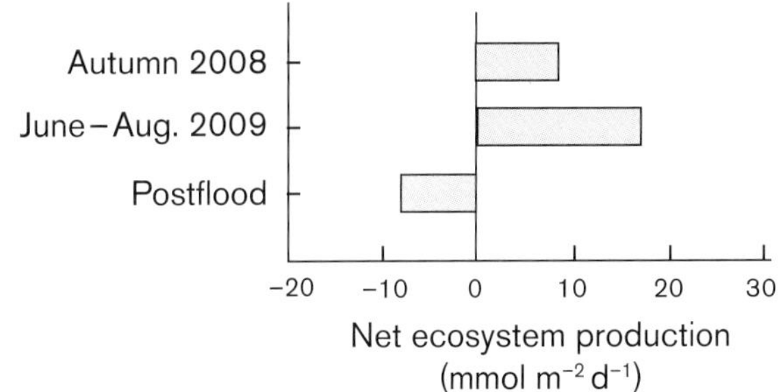

FIGURE 32.2 Whole-lake, depth-integrated net ecosystem production measured in Emerald Lake. Modified from Sadro and Melack 2012.

consequence of the loss or decline of amphibians is a decline in mountain garter snakes (*Thamnophis elegans elegans*), which feed on the frogs (Matthews et al. 2002). The demise of the mountain yellow-legged frog strikingly exemplifies the influence of multiple stressors in general, and the strong impact of invasive species in particular, on lake communities.

LAKE TAHOE: VERTICAL MIXING, CLARITY, AND RESPONSES TO INVASIVE SPECIES

Lake Tahoe, cradled between the Sierra Nevada and the Carson Range, has one of the longest limnological records in the western United States (Figure 32.4). It is the eleventh deepest lake in the world and the second deepest in the United States. A GRABEN LAKE, it is estimated to be over two million years old and was formed by tectonic activity along three major faults. While dominated by granitic geology in the southern part of the basin, the northern part of the basin is volcanic. Lake Tahoe is in the upper portion of the Truckee River watershed. It has sixty-three inflowing streams and one outflow, the Truckee River, which flows to the northeast and terminates in Pyramid Lake, Nevada, an endorheic lake. The surface area of the lake is 495 square kilometers, and it is set in a relatively small watershed of 800 square kilometers. The combination of large lake volume and small watershed area results in an exceptionally long mean residence time for water of 650 years. One consequence of this is prolonged retention of nutrients or pollutants that enter the lake.

Major anthropogenic influences in the watershed followed contact by European-American explorers in 1844; almost all vegetation in the basin has been altered since precontact times. Major influences included clearcut logging of approximately 60% of the basin during the Comstock mining era (1870s–1910s), livestock grazing (1900s–1950s), gradual urbanization of the lowest-lying parts of the basin beginning in the 1950s, and public acquisition and protection of thousands of hectares of sensitive lands since the mid-1960s. Almost 85% of the total land area of the basin is publicly owned, most of it comprised of second-growth forest. The basin's urbanized areas have a permanent population of about 60,000 (2010 Census), but tourists swell this population by an estimated 4.5 million people annually (Applied Development Economics 2010).

The thermal mass contained within the large volume of Lake Tahoe's water ensures that the lake does not freeze. As a consequence, the lake mixes deeply in the late autumn and winter. The maximum extent of vertical mixing usually occurs at the end of March and is frequently incomplete

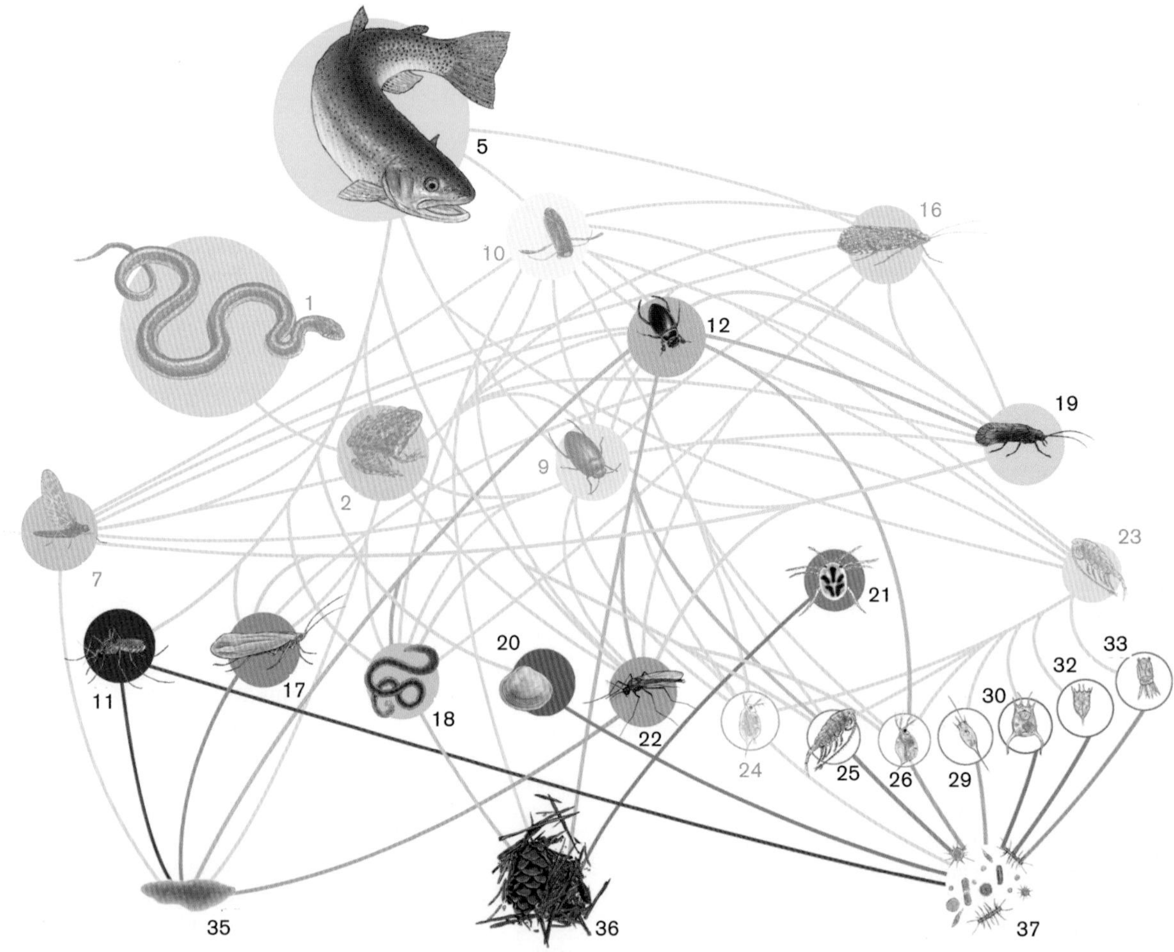

Species

1. *Thamnophis elegans elegans* (mountain garter snake)
2. *Rana muscosa* (mountain yellow-legged frog)
5. Several species of trout
7. *Ameletus edmundsi* (mayfly)
9. *Agabus* sp. (predaceous diving beetle)
10. Corixidae (water boatman)
11. *Culex* spp. (mosquitoes)
12. Hydroporini (water beetles)
16. *Polycentropis* spp. (caddisflies)
17. *Psychoglypha* spp. (caddisflies)
18. *Oligochaeta* (aquatic worms)
19. *Sialis* spp. (alderflies)
20. *Pisidium* spp. (freshwater pea clams)
21. Acari (mites)
22. Chironomidae (midges)
23. *Hesperodiaptomus shoshone* (copepod)
24. *Daphnia middendorffiana* (water flea)
25. *Leptodiaptomus signicauda* (copepod)
26. *Daphnia rosea* (water flea)
29. *Kellicottia* spp. (rotifers)
30. *Keratella quadrata* (rotifer)
32. *Keratella* spp. (rotifers)
33. *Polyartha* spp. (rotifers)
35. Benthic algae
36. Detritus
37. Pelagic algae

FIGURE 32.3 Food web of high-elevation Sierran lakes with introduced trout. Gray items are those negatively influenced by introduced trout. Illustration: Jennifer Parks with data from Harper-Smith et al. 2005.

(oligomixis), with mixing over the full depth of the lake (monomixis) occurring only about one year in four. This variability in mixing depth results in an accumulation of nutrients, particularly nitrate, in deep waters between mixing events (Jassby et al. 1992). This variable depth of mixing each year compounds uncertainty concerning the loading of nutrients and their impacts on algal growth in Lake Tahoe. Mixing depth influences the quantity of nutrients recirculated into the photic zone. Numerical modeling suggests that climate warming could result in a transition toward meromixis (Sahoo et al. 2012), which would cause anoxia in the HYPOLIMNION and elevated levels of internal nutrient loading.

Anthropogenic EUTROPHICATION in Lake Tahoe was first documented by Goldman (1967). Despite the installation of a sewage system for the entire basin and the physical removal of all wastewater, since the early 1960s annual average SECCHI DEPTH, a measure of water clarity, has decreased from approximately 30 meters to 22 meters (UC Davis 2012; Figure 32.5). This has accompanied a fivefold increase in ANNUAL PRIMARY PRODUCTIVITY, from 40 gC m^{-2} y^{-1} to 220 gC m^{-2} y^{-1} in 2011 (UC Davis 2012; Figure 32.6). The underlying causes of these changes are complex but linked to human activities. Inputs of fine inorganic particles, derived from urban stormwater runoff, account for over 70% of the observed clarity decline. The observed change in primary productivity is more complex, as

FIGURE 32.4 Lake Tahoe from the northeast shore. Photo: Geoffrey Schladow.

evidenced by the essential lack of change in mean lake chlorophyll concentration over the same period. This suggests that a shift in algal species has been occurring, fueled in part by shifting nutrient balance of the lake. While the lake had previously been nitrogen-limited, it is now either phosphorus-limited or co-limited by nitrogen and phosphorus (Jassby et al. 1994, Sahoo et al. 2010). Climate change is also influencing algal species composition, with a trend toward smaller algal species (Winder et al. 2009).

Management agencies have embraced the need to address eutrophication. The recent development and adoption of a total maximum daily load (TMDL) based on lake clarity was the culmination of over ten years of research and public review (Roberts and Reuter 2009). The calculation of a TMDL is required by the federal Clean Water Act. If a water body is determined to be impaired, the act requires that the source of the impairment be determined, the current load of contaminant be estimated, and an apportionment be made among all entities contributing to the load of the reduction needed to bring the water body back into compliance. In the case of Lake Tahoe, Roberts and Reuter (2009) determined that fine inorganic particles along with phosphorus and nitrogen were responsible for the lake's declining clarity (its "impairment"). The adoption of the findings and the recommendations by both California and Nevada represented a major step toward reversing the impacts of "cultural eutrophication."

Introduced species have significantly altered Lake Tahoe's biota. The recreational fishery in Lake Tahoe targets lake trout (*Salvelinus namaycush*), though rainbow trout (*Oncorhynchus mykiss*), brown trout (*Salmo trutta*), and kokanee salmon (landlocked sockeye salmon, *Oncorhynchus nerka*) are also caught (Moyle et al. 1996). Salmonids such as lake trout and rainbow trout are non-native, introduced following the extirpation of the native Lahontan cutthroat trout (*O. clarkii henshawi*). Prior to its extirpation, the Lahontan cutthroat trout was fished commercially and recreationally. A combination of overfishing, predation by introduced lake trout, and the blockage of Lake Tahoe's connection to Pyramid Lake likely led to its demise. Efforts are currently under way to reintroduce it. In an attempt to enhance the harvest of lake trout, opossum shrimp (*Mysis relicta*) was also introduced, which caused the loss of most large zooplankton as well as other changes to the lake's ecology (Morgan et al. 1978). While in principle the addition of opossum shrimp should have enhanced fishery yield, in hindsight it is apparent why it had the opposite effect. Opossum shrimp undertake diurnal vertical migrations, sinking below the PHOTIC ZONE during the day. There, they are invisible to the sight feeding salmonids. During the night they rise to the surface, where they are still protected from predation but can consume vast quantities of zooplankton. This has led to the virtual disappearance of *Daphnia* from Lake Tahoe.

Recent, accidental (or possibly deliberate) introductions of aquatic plants such as Eurasian watermilfoil (*Myriophyllum spicatum*), aquatic invertebrates such as Asian clams (*Corbicula fluminea*), and warm-water fishes such as largemouth bass (*Micropterus salmoides*) have further altered the lake's ecology. Management agencies have aggressively pursued control measures, particularly for Asian clams, for which concentrations in excess of 6,000 m^{-2} have been documented (Wittmann et al. 2012b). Large-scale deployments of benthic barriers to block oxygen to the sediments have successfully controlled the spread of Asian clams at Lake Tahoe (Wittmann et al. 2012a). This method has been adopted at other lakes, most notably Lake George in New York. The long-term costs of continued invasive species control remains a major challenge at Lake Tahoe. While the required programs might be fundable for an individual lake, regional invasion pressure increases as other affected lakes are left without control programs.

Gradual eutrophication due to changing land use, deliberate introductions of fish species, and the establishment of invasive species are altering the ecology of Lake Tahoe in a range of ways beyond aesthetics. One possible consequence of changing clarity in combination with invasive species introductions is reduction in the lakewide densities of benthic invertebrate taxa endemic to Lake Tahoe by 80% to 100% between the 1960s and 2009 (Caires et al. 2013). The cumulative impact played by each of these factors is still unknown, and climate change might be compounding the situation.

MONO LAKE: MIXING AND PLANKTON DYNAMICS IN A LOW DIVERSITY ECOSYSTEM

Mono Lake, located in the western Great Basin of North America, is a well-studied saline lake whose geology, geochemistry, hydrology, limnology, ecology, and microbiology have been investigated (http://www.monobasinresearch.org). Geological

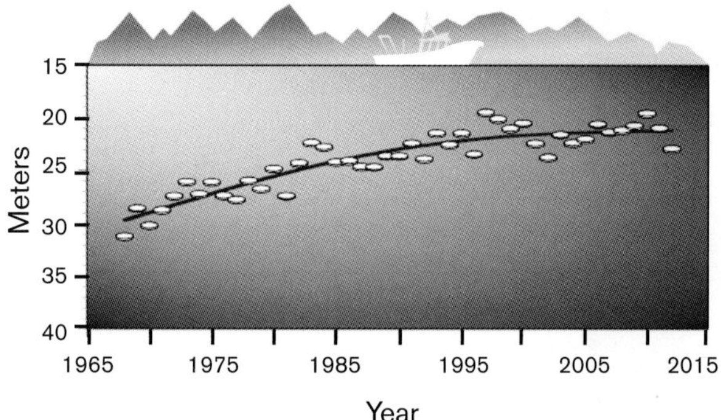

FIGURE 32.5 Annual average Secchi depth in Lake Tahoe has been measured continuously since 1968. The clarity level is the average of twenty-two to twenty-five individual readings taken throughout the year. Since approximately 1997, the rate of decline in clarity has slowed. Measurements taken by LeConte in the 1870s were consistent with those measured in the late 1960s, suggesting the recent decline is due to recent anthropogenic factors. The total maximum daily load (TMDL) goal for Lake Tahoe is to restore the annual average Secchi depth to 29.7 meters. Source: UC Davis Tahoe Environmental Research Center.

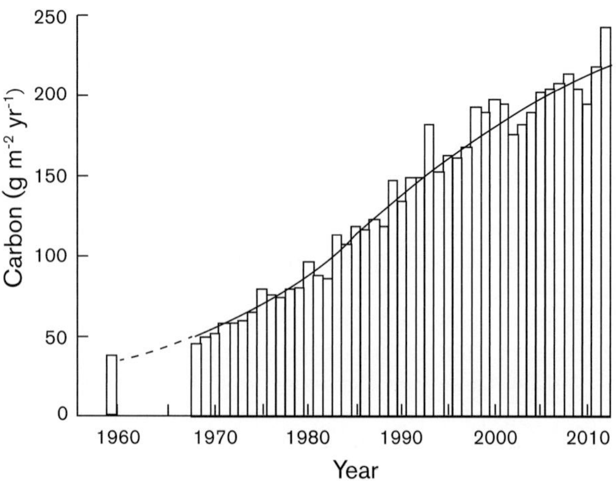

FIGURE 32.6 Primary productivity by phytoplankton was first measured at Lake Tahoe in 1959 and has been continuously measured since 1968. Primary productivity has generally increased over that time, promoted by nutrient loading to the lake, changes in the underwater light environment, and the succession of algae species. Source: UC Davis Tahoe Environmental Research Center.

evidence indicates that the lake has existed for at least five hundred thousand years (Lajoie 1968). It lies in a hydrologically closed basin, so its water levels and salinities are quite sensitive to climatic variation and diversion of inflows. The level of the contemporary lake is low compared to that in the late Pleistocene, when depths reached approximately 300 meters (Benson et al. 1998). Prolonged droughts in the last millennium resulted in low lake levels (Stine 1994). More recently, diversions to Los Angeles of freshwater streams that previously flowed into Mono Lake led to a 14 meter decline in surface elevation from 1941 to 1981 and a doubling of the lake's salinity from approximately 50 g L^{-1} to 100 g L^{-1} (Patten et al. 1987). Its waters have a pH near 10 and contain high concentrations of sodium, carbonate, bicarbonate, chloride, and sulfate. The geochemistry of Mono Lake is described by Simpson et al. (1980), Domagalski et al. (1989), and Johannesson and Lyons (1994). Finely laminated sediments provide a detailed record of organic matter accumulation and reveal a gradual doubling of rates during the recent period of increasing salinities (Jellison et al. 1996). In 1994, following two decades of litigation and environmental controversy, the State Water Resources Control Board of California issued a decision to amend Los Angeles's water rights "to protect public trust resources at Mono Lake." This decision has resulted in increased inflows with amounts primarily dependent on snowfall in the high-elevation, western portion of the watershed (see also Chapter 30, "Deserts").

The limnology of Mono Lake was first documented in the mid-1960s (Mason 1967). During this period Mono Lake had declining lake levels and increasing salinity, as it had in 1976 during the next limnological survey (Winkler 1977). Regular field studies (Melack and Jellison 1998) complemented by experiments (Dana et al. 1993, Dana et al. 1995, Herbst and Blinn 1998) and modeling (Jellison et al. 1995, Jellison et al. 1998, Bruce et al. 2008) began in 1979 and have continued to the present, producing a wealth of information about lake's ecology.

SOLUBLE REACTIVE PHOSPHORUS concentrations are high in Mono Lake (>400 μM) and do not limit phytoplankton growth. Inorganic nitrogen varies seasonally and is often low and can be limiting to algal growth (Jellison and Melack 2001). The two major sources of inorganic nitrogen are brine shrimp excretion and vertical mixing of ammonium-rich deep water, and measurements of algal photosynthetic activity show the importance of variation in vertical mixing of nutrients (Jellison and Melack 1993a, Jellison et al. 1993, Romero et al. 1998, MacIntyre et al. 1999). Nitrogen fixation by cyanobacteria makes a small additional contribution (Herbst 1999, Oremland 1990).

Chemical conditions and strong REDOX GRADIENTS associated with vertical stratification are conducive to a variety of microbial communities, and recent investigations have provided considerable information about their composition and biogeochemical functions (Budinoff and Hollibaugh 2007, Carini and Joye 2008, Fisher et al. 2008, Hollibaugh et al. 2001, Humayoun et al. 2003, Jiang et al. 2004, Oremland 1990, Scholten et al. 2005, Steward et al. 2004). To determine occurrence of biogeochemically important functional genes, Giri et al. (2004) and Lin et al. (2005) surveyed for a variety of microbial enzymes involved in chemical transformations and decomposition. Carini et al. (2005) and Joye et al. (1999) measured vertical distributions and seasonal variation in rates of aerobic and anaerobic methane oxidation and coupling between anaerobic methane oxidation and dissimilatory sulfate reduction.

Because of the high concentrations of arsenic, some prokaryotes living in the lake have evolved biochemical mechanisms to exploit arsenate and arsenite by using them either as an electron acceptor for anaerobic respiration (arsenate) or as an electron donor (arsenite) to support CHEMOAUTOTROPHIC FIXATION OF CO_2 (Oremland et al. 2004, Hoeft et al. 2002, Kulp et al. 2008, Hollibaugh et al. 2005). Phylogenetic analysis indicates that microbial arsenic metabolism is ancient and probably extends back to the primordial Earth. Arsenate and sulfate reducers are estimated to represent up to 14% and 40%, respectively, of the oxidative use of the lake's pelagic primary production (Oremland et al. 2004). Methane enters from thermogenic and biogenic sources in large quantities and supports an active community of methane oxidizers in the lake (Oremland et al. 1987).

Mono Lake is productive, harbors distinctive species but low diversity, and supports large populations of migratory

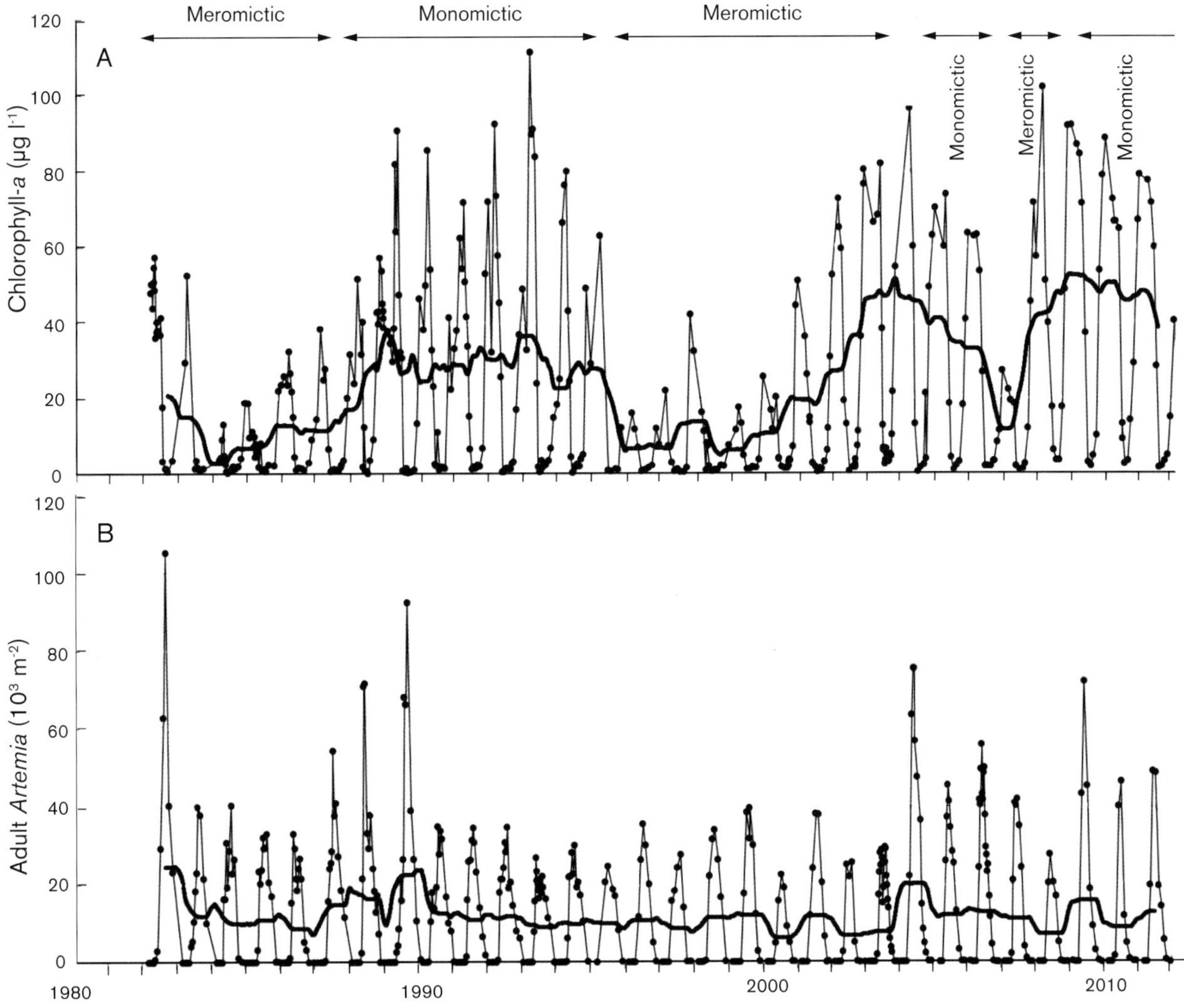

FIGURE 32.7 Long-term (A) mixed-layer chlorophyll-*a* and (B) adult *Artemia* abundance in Mono Lake. Bold lines indicate seasonally filtered (365-day) running mean. Meromictic and monomictic periods refer to periods of vertical lake stratification and top-to-bottom mixing, respectively (see chapter for details). Source: Robert Jellison and John Melack (unpublished).

and breeding birds. A recently described unicellular alga isolated from the lake occupies a niche that spans two environments: the upper OXIC waters and the deeper ANOXIC waters (Roesler et al. 2002). This organism, *Picocystis* sp. strain ML, accounts for nearly 25% of winter primary production and more than 50% at other times of the year. *Picocystis* appears to be particularly adapted to low irradiance. Growth and oxygenic photosynthesis were observed under anoxic conditions at rates comparable to those measured under oxic conditions. The ability of the organism to acclimate to and grow under a broad range of environmental conditions makes it an important component of the Mono Lake ecosystem.

The brine shrimp (*Artemia monica*) is the dominant and often sole species of zooplankton in the pelagic waters. Rotifers are present occasionally (Jellison et al. 2001), and ciliates have been reported (Mason 1967). In nearshore habitats, the alkali fly (*Ephydra hians*) is seasonally abundant (Herbst 1990). The pupae of the alkali fly were sufficiently abundant to provide a food source for local Paiute (Davis 1965). Though no fish occur in the lake, brine shrimp and alkali fly larvae support large numbers of birds including an important breeding colony of the California gull (*Larus Californicus*) and migratory eared grebes (*Podiceps nigricollis*), Wilson's phalaropes (*Phalaropus tricolor*), and red-necked phalaropes (*P. lobatus*) (Patten et al. 1987).

The seasonal variations in phytoplankton and brine shrimp abundances have a consistent pattern. Phytoplankton, as measured by concentrations of chlorophyll, are abundant in the winter and early spring then decrease in the upper waters as brine shrimp grazing increases. They then increase in the autumn as brine shrimp numbers decline (Figure 32.7a). During summer, chlorophyll levels remain high in the deeper, cold, dim, and dark waters. Brine shrimp hatch from overwintering cysts in the winter and develop through a series of NAUPLIAR and juvenile stages to become reproductive adults by late spring (Lenz 1984). These animals produce live nauplii that mature into a second generation of adults. By late summer and autumn, the adults decline in number and produce cysts (Figure 32.7b). Senescence and grebe predation contribute to the annual decrease in brine shrimp (Cooper et al. 1984).

A major perturbation to the ecology of the lake was observed in 1983 when a large influx of freshwater resulted in a condition of persistent chemical stratification (meromixis) Jellison and Melack 1993a, 1993b; Jellison et al. 1993; Miller et al. 1993). A decrease in surface salinities resulted in a strong chemical gradient between the MIXOLIMNION (upper mixing layer) and the MONIMOLIMNION (layer below persistent CHEMOCLINE). In subsequent years evaporative concentration led to a decrease in this gradient, and in November 1988 meromixis ended with mixing from top to bottom. Following the onset of meromixis, ammonium concentrations in the mixolimnion were reduced to near zero during spring 1983 and remained below 5 µM until late summer 1988. Accompanying the decrease in ammonium concentrations was a large decrease in algal abundance associated with periods when brine shrimp were less abundant (November through April). Brine shrimp dynamics were also affected by the onset of meromixis, as the size of the first generation of adult brine shrimp in 1984 was nearly ten times as large as observed in 1981 and 1982. Over the course of the next two decades the lake experienced two more episodes of meromixis interspersed with periods when the lake fully mixed during winter.

Multiyear episodes of meromixis have markedly increased the interyear variation in standing algal biomass, producing low values that contrast with periods of monomixis in which winter periods of complete mixing occur and spring chlorophyll levels are high. Seasonally averaged chlorophyll concentrations (see Figure 32.7a) show the marked impact of the three episodes of meromixis (1983–1988, 1995–2003, 2005–2007). Seasonally averaged chlorophyll ranged from a minimum of approximately 3 $\mu g\ L^{-1}$ following the onset of meromixis in 1984 to 51 $\mu g\ L^{-1}$ in late 2003 and 53 $\mu g\ L^{-1}$ in 2008 as the second and third episodes of meromixis ended.

Seasonally averaged adult brine shrimp abundances have less interyear variation than phytoplankton (see Figure 32.7b), with mean abundances ranging from 6,200 m^{-2} in 2000 to 24,000 m^{-2} in 1982. Interyear variation in climatic and hydrological conditions, vertical stratification, food availability, and salinity have led to interyear differences in brine shrimp population dynamics. During years when the first generation was small due to reduced hatching, high mortality, or delayed development (1981, 1982, and 1989), the second-generation peak of adults was 2 to 3 times the long-term average. Early season (May–June) peak abundances were also significantly higher (1.5 to 2 times the mean) in 1987 and 1988 as an episode of meromixis weakened and nutrients that had accumulated beneath the chemocline were transported upward.

The inverse correlation between the sizes of the spring and summer brine shrimp generations, observed during many years, has important consequences. Large spring generations of adult brine shrimp reduce phytoplankton to concentrations that become limiting to the growth and survival of OVOVIVIPAROUSLY produced nauplii of the spring generation. Thus recruitment into the summer population is reduced and the autumn abundance is reduced. The larger size of the first generation and subsequent earlier autumn decline is advantageous to breeding gulls (Wrege et al. 2006) and disadvantageous to migrating grebes that visit the lake in late summer and early autumn (Jehl 2007).

Coastal Ranges

CLEAR LAKE: POLYMIXIS AND MERCURY POLLUTION

Clear Lake is a large (176 square kilometers) eutrophic natural lake located 404 meters above sea level in northern California (39°00′N, 122°45′W) (Figure 32.8). It is between 0.45 million and 2 million years old (Sims et al. 1988). The lake is shallow (average depth ca. 6.5 meters), alkaline (about pH 8), and polymictic. It is located within an active volcanic region, and geothermal springs release both fluids and gases (carbon dioxide, hydrogen sulfide, and methane) from the lake bottom. It is biologically diverse and supports around 100 species of green and yellow-green algae and cyanobacteria, about 115 species of diatoms, 23 species of aquatic macrophytes, approximately 94 species of invertebrates, 34 species of fishes, numerous lake-dependent or lake-associated mammals, and an abundance of bird species (Horne 1975, Richerson et al. 1994, Moyle 2002, Suchanek et al. 2003, Suchanek et al. 2008). Massive additions of DDT to the lake took place in the late 1940s and early 1950s to control the Clear Lake gnat (*Chaoborus astictopus*), with devastating effects on breeding grebe populations. Studies of these events made Clear Lake the site where the process of pesticide bioaccumulation in food webs was first identified and subsequently popularized in Rachel Carson's book *Silent Spring* (Carson 1962, Rudd 1964, Suchanek et al. 2003).

Clear Lake is naturally divided into three distinct subbasins: the Upper Arm, Lower Arm, and Oaks Arm, with the large, shallow basin of the Upper Arm comprising almost 72% of the lake's surface and receiving more than 90% of the watershed's runoff. A narrow passage connects it with the two other arms, both of which are considerably narrower and deeper than the Upper Arm. The Lower Arm is a conduit to the lake's only outlet, Cache Creek, at the southeastern end of the lake. The lake's residence time is two to three years (Lynch 1996).

The Sulphur Bank Mercury Mine, now an Environmental Protection Agency Superfund site, is located 100 meters from the edge of the lake at the far eastern end of the Oaks Arm. The abandoned mine pit is filled with water and has a pH of 3 to 4. Seepage from the mine pit, believed to travel along preferred pathways left from abandoned underground mine shafts, transfers mercury-rich water to the lake (Schladow and Clark 2008, Suchanek et al. 2008). Once in the lake, currents driven by a complex interaction between the wind field, weak stratification, and Earth's rotation transfer the mercury-rich water from the Oaks Arm to the others (Rueda and Schladow 2003; Rueda et al. 2003). Transport of contaminants from the vicinity of the mine to the other basins takes less than a week at times when stratification is present. In 1987 the California Office of Environmental Health Hazard Assessment issued a fish consumption advisory for Clear Lake for sport fish based on mercury contamination in edible fish tissue. The Central Valley Regional Water Quality Control Board has subsequently used this dataset to develop a Total Maximum Daily Load (TMDL) for mercury for Clear Lake to lower mercury levels in the watershed to protect human and wildlife health (Gassell et al. 2005).

CASTLE LAKE: INTERANNUAL FLUCTUATIONS IN PRIMARY PRODUCTIVITY

Castle Lake has the longest time-series of limnological data of any lake in the coastal mountains (http://castlelake.ucdavis.edu). Pioneering studies by C. R. Goldman demonstrated the importance of nitrogen supply derived from alder (*Alnus incana tenuifolia*), a plant with associated nitrogen fixers, and of limitation by molybdenum (Goldman 1960, 1961). This laid the foundation for decades of subsequent work on the lake. A

FIGURE 32.8 Clear Lake viewed from the east. In the foreground is the Herman Pit, an EPA superfund site, and the remnants of the former Sulphur Bank Mercury Mine. The Oaks Arm, the deepest of Clear Lake's three basins, is immediately adjacent to it. To the left is the Lower Arm, and in the upper center is the Upper Arm. Mount Konocti, the twin volcanic peaks adjacent to the confluence of all three basins, exerts a dominant influence on wind patterns over the lake, adding considerably to its physical and ecological complexity. Photo: Tetra Tech EMI.

nearly three-decade record of summer primary productivity shows no long-term trend but considerable interannual variability, with extremes often coincident with El Ninõ Southern Oscillations (Goldman et al. 1989) (see Chapter 2, "Climate"). Preceding the spring bloom of phytoplankton, the timing of ICE-OFF, which sets the length of the growing season, is negatively correlated with total precipitation; this influences flushing rates (Jassby et al. 1990). In this regard, Castle Lake shares characteristics with high-elevation lakes in the Sierra Nevada.

COASTAL LAKES AND LAGOONS

Information about coastal lakes and lagoons scattered around California is sparse. Borax Lake, a saline water body located near Clear Lake in the northern coastal ranges, is one of the first lakes in which the contributions of higher plants, phytoplankton, and PERIPHYTON to primary productivity were all measured (Wetzel 1964; see Figure 32.8). Zaca Lake, located in the San Rafael Mountains of Santa Barbara County, is one of the few natural lakes in the central and southern California coastal ranges. It was formed by a landslide in a steep canyon. The lake is sufficiently deep to seasonally stratify, and high sulfate concentrations and anoxia in the deep water lead to production of hydrogen sulfide, in turn used by photosynthetic sulfur bacteria (Folt 1978). Sarnelle (1992) conducted zooplankton manipulations and whole-lake observations to examine how nitrogen to phosphorus ratios in SESTON are modified by zooplankton grazing, sedimentation, and WHITING (calcium carbonate precipitation) events.

Lake Elsinore, the largest natural lake in southern California (1,200 hectares in area), is a shallow (average depth about 5 meters) eutrophic lake at the base of the San Jacinto River watershed (Martinez and Anderson 2013). Pumps installed to enhance mixing and increase dissolved oxygen near the sediments have not been effective (Lawson and Anderson 2007). Variations in lake level occur in response to evaporative losses and climate conditions (Kirby et al. 2004).

Inland coastal ponds have received little attention. One of few studies surveyed the chemical composition of coastal ponds in Santa Barbara County (Melack and Setaro 1986). These water bodies had high ALKALINITY (5 to 60 meq L^{-1}) and total dissolved ion concentrations ranging from 20 to 150 meq L^{-1}. Coastal lagoons with occasional connection to the ocean occur along the coast of California. Those usually open to marine waters function as estuaries, while those closed except during runoff events have lake-like characteristics. An example is Devereux Slough, near Santa Barbara, which covers approximately 18 hectares and is impounded most of the time by a sand berm. Collins and Melack (2014) recorded over a four-year period a salinity variation in the slough from approximately 2 g L^{-1} to 64 g L^{-1} and HYPOXIC conditions near the bottom. The endangered tidewater goby (*Eucyclogobius newberyi*) was common in the Slough.

Deserts

SALTON SEA: AN ACCIDENTAL WATER BODY AND MANAGEMENT CHALLENGES

Though it lies in a basin that has held water during wetter periods in the past, the current water body constituting the Salton Sea formed between 1905 and 1907 when a diversion dam failed and allowed Colorado River water to enter the basin (Carpelan 1958, Edmondson 1963) (see also Chapter 30, "Deserts"). Subsequently, the Salton Sea's water level and salinity have varied considerably as a function of climate and runoff from the agricultural and urban lands to the south. By area the Salton Sea is the largest body of water in the state, encompassing approximately 960 square kilometers with a maximum depth of about 15 meters and a salinity of approximately 48 g L^{-1} (Cook 2000, Cook et al. 2002, Schroeder et al. 2002, Vogl and Henry 2002). The Salton Sea receives agricultural drain water from the Coachella and Imperial Valleys of California and the Mexicali Valley of Mexico.

The Salton Sea is a eutrophic water body, characterized by high nutrient concentrations, high algal biomass as demonstrated by high chlorophyll concentrations, high fish productivity, low clarity, frequent low dissolved oxygen concentrations, massive fish kills, and noxious odors (Watts et al. 2001, Holdren and Montaño 2002, Marti-Cardona et al. 2008, Robertson et al. 2008). However, the Salton Sea provides important habitat for large numbers of migratory bird species, some of which are threatened and endangered. The sea's function as bird habitat has become more important as many other habitat regions have been lost to development over the past hundred years (Carpelan 1958, Cohen et al. 1999, Holdren and Montaño 2002). However, the sea is the site of increased incidence of avian diseases including a 1996 event with unprecedented mortality of American white pelicans (*Pelecanus erythrorhynchos*) and California brown pelicans (*Pelecanus occidentalis*) (Friend 2002). This event received national attention and helped motivate a coordinated effort, the Salton Sea Restoration Project.

The Salton Sea's eutrophic condition is controlled or limited by phosphorus concentrations, with observed nitrogen to phosphorus ratios ranging from 25:1 up to 400:1 (Holdren and Montaño 2002). Most phosphorus input to the Salton Sea is from tributaries; despite the presence of persistent anoxia in the deep water, concentrations of dissolved inorganic phosphorus in the water column are usually negligible. The absence of internal loading of phosphorus during anoxia is peculiar. This hypothesized cause of this phenomenon has been the chemical sequestration of phosphorus due to precipitation of hydroxyapatite and fluorapatite (Holdren and Montaño 2002). It has been hypothesized that phosphorus may be released from the sediments during resuspension events, which are known to occur several times a year due to the sea's high winds and long fetch. Internal phosphorus loading has been related in other shallow eutrophic lakes and reservoirs to resuspension of particulate phosphorus and movement of water high in sediment phosphate into the water column (Chung et al. 2009a,b)

The Salton Sea's biota is a mixture of marine and inland species and has waxed and waned as salinity, mixing, and nutrients have varied. Approximately four hundred species have been recorded in the sea. They include a large diversity of phytoplankton and invertebrates as described in a series of recent publications (Barnum et al. 2002). Currently, because of rising salinity, the only fish remaining in the lake is a species of tilapia (*Oreochromis niloticus*). However, desert pupfish (*Cyprinodon macularius*) are found at the inlets of rivers and streams where salinity is lower.

PLAYAS

Eugster and Hardie (1978) provide a synthetic examination of the geochemistry of saline lakes worldwide that includes details about several playas in California. Deep Springs Lake, located just east of the northern Owens Valley, contains a small, hypersaline lake with a sodium-chloride-carbonate-sulfate brine. As one of the first playas studied in detail, the Deep Springs hydrological-geochemical system provides an example of a common type of brine evolution and of a system with active calcite and dolomite precipitation. In Saline Valley, an intermontane basin northeast of Owens Lake, an ephemeral, very shallow brine pool of saturated sodium chloride occurs. Searles Lake, now a dry playa, contains lake deposits that may be 1,000 meters thick and had an estimated water depth of 200 meters deep during the Pleistocene. Similar playas exist in neighboring valleys. Given the high salt content and shallow, often intermittent inundation in playas, few aquatic species are present. Branchiopods have received attention as conspicuous biota (Erikson and Belk 1999, Brostoff et al. 2010), as have algae (Brostoff 2002). Surprisingly little microbial study has been done in playas. One intriguing example is the work of Oremland et al. (2005) at Searles Lake, in which a full biogeochemical cycle of arsenic involving arsenate and arsenite plus inorganic electron donors was identified.

Owens Lake, though now only partially flooded with shallow water, was a large lake in the early 1900s until diversions of inflows by the Los Angeles Department of Water and Power desiccated it. Currently, halophilic Archaea, strikingly pink, are conspicuous at times in the lake, and abundant alkali flies feed a variety of waterfowl (http://www.ovcweb.org/owensvalley/owenslake).

Central Valley

SACRAMENTO–SAN JOAQUIN DELTA LAKES

Construction of levees and subsequent farming activities in the wetlands of the Sacramento–San Joaquin Delta led to oxidation of the peats and subsidence of the lands behind the levees. A number of these depressions have been flooded accidently or purposely, resulting in formation of shallow lakes (e.g., Franks Track, Mildred Island, Liberty Island) (Lehman et al. 2010). The Delta Wetlands Project (http://www.deltawetlands.com) proposes to add more flooded areas as temporary water storage facilities. As part of the evaluation of this proposal, possible water quality issues have arisen. In particular, dissolved organic carbon released from submerged peats could lead to production of trichloromethanes and similar compounds during water treatment. These compounds are known carcinogens and raise water quality concerns.

VERNAL POOLS

Vernal pools occur on coastal terraces and are scattered through the Central Valley, though many have been lost to agricultural and urban development. They are ephemeral, typically contain shallow water during the cool, rainy season, and are dry at other times. Hence, only a limited number of aquatic organisms have adapted to vernal pools (King et al. 1996, Ripley and Simovich 2008). Given their small size (tens of meters across and tens of centimeters in depth), vernal pools are often classified as wetlands (see Chapter 31, "Wetlands").

RESERVOIRS

Large and moderate-sized reservoirs are located on the slopes of the Sierra Nevada and in the coastal mountains. These reservoirs are operated primarily for water supply for irrigation and industrial or domestic consumption with additional uses for flood control, recreation, and generation of electricity. The most recent California Water Plan (California Department of Water Resources 2009) provides an overview of the network of major reservoirs and water conveyance systems throughout California. These facilities are operated by local, state, and federal agencies in a coordinated manner with a complex set of allocation rules derived from legal, historical, economic, and environmental factors. In addition, hundreds of small reservoirs associated with agricultural or local water supply are scattered throughout the state. Limited information about limnological conditions in California's reservoirs exists, and much of it resides within internal documents of the agencies operating the facilities.

As part of permitting requirements, the Pacific Gas and Electric Company monitors water temperatures and several water quality parameters (dissolved oxygen, conductance, pH, turbidity) in a series of reservoirs and associated rivers (e.g., Mokelumne system) (Pacific Gas and Electric 2011). These data relate to fish habitat issues, as reservoirs and their operation can alter thermal and dissolved oxygen regimes. Likewise, reservoirs operated by the U.S. Bureau of Reclamation have programs monitoring water temperatures and dissolved oxygen in the context of fish habitat (e.g., U.S. Bureau of Reclamation 2013). Measurements at Hetch Hetchy Reservoir by the San Francisco Water Department include similar information and additional measurements of dissolved nutrients and counts of plankton (Bruce McGurk, personal communication). An analysis of long-term trends in pH in Pardee and Hetch Hetchy reservoirs indicated an increase in acidity from 1954 to 1979 (McColl 1981), an analysis worth repeating with recent data.

The Los Angeles Department of Water and Power depends on snowmelt runoff from the eastern Sierra for most of its water and has a series of moderate-sized reservoirs (capacities range from 0.6×10^6 m^3 to 226×10^6 m^3) in the Mono Basin, Owens Valley, and further south. Crowley Lake is the largest and can have blooms of phytoplankton because of naturally high inputs of phosphorus and nitrogen fixing cyanobacteria (Jellison et al. 2003). Crowley Lake also has elevated concentrations of arsenic from geothermal spring inputs (Kneebone and Hering 2000).

Recreational fishing occurs in many reservoirs (Moyle et al. 1996). Those near the Sierra Nevada support mainly trout and are routinely stocked with hatchery fish. Self-sustaining warm- water fishes occur in low-elevation reservoirs. However, little evaluation of the status these fisheries is conducted.

Ecological Services Provided by Lakes

Water is essential for life, and lakes are critical sources of water. In the terminology of ecosystem services, the supply of freshwater is a provisioning service. Because of the critical importance of water quantity and quality, a large supply, treatment, and control infrastructure has been constructed at the local and state levels. Much of the data on water supply is available from the California Data Exchange Center (http://cdec.water.ca.gov/) or the U.S. Bureau of Reclamation (http://www.usbr.gov/mp/cvo/reports). Professional organizations, such as the California Lake Management Society (http://www.california-lakes.org), provide networks of individuals and public and private entities focused on lakes. Additional provisioning services provided by lakes include capture and cultivation of fish and invertebrates for food, electricity generation via hydroelectric dams, and transportation corridors. Playas are sources of mineable salts. Regulating service provided by lakes include carbon sequestration in sediments, flood modulation, and modification of local and regional climate. For example, air temperatures at Tahoe City are warmer in winter and cooler in summer than nearby Truckee due to the large heat storage capacity of the lake.

Because of the scenic beauty of lakes and their recreational opportunities, they offer cultural services to many people. An especially renowned example is Lake Tahoe, the home of the native Washoe people. Lake Tahoe was the traditional summer hunting and fishing grounds for the Washoe. Washoe used the reeds growing around the lake for baskets and ceremonial objects. During the winter they would migrate to lower altitudes. While the Lake Tahoe basin has a current permanent population of only 65,000 (2010 Census), its annual tourist population of 4.5 million makes the basin an economic region of national significance, with estimated revenues of $4.7 billion annually (Applied Development Economics 2010). The tourist economy contributes to the vitality of the local economy. With such a small population base, it is challenging to undertake the infrastructure changes needed to reduce runoff into the lake and control eutrophication. Without these improvements, lake clarity and ecosystem health are likely to decline further, jeopardizing future tourism.

The lakes of the Sierra Nevada are an important aspect of Yosemite and Sequoia-Kings Canyon National Parks and neighboring national forests as sites for recreational fishing, camping, and viewing. Between four million and five million people from around the world visit this area each year. Scenes from these parks and forests are well represented in the iconic photographs by Ansel Adams (e.g., *Moon and Half Dome*, 1960; *Clearing Winter Storm*, 1940; *Winter Sunrise*, 1944) and collected works (e.g., Adams 1979). The SNEP (1996) report includes consideration of resources values and management issues in the Sierra Nevada forests and surroundings.

Mono Lake was the focus of a significant decision by the California Supreme Court (*National Audubon Society v. Department of Water and Power of the City of Los Angeles*, February 17, 1983). The Public Trust Doctrine was invoked to state, in part, that "the public trust is an affirmation of the duty of the state to protect the people's common heritage in the streams lakes, marshlands, and tidelands." Public trust values were recognized to include "the scenic views of the lake and its shore, the use of the lake for nesting and feeding birds." Furthermore, the court ruled that water rights, even those previously awarded, had to be balanced against public trust values, which include a suite of nonuse and existence values. This decision is a rare example of a high court affirming ecosystem services as a key consideration in evaluations of resources uses. The court's decision and subsequent administrative actions, including decisions by the California State Water Resources Control Board to implement modifications to water rights of the City of Los Angeles, is a model of sustained citizen action leading to improved environmental stewardship (Hart 1996). Spearheading these efforts is the Mono Lake Committee, established in 1978 as an outgrowth of a student-led study of the lake (Winkler 1977) with leadership by David Gaines, now with sixteen thousand members (http://www.monolake.org/mlc/).

Future Scenarios as a Function of Climate and Land Use Changes

Analyses of long-term climatic and hydrological records, biogeochemical responses to observed interannual variations, and results from simulations of projected climates and limnological responses provide the basis for consideration scenarios of future conditions. Melack et al. (1997) summarized some results of these approaches for inland waters along the Pacific coast of North America. However, as noted by MacKay et al. (2009), coupled atmosphere-land surface-lake climate models at a scale appropriate for California's lakes do not exist. Nutrient-loading models that consider land use do exist on the scale of California's lakes but have seldom been applied. We present a few examples for lakes discussed earlier.

Regional climate changes include warmer temperatures and earlier timing of snowmelt with reduced snowpack

(Dettinger and Cayan 1995, Melack et al. 1997, Cayan et al. 2001, Stewart et al. 2004). Wolford and Bales (1996) modeled hydrological and geochemical conditions in Emerald Lake and its watershed for years with high and low snowfall and with current and enhanced melt rates as scenarios representing possible conditions under altered climate. Modeled concentrations of calcium, a weathering product, during spring snowmelt declined at the higher melt rate. However, because the snow disappeared sooner with higher melt rates, higher calcium concentrations occurred in late summer.

Given the importance of meromixis to the ecology of Mono Lake, Jellison et al. (1998) modeled the likelihood of meromixis persistence under simulated sequences of hydrological and climatic conditions based on historical data. Their modeling indicated a prolonged period of meromixis following its initiation in 1995. However, that episode of meromixis ended much sooner than predicted, demonstrating that the model of vertical mixing applied did not capture all mixing processes.

Hydrodynamic and water quality models formed the basis of the recently developed TMDL for Lake Tahoe. They indicated a dominant role of fine particulates on lake clarity and estimated the load reductions necessary to achieve the desired clarity (Swift et al. 2006, Sahoo et al. 2010). By combining this lake model with future climate scenarios and hydrologic modeling, the impact of future climate change on Lake Tahoe has recently been described (Coats et al. 2013 and other papers in the same special issue).

Summary

Lakes occur throughout the varied landscapes of California and include large ones, such Tahoe, Mono, and Clear Lakes and the Salton Sea; thousands of high-elevation lakes and ponds in the Sierra Nevada; playas in the deserts; vernal ponds; numerous water supply reservoirs; and a few natural lakes in coastal ranges and ponds and lagoons along the Pacific coast. Water is essential for life, and lakes are critical sources of water and of habitat for aquatic organisms.

A common denominator influencing lakes in or near the Sierra Nevada is the annual snowfall that determines the amount and timing of runoff. Small, high-elevation lakes are flushed each year by snowmelt, but inputs of nitrogen, often a nutrient-limiting biological productivity, vary considerably depending on amount of snow and duration of snow cover. The long residence time of water in Lake Tahoe buffers it against annual differences in runoff, but supplies to it of inorganic particles and nutrients depend on the amount and timing of snowmelt as well as anthropogenic loading. Large amounts of runoff into Mono Lake can alter vertical mixing enough to dramatically reduce nitrogen supply and algal abundance and productivity.

Though generally distant from the direct modifications of their watersheds by human activities (with the exceptions of tourist developments at Lake Tahoe and water diversions from the Mono Basin), freshwater lake ecology in the Sierra Nevada has been profoundly affected by introductions of non-native fishes, invasive pathogens, and aquatic plants. Removal of trout from high-elevation lakes is feasible and can result in recovery of these ecosystems, but invasions pose ongoing management challenges (Knapp et al. 2001). Though control of eutrophication by reducing phosphorus inputs is generally emphasized in North America and Europe, the lakes of the Sierra Nevada are often nitrogen-limited and require a different strategy. Reductions in atmospheric sources of nitrogen are one possibility.

The Sierra Nevada generally is considered highly vulnerable to climate change impacts. As the Sierra snowpack provides the bulk of California's surface water, regional changes pose large risks to California's economy as well as to the health of its lakes and reservoirs. Likely changes include warmer temperatures with concomitant increases in rain relative to snow and earlier timing of snowmelt. These changes will likely influence chemical conditions, seasonal mixing, and aquatic organisms.

Clear Lake, a eutrophic lake in the northern coastal mountains, received large inputs of pesticides in the mid-twentieth century, which led to bioaccumulation and strong negative effects on breeding birds. Lessons learned at Clear Lake contributed to bans of pesticides such as DDT. Mercury mining in the lake's basin led to mercury contamination of the fishes, and studies of mercury there provided valuable information about mercury transport and cycling. The Salton Sea formed between 1905 and 1907 when a diversion dam failed and allowed Colorado River water to enter the basin, and its water level and salinity have varied considerably as a function of climate and runoff from the agricultural and urban lands. The sea has high nutrient concentrations, algal biomass, and fish productivity but also frequent low dissolved oxygen concentrations, massive fish kills, and noxious odors. Its biggest threat is likely water shortage. As California is forced to reduce its consumption of Colorado River water, less water will be available for farming around the Salton Sea. This irrigation tailwater, polluted as it is, will simply not be present in the same volumes. This trend is already producing falling water levels and increasing salinity. Salinity will soon surpass the levels that fish can endure, eliminating an entire trophic level. With it, the habitat for piscivorous birds, such as the endangered brown pelican, will likewise disappear.

How does the ecosystem quality of California's lakes compare with lakes nationwide? Unfortunately, this is not possible to assess quantitatively. Nationwide, the EPA reports water quality for 43% of the more than 166,000 square kilometers of lakes, reservoirs, and ponds excluding the Great Lakes (EPA ATTAINS database, http://www.epa.gov/waters/ir/). Of these, 68% are considered impaired under the Clean Water Act. For California, less that 0.1%of the area of lakes, reservoirs, and ponds have been assessed. Though 98% of these are considered impaired, the number is likely misleading due to the extremely small sample size. Indeed, the majority of lakes in California are located in the Sierra Nevada, and these retain excellent water quality.

Acknowledgments

We thank Steven Sadro and James Sickman for information on high-elevation lakes in the Sierra Nevada, and Robert Jellison for assistance with data about Mono Lake. We also wish to thank Charles Goldman, John Reuter, Bob Richards, and Brant Allen for their foresight and perseverance in initiating and maintaining the long-term ecological record from Lake Tahoe.

Recommended Reading

Adams, A. 1979. Yosemite and the Range of Light. Little Brown & Company, Boston, Massachusetts.

California Department of Water Resources. 2009. California Water Plan—Update 2009. Bulletin 160-09. California Department of Water Resources, Sacramento, California.
Cohen, M. J., J. I. Morrison, and E. P. Glenn. 1999. Haven or hazard: The ecology and future of the Salton Sea. Pacific Institute for Studies in Development, Environment, and Security, Oakland, California.
Eugster, H. P., and L. A. Hardie. 1978. Saline lakes. Pages 237–293 in A. Lerman, editor. Lakes: Chemistry, Geology, Physics. Springer-Verlag, New York, New York.
Goldman, C. R., and A. J. Horne. 1983. Limnology. McGraw-Hill, San Francisco, California.
Knapp, R. A., and K. R. Matthews. 2000. Non-native fish introductions and the decline of the mountain yellow-legged frog from within protected areas. Conservation Biology 14:428–438.
Melack, J. M., and J. L. Stoddard. 1991. Sierra Nevada. Pages 503–530 in D. F. Charles, editor. Acidic Deposition and Aquatic Ecosystems: Regional Case Studies. Springer-Verlag, New York, New York.
Melack, J. M., J. Dozier, C. R. Goldman, D. Greenland, A. Milner, and R. J. Naiman. 1997. Effects of climate change on inland waters of the Pacific coastal mountains and western Great Basin of North America. Hydrological Processes 11:971–992.
Patten, D. T., F. P. Conte, W. E. Cooper, J. Dracup, S. Dreiss, K. Harper, G. L. Hunt, P. Kilham, H. E. Klieforth, J. M. Melack, and S. A. Temple. 1987. The Mono Basin ecosystem—Effects of changing lake level. National Academy Press, Washington, D.C.
Suchanek, T. H., P. J. Richerson, R. A. Zierenberg, C. A. Eagles-Smith, D. G. Slotton, E. J. Harner, D. A. Osleger, D. W. Anderson, J. J. Cech Jr., S. G. Schladow, A. E. Colwell, J. F. Mount, P. S. King, D. P. Adam, and K. J. McElroy. 2008. The legacy of mercury cycling from mining sources in an aquatic ecosystem: From ore to organism. Ecological Applications 18:A12–A28.

Glossary

ACID NEUTRALIZING CAPACITY The capacity of a solution to resist changes in pH associated with additions of acid; usually expressed as microequivalents per liter (μeq L^{-1}).

AEROSOLS Particulate matter composed of inorganic and organic particles suspended in the atmosphere.

AIRSHED The region from which substances that enter a lake via wet or dry atmospheric precipitation.

ALKALINITY Concentration of bicarbonate and carbonate, primarily, expresses as milliequivalents per liter (meq L^{-1}) or microequivalents per liter (μEq L^{-1}).

ANNUAL PRIMARY PRODUCTIVITY The uptake of inorganic carbon and formation of organic carbon, expressed as gC m^{-2} y^{-1}.

ANOXIC Water not containing dissolved oxygen.

AUTOTROPHY Positive net ecosystem production in terms of oxygen.

CHEMOAUTOTROPHIC FIXATION OF CO_2 The use of oxidized inorganic ions as a source of electrons to reduce carbon dioxide.

CHEMOCLINE Strong vertical gradient in concentration of solutes.

CHLOROPHYLL Plant and algal pigment associated with photosynthesis. Concentrations of chlorophyll suspended in a lake are often used as a measure of algal abundance, expressed as microgram per liter (μg L^{-1}).

DIMICTIC A common feature of lakes that develop ice cover and typically mix from top to bottom during two periods per year, after ice cover is lost in spring and before ice cover forms in autumn (e.g., Emerald Lake).

ENDORHEIC A hydrologically closed basin—that is, a watershed from which water loss is only by evaporation, not by surface or subsurface discharge.

EUTROPHICATION The addition of nutrients that can result in altered productivity, transparency, algal abundance, dissolved oxygen levels, and species composition.

EUTROPHIC High levels of nutrients usually associated with high biological productivity.

GLACIAL CIRQUE LAKE A lake lying in a basin formed by erosional processes of a montane glacial.

GRABEN LAKE A lake occupying a basin formed by block faulting associated with tectonic activity.

HETEROTROPHY Negative net ecosystem production in terms of oxygen.

HYDROLOGICALLY CLOSED BASIN A watershed from which water loss is only by evaporation, not by surface or subsurface discharge.

HYPERSALINE Total dissolved solute concentrations higher than those observed in seawater (i.e., above about 36 g L^{-1}).

HYPOLIMNION The region in a lake below the thermocline.

HYPOXIC Low concentrations of dissolved oxygen.

ICE-OFF The loss of ice from a lake.

INVERSE STRATIFICATION Under ice, water temperatures in the upper portion of a lake are near 0°C, while lower in the lake temperatures are often near 4°C, at which temperature the water has higher density than at near 0°C.

LIMNOLOGY The study of all waters contained within continental boundaries. As a synthetic science, limnology includes aspects of geology, geomorphology, hydrology, ecology, hydrodynamics, environmental chemistry, biogeochemistry, public health, and most areas of biology (Goldman and Horne 1983, Kalff 2002).

MAJOR SOLUTES Calcium, magnesium, sodium, potassium, bicarbonate-carbonate, sulfate, and chloride.

MEROMIXIS Vertical stratification of density, in part owed to dissolved solutes, that persists for multiple years. Mono Lake can be meromictic.

MIXOLIMNION The upper mixing layer in a meromictic lake.

MONIMOLIMNION The layer below persistent chemocline in a meromictic lake.

MONOMICTIC Lakes that mix from top to bottom during one season per year (e.g., sometimes Lake Tahoe and Mono Lake).

NAUPLIAR The first larval stage of invertebrates such as brine shrimp.

NET ECOSYSTEM PRODUCTION (NEP) Difference between production of oxygen (or uptake of carbon dioxide) by algae and plants and uptake of oxygen (or release of carbon dioxide) by all organisms over at least a twenty-four-hour period.

NITROGEN FIXATION The biological reduction of atmospheric nitrogen.

NUTRIENTS Major nutrients in lakes are nitrogen and phosphorus; minor nutrients can include a variety of metal (e.g., iron or molybdenum). Concentrations of nutrients are usually expressed as micromoles per liter or micromolar (μM).

OLIGOMICTIC Lakes that mix from top to bottom during one season every few years (e.g., usually Lake Tahoe).

OLIGOTROPHIC Low levels of nutrients associated with low biological productivity.

OVOVIVIPAROUS A type of reproduction in which embryos develop inside eggs that are retained within the female.

OXIC Water containing dissolved oxygen.

PERIPHYTON Alga that attaches to submerged surfaces.

pH The negative log of the hydrogen ion concentration.

PHOTIC ZONE The region of a lake in which light is sufficient for photosynthesis to occur.

PLANKTON DYNAMICS Temporal changes in the abundance and/or species composition of zooplankton, phytoplankton, or microbes.

PLAYA A basin in arid regions that is temporarily inundated and often dry and saline.

POLYMIXIS Mixing from top to bottom in lakes at least several times per year. Clear Lake is polymictic.

REDOX GRADIENTS Vertical differences in the extent of oxidizing or reducing conditions.

ROTIFER A microscopic, invertebrate characterized by rings of cilia near its mouth.

SALINITY The sum of concentrations of all dissolved solutes, expressed as grams per liter (g L^{-1}), milligrams per liter (mg L^{-1}), or milliequivalents per liter (meq L^{-1}).

SECCHI DEPTH The depth at which a white disk 20 to 50 centimeters in diameter is no longer visible to an observer at the surface.

SESTON Suspended particulate matter.

SOLUBLE REACTIVE PHOSPHORUS Dissolved phosphorus including inorganic P and compounds of small molecular weight organic P.

SPECIFIC CONDUCTANCE A measure of total dissolved solute concentrations based on the electrical conductance standardized to 25°C, expressed as microSiemens per centimeter(μS cm^{-1}).

STRATIFICATION Division of a water column by differences in density caused by temperature and/or salinity gradients.

TECTONIC PROCESSES These are movements of the earth, such as its faults, associated with earthquakes that can form basins in which lakes such as Tahoe occur.

TOTAL PHOSPHORUS The concentration of dissolved and particulate inorganic and organic phosphorus, usually expressed as micrograms per liter (μg L^{-1}).

TROPHIC STATUS The level of productivity often indicated by nutrient levels and concentrations of chlorophyll, as a measure of algal abundance.

WHITING Precipitation of calcium carbonate with particles suspended in water.

References

Adams, A. 1979. Yosemite and the Range of Light. Little Brown & Company. Boston, Massachusetts.

Applied Development Economics. 2010. Lake Tahoe Basin prosperity plan. Report prepared for the Western Nevada Development District on behalf of the Lake Tahoe Basin Prosperity Plan Steering Committee. Lake Tahoe, Nevada.

Armstrong, T. W., and R. A. Knapp. 2004. Response by trout populations in alpine lakes to an experimental halt to stocking. Canadian Journal of Fisheries and Aquatic Sciences 61:2025–2037.

Barmuta, L.A., S.D. Cooper, S.K. Hamilton, K. W. Kratz and J. M. Melack. 1990. Responses of zooplankton and zoobenthos to experimental acidification in a high-elevation lake (Sierra Nevada, California, U.S.A.). Freshwater Biology 23: 571–586.

Barum, D. A., J. F. Elder, D. Stephens, and M. Friend, editor . 2002. The Salton Sea. Hydrobiologia 473:1–306.

Benson, L. V., S. P. Lund, J. W. Burdett, M. Kashgarian, T. P. Rose, J. P. Smoot, and M. Schwartz. 1998. Correlation of late-Pleistocene lake-level oscillations in Mono Lake, California, with North American climate events. Quaternary Research 49:1–10.

Brostoff W. N. 2002. Algae of a cryptobiotic crust dominated dune/pan system in the Western Mojave Desert. Journal of Arid Environments 51:339–361.

Brostoff, W. N., J. G. Holmquist, J. M. Schmidt-Gengenbach, and P. Zimba. 2010. Fairy, tadpole, and clam shrimps (Branchiopoda) in seasonally inundated clay pans in the western Mojave Desert and effect on primary producers. Saline Systems 6:1–8.

Bruce, L. C., R. Jellison, J. Imberger and J. M Melack. 2008. Effect of benthic boundary layer transport on the productivity of Mono Lake, California. Saline Systems 4:11. <http://www.salinesystems.org/content/4/1/11>. Accessed January 2014

Budinoff, C. R., and J. T. Hollibaugh. 2007. Ecophysiology of a Mono Lake cyanobacterium. Limnology and Oceanography 52:2484–2496.

Caires, A. M., S. Chandra, B. L. Hayford, and M. Wittmann. 2013. Four decades of change: Dramatic loss of zoobenthos in an oligotrophic lake exhibiting gradual eutrophication. Freshwater Science 32:692–705.

California Department of Water Resources. 2009. California Water Plan—Update 2009. Bulletin 160-09. Department of Water Resources, Sacramento.

Carini, S. C., and S. B. Joye. 2008. Nitrification in Mono Lake, California (USA): Activity and community composition during contrasting hydrological regimes. Limnology and Oceanography 53:2546–2557.

Carini, S., N. Bano, G. LeCleir, and S. B. Joye. 2005. Patterns of aerobic methanotrophy and methanotroph community composition during seasonal stratification in a meromictic lake, Mono Lake, CA. Environmental Microbiology 7:1127–1138.

Carpelan, L. H. 1958. The Salton Sea: Physical and chemical characteristics. Limnology and Oceanography 3:373–386.

Carson, R. 1962. Silent spring. Houghton Mifflin, Boston, Massachusetts.

Cayan, D. R., S. A. Kammerdiener, M. D. Dettinger, J. M. Caprio, and D. H. Peterson. 2001. Changes in the onset of spring in the western United States. Bulletin of the American Meteorological Society 82: 399–415.

Chung, E. G., F. Bombardelli, and S. G. Schladow. 2009a. Modeling linkages between sediment resuspension and water quality in a shallow, eutrophic, wind-exposed lake. Ecological Modeling 220:1251–1265.

———. 2009b. Sediment resuspension in a shallow lake. Water Resources Research 45:W05422. <doi:10.1029/2007WR006585>.

Clow, D. W., J. O. Sickman, R. G. Striegl, D. P. Krabbenhoft, J. G. Elliott, M. Dornblaser, D. A. Roth, and D. H. Campbell. 2003. Changes in the chemistry of lakes and precipitation in high-elevation National Parks in the Western United States, 1985–1999. Water Resources Research 396:1171. <doi:10.1029/2002WR001533>.

Coats, R., M. Costa-Cabral, J. Riverson, J. Reuter, G. Sahoo, G. Schladow, and B. Wolfe. 2013. Projected 21st century trends in hydroclimatology of the Tahoe Basin. Climatic Change. <doi:10.1007/s10584-012-0425-5>.

Cohen, M. J., J. I. Morrison, and E. P. Glenn. 1999. Haven or hazard: The ecology and future of the Salton Sea. Pacific Institute for Studies in Development, Environment, and Security, Oakland, California.

Collins, D. and J. M. Melack. 2014. Biological and chemical responses in a temporarily open/closed estuary to variable freshwater inputs. Hydrobiologia 743: 97–113.

Cook, C. B. 2000. Internal dynamics of terminal basin lake: A numerical model for management of the Salton Sea. PhD dissertation University of California, Davis, California.

Cook, C. B., G. T. Orlob, and D. W. Huston. 2002. Simulation of wind-driven circulation in the Salton Sea: Implications for indigenous ecosystems. Hydrobiologia 473:59–75.

Cooper, S. D., D. W. Winkler, and P. H. Lenz.1984. The effect of grebe predation on a brine shrimp population. Journal of Animal Ecology 53:51–64.

Dana, G. L., R. Jellison, and J. M. Melack. 1995. Effects of different natural regimes of temperature and food on survival, growth, and development of *Artemia*. Journal of Plankton Research 17:2115–2128.

Dana, G. L., R. Jellison, J. M. Melack, and G. Starrett. 1993. Relationships between *Artemia monica* life history characteristics and salinity. Hydrobiologia 263:129–143.

Davidson, C., and R. A. Knapp. 2007. Multiple stressors and amphibian declines: Dual impacts of pesticides and fish on yellow-legged frogs. Ecological Applications 17:587–597.

Davis, E. L. 1965. An ethnography of the Kuzedika Paiute of Mono Lake, Mono County, California. Anthropological Papers (University of Utah) 75:1–55.

Davis, W. M. 1933. The lakes of California. California Journal of Mines Geology 29:175–236.

Dettinger, M. D., and D. R. Cayan. 1995. Large-scale atmospheric forcing of recent trends toward early snowmelt runoff in California. Journal of Climate 8:606–623.

Domagalski, J. L., W. H. Orem, and H. P. Eugster. 1989. Organic geochemistry and brine composition in Great Salt, Mono, and Walker lakes. Geochimica Cosmochimica Acta 53:2857–2872.

Edmondson, W. T. 1963. Pacific coast and Great Basin. Pages 371–392 in D. G. Frey, editor. Limnology in North America. University of Wisconsin Press, Madison, Wisconsin.

Engle, D., and J. M. Melack. 2001. Ecological consequences of infrequent events in high-elevation lakes and streams of the Sierra Nevada, California. Verhandlungen Internationale Vereinigun Limnologie 27:3761–3765.

———. 1995. Zooplankton of high-elevation lakes of the Sierra Nevada, California: Potential effects of chronic and episodic acidification. Archiv fur Hydrobiologie 1331:1–21.

Erikson C. H. and D. Belk. 1999. Fairy shrimps of California's puddles, pools, and playas. Mad River Press. Eureka, California

Eugster, H. P., and L. A. Hardie. 1978. Saline lakes. Pages 237–293 in A. Lerman, editor. Lakes: Chemistry, Geology, Physics. Springer-Verlag, New York, New York.

Fisher, J. C., D. Wallschläger, B. Planer-Friedrich, and J. T. Hollibaugh. 2008. Sulfur plays an unexpected role in the arsenic cycle of Mono Lake, CA. International Journal of Environmental Science and Technology 42:81–85.

Folt, C. L. 1978. The abundance and distribution of *Thiopedia rosea* in Zaca Lake, California. MA thesis. University of California, Santa Barbara, California.

Friend, M. 2002. Preface. Hydrobiologia 473:vii–xii.

Gassell, M., S. Klasing, R. K. Brodberg, and S. Roberts. 2005. Fish consumption guidelines for Clear Lake, Cache Creek, and Bear Creek (Lake, Yolo, and Colusa counties). Pesticide and Environmental Toxicology Section, Office of Environmental Health Hazard Assessment, California Environmental Protection Agency. Sacramento, California.

Giri, B. J., N. Bano, and J. T. Hollibaugh. 2004. Distribution of RuBisCO genotypes along a redox gradient in Mono Lake, California. Applied and Environmental Microbiology 70:3443–3448.

Goldman, C.R. 1967. The bad news from Lake Tahoe. Cry California. 3:12–23.

———. 1961. The contribution of alder trees (*Alnus tenuifolia*) to the primary productivity of Castle Lake. Ecology 42:282–288.

———. 1960. Molybdenum as a factor limiting primary productivity in Castle Lake, California. Science 132:1016–1017.

Goldman, C. R., and A. J. Horne. 1983. Limnology. McGraw-Hill. San Francisco, California.

Goldman, C. R., A. Jassby, and T. Powell. 1989. Interannual fluctuations in primary production: Meteorological forcing of two subalpine lakes. Limnology and Oceanography 34:310–323.

Harper-Smith, S., E. L. Berlow, R. A. Knapp, R. J. Williams, and N. D. Martinez. 2005. Communicating ecology through food webs: Visualizing and quantifying the effects of stocking alpine lakes with trout. Pages 407–423 in P. DeRuiter, J. C. Moore, and V. Wolters, editors. Dynamic Webs: Multispecies Assemblages, Ecosystem Development and Environmental Change. Elsevier/Academic Press, New York, New York.

Hart, J. 1996. Storm over Mono Lake: The Mono Lake battle and the California water future. University of California Press, Berkeley, California.

Herbst, D. B. 1999. Salinity limits nitrogen fixation in sediments from Mono Lake, California. International Journal of Salt Lake Research 7:261–274.

———. 1990. Distribution and abundance of the alkali fly (*Ephydra hians* Say) at Mono Lake (USA) in relation to physical habitat. Hydrobiologia 197:193–205.

Herbst, D. B., and D. W. Blinn. 1998. Experimental mesocosm studies of salinity effects on the benthic algal community of a saline lake. Journal of Phycology 34:772–778.

Hollibaugh, J. T., P. S. Wong, N. Bano, S. K. Pak, E. M. Prager, and C. Orrego. 2001. Stratification of microbial assemblages in Mono Lake, California, and response to a mixing event. Hydrobiologia 466:45–60.

Hollibaugh, J. T., S. Carini, H. Gurleyuk, R. Jellison, S. B. Joye, G. LeCleir, L. Vasquex, and D. Wallschlager. 2005. Arsenic speciation in Mono Lake, California: Response to seasonal stratification and anoxia. Geochimica Cosmochimica Acta 69:1925–1937.

Hoeft, S. E., F. Lucas, J. T. Hollibaugh, and R. S. Oremland. 2002. Characterization of microbial arsenate reduction in the anoxic bottom waters of Mono Lake, California. Geomicrobiology Journal 19:23–40.

Holdren, G. C., and A. Montaño. 2002. Chemical and physical characteristics of the Salton Sea, California. Hydrobiologia 473:1–21.

Horne, A. J. 1975. The ecology of Clear Lake phytoplankton. Special Report. Clear Lake Algal Research Unit, Lakeport, California

Humayoun, S., N. Bano, and J. T. Hollibaugh. 2003. Phylogenetic composition of the bacterioplankton from an alkaline, hypersaline lake, Mono Lake, California. Applied and Environmental Microbiology 69:1030–1042.

Iwatsubo, R. T., L. K. Britton, and R. C. Averett. 1972. Selected physical and chemical characteristics of 20 California lakes. Open file report. U.S. Department of Interior, Geological Survey. Water Resources Division, Menlo Park, California.

Jassby, A. D., C. R. Goldman, and T. M. Powell. 1992. Trend, seasonality, cycle, and irregular fluctuations in primary productivity at Lake Tahoe, California-Nevada. Hydrobiologia 246:195–203.

Jassby, A. D., J. E. Reuter, R. P. Axler, C. R. Goldman, and S. H. Hackley. 1994. Atmospheric deposition of nitrogen and phosphorus in the annual nutrient load of Lake Tahoe (California-Nevada). Water Resources Research 30:2207–2216.

Jassby, A. T. M. Powell, and C. R. Goldman. 1990. Interannual fluctuations in primary productivity: Direct physical effects and the trophic cascade at Castle Lake, California. Limnology and Oceanography 35:1021–1038

Jehl, J. R., Jr. 2007. Why do eared grebes leave hypersaline lakes in autumn? Waterbirds 30:112–115.

Jellison, R., and J. M. Melack. 2001. Nitrogen limitation and particulate elemental ratios of seston in hypersaline Mono Lake, California, USA. Hydrobiologia 466:1–12.

———. 1993a. Algal photosynthetic activity and its response to meromixis in hypersaline Mono Lake, California. Limnology and Oceanography 38:818–837.

———. 1993b. Meromixis in hypersaline Mono Lake, California I. Vertical mixing and density stratification during the onset, persistence, and breakdown of meromixis. Limnology and Oceanography 38:1008–1019.

Jellison, R., G. L. Dana, and J. M. Melack. 1995. Zooplankton cohort analysis using systems identification techniques. Journal of Plankton Research 17:2093–2115.

Jellison, R., H. Adams, and J. M. Melack. 2001. Re-appearance of rotifers in hypersaline Mono Lake, California, during a period of rising lake levels and decreasing salinity. Hydrobiologia 466:39–43.

Jellison, R., J. Romero, and J. M. Melack. 1998. The onset of meromixis during restoration of Mono Lake, California: Unintended consequences of reducing water diversions. Limnology and Oceanography 43:706–711.

Jellison, R., K. Rose, and J. M. Melack. 2003. Assessment of internal nutrient loading to Crowley Lake, Mono County. Final Report to State Water Resources Control Board #00-196-160-0. Marine Science Institute, University of California, Santa Barbara, California.

Jellison, R., L. G. Miller, J. M. Melack, and G. L. Dana. 1993. Meromixis in hypersaline Mono Lake, California II. Nitrogen fluxes. Limnology and Oceanography 38:1020–1039.

Jellison, R., R. Anderson, J. M. Melack, and D. Heil. 1996. Organic matter accumulation in Mono Lake sediments during the past 170 years. Limnology and Oceanography 41:1539–1544.

Jiang, S., G. F. Steward, R. Jellison, W. Chu, and S. Choi. 2004. Abundance, distribution, and diversity of viruses in alkaline, hypersaline Mono Lake, California. Microbial Ecology 47:9–17.

Johannesson, K. H., and W. B. Lyons. 1994. The rare earth element geochemistry of Mono Lake water and the importance of carbonate complexing. Limnology and Oceanography 39:1141–1154.

Joye, S. B., T. L. Connell, L. G. Miller, R. S. Oremland, and R. Jellison. 1999. Oxidation of ammonia and methane in an alkaline, saline lake. Limnology and Oceanography 44:178–188.

Kalff, J. 2002. Limnology: Inland water ecosystems. Prentice Hall. Upper Saddle River, New Jersey.

King, J. L., M. A. Simovich, and R. C. Brusca. 1996. Species richness, endemism, and ecology of crustacean assemblages in northern California vernal pools. Hydrobiologia 328: 85–116.

Kirby, M. E., C. J. Poulsen, S. P. Lund, W. P. Patterson, L. Reid, and D. E. Hammond. 2004. Late Holocene lake level dynamics inferred from magnetic susceptibility and stable oxygen isotope data: Lake Elsinore, southern California (USA). Journal of Paleolimnology 31:275–293.

Knapp, R. A., and K. R. Matthews. 2000. Non-native fish introductions and the decline of the mountain yellow-legged frog from within protected areas. Conservation Biology 14:428–438.

Knapp, R. A., K. R. Matthews, and O. Sarnelle. 2001. Resistance and resilience of alpine lake fauna to fish introductions. Ecological Monographs 71:401–421

Kneebone P. E., and J. G. Hering. 2000. Behavior of arsenic and other redox sensitive elements in Crowley Lake, CA: A reservoir in the Los Angeles Aqueduct system. International Journal of Environmental Science and Technology 34:4307–4312.

Kulp, T. R., S. E. Hoeft, M. Asao, M. T. Madigan, J. T. Hollibaugh, J. C. Fisher, J. F. Stolz, C. W. Culbertson, L. G. Miller, and R. S. Oremland. 2008. Arsenic(III) fuels anoxygenic photosynthesis in hot spring biofilms from Mono Lake, California. Science 321:967–970.

Lajoie, K. R. 1968. Quaternary stratigraphy and geologic history of Mono Basin, eastern California. PhD dissertation. University of California, Berkeley, California.

Lawson, R., and M. A. Anderson. 2007. Stratification and mixing in Lake Elsinore, California: An assessment of axial flow pumps for improving water quality in a shallow eutrophic lake. Water Research 41:4457–4467.

Lehman, P. W., S. Mayr, L. Mecum, and C. Enright. 2010. The freshwater tidal wetland Liberty Island, CA, was both a source and sink of inorganic and organic material to San Francisco Estuary. Aquatic Ecology 44:359–372.

LeConte, J. 1883–1884. Physical studies of Lake Tahoe—I, II and III. Overland Monthly and Out West Magazine.

Lenz, P. H. 1984. Life history analysis of an *Artemia* population in a changing environment. Journal of Plankton Research 6:967–983.

Leydecker, A., J. O. Sickman, and J. M. Melack. 1999. Episodic lake acidification in the Sierra Nevada, California. Water Resources Research 359:2793–2804.

Lin, J.-L., S. B. Joye, J.C.M. Scholten, H. Schafer, I. R. McDonald, and J. Colin Murrell. 2005. Analysis of methane monooxygenase genes in Mono Lake suggests that increased methane oxidation activity may correlate with a change in methanotroph community structure. Applied and Environmental Microbiology 71:6458–6462.

Lynch, M. G. 1996. Seasonal variations in lake mixing: Clear Lake, California. MS thesis. University of California, Davis, California.

MacIntyre, S., K. Flynn, R. Jellison, and J. Romero. 1999. Boundary mixing and nutrient fluxes in Mono Lake, California. Limnology and Oceanography 44:512–529.

MacKay, M. D., P. J. Neale, C. D. Arp, L. N. De Senerpont Domis, X. Fang, G. Gal, K. Jöhnk, G. Kirillin, J. D. Lenters, E. Litchman, S. MacIntyre, P. Marsh, J. Melack, W. M. Mooij, F. Peeters, A. Quesada, S. G. Schladow, M. Schmid, C. Spence, H. G. Stefan, and S. L. Stokes. 2009. Modeling lakes and reservoirs in the climate system. Limnology and Oceanography 54:2315–2329

Majors, J., and D. W. Taylor. 1977. Alpine. Pages 601–675 in M. G. Barbour and J. Major, editors. Terrestrial Vegetation of California. John Wiley & Sons, New York, New York.

Marti-Cardona, B., T. E. Steissberg, S. G. Schladow, and S. J. Hook. 2008. Relating fish kills to upwellings and wind patterns in the Salton Sea. Hydrobiologia 604:85–95.

Martinez, D., and M. A. Anderson. 2013. Methane production and ebullition in a shallow, artificially aerated eutrophic temperate lake (Lake Elsinore, CA). Science of the Total Environment 454/455:457–465.

Mason, D. T. 1967. Limnology of Mono Lake, California. University of California Publications in Zoology 83:1–110.

Matthews, K. R., R. A. Knapp, and K. L. Pope. 2002. Garter snake distributions in high-elevation aquatic ecosystems: Is there a link with declining amphibian populations and nonnative trout introductions? Journal of Herpetology 36:16–22.

McColl, J. G. 1981. Increasing hydrogen ion activity of water in two reservoirs supplying the San Francisco Bay area, California. Water Resources Research 17:1510–1516.

Melack, J. M., and F. Setaro. 1986. Survey of sensitivity of southern California lakes to acid deposition. Final Report. California Air Resources Board Contract A3-107-32. Sacramento, California.

Melack, J. M., and J. L. Stoddard. 1991. Sierra Nevada. Pages 503–530in D. F. Charles, editor. Acidic Deposition and Aquatic Ecosystems: Regional Case Studies. Springer-Verlag, New York, New York.

Melack, J. M., and R. Jellison. 1998. Limnological conditions in Mono Lake: Contrasting monomixis and meromixis in the 1990s. Hydrobiologia 384:21–39.

Melack, J. M., J. Dozier, C. R. Goldman, D. Greenland, A. Milner, and R. J. Naiman. 1997. Effects of climate change on inland waters of the Pacific coastal mountains and western Great Basin of North America. Hydrological Processes 11:971–992.

Melack, J. M., J. L. Stoddard, and C. A. Ochs. 1985. Major ion chemistry and sensitivity to acid precipitation of Sierra Nevada lakes. Water Resources. Research 21:27–32.

Melack, J. M., J. O. Sickman, and A. Leydecker. 1998. Comparative analyses of high-altitude lakes and catchments in the Sierra Nevada: Susceptibility to acidification. Final Report, California Air Resources Board contract A032-188. Sacramento, California.

Melack, J. M., J. O. Sickman, F. Setaro, and D. Engle. 1993. Long-term studies of lakes and watersheds in the Sierra Nevada: Patterns and processes of surface-water acidification. Final Report, California Air Resources Board, contract A9-320-60. Sacramento, California.

Miller, L. G., R. Jellison, R. S. Oremland, and C. W. Culbertson. 1993. Meromixis in hypersaline Mono Lake, California III. Breakdown of stratification and biogeochemical response to overturn. Limnology and Oceanography 38:1040–1051.

Morgan, M. D., S. T. Threlkeld, and C. R. Goldman. 1978. Impact of the introduction of kokanee (*Oncorhynchus nerka*) and opossum shrimp (*Mysis relicta*) on a subalpine lake. Journal of the Fisheries Resources Board, Canada 35:1572–1579.

Moyle, P. B. 2002. Inland fishes of California. Revised and expanded. University of California Press, Berkeley, California.

Moyle, P. B., R. M. Yoshiyama, and R. A. Knapp. 1996. Status of fish and fisheries. Pages 953–973 in Sierra Nevada Ecosystem Project: Final Report to Congress. Volume II: Assessments and scientific basis for management options. Centers for Water and Wildland Resources, University of California, Davis, California.

Oremland, R. S. 1990. Nitrogen fixation dynamics of two diazotrophic communities in Mono Lake, California. Applied and Environmental Microbiology 56:614–622.

Oremland, R. S., J. F. Stolz, and J. T. Hollibaugh. 2004. The microbial arsenic cycle in Mono Lake, California. FEMS Microbiology Ecology 48:15–27.

Oremland, R. S., L. Miller, and M. Whiticar. 1987. Sources and flux of natural gases from Mono Lake, California. Geochimica Cosmochimica Acta 51:2915–2929.

Oremland, R. S., T. R. Kulp, J. Switzer Blum, S. E. Hoeft, S. Baesman, L. G. Miller, and J. F. Stolz. 2005. A microbial arsenic cycle in a salt-saturated, extreme environment. Science 308:1305–1308.

Pacific Gas and Electric. 2011. Mokelumne River Project (FERC Project No. 137). 2010 Annual water temperature monitoring program report and 2010 Annual water quality monitoring program report. Pacific Gas and Electric Co., San Ramon, California.

Patten, D. T., F. P. Conte, W. E. Cooper, J. Dracup, S. Dreiss, K. Harper, G. L. Hunt, P. Kilham, H. E. Klieforth, J. M. Melack, and S. A. Temple. 1987. The Mono Basin Ecosystem—Effects of Changing Lake Level. National Academy Press, Washington, D.C.

Poff, N. L., and J. V. Ward. 1989. Implications of streamflow variability and predictability for lotic community structure: A regional analysis of stream flow patterns. Canadian Journal of Fisheries and Aquatic Sciences 46:1805–1818.

Porinchu, D. F., A. P. Potitio, G. M. MacDonald, and A. M. Bloom. 2007. Subfossil chironomids as indicators of recent climate change in Sierra Nevada, California, lakes. Arctic Antarctic Alpine Research 39:286–296.

Rachowicz, L. J., R. A. Knapp, J. A. T. Morgan, M. J. Stice, V. T. Vredenburg, J. M. Parker, and C. J. Briggs. 2006. Emerging infectious disease as a proximate cause of amphibian mass mortality. Ecology 87:1671–1683.

Reimers, N., J. A. Maciolek, and E. P. Pister. 1955. Limnological study of the lakes in Convict Creek Basin, Mono County, California. U.S. Fish and Wildlife Service, Fishery Bulletin 56:437–503.

Rettig, S. A., and G. C. Bortleson. 1983. Limnological study of Shasta Lake, Shasta County, California, with emphasis on the effects of the 1977 drought. USGS Water-Resources Investigations Report 82-4081.
Richerson, P. J., T. H. Suchanek, and S. J. Why. 1994. The causes and control of algal blooms in Clear Lake. Clean Lakes Diagnostic/Feasibility Study for Clear Lake, California. U.S. Environmental Protection Agency Region IX, San Francisco, California.
Ripley, B. J., and M. A. Simovich. 2008. Species richness on islands in time: Variation in ephemeral pond crustacean communities in relation to habitat duration and size. Hydrobiologia 617:181–196.
Roberts, D. M., and J. E. Reuter. 2009. Lake Tahoe total daily maximum load report—California and Nevada. California Regional Water Quality Control Board, South Lake Tahoe, California, and Nevada Department of Environmental Protection, Carson City, Nevada.
Robertson, D. M., S. G. Schladow, and G. C. Holdren. 2008. Long-term changes in the phosphorus loading to and trophic state of the Salton Sea, California. Hydrobiologia 604:21–36.
Roesler, C. S., C. W. Culbertson, S. M. Etheridge, R. Goericke, R. P. Kiene, L. G. Miller, and R. S. Oremland. 2002. Distribution, production, and ecophysiology of *Picocycstis* strain ML in Mono Lake, CA. Limnology and Oceanography 47:440–452.
Romero, J. R., R. Jellison, and J. M. Melack. 1998. Stratification, vertical mixing, and upward ammonium flux in hypersaline Mono Lake, California. Archiv fur Hydrobiologie 142:283–315.
Rudd, R. L. 1964. Pesticides and the living landscape. University of Wisconsin Press, Madison, Wisconsin
Rueda, F. J., and S. G. Schladow. 2003. The internal dynamics of a large polymictic lake. Part II: Three-dimensional numerical simulations. ASCE Journal of Hydraulic Engineering 129:92–101.
Rueda, F. J., S. G. Schladow, S. G. Monismith, and M. T. Stacey. 2003. The internal dynamics of a large polymictic lake. Part I: Field experiments. ASCE Journal of Hydraulic Engineering 129:82–91.
Sadro, S., and J. M. Melack. 2012. The effect of an extreme rain event on the biogeochemistry and ecosystem metabolism of an oligotrophic high-elevation lake (Emerald Lake, Sierra Nevada, California). Alpine, Arctic, and Antarctic Research 44:222–231.
Sahoo, G. B., S. G. Schladow, and J. E. Reuter. 2010. Effect of sediment and nutrient loading on Lake Tahoe (CA-NV) optical conditions and restoration opportunities using a newly developed lake clarity model. Water Resources Research <doi:10.1029/2009WR008447>.
Sahoo, G. B., S. G. Schladow, J. E. Reuter, R. Coats, M. Dettinger, J. Riverson, B. Wolfe, and M. Costa-Cabral. 2012. The response of Lake Tahoe to climate change. Climatic Change. <doi:10.1007/s10584-0>.
Sarnelle, O. 1992. Contrasting effects of *Daphnia* on ratios of nitrogen to phosphorus in a eutrophic, hard-water lake. Limnology and Oceanography 37:1527–1542.
Schladow, S. G., and J. F. Clark. 2008. Use of tracers to quantify subsurface flow through a mining pit. Ecological Applications 18:A55–A71.
Scholten, J.C.M, S. B. Joye, J. T. Hollibaugh, and J. C. Murrell. 2005. Molecular analysis of the sulfate reducing and Archaeal community in a meromictic lake (Mono Lake, California) by targeting 16s rRNA, mcrA, apsA, and dsrAB reductase genes. Microbial Ecology 50:29–39.
Schroeder, R. A., W. H. Orem, and Y. K. Kharaka. 2002. Chemical evolution of the Salton Sea, California: Nutrient and selenium dynamics. Hydrobiologia 473:23–45.
Sickman, J. O., A. Leydecker, and J. M. Melack. 2001. Nitrogen mass balances and abiotic controls on N retention and yield in high-elevation catchments of the Sierra Nevada, California, United States. Water Resources Research 37:1445–1461.
Sickman, J. O., A. Leydecker, C.C.Y. Chang, C. Kendall, J. M. Melack, D. M. Lucero, and J. P. Schimel. 2003. Mechanisms underlying export of N from high-elevation catchments during seasonal transitions. Biogeochemistry 64:1–32.
Sickman, J. O., D. M. Bennett, D. M. Lucero, T. J. Whitmore, and W. F. Kenney. 2013. Diatom-inference models for acid neutralizing capacity and nitrate based on 41 calibration lakes in the Sierra Nevada, California, USA. Journal of Paleolimnology 50:159–174.
Sickman, J. O., J. M. Melack, and D. W. Clow. 2003. Evidence for nutrient enrichment of high-elevation lakes in the Sierra Nevada, California. Limnology and Oceanography 48:1885–1892.
Sickman, J. O., J. M. Melack, and J. L. Stoddard. 2002. Regional analysis of inorganic nitrogen yield and retention in high-elevation ecosystems of the Sierra Nevada and Rocky Mountains. Biogeochemistry 57/58:341–374.
Simpson, H. J., R. M. Trier, C. R. Olson, D. E. Hammond, E. Ege, L. Miller, and J. M. Melack. 1980. Fallout plutonium mobility in an alkaline, saline lake. Science 207:1071–1072.
Sims, J. D., M. J. Rymer, and J. A. Perkins. 1988. Late Quarternary deposits beneath Clear Lake, California: physical stratigraphy, age, and paleogeographic implications. Pages 21–44 in J. D. Sims, editor. Late Quarternary climate, tectonism, and sedimentation in Clear Lake, northern California Coast Ranges. Special Paper 214. Geological Society of America, Menlo Park, California, USA.
SNEP. 1996. Sierra Nevada Ecosystems Project. Final Report to Congress. Volume 1: Assessment summaries and management strategies. Centers for Water and Wildland Resources, University of California, Davis, California.
Steward, G. F., J. P. Zehr, R. Jellison., J. P. Montoya, and J. T. Hollibaugh. 2004. Vertical distribution of nitrogen-fixing phylotypes in a meromictic, hypersaline lake. Microbial Ecology 47:30–40.
Stewart, I. T., D. R. Cayan, and M. D. Dettinger. 2004. Changes in snowmelt runoff timing in western North America under a "business as usual" climate change scenario. Climatic Change 62:217–232.
Stine, S. 1994. Extreme and persistent droughts in California and Patagonia during Mediaeval time. Nature 369:546–549.
Stoddard, J. L. 1987. Alkalinity dynamics in an unacidified alpine lake, Sierra Nevada, California. Limnology and Oceanography 32:825–839.
Suchanek, T. H., and others. 2003. Evaluating and managing a multiply stressed ecosystem at Clear Lake, California: A holistic ecosystem approach. Pages 1239–1271 in D. J. Rapport, W. L. Lasley, D. E. Rolston, N. O. Nielsen, C. O. Qualset, and A. B. Damania, editors. Managing for Healthy Ecosystems. Lewis, Boca Raton, Florida.
Suchanek, T. H., P. J. Richerson, R. A. Zierenberg, C. A. Eagles-Smith, D. G. Slotton, E. J. Harner, D. A. Osleger, D. W. Anderson, J. J. Cech Jr., S. G. Schladow, A. E. Colwell, J. F. Mount, P. S. King, D. P. Adam, and K. J. McElroy. 2008. The legacy of mercury cycling from mining sources in an aquatic ecosystem: From ore to organism. Ecological Applications 18:A12–A28.
Swift, T. J., J. Perez-Losada, S. G. Schladow, J. E. Reuter, A. D. Jassby, and C. R. Goldman. 2006. Water clarity modeling in Lake Tahoe: Linking suspended matter characteristics to Secchi depth. Aquatic Science 68:1–15.
University of California at Davis (UC Davis). 2012. Tahoe: State of the lake report: 2012. Tahoe Environmental Research Center, University of California, Davis, California.
U.S. Bureau of Reclamation. 2013. 2010 Annual monitoring report and trend analysis for biological opinion for operation and maintenance of the Cachuma project of the Santa Ynez River in Santa Barbara County, California. Bureau of Reclamation, Fresno, California.
Vicars, W., and J. O. Sickman. 2011. Mineral dust transport to the Sierra Nevada, California: Loading rates and potential source areas. Journal of Geophysical Research-Biogeoscience <doi:10.1029/2010JG001394>.
Vicars, W., J. O. Sickman, and P. J. Ziemann. 2010. Atmospheric phosphorus deposition at a montane site: Size distribution, effects of wildfire, and ecological implications. Atmospheric Environment 44:2813–2821.
Vogl, R. A., and R. N. Henry. 2002. Characteristics and contaminants of the Salton Sea sediments. Hydrobiologia 473:47–54.
Watts, J. M., B. K. Swan, M. A. Tiffany, and S. H. Hurlbert. 2001. Thermal, mixing, and oxygen regimes of the Salton Sea, California, 1997–1999. Hydrobiologia 466:159–176.
Wetzel, R. G. 1964. A comparative study of primary productivity of higher aquatic plants, periphyton, and phytoplankton in a large, shallow lake. International Review of Hydrobiology 49:1–61.
Williams, M. W., and J. M. Melack 1991. Precipitation chemistry in and ionic loading to an alpine basin, Sierra Nevada. Water Resources Research 277:1563–1574.
Williams, M. W., R. Bales, A. D. Brown, and J. M. Melack. 1995. Fluxes and transformations of nitrogen in a high-elevation catchment, Sierra Nevada. Biogeochemistry 28:1–31.
Winder, M., J. E. Reuter, and S. G. Schladow. 2009. Lake warming favors small-sized planktonic diatom species. Proceedings of the Royal Society B. 276:427–435.

Winkler, D. W., editor. 1977. An ecological study of Mono Lake, California. Institute of Ecology Publications 12. University of California, Davis, California.

Wittmann, M. E., S. Chandra, J. E. Reuter, A. Caires, G. Schladow, and M. Denton. 2012a. Harvesting an invasive bivalve in a large natural lake: Species recovery and impacts to native benthic macroinvertebrate community structure in Lake Tahoe, USA. Aquatic Conservation of Marine Freshwater Ecosystems. <doi:10.1002/aqc.2251>.

Wittmann, M. E., S. Chandra, J. E. Reuter, S. G. Schladow, B. C. Allen, and K. J. Webb. 2012b. The control of an invasive bivalve, *Corbicula fluminea*, using gas impermeable benthic barriers in a large natural lake. Environmental Management. <doi:10.1007/s00267-012-9850-5>.

Wolford, R. A., and R. C. Bales 1996. Hydrochemical modeling of Emerald Lake watershed, Sierra Nevada, California: Sensitivity of stream chemistry to changes in fluxes and model parameters. Limnology and Oceanography 415: 947–954.

Wrege, P. H., W. D. Shuford, D. W. Winkler, and R. Jellison. 2006. Annual variation in numbers of breeding California Gulls at Mono Lake, California: The importance of natal philopatry and local and regional conditions. Condor 108:82–96.

THIRTY-THREE

Rivers

MARY E. POWER, SARAH J. KUPFERBERG, SCOTT D. COOPER,
and MICHAEL L. DEAS

Introduction

The diverse ecosystems in and around California's river networks reflect their large latitudinal range and extreme topographic and geologic heterogeneity. California's sixty major and more than a thousand smaller river drainages contrast sharply in the amount of annual precipitation they receive (from >500 cm y^{-1} in the northwest corner of the state to <5 cm y^{-1} in its southeast corner in the Colorado Desert) (Mount 1995). The timing of runoff from this precipitation also differs markedly between coastal basins watered by rain from Pacific storms and interior basins whose runoff is derived in large part from snowmelt. In this chapter we describe watershed ecosystems of the California rivers that drain to the Pacific Ocean (Figure 33.1). We discuss how native riverine and RIPARIAN biota have adapted, or at least adjusted, to the wide variability in flow and temperature that characterizes various natural (UNIMPAIRED) HYDROLOGIC regimes (Figure 33.2). Knowing how the riverine biota and food webs once assembled and functioned is important for understanding the profound nineteenth- and twentieth-century ecological impacts of humans on California's water systems, "one of the most massive re-arrangements of Nature ever attempted" (Kahrl et al. 1979, p. iv).

We also hope to inform predictions of how California's riverine ecosystems might change, or be sustained, through shocks and directional changes in climate, land use, and biological communities faced by the state's natural and human systems. We survey general changes in river environments and biota as one travels downstream from headwaters to lowland mainstems and estuaries, and we discuss general attributes of California's riverine biota. We conclude with a description of past, current, and projected human interactions with, and impacts on, California's river systems. Four California basins or regions (Table 33.1) are used to illustrate temporal and spatial variation in natural riverine food webs (the Eel River); water quality patterns through a large river system (the Klamath River); and the impacts of land and water development on rivers and their native species (the Sacramento–San Joaquin–Lake Tulare system; and southern and central coastal rivers).

General Tendencies in River Networks and Ecosystems

Every river basin is unique, and those in California are particularly diverse, but all river networks share fundamental characteristics that constrain how their habitats and ecosystems change over space and time. From headwaters of drainage networks to lowland mainstems, rivers change in partially predictable ways that strongly influence the organisms and ecosystems they support. Streams usually begin at springs or seeps near basin divides (Montgomery and Dietrich 1988) and gather RUNOFF from larger and larger DRAINAGE AREAS as they flow from headwaters to lowlands. As discharge (flow) increases downstream, river channels widen and deepen, and average flow velocities increase. At a single site, width, depth, and velocity also increase or decrease as river flow rises and falls. These changes in width, depth, and flow velocity vary more or less predictably according to a set of empirical relationships known, respectively, as "DOWNSTREAM" and "AT-A-STATION HYDRAULIC GEOMETRY" (Leopold et al. 1964). These hydraulic adjustments with flow result in changes in sediment erosion, transport, and deposition that alter channel morphology, bed texture, and disturbance regimes (i.e., bed mobilization during floods).

As channels widen, streams receive more solar radiation, which increases water temperature and the potential for aquatic primary production (growth of aquatic plants and algae) (Vannote et al. 1980). Substrata and channel morphology change systematically downstream, with steep headwaters typified by coarse boulder and bedrock substrata, and mid-elevation rivers with gentler gradients having gravel, pebble, and cobble substrata, with occasional boulders and bedrock formations emerging as habitat islands (Dunne et al. 1991, Montgomery and Buffington 1997). Near river mouths (e.g., estuaries, confluences) and in low-gradient lowland rivers, beds are composed of mobile sands and silts. Disturbance from bed mobilization therefore increases in frequency downstream. In steep headwaters, debris flows sometimes fill channels, but these are rare events, recurring at century to millennial time scales. Lower in the drainage network, floods mobilize beds and scour rock-bound organisms, sometimes several times a year, when flows exceed BANKFULL. In lowland rivers, sand and silt beds are in constant motion, except where sediments are stabilized by large debris jams and flood-tolerant vegetation or are stored in off-channel water bodies.

As river discharge fluctuates, local ("at-a-station") habitats expand and contract, connect and fragment, and environmental gradients within and along channels change. Drought may leave channels completely dry, whereas sediments carried by large floods scour, move, and bury river beds, killing or removing the sedentary benthic (bottom) biota. Some organisms can survive scouring disturbances. Mobile organisms, such as fish, can seek refuge in channel backwaters, under banks, behind logs, bedrock formations, or large rocks. Generally only the surface layer of the river bed, about as deep as the median diameter of bed particles, is mobilized during floods. Water-filled spaces below this layer serve as refuges for organisms that seek cover there. These HYPORHEIC habitats are also refuges during droughts if they provide access to underlying groundwater. They are important refuges for prey from larger predators during biologically active periods. Hyporheic refugia are lost when coarse cobbles and pebbles in rivers become embedded within fine sand, silt, and clay sediments, or when ground water is pumped, withdrawing hyporheic flows. Excessive loading of fine sediments is one of the most widespread forms of environmental degradation of river ecosystems (Waters 1995). In California (Suttle et al. 2004), excessive fine sediments that clog river beds have been introduced by hydraulic mining, deforestation, road building, livestock grazing, construction, and agricultural practices, some of which continue to this day.

Photo on previous page: Unicorn Peak and Tuolumne River at Tuolumne Cascades, Yosemite. Photo: Carson Jeffres.

Dewatering droughts and bed-scouring floods are natural disturbances that structured stream ecosystems long before humans appeared. Sousa (1984) defined DISTURBANCE as an event that kills or removes organisms and frees space and other resources for new biota. Animals that survive drought or flood in refuges, as well as attached algae, mosses, and microbes that are not completely removed from rock surfaces, become the seeds for recovery during ecological SUCCESSION, the process that reestablishes biota after disturbance (Connell and Slatyer 1978, Fisher et al. 1982, Power et al. 2008). Surviving organisms are joined by colonists that move from other habitats into recently disturbed, sparsely populated areas. For example, an "air force reserve" of winged, terrestrial adult insects oviposit in rivers, seeding new generations of aquatic larvae to reestablish their populations (Gray and Fisher 1981). Large fish and other predators are more mobile than algae or small invertebrates and often survive disturbances that destroy organisms at lower trophic levels. As food webs recover from disturbance during succession, the first producer or prey species to recover or colonize tend to have traits that favor high dispersal and high growth rates. Later arriving taxa are often more defended against predators (e.g., toxic, armored, or tightly attached). Living within attached retreats is another common adaptation that protects stream animals from predators and parasites but requires organisms to stay in one place (a SESSILE lifestyle), and allocate energy, time, and nutrients from reproduction or growth to building protective coverings. During early stages of succession, food webs tend to have surviving predators that encounter relatively edible, vulnerable prey. Therefore, disturbances can often lengthen food chains (Power et al. 1996) by allowing energy from primary producers (algae or plants) to flow efficiently up through herbivores to feed predators. By controlling prey, these predators can indirectly alter the biomass of primary producers by reducing grazers or their predators through chains of direct and indirect interactions called TROPHIC CASCADES (Estes et al. 2011, Power 1990b).

Hydrologic Regimes in California's Rivers

Many Californian rivers experience Mediterranean seasonality, with almost all precipitation occurring during the cool winter months, followed by summer droughts with little or no rainfall. In rivers fed by snowpacks in the Sierra Nevada, Klamath, or Cascade mountains, HYDROGRAPHS (plots of discharge or flow versus time; see Figure 33.2) are typified by large spring flows during snowmelt that diminish through the summer. In other regions of California with less snow-

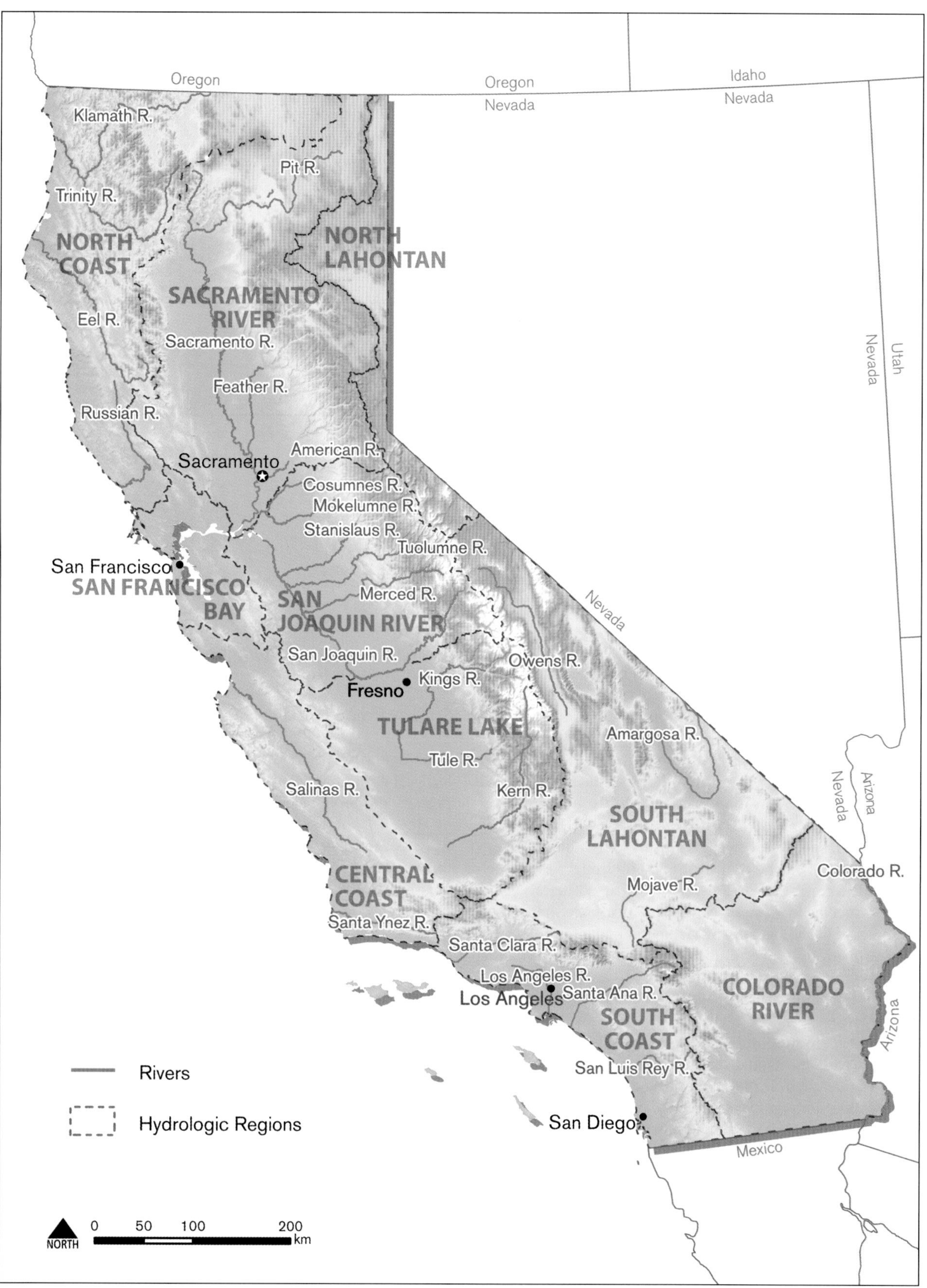

FIGURE 33.1 Major rivers and hydrologic regions of California (with permission after figure in Howard et al. 2013). Source: U.S. Geological Survey, National Hydrography Dataset (NHD). Map: Parker Welch, Center for Integrated Spatial Research (CISR).

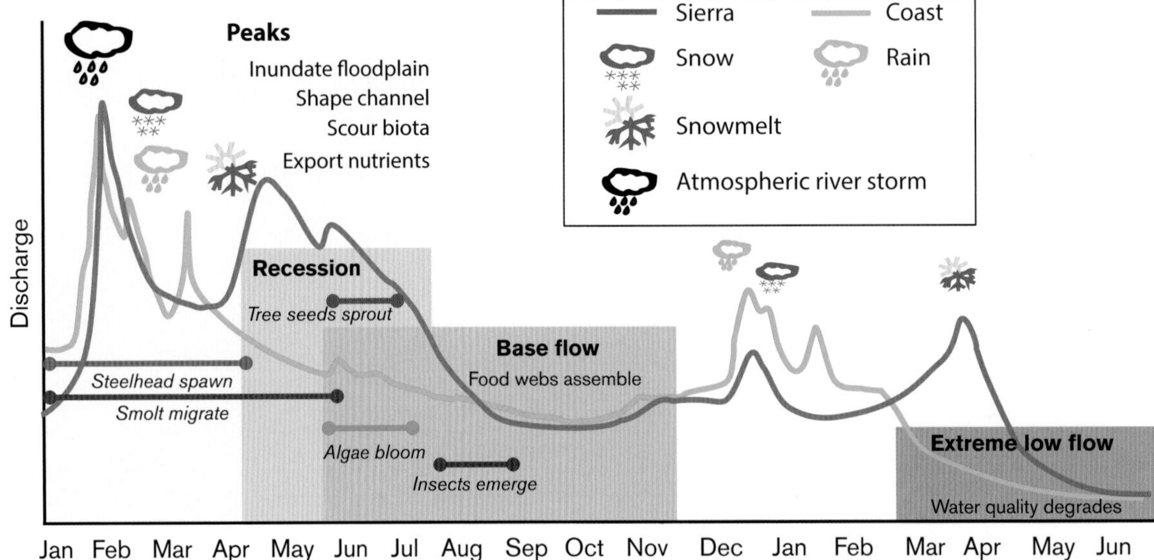

FIGURE 33.2 Stylized hydrographs indicating periods of flooding in a wet year (left); life-cycle events of representative organisms (colored bars placed with respect to time, not discharge); and periods of stress on the biota in a drought year (right) due to drying, high temperatures, and high solute and low dissolved oxygen concentrations. Discharge indicates relative volume rate of water flow. With permission after a figure from Yarnell et al. 2010.

pack, hydrographs of streams and rivers closely follow rainfall patterns, which typically follow the winter-wet, summer-drought "Mediterranean" seasonality of much of the state. On top of this strong seasonality, regions under Mediterranean climates, including California, experience large year-to-year variation in precipitation and flow patterns, ranging from frequent, intense winter storms and unseasonably late spring spates to extreme year-round drought, with many implications for the river biota (Gasith and Resh 1999, Power et al. 2008). The responses of river organisms to hydrologic disturbances depends on the timing of flood or drought events relative to the timing of organismal life history stages. Native riverine species in western North America have many morphological, physiological, and behavioral adaptations to the "deluge or drought" conditions typical of this region, such as behavioral adaptations for seeking refugia during disturbances (Meffe and Minckley 1987, Meffe et al. 1983, Lytle and Poff 2004).

An attempt to subdue and harness the variable flows of California's rivers motivated the massive rearrangement of the state's water system for flood management or prevention; for storage, diversion, and transport of water to generate electricity; and to irrigate crops and supply urban areas. By capturing much of the water from winter rains and spring snowmelt and releasing it over the summer, dam operations decrease the average magnitude of high flows, create daily pulsed flows for powerhouses to generate electricity during peak demand hours, and eliminate the gradual decline of river stage when flood waters recede (Figure 33.3). Next, we briefly describe dominant types of organisms—primary producers, invertebrates, and vertebrates—that live in and around California's rivers. We find repeated evidence that human alteration of the water cycle is a serious threat to California native, river-associated flora and fauna because they are adapted to the region's natural, albeit extremely variable, hydrologic regimes.

Overview of Key Taxa in Food Webs of Californian Rivers

Primary Producers

Consumers in rivers derive their energy (or carbon) both from terrestrial plant detritus and invertebrates and from aquatic primary producers. Primary production in rivers is carried out by diverse, phylogenetically distant photosynthetic organisms: cyanobacteria or "blue green algae" (Cyanophyta); diatoms (Bacillariophyta); green algae (Chlorophyta); aquatic mosses and liverworts (Bryophyta); and vascular plants (Tracheophyta). All riverine producers have distinct life history traits that affect their distributions and abundances in channel networks, their PHENOLOGIES (seasonal life history cycles), and their ecological roles. Aquatic vascular plants (macrophytes) may become dense in slow-moving or stagnant waters as well as during sustained periods of low, stable flow but are scoured from substrata during floods (Klose et al. 2009). These plants are often important habitats for EPIPHYTON, fish, and invertebrates. Like terrestrial plant material, aquatic macrophyte tissue enters river food webs primarily as DETRITUS (dead organic matter) (Webster and Benfield 1986), which is colonized and broken down by microbes (fungi and bacteria). The simple molecules produced and incorporated by these microbes make important nutritional contributions to the diets of detritivorous invertebrates and fish (Arsuffi and Suberkropp 1984).

"Algae" (an informal term for a diverse array of nonvascular aquatic primary producers, including single-celled and multicellular colonial taxa) are usually the dominant primary producers in sunlit streams and rivers (Box 33.1). During favorable periods, algae grow vegetatively by division of solitary or colonial cells. Spores or other resting stages are produced for dispersal and to endure periods of environmental stress, like drought (Bold and Wynne 1985). Diatoms can divide from

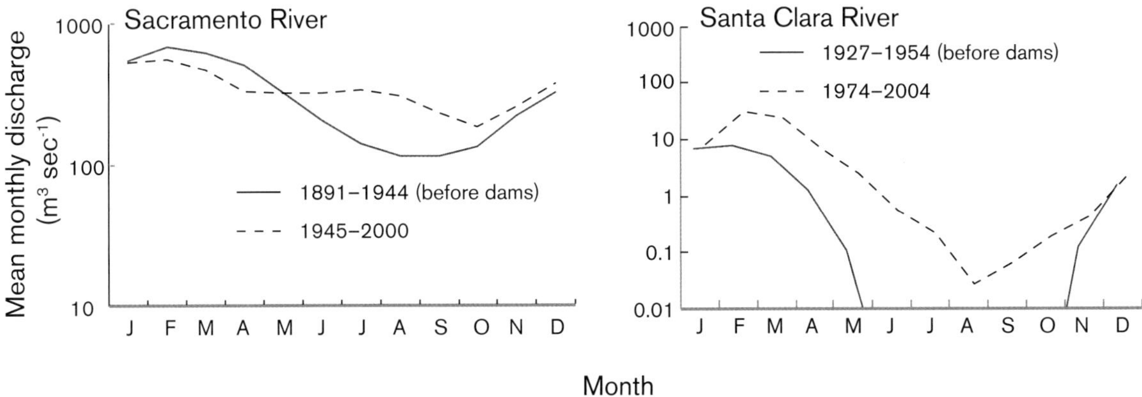

FIGURE 33.3 Seasonal flows in the Sacramento River (left) and Santa Clara River of southern California near Montalvo (right, U.S. Geological Survey gage 11114000), showing the effects of dam operations that capture and store winter precipitation, release flows during the summer, and augment discharge with agricultural return flows. Sources: With permission after figure from Kondolf and Batalla 2005.

once to several times daily, prokaryotic cyanobacteria even faster (Lowe 2011). Green algae, which can attain a high biomass as "macroalgae" in sunlit rivers (Whitton 1970, Dodds and Gudder 1992), can proliferate via cell division or episodic cloning events (Stevenson et al. 1996).

Algae also are characterized by their habitat associations. They can be planktonic (drifting in the water column) or attached. Attached algae, because they resist washout, dominate in flowing streams and rivers and are characterized by the substrata on which they grow, as EPILITHIC (on stone), EPIPELIC (on clay, sand or silt), or EPIPHYTIC (on plants, often on macroalgae) forms. METAPHYTON are algae that may initiate growth attached to substrata but then proliferate to become suspended, cloudlike, in the water column. Floating mats of detached algae can become conspicuous after proliferations start to senesce. PHYTOPLANKTON are algae suspended in the water column, which can accumulate in river pools, side channels, or floodplain waters during low flow.

Algae have strong impacts in rivers as food sources, as habitat structure, and by influencing and sometimes controlling biogeochemical cycles and water quality. Diatoms generally have the highest nutritional quality, supplying lipids and polyunsaturated fatty acids (PUFAs) that are needed but not synthesized by most animals (Brett et al. 2009). Given their rapid growth and high nutritional quality, low (inconspicuous) standing crops of diatoms can support large biomasses of consumers (Elton 1927). Their potentially high productivity, nutritional quality, and low abundance (often due to high grazing pressure) make diatoms and other edible algae sources of "hidden carbon" whose importance in river food webs is revealed only when scientists conducting experiments (Lamberti and Resh 1983, McNeely and Power 2007), or other circumstances (Kohler and Wiley 1992), remove grazers. In contrast, certain cyanobacteria, particularly those that proliferate under warm, low-flow conditions, can synthesize harmful toxins affecting the liver (e.g., microcystin) (Smith et al. 2008, Miller et al. 2010) and nervous system (e.g., anatoxin) (Kudela 2011, Paerl and Huisman 2009). Whether algae have beneficial (via food web support) or detrimental (via toxin production or oxygen depletion) effects on fish and other vertebrates (Puschner et al. 2008) depends on environmental conditions, particularly flow, light, temperature, and nutrient levels (Klose et al. 2012). In flowing rivers that are sunlit but cooled during summer by groundwater inputs and riparian shading, edible algae grow rapidly but are also typically suppressed by grazers. These algae can fuel the growth of salmonids (salmon and trout) and other desirable consumers by supporting invertebrate prey. When drought, water withdrawals, or impoundments reduce flow through sunlit California rivers, disconnected pools and backwaters warm, stagnate, and stratify. If warm stagnant habitats are enriched by decaying organic matter or other sources of nutrients, they can support blooms of cyanobacteria, including potentially toxic taxa (Paerl and Huisman 2011).

In contrast, when river flows below dams are kept artificially cold and stable during summer by releases of deep water from upstream reservoirs, other potentially harmful algae can proliferate, such as the benthic diatom *Didymosphenia geminata* (Kirkwood et al. 2009, Kumar et al. 2009). The bedrock geology and snowmelt hydrology of rivers in the mountains of California produce chemical and thermal conditions that allow *Didymosphenia* to cover rocks with a sheath of extracellular mucilage and exclude edible algal species (Rost et al. 2011). *Didymosphenia* may also benefit when hydroelectric dams are managed to follow peak energy demand, causing daily wetting and exposure of river edges (Furey et al. in press). Mucilage may keep these and other algae moist, allowing them to dominate areas that are only periodically inundated (Benenati et al. 1998). Because mucilaginous taxa are often unpalatable or have low nutritional value (Shannon et al. 1994), such algae may lower the nutritional quality of attached algal assemblages and restrict the flow of energy and nutrients up food chains to higher trophic levels (Furey et al. in press).

Invertebrates

California rivers and streams host a wide range of invertebrates: worms (flat worms, round worms, aquatic earthworms, leeches); insects; crustaceans (e.g., crayfish, amphipods or scuds, and microcrustaceans (cladocerans, copepods, and ostracods); water mites; and mollusks (snails, mussels, and clams) (Figure 33.4). Some groups are quite diverse, with at least 100 species of mollusks, 50 species of crustaceans, and more than 1,100 species of aquatic insects, excluding the Diptera (flies, midges, mosquitoes) (Ball et al. 2013). Many additional species, including many that are ENDEMIC to Cali-

(continued on page 722)

TABLE 33.1

Characteristics of river systems described in Boxes 33.1, 33.3, 33.4, and 33.5

Descriptive feature	Klamath	Eel	Sacramento	San Joaquin/ Tulare Lake	Central/southern California
Major river or tributaries (generally listed north to south)	Shasta, Scott, Salmon, Trinity (below Upper Klamath Lake)	South, Middle, North Forks, Van Duzen	McCloud, Pit, Feather, Yuba, Bear, American	San Joaquin: Mokelumne, Stanislaus, Tuolumne, Merced, Upper San Joaquin. Tulare Lake: Kaweah, Tule, Kern, Kings Rivers	Central: Pajaro, Salinas, Carmel, Arroyo Grande South: Santa Maria, Santa Ynez, Ventura, Santa Clara, Los Angeles, San Gabriel, Santa Ana, Santa Margarita, San Luis Rey, San Diego
Drainage area (km^2)	31,339	9,546	71,432	35,065	355–10,774
River length (km)	410	320	1,110 (including Pit River)	589	40–290
Peak discharge (m^3sec^{-1}, date)	15,775 (December 3, 1965)	>21,000 (December 31, 1964)	17,556 (February 19, 1986)	2,237 (December 9, 1950)	680–3,653
Mean annual discharge (m^3sec^{-1})	487	207	665[A]	127	1.9–10.3
Hydrograph type	Headwaters: Interior: snowmelt Below 1,000 m Coastal: rain	Mediterranean, precipitation as rain with coastal fog	Headwaters: snowmelt Below 1,000 m: rain	Headwaters: snowmelt Below 1,000 m: rain	Rain
Vegetation	Great Basin/High Desert, subalpine forest, mixed conifer and oak woodland, coastal mixed deciduous and conifer	Coastal mixed deciduous and conifer, eastern oak-grassland	High elevations: treeless and subalpine forest, mixed conifers Low elevations: oak savannah, deciduous riparian forest, wetlands	High elevations: coniferous forests Treeless above 3,200–3,500 m Low elevations: wetlands, grassland, chaparral, and oak woodlands	Chaparral, oak woodlands, grasslands, coastal sage scrub; mixed coniferous/redwoods in northern coastal
Land use	High elevations: wildlands, timber, livestock grazing/ rangelands. Moderate elevations: timber, agriculture, livestock grazing/ rangelands Low elevations: timber, low intensity/ sustainable agriculture	Timber, cattle ranching, gardens (marijuana and vegetable) and dairy near the mouth	High elevations: wildlands, timber, livestock grazing Low elevations: intense agriculture, urbanized around cities of Sacramento and Fresno	High Sierra: wildlands, some timber, livestock grazing Low elevations: intense agriculture	Wildlands: high elevations and inland; valley agriculture; heavily urbanized in the south (Ventura, Los Angeles to San Diego)

A. At Freeport.

The South Fork Eel River and several of its tributaries run through the 3,200 hectare forested Angelo Reserve, where biota and food webs have been studied since the 1980s. Within the reserve, tributary basins are relatively pristine, but the mainstem South Fork bed is clogged with excessive fine sediment from logging and dirt roads upstream of the reserve. Studies of the upper Eel illustrate how food web structure and species interactions change over the annual Mediterranean hydrologic cycle, and up and down drainage networks, in relatively unimpaired coastal California rivers.

Changes over Time: Seasonal Phenology of the Eel River Biota

Under "normal" Mediterranean seasonality, rainy, cool winters precede biologically active summer drought periods. The coarse boulder and bedrock beds in tributaries of the Eel remain stationary during high winter flows, but in mainstem channels with more flow, smaller (gravel, pebble, cobble) bed sediments are mobilized once or several times during winter floods, when discharges exceed bankfull (a frequency-defined discharge corresponding to flows with about 1.5 year RECURRENCE INTERVALS) (Parker 1978).

In springs following winter flood-scour, days lengthen; flows clear, subside, and warm; and attached algae proliferate. Epilithic diatoms, cyanobacteria, and green algae regrow on the river bed. The green macroalga (*Cladophora glomerata*), which dominates PRIMARY PRODUCER biomass during summer, initiates vegetative growth from basal cells that survived winter flood-scour on more stable substrates (e.g., boulders and bedrock). During the late spring/early summer period with high-nutrient fluxes and lengthening days, and before grazer populations have recovered from scour, *Cladophora* streamers can attain several meters in length, peaking in midsummer.

The first invertebrates to colonize after scouring floods are early successional PRIMARY CONSUMERS, primarily fast-growing, mobile, unarmored invertebrates like mayflies and chironomids. These are prey vulnerable to predatory invertebrates (e.g., dragonfly and damselfly nymphs) and fish. At this time, fish influence the persistence of *Cladophora* blooms through trophic cascades (Estes et al. 2011). Large fish in the Eel suppress both herbivores and small predators that eat herbivores, so their indirect effects on algae can be positive or negative depending on which pathway dominates during a given year (Power et al. 2008). In some years, an algivorous midge (*Pseudochironomus richardsoni*) that is consumed by small predators but not large fish becomes abundant enough to suppress *Cladophora*. During these years, fish have negative effects on algal biomass because they reduce small predators, releasing fish-resistant grazers to suppress algae (Power 1990a, Power et al. 2008). In years without substantial recruitment of fish-resistant grazers, fish suppress all important algivores, with a positive indirect effect on algae (Power et al. 2008).

Bed-scouring flows do not happen every winter. During drought winters without flood-scour, large, heavily armored, cased caddis flies (*Dicosmoecus gilvipes*) and sessile, attached grazers such as a common aquatic moth larva (*Petrophila* spp.) overwinter in large numbers. These grazers are susceptible to scouring floods, but not to fish and other predators, and can suppress *Cladophora* growth during the following summer (Power et al. 2008). When *Dicosmoecus* are experimentally removed during drought summers, however, algae can recover to cover substrates and form floating mats (Wootton et al. 1996). In summers following drought (scour-free) winters, fish have no indirect impact on algal biomass, receive little energy from invulnerable grazers, and grow poorly (Parker and Power 1997). Invulnerable grazers are the functionally important apex consumers in two-level food chains. In contrast, floods that remove predator-resistant grazers and release vulnerable grazers and algae are followed by summers with longer food chains, more energy flow from algae to fish, and stronger top-down effects of fish on algal biomass (Power et al. 2008) (Box 33.1 Figure 1).

Cladophora blooms can increase the surface area available for colonization by microbes, stream invertebrates, and epiphytic cyanobacteria and diatoms by approximately five orders of magnitude (Dodds 1991, Dudley et al. 1986, Power et al. 2009). Over the summer months the color of *Cladophora* blooms changes from green to yellow to rusty red as encrustations by epiphytic diatoms thicken (Power et al. 2009). During early to middle epiphyte succession (June through early July), epiphytes are dominated by monolayers of tightly adhering, low-profile taxa. Later in the season, *Cladophora* and its early epiphytes become smothered by diatoms in the family Rhopalodiacea, a family of diatoms that contain nitrogen-fixing endosymbiotic cyanobacteria that provide a nutrient source in these nitrogen-limited waters (Peterson and Grimm 1992, Hill and Knight 1988, Marks and Power 2001, Power et al. 2009, Furey et al. 2012). Unlike earlier epiphyte assemblages, *Rhopalodia* and *Epithemia* smother their

(continued)

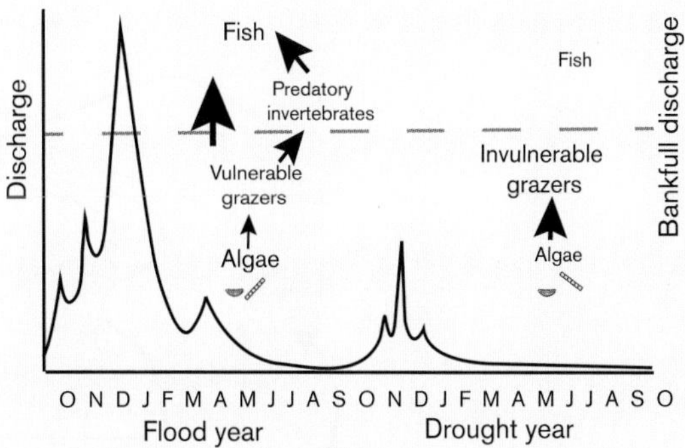

BOX 33.1 FIGURE 1 Dominant food webs in the Eel River over wet and dry years. Text sizes and arrow sizes within the food web diagrams indicate abundances of functional groups and magnitudes of trophic interactions, respectively. Illustration: Sheila Wiseman.

Cladophora host in deep layers, darkening the bloom to a deep rusty red (Power et al. 2009).

Atmospheric nitrogen fixed by cyanobacteria can be used to synthesize toxins or proteins. The endosymbionts in *Epithemia* and *Rhopalodia* appear to produce compounds of high nutritional quality, as they are strongly preferred and rapidly consumed by tadpoles (Kupferberg et al. 1994), estuarine amphipods, and isopods (Ng 2012), snails, and grazing insects (Power et al. 2009, Furey et al. 2012). Areal rates of insect emergence are up to twenty-five-fold greater over rusty-red *Epithemia*-rich *Cladophora* proliferations than over areas lacking these blooms (Power et al. 2009).

By late summer, *Cladophora*-epiphyte assemblages are reduced to short stubbles by grazing, decay, or sloughing. Much *Cladophora* biomass dries along shorelines and on emergent rocks, or floats downstream to accumulate in slack water areas and depositional zones, where it decomposes. Floating mats of algae become hot spots of insect emergence (Power 1990b), diverting riverine energy and nutrients to riparian and aerial insectivores (lizards, spiders, birds, and bats) (Power et al. 2004, Baxter et al. 2005, Ng 2012). Riverine algae that drift (or are experimentally introduced) into the estuary are rapidly consumed by the crustaceans (amphipods and isopods) that abound there. During late summer, palatable algae and algal detritus are repeatedly regrazed, passing several times through guts as the feces of snails, tadpoles, and grazing insects. These repeatedly processed algae accumulate as whitened, flour-like deposits in quiet backwaters and pools along river margins. Late-summer *Cladophora* becomes overgrown by cloudy blooms of bright green Zygnematales (*Mougeotia* and *Spirogyra* spp.) whose slimy extracellular mucopolysaccharide secretions keep them free of diatom epiphytes and, hence, grazers (Power and Matthews 1983, Power and Stewart 1987). Where heavy grazing or abrasion keeps stone surfaces clear of deposits or overgrowth, free-living, tightly attached cyanobacteria like *Rivularia* proliferate.

During the later phases of summer drought, pools and backwaters become isolated and stagnant, conditions exacerbated by water extraction for human use. Rotting algae and detritus trapped in these warm habitats release nutrients, fueling blooms of cyanobacteria (*Anabaena, Cylindrospermum, Lyngbya* or *Planktothrix*) (K. Bouma-Gregson, R. Lowe, P. Furey, and M. Power personal observations). During extremely low summer flows, isolated mainstem pools can become thermally stratified, engendering harmful blooms of toxic cyanobacteria (Paerl and Huisman 2009). At least eleven dog deaths have been linked to toxic cyanobacteria in the Eel since 2002 (Hill 2006, Puschner et al. 2008). Predicting where and when such problems arise motivates considerations of controls over river food webs and water quality from headwater tips to the terminus of the drainage network.

Spatial Energy Sources to Channel Food Webs down the Drainage Network

Headwater Tributaries

(Drainage Areas = 0.1–100 square kilometers)

Stable carbon isotopes have been used to distinguish terrestrial from aquatic sources of carbon for river resources and consumers (Finlay 2001), although information from other isotopes (e.g., of H and N) is often needed to reduce uncertainty in these analyses (Cross et al. 2013, Tsui et al. 2013) (Box 33.1 Figure 2). Using published and his own data from drainage areas ranging from 0.2 to >4,000 square kilometers, Finlay (2001) analyzed downstream trends in $\delta^{13}C$ signatures of detritus, algae, and various functional groups of consumers. Over this range, terrestrial leaf litter retained a $\delta^{13}C$ signal of ca. –28, but algae showed increasingly enriched $\delta^{13}C$ values downstream (Finlay 2001, Finlay et al. 2011). As channels widened, productive algae in sunny reaches became increasingly carbon-limited and enriched in the heavier isotope, particularly in pools (Finlay et al. 1999). Where channel drainage areas exceeded 100 square kilometers, algae were clearly $\delta^{13}C$-enriched relative to terrestrially derived carbon, allowing clear distinctions between consumer tissues built from terrestrial detritus versus instream algae.

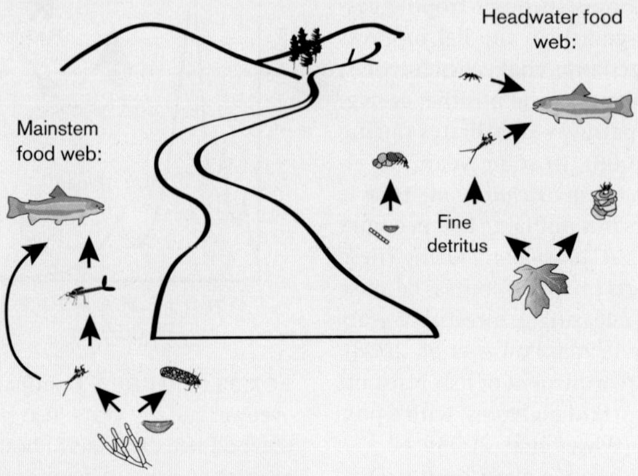

BOX 33.1 FIGURE 2 Longitudinal changes in the Eel River food web from headwaters to mouth. Illustration: Sheila Wiseman.

Carbon signatures of stream consumers, then, can indicate their dietary sources of energy (Rundel et al. 1988). Finlay et al. (1999) found that shredders, as expected, had $\delta^{13}C$ values consistently similar to those for terrestrial leaves in channels draining areas ranging from 0.2 to 4,000 square kilometers. Deposit and filter-feeders, unarmored scrapers, and invertebrate predators were also built of terrestrial carbon, but only in small headwater streams. Except for shredders, all consumer FUNCTIONAL GROUPS were substantially and increasingly supported by algal carbon downstream (Finlay 2001, McNeely et al. 2007). Fish predators did not occur in very small headwaters and showed increased $\delta^{13}C$ signatures elsewhere, suggesting substantial contributions of algal-based resources to their diets. Strikingly, armored grazing invertebrates, such as the stone-cased caddis fly (*Glossosoma penitum*), had algal carbon signatures even in the smallest headwater streams (i.e., those draining <1 square kilometers) (McNeely et al. 2007). Experimental removal of this caddis fly from replicated pools of a small, dark tributary of the Eel River shifted mayfly diets from terrestrial detritus to algae (McNeely et al. 2007).

We can use these results to illustrate "predictive mapping" of environmental or biotic changes in river channel networks. If sunlight to the channel increased (e.g., following fire or logging), or if *Glossosoma* were extirpated by parasites, as occurred in Michigan streams (Kohler and Wiley 1992), the threshold above which vulnerable grazers, and hence their fish and salamander predators, could derive their carbon from high-quality algal sources might move upstream in the drainage network. Shifts to algal energy sources should also occur further upstream in basins where riparian vegetation is reduced, either naturally (e.g., in deserts or at high elevations) (Minshall et al. 1997) or by human disturbance.

Mainstems (Drainage Areas = 100–1,000 square kilometers)

Downstream in more sunlit reaches, epilithic and epiphytic algal production is higher (Finlay et al. 2011) (see Box 33.1 Figure 2). South Fork Eel mainstem channels, draining subcatchments more than 100 square kilometers, are wide enough that solar radiation reaches the water surface for six to eight hours or more per day during the summer growing season. As a consequence, primary production increases and blooms of filamentous green macroalgae proliferate. Solar radiation is also sufficient to support a sharp increase in nitrogen fixation (Finlay et al. 2011), an energy-intensive process (Vitousek and Howarth 1991, Marcarelli et al. 2008).

Mediterranean flow seasonality and leaf phenology reduce the access of river consumers to terrestrial litter or detritus during the summer. Because winter scour denudes lateral bars of vegetation and channels are much narrower in the summer than winter, riparian vegetation is set far back from the summer wetted channel, and much of the terrestrial litter is stored on dry bars until the rainy season. In addition, dominant riparian trees along the Eel (white alders, *Alnus rhombifolia* (Nutt.); big-leafed maples, *Acer macrophyllum* Pursh; Oregon ash, *Fraxinus latifolia* Benth., willows, *Salix laevigata* Bebb, *S. lasiolepis* Benth.) retain most of their leaves until fall or winter. Leaf litter on mainstem lateral bars is swept downstream towards the ocean by the first winter floods. Despite this Mediterranean seasonality and phenology, some mainstem shredder taxa still consume primarily terrestrial detritus.

Fluxes of algae or invertebrates link river habitats longitudinally as well as laterally. The carbon signatures of filter-feeders (net-spinning caddis flies and blackflies) in sheet wash habitats tumbling over boulders indicate that they are collecting algal particles that grew in quiet upstream pools (Finlay et al. 1999, Finlay et al. 2002). Algal production in shallow pools in the South Fork of the Eel River supports invertebrate prey, which emigrate and are eaten by juvenile steelhead in riffles. These juvenile trout, in turn, can move into deep pools, where they become prey for large, cannibalistic rainbow trout (Finlay et al. 2002) and non-native pike minnows (*Ptychocheilus grandis*) that were introduced into the Eel in 1979 or 1980 (Brown and Moyle 1991, 1996).

Lowland Channels to Estuaries (Drainage Areas = 1,000–10,000 square kilometers)

Although Mediterranean riparian tree phenology and flow seasonality reduce terrestrial subsidies for river consumers in Eel River mainstems, these seasonal changes enhance links from riverine algae to terrestrial consumers directly or indirectly via insect emergence. Emerging insects deliver algal carbon and nutrients to terrestrial invertivores (spiders, beetles, lizards, birds, and bats) (Power et al. 2004, Sabo and Power 2002 a,b), and stranded algae along shorelines become food for terrestrial herbivores. Near the Eel estuary at Ferndale, the Eel Valley opens, and wide, lateral bars retain considerable biomass of locally attached and incoming drift algae stranded during receding summer flows (Power et al. 2013). Stranded algae are consumed by specialist algivores, such as tetrigid grasshoppers *Paratettix aztecus* and *P. mexicanus*, who derive 88–100% of their carbon from epilithic algae rather than terrestrial vegetation (Bastow et al. 2002). Stranded algae also are eaten by dipteran larvae, which in turn become prey for shoreline predators (carabid and staphylinid beetles, gelastocorid bugs, lycosid spiders) and riparian birds, lizards, and amphibians such as the abundant Pacific tree frog (*Pseudacris regilla*) and the once common western toad (*Bufo* [aka *Anaxyrus*] *boreas*). Frogs and toads, in turn, provide important food for birds and snakes, like the aquatic and common garter snakes (*Thamnophis atratus* and *T. sirtalis*).

Cladophora and other Eel River primary producers may constitute a trophic subsidy to the sea. Because the Eel is a relatively short, steep river, it remains largely gravel-cobble bedded all the way to its mouth. Attached filamentous and low-profile epilithic algae dominate summer energy inputs throughout the river network. They also dominate exports of organic matter to the estuary, except following the first winter storms. Ng (2012) found that copious amounts of filamentous green algae were exported from the river

(continued)

(Box 33.1 continued)

to its estuary during summer and fall, with exports of terrestrial litter becoming important only with the first winter flood. River export of high-quality algal food to the estuary may be nutritionally important to primary consumers (amphipods, isopods) in the estuary, which strongly prefer filamentous river algae over the marine green algae (*Ulva* and *Enteromorphora*) that dominate producer biomass in the estuary (Ng 2012). If estuarine grazers rapidly consume this riverine algal flux, the subsidy would be "invisible carbon," important but easy to underestimate.

In summary, the amount, composition, and fate of algae and the nutrients they cycle depend on seasonal regimes of discharge and solar radiation as well as on consequent temperatures, nutrient fluxes, and food web interactions (Stevenson et al. 1996, Power et al. 2008, Power et al. 2013). Precipitation and flow are the "master variables" (Resh et al. 1988, Power et al. 1995, Poff et al. 1997) driving temporal changes in food web structure and subsidies across seasons and years. If at least one scouring flood occurs during the winter, large blooms of algae, released from predator-resistant grazers, can proliferate during the following spring and early summer, before animal densities build up (the food chain has at this time one functional trophic level—producers). This algal biomass may rot on shores or in the water; be grazed and fuel upland, riverine, or estuarine/coastal food webs; or slough off and drift down to the coastal ocean. As time goes on, the fate of algae depends largely on how quickly summer base flows decrease. If relatively high summer flows sustain the longitudinal connection of channel habitats and maintain cooler temperatures, algal production will likely support food webs that produce salmonids and other predators valued by society, either in the river or offshore. If summer base flows drop so that stream reaches become disconnected and pools and backwaters warm and stratify, edible algae will be overtaken by inedible, or even toxic, taxa. The future of the Eel River will depend on how climate, vegetation change, and choices about land and water use affect the river's light, temperature, chemical, and hydrologic regimes.

fornia, are likely unknown or undescribed (Ball et al. 2013). Among known species, estimates of endemicity in California's Mediterranean areas range from about 2% for mollusks to 5% for insects to 21% for crustaceans. Within insect groups, estimates of endemicity for stoneflies (Order Plecoptera) and caddis flies (Order Trichoptera) were reported to be 11% and 7%, respectively, in Mediterranean areas and 25% and 19% in the Sierra Nevada (Erman 1996, Ball et al. 2013). Several endemic species have become extinct, and a number are very rare and have restricted distributions (Kabat and Hershler 1993, Erman 1996, Silldorff 2003, Herbst et al. 2009, Martin et al. 2009, Ball et al. 2013). Two species, a crayfish and a shrimp, are currently listed as endangered under the Endangered Species Act (Box 33.2). Approximately ten non-native mollusk (e.g., New Zealand mud snail [*Potamopyrgus antipodarum*]), Asiatic clam (*Corbicula fluminea*), Zebra and Quagga mussels (*Dreissena polymorpha* and *D. rostriformis bugensis*), and twenty crustacean species (e.g., the Louisiana red swamp crayfish, *Procambarus clarkii*) have been introduced to California, in some cases with substantial effects on native aquatic species (Klose and Cooper 2012, 2013; Moore et al. 2012a, 2012b).

California's native and exotic aquatic invertebrates have diverse life styles, habitat preferences, and life histories. Non-insect aquatic invertebrates and a few aquatic insects spend their entire lives in water, but most aquatic insect larvae emerge as flying terrestrial adults (Merritt et al. 2008, Thorp and Covich 2010). During their aquatic phases, many species are more abundant in either depositional (pool, back water) or erosional (riffle, run) habitats and most have one to multiple generations per year (i.e., are UNIVOLTINE to MULTIVOLTINE), with a few completing their life cycles in two or three years (SEMIVOLTINE taxa) (Bêche et al. 2006, Bonada et al. 2007, Merritt et al. 2008). The life histories and/or behavior of stream invertebrates are often timed to seasonal cycles of flooding and drought. Certain groups dominate in the wet season, when flows are high, and are replaced by other invertebrates in the dry season, when diminishing flows dry rivers to a series of isolated pools or sometimes completely (Bêche et al. 2006, Bonada et al. 2007). Because different invertebrate taxa have different susceptibilities to drying, perennial and nonperennial streams usually have different biotas (Lunde et al. 2013). Variation in river flows from year to year also drive interannual changes in the composition and abundance of invertebrate communities and in stream food webs in California (Bêche and Resh 2007a,b; Power et al. 2008). Stream reaches disturbed by fire, floods, or drying are often quickly colonized by short-lived, dispersive, small, multivoltine insect species, such as some mayflies, midges, and black flies. In contrast, invertebrates that spend their entire lives in streams or have long life cycles (e.g., some predatory stoneflies, dragonflies, and damselflies, some heavily armored caddis flies) are often extirpated by intense disturbances, and their populations may take some time to recover (Bêche et al. 2009, Verkaik et al. 2013). In some cases, early colonists are displaced by later colonists via competition or predation, particularly when colonizing taxa compete for space (Hemphill and Cooper 1983).

California's stream invertebrates also have diverse food habits (Merritt et al. 2008). Some invertebrates, called SHREDDERS, eat primarily leaf litter and associated microbes (bacteria, fungi); grazing invertebrates either browse or scrape attached algae from substrate surfaces; predatory invertebrates consume other animals; and collectors either filter fine particulate organic material (FPOM) from the water column using nets, head fans, mucus strings, or setae (filter-feeders) or ingest FPOM after it has settled on the bottom (deposit feeders) (see Figure 33.4). One insect family, the Chironomidae (midges), includes almost all of these feeding groups. Midges are generally the most abundant and diverse group of stream macroinvertebrates. Other invertebrate groups (such as the Decapods = crayfish and shrimp) are omnivorous, consuming a variety of algal, detrital, plant, and animal items (Klose and Cooper 2013). Different feeding groups abound in different types of habitats, with shredders more abundant in heav-

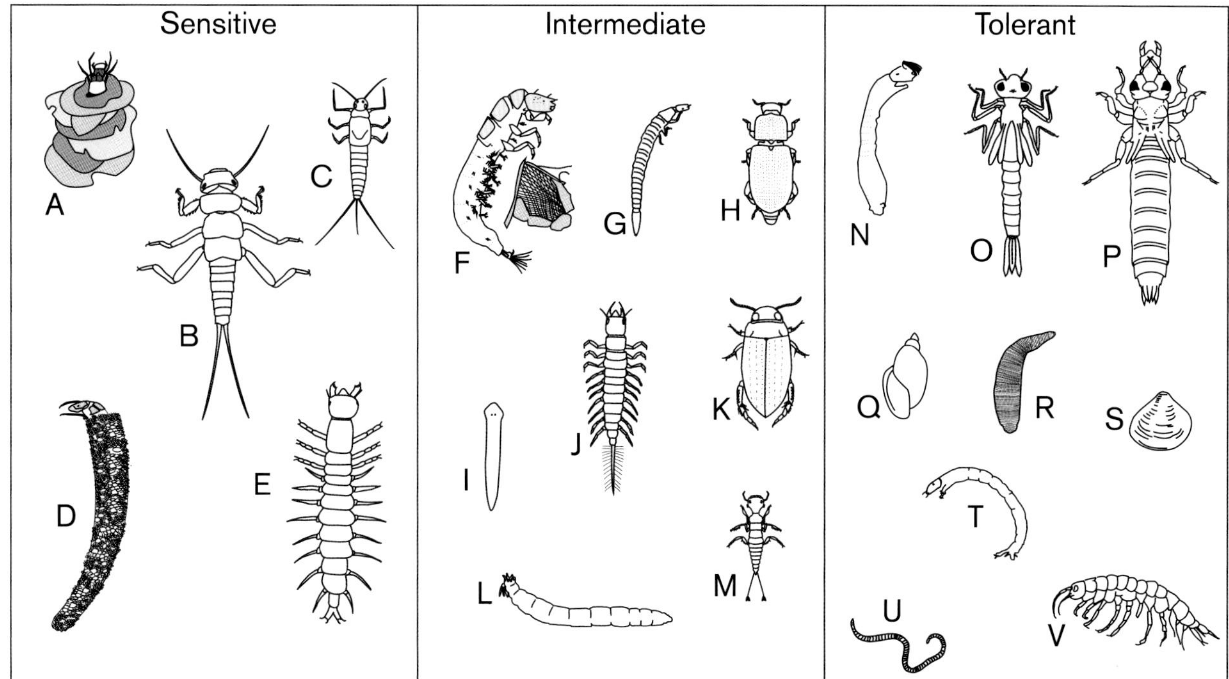

FIGURE 33.4 Major riverine invertebrate groups, classified by their sensitivity to pollution and land use change, from sensitive to tolerant. The functional feeding group designations are for the specific taxa shown. Other taxa within the same group (e.g., family) may have different feeding habits. Organisms are not drawn to scale relative to one another. Redrawn by Sheila Wiseman from Herbst et al. 2001.

(A) and (D): cased caddisflies (Order Trichoptera; A shredder, D shredder/deposit-feeder/grazer)

(B) stonefly (Order Plecoptera, predator)

(C) mayfly (Order Ephemeroptera, grazer/deposit-feeder)

(E) hellgrammite (Order Megaloptera, Family Corydalidae, predator)

(F) net-spinning caddisfly (Order Trichoptera, Family Hydropsychidae, filter feeder: net is shown); larval (G and M) and adult (H, K) aquatic beetles (Order Coleoptera; G and H deposit-feeders, K and M predators)

(I) flatworm (Phylum Platyhelminthes, Class Turbelliaria, predator)

(J) alder fly (Order Megaloptera, Family Sialidae, predator)

(L) cranefly (Order Diptera, Family Tipulidae, shredder)

(N) blackfly (Order Diptera, Family Simuliidae, filter-feeder)

(O) damselfly and (P) dragonfly (Order Odonata, predators)

(Q) snail (Phylum Mollusca, Class Gastropoda, grazer)

(R) leech (Phylum Annelida, Class Clitellata, Subclass Hirudinea, predator)

(S) fingernail clam (Phylum Mollusca, Class Bivalvia, Order Veneroida, Family Sphaeriidae, deposit-feeder)

(T) midge or chironomid (Order Diptera, Family Chironomidae, variable)

(U) aquatic earthworm (Phylum Annelida, Class Clitellata, Subclass Oligochaeta, deposit-feeder)

(V) scud or amphipod (Phylum Arthropoda, Subphylum Crustacea, Class Malacostraca, Superorder Peracarida, Order Amphipoda, deposit-feeder/grazer)

A–H, J–P, and T are insects (Phylum Arthropoda, Subphylum Hexapoda, Class Insecta).

ily shaded, headwater streams where inputs of leaf litter from riparian vegetation are substantial, and grazers more abundant in sunny, clear streams with adequate nutrient concentrations where algal production is high (Minshall et al. 1983; see Box 33.1).

Collectors are common in most streams, consuming detritus generated from leaf litter, algae, or aquatic macrophytes. Aquatic invertebrates, particularly if they lack protective armor and are exposed on substrate surfaces, are fed upon by invertebrate and vertebrate predators. Benthic aquatic invertebrates can enter the water column and drift downstream, presumably to locate new food sources or to avoid benthic predators. However, this drifting behavior makes these invertebrates vulnerable to drift-feeding fish, such as trout or juvenile salmon. Aquatic invertebrates have adapted to predation pressure from these visually-feeding fish by drifting primarily at night (Douglas et al. 1994). In addition to providing a major food source for many aquatic vertebrates (fish, newts, salamanders), aquatic insects after emergence are an important food source for riparian predators (spiders, predatory insects, salamanders, frogs, lizards, birds, bats) (Erman 1996, Nakano and Murakami 2001, Sabo and Power 2002a, Sabo and Power 2002b, Power et al. 2004, Baxter et al. 2005).

Because invertebrate taxa vary greatly in their tolerances to extreme temperatures, low oxygen concentrations, and high sediment and contaminant loads, they are often used as indicators of human impacts on stream and river systems (California Department of Fish and Wildlife Aquatic Bioassessment Laboratory 2014, SWAMP 2014). The diversity and abundances of many species in the insect orders Ephemeroptera (mayflies), Plecoptera (stoneflies), and Trichoptera (caddis flies) (EPT taxa) are reduced by pollution, excessive sediment deposition, and land use impacts on their food resources (leaf litter, algae), whereas the relative abundances of noninsects and some of the chironomids often increase in the face of human perturbations associated with agricultural, industrial,

BOX 33.2 ENDANGERED STREAM INVERTEBRATES IN CALIFORNIA

The Shasta crayfish (*Pacifastacus fortis*) and the California freshwater shrimp (*Syncaris pacifica*) are listed as endangered under the Endangered Species Act (California Department of Fish and Wildlife 2013). The Shasta crayfish once occurred throughout the upper Pit River, which flows into the Sacramento River, and its highly productive tributary, the Fall River (Daniels 1980), but has been largely displaced by the non-native signal crayfish (*P. leniusculus*). The exotic signal crayfish is more aggressive and has higher consumption rates than the Shasta crayfish, so can competitively exclude the native. This invasive species also benefits from dams and flow regulation because it is vulnerable to flood flows but can tolerate warm water (Ellis 1999, Light 2003, Pintor et al. 2009, Pintor and Sih 2011). To restrict further upstream invasion of signal crayfish in the Fall River, Pacific Gas and Electric has installed a migration barrier as a requirement of its operating license on the Pit River (Box 33.2 Figure 1). The California freshwater shrimp, native to lowland streams in Sonoma, Marine, and Napa Counties, has been severely reduced by water quality degradation, habitat loss, and the introduction of predatory fish (U.S. Fish and Wildlife Service 1998, Martin et al. 2009, Wickstein 2012). Because the preferred habitat of California freshwater shrimp is submerged, exposed tree roots; undercut banks; and terrestrial detritus in shaded streams, restoration efforts for this species have concentrated on planting riparian trees and stabilizing banks.

BOX 33.2 FIGURE 1 An underwater fence constructed on the upper Fall River in 2007 to prevent the unrestricted upstream invasion by signal crayfish into habitat occupied by Shasta crayfish. Photograph by Maria Ellis and drawing by Sheila Wiseman.

and urban development (see Figure 33.4) (Brinkman 2007, Carter et al. 2009). As a consequence, biomonitoring programs have used indices based on macroinvertebrate assemblages (composition or diversity) to evaluate environmental gradients or compare perturbed and unperturbed sites (Ode et al. 2005, 2008, Rehn et al. 2007, Rehn 2009). Such indices also are used to monitor the "health" of streams over time and under different watershed conditions or to measure the success of stream restoration efforts. These indices, however, have been criticized because of ambiguities in their interpretation, limitations in the databases used for their construction, inadequate consideration of temporal and spatial variability, and unclear presentation of basic biological data (Mazor et al. 2011, Lunde et al. 2013, Cooper et al. 2013). Furthermore, indices developed for one set of human perturbations (e.g., land use change) may not be useful indicators of other kinds of stress (e.g., climate change) (Lawrence et al. 2010).

Vertebrates

Vertebrates in California's rivers include those that are fully aquatic (e.g., fish) as well as those that use both aquatic and terrestrial habitats (e.g., mammals like water shrews, mink). Over 135 species of birds use California riparian habitats during some stage of life (RHJV 2004). Some riparian vertebrates are riverine specialists, such as the bats *Myotis yumanensis* and *M. lucifugus*, which usually feed by skimming above the water's surface at night (Brigham et al. 1992) and birds such as bank and cliff swallows (*Riparia riparia, Hirundo pyrrhonata*), which feed aerially above the water by day. Others, such as the western red bat *Lasiurus blossevillii*, roost in mature sycamores and cottonwoods and forage for insects over gravel bars and along riparian canopy margins (Pierson et al. 2006). These aerial and terrestrial insectivores are reduced by losses of riparian vegetation and declines in water quality that reduce aquatic insects (increasing water temperature, fine sediment, and toxin loading) (RHJV 2004). In Japan, riparian forest loss caused stream salmonids to switch from terrestrial to aquatic prey, reducing the biomass of insects emerging from streams and thereby abundances of streamside predators (spiders, lizards, birds, bats) (Baxter et al. 2004, 2005).

Many terrestrial vertebrate consumers in California, including humans and now-extinct grizzly bears, relied on historically large seasonal runs of ANADROMOUS fish (salmon, steelhead, Pacific lamprey), with Chinook and Coho salmon forming the basis for a commercial fishery. Only small, remnant runs of these fish remained after the construction of dams throughout the state (Moyle et al. 2002, Carlson and Satterthwaite 2011). The Central Valley supported annual runs of one to three million salmon per year, but only about forty thousand to two hundred thousand migrate today (Yoshiyama et al. 2001). Even these depleted runs, however, provide substantial amounts of food to terrestrial vertebrates. Fourteen species, mostly turkey vultures and raccoons but also gray fox, red-tailed hawks, and "herbivores" such as mule deer and squirrels, have been photographed eating Chinook salmon carcasses (Merz and Moyle 2006). These scavengers likely transport marine-derived nitrogen to riparian trees (willows, sycamores, and cottonwoods) as well as to agricultural fields. Wine grapes in vineyards near salmon spawning sites on the Mokelumne River received 18–25% of their foliar nitrogen from marine sources (Merz and Moyle 2006), probably from salmon.

FISH

Among California's 129 distinct forms of native freshwater fish (including species, subspecies, DISTINCT POPULATION SEGMENTS, and evolutionary significant units, hereafter called

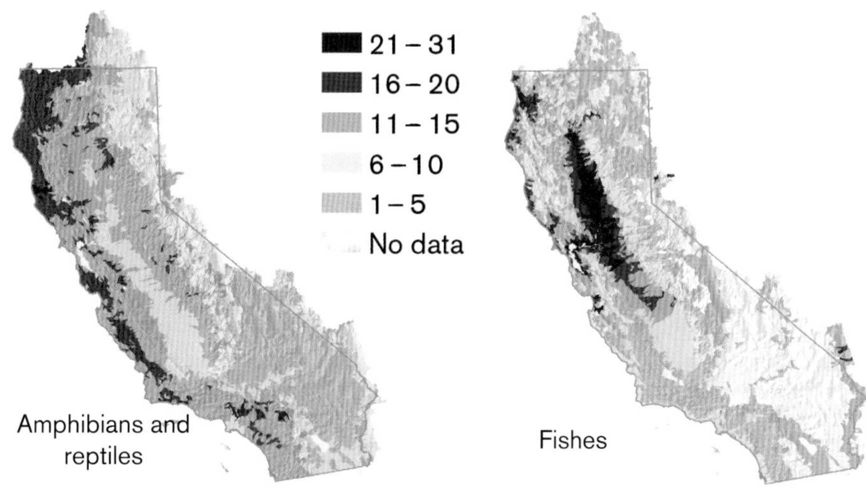

FIGURE 33.5 Total diversity of amphibians, reptiles, and fishes found in California's rivers.
Source: Data from Howard et al. 2013. Map: K. Fesenmyer.

"species"), almost two thirds (63%) are endemic. The highest fish diversity occurs in the tributaries and mainstems of the Sacramento and San Joaquin Rivers (Moyle 2002, Moyle et al. 2011) (Figure 33.5). Across the Sacramento and San Joaquin drainage basins, thirty-three distinct habitats based on patterns of fish distribution and endemism occur from montane headwaters to the rivers' confluence in the Sacramento–San Joaquin Delta (Moyle and Ellison 1991). Most native sculpins and cyprinids (minnow family: hitch, roach, hardhead, squawfish, dace) are found at low to middle elevations on the west slope of the Sierra, but native rainbow trout (*Oncorhynchus mykiss*) and Sacramento suckers (*Catotomus occidentalis*) were historically recorded at elevations over 2,000 meters in the Kings River drainage. Rainbow and golden trout subspecies (*Oncorhynchus mykiss* subspp.) in the Kern River drainage reached elevations of 2,400 to 3,000 meters. Because of glacial or volcanic activity and barriers to fish migration, most Sierra waters over 2,000 meters in elevation and many eastside streams originally lacked fish, with the exceptions noted above, but trout have been widely stocked in these waters for a recreational fishery. The unglaciated southernmost portions of the Sierra host three golden trout subspecies including the California golden trout (*Oncorhynchus mykiss aguabonita*), the state fish (Moyle 2002).

Some of the tributaries of the upper Sacramento River, such as the Pit River, drain the Modoc Plateau, a volcanic landscape containing closed basins with historically large lakes that still host a variety of unique fish species. The Lost River system is home to two endangered species, the Lost River sucker (*Deltistes luxatus*) and shortnose sucker (*Chasmistes brevirostris*), which live in warm, eutrophic systems with low dissolved oxygen concentrations. The watershed of Goose Lake, now separated from the Pit River and occasionally dry (Heck et al. 2008), contains four endemic fish taxa: the Goose Lake redband trout (*Oncorhynchus mykiss newberrii*), lamprey (*Lampetra tridentata* ssp.), sucker (*Catostomus occidentalis lacusanserinus*), and tui chub (*Gila bicolor thallassina*). These fish spend distinct life history stages in the lake and its tributaries, respectively. Similarly, fishes of arid and semiarid areas of the state, although low in number of species, have high levels of local or regional endemicity, including species or subspecies of pupfish (*Cyprinodon* spp.), tui chubs (*Siphateles bicolor* subspp.), and/or speckled dace (*Rhinichthys osculus* subspp.) in the southeastern valleys (e.g., Owens and Death Valleys) and deserts; a variety of sucker (*Catostomus santaanae*), chub (*Gila orcutti*), dace, and stickleback (*Gasterosteus aculeatus* subspp.) along the southern Coast; and the Lahontan fish fauna of the eastern Sierra and western Great Basin including Lahontan tui chubs (*Siphateles bicolor obesa*), redside (*Richardsonius egregius*), speckled dace (*Rhinichthys osculus robustus*), mountain suckers (*Catostomus platyrhynchus*), Paiute sculpin (*Cottus beldingi*), mountain whitefish (*Prosopium williamsoni*), and two subspecies of cutthroat trout (*Oncorhynchus clarki henshawi* and *seleneris*) (Swift et al. 1993, Moyle et al. 1996, Moyle 2002, Lin and Ambrose 2005, Brown et al. 2005, O'Brien et al. 2011). The native fishes of these regions are adapted for dealing with extreme hydrologic events, high summer temperatures, and low dissolved oxygen levels (Swift et al. 1993, Matthews and Berg 1997, Spina 2007, Boughton et al. 2007, Bell et al. 2011, Sloat and Osterback 2013).

Like riverine invertebrates, fish show diverse and distinct foraging modes and food and habitat preferences. Eel-like lampreys, which have cartilaginous skeletons but lack jaws, show ONTOGENETIC NICHE SHIFTS in their habitats and feeding habits. The anadromous Pacific lamprey (*Lampetra tridentata*), the most widespread California lamprey, preys on fish as adults in the ocean, attaching to hosts' bodies with suckerlike mouths and ingesting fluids from wounds made with their rasping tongues. When they spawn in rivers and streams, Pacific lamprey migrate inland as far as 440 kilometers and historically were abundant enough to be harvested by Native Americans (Moyle 2002, Brown et al. 2010, Close et al. 2002). After hatching from eggs, the larval ammocoete stage lives three to seven years within fine sediments, where it filter feeds on suspended particles. Ammocoete growth is enhanced by the presence of western pearl shell mussels (*Margaritifera falcata*) (Limm and Power 2011).

Many fish feed on insects and other macroinvertebrates, with some benthic-feeding fishes (e.g., sculpins, some minnows) relying exclusively on invertebrates for food (Erman 1996). Other fish (such as many salmonids) forage on benthic invertebrates, invertebrates drifting downstream in the water column and at the surface, and terrestrial invertebrates that fall into the water (Rundio and Lindley 2008). Some fishes that are insectivorous as small juveniles become piscivorous as adults, such as the Sacramento pikeminnow (*Ptychocheilus grandis*) and larger rainbow trout (*Oncorhynchus mykiss*). Fish 3 to 15 centimeters in length are "perfect prey" (Moyle 2002, p. 28), vulnerable in shallow water to predatory birds such as kingfishers and herons and in deep water to larger fish. Threats to small fish from aquatic predators, and to large fish from fishing birds and mammals, can set up a "bigger-deeper" size-depth distribution for fish seeking to avoid size-specific predation (Power 1987). Ontogenetic niche shifts also can shift the trophic position of fishes downward. For example, hardhead (*Mylopharadon conocephalus*), a large (up to 46 centimeters) minnow once widespread throughout Sierran foothill rivers, consume invertebrates as juveniles using hooked teeth. As adults they develop large, molar-like teeth and eat aquatic plants, macroalgae, and hard-shelled invertebrates (*Mylo-phara-don* means "mill-throat-teeth").

California's freshwater fish fauna has been severely diminished by human activities, with seven species extinct, thirty-three more (26%) at immediate risk of extinction, and another thirty-three species on a path to extinction if current trends continue (Figure 33.6; Moyle et al. 2011). Native fishes are particularly threatened by flow modifications, especially dams and diversions, the introduction of exotic species, and agricultural and urban development and operations (Box 33.3; May and Brown 2002, Kats and Ferrer 2003, Riley et al. 2005, Moyle et al. 2011). At least fifty non-native species of fish have become established in California's waterways, including many predatory species from the Mississippi River basin (e.g., black bass [*Micropterus* spp.], sunfish [*Lepomis* spp.], crappie [*Pomoxis* spp.], catfish [*Ictalurus* spp.], bullheads [*Ameiurus* spp.]) adapted to the slack water conditions that follow flow modification, rather than the strong flow variation characteristic of natural western rivers (Brown et al. 2005, Marchetti et al. 2004, Light and Marchetti 2007). The distributions of introduced fish species in California are often determined by the locations of introductions, hydrologic connections, perennial flow patterns, and dispersal limitations (Riley et al. 2005, Marchetti et al. 2006, Moyle and Marchetti 2006). These introductions have reduced native amphibian populations, altered invertebrate assemblages, and, in some cases, released algae from grazing pressure (Knapp et al. 1998, Riley et al. 2005, Herbst et al. 2009). In the case of trout introductions to montane waters that originally lacked fish, it appears that high-elevation, endemic invertebrate and amphibian prey species, which have no evolutionary history with fish, are the most vulnerable taxa (Knapp et al. 1998, Herbst et al. 2009). Introduced brown (*Salmo trutta*), brook (*Salvelinus fontinalis*), and rainbow trout also have affected native golden and cutthroat trout via hybridization, competition, and predation at high elevations, and introduced black bass have reduced native cyprinids at low elevations (Moyle et al. 1996).

AMPHIBIANS AND REPTILES

Of the more than 150 species comprising California's herpetofauna, Brode and Bury (1984) estimated that 83% of the amphibians and 40% of the reptiles occupy riparian habitat, with a smaller subset truly aquatic (see Figure 33.6). The river-dwelling frogs, toads, newts, salamanders, snakes, and turtles of California occupy various levels in food chains. Frog and toad tadpoles eat primarily algae, and most species require open sunlit channels where high primary productivity promotes rapid growth. Where locally abundant, tadpoles can reduce benthic algal biomass, but they can also facilitate the growth of less edible *Cladophora* by scraping epiphytic diatoms off this filamentous host alga (Kupferberg 1997). In small, high-gradient streams, salamanders and newts are often the dominant vertebrate predators. In forested coastal streams, larvae of the coastal giant salamander (*Dicamptodon tenebrosus*) and the endemic California giant salamander (*D. ensatus*) are top predators. Both eat macroinvertebrates and sometimes juvenile salmonids (Parker 1994).

Although juvenile salmonids recycle 1.7 times more nitrogen and 1.2 times more phosphorus than salamander larvae per unit mass, salamanders can make up a much larger proportion of total predator biomass in some streams (Munshaw et al. 2013). Salamanders are often overlooked because they are cryptic, sometimes nesting or seeking dry season refuges below the streambed surface (in the hyporheic zone) (Nussbaum 1969, Feral et al. 2005). In central and southern California streams, California newts (*Taricha torosa*) are the dominant salamanders. Newts have flexible food habits, shifting to earthworms after wildfires, which can reduce adult newt cannibalism on newt larvae (Kerby and Kats 1998). Although *Taricha* possess potent neurotoxins (tetrodotoxin) (Bradley and Klitka 1981, Ferrer and Zimmer 2013) as adults, egg masses and larvae are vulnerable to introduced predators like western mosquitofish (*Gambusia affinis*) and Louisiana swamp crayfish (*Procambarus clarkii*) (Kats and Ferrer 2003, Riley et al. 2005, Kats et al. 2013).

River-breeding amphibians illustrate a wide range of flow-regime adaptations (Lytle and Poff 2004), defined as morphological traits and life history strategies enabling persistence through extreme droughts and floods. Some adult amphibians react to seasonally predictable flood-drought cycles by migrating long distances, sometimes several kilometers, from headwaters or terrestrial refugia to specific stream segments in the spring (e.g., California red-legged frogs, *Rana draytonii* [Tatarian 2008]; red-bellied newts, *Taricha rivularis* [Twitty et al. 1964]; and foothill yellow-legged frogs, *R. boylii* [Bourque 2008]). Breeding adults gather where the channel cross-sectional shape minimizes the risks of flood disturbance or dewatering, providing safe rearing habitats with slow water velocities for sessile eggs and weakly swimming larvae (Kupferberg 1996). Other native anurans (frogs and toads), such as spadefoot toads *Spea hammondii* and *Spea intermontanus*, are adapted to xeric environments, breed in ephemeral streams, and use keratinized patches on their hind feet as "spades" to burrow into sandy sediments during dry periods. There they wait in a state of torpor with low metabolic rates (ESTIVATION) until low-frequency vibrations from rainfall trigger their emergence. The federally protected Arroyo toad (*Anaxyrus californicus*) of southern California forms a cocoon of layers of shed skin to prevent moisture loss while estivating. These toads avoid washout by laying their eggs at the end of the wet season, and their tadpole development can accelerate in response to decreasing water levels to allow early metamorphosis before stream drying (Denver et al. 1998). At the opposite extreme, tadpoles of the tailed frog (*Ascaphus truei*) may take years to reach metamorphosis in the cold, shaded headwaters of northwestern California's forests, where growth is constrained by light-limited algal productivity (Mallory and Richardson 2005). *Ascaphus* tadpoles are able to persist through multiple growing seasons because their strong suction cup mouths are used to adhere to rocks and withstand winter high flows.

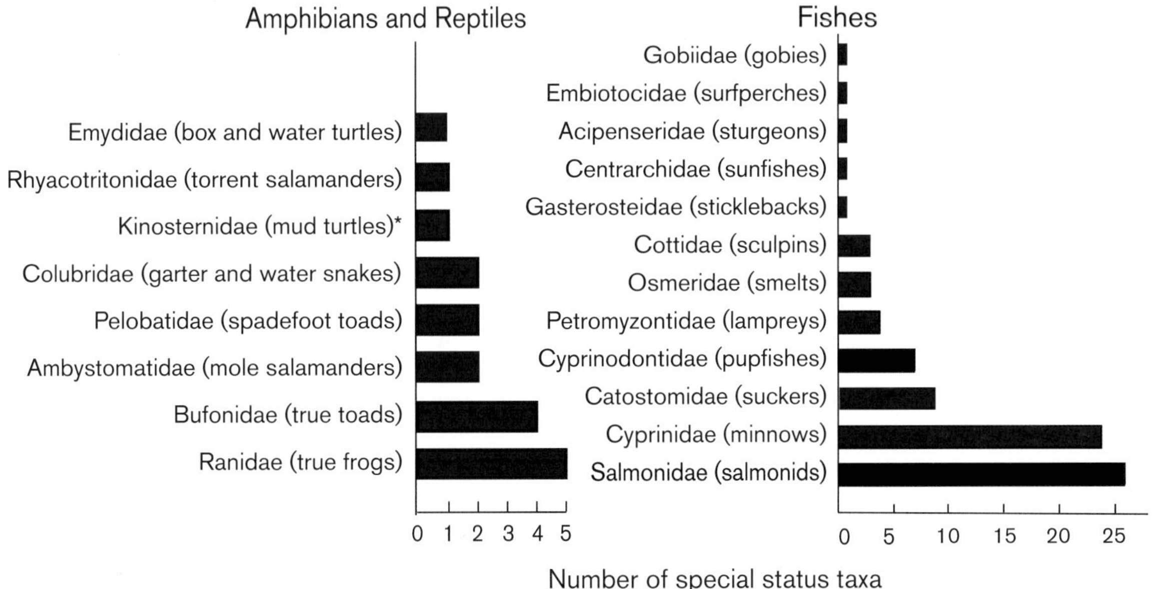

*The Sonoran mud turtle (*Kinosternon sonoriense sonoriense*) was formerly present in the Colorado River but appears to be extirpated.

FIGURE 33.6 Total family-level diversity of special status amphibians, reptiles, and fishes in California's rivers. Included taxa are California State Species of Special Concern or threatened or endangered species under the California or Federal Endangered Species Act. Sources: Moyle 2002, Stebbins and McGinnis 2012, and California Department of Fish and Wildlife 2011.

Despite these adaptations, amphibians are declining in California's rivers and streams. For example, the foothill yellow-legged frog (*Rana boylii*) was historically widespread throughout the Coast Range, the west slope of the Sierra Nevada, and the mountains of southern California but has disappeared from more than half of its range, particularly downstream from large dams (Kupferberg et al. 2012). Untimely pulsed releases from dams (e.g., for recreational whitewater boating) remove eggs and tadpoles, whereas rapid cessation of snowmelt flows blocked by dams kills them by stranding (Kupferberg et al. 2011, 2012). Reservoirs also harbor non-native predators (e.g. American bullfrog, *Lithobates catesbeiana* [Moyle 1973]), and block frog movements, creating genetic isolation (Peek 2011). Water temperature is the best predictor of the yellow-legged frog's breeding abundance (Welsh and Hodgson 2011). When dams release cold water from the depths of upstream reservoirs, frog populations shift to shadier and less productive, but relatively warmer, tributaries (Catenazzi and Kupferberg 2013). Tadpoles comprise a large portion of the diet of young garter snakes (Lind and Welsh 1994) and are a food source for predatory macroinvertebrates and fish, so the loss of tadpoles from river food webs can affect a diverse array of consumers.

California has one extant native turtle, the western pond turtle (*Actinemys marmorata,* previously *Clemmys, Emys*) (Stebbins and McGinnis 2012). Western pond turtles forage and mate in water but nest, estivate, and overwinter on land (Pilliod et al. 2013). These opportunistic predators and scavengers (Holland 1985, Bury 1986) show great flexibility in dealing with extreme hydrologic events, traveling far from rivers to avoid floods (Pilliod et al. 2013) and persisting in relictual populations in the remnants of the Mojave River (Lovich and Meyer 2002). Western pond turtles are declining due to habitat destruction, dam construction, flow regulation, and introductions of exotic species, such as the American bullfrog (Moyle 1973, Brattstrom 1988, Reese and Welsh 1998, Bury and Germano 2008, Bondi and Marks 2013). In urban settings, western pond turtles are often outnumbered by alien turtle species such as the more aggressive and fecund red-eared slider (*Trachemys sripta elegans*) that have become naturalized after being released as unwanted pets (Spinks et al. 2003).

MAMMALS

The legacy of California's fur rush, which preceded the Gold Rush, is just beginning to be appreciated. European exploration and exploitation of inland California during the 1820s were driven by the quest for beaver pelts (Dolin 2011). The California golden beaver, a subspecies of the North American beaver (*Castor canadensis subauratus*), had become rare by 1837 (Skinner 1962). Recent reexaminations of historic, ethnographic, and paleontologic evidence challenge the long-held assumption that beaver were originally absent above elevations of 350 meters, especially from the eastern Sierra Nevada, where they have been recently introduced (James and Lanman 2012, Lanman et al. 2012). Given the significance of beavers as ecosystem engineers, their true historical distribution and abundance have critical management implications. In semiarid habitats of the western United States, the reintroduction of beaver can aggrade incised streams, reconnecting them to their floodplains (Pollock et al. 2007). Beaver dams increase macroinvertebrate production (McDowell and Naiman 1986, Wright et al. 2002), increase habitat heterogeneity, enhance production of salmonid smolts, and provide fish with refuges during both low and high flows without impeding fish passage (Gard 1961, Pollock et al. 2004, Kemp et al. 2012, Lokteff et al. 2013). When managers have removed beaver dams ostensibly to facilitate fish passage, they

BOX 33.3 CHANGES IN WATER QUALITY FROM HEADWATERS TO MOUTH IN A LARGE RIVER SYSTEM: THE KLAMATH RIVER

The Klamath River Basin contains an impressive diversity of peoples, land uses, geology, topography, flora, and fauna, including remarkable anadromous fish runs (Wallace 1983). Some of the native fish species found here include Chinook (*Oncorhynchus tshawytscha*), coho (*Oncorhynchus kisuch*), and chum salmon (*Oncorhynchus keta*), steelhead (*Oncorhynchus mykiss*), coastal cutthroat trout (*Oncorhynchus clarkii clarkii*), Pacific lamprey (*Lampetra tridentata*), eulachon (*Thaleichthys pacificus*), and Green sturgeon (*Acipenser medirostris*) in the middle and lower river, and Lost River sucker (*Deltistes luxatus*), shortnose sucker (*Chasmistes brevirostris*), and redband trout (*Oncorhynchus mykiss newberrii*) in the upper river. Fisheries for these and other species are critical for cultural and subsistence uses by several Native American tribes as well as for commercial and recreational fishers. Wild salmon and steelhead populations have been in continual decline due to modified flow regimes, and degraded habitat and water quality (Moyle 2002) in response to legacy mining, forestry, water extraction and impoundment, agriculture, and other factors, some of which continue today.

The Klamath Basin's hydrology and water quality reflect its geographic, climatic, and geologic setting, as well as modifications by humans during the twentieth century. The Klamath River's headwater tributaries, the Sprague and Williamson Rivers in southern Oregon, flow into Upper Klamath Lake. Upper Klamath Lake is a large (surface area 313 square kilometers), shallow (mean depth 2.4 meters), naturally eutrophic lake that has become hypereutrophic in response to anthropogenic activities (NRC 2004, Eilers et al. 2004). The Klamath River proper then flows from near Klamath Falls, Oregon, over 400 kilometers to the Pacific Ocean south of Crescent City, California. The river has few tributaries but several hydropower impoundments in the first 100 kilometers below the lake. Over the next 300 kilometers, mean annual river flows roughly double every 100 kilometers, increasing from around 1.0 billion cubic meters below Iron Gate Dam to over 13 billion cubic meters at the estuary. Major tributaries in this section include the Salmon, Shasta, Scott, and Trinity Rivers, with extensive water development in the latter three.

Water quality affects native fishes either directly (via temperature, turbidity, dissolved oxygen) or indirectly (via nutrients and associated primary production). Due to unusual landscape and anthropogenic controls over water quality, the Klamath River is often called an "upside-down river" (Rymer 2008), with upper reaches impaired and water quality improving downstream (Kaplan and Newbold 2003) (Box 33.3 Figure 1). The distribution of native fish species reflects water quality conditions, with upstream species (e.g., suckers, redband trout) tolerating eutrophic conditions and downstream species relying on higher water quality.

Although anadromous salmonids typically require cool water temperatures, the Klamath River is not considered a cold-water stream (Bartholow 2005). The Klamath River has cool water temperatures from late fall through spring but warm water temperatures in the summer, although groundwater and other cold-water inputs provide local summer thermal refugia (Sutton et al. 2007). Large mainstem reservoirs stratify during warm seasons and, depending on the depth of reservoir water releases, alter river temperatures (Ward and Stanford 1983). Although temperature responds largely to seasonal changes in climate, dissolved oxygen levels in the upper river are reduced by large organic loads emanating from Upper Klamath Lake (Sullivan et al. 2011), then increase downstream, attaining saturation in lower river reaches. Local deviations in dissolved oxygen occur below large mainstem reservoirs, where hypolimnetic anoxia during summer stratified periods leads to subsaturated dissolved oxygen concentrations immediately below their dams (NRC 2004).

Upper river reaches below Upper Klamath Lake have total phosphorus (TP) and total nitrogen (TN) concentrations three to five times higher than those in the lower reaches in both winter and summer (see Box 33.3 Figure 1). Concentrations of inorganic nitrogen (ammonium, nitrite, nitrate) and phosphorus (orthophosphate), and dissolved and particulate organic carbon, are likewise higher in the upper basin and diminish downstream, although local deviations can occur. Reservoir impacts on river nutrient levels also are evident (Kann and Asarian 2005, Asarian et al. 2010), but their effects are modest relative to the landscape-scale nutrient changes from the upper basin to the estuary.

PERIPHYTON assemblages and aquatic macroinvertebrate distributions reflect these water quality conditions. During spring, nutrients support a wide range

have inadvertently damaged sensitive habitats. For example, when beaver dams were removed from a stream flowing into Lake Tahoe to promote the spawning migrations of introduced Kokanee salmon, stream phosphorus concentrations doubled (Muskopf 2007).

The North American river otter (*Lontra canadensis*), also once prized for its pelt, is recovering its position as the top carnivore of California's rivers as populations rebound (Black 2009). River otters are highly mobile, commonly moving > 4 km d^{-1}, with some tracked individuals moving up to 42 km d^{-1} (Melquist and Hornocker 1983). In coastal California, river otters move among freshwater, brackish, and marine habitats, feeding mainly on fish and crayfish (including non-native taxa), as well as on crabs, amphibians, insects, and birds (Grenfell 1974, Penland and Black 2009). In winter, when waterfowl migrate along the Pacific flyway, ducks and coots can make up 21% of otter diets (Cosby 2013). In the Klamath, southern Cascades, and Sierra Nevada mountain ranges, river otters occur above 3,000 meters; however, it is not clear if their occurrence at high elevations is a result of recent expansion into waters now inhabited by non-native fish and crayfish (Garwood et al. 2013).

of benthic eutrophic diatoms, but by late summer, nitrogen limitation in the lower river favors diatoms like *Epithemia sorex* that have nitrogen-fixing ENDOSYMBIONTS. Macroinvertebrates are abundant, but have low diversity, in the upper reaches of the river and in the hydropower peaking reach (PacifiCorp 2004), with diversity increasing with distance downstream of Iron Gate Dam (Malakauskas and Wilzbach 2012). One macroinvertebrate of interest is the freshwater polychaete worm, *Manayunkia speciosa*, which acts as an intermediate host to two myxozoan parasites, *Parvicapsula minibicornis* and *Ceratonova shasta*, that are potentially lethal to salmonids in the Klamath (Bartholomew et al. 1997 and 2006, Stocking and Bartholomew 2007, Nichols et al. 2007, Wilzbach and Cummins 2009).

The Klamath's naturally eutrophic condition has left the basin particularly susceptible to additional impairment from human activities. A particular worry is climate change, which is expected to increase water temperatures by several degrees Celsius in tributary and mainstem reaches that already provide only marginal summer habitat for salmonids. Currently, efforts are under way to remove four mainstem hydropower dams to foster the recovery of anadromous fishes and improve water quality as part of a basinwide agreement among a wide range of stakeholders (KBRA 2010). Additional work is needed to define problems, pose solutions, and develop clear metrics for prioritizing actions, allocating resources, and measuring success. Interim, transitional, and long-term measures, including adaptive management programs, should be developed and implemented as responsible steps towards robustly balancing the needs of aquatic ecosystems, human cultures, and enterprises in this large, complex basin.

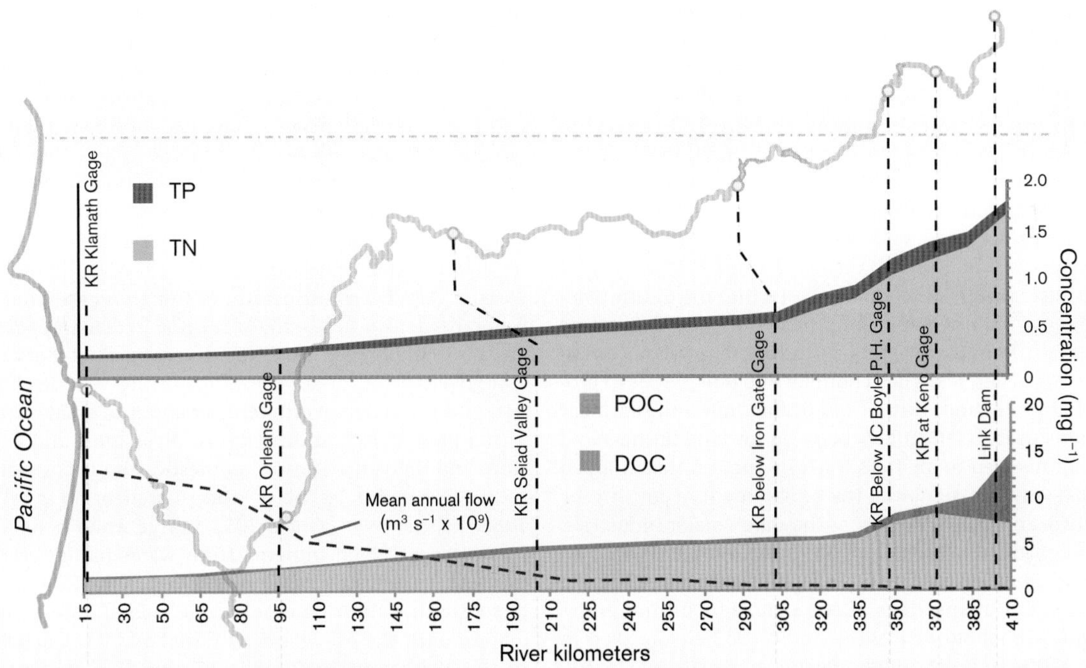

BOX 33.3 FIGURE 1 Summertime total nitrogen (TN, green), total phosphorus (TP, brown, top), and particulate (POC, brown, bottom) and dissolved organic carbon (DOC, blue) concentrations in the Klamath River, indicating higher concentrations in headwaters near Link Dam (RKM 400) and decreasing en route to the Pacific Ocean (RKM 0). Mean annual flow is shown as the dashed line in the lower graph. USGS Gage locations identified on map overlay. Klamath, Orleans, and Seiad Valley are communities; Iron Gate, J. C. Boyle, Keno, and Link are dams along the upper Klamath.

The Past and Alternative Futures of Californians and Their Rivers

Humans have had a long, intimate history with California's rivers and streams. For over twelve thousand years, these waterways have been corridors for human colonization, dispersal, and migration as well as sources of water, food, fiber, and shelter. Although early Native Californians attained a population size of more than three hundred thousand (Anderson 2005) by the time of European exploration and, in some cases, developed economies and cultures based on riverine resources (e.g., salmon in northern rivers), their environmental impacts were probably muted by their low densities and largely hunter-gatherer lifestyles (Fagan 2003; see Chapter 10, "Indigenous California"). Although the widespread use of low-intensity fire to manipulate forest structure, generate wildlife forage, and encourage useful plants may have affected river flows (Skinner and Chang 1996, Keeley 2002, Stephens et al. 2007, Lightfoot and Parrish 2009), these fires probably had much lower impacts on rivers than the severe wildfires of today (Verkaik et al. 2013). From 1769 to 1823 the Spaniards founded missions and conscripted Native Americans to build water-delivery systems, herd livestock, and farm arable land, with probable local impacts on streams. Spanish concessions and Mexican land grants dedicated large tracts to livestock grazing and introduced invasive European grasses and weeds, culminating in the Rancho period (1834–1849). Vegetation cover in catchments affects river conditions, and the conversion of California grasslands to domination by exotic plant species heavily grazed by cattle probably had many, although largely unstudied, impacts on river systems (Minnich 2008, Herbst et al. 2012, Cooper et al. 2013). At the same time, after depleting sea otter populations along the coast, Russian, English, and American fur traders and trappers exploited inland fur-bearers, greatly reducing or extirpating beaver, otters, mink, and other mammals in much of California (Lanman et al. 2012).

In 1848 the discovery of gold by James W. Marshall at Sutter's sawmill on the South Fork American River ushered in a new era of rapid economic growth and land development, shifting California from a bucolic backwater to an economic powerhouse (see Chapter 5, "Population and Land Use"). Over three hundred thousand people migrated to California in the first seven years of the Gold Rush, prospecting for gold deposits and providing the goods and services needed by miners. After depleting placer deposits in Sierra foothill stream beds, miners turned to hydraulic mining, spraying hillslopes with high-pressure jets of water and capturing runoff in sluices for gold separation. Miners denuded riparian zones of much of their timber and introduced massive amounts of sediment to rivers, with river beds, such as those in the American and Yuba Rivers, rising 10 to 30 meters (Mount 1995). Over 40 million cubic meters of sediment flowed into the Central Valley, clogging channels, blocking boat traffic, and flooding downstream floodplain farms. In response, lowland enterprises dredged and realigned channels and built levees to provide flood protection, further modifying flow and sediment conditions in rivers. Conflicts between lowland farmers and upland miners led to an 1884 court injunction that stopped hydraulic mining, signaling the replacement of mining by agriculture and timber harvest as the state's major industries.

Although the Great Flood of 1861 and 1862, followed by the drought of 1863 and 1864, devastated livestock herds and wheat farms in many parts of the state, agricultural enterprises quickly rebounded. Sheep and cattle herds peaked in the late 1800s and early 1900s, grazing most parts of California, while the expansion of row crop, orchard, and vineyard farming fueled agricultural prosperity. Private agricultural development, often based on irrigation from local surface and groundwater supplies, fostered irrigation colonies in southern California and later the Central Valley. Logging accelerated along the North Coast and later in the Sierra Nevada. All of these activities decreased or degraded river habitat for native aquatic biota by altering flow patterns and increasing erosion, sediment loading, and contaminant concentrations (Mount 1995, Cooper et al. 2013). These impacts on habitat, together with overfishing, destroyed commercial riverine fisheries such as the Chinook salmon fishery on the Sacramento River (Lichatowich 1999).

Even these nineteenth-century changes pale in comparison to the rearrangement of landscapes and waterscapes in the twentieth century. As California's human population has grown from about 1.5 million in 1900 to 38 million today, unfettered agricultural, urban, and industrial growth made California one of the ten largest economies in the world. To satisfy demands for wood, logging of private and federal lands in northern coastal California and the Sierra Nevada peaked by the 1940s and 1950s, destroying most of the old-growth forests. During the 1940s government agencies expanded rangelands using herbicides and fire. Although these practices have been discontinued, grazing still occurs on about half of the state's wildlands, and many of these areas are overgrazed (Mount 1995). Toxic runoff to river networks from nearly 2,500 abandoned mines persists (Domagalski et al. 2004, Kim et al. 2012, Davis et al. 2012). Mining of sand and gravel from river channels and floodplains increases erosion, alters channel morphology, and decreases riparian vegetation (Kondolf 1994, Downs et al. 2013). Despite mitigation measures now in place, many streams and rivers continue to be degraded by logging, grazing, and mining legacies or practices (Box 33.4).

The most massive impacts on rivers and streams in the twentieth century, however, came from the development of water and land resources to support agricultural and urban development (Kahrl 1979, Worster 1985, Mount 1995, Grace 2012). In the early 1900s, as local water supplies became inadequate to satisfy their demands, agricultural and urban interests looked further afield for water resources. Because private resources were not sufficient to construct and maintain storage and long-distance conveyance facilities, public initiatives came to the fore. Municipalities, such as the cities of Los Angeles and San Francisco, developed schemes to tap distant water sources, with Los Angeles completing the 375-kilometer Los Angeles aqueduct to the Owens Valley in 1913 and San Francisco completing the 269- kilometer Hetch Hetchy aqueduct to the Tuolumne River in 1934 (Figure 33.7). In 1928 the state legislature created the Metropolitan Water District (MWD), a consortium of fourteen cities and twelve water districts in southern California, to construct and operate the 389-kilometer Colorado River aqueduct. Both the federal government, under the terms of the 1902 Reclamation Act, and the state government set about to "make arid California bloom" by building dams, diversions, and canals to store and deliver irrigation, domestic, and industrial water, to provide hydroelectricity, and to control floods (Worster 1985, Reisner 1993, Grace 2012). Large water-delivery projects often received impetus from water panics created by drought. To deliver irrigation water from the Colorado River to southern California deserts, the federal Bureau of Reclamation built the All-American Canal and its Coachella spur in the 1940s and 1950s. The Bureau of Reclamation also built the Central Valley Project (CVP), a massive complex of dams, pumps, and canals, to store Sierra Nevada and Klamath Mountains runoff and ultimately divert it to farmlands in the Central Valley.

To circumvent restrictions on water supplied by federal reclamation projects and to serve more of southern California's water needs, the state approved the State Water Project (SWP) in 1960, subsequently constructing dams to collect Sierra Nevada meltwater and regulate downstream Sacramento flows to the northern Delta. The CVP and SWP have intake facilities just outside the southern Delta near Tracy that supply canals (Delta–Mendota Canal, California Aqueduct) that transport water to central and southern California. Although similar in design and now largely operated together, the CVP and SWP differ in their purposes, with the CVP serving agricultural developments and the SWP primarily serving urban interests (Kahrl 1979). Both projects turn an east-west flowing natural system, the Delta, into a north-south conveyance facility, creating many problems for the Delta's farms, fisheries, and ecosystems (Lund et al. 2008).

BOX 33.4 ENVIRONMENTAL CONTAMINANTS THROUGH A LONGITUDINAL CONTINUUM: THE SACRAMENTO–SAN JOAQUIN SYSTEM

The Sacramento and the San Joaquin are the largest rivers flowing entirely within California and provide water to most of the state. They face the most varied, complex, and difficult environmental problems in the region. Here we illustrate three ways that humans have affected inputs of sediment, heavy metals, pesticides, nutrients, and other contaminants, proceeding longitudinally from river headwaters in the Sierra Nevada to the rivers' mouth in the Sacramento–San Joaquin Delta.

High- and Mid-Elevation Sierra: Sediment and Nutrient Inputs from Logging, Livestock Grazing, and Fire

At mid- and high elevations in the Sierra Nevada, logging and livestock grazing have altered aquatic habitats and reduced native species by reducing or removing native vegetation, increasing runoff, erosion, and sediment inputs. Excessive deposition of fine sediment covers benthic organisms and food sources, reduces habitat heterogeneity, clogs gills, and fills interstitial pore spaces, reducing oxygen penetration and hence the survival of benthic organisms including salmonid fish eggs (Graber 1996, Kattelman 1996). Sediment inputs to streams in logged basins depend on the extent and intensity (selectivity) of timber removal, the disposition of slash and debris, and distance of these activities from streams. They can be reduced to some extent by the preservation of riparian buffer strips of adequate width (Newbold et al. 1980, Erman and Mahoney 1983, Mahoney and Erman 1984). In many cases, the roads, skid trails, and yarding areas associated with timber harvest have had larger effects on erosion and sediment deposition than the logging itself.

Sediment and nutrient inputs from cattle grazing accrue because cattle are attracted to streams and their riparian zones for shade, forage, and drink, where they trample and consume riparian vegetation, defecate and excrete nutrients, and compact soils and break down channel banks. Compaction and erosion by cattle can lead to channel incision and a lowering of the water table, desiccating riparian habitats. Streams heavily impacted by livestock often are wider, shallower, and clogged with fine sediment deposits, and they often have bare banks and low riparian shading and inputs. These changes have strong effects on stream algae, invertebrates, and vertebrates including salmonid populations (Knapp et al. 1998, Herbst and Silldorff 2006, Herbst and Blinn 2007). Reversing the effects of livestock on streams may require management on relatively large scales. For example, fencing livestock away from sections of stream, varying in length from several hundred to several thousand meters, had few effects on invertebrate communities, but removing livestock from large allotments restored natural invertebrate communities and diversity (Herbst et al. 2012).

Burned areas are another major source of sediment delivered to Sierran streams (Box 33.4 Figure 1). Although fires are widespread natural disturbances in California, their intensities and frequencies have changed due to human activities (Miller et al. 2009; see Chapter 3, "Fire as an Ecosystem Process"). By removing upland vegetation and altering soils, wildfires increase erosion and runoff, increasing loading of sediment and nutrients to streams (Jackson et al. 2012, Oliver et al. 2012). Catastrophic disturbances after fire, such as debris or mud slides and scouring floods, can have long-lasting effects on stream communities by removing or smothering most organisms in stream beds (Koetsier et al. 2010). Aquatic ecosystem recovery rates after fires can be prolonged in forested catchments, but faster in shrub or grassland habitats (Verkaik et al. 2013). In one study the geomorphology of drainage channels in forested Sierran catchments returned to prefire configurations within six years, but benthic macroinvertebrate diversity remained lower in burned than in unburned streams for up to seven to twenty-three years (Roby 1989). Although diversity can decline, the density of recolonizing species characterized by short life histories, small sizes, and high dispersal rates (i.e., midges, mayflies, blackflies) can be high. Where riparian vegetation has burned, algal-based food webs dominate, because of high nutrient and light levels, whereas streams with intact riparian vegetation have food webs based on terrestrial detritus, including higher abundances of shredders (Cooper et al. 2015, Verkaik et al. 2013). When macroinvertebrates proliferate postfire, they can provide a rich food supply for aquatic and riparian predators (e.g., fish, spiders, bats, birds) (Koetsier et al. 2007, Malison and Baxter 2010, Buchalski et al. 2013). Because low-severity prescribed fires that do not affect the riparian canopy have far fewer and shorter-lived effects (less than one year) on stream ecosystems (Stephens et al. 2004, Bêche et al. 2005), their increasing use may re-create some aspects of pre-European fire regimes and reduce fuel loads while protecting water quality.

(continued)

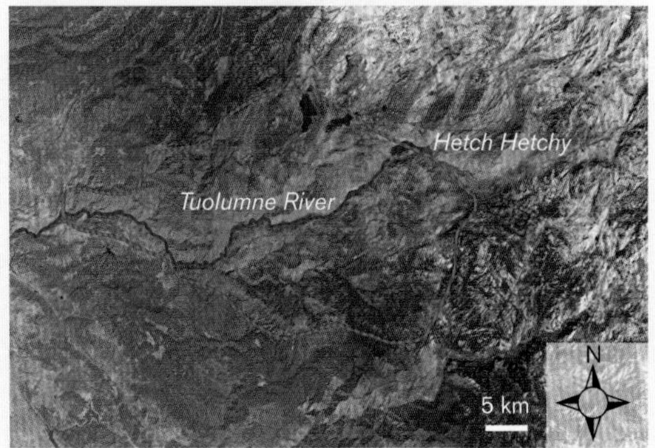

BOX 33.4 FIGURE 1: Satellite imagery of Rim Fire burn scar (red) encompassing the Tuolumne River from Hetch Hetchy to Don Pedro Reservoir (blue). Source: < http://www.nasa.gov/sites/default/files/california.a2013270.2105.721.250m_0.jpg>.

(Box 33.4 continued)

Sierra Foothills and Inner Coast Range: Heavy Metal Pollution

Legacy pollution from the California Gold Rush continues to affect the greater Sacramento River Basin. Hydraulic mining on the western slopes of the Sierra from 1853 to 1884 resulted in massive slope failures and sediment inputs, which smothered river beds (Box 33.4 Figure 2). Although these river channels have now returned to their natural forms, sediment deposits remain on terraces (Mount 1995). Eroding sediments and acid mine drainage from mine tailing piles deliver metals, such as copper, at concentrations high enough to alter the production, abundance, and composition of algal and invertebrate assemblages (Leland and Carter 1985, Leland et al. 1989). The exhumation and transport of mercury, in particular, has created widespread environmental problems (Alpers et al. 2005). Cinnabar ore (mercury sulfide, HgS) was mined in the Inner Coast Ranges and transported as liquid mercury to the Sierra Nevada for the recovery of gold. This enterprise transported more than 3 million kilograms of mercury to the northwestern Sierra (Domagalski 2001). Mercury (Hg), a potent neurotoxin, BIOACCUMULATES, increasing at each trophic level in aquatic and riparian food webs.

Periphyton in streams and rivers can BIOMAGNIFY mercury and methyl mercury (MeHg), which is converted from mercury by bacterial activity in environments with a high carbon supply and little or low oxygen levels (Bell and Scudder 2007, Moye et al. 2002). Near and downstream of abandoned cinnabar mines, tissue concentrations of mercury for insectivorous consumers, such as cliff swallows, are five to seven times greater than at reference sites (Hothem et al. 2008). Amphibians including the American bullfrog, which may be caught and consumed by humans, had concentrations above the U.S. Environmental Protection Agency's tissue residue criteria for fish (Hothem et al. 2010). In the floodplain wetlands of the Sacramento River, methyl mercury concentrations are highest where inundation is prolonged (Sacramento Slough) and where wetlands receive flow from Cache Creek (see Figure 33.5) that carries runoff from abandoned mercury mines (Domagalski et al. 2004). After the record

BOX 33.4 FIGURE 2 Water cannons at Malakoff Diggins used to erode sediment into sluice boxes for gold recovery. Mine tailings flowed into the South Yuba River. Photo: Courtesy of the Bancroft Library, UC Berkeley.

These large federal and state projects, combined with flood control and navigation projects completed by the Army Corps of Engineers and numerous other private and public water agencies, have massively changed the flow patterns, amounts, and paths of California's streams and rivers (Kahrl 1979, Worster 1985, Reisner 1993, Grace 2012). Water development projects in California, anchored by over fourteen hundred large dams, have captured nearly 60% of the state's runoff, engendering explosive agricultural and urban growth. Some of the largest components of this water system are the dams on the tributaries and mainstem of the Sacramento and San Joaquin Rivers, which store nearly 30 billion cubic meters of water and produce nearly 24 million megawatt-hours of power (see Figure 33.7). In general, dams inundate upstream areas, converting rivers to reservoirs; trap sediments; and in concert with the land use changes discussed earlier, dams have altered the hydrology, geomorphology, and chemistry of rivers and their riparian zones, often with deleterious effects on sen-

flood of January 1, 1997, concentrations of mercury were lower than expected in the water and sediments of Sacramento tributaries draining former gold-mining areas, perhaps because reservoirs on these rivers had trapped mercury-laden sediments and the mercury had then bioaccumulated in the tissues of reservoir organisms (Domagalski 2001). Mercury concentrations in game fish in reservoirs on the Yuba and Bear Rivers exceed levels considered safe for human consumption and potentially create neurotoxic effects in piscivorous mammals, such as otter and mink (Saiki et al. 2010, and references cited therein).

Central Valley Pesticides: Nutrient and Metal Contamination

Urbanization and agriculture on the Central Valley floor also deliver contaminants to fresh waters. Airborne pollutants generated in the Central Valley, including pesticides, have increased contaminant inputs to High Sierra waters with uncertain impacts on aquatic organisms (Cahill et al. 1996, Davidson and Knapp 2007, Bradford et al. 2011, 2013). Dust-borne phosphorus appears to have contributed to eutrophication and a shift from phosphorus to nitrogen limitation in High Sierra lakes (Vicars et al. 2010, Vicars and Sickman 2011). More locally, valley floor rivers receive pesticides in urban storm runoff at concentrations toxic to the aquatic biota (Weston and Lydy 2012). Wastewater effluent from urban areas in the watershed have augmented nutrient inputs to the Sacramento and San Joaquin Rivers (Jassby and Van Nieuwenhuyse 2005, Jassby 2008), stimulating problematic phytoplankton production downstream (Parker et al. 2012).

Interestingly, over the past fifty years, phytoplankton community dominance in the Sacramento River has shifted from a diverse diatom flora to small flagellates and green algae (Greenberg 1964, Parker et al. 2012 and references cited therein). The cities of Stockton and Sacramento are both under regulatory scrutiny as they install and implement new systems to reduce their considerable discharge loads to surface waters (California State Water Resources Control Board 2012). Research revealing the toxicity of PYRETHROIDS for aquatic invertebrates (Gan et al. 2008, Weston and Lydy 2012), and the widespread dissemination of antibiotics, endocrine disruptors (Colborn et al. 1993, PAN 2014), and other micropollutants, implicate urban and suburban Californians and their lawns and gardens as additional sources of harmful chemicals to aquatic habitats.

Because of extensive and intensive agriculture and water use in the San Joaquin Valley, most of the diminished flow in the lower San Joaquin River is agricultural return flow, laden with fertilizer residues, pesticides, herbicides, metals, and other potentially harmful chemicals. Some attempts to deal with environmental impacts created by polluted agricultural return flows have exacerbated the problem. For example, the Bureau of Reclamation (the Bureau) built the 137 kilometer San Luis Drain that in 1971 began delivering wastewater from areas served by the Westlands irrigation district to Kesterson Reservoir in the Kesterson National Wildlife Refuge, a migratory waterfowl refuge administered by the U.S. Fish and Wildlife Service (FWS) (Garone 2011). Drainage tiles were installed under 17,000 hectares of the Westlands service area in 1976 to collect water from saturated soils and contaminated agricultural return flows and channel it to the San Luis Drain. These subsurface waters became the primary contributors to Drain flows by 1981. From 1981 to 1985, federal agency personnel found high selenium concentrations in Kesterson waters, often far in excess of later-developed toxicity thresholds for this element (Wu 2004). In addition, they reported algal blooms and declines in emergent aquatic vegetation, fish, frogs, and waterfowl. Because selenium is incorporated into the tissues of plants and algae then bioaccumulates up the food chain, it often becomes most concentrated in top predators, like birds and fish (Hamilton 2004). Horribly deformed bird embryos associated with high selenium concentrations in tissue were observed at Kesterson (Ohlendrof et al. 1986, Wu 2004).

Because agricultural runoff is exempt from the provisions of the federal Clean Water Act, but not from the provisions of the state's Porter-Cologne Water Quality Control Act, it took the State Water Resources Control Board (SWRCB) to order the Bureau to remedy the environmental damage created by its actions. Under orders from the Department of Interior, which oversees both the FWS and Bureau, the San Luis Drain was closed and Kesterson Reservoir was sealed with a layer of soil to reduce wildlife exposure to selenium hazards (Garone 2011). With the tile drains now plugged, Westlands and other Valley agencies still suffer from soil waterlogging and salinization and have been testing mitigation measures, including drip irrigation, on-site evaporation ponds, HALOPHYTE planting to concentrate salts, and limited retirement of marginal farm lands (Garone 2011). The types of problems encountered at Kesterson now appear more ubiquitous than formerly thought, with high selenium concentrations in other parts of the western San Joaquin Valley and the Tulare Lake Basin as well as in the Salton Sea (Garone 2011, Saiki et al. 2012).

sitive native species and ecosystems (Sabo et al. 2012, Cooper et al. 2013). The direct manipulation of the water cycle through dams, canals, groundwater pumping, and interbasin transfers have devastated migratory and other sensitive species that rely on natural hydrologic cycles to survive and complete their life cycles, and have promoted the spread of alien species adapted to altered conditions (Lichatowich 1999, Moyle et al. 2008, Moyle et al. 2011, Alagona et al. 2012). Moyle et al. (2011) concluded that dams; alien species; and urban, agricultural, and industrial development were the major causes of the extensive loss of native fish species diversity in California (Box 33.5).

Concerns about human-caused damage to the environment provoked the environmental movement of the 1960s and 1970s. In the 1970s state and federal legislation—such as the Clean Water, Endangered Species (ESA), Wild and Scenic Rivers, National Environmental Policy, and California Environmental Quality Acts—inaugurated an era of increased

FIGURE 33.7 Major components of the California water storage and delivery system. Major rivers are shown with solid lines, aqueducts and canals as dashed lines, dams as bars, reservoirs as black bodies without outlines, and lakes as gray bodies outlined in black. Map by Parker Welch, Center for Integrated Spatial Research (CISR).

public awareness and governmental oversight of development activities that harmed natural resources, species, and ecosystems as well as remedies for their conservation. For example, after a decades-long legal battle, a 2006 settlement mandated the rewatering of the lower 150 mile-long San Joaquin channel as well as the construction of a conservation hatchery and reintroduction of Chinook salmon (Matthews 2007, NOAA 2013). Because of environmental concerns, increased construction costs, a scarcity of remaining sites appropriate for dams, and doubts about their economic benefits, large dams are no longer being built, although a number are proposed (e.g., Temperance Flat on the San Joaquin River) and some existing dams are slated for enlargement (e.g., Los Vaqueros, Shasta). The last large dam built in California was the New Melones Dam on the Stanislaus River in 1979. Furthermore, urban and environmental concerns during recent droughts have challenged agriculture's dominance as a user of the state's water resources. Although agriculture currently represents a small proportion of the California economy, it uses most of the state's water. Although many citizens and nongovernmental organizations agitate for the protection or restoration of natural ecosystems, and many governmental agencies are charged with monitoring and enforcing environmental laws, the legacy of massive rearrangements of waterways and landscapes in California has created overwhelming challenges for the state's rivers and their biota.

BOX 33.5 THE STEELHEAD: A DWINDLING ICONIC SPECIES IN COASTAL CENTRAL AND SOUTHERN CALIFORNIA

Steelhead (*Oncorhynchus mykiss*) precariously persist in the streams and rivers of coastal southern and central California, a region with a benign climate punctuated by catastrophic earthquakes, fires, floods, landslides, and droughts. Geologic faults, including the San Andreas fault on its eastern border, and steep coastal mountains bordered by marine terraces and coastal floodplains characterize the region's geography (Faber et al. 1989, Norris and Webb 1990, Keeley et al. 2012). Short streams drain coastal mountains, whereas longer rivers drain inland areas and flow to the sea through mountain gaps (e.g., Pajaro, Salinas, Santa Maria, Santa Ynez, Santa Clara) or large alluvial floodplains (Los Angeles, San Gabriel, Santa Ana). This topography and latitudinal range have produced strong gradients in rainfall and river flow that typically increase with increasing elevation and latitude and decrease with distance from the coast.

Because of large seasonal and interannual variation in rainfall, driven by large-scale climatic cycles (e.g., EL NIÑO/SOUTHERN OSCILLATION, PACIFIC DECADAL OSCILLATION cycles; see Chapter 2, "Climate") and steep terrain, flow regimes vary from catastrophic winter floods to summer desiccation, when many alluvial, southern, or inland reaches become intermittent or dry completely. These flow regimes also affect the estuaries at the mouths of streams and rivers, which range from conduits for strong winter floods to intermittently closed lagoons separated from the ocean by sand berms during the dry season, sometimes for prolonged periods during dry years (Jacobs et al. 2011, Rich and Keller 2013). Against this extremely dynamic backdrop, the steelhead has maintained populations for thousands of years due to flexibility in its behavior, life history, and physiological tolerances. The steelhead has a complex (nonobligate) anadromous life history, maturing in the ocean, ascending rivers during winter flood flows to spawn in mainstem reaches or tributaries, then developing as juveniles in streams over one to three years (usually two). At the end of their stream residence, juveniles undergo physiological and morphological changes (smoltification), usually in late winter or spring, that allow them to survive in the ocean. The smolts then migrate to the sea where they develop for one to four years (usually two) before returning to rivers as migrating spawners (Moyle 2002, Quinn 2005, Quinn and Meyers 2005, Boughton et al. 2006). Individual steelhead show many variations in life history. Some fish show the typical two-year freshwater, two-year marine cycle; some spend substantial time as juveniles in estuaries, where they grow faster and larger, enhancing their survival in the ocean; and some individuals (usually called rainbow trout) spend their entire lives in streams (Hayes et al. 2011, Kern and Sogard 2013, NMFS 2012, NMFS 2013).

Some studies report that resident fish can produce anadromous offspring and vice-versa, but the conditions and frequency under which this occurs may vary between populations and require more research (Thrower et al. 2004, 2008, Olsen et al. 2006, Christie et al. 2011, Hayes et al. 2012, but see Zimmerman and Reeves 2000, Pearse et al. 2009). Their remarkable life history variation can buffer steelhead populations from environmental change, for example, by allowing populations to persist as residents where downstream migration is blocked by drying or migration barriers or by allowing upstream areas decimated by severe floods or fires to be repopulated by anadromous fish (Bell et al. 2011, Thorson et al. 2013). Because adult anadromous steelhead are much larger and more fecund than resident forms, they have the potential to disproportionately augment upstream populations where their passage to the sea is maintained.

Steelhead exist near the southern limits of their range in southern California. The native populations occurring in this region have a variety of distinctive behavioral, physiological, and genetic traits warranting their designation as distinct population segments (DPSs) by the NATIONAL MARINE FISHERIES SERVICE (NMFS 2012, 2013). Because of large, interannual variation in lagoon sand berm breaching, some steelhead spawners do not have access in dry years to their natal streams, where they typically spawn, so they can disperse to nearby streams where adequate flows allow access (Boughton et al. 2006, Clemento et al. 2009, Bell et al. 2011, Jacobs et al. 2011). Steelhead populations in this region also show unusual tolerances to low flow, high temperatures, and low oxygen levels, with juveniles often oversummering in isolated or semi-isolated pools with temperatures sometimes exceeding 25°C (occasionally approaching 30°C) and oxygen levels occasionally dropping to <3 mg/L, outside tolerances reported for steelhead in other regions (Carter 2005, Richter and Kolmes 2005, Spina et al. 2005, Spina 2007, Bell et al. 2011, Sloat and Osterback 2013, S. Cooper personal communication). Furthermore, steelhead in this region are adept at seeking out cold water seeps or pockets with more suitable temperature conditions (Matthews and Berg 1997).

Despite this array of adaptations for dealing with a variable and sometimes harsh environment, widespread land conversion and water developments in this region have reduced steelhead from historical runs in the tens of thousands to current runs that amount to a few individuals (probably less than one thousand anadromous individuals regionwide) (Moyle et al. 2008, Moyle et al. 2011, Alagona et al. 2012, NMFS 2012, 2013) (Box 33.5 Figure 1). The extensive construction of dams, in particular, has blocked steelhead migrations, isolated upstream landlocked *O. mykiss* from downstream migrant populations, and altered downstream flow regimes, sometimes producing inadequate flows to breach lagoon sand berms, to provide adequate depths for spawner migrations, or to support juvenile rearing habitat (Boughton et al. 2006, Moyle et al. 2011, Petts and Grunell 2013). Numerous water diversions and intensive groundwater pumping also have dewatered channels and many rivers have been channelized for flood

(continued)

control, destroying the complex habitats, cover, and food sources required by juvenile steelhead (McEwan and Jackson 2003, Hunt & Associates 2008a, Hunt & Associates 2008b, Kier Associates and NMFS 2008).

These water structures were built to serve extensive agricultural, urban, and industrial development, which itself has changed water and chemical cycles, engendering flashier hydrographs with higher flood peaks, lower base flows, simplified stream morphologies, altered shading, and increased nutrient and pollutant loading and temperatures, with many repercussions for steelhead and the food webs that support them (Paul and Meyer 2001, Allan 2004, Ackerman and Schiff 2003, Mazor and Schiff 2008, Cooper et al. 2013). Flood control activities, including the construction and maintenance of debris dams to trap sediments, stream channelization, and clearance of in-stream and riparian vegetation often block steelhead migrations and degrade habitat (NMFS 2012).

Further, urban and agricultural development and gravel and sand mining have directly destroyed or degraded important steelhead habitat, such as estuaries and stream channels, through infilling, dredging, paving, construction, and/or the diversion of flows through pipes or tunnels (Ferren et al. 1995, Ferren et al. 1996, Kier and Associates and NMFS 2008, Grossinger et al. 2011). Although dams and diversions decrease downstream flows in some cases, depending on the time of year and operational schedules, many urban rivers of southern California have increased flows throughout the year compared to historical times. This is due to increased runoff from impervious surfaces in the wet season and return flows of water imported from other parts of the state (Delta, Colorado River, Owens Valley) for irrigation, industrial, and domestic uses in the dry season (White and Greer 2006, Townsend-Small et al. 2013). In some cases, waste water treatment plants supply most of the flow in the lower reaches of southern California's rivers in the dry season (Spina et al. 2005, Lyon and Sutula 2011). They can produce effluent water laden with nutrients, producing algal blooms that decrease oxygen at night to levels potentially harmful to steelhead (Klose et al. 2012).

Increased flows in these rivers have not enhanced steelhead stocks because existing channels do not have the complexity, cool temperatures, riparian inputs, cover, depths, or high water quality needed to support steelhead. Further, these modifications to flow regimes (dams, more perennial flows) often promote the introduction and spread of exotic fish species, which may prey on or compete with steelhead (Riley et al. 2005, Marchetti et al. 2006, Cucherousset and Olden 2011). Irrigation return flows in agricultural areas, such as those along the Pajaro, Salinas, Arroyo Grande, Santa Maria, Santa Ynez, and Santa Clara Rivers, and urban runoff in rivers such as the Los Angeles, San Gabriel, and Santa Ana can carry high loads of herbicides, pesticides, metals, oil residues, nutrients, hormones, antibiotics, and other contaminants with potential lethal and sublethal effects on aquatic life (Ackerman and Schiff 2003, Moeller et al. 2003, Busse et al. 2006, Macneale et al. 2010, Cooper et al. 2013, Sengupta et al. 2014). Many of these stresses are exacerbated in estuaries, which become downstream sumps for contaminants originating in their watersheds.

The expansion of human populations into wildland areas has increased the incidence of wildfires, which can extirpate steelhead from some reaches via accidental drops of toxic fire retardants, extreme scouring flood flows, and sediment deposition from erosion and landslides. Subsequent steelhead recolonization can then be blocked by stream barriers (dams, road crossings) (Kier and Associates and NMFS 2008, Verkaik et al. 2013). Although the California Department of Fish and Wildlife has restricted angling for listed steelhead, it still continues to stock reservoirs in this region with hatchery strains of this species (California Department of Fish and Wildlife and U.S. Fish and Wildlife Service 2010, California Department of Fish and Wildlife 2013). Genetic studies have established that hatchery

BOX 33.5 FIGURE 1 What has been lost? 1946 catch of steelhead from the Ventura River at Foster Park. Angler: John B. Colla. Photo: Robert Phelan.

stocks generally do not interbreed with native stocks (Nielsen et al. 1994, Girman and Garza 2006, Clemento et al. 2009), but concerns exist about competition with or the introduction of disease by hatchery strains.

Given all the human impacts on steelhead stocks in central and southern California, near their southern range limits where their existence was already precarious, is there hope for their restoration? Because of their unique characteristics and the numerous threats to their continued existence, NMFS designated the south-central California steelhead, ranging from the Pajaro River to Arroyo Grande Creek, as threatened and the southern California steelhead, ranging from the Santa Maria River to the U.S.-Mexico border, as endangered under the U.S. Endangered Species Act. In their recovery plans for these steelhead stocks, NMFS called for a variety of measures to protect and restore key populations, including fish passage structures around dams, removal of barriers, water regulation to ensure adequate flows for spawning migrations and nursery and rearing habitat, improvements in water quality, appropriate fuel and fire management, and restoration of in-stream and riparian habitat (NMFS 2012, 2013). Extensive research and monitoring plans assessed the changing status of the species and addressed unanswered questions regarding the species' life history and relationships between anadromous and resident *O. mykiss* (NMFS 2012, 2013). Fish passage facilities around dams and dam removal are promising because many headwater streams on federal lands in this region support resident steelhead (trout) populations (Bell 1978, O'Brien et al. 2011, NMFS 2012, NMFS 2013). Steelhead populations above and below dams are more closely related to each other than to those in other watersheds (Clemento et al. 2009), indicating that effectively reconnecting upstream and downstream populations could rehabilitate anadromous runs.

Currently, however, it is not clear that the few fish passage facilities that have been installed (e.g., around the Ventura River's Robles Dam and the Santa Clara River's Freeman Diversion Dam) are effective for both adult and juvenile migration. Plans to remove dams, such as Matilija Dam on a tributary of the Ventura River and Rindge Dam on Malibu Creek, have foundered on problems associated with the disposal of trapped reservoir sediment and concerns about impacts on downstream resources; however, the removal of San Clemente Dam on the Carmel River has begun (Capelli 1999, 2004, 2007). Recent hearings before the State Water Resources Control Board (e.g., over releases from Bradbury Dam on the Santa Ynez River) indicate that agencies are struggling to find a balance between in-stream and off-stream uses of water, particularly while considering natural resources like steelhead that are protected under California's Public Trust Doctrine. Although the State Water Resources and Regional Water Quality Control Boards have set standards and identified impaired water bodies in this region (California State Water Resources Control Board 2007a, 2007b, 2007c, 2007d), the process of setting total daily maximum load (TMDL) targets for contaminants and permitting effluent discharges from waste water treatment plants and other point sources takes many years. This has produced a large backlog of cases without addressing large contaminant loads resulting from nonpoint sources.

In short, threats to steelhead continue to grow, solutions remain elusive, basic ecological data are lacking, and many governmental agencies work at cross-purposes. Competing interests among private citizens, nongovernment groups, and a variety of government agencies over river resources in this region are likely to grow with climate and land use change. Expected increases in droughts, wildfires, sea level, storm intensity, and human population size will increase human demands for water, flood control, and coastal protection to the detriment of protecting and restoring river and estuarine ecosystems and their native biotas and natural ecological processes (Keeley et al. 2012, NMFS 2012, NMFS 2013). Further, warming water may push southern steelhead to their lethal limits, with weakened steelhead being more prone to disease.

A note of hope involves the efforts of government agencies and citizens' groups to restore river habitat and protect steelhead. For example, the City of San Luis Obispo has restored the reach of San Luis Obispo Creek passing through the heart of the city, and The Ojai Land Conservancy has acquired a large portion of the Ventura River and established the first Southern California Steelhead Preserve. Many citizens' groups have adopted particular rivers to promote their environmental qualities, expand outdoor education, and protect and restore natural resources. For example, although the Los Angeles River has been called the largest storm drain in the world with 80% of its channel paved, the FRIENDS OF THE LOS ANGELES RIVER (FOLAR) are working to restore habitat, develop recreational facilities, modify flood control practices, educate students and the public, coordinate cleanup efforts, improve water quality, participate in planning, and influence policy to better steward this river's natural and historical amenities (Gumprecht 1999). These local-scale efforts need to be better complemented by basinwide planning and management efforts to ensure adequate flows for native species and to reduce contaminant inputs (Bernhardt and Palmer 2007, 2011).

It is a testament to the steelhead's natural resilience that this species continues to persist in central and southern California, given the numerous natural and human threats it has faced. They represent precious genetic resources for maintaining salmonids in a warming world (IPCC 2014a, 2014b). Concerted, coordinated research and data-driven action by private citizens, environmental groups, and governmental agencies at all levels are needed to prevent this natural treasure from becoming an environmental tragedy.

The future of California's rivers is inextricably linked to climate change. Climate models project warming of streams and rivers, earlier peak flows, more prolonged or lower summer base flows, and autumnal and winter discharge peaks due to increased rain and rain-on-snow events, the latter associated with "pineapple express" storms (Singer 2007, Dettinger et al. 2009, Dettinger 2011, Weller et al. 2012). Hydrologic models further predict that overall river discharge will decline with increasing temperature, with more pronounced changes in the northern than the southern Sierra (Null et al. 2010). Many Sierran glaciers are expected to melt away within the next 50 to 250 years, removing water supplies during dry periods for high-elevation streams and lowland valleys (Basagic and Fountain 2011, Stock and Anderson 2012). Changes in water temperature and in the timing, duration, and magnitude of floods and droughts are likely to alter habitats and elevational distributions of organisms, challenge cold-water taxa, and shift the composition of communities (Herbst and Cooper 2010, Herbst 2013, Kadir et al. 2013). Over 80% of California's native fishes could be extinct in one hundred years if present climate trends continue (Moyle et al. 2013). Climate change also will increase human demands for water, and more calls for storing and transporting water will likely intensify competition among interest groups for increasingly limited, variable, and altered water supplies.

As a final example of California's water problems, we turn to the Sacramento–San Joaquin Delta, which is both the linchpin for California's largest water projects (CVP, SWP) and a complex agricultural, wetland, and aquatic ecosystem supporting high biodiversity and productive farms. The Delta receives half of the state's runoff, drains over 40% of the state's land area, and has been radically altered by diking and draining, island (polder) subsidence, pollution, local and regional development, upstream dams and diversions, and the introduction of many alien species (Lund et al. 2008, Whipple et al. 2012, Alagona 2013; see also Chapter 19, "Estuaries: Life on the Edge"). Water quality deteriorates as it flows from the Sacramento River through the Delta, and federal and state water agencies have faced the challenge of delivering large quantities of high-quality water from the Sacramento River in the north to intake systems for the Central Valley and State Water Projects near Tracy in the south. Past proposals to divert Sacramento water around the Delta to the Tracy intakes were opposed by groups who believed that such developments would harm the Delta's remaining wetlands, rich agricultural areas, and endemic species, such as the endangered Delta smelt, while damaging northern California ecosystems and economies to benefit primarily southern California (Lund et al. 2008, Alagona 2013).

Droughts exacerbate such conflicts, preventing the CVP and SWP from meeting their contractual water deliveries while creating conspicuous environmental impacts (e.g., saline intrusion, reduced fish habitat). Attempts to develop coordinated state, federal, and private actions to deal with the Delta's water and environmental problems, such as the CALFED Bay-Delta Program, have made little progress due to political, organizational, and funding problems (Little Hoover Commission 2005, Legislative Analyst's Office 2006, Hanemann and Dyckman 2009, Alagona 2013). The rapid decline of the Delta's pelagic fish and invertebrates and subsequent lawsuits under the ESA led to court orders to shut down the Tracy pumps for short periods, exacerbating conflicts between environmental groups and development, agricultural, and urban interests. The state Delta Reform Act of 2009 addressed wetland restoration, protections for listed species, the repair of aging levees, and new conveyances to ensure the quality and reliability of water supplies for users. Nevertheless, detailed proposals to carry Sacramento water to Tracy via tunnels or canals, even with associated environmental protection and restoration programs, have reignited concerns about the environmental and economic impacts of rerouting Delta flows.

Are there solutions to the ecological problems of California's rivers generated by water development and land use changes? Environmental laws and industry regulation have led to management changes and reduced sediment and pollutant loading to some streams and rivers, and some upland and riparian zones have been preserved or restored. Selective and/or rotational logging and changes in harvest practices (e.g., yarding methods) in the timber industry; rotational grazing and changes in the intensity (number of animals), duration, and timing of livestock grazing allotments; and preservation of riparian buffer strips also have helped to reduce environmental damage to streams (Erman and Mahoney 1983, Herbst et al. 2012). Some of the legacy and current effects of mining have been reduced by remediation practices and controls on sand and gravel mining (Kondolf 1994, Davis et al. 2012). Local zoning restrictions and regional water constraints can also affect the patterns and extent of urban and agricultural development and associated water use, although the effectiveness of these measures varies widely and is often challenged by development interests. The state's water quality is overseen by the State Water Resources Control Board, which through its regional boards aims to meet the provisions of the Clean Water Act by setting standards, identifying impaired waters, developing TOTAL MAXIMUM DAILY LOAD (TMDL) allocations for pollutants, and regulating pollutant discharge (http://www.waterboards.ca.gov/water_issues/programs/tmdl/).

Although new developments are subject to environmental review under federal and state laws (e.g., the California Environmental Quality Act [CEQA]), it is often difficult to mitigate environmental damage legacies from past developments. An exception is the process used to renew hydropower dams operating under thirty- to fifty-year licenses from the Federal Energy Regulatory Commission. In California, where hydropower accounts for approximately half of all renewable energy generation in the state (U.S. Energy Information Administration, Annual Energy Outlook 2013), approximately fifty multidam licenses were scheduled for review and renewal between 2005 and 2020 (Rehn 2009). This relicensing process provides one of the only formal opportunities to evaluate the effects of flow schedules on river ecosystems and reconfigure dam operations to achieve conservation goals. Recent court decisions have demonstrated that the California Department of Fish and Wildlife has considerable statutory authority to improve flows for fish below dams (Bork et al. 2012), as does the State Water Resources Control Board in regulating water allocations and dam operations. Other biota besides fish also are now being considered (Kupferberg et al. 2012).

Considerable recent attention has focused on the operations of dams to achieve environmental objectives. The native riverine biota of California, as in much of western North America, has had a long evolutionary history with extreme hydrology, characterized by large seasonal and interannual variation in discharge including megafloods and droughts (Moyle 2002, Waples et al. 2008). Over the long term, hydrologic variation and extreme events can enrich ecosystems and diversify habitat structure (Waples et al. 2009). As a consequence, many river scientists have postulated that native riverine species and diversity can be restored by operating dams to mimic natural hydrologic regimes (Waples et al. 2008, Poff and Zimmerman 2010). Although it could be impossible to replicate natural flow variation while meeting human water demands, it could be possible to operate dams to produce some seasonal flow characteristics required by critical life history stages (Kiernan et al. 2012, Kupferberg et al. 2012). In some cases, dams have outlived their usefulness while prolonging environmental damage, leading to calls for their removal (e.g., Searles Dam on San Francisquito Creek; Matilija Dam on Matilija Creek, a tributary to the Ventura River). The largest such demolition project in California history is currently under way on the Carmel River, where the seismically unsafe San Clemente Dam is being removed (http://www.sanclementedamremoval.org/). Because of sediment stored behind dams, however, dam removal has to be done carefully to minimize impacts on downstream areas (Stanley and Doyle 2003). Discontinuing water diversions could also recreate natural conditions that support natural communities.

Stream and river restoration has become a focus for many governmental agencies and environmental groups. By reestablishing more natural stream contours, planting native vegetation, removing exotic plant and animal species, providing passage for migratory species, reestablishing historical flow regimes, and instituting sediment and contaminant controls, restoration projects can rebuild ecosystems more hospitable for native species. Most current restoration projects lack follow-up studies to measure their effectiveness and are too small in scale (e.g., in short reaches) or with too little water to be effective (Bernhardt et al. 2005, Palmer et al. 2005, Kondolf et al. 2007, Bernhardt and Palmer 2011). Nevertheless, some effective river restoration efforts have been well documented. One example is the reestablishment of the native fish fauna in Putah Creek, a tributary to the Sacramento flowing through the Yolo Bypass (Kiernan et al. 2012). After 32 kilometers of the creek was dewatered in 1989, a lawsuit and subsequent court order mandated releases of water from Lake Berryesa / Monticello Dam to feed the creek. Flow was manipulated to provide sufficient water for spring spawning species to reestablish and to allow Chinook salmon to migrate upstream from the Yolo bypass. Native fish now numerically dominate > 20 kilometers of this reach, compared to < 2 kilometers under the old regime.

Another particularly heartening example is the restoration of Big Springs Creek, a tributary to the Shasta River in the Klamath basin. Despite contributing less than 1% of the Klamath's mean annual flow at the estuary, the Shasta River historically produced roughly half of the Chinook salmon in the lower Klamath River watershed because of cool spring flows that feed the Shasta River from Big Springs Creek (Wales 1951, NRC 2004). Poor land management practices degraded the area around Big Springs Creek, increasing daily maximum water temperatures from 11°C near the creek source to over 25°C in just 3.5 kilometers, and restricting oversummering anadromous salmonids to only about 10 meters at the head of the creek (Jeffres et al. 2009). In 2008 the Nature Conservancy purchased lands adjacent to Big Springs Creek and the Shasta River and initiated active restoration. Today, anadromous salmon again oversummer down the entire length of Big Springs Creek as well as in several kilometers of the downstream Shasta River (Nichols et al. 2013).

Lowland river floodplains are particularly promising foci for future restoration efforts. Once teeming with rich communities of native species including juveniles of valued fish, active river floodplains have been largely lost or degraded by urban and agricultural development. Originally, floodwaters in Central Valley rivers would spill over natural levees onto extensive floodplains. Flows are now diverted into canals or channels, and floodplains drained and converted to agriculture. One of the few exceptions is the 24,000 hectare Yolo bypass basin (Figure 33.8) that floods annually when the Sacramento River overtops the Fremont Weir, a 2-mile long concrete structure (Sommer et al. 2005). Because the Yolo basin has natural flood cycles, it supports fifteen native fish species and twenty-seven non-native taxa, providing appropriate seasonal habitats for several species of special concern including a recently delisted species, the cyprinid splittail (*Pogonichthys macrolepidotus*) and runs of Chinook salmon (Sommer, Harrell et al. 2001; Sommer, Nobriga et al. 2001; Feyrer et al. 2006). A complex Bay Delta Conservation Plan is under development (CALFED 2005, Mount et al. 2013). Recommendations to enhance the Yolo basin's floodplain function include placing notches or gates in the Fremont Weir to improve fish passage. Lowering the height of the weir would increase the frequency and duration of inundation, expanding the area of flooded agricultural fields. A challenging mix of grassroots environmental activism, landowner input, evolving frameworks of governance and management, and scientific research is under way to expand the successes of floodplain restoration, while addressing the economic costs of lost agricultural revenues (Salcido 2012, Howitt et al. 2013).

California's central water problem—that most of the state's precipitation falls in the north but most of its water is consumed in the central and southern regions—was addressed with the construction of one of the largest water storage and delivery systems in the world. The California water system has been vital to the state's economy but has had profound and far-ranging effects on its landscapes, waterscapes, and ecosystems. Revised dam operations or removal, the integrated management of ground and surface waters, the preservation of sensitive habitats (e.g., cold water streams, springs, oases) and species, and management practices tailored to California's unique array of freshwater ecosystems can all help to address environmental concerns (Moyle 2013). At base, however, there simply is not enough high-quality freshwater to serve all of the state's projected economic and environmental needs. This is particularly true given the current use of subsidized water by agricultural interests. Even along the relatively well-watered North Coast, rivers are overtaxed by summer withdrawals and drought and have approached thresholds at which they may flip between salmon-supporting and cyanobacterially degraded ecosystems (see Box 33.1). Some water conflicts could be reduced by conservation and recycling measures, a shift to more efficient, unsubsidized water pricing, and transfer of water contracts from low- to high-value uses (Gleick et al. 1995). Rising sea levels, altered fire intensities and frequencies, and climate change and human uses that alter hydrological cycles and thermal regimes will have many repercussions for rivers and the natural and human ecosystems they support (Hayhoe et al. 2004, Kadir et al. 2013). Native Californian cultures endured and survived droughts and megafloods as severe as those predicted to recur over the years and decades ahead (Ingram and Malamud-Roam 2013). Modern Californians will require similar adaptability, flexibility, tenacity, and

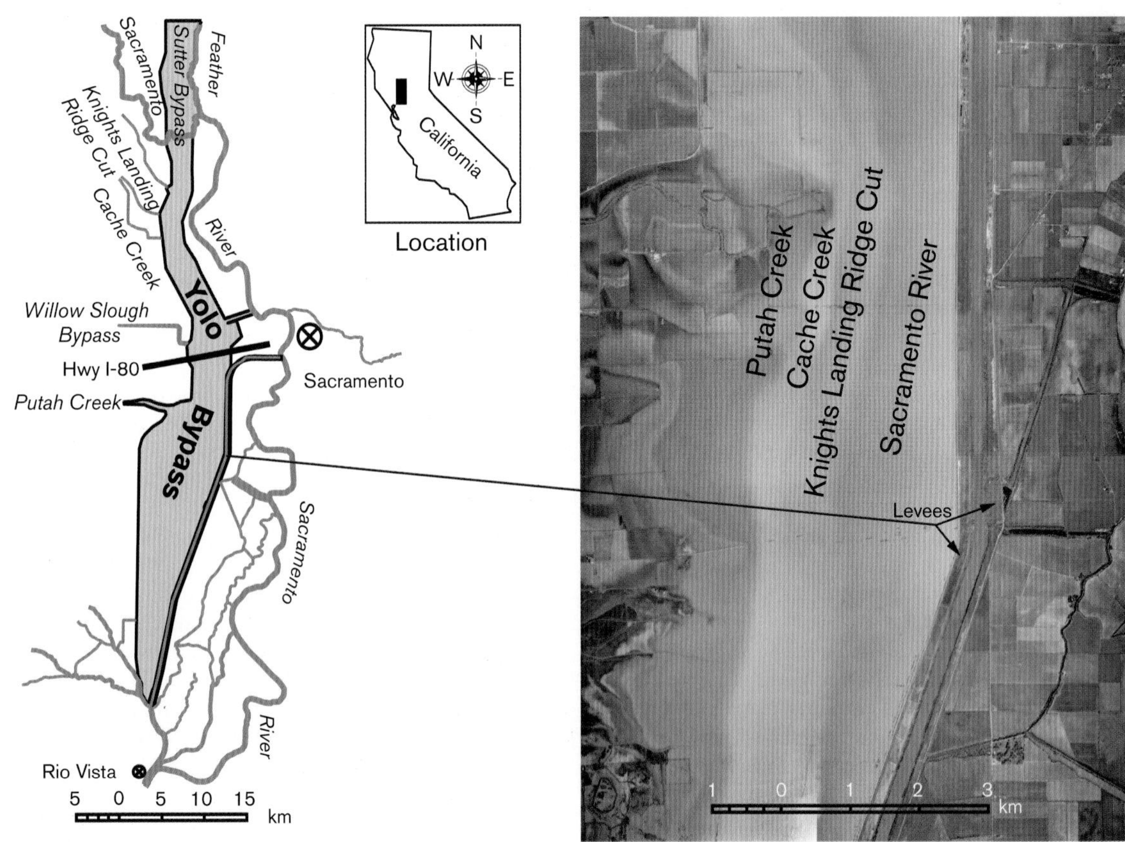

FIGURE 33.8 Schematic map and high-resolution photomosaic of the central 10 kilometers of the Yolo Bypass during a March 1998 flood event. Source: With permission from Sommer et al. 2008.

ingenuity, as well as a shift in values toward (in Wallace Stegner's phrase) "making a living not a killing" within our home watersheds.

Summary

California's river networks harbor diverse ecosystems due to their large latitudinal range and extreme topographic and geologic heterogeneity. California's sixty major and more than a thousand smaller river drainages contrast sharply in annual precipitation, from >500 cm y^{-1} in the northwest corner of the state to <5 cm y^{-1} in the southeast corner in the Colorado Desert. Coastal Californian rivers, watered by rain from Pacific storms, experience Mediterranean seasonality with almost all precipitation falling during the cool winter months and with summer droughts. Rivers of interior basins fed mainly from snowmelt have large spring flows that diminish through the summer. The native riverine biota has adapted behaviorally, morphologically, and physiologically to these seasonal rhythms and to "deluge or drought" year-to-year hydrologic variation, including superfloods and megadroughts that have occurred over centuries and millennia in this region. Repeatedly, human alterations have suppressed and rearranged this flow variation, creating more of a threat to the native flora and fauna of California's rivers than extreme natural variation to which the biota has adapted.

In "one of the most massive re-arrangements of Nature ever attempted" (Kahrl et al. 1979), humans during the nineteenth and twentieth centuries have subdued, diverted, and harnessed California's rivers, transforming them into the largest plumbing system in the world and managing it for flood protection, water storage and diversion to irrigate crops, supply urban areas, and generate electricity. Although early logging, grazing, and mining damaged river watersheds and channel networks, the most massive impacts on rivers and streams came from development of water and land resources to support agricultural and urban growth. Despite increasing demands on water supplies, encouraging cases of river restoration and improved stewardship are building on the natural resilience of some riverine landscapes and their biotas. The future of California's rivers, however, is inextricably linked to climate change and intensifying land use. Climate models project warming of streams and rivers, earlier peak flows, more prolonged or lower summer base flows, and autumnal and winter discharge peaks due to increased rain and rain-on-snow events—the latter associated with atmospheric rivers. Climate change will increase human demands for water, intensifying competition between interest groups and natural ecosystems for increasingly limited, variable, and compromised water supplies. Using the Eel, the Klamath, and the Sacramento–San Joaquin River systems as well as rivers draining the central and southern California coast, we discuss the adaptations of the native biota to variation through seasons, across years, and from headwaters to mouth. This chapter emphasizes that the state's rivers are among the most dynamic, critical, altered, and vulnerable components of California's ecosystems.

Acknowledgments

We thank Peter Moyle for an extremely helpful review; Sheila Wiseman, Carson Jeffres, Mimi Chapin, Kurt Fesenmyer of Trout Unlimited, and Kirk Klausmeyer and Jeanette Howard of The Nature Conservancy for assistance with and contributions of figures; the University of California's Natural Reserve System for providing protected sites for decades of river research; and the Eel River Critical Zone Observatory (National Science Foundation SGP 1331940) and the Santa Barbara Coastal Long Term Ecological Research Project (part of the NSF LTER network) for support.

Recommended Reading

Mount, J. F. 1995. California rivers and streams—the conflict between fluvial processes and land use. University of California Press, Berkeley, California.

Moyle, P. B. 2002. Inland fishes of California. University of California Press, Berkeley, California.

Reisner, M. 1986. Cadillac desert. Viking-Penguin, New York, New York.

Glossary

ANADROMOUS Organisms that migrate up rivers from the sea to breed in freshwater, spend early stages of their life histories in freshwater, but return to the ocean to grow and mature.

BANKFULL Discharge or stage (river depth) at which river flow in channels is level with the floodplain, which recurs on average about every 1.5 years. In rivers where there is no obvious floodplain, bankfull discharge is estimated as that delivered during the 1.5-year recurrence discharge.

BIOACCUMULATION The accumulation of a substance inside the bodies of organisms.

BIOMAGNIFICATION Increasing concentration of a substance from lower to higher trophic levels up food chains when consumers or predators accumulate and don't excrete the toxic loads of their resources or prey.

COLLECTORS Functional group of invertebrates that make their living by feeding on fine particles that they either filter from the water column (filter-feeders) or collect from deposits (deposit-feeders).

DETRITUS Dead organic matter of plant, algal, microbial, or animal origin.

DISTINCT POPULATION SEGMENT (DPS) Defined in the Endangered Species Act as a population of a species that has distinctive genetic, behavioral, physiological, and/or morphological traits.

DISTURBANCE A discrete event that kills or removes biota and frees space or other resources for recolonizing organisms (Sousa 1985). OR 1984 AS IN REFS?

DRAINAGE AREA The area of the basin (also known as catchment or watershed) that collects the water that drains into a given site within a river network. Delimited by drainage divides or ridges between basins.

EL NIÑO/SOUTHERN OSCILLATION (ENSO) El Niños result when high pressure over the western Pacific weakens equatorial trade winds, increasing sea surface temperatures in the eastern Pacific, resulting in the cessation of upwelling off Peru and California. La Niña is the reverse. On average, El Ninos produce wet conditions and La Ninas produce dry conditions in California.

ENDEMIC A species that only occurs within a defined geographic location.

ENDOSYMBIONT An organism that lives within a host organism of a different species.

EPILITHIC Living on the surface of stones.

EPIPELIC Living on the surface of sand or mud.

EPIPHYTIC Living on the surface of plants, including macroalgae.

EPIPHYTON Plants that live on the surface of other organisms.

ESTIVATION A state of torpor with lowered metabolic rates in which animals endure seasonal periods of stress.

FRIENDS OF THE EEL RIVER (FOER) A citizens group concerned with management and restoration of the Eel River.

FRIENDS OF THE LOS ANGELES RIVER (FOLAR) A citizens group concerned with management and restoration of the Los Angeles River.

FUNCTIONAL GROUPS Arbitrary groupings devised by ecologists to classify organisms into guilds that make their living in particular ways.

HALOPHYTE Salt-loving (or at least tolerant) plant.

HYDROGRAPH The graph of discharge over time (measured as volume time^{-1}, e.g. m^3s^{-1}); the amount of water flowing past a specific cross-section of a river or other channel versus time. Sometimes discharge is estimated from river stage, or depth, if rating curves that relate stage to discharge are available for the cross-section.

HYDRAULIC GEOMETRY Empirical power-law relationships that scale flow velocity (v), depth (d), and width (w) to river discharge (Q), discovered by Luna Leopold and Tom Maddox:

$$w = a\,Q^b$$

$$d = c\,Q^f$$

$$v = k\,Q^m$$

Where exponents b+f+m = 1 and coefficients a*c*k = 1. (Eq 33.1)

DOWNSTREAM HYDRAULIC GEOMETRY At a discharge with the same recurrence interval, discharge and width and depth increase from upstream to downstream locations according to hydraulic geometry relationships with approximately these exponents:

$b \sim 0.50$; $f \sim 0.40$ $m \sim 0.10$

AT-A-STATION HYDRAULIC GEOMETRY At a given cross-section, changes in discharges of different recurrence frequencies will be related to depth, width, and velocity with these exponents:

$b \sim 0.05$; $f \sim 0.35$, $m \sim 0.60$

HYPORHEIC Below the streambed, in interstitial pore water flow.

METAPHYTON Macroscopic cloudy proliferations, often algal, that accrue suspended in the water column.

NATIONAL MARINE FISHERIES SERVICE (NMFS) The federal agency within the National Oceanic and Atmospheric Administration (NOAA) in the Department of Commerce. Among other things, NMFS is responsible for overseeing provisions of the Endangered Species Act for marine and anadromous species.

NITROGEN FIXATION The reduction by bacteria or cyanobacteria of atmospheric nitrogen N_2 to ammonia (NH_4)—a form that can be used by nonfixing microbes, plants, and fungi.

ONTOGENETIC NICHE SHIFT The changes in the niche of an organism as it grows and develops.

PACIFIC DECADAL OSCILLATION (PDO) Warm and cool cycles of sea surface temperature in the northern Pacific, shifting typically at twenty- to thirty-year intervals. Discovered by Nate Mantua, a scientist trying to determine why salmonid oceanic survival was so variable across years.

PERIPHYTON An assemblage of attached algae and associated micro-organisms that live on stream plant, detrital, or mineral substrates.

PHENOLOGY The seasonal patterns of life history events of organisms.

PHYTOPLANKTON Microscopic algae that drift in the water column.

PRIMARY PRODUCERS The organisms (also known as "autotrophs") that fix their own carbon from solar radiation (photosynthesizers) or chemical bonds (chemosynthesizers).

PRIMARY CONSUMERS The organisms that eat (primarily) primary producers or their dead cells or tissues.

PYRETHROIDS A class of synthetic, organic compounds that comprise the majority of current household insecticides.

RECURRENCE INTERVAL The probability of a hydrologic event; the chance that an event during any given year will equal or exceed some given value. The hundred-year flood is a flood of a magnitude that has a 1% probability (calculated from a fairly long record) of being equaled or exceeded during any given year.

RIPARIAN Along the banks of a body of water.

RUNOFF Overland flow of water from rain, snowmelt, or surfacing groundwater.

SECONDARY CONSUMERS Animals that prey on primary consumers.

SESSILE Organisms attached permanently or semipermanently to substrates.

SHREDDERS Primary consumers that feed on particulate organic matter (e.g., dead tree leaves) that is larger than 1 millimeter in diameter.

SUCCESSION The sequential recovery of biota that recolonize habitats after disturbance.

TOTAL DAILY MAXIMUM LOAD (TMDL) The estimated amount of a pollutant that a body of water can receive per day and still meet water quality standards specified by regulatory agencies enforcing the U.S. Clean Water Act.

TROPHIC CASCADE The indirect effects of top-down changes in food web control. The alternate release and suppression of populations at odd versus even numbers of levels below trophic position x that would occur if an important consumer or predator at position x is extirpated from a food web. For example, predators may reduce grazers, causing increases in primary producers.

UNIMPAIRED HYDROGRAPH A hydrograph that depicts the natural discharge through the river that would flow without human interventions like dams or diversions. Often computed as the sum of known sources of runoff and groundwater reaching river drainages at a given point.

VOLTINISM Describes the numbers of generations per year in the life history of a species, most commonly used with aquatic invertebrates. UNIVOLTINE refers to one generation per year; BIVOLTINE, two generations per year; MULTIVOLTINE, more than two generations per year; and SEMIVOLTINE refers to organisms whose generation time is more than one year.

References

Ackerman, D., and K. Schiff. 2003. Modeling storm water mass emissions to the southern California bight. Journal of Environmental Engineering 129:308–317.

Alagona, P. S. 2013. After the grizzly: Endangered species and the politics of place in California. University of California Press, Berkeley, California.

Alagona, P. S., S. D. Cooper, M. Capelli, M. Stoecker, and P. H. Beedle. 2012. A history of steelhead and rainbow trout (*Oncorhynchus mykiss*) in the Santa Ynez River watershed, Santa Barbara County, California. Bulletin of the Southern California Academy of Sciences 111:163–222.

Allan, J. D. 2004. Landscapes and riverscapes: The influence of land use on stream ecosystems. Annual Review of Ecology, Evolution, and Systematics 35:257–284.

Alpers, C. N., M. P. Hunerlach, J. T. May, and R. L. Hothem. 2005. Mercury contamination from historic gold mining in California. U.S. Geological Survey Fact Sheet 2005-3014 Version 1.1. Sacramento, California.

Anderson, K. 2005. Tending the wild. University of California Press, Berkeley, California.

Arsuffi, T. L., and K. Suberkropp. 1984. Leaf processing capabilities of aquatic hyphomycetes: Interspecific differences and influence of shredder feeding preferences. Oikos 42:144–154.

Asarian, E., J. Kann, and W. Walker. 2010. Klamath River nutrient loading and retention dynamics in free-flowing reaches, 2005–2008. Final Technical Report to the Yurok Tribe Environmental Program. Klamath, California.

Ball, J. E., L. A. Bêche, P. K. Mendez, and V. H. Resh. 2013. Biodiversity in Mediterranean-climate streams of California. Hydrobiologia 719:187–213.

Bartholomew, J. L., M. J. Whipple, D. G. Stevens, and J. L. Fryer. 1997. The life cycle of *Ceratomyxa shasta*, a myxosporean parasite of salmonids, requires a freshwater polychaete as an alternate host. Journal of Parasitology 83:859–868.

Bartholomew, J. L., S. D. Atkinson, and S. L. Hallett. 2006. Involvement of *Manayunkia speciosa* (Annelida:Polychaeta:-Sabellidae) in the life cycle of *Parvicapsula minibicornis*, a myxozoan parasite of Pacific salmon. Journal of Parasitology 92:742–748.

Bartholow, J. M. 2005. Recent water temperature trends in the lower Klamath River, California. North American Journal of Fisheries Management 25:152–162.

Basagic, H. J., and A. G. Fountain. 2011. Quantifying 20th century glacier change in the Sierra Nevada, California. Arctic, Antarctic, and Alpine Research 43:317–330.

Bastow, J. L., J. L. Sabo, J. C. Finlay, and M. E. Power. 2002. A basal aquatic-terrestrial trophic link in rivers: Algal subsidies via shore-dwelling grasshoppers. Oecologia 131:261–268.

Baxter, C. V., K. D. Fausch, and W. C. Saunders. 2005. Tangled webs: Reciprocal flows of invertebrate prey link streams and riparian zones. Freshwater Biology 50:201–220.

Baxter, C. V., K. D. Fausch, M. Murakami, and P. L. Chapman. 2004. Fish invasion restructures stream and forest food webs by interrupting reciprocal prey subsidies. Ecology 85:2656–2663.

Bêche, L. A., and V. H. Resh. 2007a. Biological traits of benthic macroinvertebrates in California Mediterranean-climate streams: Long-term annual variability and trait diversity patterns. Fundamental and Applied Limnology 169:1–23.

———. 2007b. Short-term climatic trends affect the temporal variability of macroinvertebrates in California "Mediterranean" streams. Freshwater Biology 52:2317–2339.

Bêche, L. A., E. P. McElravy, and V. H. Resh. 2006. Long-term seasonal variation in the biological traits of benthic-macroinvertebrates in two Mediterranean-climate streams in California, U.S.A. Freshwater Biology 51:56–75.

Bêche, L. A., P. G. Connors, V. H. Resh, and A. M. Merenlender. 2009. Resilience of fishes and invertebrates to prolonged drought in two California streams. Ecography 32:778–788.

Bêche, L. A., S. L. Stephens, and V. H. Resh. 2005. Effects of prescribed fire on a Sierra Nevada (California, USA) stream and its riparian zone. Forest Ecology and Management 218:37–59.

Bell, A. H., and B. C. Scudder. 2007. Mercury accumulation in periphyton of eight river ecosystems. Journal of the American Water Resources Association 43:957–968.

Bell, E., R. Dagit, and F. Ligon. 2011. Colonization and persistence of a southern California steelhead (*Oncorhynchus mykiss*) population. Bulletin of the Southern California Academy of Sciences 110:1–16.

Bell, M. A. 1978. Fishes of the Santa Clara River system, southern

California. Natural History Museum of Los Angeles County, Contributions in Science. 295.

Benenati, P. L., J. P. Shannon., and D. W. Blinn. 1998. Desiccation and recolonization of phytobenthos in a regulated desert river: Colorado River at Lees Ferry, Arizona, USA. Regulated Rivers: Research and Management 14:519–532.

Bernhardt, E. S., and M. A. Palmer. 2011. River restoration: The fuzzy logic of repairing reaches to reverse catchment scale degradation. Ecological Applications 21:1926–1931.

———. 2007. Restoring streams in an urbanizing world. Freshwater Biology 52:738–751.

Bernhardt, E. S., M. A. Palmer, J. D. Allan, G. Alexander, K. Barnas, S. Brooks, J. Carr, S. Clayton, C. Dahm, J. Follstad Shah, D. Galat, S. Gloss, P. Goodwin, D. Hart, B. Hassett, R. Jenkinson, S. Katz, G. M. Kondolf, P. S. Lake, R. Lave, J. L. Meyer, T. K. O'Donnell, L. Pagano, B. Powell, and E. Sudduth. 2005. Synthesizing U.S. river restoration efforts. Science 308:636–637.

Black, J. M. 2009. River otter monitoring by citizen science volunteers in northern California: Social groups and litter size. Northwestern Naturalist 90:130–135.

Bold, H. C., and M. J. Wynne. 1985. Introduction to the algae. Second edition. Prentice Hall, Englewood Cliffs, New Jersey.

Bonada, N., M. Rieradevall, and N. Prat. 2007. Macroinvertebrate community structure and biological traits related to flow permanence in a Mediterranean river network. Hydrobiologia 589:91–106.

Bondi, C. A., and S. B. Marks. 2013. Differences in flow regime influence the seasonal migrations, body size, and body condition of western pond turtles (*Actinemys marmorata*) that inhabit perennial and intermittent riverine sites in northern California. Copeia 2013:142–153.

Börk, K.S. J. F. Krovoza, J. V. Katz, and P. B. Moyle. 2012. The rebirth of California Fish & Game Code 5937: Water for fish. University of California Davis Law Review 45:809–913.

Boughton, D. A., M. Gibson, R. Yedor, and R. Kelley. 2007. Stream temperature and the potential growth and survival of juvenile *Oncorhynchus mykiss* in a southern California creek. Freshwater Biology 32:1353–1364.

Boughton, D., P. Adams, E. Anderson, C. Fusaro, E. Keller, E. Kelley, L. Lentsch, J. Nielsen, K. Perry, H. Regan, J. Smith, C. Swift, L. Thompson, and F. Watson. 2006. Steelhead of the South-Central/Southern California Coast: Population characterization for recovery planning. NOAA Technical Memorandum NMFS-SWFC TM 394.

Bourque, R. M. 2008. Spatial ecology of an inland population of the foothill yellow-legged frog (*Rana boylii*) in Tehama County, California. MS thesis. Humboldt State University, Arcata, California.

Bradford, D. F., K. A. Stanley, N. G. Tallent, D. W. Sparling, M. S. Nash, R. A. Knapp, L. L. McConnell, and S. L. M. Simonich. [illegible] spatial variation of atmospherically deposited organic contaminants at high elevation in Yosemite National Park, California, USA. Environmental Toxicology and Chemistry 32:517–525.

Bradford, D. F., R. A. Knapp, D. W. Sparling, M. S. Nash, K. A. Stanley, N. G. Tallent-Halsell, L. L. McConnell, and S. M. Simonich. 2011. Pesticide distributions and population declines of California, USA, alpine frogs, *Rana muscosa* and *Rana sierrae*. Environmental Toxicology and Chemistry 30:682–691.

Bradley, S. G., and L. J. Klika. 1981. A fatal poisoning from the Oregon rough-skinned newt (*Taricha granulosa*). Journal of the American Medical Association 246:247.

Brattstrom, B. H. 1988. Habitat destruction in California with special reference to *Clemmys marmorata*: A perspective. Pages 13–24 in H. F. De Lisle, P. R. Brown, B. Kaufman, and B. M. McGurty, editors. Proceedings of the Conference on California Herpetology. Van Nuys, California: Southwestern Herpetologists Society, Special Publication No. 4.

Brett, M. T., M. Kainz, S. J. Taipale, and H. Seshan. 2009. Phytoplankton, not allochthonous carbon, sustains herbivorous zooplankton production. Proceedings of the National Academy of Sciences 106:21197–21201.

Brigham, R. M., H. Aldridge, and R. L. Mackey. 1992. Variation in habitat use and prey selection by Yuma bats, *Myotis yumanensis*. Journal of Mammalogy 73:640–645.

Brinkman, J. 2007. Influences of human disturbance and natural physical and chemical variables on biological community structure in streams of southern coastal Santa Barbara County, California, and an index of biological integrity. MA thesis. University of California, Santa Barbara, California.

Brode, J. M., and R. B. Bury. 1984. The importance of riparian systems to amphibians and reptiles. Pages 30–36 in R. E. Warner and K. M. Hendrix, editors. California riparian systems: Ecology, conservation, and productive management. University California Press, Berkeley, California.

Brown, L. R., and P. B. Moyle. 1996. Invading species in the Eel River, California: Successes, failures, and relationships with resident species. Environmental Biology of Fish 49:271–291.

———. 1991. Changes in habitat and microhabitat partitioning within an assemblage of stream fishes in response to predation by Sacramento squawfish (*Ptychocheilus grandis*). Canadian Journal of Fisheries and Aquatic Sciences 48:849–856.

Brown, L. R., C. A. Burton, and K. Belitz. 2005. Aquatic assemblages of the highly urbanized Santa Ana River basin, California. Pages 263–287 in L. R. Brown, R. H. Gray, R. M. Hughes, and M. R. Meador, editors. Effects of urbanization on stream ecosystems. Symposium 47. American Fisheries Society, Bethesda, Maryland.

Brown, L. R., S. D. Chase, M. G. Mesa, R. J. Beamish, and P. B. Moyle, editors. 2010. Biology, management, and conservation of lampreys in North America. American Fisheries Society Symposium 72. American Fisheries Society, Bethesda, Maryland.

Buchalski, M. R., J. B. Fontaine, P. A. Heady III, J. P. Hayes, and W. F. Frick. 2013. Bat response to differing fire severity in mixed-conifer forest California, USA. PloS One 8:e57884.

Bury, R. B. 1986. Feeding ecology of the turtle *Clemmys marmorata*. Journal of Herpetology 20:515–521.

Bury, R. B., and D. J. Germano. 2008. *Actinemys marmorata* (Baird and Girard 1852)—western pond turtle, Pacific pond turtle. Pages 001.1–001.9 in A. G. J. Rhodin, P. C. H. Pritchard, P. P. van Dijk, R. A. Saumure, K. A. Buhlman, and J. B. Iverson , editors. Conservation biology of freshwater turtles and tortoises. A compilation project of the IUCN/SSC tortoise and freshwater turtle specialist group. Chelonian Research Monographs 5.

Busse, L. B., J. C. Simpson, and S. D. Cooper. 2006. Relationships among nutrients, algae, and land use in urbanized southern California streams. Canadian Journal of Fisheries and Aquatic Science 63:2621–2638.

Cahill, T. A., J. J. Carroll, D. Campbell, and T. E. Gill. 1996. Chapter 48: Air quality. Pages 1227–1262 in Sierra Nevada Ecosystem Project (SNEP). Status of the Sierra Nevada. Volume II: Assessments and scientific basis for management options. Wildland Resources Center Report No. 37. University of California, Davis, California.

CALFED. 2005. CALFED Bay-Delta Program. Ecosystem restoration multiyear program plan (years 6–9) and annotated budget (year 5). Draft, June 16, 2005.

California Department of Fish and Wildlife. 2013. California supplemental fishing regulations, effective March 1, 2013, through February 28, 2014. California Natural Resources Agency.

———. 2011. Special animals list. <http://www.dfg.ca.gov/biogeodata/cnddb/pdfs/SPAnimals.pdf>. access date?

California Department of Fish and Wildlife and U.S. Fish and Wildlife Service. 2010. Final hatchery and stocking program EIR/EIS. SCH #20008082025. Prepared by ICF Jones and Stokes.

California Department of Fish and Wildlife Aquatic Bioassessment Laboratory. 2014. <https://www.dfg.ca.gov/abl/>. Accessed February 15, 2014.

California State Water Resources Control Board. 2012. Stockton wastewater treatment plant total maximum daily load progress report. <http://www.waterboards.ca.gov/about_us/performance_report_1112/plan_assess/docs/fy1112/11112_r5_stocktonshipchannel_do.pdf>. Accessed July 7, 2015.

———. 2007a. Clean Water Act Section 303(d) list of water quality limited segments requiring TMDLs: Central Coast Regional Water Quality Control Board. (U.S. EPA Approved June 28, 2007.)

———. 2007b. Clean Water Act Section 303(d) list of water quality limited segments requiring TMDLs: Los Angeles Regional Water Quality Control Board. (U.S. EPA Approved June 28, 2007).

———. 2007c. Clean Water Act Section 303(d) list of water quality limited segments requiring TMDLs: Santa Ana Regional Water Quality Control Board. (U.S. EPA Approved June 28, 2007).

———. 2007d. Clean Water Act Section 303(d) list of water quality limited segments requiring TMDLs: San Diego Regional Water Quality Control Board. (U.S. EPA Approved June 28, 2007).

Capelli, M. H. 2007. San Clemente and Matilija Dam removal: Alternative sediment management scenarios. Modernization and optimization of existing dams and reservoirs. Pages 607–620 in Proceedings, U.S. Society on Dams. U.S. Society on Dams Annual Meeting, March 5–9. Philadelphia, Pennsylvania.

———. 2004. Removing Matilija Dam: Opportunities and challenges for Ventura River restoration. Proceedings, U.S. Society on Dams. U.S. Society on Dams Annual Meeting, March 29–April 2. Saint Louis, Missouri.

———. 1999. Dams and rights: Removing Rindge and Matilija dams. Conference Proceedings, Sand Rights, '99 Bringing Back the Beaches. California Shore and Beach and Coastal Zone Foundation, September 23–26. Ventura, California.

Carlson, S. M., and W. H. Satterthwaite. 2011. Weakened portfolio effect in a collapsed salmon population complex. Canadian Journal of Fisheries and Aquatic Sciences 68:1579–1589.

Carter, J. L., A. H. Purceli, S. V. Fend, and V. H. Resh. 2009. Development of a local-scale urban stream assessment method using benthic macroinvertebrates: An example from the Santa Clara Basin, California. Journal of the North American Benthological Society 28:1007–1023.

Carter, K. 2005. The effects of dissolved oxygen on steelhead trout, Coho salmon, and Chinook salmon biology and function by life stage. California Regional Water Quality Control Board, North Coast Region. Santa Rosa, California.

Catenazzi, A., and S. J. Kupferberg. 2013. The importance of thermal conditions to recruitment success in stream-breeding frog populations distributed across a productivity gradient. Biological Conservation 168:40–48.

Christie, M. R., M. L. Marine, and M. S. Blouin. 2011. Who are the missing parents? Grandparentage analysis identifies multiple sources of gene flow into a wild population. Molecular Ecology 20:1263–1276.

Clemento, A. J., E. C. Anderson, D. Boughton, D. Girman, and J. C. Garza. 2009. Population genetic structure and ancestry of *Oncorhychus mykiss* populations above and below dams in south-central California. Conservation Genetics 10:1321–1336.

Close, D. A., M. S. Fitzpatrick, and H. W. Li. 2002. The ecological and cultural importance of a species at risk of extinction, Pacific lamprey. Fisheries 27:19–25.

Colborn T., F. S. vom Saal, and A. M. Soto. 1993. Developmental effects of endocrine-disrupting chemicals in wildlife and humans. Environmental Health Perspectives 101:378–84. <doi:10.2307/3431890>.

Connell, J. H., and R. O. Slatyer. 1977. Mechanisms of succession in natural communities and their role in community stability and organization. American Naturalist 1977:1119–1144.

Cooper, S. D., P. S. Lake, S. Sabater, J. M. Melack, and J. L. Sabo. 2013. The effects of land use changes on streams and rivers in Mediterranean climates. Hydrobiologia 719:383–425.

Cooper, S. D., H. M. Page, S. W. Wiseman, K. Klose, D. Bennett, T. Even, S. Sadro, C. E. Nelson, and T. L. Dudley. 2015. Physicochemical and biological responses of streams to wildfire severity in riparian zones. Freshwater Biology, doi:10.1111/fwb.12523.

Cosby, H. A. 2013. Variation in diet and activity of river otters (*Lontra canadensis*) by season and aquatic community. MS thesis. Humboldt State University, California.

Cross, W. F., C. V. Baxter, E. J. Rosi-Marshall, R. O. Hall, T. A. Kennedy, K. C. Donner, H. A. Wellard-Kelly, S. E. Z. Seegert, K. E. Behn, and M. D. Yard. 2013. Food-web dynamics in a large river discontinuum. Ecological Monographs 83:311–337.

Cucherousset, J., and J. D. Olden. 2011. Ecological impacts of non-native freshwater fishes. Fisheries 36:215–30.

Daniels, R. A. 1980. Distribution and status of crayfishes in the Pit River drainage, California. Crustaceana 1980:131–138.

Davidson, C., and R. A. Knapp. 2007. Multiple stressors and amphibian declines: Dual impacts of pesticides and fish on yellow-legged frogs. Ecological Applications 17:587–597.

Davis, J. A., R. E. Looker, D. Yee, M. Marvin-Di Pasquale, J. L. Grenier, C. M. Austin, L. J. McKee, B. K. Greenfield, R. Brodberg, and J. D. Blum. 2012. Reducing methyl mercury accumulation in the food webs of San Francisco Bay and its local watersheds. Environmental Research 119:3–26.

Denver, R. J., N. Mirhadi, and M. Phillips. 1998. Adaptive plasticity in amphibian metamorphosis: Response of *Scaphiopus hammondii* tadpoles to habitat desiccation. Ecology 79:1859–1872.

Dettinger, M. D. 2011. Climate change, atmospheric rivers, and floods in California—a multimodel analysis of storm frequency and magnitude changes. Journal of the American Water Resources Association 47:514–523.

Dettinger, M. D., H. Hidalgo, T. Das, D. Cayan, and N. Knowles, 2009. Projections of potential flood regime changes in California. California Energy Commission Report CEC-500-2009-050-D. California Energy Commission, Sacramento, California.

Dodds, W. K. 1991. Community interactions between the filamentous alga *Cladophora gomerata* L Kuetzling, its epiphytes and epiphyte grazers. Oecologia 85:572–580.

Dodds, W. K., and D. A. Gudder. 1992. The ecology of *Cladophora*. Journal of Phycology 28:415–427.

Dolin, E. J. 2011. Fur, fortune, and empire: The epic history of the fur trade in America. W.W. Norton & Company, New York, New York.

Domagalski, J. 2001. Mercury and methylmercury in water and sediment of the Sacramento River Basin, California. Applied Geochemistry 16:1677–1691.

Domagalski, J. L., C. N. Alpers, D. G. Slotton, T. H. Suchanek, and S. M. Ayers. 2004. Mercury and methylmercury concentrations and loads in the Cache Creek watershed, California. Science of the Total Environment 327:215–237.

Douglas, P. L., G. E. Forrester, and S. D. Cooper. 1994. Effects of trout on the diel periodicity of drifting in baetid mayflies. Oecologia 98:48–56.

Downs, P. W., S. R. Dusterhoff, and W. A. Sears. 2013. Reach-scale channel sensitivity to multiple human activities and natural events: Lower Santa Clara River, California, USA. Geomorphology 189:121–134.

Dudley, T. L., S. D. Cooper, and N. Hemphill. 1986. Effects of macroalgae on a stream invertebrate community. Journal of the North American Benthological Society 5:93–106.

Dunne, T., D. Montgomery, and W. E. Dietrich. 1991. Proposal for research in geomorphological watershed analysis. Timber Fish and Wildlife TFW-SH10-91-002.

Eilers, J. M., J. Kann, J. Cornett, K. Moser, and A. St. Amand. 2004. Paleolimnological evidence of change in a shallow, hypereutrophic lake: Upper Klamath Lake, Oregon, USA. Hydrobiologia 520:7–18.

Ellis, M. J. 1999. Species invasions and replacements in a native crayfish community. PhD dissertation. University of Michigan, Ann Arbor, Michigan.

Elton, C. S. 1927. Animal ecology. University of Chicago Press, Chicago, Illinois.

Erman, D. C., and D. Mahoney. 1983. Recovery after logging with and without bufferstrips in northern California. California Water Resources Center, University of California, Davis, California.

Erman, N. A. 1996. Status of aquatic invertebrates. Pages 987–1008 in Sierra Nevada Ecosystem Project. Final Report to Congress, volume II: Assessments and Scientific Basis for Management Options. Centers for Water and Wildland Resources, University of California, Davis, California.

Estes, J. A., J. Terborgh, J. S. Brashares, M E. Power, J. Berger, W. J. Bond, S. R. Carpenter, T.E. Essington, R. D. Holt, J. B.C. Jackson, R. J. Marquis, L. Oksanen, T. Oksanen, R. T. Paine, E. K. Pikitch, W. J. Ripple, S. A. Sandin, M. Scheffer, T. W. Schoener, J. B. Shurin, A. R. E. Sinclair, M. E. Soule, R. Virtanen, and D. A. Wardle. 2011. Trophic downgrading of Planet Earth. Science 333:301–306.

Faber, P. M., E. A. Keller, A. Sands, and B. M. Massey. 1989. The ecology of riparian habitats of the southern California region: A community profile. Biological Report 85(7.27). Prepared for the U.S. Department of the Interior Fish and Wildlife Series, Research and Development, National Wetland Research Center. Lafayette, Louisiana.

Fagan, B. M. 2003. Before California: An archaeologist looks at our earliest inhabitants. Rowman and Littlefield Publishers/AltaMira Press, Lanham, Maryland.

Feral, D., M. A. Camann, and H. H. Welsh Jr. 2005. *Dicamptodon tenebrosus* larvae within hyporheic zones of intermittent streams in California. Herpetological Review 36:26–26.

Ferren, W. R., Jr., P. Fielder, and R. Leidy. 1996. Wetlands of California. Part I: History of wetland habitat classification; Part II: Classification and description of wetlands of central and southern California coast and coastal watersheds; Part III: Key to and classification of wetlands of the central and southern California coast

and coastal watersheds. Madrono: A West American Journal of Botany 43(1)supplement:105–233.
———. 1995. Wetlands of central and southern California and coastal watersheds. Final Report. Prepared for U.S. Environmental Protection Agency, Region IX. San Francisco, California.
Ferrer, R. P., and R. K. Zimmer. 2013. Molecules of keystone significance crucial agents in ecology and resource management. Bioscience 63:428–438.
Feyrer, F., T. Sommer, and W. Harrell. 2006. Managing floodplain inundation for native fish: Production dynamics of age-0 splittail (*Pogonichthys macrolepidotus*) in California's Yolo Bypass. Hydrobiologia 573:213–226.
Finlay, J. C. 2001. Stable carbon isotope ratios of river biota: Implications for carbon flow in lotic food webs. Ecology 82:1052–1064.
Finlay, J, C., J. M. Hood, M. P. Limm, M. E. Power, J. D. Schade, and J. R. Welter. 2011. Light-mediated thresholds in stream-water nutrient composition in a river network. Ecology 92:140–150.
Finlay, J. C., M. E. Power, and G. Cabana. 1999. Effects of water velocity on algal carbon isotope ratios: Implications for river food web studies. Limnology and Oceanography 44:1198–1203.
Finlay, J. C., S. Khandwala, and M. E. Power. 2002. Spatial scales of carbon flow in a river food web. Ecology 83:1845–1859.
Fisher, S. G., L. J. Gray, N. B. Grimm, and D. E. Busch. 1982. Temporal succession in a desert stream ecosystem following flash flooding. Ecological Monographs 52:93–110.
Furey, P. C., R. L. Lowe, M. E. Power, and A. M. Campbell-Craven. 2012. Midges, *Cladophora*, and epiphytes: Shifting interactions through succession. Freshwater Science 31:93–107.
Furey, P. C., S. J. Kupferberg, , and A. J. Lind. In press. The perils of unpalatable periphyton: *Didymosphenia* and other mucilaginous stalked diatoms as food for tadpoles. Diatom Research.
Gan, J., F. Spurlock, P. Hendley, and D. Weston, editors. 2008. Synthetic pyrethroids: Occurrence and behavior in aquatic environments. Pages 26–54 in American Chemical Society Symposium Series 991. American Chemical Society, Washington, D.C.
Gard, R. 1961. Effects of beaver on trout in Sagehen Creek, California. Journal of Wildlife Management 25:220–242.
Garone, P. 2011. The fall and rise of the wetlands of California's Great Central Valley. University of California Press, Berkeley and Los Angles, California.
Garwood, J. M., R. A. Knapp, K. L. Pope, R. L. Grasso, M. L. Magnuson, and J. R. Maurer. 2013. Use of historically fishless high-mountain lakes and streams by nearctic river otters (*Lontra canadensis*) in California. Northwestern Naturalist 94:51–66.
Gasith, A., and V. H. Resh. 1999. Streams in Mediterranean climate regions: Abiotic influences and biotic responses to predictable seasonal events. Annual Review of Ecology and Systematics 30:51–81.
Girman, D., and J. C. Garza. 2006. Population structure and ancestry of *O. mykiss* populations in south-central California based on genetic analysis of microsatellite data. Final Report for California Department of Fish and Game (Project No. P0350021) and Pacific States Marine Fisheries (Contract No. AWIP-S-1). NOAA Southwester Fisheries Science Center, University of California, Santa Cruz, California.
Gleick, P. H., P. Loh, S. V. Gomez, and J. Morrison. 1995. California water 2020: A sustainable vision. Pacific Institute, Oakland, California.
Graber, D. M. 1996. Chapter 25: Status of terrestrial vertebrates. Pages 709–734 in Sierra Nevada Ecosystem Project (SNEP). Status of the Sierra Nevada. Volume II: Assessments and scientific basis for management options. Wildland Resources Center Report No. 37. University of California, Davis, California.
Grace, S. 2012. Dam nation: How water shaped the west and will determine its future. Globe Pequot Press, Guilford, Connecticut.
Gray, L. J., and S. G. Fisher. 1981. Postflood recolonization pathways of macroinvertebrates in a lowland Sonoran Desert stream. American Midland Naturalist 106:249–257.
Greenberg, A. E. 1964. Plankton in the Sacramento River. Ecology 45:40–49.
Grenfell, W. E., Jr. 1974. Food habits of the river otter in Suisin Marsh, central California. MS thesis. California State University, Sacramento, California.
Grossinger, R., E. D. Stein, K. Cavce, R. Askevold, S. Dark, and A. Whipple. 2011. Historical wetlands of southern California: An atlas of U.S. Survey T-Sheets 185101998. San Francisco Estuary Institute. Contribution #586 and Southern California Coastal Water Research Project Technical Report #859.
Gumprecht, B. 1999. The Los Angeles River: Its life, death, and possible rebirth. Johns Hopkins University Press, Baltimore, Maryland.
Hamilton, S. J. 2004. Review of selenium toxicity in the aquatic food chain. Science of the Total Environment 326:1–31.
Hanemann, M., and C. Dyckman. 2009. The San Francisco Bay-Delta: A failure of decision-making capacity. Environmental Science and Policy 12:712–721.
Hayes, S. A., C. V. Hanson, D. E. Pearse, M. H. Bond, J. C. Garza, and R. B. MacFarlane. 2012. Should I stay or should I go? The influence of genetic origin on emigration behavior and physiology of resident and anadromous juvenile *Oncorhynchus mykiss*. North American Journal of Fisheries Management 32:772–780.
Hayes, S. A., M. H. Bond, C. V. Hanson, A. W. Jones, A. J. Ammann, J. A. Harding, A. L. Collins, J. Peres, and R. B. MacFarlane. 2011. Down, up, down and "smolting" twice? Seasonal movement patterns by juvenile steelhead (*Oncorhynchus mykiss*) in a coastal watershed with a bar closing estuary. Canadian Journal of Fisheries and Aquatic Sciences 68:1341–1350.
Hayhoe, K., D. Cayan, C. B. Field, P. C. Frumhoff, E. P. Maurer, N. L. Miller, S. C. Moser, S. H. Schneider, K. N. Cahill, E. E. Cleland, L. Dale, R. Drapek, R. Hanemann, L. S. Kalkstein, J. Lenihan, C. K. Lunch, R. P. Neilson, S. C. Sheridan, and J. H. Verville. 2004. Emissions pathways, climate change, and impacts on California. Proceedings of the National Academy of Sciences 101:12422–12427.
Heck, P. M., P. D. Scheerer, S. L. Gunckel, and S. E. Jacobs. 2008. Status and distribution of native fishes in the Goose Lake Basin. Oregon Department of Fish and Wildlife. Information Report 2008-02. Corvallis, Oregon.
Hemphill, N., and S. D. Cooper. 1983. The effect of physical disturbance on the relative abundances of two filter-feeding insects in a small stream. Oecologia 58:378–382.
Herbst, D. B. 2013. A sentinel stream network for detecting the effects of climate change on hydrologic regime and aquatic ecosystems in the Sierra Nevada. Appendix A in J. Furnish, editor. Annual Report on the Monitoring of Aquatic Management Indicator Species (MIS) in the National Forests of the Sierra Nevada Province: 2009–2012. <http://www.fs.usda.gov/Internet/FSE_DOCUMENTS/stelprdb5415765.pdf>. Accessed July 7, 2015.
Herbst, D. B., and D. W. Blinn. 2007. Preliminary index of biological integrity (IBI) for periphyton in the Eastern Sierra Nevada, California. Draft report for the Lahontan Regional Water Quality Control Board.
Herbst, D. B., and E. L. Silldorff. 2006. Comparison of the performance of different bioassessment methods: Similar evaluations of biotic integrity from separate programs and procedures. Journal of the North American Benthological Society 25:513–530.
Herbst, D. B., and S. D. Cooper. 2010. Before and after the deluge: Rain-on-snow flooding effects on aquatic invertebrate communities of small streams in the Sierra Nevada, California. Journal of the North American Benthological Society 29:1354–1366.
Herbst, D. B., E. L. Silldorff, and S. D. Cooper. 2009. The influence of introduced trout on the benthic communities of paired headwater streams in the Sierra Nevada of California. Freshwater Biology 54:1324–1342.
Herbst, D. B., A. Y. Feng, and D. E. Gregorio. 2001. The California streamside biosurvey: An introduction to using aquatic invertebrates as water quality indicators. Clean Water Team Citizen Monitoring Program, Division of Water Quality, State Water Resources Control Board, Sacramento, California. <http://www.waterboards.ca.gov/water_issues/programs/bluegreen_algae/docs/workgroup110805/bgadetailedfactsheet.pdf>. Accessed August 19, 2015.
Herbst, D. B., M. T. Bogan, S. K. Roll, and H. D. Safford. 2012. Effects of livestock exclusion on in-stream habitat and benthic invertebrate assemblages in montane streams. Freshwater Biology 57:204–217.
Hill, H. 2006. Blue Green Algae (BGA) Detailed Fact Sheet. <https://www.google.com/?gws_rd=ssl#q=Hill%2C+Harriet+2006+Humboldt>. Accessed June 20, 2015.
Hill, W. R., and A. W. Knight. 1988. Nutrient and light limitation of algae in two northern California streams. Journal of Phycology 24:125–132.
Holland, D. C. 1985. Western pond turtle (*Clemmys marmorata*): Feeding. Herpetological Review 16:112–113.

Hothem, R. L., B. S. Trejo, M. L. Bauer, and J. J. Crayon. 2008. Cliff swallows *Petrochelidon pyrrhonota* as bioindicators of environmental mercury, Cache Creek Watershed, California. Archives of Environmental Contamination and Toxicology 55:111–121.

Hothem, R. L., M. R. Jennings, and J. J. Crayon. 2010. Mercury contamination in three species of anuran amphibians from the Cache Creek watershed, California, USA. Environmental Monitoring and Assessment 163:433–448.

Howard, J., K. Klausmeyer, and K. Fesenmyer. 2013. Below the surface: California's freshwater biodiversity. The Nature Conservancy of California. San Francisco, California. <http://scienceforconservation.org/projects/freshwater>. Accessed April 10, 2014.

Howitt R., D. MacEwan, C. Garnache, J. Medellín-Azuara, P. Marchand, D. Brown, J. Six, and J. Lee. 2013. Agricultural and economic impacts of Yolo Bypass fish habitat proposals. <https://watershed.ucdavis.edu/files/biblio/Yolo_0.pdf>. Accessed October 9, 2013.

Hunt & Associates Biological Consulting Services. 2008a. Southern California coast steelhead recovery planning area conservation action planning (CAP) workbooks threats assessment. Prepared for the National Marine Fisheries Service, Southwest Region, Protected Resources Division. Santa Barbara and Long Beach, California.

———. 2008b. Southern California coast steelhead recovery planning area recovery actions. Prepared for National Marine Fisheries Service, Southwest Region, Protected Resources Division. Santa Barbara and Long Beach, California.

Ingram, B. L., and F. Malamud-Roam. 2013. The West without water. University of California Press, Berkeley, California.

Intergovernmental Panel on Climate Change (IPCC). 2014a. Climate change 2014: Impacts, adaptation, and vulnerability. Working Group II. Report of the Intergovernmental Panel on Climate Change. Cambridge University Press, Cambridge, UK.

———. 2014b. Climate change 2014: Mitigation of climate change. Working Group III. Report of the Intergovernmental Panel on Climate Change. Cambridge University Press, Cambridge, UK.

Jackson, B. K., S. M. P. Sullivan, and R. L. Malison. 2012. Wildfire severity mediates fluxes of plant material and terrestrial invertebrates to mountain streams. Forest Ecology and Management 278:27–34.

Jacobs, D., E. Stein, and T. Longcore. 2011. Classification of California estuaries based on natural closure patterns: Templates for restoration and management. Technical Report 619a. Southern California Coastal Water Research Project.

James, C. D., and R. B. Lanman. 2012. Novel physical evidence that beaver historically were native to the Sierra Nevada. California Fish and Game 98:129–132.

Jassby, A. 2008. Phytoplankton in the upper San Francisco Estuary: Recent biomass trends, their causes, and their trophic significance. San Francisco Estuary and Watershed Science 6:1–24.

Jassby, A., and E. E. Van Nieuwenhuyse. 2005. Low dissolved oxygen in an estuarine channel (San Joaquin River, California): Mechanisms and models based on long-term time series. San Francisco. Estuary and Watershed Science 3:1–33.

Jeffres, C. A., R. A. Dahlgren, M. L. Deas, J. D. Kiernan, A. M. King, R. A. Lusardi, J. M. Mount, P. B. Moyle, A. L. Nichols, S. E. Null, S. K. Tanaka, and A. D. Willis. 2009. Baseline assessment of physical and biological conditions within waterways on Big Springs Ranch, Siskiyou County, California. Prepared for California State Water Resources Control Board by U.C. Davis Center for Watershed Sciences and Watercourse Engineering, Inc. Davis, California. <http://watershed.ucdavis.edu/pdf/Jeffres-et-alSWRCB-2009.pdf> Accessed July 12, 2015.

Kabat, A. R., and R. Hershler. 1993. The prosobranch snail family Hydrobiidae (Gastropoda, Rissooidea): Review of classification and supraspecific taxa. Smithsonian Contributions to Zoology 547:1–94.

Kadir, T., L. Mazur, C. Milanes, and K. Randles, editors. 2013. Indicators of climate change in California. Office of Environmental Health Hazard Assessment, California Environmental Protection Agency. Sacramento, California.

Kahrl, W. L., editor. 1979. The California water atlas. Governor's Office of Planning and Research, Sacramento, California.

Kann, J., and E. Asarian. 2005. 2002 Nutrient and hydrologic loading to Iron Gate and Copco Reservoirs, California. Kier Associates Final Technical Report to the Karuk Tribe. Department of Natural Resources, Orleans, California.

Kaplan, L. A., and J. D. Newbold. 2003. The role of monomers in stream ecosystem metabolism. Pages 97–119 in S. E. G. Findlay and R. L. Sinsabaugh, editors. Aquatic ecosystems: Interactivity of dissolved organic matter. Academic Press, San Diego, California.

Kats, L. B., and R. P. Ferrer. 2003. Alien predators and amphibian declines: Review of two decades of science and the transition to conservation. Diversity and Distributions 9:99–110.

Kats, L. B., G. Bucciarelli, T. L. Vandergon, R. L. Honeycutt, E. Mattiasen, A. Sanders, S. P. D. Riley, J. L. Kerby, and R. N. Fisher. 2013. Effects of natural flooding and manual trapping on the facilitation of invasive crayfish-native amphibian coexistence in a semi-arid perennial stream. Journal of Arid Environments 98:109–112.

Kattelmann, R. 1996. Chapter 30: Hydrology and water resources. Pages 855–920 in Sierra Nevada Ecosystem Project (SNEP). Status of the Sierra Nevada. Volume II: Assessments and scientific basis for management options. Wildland Resources Center Report No. 37, University of California, Davis, California.

Keeley, J. E. 2002. Native American impacts on fire regimes of the California coastal ranges. Journal of Biogeography 29:303–320.

Keeley, J. E., W. J. Bond, R. A. Bradstock, J. G. Pausas, and P. W. Rundel, editors. 2012. Fire in Mediterranean ecosystems: Ecology, evolution, and management. Cambridge University Press, Cambridge, UK.

Kemp, P. S., T. A. Worthington, T. E. Langford, A. R. Tree, and M. J. Gaywood. 2012. Qualitative and quantitative effects of reintroduced beavers on stream fish. Fish and Fisheries 13:158–181.

Kerby, J. L., and L. B. Kats. 1998. Modified interactions between salamander life stages caused by wildfire-induced sedimentation. Ecology 79:740–745.

Kern, C. H., and S. M. Sogard. 2013. Differential expression of gill Na+-K+-ATPase across life history pathways in two California steelhead populations. Unpublished report. National Marine Fisheries Service, Southwest Fisheries Science Center. Santa Cruz, California.

Kier Associates and National Marine Fisheries Service (NMFS). 2008. Fifty-five south-central/southern California steelhead DPS conservation action planning (CAP) workbooks (DVD). Prepared for National Marine Fisheries Service, Southwest Region, Protected Resources Division. Long Beach, California.

Kiernan, J. D., P. B. Moyle, and P. K. Crain. 2012. Restoring native fish assemblages to a regulated California stream using the natural flow regime concept. Ecological Applications 22:1472–1482.

Kim, C. S., D. H. Stack, and J. J. Ryuba. 2012. Fluvial transport and surface enrichment of arsenic in semi-arid mining regions: Examples from the Mojave Desert, California. Journal of Environmental Monitoring 14:1798–1813.

Kirkwood A. E., L. J. Jackson, and E. McCauley. 2009. Are dams hotspots for *Didymosphenia geminata* blooms? Freshwater Biology 54:1856–1863.

Klamath Basin Restoration Agreement for the Sustainability of Public Trust Resources and Affected Communities (KBRA). 2010. <http://www.doi.gov/news/pressreleases/upload/Klamath-Basin-Restoration-Agreement-2-18-10.pdf>. Accessed July 12, 2015.

Klose, K., and S. D. Cooper. 2013. Complex impacts of an invasive omnivore and native consumers on stream communities in California and Hawaii. Oecologia 171:945–960.

———. 2012. Contrasting effects of an invasive crayfish (*Procamburus clarkii*) on two temperate stream communities. Freshwater Biology 57:526–540.

Klose, K., S. D. Cooper, A. D. Leydecker, and J. Kreitler. 2012. Relationships among catchment land use and concentrations of nutrients, algae, and dissolved oxygen in a southern California river. Freshwater Science 31:908–927.

Klose, K., S. D. Cooper, and A. Leydecker. 2009. An assessment of numeric algal and nutrient targets for Ventura River watershed total maximum daily loads (TMDLs). Report to the Los Angeles Regional Water Quality Control Board. Los Angeles, California.

Knapp, R. A., V. T. Vredenburg, and K. R. Matthews. 1998. Effects of stream channel morphology on golden trout spawning habitat and recruitment. Ecological Applications 8:1104–1117.

Koetsier, P., Q. Tuckett, and J. White. 2007. Present effects of past wildfires on the diets of stream fish. Western North American Naturalist 67:429–438.

Kohler, S. L., and M. J. Wiley. 1992. Parasite-induced collapse of populations of a dominant grazer in Michigan streams. Oikos 65:443–449.

Kondolf, G. M. 1994. Environmental planning in regulation and management of instream gravel mining in California. Landscape and Urban Planning 29:185–199.

Kondolf, G. M., and R. J. Batalla. 2005. Hydrological effects of dams and water diversions on rivers of Mediterranean-climate regions: Examples from California. Developments in Earth Surface Processes 7:197–211.

Kondolf, G. M., S. Anderson, R. Lave, L. Pagano, A. Merenlender, and E. S. Bernhardt. 2007. Two decades of river restoration in California: What can we learn? Restoration Ecology 15:516–523.

Kudela, R. M. 2011. Characterization and deployment of Solid Phase Adsorption Toxin Tracking (SPATT) resin for monitoring of microcystins in fresh and saltwater. Harmful Algae 11:117–125.

Kumar S., S. A. Spaulding, T. J. Stohlgren, K. A. Hermann, T. S. Schmidt, and L. L. Bahls. 2009. Potential habitat distribution for the freshwater diatom *Didymosphenia geminata* in the continental U.S. Frontiers in Ecology and the Environment 7:415–420.

Kupferberg, S. J. 1997. Facilitation of primary production by grazing: Functionally important differences among species. Freshwater Biology 37:427–439.

———. 1996. Hydrologic and geomorphic factors affecting conservation of the foothill yellow legged frog (*Rana boylii*). Ecological Applications 6:1332–1344.

Kupferberg, S. J., A. J. Lind, V. Thill, and S. Yarnell. 2011. Water velocity tolerance in tadpoles of the foothill yellow-legged frog (*Rana boylii*): Swimming performance, growth, and survival. Copeia 2011:141–152.

Kupferberg, S. J., J. C. Marks, and M. E. Power. 1994. Effects of variation in natural algal and detrital diets on larval anuran (*Hyla regilla*) life-history traits. Copeia 1994:446–457.

Kupferberg, S. J., W. J. Palen, A. J. Lind, S. Bobzien, A. Catenazzi, J. Drennan, and M. E. Power. 2012. Effects of flow regimes altered by dams on survival, population declines, and range-wide losses of California river-breeding frogs. Conservation Biology 26:513–524.

Lamberti, G. A., and V. H. Resh. 1983. Stream periphyton and insect herbivores: An experimental study of grazing by a caddisfly population. Ecology 64:1124–1135.

Lanman, R. B., H. Perryman, B. Dolman, and C. D. James. 2012. The historical range of beaver in the Sierra Nevada: A review of the evidence. California Fish and Game 98:65–80.

Lawrence, J. E., K. B. Lunde, R. D. Mazor, L. A. Bêche, E. P. McElravy, and V. H. Resh. 2010. Long-term macroinvertebrate responses to climate change: Implications for biological assessment in Mediterranean-climate streams. Journal of the North American Benthological Society 29:1424–1440.

Legislative Analyst's Office. 2006. Analysis of the 2006–07 budget bill: Reforming the CALFED Bay-Delta Program. February 2006. Sacramento, California.

Leland, H. V., and J. L. Carter. 1985. Effects of copper on production of periphyton, nitrogen fixation, and processing of leaf litter in a Sierra Nevada, California, stream. Freshwater Biology 15:155–173.

Leland, H. V., S. V. Fend, T. L. Dudley, and J. L. Carter. 1989. Effects of copper on species composition of benthic insects in a Sierra Nevada, California, stream. Freshwater Biology 21:163–179.

Leopold, L. B., M. G. Wolman, and J. P. Miller. 1964. Fluvial processes in geomorphology. Freeman, San Francisco, California.

Lichatowich, J. 1999. Salmon without rivers: A history of the Pacific salmon crisis. Island Press, Washington, D.C.

Light, T. 2003. Success and failure in a lotic crayfish invasion: The roles of hydrologic variability and habitat alteration. Freshwater Biology 48:1886–1897.

Light, T., and M. P. Marchetti. 2007. Distinguishing between invasions and habitat changes as drivers of biodiversity loss among California's freshwater fishes. Conservation Biology 21:434–446.

Lightfoot, K. G., and O. Parrish. 2009. California Indians and their environment. University of California Press, Berkeley, California.

Limm, M. P., and M. E. Power. 2011. Effect of the western pearlshell mussel *Margaritifera falcata* on Pacific lamprey *Lampetra tridentata* and ecosystem processes. Oikos 120:1076–1082.

Lin, C. J., and R. F. Ambrose. 2005. Relations between fish assemblages and urbanization in southern California coastal streams. Pages 229–238 in L. R. Brown, R. H. Gray, R. H. Hughes, and M. R. Meador, editors. Effects of urbanization on stream ecosystems. American Fisheries Society Symposium 47. American Fisheries Society, Bethesda, Maryland.

Lind, A. J., and H. H. Welsh Jr. 1994. Ontogenetic changes in foraging behaviour and habitat use by the Oregon garter snake, *Thamnophis atratus hydrophilus*. Animal Behaviour 48:1261–1273.

Little Hoover Commission. 2005. Still imperiled, still important: The Little Hoover Commission's Review of the CALFED Bay-Delta Program. Sacramento, California.

Lokteff, R. L., B. B. Roper, and J. M. Wheaton. 2013. Do beaver dams impede the movement of trout? Transactions of the American Fisheries Society 142:1114–1125.

Lovich, J., and K. Meyer. 2002. The western pond turtle (*Clemmys marmorata*) in the Mojave River, California, USA: Highly adapted survivor or tenuous relict? Journal of Zoology 256:537–545.

Lowe, R. L. 2011. The importance of scale in understanding the natural history of diatom communities. Pages 293–311 in J. Seckbach and J. P. Kociolek, editors. The Diatom World. Springer, New York, New York.

Lunde, K. B., M. R. Cover, R. D. Mazor, C. A. Sommers, and V. H. Resh. 2013. Identifying reference conditions and quantifying biological variability within benthic macroinvertebrate communities in perennial and non-perennial northern California streams. Environmental Management 51:1262–1273.

Lund, J., E. Hanak, W. Fleenor, W. Bennett, R. Howitt, J. Mount, and P. Moyle. 2008. Comparing futures for the Sacramento–San Joaquin Delta. Public Policy Institute of California, San Francisco, California.

Lyon, G. S., and M. A. Sutula. 2011. Effluent discharges to the Southern California Bight from large municipal wastewater treatment facilities from 2005 to 2009. Pages 223–236 in S. B. Weisberg and K. Miller, editors. Southern California Coastal Watershed Research Project Annual Report 2011.

Lytle, D. A., and N. L. Poff. 2004. Adaptation to natural flow regimes. Trends in Ecology and Evolution 19:94–100.

Macneale, K. H., P. M. Kiffney, and N. L. Scholz. 2010. Pesticides, aquatic food webs, and the conservation of Pacific salmon. Frontiers in Ecology and Environment 8:475–482.

Mahoney, D. L., and D. C. Erman. 1984. The role of streamside bufferstrips in the ecology of aquatic organisms. Pages 168–176 in R. E. Warner and K. M. Hendrix, editors. Proceedings, California Riparian Systems. University of California Press, Berkeley, California.

Malakauskas, D. M., and M. A. Wilzbach. 2012. Invertebrate assemblages in the lower Klamath River, with reference to *Manayunkia speciosa*. California Fish and Game 98:214–235.

Malison, R. L., and C. V. Baxter. 2010. The fire pulse: Wildfire stimulates flux of aquatic prey to terrestrial habitats driving increases in riparian consumers. Canadian Journal of Fisheries and Aquatic Sciences 67:570–579.

Mallory, M. A., and J. S. Richardson. 2005. Complex interactions of light, nutrients and consumer density in a stream periphyton-grazer (tailed frog tadpoles) system. Journal of Animal Ecology 74:1020–1028.

Marcarelli, A. M., M. A. Baker, and W. A. Wurtsbaugh. 2008. Is instream N_2 fixation an important N source for benthic communities and stream ecosystems? Journal of the North American Benthological Society 27:186–211.

Marchetti, M. P., J. L. Lockwood, and T. Light. 2006. Effects of urbanization on California's fish diversity: Differentiation, homogenization and the influence of spatial scale. Biological Conservation 127:310–318.

Marchetti, M. P., T. Light, P. B. Moyle, and J. H. Viers. 2004. Fish invasions in California watersheds: Testing hypotheses using landscape patterns. Ecological Applications 14:1507–1525.

Marks, J. C., and M. E. Power. 2001. Nutrient induced changes in the species composition of epiphytes on *Cladophora glomerata* Kutz. (Chlorophyta). Hydrobiologia 450:187–2001.

Martin, B. A., M. K. Saiki, and D. Fong. 2009. Habitat requirements of the endangered California freshwater shrimp (*Syncaris pacifica*) in Lagunitas and Olema Creeks, Marin County, California, USA. Journal of Crustacean Biology 29:595–604.

Matthews, K. R., and N. H. Berg. 1997. Rainbow trout responses to water temperature and dissolved oxygen stress in two southern California stream pools. Journal of Fish Biology 50:50–67.

Matthews, N. 2007. Rewatering the San Joaquin River: A summary of the Friant Dam litigation. Ecology Law Quarterly 34:1109–1136.

May, J. T., and L. R. Brown. 2002. Fish communities of the Sacramento Basin: Implications for conservation of native fishes in

the Central Valley, California. Environmental Biology of Fishes 63:373–388.
Mazor, R. D., and K. Schiff. 2008. Surface Water Ambient Monitoring Program (SWAMP) synthesis report on stream assessments in the San Diego region. Prepared for the California Regional Water Quality Control Board, San Diego Region (Region 9). Southern California Coastal Water Research Project. Technical Report 527.
Mazor, R. D., D. J. Gillett, K. Schiff, K. Ritter, and E. D. Stein. 2011. Ecological condition of watersheds in coastal southern California: Summary of the Stormwater Monitoring Coalition's Stream Monitoring Program First Year (2009). Prepared for the Stormwater Monitoring Coalition Bioassessment Workgroup. Southern California Coastal Water Research Project. Technical Report 639.
McDowell, D. M., and R. J. Naiman. 1986. Structure and function of a benthic invertebrate stream community as influenced by beaver (*Castor canadensis*). Oecologia (Berlin) 68:481–489.
McEwan, D., and T. A. Jackson. 2003. Steelhead restoration and management plan for California. California Department of Fish and Game, Sacramento, California.
McNeely, C., J. C. Finlay, and M. E. Power. 2007. Grazer traits, competition, and carbon sources to a headwater-stream food web. Ecology 88:391–401.
McNeely, F. C., and M. E. Power. 2007. Spatial variation in caddisfly grazing regimes within a northern California watershed. Ecology 88:2609–2619.
Meffe, G. K., and W. L. Minckley. 1987. Persistence and stability of fish and invertebrate assemblages in a repeatedly disturbed Sonoran Desert stream. American Midland Naturalist 117:177–191.
Meffe, G. K., D. A. Hendrickson, W. L. Minckley, and J. N. Rinne. 1983. Factors resulting in decline of the endangered Sonoran topminnow *Poeciliopsis occidentalis* (Atheriniformes:Poeciliidae) in the United States. Biological Conservation 25:135–159.
Melquist, W. E., and M. G. Hornocker. 1983. Ecology of river otters in west central Idaho. Wildlife Monographs 1983:3–60.
Merritt, R. W., K. W. Cummins, and M. B. Berg, editors. 2008. An introduction to the aquatic insects of North America. Fourth edition. Kendall/Hunt Publishing Company, Dubuque, Iowa.
Merz, J. E., and P. B. Moyle. 2006. Salmon, wildlife, and wine: Marine-derived nutrients in human-dominated ecosystems of central California. Ecological Applications 16:999–1009.
Miller, J. D., H. D. Safford, M. Crimmins, and A. E. Thode. 2009. Quantitative evidence for increasing forest fire severity in the Sierra Nevada and southern Cascade Mountains, California and Nevada, USA. Ecosystems 12:16–32.
Miller, M. A., R. M. Kudela, A. Mekebri, D. Crane, S. C. Oates, M. T. Tinker, M. Staedler, W. A. Miller, S. Toy-Choutka, C. Dominik, D. Hardin, G. Langlois, M. Murray, K. Ward, and D. A. Jessup. 2010. Evidence for a novel marine harmful algal bloom: Cyanotoxin (Microcystin) transfer from land to sea otters. PLoS One 5(9):e12576. <doi:10.1371/journal.pone.0012576.t003>.
Minnich, R. A. 2008. California's fading wildflowers: Lost legacy and biological invasions. University of California Press, Berkeley, California.
Minshall, G. W., C. T. Robinson, and D. E. Lawrence. 1997. Immediate and mid-term responses of lotic ecosystems in Yellowstone National Park, USA to wildfire. Canadian Journal of Fisheries and Aquatic Science 54:2509–2525.
Minshall, G. W., R. C. Petersen, K. W. Cummins, T. L. Bott, J. R. Sedell, C. E. Cushing, and R. L. Vannote. 1983. Interbiome comparison of stream ecosystem dynamics. Ecological Monographs 53:1–25.
Moeller, A., S. D. MacNeil, R. F. Ambrose, and S. S. Que Hee. 2003. Elements in fish of Malibu Creek and Malibu Lagoon near Los Angeles, California. Marine Pollution Bulletin 46:424–429.
Montgomery, D. R., and J. S. Buffington. 1997. Channel-reach morphology in mountain drainage basins. Geological Society of America Bulletin 109:596–611.
Montgomery, D. R., and W. E. Dietrich. 1988. Where do channels begin? Nature 336:232–234.
Moore, J. W., D. B. Herbst, W. N. Heady, and S. M. Carlson. 2012a. Stream community and ecosystem responses to the boom and bust of an invading snail. Biological Invasions 14:2435–2446.
Moore, J. W., S. M. Carlson, L. A. Twardochleb, J. L. Hwan, J. M. Fox, and S. A. Hayes. 2012b. Trophic tangles through time? Opposing direct and indirect effects of an invasive omnivore on stream ecosystem processes. PLoS One 7:e50687. <doi:10.1371/journal.pone.0050687>.
Mount, J. F. 1995. California rivers and streams. University of California Press, Berkeley, California.
Mount. J. F., W. Fleenor, B. Gray, B. Herbold, and W. W. Kimmerer. 2013. Panel review of the Draft Bay Delta Conservation Plan. <https://watershed.ucdavis.edu/files/biblio/FINAL-BDCP-REVIEW-for-TNC-and-AR-Sept-2013.pdf>. Accessed October 14, 2013.
Moye, H. A., C. J. Miles, E. J. Philips, B. Sargent, and K. K. Merritt. 2002. Kinetics and uptake mechanisms for monomethylmercury between freshwater algae and water. Environmental Science and Technology 36:3550–3555.
Moyle, P. B. 2013. Novel aquatic ecosystems: The new reality for streams in California and other Mediterranean climate regions. River Research and Applications. <doi:10.1002/rra.2709>.
———. 2002. Inland fishes of California. University of California Press, Berkeley, California.
———. 1973. Effects of introduced bullfrogs, *Rana catesbeiana*, on the native frogs of the San Joaquin Valley, California. Copeia 1973:18–22.
Moyle, P. B., and J. P. Ellison. 1991. A conservation-oriented classification system for the inland waters of California. California Fish and Game 77:161–180.
Moyle, P. B., J. A. Israel, and S. E. Purdy. 2008. Salmon, steelhead, and trout in California: Status of an emblematic fauna. Center for Watershed Sciences, University of California, Davis, California.
Moyle, P. B., J. D. Kiernan, P. K. Crain, and R. M. Quiñones. 2013. Climate change vulnerability of native and alien freshwater fishes of California: A systematic assessment approach. PLoS ONE 8(5): e63883. <doi:10.1371/journal.pone.0063883>. <http://dx.plos.org/10.1371/journal.pone.0063883>.
Moyle, P. B., J. V. E. Katz, and R. M. Quinones. 2011. Rapid decline of California's native inland fishes: A status assessment. Biological Conservation 144:2414–2423.
Moyle, P. B., R. M. Yoshiyama, and R. A. Knapp. 1996. Chapter 33: Status of fish and fisheries. Pages 953– 974 in Sierra Nevada Ecosystem Project (SNEP). Status of the Sierra Nevada. Volume II: Assessments and scientific basis for management options. Wildland Resources Center Report No. 37. University of California, Davis, California.
Munshaw, R. G., W. J. Palen, D. M. Courcelles, and J. C. Finlay. 2013. Predator-driven nutrient recycling in California stream ecosystems. PloS One 8:e58542.
Muskopf, S. A. 2007. The effect of beaver (*Castor canadensis*) dam removal on total phosphorus concentration in Taylor Creek and Wetland, South Lake Tahoe, California. MS thesis. Humboldt State University, California.
Nakano, S., and M. Murakami. 2001. Reciprocal subsidies: Dynamic interdependence between terrestrial and aquatic food webs. Proceedings of the National Academy of Sciences 98:166–170.
National Marine Fisheries Service (NMFS). 2013. South-central California coast steelhead recovery plan. NMFS, West Coast Region, Long Beach, California.
———. 2012. Southern California steelhead recovery plan. NMFS, Southwest Regional Office, Long Beach, California.
———. 2008. NOAA's National Marine Fisheries Service's reinitiated biological opinion on the effects of the U.S. Forest Service's National Fire Retardant Programmatic Consultation, issued under the authority of section 7(a)(2) of the Endangered Species Act. NMFS Office of Protected Resources, Silver Spring, Maryland: 8.
National Oceanic and Atmospheric Administration (NOAA). 2013. Endangered and threatened Species: Designation of a nonessential experimental population of Central Valley spring-run Chinook salmon below Friant Dam in the San Joaquin River, CA. Federal Register 78:79622–79633.
National Research Council (NRC). 2004. Endangered and threatened fishes in the Klamath River basin. National Academies Press, Washington D.C.
Newbold, J. D., D. C. Erman, and K. B. Roy. 1980. Effects of logging on macroinvertebrates in streams with and without buffer strips. Canadian Journal of Fisheries and Aquatic Science 37:1076–1085.
Ng, C. 2012. The transport of chemicals and biota into coastal rivers and marine ecosystems. PhD dissertation. University of California, Berkeley, California.

Nichols, A. L., A. D. Willis, C. A. Jeffres, and M. L. Deas. 2013. Water temperature patterns below large groundwater springs: Management implications for coho salmon in the Shasta River, California. River Research and Applications 14. <doi:10.1002/rra.2655>.

Nichols, K., K. True, E. Wiseman, and J. S. Foott. 2007. FY 2005 investigational report: Incidence of *Ceratomyxa shasta* and *Parvicapsula minibicornis* infections by QPCR and histology in juvenile Klamath River Chinook Salmon. U.S. Fish and Wildlife Service California-Nevada Fish Health Center, Anderson, California.

Nielsen, J. L., C. Gan, and W. K. Thomas. 1994. Differences in genetic diversity for mitochondrial DNA between hatchery and wild populations of *Oncorhynchus*. Canadian Journal of Fisheries and Aquatic Science 51(suppl. 1):290–297.

Norris, R. M., and R. W. Webb. 1990. Geology of California. John Wiley & Sons, Inc. 2nd edition, Somerset, New Jersey.

Null, S. E., J. H. Viers, and J. F. Mount. 2010. Hydrologic response and watershed sensitivity to climate warming in California's Sierra Nevada. PLoS One 5:e9932.

Nussbaum, R. A. 1969. Nests and eggs of the Pacific giant salamander, *Dicamptodon ensatus* (Eschscholtz). Herpetologica 1969:257–262.

O'Brien, J. W., H. K. Hansen, and M. E. Stephens. 2011. Status of fishes in the Upper San Gabriel River Basin, Los Angeles County, California. California Fish and Game 97:149–163.

Ode, P. R., A. C. Rehn, and J. T. May. 2005. A quantitative tool for assessing the integrity of southern coastal California streams. Environmental Management 35:493–504.

Ode, P. R., C. P. Hawkins, and R. D. Mazor. 2008. Comparability of biological assessments derived from predictive models and multimetric indices of increasing geographic scope. Journal of the North American Benthological Society 27:967–985.

Ohlendrof, H. M., R. L. Hoffman, T. W. Aldrich, and J. F. Moore. 1986. Relationships between selenium concentrations and avian reproduction. Transactions of the North American Wildlife Natural Resources Conference 5:330–342.

Oliver, A. A., J. E. Reuter, A. C. Heyvaert, and R. A. Dahlgren. 2012. Water quality response to the Angora Fire, Lake Tahoe, California. Biogeochemistry111:361–376.

Olsen, J. B., K. Wuttig, D. Fleming, E. J. Kretschmer, and J. K. Wenburg. 2006. Evidence of partial anadromy and resident-form dispersal bias on a fine scale in populations of *Oncorhynchus mykiss*. Conservation Genetics 7:613–619.

PacifiCorp. 2004. Water Resources Final Technical Report. Klamath Hydroelectric Project (FERC Project No. 2082). Portland, Oregon.

Paerl, H. W., and J. Huisman. 2009. Climate change: A catalyst for global expansion of harmful cyanobacterial blooms. Environmental Microbiology Reports 1:27–37.

Palmer, M. A., E. S. Bernhardt, J. D. Allan, P. S. Lake, G. Alexander, S. Brooks, J. Carr, S. Clayton, C. N. Dahm, J. F. Shah, D. L. Galat, S. G. Loss, P. Goodwin, D. D. Hart, B. Hassett, R. Jenkinson, G. M. Kondolf, R. Lave, J. L. Meyer, T. K. O'Donnell, L. Pagano and E. Sudduth. 2005. Standards for ecologically successful river restoration. Journal of Applied Ecology 42:208–217.

Parker, A. E., R. C. Dugdale, and F. P. Wilkerson. 2012. Elevated ammonium concentrations from wastewater discharge depress primary productivity in the Sacramento River and the northern San Francisco Estuary. Marine Pollution Bulletin 64:574–586.

Parker, G. 1978. Self-formed straight rivers with equilibrium banks and mobile bed. Part q. The gravel river. Journal of Fluid Mechanics 89:127–146.

Parker, M. S. 1994. Feeding ecology of stream-dwelling Pacific giant salamander larvae (*Dicamptodon tenebrosus*). Copeia 1994:705–718.

Parker, M. S., and M. E. Power. 1997. Effect of stream flow regulation and absence of scouring floods on trophic transfer of biomass to fish in Northern California rivers. In University of California Water Resources Center Technical Completion Report, UCAL-WRC-W-825. University of California, Davis, California.

Paul, M. J., and J. L. Meyer. 2001. Streams in the urban landscape. Annual Review of Ecology and Systematics 32:333–365.

Pearse, D. E., S. A. Hayes, M. H. Bond, C.V. Hanson, E. C. Anderson, R. B. MacFarlane, and J. C. Garza. 2009. Over the falls? Rapid evolution of ecotypic differentiation in steelhead/rainbow trout (*Oncorhynchus mykiss*). Journal of Heredity 100:515–525.

Peek, R. A. 2011. Landscape genetics of Foothill yellow-legged frogs (*Rana boylii*) in regulated and unregulated rivers: assessing connectivity and genetic fragmentation. MS Thesis, University of San Francisco, California.

Penland, T. F., and J. M. Black. 2009. Seasonal variation in river otter diet in coastal northern California. Northwestern Naturalist 90:233–237.

Pesticide Action Network North America (PAN). 2013. Organophosphates. <http://www.panna.org/resources/organophosphates>. Accessed March 5 2013.

Peterson, C. G., and N. B. Grimm. 1992. Temporal variation in enrichment effects during periphyton succession in a nitrogen-limited desert stream ecosystem. Journal of the North American Benthological Society 11:20–36.

Petts, G., and A. Gurnell. 2013. Hydrogeomorphic effects of reservoirs, dams, and diversions. Treatise on Geomorphology 13:96–114.

Pierson, E. D., W. E. Rainey, and C. Corben, C. 2006. Distribution and status of western red bats (*Lasiurus blossevillii*) in California. California Department of Fish and Game, Habitat Conservation Planning Branch, Species Conservation and Recovery Program Report, 2006–04. California Department of Fish and Game, Sacramento, California.

Pilliod, D. S., J. L. Welty, and R. Stafford. 2013. Terrestrial movement patterns of western pond turtles (*Actinemys marmorata*) in central California. Herpetological Conservation and Biology 8:207–221.

Pintor, L. M., and A. Sih. 2011. Scale dependent effects of native prey diversity, prey biomass, and natural disturbance on the invasion success of an exotic predator. Biological Invasions 13:1357–1366.

Pintor, L. M., A. Sih, and J. L. Kerby. 2009. Behavioral correlations provide a mechanism for explaining high invader densities and increased impacts on native prey. Ecology 90:581–587.

Poff, N. L., and J. K. H. Zimmerman. 2010. Ecological responses to altered flow regimes: A literature review to inform the science and management of environmental flows. Freshwater Biology 55:194–205.

Poff, N. L., J. D. Allan, M. B. Bain, J. R. Karr, K. L. Prestegaard, B. D. Richter, R. E. Sparks, and J. C. Stromberg. 1997. The natural flow regime. Bioscience 47:769–784.

Pollock, M. M., G. R. Pess, T. J. Beechie, and D. R. Montgomery. 2004. The importance of beaver ponds to Coho salmon production in the Stillaguamish River basin, Washington, USA. North American Journal of Fisheries Management 24:749–760.

Pollock, M. M., T. J. Beechie, and C. E. Jordan. 2007. Geomorphic changes upstream of beaver dams in Bridge Creek, an incised stream channel in the interior Columbia River basin, eastern Oregon. Earth Surface Processes and Landforms 32:1174–1185.

Power, M. E. 1990a. Benthic turfs vs. floating mats of algae in river food webs. Oikos 58:67–79.

———. 1990b. Effects of fish in river food webs. Science 250:411–415.

———. 1987. Predator avoidance by grazing fishes in temperate and tropical streams: Importance of stream depth and prey size. Pages 333–351 in W. C. Kerfoot and A. Sih, editors. Predation: Direct and indirect impacts on aquatic communities. University Press of New England, Hanover, New Hampshire.

Power, M. E., and A. J. Stewart. 1987. Disturbance and recovery of an algal assemblage following flooding in an Oklahoma [USA] stream. American Midland Naturalist 117:333–345.

Power, M. E., A. Sun, G. Parker, W. E. Dietrich, and J. T. Wootton. 1995. Hydraulic food-chain models. BioScience 1995:159–167.

Power, M. E., and W. J. Matthews. 1983. Algae-grazing minnows (*Campostoma anomalum*), piscivorous bass (*Micropterus* spp.) and the distribution of attached algae in a prairie-margin stream. Oecologia 60:328–332.

Power, M. E., J. R. Holomuzki, and R. L. Lowe. 2013. Food webs in Mediterranean rivers. Hydrobiologia 719:119–136. Featured in N. Bonada and V. H. Resh, editors. Streams in Mediterranean climate regions: Lessons learned from the last decade. <doi:10.1007/s10750-013-1510-0>.

Power, M. E., M. S. Parker, and J. T. Wootton. 1996. Disturbance and food chain length in rivers. Pages 286–297 in G. A. Polis and K. O. Winemiller, editors. Food webs. Chapman and Hall, New York, New York.

Power, M. E., M. S. Parker, and W. E. Dietrich. 2008. Seasonal reassembly of a river food web: Floods, droughts, and impacts of fish. Ecological Monographs 78:263–282.

Power, M. E., R. Lowe, P. C. Furey, J. Welter, M. Limm, J. C. Finlay, C.

Bode, S. Chang, M. Goodrich, and J. Sculley. 2009. Algal mats and insect emergence in rivers under Mediterranean climates: Towards photogrammetric surveillance. Freshwater Biology 54: 2101–2115.

Power, M. E., W. E. Rainey, M. S. Parker, J. L. Sabo, A. Smyth, S. Khandwala, J. C. Finlay, F. C. McNeely, K. Marsee, and C. Anderson. 2004. River-to-watershed subsidies in an old-growth conifer forest. Pages 217–240 in G. A. Polis, M. E. Power, and G. R. Huxel, editors. Food webs at the landscape level. University of Chicago Press, Chicago, Illinois.

Puschner, B., B. Hoff, and E. R. Tor. 2008. Diagnosis of anatoxin-a poisoning in dogs from North America. Journal of Veterinary Diagnostic Investigation 20:89–92.

Quinn, T. P. 2005. The behavior and ecology of Pacific salmon and trout. American. Fisheries Society and University of Washington Press, Seattle, Washington.

Quinn, T. P., and K. W. Meyers. 2005. Anadromy and the marine migration of Pacific salmon and trout: Rounsefell revisited. Reviews in Fish Biology and Fisheries 14:421–42.

Reese, D. A., and H. H. Welsh Jr. 1998. Comparative demography of *Clemmys marmorata* populations in the Trinity River of California in the context of dam-induced alterations. Journal of Herpetology 1998:505–515.

Rehn, A. C. 2009. Benthic macroinvertebrates as indicators of biological condition below hydropower dams on west slope Sierra Nevada streams, California, USA. River Research and Applications 25:208–228.

Rehn, A. C., P. R. Ode, and C. P. Hawkins. 2007. Comparisons of targeted-riffle and reach-wide benthic macroinvertebrate samples: Implications for data sharing in stream-condition assessments. Journal of the North American Benthological Society 26:332–348.

Reisner, M. 1993. Cadillac desert: The American West and its disappearing water. Revised edition. Penguin Books, New York, New York.

Resh, V. H., A. V. Brown, A. P. Covich, M. E. Gurtz, H. W. Li, G. W. Minshall, S. R. Reice, A. L. Sheldon, J. B. Wallace, and . C. Wissmar. 1988. The role of disturbance in stream ecology. Journal of the North American Benthological Society 7:433–455.

Rich, A., and E. A. Keller. 2013. A hydrologic and geomorphic model of estuary breaching and closure. Geomorphology 191:64–74.

Richter, A., and S. A. Kolmes. 2005. Maximum temperature limits for Chinook, Coho, and chum salmon, and steelhead trout in the Pacific Northwest. Reviews in Fisheries Science 13:23–49.

Riley, S. P. D., G. T. Busteed, L. B. Kats, T. L. Vandergon, L. F. S. Lee, R. G. Dagit, J. L. Kerby, R. N. Fisher, and R. M. Sauvajot. 2005. Effects of urbanization on the distribution and abundance of amphibians and invasive species in southern California streams. Conservation Biology 2005:1894–1907.

Riparian Habitat Joint Venture (RHJV). 2004. The riparian bird conservation plan: A strategy for reversing the decline of riparian associated birds in California. California Partners in Flight. <http://www.prbo.org/calpif/pdfs/riparian_v-2.pdf>. Accessed October 8, 2013.

Roby, K. B. 1989. Watershed response and recovery from the Will Fire: Ten years of observation. U.S. Forest Service General Technical Report Pacific South West 109:131–136.

Rost A. L., C. H. Fritsen, and C. J. Davis. 2011. Distribution of the freshwater diatom *Didymosphenia geminata* in streams in the Sierra Nevada, USA, in relation to water chemistry and bedrock geology. Hydrobiologia 665:157–167.

Rundel, P. W., J. R. Ehleringer, and K. A. Nagy. 1988. Stable isotopes in ecological research. Springer, Berlin, Germany.

Rundio, D. E., and S. T. Lindley. 2008. Seasonal patterns of terrestrial and aquatic prey abundance and use by *Oncorhynchus mykiss* in a California coastal basin with a Mediterranean climate. Transactions of the American Fisheries Society 137:467–480.

Rymer, R. 2008. Reuniting a river: After fighting for years over its water, farmers, Indians, and fishermen are joining forces to let the troubled Klamath River run wild again. National Geographic December 2008:134–155.

Sabo, J., K. Bestgen, T. Sinha, W. L. Graf, and E. E. Wohl. 2012. Dams in the Cadillac Desert: Downstream effects in a geomorphic context. Annals of the New York Academy of Sciences 1249:227–246.

Sabo, J. L. and M. E. Power. 2002a. Numerical response of lizards to aquatic insects and short-term consequences for terrestrial prey. Ecology 11:3023–3036.

———. 2002b. River-watershed exchange: Effects of riverine subsidies on riparian lizards and their terrestrial prey. Ecology 7:1860–1869.

Saiki, M. K., B. A. Martin, T. W. May, and C. N. Alpers. 2010. Mercury concentrations in fish from a Sierra Nevada foothill reservoir located downstream from historic gold-mining operations. Environmental Monitoring and Assessment 163:313–326.

Saiki, M. K., B. A. Martin, and T. W. May. 2012. Selenium in aquatic biota inhabiting agricultural drains in the Salton Sea Basin, California. Environmental Monitoring and Assessment 184:5623–5640.

Salcido, R. E. 2012. The success and continued challenges of the Yolo Bypass Wildlife Area: A grassroots restoration. Ecology Law Quarterly 39:1085–1085.

Sengupta, A., J. M. Lyons, D. J. Smith, J. E. Drewes, S. A. Snyder, A. Heil, and K. A. Maruya. 2014. The occurrence and fate of chemicals of emerging concern in coastal-urban rivers receiving discharge of treated municipal wastewater effluent. Environmental Toxicology and Chemistry 35:350–358.

Shannon J. P., D. W. Blinn, and L. E. Stevens. 1994. Trophic interactions and benthic animal community structure in the Colorado River, Arizona, USA. Freshwater Biology 31:213–220.

Silldorff, E. 2003. Stream invertebrate responses to trout introductions: Results from large-scale studies in the central Sierra Nevada and Yosemite National Park. PhD thesis. University of California, Santa Barbara, California.

Singer, M. B. 2007. The influence of major dams on hydrology through the drainage network of the Sacramento River basin, California. River Research and Applications 23:55–72.

Skinner, C. N., and C. Chang. 1996. Chapter 38: Fire regimes: Past and present. Pages 1041–1070 in Sierra Nevada Ecosystem Project (SNEP). Status of the Sierra Nevada. Volume II: Assessments and scientific basis for management options. Wildland Resources Center Report No. 37. University of California, Davis, California.

Skinner, J. E. 1962. An historical review of the fish and wildlife resources of the San Francisco Bay area. Water Projects Branch Report No.1. California Department of Fish and Game Water Projects Branch, Sacramento, California.

Sloat, M. R., and A.-M. K. Osterback. 2013. Maximum stream temperature and the occurrence, abundance, and behavior of steelhead trout (*Oncorhynchus mykiss*) in a southern California stream. Canadian Journal of Fisheries and Aquatic Science 70:64–73.

Smith, J. L., G. L. Boyer, E. Mills, and K. L. Schulz. 2008. Toxicity of microcystin, a cyanobacterial toxin, to multiple life stages of the burrowing mayfly, Hexagenia, and possible implications for recruitment. Environmental Toxicology 23(4):499–506. <doi:10.1002/tox.20369>.

Sommer, T. R., M. L. Nobriga, W. C. Harrell, W. Batham, and W. J. Kimmerer. 2001. Floodplain rearing of juvenile Chinook salmon: Evidence of enhanced growth and survival. Canadian Journal of Fisheries and Aquatic Sciences 58:325–333.

Sommer, T. R., W. C. Harrell, and M. L. Nobriga. 2005. Habitat use and stranding risk of juvenile Chinook salmon on a seasonal floodplain. North American Journal of Fisheries Management 25:1493–1504.

Sommer, T. R., W. C. Harrell, and T. J. Swift. 2008. Extreme hydrologic banding in a large-river Floodplain, California, USA. Hydrobiologia 598:409–415.

Sommer, T. R., W. C. Harrell, M. Nobriga, R. Brown, P. Moyle, W. Kimmerer, and L. Schemel. 2001. California's Yolo Bypass: Evidence that flood control can be compatible with fisheries, wetlands, wildlife, and agriculture. Fisheries 26:6–16.

Sousa, W. P. 1984. The role of disturbance in natural communities. Annual Review Ecology and Systematics 15:353–391.

Spina, A. P. 2007. Thermal ecology of juvenile steelhead in a warm-water environment. Environmental Biology of Fishes 80:23–34.

Spina, A. P., M. A. Allen, and M. Clarke. 2005. Downstream migration, rearing abundance, and pool habitat associations of juvenile steelhead in the lower main stem of a south-central California stream. North American Journal of Fisheries Management 25:919–930.

Spinks, P. Q., G. B. Pauly, J. J. Crayon, and H. Bradley Shaffer. 2003. Survival of the western pond turtle (*Emys marmorata*) in an urban California environment. Biological Conservation 113:257–267.

Stanley, E. H., and M. W. Doyle. 2003. Trading off: The ecological effects of dam removal. Frontiers in Ecology and Environment 1:15–22.

Stebbins, R. C., and S. McGinnis. 2012. Field guide to amphibians and reptiles of California. University of California Press, Berkeley, California.

Stephens, S. L., R. E. Martin, and N. E. Clinton. 2007. Prehistoric fire area and emissions from California's forests, woodlands, shrublands, and grasslands. Forest Ecology and Management 251:205–216.

Stephens, S. L., T. Meixner, M. Poth, B. McGurk, and D. Payne. 2004. Prescribed fire, soils, and stream water chemistry in a watershed in the Lake Tahoe Basin, California. International Journal of Wildland Fire 13:27–35.

Stevenson, R. J., M. J. Bothwell, and R. L. Lowe. 1996. Algal ecology. Academic Press, San Diego, California.

Stock, G., and R. Anderson. 2012. Yosemite's melting glaciers. <http://www.cfc.umt.edu/CESU/Reports/NPS/CU/2009/09_11Anderson_YOSE_glaciers_fnl%20rpt.pdf>. Accessed October 9, 2013.

Stocking, R. W., and J. L. Bartholomew. 2007. Distribution and habitat characteristics of *Manayunkia speciosa* and infection prevalence with the parasite *Ceratomyxa shasta* in the Klamath River, Oregon—California. Journal of Parasitology 93:78–88.

Sullivan, A. B., S. A. Rounds, M. L. Deas, J. R. Asbill, R. E. Wellman, M. A. Stewart, M. W. Johnston, and I. E. Sogutlugil. 2011. Modeling hydrodynamics, water temperature, and water quality in the Klamath River upstream of Keno Dam, Oregon, 2006–09. U.S. Geological Survey Scientific Investigations Report 2011–5105.

Surface Water Ambient Monitoring Program (SWAMP). 2014. California Environmental Protection Agency, State Water Resources Control Board. <http://www.waterboards.ca.gov/water_issues/programs/swamp/>. Accessed February 15, 2014.

Suttle, K. B., M. E. Power, J. A. Levine, and F. C. McNeely. 2004. How fine sediment in river beds impairs growth and survival of juvenile salmonids. Ecological Applications 14:969–974.

Sutton, R. J., S. K. Tanaka, M. L. Deas, T. Soto, and A. Corum. 2007. Salmonid observations at a Klamath River thermal refuge under various hydrological and meteorological conditions. River Research and Applications 23:775–785.

Swift, C. C., T. R. Haglund, M. Ruiz, and R. N. Fisher. 1993. The status and distribution of freshwater fishes of southern California. Bulletin of the Southern California Academic of Sciences 92:101–167.

Tatarian, P. J. 2008. Movement patterns of California red-legged frogs (*Rana draytonii*) in an inland California environment. Herpetological Conservation and Biology 3:155–169.

Thorp, J. H., and A. P. Covich, editors. 2010. Ecology and classification of North American freshwater invertebrates. Third edition. Academic Press, Elsevier, San Diego, California.

Thorson, J. T., M. D. Scheuerell, E. R. Buhle, and T. Copeland. 2013. Spatial variation buffers temporal fluctuations in early juvenile survival for an endangered Pacific salmon. Journal of Animal Ecology 83:157–167.

Thrower, F. P., J. E. Joyce, A. G. Clewycz, and P. W. Malecha. 2008. The potential importance of reservoirs in the western United States for recovery of endangered populations of anadromous steelhead. American Fisheries Society Symposium 62:309–324.

Thrower, F. P., J. J. Hard, and J. E. Joyce. 2004. Genetic architecture of growth and early life-history transitions in anadromous and derived freshwater populations of steelhead. Journal of Fish Biology 65(suppl. A):286–307.

Townsend-Small, A., D. E. Patak, H. Liu, Z. Li, Q. Wu, and B. Thomas. 2013. Increasing summer river discharge in southern California, USA, linked to urbanization. Geophysical Research Letters 40:4643–4647.

Tsui, M. T. K., J. D. Blum, J. C. Finlay, S. J. Balogh, Y. H. Nollet, W. J. Palen, and M. E. Power. 2013. Tracing sources of methylmercury to stream predators using stable mercury isotopes. Submitted to Environmental Science and Chemistry.

Twitty, V., D. Grant, and O. Anderson. 1964. Long distance homing in the newt *Taricha rivularis*. Proceedings of the National Academy of Sciences 51:51–58.

U.S. Energy Information Administration. 2013. Renewable generation provides a growing share of California's electricity. <http://www.eia.gov/todayinenergy/detail.cfm?id=13071>. Accessed February 2014.

U.S. Fish and Wildlife Service. 1998. California freshwater shrimp (*Syncaris pacifica* Holmes) recovery plan. U.S. Fish and Wildlife Service, Portland, Oregon.

Vannote, R. L., G. W. Minshall, K. W. Cummins, J. R. Sedell, and C. E. Cushing. 1980. The river continuum concept. Canadian Journal of Fisheries and Aquatic Sciences 37:130–137.

Verkaik, I., M. Rieradevall, S. D. Cooper, J. M. Melack, T. L. Dudley, and N. Prat. 2013. Fire as a disturbance in Mediterranean climate streams. Hydrobiologia 719:353–382.

Vicars, W. C., and J. O. Sickman. 2011. Mineral dust transport to the Sierra Nevada, California: Loading rates and potential source areas. Journal of Geophysical Research 116:G01018. <doi:10.1029/2010JG001394>.

Vicars, W. C., J. O. Sickman, and P. J. Ziemann. 2010. Atmospheric phosphorus deposition at a montane site: Size distribution, effects of wildfire, and ecological implications. Atmospheric Environment 44:2813–2821.

Vitousek, P. M., and R. W. Howarth. 1991. Nitrogen limitation on land and in the sea: How can it occur? Biogeochemistry 13:87–115.

Wales, J. H. 1951. The decline of the Shasta River king salmon run. Bureau of Fish Conservation, California Division of Fish and Game. Sacramento, California.

Wallace, David Rains. 1983. The Klamath knot. Yolla Bolly Press, San Francisco, California.

Waples, R. S., G. R. Pess, and T. Beechie. 2008. SYNTHESIS: Evolutionary history of Pacific salmon in dynamic environments. Evolutionary Applications 1:189–206.

Waples, R. S., T. Beechie, and G. R. Pess. 2009. Evolutionary history, habitat disturbance regimes, and anthropogenic changes: What do these mean for resilience of Pacific salmon populations? Ecology and Society 14:3. <http://www.ecologyandsociety.org/vol14/iss1/art3/>. Accessed June 20, 2015.

Ward, J. V., and J. A. Stanford. 1983. The serial discontinuity concept of lotic ecosystems. Pages 29–41 in T. D. Fontaine III and S. M. Bartell, editors. Dynamics of lotic ecosystems. Ann Arbor Science, Ann Arbor, Michigan.

Waters, T. F. 1995. Sediment in streams: Sources, biological effects, and control. American Fisheries Society Monograph. Bethesda, Maryland.

Webster, J. R., and E. F. Benfield. 1986. Vascular plant breakdown in freshwater ecosystems. Annual Review of Ecology and Systematics 17:567–594.

Weller, G. B., D. S. Cooley, and S. R. Sain. 2012. An investigation of the pineapple express phenomenon via bivariate extreme value theory. Environmetrics 23:420–439.

Welsh, H. H., Jr., and G. R. Hodgson. 2011. Spatial relationships in a dendritic network: The herpetofaunal metacommunity of the Mattole River catchment of northwest California. Ecography 34:49–66.

Weston, D. P., and M. J. Lydy. 2012. Stormwater input of pyrethroid insecticides to an urban river. Environmental Toxicology and Chemistry 31:1579–1586.

Whipple A. A., R. M. Grossinger, D. Rankin, B. Stanford, and R. A. Askevold. 2012. Sacramento–San Joaquin Delta historical ecology investigation: Exploring pattern and process. Prepared for the California Department of Fish and Game and Ecosystem Restoration Program. A Report of SFEI-ASC's Historical Ecology Program, Publication #672. San Francisco Estuary Institute–Aquatic Science Center, Richmond, California.

White, M. D., and K. A. Greer. 2006. The effects of watershed urbanization on the stream hydrology and riparian vegetation of Los Penasquitos Creek, California. Landscape and Urban Planning 74:125–138.

Whitton, B. A. 1970. Biology of *Cladophora* in freshwaters. Water Research 4:457–476.

Wickstein, M. K. 2012. Decapod crustacean of the Californian and Oregonian zoogeographic provinces. Zootaxa 3371:1–307.

Wilzbach, M. A., and K. W. Cummins. 2009. Recommendations for study of the distribution and population dynamics of the freshwater polychaete, *Manayunkia speciosa* in the Lower Klamath River. Final report, USGS Research Work Order 77, February 2009. <http://www.humboldt.edu/cuca/documents/reports/RWO77FinalReport.pdf>. Accessed July 25, 2013.

Wootton, J. T., M. S. Parker, and M. E. Power. 1996. Effects of disturbance on river food webs. Science 273:1558–1561.

Worster, D. 1985. Rivers of empire: Water, aridity, and the growth of the American West. Oxford University Press, Oxford, UK.

Wright, J. P., C. G. Jones, and A. S. Flecker. 2002. An ecosystem engineer, the beaver, increases species richness at the landscape scale. Oecologia 132:96–101.

Wu, L. 2004. Review of 15 years of research on ecotoxicology and remediation of land contaminated by agricultural drainage sediment rich in selenium. Ecotoxicology and Environmental Safety 57:257–269.

Yarnell, S. M., J. H. Viers, and J. F. Mount. 2010. Ecology and management of the spring snowmelt recession. BioScience 60:114–127.

Yoshiyama, R. M., E. R. Gerstung, F. W. Fisher, and P. B. Moyle. 2001. Historical and present distribution of Chinook salmon in the Central Valley drainage of California. Pages 71–176 in R. L. Brown, editor. Contributions to the biology of Central Valley salmonids. Fish Bulletin. California Department of Fish Game 179. Sacramento, California.

Zimmerman, C. E., and G. H. Reeves. 2000. Population structure of sympatric anadromous and nonanadromous *Oncorhynchus mykiss*: Evidence from spawning surveys and otolith microchemistry. Canadian Journal of Fisheries and Aquatic Science 57:2152–2162.

PART FIVE

MANAGED SYSTEMS

THIRTY-FOUR

Managed Island Ecosystems

KATHRYN MCEACHERN, TANYA ATWATER, PAUL W. COLLINS, KATE FAULKNER, and DANIEL V. RICHARDS

Introduction

The California Islands are mainland California in a microcosm. They harbor incredible biodiversity. They have been exploited and managed for nearly all of the same human uses discussed throughout this book. Alien annual grasslands have replaced native scrub vegetation, soils have eroded to the sea, hydrologic functions have been disrupted, marine ecosystems have been depleted of harvested species, and some species have been pushed to extinction or near-extinction. However, land managers are working to reduce historical stressors on the state's island ecosystems. Many non-native animals and aggressive introduced plants have been removed, at-risk species have been identified, and restoration is under way. No-harvest areas have been established in the marine waters around the islands in the United States (U.S.), and science now plays a bigger role in marine harvest decisions.

The California islands are on trajectories toward a future of dominance by natives that sustains island endemics and conserves biodiversity. Oil and gas exploration is exhausted onshore and diminished offshore, the military has increased its environmental stewardship, agriculture is reduced in acreage, urban development is managed for limited impact, and the history of Native American life and European ranching has been preserved for research and education. These islands are among the only places in the world to witness ecosystems putting themselves back together. How did they get here, and what raw materials are left for recovery? How RESILIENT are these ecosystems? Will ecological restoration better position these islands to face the threats of rapidly changing climate and ocean acidification? Can management foster islands resilient to a variety of perturbations and requiring of less dramatic intervention in an uncertain future? In these islands lie lessons for all of California.

California Islands

The California Islands comprise eighteen named islands extending from 38 to 27.5 degrees north latitude, from California in the U.S. southward to central Baja California, Mexico (Figure 34.1). They range in size from Cedros Island at 348 square kilometers (km^2) (134 square miles [mi^2]) to tiny San Geronimo at less than 0.05 km^2 (99 acres or 0.4 mi^2) (Table

34.1). Ten islands belong to the U.S., including the Farallon Islands, Año Nuevo, San Miguel, Santa Rosa, Santa Cruz, Anacapa, San Nicolas, Santa Barbara, Santa Catalina, and San Clemente. Eight more islands off the coast of northern and central Baja California are included in the archipelago. These Baja Islands include Los Coronados, Todos Santos, San Martin, San Geronimo, Guadalupe, San Benito, Cedros, and Natividad. Small islets also occur near some of the islands; typically these are included in land ownership and management plans along with their neighboring island. Some of the California Islands have never been connected to the mainland and others have only intermittently in prehistoric times, resulting in high numbers of endemic species and great contributions to the overall biodiversity of the State of California.

All of these islands have been used for commercial gains, but most are now managed as public lands (see Table 34.1). In both the U.S. and Mexico, management now focuses on conservation of the island ecosystems, in recognition of their uniqueness and impressive biodiversity. This chapter focuses on the Channel Islands—eight of the ten U.S. islands, located in the marine waters of the Southern California Bight from Point Conception to the U.S.-Mexico border. A wealth of information on the natural and cultural history of these islands exists to guide management. In many ways these eight Channel Islands illustrate issues shared by all eighteen California Islands as land managers seek diverse solutions to shared conservation concerns.

Channel Islands in the Southern California Bight

The California Channel Islands range in size from Anacapa and Santa Barbara Islands, at about 2.9–2.6 km^2 each (1 mi^2), to Santa Cruz and Santa Rosa Islands at 244 km^2 and 217 km^2 (96 mi^2 and 83 mi^2), respectively. Like nearby mainland coastal southern California, the islands experience a Mediterranean climate with warm, wet winters and hot, dry summers. The islands are among the first sites in the state known to have been occupied by modern humans—some of the oldest human remains documented on the North American continent come from Santa Rosa Island, dating from about thirteen thousand years ago (Johnson et al. 2002, Erlandson et al. 2011; see Chapter 10, "Indigenous California"). The Chumash and Gabrieleño people may have had permanent settlements on the islands as early as eight thousand years ago, subsisting primarily on marine resources and supplemented by plants gathered seasonally. The era of European exploration from the 1500s to the early 1800s was a period of transition that ended with the removal of Native Americans from the islands and the beginning of ranching land use. A number of non-native animals were introduced (Table 34.2); and sustained grazing pressure, primarily by domestic European mouflon sheep (domestic sheep, *Ovis aries*) and domestic cattle (*Bos taurus*), lasted nearly 150 years. During that time much of the native island scrub was destroyed and replaced by non-native annual grasses, a phenomenon known throughout California as vegetation type conversion. Concurrently, harvest pressure increased on fishes, lobsters (*Panulirus interruptus*), and shellfish; seabird populations declined; and several species of PINNIPEDS were hunted to near extinction (Cass 1985, Stewart et al. 1993, Stewart et al. 1994). Unlike the mainland, few people live on the islands now, which are managed for conservation, recreation, and national defense.

Photo on previous page: Looking eastward toward Prince Island from San Miguel Island to Santa Rosa and Santa Cruz Islands, 2011: a view across the Pleistocene island Santa Rosae. Photo: Daniel Richards.

Unique Flora and Fauna

The lack of a "land bridge" connecting the California Channel Islands to the mainland throughout their existence has strong ecological consequences apparent today (Wenner and Johnson 1980). First, the flora and fauna of the islands derive from a subset of mainland species that managed to cross the channels, establish permanently, and expand as they adapted to island conditions. Many changed genetically and morphologically from their mainland types into new, endemic species and subspecies. Second, because the plants and animals stem from a subset of the mainland flora and fauna, island native plant and animal communities are correspondingly simpler in structure. Island coastal sage scrub, for example, lacks several species that dominate coastal sage scrub on the nearby mainland. As a result, most vegetation cover in island coastal sage scrub is composed of just one or two species. Damage to those species can place the entire community at risk. Because vegetation provides habitat for island animals, its loss can cascade through the system with potentially devastating effects on both invertebrates and vertebrates. Reference to islands as fragile ecosystems most often reflects islands' smaller community-wide set of species, because reduced complexity can confer greater vulnerability. On the other hand, this reduced complexity might also allow island ecosystems to recover quickly once stressors are removed, provided that key island species still exist in sufficient numbers to recover.

Why So Diverse?

As a group, the California Channel Islands constitute an area of extraordinary biological diversity with more unique marine and terrestrial taxa per square kilometer than most temperate islands of the world. A number of factors help explain why this is so. First, only five regions in the world have a Mediterranean-type climate—a globally rare setting for the evolution of novel plants and animals. Second, wind and oceanic currents often drive deep, nutrient-rich waters toward the surface near the Channel Islands. This deep-water upwelling sustains high biomass and diversity of phytoplankton, zooplankton, marine algae, and the organisms that depend upon them. Third, the Southern California Bight is a unique transition zone where cold water carried from the north Pacific by the California Current meets warm water brought from the south on the southern California Countercurrent. Strong air and water temperature gradients run across the island archipelago driven by these regional currents; each island and its nearshore marine environment has a slightly different climate. Plants and animals to the northwest are exposed to year-round wind and fog; air and water temperatures are lower here than in the southeastern part of the Bight (Engle 1994, Channel Islands National Park Weather Monitoring Program unpublished data). On land this climate gradient drives the evolution of genetically distinct species, subspecies, and ecotypes across the islands. Marine life differences among the islands are also related largely to variation in exposure to northern and southern currents carrying warm-water and cool-water larvae. Finally, compounding the effect of strong

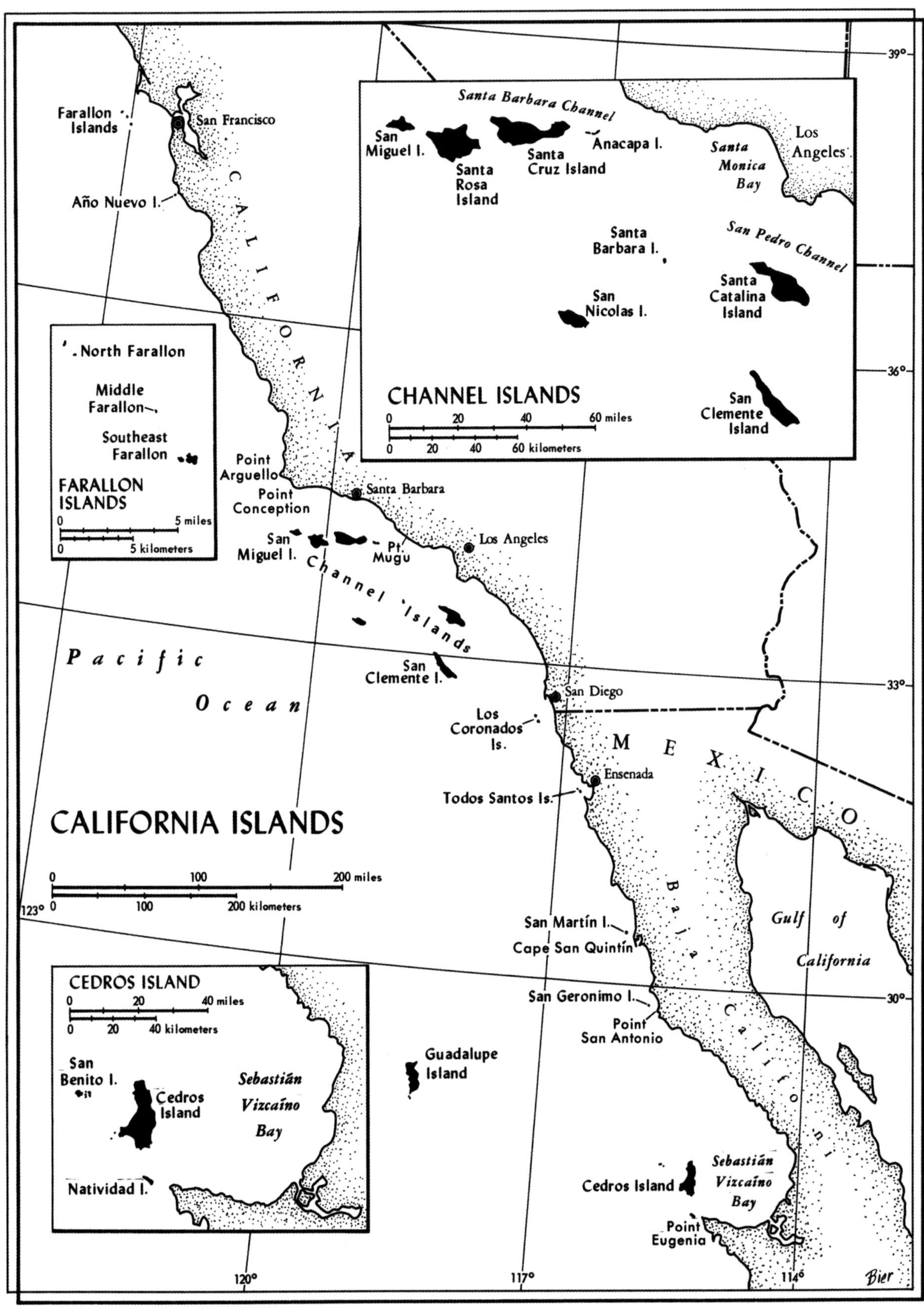

FIGURE 34.1 Eighteen California Islands. Source: Power 1980. Reproduced by permission of the Santa Barbara Museum of Natural History, Santa Barbara, California.

TABLE 34.1
Physical characteristics and land ownership of the eighteen California Islands

Island	Area km²	Area mi²	Distance to mainland km (mi)	Distance to nearest island km (mi)	Number of plant taxa	Percentage of native plants	Land owners
Northern California Islands, U.S.							
Farallon Group	0.9	0.3	32 (20)	88 (54)	NA	NA	U.S. Fish and Wildlife Service
Año Nuevo	0.05	0.02	0.5 (0.3)	88 (54)	NA	NA	State of California
Northern Channel Islands, U.S. (formerly connected as Pleistocene Santa Rosae)							
San Miguel	37	14.5	42 (26)	5 (3)	270	74	U.S. Navy (managed by the U.S. National Park Service)
Santa Rosa	217	83.1	43 (27)	5 (3)	500	80	U.S. National Park Service
Santa Cruz	244	96.5	30 (19)	8 (5)	680	72	The Nature Conservancy, U.S. National Park Service
Anacapa	2.9	1.1	19 (12)	8 (5)	265	72	U.S. National Park Service
Southern Channel Islands, U.S. (never connected to other islands)							
San Nicolas	58	22.7	98 (61)	45 (28)	277	49	U.S. Navy
Santa Barbara	2.6	1.0	61 (38)	39 (24)	135	67	U.S. National Park Service
Santa Catalina	194	75.0	32 (20)	34 (21)	650	66	Catalina Island Conservancy, Santa Catalina Island Company
San Clemente	145	56.8	79 (49)	34 (21)	435	69	U.S. Navy
Baja California Islands, Mexico (administered by the Ministry of the Interior, Mexico)							
Coronados	2.5	1.0	13 (8)	76 (47)	126	76	Mexican Federal Territory
Todos Santos	1.2	0.5	6 (4)	76 (47)	142	76	Mexican Federal Territory
San Martin	2.3	0.9	5 (3)	82 (51)	98	82	Mexican Federal Territory
San Geronimo	0.4	0.2	9 (6)	82 (51)	–	50	Mexican Federal Territory
Guadalupe	249	98	252 (157)	249 (155)	216	72	Mexican Federal Territory
San Benito	6.4	2.5	66 (41)	25 (16)	51	83	Mexican Federal Territory
Cedros	348	134	23 (14)	16 (10)	267	86	Mexican Federal Territory
Natividad	7.2	2.8	7 (5)	16 (10)	77	82	Mexican Federal Territory

SOURCES: Data from Junak and Philbrick 1999a, Junak and Philbrick 1999b, Moran 1996, Oberbauer 1987, Oberbauer 1999a, Oberbauer 1999b, Power 1980, Raven 1967, Channel Islands National Park Geographic Information Systems Program 2014.

climate gradients is the serendipitous pattern in which plants and animals came to the islands, yielding different subsets of mainland plants and animals as each island subsampled the nearby mainland.

Ownership and Land Use

Most of the California Channel Islands are now in the public trust, owned by federal agencies including the U.S. Navy (Navy) and the National Park Service (NPS); or by private organizations including The Nature Conservancy, the Santa Catalina Island Company, and the Catalina Island Conservancy. The Navy owns San Clemente and San Nicolas and manages a small facility on Santa Cruz Island. While the Navy also owns San Miguel Island, it falls within the boundaries of Channel Islands National Park and is managed by the NPS by mutual agreement. Channel Islands National Park encompasses the four northern islands of Anacapa, Santa Rosa, Santa Cruz, and San Miguel; and the southern Channel Island of Santa Barbara. The park maintains housing for staff on these five islands along with public campgrounds open year-round. The Nature Conservancy owns 76% of Santa Cruz Island and maintains a historic ranch complex used for housing; the remaining 24% of the island is owned by the NPS. The University of California Natural Reserve System manages the Santa Cruz Island Reserve from a research station on the island, and California State University Channel Islands

TABLE 34.2
Timeline of terrestrial mammal introductions and eradications on the California Channel Islands that accompanied European settlement

Species	San Miguel	Santa Rosa	Santa Cruz	Anacapa	Santa Barbara	San Nicolas	Santa Catalina	San Clemente
				Rabbits (*Lagomorpha*)				
European rabbit					1942–1981		2000–present (pets)	
European hare				1930s–mid-1960s	1918–1930s			
				Rodents (*Rodentia*)				
Western harvest mouse								1930s–present?
California vole								1930s–present?
House mouse							Early 1900s–present	Post-1943–present
Black rat	Early 1900s–present			1853?–2002			Early 1900s–present	Post-1943–present
Norway rat							1939–present?	
				Carnivores (*Carnivora*)				
Dogs								
Domestic dog	1884–1940s	1888–1993	1880s–1980			1853–1857, early 1940s	Late 1800s–present (pets)	1870s–1940s
Cats								
Feral cat	1884–Early 1940s	Late 1930s	Early 1920s–1939	Late 1920s–late 1940s	Pre-1863–1978	1901–2010	Pre-1932–present	1863–present
				Herbivores: Odd-toed ungulates (*Perissodactyla*)				
Horse	1851–1948	1844–present	1830–2009		1915–1919	1857–1943	1863–present	1860s–1958, 1972–1977
Mule/burro/donkey	Early 1950s–1976	1880s			1915–1922	1900s–early 1940s	1886–1903?	1913–1930s
				Herbivores: Even–toed ungulates (*Artiodactyla*)				
Pigs								
Feral pig	1851–1897?	1853–1993	1852–2006				1932–2004	1951–1990
Deer								
Fallow deer		1890–1949						

(continued)

TABLE 34.2 *(continued)*

Species	San Miguel	Santa Rosa	Santa Cruz	Anacapa	Santa Barbara	San Nicolas	Santa Catalina	San Clemente
Mule deer		1880–2015					1928–present	1955, 1962–1990
Elk		1879–2011						
Cattle, Sheep, Goats								
American bison							1924–present	
Domestic cattle	1851–1917?	1844–1998	1830–1999			1856–1870, late 1930s	1854–1970s	1890s–1934
Blackbuck							1972–2011	
Goat	Late 1880s–1890?	1883–early 1900s	Late 1880s, 1919–1920				Pre-1827–2005	1875–1993
European mouflon sheep	Pre-1850–early 1970s	1844–early 1960s	1853–2001	1869–1937	Pre-1863–1926, 1942–1946	1856–1949	1850s–mid-1920s	1853–1941
Barbary sheep							1973–late 1970s	

SOURCES: Data from Von Bloeker 1967, Garcelon et al. 2005, Keegen et al. 1994, Livingston 2006, Paul Collins unpublished data, Channel Islands National Park unpublished data, Catalina Island Conservancy unpublished data, U.S. Navy unpublished data, Santa Barbara Museum of Natural History Channel Islands unpublished archives, Santa Cruz Island Foundation unpublished archives.

recently established a research station on Santa Rosa Island. The Catalina Island Conservancy owns and manages 88% of Santa Catalina Island, while 11% is owned by the Santa Catalina Island Company and 1% is the City of Avalon. Currently, the NPS islands are accessible to the public through boat and airplane concessions and private boat transportation. Catalina Island is served by ferry service and a small airport. San Clemente and San Nicolas are closed to the public.

The boundaries of Channel Islands National Park extend 1.8 kilometers (1 nautical mile) into the ocean from each of the five islands, and the U.S. National Oceanic and Atmospheric Administration's (NOAA) Channel Islands National Marine Sanctuary protects resources up to 11.1 kilometers (6 nautical miles) from shore (Figure 34.2). In 2003 a system of MARINE PROTECTED AREAS (MPAs) was established by the State of California (2002) and NOAA around the park islands, expanded to the remaining three Channel Islands in 2012. These management agencies work together to fulfill their individual missions, but they also work together by mutual agreement for the recovery and conservation of the unique biota of the islands and the processes that support them.

Southern California's Geologic History

Creation and Disruption of the Continental Rim

The distinct geography of the California Bight and Channel Islands results from regional plate tectonics (Figure 34.3; see Chapter 4, "Geomorphology and Soils"). Presently, the San Andreas Fault system is the plate boundary between the Pacific and North American plates. For more than one hundred million years, however, the rim of western North America was a SUBDUCTION ZONE, with the Farallon and other oceanic plates diving beneath this rim. Starting approximately twenty-five million years ago, the continent overran these plates and came into contact with the huge Pacific plate for the first time. This new plate boundary lengthened until about five million years ago, when it reached its present span of about 1,500 miles from Cape Mendocino to the mouth of the Gulf of California (Atwater 1998, Atwater and Stock 1998).

That first Pacific plate contact region sat along the continental edge offshore of southern California, and the great geological complexity there reflects the gradual transfer of pieces of the continental rim from the North American plate to the Pacific plate. The continental shelf off southern California, "the California Borderland" (Figure 34.4), is therefore both broad and broken up in stark contrast to nearly every other continental shelf in the world. The islands are the tops of some of the broken blocks that happen to be taller than present sea level.

Rotation of the Transverse Ranges Block

The most unusual aspect of the continental breakup off southern California is the rotation of the Transverse Ranges block (Crouch and Suppe 1993; see Figure 34.4). The Pacific plate was moving northwestward, upcoast and a little offshore. As the Pacific plate scraped against North America, it plucked off pieces of the continental edge and carried them away. Most pieces simply pulled away and slid along, but one piece had its southern end pulled out while its northern end remained embedded in the continent. That piece rotated, eventually

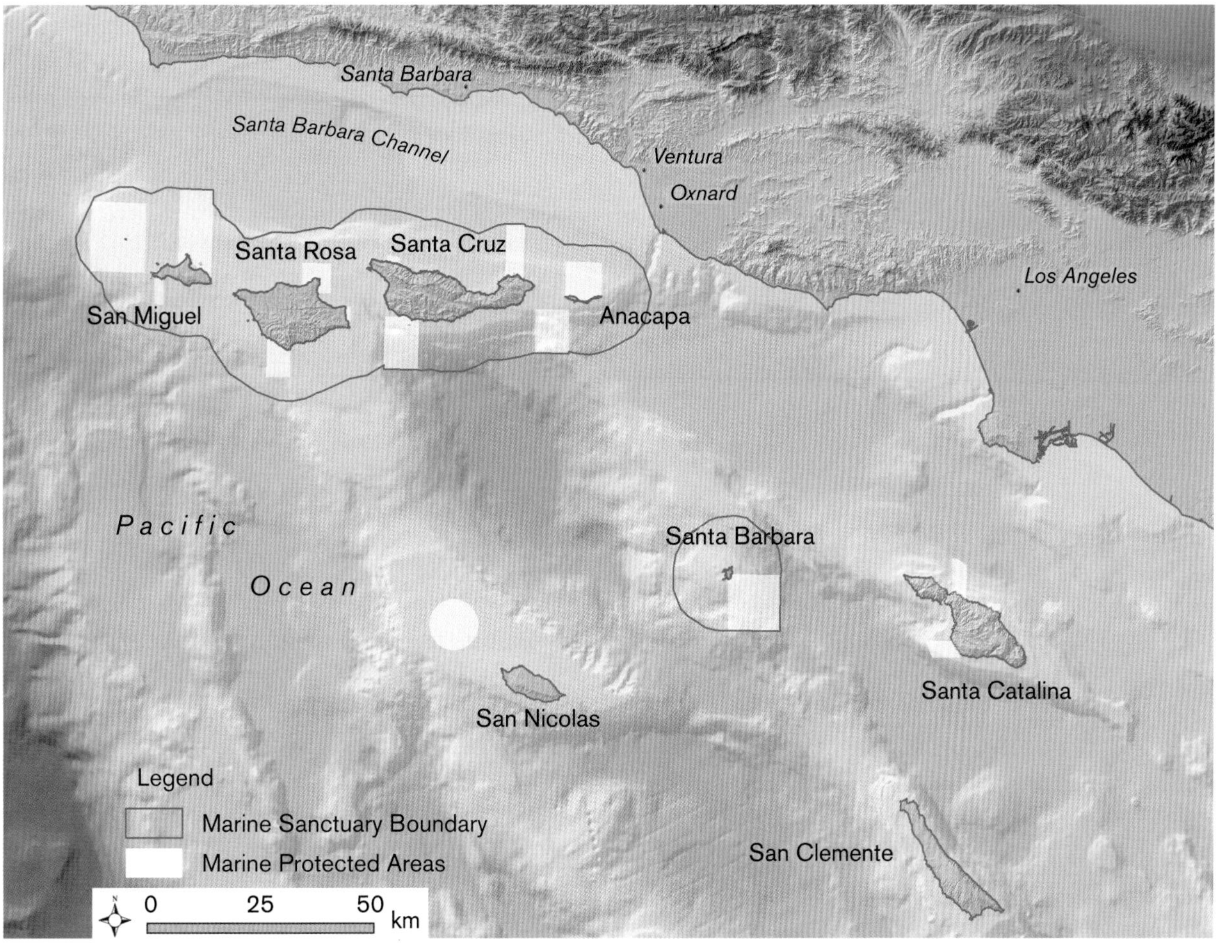

Santa Barbara
Santa Barbara Channel
Ventura
Oxnard
Santa Rosa
Santa Cruz
San Miguel
Anacapa
Los Angeles
Pacific
Ocean
Santa Barbara
San Nicolas
Santa Catalina
Legend
Marine Sanctuary Boundary
Marine Protected Areas
San Clemente
0 25 50 km

FIGURE 34.2 The eight U.S. Channel Islands, California Borderlands, and subsurface bathymetry, showing the National Marine Sanctuary and Channel Islands Marine Protected Areas. Source: Redrawn from National Park Service files and California Department of Fish and Wildlife 2013.

NORTH AMERICAN PLATE
PACIFIC PLATE
Transform fault
Spreading center
Subduction zone
Ma = million years ago
25 Ma
12.5 Ma
Present

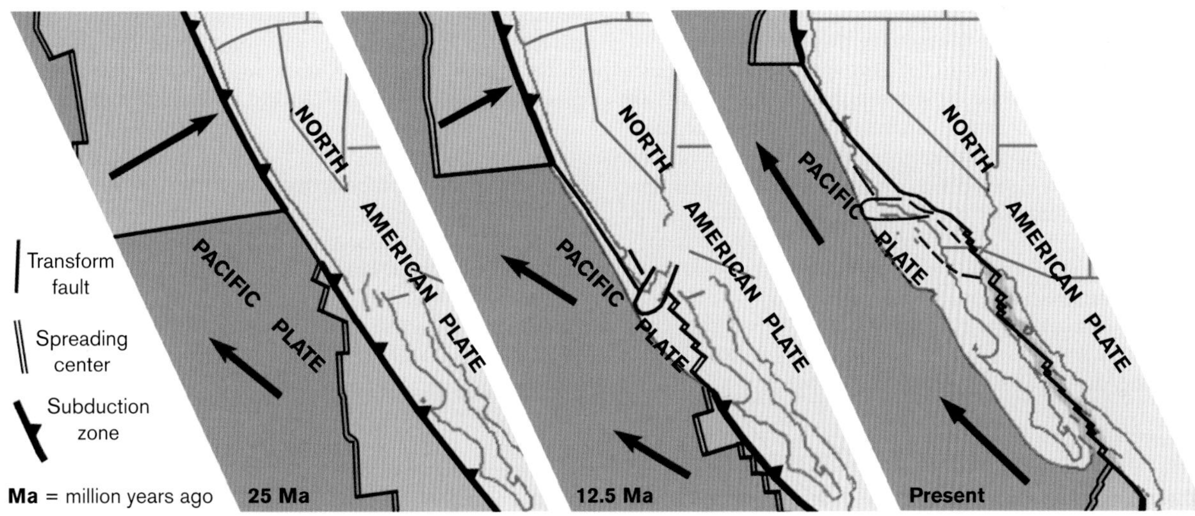

FIGURE 34.3 The southern California continental rim was broken up to form the California Borderland during the development of the San Andreas plate boundary. Source: After Atwater and Stock 1998.

25 MA: The Pacific and North American plates first make contact, establishing a plate boundary along the rim of the continent.

12.5 MA: The contact region has lengthened and the plate boundary has moved inland, obliquely pulling open the Borderland region.

PRESENT: The plate boundary has moved farther inland into the Gulf of California and to the present location of the San Andreas Fault, putting most of southern California into a compressive condition. To view or download various animations of this evolution, see Atwater 2007.

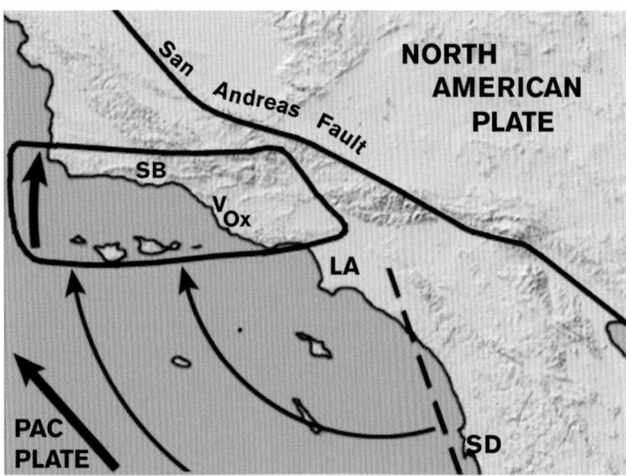

FIGURE 34.4 During the formation of the southern California Borderland, the Transverse Ranges block, outlined, has been turned clockwise about 110 degrees and compressed, forming the east-west trending coastlines, mountains, and the northern Channel Islands. Source: Atwater and Stock 1998.

SB = Santa Barbara, **V** = Ventura, **Ox** = Oxnard, **LA** = Los Angeles, **SD** = San Diego, California.

turning about 110 degrees clockwise (Luyendyk 1991, Hornafius et al. 1986). The bight at Point Conception and the present east-west orientation of the mountains, coastlines, and islands south of the bight result directly from this rotation.

Interactions between the rotating Transverse Ranges block and its neighbors generated much of the topography of southwestern California, both onshore and in the offshore Borderland. Along the block's northern edge collisions push upward, forming the Santa Ynez, Topa Topa, and other mountains. Along its southern edge, other blocks following the rotating block northwestward are running into and under it, pushing up land to form the four northern Channel Islands, the Santa Monica Mountains, and the Hollywood Hills. As the rotation of the Transverse Ranges block proceeds, the regions north and south of the block have to constantly readjust their shapes to fill the ever-changing space. These readjustments are accomplished by slip along numerous faults in those regions. The southern Channel Islands and the Palos Verdes Peninsula appear to be the results of oblique collisions along those faults (Legg 1991). About five million years ago, Baja California came off the continent as one intact piece and joined the Pacific plate. This moved the plate boundary inland to the Gulf of California, forming a "big bend" and putting southern California under compression.

Sculpting during the Pleistocene Ice Ages

CLIMATE BELT SHIFTS

Although no glacial ice occurred in southwestern California during the Pleistocene, the alternating glacials (ice ages) and interglacials of that period caused global climate belts to fluctuate south and north across the region and down and up in elevation. The flora followed these belts, shifting in latitude and elevation. The effects of climate shifts on the island flora are not well studied, but major shifts could have eliminated some of the more marginal, climate-sensitive species and made available habitat for new, chance arrivals.

SEA LEVEL FLUCTUATIONS AND COASTLINES

Among the most important effects of the ice ages were great fluctuations in sea level resulting from periodic changes in the global volume of water stored as ice. These sea level changes caused large shifts in the locations of coastlines. For example, at the time of the last glacial maximum (about 26,500 to 19,000 years ago) (Clark et al. 2009), global sea level was about 120 m (394 ft) lower than present (Muhs et al. 2012); the land around and between the four northern Channel Islands was uncovered, and they formed one large island known as Santa Rosae. The coastline of the nearby mainland shifted outward, but a deep, narrow channel remained between the mainland and the island so that no dry land connected them. The shortest distance across the channel was reduced to about 8 km (5 mi) as compared to the present 18 km (11 mi). Humans, having arrived in the Channel Islands about thirteen thousand years ago (Erlandson et al. 1996, Johnson et al. 2002), would have experienced the last parts of the glacial climate and a sea level as much as 70 m (230 ft) lower than present.

CONTINUOUS DRY LAND OR SUBMERGENCE?

Terrestrial organisms could not likely have survived on the islands from the time of the original breakup of the continental rim nearly twenty million years ago. The present islands most likely spent most of that time submerged. The tops of most of the islands are marine terrace surfaces, ground down to below sea level at the times the terraces were formed. Furthermore, many of the islands contain wide outcroppings of the Monterey Formation, rocks deposited on the seafloor well below the waves. The similar but more complete rock record on the nearby mainland contains only marine rocks during most of this period. Finally, tectonic history implies that the Borderland was rifted and extended during most of its history such that the crust thinned and probably subsided. The present regime of compressions and collisions began about five million to six million years ago when Baja California was transferred to the Pacific plate and began to collide with southern California. The island flora and fauna hence probably crossed the water and arrived within the last few million years.

Patterns of Variability among Islands

Geographic Distinctions and Commonalities Based on Geologic History

The theory of ISLAND BIOGEOGRAPHY holds that the larger and more topographically complex an island, the more diverse its biota (MacArthur and Wilson 1967). It also predicts that the closer an island is to the mainland or another island, the more species rich it should be. The Channel Islands generally conform to these predictions (see Table 34.1), but their patterns of biological diversity also reflect the geologic and human history of the islands as well as their current configurations and climate gradients (Oberbauer 1999a). The larger islands have more plant and animal species. The northern islands also have more species in common with each other, due to both their proximity and their common history as ancient Santa Rosae. Small Anacapa was once part of Santa Rosae and is closer to the mainland and other islands than similarly sized Santa Barbara; it has twice as many species as

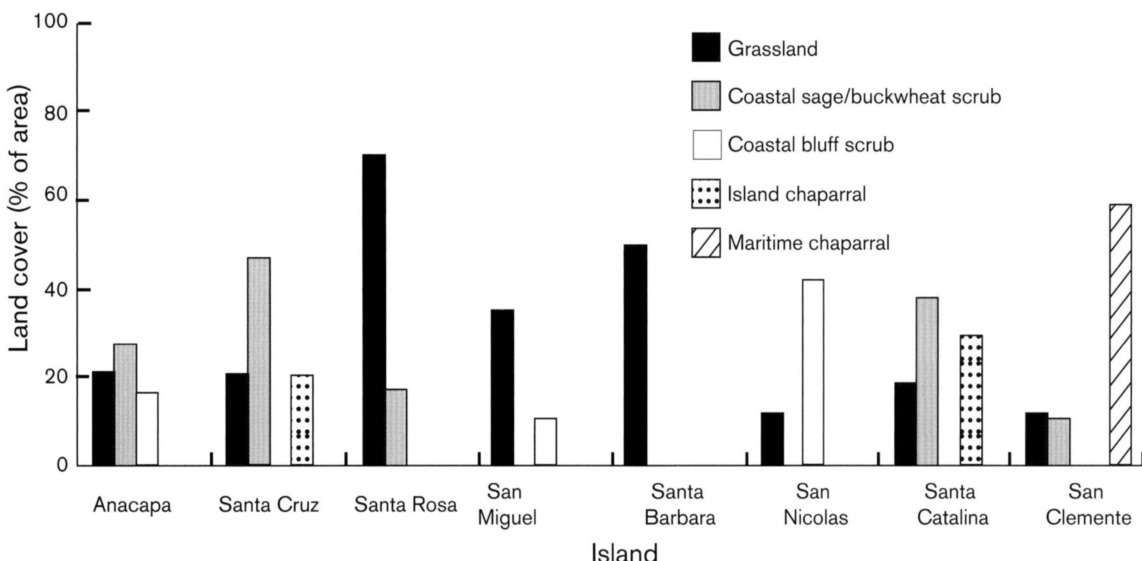

FIGURE 34.5 Percentage land cover of major Channel Island vegetation types for communities occupying greater than 10% of the total island area. Sources: Data from Hochberg et al. 1979 (Anacapa, Santa Barbara, San Miguel), Cohen et al. 2009 (Santa Cruz), Clark et al. 1990 (Santa Rosa), Halvorson et al. 1996 (San Nicolas), Knapp 2005 (Santa Catalina), NALF 2013 (San Clemente Island).

Santa Barbara. Conversely, small Santa Barbara hosts twice as many single-island endemic plants, influenced by its greater isolation.

Vegetation Bears the Imprint of Physical Environment and Past Land Use

Superimposed on patterns driven by physical factors are patterns in plant community composition and structure reflecting past land use. The "outer" islands of San Miguel and San Nicolas are cool and windy, composed of low-elevation marine terraces with sandy soils. Their native vegetation was likely a short form of island chaparral with wind-tolerant plants requiring cool and foggy conditions for growth. Conversely, the southern islands of Santa Barbara and San Clemente are much hotter and drier, with succulent plants and cacti as significant members of their island shrub communities. The larger, more topographically complex islands have a greater variety of microclimates and host a range of island variants of native community types found on the mainland including chaparral, coastal scrub, herbaceous and woody streamside vegetation and a range of woodland types. The island communities generally lack some species common on the mainland, and a large part of their cover is comprised of endemic shrubs. In testament to the effects of past land use, about 20% to 50% of the plant species list for any one island is non-native (see Table 34.1), and vegetation mapping shows that non-native annual grassland cover approximately 20% to 70% of total island area (Figure 34.5).

Vegetation Changes

A major management goal for the Channel Islands is to shift vegetation toward dominance by native plants. In general, this has been happening since feral animals were removed (see Table 34.2), but changes have been uneven in space and time, influenced by both physical characteristics of the landscape and the abilities of individual species to exploit the altered conditions. On both Santa Cruz (Klinger et al. 1994) and Santa Catalina Islands (Laughrin et al. 1994), herbivore removal initially was followed by increased annual grass cover. However, repeat mapping of plant community boundaries in 1985 and 2005 on Santa Cruz Island (Cohen et al. 2009), and repeat transect sampling and photograph analysis (Beltran et al. 2014) show a longer-term decrease in annual grassland area of about 30%, accompanied by a 30% increase in island chaparral and a nearly fifteen-fold increase in coastal sage scrub. By contrast, vegetation remained fairly static on Santa Catalina from 1975 to 2000 under a continued mule deer (*Odocoileus hemionus*), American bison (*Bos bison*), goat (*Capra hircus*), and feral pig (*Sus scrofa*) grazing regime (Knapp 2005).

Vegetation transect monitoring conducted by Channel Islands National Park on Santa Barbara Island from 1984 to 2005 showed that rates of recovery are fastest in areas with coarse-grained, deep soils—especially on northerly slopes in response, perhaps, to more favorable moisture conditions in those locations (Corry and McEachern 2009). However, these areas also had the highest proportion of natives at the time of European rabbit (*Oryctolagus cuniculus*) removal, perhaps setting the stage for more rapid recovery because native plant propagules were readily available. Extension of these analyses into 2012 showed that sites on thin, clayey soils that were dominated by non-native annuals tended to stay that way on Santa Barbara Island (U.S. Geological Survey Channel Islands Field Station, unpublished). Similar analyses of Santa Rosa Island data collected from 1989 through 2012 indicated highest rates of recovery in coastal sage and coyote brush scrub and nearby grassland sites, and in riparian areas. Rates of change on both Santa Barbara and Santa Rosa were most significantly related to precipitation in the current year and the previous two years combined. Recovery is slow to nonexistent in areas of exposed bedrock, thin or clayey soils, steep slopes, and south- and west- facing slopes. Moisture, influenced by precipitation, evaporation, and soil moisture-holding capacity, stands out as a key driver that interacts with other factors to encourage recovery.

TABLE 34.3
Numbers of endemic species, subspecies, and varieties of terrestrial plants found on the California Channel Islands

Island	Endemic to one island only	Endemic to more than one island	Endemic presumed extirpated	Island total
San Miguel Island	1	18	2	20
Santa Rosa Island	5	38	1	44
Santa Cruz Island	7	45	3	55
Anacapa Island	2	22	1	25
Santa Barbara Island	4	13	0	17
San Nicolas Island	2	15	1	18
Santa Catalina Island	8	26	1	35
San Clemente Island	15	47	1	63

SOURCES: Data from Channel Islands National Park and U.S. Geological Survey, Channel Islands Field Station unpublished data, Catalina Island Conservancy 2014, Santa Barbara Botanic Garden 2014, Center for Plant Conservation 2014.

Studies focused on single species provide insights into some mechanisms that influence population growth and spread as plants respond to feral animal reduction and environmental change. For example, on Santa Cruz Island, Yelenik and Levine (2010) showed that the native shrubs Santa Cruz Island buckwheat (*Eriogonum arborescens*) and California sagebrush (*Artemisia californica*) can alter soil nutrient cycling, possibly influencing the abilities of grasses and other shrubs to recruit with them. However, climate and plant competition also affected recruitment (Yelenik and Levine 2011) in complex feedback patterns that varied with year, soil, and the plant species involved. The presence of biological SOIL CRUSTS altered nutrient cycling on recovering dunes of San Nicolas Island (Belnap 1994), facilitating establishment of certain native plants. Repeat mapping of sixty-four rare plant species on Santa Rosa Island in 1994 and 2010 showed two-hundred- to seven-hundred-fold increases in plant numbers and expansion of population boundaries in the island's major canyons for a subset of the species (McEachern and Thomson, unpublished).

Genetic studies of endemic plants similarly colonizing canyons on San Clemente and Santa Catalina indicated that new individuals are coming into populations from long-buried seeds following reduction in grazing pressure (Furches et al. 2009, Helenurm 2003). Field studies of two endemic native annuals of Santa Rosa Island (Levine et al. 2010) showed that population growth is driven first by seed germination in response to infrequent and specific combinations of rainfall and minimum temperatures, but that once germination occurs, competition with the dense non-native grasses now occupying their habitats becomes the driving force that ultimately determines how many of those seedlings live to reproduce. Long-term demographic studies from 1995 through 2007 of an endemic Santa Rosa perennial showed that small-plant mortality increased with average air temperature, ultimately resulting in population decline even after feral herbivore reduction as the larger plants died of old age (McEachern et al. 2009). These island studies, along with many others from mainland areas, clearly indicate that vegetation recovery responds to factors beyond reduction in trampling, rooting, and herbivory; and that species are responding individually to the removal of these stressors. These and other studies provide insights into patterns and mechanisms of recovery that can help managers direct their limited resources for restoration of island vegetation.

Endemism, Vulnerability, and Resilience

Endemism among Plants and Animals

Currently considered endemic to the Channel Islands are 281 plant taxa, including full species, subspecies, and varieties (Table 34.3). They include single-island endemic plants restricted to one or more sites on an island (e.g., the NEOENDEMIC Hoffmann's slender-flowered gilia, *Gilia tenuiflora* ssp. *hoffmannii*) (Figure 34.6), multi-island endemics growing in similar places on several of the Channel Islands (e.g., the relictual island oak, *Quercus tomentella*) (see Figure 34.6), and regional island-mainland endemic plants that grow on one or more islands plus in similar habitats in small numbers on the nearby mainland (e.g., giant coreopsis, *Leptosyne gigantea*). Endemism is the result of at least two features: the uniqueness of a particular location and the genetic potential of individuals making up populations to thrive in that place. Channel Islands endemic plants can range from short-lived annual herbs that complete their entire life cycle in one growing season to shrubs or trees that live for decades or even centuries.

The vertebrate fauna of the Channel Islands is depauperate, and species occur in unusual patterns when compared to the adjacent southern California mainland. Common, widespread mainland species like rabbits (family Leporidae), gophers (family Geomyidae), moles (family Talpidae), woodrats (*Neotoma* spp.), coyotes (*Canis latrans*), mule deer, and a wide diversity of amphibians, reptiles, and birds are not native to the islands. However, some species like Channel Islands slender salamanders (*Batrachoseps pacificus*), island foxes (*Urocyon littoralis*), island scrub-jays (*Aphelocoma insu-

FIGURE 34.6 Four endemic plants and animals of the Channel Islands. Photos: (A–B) Denise Knapp, (C–D) Matt Victoria.

A Hoffmann's slender-flowered gilia (*Gilia tenuiflora* spp. *Hoffmannii*)

B Island oak (*Quercus tomentella*)

C Island night lizard (*Xantusia riversiana*)

D Island scrub-jay (*Aphelocoma insularis*)

laris), and Channel Islands spotted skunks (*Spilogale gracilis amphiala*) have reached one or more of the islands. The Chumash and Gabrieleño (Tongva) likely played a role in the transport of a number of native mammals (e. g., island fox, Channel Islands spotted skunk, deer mouse (*Peromyscus maniculatus*), and western harvest mouse (*Reithrodontomys megalotis*) and some reptiles and amphibians, to or between islands (Collins 1991, Rick et al. 2009, 2011, Walker 1980, Wenner and Johnson 1980).

Forty-three endemic terrestrial vertebrates (including species and subspecies) have been described for the Channel Islands (Table 34.4). One species of amphibian, two lizards, one snake, fourteen birds, and six mammals are endemic to one or more of the Channel Islands. The island fox is found on the six largest of the Channel Islands, classified as a unique subspecies on each island. The Channel Island slender salamander occurs only on the northern Channel Islands, while the relict endemic island night lizard (*Xantusia riversiana*, see Figure 34.6) is found only on three of the southern Channel Islands (Santa Barbara, San Nicolas, and San Clemente). The island scrub-jay (see Figure 34.6) today is found only on Santa Cruz Island but occurred prehistorically on Santa Rosa and San Miguel. Several species with described endemic subspecies are found on all of the islands, like the island horned lark (*Eremophila alpestris insularis*), or with unique described subspecies on each of the eight islands, such as the deer mouse. Several of the island endemics, including the nonmigratory Allen's hummingbird (*Selasphorus sasin sedentarius*) and the dusky orange-crowned warbler (*Oreothlypis celata sordida*), occur as resident breeders on one or more of the Channel Islands but also breed in a restricted range along the immediate mainland coast of southern California.

Paleoendemics and Neoendemics

We know from genetic and fossil records that island endemic plants have taken at least two vastly different paths toward endemism. There are PALEOENDEMICS: RELICTS of bygone times that persist today in small populations in a few places where the microclimate resembles past climate regimes. Island ironwood (*Lyonothamnus floribundus*) is a relictual endemic species found as two subspecies occurring on four of the California Channel Islands. It is known from the fossil record to have been widespread on the mainland, ranging from near Truckee, Nevada, to near the U.S. border with Mexico during

TABLE 34.4
Numbers of endemic species and subspecies of terrestrial vertebrates found on the California Channel Islands

Island	Endemic to one island only	Endemic to more than one island	Endemic presumed extirpated	Island total
San Miguel Island	3	7	1	10
Santa Rosa Island	2	12	0	14
Santa Cruz Island	4	12	0	16
Anacapa Island	1	8	2	9
Santa Barbara Island	2	4	2	6
San Nicolas Island	2	4	0	6
Santa Catalina Island	8	7	0	15
San Clemente Island	6	7	3	13

SOURCES: Data from Johnson 1972, Power 1994, and Paul Collins unpublished data.

the Miocene about twenty-three million years ago (Raven and Axelrod 1995). Today it persists in shaded glens under the cool, moist maritime conditions of the offshore islands. On the other hand, neoendemics like island Phacelia (*Phacelia insularis*), found on San Miguel and Santa Rosa Islands, evolved into varieties distinct from their mainland ancestors by radiating into new habitats and rapidly adapting to them once on the islands (Raven and Axelrod 1995).

The island night lizard is one of the oldest of the Channel Island endemic vertebrates, having reached San Clemente as early as the late Miocene or Pliocene and then dispersing to Santa Barbara and San Nicolas Islands within the last half million years (Bezy et al. 1980). It was once more widespread in North America north of the Isthmus of Tehuantepec in southern Mexico, but it died out on the mainland prior to approximately 2.58 million years ago (Gehlbach 1965). The outer southern islands lack competing lizards and predatory snakes and offer an equable climate, allowing island night lizard persistence. Regardless of origin, these endemics are now rare, pushed to their limits by the erosion, trampling, grazing, and habitat change that accompanied ranching. Few refugia exist for plants and animals on islands; migration strategies available for dealing with change on the mainland do not exist for them. Their rarity makes them appear fragile, but they are survivors and opportunists, resilient in the face of past change and illustrating the potential to weather an uncertain future. Patterns of endemism provide a window into the deeper past, reflecting complex interactions among physical landscapes, sea level, and climate variations during the ice ages as well as the influences of island drift, colonization opportunities, extinction pressures, and genetic capacity.

Human History

Earliest North Americans

Growing evidence indicates that the earliest North Americans traveled to the west coast by boat, following ocean currents and a food-rich nearshore marine "kelp highway" (*Macrocystis pyrifera*) from Asia across the Alaskan Peninsula and down to the Channel Islands (Erlandson et al. 2008, 2011). Permanent Chumash and Gabrieleño villages were present on the larger islands from about eight thousand years ago to the early 1800s (Rick et al. 2005). Many of these villages were very large, inhabited for centuries. Freshwater would have been a necessity, and indeed the village sites are near drainages, seeps, and springs; some inland hearths, middens, and villages with house pits have been found near what might have been intermittent or permanent seeps as well. The Chumash and Gabrieleño were mainly maritime cultures with a sophisticated trade network throughout the Southern California Bight. For currency they used *Olivella* beads, which have been found in archaeological sites throughout parts of western North America. The mineral steatite was mined on the islands and made into bowls and artifacts that have been found along the coast from Santa Barbara to Orange Counties in California (Cameron 2000).

Midden remains (Figure 34.7) show that the Chumash and Gabrieleño harvested their food mainly from the intertidal and from nearshore marine fisheries and supplemented this with fruits, seeds, and roots gathered from the island interiors (Glassow 1988, Timbrook 2007). They caused SERIAL DEPLETION of the local marine food resource (Braje et al. 2012) as we have with our fisheries today, albeit at a much smaller scale. Mainland Chumash burned the landscape for vegetation management (Timbrook et al. 1982), and Anderson et al. (2010) documented an increase in burning starting about four thousand years ago attributable to Native Americans. However, it is unknown whether this was a regular practice on the islands, since archaeologists are just starting to seek evidence of fire use on the islands. Island soils lack evidence of widespread cultivation, although this too needs more study (Kennet 2005). The exact mechanisms that regulated human population sizes on the individual islands remain unclear. A period of tumult began around AD 1100 with declining resource productivity and violence, and people may have moved to more favorable locations. Conditions improved by the 1400s, persisting until widespread decline from introduced disease and other factors during the historic period (Kennet 2005). The

FIGURE 34.7 Shell midden, 2012, southwest Santa Rosa Island. Photo: Daniel Richards.

last Native Americans left the islands in the early 1800s, displaced or removed to the mainland by European traders, fishermen, and settlers. Their descendants today live mostly in Ventura and Santa Barbara Counties.

Early Maritime Hunting and Fishing

Asian and European traders and fishermen used the islands as early as the mid-1700s (Ogden 1941). Fur traders hunted fur-seals (*Arctocephalus townsendii* and *Callorhinus ursinus*) and southern sea otters (*Enhydra lutris nereis*), completely extirpating sea otters around the Channel Islands by the early 1900s. California sea lions (*Zalophus californianus*) were hunted for their whiskers (prized as pipe cleaners). Whalers and sealers hunted northern elephant seals (*Mirounga angustirostris*) and whales relentlessly in the nineteenth century for their oil, and elephant seals were nearly exterminated (Stewart et al. 1994). Chinese fishermen set up semipermanent abalone (*Haliotis spp.*) harvesting camps on the larger islands (Livingston 2006) during the late nineteenth century, persisting until about 1913. Divers began harvesting abalone in the 1930s; that fishery was closed in 1997 due to overfishing and disease. A lobster fishery began in the late 1800s, but by 1900 dwindling stocks required new management restrictions. Despite these, the fishery was closed for two years in 1909 and 1910. Seabirds were also heavily affected by harvest.

Ranching and Agriculture

Ranching began on the Channel Islands as individuals were granted land deeds or land use permits by the Mexican government beginning in the early 1800s (Junak et al. 1995, Livingston 2006) in parallel with development of ranching infrastructure on the mainland. Each island has a slightly different ranching history, but nearly all were stocked with free-ranging livestock for meat and wool and with game animals for sport (see Table 34.2). Generally, domestic European mouflon sheep or goats (*Capra hircus*) were introduced first, cultivated for their wool and later for meat to supply markets during the Gold Rush, Civil War, and after World War I. Initially island vegetation provided ample food for the industry, and livestock herds grew to more than one hundred thousand on each of the larger islands of Santa Cruz, Santa Rosa, Santa Catalina, and San Clemente by the 1890s. This stocking rate averaged about two animals per hectare (one per acre) across those islands and was not sustainable for more than a decade. Herd populations crashed; ranchers reduced sheep numbers; and periodic, multiyear droughts in the 1870s, 1890s, and 1940s exacerbated the island sheep industry's decline.

Ranches on the larger islands switched to cattle operations by the early 1900s. Island cattle ranches were generally rotational stocker operations, in which young cattle were brought to the islands to be prepared for market for about a year before being rotated off again. This livestock management system was more sustainable than sheep ranching had been, especially when combined with income from big-game hunting. Concerted efforts to remove non-native ungulates began in the late 1900s. The last non-native ungulates were removed from Santa Cruz in 2006 and Santa Rosa Island by 2015, but deer and bison remain on Santa Catalina today. Sheep ranching was unsustainable and ended earlier on Anacapa and Santa Barbara Islands, small islands with no freshwater. The U.S. Air Force put rabbits on Santa Barbara Island in 1940 as a source of emergency food, and they were eliminated by the National Park Service in 1981.

Small-scale viticulture (grape farming) was pursued for profit on Santa Catalina and Santa Cruz Islands for ten to twenty years, ending with Prohibition in 1920. In 2007 a small, 2.4 hectare (6 acre) vineyard was planted from that old stock in a revival of island viticulture on Santa Catalina Island. European honey bees (*Apis mellifera*) were tended for honey production concurrent with grape farming on those islands. Otherwise, agriculture was pursued mainly in the form of hayfields and produce gardens to support the ranches.

Oil Exploration, Military Uses, Tourism, and Recreation

Other activities were pursued in the Channel Islands concurrent with ranching, and some continue today. In particular, a flurry of unproductive exploratory oil drilling on the islands took place from about 1929 to the 1960s (Livingston 2006).

The U.S. Department of Defense established operations bases on several islands, and some of these remain as permanent facilities. Tourism and public recreation persist in Avalon and Two Harbors on Santa Catalina Island and in the Channel Islands National Park. Finally, the coves, sea caves, uplands, canyons, and terraces of the Channel Islands have been visited throughout history by bootleggers and sailors, gentlemen hunters and their families, divers and anglers, movie stars and film production studios, scientists, hikers, birders, campers, and explorers of all ages and nationalities. In sum, most of the land uses pursued on the southern California mainland, except for intense urban development, have occurred on the islands as well.

How Development Changed the Functioning of Island Ecosystems

The Chumash Era

During Chumash and Gabrieleño occupation of the islands, the climate was in a continuing, post-Pleistocene warming phase. Pollen analyses (Anderson et al. 2010) showed that island vegetation transitioned from moist forest to vegetation more tolerant of dry conditions including herbs and shrubs in the sunflower family (Asteraceae), oak (*Quercus* spp.) scrub, pines (*Pinus* spp.), and grasses. While we cannot reconstruct its particular species composition, the vegetation toward the end of Chumash occupation was likely a form of open coastal scrub and oak chaparral, with pine and oak groves emerging from scrub canopies wherever sufficiently moist conditions occurred to support growing tree saplings. The Chumash, Gabrieleño, and their ancestors occupied the islands for thousands of years, and this population pressure affected the island resources. Most evident is the depletion of nearshore marine resources, potentially disrupting food webs. However, their activities generally did not disrupt the soils, leaving terrestrial ecosystem functions, like water retention and nutrient cycling, largely intact.

Ranching

Ranching, on the other hand, had profound and long-lasting effects on island ecosystem processes. Soil cores and eyewitness reports (Johnson 1980, Cole and Liu 1994), newspapers, tax documents, and ranch account ledgers (Junak et al. 1995, Livingston 2006) make clear that sheep grazing had nearly denuded island landscapes by the late 1800s (Johnson 1980). Accounts describe barren slopes and starving sheep during the droughts of the late 1800s and early 1900s, when ranch foremen staged periodic roundups to dispose of sheep and pigs and reduce the pressure on Santa Cruz and Santa Rosa Islands (Livingston 2006). Prickly pear cactus (*Opuntia* spp.), unpalatable to grazing animals, became so common on those two islands by 1940 that ranch managers introduced the cochineal scale (*Dactylopius* sp.) in an early and successful attempt at cactus biocontrol. Non-native annual grasslands took the place of native scrub, becoming the dominant vegetation cover of all the islands.

Several factors contributed to the swift failure of native island vegetation at that time. One is the sheer numbers of animals grazing, browsing, and trampling the vegetation. Another is the palatability of the island forms of many dominant chaparral shrubs. Endemic island plants have lower concentrations of unpalatable compounds in their leaves than their mainland relatives (Bowen and Van Vuren 1987, Carlquist 1974). No large, native herbivores inhabited the islands after pygmy mammoths (*Mammuthus exilis*) went extinct approximately thirteen thousand years ago (Agenbroad 2012). In the absence of herbivory, natural selection favored plants not investing in the production of these energetically expensive, protective compounds. Thus poorly defended, island-adapted plants were sought out by non-native livestock. Feeding trials have shown that sheep and other ungulates preferred to eat many island plants over their mainland relatives (Van Vuren and Bowen 1999), and field studies have shown that island endemic shrubs are browsed more heavily than nonendemics growing nearby in the same area (Van Vuren and Coblentz 1987, Manuwal and Sweitzer 2010). Where ungulates were and still are present on the islands, it is not uncommon to see these shrubs grazed to bare rootstock, repeatedly resprouting and then browsed again. Finally, because these shrubs made up a large proportion of the cover in the islands' simplified plant communities, damage to them exposed the entire community to soil erosion and invasion by non-native plants. These in turn exacerbated vegetation change and loss. A soil core taken from a Santa Rosa Island marsh showed mean sedimentation rates increasing from 0.7 millimeters per year prior to herbivore introductions to 23.0 millimeters per year between 1874 and 1920, more than a thirtyfold increase within twenty years of sheep introduction (Cole and Liu 1994).

From a range management perspective, the islands rapidly exceeded their livestock carrying capacities, resulting in unsustainable sheep ranching operations. In ecological terms, island ecosystems were pushed over a threshold into a disequilibrium state dominated by disturbance and erosion. This yielded upland areas denuded of vegetation with soils washed away, bedrock exposed on the surface, and continuing erosion (Johnson 1980). With soils no longer there to hold moisture, water from rain, dew, and fog ran off across the surface rather than percolating into the soil; and streams cut vertically down through their terraces. Riparian vegetation that depended upon a reservoir of water was stranded on high and dry terraces. Having lost the ability to hold nutrients and shelter soil microorganisms, island uplands became dry and barren. The low-elevation, sandy islands of San Nicolas and San Miguel became blowing and eroding sand dunes (Figure 34.8). Lower-elevation streams, alluvial fans, and terraces received unusually high sediment loads, and some rocky intertidal areas and giant kelp beds were buried with new sediment. Where soils persisted in these lowland areas, non-native annual grasses brought to the islands on the fur of animals invaded and replaced the native shrub stands. Native vegetation was reduced to small remnant patches on steep slopes and cliffs inaccessible to ungulates.

Introduced Species

The effects of native habitat loss through livestock use were exacerbated by introductions of other non-native plants and animals. Several endemic plant taxa are presumed extirpated from the islands as a result of these introductions (see Table 34.3). At least ten endemic populations of land birds have been extirpated from the Channel Islands in historic times, probably as a direct result of suitable habitat loss to

FIGURE 34.8 Arlington Canyon, Santa Rosa Island, in (A) 1994 and (B) 2012. See Table 34.2 for dates of feral livestock removal. Note recovery of riparian vegetation in the foreground and coastal sage scrub (*Artemisia californica* and *Baccharis pilularis*) in the background. Source: National Park Service files.

overgrazing by introduced herbivores (see Table 34.4). A small, ground-feeding endemic population of a song sparrow (*Melospiza melodia graminea*) found on Santa Barbara Island declined as stands of giant coreopsis and boxthorn (*Lycium californicum*) scrub were eliminated by farming, sheep grazing, browsing from introduced European rabbits, and wildfire. Following the elimination of protective vegetative cover on the island, the bird was ultimately eliminated by feral cat (*Felis catus*) predation. The Santa Barbara Island song sparrow was declared extinct in 1983 after repeated searches failed to find any individuals. The extant but endangered San Clemente Island loggerhead shrike (*Lanius ludovicianus mearnsi*) is similarly threatened by black rats (*Rattus rattus*) and feral cats. Ornate shrews (*Sorex ornatus*), present on San Miguel Island for over nine thousand years, recently became extinct, possibly as a result of habitat changes wrought by introduced herbivores (Guthrie 1993). Predatory black rats threatened populations of burrow-nesting seabird species (Scripps's murrelets [*Synthiboramphus scrippsi*]) and ashy storm-petrels (*Oceanodroma homochroa*) on Anacapa Island until their removal in 2002 (Howald et al. 2005).

Maritime Hunting

The giant kelp marine forests that sustained early maritime cultures also attracted European hunters and traders, resulting in cascading changes that reverberate through the nearshore marine ecosystem today (see Chapter 17, "Shallow Rocky Reefs and Kelp Forests"). Southern sea otters, a KEYSTONE SPECIES in the kelp forest community, were extirpated from southern California through overharvesting by the early 1900s. This probably led to increased abundance of their prey species, including abalone and sea urchins (*Strongylocentrotus* spp.). For about fifty years, increased abalone numbers supported a thriving diver-based fishery. However, overfishing and disease led white abalone (*H. sorenseni*) and black abalone (*H. cracherodii*) to became the first marine invertebrates placed on the federal endangered species list. As abalone became less abundant, divers switched to harvesting large red sea urchins, *Strongylocentrotus franciscanus*, but not the small purple urchins, *S. purpuratus* (Dugan and Davis 1993). In the absence of predators, these urchins can overgraze kelp and other seaweeds, creating low-diversity "barrens" devoid of the kelp forests essential for a wide variety of algae, invertebrates, and fishes. The cascading effects on kelp forest ecosystems resulting from losses of sea otters and overgrazing by urchins continue today. Southern sea otters were protected as a threatened species in 1977 (U.S. Fish and Wildlife Service), and populations are now increasing in northern and central California (U.S. Fish and Wildlife Service 2003). Sea otters were also reintroduced to San Nicolas Island nearly thirty years ago; that small population has been increasing gradually.

Fishing

Even though the Channel Islands represent about 5% of California's total shoreline, approximately 20% of the state's total fishery and around 80% of the market squid (*Loligo opalescens*) catch comes from the islands (California Department of Fish and Wildlife 2014, unpublished California Fish and Wildlife Block Landings). Formerly a seasonal fishery in southern California, squid harvest is now open nearly year-round and has become the most economically valuable fishery in California. The harvest was little-managed for many years. However, squid are food for California sea lions (Lowry and Carretta 1999) and large fish like California halibut (*Paralichthys californicus*) and blue sharks (*Prionace glauca*). The fishery uses powerful lights to attract squid to the surface, raising concerns over possible effects on nocturnal seabirds. An annual market squid quota was established in 2005, and its limit has been reached earlier every year since 2010. The future effects of this fishery remain unclear. The red sea urchin is another relatively new commercial fishery, one of California's most valuable fisheries for more than a decade (California Department of Fish and Wildlife 2004).

New technologies enhance our harvest capacity. For species that grow slowly for decades and reproduce infrequently, such as the rockfish (*Sebastes* spp.), increasing harvest pressure is unsustainable. The recent popularity of fish in a healthy diet promoted a rockfish harvest that evolved faster than regulations to manage it; rockfish populations declined beginning in the 1980s and have yet to recover. Earlier, in the 1900s new gillnet technology replaced a sustainable harpoon fishery for swordfish (*Xiphias gladius*), depleting several shark species. Gillnets likely also limited recovery of giant sea bass (*Stereolepis gigas*), a species regulated since 1982 because of overfishing. In 1992 California voters, motivated in part by images of pinnipeds being drowned in the nets, banned gillnets off California within three miles of the coast and one mile of the islands.

Islands in Transition

With the exception of Santa Catalina Island, the Channel Islands are in transition from ranching to conservation or managed military use. At least nine entities, each with individual mandates and management goals, own land in the California Channel Islands (see Table 34.1). In general, long-term management plans place conservation of natural and cultural resources as a high priority within a broad, multiple-use context. Human populations have not expanded much on the islands, ranching has ceased, many developments are being dismantled, and active ecological recovery is under way. For the first time in thousands of years, except for increased military operations in the 2000s at San Clemente Island, the footprint of humanity has declined on land in the islands. On the other hand, broader contexts are in rapid flux: climates are changing, oceans acidifying, sea level rising, and marine resources increasingly overharvested. Parts of the island ecosystems are missing, such as extinct and extirpated species, and some invasive plants are here to stay. Is it possible to reestablish a natural regime governed by ecological processes, and what will that look like? We do not have many good examples where entire landscapes, let alone entire archipelagos, have been allowed to revert to nature. Ecological theory, however, does allow us to formulate some basic principles and predictions:

1. Recovery will not occur until the major stressors are removed.
2. The islands will not be exactly as they once were; for example, native plants will coexist with many non-natives. Biophysical drivers are changing, making the past an imperfect guide to the future.
3. Outcomes and recovery rates will depend on initial conditions, including each island's position along physical and climatic regional gradients. Starting points for recovery vary with each site's state in relation to bio-physical thresholds, such as slowing of erosion to allow development of soil crust for stability, and reduction of non-native grass thatch so that native seeds can germinate.
4. Processes that are broken may not self-repair quickly, such as soil development from bedrock; in barren areas, recovery will have to start with soil formation.
5. Recovery will be uneven through time, slowing during droughty conditions, accelerating in wetter years.
6. Rates of native plant community expansion will vary across island landscapes in relation to site-specific conditions, and animal recovery will depend in some part on vegetation recovery.
7. Some animals that benefited from the open grassland disturbance state will decline as island vegetation recovers.
8. Population recovery of wide-ranging animals that use the islands for breeding, like seabirds and pinnipeds, will depend on conditions across the globe far from the islands as well as on the islands.
9. Ocean warming and acidification will alter currents, distribution of species, and persistence of shelled organisms.
10. The unexpected is to be expected—new interactions and climate changes will produce heretofore unseen combinations of soils, plants, animals, and processes on the landscape.

Managing for conservation in such damaged ecosystems under such uncertainty and with very little funding can be daunting. However, recovery actions and research priorities have already been set by these principles and guide when and where to focus effort, what to measure to gauge outcomes, and how long to wait for results.

Conservation Management Actions

REMOVAL OF NON-NATIVE SPECIES

Introductions of non-native herbivores and predators to the islands were paramount among stressors and led to a range of devastating changes. Each Channel Islands management agency has worked to remove or reduce ranch and introduced game animals (see Table 34.2). Several accidental or unanticipated animal introductions occurred in the decades since European settlement; many of these have been or are being addressed as well. Accidental introductions include organisms as diverse as Argentine ants (*Linepithema humile*), northern raccoon (*Procyon lotor*), giant reed (*Arundo donax*), and sargassum seaweed (*Sargassum horneri*). The single best management action that island agencies have taken is the removal of non-native animals. Without that first step, further recovery would be impossible.

The elimination of the black rat from Anacapa Island exemplifies such a removal project. Rats were first recorded on Anacapa in the late 1800s, possibly arriving on the island from the shipwreck of the Winfield Scott in 1853 (as reported in the Santa Barbara Morning Press, June 27, 1907). Black rat removal was identified as necessary for recovery of decimated nesting seabird populations, particularly the Scripps's murrelet, Cassin's auklet (*Ptychoramphus aleuticus*), and ashy storm-petrel. In 2001 and 2002 the National Park Service, in partnership with the nongovernmental organization Island Conservation and with funding from the American Trader Trustees, applied the anticoagulant rodenticide brodificaum to Anacapa Island. The project included substantial mitigation actions to minimize impacts to nontarget species, and black rats were completely eliminated. Posteradication monitoring has shown significant increases in the number, success, and extent of nesting Scripps's murrelet and the return of nesting Cassin's auklets and ashy storm-petrels. In spite of mitigations, short-term and local impacts to nontarget species occurred, particularly to landbirds and the native Anacapa deer mouse (*P. maniculatus anacapae*), from the eradication. Following the successful eradication of rats from Anacapa Island, similar projects have been carried out or are planned on other U.S. islands.

Some invasive plants reached the islands before widespread ranching, such as crystalline iceplant (*Mesymbryanthemum crystallinum*), which washed ashore from the ballast of ships coming around the Horn of Africa from Europe. However, invasive plants exploded onto the islands with the advent of ranching. Many appear here to stay, such as ripgut brome

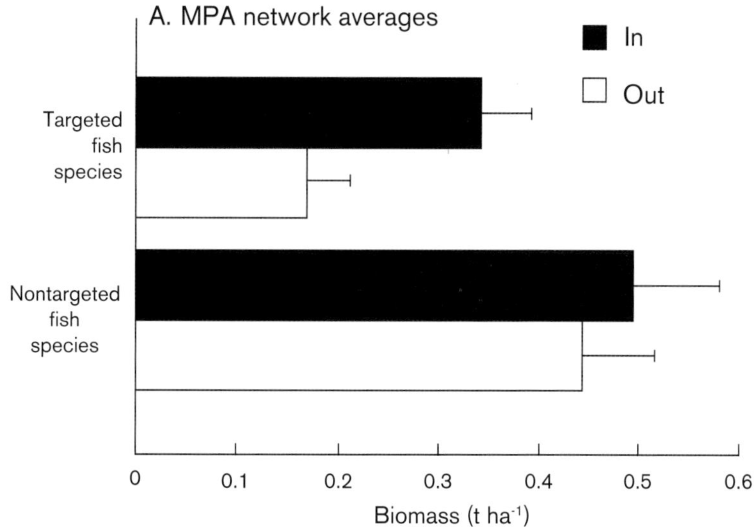

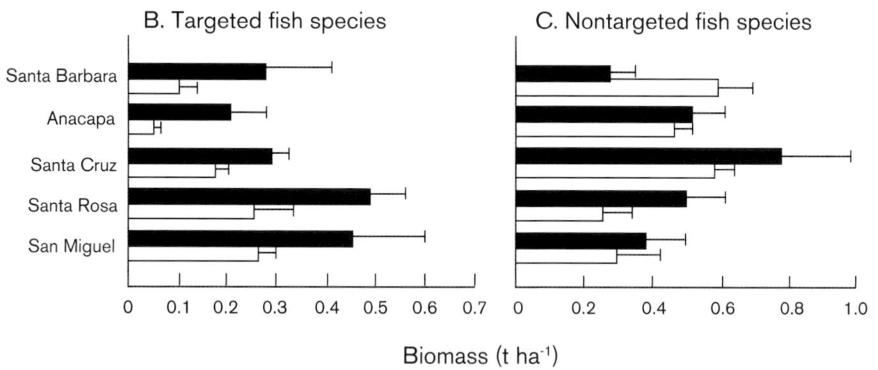

FIGURE 34.9 Spatial patterns of biomass (t ha^{-1}) for targeted and nontargeted fish species inside (black bars) and outside (white bars) of marine reserves in the Channel Islands, 2003–2008. (A) Averages across all islands in the reserve network, (B) targeted fish species biomass for each island, and (C) nontargeted fish species biomass for each island. Source: Hamilton et al. 2010.

grass (*Bromus diandrus*) and wild oats (*Avena* spp.). Others are dwindling as soil disturbance abates, such as cheeseweed (*Malva parviflora*) and spiny clotbur (*Xanthium strumarium*) that thrived on cattle-trampled stream terraces. Some exotic plants, however, are aggressive invaders still small in numbers or discrete enough in distribution that they could be eradicated. Early detection and removal efforts have been undertaken to find and destroy these plants, and plans are in place on most islands to guard against future accidental introductions. Biosecurity, or the prevention of new introductions, is now a paramount management tool for the islands.

ESTABLISHMENT OF MARINE RESERVES

Kelp forest monitoring begun by Channel Islands National Park in 1982 (Davis 2005), showed the value of a small, 15 hectare (37 acre), no-take reserve at Anacapa Island relative to nearby fished areas. The program demonstrated that fishing reduced the average size and abundance of the targeted fish species, reducing their ability to rebound and disperse after natural perturbations like those associated with El Niño events. In 2003, the California Fish and Game Commission designated a network of MPAs (Lubchenco et al. 2003) in state waters around the northern Channel Islands. NOAA extended these into federal waters in 2007 (California Department of Fish and Game Partnership for Interdisciplinary Studies 2008), and in 2012 new MPAs were established at the three nonpark Channel Islands.

The goal of the MPA network is to provide areas that include seaweeds, invertebrates, fishes, seabirds, and marine mammals and allow species to grow and reproduce. Ideally, in the MPA large individuals can produce young that repopulate nearby areas outside the MPAs. After five years of protection at the northern Channel Islands, monitoring showed significant increases in densities and biomass of many targeted fish within (Figure 34.9) and near no-take reserves (Hamilton et al. 2010).

LEGISLATION FOR PROTECTION OF AT-RISK SPECIES

Some species that use the islands are put at risk by fishing, hunting, habitat alterations, and climate changes ranging far from the Channel Islands and beyond the jurisdictional control of island managers. For example, seabirds such as the Scripps's murrelet and Cassin's auklet breed on the Channel Islands, yet they spend most of their time at sea in other habitats. For them, sustainable recovery requires a collaborative effort among many managers across the globe. In some cases, international legislation has led to recovery as habitats are protected, restored, and conserved.

Northern elephant seals were hunted extensively in the eighteenth and nineteenth centuries, prized for oil from their blubber (Stewart et al. 1994). Thought to be extinct by 1884, a small colony of fewer than one hundred survived on Guadalupe Island off Mexico (Huey 1930). The Marine Mammal Protection Act, passed in 1972, provided all marine mammals in U.S. waters with protection from take (pursuit, harassment, capture, or harvest). The current population now exceeds one hundred thousand (Stewart et al. 1994), perhaps even higher than during the period of occupation by prehistoric humans (Rick et al. 2011). Diving to great depths in the north Pacific to feed on deep-water fish and squid, elephant seals have been able to escape conflicts with fisheries. They visit remote island beaches in the winter to breed, swim to the Bering Sea to feed, return to the beaches in the spring to molt, and make a second migration to feed through the summer. The population has grown at about 20% per year, though in El Niño years a large proportion of pups can perish in storm events. Colonies have expanded among the Baja and Channel Islands since the 1950s, to Año Nuevo Island followed by the Farallons, and recently to mainland colonies along the Big Sur coast (Stewart et al. 1994).

INFRASTRUCTURE REMOVAL AND AMELIORATION OF CONTAMINANTS

As developments were abandoned, some landowners left buildings, roads, and piers. The NPS has removed infrastructure left by the U.S. Coast Guard, the U.S. Navy, and the U.S. Air Force from Anacapa, Santa Barbara, Santa Rosa, and Santa Cruz Islands. The Nature Conservancy removed abandoned equipment from Santa Cruz Island, and the U.S. Navy has dismantled hazardous piers and buildings on San Nicolas and San Clemente Islands. Early roads followed horse trails on many of the islands. This resulted in deep erosion when they were later used for vehicular travel. Road management plans now help to reduce erosion from regularly traveled roads, and some roads have been closed altogether.

Chemical legacies have also diminished over time. BIOACCUMULATION of the pesticide dichlorodiphenyltrichloroethane (DDT) released into the San Pedro Basin in the 1950s and 1960s resulted in thinning of eggshells of many birds, particularly at high trophic levels. Breeding California brown pelicans (*Pelecanus occidentalis californicus*), bald eagles (*Haliaeetus leucocephalus*), and peregrine falcons (*Falco peregrinus*) disappeared from the islands (Kiff 1980) and were listed as threatened or endangered under the Endangered Species Act. Recently, DDT concentrations have dropped, the birds have been delisted (Sharpe and Garcelon 2005), and those species are currently breeding on the Channel Islands (Walton 1990).

REESTABLISHING FOG DRIP

Some biophysical processes that sustain island ecosystems need to be repaired. On San Clemente and Santa Rosa Islands, researchers and managers are investigating ways to harness fog drip to restore hydrologic function and help vegetation recovery. Uplands of these islands, denuded of their native shrubs, now have exposed bedrock in the absence of roots to hold soil in place. Native trees and shrubs cannot establish because the thin remaining soils are too dry, yet these highlands are bathed in fog almost every day. When shrubs were present, fog condensed on their leaves and branches, dripped to the ground, and soaked the soil, providing a water reservoir for seedling establishment and sustained growth. Without vegetation the islands do not "harvest" fog water, and without fog water the vegetation cannot establish. Managers are experimenting with recovering upland chaparral using artificial structures to harness fog drip to jumpstart vegetation growth.

PASSIVE RECOVERY

Removal of introduced animals and invasive plants has allowed some areas to recover further on their own, a process of passive recovery. For example, native bunchgrasses are increasing on marine terraces on all of the islands. Pioneering native shrubs including coyote brush (*Baccharis pilularis*) and island buckwheat (*Eriogonum* spp.) are moving into nonnative annual grasslands on alluvial fans and slopes where soils still persist (see Figure 34.9), facilitating increases in native herbs and some other shrubs. The federally listed island rush-rose (*Crocanthemum greenei*) is appearing in greater numbers in patches across the larger islands now that it is no longer trampled; and the diminutive, native Catalina grass (*Poa thomasii*), thought to be extirpated, was found recently on Santa Catalina and San Clemente Islands. Plants with underground bulbs that were extremely tasty to feral pigs are now increasing, such as the endemic Humboldt lily (*Lilium humboldtii*) and island Jepsonia (*Jepsonia malvifolia*). Riparian and freshwater marsh vegetation is recolonizing stream bottoms that had been reduced to mud and cobble (see Figure 34.8). As a result, some streams have begun to regain sinuosity and greater periods of flow, leading to decreasing flow velocities and increased sediment capture. All of these features are precursors to increased water-holding capacities in stream alluvium and better hydrological functioning.

Areas like these might not need more intensive management to reach the conservation goals set by management agencies. The trick for managers, however, is to ensure that these trends continue unabated. Therefore, inventory and monitoring programs track changes using methods including repeat transect sampling, aerial photography, remote sensing, demographic studies, animal tracking, periodic surveys, and photographic documentation.

ACTIVE RESTORATION

Further, ACTIVE RESTORATION is necessary to recover some processes, functions, and species on the California Channel Islands, and a growing number of such efforts have generated successful outcomes. With the exception of Catalina Island, where deer, bison, feral cats, domestic dogs, and black rats still occur (see Table 34.2), active restoration in the Channel Islands has turned from feral animal removal to projects targeting specific processes and functions. For the most part, these projects address remaining barriers to ecosystem functioning, or they catalyze self-perpetuating processes for sustained recovery in the face of changing climate conditions.

The smaller islands generally have lost more resources than the larger ones and likely will require greater effort per hectare. For example, San Miguel had island chaparral communities that do not exist at all today (Johnson 1980). Remains of island scrub-jay and spotted towhee (*Pipilo maculatus*), both chaparral residents, have been found on San Miguel in recent archeological-paleontological research (P. Collins, unpublished data). None of the chaparral plants have reappeared spontaneously in the forty years since feral animal removal, making clear that active restoration is needed for chaparral recovery. Likewise, native seed banks are gone from the uplands of Santa Barbara Island, and colonization has to come from plants growing on the cliff faces. A multiyear project on Santa Barbara is under way to plant native shrubs so that seabirds depending upon them for nesting cover can expand their use of the island.

Alterations to island ecosystems can sometimes have surprising and INDIRECT EFFECTS. For example, the disappearance of bald eagles made room for golden eagles (*Aquila chrysaetos*) to establish on the northern islands. While bald eagles fed in the marine ecosystem, golden eagles are terrestrial predators and were sustained by non-native feral pigs on Santa Cruz Island and mule deer on Santa Rosa Island (Collins and Latta 2009, Roemer et al. 2001, Roemer et al. 2002). Subsidies from these non-native prey allowed golden eagle populations to grow large enough that they posed a substantial threat to the endemic island fox. Island foxes evolved without large predators and are often active during the day; in the early 1990s their populations plummeted in response to golden eagle predation. Swift recovery actions prevented extinction (Coonan et al. 2009), but only after foxes were taken into captivity for their own protection, golden eagles were removed (Latta et al. 2005), and feral pigs were eliminated (Morrison et al. 2007). Island fox recovery required both direct actions (captive breeding of foxes and live removal of golden eagles) and indirect actions (elimination of feral pigs and mule deer to eliminate golden eagle prey subsidies, and reintroduction of bald eagles to discourage golden eagle establishment).

The Santa Catalina Island fox (*U. littoralis catalinae*) declined in the late 1990s for a very different reason: canine distemper, a virus likely introduced by a non-native northern raccoon. The virus spread rapidly, killing most exposed animals. Fortunately, geography limited movement of foxes across an isthmus at the western end of the island, and enough foxes remained to establish a captive breeding population and support implementation of a vaccination program. Although the causes of island fox declines on the northern Channel Islands and Santa Catalina Island were very different, the restoration projects required both immediate action to protect remaining individuals and broader actions to ensure sustained recovery.

San Clemente Island supports a single-island endemic subspecies of loggerhead shrike that declined to a low of seven to thirteen birds in the mid-1990s due to predation by feral cats and rats (Scott and Morrison 1990). Since then, the U.S. Navy has implemented captive breeding, population monitoring, predator control, and habitat restoration; and by 2010 the estimated population of shrikes on San Clemente had increased to roughly seventy breeding pairs in the wild (USDOD 2010).

Another successful active restoration effort involved one of the two largest wetlands on all the Channel Islands, at the mouth of Cañada del Puerto Creek at Prisoners Harbor on Santa Cruz Island. The wetland is fed by alluvial groundwater, recharged from an upland drainage area of 37 km^2 (13 mi^2). The wetland was filled in the 1880s to make a level loading area for shipment of goods on and off the island. At the same time, the Cañada del Puerto Creek was channelized, disconnecting the creek from its floodplain wetland. This inadvertently caused erosion to a nearby, archaeologically significant Chumash village site. Over the last 150 years eucalyptus (*Eucalyptus globulus* and *E. camaldulensis*) trees escaped from nearby landscaping, formed a thicket extending the length of the drainage bottom and altered the hydrology of the lower Cañada del Puerto Creek. As a result, wetland plants and animals lost their only habitat on the island, the wetland stopped filtering water as it ran to the sea and an entire riparian forest disappeared. Since 2010, the NPS, the Nature Conservancy, and partners have worked to remove the wetland fill, plant native wetland species, protect the ancient village site, cut the eucalyptus, and plant native riparian species. Activities will continue for several more years before the project's completion. Although this wetland had clearly passed beyond a threshold into a state from which it could not recover without assistance, wetland plants are now reestablishing and birds not seen in decades are using the site.

RECOVERY IN AN UNCERTAIN FUTURE

Recovery is uneven as species and processes adjust to new conditions. Island plant communities are forever altered as non-native and native plants establish new blended vegetation types on the islands. Rising mean minimum temperatures on the islands (Channel Islands National Park unpublished weather monitoring data) foretell continued climate changes that could affect species persistence and ecosystem recovery (e.g., McEachern et al. 2009, Cayan et al. 2008). Ironically, some species that survived or even thrived in the recent past could find themselves challenged by future conditions.

Some island endemics represent conservation-reliant species: threats from external processes like climate change may not be fully abated, perhaps requiring human intervention for the species' long-term survival. For example, Island scrub-jays (see Figure 34.6), the only endemic full species of bird found on the Channel Islands, are today confined to Santa Cruz Island with fewer than three thousand individuals (Morrison et al. 2011). In the Pleistocene, when the northern Channel Islands were connected as Santa Rosae, their ancestors inhabited areas that became Santa Rosa and San Miguel Islands (Delaney and Wayne 2005). Like other poorly dispersed, single-island endemics, loss of the jay from Santa Cruz Island would mean loss of the entire species. Future considerations and active discussions for scrub-jay conservation include such measures as off-site captive breeding, vaccination against novel diseases like West Nile virus (Boyce et al. 2011, LaDeau et al. 2008), implementation of biosecurity measures to reduce risk of infection, and establishment of a population on nearby Santa Rosa Island. Whatever the outcome, the Island scrub-jay is a great example of the challenges faced by island managers now and into the future.

Removing non-native species that have adversely affected island ecosystems does not ensure that all island endemics will benefit. A few island birds appear to have thrived in the open grassland plant communities that resulted from intensive grazing, such as the multi-island endemic Island loggerhead shrike (*L. ludovicianus anthonyi*) and the Island horned lark. These subspecies were common and widespread while the islands were grazed (Collins 2008, P. Collins unpublished

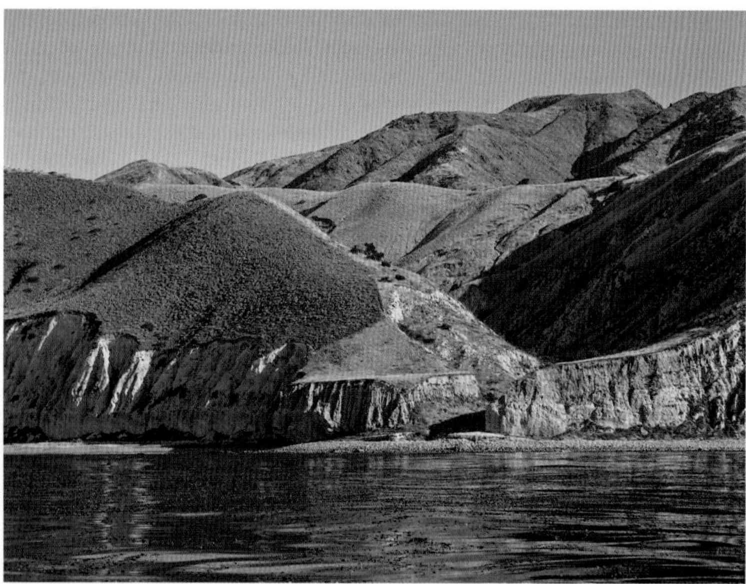

FIGURE 34.10 Recovering landscape along a fence line at Yellowbanks, Santa Cruz Island, 2005. The area to the right of the fence line was grazed by sheep from 1853 through 2001; grazing ended in the similarly denuded coastal sage scrub on the left in about 1950 (L. Laughrin personal communication). Photo: Daniel Richards.

data). Following herbivore removal and the concomitant increase in shrub cover, Island loggerhead shrikes disappeared as breeders from San Miguel and West Anacapa Islands (P. Collins, unpublished data) and declined on Santa Cruz and Santa Catalina Islands (Hicks and Walter 2009, Stanley et al. 2012). Island horned larks have shown similar declines with shrub recovery on the Northern Channel Islands and Santa Catalina Island, and they have been extirpated from Anacapa Island (P. Collins, unpublished data). Land managers have the difficult task of balancing island vegetation restoration against maintenance of viable island endemic populations like these.

How Resilient Are the Islands?

The Channel Islands have already displayed surprising RESILIENCE given the devastating effects of the ranching era and the rate at which they fell apart. At this point, several factors contribute to this resilience and recovery. First, total rather than just partial removal of exotic grazing and browsing animals has allowed native island plants to produce flowers and seeds in amounts unseen in past decades. Even when herd sizes were reduced, the tender roots, shoots, and flowers of the highly palatable island plants were browsed at much greater rates than their nonendemic neighbors. Thus, we are now seeing seed production and seedling establishment not possible before. Second, many of the native island chaparral shrubs also persisted through the ranching era as living underground rootstocks. Their adaptation for resprouting after fire from a root or burl allowed them to persist under a regimen of constant browsing and to recover relatively quickly following removal of herbivore pressure. Third, livestock were removed before all the parts were lost on the larger islands—remnant stands of vegetation and small populations of endemic plants and animals were still present, albeit sometimes near extirpation. The rugged terrain of some islands provided refugia for plants in areas that grazers and browsers could not easily access. Surprisingly, seed banks persisted for many of the rare and endemic herbaceous plants that contribute to the total biodiversity of island floras. Surveys show more than a hundred-fold increase in individuals of some species in island canyons. Some new plants arise by seed dispersal from remnant populations, while many are germinating from buried seed banks. Finally, the islands lack many of the native root and seed herbivores that limit plant productivity on the mainland and some of the natural predators and competitors that constrain animal population growth. Growing free of native herbivores and predators gives island organisms a capacity to rebound not present elsewhere.

Uncertainty persists about the capacity of island systems to rebound from past human impacts. Biophysical drivers are shifting, parts are missing and new additions and physical conditions constrain growth in unusual ways. It is clear, however, that these island ecosystems possess great resilience, retain their uniqueness, and can continue to contribute disproportionately to the incredible diversity found in California.

Summary

Eighteen islands make up the California Islands in the Pacific Ocean from near San Francisco, California, to central Baja California, Mexico. Their geologic history of isolation, and their size, topographic complexity, and distance from other islands and the mainland lead to high endemism in the flora and fauna. Because of their isolation, island plant communities tend to have fewer total plant species than the mainland and are often dominated by local endemics that evolved in the unique island environments. In turn, these habitats support both endemic animals and global travelers such as seabirds and pinnipeds. The larger islands in particular were home for at least thirteen thousand years to Native Americans who eventually established large, permanent villages; had complex interactions and trade networks with other islands and the mainland; and strongly influenced island ecosystem structure and function.

For the most part, these Native Americans practiced hunting and gathering lifestyles that did not have the widespread, devastating effects produced by later ranching activities that came with European settlement. Ecosystem collapse came quickly with the advent of ranching activities, as native scrub communities were replaced by non-native annual grasslands;

erosion and sedimentation rates increased; and water-holding capacity declined. Still, this archipelago preserves some of the last remnants of native California, now managed by federal agencies and private conservation organizations for recovery and conservation of native ecosystems. They are places of incredible biodiversity and unparalleled natural beauty. The California Islands are recovering from conditions not unlike what most of southern California faces right now and will face in the future. They provide a living laboratory for recovery of native ecosystems (Figure 34.10), as well as a rare and valuable global resource.

Acknowledgments

We thank our reviewers, Julie King and Torrence Rick, as well as an anonymous reviewer, for their helpful insights.

Recommended Reading

California Island symposium proceedings, 1980–2010. Coastal southern California science and learning. <http://www.medn science.org/California Islands Symposium> Accessed July 16, 2015.

Daily, M. 2012. The California Channel Islands (images of America). Santa Cruz Island Foundation. Santa Barbara, California.

Eaton, M. H. 1980. Diary of a sea captain's wife: Tales of Santa Cruz Island. McNally and Loftin, Santa Barbara, California.

Junak, S., T. Ayers, R. Scott, D. Wilken, and D. Young. 1995. A flora of Santa Cruz Island. Santa Barbara Botanic Garden and the California Native Plant Society. Santa Barbara, California.

Riedman, M. 1990. The pinnipeds: Seals, sea lions, and walruses. University of California Press, Berkeley, California.

Schoenherr, A. A., C. R. Feldmeth, and M. J. Emerson. 1999. Natural history of the islands of California. University of California Press, Berkeley, California.

Timbrook, J. 2007. Chumash ethnobotany: Plant knowledge among the Chumash people of southern California. Santa Barbara Museum of Natural History. Santa Barbara, California.

Glossary

ACTIVE RESTORATION Directed work focused on restoring processes, functions, or species.

BIOACCUMULATION A process in which a chemical becomes more and more concentrated in animal tissues with each step up the food chain.

ENDEMIC A species that only exists in a specified locale, as in "endemic to Santa Rosa Island."

INDIRECT EFFECT Something that causes a change in another part of a system—not by contact or proximity but by affecting something that then in turn causes the change.

ISLAND BIOGEOGRAPHY An ecological theory developed in the 1960s that predicts how many species will occur on an island given its size, the source pool for immigrants, distance from the source, diversity of the habitats and competition for those habitats, intrinsic ability of the colonizing individuals to use the new resources, and changes occurring on the island as it becomes densely populated.

KEYSTONE SPECIES A species within an ecosystem that disproportionately influences many of the other species and processes in the system.

MARINE PROTECTED AREA An area of the ocean where the taking (e.g., fishing, harvesting) of marine resources is prohibited or restricted to conserve marine ecosystems.

NEOENDEMIC A plant or animal taxon that developed into a genetic variety distinct from its ancestors by moving into new habitats and rapidly adapting to them.

PALEOENDEMIC OR RELICT A plant or animal taxon seen from the fossil record to be more widespread in ancient times that persists today in small populations in only a few places.

PINNIPED A group (order) of aquatic mammals including seals, sea lions, and the walrus.

RESILIENCE The capacity of a system to respond to and maintain its character in the face of shocks and perturbations.

SERIAL DEPLETION Use of the best and biggest prey first, then switching to less desirable prey as the previous targets are depleted.

SOIL CRUST A community of biological organisms living in the top few millimeters of the soil, consisting of cyanobacteria, green algae, microfungi, mosses, liverworts, and lichens; these organisms break down mineral soil and rock and recycle them into nutrients available to other flora and fauna.

SUBDUCTION ZONE An area of the Earth's crust where tectonic plates meet and one rides over the other.

References

Agenbroad, L. 2012. Giants and pygmies: Mammoths of Santa Rosa Island, California (USA). Quaternary International 255:2–8.

Anderson, R. S., S. Stewart, R. M. Brunner, and N. Pinter. 2010. Fire and vegetation history on Santa Rosa Island, Channel Islands, and long-term environmental change in southern California. Journal of Quaternary Science 25:782–797.

Atwater, T. M. 2007. The Educational Multimedia Visualization Center of the Department of Earth Science, University of California, Santa Barbara. 4–N.E. Pacific and W. North America. <http://emvc.geol.ucsb.edu/1_DownloadPage/Download_Page.html#WNATectGeolHist>. Accessed February 24, 2014.

———. 1998. Plate tectonic history of southern California with emphasis on the western Transverse Ranges and Santa Rosa Island. Pages 1–8 in P. W. Weigand, editor. Contributions to the geology of the Northern Channel Islands, Southern California. American Association of Petroleum Geologists, Pacific Section, MP 45. Bakersfield, California.

Atwater, T. M., and J. Stock. 1998. Pacific-North America plate tectonics of the Neogene southwestern United States—an update. International Geological Review 40:375–402. Reprinted, 1998, Pages 393–420 in W. G. Ernst and C. A. Nelson, editors. Integrated Earth and The Clarence A. Hall Jr. Volume. Bellwether Publishing, Columbia, Maryland.

Belnap. J. 1994. Cyanobacterial-lichen soil crusts of San Nicolas Island. Pages 491–495 in W. L. Halvorson and G. J. Maender, editors. The Fourth California Islands Symposium: Update on the Status of Resources. Santa Barbara Museum of Natural History, Santa Barbara, California.

Beltran, R. S., N. Kreidler, D. H. Van Vuren, S. A. Morrison, E. S. Zavaleta, K. Newton, B. R. Tershy, and D. A. Croll. 2014. Passive recovery of vegetation after herbivore eradication on Santa Cruz Island, California. Restoration Ecology 22(6):790–727.

Bezy, R. L., G. C. Gorman, G. A. Adest, and Y. J. Kim. 1980. Divergence in the Island night lizard *Xantusia riversiana* (Sauria: Xantusiidae). Pages 565–583 in D. M. Power, editor. The California Islands: Proceedings of a Multidisciplinary Symposium. Santa Barbara Museum of Natural History, Santa Barbara, California.

Boyce, W. M., W. Vickers, S. A. Morrison, T. S. Sillett, L. Caldwell, S. S. Wheeler, C. M. Baker, R. Cummings, and W. K. Reisen. 2011. Surveillance for West Nile virus and vaccination of free-ranging island scrub-jays (*Aphelocoma insularis*) on Santa Cruz Island, California. Vector-Borne Zoonotic Diseases 11:1063–1068.

Bowen, L., and D. Van Vuren. 1997. Insular endemic plants lack defenses against herbivores. Conservation Biology 11:1249–1254.

Braje, T. J., C. R. Torben, and J. M. Erlandson. 2012. A Trans-Holocene historical ecological record of shellfish harvesting on the northern Channel Islands. Quaternary International 264:109–120.

California Department of Fish and Wildlife. 2014. Commercial Market Squid Landing Receipt data. <http://www.dfg.ca.gov/marine/cpshms/marketsquidlanding.asp>. Accessed February 24, 2014.

———. 2013. South Coast MPAs. Marine Region GIS Lab, September 16, 2013. <http://www.dfg.ca.gov/marine/images/mpamaps/scmpas.jpg>. Accessed February 24, 2014.

———. 2011. Review of selected California fisheries for 2010: Coastal pelagic finfish, market squid, ocean salmon, groundfish, highly migratory species, Dungeness crab, spiny lobster, spot prawn, Kellet's whelk, and white sea bass. CalCOFI Rep. Vol. 52, 2011. <http://calcofi.org/publications/calcofireports/v52/Vol_52_13-35.Fisheries.pdf>. Accessed February 24, 2014

———. 2004. Annual status of the fisheries report through 2003. California Department of Fish and Game Marine Region. <https://www.dfg.ca.gov/marine/status/>. Accessed February 24, 2014.

California Department of Fish and Wildlife, Partnership for Interdisciplinary Studies of Coastal Oceans, Channel Islands National Marine Sanctuary, and Channel Islands National Park. 2008. Channel Islands Marine Protected Areas: First 5 Years of Monitoring: 2003–2008. S. Airamé and J. Ugoretz, editors. <http://www.dfg.ca.gov/marine/mpa/scmpas_list.asp>. Accessed February 24, 2014.

Cameron, C. 2000. Animal effigies from coastal southern California. Pacific Coast Archaeological Society Quarterly 36(2):30–52.

Carlquist, S. 1974. Island biology. Columbia University Press, New York, New York.

Cass, V. L. 1985. Exploitation of California sea lions, *Zalophus californianus*, prior to 1972. Marine Fisheries Review 47:36–38.

Catalina Island Conservancy. 2014. Endemic plants. <http://www.catalinaconservancy.org/index.php?s=wildlife&p=endemic_species>. Accessed January 16, 2014.

Cayan, D. R., E. P. Maurer, M. D. Dettinger, M. Tyree, and K. Hayhoe. 2008. Climate change scenarios for the California region. Climate Change 87:S21–S42.

Center for Plant Conservation. 2014. Search CPC. <http://www.centerforplantconservation.org/collection/NationalCollection.asp>. Accessed January 16, 2014.

Clark, P. U., A. S. Dyke, J. D. Shakun, A. E. Carlson, J. Clark, B. Wohlfarth, J. X. Mitrovica, S. W. Hostetler, and A. M. McCabe. 2009. The last glacial maximum. Science 325(5941):710–714.

Clark, R. A., W. L. Halvorson, A. A. Sawdo, and K. C. Danielson. 1990. Plant communities of Santa Rosa Island, Channel Islands National Park. Technical Report No. 42. Cooperative National Park Resources Study Unit, University of California, Davis, California.

Cohen, B., C. Cory, J. Menke, and A. Hepburn. 2009. A spatial database of Santa Cruz island vegetation. Pages 229–244 in C. C. Damiani and D. K. Garcelon, editors. 2009. Proceedings of the Seventh California Islands Symposium. Institute for Wildlife Studies, Arcata, California.

Cole, K. L., and G. W. Liu. 1994. Holocene paleoecology of an estuary on Santa Rosa Island, California. Quaternary Research 41:326–335.

Collins, P. W. 2008. Island loggerhead shrike (*Lanius ludovicianus anthonyi*). Pages 278–283 in W. D. Shuford and T. Gardali, editors. California Bird Species of Special Concern: A ranked assessment of species, subspecies, and distinct populations of birds of immediate conservation concern in California. Studies of Western Birds 1. Western Field Ornithologists, Camarillo, California, and California Department of Fish and Game, Sacramento, California.

———. 1991. Interaction between island foxes (*Urocyon littoralis*) and Indians on islands off the coast of southern California I: Morphological and archaeological evidence of human assisted dispersal. Journal of Ethnobiology 11:51–81.

Collins, P. W., and B. C. Latta. 2009. Food habits of nesting golden eagles (*Aquila chrysaetos*) on Santa Cruz and Santa Rosa Islands, California. Pages 255–268 in C. C. Damiani and D. K. Garcelon, editors. Proceedings of the Seventh California Islands Symposium, Oxnard, California, February 5–8, 2008. Institute for Wildlife Studies, Arcata, California.

Coonan, T. J., C. A. Schwemm, and D. K. Garcelon. 2009. Decline and recovery of the Island Fox: A case study of population recovery. Cambridge University Press, New York, New York.

Corry, P. M., and K. McEachern. 2009. Patterns in post-grazing vegetation changes among species and environments, San Miguel and Santa Barbara Islands. Pages 201–214 in C. C. Damiani and D. K. Garcelon, editors. 2009. Proceedings of the Seventh California Islands Symposium. Institute for Wildlife Studies, Arcata, California.

Crouch, J. K., and J. Suppe. 1993. Late Cenozoic tectonic evolution of the Los Angeles basin and California borderland: A model for core complex-like crustal extension. Geological Society of America Bulletin 105:1415–1434.

Davis, G. E. 2005. Science and society: Marine reserve design for the California Channel Islands. Conservation Biology 19:1745–1751.

Delaney, K. S., and R. K. Wayne. 2005. Adaptive units for conservation: Population distinction and historic extinctions in the island scrub-jay. Conservation Biology 19:523–533.

Dugan J. E., and G. E. Davis. 1993. Applications of marine refugia to coastal fisheries management. Canadian Journal of Fisheries and Aquatic Science 50:2029–2042.

Engle, J. M. 1994. Perspectives on the structure and dynamics of nearshore marine assemblages of the California Channel Islands. Pages 13–26 in W. L. Halvorson and G. J. Maender, editors. The Fourth California Islands Symposium: Update on the Status of Resources. Santa Barbara Museum of Natural History, Santa Barbara, California.

Erlandson, J. M., D. J. Kennett, B. L. Ingram, D. A. Guthrie, D. P. Morris, M. A. Tveskov, G. J. West, and P. L. Walker. 1996. An archaeological and paleontological chronology for Daisy Cave (CA-SMI-261), San Miguel Island, California. Radiocarbon 38:355–373.

Erlandson, J. M., M. L. Moss, and M. DesLauriers. 2008. Life on the edge: Early maritime cultures of the Pacific Coast of North America. Quaternary Science Reviews 27:2232–2245.

Erlandson, J. M., T. C. Rick, T. J. Braje, M. Casperson, B. Culleton, B. Fulfrost, T. Garcia, D. A. Guthrie, N. Jew, D. J. Kennett, M. L. Moss, L. Reeder, C. Shinner, J. Watts, and L. Willis. 2011. Paleoindian seafaring, maritime technologies, and coastal foraging on California's Channel Islands. Science 441:1181–1185.

Furches, M. S., K. E. Wallace, and K. Helernurm. 2009. High genetic divergence characterizes populations of the endemic plant *Lithophragma maximum* (Saxifragaceae) on San Clemente Island. Conservation Genetics 10:115–126.

Garcelon, D. K., K. P. Ryan, and P. T. Schulyer. 2005. Application of techniques for feral pig eradication on Santa Catalina Island, California. Pages 331–340 in D. K. Garcelon and C. A. Schwemm, editors. Proceedings of the Sixth California Islands Symposium. National Park Service Technical Publication CHIS-05-01, Institute for Wildlife Studies, Arcata, California.

Gehlbach, F. R. 1965. Amphibians and reptiles from the Pliocene and Pleistocene of North America: A chronological summary and selected bibliography. Texas Journal of Science 17:56–70.

Glassow, M. A., and L. R. Wilcoxon. 1988. Coastal adaptations near Point Conception, California, with particular regard to shellfish exploitation. American Antiquity 53:36–51.

Guthrie, D. A. 1993. New information on the prehistoric fauna of San Miguel Island, California. Pages 405–416 in F. G. Hochberg, editor. Third California Islands Symposium: Recent Advances in Research on the California Islands. Santa Barbara Museum of Natural History, Santa Barbara, California.

Halvorson, W., S. Junak, C. Schwemm, and T. Keeney. 1996. Plant communities of San Nicolas Island. Technical Report No. 55. USDI Cooperative Park studies Unit, University of Arizona, Tucson, Arizona.

Hamilton, S. L., J. E. Caselle, D. P. Malone, and M. H. Carr. 2010. Incorporating biogeography into evaluations of the Channel Islands marine reserve network. Proceedings of the National Academy of Sciences 107(43):18272–18277.

Helenurm, K. 2003. Genetic diversity in the rare insular endemic *Sibara filifolia* (Brassicaceae). Madrono 50(3):181–186.

Hicks, J. J., and H. S. Walter. 2009. Population decline of the island loggerhead shrike (*Lanius ludovicianus anthonyi*) in the California Channel Islands. Wilson Journal of Ornithology 121:184–187.

Hochberg, M. C., S. A. Junak, R. N. Philbrick, and S. Timbrook. 1979. Botany. Pages 5.1–5.85 in D. M. Power, editor. Natural Resources Study of the Channel Islands National Monument, California. Technical Report. Santa Barbara Museum of Natural History, Santa Barbara, California.

Hornafius, J. S., B. P. Luyendyk, R. R. Terres, and M. J. Kamerling. 1986. Timing and extent of Neogene tectonic rotation in the western Transverse Ranges, California. Geological Society of America Bulletin 97:1476–1487.

Howald, G. R., K. R. Faulkner, B. Tershy, B. Keitt, H. Gellerman, E. M.

Creel, M. Grinnell, S. T. Ortega, and D. A. Croll. 2005. Eradication of black rats from Anacapa Island: Biological and social considerations. Pages 299–312 in D. K. Garcelon and C. A. Schwemm, editors. Proceedings of the Sixth California Islands Symposium. National Park Service Technical Publication CHIS-05-01. Institute for Wildlife Studies, Arcata, California.

Huey, L. H. 1930. Past and present status of the northern elephant seal with a note on the Guadalupe fur seal. Journal of Mammalogy 11:188–194.

Johnson, D. 1980. Episodic vegetation stripping, soil erosion, and landscape modification in prehistoric and recent historic time. Pages 103–121 in D. M. Power, editor. The California Islands: Proceedings of a Multidisciplinary Symposium. Santa Barbara Museum of Natural History, Santa Barbara, California.

Johnson, J. R., T. W. Stafford Jr., H. O. Ajie, and D. P. Morris. 2002. Arlington Springs revisited. Pages 541–545 in D. K. Browne, K. L. Mitchell, and H.W. Chaney, editors. Proceedings of the Fifth California Islands Symposium. Santa Barbara Museum of Natural History, Santa Barbara, California.

Johnson, N. K. 1972. Origin and differentiation if the avifauna of the Channel Islands, California. Condor 74:295–315.

Junak, S. A., and R. Philbrick. 1999a. Flowering plants of the Natividad Island, Baja California, Mexico. Pages 224–234 in D. K. Browne, K. L. Mitchell, and H. W. Chaney, editors. Proceedings of the Fifth California Islands Symposium. U.S. Department of the Interior, Minerals Management Service, Pacific OCS Region. Camarillo, California.

———. 1999b. Flowering plants of the San Benito Islands, Baja California, Mexico. Pages 235–246 in D. K. Browne, K. L. Mitchell, and H. W. Chaney, editors. Proceedings of the Fifth California Islands Symposium. U.S. Department of the Interior, Minerals Management Service, Pacific OCS Region. Camarillo, California.

Junak, S., T. Ayers, R. Scott, D. Wilken, and D. Young. 1995. A flora of Santa Cruz Island. Santa Barbara Botanic Garden and the California Native Plant Society. Santa Barbara, California.

Keegen, D. R., B. E. Coblentz, and C. S. Winchell. 1994. Ecology of feral goats eradicated on San Clemente Island, California. Pages 323–330 in W. L. Halvorson and G. J. Maender, editors. The Fourth California Islands Symposium: Update on the Status of Resources. Santa Barbara Museum of Natural History, Santa Barbara, California.

Kennett, D. J. 2005. The Island Chumash: Behavioral ecology of a maritime society. University of California Press, Berkeley, California.

Kiff, L. F. 1980. Historical changes in resident populations of California Islands raptors. Pages 651–673 in D. M. Power, editor. The California Islands: Proceedings of a Multidisciplinary Symposium. Santa Barbara Museum of Natural History, Santa Barbara, California.

Klinger, R. C., P. T. Schuyler, and J. D. Sterner. 1994. Vegetation response to the removal of feral sheep from Santa Cruz Island. Pages 341–350 in W. L. Halvorson and G. J. Maender, editors. The Fourth California Islands Symposium: Update on the Status of Resources. Santa Barbara Museum of Natural History, Santa Barbara, California.

Knapp, D. 2005. Vegetation community mapping on Santa Catalina Island using orthorectification and GIS. Pages 193–204 in D. K. Garcelon and C. A. Schwemm, editors. Proceedings of the Sixth California Islands Symposium. National Park Service Technical Publication CHIS-05-01, Institute for Wildlife Studies, Arcata, California.

LaDeau, S. L., P. P. Marra, A. M. Kilpatrick, and C. A. Calder. 2008. West Nile virus revisited: Consequences for North American ecology. BioScience 58:937–946.

Latta, B. C., D. E. Driscoll, J. L. Linthicum, R. E. Jackman, and G. Doney. 2005. Capture and translocation of golden eagles from the California Channel Islands to mitigate depredation of endemic island foxes. Pages 341–350 in D. K. Garcelon and C. A. Schwemm, editors. Proceedings of the Sixth California Islands Symposium. National Park Service Technical Publication CHIS-05-01. Institute for Wildlife Studies, Arcata, California.

Laughrin, L., M. Carroll, A. Bromfield, and J. Carrow. 1994. Pages 523–530 in W. L. Halvorson and G. J. Maender, editors. The Fourth California Islands Symposium: Update on the Status of Resources. Santa Barbara Museum of Natural History, Santa Barbara, California.

Legg, M. R. 1991. Developments in understanding the tectonic evolution of the California Continental Borderland Pages 291–312 in R. H. Osborne, editor. From shoreline to abyss. Society of Economic Paleontologists and Mineralogists, Special Paper 46.

Levine, J. M., K. McEachern, and C. Cowan. 2010. Do competitors modulate rare plant response to precipitation change? Ecology 91(1):130–140.

Livingston, D. S. 2006. Historic resource study: A history of the islands within Channel Islands National Park. Technical Report to Channel Islands National Park, Ventura, California.

Lowry, M. S., and J. V. Carretta. 1999. Market squid (*Loligo opalescens*) in the diet of California sea lions (*Zalophus californianus*) in southern California (1981–1995). CalCOFI Report 40:196–207.

Lubchenco, J., S. R. Palumbi, S. D. Gaines, and S. Andelman. 2003. Plugging a hole in the ocean: The emerging science of marine reserves. Ecological Applications 13:S3–S7.

Luyendyk, B. P. 1991. A model for Neogene crustal rotations, transtension, and transpression in southern California. Geological Society of America Bulletin 103:1528–1536.

Manuwal, T., and R. Sweitzer, R. 2010. Impacts of introduced mule deer to island scrub oak habitats of Santa Catalina Island, California. Pages 19–34 in D. Knapp, editor. Oak Ecosystem Restoration on Santa Catalina Island, California: Proceedings of an On-Island Workshop February 2–4, 2007. Catalina Island Conservancy, Avalon, California.

MacArthur, R. H., and E. O. Wilson. 1967. A theory of island biogeography. Princeton University Press, Princeton, New Jersey.

McEachern, K., D. Thomson, and K. Chess. 2009. Climate alters response of an endemic island plant to removal of invasive herbivores. Ecological Applications 19(6):1574–1584.

Moran, R. V. 1996. The flora of Guadalupe Island, Mexico. Memoirs California Academy of Sciences 19:1–190.

Morrison, S. 2007. Reducing risk and enhancing efficiency in non-native vertebrate removal efforts on islands: A 25 year multi-taxa retrospective from Santa Cruz Island, California. Pages 398–409 in G. W. Witmer, W. C. Pitt, and K. A. Fagerstone, editors. Managing Vertebrate Invasive Species: Proceedings of an International Symposium. USDA/APHIS/WS. National Wildlife Research Center, Fort Collins, Colorado.

Morrison, S., N. Macdonald, K. Walker, L. Lozier, and R. M. Shaw. 2007. Facing the dilemma at eradication's end: Uncertainty of absence and the Lazarus effect. Frontiers in Ecology and the Environment 5(5):271–276.

Morrison, S. A., T. S. Sillett, C. K. Ghalambor, J. W. Fitzpatrick, D. M. Graber, V. J. Bakker, R. Bowman, C. T. Collins, P. W. Collins, K. S. Delaney, D. F. Doak, W. D. Koenig, L. Laughrin, A. A. Lieberman, J. M. Marzluff, M. D. Reynolds, J. M. Scott, J. A. Stallcup, W. Vickers, and W.M. Boyce. 2011. Proactive conservation management of an island-endemic bird species in the face of global change. BioScience 61:1-13-1021.

Muhs, D. R., K. R. Simmons, R. R. Schumann, L. T. Groves, J. X. Mitrovica, and D. Laurel. 2012. Sea-level history during the last interglacial complex on San Nicolas Island, California: Implications for glacial isostatic adjustment processes, paleozoogeography and tectonics. Quaternary Science Reviews 37:1–25.

NALF (Naval Auxiliary Landing Field). 2013. Integrated natural resources management plan. U.S. Navy, Naval Auxiliary Landing Field, San Clemente Island, California.

Oberbauer, T. A. 1987. Floristic analysis of vegetation communities on Isla de Cedros, Baja California, Mexico. Pages 115–131 in F. G. Hochberg, editor. Third California Island Symposium: Recent Advances in Research on the California Islands. Santa Barbara Museum of Natural History, Santa Barbara, California.

Oberbauer, T. A. 1999a. Analysis of vascular plant species diversity of the Pacific Coast Islands of Alta and Baja California. Pages 201–211 in D. K. Browne, K. L. Mitchell, and H. W. Chaney, editors. Proceedings of the Fifth California Islands Symposium. U.S. Department of the Interior, Minerals Management Service, Pacific OCS Region. Camarillo, California.

———.1999b. Vegetation and flora of Islas Los Coronados Baja California, Mexico. Pages 212–223 in D. K. Browne, K. L. Mitchell, and H. W. Chaney, editors. Proceedings of the Fifth California Islands Symposium. U.S. Department of the Interior, Minerals Management Service, Pacific OCS Region. Camarillo, California.

Ogden, A. 1941. The California sea otter trade, 1784–1848. University of California Press, Berkeley, California.

Power, D. M. 1994. Avifaunal change on California's Coastal Islands. Pages 75–90 in J. R. Jehl Jr. and N. K. Johnson, editors. A Century of Avifaunal Change in Western North America. Studies in Avian Biology No. 15.
———. 1980. Introduction. Pages 1–4 in D. M. Power, editor. The California Islands: Proceedings of a multidisciplinary symposium. Santa Barbara Museum of Natural History, Santa Barbara, California.
Raven, P. H. 1967. The floristics of the California Islands. Pages 57–67 in R. Philbrick, editor. Proceedings of the Symposium on the Biology of the California Islands, Santa Barbara Botanic Garden, Santa Barbara, California.
Raven P. H., and D. I. Axelrod. 1995. Origins and relationships of the California flora. University of California Press, Berkeley, California.
Rick, T. C., J. M. Erlandson, R. L. Vellanoweth, and T. J. Braje. 2005. From Pleistocene mariners to complex hunter-gatherers: The archaeology of the California Channel Islands. Journal of World Prehistory 19:169–228.
Rick, T. C., J. M. Erlandson, R. L. Vellanoweth, T. J. Braje, P. W. Collins, D. A. Guthrie, and T. W. Stafford Jr. 2009. Origins and antiquity of the island fox (*Urocyon littoralis*) on California's Channel Islands. Quaternary Research 71:93–98.
Rick, T., R. DeLong, J. M. Erlandson, T. J. Braje, T. L. Jones, J. E. Arnold, R. Des Lauriers, W. R. Hildebrandt, D. J. Kennett, R. L. Vellanoweth, and T. A. Wakes. 2011. Where were the northern elephant seals? Holocene archaeology and biogeography of *Mirounga angustirostris*. The Holocene 21(7):1159–1166.
Roemer, G. W., C. J. Donlan, and F. Courchamp. 2002. Golden eagles, feral pigs, and insular carnivores: How exotic species turn native predators into prey. Proceedings of the National Academy of Sciences USA 99:791–796.
Roemer, G. W., T. J. Coonan, D. K. Garcelon, J. Bascompte, and L. Laughrin. 2001. Feral pigs facilitate hyperpredation by golden eagles and indirectly cause the decline of the island fox. Animal Conservation 4:307–318.
Santa Barbara Botanic Garden. 2013. Channel Islands. <http://www.sbbg.org/conservation-research/channel-islands/>. Accessed January 16, 2014.
Scott, T. A., and M. L. Morrison. 1990. Natural history and management of the San Clemente loggerhead shrike. Proceedings of the Western Foundation of Vertebrate Zoology 4:23–57.
Sharpe, P. B., and D. K. Garcelon. 2005. Restoring and monitoring bald eagles in southern California: The legacy of DDT. Pages 323–330 in D. K. Garcelon and C. A. Schwemm, editors. Proceedings of the Sixth California Islands Symposium. National Park Service Technical Publication CHIS-05-01. Institute for Wildlife Studies, Arcata, California.
Stanley, T. R., S. Teel, L. S. Hall, L. C. Dye, and L. L. Laughrin. 2012. Population size of island loggerhead shrikes on Santa Rosa and Santa Cruz Islands. Wildlife Society Bulletin 36(1):61–69.
State of California. 2002. Final environmental document marine protected areas in NOAA's Channel Islands National Marine Sanctuary (Sections 27.82, 630, and 632 Title 14, California Code of Regulations) Volume I.
Stewart, B. S., P. K. Yochem, D. L. DeLong Jr., and G. A. Antonelis. 1993. Trends in abundance and status of pinnipeds on the southern California Islands. Pages 501–516 in F. G. Hochberg, editor. Third California Islands Symposium: Recent Advances in Research on the California Islands. Santa Barbara Museum of Natural History, Santa Barbara, California.
Stewart, B. S., P. K. Yochem, H. R. Huber, D. L. DeLong Jr., R. J. Jameson, W. J. Sydeman, S. G. Allen, and B. J. LeBoeuf. 1994. History and present status of the northern elephant seal population. Pages 29–48 in B. J. LeBoeuf and R. M. Laws, editors. Elephant Seals: Population ecology, behavior and physiology. University of California Press, Berkeley, California.
Timbrook, J. 2007. Chumash ethnobotany. Santa Barbara Museum of Natural History. Santa Barbara, California.
Timbrook, J., J. R. Johnson, and D. Earle. 1982. Vegetation burning by the Chumash. Journal of California and Great Basin Anthropology 4:163–186.
U.S. Department of Defense (USDOD). 2010. Threatened and endangered species on DOD lands. USDOD Natural Resources Conservation Program. <http://www.dodnaturalresources.net/files/T_E_s_fact_sheet_1-15-10_final_.pdf>. Accessed August 30, 2011.
U.S. Fish and Wildlife Service. 2003. Final revised recovery plan for the southern sea otter (*Enhydra lutris nereis*). Portland, Oregon. <http://www.fws.gov/ventura/species_information/so_sea_otter/ssorecplan.pdf>. Accessed February 24, 2014.
———. 1977. Determination that the southern sea otter is a threatened species. 42 FR 2965 2968 (*Enhydra lutris nereis*).
von Bloeker, J. C., Jr. 1967. Land mammals of the southern California Islands. Pages 245–263 in R. Philbrick, editor. Proceedings of the Symposium on the Biology of the California Islands. Santa Barbara Botanic Garden, Santa Barbara, California.
Van Vuren, D., and B. Coblentz. 1987. Some ecological effects of feral sheep on Santa Cruz Island, California. Biological Conservation 41:253–268.
Van Vuren, D., and E. Bowen. 1999. Reduced defenses in insular endemic plants: An evolutionary time frame. Conservation Biology 13:211–212.
Walker, P. L. 1980. Archaeological evidence for the recent extinction of three terrestrial mammals on San Miguel Island. Pages 703–717 in D. M. Power, editor. The California Islands: Proceedings of a Multidisciplinary Symposium. Santa Barbara Museum of Natural History, Santa Barbara, California.
Walton, B. 1990. Peregrine falcon recovery in California. Pages 69–77 in P. J. Bryant and J. Remington, editors. Endangered Wildlife and Habitats in Southern California. Memoirs of the Natural History Foundation of Orange County No. 3. Irvine, California.
Wenner, A. M., and D. L. Johnson. 1980. Land vertebrates on the islands: Sweepstakes or landbridges? Pages 497–530 in D. M. Power, editor. The California Islands: Proceedings of a Multidisciplinary Symposium. Santa Barbara Museum of Natural History, Santa Barbara, California.
Yelenik, S. G., and J. M. Levine. 2011. The role of plant-soil feedbacks in driving native-species recovery. Ecology 92(1):66–74.
———. 2010. Native shrub reestablishment in exotic annual grasslands: Do ecosystem processes recover? Ecological Applications 20(3):716–727.

THIRTY-FIVE

Marine Fisheries

ERIC P. BJORKSTEDT, JOHN C. FIELD, MILTON LOVE, LAURA ROGERS-BENNETT, and RICK STARR

Introduction

The marine ecosystems off the coast of California are among the most productive in the world, fueled by upwelling of cool, nutrient-rich waters. They are also among the most dynamic, responding dramatically to large-scale fluctuations in the winds that drive upwelling and govern the flow of the California Current (Checkley and Barth 2009; see Chapter 6, "Oceanography"). Commercial, recreational, and traditional fishers harvest over 350 species of fish and invertebrates from these ecosystems, of which some 200 or so are landed almost entirely by commercial fleets (Leet et al. 2001, Allen et al. 2006). Fisheries operate in nearly every major marine ecosystem off the California coast, from intertidal beaches and rocky shores to offshore PELAGIC waters and deep, DEMERSAL habitats on the upper reaches of the continental slope. These fisheries range from highly technical commercial operations to the hands-only pursuit of grunion (*Leuresthes tenuis*) as they make their spawning runs onto beaches.

With rare exception, California's fisheries are now regulated in the recognition that carried too far, fishing can degrade the structure and productivity of the STOCKS and ecosystems on which fisheries depend. Historically, however, effective fisheries management has not been the rule. California has experienced numerous fisheries collapses throughout the past century, including collapse of the sardine fishery in the 1940s and the widespread and ongoing closure of the groundfish fishery that has marked the early years of the twenty-first century. Such crises have triggered widespread and lasting ecological and economic consequences, and growing concern about the long-term sustainability of fisheries and the ecosystems in which they operate (Halpern et al. 2009). Crisis and concern have inspired deeper study and understanding of fisheries and their ecosystems. More recently, they have spurred legislative action and an ongoing transition in how marine fisheries and ecosystems are managed (U.S. Commission on Ocean Policy 2004, Methot et al. 2013).

In this chapter we examine California's marine fisheries as managed ecosystems to understand how this process has unfolded and what lessons can be learned as we look to the future. We begin by defining what we mean by "a fishery" and the diverse perspectives on how fisheries and marine ecosystems ought to be managed. We then introduce some fundamental concepts of fisheries management and consider ecological consequences of fishing key to understanding the inherent trade-offs of fisheries. Next we summarize the current state of California's marine fisheries and the history of these fisheries as a crude means of assessing their impact on marine ecosystems; broader consideration of the state of several ecosystems in which fisheries operate is covered elsewhere (see Chapters 16–20 and 33). Finally, our attention turns to the ongoing and emerging challenges that fisheries managers must anticipate and to several nascent, potentially complementary approaches to fisheries management intended to support progress towards sustainable, resilient fisheries, communities, and ecosystems. We reach no final answers, as the management of California's marine fisheries is in the early stages of a profound transition whose ecological, economic, and social consequences are only beginning to be apparent. Indeed, although the initial steps towards a more sustainable future have been taken and we can see signs of progress, the path forward remains challenging.

What Is a Fishery? How Should Fisheries and Ecosystems Be Managed?

For most people, the term "fishery" brings to mind a vision of a fleet of fishing boats heading to sea and bringing their catch to market. However, fisheries have a more complex structure that must be understood for effective management. McEvoy (1996) proposes: "What a fishery is, descriptively, and what management ought to sustain, prescriptively, is an interaction between three variables: an ecosystem, a group of people working, and the system of social control within which the work takes place. Each of the three variables has a good bit of its own dynamism, but each varies continually in response to changes in the other two." This perspective implies that successful strategies for maintaining resilient ecosystems, including fisheries, are likely to be less about controlling the system and more about facilitating the processes, variability, and interactions that make up the whole (Holling and Meffe 1996, McEvoy 1996, Gunderson et al. 2008, Gaichas 2008). It may well be true that "the best that fisheries managers can do is to monitor and adjust the interaction between a volatile ecology, a creative economy, and society's understanding and control as they go along" (McEvoy 1996).

The challenge to managers lies in balancing the diverse trade-offs between ecological, economic, and social elements of a fishery (Hilborn 2007d, Rice and Garcia 2011). Because of its power to alter the structure and function of marine ecosystems, fishing is commonly viewed as in conflict with stewardship and conservation of marine environments and ecosystems, and as potentially diminishing the value gained from nonextractive uses and services of marine ecosystems (e.g., ecotourism, existence values, scientific and educational opportunities). Yet fisheries are themselves a major service humans derive from marine ecosystems. Fisheries provide employment and revenue (and are often a primary source of the same) for many coastal communities; they generate protein, oils, and other material for human nutrition, agriculture, and industry; and fishing is a much enjoyed form of recreation. As history has shown, past attempts to balance these trade-offs have often proven untenable, leading to undesirable ecological conditions and ultimately to economic hardship.

Photo on previous page: A purse seiner hauls in its catch on Monterey Bay. Vessels like this fish sardine, anchovy, squid, and mackerel in California's waters. Photo: Rick Starr.

Increasing concern about the present and future ability of marine ecosystems to provide essential services has motivated vigorous debate within the scientific community about how fisheries have affected marine ecosystems and ought to be managed. One view is that fishing has had and continues to have devastating effects on marine ecosystems and is a major risk to the sustainability and resilience of the world oceans (Pauly et al. 1998, Jackson et al. 2001, Worm et al. 2006). Counterarguments point out that modern approaches to fisheries management can support sustainable, resilient systems—at least in regions where FISHERIES SCIENCE is reasonably well developed and fisheries management is practiced and enforced (Hilborn et al. 2003, Essington et al. 2006, Murawski et al. 2007, Hilborn 2007c, Branch et al. 2010, Worm et al. 2009, Murawski 2010).

This debate reflects diverse perspectives and assumptions regarding the goals of ecosystem management and what constitutes a "healthy ecosystem" (Callicott et al. 1999). On the one hand, the "compositionalist" worldview is decidedly biocentric, emphasizing the importance of taking the long view in maintaining ecological and evolutionary processes by preserving intact ecosystems (at least within protected areas) and maintaining viable populations of native species, while accommodating human activities consistent with these goals (Grumbine 1994, Callicott et al. 1999, Field and Francis 2006). This view rests on two concepts: first, that prior to human fisheries and removals all production was recycled within marine ecosystems (including export to deep-sea and coastal terrestrial ecosystems); and second, that having evolved in response to natural variability and trends in environmental and climate conditions, undisturbed populations and ecosystems are expected to be more resilient than those altered by fishing and other human activities.

In contrast, traditional fisheries management is more consistent with anthropocentric or "functionalist" perspectives, in which ecosystems are manipulated to maximize sustainable transfer of energy and nutrients to human uses (Callicott et al. 1999). Although it is recognized that fisheries can ultimately damage the resources on which they depend, depletion of populations is intentional, related fisheries-driven changes in marine ecosystems are to be expected, and healthy ecosystems are identified by their ability to support sustainable production. In a sense, this view of a healthy ecosystem is one that can endure the stress of fisheries or other extractive human uses (Gaichas 2008). More recently, the role of biodiversity as a foundation for greater, more stable aggregate production and yield has been recognized as central to this resilience (Stachowicz et al. 2007, Schindler et al. 2010).

This debate is part of the ongoing evolution of fisheries management and outlines the trade-offs between harvest and conservation that must be balanced in finding our way to a sustainable future. McEvoy's definition of a fishery reminds us to look beyond the ecosystem to recognize the roles economic incentives and social structure play in driving fishery dynamics (Hilborn 2007b, Gutiérrez et al. 2011). Taken together, these perspectives yield a conceptual view in which the direct interactions between ecology, economy, and governance that comprise a fishery are considered in the context of the entire ecosystem. This view also highlights the role of climate in controlling ecosystem structure and the flow of energy and nutrients throughout the system (Figure 35.1).

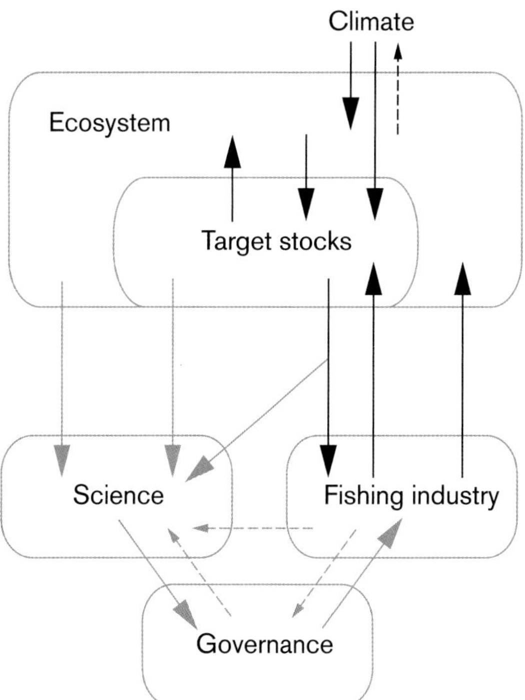

FIGURE 35.1 A simplified conceptual view of a fisheries ecosystem illustrating the major relationships between human components of fisheries and the ecosystems in which fisheries operate. Dark arrows indicate connections involving or affecting production or transfer of biomass. Gray arrows indicate connections based primarily on collection or communication of data, scientific information or advice, regulation, and feedback. Dashed lines indicate potential feedbacks. Sources: Adapted from McEvoy 1996, Field and Francis 2006, Brander 2007, Crowder et al. 2008, and Methot et al. 2013.

An Introduction to Fisheries Science and Management

In the following sections, we introduce the general principles of fisheries science and its application to management, then touch upon several challenges associated with management of particular stocks. Fisheries management has traditionally focused on individual stocks. This remains the foundation today, even as management of particular fisheries increasingly accounts for impacts across multiple species and on the whole ecosystem (MacCall 2002, Mangel and Levin 2005, Kaplan, Gray, et al. 2012). We discuss progress towards more comprehensive management schemes later in the chapter.

Management of a particular stock depends strongly on the species' LIFE HISTORY, which underpins the natural dynamics of the stock and how it will respond to fishing. Species with similar life histories typically exhibit similar responses to fishing, even though they might come from highly divergent evolutionary lineages (Winemiller and Rose 1992, Jennings and Reynolds 1998, King and MacFarlane 2003). This pattern is so robust that simple life history data can be a foundation for precautionary fisheries management in the absence of more detailed information (Froese 2004, Patrick et al. 2010, Thorson et al. 2012). In general, long-lived, low-productivity species tend to be most sensitive to the effects of fishing, while highly productive, short-lived species may be able to sustain more intense harvest rates—at least under favorable environmental conditions. The following discussion focuses on the question of how stocks generally respond to fishing and why fisheries can happen. These underlying principles also apply to species not targeted for harvest.

Surplus Production, Sustainable Yields, and Stability

The theory of sustainable fishing is grounded in the tendency for populations depleted by harvest to grow back towards their unfished state. Fishing induces this growth by "fishing a stock down": increasing mortality, thereby reducing stock biomass (B, which is commonly scaled by age- or size-specific per capita reproductive output to represent the total population's spawning output). This increases the proportion of smaller, younger, faster-growing individuals in the population. Faster per capita growth, combined with increased average per capita production of recruits (offspring), gives rise to SURPLUS PRODUCTION that can be removed over and over as sustainable yield to a fishery. The relationship between biomass and surplus production is referred to as a stock's PRODUCTION CURVE (Figure 35.2). STOCK-RECRUITMENT RELATIONSHIPS describe the average response of recruitment (the addition of new individuals to a population) to changes in stock size. However, recruitment tends to be highly variable in most fish and invertebrate stocks. MAXIMUM SUSTAINABLE YIELD (MSY) is the maximum harvest a stock can sustain without inevitable decline and is achieved at a stock size termed B_{MSY} that is typically substantially lower than the unfished biomass, termed B_0. The rate of fishing mortality that leads to B_{MSY} is similarly designated as F_{MSY}. Fishing

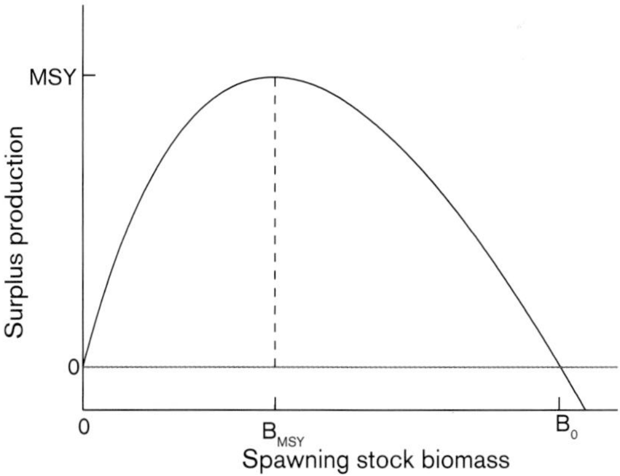

FIGURE 35.2 A hypothetical production curve showing surplus production as a function of stock size. Positive surplus production arises as a population grows back towards its unfished state, B_0. In this example, the shape of the production curve is similar to those estimated for relatively long-lived (low mortality), low-productivity species like rockfish, in which B_{MSY} (biomass at maximum sustainable yield) is about 40% of B_0 and MSY (maximum sustainable yield) is a small percentage of the standing stock. Values along the y-axes are an order of magnitude smaller than those along the x-axes.

more intensely than F_{MSY}—OVERFISHING—will drive a stock to a level below B_{MSY}. In extreme cases, fishing more intensely than some critical level (F_{crit}) will drive a population towards extinction.

Any combination of biomass and yield on a stock's production curve is theoretically sustainable. However, when B is less than or equal to B_{MSY}, persistent errors in controlling fishing mortality (F), if left uncorrected for any length of time, can lead to substantial departure from the target stock biomass. If $B<B_{MSY}$, fishing more intensely than the target level F, even if still less than F_{MSY}, will lead to further depletion and lower surplus production. It will increase disparity between how hard the stock is fished and what it can sustain. Conversely, if the stock at $B>B_{MSY}$ is fished more intensely than the target F, the stock will decline in size, but surplus production will increase, partially countering the decline in biomass.

Practical Applications: Stock Assessments and Management Advice

In practice, stock size, spawning output, recruitment, and productivity are estimated by fitting a population model to available data (Quinn and Deriso 1999). This forms the basis for management advice conveyed in a STOCK ASSESSMENT. The key information provided in a stock assessment are MANAGEMENT REFERENCE POINTS (such as F_{MSY}, B_{MSY}, MSY, or their proxies) that managers use to set catch limits and other regulations (e.g., fishing seasons, gear designs, etc.) for a fishery. The population models used in stock assessments have their origins in the early days of quantitative fisheries science (Schaefer 1954, Ricker 1954, Beverton and Holt 1957; see reviews by Smith 1994, Needle 2001, and Hilborn 2012). They range in complexity from relatively simple biomass production models (e.g., Fox 1970) to detailed models in which abundance, demographic information (sex-, size- and age-structure), and reproductive output are all explicitly estimated from detailed (and costly) data sets (e.g., Methot and Wetzel 2012). Assessments for salmon in particular likewise vary in complexity, ranging from simple abundance indices for data-poor stocks to run-reconstructions based on detailed data about the number of fish of each age (e.g., two-, three, or four-year-olds) captured in the fishery (catch-at-age) and age-specific ESCAPEMENT (Hilborn and Walters 1992, O'Farrell et al. 2013).

In the early days of fisheries management, MSY (or, in the case of salmon, an escapement threshold) was treated as a target rather than a limit. This practice involved some risk of overfishing and ensuing stock depletion. In many cases, this risk was magnified by the combination of inadequate data and poor control of actual fishing effort, especially during the development of a fishery (see Box 35.1). More recently, management reference points and biomass thresholds have accounted for statistical uncertainty in estimated stock-recruit relationships and the productive capacity of stocks (Ralston 2002, Punt et al. 2008), and we continue to develop our understanding of how other sources of error and uncertainty pervade even the best model-based assessments (see e.g., Ralston et al. 2011, Mangel et al. 2013). Current federal law requires that stock assessments provide biomass thresholds below which stocks are declared either in a precautionary zone or overfished. Federal law also requires that for federally managed stocks, overfishing limits (OFLs) are set at the best estimate of stocks' MSY (or its proxy). Finally, federally managed stocks must have target catch (the annual catch limit, or ACL) set as a fraction of the OFL (often approximately 75%) in order to account for multiple sources of uncertainty (Figure 35.3; Methot et al. 2013).

BOX 35.1 TEMPTING TRAPS: WINDFALL HARVESTS IN DEVELOPING FISHERIES

Yield in a developing fishery is not dependent solely on new (surplus) production but also includes additional harvest required to fish the stock down to increase surplus production (the difference between B_0 and B_{MSY} in Figure 35.2). These "windfall" harvests (sensu MacCall 2009b) present a particularly difficult management challenge. As a fishery matures, biomass, the average size of fish captured, and yields all must eventually decline, yet this is not readily apparent in aggregated catch data. Instead, high catches during the development of a fishery can obscure the consequences of low (or declining) productivity in a stock. Local depletions have little effect on landings as fisheries spread through space or across species. High catch rates during the early days of a fishery can induce rapid development of a fleet too large to be supported by surplus production once the fishery has fully developed.

This dynamic sets up conditions for sharp ecological feedbacks and fishery collapse, as the necessary reduction in fishing can be substantial. In fisheries that target low-productivity, long-lived stocks, exhaustion of windfall harvests over a short period of fishery growth (e.g., five years) can result in annual landings double or triple what the stock can maximally sustain. Even when it becomes clear that a fishery has outgrown its stock, strong socioeconomic pressures typically exist to protect the fleet from the natural consequences of declining yields. This is often to the detriment of the harvested stocks and ultimately to the fishery as a whole (Cochrane 2000). Such dynamics can be especially challenging in fisheries on coastal, pelagic species that naturally undergo extreme fluctuations, in which the temptation to build a fleet is strong during a stock's expansion phase even though natural stock decline and fishery contraction is inevitable (Fréon et al. 2005).

Sources of Uncertainty and Bias

RECRUITMENT VARIABILITY AND CLIMATE-DEPENDENT SURPLUS PRODUCTION

Stock assessments (when they can be developed) estimate average productivity. However, most marine species exhibit substantial, sometimes dramatic, interannual fluctuations in recruitment, growth, mortality, and reproductive output driven by variability in oceanographic conditions (Wells et al. 2007, Williams et al. 2007, Black et al. 2010, Harvey et al. 2011, Koslow and Allen 2011, Ralston et al. 2013, Thorson et al. 2013). Variability in recruitment generates strong and weak year-classes that propagate through a stock over time (Figure 35.4). Variability in recruitment also contrib-

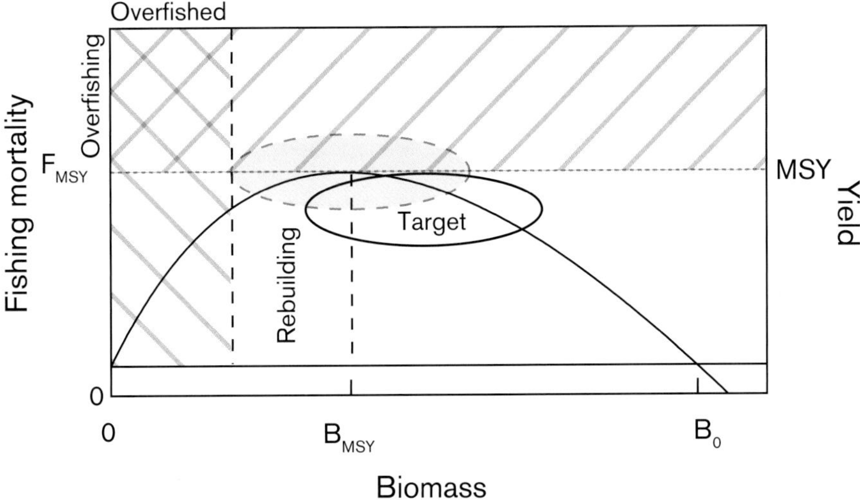

FIGURE 35.3 Schematic of fisheries management definitions, showing combinations of fishing mortality (left y-axis), corresponding yield (right y-axis) and biomass (an index of stock status). Hatched regions of the figure correspond to overfishing and to overfished status; the labeled zone to the right of the overfished region corresponds to rebuilding of overfished stocks. Under present law, management targets (open oval) are more conservative than in the past (shaded oval), when management focused on achieving maximum sustainable yield (MSY). B_0 indicates unfished biomass, B_{MSY} and F_{MSY} indicate biomass and fishing mortality at MSY. Source: Adapted from Methot et al. 2013.

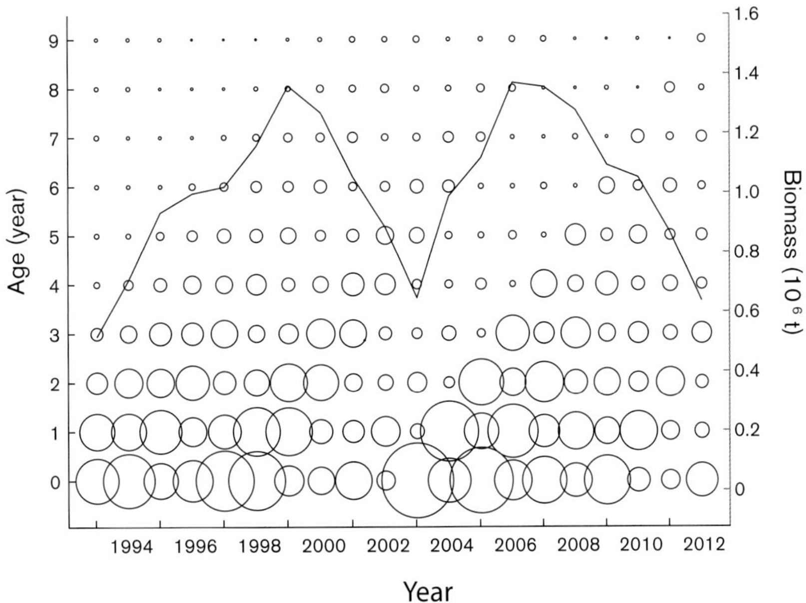

FIGURE 35.4 Illustration of recruitment variability and subsequent contributions of year-classes to stock biomass based on data from the stock assessment for Pacific sardine (Hill et al. 2012). Circles show relative recruitment strength (bottom row), attrition of each cohort over time (rising diagonal tracks), and annual age structure (vertical columns; left y-axis) in the Pacific sardine stock. Line shows total biomass of sardine stock (right y-axis). Increases in biomass reflect early growth of strong year classes, and declines in biomass follow years of poor recruitment as natural mortality and fishing reduce strong year classes. Note how strong year classes, although declining over time, can persist across periods of poor recruitment.

utes to uncertainty in the estimates of stock productivity that underpin management reference points. This uncertainty has motivated research into how recruitment indices based on late-stage larvae or settling juveniles might be usefully incorporated into stock assessments (e.g., Field, MacCall, Ralston et al. 2010, White and Rogers-Bennett 2010). It has also led to more general efforts to incorporate environmental proxies into stock assessments (e.g., Jacobson and MacCall 1995, Shirippa and Colbert 2006). Some species, like Pacific sardine (*Sardinops sagax*), respond so strongly to large-scale climate variability that substantial surplus production may only be possible during favorable climate regimes (MacCall 1996, Schwartzlose et al. 1999, Chavez et al. 2003, Lindegren et al. 2013). For such stocks, relatively nimble approaches to monitoring and management are required (MacCall 2002). For others (e.g., long-lived rockfish), longevity can temper a stock's response to low-frequency climate variability, allowing steadier management (MacCall 2002). Still, questions such as whether to base management on "poor" conditions or to allow (presumably temporary) overfishing during periods of low productivity must be considered (Parma 2002). Density-dependent ecological interactions (e.g., predation and competition) on juvenile stages can modulate recruitment variability (Hobson et al. 2001, Iles and Beverton 2000).

DATA LIMITATIONS

Typically, complex stock assessment models tend to be "data-hungry." Because the costs of obtaining sufficiently rich data sets can be very substantial, highly detailed assessments have been developed for relatively few stocks, with emphasis on those that support highly valuable fisheries or are the subject of conservation concerns. Data are much sparser for numerous stocks that individually represent relatively modest contributions to total landings and value of fisheries but that are important cumulatively and contribute to biodiversity. Recently developed assessment methods (e.g., MacCall 2009b, Dick and MacCall 2011, Carruthers et al. 2014; see also the discussion of marine protected areas below) have greatly expanded the scope for managers to link allowable catches for such "data-poor" species to estimates of management reference points related to sustainable yields and biomass trends, rather than relying on riskier approaches based solely on historical catches (see Branch et al. 2010, 2011 for discussion of the dangers of relying too strongly on landings trends alone).

In particular, fishery-dependent catch data may be a negatively biased indicator of stock status if these data reflect the effects of localized depletion near ports, other access points, or preferred fishing locations (e.g., known reefs). Like seabirds and other place-based foragers, fishers base the range of their fishing trips by setting expected catches against costs, such as for fuel, and safety risk. This leads to localized depletion near ports that spreads as fishers are forced to venture further afield to maintain catch rates (Karpov et al. 2000, Koslow et al. 2000, Smith and Wilen 2003, Morato et al. 2006, Miller et al. in press). Such depletions are difficult to manage or prevent given the mismatch between the scales at which depletions occur and over which management operates (Prince 2010, Prince et al. 2011). Nevertheless, these depletions give rise to uncertainty that must be accommodated under precautionary management by reducing overall allowable catches. Developing assessment models to support management of long-lived invertebrates such as abalone (*Haliotus* sp.) is further constrained by difficulty in obtaining reliable age data and by indeterminacy in their growth patterns.

Management of Volatile, Short-lived Stocks

Life history can also be a constraint on the sort of management that can be developed, in that accurate population dynamics models are difficult to estimate for species with highly variable population dynamics and relatively short life spans such as market squid (*Doryteuthis opalescens*, formerly *Loligo opalescens*), Dungeness crab (*Metacarcinus magister*, formerly *Cancer magister*), and ocean shrimp (*Pandalus jordani*). For these species, management measures that regulate the spatial and temporal distribution of effort (and in cases like market squid, total allowable catch) or regulate retention by size or sex (as in the Dungeness crab fishery) to preserve the productive capacity of the stock appear to suffice. Test-fisheries or other short-term forecasts based on environmental or juvenile abundance indices or preseason assessments (e.g., Shanks et al. 2010, Hannah 2011, Koslow and Allen 2011, Burke et al. 2013) also help fishers' short-term planning with information about likely returns on effort.

Ecological Effects of Fishing

Fishing has the potential to substantially alter the structure and function of marine ecosystems, through both direct and indirect pathways (see reviews by Dayton et al. 1995, Goñi 1998, Jennings and Kaiser 1998, Dayton et al. 2003, Crowder et al. 2008, Jensen et al. 2012). The broader, ecological effects of fishing depend largely on four factors:

- The suite of species directly affected by fishing (and how they are affected)—a function of the fishing methods used (Box 35.2).
- How fisheries-induced changes in affected stocks alter their ecological roles.
- The effective trophic level(s) of individual fisheries—that is, where a fishery fits into an ecosystem's food web—and of fisheries in aggregate.
- The intensity and extent of fishing effort.

Population Responses to Fishing: Conservation-Yield Trade-offs

Recall that sustainable fisheries are based on the concept of surplus production, in which stocks become more productive in response to harvest through increased growth and enhanced recruitment. This fundamental characteristic of fisheries sets up trade-offs between conservation and yield within the management of individual stocks. For example, with the exception of MSY, a given level of sustainable surplus production (i.e., yield or fishing mortality) can be produced by a stock at one of two states: one with biomass above B_{MSY} and one below. While a greater amount of biomass can be removed at the start of the fishery to achieve the lower B, this comes at the cost of greater risk of fishery collapse. This is because errors in controlling fishing effort tend to be magnified in heavily depleted stocks, and because fishery-driven

BOX 35.2 SELECTED FISHING TECHNIQUES

A broad range of fishing gears and techniques has been used in California's marine fisheries. Each method was developed to fish one or more target species from a particular habitat. Each method thus affects the ecosystem (via bycatch or disturbance) in a particular way. While all methods of fishing involve selecting waters to be fished, some (e.g., harpoon, trawling) involve active pursuit (or search for) and capture of target species while others (e.g., baited traps and gillnets) are more passive. In contrast to highly selective techniques, in which fish or invertebrates are selected and taken individually, most methods' selectivity varies and can be controlled only partially through design and technique.

LONGLINE techniques use a series of baited hooks (or less commonly lures) attached at intervals to a main line. Setlines are anchored to the seafloor and fished for (typically) one to several days. A variant of this technique uses small number of baited hooks attached to weighted pipes. Pelagic longlines are suspended at depths from several tens to hundreds of meters and are closely attended as they drift. Historically, vertical longlines suspended from drifting floats have been used to fish around high-relief rocky pinnacles.

TROLLING techniques involve pulling flashy lures or bait behind a moving vessel at depths and speeds that depend on the target species. Recreational troll fisheries typically use rod-and-reel (often with downriggers). Commercial trollers typically deploy multiple rigs simultaneously, using heavy weights and outriggers, and retrieve the gear using hydraulic winches or gurdies.

HOOK-AND-LINE methods vary widely but typically involve traditional rod-and-reel equipment of various designs tailored to the habitat and size of the target species.

TRAPS AND POTS are deployed individually or in series attached to a main ground line in benthic habitats. They allow organisms attracted by the bait to enter the trap, then prevent or hinder their escape. Upon retrieval, legal animals are retained and others are returned to the water.

GILLNETS consist of a single wall of loose, webby mesh, usually made of monofilament line, with a float line along the top and a weighted line along the bottom. This gear is designed to be nearly invisible and captures fish by entanglement. Drift gillnets are typically deployed near the surface or in midwater (suspended from buoys). Demersal gillnets are anchored to the seafloor.

TRAWLING includes bottom trawls dragged along soft or low-relief seafloor habitats and midwater trawls fished off the bottom. Both designs include a weighted leadline and floats along the headrope to keep the net open vertically, and wood or steel panels ("doors") and bridles attached to the towing cables that keep the net open laterally. Net designs and dimensions vary with the target species and method of fishing.

PURSE SEINES are fine-meshed, rectangular nets typically 200 to 400 meters long and up to 50 meters in depth, with a weighted bottom line along one edge and a float line opposite. These nets are deployed to encircle a school of fish—one end of the net is held in place by a skiff, effectively drawing the net off the main vessel as it steams in a wide circle around the targeted school—and then closed from below (pursed) and hauled aboard to concentrate the catch, which is then transferred by pump or large dip nets ("brails") to the hold of the main fishing vessel. In the California market squid fishery, a second vessel fitted with high-intensity lights attracts the animals to the surface to facilitate capture.

HAND-HARVEST methods include take by hand, with or without the use of simple tools such as abalone irons, spears, or harpoons, and with or without the use of diving gear. These methods typically are highly selective, as the fisher identifies individual organisms for harvest.

changes in stock structure may lead to reduced productivity or greater sensitivity to environmental variability. These dynamics also arise in considering trade-offs that emerge in more complex fisheries and the ecosystem as a whole.

AGE-STRUCTURE TRUNCATION, MATERNAL EFFECTS, AND FISHERIES-INDUCED EVOLUTION

As a consequence of increasing mortality rates, fishing truncates the natural age-structure (and in some cases size-structure) of a population—proportionally fewer individuals survive to larger and older ages (Berkeley et al. 2004). Because reduced mean longevity compromises individuals' chances to contribute to a strong year-class, the depletion of older age-classes reduces a stock's ability to weather extended periods of poor recruitment. This effect can be especially acute in long-lived species (Berkeley et al. 2004, Zabel et al. 2011). Truncation of age-structure can also increase fish populations' sensitivity to climate variability as a consequence of reduced breadth of spawning seasons and locations, depletion of more effective (experienced) spawners, COHORT RESONANCE, and other mechanisms (e.g., Hseih et al. 2006, Ottersen et al. 2006, Anderson et al. 2008, Worden et al. 2010, Shelton and Mangel 2011, Botsford et al. 2011). There has been concern that size-selective fishing mortality has the potential to drive evolutionary responses towards slower growth rates, reduced maximum size, or earlier maturation (Grift et al. 2003, Olsen et al. 2004, Kuparinen and Merilä 2007), but it is not clear that such evolution is widespread or occurs rapidly (Brown et al. 2008, Andersen and Brander 2009).

The consequences of age-structure truncation can be exacerbated in species (including, for example, several rockfishes) that exhibit maternal effects on reproductive capacity. In such cases species, older, larger individuals are disproportionately fecund or produce higher-quality larvae (Bobko and

Berkeley 2004, Berkeley et al. 2004, Sogard et al. 2008, Beyer et al. 2015). Where appropriate data are available, stock assessments are being extended to include maternal effects in the underlying population model. This accounts more comprehensively for how harvest affects the productivity of fished stocks and helps to identify cases where maternal effects generate acute management concerns (O'Farrell and Botsford 2006, Dick 2009, Lucero 2009, Spencer and Dorn 2013, Spencer et al. 2013). Even in species where fecundity appears to be a simple function of individual size (e.g., squid, sea urchins, and abalone), fishing tends to remove the individuals that make the greatest per capita contributions to reproductive effort.

"Omnivorous" Fisheries: Effects and Trade-offs

With the exception of a few highly selective fisheries, fisheries typically affect a suite of target species as well as numerous other species that co-occur in the ecosystem. In some cases, the ecological footprint of such fisheries can be quite extensive, which presents a distinctly challenging set of trade-offs to fisheries managers.

MIXED-STOCK FISHERIES

Several fisheries operating off California intentionally operate as mixed-stock fisheries. Commercial trawl, longline, and trap fisheries use gears that by design or coincidence are able to capture any of a diverse suite of species encountered. In some cases, simply delineating the stocks that comprise such mixed-stock fisheries in a manner relevant to management can be a challenge (Cope et al. 2011). Recreational fishers likewise typically target and capture a diverse assemblage of species. Ocean salmon fisheries target Chinook salmon (*Oncorhynchus tschwytscha*) from robust, hatchery-supplemented, stocks yet also contact salmon from protected stocks of Chinook salmon and coho salmon (*O. kisutch*) in coastal waters (Satterthwaite et al. 2013). In some fisheries, serendipitous captures of species encountered too rarely to support a directed fishery (e.g., opah [*Lampris guttatus*] in pelagic longline fisheries) yield high economic returns dockside.

Mixed-stock fisheries present challenging trade-offs between conservation and economic performance arising from differences among stocks' ability to support sustained harvest. For example, fishing effort in bottom-trawl fisheries off California and the rest of the U.S. West Coast has been dramatically reduced to allow overfished stocks of less-productive species (e.g., cowcod [*Sebastes levis*], bocaccio [*S. paucispinus*], yelloweye rockfish [*S. ruberimus*], and canary rockfish [*S. pinniger*]) to rebuild. These fisheries will remain below historical levels to prevent renewed overfishing of these stocks. As a consequence, co-occurring, more productive stocks (e.g., chilipepper [*S. goodei*], yellowtail rockfish [*S. flavidus*], many flatfishes, and, since the mid-2000s, lingcod [*Ophiodon elongatus*]) are fished lightly relative to what they can sustain, resulting in substantial underfishing and foregone aggregate yield (Hilborn et al. 2012). Likewise, in the ocean salmon fishery, managers set harvest regulations to limit fishery impacts on stocks currently protected under the Endangered Species Act (ESA) (e.g., coho salmon throughout California, California coastal Chinook salmon, and Sacramento River winter- and spring-run Chinook salmon) and to ensure adequate escapements to the Klamath River in accordance with tribal harvest allocation rights. On occasion, these constraints on ocean harvest have resulted in large escapements for hatchery-augmented stocks in California's Central Valley—fish that are seen as "wasted" by commercial and recreational ocean salmon fishers. These approaches to fisheries management are commonly referred to as weak stock management, in which mixed-stock fisheries are constrained by what the least productive stock can sustain.

In mixed-stock fisheries in general, multiple species are susceptible to capture, and the fishing method does not effectively discriminate among those species present when and where fishing takes place. Similar dynamics can also occur in more selective fisheries, such as dive fisheries, that target multiple, co-occurring species. In extreme cases, multiple-target fisheries can lead to "subsidized depletion," in which increasingly rare, high-value species continue to be taken in the course of parallel fisheries on less-valued but more abundant species (Karpov et al. 2000, Branch et al. 2013). This appears to have occurred in the commercial abalone fishery, in which SEQUENTIAL DEPLETION—first of red abalone (*Haliotis rufescens*), then of other stocks—did not reduce harvest pressure on previously depleted stocks. Moreover, abalone continued to be taken in urchin fisheries (under dual permits) well after abalone stocks were reduced to levels that would not have supported an independent fishery (Karpov et al. 2000, Dugan and Davis 1993).

BYCATCH

Fisheries also affect a broad suite of nontarget species—some killed or damaged in situ but never brought aboard the fishing vessel, and others hauled aboard only to be discarded at sea. Such bycatch might include species that are retained for market, but greater concern generally attaches to bycatch of species for which there is no market, or that occurs when regulatory prohibitions on landings require fishers to discard catch when trip- or bag-limits have been reached in order to continue fishing for other species, or when fishers "high-grade" their catch by discarding smaller individuals as larger ones are caught. Regulations increasingly prohibit these wasteful practices. Some fishing techniques are particularly prone to unintentional bycatch, especially longlines, gillnets, and trawl nets that have limited or no ability to select for target species. In this regard, trap fisheries tend to have relatively low impacts—they can be moderately selective (through trap design), and undesirable or sublegal individuals that are captured can typically be released with little harm.

Acute trade-offs arise in fisheries for which the bycatch and mortality of seabirds, marine mammals, sea turtles, and other charismatic megafauna is a serious conservation concern (Forney et al. 2001, Carretta et al. 2004, Moore et al. 2009). Bycatch of these species typically has no value to a fishery and can even have negative value due to gear damage or lost fishing opportunity should excessive bycatch trigger a fishery closure. However, these species are highly valued (when alive) by certain stakeholder constituencies and in many cases have been placed under strict legal protections. Regulatory approaches to minimizing bycatch of birds, mammals, and turtles include time and area closures to minimize interactions during the seasons and areas of greatest vulnerability to bycatch (Carretta et al. 2004). In California, high bycatch of seabirds and marine mammals motivated the prohibition of gillnet and longline fisheries in shallow coastal waters (Julian and Beeson 1998). These prohibitions also benefited efforts to restore depleted stocks of large predatory fishes in nearshore habitats (Pondella and Allen 2008). Concerns over turtle and mammal bycatch have resulted in large time-area closures for fisheries that target swordfish (*Xiphias gladius*), tunas, and other highly migratory species (Carretta et al. 2004).

In some cases, technological innovations have helped to mitigate trade-offs between conservation and fishing effort (yield) by reducing unwanted bycatch. Technological approaches to reducing bycatch in commercial fisheries include:

- Redesigned trawl nets with lower vertical profiles and headropes that trail behind the footrope, to allow fishing on highly productive flatfish stocks while enhancing the ability of rockfishes and other species to evade capture (King et al. 2004).
- "Excluder devices" fitted on shrimp trawls that shunt larger organisms through an escape hatch while passing shrimp through to the cod-end (Hannah and Jones 2007).
- Pingers attached to drift gillnets to reduce entanglement mortality of marine mammals (Barlow and Cameron 2003).
- New techniques for deploying longlines to ensure that baited hooks sink rapidly and are not accessible to seabirds (Melvin et al. 2001).

Methods for rapid, genetic assessment of stock composition in ocean salmon fisheries are also being developed so that managers can adjust zone-specific openings and closings in nearly real-time to enhance opportunities for harvest on hatchery-augmented stocks while minimizing impacts on stocks of conservation concern (Satterthwaite et al. 2014). In recreational bottom-fisheries, various devices are used to return unwanted fish (including currently protected species like yelloweye rockfish for which retention is prohibited) rapidly to depth prior to release. This reduces the risk of mortality in fish affected by acute barotrauma (rapid depressurization when brought to the surface) (Rogers et al. 2011, Pribyl et al. 2012).

HABITAT DISTURBANCE

Fishing methods that contact the seafloor like bottom trawling (dragging) and (in some settings) set-line traps can damage and degrade both physical and biogenic habitat structure, especially benthic organisms that extend from the seafloor and provide three-dimensional structure used as cover by juvenile fishes (Tissot et al. 2006) yet are highly susceptible to fishing disturbances (Thrush and Dayton 2002, Chuenpagdee et al. 2003, Asch and Collie 2008, de Marignac et al. 2009). In some habitats, structure-forming communities can recover within a few years of disturbance (Asch and Collie 2008). In the case of deep-water corals and sponges, however, recovery may take decades to centuries (Morgan et al. 2005). Fishery stocks themselves can provide important structure: sea urchins' spine canopies provide important habitat for small invertebrates and fishes, including juvenile stages of some target species, as did native oyster reefs before they were depleted (Rogers-Bennett and Pearse 2001, Coleman and Williams 2002, Brumbaugh and Coen 2009).

Protecting three-dimensional biogenic structure from such disturbance (or allowing it to recover) could be essential to maintaining (or rebuilding) populations of species that rely on such structure to provide refuge from predation and to harbor prey resources. For example, areas with more deep-water corals were found to be more productive for fisheries including sablefish (*Anoplopoma fimbria*) and other groundfish (Bracken et al. 2007). Approaches to deal with this issue include adopting other methods of fishing (such as shifting from trawling to longlines) or curtailing the spatial distribution or frequency of fishing. For habitats that require a long time to recover from disturbance, simple effort restrictions might be impractical. In these cases, gear restrictions or spatial closures may be preferred as an effective means for protection.

Some fisheries can benefit from efforts to protect or restore critical nursery habitats shoreward of the fishing grounds (Beck et al. 2001). During the critical transition from pelagic to demersal habitats, several species of rockfish settle to tidepools, estuaries, kelp beds, and nearshore rocky reefs before migrating to deeper habitats as they grow (Carr et al. 1991, Love et al. 1991, Studebaker and Mulligan 2008). Juvenile spiny lobster (*Panulirus interruptus*) use nearshore surfgrass beds and mussel beds as nursery habitats before moving into deeper, rocky habitats (Booth and Phillips 1994). Dungeness crab and many species of flatfish also settle to shallow or estuarine habitats, eventually migrating to deeper habitats as they grow. Restoration of native oyster reefs is likely to increase fish production in estuaries. Ocean salmon fisheries stand to benefit from conservation and restoration of freshwater and estuarine habitats, which can buffer populations' sensitivity to variability in marine productivity (Reeves et al. 1995, Nicholson and Lawson 1998, Spence and Hall 2010).

Indirect Ecosystem Effects of Fisheries

Depletion of biomass in fished stocks can be substantial, often on the order of 40% to 60% in well-managed stocks and sometimes greater in cases where stocks have been overfished. These changes affect both abundance and the average size of individuals in a population, both of which can alter a species' role within an ecosystem. Moreover, increased variability in individual stocks can propagate into other elements of the ecosystem, and pervasive depletions can degrade an ecosystem's ability to buffer such perturbations (Stachowicz et al. 2007).

Fisheries are novel predators in marine ecosystems that can directly alter ecosystem structure. This is especially true in the cases of fisheries that target apex or intermediate predators, where the fishery represents a new, higher trophic level. Fisheries that target "forage species" can compete with predator species including birds, mammals, other fishes. Several fisheries target herbivores or low-level consumers such as molluscs or echinoderms that feed on algae, plankton, or detritus. Some of these organisms play major roles in the ecosystem, such as the role of sea urchins as "ecosystem engineers" that affect the structure and function of kelp communities (Rogers-Bennett and Pearse 2001, Coleman and Williams 2002).

CONSEQUENCES OF PREDATOR REMOVAL

Fisheries that preferentially target larger species within an ecosystem can "fish down the food web" as upper trophic levels are depleted and fisheries shift to smaller species (Pauly et al. 1998, Essington et al. 2006, but see Branch et al. 2010). Fisheries that remove large and intermediate predators from an ecosystem can trigger a trophic cascade, in which prey species increase in abundance in response to reduced predation and might adopt bolder behavior under reduced predation risk. This in turn leads to stronger predation or grazing pressure on the next lower trophic level (Pinnegar et al. 2000).

The classic example of such a cascade links sea otters (*Enhydra lutris*), sea urchins, and kelp: in the absence of otters (a top predator), urchin populations can reach densities where they degrade kelp forests. Conversely, the presence of otters suppresses urchin densities and allows kelps to thrive (Estes and Duggins 1995). Although this dynamic appears to be less important in controlling kelp forest dynamics in California (Harrold and Reed 1985, Foster and Schiel 1988), depletion and recovery of other urchin predators, such as spiny lobster and California sheephead may have had comparable ecosystem effects (Tegner and Levin 1983, Tegner and Dayton 2000, Byrnes et al. 2006, Halpern et al. 2006, but see Foster and Schiel 2010).

Studies focused on understanding the dynamics of marine protected areas indicate similar responses to predator depletion in fish communities. Biomass of small fish species tend to increase following removal by fishing of predatory fishes; conversely, biomass of small fish species tends to decline as piscivore populations increase following protection from harvest (Micheli et al. 2004, CDFG Partnership for Interdisciplinary Studies 2008, Love et al. 2009).

These effects also reflect, and may be exacerbated by, fishing-driven changes in the size-structure of predator populations. Such changes in size-dependent predation have been observed in rockfish populations (Mason 1998, Harvey et al. 2006) and other heavily fished stocks. Likewise, intense harvest of spiny lobster over several decades has transformed a lobster exceeding 2–3 kilograms into a "trophy catch," even though lobster can and historically did reach sizes in excess of 10 kilograms and 1 meter in length. These dramatic changes in size structure greatly altered the size range of prey that lobster, an important predator in kelp forest ecosystems, can take (Tegner and Levin 1983). This can have broader consequences that propagate through the food web.

Depletion of large predators has potential to cause irreversible ecosystem changes—shifts to alternative stable states from which the ecosystem might not recover even if fishing pressure is reduced. This is especially a concern in ecosystems where almost every species is prey for or competes with other species at some point in its life cycle. For example, the deep-water rockfish community includes large, long-lived apex predators (e.g., cowcod) and several species of small, shorter-lived "dwarf" rockfishes (e.g., pygmy rockfish [*S. wilsoni*]). All of these species settle to benthic habitats as juveniles a few centimeters long, potentially compete for the same prey base of small invertebrates, and are susceptible to predation by adults. Depletion of the larger predators in these systems has allowed densities of unfished dwarf species to increase (O'Farrell et al. 2009). Increased densities of smaller rockfishes may increase predation and competition on the apex predators' young, suppressing the already-low productivity of the larger predator species. In extreme cases, disruption of such a "cultivation effect" (Walters and Kitchell 2001, MacCall 2002) can, in theory, constrain the growth of a predator population even after fishing mortality has been dramatically reduced (Baskett et al. 2006). A similar dynamic might be reinforcing or exacerbating fishery-driven shifts in groundfish assemblages that inhabit the continental shelf off the U.S. West Coast (Levin et al. 2006).

FISHERIES AS COMPETITORS: CONSEQUENCES OF DEPLETING FORAGE STOCKS

In the California Current, as in other upwelling systems, much of the primary productivity that reaches higher trophic levels is channeled through a small number of intermediate forage species such as krill, small planktivorous fishes, and young-of-the-year pelagic juvenile rockfish (Fréon et al. 2009, McClatchie et al. 2012). Thus fisheries that target forage species potentially compete with predators that rely on these same species as prey, especially seabirds and pinnipeds that can be affected by fluctuations in prey abundance during their reproductive seasons. For example, reproductive success in brown pelicans (*Pelecanus occidentalis*) has been linked to the abundance of northern anchovy (*Engraulis mordax*) at scales that match brooding adults' foraging range (Anderson et al. 1982). Reduced production of pelagic juvenile rockfish (due to depletion of rockfish stocks) has been implicated in reduced reproductive success in seabirds on the Farallon Islands (Field, MacCall, Bradley et al. 2010). Simple calculations of energetic requirements suggest that ongoing recovery of marine mammals, especially of depleted whale populations, could have increasing and substantial effect on fisheries for forage fishes like Pacific sardine and northern anchovy that are key prey for these species (Estes et al. 2006).

REDIRECTED TROPHIC PATHWAYS: SUBSIDIZING SCAVENGERS

Fisheries also alter trophic transfers within marine ecosystems by subsidizing scavengers (including opportunistic predators) through at-sea discards and organisms damaged or killed in situ by fishing gear (Kaiser and Hiddink 2007). Discards and fishery offal represent major subsidies to several seabird species (Wagner and Boersma 2011). These effects are not entirely detrimental, as discards and disturbance can enhance production in fisheries that target crabs and other demersal crustaceans (Zhou 2008).

California's Marine Fisheries: Now and Then

Management Structure and Guiding Legislation

The history of fisheries management since the middle of the twentieth century has unfolded in three overlapping phases (Fréon et al. 2005, MacCall 2009):

- Expansion of industrial-scale harvests that quickly dispelled (contemporary) conventional views that the seas' resources are inexhaustible and immune to depletion.

BOX 35.3 MANAGEMENT OF MARINE FISHERIES AND ECOSYSTEMS: LAWS AND AGENCIES

At the federal level, modern fisheries management stems from the Fishery Conservation and Management Act (FCMA) of 1976. The act established the 200-mile Exclusive Economic Zone (EEZ), established the regional fishery management councils, and mandated development of management focused on protecting fish stocks while maintaining sustainable commercial and recreational harvest. In 1996 the FCMA was reauthorized and amended as the Magnuson-Stevens Fishery Conservation and Management Act (MSA, also known as the Sustainable Fisheries Act [SFA]) to address the issues of overfishing, rebuilding stocks, reduction of bycatch, and protection of fish habitat; and to establish national standards for fisheries management that emphasize conservation, fair allocation, the use of best available scientific data, optimum yield, and sustainability of resources. In 2006 the MSA was further revised and reauthorized to broadly strengthen the role of scientific advice in the management and implementation of conservation measures (Tromble 2009, Methot et al. 2013).

At the state level, the passage in 1999 of the Marine Life Management Act (MLMA) and Marine Life Protection Act (MPLA) dramatically changed California's approach to management of marine ecosystems (Weber and Heneman 2000, Kirlan et al. 2013). While the two acts differ substantially in their specific mandates and effects, they both support establishing sustainable fisheries through the restoration and conservation of fisheries and ecosystems, greatly expand the scope of management beyond fishery stocks to encompass all marine wildlife that affect and are affected by fisheries, and recognize that the value of living marine resources goes beyond fisheries. In contrast to the broader scope of the MLMA, the MLPA explicitly mandated the design and implementation of marine protected areas (MPAs) as part of California's strategy for managing and conserving marine resources.

Fisheries are also constrained by several laws and treaties that grant protections to marine mammals, sea birds, sea turtles, and other species that can be adversely affected directly or indirectly by fisheries. These include federal and state Endangered Species Acts, the Marine Mammal Protection Act, and the North American Migratory Bird Treaty, among others. Tribal regulations and treaties are an integral part of salmon fisheries management, especially with respect to salmon stocks returning to the Klamath and Trinity Rivers in northern California.

Five major entities have broad roles in the management of fisheries and marine ecosystems off California. The Pacific Fishery Management Council (PFMC) leads the development of fishery management plans (FMPs) that underpin fishery regulations and advises the federal government on fisheries management issues along the U.S. West Coast. The California Fish and Game Commission (CFGC) develops management plans for recreational and commercial fisheries within state waters (marine waters within three nautical miles of the coast) and implements state fishery regulations consistent with NMFS management of fisheries with broader extents. NOAA's National Marine Fisheries Service (NMFS) and the California Department of Fish and Wildlife (CDFW) collect data essential to fisheries management, conduct extensive research and population modeling (stock assessment) to inform development of fisheries regulations by the PFMC and CGFC, and share primary responsibility for enforcement of fisheries regulations. The Pacific States Marine Fisheries Commission (PSFMC) supports this process as a forum for seeking consensus on coordinated regional strategies for research and management of shared fisheries resources, and by collating and serving fishery data for coastwide analysis. Several tribal agencies, fisheries groups, nongovernmental organizations, and the general public contribute substantial input and information to the management process.

- Subsequent development of fisheries science and management that, even as technical sophistication increased, revealed the limitations of conventional scientific approaches and renewed focus on climate as a driver of population and fishery dynamics.
- Gradual recognition that effective management of fisheries (and other living marine resources) requires a holistic consideration of the ecosystem.

We are well into the second phase of this evolution and in the early days of the third, as our growing understanding of climate's role in fisheries ecosystems and the importance of spatial context supports nascent ecosystem-based approaches to fisheries management (Levin et al. 2009, Levin et al. 2013). Management priorities have likewise evolved, with mandates to emphasize conservation and long-term sustainability made explicit in laws that govern how marine fisheries and ecosystems are to be managed (Box 35.3). As a consequence, fisheries and fishery management in California and elsewhere in the United States are in a period of dynamic transition, as recently implemented regulations dramatically alter the scale and scope of many fisheries and initiate ecological responses expected to take decades to centuries to fully manifest (Moffitt et al. 2013, White et al. 2013).

Recent Landings and Value

Commercial fisheries operate out of ports all along the coast of California, with different fisheries tending to be concentrated in particular regions (Figure 35.5). From 2000 through 2012, commercial fisheries have annually landed an average of approximately 2.2 million tons of marine fishes and invertebrates to California's coastal ports, with a combined ex-vessel value of approximately $3.4 billion (all values reported herein have been adjusted to 2010 dollars). Market squid supported

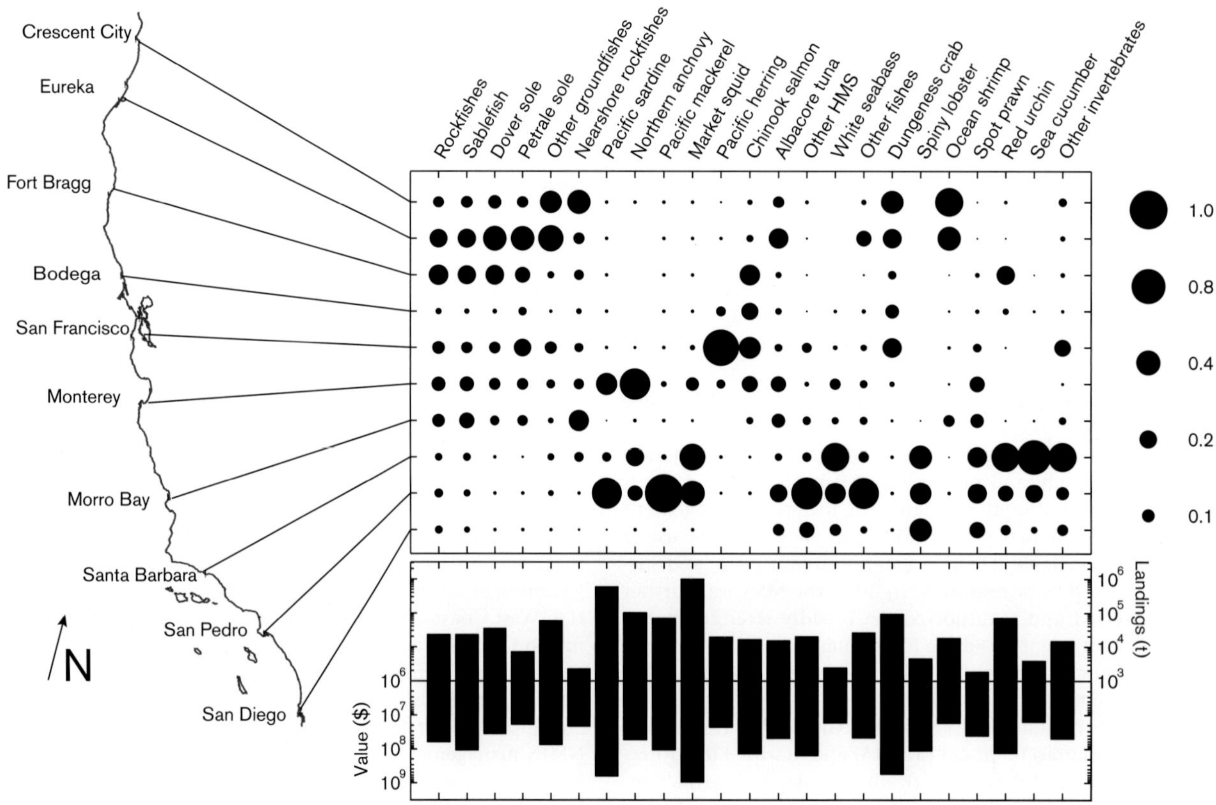

FIGURE 35.5 Commercial fisheries operate out of ports along the California coast, with different fisheries concentrated in particular regions. Source: Data collated from the PacFIN database maintained by the Pacific States Marine Fisheries Commission.

TOP: Spatial distribution of cumulative commercial marine fisheries landings to ports in California for major species or species groups, for the period 2000–2012. Circles indicate the proportion of landings across port groups by species or species group (scale to the right). Port groups are centered on major ports and include nearby smaller ports. HMS=highly migratory species.

BOTTOM: Comparison of landings (bars extending above center line) and ex-vessel value (bars extending below center line) by species or species groups. Note that center line is not zero for either bar plot.

the largest fishery during this period, in both volume and total value, with landings to southern California approaching 1 million tons worth over $950 million. Sardine landings were also substantial through this period (about 585,000 tons worth nearly $121 million), and commercial crabbers landed 1.5 million tons of Dungeness crab worth nearly $550 million dockside, mostly to ports in northern California. Several fisheries with small landings by weight, such as spiny lobster, spot prawn (*Pandalus platyceros*), and nearshore rockfish (primarily landed as live-fish for restaurants) yielded high revenues, reflecting the premium value placed on these seafoods.

Landings in recreational fisheries during a comparable period (2000–2010) were a small fraction of commercial landings in terms of biomass, amounting to nearly 70,000 tons. However, recreational landings are major fraction of total landings for several species. Since 2001, 80% of lingcod, over 68% of bocaccio, and more than 90% of blue rockfish (*S. mystinus*) caught in California have been taken by recreational fishers. Likewise, for many fishes classified as "game fishes" (e.g., white sea bass [*Atractoscion nobilis*] and California halibut [*Paralichthys californicus*]) and various species of surfperch (Embiotocidae), landings are dominated by recreational fisheries—for several species, the catch is taken entirely by recreational anglers. Recreational fishers also landed nearly half of the legal spiny lobster and all of the red abalone taken during this period. Recreational landings tend to be concentrated near population centers and are an important driver of localized depletions in some stocks. Not surprisingly, regional patterns of recreational fishing pressure reflect patterns of human populations and weather: recreational fisheries as a whole are much larger off southern California than in the north.

In any given year, these fisheries support substantial economic activity. For example, in 2011, California fishermen landed 185,000 tons of fish and invertebrates worth over $200 million dockside. These landings are a substantial fraction of the seafood handled by processors and other value-adding operations, thereby contributing substantially to the California seafood industry—a $20 billion-per-year sector of the state's economy—and supporting about 122,000 jobs (NMFS 2012). The economic impact of recreational fisheries can be gauged in terms of associated economic activity. For example, in 2011 a total of 1.5 million recreational saltwater anglers took at least 6.1 million trips, fished from beaches and piers and aboard commercial passenger fishing vessels and private boats, spent $1.7 billion, and supported approximately 7,700 jobs (NMFS 2012). In relation to the entire state economy these are modest amounts, but this economic activ-

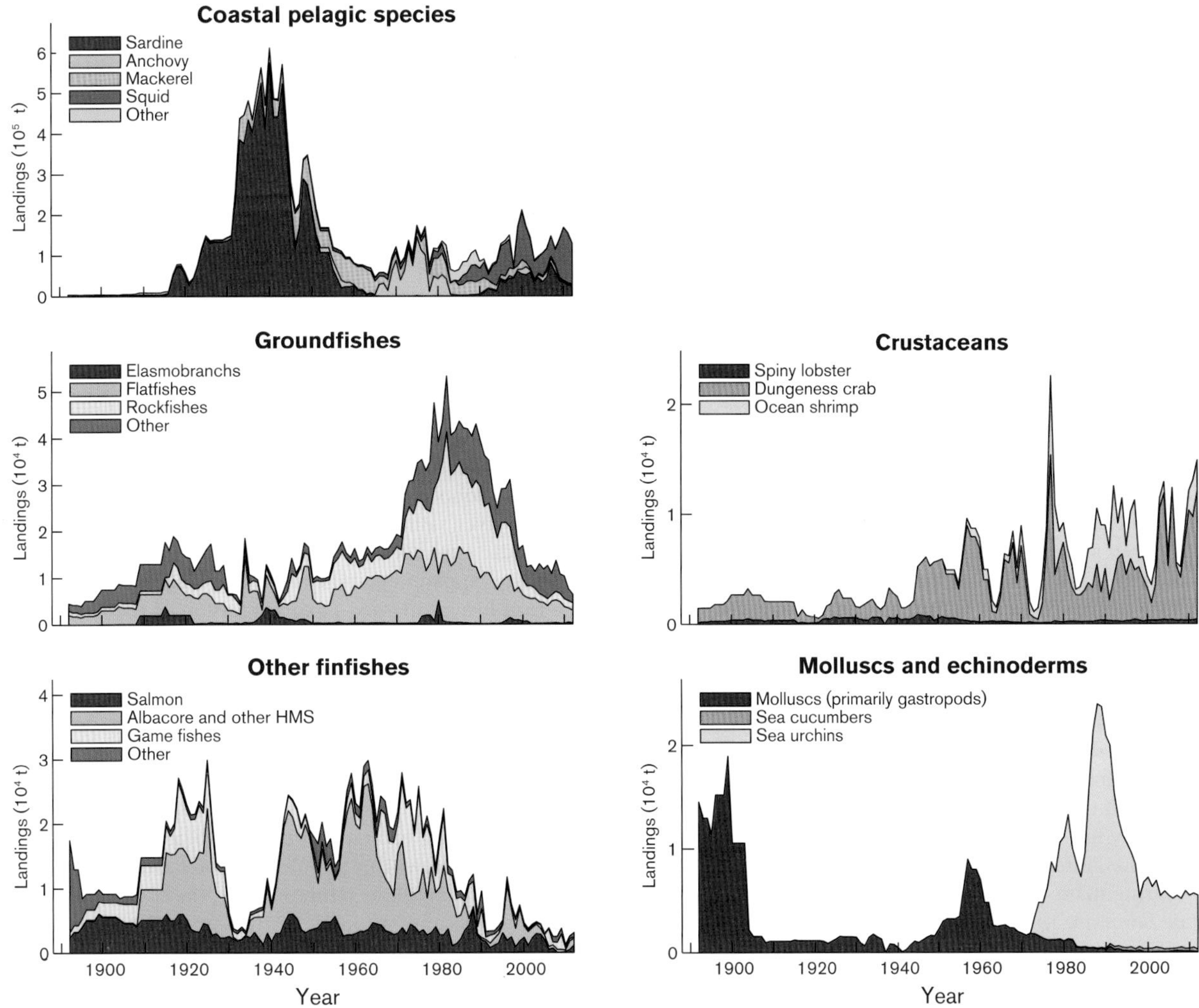

FIGURE 35.6 Historical landings of coastal pelagic species, groundfishes, other finfishes, crustaceans, and invertebrates (molluscs and echinoderms). Landings data collated from landing receipts (1950–present) and historical summaries (e.g., Heimann and Carlisle 1970, Sette and Fiedler 1928). Data on highly migratory species (HMS) exclude species commonly or primarily caught outside of California waters (e.g., Eastern Tropical Pacific tuna fisheries) but landed in California ports.

ity tends to be concentrated near the coast and contributes substantially to the economic well-being and social stability of smaller coastal communities.

Buoyed largely by record and near-record landings of Dungeness crab in recent years and a booming squid fishery, average annual landings through the early part of the twenty-first century are on the same order of annual landings during the preceding century—cumulative landings of fishes and invertebrates through the twentieth century approached 20 million tons. However, the composition of these landings has shifted dramatically over time as new fisheries developed and others declined or collapsed, sometimes spectacularly (Figure 35.6). Recent decades have seen a marked shift in the fraction of landings (by value) from finfish to invertebrate fisheries—a pattern consistent with worldwide trends (Anderson et al. 2011). This transition reflects emerging foreign markets for several invertebrates as well as regulation-driven contraction of major finfish fisheries. Similar shifts have occurred within fisheries as well; new stocks are discovered or support new fisheries as other stocks are depleted. For many stocks, landings have declined under regulations designed to rebuild depleted stocks. However, even after stocks have recovered, sustainable landings will remain lower than those inflated by windfall harvests during the development of a fishery.

Historical Landings and Impacts

To put recent fishery landings into context, we summarize the history of California's marine fisheries—including some that are no longer active yet have had lingering effects—by drawing upon and updating work by McEvoy (1986), Mason (2004), and Field and Francis (2006) (and species-specific summaries in Leet et al. [2001]). A diverse suite of marine species were (and remain) important to Native American peoples of the coast and inland peoples who migrated to the coast for seasonal harvests or who traded with their coastal counterparts (McEvoy 1986, Lyman 1989, Gobalet and Jones 1995, Rick and Erlandson 2000, Erlandson et al. 2005). Despite archaeological evidence that harvest by Native peoples affected the local abundance and structure of some of their fishery resources (Hildebrandt and Jones 1992, Erlandson et al. 2008, Whitaker 2008; see also Chapter 10, "Indigenous Californians"), it is clear these harvests were far more sustainable than what was to follow.

MARINE MAMMALS

Intensive commercial harvest of marine mammals for pelts, oil, and meat began in the late eighteenth and early nineteenth centuries, causing dramatic declines in abundance and major shifts in ecosystem structure (Springer et al. 2003, Estes et al. 2006). By the early 1900s, commercial hunters had nearly extirpated sea otters, elephant seals (*Mirounga angustirostris*), and Guadalupe fur seals (*Arctocephalus townsendi*) and had driven massive declines in abundance of other several pinnipeds, including Steller's sea lions (*Eumetopias jubatus*) and California sea lions (*Zalophus californianus*). Even after commercial hunting had ceased, substantial numbers of pinnipeds continued to be killed due to interactions with commercial fishing well into the twentieth century. Commercial whale fisheries removed several thousand whales of diverse species (e.g., gray [*Eschrichtius robustus*], humpback [*Megaptera novaeangliae*), blue [*Balaenoptera musculus*], fin [*B. physalus*], sei [*B. borealis*], and sperm (*Physeter macrocephalus*] whales) during each of three boom-and-bust fisheries that operated in California waters between the mid-1800s and the late 1960s, in each case driving the stocks to extremely low levels (Tønnesson and Johnsen 1982, Springer et al. 2003, Estes et al. 2006).

Marine mammals have been protected under federal and state law since the early 1970s. Gray whales, sea otters, and northern elephant seals have since recovered from the brink of extinction (Buckland et al. 1993, Estes 1990, Stewart et al. 1994, Carretta et al. 2009). Recovery of northern elephant seals, which had been extirpated from California waters, stems from Mexico's protection in 1922 of the last remaining seals on Guadalupe Island and the subsequent growth and northward spread of the population. Many, but not all, other depleted stocks have shown signs of local or regional recovery (Sydeman and Allen 1999, Carretta et al. 2009). Interactions with fisheries such as entanglement risks remain a concern and have in some cases forced changes in fisheries management (Forney et al. 2001, Carretta et al. 2009). In most cases, however, attention has shifted to the broader ecosystem and fisheries implications of rebounding marine mammal populations and to greater appreciation for the ecosystem impacts of historical depletions (Springer et al. 2003, Estes et al. 2006).

SEABIRDS

During the latter half of the 1800s, egg harvesters drove a massive decline in the common murre (*Uria aalge*) population on the Farallons, from perhaps half a million birds to fewer than five thousand by the 1920s (Ainley and Lewis 1974). Egg harvesting likely caused similar declines in other seabird colonies as well. Although directed harvest of seabirds in California was short-lived, fishery-seabird interactions remain a concern, causing changes in fisheries management to avoid direct mortality due to bycatch in gillnet or longline fisheries (Julian and Beeson 1998, Forney et al. 2001) and to minimize potentially adverse effects of prey depletion on reproductive success (Anderson et al. 1982).

SALMON

Commercial salmon fishing in California began during the 1850s and rapidly developed into intensive gillnet fisheries in the Sacramento and San Joaquin Rivers and rivers north of San Francisco. These fisheries sequentially depleted runs, leading to repeated collapses and ultimately to closure of inland commercial salmon fisheries (McEvoy 1986). Decline of these fisheries was exacerbated by degradation of freshwater spawning and rearing habitats associated with mining operations, agricultural practices, and timber harvest. The primary targets for these fisheries were the diverse runs of Chinook salmon in California's Central Valley and the Chinook and coho salmon in coastal rivers.

As in-river salmon fisheries collapsed, ocean troll fisheries rapidly expanded northward from their origin in Monterey Bay. Apparent stability in the aggregate landings from the troll fishery masked rapid expansion of the commercial trolling fleet, explosive growth of fishing effort, and the rise of a substantial recreational ocean salmon fishery (especially following World War II). As declines in wild salmon stocks were occurring, fisheries depended increasingly on salmon reared in hatcheries that were constructed to offset the loss of production from freshwater habitat upstream of impassable dams. Ultimately, the combined pressures of overfishing and loss of spawning habitat contributed to precipitous declines of naturally spawning populations of Pacific salmon and steelhead (anadromous rainbow trout, *Onchorhynchus mykiss*) in California and throughout the Pacific Northwest. This decline led to extensive listings under the Federal and state Endangered Species Acts and stringent constraints on ocean fisheries, including prohibition of fishing for coho salmon. The decline also spurred the direction of substantial resources towards recovery planning and restoration (e.g., McElhany et al. 2000, Ruckelshaus et al. 2002, Good et al. 2007, Lindley et al. 2007, Spence et al. 2008).

Ocean salmon fisheries are now intensively managed to maximize opportunity for harvest on strong, generally hatchery-supplemented salmon stocks while meeting mandated allocations to tribal and in-river fishers for Klamath River fall Chinook and controlling incidental take of protected stocks. The ocean salmon fishery experienced a massive collapse in 2008, presumably as a consequence of extremely poor ocean conditions causing very low survival of juvenile Central Valley fall-run Chinook salmon entering the ocean in 2005 and 2006 (Lindley et al. 2009). Although the stock has since rebounded; this fishery disaster spurred renewed study of how hatcheries, freshwater habitat, ocean conditions, and fisheries management interact to shape productivity and variability in these stocks. Particular concerns stem from the decline of average age-at-return in Chinook salmon returning to California rivers—most fish return at age three with reduced contributions of four- and five-year-old fish—as this increases stock sensitivity to environmental and fishery perturbations. The ocean troll fishery, which exposes salmon that remain at sea for additional years to repeated bouts of intensive fishing, has been implicated in this shift, as have hatchery practices that deviated from natural assortative mating patterns (Hankin and Healy 1986, Hankin et al. 2009). Similar concerns arise from the loss in habitat and life history diversity (especially in the timing of ocean entry) in juvenile salmon (Lindley et al. 2009, Spence and Hall 2010, Carlson and Satterthwaite 2011).

COASTAL PELAGIC FISHES

California's commercial fishery for Pacific sardine began in the mid-1800s. It grew rapidly around World War I to meet increasing demand for canned sardines (and to replace salmon in the canneries) and for the development of lucrative markets for fishmeal and fertilizer. At its height in the late 1930s, the fishery spanned the entire west coast from British Columbia to southern California, landing in excess of 700,000 metric tons annually during peak years (of which over 500,000 metric tons per year were landed to California's ports) (see Figure 35.6). Signs of overfishing were recognized by some as early as the late 1920s, and the population began to decline by the mid-1930s under the combined influence of a shift to less favorable climate and intense harvest (Box 35.4). However, the schooling behavior of the fish allowed the fishery to continue to grow and sustain high catch rates (a phenomenon called "catch hyperstability") (MacCall 1976) and the fishery remained largely unregulated (McEvoy 1996). Landings declined sharply just after World War II, as sardines disappeared sequentially from north to south, until all that remained in the 1950s was a tiny (yet lucrative) fishery in the Southern California Bight that supplied sardine as bait to recreational fisheries (McEvoy 1986). By 1968, when the directed fishery was closed, sardine biomass had declined by several orders of magnitude to only a few thousand metric tons (Murphy 1966, MacCall 1979).

Following a dramatic recovery, from a biomass of several tens of thousands of tons in the mid-1980s to over 1 million tons by the mid-1990s, directed fishing has been resumed at a much reduced intensity. Harvest reached substantial levels in the 1990s, averaging about 38,000 tons per year or 5–10% of the annual harvest during the 1930s to 1950s, due to both lower abundances relative to the 1930s and far more conservative management strategies. As of 2013, signs indicate that environmental conditions are once again causing sardine biomass to decline without having reached a level approaching that of the 1920s and 1930s (Hill et al. 2012). This time, however, the fishery is scaling back in response to more precautionary management rules.

In contrast to sardine (and the parallel but less dramatic fluctuations of Pacific mackerel [*Scomber japonicus*]), landings of northern anchovy increased during the 1970s when anchovy biomass was high and directed fishing for sardine and mackerel was prohibited. As this fishery developed in the late 1970s and early 1980s, management strategies evolved to avoid adverse effects on (then critically endangered) brown pelicans by "maintain[ing] an anchovy population . . . of sufficient size to sustain adequate levels of predator fish, birds and mammals" (Northern Anchovy FMP 1983). This management plan is one of the earliest cases of action being taken as part of an ecosystem-based approach to fisheries management. Presently little economic incentive exists to fish anchovy intensively (although modest fisheries for bait have continued), and ongoing fluctuations in population size appear to be driven more by species interactions and environmental factors than by fishing.

BOX 35.4 CLIMATE-DEPENDENT PRODUCTIVITY IN PACIFIC SARDINE

The spectacular collapse of the sardine fishery in the 1940s triggered enormous debates among fishery biologists over whether a change in predominant climate conditions or fishing was to blame (Clark and Marr 1955, McEvoy 1986). It motivated what has become one of the longest-running oceanographic research programs in the world: the California Cooperative Fisheries Oceanography Investigation (CalCOFI) (McClatchie 2014). We now understand that intense fishing exacerbated what would have likely been a natural (climate-driven) decline in the abundance of Pacific sardine in the 1950s and 1960s (MacCall 1996, Schwartzlose et al. 1999, Chavez et al. 2003, Lindegren et al. 2013). Indeed, coastal pelagic species' sensitivity to climate conditions is well documented throughout the world and, through paleo-oceanographic studies off California, over the past several millennia (Baumgartner et al. 1992). Box 35.4 Figure 1 illustrates the relationship between surplus production in Pacific sardine and an oceanographic index of the quality and extent of sardine habitat developed by Jacobson and MacCall (1995)—and recently updated by Lindegren et al. (2013)—as one of the few robust environment-production models used in stock assessment and management.

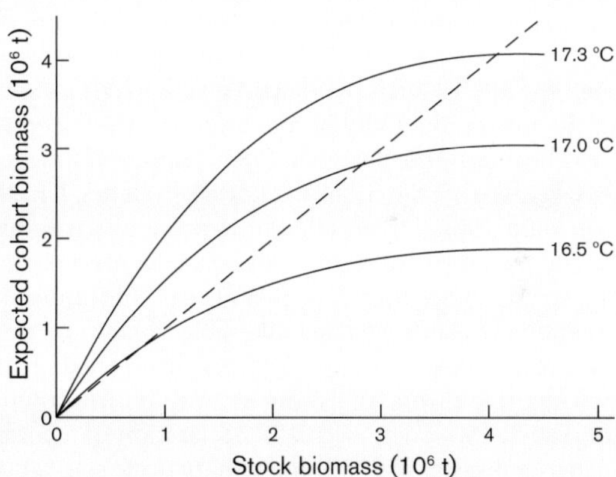

BOX 35.4 FIGURE 1: Relationship between temperature measured at the Scripps Institute of Oceanography Pier in La Jolla, California (a proxy index for ocean conditions affecting sardine productivity) and production in Pacific sardine (Jacobson and MacCall 1995; see also Lindegren et al. 2013 for updated analysis based on a broader spatial index of sea surface temperature). During warm periods the stock is expected to be highly productive and to increase in size. Under such conditions the stock is capable of supporting substantial surplus production (production in excess of the dashed diagonal "replacement line") and sustainable yields to the fishery. During cool periods sardine production is reduced, surplus production is nearly eliminated, and the stock is expected to contract, even in the absence of directed harvest. Redrawn with permission from Jacobson and MacCall 1995.

GROUNDFISH

Rockfishes (*Sebastes* spp.), nearshore flatfishes, and other groundfish have been fished commercially with hook-and-line and paranzellas (two-boat trawls) in San Francisco Bay and nearby coastal waters since at least the 1870s. The development of the otter trawl (which requires only a single vessel) and the demand for inexpensive protein spurred rapid growth of these fisheries during World War II (Scofield 1948). The war also prompted an intensive fishery on soupfin sharks (*Galeorhinus zyopterus*) that depleted the stock in pursuit of vitamin-rich oils to replace the loss of cod-liver imports from Europe. Growth of the commercial groundfish fishery resumed in the 1950s and 1960s, driven in part by foreign fleets, fishers exiting the declining whaling industry, and (following the establishment of the 200-mile Exclusive Economic Zone [EEZ] in 1976) a growing domestic fleet. As the fishery grew, fleets sought to maintain high catch rates by spreading out from their home ports into more distant, offshore, and deeper habitats. Fleets took advantage of technological innovations that allowed trawling in deeper or more rough-bottomed habitats and exploited the discovery of massive stocks of midwater species (e.g., widow rockfish, *Sebastes entomelas*). All of this led to rapid development (and depletion) of new fishing opportunities (Gunderson 1984, Miller et al. 2014). Recreational anglers shifted to rockfish, lingcod, and the like as catches of desirable game fishes declined, especially off southern California, fishing deeper and deeper waters with the benefit of improvements in angling technology (MacCall 1996).

Continued fishing pressure drove declining trends in mean sizes of rockfishes, especially in longer-lived species (Mason 1998, Harvey et al. 2006), and changes in the composition of landings (e.g., Mason 1995, 2004). Stock assessments documented steep declines in biomass of several groundfish species through the 1990s. These, combined with emerging concerns about the low-productivity of rockfish and other deep-water species (Leaman and Beamish 1984, Francis 1986), led to increasingly sharp reductions in allowable catches. Landings-per-trip were limited in an attempt to preserve participation in the fishery, but these regulations created a perverse incentive to discard "trip-limited" stocks at-sea. This undermined the intended effect of reducing allowable catches. By the late 1990s several stocks were recognized as overfished. This led to the extensive closure of fishing grounds on the outer continental shelf (Mason et al. 2012), declaration of a commercial fisheries disaster in 2000, and a sharp decline in landings (see Figure 35.6).

As a consequence, commercial fishing effort was displaced to the upper slope, where effort shifted to target thornyheads (*Sebastolobus* spp.) and sablefish. The recreational fishery was also regulated more strongly through shorter seasons, reduced bag limits, and maximum-depth boundaries that generally shifted the fishery closer to shore. A commercial nearshore fishery expanded rapidly in the 1990s as well, driven by growing demand for plate-sized live fish in the restaurant trade. Landings in nearshore recreational fisheries decreased substantially over the 1980s and 1990s as nearshore landings shifted strongly towards commercial fisheries (Figure 35.7) (Love et al. 1998; Schroeder and Love 2002). More recently, the proliferation of kayak fishing has allowed fishing in nearshore areas that had previously been inaccessible.

In the past decade, combined commercial and recreational catches of rockfish in California have been approximately

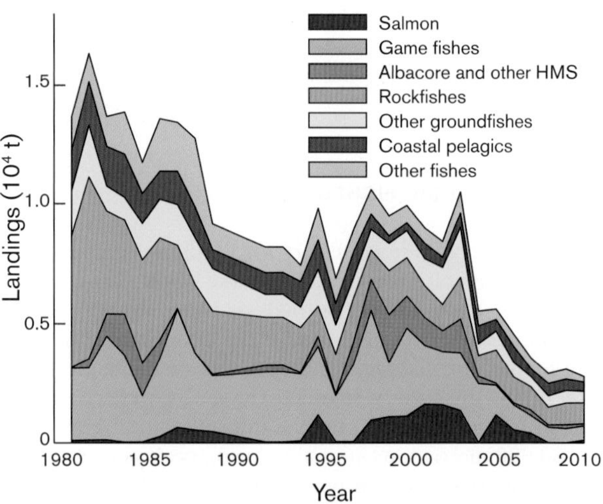

FIGURE 35.7 Recreational finfish landings by major group. Data are based on Recreational Fisheries Information Network (RecFIN) estimates of catches and discards recorded in RecFIN <http://www.recfin.org>. RecFIN data on landings may be less reliable for some fisheries, such as the salmon fishery. Aggregated groundfish and rockfish landings shown here do not show shifts in species composition towards a greater representation of nearshore species of rockfish and other groundfish that occurred following closure of deeper waters to recreational fisheries. HMS=highly migratory species.

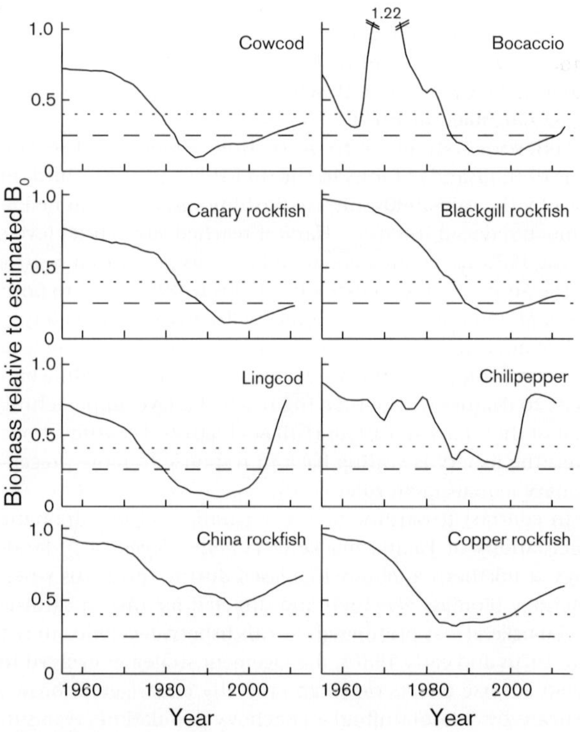

FIGURE 35.8 Biomass trajectories (relative to estimates of average unfished biomass, B_0) for selected rockfish stocks and lingcod off the U.S. West Coast, illustrating declines from 1970s through 1990s and progress towards rebuilding following dramatic reduction in fishing effort in the late 1990s and early 2000s. Dotted lines indicate the rebuilding target of B_{40} (40% of B_0) and the dashed lines indicate the "overfished" threshold of B_{25} (25% of B_0). Source: Data are collated from species-specific assessments available through the Pacific Fisheries Management Council <http://www.pcouncil.org/groundfish/stock-assessments/>.

10% of what they were during the peak of the fishery, reflecting both the exhaustion of substantial windfall harvests in these large, low-productivity stocks and regulatory reductions in fishing mortality. Reduction in fishing mortality has allowed recovery of more productive species (e.g., chilipepper, yellowtail rockfish, and lingcod), which are now considered robust, and steady progress on stock recovery of longer-lived species (e.g., boccacio, cowcod, and canary rockfish) (Figure 35.8), but at the cost of severe impacts on fishers and fishing communities that had depended on groundfish. As noted earlier, one of the greatest challenges in groundfish management along the West Coast is the fact that fishing on healthy stocks must be constrained to limit impacts on less productive species. Changes in size structure and relative abundance in the groundfish assemblage have raised concerns that ecological interactions could retard progress towards recovery of larger, longer-lived species (Levin et al. 2006). One study has documented a shift to younger age-at-maturity in blue rockfish (Schmidt 2014), but there is limited evidence for widespread fishery-induced evolution in these stocks, even among long-lived rockfishes.

HIGHLY MIGRATORY SPECIES

Albacore (*Thunnus alalunga*) and other tunas (*Thunnus* spp. and *Euthynnus* spp.) have been enormously important fisheries to California, although they are only in U.S. waters for limited seasons as they circumnavigate the north Pacific Ocean. Despite the fact that the California share of the total catch is modest, the California Current more generally appears to be a key habitat for both exploited highly migratory species as well as unexploited fishes, marine mammals, and seabirds (Block et al. 2011; see Chapter 16, "The Offshore Ecosystem"). Many of these stocks are of high and increasing conservation concern; as of 2014, Pacific stocks of bigeye (*T. obesus*), yellowfin (*T. albacares*), and Pacific bluefin (*T. thynnus*) tuna in the Pacific have been formally declared subject to overfishing. However, management response is complicated by the tremendous spatial range of these populations, the large number of international participants in fisheries, and a suite of management bodies. Some evidence suggests that declines in these populations (as well as marlin and possibly shark populations, which remain unassessed) have led to increased productivity for more mid-trophic-level pelagic species, such as skipjack (*Katsuwonus pelamis*), mahimahi (*Coryphaena hippurus*), pomfrets (family Bramidae), and snake mackerel (*Gempylus serpens*) (Sibert et al. 2006, Polovina et al. 2009). Moreover, fisheries on tunas and billfish are the focus of high-profile concerns regarding bycatch of sea turtles, sharks, seabirds, and other species of conservation value (Forney et al. 2001, Carretta et al. 2004, Moore et al. 2009). From an economic perspective, tuna fisheries off Mexico and in more distant waters (the Eastern Tropical Pacific) were historically very valuable to the California economy (see Figure 35.5), but they no longer operate in the United States as a consequence of regulations put in place to support conservation of marine mammals (Francis et al. 1992).

GAMEFISHES

Gamefish (a catch-all classification for species targeted primarily or entirely by recreational fisheries) include a diverse suite of larger, typically piscivorous species from a broad range of taxonomic families, including white sea bass, California halibut, Pacific bonito (*Sarda chiliensis lineolata*), California sheephead (*Semicossyphus pulcher*), yellowtail (*Seriola lalandi*), Pacific barracuda (*Sphyraena argentea*), giant sea bass (*Stereolepis gigas*), and several basses (barred sand bass [*Paralabrax nebulifer*], spotted sand bass [*P. maculatofasciatus*], and kelp bass [*P. clathratus*]). Many of these species were targeted by early fisheries (including recreational fisheries) that developed off southern California (see Figures 35.6, 35.7), with giant sea bass, yellowtail, white sea bass, and Pacific barracuda among the earliest stocks to show clear signs of overexploitation in the 1920s and 1930s (MacCall 1996).

Some of these stocks are targeted by both commercial and recreational fishermen; giant sea bass is not targeted, but limited incidental take is allowed in some commercial fisheries. Although total commercial landings have typically been less than 1,000 tons yr^{-1} in recent years, the more valuable species can fetch up to \$22 kg^{-1} dockside, with live fish of desirable species (e.g., California sheephead, opaleye [*Girella nigricans*]) commanding premium prices. For many of these species, however, recreational fisheries account for all (or nearly all) recent landings. White sea bass (Allen et al. 2007) and giant sea bass (Allen and Andrews 2012, Hawk and Allen 2014) have increased in abundance in the past two decades. The closure of nearshore gillnet fisheries appears to have contributed to these recoveries (Pondella and Allen 2008).

Past declines in several species in this group have been linked to fisheries that targeted spawning aggregations. For example, fishers in pursuit of giant sea bass would repeatedly return to specific reefs where these fish were known to aggregate, taking scores of fish at a time. In one case, fishers landed 225 of these massive, slow-growing fish off a single reef in a single weekend (Leet et al. 2001). This strategy led to extensive depletion of giant black sea bass throughout the Southern California Bight. Even when seasonal closures protect spawning aggregations, more diffuse fishing can diminish the integrity of spawning aggregations through depletion of older fishes that "lead the way" during spawning migrations—a form of cultural transfer to younger fishes (Petigas et al. 2010, MacCall 2012). This may be a major factor explaining the recent decline in barred sand bass and kelp bass populations in the Southern California Bight (Erisman et al. 2011).

ELASMOBRANCHS

Several species of sharks, skates, and rays are captured in groundfish, pelagic, and nearshore fisheries. We draw special attention to these taxa because of the important roles they play in marine ecosystems and because they share a low-fecundity, late-maturing life history that makes many of them highly susceptible to overfishing. Landings of several species of skates (*Raja* spp.) in trawl fisheries increased sharply in the late 1990s, possibly in response to decreasing limits on landings of other groundfish, but dropped again following closure of much of the continental shelf to trawling in the early 2000s. Several pelagic sharks, including common thresher shark (*Alopus vulpinus*) and shortfin mako shark (*Isurus oxyrinchus*), are taken as valuable bycatch in several pelagic fisheries and are targeted directly by recreational fishers. Others, such as blue shark (*Prionace glauca*), are also taken in these fisheries but are less marketable. Angel shark (*Squatina cali-*

fornica) and leopard shark (*Triakis semifaciata*) were taken in (now-prohibited) nearshore demersal gillnet fisheries, and leopard shark and bat rays (*Myliobatis californica*) are popular recreational species. Landings for most sharks have declined since the development of fisheries in the 1970s and 1980s. Several stocks, such as angel shark, soupfin shark, white shark (*Carcharodon carcharias*), basking shark (*Cetorhinus maximus*), shortfin mako, and common thresher shark (*Alopus vulpinus*), have declined in abundance or average size consistent with the effects of intense fishing and are considered threatened under IUCN criteria (reviewed in Holts et al. 1998, Stevens et al. 2000, Dulvy et al. 2008). Harvest moratoria and other protections have been put in place for species of conservation concern, including white shark and basking shark. Size limits and bag-limits have been implemented for several other species, and the prohibition of nearshore gillnet fisheries appear to be allowing several stocks to rebuild or to maintain consistent yields.

MARKET SQUID

Present-day landings of market squid are among the highest on record. They regularly meet or exceed catch quotas established as much to maintain demand (and thus price) for squid from California fisheries as to complement other regulations (e.g., weekend fishery closures to allow undisturbed spawning activity) that support the sustainability of the fishery. Small commercial landings of market squid have occurred since the late 1800s, but the fishery remained small until the 1980s (Vojkovich 1998). From the 1980s on, the squid fishery grew rapidly in both volume and value. This was a result of growing demand in international markets ranging from Europe to Asia and of growth in domestic demands for consumption and bait. Fluctuations in the fishery reflect the sensitivity of the stock to climate variability—landings decline dramatically, sometimes to zero, during warm El Niño events but recover rapidly following the onset of more productive ocean conditions (Jackson and Domeier 2003, Koslow and Allen 2011)—and reflect the dynamics of squid fisheries worldwide.

BOX 35.5 DEPENSATION

Depletion in fisheries is intended to spur compensatory population growth. However, the opposite response, a depensatory decline in populations' per capita productivity with continued decline in density, can arise if densities fall below a critical level. Strong evidence for depensation in marine finfishes is rare (Liermann and Hilborn 1997, Jensen et al. 2012), but such dynamics are a concern for several valuable species fished in California waters. Foremost is the potential for localized depletions to reduce (or eliminate) larval production, at least at local scales, in sedentary, broadcast-spawning invertebrates (Babcock and Keesing 1999, Button 2008). This is an especially acute issue for white abalone, which have been depleted to such low densities that eggs and sperm are rapidly diluted to infinitesimal concentrations, fertilization is at best an extremely rare event, and natural recruitment is effectively zero (Stierhoff et al. 2012).

Depensation can also arise in species where adults play roles in facilitating juveniles' survival. For example, the spine canopies of adult sea urchins serve as important refugia from benthic predators and intense wave action for newly settled juveniles (Rogers-Bennett et al. 1995, Nishizaki and Ackerman 2007); this effect can also benefit juvenile abalone (Rogers-Bennett and Pearse 2001). Shells of adult oysters are preferred settlement habitat for oyster larvae; degradation of oyster reefs thus has negative feedbacks for recruitment. Potential depensatory mechanisms in fish populations include the "cultivation effect" through which large predators indirectly facilitate survival of their offspring (Walters and Kitchell 2001, MacCall 2002), enrichment of freshwater habitats by marine nutrients derived from the carcasses of anadromous salmon (Merz and Moyle 2006), and reproductive strategies that include spawning aggregations (Petigas et al. 2010, MacCall 2012). In all these cases, declining abundance can disproportionately reduce population productivity and hinder rebuilding of depleted stocks.

MOLLUSC AND ECHINODERM FISHERIES

Several species of molluscs and echinoderms have historically been harvested by hand from California waters and have exhibited boom-and-bust dynamics typical of long-lived, low-productivity species (see Figure 35.6). For some of these species, fisheries management must consider the potential for depensation (Box 35.5) to undermine population productivity, connectivity, and the ability of depleted stocks to recover.

Stocks of the native oysters (*Ostrea conchaphila*, formerly *O. lurida*) in San Francisco Bay were rapidly depleted in the 1840s and 1850s, followed by sequential depletion of stocks to the north in Humboldt Bay, Oregon, and Washington (Kirby 2004). While there is interest in reestablishing these stocks, particularly for their value as habitat (Polson and Zacherl 2009), recovery has been hindered by loss of the oyster reefs themselves, which represent prime settlement habitat for larval oysters, and by competition from introduced species (Trimble et al. 2009). Present-day mariculture operations rely on non-native species of oyster.

Abalone have been harvested intensively since the mid-1800s, first from intertidal and shallow nearshore habitats by Chinese fishers (who were displaced through discriminatory legislative action [McEvoy 1990]), then by Japanese divers, and finally by a commercial dive fishery that lasted into the mid-1900s. This fishery sequentially depleted several species of abalone, starting with the largest (red abalone). Catches of each new species masked declines of the former in combined landings data, just as the spread of the fishery to deeper waters and grounds further from port obscured the effects of local depletion (Karpov et al. 2000). The fishery peaked in the 1960s, after which landings declined to the point that the commercial fishery—already in transition to sea urchins—was closed. A highly regulated recreational fishery for red abalone continues in waters north of San Francisco, and poaching (driven by the high black-market value of abalone) is a serious and ongoing threat all along the coast. Severe depletion led white abalone (*Haliotis sorensi*) to become the first marine invertebrate placed on the Endangered Species List and was a major cause for subsequent listing of black abalone (*H. cracherodii*).

Sea urchins (primarily red sea urchin [*Strongylocentrotus franciscanus*] but also purple sea urchin [*S. purpurescens*]) have been harvested intensively since the early 1970s in a southern fishery by divers who fished the northern Channel Islands out of Santa Barbara and have since spread south, and in a northern fishery centered on Fort Bragg that ranges from Bodega to Crescent City. Urchin populations along the intervening Central Coast are too low to support commercial fishing, presumably due to intense predation by sea otters. Following peak landings in the 1980s, abundance of large individuals has remained low. Especially in the north, the fishery depends increasingly on episodic recruitment events, fishing down each year-class as individuals grow to legal size, and moving among fishing grounds as local catches decline.

Landings of sea cucumber (primarily the warty sea cucumber [*Parastichopus parvimensis*] in the Channel Islands and the giant red sea cucumber [*P. californicus*] in both the north and south) first reached substantial levels in the 1980s and grew rapidly in the 1990s. Landings in these fisheries appear to have peaked recently and to be in decline, despite sharp increases in ex-vessel value by weight. As for urchins and abalone, intensive harvest appears to have caused substantial reductions of cucumber density in fished areas (Leet et al. 2001). Landings in emerging fisheries on Kellet's whelk (*Kelletia kelletii*), which are captured primarily in lobster and rock crab trap fisheries off southern California, and wavy turban snails (*Megastrea undosa*), which are taken in urchin dive fisheries, show similar boom-bust dynamics. Both snails appear to be relatively long-lived, and the fisheries appear to have rapidly depleted the standing stock in fished areas. Kellet's whelk were found to be especially susceptible to depletion during springtime mating aggregations, which prompted seasonal closure of the fishery to protect the stock.

CRUSTACEAN FISHERIES

Dungeness crab have long supported a large and valuable commercial fishery off central and northern California that appears robust and sustainable despite high variability in landings over time. Recent years have seen record or near-record landings (see Figure 35.6). Recreational fishing for Dungeness crab, though popular, typically contributes a very minor fraction of the catch. California spiny lobster have been harvested in a high-value commercial fishery off southern California throughout the last half-century, even as the recreational fishery has increased over time to the point that it now comprises approximately half of the landings. In both of these fisheries, harvest is intensive: harvest of legal-size, male Dungeness crab typically exceeds 90% in any given year, approximately 75% of the lobsters handled by commercial fishers are sublegal (and released), and a high frequency (approximately 40%) of recreational trips fail to land legal-size lobster. In both fisheries, however, the combination of low mortality of released, sublegal individuals; seasonal closures intended to protect gravid and molting females; minimum size limits for retention that exceed typical size-at-maturation; and (in the case of Dungeness crab) male-only retention appears to effectively protect the productivity of the stock (e.g., Hankin et al. 1997).

Other important (and often high-value) crustacean fisheries target prawns and ocean shrimp with trawls, and prawns and several crab species with traps. Of these smaller crustacean fisheries, the ocean shrimp fishery has the most substantial landings—on the order of several thousand tons a year taken from California waters (some of which are landed in ports in southern Oregon)—but the spot prawn fishery is the most valuable. See Leet et al. (2001) for more information on these species.

Continuing Pressures

California's marine fisheries face several challenges with roots in the past, not least of which is the task of rebuilding depleted stocks and finding a suitable balance between ecological and economic measures of fishery performance. However, managers must also look into the future to identify and plan for the potential consequences of threats (and opportunities) emerging from processes largely or entirely independent of fisheries management. Two major challenges in particular—increasing pressure from diverse human uses of marine systems, and the consequences of climate change—are increasingly integrated directly into strategic management planning and have helped motivate development of new management tools and sources of science-based information.

Increasing Human Use of Fisheries and Marine Habitats

California's marine fisheries will almost certainly never see the levels of landings observed during their development and during the periods when stocks were being overfished (although there may be scope for modest growth in landings from present levels) (Hilborn 2010). For some species, domestic and foreign demand has driven higher prices and maintained pressure on the fishery. Several high-value species (e.g., abalone, spiny lobster) are tempting targets for poachers. Historical changes in fishing linked to global conflicts such as World War II illustrate that less predictable but potentially large challenges to national and global food security could exacerbate pressures on fished stocks and ecosystems in the future.

Aquaculture and mariculture industries have developed in response to increasing demands for seafood (Box 35.6) and (at least in theory) hold out the promise of eventually reducing or shifting pressures on marine ecosystems. However, aquaculture industries also generate environmental concern. For example, oyster farming affects estuarine habitats in areas where oysters are placed for grow-out. Intensive forms of aquaculture presently require marine-derived sources of feed and can be a source of local pollution due to concentrated wastes.

Likewise, although California has relatively strong regulation of coastal development and water discharges by the Coastal Commission and the State Water Resources Control Board, continued growth and coastward migration of human populations will occur. These trends are expected to drive ongoing development of coastal regions and risks of increased pollution of coastal waters, threatening fisheries and important nursery grounds in nearshore and coastal hab-

BOX 35.6 MARICULTURE IN CALIFORNIA

In conjunction with global trends, mariculture in California has grown substantially over the past several decades. Present-day mariculture operations raise several species of oyster, abalone, and mussels (CDFG 2010). Several anadromous fishes are also cultured intensively in freshwater, including Chinook and coho salmon, steelhead, and white sturgeon (*Acipenser transmontanus*). Oyster mariculture in particular has grown substantially since 2000, with reported production valued at approximately $5 million (in 2010 dollars) annually in the early 2000s growing to nearly $20 million annually by the early 2010s. This industry rears non-native species (e.g., Pacific oyster [*Crassostrea gigas*], kumamoto oyster [*C. sikamea*], Atlantic oysters [*C. virginicas*], and European flat oyster [*Ostrea edulis*]) that are produced in onshore, laboratory culture facilities and transferred to marine and estuarine environments for grow-out. Culture of red abalone yields production worth several million dollars a year. Production of clams and mussels is relatively small by comparison. These industries face several challenges stemming from degraded coastal water quality and interacting effects of climate change (e.g., ocean warming, sea level rise, changes in ocean productivity, and ocean acidification) that threaten the growth, survival, and reproduction of reared organisms and marketability of the product.

itats. Several nearshore fisheries (and mariculture operations) are susceptible to pollutants, with obvious consequences for human health (Davis et al. 2010). Increased sediment loading linked to land use practices can also degrade nearshore habitats. Nutrient loading can alter plankton communities and increase the risk of harmful algal blooms with adverse effects on human health and profound ecosystem consequences (Lewitus et al. 2012).

Climate Change

Climate change is expected to have wide-ranging and profound consequences for marine fisheries and ecosystems (Osgood 2008, Brander 2010, Perry et al. 2010, Hollowed et al. 2011, King et al. 2011, Doney et al. 2012, Poloczanska et al. 2013). Growth and reproduction of key fishery stocks could be affected by changes in timing, variability, and magnitude of environmental forcing that govern ecosystem productivity and structure at seasonal and longer time scales (Sydeman et al. 2009, Black et al. 2010, DiLorenzo et al. 2013, Burke et al. 2013). Rapid sea level rise will alter coastal habitats and could affect especially those species that rely on nearshore or estuarine habitats during critical life history stages.

Increasing acidification of ocean waters is especially concerning, as reduced pH has direct detrimental effects on shell-forming invertebrates (a serious concern in the aquaculture industry). Demersal habitats over the continental shelf will be increasingly exposed to hypoxic, corrosive, low pH water (Grantham et al. 2004, Chan et al. 2008), with direct effects on fisheries resources (Keller et al. 2010) and the potential to substantially reduce the available habitat extent for important fishery stocks (McClatchie et al. 2010). This is especially the case for sensitive larval stages and taxa such as pteropods that are important prey for salmon and other fished species (Fabry et al. 2008, Byrne 2011, Kroeker et al. 2013).

Warming or other changes in ocean structure related to climate change could drive to shifts in species distributions, such as poleward contractions of the ranges of several abalone species (Vilchis et al. 2005, Rogers-Bennett 2007). Climate change could increase the likelihood of unusual ecological events, such as the explosive range expansion of jumbo squid (*Doscidicus gigas*) throughout the California Current (Stewart et al. 2014) or harmful algal blooms (Lewitus et al. 2012). Fishing could exacerbate the effects of climate change by increasing variability in the dynamics of stocks and ecosystems (Brander 2007, Ling et al. 2009). The already challenging goal of maintaining sustainable fisheries and resilient ecosystems could become more difficult to achieve if fisheries do not shift in concert with climate-driven changes in the distribution of their target stocks (Pinsky and Fogarty 2012).

Pathways to Sustainable, Resilient Fisheries

So far in this chapter, we have described the history of California's marine fisheries, how fisheries function and affect populations and ecosystems, the emergence of conservation as a central priority in fisheries management, and powerful emerging challenges associated with climate change and food security. With this in mind, we return to the question: What steps can we take to establish and support fisheries that are sustainable for generations to come? Fundamentally, the answer lies in adopting a holistic, ecosystem-based approach to fisheries management that integrates economics and other elements of human behavior. Such an approach must effectively rebalance trade-offs within fisheries to reflect and support a renewed emphasis on conservation, and must incentivize participants to invest in the long-term sustainability of their fishery. This type of approach is already emerging in California and other West Coast states, spurred by explicit and implicit language in the legislation that collectively governs how fisheries and marine ecosystems are to be managed.

Ecosystem-based Fisheries Management

Ecosystem-based fisheries management (EBFM) builds on traditional, single-species management by providing managers and stakeholders with information needed to understand both how their decisions influence target stocks and how their decisions are likely to affect the ecosystem, including indirect effects on other managed fisheries (Pikitch et al. 2004, Francis et al. 2007, Crowder et al. 2008, Link 2010). EBFM is enabled by information on the current state of the system in its historical context, long-term and short-term trends in environmental and climate conditions, the structure of trophic interactions within an ecosystem, the broader structure of trade-offs among ecosystem and economic attributes of a fishery, and the ways these various interactions might be affected by fishing or other uses of marine ecosystems.

Modern-day stock assessments already include estimates of

historical, unfished biomass as part of the context for fisheries management decisions. Historical perspective is likewise essential to EBFM to avoid acceptance of the altered state of ecosystems as the new norm. Without it, managers risk tolerating further degradation from each "shifted baseline" without appreciating the full magnitude of the damage already done (Dayton et al. 1998, Jackson et al. 2001, Frank et al. 2005, Collie et al. 2008, Baum and Worm 2009) or counting themselves successful in "managing to the present misery" (Pitcher 2001). A long-term view also helps put into perspective the sometimes dramatic fluctuations in fisheries ecosystems related to climate variability, inform what to expect going forward, and even to gain some insight to how fisheries ecosystems might respond to climate change (Planque et al. 2010, Doney et al. 2012). Ongoing global changes mean that ecosystems will recover towards a "pristine" state that differs from conditions that existed prior to substantial human influence.

The data and analysis required for a fully comprehensive EBFM are daunting. The lack of ecological or fisheries data sets with sufficient resolution to support spatially explicit stock assessments, much less ecosystem assessments, presents a long-term challenge for extending quantitative EBFM to local scales (Hilborn 2011). Similar challenges face efforts to forecast and evaluate ecosystem and fishery responses to implementation of MPAs (Smith and Wilen 2003; White, Scholz et al. 2012; White et al. 2013), and to manage multispecies fisheries (Hollowed et al. 2000, Mangel and Levin 2005). Increasingly sophisticated models (e.g., Fulton et al. 2011) continue to enhance managers' capacity to compare alternative management strategies based on forecasts of long-term ecosystem and fishery responses to management actions (Kaplan, Horne, et al. 2012). While all aspects of data collection and model development continue to be refined, information on ecological relationships among species (and how these vary over time and space) and behavior (primarily in terms of movement) of both organisms and fleets remains a major challenge and source of uncertainty (Fulton et al. 2011).

This need not prevent progress being made now. Fundamentally, effective EBFM requires little more than that managers, scientists, and stakeholders take a holistic view of fisheries as elements of a larger system and that they accommodate uncertainty by adopting risk-averse strategies and maintaining a flexible, adaptive approach to management (Francis et al. 2007). To this end, carefully designed or selected "indicators" can be useful metrics of the state of the ecosystem (Cury and Christiansen 2005, Fulton et al. 2005, Link 2005 and 2010, Hilborn 2011). EBFM leads managers to (1) accept dynamic change and (2) focus on maintaining connections and adjusting interactions so that various ecosystem components and their dynamics are not perturbed beyond their natural ranges of variability, rather than on the impossible task of constraining the ecosystem towards a particular state.

Together, these two aspects of EBFM require that managers "protect structure and diversity" throughout the system (Francis et al. 2007). Biodiversity hedges against uncertainty and has been recognized as a useful measure for evaluating whether the system has been pushed too far by the combined uses it serves (Murawksi 2000, Palumbi et al. 2008). A set of principles developed with the objective of implementing EBFM to achieve long-term sustainability and resilience might call for the following actions (Francis et al. 2007):

- The age-structure and spatial-structure of species be conserved in a manner consistent with supporting the life history of a species.
- Connections among species (especially trophic connections) within ecological communities remain intact, and species serve in their ecological role(s).
- Habitats retain (or recover) the physical and biogenic attributes that support the ecosystem.

These principles clearly relate to the "compositionalist" emphasis on biodiversity as essential to population and ecosystem resilience and adaptability, yet they also speak to "functionalist" definitions of healthy ecosystems as those that can accommodate fishing and other human impacts. EBFM based on these principles is a means for finding ways to ease the stresses placed on ecosystems or to structure these pressures in ways that maintain a robust ecosystem that supports human uses. For example, one proffered definition of sustainability in fisheries suggests that fishing mortality should fall within the range of mortality a stock might experience from natural sources (Fowler 1999). Others have suggested that ecosystem-based approaches might help to structure fisheries in a way that scales removals across trophic levels to maintain balance in ecosystem structure (Crowder et al. 2008, Zhou et al. 2010). More concretely, ecosystem models have supported EBFM approaches to evaluating the relative impacts of forage species fisheries on other components of the ecosystem, in order to more explicitly understand the trade-offs between yield and impacts to higher predators that include other fishery stocks (Smith et al. 2011; Kaplan, Holland et al. 2013).

Changes from Within: Enriching Traditional Management with EBFM

EBFM is being implemented now based on what we already understand about how marine ecosystems function and the how fishing affects marine populations and ecosystems. For example, the Pacific Fisheries Marine Council (PFMC) in 2006 implemented a preemptive moratorium on krill harvest based on the critical ecological role these species play in the California Current ecosystem. More recently, the PFMC has adopted a "Fisheries Ecosystem Plan" to support coordination of species- or assemblage-specific management measures and to more explicitly consider the trade-offs of alternative management decisions (deReynier 2012, PFMC 2013). As of 2014, the PFMC was also considering options to ban, in the absence of robust scientific information, fisheries for forage species not currently targeted by major fisheries (such as myctophids, smelts, deep-sea squids). Management for sardine is already structured to constrain harvest to rates well below those associated with the famous collapse of the 1940s and to scale down and even eliminate directed harvest during periods when sardine biomass is low. That said, considerable debate remains about what level of harvest is consistent with preserving the role of sardine and other forage fishes in coastal food webs, and more generally how fisheries on species that are integral to food webs ought to be managed (Smith et al. 2011; Cury et al. 2011; Zwolinski and Demer 2012; Kaplan, Brown et al. 2013).

EBFM concepts also inform several actions that are traditionally implemented within fisheries management. Management reference points used to set catch limits increasingly

BOX 35.7 MARINE PROTECTED AREAS: INTERACTIONS AND TRADE-OFFS WITH FISHERIES

Between 2004 and 2013, California established a coastwide network of MPAs intended to serve several purposes outlined in the Marine Life Protection Act (MLPA) of 1999. These purposes include conservation of marine ecosystems and restoration of depleted populations (Gleason et al. 2010, Kirlan et al. 2012, Saarman and Carr 2013). Design of this network was informed by substantial scientific study and enhanced by consideration of economic impacts (e.g., Scholz et al. 2004; White, Scholz et al. 2012), some results of which are summarized here.

MPAs are intended to have conservation benefits measurable as increased abundance, increased average individual size, restoration of age- and size-structure in species that have been depleted by fishing, and a concurrent shift in ecosystem structure towards its undisturbed state (Micheli et al. 2004). MPAs designed to achieve these goals for a particular species must (1) include the appropriate habitat; (2) individually be sufficiently large, relative to individuals' movement patterns, to provide partial or complete protection from harvest for some portion of the population; and (3) cumulatively be sufficiently large and arranged in such a way that enough larvae settle into protected areas (Botsford et al. 2001, Kaplan et al. 2009, Mitarai et al. 2009). Conservation benefits tend to increase with larger or more closely spaced MPAs. MPAs established off California are expected to be effective in protecting species that are largely sedentary as adults and disperse as planktonic larvae (e.g., abalone, urchin, numerous reef and demersal fishes) but are too small to provide much protection of highly mobile species such as salmon or sardine. Conventional fisheries management approaches are typically more appropriate in the latter cases (Hilborn et al. 2004).

Potential direct benefits to a fishery depend on "spillover" from MPAs to areas open to fishing (Botsford et al. 2001). Because fished and protected areas are connected, the progress of MPAs towards conservation goals and thus their relative benefit or cost to fisheries depends on how fisheries operating outside of MPAs are managed (and on the life history of the species in question [Ralston and O'Farrell 2008, Hart and Sissenwine 2009]) (White et al. 2010, 2013). In cases where fishing is intense ($F > F_{MSY}$), biomass within MPAs is expected to increase substantially and to subsidize the fishery through spillover (primarily through larval supply) to areas open to fishing, but overall depletion of the stock limits larval supply and the biomass that can be achieved in the MPAs. (In extreme cases, localized depletion sufficient to cause depensation could greatly exacerbate these effects and undermine the utility of MPAs as a conservation tool [Bell et al. 2008]). The subsidy from MPAs to the fishery sets up a synergistic response to modest increases in area placed under protection: not only does more area support increased biomass, these protected populations in MPAs are increasingly robust (through mutual subsidy, or a "network effect" (Kaplan et al. 2009, White et al. 2010), and fisheries benefits increase with enhanced recruitment to open areas (White et al. 2013). Conversely, when open areas are managed more conservatively (i.e., fished at or below F_{MSY}), differences between protected and open areas becomes less stark and open areas are more productive (Box 35.7 Figure 1). This can set up a trade-off for conservatively managed fisheries with increasing protected area in that although fish biomass benefits, these conservation benefits are smaller and are accompanied by reduced yield as well as reduced fishing opportunities as fishers are excluded from MPAs (Box 35.7 Figure 2).

account for uncertainty in spawner-recruit relationships and the productive capacity of stocks (Ralston 2002, Punt et al. 2008, Methot et al. 2013). Larger buffers are included in harvest policies for stocks with little scientific information to support assessment, while this lack of information is being actively addressed through novel approaches to data collection and assessment methods that can handle sparse data and use basic life-history information to improve the basis for setting catch allocations (MacCall 2009b, Dick and MacCall 2010, Dick and MacCall 2011). Strict policies require that overfished stocks be rebuilt to target levels as fast as possible, while maintaining some access to healthy stocks by fisheries. Mixed-stock fisheries remain a serious management challenge (Punt and Ralston 2007). Over time, more and more fished species have been brought under risk-adverse management, reflecting widespread agreement that state-of-the-art fisheries assessment models—combined with sufficient will on the part of managers and stakeholders to achieve conservation objectives and a shared understanding of the limitations and uncertainties associated with assessments and management actions—provide the most robust basis available for managing marine populations (Mace 2001, Worm et al. 2009).

Nevertheless, the sheer diversity of species, stocks, and populations that inhabit the wide range of marine habitats and ecotones off the California coast means that large numbers of species still remain for which the best available science is poorly developed. This is particularly true for nearshore species and smaller-scale fisheries, where management science is constrained by available funding and traditional data streams do not supply the information required for more detailed assessments. Efforts to prioritize science needs through use of life history characteristics to rank species' and assemblages' vulnerability to fishing could become particularly important under tight budgetary constraints (Patrick et al. 2010, Cope et al. 2011), as will creative, collaborative approaches to collecting essential data (Starr, Carr, et al. 2010).

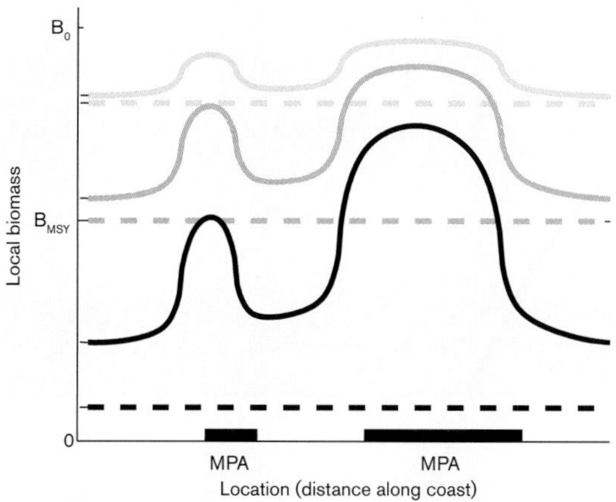

BOX 35.7 FIGURE 1: Hypothetical illustration of how protection in a marine protected area (MPAs, indicated by black bars on x-axis) interacts with fishing in open areas (other x-axis locations). Dashed lines indicate local biomass of fished stock in absence of MPAs for overfishing (dark gray), fishing to obtain maximum sustainable yield (MSY) (medium gray), and conservatively fishing (light gray). Solid lines indicate local biomass after steady state has been achieved following implementation of MPAs. This example assumes that fishing intensity remains constant in open areas but is not displaced from MPAs into open areas. Note that MPAs increase biomass, but that fishing intensity controls how closely stocks within MPAs approximate the unfished state (B_0). Note that larger MPAs are less sensitive to effects of fishing in open areas due to reduced susceptibility to capture along MPA edges and greater retention of locally produced larvae. B_{MSY}=biomass at maximum sustainable yield. Based on Wilson et al. 2013 and others. Source: White et al. 2013.

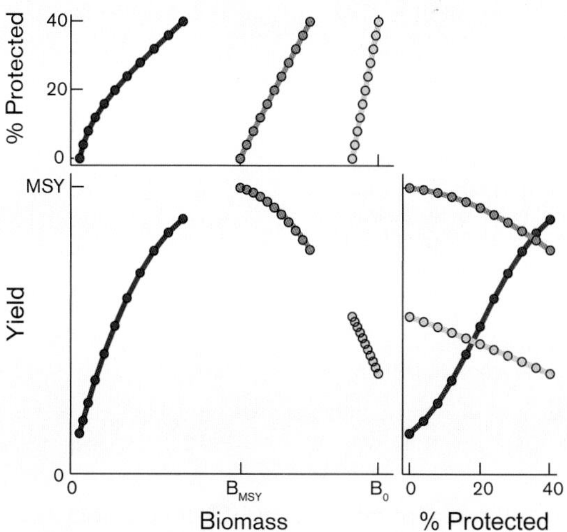

BOX 35.7 FIGURE 2: Illustration of tradeoffs between measures of conservation (biomass) and economic output (yield) of a hypothetical fishery as a function of how much of the fishing grounds are put into MPAs ("% protected") and of fishery management in areas open to fishing (black=overfishing, gray=moderate intensity of fishing, light gray=lowest intensity). Upper-left panel shows total biomass of the stock (relative to unfished biomass, B_0) for a range of MPA coverages, illustrating the general tendency for protection in MPAs to increase biomass of fished stocks with the strongest effects at high intensity of fishing in open areas. Lower-right panel shows yield (landings) by the fishery (relative to MSY for the stock), illustrating the potential for greater coverage by MPAs to increase yield from an overfished stock (black) and the converse effect of foregone yield in a conservatively managed fishery (light gray). Lower-left panel illustrates the tradeoff between conservation (biomass) and economic (yield) performance as a function of how much of the fishing grounds are put into MPAs (moving right to left along each set of points). Note how MPAs have a potentially synergistic effect (a positive relationship between conservation and yield) in overfished stocks but present a clear tradeoff in well-managed stocks. Other conservation benefits (see Box 35.7) are not included in this simple model. Source: Based on Wilson et al. 2013 and others. Source: White et al. 2013.

Marine Protected Areas

Spatial management of marine systems has strong potential to yield greater cumulative benefits by allowing different uses to approach optimal effectiveness in different areas (White, Scholz et al. 2012). MARINE PROTECTED AREAS (MPAs)—areas where some or all forms of harvest are prohibited—embody this strategy. Over the past two decades, MPAs have become a core element in California's approach to management of marine resources; the handful of marine reserves established in the 1970s are now part of an extensive network of MPAs that spans the entire coastline of California (Kirlan et al. 2012; see Chapters 16–18 in this volume).

Effectively designed and enforced MPAs can be a powerful, and in some cases essential, component of broader strategies for conserving marine resources and supporting sustainable fisheries (Allison et al. 1998, Murray et al. 1999, NRC 2001, Berkeley et al. 2004). However, MPAs alter the balance between conservation and economic activity, leading to uncertainty regarding whether placing more or less area into MPAs is to a fishery's advantage (Murray et al. 1999, Klein et al. 2008, White et al. 2010, White et al. 2013; Box 35.7). In general, the combination of MPA configurations, species life histories, and fishery characteristics that yield a net benefit to fisheries can be narrow (Ralston and O'Farrell 2008; Hart and Sissenwine 2009; White et al. 2009; Ono et al. 2013). Although it is not entirely clear how MPAs will be incorporated into conventional fisheries management (Field et al. 2006, Hillborn and de Leo 2006, Botsford et al. 2009), it is likely that direct economic benefits from MPAs to fisheries will be limited.

However, MPAs offer several other, indirect benefits that must be considered in any cost-benefit analysis (Hilborn 2004). Allowing ecosystems within MPAs to recover towards their undisturbed state can enhance their resilience to climate change and other stressors (Ling et al. 2009). MPAs can

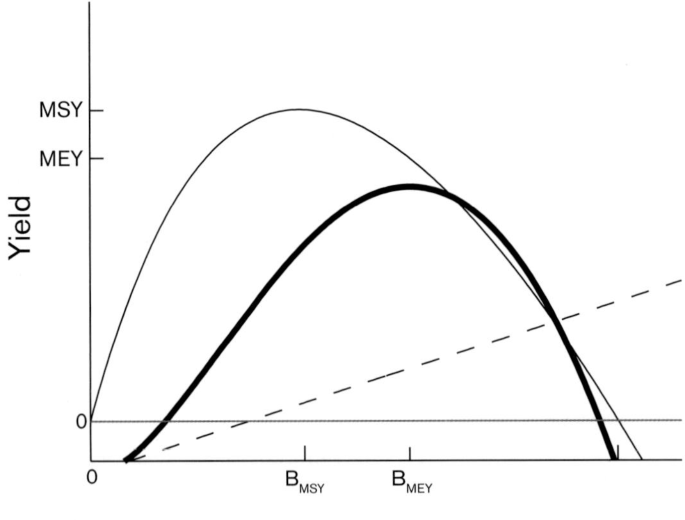

FIGURE 35.9 Schematic comparison of maximum sustainable yield (MSY) and maximum economic yield (MEY). The lighter solid line shows traditional surplus production curve as the basis for MSY. The dashed diagonal line is a hypothetical relationship linking the profit per landed fish to stock biomass, with the following assumptions: (1) fixed cost of buying and maintaining fishing vessel and permits, (2) fish are more valuable (larger) and easier to locate when the stock is larger, so that less fuel and time must be spent fishing, and (3) price increases when fewer fish are landed to meet market demand. The heavy black curve is the economic yield or total profit, calculated as a product of the fish landed and the profit on each. Note that total profit peaks to the right of B_{MSY}, indicating that managing for maximum profit yields a conservation benefit. B_0 = estimated unfished biomass. Source: Based on Grafton et al. 2007 and others.

bolster the resilience of fished stocks by allowing rebuilding of age-structure and size-structure and reproductive potential (Berkeley et al. 2004), protecting critical habitat (especially for juveniles), and mitigating against selective pressures of fishing on species' life history (Baskett et al. 2005). Demographic data from populations within protected areas can inform stock assessments, especially with respect to disentangling the effects of fishing and climate on stock status and dynamics and supporting alternative management approaches for "data-poor" species (Babcock and MacCall 2011, McGilliard et al. 2011, Wilson et al. 2010, Prince et al. 2011). MPAs also provide (imperfect) insight to "undisturbed" ecosystem structure as fished populations recover locally (Micheli et al. 2004, CDFG et al. 2008). Finally, the monitoring necessary to evaluate and adaptively manage MPAs can support efforts to develop and test methods for managing fisheries at higher spatial resolution.

Managing for Economic Efficiency to Support Conservation

Fisheries management has traditionally emphasized maximizing biomass yield from a fishery, a justifiable goal if fisheries are to maximize total revenue, maintain employment in fisheries, and supply maximum food (or other resources) to society (Hilborn 2007a). More recently, increasing attention has gone to strategies for achieving maximum economic yield (MEY, i.e., profit), from fisheries using methods that more fully account for the costs of fishing as well as the value of what is landed (Grafton et al. 2007). These analyses typically find that B_{MEY} is larger than B_{MSY}, suggesting an economic benefit to conservation-oriented management (Figure 35.9). The specifics are hard to quantify robustly, and economically optimal paths (e.g., temporary fishing moratoria) are not always socially acceptable or tractable (Dichmont et al. 2010). Fortunately, being "off the peak" for several measures of fisheries performance does not necessarily imply catastrophic loss (Hilborn 2010). For example, in California and along the West Coast, petrale sole (*Eopsetta jordani*) have been below the (current) management target (25% of B_0) since the 1960s, and below the overfished threshold (12.5% of B_0) since the early 1980s, yet the stock has supported consistent catches of approximately half of the peak values for nearly five decades, an indication of a highly resilient population (Haltuch et al. 2013).

Regardless of the broader target of fisheries management, a sustainable path must correct the conditions that underpinned historical failures of fisheries management: severe mismatch between fishers' short-term economic incentives and the long-term sustainability of the ecological system, and lack (or disruption of) governance structures that might have otherwise constrained the intensity and growth of fishing (McEvoy 1996). With the exception of fisheries that maintained informal forms of social governance, the race to catch fish in open-access fisheries led to a "tragedy of the commons" (Hardin 1968) in which communal, long-term interest in a sustainable, high-yield fishery was under-

BOX 35.8 CATCH SHARES IN THE U.S. WEST COAST GROUNDFISH FISHERY

In January 2011 federal management of groundfish trawl fisheries along the U.S. West Coast implemented the West Coast Shore–based Individual Fishing Quota (IFQ) Program as part of the broader Pacific Groundfish Trawl Rationalization Program (http://www.westcoast.fisheries.noaa.gov/fisheries/groundfish_catch_shares/). The IFQ program replaced a system based on bimonthly, cumulative trip limits, which had long been criticized for being economically inefficient and driving regulatory discards (i.e., discards of fish captured in excess of what could be legally landed) to high levels during the late 1990s and 2000s (Branch 2006, Branch et al. 2006).

Under the new program, IFQs have been established for twenty-nine stocks (species or species groups, some of which are demarcated into northern and southern units), as have rules for determining initial allocations and constraining how much of quota share an entity may control. Several species within this mixed-stock fishery are or have recently been considered "overfished" and thus have very limited total allocated catch (TAC) and individual quotas; however, fishers may share quota for these species through "risk pools" as a way spread the risk of an unintentional large catch of a species for which quotas are low. Accounting of landings against quota is accomplished through full coverage of the fleet by at-sea observers and by requirements that landings be made to licensed receivers and be verified by dockside monitors.

Several challenges remain with respect to the continued implementation and troubleshooting of this complex program, including how the (presently subsidized) cost of the observer program will be supported in the future, whether electronic monitoring technology might suffice to replace at-sea observers, and what the broader consequences are of apparent regional shifts in fishery effort and landings (see, e.g., Toft et al. 2011 and Mason et al. 2012). Nevertheless, the program has clearly altered the future course of the groundfish fishery with the ultimate goal of benefitting both fishery participants and the marine resources on which they depend.

mined by individual incentives to catch what fish one can quickly, lest someone else catch those fish first. Competition among fishers and spatial depletion of stocks also sets up a cycle in which fishers take loans to finance larger vessels and more advanced equipment, which in turn increases the pressure to fish in order to service the loans (Ludwig et al. 1993, Pitcher 2001).

One approach to changing this dynamic is to restructure fishery management so that the total allowable catch is partitioned and allocated among fishers (or vessels, communities, or cooperatives) in the form of CATCH SHARES, typically as some form of individually transferrable quota (ITQ). The groundfish fishery off the U.S. West Coast is one of the first such U.S. fisheries (Box 35.8). Individuals who participate in such a fishery are expected to enjoy increased profits as a result of strategically distributing their effort over space and time, landing a better product, and matching the timing of supply to demand (Costello et al. 2010, Melnychuk et al. 2012). Moreover, by holding a diverse portfolio of quotas, fishers can enhance income stability in the face of fluctuations in stock size (Kasperski and Holland 2013). In return, fishers are held individually accountable for their impact on managed stocks, including discards and bycatch, and must stop fishing (or acquire additional quota) upon reaching their allocation. Extending fishing rights to explicitly include spatial rights, or assigning rights to fisheries cooperatives, can likewise enhance the economic performance of a fishery by reducing competition for preferred fishing grounds and encouraging coordination of effort (Costello and Deacon 2007, Ovando et al. 2013).

By allowing fishers to "own" part of the stock, catch shares (or other forms of dedicated access) arguably bring fishers' longer-term economic interests into closer alignment with the conditions required to establish and maintain ecological sustainability (Hilborn et al. 2005, Grafton et al. 2006, Costello et al. 2008, NOAA 2010). In some cases, catch-share schemes might provide means for conservation interests to play more active roles in how fisheries operate or to facilitate large-scale collaborative research on economic and ecological responses to changes in fisheries practices (Gleason et al. 2013), but these are not typically stated goals of catch-share programs.

Fisheries managed through catch shares tend to exhibit better and more consistent compliance with total catch limits (Essington 2010, Melnychuk et al. 2012), including reduction in at-sea discards in mixed-stock fisheries (Branch et al. 2006). This reduces uncertainty for both fishers and managers and can increase efficacy of other management efforts. However, conservation does not emerge automatically from management based on catch shares (Essington et al. 2012, Melnychuk et al. 2012). Managers must still rationalize fisheries and set allowable catches and other regulations appropriately to achieve conservation goals and to rebuild overfished stocks (Parslow 2010, Sumaila 2010); RATIONALIZATION means that each fishery much be scaled to the productivity of its stock(s). Moreover, management based on catch shares might not effectively support conservation in a broader ecosystem sense unless a sufficiently extensive suite of affected species are brought into consideration (Gibbs 2010, Gibbs and Thebaud 2013).

Economic benefits of catch-share fisheries are also not guaranteed. The ability to sell or lease catch shares is fundamental to increasing economic efficiency in a fishery, yet constraints on transfer and aggregation of quota might be required to reduce the likelihood of undesirable ecological or social consequences. Absent such constraints, an ITQ fishery might favor marked regional shifts in fishing effort that reduce opportunities to actively participate in a fishery in some areas while (local) overfishing continues elsewhere, even as total stock biomass rebuilds (Toft et al. 2011). Strong social or cultural pressures to participate in a fishery can affect the ability of individual fishers and communities to achieve economically efficient outcomes (Marchal et al. 2009, Olson 2011). Opportunities to establish or maintain diverse portfolios can also be limited: initial allocations of catch shares might discriminate against historically minor or inconsistent participants in a fishery, capital requirements for acquiring quota to enter a fishery can be substantial, and catch-share programs by design establish incentives for less efficient, generalist fishers to transfer quota to more efficient, specialized operations (Kasperski and Holland 2013).

Collaboratively Transforming Management of Marine Fisheries

Even in their nascent forms, both EBFM and dedicated-access fisheries management represent major conceptual shifts in fisheries management and important progress towards ensuring that sustainable, productive fisheries are part of California's future. Progress towards more comprehensive EBFM will almost certainly benefit from effective communication and more complete integration of managers, scientists, and stakeholders in management, as such interactions can provide efficient access to critical information while broadening engagement (Levin et al. 2009, Wendt and Maruska 2009, Gleason et al. 2013). Cooperative fisheries research is one strategy for doing this. It offers several advantages (and risks) with respect to cost, data resolution, and event or trend detection, as well as opportunities to enhance communication, trust, and a shared sense of investment in a fishery (NRC 2004, Yochum et al. 2011). Truly collaborative research can yield even greater benefit, as involving fishers in each step of the research process helps them better understand and accept scientific findings and facilitates incorporation of fishers' knowledge into research (Wendt and Starr 2009). Fishers' knowledge can be highly informative in several aspects of marine resource management (e.g., MPA planning; Scholz et al. 2004).

Outlook for Marine Fisheries and Ecosystems of California

Where are California's marine fisheries headed? Predictions are fraught with uncertainty, especially for a complex system strongly dependent on climate change and political will. Yet we see cause for cautious optimism. Based on current trajectories and recent changes in how California and the United States manage and protect their marine ecosystems, the state's marine fisheries appear to be on a path towards increased resilience and capacity to adapt to changing conditions.

Foremost among the encouraging signs is evidence that for most stocks, depletions were not so grave or sustained that the potential for rebuilding and recovery is severely compromised (Neubauer et al. 2013). For rockfish and similar groundfish there is a strong case to be made that population responses to the dramatic reduction in fishing pressure has improved the status of several depleted stocks and that the timely arrival of several successful year-classes has moved them more rapidly than initially expected towards rebuilding goals established in their respective assessments. Stocks of long-lived fishes that were once thought all but lost, like the giant sea bass are now rebuilding. There remain difficult cases, of course, in which massive depletions driven by intensive fishing and other challenges (e.g., disease) have greatly compromised chances of recovery under natural conditions (e.g., white abalone). Nevertheless, as a whole, fisheries ecosystems appear to be on a trajectory towards greater sustainability.

For the groundfish fishery off the U.S. West Coast, progress has been bolstered by a recent (but temporary) shift to cooler, more productive conditions in the California Current. This progress has yielded strong recruitment in diverse species but also reflects consequences of dramatic changes in how tradeoffs between conservation and harvest are being balanced—often to the long-term benefit of both. In contrast to groundfish, the sardine stock is presently experiencing a dramatic contraction, presumably in response to cooler conditions in the California Current that are less favorable for sardine production. Yet in this case, too, management of the fishery is proving to be more responsive and precautionary than was the case during its spectacular collapse in the 1940s. Management strategies are increasingly guided by broader ecosystem-based principles, and managers increasingly make use of strategies for altering incentives rather than relying solely on "command-and-control" approaches to fisheries management.

As we go forward, we must keep in mind that getting on this path was difficult and painful for many who directly participate in fisheries, that the way forward will remain challenging for some time, and that future fisheries will of necessity be more limited in scale than their historical peaks. Future fisheries, however, will be better structured to generate economic yield while limiting the stresses imposed on the ecosystem. Continued progress requires that even as we adapt our approaches based on ongoing learning, we stay the course towards rebuilding depleted stocks and implementing strategies for ecosystem recovery and protection. As Shepherd (1990) observes: "It is important to recognise that the benefits of reducing fishing effort—larger stocks, higher yields, improved stability, and higher profitability—can only be maintained if the fishing effort is kept down indefinitely. The reductions required are permanent: the effort cannot be allowed to increase again, and no more fishing boats will be needed, even when the stocks have rebuilt. The price of profitability is eternal regulation." Our optimism is buoyed by the emergence of collaborative approaches and greater communication within fisheries communities. Success in achieving a sustainable future will require the shared efforts of fishers, conservationists, scientists, managers, and all who use and value marine ecosystems.

Summary

Over the last two centuries, fishers have used a diverse suite of methods and gear to harvest some 350 species from California's ocean waters. Over time they have affected nearly every marine ecosystem through direct impacts of harvest, bycatch, and habitat damage and indirect effects mediated by ecological interactions and dispersal. In some cases, such as the historic depletion of marine mammals, the effects of fisheries on marine ecosystems have only become apparent as depleted stocks have recovered. The history of California's marine fisheries, like fisheries elsewhere in the world, includes numerous cases of rapid development as fleets expand (or shift) to exploit new fishing opportunities, followed by collapse when harvests exceed what stocks and ecosystems can sustainably produce. Recent legislative mandates and policies, however, seek to break this pattern by emphasizing conservation as the foundation for sustainable, resilient fisheries. Management of marine fisheries has become more precautionary and adopted a more holistic, ecosystem-based perspective supported by growing understanding of interactions among the ecological, economic, and social elements of fisheries ecosystems. Dramatic reductions in fishing effort triggered by shifts in management goals have had profound economic and social consequences but in many cases have also contributed to rebuilding of depleted stocks and shifts in ecosystem structure towards less disturbed states. Conservation concerns have also motivated the implementation of a network of marine protected areas (MPAs) along the California coast.

Looking forward, new techniques for assessing the status and productivity of fishery (and nonfishery) stocks, insights from comparisons of ecosystems in fished areas to those in MPAs, and increasingly sophisticated ecosystem models will enhance information available to managers. These managers are tasked with balancing the diverse trade-offs inherent to fisheries and identifying approaches for adapting to the growing challenges of climate change and other pressures related to a growing human population. Greater emphasis on economic efficiency has spurred development and implementation of management tools such as catch shares that adjust fishers' incentives to increase profitability, reduce risk, and promote closer alignment between economic interests and ecological sustainability. Such approaches still require managers to set appropriate science-based harvest policies. Disparity in spatial scales of management and fisheries effects also presents an ongoing challenge. Continued progress towards sustainable, resilient fisheries will require steadfast, yet adaptive, adherence to the hard lessons of the past, ideally supported by effective collaborations among scientists, managers, fishers, conservationists, and other stakeholders.

Acknowledgments

We thank Larry Allen, Michael O'Farrell, Alec MacCall, Steve Ralston, Cindy Thompson, and Will White for thoughtful reviews; Don Pearson, Christy Juhasz, and Kirsten Ramey for assistance with compiling fisheries and mariculture data; and Rebecca Miller for assistance in preparing Figure 35.5.

Recommended Reading

Hilborn, R., with U. Hilborn. 2012. Overfishing: What everyone needs to know. Oxford University Press, Oxford UK.

Link, J. S. 2010. Ecosystem-based fisheries management: Confronting tradeoffs. Cambridge University Press, Cambridge, UK.

McEvoy, A. F. 1990. The fisherman's problem: Ecology and law in the California fisheries, 1850–1980. Cambridge University Press, Cambridge, UK.

Palumbi, S. R., and C. Sotka. 2010. The death and life of Monterey Bay: A story of revival. Island Press, Washington, D.C.

Walters, C. J., and S. J. D. Martell. 2004. Fisheries ecology and management. Princeton University Press, Princeton, New Jersey.

Glossary

CATCH SHARE A form of designated-access to a fishery resource, in the form of a set fraction of the total allowable catch for a fishery that has been allocated to an individual fisher (or another entity eligible to hold shares).

COHORT RESONANCE The increased sensitivity of fish populations to environmental variability occurring on time scales near the length of a generation (time between birth of a fish and birth of its offspring). Fishing increases cohort resonance across all species, but especially in those that are longer-lived.

DEMERSAL Associating closely with the sea floor.

ESCAPEMENT The number of salmon that return to freshwater habitats to spawn or to become accessible to in-river fisheries (i.e., that have survived their oceanic life history phase, including evading capture in marine fisheries). "Spawning escapement" is sometimes used to refer specifically to salmon that reach spawning habitats.

FISHERIES SCIENCE A multidisciplinary blend of oceanography, biology, population dynamics, ecology, economics, social sciences, and other fields focused on developing an integrated understanding of fisheries and providing information to decision makers charged with management of marine resources.

LIFE HISTORY The suite of traits including but not limited to potential longevity, maturation schedule, growth rate, reproductive strategy, movement and migration, and so on that affect an organism's survival and reproductive success.

MANAGEMENT REFERENCE POINTS Values of stock biomass, potential yield, and other key parameters developed in a stock assessment and used by fisheries managers as targets or limits in setting harvest rates, catch quotas, and fisheries regulations.

MARINE PROTECTED AREA An area of the ocean in which one or more human uses (typically extractive uses like fishing or mining) are prohibited.

MAXIMUM SUSTAINABLE YIELD (MSY) The maximum amount of harvest (yield) a population can (theoretically) sustain indefinitely.

OVERFISHING Fishing that harvests fish at rates greater than a stock can sustain and that puts at risk the long-term productivity of a stock.

PELAGIC Inhabiting the water column, away from solid structure.

PRODUCTION CURVE The relationship describing surplus production as a function of stock size (biomass).

RATIONALIZATION The process of scaling a fishery's infrastructure and activity to the productivity of the stock, as a means of meeting conservation and sustainability goals while reducing economic inefficiency.

SEQUENTIAL DEPLETION The process of depleting (overfishing) target stocks, one after the other, often in order of value or profit to the fishery.

STOCK A biologically distinct and sufficiently mixed population of a particular species of fish or invertebrate.

STOCK ASSESSMENT A statistical analysis of the status of a stock, focused on estimating existing biomass, reproductive potential, productivity, and fishing mortality of a stock as a basis for informing management decisions on allowable catch and other harvest regulation.

STOCK-RECRUITMENT RELATIONSHIP The relationship describing recruitment (addition of new individuals to the population) as a function of stock size. Sometimes referred to as a spawner-recruit relationship in the context of salmon fisheries.

SURPLUS PRODUCTION Production by a population in excess of that required to maintain the population at its present size; production that would lead to population growth if not harvested.

References

Ainley, D. G., and T. J. Lewis. 1974. The history of Farallon Island marine bird populations, 1954–1972. Condor 76:432–446.

Allen, L. G., and A. H. Andrews. 2012. Bomb radiocarbon dating and estimated longevity of Giant Sea Bass (*Stereolepis gigas*). Bulletin of Southern California Academy of Science 111:1–14.

Allen, L. G., D. J. Pondella, and M. A. Shane. 2007. Fisheries independent assessment of a returning fishery: Abundance of juvenile white seabass (*Atractoscion nobilis*) in the shallow nearshore waters of the Southern California Bight, 1995–2005. Fisheries Research 88:24–32.

Allen, L. G., D. J. Pondella, and M. H. Horn. 2006. The ecology of marine fishes: California and adjacent waters. University of California Press, Berkeley, California.

Allison, G. W., J. Lubchenco, and M. H. Carr. 1998. Marine reserves are necessary but not sufficient for marine conservation. Ecological Applications 8:S79–S92.

Andersen, K. H., and K. Brander. 2009. Expected rate of fisheries-induced evolution is slow. Proceedings of the National Academy of Sciences 106:11657–11660.

Anderson, C. N. K., C. Hsieh, S. A. Sandin, R. Hewitt, A. Hollowed, J. Beddington, R. May, and G. Sugihara. 2008. Why fishing magnifies fluctuations in fish abundance. Nature 452:835–839.

Anderson, D. W., F. Gress, and K. F. Mais. 1982. Brown pelicans: Influence of food supply on reproduction. Oikos 39:23–31.

Anderson, S. C., J. M. Flemming, R. Watson, and H. K. Lotze. 2011. Rapid global expansion of invertebrate fisheries: Trends, drivers, and ecosystem effects. PLoS One 6:e14735.

Asch, R. G., and J. S. Collie. 2008.Changes in a benthic megafaunal community due to disturbance from bottom fishing and the establishment of a fishery closure. Fishery Bulletin 106:438–456.

Babcock, E. A., and A. D. MacCall. 2011. How useful is the ratio of fish density outside versus inside no-take marine reserves as a metric for fishery management control rules? Canadian Journal of Fisheries and Aquatic Sciences 68:343–359.

Babcock, R., and J. Keesing. 1999. Fertilization biology of the abalone *Haliotis laevigata*: Laboratory and field studies. Canadian Journal of Fisheries and Aquatic Sciences 56:1668–1678.

Barlow, J., and G. A. Cameron. 2003. Field experiments show that acoustic pingers reduce marine mammal bycatch in the California drift gill net fishery. Marine Mammal Science 19:265–283.

Baskett, M. L., M. Yoklavich, and M. S. Love. 2006. Predation, competition, and the recovery of overexploited fish stocks in marine reserves. Canadian Journal of Fisheries and Aquatic Sciences 63:1214–1229.

Baskett, M. L., S. A. Levin, S. D. Gaines, and J. Dushoff. 2005. Marine reserve design and the evolution of size at maturation in harvested fish. Ecological Applications 15:882–901.

Baumgartner, T. R., A. Soutar, and V. Ferreira-Bartrina. 1992. Reconstructions of the history of Pacific sardine and northern anchovy populations over the past two millennia from sediments of the Santa Barbara Basin, California. California Cooperative Oceanic Fisheries Investigations Reports 33:24–40.

Baum, J. K., and B. Worm. 2009. Cascading top-down effects of changing oceanic predator abundances. Journal of Animal Ecology 78:699–714.

Beck, M. W., K. L. Heck Jr., K. W. Able, D. L. Childers, D. B. Eggleston, B. M. Gillanders, B. Halpern, C. G. Hays, K. Hoshino, T. J. Minello, R. J. Orth, P. F. Sheridam, and M. P. Weinstein. 2001. The Identification, conservation, and management of estuarine and marine nurseries for fish and invertebrates: A better understanding of the habitats that serve as nurseries for marine species and the factors that create site-specific variability in nursery quality will improve conservation and management of these areas. Bioscience 51(8):633–641.

Bell, J. D., S. W. Purcell, and W. J. Nash. 2008. Restoring small-scale fisheries for tropical sea cucumbers. Ocean and Coastal Management 51(8):589–593.

Berkeley, S. A., M. A. Hixon, R. J. Larson, M. S. Love. 2007. Fisheries sustainability via protection of age structure and spatial distribution of fish populations. Fisheries 29:23–32.

Beverton, R.J.H., and S. J. Holt. 1957. On the dynamics of exploited fish populations. Ministry of Agriculture, Fisheries, and Food (UK) Fisheries Investigations 2:19.

Beyer, S. G., S. M. Sogard, C. J. Harvey, and J. C. Field. 2015. Variability in rockfish (*Sebastes* spp.) fecundity: Species contrasts, maternal size effects, and spatial differences. Environmental Biology of Fishes 98: 81–100.

Black, B. A., I. D. Schroeder, W. J. Sydeman, S. J. Bograd, and P. W. Lawson. 2010. Wintertime ocean conditions synchronize rockfish growth and seabird reproduction in the central California Current ecosystem. Canadian Journal of Fisheries and Aquatic Sciences 67:1149–1158.

Block, B. A., I. D. Jonsen, S. J. Jorgensen, A. J. Winship, S. A. Shaffer, S. J. Bograd, E. L. Hazen, D. G. Foley, G. A. Breed, A.-L. Harrison, J. E. Ganong, A. Swithenbank, M. Castleton, H. Dewar, B. R. Mate, G. L. Shillinger, K. M. Schaefer, S. R. Benson, M. J. Weise, R. W. Henry, and D. P. Costa. 2011. Tracking apex marine predator movements in a dynamic ocean. Nature 475:86–90.

Bobko, S. J., and S. A. Berkeley. 2004. Maturity, ovarian cycle, fecundity, and age-specific parturition of black rockfish, *Sebastes* melanops. Fishery Bulletin 102:418–429.

Booth, J. D., and B. F. Phillips. 1994. Early life history of spiny lobster. Crustaceana 66:271–294.

Botsford, L.W., A. Hastings, and S. Gaines. 2001. Dependence of sustainability on the configuration of marine reserves and larval dispersal distance. Ecological Letters 4:144–150

Botsford, L. W., D. R. Brumbaugh, C. Grimes, J. B. Kellner, J. Largier, M. R. O'Farrell, S. Ralston, E. Soulanille, and V. Wespestad. 2009. Connectivity, sustainability, and yield: Bridging the gap between conventional fisheries management and marine protected areas. Reviews in Fish Biology and Fisheries 19:69–95.

Botsford, L. W., M. D. Holland, J. F. Samhouri, J. Wilson White, and A. Hastings. 2011. Importance of age structure in models of the response of upper trophic levels to fishing and climate change. ICES Journal of Marine Science 68:1270–1283.

Bracken, M.E.S., B. E. Bracken, and L. Rogers-Bennett. 2007. Species diversity and foundation species: Potential indicators of fisheries yields and marine ecosystem functioning. CalCOFI Reports 48:82–89.

Branch, T. A. 2006. Discards and revenues in multispecies groundfish trawl fisheries managed by trip limits on the U.S. West Coast and by ITQs in British Columbia. Bulletin of Marine Science 78(3):669–689.

Branch, T. A., A. S. Lobo, and S. W. Purcell. 2013. Opportunistic exploitation: An overlooked pathway to extinction. Trends in Ecology and Evolution 28:409–413.

Branch, T. A., K. Rutherford, and R. Hilborn. 2006. Replacing trip limits with individual transferable quotas: Implications for discarding. Marine Policy 30(3):281–292.

Branch, T. A., O. P. Jensen, D. Ricard, Y. Ye, and R. Hilborn. 2011. Contrasting global trends in marine fishery status obtained from catches and from stock assessments. Conservation Biology 25(4):777–786.

Branch, T. A., R. Watson, E. A. Fulton, S. Jennings, C. R. McGilliard, G. T. Pablico, D. Ricard, and S. R. Tracey. 2010. The trophic fingerprint of marine fisheries. Nature 468:431–435.

Brander, K. 2010. Impacts of climate change on fisheries. Journal of Marine Systems 79(3):389–402.

Brander, K. M. 2007. Global fish production and climate change. Proceedings of the National Academy of Sciences 104: 19709–19714.

Brown, C. J., A. J. Hobday, P. E. Ziegler, and D. C. Welsford. 2008. Darwinian fisheries science needs to consider realistic fishing pressures over evolutionary time scales. Marine Ecology Progress Series 369:257–266.

Brumbaugh, R. D., and L. D. Coen. 2009. Contemporary approaches for small-scale oyster reef restoration to address substrate versus recruitment limitation: A review and comments relevant for the

Olympia oyster, *Ostrea lurida* Carpenter 1864. Journal of Shellfish Research 281:147–161.

Buckland, S. T., J. M. Breiwick, K. L. Cattanach, and J. L. Laake. 1993. Estimated population size of the California gray whale. Marine Mammal Science 9(3):235–249.

Burke, B. J., W. T. Peterson, B. R. Beckman, C. Morgan, E. A. Daly, and M. Litz. 2013. Multivariate models of adult Pacific salmon returns. PloS One 8:e54134.

Button, C. A. 2008. The influence of density-dependent aggregation characteristics on the population biology of benthic broadcast-spawning gastropods: Pink abalone (*Haliotis corrugata*), red abalone (*Haliotis rufescens*), and wavy turban snails (*Megastraea undosa*). UC San Diego California Sea Grant College Program. <http://escholarship.org/uc/item/4xk8j75t>. Accessed November 30, 2013.

Byrne, M. 2011. Impact of ocean warming and ocean acidification on marine invertebrate life history stages: vulnerabilities and potential for persistence in a changing ocean. 2011. Oceanography and Marine Biology: an Annual Review 49: 1–42.

Byrnes, J., J. J. Stachowicz, K. M. Hultgren, A. R. Hughes, S. V. Olyarnik, and C. S. Thornber. 2006. Predator diversity strengthens trophic cascades in kelp forests by modifying herbivore behaviour. Ecology letters 9:61–71.

California Department of Fish and Game (CDFG). 2013. Status of the fisheries report: An update through 2008. <http:// www.dfg.ca .gov/marine/status>. Accessed November 20, 2014.

California Department of Fish and Game (CFDG) Partnership for Interdisciplinary Studies of Coastal Oceans, Channel Islands National Marine Sanctuary, and Channel Islands National Park. 2008. Channel Islands Marine Protected Areas: First 5 Years of Monitoring: 2003–2008. S. Airamé and J. Ugoretz, editors. <http:// www.dfg.ca.gov/marine>. Accessed January 10, 2014.

Callicott, J. B., L. B. Crowder, and K. Mumford. 1999. Current normative concepts in conservation. Conservation Biology 13:22–35.

Carlson, S. M., and W. H. Satterthwaite. 2011. Weakened portfolio effect in a collapsed salmon population complex. Canadian Journal of Fisheries and Aquatic Sciences 68:1579–1589.

Carr, M. H., et al. 1991. Habitat selection and recruitment of an assemblage of temperate zone reef fishes. Journal of Experimental Marine Biology and Ecology 146:113–137.

Carretta, J. V., K. A. Forney, M. S. Lowry, J. Barlow, J. Baker, D. Johnston , B. Hanson, R. L. Brownell Jr., J. Robbins, D. K. Mattila, K. Ralls, M. M. Muto, D. Lynch, and L. Carswell. 2009. U.S. Pacific marine mammal stock assessments: 2009. Publications, Agencies and Staff of the U.S. Department of Commerce. Paper 114. <http:// digitalcommons.unl.edu/usdeptcommercepub/114>. Accessed February 19, 2014.

Carretta, J. V., T. Price, D. Petersen, and R. Read. 2004. Estimates of marine mammal, sea turtle, and seabird mortality in the California Drift Gillnet Fishery for swordfish and thresher shark, 1996–2002. Marine Fisheries Review 66:21–30.

Carruthers, T. R., A. E. Punt, C. J. Walters, A. MacCall, M. K. McAllister, E. J. Dick, and J. Cope. 2014. Evaluating methods for setting catch limits in data-limited fisheries. Fisheries Research 153:48–68.

Chan, F., J. A. Barth, J. Lubchenco, A. Kirincich, H. Weeks, W. T. Peterson, and B. A. Menge. 2008. Emergence of anoxia in the California current large marine ecosystem. Science 319: 920–920.

Chavez F. P., J. Ryan, S. E. Lluch-Cota, and M. Niquen. 2003. From anchovies to sardines and back: Multi-decadal change in the Pacific Ocean. Science 299:217–221.

Checkley, D. M., and J. A. Barth. 2009. Patterns and processes in the California Current System. Progress in Oceanography 83:49–64.

Chuenpagdee, R., L. E. Morgan, S. M. Maxwell, E. A. Norse, and D. Pauly. 2003. Shifting gears: Assessing collateral impacts of fishing methods in U.S. waters. Frontiers in Ecology and the Environment 1:517–524.

Clark, F. N., and J. C. Marr. 1955. Population dynamics of the Pacific sardine. California Cooperative Oceanic Fisheries Investigations Reports 4:12–46.

Cochrane, K. L. 2000. Reconciling sustainability, economic efficiency, and equity in fisheries: The one that got away? Fish and Fisheries 1:3–21.

Coleman, F. C., and S. L. Williams. 2002. Overexploiting marine ecosystem engineers: Potential consequences for biodiversity. Trends in Ecology and Evolution 17:40–44.

Collie J. S., A. D. Wood, and H. P. Jeffries. 2008. Long-term shifts in the species composition of a coastal fish community. Canadian Journal of Fisheries and Aquatic Sciences 65:1352–1365.

Cope, J. M., J. DeVore, E. J. Dick, K. Ames, J. Budrick, D. L. Erickson, J. Grebel, G. Hanshew, R. Jones, L. Mattes, C. Niles, and S. Williams. 2011. An approach to defining stock complexes for U.S. West Coast groundfishes using vulnerabilities and ecological distributions. North American Journal of Fisheries Management 31:589–604.

Costello, C., S. D. Gaines, and J. Lynham. 2008. Can catch shares prevent fisheries collapse? Science 321:1678–1681.

Costello, C., J. Lynham, S. E. Lester, and S. D. Gaines. 2010. Economic incentives and global fisheries sustainability. Annual Review of Resource Economics 2:299–318.

Costello, C. J, and R. T. Deacon. 2007. The efficiency gains from fully delineating rights in an ITQ Fishery. Department of Economics, University of California, Santa Barbara. <http://escholarship.org/ uc/item/56n8x9qb>. Accessed January 31, 2014.

Crowder, L. B., E. L. Hazen, N. Avissar, R. Bjorkland, C. Latanich, and M. B. Ogburn. 2008. The impacts of fisheries on marine ecosystems and the transition to ecosystem-based management. Annual Review of Ecology, Evolution, and Systematics 39:259–278.

Cury, P. M., and V. Christensen. 2005. Quantitative ecosystem indicators for fisheries management. Journal of Marine Science 62:307–310.

Cury, P. M., I. L. Boyd, S. Bonhommeau, T. Anker-Nilssen, R. J. M. Crawford, R. W. Furness, J. A. Mills, E. J. Murphy, H. Österblom, M. Paleczny, J. F. Piattt, P.-P. Roux, L. Shannon, and W. Sydeman. 2011. Global seabird response to forage fish depletion—one-third for the birds. Science 334:1703–1706.

Davis, J. A., J. R. M. Ross, S. N. Bezalel, J. A. Hunt, A. R. Melwani, R. M. Allen, G. Ichikawa, A. Bonnema, W. A. Heim, D. Crane, S. Swenson, C. Lamerdin, M. Stephenson, and K. Schiff. 2010. Contaminants in Fish from the California Coast, 2009–2010: Summary Report on a Two-Year Screening Survey. A Report of the Surface Water Ambient Monitoring Program (SWAMP). California State Water Resources Control Board, Sacramento, California.

Dayton, P. K., S. Thrush, and F. C. Coleman. 2003. Ecological Effects of Fishing. Report to the Pew Oceans Commission, Arlington, Virginia.

Dayton, P. K., M. J. Tegner, P. B. Edwards, and K. L. Riser. 1998. Sliding baselines, ghosts, and reduced expectations in kelp forest communities. Ecological Applications 8:309–322.

Dayton, P. K., S. F. Thrush, M. T. Agardy, and R. J. Hofman. 1995. Environmental effects of marine fishing. Aquatic conservation: Marine and freshwater ecosystems 5:205–232.

de Marignac, J., J. Hyland,. J. Lindholm, A. DeVogelaere, W. L. Balthis, and D. Kline. 2009. A comparison of seafloor habitats and associated benthic fauna in areas open and closed to bottom trawling along the central California Continental Shelf. Marine Sanctuaries Conservation Series, ONMS-0. NOAA/National Ocean Service/Office of National Marine Sanctuaries, Silver Spring, Maryland.

deReynier, Y. 2012. Making ecosystem-based management a reality: The Pacific Fishery Management Council and the California Current Integrated Ecosystem Assessment. CalCOFI Reports 53:81–88.

Dichmont, C. M., S. Pascoe, T. Kompas, A. E. Punt, and R. Deng. 2010. On implementing maximum economic yield in commercial fisheries. Proceedings of the National Academy of Sciences 107:16–21.

Dick, E. J. 2009.Modeling the reproductive potential of rockfishes (*Sebastes* spp.). PhD dissertation. University of California, Santa Cruz, California.

Dick, E. J., and A. D. MacCall. 2011. Depletion-based stock reduction analysis: A catch-based method for determining sustainable yields for data-poor fish stocks. Fisheries Research 1102:331–341.

———. 2010. Estimates of sustainable yield for 50 data-poor stocks in the Pacific coast groundfish fishery management plan. NOAA Technical Memorandum NMFS-SWFSC-460.

Di Lorenzo, E., V. Combes, J. E. Keister, P. T. Strub, A. C. Thomas, P. J. S. Franks, M. D. Ohman, J. C. Furtado, A. Bracco, S. J. Bograd,

W. T. Peterson, F. B. Schwing, S. Chiba, B. Taguchi, S. Hormazabal, and C. Parada. 2013. Synthesis of Pacific Ocean climate and ecosystem dynamics. Oceanography 26:68–81.

Doney, S. C., M. Ruckelshaus, J. E. Duffy, J. P. Barry, F. Chan, C. A. English, H. M. Galindo, J. M. Grebmeier, A. B. Hollowed, N. Knowlton, J. Polovina, N. N. Rabalais, W. J. Sydeman, and L. D. Talley. 2012. Climate change impacts on marine ecosystems. Annual Review of Marine Science 4:11–37.

Dugan, J. E., and G. E. Davis. 1993. Application of marine refugia to coastal fisheries management. Canadian Journal of Fisheries and Aquatic Sciences 50:2029–2042.

Dulvy, N. K., J. K. Baum, S. Clarke, L. J. Compagno, E. Cortés, E., A. Domingo, S. Fordhan, S. Fowler, M. P. Francis, C. Gibson, J. Martínez, J. A. Musick, A. Soldo, J. D. Stevens, and S. Valenti. 2008. You can swim but you can't hide: The global status and conservation of oceanic pelagic sharks and rays. Aquatic Conservation: Marine and Freshwater Ecosystems 18:459–482.

Erisman, B. E., L. G. Allen, J. T. Claisse, D. J. Pondella, E. F. Miller, and J. H. Murray. 2011. The illusion of plenty: Hyperstability masks collapses in two recreational fisheries that target fish spawning aggregations. Canadian Journal of Fisheries and Aquatic Sciences 68:1705–1716.

Erlandson, J. M., T. C. Rick, J. A. Estes, M. H. Graham, T. J. Braje, and R. L. Vellanoweth. 2005. Sea otters, shellfish, and humans: 10,000 years of ecological interaction on San Miguel Island, California. Proceedings of California Island Symposium 6:58–68.

Erlandson, J. M., T. C. Rick, T. J. Braje, A. Steinberg, and R. L. Vellanoweth. 2008. Human impacts on ancient shellfish: A 10,000 year record from San Miguel Island, California. Journal of Archaeological Science 35:2144–2152.

Essington, T. E. 2010. Ecological indicators display reduced variation in North American catch share fisheries. Proceedings of the National Academy of Sciences 107:754–759.

Essington, T. E., A. H. Beaudreau, and J. Wiedenmann. 2006. Fishing through marine food webs. Proceedings of the National Academy of Sciences of the United States of America 103:3171–3175.

Essington, T. E., M. C. Melnychuk, T. A. Branch, S. S. Heppell, O. P. Jensen, J. S. Link, S. J. D. Martell, A. M. Parma, J. G. Pope, and A. D. Smith. 2012. Catch shares, fisheries, and ecological stewardship: A comparative analysis of resource responses to a rights-based policy instrument. Conservation Letters 5:186–195.

Estes, J. A. 1990. Growth and equilibrium in sea otter populations. Journal of Animal Ecology 59:385–401.

Estes, J. A., and D. O. Duggins. 1995. Sea otters and kelp forests in Alaska: Generality and variation in a community ecological paradigm. Ecological Monographs 65:75–100.

Estes, J. A., D. P. DeMaster, D. F. Doak, T. M. Williams, and R. L. Brownell. 2006. Whales, whaling, and ocean ecosystems. University of California Press, Berkeley, California.

Fabry, V. J., B. A. Seibel, R. A. Feely, and J. C. Orr. 2008. Impacts of ocean acidification on marine fauna and ecosystem processes. ICES Journal of Marine Science: Journal du Conseil 65(3): 414–432.

Field, J. C., A. D. MacCall, R. W. Bradley, and W. J. Sydeman. 2010. Estimating the impacts of fishing on dependent predators: A case study in the California Current. Ecological Applications 20:2223–2236.

Field, J. C., A. D. MacCall, S. Ralston, M. S. Love, E. F. Miller, L. Rogers-Bennett, and J. W. White. 2010. Bocaccionomics: The effectiveness of pre-recruit indices for assessment and management of bocaccio. California Cooperative Oceanic Fisheries Investigations Report 51:77–90.

Field, J. C., A. E. Punt, R. D. Methot, and C. J. Thomson. 2006. Does MPA mean "major problem for assessments"? Considering the consequences of place-based management systems. Fish and Fisheries 7:284–302.

Field, J. C., and R. C. Francis. 2006. Considering ecosystem-based fisheries management in the California Current. Marine Policy 30:552–569.

Forney, K. A., S. R. Benson, G. A. Cameron. 2001. Central California gillnet effort and bycatch of sensitive species, 1990–1998. Pages 141–160 in Seabird bycatch: Trends, roadblocks, and solutions. University of Alaska Sea Grant, Fairbanks, Alaska.

Foster, M. S., and D. R. Schiel. 2010. Loss of predators and the collapse of southern California kelp forests (?): Alternatives, explanations, and generalizations. Journal of Experimental Marine Biology and Ecology 393:59–70.

———. 1988. Kelp communities and sea otters: Keystone species or just another brick in the wall? Pages 92–115 in The community ecology of sea otters. Springer, Berlin and Heidelberg, Germany.

Fowler, C. W. 1999. Management of multi-species fisheries: From overfishing to sustainability. ICES Journal of Marine Science 56:927–932.

Fox, W. W., Jr. 1970. An exponential surplus-yield model for optimizing exploited fish populations. Transactions of the American Fisheries Society 991:80–88.

Francis, R. C. 1986. Two fisheries biology problems in west coast groundfish management. North American Journal of Fisheries Management 6:453–462.

Francis, R. C., F. T. Awbrey, C. A. Goudey, M. A. Hall, D. M. King, H. Medina, K. S. Norris, M. K. Orbach, R. Payne, and E. Pikitch. 1992. Dolphins and the tuna industry. National Research Council, National Academy Press, Washington, D.C.

Francis, R. C., M. A. Hixon, M. E. Clarke, S. A. Murawski, and S. Ralston. 2007. Ten commandments for ecosystem-based fisheries scientists. Fisheries 32:217–233.

Frank, K. T., B. Petrie, J. S. Choi, and W. S. Leggett. 2005. Trophic cascades in a formerly cod-dominated ecosystem. Science 308:1621–1623

Fréon, P., J. Arístegui, A. Bertrand, R. J. Crawford, J. C. Field, M. J. Gibbons, L. Hutchings, H. Masski, C. Mullon, M. Ramdani, B. Seret, M. Simier, and J. Tam. 2009. Functional group biodiversity in Eastern Boundary Upwelling Ecosystems questions the wasp-waist trophic structure. Progress in Oceanography 83:97–106.

Fréon, P., P. Cury, L. Shannon, and C. Roy. 2005. Sustainable exploitation of small pelagic fish stocks challenged by environmental and ecosystem changes: A review. Bulletin of Marine Science 76:385–462.

Froese, R. 2004. Keep it simple: Three indicators to deal with overfishing. Fish and Fisheries 5:86–91.

Fulton, E. A., A. D. Smith, and A. E. Punt. 2005. Which ecological indicators can robustly detect effects of fishing? ICES Journal of Marine Science 62:540–551.

Fulton, E. A., A. D. Smith, D. C. Smith, and I. E. van Putten. 2011. Human behaviour: The key source of uncertainty in fisheries management. Fish and Fisheries 12:2–17.

Gaichas, S. K. 2008. A context for ecosystem-based fishery management: Developing concepts of ecosystems and sustainability. Marine Policy 32:393–401.

Gibbs, M. T. 2010. Why ITQs on target species are inefficient at achieving ecosystem based fisheries management outcomes. Marine Policy 34:708–709.

———. 2009. Individual transferable quotas and ecosystem-based fisheries management: It's all in the T. Fish and Fisheries 10:470–474.

Gibbs, M. T., and O. Thebaud. 2012. Beyond individual transferrable quotas: Methodologies for integrating ecosystem impacts of fishing into fisheries catch rights. Fish and Fisheries 13:434–449.

Gleason, M., E. M. Feller, M. Merrifield, S. Copps, R. Fujita, M. Bell, S. Rienecke, and C. Cook. 2013. A transactional and collaborative approach to reducing effects of bottom trawling. Conservation Biology 27:470–479.

Gleason, M., S. McCreary, M. Miller-Henson, J. Ugoretz, E. Fox, M. Merrifield, W. McClintock, and K. Hoffman. 2010. Science-based and stakeholder-driven marine protected area network planning: A successful case study from north central California. Ocean and Coastal Management 53:52–68.

Gobalet, K. W., and T. L. Jones. 1995. Prehistoric Native American fisheries of the central California coast. Transactions of the American Fisheries Society 124:813–823.

Good, T. P., T. J. Beechie, P. McElhany, M. M. McClure, and M. H. Ruckelshaus. 2007. Recovery planning for Endangered Species Act–listed Pacific salmon: Using science to inform goals and strategies. Fisheries 32:426–440.

Goñi, R. 1998. Ecosystem effects of marine fisheries: An overview. Ocean Coastal Management 40:37–64.

Grafton, R. Q., R. Arnason, T. Bjørndal, D. Campbell, H. F. Campbell, C. W. Clark, R. Connor, D. P. Dupont, R. Hannesson, R. Hilborn, J. E. Kirkley, T. Kompas, D. E. Lane, G. R. Munro, S. Pascoe, D. Squires, S. I. Steinshamm, B. R. Turris, and Q. Weninger. 2006.

Incentive-based approaches to sustainable fisheries. Canadian Journal of Fisheries and Aquatic Sciences 63:699–710.
Grafton, R. Q., T. Kompas, and R. W. Hilborn. 2007. Economics of overexploitation revisited. Science 318:1601–1601.
Grantham, B. A., F. Chan, K. J. Nielsen, D. S. Fox, J. A. Barth, A. Huyer, J. Lubchenco, and B. A. Menge. 2004. Upwelling-driven nearshore hypoxia signals ecosystem and oceanographic changes in the northeast Pacific. Nature 429: 749–754.
Grift, R. E., A. D. Rijnsdorp, S. Barot, M. Heino, and U. Dieckmann. 2003. Fisheries-induced trends in reaction norms for maturation in North Sea plaice. Marine Ecology Progress Series 257:247–257.
Grumbine, R. E. 1994. What is ecosystem management? Conservation Biology 81:27–38.
Gunderson, D. R. 1984. Great widow rockfish hunt of 1980–1982. North American Journal of Fisheries Management 4:465–468.
Gunderson, D. R., A. M. Parma, R. Hilborn, J. M. Cope, D. L. Fluharty, M. L. Miller, H. G. Greene et al. 2008. The challenge of managing nearshore rocky reef resources. Fisheries 33:172–179.
Gutiérrez, N. L., R. Hilborn, and O. Defeo. 2011. Leadership, social capital, and incentives promote successful fisheries. Nature 470:386–389.
Halpern, B. S., C. V. Kappel, K. A. Selkoe, F. Micheli, C. M. Ebert, C. Kontgis, C. M. Crain, R. G. Martone, C. Shearer, and S. J. Teck. 2009. Mapping cumulative human impacts to California Current marine ecosystems. Conservation Letters 2:138–148.
Halpern, B. S., K. Cottenie, and B. R. Broitman. 2006. Strong top-down control in southern California kelp forest ecosystems. Science 312:1230–1232.
Haltuch, M. A., K. Ono, and J. Valero. 2013. Status of the U.S. petrale sole resource in 2012. Pacific Fishery Management Council, Portland, Oregon. <http://www.pcouncil.org/wp-content/uploads/Petrale_2013_Assessment.pdf>. Accessed March 10, 2014.
Hankin, D. G., and M. C. Healey. 1986. Dependence of exploitation rates for maximum yield and stock collapse on age and sex structure of Chinook salmon (*Oncorhynchus tshawytscha*) stocks. Canadian Journal of Fisheries and Aquatic Sciences 43:1746–1759.
Hankin, D. G., J. Fitzgibbons, and Y. Chen. 2009. Unnatural random mating policies select for younger age at maturity in hatchery Chinook salmon (*Oncorhynchus tshawytscha*) populations. Canadian Journal of Fisheries and Aquatic Sciences 66:1505–1521.
Hankin, D. G., T. H. Butler, P. W. Wild, and Q. L. Xue. 1997. Does intense fishing on males impair mating success of female Dungeness crabs. Canadian Journal of Fisheries and Aquatic Sciences 54:655–669.
Hannah, R. W. 2011. Variation in the distribution of ocean shrimp (*Pandalus jordani*) recruits: Links with coastal upwelling and climate change. Fisheries Oceanography 20:305–313.
Hannah, R. W., and S. A. Jones. 2007. Effectiveness of bycatch reduction devices (BRDs) in the ocean shrimp (*Pandalus jordani*) trawl fishery. Fisheries Research 85:217–225.
Hannah, R. W., S. J. Parker, and T. V. Buell. 2005. Evaluation of a selective flatfish trawl and diel variation in rockfish catchability as bycatch reduction tools in the deepwater complex fishery off the U.S. West Coast. North American Journal of Fisheries Management 25:581–593.
Hardin, G. 1968. The tragedy of the Commons. Science 162:1243–1248.
Harrold, C. and D. C. Reed. 1985. Food availability, sea urchin grazing, and kelp forest community structure. Ecology 66: 1160–1169.
Hart, D. R., and M. P. Sissenwine. 2009. Marine reserve effects on fishery profits: A comment on White et al. 2008. Ecology Letters 12:E9–E11.
Harvey, C. J., J. C. Field, S. G. Beyer, and S. M. Sogard. 2011. Modeling growth and reproduction of chilipepper rockfish under variable environmental conditions. Fisheries Research 109:187–200.
Harvey, C. J., N. Tolimieri, and P. S. Levin. 2006. Changes in body size, abundance, and energy allocation in rockfish assemblages of the northeast Pacific. Ecological Applications 16:1502–1515.
Hawk, H. A., and L. G. Allen. 2014. Age and growth of the giant sea bass, *Stereolepis gigas*. CalCOFI Report 55: 1–7.
Heimann, R.F.G., and J. G. Carlisle Jr. 1970. The California marine fish catch for 1968 and historical review 1916–68. State of California Department of Fish and Game, Fish Bulletin 149.
Hilborn, R. 2012. The evolution of quantitative marine fisheries management 1985–2010. Natural Resource Modeling 25:122–144.
———. 2011. Future directions in ecosystem based fisheries management: a personal perspective. Fisheries Research 108: 235–239.
———. 2010. Pretty good yield and exploited fishes. Marine Policy 34:193–196.
———. 2007a. Defining success in fisheries and conflicts in objectives. Marine Policy 31:153–158.
———. 2007b. Managing fisheries is managing people: What has been learned? Fish and Fisheries 8:285–296.
———. 2007c. Moving to sustainability by learning from successful fisheries. AMBIO: A Journal of the Human Environment 36:296–303.
———. 2007d. Reinterpreting the state of fisheries and their management. Ecosystems 10:1362–1369.
Hilborn, R., and C. J. Walters. 1992. Quantitative fisheries stock assessment. Choice, dynamics and uncertainty. Chapman and Hall, New York, New York.
Hilborn, R., F. Micheli, and G. A. De Leo. 2006. Integrating marine protected areas with catch regulation. Canadian Journal of Fisheries and Aquatic Sciences 63:642-649.
Hilborn, R., I. J. Stewart, T. A. Branch, and O. P. Jensen. 2012. Defining trade-offs among conservation, profitability, and food security in the California Current bottom-trawl fishery. Conservation Biology 26:257–268.
Hilborn, R., J. L. Orensanz, and A. M. Parma. 2005. Institutions, incentives, and the future of fisheries. Philosophical Transactions of the Royal Society B: Biological Sciences 360:47–57.
Hilborn, R., K. Stokes, J. J. Maguire, T. Smith, L. W. Botsford, M. Mangel, J. Oresanz, A. Parma, J. Rice, J. Bell, K. L. Cochrane, S. Garcia, S. J. Hall, G. P. Kirkwood, K. Sainsbury, G. Stefansson, and C. Walters. 2004. When can marine reserves improve fisheries management? Ocean and Coastal Management 47:197–205.
Hilborn, R., T. A. Branch, B. Ernst, A. Magnusson, C. V. Minte-Vera, M. D. Scheuerell, and J. L. Valero. 2003. State of the world's fisheries. Annual review of Environment and Resources 28:359–399.
Hildebrandt, W. R., and T. L. Jones. 1992. Evolution of marine mammal hunting: A view from the California and Oregon coasts. Journal of Anthropological Archaeology, 11(4), 360-401.
Hill, K. T., P. R. Crone, N. C. Lo, D. A. Demer, J. P. Zwolinski, and B. J. Macewicz. 2012. Assessment of the Pacific sardine resource in 2012 for U.S. management in 2013. Pacific Fishery Management Council, 7700. <http://www.pcouncil.org/wp-content/uploads/MAIN_DOC_G3b_ASSMNT_RPT2_WEB_ONLY_NOV2012BB.pdf>. Accessed January 14, 2014.
Hobson, E. S., J. R. Chess, and D. F. Howard. 2001. Interannual variation in predation on first-year *Sebastes* spp. by three northern California predators. Fishery Bulletin 99:292–302.
Holling, C. S., and G. K. Meffe. 1996. Command and control and the pathology of natural resource management. Conservation Biology 10:328–337.
Hollowed, A. B., N. Bax, R. Beamish, J. Collie, M. Fogarty, P. Livingston, J. Pope, and J. C. Rice. 2000. Are multispecies models an improvement on single-species models for measuring fishing impacts on marine ecosystems? ICES Journal of Marine Science 57:707–719.
Hollowed, A. B., M. Barange, S. I. Ito, S. Kim, H. Loeng, and M. A. Peck. 2011. Effects of climate change on fish and fisheries: Forecasting impacts, assessing ecosystem responses, and evaluating management strategies. ICES Journal of Marine Science 68:984–985.
Holts, D. B., A. Julian, O. Sosa-Nishizaki, and N. W. Bartoo. 1998. Pelagic shark fisheries along the west coast of the United States and Baja California, Mexico. Fisheries Research 39:115–125.
Hsieh, C. H., C. S. Reiss, J. R. Hunter, J. R. Beddington, R. R. May, and G. Sugihara. 2006. Fishing elevates variability in the abundance of exploited species. Nature 443:859–862.
Iles, T. C., and R. J. H. Beverton. 2000. The concentration hypothesis: The statistical evidence. ICES Journal of Marine Science 57:216–227.
Jackson, G. D., and M. L. Domeier. 2003. The effects of an extraordinary El Niño / La Niña event on the size and growth of the squid *Loligo opalescens* off southern California. Marine Biology 142:925–935.
Jackson, J. B. C., M. X. Kirby, W. H. Bergner, K. A. Bjorndal, L. W. Botsford, B. J. Bourque, R. H. Bradbury, R. Cooke, J. Erlandson, J. A. Estes, T. P. Hughes, S. Kidwell, C. B. Lange, H. S. Lenihan,

J. M. Pandolfi, C. H. Peterson, R. S. Steneck, M. J. Tenger, and R. R. Warner. 2001. Historical overfishing and the recent collapse of coastal ecosystems. Science 293:629–638.

Jacobson, L. D., and A. D. MacCall. 1995. Stock-recruitment models for Pacific sardine (*Sardinops sagax*). Canadian Journal of Fisheries and Aquatic Sciences 52:566–577.

Jennings, S., and M. J. Kaiser. 1998. The effects of fishing on marine ecosystems. Advances in Marine Biology 34:201–351.

Jennings, S., J. D. Reynolds, and S. C. Mills. 1998. Life history correlates of responses to fisheries exploitation. Proceedings of the Royal Society of London. Series B: Biological Sciences 265:333–339.

Jensen, O. P., T. A. Branch, and R. Hilborn. 2012. Marine fisheries as ecological experiments. Theoretical Ecology 5:3–22.

Julian, F., and M. Beeson. 1998. Estimates of marine mammal, turtle, and seabird mortality for two California gillnet fisheries: 1990–1995. Fishery Bulletin 96:271–284.

Kaiser, M. J., and J. G. Hiddink. 2007. Food subsidies' from fisheries to continental shelf benthic scavengers. Marine Ecology Progress Series 350:267–276.

Kaplan, D. M., L. W. Botsford, M. R. O'Farrell, S. D. Gaines, and S. Jorgensen. 2009. Model-based assessment of persistence in proposed marine protected area designs. Ecological Applications 19:433–448.

Kaplan, I. C., C. J. Brown, E. A. Fulton, I. A. Gray, J. C. Field, and A. D. Smith. 2013. Impacts of depleting forage species in the California Current. Environmental Conservation 40:380–393.

Kaplan, I. C., D. S. Holland, and E. A. Fulton. 2013. Finding the accelerator and brake in an individual quota fishery: Linking ecology, economics, and fleet dynamics of U.S. West Coast trawl fisheries. ICES Journal of Marine Science 71:308–319.

Kaplan, I. C., I. A. Gray, and P. S. Levin. 2012. Cumulative impacts of fisheries in the California Current. Fish and Fisheries 14:515–527.

Kaplan, I. C., P. J. Horne, and P. S. Levin. 2012. Screening California Current fishery management scenarios using the Atlantis end-to-end ecosystem model. Progress in Oceanography 102:5–18.

Karpov, K. A., P. L. Haaker, I. K. Taniguchi, and L. Rogers-Bennett. 2000. Serial depletion and the collapse of the California abalone (*Haliotis* spp.) fishery. Pages 11–24 in A. Campbell, editor. Workshop on Rebuilding Abalone Stocks in British Columbia Canadian Special Publication of Fisheries and Aquatic Sciences 130 (Proceedings of Workshop on Rebuilding Abalone Stocks in British Columbia, Nanaimo, 23 February–26 February, 1999. NRC Research Press, Ottawa.

Kasperski, S., and D. S. Holland. 2013. Income diversification and risk for fishermen. Proceedings of the National Academy of Sciences 110:2076–2081.

Keller, A. A., V. Simon, F. Chan, W. W. Wakefield, M. E. Clarke, J. A. Barth, D. A. N. Kamikawa, and E. L. Fruh. 2010. Demersal fish and invertebrate biomass in relation to an offshore hypoxic zone along the US West Coast. Fisheries Oceanography 19: 76–87.

King, J. R., and G. A. McFarlane. 2003. Marine fish life history strategies: Applications to fishery management. Fisheries Management and Ecology 10:249–264.

King, J. R., V. N. Agostini, C. J. Harvey, Gordon A. McFarlane, M. G. G. Foreman, J. E. Overland, E. Di Lorenzo, N. A. Bond, and K. Y. Aydin. 2011. Climate forcing and the California Current ecosystem. ICES Journal of Marine Science: Journal du Conseil 68: 1199–1216.

King, S. E., R. W. Hannah, S. J. Parker, K. M. Matteson, and S. A. Berkeley. 2004. Protecting rockfish through gear design: development of a selective flatfish trawl for the US west coast bottom trawl fishery. Canadian Journal of Fisheries and Aquatic Sciences 61: 487–496.

Kirby, M. X. 2004. Fishing down the coast: Historical expansion and collapse of oyster fisheries along continental margins. Proceedings of the National Academy of Sciences of the United States of America 101:13096–13099.

Kirlin, J., M. Caldwell, M. Gleason, M. Weber, J. Ugoretz, E. Fox, and M. Miller-Henson. 2012. California's Marine Life Protection Act Initiative: Supporting implementation of legislation establishing a statewide network of marine protected areas. Ocean and Coastal Management 74:3–13.

Klein, C. J., A. Chan, L. Kircher, A. J. Cundiff, N. Gardner, Y. Hrovat, A. Scholz, B. E. Kendall, and S. Airame. 2008. Striking a balance between biodiversity conservation and socioeconomic viability in the design of marine protected areas. Conservation Biology 22:691–700.

Koslow, J. A., and C. Allen. 2011. The influence of the ocean environment on the abundance of market squid, *Doryteuthis* (Loligo) *opalescensparalarvae* in the Southern California Bight. CalCOFI Reports 52:205–213.

Koslow, J. A., G. W. Boehlert, J. D. M. Gordon, R. L. Haedrich, P. Lorance, and N. Parin. 2000. Continental slope and deep-sea fisheries: Implications for a fragile ecosystem. ICES Journal of Marine Science 57:548–557.

Kroeker, K. J., R. L. Kordas, R. Crim, I. E. Hendriks, L. Ramajo, G. S. Singh, C. M. Duarte, and J.-P. Gattuso. 2013. Impacts of ocean acidification on marine organisms: Quantifying sensitivities and interaction with warming. Global Change Biology 19:1884–1896.

Kuparinen, A., and J. Merilä. 2007. Detecting and managing fisheries-induced evolution. Trends in Ecology and Evolution 22:652–659.

Leaman, B. M., and R. J. Beamish. 1984. Ecological and management implications of longevity in some northeast Pacific groundfish. Bulletin of the International North Pacific Fisheries Commission 42:85–97.

Leet, W. S., C. M. Dewees, R. Klingbeil, and E. Larson. 2001. California's living marine resources: A status report. California Department of Fish and Game. Sacramento, California.

Levin, P. S., B. K. Wells, and M. B. Sheer. 2013. California Current Integrated Ecosystem Assessment: Phase II Report. Available from <http://www.noaa.gov/iea/CCIEA-Report/index>.

Levin, P. S., E. E. Holmes, K. R. Piner, and C. J. Harvey. 2006. Shifts in a Pacific Ocean fish assemblage: The potential influence of exploitation. Conservation Biology 20:1181–1190.

Levin, P. S., M. J. Fogarty, S. A. Murawski, and D. Fluharty. 2009. Integrated ecosystem assessments: Developing the scientific basis for ecosystem-based management of the ocean. PLoS Biology 7:e1000014.

Lewitus, A. J., R. A. Horner, D. A. Caron, E. Garcia-Mendoza, B. M. Hickey, M. Hunter, D. D. Huppert, R. M. Kudela, G. W. Langlois, J. L. Largier, E. J. Lessard, R. RaLonde, J. E. J. Rensel, P. G. Strutton, V. L. Trainer, and J. F. Tweddle. 2012. Harmful algal blooms along the North American west coast region: History, trends, causes, and impacts. Harmful Algae 19:133–159.

Liermann, M., and R. Hilborn. 1997. Depensation in fish stocks: A hierarchic Bayesian meta-analysis. Canadian Journal of Fisheries and Aquatic Sciences 54:1976–1984.

Lindegren, M., D. M. Checkley, T. Rouyer, A. D. MacCall, and N. C. Stenseth. 2013. Climate, fishing, and fluctuations of sardine and anchovy in the California Current. Proceedings of the National Academy of Sciences 110:13672–13677.

Lindley, S. T., C. B. Grimes, M. S. Mohr, W. Peterson, J. Stein, J. T. Anderson, L. W. Botsford, D. L. Bottom, C.A. Busack, T. K. Collier, J. Ferguson, J. C. Garza, A. M. Grover, D. G. Hankin, R. G. Kope, P. W. Lawson, A. Low, R. B. MacFarlane, K. Moore, M. Palmer-Zwahlen, F. B. Schwing, J. Smith, C. Tracy, R. Webb, B. K. Wells, and T. H. Williams. 2009. What caused the Sacramento River fall Chinook stock collapse? NOAA Tech. Memo. NMFS NOAA-TM-NMFS-SWFSC-447.

Lindley, S. T., R. S. Schick, E. Mora, P. B. Adams, J. J. Anderson, S. Greene, C. Jamspm, B. P. May, D. R. McEwan, R. B. MacFarlane, C. Swanson, and J. G. Williams. 2007. Framework for assessing viability of threatened and endangered Chinook salmon and steelhead in the Sacramento–San Joaquin Basin. San Francisco Estuary and Watershed Science 5(1). jmie_sfews_10986. <http://escholarship.org/uc/item/3653x9xc>. Accessed November 12, 2013.

Ling, S. D., C. R. Johnson, S. D. Frusher, and K. R. Ridgway. 2009. Overfishing reduces resilience of kelp beds to climate-driven catastrophic phase shift. Proceedings of the National Academy of Sciences 106:22341–22345.

Link, J. 2010. Ecosystem-based fisheries management: Confronting tradeoffs. Cambridge University Press, Cambridge, UK.

Link, J. S. 2005.Translating ecosystem indicators into decision criteria. Journal of Marine Science 62:569–576.

Love, M. S., J. E. Caselle, and W. Van Buskirk. 1998. A severe decline in the commercial passenger fishing vessel rockfish (*Sebastes* spp.) catch in the Southern California Bight, 1980–1996. CalCOFI Reports 39:180–195.

Love, M. S., M. H. Carr, and L. J. Haldorson. 1991. The ecology of substrate-associated juveniles of the genus *Sebastes*. Environmental Biology of Fishes 30:225–243.

Love, M. S., M. Yoklavich, and D. M. Schroeder. 2009. Demersal fish assemblages in the Southern California Bight based on visual surveys in deep water. Environmental Biology of Fishes 84:55–68.

Lucero, Y. 2009. A multivariate stock-recruitment function for cohorts with sympatric subclasses: Application to maternal effects in rockfish (genus *Sebastes*). Canadian Journal of Fisheries and Aquatic Sciences 66:557–564.

Ludwig, D., R. Hilborn, and C. Walters. 1993. Uncertainty, resource exploitation, and conservation: Lessons from history. Science 260:17.

Lyman, R. L. 1989. Seal and sea lion hunting: A zooarchaeological study from the southern northwest coast of North America. Journal of Anthropological Archaeology 8: 68–99.

MacCall, A. D. 2012. Data-limited management reference points to avoid collapse of stocks dependent on learned migration behaviour. ICES Journal of Marine Science 69:267–270.

———. 2010.

———. 2009a. A short scientific history of the fisheries. Pages 6–11 in D. Checkley et al., editors. Climate change and small pelagic fish. Cambridge University Press, Cambridge, UK.

———. 2009b. Depletion-corrected average catch: A simple formula for estimating sustainable yields in data-poor situations. ICES Journal of Marine Science 66:2267–2271.

———. 2002. Fishery-management and stock-rebuilding prospects under conditions of low-frequency environmental variability and species interactions. Bulletin of Marine Science 70:613–628.

———. 1996. Patterns of low-frequency variability in fish populations of the California Current. California Cooperative Oceanic Fisheries Investigations Reports 37:100–110.

———. 1979. Population estimates for the waning years of the Pacific sardine fishery. California Cooperative Oceanic Fisheries Investigations Reports 20:72–82.

———. 1976. Density dependence of catchability coefficient in the California Pacific sardine, *Sardinops sagax caerulea*, purse seine fishery. California Cooperative Oceanic Fisheries Investigations Reports 18:136–148.

Mace, P. M. 2001. A new role for MSY in single-species and ecosystem approaches to fisheries stock assessment and management. Fish and Fisheries 2:2–32.

Mangel, M., and P. S. Levin. 2005. Regime, phase, and paradigm shifts: Making community ecology the basic science for fisheries. Philosophical Transactions of the Royal Society B: Biological Sciences 360:95–105.

Mangel, M., A. D. MacCall, J. K. Brodziak, E. J. Dick, R. E. Forrest, R. Pourzand, and S. Ralston. 2013. A perspective on steepness, reference points, and stock assessment. Canadian Journal of Fisheries and Aquatic Sciences 70:930–940.

Marchal, P., P. Lallemand, and K. Stoke. 2009. The relative weight of traditions, economics, and catch plans in New Zealand fleet dynamics. Canadian Journal of Fisheries and Aquatic Sciences 66:291–311.

Mason, J. E. 2004. Historical patterns from 74 years of commercial landings from California waters. CalCOFI Reports 45:180–190.

———. 1998. Declining rockfish lengths in the Monterey Bay, California, recreational fishery. Marine Fisheries Review 60:15–28.

———. 1995. Species trends in sport fisheries, Monterey, CA, 1959–86. Marine Fisheries Review 57:1–16.

Mason, J., R. Kosaka, A. Mamula, and C. Speir. 2012. Effort changes around a marine reserve: The case of the California Rockfish Conservation Area. Marine Policy 36:1054–1063.

McClatchie, S., et al. 2014. Regional fisheries oceanography of the California Current System: The CalCOFI program. Springer Science and Business, Dordrecht, Germany.

McClatchie, S., R. Goericke, R. Cosgrove, G. Auad, and R. Vetter. 2010. Oxygen in the Southern California bight: multidecadal trends and implications for demersal fisheries. Geophysical Research Letters, 37: L19602

McElhany, P., M. H. Ruckelshaus, M. J. Ford, T. C. Wainwright, and E. P. Bjorkstedt. 2000. Viable salmon populations and the recovery of evolutionarily significant units. NOAA Technical Memorandum NMFS-NWFSC, 42. U.S. Department of Commerce.

McEvoy, A. F. 1996. Historical interdependence between ecology, production, and management in California fisheries. Pages 45–53 in D. Bottom, G. Reeves, and M. Brookes, editors. Sustainability Issues for Resource Managers. USDA Forest Service Tech Rep. PNW-GTR-370.

———. 1986. The fisherman's problem: Ecology and law in the California fisheries, 1850–1980. Cambridge University Press, Cambridge, UK.

McGilliard, C. R., R. Hilborn, A. MacCall, A. E. Punt, and J. Field. 2011. Can information from marine protected areas be used to inform control rule-based management of small-scale, data-poor stocks? ICES Journal of Marine Science 68:201–211.

Melnychuk, M. C., T. E. Essington, T. A. Branch, S. S. Heppell, O. P. Jensen, J. S. Link, S. J. D. Martell, A. M. Parma, J. G. Pope, and A. D. Smith. 2012. Can catch share fisheries better track management targets? Fish and Fisheries 13:267–290.

Melvin, E. F., J. K. Parrish, K. S. Dietrich, and O. S. Hamel. 2001. Solutions to seabird bycatch in Alaska's demersal longline fisheries. Washington Sea Grant Program, University of Washington, Seattle, Washington.

Merz, J. E., and P. B. Moyle. 2006. Salmon, wildlife, and wine: Marine-derived nutrients in human-dominated ecosystems of central California. Ecological Applications 16:999–1009.

Methot, R. D., G. R. Tromble, D. M. Lambert, and K. E. Greene. 2013. Implementing a science-based system for preventing overfishing and guiding sustainable fisheries in the United States. ICES Journal of Marine Science 71: 183–194.

Methot, R. D., Jr., and C. R. Wetzel. 2012. Stock synthesis: A biological and statistical framework for fish stock assessment and fishery management. Fisheries research 142:86–99.

Micheli, F., B. S. Halpern, L. W. Botsford, and R. R. Warner. 2004. Trajectories and correlates of community change in no-take marine reserves. Ecological Applications 14:1709–1723.

Miller, R. R., J. C. Field, J. Santora, I. Schroeder, D. D. Huff, M. Key, D. Pearson, and A. D. MacCall. 2014. A spatially distinct history of the development of California Groundfish Fisheries. Public Library of Science (PLOS ONE) 9:6: e99758.

Mitarai, S., D. A. Siegel, J. R. Watson, C. Dong, and J. C. McWilliams. 2009. Quantifying connectivity in the coastal ocean with application to the Southern California Bight. Journal of Geophysical Research: Oceans 114 (C10):2156–2202.

Moffitt, E. A., J. W. White, and L. W. Botsford. 2013. Accurate assessment of marine protected area success depends on metric and spatioatemporal scaling of monitoring. Marine Ecology Progress Series 489:17–28.

Moore, J. E., B. P. Wallace, R. L. Lewison, R. Žydelis, T. M. Cox, and L. B. Crowder. 2009. A review of marine mammal, sea turtle, and seabird bycatch in USA fisheries and the role of policy in shaping management. Marine Policy 33:435–451.

Morato, T., R. Watson, T. J. Pitcher, and D. Pauly. 2006. Fishing down the deep. Fish and Fisheries 7:24–34.

Morgan, L. E., P. Etnoyer, A. J. Scholz, M. Mertens, and M. Powell. 2005. Conservation and management implications of deep-sea coral and fishing effort distributions in the Northeast Pacific Ocean. Pages 1171–1187 in Cold-water corals and ecosystems. Springer, Berlin and Heidelberg, Germany.

Murawski, S. A. 2010. Rebuilding depleted fish stocks: The good, the bad, and, mostly, the ugly. ICES Journal of Marine Science: Journal du Conseil 67:1830–1840.

———. 2000. Definitions of overfishing from an ecosystem perspective. ICES Journal of Marine Science: Journal du Conseil 57:649–658.

Murawski, S., R. Methot, G. Tromble, R. W. Hilborn, and J. C. Briggs. 2007. Biodiversity loss in the ocean: How bad is it? Science 316:1281.

Murphy, G. I. 1966. Population biology of the Pacific sardine (*Sardinops cuerulea*). Proceedings of the California Academy of Sciences 34:1–84.

Murray, S. N., R. F. Ambrose, J. A. Bohnsack, L. W. Botsford, M. H. Carr, G. E. Davis, P. K. Dayton, D. Gotshall, D. R. Gunderson, M. A. Hixon, J. Lubchenco, M. Mangel, A. MacCall, D. A. McArdle, J. C. Ogden, J. Roughgarden, R. M. Starr, M. J. Tenger, and M. M. Yoklavich. 1999. No-take reserve networks: Sustaining fishery populations and marine ecosystems. Fisheries 24:11–25.

Needle, C. L. 2001. Recruitment models: Diagnosis and prognosis. Reviews in Fish Biology and Fisheries 11:95–111.

Neubauer, P., O. P. Jensen, J. A. Hutchings, and J. K. Baum. 2013. Resilience and recovery of overexploited marine populations. Science 340:347–349.

Nickelson, T. E., and P. W. Lawson. 1998. Population viability of coho salmon, *Oncorhynchus kisutch*, in Oregon coastal basins: application of a habitat-based life cycle model. Canadian Journal of Fisheries and Aquatic Sciences 55: 2383–2392.

Nishizaki, M. T., and J. D. Ackerman. 2007. Juvenile–adult associations in sea urchins (*Strongylocentrotus franciscanus* and *S. droebachiensis*): Protection from predation and hydrodynamics in *S. franciscanus*. Marine Biology 151:135–145.

NMFS (National Marine Fisheries Service). 2012. Fisheries economics of the United States, 2011. U.S. Department of Commerce, NOAA Technical Memorandum NMFS-F/SPO-128. <https://www.st.nmfs.noaa.gov/st5/publication/index.html>. Accessed January 15, 2014.

NOAA Catch Share Policy. <http://www.nmfs.noaa.gov/sfa/management/catch_shares/about/documents/noaa_cs_policy.pdf> Accessed January 15, 2014.

Northern Anchovy Fishery Management Plan (FMP). 1983. Final Supplementary Environmental Impact Statement and Draft Regulatory Impact Review/Initial Regulatory Flexibility Analysis. Pacific Fishery Management Council, Portland, Oregon.

NRC (National Research Council). 2004. Cooperative research in the National Marine Fisheries Service. National Academies Press, Washington, D.C.

———. 2001. Marine protected areas: Tools for sustaining ocean ecosystems. National Academy Press, Washington, D.C.

O'Farrell, M. R., and L. W. Botsford. 2006. The fisheries management implications of maternal–age-dependent larval survival. Canadian Journal of Fisheries and Aquatic Sciences 63:2249–2258.

O'Farrell et al. 2013. Klamath River Fall Chinook Salmon Age-Specific Escapement, River Harvest, and Run Size Estimates, 2012 Run. <http://www.pcouncil.org/wp-content/uploads/age_comp_final_27Feb2013.pdf>. Accessed February 19, 2014.

O'Farrell, M. R., M. M. Yoklavich, and M. S. Love. 2009. Assessment of habitat and predator effects on dwarf rockfishes (*Sebastes* spp.) using multi model inference. Environmental biology of fishes 85:239–250.

Olsen, E. M., M. Heino, G. R. Lilly, M. J. Morgan, J. Brattey, B. Ernande, and U. Dieckmann. 2004. Maturation trends indicative of rapid evolution preceded the collapse of northern cod. Nature 428:932–935.

Olson, J. 2011. Understanding and contextualizing social impacts from the privatization of fisheries: An overview. Ocean and Coastal Management 54:353–363.

Ono, K., D. S. Holland, and R. Hilborn. 2013. How does species association affect mixed stock fisheries management? A comparative analysis of the effect of marine protected areas, discard bans, and individual fishing quotas. Canadian Journal of Fisheries and Aquatic Sciences 70:1792–1804.

Osgood, K. E.. 2008. Climate Impacts on U.S. Living Marine Resources: National Marine Fisheries Service Concerns, Activities and Needs. U.S. Department of Commerce, NOAA Technical Memorandum. NMFSF/SPO-89, 118 pages.

Ottersen, G., D. Ø. Hjermann, and N. C. Stenseth. 2006. Changes in spawning stock structure strengthen the link between climate and recruitment in a heavily fished cod (*Gadus morhua*) stock. Fisheries Oceanography 15:230–243.

Ovando, D. A., R. T. Deacon, S. E. Lester, C. Costello, T. Van Leuvan, K. McIlwain, C. K. Strauss, M. Arbuckle, R. Fujita, S. Gelcich, and H. Uchida. 2013. Conservation incentives and collective choices in cooperative fisheries. Marine Policy 37:132–140.

Pacific Fishery Management Council (PFMC). 2013. Pacific Coast Fishery Ecosystem Plan for the U.S. Portion of the California Current Large Marine Ecosystem. Pacific Fishery Management Council, Portland, Oregon. <http://www.pcouncil.org/ecosystem-based-management/fep/>. Accessed February 26, 2014.

Palumbi, S. R., P. A. Sandifer, J. D. Allan, M. W. Beck, D. G. Fautin, M. J. Fogarty, B. S. Halpern, L. S. Incze, J.-A. Leong, E. Norse, J. J. Stachowicz, and D. H. Wall. 2008. Managing for ocean biodiversity to sustain marine ecosystem services. Frontiers in Ecology and the Environment 7:204–211.

Parma, A. M. 2002. In search of robust harvest rules for Pacific halibut in the face of uncertain assessments and decadal changes in productivity. Bulletin of Marine Science 70:423–453.

Parslow, J. 2010. Individual transferable quotas and the "tragedy of the commons." Canadian Journal of Fisheries and Aquatic Sciences 67:1889–1896.

Patrick, W. S., P. Spencer, J. Link, J. Cope, J. Field, D. Kobayashi, P. Lawson, T. Gedamke, E. Cortés, O. Ormseth, K. Bigelow, and W. Overholtz. 2010. Using productivity and susceptibility indices to assess the vulnerability of United States fish stocks to overfishing. Fishery Bulletin 108:305–322.

Pauly, D., V. Christensen, J. Dalsgaard, R. Froese, and F. Torres. 1998. Fishing down marine food webs. Science 279:860–863.

Perry, R. I., P. Cury, K. Brander, S. Jennings, C. Möllmann, and B. Planque. 2010. Sensitivity of marine systems to climate and fishing: Concepts, issues, and management responses. Journal of Marine Systems 79:427–435.

Petitgas, P., D. H. Secor, I. McQuinn, G. Huse, and N. Lo. 2010. Stock collapses and their recovery: Mechanisms that establish and maintain life-cycle closure in space and time. ICES Journal of Marine Science 67:1841–1848.

Pikitch, E. K., C. Santora, E. A. Babcock, A. Baku, R. Bonfil, D. O. Conover, P. Dayton, P. Doukakis, D. Fluharty, B. Heneman, E. D. Houde, J. Link, P. A. Livingston, M. Mangel, M. K. McAllister, J. Pope, and K. J. Sainsbury. 2004. Ecosystem-Based Fishery Management. Science 305: 346–347.

Pinnegar, J. K., N. V. C. Polunin, P. Francour, F. Badalamenti, R. Chemello, M. L. Harmelin-Vivien, B. hereu, M. Milazzo, M. Zabala, G. D'Anna, and C. Pipitone. 2000. Trophic cascades in benthic marine ecosystems: Lessons for fisheries and protected-area management. Environmental Conservation 27:179–200.

Pinsky, M. L., and M. Fogarty. 2012. Lagged social-ecological responses to climate and range shifts in fisheries. Climatic Change 115: 883–891.

Pitcher, Tony J. 2001. Fisheries managed to rebuild ecosystems? Reconstructing the past to salvage the future. Ecological Applications 11:601–617.

Planque, B., J. M. Fromentin, P. Cury, K. F. Drinkwater, S. Jennings, R. I. Perry, and S. Kifani. 2010. How does fishing alter marine populations and ecosystems sensitivity to climate? Journal of Marine Systems 79:403–417.

Poloczanska, E. S., C. J. Brown, W. J. Sydeman, W. Kiessling, D. S. Schoeman, P. J. Moore, K. Brander, J. F. Bruno, L. B. Buckley, M. T. Burrows, C. M. Duarte, B. S. Halpern, J. Holding, C. V. Kappel, M. I. O'Connor, J. M. Pandolfi, C. Parmesan, F. Schwing, S. A. Thompson, and A. J. Richardson. 2013. Global imprint of climate change on marine life. Nature Climate Change 3: 919–925.

Polovina, J. J., M. Abecassis, E. A. Howell, and P. Woodworth. 2009. Increases in the relative abundance of mid-trophic level fishes concurrent with declines in apex predators in the subtropical North Pacific, 1996-2006. Fishery Bulletin 107:532–531.

Polson, M. P., and D. C. Zacherl. 2009. Geographic distribution and intertidal population status for the Olympia oyster, *Ostrea lurida* Carpenter 1864, from Alaska to Baja. Journal of Shellfish Research 28:69–77.

Pondella, D. J., II, and L. G. Allen. 2008. The decline and recovery of four predatory fishes from the Southern California Bight. Marine Biology 154:307–313.

Pribyl, A. L., C. B. Schreck, M. L. Kent, K. M. Kelley, and S. J. Parker. 2012. Recovery potential of black rockfish, *Sebastes melanops* Girard, recompressed following barotrauma. Journal of Fish Diseases 35:275–286.

Prince, J. 2010. Rescaling fisheries assessment and management: A generic approach, access rights, change agents, and toolboxes. Bulletin of Marine Science 86:197–219.

Prince, J. D., N. A. Dowling, C. R. Davies, R. A. Campbell, and D. S. Kolody. 2011. A simple cost-effective and scale-less empirical approach to harvest strategies. ICES Journal of Marine Science 68:947–960.

Punt, A. E., and S. Ralston. 2007. A management strategy evaluation of rebuilding revision rules for overfished rockfish stocks. Pages 329–351 in J. Heifetz, J. Dicosimo, A. J. Gharrett, M. S. Love, V. M. O'Connell, and R. D. Stanley, editors. Proceedings of the 2005 Lowell Wakefield Symposium—Biology, Assessment, and Management of North Pacific Rockfishes. Alaska Sea Grant College Program AK-SG-07-01. University of Alaska, Fairbanks, Alaska.

Punt, A. E., M. W. Dorn, and M. A. Haltuch. 2008. Evaluation of threshold management strategies for groundfish off the U.S. West Coast. Fisheries Research 94:251–266.

Quinn, T. J., II, and R. B. Deriso. 1999. Quantitative fish dynamics. Oxford University Press, Oxford, UK.

Ralston, S. 2002. West Coast groundfish harvest policy. North American Journal of Fisheries Management 22:249–250.

Ralston, S., A. E. Punt, O. S. Hamel, J. D. DeVore, and R. J. Conser. 2011. A meta-analytic approach to quantifying scientific uncertainty in stock assessments. Fishery Bulletin 109:217–231.

Ralston, S., and M. R. O'Farrell. 2008. Spatial variation in fishing intensity and its effect on yield. Canadian Journal of Fisheries and Aquatic Sciences 65:588–599.

Ralston, S., K. M. Sakuma, and J. C. Field. 2013. Interannual variation in pelagic juvenile rockfish abundance—going with the flow. Fisheries Oceanography 22:288–308.

Reeves, G. H., L. E. Benda, K. M. Burnett, P. A. Bisson, and J. R. Sedell. 1995. A disturbance-based ecosystem approach to maintaining and restoring freshwater habitats of evolutionarily significant units of anadromous salmonids in the Pacific Northwest. In American Fisheries Society Symposium 17:334–349.

Rice, J. C., and S. M. Garcia. 2011. Fisheries, food security, climate change, and biodiversity: Characteristics of the sector and perspectives on emerging issues. ICES Journal of Marine Science 68:1343–1353.

Ricker, W E. 1954. Stock and recruitment. Journal of the Fisheries Board of Canada 11: 559–623.

Rick, T. C., and J. M. Erlandson. 2000. Early Holocene fishing strategies on the California coast: Evidence from CA-SBA-2057. Journal of Archaeological Science 27:621–633.

Rogers-Bennett, L., and J. S. Pearse. 2001. Indirect benefits of marine protected areas for juvenile abalone. Conservation Biology 15: 642–647.

Rogers-Bennett, L. 2007. Is climate change contributing to range reductions and localized extinctions in northern (*Haliotis kamtschatkana*) and flat (*Haliotis walallensis*) abalones? Bulletin of Marine Science 81:283–296.

Rogers-Bennett, L., K. E. Hubbard, C. I. Juhasz. 2013. Dramatic declines in red abalone populations after opening a *de facto* marine reserve to fishing: Testing temporal reserves. Biological Conservation 157: 423–431.

Rogers-Bennett, L., R. F. Dondanville, J. D. Moore, and L. I. Vilchis. 2010. Response of red abalone reproduction to warm water, starvation, and disease stressors: Implications of ocean warming. Journal of Shellfish Research 29:599–611.

Rogers-Bennett, L., W. A. Bennett, H. C. Fastenau, and C. M. Dewees. 1995. Spatial variation in red sea urchin reproduction and morphology: implications for harvest refugia. Ecological Applications 5:1171–1180.

Rogers, B. L., C. G. Lowe, and E. Fernández-Juricic. 2011. Recovery of visual performance in rosy rockfish (*Sebastes* rosaceus) following exophthalmia resulting from barotrauma. Fisheries Research 112:1–7.

Ruckelshaus, M. H., P. Levin, J. B. Johnson, and P. M. Kareiva. 2002. The Pacific salmon wars: What science brings to the challenge of recovering species. Annual Review of Ecology and Systematics 33:665–706.

Saarman, E. T., and M. H. Carr. 2013. The California Marine Life Protection Act: A balance of top down and bottom up governance in MPA planning. Marine Policy 41:41–49.

Satterthwaite, W. H., M. S. Mohr, M. R. O'Farrell, E. C. Anderson, M. A. Banks, S. J. Bates, M. R. Bellinger, L. A. Borgerson, E. D. Crandall, J. C. Garza, B. J. Kormos, P. W. Lawson, and M. L. Palmer-Zwahlen. 2014. Use of genetic stock identification data for comparison of the ocean spatial distribution, size at age, and fishery exposure of an untagged stock and its indicator: California coastal versus Klamath River Chinook salmon. Transactions of the American Fisheries Society 143:117–133.

Satterthwaite, W. H., M. S. Mohr, M. R. O'Farrell, and B. K. Wells. 2013. A comparison of temporal patterns in the ocean spatial distribution of California's Central Valley Chinook salmon runs. Canadian Journal of Fisheries and Aquatic Sciences 70:574–584.

Schaefer, M. B. 1954. Some aspects of the dynamics of populations important to the management of the commercial marine fisheries. Bulletin of the Inter-American Tropical Tuna Commission 1:27–56.

Schindler, D. E., R. Hilborn, B. Chasco, C. P. Boatright, T. P. Quinn, L. A. Rogers, and M. S. Webster. 2010. Population diversity and the portfolio effect in an exploited species. Nature 465:609–612.

Schirripa, M. J., and J. J. Colbert. 2006. Interannual changes in sablefish (*Anoplopoma fimbria*) recruitment in relation to oceanographic conditions within the California Current System. Fisheries Oceanography 15: 25–36.

Schmidt, K. T. 2014. Life history changes in female blue rockfish, *Sebastes mystinus*, before and after overfishing, in central California. M.S. thesis. California State University, Monterey Bay. 94 pp.

Scholz, A., K. Bonzon, R. Fujita, N. Benjamin, N. Woodling, P. Black, and C. Steinback. 2004. Participatory socioeconomic analysis: Drawing on fishermen's knowledge for marine protected area planning in California. Marine Policy 28:335–349.

Schroeder, D. M., and M. S. Love. 2002. Recreational fishing and marine fish populations in California. California Cooperative Oceanic Fisheries Investigations Report 43: 182–190.

Schwartzlose, R.A., J. Alheit, A. Bakun, T. R. Baumgartner, R. Cloete, R. J. M. Crawford, W. J. Fletcher, Y Green-Ruiz, E. Hagen, T. kawasaki, D. Lluch-Belda, S.E. Lluch-Cota, A. D. MacCall, Y. Matsuura, M. O. Nevárez-Martínez, R. H. Parrish, C. Roy, R. Serra, K. V. Schust, M. N. Ward, and J. Z. Zuzunaga. 1999. Worldwide large-scale fluctuations of sardine and anchovy populations. South African Journal of Marine Science 21: 289–347.

Scofield, W. L. 1948. Trawling gear in California. California Division of Fish and Game. Fish Bulletin No. 72.

Sette, O. E., and R. H. Fiedler. 1928. Fishery Industries of the United States, 1927. In Report of the United States Commissioner of Fisheries for the Fiscal Year 1928. U.S. Department of Commerce.

Shanks, A. L., G. C. Roegner, and J. Miller. 2010. Using megalopae abundance to predict future commercial catches of Dungeness crabs (*Cancer magister*) in Oregon. CalCOFI Reports 51-106-118.

Shelton, A. O., and M. Mangel. 2011. Fluctuations of fish populations and the magnifying effects of fishing. Proceedings of the National Academy of Science 108:775–780.

Shepherd, J. G. 1990. Stability and the objectives of fisheries management: The scientific background. Ministry of Agriculture, Fisheries and Food, Directorate of Fisheries Research.

Sibert, J., J. Hampton, P. Kleiber, and M. Maunder. 2006. Biomass, size, and trophic status of top predators in the Pacific Ocean. Science 314:1773–1776.

Smith, A. D., C. J. Brown, C. M. Bulman, E. A. Fulton, P. Johnson, I. C. Kaplan, H. Lozano-Montez, S. Mackinson, M. Marzloff, L. J. Shannon, Y.-J. Shin, and J. Tam. 2011. Impacts of fishing low-trophic level species on marine ecosystems. Science 333:1147–1150.

Smith, M. D., and J. E. Wilen. 2003. Economic impacts of marine reserves: The importance of spatial behavior. Journal of Environmental Economics and Management 46:183–206.

Smith, T. D. 1994. Scaling fisheries. Cambridge University Press, Cambridge, UK.

Sogard, S. M., S. A. Berkeley, and R. Fisher. 2008. Maternal effects in rockfishes *Sebastes* spp.: A comparison among species. Marine Ecology Progress Series 360:227–236.

Spence, B. C., and J. D. Hall. 2010. Spatiotemporal patterns in migration timing of coho salmon (*Oncorhynchus kisutch*) smolts in North America. Canadian Journal of Fisheries and Aquatic Sciences 67:1316–1334.

Spence, B. C., E. P. Bjorkstedt, J. C. Garza, J. J. Smith , D. G. Hankin, D. Fuller, W. E. Jones, R. Macedo, T. H. Williams, and E. Mora. 2008. A framework for assessing the viability of threatened and endangered salmon and steelhead in the North Central California Coast recovery domain. NOAA Tech. Memo. NMFS-SWFSC-423. U.S. Department of Commerce.

Spencer, P. D., and M. W. Dorn. 2013. Incorporation of weight-specific relative fecundity and maternal effects in larval survival into stock assessments. Fisheries Research 138:159–167.

Spencer, P. D., S. B. Kraak, and E. A. Trippel. 2013. The influence of maternal effects in larval survival on fishery harvest reference points for two life-history patterns. Canadian Journal of Fisheries and Aquatic Sciences 70:1–11.

Springer, A. M., J. A. Estes, G. B. van Vliet, T. M. Williams, D. F.

Doak, E. M. Danner, K. A. Forney, and B. Pfister. 2003. Sequential megafaunal collapse in the North Pacific Ocean: An ongoing legacy of industrial whaling? Proceedings of the National Academy of Sciences 100:12223–12228.

Stachowicz, J. J., J. F. Bruno, and J. E. Duffy. 2007. Understanding the effects of marine biodiversity on communities and ecosystems. Annual Review of Ecology, Evolution, and Systematics 38:739–766.

Starr, R. M., C. Culver, C. Pomeroy, S. McMillan, T. Barnes, and D. Aseltine-Neilson. 2010. Proceedings of 2008 managing data-poor fisheries workshop: Case studies, models, and solutions. UC San Diego: California Sea Grant Program. San Diego, California.

Starr, R. M., M. Carr, D. Malone, A. Greenley, and S. McMillan. 2010. Complementary sampling methods to inform ecosystem-based management of nearshore fisheries. Marine and Coastal Fisheries 2:159–179.

Stevens, J. D., R. Bonfil, N. K. Dulvy, and P. A. Walker. 2000. The effects of fishing on sharks, rays, and chimaeras (chondrichthyans), and the implications for marine ecosystems. Journal of Marine Science 57:476–494.

Stewart, J. S., E. L. Hazen, S. J. Bograd, J.E.K. Byrnes, D. G. Foley, W. F. Gilly, B. H. Robison, and J. C. Field. 2014. Combined climate-and prey-mediated range expansion of Humboldt squid (*Dosidicus gigas*), a large marine predator in the California Current System. Global Change Biology 20:1832–1843.

Stewart, B. S., P. K. Yochem, H. R. Huber, R. L. DeLong, R. J. Jameson, W. J. Sydeman, S. G. Allen, and B. J. Le Boeuf. 1994. p. 29–48 in Le Boeuf, B. J., and R. M. Laws. Elephant seals: population ecology, behavior, and physiology. University of California Press. Berkeley, California.

Stierhoff, K. L., M. Neuman, and J. L. Butler. 2012. On the road to extinction? Population declines of the endangered white abalone, *Haliotis sorenseni*. Biological Conservation 152:46–52.

Studebaker, R. S., and T. J. Mulligan. 2008. Temporal variation and feeding ecology of juvenile *Sebastes* in rocky intertidal tidepools of northern California, with emphasis on *Sebastes* melanops Girard. Journal of Fish Biology 72:1393–1405.

Sumaila, U. R. 2010. A cautionary note on individual transferable quotas. Ecology and Society 15:1–8.

Sydeman, W. J., and S. G. Allen. 1999. Pinniped population dynamics in central California: correlations with sea surface temperature and upwelling indices. Marine Mammal Science 15: 446–461.

Sydeman, W. J., K. L. Mills, J. A. Santora, S. A. Thompson, D. F. Bertram, K. H. Morgan, J. M. Hipfner, B. K. Wells, and S. G. Wolf. 2009. Seabirds and climate in the California Current—a synthesis of change. California Cooperative Fisheries Investigative Reports 50: 82–104.

Tegner, M. J., and L. A. Levin. 1983. Spiny lobsters and sea urchins: Analysis of a predator-prey interaction. Journal of Experimental Marine Biology and Ecology 73:125–150.

Tegner M. J., and P. K. Dayton. 2000. Ecosystem effects of fishing in kelp forest communities. ICES Journal of Marine Science 57:579–589.

Thorson, J. T., I. J. Stewart, I. G. Taylor, and A. E. Punt. 2013. Using a recruitment-linked multispecies stock assessment model to estimate common trends in recruitment for US West Coast groundfishes. Marine Ecology Progress Series 483:245–256.

Thorson, J. T., J. M. Cope, T. A. Branch, and O. P. Jensen. 2012. Spawning biomass reference points for exploited marine fishes, incorporating taxonomic, and body size information. Canadian Journal of Fisheries and Aquatic Sciences 69:1556–1568.

Thrush, S. F., and P. K. Dayton. 2002. Disturbance to marine benthic habitats by trawling and dredging: implications for marine biodiversity. Annual Review of Ecology and Systematics 33:449–473.

Tissot, B. N., M. M. Yoklavich, M. S. Love, K. York, and M. Amend. 2006. Benthic invertebrates that form habitat on deep banks off southern California, with special reference to deep sea coral. Fishery Bulletin 104:167–181.

Toft, J. E., A. E. Punt, and L. R. Little. 2011. Modelling the economic and ecological impacts of the transition to individual transferable quotas in the multispecies U.S. West Coast groundfish trawl fleet. ICES Journal of Marine Science 68:1566–1579.

Tønnessen, J. N., and A. O. Johnsen. 1982. The history of modern whaling. University of California Press, Berkeley, California.

Trimble, A. C., J. L. Ruesink, and B. R. Dumbauld. 2009. Factors preventing the recovery of a historically overexploited shellfish species, *Ostrea lurida* Carpenter 1864. Journal of Shellfish Research 28:97–106.

Tromble G. R., D. M. Lambert, and L. R. Benaka. 2009. Prelude to sustainability: ending overfishing in U.S. fisheries; p. 57–66. in Our Living Oceans, Report on the Status of U.S. Living Marine Resources. 6th ed. U.S. Department of Commerce, NOAA Technical Memorandum, NMFS-F/SPO-80.

U.S. Commission on Ocean Policy. 2004. An ocean blueprint for the 21st century. USCOP, Washington, D.C.

Vilchis, L. I., M. J. Tegner, J. D. Moore, C. S. Friedman, K. L. Riser, T. T. Robbins, and P. K. Dayton. 2005. Ocean warming effects on growth, reproduction, and survivorship of southern California abalone. Ecological Applications 15:469–480.

Vojkovich, M. 1998. The California fishery for market squid (*Loligo opalescens*). CalCOFI Reports 39:55–60.

Wagner, E. L., and P. D. Boersma. 2011. Effects of fisheries on seabird community ecology. Reviews in Fisheries Science 19:157–167.

Walters, C., and J. F. Kitchell. 2001. Cultivation/depensation effects on juvenile survival and recruitment: Implications for the theory of fishing. Canadian Journal of Fisheries and Aquatic Sciences 58: 39–50.

Weber, M. L., and B. Heneman. 2000. Guide to the California's Marine Life Management Act. Common Knowledge Press, Bolinas, California.

Wells, B. K., C. B. Grimes, and J. B. Waldvogel. 2007. Quantifying the effects of wind, upwelling, curl, sea surface temperature, and sea level height on growth and maturation of a California Chinook salmon (*Oncorhynchus tshawytscha*) population. Fisheries Oceanography16:363–382.

Wendt, D. E., and R. M. Starr. 2009. Collaborative research: An effective way to collect data for stock assessments and evaluate marine protected areas in California. Marine and Coastal Fisheries: Dynamics, Management, and Ecosystem Science 1:315–324.

Wendt, D. E, L. Pendleton, and D. L. Maruska. 2009. Morro Bay, California: A case study of ecosystem-based management through community action. Pages 183–200 in K. L. McLeod and H. M. Leslie, editors. Ecosystem-based Management for the Oceans. Island Press, Washington, D.C.

Whitaker, A. R. 2008. Incipient aquaculture in prehistoric California?: Long-term productivity and sustainability vs. immediate returns for the harvest of marine invertebrates. Journal of Archaeological Science 35:1114–1123.

White, J. W., L.W. Botsford, A. Hastings, M. L. Baskett, D. M. Kaplan, and L. A. K. Barnett. 2013. Transient responses of fished population to marine reserve establishment. Conservation Letters 6:180–191.

White, J. W., L. W. Botsford, A. Hastings, and J. L. Largier. 2010. Population persistence in marine reserve networks: Incorporating spatial heterogeneities in larval dispersal. Marine Ecology Progress Series 38:49–67.

White, C., B. E. Kendall, S. Gaines, D. A. Siegel, and C. Costello. 2008. Marine reserve effects on fishery profit. Ecology Letters 11:370–379.

White, J. W., and L. Rogers-Bennett. 2010. Incorporating physical oceanographic proxies of recruitment into population models to improve fishery and marine protected area management. Cal COFI Reports 51:128–149.

White, J. W., A. J. Scholz, A. Rassweiler, C. Steinback, L. W. Botsford, S. Kruse, C. Costello, S. Mitarai, D. A. Siegel, P. T. Drake, and C. A. Edwards. 2012. A comparison of approaches used for economic analysis in marine protected area network planning in California. Ocean Coastal Management 74:77–89.

———. 2013. A comparison of approaches used for economic analysis in marine protected area network planning in California. Ocean and Coaastal Management 74: 77–89.

Williams, J. P., L. G. Allen, M. A. Steele, and D. J. Pondella II. 2007. El Niño/Southern Oscillation events increase growth of juvenile white seabass (*Atractoscion nobilis*) in the Southern California Bight. Marine Biology 152:193–200.

Wilson, J. R., J. D. Prince, and H. S. Lenihan. 2010. A management strategy for sedentary nearshore species that uses marine protected areas as a reference. Marine and Coastal Fisheries 2:14–27.

Winemiller, K. O., and K. A. Rose. 1992. Patterns of life-history diversification in North American fishes: Implications for population regulation. Canadian Journal of Fisheries and Aquatic Sciences 49:2196–2218.

Worden, L., L. W. Botsford, A. Hastings, and M. D. Holland. 2010. Frequency responses of age-structured populations: Pacific salmon as an example. Journal of Theoretical Population Biology 78:239–249.

Worm, B., E. B. Barbier, N. Beaumont, J. E. Duffy, C. Folke, B. S. Halpern, J. B. C. Jackson, H. K. Lotke, F. Micheli, S. R. Palumbi, E. Sala, K. A. Selkoe, J. J. Stachowicz, and R. Watson. 2006. Impacts of biodiversity loss on ocean ecosystem services. Science 314:787–790.

Worm, B., R. Hilborn, J. K. Baum, T. A. Branch, J. S. Collie, C. Costello, M. J. Fogarty, E. A. Fulton, J. A. Hutchings, S. Jennings, O. P. Jensen, H. K. Lotke, P. M. Mace, T. R. McClanahan, C. Minto, S. R. Palumbi, A. M. Parma, D. Ricard, A. A. Rosenberg, R. Watson, and D. Zeller. 2009. Rebuilding global fisheries. Science 325:578–585.

Yochum, N., R. M. Starr, and D. E. Wendt. 2011. Utilizing fishermen knowledge and expertise: Keys to success for collaborative fisheries research. Fisheries 36:593–605.

Yoshiyama, R. M., F. W. Fisher, and P. B. Moyle. 1998. Historical abundance and decline of Chinook salmon in the Central Valley region of California. North American Journal of Fisheries Management 18:487–521.

Zabel, R. W., P. S. Levin, N. Tolimieri, and N. J. Mantua. 2011. Interactions between climate and population density in the episodic recruitment of bocaccio, *Sebastes paucispinis*, a Pacific rockfish. Fisheries Oceanography 20:294–304.

Zhou, S. 2008. Fishery by-catch and discards: A positive perspective from ecosystem-based fishery management. Fish and Fisheries 9(3):308–315.

Zhou, S., A. D. Smith, A. E. Punt, A. J. Richardson, M. Gibbs, M., E. A. Fulton, S. Pascoe, C. Bulma, P. Bayliss, and K. Sainsbury. 2010. Ecosystem-based fisheries management requires a change to the selective fishing philosophy. Proceedings of the National Academy of Sciences 107:9485–9489.

Zwolinski, J. P., and D. A. Demer. 2012. A cold oceanographic regime with high exploitation rates in the northeast Pacific forecasts a collapse of the sardine stock. Proceedings of the National Academy of Sciences 109:4175–4180.

THIRTY-SIX

Forestry

WILLIAM STEWART, BENKTESH SHARMA, ROB YORK, LOWELL DILLER,
NADIA HAMEY, ROGER POWELL, and ROBERT SWIERS

Introduction

Forestry is the practice of creating, managing, using, and conserving forests to sustainably meet desired social goals, needs, and values. In California, active forest management is currently limited to productive timberlands that are not in parks or preserves. Timberlands are forests that can be managed for the sustainable production of wood products. The 1.65 million hectares of private timberlands and 2.55 million hectares of National Forest timberlands represent 30% of California's total forest area (Table 36.1). Forest lands not classified as timberlands either have low site productivity or are reserved forest lands. An additional 0.88 million hectares of ecologically similar forests are permanently reserved from wood products utilization through statute or administrative designation. The reserved forest lands provide an example of what timberlands could look like without harvesting. From an economic standpoint, economic timberlands can be described as lands that, under guidance by local, state, and federal environmental regulations, can sustain positive revenues from the sale of wood products such as building materials, fuelwood, and paper products after deducting resource management expenses. If they do not provide positive net revenues, private timberlands can be converted to residential or recreational land uses, and public timberlands need to be financed like parks through general government revenues and user fees. In addition to the global ecosystem service of carbon sequestration that the forest and wood products provide, different forest management approaches also affect other ecosystem services such as biodiversity, water quality and quantity, and amenity values. The goal of this chapter is to describe how different management regimes affect California's forest ecosystems and their provision of ecosystem services.

Most of California's timberlands fall into four of the ten major forest type groups defined by the Forest Inventory and Analysis (FIA) program (Christensen 2008). California mixed conifer, ponderosa pine, Douglas-fir, and redwood forest types contain commercially valuable tree species such as ponderosa pine (*Pinus ponderosa*), Jeffrey pine (*P. jeffreyii*), sugar pine (*Pinus lambertiana*), Douglas-fir (*Pseudotsuga menziesii*), white fir (*Abies concolor*), incense cedar (*Calocedrus decurrens*), and coast redwood (*Sequoia sempervirens*). The California mixed conifer forests are the most extensive type and are intermixed with ponderosa pine forests on drier and less

TABLE 36.1
Forest area by owner of all forests in California (hectares)

Forest types	Private forest land	National forest timberland	Reserved forest land	Total
Major timberland forests (California mixed conifer, ponderosa pine, Douglas-fir, redwood)	1,653,000	2,255,000	878,000	4,785,000
Other coniferous forests	414,000	632,000	1,857,000	2,903,000
Hardwood forests and nonstocked forest lands	3,075,000	811,000	1,626,000	5,512,000
TOTAL FOREST	**5,141,000**	**3,698,000**	**4,361,000**	**13,200,000**

SOURCE: PNW-FIA 2013.

productive sites. The redwood forests type hugs the Pacific Ocean and grades into Douglas-fir forests on drier and more interior sites. The FIA network consists of thousands of forest plots that are remeasured every decade. This provides an unbiased database of vegetation across wide ranges of physiographic and ownership conditions (Figure 36.1).

A Natural Experiment

California's timberlands have been shaped by a long and varied history of anthropogenic and natural influences. Private and public ownership classes within timberlands of each forest type share broadly similar geology, climate, fire regimes, fauna and flora. These characteristics are described in other chapters in this book (see Chapters 26–28). The current mosaic of vegetation and habitat diversity on the timberlands reflects a long legacy of active timber harvesting since the 1850s, effective fire suppression since the 1920s, a dependence on natural regeneration rather than plantation plantings, and the ongoing impact of large wildfires and other disturbance agents such as insects and pathogens. The FIA program provides plot-level and aggregated data that includes forest area, detailed tree demographics, basic life form information on forbs and shrubs, and other soils, disturbances, and air pollution data (Christensen 2008). The amount of wood products removed or potentially removable is commonly measured in terms of the amount of final product. Board foot measurements refer to the amount of lumber, or sawn wood, that could be extracted from a tree or forest stand (Tappeiner et al. 2007). This represents about half of the total usable volume measured in board feet of wood that is currently utilized for lumber, energy, pulpwood, and other wood products (Morgan et al. 2012). Harvest volumes in this chapter have been converted to metric units from the more widely used estimates based on board foot measurements unless noted otherwise.

Harvests, fires, grazing, and biotic disturbances such as disease and insect outbreaks have extensively altered current and historical timberlands since the California Gold Rush. Historical harvesting and fires followed by natural regeneration often involved significant levels of soil erosion and impacts to other forest characteristics such as fish and wildlife habitats. Forest harvesting and regeneration on private timberlands are regulated under California's Forest Practice Rules (California Department of Forestry and Fire Protection 2013), where Section 897 describes how landowners who desire a harvesting permit are required to "achieve a balance between growth and harvest over time consistent with the harvesting methods within the rules of the Board, maintain functional wildlife habitat . . . , retain or recruit late and diverse seral stage habitat components . . . , and maintain growing stock, genetic diversity, and soil productivity." Management of timberlands in federal ownership depends on the land management plans that direct management actions (U.S. Forest Service and U.S. Bureau of Land Management 2000, U.S. Forest Service Pacific Southwest Region 2004), legal definitions on some areas that prohibit commercial timber harvesting, and budget constraints. Since 2000, most National Forest timberlands have experienced very limited management actions except for fire suppression (USDA Forest Service PSW Region Remote Sensing Lab 2007) (in Christensen 2008). The reserved forest land category may have had some historical harvests but are now mainly in state parks, national parks, wilderness, or roadless areas where commercial timber harvesting is not permitted. For simplicity, the minor amounts of forest under Bureau of Land Management, Department of Defense, and U.S. Fish and Wildlife Service management are also placed in the reserved forest land statistics.

For the timberlands at the focus of this chapter, government ownership dominates the interior California mixed conifer and ponderosa pine forest types while private ownership dominates the Douglas-fir forests and the redwood forest type closer to the coast (Table 36.2). The highly productive redwood forests are in either private ownership or public parks after being purchased by private, state, and federal entities. Private timberlands in interior forest types generally produce 10–15% more timber than public timberlands and currently have 25% lower inventories due to more harvests over time (Tables 36.3 and 36.4).

Having three distinct management regimes—private timberlands, National Forest timberlands, and reserved forest land—on forests that all have the biological capacity to be managed to produce wood products is essentially a broadly applied, ongoing natural experiment (Walters and Holling 1990). Comparing these three regimes can provide retrospec-

Photo on previous page: Ten- to one-hundred-year-old regenerating forest stands in a central Sierra mixed conifer forest. Photo: Rob York.

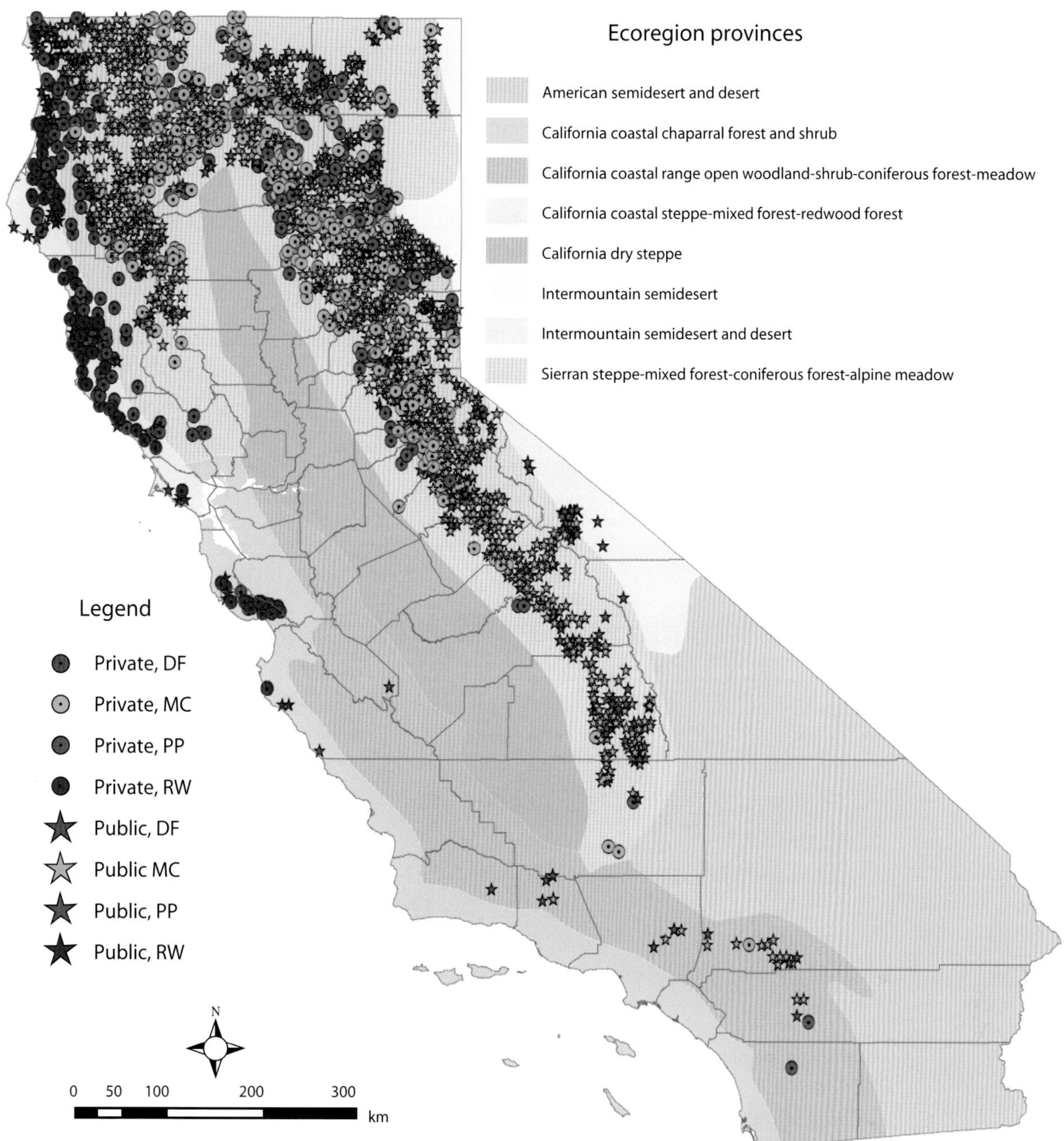

FIGURE 36.1 Locations of FIA (Forest Inventory and Analysis) plots of the four major production forest types by ownership class (private, public). Source: PNW-FIA 2013.

DF: Douglas-fir, **MC**: mixed conifer, **PP**: ponderosa pine, **RW**: redwood.

tive insights into how historic and current forestry activities affect both global and local ecosystem services. As with many natural experiments, consistency of initial conditions, replications, and controls are somewhat constrained. The most significant global ecosystem services provided by timberlands are the global carbon cycle impacts of maintaining high forest carbon stocks (Hayes et al. 2012); and the sustainable supply of products that can replace fossil-fuel based alternatives such as coal, cement, steel, and plastics as well as provide additional carbon storage (Nabuurs et al. 2007, Canadell and Raupach 2008, Malmsheimer et al. 2011). While historic conversion efficiencies of trees to products were low (Harmon et al. 1996), they are increasing (Skog 2008, Smith et al. 2009, Morgan et al. 2012) and further improvements are feasible. Different forest management practices also affect localized ecosystem services such as plant and animal biodiversity, protection of clean air and clean water resources, and the maintenance of soil resources. The amenity values of forests are primarily a function of visitation and visibility. Amenity values are highest for scenic forests near urban areas and in accessible parks, moderate on public forests and family-owned forests, and lowest on industrial forest lands where recreational infrastructure is limited (Fire and Resource Assessment Program 2003).

TABLE 36.2

Forest area by owner of the four major timberland types (hectares)

Forest type	Private timberland	National forest timberland	Reserved forest land	Total
California mixed conifer	847,000	1,680,000	630,000	3,157,000
Ponderosa pine	304,000	477,000	119,000	900,000
Douglas-fir	273,000	98,000	71,000	441,000
Redwood	229,000	–	58,000	287,000
TOTAL FOREST	**1,653,000**	**2,255,000**	**878,000**	**4,785,000**

SOURCE: PNW-FIA 2013.

TABLE 36.3

Average site productivity by forest type and owner (m^3 ha^{-1} $year^{-1}$) based on FIA estimates of potential annual commercial wood volume production

Forest type	Private timberland	National forest timberland	Reserved forest land
California mixed conifer	7.7	7.0	6.8
Ponderosa pine	6.4	4.8	5.4
Douglas-fir	9.2	5.8	9.1
Redwood	12.9	–	12.2
Area weighted average for four timberland forest types	8.4	6.4	7.1
Area weighted average for nonredwood forests	7.7	6.5	6.8

SOURCE: PNW-FIA 2013.

TABLE 36.4

Average and interquartile range for carbon mass (MgC ha^{-1}) by forest type and owner

Forest type	Private timberland	National forest timberland	Reserved forest land
California mixed conifer	70 (31–92)	108 (46–150)	104 (54–137)
Ponderosa pine	51 (22–71)	59 (18–69)	63 (22–64)
Douglas-fir	118 (64–140)	142 (43–208)	157 (83–240)
Redwood	153 (61–227)	N/A	435 (205–552)

SOURCE: PNW-FIA 2013.

History of California's Timberlands

1849–1949

The Gold Rush set off a huge growth in the demand for lumber to build flumes, mining towns, new cities, and railroads. The first sawmills were built in the Sierra Nevada near gold-mining regions where wood was also the main source of heat. When John Leiberg surveyed the forests of the Feather, Yuba, Bear, American, and Truckee watersheds in the 1890s, he estimated that 42% of the forests had been harvested for lumber or fuel and that 24% of the forests had been severely burned by wildfires that were intentionally or accidentally set by the new residents (Leiberg 1902).

Access to the enormous redwood forests along the North Coast started in the 1860s, leading to the development of many sawmills that sent much of their production to San Francisco, which then became the hub of a maritime-lumber market. The San Francisco–based lumber market delivered wood around the Pacific Rim (Williams 1989). In addition, large areas of forests were given to companies by the federal government in a checkerboard pattern to entice them to build railroads. The federal forest reserve system brought an end to the policy of the federal government selling forest lands and resulted in large areas of forest eventually becoming managed as National Forests and National Parks (Dana and Fairfax 1980).

California's sawmill production surveys from 1849 to 1946 record harvests of 2.4 million cubic meters (1.0 billion board feet) of lumber per year (Steer 1948). Oregon and Washington produced 10.4 million cubic meters (4.4 billion board feet) of lumber per year over this span and exported much of their production to California (Steer 1948). Sawmill- and forest-based volume estimates reported in board feet of lumber refer to the volume of finished products rather than the volume of trees harvested. It is estimated that at least an equivalent amount of biomass was removed for products such as fuel (Figure 36.2), other building products, and pulpwood (Hair and Ulrich 1967). Tops, branches, and small trees were left at the logging sites where there was not a strong demand for fuelwood. Preferential harvesting of pines shifted the species balance towards less valuable white fir and incense cedar across much of California's mixed conifer and pine forests. During this era, statewide output was mainly pine (53%), redwood (23%), and Douglas-fir (11%) with the shade-tolerant true firs and incense cedar making up only 10% of the total lumber harvest (Steer 1948).

FIGURE 36.2 Logging railroad of the Michigan–California Lumber Company close to Pino Grande, El Dorado County, California, showing piles of slab wood fuel for the railroad engines, May 1925. Though slab wood was an expensive form of fuel, its use meant closer utilization of the forest products. Photo: Courtesy of the Marian Koshland Bioscience and Natural Resources Library, UC Berkeley <http://lib.berkeley.edu/BIOS>.

1950–1999

Increased demand from a growing economy and the opening up of National Forests to more timber harvesting characterized this half-century. Annual timber output during this period averaged 8.5 million cubic meters (3.6 billion board feet) per year of lumber with roughly equivalent removals for pulp chips and energy (Hair and Ulrich 1967). Private timber production peaked in the early 1950s, but newly roaded areas of the National Forests kept statewide harvest levels high through the 1970s. Beginning in the 1970s, large areas of National Forest lands with forest cover, some of which had been harvested, received wilderness and roadless designations and were then removed from the production base. While reductions in forest cover and biomass have been documented to increase water yields (Zhang et al. 2001) that are highly valued in California when they can be diverted to farms and cities, damages to water quality led to major efforts to strengthen regulations and to improve best management practices (Ice et al. 2004, Rice et al. 2004) to limit erosion from logging operations and roads.

As the century ended, concerns over a number of endangered animal and fish species associated with forests and forest streams led to sharp reductions in harvests on both federal and private timberlands. The expansion of the temporary and permanent road and skid trail networks related to timber harvesting during this period had led to significant increases in soil erosion into streams. The most significant negative impacts occurred in the highly erosive North Coast, where road building and mechanical timber harvesting generated huge pulses of sediment into streams and rivers that severely impacted salmonid populations (Yoshiyama and Moyle 2010; see Chapter 33, "Rivers"). Expensive restoration efforts to improve salmonid habitats began near the end of the century.

2000–2013

After a fifty-year era of significant harvests from both private and federal lands, harvest volumes now come primarily from private lands. Annual timber harvests have declined to 2.6 million cubic meters (1.1 billion board feet) with two-thirds of the current timber harvest consisting of high-value species such as redwood, Douglas-fir, and pines, and the remaining one-third consisting mainly of lower-value white fir (Morgan et al. 2012). Harvest methods on private timberlands in California are unique on the West Coast in that they are dominated by selection and intermediate harvests rather than clearcut harvests to produce timber. Harvesting only some of the trees in any given area leaves the majority of the trees and other vegetation but also involves more frequent entries into the forest. However, in the years preceding the economic slowdown of 2008, the area permitted for selection harvest prescriptions on private lands declined more rapidly than that permitted for 1–20 hectare units of clearcut harvests (Figures 36.3, 36.4).

Private landowners who want to reduce numbers of small trees to reduce fire risk or shift resource availability to more commercially valuable trees typically bundle these activities with commercial harvests (Stewart and Nakamura 2012). By the end of this period, the U.S. Forest Service restated their mission around the concept of ecological restoration, which limited the amounts of harvested products (U.S. Forest Service Pacific Southwest Region 2013). On the North Coast, ecological restoration related to protecting and improving salmonid habitats has been accomplished with considerable investment of public funds. In addition, projects such as the creation of the 9,000 hectare Yurok Tribal Community Forest from lands previously owned by Green Diamond Resources Company create forests where fisheries and wildlife habitat protection become the dominant management goals.

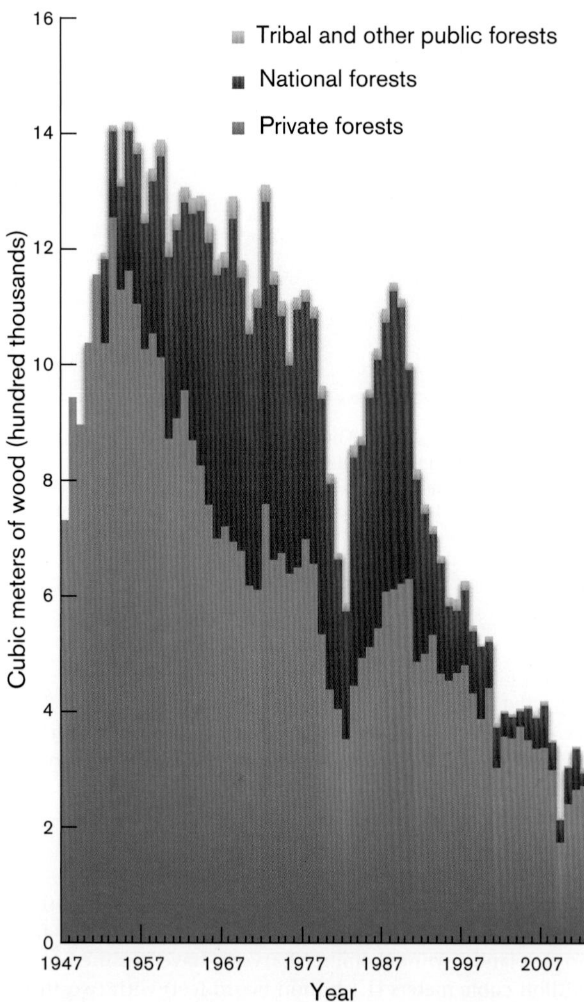

FIGURE 36.3 California timber harvest by ownership class, 1947–2012. Morgan et al. 2012.

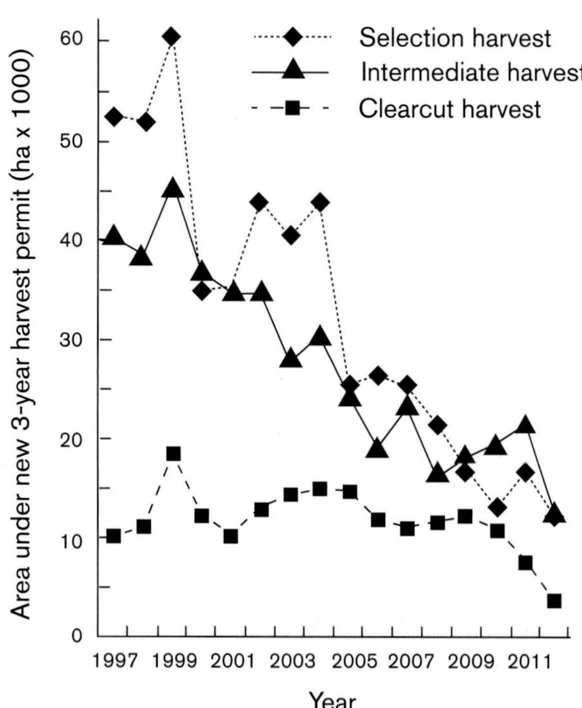

FIGURE 36.4 Area of private harvest by major silvicultural types. Source: Cal Fire 2013b.

Global Ecosystem Services under Different Forest Management Regimes

Temperate forests are major carbon sinks (Ciais et al. 2013) even with the majority of these forests periodically harvested for products (Smith et al. 2009, Nabuurs et al. 2013, Canadian Forest Services 2013). Different forest types as well as management regimes have unique net tree growth, natural emissions, and harvest patterns that influence forest carbon sequestration estimates (Hayes et al. 2012). Private timberland owners typically have a greater focus on maximizing net growth than managers of National Forest timberlands. Within each major forest type, private timberlands maintain lower inventory per hectare (see Table 36.4) but produce considerably more wood products (Tables 36.5 and 36.6). Losses to fires, insects, and disease are more pronounced in California's dry interior forests than in the moister redwood and Douglas-fir forests along the Coast. How effectively society uses the harvested wood products to reduce fossil fuel–related emissions and maintain carbon storage during wood product use lifetimes as well as in landfills depends on regulations, resource use practices, and the costs of new product and of old product disposal.

California's three major forest management regimes provide different levels of products (see Table 36.5). Private timberlands account for 42% of California's timberlands (see Table 36.1) and now produce 85% of forest products (Morgan et al. 2012; see Table 36.6) in California. The larger area of National Forest timberlands produces most of the remainder, with only small amounts coming from other public lands. Although the common board foot measurement of forest inventories refers to the volume of sawn lumber, over half of all the harvested volume is wood chips used for bioenergy or shipped to pulpmills in Oregon (Morgan et al. 2012). While some accounting systems consider wood used for energy to be "lost" to the forest/forest products sector and do not account for it in the energy sector (e.g., Hayes et al. 2012), we follow the IPCC guidelines used in the national greenhouse gas accounting (U.S. Environmental Protection Agency 2013), where wood used for bioenergy is considered carbon-neutral if forest inventories are stable. When corrected for differences in site productivity, private timberlands are producing about six times as much harvested product per hectare as National Forest timberlands (see Table 36.6).

Local Ecosystem Services under Different Forest Management Regimes

In addition to the significant global ecosystem benefits of forest carbon inventories (Hayes et al. 2012, PNW-FIA 2013) as well as the direct carbon storage and substitution benefits when harvested products are used instead of fossil-fuel intensive products (Malmsheimer et al. 2011, Fried 2013), stand- and tree-level characteristics influence plant diversity, animal biodiversity, and amenity benefits. All three are often positively associated with a mosaic of diverse forest structures with trees of all sizes and ages. Christensen et al. (2008)

TABLE 36.5
Harvested products from private and U.S. Forest Service timberlands in California in 2006 in (MgC)

Land ownership	Sawn wood products	Pulp	Bioenergy	Total
Private	708,633	253,083	506,166	1,467,882
National forest	105,835	36,812	115,038	257,685
TOTAL	**814,468**	**289,895**	**621,204**	**1,725,567**
Percentage of total	47%	17%	36%	100%

SOURCE: Morgan et al. 2012.
NOTE: The cubic foot harvest volumes in Morgan et al. 2012 have been converted to MgC based on Food and Agriculture Organization (FAO 1947) conversions to make them comparable to in-forest carbon stocks data in these sections.

TABLE 36.6
Median and mean values for forest metrics for four production forests by management regime

	Private timberland (n = 602)		National forest timberland (n = 980)		Reserved forest land (n = 329)	
Metric	Median	Mean	Median	Mean	Median	Mean
All live trees (MgC ha^{-1})	63.55	85.21^{A}	75.01	98.24^{B}	93.59	121.07^{C}
<=25 cm dbh (MgC ha^{-1})	8.65	11.32^{A}	6.40	9.02^{B}	4.14	7.14^{C}
26–64 cm dbh (MgC ha^{-1})	32.47	41.84^{A}	31.80	$38.32^{A,B}$	26.71	35.22^{B}
>65 cm dbh (MgC ha^{-1})	10.38	32.05^{A}	24.88	50.90^{B}	46.82	78.72^{C}
All standing dead trees (MgC ha^{-1})	1.26	3.89^{A}	2.72	7.17^{B}	5.21	11.65^{C}
<=38 cm dbh standing (MgC ha^{-1})	0.19	1.02^{A}	0.30	1.41^{B}	0.38	2.04^{C}
>38 cm dbh standing (MgC ha^{-1})	0.00	2.87^{A}	1.45	5.76^{B}	3.84	9.62^{C}
Downed wood (MgC ha^{-1})	8.95	12.72^{A}	7.60	10.86^{B}		
Shrub cover (%)	12	18	11	18		
Forb cover (%)	4	8	3	5		
Graminoid cover (%)	2	5	2	4		
2006 removals (MgC ha^{-1})		0.89		0.11		

NOTE: Means with different letters are statistically significantly different from each other (Wilcoxon signed-rank test, $p < 0.05$). One-tenth of the plots were measured each year between 2002 and 2011.

provides detailed FIA plot-based analyses of disturbances, stressors, trees, and understory vegetation for all forest types. The following section focuses on the interactions of harvests, natural disturbances, and forest regeneration under different management regimes.

One metric for assessing forest stand diversity is the mix of stand ages, measured by the age of the dominant trees that are assumed to represent the oldest trees. In California's timberlands, private stands have an average age of 71 years, National Forest timberlands have an average age of 104 years, and reserved forest lands have an average stand age of 115 years. The distribution of forest area by forest stand age (Figure 36.5) is often used as a proxy for structural classes (Oliver and Larson 1996) or seral classes (Hall et al. 1995) that are important to the food web and habitat requirements of many animal species (Spurr and Barnes 1980).

We analyzed plot-level tree lists and vegetative cover percentages from hundreds of FIA plots to provide a comparison across the different management regimes. Median and mean values are both presented (see Table 36.6), as high-value outliers for many attributes are common across management regimes. The interquartile and the full range of forest plot biomass densities illustrate the similarities and differences among forest stands under the three primary manage-

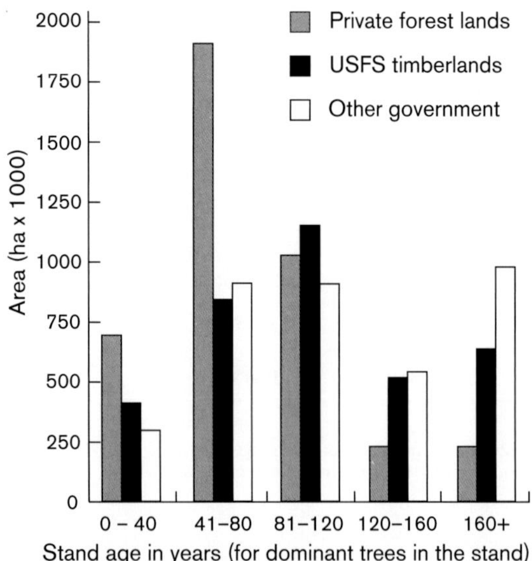

FIGURE 36.5 Age of dominant trees in stands for the private forest lands, U.S. Forest Service (USFS) timberlands, and ecologically similar forests in government parks and roadless areas (other government). Source: PNW-FIA 2013.

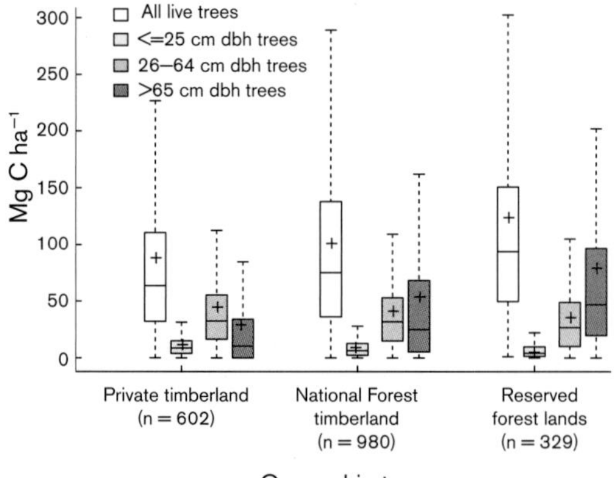

FIGURE 36.6 Carbon stocks in live trees in timberlands and ecologically similar forests under different management regimes; 1 Mg = 1,000 kg. The box defines the interquartile range (IQR) around the median value. The whiskers are 1.5 × IQR. Outliers are not shown for clarity. The population mean is shown by the (+); *n* is the number of plots in each group. Plot data were collected from 2002 through 2011. Source: PNW-FIA 2013.

ment regimes (Figures 36.6 and 36.7). The range, median, and mean values for small trees, medium trees, and small snags are similar across management regimes. Differences in overall, stand-level tree biomass densities across management regimes were driven primarily by the biomass in live trees larger than 65 centimeters in diameter and in snags larger than 38 centimeters in diameter. Downed wood densities and understory vegetation cover were similar between private timberlands and National Forest timberlands. The upper quartile of private timberland plots had considerable biomass in large snags, but many plots had few if any large snags, which are important habitat elements for some birds and mammals.

Understory vegetation is important for floristic diversity and is an important source of food and cover for many animals that live on the forest floor. The use of clearcut harvest followed by systematic replanting is practiced on a minor portion of private timberlands, but overall life form abundance of shrubs, forbs, and graminoids is similar for private timberlands and public timberlands (Figure 36.8). Detailed floristic surveys comparing plantations to adjacent mixed-age stands across seventy-three paired plantation/natural forest sites in northern California showed that the plantations can rapidly acquire floristic diversity and can eventually achieve similar levels of floristic diversity after their initial establishment (James et al. 2012).

Beyond meeting the regulatory requirements of water quality and wildlife agencies, relatively little is published on how owners of private timberlands manage their resources to achieve positive outcomes. In the following section, we provide examples of forest management with goals for both long-term timber productivity and broader forest ecosystem attributes. While some of the examples described lack the certainty that can come from well-designed experiments, they illustrate forest management approaches that are able to meet both economic and ecological goals. The first example highlights results from an experimental forest where a broad range of management approaches have been used for

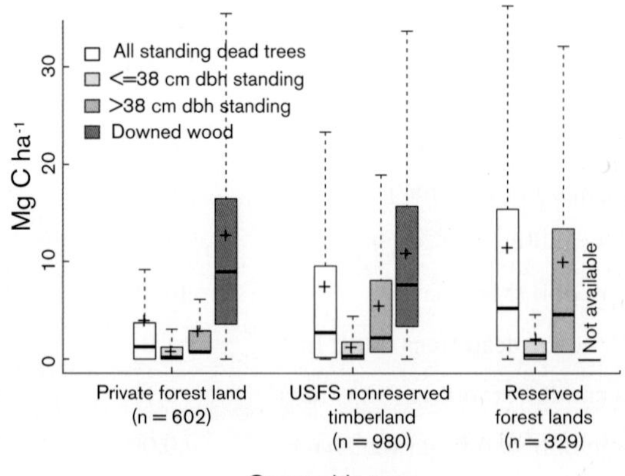

FIGURE 36.7 Carbon stocks in dead standing and downed trees in private and federal timberlands and ecologically similar reserved forest lands. Source: PNW-FIA 2013.

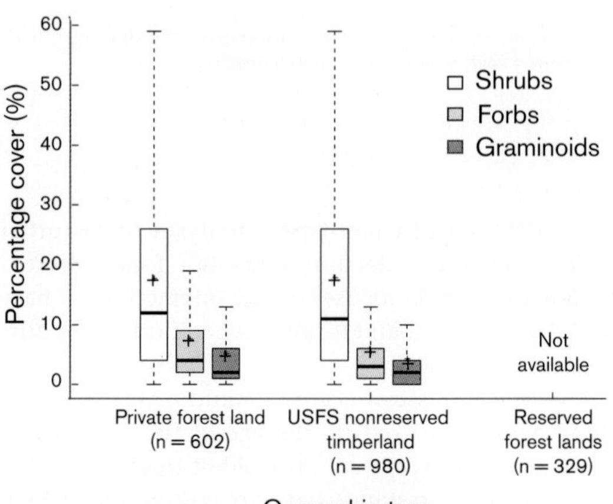

FIGURE 36.8 Understory cover in timberlands and ecologically similar forests. Source: PNW-FIA 2013.

decades on adjacent stands. The second summarizes the ecologically oriented actions of family forest owners who own half the private timberlands in California. The third example summarizes an innovative effort to introduce a rare mammal onto managed timberlands within its historic range. The fourth describes major efforts to address floral and faunal biodiversity within the construction of approved habitat conservation plans of a large timber company. The final example illustrates the challenge of managing for rare plants whose growth requirements are not necessarily aligned with local forest management regulations.

Experimental Managed Forests

Experimental forests with a designed range of treatments can act as "Rosetta Stones" to translate differences in global and local ecosystem services across different forest management approaches. The 12 square kilometer Blodgett Forest Research Station of the University of California (Blodgett) is one of the few locations in California where a gradient of forest management approaches is applied and evaluated within a long-term experimental framework. A primary focus of Blodgett management over the past fifty years has been to achieve and document the creation of a sustained timber yield while also sustaining wildlife, water, soil, archaeological, and visual resources as required by the California Forest Practices Rules. Similar research results for ponderosa pine forests in northern California have come from experimental forests managed by the U.S. Forest Service (Zhang et al. 2008, Youngblood 2011, Zhang et al. 2012). In both cases, well-documented and diverse stand conditions can be a template for research on tree-related and non-tree-related resources under different disturbance conditions.

Blodgett (approximately at 38.9102°N, 120.6627°W) lies between 1,200 and 1,500 meter elevation on the western slope of the Sierra Nevada, where annual precipitation averaged 158 centimeters per year. Soils are productive, with canopy trees typically reaching 27–34 meters tall in fifty to sixty years. Following extensive logging with railroads and steam engines from 1900 to 1933, the young stands were compartmentalized and assigned to a wide range of management alternatives that span all silvicultural systems including reserves, even-aged, and uneven-aged methods. Harvest activity on the regenerating forest began in earnest in 1962 and has continued annually to the present. The wide range of treatments applied consistently over time, coupled with comprehensive permanent plots established in 1974, has enabled the longest available empirical assessment of diverse forest management impacts and trade-offs in productive forests of the Sierra Nevada in the context of fire exclusion. Even-aged stands consist of both mature stands that have been thinned (i.e., "second-growth") and regenerated plantations (i.e., "third-growth") ranging from one to thirty-five years of age. Uneven-aged stands consist of complex canopy structures created with periodic selection harvests. From an overhead view, uneven-aged stands have a rougher texture and are more open than the high-density canopies of reserve stands (Figure 36.9).

The combination of productive soils, active management, and long rotations of one hundred years or more has resulted in forest biomass densities greater than those on public lands in mixed conifer forests that had considerably less harvesting. Active management typically involves reductions in the number of trees less than 25 centimeters in diameter. Compared to the other management regimes, Blodgett also has the highest proportion of total biomass in the large-tree class. While the median values for large-tree carbon densities are similar across these three management regimes, overall variability among stands is inversely related to forest management intensity. Considerably more small-diameter trees are found on the National Forest timberlands and private timberlands than on reserved forest lands and at Blodgett (Figure 36.10). The small trees represent less than 10% of the total stand biomass but constitute a significant component of the ladder fuels in fire-prone forests (Collins et al. 2007).

A comparison of treatment effects on productivity and species composition at Blodgett (Olson and Helms 1996) concluded that:

1. Standing volume and basic structural diversity increased as a result of postdisturbance stand development and thirty years of active management.
2. Timber productivity across various partial harvest methods was similar in terms of net growth and harvest.
3. Natural regeneration of all species was adequate to sustain tree diversity in all of the silvicultural methods.
4. Clearcutting and overstory removal had the least amount of fuels after treatment; individual tree selection and reserves had the most.

The continuation of treatments since this last comparison, coupled with repeated measurement of permanent plots and new analytical tools, allows an update on the productivity, composition, and structure after what is now fifty years of active management at Blodgett. Unless otherwise cited, values are from the Blodgett vegetation database. Between 1995 and 2009, standing tree volume increased while 75% of gross growth was harvested. Structural diversity in terms of patch size and age has increased greatly as clearcut and regeneration harvests have created openings ranging in size from 0.01 to 8 hectares. Numerous small openings in uneven-aged stands create a complex structure across the whole ownership, with a wide variety of openings and edges between stands with trees of very different ages (Figure 36.11).

A shift in species composition is clearly occurring in the forests managed as reserves. Similar to other undisturbed mixed conifer forests (e.g., Ansley and Battles 1998), the reserves have experienced a reduction in ponderosa pine recruitment and a relative increase in white fir and incense cedar. A similar pattern within young SINGLE-TREE SELECTION stands led to adjustments in harvest patterns that regenerated a more balanced mix of species (York et al. 2012). Even-aged methods involve planting and density management and include all native tree species. Total species richness (including understory plants) generally increases with canopy openness at Blodgett (Battles et al. 2001). Young even-aged and GROUP SELECTION stands tended to have the highest levels of species richness but also had a higher richness of exotic species. Large wildfires have been effectively excluded from Blodgett since the 1930s with substantial surface and ladder fuel loads as a result. The fire and fire surrogate studies compared the use of prescribed fire and mechanical treatments to reduce high fuel loads in mature forest stands. The results demonstrated that fire risks can be reduced with both mechanical and prescribed fire approaches with few negative ecological impacts (Hartsough et al. 2008, Moghaddas et al. 2008, Stephens et al. 2009, Stephens et al. 2012).

FIGURE 36.9 Even aged, uneven aged, and reserve forest stands at Blodgett Forest (center: 38.9099°N, 120.6571°W). Sources: Imagery ©2014 Google, DigitalGlobe, U.S. Geological Survey, USDA Farm Service Agency.

A = reserve (no management except fire suppression), B = single tree selection, C = group selection, D = shelterwood, post seed-step, E = ten-year-old plantation, F = twenty-five-year-old plantation.

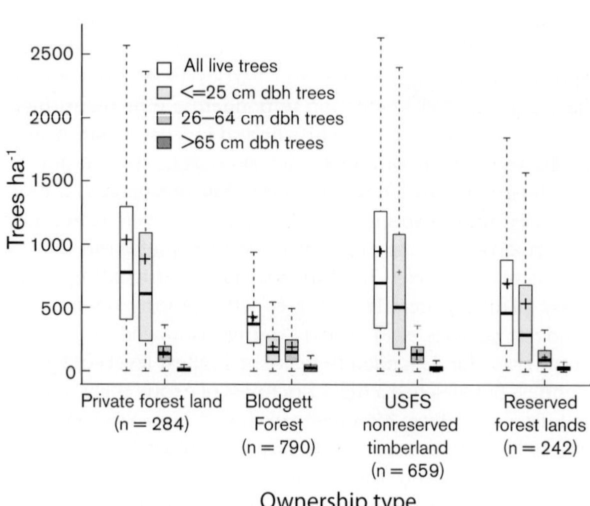

FIGURE 36.10 Tree density in California mixed conifer forests by management regime. The box defines the interquartile range (IQR) around the median value. The whiskers are 1.5× the IQR. Outliers are not shown for clarity. The population mean is shown by the (+). Source: PNW-FIA 2013 and Blodgett Forest Research Station 2013.

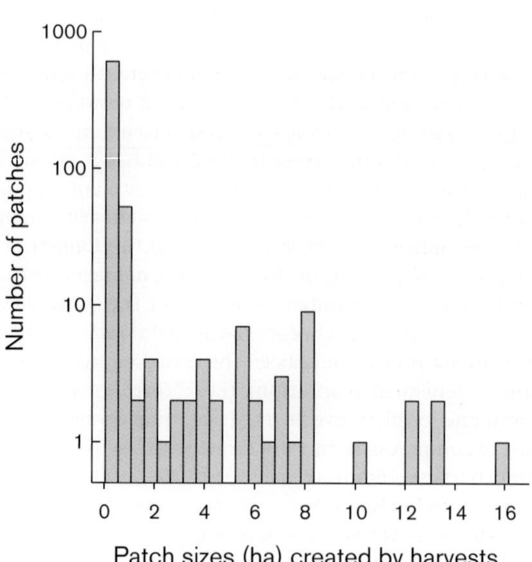

FIGURE 36.11 Distribution (y-axis transformed with log scale) of patch sizes across Blodgett Forest following fifty years of annual harvests, including both even-aged and uneven-aged harvests. Only patches created by harvests were included. The smallest patch size considered was 0.04 ha. Source: Blodgett Forest Research Station 2013.

Increasing forest resilience to projected dramatic yet uncertain climatic changes is a key long-term goal for the forest. The two primary assumptions driving this new objective are that a changing climate will have significant yet uncertain effects and that the primary management tool available at Blodgett is the application of silvicultural treatments to influence stand density, species composition, genetic composition, and fuel structure. The limitations of models for predicting ecosystem responses to climate change (e.g., Chmura et al. 2011) force a focus on hedging against uncertainty with active adaptive management (Walters and Holling 1990). The establishment at Blodgett of a wide variety of stand structures and age classes provides an opportunity to test alternative strategies for building resilient forest stand structures. A high-diversity seed bank is being built that includes seeds from hotter/wetter and hotter/drier climates large enough to replant all of Blodgett in the event of a high-severity fire.

The current gradient of stand densities and age classes will be maintained by continuing all forms of basic regeneration methods (even-aged and uneven-aged methods), while testing new approaches for reducing fire severity and increasing drought resistance. Stands with a low density of large trees and high frequency of pine species will be developed with the objective of producing stands resistant to extended periods of exceptionally high climatic water deficit. The reserves will be maintained to illustrate how a "hands-off" approach will influence shifts in tree species composition, differential response to drought, and changing fire-risk levels common to stands harvested once with minimal ongoing manipulation. Managing for high levels of timber productivity from forest stands with high levels of within-stand and across-stand diversity creates a forest that is more ecologically complex than high-yield forest plantations while still providing significant volumes of wood products and revenue for landowners. Finally, the research focus at Blodgett provides an opportunity to study the interactions of various ecosystem services across a wide range of forest structures.

Family Forests

While large timber companies are more visible, around half of private timberland in California is owned by families where revenue, stewardship, amenity, and aesthetic values are more varied (Butler 2008, Christensen et al. 2008, Ferranto et al. 2011). Compared to industrial and national forest timberlands, family ownerships have lower total inventories per hectare and lower proportions of more commercially valuable species (Christensen et al. 2008). Timber harvesting was reported by 80% of the ownerships with more than 200 hectares but becomes progressively less common for smaller ownerships (Stewart et al. 2012). Owners that harvested timber were nearly twice as likely as those who did not harvest timber to undertake non-revenue-generating stewardship activities such as protection of water quality, improvement of fish and wildlife habitats, and removal of individual trees to promote forest health (Table 36.7).

Sustainable timber production is the primary revenue-generating alternative to real estate development for forest properties. However, the higher regulatory costs of timber production in California compared to other states and Canadian provinces are often cited as a significant challenge by forest land owners (Stewart et al. 2012). Where additional costs make a timber harvest uneconomical, associated investments in road and drainage infrastructures, water quality improvements, and wildlife habitat improvements are delayed or not undertaken (Ferranto et al. 2011).

TABLE 36.7

Correlation between environmental stewardship activities and timber harvesting for forest ownerships larger than 20 hectares (n=96)

Environmental stewardship activity	Harvest timber	Do not harvest timber	*p* value
Remove exotics	.525	.457	.5245
Improve water quality	.738	.389	.0007
Improve riparian habitat	.721	.389	.0012
Improve wildlife habitat	.836	.486	.0003
Cut trees for forest health	.921	.500	.0001

SOURCE: Stewart et al. 2012.

Managing Landscape-scale Biodiversity on Private Timberlands

The following case studies of various ecological restoration projects, programs, and approaches illustrate ways in which owners of private production forests address the maintenance and often the expansion of the populations of rare plant species as well as candidate or listed species under the federal Endangered Species Act (ESA) or the California Endangered Species Act (CESA). Assessments of how different forest management regimes affect wildlife populations are difficult and expensive when they involve monitoring and analysis of populations, food webs, specific habitat elements such as snag trees with cavities, and predator populations. In forest areas with significant numbers of threatened or endangered species, a number of the larger timber companies have been required to provide considerable documentation to regulating state and federal agencies when they propose forest management practices more active than the default precautionary or no-action approaches.

Expanding Fishers into Their Historical Range

An innovative fisher (*Pekania* [formerly *Martes*] *pennanti*) reintroduction project (Lewis et al. 2012) involves the formal cooperation of the California Department of Fish and Wildlife, the U.S. Fish and Wildlife Service, Sierra Pacific Industries, and North Carolina State University. When the project was conceived, the fisher was a candidate for endangered or threatened status under both the U.S. Endangered Species Act and the California Endangered Species Act. Each cooperator contributed its particular capacity to planning, capture and release, and monitoring. The long-term project started with a formal assessment of the sustainability of potential donor populations and likelihood of successful establishment of the introduced population under different scenarios.

The selection goal was healthy females at the beginning of their reproductive lives and males at the peak of their ability to breed with many females. Fishers in some source populations were infected with eye worms (*Thelazia californica*), and some fishers from Humboldt and western Trinity Counties were infected with a previously undescribed trematode that could negatively affect fisher survival. These fishers were rejected as candidates for translocation. The source population eventually selected in the eastern Klamath Region of northern California had been previously monitored and its population dynamics modeled (Swiers 2013). Because of ongoing monitoring in the eastern Klamath Region, for the first time the effects on a source population of having animals removed could be documented (Swiers 2013). Researchers found that removing ten adult fishers with the highest reproductive values from the eastern Klamath population had no statistically discernible effect on population growth, annual reproduction, or annual survival of that source population. The project also included modeling of habitat quality of potential release sites before reintroduction (Callas and Figura 2008).

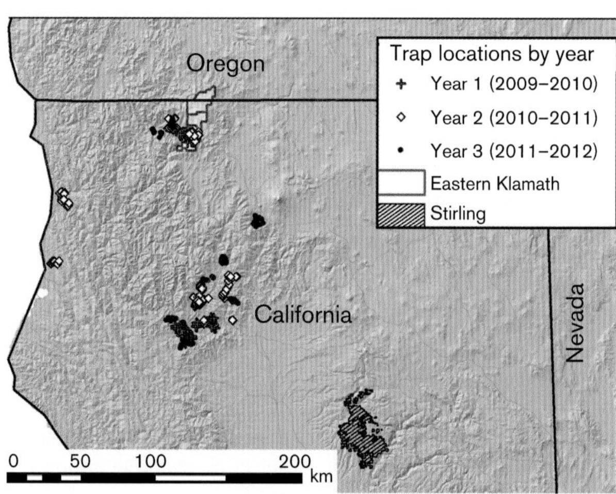

FIGURE 36.12 Location of fisher collection trap sites including the Eastern Klamath Study Area (EKSA) and relocation site on the Stirling Management Area owned by Sierra Pacific Industries. Source: Robert Swiers.

From late 2009 through late 2011, the cooperators released forty fishers (24F, 16M) onto the Stirling Management Area owned by Sierra Pacific Industries (SPI) in the northern Sierra Nevada and southern Cascade Mountains (Figure 36.12) (Powell et al. 2012). Personnel from North Carolina State University and the California Department of Fish and Wildlife have since conducted monitoring and research on the reintroduced population. They have, to date, monitored all fishers for survival, reproduction, dispersal, and home range development. All released fishers established home ranges and, as in other established populations studied, males had larger home ranges and traveled further than females. The majority of the fishers stayed on the Stirling Management Area rather than move to adjacent national forest lands. The released fishers enjoyed high survival during both the initial postrelease period (four months) and for up to two years after release. Through 2013, sixteen fishers were known to have died. Females from all annual release cohorts reproduced in all years. Approximately 75–80% of females each year were tracked to natal dens where they gave birth, producing approximately two kits apiece each year. The estimated minimum population in that area was thirty-seven fishers, representing a growing population. On average, released female fishers upon recapture had increased their weights by 0.1 kilogram and males by 0.4 kilogram. Juvenile fishers captured on Stirling weighed more than similarly aged juveniles from other parts of California. These data, though early, indicate that the reintroduced population is healthy and potentially self-sustaining. The overall process also illustrates the institutional complexity, extensive resources, and expertise necessary to undertake an experiment to expand the sustainable population of a wildlife species for which there is limited information.

Habitat Conservation Plans on Private Timberlands

Many of the larger timber ownerships in California use habitat conservation plans or similar agreements to address the habitat requirements of rare plants and animals. Green Diamond Resource Company (Green Diamond) owns approximately 2,000 square kilometers of forested land in northwestern California and has developed multiple habitat conservation plans to address the numerous species of concern on its lands. It developed a habitat conservation plan (HCP) for northern spotted owls in cooperation with the U.S. Fish and Wildlife Service in 1992, a Deadwood Management Plan and a Sensitive Plant Conservation Plan in cooperation with California Department of Fish and Game in 2005, a second HCP covering six listed or sensitive aquatic species with dual jurisdictions approved by the U.S. Fish and Wildlife Service and National Marine Fisheries Service in 2007, a consistency determination issued for coho salmon by the California Department of Fish and Game in 2008, and an incidental take permit for the Trinity bristle snail (*Monadenia setosa*) in 2009. A new forest HCP (FHCP) is expected to be completed in the near future and will include updated conservation measures for the northern spotted owl (*Strix occidentalis caurina*), the fisher, and two species of tree voles. The approved plans, maps, and monitoring reports are available on Green Diamond's website.

The earliest plans covered active forest management in areas that overlapped with the ranges of many plant species and the home ranges of animals of many species that are threatened, endangered, or are under consideration for designation. Northern spotted owls are generally associated with old-growth or late seral forests (USFWS 1990, Powell and Zielinksi 1994, Carroll et al. 1999, Courtney et al. 2004, Zielinski 2004). Genetic exchange occurs among owls throughout coastal California and the Klamath Province (Haig et al. 2004), where a variety of forest management regimes are used. In the 1990s the estimated density of northern spotted owls on Green Diamond's lands was among the highest reported in the scientific literature (Diller and Thome 1999). Green Diamond's mark-recapture study over the last twenty-two years has indicated that juvenile spotted owls disperse to and from Green Diamond's lands to the Eel River drainage to the south, north into southern Oregon, and to the Hoopa and Willow Creek study areas to the east.

Demographic analysis found that the spotted owl population on Green Diamond's timberlands was stable from 1990 to 2001 but then decreased. Growing evidence strongly suggests that the invasion of barred owls (*Strix varia*) into northern California is responsible for the decline. Preliminary results of a recently initiated removal experiment suggest that control of barred owls is operationally feasible and that spotted owls respond rapidly and favorably where barred owls are removed. When barred owls were removed from historical spotted owl sites covering half of a study area, the sites were recolonized by spotted owls (Diller et al. 2012). While spotted owls prefer to roost and nest in old forests in coastal California, their primary small mammal prey occur in young forests such as the ones found on Green Diamond's land. Long-term demographic studies of spotted owls using mark-recapture data have found that habitat heterogeneity in the form of a mosaic of young and old forests likely contributes to maintaining spotted owls in northern California (Franklin et al. 2000, Diller et al. 2010). Given that fire has largely been eliminated from managed forests in the redwood region (Skinner et al. 2006, Stuart and Stephens 2006), creating openings of diverse sizes through timber management with retention of some larger live and dead trees could provide valuable ecotone habitat for spotted owls.

One reason for the prevalence of spotted owls near younger forest plantations may be the high density of dusky-footed woodrats (*Neotoma fuscipes*). Dusky-footed woodrats tend to be associated with early seral shrub and pole-staged stands (Sakai and Noon 1993, Hamm 1995, Hughes 2005) and are an important food source for spotted owls. Sustaining a mosaic of early seral stands with significant woodrat populations within a forest environment can be accomplished with harvest blocks or wildfires. Woodrat habitat appears to depend on having sufficient sunlight to promote the growth of early seral plant species that are eaten by woodrats. Under low light levels, unpalatable, shade-tolerant shrubs—such as salal (*Gaultheria shallon*), evergreen huckleberry (*Vaccinium ovatum*), and Pacific rhododendron (*Rhododendron macrophyllum*)—dominate understory vegetation. In one study of woodrats living in areas with various levels of thinning, woodrats did not colonize stands until they reached a level of thinning equivalent to clearcutting or variable retention standards in California (Hamm and Diller 2009). In the portion of their range on company lands, Green Diamond has concluded that spotted owls appear to be compatible with even-age management where openings, dense stands, and large residual trees maintain habitat heterogeneity (Diller et al. 2010).

Fishers are another rare animal that no longer occupies its historic range and is generally associated with old-growth or late seral forests (USFWS 1990, Powell and Zielinksi 1994, Carroll et al. 1999, Courtney et al. 2004, Zielinski et al. 2004). No barriers inhibit genetic exchange among fishers within the coastal redwood region and the western Klamath Province, a contiguous population of fishers in forests from southern Oregon to the Eel River. Fisher densities on Green Diamond's lands are similar to some densities reported elsewhere in North America (Thompson 2008) but are considerably lower than those recently reported for the Hoopa Indian Reservation located to the east of Green Diamond's lands (Matthews et al. 2011, Matthews et al. 2013).

A key to creating a forest matrix used by fishers is identifying and maintaining elements such as large-diameter snags and retained live trees with cavities across an ownership where even-aged silviculture is practiced. Unharvested live trees and snags eventually become downed logs and coarse woody debris that are important to some late-seral wildlife species. In addition to late-seral habitat elements, structural complexity of the stand layers (i.e., shrub, intermediate canopy, and overstory canopy) and diversity of tree species are important. In particular, conifer stands with a mix of hardwood species tend to be important to selected species of wildlife such as fishers (Zielinski et al. 2013). A combination of monitoring and managing individual legacy trees and other forms of structural complexity along with recruitment of future habitat elements is central to an information-based approach to timber management. Maintaining noncommercial species such as tanoak (*Lithocarpus densiflorus*), California bay (*Umbellularia californica*), and Pacific madrone (*Arbutus menziesii*) that exhibit coppice growth create high structural and species diversity in timberland units in a manner similar to some attributes of late-seral forests. Over time, the spread of sudden oak death (*P. ramorum*) (Filipe et al. 2010) into some of these host trees could have negative impacts on some hardwood trees in the region.

Habitat conservation plans have also been implemented on Green Diamond's lands for a number of salmonids and amphibians. Across California, erosion from historical land uses, water diversions, and pollution have negatively impacted salmonid populations. Fish surveys on Green Diamond's lands revealed that historical salmonid streams continue to support significant populations of these fish (Green Diamond Resources Company 2013). The initial foci of surveys initiated in 1993 were coho and Chinook salmon (*Oncorhynchus kisutch* and *O. tshawytscha*), steelhead (*O. mykiss*), and cutthroat trout (*O. clarki*) with annual monitoring of juvenile populations and outmigrant smolt populations in key watersheds throughout the ownership. Two potential contributors to the persistence of healthy salmonid populations are the maintenance of best management practices for reducing sediment delivery from roads and harvest operations into streams, and the productivity-enhancing role of additional sunlight on resident salmonids populations. Experiments with different levels of sunlight on streams on Green Diamond's lands showed a positive impact from increased sunlight onto stream reaches on salmonid biomass, density, and growth (Wilzbach et al. 2005).

Managing Sun-demanding Plants within Shade-tolerant Forests

The Santa Cruz Mountains historically provided some of the most accessible timber source for the expanding human population of the San Francisco Bay area and nearby agricultural areas. Consequently, they were the first forested region in California where nearly all private land was harvested by the 1930s. Forest regrowth and limited harvesting have led to the presence in the Santa Cruz Mountains of the densest forests in the state (Christensen et al. 2008). In some cases, dense forests without the disturbances historically created by wildfires will not necessarily support the full range of plants that are native to the area (Land Trust of Santa Cruz County 2011).

County-specific regulations (California Department of Forestry and Fire Protection 2013) allow only single-tree selection and small-group selection harvests. Single-tree selection has been practiced on approximately 40% of the land within the Timberland Production Zone (TPZ) area in the Santa Cruz Mountains. A common characteristic of forests managed by single-tree selection is that only limited light reaches the forest floor. The central part of this region is home to a number of species that evolved in high-sunlight patches within larger forest areas. Santa Cruz manzanita (*Arctostaphylos anderso-*

nii) inhabits an ecological niche on the edge of southern redwood–Douglas-fir forests in association with blue-blossom ceanothus (*Ceanothus thrysiflorus*), madrone (*Arbutus menziesii*), California coffeeberry (*Frangula californica*), and toyon (*Heteromeles arbutifolia*).

Santa Cruz manzanita is an obligate seeder that produces seed at an early age. More than a dozen manzanita species occur in the Santa Cruz Mountains, occupying a wide variety of niches. Only a few have burls and sprout after fire, but all depend on fire (or mechanical clearing) to provide openings for sunlight and bare mineral soil for germination. In the absence of fires or management, there is a lack of recruitment of a wide variety of understory species, including Santa Cruz manzanita and several other rare species. The selective removal of small groups of redwood and Douglas-fir trees can provide the light penetration to the forest floor necessary to trigger regeneration of many of these understory species. In unmanaged stands, Santa Cruz manzanita is frequently shaded out by an increasing overstory canopy. Perhaps as a result, many of the private lands historically managed for timber production have more of the Santa Cruz manzanita than parks, residential, and recreational parcels with no harvests. However, the disturbances associated with harvesting also have the potential to introduce and spread exotic species.

Summary

Timberlands are forests that can be managed for the sustainable production of wood products. California's principal timberlands are the California mixed conifer, ponderosa pine, and Douglas-fir forests of the interior and redwood forests close to the Pacific Ocean. They cover slightly less than 4 million of the 13 million hectares of forests in California. Differences in timberland ownership and management, including practices on the roughly 1 million hectares of reserved forest lands ecologically similar to harvested areas, create a natural experiment that provides insights into how different combinations of managed disturbances (harvests, regeneration, thinning) and natural disturbances (fires, insects, diseases, droughts) affect the provision of global and local ecosystem services.

Redwood forests are nearly twice as productive as other timberlands in California and are now mainly private timberlands or parks. More than half of California mixed conifer, ponderosa pine, and Douglas-fir forest types are managed as National Forests, with the rest mainly in private ownership. These mixed conifer forests experience considerably more natural disturbance such as fires, insect and disease infestations, and droughts. Private timberlands, National Forest timberlands, and reserve forest lands all have high levels of forest carbon storage but very different flows of wood products. After correcting for site primary productivity differences, mean inventories on private timberlands are 25% lower than those on similar National Forest timberlands and reserved forest lands. The total carbon cycle benefits derived from forest products depend on how efficiently consumers use, reuse, and recycle wood products. Private timberlands annually harvest approximately six times as much product per hectare as National Forest timberlands while sustaining their inventories. The revenues from products and services are important to private timberland owners to keep them from accepting more lucrative offers to sell land for residential and recreational uses.

Private timberlands have similar vegetation characteristics to the less intensively managed National Forest timberlands and reserve forest lands in many respects, with the exceptions of live trees larger than 65 centimeters in diameter and large snags. Successful efforts to maintain and enhance biodiversity while still producing revenue have been demonstrated on some experimental forests, through habitat conservation plans, and through voluntary stewardship actions on family-owned forests. Achieving high levels of biodiversity and resilience requires considerable investment in intensive monitoring of specific species of interest, protection of key habitat elements, and attention to disease and disturbance threats. Active management through harvesting, planned regeneration, and managed fire can increase overall resilience to unknown but changing future conditions. Our understanding of forests would benefit from more explicit experiments on both private and National Forest timberlands as we move towards a more uncertain future.

Acknowledgments

The authors want to thank all the research foresters and wildlife biologists from the University of California, the U.S. Forest Service, and many of the private timber companies in California who provided documents, publications, and valuable review comments. The careful comments of four anonymous reviewers also improved the manuscript.

Recommended Reading

Christensen, G. A., S. J. Campbell, and J. S. Fried, technical editors. 2008. California's forest resources, 2001–2005: Five-year forest inventory and analysis report. PNW GTR 763. U.S. Forest Service, Pacific Northwest Research Station, Portland, Oregon.

Christensen, G. A., K. Waddell, S. Stanton, O. Kuegler, technical editors. 2015. California's forest resources: Forest inventory and analysis, 2001–2010. U.S. Forest Service, Pacific Northwest Research Station, Portland, Oregon.

Lanner, R. M. 1999. Conifers of California. Cachuma Press, Los Olivios, California.

Tappeiner, J. C., II, D. A. Maguire, and T. B. Harrington. 2007. Silviculture and ecology of western U.S. Forests. Oregon State University Press, Corvallis, Oregon.

Glossary

DBH Diameter of the stem of a tree measured at breast height (1.37 m or 4.5 feet) from the ground.

GROUP SELECTION Trees are harvested within discrete locations within stands to create cleared canopy gaps large enough to facilitate high levels of resource availability for regeneration of all species, including those adapted to colonizing disturbed forests. Group sizes generally range from 0.1 hectare to 1.0 hectare.

SINGLE TREE SELECTION Individual or small groups of trees of all size classes are removed to create growing space for new regeneration and to create highly complex stand structures diffusely across entire stands.

References

Ansley, J. S. and J. J. Battles. 1998 Forest composition, structure, and change in an old growth mixed conifer forest in the northern Sierra Nevada. Journal of the Torrey Botanical Society 125: 297–308.

Battles, J. J., A. J. Shlisky, R. H. Barrett, R. C. Heald, and B. H. Allen-Diaz. 2001. The effects of forest management on plant species diversity in a Sierran conifer forest. Forest Ecology and Management 146: 211–222.

Blodgett Forest Research Station. 2013. Continuous Forest Inventory Database. University of California Center for Forestry, Berkeley, California.

Butler, Brett J. 2008. Family Forest Owners of the United States, 2006. NRS-GTR-27. Newtown Square, PA: U.S. Department of Agriculture, Forest Service, Northern Research Station. 72 p.

California Department of Forestry and Fire Protection (Cal Fire). 2013a. California forest practice rules 2013. Page 306. Sacremento, California.

California Department of Forestry and Fire Protection. 2013b. Forest Practice Geographical Information System (GIS). Statewide Timber Harvest Data.

Callas, R. L., and P. Figura. 2008. Translocation plan for the reintroduction of fishers (*Martes pennanti*) to lands owned by Sierra Pacific Industries in the northern Sierra Nevada of California. California Department of Fish and Game. Sacramento, California.

Canadell, J. G., and M. R. Raupach. 2008. Managing forests for climate change mitigation. Science 320:1456–1457.

Canadian Forest Service. 2013. The State of Canada's Forests: Annual Report 2013. Natural Resources Canada. Ottawa, Canada.

Carroll, C. R., W. J. Zielinski, and R. F. Noss. 1999. Using presence-absence data to build and test spatial habitat models for the fisher in the Klamath Region, U.S.A. Conservation Biology 13:1344–1359.

Chmura, D. J., P. D. Anderson, G. T. Howe, C. A. Harrington, J. E. Halofsky, D. L. Peterson, D. C. Shaw, and J. B. St. Clair. 2011. Forest responses to climate change in the northwestern United States: Ecophysiological foundations for adaptive management. Forest Ecology and Management 261:1121–1142.

Christensen, G., J. Fried, and S. Campbell, technical editors. 2008. California's forest resources, 2001–2005: Five-year forest inventory and analysis report. PNW-GTR-763. U.S. Forest Service, Pacific Northwest Research Station, Portland, Oregon.

Ciais, P., C. Sabine, G. Bala, L. Bopp, V. Brovkin, J. Canadell, A. Chhabra, R. DeFries, J. Galloway, M. Heimann, C. Jones, C. Le Quéré, R. B. Myneni, S. Piao, and P. Thornton. 2013. Carbon and other biogeochemical cycles. Pages 465–570 in T. F. Stocker, D. Qin, G.-K. Plattner, M. Tignor, S. K. Allen, J. Boschung, A. Nauels, Y. Xia, V. Bex, and P. M. Midgley, editors. The Physical Science Basis. Contribution of Working Group I to the Fifth Assessment Report of the Intergovernmental Panel on Climate Change. Cambridge University Press, Cambridge, UK, and New York, New York.

Collins, B. M., J. J. Moghaddas, and S. L. Stephens. 2007. Initial changes in forest structure and understory plant communities following fuel reduction activities in a Sierra Nevada mixed conifer forest. Forest Ecology and Management 239:102–111.

Courtney, S. P., J. A. Blakesley, R. E. Bigley, M. L. Cody, J. P. Dumbacher, R. C. Fleisher, A. B. Franklin, J. F. Franklin, R. J. Gutiérrez, J. M. Marzluff, and L. Sztukowski. 2004. Scientific evaluation of the status of the northern spotted owl. Sustainable Ecosystems Institute, Portland, Oregon.

Dana, S. T., and S. K. Fairfax. 1980. Forest and range policy: Its development in the United States. McGraw-Hill Book Company, New York, New York.

Diller, L., K. Hamm, D. Lamphear, and T. McDonald. 2012. Two decades of research and monitoring of the northern spotted owl on private timberlands in the Redwood region: What do we know and what challenges remain? Pages 399–408 in R. B. Standiford, T. J. Weller, D. D. Piirto, J. D. Stuart, editors. Proceedings of coast redwood forests in a changing California: A symposium for scientists and managers. PSW-GTR-238. Pacific Southwest Research Station, Forest Service, U.S. Department of Agriculture, Albany, California, and Santa Cruz, California.

———. 2010. Green Diamond Resource Company, northern spotted owl habitat conservation plan, ten-year review report. Report available from U.S. Fish and Wildlife Service, Arcata Fish and Wildlife Office, Arcata, California.

Diller, L. V., and D. M. Thome. 1999. Population density of northern spotted owls in managed young-growth forests in coastal northern California. Journal of Raptor Research 33:275–286.

Ferranto, S., L. Huntsinger, C. Getz, G. Nakamura, W. Stewart, S. Drill, Y. Valachovic, M. DeLasaux, and M. Kelly. 2011. Forest and rangeland owners value land for natural amenities and as financial investment. California Agriculture 65:184–191.

Filipe, J. A. N., R. C. Cobb, D. M. Rizzo, R. K. Meetemeyer, and C. A. Gilligan. 2010. Strategies for control of sudden oak death in Humboldt County—Informed guidance based on a parameterized epidemiological model. Pages 122–125 in S. J. Frankel, J. T. Kliejunas, and K. M. Palmieri, editors. Proceedings of the Sudden Oak Death Fourth Science Symposium. PSW-GTR-229. U.S. Department of Agriculture, Forest Service, Pacific Southwest Research Station, Albany, California.

Fire and Resource Assessment Program. 2003. The changing California: Forest and range 2003 assessment. Department of Forestry and Fire Protection, Sacramento, California.

Food and Agriculture Organization. 1947. Conversion factors. Unasylva 1:1:62–63.

Franklin, A. B., D. R. Anderson, R. J. Gutierrez, and K. P. Burnham. 2000. Climate, habitat quality, and fitness in northern spotted owl populations in northwestern California. Ecological Monographs 70:539–590.

Fried, J. 2013. Do carbon offsets work?: The role of forest management in greenhouse gas mitigation. Science Findings 155. U.S. Department of Agriculture, Forest Service, Pacific Northwest Research Station, Portland, Oregon.

Green Diamond Resources Company. 2013. Aquatic habitat conservation plan: 2013 biennial report. Korbel, California.

Haig, S. M., T. D. Mullins, E. D. Forsman, P. W. Trail, and L. I. V. Wennerberg. 2004. Genetic Identification of spotted owls, barred owls, and their hybrids: Legal implications of hybrid identity. Conservation Biology 18:1347–1357.

Hair, D., and A. H. Ulrich. 1967. The demand and price situation for forest products 1964. Miscellaneous. Publication 983. U.S. Department of Agriculture Forest Service, Washington, D.C.

Hall, F. C., L. Bryant, R. Claunitzer, K. Geier-Hayes, R. Keane, J. Kertis, and A. Shlisky. 1995. Definitions and codes for seral status and structure of vegetation. PNW-GTR-363. U.S. Department of Agriculture, Forest Service, Pacific Northwest Research Station, Portland, Oregon.

Hamm, K. A. 1995. Abundance of dusky-footed woodrats in managed forests of north coastal California. MS thesis. Humboldt State University, Arcata, California.

Hamm, K. A., and L. V. Diller. 2009. Forest management effects on abundance of woodrats in northern California. Northwestern Naturalist 90:97–106.

Harmon, M. E., J. M. Harmon, W. K. Ferrell, and D. Brooks. 1996. Modeling carbon stores in Oregon and Washington forest products: 1900–1992. Climatic Change 33:521–550.

Hartsough, B. R., S. Abrams, R. J. Barbour, E. S. Drews, J. D. McIver, J. J. Moghaddas, D. W. Schwilk, and S. L. Stephens. 2008. The economics of alternative fuel reduction treatments in western United States dry forests: Financial and policy implications from the National Fire and Fire Surrogate Study. Forest Policy and Economics 10:344–354.

Hayes, D. J., D. P. Turner, G. Stinson, A. D. McGuire, Y. Wei, T. O. West, L. S. Heath, B. de Jong, B. G. McConkey, R. A. Birdsey, W. A. Kurz, A. R. Jacobson, D. N. Huntzinger, Y. Pan, W. M. Post, and R. B. Cook. 2012. Reconciling estimates of the contemporary North American carbon balance among terrestrial biosphere models, atmospheric inversions, and a new approach for estimating net ecosystem exchange from inventory-based data. Global Change Biology 18:1282–1299.

Hughes, K. D. 2005. Habitat associations of dusky-footed woodrats in managed Douglas-fir / hardwood forests of northern California. MS thesis. Humboldt State University, Arcata, California.

Ice, G. G., P. W. Adams, R. L. Beschta, H. A. Froelich, and G. W. Brown. 2004. Forest management to meet water quality and fisheries objectves: Watershed studies and assessment tools in the Pacific Northwest. Pages 239–261 in G. G. Ice and J. D. Stednick, editors. A Century of Forest and Wildland Watershed Lessons. Society of American Foresters, Bethesda, Maryland.

James, C. E., B. Krumland, and D. W. Taylor. 2012. Comparison of floristic diversity between young conifer plantations and second-growth adjacent forests in California's northern interior. Western Journal of Applied Forestry 27:60–71.

Land Trust of Santa Cruz County. 2011. A conservation blueprint: An assessment and recommendations from the Land Trust of Santa Cruz County. Santa Cruz, California.

Leiberg, J. R. 1902. Forest conditions in the northern Sierra Nevada, California. United States Geological Survey, Department of the Interior, Washington, D.C.

Lewis, J. C., R. A. Powell, and W. J. Zielinski. 2012. Carnivore translocations and conservation: Insights from population models and field data for fishers ("Martes pennanti"). PLoS One 7:e32726.

Malmsheimer, R. W., J. L. Bowyer, J. S. Fried, E. Gee, R. L. Izlar, R. A. Miner, I. A. Munn, E. Oneil, and W. C. Stewart. 2011. Managing forests because carbon matters: Integrating energy, products, and land management policy. Journal of Forestry 109:S7–S51.

Matthews, S. M., J. M. Higley, J. S. Yaeger, and T. K. Fuller. 2011. Density of fishers and the efficacy of relative abundance indices and small-scale occupancy estimation to detect a population decline on the Hoopa Valley Indian Reservation, California. Wildlife Society Bulletin 35:69–75.

Matthews, S. M., J. M. Higley, K. M. Rennie, R. E. Green, C. A. Goddard, G. M. Wengert, M. W. Gabriel, and T. K. Fuller. 2013. Reproduction, recruitment, and dispersal of fishers (Martes pennanti) in a managed Douglas-fir forest in California. Journal of Mammalogy 94:100–108.

Moghaddas, J. J., R. A. York, and S. L. Stephens. 2008. Initial response of conifer and California black oak seedlings following fuel reduction activities in a Sierra Nevada mixed conifer forest. Forest Ecology and Management 255:3141–3150.

Morgan, T. A., J. P. Brandt, K. E. Songster, C. E. Keegan III, and G. A. Christensen. 2012. California's forest products industry and timber harvest, 2006. PNW-GTR-866. U.S. Department of Agriculture, Forest Service, Pacific Northwest Research Station, Portland, Oregon.

Nabuurs, G.-J., M. Lindner, P. J. Verkerk, K. Gunia, P. Deda, R. Michalak, and G. Grassi. 2013. First signs of carbon sink saturation in European forest biomass. Nature Climate Change 3:792–796.

Nabuurs, G. J., O. Masera, K. Andrasko, P. Benitez-Ponce, R. Boer, M. Dutschke, E. Elsiddig, J. Ford-Robertson, P. Frumhoff, T. Karjalainen, O. Krankina, W. A. Kurz, M. Matsumoto, W. Oyhantcabal, N. H. Ravindranath, M. J. Sanz Sanchez, and X. Zhang. 2007. Forestry. In Climate Change 2007: Mitigation. Contribution of Working Group III to the Fourth Assessment Report of the Intergovernmental Panel on Climate Change. B. Metz, O. R. Davidson, P. R. Bosch, R. Dave, L. A. Meyer (eds), Cambridge University Press, Cambridge.

Oliver, C. D., and B. C. Larson. 1996. Forest stand dynamics. John Wiley and Sons, New York, New York.

Olson, C. M., and J. A. Helms. 1996. Forest growth and stand structure at Blodgett Forest Research Station 1933–1955. Pages 681–732 in Sierra Nevada Ecosystem Project: Final Report to Congress. Volume II, Assessments and Scientific Basis for Management Options. Centers for Water and Wildland Resources, University of California, Davis, California.

Pacific Northwest Research Station Forest Inventory and Analysis (PNW-FIA). 2013. The Pacific Northwest forest inventory and analysis database annual inventory data, 2001–2011. U.S. Department of Agriculture, Forest Service, Pacific Northwest Research Station, Portland, Oregon.

Powell, R. A., and W. J. Zielinksi. 1994. Fisher. Pages 38–73 in L. F. Ruggiero, K. B. Aubry, S. W. Buskirk, L. J. Lyon, and W. J. Zielinski, editors. The scientific basis for conserving forest carnivores: American marten, fisher, lynx, wolverine in the western United States. U.S. Department of Agriculture Forest Service, Rocky Mountain Forest and Range Experiment Station, Fort Collins, Colorado.

Powell, R. A., J. C. Lewis, B. G. Slough, Scott M. Brainerd, N. R. Jordan, A. V. Abramov, V. Monakhov, P. A. Zollner, and T. Murakami. 2012. Evaluating translocation of martens, sables, and fishers. Pages 93–137 in W. J. Z. Keith B. Aubry, Martin G. Raphael, Gilbert Proulx, and Steven W. Buskirk, editors. Biology and Conservation of Martens, Sables, and Fishers. Cornell University Press, Ithaca, New York.

Rice, R. M., R. R. Ziemer, and J. Lewis. 2004. Evaluating forest management effects on erosion, sediment, and runoff: Caspar Creek and northwestern California. Pages 223–238 in G. G. Ice and J. D. Stednick, editors. A Century of Forest and Wildland Watershed Lessons. Society of American Foresters, Bethesda, Maryland.

Sakai, H. F., and B. R. Noon. 1993. Dusky-footed woodrat abundance in different-aged forests in northwestern California. Journal of Wildlife Management 57:373–382.

Skinner, C. N., A. H. Taylor, and J. K. Agee. 2006. Klamath Mountains bioregion. Page 596 in N. G. Sugihara, J. W. v. Wagtendonk, K. E. Shaffer, J. Fites-Kaufman, and A. E. Thode, editors. Fire in California's Ecosystems. University of California Press, Berkeley, California.

Skog, K. E. 2008 Sequestration of carbon in harvested wood products for the United States. Forest Products Journal 58:56–72.

Smith, W. B., technical coordinator; P D. Miles, data coordinator; C. H. Perry, map coordinator; and S. A. Pugh, data coordinator. 2009. Forest resources of the United States, 2007. GTR-WO-78. U.S. Department of Agriculture, Forest Service, Washington, D.C.

Spurr, S. H., and B. V. Barnes. 1980. Forest ecology. John Wiley and Sons, New York, New York.

Steer, H. B. 1948. Lumber production in the United States, 1799–1946. U.S. Department of Agriculture Miscellaneous Publication no. 669. Government Printing Office, Washington, D.C.

Stephens, S. L., B. M. Collins, and G. Roller. 2012. Fuel treatment longevity in a Sierra Nevada mixed conifer forest. Forest Ecology and Management 285:204–212.

Stephens, S. L., J. J. Moghaddas, C. Edminster, C. E. Fiedler, S. Haase, M. Harrington, et al. 2009. Fire treatment effects on vegetation structure, fuels, and potential fire severity in western U.S. forests. Ecological Applications 19:305–320.

Stewart, W. C., and G. Nakamura. 2012. Documenting the full climate benefits of harvested wood products in northern California: Linking harvests to the U.S. greenhouse gas inventory. Forest Products Journal 62:340–353.

Stewart, W., S. Ferranto, G. Nakamura, C. Getz, L. Huntsinger, and M. Kelly. 2012. Subdivide or silviculture: Choices facing family forest owners in the Redwood region. Page 626 in R. B. Standiford, T. J. Weller, D. D. Piirto, and J. D. Stuart, editors. Proceedings of coast redwood forests in a changing California: A symposium for scientists and managers. PSW-GTR-238. Pacific Southwest Research Station, Forest Service, U.S. Department of Agriculture, Albany, California, and Santa Cruz, California.

Stuart, J. D., and S. L. Stephens. 2006. North Coast bioregion. Page 596 in N. G. Sugihara, J. W. v. Wagtendonk, K. E. Shaffer, J. Fites-Kaufman, and A. E. Thode, editors. Fire in California's Ecosystems. University of California Press, Berkeley, California.

Swiers, R. C. 2013. Non-invasive genetic sampling and mark-recapture analysis of a fisher (*Martes pennanti*) population in northern California used as a reintroduction source. MS thesis. North Carolina State University, Raleigh, North California.

Tappeiner, J. C., II, D. A. Maguire, and T. B. Harrington. 2007. Silviculture and ecology of western U.S. Forests. Oregon State University Press, Corvallis, Oregon.

Thompson, J. L. 2008. Density of fisher on managed timberlands in north coastal California. MS thesis. Humboldt State University, Arcata, California.

U.S. Department of Agriculture (USDA), Forest Service, Pacific Southwest Research Station (PSW) Region Remote Sensing Lab. 2007. Western core table reports. Sacramento, California.

U.S. Environmental Protection Agency. 2013. Inventory of U.S. greenhouse gas emissions and sinks: 1990–2011. Washington, D.C.

U.S. Forest Service and U.S. Bureau of Land Management. 2000. Final supplemental environmental impact statement for amendment to the survey and manage, protection buffer, and other mitigating measures standards and guidelines. U.S. Forest Service. Portland, Oregon.

U.S. Forest Service Pacific Southwest Region. 2013. Ecological restoration implementation plan. R5-MB-249. U.S. Department of Agriculture Forest Service, Vallejo, California.

———. 2004. Sierra Nevada forest plan amendment, final supplemental environmental impact statement. R5-MB-046. U.S. Department of Agriculture Forest Service, Vallejo, California.

USFWS (U.S. Fish and Wildlife Service). 1990. The 1990 status review: Northern spotted owl: Strix occidentalis caurina. U.S. Department of the Interior Fish and Wildlife Service, Portland, Oregon.

Walters, C. J., and C. S. Holling. 1990. Large-scale management experiments and learning by doing. Ecology 71:2060–2068.

Williams, M. 1989. American and their forests: A historical geography. Cambridge University Press, Cambridge, UK.

Wilzbach, M. A., B. C. Harvey, J. L. White, and R. J. Nakamoto. 2005. Effects of riparian canopy opening and salmon carcass addition on the abundance and growth of resident salmonids. Canadian Journal of Fisheries and Aquatic Sciences 62:58–67.

York, R.A., J. J. Battles, R. C. Wenk, and Saah. 2012. A gap-based approach for regenerating pine species and reducing surface fuels in multi-aged mixed conifer stands in the Sierra Nevada, California. Forestry, 85:203–213.

Yoshiyama, R. N., and P. B. Moyle. 2010. Historical review of eel river anadromous salmonids, with emphasis on Chinook salmon, coho salmon, and steelhead. Center for Watershed Sciences Working Paper. University of California, Davis, California.

Youngblood, A. 2011. Ecological lessons from long-term studies in experimental forests: Ponderosa pine silviculture at Pringle Falls Experimental Forest, central Oregon. Forest Ecology and Management 261:937–947.

Zhang, J., J. Webster, R. F. Powers, and J. Mills. 2008. Reforestation after the Fountain fire in northern California: An untold success story. Journal of Forestry 106:425–430.

Zhang, J., R. F. Powers, W. W. Oliver, and D. H. Young. 2013. Response of ponderosa pine plantations to competing vegetation control in northern California, USA: A meta-analysis. Forestry. 86:3–11.

Zhang, L., W. R. Dawes, and G. R. Walker. 2001. Response of mean annual evapotranspiration to vegetation changes at catchment scale. Water Resources Research 37:701–708.

Zielinski, W. J., C. M. Thompson, K. L. Purcell, and J. D. Garner. 2013. An assessment of fisher (*Pekania pennanti*) tolerance to forest management intensity on the landscape. Forest Ecology and Management 310:821–826.

Zielinski, W. J., R. L. Truex, G. A. Schmidt, F. V. Schlexer, K. N. Schmidt, and R. H. Barrett. 2004. Home range characteristics of fishers in California. Journal of Mammalogy 85:649–657.

THIRTY-SEVEN

Range Ecosystems

SHERI SPIEGAL, LYNN HUNTSINGER, PETER HOPKINSON, and JAMES W. BARTOLOME

Introduction

Livestock grazing on woodlands and grasslands make up a typical pastoral scene in California, where the Mediterranean climate supports abundant grass growth in response to cool-season rains. Prior to European colonization, post-Pleistocene grasslands were grazed by elk, deer, bison, and other native large herbivores. The first European settlers, from Spain, in 1769 added domestic livestock to the mix, and they have flourished ever since in the mild climate and varied ecosystems of the state. The chief limit on the state's livestock production was once drought; today it is the conversion and fragmentation of the landscape. Where once the ranching and environmental communities were largely at odds, today new opportunities for collaboration, based on ecological science and social demand for the multiple benefits of wide, open spaces, are emerging. The generation of ecological knowledge about how vegetation responds to grazing has increased the emphasis on understanding and coping with the influences of unpredictable abiotic factors. In this chapter, we present an overview of livestock grazing in the California landscape.

Discussions of grazing are often plagued by poorly defined and confusing terms (Box 37.1). RANGELANDS are the state's uncultivated or undeveloped ecosystems that are not in dense trees or barren desert, and where the landscape is vegetated by grasses or shrubs. Rangelands can include scattered trees; the oak woodlands of California are a classic California rangeland type. Rangelands make up about two-thirds of the California landscape. The traditional, agricultural use of rangeland, where lack of water limits cultivation and lack of trees limits forestry, has been livestock grazing. RANGE, defined as land grazed by livestock, spans over a third of California, and grazing remains the state's most extensive land use (FRAP 2010). This chapter focuses on range ecosystems: managed ecosystems grazed by livestock.

Rangelands cover an estimated 50–70% of the earth's land surface and 40–50% of the United States. Because rangelands are so extensive, understanding the consequences of human activities on them has implications for subjects as diverse as water and food security, biodiversity conservation, and global

BOX 37.1 RANGE AND RANGELANDS

Terms describing grazing and its land base can be confusing and are often inconsistently applied. Although range managers commonly use "rangeland" and "range" interchangeably, a useful distinction exists between the two terms. "Rangeland" is a type of land, generally delineated by vegetation. "Range," in contrast, is land grazed by livestock. The term "pasture" is also used for lands grazed by livestock, and "range" is usually but not always synonymous with open or unfenced pasture (von Richthofen 1885).

A typical definition for rangeland is: Land on which the vegetation is predominately grasses, grass-like plants, forbs (herbaceous dicots), or shrubs, and which is managed as a natural ecosystem, even if the dominant plants are non-native. The vegetation may include scattered trees (canopy cover ≤30%). Rangelands include natural grasslands, savannas, shrublands, many deserts, tundras, alpine communities, marshes, and meadows (modified from Society for Range Management 1998). One outcome from inconsistent definitions has been inaccurate numbers for both the extent of grazed lands and count of grazing livestock (Lund 2007), but range is estimated to cover between 50% to 70% of the earth's land surface and 40% to 50% of the United States (Holechek et al. 2011).

In California, rangelands cover approximately 60% of the land (23 million hectares), while range covers about 33% (13.8 million ha; Heady and Child 1994, FRAP 2010). Rangeland vegetation types within California include valley grassland (also known as annual grassland), coastal prairie, serpentine grassland, vernal pool grassland (Chapter 23, "Grasslands"), montane meadow (Chapter 27, "Montane Forests"), chaparral (Chapter 24, "Chaparral"), coastal scrub (Chapter 22, "Coastal Sage Scrub"), desert grassland and shrubland (Chapter 30, "Deserts"), and oak savanna (Chapter 25, "Oak Woodlands"). Forests, dense woodlands (>30% tree cover), ice-covered areas, water, or areas that are cultivated or irrigated (Chapter 38, "Agriculture") are not generally classified as rangelands. Some forested lands (Chapters 26, "Coast Redwood Forests"; 27, "Montane Forests"; and 28, "Subalpine Forests") are grazed by livestock and so, although not rangeland, are still considered range.

climate change (Heady and Child 1994, FRAP 2010, Holechek et al. 2011). Rangeland ecosystems of the world have some things in common:

1. Rainfall tends to be limited and highly variable in amount and timing.
2. Range soils tend to be low in fertility, shallow, and often rocky.
3. Grazing and browsing by large herbivores, often ruminants, cycles a significant portion of net primary productivity (Holechek et al. 2011).

While rangelands generally cannot sustain crop agriculture without irrigation and costly soil modifications, rangeland livestock, with digestive systems similar to those of native, large herbivores, can convert low-quality, fibrous plants into products such as meat, milk, and blood that humans can readily digest. As a result, harvesting products from herbivores has been a defining element in the relationship between humans and rangelands worldwide for millennia (Briske and Heitschmidt 1991).

Managing range ecosystems is challenging because they are strongly affected by unpredictable factors like rainfall, temperature, and fire. Rangeland ecosystems are often referred to as NONEQUILIBRIUM ECOSYSTEMS because conditions can change rapidly, regardless of livestock grazing activities, and no long-term equilibrium can be struck between livestock numbers and FORAGE production (Box 37.2, Box 37.3). Livestock management can protect soils and influence biomass production but beyond that generally only has limited influence on the ecosystem (Jackson and Bartolome 2002), although many grazing systems have been devised in an attempt to overcome this limitation (Heitschmidt and Taylor 1991, Briske et al. 2008). Instead, an adaptive and flexible approach is needed, whether through formal experimentation and monitoring (Reever Morghan et al. 2006); the skilled, long-term observations of managers and graziers; or the cultural practices of pastoralist societies. In California, forage production can vary by orders of magnitude from year to year, posing challenges to matching animal needs to production and stimulating a variety of creative solutions.

This chapter begins with a description of the distribution of range ecosystems in California, focusing on types of livestock as well as regional patterns of grazing land ownership and herd and rancher characteristics. Next we offer a brief account of the history of grazing lands management in California. A subsequent discussion about the ecological dimensions of range ecosystems features models describing how range ecosystems work and implications for management in California. The effects of livestock grazing take many forms. We compare these effects before closing the chapter with a discussion of future directions for range ecosystems and managers.

The Geography of Livestock Grazing

The use of Californian rangelands for domestic livestock production began with Spanish colonization in 1769 and establishment of missions, individual land grants, and presidios along the coast, with significant livestock grazing by 1773. Livestock grazing spread inland beginning in 1824, when the Mexican government granted land for vast cattle ranches

Photo on previous page: Cattle graze annual range in spring before a backdrop of oak savanna and woodland on the Tehachapi foothills. Spatial and temporal vegetation patterns are most strongly associated with soils and weather. Photo: Rebecca C. Wenk.

BOX 37.2 EQUILIBRIUM AND NONEQUILIBRIUM MODELS OF COMMUNITY DYNAMICS IN RANGE ECOSYSTEMS

A useful approach to understanding and predicting community dynamics of a particular range ecosystem is to place that ecosystem on a theoretical continuum with two types of models at its extremes: equilibrium community models and nonequilibrium community models (Wiens 1984).

In equilibrium models, interactions among the biota internal to the community regulate community dynamics so that an equilibrium is achieved (Briske et al. 2003). In these models, community succession proceeds linearly and has a single endpoint or stable equilibrium state. Examples of equilibrium models are the plant-herbivore population model that emphasizes herbivory as structuring plant and herbivore communities (Caughley 1976) and Clements's succession model that emphasizes plant competition and facilitation as the main drivers of vegetation change (Clements 1916). Nonequilibrium models include the persistent nonequilibrium model (Briske et al. 2003), representing systems in which the effects of external factors like low and erratic rainfall prevent organisms internal to the community from reaching an equilibrium through competition or grazing (Wiens 1984, Ellis and Swift 1988). Threshold models that describe alternative stable states (e.g., Scheffer et al. 2001) are also considered to be nonequilibrium-type models (Briske et al. 2003). However, these threshold models can accommodate states that are regulated by biotic processes of competition and grazing. State-and-transition models, though designed to describe nonequilibrium dynamics, can be used to describe either equilibrium or nonequilibrium systems (Westoby et al. 1989).

Two main foci of the models—(1) the relative effects on vegetation of grazing versus a highly variable environment, and (2) the potential for multiple stable states—are important considerations for understanding and managing range ecosystems. On range, as described throughout this chapter, spatial and temporal variation in water and forage resources is high, annual production is as unpredictable as rainfall and temperature patterns, and extremes of precipitation or temperature are not uncommon. While specific applications of these models are still contested due to issues of spatial and temporal scale (see Box 37.3; Briske et al. 2003), there is now broad scientific consensus that nonequilibrium models better explain the community dynamics of arid rangelands in the U.S. and throughout the world than equilibrium models do (Briske et al. 2005, Vetter 2005, Booker et al. 2012).

The current consensus represents a shift in thinking over the past hundred years. The severe damage to western U.S. rangelands caused by unregulated and excessive livestock use in the late 1800s was explained by models emphasizing changes in community structure (Booker et al. 2012). Those early models employed the then new CLEMENTSIAN EQUILIBRIUM ECOLOGY (Clements 1916, Sampson 1919) to describe successional changes on range. Early workers assumed that competition-driven plant succession and livestock grazing were the strongest controls on vegetation succession and that there is a single climax or equilibrium state for range in a particular climate region. Livestock grazing was identified as the cause of "range retrogression." It was thought that the removal of livestock would allow for competition and other processes internal to the system to take over and result in succession to the climax state. This approach persisted with modifications through the 1970s. The application of nonequilibrium models to arid and semiarid rangelands began in earnest in the 1980s. This conceptual evolution occurred due to the recognition that equilibrium climax models fail to describe rangelands well at most scales (Wiens 1984, Ellis and Swift 1988, Behnke et al. 1993, Briske et al. 2003) and that assessments of range condition work better when decoupled from the use of linear distance to a purported climax state.

(Bartolome, Barry et al. 2007). The Gold Rush of 1849 not only brought large numbers of livestock into the state to feed miners but also accelerated the movement of ranching inland and into the Sierra (Burcham 1982). In the mid-nineteenth century, patterns of TRANSHUMANCE, or herding of livestock to the mountains for the summer to graze green meadows, became a common strategy for coping with California's long, dry summers. In the later nineteenth century, as crop production and irrigation spread through the Central Valley and other fertile lowlands (see Chapter 38, "Agriculture"), the foothill and coastal grasslands and oak woodlands became the focus of rangeland grazing. Large areas of high-elevation range were taken out of production in the late twentieth century as government priorities for these mostly federal lands shifted and as widespread fire suppression led to an increase in tree density and loss of open areas suitable for range use (SNEP 1997, Forero 2002). Conversion of foothill lands for viticulture, orchards, urbanization, and semirural housing development today continues the trend of reducing California range area (see Chapter 5, "Population and Land Use").

Today, livestock commonly graze the oak woodlands and grasslands that occupy the elevational band between California's lower valleys and higher mountains. Some producers still use montane range in the summer, and cattle are frequently supplemented with hay and crop by-products. Livestock graze in the Central Valley, the Sierran foothills, Sierra Nevada meadows, along the coastal mountain ranges from San Diego to Mendocino, on the Modoc Plateau, and in the deserts of southeastern California (Figure 37.1). The geography of the industry extends beyond state borders because livestock are moved between California and Mexico, Canada, and other western states including Hawaii. Expanding cultivation has displaced grazing from valleys and replaced many irrigated pastures, but it has also produced livestock feed in the forms of agricultural by-products, hay, grain, and crop

BOX 37.3 CALIFORNIA GRASSLAND SYSTEMS ON THE CONTINUUM FROM EQUILIBRIUM TO NONEQUILIBRIUM

Understanding where a range system sits on the theoretical continuum from equilibrium to nonequilibrium can guide managers as they describe, understand, and predict the factors that will likely control community dynamics in that range system (see Box 37.2). No system is purely nonequilibrium or equilibrium; rather, each comprises a blend of dynamics (Wiens 1984). Placing systems to be understood and managed along a conceptual continuum can be a launching point for discussion and verification through experimentation and monitoring. Here, we propose two sample continuums representing degree of departure from the "persistent nonequilibrium model" (see Box 37.2). Continuum endpoints reflect two possible extremes: one, that temporal changes in species composition are regulated by livestock grazing; and the other, that temporal changes in species composition are regulated by variable rainfall. Species composition is the focal metric here, but vegetation productivity or herbivore population dynamics could also be used to arrange the systems, with potentially different outcomes.

The influences of edaphic (soil) and topographic properties on the spatial arrangement of plant species across semiarid and arid rangelands cannot be understated (Moseley et al. 2010). As the persistent nonequilibrium model focuses more on temporal rather than spatial change, managers can use the continuum in our example to ask: "Once species from the regional species pool colonize particular soils, which factors or processes will have the strongest influence over community dynamics through time?"

Spatial and temporal scales of observation greatly influence whether nonequilibrium or equilibrium patterns are prevalent and detectable (Wiens 1989, Friedel 1994, Fulendorf and Smeins 1996, Ryerson and Parmenter 2001). In Box 37.3 Figure 1, we arrange along the theoretical continuum the three major California grassland subtypes of California's Mediterranean climate zone (regional scale, top line), as well as particular types of sites found within the valley grassland subtype (site scale, bottom line). The scale of temporal change in species composition represented by both continuums is interannual. Perennial-dominated coastal prairie occurs along the coast. Annual-dominated valley grassland occurs on the edges of the Central Valley and into the eastern slopes of the Coast Ranges and western slopes of the Sierra Nevada (Bartolome, Barry et al. 2007). Jackson and Bartolome (2002) proposed a third, floristically distinct subtype called coast range grassland, a mix of annuals and perennials. It is typified in the hills east of the San Francisco Bay (Bartolome et al. 2004). We propose that valley grassland sits closest to the nonequilibrium side of the continuum and is well-described by the persistent nonequilibrium model. Two multiyear studies of plots arranged across large expanses of valley grassland concluded that most temporal variability in species composition was linked to changes in rainfall timing and amount, with only very weak links to grazing intensity and effects (Jackson and Bartolome 2002, Spiegal et al. 2014). A study conducted in coast range grassland revealed that rainfall and grazing play somewhat equivalent roles in temporal changes in species composition in this subtype (Bartolome et al. 2004). Regional-scale studies of coastal prairie suggest this system can, with some regularity, depart from the persistent nonequilibrium model because the biotic interactions between livestock and plants strongly influence species composition (Jackson and Bartolome 2002, Hayes and Holl 2003). Accordingly, we have placed coastal prairie nearer the equilibrium end of the continuum.

On the bottom continuum, we arrange ecosystems at the spatial scale of site and the interannual temporal scale, using the example of Beale Air Force Base (AFB) in Yuba County. If conceptualized only at the regional scale, Beale Air Force Base would be classified as valley grassland. However, it comprises sites of valley grassland dominated by exotic annual grasses and forbs, sites with stands of the native perennial bunchgrass purple needlegrass (*Stipa pulchra*), and sites with vernal pools (Platenkamp 1998, Marty et al. 2005). Some sites within this spatially variable location therefore sit closer to the equilibrium end than does its regional landscape on the whole.

We extrapolated from other studies conducted about the site types to build a working hypothesis for their arrangement on the continuum. Valley grassland and sites dominated by exotic annual grasses and forbs are placed to the right in the regional-scale and site-scale continuums, respectively, because abiotic controls over temporal variation in species composition are prevalent at both scales (Jackson and Bartolome 2002, Spiegal et al. 2014). In contrast, at a purple needlegrass site at Beale AFB, the reduction of height and reproduction of mature bunchgrasses over a three-year period were linked to changes in rainfall and temperature as well as to grazing (Marty et al. 2005). Because the reduction in the purple needlegrass population size, partially effected by grazing, will potentially impact community composition, we placed purple needlegrass sites further from the nonequilibrium end of the spectrum. Vernal pool sites sit closest to the equilibrium end of the spectrum, based on evidence from a ranch in nearby eastern Sacramento County on geologic formations similar to those found at Beale AFB (Platenkamp 1998, Pyke and Marty 2005). Researchers found that grazing is necessary to reduce exotic annual grasses and maintain the standing water critical to the existence of native vernal pool plants and invertebrates (Marty 2005, Pyke and Marty 2005).

The arrangements in the two examples generate an important hypothesis: wetter range ecosystems may not be well described by the persistent nonequilibrium model. The fog-influenced coastal prairie and seasonally inundated vernal pools are regulated to some degree by the biotic interaction between livestock and plants. It is possible that the more persistent water in these systems buffers the communities from the impacts of California's rainfall variability. The degree of annual plant dominance also appears to influence whether the persistent nonequilibrium model is suitable. Because perennial plants' survival and reproduction are not as dependent on annual germination conditions as are annual plants' survival, perennial-dominated coastal prairie and perennial native bunchgrass sites within the valley grassland may be less impacted by fluctuations in climate and more impacted by biotic interaction with grazers.

These arrangements are hypothetical but can be used to inform management planning and monitoring. Knowing where a grassland system sits on the continuum can help managers predict the factors that will most strongly influence management actions. For instance, managers of valley grassland whose primary vegetation management tool is livestock grazing can opportunistically time grazing to coincide with rainfall that is known to support desired changes in species composition and thereby augment the strength of rainfall to meet management objectives (Westoby et al. 1989, Spiegal et al. 2014). This knowledge can also provide insight into the selection of factors for study and monitoring and the spatial scales at which to conduct these activities.

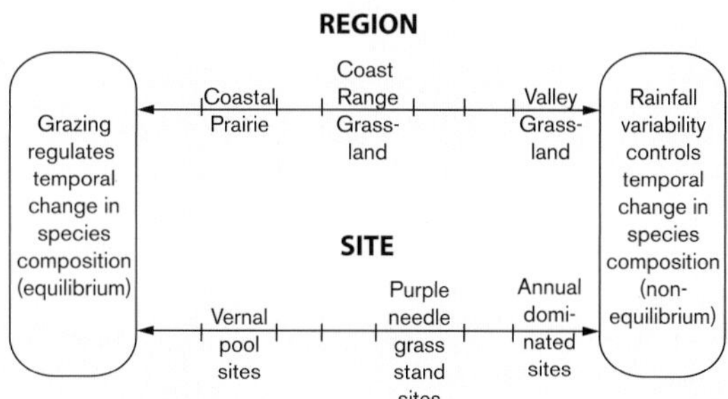

BOX 37.3 FIGURE 1 Valley grassland and sites dominated by exotic annual grasses and forbs are placed to the right in the regional-scale and site-scale continuums, respectively, because abiotic controls over temporal variation in species composition are prevalent at both scales. Sources: Weins 1984, Jackson and Bartolome 2002, Spiegal et al. 2014.

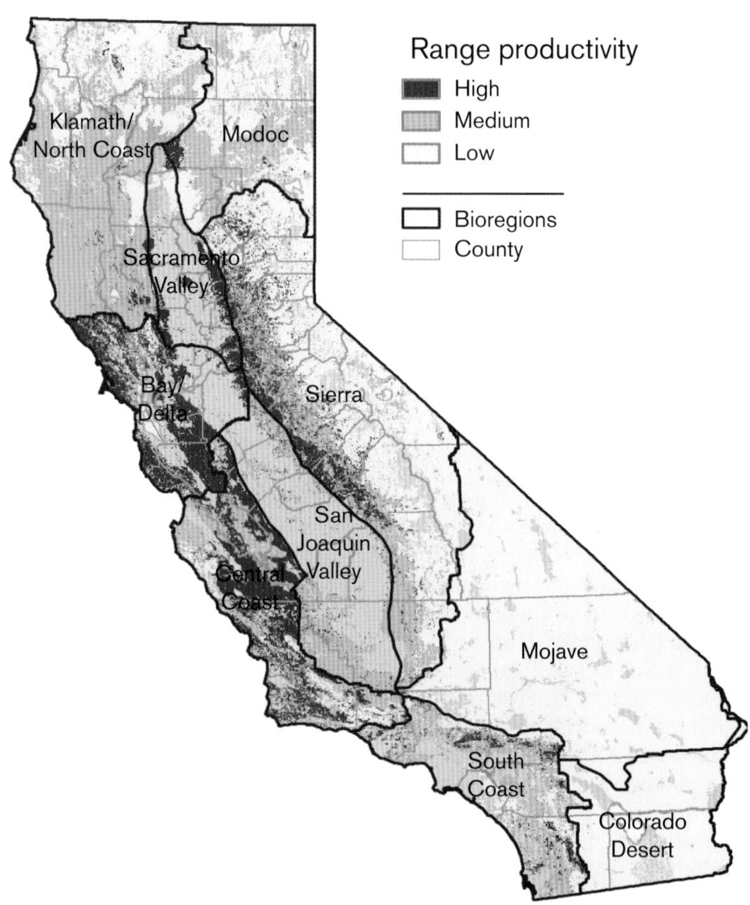

FIGURE 37.1 Estimated average forage productivity. Availability of vegetation for consumption by grazing or browsing animals varies across the state. Source: Adapted from the FRAP 2010 Assessment, which recompiled data from the NRCS Forage Production and Soil Survey.

TABLE 37.1
Management systems, land tenure, and other major influences affecting range production in major Californian climate regions

Range type	Typical management system	Land tenure: percentage public	Major influences on the range industry
Mediterranean inland, coastal	Cow-calf and stocker, fall calving, may not lease or may use a diversity of leases and permits, and a variety of feeding options, to meet year-round forage needs Forage: annual grass and browse Greatest forage constraints: fall when forage deteriorates, recurrent droughts	15%	Development along the coast, shrub encroachment, wildfire, spread of vineyards and other intensive agriculture, lack of packing plants, endangered species, niche marketing opportunities, loss of producer communities
Intermountain cold desert	Cow-calf, spring calving, small privately owned base properties with grazing permits on federal land Forage: bunchgrasses, shrubs Greatest forage constraints: winter range, drought	80%	Public policy, wildfires, development in riparian private lands, mining, wild horses, invasive species
Mojave and Sonoran hot desert	Cow-calf and stocker, winter and spring use, often on ephemeral permits Forage: desert grasses Greatest forage constraints: drought	80%	Public policy, endangered species, bighorn sheep
Montane	Cow-calf, summer seasonal use via transhumance; agencies may stipulate management approach Forage: montane meadows, shrubs Greatest forage constraint: short grazing season, access	Mostly public or corporate	Public policy, competition with recreational use, forest encroachment, wildfire, lack of ability to live in mountains for summer herding because of employment, loss of skills

stubble. The feedlot industry in California has its origins in converting unused portions of crops, and low-priced grains, to meat for the market (see Chapter 38, "Agriculture").

Patterns of Range Ownership

Land ownership influences the distribution of livestock production, as landowners can have vastly different goals and practices (Huntsinger et al. 2007). Most annual grasslands and oak woodlands in California are privately owned (Table 37.1), and about 80% of the oak woodland properties over 80 hectares are used for grazing (Huntsinger, Johnson et al. 2010). The U.S. Forest Service, Bureau of Land Management, National Park Service, and Department of Defense also own a small but significant amount of California grassland and oak woodland habitat that are leased for grazing, as do state, local, and regional agencies and watershed, utility, and recreation districts. A growing phenomenon in California is ownership by land trusts (Huntsinger et al. 2007). Although these various owners tend to have different management goals for livestock grazing, maintaining grassland "sustainability" is a common theme (Huntsinger et al. 2007). Private landowner goals are usually more influenced by the need to generate income, while agencies and land trusts can be more focused on goals related to their particular mandates such as fire hazard reduction, restoration of native species, water quality protection, and conservation of endangered species. However, goals overlap and blend considerably. Moreover, agencies and land trusts that use grazing to manage vegetation need to accommodate the goals and needs of those who supply the livestock, just as the livestock provider needs to accommodate the goals of the agency or trust.

Characteristics and Distribution of Livestock

The California range livestock industry is overwhelmingly dominated by beef cattle production, although sheep, dairy cattle, horses, goats, and small numbers of exotic species such as llamas and ostriches are also raised on California range (de Dios Vargas et al. 2013). Calving and lambing are timed to take advantage of spring forage growth (George, Bartolome et al. 2001; George, Nader et al. 2001). Supplemental feeds, selling of calves, transhumance, irrigated pasture, leased pastures, and shipping livestock to distant pastures help to cope with unpredictability and the summer dry period (Huntsinger, Forero et al. 2010). A fattening period for livestock, using crop by-products and eventually grains, is now part of the standard production cycle.

CATTLE

The vast majority of livestock producers relying on range produce only beef cattle and are known as ranchers. Most are "cow-calf producers" with a stable base herd of brood cows whose calves are sold at weaning each year. Owners might retain weaned calves for further weight gain if they have adequate forage or feed, or sell them to other ranches or feedlots. About 710,000 beef cows and heifers grazed California rangelands in 2011, down from 920,000 in 2001, with an additional 0.5 million to 1 million weaned calves, known as "stockers" (Figure 37.2). The number of stockers in a given year depends on rainfall, markets, and other factors. To gain weight on grass before entering a feedlot for the last few months before slaughter, stockers are grazed for about six months after weaning. Most stockers are grazed by ranchers who also have a cow-calf herd; fewer than a tenth of oak woodland cattle producers grazed only stockers in 2004 (Huntsinger et al. 2007). Dairy steers are also used as stockers in some cases, and rarely, dairies are range-based, especially along the north coast. Cow-calf herds are the animals that most commonly use open or mountain range. Cows pass knowledge of their particular ranges on to their calves (George et al. 2007). Accordingly, herd behavior is more predictable, allowing for minimal interaction with cowhands. In contrast, stockers, who do not have intergenerational "herd knowledge," require more control and fencing.

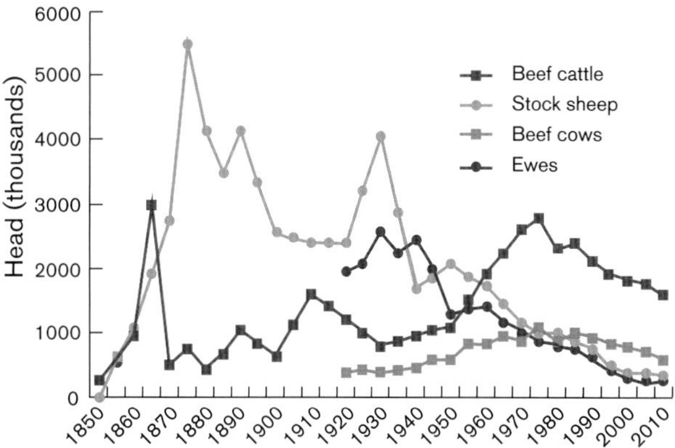

FIGURE 37.2 Range cattle and sheep in California, 1850–2010. Beef cows are brood cows, ewes are brood ewes, and both are often on rangeland. Beef cattle includes cows; the gap between the number of beef cows and beef cattle indicates the presence of yearlings (stockers) on rangelands or in feedlots within the "cattle" category. Separate data for cows and ewes were not provided until 1920. Source: Adapted from de Dios Vargas et al. 2013, in which data were recompiled from Burcham 1982, NASS 2011a, NASS 2011c, CDFA 2012.

SHEEP, GOATS, PIGS, AND HORSES

In 2010, California had 263,000 ewes, mostly in the Central Valley, down from 770,000 in 1985 (NASS 2011c). The drop is attributed to low profits due to competition from imported lamb, high labor costs, low wool prices, and a decline in lamb consumption. In oak woodlands, predators have increased with wildlife protection (Conner et al. 1998, Neale et al. 1998); and with widespread development of the wildland-urban interface, domestic dogs are a growing problem. Lambing takes place in late fall and winter, with lamb sales in spring.

About 140,000 goats resided in California in 2011, including 38,000 dairy animals (NASS 2011c). Goats are used for meat, dairy, and vegetation management. Goats may be herded to control weeds and reduce fire hazard, often on steep hills where other brush control methods would be expensive and difficult. Free-ranging pigs are rare, but the practice has undergone a recent revival for the gourmet market, with a few producers working on rearing acorn-fed pigs (Reed 2010, O'Rourke 2012). Horses have been a significant presence on California range since the Spanish Mission era (Denhardt 1940, Allen 1989). A survey of horse owners in 2004 generated an estimate of almost 700,000 horses in California, although how many of those graze range is unreported (American Horse Council Foundation 2005).

Regional Differences

The characteristics of range use are a function not only of land ownership but also of the geography and demographics of each region containing range. Range production is shaped by topographical features, local soils and climate, proximity to highways and settlements, local farming, and other factors (see Table 37.1). In the cold, desert steppes of the intermountain range, the growing season is in summer, but the dry grass retains good quality in the winter. The Bureau of Land Management manages most of the steppe regions, while the pattern of transhumance common in the region often means that animals are herded to Forest Service montane range during the summer. After a summer in the mountains, animals return to the steppe and to ranch pasture for the winter. In the southern deserts, forage might be available whenever sufficient rain falls, leading to "ephemeral" grazing permits from the Bureau of Land Management that are used only during those periods.

A 2000 study comparing northern and central California ranchers in three Mediterranean-climate counties found similar management goals but varying grazing practices and range uses (Liffmann et al. 2000). The impact of geographical differences, even within the Mediterranean region, is apparent. In Tehama County the summer climate is very dry and hot and high-elevation mountain ranges are nearby, so moving stock to upland or irrigated pastures during the summer is common. In the cooler, more coastal climates of Alameda and Contra Costa Counties, livestock can be maintained on grassland year-round, but as a result, ranchers need to actively manage and develop water sources on low-elevation range throughout the summer and early fall.

History of Range Management in California

Prior to European contact, tule elk (*Cervus canadensis nannodes*) and pronghorn (*Antilocapra americana*) ranges were managed by Native Californians for hunting (see Chapter 10, "Indigenous California"). Fire was used to create grassy areas that attracted large herbivores (Huntsinger and McCaffrey 1995), and the seeds of herbaceous species and acorns were gathered for food. Some native Californians used fire to renew grasslands, drive and trap wild grazing animals, produce goods, and control insects and disease, as well as in warfare (Anderson 2005). Planting, irrigation, and pruning might also have influenced plant communities (Anderson 2005). Lightning frequency records, oral histories, and tree-ring data confirm that Native Californians in some areas shortened wildfire intervals from natural cycles of about once a century to a frequency of a decade or less (Keeley et al. 2005, Syphard et al. 2007). Indigenous burning continues where allowed, sometimes as part of efforts to restore native vegetation.

The early Spanish and Mexican colonists, known as Californios, blended Spanish and Mexican tradition with New World imperatives and established unique cattle handling practices, many of which persist to this day (Starrs and Huntsinger 1998, Alagona et al. 2013). Through the early nineteenth century, the major livestock products were hides and tallow for export to Europe. The condition of the livestock or range was not a major concern, and in most years animals thrived in a semiwild state. Feral horses and cattle became common. Between 1833 and 1836, under the Mexican government, the missions were secularized, allowing the transfer of most of their lands into private hands.

At the end of the Mexican-American War in 1848, California was annexed by the United States and became a state in 1850. In the decades that followed, Anglo-American settlers used the courts to dispossess most Mexican grantees of their lands, and ranchos were often broken into smaller parcels (Hornbeck 1983). The few original ranchos in existence today cover thousands of hectares. After statehood, the government made numerous land grants to individuals and investors to drain the state's vast wetlands, produce timber, and construct railroads. Although smaller parcels on the scale of hundreds of hectares are more numerous, the large, remnant parcels of the Mexican and U.S. land grant systems remain important influences on the characteristics of California's range industry. For instance, California has a lower proportion of public range than surrounding western states.

The 1849 Gold Rush brought a huge influx of people into the state, creating local markets for meat that stimulated imports of large numbers of beef cattle (see Figure 37.2), including the English breeds, Hereford and Angus, that still predominate. Cattle and sheep were driven to Sierran foothill town markets and eventually to montane meadows for summer grazing. Livestock numbers and grazing pressure peaked and crashed more than once in the 1860s with severe drought and as population centers moved (Burcham 1982). The Gold Rush left a legacy of the use of montane meadows for grazing in summertime; as barbed wire and enclosure laws began to restrict winter access of livestock to valley croplands, montane summer range helped compensate (Alagona et al. 2013) and provided some relief from drought. Most high-elevation lands remained in the public domain, eventually leading to the annual, highly competitive rush to the uplands by sheepherders and cattle producers described by John Muir (1911). Herders and farmers frequently used fire to clear lands and reduce brush. Fire-return intervals were often shorter than decadal (McClaran and Bartolome 1989a), although where grazing pressure was high, there was often little to burn. In this period the federal government was an absentee landlord.

At the turn of the nineteenth century, the federal government began to take a more active role in management of public forests, establishing forest reserves (eventually to become National Forests) to protect timber and watersheds from uncontrolled timber harvest, fire, and grazing (Alagona et al. 2013). After 1906, graziers were required to get a permit from the U.S. Forest Service and to pay a per-head fee to graze in specified areas or allotments. The numbers of animals allowed on the forests was reduced. Permits were preferentially given to those owning adjacent foothill properties; migratory sheepherders, including many of Basque or Irish heritage, often lost out, especially on the west slope of the Sierra. The establishment of National Parks, such as Yosemite and Sequoia-Kings Canyon, further restricted high-country grazing. The World War I push for increased agricultural production caused a spike in grazing, including in the amount allowed on forests, that was not repeated again (see Figure 37.2). Since World War II, transhumance has continued to decline due to fire suppression efforts that have led to denser woody vegetation and reduced livestock forage, shifting land use priorities for public lands with stringent and constantly changing constraints on livestock producers, reductions of grazing permits on public lands, and land development patterns that interfere with traditional stock routes (Huntsinger, Forero et al. 2010).

Beginning around 1930, a shift from sheep to cattle production began that still continues. Over the next twenty-five years, California's beef cattle population rose to approximately 3.2 million head in 1976 (see Figure 37.2; Burcham 1981). California's ranchers benefited from financial and technical support provided by the state and federal governments, corporations, private donors, and a new generation of range managers who launched ambitious research, education, and outreach programs. Postwar range managers were advocates for the use of herbicides, heavy machinery, and other tools to increase forage availability, improve streamflow, and raise livestock carrying capacity through "range improvement" (Alagona et al. 2013). Using state annual range improvement reports, Bolsinger (1988) found that from 1945 to 1974 about 0.8 million hectares of hardwoods and chaparral were cleared in the cause of range improvement (Chapter 24, "Chaparral"). Since then, rangeland management has increasingly emphasized multiple goals, including oak conservation and production of ecosystem services—the benefits people derive from the ecosystem (de Groot et al. 2010). Awareness is growing that while the returns from livestock production are often modest, range and ranches are in fact multifunctional, producing diverse goods and services for their owners and society.

Today, except in specialty operations, weaned range calves or yearlings are sold to feedlots where they are fed agricultural by-products, hay, grain, and other rations for 100 to 150 days and slaughtered at 18 to 24 months of age and weights of 475 to 520 kilograms. The largest feedlots are near the grain production centers in the middle of the U.S., though California has a few. The great majority of Californian livestock producers live on their properties and manage the land themselves. Most have owned their land for a long time: in one survey, 63% of ranchers with public land grazing permits for summer grazing reported that their families owned their home ranch in the oak woodlands for more than one hundred years (Sulak and Huntsinger 2002). In 2005 only one quarter of oak woodland ranchers in a statewide survey reported that the majority of household income came from ranching, while 10% reported farming as their major source of income. About 22% cited off-ranch wages as their major income source, and another 22% earned most of their income from other forms of "self-employment" including investments, pensions, and so forth (Huntsinger et al. 2007, de Dios Vargas et al. 2013). What ranchers say makes ranching worthwhile is experiencing the lifestyle, raising a family on a ranch, working with livestock, and enjoying the natural environment. This is common throughout the West (Martin and Jeffries 1966, Smith and Martin 1972, Bartlett et al. 1989, Rowe et al. 2001, Gentner and Tanaka 2002, Sulak and Huntsinger 2002, Tanaka et al. 2005). In a three-county California survey, more than 90% of ranchers agreed that ranching "makes them feel closer to the earth" and that it is a "good place for family life," and about a third reported that they belonged to some sort of "environmental organization" (Liffmann et al. 2000). Most consider land appreciation an important, long-term financial asset and have planned retirements and estates accordingly. Selling off small parcels is a traditional means of escaping a financial crisis. As a result, ranchers strongly defend the right to market their land at a good price.

Range Ecology

A critical part of understanding the ecological dynamics of rangelands, and predicting the outcomes of management or changes in the environment, is developing models for how rangeland ecosystems work. The field of rangeland management in the United States has its roots in the need of Forest Service managers to manage livestock grazing on the National Forests starting in the early twentieth century. Models that explained the relationship between the number of grazing animals and vegetation response were sought in order to set appropriate stocking levels. California's highly variable rainfall, and its dramatic effects on forage production, makes clear that effective rangeland ecological models must recognize high levels of unpredictability and strong abiotic influences.

Range Ecosystem Models

The models presented here (Figure 37.3) identify and simplify important interactions in rangeland and range ecosystems. The models provide a useful framework for understanding changes over time, processes like energy and nutrient flows, and influences of herbivory, as well as consequences of different management goals.

In the basic rangeland ecosystem model (see Figure 37.3a), meat-eating predators take advantage of the ability of grazing herbivores like livestock and elk to consume low-quality grasses and other forages and convert them to high-quality protein and energy-rich fats. Large-bodied grazing animals have evolved complex digestive systems that draw on the ability of some microbes to break down cellulose for energy and to construct proteins without consuming specific amino acids. In this model, humans can be considered secondary consumers that do not directly use primary production, relying instead on rangeland herbivores to capture dispersed and low-quality primary production, process it via their symbiotic relationship with microbes in their digestive systems, and concentrate it in conveniently edible and high-quality forms like milk and meat.

A few modifications to the basic rangeland ecosystem model illustrate the important role of humans as providers and recipients of ecosystem services in contemporary range ecosystems (see Figure 37.3b). Though livestock producers have long recognized and consumed a constellation of nonmarket benefits from rangeland livestock production, which in fact have been known for decades as strong motivators for participating in ranching (Smith and Martin 1972), the benefits that the public derives from range ecosystems have more recently gained wider recognition: irrigation and drinking water, recreational and lifestyle opportunities, wildlife habitat, open pastoral landscapes, biodiversity, and carbon storage. It might even be argued that the most important role of ranching in twenty-first-century California is not providing the traditional livestock products of meat, milk, and fiber but rather acting as a bulwark against the conversion of range into housing developments, vineyards, orchards, and other, more intensive land uses that do not provide the same multiple ecosystem services.

A. Rangeland ecosystem model

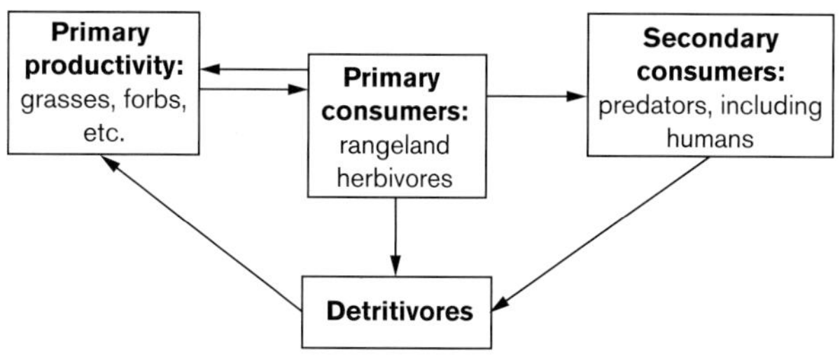

B. Range production systems in California

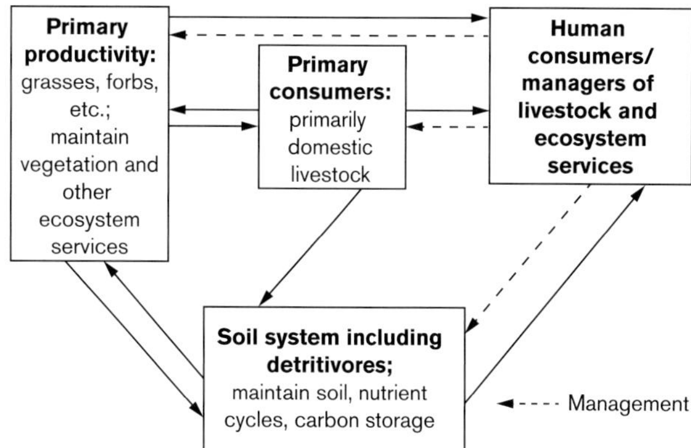

FIGURE 37.3 (A) Basic rangeland ecosystem model and (B) contemporary range production system model for California. Boxes represent the major components of the system, and solid arrows symbolize interactions (transfer of energy or materials) between components. In (B) text within boxes describes management goals as well as system constituents. Dotted arrows represent interactions pertaining to management.

Forage in Californian Range Ecosystems

The portion of net primary productivity available for grazing use is called the available forage and differs considerably among and within California's diverse ecosystems. Here we describe the year-round forage productivity in four major Californian range ecosystem types: inland Mediterranean grassland, inland Mediterranean grassland with oak canopy, coastal Mediterranean grassland, and cold and hot deserts. These range types differ in net primary productivity (Figure 37.4) but are interrelated across the Californian landscape. Grasslands of California's Mediterranean climate zone are classified into two main subtypes: perennial grass–dominated coastal prairie, and annual grass–dominated valley grassland (Bartolome, Barry et al. 2007; see Chapter 23,

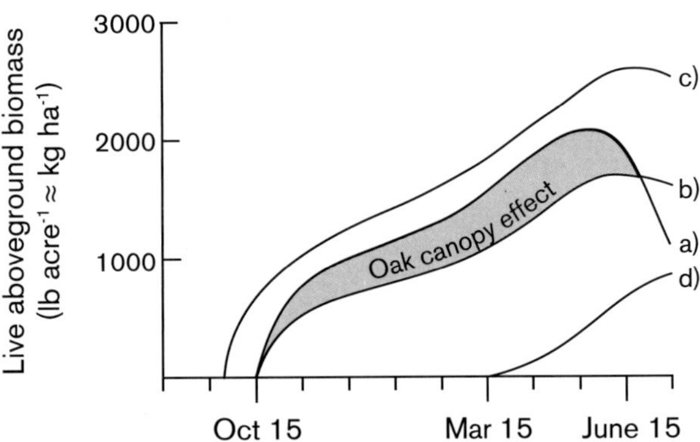

FIGURE 37.4 Conceptualized figure of seasonal changes in aboveground biomass for four California range types. (A) Inland Mediterranean annual grassland; (B) inland Mediterranean annual grassland with oak canopy (here, with >50 cm yr^{1} precipitation); (C) coastal Mediterranean grassland; and (D) hot and cold desert range. The oak canopy effect (shaded area) indicates the difference exerted by the presence of oaks in (B) versus (A), where oaks suppress biomass during the wet season but extend forage productivity longer into the dry season. 1 kg ha^{-1} ≈ 1 lb. ac^{-1}.

"Grasslands"). With little change in its herbaceous character, valley grassland and coastal prairie extend into the understory of oak SAVANNA, oak woodland, chaparral, and other scrub vegetation types (Allen-Diaz et al. 2007). The northern coastal shrub dominant, the short-lived shrub coyote brush (*Baccharis pilularis*), invades and modifies coastal prairie but also is common quite far inland (Hobbs and Mooney 1986, Williams et al. 1987).

Outside of California's Mediterranean climate zone, grassland and woodland ecosystems are less widespread, replaced mainly by forests and shrublands. Grazing was formerly more important on transitory openings in forests but has greatly declined in recent decades. Use of middle- to high-elevation meadow systems is still common. Montane forage characteristics are quite different from that of the lowlands, with many native perennial grasses and sedges and a short summer grazing season. While the impenetrable and unpalatable chaparral of the Mediterranean zone is little grazed, cold and hot desert shrublands in northeastern and southern California furnish important perennial grass forage and ephemeral annual forage, respectively.

INLAND MEDITERRANEAN ANNUAL GRASSLAND

Grasslands of the inland Mediterranean climate zone (i.e., valley grassland) comprise largely exotic annual grass and forb species from the Mediterranean basin and surrounding areas (Bartolome, Barry et al. 2007). Factors at many spatial and temporal scales interact to control herbaceous productivity of California's annual grasslands (Bartolome 1989). Aboveground biomass at the time of late spring seed set varies interannually as a function of the timing and amount of rainfall, temperature (Talbot et al. 1939, Bentley and Talbot 1948, Heady 1958, George et al. 1988), and edaphic and topographic characteristics (Jackson et al. 1988, Callaway et al. 1991). A typical yearly production curve for annual grassland starts with the onset of autumn germination following fall rains of more than 2.5 centimeters in a one-week period (see Figure 37.4a). Winter growth slowly progresses as temperatures decline, followed by rapid spring growth as soil temperatures increase while there is adequate soil moisture (Chiariello 1989). During spring, forage production usually exceeds the ability of grazing animals to consume it. Peak standing crop of the herbaceous vegetation generally occurs between April 1 and May 15, followed by the death of the annual plants. Standing dead biomass slowly decomposes as summer drought limits microbial activity until the ensuing autumn rains stimulate decomposition. Sufficient fall rainfall also brings about new annual plant germination (Jackson et al. 1988).

INLAND MEDITERRANEAN ANNUAL GRASSLAND WITH OAK CANOPY

Adding tree canopy cover to the annual grassland alters the local environment and affects both forage production and utilization. The type and amount of tree cover (evergreen or deciduous), geographic location (high or low rainfall), and local soil factors can be important variables (Frost and McDougald 1989, Frost et al. 1997, Rolo and Moreno 2012). Dahlgren et al. (1997) described soils beneath oak canopy as "islands of fertility" because of their greater carbon, nitrogen, and phosphorus stocks compared to adjacent open grassland sites. The patchy distribution of oak trees might be enhanced by the ability of oaks to garner water and nutrients from the open spaces between trees and then concentrate them by way of leaf fall to the area beneath the canopy (Schlesinger and Pilmanis 1998, Cross and Schlesinger 1999, Huenneke et al. 2002). An untested hypothesis is that herbivores provide a check on this effect by harvesting plant nutrients from beneath the canopy and redistributing them in a more homogeneous way across the landscape.

Shade from trees usually inhibits herbaceous production in areas of California receiving more than 50 centimeters of annual precipitation (see Figure 37.4b; McClaran and Bartolome 1989b). The opposite generally holds for drier portions of the state, where shade reduces drought stress, moderates temperatures, and can increase forage growth. Frost et al. (1997) reported that an increase in tissue and litter nutritional quality under oaks in drier regions more than compensated for any possible reductions in forage amount. The differences in species found in shade as opposed to full sun explained differences of forage nutrient quality more than changes in the nutritional content of individual plants.

COASTAL MEDITERRANEAN GRASSLAND

Coastal prairie grasslands occur in climate zones with significant coastal fog. Native perennial bunchgrasses are more prevalent there than in inland grasslands. More summer moisture allows perennial grasses to continue growing in the summer when exotic annuals have gone to seed (Corbin et al. 2007; see Chapter 23, "Grasslands"). The growth/production curve for coastal prairie (see Figure 37.4c) is quite different from more seasonally arid grasslands. The shorter period of water deficiency in summer, more moderate winter temperatures, and different growth patterns of perennial and annual grasses influence the growth curve. Typically, fall and peak biomass production are greater than for annual-dominated valley grasslands (George, Bartolome et al. 2001; Bartolome, Barry et al. 2007). The decline in forage amount and quality after the spring peak is slower as perennials go dormant later. Coastal grasslands are among the most productive in North America both in net primary productivity and livestock production (Huntsinger et al. 2007).

HOT AND COLD DESERT RANGE

Outside of the Mediterranean zone, lower total rainfall and cold winters limit forage (see Figure 37.4d). On intermountain cold desert steppe where perennial grasses like blue-bunch wheatgrass (*Elymus spicatus*) are common, forage quality is high even during the dormant season in winter, and beef cattle are often raised without supplementation but at low stocking levels. Invasive annual grasses can increase production in some years but reduce forage quality and increase fire hazard. On warm desert range, annuals like red-stem filaree (*Erodium cicutarium*) form the basis for ephemeral grazing permits (Holechek et al. 2011). Forage growth in mountain meadows is rapid but short-lived and available only in summer.

Range Ecology and Management

Grazing is an ecosystem process broadly defined as feeding on herbaceous plants, algae, fungi, or phytoplankton (Begon et al. 1996). While livestock grazing started in California less than 250 years ago, the rangelands have always been grazed by large and small animals, albeit in many different ways. Grazing (shown in Figure 37.3 as the interaction between primary production and primary consumption) includes three primary phenomena affecting ecosystems: defoliation, trampling, and nutrient redistribution (Jackson and Bartolome 2007). These can be precisely described using the terms "grazing pressure" (the amount of forage removed relative to availability); "grazing distribution" (where grazing occurs); "grazing period" (when grazing occurs); "selectivity" (what is grazed); and "kind and class" of animal (what kind of animal does the grazing and what is its phenological state). When described in these terms, it is apparent that for any given landscape, ecosystem, community, or management unit, grazing can be spatially and temporally complex.

The needs of primary producers and consumers fundamentally conflict. Plants capture energy and support growth by growing leaves, but herbivores capture energy and protein by removing the leaves. This observation has led to the principle that the grazing manager cannot simultaneously optimize primary production and primary consumption (Heitschmidt and Stuth 1991). This principle has held up well despite observations that can be loosely grouped as describing COMPENSATORY PLANT GROWTH (Bartolome 1993). Attempts to use highly complex SPECIALIZED GRAZING SYSTEMS to circumvent this principle have been many, costly, and mostly failures (Briske et al. 2008, Briske et al. 2011).

Range Livestock Production in the Mediterranean Climate Zone

In the most typical range cattle production system (cow-calf), the animals present during the grazing year consist of a mix of older cows in various states of pregnancy and lactation, breeding bulls, and calves. Yearlings can also be present. These classes of cattle each have very different nutritional requirements. In the inland zone the period between roughly March 1 and June 1 is referred to as the "adequate green feed period" (George, Bartolome et al. 2001) because animal needs for energy, protein, and vitamins can be met by range forage. During the rest of the year, range cattle need to either be supplemented or draw on reserves stored in their bodies.

California ranchers have devised ways to adapt to the nutritional needs of livestock production. Their basic approach is to time calving in fall to allow the growing calves to take advantage of the later adequate green feed period in spring on annual range. Young nursing calves in fall utilize milk produced by the cow, which is generally allowed to lose weight and use fat reserves. Often the pregnant cows are fed a protein supplement to overcome lower forage quality during the late summer and fall dry season. Historically, ranchers with access to higher-elevation range could extend the green feed period by moving animals to mountain pastures (Huntsinger, Forero et al. 2010; Brownsey et al. 2013). Another way to effectively extend the quality of feed is to use irrigated pastures (Huntsinger et al. 2007). In the inevitable years when forage production is low, hay may be fed to maintain adequate nutritional levels in cows. Similar production schedules to adapt nutritional needs to range forage quality are seen in sheep operations and on coastal prairie, where a longer green feed season is typical.

Models for Range Community Dynamics

To understand grazing, ecological models must incorporate the dynamics of vegetation change. Understanding how changes in grazing might influence the ecosystem requires understanding the many, interacting factors that shape plant communities. As the influences of relatively unpredictable and unmanageable abiotic forces like rainfall have come to be better understood, vegetation change models have shifted away from the idea that there is a single, equilibrial, CLIMAX COMMUNITY that represents the potential, or most pristine, community for a given site. Instead, newer models emphasize that unpredictability in vegetation change means there is no single "equilibrial" state and that several "stable" vegetation states are possible on a given site with different potentials to produce ecosystem services. While equilibrium models posit that biotic interactions such as competition and herbivory are key drivers of plant community structure, nonequilibrium models posit that plant-plant and plant-animal interactions are of minimal importance relative to abiotic constraints (Wiens 1984, Ellis and Swift 1988, Briske et al. 2003). The choice of model is critical to describing, understanding, and predicting range dynamics. (We discuss equilibrium and nonequilibrium models with more detail in Box 37.2.)

Ecological Site Classifications, State-and-Transition Models, and Adaptive Management: Conceptual Tools for Range Management

Just as different definitions of the term "rangeland" can lead to vastly different estimates of how much rangeland there is, overgeneralization of ecological knowledge can lead to incorrect assumptions about possible management outcomes. Site specificity is important because rangelands are so widespread and so diverse. Over the past century, rangeland managers in the western U.S. have worked to identify and define "sites" that are similar enough to have the same potential ecological dynamics. A site is typically conceptualized as an area of homogenous soil and topography that spans 10^4 to 10^5 m^2 within a zone of a relatively singular climate (Fuhlendorf and Smeins 1996; Bestelmeyer, Brown et al. 2011). The goal of this work is to allow managers to predict with some certainty that similar sites will react similarly to management treatment (Brown 2010).

Rangeland ecologists have promoted various elements of range ecosystems as predictors of potential vegetation and response to management on a given site. By 1919, Arthur Sampson, one of the first Forest Service range scientists, had adapted the equilibrial succession model developed by grassland ecologist Frederick Clements (Clements 1916) to rangelands as the "range condition model" (Sampson 1919). This model represented the idea that there is a single climax or equilibrium state for grasslands of a particular climate region. Livestock grazing was the cause of "range retrogression" away from the climax state, and the removal of livestock would allow for competition and other processes internal to the system to drive succession to the climax state. The status of a zone within the climatic region relative to the general, regional climax was used to predict the potential of that zone. Differences among soils across the landscape were mostly attributed to soil depletion (a result of grazing) or soil succession (a result of the plant community on the soil).

Later, Dyksterhuis (1949) emphasized the importance of delineating sites by their inherent edaphic and topographic characteristics. He retained but improved climax theory by positing that each range landscape had a "polyclimax," with each site class (known then as a "range site") having its own climax. Grazing remained the primary posited cause for a range site's departure from its climax. Through his "quantitative range condition model," Dyksterhuis recommended measuring the abundance of plant species considered indicators of range condition on each site. Subsequently, advances in observation and manipulative experimentation have verified the basic idea that geology, topography, and soils are the primary governing agents of a site's potential within a particular climate region (Grigal et al. 1999, Bestelmeyer et al. 2009, Brown 2010) and that rangeland sites have the potential to support alternative stable states (Briske et al. 2003). Consequently, using the current vegetation of a site to define that site's potential, and the vegetation's departure from the climatic climax or polyclimax as an indicator of the effect of livestock grazing, has been largely abandoned. Today, defining site classes using soils and topography is increasingly accepted for the rangelands of the American West (Caudle et al. 2013). This shift is reflected by the change in name of site classifications from "range sites," used in the 1950s through the 1990s, to ECOLOGICAL SITES, used today (Booker et al. 2012).

With the state-and-transition model, Westoby et al. (1989) provided a flexible approach to describing the dynamics of managed ecological sites. These are box-and-arrow diagrams in which boxes represent theoretical or observed ecosystem states and arrows represent the theoretical or observed transitions among these states. The transitions usually describe changes through time instead of space (Bestelmeyer, Goolsby et al. 2011). A state-and-transition model can help the range manager describe, understand, and predict potential states as well as potential management impacts on those states. The models are flexible in that they can be used to describe succession resulting from both nonequilibrium and equilibrium dynamics; as explained in Box 37.2, nonequilibrium dynamics are generally more prevalent on rangelands.

The three major U.S. land management agencies are working toward creating ecological site descriptions, and pairing each with a state-and-transition model, for the rangelands of the West (Caudle et al. 2013). Currently, federal agencies emphasize the concepts of stable states and thresholds and use recent advances in soil information and Geographic Information System technology (Brown 2010). Each federal ecological site description is linked to a particular soil type. Problematically, each soil map unit in a given soil survey contains multiple soil types that are not differentiated (Soil Survey Staff 1999), resulting in a situation in which the size of the map unit is almost always larger than the size of the ecological sites in that map unit.

The main factors limiting management of California range ecosystems are patchy availability and applicability of published ecological site descriptions, largely untested management practices with poor economic justification, and unknown responses to rapid environmental change. The more traditional goals of sustainable grazing management and enhanced forage production have been joined by the need to evaluate and anticipate response of rangelands to global change and the potential for enhancing carbon sequestration and other ecosystem services. This enlarged set of goals requires an approach that incorporates realistic predictive models, improved monitoring, and well-structured adaptive management. Monitoring and assessment of range condition, using the ecological site as the basic spatial unit and state-and-transition models to understand the dynamics of the system, is recommended for semiarid and arid rangelands of the western U.S. (Herrick et al. 2006). Incorporating best-available information about how to define ecological sites, understanding their potential states through state-and-transition models, and monitoring and assessment linking the models to an adaptive management framework is an approach also gaining prominence, especially on public lands (Herrick et al. 2012, Spiegal et al. 2014). This approach recognizes the synergies and trade-offs inherent to natural resource management and emphasizes "learning by doing."

Ecosystem Services and Livestock Production

Range production depends on many ecosystem services, often with relatively little direct human manipulation, including supporting and regulating services like water flow regulation and soil nutrient cycling. The "seminatural" appearance of range is responsible for many of the values that conservation and environmental policies seek to enhance or maintain. Rangeland owners and the public both consume ecosystem services from rangelands, benefiting from the market and nonmarket benefits of seeing and living in rangeland landscapes. In California the relationship of livestock grazing to ecosystem services such as biodiversity and oak regeneration is increasingly studied, and there is strong recent interest in understanding the dynamics of rangeland carbon storage and sequestration (Booker et al. 2012).

A growing body of research and management experience shows that livestock grazing can enhance biodiversity (Barry 2011, Huntsinger and Oviedo 2014). Some species can benefit from grazing that alters grassland structure to create shorter vegetation, more openings, or more structural heterogeneity in general than when livestock are excluded. Those species include burrowing owls (*Athene cunicularia*; Nuzum 2005), a variety of beetles (Dennis et al. 1997), kit fox (*Vulpes macrotis mutica*; USFWS 2010), kangaroo rats (*Dipodomys stephensi*; USFWS 1997, Kelt et al. 2005, Germano et al. 2012), blunt-nosed leopard lizards (*Gambelia sila*), and San Joaquin antelope squirrel (*Ammospermophilus nelsoni*; Germano et al. 2012). To a surprising degree, this understanding stems from cases where, as part of conservation efforts, livestock grazing was removed and species or habitats of interest subsequently disappeared.

Trade-offs, however, are integral to managing range for livestock production. While livestock production can provide and enhance many ecosystem services, it can also be the source of "disservices," including adverse impacts to particular habitats, soil erosion, and nutrient and pathogen runoff. The responses of a site and its organisms to grazing are influenced by complex interaction of the abiotic environment, regional species pool, and land management of the past and present (Heady 1984). Untangling background site- and time-specific processes from the effects of management can be expensive and time-consuming, and such untangling is unfortunately often not achieved in grazing studies (but see Langstroth 1991, Dyer et al. 1996, Jackson and Bartolome 2002). The complexity of isolating the effects of grazing is exacerbated by the heterogeneity of range landscapes: grazing on one site might provide services for one suite of organisms, while grazing another site in the same landscape can result in disservices to a different suite of organisms. Moreover, the grazing process occurs at multiple spatial and temporal scales. The process affects organisms that operate at these varied scales differently.

While such complexity prohibits broad generalizations, below we offer the "state of the knowledge" about the links between production of livestock and ecosystem services. We organize this discussion around the components of range and rangeland ecosystems conceptualized in Figure 37.3, including plant communities (primary producers), herbivores (primary consumers), carnivores (secondary consumers), soils, water, and the atmosphere. We highlight the relationship of livestock production to maintaining and enhancing ecosystem services as applied to different range regions and, at times, particular ecological sites within those regions.

Native Plants and Livestock Production

MEDITERRANEAN CLIMATE INLAND AND COASTAL GRASSLANDS

Widespread cultivation by eager homesteaders, livestock, and drought in the late 1800s contributed to the rapid spread of highly competitive species from the Mediterranean Basin into Californian grasslands. Conversion from the original vegetation to the exotics that now characterize the majority of Mediterranean climate grasslands in California has been nearly total (see Chapter 23, "Grasslands"). In many areas, native species form only a small percentage of the herbaceous cover (Biswell 1956, Heady et al. 1991, Hamilton et al. 2002). Many rangeland ecologists view this conversion as irreversible (Heady 1977, Heady et al. 1991); however, persistent native species richness, the dominant cover of natives in some areas, and the success of native species restoration on some sites is tempering that view (Bartolome, Barry et al. 2007).

A statewide assessment of the changes in the California grassland since colonization is impossible, because the spread of livestock largely coincided with dramatic nineteenth-century species invasion, and community structure prior to these events was not scientifically recorded (see Chapter 23, "Grasslands"; Schiffman 2007b). Also lacking for California grasslands is research directly linking grazing to plant responses at the individual, population, and site levels of ecological organization. Our understanding relies largely on results from more general research conducted by range scientists studying productivity and community composition responses to grazing management (Jackson and Bartolome 2007). Early ecological research in the grasslands of California's Mediterranean climate zone was directed toward understanding the forage base for livestock grazing (Bentley and Talbot 1948, Sampson et al. 1951, Biswell 1956). Much of this work established the primacy of location and weather as factors controlling herbaceous production and composition (Talbot et al. 1939, Heady 1958). Later studies and management practice have shown that effects of grazing are strongly related to the abundance of litter or RESIDUAL DRY MATTER remaining at the time of autumn germination (Hedrick 1948, Heady 1956 and 1965, Bartolome et al. 1980, Bartolome et al. 2006).

That body of work has quantified the experience shared by California ranchers and grassland managers: management activities are successful only within the constraints of the California climate. Forage productivity can be effectively managed for livestock production via manipulation of the amount of fall residual dry matter through grazing intensity (Bartolome et al. 1980), but species composition is more or less entrained by intra- and interannual weather. A working hypothesis is that grasslands so constrained by highly variable weather are best described using nonequilibrium models (see Box 37.2, Jackson and Bartolome 2002). However, at smaller-scale sites within the grassland, such as serpentine soils and vernal pools, biotic interactions like grazing can impose stronger controls on species composition than weather (see Box 37.3).

Despite the challenges presented by erratic climate and weather, California grassland managers are increasingly using livestock as a management tool for native species restoration (Stahlheber and D'Antonio 2013). Here we describe responses of native plants to grazing as identified in studies that did not explicitly compare the effects of rainfall fluctuations over time with the effects of grazing over time (but see Box 37.3). Stahlheber and D'Antonio (2013) used meta-analysis to identify impacts of livestock grazing on diversity and cover of natives in the grasslands of California's Mediterranean climate zone. They chose to analyze valley grassland and coastal prairie together despite the differences between the two grassland types because both have been dramatically invaded by exotic species, and as a result, managers of both have comparable restoration goals. Grazing increased forb (broad-leaved herb) cover, most reliably exotic low-growing forbs like filaree and cat's ear (*Hypochaeris* spp.), especially at the more arid study sites. Native forb cover responded more variably than exotic forb cover, increasing more in response to wet- and dry-season grazing as opposed to continuous/year-round grazing, and more in inland sites than in coastal sites. The authors hypothesize that the difference between coastal and inland site responses stems from the presence of native perennial forbs on the coast and their absence inland. Although the effect of grazing on grass cover was variable, grazing increased cover of native perennial grasses more reliably than cover of exotic annual grasses. Wet-season grazing produced a strong response, diminishing exotic annual grass cover and increasing native perennial grass cover. The authors conclude that site specificity is a critical consideration but that grazing can be compatible with efforts on some sites to enhance and restore native forb and grass abundance, if an increase in exotic forbs is acceptable.

The extent and richness of native species growing in particular types of sites within the grasslands of the Mediterranean climate zone appear to increase with grazing. For instance, serpentine-derived soils are refugia for native species (Harrison and Viers 2007), and grazing appears to enhance native forb species richness in these soils (Harrison et al. 2003, Pasari et al. 2014). Vernal pools, specialized seasonal wetlands nested within the grasslands of the Central Valley, are another specific site type in which grazing enhances the native community. Vernal pools are depressions underlain by soils with an impermeable layer of claypan, hardpan, cemented mudflow, and/or rock that fill with fall and winter rains and runoff (see Chapter 31, "Wetlands"; Rains et al. 2008). As temperatures warm in the spring, the standing water evaporates and concentric rings dry individually over time, exhibiting remarkable wildflower shows by plants specifically adapted to the water regime of particular bands. By summer, the pools are dry and the soils are at permanent wilting point until the rains come again in the fall (O'Geen et al. 2008). Vernal pools are highly valued as habitat for endemic, rare, and endangered plant and animal species specifically adapted to the inundation regimes. They also prevent regional flooding, regulate groundwater recharge, contribute to the phosphorus and nitrogen cycles, and provide prey for migratory birds (Hobson and Dahlgren 1998).

Marty (2005) investigated the effects of cattle grazing on the native flora and fauna of pools in valley grassland in eastern Sacramento County. Removal of livestock grazing for three years increased cover of exotic annual grasses. Endemic plants, largely annuals, were "choked out" by the exotic grasses, and native species cover and richness declined. Reintroducing grazing resulted in increased native vegetation species richness and cover. Grassland patches in the uplands between the pools also supported higher richness and cover of native species when grazed. Within-pool aquatic invertebrates species benefited from grazing as well, because exotic annual grasses were removed and inundation could occur. The grazing regime with the strongest effect was continuous October–June grazing rather than wet-season or dry-season grazing.

In an example of an unexpected synergistic relationship, rancher-created stock ponds provide habitat to replace the many lost vernal pools. Half of the remaining habitat for the endangered California tiger salamander (*Ambystoma californiense*) in the San Francisco Bay area is found in stock ponds (USFWS 2004), and a variety of "payment for ecosystem services" and mitigation initiatives help ranchers to maintain the ponds and support the species. Some amphibian species, including the endangered California red-legged frog (*Rana draytonii*) and the California tiger salamander, also seem to benefit from grazing that reduces vegetation near the ponds (DiDonato 2007).

MOJAVE DESERT GRASSLANDS

The Californian portion of the Mojave Desert (see Chapter 30, "Deserts") has undergone drastic land use change over the last fifty years. The region's human population increased by 350% between 1970 and 1990 (Hunter et al. 2003, Berry et al. 2006). Human use, often characterized as a "disturbance," is associated with dramatic invasions of annual grasses and forbs and their attendant altered fire regimes (Brooks and Matchett 2006), dangerous dust storms (Grantz et al. 1998), and loss of habitat for valued species (Inman et al. 2013). Livestock grazing is often considered a disturbance in line with fast-paced urbanization, off-highway vehicle use, wind and solar energy developments, and crop agriculture (Brooks et al. 2006, Lovich and Bainbridge 1999). The effects of grazing, however, have not been investigated nearly as thoroughly as they have been in the grasslands of the Mediterranean climate zone to the west.

Grasslands cover approximately 85,000 hectares of the Californian Mojave, located mostly in the western portion known as the Antelope Valley (Menke et al. 2013). Like in their westerly counterparts, different scales of observation reveal different responses to grazing. For instance, Brooks et al. (2006) found significant effects of cattle grazing on species composition within 200 meters of artificial livestock watering sites in the west-central Californian Mojave, whereas a multiyear observational study across 20,000 hectares of grasslands on Tejon Ranch in the western Mojave Desert indicated that grazing did not affect species composition nearly as much as did interannual rainfall timing and amount (Spiegal and Bartolome unpublished data). A pressing need exists to describe and understand the effects of grazing on Mojave Desert grasslands before changes intensify.

MONTANE MEADOWS

Grazing impacts in California's montane meadows have been a concern since the late 1800s, when John Muir famously described sheep in the Sierra Nevada as "hoofed locusts" (Muir 1894). Teasing apart the specific impacts of grazing has proven difficult, however, as montane meadow systems are immensely complex (Ratliffe 1985) and grazing introductions coincided with widespread water diversion, water application for mining, a huge population boom as mining camps populated the high country, and burning for clearing by miners, farmers, and graziers. Abiotic factors, especially hydrology, elevation, and weather, control the systems to a large degree, and vegetation varies from year to year and over small spatial scales even within a single meadow (see Chapter 29, "Alpine Ecosystems"; Fites-Kaufman et al. 2007).

Despite this complexity, studies have illustrated trends in grazing effects on montane meadow vegetation. Livestock grazing can change plant species composition and production both directly, through grazing and trampling, and indirectly, through stream incision and lowered water tables. Important factors affecting whether species composition or productivity will more strongly respond to grazing in Sierra Nevada montane meadows appear to be location (northern, central, or southern) and grazing intensity.

Grazing-induced changes in species composition have been detected over both long and short time scales. Stratigraphic pollen records from a montane meadow complex in the upper reaches of the South Fork Kern River, on the Kern Plateau, show that species composition changed in the region during the last 150 years following the widespread introduction of livestock. Willows (*Salix* spp.) and liverwort (*Riccia* sp.) declined significantly coincident with the introduction of livestock during the Gold Rush period. Pollen from sedges (Cyperaceae) and silver sagebrush *(Artemisia cana)* increased over this period (Dull 1999). In the same area, on a shorter time scale, Stevenson (2004) examined the impacts of seasonal cattle grazing on montane meadow hydrology and flora in nine pairs of grazed and ungrazed meadows. Her observational study found that livestock grazing was associated with changes in channel morphology and soil-moisture class distribution. Although plant species richness was not affected by grazing, species composition differed between ungrazed and grazed meadows, with tall forbs less common in the latter.

A study further north, in Yosemite National Park of the central Sierra Nevada, found that whether grazing affects productivity or species composition can be most related to grazing intensity. Using a five-year recreational packstock grazing experiment, Cole et al. (2004) concluded that when grazing impact is light, productivity and ground cover are more strongly affected than species composition. In three characteristic meadow types, they found that productivity was reduced by about 20%, vegetative cover was also reduced, and bare ground increased in grazed as compared to ungrazed plots.

SHRUBLANDS

California's chaparral and coastal sage scrub communities are managed as range to a lesser degree than other rangeland types such as grasslands and oak savanna. Shrublands of California's southern coast were converted to grassland to improve forage by European settlers, but the climate and short growing season proved to be less than ideal for livestock production (see Chapter 22, "Coastal Sage Scrub"). Some evidence indicates that these converted areas have largely changed back to coastal sage scrub.

Like the coastal sage scrub, conversion of chaparral to grassland has been attempted, especially by seeding grasses after fires (Mooney et al. 1986; see Chapter 24, "Chaparral"). Compared with other Mediterranean climate regions globally, such conversions have been largely unsuccessful (Mooney and Parsons 1973). Because livestock grazing is somewhat uncommon on chaparral itself, understanding the impacts of grazing on chaparral vegetation might require expansion to a landscape view. Again, disentangling the effects of grazing from other factors can complicate this understanding. For instance, in a 2003 study Keeley and others posited that blue oak (*Quercus douglasii*) savannas, which grow in close proximity to chaparral in the southern Sierra Nevada, provide an important source of alien annual grass seeds that colonize chaparral sites postfire (Keeley et al. 2003). They were not able to find differences between grazed and ungrazed savanna, however; alien species richness and cover do not differ much between oak woodlands that are grazed and those in which grazing was removed a century ago. Accordingly, the effects of grazing on postfire chaparral could not be isolated.

OAK SAVANNA

Grazing might influence oak recruitment and survival in oak woodlands, a concern because replacement of oaks lost to age, disease, and harvest is suspected to be inadequate in some areas. In the Sierra Nevada foothills, for example, blue oak–foothill pine (*Pinus sabiniana*) woodland/savanna is the characteristic landscape. Blue oak woodland/savanna is also widespread through the Coast Range and Cascade foothills. Its herbaceous understory is for the most part non-native, annual grasses and forbs. Some surveys over the last few decades have noted a lack of sapling-sized blue oaks (Allen-Diaz et al. 2007, Zavaleta et al. 2007); if inadequate sapling recruitment persists, blue oak stands could begin to thin and disappear as adult trees die but are not replaced.

Research has shown that grazing by both livestock and wildlife reduces growth and survival of blue oaks. Especially when range is grazed during the summer, livestock may browse on seedlings (McCreary and George 2005). Protection of seedlings as they move into the sapling stage might be necessary for successful maintenance of blue oak stands (Allen-Diaz et al. 2007); use of "treeshelters"—individual, translucent plastic protectors that fit over oak seedlings and are secured with a metal fence post—have proved successful (McCreary 2001). Grazing might indirectly help blue oak seedlings by reducing competition with annual grasses and forbs (Tyler et al. 2006).

Coast live oak (*Quercus agrifolia*) woodland/savanna occurs within 100 kilometers of the coast (see Chapter 25, "Oak Woodlands"). Canopy cover can vary from open to dense, and the herbaceous understory, if present, comprises largely non-native grasses and forbs. The evergreen coast live oak appears fairly resistant to livestock grazing and could replace less resistant deciduous oaks in areas with high grazing pressure. However, the sudden oak death pathogen (*Phytopthora ramorum*) (see Box 13.2 in Chapter 13, "Biological Invasions") has caused widespread mortality of coast live oak, which will likely affect this woodland type in the future (Allen-Diaz et al. 2007).

In the past, oaks were removed to increase forage production. The University of California and other range management advisers encouraged this. As described earlier, studies have subsequently shown that forage can remain green longer under an open oak canopy and production is just as high as in the open. As part of the Integrated Hardwood Range Management Program, from 1985 to 2010 University of California outreach promoted the benefits of oaks. These include the contribution of oaks to maintaining property values, increasing wildlife habitat, and in some cases, extending the green forage season for grazing. Outreach efforts were linked to an understanding of rancher needs and values derived from survey research. Over the period of the program's duration, oak planting by landowners there increased and cutting declined (Huntsinger, Johnson et al. 2010).

RANGE RIPARIAN ZONES

Use by livestock of riparian areas is more often spatially concentrated than their use of upland or dryland range. Riparian areas can include the only sources of water on the range and offer shady or cooler places to rest. Cattle in particular also resist climbing steep slopes and may congregate in low or flat areas. On the other hand, they will usually avoid muddy areas if possible.

Widespread concern about the impacts of grazing on riparian ecosystems in the American West (Belsky et al. 1999) has inspired much study. Care should be taken when extrapolating study results from climates that differ from the arid and/or semiarid Mediterranean climates of Californian rangelands (Jackson and Bartolome 2007). In addition, landscape heterogeneity is a critical consideration when assessing the impacts of livestock on riparian zones. In the grassland landscapes of California's inland Mediterranean climate zone, trampling effects are stronger in riparian zones than in grassy uplands because livestock preferentially use areas near shade and water sources (Tate et al. 2003). This effect can be patchy, however, because oak tree canopy can mitigate trampling effects by increasing organic matter through litterfall (Tate, Dudley et al. 2004). In addition, at spatial scales nested within landscapes, for instance within riparian zones, abiotic factors like flooding—not biotic interactions like livestock grazing—are primary controls of vegetation patterns (Stringham and Repp 2010).

INVASIVE GRASSES AND FORBS

Controlling invasive plants has proven to be one of the greatest challenges facing California range managers (Stromberg et al. 2007). In valley grasslands and coastal and foothill oak savannas, cover of non-native grasses and forbs commonly exceeds 90% (Bartolome, Jackson et al. 2007). The effects of plant invasions on California's range ecosystems have been profound and continue today. Obviously, species composition and dominance have changed, but so have many ecosystem processes, including hydrologic and nutrient cycles and fire regimes (D'Antonio et al. 2007). However, most common, non-native grasses and forbs are no longer invasive; rather, they have completely taken over and are NATURALIZED SPECIES. Of greater concern to range managers is the expansion and increasing abundance of newer species that continue to invade California rangelands. The three most troublesome invasive rangeland plants in California at present are yellow starthistle (*Centaurea solstitialis*; see Box 13.1 in Chapter 13, "Biological Invasions"), meadusahead (*Elymus caput-medusae*), and barbed goatgrass (*Aegilops triuncialis*). Range dominated by these species often has greatly reduced forage value for both livestock and wildlife. In addition, native plant populations, wildlife habitat, recreation, and other ecosystem services are often negatively affected (D'Antonio et al. 2007).

Livestock have both positive and negative impacts on invasive species control. Livestock production has been implicated in the introduction of weeds into noninvaded areas, as invaders either hitch rides on livestock or contaminate hay fed to livestock. Concentrated livestock use can increase the cover of bare ground, which can provide favorable germination sites for weeds. On the positive side, livestock grazing is an invasive plant management tool available to range managers; however, a single weed management tool often does not result in successful control (DiTomaso et al. 2007). To increase likelihood of successful long-term control, experts recommend combining several weed management methods tailored to situation-specific goals, constraints, and opportunities (DiTomaso et al. 2007).

Using livestock to control invasive plants often requires prescription grazing, which is the application of specific livestock grazing actions to accomplish specific vegetation management goals. Grazing intensity, animal distribution, and grazing period often differ from standard grazing practice, and livestock performance can be significantly reduced (Germano et al. 2012). Consequently, finding a livestock operator willing to implement a grazing prescription can prove difficult and might require reduced grazing fees or even payment to the operator. Intensive grazing, sometimes necessary for successful weed control, can have undesirable consequences. For example, concentrated hoof impacts and greatly reduced vegetative cover could result in increased soil erosion; as noted earlier, greater bare ground might also allow other weed species to thrive. In addition, intensive grazing can significantly impact desirable species in the weed-infested area.

Those caveats noted, prescription grazing can work well in controlling some invasive species (DiTomaso et al. 2007). An essential planning factor is that prescription grazing needs to be timed to the target weed species' PHENOLOGY. Grazing must occur when weeds are most vulnerable to defoliation; poorly timed grazing can actually benefit target species (Huntsinger et al. 2007). Correctly timed livestock grazing can be used to control yellow starthistle effectively (DiTomaso et al. 2006). Reducing residual dry matter through livestock grazing (or fire) creates unfavorable conditions for medusahead, providing some measure of control. Goatgrass is only palatable to livestock in early spring, so it typically must be managed with other methods such as fire or herbicide application. Grazing can also be used to manage velvet grass (*Holcus lanatus*), one of the most troublesome perennial grass weeds in the coastal prairie grassland type (Hayes and Holl 2003).

FUEL MANAGEMENT AND WOODY PLANT ENCROACHMENT

Woody plant encroachment and the fine fuels created by dry grasses can exacerbate fire hazard. Fine fuels left on range in summer and fall promote a higher probability of ignition and rapid fire spread. Cattle, sheep, goats, and horses can all be used to reduce fine-fuel loads. The effectiveness of grazing on fire behavior has not at this point been quantified but is inferred from the removal and alteration of fuels (Stechman 1983). Grazing is an alternative to prescribed fire for fire hazard reduction at wildland-urban interfaces and in other situations where risk of fire escape cannot be tolerated. Goat herders usually charge to graze for vegetation management, and goats will concentrate on shrubs, while cattle and sheep graziers typically pay for grazing leases, and cattle and sheep concentrate on grasses and forbs. Management emphasizes control of shrub encroachment and fine fuels while protecting other resources.

Control of woody vegetation can be desirable from a conservation or biodiversity perspective as well. Coastal prairie grasslands are highly subject to woody plant invasion, reducing the extent of native perennial grasslands. Grazing can help prevent encroachment of shrubs and trees. Coastal prairie intergrades with several shrub and forest community types that tend to encroach on open grassland in the absence of grazing and fire (Ford and Hayes 2007). The native shrub coyote brush is a primary offender in this regard, and cattle (McBride and Heady 1968, McBride 1974) as well as the native grazer tule elk (Johnson and Cushman 2007) significantly reduce cover of coyote brush in open grasslands if grazing takes place when shrubs are small.

RANGE MANAGEMENT IMPLICATIONS

The wildlife and plants present on Californian range today have coexisted with more than two hundred years of livestock grazing that has at some times been extreme. These species have also persisted despite increases and decreases in fire frequencies and extensive water diversions. The most unprecedented ecological change on rangelands today is that the range is subject to reduced intensity and even removal of livestock grazing from areas for various purposes, while at the same time these areas rarely are able to duplicate the levels or types of grazing that occurred before the introduction of livestock. No real knowledge base is available for predicting the long-term impact of reductions in herbivory and fire over large areas. The primary message could be that changing traditional grazing practices, whether to increase, reduce, change the season of or eliminate grazing, should be approached with caution and carried out incrementally.

The secondary message is that grazing effects, desirable or undesirable, depend on multiple, site-specific factors—another reason for incremental, adaptive management and for avoiding generalization. The interannual variability of rainfall is also a constant and very powerful factor modifying the effects of grazing on the California range, and desirable outcomes in one year might very well be followed by undesirable outcomes the next. Clear opportunities for livestock-related ecosystem services in California involve restoration in Mediterranean climate grasslands, conservation of oak savanna, weed management, and rancher husbandry and management. Researchers and managers must document results and link outcomes to specific ecological sites for them to be useful in future management. Managers need to draw on this information and use adaptive, incremental approaches.

Finally, there are ways to manipulate grazing impacts on vegetation. Keeping many animals in a small area—for example, in a rotational grazing plan with high stocking rates—can result in more even grazing. Because each animal has less choice about what to eat, animals will eat less preferred plants. This could be a useful strategy if a manager wants animals to graze weedy plants that are not preferred or when an even level of utilization is desired. On the other hand, when managing for diverse vegetation structure, or when animal selectivity or choice is beneficial in meeting management goals, allowing fewer animals to graze longer on larger areas can be useful, as in a year-round or season-long grazing plan. For example, in grazing vernal pools, giving animals time and space to make the choice of when to use the plants in the pools and to select grass rather than rare forbs is important. High-intensity, short-duration grazing that crowds animals in small areas for short periods of time would be inappropriate. In general, the more the animals prefer or select a target species, the easier it is to use grazing to manage that species. Knowledge of the preferences of different types of animals is very useful in developing these kinds of prescriptions.

Native Herbivores and Livestock Production

Research has shown that livestock grazing can compete with, facilitate, or not affect native herbivores. Burrowing mammals, as well larger grazing animals, are perhaps most directly influenced. Whether livestock grazing has beneficial or harmful effects depends on the wild herbivore species under consideration. Small burrowing mammals are important players in the function of California's grassland ecosystems. While gophers do not increase with livestock grazing, ground squirrels and kangaroo rats do. Among the larger wildlife species, a comparison of wild ungulates with their domestic counterparts indicates that they share preferences for forage. In range operations in which wildlife conservation is a goal, these interactions should inform management planning.

BURROWING MAMMALS

In 1923, Grinnell estimated that 1 billion burrowing mammals lived in California (Grinnell 1923). These small mammals are considered ecosystem engineers because of their contributions to soil disturbance, seed dispersal, granivory, and herbivory (Schiffman 2007a). Prevalent species include the California Beechey ground squirrel (*Spermophilus beecheyi*), pocket gopher (*Thomomys bottae*), and kangaroo rat (*Dipodomys* spp.). Responses to livestock grazing tend to be species- and site-specific.

Ground squirrel populations increase with livestock grazing in inland grasslands (Fitch and Bentley 1949, Howard et al. 1959), coastal grasslands (Linsdale 1946), and blue oak savanna with annual grass understory (Bartolome 1997). Howard (1953) hypothesized that livestock-induced litter reduction favors the germination of broadleaved plants that are desirable to squirrels. A reevaluation could be appropriate, incorporating knowledge about nonequilibrium dynamics prevalent on drier rangelands (see Box 37.2). Concern that ground squirrels compete with livestock for forage (Fitch and Bentley 1949, Howard et al. 1959) and create leg-breaking burrows dangerous to livestock and humans (Marsh 1998) resulted in eradication efforts (Howard 1953). Ground squirrel eradication has been controversial because of the ecological services they provide, including soil formation; burrow habitat for rare wildlife species like burrowing owls and California tiger salamanders; and prey for raptors, coyotes, and rattlesnakes (Davidson et al. 2012).

Pocket gopher activity is spatially and temporally complex but pervasive in California grasslands. In nonserpentine, annual-dominated grasslands in Monterey County, gophers occur at densities of 26–125 ha^{-1} (Lidicker 1989, Stromberg and Griffin 1996). Hobbs and Mooney (1995) found that no part of the soil was left undisturbed for more than five years during their eleven-year study of gopher disturbance in coastal grasslands on serpentine-derived soils. Gophers affect the composition and arrangement of vegetation in grasslands (Hobbs et al. 2007). Native bunchgrass seeds have low success rates on gopher tailings (Stromberg and Griffin 1996); soil disturbance by burrowing mammals in general tends to favor annuals (Schiffman 2000). In a study on interactions of cultivation, gopher disturbance, and cattle grazing on grassland composition and structure in Monterey County coastal range, Stromberg and Griffin (1996) found gophers inhabit a wide variety of soil textures, produce the same amount of tailings in cultivated as they do in uncultivated areas, and produce more tailings in ungrazed areas than in grazed areas. An increase in gopher activity with livestock removal also occurred in Vina Plains (Hunter 1991) and Jasper Ridge (Hobbs and Mooney 1991).

Population densities of kangaroo rats tend to increase in grazed areas (Reynolds and Trost 1980, Bock et al. 1984, Jones and Longland 1999, Germano et al. 2012). Research conducted at the Carrizo Plain National Monument indicates that the giant kangaroo rat (*Dipodomys ingens*) decreases the abundance of exotic annual grasses due to preferential granivory on their seeds. Depending on plant-plant interactions and the importance of these interactions at a particular site, the suppression of these exotics could enhance native species communities (Gurney 2012). Intensive livestock grazing benefits kangaroo rats and an associated suite of special-status vertebrates that inhabit grasslands of the San Joaquin Valley, including the San Joaquin kit fox and blunt-nosed leopard lizard (Germano et al. 2012).

LARGE NATIVE HERBIVORES

Ungulates and other range herbivores graze selectively, meaning they choose some plants over others. Livestock and large native herbivores overlap in their dietary preferences. Cattle, horses, and tule elk prefer grasses (McCullough 1969, Heady and Child 1994); sheep prefer forbs (Bartolome and McClaran 1992); deer (*Odocoileus hemionus*) prefer browse (Gogan and Barrett 1995); and pronghorn can overlap with all the other species because they prefer grasses, forbs, or shrubs depending on season (Yoakum and O'Gara 2000). Interactions between livestock and native ungulates vary widely but are not addressed here due to space constraints. An extensive review of studies on impacts of livestock grazing and other range management practices on wildlife in the West was recently conducted by Krausman et al. (2011).

Native Carnivores and Livestock Production

During the late Pleistocene (19,000–17,000 ya), mammalian carnivores were diverse, and at least eleven species were as large or larger than the coyote (*Canis latrans*; Edwards 1996; see Chapter 9, "Paleovertebrate Communities"). In large part, the carnivores' food base comprised small burrowing mammals (Schiffman 2000) and large mammalian herbivores, which were also diverse with at least eighteen species (Edwards 1996). A massive extinction occurred during the dramatic climatic changes of the early Holocene approximately 10,000 years ago (Edwards 1992, 1996). A handful of carnivore species, most of the small burrowing mammal species, as well as three (elk, deer, and pronghorn) of the eighteen large herbivores, survived the extinction (Bartolome, Barry et al. 2007). Throughout the Holocene, Native Californians hunted these animals, possibly intensively enough to have kept their populations down (see Chapter 10, "Indigenous California"). Archeological evidence suggests that populations of large herbivores and predators were larger at the time of European contact than the long-term norm, possibly due to the concurrent decimation of indigenous peoples and their hunting practices (Schiffman 2007a). The earliest historical accounts of California's natural resources convey a high abundance and widespread distribution of burrowing mammals, large herbivores, and carnivores (Minnich 2008, Schiffman 2007a).

Concerns about predation on livestock have led livestock producers and government predator control agents to use lethal methods to suppress predators. In 2010 in California, about 9,600 head of cattle (including calves) were lost to predators, equaling about 1% of the total head of cattle in California. Coyotes were responsible for 57% of the deaths, while mountain lions (*Puma concolor*) and bobcats (*Lynx rufus*) were responsible for 33% (NASS 2011b). During the nineteenth and twentieth centuries, regulations on control methods were few, and poison, trapping, and shooting were employed. Many lament the resulting extirpation of the grizzly bear (*Ursus arctos*), which was likely a keystone species before European settlement (Schiffman 2007a). With the 1998 passage of Proposition 4, poison and leg traps were banned (Timm et al. 2007). Today the law stipulates that a person may kill a coyote on sight, using approved methods, but a depredation permit must be obtained to kill a mountain lion.

The predators that survived the extinction event between the Pleistocene and Holocene can cause problems for people making their living from California's natural resources. As a result, predator control efforts, both off the record and official, have been extensive over the past two centuries. However, lethal predator control is controversial in California. Along with the ecological services that predator species provide, Californians also tend toward conserving predators for their intrinsic value (Wolch et al. 1997, Fox 2006). Ranchers and other rangeland managers are mitigating this conflict by employing innovative, nonlethal control methods (Andelt 2004, NASS 2011b, Shivik 2006).

The Soil System and Livestock Production

Livestock grazing can influence physical, biological, and chemical components of the soil. One way is through the amount of dry plant matter left on the soil after the grazing season. Research has shown that residual dry matter can protect the soil from erosive forces (Bartolome et al. 2006, Tate et al. 2006), return organic matter to the soil, and affect the next year's plant germination (Heady 1956). By managing grazing to leave particular amounts and patterns of ungrazed plant matter behind at the conclusion of an annual grazing cycle, the manager has the best opportunity, within the confines of weather conditions and other abiotic factors, to influence the next year's germination and to protect the soil. The amount of residual dry matter recommended for protecting soils and forage quality varies with rainfall, slope, soil characteristics, and other factors (Bartolome et al. 1980). Prescriptions are necessarily unique to the ecosystem and the goals of the manager.

BULK DENSITY

The weight of a beef cow is approximately 450 kilograms; this can compact the soil, reducing porosity and increasing bulk density (mass of soil particles/volume of soil). Undesirable effects of increased bulk density on rangelands include reduced root growth (Brady and Weil 2002) and infiltration rates (Daniel et al. 2002, Pietola et al. 2005), both of which can increase surface runoff (with and without pollutants) and erosion (Blackburn 1984). Site specificity strongly influences livestock impacts on bulk density. Soil texture, which varies widely over short distances in California, is a major control on bulk density and its response to grazing. For example, clay-rich soils naturally tend toward lower bulk densities because clay-sized particles decrease average pore size, increasing the "volume of soil" factor in the bulk density equation (Brady and Weil 2002). No meta-analysis quantifying the impacts of livestock trampling on soils of different textures has been conducted, but increases in bulk density in grazed compared to ungrazed sites on Mediterranean climate range have been found on coarse sandy loams of the San Joaquin Valley (Tate, Dudley et al. 2004), sandy loams of Salinas and Carmel Valleys (Steenwerth et al. 2002), and clay loams east of Berkeley (Liacos 1962). Changes in bulk density can persist for centuries in some soils (Sharratt et al. 1998), but bulk density decreased after just six years of grazing removal in the coarse sandy loams of the San Joaquin Valley.

SOIL BIOTA

The impacts of livestock grazing on soil biota vary. The microbial community appears largely unaffected, at least in some sites, while cryptogamic crusts are generally negatively affected. An investigation in the Salinas and Carmel Valleys of the Central Coast of land-use effects on soil microbial biomass and composition indicated that total microbial biomass and composition vary more as a function of grassland vegetation growth habit (annual versus perennial) and cultivation history than of grazing history (Steenwerth et al. 2002). Cryptogamic soil crusts—assemblages of algae, fungi, mosses, bacteria, and/or liverworts coexisting mutualistically—provide nutrient cycling, nitrogen fixing, water conservation, and primary productivity (Brady and Weil 2002). Though often associated with arid rangelands and deserts (see Chapter 30, "Deserts"; Dunne 1989), they are also found on Californian Mediterranean climate (Fierer and Gabet 2002) and montane range sites. For instance, in his study of the pollen record of the Kern Plateau, Dull (1999) found that a liverwort decreased dramatically in the period after cattle and sheep grazing was initiated and proposed that cryptogamic crusts likely disappeared from his site due to direct (e.g., grazing, trampling) and indirect (e.g., stream incision and lowered water table) effects of livestock.

BIOGEOCHEMICAL CYCLES

Grazing alters biogeochemical cycles because herbivores mineralize organic matter and return it to the environment in solid, liquid, and gaseous forms (Hack-Ten Broeke and Van der Putten 1997). In general, grazing in grasslands accelerates carbon and nutrient cycling by effectively bypassing the microbial decomposition pathway (see Figure 37.3a; Singer and Schoenecker 2003). This acceleration happens in a spatially heterogeneous manner because livestock use some areas preferentially and because their excreta is deposited in patches that make up a small fraction of the grazed landscape (Tate et al. 2003).

Water Quality and Livestock Production

Protecting water quality is an important range management concern. The location of significant areas of California's rangelands between the Sierra Nevada snowpack and the state's major river systems means that almost all surface water in California passes through rangeland; in addition, two-thirds of the state's major reservoirs are located on rangeland (Harper et al. 1996a). Nonpoint source pollution, the diffuse discharge of pollutants throughout the environment, is the primary pollution problem on rangelands. Four main nonpoint source pollutants occur on rangelands: sediment, nutrients, heat that causes elevated water temperatures, and pathogenic organisms. All four can degrade water quality for fish, wildlife, and human uses (Harper et al. 1996b). In general, concentrations of livestock in and near water should be minimized unless such concentrations meet specific management goals. Herding and fencing can both be used to better distribute livestock. Buffer strips can be used to filter out pollutants before they reach water. Research shows that normal grazing management practices may be adequate to protect water quality and aquatic habitat in some cases.

Sediment is the pollutant most common on rangelands (George, Larson-Praplan et al. 2011) and often results from improperly constructed roads or animal confinement areas located too close to water bodies, rather than directly from livestock grazing (Weaver and Hagans 1994). Existing road building and corral placement methods can significantly reduce rangeland sediment pollution if applied (George and Jolley 1995). Direct livestock impacts on water quality are a concern, but generalizations should be avoided. While direct inputs of animal excrement in small ponds in areas with intensive grazing can increase ammonia and nitrite (Clausnitzer and Huddleston 2002, Knutson et al. 2004), grazing can actually enhance the ability of riparian vegetation to filter nitrate out of surface waters. In a grazing removal experiment in the Sierran foothills grassland–oak savanna, soil water nitrate was five times higher in plots from which grazing had been removed for two years than in grazed plots, perhaps because of reduced nitrate use by plants (Jackson et al. 2006). Livestock impacts on overhanging riparian vegetation can raise water temperature, but properly managed livestock grazing practices should be able to minimize such impacts.

A study of montane meadows at Yosemite National Park compared grazed pools to pools where grazing was excluded to evaluate effects on Yosemite toads (*Anaxyrus canorus*). Overall water quality was high and unaffected by fencing, and conditions for toad breeding pool habitat did not improve following fencing and cattle exclusion compared to standard U.S. Forest Service grazing management. Toads were more likely to use warmer, shallower, and more nitrogen-enriched pools, contrary to the expectations of the researchers (Roche et al. 2012). Studies in the same area found no detectable effects of grazing treatments on tadpole, young of the year, or pool occupancy (Allen-Diaz et al. 2010, Lind et al. 2011).

As with wildlife and human feces, livestock feces can contaminate drinking water with pathogenic organisms such as *E. coli*, *Giardia*, *Salmonella*, and *Cryptosporidium*, all of which can cause serious disease in humans. Leaving several meters of ungrazed vegetation around water bodies greatly reduces any movement of pathogens into water, so a fenced buffer strip is an effective management practice (Tate, Pereira et al. 2004; Tate et al. 2006); buffer strips can also reduce nutrient and sediment transport into water bodies. In general, practices that reduce livestock concentration in riparian areas will also help minimize nonpoint source pollution in areas where it is a concern (George, Jackson et al. 2011).

To comply with the 1972 Clean Water Act, the Environmental Protection Agency and state water resources boards developed total maximum daily load (TMDL) standards, the maximum amount of a pollutant that a water body can receive and still meet water quality standards. In response, the California livestock industry and public agencies worked with the State Water Resources Control Board to address water quality impacts on rangelands, resulting in the 1995 California Rangeland Water Quality Management Plan. The plan detailed voluntary rangeland livestock production "Best Management Practices" to protect water quality from nonpoint source pollution. In 2004 the State Water Resources Control Board adopted new nonpoint source pollution policies, which replaced voluntary compliance with regulatory programs that implemented TMDL requirements on agricultural lands including rangelands (George, Larson-Praplan et al. 2011). Watershed and agricultural groups, with assistance from state and federal agencies, are working with Regional Water Quality Control Boards to meet these TMDL standards.

Atmosphere and Livestock Production

Worldwide, livestock meat and milk production processes represent approximately 7.1 gigatonnes CO_2-equivalent yr^{-1}, or 14.5% of all anthropogenic greenhouse gas emissions (Gerber et al. 2013). Generally, systems that include more grass-based, extensive production (range) emit less total greenhouse gas than systems with more intensive feeding (feedlots) (Subak 1999, Casey and Holden 2006). Primarily because they are so extensive, rangelands contain significant carbon stocks. Grasslands alone have the potential to partially offset the emissions of meat and milk production by sequestering 0.6 gigatonnes CO_2-equivalent yr^{-1}. Factors currently hindering the realization of the potential include lack of reliable measurement techniques and questions about economic viability (Gerber et al. 2013).

In terms of long-term carbon storage, rangelands can be superior to forests because relatively more of total carbon is stored in the soil (White et al. 2000, Paruelo et al. 2010) where it is usually better protected from atmospheric release (for example, by wildfire) than carbon stored in vegetation. However, carbon inputs in rangelands—i.e., net carbon flows from the atmosphere—are comparatively small, and soil carbon is more difficult to measure than carbon in trees. The nonequilibrium characteristics of arid ranges mean that year-to-year sequestration is difficult to predict and that in many years carbon may actually be emitted rather than stored, as plants decompose on the surface (Booker et al. 2012). Timing and amount of rainfall, temperature variations, and soil type—the most important factors influencing carbon sequestration on such ranges—are not amenable to management (Westoby et al. 1989, Parton et al. 1994, Briske et al. 2003 and 2005, Booker et al. 2012). Opportunities to increase carbon sequestration on rangelands are highly variable and best predicted at a coarse scale by the position of an ecological site along an aridity gradient. The magnitude of carbon sequestration and management influences diminishes with decreasing rainfall (Booker et al. 2012).

Nevertheless, proposals for managing rangelands for climate change mitigation are gaining attention at state and federal levels in the United States. Rangeland livestock producers, generally operating with low and variable financial returns, continue to express considerable interest in diversifying income streams to include payments related to carbon sequestration (Diaz et al. 2009). Range managers are in a unique position to offset emissions from livestock production through carbon sequestration. More work is needed to develop reliable measuring techniques and an economic system that appropriately compensates those enhancing carbon sequestration. In the meantime, manipulating the amount of woody vegetation through grazing, where feasible, remains an intervention opportunity that is manageable, tractable, and likely has a significant effect on carbon stocks. However, more needs to be known about the effects of these vegetation state changes on carbon, especially soil carbon, in different ecological sites, and how to balance increases in aboveground carbon stores with possibly higher fire probabilities. The consequences of altered disturbance regimes also must be evaluated, or short-term gains may result in long-term loss (Booker et al. 2012). As carbon is stored in rangeland soils, management that protects soils is crucial.

Livestock Operators and Ecosystem Services

Livestock producers own the majority of the Mediterranean rangelands of California. While many of the ecosystem services that ranchers seek from their own land are consumed only by them—the ability to leave land to their heirs, host people at the ranch, enjoy a rural lifestyle, and work with animals—many of the ecosystem services produced on private land are shared with and valued by the public. These include wildlife habitat; beautiful, seminatural landscapes; watersheds; livestock products; and recreation.

Through the decisions they make, ranchers shape the characteristics and rate of ecosystem service production from rangelands (Huntsinger and Oviedo 2014). The construction of stock ponds can benefit tiger salamanders and red-legged frogs, and control of weeds and managed grazing can offer ecosystem benefits. Irrigation canals and pasture runoff create favorable habitat conditions for some species, including the California black rail (*Laterallus jamaicensis coturniculus*; Richmond et al. 2010, 2012). Ranchers can offer ecosystem services like bird-watching, hunting, and other recreational opportunities on the market. In California, production of organic and grass-fed livestock products from rangelands is increasing, providing a way for ranchers to increase the market value of range products. Considerable interest exists among ranchers in finding ways to diversify income streams by marketing additional ecosystem services or participating in payment-for-services programs (Cheatum et al. 2011).

As studies have evinced the capacity of grazing to improve certain kinds of habitat, interest in using grazing for conservation benefits has grown. However, even when convinced that livestock grazing is essential for achieving conservation goals, managers and planners often fail to consider the ranches or people that produce livestock. As in many parts of the world, government and nongovernmental organizations often hire "professional land managers" or "environmental consultants" who do not know the rancher perspective, respect rancher knowledge, or understand the imperatives of the pastoralist operation. They might ask ranchers to graze for a month here or a month there at limited times, making an economic enterprise infeasible. The following section explores some of the challenges and creative solutions being implemented as range management moves into the future.

Future of Range Management in California

California ranchers face serious challenges including those associated with inheritance, increasing property taxes, worsening industry economics, loss of infrastructure, increasing conflicts with urban neighbors, fragmentation, development, and agricultural intensification of grazing lands. Livestock prices do not necessarily reflect conditions affecting the range industry, as ranchers are at the bottom of a multilayered industry where livestock prices are determined by large-scale feedlot, processing, and retail enterprises. Drought and the prospect of its increased likelihood also confront rangeland producers. Animals permitted on public rangelands have generally declined, as have livestock numbers overall (see Figure 37.2).

The likelihood that a ranch will persist is higher if the rancher is able to conduct a profitable business, and this has a direct impact on the conservation of rangeland landscapes. Average returns of only 2% to 3% from livestock production on western rangelands (Workman 1986, Torell et al. 2001) mean that ranchers often must depend on returns from land appreciation to recoup their long-term investment and to obtain capital, which means selling the land to development interests. In some areas conversion to more intensive, high-value agriculture, such as grains, viticulture or horticulture, is an option. With agricultural intensification, carbon emissions increase and wildlife habitat is lost.

Further challenges for ranching in California include a critical shortage of packing and processing facilities within the state, federal food safety regulations that forbid on-farm slaughter for sale, and competition for grazing lands from California's large dairy industry, where young females may be raised to milking age on rangelands. Finally, variability in forage production remains an annual challenge and adds an element of risk to livestock operations (Brownsey et al. 2013). While years of abundance interspersed with years of below-average rainfall are expected and incorporated into the management of California ranches, long-term drought can create huge costs through feed purchases made in an attempt to maintain the herd. The multi-year drought beginning in 2012, for example, caused liquidation of many herds as ranchers found themselves without forage or affordable feed. Interest in acquiring and feeding agricultural by-products like waste squash, corn stalks, tomatoes, and crop aftermath skyrocketed.

Cow-calf operators maintain a base cow herd to produce calves, which limits their ability to reduce numbers in drought. Standard practice is to reduce brood herds by selling older, less productive animals first. Brood herds are often the result of decades of breeding and selection, with cows that do best on a ranch's unique configuration of forage resources persisting in the herd. The genetic resources lost from these "adapted" herds take a long time to recover. For those in the business of grazing yearlings for a few months annually, it becomes a matter of weighing how long the animals can be kept in a drought year versus opportunities to maximize price. If range has been contracted for, the operator might still have to pay grazing rents even when the animals are gone. Depending on concurrent livestock prices, operators might have to sell at or below cost. Beyond the loss of income from having fewer or no cows, ranchers need capital to purchase replacement animals when drought ends.

The amount of land a California rancher leases to complete the annual forage requirements for a herd of cows is substantial. Leasing of public and private land is common, with public land usually about a third to half of the rangeland portfolio (Liffmann et al. 2000, Sulak and Huntsinger 2007; Huntsinger, Johnson et al. 2010; Lubell et al. 2013). Studies have shown that without such leases, a large proportion of operators believe they cannot sustain their ranches (Sulak and Huntsinger 2007). In an interview, one central Sierra permittee put his family's dilemma eloquently into words: "Public lease versus private lease? Where is the opportunity? How will we pass on this ranching operation to the next generation? These questions will be resolved over the next ten years—without public lands as an option the answers may be harder to come by for the next generation." Agency lessors, on the other hand, find themselves in the position of selecting the surviving generation of ranchers by way of their leasing decisions.

The California Rangeland Conservation Coalition has developed a "rangeland resolution" with more than one hundred public agency, ranching groups, and environmental organization signatories that commits them to working for rangeland conservation in concert with livestock production in the state (CRCC 2014). These and other similar efforts in the western United States argue for sustaining "working landscapes" that combine livestock production and ecosystem service production (Huntsinger and Sayre 2007, Huntsinger et al. 2014). There are initiatives at multiple scales, from mitigation markets and planning that support landscape conservation through maintaining ranching as a widespread land use, to environmental payment-for-services programs and outreach efforts that encourage specific management practices and help sustain extensive rural land uses.

Ecosystem Service Initiatives

Public acquisition is one way to protect grasslands from development, but it is costly and controversial (Merenlender et al. 2004). Regulations protecting endangered species, water quality, air quality and wildlife in general can also protect ecosystem services but can have negative impacts on ranchers and therefore on extensive rangelands. They may increase costs and imply social disapproval of ranching. While ranchers overwhelmingly responded that they valued the natural beauty of California oak woodlands, the majority in a survey of two California counties responded that "being over-regulated" was a good reason to quit ranching altogether (Liffmann et al. 2000). Regulatory efforts can also have unfortunate unintended consequences. Researchers in North Carolina documented landowner destruction of forest habitat to prevent occupation by a rare species in an effort to avoid the restrictions of the Endangered Species Act (Lueck and Michael 2003). Overall, the Endangered Species Act and regulations like it, while a valuable component of environmental protection, do little to increase habitat extent or quality from private lands (Bean and Wilcove 1997) or to stimulate ecosystem service flows in general.

As an alternative, in recent years efforts have been made by the conservation community to offer incentives to private landowners for maintaining the natural characteristics of their land as a way to conserve open space and wildlife habitat (Barry and Huntsinger 2002, Huntsinger and Hopkinson 1996). The rancher provides on-site management for these "working landscapes," and the land remains agriculturally productive. Efforts to define and measure range ecosystem services are part of this effort. Ranchers have considerable interest in payment for ecosystem services, though they may not recognize it by name (Cheatum et al. 2011). Interest has been expressed in habitat improvement, carbon sequestration, and other possibilities that can complement livestock grazing. Fee hunting, in that it encourages landowners to manage habitat for wildlife, is an existing market for ecosystem services.

Examples of payment for ecosystem services programs available for privately owned range include the federal Environmental Quality Incentives Program (EQIP) and Conservation Stewardship Program (CSP). These programs, administrated by the U.S. Department of Agriculture's Natural

Resources Conservation Service (NRCS), offer cost-sharing and payments for certain conservation projects and practices, including managing ponds and water developments to conserve aquatic species, improving wildlife habitat, and protecting water quality. These federal benefits are founded on the idea that the benefit received by the public from the conservation activities of farmers and ranchers makes public investment in these activities worthwhile. In 2012, EQIP paid $117 million, CSP paid $8 million, the Grassland Reserve Program (incorporated into the Agricultural Conservation Easement Program [ACEP] in 2014) paid $0.3 million, and the Wildlife Habitat Incentive Program, now folded into EQIP, paid $0.6 million for conservation projects on California farms and ranches. In addition, the NRCS spent $42.6 million on technical assistance in California in 2012 (USDA 2013).

Markets, payments, and cost-shares for ecosystem services help support enterprises financially. Payment for ecosystem services may also transmit a sense of social approval to the landowner, feeding back to greater interest in ecosystem service production. However, equally important is building partnerships with ranchers and landowners based on a mutual interest in maintaining a healthy, pleasant environment. In fact, ranchers and rangeland landowners in numerous studies emerge as strongly motivated by environmental factors; building on that affection for the land and appreciation for responsible stewardship is perhaps one of the most effective ways of conserving rangelands (Smith and Martin 1972; Huntsinger, Johnson et al. 2010).

Conservation easements are also a market for ecosystem services, with willing purchasers and sellers. They are now the most widely used, private-sector land conservation method in the United States (Gustanski and Squires 2000). In exchange for tax benefits or outright payment, a landowner voluntarily agrees to a permanent deed restriction on the property title that prohibits development. This right is then held by a third party, sometimes a public agency, but often a nongovernmental organization known as a land trust. Although far from perfect as a conservation strategy (Merenlender et al. 2004, Reiner and Craig 2011), easements allow ranchers to continue providing ecosystem services from the property, while extracting some of the capital value of the land by donating or selling the right to develop (Sulak et al. 2004). This market is subsidized through tax benefits and the U.S. Farm Bill, with the NRCS, for example, allocating $4 million in California for purchase of easements on farms and ranches in 2012 through the Farm and Ranch Lands Protection Program incorporated into the ACEP in 2014 (USDA 2013).

A 2005 survey of oak woodland landowners found that approximately 6% of properties had a conservation easement on them (Huntsinger, Johnson et al. 2010). Ferranto and colleagues found in 2011 that 6% of California forest and rangeland owners in ten representative California counties had a conservation easement in place in 2008 (Ferranto et al. 2011). Mitigation easements are similar but are purchased using the funds of property developers to preserve specific types of habitat lost as a result of development. A landowner might have one part of a property designated as a "mitigation easement" for a particular threatened or endangered species, for example. To meet the requirements of the law, easements must be regularly monitored to make sure that the landowner is complying with the terms of the easement. A challenge for conservationists is how to keep the cost of monitoring down. Costs are partly related to how complex the easement requirements are. In some cases, simple site visits or aerial monitoring to check for construction have been effective. Many organizations now emphasize that they use the monitoring process to build a partnership with the landowner.

Niche Markets for Ecosystem Services

Advertising or certifying that agricultural products also offer ecosystem service benefits can raise their value on the market. While the main motivation for purchasers of meat, milk, and leather probably lies in the quality and characteristics of the product itself, heritage values, belief in "sustainable" uses of land, and the appeal of woodland and local landscapes undoubtedly also have a positive impact on many consumers, and interest in various product designations is on the increase. Some producers market to the public by stating that they manage for ecosystem services and "sustainability," incorporating this into the price. Nongovernmental certification programs play a growing role in informing consumers of the ecosystem services associated with buying various products or brands. California livestock operators have been fairly innovative in developing alternative livestock production systems, especially as alternative production may become an increasingly important part of the industry. Producers are known to market products over the Internet, shipping frozen products or meeting up with purchasers in designated places in urban areas to complete transactions. Farmers' markets have also become an important outlet for local, organic, and grass-fed products.

Finally, grazing as an ecosystem service has also found a market. Grazing for control of fire and invasive weeds can be lucrative. Companies have sprung up offering to provide goats specifically for vegetation management, and they charge as much as $1,300 per hectare for this service. Cattle are also used for fire hazard management, and in fact this is one rationale for grazing on some public lands (Byrd et al. 2009).

Climate Change

The implications of climate change for California range are likely to be profound (see Chapter 14, "Climate Change Impacts"). Changes in temperature, precipitation, and carbon dioxide will likely alter forage production and timing, plant species composition and phenology, non-native plant invasions, frequency of drought and wildfire, livestock performance, and many other range attributes (Polley et al. 2013). A good deal of uncertainty still surrounds the magnitude and even direction of change in range attributes at state and local scales, but it appears highly likely that California will experience increased ecosystem variability and more frequent extreme weather events (Polley et al. 2013, Chaplin-Kramer and George 2013). Although California range managers have long experience working in variable and uncertain ecosystems, the potential for adverse consequences presents a significant challenge for everyone interested in California's range landscapes.

For example, Shaw et al. (2011) projected the impact of several climate change scenarios on forage production in California. They found that under most scenarios, statewide forage production would decline significantly by the end of the century, with a corresponding reduction in profits for California ranchers. Another model that incorporated the effects of temperature as well as precipitation changes on forage production and that focused on the San Francisco Bay Area suggested climate change effects on Bay Area forage production might be less grim (Chaplin-Kramer and George 2013). This model projected that in most years, annual forage production could actually increase, although this news was tempered by the likelihood that the growing season could be shorter and that the frequency of extremely dry years would increase (both changes necessitating the potentially costly provision of additional food for livestock). These findings suggest that climate change could bring range managers some opportunities, such as the increase in Bay Area forage, as well as anticipated difficulties.

Whatever changes are wrought by climate change, those interested in the maintenance of California's range ecosystems and the services they provide must start planning and implementing effective adaptation and transformation strategies. Alternative livestock breeds/species and production methods, diversified businesses, innovative pest management, geographic relocation, alternative ecosystem services, and new policies, incentives, and social networks have been proposed as potential strategies (Joyce et al. 2013). Technical outreach to ranchers to encourage the development of drought plans and strategies is important, as is exploration of alternative feed sources such as agricultural by-products. The creation of grass banks—areas set aside for grazing only during drought—could also increase flexibility in response to growing uncertainty. Because temporal and spatial changes in California range ecosystems interact at the scale of the range site (Bartolome et al. 2009), it is very difficult to predict how projected climate change will unfold. Practices will undoubtedly need to adapt, and they will need to be developed within a realistic adaptive management framework.

Summary

Range forms a diverse class of managed ecosystems covering about a third of California, primarily in natural and seminatural grasslands, savannas, and shrublands. Characteristic of range ecosystems are aridity, nonarable soils, and the important ecological and economic roles of grazing and browsing animals. After more than two hundred years, grazing remains California's most extensive land use, with goals and management strongly affected by patterns of land ownership. After peaking in 1970, beef cattle numbers have slowly declined along with sheep numbers, leading to social and economic stresses within the producer community. Grazing management differs considerably among the Mediterranean, desert, and montane regions of the state. Models for the principal functional components of range ecosystems (primary producers, primary consumers, secondary consumers, and detritivores) provide a foundation for understanding the basic system and how it can best be managed and sustained. Forage growth patterns drive seasonal livestock production practices in different range areas.

Cattle are the most numerous kind of range livestock at present, producing calves in fall in the Mediterranean climate zone and in spring in the intermountain zone. Warm desert grazing is less linked to season. Forage production is heavily influenced by local climate and soils. Models predicting range community responses to grazing currently emphasize nonequilibrium dynamics and integrated management goals as opposed to older, equilibrium-type models focusing on livestock production or grazing impacts. Livestock management goals today include maintaining biodiversity, controlling invasive plants, managing fuels, and protecting soil, water, and air quality. Management of public range must now consider impacts on private range, as forage resources have become limited statewide. Partnerships with ranchers and rangeland landowners are essential to conserving the extensive landscapes cherished in California.

Acknowledgments

Thanks to Rebecca C. Wenk (1979–2011) for the livestock and wildflowers photograph, one of many beautiful images she created while working with the University of California–Berkeley Range Group.

Recommended Reading

Briske, D. D., editor. 2011. Conservation benefits of rangeland practices: Assessment, recommendations, and knowledge gaps. U.S. Department of Agriculture Natural Resources Conservation Service.

Bush, L. 2006. Grazing handbook: A guide for resource managers in coastal California. Sotoyome Resource Conservation District, Santa Rosa, California.

California Rangeland Conservation Coalition. <http://www.carangeland.org/>.

Campos, P., L. Huntsinger, J. L. Oviedo, P. F. Starrs, M. Diaz, R. B. Standiford, and G. Montero, editors. 2013. Mediterranean oak woodland working landscapes: Dehesas of Spain and ranchlands of California. Landscape Series 16. Springer Science+Business Media, Dordrecht, Netherlands.

Holechek, J. L., R. D. Pieper, and C. H. Herbel. 2011. Range management: Principles and practices. Sixth edition. Prentice Hall, Upper Saddle River, New Jersey.

Stromberg, M. R., J. D. Corbin, and C. M. D'Antonio, editors. 2007. California grasslands: Ecology and management. University of California Press, Berkeley, California.

University of California Division of Agriculture and Natural Resources. 2014. Annual rangeland handbook. <http://californiarangeland.ucdavis.edu/Annual_Rangeland_Handbook/>.

Glossary

CLEMENTSIAN EQUILIBRIUM ECOLOGY Theory developed by Frederic Clements (1874–1945) and followers describing the predictable development of vegetation over time, based on equilibrium concepts.

CLIMAX COMMUNITY The cornerstone of Clementsian equilibrium ecology. The stable vegetation endpoint in a successional series as determined by climate.

COMPENSATORY PLANT GROWTH The increase in net primary productivity as a result of herbivory.

ECOLOGICAL SITE An assemblage of basic land units, defined by topographic, soil, and climatic characteristics, that share potential vegetation and react similarly to management.

FORAGE Vegetation available for consumption by grazing or browsing animals.

NATURALIZED SPECIES A well-established, common, and widespread non-native species that survives and reproduces in the wild without human assistance.

NONEQUILIBRIUM ECOSYSTEM An ecosystem that displays biotic decoupling, nonlinear succession, and multiple stable states. In contrast, in an equilibrium ecosystem, succession is controlled by biotic interactions, passes from stage to stage in a linear fashion, and has a predictable endpoint.

PHENOLOGY The stages of seasonal plant growth, development, and reproduction.

RANGE Refers to land grazed by livestock

RANGELAND According to the Society for Range Management (1998), this refers to land on which the indigenous vegetation (climax or natural potential) is predominantly grasses, grasslike plants, forbs, or shrubs, and is managed as a natural ecosystem. If plants are introduced, they are managed similarly. Rangelands include natural grasslands, savannas, shrublands, many deserts, tundras, alpine communities, marshes, and meadows.

RESIDUAL DRY MATTER Refers to old, aboveground herbaceous plant material left standing or on the ground at the beginning of a new growing season.

SAVANNA This is grassland with scattered trees (usually less than 30% tree cover).

SPECIALIZED GRAZING SYSTEMS Grazing management employing recurring periods of grazing and removal of grazing in at least two pastures or management units.

TRANSHUMANCE The practice of seasonally moving animals to take advantage of forage, often along an elevational gradient.

References

Alagona, P. S., A. Linares, P. Campos, and L. Huntsinger. 2013. History and recent trends. In P. Campos, L. Huntsinger, J. L. Pro Oviedo, P. F. Starrs, M. Diaz, R. B. Standiford, and G. Montero, editors. Mediterranean oak woodland working landscapes: Dehesas of Spain and ranchlands of California. Landscape Series 16. Springer Science+Business Media, Dordrecht, Netherlands.

Allen, B. H. 1989. Historical change in California landscapes: A perspective for land managers. Pages 33–48 in W. J. Clawson, editor. Proceedings of Man and the Biosphere Symposium, XVI International Grassland Congress. Landscape Ecology: Study of Mediterranean Grazed Ecosystems. Program International L'Homme et la Biosphere, Comite Francais, Neuilly-sur-Seine, France.

Allen-Diaz, B., R. Standiford, and R. D. Jackson. 2007. Oak woodlands and forest. Pages 313–338 in M. G. Barbour, T. Keeler-Wolf, and A. A. Schoenherr, editors. Terrestrial vegetation of California. Third edition. University of California Press, Berkeley, California.

Allen-Diaz, B., S. K. McIlroy, L. M. Roche, K. W. Tate, and A. J. Lind. 2010. Determining the effects of livestock grazing on Yosemite toads (*Bufo canorus*) and their habitat: Final report. Page 45. U.S. Department of Agriculture Forest Service—Region 5, Vallejo, California.

American Horse Council Foundation. 2005. The economic impact of the horse industry on the United States. American Horse Council Foundation, Washington, D.C..

Andelt, W. F. 2004. Use of livestock guarding animals to reduce predation on livestock. Sheep and Goat Research Journal 19:72–75.

Anderson, K. 2005. Tending the wild: Native American knowledge and the management of California's natural resources. University of California Press, Berkeley, California.

Barry, S., and L. Huntsinger. 2002. Will California's landscapes keep working? Rangelands 24:6–10.

Barry, S. J. 2011. Current findings on grazing impacts of California's special status species. Keeping Landscapes Working: A Newsletter for Managers of Bay Area Rangelands. University of California Cooperative Extension 7:2–6.

Bartlett, E. T., R. G. Taylor, J. R. McKean, and J. G. Hof. 1989. Motivation of Colorado ranchers with federal grazing allotments. Journal of Range Management 24. 6:454–457.

Bartolome, J. W. 1997. The influence of cattle grazing on California ground squirrels in a blue oak savanna. Pages 327–330 in N. H. Pillsbury, W. D. Tietje, and J. Verner, editors. Proceedings of a Symposium on Oak Woodlands: Ecology, Management, and Urban Interface. San Luis Obispo, California.

———. 1993. Application of herbivore optimization theory to rangelands of the western United States. Ecological Applications 3. 1:27–29.

———. 1989. Ecological history of the California Mediterranean-type landscape. Pages 2–14 in W. J. Clawson, editor. Proceedings of Man and the Biosphere Symposium, XVI International Grassland Congress. Landscape Ecology: Study of Mediterranean Grazed Ecosystems. Program International L'Homme et la Biosphere, Comite Francais, Neuilly-sur-Seine, France.

Bartolome, J. W., and M. P. McClaran. 1992. Composition and production of California oak savanna seasonally grazed by sheep. Journal of Range Management. Volume 45. 1:103–107.

Bartolome, J. W., J. S. Fehmi, R. D. Jackson, and B. Allen-Diaz. 2004. Response of a native perennial grass stand to disturbance in California's Coast Range Grassland. Restoration Ecology 12:279–289.

Bartolome, J. W., M. C. Stroud, and H. F. Heady. 1980. Influence of natural mulch on forage production on differing California annual range sites. Journal of Range Management 33. 1:4–8.

Bartolome, J. W., R. D. Jackson, A. D. K. Betts, J. M. Connor, G. A. Nader, and K. W. Tate. 2007. Effects of residual dry matter on net primary production and plant functional groups in Californian annual grasslands. Grass and Forage Science 62:445–452.

Bartolome, J. W., R. D. Jackson, and B. Allen-Diaz. 2009. Developing data-driven descriptive models for Californian grasslands. Pages 124–138 in R. J. Hobbs and K. N. Suding, editors. New models for ecosystem dynamics and restoration. Island Press, Washington, D.C.

Bartolome, J. W., W. E. Frost, and N. K. McDougald. 2006. Guidelines for residual dry matter on coastal and foothill rangelands in California. Rangeland Management Series Publication 8092. Page 6. Division of Agriculture and Natural Resources, University of California, Oakland, California.

Bartolome, J. W., W. J. Barry, T. Griggs, and P. Hopkinson. 2007. Valley grassland. Pages 367–393 in M. Barbour, T. Keeler-Wolf, and A. A. Schoenherr, editors. Terrestrial vegetation of California. Third edition. University of California Press, Berkeley, California.

Bean, M. J., and D. S. Wilcove. 1997. The private land problem. Conservation Biology 11:1–2.

Begon, M., J. L. Harper, and C. R. Townsend. 1996. Ecology: Individuals, populations, and communities. Third edition. Blackwell Science, Oxford, UK.

Behnke, R. H., I. Scoones, and C. Kerven. 1993. Range ecology at disequilibrium: New models of natural variability and pastoral adaptation in African savannas. Overseas Development Institute, London, UK.

Belsky, A. J., A. Matzke, and S. Uselman. 1999. Survey of livestock influences on stream and riparian ecosystems in the western United States. Journal of Soil and Water Conservation 54:419–431.

Bentley, J. R., and M. W. Talbot. 1948. Annual-plant vegetation of the California foothills as related to range management. Ecology 29:72–79.

Berry, K. H., R. W. Murphy, J. Mack, and W. Quillman. 2006. Introduction to the special issue on the changing Mojave Desert. Journal of Arid Environments 67:5–10.

Bestelmeyer, B., J. Brown, S. Fuhlendorf, G. Fults, and X. B. Wu. 2011. A landscape approach to rangeland conservation practices. Pages 337–370 in D. D. Briske, editor. Conservation benefits of rangeland practices: Assessment, recommendations, and knowledge gaps. U.S. Department of Agriculture—Natural Resources Conservation Service.

Bestelmeyer, B. T., A. J. Tugel, G. L. Peacock Jr., D. G. Robinett, P. L. Shaver, J. R. Brown, J. E. Herrick, H. Sanchez, and K. M. Havstad. 2009. State-and-transition models for heterogeneous landscapes: A strategy for development and application. Rangeland Ecology and Management 62:1–15.

Bestelmeyer, B. T., D. P. Goolsby, and S. R. Archer. 2011. Spatial perspectives in state-and-transition models: A missing link to land management? Journal of Applied Ecology 48:746–757.

Biswell, H. H. 1956. Ecology of California grasslands. Journal of Range Management 9:19–24.

Blackburn, W. H. 1984. Impacts of grazing intensity and specialized grazing systems on watershed characteristics and responses. Developing strategies for rangeland management: A report of the Committee on Developing Strategies for Rangeland Management of the National Research Council National Academy of Sciences. Pages 927–933. Westview Press, Boulder, Colorado.

Bock, C. E., J. H. Bock, W. R. Kenney, and V. M. Hawthorne. 1984. Responses of birds, rodents, and vegetation to livestock exclosure

in a semidesert grassland site. Journal of Range Management 37. 3:239–242.
Bolsinger, C. L. 1988. The hardwoods of California's timberlands, woodlands, and savannas. Res. Bull. PNW-RB-148. U.S. Department of Agriculture Forest Service, Pacific Northwest Research Station, Portland, Oregon.
Booker, K., L. Huntsinger, J. W. Bartolome, N. F. Sayre, and W. Stewart. 2012. What can ecological science tell us about opportunities for carbon sequestration on arid rangelands in the United States? Global Environmental Change 23:240–251.
Brady, N. C., and R. R. Weil. 2002. The nature and properties of soils. Thirteenth edition. Pearson Education, Upper Saddle River, New Jersey.
Briske, D. D., and R. K. Heitschmidt. 1991. An ecological perspective. Pages 11–26 in R. K. Heitschmidt and J. W. Stuth, editors. Grazing: An ecological perspective. Timber Press, Portland, Oregon.
Briske, D. D., J. D. Derner, J. R. Brown, S. D. Fuhlendorf, W. R. Teague, K. M. Havstad, R. L. Gillen, A. J. Ash, and W. D. Willms. 2008. Rotational grazing on rangelands: Reconciliation of perception and experimental evidence. Rangeland Ecology and Management 61:3–17.
Briske, D. D., J. D. Derner, D. G. Milchunas, and K. W. Tate. 2011. An evidence-based assessment of prescribed grazing practices. Pages 21–74 in D. D. Briske, editor. Conservation benefits of rangeland practices: Assessment, recommendations, and knowledge gaps. U.S. Department of Agriculture Natural Resources Conservation Service.
Briske, D. D., S. D. Fuhlendorf, and F. E. Smeins. 2005. State-and-transition models, thresholds, and rangeland health: A synthesis of ecological concepts and perspectives. Rangeland Ecology and Management 58:1–10.
———. 2003. Vegetation dynamics on rangelands: A critique of the current paradigms. Journal of Applied Ecology 40:601–614.
Brooks, M. L., and J. R. Matchett. 2006. Spatial and temporal patterns of wildfires in the Mojave Desert, 1980–2004. Journal of Arid Environments 67:148–164.
Brooks, M. L., J. R. Matchett, and K. H. Berry. 2006. Effects of livestock watering sites on alien and native plants in the Mojave Desert. Journal of Arid Environments 67:125–147.
Brown, J. R. 2010. Ecological sites: Their history, status, and future. Rangelands 32:5–8.
Brownsey, P., J. L. Oviedo, L. Huntsinger, and B. Allen-Diaz. 2013. Historic forage productivity and cost of capital for cow-calf production in California. Rangeland Ecology and Management 66:339–347.
Burcham, L. T. 1982 [1957]. California range land: An historico-ecological study of the range resource of California. Center for Archaeological Research at Davis Publication 7. University of California, Davis, California.
———. 1981. California rangelands in historical perspective. Rangelands 3:95–104.
Byrd, K. B., A. R. Rissman, and A. M. Merenlender. 2009. Impacts of conservation easements for threat abatement and fire management in a rural oak woodland landscape. Landscape and Urban Planning 92:106–116.
California Rangeland Conservation Coalition (CRCC). 2014. <http://www.carangeland.org/>. June 2015.
Callaway, R. M., N. M. Nadkarni, and B. E. Mahall. 1991. Facilitation and interference of *Quercus Douglasii* on understory productivity in central California. Ecology 72:1484–1499.
Casey, J. W., and N. M. Holden. 2006. Quantification of GHG emissions from sucker-beef production in Ireland. Agricultural Systems 90:79–98.
Caudle, D., J. DiBenedetto, M. Karl, H. Sanchez, and C. Talbot. 2013. Interagency Ecological Site handbook for rangelands. U.S. Department of the Interior, Bureau of Land Management; U.S. Department of Agriculture, Forest Service; and U.S. Department of Agriculture, Natural Resources Conservation Service.
Caughley, G. 1976. Plant-herbivore systems. Pages 94–113 in R. M. May, editor. Theoretical ecology: Principles and applications. Saunders, Philadelphia, Pennsylvania.
CCRC (California Rangeland Conservation Coalition). 2014. <http://www.carangeland.org/>. Accessed February 1, 2014.
CDFA (California Department of Food and Agriculture). 2012. California agricultural production statistics, 1981–2010. California Department of Food and Agriculture, Sacramento, California. <http://www.cdfa.ca.gov/statistics/>. Accessed June 1, 2012.
Chaplin-Kramer, R., and M. R. George. 2013. Effects of climate change on range forage production in the San Francisco Bay Area. PloS One 8:e57723.
Cheatum, M., P. Alvarez, and B. Parkhurst. 2011. Payments for ecosystem services: A California rancher perspective. Duke University Nicholas Institute for Environmental Policy Solutions, Washington, D.C..
Chiariello, N. R. 1989. Phenology of California grasslands. Pages 47–58 in L. F. Huenneke and H. A. Mooney, editors. Grassland structure and function: California annual grassland. Kluwer Academic Publishers, Dordrecht, Netherlands.
Clausnitzer, D., and J. H. Huddleston. 2002. Wetland determination of a southeast Oregon vernal pool and management implications. Wetlands 22:677–685.
Clements, F. E. 1916. Plant succession; an analysis of the development of vegetation. Publication 242. Pages 1–512. Carnegie Institution of Washington, Washington, D.C..
Cole, D. N., J. W. Van Wagtendonk, M. P. McClaran, P. E. Moore, and N. K. McDougald. 2004. Response of mountain meadows to grazing by recreational pack stock. Rangeland Ecology and Management 57:153–160.
Conner, M. M., M. M. Jaeger, T. J. Weller, and D. R. McCullough. 1998. Effect of coyote removal on sheep depredation in northern California. Journal of Wildlife Management 62:690–699.
Corbin, J. D., A. R. Dyer, and E. Seabloom. 2007. Competitive interactions. Pages 156–168 in M. R. Stromberg, J. D. Corbin, and C. D'Antonio, editors. California grasslands: Ecology and management. University of California Press, Berkeley, California.
Cross, A. F., and W. H. Schlesinger. 1999. Plant regulation of soil nutrient distribution in the northern Chihuahuan Desert. Plant Ecology 145:11–25.
Dahlgren, R. A., M. J. Singer, and X. Huang. 1997. Oak tree and grazing impacts on soil properties and nutrients in a California oak woodland. Biogeochemistry 39:45–64.
Daniel, J. A., K. Potter, W. Altom, H. Aljoe, and R. Stevens. 2002. Long-term grazing density impacts on soil compaction. Transactions of the ASAE (American Society of Agricultural Engineers) 45:1911–1915.
D'Antonio, C. M., C. Malmstrom, S. A. Reynolds, and J. Gerlach. 2007. Ecology of invasive non-native species in California grassland. Pages 67–83 in M. R. Stromberg, J. D. Corbin, and C. M. D'Antonio, editors. California grasslands: Ecology and management. University of California Press, Berkeley, California.
Davidson, A. D., J. K. Detling, and J. H. Brown. 2012. Ecological roles and conservation challenges of social, burrowing, herbivorous mammals in the world's grasslands. Frontiers in Ecology and the Environment 10:477–486.
de Dios Vargas, J., L. Huntsinger, and P. F. Starrs. 2013. Raising livestock in oak woodlands. Pages 273–310 in P. Campos, L. Huntsinger, J. L. Oviedo, P. F. Starrs, M. Diaz, R. B. Standiford, and G. Montero, editors. Mediterranean oak woodland working landscapes: Dehesas of Spain and ranchlands of California Landscape Series 16. Springer Science+Business Media, Dordrecht, Netherlands.
de Groot, R. S., R. Alkemade, L. Braat, L. Hein, and L. Willemen. 2010. Challenges in integrating the concept of ecosystem services and values in landscape planning, management and decision making. Ecological Complexity 7:260–272.
Denhardt, R. M. 1940. The role of the horse in the social history of early California. Agricultural History 14:13–22.
Dennis, P., M. R. Young, C. L. Howard, and I. J. Gordon. 1997. The response of epigeal beetles (Col.: Carabidae, Staphylinidae) to varied grazing regimes on upland *Nardus stricta* grasslands. Journal of Applied Ecology 34. 2:433–443.
Díaz, S., A. Hector, and D. A. Wardle. 2009. Biodiversity in forest carbon sequestration initiatives: Not just a side benefit. Current Opinion in Environmental Sustainability 1:55–60.
DiDonato, J. 2007. Endangered amphibian research within grazed grasslands. Keeping Landscapes Working: A Newsletter for Managers of Bay Area Rangelands. University of California Cooperative Extension:4–6.
DiTomaso, J. M., G. B. Kyser, and M. J. Pitcairn. 2006. Yellow starthistle management guide. California Invasive Plant Council, Berkeley, California.
DiTomaso, J. M., S. F. Enloe, and M. J. Pitcairn. 2007. Exotic plant management in California annual grasslands. Pages 281–296 in M. R. Stromberg, J. D. Corbin, and C. D'Antonio, editors. Califor-

nia grasslands: Ecology and management. University of California Press, Berkeley, California.

Dull, R. A. 1999. Palynological evidence for nineteenth century grazing-induced vegetation change in the southern Sierra Nevada, California, U.S.A. Journal of Biogeography 26:899–912.

Dunne, J. 1989. Cryptogamic soil crusts in arid ecosystems. Rangelands 11. 4:180–182.

Dyer, A. R., H. C. Fossum, and J. W. Menke. 1996. Emergence and survival of *Nassella pulchra* in a California grassland. Madroño 43. 316–333.

Dyksterhuis, E. J. 1949. Condition and management of range land based on quantitative ecology. Journal of Range Management 2. 3:104–115.

Edwards, S. W. 1996. A Rancholabrean-age, latest Pleistocene bestiary for California botanists. Four Seasons 10:5–34.

———. 1992. Observations on the prehistory and ecology of grazing in California. Fremontia 20:3–11.

Ellis, J. E., and D. M. Swift. 1988. Stability of African pastoral ecosystems: Alternate paradigms and implications for development. Journal of Range Management 41:450–459.

Ferranto, S., L. Huntsinger, C. Getz, G. Nakamura, W. Stewart, S. Drill, Y. Valachovic, M. DeLasaux, and M. Kelly. 2011. Forest and rangeland owners value land for natural amenities and as financial investment. California Agriculture 65:184–191.

Fierer, N. G., and E. J. Gabet. 2002. Carbon and nitrogen losses by surface runoff following changes in vegetation. Journal of Environmental Quality 31:1207–1213.

Fitch, H. S., and J. R. Bentley. 1949. Use of California annual-plant forage by range rodents. Ecology 30:306–321.

Fites-Kaufman, J. A., P. Rundel, N. Stephenson, and D. A. Weixelman. 2007. Montane and subalpine vegetation of the Sierra Nevada and Cascade ranges. Pages 456–501 in M. G. Barbour, T. Keeler-Wolf, and A. A. Schoenherr, editors. Terrestrial vegetation of California. Third edition. University of California Press, Berkeley, California.

Ford, L. D. and G. F. Hayes. 2007. Northern coastal scrub and coastal prairie. Pages 180–207 in M. G. Barbour, T. Keeler-Wolf, and A. A. Schoenherr, editors. Terrestrial vegetation of California. Third edition. University of California Press, Berkeley, California.

Forero, L. C. 2002. Grass, graziers, and tenure: A case study on the Shasta-Trinity National Forest. PhD dissertation. University of California, Berkeley, California.

Fox, C. H. 2006. Coyotes and humans: Can we coexist? Pages 287–293 in R. M. Timm and J. M. O'Brien, editors. Proceedings of the 22nd Vertebrate Pest Conference. Berkeley, California.

FRAP (Fire and Resource Assessment Program). 2010. California's forests and rangelands: 2010 assessment. California Department of Forestry and Fire Protection Fire and Resource Assessment Program, Sacramento, California. <http://frap.fire.ca.gov/assessment/2010/assessment2010.php>. Accessed January 15, 2014.

Friedel, M. 1994. How spatial and temporal scale affect the perception of change in rangelands. The Rangeland Journal 16:16–25.

Frost, W. E., and N. K. McDougald. 1989. Tree canopy effects on herbaceous production of annual rangeland during drought. Journal of Range Management 42:281–283.

Frost, W. E., J. W. Bartolome, and J. M. Connor. 1997. Understory-canopy relationships in oak woodlands and savannas. Pages 183–90 in Oak Woodlands: Ecology, Management, and Urban Interface Issues. General Technical Report PSW-GTR-160. U.S. Department of Agriculture Forest Service, Berkeley, California.

Fuhlendorf, S. D., and F. E. Smeins. 1996. Spatial scale influence on longterm temporal patterns of a semi-arid grassland. Landscape Ecology 11:107–113.

Gentner, B. J., and J. A. Tanaka. 2002. Classifying federal public land grazing permittees. Journal of Range Management 55. 1:2–11.

George, M., and L. Jolley. 1995. Management measures and practices. Rangeland Watershed Program Fact Sheet 9. University of California Cooperative Extension, Davis, California.

George, M., D. Bailey, M. Borman, D. Ganskopp, G. Surber, and N. Harris. 2007. Factors and practices that influence livestock distribution. Rangeland Management Series Publication 8217. Division of Agriculture and Natural Resources, University of California, Oakland, California.

George, M., G. Nader, N. McDougald, M. Connor, and W. Frost. 2001. Forage quality. Rangeland Management Series Publication 8022. University of California Division of Agriculture and Natural Resources, Oakland, California.

George, M., J. W. Bartolome, N. McDougald, M. Connor, C. Vaughn, and G. Markegard. 2001. Annual range forage production. Rangeland Management Series Publication 8018. University of California Division of Agriculture and Natural Resources, Oakland, California.

George, M. R., S. Larson-Praplan, J. Harper, D. Lewis, and M. Lennox. 2011. California's rangeland water quality management plan: An update. Rangelands 33:20–24.

George, M. R., C. A. Raguse, W. J. Clawson, C. B. Wilson, R. L. Willoughby, N. K. McDougald, D. A. Duncan, and A. H. Murphy. 1988. Correlation of degree-days with annual herbage yields and livestock gains. Journal of Range Management 41. 3:193–197.

George, M. R., R. D. Jackson, C. S. Boyd, and K. W. Tate. 2011. A scientific assessment of the effectiveness of riparian management practices. Pages 215–252 in D. D. Briske, editor. Conservation benefits of rangeland practices: Assessment, recommendations, and knowledge gaps. U.S. Department of Agriculture Natural Resources Conservation Service.

Gerber, P. J., H. Steinfeld, B. Henderson, A. Mottet, C. Opio, J. Dijkman, A. Falcucci, and G. Tempio. 2013. Tackling climate change through livestock: A global assessment of emissions and mitigation opportunities. United Nations Food and Agriculture Organization, Rome, Italy.

Germano, D. J., G. B. Rathbun, and L. R. Saslaw. 2012. Effects of grazing and invasive grasses on desert vertebrates in California. Journal of Wildlife Management 76:670–682.

Gogan, P. J. P., and R. H. Barrett. 1995. Elk and deer diets in a coastal prairie-scrub mosaic, California. Journal of Range Management 48:327–335.

Grantz, D., D. Vaughn, R. Farber, B. Kim, T. VanCuren, R. Campbell, D. Bainbridge, and T. Zink. 1998. DustBusters reduce pollution, wind erosion: Though difficult to achieve, revegetation is best way to stabilize soil. California Agriculture 52:8–13.

Grigal, D. F., J. C. Bell, R. J. Ahrens, R. D. Boone, E. F. Kelly, H. C. Monger, and P. Sollins. 1999. Site and landscape characterization for ecological studies. Pages 29–51 in G. P. Robertson, D. C. Coleman, and C. S. Bledsoe, editors. Standard soil methods for Long-Term Ecological Research. Oxford University Press, Cary, North Carolina.

Grinnell, J. 1923. The burrowing rodents of California as agents in soil formation. Journal of Mammalogy 4:137–149.

Gurney, C. M. 2012. Giant kangaroo rats (*Dipodomys ingens*) and plant ecology at Carrizo Plain National Monument. MS thesis. University of California, Berkeley, California.

Gustanski, J. A., and R. H. Squires. 2000. Protecting the land: Conservation easements past, present, and future. Island Press, Washington, D.C..

Hack-Ten Broeke, M. J. D., and A. H. J. Van der Putten. 1997. Nitrate leaching affected by management options with respect to urine-affected areas and groundwater levels for grazed grassland. Agriculture, Ecosystems, and Environment 66:197–210.

Hamilton, J. G., J. R. Griffin, and M. R. Stromberg. 2002. Long-term population dynamics of native Nassella (Poaceae) bunchgrasses in Central California. Madroño 49:274–284.

Harper, J., M. George, and K. Tate. 1996a. California rangeland water quality management program. Rangeland Watershed Program Fact Sheet 1. University of California Cooperative Extension, Davis, California.

———. 1996b. Nonpoint sources of pollution on rangeland. Rangeland Watershed Program Fact Sheet 3. University of California Cooperative Extension, Davis, California.

Harrison, S., B. D. Inouye, and H. D. Safford. 2003. Ecological heterogeneity in the effects of grazing and fire on grassland diversity. Conservation Biology 17:837–845.

Harrison, S. P., and J. H. Viers. 2007. Serpentine grasslands. Pages 145–155 in M. R. Stromberg, J. D. Corbin, and C. D'Antonio, editors. California grasslands: Ecology and management. University of California Press, Berkeley, California.

Hayes, G. F., and K. D. Holl. 2003. Cattle grazing impacts on annual forbs and vegetation composition of mesic grasslands in California. Conservation Biology 17:1694–1702.

Heady, H. F. 1984. Concepts and principles underlying grazing systems. Developing strategies for rangeland management: A report of the Committee on developing strategies for rangeland management of the National Research Council National Academy of Sciences. Westview Press, Boulder, Colorado.

———. 1977. Valley Grassland. Pages 491–514 in M. G. Barbour and J. Major, editors. Terrestrial vegetation of California. Wiley, New York, New York.

———. 1965. The influence of mulch on herbage production in an annual grassland. Papers from the Ninth International Grasslands Congress. San Paulo, Brazil.

———. 1958. Vegetational changes in the California annual type. Ecology 39:402–416.

———. 1956. Changes in a California annual plant community induced by manipulation of natural mulch. Ecology 37:798–812.

Heady, H. F., and R. D. Child. 1994. Rangeland ecology and management. Westview Press, Boulder, Colorado.

Heady, H. F., J. W. Bartolome, M. D. Pitt, M. G. Stroud, and G. D. Savelle. 1991. California prairie. Pages 313–335 in R. T. Coupland, editor. Natural grasslands. Elsevier Science Publishing Company, Amsterdam, Netherlands.

Hedrick, D. W. 1948. The mulch layer of California annual ranges. Journal of Range Management 1:22–25.

Heitschmidt, R. K., and C. A. Taylor. 1991. Livestock production. Pages 161–177 in R. K. Heitschmidt and J. W. Stuth, editors. Grazing: An ecological perspective. Timber Press, Portland, Oregon.

Heitschmidt, R. K., and J. W. Stuth, editors. 1991. Grazing: An ecological perspective. Timber Press, Portland, Oregon.

Herrick, J. E., B. T. Bestelmeyer, S. Archer, A. J. Tugel, and J. R. Brown. 2006. An integrated framework for science-based arid land management. Journal of Arid Environments 65:319–335.

Herrick, J. E., M. C. Duniway, D. A. Pyke, B. T. Bestelmeyer, S. A. Wills, J. R. Brown, J. W. Karl, and K. M. Havstad. 2012. A holistic strategy for adaptive land management. Journal of Soil and Water Conservation 67:105–113.

Hobbs, R. J., and H. A. Mooney. 1995. Spatial and temporal variability in California annual grassland—results from a long-term study. Journal of Vegetation Science 6:43–56.

———. 1991. Effects of rainfall variability and gopher disturbance on serpentine annual grassland dynamics. Ecology 72:59–68.

———. 1986. Community changes following shrub invasion of grassland. Oecologia 70:508–513.

Hobbs, R. J., S. Yates, and H. A. Mooney. 2007. Long-term data reveal complex dynamics in grassland in relation to climate and disturbance. Ecological Monographs 77:545–568.

Hobson, W. A., and R. A. Dahlgren. 1998. Soil forming processes in vernal pools of northern California, Chico area. Pages 24–37 in C. W. Witham, E. T. Bauder, D. Belk, W. R. Ferren Jr., and R. Ornduff, editors. Ecology, Conservation, and Management of Vernal Pool Ecosystems—Proceedings from a 1996 Conference. California Native Plant Society, Sacramento, California.

Holechek, J. L., R. D. Pieper, and C. H. Herbel. 2011. Range management: Principles and practices. Sixth edition. Pearson/Prenctice Hall, Upper Saddle River, New Jersey.

Hornbeck, D. 1983. California patterns: A geographical and historical atlas. Mayfield Publishing Company, Palo Alto, California.

Howard, W. E. 1953. Rodent control on California ranges. Journal of Range Management 6:423–434.

Howard, W. E., K. A. Wagnon, and J. R. Bentley. 1959. Competition between ground squirrels and cattle for range forage. Journal of Range Management 12:110–115.

Huenneke, L. F., J. P. Anderson, M. Remmenga, and W. H. Schlesinger. 2002. Desertification alters patterns of aboveground net primary production in Chihuahuan ecosystems. Global Change Biology 8:247–264.

Hunter, J. E. 1991. Grazing and pocket gopher abundance in a California annual grassland. Southwestern Naturalist 36.

Hunter, L. M., M. Stevenson, K. S. Karish, R. Toth, T. C. Edwards Jr., R. J. Lilieholm, and M. Cablk. 2003. Population and land use change in the California Mojave: Natural habitat implications of alternative futures. Population Research and Policy Review 22:373–397.

Huntsinger, L., and J. L. Oviedo. 2014. Ecosystem services are social-ecological services in a traditional pastoral system: The case of California's Mediterranean rangelands. Ecology and Society 19:8.

Huntsinger, L., and N. F. Sayre. 2007. Introduction: The working landscapes special issue. Rangelands 29:3–4.

Huntsinger, L., and P. Hopkinson. 1996. Viewpoint: Sustaining rangeland landscapes: A social and ecological process. Journal of Range Management 49:167–173.

Huntsinger, L., and S. McCaffrey. 1995. A forest for the trees: Forest management and the Yurok Environment, 1850 to 1994. American Indian Culture and Research Journal 19:155–192.

Huntsinger, L., J. W. Bartolome, and C. D'Antonio. 2007. Grazing management on California's Mediterranean grasslands. Pages 233–253 in M. R. Stromberg, J. D. Corbin, and C. D'Antonio, editors. California grasslands: Ecology and management. University of California Press, Berkeley, California.

Huntsinger, L., L. Forero, and A. Sulak. 2010. Transhumance and pastoralist resilience in the western United States. Pastoralism: Research, Policy, and Practice 1:1–15.

Huntsinger, L., M. Johnson, M. Stafford, and J. Fried. 2010. Hardwood rangeland landowners in California from 1985 to 2004: Production, ecosystem services, and permanence. Rangeland Ecology and Management 63:324–334.

Huntsinger, L., N. Sayre, and L. Macaulay. 2014. Ranchers, Land Tenure, and Grass-Roots Governance: Maintaining Pastoralist Use of Rangelands in the U.S. in Three Different Settings. Pages 62–93 in P. M. Herrera, J. Davies, and P. M. Baena, editors. The Governance of Rangelands: Collective Action for Sustainable Pastoralism, Routledge, New York.

Inman, R. D., T. C. Esque, K. E. Nussear, P. Leitner, M. D. Matocq, P. J. Weisberg, T. E. Dilts, and A. G. Vandergast. 2013. Is there room for all of us? Renewable energy and *Xerospermophilus mohavensis*. Endangered Species Research 20:1–18.

Jackson, L. E., R. B. Strauss, M. K. Firestone, and J. W. Bartolome. 1988. Plant and soil nitrogen dynamics in California annual grassland. Plant and Soil 110:9–17.

Jackson, R. D., and J. W. Bartolome. 2007. Grazing ecology of California grasslands. Pages 197–206 in M. R. Stromberg, J. D. Corbin, and C. D'Antonio, editors. California grasslands: Ecology and management. University of California Press, Berkeley, California.

———. 2002. A state-transition approach to understanding nonequilibrium plant community dynamics in Californian grasslands. Plant Ecology 162:49–65.

Jackson, R. D., B. Allen-Diaz, L. G. Oates, and K. W. Tate. 2006. Spring-water nitrate increased with removal of livestock grazing in a California oak savanna. Ecosystems 9:254–267.

Johnson, B. E., and J. Cushman. 2007. Influence of a large herbivore reintroduction on plant invasions and community composition in a California grassland. Conservation Biology 21:515–526.

Jones, A. L., and W. S. Longland. 1999. Effects of cattle grazing on salt desert rodent communities. American Midland Naturalist 141:1–11.

Joyce, L. A., D. D. Briske, J. R. Brown, H. W. Polley, B. A. McCarl, and D. W. Bailey. 2013. Climate change and North American rangelands: Assessment of mitigation and adaptation strategies. Rangeland Ecology and Management 66:512–528.

Keeley, J. E., et al. 2005. Fire history of the San Francisco East Bay region and implications for landscape patterns. International Journal of Wildland Fire 14:285–296.

Keeley, J. E., D. Lubin, and C. J. Fotheringham. 2003. Fire and grazing impacts on plant diversity and alien plant invasions in the southern Sierra Nevada. Ecological Applications 13:1355–1374.

Kelt, D. A., E. S. Konno, and J. A. Wilson. 2005. Habitat management for the endangered Stephens' kangaroo rat: The effect of mowing and grazing. Journal of Wildlife Management 69:424–429.

Knutson, M. G., W. B. Richardson, D. M. Reineke, B. R. Gray, J. R. Parmelee, and S. E. Weick. 2004. Agricultural ponds support amphibian populations. Ecological Applications 14:669–684.

Krausman, P. R., V. C. Bleich, W. M. Block, D. E. Naugle, and M. C. Wallace. 2011. An assessment of rangeland activities on wildlife populations and habitats. Pages 253–290 in D. D. Briske, editor. Conservation benefits of rangeland practices: Assessment, recommendations, and knowledge gaps. U.S. Department of Agriculture Natural Resources Conservation Service.

Langstroth, R. P. 1991. Fire and grazing ecology of *Stipa pulchra* grassland: A field study at Jepson Prairie, California. University of California, Davis, California.

Liacos, L. G. 1962. Water yield as influenced by degree of grazing in the California winter grasslands. Journal of Range Management 15. 1:34–42.

Lidicker, W. Z., Jr. 1989. Impacts of non-domesticated vertebrates on California grasslands. Pages 135–150 in L. F. Huenneke and H. A. Mooney, editors. Grassland structure and function: California annual grassland. Kluwer Academic Publishers, Dordrecht, Netherlands.

Liffmann, R. H., L. Huntsinger, and L. C. Forero. 2000. To ranch or not to ranch: Home on the urban range? Journal of Range Management 53:362–370.

Lind, A. J., R. Grasso, J. Nelson, K. Vincent, and C. Liang. 2011. Determining the effects of livestock grazing on Yosemite toads (*Bufo canorus*) and their habitat: Final report addendum. Page 25. U.S. Department of Agriculture Forest Service, Region 5, Vallejo, California.

Linsdale, J. M. 1946. The California ground squirrel: A record of observations made on the Hastings Natural History Reservation. University of California Press, Berkeley, California.

Lovich, J. E., and D. Bainbridge. 1999. Anthropogenic degradation of the southern California desert ecosystem and prospects for natural recovery and restoration. Environmental Management 24:309–326.

Lubell, M. N., B. B. Cutts, L. M. Roche, M. Hamilton, J. D. Derner, E. Kachergis, K. W. Tate. 2013. Conservation program participation and adaptive rangeland decision-making. Rangeland Ecology and Management 66:609–620.

Lueck, D., and J. A. Michael. 2003. Preemptive habitat destruction under the Endangered Species Act. Journal of Law and Economics 46:27–60.

Lund, H. G. 2007. Accounting for the world's rangelands. Rangelands 29:3–10.

Marsh, R. E. 1998. Historical review of ground squirrel crop damage in California. International Biodeterioration and Biodegradation 42:93–99.

Martin, W. E., and G. L. Jefferies. 1966. Relating ranch prices and grazing permit values to ranch productivity. Journal of Farm Economics 48:233–242.

Marty, J. T. 2005. Effects of cattle grazing on diversity in ephemeral wetlands. Conservation Biology 19:1626–1632.

Marty, J. T., S. K. Collinge, and K. J. Rice. 2005. Responses of a remnant California native bunchgrass population to grazing, burning, and climatic variation. Plant Ecology 181:101–112.

McBride, J., and H. F. Heady. 1968. Invasion of grassland by *Baccharis pilularis* DC. Journal of Range Management 21:106–108.

McBride, J. R. 1974. Plant succession in the Berkeley hills, California. Madroño 22:317–329.

McClaran, M. P., and J. W. Bartolome. 1989a. Effect of *Quercus douglasii* (Fagaceae) on herbaceous understory along a rainfall gradient. Madroño 36:141-153.

———. 1989b. Fire-related recruitment in stagnant *Quercus douglasii* populations. Canadian Journal of Forest Research 19:580–585.

McCreary, D. D. 2001. Regenerating rangeland oaks in California. Publication 21601. University of California Division of Agriculture and Natural Resources, Oakland, California.

McCreary, D. D., and M. R. George. 2005. Managed grazing and seedling shelters enhance oak regeneration on rangelands. California Agriculture 59:217–222.

McCullough, D. R. 1969. The tule elk: Its history, behavior, and ecology. University of California Press, Berkeley, California.

Menke, J., E. Reyes, A. Glass, D. Johnson, and J. Reyes. 2013. 2013 California vegetation map in support of the Desert Renewable Energy Conservation Plan. Final Report. California Department of Fish and Wildlife Renewable Energy Program and California Energy Commission. Prepared by Aerial Information Systems, Inc., Redlands, California.

Merenlender, A. M., L. Huntsinger, G. Guthey, and S. K. Fairfax. 2004. Land trusts and conservation easements: Who is conserving what for whom? Conservation Biology 18:65–75.

Minnich, R. A. 2008. California's fading wildflowers: Lost legacy and biological invasions. University of California Press, Berkeley, California.

Mooney, H., and D. Parsons. 1973. Structure and function of the California chaparral—an example from San Dimas. Pages 83–112 in F. Castri and H. Mooney, editors. Mediterranean type ecosystems. Ecological Studies. Volume 7. Springer New York, New York, New York.

Mooney, H. A., S. P. Hamburg, and J. A. Drake. 1986. The invasions of plants and animals into California. Pages 250–272 in H. Mooney and J. Drake, editors. Ecology of biological invasions of North America and Hawaii. Ecological Studies. Volume 58. Springer New York, New York, New York.

Muir, J. 1911. My first summer in the Sierra. Houghton Mifflin Company, Boston, Massachusetts.

———. 1894. The mountains of California. Century Company, New York, New York.

NASS (National Agricultural Statistics Service). 2011a. California agricultural statistics, Crop Year 2010, Livestock and Dairy. October 28, 2011. U.S. Department of Agriculture Agricultural Statistics Board, Washington, D.C..

———. 2011b. Cattle death loss 2010, May 12, 2011. Page 17. U.S. Department of Agriculture Agricultural Statistics Board, Washington, D.C..

———. 2011c. Sheep and goat review report, January 27, 2012. U.S. Department of Agriculture Agricultural Statistics Board, Washington, D.C..

Neale, J. C. C., B. N. Sacks, M. M. Jaeger, and D. R. McCullough. 1998. A comparison of bobcat and coyote predation on lambs in north-coastal California. Journal of Wildlife Management 62:700–706.

Nuzum, R. C. 2005. Using livestock grazing as a resource management tool in California. Contra Costa Water District, Concord, California.

O'Geen, A. T., W. A. Hobson, R. A. Dahlgren, and D. B. Kelley. 2008. Evaluation of soil properties and hydric soil indicators for vernal pool catenas in California. Soil Science Society of America Journal 72:727–740.

O'Rourke, T. 2012. Sustainable ranching renaissance takes hold in northern California. May 2. San Jose Mercury News.

Parton, W. J., D. S. Ojima, and D. S. Schimel. 1994. Environmental change in grasslands: Assessment using models. Pages 111–141 in K. D. Frederick and N. J. Rosenberg, editors. Assessing the impacts of climate change on natural resource systems. Springer Science+Business Media, Dordrecht, Netherlands.

Paruelo, J. M., G. Piñeiro, G. Baldi, S. Baeza, F. Lezama, A. Altesor, and M. Oesterheld. 2010. Carbon stocks and fluxes in rangelands of the Rio de la Plata basin. Rangeland Ecology and Management 63:94–108.

Pasari, J. R., D. L. Hernandez, and E. S. Zavaleta. 2014. Interactive effects of nitrogen deposition and grazing on plant species composition in a serpentine grassland. Rangeland Ecology and Management. 67:693–700.

Pietola, L., R. Horn, and M. Yli-Halla. 2005. Effects of trampling by cattle on the hydraulic and mechanical properties of soil. Soil and Tillage Research 82:99–108.

Platenkamp, G. A. J. 1998. Patterns of vernal pool biodiversity at Beale Air Force Base. Pages 151–160 in C. W. Witham, E. T. Bauder, D. Belk, W. R. Ferren Jr., and R. Ornduff, editors. Ecology, Conservation, and Management of Vernal Pool Ecosystems—Proceedings from a 1996 Conference. California Native Plant Society, Sacramento, California.

Polley, H. W., D. D. Briske, J. A. Morgan, K. Wolter, D. W. Bailey, and J. R. Brown. 2013. Climate change and North American rangelands: Trends, projections, and implications. Rangeland Ecology and Management 66:493–511.

Pyke, C. R., and J. Marty. 2005. Cattle grazing mediates climate change impacts on ephemeral wetlands. Conservation Biology 19:1619–1625.

Rains, M. C., R. A. Dahlgren, G. E. Fogg, T. Harter, and R. J. Williamson. 2008. Geological control of physical and chemical hydrology in California vernal pools. Wetlands 28:347–362.

Ratliffe, R. D. 1985. Meadows in the Sierra Nevada of California: State of knowledge. General Technical Report PSW-84. U.S. Department of Agriculture Forest Service, Berkeley, California.

Reed, B. 2010, January 7. Magruder Ranch slideshow. <http://ethicalbutcher.blogspot.com/2010/07/magruder-ranch-slideshow.html>. Accessed June 1, 2012.

Reever Morghan, K. J., R. L. Sheley, and T. J. Svejcar. 2006. Successful adaptive management—the integration of research and management. Rangeland Ecology and Management 59:216–219.

Reiner, R., and A. Craig. 2011. Conservation easements in California blue oak woodlands: Testing the assumption of livestock grazing as a compatible use. Natural Areas Journal 31:408–413.

Reynolds, T. D., and C. H. Trost. 1980. The response of native vertebrate populations to crested wheatgrass planting and grazing by sheep. Journal of Range Management 32. 122–125.

Richmond, O. M., B. B. Risk, J. Tecklin, and S. R. Beissinger. 2010. California black rails depend on irrigation-fed wetlands in the Sierra Nevada foothills. California Agriculture 64:85–93.

Richmond, O. M. W., J. Tecklin, and S. R. Beissinger. 2012. Impact of cattle grazing on the occupancy of a cryptic, threatened rail. Ecological Applications 22:1655–1664.

Roche, L. M., B. Allen-Diaz, D. J. Eastburn, and K. W. Tate. 2012. Cattle grazing and Yosemite toad (*Bufo canorus* Camp) breeding habitat in Sierra Nevada meadows. Rangeland Ecology and Management 65:56–65.

Rolo, V., and G. Moreno. 2012. Interspecific competition induces asymmetrical rooting profile adjustments in shrub-encroached open oak woodlands. Trees 26:997–1006.

Rowe, H. I., E. T. Bartlett, and L. E. Swanson Jr. 2001. Ranching motivations in two Colorado counties. Journal of Range Management 54:314–321.

Ryerson, D. E., and R. R. Parmenter. 2001. Vegetation change following removal of keystone herbivores from desert grasslands in New Mexico. Journal of Vegetation Science 12:167–180.

Sampson, A., A. Chase, and D. Hedrick. 1951. California grasslands and range forage grasses. California Agricultural Experiment Station Bulletin 724:3–130.

Sampson, A. W. 1919. Plant succession in relation to range management. U.S. Government Printing Office, Washington, D.C..

Scheffer, M., S. Carpenter, J. A. Foley, C. Folke, and B. Walker. 2001. Catastrophic shifts in ecosystems. Nature 413:591–596.

Schiffman, P. M. 2007a. Ecology of native animals in California grasslands. Pages 180–190 in M. R. Stromberg, J. D. Corbin, and C. M. D'Antonio, editors. California grasslands: Ecology and management. University of California Press, Berkeley, California.

———. 2007b. Species composition at the time of first European settlement. Pages 52–56 in M. R. Stromberg, J. D. Corbin, and C. M. D'Antonio, editors. California grasslands: Ecology and management. University of California Press, Berkeley, California.

———. 2000. Mammal burrowing, erratic rainfall, and the annual lifestyle in the California prairie: Is it time for a paradigm shift? Second Interface Between Ecology and Land Development in California. U.S. Geological Survey Open File Report 00-62. Pages 153–159. U.S. Geological Survey, Denver, Colorado.

Schlesinger, W. H., and A. M. Pilmanis. 1998. Plant-soil interactions in deserts. Developments in Biogeochemistry 4. Pages 169–187 in N. V. Breemen, editor. Plant-induced soil changes: Processes and feedbacks. Springer Netherlands, Dordrecht, Netherlands.

Sharratt, B., W. Voorhees, G. McIntosh, and G. Lemme. 1998. Persistence of soil structural modifications along a historic wagon trail. Soil Science Society of America Journal 62:774–777.

Shaw, M. R., L. Pendleton, D. R. Cameron, B. Morris, D. Bachelet, K. Klausmeyer, J. MacKenzie, D. R. Conklin, G. N. Bratman, and J. Lenihan. 2011. The impact of climate change on California's ecosystem services. Climatic Change 109:465–484.

Shivik, J. A. 2006. Tools for the edge: What's new for conserving carnivores. BioScience 56:253–259.

Singer, F. J., and K. A. Schoenecker. 2003. Do ungulates accelerate or decelerate nitrogen cycling? Forest Ecology and Management 181:189–204.

Smith, A. H., and W. E. Martin. 1972. Socioeconomic behavior of cattle ranchers, with implications for rural community development in the West. American Journal of Agricultural Economics 54:217–225.

SNEP (Sierra Nevada Ecosystem Project). 1997. Status of the Sierra Nevada: The Sierra Nevada Ecosystem Project Final Report to Congress. University of California Centers for Water and Wildland Resources, Davis, California.

Society for Range Management. 1998. Glossary of terms used in range management: A definition of terms commonly used in range management. The Society for Range Management, Denver, Colorado.

Soil Survey Staff. 1999. Soil taxonomy: A basic system of soil classification for making and interpreting soil surveys. Second edition. U.S. Department of Agriculture, Natural Resources Conservation Service, Washington D.C.

Spiegal, S., L. Larios, J. W. Bartolome, and K. N. Suding. 2014. Restoration management for spatially and temporally complex Californian grassland. Pages 69–104 in P. Mariotte and P. Kardol, editors. Grasslands: Biodiversity and conservation in a changing world. Nova Science Publishers, Hauppauge, New York.

Stahlheber, K. A., and C. M. D'Antonio. 2013. Using livestock to manage plant composition: A meta-analysis of grazing in California Mediterranean grasslands. Biological Conservation 157:300–308.

Starrs, P. F., and L. Huntsinger. 1998. The cowboy and buckaroo in American ranch hand styles. Rangelands 20:36–40.

Stechman, J. V. 1983. Fire hazard reduction practices for annual-type grassland. Rangelands 5:56–58.

Steenwerth, K. L., L. E. Jackson, F. J. Calderon, M. R. Stromberg, and K. M. Scow. 2002. Soil microbial community composition and land use history in cultivated and grassland ecosystems of coastal California. Soil Biology and Biochemistry 34:1599–1611.

Stevenson, K. M. 2004. Conservation of plant and abiotic diversity in grazed and ungrazed meadows of the Sierra Nevada. PhD dissertation. University of California, Davis, California.

Stringham, T. K., and J. P. Repp. 2010. Ecological site descriptions: Consideration for riparian systems. Rangelands 32:43–48.

Stromberg, M. R., and J. R. Griffin. 1996. Long-term patterns in coastal California grasslands in relation to cultivation, gophers, and grazing. Ecological Applications 6:1189–1211.

Stromberg, M. R., C. M. D'Antonio, T. P. Young, J. Wirka, and P. R. Kephart. 2007. California grassland restoration. Pages 254–280 in M. R. Stromberg, J. D. Corbin, and C. D'Antonio, editors. California grasslands: Ecology and management. University of California Press, Berkeley, California.

Subak, S. 1999. Global environmental costs of beef production. Ecological Economics 30:79–91.

Sulak, A., and L. Huntsinger. 2007. Public land grazing in California: Untapped conservation potential for private lands? Rangelands 29:9–12.

———. 2002. Sierra Nevada grazing in transition: The role of Forest Service grazing in the foothill ranches of California. A report to the Sierra Nevada Alliance, the California Cattlemen's Association, and the California Rangeland Trust. <http://www.sierranevadaalliance.org/publications>. Accessed August 9, 2006.

Sulak, A., L. Huntsinger, R. Standiford, A. Merenlender, and S. K. Fairfax. 2004. A Strategy for Oak Woodland Conservation: The Conservation Easement in California. Pages 353-364 in S. Schnabel and A. Ferreira, editors. Sustainability of Agrosilvopastoral Systems: Dehesas, Montados. Advances in Geoecology 37. Catena Verlag, Reiskirchen, Germany.

Syphard, A. D., V. C. Radeloff, J. E. Keeley, T. J. Hawbaker, M. K. Clayton, S. I. Stewart, and R. B. Hammer. 2007. Human influence on California fire regimes. Ecological Applications 17:1388–1402.

Talbot, M. W., H. H. Biswell, and A. L. Hormay. 1939. Fluctuations in the annual vegetation of California. Ecology 20:394–402.

Tanaka, John A., L. Allen Torell, and Neil R. Rimbey. 2005. Who Are Public Land Ranchers and Why Are They out There? Western Economics Forum 4: 14–20.

Tate, K. W., D. M. Dudley, N. K. McDougald, and M. R. George. 2004. Effect of canopy and grazing on soil bulk density. Rangeland Ecology and Management 57:411–417.

Tate, K. W., E. R. Atwill, J. W. Bartolome, and G. Nader. 2006. Significant *E. coli* attenuation by vegetative buffers on annual grasslands. Journal of Environmental Quality 35:795–805.

Tate, K. W., E. R. Atwill, N. K. McDougald, and M. R. George. 2003. Spatial and temporal patterns of cattle feces deposition on rangeland. Journal of Range Management 56:432–438.

Tate, K. W., M. D. G. C. Pereira, and E. R. Atwill. 2004. Efficacy of vegetated buffer strips for retaining *Cryptosporidium parvum*. Journal of Environmental Quality 33:2243–2251.

Timm, R. M., C. C. Coolahan, R. O. Baker, and S. F. Beckerman. 2007. Coyotes. Pest Notes Publication 74135. University of California Division of Agriculture and Natural Resources, Statewide Integrated Pest Management Program, Oakland, California.

Torell, L. A., N. R. Rimbey, J. A. Tanaka, and S. A. Bailey. 2001. The lack of a profit motive for ranching: Implications for policy analysis. Proceedings of a Symposium Sponsored by the Western Coordinating Committee. Current Issues in Rangeland Resource Economics. Kailua-Kona, Hawaii.

Tyler, C. M., B. Kuhn, and F. W. Davis. 2006. Demography and recruitment limitations of three oak species in California. Quarterly Review of Biology 81:127–152.

USDA (U.S. Department of Agriculture). 2013. California NRCS conservation programs. Financial Management Modernization Initiative (FMMI) April 2013; Foundation Financial Information System (FFIS) December 2011; National Conservation Planning Database November 2012; ProTracts Program Contracts System October 2012. <http://www.nrcs.usda.gov/Internet/NRCS_RCA/reports/cp_ca.html>. Accessed February 1, 2014.

USFWS (U.S. Fish and Wildlife Service). 2010. San Joaquin kit fox (*Vulpes macrotis mutica*), five year review: Summary and evaluation. U.S. Department of the Interior Fish and Wildlife Service, Sacramento Fish and Wildlife Office, Sacramento, California.

———. 2004. Determination of threatened status for the California tiger salamander; and special rule exemption for existing routine ranching activities; final rule. Federal Register 69 (149): 47211-47248. U.S. Department of the Interior Fish and Wildlife Service, Washington, D.C.

———. 1997. Draft recovery plan for the Stephen's kangaroo rat, Region 1. U.S. Department of the Interior Fish and Wildlife Service, Portland, Oregon.

Vetter, S. 2005. Rangelands at equilibrium and non-equilibrium: Recent developments in the debate. Journal of Arid Environments 62:321–341.

von Richthofen, W. B. 1885. Cattle-raising on the Plains of North America. D. Appleton and Company, New York, New York.

Weaver, W. E., and D. K. Hagans. 1994. Handbook for forest and ranch roads. Mendocino County Resource Conservation District, Ukiah, California.

Westoby, M., B. Walker, and I. Noy-Meir. 1989. Opportunistic management for rangelands not at equilibrium. Journal of Range Management 42:266–274.

White, A., M. G. Cannell, and A. D. Friend. 2000. CO_2 stabilization, climate change, and the terrestrial carbon sink. Global Change Biology 6:817–833.

Wiens, J. A. 1989. Spatial scaling in ecology. Functional Ecology 3:385–397.

———. 1984. On understanding a non-equilibrium world: Myth and reality in community patterns and processes. Pages 439–458 in D. R. Strong, D. Simberloff, L. G. Abele, and A. B. Thistle, editors. Ecological communities: Conceptual issues and the evidence. Princeton University Press, Princeton, New Jersey.

Williams, K., R. J. Hobbs, and S. P. Hamburg. 1987. Invasion of an annual grassland in Northern California by *Baccharis pilularis* ssp. *consanguinea*. Oecologia 72:461–465.

Wolch, J. R., A. Gullo, and U. Lassiter. 1997. Changing attitudes toward California's cougars. Society and Animals 5:95–116.

Workman, J. P. 1986. Range economics. Macmillan, New York, New York.

Yoakum, J. D., and B. W. O'Gara. 2000. Pronghorn. Pages 559–577 in S. Demarais and Paul R. Krausman. Ecology and management of large mammals in North America. Prentice Hall, Upper Saddle River, New Jersey.

Zavaleta, E. S., K. Hulvey, and B. Fulfrost. 2007. Regional patterns of recruitment success and failure in two endemic California oaks. Diversity and Distributions 13:735–745.

THIRTY-EIGHT

Agriculture

ALEX MCCALLA and RICHARD HOWITT

Introduction

The task of this chapter is to provide a comprehensive overview of California agriculture as a managed ecosystem. It is a highly productive, complex, ever-changing system that is fragile and, in the judgment of many, unsustainable. Whole books have been written to cover the same terrain (Starrs and Goin 2010), as it comprises the largest and most diverse agriculture in the U.S. We begin with a description of the broad dimensions of California agriculture in terms of land and water use, value and diversity of production, scale and distribution of production, and the relative importance of crop and livestock production. We focus on irrigated and rain-fed crop production and confined livestock production operations.

The second section of this chapter provides a history of the rather short life of California agriculture. In less than 250 years, the state's agricultural system has grown to be a modern, large-scale, technologically intense commercial enterprise. Commercial agriculture is slightly over 150 years old, but most recently it has been transformed from an extensive, dryland, livestock and cereals economy to a diverse, intensively farmed irrigated agriculture. The section closes by describing how California agriculture is distributed on one-tenth of California's land mass. Most of it is in river valleys, large (the Great Central Valley) and small (the Coachella Valley), running 1,125 kilometers southeast to northwest from Mexico to the Oregon border.

The third section deals with the functioning of California's agricultural system in its current form as a managed ecosystem, looking at components such as fertility, salinity, urbanization, groundwater depletion, water quality, and expansion and contraction of the irrigated area. Section four explores how this managed ecosystem has impacted natural ecosystems by looking at three major cases: loss of wetlands to agriculture, restrictions on salmon habitat, and changes in the food base for birds in the Pacific flyway. Section five looks at synergies and trade-offs with other parts of California's ecosystems and points out that not all interactions are negative. We discuss two emerging, positive interactions: flooded rice fields and expanded bird food availability in the Sacramento Valley, and agriculture as fish habitat in the flood plains of the Yolo Bypass. The chapter closes with our thoughts about the future of the California agricultural ecosystem.

Overview of California Agriculture

General Parameters

LAND

The majority of California's 40 million hectares is mountains and desert. About 17.5 million hectares are classified as having some possible use for agriculture: 6.5 million hectares potentially available for grazing and 11 million hectares for cropland. Actual land in farms in 2007 (according to the 2014 U.S. Census of Agriculture) was identified as 10.25 million hectares, down from a high of over 14 million hectares in the 1950s. In 2007 slightly less than 4 million hectares were identified as cropland, of which 3.25 million hectares were irrigated. Because of urban encroachment, conversion to conservation uses, and land degradation, both of these numbers have been declining. Cropland is down from its peak in 1950 of 5.5 million hectares and irrigated area down from its peak in 1997 of 3.6 million hectares. Crop and irrigated land is located primarily in river valleys, with most of it in the Great Central Valley (Figure 38.1).

CLIMATE AND AGROECOLOGY

California is blessed with a rich and diverse agroecological endowment. Its climatic conditions range from cool temperate to subtropical hot, and its elevations range from below sea level to high plateaus. These features give it the potential to produce a diverse menu of products (claimed to exceed four hundred in 2013 by the California Department of Food and Agriculture). The critical constraint on fulfilling that potential is water availability—in sufficient quantities, at the right places, at the right times. Average annual precipitation varies from 5 centimeters in the Imperial Valley to 173 centimeters at Blue Canyon in the Sierras near Lake Tahoe. Almost all falls in November through March. Sixty percent of the water used in California comes from Sierra snowmelt.

WATER AND IRRIGATION

The development of California agriculture therefore is inextricably linked to water control, capture, management, and transport. Early water challenges included controlling flooding of the Sacramento River and managing hydraulic mining debris in the Sacramento Valley 1860–1920 (see Kelley 1989), control of the rivers feeding Tulare Lake, and ultimately converting the Tulare lake bed into farm land (Arax and Wartzman 2005). Reclamation of wetlands also played a major role. Of the wetlands that existed in California in 1900, only 4.9% remain today (see Chapter 31, "Wetlands"). For example, a total of 179,000 hectares were drained in the Sacramento River Delta alone between the 1850s and the 1930s.

California's irrigation expansion occurred in three waves: small, within-basin development; then groundwater extraction; then large-scale, interbasin surface water transfers. Early expansion was primarily small-scale, private sector, within-basin development on the western slopes of the Sierras (1870s through the 1930s). The second wave was again private sector expansion of groundwater use, with the application of new centrifugal pump technologies in the early 1900s. This expansion occurred primarily in 1900–1930 and in the 1940s. Irrigated acreage in 1940 was just over 1.6 million hectares and rose to exceed 2.4 million hectares by 1950. Large-scale, interbasin transfers of water, funded by the public sector, rapidly expanded as the Central Valley Project (CVP) came fully on board in the 1950s, 1960s, and early 1970s when 0.8 million additional hectares were added. The completion of the Tehama-Colusa Canal and the California Water Project (CWP) in the 1970s and early 1980s brought irrigated area to its peak of almost 3.6 million hectares (Figure 38.2).

California's rise to become the top agricultural producing state after World War II paralleled public sector irrigation development, including the rapid expansion interbasin transfers of surface water. California agriculture consumes the vast majority of human water used in California, though agriculture's share has steadily eroded from about 90% in the 1960s to less than 80% in recent years. This declining share, coupled with a steady decline in total water available (from 53 billion cubic meters in 1995 to 44 billion cubic meters in 2005), means agricultural use has fallen from an annual peak of over 43 billion cubic meters in 1980 to 33 billion cubic meters in 2005.

AGRICULTURAL PRODUCTION

The state of California is by far the largest producer of agricultural products in the U.S., with a FARM GATE VALUE of $43.5 billion in 2011. This exceeded the next two largest producing states, Iowa ($29.9 billion) and Texas ($22.7 billion), by significant margins. California has been the leading state since the late 1940s, with its share of U.S. production rising from 8% in 1950 to a high of 13.3% in 2005. High grain and oilseed prices since 2007, which dominate farm value of production in the Midwest, lowered California's share to 11.6% in 2011.

Crop production increasingly dominates California agriculture, with the share of output coming from the crop sector increasing from 61% in 1950 to 75% in the first decade of the twenty-first century. Running counter to this shift towards crop production, California's dairy industry has grown to become the largest commodity sector in the state's agriculture, accounting for more than 17% of the value of California farm output, more than twice the value of each of the next two most important commodities: almonds and grapes. In recent years, California has produced about 15% of the value of U.S. crop production and 7.4% of U.S. livestock production.

FARM SIZE

California agriculture is characterized by a highly skewed distribution of farm size as measured by farm sales. The 2007 Census of Agriculture counted just over 81,000 farms in California (for census purposes a farm is an enterprise that sells over $1,000 yr^{1} of product); 69% of those farms sell less than $50,000 yr^{1} of product and account for only 1.5% of the total value of California output, while 8,580 farms (10.6%) who sell over $500,000 yr^{1} account for 90.1% of the value of California output ($33.8 billion on 2007). This is even more skewed than overall U.S. figures, where farms selling over $500,000 make up 5% of U.S. farms and sell 73% of U.S. output. Finally, California agriculture has become increasingly foreign-trade

Photo on previous page: Intensive cropping around the Salinas River, Monterey County, California. Photo: Aerial Archives / Alamy.

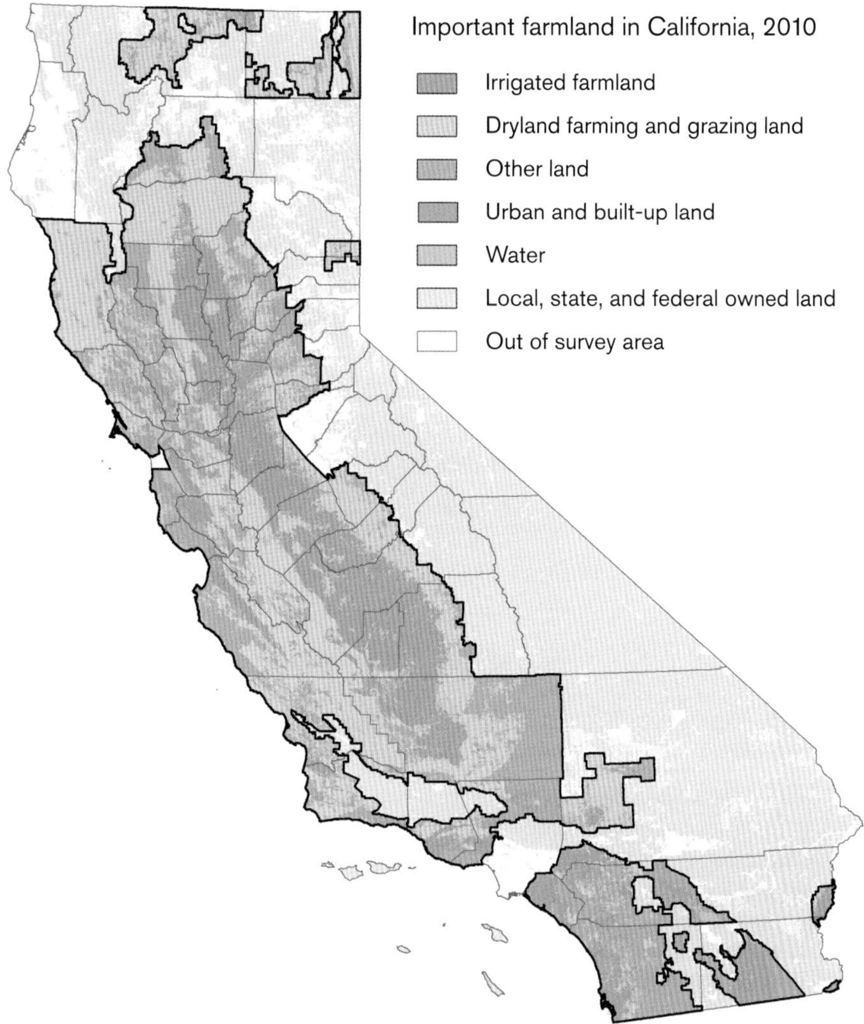

FIGURE 38.1 Cropland and irrigated agricultural areas in California. Map: California Department of Conservation, Farmland Mapping and Monitoring Program, 1984–2013.

oriented, exporting now nearly 40% of the value of farm output (whereas the U.S. value is approximately 33%). For example, more than two-thirds of California almond, walnut, and pistachio production is exported.

The Scope of California's Agriculture

This chapter focuses on irrigated and dry land crops as well as confined animal operations—principally dairy, beef, and poultry production. The area utilized as rain-fed range pasture for cattle and sheep is dealt with in Chapter 37, "Range Ecosystems." The vast majority of the value of California crop production is derived from irrigated acreage. Irrigated area varies by year depending on water availability, but total area has been declining in recent years. It peaked at 8.9 million hectares in 1997 and declined to 3.6 million hectares in 2007.

Precisely separating the value of irrigated production from the value of total crop production is difficult in California because county reports are based on volumes marketed, not on the source of water used in production. Some field crop production of barley, wheat, and hay, and perhaps still a few acres of almonds and grapes, are produced under rain-fed

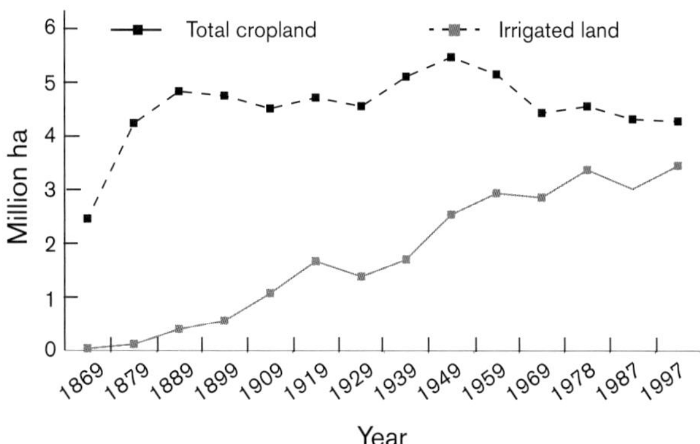

FIGURE 38.2 Total cropland and irrigated land in farms, California, 1869–2002. Sources: Data from Olmstead and Rhode 1997 (1869–1919), U.S. Department of Commerce Bureau of Census 1967 (1929–1959), and U.S. Census of Agriculture (1969–2007).

TABLE 38.1
Proportion of total value of agricultural output in California, 2011

Category	2011 Total value ($1,000)	Share included	Included value ($1,000)
Field crops	4,927,714	93%	4,582,774
Fruit and nut crops	15,322,511	97%	14,862,835
Nursery, greenhouse, and floriculture	3,687,630	100%	3,687,630
Vegetable crops	7,241,252	100%	7,241,252
Livestock, poultry, and products	12,357,994	92%	11,336,483
Milk and cream	7,680,566	95%	7,296,357
Chickens, eggs, and turkeys	1,381,092	100%	1,381,092
Hogs	39,196	100%	39,196
Sheep and lambs	287,463	50%	143,731
Cattle and calves	2,825,125	80%	2,260,100
Other	432,015	50%	216,007
TOTALS	**43,544,001**	**95%**	**41,710,974**

SOURCE: California Department of Food & Agriculture 2013, and authors' calculations.

conditions; and some irrigated pasture is used in the dairy industry. However, it is highly unlikely that rain-fed agriculture produces even 5–7% of the value of plant production (less than $2 billion in 2011). We can only conclude that the vast majority of the value of field crop, fruit and nut, and vegetable production is produced under irrigation of some form. In 2011 this totaled $27.5 billion (63% of the value of California agriculture sales). The nursery sector (value almost $3.7 billion in 2011), which is not counted as a crop per se, also uses irrigation. Beyond plant products produced, the livestock sector, especially the dairy, poultry, and beef feed lot subsectors, also depend highly on the irrigated sector for feed stocks.

It is also difficult to sort out what share of the value of livestock, poultry, and products comes from confined animal operations. Virtually all of California's dairy operations are now large-scale, confinement operations. There are still a few nonconfinement operations on the North Coast, but we estimate the share of confinement dairy production at 95% of the value of milk and cream. Essentially all of poultry production is confinement, as is what little hog production there is. This leaves the problem of segregating the value of rain-fed range cow-calf operations from the aggregate 2011 value of $2.825 billion reported for cattle and calves. NASS statistics do segregate out sales from feed lots of 630,000 head with a value of $780 million. But these numbers exclude cows culled from dairy herds, which likely number as many as 500,000 head per year out of a dairy herd of 1.8 million milking cows. The sum of those two would be 1.13 million head out of 1.7 million slaughtered in 2011, yielding a minimum of 67% of value that comes from confinement operations. The 2007 census data also show that 80% of cattle and calf sales come from operations of 5,000 head or more. As these are highly likely to be confinement operations, we can estimate that up to 80% of the cattle and calves value comes from confinement operations (Table 38.1). The vast majority (95%) of the real value of California agriculture is thus included in our analysis.

A Brief History of California Agriculture

California, until well into the eighteenth century, was one of the few remaining major "hunter-gatherer" societies left in the world (Adams 1946, Diamond 1999, and Smith 1998). The origins of sedentary California agriculture came with the development of Spanish missions over the period 1769–1823. Over its brief history of 250 years, the character of California agriculture has been in a perpetual state of transition and adjustment: from early mission attempts to raise livestock, grow grains, and develop horticulture; to the era of ruminants (i.e., cattle and sheep); to the development of large-scale, extensive wheat and barley production; to the beginnings of intensive fruit, nut, and vegetable agriculture based on ditch irrigation and groundwater; to pioneering large-scale beef feedlot and dairy production; to the intensified and expanded production of an increasingly diverse portfolio of crops resulting from massive public irrigation schemes; to today's highly sophisticated, technologically advanced, management-intensive agricultural industry, which is embedded in a rich, urban state of thirty-eight million people. It is a history of perpetual, profound, and often painful change.

California agriculture has always battled economic adversity. While blessing California with good weather and fertile soils, nature did not provide adequate rainfall in the right places or times. Substantial investments are therefore needed to bring water to the soil to grow crops. The upside is that irrigation potentially allows watering of crops at the precise time of need and in the correct amounts, greatly increasing the range of production options. Thus water management is a critical additional dimension of complexity for California agriculture. California is a long distance from everywhere; therefore, importing and exporting have always been expensive in terms of both money and time. Finally, California, because of its mild, Mediterranean climate, has different and more complex problems with pests and diseases than does the rest of mainland agriculture.

Despite continuous change, Johnston and McCalla (2004) argue that at least seven constants have driven California agriculture.

1. California agriculture has always been "demand driven." It was never subsistence, family-farm agriculture like that which characterized much of early U.S. agriculture.
2. California agriculture is resource-dependent (land and water). Its history includes aggressive development of new land and water resources along with cases of soil and groundwater exploitation.
3. California agriculture has been shaped by the absence of water in the right place. It has always been in search of more water and has been an aggressive participant in water disputes with both internal and external competing interests.
4. California agriculture has always depended on a large supply of agricultural labor for planting, cultivating, and harvesting its abundant produce from both relatively large-scale operations and specialty-crop farms. The source of a stable supply of field labor has varied over time from countries of Asia and the Americas.
5. California agriculture has grown rapidly and almost continuously, although it has been periodically buffeted by natural catastrophes (e.g., floods, droughts) and adverse economic shocks (e.g., the Great Depression, various recessions).
6. California agriculture, at least since the Gold Rush, has required very high levels of technical and economic management skills. It has always been dominated by large-scale operations that have grown in complexity and sophistication.
7. It has always been on the technological frontier in developing, modifying, or stealing new technologies, such as large-scale mechanical technology, irrigation equipment, plant varieties, pest control, food processing, and wine making.

If we are to understand where California agriculture might go in the twenty-first century, we must understand the forces that have shaped California agriculture to date. Therefore we trace that evolution in more detail in terms of eight episodes grouped into three clusters—pre-twentieth century and the first and the second halves of the twentieth century. This review focuses on the impacts of five critical drivers of California agricultural development:

- Changes in the market demand for California agricultural products, driven by population and income growth in and outside of California.
- The constant search for ways to control, manage, and access more water.
- The seeking of biological, mechanical, and engineering technology to better manage the complexities and opportunities of the natural ecosystem.
- People pressure: competition for resources, especially water and land as rapid economic growth and urbanization forced agriculture out of preferred locations.
- Public investments in infrastructure, education, research, and development; and public policy interventions that foster agricultural development such as the Wright Act, marketing boards, cooperatives, and the University of California agricultural sciences.

Pre-twentieth Century

SPANISH-MEXICAN PERIOD, 1760–1848

The Franciscan Order extended its missionary activities to Alta California in the 1760s. Led by the pioneering efforts of Fathers Portola, Serra, and others, the order developed a string of twenty-one Spanish Missions from San Diego to Sonoma over the period 1769–1823. The Spanish Church missionary strategy included, in addition to its missions (spiritual), the presidio (military) and the pueblo (commercial) as components of early development. Livestock, field crops, and horticulture were introduced to feed the settlers and to provide economic activity for the converted natives. But Alta California was never much more than self-sufficient, as total acreage of all cultivated field crops in all missions never exceeded 2,000–4,100 hectares and livestock numbers varied between 285,000 and 400,000 head in the period 1807–1834 (Adams 1946). Mission agriculture was small, and much of it disappeared in the subsequent Mexican period.

Until Mexican independence in 1821, land was vested in the church, and few land grants were given out in the Spanish-California period. Mexican independence was followed by a period of uncertainty as to the role of the church in secular affairs. This was not settled until the secularization of all missions in 1834, which stripped the church of land ownership and established the principle (unrealized) of the division of land between settlers and natives. Prior to 1822, there had been some thirty large "Rancho" land grants, and that number had risen to fifty by 1834. But after secularization (1834) and before the Bear Flag Rebellion (1846), 813 additional land grants were issued, totaling 5 million to 6 million hectares (Jelinek 1982). This was the period of the California Rancho—large spreads of land acquired by grants to Mexican citizens where cattle ranged largely untended (Jelinek 1982). Periodically cattle were slaughtered on the range to meet an East Coast and international demand for tallow and hides.

GOLD, STATEHOOD, CATTLE, AND GROWTH, 1848–1860S

The discovery of gold in 1848 and the Gold Rush of 1849 shaped the new state of California (which entered the Union in 1850) and fundamentally altered California agriculture. The European population of California was estimated at 7,000 in 1845. In January 1849 it was estimated to be 26,000. By December 1849 it was 92,000, and it multiplied to 255,000 by 1852 and to 380,000 by 1860 (Jelinek 1982). This explosive growth increased population tenfold between early 1849 and 1860. The numerous gold miners, and an even larger numbers of people who came to profit by serving the miners, needed to eat, and a strong demand for food (especially meat) emerged. Rancheros reaped first advantage from the population surge: "Hides hides gave way to beef as the price of cattle rose from under $4 a head before the rush to $500 a head at one point in 1849, leveling off at $50–$150 a head during the 1850's" (Jelinek 1982, pp. 23–24). Southern herds were driven up the Central Valley or along the coast and sold to Americans who drove them into northern and MOTHER LODE towns for processing.

Competition soon came from American cattlemen from the Midwest and Texas, who in the 1850s drove herds west to California. By mid-decade, "up to 40,000 head entered annually" (Jelinek 1982). Large numbers of sheep were also driven in from the Southwest. In the peak year of 1856, 200,000 head of sheep entered California. But the rancheros lost out to American entrepreneurs who better understood the nature of the demand for meat and the need for improved herds. By the end of the decade, an American-owned cattle and sheep business had flourished in California. Estimates of the number of cattle vary from 1,234,000 head recorded in the 1860 census (Hart et al. 1946) to 3 million head estimated by Jelinek (1982).

Weather, the ever-threatening wild card of California agriculture, dealt a near-death blow to the cattle industry in the first half of the 1860s. In 1861–1862 a huge flood in the Central Valley created a lake 400–485 kilometers long and 32–100 kilometers wide that drowned perhaps 200,000 head of cattle (Jelinek 1982, McClurg 2000). Immediately following the flood was a two-year drought in 1863–1864. Durrenberger (1999) claimed that droughts of the 1860s "resulted in the death of millions of head of cattle." Thus, even with some recovery in population, there were only 630,000 head of cattle left in California in 1870.

SHEEP, WHEAT, AND EARLY HORTICULTURE (1860s–1890s)

The cattle industry was briefly overtaken in the 1860s by the sheep industry as California's major agricultural enterprise. The first census in 1850 identified 17,514 head of sheep. By 1860 it had climbed to a million head, and the industry peaked in 1876 at 6,406,465 head (Hart et al. 1946). But even before the sheep population peaked, wheat acreage was growing rapidly on extensive ranches (Scheuring 2010). California already had significant wheat production in 1859 and had begun to export wheat. The combined acreage of wheat and barley soared in the 1860s, exceeding 0.5 million hectares in 1867 and peaking at nearly two million hectares in the late 1880s (Olmstead and Rhode 1997).

However, as quickly as wheat (and barley) had grown to dominate valley agriculture, it crashed to the point that "by the end [of the first decade] of the 1900s only about 0.5 million acres of wheat were cut, and the state became a net importer of wheat" (Olmstead and Rhode 1997, p 2.). Three causes are often postulated to explain the demise of the wheat industry, though there is some disagreement on the third. The first was soil exhaustion. Yields were declining as large-scale wheat growers simply mined natural soil fertility and moved on (Stoll 1998). Second, a severe depression in agricultural prices occurred in the 1880s, and it was acute in wheat. California's distance from European markets resulted in very low farm prices. Third, development of a small but diversified fruit, nut, and vegetable industry provided an alternative land use. In the same period (the 1890s) irrigated acreage was increasing rapidly. It is tempting to argue that horticulture replaced, if not displaced, wheat. But some scholars argue that wheat declined and fell on its own (Stoll 1998). It is safe to say that the expansion of horticulture occurred simultaneously with the decline of wheat, thus staving off a severe depression in California agriculture.

CALIFORNIA AGRICULTURE AT THE TURN OF THE CENTURY

California agriculture at the end of the nineteenth century had already experienced several transformations of phenomenal magnitude and speed—from mission agriculture to cattle, to sheep, to wheat (Figure 38.3). Another transformation was under way that would forever shift California agriculture from extensive, dryland agriculture to intensive, irrigated agriculture. The cattle and sheep booms each lasted less than twenty years, and the wheat (and barley) peak had passed before the beginning of the 1900s. The rapid growth of irrigated land started in 1880 and tripled between 1900 and 1930. This is a proxy for the growth of irrigated horticulture and vegetable production. Thus the major outlines of the state's agriculture were fairly well established by the beginning of the twentieth century (Benedict 1946).

The First Half of the Twentieth Century

EXTENSIVE TO INTENSIVE AGRICULTURE (1890–1930)

According to Olmstead and Rhode (1997, p. 5), "The share of intensive crops in the value of total output climbed from less than 4 percent in 1879 to over 20 percent in 1889. By 1909 the intensive share reached nearly one-half, and by 1929, it was almost four-fifths of the total." The growth in fruit shipments was rapid, increasing fivefold between 1890 and 1910. The most phenomenal growth was in oranges, from two navel orange trees planted in 1873 to 5.5 million orange-bearing trees in 1900.

California, aided by the transcontinental railroad and new cooling technology, soon expanded from servicing local needs to shipping products to eastern U.S. markets and abroad. Those who analyzed the phenomenal transformation of California agriculture between 1890 and 1930 postulated a particular set of drivers. Jelinek (1982) argued the process was stimulated by prominent individuals, but success really depended on four critical factors:

- Available agricultural labor from a succession of international sources—China, Japan, the Philippines, India, Mexico.
- Irrigation development—about 0.5 million irrigated hectares in 1890 and almost 2 million by 1930.
- Improved transportation services—refrigerated rail shipping, trucking and rural roads, and improved handling, storage, and transportation technology.
- The development of marketing cooperatives that provided innovation in selling, rapidly increasing production outside of California and to the world.

Rhode (1995) argues that two dominant factors, usually not discussed, were (1) rapid decreases in credit costs (interest

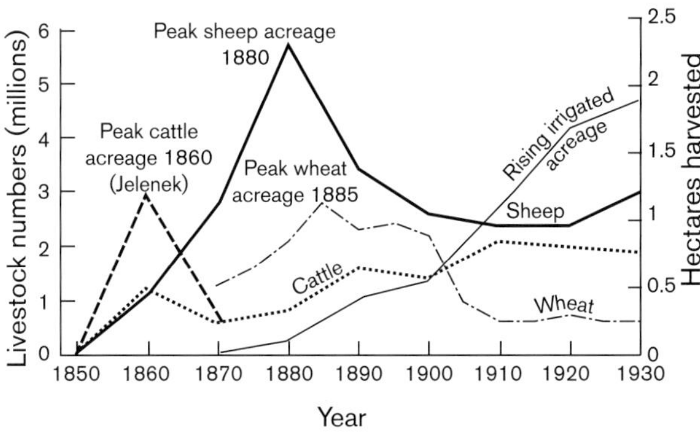

FIGURE 38.3 Selected waves of agricultural development in California, 1850–1930. Source: Johnston & McCalla (2004).

rates declined significantly around 1890) and (2) horticultural productivity that was substantially improved by "biological learning." Rhode (1995) also identified four other drivers of importance, three of which are the same as Jelinek's:

- Mechanization (California was always a leader). Among other innovations, California was home to the first commercial combine harvester, track-laying tractor, orchard sprayers, and mechanical fruit and nut harvesters.
- Irrigation. Small-ditch irrigation schemes and newly formed irrigation districts, under the Wright Act of 1897, fostered expansion of surface-water irrigated acreage, and the 1890 invention of the centrifugal pump allowed greatly expanded groundwater use in the early 1900s.
- Labor. California had access to large supplies of quality labor at low cost.
- Cooperatives. California had innovative forms of collective grower action.

The major point is that the transformation from extensive grain growing and livestock grazing occurred relatively quickly and resulted from a complex interaction of many factors.

From 1890 to 1930 the population of California increased fivefold (1 million to 5 million). Incomes rose rapidly from 1910 to 1929, which drove consumer demand toward fruits, vegetables, and livestock products and away from grains and field crops. A world-class agricultural research and extension system was established. Californians continued to import biological technology, to test and modify it, and to apply it quickly. The 1920s, according to Benedict (1946), was a period of relative optimism and rapid development. In the period 1919–1929, grape acreage expanded 94%; subtropical fruit and nut acreage 82%; vegetable acreage 91%; and temperate-zone fruit acreage 63%. In contrast, acreage of cereals, hay, and other field crops fell (Benedict 1946). In part, this transition was responsive to changes in relative agricultural prices in the 1920s. All agricultural prices fell sharply in 1919 at the end of World War I, and grain prices stayed relatively low throughout the 1920s before plunging again in 1930. Prices of fruits, vegetables, nuts, and cotton, however, recovered substantially in the 1920s, fueled, no doubt, by rising incomes and a growing California population. Immigration in the 1920s amounted to 1.25 million people, who came for well-paying jobs in growing cities.

Thus, by 1930, California seemed on the way to agricultural riches, but ominous events were beginning to cause worry. Much of the expansion of irrigation in the period 1900–1930 came from groundwater sources; in 1902 less than 10% of irrigation water came from groundwater sources. The fastest expansion in groundwater exploitation occurred in 1910–1930, driven, in part, by widespread adoption of the centrifugal pump. The number of pumping units increased from approximately 10,000 in 1910 to almost 50,000 in 1930. Groundwater use again expanded in the 1940s, rising to 75,000 units in 1950 (Olmstead and Rhode 1997). Groundwater had been perceived as an unlimited resource, but by 1930 problems with falling water tables, subsidence, and salinization were steadily approaching levels that Riesner (1993) called an ecological time bomb.

DEPRESSION AND WAR (1930–1949)

The threat of water shortages was only one of the pending shocks facing California agriculture. The 1920s was a period of rapid expansion in many perennial crops, as perennial-crop prices had fared better than grain prices. Therefore the crash into the Depression was even more precipitous and shocking. Failing prices, exacerbated by significant droughts in 1929, 1931, 1933, and 1934, led to sharp contractions of farm income. Irrigated area dropped by 0.5 million hectares between 1929 and 1935. The INDEX OF FARMLAND VALUES, which had been at 160 in 1930, plunged to 109 in 1933 (Benedict 1946).

Unemployment rose rapidly, and job-induced in-migration, which virtually stopped in the early 1930s, was soon replaced by an influx of poor farmers displaced by the Dust Bowl and the Depression. These new migrants, poor and unemployed, settled mainly in rural California, adding to an already volatile and sometimes violent labor situation. Contractions in demand hammered farm prices, drought reduced farm production (and income), surplus labor put downward pressure on wages, and poverty rates soared among both farmers and farm workers. The crisis of the 1930s fundamentally altered the policy environment in which California agriculture operated. Prior to 1930, California farmers opposed federal participation in agricultural affairs and were little affected by it, but the Depression changed that. Federal intervention came on several fronts, including new forms of credit under the Farm Credit Administration. The Agricultural Adjustment Administration (AAA) was a comprehensive program designed to reduce production and provide floor prices. Relatively generous support prices, coupled with California's efficiency in producing rice, cotton, and milk, no doubt contributed to rapid expansion of production of these commodities in the 1940s.

The 1930s also saw major efforts by California agriculture to enlist state assistance in constructing a major water scheme to capture and transport northern Sierra water south to Central Valley agriculture. The original Central Valley Water Project was proposed as a state operation to be financed by a voluntary bond sale. It quickly received legislative approval, but the deepening Depression prevented the bond sale from being initiated. Attention turned to the federal government, where the idea of spending to help agriculture while creating public works employment appealed to New Dealers in the early 1930s. In 1935 the Central Valley Project (CVP) became a federal Bureau of Reclamation project, and after 1937 a massive dam and conveyance system began to be constructed. The major impact on California agriculture would not, however, occur until after World War II. Prior to the 1930s, irrigation development in California was almost exclusively financed privately. Less than 1% of irrigated acreage in California had been developed through federal action (Benedict 1946). The takeover of the CVP by the Bureau of Reclamation in 1935; subsequent bureau projects such Monticello, New Melones, and San Luis; and the state's subsequent development of the California State Water Project (SWP) in the 1960s meant that a very large share of all subsequent surface-water development was publicly financed.

The 1940s saw a rapid return to prosperity and growth. This recovery was mainly a product of developments in the California and U.S. economies that were driven by the war effort. Durrenberger (1999) argued that World War II transformed California from a rural, natural resource–based economy to a leading industrial and military state in just five years. The population in California almost doubled, from 5.6 million in 1930 to 10.6 million in 1950—with nearly 4 million of the increase occurring in the 1940s. In-migration resumed and, at its peak in the early 1940s, amounted to about 0.5 million people per year. California led all states in receipt of federal wartime expenditures. According to Durrenberger (1999, p. 101), "Over 90% of federal expenditure to promulgate the war in the Southwest Pacific was allocated to California."

Unlike after World War I, no sharp fall in agricultural prices and incomes followed World War II. California agriculture continued to grow and diversify due to a combination of federal policy and a rapidly growing economy. The value of farm output in California grew 24% in 1945–1950. Expansion and its labor requirements made labor the dominant issue in California agriculture in the postwar 1940s and 1950s. The wartime boom had siphoned excess labor out of agriculture. California agriculture, facing rising wage rates, pressed for and received a program that allowed importing of Mexican labor. The federal Bracero Program, initiated in 1942, supplied significant quantities of farm labor through the boom years of the war and the postwar expansion of California agriculture. Water then replaced labor as the dominant issue in California agriculture. Expansion of production caused groundwater overdrafts to resume in the 1940s. However, construction on the CVP was suspended during the war years (1942–1944), delaying the availability of new surface-water supplies to production areas with overdrafted groundwater supplies. In 1948, California permanently took over as the largest agricultural state in the Union in terms of value of production (Bradley 1997).

The Second Half of the Twentieth Century to the Present

California emerged from the first half of the twentieth century as the leading state in the U.S. military/industrial complex. Its agriculture had weathered the Depression, had regained health during World War II, and was poised to expand as the CVP came online. At midcentury, the future must have been seen as a time of great promise for the state. The second half of the century, at least until the 1990s, met that promise. California's population grew in fifty years post–World War II from 10 million to 35 million people. California gross domestic product (GDP) generally grew faster than that of the United States, meaning per capita California GDP exceeded the U.S. GDP in most years. The growth was fueled by rapid expansion, first in the aerospace industry and then in electronics and computers. California led the nation in both fields. Military expenditures also remained high through the 1980s.

Accordingly, when defense cutbacks came in the 1990s, California suffered a disproportionately high share of defense reduction. Immigration slowed substantially, a severe recession struck the state in the early 1990s, and the state continued to suffer through a prolonged and severe drought. A rapid recovery in the second half of the 1990s, fueled in part by the "dot com" boom, quickly collapsed into a recession in the first years of the twenty-first century, bringing with it severe financial difficulties for the state. A modest recovery marked the middle of the first decade of the twenty-first century, but it then collapsed—beginning with the housing sector in 2008 and then spreading rapidly into a prolonged, deep recession. Agricultural prices spiked upward in 2007 and 2008 but fell when the general economy collapsed in late 2008. They rose somewhat in 2010 and have been volatile since, but as of 2014 they remain at levels much above the early years of this century.

BIG WATER, GROWTH, RELOCATION, AND DIVERSIFICATION (1950–1970)

The decades of the 1950s and 1960s were boom periods in California. Massive investments in infrastructure continued in water projects, highways, airports, ports, higher education, and urban development. Virtually all of the increase in population was in burgeoning urban areas on the south coast, particularly in the Los Angeles Basin and the San Francisco Bay Area.

Rapidly expanding housing growth, mostly in sprawling single-home subdivisions, accelerated urban takeover of agricultural land. In just twenty years, Los Angeles County went from generating the highest value of agricultural production in the state (and nation) to falling out of the "top ten" California counties in 1970 and falling below twenty-eighth after 2000. Vast stretches of Orange and San Diego Counties, longtime major producers of citrus and subtropical fruits and vegetables, were developed quickly. In the north, rapid urbanization quickly consumed much of Santa Clara County's agriculture, pushing fresh- and dried-fruit production into the Sacramento and northern San Joaquin Valleys. This rapid relocation of production was abetted, in part, because the state's stock of irrigated land increased from less than 2 million hectares in 1945 to more than 3 million hectares in 1970, peaking at approximately 3.6 million hectares in the 1990s.

The cumulative impacts of population and income growth and urbanization, coupled with new production opportunities opened by new water transfers, led to rapid and significant changes in California agriculture. These changes included expansion in the suite of crops produced and changes in the location of production. Three examples illustrate the process. First, southern California's dairy industry moved from southern Los Angeles and northern Orange Counties to eastern Los Angeles County (Chino and Pomona) and then to western San Bernardino and Riverside Counties in the 1950s and 1960s. The dairy industry eventually migrated north into the southern San Joaquin Valley, where it is now concentrated in Tulare and Merced Counties. Each time farmers moved, they recapitalized using the proceeds of urban land sales prices to expand and modernize their operations. Second, the citrus industry experienced a similar migration, first east to Riverside and San Bernardino, then north. Today, more than 50% of the state's production is in Tulare County, compared to nearly 45% of production in Los Angeles and Orange Counties in 1950 (Figure 38.4).

Third, rapid urban development in the South San Francisco Bay Area pushed deciduous fruit production out of the Santa Clara Valley into the Sacramento and northern San Joaquin Valleys. For example, in 1950 nearly 80% of the 40,000 bearing hectares of prunes were on the Central Coast. Prunes in the Sacramento Valley increased from 8,000 hectares to 20,000 hectares in the 1960s. By the end of the century, nearly all prunes were grown in the upper Sacramento Valley. This massive relocation resulted in high-priced buyouts of farm land at urban prices, allowing relocating farmers to recapitalize with larger operations that experienced substantial yield increases because of new trees, better varieties, higher planting densities, and new cultural practices. Prune yield was 3,212 kg ha^{-1} in 1950, 4,695 kg ha^{-1} in 1970, and over 6,672 kg ha^{-1} by 1987.

Crops also moved and expanded as new water became available. One significant example is almonds. In 1950 half of the state's almonds were grown in the Sacramento Valley, 25% in the San Joaquin Valley, and the remainder in coastal counties. Bearing hectares totaled 36,000 and yields averaged 940 kg ha^{-1}. Almonds were aggressively planted in the San Joaquin Valley beginning in the late 1960s, and by 1970 the state had 60,000 bearing hectares. This area increased to 160,000 hectares by the mid-1980s, to 214,000 hectares by 2001, and to 310,000 by 2011. Yields approached 1,800 kg ha^{-1} by 2000 and have exceeded 2,200 kg ha^{-1} in five of the six years between 2005 and 2011. Average production has doubled since 2000. Exports expanded as rapidly as supplies increased, accounting for about two-thirds of the crop in recent years. By 2000, 80% of production was in the San Joaquin Valley, 20% in the Sacramento Valley, and virtually none on the coast (Figure 38.5).

The 1950s and 1960s saw the beginning of a second fundamental transformation of California crop agriculture in terms of expansion, changing composition, relocation, and greatly enhanced yields. The dominant driver of this transformation was productivity growth funded in part by land profits from relocation to lower land-price areas. Traditional field crops, as a share of production, declined steadily, to be replaced by higher-valued, income-sensitive crops. Higher incomes plus urbanization accounted for the rising importance of fresh vegetables and horticulture products in California agriculture. These trends have contributed to significant changes in the relative shares of crop production over the last sixty years (Figure 38.6).

Rising incomes after World War II also fueled a rapid expansion in consumer demand for beef. U.S. consumption rose from somewhat more than 20 kilograms per capita in 1950 to almost 40 kilograms in the mid-1970s. California's livestock sector responded strongly to that demand expansion. One of the most phenomenal growth patterns observed was the practice of fattening slaughter beef in confined feedlots. Cattle numbers in California had been flat from 1900 to 1940, at approximately 1.4 million head. Numbers increased to 3.9 million head in 1969—a 250% increase (Olmstead and Rhode 1997). Overall, the state's feedlot industry exploded after World War II, increasing from 125,000 head in 1945 to 1 million head in 1965 (Scheuring 2010). Again, California had led the nation in new approaches to large-scale agricultural production. However, by the 1970s large-scale feedlots were established in Arizona, Colorado, Texas, and the Midwest, areas generally more proximate to Great Plains and Midwestern feed supplies. California feedlot numbers declined. Per capita beef consumption also steadily declined after the 1970s, stabilizing around 30 kilogram per capita in the 1990s and early 2000s.

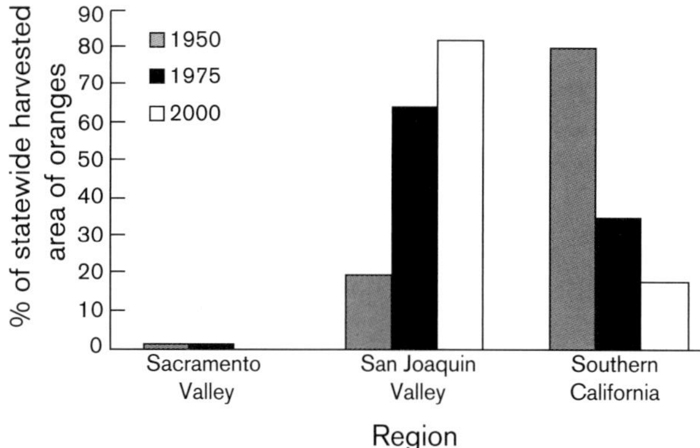

FIGURE 38.4 Oranges, share of harvested area by major agricultural production region, in 1950, 1975, 2000. Source: Johnston & McCalla 2014.

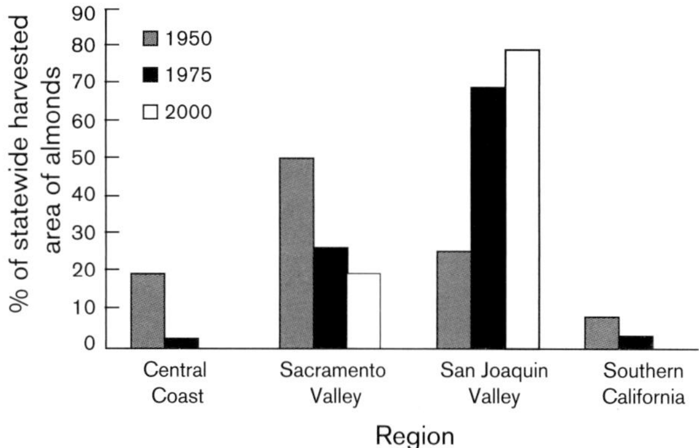

FIGURE 38.5 Almonds, share of harvested area by major agricultural production region, in 1950, 1975, 2000. Source: Johnston & McCalla 2014.

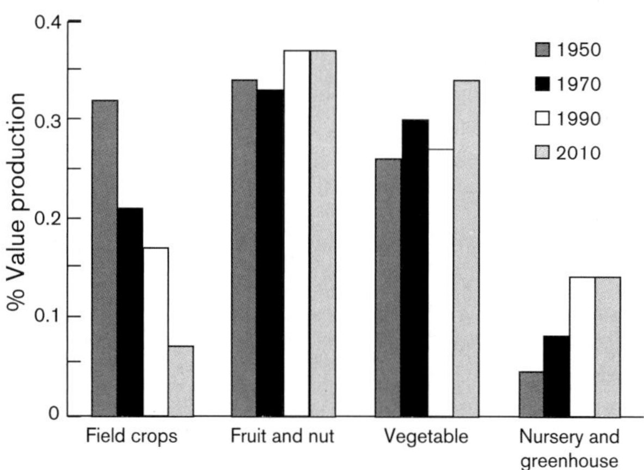

FIGURE 38.6 Relative shares of crop production, California, 1950–2010. Source: Johnston and McCalla 2014.

TABLE 38.2
Transformation of California's dairy industry, 1950–2011

Year	Number of cows	Number of farms	Average number of cows per farm	kg / cow
1950	780,000	19,428	40	3,500
1970	750,000	5,000	150	6,000
2011	1,769,000	1,668	1,101	10,600

SOURCE: California Department of Food & Agriculture 2013.

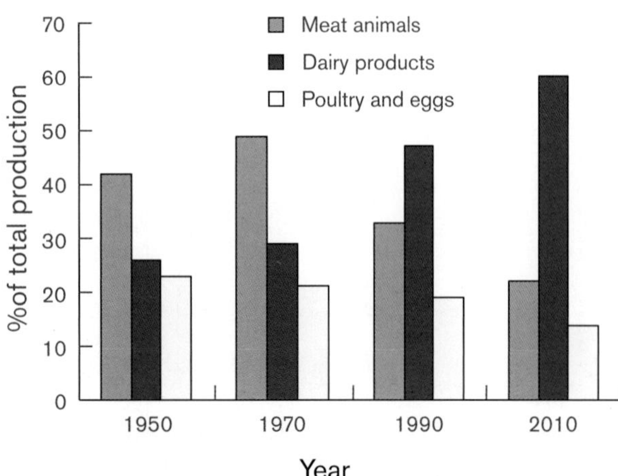

FIGURE 38.7 Relative shares of livestock and livestock products, California, 1950–2010. Source: Johnston and McCalla 2010, California Department of Food & Agriculture 2013.

California then underwent a phenomenal transformation of the dairy industry (Table 38.2, Figure 38.7). In just over sixty years cow numbers have more than doubled and milk yields per cow have tripled. The number of farms has dropped tenfold as average herd size has grown from 40 to 1,101 animals. The dairy industry emerged as the dominant commodity in the agricultural portfolio of California. In 1993, California overtook Wisconsin as the number one milk producer in the nation.

UPS AND DOWNS, INTENSIFICATION AND INTERNATIONALIZATION (1970–2010)

Despite this record of rapid growth, the next four decades were to be even more explosive and also more unstable. Whereas the 1950s and 1960s were characterized by relatively stable prices, increased price volatility in the next four decades would lead to substantial swings in the profitability and economic sustainability of firms in California agriculture. The early 1970s can be characterized as a period of aggressive expansion fueled by improving world markets and concern about "feeding a hungry world." Product prices were strong for food commodities. With strong prices came a rapid run-up in U.S. farm asset values. Worldwide market demands slowed later in the 1970s, but U.S. farmland values continued to rise into the early 1980s.

This period witnessed an eroding of California's heavy reliance on production of undifferentiated commodities toward a more diverse, specialized agriculture involving higher-valued, more capital-intensive crops. The mass of production for many products shifted into the San Joaquin Valley from both the south and the north, and the number of commodities produced grew from two hundred to four hundred. The period included two contrasting water-resource trends that greatly influenced by population growth. First, California agriculture seemed flush with new surface-water supplies at the end of the 1970s. Increased surface-water deliveries occurred following completion of Oroville Dam and San Luis Reservoir in 1967 and 1968, respectively, and with extensions of the California Aqueduct serving westside and southern San Joaquin agriculture in the 1970s. The Kern County Intertie Canal, which connected the east side of the valley with the aqueduct, was completed in 1977. A second significant increment in surface-water availability followed the extension of the CVP's Tehama-Colusa Canal, enabling intensification of production on the west side of the Sacramento Valley (e.g., of tomatoes, almonds, and vegetable seeds). These completions signaled the end of the decades-long expansion of major surface-water delivery systems.

Second, two of the century's more severe droughts occurred during this period—the first in 1976–1977 and the second over the period 1987–1992. The former was more severe, but the latter, longer drought had a far greater impact on agriculture. Both droughts sharply reduced water deliveries from the north to meet the growing needs of San Joaquin Valley agriculture. Average runoff in the Sacramento and San Joaquin hydrological areas fell to half of normal levels in the 1987–1992 drought. At the turn of the century, agriculture, in the face of resource competition from urban and environmental demands, was confronted with increasing water-resource scarcity and uncertainty.

Into a New Century

By the century's end, California agriculture was more diverse in production and less dependent on field-crops and livestock (except for dairy) production than in 1970. Contractual marketing arrangements for agricultural production had become the norm in this new, higher-valued production system, changing marketing channels and risk exposures of producers and contracting firms. Yet in the early years of the twenty-first century, prices were low and California agriculture was again concerned about its future. Some price recovery occurred in 2004 before basic commodity prices spiked wildly in 2007. Wheat, rice, corn, and soybeans prices nearly tripled. They began to fall in 2008, then collapsed with the severe economic recession that began in 2008 and lingered for over five years. As of 2014, agricultural prices in general have been very volatile but have not returned to pre-2006 levels. California's agriculture, especially the dairy industry, suffered through this instability. Federally mandated expansion of biofuel production has pushed 2014 corn and soybean prices well above 2007–2008 peaks, impacting heavily the costs of feeding livestock.

Competitive pressures have increased for water resources throughout the state and for land in some areas, particularly in the northern San Joaquin and southern Sacramento Valleys. Environmental issues continue to command attention, with more emphasis on instream water use, dairy-waste management, new chemical standards, water quality, and particulate matter (air-pollution) concerns. The two dominant underlying forces affecting regional shifts in the location of agricultural production remain population growth and water-supply conditions.

Defining the Agricultural and Ecosystem Regions of California

In many ways, the development of California agriculture has mirrored its highly variable ecosystems. This is hardly surprising, as both natural and managed ecosystem performance are driven by the resource base and soils, topography, water resources, and microclimates. We define nine regions of California agriculture in terms of the agricultural ecology that occurs in each region rather than geographic location (see Figure 38.1). The North Coast region was one of the earliest settled but was never a major force in agricultural production since its principal products were originally fur, fisheries, and lumber. More recently, the region developed sporadically with the concentration of livestock production in beef herds, dairy cows, and, for a while, chickens on the coastal plain. Agricultural value in the North coast more recently has become dominated by wine production and, unofficially, marijuana production, which one government official correctly listed as the most valuable crop in Mendocino County for one year.

The Central Coast was first developed with large, extensive cattle ranches that took advantage of the differences in growing season microclimate among the coastal, Coast Range, and Central Valley environments to move cattle seasonally from west to east and back again. However, these cattle operations depended heavily on rainfall, and many did not survive the climatic fluctuations that led to inevitable booms and busts of stocking rates. Nowhere is this more aptly described in John Steinbeck's *East of Eden* (1952). During the early 1900s, more intensive agriculture emerged in the fertile, alluvial Salinas and Santa Maria Valleys, largely based on groundwater extraction. The Salinas Valley became renowned for vegetable production—in particular, lettuce. Watsonville was the center for artichoke production given its unique microclimate. Over the last thirty years, grazing has given way to wine grape production in many of the Central Coastal valleys, which are increasingly recognized for the quality of many of their wines.

We divide the Sacramento Valley lengthwise into eastside and westside ecological regions on the basis of soils, crops and, in particular, water sources and development. The eastside region includes both sides of the Sacramento River, which were the first to be developed in the early parts of the previous century as local surface irrigation districts used tributary streams and river water. These irrigation districts were formed by groups of farmers to mutually finance and develop county-based, surface-water distribution systems. A wide range of perennial crops was grown, from peaches, plums, and nectarines to olives and some field crops. Agricultural development and ecological conversion of the westside was initially dominated by extensive dryland wheat production, mechanized as much as animal power would allow. Photographs of combine harvesters drawn by forty mules show the lengths to which these large extensive farms had to go to obtain timely wheat harvests. Irrigated agriculture in the westside valley region occurred thirty years later than on the eastside and was stimulated by both the development of heavy agricultural machinery for rice production and the Tehema Colusa and Glenn Colusa canal systems. Heavy soils and ample water supplies made the northern part of this region very well suited for rice production, much of which was exported to Japan and Korea. Further south on the westside of the Sacramento Valley, irrigation districts based on Clear Lake and Lake Berryessa, developed in the 1940s, expanded grain and row crop acreage in Yolo and Solano Counties.

The Sacramento River Delta is approximately 0.25 million hectares and occupies a unique natural and agricultural ecosystem. Originally, the Delta was a fertile, tideland marsh. In the 1840s the explorer Kit Carson remarked on the extraordinary number of birds and beavers he encountered in his journey up the San Joaquin River and through the Sacramento Delta. In the latter part of the 1800s, levee-building began in the Delta to improve riverboat transportation to the gold fields. The levees quickly became necessary for water control, which allowed the agricultural development of the Delta's fertile peat soils. This drainage of the Delta completely transformed it ecologically but also allowed extensive cropping of field crops, pears, asparagus, and other specialty crops. The new agricultural ecology in the Delta was not stable. Drainage and cultivation of the soils induces oxidization, which removes topsoil at a rate of up to 0.5 cm yr^{-1}. As a result, Delta soils have subsided by up to 4.5 meters in some places. This soil loss both reduces agricultural potential and further weakens the levees that retain the water from fields and are now below sea level.

The ecology of the Delta channels has been further modified over the past fifty years through use as part of the conveyance infrastructure moving water from northern California to the San Joaquin Valley in southern California. This use means that most of the Delta has to be kept at the lowest possible salinity levels. Thus the Delta's historical, seasonal salinity fluctuations have been replaced by a constant medium-salinity regime. This shift has favored invasive species, so much so that more than 80% of its marine biomass now comprises exotic species (Hanak et al. 2011). In short, the Sacramento River Delta's natural and managed ecosystems are neither stable nor reliable for the support of either the remaining ecosystem or its use for water conveyance.

Like the Sacramento Valley, we divide the San Joaquin Valley into eastside and westside, each with distinct development history, microclimates, water sources, and cropping patterns. Irrigation districts on the eastside developed mostly around the turn of the past century. The three main river systems supplying this area—the Merced, Tuolumne, and Mokelumne—have catchments on the western slopes of the Sierras. All three flow into the San Joaquin River, containing headwaters in the southern part of the valley and flowing north to the Sacramento River Delta. With the formation of irrigation districts on the eastside, oak savanna gave way to irrigation canals, perennial crops, dairies, grapes for table consumption, and raisins. Further east in this region, the foothills retain many features of the original oak savanna, but with a lower oak density due to cattle grazing and firewood harvesting. Because the historical settlement of this area occurred about eighty years before the westside, farm sizes and degree of mechanization were much smaller.

Many crops that lend themselves to smaller-scale production persist in this region. The west side of the San Joaquin Valley was very unproductive until the introduction of the centrifugal groundwater pump in the 1920s. Given the low productivity and extensive nature of the region, landholdings were extremely large and concentrated in few hands. The introduction of groundwater for irrigation led to the classic common property problem of excess pumping. Over a period of forty years, groundwater levels on the west side of the San Joaquin Valley fell by 60 meters. By the late 1930s the unreliability of groundwater supplies made westside land owners more than willing to step in and take contracts in the newly proposed state water project, when established irrigators on the eastside backed out of the project for fear of indebtedness under Depression conditions.

As state and federal water projects developed in the 1950s and 1960s, new large areas of westside irrigated land came into production. Despite discussion and planning, no formal drainage system was established. This rapidly led to significant environmental drainage problems. With expansion of the federal government's role in irrigation projects under the National Reclamation Act, several districts on the westside came under federal jurisdiction. However, its attendant restrictions on irrigated land ownership were blatantly ignored for many years. Because of the almost complete absence of natural water supplies on the westside, growers are always acutely aware of the scarcity value of water, particularly during drought periods. This scarcity has generated both efficient distribution systems and highly efficient, large-scale farming in this region—both criticized at times for their management.

The remaining two regions include south of the Tehachapi Mountains along the South Coast and the southern desert area near the Mexican border. The South Coast region, stretching from Ventura to San Diego, was the original agricultural development in California associated with the missions. These areas rapidly developed crop specializations—for example, Orange County was a center of citrus production until uprooted by urban development. Ventura specialized in lemons, and San Diego and San Clemente in avocados and ornamental plants. Water sources included both local surface water and groundwater until the 1930s, when the introduction of water from the east side of the Sierras into the San Fernando Valley expanded both irrigation and urban development. Once the most agriculturally productive region in the state, the South Coast counties' agriculture now struggles with urbanization pressures and extraordinarily high water costs that threaten even high-value crops such as avocados.

In contrast to the South Coast, the southern desert regions have strong water supply endowments from the Colorado River water irrigation. In particular, the Imperial Valley, with 172,000 hectares of irrigated land, arose in the early part of the century and dominates agricultural production in this region despite its large area of relatively low-value fodder crops. The Coachella Valley, known for dates, vegetables, and other high-value produce, is a smaller but highly productive area, while the Palo Verde area's production is dominated by fodder crops, mainly alfalfa.

The Balance of Water Use and Supply in California

Sources of water supply in California fluctuate strongly with rainfall and climate (see Chapter 2, "Climate"). The years 1998–2006 represent the typical range of California's water years (Figure 38.8, right side). The 2001 drought significantly reduced supplies from streamflows, which were partially compensated by increased groundwater pumping and releases from storage in state, federal, and local projects. In normal water years the ratio of supply between groundwater and recycled water is approximately equal. However, in drought years like 2001 this ratio changes significantly with escalated pumping and much less recycled water available. Groundwater is the main stabilizing source in dry years. However, the current institution of CORRELATIVE RIGHTS puts few restrictions on pumping by overlying landowners, resulting in excessive extraction. Over the last twenty years, the annual rate of overdraft (pumping excess over natural and artificial recharge rate) averaged 1.5 billion m^3 yr^1. This is clearly unsustainable and a source of significant social costs in the forms of water-quality degradation and the threat of supply loss for shallow wells. Water diverted from the Colorado River also makes up an essential part of the overall California supply, particularly to the predominantly urban area in southern California managed by the Metropolitan Water District.

Use of California's water resources is dominated by irrigated agriculture (Figure 38.8, left side). The next largest use is allocation to flows in federally designated Wild and Scenic Rivers; however, this water use fluctuates much more than irrigated agriculture use or water allocated to maintain Delta outflow standards and instream fish requirements (e.g., see Figure 38.8, 1998 versus 2001 uses). Two dominant problems with the current imbalance between demand and supply of California water resources are, first, continuing overdraft of scarce groundwater reserves; and, second, the continued declines of many fish species despite significant recent increases in instream water allocations.

Principal Functions of the California Agricultural Ecosystem

The California agricultural ecosystem functions very well for agriculture but malfunctions for other ecological values. The main reason for this difference is that on the agricultural side, a wide range of efficient prices and institutions dictate production and technologies. In contrast, the ecological side is marked by sustained disinterest by the agricultural industry and a complete lack of price signals for all ecological functions except those that directly impact the costs of farming operations, such as groundwater levels.

Agricultural market prices are, as noted earlier, the dominant driver of the levels, locations, and quantities of crop production. Many of California's specialty crops supply a sufficient proportion of national and international demands to significantly influence the global market. For almonds, table wine, artichokes, and many other crops, California is by far the dominant U.S. producer; thus crop cooperatives, wholesalers, and marketing boards have strong incentives to promote their crops nationally and internationally. The most prominent recent example is the Blue Diamond almond cooperative, which has steadily expanded national and world consumption of almonds without sacrificing real prices. From the 1930s through the 1970s, many California specialty crops were marketed predominantly through cooperatives. However, for the last thirty years the difficulties of running a cooperative have in many cases outweighed the advantages. In industries such as rice, citrus, and canned fruits, the role of cooperatives has been usurped by larger, efficient, wholesale marketing firms. The demand-driven, commodity-specific signals from these wholesalers and cooperatives cut across several different producing areas in California.

The other main driver of the California agricultural production function, water, has a very different functional structure. It is composed of more than a thousand water and flood

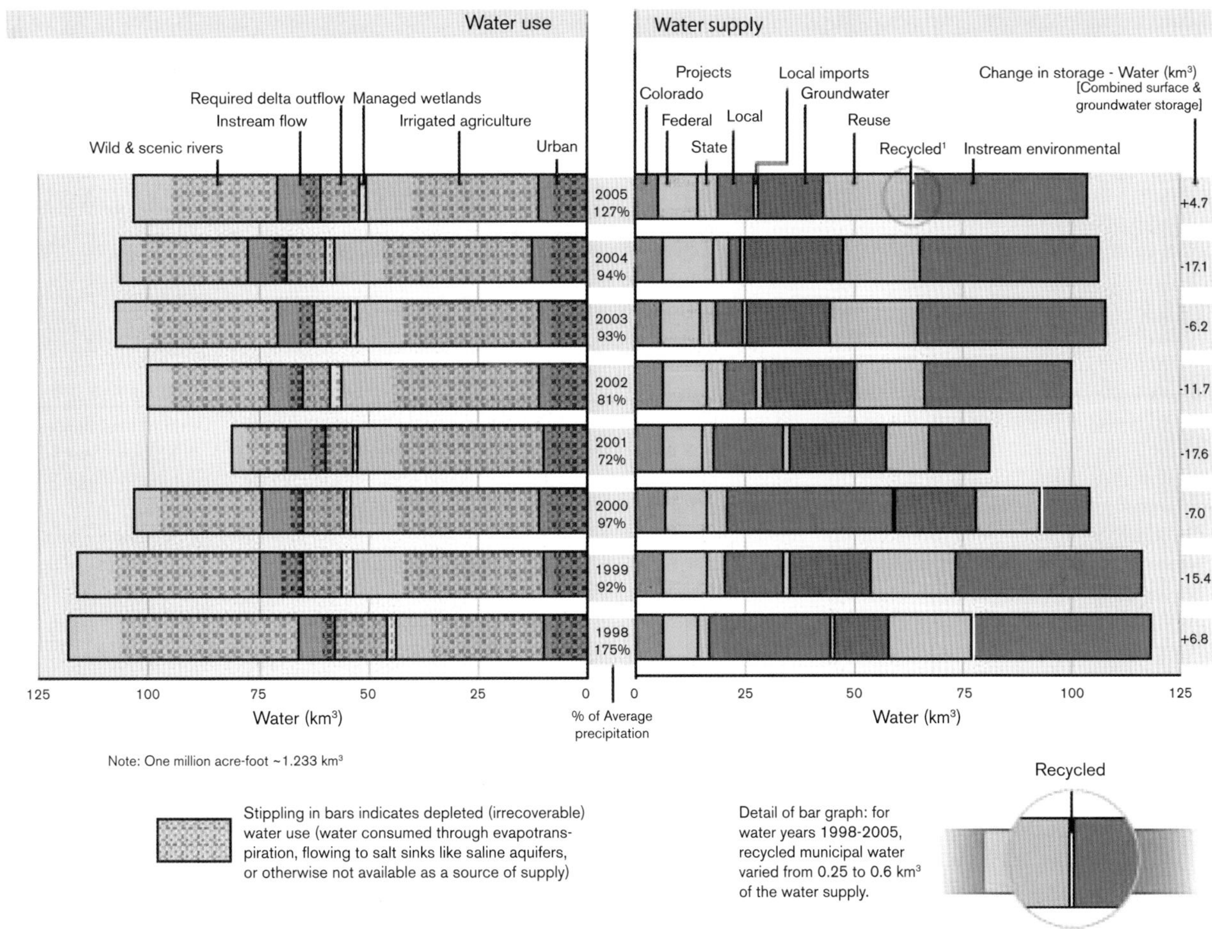

FIGURE 38.8 The balance of water use and supply in California, colloquially known as the butterfly diagram. Source: California Department of Water Resources.

control districts constituted and empowered under strict local benefit conditions. Each districts acts as the retailer of water for, typically, approximately 50,000 hectares of land linked to a particular river catchment or water supply project delivery branch. As such, water districts are fervent about local values and perceive themselves to be arbiters of the local public good, with powers over water supply that cut across many different crops produced in a district. California water districts are concerned almost exclusively with supplying surface water, while groundwater pumping is almost never regulated, recorded, or even measured in a meaningful way.

As discussed earlier, another highly important input to California agriculture is labor. Farm labor takes two distinct forms: permanent, more skilled labor; and temporary, seasonal, piecework labor performed by migrant workers. Permanently employed labor is usually concentrated among managers, irrigators, tractor drivers, and other skilled field hands. Seasonal migrant labor is almost all contracted through a system of independent labor contractors who organize employees and transport gangs of laborers to particular fields for precisely defined tasks such as weeding, harvesting, or pruning. Since many of the migrant laborers are undocumented, the system of loosely regulated labor contractors has the potential to malfunction. Recently, the United Farm Workers union has increased facilities available for laborers in the field and provided a safer working environment from hazards such as pesticide contamination.

Management training for California agriculture and agribusiness is concentrated at three universities: Fresno State, California State Polytechnic University, and University of California–Davis. A large, progressive research sector exists on agricultural technology, agronomy, livestock husbandry, and marketing. Early in the previous century, agricultural research was concentrated at the land-grant universities UC Davis and UC Berkeley. More recently, the state universities have taken a strong role in applied research, as have the private sector interests and the agricultural biotechnology industry.

The Structure of California's Organic Agricultural Production

Statistics on the recent growth in size of California organic agricultural production are based on the registration of growers and processors of organic products under the California Organic Products Act (COPA). The Agricultural Issues Center at UC Davis reports the very long list of crops produced under organic conditions in six major commodity groups: field crops; fruit and nut crops; livestock, dairy, poultry, and apiary products; nursery, greenhouse, and floriculture; pasture and rangeland; and vegetable crops (Klonsky and Healey 2012). From 2009 to 2012 the number of organic growers increased 16% to 2,693, crop area increased 36% to 238,455 hectares, and gross sales increased 55% to $1.5 billion. This expansion has taken place across all the commodity groups with the exception of floriculture and greenhouse products. Sales of fluid organic milk showed the fastest growth over the four years surveyed.

Contrary to popular perception, California's highly successful organic agricultural industry is dominated by large growers (Figure 38.9). In 2012, 9% of the growers, each producing more than \$1 million of product, accounted for 78% of the total production value in the state. In contrast, 50% of the growers with the smallest production value accounted for about 2% of the value produced. While this may challenge social preconceptions, it does show that California's organic industry has matured to a highly successful sector where specialized knowledge and economies of scale of operation have pushed towards large farming units as seen with conventional production systems. In many instances the same farm management units simultaneously produce both organic and conventional crops on different lands. This shift in the structure of organic production reflects strong and growing consumer preference for organic foods based on marketable commodities and characteristics rather than method of production. Given the increasing complexity of organic production, with the exception of some niche products, this concentration of organic production by the larger growers will likely be maintained into the future.

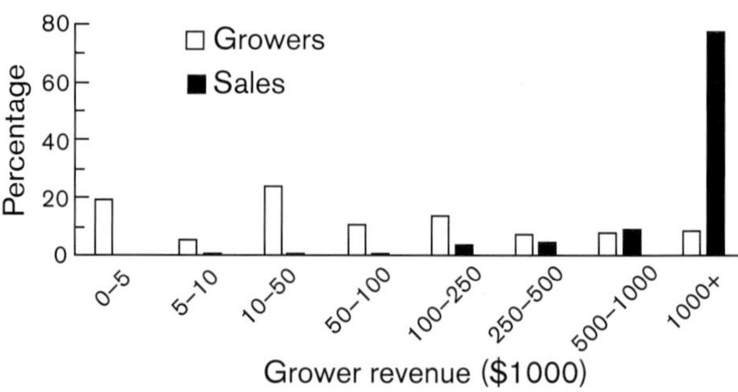

FIGURE 38.9 Structure of California organic agriculture. Source: Based on Klonsky and Healy 2012.

FIGURE 38.10 Demonstrating the effect of land subsidence. Photo: Ireland, Poland and Riley 1984.

Ecological Malfunctions of the System

Groundwater Overdraft

The COMMON-POOL nature of most California groundwater basins coupled with the concept of correlative rights to pump groundwater, which in many cases practically means unlimited rights, has led to the classic resource exploitation problem known as the tragedy of the commons (Hardin 1968). The overcrowding of groundwater resources continues, albeit at the reduced rate; the California Department of Water Resources estimates that the average annual overdraft in California is 1.8 billion m^3, or approximately 5% of the developed water supply. In the 1920s and 1930s, overdrafting on the west side of the San Joaquin Valley was so extensive that it caused the surface of the land to subside by 11 meters in fifty years (Figure 38.10). Subsidence can lead to substantial costs of upgrading and repairing infrastructure such as dikes, canals, roads, bridges, and buried gas lines. Groundwater overdrafting can also degrade of aquifer water by driving inflow of neighboring saline waters.

More recently, aquifers have been recognized as a possible solution to the water storage problem in the southern part of the state. Recharging these aquifers is termed "groundwater banking"; in the southern San Joaquin Valley, three active groundwater banks have been in operation for more than ten years and proved extremely useful in the 2009 drought. While active groundwater banking does in some sense offset the costs of overdrafting, it by no means compensates for the lost stock of groundwater and the additional pumping cost that this generates. In several cases, California groundwater basins have been adjudicated and carefully managed and controlled, but these are invariably where the aquifer is threatened by an outside appropriation or salinity intrusion. Until wider adoption of monitoring and measurement of groundwater and clear, quantitative specification of overlying rights occur, the problem of overdrafting will continue.

Irrigation Water Drainage

The twentieth-century expansion of irrigation resulted in several associated agricultural drainage problems. These were especially severe on the west side of the San Joaquin Valley, which had no natural drainage in the past due to a subterranean, impermeable marine layer. The region experienced accumulating concentrations of selenium and other elements in agricultural drainwater along with the normal salinity load. The toxic nature of this agricultural drainwater became apparent in 1981 when it emerged that waterfowl liv-

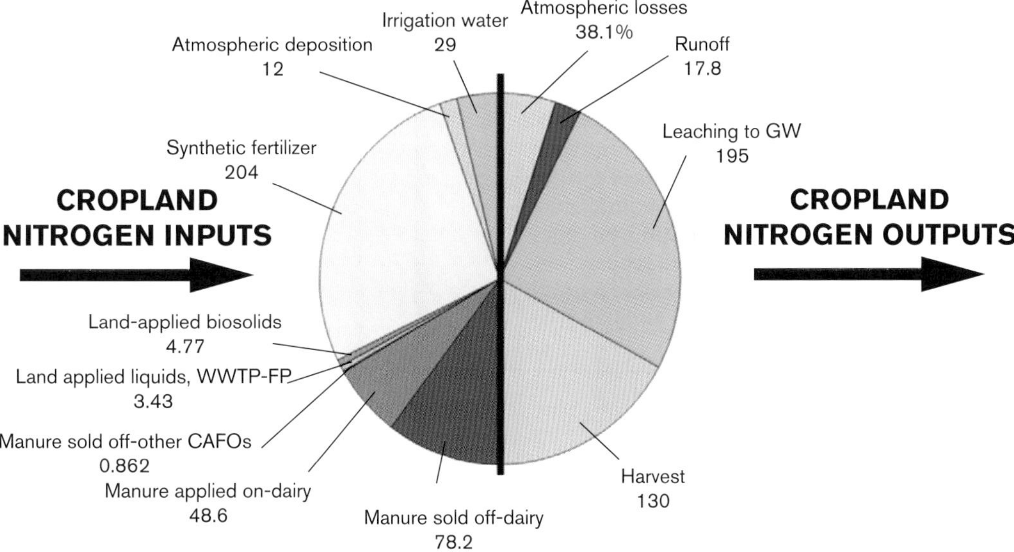

FIGURE 38.11 Cropland nitrogen sources and fates. Source: Harter et al. 2012.
GW = groundwater, CAFO = Confined Animal Feeding Operation, WWTP = Waste Water Treatment Plant.
FP= Food Processor.

ing in Kesterson Lake were suffering from toxic exposure to selenium (see Chapter 31, "Wetlands"). The central problem was that Kesterson was essentially a sump into which drainage water was dumped to evaporate and thus concentrate any contaminants in it. Earlier plans had called for a drain to take drainage water north to San Francisco Bay. Completion of this plan was prevented by opposition to having agricultural drainage water from the San Joaquin Valley drain out through the Delta and the San Francisco Bay. Kesterson was decommissioned as a drainage sump, and a satisfactory alternative has not yet been found. As a result, most of the area's highly saline drainwater is conveyed to evaporation ponds, where salt and other undesirable trace elements are concentrated and await disposal or use.

Groundwater Contamination by Nitrogen

Nitrates are the predominant contaminant of groundwater in rural areas; more than 90% of these nitrates leach from irrigated crops and confined animal feeding operations (CAFOs). Harter et al. (2012) estimate that less than 40% of total nitrate input to fields is removed by harvested crops (Figure 38.11).

Much of this section is drawn from a recent study by Harter et al. (2012) of the sources and causes of nitrate pollution in groundwater. The study focuses on two areas in California known to have significant nitrate pollution of groundwater: the Tulare Basin in the southern San Joaquin Valley and the Salinas Valley. As a result of leaching of nitrates into groundwater, 250,000 people in these regions are at risk from nitrates in drinking water, and 1.3 million people are affected by nitrate pollution in less threatening ways. The level of nitrate pollution in groundwater is expected to increase because of the long period of time required for nitrates to percolate down to active groundwater areas. Direct remediation of nitrate-polluted aquifers is economically prohibitive given currently available methods. However, nitrate levels can be reduced slowly over time using a simple "pump and fertilize" approach that involves persuading farmers to use the nitrates present in groundwater as part of their fertilization requirements. Deep percolation from irrigation systems would reduce concentrations of nitrates or at least not increase them. Economic studies have shown that the modest reductions possible through the pump-and-fertilize approach can be achieved at a cost that can be accommodated by the agricultural industry. However, radical reductions in the amount of nitrogen applied would result in radical increases in the cost of production and an economic downshift in the agricultural industry, a critical source of livelihoods for many of the people who suffer from nitrate pollution (Harter et al. 2012).

The optimal policy combination thus seems to be a subsidized program of monitoring and treatment for moderate-sized, local water utilities and bottled water as an alternative drinking supply for the smallest water systems that exceed the state's contamination standards. The cost of the programs should be borne by nitrate users; nitrate-use charges would both raise funds for remediation and monitoring and provide an incentive for farmers to reduce their nitrate use. Currently, farmers are exempt from state taxes on nitrate purchases. The first step would be to eliminate this exemption and add a small nitrate-use charge similar to fees already imposed on other commodities such as automobile tires, batteries, and some electronic goods—all of which have higher-than-average disposal and social costs that generate social externalities. Harter et al. (2012) identify many practices that would reduce both the rate of nitrate accumulations in groundwater and applied quantities of nitrate on the surface. The impact of nitrates on groundwater can be reduced by more efficient irrigation practices, which would reduce the transfer rate of nitrates to groundwater and, because the water would reside longer in the root zone, allow a greater proportion of the dissolved nitrates to be taken up by plants. Thus, improved fertilizer use and irrigation efficiency combined with a deliberate pump-and-fertilize policy could stabilize the level of nitrogen currently contaminating groundwater. However, alternative water supply systems must be developed and financed for small rural communities.

Waste Disposal from Livestock Confined Animal Feeding Operations (CAFOs)

The California livestock industry overwhelmingly functions through CAFOs; 1.7 million dairy cows are concentrated, mostly in the San Joaquin Valley, in confined conditions (see Table 38.2). In addition are several large beef feedlots and significant chicken operations. This animal production produces a substantial load of waste high in nitrogen, phosphates, and other nutrients (see Figure 38.11). As described earlier, increasing nitrates in drinking water present a health hazard and a significant health risk for young children (Harter et al. 2012).

Agricultural Interactions with Natural Ecosystems

California's wide-ranging topography and Mediterranean climate give it a widely varied natural ecology. The introduction of European settlers and their resource-based economic activities has affected all but the high Sierra regions. Here, we examine the effect that the development of California agriculture has had on the natural ecosystems in the Central Valley and to a lesser extent in the coastal regions and temperate oak woodlands and savannas. The original Spanish land-grant ranches that produced cattle for tallow and hides fell on an east-west transect that ran from the coast to the Sierras, since the full range of California's cross-section was needed to ensure some productive grazing at all times of the year. When first considered for agriculture, California's Central Valley was both unproductive and unhealthy, with periodic flooding and droughts and endemic diseases such as malaria and dengue. The Central Valley needed effective control of floods, drainage, and irrigation to be feasible for crop agriculture.

Initial development of irrigated agriculture took place along the Sacramento River with the development of orchards and crops. The extreme floods of 1862 were exacerbated by the residual sediment from hydraulic mining, and in 1868 water reclamation districts were authorized. Irrigation districts for additional water development were authorized in 1887. Both of these local institutions were used to finance and construct levees systems to control floods and drain farming areas. The extent of native wetlands was significant as recently as 1900 (Figure 38.12). Between 1900 and 2000, 95% of California's natural wetlands that existed in 1900 were drained and converted to use in irrigated agriculture.

This conversion of wetlands to irrigated agriculture has significantly affected many species. Most affected are the migratory birds using the Central Valley as part of the Pacific flyway. There have been some slight compensations, first of which was the inadvertent creation of the Salton Sea in the far south of the state by a misguided attempt to irrigation development in 1906, and second of which is the introduction of rice production, mostly concentrated in the Sacramento Valley, which produced significant habitat and food sources in the forms of rice tailings and flooded stubble fields.

Nowhere has the change wrought by agricultural development been greater than in the Sacramento–San Joaquin River Delta. Not only was the area diked, drained, and leveled for agriculture, but the elevation of the land was changed so drastically over the last hundred years that in some parts of the Delta fields are being farmed 4–5 meters below sea level. In the southern San Joaquin Valley, the natural lake in Tulare Lake Basin that was originally 130 kilometers long and 56 kilometers wide was completely controlled and drained during the early twentieth century. Folklore has it that the rusting remains of the engine of the paddle steamer that used to ply the lake remains landlocked in the corner of some irrigated field. Another dramatic ecological change caused by agricultural development was the damming of most of the upstream parts of the rivers leading into the Central Valley from the surrounding mountain ranges. These dams prevented the migration of salmon and other fishes to upstream spawning grounds. Overall, the loss of fish spawning and rearing habitat over the past hundred years due to damming and irrigation development has been substantial (Figure 38.13).

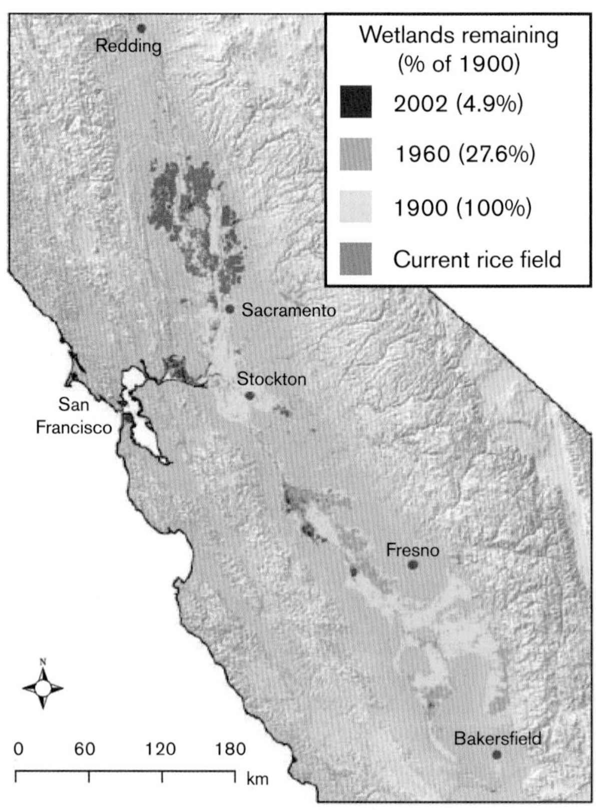

FIGURE 38.12 A historical perspective on California's wetlands. The red shaded areas show those wetlands that still remain one hundred years later. 1900 wetlands include the yellow, orange and red areas, and 1960 wetlands include the orange and red areas. Sacramento Valley rice fields provide some seasonal wetlands function for migrating birds and terrestrial and riparian species such as the giant garter snake. Sources: California State University, Chico (2003): Dahl and Allord 1997; by Hanak et al. 2011.

In addition, exotic species have been introduced for fishing, through ship ballast water and aquarium releases, and from ponds and nurseries, making the San Francisco Bay-Delta one of the most invaded estuaries in the world (Cohen and Carlton 1998; see Chapter 19, "Estuaries: Life on the Edge"). Some exotics thrive in this highly altered ecosystem, competing with natives for food, preying upon them, and degrading their habitat. The combined result of changes in water quality, habitat, access upstream, and competition from invasive species, along with other stressors, includes widespread

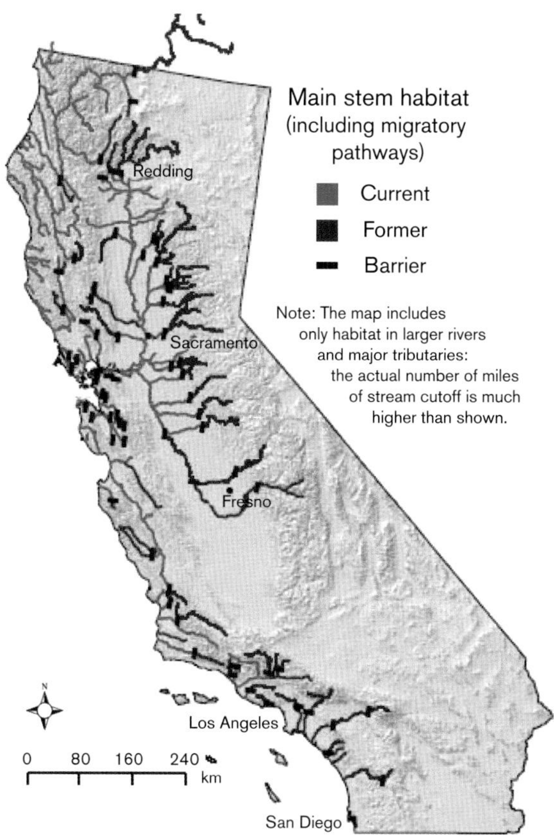

FIGURE 38.13 Loss of salmon spawning grounds. Source: Moyle et al. 2005.

impacts to California's native fishes. Hanak et al. (2011) estimate that 73% of these native species are in decline. In contrast, populations of exotic black bass (*Micropterus* sp.) in the Delta have increased rapidly, and the Sacramento–San Joaquin Delta is now regarded as one of the premier bass fishing locations in the country (Bass Master Magazine 2013). The irony of an estuarine system being defined as among the top "lakes" in the country, based on the prevalence of an invasive species, has not escaped those concerned with sustaining what is left of a California estuarine system.

Synergies and Trade-offs

After his seminal book *Cadillac Desert*, Mark Reisner (1986) thought that it was possible for irrigated agriculture to yield ecosystem benefits as well as costs. Accordingly, he turned his attention to the potential for joint production of agricultural and environmental services. Reisner focused on rice, a surprise since he had once described California rice as a tropical crop being grown in an arid environment. He focused on the potential for producing duck habitat as well as rice through additional flooding in the fall season. An additional motivation for the farmers to shift to fall flooding was a need to incorporate rice straw into the heavy, rice-growing soils. Beginning in 1992, rice farmers had to reduce use of burning to remove rice straw in order to mitigate significant air pollution effects from smoke. The phaseout of rice straw burning reduced the total area burned by 75% over ten years. Currently, only 12% of the total rice area is burned. This reduction in burning required that an alternative straw disposal mechanism be developed. Fall flooding of rice fields significantly aided decomposition of straw and its incorporation into the soil before planting the following season. In this case, a shift in agricultural production technology simultaneously reduced air pollution and enhanced waterfowl habitat. The shift was not without cost to farmers, but the production of an environmental service while reducing pollution conferred ecosystem services with economic efficiency.

A second example of joint ecosystem production with agriculture is emerging in the alternative management of floodplains. The Yolo Bypass in northern California has acted effectively as a flood control mechanism, in part protecting Sacramento, for the past seventy years. As part of its original design, the Bypass floodplain area is under active cropping by farmers who grow products ranging from processing tomatoes and rice to dryland and irrigated pasture. In addition, 6,800 hectares of the Bypass floodplain have been used for a wildlife reserve over the past twenty years, partially funded by revenues from the crop area. Most of the floodplain is farmed on crop leases reduced in price to compensate for the flood easement that occurs when a fixed weir, in the northern part of the Bypass, is overtopped by a rising river. The Bypass has flooded naturally in about half of the last twenty-six years, with some of the floods extending into the April–May planting season. Over the past three years an additional ecosystem service, namely the provision of a short-term rearing ground for young salmonids from the winter salmon run, is emerging as potential and very valuable use for the Bypass floodplains.

Ongoing experiments, in which the growth of tagged young salmon is compared in the artificial floodplains versus the river mainstem, show a growth advantage from floodplains covering crop stover from the previous year (Jeffres et al. 2008). Waterborne daphnia, food for the salmonids, thrive on the decomposing rice stubble in the floodplain. In short, some of the excess energy from floodplain cropping activity appears to be transferred over a short period to subsidize young salmon, allowing agricultural operations on the floodplain to provide an additional ecosystem. In addition to the fishery benefits, flooding at different depths and times supports waders, divers, and shorebirds that use the area at different times of year. In this form the Yolo Bypass and possibly other floodplains in California represent a truly multi-output system producing food, flood protection, salmonid habitat, and bird habitat in an interdependent system.

The Future of California's Agroecosystem

We judge the future of California agriculture as a managed ecosystem from two perspectives: the stability and sustainability of the current system and whether institutional and physical characteristics of the system provide enough feedback for it to adjust to future shocks such as climate change and market shifts. The past hundred years have shown that California agriculture is both highly productive and remarkably adept at adjusting to shifts in its resource base and the market demand on which it depends. Despite its rapid and successful development, several resources essential to California agriculture remain unsustainable. Groundwater stocks continue to suffer from overdraft, and many freshwater fish species in California are listed under the Endangered Species Act or declining—a situation that recently has severely constrained producers' ability to divert water from the Delta.

While the reasons for declines in these fish populations are complex and varied, it is generally accepted that the amount of water exported from the Delta is a significant contributor, and recent legal decisions have tied exports of water for southern agricultural and urban uses to recovery of some of the Delta's significant fish species. In addition, the salinity of groundwater in the Central Valley continues to rise. In particular, the large, productive Tulare Basin region has no natural outlet for drainage and presents the substantial challenge of identifying methods of extracting and storing the excess salt, which is imported into the basin via irrigation water and mobilized by agricultural drainage. The final, primary imbalance is in nitrates and other pollutants in groundwater. As discussed earlier in this chapter, contaminated groundwater is a significant but not insurmountable problem for the future.

Johnston and McCalla (2004) identified six drivers of agricultural development in the past. Note that of those six, four—public investment in water development, ready access to capital for agricultural development, a strong infrastructure of producer-based cooperatives and marketing institutions, and a mobile, plentiful, and low-cost labor supply—are unlikely to continue to drive agricultural development in the future. Two new entrants—environmental and safety regulations and urban and environmental competition for resources—will have a dampening effect on development of irrigated agriculture. This change in the drivers of development of irrigated agriculture is likely to result in several broad trends over the next twenty-five years.

First, the growing scarcity of water will force producers to downsize irrigated agriculture in some parts of the state in terms of land area irrigated and amount of water used. However, there will be countervailing growth in demand for California agricultural products, which have the unique advantage of being upmarket products for which demand increases as personal incomes rise. Standard projections show that agriculture in the state can grow in economic value, profitability, and market influence in the foreseeable future. This increase in the proportion of high-value fruit, nut, and vegetable crops demanded by the market will influence how farmers can respond to California's seasonal water scarcities and will place a premium on quality farm labor and increased mechanization. Another trend foreseen in the food market is an emphasis on the safety and quality of the commodities produced, even requiring traceability of products. This approach to food safety favors the kind of large-scale, organized production found in California over dispersed, small-scale peasant production from competing nations such as China.

Another trend that favors California agricultural production and the resulting agroecosystem is the shift in public support away from commodity price-support programs and towards agricultural programs that generate public environmental goods. This trend, which has been predominant in Europe for the past fifteen years, is showing signs of traction in the United States in recent federal farm bills. To reconcile the current price-based structure, which made the California agriculture system what it is today, with increasing demand for environmental goods, transparency in production, and food safety, several shifts in institutional priorities will have to occur. Water is the driving and defining resource for both environmental goods and irrigated agriculture, so the institutions that have arisen over the past 150 years to control water allocation and development will have to adapt. Those institutions worked very well in the past but will be too rigid to accommodate future increases in scarcity and requirements for equitable reallocation among sectors and locations.

The inherent tension between agricultural and environmental water use can be modified only if the environmental sector has some degree of control over its water resources, allowing it to actively respond to varying interannual scarcity, using trade-offs and triage to ensure stable environmental systems. Past interactions between California agriculture and demands for ecosystem services have often been adversarial, and conflicts over resource allocation between agricultural and environmental uses are often perceived as requiring substitution of one use for another. An alternative approach is to look for opportunities for joint production of ecosystem services and agricultural crops. It is likely that this approach, which can be incorporated into the structure of California agriculture, will be needed to accommodate the increasing demand for ecosystem goods in the future.

Summary

The managed ecosystem that is California agriculture is highly variable in both the types and productivity levels of crops grown. This reflects the diversity of the soil and water resources and the microclimates that support California agricultural production. The development of the system has been driven predominantly by three factors: changing market demand for crops, water availability and its development, and technological improvements in both crops and growing methods. This massive managed ecosystem has not evolved without severe impacts on California's natural ecosystem. Irrigated agricultural development on this scale has had a major impact on historical wetland areas and riparian corridors. The first major change in the ecosystem was the drainage of about 85% of California's natural wetlands over an eighty-year period. Some partial compensation for this receding habitat occurred through the development of rice stubble as a food source for the Pacific flyway birds in the north and the mistakenly created Salton Sea as a source of food in the south. However, many of the other ecosystem services from wetlands were lost. Construction of dams for surface water storage on most of the state's major rivers led to severe reductions in aquatic ecosystem functioning, such as the loss of natural salmon spawning grounds. The development of fish hatcheries has not compensated for this loss of spawning grounds.

In addition, the development of highly sophisticated irrigated agriculture has led to a number of unintentional, byproduct pollutants in the ecosystem. Among these are nitrogen, selenium, and salts. Pesticide residues and metals are also a serious concern. The overdevelopment of groundwater pumping in some regions has led to land subsidence and loss of some vernal pools. On the positive side, California agriculture is immensely valuable in terms of the products produced, jobs and welfare generated, and the development of the California economy. In recent years the agricultural industry has become more conscious of both ecological impacts and values and has reduced its ecological impacts in some areas by reducing excessive pesticide use and agricultural burning. In addition, some crops are now grown in ways that enhance ecosystem benefits from their production. Notable examples include rice production in the Sacramento Valley and field crop production on floodplains, which have both been shown to directly contribute to the food webs of wild fishes and birds. We anticipate that this trend towards reconciling agricultural production and ecosystem benefits will continue at an increasing rate in the future.

Recommended Reading

Hanak, E., J. Lund, A. Dinar, B. Gray, R. Howitt, J. Mount, P. Moyle, and B. Thompson. 2011. Managing California's water: From conflict to reconciliation. Public Policy Institute of California, San Francisco, California.

Olmstead, A. L., and P. W. Rhode. 2004. The evolution of California agriculture, 1850–2000. Pages 1–28 in J. B. Siebert, editor. California Agriculture: Dimensions and Issues. Giannini Foundation of Agricultural Economics, Berkeley, California.

Reisner, M. 1993. Cadillac desert: The American West and its disappearing water. Revised and updated. Penguin Books, New York, New York.

Glossary

COMMON-POOL Term describes a resource or good that—whether owned and/or regulated by government, communal group, private entity or no one—is costly and difficult to exclude potential users from.

CORRELATIVE RIGHTS A system under California law in which groundwater is held in common by the overlying landowners, who are allowed to use any water that can be put to "beneficial use."

FARM GATE VALUE The price of a product at which it is sold by a farm.

INDEX OF FARMLAND VALUES A measure based on an initial index value of 100 for farmland in 1912–1914. For example, an index of 160 means that farm values have appreciated 60% over 1912–1914 values.

MOTHER LODE The California Mother Lode was a narrow region rich in gold deposits and extending about 190 kilometers north to south along the Sierra Nevada, through El Dorado, Amador, Calaveras, and Tuolumne Counties, along the edge of a geologic terrane called the Smartville Block.

References

100 Best Bass Lakes. <http://www.bassmaster.com/top100>. Accessed July 14, 2015.

Adams, F. 1946. The historical background of California agriculture. Pages 1–50 in C. B. Hutchison, editor. California Agriculture. University of California Press, Berkeley, California.

Arax, M., and R. Wartzman. 2005. King of California: J. G. Boswell and the making of a secret American empire. Public Affairs, New York, New York.

Benedict, M. R. 1946. The economic and social structure of California agriculture. Pages 395–435 in C. B. Hutchison, editor. California Agriculture. University of California Press, Berkeley, California.

Bradley, K. J. 1997. Cultivating the terrain: Public image and politics of California farming from the Depression to the post war years. UMI Dissertation Services, Ann Arbor, Michigan.

California Department of Water Resources. 2009. California water plan. Bulletin 160-04. Sacramento, California.

California Department of Food & Agriculture. 2013. California Agricultural Statistics Review, 2012-2013. Sacramento, California.

Cohen, A. N., and J. T. Carlton. 1998. Accelerating invasion rate in a highly invaded estuary. Science 279:555–57.

Diamond, J. 1999. Guns, germs, and steel: The fates of human societies. W.W. Norton and Co., New York, New York.

Durrenberger, R. 1999. California: The last frontier. Van Nostram and Reinhold Company, New York, New York.

Hanak, E., J. Lund, A. Dinar, B. Gray, R. Howitt, J. Mount, P. Moyle, and B. Thompson. 2011. Managing California's water: From conflict to reconciliation. Public Policy Institute of California, San Francisco, California.

Hardin, G. 1968. The Tragedy of the Commons. Science 13:1243–1248

Harter, T., J. Lund, J. Darby, G. E. Fogg, R. E. Howitt, K. K. Jessoe, G. S. Pettygrove, J. F. Quinn, and J. H. Viers. 2012. Addressing nitrate in California's drinking water. Center for Watershed Science, University of California, Davis, California.

Hart, G. H., et al. 1946. Wealth pyramiding in the production of livestock. Pages 51–112 in C. B. Hutchison, editor. California Agriculture. University of California Press, Berkeley, California.

Ireland, R. L., J. F. Poland, and F. S. Riley. 1984. Land subsidence in the San Joaquin Valley, California, as of 1980. U.S. Geological Survey Professional Paper 437-I.

Jeffres, C. A., J. J. Opperman, and P. B. Moyle. 2008. Ephemeral floodplain habitats provide best growth conditions for juvenile Chinook salmon in a California river. Environmental Biology of Fishes 83:449–458.

Jelinek, L. J. 1982. Harvest empire: A history of California agriculture. Second edition. Boyd and Fraser Publishing Company, San Francisco, California.

Johnston, W. E., and A. F. McCalla. 2004. Whither California agriculture: Up, down, or out? Some thoughts about the future. Giannini Foundation Special Report 4.

Kelley, R. 1989. Battling the inland sea. University of California Press, Berkeley, California.

Klonsky, K., and B. D. Healy. 2012. Statistical review of California's organic agriculture 2009—2012. Agricultural Issues Center, University of California, Davis, California.

McClurg, S. 2000. Water and the shaping of California. Water Education Foundation, Sacramento, California.

Moyle, P. B., J. A. Israel, and S. E. Purdy. 2008. Salmon, Steelhead and Trout in California. Watershed Science Center, University of California, Davis.

Olmstead, A. L., and P. W. Rhode. 1997. An overview of the history of California agriculture. California agriculture: Issues and challenges. Pages 1–27 in J. B. Siebert, editor. Giannini Foundation of Agricultural Economics, Berkeley, California.

Reisner, M. 1993. Cadillac desert: The American West and its disappearing water. Revised and updated. Penguin Books, New York, New York.

Rhode, P. W. 1995. Learning, capital accumulation, and the transformation of California agriculture. Journal of Economic History 55:773–800.

Scheuring, A. F. 2010. Valley empires: Hugh Glenn and Henry Miller in the shaping of California. Gold Oaks Press, Rumsey, California.

Smith, B. D. 1998. The emergence of agriculture. American Scientific Library, New York, New York.

Starrs, P., and P. Goin. 2010. Field guide to California agriculture. University of California Press, Berkeley, California.

Stoll, S. 1998. The fruits of natural advantage: Making the industrial countryside in California. University of California Press, , Berkeley, California.

U.S. Census of Agriculture. 1969–2007. Page 866. <https://www.census.gov/econ/www/agrimenu.html>. Accessed 7/18/2015.

U.S. Department of Commerce Bureau of Census. 1967. Economics and Statistics Administration < http://www.esa.doc.gov/>. Accessed July 18,2015.

THIRTY-NINE

Urban Ecosystems

DIANE E. PATAKI, G. DARREL JENERETTE, STEPHANIE PINCETL,
TARA L. E. TRAMMELL, and LA'SHAYE ERVIN

Introduction

The twentieth-century history of California is a history of urbanization. Yet until quite recently textbooks and field guides about California's ecology omitted most mention of urban ecosystems except in the context of destruction of native habitat. Urban areas are ecosystems by virtually every definition. In addition to dynamic and complex human-environment relationships, cities host diverse plant, faunal, and microbial species, sometimes with greater species richness than in natural ecosystems (Luck 2007, Kowarik 2011). While some argue that many of these species are non-native and therefore of little value, urban residents and land managers invest enormous resources in creating and maintaining "novel" ecosystems—species assemblages and environmental conditions that may not occur in non-urban ecosystems (Kowarik 2011, Hobbs et al. 2013). A body of literature is emerging on the many benefits that urban residents enjoy from proximity to novel, diverse habitats in cities such as private yards, parks, and other types of greenspace (Dunnett and Qasim 2000, Jackson 2003, Tzoulas et al. 2007, Musacchio 2009). An understanding of the ecology of these spaces is vital for optimizing their design and management and for understanding their broader functioning in the context of local and regional sustainability.

In this chapter we address three issues: (1) a review of current knowledge about the ecology of novel urban ecosystems in California; (2) a discussion of the known consequences, both intended and unintended, of creating and maintaining these novel ecosystems; and (3) some pathways toward integrating an understanding of the ecology of cities in planning a sustainable future for California.

Urban Ecosystems of California

Urban ecosystems differ markedly from natural ecosystems in several critical ways. Like agricultural systems, they are strongly influenced by human choices and management. Unlike most of the other ecosystems described in this book, the BUILT ENVIRONMENT plays a central role in urban ecosystems. Built structures such as roads, buildings, and water and energy infrastructure dominate cities, and their functions and impacts both within cities and in the larger regional and global context can be considered from an ecological perspective. In addition to the prominent role of humans in both the built environment and the biotic components of land cover in cities, the very definition of urban ecosystems is uniquely fluid compared to the ways natural ecosystems are defined. Urban ecosystems can be found within virtually every biome in California, from the coastal regions to the mountains and deserts. Spatial delineations of the location and extent of urban ecosystems in California vary, but common classifications include the extent of urban area itself as defined by political boundaries, U.S. census definitions of urban areas, and land cover classifications (Figure 39.1). More broadly, the larger area that encompasses both the urban area and its resource base is based in the ECOLOGICAL FOOTPRINT concept, which was developed to determine the area of land required to sustain a given urban area. Given that California cities are sustained by resources imported from many regions nationally and internationally, the determination of specific ecological footprints can be complex (Wackernagel and Rees 1996, Luck et al. 2001).

According to the U.S. Census, as of 2010 California was the most urban state in the nation with almost 95% of its population living in urban areas. More than half of this population lives in the state's three largest metropolitan areas, all of which are located on the coast: the Los Angeles–Long Beach–Santa Ana METROPOLITAN STATISTICAL AREA (MSA), the San Francisco–Oakland–Fremont MSA, and the San Diego–Carlsbad–San Marcos MSA. These urban areas are located in coastal plains and valleys and tend to be surrounded by mountain ranges and public lands. For the most part, the major coastal cities of California have almost entirely displaced the low-elevation shrublands and now border montane forested lands. This has several important consequences: as undeveloped land has become scarce on the coast, population densities have increased, housing costs have risen, and population growth has shifted to inland areas in the Central Valley and the Mojave Desert.

In addition, the urban expansion of the twentieth and early twenty-first centuries has placed larger numbers of people in close proximity to the URBAN-WILDLAND INTERFACE near U.S Forest Service and other public lands. As a result, forested ecosystems near coastal cities have experienced increased fire frequencies, pollution, and EX-URBAN development. Within and surrounding California's major urban areas, other notable environmental conditions include URBAN HEAT ISLANDS, highly altered and/or contaminated soils, unique species composition, contamination of coastal and aquatic habitats, and rerouting of hydrologic flows, sometimes over hundreds of kilometers (Taha 1997; Dwight et al. 2002; Steiner et al. 2006; Lau et al. 2009; Fenn et al. 2010; Pataki, Boone et al. 2011). We describe these features in greater detail below.

The Biotic Environment of California's Cities

Cities are commonly assumed to reduce biodiversity due to extirpations and extinctions resulting from habitat destruction (Thompson and Jones 1999) and introduction of exotic species (Hobbs and Mooney 1998). Both processes contribute to BIOTIC HOMOGENIZATION across regions—that is, convergence in the species compositions of different urban areas (McKinney 2006). However, several synthetic studies have reported that for plant and bird taxa, species richness (the number of species) tends to increase with human population density (McKinney 2002, Gaston 2005, Pautasso and McKinney 2007, Luck 2007, Kowarik 2011). While exotic invasive species contribute to this pattern, other mechanisms also increase species richness in densely populated areas, such as cultivation of garden and domesticated species across regions (Kendal et al. 2012) as well as the tendency for cities to be located in native biodiversity hotspots (Kühn et al. 2004). There is additional evidence that these processes result in biotic homogenization (Chace and Walsh 2006, McKinney 2006). In contrast to floral and bird species, other taxa such as butterflies decline in species richness with increasing urbanization density (Lizée et al. 2011).

To date, these general patterns are consistent with studies of the urban biodiversity of California, where urbanization appears to have resulted in an increase in local species richness for some taxa at a cost of increasing prevalence of exotic species. Local studies of insect and bird species have shown this pattern (Frankie et al. 2005, Pawelek et al. 2009, Blair 2001, Connor et al. 2002). The pattern is particularly prevalent for plant species because unlike most faunal species, plant diversity is heavily affected by the continual introduction of new horticultural cultivars and exotic garden species imported to California from all over the world (Clarke et al. 2013; Pincetl, Prabhu et al. 2013). Some intentionally introduced species have gone on to become highly invasive in more natural ecosystems, resulting in a homogenization of the flora of urban localities in the state (Schwartz et al. 2006).

Nevertheless, at the local scale, floral ALPHA DIVERSITY of urban ecosystems can far exceed the native habitat they replaced. Clarke et al. (2013) found 140 tree species by direct inventory and 214 (±10) by RAREFACTION in the city of Los Angeles. Pincetl, Prabhu et al. (2013) found more than 500 tree species available for purchase in plant nurseries in Los Angeles County. This is in comparison to the approximately 14 tree species native to the lower elevations of southern California, where urbanization has been concentrated (Schoenherr 1995, Rundel and Gustafson 2005). The Los Angeles urban forest contains several exotic species that have become naturalized or invasive, such as *Schinus terebinthifolius*, which disrupts natural riparian ecosystems (Clarke et al. 2013). Exotic disease-causing organisms are also prevalent in California cities; a current concern is Huanglongbing (HLB), a citrus virus spread by the Asian Citrus Psyllid that has already decimated citrus production in Florida (Stokstad 2012).

In Los Angeles, tree diversity is highest in older neighborhoods, and plant cover increases with neighborhood income (Clarke et al. 2013), a phenomenon known as the "luxury effect" (Hope et al. 2003 and 2006, Kinzig et al. 2005). This effect has been reported throughout the southwestern U.S. (Jenerette et al. 2013) and could be associated with a HIERARCHY OF NEEDS rather than differences in residents' desires (Avolio et al. in review, Wu 2013). In other words, residents of varying incomes could have similar desires for biodiversity, but only high-income residents are able to fully express these desires through investments in urban landscaping and its maintenance. It is therefore appropriate to consider adding these amenities to urban public spaces instead of relying largely on private spaces and remote public lands to provide access to biodiversity. In general, the resources required to maintain irrigated, non-native vegetation in this region appear to influence social and neighborhood inequities in tree and vegetation amenities.

Photo on previous page: The San Francisco Bay Area at night. Photo: Shutterstock.

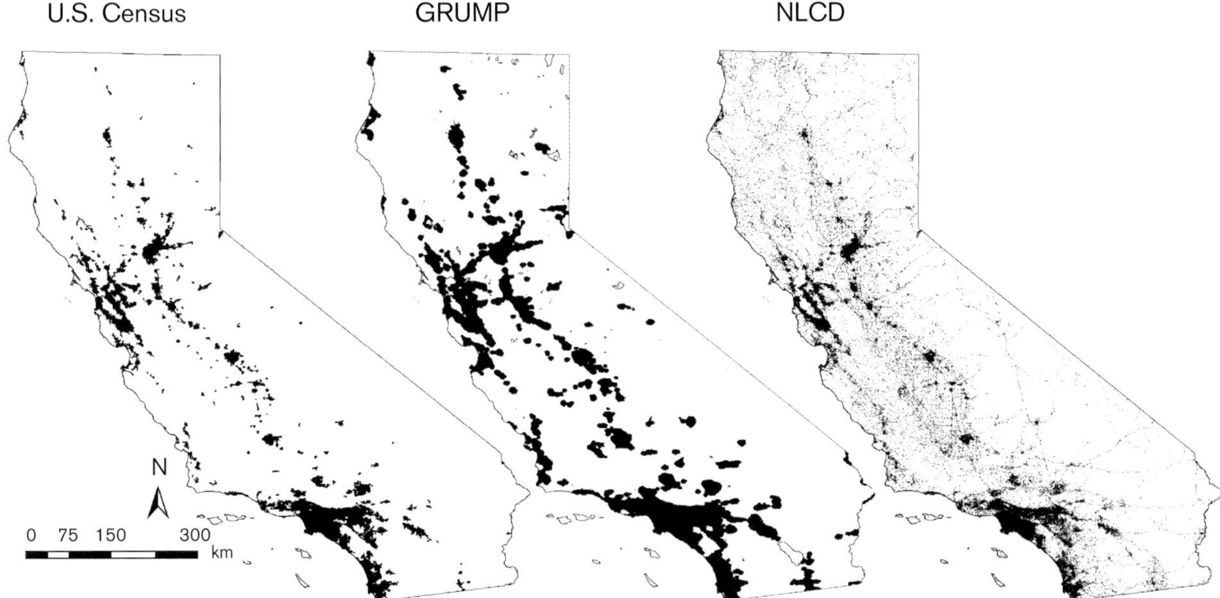

FIGURE 39.1 The urbanized areas of California as defined by the U.S. Census. Because there is no single, standard definition of what constitutes "urban" land cover, a number of different classifications have been developed based on population density, political boundaries, remote sensing data, or a combination of approaches. The extent of urban land in the three estimates depicted here range from 5% of the area of the state (U.S. Census) to 7% (U.S. National Land Cover Database, NLCD) to 14% (Global Rural-Urban Mapping Project, GRUMP). Sources: U.S. Census, <http://www.census.gov/geo/reference/ua/urban-rural-2010.html>; GRUMP, <http://sedac.ciesin.columbia.edu/data/collection/grump-v1>; NLCD, <http://www.mrlc.gov/nlcd2001.php>.

Ecologists and social scientists are jointly studying the factors that influence decisions about planting and managing urban vegetation, soils, and wildlife. In Los Angeles a complex set of institutional factors determine the nature and fate of tree planting programs. As in most cities in the United States, Los Angeles has many agencies but few resources allocated to the planting and maintenance of city trees, which now tend to be associated with public-private partnerships and diverse sources of funding and fundraising (Pincetl 2010b). At the household level, Alvolio et al. (2015) reported that both socioeconomic and environmental factors influence residents' preferences for urban trees in the Los Angeles metropolitan area. Affluent residents are more likely to prefer trees, and older residents are more likely to be concerned with their maintenance costs. Residents of urban areas in the Mojave Desert portion of southern California are more likely to value shade but less likely to consider public trees important than are residents of the naturally forested, montane region.

Pataki et al. (2013) used surveys of residents in the Los Angeles area to develop a classification of the factors that influence the selection of garden tree species, such as their size, water use, phenology, and presence of showy flowers. They found that these factors were related to easily measurable leaf functional traits as well as each species' biogeographic region of origin (the continent, climate, or habitat from which the species was imported to Los Angeles). Hence, it is increasingly possible to understand the relationships between institutions, household decisions, biodiversity, and ecosystem function in the highly urbanized regions of California. This can facilitate development of urban landscaping options and designs that meet criteria for both environmental performance and social acceptance, particularly if ecologists are integrated into the design process (Felson and Pickett 2005, Felson et al. 2013).

Fewer data exist for California on how patterns of biodiversity, species composition, and other alterations to urban environments influence ecosystem processes such as biogeochemistry, nutrient cycling, and mass/energy exchange. In general, urban landscapes in California tend to be irrigated, resulting in urban forest transpiration rates that can be similar to MESIC natural forests depending on tree planting density (Pataki, McCarthy et al. 2011) and lawn evapotranspiration rates close to POTENTIAL EVAPOTRANSPIRATION (Litvak et al. 2014). These enhanced water fluxes alter climate on local to regional scales (Kueppers et al. 2007, Lobell et al. 2009). Although newly urbanized land cover tends to be associated with construction fill that is low in soil organic matter (Pouyat et al. 2006, Raciti et al. 2012), intensive resource inputs from irrigation and fertilization accelerate the soil carbon and nitrogen cycles (Kaye et al. 2005; Jenerette, Wu et al. 2006; Raciti et al. 2008).

In southern California lawn soils that are not frequently tilled rapidly accumulate carbon for several decades (Townsend-Small and Czimczik 2010). However, the benefits of lawn soil carbon sequestration for mitigating global warming are offset by greenhouse gas emissions from lawn maintenance and fertilization (Townsend-Small and Czimczik 2010). Furthermore, the impacts of urban vegetation and soils on greenhouse gases and other types of pollution must be considered in the context of overall anthropogenic emissions. The direct carbon sequestration of urban vegetation is a negligible fraction of CO_2 emissions from fossil fuel combustion, but urban plants and soils can substantially impact local urban air temperatures through evaporative cooling and shading, providing an ecosystem service. NO_2 and N_2O emissions and nitrate and pesticide leaching from fertilized soils are costs, however, of fertilized and chemically treated landscapes (Pataki, Carreiro et al. 2011).

TABLE 39.1

Imports, local sources, and outputs of energy, water, and food in Los Angeles County, 2000

Energy reported in terajoules (TJ) of production from imported fuels, local solar radiation, and waste heat of combustion

	Imports	Local sources	Outputs
Energy and GHG emissions[A]	2,362,300 TJ	9,500 TJ	2,371,800 TJ waste heat 124 MMT CO_2Eq
Water[B]	1,600 MMT	3,100 MMT precipitation 775 MMT groundwater	930 MMT wastewater 4,500 MMT runoff + ET + recharge
Materials[C]	8.3 MMT food	0.1 MMT food	8.3 MMT solid waste

SOURCE: Ngo and Pataki 2008.

A. Greenhouse gas (GHG) emissions are reported in million metric tonnes (MMT) of CO_2 equivalents (CO_2Eq), which is the effective warming of the atmosphere that would result from the equivalent amount of carbon dioxide (CO_2).

B. Water is reported as MMT imported from areas outside of Los Angeles County, as well as local precipitation and groundwater pumping. Some outputs of water are accounted for in wastewater discharge from sewage treatment plants; the remainder must be found either in surface runoff, evapotranspiration (ET) from vegetation and surfaces, or recharge of local groundwater.

C. Only estimates of material imports and local production of food are available, while solid waste includes food plus other materials.

Urban Metabolism, Ecological Footprints, and Life Cycle Assessment

For at least the last decade, urban ecologists have distinguished between the study of ecology *in* cities—that is, biological or biophysical processes that happen to occur within cities—and the ecology *of* cities, in which urban areas are studied more broadly as ecosystems that involve complex interactions between biophysical and social processes (Pickett et al. 1997, Grimm et al. 2000). The shift to studying the ecology of cities has caused a need for new tools and approaches and for modifications of approaches from other disciplines in order to understand ecological processes within cities as well as the interaction of cities with regional landscapes, climate, and resource availability. The challenge going forward in the twenty-first century is to understand cities as ecosystems in which human actions, the biophysical environment, the biotic environment, and the built environment all interact (Collins et al. 2000, Pickett et al. 2001, Alberti et al. 2003). Cities are complex systems in which many different social and natural processes operate simultaneously and influence each other at varying spatial and temporal scales. The sum total of these processes yields the total flows and transformations of energy and materials into and out of cities. Ecologists and urban planners alike are very interested in minimizing the environmental impacts of cities and maximizing the positive outcomes for human well-being. This requires understanding of the total resource use of cities, the impacts of the urban environment, and social and health outcomes—in other words, the ecology *of* cities.

Cities are highly HETEROTROPHIC ecosystems in that they depend on enormous inputs of energy and materials to sustain urban functions. To put this in ecological terms, most natural ecosystems capture more energy in primary production (photosynthesis) than they consume in respiration. However, in cities primary production is orders of magnitude smaller than the energy consumed in transportation, electricity, and heat production. In addition, far more materials are imported into cities for building materials, food, and consumer goods than can be produced locally (Collins et al. 2000). For example, Los Angeles imports far more energy and materials than are available locally (Table 39.1). Several related methods have been developed to quantify the total amount of energy, materials, and land necessary to sustain cities. URBAN METABOLISM describes the total inputs of energy and materials and the export of waste from a given urban area (Wolman 1965, Hanya and Ambe 1976, Newman 1999). The concept originally arose as an analogy in which the city was described as a living organism that consumes energy and produces waste. From an ecological perspective, this analogy is fairly limited because more strictly speaking, cities are complexes of organisms that interact with their environment and therefore are better described as "ecosystems" rather than "organisms" (Golubiewski 2012). Nevertheless, studies of urban metabolism introduced useful methods of quantifying total imports of energy, food, and/or other materials and exports of greenhouse gas emissions, solid waste, and other pollutants from various urban areas. These analyses tend to be quite data-limited, as energy and material consumption statistics are seldom easily available at the municipal scale (Pataki et al. 2006, Kennedy et al. 2007).

However, Ngo and Pataki (2008) conducted an urban metabolism study of Los Angeles County from 1990 to 2000 and found that with the exception of food imports and wastewater outputs, inflows and outflows of energy and materials generally declined per capita over the study period, reflecting improvements in urban efficiency. Kennedy et al. (2009) used these results to compare energy use and greenhouse gas emissions from Los Angeles County to nine other metropolitan regions globally and found that per capita energy consumption was relatively low in Los Angeles, likely due to its mild climate and low energy demands, while per capita emissions from the transportation sector were quite high relative to Barcelona, Cape Town, London, Geneva, New York City, and Prague. Population density, one measure of URBAN SPRAWL, explained much of the variation in transportation emissions among cities (Figure 39.2). Hence, the perception of Los Angeles as a center of "car culture" (Selby 2012) and sprawl is borne out in urban metabolic analysis. These data provide insight into the mechanisms underlying patterns of emissions, which provides a means of prioritizing emissions reductions strategies. They also establish a baseline to evaluate future improvements in land use transportation planning and design.

In studies of ecological footprints, estimates of urban energy and material consumption are used to calculate the total land area needed to support urban functions. The con-

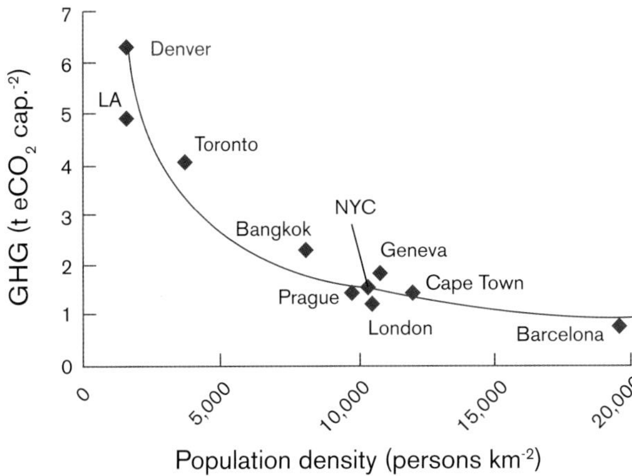

FIGURE 39.2 The relationship between per capita (cap.) greenhouse gas emissions (GHG) from ground transportation and population density in Los Angeles (LA) in comparison to nine other cities worldwide. Source: Reprinted with permission from Kennedy et al. 2009. Copyright 2009 American Chemical Society.

cept was originally applied at the national scale to show inequities in resource use among countries (Wackernagel and Rees 1996, Wackernagel et al. 1999, Lenzen and Murray 2001) but has also been applied to cities (Luck et al. 2001; Jenerette, Marussich et al. 2006). At the urban scale, the classic ecological footprint concept has been criticized for its simplifying assumptions (Luck et al. 2001) and for implying in a general sense that cities are "bad" for the environment and natural resource consumption when, in fact, concentrating populations in small urban areas is probably more efficient than distributing the human population across the landscape (Kaye et al. 2006). Nevertheless, it is informative to establish a baseline for current urban resource and land consumption against which to evaluate future change. To do this, the assumptions underlying ecological footprint calculations must be considered very carefully. Studies of both urban metabolism and ecological footprints are highly sensitive to decisions about the size and scope of the urban region, which flows to consider, and the specific source regions for energy and waste. For example, Luck et al. (2001) showed that the estimated ecological footprint of Phoenix, Arizona, can vary by almost an order of magnitude depending on these embedded assumptions.

Outside of Los Angeles, few if any studies of urban metabolism and ecological footprints have taken place in California to date. The most current approaches combine several methods: urban metabolism and ecological footprints as well as LIFE CYCLE ASSESSMENT (LCA). LCA has been used extensively in analyses of industrial processes, services, and consumer products. Applied to an urban area, LCA involves inventories and impact assessments similar to urban metabolism but coupled with a "cradle-to-grave" analysis of urban activities and infrastructure including material supply chains, remote ecosystem and health impacts, and end-of-life waste disposal (Chester et al. 2012). For example, while urban metabolism studies have quantified direct greenhouse emissions from the urban transportation sector (Kennedy et al. 2009), Chester and Horvath (2009) showed that non-tailpipe emissions, such as those associated with vehicle and road construction, actually dominate total LCA passenger transportation emissions in the United States.

They used this methodology to compare scenarios of passenger car vehicle occupancy and air transportation with and without the construction of California's proposed high-speed rail line. They found that high-speed rail was advantageous for greenhouse gas emissions under high-occupancy scenarios but potentially disadvantageous for sulphur dioxide emissions due to California's current reliance on coal for electrical energy (Chester and Horvath 2010). This method shows great promise for evaluating sustainability options in California. A movement has begun, spurred by these studies, to establish a central repository of the data needed to conduct combined studies of urban metabolism and LCA in the state. Life cycle analysis can also account for the supply chain impacts of resource flows into cities. Chester et al. (2012) estimated the environmental impacts of materials embedded in existing buildings and roads in in Los Angeles County. This more complete approach leads to fuller accounting of the requirements for sustaining cities (Pincetl et al. 2012).

Integrating Biotic and Abiotic Components of Cities

So far we have discussed the biotic features of cities—their faunal and floral diversity and composition—separately from other environmental dimensions such as resource appropriation and pollution emissions. This is because, to date, studies of biotic and built components of cities have not been well integrated. Conceptually, recognition exists that this integration is necessary. There has been a call to better incorporate the biotic environment—parks, outdoor landscaping, street trees, and greenspace—into calculations of urban metabolism, ecological footprints, and LCA (Chester et al. 2012). Conversely, a variety of urban planning tools available are currently available that consider scenarios and outcomes associated with the built environment, but these tools do yet explicitly consider the form and function of greenspace. Enormous interest exists in California in replacing "gray" or built infrastructure in cities with "green" or biologically-based infrastructure to facilitate urban and regional sustainability. The many possible cobenefits of appropriate design and maintenance of urban GREEN INFRASTRUCTURE have been described as ranging from pollution removal in air, soils, and water (Freer-Smith et al. 1997; Beckett et al. 2000; Davis et al. 2001; Nowak et al. 2006; Pataki, Carreiro et al. 2011) to food and water provision (Smit and Nasr 1992, Alaimo et al. 2008, Draper and Freedman 2010, Litt et al. 2011); habitat provision for native and rare species (Rudd et al. 2002, Matteson et al. 2008, Goddard et al. 2010); economic impacts, particularly in the real estate market (Tyrväinen 1997, Morancho 2003, Conway et al. 2010, Li and Saphores 2012); and more general benefits to human health and well-being.

Common urban features in California designed to utilize biological processes to serve these functions include BIOSWALES and BIORETENTION basins for stormwater infiltration, urban farms and community gardens for food provision, greenbelts and corridors for wildlife habitat, green roofs, and a variety of other spaces that serve multiple functions. These features are hybrids of the built and biological environments, and developing science-based approaches for designing, implementing, and monitoring urban green infrastructure is an emerging research area (Pincetl 2010a; Pataki, Carreiro et al. 2011; Felson et al. 2013). Burian and Pomeroy (2010) and Pataki, Carreiro et al. (2011) have pointed out that much of the literature on urban green infrastructure originates from wetter environments and that appropriate designs for more arid environments in California cities remain to be tested.

Design, construction, and maintenance of urban green infrastructure is associated with environmental costs as well as ecosystem services. Such costs have been termed ECOSYSTEM DISSERVICES and include monetary costs; negative environmental impacts such as energy, water, and fertilizer inputs to urban landscapes; and negative health impacts such as the release of allergens in pollen (Lyytimaki et al. 2008). Most studies have not yet evaluated the materials and embedded energy and emissions costs necessary to build and maintain these infrastructures. In general, far fewer studies of urban ecosystems address disservices than services, so the extent of these costs is usually uncertain. Most studies of urban ecosystem services in California have focused on a set of calculators about urban trees that was developed by the U.S. Forest Service (http://itree.org). To date, these tools have been used in several California cities to estimate various benefits of urban trees including carbon sequestration, air pollution removal, stormwater mitigation, and energy savings (McPherson 1996 and 2003, Maco and McPherson 2003, McPherson et al. 2005).

However, these tools are very limited in their ability to evaluate urban ecosystem services as a whole, as they have been poorly constrained by available data and currently consider only the urban forest components of urban ecosystems. The next steps in these types of quantitative analyses are tools that integrate planning and assessment of greenspace and the built environment to more explicitly consider costs as well as benefits of alternative urban designs and can therefore contribute to SCENARIO PLANNING and ADAPTIVE GOVERNANCE. A variety of quantitative tools is available for land use and transportation in cities (Bartholomew 2007), but most do not currently incorporate greenspace planning. Integrating multiple aspects of ecosystem functioning in the built and nonbuilt environments is a promising future direction in urban ecological planning.

Impacts of Urban Activities on Surrounding Areas

As urban metabolism studies have shown, urbanization can greatly impact adjacent or embedded undeveloped ecosystems through increased fire, pollution, species introductions, resource extraction, and altered climate and water availability. These effects occur through production within the city and transport to other regions (pollution, invasive species, altered climate), actions of urban residents within adjacent wildlands (fire), and direct appropriation of wildland resources (water) and other resources such as building materials, fossil fuels, and other materials. Interactions among these effects are pervasive, with urban-derived nitrogen pollution (see Chapter 7, "Atmospheric Chemistry") leading to increased fire risk in adjacent deserts (Rao et al. 2010), fires leading to increased ozone (O_3) precursor production (Bytnerowicz et al. 2010), and appropriations of water for urban uses leading to plant species and associated community changes (Elmore et al. 2003). At broader scales, urban areas are dominant contributors of greenhouse gas emissions through emissions of CO_2 from buildings, industry, and transportation (Pataki et al. 2006) as well as emissions of N_2O from irrigated and fertilized lawns (Townsend-Small and Czimczik 2010).

Fire at the urban-wildland interface (UWI) is a perennial challenge in much of California. The state's chaparral and forested regions are fire-prone, with a high risk of large fires near urban areas. The most recent five-year average (2011–2006) had 5,084 fires that burned 8,439 hectares annually within California. The fire most destructive of infrastructure in California, the 1991 Tunnel Fire, was only 648 hectares but burned twenty-nine hundred structures (according to Cal-Fire). Weather patterns of unusually high precipitation (leading to more fuel) or low precipitation (leading to more flammable fuel) both increase fire risks. Increasing fire risk near urbanized areas is linked with increasing ignition sources (Keeley et al. 1999), past practices of suppression that have increased standing fuel loads (Minnich 1983), and an increasingly complex matrix of low-density urban development in high-risk fire areas (Syphard et al. 2012).

Pollution from urban areas is a major contributor to degradation of wildland ecosystems, with both extensive air and water pollution. Airborne urban pollutants that affect surrounding areas are dominated by nitrogen, O_3, and particulates. The majority of NO_x pollutants are produced by transportation (86%) and industrial activities (Fenn et al. 2010). On-road nitrogen emissions also likely include substantial NH_3 beyond what is included in existing inventories (Battye et al. 2003, Bishop et al. 2010, Fenn et al. 2010). Correspondingly, emissions of nitrogenous pollutants differ greatly between weekday and weekend periods. For many urban sources, pollution emissions have declined since the enactment of vehicular emission controls despite increases in vehicle kilometers traveled (Fenn et al. 2003, Cox et al. 2009). At present, nitrogen emissions have led 29–54% of nonurban vegetation cover to exceed biologically determined nitrogen deposition critical loads (Fenn et al. 2010).

Tropospheric ozone formation is complex and related to NOx, temperature, water vapor, light, and volatile organic compounds (VOCs). These atmospheric drivers lead to diel and seasonal variations in O_3 production. O_3 concentrations in forests adjacent to urban areas, for example, in the San Bernardino Mountain forests adjacent to Los Angeles, can have severe effects (Bytnerowicz et al. 2008; see Chapter 7, "Atmospheric Chemistry"). High O_3 concentrations near urban areas have led to declines of several native conifer trees through mortality and reduced recruitment (Bytnerowicz et al. 2007). O_3 concentrations in the regions adjacent to Los Angeles have shown marked decreases from 1970 to the present with much larger decreases in peak concentrations compared to weekly means (Bytnerowicz et al. 2007). The Sierra Nevada are also affected by O_3 emissions from urban areas, with the highest concentrations often driven by airflows from San Francisco (Bytnerowicz et al. 2013). Future projections suggest a potential for reduced tropospheric O_3 but with large uncertainties and spatial variation (Steiner et al. 2006).

Urban discharge of water pollutants to surrounding areas including surface water, groundwater, and coastal ecosystems can be substantial. Water pollutants include sewage, nutrients, pharmaceuticals, toxins, and growing amounts of nanoparticles. Sewage contamination of bacteria and viruses from urbanization into many coastal areas presents recurring human health issues (Dwight et al. 2002, Ahn et al. 2005). Urban inputs of nutrients including nitrogen, phosphorus, and carbon into waterways can contribute to disproportionately large total loads. For example, up to 17% of total organic carbon inputs to the Sacramento River might originate from urban lands (Sickman et al. 2007). Improvements in analytical capabilities have allowed increasing detection of pharmaceuticals and personal care products in surface water and groundwater (Kolpin et al. 2002, Loraine and Pettigrove 2006). These materials likely have health consequences for humans (Santos et al. 2010) as well as wildlife (Nash et al. 2004). Metals and polycyclic aromatic hydrocarbon contamination of stormwater runoff are associated with transportation corridors (Lau et al. 2009, Kayhanian et al. 2012). Nanoparticles, a diverse class of materials defined solely by size, are increasingly of interest in urban discharge. Recent findings have shown direct movement of a widely used nanoparticle into urban waterways (Kaegi et al. 2008). Pollutant runoff patterns can interact with fires because airborne pollutants accumulate between fire intervals and become mobilized after fire events, causing large rates of surface water contamination (Stein et al. 2012).

Urbanization is associated with several mechanisms for altering species communities in surrounding areas. Habitat fragmentation in wildlands adjacent to cities can reduce animal population sizes, decrease metapopulation connectivity, and increase invasive species, leading to increased risk of native species extirpations (Bolger et al. 1997, Suarez et al. 1998). Interactions between fragmentation and altered fire regimes can exacerbate these effects (Regan et al. 2010). Pollution by both nitrogen and O_3 can alter plant communities, favoring species that can either use additional nitrogen inputs or tolerate higher O_3 concentrations (Allen et al. 2007, Vourlitis and Pasquini 2009, Vallano et al. 2012). As discussed earlier, cities are also frequently sources of exotic species cultivated as landscape plants. Future studies of ecological footprints and LCA might be better able to incorporate the impacts of urban activities on wildland health (Chester et al. 2012). This information can then be used in regional planning and in "conservation development"—a form of controlled development intended to preserve or restore natural ecosystems while allowing limited growth (Arendt 1999, Milder 2007).

The Future of California's Urban Areas

California has seen rapid changes in urbanization throughout its history. Following the Gold Rush, California urbanized far more rapidly than the rest of the United States, with particularly rapid population growth in the Bay Area (see Chapter 5, "Population and Land Use"). The early twentieth century saw a rapid increase in urbanization in and around Los Angeles, while the growth of outlying suburbs and smaller settlements dominated after World War II. In recent years there has been an effort to revive and repopulate California's urban cores and central business districts.

Today, California cities are moving in several directions with a growing emphasis on sustainable development. As we have discussed, interest has grown in urban greening activities, directed primarily towards increasing tree and greenspace cover. However, these activities are not necessarily compatible with efforts to reduce water demands and curtail outdoor irrigation. It will take careful planning to select species and designs for greening efforts that minimize water costs and other unintended consequences. Another emphasis for California's cities is to increase reliance on renewable energy sources, with both large scale solar and wind power plants adjacent to urban centers as well as broad adoption of rooftop solar collectors. In 2013 the Los Angeles Department of Water and Power began its largest rooftop feed-in tariff program (100 MW) for rooftop solar energy (http://www.ladwp.com/fit). These large-scale programs have potential monetary as well as environmental costs and require careful consideration (Hernandez et al. 2014). Interest is also increasing in mass transit options to increase connections within and between urban centers of California. Both San Francisco and Los Angeles metropolitan regions are expanding commuter rail services. Planned for current construction are high-speed rail lines connecting Los Angeles with San Francisco and Sacramento (California High Speed Rail Authority, http://www.hsr.ca.gov/).

Land cover changes will continue to be a dominant component of urban ecosystems in the future. Within the Los Angeles region and the Bay Area, densities will likely increase because of the scarcity of available land. The age of these cities will also require retrofitting of existing infrastructure, with many opportunities for incorporating new designs. In the last few decades a shift has occurred away from single-use zoning of urban areas in which residential, commercial, and industrial land covers are spatially separated, resulting in heavy dependence on automobile transit. Increasingly, alternative planning models such as TRANSIT-ORIENTED DEVELOPMENT and NEW URBANISM incorporate mixed land uses and increased reliance on walking and alternative transportation (Fulton 1996, Cervero et al. 2002, Lund 2003). However, urban development is still associated with suburban and periurban residential expansion. Urban land cover types are likely to continue ongoing expansion into historically agricultural and desert regions of California (see Chapter 5, "Population and Land Use").

Planning and decision making increasingly consider climate changes both exogenous and endogenous to California's urban areas. Rising temperatures accompany both global warming trajectories and expansion of urban heat islands (Jenerette et al. 2011). These warming trends directly affect human health, electricity usage, and evaporation rates, with further indirect effects on air quality and fire frequency and intensity (Pincetl, Franco et al. 2013). Climate changes are also altering water availability for California's urban areas (Tanaka et al. 2006, O'Hara and Georgakakos 2008). While urban areas are a relatively small component of total water demands, they are a rapidly growing water use sector (Christian-Smith et al. 2012). Reduced snowpack in the mountains and earlier snowmelt could have large effects on water availability. Reductions in available water could lead to reduced urban irrigation and some reductions of in-home, commercial, and industrial uses via increases in water rates and/or through other incentives to reduce urban water consumption. Notably, water availability is tightly connected to energy consumption; reductions in available water resources will likely increase energy demands to pump groundwater and reduce energy production from hydroelectric sources (Klein et al. 2005; Pincetl, Franco et al. 2013).

Urban-driver effects on biotic communities will likely also grow. The availability of species imported from other regions and continents into California nurseries is increasing, and plant communities seem to follow "fads" in desirability that change at decadal scales (Pincetl, Prabhu et al. 2013). The once iconic palm trees of southern California are now frequently being replaced by other species (Figure 39.3). *Eucalyptus* species, once widely popular, are now less desirable (http://www.laparks.org/dos/forest/eucalyptus.htm). We expect different species to supplant current favorites in their desirability over time. As a result, new exotics and invasive plants will likely arrive in California cities and increase in prominence in less developed areas.

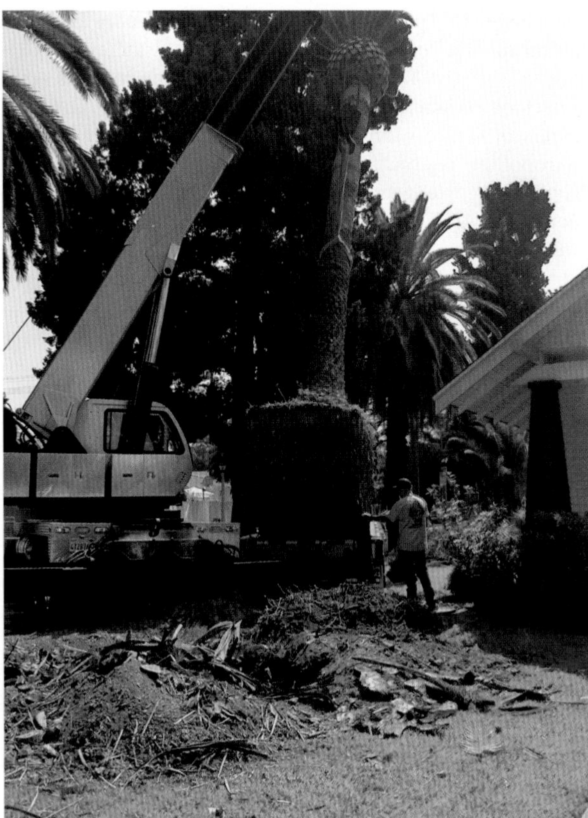

FIGURE 39.3 Removal of a palm tree in Riverside, California. Photo: G. D. Jenerette.

In summary, California's urban areas continue to rapidly change, with evolving decision making, implementation of new technologies, and sensitivity to the dynamic environment. Land cover changes will continue both within and outside of existing urban areas. While many coastal regions have been nearly completely developed, such as Los Angeles and San Francisco, more inland regions are sites of rapid urban expansion, such as Riverside and Fresno. Within all of these existing urban and urbanizing regions, future cities in California will not likely look like the cities of today, which themselves are quite different from the cities of fifty years ago. Climate change, increasing pollution loads, and declining resources now place pressure on cities to reduce their water, energy, and resource consumption. Significant changes in material and energy flow into and out of cities will likely require large changes in both infrastructure and governance. We have shown that there are many unanticipated consequences of urbanization for other aspects of California ecosystems, such as biodiversity, biogeochemistry, fire frequency and severity, and feedbacks to local climate. It has been difficult to predict these effects a priori, as some effects of urban development such as the prevalence of novel and diverse floral and floral communities have been surprising. To better anticipate the impacts of urban development choices on the complex landscapes of California, ecologists should play a role in informing urban planning and design. However, ecological science is only one of the many factors that determine land use decisions and outcomes. The sustainable future of California will require continual advancements and refinements in theories and concepts concerning coupled human-environment interactions and the functioning of novel ecosystems, as well as effective consortia of ecologists, engineers, planners, designers, and decision makers in California cities.

Summary

California is the most highly urbanized state in the U.S., with almost 95% of its population living in U.S. Census–defined urban areas. Historically, most urban development took place on the coast, displacing native coastal ecosystems. Recently, urban development is taking place in higher-elevation areas and inland in the southern deserts and the Central Valley. Urban development has created hybrid ecosystems that consist of the built environment as well as novel assemblages of floral and faunal species. Floral diversity, as well the diversity of some animal taxa, is surprisingly high in California's cities. However, some of these species are exotic invasives that have escaped from cities to impact California's natural ecosystems. Numerous other unanticipated consequences of rapid urban development can occur, such as air and water pollution and changes in fire frequencies. Scientists are attempting to quantify these effects with studies of urban metabolism, ecological footprints, and life cycle assessment. These studies will help evaluate the effectiveness of new programs to reduce the negative environmental impacts of urbanization.

California's cities are now implementing new programs in alternative energy generation, green infrastructure, and restrictions on outdoor water use. A major uncertainty in designing these new elements of urban landscapes is the relationship between the built and the biological environment. The extent to which biological characteristics such as biodiversity and species composition influence urban functioning and pollution is unknown. Many questions also persist as to how aspects of the urban environment influence human health and well-being. Overall, increasing walkability, reducing carbon-based energy use, and replacing some features of the built environment of cities with green infrastructure hopefully will contribute to mitigating environmental problems and improving quality of life. New strategies and policies in urban planning in California are attempting to integrate greenspace, open space, and ecosystem services into land use and transportation planning, which requires new consortia of urban planners, engineers, policy experts, ecologists, and other scientists. California is continuing to test new policies and strategies for urban sustainability, and the results of current programs will inform the future for both the state and beyond.

Acknowledgments

This work was supported by U.S. National Science Foundation grants EAR 1204442, EAR 1204235, and EF 1065831.

Recommended Reading

Adler, F. R., and C. J. Tanner. 2013. Urban ecosystems: Ecological principles for the built environment. Cambridge University Press, Cambridge, UK.

Collins, J., A. Kinzig, N. B. Grimm, W. F. Fagan, D. Hope, J. Wu, and E. T. Borer. 2000. A new urban ecology: Modeling human communities as integral parts of ecosystems poses special problems for

the development and testing of ecological theory. American Scientist 88:416–425.
Kennedy, C. A., J. Steinberger, B. Gasson, Y. Hansen, T. Hillman, and M. Havrenak. 2009. Greenhouse gas emissions from global cities. Environmental Science and Technology 43:7292–7302.
Pincetl, S., P. Bunje, and T. Holmes. 2012. An expanded urban metabolism method: Toward a systems approach for assessing urban energy processes and causes. Landscape and Urban Planning 107:193–202.
Schwartz, M. W., J. H. Thorne, and J. H. Viers. 2006. Biotic homogenization of the California flora in urban and urbanizing regions. Biological Conservation 127:282–291.
Selby, W. A. 2012. Rediscovering the Golden State: California geography. Third edition. Wiley, Hoboken, NJ.

Glossary

ADAPTIVE GOVERNANCE A dynamic method of managing complex ecosystems in which decision-making and management change in response to experimentation and new information.

ALPHA DIVERSITY The number of species at a specific location, in contrast to the diversity of multiple locations or a region as a whole.

BIORETENTION A landscape designed to infiltrate stormwater into soil.

BIOSWALES A type of bioretention feature, usually linearly designed to infiltrate stormwater into soil along streets, sidewalks, parking lots, or other paved areas.

BIOTIC HOMOGENIZATION A process in which localities become more similar in terms of biodiversity, ecosystem function, and other biological characteristics.

BUILT ENVIRONMENT The human engineered and constructed environment, which includes roads, buildings, pavements, and other human-built structures.

ECOLOGICAL FOOTPRINT The area needed to supply resources to a given local population.

ECOSYSTEM DISSERVICES The costs or negative impacts of creating or managing a given ecosystem.

EX-URBAN Very low-density urban development, generally lower in population and housing density than suburban areas.

GREEN INFRASTRUCTURE Human-designed and -engineered features that rely on biological processes to provide environmental services.

HETEROTROPHIC An organism or ecosystem that cannot synthesize its own sustenance. Cities are considered heterotrophic because their food, energy, and materials cannot be supplied entirely locally and must be imported from outside the city boundaries.

HIERARCHY OF NEEDS A ranking of human needs proposed by Maslow (1943) in which humans fulfill basic needs in a certain order, beginning with basic physiological requirements and moving to other social and psychological needs only when basic needs have been fulfilled. This pattern is proposed to explain the relationship between urban biodiversity and affluence, in which high levels of biodiversity are only planted and maintained by residents who can afford to fulfill other basic needs.

LIFE CYCLE ASSESSMENT A cradle-to-grave assessment of the total environmental impacts of a given process, product, or urban area.

MESIC A moist climate with adequate rainfall for forest growth.

METROPOLITAN STATISTICAL AREA (MSA) A U.S. Census–defined core urban area of fifty thousand or more residents that includes: (1) the counties containing the urban area, and (2) the adjacent counties with a high degree of social and economic integration measured by commutes to work in the urban core.

NEW URBANISM A revival of older, preautomobile neighborhood designs that encourage pedestrian and nonautomobile transit.

POTENTIAL EVAPOTRANSPIRATION The amount of water that can be evaporated from a moist surface given atmospheric conditions.

RAREFACTION A method of estimating numbers of species by the relationship between the area sampled and the numbers of species found in sampled plots.

SCENARIO PLANNING A process of testing the form and impacts of alternative futures for urban growth in order to develop a shared community vision for local planning.

TRANSIT-ORIENTED DEVELOPMENT High-density urban development focused on public transportation hubs.

URBAN HEAT ISLANDS Areas of elevated temperature and other alterations to local climate caused by urban materials and processes. These include heat retention by buildings and pavement, heat generation from combustion, and reductions in vegetation cover.

URBAN METABOLISM Energy and materials inflows, transformations, and outflows from urban areas.

URBAN SPRAWL Low-density urban development that may have a number of characteristics including low population density, reliance on automobile transportation, and single-use land use and building types as opposed to mixed commercial and residential development.

URBAN-WILDLAND INTERFACE The encroachment of urban development into largely natural areas. In California this interface often occurs in foothills and higher-elevation areas that developed more recently after valleys and lower-elevation agricultural lands were fully developed.

References

Ahn, J. H., S. B. Grant, C. Q. Surbeck, P. M. DiGiacomo, N. P. Nezlin, and S. Jiang. 2005. Coastal water quality impact of stormwater runoff from an urban watershed in southern California. Environmental Science and Technology 39:5940–5953.
Alaimo, K., E. Packnett, R. A. Miles, and D. J. Kruger. 2008. Fruit and vegetable intake among urban community gardeners. Journal of Nutrition Education and Behavior 40:94–101.
Alberti, M., J. M. Marzluff, E. Shulenberger, G. Bradley, C. Ryan, and C. Zumbrunen. 2003. Integrating humans into ecology: Opportunities and challenges for studying urban ecosystems. BioScience 53:1169–1179.
Allen, E. B., P. J. Temple, A. Bytnerowicz, M. J. Arbaugh, A. G. Sirulnik, and L. E. Rao. 2007. Patterns of understory diversity in mixed coniferous forests of southern California impacted by air pollution. Scientific World Journal 7:247–263.
Arendt, R. G. 1999. Growing greener: Putting conservation into local plans and ordinances. Island Press, Washington, D.C..
Avolio, M. L., D. E. Pataki, S. Pincetl, T. W. Gillespie, G. D. Jenerette, and H. R. McCarthy. 2015. Understanding preferences for tree attributes: The relative effects of socio-economic and local environmental factors. Urban Ecosystems 18:73–86.
Bartholomew, K. 2007. Land use-transportation scenario planning: Promise and reality. Transportation 34:397–412.
Battye, W., V. P. Aneja, and P. A. Roelle. 2003. Evaluation and improvement of ammonia emissions inventories. Atmospheric Environment 37:3873–3883.
Beckett, K. P., P. H. Freer-Smith, and G. Taylor. 2000. The capture of particulate pollution by trees at five contrasting urban sites. Arboricultural Journal 24:209–230.
Bishop, G. A., A. M. Peddle, D. H. Stedman, and T. Zhan. 2010. On-road emission measurements of reactive nitrogen compounds

from three California cities. Environmental Science and Technology 44:3616–3620.

Blair, R. B. 2001. Birds and butterflies along urban gradients in two ecoregions of the United States: Is urbanization creating a homogeneous fauna? Pages 33-56 in J. Lockwood and M. McKinney, editors. Biotic Homogenization. Kluwer Academic/Plenum Publishers, New York, NY.

Bolger, D. T., A. C. Alberts, R. M. Sauvajot, P. Potenza, C. McCalvin, D. Tran, S. Mazzoni, and M. E. Soulé. 1997. Response of rodents to habitat fragmentation in coastal southern California. Ecological Applications 7:552–563.

Burian, S. J., and C. A. Pomeroy. 2010. Urban impacts on the water cycle and potential green infrastructure implications. Pages 277–296 in J. Aitkenhead-Peterson and A. Volder, editors. Urban Ecosystem Ecology. American Society of Agronomy, Crop Science Society of America, Soil Science Society of America. Madison, WI.

Bytnerowicz, A., D. Cayan, P. Riggan, S. Schilling, P. Dawson, M. Tyree, L. Wolden, R. Tissell, and H. Preisler. 2010. Analysis of the effects of combustion emissions and Santa Ana winds on ambient ozone during the October 2007 southern California wildfires. Atmospheric Environment 44:678–687.

Bytnerowicz, A., J. D. Burley, R. Cisneros, H. K. Preisler, S. Schilling, D. Schweizer, J. Ray, D. Dulen, C. Beck, and B. Auble. 2013. Surface ozone at the Devils Postpile National Monument receptor site during low and high wildland fire years. Atmospheric environment 65:129–141.

Bytnerowicz, A., M. Arbaugh, S. Schilling, W. Frączek, and D. Alexander. 2008. Ozone distribution and phytotoxic potential in mixed conifer forests of the San Bernardino Mountains, southern California. Environmental Pollution 155:398–408.

Bytnerowicz, A., M. Arbaugh, S. Schilling, W. Fraczek, D. Alexander, and P. Dawson. 2007. Air pollution distribution patterns in the San Bernardino Mountains of southern California: A 40-year perspective. Scientific World Journal 7(suppl. 1):98–109.

Cal Fire 2015. Twenty most damaging California wildfires. <http://cdfdata.fire.ca.gov/incidents/incidents_statsevents>. Accessed July 10, 2015.

Cervero, R., C. Ferrell, and S. Murphy. 2002. Transit-oriented development and joint development in the United States: A literature review. TCRP Research Results Digest. Transportation Research Board, Washington, DC.

Chace, J. F., and J. J. Walsh. 2006. Urban effects on native avifauna: A review. Landscape and urban planning 74:46–69.

Chester, M., and A. Horvath. 2010. Life-cycle assessment of high-speed rail: The case of California. Environmental Research Letters 5:014003.

Chester, M., S. Pincetl, and B. Allenby. 2012. Avoiding unintended tradeoffs by integrating life-cycle impact assessment with urban metabolism. Current Opinion in Environmental Sustainability 4:451–457.

Chester, M. V., and A. Horvath. 2009. Environmental assessment of passenger transportation should include infrastructure and supply chains. Environmental Research Letters 4:024008.

Christian-Smith, J., M. Heberger, and L. Allen. 2012. Urban water demand in California to 2100: Incorporating climate change. Pacific Institute, Oakland, California.

Clarke, L. W., G. D. Jenerette, and A. Davalia. 2013. The luxury of vegetation and the legacy of tree biodiversity in Los Angeles, CA. Landscape and Urban Planning 116:48–59.

Collins, J. ., A. Kinzig, N. B. Grimm, W. F. Fagan, D. Hope, J. Wu, and E. T. Borer. 2000. A new urban ecology: Modeling human communities as integral parts of ecosystems poses special problems for the development and testing of ecological theory. American Scientist 88:416–425.

Connor, E. F., J. Hafernik, J. Levy, V. L. Moore, and J. K. Richman. 2002. Insect conservation in an urban biodiversity hotspot: The San Francisco Bay area. Journal of Insect Conservation 6: 247–259.

Conway, D., C. Q. Li, J. Wolch, C. Kahle, and M. Jerrett. 2010. A spatial autocorrelation approach for examining the effects of urban greenspace on residential property values. Journal of Real Estate Finance and Economics 41:150–169.

Cox, P., A. Delao, A. Komorniczak, and R. Weller. 2009. The California almanac of emissions and air quality, 2009 edition. California Environmental Protection Agency, Air Resources Board, Sacramento, California.

Davis, A. P., M. Shokouhian, H. Sharm, and C. Minami. 2001. Laboratory study of biological retention for urban stormwater management. Water Environment Research 73:5–14.

Draper, C., and D. Freedman. 2010. Review and analysis of the benefits, purposes, and motivations associated with community gardening in the United States. Journal of Community Practice 18:458–492.

Dunnett, N., and M. Qasim. 2000. Perceived benefits to human well-being of urban gardens. HortTechnology 10:40–45.

Dwight, R. H., J. C. Semenza, D. B. Baker, and B. H. Olson. 2002. Association of urban runoff with coastal water quality in Orange County, California. Water Environment Research 74:82–90.

Elmore, A. J., J. F. Mustard, and S. J. Manning. 2003. Regional patterns of plant community response to changes in water: Owens Valley, CA. Ecological Applications 13:443–460.

Felson, A. J., and S. T. Pickett. 2005. Designed experiments: New approaches to studying urban ecosystems. Frontiers in Ecology and the Environment 3:549–556.

Felson, A. J., M. A. Bradford, and T. M. Terway. 2013. Promoting Earth stewardship through urban design experiments. Frontiers in Ecology and the Environment 11:362–367.

Fenn, M. E., E. B. Allen, S. B. Weiss, S. Jovan, L. H. Geiser, G. S. Tonnesen, R. F. Johnson, L. E. Rao, B. S. Gimeno, F. Yuan, T. Meixner, and A. Bytnerowicz. 2010. Nitrogen critical loads and management alternatives for N-impacted ecosystems in California. Journal of Environmental Management 91:2404–2423.

Fenn, M. E., R. Haeuber, G. S. Tonnesen, J. S. Baron, S. Grossman-Clarke, D. Hope, D. A. Jaffe, S. Copeland, L. Geiser, H. M. Rueth, and J. O. Sickman. 2003. Nitrogen emissions, deposition, and monitoring in the western United States. BioScience 53:391–403.

Frankie, G.W., R.W. Thorp, M. Schindler, J. Hernandez, B. Ertter, and M. Rizzardi. 2005. Ecological patterns of bees and their host ornamental flowers in two northern California cities. Journal of the Kansas Entomological Society 78(3):227–246.

Freer-Smith, P. H., S. Holloway, and A. Goodman. 1997. The uptake of particulates by an urban woodland: Site description and particulate composition. Environmental Pollution 95:27–35.

Fulton, W. 1996. The new urbanism: Hope or hype for American communities? Lincoln Institute of Land Policy, Cambridge, MA.

Gaston, K. J. 2005. Biodiversity and extinction: Species and people. Progress in Physical Geography 29:239–247.

Goddard, M. A., A. J. Dougill, and T. G. Benton. 2010. Scaling up from gardens: Biodiversity conservation in urban environments. Trends in Ecology and Evolution 25:90–98.

Golubiewski, N. 2012. Is there a metabolism of an urban ecosystem? An ecological critique. AMBIO 41:751–764.

Grimm, N. B., J. M. Grove, S. T. A. Pickett, and C. L. Redman. 2000. Integrated approaches to long-term studies of urban ecological systems. Bioscience 50:571–584.

Hanya, T., and Y. Ambe. 1976. A study on the metabolism of cities. Science for better environment: Proceedings of the International Congress on the Human Environment. Science Council of Japan, Kyoto.

Hernandez, R. R., S. B. Easter, M. L. Murphy-Mariscal, F. T. Maestre, M. Tavassoli, E. B. Allen, C. W. Barrows, J. Belnap, R. Ochoa-Hueso, S. Ravi, and M. F. Allen. 2014. Environmental impacts of utility-scale solar energy. Renewable and Sustainable Energy Reviews 29:766–779.

Hobbs, R. J., and H. A. Mooney. 1998. Broadening the extinction debate: Population deletions and additions in California and western Australia. Conservation Biology 12:271–283.

Hobbs, R. J., E. S. Higgs, and C. Hall. 2013. Novel ecosystems: Intervening in the new ecological world order. Wiley-Blackwell. Oxford, UK.

Hope, D., C. Gries, D. Casagrande, C. L. Redman, N. B. Grimm, and C. Martin. 2006. Drivers of spatial variation in plant diversity across the central Arizona, Phoenix ecosystem. Society and Natural Resources 19:101–116.

Hope, D., C. Gries, W.-X. Zhu, W. F. Fagan, C. L. Redman, N. B. Grimm, A. L. Nelson, C. Martin, and A. Kinzig. 2003. Socioeconomics drive urban plant diversity. Proceedings of the National Academy of Sciences 100:8788–8792.

Jackson, L. E. 2003. The relationship of urban design to human health and condition. Landscape and Urban Planning 64:191–200.

Jenerette, G. D., G. Miller, A. Buyantuyev, D. E. Pataki, T. W. Gillespie, and S. Pincetl. 2013. Urban vegetation dynamics and income segregation in drylands: A synthesis of seven metropolitan regions in the southwestern United States. Environmental Research Letters 8:044001.

Jenerette, G. D., J. Wu, N. B. Grimm, and D. Hope. 2006. Points, patches, and regions: Scaling soil biogeochemical patterns in an urbanized arid ecosystem. Global Change Biology 12:1532–1544.

Jenerette, G. D., S. L. Harlan, W. L. Stefanov, and C. A. Martin. 2011. Ecosystem services and urban heat riskscape moderation: Water, green spaces, and social inequality in Phoenix, USA. Ecological Applications 21:2637–2651.

Jenerette, G. D., W. A. Marussich, and J. Newell. 2006. Linking ecological footprints with ecosystem service valuation in the urban consumption of freshwater. Ecological Economics 59:38–47.

Kaegi, R., A. Ulrich, B. Sinnet, R. Vonbank, A. Wichser, S. Zuleeg, H. Simmler, S. Brunner, H. Vonmont, M. Burkhardt, and M. Boller. 2008. Synthetic TiO_2 nanoparticle emission from exterior facades into the aquatic environment. Environmental Pollution 156:233–239.

Kaye, J. P., P. M. Groffman, N. B. Grimm, L. A. Baker, and R. V. Pouyat. 2006. A distinct urban biogeochemistry? Trends in Ecology and Evolution 21:192–199.

Kaye, J. P., R. L. McCulley, and I. C. Burke. 2005. Carbon fluxes, nitrogen cycling, and soil microbial communities in adjacent urban, native, and agricultural ecosystems. Global Change Biology 11:575–587.

Kayhanian, M., B. D. Fruchtman, J. S. Gulliver, C. Montanaro, E. Ranieri, and S. Wuertz. 2012. Review of highway runoff characteristics: Comparative analysis and universal implications. Water Research 46:6609–6624.

Keeley, J. E., C. J. Fotheringham, and M. Morais. 1999. Reexamining fire suppression impacts on brushland fire regimes. Science 284:1829–1832.

Kendal, D., N. S. G. Williams, and K. J. H. Williams. 2012. A cultivated environment: Exploring the global distribution of plants in gardens, parks, and streetscapes. Urban Ecosystems 15:637–652.

Kennedy, C. A., J. Cuddihy, and J. Engel-Yan. 2007. The changing metabolism of cities. Journal of Industrial Ecology 11:43–59.

Kennedy, C. A., J. Steinberger, B. Gasson, Y. Hansen, T. Hillman, and M. Havrenak. 2009. Greenhouse gas emissions from global cities. Environmental Science and Technology 43:7292–7302.

Kinzig, A., P. Warren, C. Martin, D. Hope, and M. Katti. 2005. The effects of human socioeconomic status and cultural characteristics on urban patterns of biodiversity. Ecology and Society 10:23.

Klein, G., M. Krebs, V. Hall, T. O'Brien, and B. B. Blevins. 2005. California's water-energy relationship. California Energy Commission. CEC-700-2005-011-SF, California.

Kolpin, D. W., E. T. Furlong, M. T. Meyer, E. M. Thurman, S. D. Zaugg, L. B. Barber, and H. T. Buxton. 2002. Pharmaceuticals, hormones, and other organic wastewater contaminants in U.S. streams, 1999–2000: A national reconnaissance. Environmental Science and Technology 36:1202–1211.

Kowarik, I. 2011. Novel urban ecosystems, biodiversity, and conservation. Environmental Pollution 159:1974–1983.

Kueppers, L. M., M. A. Snyder, and L. C. Sloan. 2007. Irrigation cooling effect: Regional climate forcing by land-use change. Geophysical Research Letters 34.

Kühn, I., R. Brandl, and S. Klotz. 2004. The flora of German cities is naturally species rich. Evolutionary Ecology Research 6:749–794.

Lau, S.-L., Y. Han, J.-H. Kang, M. Kayhanian, and M. K. Stenstrom. 2009. Characteristics of highway stormwater runoff in Los Angeles: Metals and polycyclic aromatic hydrocarbons. Water Environment Research 81:308–318.

Lenzen, M., and S. A. Murray. 2001. A modified ecological footprint method and its application to Australia. Ecological Economics 37:229–255.

Li, W., and J.-D. Saphores. 2012. A spatial hedonic analysis of the value of urban land cover in the multifamily housing market in Los Angeles, CA. Urban Studies 49:2597–2615.

Litt, J. S., M.-J. Soobader, M. S. Turbin, J. W. Hale, M. Buchenau, and J. A. Marshall. 2011. The influence of social involvement, neighborhood aesthetics, and community garden participation on fruit and vegetable consumption. American Journal of Public Health 101:1466–1473.

Litvak, E., N. S. Bijoor, and D. E. Pataki. 2014. Adding trees to irrigated turfgrass lawns may be a water-saving measure in semi-arid environments. Ecohydrology. 7(5):1314-1330.

Lizée, M.-H., J.-F. Mauffrey, T. Tatoni, and M. Deschamps-Cottin. 2011. Monitoring urban environments on the basis of biological traits. Ecological Indicators 11:353–361.

Lobell, D., G. Bala, A. Mirin, T. Phillips, R. Maxwell, and D. Rotman. 2009. Regional differences in the influence of irrigation on climate. Journal of Climate 22:2248–2255.

Loraine, G. A., and M. E. Pettigrove. 2006. Seasonal variations in concentrations of pharmaceuticals and personal care products in drinking water and reclaimed wastewater in southern California. Environmental Science and Technology 40:687–695.

Luck, G. W. 2007. A review of the relationships between human population density and biodiversity. Cambridge Philosophical Society 82:607–645.

Luck, M. A., G. D. Jenerette, J. Wu, and N. B. Grimm. 2001. The urban funnel model and the spatially heterogenous ecological footprint. Ecosystems 4:782–796.

Lund, H. 2003. Testing the claims of New Urbanism: Local access, pedestrian travel, and neighboring behaviors. Journal of the American Planning Association 69:414–429.

Lyytimaki, J., L. K. Peterson, B. Normander, and P. Bezak. 2008. Nature as a nuisance? Ecosystem services and disservices to urban lifestyle. Environmental Sciences 5:161–172.

Maco, S. E., and E. G. McPherson. 2003. A practical approach to assessing structure, function, and value of street tree populations in small communities. Journal of Arboriculture 29:84–97.

Maslow, A. H. 1943. A theory of human motivation. Psychological Review 50:370–396.

Matteson, K. C., J. S. Ascher, and G. A. Langellotto. 2008. Bee richness and abundance in New York City urban gardens. Annals of the Entomological Society of America 101:140–150.

McKinney, M. L. 2006. Urbanization as a major cause of biotic homogenization. Biological Conservation 127:247–260.

———. 2002. Do human activities raise species richness? Contrasting patterns in United States plants and fishes. Global Ecology and Biogeography 11:343–348.

McPherson, E. G. 2003. A benefit-cost analysis of ten street tree species in Modesto, California, U.S. Journal of Arboriculture 29:1–8.

———. 1996. Urban forest landscapes, how greenery saves greenbacks. Pages 27–29 in C. Wagner, editor. Annual Meeting Proceedings of the American Society of Landscape Architects. publisher? pub city/state?

McPherson, E. G., J. R. Simpson, P. F. Peper, S. E. Maco, and Q. Xiao. 2005. Municipal forest benefits and costs in five U.S. cities. Journal of Forestry 104:411–416.

Milder, J. C. 2007. A framework for understanding conservation development and its ecological implications. BioScience 57:757–768.

Minnich, R. A. 1983. Fire mosaics in southern California and northern Baja California. Science 219:1287–1294.

Morancho, A. B. 2003. A hedonic valuation of urban green areas. Landscape and Urban Planning 66:34–41.

Musacchio, L. R. 2009. The scientific basis for the design of landscape sustainability: A conceptual framework for translational landscape research and practice of designed landscapes and the six Es of landscape sustainability. Landscape Ecology 24:993–1013.

Nash, J. P., D. E. Kime, L. T. M. Van der Ven, P. W. Wester, F. Brion, G. Maack, P. Stahlschmidt-Allner, and C. R. Tyler. 2004. Long-term exposure to environmental concentrations of the pharmaceutical ethynylestradiol causes reproductive failure in fish. Environmental Health Perspectives 112:1725–1733.

Newman, P. W. G. 1999. Sustainability and cities: Extending the metabolism model. Landscape and Urban Planning 44:219–226.

Ngo, N. S., and D. E. Pataki. 2008. The energy and mass balance of Los Angeles County. Urban Ecosystems 11:121–139.

Nowak, D. J., D. E. Crane, and J. C. Stevens. 2006. Air pollution removal by urban trees and shrubs in the United States. Urban Forestry and Urban Greening 4:115–123.

O'Hara, J. K., and K. P. Georgakakos. 2008. Quantifying the urban water supply impacts of climate change. Water Resources Management 22:1477–1497.

Pataki, D. E., C. G. Boone, T. Hogue, G. D. Jenerette, J. P. McFadden, and S. Pincetl. 2011. Socio-ecohydrology and the urban water challenge. Ecohydrology 4:341–347.

Pataki, D. E., H. R. McCarthy, and E. Litvak. 2011. Transpiration of

urban forests in the Los Angeles metropolitan area. Ecological Applications 21:661–677.
Pataki, D. E., H. R. McCarthy, T. W. Gillespie, G. D. Jenerette, and S. Pincetl. 2013. A trait based ecology of the Los Angeles urban forest. Ecosphere. 4(6):art72.
Pataki, D. E., M. M. Carreiro, J. Cherrier, N. E. Grulke, V. Jennings, S. Pincetl, R. V. Pouyat, T. H. Whitlow, and W. C. Zipperer. 2011. Coupling biogeochemical cycles in urban environments: Ecosystem services, green solutions, and misconceptions. Frontiers in Ecology and the Environment 9:27–36.
Pataki, D. E., R. J. Alig, A. S. Fung, N. E. Golubiewski, C. A. Kennedy, E. G. McPherson, D. J. Nowak, R. V. Pouyat, and P. Romero Lankao. 2006. Urban ecosystems and the North American carbon cycle. Global Change Biology 12:2092–2102.
Pautasso, M., and M. L. McKinney. 2007. The botanist effect revisited: Plant species richness, county area, and human population size in the United States. Conservation Biology: The journal of the Society for Conservation Biology 21:1333–1340.
Pawelek, J.C., G. W. Frankie, R. W. Thorp, and M. Przybylski. 2009. Modification of a community garden to attract native bee pollinators in urban San Luis Obispo, California. Cities and the Environment 2(1): Article 7.
Pickett, S. T. A., M. L. Cadenasso, J. M. Grove, C. H. Nilon, R. V. Pouyat, W. C. Zipperer, and R. Costanza. 2001. Urban ecological systems: Linking terrestrial ecological, physical, and socioeconomic components of metropolitan areas. Annual Review of Ecology and Systematics 32:127–157.
Pickett, S. T. A., W. R. Burch, S. E. Dalton, and T. W. Foresman. 1997. Integrated urban ecosystem research. Urban Ecosystems 1:183–184.
Pincetl, S. 2010a. From the sanitary city to the sustainable city: Challenges to institutionalising biogenic ("nature's services") infrastructure. Local Environment 15:43–58.
———. 2010b. Implementing municipal tree planting: Los Angeles Million Tree Initiative. Environmental Management 45:227–238.
Pincetl, S., G. Franco, N. B. Grimm, T. Hogue, S. Hughes, E. R. Pardyjak, A. M. Kinoshita, and P. Jantz. 2013. Urban areas. Pages 4(6):art72 in G. Garfin, A. Jardine, R. Merideth, M. Black, and S. LeRoy, editors. Assessment of the climate change in the southwest United States: A report prepared for the National Climate Assessment. Island Press, Washington, D.C.
Pincetl, S., P. Bunje, and T. Holmes. 2012. An expanded urban metabolism method: Toward a systems approach for assessing urban energy processes and causes. Landscape and Urban Planning 107:193–202.
Pincetl, S., S. Prabhu, T. W. Gillespie, G. D. Jenerette, and D. E. Pataki. 2013. Evolution of tree nursery offerings and the cultivated urban forest of Los Angeles. Landscape and Urban Planning. 118:10–17.
Pouyat, R. V., I. D. Yesilonis, and D. J. Nowak. 2006. Carbon storage by urban soils in the United States. Journal of Environmental Quality 35:1566–1575.
Raciti, S. M., L. Hutyra, and A. C. Finzi. 2012. Depleted soil carbon and nitrogen pools beneath impervious surfaces. Environmental Pollution 164:248–251.
Raciti, S. M., P. M. Groffman, and T. J. Fahey. 2008. Nitrogen retention in urban lawns and forests. Ecological Applications 18:1615–1626.
Rao, L. E., E. B. Allen, and T. Meixner. 2010. Risk-based determination of critical nitrogen deposition loads for fire spread in southern California deserts. Ecological Applications 20:1320–1335.
Regan, H. M., J. B. Crookston, R. Swab, J. Franklin, and D. M. Lawson. 2010. Habitat fragmentation and altered fire regime create trade-offs for an obligate seeding shrub. Ecology 91: 1114-1123.
Rudd, H., J. Vala, and V. Schaefer. 2002. Importance of backyard habitat in a comprehensive biodiversity conservation strategy: A connectivity analysis of urban green spaces. Restoration Ecology 10:368–375.
Rundel, P. W., and J. R. Gustafson. 2005. Introduction to the plant life of southern California: Coast to foothills. University of California Press, Berkeley, California.
Santos, L. H. M. L. M., A. N. Araújo, A. Fachini, A. Pena, C. Delerue-Matos, andM. C. B. S. M. Montenegro. 2010. Ecotoxicological aspects related to the presence of pharmaceuticals in the aquatic environment. Journal of Hazardous Materials 175:45–95.
Schoenherr, A. A. 1995. A natural history of California. University of California Press, Berkeley, California.
Schwartz, M. W., J. H. Thorne, and J. H. Viers. 2006. Biotic homogenization of the California flora in urban and urbanizing regions. Biological Conservation 127:282–291.
Selby, W. A. 2012. Rediscovering the Golden State: California geography. Third edition. Wiley. Hoboken, NJ.
Sickman, J. O., M. J. Zanoli, and H. L. Mann. 2007. Effects of urbanization on organic carbon loads in the Sacramento River, California. Water Air and Soil Pollution 43.
Smit, J., and J. Nasr. 1992. Urban agriculture for sustainable cities: Using wastes and idle land and water bodies as resources. Environment and Urbanization 4:141–152.
Stein, E. D., J. S. Brown, T. S. Hogue, M. P. Burke, and A. Kinoshita. 2012. Stormwater contaminant loading following southern California wildfires. Environmental Toxicology and Chemistry 31:2625–2638.
Steiner, A. L., S. Tonse, R. C. Cohen, A. H. Goldstein, and R. A. Harley. 2006. Influence of future climate and emissions on regional air quality in California. Journal of Geophysical Research: Atmospheres 111.
Stokstad, E. 2012. Dread citrus disease turns up in California, Texas. Science 336:367–367.
Suarez, A. V., D. T. Bolger, and T. J. Case. 1998. Effects of fragmentation and invasion on native ant communities in coastal southern California. Ecology 79:2041–2056.
Syphard, A. D., J. E. Keeley, A. B. Massada, T. J. Brennan, and V. C. Radeloff. 2012. Housing arrangement and location determine the likelihood of housing loss due to wildfire. PLoS One 7:e33954.
Taha, H. 1997. Modeling the impacts of large-scale albedo changes on ozone air quality in the South Coast Air Basin. Atmospheric Environment 31:1667–1676.
Tanaka, S. K., T. Zhu, J. R. Lund, R. E. Howitt, M. W. Jenkins, M. A. Pulido, M. Tauber, R. S. Ritzema, and I. C. Ferreira. 2006. Climate warming and water management adaptation for California. Climatic Change 76:361–387.
Thompson, K., and A. Jones. 1999. Human population density and prediction of local plant extinction in Britain. Conservation Biology 13:185–189.
Townsend-Small, A., and C. I. Czimczik. 2010. Carbon sequestration and greenhouse gas emissions in urban turf. Geophysical Research Letters 37.
Tyrväinen, L. 1997. The amenity value of the urban forest: An application of the hedonic pricing method. Landscape and Urban Planning 37:211–222.
Tzoulas, K., K. Korpela, S. Venn, V. Yli-Pelkonen, A. KaÅºmierczak, J. Niemela, and P. James. 2007. Promoting ecosystem and human health in urban areas using Green Infrastructure: A literature review. Landscape and Urban Planning 81:167–178.
Vallano, D. M., P. C. Selmants, and E. S. Zavaleta. 2012. Simulated nitrogen deposition enhances the performance of an exotic grass relative to native serpentine grassland competitors. Plant Ecology 213:1015–1026.
Vourlitis, G. L., and S. C. Pasquini. 2009. Experimental dry-season N deposition alters species composition in southern Californian Mediterranean-type shrublands. Ecology 90:2183–2189.
Wackernagel, M., and W. E. Rees. 1996. Our ecological footprint: Reducing human impact on the earth. New Society Publishers, Gabriola Island, British Columbia, Canada.
Wackernagel, M., L. Onisto, P. Bello, A. C. Linares, I. S. L. Falfan, J. M. Garcia, A. I. S. Guerrero, and M. G. S. Guerrero. 1999. National natural capital accounting with the ecological footprint concept. Ecological Economics 29:375–390.
Wolman, A. 1965. The metabolism of cities. Scientific American 213:179–190.
Wu, J. 2013. Landscape sustainability science: Ecosystem services and human well-being in changing landscapes. Landscape Ecology 28:999–1023.

PART SIX

POLICY AND STEWARDSHIP

FORTY

Land Use Regulation for Resource Conservation

STEPHANIE PINCETL, TERRY WATT, and MARIA J. SANTOS

Introduction

Over the past 150 years a great deal of California's most scenic landscapes has been conserved because of California's exceptional biodiversity. In this chapter we review the history of land conservation in California from a land use and governance perspective. We first introduce some key concepts in land use planning relevant to California, then we review and describe the historical process of conservation land acquisition and land use policies. Finally, we explain how and why land use regulations, fiscal constraints, and regulatory requirements today create a complex terrain for future land conservation. One important factor is that with urbanization, ecosystems that were once isolated are now close to the state's cities (See Chapter 5, "Population and Land Use").

These lands are the new frontier for conservation efforts but also face unprecedented, unmet challenges such as those likely posed by climate change. New legislative and funding tools are emerging for protection, as we explain below, but a legacy of structural constraints remains in place. Surely, better land use is at the heart of conservation of the state's magnificent heritage. In the end conservation rests upon political will and the support of the state's residents. The state legislature will have to restructure the state's taxation system and the way in which private property rights are interpreted and will need to create new governmental regulations that ensure the state's social and ecological resilience to climate change. This will require a change in land development patterns and fundamentally in the way California's residents live on the land.

Key Concepts in Land Use Planning

Regulations

Federal, state, and local regulations all affect California's ecosystems and land uses. Regulations are rules adopted to implement legislation passed by elected officials to guide public policies. These regulations can be prescriptive (for example, stipulating that houses cannot be built on flood plains) or procedural (for instance, requiring one to conduct an environmental impact statement before a decision can be made). Other legislative activities, such as establishing taxation rates, also are significant as they constrain or enable activities by governments and influence private behavior. Taxation rates influence financial resource availability: fewer resources are available when tax rates are low, and more are available when tax revenues are higher. All of these are important factors in shaping natural resource conservation policies and outcomes in California.

Land Use Planning

Land use planning stems from the need to plan for competing interests for land: land for housing, roads, commercial establishments, and schools as well as for the conservation of ecosystems, public open space, water, and other resources and values. Today, this competition takes place over privately held land. For greater conservation to occur, more land must be set aside from other uses; more often than not, this requires its purchase. This task is generally undertaken by a governmental entity, as private entities generally do not take on long-term conservation landownership and management as they typically lack the institutional infrastructure or funding to do so. The obligation to protect endangered fauna and flora imposed by the 1973 ENDANGERED SPECIES ACT (ESA) has added another dimension to local land use planning that must be balanced with the protection of private property rights, requiring new strategies and approaches to land use planning and financing for conservation land acquisition.

As for any land purchased by government, the Fifth Amendment of the U.S. Constitution ensures that private landowners are compensated fairly by the governmental entity in question. Government is constitutionally authorized to regulate land use, known as its POLICE POWER. It can, for example, through land use zoning, prevent building in flood zones. Zoning is how land use is designated, and in California this power is in the hands of city and county elected officials. Land use designations include residential, industrial, commercial, institutional, open space (i.e., undeveloped land), and so forth. Land use designations change over time reflecting public opinion, pressures for urbanization, the need for additional tax revenues, and various other conditions because land uses generate value including tax revenues. The development potential of near-urban lands with conservation value makes them more expensive to purchase than distant rural lands as the former's price reflects the potential for urban uses.

Management of Public Lands

Congress recognized the value of public lands, declaring that they should remain in public ownership. However, federal lands in public ownership are managed by different laws depending on the land type and jurisdictional management. Most are managed by ORGANIC ACTS that allow for multiple uses and for the most part do not recognize conservation as an exclusive use. This means there can be hiking, hunting, logging, grazing, mining, or other uses allowed. Lands with designations such as Wilderness or National Park allow no extractive uses—only recreation such as hiking and camping. The U.S. Forest Service (USFS) is subject to the NATIONAL FOREST MANAGEMENT ACT (NFMA) and the MULTIPLE USE SUSTAINED YIELD ACT (MUSYA). Bureau of Land Management (BLM) lands are commissioned in FEDERAL LAND POLICY AND MANAGEMENT ACT (FLPMA) (Pub. L. 94-579)—the least restrictive in terms of uses—to allow a variety of uses on the agency's land while simultaneously trying to preserve their natural resources. This concept is best summarized by the term MULTIPLE-USE, defined in MUSYA as "management of the public lands and their various resource values so that they are utilized in the combination that will best meet the present and future needs of the American people." As a result, much of these public lands have a myriad of uses including large-scale renewable energy facilities, transmission, roads, and recreation including parks and off-road vehicles.

Land Use Planning Regulation in California

State planning law requires that local General Plans contain seven mandatory topical elements and meet other statutory criteria, which were added throughout the years. The elements include: noise, land use, circulation, conservation, safety, open space, and housing. Mandatory elements of a General Plan can be broken into two categories with some overlaps: the built environment (land use, housing, noise, and infrastructure) and the natural environment (open space and conservation). All elements of a General Plan are considered equal and must comprise an integrated, internally consistent statement of policies (Government Code Section 65300.5). The housing element, however, is the only element required to be updated, reviewed, and *certified* by the CALIFORNIA STATE OFFICE OF PLANNING AND RESEARCH (OPR). In some respects, the housing element has been elevated above other elements of the General Plan as California has experienced high levels of population growth through the early 2000s and suffered from insufficient affordable housing for its inhabitants. Cities may not deny or conditionally approve certain housing projects in a manner that renders the project infeasible without making efforts to curb discriminatory practices. (This requirement is often violated in practice). No similar certification exists for other land use actions otherwise consistent with the General Plan.

The core natural environment components of a General Plan include the open space and conservation elements, which must together plan for the comprehensive and long-term conservation of open space and resource-providing lands. However, even though state law mandates ambitious and detailed planning efforts for open space, including an action program that the local government intends to pursue, the majority of elements developed by cities have increasingly shied away from mapping "proposed" parks and open space on private lands. Thus we see a trend away from a commitment to parks and open space. This is likely due to fear of lawsuits following *Nollan vs. California Coastal Commission* (483 U.S. 825). In essence, for a local government to require public access to public land from a landowner (for example, access to the beach or zoning of private land for open space), the Court requires the demonstration of a clear relationship between the regulation and the resulting access or use.

In 1987 the Court determined there must be a logical relationship between the negative impact of the project and the need for a public easement across the owner's property (a nexus). In the *Nollan* case, the Court rejected the requirement of an easement along the beach in southern California because it was not related to restoration of the view from the road—a type of access—and constituted a governmental TAK-

Photo on previous page: The urban-wildland interface in Solano County, California. Photo: Larry Ford.

ING of private property rights. This has had a strong effect on local government's willingness to plan for the zoning of private lands for open space, even when those lands are not currently adjacent to urbanized areas. The Court was concerned with the protection of private property interests under the Fifth Amendment of the U.S. Constitution. *Nollan vs. California Coastal Commission*, however, also had a significant chilling effect, as local governments have now shied away from even designating lands for future parks and open space, or preservation, for fear of landowner lawsuits. Local governments also expressed concerns about designating lands as open space, as designation could preclude the ability of these lands to be developed and thus generate future tax revenues. This marks a change in political culture away from government regulation and towards more "voluntary" approaches, such as one in which property owners themselves enter into agreements to preserve public access or to refrain from developing their lands in exchange for property tax relief or other tax relief. Such agreements can actually then be part of the property deed in perpetuity (Crew 1990).

This brief overview of land use planning in California already hints at the paradox that the state faces: to be able to create revenue for land purchases, cities or regional governments must grow; in turn, this quest for growth limits the land available for conservation. In the next section we describe and illustrate the historical process of conservation land acquisition. We then describe the evolution of land use policies in the state and their current status and assess whether they will be able to meet the challenges ahead.

History of Conservation Land Acquisition

Conservation of California's remarkable natural resources was under way by the later decades of the nineteenth century. After the American Revolution, the U.S. federal government inherited all lands west of the Alleghenies with its new territories. It established a policy of selling and distributing these lands through many public land distribution acts (including the HOMESTEAD ACT 1862). By the mid-nineteenth century, much land had shifted to private ownership, but mountains and desert lands often remained undesired by the public. A movement to protect some of these lands arose, and in 1864 Yosemite Valley and the Mariposa Grove of Giant Sequoia trees were protected by Abraham Lincoln, with a grant of 8,100 hectares of federal land to the state of California. Yosemite Valley protection was the first example of the president withdrawing lands of exceptional beauty from the possibility of sale to the public, and the same mechanism was used to reserve National Forests for conservation purposes. At this time, many of the nation's forests had been purchased by private companies and logged. Fear of timber shortages over time, as well as a growing understanding of forests' importance for watershed functioning, led to presidential acts to reserve remaining forests in public ownership, especially in the western states. Much of California's early conserved land became the backbone of the lands of the National Park Service and the National Forest Service.

California is arguably the state that led the implementation of the concept of resource reserves beginning in the nineteenth century (Barton 2000). Californians lobbied Congress and the president about the public interest in the public lands: that they should be conserved, not sold. The San Gabriel and San Bernardino Forest reserves, for example, were created from the public domain in 1892 and 1893, respectively, by President Harrison for their watershed function. California is the birthplace of the Sierra Club (1892) and the Sempervirens Fund (1900), aimed at preserving redwood forests. Without question, interest in protecting the state's scenic beauty has been important for nearly a century and a half. Local organization actions are exemplified by the early acquisition of remaining redwood forests in Santa Cruz County—Big Basin State Park—in 1902 by the Sempervirens Fund, whose ownership was then transferred to the State Parks Commission (see Chapter 26, "Coast Redwood Forests"). State interest in land conservation was reflected in 1927 by the then recently created State Parks Commission, which instructed Frederick Law Olmsted Jr. "to make a survey to determine what lands are suitable and desirable for the ultimate development of a comprehensive, well-balanced state park system, and to define the relation of such a system to other means of conserving and utilizing the scenic and recreational resources of the state" (Olmsted 1929). The resulting survey set the vision for the creation of the state parks system.

California is not only one of the most biodiverse areas in the United States, it is one of the most biodiverse regions on Earth (Brooks et al. 2002; see Chapter 11, "Biodiversity"). Today, 25% to over 40% of California land is designated as OPEN SPACE depending on the definition used thereof (see Box Figure 1a). Open Space corresponds broadly to "lands protected through fee title ownership (absolute ownership) by a public agency or non-profit land conservation organization" (GreenInfo Network 2013). Open Space includes a wide array of property types, from city parks to National Parks, Bureau of Land Management (BLM) lands used for recreation and resource extraction, and Department of Defense lands. However, Open Space does not include private land in CONSERVATION EASEMENTS. A conservation easement is an agreement by a property owner to maintain his or her land in private open space—no development will occur—in exchange for a tax rebate on that property. Conservation easements can have a time limit, after which they must be renewed or not. They are permanently tied to the title to the land and inhere at the sale of a property. Arriving at a definitive estimate of conserved land area is not easy as there are many types of land conservation in the state, including those just described as well as contracts under the Williamson Act (that can be exited after ten years) to keep agricultural lands in agriculture.

Large tracts of land were set aside from the remaining public domain at the turn of the twentieth century. After that, additional park land had to be acquired (mostly by federal agencies) from the remaining, privately owned open space (see Box Figure 1a–b). This is the process we describe below—the evolution of land use policies, their land development implications, and the revenue streams for conservation land acquisition.

Geographically, early land conservation focused on mountain regions, mostly in the central and southern Sierras and in the mountains surrounding Los Angeles (see Box Figure 1a). Land set-asides and early acquisitions then expanded to the northern California mountain ranges until the 1920s (see Box Figures 1a and 4). In the 1930s, California State Parks took the lead on land acquisition for additional parks. In the 1940s, funded by the recently formed State Park system, large tracts in southern California were purchased; this pattern continued into the 1950s. These acquisitions were also greatly aided by regulations passed by the state legislature in the 1940s

(continued on page 906)

BOX 40.1 RECONSTRUCTING CALIFORNIA'S LAND CONSERVATION HISTORY

Maria J. Santos

Today, fully one quarter of all land in California is protected in some form or another, but our knowledge of how this came to be is fragmentary. In 1864, Abraham Lincoln granted approximately 8,100 hectares (20,000 acres) of land to the State of California—land that would become Yosemite National Park and the Mariposa Big Tree Grove (Barton 2000). In the 1880s the state made initial steps to impose limits on the logging of its redwood forests. In the 1930s, U.S. Forest Service scientist Albert Wieslander painstakingly documented California forest resources (Wieslander 1935). Urban sprawl in the latter half of the twentieth century prompted communities to secure Open Space amenities close to residential areas (Pincetl 2004). All of these seemingly disparate actions have, in concert with hundreds of other actions over the past century and a half, shaped the current conservation network in the state.

Since conservation decisions are intrinsically a human decision-making process, the likely future behavior of a human society is strongly tied with its past (Szabó and Hédl 2011). Unprecedented rates of change in land cover and climate over the past century challenge the ability of conservation networks to conserve biodiversity, among other goals. The timing of historic land acquisitions may have had an effect on whether conservation goals as currently defined have been met (Meir et al. 2004). The timing of conservation acquisitions may be a function of multiple factors, such as delays linked to requests for more information, the inherent dynamics of natural systems, and insufficient traction (funding, policies, etc.), among others (Czech 2004, Grantham et al. 2010, Knight et al. 2008). I thus took a step back to reconstruct the conservation land acquisition history of California and to assess the contribution of land additions at different time periods to the overall conservation network of the state.

Conservation history describes the processes that created today's parks, preserves, and refuges. It entails both a spatial and temporal depiction of conservation activities, implementation, and achievement. Once constructed, this history can point to past successes and shortcomings, aiding future conservation efforts. Many parks or Open Spaces have documented who inspired their acquisition, the steps towards their establishment, and the observed changes in them over time—but this knowledge is not scalable to a region, state, or country. A sober appraisal of past efforts can galvanize future action, yet much work on the topic remains to be done.

As a potentially emerging field, conservation history aims at linking historical ecology and environmental history. Historical ecology answers ecological questions using historical data, while environmental history looks into the effects of human presence on the environment they experience and modify. By their integration we can benefit from the quantitative perspective added by historical ecology (here narrowed to historical conservation biology) and the qualitative and legacy perspective from environmental history. Conservation decisions are more often than not a political decision, and thus the integration of both fields is only a necessary requirement to be able to assess the success of conservation. We know that conservation success is geographically and temporally concentrated in HOTSPOTS (Brooks et al. 2002) and HOTTIMES (Radeloff et al. 2013).

The process of reconstructing the state conservation history involved three steps: the spatial location of the Open Space properties, attribution of the time of acquisition and establishment, and data quality control and assessment. Open Space corresponds to "lands protected through fee title ownership by a public agency or nonprofit land conservation organization" (GreenInfo Network 2013). Below I describe the process and data sets used for such reconstruction and the resulting outputs.

Over fifty thousand Open Space parcels exist in California. They are managed by over eight hundred agencies with varied archival structures. The development of geospatial data for all Open Spaces in the state has been a large effort lead by the GreenInfo Network, and it is now systematized in the California Protected Area Database (CPAD) (GreenInfo Network 2013). CPAD is a GIS inventory of all fee-protected Open Space properties in California assembled by collating and curating data from management agencies. Open Space management agencies retain FEE TITLE OWNERSHIP—that is, property rights over the land designated as Open Space. I selected this database rather than the World Protected Areas database (IUCN and UNEP-WCMC 2013) because the former has a more comprehensive representation of the Open Space properties in California. It includes properties that range from city parks to national parks, thus it is likely to better reflect the state's conservation history. However, this database does not include attributes that describe the acquisition and establishment dates of every Open Space property in the state.

To complement this information gap, my research team and I obtained from the federal and state agencies and nongovernmental organizations that manage Open Space properties data on acquisition date (when the fee title was purchased) and establishment date (when the property was open to the public). After one year of contacting agencies, we got an enormous amount of data. We retrieved information on acquisition date for a total of 35,807 properties (67%), corresponding to 110,300 square kilometers (98.85%) of the state's Open Space (Figure 1a–b). Merced, Orange, San Joaquin, Stanislaus, and Sutter Counties were harder to collect information from (dates were acquired for ca. 70% of their Open Space area). To complement this data gap, in collaboration with GreenInfo Network, we developed an online crowdsourcing platform for data collection, launched

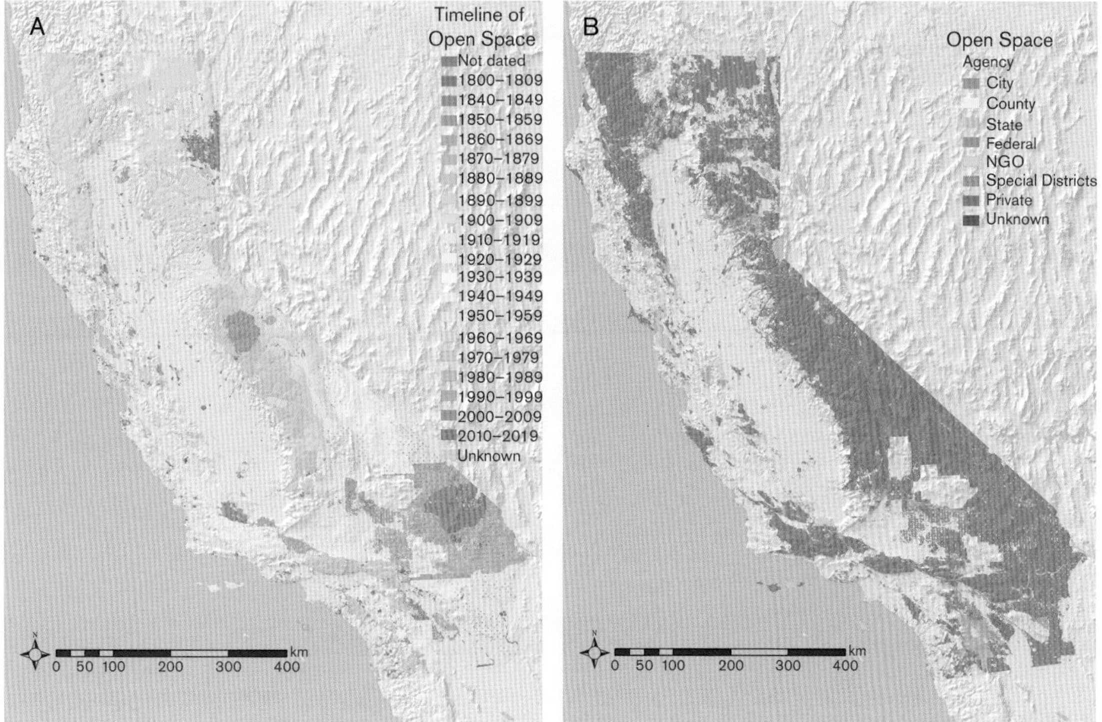

BOX 40.1 FIGURE 1 Timeline of Open Space acquisition and establishment in California over the past 150 years: (A) timeline of California current Open Space extent; and (B) Open Space land ownership/management responsibility, with governance types represented by different colors (city, special district, county, state, federal, nongovernmental organization [NGO], private, and unknown).

in mid-2013. It is geared to harvest the knowledge of the public on the dates and history of each Open Space property (http://www.mapsportal.org/mapcollab_dates/). I used only data from the management agencies to construct the mapped history herein, amounting to 99% of the area of Open Space in the state.

Sixteen thousand Open Space properties were acquired in California throughout the past 150 years as 53,337 parcels. These properties cover a quarter of the state's area (112,156 square kilometers). The first hotspots of California conservation history were the mountains, followed by the southern coast and finally the deserts. The first hotspot of conservation also corresponds to the first hottime for conservation, which occurred at the turn of the twentieth century. However, throughout the twentieth century, hotspots and hottimes were not matched. During this time, hottimes in 1930s and 1970s corresponded to acquisition of land in many parts of the state but not in particular areas of the state (see Figure 1a–b). The hotspots and hottimes of conservation are a result of the push and pull of pro-development and pro-conservation policies and action in the state's history, as described elsewhere in this chapter (see Table 40.2).

The growth of the conservation land networks in the state's first most populous counties varied among locations. The early, most populous counties include Los Angeles, San Diego, San Francisco, Alameda, San Mateo, Santa Clara, and Sacramento (Figure 2a–g, Figure 3). While the counties vary in their area and proportion of Open Space (see Table 40.1), the earliest acquisitions occurred in the county of San Francisco with the reservation of the Presidio first by the Department of Defense and then with fee ownership transferred to Golden Gate Park (Figure 2c). Temporal Open Space acquisition patterns differ across locations, with (1) a stepwise pattern of acquisition in southern counties of Los Angeles and San Diego, (2) a steady acquisition rate for San Francisco, and (3) a very fast and more recent acquisition rate for other Bay Area counties and Sacramento (Figure 2a–g, Figure 3). Despite these differing patterns, northern and southern California counties have similar proportions of Open Space land. While the southern coast of California was a hotspot of land conservation, its acquisition was phased, with an earlier history of less conservation followed by more recent acquisitions and the parallel development of systematic plans for biodiversity and their natural habitats. Today, counties like San Diego are leading the state in the development of Habitat Conservation Plans (HCPs) and Natural Community Conservation Plans (NCCPs). The outcomes of such experimentation with scientifically sound plans are commendable, but these actions are still of voluntary nature. They also unfold gradually; some of these HCPs and NCCPs took over ten years just in the planning phase.

The hotspots and hottimes of land conservation in the

(continued)

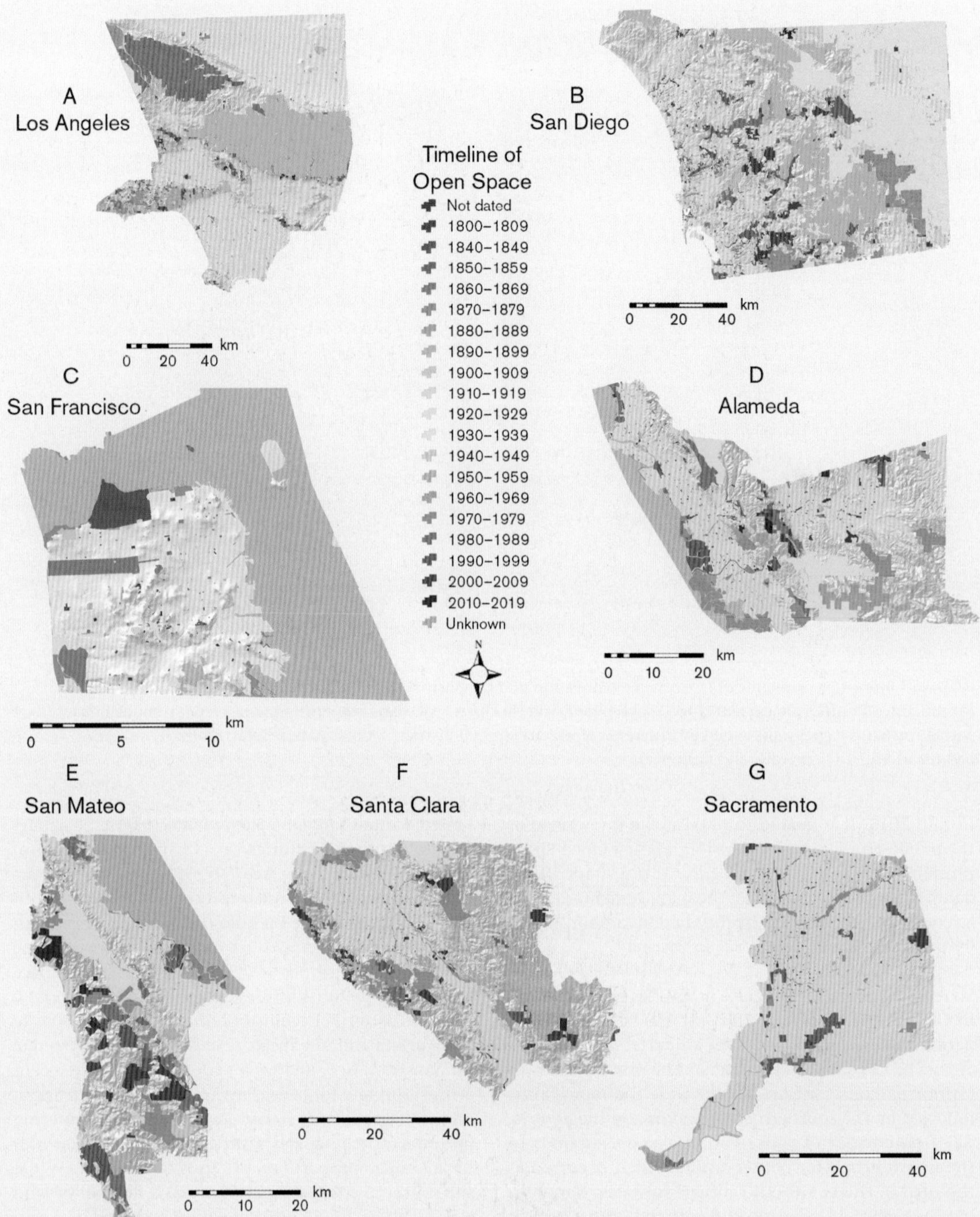

BOX 40.1 FIGURE 2 Timeline of conservation land acquisition in the most populous counties. Light blue areas indicate water. Sources: Santos et al. 2014a and 2014b.

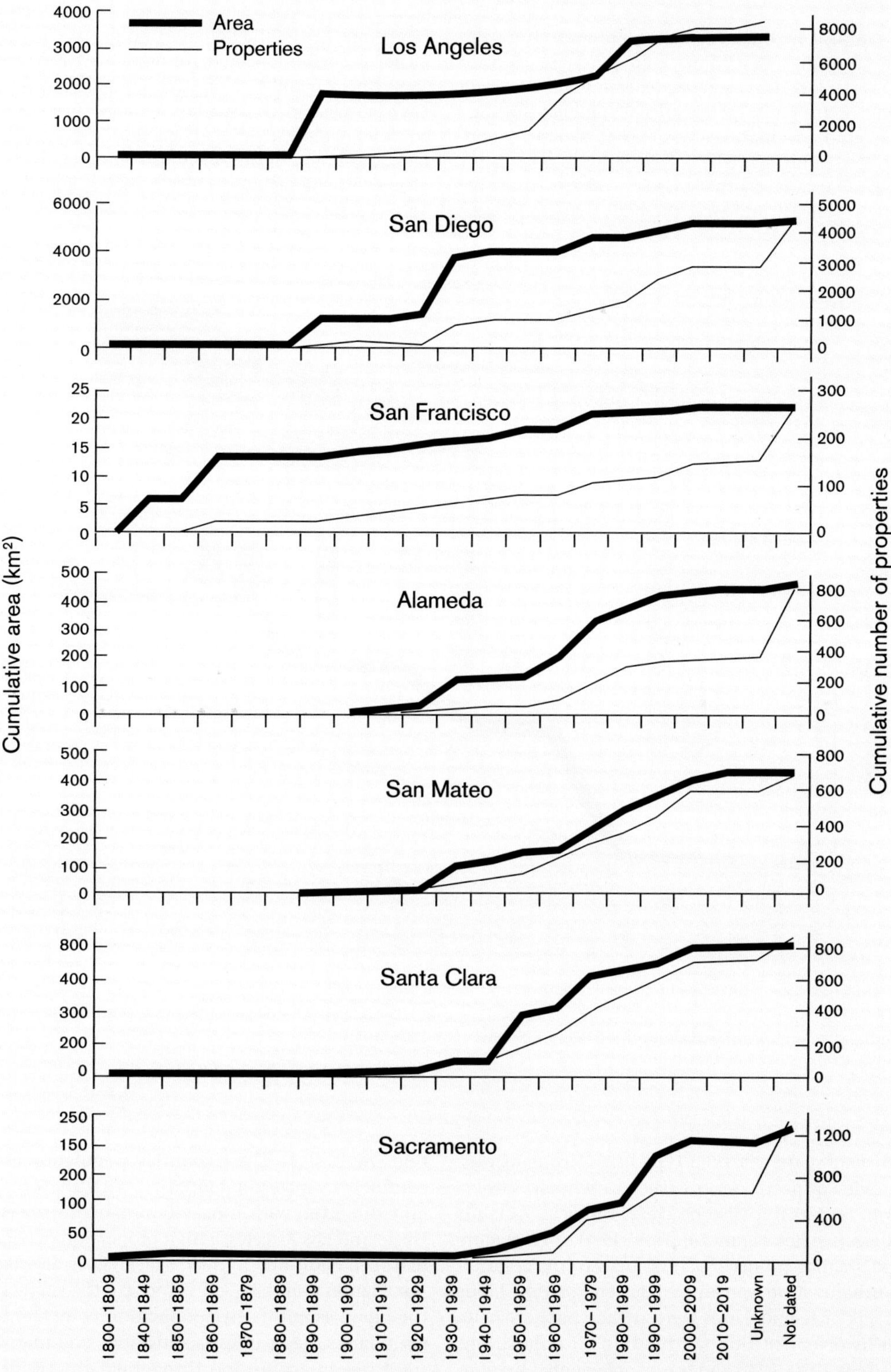

BOX 40.1 FIGURE 3 Timeline of area and number of parcels conserved for the most populous counties as of 1910. The thick line represents the cumulative area in Open Space acquired. The fine line is the cumulative number of parcels acquired. Source: Santos et al. 2014a.

(continued)

(continued)

state can also be linked with the presence of governance structures that allow land purchase. Governance is the level (for example, federal, state, city, etc.) within which a given agency operates and has jurisdiction. Not all governance levels existed a century and a half ago (Figure 4). Federal agencies were one of the few governance levels that existed at the turn of the twentieth century and were the ones that could take land from the public domain into private ownership. Other agencies appeared through the history of the state with a mandate to acquire land for conservation. For example, "special districts" emerged in the 1940s as a result of political victories over pro-development policies. Regulation in the 1970s also required Open Space elements to be included in land use General Plans (see Table 40.2).

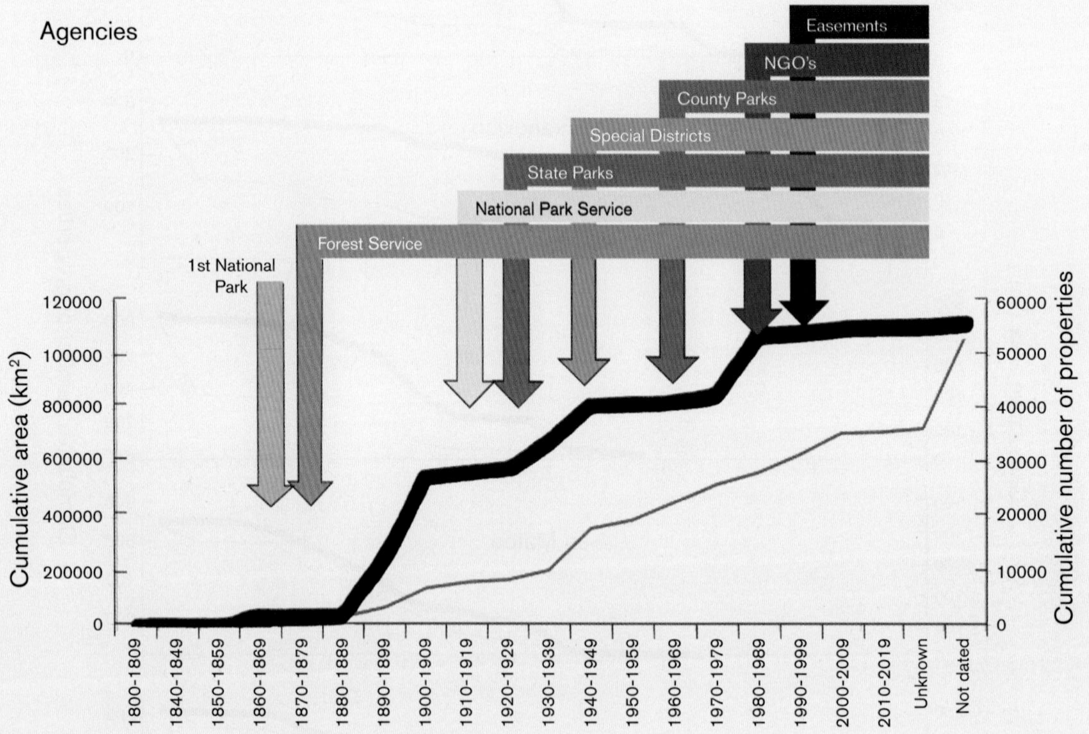

BOX 40.1 FIGURE 4 Timeline of California conservation land acquisition and dates in which natural resource management agencies were created. The broad colored line represents the cumulative area in Open Space acquired. The fine gray line is the cumulative number of parcels acquired. Source: Santos et al. 2014a.

that allowed SPECIAL DISTRICTS (a type of government unit formed to provide a specific service, such as schools, sewers, street lighting, or parks) to also be created to acquire lands for conservation (see Box Figure 5a). From 1950 to 1980 more scattered and smaller properties filled in the conservation network as urbanization spread to adjacent private lands and larger tracts of remote lands were already publicly held. High federal involvement through funding for acquisitions occurred again in 1970–1990 and was supplemented by nonprofit organizations' land acquisitions (see Box Figure 5b). From the 1980s to today large tracts of desert lands have been acquired that had not been considered valuable until then (see Box Figure 1a–b).

While a great deal of land has been protected and kept or placed in the public domain, ecosystem losses continue as urbanization encroaches onto unprotected private lands. The most populous counties in 1910 showed very different processes and proportions of conservation land acquisition (Table 40.1). These counties' population is today mostly confined to incorporated cities, with the exception of Sacramento. Even within heavily urbanizing areas, such as San Diego and Los Angeles, a high proportion of county land area has been dedicated to open space via a stepwise process (see Box Figures 2 and 3). San Francisco, the smallest county and the one with all its city population coincident with county boundaries, had earliest acquisitions and maintained a constant rate of acquisition throughout the twentieth century. San Francisco is also geographically bounded, and conservation options are limited. It is in this part of California—the Bay Area—that the first ideas for regional planning were implemented. Alameda, San Mateo, and Santa Clara showed a peak of conservation land acquisition in 1950s.

While California's policies lead the nation in ecosystem conservation, they are inadequate to meet future challenges such as climate change and potential urban growth. This is because regulation in California is piecemeal, fragmented,

Prior to this time, General Plans could voluntarily include Open Space elements, but only in the 1970s did this requirement become mandatory. This created a way for the state to supervise development planning (which remains within the jurisdiction of the cities) and to be able to force the protection of natural resources at a state level. Finally, some of these governance levels appeared as a reaction to legislation such as Proposition 13, which affected the way funds were gathered for conservation land acquisition. Prior to Proposition 13, a part of development fees were set aside for land acquisition by special districts or other agencies. Proposition 13 altered the redistribution of development fees, greatly reducing the amount directed to conservation land acquisition. A supermajority vote was also included in the legislation, which requires a two-thirds' vote in favor to change tax funds distribution. To respond to these decreases in development funds directed towards conservation land acquisition, an increase in land purchases by nongovernmental organizations took place (Figure 5a, b). Later legislation enabled conservation easements. These were innovations towards the maintenance of land as Open Space and the acquisition of its fee title at a time when conservation science was already advocating strategic planning. These forces led to complementary acquisitions of ecosystems that were yet to be included in the conservation lands network. For example, in the San Francisco Bay Area nonprofit organizations (NGOs), special districts, cities, and counties focused on grasslands, and federal agencies focused on coastal salt marsh, while all agencies acquired large extents of agricultural land.

From this quick exploration of the state's conservation history, it can be argued that a great deal of the state's most spectacular and biodiverse areas have been conserved. Some of them were protected as early as the late nineteenth century, and early ideas from California about land conservation have been exported to varying extents to other parts of the state, nation, and world.

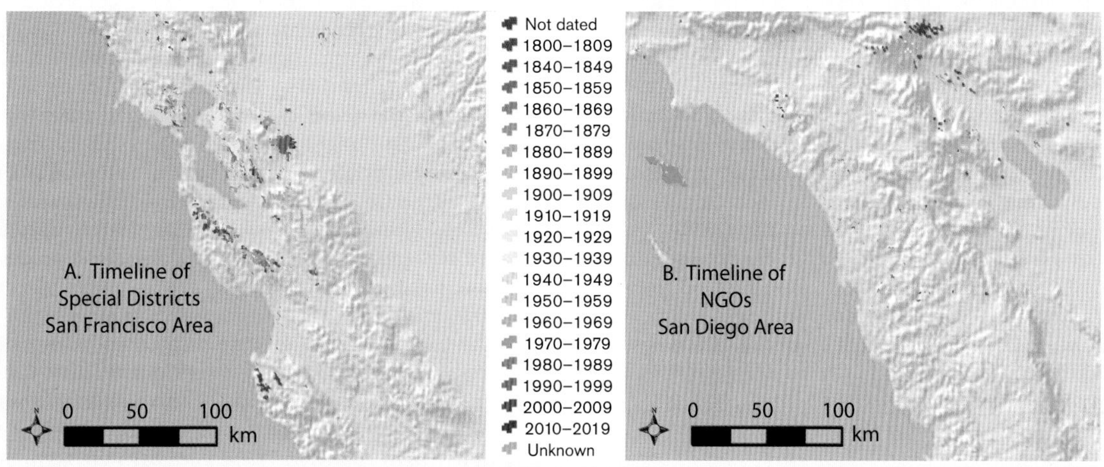

BOX 40.1 FIGURE 5 Timeline of special districts in the San Francisco (A) area and nongovernmental organizations in the San Diego (B) area. Source: Santos et al. 2014a.

and often too weak. There are, as we explain in this chapter, deep conflicting interests in funding allocation and priorities in the state. The following discussion reviews resource conservation issues in the state, the history of urban growth and land use regulation since the postwar period, and the rise and evolution of targeted conservation tools since the 1990s. The chapter addresses continued and new conservation challenges and innovative ideas and tools for conservation that emerge from the state's history of land use planning and attempts to best preserve the state's natural heritage.

Evolution of Land Use Planning and Policy in California

Land use (and its planning) is at the heart of conservation of California's magnificent heritage. As introduced earlier, land use planning stems from the need to plan for the competing interests for land. For greater conservation to occur into the future, more land must be set aside from other uses; more often than not, this requires its purchase. Next we review the historical process through which that came to be the case. We start with the Progressive Era (pre-1940s) when pro-development policies, such as the attribution of land use regulatory power to local entities, created the building blocks of California's land use policy and established a legacy carried on until the twenty-first century. We then review the attempts to regulate urban growth when the boom of post–World War II, pro-growth policies began to be contested as impacts of local land use and planning "power" led to suburban expansion onto agricultural lands, creating inefficient and often segregated urban land use patterns.

By the late 1970s a major change in revenue policies for local governments greatly affected their fiscal capacity, threatening the future of conservation land acquisition and adding a contradictory tension. While urban growth was

TABLE 40.1
Open space area in urban California counties

County	County area (km²)	Open space area (km²)	Area of county in open space (%)
San Diego	10,973.57	5,286.147	48.17
Los Angeles	10,242.41	3,375.847	32.96
San Mateo	1,430.55	435.12	30.42
Santa Clara	3,378.21	811.63	24.03
Alameda	2,126.87	469.39	22.07
Sacramento	2,580.21	225.94	8.76
San Francisco	277.02	22.12	7.98

SOURCE: Santos et al. 2014a.

contested, a citizen-passed ballot initiative, Proposition 13, greatly decreased the property tax rate. This dramatically reduced city budgets and pushed land use zoning choices by cities and counties away from housing toward sales tax–generating land uses. Today the property tax rate can only be changed by a supermajority vote, which means that at least two-thirds of the state population would have to approve the change. This has led to innovative solutions to raise funds for conservation land acquisition. A diversification of the portfolio of funding streams has occurred, including the participation of nongovernmental organizations (NGOs) and use of private philanthropic funds. Newer funding streams are also coming from impact MITIGATION BANKS and from CARBON CREDITS, but these are just emerging and little is known about how effective they will be. This history of land use policies and their cascading effects sets the stage for where California is today (Table 40.2).

Progressive Era Legacy: Pre-1940s

A century-long series of efforts has occurred to create effective institutions to help guide metropolitan growth and development in California (Schrag 1998, Pincetl 1999b, Barbour 2002). Such institutions were proposed to operate at a regional or metropolitan scale, regulating where development could occur, infrastructure (like roads) would be built, and so forth. However, metropolitan-level approaches were pursued early and then consistently rejected in favor of local jurisdictional independence for cities and counties. Beginning in 1914, state legislation authorized charter cities to make and enforce all laws and regulations pertaining to municipal affairs, city-by-city and county-by-county (Silva and Barbour 1999), meaning that the state government could not tell cities what to do. Charter cities are cities that have developed a kind of constitution (a charter) that details its governmental arrangements, including the types of agencies and departments of the city, their roles, the role of the mayor, whether the mayor is elected or appointed, and other rules. Cities and counties have the authority to institute local control over land use, developing individual land use plans, zoning regulations, and so forth. Such local autonomy remains strong today. Local jurisdictional independence means the state government has no authority over local land use decisions, including, in our case, preserving land for conservation.

In order to understand the pressures facing the state's ecosystems, it is important to review the patterns and governance structures of urban growth—determined at the local level, as just explained—in the state (see also Chapter 41, "Stewardship, Conservation, and Restoration in the Context of Environmental Change," for additional pressures on the state's ecosystems). Many of these patterns have not been significantly altered since the Progressive Era that set up the state government's architecture in the period of 1912–1918. This included local governmental autonomy in determining land uses and services (such as police and fire) and establishing elected representation in the form of city councils, county boards of supervisors, and planning and other representative bodies. General Plans for land use of cities and counties were required in 1937 by the state legislature—though for charter cities they were voluntary—and are documents that essentially establish the framework for directing the allowed uses of land as residential, industrial, commerce, or for institutions like schools and hospitals.

General Plans guide where and what kind of development takes place over time. These documents are important legally for cities and counties and are the documents of reference when developments are proposed. They often can be amended to reflect changes in thinking by elected officials about land uses over time. For example, a development might be proposed that seems useful or appropriate, but the existing General Plan might show that land as Open Space. The local elected officials will then hold hearings and debate a change in the General Plan to accommodate that new proposal (see Fulton and Shigley 2012). These changes can be contentious and are the subject of democratic processes of decision making.

With continued high urban population growth the state's cities grew, and new cities were created and General Plans developed and revised. In the twentieth century, a time of seemingly abundant land and resources, inexpensive fossil fuels and building materials, land development was extensive rather than compact. These patterns were facilitated by urban and state policies including uniform subdivision regulations in 1929 (Fogelson 1967, Dear 1996, Hise 1997, Pincetl 1999b). Such subdivision regulations set out suggested patterns for subdivisions, including numbers of houses per area, sizes of roads, and other infrastructure patterns that were based on a perception of abundance. General Plans struggled to keep up with the pace of development, often overwhelmed by the tenacity of local developers and the proliferation of new municipalities, each with its own planning authority (Pincetl 1999b).

California's divestment of responsibility to localities during the Progressive Era continues to shape land use. Local governments base their ability to zone land and conduct business on "police power" as set forth in the California Constitution. This is an elastic power allowing cities and counties to broadly tailor policies and regulations to suit their community needs (California Constitution Article XI Section 7). Because each city and county controls its own land uses and development processes, governance is fragmented among many cities, none of which must coordinate with the others even when they are adjacent and when infrastructure deployment (like roads or sewers) would be more efficient through collaboration. While they often do collaborate, it is not required. Beyond local control over land use, land in the U.S. is parcelized, as parcels

TABLE 40.2
Timeline of California legislation and regulation affecting open space, land use, and conservation

Year	Regulation	Purpose	Accomplishments	Unintended consequences
1914	Charter City Regulation	Codifies city control over municipal affairs	Regulate over where development could occur, infrastructure would be built, etc.	Lack of regional coordination for land use planning, mixed messages
1929	Uniform subdivision regulations	Codifies how subdivisions are to be defined	Extensive land development	Fragmentation of the land, encroachment on agriculture and natural ecosystems
1935	Central Valley Project	Water diversion project	Distribute water to agricultural areas in the Central Valley	Water rights, water dependencies
1937	General Plan	Comprehensive plan needs to be authorized for cities	Comprehensive plants that are guiding documents for cities and unincorporated land in counties that set out a general vision for the land in the jurisdiction of the city or county, and how it should be utilized	Charter cities receive autonomy from the requirement to adopt comprehensive plans
1947	State Highway Act	Determines regulations, plan and funds for the development of state highways	Growth of the road network	Exurban development towards agricultural and natural areas
1956	Federal Highway Act	Determines regulations, plan and funds for the development of federal highways		Exurban development towards agricultural and natural areas
1956	Department of Water Resources	To manage state agencies over water use	Manages many water rights and water quality agencies	
1957	California Water Plan	Determines who, where, and how much water can be used	New set of water projects including damming the Feather River and the State Water Project	Overallocated existing available water resources; contributed to urban growth and the expansion of agriculture in the Central Valley
1958	Bay Area Greenbelt Alliance	Regional planning and control growth through densification	Conservation of agriculture and open space	
1959	State Planning Office	Centralized planning for land use	Reviews planning decisions; attempts to regional coordination of plans	Advisory power
1962	Federal Highway Act	Determines regulations, plan and funds for the development of federal highways		Exurban development towards agricultural and natural areas
1962	California Tomorrow	NGO responsible for assessing federal and state actions over natural resources	Proposals to reform state government and creation of regional government; impacts of sprawl on agricultural and natural lands	
1963	Local Area Formation Commission Act	County-level entity that reviews proposals to incorporate new cities, annex new territory to existing cities and create new special districts		No incentive to dissolve poorly functioning governments or take regional issues into consideration

(continued)

TABLE 40.2 *(continued)*

Year	Regulation	Purpose	Accomplishments	Unintended consequences
1965	Bay Area Conservation and Development Commission	To overview development proposals towards a regional development plan	Stop Bay Infill projects; control development around the San Francisco Bay Area	
1965	Williamson Act	Conservation of agricultural land	Allows farmers and ranchers to qualify for lower property taxes by keeping land as agriculture for ten years	Did not provide permanent protection because a termination fee can be used
1965	Quimby Act	Open space is required	Requires developers to set aside land as open space	Not a proactive planning tool or financial instrument thus cannot meet the open space needs; only helps new areas
1970	Update in General Plans	Requires open space elements	Open space elements are integrated in the general plans	OPR has little regulatory authority to impose them
1970	CEQA	California Environmental Quality Act	Requires state and local agencies to follow a protocol of analysis and public disclosure of environmental impacts of proposed projects and identify mitigation measures	
1971	Update in General Plans	Become required for cities and counties	Require the inclusion of separate chapters—or elements—on transportation, open space, zoning, noise, housing, etc.; general plans are reviewed by the California State Office of Planning and Research (OPR)	Localities are still in charge of writing the general plans; there are no sanctions if the elements are poorly written, inconsistent, or out of date; the state has no substantive requirements for the plan's elements
1972	California Wild and Scenic Rivers Act		Protection of rivers of extreme scenic beauty	No commitment from the state to provide water flows for maintenance of ecological processes
1972	Coastal Protection Act	Protection of California's coast	Protection of the coast from development	
1972	Coastal Commission	Protection of California's coast		
1972	Golden Gate National Recreation Area	Protection of San Francisco's park and surroundings	Prior was land from the Department of Defense	
1973	Federal Endangered Species Act	Protection of Endangered Species and their habitat	Strong regulatory power; defines take	
1978	Proposition 13	Property tax reduction initiative	Cuts budgets for local governments dramatically	Growth management efforts were hampered by the need for revenues; no funding for open space acquisition available
1978	Santa Monica National Recreation Area			

TABLE 40.2 *(continued)*

Year	Regulation	Purpose	Accomplishments	Unintended consequences
1978	AB857 Urban Strategy	Infill versus further growth	Aimed to curb sprawl	No enforcement
1979	Proposition 4	Ceiling on state and local government expenditures	Further reduces local funds	Further constrains habitat acquisition
1982	Federal HCPs added to ESA	Habitat Conservation Plans		Unfunded mandate of the federal government
1988	Proposition 70	Specific park and recreation area projects	Sixty new specified projects were approved; sets the new era of voters approving specific and identified activities; voter trust, role of NGOs	No long-term funding
1991	NCCP	Natural Communities Conservation Planning	Voluntary participation necessary	Works best for large scale developers and large land areas
1996	Proposition 62 and 268	Control on local government spending	Extend supermajority rule (two-thirds) to all types of assessments, fees, or taxes used by local government	
2000	AB 1427	Cortese Knox Hertzberg Local Government Reauthorization Act	Annexations must account for the protection of prime farmland	Procedural, no sanctions or consequences
2001	AB 857	Farmland Protection Act	Promote infill, protect environmental and agricultural resources, efficient development patterns	Same as above
2006	AB32	Global Warming Solutions Act	Set the new 2020 greenhouse gas emissions reduction goal	
2007	SB 97	CEQA and Greenhouse Gas Emissions	Required OPR to develop, and the Natural Resources Agency to adopt, amendments to the CEQA Guidelines addressing the analysis and mitigation of greenhouse gas emissions	Procedural
2008	SB 375	Sustainable Communities and Climate Protection Act		Does not change land use law and local control over local land use

are what can be bought and sold. While this may seem like an obvious division of land, as we are accustomed to land regulated and on the market in parcels, this scale rarely is commensurate with ecosystems or habitats for ecosystem management and conservation purposes.

Progressive Era land use and government frameworks set the stage for the rest of the century. At the same time, this new era brought increased public awareness and demands to curb development and preserve the natural resources of the state, including ecosystems and rivers as well as agricultural lands.

Attempts to Regulate Urban Growth: 1940s–1980

Federal investments in World War II military industries greatly contributed to urban growth from the 1940s through the 1950s as jobs were plentiful, attracting people to the state (McWilliams 1979). War and postwar industries, including the aerospace and automobile industries, made Los Angeles a manufacturing and industrial powerhouse. Mass building of Los Angeles suburbs like Winsor Hills, Westside Village, Toluca Lake, and Westchester was accompanied by new types of retail outlets such as supermarkets and malls, creating land use patterns still familiar today that are land-intensive and automobile-dependent. This pattern was replicated across the state (Hise 1997). Between 1950 and 1960 one hundred new California cities were incorporated in the state, with most of the growth located in suburban communities (Barbour 2002). Highways were also being built, launched and funded with the passage of the 1947 State Highway Act and the 1956 and 1962 Federal Highway Acts. These roads played critical roles in supporting suburban growth away from city centers

(Gregor 1957, Nash 1972). Federal subsidies aimed at supporting economic growth and modernizing the nation greatly assisted suburban expansion, an expansion that transformed agricultural lands, open spaces, and ecosystems.

Post–World War II urban growth also stressed the state's existing water infrastructure and led to changes in it, affecting watersheds and groundwater resources. While we often think of conservation as the setting aside of lands for ecosystem preservation, water diversion and extraction also has significant impacts on ecosystem health. Water diversion and extraction from far-flung areas of the state has enabled the state's urban growth to occur and agriculture to thrive (Reisner 1986, Hundley 1992). To meet new demand, water management entities proliferated (Pincetl 1999b). By the mid-1950s California had at least 165 irrigation districts, 69 county water districts, 55 reclamation districts, 39 water districts, 35 county water-works districts, 19 municipal water districts, 1,460 mutual water corporations, 456 commercial water companies, and 207 municipal water operations. In response, in 1956 a single state agency, the Department of Water Resources (DWR), was created by a special session of the legislature to bring together all of the state-level water agencies, and an appointed state water board was created. DWR was not given authority, however, over the myriad water management entities that had been created previously or over any subsequent water entities. In addition, groundwater pumping was excluded from regulatory purview and remains unregulated (pumping rate reporting has recently been required). A few urban groundwater basins are "adjudicated" or managed for safe yield, but this is recent and exceptional (see Chapter 38, "Agriculture").

In 1957, DWR issued a California Water Plan to call for a new set of water projects, including the damming of the Feather River and a new canal to bring water to the San Joaquin Valley conveyed through the San Francisco Bay-Delta. This ushered in the State Water Project (SWP), narrowly passed by the voters. The SWP has strongly contributed to urban growth in southern California and to expansion of agriculture in the Central Valley onto lands that had not previously been cultivated and are considered marginal. This resulted in severe impacts on the health of the Bay Delta as well as on the lands and groundwater of the west side of the San Joaquin Valley (Taylor 1975, Pincetl 1999a).

By 1962, California had more than four thousand public and private water-related corporations, of which more than three thousand were concerned with some phase of water distribution while the rest were dedicated to flood control, drainage, and reclamation. This fragmentation of water responsibilities was not accompanied by any accounting of groundwater pumping, water sales, or monitoring of discharges. The State Water Rights Board existed at this time, but the dominant legal regime of "reasonable and beneficial use" limited its authority to incorporate public trust values in decisions. This situation since has proven difficult to remedy and is an important issue for the preservation of headwater ecosystems (ecosystems where water resources originate) and for determining how much water exists for ecosystem functions in the state. Unfortunately, current and future estimates of water volumes show that the State Water Project and the 1935 Central Valley Project (constructed earlier to provide farmers water in the Central Valley) lack adequate water to back up promised water contract deliveries (Table 40.3).

Both the State Water Project and the Central Valley Project have allocated water contract rights that are a form of property right—a USUFRUCTORY RIGHT (right to use). The shortage of committed water—even in average rainfall years—means that the rights in contract could be breached, leading to potential lawsuits and perhaps compensation requirements. The long-term impacts of these projects are already being felt. In headwaters with significant water diversions for agricultural and urban use, rivers and streams no longer fully support fisheries and local fauna and flora. Lack of groundwater pumping regulations means heavy pumping, especially in drought years, is leading to subsidence and depletion, especially in the Central Valley. All in all, between the state and federal water projects and the limited authority of the Water Rights Board, not only are the state's water resources severely overallocated, but groundwater resources are also poorly protected. Still, in recognition of the importance of the state's natural resources, the 1972 California Wild and Scenic Rivers Act was passed to preserve the few, nondiverted, undammed remaining rivers possessing extraordinary scenic, recreation, fishery, or wildlife values. The act required the state to limit activities that might threaten flow, such as dam building or other diversions, on these wild rivers.

TABLE 40.3

River flow and water right allocations in three major California river basins

River basin	Annual flows km³(MAF)	Water rights km³(MAF)[D]	Ratio
Sacramento[A]	26.6 (21.6)	148.6 (120.5)	5.58
San Joaquin[B]	7.6 (6.2)	40.3 (32.7)	5.28
Trinity[C]	1.6 (1.283)	10.8 (8.725)	6.7

SOURCE: Adapted from California Water Impact Network: http://www.c-win.org/webfm_send/270, downloaded 3/4/12

MAF = million acre-feet.

A. Includes the Sacramento, Trinity, Feather, Yuba, Bear, and American Rivers.

B. Includes the San Joaquin, Merced, Tuolumne, and Stanislaus Rivers.

C. Trinity River at Lewiston.

D. Nonconsumptive hydropower rights are not included in this analysis.

Stress on water resources has polarized debate between agricultural users and those advocating for ecosystem water as well as between urban and agricultural water uses. Fragmented water management in all parts of the state, absence of water meters at residences in cities in the Central Valley, lack of central reporting of water use in urban areas, and weak reporting from agriculture all make it nearly impossible to accurately account for water use by different sectors. Only recently are farmers required to report groundwater pumping amounts. With growing concerns about climate impacts on the state's water resources and recurring, serious drought episodes, such lack of data hampers better water management and exacerbates conflict among users.

There have been efforts to better coordinate urban growth and water use in the state. Acknowledging these efforts and understanding why they were not implemented can inform future such efforts. The postwar growth boom spurred concern in the early 1960s from state policy makers and Governor Pat Brown about the effects of added fragmentation at the local level caused by increasing numbers of special districts formed to service urban growth (see Box Figure 5a) and the creation of new cities. The state legislature created a state Planning Office in 1959, located in the governor's office, and in 1960, Governor Brown appointed the Coordinating Council on Urban Policy to develop proposals to improve planning and coordination of growth. This emerged from the perceived need to prevent competition among local governments for new development and to mitigate adverse regional effects resulting from lack of development coordination. Adverse impacts included poor regional road integration, potentially redundant water agencies, duplication of services such as shopping malls authorized by individual cities and resulting competition between malls that undercut their financial viability, and competition for land uses that generate high tax revenues.

The COORDINATING COUNCIL's report urged the creation of one multipurpose district in each of the state's metropolitan areas to deal with regional issues such as air pollution, water supply, sewage, parks, and more. Today, regions have limited districts, including air quality management districts and flood control districts, though they are not elected and lack some of the initial far-reaching vision of the coordinating Council's efforts. The council also suggested that INCORPORATION, ANNEXATION, and the creation of special districts—such as the myriad water districts mentioned earlier—be coordinated and regulated at the *state* level to ensure more equitable growth throughout the state and better planning. Such an approach would have centralized decision making around creating new cities (incorporation), adding new land to a city (annexation), and the creation of new single-purpose agencies to provide a service (for example, a water district, a school district, a sanitation district).

These proposals were opposed by cities and counties concerned about maintaining local authority over all aspects of urban growth and management. In 1963 the state legislature instead created watered-down, county-level LOCAL AGENCY FORMATION COMMISSIONS (LAFCOs) that consist of five appointed commissioners empowered to approve or disapprove any petition for incorporation, special-district formation or dissolution, or annexation in each county. This was seen as a way to prevent some of the worst proposals—for example, for new cities or districts that would not be able to generate sufficient taxes or fees to support necessary services, or for new cities too far away from existing infrastructure to be economically viable (Martin and Wagner 1978, Lewis 2000)

One exception to the local-government rejection of coordinated regional planning was the creation in 1965 of the Bay Area Conservation and Development Commission (BCDC), a singe-purpose regional, land use planning entity. In this specific case the state legislature took initiative and designated a new entity to regulate and supervise land use and development around the San Francisco Bay, going against local government opposition (Dowall 1984). A strong citizen movement concerned about development impacts on the health of San Francisco Bay, including infill of the Bay to facilitate land creation for further development, had excellent relations with state legislative leaders and were able to convince the legislature to act.

With continued urbanization pressure, additional grassroots movements to curb growth and to protect natural resources started to mobilize across the state in the 1960s and into the 1970s. The Sierra Club defeated an attempt by the state Highway Commission to improve Highway 101 by cutting through portions of the Prairie Creek Redwoods and Jedediah Smith Redwoods State Parks. Projects proposed by the Highway Commission often targeted state park lands for transportation projects, as the land belonged to the state. The alternative was purchase of privately held lands. The many specific struggles are too numerous to enumerate here, but it is notable how conservation and land use issues became the subject of innovative proposals. One of the most significant, prescient organizations of the time leading these efforts and developing proposals to change California's land use governance was California Tomorrow.

In 1962 this nonprofit, educational institution began a decade-long effort of developing innovative proposals to reform state government and create regional government to manage growth. California Tomorrow published a monthly magazine; in 1967 it wrote: "Regional governments have not been created, in part because the white majority doesn't want to face the full range of economic and social problems of the regional cities where, in fact, they live." In essence, California Tomorrow pointed out the many challenges of suburbanization for good planning and also called out the role of white flight from inner-city neighborhoods that fueled the incorporation of suburban cities. California Tomorrow pointed out how sprawled urbanization patterns impacted agricultural and natural lands of the state and had negative effects on the fiscal health of older cities. It suggested infill development (using the unbuilt land in already urbanized areas) as an alternative, as well as curbs on incorporation despite the creation of the LAFCOs and their intended mission. Today these ideas are echoed in policies to develop more compact, transit-friendly cities to reduce greenhouse gas emissions.

The Bay Area saw the rise of the Greenbelt Alliance in 1958 (then called People for Open Space), also organized around regional planning but with a focus on the conservation of both agricultural and open spaces and with the aim to control growth and encourage densification. This was a sophisticated approach that we can recognize today: to place further urbanization where it already exists and to maintain other lands for their ecosystem services, whether for food production or conservation. Other nongovernmental organizations that emerged during this period included the Planning and Conservation League (PCL) established in 1965 and the Trust for Public Land (TPL) created in 1972. TPL had been created in response to a development planned for the Marin Headlands north of San Francisco (TPL 2000). TPL pioneered the development of private land trusts that retain land in permanent open space and set a model for the rest of the country (see Box Figure 5b). In addition, the federal Golden Gate National Recreation Area (GGNRA) was created in 1972 partly as a result of the land conservation advocacy of the aforementioned nonprofit organizations but also reflecting the vigorous grassroots efforts to conserve important open space lands endangered by encroaching urbanization. In southern California citizen efforts led to the creation of the federal Santa Monica Mountains National Recreation Area (1978) in an attempt to preserve the unique ecosystem, one of the only east-west transverse mountains range in the U.S.

The state legislature created additional opportunities for local governments to create open spaces, employing incentive-based approaches rather than regulatory requirements. The 1965 state legislature passed the Quimby Act, for example, which allowed local governments to require developers to set aside a portion of new subdivisions as parks or open space or to pay fees for park land acquisition and maintenance. The Quimby Act preserves open space as a condition of development and thus is not a proactive planning tool and financing instrument for open-space protection. In 1970 the legislature also required open-space elements in city and county General Plans, but the numbers, sizes, and locations of these open spaces are at the discretion of cities and counties.

In 1965 the state legislature also passed the California Land Conservation Act (the Williamson Act). This was once again an incentive program, and it reflected the legislature's concern with urban growth impacts on the state's agricultural lands. The Williamson Act allowed farmers and ranchers to qualify for lower property tax rates if they entered into contracts to keep their lands in agriculture for a minimum of ten years, and it provided counties financial compensation from the state for lost revenue. At the same time, the Williamson Act did not provide permanent agricultural land protection, as the contract could be abrogated by the property owner through payment of a termination fee (Sokolow 1990). Thus neither of these well-intentioned acts nor the open-space General Plan requirement met the need to protect open space and ecosystems through strategic planning and strong mechanisms for land conservation. Rather, they merely enabled the possibility of conservation, whether of agricultural or park lands. Today, counties are not compensated by the state for lost Williamson Act revenues.

The 1969 Santa Barbara oil spill had a jarring effect on the state, prompting a number of legislative initiatives including the passage of the CALIFORNIA ENVIRONMENTAL QUALITY ACT (CEQA) in 1970. Modeled on the federal National Environmental Policy Act, it requires state and local agencies within California to follow a protocol of analysis and public disclosure of environmental impacts of proposed projects and to adopt feasible measures for mitigating those impacts. It is a mandatory part of every California state and local agency process. Its passage was prompted by increased land development on the urban fringe and by the belief that greater transparency of impacts through their documentation would enable citizens to participate and demand better land use planning to protect critical resources (Pincetl 1999b).

By the mid- to late 1960s the lack of integrated regional transportation infrastructure across metropolitan areas in the U.S. prompted Congress to incentivize the creation of metropolitan planning agencies (MPOs) or COUNCILS OF GOVERNMENT (COGs). Congress did so by offering transportation infrastructure grants to the regions that created these organizations—another example of an incentive-based approach. California COGs were created in Los Angeles (the Southern California Council of Governments, SCAG), the San Francisco Bay Area (the Association of Bay Area Governments, ABAG), Sacramento, San Diego, and eventually the Central Valley. These voluntary organizations consist of local cities and counties, coordinate and collaborate across jurisdictions to plan and implement regional transportation projects, and can therefore qualify for federal funds to build them.

In the early 1970s another regional governance organization also came about due to congressional law making—air quality management districts. In California these were created by the state to implement the Clean Air Act at the air basin scale. Other regional governments, such as flood control districts, tend to be organized around single issues that might transcend jurisdictional boundaries but do not serve multiple purposes, certainly short of Pat Brown Coordinating Council proposals. Some have regulatory authority, such as air quality management districts; others are based on voluntary participation. While their actions affect ecosystems and environmental quality and must comply with the California Environmental Quality Act, none can facilitate land conservation and thus have only indirect ability to protect ecosystem health.

In 1971 the state legislature also required all local governments to develop, adopt, and follow General Plans—which previously existed but were advisory for city planning. The General Plan was to be a city and county's premier policy document and is now often referred to as the local constitution or blueprint for development. In 1990 the California Supreme Court held that the General Plan was the "constitution for all future development" (*Lesher Communications, Inc. v. City of Walnut Creek*, 52 Cal. 3d 531, 540 [1990]). After 1971 the government code was expanded to require that all land use approvals be consistent with the adopted General Plan and that all its elements be consistent with one another and the plan overall. At the time, this was seen as a great improvement in local planning processes. All General Plans and their elements were to be reviewed for consistency by the Office of Planning and Research (OPR) and revised every ten years. Unfortunately, the OPR has little regulatory authority to reject General Plans or demand revisions. It is often understaffed and unable to review plans in a timely manner, and no real sanctions exist for poor compliance.

In another major, citizen-led change inspired by concerns over urban growth, state voters created the California Coastal Commission in 1972 by ballot initiative. The commission, an entity appointed by the governor, was given regulatory authority to protect California's coast from overdevelopment. This was one of the strongest measures to emerge from a period described by Press (2002) as the state's first slow-growth era, and a clear reaction to the increased pace of urbanization that was occurring. The 1970s were a period of active citizen initiatives to preserve land and environmental quality, both at the state level, as with the Coastal Commission, and at the local level with over one hundred ballot initiatives aimed to restrict or slow growth throughout the state. It was widely perceived that—for different reasons in different parts of the state—the pace of growth was having negative effects. Reasons included concern about preserving agricultural land, impacts of sprawl on the environment, increased length of commuting, and desire to maintain property values. Citizens created ballot initiatives to attempt to change land-use designations to curb further sprawl. Some succeeded in passing while others did not, but overall they did little to curb the pace of urban growth fueled by population and economic growth. With the establishment of the suburban land use pattern, most new urbanization was land-intensive and car-dependent, intruding further and further into the countryside.

Unease about land development made increasingly profitable by the inflation of property values and leading to higher and higher property taxes led to another outcome: the passage in 1978 by state voters of Proposition 13, the property tax reduction initiative. Proposition 13 lowered the taxation rate for property and required a two-thirds majority vote for any new taxes. Local government revenues plummeted from about $10 billion just prior to the passage of the measure to approximately half of that shortly thereafter. In 1979, Proposition 4 furthermore placed a ceiling on both state and local government expenditures (Press 2002). The impacts of Proposition 13 on local government budgets and land use planning were immense. Growth management efforts were hampered by the need for revenues to purchase lands for conservation. Due to the cut in revenues from property taxes, cities and counties went the opposite direction, adopting land use policies most likely to replenish their depleted budgets: zoning for high sales tax businesses and annexing farmland and open space to add to developable land resources so as to increase their tax base (Pincetl 2004 and 2006, Wolch et al. 2004).

In summary, the 1940s through the 1970s were complex and sometimes contradictory years. The era started with pro-development policies aided by the Federal and State Highway Acts that increased accessibility and further promoted development. But this huge growth and its impacts on the state's scenic resources and agricultural lands, as well as on quality of life, led to ballot initiatives to guide and curb growth and to protect the environment. These efforts in turn encountered the entrenched interest of cities and counties in maintaining control over land use and the need to generate revenue to fund city and county services, revenues derived from developed land. Growth pressures ultimately led to the creation of some regional governance entities, including councils of government, air quality management districts, and others. At the same time, desire for the protection of habitat and species led to federal and state Endangered Species Acts, adding to the complexity of land use regulation. With the advent of property tax reductions, local governments found themselves increasingly squeezed among regulatory requirements, frameworks and voter sentiments. The next phase of California's regulatory development was in part an attempt to overcome some of these contradictions in policy direction.

The 1980s and 1990s

This abrupt shift in attitude and relationship towards government and governmental resources by the public—that of reducing taxes, and radically reducing revenues while also wanting environmental protections—led to new conservation strategies and approaches as the effects of Proposition 13's tax reductions and of continued growth played out on the landscape. Ballot measures for open space funding using bonds became popular, and these measures had habitat and wildlife protection goals as their focus, earmarking substantial funds for acquisition of valuable ecosystems. Changes in intergovernmental relations and in the relations between government and civil society emerged as well (Press 2002). With the decline in local governments' ability to fund land preservation with tax dollars, new mechanisms emerged. One such new strategy was developed successfully by the Planning and Conservation League (PCL) under the leadership of Gerald Meral (from 1983 to 2003). The PCL developed a set of inventive campaign funding tactics and ballot initiatives to finance the acquisition and development of park and recreation areas. Meral's first successful measure (Proposition 70) in 1988 included sixty individually defined projects, each with a specified amount, in every corner of the state (Pincetl 2003). Never before had specific projects been prescribed in a ballot initiative, and each one was chosen with an eye to maximizing local voter appeal and was based on negotiations for support with local environmental groups and others ranging from homeowners to local governments (Schrag 1998, in Pincetl 2003).

This marked a departure from having the state legislature determine where park or open space bond funds would be spent. It was part of the shift toward appealing to voters based on pre-specified projects, and it reassured voters that funding would go to projects they preferred. What was also novel in this approach was that the unallocated, but prescribed, funds could be used by NGOs for certain types of projects. While a smaller percentage of the bond funding, these funds allowed the precedent of local groups participating in creating parks of their choosing rather than having parks established by the state legislature or state parks department. Unfortunately, this funding did not come with maintenance monies, thus creating longer-term financing problems for local nonprofits or governmental agencies responsible for managing the new parks.

Nongovernmental organizations and quasi-governmental agencies thus emerged from this period as new stewards of public spaces, including ecosystems. State conservancies funded by grants and donations were created, such as the Coachella Valley Mountains Conservancy in 1991. State-chartered, with an appointed board approved by the governor and with nominal state funding, these conservancies are now found across the state working to preserve critical ecosystems. More nonprofit organizations including local land trusts were created and stepped in to raise funds for land conservation. Empowered by the new conservation regime established by the PCL, they also applied for state bond funds to purchase land (see Box Figure 5), often turning them over to public agencies to manage.

In parallel, voters passed Propositions 62 and 218 in 1996, extending the supermajority approval requirement of Proposition 13 to virtually all types of assessments, fees, or taxes used by local government. This further constricted local government's flexibility to raise funds for necessary services outside of voter-approved bond propositions, let alone to directly purchase additional lands for conservation purposes. Open space preservation efforts have therefore since been further squeezed by lack of state funds, creating new and different relationships between state and local governments and nonprofit organizations. For example, private conservation easements emerged in this period (Merenlender et al. 2004). Conservation easements are entirely private agreements that have little or no state or local public governmental supervision or regulation. These, and other new land conservation approaches like state-created but independently funded land conservancies, are still relatively novel; their consequences for long-term land preservation, management, and the funding of both remain to be examined over time.

In the big picture the historical contribution of federal agencies to California open space has been quite disproportionate when compared to other levels of government (see Box Figure 1b). This is an artifact of California having a lot of spectacular public lands that had not been claimed for private ownership in the nineteenth and early twentieth centuries. It also reflects the dilemma of the fundamental mechanism for conserving land once the state grew—the necessity for land to be purchased when state and local land use regulators are unable or unwilling to conserve important ecosystem values through regulation or are constrained by the need for revenues.

The 1980s and 1990s started off with an abrupt reduction in allocated governmental resources for conservation land acquisition and for local government operations in general. Rather than stalling conservation, it led to the development of innovative funding streams for land acquisition and the emergence of conservation easements. Ballot measures and bonds earmarked substantial funds for land acquisitions, and for the first time individual projects were identified in ballot initiatives. This era also saw the blossoming of nongovernmental organization land purchases. These innovations set the stage for the twenty-first-century conservation.

Twenty-first Century: Continued Conservation Challenges

Given the historical antagonism of localities to state land use regulation, increasing fiscal pressure on local governments, and the simultaneous persistence of support for land conservation, the state has developed reactive and voluntary approaches to meet conservation demands. These create tensions and mixed messages between local power and regional planning efforts, and mismatches between policy goals and instruments for their implementation.

Tensions between Local Authority and Regional Planning

Land use designations are an important part of municipal powers (the powers of city and county governments), as land use determines the character of cities and counties, their revenues, and their attractiveness for investors and businesses. Local tax revenues depend upon the way land is zoned or allocated among uses—residential, commercial, and industrial. Zoning land is one of the main responsibilities of local governments and the way they control what goes on in their cities. Elected officials can zone for medical uses, auto body repair shops, single-family dwellings or apartments, parks and open space, and so forth. Since retail sales generate a great deal of tax revenue, zoning for this use has become very popular, and cities and counties do not want to give up any authority over zoning of their lands. Cities prefer to avoid zoning land uses that do not generate tax revenues—like parks—or that require high levels of expensive public services.

As Nicolaides and Wiese (2013) point out, zoning can perpetuate inequality among cities and suburbs. Cities, in contrast to suburbs, are often older and have less flexibility to change their land uses to attract land uses that generate higher revenues. They have historic infrastructure like existing buildings and roads that are complex and expensive to change. Suburbs, which are newer, have planned their land uses to generate revenue. In essence, "the places themselves help to create wealth and poverty. . . . Adding to these [fiscal] advantages, each is carefully controlled by land-use restrictions that freeze in place their landscapes of high-end homes and freeze out almost everyone else" (Nicolaides and Wiese 2013). This is because localities have no incentive to be inclusionary (that is, to include people and land uses that generate little revenue), as that might reduce the already-fragile revenue stream. This is why a requirement now exists of state review through the state Office of Planning and Research of the housing element of General Plans, but its enforcement is very weak.

There have been numerous attempts to create regional governments with regulatory authority and to encourage greater collaboration among local governments. A regional government would transcend individual city governments in a region. For example, Los Angeles County has eighty-eight cities. The county can only govern its own lands—the lands that are not in the eighty-eight cities. Thus in Los Angeles County each city runs itself as though it was an island and its decisions had no impact on its neighbors. Funding is not shared, infrastructure projects are rarely coordinated, and each city tries to increase its own revenues through zoning decisions at the expense of its neighbor. Common goods like parks do not generate income; at the regional scale little incentive exists for a city to create them, as park land is withdrawn from the taxable pool and the city is responsible for maintenance of the park even if it is a regional asset or benefit.

Existing regional "special districts" like air quality management and flood control have narrow, single-issue mandates and do not serve to coordinate regional decisions outside their purviews. Notwithstanding prior attempts to create regional government entities with land use authority, today only the Tahoe Regional Planning Agency (with bistate jurisdiction) has land use authority. Even this organization has many difficulties, as the Nevada side is much more pro-development than the California side. Nevada's position is driven primarily by the desire for more revenues, and Nevada has threatened to withdraw from the compact over stricter land use requirements proposed by California. Meanwhile the water quality of the Lake Tahoe—the issue the agency was created to address—continues to deteriorate due to land use impacts. This has led to something of an impasse.

Conservation needs and ecosystems do not observe political boundaries; they are regional and even statewide. One could argue that many urban regional issues are similar, such as transportation, housing, water supply and reuse, and air quality. Ecosystem conservation often calls for landscape or regional conservation, keeping parcels together to provide connectivity and enough space for ecosystems to achieve full functioning and to preserve watersheds (see Chapter 41, "Stewardship, Conservation, and Restoration in the Context of Environmental Change"). This generates a fundamental mismatch and contradiction between how land use is planned and regulated and the scales at which conservation needs to occur. In addition, parcel-oriented planning is inimical to orderly urban growth, as it is not really possible to develop large and proactive plans for cities when the process that allocates land is piecemeal. Nothing in current planning law recognizes this fundamental incapacity to treat a region more holistically, including its ecosystems and topography, with the exception of the NATURAL COMMUNITIES CONSERVATION PLANNING (NCCP) process discussed below. One could argue that contemporary, parcel-based planning is anachronistic for the needs of more sustainable cities and landscape preservation and conservation.

Mixed Messages to Localities, and No Additional Resources

With the decline in property taxes, cities and counties became increasingly reliant on impact fees (charging new development a special surcharge to mitigate its impact, for example, on habitat) and alternative property assessments to finance public infrastructure (Matute and Pincetl 2013). Impact fees charged at the time a development is authorized can be used to mitigate impacts from developments, and cities and counties often encourage large developments to reap significant impact fees. Often these fees are used to build schools and local parks, projects necessary to satisfy the additional population growth. Another strategy to increase local revenues has been to zone more land for retail sales, especially for high-priced items such as automobiles or high-volume sales from big-box developments since sales tax was not been affected by Proposition 13. These land uses have generated still greater consumption of land, especially on the urban fringe since big-box developments need big areas. This has been described by a number of observers as the "fiscalization of land use" (Matute and Pincetl 2013, Barbour 2002, Pincetl 1999b, Schrag 1998, Fulton 1997).

The fiscalization of land use has been a known barrier to sustainable land use outcomes for decades. This issue cannot be overstated; simply put, the tax structure resulting from Proposition 13 favors sprawl over infill since large-format retail and auto malls that generate high tax revenue better fill local government coffers. Paradoxically, while retail development is considered fiscally positive, it often generates a net fiscal drain due to impacts such as traffic, costly ongoing maintenance of an expanded road system, and induced growth in the form of residential development (Pincetl 1999a). Other policies reinforce current land use patterns and are deeply embedded in how cities do their business, such as school funding formulas that reward suburban schools and lender's aversion to new housing formulas (for example, for infill or mixed-use development). These too are well-known, but policy remedies have not been adopted into law.

Localities are now also being asked to consider development and transportation impacts on greenhouse gases by Senate Bill 375, to include greenhouse gas (GHG) impacts in CEQA documents, and to create climate actions plans. However, within an unchanged regulatory context no sanctions occur if these new requirements are not met, and no changes have been made to General Plan guidelines that require GHG reduction measures. Individual-city General Plans need not be consistent with those of adjoining cities in the region. Finally, no new sources of revenue mitigate the pressures towards further development (and especially retail development) for revenue. Thus localities have not been given any new tools that might encourage greater infill development, relieving pressure on undeveloped agricultural land and impacts on natural habitats nearby and in the hinterlands.

Mismatches between Policy Goals and Legislative Tools

California has long recognized the costs of sprawl; it has identified the need for specific land use outcomes including orderly and efficient land use, infill, farmland protection, and conservation of resource lands. But the fundamental way in which land (and water) is regulated has not changed, only the urgency of state priorities. With the advent of climate change, priorities have expanded to include renewable energy and land use that reduces greenhouse gas emissions. All of these concerns are embodied in adopted state law and policy. Examples include the 1978 Urban Strategy turned into state law under Assembly Bill 857 (Wiggins codified at Section 65041.1 of the Government Code) in 2001; Assembly Bill 32 (California Global Warming Solutions Act), 2006; and Senate Bill 375 (Sustainable Communities and Climate Protection Act), 2008—none of which actually alters land use planning.

Among the broad goals in the adopted the 1978 Urban Strategy developed by Governor Brown's Office of Planning and Research during his first administration (second term) were curbing urban sprawl and directing new urban growth to existing cities and suburbs, revitalizing central cities and neighborhoods, and protecting resource lands, in alignment with the proposals put forward by California Tomorrow and others. This was before understanding had emerged about climate change and was simply a strategy to deal with the state's urban growth. The Urban Strategy laid out a framework for how planning *should* be done; it had no legal requirements for implementation. In 2001, Assembly Bill 857 (the Farmland Protection Act) codified these planning objectives by establishing three priorities that encourage all state agencies to (1) promote infill development within existing communities, (2) protect the state's most valuable environmental and agricultural resources, and (3) encourage efficient development patterns overall.

It required the governor, in conjunction with the governor's budget, to submit annually to the state legislature a proposed five-year infrastructure plan. The plan would have to show how all proposed infrastructure expenditures were consistent with these state planning priorities. There is little evidence that Assembly Bill 857 is being implemented, with the small exception of the current Strategic Growth Council's use of the act's planning principles as a prerequisite for grant giving. The current Strategic Growth Council was created in 2008 as part of the state legislature's package of incentives to help localities plan for climate impacts. The council leadership embraced Assembly Bill 857's languishing principles as good guidelines for their own grant funding (to which funds are provided by the state legislature).

In 2006 the state legislature passed and Governor Arnold Schwarzenegger signed Assembly Bill 32, the Global Warming Solutions Act of 2006, which set into law a 2020 greenhouse gas emissions reduction goal to return overall emissions to 1990 levels. This law directed the California Air Resources Board to begin developing discrete, early actions to reduce greenhouse gases while also preparing a scoping plan to identify how best to reach the 2020 limit. Strategies in the scoping plan include *recommendations* for local policies that promote infill and more compact urban growth to reduce vehicle miles traveled (VTM) and greenhouse gas emissions. Senate Bill 97 (CEQA and Greenhouse Gas Emissions), passed in 2007, expressly added greenhouse gas emissions *analysis* as part of the CEQA process. Senate Bill 97 required the state Office of Planning and Research to develop, and the Natural Resources Agency to adopt, amendments to the CEQA guidelines addressing the analysis and mitigation of greenhouse gas emissions. These are targets and analyses requirements that do not have explicit required implementation steps and can be met however is deemed appropriate. Building on Assembly Bill 32, Senate Bill 375 (2008) then linked reduction of greenhouse gas emissions to land use and regional transportation planning. While this statute is possibly the closest California has come to requiring regional planning and *encourages* urban and suburban infill, clustered development, mixed land uses, transit-oriented development to reduce GHGs (California Transportation Commission 2010), Senate Bill 375 does not change land use law and local control over local land use. Compliance is not mandatory.

All of the aforementioned statutes are aimed at the same overarching policy direction and land use strategies—creating more compact development, achieving greater regional integration of land use, infrastructure, and transportation planning—but the fundamental structures of local control over land use were not touched, nor were the guidelines for General Plan. No additional sanctions or rules were created, nor revenue streams, with the exception of a "sleeper" provision that creates legal claims and remedies for violation of housing policies. Unfortunately, as in previous attempts to regulate land use in the state, the gap between these state policy guidance regulations and local land use planning and actions was not filled. For example, Cordova Hills, a 1,100-hectare housing development not adjacent to any current development and inconsistent with the recently adopted Sacramento regional plan and with the goals of SB 375, was approved by the Sacramento County Board of Supervisors as a measure to encourage economic activity and growth in March 2013. Local governments opposed regulatory requirements for the consistency of local plans with SB 375, and for good reason. They did not want to be constrained in land use decisions they consider their prerogative. As a result, SB 375 contains incentives rather than penalties that fall short of what is necessary to align state and local policy and state desired outcomes.

Innovations toward a Change

Current and recent policy innovations have developed to try to improve conservation planning in lieu of strong state and regional planning (see also Chapter 41, "Stewardship, Conservation, and Restoration in the Context of Environmental Change"). They are speculative—that is, not yet fully tried out—complex, and highly technical. They are often predicated on large-scale transportation infrastructure (to accommodate assumed future growth), tying funding for habitat preservation and compliance with the Endangered Species Act with the construction of freeways to service future and further urbanization. These innovations demonstrate the direction of habitat conservation going forward—finding opportunities for funding in continued urban growth, and using existing programs and infrastructure plans rather than regulatory reform or the creation of new funding streams.

Habitat Conservation Plans and Natural Communities Conservation Plans

California, due to its unique geography, has more endemic species than any other state in the continental U.S. (see Chapter 11, "Biodiversity"). With urbanization pressures throughout the state, developments have thus been held up by the federal Endangered Species Act (ESA), passed in 1973 with the aim to preserve threatened and endangered species and their habitat. Development conflicts began to abound. Environmental organizations used the ESA to challenge development with some success, and developers found themselves stymied and slowed down by ESA challenges to development projects. ESA challenges were based on a species-by-species threat reflecting the law, and it became clear that policies based on protecting individual species would scarcely achieve the goal of preserving species as they relied on habitats that needed to be preserved as well.

HABITAT CONSERVATION PLANS (HCPS) were added to the ESA by Congress in 1982. Congress viewed HCPs as a win-win for imperiled species. HCPs took habitat into consideration and created incidental take permits (ITPs), which allowed—for the first time—the taking of a limited amount of habitat via permit. This *take* permit would be issued in exchange for a commitment to protect and manage other habitat areas, maintaining the species' chances of overall recovery (Kostyack 2001). Kostyack (2001) describes: "Facing the possibility of significant development restrictions due to the ESA's prohibition against taking of listed species and the possibility of liability for issuing permits in violation of this prohibition, local governments have negotiated with federal agencies to ensure that their development plans are consistent with ESA standards," thus allowing development to go forward. However, habitat conservation is fundamentally an issue of how much habitat is required and where it must be located to ensure a species' long-term viability. As HCPs were created to protect one species at time, California, under Governor Pete Wilson, created Multiple Species Habitat Conservation Planning (MSHCP) and the 1991 Natural Communities Conservation Planning (NCCP) process in an effort to encompass entire ecosystems and their processes.

The NCCP process was predicated on volunteer landowner participation. It was launched to construct preserves for coastal sage scrub habitat in southern California as a way to enable large-scale developers in Orange County to proceed with development but to also preserve the coastal sage scrub habitat and its fauna. It was intended to bring all stakeholders to the table in order to set aside coherent, regional habitat preserves (Fulton 1997, Pincetl 1999a). NCCPs were endorsed by secretary of the interior at the time, Bruce Babbitt, as a legitimate implementation of the ESA that would allow the protection of endangered species but not halt development. At that point, some feared that the ESA would be challenged by hostile forces in Congress. If the NCCP could be shown to work, it would obviate the calls for reform or deauthorization of the ESA.

The NCCP process is similar to the HCP process in that it allows the taking of habitat and individual species in exchange for habitat set-asides. It differs from the federal HCP in that it is a state-led program that is voluntary, locally initiated, potentially applicable at a county or regional scale, and initiated before the landscape becomes degraded and to protect ecosystems at the landscape scale while accommodating compatible development. It is a landscape-oriented approach that can potentially resolve habitat fragmentation while also ensuring development. NCCPs have been successful in creating conservation set-asides where there have been *willing* landowners and funding to purchase lands as the process is voluntary.

The NCCP process was an important attempt to address the scale mismatch between land use policies and natural resource protection discussed earlier. Because land planning is done parcel by parcel, and habitat often needs to be protected at a much larger scale that often transcends several local political jurisdictions, implementing the NCCP opened up new conservation options to draw in participants at multiple scales and different political jurisdictions. Nongovernmental organizations' land acquisitions (see Box Figure 4) post-1980s also resulted in large tracts of land in southern California being added to the conservation network (see Box Figures 1a, 4, and 5).

Landscape-level planning provides a wide range of benefits, particularly when in the form of HCPs and NCCPs:

- It permanently protects large, interconnected, and biologically rich blocks of habitat—a strategy for conserving species and habitats far more effective than protecting small and isolated reserves.
- It increases efficiency and provides more certainty to project proponents seeking state and federal permits from wildlife agencies.
- It provides economic incentives and fair compensations to private landowners for permanently protecting natural resources on their lands.
- It establishes partnerships among local government agencies and state and federal wildlife agencies for the conservation of natural resources.

- It establishes partnerships between state conservation agencies and state infrastructure agencies to align conservation goals and implementation and to plan for California's water, transportation, and energy needs, for example, while avoiding its most sensitive resources and reducing the further fragmentation of habitat.

General Plans: The Blueprint Process

Not to be confused with local General Plans, the California Department of Transportation (CALTRANS) developed a Regional Blueprint program that preceded Senate Bill 375. Regional Blueprints came about as a result of increasing traffic congestion and the long-term inability of CALTRANS to build sufficient road infrastructure to address the state's needs. Not only are funds insufficient, but growing evidence also shows that building more road capacity simply induces more traffic. Regional blueprints are collaborative planning processes that engage residents in articulating a vision for the long term of their region and assessing trade-offs. Regional visioning efforts used advanced Geographic Information Systems (GIS) scenario mapping to demonstrate the comparative impacts of different regional development scenarios. They involved numerous stakeholders who were challenged to allocate projected growth across each transportation region. The concept was that if people—stakeholders—were involved and learned of the difficult trade-offs by trying to make projected growth fit in an existing region, good policy would emerge from the ground up.

These early blueprints inspired the Sustainable Communities Strategies (SCS) planning requirements under SB 375 and have become a touchstone for local general planning. However, the blueprints and SCS requirements have no implementation and enforcement mechanisms, and they focus on the existing built environment, leaving aside existing open space lands and their future (CALTRANS 2013). Few regions have exhibited ground-up results from these processes. Sustainable Communities Strategies under SB 375 require the state's regional metropolitan planning organizations (MPOs) to develop plans for how to reduce vehicle miles traveled and better match housing locations to jobs. SB 375 does not provide the MPOs with any greater authority to require their members to implement the SCS, however, nor are there any penalties if the SCS is not abided by. Further, neither Regional Blueprints nor SCSs under SB 375 are required to be consistent with local General Plans. Consistency would, at a minimum, oblige localities to address how their land use decisions might affect what is outlined in the SCSs and/or Blueprints. But only the state legislature has the authority to require consistency through legislation, and it has not chosen thus far to exercise this authority.

General Plan guidelines were last updated by the California Office of Planning and Research (OPR) in 2003. OPR has recently initiated an update with a focus on the policy outcomes of the state—as articulated in AB 857 and the 1978 Urban Strategy for California—and specific "metrics or measures" General Plans should meet to do so. Under the Brown administration, enforcing existing rules is seen as a way to address climate impacts and encourage better planning. Creating metrics or measures that General Plans should meet could provide a pathway to effective change in land use decision making.

Regional Advance Mitigation Planning (RAMP)

Another recent innovation is the Regional Advance Mitigation Planning (RAMP) in 2010. This is being implemented with an early example in Transnet, San Diego's sales tax for local transportation, and Measure M2, Orange County's reauthorized sales tax measure. These are parallel and nearly invisible efforts (probably because of their novelty) that might provide a new framework for conservation. RAMP is an effort to develop a more comprehensive approach to mitigate biological resource impacts caused by major infrastructure projects. It allows for natural resources to be protected or restored as compensatory mitigation before projects are constructed, and often years in advance (Thorne et al. 2014). However, the fear of takings looms, and it remains to be seen if this approach will obviate that concern.

Sustainable Communities Strategies, Conservation, and Open Space Plans: The Greenprint

As discussed earlier, the Endangered Species Act has been a driver of habitat conservation in the state. The Natural Communities Conservation Plan process created a more comprehensive, regional approach to conserve habitats based on science. Yet the NCCP does little to address the fiscal pressures on localities, and in fact NCCP success is often predicated on growth because land preservation is possible only through development fees that can fund land acquisition. Localities, given the dearth of tax revenue financing, use growth opportunities to leverage new infrastructure and to levy fees that go to paying for habitat conservation or other programs. While some localities might want to plan proactively, including for conservation, this is difficult where other cities continue to plan for growth and in a time of tax revenue scarcity.

An emerging concept to creating sustainable communities is inclusion of Regional Greenprints (different from the Blueprints just discussed) as an integral part of local General Plans and Sustainable Community Strategies. While Greenprints are still conceptual, they would offer a new way to improve conservation planning by providing a process to map a region's important open space for a full range of ecosystem services, including habitat, farmland, recreation, water resources, and more. Greenprints go beyond conservation plans because they are inclusive of all open space values. Since a region's natural systems provide the basis for ecosystem services, planning for and integrating green infrastructure with the planning of hard infrastructures like freeways would serve to identify natural areas that should be protected or managed appropriately. This concept is not new; Ian McHarg (1970) laid out a compelling vision for this approach to planning and development. Today, with GIS tools, advances in conservation biology and interest in sustainability and resilience, more and better tools for protecting ecosystems are available.

Conservation planning could provide a baseline from which land use plans are developed and could be linked to CO_2 sequestration—a new and popular idea. Requiring conservation priorities to be respected in land use and transportation planning would provide a number of important benefits. These include:

1. Promoting strategies that would reduce risk and project delays for infrastructure agencies and development, as plans would be based on better information

about landscapes, water resources, and working lands, to help guide decisions on infrastructure investment.
2. Driving mitigation (e.g., regional advanced mitigation) and conservation dollars to protect priority conservation areas.
3. Directing development to areas more suitable for development and avoiding hazards such as infill development.
4. Preserving lands that will sequester CO_2.
5. Reducing conflicts by incorporating conservation planning into infrastructure and land use scenarios, providing an element of certainty for development and allowing for more systematic economic growth.

CO_2 sequestration credits or land preservation, currently another land use conservation strategy under consideration, is associated with a number of uncertainties and caveats. These include the uncertain science regarding CO_2 sequestration by specific lands in specific places in the state, including the state's forests; whether carbon offsets for forestry or land use conservation represents "additional" sequestration; and long-term management of these lands and forces such as fire, floods, and other potentially destructive events. Further, many CO_2 sequestration estimates are based on data from lands outside California and not previously degraded. The idea of linking Greenprints to CO_2 sequestration is new and may take time to learn how to implement. It could also be funded by California's new carbon market, helping relieve the pressure on development fees to fund conservation.

Future Challenges

Other ongoing activities will also challenge habitat preservation. Paradoxically, concern about greenhouse gas emissions is fueling Governor Jerry Brown's drive to have a high-speed rail line link southern California to the Bay Area and Sacramento. This project is highly contentious. Its route, as currently designed, goes through some of the state's prime agricultural land and could support even more suburbanization in the already urbanizing Central Valley. More suburbanization will likely bring more air pollution, demand for more water, and impacts on the Sierra Nevada mountain ecosystems and water areas of origin, undermining GHG reductions. Without strong land use controls, this outcome is likely.

Governor Brown is also pursuing more energy resources, including oil and natural gas fracking. "Fracking" is the fracturing of rock by a pressurized liquid, often water-based and supplemented by chemicals that increase pressure and keep fractures open such that the oil or gas can be pumped. A great deal of the state's natural gas and petroleum resources are found in the Central Valley and compete for water, adding another demand to the state's scarce water resources in addition to agriculture, cities, and places of origin. Fracking will also produce highly problematic wastewater, which will have to be disposed of, and could pose threats to fauna and flora as well as contribute to already contaminated groundwater. Fracking activities will increase air pollution, which in the Central Valley affects ecosystem functioning in the Sierras (see Chapter 7, "Atmospheric Chemistry").

As with many water extractions in the state, little accounting is taking place of the quantities of water being used for fracking or of current quantities of water used by the active petroleum extraction industry in the southern Joaquin Valley. Another important potential area of energy exploitation is the Monterey Formation in the California Coast Ranges and Peninsular Ranges. The formation was first considered by the U.S. Energy Information Administration to have yield potential of approximately 15.5 billion barrels of oil. Though this estimate has been downgraded considerably, it still illustrates the pressure resources are under for multiple use. While recent legislation (SB 4, 2013) has been passed to regulate fracking in the state, it is considered by some as not strong enough.

Protected Forest Service and BLM federal lands are not exempt from other energy projects in California. Large-scale renewable electricity generation projects in the high desert of the Mojave have been given the green light by the Department of the Interior despite documented impacts on the desert tortoise (*Goperhus agassizii*), among other species (see Chapter 11, "Biodiversity"). Addressing climate change policy through renewable energy development is therefore in tension with land conservation in some areas.

Climate Change

Climate change is an important emerging factor affecting conservation (see Chapters 14, "Climate Change Impacts"; 41, "Stewardship, Conservation, and Restoration in the Context of Environmental Change"; and other chapters throughout this volume). Its impacts on California, which will likely include reduced snowpack, increased temperatures, sea level rise, and other less understood changes, have significant implications for the state's future. As elsewhere in the world, changes in temperature affect fauna and flora dramatically, and accompanying changes in the hydrologic regime will exacerbate those impacts. Greater competition for water is probable among existing users and will also increase for reserved water for ecosystems and places of origin. Ironically, transportation is the single highest contributor to GHGs in the state, a result of the state's still predominantly automobile-oriented urbanization process. This means that cities remain one of the biggest contributors to GHG emissions, affecting habitat in this way as well as competing for land.

Increased temperatures will also aggravate air pollution, affecting human and ecosystem health. Places like southern California and the Central Valley will see much worse air quality, with increased ozone levels impairing ecosystem health in adjacent national forests and parks. Climate change is the culminating phenomenon resulting from human reliance on fossil energy, an energy source that is deeply intertwined in all aspects of daily life and the economy.

Where Do We Go from Here?

California has been one of the most urbanized states in the nation since its early days. Local control over local land use is strongly protected by localities and local elites who defend their prerogatives to maintain the character and type of housing, and thus the population that can live in that locality. However, to improve the future of conservation of the state's biodiversity and unique habitats and to address other important regional and statewide issues, new approaches are necessary. As recommended throughout this book, it is necessary to take an ecosystem stewardship approach—"a strategy to respond to and shape social-ecological systems under conditions of uncertainty and change to sustain the supply and opportunities for use of ecosystem services to support human well-being" (Chapin et al. 2010). A renewed commitment to stewardship of the state's public lands is needed. This will not be easy given the current regulatory framework—local control over local land use, fiscal constraints, and protection of private property rights, among other regulatory structures. This chapter has outlined some newer initiatives that attempt to use infrastructure development to advance habitat conservation on a landscape level as well as potential funding from carbon credits. Admittedly these initiatives are tentative and complex; they rely on voluntary willingness to implement them.

Ultimately, conservation of the state's resources is predicated upon better state urban policy, directing growth inward and constraining further growth on greenfields. While the state has a few tools at its disposal, such as Assembly Bill 857, the GHG requirements in CEQA, and the nudging requirements in Senate Bill 375, real progress will require the state legislature to reform General Plan requirements and elements. It will require changing the fiscal rewards of cities and the provision of new funding streams for conservation. Fundamentally, conservation will be successful only by virtue of better urbanization patterns. This chapter has not even considered impacts on habitat of development in the wildland-urban interface, another artifact of local land use regulations. Many of the arising issues from that phenomenon—such as fire, habitat fragmentation, flooding, and the spread of invasive species—are covered elsewhere in this book in the chapters exploring the affected ecosystems.

Summary

California has been fortunate to have had some of its magnificent ecosystems conserved starting in the late nineteenth century. At the same time, the state has experienced tremendous population growth and urbanization. This has led to conflicts between land conservation and development. These conflicts are local because land use planning—determining zoning and where development will occur—is the prerogative of cities and counties, and there is no regional coordination or goal setting for future growth. Urban growth is still seen as the key to the prosperity of localities, so little incentive exists to conserve land, to build denser more contained cities, and to collaborate across jurisdictions for infrastructure, land use, or revenue sharing. This is further complicated by the legacy of the Fifth Amendment of the Constitution, which stipulates that in order for land to be conserved, it must be purchased at fair price from its legal owners, in the context of increasing constraints on local government's ability to raise taxes or other funds.

This chapter describes how the state legislature, and voters through the ballot initiative process, have passed a number of laws and created new agencies to attempt to improve conservation planning and to protect conservation lands. These include the California Coastal Act and the creation of the Coastal Conservancy, the California Environmental Quality Act, HCPs and NCCPs, the Williamson and Quimby Acts, and public involvement via voting or lobbying to protect the state's natural resources, as with the Bay Conservation and Development Commission. But with the reduction of funding since the early 1980s due to ballot initiatives, conserving California's lands has been more difficult. Because government must purchase its land, and since land in California is expensive, conserving more lands is costly. Despite this challenge, innovative funding streams have emerged—especially with the greater participation of public parties in conservation land acquisition—as well as alternative forms of land conservation such as conservation easements.

Better land use is at the heart of conservation of California's magnificent heritage. In the end, conservation rests upon political will and the support of the state's residents. The state legislature will have to restructure the state's taxation system and the way in which private property rights are interpreted, and create new governmental regulations to ensure the state's social and ecological resilience to climate change. Successful conservation will require a change in land development patterns and fundamentally in the way people live on the land.

Acknowledgments for Box 40.1

"Reconstructing California's Land Conservation History" (page 902) would have not been possible without the funding from the Spatial History Project (Wallenberg Foundation) and the Bill Lane Center for the American West, and the Vice-Provost Undergraduate Education program at Stanford University. Several acknowledgments are also due to individuals and institutions for valuable contributions and data: Jon Christensen at the University of California at Los Angeles and Zephyr Frank at Stanford University for their support, mentorship, and insights to the development of the idea of the reconstruction of California conservation history. Jon Christensen for the access to the Herbarium records data sets, and Zephyr Frank and Richard White for the access to Spatial History's data sets.

James H. Thorne at the Information Center for the Environment at the University of California at Davis for the access to the Wieslander project, especially the historic and modern vegetation data. Maggie Kelly and David Ackerly at the University of California at Berkeley for their insights on Wieslander data and collections, and the conservation environment of the Bay Area. Open Space Council for providing the inspiration and the connections between academic research and the on-the-ground managers. GreenInfo Network for creating and making available the invaluable California Protected Areas Database, one of the building blocks of this work. Jake Coolidge, Erik Steiner, and Geoff McGhee for their insights on cartographic design and how to visualize this type of information.

And last but not least, to all the students and collaborators who contributed to the collection of the data set herein presented: Alice Avery, Alexandra Peers, Emily Francis, Claudia Preciado, Taz George, Matthew Walter, Alex Powel, Ma'ayan Dembo, and Salma Zahedi.

Recommended Reading

Curtin, D. J., and C. T. Talbert. 2004. Curtin's California land use and planning law. 24th edition. Solano Press Books, Point Arena, California.

Fairfax, S. K., L. Gwin, M. A. King, L. Raymond, and L. A. Watt. 2005. Buying nature: The limits of land acquisition as a conservation strategy. MIT Press, Cambridge, Massachusetts.

Fulton, W. 1997. The reluctant metropolis: The politics of urban growth in Los Angeles. Solano Press Books, Point Arena, California.

Jensen, D. B., M. S. Torn, and J. Harte. 1993. In our own hands: A

strategy for conserving California's biological diversity. University of California Press, Oakland, California.
Meyer, A. 2006. New guardians for the golden gate: How America got a great national park. University of California Press, Oakland, California.
Schrag, P. 1999. Paradise lost: California's experience, America's future. University of California Press, Oakland, California.
Sellers, C. C. 2012. Crabgrass crucible, suburban nature, and the rise of environmentalism in twentieth-century America. University of North Carolina Press, Chapel Hill, North Carolina.
Walker, R. 2007. The country in the city: The greening of the San Francisco Bay Area. University of Washington Press, Seattle, Washington.

Glossary

ANNEXATION The addition of new land to a city.

CALIFORNIA ENVIRONMENTAL QUALITY ACT (CEQA) This act requires that state and local agencies follow a protocol for analysis and public disclosure of environmental impacts of proposed projects and adopt feasible measures for mitigating those impacts.

CALIFORNIA STATE OFFICE OF PLANNING AND RESEARCH (OPR) This was created by statute in 1970 and constitutes the state planning agency.

CARBON CREDITS Refers to funds or credit in carbon markets, originated from offsetting carbon emissions from operations such as air travel, industries, and so on.

CONSERVATION EASEMENT An agreement by a property owner to maintain his or her land in private open space—no development will occur—in exchange for a tax rebate on that property. Conservation easements may have a time limit, after which they must be renewed or not. They are permanently tied to the title to the land and inhere at the sale of a property.

COORDINATING COUNCIL Refers to a council created to develop policy proposals to improve planning and coordination of growth.

COUNCILS OF GOVERNMENT Metropolitan planning agencies that coordinate regional transportation infrastructure.

ENDANGERED SPECIES ACT (ESA) Act passed in 1973 with the aim to preserve threatened and endangered species such as eagles, wolves, and grizzly bears and their habitat. The ESA can be (and has been) used to challenge development. The ESA aims to preserve species and the habitats they depend on.

FEDERAL LAND POLICY AND MANAGEMENT ACT (FLPMA) Passed in 1976, the FLPMA is the driving force behind the Bureau of Land Management (BLM), and it establishes the multiple use of the bureau. According to BLM's website (http://www.blm.gov/flpma/FLPMA.pdf), the act states that "the public lands be retained in Federal ownership [. . .] disposal of a particular parcel will serve the national interest" and also that "the public lands be managed in a manner that will protect the quality of scientific, scenic, historical, ecological, environmental, air and atmospheric, water resource, and archaeological values; that, were appropriate, will preserve and protect certain public lands in their natural condition; that will provide food and habitat for fish and wildlife and domestic animals; and that will provide for outdoor recreation and human occupancy and use."

FEE TITLE OWNERSHIP Refers to when an Open Space management agency owns the title of that property (which means it has its property rights).

HABITAT CONSERVATION PLANS (HCPS) Plans to implement the mandates of the ESA for the protection of threatened and endangered species and their habitat. HCPs took habitat into consideration, and they created incidental take permits (ITPs), which allowed—for the first time—the taking of a limited amount of habitat via permit.

HOMESTEAD ACT Passed in 1862, this act secured homesteads to actual settlers on the public domain.

HOTSPOTS Spatial locations with high frequency of conservation areas.

HOTTIMES Time periods with high concentration of conservation activity, as, for example, acquisition of land for conservation.

INCORPORATION The addition of new cities with a threshold in the number of residents.

LOCAL AGENCY FORMATION COMMISSION County-level agencies with the responsibility to approve or disapprove any petition for incorporation, annexation, and special district formation or dissolution.

MITIGATION BANKS Funds from development fees, mitigation, and other sources are held in these "banks" for purchasing land in the future.

MULTIPLE USE Defined in the Multiple Use Sustained Yield Act as "management of the public lands and their various resource values so that they are utilized in the combination that will best meet the present and future needs of the American people."

MULTIPLE USE SUSTAINED YIELD ACT (MUSYA) Passed in 1960, this act authorizes and directs "that the national forests be managed under principles of multiple use and to produce a sustained yield of products and services, and for other purposes," according to the act's website (http://www.fs.fed.us/emc/nfma/includes/musya60.pdf).

NATIONAL FOREST MANAGEMENT ACT (NFMA) Passed in 1976, this act mandates that "the public interest is served by the Forest Service, Department of Agriculture, in cooperation with other agencies, assessing the Nation's renewable resources, and developing and preparing a national renewable resource and program, which is periodically reviewed and updated," according to the act's website (http://www.fs.fed.us/emc/nfma/includes/NFMA1976.pdf).

NATURAL COMMUNITIES CONSERVATION PLANS (NCCP) These are an effort to encompass entire ecosystems and their processes, in contrast to HCPs (which are aimed at protecting one species at a time).

OPEN SPACE Open Space (as opposed to open space, or undeveloped land) refers to "lands protected through fee title ownership by a public agency or non-profit land conservation organization" (GreenInfo Network 2013). Open Spaces include a wide array of types of properties from city parks to national parks, Bureau of Land Management lands used for recreation and resource extraction, or Department of Defense lands. However, Open Space does *not* include private land in conservation easements.

ORGANIC ACT A law that regulates how a certain agency acts on behalf of the public good.

POLICE POWER Constitutional right provided to regulate land use. It follows from the Tenth Amendment to the Constitution and gives state rights and powers not delegated to the United States.

SPECIAL DISTRICTS A type of government unit to provide a specific service—such as schools, sewers, street lighting, parks, or acquisition of lands—for conservation

TAKING LAW Habitat taking is a component of the Endangered Species Act. It means that in specific cases habitat of listed species can be taken (for other use) with the trade-off of mitigation land.

USUFRUCTORY RIGHT A right to use.

References

Barbour, E. 2002. Metropolitan growth planning in California, 1900–2000. Public Policy Institute of California, San Francisco, California.

Barton, G. A. 2000. Empire forestry and American environmentalism. Environment and History 6:187–203.

Brooks, T. M., R. A. Mittermeir, C. G. Mittermeier, G.A.B. da Fonseca, A. B. Rylands, W. R. Konstant, P. Flick, J. Pilgrim, S. Oldfield, G. Magin, and C. Haig-Taylor. 2002. Habitat loss and extinction in the hotspots of biodiversity. Conservation Biology 16:909–923.

California Department of Transportation (CALTRANS). 2013. Regional blueprints. <http://calblueprint.dot.ca.gov>. Accessed March 12, 2013.

California Transportation Commission. 2010. Regional Transportation Guidelines. <http://www.catc.ca.gov/programs/rtp/2010_RTP_Guidelines.pdf>. Accessed March 12, 2013.

Chapin, F. S.,S. R. Carpenter, G. P. Kofinas, C. Folke, N. Abel, W.C. Clark, P. Olsson, D. M. Stafford Smith, B. H. Walker, O. R. Young, F. Berkes, R. Biggs, J. M. Grove, R. L. Naylor, E. Pinkerton, W. Steffen, and F. J. Swanson. 2010. Ecosystem stewardship: Sustainability strategies for a rapidly changing planet. Trends in Ecology and Evolution 25:241–249.

Crew, M. H. 1990. Development agreements after Nollan vs. California Coastal Commission, 483 US 825 (1987). The Urban Lawyer 22:23–58.

Czech, B. 2004. A transdisciplinary approach to conservation land acquisition. Conservation Biology 16:1488–1497.

Dear, M. 1996. In the city, time becomes visible: Intentionality and urbanism in Los Angeles, 1781–1991. Pages 760105 in Allen J. Scott and Edward W. Soja, editors. The City: Los Angeles and Urban Theory at the End of the Twentieth Century. University of California Press, Berkeley, California.

Dowall, D. E. 1984. The suburban squeeze: Land conversion and regulation in the San Francisco Bay Area. University of California Press, Berkeley, California.

Fogelson, R. M. 1967. The fragmented metropolis Los Angeles, 1850–1930. University of California Press, Berkeley, California.

Fulton, W. 1997. The reluctant metropolis: The politics of urban growth in Los Angeles. Solano Press Books, Point Arena, California.

Fulton, W., and P. Shigley. 2012. Guide to California planning. Fourth edition. Solano Press Books, Point Arena, California.

Grantham, H. S., M. Bode, E. McDonald-Madden, E. T. Game, A. T. Knight, and H. P. Possingham. 2010. Effective conservation planning requires learning and adaptation. Frontiers in Ecology and the Environment 8:431–437.

GreenInfo Network. 2013. Bay Area protected areas database (BPAD). <http://www.openspacecouncil.org/programs/index.php?program=6>. Accessed November 20, 2013.

Gregor, H. F. 1957. Urban pressures on California land. Land Economics 33:311–325.

Hise, G. 1997. Magnetic Los Angeles: Planning the twentieth century metropolis. Johns Hopkins University Press, Baltimore, Maryland.

Hundley, N. 1992. The great thirst: Californians and water, 1770s–1990s. University of California Press, Berkeley, California.

IUCN - International Union for Nature Conservation and UNEP-WCMC - United Nations Environmental Program - World Conservation Monitoring Center. 2013. The world database on protected areas (WDPA). UNEP-WCMC, Cambridge, UK. <http://www.protectedplanet.net>. Accessed November 20, 2013.

Knight, A. T., R. M. Cowling, M. Rouget, A. Balmford, A. T. Lombard, and B. M. Campbell. 2008. Knowing but not doing: Selecting priority conservation areas and the research-implementation gap. Conservation Biology 22:610–617.

Kostyack, J. 2001. NWF v. Babbitt: Victory of smart growth and imperiled wildlife. Environmental Law Reporter 31:10712–10718.

Lewis, P. G. 2000. The durability of local government structure: Evidence from California. State and Local Government Review 32:34–48.

Martin, D. T., and R. E. Wagner. 1978. The institutional framework for municipal incorporation: An economic analysis of Local Agency Formation Commissions in California. Journal of Law and Economics 21:409–425.

Matute, J., and S. Pincetl. 2013. Unraveling petroleum. Report for Next Ten. <www.next10.org>. Accessed October 10, 2014.

McHarg, I. 1969. Design with nature. American Museum of Natural History, New York, New York.

McWilliams, C. 1979 [1949]. California, the great exception. Peregrine Smith, Santa Barbara, California.

Meir, E., S. Andelman, and H. P. Possingham. 2004. Does conservation planning matter in a dynamic and uncertain world? Ecology Letters 7:615–622.

Merenlender, A. M., L. Huntsinger, G. Guthey, and S. K. Fairfax. 2004. Land trusts and conservation easements: Who is conserving what for whom? Conservation Biology 18:65–76.

Nash, G. D. 1972. Stages of California's economic growth, 1870–1970: An interpretation. California Historical Quarterly 51:315–330.

Nicolaides, B. M., and A. Wiese. 2013. Suburban Disequilibrium. New York Times. Week in Review. April 7. Page 5.

Olmsted, F. L. 1929. Report of state parks survey of California. California State Park Commission. Sacramento, CA.

Pincetl, S. 2006. Conservation planning in the West: Problems, new strategies, and entrenched obstacles. Geoforum 37(2):246–255.

———. 2004. The preservation of nature at the urban fringe. Pages 225–254 in J. Wolch, M. Pastor, and P. Drier, editors. Up against the Sprawl: Public Policy and the Making of Southern California. University of Minnesota Press, Minneapolis, Minnesota.

———. 2003. Nonprofits and park provision in Los Angeles: An exploration of the rise of governance approaches to the provision of local services. Social Science Quarterly 84(4):989–1001.

———. 1999a. The politics of influence: Democracy and the growth machine in Orange County, U.S. Pages 195–212 in A. Jonas and D. Wilson, editors. The Urban Growth Machine: Critical Perspectives, Two Decades Later. State University of New York Press, Buffalo, New York.

———. 1999b. Transforming California: The political history of land use in the state. Johns Hopkins University Press, Baltimore, Maryland.

Press, D. 2002. Saving Open Space: The politics of local preservation in California. University of California Press, Berkeley, California.

Radeloff, V. C., F. Beaudry, T. M. Brooks, V. Butsic, M. Dubinin, T. Kuermmerle, and A. M. Pidgeon. 2013. Hot moments for biodiversity conservation. Conservation Letters 6:58–66.

Reisner, M. 1986. Cadillac desert. Viking, New York, New York.

Santos, M. J., T. Watts, and S. Pincetl. 2014a. The push and pull of Land Use Policy: Reconstructing 150 Years of Development and Conservation Land Acquisition. PlosONE. doi: 10.1371/journal.pone.0103489.

Santos, M. J., J. H. Thorne, J. Christensen, and Z. Frank. 2014b. An historical land conservation analysis in the San Francisco Bay Area, USA: 1850 to 2010. Landscape and Urban Planning. 127:114–123.

Schrag, P. 1998. Paradise lost: California's experience, America's future. University of California Press, Berkeley, California.

Silva, F. J., and E. Barbour. 1999. The state-local fiscal relationship in California: A changing balance of power. Public Policy Institute of California, San Francisco, California.

Sokolow A. D. 1990. The Williamson Act: Twenty-five years of land conservation. The Resources Agency, Department of Conservation, Sacramento, California.

Szabó, P., and R. Hédl. 2011. Advancing the integration of history and ecology for conservation. Conservation Biology 25:680–687.

Taylor, P. S. 1975. California Water Project: Law and politics. Ecology Law Quarterly 5:1–52.

Thorne, J. H., P. R. Huber, E. O'Donoghue, and M. J. Santos. 2014. The use of regional advance mitigation planning (RAMP) to integrate transportation infrastructure impacts with sustainability: A perspective from the USA. Environmental Research Letters 9: 065001.

Trust for Public Lands (TPL). 2000. Building green infrastructure. TPL, San Francisco, California. <http://www.tpl.org>. Accessed October 10, 2014.

Wieslander, A. E. 1935. A vegetation type map for California. Madroño 3:140–144.

Wolch, J., M. Pastor, and P. Drier, editors. 2004. Up against the sprawl: Public policy and the making of southern California. University of Minnesota Press, Minneapolis, Minnesota.

FORTY-ONE

Stewardship, Conservation, and Restoration in the Context of Environmental Change

ADINA M. MERENLENDER, DAVID D. ACKERLY, KATHARINE SUDING, M. REBECCA SHAW, and ERIKA ZAVALETA

Introduction

California's ecosystems are diverse and dynamic; they have always experienced change. However, unprecedented human activity and impacts have brought about increasingly dramatic changes that require our attention. California's rapidly growing human system will include inevitable increases in land and water use. In the next fifteen years we expect California's population to grow by more than eight million people, a number as large as the current size of New York City. Continued development at current, low densities—with only 10% infill—will consume an estimated 2.1 million hectares (5.1 million acres) of undeveloped land in that time (Landis and Reilly 2003). The existing water supply cannot accommodate this expected growth while also sustaining California's diverse and important agricultural sector. Global climate change will exacerbate this shortfall, with expected 30% declines in snowfall and a further increase of 0.5°C to 1.0°C by 2025 and even more dramatic changes through the rest of the century (see Chapter 14, "Climate Change Impacts"). The rising likelihood of extreme rainfall events and intensifying drought, as we experienced in the winter of 2013–2014, will profoundly affect California's natural and human systems. We must anticipate and prepare for change to California's ecosystems from both old forces like development and new, interactive forces like climate change.

A range of anthropogenic changes—including climate change and other changes related to human development such as ocean acidification, biodiversity loss, land use change, freshwater use, and higher nitrogen and phosphorus levels—are all on the rise around the world (Fenn et al. 2010, Hayhoe et al. 2004). With the widespread recognition of these dramatic changes and the documented accelerating rates of change, many argue that Earth has experienced a decisive break from what it experienced during most of the Holocene and we have entered a new epoch: the Anthropocene (Crutzen 2002). This new epoch could be dated as early as the beginning of the Industrial Revolution, or when the great acceleration in population began in the 1950s, or at the start of the current trajectory of anthropogenic climate change around 1970 (Zalasiewicz et al. 2010). While the question of whether this current time in history is distinct and lasting enough to be designated a new epoch on a geological time scale is still in debate, humans are indisputably leaving their mark across the planet and changing the trajectory of Earth's biological and physical systems (Vince 2011).

This recent period of industrialization and globalization has led to increasing homogenization of natural communities at unprecedented rates because humans have facilitated massive biotic exchanges among regions (Olden et al. 2004). Biotic homogenization refers to simplification of a community's composition and happens when native ecosystems are assimilated by widespread exotic or weedy species reducing diversity (McKinney and Lockwood 1999). In California this is best illustrated in the prairies and grasslands, where nonnative species make up over half of the California flora (Bartolome et al. 2007, Stromberg et al. 2007; see Chapter 13, "Biological Invasions"). Given the trajectory of projected change in the state, our greatest challenge is to ensure that California's ecosystems persist and retain their capacity to sustain vital ecosystem services and biological diversity while building a sustainable and resilient society.

Rates of change in California's ecosystems will increase in this century unless dramatic action is taken to limit land conversion, realign water management, and dramatically slow greenhouse gas emissions into the atmosphere. Growth and conservation policies related to land use, such as increasing urban infill, could greatly enhance conservation outcomes in California. Land use patterns reflect land economics, which in turn reflect taxation structures; for example, Proposition 13 reduced local government's ability to keep up with urban infrastructure, stimulated growth in suburban communities, and reduced options to finance infill developments (see Chapter 40, "Land Use Regulation for Resource Conversation"). However, even with dramatic improvements to land and water use patterns, we face the highest rates of climate change recorded in human history. This means that California's ecosystems that we observe today, as detailed throughout this book, could be transient, albeit on the scale of thousands of years, and that the trajectories of the transitions they will undergo are dramatic and highly uncertain. For example, forecasted increases in summer temperatures suggest that desert plants could grow in Bakersfield and the Central Valley; and in the San Francisco Bay Area the vegetation is expected to be more similar to what we currently observe in southern California (Loarie et al. 2008).

This reality requires that researchers, managers, decision makers, and the public make a concerted break from the notion of equilibria or stationary ecosystems. Recognizing increased dynamism in ecosystems does not imply abandoning biodiversity conservation. Rather, a more concerted conservation effort and improvements to ecosystem management that incorporate an increased understanding of global and local forces of change are more important than ever to increase social and ecological system resilience to rapid change. In this chapter we examine the challenges environmental change presents to conservation, stewardship, and restoration in California. Many of these have been raised in earlier chapters of this book. We attempt to emphasize and integrate the actions various authors have suggested to best address future protection and management of California's ecosystems through the lens of inevitable change.

Photo on previous page: Environmental stewards of all ages at Pepperwood Preserve, in Sonoma County. Photo: Greg Damron, <www.wildvinestudios.com>.

Ecological Responses to Environmental Change

Protection and management begin with understanding of how ecosystems respond to environmental changes. While land use and other changes have been occurring for centuries, rates of change and associated responses such as species introductions are accelerating. Other changes are essentially new and unprecedented, such as accelerating climate changes to which we are already committed. Ecological responses to these growing challenges can take millennia to be fully realized. Inertia within ecosystems resists change; systems can appear to be in equilibrium when in fact they are simply experiencing lags preceding more radical ecosystem reorganization. One of the most important lessons from the paleoecological record is that time lags of one thousand to five thousand years after episodes of major changes, such as in climate, are expected in the observed responses of ecosystems (see Chapter 8, "Ecosystems Past: Vegetation Prehistory"). For example, climate change induces disequilibria at both leading and trailing edges of species ranges—with time lags at the leading edge due to delays in migration, succession, and evolutionary adaptation, and on the trailing-edge due to delayed local extinctions and disruptions of species interactions (Svenning and Sandel 2013).

Species respond to change at varying rates depending on their life history characteristics, tolerances to environmental variation, and degrees of interaction with and dependence on other species in the community. For example, species' lifespan and dispersal ability influence their response rates and the duration of lag effects. Species responses can also lag shifts in ecosystem processes such as soil formation and biochemical cycles (Jackson and Sax 2010). At the community level, ecological responses to multiple stressors can interact as well as lag changes in drivers. In some California ecosystems, climate change will likely favor exotic species that are more productive under the new climate conditions, with cascading ecosystem effects such as increased carbon storage rates and community effects such as displacement of native species (Ehrenfeld 2003).

Lags in species and community effects are reflected by the fact that only twenty documented extinctions of California's plant species have occurred in the past hundred or so years despite the conversion of about 43% of the land to agriculture and development throughout the twentieth century (see Chapter 11, "Biodiversity"). With an estimated 612 plant species now considered threatened across the state, far more extinctions are expected. Plant species extinctions are observed as they gradually unfold over human lifetimes through long-term monitoring at university research stations. For example, ecologists over a decade ago witnessed what could have been the last observation of beaked tracyina (Tracyina rostrata) at the Hopland Research and Extension Center (Heise and Merenlender 2002).

Attribution of ecological changes to particular stressors, while more often straightforward in the past—such as the demise through overexploitation of animals like the California grizzly bear (*Ursus arctos californicus*)—has also become more challenging in some cases. For example, it is clear that climate change is driving extinctions worldwide. However, attributing biotic response to even the most well-documented aspect of climate change—warming—is difficult. The complexity inherent in natural ecosystems and the disconnection between the temporal and spatial scales that global change operates on and those at which ecosystems respond makes it especially difficult to attribute ecological changes to global-scale drivers alone. Some notable successes documenting climate-driven transitions discussed previously are worth replicating, such as documented shifts in distributions of small mammals in the Sierra Nevada and intertidal invertebrates at the coast (see Chapter 14, "Climate Change Impacts"). The topographic complexity of California makes it harder to generalize how species ranges may shift, as widely anticipated shifts northward and to higher elevations might also be accompanied by some downward movements, such as towards moister locations, and westward to cooler coastal areas.

Detection and attribution of change will almost certainly improve as we combine high-quality baseline data and real-time tracking of ecological responses to change. Still, Mediterranean climates pose considerable challenges to climate change response detection because of their inherently high interannual variability in precipitation patterns and the potential for biotic changes to be strongly driven by climatic change during any season. A wide range of climate change responses have been documented in California and attributed to contrasting effects of temperature and precipitation (Rapacciuolo et al. 2014). California's diversity of ecosystems and concomitant diversity of responses and feedback loops also complicate generalized predictions about the outcomes of global change forces. In California's deserts, for example, increases in atmospheric carbon dioxide (CO_2) and nitrogen are of concern as they could facilitate the proliferation of non-native species and associated wildfires at the expense of native species more tolerant to nutrient-poor conditions (see Chapter 30, "Deserts"). This potential shift could be counterbalanced by soil moisture reductions that limit non-native grass invasion, but other interactions between elevated atmospheric CO_2 and both water use and temperature-sensitivity of different species might further complicate these responses (Dole et al. 2003). Alterations to water and land management required for humans to adapt will make predicting ecosystem response still more challenging. In sum, California's current ecosystems will continue to change at varying rates; while strong lags may dampen initial rates of extinction, introduction, and disruption, ecosystem shifts and novel community types will eventually result. The future of California's ecosystems remains unknown, but change is certain. Tackling these changes despite some areas of increased uncertainty are essential to guide effective stewardship and conservation.

Stewardship, Conservation, and Restoration

The time lags and uncertainties inherent in ecosystem responses to climate and other environmental changes require us to rethink how we approach conservation and restoration and necessitate nimble adaptive management strategies to manage inherently transient ecosystems. Despite these challenges, there is much we can do to conserve, restore, and manage California's ecosystems to safeguard biodiversity and human welfare into the future (Caro et al. 2012). Conservation in an era of change will need to: (1) manage toward a dynamic future rather than a static past; (2) be open to the challenge of reconsidering long-held conservation goals and objectives; and (3) extend collaboration to nontraditional private and institutional partners. Equally important, it requires that we reexamine and amend the scaffold of environmental, regulatory, and institutional policies that have begun to constrain our ability to respond effectively and that we build in sufficient flexibility to meet the future needs of conservation.

Defining and obtaining consensus on achievable goals, measuring and monitoring conservation success against those goals, implementing adaptive responses and partnering with diverse institutions have all proven difficult in the conservation community even without considering climate change (Salafsky et al. 2002, Ferraro and Pattanayak 2006). Successful conservation will require "managing according to clear goals by which decisions are made and modified as a function of what is known and learned about the system, including information about the effect of previous management actions" (Parma et al. 1998). Stating achievable goals and building adaptive plans to achieve those goals are essential. In the future there will likely need to be a shift from a focus on maintaining specific patterns of species and habitat diversity towards sustaining underlying ecological and evolutionary processes that promote continued ecological functioning in the face of change. Conservation will be defined less by the persistence of current patterns and conditions, and more by managing change in ways that sustain core conservation values and human needs.

An Ecosystem Stewardship Framework

In this period of unprecedented change, intervention may be needed simply to remain in the same spot along a degradation/transformation trajectory. Much as Lewis Carroll wrote in *Through the Looking Glass* (1871), "Now, here, you see, it takes all the running you can do, to keep in the same place. If you want to get somewhere else, you must run at least twice as fast as that!" This context of directional environmental changes forces us to consider new management approaches not premised on maintaining a particular community or genetic composition, but rather capable of shifting to maintain diversity as well as core ecosystem functions and important services over time (Choi et al. 2008). Although this type of approach has been discussed for some time among researchers, in practice it remains relatively new to explicitly incorporate ecosystem dynamism into land management strategies and to target outcomes that might vary and potentially include novel ecosystems (discussed later in this chapter).

Ecosystem stewardship has been defined as "a strategy to respond to and shape social-ecological systems under conditions of uncertainty and change to sustain the supply and opportunities for use of ecosystem services to support human well-being" (Chapin et al. 2010). Defined in this way, the framework relies less on maintaining historical conditions of a community and more on managing the dynamics, pathways, and rates of ecological change. If the current community status is viewed as desirable, efforts should be made to maintain the components of the current system by increasing stabilizing feedbacks that contribute to community persistence, and/or to maintain components of the system in shifting distribution over time. These goals should be defined and articulated as part of the ecosystem resilience concept. Resilience is conceptualized as the amount of change a system can undergo and still maintain similar function and structure with minimal intervention (Gunderson and Holling 2002). It is a critically and widely invoked concept, though still difficult to translate into practice in specific instances (Zavaleta and Chapin 2010).

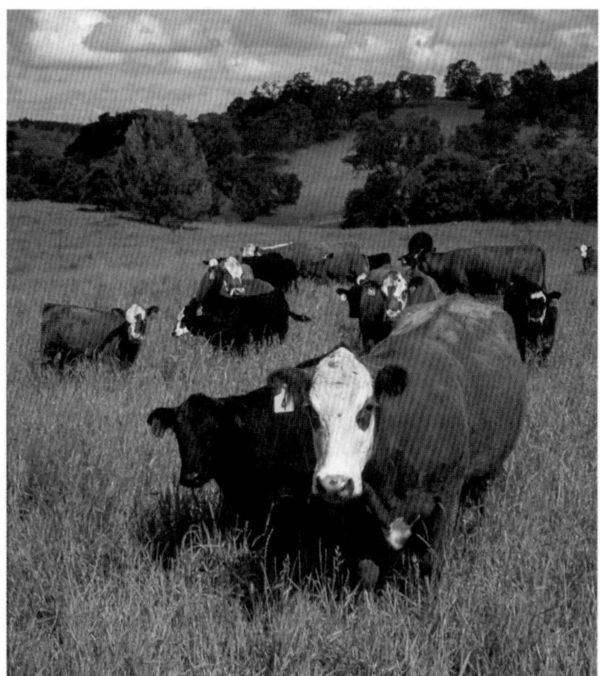

FIGURE 41.1 Many rangelands in California can be considered novel ecosystems due to the abundance of non-native grasses. These grasslands provide important ecosystem services, including forage. Conserving native species in these ecosystems is sometimes facilitated by livestock grazing, which can reduce competition from annual grasses that otherwise dominate. Photo: Jack Kelly Clark.

Stewardship on California's Tahoe National Forest (TNF) illustrates this approach. Here, as with many forest systems in the western United States, drought concerns, amplified by rising temperatures and lowered snowpacks, interact with dense forest structure from fire suppression to create severe forest hazards, extreme flood events, and new opportunities for invasive species spread (see Chapter 27, "Montane Forests"). Managers on the TNF recognized several general principles as opportunities for stewardship in the face of rapidly changing climate: (1) managing for drought- and heat-tolerant species and ecotypes, (2) reducing impact of current anthropogenic stressors, (3) managing for diverse successional stages, (4) spreading risks by including buffers and redundancies in natural environments and plantations, and (5) increasing collaboration with interested stakeholders. In addition, for reforestation they considered more drought-tolerant germplasm and species mixes and prioritized sensitive-species management actions at the "leading edges" of species ranges (likely favorable future habitats) rather than at "trailing edges" (Joyce et al. 2008). North and colleagues place a similar emphasis on forest resilience in this volume (Chapter 27, "Montane Forests"), in which large trees are recognized as providing more secure carbon storage compared to high-density, small trees that are prone to pests, pathogens, and fire.

The ecosystem stewardship framework also emphasizes the value of expecting and exploiting disturbances such as fires, floods, and high rates of nitrogen deposition rather than attempting to prevent such events. Managing for disturbance is an important aspect of maintaining healthy ecosystems (see, e.g., Chapter 3, "Fire as an Ecosystem Process"). Natural disturbance plays a well-documented, essential role in developing ecosystem structure and function (Attiwill 1994). Fire is one of the most widespread and intense sources of disturbance. Prescribed fire has been a preferred management strategy for thousands of years in California, and in some areas the use of fire by Native people has influenced the composition of ecosystems we see today (see Chapter 10, "Indigenous California").

Maintaining fire as a management tool is critical to the protection of many ecosystems, and when fire is not feasible, other types of disturbance such as selective harvesting and grazing could be required (Stromberg et al. 2007). In California's serpentine grasslands, for example, selective grazing on nitrogen-rich exotic grasses has been used with success to combat effects of nitrogen deposition (Weiss 1999) (Figure 41.1). However, this same method in coastal sage scrub is less effective because sufficient grass forage occurs only in very wet years (see Chapter 22, "Coastal Sage Scrub"). In many valley grasslands, however, invasions occurred so long ago and are spatially so extensive that fire and mowing often no longer suffice for large-scale restoration (see Chapter 23, "Grasslands"). Though grazing or mowing have been successfully used to mitigate the effects of nitrogen deposition in some grasslands, they might not be effective or feasible in other systems. Here, new management techniques need to be developed or goals altered to reflect the transformation of the systems in question to new states. Adopting an ecosystem stewardship framework acknowledges the need to incorporate expected changes into interventions and to consider how to maintain system integrity over large potential ranges of variability rather within narrow bounds.

Conservation

Halting habitat loss for all of California's ecosystems is crucial to maintain biological diversity. Diversity of genotypes, species, and functional groups influences a range of biogeochemical processes, trophic interactions, resistance to biological invasions, and dimensions of temporal ecosystem variability (Hillebrand and Matthiessen 2009, Hughes et al. 2008, Báez and Collins 2008, Isbell et al. 2009; see Chapter 15, "Introduction to Concepts of Biodiversity, Ecosystem Functioning, Ecosystem Services, and Natural Capital").

A review of over two hundred studies worldwide revealed that species losses result in decreases in productivity and influence decomposition and can be as disruptive to ecosystems as warming temperatures and other global change factors (Hooper et al. 2012). Habitat loss can thus, in addition to increasing risks of species extirpations and extinctions (see Chapter 11, "Biodiversity"), have biophysical impacts on ecosystems. For example, tree removal in oak woodland ecosystems can affect local climate, hydrology, and ecosystem processes. Trees in oak woodlands create microclimates distinct from grasslands, influencing soil development as well as nutrient cycling (see Chapter 25, "Oak Woodlands"). Avoiding land development patterns that continue to increase habitat loss and fragmentation is critical to maintain biodiversity, ecosystem processes, functions, and services. All development involves trade-offs, including green energy efforts such as planned solar development that threatens sensitive valley and desert habitat for a number of listed species (see Chapter 11, "Biodiversity").

International agreements provide a guide to setting large-scale conservation goals for the state. While the United States has not signed the International Convention on Biodiversity

TABLE 41.1
Percentage of surface area protected, selected regions

Region	Percentage
Antarctic	0.50
Australia/New Zealand	16.87
Brazil	18.70
Caribbean	8.17
Central America	22.45
East Asia	13.99
Eastern and Southern Africa	14.06
Europe	12.37
North Africa and Middle East	9.79
North America	16.21
North Eurasia	7.74
Pacific	1.89
South America	19.33
South Asia	6.53
South East Asia	9.55
Western and Central Africa	8.65
TOTAL	**11.58**

SOURCE: UNEP–World Conservation Monitoring Centre 2006.

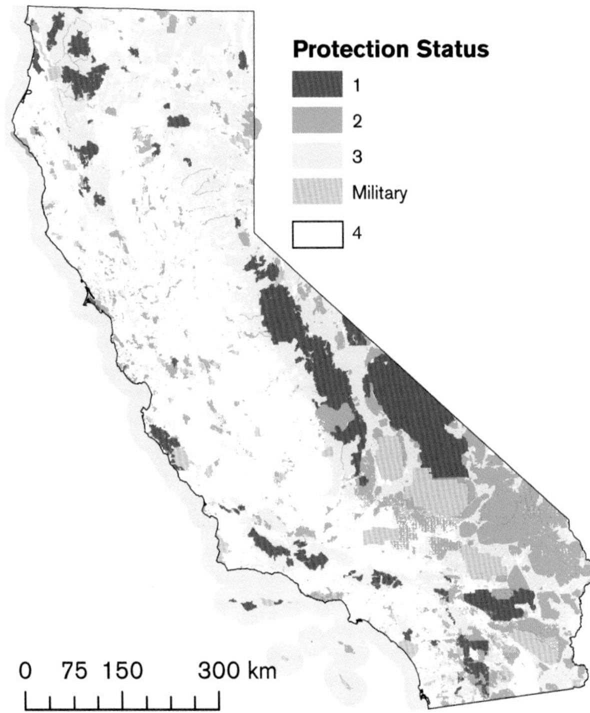

FIGURE 41.2 Management status of protected lands in California, as categorized by the U.S. Geological Survey Gap Analysis Program (GAP), Protected Area Database v1.3 (2012). Map: Frank Davis.

STATUS 1 LANDS: Permanently protected and managed to maintain a natural state (e.g., national parks and wilderness areas).

STATUS 2 LANDS: Permanently protected and maintained primarily in a natural state but may include some management actions such as wildfire suppression.

STATUS 3 LANDS: Permanent protection but subject to extractive uses such as logging, Off Highway Vehicle recreation and mining.

STATUS 4 LANDS: Includes private lands of California that lack formal protection (such as legally recognized easements or other known mandates) and where development and conversion of natural habitats and development are generally allowed.

(ICB) (Convention on Biological Diversity 2011), California could play a leadership role in meeting these standards much the way it has in reducing carbon emissions following the adoption of the Kyoto Protocol. To meet the IBC standards, California would need to bring its rate of natural habitat loss to zero where possible and commit to reducing current carbon emissions by at least one half. California would need to ensure that 17% or more of every terrestrial ecosystem has full protection, along with 10% of the state's marine and coastal areas. The international standards also require restoration of at least 15% of degraded areas within each ecosystem. Meeting these conservation targets is a critical step to protecting California's spectacular biodiversity that took millions of years to evolve (see Chapter 11, "Biodiversity").

The California GAP analysis (1998) provides an estimate on the amount of protection afforded to each of California's ecosystems. As part of this effort, levels of protection were ranked from 1 to 4, with 1 the highest, most permanent level of protection against habitat conversion and use and 4 the lowest level of protection. Approximately 15% of California currently falls under the most protected status (1), with an additional 3% in the second-highest protective category (Figure 41.2). Over half of the state lacks protection from habitat conversion; most of this is privately owned. The remaining 30% is managed for multiple uses by agencies such as the U.S. Forest Service and the Bureau of Land Management. While 15% might seem high compared to other areas of the world (Table 41.1), these protected areas in California are almost entirely in high-elevation Sierra Nevada or in Mojave and Sonoran Desert ecosystems. Other low-elevation areas in the Great Valley and along the coast, along with many rare habitat types, have very little protection to date.

The nearshore marine ecosystems present a different story. Under the Marine Life Protection Act of 1999, a public-private partnership established marine protected areas using the best available scientific methods. As a result, 16.4% of the marine ecosystems are captured in protected areas with varying goals as compared to the 2% global average. For example, five National Marine Sanctuaries now lie along the West Coast, protecting over 31,263 square kilometers in the California Current system and especially benefiting kelp conservation (see Chapter 17, "Shallow Rocky Reefs and Kelp Forests"). With approximately 18% of state marine area under designated protected status, however, only 243 square kilometers (94 square miles) fall under the highest level of protection, which prevents all fishing or habitat loss. Current conservation actions required to fill the gaps among these areas remain piecemeal and reliant on private sector investment.

To meet and hopefully exceed these conservation goals, California will need to continue to embrace the importance of biodiversity for human well-being and the moral, ethical,

FIGURE 41.3 California's Essential Habitat Connectivity Project. Proposed linkages across California based on expert opinion of habitat requirements for a select group of focal species. Data and map: California Department of Fish and Wildlife, Spencer et al. 2010.

and practical responsibility to protect species and their habitats, as well as to strengthen public connections to nature and increase general understanding of the role that species and natural systems serve in supporting society. All of these elements are important to increase public and political support for conservation.

Habitat Connectivity

Remnant protected areas are often too small to allow persistence of viable species populations. Connecting protected areas into networks can increase persistence; in particular, the need to recover endangered species and rare habitat types has driven much of the demand for habitat connectivity. Plans to increase connectivity through corridors, ecological networks, and other landscape features to minimize continued fragmentation and associated species extinctions are widespread. The most common approach to connectivity is to maintain and restore habitat that will provide pathways among protected natural areas for wildlife movement. However, it is not always clear that connecting wildlands through linear habitat features across disturbed landscapes really does enhance species persistence within reserves. The goal of reconnecting landscapes comes from our theoretical and empirical understanding of how habitat fragmentation contributes to rates and patterns of species extinction. Fragmentation is defined as the transformation of a continuous habitat into habitat patches varying in size and configuration (Fahrig 2003). Habitat loss and consequential fragmentation is the largest current threat to the world's biodiversity (e.g., Dirzo and Raven 2003).

The extent to which species distributions are expected to shift due to climate change has increased the justification for additional protected areas. Many existing protected areas are currently too small to be resilient in the face of today's changes, let alone those projected into the future (Heller and Zavaleta 2009). Climate change compounded by habitat loss and fragmentation could impede species' range shifts to such an extent that population and species extinctions could result (Nuñez et al. 2013). The built environment poses barriers to species movement between protected and unprotected remnant natural areas, and even areas with high habitat connectivity could prevent species to adapt to a changing climate and shifting ecological zones for a variety of reasons. In particular, as conditions warm, alpine plants will have nowhere to go, and those occurring at the edges of their ranges or within small isolated patches might not survive. Species' ability to move through landscapes of varying composition and through corridors of varying size and configuration range widely; what constitutes connectivity for one group of organisms might not for another (Chester and Hilty 2010). Many scientists and land managers have assumed that improving the connectivity of existing protected area networks will improve the chances of species movement and adaptation. In California, consultants have proposed linkages between many protected lands across the state using simplified rule-based models of species habitat preferences (California Essential Habitat Connectivity Project 2010) (Figure 41.3).

Habitat connectivity to facilitate animal and plant movement is one of the most frequently promoted strategies addressing rapid climate change resulting from anthropogenic disturbance (Heller and Zavaleta 2009). As part of this strategy, habitat corridors have been adopted to make protected area networks more resilient to climate change (Vos et al. 2008). Despite the fact that habitat connectivity is the go-to solution for increasing reserve resilience to climate change, most methods remain untested. The most common approach is to establish corridors that track the species expected range shifts due to climate change in order to permit the expected movement of the species to more suitable habitat in the future (Lawler et al. 2013). This approach depends on models that have high levels of uncertainty about species climate sensitivity as well as the climate change models themselves. A more problematic aspect of this species modeling approach is forecasting the distribution of species across novel climates when we lack information about whether these novel climates and the vegetation they support in both the near- and long-term will provide suitable habitat.

A simpler alternative that avoids the inherent uncertainties in a species-based approach is to design linkages based on expected rates of climate change and the distributions of climates across space and time (Loarie et al. 2009, Ackerly et al. 2010). This approach can take advantage of high-resolution, downscaled climate models (e.g., Flint 2013) and avoids some of the pitfalls associated with species habitat modeling. It focuses on features of climate that could influence reserve network resilience, based on the following assumptions: (1) the advantages of connectivity are greatest for areas that will experience faster rates of change, (2) a reserve network that harbors greater climatic diversity will allow greater adaptation, (3) maintaining access to cooler climates is a high priority, and (4) corridors that track isotherm movement will facilitate climate migrants trying to remain in the same climate analog over time. In other words, it is useful to think about climate space and diversity across the entire landscape as well as how fast organisms will need to move to stay in the current climate (Loarie et al. 2009; Burrows et al. 2014).

Unique physiographic features could be important to protect in order to maintain landscape connectivity for multiple species. These include alluvial valleys, river mouths, and other places where hydrologic flow paths provide conditions that promote increased diversity and are often restricted geographically (Klausmeyer et al. 2011). Rarely are these different goals for maintaining connectivity met by the same corridors across the landscape, and it is not possible to secure corridors among all habitat fragments. Hence it could be more important to enhance the permeability of the matrix landscape surrounding protected areas through measures such as diversifying agricultural landscapes, adding highway crossings, and removing fences to facilitate as much species movement as possible across moderately modified landscapes. In some cases, species might only require short-distance movement to persist. In these cases, enlarging core reserves could be more effective than establishing corridors between reserves. More research is needed to examine the ecological and economic trade-offs between augmenting and acquiring new reserves and conserving habitat corridors (Shaw et al. 2012). Conservation planning needs to be coupled with land use planning. Conservation strategies that include multiple environmental benefits, reduce time delays, and increase predictability for the development community are desirable and will be implemented more readily.

Ecological Restoration

The chapters in this book describe many ecosystems that persist in California today. Yet we know that land use change over the years has taken its toll and that large areas have been converted to urban and agricultural land. Some ecosystem loss stands out as particularly severe, such as the loss of 90% of California's wetlands (Dahl 1990; see Chapter 31, "Wetlands"). With less than 10% of this ecosystem remaining, wetland restoration is essential to recover some of what has been lost. Other ecosystems in the state remain widespread but have been greatly modified by agriculture and residential development, such as California's oak woodlands (Chapter 25). In oak woodlands, field surveys show that 67% of trees on average are greater than 13 centimeters in diameter at breast height (cm dbh) and 37% of trees were found to be greater than 61 cm dbh (Gaman and Firman 2008). Inadequate regeneration could be affecting at least three oak species (blue oak Quercus douglasii, valley oak Q. lobata, and Engelmann oak Q. engelmannii) (Koenig and Ashley 2003, Zavaleta et al. 2007, McLaughlin and Zavaleta 2013). Oak restoration is often required to mitigate for continued habitat loss, degradation, and lack of regeneration (McCreary 2009).

Today, much restoration is shifting away from goals of returning communities to particular reference assemblages and towards rehabilitating systems to a point along a development trajectory that allows for self-sustaining population, community, and ecosystem processes (Suding 2011, Choi et al. 2008, Hobbs and Cramer 2007). Restoration of these processes can also lead to higher or desired levels of particular functions or services, such as erosion control and drinking water quality. However, we lack experience in implementing ecosystem management goals other than the traditional goals that emphasize native species and permanence.

In some cases, ecosystems have been so strongly impacted that it is not an option to use a historical analogue as a target for restoration. These systems are often termed "novel ecosystems." Hobbs and others (Hobbs et al. 2006, Hobbs et al. 2009) have defined a novel ecosystem as one that lacks a historical analog and has crossed a threshold to where reversing these impacts is not feasible. In these cases, goals based on historical conditions can be impossible to attain or require more intensive and continual management than can be reasonably accomplished. Eventual failure in cases like this can both waste valuable public investment and leave ecosystems in poor condition. Instead, consideration of how these "novel" systems can have value and of how to manage these systems for other goals, such as providing ecosystem services or natural areas for recreation and enjoyment, is warranted (Daily et al. 2009; see Chapter 39, "Urban Ecosystems").

The widespread existence of and forecasted increase in novel California ecosystems impels us to adopt equally novel approaches to restoration and to make increased investments in managing ecosystems. For example, an approach to protect important ecosystem processes, functions, and services could focus on ensuring persistence of diverse functional groups (Suding et al. 2008). A functional group is a set of species that have similar traits and that thus are likely to be similar in their effects on ecosystem functioning. Functional diversity can be very important because it goes beyond diversity and community composition and focuses on how species influence ecosystem dynamics, stability, productivity, nutrient balance, and other functions (Tilman 2001).

Some express concern that by recognizing the role of novel ecosystems we will abandon efforts to prevent continued modification of natural ecosystems. However, acknowledging that novel ecosystems are providing essential ecosystem services and might not warrant investment to recover to their historical composition can free resources to protect more pristine ecosystems and restore native plant and animal communities where they are more vital for biodiversity conservation. An increased level of uncertainty is associated with trying to predict how animal populations will respond to future change; models are aimed at forecasting changes to California's bird communities involving novel communities as a result of climate change (see Chapter 11, "Biodiversity").

Biodiversity goals such as native species persistence and diversity require more and innovative attention in the context of accelerating environmental change. Intensive and continued management (essentially gardening) can be justified in rare cases due to unique aspects of natural heritage or place, but more of biodiversity protection will need to emphasize movement and change, and limited resources may often be better used targeting less-affected areas with more certain recovery trajectories. Generally, we should not expect to be able to maintain existing communities in their current, static form. A long-term perspective, including paleohistory, can provide useful information on how species migrated under specific climate conditions in the past and provides a rich context from which to consider current possibilities. Understanding what stakeholders need and involving them in planning and implementation also encourages long-term public investment in site stewardship even as sites change. Often, both historical and stakeholder perspectives can be achieved with minimal trade-offs. For instance, urban creek restoration can generate high native plant diversity and abundant wildlife habitat while providing an open understory that allows children to explore (Lyytimaki and Sipila 2009). Even in more protected wilderness areas, where emphasis shifts towards historical goals, anticipation of and reconciliation with future climate and disturbance regimes are critical (Baron et al. 2009).

Assisted migration is a controversial approach to conserving biodiversity under climate change (Vitt et al. 2010). It involves the purposeful introduction of genotypes or species not part of any (past) reference condition but adaptable to current and future likely conditions. Although thousands of conservation translocations have taken place in the past for other purposes (Godefroid et al. 2011.), assisted migration is a new approach to preventing species losses under climate change and pursuing increased ecosystem resilience. Some assisted migration efforts aim to prevent extinctions by deliberately expanding the ranges of endangered species, while others might pursue improved future vegetation cover and plant survivorship at a restored site by planting more drought-tolerant varieties. The latter contrasts starkly with the standard approach of relying on local genetic stock for planting efforts (Vander Mijnsbrugge et al. 2010). Hence, assisted migration is contentious because it can place different conservation objectives at odds with one another (McLachlan et al. 2007).

While in some contexts it is time to rethink the focus on local genetic stock for plant restoration projects (as has begun to take place, for instance, in reforestation efforts in British Columbia, Canada), the risks of using alternative genetic stocks should be considered carefully before implementation. In particular, those that could dilute locally adapted gene pools could present greater biodiversity risks than introductions of more distinct southerly or lower-elevation taxa. Given the effort made to care for and maintain early restoration efforts, strong natural selection to maintain locally adapted

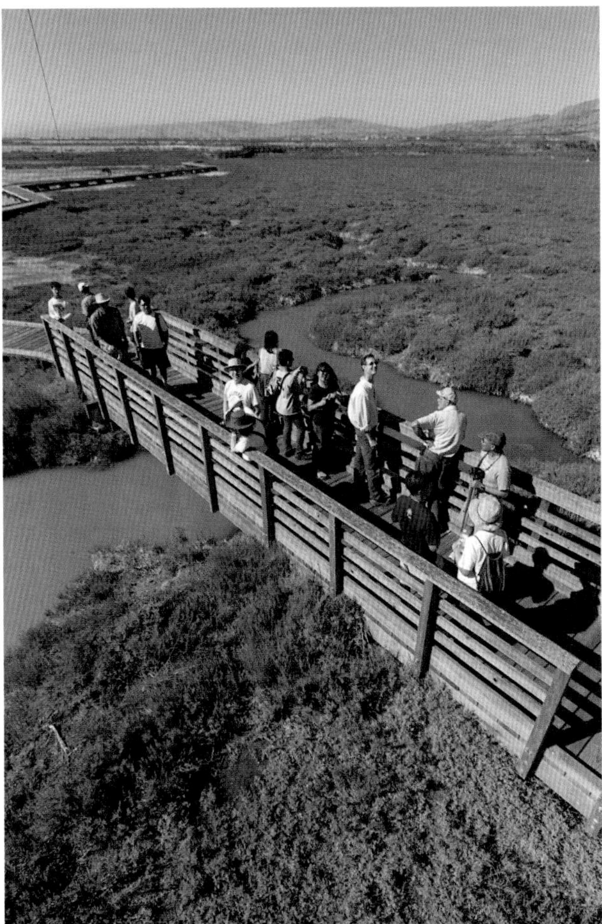

FIGURE 41.4 Don Edwards National Wildlife Refuge workshop participants viewing restored wetlands at the Environmental Education Center in New Chicago Marsh near Alviso, California. Photo: Cris Benton.

FIGURE 41.5 South Bay Salt Pond Restoration in San Francisco Bay. The lighter color areas surrounding the bay are urban. Because both the salt flats and the tidal marshes provide critical bird habitat, the restoration project is taking a piecewise approach, restoring tidal flow in some areas while maintaining drier salt flats in others. The diversified approach is allowing multiple restoration goals to be achieved. Photo: Cris Benton.

genotypes is less likely, thus newly introduced genotypes could degrade remnant native genotypes through hybridization or competition under temporarily subsidized conditions. Maintaining relatively local genetic solutions, such as by using genotypes and ecotypes found within a larger, given watershed area and in similar microclimates, is the safest option for restoring and maintaining local biodiversity.

While the extent of invasion and land use impacts in California may pose serious challenges to ecological restoration, several large-scale solutions and innovative strategies have successfully overcome these impacts. As part of one of the largest wetland restoration programs in the western United States, 6,100 hectares of former commercial-production salt ponds are being reconnected to the South San Francisco Bay (Thebault et al. 2008) (Figures 41.4, 41.5). Restoration program managers are balancing salt pond retention with reconversion to tidal salt marsh because both currently provide critical habitat for endangered bird species. Given the uncertainties inherent in restoring a mixed complex of wetland types without historical analog, the project developed targets for a range of restoration goals, with predefined triggers for reevaluation if monitored components deviate from the desired range. This approach allows both specificity in restoration planning and the ability to adapt and address uncertainty. This is a good example of a large-scale project, that along with the estuarine habitat being protected under the marine protected area (MPA) and 26,000 hectares of tidal habitat recovery being planned for the Sacramento–San Joaquin Delta, takes us in the direction of restoring and protecting large-scale ecosystems rather than the more typical small-scale or piecemeal approach to mitigation of endangered species habitat loss (see Chapter 19, "Estuaries: Life on the Edge").

The Channel Islands represent the largest experiment in California testing how a combination of active management, mostly of invasive species, and passive restoration, resulting from human depopulation and declining land use, is leading to the ecological recovery of unique habitats (see Chapter 34, "Managed Island Ecosystems"). While the recovering island ecosystems are not identical in composition to their historical counterparts, with certain elements entirely missing and with well-established new species, the dynamics of recovery and change on the islands are remarkable and critical to observe as they "revert back to nature." Guided by a desire to recover ecological processes, managers have ended livestock grazing, reduced human population densities, and removed feral non-native animals from the islands, including some voracious herbivores that have greatly affected plant growth and soil structure. Removal of ranch animals was an essential first step to trigger restoration of these islands, which has progressed considerably without additional interventions (Beltran et al. 2014). Some efforts have also successfully removed invasive plants that represent a high risk to restricted native communities. Other invasive plant populations are waning due to declines in disturbance from intensive land use and overgrazing; still others, such as common, naturalized annual grasses found throughout California, have been left untreated and will likely remain on the islands indefinitely.

Positive outcomes apparent today on the islands include intact riparian vegetation along stream corridors that had been reduced to exposed cobble and mud, and increased channel sinuosity, which together reduce flow velocities and increase sediment capture. Early colonizing shrub species are now facilitating establishment of native herbs over annual exotics along with increases in rare species that were reduced to low numbers by trampling by non-native animals. Clear goals and working assumptions have been critical to the success of the Channel Islands restoration approach. Land managers recognized that some change is inevitable, and some human-caused changes are irreversible, alleviating expectations that the islands will return to a particular historical baseline. They also acknowledge that restoration outcomes depend on initial ecosystem and weather conditions (precipitation in particular) and that self-repair might be slow, especially for soil development and other processes that operate on longer time scales. Finally, the importance of local, regional, and global contexts for the recovery of wide-ranging species on the islands has been clearly articulated, clarifying the role of the Channel Islands in broader, mutually contingent efforts to conserve these taxa.

Restoration is not only essential for maintaining many of California's ecosystems but also for enhancing quality of life; it can reconnect people with nature and improve air and water quality. Restoration of degraded habitat and conservation of intact habitats are both essential, with the latter in part providing the source propagules for future biodiversity. Restoration requires source material, and its success is greatly influenced by the configuration of natural areas and their composition present in the surrounding landscape. Scientists increasingly appreciate the value of participatory research and collaborate with land stewards, managers, and citizen naturalists to implement realistic restoration and management goals for most of California's wildlands.

Future Directions for Stewardship and Policy across California's Ecosystems

Interwoven in many of the chapters in this volume are important suggestions for land management, research directions, and revisions to policy. These focus largely on increasing ecosystem resilience to help California's ecosystems adapt to global environmental changes. This focus is critical to minimize future regrets and provide desired outcomes and benefits no matter how climate and other changes proceed, to provide environmental co-benefits including the alleviation of potential threats to human communities associated with climate and other environmental changes, to dynamically restoring natural processes, and to address the areas of greatest risk in the state. With this in mind we review and augment the calls to action presented throughout this book for the benefit of California's ecosystems and the people who inhabit them. We emphasize the importance of fire management, managing for natural hydrologic flow regimes, emerging challenges to open space stewardship, and ecological monitoring as essential elements of adaptive management that each apply to a diversity of ecosystem types in the state.

Fire Management

Many of the authors in this book point to the challenges and importance of fire as a disturbance agent integral to California's plant community dynamics and an essential management tool for replicating natural ecological processes. Native Californians used fire to drive and concentrate game, open paths for travel, alter habitat mosaics, protect against enemies, safeguard villages, and promote the growth of desirable plants and specific plant parts (see Chapter 10, "Indigenous California") (DeNevers et al. 2013). These prescribed burns certainly enhanced habitat diversity in some parts of California; however, the influence of prescribed burning on plant communities by indigenous people may be less widespread than is sometimes asserted.

From the forests to the deserts, authors stress that the combined effects of warming, decreases in rainfall, increases in the extent and intensity of human land use, and atmospheric changes due to pollution could increase fuel loads and fire frequencies, which in turn could greatly alter plant community composition. In particular, fire suppression over the past century has produced dense, even-aged forests that, in combination with increased human ignitions and increased tree mortality from a variety of sources such as beetle kill, present a "perfect storm" for catastrophic fire (see Chapter 3, "Fire as an Ecosystem Process"). Most models predict that the frequency and severity of fire will rise, with 5–8% increases in area burned (see Chapter 27, "Montane Forests"). The chaparral ecosystem, characterized by drought-tolerant, fire-adapted species, is expected to expand as conditions warm and fire intervals increase. California's already extensive urban-wildland interface in chaparral ecosystems continues to grow; damage to structure and loss of life could get much worse without immediate attention to land use policies that encourage expansion of development into these wildlands (see Chapter 24, "Chaparral"). Montane forests face similar challenges.

Changing fire regimes across the state could be the most important consequence for California's coupled human and natural systems of changing climate and continued sprawl. Ecological restoration requires fire in many ecosystems, but many issues lamentably limit or prevent use of prescribed burns. These include potential threats from escaped fires to structures and lives, air quality restrictions, and a lack of resources to conduct controlled burns. Alternatives to fire such as mechanical tree or shrub removal can benefit tree stand management and reduce risk of future fires, but these alternatives do not restore important ecological processes such as nutrient cycling that accompany fire. Prescribed fire is described as the most efficient means to promote montane forest resilience, especially in the face of climatic stress (see Chapter 27, "Montane Forests").

Freshwater Landscapes

Water is one of California's most important natural resources. A central need to improve conditions in several important California ecosystems is to address past and continued hydrological alterations and improve freshwater conservation for environmental processes, functions, and species. Water has long been a critical resource in California whose natural capture and delivery have been impacted by dams and other water management projects. Many threatened and endangered species in the state rely on freshwater ecosystems. Of the California species that went extinct in the past hundred years, 19% occupied freshwater systems (see Chapter 11, "Biodiversity"), and close to 80% of California's 129 native freshwater fishes are at risk of becoming extinct (Moyle et al. 2011; see Chapter 33, "Rivers"). A remarkable 82% of California's native fish species are considered highly vulnerable to climate change (Moyle et al. 2013). Conflicts surrounding water management are at the heart of many divisive political agendas, contrasting cultural and ecological values. It is hard to imagine how California's ecosystems, especially those highly dependent on dynamic hydrologic processes, will fare as the state's population approaches fifty million and drought increases.

For example, wetlands are highly sensitive to alterations throughout both the terrestrial and the aquatic components of watersheds. Landscape configuration and seasonal flow conditions affect wetlands; thus watershed alterations that create hydrologic rerouting and change flow dynamics can greatly affect wetland processes and lead to dysfunction and species extirpation. Wetland features technically protected under the Clean Water Act can be severely degraded by hydrological alterations caused by permitted, adjacent, or nearby development. The same can be said for riparian communities that rely on seasonal streamflow variation. For example, germination of Fremont cottonwood (*Populus fremontii*) in riparian areas depends on the spring and early summer inundation associated with floods from Sierran snowmelt (Mahoney and Rood 1998). These large, overstory trees provide vital habitat and shade for salmon and other freshwater species. The magnitude, frequency, and duration of flooding have been widely altered by reservoir management specifically to avoid flooding and to provide a more constant water supply.

The problems of addressing wetland management independent from the management of surrounding, often highly modified, landscapes has crippled many ecosystems (see Chapter 31, "Wetlands"). Managing wetlands and fresh water at a larger scale requires balancing socioeconomic demands on the system, often expressed as political influence, with protecting the dynamic hydrologic processes required for ecosystem function and self-maintenance. California's water policies are completely inadequate to structure effective allocation of this resource (see Chapter 40, "Land Use Regulation for Resource Conversation"). This fact has severely hampered attempts to protect streamflows for environmental benefits including endangered species recovery. In rare instances such as the Mono Lake case (see Chapter 32, "Lakes"), fresh water was returned to an ecosystem for public trust benefits. However, other fresh waters such as coastal streams around the San Francisco Bay have been the subjects of long legal struggles pitting urban, agricultural, and environmental interests against each other without clear resolution.

Protected Area Challenges

Many of California's parks and preserves face a growing number of management challenges. A renewed commitment and stewardship to these precious public lands is needed. The recent establishment of marine protected areas (MPA) along California is one of the most promising conservation actions recently taken in the region. These reserves are intended to provide refuge from fishing, creating core habitat areas for fish and other marine species to reproduce and grow, and providing a source for replenishment of currently overharvested areas. Performance of marine protected areas is rather mixed, mostly due to a lack of enforcement and monitoring. This underscores the importance of building capacity to better manage MPAs and to effectively manage and evaluate their strategies and actions (Pomeroy et al. 2005). Effective marine protected area management along with implementation of the catch shares or individual transferable quotas in fisheries management can go a long way towards restoring both marine biodiversity, habitats, and productive fisheries (Costello et al. 2008).

While large areas of California's public lands are designated as parks, preserves, and wilderness areas, activities still occur within these lands that can degrade ecosystems. Demand continues to grow for multiple-use considerations in California's open spaces, and particular tensions surround off-road vehicle use. The impacts on natural ecosystems of rapidly growing recreation can be extensive yet remain understudied and underappreciated. In the United States the popularity of outdoor recreation activities—such as hiking, backpacking, and birdwatching—has doubled in the past twenty years (Cordell et al. 2005). In California a majority of residents (65%) prefer to recreate in undeveloped and nature-oriented parks, a trend that has increased over the past fifteen years. Public forested lands in California receive an average annual total of fifty million to sixty million visitor-days. Yosemite National Park received four million visitors in 2010; while not all activities equally affect ecological systems, these sheer numbers present concerns for montane forest health.

On the other hand, access for recreation is a key component of plans to generate public support and revenue for land conservation. Public parks and open space preserves are the primary places where most people access nature, and contact with nature has a range of human health benefits (Frumkin 2001). Ecologists have identified recreation as an ecosystem service supporting human populations (Costanza et al. 1997), estimating the monetary value of recreation opportunities that are provided when land is protected from development (Chan et al. 2006). The Lake Tahoe Basin has a tourist population of 4.5 million yr^{1}, and with revenues of $4.7 billion annually, tourism is at the heart of the region's economy (see Chapter 32, "Lakes"). Outdoor recreation enthusiasts are vocal advocates for land conservation, and public access is an important platform for generating tax and bond revenue for protected area acquisition. For example, California voters passed Proposition 84 in 2006, which as part of over $5 billion in bond commitments included nearly $2.5 billion for conservation ranging from park facilities to forest and coastal protection. In the same year voters passed Measure F in Sonoma County, extending a quarter-cent sales tax in the county entirely dedicated to open space protection.

Still, recreation is not always compatible with other conservation objectives. Recreational activities are the second largest cause of endangerment to species occurring on U.S. federal lands (Losos et al. 1995). California is the state with the greatest number of listed species threatened by recreation. This is in part because the threat of recreation is most frequently associated with urbanization, another important cause of endangerment (Czech et al. 2000). Growing evidence indicates that nonmotorized activities have negative impacts on a wide range of wildlife species (Knight and Gutzwiller 1995). For example, recreational activity correlates with decreases in species abundances and activity levels (Garber and Burger 1995), causes wildlife to flee (Papouchis et al. 2001) or avoid otherwise suitable habitat (Taylor and Knight 2003), and alters species composition and behavior (Ikuta and Blumstein 2003). Reed and Merenlender (2008) found that the key factors associated with recreational effects on carnivores appear to be the presence and number of human visitors to protected areas in California oak woodlands. In this study abundances of native coyotes (*Canis latrans*) and bobcats (*Lynx rufus*) were over four times greater in sites not open for public access than in adjacent park lands. Expanding human communities demand additional land and public access for recreation, underscoring the need for refined understanding of the consequences of recreation for ecosystems and biodiversity that can guide co-development of management strategies with park managers to minimize these impacts while providing opportunities for people to experience nature in a diversity of ways.

Ecological Monitoring for Adaptive Management

Active ecosystem stewardship requires increased attention to ecological monitoring in California. Monitoring is integral to adaptive management and is stressed by authors throughout this volume as a vital and undersupported activity. Only through monitoring biodiversity is early detection of invasive species possible and equally important is impact monitoring to assess the effectiveness of eradication efforts, which generally require ongoing efforts to achieve long-term control (see Chapter 13, "Biological Invasions"). For instance, multimillion-dollar restoration efforts in the San Francisco Bay-Delta and elsewhere to recover estuaries and wetlands in general still lack effective monitoring and evaluation programs to measure the environmental and social benefits of these efforts and to determine whether management or policy changes are required to improve success (see Chapter 19, "Estuaries: Life on the Edge"). Effective management requires clear identification of monitoring objectives, stressors that contribute to ecosystem degradation, and indicators that can be used to monitor ecosystem responses to change (see Chapter 30, "Deserts"). Monitoring is especially critical given the uncertainties associated with increased rates of change. In some systems, such as oak woodlands, the dominance of private ownership and growing prevalence of small individual land parcels pose special challenges (see Chapter 25, "Oak Woodlands"). These include lack of landowner experience, training, financial incentives, and general willingness to participate and mean that improving stewardship in these privately owned landscapes can only be done with outreach and education. Remote monitoring technologies are also increasingly important tools to assess the condition, composition, and changes that will occur on woodlands and other privately owned landscapes.

While monitoring protocols are well developed for some systems, such as wetlands and watersheds, less information exists in other ecosystems to build on to inform monitoring programs. For example, reliable methods for restoration and monitoring under different environmental contexts are largely undeveloped for desert systems (see Chapter 30, "Deserts"). Likewise, effective management of newly established marine protected areas requires monitoring, evaluation, communication, and adaptation. Evaluation involves quantitative tracking of ecosystems before and after management actions are taken and assessing whether these actions are producing the desired outcomes. Evaluation is a routine part of the management process yet is underdeveloped for most managed ecosystems. Even in places that are rebounding and might require less new action, such as the Channel Islands, monitoring remains crucial for detecting changes over time.

Beyond resources and will, monitoring and assessing management effectiveness rely on sound, scientifically based design. Much can be learned from well-documented experiments designed to test hypotheses and provide information for natural resource management. Research forests and field stations exist throughout California that could be used to compare management alternatives as well as to monitor global change within and between the ecosystems that span the state. Intensive climate monitoring efforts are under way on sites such as Blue Oak Ranch Reserve, a University of California reserve in the Mount Hamilton Range, Santa Clara County, California (Blue Oak Ranch 2008). Here, a wireless environmental monitoring system has been deployed to collect fine-resolution data on spatial and temporal variability in the landscape. This type of passive monitoring system provides an excellent opportunity to understand how environmental changes impact biophysical processes and functions and, ultimately, organismal and community responses. This type of intensive, fine-scale monitoring provides an important complement to the more coarse-grained monitoring feasible over larger spatial extents.

Policy

Shifting and expanding stewardship goals will create an enormous challenge for business-as-usual conservation policy making. Existing policies (e.g., the National Environmental Protection Act [NEPA], the California Environmental Quality Act [CEQA], the federal Endangered Species Act [ESA], and the California ESA [CESA]) and their current implementation offer few options for future flexibility and adaptation. There is a critical need to analyze existing policy tools and define future policy needs from four perspectives: (1) the extent to which existing state and federal policies hinder the reevaluation of conservation goals in the context of directional change, (2) the degree to which existing state and federal laws across multiple sectors hinder or facilitate implementation of conservation goals, (3) whether existing state and federal programs that provide financial resources are aligned to help conservation adapt to directional change, and (4) the extent to which tools for state agencies, local governments, and nonprofit organizations are available or under development to facilitate conservation implementation in the context of regional change.

The California Natural Resources Agency has made statewide adaptation planning for climate change a priority for addressing complex and large-scale challenges to conserving biodiversity and habitats (California Climate Adaptation Strategy for Biodiversity and Habitat 2009). Initial planning efforts focus on helping species persist in a changing environment. Towards this goal, the state agencies responsible for stewarding the state's biological diversity, the Department of Fish and Wildlife and California State Parks, have committed to evaluate internal policies related to regulatory responsibilities and to communicate openly with other agencies and the public. In their adaptation plan, these agencies outline near- and long-term climate adaptation strategies that will require additional collaborative efforts with multiple state agencies as well as sustainable funding and long-term state support.

The California Global Warming Solutions Act of 2006, AB 32, SB 375, and the Sustainable Communities and Climate Protection Act of 2008 set statewide and regional targets for GHG emissions reductions and demonstrate a willingness to address climate change in California. While deep structural change is needed to address the environmental improvements needed in California, demands for mitigation and conservation protection that are emerging to support greenhouse gas emission reductions could provide a way forward through climate change policy (see Chapter 40, "Land Use Regulation for Resource Conservation"). Climate mitigation funds and efforts should be directed or incentivized to protect the conservation priorities outlined in existing regional and state conservation plans. Climate mitigation needs to avoid restoration projects that fail to deliver functioning ecosystems and conservation of small, unconnected mitigation sites and projects disconnected from existing conservation priorities and unlikely to contribute lasting conservation value. The state needs to expand the approach used by regional transportation plans that fully assess cumulative and site impacts of development and that aggregate proposed greenhouse gas offsets and direct them toward meaningful conservation investments.

Equally important, counties need resources to improve urban services and incentives to direct development toward infill and other suitable areas in order to avoid habitat conversion and fragmentation. We focus on aligning local land use planning and state conservation with the changing needs of the state's biological resources, but the state will require support from academic and other science institutions to rethink policy and implementation in the context of the changes we are now experiencing.

Future Research, Education, and Outreach for Addressing Environmental Change

Fundamental to future actions is the need for sound science and adaptive, effective management, along with knowledge sharing and comprehensive and sustainable data collection and monitoring systems. We bring the following areas of investigation into focus because of their importance in improving our understanding of how to best steward California's ecosystems given future environmental change and the increased uncertainty that this presents for biodiversity conservation and ecosystem services. Most of these priorities span more than one ecosystem, and all reflect the scholarship contained in this volume. The following specific areas are loosely divided into biophysical research, interdisciplinary and applied research, and public participatory efforts.

Biophysical Research

Understanding interactions among climate conditions, ecosystem processes, and vegetation dynamics is the foundation for the stewardship approach we propose as a framework for ecosystem conservation in California. The impacts of climate change will be mediated largely through extreme physical events, including drought, wildfire, heat waves, loss of chilling hours, and relaxation of freezing events. Continued efforts to enhance and validate downscaling methods, coupled with enhanced understanding of biological responses at all levels to changing abiotic and biotic conditions, will be important for bringing the large-scale projections of GCMs to the local scale of organismal and population responses (e.g., Flint et al. 2013). Large-scale tree mortality due to heat or drought has already been observed on all continents (Allen et al. 2010), including increased mortality of large trees in California and the American West (van Mantgem et al. 2009). In California's Mediterranean-type climate, changes in precipitation and water balance will in many cases be more important than increased temperatures, leading to heterogeneous responses across complex gradients and microclimates (Crimmins et al. 2011, Rapacciuolo et al. in review). Specific research needs that emphasize climate change as an emerging driver include:

- Food webs and species interactions, including the top-down roles of meso- and top predators such as mountain lions, bobcats, and coyotes in community dynamics; the bottom-up impacts of invasive plants on animal community composition; and mechanisms controlling community invasibility.
- Disturbance regimes and successional dynamics in nonstationary environments, including identification of leading and trailing edges of existing ecosystems and emergence of novel ecosystems.
- Interactions between climate, including extreme drought events, and disease.
- Ecosystem inventory to identify remnant native grasslands; species assemblages associated with hot, dry microclimates within each ecosystem type to pinpoint likely beneficiaries of future change; species assemblages in cool climate areas across each ecosystem type that are not likely to change; and potential refugia in need of protection.
- Paleoecology and historical ecology to provide historical context on recovery and dynamics of vegetation change across ecosystems and historical responses to drought.
- Improved understanding of current and likely future fog patterns and how coastal microclimates and fog-reliant communities respond to changes in fog timing and extent.
- Ecophysiology and climate change biology of California's dominant woody plant species, including climate and microclimate controls on seedling establishment, early growth, and mortality; and patterns and scales of genetic climate adaptation.
- Ecohydrology, including interactions among major plant growth forms, associated spatio-temporal patterns of water availability, and spatial and temporal variation in soil moisture available across complex geologies and landforms.
- Belowground processes, including the influence of water deficit on microbial processes; and root function and climate sensitivity.
- Microevolutionary dynamics and rapid evolution in relation to dispersal rates and gene flow in spatially heterogeneous environments.
- Carbon, water, and energy exchange of California's ecosystems, including rates of carbon sequestration.

Interdisciplinary and Applied Research

While many of our identified priorities for biological research focus on mechanisms of response to climate, research on and experimental tests of conservation and climate adaptation strategies and their effectiveness are equally needed. Conservation and restoration biology lead the way in this regard. The urgency to intervene, conserve threatened species, and improve degraded systems should not preclude capitalizing

FIGURE 41.6 Inland Mendocino California Naturalists monitor a nest cavity at the Hopland Research and Extension Center as part of NestWatch <http://www.nestwatch.org>, a citizen science project. Photo: Brook Gamble.

on opportunities to conduct long-term studies and controlled, experimental research on intervention effectiveness. Truly interdisciplinary research, designed from the outset by collaborations of physical, biological, and social scientists and non-academic partners, requires significant investments to build professional relationships and bridge intellectual domains. However, such collaborations hold great potential to address conservation and climate impacts; design and evaluate solutions; and identify the costs of, barriers to, and opportunities for implementation. Priorities for interdisciplinary conservation science include:

- Experimental study of how systems respond to interventions such as invasive animal or plant removal, prescribed burning, and other actions that could enhance ecosystem recovery and resilience, where possible with controls, replication, and time depth.
- Retrospective analysis of outcomes of past actions, including restoration projects, effectiveness of mitigation banks and projects, and conservation easements.
- Study of recreation impacts, including risk analyses for threatened species in high-visitation areas, changes in animal movement patterns to avoid people, and effect zones around trails.
- Integrated, large-scale models examining relationships among development patterns, fire regime, and ecosystem resilience; effects of low-density residential housing on community composition and ecosystem processes; and biophysical dynamics such as through models that link climate and vegetation structure and dynamics to transfers of energy, water, carbon, and other nutrients.
- Risk assessment of the potential for and consequences of change for rare habitat types.
- Valuation of regulating, supporting, and amenity services flowing from natural ecosystems and design of markets to incentivize private landowners to conserve or increase provision of ecosystem services on their properties.
- Conservation planning and trade-off analyses of the implications of targeting ecosystem services versus biodiversity, prioritizing physiographic landscape features versus habitat types; prioritizing for conservation areas with lower climate water deficit; improving habitat connectivity through increasing reserve size and number versus corridor conservation or diversifying moderately modified habitat surrounding reserves; and enhancing corridors versus facilitating broader movement through matrix lands.

Ecological Monitoring and Public Participation

The need has never been greater to implement broad networks of monitoring and early detection sites and to acquire baseline data in the short term. Increasingly, advances in remote sensing will provide more complete coverage with enhanced spatial and temporal resolution for many variables of conservation interest. Ecological monitoring efforts nationwide span the gamut from the multimillion-dollar National Environmental Observatory Network (NEON) to dispersed citizen-science initiatives such as the National Phenology Network and biodiversity observations collected by the public through systems such as iNaturalist.org. Hundreds of active citizen-science programs exist in California, with details for each provided through the UC California Naturalist Program website (UC California Naturalist Program 2013) (Figure 41.6).

Trade-offs in investment, data consistency, and long-term reliability must be addressed in each case to identify the optimal balance of dispersed, low-cast networks and more concentrated sites with institutional support. Rapid data processing and availability are critical for adaptive management, especially given rapid rates of change. Local Cooperative Weed Management Areas also demonstrate the power of ecological monitoring by volunteer stewards to increase effectiveness of invasive species detection and control while reducing its cost (see Chapter 13, "Biological Invasions"). Preventing mass extinction will require comprehensive science, adaptive management, and a committed public. Priorities for advancing ecological monitoring and public participation include:

- A statewide, open-access database on restoration outcomes monitoring to foster evidence-based restoration and management actions.
- Networks of "sentinel" sites spanning bioregions and ecosystems across the state, providing continuous monitoring and early detection of changes.
- Participatory research through improved usability of existing mobile and online applications for crowd-sourced data acquisition; improved detection of local species declines and extirpations; and new statistical approaches to weight-contributed data based on estimates of reliability (e.g., bird list length).
- Citizen monitoring of early detection of new arrivals and diseases; changes in flowering timing, seed set, and other life-cycle events in relation to environmental cues; citizen rephotography of historic photo points; and citizen supervision of monitoring instruments.
- Education of small-parcel landowners about sustainable land management practices, including ways to maintain appropriate grazing levels, enhance riparian vegetation and woody debris, control invasive species, manage pests, and minimize movement barriers such as fencing.

Summary

Given continued rates of land use change, increasing influence of climate change, and the transient nature of California's ecosystems, it is time to reconsider some of our current approaches to conservation, stewardship, and restoration. Time lags between our actions today and species and ecosystem responses in the future make even more critical efforts to anticipate and conserve now. We need renewed, immediate protection against habitat loss and fragmentation from continued urban and agricultural development throughout California. Given increased rates of change and the resulting widespread existence of novel communities, we must adopt and pursue novel approaches to restoration and increase investment in stewardship.

Ecological restoration efforts should acknowledge ecosystem disequilibrium associated with directional global changes, take advantage of information on historical ecology and consider human needs to set achievable goals and produce realistic outcomes. A new stewardship framework founded in resilience to guide future interventions will help maintain ecosystem integrity over a large range of variability in climatic conditions and perturbation frequency and intensity. Many successful interventions described throughout this book make clear that we have substantial successes to build on, learn from, and advance further stewardship efforts. Based on the concerns and strategies raised in many of the ecosystem chapters, we emphasize the importance for California of managing fire and natural hydrologic flow regimes, tackling emerging challenges to open space stewardship, and ecological monitoring as part of this stewardship framework.

Advancing our understanding of California's ecosystems and their responses to environmental changes, primarily mediated through extreme physical events, is at the heart of advancing our stewardship goals. This requires a stronger state funding stream for targeted biophysical research on ecosystem dynamics and applied, interdisciplinary research on environmental disturbances, restoration, and management. Equally important, we must implement monitoring networks within and across California's ecosystems and take advantage of new technologies as well as public participation to be successful in this endeavor. New stewardship strategies and research should not overshadow the need to protect California's ecosystems. An emerging part of this is the growing need for climate change adaptation and resilience, particularly as efforts to prepare other systems for climate change—such as California's water storage and delivery—affect ecological systems. The state should set clear targets that meet or exceed international standards for conservation and restoration of every ecosystem type. This type of conservation planning and ecological restoration needs to be coupled with land use planning and considerations for carbon dioxide sequestration. In sum, coping with rapid environmental changes requires increased focus on strategic conservation planning, collaborative stewardship efforts, new approaches to restoration that improve the returns on our investment, and an integrated, targeted research and extension agenda.

Acknowledgments

We would like to acknowledge Cris Benton, Dylan Chapple, Greg Damron, Frank Davis, Brook Gamble, Kerry Heise, and Heather Rustigian-Romsos for assistance with some figures and photographs that help to bring this chapter alive.

Recommended Reading

Barnosky, A. 2009. Heatstroke. Island Press, Washington, D.C.

Chapin, F. S., III, G. Kofinas and C. Folke, editors. 2009. Principles of ecosystem stewardship. Springer. New York.

Cole, D. and L. Yung, editors. 2010. Beyond naturalness: Rethinking park and wilderness stewardship in an era of rapid change. Island Press, Washington, D.C.

De Nevers, G., D. S. Edelman, and A. M. Merenlender. 2013. The California naturalist handbook. University of California Press, Berkeley, California.

Hobbs, R., and E. Higgs, editors. 2013. Novel ecosystems. Wiley–Blackwell: A John Wiley & Sons Ltd. Oxford, UK.

Hobbs, R., and K. Suding, editors. 2009. New models for ecosystem dynamics. Island Press, Washington, D.C.

Interdisciplinary Research Team Summaries. 2011. Ecosystem Services: Charting a Path to Sustainability. The National Academies Keck Futures Initiative. Arnold and Mabel Beckman Center, Irvine, California, November 10–11, 2011.

Jensen, D. B., M. S. Torn, and J. Harte. 1993. In our own hands: A strategy for conserving California's biological diversity. University of California Press, Berkeley, California.

References

Ackerly, D. D., S. R. Loarie, W. K. Cornwell, S. B. Weiss, H. Hamilton, R. Branciforte, and N.J.B. Kraft. 2010. The geography of climate change: Implications for conservation biogeography. Diversity and Distributions 16:476–487.

Allen, C. D., A. K. Macalady, H. Chenchouni, D. Bachelet, N. McDowell, M. Vennetier, T. Kitzberger, A. Rigling, D. D. Breshears, E. H. Hogg, P. Gonzalez, R. Fensham, Z. Zhang, J. Castro, N. Demidova, J. H. Lim, G. Allard, S. W. Running, A. Semerci, and N. Cobb. 2010. A global overview of drought and heat-induced tree mortality reveals emerging climate change risks for forests. Forest Ecology and Management 259:660–684.

Attiwill, P. M. 1994. The disturbance of forest ecosystems: The ecological basis for conservative management. Forest Ecology and Management 63(2–3):247–300.

Báez S., and S. L. Collins. 2008. Shrub invasion decreases diversity and alters community stability in northern Chihuahuan desert plant communities. Plos One 3(6):e2332.

Baron, J. S., L. Gunderson, C. D. Allen, E. Fleishman, D. McKenzie, L. A. Meyerson, J. Oropeza, and N. Stephenson. 2009. Options for national parks and reserves for adapting to climate change. Environmental Management 44(6):1033–1042.

Bartolome, J. W., W. J. Barry, T. Griggs, and P. Hopkinson. 2007. Valley grassland. Pages 367–393 in M. G. Barbour, T. Keeler-Wolf, and A. A. Schoenherr, editors. Terrestrial vegetation of California. Third edition. University of California Press, Berkeley, California.

Beltran, R. S., N. Kreidler, D. H. Van Vuren, S. A. Morrison, E. S. Zavaleta, K. Newton, B. R. Tershy, and D. Croll. 2014. Passive recovery of vegetation after herbivore eradication on Santa Cruz Island, California. Restoration Ecology, 22:790–797.

Blue Oak Ranch. 2008. Climate and atmosphere. <http://www.blueoakranchreserve.org/borr/Information/Entries/2008/1/6_Climate_and_Atmosphere.html>. Accessed January 23, 2014.

Burrows, M. T., D. S. Schoeman, A. J. Richardson, J. G. Moinos, A. Hoffmann, L. B. Buckley, P. J. Moore, C. J. Brown, J. F. Bruno, C. M Duarte, B. S. Halpern, O. Hoegh-Guldberg, C. V. Kappel, W. Kiessling, M. I O'Connor, J. M. Pandolfi, C. Parmesan, W. J. Sydeman, S. Feirrier, K. J. Williams, and E. S. Poloczanska. 2014. Geographical limits to species-range shifts are suggested by climate velocity. Nature 507:492–495.

California Climate Adaptation Strategy for Biodiversity and Habitat. 2009. <http://www.climatechange.ca.gov/adaptation/documents/Statewide_Adaptation_Strategy_-_Chapter_5_-_Biodiversity_and_Habitat.pdf>. Accessed February 2, 2014.

California Essential Habitat Connectivity Project. 2010. Strategy for Conserving a Connected California. <http://www.dfg.ca.gov/

habcon/connectivity/#CaliforniaEssential>. Accessed February 2, 2014.

California GAP Analysis. 1998. Executive summary. <http://www.biogeog.ucsb.edu/projects/gap/report/gap_rep_sum.html>. Accessed January 22, 2014.

California Naturalist Program. 2013. Citizen Science for Naturalists. <http://calnat.ucanr.edu/California_PPSR/>. Accessed January 23, 2014.

Caro, T., J. Darwin, T. Forrester, C. Ledoux-Bloom, and C. Wells. 2012. Conservation in the Anthropocene. Conservation Biology 26:185–188.

Chan, K. M. A., M. R. Shaw, D. R. Cameron, E. C. Underwood, and G. C. Daily. 2006. Conservation planning for ecosystem services. Public Library of Science Biology 4:2138–2152.

Chapin, F. S., S. R. Carpenter, G. P. Kofinas, C. Folke, N. Abel, W. C. Clark, P. Olsson, D. M. Stafford Smith, B. H. Walker, O. R. Young, F. Berkes, R. Biggs, J. M. Grove, R. L. Naylor, E. Pinkerton, W. Steffen, and F. J. Swanson 2010 Ecosystem stewardship: Sustainability strategies for a rapidly changing planet. Trends in Ecology and Evolution 25:241–249.

Chester, C., and J. Hilty. 2010. Connectivity conservation concepts. Pages 22–33 in G. L. Worboys, W. L. Francis, M. Lockwood, editors. Connectivity Conservation Management: A Global Guide. IUCN/Earthscan, New York, New York.

Choi, Y. D., V. M. Temperton, E. B. Allen, A. P. Grootjans, M. Halassy, R. J. Hobbs, M. A. Naeth, and K. Torok. 2008. Ecological restoration for future sustainability in a changing environment. Ecoscience 15(1):53–64.

Convention on Biological Diversity. 2011. Strategic plan for biodiversity 2011–2020. <https://www.cbd.int/sp/default.shtml>. Accessed January 22, 2014.

Cordell, H. K., G. T. Green, V. R. Leeworthy, R. Stephens, M. J. Fly and C. J. Betz. 2005. United States of America: Outdoor recreation. Pages 245–264 in G. Cushman, A. J. Veal, and J. Zuzanek, editors. Free time and leisure participation: International perspectives. CABI Publishing, Wallingford, UK.

Costanza, R., R. d'Arge, R. de Groot, S. Farber, M. Grasso, B. Hannon, K. Limburg, S. Naeem, R. V. O'Neill, J. Paruelo, R. G. Raskin, P. Sutton, and M. van den Belt. 1997. The value of the world's ecosystem services and natural capital. Nature 387:253–260.

Costello, C., S. D. Gaines, and J. Lyanham. 2008. Can catch shares prevent fisheries collapse? Science 321:1678—1681

Crimmins, S. M., S. Z. Dobrowski, J. A. Greenberg, J. T. Abatzoglou, and A. R. Mynsberge. 2011. Changes in climatic water balance drive downhill shifts in plant species' optimum elevations. Science 331:324–327.

Crutzen, P. J. 2002. Geology of mankind. Nature 415:23.

Czech, B., P. R. Krausman, and P. K. Devers. 2000. Economic associations among causes of species endangerment in the United States. Bioscience 50:593–601.

Dahl, T. E. 1990. Wetlands losses in the United States 1780's to 1980's. U.S. Department of the Interior, Fish and Wildlife Service, Washington, D.C.

Daily, G. C., S. Polasky, J. Goldstein, P. M. Kareiva, H. A. Mooney, L. Pejchar, T. H. Ricketts, J. Salzman, and R. Shallenberger. 2009. Ecosystem services in decision making: Time to deliver. Frontiers in Ecology and the Environment 7(1):21–28.

DeNevers, G., D. S. Edelman, and A. M. Merenlender. 2013. The California naturalist handbook. University of California Press, Berkeley, California.

Dirzo, R., and P. H. Raven. 2003. Global state of biodiversity and loss. Annual Review of Environment and Resources 28:137–167.

Dole, K. P., M. E. Loik, and L. C. Sloan. 2003. The relative importance of climate change and the physiological effects of CO^2 on freezing tolerance for the future distribution of Yucca brevifolia. Global and Planetary Change 36:137–146.

Ehrenfeld, J. G. 2003. Effects of exotic plant invasions on soil nutrient cycling processes. Ecosystems 6(6):503–523.

Fahrig, L. 2003. Effect of habitat fragmentation on biodiversity. Annual Review of Ecology, Evolution, and Systematics 34:487–515.

Fenn, M. E., E. B. Allen, S. B. Weiss, S. Jovan, L. H. Geiser, G. S. Tonnesen, R. F. Johnson, L. E. Rao, B. S. Gimeno, F. Yuan, T. Meixner, and A. Bytnerowicz. 2010. Nitrogen critical loads and management alternatives for N-impacted ecosystems in California. Journal of Environmental Management 91(12):2404–2423.

Fenn, M. E., R. Haeuber, G. S. Tonnesen, J. S. Baron, S. Grossman-Clarke, D. Hope, D. A. Jaffe, S. Copeland, L. Geiser, H. M. Rueth, and J. O. Sickman. 2003. Nitrogen emissions, deposition, and monitoring in the western United States. Bioscience 53(4):391–403.

Ferraro, P. J., and S. K. Pattanayak. 2006. Money for nothing? A call for empirical evaluation of biodiversity conservation investments. PLoS Biology 4:e105.

Flint, L. E., A. Flint, J. H. Thorne, and R. Boynton. 2013. Fine-scale hydrologic modeling for regional landscape applications: The California Basin Characterization Model development and performance. Ecological Processes 2:2–25.

Frumkin, H. 2001. Beyond toxicity: Human health and the natural environment. American Journal of Preventative Medicine 20:234–240.

Gaman, T., and J. Firman. 2008. Oaks 2040: The status and future of oaks in California. Pages 603–616 in Proceedings of the sixth California oak symposium. General technical report PSW. GTR-217.

Garber, S. D., and J. Burger. 1995. A twenty-year study documenting the relationship between turtle decline and human recreation. Ecological Applications 5:1151–1162.

Godefroid, S., C. Piazza, G. Rossi, S. Buord, A. Stevens, R. Aguraiuja, C. Cowell, C. W. Weekley, G. Vogg, J. M. Iriondo, I. Johnson, B. Dixon, D. Gordon, S. Magnanon, B. Valentin, K. Bjureke, R. Koopman, M. Vicens, M. Virevaire, and T. Vanderborght. 2011. How successful are plant species reintroductions? Biological Conservation 144:672–682.

Gunderson, L. H., and C. S. Holling. 2002. Panarchy: Understanding transformations in human and natural systems. Island Press, Washington, D.C.

Hayhoe, K., D. Cayan, C. B. Field, P. C. Frumhoff, E. P. Maurer, N. L. Miller, S. C. Moser, S. H. Schneider, K. N. Cahill, E. E. Cleland, L. Dale, R. Drapek, R. M. Hanemann, L. S. Kalkstein, J. Lenihan, C. K. Lunch, R. P. Neilson, S. C. Sheridan, and J. H. Verville. 2004. Emissions pathways, climate change, and impacts on California. Proceedings of the National Academy of Sciences USA 101(34):12422–12427.

Heise, K., and A. M. Merenlender 2002. Monitoring a half-century of change in a hardwood rangeland. Journal of Range Management 55(4):412–419.

Heller, N. E., and E. S. Zavaleta. 2009. Biodiversity management in the face of climate change: A review of twenty-two years of recommendations. Biological Conservation 142:14–32.

Hillebrand, H., and B. Matthiessen. 2009. Biodiversity in a complex world: Consolidation and progress in functional biodiversity research. Ecology Letters 12(12):1405–1419.

Hobbs, R. J., and V. A. Cramer. 2007. Old field dynamics: Regional and local differences, and lessons for ecology and restoration. Pages 309–318 in V. A. Cramer and R. J. Hobbs, editors. Old fields: Dynamics and Restoration of Abandoned Farmland. Island Press, Washington, D.C.

Hobbs, R. J., E. Higgs, and J. A. Harris. 2009. Novel ecosystems: Implications for conservation and restoration. Trends in Ecology and Evolution 24(11):599–605.

Hobbs, R. J., S. Arico, J. Aronson, J. S. Baron, P. Bridgewater, V. A. Cramer, P. R. Epstein, J. J. Ewel, C. A. Klink, A. E. Lugo, D. Norton, D. Ojima, D. M. Richardson, E. W. Sanderson, F. Valladares, M. Vilà, R. Zamora, and M. Zobel. 2006. Novel ecosystems: Theoretical and management aspects of the new ecological world order. Global Ecology and Biogeography 15(1):1–7.

Hooper, D. U., E. C. Adair, B. J. Cardinale, J. E. K. Byrnes, B. A. Hungate, K. L. Matulich, A. Gonzalez, J. E. Duffy, L. Gamfeldt, and M. I. O'Connor. 2012. A global synthesis reveals biodiversity loss as a major driver of ecosystem change. Nature 486:105–108.

Hughes, A. R., B. D. Inouye, M. T. J. Johnson, N. Underwood, and M. Vellend. 2008. Ecological consequences of genetic diversity. Ecology Letters 11(6):609–623.

Ikuta, L. A., and D. T. Blumstein. 2003. Do fences protect birds from human disturbance? Biological Conservation 112(3):447–452.

Isbell, F. I., H. W. Polley, and B. J. Wilsey. 2009. Species interaction mechanisms maintain grassland plant diversity. Ecology 90(7):1821–1830.

Jackson, S. T., and D. F. Sax. 2010. Balancing biodiversity in a changing environment: Extinction debt, immigration credit, and species turnover. Trends in Ecology and Evolution 25(3):153–160.

Joyce, L. A., G. M. Blate, S. G. McNulty, C. I. Millar, S. Moser, R. P. Neilson, and D.L. Peterson. 2008. Managing for multiple resources under climate change: National forests. Environmental Management 44(6):1022–1032.

Klausmeyer, K. R., M. R. Shaw, J. B. MacKenzie, and D. R. Cameron. 2011. Landscape-scale indicators of biodiversity's vulnerability to climate change. Ecosphere 2(8):1–18.

Knight, R. L., and K. J. Gutzwiller. 1995. Wildlife and recreationists: Coexistence through management and research. Island Press, Washington, D.C.

Koenig, W. D., and M. V. Ashley 2003. Is pollen limited? The answer is blowin' in the wind. TRENDS in Ecology and Evolution 18(4):157–159.

Landis, J. D., and M. Reilly. 2003. How we will grow: Baseline projections of the growth of California's urban footprint through the year 2100. Institute of Urban and Regional Development, University of California, Berkeley, California.

Lawler, J. J., A. S. Ruesch, J. D. Olden, and B. H. McRae. 2013. Projected climate-driven faunal movement routes. Ecology Letters 16:1014–1022.

Loarie S. R., B. E. Carte, K. Hayhoe, S. McMahon, R. Moe, C. A. Knight, and D. D. Ackerly. 2008. Climate change and the future of California's endemic flora. PLoS ONE 3(6):2502.

Loarie, S. R., P. B. Duffy, H. Hamilton, G. P. Asner, C. B. Field, and D. Ackerly. 2009. The velocity of climate change. Nature 462(7276):1052–1055.

Losos, E., J. Hayes, A. Phillips, D. Wilcove, and C. Alkire. 1995. Taxpayer-subsidized resource extraction harms species. Bioscience 45:446–455.

Lyytimaki, J., and M. Sipila. 2009. Hopping on one leg—The challenge of ecosystem disservices for urban green management. Urban Forestry and Urban Greening 8(4):309–315.

Mahoney, J. M., and S. B. Rood. 1998. Streamflow requirements for cottonwood seedling recruitment—an integrative model. Wetlands 18:634–645.

McCreary, D. D. 2009. Regenerating rangeland oaks. University of California Agriculture and Natural Resources Publication 21601e.

McKinney, M. L., and J. L. Lockwood. 1999. Biotic homogenization: A few winners replacing many losers in the next mass extinction. Trends in Ecology and Evolution 14(11):450–453.

McLachlan, J. S., Hellmann, J. J., and M. W. Schwartz. 2007. A framework for debate of assisted migration in an era of climate change. Conservation Biology 21:297–302.

McLaughlin, B., and E. Zavaleta. 2013. Regional and temporal patterns of natural recruitment in a California endemic oak and a potential "research reserve effect." Diversity and Distributions 19:1440–1449.

Moyle, P. B., J. D. Kiernan, P. K. Crain, and R. M. Quiñones. 2013. Climate change vulnerability of native and alien freshwater fishes of California: A systematic assessment approach. PLoS ONE 8(5):63883.

Moyle, P. B., J. V. E. Katz, and R. M. Quiñones. 2011. Rapid decline of California's native inland fishes: A status assessment. Biological Conservation 144:2414–2423.

Nuñez T. A., J. J. Lawler, B. H. McRae, D. J. Pierce, M. B. Krosby, D. M. Kavanagh, P. H. Singleton, and J. J. Tewksbury. 2013. Connectivity planning to address climate change. Conservation Biology 27(2):407–416.

Olden, J. D., N. LeRoy Poff, M. R. Douglas, M. E. Douglas, and K. D. Fausch. 2004. Ecological and evolutionary consequences of biotic homogenization. Trends in Ecology and Evolution 19(1):18–24.

Papouchis, C. M., F. J. Singer, and W. B. Sloan. 2001. Responses of desert bighorn sheep to increased human recreation. Journal of Wildlife Management 65(3):573–582.

Parma, A. M., P. Amarasekare, M. Mangel, J. L. Moore, W. M. Murdoch, E. Noonburg, M. Pascual, H. P. Possingham, K. Shea, C. Wilcox, and D. W. Yu. 1998. What can adaptive management do for our fish, forests, food, and biodiversity? Integrative Biology—Issues, News, and Reviews 1:16–26.

Pomeroy, R. S., L. M. Watson, J. E. Parks, and G. A. Cid. 2005. How is your MPA doing? A methodology for evaluating the management effectiveness of marine protected areas. Ocean and Coastal Management 48(7–8):485–502.

Rapacciuolo, G., S. P. Maher, A. C. Schneider, T. T. Hammond, M. D. Jabis, R. Walsh, K. J. Iknayan, G. K. Walden, M. F. Oldfather, D. D. Ackerly, and S. R. Beissinger. 2014. Beyond a warming fingerprint: Individualistic biogeographic responses to heterogeneous climate change in California. Global Change Biology. 20:2841–2855.

Reed, S. E., and A. M. Merenlender. 2008. Quiet, nonconsumptive recreation reduces protected area effectiveness. Conservation Letters 1(3):146–154.

Salafsky, N., R. Margolius, K. H. Redford, and J. G. Robinson. 2002. Improving the practice of conservation: A conceptual framework and research agenda for conservation science. Conservation Biology 16:1469–1479.

Shaw, M. R., D. Cameron, K. Klausmeyer, J. MacKenzie, and P. Roehrdanz. 2012. Economic costs of achieving current conservation goals as climate changes. Conservation Biology 26:385–396.

Spencer, W. D, P. Beier, K. Penrod, K. Winters, C. Paulmann, H. Rustigian-Romsos, J. Strittholt, M. Parisi, and A. Pettler. 2010. California Essential Habitat Connectivity Project: A strategy for conserving connected California. Prepared for California Department of Transportation, California Department of Fish and Game, and Federal Highways Administration. Sacramento, CA.

Stromberg, M. R., J. D. Corbin, and C. M. D'Antonio. 2007. California grasslands: Ecology and management. University of California Press, Berkeley, California.

Suding, K. N. 2011. Toward an era of restoration in ecology: Successes, failures, and opportunities ahead. Pages 465–487 in D. J. Futuyma, H. B. Shaffer, and D. Simberloff, editors. Annual Review of Ecology, Evolution, and Systematics. Volume 42.

Suding, K. N., S. Lavorel, F. S. Chapin, J. H. C. Cornelissen, S. Diaz, E. Garnier, D. Goldberg, D. U. Hooper, S. T. Jackson, and M. L. Navas. 2008. Scaling environmental change through the community-level: A trait-based response-and-effect framework for plants. Global Change Biology 14(5):1125–1140.

Svenning, J., and B. Sandel. 2013. Disequilibrium vegetation dynamics under future climate change. American Journal of Botany 100(7):1266–1286.

Taylor, A. R., and R. L. Knight. 2003. Wildlife responses to recreation and associated visitor perceptions. Ecological Applications 13:951–963.

Thebault, J., T. S. Schraga, J. E. Cloern, and E. G. Dunlavey. 2008. Primary production and carrying capacity of former salt ponds after reconnection to San Francisco Bay. Wetlands 28(3):841–851.

Tilman, D. 2001. Functional diversity. Encyclopedia of biodiversity. Volume 3. Academic Press, San Diego, California.

van Mantgem, P. J., N. L. Stephenson, J. C. Byrne, L. D. Daniels, J. F. Franklin, P. Z. Fule, M. E. Harmon, A. J. Larson, J. M. Smith, A. H. Taylor, and T. T. Veblen. 2009. Widespread increase of tree mortality rates in the western United States. Science 323:521–524.

Vander Mijnsbrugge, K., A. Bischoff, and B. Smith. 2010. A question of origin: Where and how to collect seed for ecological restoration. Basic and Applied Ecology 11(4):300–311.

Vince, G. 2011. An epoch debate. Science 334(6052):32–37.

Vitt, P., K. Havens, A. T. Kramer, D. Sollenberger, and E. Yates. 2010. Assisted migration of plants: Changes in latitudes, changes in attitudes. Biological Conservation 143(1):18–27.

Vos, C. C., P. Berry, P. Opdam, H. Baveco, B. Nijhof, J. O'Hanley, C. Bell, and H. Kuipers. 2008. Adapting landscapes to climate change: Examples of climate-proof ecosystem networks and priority adaptation zones. Journal of Applied Ecology 45:1722–1731.

Weiss, S. B. 1999. Cars, cows, and checkerspot butterflies: Nitrogen deposition and management of nutrient-poor grasslands for a threatened species. Conservation Biology 13(6):1476–1486.

Zalasiewicz, J., M. Williams, W. Steffen, and P. Crutzen. 2010. The new world of the Anthropocene. Environmental Science and Technology 44(7):2228–2231.

Zavaleta, E., and F. S. Chapin III. 2010. Resilience frameworks: Enhancing the capacity to adapt to change. Pages 142–158 in D. N. Cole and L. Yung, editors. Beyond Naturalness: Conserving Parks and Wilderness in the Twenty-first Century. Island Press, Washington, D.C.

Zavaleta, E. S., K. Hulvey, and B. Fulfrost. 2007. Regional patterns of recruitment success and failure in two endemic California oaks. Diversity and Distributions 13:735–745.

INDEX